W9-CHE-859

WITHDRAWN

Features

Visit us on the Web at
http://www.census.gov/statab/www/

ACKNOWLEDGMENTS

Lars B. Johanson was responsible for the technical supervision and coordination of this volume under the general direction of **Glenn W. King**, Chief, Statistical Compendia Branch. Assisting in the research and analytical phases of assigned sections and in the development aspects of new tables were **Rosemary E. Clark**, **Richard P. Kersey**, **Stacey M. Lowe**, and **Jean F. Maloney**. **Catherine Lavender** provided primary editorial assistance. Other editorial assistance was rendered by **Susan Antroinen**, **Samuel E. Santos**, and **Barbara Shugart**.

Maps were designed and produced by **Connie Beard** and **Jessica Dobrowolski** of the Cartographic Operations Branch within the Geography Division.

Catherine M. Raymond, **Patricia Edwards**, **Wanda Cevis**, **Linda Chen**, and **Diane Oliff-Michael** of the Administrative and Customer Services Division, **Walter C. Odom**, Chief, provided publications and printing management, graphics design and composition, and editorial review for print and electronic media. General direction and production management were provided by **James R. Clark**, Assistant Division Chief, and **Susan L. Rappa**, Chief, Publications Services Branch.

The cooperation of many contributors to this volume is gratefully acknowledged. The source note below each table credits the various government and private sector agencies that have collaborated in furnishing the information for the *Statistical Abstract*.

Statistical Abstract
of the United States: 2006

The National Data Book

125TH
EDITION

Issued October 2005

U.S. Department of Commerce
Carlos M. Gutierrez,
Secretary

David A. Sampson,
Deputy Secretary

Economics and Statistics
Administration
Kathleen B. Cooper,
Under Secretary for Economic Affairs

U.S. CENSUS BUREAU
Charles Louis Kincannon,
Director

SUGGESTED CITATION

U.S. Census Bureau,
*Statistical Abstract of the
United States: 2006*
(125th Edition)
Washington, DC,
2005

ECONOMICS
AND STATISTICS
ADMINISTRATION

Economics and Statistics Administration

Kathleen B. Cooper,
Under Secretary
for Economic Affairs

U.S. CENSUS BUREAU

Charles Louis Kincannon,
Director

Hermann Habermann,
Deputy Director and
Chief Operating Officer

Ted A. Johnson, Associate Director
for Administration
and Chief Financial Officer

Walter C. Odom, Chief, Administrative
and Customer Services Division

U.S. GOVERNMENT PRINTING OFFICE OFFICIAL EDITION NOTICE

This is the Official U.S. Government edition of this publication and is herein identified to certify its authenticity. The Superintendent of Documents of the U.S. Government Printing Office requests that any reprinted edition clearly be labeled as a copy of the authentic work. Use of the 0-16 ISBN prefix is for U.S. Government Printing Office Official Editions only.

ISBN: 0-16-074007-X

NATIONAL BIBLIOGRAPHY OF U.S. GOVERNMENT PUBLICATIONS

Statistical Abstract of the United States : 2006.—125 ed.
  Includes index.
  ISBN 0-16-074007-X
  ISSN 0081-4741
1. United States—Statistics. I. United States. Census Bureau.

HA 202.S8 2006
317.3

Library of Congress Card No. 0418089

http://purl.access.gpo.gov/GPO/LPS2878

3 9082 10103 2368

For sale by the Superintendent of Documents, U.S. Government Printing Office
Internet: bookstore.gpo.gov Phone: toll free (866) 512-1800; DC area (202) 512-1800
Fax: (202) 512-2250 Mail: Stop SSOP, Washington, DC 20402-0001

ISBN 0-16-074007-X

Preface

The *Statistical Abstract of the United States*, published since 1878, is the standard summary of statistics on the social, political, and economic organization of the United States. It is designed to serve as a convenient volume for statistical reference and as a guide to other statistical publications and sources. The latter function is served by the introductory text to each section, the source note appearing below each table, and Appendix I, which comprises the Guide to Sources of Statistics, the Guide to State Statistical Abstracts, and the Guide to Foreign Statistical Abstracts.

This volume includes a selection of data from many statistical sources, both government and private. Publications cited as sources usually contain additional statistical detail and more comprehensive discussions of definitions and concepts. Data not available in publications issued by the contributing agency but obtained from the Internet or unpublished records are identified in the source notes. More information on the subjects covered in the tables so noted may generally be obtained from the source.

Except as indicated, figures are for the United States as presently constituted. Although emphasis in the *Statistical Abstract* is primarily given to national data, many tables present data for regions and individual states and a smaller number for metropolitan areas and cities. Appendix II, Metropolitan and Micropolitan Statistical Areas: Concepts, Components, and Population, presents explanatory text, a complete current listing and population data for metropolitan and micropolitan areas defined as of November 2004. Statistics for the Commonwealth of Puerto Rico and for island areas of the United States are included in many state tables and are supplemented by information in Section 29. Additional information for states, cities, counties, metropolitan areas, and other small units,

as well as more historical data are available in various supplements to the *Abstract* (see inside back cover).

Statistics in this edition are generally for the most recent year or period available by summer 2005. Each year over 1,400 tables and charts are reviewed and evaluated; new tables and charts of current interest are added, continuing series are updated, and less timely data are condensed or eliminated. Text notes and appendices are revised as appropriate.

Several special features such as *USA Statistics in Brief*, *Mini Historical Statistics*, and *State Rankings* can be found on our Web site: <http://www.census.gov/statab/www/>.

Changes in this edition—In recognition of this being the 125th edition of the *Statistical Abstract*, historical tables will be included at the beginning of each section in order to highlight related data when they first appeared in earlier editions. These cover topics such as: the number of alien passengers arriving in the U.S. (1819 to 1870); the number of juvenile delinquents (1890 and 1904); apportionment of congressional representation (1790 to 1900); number of pension claims filed and allowed each year (1861); and imports and exports of merchandise into and out of Alaska (1879 to 1905).

We have introduced 80 new tables in this edition, including several from the American Community Survey. These cover a variety of topics including select family planning and medical services, asthma incidence among children under 18 years of age, public schools with broadband and wireless connections, state trends in identity theft, hazardous waste generated, shipped, and received by state, retail gasoline prices by selected areas, and a profile of second-home buyers. In addition, a number of new tables have been added that contain data from the 2002 Economic Census. For a complete

v

list of new tables, see Appendix VI, p. 965. Section 10 has a new title (National Security and Veterans Affairs) that reflects its reorganization and 13 new tables on the subject of homeland security.

Statistical Abstract on other media— The *Abstract* is available on the Internet and on CD-ROM. Both versions contain the same material as the book, except for a few copyrighted tables for which we did not receive permission to release in these formats. Our Internet site <http://www .census.gov/statab/www> contains this 2006 edition plus selected earlier editions in Adobe Acrobat .pdf format. The CD-ROM version also includes spreadsheet files for each table and links to the Web sites of each source. Many of the spreadsheet files on the CD-ROM contain more historical and/or detailed data than are found in the book.

Statistics for states and metropolitan areas—Extensive data for the states and metropolitan areas of the United States can be found in the *State and Metropolitan Area Data Book: 1997–98.* This publication minus some data items, as well as selected rankings of the states and metropolitan areas, is available on our Internet site at <http://www.census .gov/statab /www/smadb.html>. The CD-ROM version is also available.

Statistics for counties and cities— Extensive data for counties can be found in the *County and City Data Book: 2000.* It features 191 data items covering everything from age and agriculture to water use and wholesale trade for all states and counties with U.S. totals for comparison. Also included are 103 data items for cities with population of 25,000 or more. The primary sources are Census 2000 and the 1997 Economic Census. Two tables present 11 data items from Census 2000 for all places and minor civil divisions with a population of 2,500 or more.

This publication, as well as selected rankings, is available on our Internet site at <http://www.census.gov/statab/www /ccdb.html>. Some data items that appear in the book from private sources are not available on the Internet or CD-ROM versions because we did not receive copyright permission to release the data items in these formats. For a database with over 5,000 county items, check out USA Counties at <http://www .census.gov/statab /www/county.html>.

Statistical Abstract Postcard User Survey—Inserted in this edition is the ninth user survey taken periodically to ask for your suggestions on various aspects of the *Abstract.* Your input will help us to maintain the usefulness of the *Abstract.* If the postcard is missing and you would like to participate in the Survey, you may obtain one by writing us at: U.S. Census Bureau, Statistical Compendia Staff, ACSD, Room 1051-4, Washington, DC 20233, or e-mail us at <ACSD.US.Data@census.gov>.

Limitations of the data—The contents of this volume were taken from many sources. All data from either censuses and surveys or from administrative records are subject to error arising from a number of factors: Sampling variability (for statistics based on samples), reporting errors in the data for individual units, incomplete coverage, nonresponse, imputations, and processing error. (See also Appendix III, pp. 941.) The Census Bureau cannot accept the responsibility for the accuracy or limitations of the data presented here, other than those for which it collects. The responsibility for selection of the material and for proper presentation, however, rests with the Census Bureau.

For additional information on data presented—Please consult the source publications available in local libraries or write to the agency indicated in the source notes. Write to the Census Bureau only if it is cited as the source.

Suggestions and comments—Users of the Statistical Abstract and its supplements (see inside back cover) are urged to make their data needs known for consideration in planning future editions. Suggestions and comments for improving coverage and presentation of data should be sent to the Director, U.S. Census Bureau, Washington, DC 20233.

vi

Contents

[Numbers following subjects are page numbers]

Historical Tables

Guide to Tabular Presentation

Example of Table Structure

Table 521. **Border Patrol Enforcement Activities: 2000 to 2004**

[As of September 30. Excludes Immigration and Customs Enforcement (ICE) investigations' data. The source of the data is administrative records that come from the Performance Analysis System (PAS)]

Activities	2000	2001	2002	2003	2004
Persons processed by the Border Patrol [1]	1,689,195	1,277,577	967,044	946,684	1,179,296
Deportable aliens located by the Border Patrol	1,676,438	1,266,214	955,310	931,557	1,160,395
Mexican aliens	1,636,883	1,224,046	917,994	882,012	1,085,006
Working in agriculture	1,330	1,248	1,821	1,908	1,647
Working in trades, crafts, industry, and service	2,167	2,678	2,897	3,856	3,634
Seeking employment	1,525,422	1,107,550	822,161	810,671	997,986
Canadian aliens	2,211	2,539	1,836	1,611	1,497
All others	37,344	39,629	35,480	47,934	73,892
Smugglers of aliens located	14,406	8,720	8,701	11,128	16,074
Aliens located who were smuggled into the United States	236,782	112,927	68,192	110,575	193,122
Seizures (conveyances)	17,269	5,892	7,250	9,355	18,024
Value of seizures (mil. dol.)	1,945	1,581	1,564	1,680	1,696
Narcotics	1,848	1,519	1,499	1,608	1,620
Other	97	62	65	72	75

[1] Includes deportable aliens located and non-deportable (e.g., U.S. citizens).

Source: U.S. Department of Homeland Security, Office of Immigration Statistics, *Yearbook of Immigration Statistics, 2004.* See also <http://uscis.gov/graphics/shared/aboutus/statistics/ybpage.htm>.

Headnotes immediately below table titles provide information important for correct interpretation or evaluation of the table as a whole or for a major segment of it.

Footnotes below the bottom rule of tables give information relating to specific items or figures within the table.

Unit indicators show the *specified quantities* in which data items are presented. They are used for two primary reasons. Sometimes data are not available in absolute form and are estimates (as in the case of many surveys). In other cases we round the numbers in order to save space to show more data, as in the case above.

EXAMPLES OF UNIT INDICATOR INTERPRETATION FROM TABLE

Year	Item	Unit Indicator	Number shown	Multiplier
2000	Value of seizures	$ Millions	1,945	1,000,000

To Determine the Figure It Is Necessary to Multiply the Number Shown by the Unit Indicator:

Value of seizures by Border Patrol – 1,945 x $1,000,000 – $1,945,000,000
(over $1.9 billion)

When a table presents data with more than one unit indicator, they are found in the headnotes and column headings (Tables 2 and 29), spanner (Table 40), stub (Table 25), or unit column (Table 127). When the data in a table are shown in the same unit indicator, it is shown in boldface as the first part of the headnote (Table 2). If no unit indicator is shown, data presented are in absolute form (Table 1).

Vertical rules are used to separate independent sections of a table (Table 1), or in tables where the stub is continued into one or more additional columns (Table 2).

Averages—An average is a single number or value that is often used to represent the "typical value" of a group of numbers. It is regarded as a measure of "location" or "central tendency" of a group of numbers.

The *arithmetic mean* is the type of average used most frequently. It is derived by summing the individual item values of a particular group and dividing the total by the number of items. The arithmetic mean is often referred to as simply the "mean" or "average."

The *median* of a group of numbers is the middle number or value when each item in the group is arranged according to size (lowest to highest or visa versa); it generally has the same number of items above it as well as below it. If there is an even number of items in the group, the median is taken to be the average of the two middle numbers.

Per capita (or per person) quantities—a per capita figure represents an average computed for every person in a specified group (or population). It is derived by taking the total for an item (such as income, taxes, or retail sales) and dividing it by the number of persons in the specified population.

Index numbers—An index number is the measure of difference or change, usually expressed as a percent, relating one quantity (the variable) of a specified kind to another quantity of the same kind. Index numbers are widely used to express changes in prices over periods of time, but may also be used to express differences between related subjects for a single point in time.

To compute a price index, a base year or period is selected. The base year price (of the commodity or service) is then designated as the base or reference price to which the prices for other years or periods are related. Many price indexes use the year 1982 as the base year; in tables this is shown as "1982 = 100." A method of expressing the price relationship is: The price of a set of one or more items for a related year (e.g. 1990) **divided by** the price of the same set of items for the base year (e.g. 1982). The result multiplied by 100 provides the index number. When 100 is subtracted from the index number, the result equals the percent change in price from the base year.

Average annual percent change—Unless otherwise stated in the *Abstract* (as in Section 1, Population), average annual percent change is computed by use of a *compound interest formula*. This formula assumes that the rate of change is constant throughout a specified compounding period (1 year for average annual rates of change). The formula is similar to that used to compute the balance of a savings account that receives compound interest. According to this formula, at the end of a compounding period the amount of accrued change (e.g., school enrollment or bank interest) is added to the amount that existed at the beginning of the period. As a result, over time (e.g., with each year or quarter), the same rate of change is applied to a larger and larger figure.

The *exponential formula*, which is based on continuous compounding, is often used to measure population change. It is preferred by population experts, because they view population and population-related subjects as changing without interruption, ever ongoing. Both exponential and compound interest formulas assume a constant rate of change. The former, however, applies the amount of change continuously to the base rather than at the end of each compounding

period. When the average annual rates are small (e.g., less than 5 percent) both formulas give virtually the same results. For an explanation of these two formulas as they relate to population, see U.S. Census Bureau, *The Methods and Materials of Demography*, Vol. 2, 3d printing (rev.), 1975, pp. 372–381.

Current and constant dollars—Statistics in some tables in a number of sections are expressed in both current and constant dollars (see, e.g., Table 662 in Section 13, Income, Expenditures, and Wealth). Current dollar figures reflect actual prices or costs prevailing during the specified year(s). Constant dollar figures are estimates representing an effort to remove the effects of price changes from statistical series reported in dollar terms. In general, constant dollar series are derived by dividing current dollar estimates by the appropriate price index for the appropriate period (e.g., the Consumer Price Index). The result is a series as it would presumably exist if prices were the same throughout, as in the base year—in other words, as if the dollar had constant purchasing power. Any changes in this constant dollar series would reflect only changes in real volume of output, income, expenditures, or other measure.

Explanation of Symbols

The following symbols, used in the tables throughout this book, are explained in condensed form in footnotes to the tables where they appear:

- Represents zero or rounds to less than half the unit of measurement shown.

B Base figure too small to meet statistical standards for reliability of a derived figure.

D Figure withheld to avoid disclosure pertaining to a specific organization or individual.

NA Data not enumerated, tabulated, or otherwise available separately.

S Figure does not meet publication standards for reasons other than that covered by symbol B, above.

X Figure not applicable because column heading and stub line make entry impossible, absurd, or meaningless.

Z Entry would amount to less than half the unit of measurement shown.

In many tables, details will not add to the totals shown because of rounding.

Telephone & Internet Contacts

To help *Abstract* users find more data and information about statistical publications, we are issuing this list of contacts for Federal agencies with major statistical programs. The intent is to give a single, first-contact point-of-entry for users of statistics. These agencies will provide general information on their statistical programs and publications, as well as specific information on how to order their publications. We are also including the Internet (World Wide Web) addresses for many of these agencies. These URLs were current in July 2005.

Executive Office of the President
Office of Management and Budget
Administrator
Office of Information and Regulatory
Affairs
Office of Management and Budget
725 17th Street, NW
Washington, DC 20503
Information: 202-395-3080
Internet address:
http://www.whitehouse.gov/omb

Department of Agriculture
Economic Research Service
Information Center
U.S. Department of Agriculture
1800 M Street, NW
Washington, DC 20036-5831
Information and Publications:
202-694-5050
Internet address:
http://www.ers.usda.gov/

National Agricultural Statistics Service
National Agricultural Statistics Service
USDA–NASS
Room 5038-South
Washington, DC 20250
Information hotline: 1-800-727-9540
Internet address:
http://www.usda.gov/nass/

Department of Commerce
U.S. Census Bureau
Customer Services Branch
U.S. Census Bureau
4700 Silver Hill Road
Washington, DC 20233-0001
Information and Publications:
301-763-4636
Internet address:
http://www.census.gov/

Bureau of Economic Analysis
Bureau of Economic Analysis
1441 L Street, NW
Washington, DC 20230
Information and Publications:
202-606-9900
Internet address: http://www.bea.gov/

Department of Commerce —Con.
International Trade Administration
Office of Trade and Economic Analysis
International Trade Administration
Room 2814 B
U.S. Department of Commerce
Washington, DC 20230
Information: 1-800-872-8723
Internet address:
http://www.ita.doc.gov/td/industry/otea

National Oceanic and Atmospheric Administration
National Oceanic and Atmospheric
Administration Central Library
U.S. Department of Commerce
1315 East-West Highway
2nd Floor, SSMC
Silver Spring MD 20910
Library: 301-713-2600
Internet address:
http://www.lib.noaa.gov/

Department of Defense
Department of Defense
Office of the Assistant Secretary of
Defense, Public Affairs, (DPO)
Room 2E588
Attention: Press Operations
1400 Defense Pentagon
Washington, DC 20301-1400
Information: 703-428-0711
Internet address:
http://www.defenselink.mil

Department of Education
National Library of Education
U.S. Department of Education
400 Maryland Avenue, SW
Washington, DC 20202
Education Information and Statistics:
1-800-424-1616
Education Publications:
1-877-433-7827
Internet address:
http://www.ed.gov/

Department of Energy
Energy Information Administration
National Energy Information Center
U.S. Department of Energy
1000 Independence Ave., SW
Room EI-30
Washington, DC 20585
Information and Publications:
202-586-8800
Internet address:
http://www.eia.doe.gov/

Department of Health and Human Services
Health Resources and Services Administration
HRSA Office of Communications
Parklawn Building
5600 Fishers Lane
Rockville, MD 20857
Information Center: 1-888-275-4772
Internet address: http://www.hrsa.gov/

Substance Abuse and Mental Health Services Administration
U.S. Department of Health and Human Services
1 Choke Cherry Road
Room 8-1054
Rockville, MD 20857
Information: 240-276-2000
Publications: 1-800-729-6686
Internet address:
http://www.samhsa.gov/

Centers for Disease Control and Prevention
Public Inquiries/MASO
1600 Clifton Road
Atlanta, GA 30333
Public Inquiries: 1-800-311-3435
Internet address: http://www.cdc.gov/

Centers for Medicare and Medicaid Services (CMS)
U.S. Department of Health and Human Services
7500 Security Boulevard
Baltimore, MD 21244-1850
1-877-267-2323
Internet address:
http://www.cms.hhs.gov/

National Center for Health Statistics
U.S. Department of Health and Human Services - Centers for Disease Control and Prevention
National Center for Health Statistics
Hyattsville, MD 20782
301-458-4000
Internet address:
http://www.cdc.gov/nchs

Department of Homeland Security
U.S. Citizenship and Immigration Services
20 Massachusetts Avenue, NW
Washington, DC 20529
Information and Publications:
1-800-375-5283
Internet address:
http://uscis.gov/graphics/

Department of Housing and Urban Development
Office of the Assistant Secretary for Community Planning and Development
451 7th Street, SW
Washington, DC 20410
Information and Publications:
1-800-998-9999
Internet address:
http://www.hud.gov/

Department of the Interior
U.S. Geological Survey
Earth Science Information Center
12201 Sunrise Valley Drive
Reston, VA 20192
Information and Publications:
1-888-275-8747
Internet address for minerals:
http://minerals.usgs.gov/
Internet address for other materials:
http://ask.usgs.gov/

Department of Justice
Bureau of Justice Statistics
Statistics Division
810 7th Street, NW
Washington, DC 20531
Information and Publications:
1-800-851-3420
Datasets and Codebooks: 1-800-999-0960
Internet address:
http://www.ojp.usdoj.gov/bjs/

National Criminal Justice Reference Service
P.O. Box 6000
Rockville, MD 20849-6000
Information and Publications:
301-519-5500
Publications: 1-800-851-3420
Internet address: http://www.ncjrs.org/

Federal Bureau of Investigation
U.S. Department of Justice
J. Edgar Hoover Building
935 Pennsylvania Avenue, NW
Washington, DC 20535-0001
National Press Office: 202-324-3000
Internet address: http://www.fbi.gov/

Department of Labor
Bureau of Labor Statistics
Office of Publications and Special Studies
Services
Bureau of Labor Statistics
Postal Square Building
2 Massachusetts Avenue, NE
Washington, DC 20212-0001
Information and Publications:
202-691-5200
Internet address: http://www.bls.gov/

Employment and Training Administration
U.S. Department of Labor
Francis Perkins Building
200 Constitution Avenue, NW
Washington, DC 20210
Information and Publications:
1-877-872-5627
Internet address: http://www.doleta.gov/

Department of Transportation
Federal Aviation Administration
U.S. Department of Transportation
800 Independence Avenue, SW
Washington, DC 20591
Information and Publications:
202-267-3484
Internet address: http://www.faa.gov/

Bureau of Transportation Statistics
400 7th Street, SW, Room 3430
Washington, DC 20590
Products and Statistical Information:
800-853-1351
Internet address: http://www.bts.gov/

Federal Highway Administration
Office of Public Affairs
U.S. Department of Transportation
400 7th Street, SW
Washington, DC 20590
Information: 202-366-0660
Internet address:
http://www.fhwa.dot.gov/

*National Highway Traffic Safety
Administration*
Office of Public & Consumer Affairs
U.S. Department of Transportation
400 7th Street, SW
Washington, DC 20590
Information and Publications:
1-888-327-4236
Internet address:
http://www.nhtsa.dot.gov/

Department of the Treasury
Internal Revenue Service
Statistics of Income Division
Internal Revenue Service
P.O. Box 2608
Washington, DC 20013-2608
Information and Publications:
202-874-0410
Internet address:
http://www.irs.gov/taxstats/

Department of Veterans Affairs
Office of Public Affairs
Department of Veterans Affairs
810 Vermont Avenue, NW
Washington, DC 20420
Internet address: http://www.va.gov/

Independent Agencies
Administrative Office of the U.S. Courts
Statistics Division
Washington, DC 20544
Information: 202-502-2600
Internet address:
http://www.uscourts.gov/

Environmental Protection Agency
Environmental Protection Agency Library
1200 Pennsylvania Avenue, NW (3404T)
Washington, DC 20460
Information: 202-566-0556
Internet address: http://www.epa.gov/

Federal Reserve Board
Division of Research and Statistics
Federal Reserve Board
20th & C Streets, NW
Washington, DC 20551
Information: 202-452-3301
Publications: 202-452-3245
Internet address:
http://www.federalreserve.gov/

National Science Foundation
Office of Legislation and Public Affairs
National Science Foundation
4201 Wilson Boulevard
Arlington, VA 22230
Information: 703-292-5111
Publications: 703-292-7827
Internet address: http://www.nsf.gov/

Securities and Exchange Commission
Office of Public Affairs
Securities and Exchange Commission
100 F Street, NE
Washington, DC 20549
Information: 202-942-8088
Publications: 202-551-4040
Internet address: http://www.sec.gov/

Social Security Administration
Social Security Administration
Office of Research, Evaluation and
Statistics
6401 Security Boulevard
Baltimore, MD 21235
Information and Publications: 1-800-772-1213
Internet address:
http://www.socialsecurity.gov/

U.S. Census Bureau, Statistical Abstract of the United States: 2006

Section 1
Population

This section presents statistics on the growth, distribution, and characteristics of the U.S. population. The principal source of these data is the U.S. Census Bureau, which conducts a decennial census of population, a monthly population survey, a program of population estimates and projections, and a number of other periodic surveys relating to population characteristics. For a list of relevant publications, see the Guide to Sources of Statistics in Appendix I.

Decennial censuses—The U.S. Constitution provides for a census of the population every 10 years, primarily to establish a basis for apportionment of members of the House of Representatives among the states. For over a century after the first census in 1790, the census organization was a temporary one, created only for each decennial census. In 1902, the Census Bureau was established as a permanent federal agency, responsible for enumerating the population and also for compiling statistics on other population and housing characteristics.

Historically, the enumeration of the population has been a complete count. That is, an attempt is made to account for every person, for each person's residence, and for other characteristics (sex, age, family relationships, etc.). Since the 1940 census, in addition to the complete count information, some data have been obtained from representative samples of the population. In the 1990 and 2000 censuses, variable sampling rates were employed. For most of the country, 1 in every 6 households (about 17 percent) received the long form or sample questionnaire; in governmental units estimated to have fewer than 2,500 inhabitants, every other household (50 percent) received the sample questionnaire to enhance the reliability of sample data for small areas. Exact agreement is not to be expected between sample data and the 100-percent count. Sample data may be used with confidence where large numbers are involved and assumed to indicate trends and relationships where small numbers are involved.

Current Population Survey (CPS)—This is a monthly nationwide survey of a scientifically selected sample representing the noninstitutionalized civilian population. The sample is located in 754 areas with coverage in every state and the District of Columbia and is subject to sampling error. At the present time, about 60,000 occupied households are eligible for interview every month; of these between 6 and 7 percent are, for various reasons, unavailable for interview.

While the primary purpose of the CPS is to obtain monthly statistics on the labor force, it also serves as a vehicle for inquiries on other subjects. Using CPS data, the Census Bureau issues a series of publications under the general title of *Current Population Reports*, which cover population characteristics (P20), consumer income (P60), special studies (P23), and other topics.

Estimates of population characteristics based on the CPS will not agree with the counts from the census because the CPS and the census use different procedures for collecting and processing the data for racial groups, the Hispanic population, and other topics. Caution should also be used when comparing estimates for various years because of the periodic introduction of changes into the CPS. Beginning in January 1994, a number of changes were introduced into the CPS that effect all data comparisons with prior years. These changes included the results of a major redesign of the survey questionnaire and collection methodology and the introduction of 1990 census population controls, adjusted for the estimated undercount. Beginning with the 2001 CPS Annual Demographic Supplement, the independent estimates used as control totals for the CPS are based on civilian population benchmarks consistent with Census 2000. In March 2002, the sample size of the Annual Demographic Supplement was increased to approximately 78,000. In 2003 the name of the March supplement was changed to Annual Social and Economic Supplement. These changes in population controls had relatively little impact on derived measures such as means, medians, and percent distribution, but did have a significant impact on levels.

American Community Survey (ACS)—This is a nationwide survey to obtain data about demographic, social, economic, and housing information of people, households, and housing units. The survey collects the same type of information that has been collected every 10 years from the long-form questionnaire of the census, which the American Community Survey will replace. The estimates are limited to the household population and exclude the population living in institutions, college dormitories, and other group quarters.

Population estimates and projections—Estimates of the United States population are derived by updating the resident population enumerated in Census 2000 with information on the components of population change: births, deaths, and net international migration. The April 1, 2000, population used in these estimates reflects modifications to the Census 2000 population as documented in the Count Question Resolution program.

Registered births and deaths are estimated from data supplied by the National Center for Health Statistics. The net international component combines three parts: (1) net migration of the foreign-born, (2) emigration of natives, and (3) net movement from Puerto Rico to the United States. The American Community Survey (ACS) is used as the basis for the level of net migration of the foreign-born between 2000 to 2001 and 2001 to 2002 along with estimates developed from the Demographic Analysis and Population Estimates (DAPE) project. (See Deardorff and Blumerman, 2001, "Evaluation Components of International Migration: Estimates of the Foreign-Born Population by Migrant Status in 2000," Population Division Working Paper Series, No. 58.)

Estimates for state and county areas are based on the same components of change data and sources as the national estimates with the addition of net internal migration. School enrollment statistics from state departments of education and parochial school systems, federal income tax returns from the Internal Revenue Service, group quarters data from the Federal-State Cooperative Program, and Medicare data from the Centers for Medicare and Medicaid Services are also included.

The population by age for April 1, 1990, (shown in Table 11) reflects modifications to the 1990 census data counts. The review of detailed 1990 information indicated that respondents tended to report age as of the date of completion of the questionnaire, not as of April 1, 1990. In addition, there may have been a tendency for respondents to round up their age if they were close to having a birthday. A detailed explanation of the age modification procedure appears in 1990 Census of Population and Housing, Data Paper Listing CPH-L74.

Population estimates and projections are available on the Census Bureau Internet site <http://www.census.gov>. These estimates and projections are consistent with official decennial census figures with no adjustment for estimated net census coverage. However, the categories for these estimates and projections by race have been modified and are not comparable to the census race categories (see section below under "Race"). For details on methodology, see the sources cited below the individual tables.

Immigration—Immigration (migration *to* a country) is one component of international migration; the other component is emigration (migration *from* a country). In its simplest form, international migration is defined as any movement across a national border. In the United States, federal statistics on international migration are produced primarily by the U.S. Census Bureau and the Office of Immigration Statistics (located in the Department of Homeland Security).

The Census Bureau collects data used to estimate international migration through its decennial censuses and numerous surveys of the U.S. population.

2 Population

The Office of Immigration Statistics publishes immigration data in the *Yearbook of Immigration Statistics* and collects these data from several administrative records such as the Immigrant Visa and Alien Registration (OF-155, U.S. State Department) for new arrivals, and the Memorandum of Creation of Record of Lawful Permanent Residence (I-181, INS) for persons adjusting migrant status. Immigrants are aliens admitted for legal permanent residence in the United States. The category, immigrant, includes persons who may have entered the United States as nonimmigrants or refugees, but who subsequently changed their status to that of a permanent resident. Nonresident aliens admitted to the United States for a temporary period are nonimmigrants. Refugees are considered nonimmigrants when initially admitted into the United States but are not included in nonimmigrant admission data. A refugee is an alien outside the United States who is unable or unwilling to return to his or her country of nationality because of persecution or a well-founded fear of persecution. After 1 year of residence in the United States, refugees are eligible for immigrant status.

U.S. immigration law gives preferential immigration status to persons with a close family relationship with a U.S. citizen or legal permanent resident, persons with needed job skills, or persons who qualify as refugees. Immigration to the United States can be divided into two general categories: (1) those subject to the annual worldwide limitation and (2) those exempt from it. Numerical limits are imposed on visas issued and not on admissions. The maximum number of visas allowed to be issued under the preference categories in 2004 was 430,422—226,000 for family-sponsored immigrants and 204,422 for employment-based immigrants. Those exempt from the worldwide limitation include immediate relatives of U.S. citizens, refugees and asylees adjusting to permanent residence, and other various classes of special immigrants (see Table 6).

Metropolitan and micropolitan areas—The United States Office of Management and Budget (OMB) defines metropolitan and micropolitan statistical areas according to published standards that are applied to Census Bureau data. The general concept of a metropolitan or micropolitan statistical area is that of a core area containing a substantial population nucleus, together with adjacent communities having a high degree of economic and social integration with that core. Currently defined metropolitan and micropolitan statistical areas are based on application of 2000 standards to 2000 decennial census data as updated by application of those standards to more recent Census Bureau population estimates. The term "metropolitan area" (MA) was used to refer collectively to metropolitan statistical areas (MSAs), consolidated metropolitan statistical areas (CMSAs), and primary metropolitan statistical areas (PMSAs) as defined according to 1980 and 1990 standards. The term "core-based statistical area" (CBSA) became effective in 2003 and refers collectively to metropolitan and micropolitan areas.

Over time, new statistical areas are created and the components of others change. Because of historical changes in geographic definitions, users must be cautious in comparing data for these statistical areas from different dates. For some purposes, comparisons of data for areas as defined at given dates may be appropriate; for other purposes, it may be preferable to maintain consistent area definitions. For descriptive details and a list of titles and components of metropolitan and micropolitan statistical areas, see Appendix II.

Urban and rural—For Census 2000, the Census Bureau classified as urban all territory, population, and housing units located within urbanized areas (UAs) and urban clusters (UCs). A UA consists of densely settled territory that contains 50,000 or more people, while a UC consists of densely settled territory with at least 2,500 people but fewer than 50,000 people. (UCs are a new type of geographic entity for Census 2000.) From the 1950 census through the 1990 census, the urban population consisted of all people living in UAs and most places outside of UAs with a census population of 2,500 or more.

UAs and UCs encompass territory that generally consists of:

U.S. Census Bureau, Statistical Abstract of the United States: 2006

- A cluster of one or more block groups or census blocks each of which has a population density of at least 1,000 people per square mile at the time.
- Surrounding block groups and census blocks each of which has a population density of at least 500 people per square mile at the time.
- Less densely settled blocks that form enclaves or indentations, or are used to connect discontiguous areas with qualifying densities.

They also may include an airport located adjacent to qualifying densely settled area if it has an annual enplanement (aircraft boarding) of at least 10,000 people.

"Rural" for Census 2000 consists of all territory, population, and housing units located outside of UAs and UCs. Prior to Census 2000, rural consisted of all territory, population, and housing outside of UAs and outside of other places designated as "urban." For Census 2000, many more geographic entities, including metropolitan areas, counties, county subdivisions, and places, contain both urban and rural territory, population, and housing units.

Residence—In determining residence, the Census Bureau counts each person as an inhabitant of a usual place of residence (i.e., the place where one usually lives and sleeps most of the time). While this place is not necessarily a person's legal residence or voting residence, the use of these different bases of classification would produce the same results in the vast majority of cases.

Race—For the 1990 census, the Census Bureau collected and published racial statistics as outlined in Statistical Policy Directive No. 15 issued by the U.S. Office of Management and Budget (OMB). This directive provided standards on ethnic and racial categories for statistical reporting to be used by all federal agencies. According to the directive, the basic racial categories were American Indian or Alaska Native, Asian or Pacific Islander, Black, and White. (The directive identified Hispanic origin as an ethnicity.) The question on race for Census 2000 was different from the one for the 1990 census in several ways. Most significantly, respondents were given the option of selecting one or more race categories to indicate their racial identities. Because of these changes, the Census 2000 data on race are not directly comparable with data from the 1990 census or earlier censuses. Caution must be used when interpreting changes in the racial composition of the United States population over time. Census 2000 adheres to the federal standards for collecting and presenting data on race and ethnicity as established by OMB in October 1997. Starting with Census 2000, the OMB requires federal agencies to use a minimum of five race categories: White, Black or African American, American Indian or Alaska Native, Asian, and Native Hawaiian or Other Pacific Islander. Additionally, to collect data on individuals of mixed race parentage, respondents were allowed to select one or more races. For respondents unable to identify with any of these five race categories, OMB approved and included a sixth category— "Some other race" on the Census 2000 questionnaire. The Census 2000 question on race included 15 separate response categories and three areas where respondents could write in a more specific race group. The response categories and write-in answers can be combined to create the five minimum OMB race categories plus "Some other race." People who responded to the question on race by indicating only one race are referred to as the *race alone* population, or the group that reported only one race category. Six categories make up this population: White alone, Black or African American alone, American Indian and Alaska Native alone, Asian alone, Native Hawaiian and Other Pacific Island alone, and Some other race alone. Individuals who chose more than one of the six race categories are referred to as the *Two or More Races* population, or as the group that reported more than one race. Additionally, respondents who reported one race together with those who reported the same race plus one or more other races are combined to create the *race alone or in combination* categories. For example, the *White alone or in combination group* consists of those respondents who reported White combined with one or more other race groups, such as "White and Black or African American," or "White and Asian and American Indian and Alaska Native." Another way to think of the group who reported White alone or in combination is as the total number of people who identified entirely or partially as White. This group is also described as people who reported White, whether or not they reported any other race.

The *alone or in combination* categories are tallies of *responses* rather than *respondents*. That is, the alone or in combination categories are not mutually exclusive. Individuals who reported two races were counted in two separate and distinct alone or in combination race categories, while those who reported three races were counted in three categories, and so on. Consequently, the sum of all alone or in combination categories equals the number of races reported (i.e., responses) which exceeds the total population.

The concept of race, as used by the Census Bureau, reflects self-identification by people according to the race or races with which they most closely identify. These categories are sociopolitical constructs and should not be interpreted as being scientific or anthropological in nature. Furthermore, the race categories include both racial and national-origin groups.

Data for the population by race for April 1, 2000, (shown in Tables 13, 14, and 16) are modified counts and are not comparable to Census 2000 race categories. These numbers were computed using Census 2000 data by race that had been modified to be consistent with the 1997 Office of Management and Budget's, "Revisions to the Standards for the Classification of Federal Data on Race and Ethnicity," (Federal Register Notice, Vol. 62, No 210, October 1997). A detailed explanation of the race modification procedure appears on the Census Web page <http://www.census.gov/popest/topics/methodology/2003_nat_char_meth.html>.

In the CPS and other household sample surveys in which data are obtained through personal interview, respondents are asked to classify their race as: (1) White; (2) Black, African American or Negro; (3) American Indian or Alaska Native; (4) Asian; (5) Native Hawaiian or Other Pacific Islander. Beginning January 2003, respondents were allowed to report more than one race to indicate their mixed racial heritage.

Hispanic population—The Census Bureau collected data on the Hispanic origin population in the 2000 census by using a self-identification question. Persons of Spanish/Hispanic/Latino origin are those who classified themselves in one of the specific Hispanic origin categories listed on the questionnaire—Mexican, Puerto Rican, Cuban, as well as those who indicated that they were of Other Spanish/ Hispanic/Latino origin. Persons of Other Spanish/Hispanic/Latino origin are those whose origins are from Spain, the Spanish-speaking countries of Central or South America, or the Dominican Republic.

In the CPS, information on Hispanic persons is gathered by using a self-identification question. Based on a two-part question, the respondent is first asked whether or not they are of Hispanic, Spanish, or Latino origin and based on their response are further classified into the following categories: Mexican or Mexican-American or Chicano; Puerto Rican; Cuban; Central or South American; or Other Hispanic, Spanish, or Latino origin group.

Traditional and current data collection and classification treat race and Hispanic origin as two separate and distinct concepts in accordance with guidelines from the OMB. Race and Hispanic origin are two separate concepts in the federal statistical system. People who are Hispanic may be any race and people in each race group may be either Hispanic or Not Hispanic. Also, each person has two attributes, their race (or races) and whether or not they are Hispanic. The overlap of race and Hispanic origin is the main comparability issue. For example, Black Hispanics (Hispanic Blacks) are included in both the number of Blacks and in the number of Hispanics. For further information, see Census Web page <http://www.census.gov/population/www/socdemo/compraceho.html>.

Foreign-born and native populations—The Census Bureau separates the U.S. resident population into two groups based on whether or not a person was a U.S. citizen at the time of birth. Anyone born in the United States or a U.S. Island Area (such as Puerto Rico) or born abroad to a U.S. citizen parent is a U.S. citizen at the time of birth and consequently included in the *native population*. The term *foreign-born population* refers to anyone who is not a U.S. citizen at birth. This includes naturalized U.S. citizens, legal permanent resident aliens (immigrants), temporary migrants (such as foreign students), humanitarian migrants (such as refugees), and people illegally present in the United States. The Census Bureau provides a variety of demographic, social, economic, geographic, and housing information on the foreign-born population in the United States. More information on the foreign-born population collected from censuses and surveys is available at <http://www.census.gov /population /www/socdemo/foreign .html>.

Mobility status—The U.S. population is classified according to mobility status on the basis of a comparison between the place of residence of each individual at the time of the survey or census and the place of residence at a specified earlier date. Nonmovers are all persons who were living in the same house or apartment at the end of the period as at the beginning of the period. Movers are all persons who were living in a different house or apartment at the end of the period than at the beginning of the period. Movers are further classified as to whether they were living in the same or different county, state, or region or were movers from abroad. Movers from abroad include all persons, either U.S. citizens or noncitizens, whose place of residence was outside the United States at the beginning of the period; that is, in Puerto Rico, another U.S. Island Area, or a foreign country.

Living arrangements—Living arrangements refer to residency in households or in group quarters. A "household" comprises all persons who occupy a "housing unit," that is, a house, an apartment or other group of rooms, or a single room that constitutes "separate living quarters." A household includes the related family members and all the unrelated persons, if any, such as lodgers, foster children, wards, or employees who share the housing unit. A person living alone or a group of unrelated persons sharing the same housing unit is also counted as a household. See text, Section 20, Construction and Housing, for definition of housing unit.

All persons not living in housing units are classified as living in group quarters. These individuals may be institutionalized, e.g., under care or custody in juvenile facilities, jails, correctional centers, hospitals, or nursing homes; or they may be residents in noninstitutional group quarters such as college dormitories, group homes, or military barracks.

Householder—The householder is the person in whose name the home is owned or rented. If a home is owned or rented jointly by a married couple, either the husband or the wife may be listed first.

Family—The term family refers to a group of two or more persons related by birth, marriage, or adoption and residing together in a household. A family includes among its members the householder.

Subfamily—A subfamily consists of a married couple and their children, if any, or one parent with one or more never-married children under 18 years old living in a household. Subfamilies are divided into "related" and "unrelated" subfamilies. A related subfamily is related to, but does not include, the householder. Members of a related subfamily are also members of the family with whom they live. The number of related subfamilies, therefore, is not included in the count of families. An unrelated subfamily may include persons such as guests, lodgers, or resident employees and their spouses and/or children; none of whom is related to the householder.

Married couple—A married couple is defined as a husband and wife living together in the same household, with or without children and other relatives.

Statistical reliability—For a discussion of statistical collection and estimation, sampling procedures, and measures of statistical reliability applicable to Census Bureau data, see Appendix III.

No. 127.—Number of Alien Passengers Arrived in the United States from Foreign Countries from October 1, 1819, to December 31, 1870.

COUNTRIES.	DECADES.					AGGRE- GATE.
	1820 to 1830.	1831 to 1840.	1841 to 1850.	1851 to 1860.	1861 to 1870.	
England	15,837	7,611	32,092	247,125	213,527	516,192
Ireland a	57,278	198,233	733,434	936,665	714,883	2,700,493
Scotland	3,180	2,667	3,712	38,331	36,733	84,623
Wales	170	185	1,261	6,319	4,500	12,435
Great Britain, not specified	5,362	74,405	277,964	109,653	77,333	544,107
Total from British Isles	81,827	283,191	1,047,763	1,338,093	1,106,976	3,857,850
Germany	7,583	148,204	422,477	907,780	781,456	2,267,500
Prussia	146	4,250	12,149	43,887	40,551	100,983
Austria					9,398	9,398
Sweden and Norway	94	1,201	13,903	20,931	117,799	153,928
Denmark	189	1,063	539	3,749	17,885	23,425
Holland	1,127	1,412	8,251	10,789	9,539	31,118
France	8,868	45,575	77,262	76,358	37,749	245,812
Switzerland	3,257	4,821	4,644	25,011	23,839	61,572
Belgium	28	22	5,074	4,738	7,416	17,278
Spain	2,616	2,125	2,209	9,298	6,966	23,214
Portugal	180	829	550	1,055	2,081	4,695
Italy	389	2,211	1,590	7,012	12,796	23,998
Sardinia	32	7	201	1,790	73	2,103
Sicily	17	35	79	429	115	675
Malta	1	35	78	5	8	127
Corsica	2	5	2		3	12
Greece	20	49	16	31	82	198
Russia in Europe	89	277	551	457	2,671	4,045
Poland	21	369	105	1,164	2,379	4,038
Hungary					488	488
Turkey in Europe	21	7	50	83	137	307
Total from Europe, other than Great Britain	24,680	212,497	549,739	1,114,567	1,073,431	2,974,914
Total from Europe	106,507	495,688	1,597,502	2,452,660	2,180,407	6,832,764

SUMMARY.

Europe	106,507	495,688	1,597,502	2,452,660	2,180,407	6,832,764
Asia	15	48	82	41,455	68,448	110,048
Africa	358	111	62	420	353	1,304
America	11,951	33,424	62,469	74,720	121,041	363,605
Pacific	82	9	29	158	255	533
All other	32,911	69,845	53,107	28,801	60,947	245,611
Aggregate	151,824	599,125	1,713,251	2,598,214	2,491,451	7,553,865

a The natives of Ireland are partly estimated on the basis of data obtained by the Commissioners of Emigration of New York, who have made careful inquiries on this subject. The total from the British Isles, given above, is from official returns to the Bureau of Statistics.

Note.—It is estimated that the number of alien passengers arrived in the United States from 1789 to 1820 amounted to 250,000.

Source: Statistical Abstract of the United States: 1878 Edition.

Table 1. Population and Area: 1790 to 2000

[Area figures represent area on indicated date including in some cases considerable areas not then organized or settled, and not covered by the census. Total area figures for 1790 to 1970 have been recalculated on the basis of the remeasurement of states and counties for the 1980 census, but not on the basis of the 1990 census. The land and water area figures for past censuses have not been adjusted and are not strictly comparable with the total area data for comparable dates because the land areas were derived from different base data, and these values are known to have changed with the construction of reservoirs, draining of lakes, etc. Density figures are based on land area measurements as reported in earlier censuses]

Census date	Resident population					Area (square miles)		
	Number	Per square mile of land area	Increase over preceding census			Total	Land	Water [1]
			Number	Percent				
1790 (Aug. 2).......	3.929.214	4.5	(X)	(X)		891,364	864,746	24,065
1800 (Aug. 4).......	5,308,483	6.1	1,379,269	35.1		891,364	864,746	24,065
1810 (Aug. 6).......	7,239,881	4.3	1,931.398	36.4		1,722.685	1,681.828	34,175
1820 (Aug. 7).......	9,638,453	5.5	2,398,572	33.1		1,792,552	1,749,462	38,544
1830 (June 1)	12,866,020	7.4	3,227,567	33.5		1,792,552	1,749,462	38,544
1840 (June 1)	17,069,453	9.8	4,203.433	32.7		1,792,552	1,749,462	38,544
1850 (June 1)	23,191,876	7.9	6.122,423	35.9		2,991.655	2.940,042	52,705
1860 (June 1)	31,443,321	10.6	8,251,445	35.6		3,021,295	2,969,640	52,747
1870 (June 1)	[2]39,818,449	[2]11.2	8,375,128	26.6		3,612,299	3,540,705	52,747
1880 (June 1)	50,189,209	14.2	10,370,760	26.0		3,612,299	3,540.705	52,747
1890 (June 1)	62,979,766	17.8	12,790.557	25.5		3,612,299	3,540.705	52,747
1900 (June 1)	76,212,168	21.5	13.232,402	21.0		3,618,770	3,547,314	52,553
1910 (Apr. 15)	92,228,496	26.0	16,016,328	21.0		3,618,770	3,547,045	52,822
1920 (Jan. 1).......	106,021,537	29.9	13,793,042	15.0		3,618,770	3,546,931	52,936
1930 (Apr. 1).......	123,202,624	34.7	17,181.087	16.2		3,618,770	3,551,608	45,259
1940 (Apr. 1).......	132,164,569	37.2	8,961,945	7.3		3,618,770	3,551,608	45,259
1950 (Apr. 1).......	151,325,798	42.6	19,161,229	14.5		3,618,770	3,552,206	63,005
1960 (Apr. 1).......	179,323,175	50.6	27,997,377	18.5		3,618,770	3,540,911	74,212
1970 (Apr. 1).......	203,302,031	57.5	23,978,856	13.4		3,618,770	3,536,855	78,444
1980 (Apr. 1).......	[3]226,542,199	64.0	23,240.168	11.4		3,618,770	3,539,289	79,481
1990 (Apr. 1).......	[4]248,718,302	70.3	22,176,103	9.8		[5]3,717,796	3,536,278	[5]181,518
2000 (Apr. 1).......	[6]281,424,602	79.6	32,706,300	13.1		3,794,083	3,537,438	256,645

X Not applicable.   [1] Data for 1790 to 1980 cover inland water only. Data for 1990 comprise Great Lakes, inland, and coastal water. Data for 2000 comprise Great Lakes, inland, territorial, and coastal water.   [2] Revised to include adjustments for underenumeration in southern states; unrevised number is 38,558,371 (10.9 per square mile).   [3] Total population count has been revised since the 1980 census publications. Numbers by age, race, Hispanic origin, and sex have not been corrected.   [4] The April 1, 1990, census count includes count question resolution corrections processed through December 1997, and does not include adjustments for census coverage errors.   [5] Data reflect corrections made after publication of the results.   [6] Reflects modifications to the Census 2000 population as documented in the Count Question Resolution program.

Source: U.S. Census Bureau, 2000 Census of Population and Housing, *Population and Housing Counts*, Series PHC-3-1, United States Summary; and "Table NA-EST2004-01—Monthly Population Estimates for the United States: April 1, 2000, to May 1, 2005"; published 22 December 2004; <http://www.census.gov/popest/national/NA-EST2004-01.html>. Area data for 1990: unpublished data from TIGER (R).

Table 2. Population: 1960 to 2004

[In thousands, except percent (180,671 represents 180,671,000). Estimates as of July 1. Total population includes Armed Forces abroad; civilian population excludes Armed Forces. For basis of estimates, see text of this section]

Year	Total		Resident population	Civilian population	Year	Total		Resident population	Civilian population
	Population	Percent change [1]				Population	Percent change [1]		
1960	180,671	1.60	179,979	178,140	1983	234,307	0.91	233,792	232,097
1961	183,691	1.67	182,992	181,143	1984	236,348	0.87	235,825	234,110
1962	186,538	1.55	185,771	183,677	1985	238,466	0.90	237,924	236,219
1963	189,242	1.45	188,483	186,493	1986	240,651	0.92	240,133	238,412
1964	191,889	1.40	191,141	189,141	1987	242,804	0.89	242,289	240,550
1965	194,303	1.26	193,526	191,605	1988	245,021	0.91	244,499	242,817
1966	196,560	1.16	195,576	193,420	1989	247,342	0.95	246,819	245,131
1967	198,712	1.09	197,457	195,264	1990	250,132	1.13	249,623	247,983
1968	200,706	1.00	199,399	197,113	1991	253,493	1.34	252,981	251,370
1969	202,677	0.98	201,385	199,145	1992	256,894	1.34	256,514	254,929
1970	205,052	1.17	203,984	201,895	1993	260,255	1.31	259,919	258,446
1971	207,661	1.27	206,827	204,866	1994	263,436	1.22	263,126	261,714
1972	209,896	1.08	209,284	207,511	1995	266,557	1.18	266,278	264,927
1973	211,909	0.96	211,357	209,600	1996	269,667	1.17	269,394	268,108
1974	213,854	0.92	213,342	211,636	1997	272,912	1.20	272,647	271,394
1975	215,973	0.99	215,465	213,789	1998	276,115	1.17	275,854	274,633
1976	218,035	0.95	217,563	215,894	1999	279,295	1.15	279,040	277,841
1977	220,239	1.01	219,760	218,106	2000	282,402	1.11	282,192	280,968
1978	222,585	1.06	222,095	220,467	2001	285,329	1.04	285,102	283,887
1979	225,055	1.11	224,567	222,969	2002	288,173	1.00	287,941	286,695
1980	227,726	1.19	227,225	225,621	2003	291,028	0.99	290,789	289,538
1981	229,966	0.98	229,466	227,818	2004	293,907	0.99	293,655	292,414
1982	232,188	0.97	231,664	229,995					

[1] Percent change from immediate preceding year.

Source: U.S. Census Bureau, 1960 to 1979: *Current Population Reports* P25-802 and P25-917; 1980 to 1989: "Monthly Estimates of the United States Population: April 1, 1980, to July 1, 1999, with Short-Term Projections to November 1, 2000"; published 2 January 2001; <http://www.census.gov/popest/archives/1990s/nat-total.txt>; 1990 to 1999: "national intercensal estimates (1990-2000)"; published 13 August 2004; <http://www.census.gov/popest/archives/EST90INTERCENSAL/US-EST90INT-datasets.html>; 2000 to 2004: "Table NA-EST2004-01—Monthly Population Estimates for the United States: April 1, 2000, to May 1, 2005"; published 22 December 2004; <http://www.census.gov/popest/national/NA-EST2004-01.html>.

Table 3. Resident Population Projections: 2005 to 2050

[295,507 represents 295,507,000. As of July 1. The projections are based on assumptions about future childbearing, mortality, and migration. The level of childbearing among women is assumed to remain close to present levels, with differences by race and Hispanic origin diminishing over time. Mortality is assumed to decline gradually with less variation by race and Hispanic origin than at present. International migration is assumed to vary over time and decrease generally relative to the size of the population]

Year	Number (1,000)	Percent change [1]	Year	Number (1,000)	Percent change [1]	Year	Number (1,000)	Percent change [1]
2005	295,507	0.9	2020	335,805	0.8	2035	377,886	0.8
2006	298,217	0.9	2021	338,490	0.8	2036	380,716	0.7
2007	300,913	0.9	2022	341,195	0.8	2037	383,537	0.7
2008	303,598	0.9	2023	343,921	0.8	2038	386,348	0.7
2009	306,272	0.9	2024	346,669	0.8	2039	389,151	0.7
2010	308,936	0.9	2025	349,439	0.8	2040	391,946	0.7
2011	311,601	0.9	2026	352,229	0.8	2041	394,734	0.7
2012	314,281	0.9	2027	355,035	0.8	2042	397,519	0.7
2013	316,971	0.9	2028	357,862	0.8	2043	400,301	0.7
2014	319,668	0.9	2029	360,711	0.8	2044	403,081	0.7
2015	322,366	0.8	2030	363,584	0.8	2045	405,862	0.7
2016	325,063	0.8	2031	366,466	0.8	2046	408,646	0.7
2017	327,756	0.8	2032	369,336	0.8	2047	411,435	0.7
2018	330,444	0.8	2033	372,196	0.8	2048	414,230	0.7
2019	333,127	0.8	2034	375,046	0.8	2049	417,035	0.7
						2050	419,854	0.7

[1] Percent change from immediate preceding year. 2005, change from 2004.

Source: U.S. Census Bureau, "U.S. Interim Projections by Age, Sex, Race, and Hispanic Origin"; published 18 March 2004; <http://www.census.gov/ipc/www/usinterimproj/>.

Table 4. Components of Population Change: 2000 to 2004

[In thousands (281,425 represents 281,425,000), except as indicated. Resident population]

Period	Population as of beginning of period	Net increase		Births	Deaths	Net inter-national migration [2]	Population as of end of period
		Total	Percent [1]				
April 1, 2000 to July 1, 2000 [3]	281,425	768	0.3	989	561	339	282,192
July 1, 2000 to July 1, 2001	282,192	2,910	1.0	4,047	2,419	1,282	285,102
July 1, 2001 to July 1, 2002	285,102	2,839	1.0	4,007	2,430	1,262	287,941
July 1, 2002 to July 1, 2003	287,941	2,848	1.0	4,055	2,433	1,225	290,789
July 1, 2003 to July 1, 2004	290,789	2,866	1.0	4,099	2,454	1,221	293,655

[1] Percent of population at beginning of period.   [2] Includes net migration of the foreign-born, emigration of natives, net movement from Puerto Rico to the United States, and Armed Forces movement.   [3] The April 1, 2000, population estimates base reflects changes to the Census 2000 population from the Count Question Resolution program and geographic program revisions.

Source: U.S. Census Bureau, "Population, Population change and estimated components of population change: April1, 2000 to July1, 2004"; published December 2004; <http://www.census.gov/popest/datasets.html>.

Table 5. Immigration: 1901 to 2004

[In thousands, except rate (8,795 represents 8,795,000). For fiscal years ending in year shown; see text, Section 8. For definition of immigrants, see text of this section. Data represent immigrants admitted. Rates based on Census Bureau estimates as of July 1 for resident population through 1929 and for total population thereafter (excluding Alaska and Hawaii prior to 1959)]

Period	Number	Rate [1]	Year	Number	Rate [1]
1901 to 1910	8,795	10.4	1990	1,536	6.1
1911 to 1920	5,736	5.7	1991	1,827	7.2
1921 to 1930	4,107	3.5	1992	974	3.8
			1993	904	3.5
1931 to 1940	528	0.4	1994	804	3.1
1941 to 1950	1,035	0.7	1995	720	2.7
1951 to 1960	2,515	1.5	1996	916	3.4
			1997	798	2.9
1961 to 1970	3,322	1.7	1998	654	2.4
1971 to 1980	4,493	2.1	1999	647	2.3
1981 to 1990	7,338	3.1	2000	850	3.0
			2001	1,064	3.7
1991 to 2000	9,095	3.4	2002	1,064	3.7
2001 to 2004	3,780	3.3	2003	706	2.4
			2004	946	3.2

[1] Annual rate per 1,000 U.S. population. Rate computed by dividing sum of annual immigration totals by sum of annual U.S. population totals for same number of years.

Source: U.S. Department of Homeland Security, Office of Immigration Statistics, 2004 Yearbook of Immigration Statistics. See also <http://uscis.gov/graphics/shared/statistics/yearbook/index.htm>.

Table 6. Immigrants Admitted by Class of Admission: 1990 to 2004

[For fiscal year ending September 30. For definition of immigrants, see text of this section]

Class of admission	1990	2000	2001	2002	2003	2004
Immigrants, total	1,536,483	849,807	1,064,318	1,063,732	705,827	946,142
New arrivals.	435,729	407,402	411,059	384,427	358,411	362,221
Adjustments.	1,100,754	442,405	653,259	679,305	347,416	583,921
Preference immigrants, total.	272,742	342,304	411,338	362,037	241,031	369,685
Family-sponsored immigrants, total	214,550	235,280	232,143	187,069	158,894	214,355
Unmarried sons/daughters of U.S. citizens and their children	15,861	27,707	27,098	23,567	21,503	26,380
Spouses, unmarried sons/daughters of alien residents and their children.	107,686	124,595	112,260	84,860	53,229	93,609
Married sons/daughters of U.S. citizens [1].	26,751	22,833	24,878	21,072	27,303	28,695
Brothers or sisters of U.S. citizens [1]	64,252	60,145	67,907	57,570	56,859	65,671
Employment-based immigrants, total	58,192	107,024	179,195	174,968	82,137	155,330
Priority workers [1].	(X)	27,706	41,801	34,452	14,544	31,291
Professionals with advanced degrees [1]	(X)	20,304	42,620	44,468	15,459	32,534
Skilled workers, professionals, unskilled workers [1]	(X)	49,736	86,058	88,555	46,613	85,969
Special immigrants [1]	4,463	9,052	8,523	7,344	5,456	5,407
Employment creation [1]	(X)	226	193	149	65	129
Professional or highly skilled immigrants [1, 2] . . .	26,546	(X)	(X)	(X)	(X)	(X)
Needed skilled or unskilled workers [1, 2]	27,183	(X)	(X)	(X)	(X)	(X)
Immediate relatives.	231,680	347,870	443,035	485,960	332,657	406,074
Spouses of U.S. citizens	125,426	197,525	270,545	294,798	184,741	252,193
Children of U.S. citizens.	46,065	82,726	91,526	97,099	78,024	76,347
Orphans	7,088	18,120	19,087	21,100	21,320	11,170
Parents of U.S. citizens	60,189	67,619	80,964	94,063	69,892	77,534
Refugees and asylees.	97,364	65,941	108,506	126,084	44,927	71,230
Refugee adjustments.	92,427	59,083	97,305	115,832	34,496	61,013
Asylee adjustments.	4,937	6,858	11,201	10,252	10,431	10,217
Immigration Reform and Control Act of 1986 legalization adjustments.	880,372	421	263	55	39	128
Other immigrants	54,325	93,271	101,176	89,596	87,173	99,025
Diversity programs [3]	29,161	50,945	42,015	42,829	46,347	50,084
Amerasians (P.L. 100-202) [4]	13,059	943	376	348	120	32
Children born abroad to alien residents.	2,410	1,009	929	788	746	707
Legalization dependents [5]	(X)	55	37	57	21	22
Nicaraguan Adjustment and Central American Relief, Sec. 202 entrants (P.L. 105-100)	(X)	23,641	18,926	9,495	2,577	2,292
Cancellation of removal [6]	889	12,349	22,506	23,827	29,109	32,702
Other	8,806	4,329	16,387	12,252	8,253	13,186

X Not applicable. [1] Includes spouses and children. [2] Category was eliminated in 1992 by the Immigration Act of 1990. [3] Includes categories of immigrants admitted under three laws intended to diversify immigration: P.L. 99-603, P.L. 100-658, and P.L. 101-649. [4] Under Public Law 100-202, Amerasians are aliens born in Vietnam between January 1, 1962, and January 1, 1976, who were fathered by U.S. citizens. [5] Spouses and children of persons granted permanent resident status under provisions of the Immigration Reform and Control Act of 1986. [6] Was suspension of deportation prior to April 1, 1997.

Source: U.S. Department of Homeland Security, Office of Immigration Statistics, *2004 Yearbook of Immigration Statistics.* See also <http://uscis.gov/graphics/shared/statistics/yearbook/index.htm>.

Table 7. Estimated Unauthorized Immigrants by Selected States and Countries of Origin: 2000

[In thousands (7,000 represents 7,000,000). As of January. Unauthorized immigrants refers to foreign-born persons who entered without inspection or who violated the terms of a temporary admission and who have not acquired legal permanent resident status or gained temporary protection against removal by applying for an immigration benefit. The estimates were derived using the residual technique: the legally-resident population was estimated and then subtracted from the census-based foreign-born population, leaving estimated unauthorized residents as a residual. The estimates rely primarily on data from two sources: 1) annual INS statistics (immigrants admitted, deportable aliens removed, and nonimmigrant residents admitted); and 2) data for the foreign-born population from the 2000 census. Estimates were derived separately for: (1) unauthorized residents who entered the United States in the 1990s; and (2) those who entered before 1990 and still lived here illegally in January 2000]

State	Number	Country	Number
United States, total [1]	7,000	Total [1]	7,000
California	2,209	Mexico	4,808
Texas.	1,041	El Salvador	189
New York	489	Guatemala	144
Illinois	432	Colombia	141
Florida	337	Honduras.	[2]138
Arizona.	283	China	115
Georgia	228	Ecuador	108
New Jersey.	221	Dominican Republic.	91
North Carolina	206	Philippines	85
Colorado.	144	Brazil	77
Washington.	136	Haiti	76
Virginia.	103	India	70
Nevada	101	Peru	61
Oregon.	90	Korea	55
Massachusetts.	87	Canada	47

[1] Includes other states and countries not shown separately. [2] Includes 105,000 Hondurans granted temporary protected status in December 1998.

Source: U.S. Department of Homeland Security, Office of Immigration Statistics, *2002 Yearbook of Immigration Statistics.* See also <http://uscis.gov/graphics/shared/aboutus/statistics/ybpage.htm>.

10   Population

U.S. Census Bureau. Statistical Abstract of the United States: 2006

Table 8. Immigrants by Country of Birth: 1981 to 2004

[In thousands (7,338.1 represents 7,338,100). For fiscal years ending September 30. For definition of immigrants, see text, this section]

Country of birth	1981-1990, total	1991-2000, total	2001-2003, total	2004	Country of birth	1981-1990, total	1991-2000, total	2001-2003, total	2004
All countries. . . .	7,338.1	9,095.4	2,833.9	946.1	Philippines	495.3	505.6	149.9	57.8
					Syria	20.6	26.1	7.9	2.3
Europe [1]	705.6	1,311.4	450.3	127.7	Taiwan	([5])	106.4	29.0	9.0
Albania	(NA)	26.2	11.5	3.8	Thailand	64.4	48.4	11.6	4.3
Armenia	(X)	[2]26.6	4.9	1.8	Turkey	20.9	26.3	9.7	3.8
Belarus	(X)	[2]29.0	7.7	2.1	Vietnam	401.4	421.1	91.3	31.5
Bosnia and					Africa [1]	192.3	383.0	163.0	66.3
Herzegovina	(X)	[2]39.1	55.2	10.6	Egypt.	31.4	46.7	13.4	5.5
Bulgaria	(NA)	23.2	11.9	4.2	Ethiopia	27.2	49.3	19.3	8.2
France.	23.1	27.5	10.8	3.6	Ghana	14.9	35.6	12.7	5.3
Germany	70.1	67.7	23.9	7.1	Nigeria	35.3	67.3	24.3	9.4
Ireland	32.8	59.0	3.9	1.5	Somalia	(NA)	20.2	10.0	3.9
Italy.	32.9	22.6	7.4	2.3	Oceania	(NA)	48.0	16.0	6.0
Poland.	97.4	169.6	35.1	14.3	North America [1]. . . .	3,125.0	3,917.4	1,063.1	341.2
Portugal.	40.0	22.8	3.8	1.1	Canada	119.2	137.6	52.9	15.6
Romania	38.9	57.5	15.2	4.6	Mexico.	1,653.3	2,251.4	541.7	175.4
Russia	(X)	[2]128.0	55.2	13.4	Caribbean [1]	892.7	996.1	268.9	88.9
Serbia and					Cuba	159.2	180.9	65.3	20.5
Montenegro [3, 4] . . .	19.2	25.9	19.6	3.3	Dominican				
Soviet Union [3]	84.0	[?]103.9	6.2	0.9	Republic	251.8	340.9	70.1	30.5
Ukraine	(X)	[2]141.3	53.9	13.7	Haiti.	140.2	181.8	59.7	14.0
United Kingdom. . . .	142.1	[?]135.8	44.5	14.9	Jamaica	213.8	173.5	43.7	14.4
Uzbekistan	(X)	[2]22.9	5.8	2.0	Trinidad and				
Asia [1]	2,817.4	2,892.2	936.6	330.0	Tobago	39.5	63.3	16.6	5.4
Bangladesh	15.2	66.0	17.3	8.1	Central America [1] . . .	458.7	531.8	199.5	61.3
Cambodia.	116.6	18.5	7.6	3.5	El Salvador	214.6	217.4	90.7	29.8
China	[5]388.8	424.6	158.4	51.2	Guatemala	87.9	103.1	44.2	18.0
Hong Kong	63.0	74.0	18.0	4.0	Honduras	49.5	66.8	17.7	5.5
India	261.9	383.3	191.8	70.1	Nicaragua	44.1	97.7	34.9	4.0
Iran	154.8	112.6	30.8	10.4	Panama	29.0	24.0	4.8	1.4
Iraq	19.6	40.7	12.6	3.5	South America [1]	455.9	539.9	198.6	71.8
Israel.	36.3	32.0	10.4	4.2	Argentina	25.7	24.3	10.2	4.8
Japan	43.2	61.5	23.9	7.7	Brazil.	23.7	52.3	25.3	10.5
Jordan [6].	32.6	39.7	11.5	3.4	Colombia	124.4	131.0	50.4	18.7
Korea	338.8	171.3	54.3	19.8	Ecuador	56.0	76.4	27.4	8.6
Laos	145.6	43.6	3.6	1.1	Guyana	95.4	73.9	25.1	6.3
Lebanon.	41.6	43.5	11.5	3.8	Peru	64.4	105.7	32.6	11.8
Pakistan.	61.3	124.6	39.6	12.1	Venezuela	17.9	29.9	14.5	6.2

NA Not available.   X Not applicable.   [1] Includes countries not shown separately.   [2] Covers years 1992-2000.   [3] Prior to 1992, data include independent republics; beginning in 1992, data are for unknown republic only.   [4] Yugoslavia (unknown republic) prior to February 7, 2003.   [5] Data for Taiwan included with China.   [6] Prior to 2003, includes Palestine; beginning in 2003, Palestine included in Unknown.

Source: U.S. Department of Homeland Security, Office of Immigration Statistics, 2004 Yearbook of Immigration Statistics. See also <http://uscis.gov/graphics/shared/statistics/yearbook/index.htm>.

Table 9. Immigrants Admitted as Permanent Residents Under Refugee Acts by Country of Birth: 1991 to 2003

[For fiscal years ending September 30]

Country of birth	1991-2000, total	2001-2002, total	2003	Country of birth	1991-2000, total	2001-2002, total	2003
Total [1]	1,021,266	234,590	44,927	Cambodia	6,388	122	38
				China [5]	7,608	1,508	805
Europe [1]	426,565	118,736	17,290	India	2,544	2,500	1,517
Albania.	3,255	284	350	Iran	24,313	6,170	2,030
Azerbaijan.	[2]12,072	973	275	Iraq	22,557	6,494	1,223
Belarus.	[2]24,581	2,994	523	Laos	37,265	894	191
Bosnia and				Syria	2,125	588	308
Herzegovina	[2]37,591	48,336	5,847	Thailand	22,759	1,151	224
Croatia	1,807	5,652	814	Vietnam	206,857	17,277	1,581
Germany	1,093	3,234	484	Africa [1]	51,649	20,360	7,723
Kazakhstan	[2]4,269	1,307	176	Ethiopia [6]	17,865	2,778	1,225
Latvia.	2,757	329	54	Liberia	3,839	2,656	883
Moldova	[2]11,717	2,658	422	Somalia	16,837	6,568	2,157
Poland	7,500	125	31	Sudan	5,191	2,580	1,107
Romania.	15,708	204	94	Oceania	291	52	18
Russia	60,404	9,847	1,738	North America [1]	185,333	51,503	8,454
Serbia and				Cuba	144,612	47,580	7,047
Montenegro [3, 4] . . .	6,274	12,746	1,513	Haiti	9,364	1,504	472
Soviet Union [3]	90,533	3,129	610	El Salvador	4,073	382	194
Ukraine.	[2]109,739	21,731	3,350	Guatemala	2,033	809	294
Uzbekistan	[2]19,539	2,137	318	Nicaragua	22,486	631	169
Asia [1]	351,347	41,406	9,885	South America [1]	5,857	2,158	1,518
Afghanistan	9,725	1,301	716	Peru	2,507	801	457

[1] Includes other countries and unknown, not shown separately.   [2] Covers years 1992-2000.   [3] Prior to 1992, data include independent republics; beginning in 1992, data are for unknown republic only.   [4] Yugoslavia (unknown republic) prior to February 7, 2003.   [5] Includes Taiwan.   [6] Prior to 1993, data include Eritrea.

Source: U.S. Department of Homeland Security, Office of Immigration Statistics, 2003 Yearbook of Immigration Statistics. See also <http://uscis.gov/graphics/shared/statistics/yearbook/index.htm>.

Population   11

Table 10. **Immigrants Admitted by State and Leading Country of Birth: 2003**

[For year ending September 30. Revised data; numbers won't agree with Tables 5, 6, and 8. For definition of immigrants, see text of this section]

State and other area	Total [1]	Mexico	India	Philip-pines	China	El Salvador	Domini-can Republic	Vietnam	Colombia
Total	703,542	115,585	50,228	45,250	40,568	28,231	26,159	22,087	14,720
Alabama...........	1,689	250	114	77	113	13	8	65	37
Alaska	1,188	69	14	405	43	11	33	22	35
Arizona............	10,955	5,722	322	433	299	146	18	278	104
Arkansas...........	1,903	688	84	72	63	351	-	74	8
California	175,579	51,269	9,508	18,134	11,573	13,683	86	9,230	1,077
Colorado...........	10,661	3,275	468	240	632	156	10	418	129
Connecticut.........	8,274	84	722	299	403	46	298	129	399
Delaware	1,487	101	244	61	99	26	23	21	19
District of Columbia	2,491	29	85	215	132	416	63	28	28
Florida............	52,770	1,567	1,219	1,668	694	411	1,627	571	4,983
Georgia	10,794	1,482	1,023	340	387	133	74	447	219
Hawaii	4,899	51	13	3,050	397	3	-	175	7
Idaho.............	1,686	586	38	56	107	12	3	25	16
Illinois	32,413	6,044	4,536	2,116	1,609	251	68	391	237
Indiana............	5,241	901	437	230	346	100	31	105	56
Iowa.............	3,419	693	215	77	307	86	5	190	28
Kansas............	3,804	883	415	134	212	77	13	240	49
Kentucky	3,038	232	248	150	194	11	11	81	37
Louisiana	2,214	133	171	101	118	16	16	225	51
Maine.............	992	17	28	84	95	17	6	37	8
Maryland	17,770	324	1,339	1,284	1,071	1,440	180	329	200
Massachusetts........	20,127	124	1,463	350	1,718	829	1,958	683	372
Michigan...........	13,515	625	1,864	451	762	37	53	237	63
Minnesota..........	8,406	398	651	419	386	57	18	364	96
Mississippi	729	77	74	49	44	8	(D)	57	18
Missouri...........	6,160	439	449	261	379	25	27	265	56
Montana...........	453	23	4	30	28	-	(D)	3	7
Nebraska	2,827	882	119	70	108	93	(D)	212	28
Nevada	6,336	1,730	83	1,159	232	420	17	87	70
New Hampshire......	1,868	22	206	101	174	9	69	23	46
New Jersey.........	40,699	569	7,442	2,639	1,688	631	3,956	431	1,922
New Mexico.........	2,336	1,256	77	65	56	12	3	84	27
New York	89,538	1,198	4,138	1,830	8,356	4,065	13,335	463	2,069
North Carolina.......	9,451	1,175	868	419	749	181	68	323	222
North Dakota........	331	9	14	14	11	-	(D)	12	7
Ohio	9,787	274	1,743	417	767	29	64	182	78
Oklahoma...........	2,385	543	175	107	91	10	6	191	35
Oregon............	6,946	1,487	336	301	503	71	3	430	35
Pennsylvania........	14,606	514	1,964	473	1,314	71	551	567	232
Rhode Island........	2,492	30	71	48	94	56	621	28	160
South Carolina.......	1,942	186	198	209	105	6	7	44	72
South Dakota	487	33	27	24	26	(D)	-	15	(D)
Tennessee	3,367	281	308	221	203	66	12	110	28
Texas.............	53,412	25,342	2,770	1,995	1,221	2,369	136	2,201	734
Utah	3,159	755	65	74	166	78	10	129	39
Vermont	550	5	30	16	38	3	(D)	19	6
Virginia............	19,726	474	2,036	1,154	1,000	1,581	91	691	280
Washington.........	17,935	1,965	1,231	1,626	960	86	15	1,076	96
West Virginia........	483	13	87	32	32	3	4	10	6
Wisconsin..........	4,357	603	453	228	345	15	26	56	49
Wyoming	253	75	4	17	21	-	-	5	3
Armed Services posts ...	117	(D)	(D)	27	7	(D)	(D)	3	3
U.S. Possessions......	5,488	77	31	1,197	90	11	2,523	8	132
Unknown	7	-	(D)	(D)	-	-	3	-	-

- Represents zero.   D Data withheld to avoid disclosure.   [1] Includes other countries, not shown separately.

Source: U.S. Dept. of Homeland Security, Office of Immigration Statistics, *2003 Yearbook of Immigration Statistics,* Supplemental Tables, Table 1; <http://uscis.gov/graphics/shared/statistics/yearbook/YrBk03lm.htm>.

Table 11. Resident Population by Age and Sex: 1980 to 2004

[In thousands, except as indicated (226,546 represents 226,546,000). 1980, 1990, and 2000 data are enumerated population as of April 1; data for other years are estimated population as of July 1. Excludes Armed Forces overseas. For definition of median, see Guide to Tabular Presentation]

Age group	1980[1] Total	1980 Male	1980 Female	1990[2] Total	1990 Male	1990 Female	1995 total	1998 total	1999 total	2000[3] Total	2000 Male	2000 Female	2001 total	2002 total	2003 total	2004 Total	2004 Male	2004 Female
Total	226,546	110,053	116,493	248,791	121,284	127,507	266,278	275,854	279,040	281,425	138,056	143,368	285,102	287,941	290,789	293,655	144,537	149,118
Under 5 years	16,348	8,362	7,986	18,765	9,603	9,162	19,627	19,145	19,136	19,185	9,816	9,370	19,361	19,548	19,791	20,071	10,263	9,808
5 to 9 years	16,700	8,539	8,161	18,042	9,236	8,806	19,438	20,510	20,606	20,550	10,524	10,027	20,234	19,961	19,745	19,606	10,029	9,576
10 to 14 years	18,242	9,316	8,926	17,067	8,742	8,325	19,207	19,825	20,213	20,530	10,521	10,009	20,890	21,117	21,208	21,145	10,831	10,314
15 to 19 years	21,168	10,755	10,413	17,893	9,178	8,714	18,374	19,840	20,085	20,221	10,392	9,829	20,294	20,351	20,472	20,730	10,635	10,094
20 to 24 years	21,319	10,663	10,655	19,143	9,749	9,394	18,300	18,167	18,591	18,961	9,687	9,274	19,799	20,329	20,758	20,971	10,803	10,168
25 to 29 years	19,521	9,705	9,816	21,336	10,708	10,629	18,680	18,804	19,575	19,384	9,800	9,583	18,936	18,907	19,123	19,561	9,995	9,566
30 to 34 years	17,561	8,677	8,884	21,838	10,866	10,973	22,372	20,953	20,603	20,511	10,322	10,189	20,730	20,520	20,341	20,471	10,341	10,130
35 to 39 years	13,965	6,862	7,104	19,851	9,879	10,014	22,492	22,926	22,883	22,709	11,320	11,389	22,279	21,837	21,408	21,052	10,571	10,482
40 to 44 years	11,669	5,708	5,961	17,593	8,679	8,914	20,219	21,822	22,184	22,441	11,129	11,312	22,843	22,945	22,988	23,056	11,463	11,593
45 to 49 years	11,090	5,388	5,702	13,747	6,741	7,006	17,624	19,114	19,654	20,091	9,889	10,202	20,709	21,273	21,763	22,123	10,918	11,205
50 to 54 years	11,710	5,621	6,089	11,315	5,494	5,821	13,856	16,118	16,924	17,583	8,606	8,976	18,662	18,695	19,039	19,496	9,535	9,961
55 to 59 years	11,615	5,482	6,133	10,489	5,009	5,480	11,182	12,589	13,085	13,469	6,508	6,960	13,933	15,082	15,722	16,490	8,001	8,488
60 to 64 years	10,088	4,670	5,418	10,627	4,947	5,679	10,138	10,422	10,693	10,804	5,136	5,668	11,104	11,500	12,110	12,589	5,998	6,591
65 to 74 years	15,581	6,757	8,824	18,048	7,908	10,140	18,866	18,570	18,419	18,390	8,303	10,087	18,321	18,280	18,344	18,463	8,428	10,036
75 to 84 years	7,729	2,867	4,862	10,014	3,745	6,268	11,222	12,016	12,225	12,359	4,878	7,481	12,590	12,759	12,881	12,971	5,218	7,753
85 years and over	2,240	682	1,559	3,022	841	2,181	3,681	4,033	4,154	4,237	1,226	3,011	4,417	4,546	4,718	4,860	1,508	3,352
5 to 13 years	31,159	15,923	15,237	31,839	16,301	15,538	34,825	36,454	36,804	37,028	18,965	18,063	37,077	36,966	36,757	36,376	18,617	17,759
14 to 17 years	16,247	8,298	7,950	13,345	6,860	6,485	15,013	15,829	16,007	16,094	8,285	7,809	16,172	16,350	16,502	16,831	8,625	8,206
18 to 24 years	30,022	15,054	14,969	26,961	13,744	13,217	25,482	26,059	26,685	27,139	13,872	13,267	27,968	28,442	28,924	29,245	15,057	14,189
18 years and over	162,791	77,473	85,321	184,841	88,519	96,322	196,814	204,426	207,094	209,117	100,990	108,127	212,492	215,077	217,739	220,377	107,032	113,345
55 years and over	47,253	20,458	26,796	52,200	22,450	29,748	55,089	57,630	58,576	59,259	26,051	33,208	60,366	62,167	63,776	65,373	29,153	36,220
65 years and over	25,550	10,306	15,245	31,084	12,494	18,589	33,769	34,619	34,798	34,986	14,407	20,579	35,328	35,585	35,943	36,294	15,154	21,140
75 years and over	9,969	3,549	6,421	13,036	4,586	8,449	14,903	16,049	16,379	16,596	6,104	10,492	17,007	17,305	17,599	17,831	6,726	11,104
Median age (years)	30.0	28.8	31.3	32.8	31.6	34.0	34.2	34.9	35.2	35.3	34.0	36.5	35.6	35.7	35.9	36.0	34.7	37.4

[1] Total population count has been revised since the 1980 census publications. Numbers by age and sex have not been corrected. [2] The data shown have been modified from the official 1990 census counts. See text of this section for explanation. The April 1, 1990, estimates base (248,790,925) includes count resolution corrections processed through August 1997. It generally does not include adjustments for census coverage errors. However, it includes adjustments estimated for the 1995 Test Census in various localities in California, and Louisiana; and the 1998 census dress rehearsals in localities in California and Wisconsin. These adjustments amounted to a total of 81,052 persons. [3] The April 1, 2000, population. Population Estimates base reflects changes to the Census 2000 population from the Count Question Resolution program and geographic program revisions.

Source: U.S. Census Bureau, Current Population Reports, P25-1095; "Table US-EST90INT-04 - Intercensal Estimates of the United States Resident Population by Age Groups and Sex: 1990-2000: Selected Months"; published 13 September 2002; <http://www.census.gov/popest/archives/EST90INTERCENSAL/US-EST90INT-04.html>; "Table 1: Annual Estimates of the Population by Sex and Five-Year Age Groups for the United States: April 1, 2000, to July 1, 2004"; published 9 June 2005; <http://www.census.gov/popest/national/asrh/NC-EST2004-sa.html>.

Table 12. Resident Population Projections by Sex and Age: 2005 to 2050

[In thousands, except as indicated (295,507 represents 295,507,000). As of July 1. For assumptions, see Table 3. For definition of median, see Guide to Tabular Presention]

Age	2005 Total	2005 Male	2005 Female	2010 Total	2010 Male	2010 Female	2015	2020	2025	2030	2035	2040	2045	2050	% 2005	% 2010	% 2015	% 2020	% 2025	% 2030	% 2035	% 2040	% 2045	% 2050
Total	295,507	145,113	150,394	308,936	151,815	157,121	322,366	335,805	349,439	363,584	377,886	391,946	405,862	419,854	100.0	100.0	100.0	100.0	100.0	100.0	100.0	100.0	100.0	100.0
Under 5 years	20,495	10,471	10,024	21,426	10,947	10,479	21,623	22,932	23,518	24,272	25,262	26,299	27,233	28,080	6.9	6.9	6.7	6.8	6.7	6.7	6.7	6.7	6.7	6.7
5 to 9 years	19,467	9,954	9,512	20,706	10,575	10,131	20,984	21,478	22,888	23,790	24,562	25,550	26,586	27,521	6.6	6.7	6.5	6.4	6.5	6.5	6.5	6.5	6.6	6.6
10 to 14 years	20,838	10,670	10,167	19,767	10,109	9,658	20,243	20,984	22,457	23,163	24,186	24,953	25,938	26,974	7.1	6.4	6.3	6.2	6.4	6.4	6.4	6.4	6.4	6.4
15 to 19 years	21,172	10,862	10,310	21,336	10,938	10,398	21,810	20,751	22,052	23,503	24,182	24,824	25,587	26,572	7.2	6.9	6.8	6.2	6.3	6.5	6.4	6.3	6.3	6.3
20 to 24 years	20,823	10,657	10,166	21,676	11,075	10,602	21,858	22,361	22,955	23,136	23,943	24,897	25,534	26,297	7.0	7.0	6.8	6.7	6.6	6.4	6.3	6.4	6.3	6.3
25 to 29 years	19,753	10,016	9,737	21,375	10,868	10,507	22,195	22,704	23,046	22,810	23,605	25,024	25,690	26,327	6.7	6.9	6.9	6.8	6.6	6.3	6.2	6.4	6.3	6.3
30 to 34 years	19,847	9,987	9,860	20,272	10,238	10,034	20,543	22,143	23,399	23,399	22,627	24,731	25,808	26,477	6.7	6.6	6.4	6.6	6.7	6.4	6.0	6.3	6.4	6.3
35 to 39 years	20,869	10,449	10,420	20,137	10,091	10,046	20,250	20,673	23,277	23,277	23,669	24,101	25,223	26,300	7.1	6.5	6.3	6.2	6.7	6.4	6.3	6.1	6.2	6.3
40 to 44 years	22,735	11,282	11,452	20,985	10,462	10,523	20,926	20,219	20,678	23,669	23,350	22,907	25,808	26,476	7.7	6.8	6.5	6.0	5.9	6.5	6.2	5.8	6.4	6.3
45 to 49 years	22,453	11,076	11,377	22,654	11,190	11,464	22,376	20,702	20,043	23,350	23,641	23,747	24,376	24,466	7.6	7.3	6.9	6.2	5.7	6.4	6.3	6.1	6.0	6.3
50 to 54 years	19,983	9,771	10,212	22,173	10,874	11,299	22,654	22,143	20,291	20,550	20,241	23,234	23,001	24,917	6.8	7.2	7.0	6.6	5.8	5.7	5.4	5.9	5.7	6.1
55 to 59 years	17,359	8,415	8,944	19,507	9,456	10,051	21,649	21,876	21,128	19,702	19,156	21,910	22,916	24,352	5.9	6.3	6.7	6.5	6.0	5.4	5.1	5.6	5.6	5.8
60 to 64 years	13,017	6,203	6,814	16,679	7,982	8,696	18,761	20,856	19,647	19,676	18,683	19,719	21,370	23,337	4.4	5.4	5.8	6.2	5.6	5.4	4.9	5.0	5.3	5.6
65 to 69 years	10,123	4,712	5,412	12,172	5,686	6,486	15,621	17,618	16,041	19,980	18,350	17,233	18,829	22,384	3.4	3.9	4.8	5.2	4.6	5.5	4.9	4.4	4.6	5.3
70 to 74 years	8,500	3,804	4,697	9,097	4,111	4,987	10,987	14,161	12,268	13,989	15,764	16,192	16,879	20,444	2.9	2.9	3.4	4.2	3.5	3.8	4.2	4.1	4.2	4.9
75 to 79 years	7,376	3,094	4,282	7,186	3,066	4,120	7,761	9,450	7,557	9,914	11,414	12,978	15,304	15,067	2.5	2.3	2.4	2.8	2.2	2.7	3.0	3.3	3.8	3.6
80 to 84 years	5,576	2,117	3,459	5,665	2,206	3,459	5,600	6,134	4,353	5,451	7,259	8,476	13,449	12,835	1.9	1.8	1.7	1.8	1.2	1.5	1.9	2.2	3.3	3.1
85 to 89 years	3,206	1,072	2,135	3,713	1,274	2,439	3,857	3,897	2,312	2,651	3,395	4,621	9,768	10,254	1.1	1.2	1.2	1.2	0.7	0.7	0.9	1.2	2.4	2.4
90 to 94 years	1,431	397	1,034	1,727	510	1,218	2,069	2,221	1,018	1,102	1,310	1,581	5,510	6,473	0.5	0.6	0.6	0.7	0.3	0.3	0.3	0.4	1.4	1.5
95 to 99 years	412	91	321	569	137	432	723	909	327	399	467	581	2,440	2,984	0.1	0.2	0.2	0.3	0.1	0.1	0.1	0.1	0.6	0.7
100 years and over	71	12	58	114	21	93	173	241	280	399	467	581	790	1,150	(Z)	(Z)	0.1	0.1	0.1	0.1	0.1	0.1	0.2	0.3
5 to 13 years	35,968	18,402	17,566	36,439	18,618	17,821	38,418	40,148	41,501	42,627	43,922	45,536	47,379	49,138	12.2	11.8	11.9	12.0	11.9	11.7	11.6	11.6	11.7	11.7
14 to 17 years	17,175	8,809	8,366	16,566	8,492	8,074	16,243	17,220	18,079	18,809	19,311	19,847	20,505	21,330	5.8	5.4	5.0	5.1	5.2	5.2	5.1	5.1	5.1	5.1
18 to 24 years	29,156	14,931	14,225	30,481	15,587	14,894	30,000	29,339	30,980	32,533	33,924	34,841	35,763	36,895	9.9	9.9	9.3	8.7	8.9	8.9	9.0	8.9	8.8	8.8
16 years and over	230,335	111,774	118,561	242,936	118,082	124,854	253,361	264,085	275,339	287,281	299,051	310,182	320,974	331,940	77.9	78.6	78.6	78.6	78.8	79.0	79.1	79.1	79.1	79.1
18 years and over	221,868	107,430	114,438	234,504	113,758	120,746	245,347	255,505	266,341	277,877	289,391	300,264	310,746	321,305	75.1	75.9	76.1	76.1	76.2	76.4	76.6	76.6	76.6	76.5
16 to 64 years	193,639	96,475	97,164	202,693	101,071	101,622	206,570	209,453	211,815	215,828	222,410	230,132	238,015	245,234	65.5	65.6	64.1	62.4	60.6	59.4	58.9	58.7	58.6	58.4
55 years and over	67,072	29,916	37,156	76,429	34,450	41,980	87,201	97,363	104,944	110,831	116,039	121,679	127,245	132,427	22.7	24.7	27.1	29.0	30.0	30.5	30.7	31.0	31.4	31.5
65 years and over	36,696	15,299	21,397	40,244	17,011	23,233	46,791	54,632	63,524	71,453	76,641	80,050	82,959	86,706	12.4	13.0	14.5	16.3	18.2	19.7	20.3	20.4	20.4	20.7
75 years and over	18,072	6,783	11,289	18,974	7,214	11,760	20,183	22,852	27,835	33,506	39,609	44,579	47,251	48,763	6.1	6.1	6.3	6.8	8.0	9.2	10.5	11.4	11.6	11.6
85 years and over	5,120	1,572	3,548	6,123	1,942	4,182	6,822	7,269	8,011	9,603	12,430	15,409	18,498	20,861	1.7	2.0	2.1	2.2	2.3	2.6	3.3	3.9	4.6	5.0
Median age (years)	35.2	34.0	36.6	36.0	34.6	37.4	36.4	37.0	37.5	38.0	38.2	38.1	38.1	38.1	(X)	(X)	(X)	(X)	(X)	(X)	(X)	(X)	(X)	(X)

X Not applicable. Z Less than 0.05 percent.

Source: U.S. Census Bureau. "U.S. Interim Projections by Age, Sex, Race, and Hispanic Origin"; published March 2004; <http://www.census.gov/ipc/www/usinterimproj/>.

14   Population

Table 13. **Resident Population by Sex, Race, and Hispanic Origin Status: 2000 to 2004**

[281,425 represents 281,425,000. **As of July, except as noted.** Data shown are modified race counts: see text, this section]

Characteristic	Number (1,000)					Percent change, 2000 to 2004
	2000 [1] (April 1)	2001	2002	2003	2004	
BOTH SEXES						
Total	281,425	285,102	287,941	290,789	293,655	4.3
One race	277,527	281,048	283,761	286,481	289,217	4.2
White	228,107	230,506	232,348	234,199	236,058	3.5
Black or African American	35,705	36,249	36,667	37,082	37,502	5.0
American Indian and Alaska Native	2,664	2,711	2,749	2,787	2,825	6.0
Asian	10,589	11,107	11,512	11,919	12,326	16.4
Native Hawaiian and Other Pacific Islanders	463	475	485	495	506	9.3
Two or more races	3,898	4,054	4,180	4,308	4,439	13.9
Race alone or in combination: [2]						
White	231,436	233,978	235,935	237,901	239,880	3.6
Black or African American	37,105	37,744	38,238	38,732	39,232	5.7
American Indian and Alaska Native	4,225	4,280	4,323	4,366	4,409	4.4
Asian	12,007	12,586	13,041	13,498	13,957	16.2
Native Hawaiian and Other Pacific Islanders	907	927	944	960	976	7.7
Not Hispanic or Latino	246,118	248,042	249,464	250,887	252,333	2.5
One race	242,712	244,506	245,824	247,141	248,478	2.4
White	195,577	196,320	196,822	197,325	197,841	1.2
Black or African American	34,314	34,813	35,196	35,577	35,964	4.8
American Indian and Alaska Native	2,097	2,130	2,155	2,181	2,207	5.2
Asian	10,357	10,867	11,267	11,667	12,068	16.5
Native Hawaiian and Other Pacific Islanders	367	376	383	391	398	8.5
Two or more races	3,406	3,536	3,641	3,747	3,855	13.2
Race alone or in combination: [2]						
White	198,477	199,338	199,935	200,534	201,148	1.3
Black or African American	35,499	36,078	36,526	36,972	37,426	5.4
American Indian and Alaska Native	3,456	3,491	3,518	3,546	3,574	3.4
Asian	11,632	12,196	12,639	13,083	13,530	16.3
Native Hawaiian and Other Pacific Islanders	752	767	779	791	803	6.8
Hispanic or Latino	35,306	37,060	38,477	39,902	41,322	17.0
One race	34,815	36,543	37,937	39,340	40,739	17.0
White	32,530	34,186	35,526	36,873	38,217	17.5
Black or African American	1,391	1,436	1,470	1,505	1,539	10.6
American Indian and Alaska Native	566	582	594	606	618	9.1
Asian	232	240	246	252	258	10.9
Native Hawaiian and Other Pacific Islanders	95	99	102	105	107	12.6
Two or more races	491	518	539	561	583	18.7
Race alone or in combination: [2]						
White	32,959	34,641	36,000	37,368	38,732	17.5
Black or African American	1,606	1,666	1,713	1,760	1,806	12.5
American Indian and Alaska Native	770	789	805	820	835	8.6
Asian	375	390	402	414	427	13.8
Native Hawaiian and Other Pacific Islanders	155	160	165	169	174	12.0
MALE						
Total	138,056	140,013	141,519	143,024	144,537	4.7
One race	136,146	138,023	139,465	140,906	142,352	4.6
White	112,478	113,798	114,810	115,820	116,832	3.9
Black or African American	16,972	17,246	17,455	17,662	17,873	5.3
American Indian and Alaska Native	1,333	1,357	1,376	1,396	1,415	6.2
Asian	5,128	5,380	5,578	5,776	5,975	16.5
Native Hawaiian and Other Pacific Islanders	235	242	247	252	257	9.4
Two or more races	1,910	1,990	2,054	2,119	2,185	14.4
Race alone or in combination: [2]						
White	114,116	115,508	116,578	117,647	118,720	4.0
Black or African American	17,644	17,966	18,214	18,461	18,713	6.1
American Indian and Alaska Native	2,088	2,116	2,138	2,160	2,182	4.5
Asian	5,834	6,118	6,341	6,565	6,789	16.4
Native Hawaiian and Other Pacific Islanders	456	466	475	483	491	7.7
Not Hispanic or Latino	119,894	120,919	121,675	122,428	123,190	2.7
Hispanic or Latino	18,162	19,094	19,844	20,597	21,347	17.5
FEMALE						
Total	143,368	145,089	146,422	147,765	149,118	4.0
One race	141,381	143,025	144,296	145,576	146,865	3.9
White	115,628	116,708	117,538	118,379	119,225	3.1
Black or African American	18,733	19,003	19,212	19,420	19,630	4.8
American Indian and Alaska Native	1,331	1,354	1,372	1,391	1,410	5.9
Asian	5,461	5,727	5,935	6,143	6,352	16.3
Native Hawaiian and Other Pacific Islanders	227	233	238	243	248	9.2
Two or more races	1,987	2,064	2,126	2,189	2,253	13.4
Race alone or in combination: [2]						
White	117,321	118,470	119,357	120,254	121,160	3.3
Black or African American	19,461	19,778	20,024	20,271	20,520	5.4
American Indian and Alaska Native	2,137	2,164	2,185	2,206	2,227	4.2
Asian	6,173	6,468	6,701	6,933	7,168	16.1
Native Hawaiian and Other Pacific Islanders	451	461	469	477	485	7.6
Not Hispanic or Latino	126,224	127,123	127,789	128,460	129,143	2.3
Hispanic or Latino	17,144	17,967	18,633	19,305	19,975	16.5

[1] See footnote 3, Table 11. [2] In combination with one or more other races. The sum of the five race groups adds to more than the total population because individuals may report more than one race.

Source: U.S. Census Bureau, "Annual Estimates of the Population by Sex, Race and Hispanic or Latino Origin for the United States: April 1, 2000 to July 1, 2004 (NC-EST2004-03)"; published 9 June 2005; <http://www.census.gov/popest/national/asrh/NC-EST2004-srh.html>.

Population 15

Table 14. Resident Population by Race, Hispanic Origin, and Age: 2000 and 2004

[In thousands (281,425 represents 281,425,000); except as indicated. 2000, as of April and 2004, as of July. For definition of median, see Guide to Tabular Presentation]

Age group	Total 2000[2]	Total 2004	White alone 2000[2]	White alone 2004	Black or African American alone 2000[2]	Black or African American alone 2004	American Indian, Alaska Native alone 2000[2]	American Indian, Alaska Native alone 2004	Asian alone 2000[2]	Asian alone 2004	Native Hawaiian, Other Pacific Islander alone 2000[2]	Native Hawaiian, Other Pacific Islander alone 2004	Two or more races 2000[2]	Two or more races 2004	Hispanic or Latino origin[1] 2000[2]	Hispanic or Latino origin[1] 2004	Not Hispanic or Latino White alone 2000[2]	Not Hispanic or Latino White alone 2004
Total	281,425	293,655	228,107	236,058	35,705	37,502	2,664	2,825	10,589	12,326	463	506	3,898	4,439	35,306	41,322	195,577	197,841
Under 5 years	19,185	20,071	14,663	15,345	2,926	3,029	233	203	708	824	41	35	613	636	3,720	4,370	11,293	11,246
5 to 9 years	20,550	19,606	15,688	14,973	3,320	2,979	258	236	716	775	44	43	524	600	3,624	3,878	12,393	11,448
10 to 14 years	20,530	21,145	15,844	16,125	3,221	3,407	264	267	715	782	42	46	443	519	3,163	3,784	12,963	12,676
15 to 19 years	20,221	20,730	15,746	16,014	3,024	3,186	251	265	776	789	44	43	380	434	3,172	3,333	12,837	12,967
20 to 24 years	18,961	20,971	14,824	16,311	2,728	3,064	218	255	848	915	46	48	297	379	3,409	3,765	11,680	12,839
25 to 29 years	19,384	19,561	15,219	15,236	2,645	2,697	204	219	1,019	1,068	42	48	254	294	3,385	3,915	12,079	11,605
30 to 34 years	20,511	20,471	16,349	16,000	2,710	2,722	202	209	980	1,236	39	43	231	261	3,125	3,701	13,451	12,559
35 to 39 years	22,709	21,052	18,373	16,735	2,910	2,746	217	205	937	1,094	38	40	233	233	2,825	3,272	15,754	13,698
40 to 44 years	22,441	23,056	18,345	18,645	2,771	2,902	202	217	870	1,018	33	39	219	236	2,304	2,888	16,213	15,966
45 to 49 years	20,091	22,123	16,614	18,098	2,330	2,664	169	196	769	918	27	32	183	215	1,775	2,284	14,972	15,983
50 to 54 years	17,583	19,496	14,791	16,138	1,845	2,200	135	161	641	796	21	26	149	176	1,361	1,744	13,528	14,523
55 to 59 years	13,469	16,490	11,478	13,928	1,332	1,656	95	125	443	621	15	20	106	140	960	1,300	10,581	12,719
60 to 64 years	10,804	12,589	9,213	10,740	1,082	1,206	70	87	350	443	11	14	78	99	750	922	8,510	9,879
65 to 69 years	9,533	9,956	8,238	8,508	895	957	52	63	279	346	8	10	61	71	599	716	7,675	7,837
70 to 74 years	8,857	8,507	7,798	7,373	741	756	38	46	224	271	6	8	49	54	477	555	7,348	6,852
75 to 79 years	7,415	7,411	6,633	6,545	557	584	27	33	159	202	4	5	36	41	327	418	6,324	6,150
80 to 84 years	4,944	5,560	4,465	4,977	350	399	15	21	90	131	2	3	22	28	179	266	4,295	4,725
85 to 89 years	2,789	3,079	2,524	2,778	200	210	8	11	43	64	1	2	12	15	98	128	2,431	2,657
90 to 94 years	1,112	1,350	1,006	1,210	82	101	3	5	15	26	1	1	4	7	39	60	970	1,153
95 to 99 years	287	370	253	328	27	31	1	2	4	7	-	1	4	2	11	18	243	311
100 years and over	50	61	41	50	7	8	1	1	1	1	-	-	1	1	3	4	39	47
5 to 13 years	37,028	36,376	28,384	27,754	5,924	5,678	471	447	1,288	1,399	78	79	885	1,019	6,186	6,926	22,756	21,450
14 to 17 years	16,094	16,831	12,524	12,935	2,426	2,650	205	216	590	627	33	35	315	368	2,439	2,746	10,291	10,431
18 to 24 years	27,139	29,245	21,195	22,734	3,943	4,307	315	359	1,178	1,235	64	66	443	544	4,744	5,088	16,826	18,049
16 years and over	217,139	228,622	178,782	186,386	25,632	27,419	1,857	2,065	8,304	9,787	328	374	2,237	2,591	24,202	28,606	156,345	159,866
18 years and over	209,117	220,377	178,536	180,042	24,429	26,146	1,755	1,959	8,003	9,476	311	357	2,084	2,416	22,962	27,280	151,237	154,714
16 to 64 years	182,153	192,328	147,823	154,617	22,772	24,372	1,713	1,883	7,489	8,739	305	345	2,051	2,372	22,469	26,441	127,021	130,134
55 years and over	59,259	65,373	51,650	56,438	5,273	5,909	309	393	1,608	2,112	48	63	370	457	3,443	4,387	48,416	52,330
65 years and over	34,986	36,294	30,959	31,770	2,859	3,047	144	182	815	1,048	22	29	186	219	1,733	2,165	29,324	29,732
75 years and over	16,596	17,831	14,922	15,888	1,223	1,334	55	72	312	431	8	11	77	94	657	895	14,302	15,043
85 years and over	4,237	4,860	3,825	4,366	316	350	13	18	63	97	2	3	18	24	151	210	3,683	4,168
Median age (yrs)	35.3	36.0	36.6	37.5	30.0	30.8	27.7	29.2	32.5	34.1	26.8	28.9	19.8	20.4	25.8	26.9	38.6	40.0

- Represents or rounds to zero. [1] Persons of Hispanic origin may be of any race. [2] April 1, 2000, population estimates base reflects changes to the Census 2000 population from the Count Question Resolution program and geographic program revisions.

Source: U.S. Census Bureau, "National Population Estimates—Characteristics"; published 9 June 2005: <http://www.census.gov/popest/national/asrh/NC-EST2004-asrh.html>.

Table 15. Resident Population by Race, Hispanic Origin Status, and Age—Projections: 2005 and 2010

[In thousands (295,507 represents 295,507,000), except as indicated. As of July 1. For definition of median, see Guide to Tabular Presentation. Projections are based on middle series of assumptions; see headnote. Table 3]

Age group	Total 2005	Total 2010	White alone 2005	White alone 2010	Black alone 2005	Black alone 2010	Asian alone 2005	Asian alone 2010	All other races alone 2005	All other races alone 2010	Hispanic origin [1] 2005	Hispanic origin [1] 2010	White alone, not of Hispanic origin 2005	White alone, not of Hispanic origin 2010
Total	**295,507**	**308,936**	**236,924**	**244,995**	**38,056**	**40,454**	**12,419**	**14,241**	**8,108**	**9,246**	**41,801**	**47,756**	**198,451**	**201,112**
Under 5 years	20,495	21,426	15,503	15,995	3,113	3,332	833	919	1,046	1,181	4,397	4,824	11,528	11,647
5 to 9 years	19,467	20,706	14,862	15,639	2,941	3,127	763	888	901	1,052	3,892	4,515	11,330	11,553
10 to 14 years	20,838	19,767	15,881	15,049	3,332	2,976	787	834	838	909	3,853	4,057	12,370	11,361
15 to 19 years	21,172	21,336	16,281	16,203	3,306	3,357	815	886	770	851	3,576	4,162	13,013	12,401
20 to 24 years	20,823	21,676	16,153	16,591	3,078	3,396	898	943	695	785	3,604	3,878	12,836	12,992
25 to 29 years	19,753	21,375	15,377	16,495	2,807	3,130	985	1,041	584	709	3,781	3,927	11,881	12,919
30 to 34 years	19,847	20,271	15,466	15,654	2,678	2,856	1,190	1,166	514	595	3,666	3,973	12,060	11,977
35 to 39 years	20,869	20,137	16,538	15,597	2,732	2,701	1,117	1,319	482	520	3,297	3,769	13,480	12,096
40 to 44 years	22,735	20,984	18,312	16,566	2,892	2,724	1,033	1,208	457	486	2,926	3,343	15,606	13,466
45 to 49 years	22,453	22,654	18,318	18,213	2,736	2,844	948	1,105	379	492	2,375	2,939	16,113	15,489
50 to 54 years	19,983	22,173	16,499	18,006	2,276	2,657	828	997	305	453	1,823	2,371	14,812	15,870
55 to 59 years	17,359	19,507	14,582	16,102	1,788	2,176	685	857	212	372	1,393	1,806	13,289	14,431
60 to 64 years	13,071	16,679	11,075	14,004	1,250	1,674	480	706	152	295	978	1,365	10,161	12,736
65 to 69 years	10,123	12,172	8,629	10,357	972	1,127	370	489	110	199	745	941	7,931	9,477
70 to 74 years	8,500	9,097	7,348	7,767	767	838	275	355	79	138	571	694	6,811	7,117
75 to 79 years	7,376	7,186	6,506	6,226	591	622	200	244	51	94	433	510	6,097	5,747
80 to 84 years	5,576	5,665	4,993	5,005	407	440	125	158	26	61	275	359	4,733	4,666
85 to 89 years	3,206	3,713	2,890	3,321	231	274	59	83	11	34	135	204	2,763	3,128
90 to 94 years	1,431	1,727	1,286	1,546	112	136	22	31	3	14	60	84	1,230	1,467
95 to 99 years	412	569	366	503	37	53	5	8	1	4	18	28	349	476
100 years and over	71	114	60	98	9	14	1	1		1	3	6	57	92
5 to 13 years	35,968	36,439	27,432	27,613	5,575	5,491	1,389	1,550	1,571	1,786	6,975	7,760	21,091	20,580
14 to 17 years	17,175	16,566	13,150	12,589	2,735	2,597	648	695	642	685	2,956	3,291	10,453	9,586
18 to 24 years	29,156	30,481	22,594	23,280	4,347	4,768	1,226	1,307	990	1,125	4,994	5,611	18,005	18,142
16 years and over	230,335	242,936	187,339	195,194	27,964	30,383	9,874	11,427	5,159	5,933	28,904	33,541	160,572	164,179
18 years and over	221,868	234,504	180,839	188,799	26,632	29,034	9,549	11,077	4,848	5,594	27,473	31,881	155,378	159,300
16 to 64 years	193,639	202,693	155,261	160,372	24,837	26,877	8,816	10,056	4,725	5,387	26,663	30,715	130,601	132,007
55 years and over	67,072	76,429	57,734	64,928	6,165	7,355	2,223	2,934	950	1,213	4,611	5,997	53,421	59,339
65 years and over	36,696	40,244	32,078	34,821	3,127	3,505	1,058	1,371	433	546	2,240	2,826	29,971	32,171
75 years and over	18,072	18,974	16,101	16,698	1,388	1,540	413	527	171	209	924	1,191	15,228	15,577
85 years and over	5,120	6,123	4,602	5,467	390	478	87	125	41	54	216	322	4,398	5,163
Median age (yrs)	35.2	36.0	36.7	37.6	29.9	30.5	33.8	35.7	22.6	23.0	26.1	27.1	39.3	40.3

[1] Persons of Hispanic origin may be of any race.

Source: U.S. Census Bureau. "U.S. Interim Projections by Age, Sex, Race, and Hispanic Origin"; published March 2004; <http://www.census.gov/ipc/www/usinterimproj/>.

Population 17

Table 16. Resident Population by Race, Hispanic Origin, and Single Years of Age: 2004

[In thousands, except as indicated (293,655 represents 293,655,000). As of July 1. For derivation of estimates, see text of this section]

Age	Total	Race						Hispanic or Latino origin [1]	Non-Hispanic or Latino White alone
		White alone	Black or African American alone	American Indian, Alaska Native alone	Asian alone	Native Hawaiian and Other Pacific Islander alone	Two or more races		
Total	**293,655**	**236,058**	**37,502**	**2,825**	**12,326**	**506**	**4,439**	**41,322**	**197,841**
Under 5 yrs. old	20,071	15,345	3,029	203	824	35	636	4,370	11,246
Under 1 yr. old	4,077	3,116	612	40	171	7	131	907	2,261
1 yr. old	4,038	3,088	605	40	171	7	127	907	2,233
2 yrs. old	3,998	3,060	604	39	164	7	125	879	2,230
3 yrs. old	4,051	3,096	619	39	167	7	123	862	2,283
4 yrs. old	3,907	2,985	588	45	152	8	130	815	2,239
5 to 9 yrs. old	19,606	14,973	2,979	236	775	43	600	3,878	11,448
5 yrs. old	3,852	2,941	577	47	149	9	129	777	2,237
6 yrs. old	3,863	2,945	586	47	153	8	124	773	2,244
7 yrs. old	3,889	2,970	589	47	156	8	119	772	2,269
8 yrs. old	3,963	3,032	599	48	159	9	116	777	2,324
9 yrs. old	4,039	3,085	628	48	157	9	113	779	2,375
10 to 14 yrs. old	21,145	16,125	3,407	267	782	46	519	3,784	12,676
10 yrs. old	4,074	3,101	649	50	156	9	109	770	2,399
11 yrs. old	4,158	3,163	673	52	156	9	105	767	2,464
12 yrs. old	4,242	3,235	684	54	157	9	104	763	2,539
13 yrs. old	4,296	3,281	694	55	156	9	101	748	2,600
14 yrs. old	4,375	3,344	707	56	158	9	100	737	2,673
15 to 19 yrs. old	20,730	16,014	3,186	265	789	43	434	3,333	12,967
15 yrs. old	4,212	3,228	669	54	158	9	93	684	2,605
16 yrs. old	4,144	3,191	645	53	156	9	89	670	2,580
17 yrs. old	4,100	3,171	628	52	154	9	86	656	2,572
18 yrs. old	4,124	3,197	623	52	158	9	84	656	2,597
19 yrs. old	4,150	3,225	620	52	162	9	82	667	2,613
20 to 24 yrs. old	20,971	16,311	3,064	255	915	48	379	3,765	12,839
20 yrs. old	4,076	3,166	605	52	166	9	79	680	2,541
21 yrs. old	4,166	3,242	611	53	173	9	78	726	2,573
22 yrs. old	4,211	3,276	614	51	183	10	77	764	2,571
23 yrs. old	4,263	3,318	616	50	194	10	74	785	2,594
24 yrs. old	4,255	3,308	618	49	199	10	71	811	2,559
25 to 29 yrs. old	19,561	15,236	2,697	219	1,068	48	294	3,915	11,605
25 yrs. old	4,053	3,152	579	46	200	10	65	785	2,427
26 yrs. old	3,935	3,073	547	44	200	10	61	786	2,345
27 yrs. old	3,884	3,028	535	44	209	10	58	785	2,300
28 yrs. old	3,788	2,947	513	42	221	9	55	780	2,223
29 yrs. old	3,901	3,035	523	42	238	9	54	780	2,310
30 to 34 yrs. old	20,471	16,000	2,722	209	1,236	43	261	3,701	12,559
30 yrs. old	3,793	2,946	506	40	240	9	52	749	2,248
31 yrs. old	3,889	3,012	527	41	249	9	51	747	2,317
32 yrs. old	4,079	3,180	545	42	251	9	52	739	2,493
33 yrs. old	4,312	3,391	569	43	246	9	53	732	2,711
34 yrs. old	4,398	3,471	574	43	249	9	53	733	2,790
35 to 39 yrs. old	21,052	16,735	2,746	205	1,094	40	233	3,272	13,698
35 yrs. old	4,156	3,296	530	41	233	8	49	679	2,666
36 yrs. old	4,083	3,232	533	40	224	8	46	665	2,614
37 yrs. old	4,095	3,263	531	40	209	8	45	639	2,670
38 yrs. old	4,214	3,349	558	41	211	8	46	641	2,755
39 yrs. old	4,505	3,595	594	44	217	8	48	648	2,994
40 to 44 yrs. old	23,056	18,645	2,902	217	1,018	39	236	2,888	15,966
40 yrs. old	4,577	3,676	587	44	214	8	48	623	3,098
41 yrs. old	4,564	3,677	577	43	212	8	47	592	3,128
42 yrs. old	4,579	3,713	571	43	197	8	47	572	3,182
43 yrs. old	4,627	3,766	571	43	193	7	47	548	3,257
44 yrs. old	4,710	3,814	595	44	202	8	47	553	3,301
45 to 49 yrs. old	22,123	18,098	2,664	196	918	32	215	2,284	15,983
45 yrs. old	4,519	3,682	557	41	188	7	45	498	3,221
46 yrs. old	4,522	3,696	546	40	189	7	44	474	3,257
47 yrs. old	4,469	3,660	538	39	182	6	43	456	3,238
48 yrs. old	4,296	3,520	512	38	180	6	42	432	3,120
49 yrs. old	4,316	3,541	510	37	181	6	41	424	3,148

See footnote at end of table.

Table 16. **Resident Population by Race, Hispanic Origin, and Single Years of Age: 2004—Con.**

[In thousands, except as indicated (293,655 represents 293,655,000). As of July 1. Resident population. For derivation of estimates, see text of this section]

Age	Total	Race						Hispanic or Latino origin [1]	Non-Hispanic or Latino White alone
		White alone	Black or African American alone	American Indian, Alaska Native alone	Asian alone	Native Hawaiian and Other Pacific Islander alone	Two or more races		
50 to 54 yrs. old. . . .	19,496	16,138	2,200	161	796	26	176	1,744	14,523
50 yrs. old	4,130	3,407	476	35	168	6	38	387	3,049
51 yrs. old	3,994	3,308	448	33	163	5	37	363	2,972
52 yrs. old	3,862	3,208	428	32	155	5	34	340	2,893
53 yrs. old	3,762	3,119	424	31	150	5	33	328	2,815
54 yrs. old	3,748	3,096	425	30	160	5	33	326	2,793
55 to 59 yrs. old. . . .	16,490	13,928	1,656	125	621	20	140	1,300	12,719
55 yrs. old	3,603	3,008	387	28	145	5	31	294	2,735
56 yrs. old	3,572	3,009	364	27	136	4	30	281	2,749
57 yrs. old	3,744	3,210	345	27	127	4	31	267	2,962
58 yrs. old	2,791	2,353	280	21	109	4	24	235	2,134
59 yrs. old	2,779	2,348	279	21	105	3	23	224	2,139
60 to 64 yrs. old. . . .	12,589	10,740	1,206	87	443	14	99	922	9,879
60 yrs. old	2,735	2,329	263	20	98	3	22	207	2,136
61 yrs. old	2,824	2,428	260	19	91	3	22	197	2,245
62 yrs. old	2,488	2,125	235	17	88	3	19	179	1,957
63 yrs. old	2,305	1,962	223	16	83	3	18	170	1,803
64 yrs. old	2,238	1,895	225	15	83	3	17	168	1,737
65 to 69 yrs. old. . . .	9,956	8,508	957	63	346	10	71	716	7,837
65 yrs. old	2,123	1,814	202	14	75	2	16	156	1,668
66 yrs. old	2,076	1,773	199	13	73	2	15	150	1,633
67 yrs. old	1,949	1,665	187	12	69	2	14	140	1,533
68 yrs. old	1,907	1,629	185	12	66	2	13	135	1,502
69 yrs. old	1,902	1,628	184	11	64	2	13	134	1,501
70 to 74 yrs. old. . . .	8,507	7,373	756	46	271	8	54	555	6,852
70 yrs. old	1,733	1,486	165	10	59	2	12	119	1,374
71 yrs. old	1,726	1,486	161	10	57	2	11	113	1,379
72 yrs. old	1,696	1,473	149	9	53	1	11	110	1,370
73 yrs. old	1,670	1,461	138	8	51	1	10	106	1,361
74 yrs. old	1,681	1,467	143	9	51	1	10	106	1,367
75 to 79 yrs. old. . . .	7,411	6,545	584	33	202	5	41	418	6,150
75 yrs. old	1,572	1,381	128	7	46	1	9	96	1,291
76 yrs. old	1,551	1,368	123	7	44	1	9	90	1,283
77 yrs. old	1,491	1,319	117	7	40	1	8	82	1,241
78 yrs. old	1,414	1,251	111	6	37	1	8	77	1,178
79 yrs. old	1,382	1,225	107	6	36	1	7	73	1,157
80 to 84 yrs. old. . . .	5,560	4,977	399	21	131	3	28	266	4,725
80 yrs. old	1,290	1,151	95	5	32	1	7	65	1,089
81 yrs. old	1,187	1,059	87	5	29	1	6	58	1,004
82 yrs. old	1,121	1,005	79	4	26	1	6	53	954
83 yrs. old	1,029	928	69	4	23	1	5	47	884
84 yrs. old	933	835	69	4	21	-	5	43	794
85 to 89 yrs. old. . . .	3,079	2,778	210	11	64	2	15	128	2,657
90 to 94 yrs. old. . . .	1,350	1,210	101	5	26	1	7	60	1,153
95 to 99 yrs. old . . .	370	328	31	2	7	-	2	18	311
100 yrs. old and over	61	50	8	1	1	-	1	4	47
Median age (yr.) . . .	36.0	37.5	30.8	29.2	34.1	28.9	20.4	26.9	40.0

- Represents or rounds to zero.   [1] Persons of Hispanic origin may be of any race.

Source: U.S. Census Bureau, "National Population Estimates—Characteristics"; published 9 June 2005; <http://www.census.gov/popest/national/asrh/NC-EST2004-asrh.html> and "National Population Estimates for the 2000s: Monthly Postcensal Resident Population, by single year of age, sex, race and Hispanic origin"; published 9 June 2005; <http://www.census.gov/popest/national/asrh/2004natres.html>.

U.S. Census Bureau, Statistical Abstract of the United States: 2006

Figure 1.1
Center of Population: 1790 to 2000

[Prior to 1960, excludes Alaska and Hawaii. The median center is located at the intersection of two median lines, a north-south line constructed so that half of the nation's population lives east and half lives west of it, and an east-west line selected so that half of the nation's population lives north and half lives south of it. The mean center of population is that point at which an imaginary, flat, weightless, and rigid map of the United States would balance if weights of identical value were placed on it so that each weight represented the location of one person on the date of the census]

Year	Median center		Mean center		
	Latitude-N	Longitude	Latitude-N	Longitude-W	Approximate location
1790 (August 2)	(NA)	(NA)	39 16 30	76 11 12	In Kent County, MD, 23 miles E of Baltimore MD
1850 (June 1). .	(NA)	(NA)	38 59 00	81 19 00	In Wirt County, WV, 23 miles SE of Parkersburg, WV[1]
1900 (June 1). .	40 03 32	84 49 01	39 09 36	85 48 54	In Bartholomew County, IN, 6 miles SE of Columbus, IN
1950 (April 1). .	40 00 12	84 56 51	38 50 21	88 09 33	In Richland County, IL, 8 miles NNW of Olney, IL
1960 (April 1). .	39 56 25	85 16 60	38 35 58	89 12 35	In Clinton County, IL, 6.5 miles NW of Centralia, IL
1970 (April 1) . .	39 47 43	85 31 43	38 27 47	89 42 22	In St. Clair County, IL, 5.3 miles ESE of Mascoutah, IL
1980 (April 1). .	39 18 60	86 08 15	38 08 13	90 34 26	In Jefferson County, MO, .25 mile W of DeSoto, MO
1990 (April 1) . .	38 57 55	86 31 53	37 52 20	91 12 55	In Crawford County, MO, 10 miles SE of Steelville, MO
2000 (April 1). .	38 45 23	86 55 51	37 41 49	91 48 34	In Phelps County, MO, 3 miles E of Edgar Springs, MO

NA Not available. [1]West Virginia was set off from Virginia, Dec. 31, 1862, and admitted as a state, June 19, 1863.

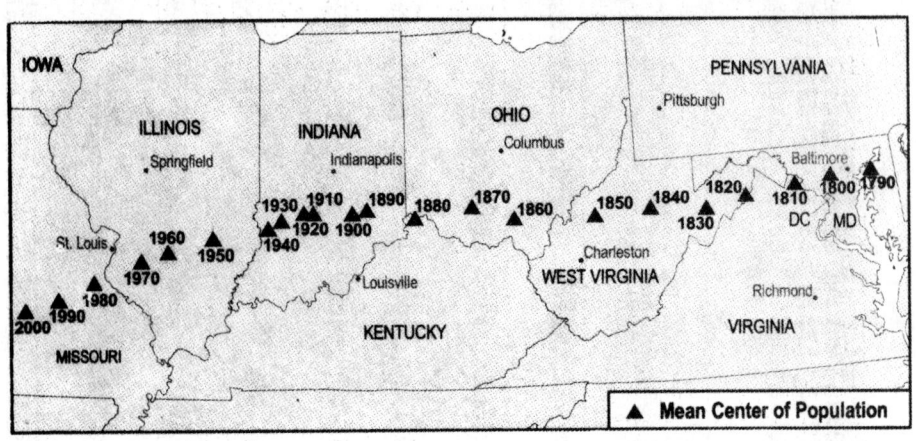

U.S. Census Bureau, Statistical Abstract of the United States: 2006

Table 17. **Resident Population—States: 1980 to 2004**

[In thousands (226,546 represents 226,546,000). 1980, 1990, and 2000 data as of April 1, data for other years as of July 1. Insofar as possible, population shown for all years is that of present area of state. See Appendix III]

State	1980 [1]	1990 [2]	1995	1999	2000 [3]	2001	2002	2003	2004
United States	226,546	248,791	266,278	279,040	281,425	285,102	287,941	290,789	293,655
Alabama.	3,894	4,040	4,297	4,430	4,447	4,468	4,481	4,504	4,530
Alaska	402	550	604	625	627	632	641	648	655
Arizona.	2,718	3,665	4,432	5,024	5,131	5,297	5,439	5,579	5,744
Arkansas	2,286	2,351	2,535	2,652	2,673	2,692	2,708	2,728	2,753
California	23,668	29,811	31,697	33,499	33,872	34,532	34,988	35,463	35,894
Colorado.	2,890	3,294	3,827	4,226	4,302	4,427	4,498	4,548	4,601
Connecticut.	3,108	3,287	3,324	3,386	3,406	3,433	3,459	3,487	3,504
Delaware	594	666	730	775	784	796	806	818	830
District of Columbia	638	607	581	570	572	569	565	558	554
Florida	9,746	12,938	14,538	15,759	15,983	16,354	16,681	16,999	17,397
Georgia	5,463	6,478	7,328	8,046	8,187	8,391	8,540	8,676	8,829
Hawaii	965	1,108	1,197	1,210	1,212	1,222	1,235	1,249	1,263
Idaho	944	1,007	1,177	1,276	1,294	1,321	1,343	1,367	1,393
Illinois	11,427	11,431	12,008	12,359	12,420	12,518	12,585	12,649	12,714
Indiana.	5,490	5,544	5,851	6,045	6,081	6,128	6,158	6,200	6,238
Iowa	2,914	2,777	2,867	2,918	2,926	2,932	2,935	2,942	2,954
Kansas.	2,364	2,478	2,601	2,678	2,689	2,701	2,713	2,725	2,736
Kentucky	3,661	3,687	3,887	4,018	4,042	4,068	4,090	4,118	4,146
Louisiana	4,206	4,222	4,379	4,461	4,469	4,467	4,477	4,494	4,516
Maine.	1,125	1,228	1,243	1,267	1,275	1,287	1,298	1,309	1,317
Maryland	4,217	4,781	5,070	5,255	5,297	5,379	5,442	5,512	5,558
Massachusetts.	5,737	6,016	6,141	6,317	6,349	6,395	6,413	6,420	6,417
Michigan.	9,262	9,295	9,676	9,897	9,938	10,005	10,042	10,082	10,113
Minnesota.	4,076	4,376	4,660	4,873	4,919	4,986	5,025	5,064	5,101
Mississippi	2,521	2,575	2,723	2,828	2,845	2,858	2,868	2,883	2,903
Missouri	4,917	5,117	5,378	5,562	5,597	5,643	5,680	5,719	5,755
Montana	787	799	877	898	902	906	911	918	927
Nebraska	1,570	1,578	1,657	1,705	1,711	1,719	1,726	1,737	1,747
Nevada	800	1,202	1,582	1,935	1,998	2,095	2,168	2,242	2,335
New Hampshire	921	1,109	1,158	1,222	1,236	1,259	1,276	1,289	1,300
New Jersey.	7,365	7,748	8,083	8,360	8,414	8,506	8,577	8,642	8,699
New Mexico	1,303	1,515	1,720	1,808	1,819	1,832	1,855	1,879	1,903
New York	17,558	17,991	18,524	18,883	18,977	19,086	19,151	19,212	19,227
North Carolina	5,882	6,632	7,345	7,949	8,046	8,198	8,312	8,421	8,541
North Dakota.	653	639	648	644	642	636	634	633	634
Ohio	10,798	10,847	11,203	11,335	11,353	11,388	11,410	11,438	11,459
Oklahoma.	3,025	3,146	3,308	3,437	3,451	3,467	3,488	3,506	3,524
Oregon.	2,633	2,842	3,184	3,316	3,421	3,474	3,523	3,564	3,595
Pennsylvania.	11,864	11,883	12,198	12,264	12,281	12,298	12,328	12,371	12,406
Rhode Island.	947	1,003	1,017	1,040	1,048	1,059	1,069	1,076	1,081
South Carolina	3,122	3,486	3,749	3,975	4,012	4,061	4,106	4,149	4,198
South Dakota	691	696	738	750	755	758	760	765	771
Tennessee	4,591	4,877	5,327	5,639	5,689	5,748	5,792	5,845	5,901
Texas.	14,229	16,986	18,959	20,558	20,852	21,335	21,723	22,103	22,490
Utah	1,461	1,723	2,014	2,203	2,233	2,281	2,320	2,352	2,389
Vermont	511	563	589	605	609	613	617	619	621
Virginia.	5,347	6,189	6,671	7,000	7,079	7,186	7,274	7,365	7,460
Washington.	4,132	4,867	5,481	5,843	5,894	5,993	6,067	6,131	6,204
West Virginia	1,950	1,793	1,824	1,812	1,808	1,802	1,805	1,811	1,815
Wisconsin.	4,706	4,892	5,185	5,333	5,364	5,406	5,440	5,474	5,509
Wyoming	470	454	485	492	494	494	499	502	507

[1] See footnote 3, Table 1.   [2] The April 1, 1990, census counts include corrections processed through August 1997, results of special censuses and test censuses, and do not include adjustments for census coverage errors.   [3] Reflects modifications to the Census 2000 population as documented in the Count Question Resolution program, updates to the Boundary and Annexation Survey, and geographic program revisions.

Source: U.S. Census Bureau, Current Population Reports, P25-1106; "Table CO-EST2001-12-00 - Time Series of Intercensal State Population Estimates: April 1, 1990 to April 1, 2000"; published 11 April 2002; <http://www.census.gov/popest/archives/2000s/vintage_2001/CO-EST2001-12/CO-EST2001-12-00.html>; and "Table NST-EST2004-01 - Annual Estimates of the Population for the United States and States, and for Puerto Rico: April 1, 2000 to July 1, 2004"; published 22 December 2004; <http://www.census.gov/popest/states/NST-ann-est.html>.

U.S. Census Bureau, Statistical Abstract of the United States: 2006

Table 18. **State Population—Rank, Percent Change, and Population Density: 1980 to 2004**

[As of April 1, except 2004 as of July 1. Insofar as possible, population shown for all years is that of present area of state. For area figures of states, see Table 347. Minus sign (-) indicates decrease. See Appendix III]

State	Rank				Percent change			Population per sq. mile of land area[1]		
	1980	1990	2000	2004	1980- 1990	1990- 2000	2000- 2004	1990	2000	2004
United States.	(X)	(X)	(X)	(X)	9.8	13.1	4.3	70.3	79.6	83.0
Alabama	22	22	23	23	3.8	10.1	1.9	79.6	87.6	89.3
Alaska	50	49	48	47	36.9	14.0	4.5	1.0	1.1	1.1
Arizona.	29	24	20	18	34.8	40.0	12.0	32.3	45.2	50.5
Arkansas.	33	33	33	32	2.8	13.7	3.0	45.1	51.3	52.9
California.	1	1	1	1	26.0	13.6	6.0	191.1	217.2	230.1
Colorado	28	26	24	22	14.0	30.6	7.0	31.8	41.5	44.4
Connecticut	25	27	29	29	5.8	3.6	2.9	678.5	702.9	723.2
Delaware.	47	46	45	45	12.1	17.6	6.0	341.0	401.1	425.1
District of Columbia. . .	(X)	(X)	(X)	(X)	-4.9	-5.7	-3.2	9,884.4	9,316.4	9,015.0
Florida	7	4	4	4	32.7	23.5	8.8	239.9	296.4	322.6
Georgia	13	11	10	9	18.6	26.4	7.8	111.9	141.4	152.5
Hawaii	39	41	42	42	14.9	9.3	4.2	172.6	188.6	196.6
Idaho	41	42	39	39	6.7	28.5	7.7	12.2	15.6	16.8
Illinois.	5	6	5	5	(Z)	8.7	2.4	205.6	223.4	228.7
Indiana	12	14	14	14	1.0	9.7	2.6	154.6	169.5	173.9
Iowa.	27	30	30	30	-4.7	5.4	1.0	49.7	52.4	52.9
Kansas	32	32	32	33	4.8	8.5	1.7	30.3	32.9	33.4
Kentucky.	23	23	25	26	0.7	9.6	2.6	92.8	101.7	104.4
Louisiana	19	21	22	24	0.4	5.9	1.0	96.9	102.6	103.7
Maine	38	38	40	40	9.2	3.8	3.3	39.8	41.3	42.7
Maryland.	18	19	19	19	13.4	10.8	4.9	489.1	541.9	568.7
Massachusetts	11	13	13	13	4.9	5.5	1.1	767.4	809.8	818.4
Michigan	8	8	8	8	0.4	6.9	1.8	163.6	175.0	178.0
Minnesota	21	20	21	21	7.4	12.4	3.7	55.0	61.8	64.1
Mississippi.	31	31	31	31	2.2	10.5	2.0	54.9	60.6	61.9
Missouri	15	15	17	17	4.1	9.4	2.8	74.3	81.2	83.5
Montana	44	44	44	44	1.6	12.9	2.7	5.5	6.2	6.4
Nebraska	35	36	38	38	0.5	8.4	2.1	20.5	22.3	22.7
Nevada.	43	39	35	35	50.1	66.3	16.8	10.9	18.2	21.3
New Hampshire	42	40	41	41	20.5	11.4	5.2	123.7	137.8	144.9
New Jersey	9	9	9	10	5.2	8.6	3.4	1,044.5	1,134.4	1,172.8
New Mexico.	37	37	36	36	16.3	20.1	4.6	12.5	15.0	15.7
New York	2	2	3	3	2.5	5.5	1.3	381.0	401.9	407.2
North Carolina	10	10	11	11	12.8	21.3	6.1	136.2	165.2	175.3
North Dakota	46	47	47	48	-2.1	0.5	-1.2	9.3	9.3	9.2
Ohio.	6	7	7	7	0.5	4.7	0.9	264.9	277.3	279.8
Oklahoma	26	28	27	28	4.0	9.7	2.1	45.8	50.3	51.3
Oregon	30	29	28	27	7.9	20.4	5.1	29.6	35.6	37.4
Pennsylvania	4	5	6	6	0.2	3.4	1.0	265.1	274.0	276.8
Rhode Island	40	43	43	43	5.9	4.5	3.1	960.3	1,003.2	1,034.2
South Carolina	24	25	26	25	11.7	15.1	4.6	115.8	133.2	139.4
South Dakota	45	45	46	46	0.8	8.5	2.1	9.2	9.9	10.2
Tennessee.	17	17	16	16	6.2	16.7	3.7	118.3	138.0	143.2
Texas	3	3	2	2	19.4	22.8	7.9	64.9	79.6	85.9
Utah.	36	35	34	34	17.9	29.6	7.0	21.0	27.2	29.1
Vermont	48	48	49	49	10.0	8.2	2.1	60.8	65.8	67.2
Virginia	14	12	12	12	15.8	14.4	5.4	156.3	178.8	188.4
Washington	20	18	15	15	17.8	21.1	5.3	73.1	88.6	93.2
West Virginia	34	34	37	37	-8.0	0.8	0.4	74.5	75.1	75.4
Wisconsin	16	16	18	20	4.0	9.6	2.7	90.1	98.8	101.4
Wyoming.	49	50	50	50	-3.4	8.9	2.6	4.7	5.1	5.2

X Not applicable.   Z Less than 0.05 percent.   [1] Persons per square mile were calculated on the basis of land area data from the 2000 census.

Source: U.S. Census Bureau, Current Population Reports, P25-1106; "ST-99-3 State Population Estimates: Annual Time Series, July 1, 1990, to July 1, 1999"; published 29 December 1999; <http://www.census.gov/population/estimates/state/st-99-3.txt>; Population Change and Distribution: 1990 to 2000, Census 2000 Brief. (C2KBR/01-2), April 2001; and "Table 2 - Cumulative Estimates of Population Change for the United States and States, and for Puerto Rico and State Rankings: April 1, 2000 to July 1, 2004 (NST-EST2004-02)"; published 22 December 2004; <http://www.census.gov/popest/states/NST-pop-chg.html>.

Table 19. **State Resident Population—Projections: 2005 to 2030**

[As of July 1. These projections were produced in correspondence with the U.S. interim projections released in March 2004 (see Tables 3 and 11). They were developed for each of the 50 states and the District of Columbia by age and sex for the years 2000 to 2030, based on Census 2000 results. These projections differ from forecasts in that they represent the results of the mathematical projection model given that current state-specific trends in fertility, mortality, internal migration and international migration continue. The projections to 2004 have been superseded by population estimates which are shown in Table 17. Minus sign (-) indicates decrease]

State	Number (1,000)						Change, 2000-2030		Rank	
	2005	2010	2015	2020	2025	2030	Number (1,000)	Percent	Total population 2030	Percent change 2000-2030
U.S.	295,507	308,936	322,366	335,805	349,439	363,584	82,163	29.2	(X)	(X)
AL............	4,527	4,596	4,663	4,729	4,800	4,874	427	9.6	24	35
AK............	661	694	733	774	821	868	241	38.4	46	12
AZ............	5,868	6,637	7,495	8,456	9,532	10,712	5,582	108.8	10	2
AR............	2,777	2,875	2,969	3,060	3,151	3,240	567	21.2	32	21
CA............	36,039	38,067	40,123	42,207	44,305	46,445	12,573	37.1	1	13
CO	4,618	4,832	5,049	5,279	5,523	5,792	1,491	34.7	22	14
CT............	3,503	3,577	3,635	3,676	3,691	3,689	283	8.3	30	38
DE............	837	884	927	963	991	1,013	229	29.2	45	18
DC	551	530	506	481	455	433	-139	-24.2	(X)	(X)
FL	17,510	19,252	21,204	23,407	25,912	28,686	12,703	79.5	3	3
GA	8,926	9,589	10,231	10,844	11,439	12,018	3,831	46.8	8	8
HI	1,277	1,341	1,386	1,412	1,439	1,466	255	21.0	41	22
ID	1,407	1,517	1,630	1,741	1,853	1,970	676	52.2	37	6
IL	12,699	12,917	13,097	13,237	13,341	13,433	1,014	8.2	5	39
IN	6,250	6,392	6,518	6,627	6,721	6,810	730	12.0	18	31
IA............	2,974	3,010	3,026	3,020	2,993	2,955	29	1.0	34	48
KS............	2,752	2,805	2,853	2,891	2,919	2,940	252	9.4	35	36
KY............	4,163	4,265	4,351	4,424	4,490	4,555	513	12.7	27	30
LA............	4,534	4,613	4,674	4,719	4,762	4,803	334	7.5	26	41
ME	1,319	1,357	1,389	1,409	1,414	1,411	136	10.7	42	32
MD............	5,601	5,905	6,208	6,498	6,763	7,022	1,726	32.6	16	16
MA............	6,519	6,649	6,759	6,856	6,939	7,012	663	10.4	17	33
MI............	10,207	10,429	10,599	10,696	10,714	10,694	756	7.6	11	40
MN............	5,175	5,421	5,668	5,901	6,109	6,306	1,387	28.2	20	20
MS	2,916	2,971	3,014	3,045	3,069	3,092	248	8.7	33	37
MO	5,765	5,922	6,070	6,200	6,315	6,430	835	14.9	19	27
MT............	933	969	999	1,023	1,037	1,045	143	15.8	44	25
NE............	1,744	1,769	1,789	1,803	1,813	1,820	109	6.4	38	42
NV............	2,352	2,691	3,058	3,452	3,863	4,282	2,284	114.3	28	1
NH............	1,315	1,386	1,457	1,525	1,586	1,646	411	33.2	40	15
NJ............	8,745	9,018	9,256	9,462	9,637	9,802	1,388	16.5	13	24
NM............	1,902	1,980	2,042	2,084	2,107	2,100	281	15.4	36	26
NY............	19,258	19,444	19,547	19,577	19,540	19,477	501	2.6	4	46
NC............	8,702	9,346	10,011	10,709	11,449	12,228	4,178	51.9	7	7
ND............	635	637	635	630	621	607	-36	-5.5	49	50
OH	11,478	11,576	11,635	11,644	11,606	11,551	197	1.7	9	47
OK	3,521	3,592	3,662	3,736	3,821	3,913	463	13.4	29	29
OR	3,596	3,791	4,013	4,260	4,536	4,834	1,413	41.3	25	10
PA............	12,427	12,584	12,711	12,787	12,802	12,768	487	4.0	6	45
RI............	1,087	1,117	1,140	1,154	1,158	1,153	105	10.0	43	34
SC............	4,239	4,447	4,642	4,823	4,990	5,149	1,137	28.3	23	19
SD............	772	786	797	802	802	800	46	6.0	47	43
TN............	5,965	6,231	6,502	6,781	7,073	7,381	1,691	29.7	15	17
TX............	22,775	24,649	26,586	28,635	30,865	33,318	12,466	59.8	2	4
UT............	2,418	2,595	2,783	2,990	3,226	3,485	1,252	56.1	31	5
VT............	631	653	673	691	703	712	103	16.9	48	23
VA............	7,553	8,010	8,467	8,917	9,364	9,825	2,747	38.8	12	11
WA............	6,205	6,542	6,951	7,432	7,996	8,625	2,731	46.3	14	9
WV............	1,819	1,829	1,823	1,801	1,766	1,720	-88	-4.9	39	49
WI............	5,554	5,727	5,883	6,005	6,088	6,151	787	14.7	21	28
WY............	507	520	528	531	529	523	29	5.9	50	44

X Not applicable.

Source: U.S. Census Bureau, "Table A1: Interim Projections of the Total Population for the United States and States: April 1, 2000 to July 1, 2030"; published 21 April 2005: <http://www.census.gov/population/www/projections/projectionsagesex.html>

Population 23

Table 20. State Resident Population—Components of Change: 2000–2004

[Covers period April 1, 2000, to July 1, 2004. Minus sign (-) indicates net decrease]

State	Numeric population change [1]	Births	Deaths	Natural increase (births minus deaths)	Net internal migration	Net international migration
United States	12,230,802	17,198,187	10,297,024	6,901,163	(X)	5,329,639
Alabama.	82,831	258,878	196,032	62,846	-703	21,712
Alaska	28,504	42,755	13,986	28,769	-4,481	4,512
Arizona.	613,202	371,351	178,046	193,305	281,625	141,175
Arkansas	79,231	159,897	118,535	41,362	20,949	18,427
California	2,022,146	2,244,263	983,736	1,260,527	-415,313	1,192,430
Colorado.	299,388	285,656	121,297	164,359	42,100	94,620
Connecticut.	98,002	181,064	127,067	53,997	-18,255	63,771
Delaware	46,764	47,020	29,651	17,369	20,184	9,621
District of Columbia	-18,536	33,197	25,203	7,994	-43,304	17,156
Florida	1,414,337	893,447	708,259	185,188	791,904	444,726
Georgia	642,567	577,914	279,352	298,562	181,296	161,522
Hawaii	51,303	78,349	38,712	39,637	-11,986	24,204
Idaho	99,306	88,369	42,609	45,760	40,761	12,208
Illinois	293,987	774,574	453,342	321,232	-304,775	276,890
Indiana.	157,052	365,221	236,937	128,284	-18,818	47,067
Iowa	28,069	159,235	118,027	41,208	-37,315	24,975
Kansas.	46,678	165,737	104,107	61,630	-48,141	32,289
Kentucky	103,637	230,345	170,046	60,299	22,512	22,745
Louisiana	46,812	284,740	177,971	106,769	-74,776	16,680
Maine.	42,330	57,576	53,238	4,338	34,356	4,182
Maryland	261,552	318,169	188,517	129,652	21,969	91,278
Massachusetts.	67,400	347,124	241,265	105,859	-173,062	137,394
Michigan.	174,140	560,624	370,460	190,164	-116,477	103,785
Minnesota.	181,466	287,611	160,686	126,925	-7,728	60,274
Mississippi	58,310	183,404	121,865	61,539	-10,423	8,717
Missouri	157,935	322,858	234,051	88,807	20,077	35,880
Montana.	24,670	46,230	35,951	10,279	13,014	1,741
Nebraska	35,949	106,706	65,074	41,632	-23,672	18,789
Nevada	336,514	135,588	71,296	64,292	216,322	55,710
New Hampshire	63,714	60,933	40,203	20,730	33,774	9,624
New Jersey.	284,532	491,048	311,614	179,434	-135,483	244,994
New Mexico	84,243	115,818	58,010	57,808	3,985	23,267
New York	250,267	1,093,899	662,269	431,630	-771,944	562,265
North Carolina	494,730	505,789	310,001	195,788	166,864	131,807
North Dakota.	-7,838	32,391	25,209	7,182	-17,742	3,023
Ohio	105,866	637,404	465,064	172,340	-133,416	63,691
Oklahoma.	72,899	213,108	150,892	62,216	-18,211	30,484
Oregon.	173,150	191,214	130,648	60,566	52,944	61,482
Pennsylvania.	125,238	613,270	552,078	61,192	-19,365	86,811
Rhode Island.	32,313	52,551	41,587	10,964	5,826	15,990
South Carolina.	186,252	239,064	160,520	78,544	79,476	30,218
South Dakota	16,043	45,137	29,911	15,226	-1,973	3,259
Tennessee	211,700	334,641	238,191	96,450	71,204	42,226
Texas	1,638,232	1,570,403	639,884	930,519	157,893	558,004
Utah	155,841	204,213	55,349	148,864	-39,856	42,176
Vermont	12,567	26,841	21,842	4,999	4,118	3,722
Virginia.	380,797	423,268	241,784	181,484	87,546	115,538
Washington.	309,648	333,188	191,793	141,395	52,965	112,580
West Virginia.	7,004	87,308	89,352	-2,044	6,794	3,114
Wisconsin	145,311	291,703	198,158	93,545	15,381	39,044
Wyoming	12,747	27,094	17,347	9,747	1,380	1,840

X Not applicable.   [1] The estimated components of population change will not sum to the numerical population change due to the process of controlling to national totals.

Source: U.S. Census Bureau, "Table 4 - Cumulative Estimates of the Components of Population Change for the United States and States: April 1, 2000 to July 1, 2004 (NST-EST2004-04)"; published 22 December 2004; <http://www.census.gov/popest/states /NST-comp-chg.html>.

U.S. Census Bureau, Statistical Abstract of the United States: 2006

Table 21. **Resident Population by Age and State: 2004**

[In thousands, except percent (293,655 represents 293,655,000). As of July. Includes Armed Forces stationed in area]

State	Total	Under 5 years	5 to 17 years	18 to 24 years	25 to 34 years	35 to 44 years	45 to 54 years	55 to 64 years	65 to 74 years	75 to 84 years	85 years and over	Percent 65 years and over
U.S. . .	293,655	20,071	53,207	29,245	40,032	44,109	41,619	29,079	18,463	12,971	4,860	12.4
AL	4,530	296	798	456	603	651	648	480	325	207	66	13.2
AK	655	50	138	74	81	102	107	61	26	13	4	6.4
AZ	5,744	450	1,097	571	830	800	719	545	396	250	86	12.7
AR	2,753	186	491	280	360	385	376	294	205	128	48	13.8
CA	35,894	2,634	6,962	3,596	5,253	5,541	4,860	3,225	1,950	1,359	514	10.7
CO	4,601	339	840	457	717	709	668	421	241	154	56	9.8
CT	3,504	213	626	311	409	565	532	374	217	175	82	13.5
DE	830	54	140	84	110	128	119	87	58	38	13	13.1
DC	554	35	75	58	108	82	72	56	34	24	9	12.1
FL	17,397	1,091	2,912	1,549	2,142	2,530	2,380	1,865	1,475	1,073	380	16.8
GA	8,829	679	1,654	902	1,364	1,392	1,189	803	477	275	95	9.6
HI	1,263	89	210	126	161	180	186	138	79	68	25	13.6
ID	1,393	103	269	157	185	192	194	135	83	53	22	11.4
IL	12,714	891	2,348	1,260	1,798	1,905	1,782	1,210	761	540	219	12.0
IN	6,238	431	1,170	632	826	907	886	614	388	279	105	12.4
IA	2,954	181	500	316	369	418	436	301	203	158	72	14.7
KS	2,736	189	495	299	359	388	392	260	170	129	55	13.0
KY	4,146	267	714	413	568	621	605	439	281	179	59	12.5
LA	4,516	324	841	503	598	642	639	441	280	188	60	11.7
ME	1,317	68	215	124	146	205	216	155	95	69	25	14.4
MD	5,558	375	1,020	521	711	895	829	573	326	226	83	11.4
MA	6,417	396	1,069	598	880	1,030	937	652	396	322	136	13.3
MI	10,113	650	1,884	997	1,306	1,514	1,496	1,020	612	460	175	12.3
MN	5,101	332	908	531	678	793	755	488	300	217	98	12.1
MS	2,903	208	541	323	391	405	397	284	193	121	40	12.2
MO	5,755	371	1,013	589	751	845	826	592	392	274	100	13.3
MT	927	53	156	99	107	128	152	107	66	42	18	13.7
NE	1,747	122	313	191	229	244	249	167	111	85	36	13.3
NV	2,335	169	435	210	355	355	310	239	154	84	24	11.2
NH	1,300	73	232	122	149	216	209	141	79	56	22	12.1
NJ	8,699	581	1,575	744	1,095	1,416	1,275	886	543	420	163	12.9
NM	1,903	133	359	206	236	266	275	199	126	77	27	12.1
NY	19,227	1,246	3,326	1,825	2,633	2,993	2,741	1,970	1,226	913	354	13.0
NC	8,541	600	1,518	828	1,242	1,289	1,175	856	555	356	121	12.1
ND	634	36	103	77	81	85	97	63	43	34	16	14.7
OH	11,459	730	2,049	1,128	1,464	1,684	1,702	1,177	747	570	208	13.3
OK	3,524	242	618	385	470	488	493	363	249	161	54	13.2
OR	3,595	226	626	350	506	511	537	379	227	163	70	12.8
PA	12,406	719	2,118	1,185	1,471	1,823	1,869	1,325	864	742	291	15.3
RI	1,081	62	182	112	139	166	159	110	65	60	26	13.9
SC	4,198	280	744	429	568	611	594	451	286	175	59	12.4
SD	771	52	139	87	93	106	111	74	52	39	18	14.2
TN	5,901	385	1,007	576	828	887	852	629	407	248	84	12.5
TX	22,490	1,843	4,424	2,400	3,336	3,338	2,981	1,952	1,214	756	246	9.9
UT	2,389	233	507	313	399	291	268	170	111	71	26	8.7
VT	621	31	104	62	70	95	105	74	41	28	11	13.0
VA	7,460	498	1,307	748	1,015	1,173	1,093	778	453	291	103	11.4
WA	6,204	387	1,099	635	859	956	933	631	357	243	103	11.3
WV	1,815	101	284	173	227	252	284	217	144	102	33	15.3
WI	5,509	338	970	575	696	840	826	550	349	256	111	13.0
WY	507	31	86	57	61	69	84	57	33	21	7	12.1

Source: U.S. Census Bureau, "Population estimates by State, Age and Sex for States and for Puerto Rico: April 1, 2000 to July 1, 2004"; published March 2005; <http://www.census.gov/popest/states/asrh/SC-est2004-02.html>

Population 25

Table 22. **Resident Population by Age and State—Projections: 2005 and 2010**

[As of July 1. These projections were produced in correspondence with the U.S. interim projections released in March 2004 (see Tables 3 and 11). They were developed for each of the 50 states and the District of Columbia by age and sex for the years 2000 to 2030, based on Census 2000 results. These projections differ from forecasts in that they represent the results of the mathematical projection model given that current state-specific trends in fertility, mortality, internal migration and international migration continue. The projections to 2004 have been superseded by population estimates which are shown in Table 21]

State	Population (1,000)										Percent of population, 2010	
	Under 18 years old		18 to 44 years old		45 to 64 years old		65 to 74 years old		75 years old and over		Under 18 years old	65 years old and over
	2005	2010	2005	2010	2005	2010	2005	2010	2005	2010	2005	2010
U.S.	73,639	74,432	112,360	113,248	72,812	81,012	18,624	21,270	18,072	18,974	24.1	13.0
AL	1,112	1,092	1,657	1,605	1,155	1,251	321	354	281	295	23.8	14.1
AK	183	184	264	270	170	184	27	35	17	21	26.5	8.1
AZ	1,533	1,688	2,185	2,349	1,384	1,678	406	516	359	406	25.4	13.9
AR	691	703	1,007	996	697	765	201	227	181	185	24.4	14.3
CA	9,462	9,497	14,357	14,787	8,319	9,391	1,990	2,333	1,910	2,060	24.9	11.5
CO	1,153	1,189	1,861	1,863	1,148	1,263	240	282	216	235	24.6	10.7
CT	838	814	1,277	1,257	909	990	223	253	256	262	22.8	14.4
DE	199	202	311	309	216	249	59	68	52	57	22.9	14.1
DC	117	114	246	237	124	118	32	32	32	29	21.5	11.5
FL	3,863	4,086	6,089	6,315	4,541	5,431	1,484	1,773	1,533	1,646	21.2	17.8
GA	2,361	2,502	3,623	3,724	2,086	2,382	473	564	383	417	26.1	10.2
HI	307	316	471	477	329	357	85	101	85	90	23.6	14.3
ID	380	400	531	554	338	381	82	99	76	82	26.4	12.0
IL	3,230	3,197	4,916	4,842	3,033	3,277	756	826	765	774	24.7	12.4
IN	1,596	1,596	2,354	2,328	1,533	1,656	386	425	380	386	25.0	12.7
IA	721	711	1,076	1,049	741	800	203	217	233	233	23.6	14.9
KS	702	699	1,024	1,004	667	727	171	185	188	190	24.9	13.4
KY	1,005	1,002	1,573	1,540	1,066	1,165	278	309	242	249	23.5	13.1
LA	1,185	1,172	1,706	1,665	1,104	1,194	282	313	257	270	25.4	12.6
ME	282	269	470	462	374	413	97	110	96	102	19.8	15.6
MD	1,384	1,406	2,153	2,212	1,421	1,568	331	386	311	332	23.8	12.2
MA	1,525	1,484	2,486	2,440	1,649	1,817	406	454	452	454	22.3	13.7
MI	2,555	2,487	3,833	3,822	2,573	2,785	624	699	622	635	23.8	12.8
MN	1,277	1,290	2,003	2,027	1,278	1,433	301	343	316	327	23.8	12.4
MS	771	759	1,084	1,052	706	781	189	209	165	170	25.6	12.8
MO	1,418	1,411	2,134	2,111	1,443	1,578	391	432	379	390	23.8	13.9
MT	215	212	326	324	263	287	66	77	64	68	21.9	15.0
NE	445	446	642	619	425	460	111	119	122	125	25.2	13.8
NV	593	665	894	961	598	735	157	199	110	131	24.7	12.3
NH	307	304	489	494	360	408	82	97	76	82	22.0	12.9
NJ	2,103	2,088	3,285	3,252	2,212	2,446	564	632	582	600	23.2	13.7
NM	488	479	684	669	491	553	129	153	111	126	24.2	14.1
NY	4,607	4,421	7,380	7,227	4,762	5,144	1,243	1,346	1,266	1,306	22.7	13.6
NC	2,152	2,269	3,363	3,471	2,150	2,445	554	641	483	520	24.3	12.4
ND	149	142	231	223	161	174	43	46	50	51	22.3	15.3
OH	2,819	2,744	4,220	4,123	2,917	3,121	758	816	763	771	23.7	13.7
OK	890	895	1,293	1,264	873	938	243	266	222	229	24.9	13.8
OR	844	863	1,360	1,412	944	1,022	220	263	228	231	22.8	13.0
PA	2,844	2,748	4,444	4,385	3,242	3,496	893	960	1,004	997	21.8	15.5
RI	256	249	408	410	271	300	68	76	83	82	22.3	14.1
SC	1,038	1,036	1,577	1,579	1,095	1,226	289	343	240	263	23.3	13.6
SD	195	194	278	269	189	209	51	55	58	60	24.7	14.6
TN	1,449	1,479	2,248	2,249	1,522	1,673	403	461	345	368	23.7	13.3
TX	6,317	6,785	9,068	9,417	5,122	5,859	1,216	1,426	1,052	1,162	27.5	10.5
UT	771	819	979	1,021	460	520	108	127	99	108	31.6	9.0
VT	140	132	230	232	179	195	42	50	41	43	20.3	14.3
VA	1,827	1,880	2,940	2,997	1,918	2,139	463	554	404	441	23.5	12.4
WA	1,491	1,488	2,410	2,481	1,602	1,777	353	429	350	367	22.8	12.2
WV	392	382	640	618	508	536	145	156	135	136	20.9	16.0
WI	1,334	1,319	2,095	2,076	1,404	1,561	351	392	369	380	23.0	13.5
WY	119	116	183	177	142	154	34	40	30	33	22.4	14.0

Source: U.S. Census Bureau, "File 2. Annual projections by 5-year and selected age groups by sex"; published 21 April 2005; <http://www.census.gov/population/www/projections/projectionsagesex.html>.

Table 23. **Resident Population by Race, Hispanic or Latino Origin, and State: 2004**

[In thousands (293,655 represents 293,655,000). As of July. Persons of Hispanic or Latino origin may be of any race. Due to the complexities associated with the production of detailed characteristics' estimates at the state and county levels, the values of the estimates at lower levels of geography may not necessarily sum to estimates at higher levels of geography]

| State | Total population | One race | | | | | Two or more races | Hispanic or Latino origin | Non-Hispanic White alone |
		White alone	Black or African American alone	American Indian, Alaska Native alone	Asian alone	Native Hawaiian and Other Pacific Islander alone			
U.S....	293,655	236,058	37,502	2,825	12,326	506	4,439	41,322	197,841
AL	4,530	3,235	1,194	23	37	2	39	98	3,148
AK	655	464	24	104	30	4	31	32	438
AZ	5,744	5,033	203	289	123	10	86	1,609	3,510
AR	2,753	2,238	434	20	26	2	32	121	2,126
CA	35,894	27,710	2,437	417	4,326	149	855	12,443	15,982
CO	4,601	4,154	189	52	116	6	82	879	3,334
CT	3,504	2,983	352	12	108	3	46	372	2,658
DE	830	625	169	3	21	(Z)	11	48	583
DC	554	207	319	2	17	(Z)	8	47	168
FL	17,397	14,022	2,726	74	352	14	209	3,305	10,920
GA	8,829	5,863	2,613	27	230	7	90	598	5,319
HI	1,263	335	28	4	528	114	254	100	295
ID	1,393	1,331	8	20	14	2	19	124	1,215
IL	12,714	10,101	1,926	39	505	8	135	1,775	8,414
IN	6,238	5,530	548	18	73	3	66	269	5,280
IA	2,954	2,807	68	10	42	1	26	104	2,710
KS	2,736	2,445	161	26	57	2	44	220	2,239
KY	4,146	3,747	311	9	37	2	40	77	3,678
LA	4,516	2,896	1,492	27	62	2	37	124	2,789
ME	1,317	1,277	10	7	11	(Z)	12	12	1,266
MD	5,558	3,583	1,615	18	258	3	81	298	3,325
MA	6,417	5,581	435	18	295	5	83	494	5,181
MI	10,113	8,232	1,451	60	220	4	146	375	7,896
MN	5,101	4,583	212	59	172	3	72	179	4,421
MS	2,903	1,780	1,069	13	21	1	18	49	1,739
MO	5,755	4,916	661	26	75	4	73	148	4,781
MT	927	844	3	60	5	1	14	22	826
NE	1,747	1,609	75	17	27	1	19	120	1,497
NV	2,335	1,927	176	33	128	12	58	532	1,429
NH	1,300	1,250	12	3	22	1	12	28	1,225
NJ	8,699	6,690	1,260	27	607	7	108	1,294	5,549
NM	1,903	1,612	45	192	24	2	28	823	827
NY	19,227	14,216	3,361	103	1,249	18	279	3,077	11,746
NC	8,541	6,332	1,861	110	148	6	83	518	5,861
ND	634	586	5	33	4	(Z)	6	10	578
OH	11,459	9,768	1,362	26	159	4	140	252	9,547
OK	3,524	2,770	272	284	54	3	140	223	2,570
OR	3,595	3,267	64	49	122	10	83	343	2,948
PA	12,406	10,693	1,304	22	267	5	115	476	10,288
RI	1,081	962	66	6	29	1	16	112	870
SC	4,198	2,868	1,233	16	44	2	35	130	2,753
SD	771	684	6	67	5	(Z)	9	15	671
TN	5,901	4,763	991	17	71	3	56	167	4,611
TX	22,490	18,726	2,633	153	718	24	235	7,781	11,190
UT	2,389	2,241	23	32	45	17	31	253	2,003
VT	621	602	4	2	6	(Z)	7	6	597
VA	7,460	5,502	1,483	24	330	5	115	426	5,122
WA	6,204	5,290	216	101	388	28	180	527	4,809
WV	1,815	1,728	58	4	10	(Z)	15	15	1,714
WI	5,509	4,967	328	51	106	2	56	237	4,749
WY	507	480	4	12	3	(Z)	6	34	449

Z Less than 500.

Source: U.S. Census Bureau, "Table 4: Annual Estimates of the Population by Race Alone and Hispanic or Latino Origin for the United States and States: July 1, 2004 (SC-EST2004-04)"; published 11 August 2005; <http://www.census.gov/popest/states/asrh/SC-EST2004-04.html>.

Population 27

Table 24. Resident Population by Region, Race, and Hispanic Origin: 2000

[As of April (281,422 represents 281,422,000). For composition of regions, see map. inside front cover]

Race and Hispanic origin	Population (1,000)					Percent distribution				
	United States	North-east	Midwest	South	West	United States	North-east	Midwest	South	West
Total population	281,422	53,594	64,393	100,237	63,198	100.0	19.0	22.9	35.6	22.5
One race	274,596	52,366	63,370	98,390	60,470	100.0	19.1	23.1	35.8	22.0
White	211,461	41,534	53,834	72,819	43,274	100.0	19.6	25.5	34.4	20.5
Black or African American	34,658	6,100	6,500	18,982	3,077	100.0	17.6	18.8	54.8	8.9
American Indian and Alaska Native	2,476	163	399	726	1,188	100.0	6.6	16.1	29.3	48.0
Asian	10,243	2,119	1,198	1,922	5,004	100.0	20.7	11.7	18.8	48.8
Asian Indian	1,679	554	293	441	391	100.0	33.0	17.5	26.3	23.3
Chinese	2,433	692	212	343	1,186	100.0	28.4	8.7	14.1	48.8
Filipino	1,850	202	151	245	1,253	100.0	10.9	8.2	13.2	67.7
Japanese	797	76	63	77	580	100.0	9.6	7.9	9.7	72.8
Korean	1,077	246	132	224	474	100.0	22.9	12.3	20.8	44.0
Vietnamese	1,123	115	107	336	564	100.0	10.3	9.5	29.9	50.3
Other Asian [1]	1,285	233	239	257	556	100.0	18.2	18.6	20.0	43.2
Native Hawaiian and Other Pacific Islander	399	21	22	51	304	100.0	5.2	5.6	12.8	76.3
Native Hawaiian	141	4	6	12	118	100.0	3.2	4.1	8.9	83.8
Guamanian or Chamorro	58	5	5	15	34	100.0	7.9	7.9	25.1	59.1
Samoan	91	4	5	9	73	100.0	4.2	5.6	9.7	80.5
Other Pacific Islander [2]	109	8	7	15	79	100.0	7.3	6.4	14.0	72.2
Some other race	15,359	2,430	1,417	3,889	7,623	100.0	15.8	9.2	25.3	49.6
Two or more races	6,826	1,228	1,022	1,847	2,728	100.0	18.0	15.0	27.1	40.0
Hispanic or Latino (of any race)	35,306	5,254	3,125	11,587	15,341	100.0	14.9	8.8	32.8	43.5
Mexican	20,641	479	2,200	6,548	11,413	100.0	2.3	10.7	31.7	55.3
Puerto Rican	3,406	2,075	325	759	247	100.0	60.9	9.6	22.3	7.2
Cuban	1,242	169	45	921	106	100.0	13.6	3.6	74.2	8.5
Other Hispanic or Latino	10,017	2,531	554	3,358	3,574	100.0	25.3	5.5	33.5	35.7
Not Hispanic or Latino	246,116	48,340	61,268	88,650	47,857	100.0	19.6	24.9	36.0	19.4
White alone	194,553	39,327	52,386	65,928	36,912	100.0	20.2	26.9	33.9	19.0

[1] Other Asian alone, or two or more Asian categories. [2] Other Pacific Islander alone, or two or more Native Hawaiian and Other Pacific Islander categories.

Source: U.S. Census Bureau, "Demographic Profiles: Census 2000"; <http://www.census.gov/Press-Release/www/2001/demoprofile.html>.

Table 25. Population in Coastal Counties: 1970 to 2003

[Population as of April 1, except as indicated (3,536 represents 3,536,000). Areas as defined by U.S. National Oceanic and Atmospheric Agency, 1992. Covers 673 counties and equivalent areas with at least 15 percent of their land area either in a coastal watershed (drainage area) or in a coastal cataloging unit (a coastal area between watersheds). See Appendix III]

Year	Total	Counties in coastal regions					Balance of United States
		Total	Atlantic	Gulf of Mexico	Great Lakes	Pacific	
Land area, 1990 (1,000 sq. mi.)	3,536	888	148	114	115	510	2,649
POPULATION							
1970 (mil.)	203.3	110.0	51.1	10.0	26.0	22.8	93.3
1980 (mil.)	226.5	119.8	53.7	13.1	26.0	27.0	106.7
1990 (mil.)	248.7	133.4	59.0	15.2	25.9	33.2	115.3
2000 (mil.)	281.4	148.3	65.2	18.0	27.3	37.8	133.1
2001 (July 1) (mil.)	285.1	150.2	66.0	18.3	27.4	38.5	134.9
2002 (July 1) (mil.)	288.0	151.6	66.6	18.6	27.5	38.9	136.4
2003 (July 1) (mil.)	290.8	152.9	67.1	18.9	27.5	39.4	137.9
1970 (percent)	100	54	25	5	13	11	46
1980 (percent)	100	53	24	6	11	12	47
1990 (percent)	100	54	24	6	10	13	46
2000 (percent)	100	53	23	6	10	13	47
2003 (July 1) (percent)	100	53	23	6	9	14	47

Source: U.S. Census Bureau, U.S. Census of Population: 1970; 1980 Census of Population, Vol. 1, Chapter A (PC80-1-A-1). *U.S. Summary*; 1990 Census of Population and Housing (CPH1); and unpublished data.

Table 26. **Large Metropolitan Statistical Areas—Population: 1990 to 2004**

[1990 and 2000, as of April 1; beginning 2002 as of July 1 (658 represents 658,000). Covers metropolitan statistical areas with 250,000 and over population in 2004, as defined by the U.S. Office of Management and Budget as of November 2004. For definitions and components of all metropolitan and micropolitan areas, see Appendix II. Minus sign (-) indicates decrease]

Metropolitan statistical area	Number (1,000)					Percent change		Rank, 2004
	1990	2000	2002	2003	2004	1990-2000	2000-2004 [1]	
Akron, OH.	658	695	700	701	702	5.7	1.0	69
Albany-Schenectady-Troy. NY	810	826	834	841	845	2.0	2.3	59
Albuquerque, NM.	599	730	754	767	781	21.7	7.1	62
Allentown-Bethlehem-Easton. PA-NJ	687	740	758	769	780	7.8	5.3	63
Anchorage; AK	266	320	333	339	345	20.1	7.9	140
Ann Arbor, MI	283	323	332	336	339	14.1	5.1	141
Asheville. NC.	308	369	378	383	387	19.9	4.9	124
Atlanta-Sandy Springs-Marietta, GA.	3,069	4.248	4,504	4,605	4,708	38.4	10.8	9
Atlantic City, NJ	224	253	259	264	269	12.6	6.4	164
Augusta-Richmond County, GA-SC	436	500	507	510	515	14.7	3.1	93
Austin-Round Rock, TX	846	1,250	1,347	1,377	1,412	47.7	13.0	38
Bakersfield, CA	545	662	693	713	735	21.4	11.1	66
Baltimore-Towson. MD	2,382	2,553	2,596	2,627	2,639	7.2	3.4	19
Baton Rouge, LA	624	706	715	721	729	13.2	3.2	67
Beaumont-Port Arthur, TX	361	385	383	383	383	6.6	-0.4	126
Birmingham-Hoover, AL.	957	1,052	1,066	1,074	1,082	10.0	2.9	48
Boise City-Nampa, ID	320	465	499	512	525	45.4	12.9	88
Boston-Cambridge-Quincy, MA-NH	4,134	4,391	4,433	4,430	4,425	6.2	0.7	11
Boulder, CO [2]	209	270	278	277	279	29.1	3.4	160
Bridgeport-Stamford-Norwalk, CT	828	883	895	900	903	6.6	2.3	53
Brownsville-Harlingen, TX	260	335	353	362	372	28.9	10.9	129
Buffalo-Niagara Falls. NY.	1,189	1,170	1,160	1,158	1,154	-1.6	-1.3	45
Canton-Massillon, OH	394	407	409	410	411	3.3	1.0	113
Cape Coral-Fort Myers. FL.	335	441	476	492	514	31.6	16.6	94
Charleston, WV	308	310	307	307	308	0.6	-0.6	148
Charleston-North Charleston, SC	507	549	564	572	583	8.3	6.3	84
Charlotte-Gastonia-Concord, NC-SC	1,025	1,330	1,407	1,439	1,475	29.8	10.8	37
Chattanooga, TN-GA	433	477	483	487	490	10.0	2.8	98
Chicago-Naperville-Joliet, IL-IN-WI	8,182	9,098	9,267	9,330	9,392	11.2	3.2	3
Cincinnati-Middletown, OH-KY-IN	1,845	2,010	2,036	2,047	2,058	8.9	2.4	25
Cleveland-Elyria-Mentor. OH	2,102	2,148	2,142	2,140	2,137	2.2	-0.5	23
Colorado Springs. CO.	409	537	563	570	576	31.3	7.2	85
Columbia, SC	549	647	663	671	679	17.9	5.0	71
Columbus, GA-AL	266	282	286	278	280	5.7	-0.8	159
Columbus, OH.	1,405	1,613	1,657	1,677	1,694	14.8	5.0	31
Corpus Christi, TX	368	403	404	406	410	9.7	1.6	114
Dallas-Fort Worth-Arlington, TX.	3,989	5,162	5,473	5,586	5,700	29.4	10.4	5
Davenport-Moline-Rock Island, IA-IL	368	376	375	375	375	2.1	-0.2	128
Dayton, OH.	844	848	845	846	846	0.5	-0.3	58
Deltona-Daytona Beach-Ormond Beach, FL	371	443	459	468	479	19.6	8.0	100
Denver-Aurora, CO [2]	1,667	2.179	2,276	2,302	2,330	30.7	6.9	22
Des Moines, IA	416	481	496	504	512	15.6	6.3	95
Detroit-Warren-Livonia, MI	4,249	4,453	4,479	4.487	4,493	4.8	0.9	10
Duluth, MN-WI.	269	275	276	276	276	2.3	0.1	162
Durham, NC	345	426	441	445	451	23.7	6.5	104
El Paso, TX.	592	680	694	703	713	14.9	4.9	68
Erie, PA	276	281	282	283	282	1.9	0.5	157
Eugene-Springfield. OR.	283	323	327	330	332	14.2	2.7	144
Evansville, IN-KY	325	343	345	347	348	5.5	1.6	137
Fayetteville, NC	298	337	341	345	348	13.1	3.3	138
Fayetteville-Springdale-Rogers, AR-MO	239	347	367	378	391	44.9	12.6	123
Flint, MI	430	436	441	443	444	1.3	1.8	105
Fort Collins-Loveland, CO	186	251	264	267	269	35.1	6.9	163
Fort Smith, AR-OK	234	273	278	280	282	16.7	3.3	158
Fort Wayne. IN	354	390	397	400	402	10.1	3.1	115
Fresno. CA	667	799	832	851	867	19.8	8.4	56
Grand Rapids-Wyoming, MI	646	740	757	763	768	14.6	3.7	65
Green Bay. WI.	244	283	289	292	295	16.0	4.6	153
Greensboro-High Point, NC	540	643	657	662	668	19.1	3.7	72
Greenville, SC.	472	560	573	578	584	18.6	4.3	83
Gulfport-Biloxi, MS	208	246	249	250	253	18.4	2.7	169
Harrisburg-Carlisle, PA	474	509	514	517	519	7.3	2.0	91
Hartford-West Hartford-East Hartford, CT	1,124	1,149	1,169	1,180	1,185	2.2	3.1	44
Hickory-Lenoir-Morganton. NC	292	342	349	351	353	16.9	3.2	136
Holland-Grand Haven. MI	188	238	246	250	252	26.9	5.9	170
Honolulu, HI	836	876	886	893	900	4.8	2.7	54
Houston-Sugar Land-Baytown, TX.	3,767	4,715	4,967	5,073	5,180	25.2	9.9	7
Huntington-Ashland, WV-KY-OH	288	289	287	287	287	0.2	-0.6	156
Huntsville, AL	293	342	353	358	362	16.8	5.8	134
Indianapolis, IN	1,294	1,525	1,578	1,601	1,622	17.8	6.3	35
Jackson, MS	447	497	505	510	517	11.2	4.0	92
Jacksonville, FL	925	1,123	1,174	1,197	1,225	21.4	9.1	42
Kalamazoo-Portage, MI	293	315	318	320	319	7.3	1.4	145
Kansas City, MO-KS	1,637	1,836	1,887	1,906	1,925	12.2	4.8	27
Killeen-Temple-Fort Hood, TX.	269	331	338	344	346	23.0	4.7	139
Kingsport-Bristol-Bristol, TN-VA.	276	298	299	300	301	8.3	0.7	150
Knoxville, TN.	535	616	632	641	647	15.2	5.0	79
Lakeland, FL	405	484	500	511	524	19.4	8.4	89
Lancaster, PA	423	471	479	483	487	11.3	3.5	99

See footnotes at end of table.

Population 29

[1990 and 2000, as of April 1; beginning 2002 as of July 1 (658 represents 658,000). Covers metropolitan statistical areas with 250,000 and over population in 2004, as defined by the U.S. Office of Management and Budget as of November 2004. For definitions and components of all metropolitan and micropolitan areas, see Appendix II. Minus sign (-) indicates decrease]

Metropolitan statistical area	Number (1,000)					Percent change		Rank, 2004
	1990	2000	2002	2003	2004	1990-2000	2000-2004 [1]	
Lansing-East Lansing, MI	433	448	452	454	456	3.5	1.8	103
Las Vegas-Paradise, NV	741	1,376	1,516	1,575	1,651	85.6	20.0	32
Lexington-Fayette, KY	348	408	415	421	425	17.2	4.0	109
Lincoln, NE	229	267	273	277	278	16.5	4.3	161
Little Rock-North Little Rock, AR	535	611	622	629	637	14.1	4.3	80
Los Angeles-Long Beach-Santa Ana, CA	11,274	12,366	12,692	12,821	12,925	9.7	4.5	2
Louisville, KY-IN	1,056	1,162	1,180	1,190	1,201	10.0	3.3	43
Lubbock, TX	230	250	254	257	258	8.6	3.2	167
Madison, WI	432	502	518	525	532	16.1	6.0	87
Manchester-Nashua, NH	336	381	392	395	399	13.4	4.7	120
McAllen-Edinburg-Mission, TX	384	569	613	635	658	48.5	15.6	74
Memphis, TN-MS-AR	1,067	1,205	1,227	1,239	1,250	12.9	3.7	41
Miami-Fort Lauderdale-Miami Beach, FL	4,056	5,008	5,206	5,277	5,362	23.5	7.1	6
Milwaukee-Waukesha-West Allis, WI	1,432	1,501	1,510	1,514	1,516	4.8	1.0	36
Minneapolis-St. Paul-Bloomington, MN-WI	2,539	2,969	3,055	3,085	3,116	16.9	5.0	16
Mobile, AL	379	400	400	400	401	5.6	0.2	119
Modesto, CA	371	447	480	491	498	20.6	11.5	97
Montgomery, AL	305	347	351	353	355	13.6	2.5	135
Naples-Marco Island, FL	152	251	276	286	297	65.3	18.0	152
Nashville-Davidson–Murfreesboro, TN	1,048	1,312	1,353	1,372	1,396	25.1	6.4	39
New Haven-Milford, CT	804	824	835	841	846	2.5	2.6	57
New Orleans-Metairie-Kenner, LA	1,264	1,317	1,313	1,316	1,320	4.1	0.2	40
New York-Northern New Jersey-Long Island, NY-NJ-PA	16,846	18,323	18,590	18,670	18,710	8.8	2.1	1
Norwich-New London, CT	255	259	263	265	266	1.6	2.8	165
Ocala, FL	195	259	273	281	291	32.9	12.5	154
Ogden-Clearfield, UT	352	443	460	469	477	25.8	7.9	101
Oklahoma City, OK	971	1,095	1,120	1,133	1,144	12.8	4.5	47
Omaha-Council Bluffs, NE-IA	686	767	783	793	804	11.8	4.8	60
Orlando-Kissimmee, FL	1,225	1,645	1,755	1,802	1,862	34.3	13.2	28
Oxnard-Thousand Oaks-Ventura, CA	669	753	781	791	798	12.6	5.9	61
Palm Bay-Melbourne-Titusville, FL	399	476	496	506	519	19.4	9.1	90
Pensacola-Ferry Pass-Brent, FL	344	412	424	429	437	19.7	6.1	107
Peoria, IL	359	367	366	366	368	2.3	0.3	131
Philadelphia-Camden-Wilmington, PA-NJ-DE-MD	5,436	5,687	5,742	5,772	5,801	4.6	2.0	4
Phoenix-Mesa-Scottsdale, AZ	2,238	3,252	3,489	3,593	3,715	45.3	14.3	14
Pittsburgh, PA	2,468	2,431	2,415	2,410	2,402	-1.5	-1.2	21
Port St. Lucie-Fort Pierce, FL	251	319	337	349	365	27.2	14.2	133
Portland-South Portland-Biddeford, ME	441	488	502	507	511	10.5	4.8	96
Portland-Vancouver-Beaverton, OR-WA	1,524	1,928	2,013	2,041	2,064	26.5	7.1	24
Poughkeepsie-Newburgh-Middletown, NY	567	622	644	656	664	9.6	6.8	73
Providence-New Bedford-Fall River, RI-MA	1,510	1,583	1,613	1,623	1,629	4.8	2.9	34
Provo-Orem, UT	269	377	400	406	412	39.9	9.4	112
Raleigh-Cary, NC	544	797	861	888	915	46.5	14.8	51
Reading, PA	337	374	382	387	392	11.0	4.8	121
Reno-Sparks, NV	257	343	365	375	384	33.3	12.1	125
Richmond, VA	949	1,097	1,125	1,138	1,154	15.6	5.2	46
Riverside-San Bernardino-Ontario, CA	2,589	3,255	3,504	3,645	3,793	25.7	16.5	13
Roanoke, VA	269	288	289	290	291	7.4	1.0	155
Rochester, NY	1,002	1,038	1,039	1,041	1,041	3.5	0.4	49
Rockford, IL	284	320	327	331	335	12.9	4.7	142
Sacramento–Arden-Arcade–Roseville, CA	1,481	1,797	1,926	1,975	2,017	21.3	12.2	26
Salem, OR	278	347	360	365	369	24.9	6.4	130
Salinas, CA	356	402	412	414	415	13.0	3.2	110
Salt Lake City, UT	768	969	995	1,006	1,019	26.1	5.2	50
San Antonio, TX	1,408	1,712	1,781	1,816	1,854	21.6	8.3	29
San Diego-Carlsbad-San Marcos, CA	2,498	2,814	2,896	2,919	2,932	12.6	4.2	17
San Francisco-Oakland-Fremont, CA	3,684	4,124	4,163	4,156	4,154	11.9	0.7	12
San Jose-Sunnyvale-Santa Clara, CA	1,534	1,736	1,730	1,732	1,741	13.1	0.3	30
San Luis Obispo-Paso Robles, CA	217	247	252	253	255	13.6	3.2	168
Santa Barbara-Santa Maria, CA	370	399	401	403	402	8.0	0.6	116
Santa Cruz-Watsonville, CA	230	256	253	252	251	11.3	-1.9	171
Santa Rosa-Petaluma, CA	388	459	466	467	468	18.1	2.1	102
Sarasota-Bradenton-Venice, FL	489	590	620	634	652	20.5	10.5	77
Savannah, GA	258	293	301	305	311	13.6	5.9	147
Scranton–Wilkes-Barre, PA	575	561	554	553	552	-2.6	-1.6	86
Seattle-Tacoma-Bellevue, WA	2,559	3,044	3,122	3,142	3,167	18.9	4.0	15
Shreveport-Bossier City, LA	360	376	377	379	382	4.5	1.6	127
South Bend-Mishawaka, IN-MI	297	317	317	317	318	6.8	0.5	146
Spartanburg, SC	227	254	259	262	264	11.9	4.1	166
Spokane, WA	361	418	427	431	436	15.7	4.2	108
Springfield, MA	673	680	684	687	688	1.0	1.2	70
Springfield, MO	299	368	379	384	391	23.3	6.1	122
St. Louis, MO-IL [3]	2,581	2,699	2,736	2,754	2,764	4.6	2.4	18
Stockton, CA	481	564	613	632	650	17.3	15.3	78
Syracuse, NY	660	650	651	653	654	-1.5	0.6	76
Tallahassee, FL	259	320	324	327	332	23.6	3.5	143
Tampa-St. Petersburg-Clearwater, FL	2,068	2,396	2,487	2,531	2,588	15.9	8.0	20
Toledo, OH	654	659	659	659	658	0.8	-0.1	75
Trenton-Ewing, NJ	326	351	358	361	365	7.7	4.1	132

See footnotes at end of table.

Table 26. **Large Metropolitan Statistical Areas—Population: 1990 to 2004—Con.**

[1990 and 2000, as of April 1; beginning 2002 as of July 1 (658 represents 658,000). Covers metropolitan statistical areas with 250,000 and over population in 2004, as defined by the U.S. Office of Management and Budget as of November 2004. For definitions and components of all metropolitan and micropolitan areas, see Appendix II. Minus sign (-) indicates decrease]

Metropolitan statistical area	Number (1,000)					Percent change		Rank, 2004
	1990	2000	2002	2003	2004	1990-2000	2000-2004 [1]	
Tucson, AZ	667	844	878	891	907	26.5	7.5	52
Tulsa, OK	761	860	876	880	882	12.9	2.6	55
Utica-Rome, NY	317	300	298	298	299	-5.3	-0.4	151
Vallejo-Fairfield, CA	339	395	410	412	413	16.2	4.7	111
Virginia Beach-Norfolk-Newport News, VA-NC	1,451	1,576	1,605	1,625	1,644	8.7	4.3	33
Visalia-Porterville, CA	312	368	381	391	402	18.0	9.1	118
Washington-Arlington-Alexandria, DC-VA-MD-WV	4,122	4,796	5,000	5,071	5,140	16.3	7.2	8
Wichita, KS	511	571	580	582	585	11.7	2.4	82
Wilmington, NC	200	275	288	294	303	37.2	10.5	149
Winston-Salem, NC	361	422	433	437	442	16.7	4.7	106
Worcester, MA	710	751	770	776	779	5.8	3.9	64
York-Hanover, PA	340	382	390	396	402	12.4	5.2	117
Youngstown-Warren-Boardman, OH-PA	614	603	596	593	590	-1.7	-2.1	81

[1] Based on the April 1, 2000 Population Estimates base which reflects changes to the Census 2000 population from the Count Question Resolution program and geographic program revisions. [2] Broomfield County, CO was formed from parts of Adams, Boulder, Jefferson, and Weld Counties, CO, on November 15, 2001 and is coextensive with Broomfield city. For purposes of defining and presenting data for metropolitan statistical areas, Broomfield city is treated as if it were a county at the time of the 1990 and 2000 censuses. [3] The portion of Sullivan city in Crawford County, Missouri, is legally part of the St. Louis, MO-IL MSA. Data shown here do not include this area.

Source: U.S. Census Bureau, 2000 Census of Population and Housing, *Population and Housing Unit Counts* PHC-3-1, United States Summary and unpublished data.

Table 27. **Urban and Rural Population by State: 1990 and 2000**

[222,361 represents 222,361,000. As of April 1. Resident population. For urban definitions; see text, this section]

State	Urban population				Rural population, 2000 (1,000)	State	Urban population				Rural population, 2000 (1,000)
	1990		2000, current definition				1990		2000, current definition		
	Former definition (percent)	Current definition (percent)	Number (1,000)	Percent			Former definition (percent)	Current definition (percent)	Number (1,000)	Percent	
US, total	75.2	78.0	222,361	79.0	59,061	MS	47.1	49.1	1,387	48.8	1,457
						MO	68.7	69.6	3,883	69.4	1,712
						MT	52.5	56.4	488	54.1	414
AL	60.4	56.8	2,466	55.4	1,981	NE	66.1	67.2	1,194	69.8	518
AK	67.5	61.0	411	65.6	216	NV	88.3	87.4	1,829	91.5	170
AZ	87.5	86.5	4,524	88.2	607	NH	51.0	57.2	732	59.3	503
AR	53.5	52.0	1,404	52.5	1,269	NJ	89.4	93.5	7,939	94.4	475
CA	92.6	93.7	31,990	94.4	1,882	NM	73.0	75.0	1,364	75.0	456
CO	82.4	83.8	3,633	84.5	668	NY	84.3	87.4	16,603	87.5	2,374
CT	79.1	87.0	2,988	87.7	418	NC	50.4	57.8	4,849	60.2	3,200
DE	73.0	79.2	628	80.1	156	ND	53.3	53.4	359	55.9	283
DC	100.0	100.0	572	100.0	-						
FL	84.8	88.0	14,270	89.3	1,712	OH	74.1	77.5	8,782	77.4	2,571
						OK	67.7	65.2	2,255	65.3	1,196
GA	63.2	68.7	5,864	71.6	2,322	OR	70.5	74.9	2,694	78.7	727
HI	89.0	90.5	1,108	91.5	103	PA	68.9	76.8	9,464	77.1	2,817
ID	57.4	62.2	859	66.4	434	RI	86.0	89.9	953	90.9	95
IL	84.6	86.4	10,910	87.8	1,510	SC	54.6	61.5	2,427	60.5	1,585
IN	64.9	69.1	4,304	70.8	1,776	SD	50.0	50.3	391	51.9	363
IA	60.6	59.4	1,787	61.1	1,139	TN	60.9	62.7	3,620	63.6	2,069
KS	69.1	69.5	1,921	71.4	768	TX	80.3	81.2	17,204	82.5	3,648
KY	51.8	55.9	2,254	55.8	1,788	UT	87.0	86.8	1,970	88.2	263
LA	68.1	72.9	3,246	72.6	1,223						
ME	44.6	42.6	513	40.2	762	VT	32.2	40.2	232	38.2	376
						VA	69.4	71.5	5,170	73.0	1,909
MD	81.3	85.0	4,559	86.1	738	WA	76.4	79.9	4,831	82.0	1,063
MA	84.3	90.5	5,801	91.4	548	WV	36.1	46.9	833	46.1	976
MI	70.5	75.2	7,419	74.7	2,519	WI	65.7	67.3	3,664	68.3	1,700
MN	69.9	69.0	3,490	70.9	1,429	WY	65.0	67.1	321	65.1	172

- Represents zero.

Source: U.S. Census Bureau, 2000 Census of Population and Housing, *Population and Housing Unit Counts* PHC-3.

U.S. Census Bureau, Statistical Abstract of the United States: 2006

Table 28. Incorporated Places by Population Size: 1980 to 2004

[140.3 represents 140,300,000. See Appendix III]

Population size	Number of incorporated places				Population (mil.)				Percent of total			
	1980	1990	2000	2004	1980	1990	2000	2004	1980	1990	2000	2004
Total	19,097	19,262	19,452	19,465	140.3	152.9	173.5	182.0	100.0	100.0	100.0	100.0
1,000,000 or more. . . .	6	8	9	9	17.5	20.0	22.9	23.4	12.5	13.0	13.2	12.9
500,000 to 999,999 . . .	16	15	20	23	10.9	10.1	12.9	14.7	7.8	6.6	7.4	8.1
250,000 to 499,999 . . .	33	41	37	37	11.8	14.2	13.3	13.4	8.4	9.3	7.7	7.4
100,000 to 249,999 . . .	114	131	172	182	16.6	19.1	25.5	27.4	11.8	12.5	14.7	15.1
50,000 to 99,999	250	309	363	407	17.6	21.2	24.9	28.1	12.3	13.9	14.3	15.4
25,000 to 49,999	526	567	644	664	18.4	20.0	22.6	23.1	13.1	13.0	13.0	12.7
10,000 to 24,999.	1,260	1,290	1,435	1,476	19.8	20.3	22.6	23.3	14.1	13.3	13.0	12.8
Under 10,000	16,892	16,901	16,772	16,667	28.0	28.2	28.7	28.8	20.0	18.4	16.6	15.8

Source: U.S. Census Bureau, *Census of Population: 1980*, Vol. I; *1990 Census of Population and Housing, Population and Housing Unit Counts* (CPH-2-1); and "Population Estimates for All Places: 2000 to 2004"; published 30 June 2005; <http://www.census.gov/popest/cities/SUB-EST2004-4.html>.

Table 29. Incorporated Places With 100,000 or More Inhabitants in 2004—Population, 1980 to 2004, and Land Area, 2000

[2004 data refer to boundaries in effect on January 1, 2004; 1990 and 2000 data, boundaries in effect on January 1, 2000; 1980 data, boundaries in effect for 1980 census. Minus sign (-) indicates decrease. See Appendix III]

Incorporated place	1980, total population (1,000)	1990, total population (1,000)	Population, 2000		Population, 2004			Land area, 2000 (square miles)
			Total (1,000)	Percent change, 1990-2000	Total (1,000)	Rank	Percent change [1], 2000-2004	
Abilene, TX	98	107	116	8.6	115	206	-1.0	105.1
Akron, OH	237	223	217	-2.7	212	88	-2.3	62.1
Albuquerque, NM	332	385	449	16.6	484	33	7.8	180.6
Alexandria, VA	103	111	128	15.4	128	179	-0.1	15.2
Allentown, PA.	104	105	107	1.3	107	223	0.1	17.7
Amarillo, TX.	149	158	174	10.2	181	118	4.1	89.9
Anaheim, CA	219	266	328	23.1	334	54	1.8	48.9
Anchorage, AK.	174	226	260	15.0	273	68	4.8	1,697.2
Ann Arbor, MI.	108	110	114	4.0	114	208	-0.5	27.0
Antioch, CA	43	62	91	45.6	101	246	11.5	26.9
Arlington, VA [2]	153	171	189	10.9	186	113	-1.8	26.0
Arlington, TX	160	262	333	27.2	359	50	8.0	95.8
Arvada, CO	85	89	102	14.5	103	238	0.4	32.7
Athens-Clarke County, GA [3]	[4]43	[4]46	100	119.3	103	237	2.5	117.8
Atlanta, GA	425	394	416	5.7	419	42	0.6	131.7
Augusta-Richmond County, GA [3] . . .	[4]48	[4]45	195	337.2	191	111	-2.0	302.1
Aurora, CO	159	222	276	24.4	292	60	5.8	142.5
Aurora, IL	81	100	143	43.6	167	128	16.4	38.5
Austin, TX	346	466	657	41.0	682	16	3.3	251.5
Bakersfield, CA	106	175	247	41.2	284	62	16.8	113.1
Baltimore, MD	787	736	651	-11.5	636	18	-2.3	80.8
Baton Rouge, LA	220	220	228	3.8	224	80	-1.9	76.8
Beaumont, TX	118	114	114	-0.4	112	211	-1.4	85.0
Bellevue, WA	74	87	110	26.1	117	203	3.9	30.7
Berkeley, CA	103	103	103	(Z)	102	241	-1.2	10.5
Birmingham, AL	284	265	243	-8.5	233	76	-4.0	149.9
Boise City, ID.	102	126	186	48.0	190	112	2.2	63.8
Boston, MA	563	574	589	2.6	569	24	-3.4	48.4
Bridgeport, CT	143	142	140	-1.5	140	166	0.3	16.0
Brownsville, TX	85	99	140	41.2	161	134	15.4	80.4
Buffalo, NY	358	328	293	-10.8	283	63	-3.3	40.6
Burbank, CA	87	94	100	7.1	104	229	3.8	17.3
Cambridge, MA	95	96	101	5.8	101	249	-0.6	6.4
Cape Coral, FL.	32	75	102	36.4	128	181	25.1	105.2
Carrollton, TX.	41	82	110	33.4	118	200	7.5	36.5
Cary, NC	22	44	95	112.9	101	243	6.9	43.5
Cedar Rapids, IA	110	109	121	11.0	122	190	0.7	63.1
Chandler, AZ	30	90	177	96.5	224	81	26.6	57.9
Charleston, SC.	70	80	97	20.9	105	226	7.6	97.0
Charlotte, NC.	315	396	541	36.6	594	20	6.5	242.3

See footnotes at end of table.

Table 29. **Incorporated Places With 100,000 or More Inhabitants in 2004—Population, 1980 to 2004, and Land Area, 2000—Con.**

2004 data refer to boundaries in effect on January 1, 2004; 1990 and 2000 data, boundaries in effect on January 1, 2000; 1980 data, boundaries in effect for 1980 census. Minus sign (-) indicates decrease. See Appendix III]

Incorporated place	1980, total population (1,000)	1990, total population (1,000)	Population, 2000		Population, 2004			Land area, 2000 (square miles)
			Total (1,000)	Percent change, 1990-2000	Total (1,000)	Rank	Percent change [1], 2000-2004	
Chattanooga, TN	170	152	156	2.1	155	144	-0.5	135.2
Chesapeake, VA	114	152	199	31.1	215	86	7.8	340.7
Chicago, IL	3,005	2,784	2,896	4.0	2,862	3	-1.2	227.1
Chula Vista, CA	84	135	174	28.4	205	92	18.0	48.9
Cincinnati, OH	385	364	331	-9.0	314	58	-5.2	78.0
Clarksville, TN	55	76	103	37.0	109	217	5.3	94.9
Clearwater, FL	85	99	109	10.3	109	220	-0.3	25.3
Cleveland, OH	574	506	478	-5.4	459	36	-3.9	77.6
Colorado Springs, CO	215	280	361	28.7	369	49	2.3	185.7
Columbia, SC	101	103	116	12.4	116	204	0.4	125.2
Columbus, GA	[3]169	[3]179	[3]186	4.0	183	116	-1.8	216.1
Columbus, OH	565	633	711	12.4	730	15	2.5	210.3
Concord, CA	104	111	122	9.4	124	189	2.0	30.1
Coral Springs, FL	37	79	118	49.1	128	178	9.2	23.9
Corona, CA	38	76	125	64.6	145	154	16.1	35.1
Corpus Christi, TX	232	257	277	7.8	281	64	1.3	154.6
Costa Mesa, CA	83	96	109	12.8	110	214	1.0	15.6
Dallas, TX	905	1,008	1,189	18.0	1,210	9	1.8	342.5
Daly City, CA	79	92	104	12.5	101	251	-2.9	7.6
Dayton, OH	194	182	166	-8.7	160	136	-3.6	55.8
Denver, CO	493	468	555	18.6	557	25	0.6	153.4
Des Moines, IA	191	193	199	2.8	194	107	-2.3	75.8
Detroit, MI	1,203	1,028	951	-7.5	900	11	-5.4	138.8
Downey, CA	83	91	107	17.4	110	215	2.8	12.4
Durham, NC	101	137	187	36.9	202	95	7.5	94.6
El Monte, CA	79	106	116	9.2	122	191	5.3	9.6
El Paso, TX	425	515	564	9.4	592	21	5.0	249.1
Elizabeth, NJ	106	110	121	9.6	125	188	3.4	12.2
Elk Grove, CA	[5]	[5]	[5]	[5]	101	250	24.2	[6]41.9
Erie, PA	119	109	104	-4.6	104	233	0.2	22.0
Escondido, CA	64	109	134	22.9	135	169	1.3	36.3
Eugene, OR	106	113	138	22.3	143	161	3.1	40.5
Evansville, IN	130	126	122	-3.7	117	201	-3.6	40.7
Fairfield, CA	58	79	96	22.3	104	232	8.1	37.7
Fayetteville, NC	60	76	121	59.5	125	184	0.1	58.8
Flint, MI	160	141	125	-11.3	120	195	-4.2	33.6
Fontana, CA	37	88	129	47.3	159	139	23.1	36.1
Fort Collins, CO	65	87	119	35.6	127	183	6.7	46.5
Fort Lauderdale, FL	153	149	152	2.1	165	131	6.7	31.7
Fort Wayne, IN	172	173	206	18.9	219	84	-0.5	79.0
Fort Worth, TX	385	448	535	19.5	603	19	11.5	292.5
Fremont, CA	132	173	203	17.3	202	94	-0.5	76.7
Fresno, CA	217	354	428	20.8	458	37	6.7	104.4
Fullerton, CA	102	114	126	10.4	133	171	5.9	22.2
Gainesville, FL	81	85	95	12.2	109	218	-2.3	48.2
Garden Grove, CA	123	143	165	15.5	167	127	1.3	18.0
Garland, TX	139	181	216	19.4	217	85	0.6	57.1
Gilbert, AZ	6	29	110	276.7	157	140	42.6	43.0
Glendale, AZ	97	148	219	48.0	236	75	7.7	55.7
Glendale, CA	139	180	195	8.3	201	96	3.3	30.6
Grand Prairie, TX	71	100	127	27.9	140	164	10.1	71.4
Grand Rapids, MI	182	189	198	4.6	195	105	-1.4	44.6
Green Bay, WI	88	96	102	6.1	101	244	-1.6	43.9
Greensboro, NC	156	184	224	21.8	232	77	3.2	104.7
Hampton, VA	123	134	146	9.4	146	153	-0.3	51.8
Hartford, CT	136	140	122	-13.0	125	186	0.6	17.3
Hayward, CA	94	111	140	25.8	141	163	0.5	44.3
Henderson, NV	24	65	175	170.0	225	78	28.2	79.7
Hialeah, FL	145	188	226	20.4	225	79	-0.8	19.2
Hollywood, FL	121	122	139	14.5	145	156	3.7	27.3
Honolulu, HI [2]	365	365	372	1.7	377	47	1.5	85.7
Houston, TX	1,595	1,631	1,954	19.8	2,013	4	2.8	579.4
Huntington Beach, CA	171	182	190	4.4	195	104	3.0	26.4
Huntsville, AL	143	160	158	-1.0	164	132	3.4	174.0
Independence, MO	112	112	113	0.9	111	213	-2.0	78.3
Indianapolis, IN [3]	701	731	782	6.9	784	12	0.3	361.5
Inglewood, CA	94	110	113	2.7	115	205	2.4	9.1
Irvine, CA	62	110	143	29.7	178	121	24.6	46.2
Irving, TX	110	155	192	23.6	195	106	1.5	67.2
Jackson, MS	203	197	184	-6.3	179	119	-2.7	104.9

See footnotes at end of table.

Population 33

Table 29. Incorporated Places With 100,000 or More Inhabitants in 2004—Population, 1980 to 2004, and Land Area, 2000—Con.

[2004 data refer to boundaries in effect on January 1, 2004; 1990 and 2000 data, boundaries in effect on January 1, 2000; 1980 data, boundaries in effect for 1980 census. Minus sign (-) indicates decrease. See Appendix III]

Incorporated place	1980, total population (1,000)	1990, total population (1,000)	Population, 2000		Population, 2004			Land area, 2000 (square miles)
			Total (1,000)	Percent change 1990-2000	Total (1,000)	Rank	Percent change [1] 2000-2004	
Jacksonville, FL	541	635	736	15.8	778	13	5.7	757.7
Jersey City, NJ	224	229	240	5.0	239	72	-0.4	14.9
Joliet, IL	78	77	106	37.6	130	176	21.4	38.1
Kansas City, KS	161	150	147	-2.0	145	155	-1.3	124.3
Kansas City, MO	448	435	442	1.5	444	39	0.6	313.5
Knoxville, TN	175	165	174	5.4	178	123	1.6	92.7
Lafayette, LA	81	94	110	16.8	112	212	0.1	47.6
Lakewood, CO	114	126	144	14.0	141	162	-2.0	41.6
Lancaster, CA	48	97	119	22.0	129	177	8.6	94.0
Lansing, MI	130	127	119	-6.4	117	202	-2.0	35.0
Laredo, TX	91	123	177	43.7	203	93	14.6	78.5
Las Vegas, NV	165	258	478	85.3	535	29	11.5	113.3
Lexington-Fayette, KY	204	225	261	15.6	266	69	2.2	284.5
Lincoln, NE	172	192	226	17.5	236	74	4.6	74.6
Little Rock, AR	159	176	183	4.2	184	114	0.5	116.2
Long Beach, CA	361	429	462	7.5	477	34	3.3	50.4
Los Angeles, CA	2,969	3,486	3,695	6.0	3,846	2	4.1	469.1
Louisville-Jefferson County, KY	[7]299	[7]270	[7]256	-4.9	556	26	0.9	[7]62.1
Lowell, MA	92	103	105	1.7	104	234	-1.4	13.8
Lubbock, TX	174	186	200	7.2	208	89	4.1	114.8
Madison, WI	171	191	208	9.1	220	83	5.4	68.7
Manchester, NH	91	99	107	7.7	109	216	2.2	33.0
McAllen, TX	66	84	106	26.7	121	193	13.4	46.0
Memphis, TN	646	610	650	6.5	672	17	-1.2	279.3
Mesa, AZ	152	288	396	37.6	437	41	10.0	125.0
Mesquite, TX	67	101	125	22.7	130	175	4.2	43.4
Miami, FL	347	359	362	1.1	380	46	4.8	35.7
Miami Gardens, FL	(5)	(5)	(5)	(5)	101	248	0.4	[6]19.1
Milwaukee, WI	636	628	597	-5.0	584	22	-2.2	96.1
Minneapolis, MN	371	368	383	3.9	374	48	-2.3	54.9
Miramar, FL	33	41	73	78.9	101	242	39.5	31.0
Mobile, AL	200	196	199	1.4	193	108	-3.2	117.9
Modesto, CA	107	165	189	14.6	207	90	9.5	35.8
Montgomery, AL	178	188	202	7.5	201	97	-0.4	155.4
Moreno Valley, CA	(5)	119	142	19.9	166	129	16.8	51.2
Naperville, IL	43	86	128	49.6	140	165	8.9	35.4
Nashville-Davidson, TN 3	456	488	546	11.7	547	28	0.2	473.3
New Haven, CT	126	130	124	-5.2	125	187	0.9	18.9
New Orleans, LA	558	497	485	-2.5	462	35	-4.6	180.6
New York, NY	7,072	7,323	8,008	9.4	8,104	1	1.2	303.3
Newark, NJ	329	275	274	-0.6	280	65	2.9	23.8
Newport News, VA	145	171	180	5.1	182	117	0.7	68.3
Norfolk, VA	267	261	234	-10.3	238	73	1.5	53.7
Norman, OK	68	80	96	19.5	101	246	4.3	189.5
North Las Vegas, NV	43	48	115	141.4	159	138	37.5	78.5
Norwalk, CA	85	94	103	9.6	107	224	2.3	9.7
Oakland, CA	339	372	399	7.3	398	44	-0.4	56.1
Oceanside, CA	77	128	161	25.7	167	126	4.0	40.6
Oklahoma City, OK	404	445	506	13.8	528	31	4.3	607.0
Olathe, KS	37	63	93	46.6	108	222	16.5	54.2
Omaha, NE	314	336	390	16.2	409	43	4.7	115.7
Ontario, CA	89	133	158	18.6	170	125	7.6	49.8
Orange, CA	91	111	129	16.4	134	170	3.1	23.4
Orlando, FL	128	165	186	12.9	206	91	7.7	93.5
Overland Park, KS	82	112	149	33.4	163	133	8.9	56.7
Oxnard, CA	108	143	170	19.5	184	115	7.8	25.3
Palmdale, CA	12	69	117	69.2	131	173	12.2	105.0
Pasadena, CA	118	132	134	1.8	144	158	7.6	44.2
Pasadena, TX	113	120	142	18.5	144	157	1.8	23.1
Paterson, NJ	138	141	149	5.9	151	148	1.1	8.4
Pembroke Pines, FL	36	66	137	109.6	150	150	9.2	33.1
Peoria, AZ	12	51	108	113.8	132	172	21.6	138.2
Peoria, IL	124	114	113	-0.5	113	209	-0.3	44.4
Philadelphia, PA	1,688	1,586	1,518	-4.3	1,470	5	-3.1	135.1
Phoenix, AZ	790	983	1,321	34.3	1,418	6	7.3	474.9
Pittsburgh, PA	424	370	335	-9.5	322	56	-3.6	55.6
Plano, TX	72	128	222	73.6	245	71	10.5	71.6
Pomona, CA	93	132	149	13.5	155	142	4.0	22.8
Port St. Lucie, FL	15	56	89	59.2	118	197	33.4	75.5
Portland, OR	368	439	529	20.6	533	30	0.8	134.3

See footnotes at end of table.

U.S. Census Bureau, Statistical Abstract of the United States: 2006

[2004 data refer to boundaries in effect on January 1, 2004; 1990 and 2000 data, boundaries in effect on January 1, 2000; 1980 data, boundaries in effect for 1980 census. Minus sign (-) indicates decrease. See Appendix III]

Incorporated place	1980, total population (1,000)	1990, total population (1,000)	Population, 2000		Population, 2004			Land area, 2000 (square miles)
			Total (1,000)	Percent change, 1990-2000	Total (1,000)	Rank	Percent change [1], 2000-2004	
Providence, RI	157	161	174	8.0	178	122	2.6	18.5
Pueblo, CO	102	99	102	3.5	104	235	1.5	45.1
Raleigh, NC	150	212	276	30.2	327	55	15.4	114.6
Rancho Cucamonga, CA	55	101	128	26.0	159	137	24.7	37.4
Reno, NV	101	134	180	34.8	198	100	9.4	69.1
Richmond, CA	75	86	99	15.3	102	239	3.1	30.0
Richmond, VA	219	203	198	-2.5	192	109	-2.7	60.1
Riverside, CA	171	227	255	12.6	288	61	13.0	78.1
Rochester, NY	242	230	220	-4.6	212	87	-3.3	35.8
Rockford, IL	140	140	150	7.2	152	146	1.3	30.5
Roseville, CA	24	45	80	78.9	104	236	29.6	56.0
Sacramento, CA	276	369	407	10.2	454	38	11.6	97.2
Salem, OR	89	108	137	27.0	146	152	6.6	45.7
Salinas, CA	80	109	151	38.9	148	151	3.7	19.0
Salt Lake City, UT	163	160	182	13.6	179	120	-1.7	109.1
San Antonio, TX	786	935	1,145	22.4	1,236	8	7.4	407.6
San Bernardino, CA	119	165	185	12.6	198	99	7.1	58.8
San Buenaventura (Ventura), CA	74	93	101	9.0	104	230	3.1	21.1
San Diego, CA	876	1,111	1,223	10.2	1,264	7	3.3	324.3
San Francisco, CA	679	724	777	7.3	744	14	-4.2	46.7
San Jose, CA	629	782	895	14.4	905	10	1.0	174.9
Santa Ana, CA	204	294	338	15.0	343	53	1.4	27.1
Santa Clara, CA	88	94	102	9.3	104	231	1.6	18.4
Santa Clarita, CA	(5)	111	151	36.5	165	130	9.0	47.8
Santa Rosa, CA	83	113	148	30.3	154	145	3.9	40.1
Savannah, GA	142	138	132	-4.6	130	174	-2.6	74.7
Scottsdale, AZ	89	130	203	55.8	222	82	9.5	184.2
Seattle, WA	494	516	563	9.1	571	23	1.4	83.9
Shreveport, LA	206	199	200	0.8	199	98	-0.7	103.1
Simi Valley, CA	78	100	111	11.1	119	196	6.8	39.2
Sioux Falls, SD	81	101	124	22.9	137	167	9.7	56.3
South Bend, IN	110	106	108	2.2	105	225	-2.3	38.7
Spokane, WA	171	177	196	10.4	197	102	0.6	57.8
Springfield, IL	100	105	111	5.7	115	207	2.9	54.0
Springfield, MA	152	157	152	-3.1	152	147	(Z)	32.1
Springfield, MO	133	140	152	7.9	151	149	-0.9	73.2
Stamford, CT	102	108	117	8.4	120	194	2.7	37.7
Sterling Heights, MI	109	118	124	5.7	127	182	2.4	36.6
Stockton, CA	150	211	244	15.6	280	66	14.8	54.7
St. Louis, MO	453	397	348	-12.2	343	52	-1.4	61.9
St. Paul, MN	270	272	287	5.5	277	67	-3.4	52.8
St. Petersburg, FL	239	240	248	3.3	249	70	0.1	59.6
Sunnyvale, CA	107	117	132	12.3	128	180	-2.9	21.9
Syracuse, NY	170	164	147	-10.1	143	159	-2.3	25.1
Tacoma, WA	159	177	194	9.6	196	103	1.3	50.1
Tallahassee, FL	82	125	151	20.7	157	141	2.8	95.7
Tampa, FL	272	280	303	8.4	322	57	6.0	112.1
Tempe, AZ	107	142	159	11.7	161	135	1.3	40.1
Thornton, CO	42	55	82	49.7	102	240	23.6	27.2
Thousand Oaks, CA	77	104	117	12.1	125	185	6.9	54.9
Toledo, OH	355	333	314	-5.8	305	59	-2.8	80.6
Topeka, KS	119	120	122	2.1	122	192	-0.9	56.0
Torrance, CA	130	133	138	3.6	143	160	3.5	20.5
Tucson, AZ	331	405	487	20.1	512	32	5.1	194.7
Tulsa, OK	361	367	393	7.0	384	45	-2.4	182.6
Vallejo, CA	80	109	117	6.9	118	198	1.4	30.2
Vancouver, WA	43	46	144	209.5	155	143	8.0	42.8
Virginia Beach, VA	262	393	425	8.2	440	40	3.5	248.3
Visalia, CA	50	76	92	21.0	105	228	13.8	28.6
Waco, TX	101	104	114	9.8	118	199	3.7	84.2
Warren, MI	161	145	138	-4.6	136	168	-1.5	34.3
Washington, DC	638	607	572	-5.7	554	27	-3.2	61.4
Waterbury, CT	103	109	107	-1.6	108	221	1.1	28.6
West Covina, CA	80	96	105	9.2	109	219	3.4	16.1
West Valley City, UT	(5)	87	109	25.2	113	210	3.5	35.4
Westminster, CO	50	75	101	35.3	105	227	3.7	31.5
Wichita, KS	280	304	344	13.2	354	51	0.7	135.8
Wichita Falls, TX	94	96	104	8.2	101	245	-3.1	70.7
Winston-Salem, NC	132	143	186	29.5	192	110	3.1	108.9
Worcester, MA	162	170	173	1.7	176	124	1.9	37.6
Yonkers, NY	195	188	196	4.3	197	101	0.6	18.1

Z Less than 0.05 percent.   [1] The April 1, 2000 Population Estimates base reflects changes to the Census 2000 population from the Count Question Resolution program and geographic program revisions.   [2] The population shown is for the census designated place (CDP).   [3] Represents the portion of a consolidated city that is not within one or more separately incorporated places.   [4] Data are for the incorporated places of Athens city and Augusta city before consolidation of the city and county governments.   [5] Not incorporated.   [6] Area as of January 1, 2004.   [7] Data are for the incorporated place of Louisville city before consolidation of the city and county governments.

Source: U.S. Census Bureau, 2000 Census of Population and Housing, *Population and Housing Unit Counts* PHC-3; and "Population Estimates for Places Over 100,000: 2000 to 2004"; published 30 June 2005; <http://www.census.gov/popest/cities/SUB-EST2004.html>.

Population   35

Table 30. Mobility Status of the Population by Selected Characteristics: 1980 to 2004

[As of March (221,641 represents 221,641,000). For persons 1 year old and over. Excludes members of the Armed Forces except those living off post or with their families on post. Based on Current Population Survey, Annual Social and Economic Supplement; see text of this section and Appendix III. For composition of regions, see map, inside front cover]

Mobility period and characteristic	Total (1,000)	Non-movers	Percent distribution — Movers (different house in United States) Total	Same county	Different county Total	Same state	Different state	Movers from abroad
1980–1981	221,641	83	17	10	6	3	3	1
1990–1991	244,884	83	16	10	6	3	3	1
2000–2001	275,611	86	14	8	6	3	3	1
2003–2004, total	284,367	86	13	8	5	3	3	(Z)
1 to 4 years old	16,026	79	20	13	7	4	3	(Z)
5 to 9 years old	19,636	84	15	10	6	3	2	(Z)
10 to 14 years old	21,176	87	12	8	5	2	2	(Z)
15 to 19 years old	20,314	87	13	7	5	3	2	(Z)
20 to 24 years old	20,339	71	28	16	11	6	5	1
25 to 29 years old	19,008	72	26	16	11	5	5	1
30 to 44 years old	63,766	85	14	9	6	3	3	1
45 to 64 years old	69,443	93	7	4	3	1	2	(Z)
65 to 74 years old	18,238	96	4	2	2	1	1	(Z)
75 to 84 years old	12,851	96	4	2	2	1	1	(Z)
85 years old and over	3,571	96	4	3	2	1	1	(Z)
Northeast	53,084	90	10	6	4	2	2	(Z)
Midwest	63,924	87	12	7	5	3	2	(Z)
South	102,021	85	14	8	6	3	3	(Z)
West	65,337	84	15	10	6	3	3	1
Persons 16 years old and over	223,422	87	13	7	5	3	3	(Z)
Civilian labor force	146,062	85	14	9	6	3	3	(Z)
Employed	137,152	86	14	8	5	3	3	(Z)
Unemployed	8,910	77	22	13	9	4	4	1
Armed Forces	912	66	28	10	18	4	15	6
Not in labor force	76,448	90	10	5	4	2	2	(Z)
Employed civilians, 16 years old and over	137,152	86	14	8	5	3	3	(Z)
Management, business, and financial	20,030	88	12	7	5	3	2	(Z)
Professional	28,182	87	13	7	6	3	3	(Z)
Service	22,148	83	17	11	6	3	3	1
Sales	15,909	85	15	8	6	3	3	(Z)
Office and administrative support	19,358	87	13	8	5	3	2	(Z)
Farming, fishing, and forestry	885	87	12	6	6	5	1	1
Construction and extraction	7,958	84	16	10	5	3	3	1
Installation, maintenance, and repair	4,946	87	12	8	5	3	2	(Z)
Production	9,402	87	12	7	5	3	2	1
Transportation and material moving	8,335	86	14	9	5	3	2	(Z)
Tenure:								
Owner-occupied units	203,302	93	7	4	3	2	1	(Z)
Renter-occupied units	81,065	70	29	18	11	5	6	1

Z Less than 0.5 percent.

Source: U.S. Census Bureau, "Geographical Mobility/Migration"; <http://www.census.gov/population/www/socdemo/migrate.html>.

Table 31. Movers by Type of Move and Reason for Moving: 2003-2004

[As of March (38,994 represents 38,994,000). For persons 1 year old and over. Excludes members of the Armed Forces except those living off post or with their families on post. Based on Current Population Survey, Annual Social and Economic Supplement; see text of this section and Appendix III]

Reason for move	All movers	Intra-county	Inter-county	From abroad	Reason for move	All movers	Intra-county	Inter-county	From abroad
2003-2004, total (1,000)	38,994	22,551	15,171	1,272	Retired	0.3	0.2	0.6	0.3
					Other job-related reason	1.4	0.5	2.2	8.2
PERCENT DISTRIBUTION					Housing-related reasons	52.8	67.6	34.4	9.1
					Wanted to own home/not rent	9.3	11.4	7.0	0.2
Total	100.0	100.0	100.0	100.0	New/better house/apartment	21.1	28.0	12.2	4.2
Family-related reasons	24.3	23.3	25.6	26.8	Better neighborhood/less crime	4.7	5.7	3.6	0.2
Change in marital status	6.2	5.8	6.7	5.7	Cheaper housing	7.3	9.4	4.8	1.1
To establish own household	7.0	8.5	5.0	3.4	Other housing	10.3	13.1	6.7	3.5
Other family reasons	11.2	8.9	14.0	17.7	Other reasons	5.9	3.1	9.1	17.2
Work-related reasons	17.0	6.0	30.9	46.7	Attend/leave college	2.9	1.2	4.6	11.9
New job/job transfer	9.2	1.7	19.0	24.6	Change of climate	0.6	0.2	1.3	-
To look for work/lost job	2.4	0.7	4.0	12.7	Health reasons	1.0	0.8	1.3	0.3
Closer to work/easier commute	3.7	2.9	5.1	0.9	Other reason	1.5	1.0	1.9	5.0

- Represents zero.

Source: U.S. Census Bureau, "Geographic Mobility: 2004, Detailed Tables"; published 22 June 2005; <http://www.census.gov/population/www/socdemo/migrate/cps2004.html>.

Table 32. Mobility Status of Households by Household Income: 2003-2004

[As of March (112,015 represents 112,015,000). Covers householders 15 years old and over. Excludes members of the Armed Forces except those living off post or with their families on post. Based on Current Population Survey, Annual Social and Economic Supplement; see text of this section and Appendix III]

Household income in 2003	Total (1,000)	Non-movers	Percent distribution						
			Movers (different house in United States)						Movers from abroad
			Total	Same county	Different county				
					Total	Same state	Different state		
Householders, 15 years and over...	112,015	87	13	8	5	3	3		(Z)
Less than $5,000	3,800	77	21	13	8	3	5		2
$5,000 to $9,999.	6,312	83	16	11	6	3	3		(Z)
$10,000 to $14,999	7,740	85	15	9	6	3	3		(Z)
$15,000 to $24,999	14,650	84	16	10	6	3	3		(Z)
$25,000 to $34,999	13,285	85	15	9	6	3	3		(Z)
$35,000 to $49,999	16,771	86	14	8	6	4	3		(Z)
$50,000 to $74,999	20,197	88	11	7	4	2	2		(Z)
$75,000 and over	29,259	91	9	5	4	2	2		(Z)

Z Less than 0.5 percent.

Source: U.S. Census Bureau, "Geographic Mobility: 2004, Detailed Tables"; published 22 June 2005; <http://www.census.gov /population/www/socdemo/migrate/cps2004.html>.

Table 33. Mobility Status of Resident Population by State: 2003

[In percent, except as indicated (279,118 represents 279,118,000). Based on comparison of place of residence in 2002 and 2003. The American Community Survey universe is limited to the household population and excludes the population living in institutions, college dormitories, and other group quarters. Based on a sample and subject to sampling variability; see text of this section and Appendix III]

State	Population 1 year old and over [1] (1,000)	Same house in 2002	Different house in United States in 2002		State	Population 1 year old and over [1] (1,000)	Same house in 2002	Different house in United States in 2002	
			Same county	Different county				Same county	Different county
U.S. ...	279,118	84.9	9.4	5.1					
AL......	4,331	85.2	9.9	4.7	MO	5,459	83.7	9.3	6.7
AK......	620	80.8	11.0	7.6	MT	883	85.7	8.1	6.0
AZ......	5,376	80.4	13.3	5.6	NE	1,664	82.4	9.8	7.6
AR......	2,614	81.9	11.2	6.6	NV	2,175	81.7	12.3	5.4
CA......	34,161	84.7	10.2	4.4	NH	1,237	86.8	7.1	5.8
CO......	4,385	81.6	10.1	7.7	NJ	8,335	88.2	6.9	4.1
CT......	3,322	87.7	8.2	3.7	NM	1,810	83.1	10.6	5.7
DE......	781	86.8	8.1	4.7	NY	18,378	89.5	6.8	3.2
DC......	523	84.3	8.4	6.0	NC	8,037	84.3	9.8	5.3
FL	16,419	82.4	10.5	6.3	ND	602	87.3	8.1	4.2
GA......	8,324	84.2	8.4	7.0	OH	10,988	85.6	10.0	4.1
HI	1,205	85.0	10.1	4.0	OK	3,354	83.6	10.0	5.9
ID	1,310	81.4	10.2	7.5	OR	3,435	80.8	12.3	6.6
IL.......	12,166	85.9	9.6	4.0	PA	11,783	88.5	7.7	3.4
IN	5,933	83.6	11.0	5.2	RI	1,027	88.5	6.9	4.2
IA	2,807	85.1	9.5	5.2	SC	3,962	84.3	9.5	5.9
KS......	2,605	81.6	10.8	7.3	SD	726	85.4	8.7	5.6
KY......	3,948	85.3	8.6	5.8	TN	5,613	84.4	9.5	5.8
LA	4,300	85.8	9.2	4.4	TX	21,203	83.1	10.8	5.4
ME......	1,260	87.1	7.9	4.7	UT	2,264	82.3	10.8	6.2
MD......	5,306	86.6	7.0	5.8	VT	593	86.9	8.1	4.8
MA......	6,141	87.8	7.4	4.2	VA	7,054	84.4	6.5	8.3
MI	9,697	86.5	8.8	4.3	WA	5,915	81.1	12.3	5.9
MN......	4,855	85.6	7.5	6.5	WV	1,746	89.0	6.5	4.4
MS......	2,747	84.8	9.5	5.6	WI	5,256	84.9	9.5	5.1
					WY	481	82.2	10.2	7.1

[1] Includes persons moving from abroad, not shown separately.

Source: U.S. Census Bureau, "American Community Survey, Multi-Year Profiles 2003 - Social Characteristics"; <http://www.census.gov /acs/www/Products/Profiles/Chg/2003/ACS/index.htm>; accessed 24 June 2005.

Population 37

Table 34. **Persons 65 Years Old and Over—Characteristics by Sex: 1990 to 2004**

[As of March, except as noted (29.6 represents 29,600,000). Covers civilian noninstitutional population. Excludes members of Armed Forces except those living off post or with their families on post. Data for 1990 are based on 1980 census population controls; 1995 and 2000 data based on 1990 census population controls; 2004 data based on 2000 census population controls and an expanded sample of households. Based on Current Population Survey; see text of this section and Appendix III]

Characteristic	Total				Male				Female			
	1990	1995	2000	2004	1990	1995	2000	2004	1990	1995	2000	2004
Total (million)	**29.6**	**31.7**	**32.6**	**34.6**	**12.3**	**13.2**	**13.9**	**14.8**	**17.2**	**18.5**	**18.7**	**19.8**
PERCENT DISTRIBUTION												
Marital status:												
Never married	4.6	4.2	3.9	3.9	4.2	4.2	4.2	4.1	4.9	4.2	3.6	3.7
Married.................	56.1	56.9	57.2	57.2	76.5	77.0	75.2	75.2	41.4	42.5	43.8	43.9
Spouse present	54.1	54.7	54.6	54.7	74.2	74.5	72.6	72.4	39.7	40.6	41.3	41.6
Spouse absent	2.0	2.2	2.6	2.5	2.3	2.5	2.6	2.8	1.7	1.9	2.5	2.3
Widowed.................	34.2	33.2	32.1	30.8	14.2	13.5	14.4	13.7	48.6	47.3	45.3	43.5
Divorced.................	5.0	5.7	6.7	8.1	5.0	5.2	6.1	7.0	5.1	6.0	7.2	8.9
Educational attainment:												
Less than ninth grade	28.5	21.0	16.7	13.9	30.0	22.0	17.8	13.8	27.5	20.3	15.9	14.0
Completed 9th to 12th grade, but no high school diploma.....	[1]16.1	15.2	13.8	13.0	[1]15.7	14.5	12.7	12.1	[1]16.4	15.6	14.7	13.7
High school graduate	[2]32.9	33.8	35.9	36.0	[2]29.0	29.2	30.4	30.9	[2]35.6	37.1	39.9	39.8
Some college or associate's degree	[3]10.9	17.1	18.0	18.4	[3]10.8	17.1	17.8	17.8	[3]11.0	17.0	18.2	18.8
Bachelor's or advanced degree...	[4]11.6	13.0	15.6	18.7	[4]14.5	17.2	21.4	25.4	[4]9.5	9.9	11.4	13.7
Labor force participation: [5]												
Employed	11.5	11.7	12.4	13.9	15.9	16.1	16.9	18.3	8.4	8.5	9.1	10.7
Unemployed	0.4	0.5	0.4	0.5	0.5	0.7	0.6	0.7	0.3	0.3	0.3	0.4
Not in labor force	88.1	87.9	87.2	85.6	83.6	83.2	82.5	81.0	91.3	91.2	90.6	88.9
Percent below poverty level [6].....	11.4	11.7	9.7	10.2	7.8	7.2	6.9	7.3	13.9	14.9	11.8	12.5

[1] Represents those who completed 1 to 3 years of high school. [2] Represents those who completed 4 years of high school.
[3] Represents those who completed 1 to 3 years of college. [4] Represents those who completed 4 years of college or more.
[5] Annual averages of monthly figures. Source: U.S. Bureau of Labor Statistics, *Employment and Earnings*, January issues. See footnote 2, Table 576. [6] Poverty status based on income in preceding year.

Source: Except as noted, U.S. Census Bureau, *Current Population Reports*, P20-546, and earlier reports; P60-226; "Educational Attainment in the United States: 2004, Detailed Tables"; published March 2005; <http://www.census .gov/population/www/socdemo/education/cps2004.html>; "Table A1. Marital Status of People 15 Years and Over, by Age, Sex, Personal Earnings, Race, and Hispanic Origin, 2004"; published June 2005; <http://www.census.gov/population/www /socdemo/hh-fam/cps2004.html>; and "POV01. Age and Sex of All People, Family Members and Unrelated Individuals Iterated by Income-to-Poverty Ratio and Race"; published August 2004; <http://ferret.bls.census.gov/macro/032004/pov/new01_000.htm>.

Table 35. **Persons 65 Years Old and Over—Living Arrangements and Disability Status: 2003**

[In thousands (33,896 represents 33,896,000), except as indicated. The American Community Survey universe is limited to the household population and excludes the population living in institutions, college dormitories, and other group quarters. Based on a sample and subject to sampling variability; see text of this section and Appendix III]

Relationship by household type	Number	Percent distribution	Type of disability	Number
Total	**33,896**	**100.0**	**Total disabilities tallied for**	
In family households	22,930	67.6	**people 65 years and over ......**	**28,231**
Householder	11,757	34.7		
Spouse	8,352	24.6	Sensory disability	5,453
Parent	1,535	4.5	Physical disability	10,301
Other relatives	1,147	3.4	Mental disability	3,713
Nonrelatives.............	139	0.4	Self-care disability	3,188
In nonfamily households	10,966	32.4	Go-outside home disability	5,576
Householder	10,566	31.2		
Living alone	10,091	29.8		
Not living alone	475	1.4		
Nonrelatives.............	400	1.2		

Source: U.S. Census Bureau, American FactFinder, 2003 American Community Survey Summary Tables, P015. Relationship by Household Type (Including Living Alone) for the Population 65 Years and Over, and P058. Total Disability Tallied by Age for the Civilian Noninstitutionalized Population 5 Years and Over With Disabilities; <http://factfinder.census.gov/>; (accessed: 8 March 2005).

[As of March, except labor force status, annual average (134,687 represents 134,687,000). Excludes members of Armed Forces except those living off post or with their families on post. Data for 1990 are based on 1980 census population controls; 2000 data (except for income and poverty) based on 1990 census population controls; 2004 data and 2000 data for income and poverty based on 2000 census population controls and an expanded sample of households. Based on Current Population Survey; see text of this section and Appendix III]

Characteristic	Number (1,000)						Percent distribution			
	White		White alone [1]	Black		Black alone [1]	White	White alone [1]	Black	Black alone [1]
	1990	2000	2004	1990	2000	2004	2000	2004	2000	2004
EDUCATIONAL ATTAINMENT										
Persons 25 years old and over	134,687	147,067	154,150	16,751	20,036	20,812	100.0	100.0	100.0	100.0
Less than ninth grade	14,131	10,035	9,566	2,701	1,417	1,197	6.8	6.2	7.1	5.8
Completed 9th to 12th grade, but no high school diploma	[2]14,080	12,153	12,292	[2]2,969	2,899	2,833	8.3	8.0	14.5	13.6
High school graduate	[3]52,449	49,105	49,579	[3]6,239	7,050	7,493	33.4	32.2	35.2	36.0
Some college or associate's degree	[4]24,350	37,353	39,311	[4]2,952	5,366	5,623	25.4	25.5	26.8	27.0
Bachelor's or advanced degree	[5]29,677	38,421	43,402	[5]1,890	3,303	3,667	26.1	28.2	16.5	17.6
LABOR FORCE STATUS [6]										
Civilians 16 years old and over	160,625	176,220	182,643	21,477	24,902	26,065	100.0	100.0	100.0	100.0
Civilian labor force	107,447	118,545	121,086	13,740	16,397	16,638	67.3	66.3	65.8	63.8
Employed	102,261	114,424	115,239	12,175	15,156	14,909	64.9	63.1	60.9	57.2
Unemployed	5,186	4,121	5,847	1,565	1,241	1,729	2.3	3.2	5.0	6.6
Unemployment rate [7]	4.8	3.5	4.8	11.4	7.6	10.4	(X)	(X)	(X)	(X)
Not in labor force	53,178	57,675	61,558	7,737	8,505	9,428	32.7	33.7	34.2	36.2
FAMILY TYPE										
Total families	56,590	60,251	62,609	7,470	8,664	8,912	100.0	100.0	100.0	100.0
With own children [8]	26,718	28,107	28,410	4,378	4,782	4,973	46.6	45.4	55.2	55.8
Married couple	46,981	48,790	50,021	3,750	4,144	4,146	81.0	79.9	47.1	46.5
With own children [8]	21,579	21,809	21,769	1,972	2,093	2,035	36.2	34.8	24.2	22.8
Female householder, no spouse present	7,306	8,380	9,050	3,275	3,814	3,984	13.9	14.5	45.1	44.7
With own children [8]	4,199	4,869	5,203	2,232	2,409	2,582	8.1	8.3	27.8	29.0
Male householder, no spouse present	2,303	3,081	3,537	446	706	782	5.1	5.6	7.8	8.8
With own children [8]	939	1,429	1,438	173	280	356	2.4	2.3	3.2	4.0
FAMILY INCOME IN PREVIOUS YEAR IN CONSTANT (2003) DOLLARS										
Total families [9]	56,590	61,074	62,620	7,470	8,653	8,914	100.0	100.0	100.0	100.0
Less than $5,000	(NA)	(NA)	1,382	(NA)	(NA)	593	(NA)	2.2	(NA)	6.7
$5,000 to $9,999	(NA)	(NA)	1,302	(NA)	(NA)	627	(NA)	2.1	(NA)	7.0
$10,000 to $14,999	(NA)	(NA)	2,235	(NA)	(NA)	692	(NA)	3.6	(NA)	7.8
$15,000 to $24,999	(NA)	(NA)	6,610	(NA)	(NA)	1,407	(NA)	10.6	(NA)	15.8
$25,000 to $34,999	(NA)	(NA)	7,049	(NA)	(NA)	1,187	(NA)	11.3	(NA)	13.3
$35,000 to $49,999	(NA)	(NA)	9,367	(NA)	(NA)	1,402	(NA)	15.0	(NA)	15.7
$50,000 or more	(NA)	(NA)	34,675	(NA)	(NA)	3,005	(NA)	55.4	(NA)	33.7
Median income (dol.) [10]	51,539	56,383	55,768	28,952	35,157	34,369	(X)	(X)	(X)	(X)
POVERTY										
Families below poverty level [11]	4,409	4,377	5,058	2,077	1,898	1,985	7.3	8.1	21.9	22.3
Persons below poverty level [11]	20,785	21,922	24,280	9,302	8,360	8,801	9.8	10.5	23.6	24.5
HOUSING TENURE										
Total occupied units	80,163	87,671	91,962	10,486	12,849	13,629	100.0	100.0	100.0	100.0
Owner-occupied	54,094	62,077	66,681	4,445	6,055	6,749	70.8	72.5	47.1	49.5
Renter-occupied	24,685	24,253	24,045	5,862	6,563	6,687	27.7	26.1	51.1	49.1
No cash rent	1,384	1,340	1,234	178	231	193	1.5	1.3	1.8	1.4

NA Not available.   X Not applicable.   [1] Beginning 2003, the Current Population Survey asked respondents to choose one or more races. Refers to people who reported specified race and did not report any other race category.   [2] Represents those who completed 1 to 3 years of high school.   [3] Represents those who completed 4 years of high school.   [4] Represents those who completed 1 to 3 years of college.   [5] Represents those who completed 4 years of college or more.   [6] Source: U.S. Bureau of Labor Statistics, *Employment and Earnings*, January issues. See footnote 2, Table 576.   [7] Total unemployment as percent of civilian labor force.   [8] Children under 18 years old.   [9] Includes families in group quarters.   [10] For definition of median, see Guide to Tabular Presentation.   [11] For explanation of poverty level, see text, Section 13.

Source: Except as noted, U.S. Census Bureau, Current Population Reports, P60-226 and earlier reports; "Educational Attainment"; <http://www.census.gov/population/www/socdemo/educ-attn.html>; "Families and Living Arrangements"; <http://www.census.gov/population/www/socdemo/hh-fam.html>; "Table F-5. Race and Hispanic Origin of Householder—Families by Median and Mean Income: 1947 to 2003": published 13 May 2005; <http://www.census.gov/hhes/www/income/histinc/f05.html>; "Table FINC-01. Selected Characteristics of Families, by Total Money Income in 2003": published 26 August 2004; <http://pubdb3.census.gov/macro/032004/faminc/new01_000.htm>; "Table 4. Poverty Status Status of Families, by Type of Family, Presence of Related Children, Race, and Hispanic Origin: 1959 to 2003"; published 26 August 2004; <http://www.census.gov/hhes/www/poverty/histpov/hstpov4.html>; and unpublished data.

Table 37. **Selected Characteristics of Racial Groups and Hispanic/Latino Population: 2003**

[In thousands (184,395 represents 184,395,000), except as indicated. The American Community Survey universe is limited to the household population and excludes the population living in institutions, college dormitories, and other group quarters. Based on a sample and subject to sampling variability; see text of this section and Appendix III]

Characteristic	Total population	White alone	Black or African American alone	American Indian and Alaska Native alone	Asian alone
EDUCATIONAL ATTAINMENT					
Persons 25 years old and over, total	**184,395**	**145,606**	**19,934**	**1,289**	**7,940**
Less than 9th grade	11,892	7,827	1,244	114	684
9th to 12th grade, no diploma	18,321	13.034	3,012	197	522
High school graduate (includes equivalency)	54,954	44.199	6,445	400	1,333
Some college, no degree	37,407	29,863	4,465	302	1,048
Associate's degree	12.883	10,356	1,383	98	532
Bachelor's degree	31,138	25.557	2,277	122	2,344
Graduate degree	17,799	14,770	1,106	57	1,477
Percent high school graduate or higher.	83.6	85.7	78.6	75.9	84.8
Percent bachelor's degree or higher.	26.5	27.7	17.0	13.9	48.1
OCCUPATION					
Employed civilian population, 16 years old and over, total	**132,422**	**104,432**	**13,791**	**859**	**5,596**
Management, professional, and related occupations	45,215	37,205	3,716	225	2,582
Service occupations	21,351	15,200	3,328	181	810
Sales and office occupations.	34,753	27,831	3,587	196	1,340
Farming, fishing, and forestry occupations.	936	715	41	9	16
Construction, extraction, and maintenance occupations . . .	12,613	10,458	838	111	206
Production, transportation, and material moving occupations	17,554	13,021	2,280	138	642
FAMILY INCOME IN THE PAST 12 MONTHS					
Total families.	**73,058**	**57,543**	**8,302**	**549**	**2,779**
Less than $10,000	3,981	2,306	1,124	67	135
$10,000 to $19,999.	6,622	4,450	1,318	81	211
$20,000 to $29,999.	8,133	5,987	1,202	88	232
$30,000 to $39,999.	8,226	6,309	1,024	75	265
$40,000 to $49,999.	7,668	6,135	803	60	236
$50,000 to $59,999.	6,919	5,652	663	44	213
$60,000 to $74,999.	8,798	7,299	752	51	327
$75,000 to $99,999.	9,731	8,216	730	41	409
$100,000 to $124,999	5,515	4,696	351	21	281
$125,000 to $149,999	2,764	2,363	153	10	174
$150,000 to $199,999	2,489	2,144	126	6	162
$200,000 or more	2.213	1,986	57	4	133
Median family income in the past 12 months (dol.)	52,273	55.938	34,608	34,641	63,883
POVERTY STATUS IN THE PAST 12 MONTHS					
Persons below poverty level	35,846	21.652	8,441	530	1,348
Percent below poverty level.	12.7	10.1	24.7	24.5	11.5
Families below poverty level	7,143	4,228	1,821	112	256
Percent below poverty level.	9.8	7.3	21.9	20.4	9.2
HOUSING TENURE					
Total householders	108,420	86,084	12,686	784	3,768
Owner-occupied	72,419	61.557	5,878	432	2,110
Renter-occupied	36,001	24.526	6,808	352	1,658

See footnotes at end of table.

U.S. Census Bureau. Statistical Abstract of the United States: 2006

Table 37. **Selected Characteristics of Racial Groups and Hispanic/Latino Population: 2003—Con.**

[See headnote, page 40]

Characteristic	Native Hawaiian and Other Pacific Islander alone	Some other race alone	Two or more races	Hispanic/ Latino [1]	White alone, not Hispanic or Latino
EDUCATIONAL ATTAINMENT					
Persons 25 years old and over, total.	237	7,208	2,180	20,899	132,780
Less than 9th grade	16	1,856	152	5,058	4,761
9th to 12th grade. no diploma	27	1.293	235	3,569	10,890
High school graduate (includes equivalency). . . .	90	1,899	588	5,456	40.880
Some college, no degree	53	1,129	547	3.290	27,895
Associate's degree.	14	330	169	1,028	9,722
Bachelor's degree	27	492	319	1,672	24,443
Graduate degree	10	210	171	825	14,188
Percent high school graduate or higher	81.7	56.3	82.3	58.7	88.2
Percent bachelor's degree or higher	15.7	9.7	22.4	11.9	29.1
OCCUPATION					
Employed civilian population, 16 years old and over, total	203	5,795	1,746	16,449	94,468
Management, professional, and related occupations	41	916	530	2,880	35,363
Service occupations	47	1,423	361	3,909	12,902
Sales and office occupations	63	1,276	460	3,641	25,633
Farming, fishing. and forestry occupations	2	144	9	381	485
Construction. extraction, and maintenance occupations	21	819	158	2,443	8,920
Production, transportation, and material moving occupations	30	1,217	228	3,195	11.165
FAMILY INCOME IN THE PAST 12 MONTHS					
Total families	86	2,942	858	8,482	52,368
Less than $10,000	7	268	73	774	1,848
10,000 to $19,999	9	445	108	1,333	3,621
20,000 to $29,999	10	496	118	1,413	5,129
30,000 to $39,999	11	437	105	1,184	5,615
40,000 to $49,999	7	337	90	932	5,574
50,000 to $59,999	8	266	73	716	5,231
60,000 to $74,999	13	264	93	769	6,823
75,000 to $99,999	11	232	93	692	7,780
100,000 to $124,999	6	110	50	332	4,488
125,000 to $149,999	2	43	18	153	2,259
150,000 to $199,999	2	30	20	110	2,069
200,000 or more	1	16	16	74	1,932
Median family income in the past 12 months (dol.)	48,908	35,611	42,227	35,600	58,131
POVERTY STATUS IN THE PAST 12 MONTHS					
Persons below poverty level	71	2,872	933	8,544	16,436
Percent below poverty level	17.7	21.4	17.6	21.9	8.6
Families below poverty level	12	585	129	1,706	3,193
Percent below poverty level	14.1	19.9	15.1	20.1	6.1
HOUSING TENURE					
Total householders	121	3,644	1,333	10.791	79,439
Owner-occupied	51	1,699	691	5,104	58,336
Renter-occupied	70	1,945	641	5,686	21,103

[1] Persons of Hispanic/Latino origin may be of any race.

Source: U.S. Census Bureau. American FactFinder, 2003 American Community Survey Summary Tables, PCT035. Sex by Educational Attainment for the Population 25 Years and Over. PCT049. Sex by Occupation for the Employed Civilian Population 5 Years and Over, P100. Family Income in the Past 12 Months (In 2003 Inflation-Adjusted Dollars), P101. Median Family Income in the Past 12 Months (In 2003 Inflation-Adjusted Dollars), P115. Poverty Status in the Past 12 Months by Age. P116. Poverty Status in the Past 12 Months of Families by Family Type by Presence of Related Children Under 18 Years by Age of Related Children. H007. Tenure by Race of Householder; <http://factfinder.census.gov/>; (accessed: 26 July 2005).

Population 41

Table 38. American Indian and Alaska Native Population by Tribe: 2000

[As of April. This table shows data for American Indian and Alaska Native tribes alone or in combination of tribes or races. Respondents who identified themselves as American Indian or Alaska Native were asked to report their enrolled or principal tribe. Therefore, data shown here reflect the written tribal entries reported on the questionnaire. Some of the entries (for example, Iroquois, Sioux, Colorado River, and Flathead) represent nations or reservations. The information on tribe is based on self-identification and includes federally- or state-recognized tribes, as well as bands and clans]

American Indian and Alaska Native tribe	Number	American Indian and Alaska Native tribe	Number
Total persons [1]	4,119,301	Osage	15,897
Apache	96,833	Ottawa	10,677
Blackfeet	85,750	Paiute	13,532
Cherokee	729,533	Pima	11,493
Cheyenne	18,204	Potawatomi	25,595
Chickasaw	38,351	Pueblo	74,085
Chippewa	149,669	Puget Sound Salish	14,631
Choctaw	158,774	Seminole	27,431
Colville	9,393	Shoshone	12,026
Comanche	19,376	Sioux	153,360
Cree	7,734	Tohono O'odham	20,087
Creek	71,310	United Houma Nation	8,713
Crow	13,394	Ute	10,385
Delaware	16,341	Yakama	10,851
Iroquois	80,822	Yaqui	22,412
Kiowa	12,242	Yuman	8,976
Latin American Indian	180,940	Alaskan Athabascan	18,838
Lumbee	57,868	Aleut	10,548
Menominee	9,840	Eskimo	54,761
Navajo	298,197	Tlingit-Haida	22,365

[1] Includes other tribes not shown separately.

Source: U.S. Census Bureau, The American Indian and Alaska Native Population: 2000, Census 2000 Brief (C2KBR/01-15), February 2002.

Table 39. Population Living on Selected Reservations and Trust Lands: 2000

[As of April. OTSA = Oklahoma Tribal Statistical Area; SDAISA = State Designated American Indian Statistical Area; ANRC = Alaska Native Regional Corporation]

Reservation, Trust Land, or Other Area	Total population	American Indian and Alaska Native population alone	American Indian and Alaska Native population alone or in combination with one or more races
Navajo Nation Reservation and Off-Reservation Trust Land, AZ—NM—UT	180,462	173,987	175,228
Cherokee OTSA, OK	462,327	76,041	104,482
Creek OTSA, OK	704,565	51,296	77,253
Lumbee SDAISA, NC	474,100	58,238	62,327
Choctaw OTSA, OK	224,472	29,521	39,984
Cook Inlet ANRC, AK	364,205	24,923	35,972
Chickasaw OTSA, OK	277,416	22,946	32,372
Calista ANRC, AK	23,032	19,617	20,353
United Houma Nation SDAISA, LA	839,880	11,019	15,305
Sealaska ANRC, AK	71,507	11,320	15,059
Pine Ridge Reservation and Off-Reservation Trust Land, SD—NE	15,521	14,304	14,484
Doyon ANRC, AK	97,190	11,182	14,128
Kiowa-Comanche-Apache-Fort Sill Apache OTSA, OK	193,260	9,675	13,045
Fort Apache Reservation, AZ	12,429	11,702	11,854
Citizen Potawatomi Nation-Absentee Shawnee OTSA, OK	106,624	6,733	10,617
Gila River Reservation, AZ	11,257	10,353	10,578
Cheyenne-Arapaho OTSA, OK	157,869	7,402	10,310
Tohono O'odham Reservation and Off-Reservation Trust Land, AZ	10,787	9,718	9,794
Osage Reservation, OK	44,437	6,410	9,209
Rosebud Reservation and Off-Reservation Trust Land, SD	10,469	9,040	9,165
San Carlos Reservation, AZ	9,385	8,921	9,065
Blackfeet Reservation and Off-Reservation Trust Land, MT	10,100	8,507	8,684
Yakama Reservation and Off-Reservation Trust Land, WA	31,799	7,411	8,193
Turtle Mountain Reservation and Off-Reservation Trust Land, MT—ND—SD	8,331	8,009	8,043
Flathead Reservation, MT	26,172	6,999	7,883
Zuni Reservation and Off-Reservation Trust Land, NM—AZ	7,758	7,426	7,466
Bering Straits ANRC, AK	9,196	6,915	7,274
Sac and Fox OTSA, OK	55,690	5,334	7,232
Eastern Cherokee Reservation, NC	8,092	6,665	6,898
Wind River Reservation and Off-Reservation Trust Land, WY	23,250	6,544	6,864
Hopi Reservation and Off-Reservation Trust Land, AZ	6,946	6,573	6,633
Fort Peck Reservation and Off-Reservation Trust Land, MT	10,321	6,391	6,577
Cheyenne River Reservation and Off-Reservation Trust Land, SD	8,470	6,249	6,346
NANA ANRC, AK	7,208	5,944	6,181
Standing Rock Reservation, SD—ND	8,250	5,946	6,054
Bristol Bay ANRC, AK	7,892	5,336	5,749
Arctic Slope ANRC, AK	7,385	5,050	5,453
Crow Reservation and Off-Reservation Trust Land, MT	6,894	5,165	5,275
Red Lake Reservation, MN	5,162	5,071	5,087

Source: U.S. Census Bureau, 2000 Census of Population and Housing. Profiles of General Demographic Characteristics. See also <http://factfinder.census.gov/home/aian/index.html>

42   Population

Table 40. Social and Economic Characteristics of the Hispanic Population: 2003

[As of March, except labor force status, annual average (39,384 represents 39,384,000). Excludes members of the Armed Forces except those living off post or with their families on post. Based on Current Population Survey; see text of this section and Appendix III]

Characteristic	Number (1,000)				Percent distribution			
	His-panic, total [1]	Mexican	Puerto Rican	Cuban	His-panic, total [1]	Mexican	Puerto Rican	Cuban
Total persons	39,384	26,293	3,851	1,436	100.0	100.0	100.0	100.0
Under 5 years	4,053	2,981	340	75	10.3	11.3	8.8	5.2
5 to 14 years old	7,381	5,239	810	174	18.7	19.9	21.0	12.1
15 to 44 years old	20,125	13,507	1,866	511	51.0	51.3	48.5	35.6
45 to 64 years old	5,772	3,464	628	335	14.6	13.2	16.3	23.3
65 years old and over	2,053	1,102	207	342	5.2	4.2	5.4	23.8
EDUCATIONAL ATTAINMENT								
Persons 25 years old and over	21,189	13,443	2,072	1,052	100.0	100.0	100.0	100.0
High school graduate or more	12,087	6,846	1,444	745	57.0	50.9	69.7	70.8
Bachelor's degree or more	2,414	1,055	256	227	11.4	7.8	12.3	21.6
LABOR FORCE STATUS [2]								
Civilians 16 years old and over	27,551	17,464	2,652	1,191	100.0	100.0	100.0	100.0
Civilian labor force	18,813	12,081	1,649	679	68.3	69.2	62.2	57.0
Employed	17,372	11,151	1,495	638	63.1	63.9	56.4	53.6
Unemployed	1,441	930	154	41	5.2	5.3	5.8	3.4
Unemployment rate [3]	7.7	7.7	9.3	6.0	(X)	(X)	(X)	(X)
Male	7.2	7.2	9.0	6.9	(X)	(X)	(X)	(X)
Female	8.4	8.6	9.7	4.9	(X)	(X)	(X)	(X)
Not in labor force	8,738	5,383	1,003	512	31.7	30.8	37.8	43.0
HOUSEHOLDS								
Total	11,339	7,126	1,256	551	100.0	100.0	100.0	100.0
Family households	9,090	5,832	964	415	80.2	81.8	76.8	75.3
Married-couple families [4]	6,189	4,126	538	309	54.6	57.9	42.8	56.1
Male householder, no spouse present	872	567	70	36	7.7	8.0	5.6	6.5
Female householder, no spouse present	2,029	1,139	356	69	17.9	16.0	28.3	12.5
Nonfamily households	2,249	1,294	292	136	19.8	18.2	23.2	24.7
Male householder	1,228	742	165	50	10.8	10.4	13.1	9.1
Female householder	1,021	552	127	86	9.0	7.7	10.1	15.6
Size:								
One person	1,600	894	226	116	14.1	12.6	18.0	21.1
Two people	2,567	1,430	322	198	22.6	20.1	25.6	35.9
Three people	2,151	1,329	252	96	19.0	18.7	20.0	17.5
Four people	2,367	1,538	248	94	20.9	21.6	19.8	17.1
Five people	1,440	998	131	30	12.7	14.0	10.4	5.5
Six people	724	558	46	10	6.4	7.8	3.7	1.9
Seven people or more	490	379	32	6	4.3	5.3	2.5	1.1
FAMILY INCOME IN 2002								
Total families [5]	9,094	5,832	964	416	100.0	100.0	100.0	100.0
Less than $5,000	378	230	65	12	4.2	4.0	6.8	2.8
$5,000 to $14,999	1,136	729	137	60	12.5	12.5	14.2	14.4
$15,000 to $24,999	1,661	1,112	156	78	18.3	19.1	16.2	18.8
$25,000 to $34,999	1,454	986	144	52	16.0	16.9	14.9	12.5
$35,000 to $49,999	1,520	983	153	61	16.7	16.9	15.9	14.7
$50,000 to $74,999	1,561	1,007	149	61	17.2	17.3	15.4	14.8
$75,000 and over	1,385	784	160	92	15.2	13.4	16.6	22.1
POVERTY STATUS IN 2002								
Families below poverty level [6]	1,792	1,221	220	54	19.7	20.9	22.8	12.9
Persons below poverty level [6]	8,549	5,956	952	238	21.8	22.8	24.8	16.7
HOUSING TENURE								
Total occupied units	11,339	7,126	1,256	551	100.0	100.0	100.0	100.0
Owner-occupied	5,385	3,549	482	339	47.5	49.8	38.4	61.6
Renter-occupied [7]	5,955	3,578	773	211	52.5	50.2	61.6	38.4

X Not applicable.   [1] Includes other Hispanic groups not shown separately.   [2] Source: U.S. Bureau of Labor Statistics, *Employment and Earnings*, January 2004. See Table 578 for 2004 data.   [3] Total unemployment as percent of civilian labor force.   [4] In married-couple families, Hispanic origin refers to the householder.   [5] Includes families in group quarters.   [6] For explanation of poverty level, see text, Section 13.   [7] Includes no cash rent.

Source: Except as noted, U.S. Census Bureau, Current Population Reports, P20-550 and P20-553; "Table FINC-01. Selected Characteristics of Families, by Total Money Income in 2002"; published 14 July 2004:<http://pubdb3.census.gov/macro/032003/faminc/new01_000.htm>; "POV01. Age and Sex of All People, Family Members and Unrelated Individuals Iterated by Income-to-Poverty Ratio and Race"; and "POV04. Families by Age of Householder, Number of Children, and Family Structure"; published 14 July 2004; <http://pubdb3.census.gov/macro/032003/pov/toc.htm>; and unpublished data.

Population 43

Table 41. Native and Foreign-Born Population by State: 2003

[In thousands, except percent (249,376 represents 249,376,000). The American Community Survey universe is limited to the household population and excludes the population living in institutions, college dormitories, and other group quarters. Based on a sample and subject to sampling variability; see text of this section and Appendix III]

State	Native popula-tion	Foreign-born population Number	Percent of total popula-tion	Percent entered 2000 or later	State	Native popula-tion	Foreign-born population Number	Percent of total popula-tion	Percent entered 2000 or later
U.S., total...	249,376	33,534	11.9	15.0					
					MO	5,347	188	3.4	24.6
AL	4,280	105	2.4	30.1	MT	876	16	1.8	12.2
AK	592	38	6.1	12.9	NE	1,607	80	4.8	24.5
AZ	4,714	757	13.8	15.4	NV	1,828	380	17.2	13.6
AR	2,567	83	3.1	20.9	NH	1,188	63	5.0	18.1
CA	25,463	9,187	26.5	11.6					
					NJ	6,823	1,621	19.2	16.1
CO	4,015	433	9.7	22.0	NM	1,654	184	10.0	15.8
CT	2,987	385	11.4	16.6	NY	14,727	3,874	20.8	10.2
DE	744	49	6.1	18.6	NC	7,644	503	6.2	26.6
DC	450	79	14.9	22.4	ND	593	16	2.7	25.7
FL	13,690	2,928	17.6	16.2					
					OH	10,756	377	3.4	18.6
GA	7,771	667	7.9	19.3	OK	3,244	153	4.5	23.1
HI	1,014	208	17.0	13.3	OR	3,181	301	8.7	15.5
ID	1,254	79	5.9	24.1	PA	11,369	553	4.6	16.2
IL	10,694	1,634	13.3	13.9	RI	917	120	11.6	9.9
IN	5,797	221	3.7	26.1					
					SC	3,874	135	3.4	22.0
IA	2,746	94	3.3	26.4	SD	723	13	1.7	14.3
KS	2,498	144	5.5	26.4	TN	5,511	178	3.1	31.4
KY	3,911	92	2.3	26.3	TX	18,190	3,358	15.6	15.4
LA	4,231	130	3.0	19.8	UT	2,142	167	7.2	16.6
ME	1,232	38	3.0	8.5					
					VT	577	21	3.5	16.8
MD	4,802	571	10.6	19.3	VA	6,495	657	9.2	19.8
MA	5,369	850	13.7	13.7	WA	5,376	614	10.3	13.6
MI	9,244	582	5.9	23.5	WV	1,740	26	1.5	26.0
MN	4,620	299	6.1	20.7	WI	5,091	225	4.2	20.0
MS	2,741	44	1.6	30.7	WY	477	11	2.2	23.6

Source: U.S. Census Bureau, American FactFinder, 2003 American Community Survey Summary Tables, P038. Place of Birth by Citizenship Status and P040. Year of Entry by Citizenship Status for the Foreign-Born Population. <http://factfinder.census.gov/>: (accessed: 11 July 2005).

Table 42. Nativity and Place of Birth of Resident Population—25 Largest Cities: 2003

[In thousands except percent (659 represents 659,000). The American Community Survey universe is limited to the household population and excludes the population living in institutions, college dormitories, and other group quarters. Based on a sample and subject to sampling variability; see text of this section and Appendix III]

City	Total population	Native population Total	Born in United States	Born outside United States	Foreign-born population Total Number	Foreign-born population Total Percent of total population	Entered 2000 or later Number	Entered 2000 or later Percent of foreign-born population
Austin, TX	659	528	512	16	131	19.9	26	19.5
Baltimore, MD	603	573	568	4	30	5.0	7	22.7
Boston, MA	541	378	364	14	163	30.1	17	10.6
Charlotte, NC	567	492	490	3	75	13.2	20	26.7
Chicago, IL	2,723	2,136	2,078	58	587	21.6	61	10.5
Columbus, OH	698	633	629	4	65	9.4	19	29.6
Dallas, TX	1,207	890	880	9	317	26.3	74	23.3
Denver, CO	545	458	455	4	86	15.9	18	21.0
Detroit, MI	880	828	819	9	52	5.9	17	32.7
El Paso, TX	567	416	399	17	151	26.7	21	14.2
Fort Worth, TX	551	455	450	5	96	17.4	12	12.2
Houston, TX	1,939	1,418	1,401	16	521	26.9	85	16.3
Indianapolis, IN [1]	763	713	709	4	50	6.5	12	24.3
Jacksonville, FL	748	686	674	12	62	8.2	14	22.7
Los Angeles, CA	3,719	2,226	2,190	35	1,494	40.2	188	12.6
Memphis, TN	600	570	568	2	30	5.1	11	37.5
Milwaukee, WI	560	509	498	11	51	9.1	11	20.7
New York, NY	7,903	5,101	4,773	328	2,802	35.5	277	9.9
Philadelphia, PA	1,424	1,274	1,232	42	150	10.5	19	12.9
Phoenix, AZ	1,319	1,027	1,015	13	292	22.1	47	16.1
San Antonio, TX	1,194	1,022	1,002	20	172	14.4	23	13.5
San Diego, CA	1,221	910	890	21	311	25.4	46	14.7
San Francisco, CA	732	472	460	12	260	35.5	30	11.6
San Jose, CA	853	507	501	7	345	40.5	47	13.6
Seattle, WA	530	443	435	8	87	16.4	11	12.5

[1] Represents the portion of a consolidated city that is not within one or more separately incorporated places.

Source: U.S. Census Bureau, American FactFinder, 2003 American Community Survey Summary Tables, P038. Place of Birth by Citizenship Status and P040. Year of Entry by Citizenship Status for the Foreign-Born Population; <http://factfinder.census.gov/>; (accessed: 11 July 2005).

Table 43. Foreign-Born Population—Selected Characteristics by Region of Origin: 2004

[In thousands (34,244 represents 34,244,000). As of March. The term foreign-born refers to anyone who is not a U.S. citizen at birth. This includes naturalized U.S. citizens, legal permanent residents (immigrants), temporary migrants (such as foreign students), humanitarian migrants (such as refugees), and persons illegally present in the United States. Based on Current Population Survey, Annual Social and Economic Supplement: see text this section and Appendix III]

Characteristic	Total foreign-born	Europe	Asia	Latin America Total	Carib-bean	Central America [1]	South America	Other areas
Total.......................	34,244	4,661	8,685	18,314	3,323	12,924	2,066	2,584
Under 5 years old...................	334	37	86	181	13	142	26	32
5 to 14 years old..................	1,822	186	339	1,135	134	866	135	162
15 to 24 years old.................	4,561	411	894	2,909	368	2,255	287	347
25 to 34 years old.................	7,784	614	1,843	4,795	521	3,842	431	532
35 to 44 years old.................	7,559	799	2,007	4,189	749	2,962	479	565
45 to 54 years old.................	5,316	707	1,587	2,568	643	1,566	359	454
55 to 64 years old.................	3,171	639	989	1,309	394	714	200	235
65 to 74 years old.................	2,092	611	593	764	286	366	112	123
75 to 84 years old.................	1,231	507	262	370	167	176	27	92
85 years old and over.............	374	151	85	94	49	34	10	44
EDUCATIONAL ATTAINMENT								
Persons 25 years old and over......	27,527	4,028	7,366	14,089	2,809	9,661	1,619	2,044
Less than ninth grade...............	5,854	375	645	4,659	458	4,034	167	175
Ninth to twelfth grade (no diploma)......	3,170	201	389	2,423	398	1,878	146	157
High school graduate................	6,748	1,173	1,470	3,613	897	2,218	498	492
Some college or associate's degree......	4,247	814	1,202	1,781	509	945	327	450
Bachelor's degree..................	4,695	823	2,206	1,158	372	453	332	508
Advanced degree...................	2,814	641	1,454	456	175	133	148	263
High school graduate or more..........	18,504	3,452	6,332	7,007	1,953	3,749	1,305	1,712
Bachelor's degree or more............	7,509	1,465	3,660	1,613	547	586	480	771
INCOME IN 2003								
Total family households............	11,016	1,517	2,860	5,852	1,132	4,084	636	787
Under $15,000....................	1,328	133	276	863	161	646	56	56
$15,000 to $24,999...............	1,648	182	251	1,116	170	870	77	99
$25,000 to $34,999...............	1,483	164	186	1,028	167	781	80	104
$35,000 to $49,999...............	1,763	208	410	1,024	174	742	107	121
$50,000 to $74,999...............	1,971	289	581	953	216	605	132	148
$75,000 and over.................	2,824	541	1,156	868	243	440	185	259
Median income (dol.) [2]...........	42,677	55,714	62,551	33,962	38,687	31,451	49,669	51,771
POVERTY STATUS IN 2003 [3]								
Persons below poverty level...........	5,897	462	1,045	4,044	581	3,204	259	346
Persons above poverty level..........	28,325	4,199	7,640	14,251	2,739	9,704	1,807	2,235

[1] Includes Mexico.   [2] For definition of median, see Guide to Tabular Presentation.   [3] Persons for whom poverty status is determined. Excludes unrelated individuals under 15 years old.

Source: U.S. Census Bureau, "Foreign-Born Population of the United States Current Population Survey – March 2004 Detailed Tables (PPL-176)"; published 17 February 2005; <http://www.census.gov/population/www/socdemo/foreign/ppl-176.html>.

Table 44. Foreign-Born Population by Place of Birth and Citizenship Status: 2003

[In thousands, except percent (33,534 represents 33,534,000). The term foreign-born refers to anyone who is not a U.S. citizen at birth. This includes naturalized U.S. citizens, legal permanent residents (immigrants), temporary migrants (such as foreign students), humanitarian migrants (such as refugees), and persons illegally present in the United States. Based on a sample and subject to sampling variability; see text of this section and Appendix III. The survey universe is limited to the household population and excludes the population living in institutions, college dormitories, and other group quarters]

Region	Foreign-born population, total	Naturalized citizen	Not U.S. citizen Number	Percent of foreign-born
Total.......................................	33,534	13,896	19,640	59
Latin America................................	17,534	5,417	12,118	69
Caribbean.................................	3,108	1,684	1,424	46
Central America..........................	12,126	2,848	9,279	77
Mexico................................	10,011	2,239	7,772	78
Other Central America.................	2,115	609	1,507	71
South America...........................	2,300	885	1,415	62
Asia..	9,147	4,917	4,230	46
Europe.....................................	4,776	2,733	2,043	43
Africa......................................	1,039	397	643	62
Northern America..........................	847	367	480	57
Oceania....................................	191	65	126	66

Source: U.S. Census Bureau, American FactFinder. 2003 American Community Survey Summary Tables, P039. Place of Birth by Citizenship Status for The Foreign-Born Population; <http://factfinder.census.gov>; (accessed: 28 March 2005).

Population   45

Table 45. **Native and Foreign-Born Populations by Selected Characteristics: 2004**

[In thousands (288,280 represents 288,280,000). As of March. The foreign-born population includes anyone who is not a U.S. citizen at birth. This includes legal permanent residents (immigrants), temporary migrants (such as students), humanitarian migrants (such as refugees), and persons illegally present in the United States. Based on Current Population Survey, Annual Social and Economic Supplement which includes the civilian noninstitutional population plus Armed Forces living off post or with their families on post; see text of this section, and Appendix III]

Characteristic	Total population	Native population	Foreign-born population			
			Total	Natural-ized citizen	Not U.S. citizen	Year of entry: 2000 to March 2004
Total.	**288,280**	**254,037**	**34,244**	**13,128**	**21,116**	**6,052**
Under 5 years old	19,932	19,597	334	75	259	321
5 to 14 years old	40,764	38,943	1,822	219	1,603	797
15 to 24 years old.	40,708	36,147	4,561	831	3,730	1,498
25 to 34 years old.	39,201	31,417	7,784	1,705	6,079	1,923
35 to 44 years old.	43,573	36,014	7,559	2,914	4,646	883
45 to 54 years old.	41,069	35,752	5,316	2,807	2,509	365
55 to 64 years old.	28,375	25,204	3,171	1,941	1,229	132
65 to 74 years old.	18,239	16,146	2,092	1,396	696	87
75 to 84 years old.	12,851	11,620	1,231	946	285	38
85 years old and over	3,571	3,197	374	293	81	9
Median age (years).	35.9	35.3	38.4	47.7	33.2	26.9
Male.	141,227	124,006	17,221	6,243	10,979	3,258
Female.	147,053	130,031	17,023	6,886	10,137	2,794
MARITAL STATUS						
Persons 15 years old and over	**227,584**	**195,496**	**32,088**	**12,834**	**19,254**	**4,934**
Married.	121,359	101,842	19,518	8,435	11,083	2,620
Widowed.	13,816	12,254	1,562	975	587	91
Divorced.	21,833	19,901	1,932	1,061	871	154
Separated.	4,551	3,689	862	317	545	85
Never married	66,025	57,811	8,214	2,046	6,168	1,984
EDUCATIONAL ATTAINMENT						
Persons 25 years old and over	**186,876**	**159,350**	**27,527**	**12,002**	**15,525**	**3,435**
Not high school graduate	27,746	18,722	9,024	2,718	6,306	1,055
High school graduate/some college	107,382	96,388	10,995	5,444	5,551	1,201
Bachelor's degree.	33,766	29,071	4,695	2,390	2,306	761
Advanced degree	17,983	15,169	2,814	1,451	1,362	417
EARNINGS IN 2003 [1]						
Persons 15 yrs old and over with earnings—	**100,680**	**85,566**	**15,114**	**6,322**	**8,792**	**1,858**
Under $15,000.	8,924	6,676	2,248	525	1,723	455
$15,000 to $24,999.	19,597	15,259	4,337	1,326	3,011	613
$25,000 to $34,999.	20,030	17,336	2,694	1,202	1,492	253
$35,000 to $49,999.	21,515	19,112	2,403	1,268	1,135	255
$50,000 to $74,999.	17,421	15,566	1,855	1,060	795	155
$75,000 and over	13,194	11,616	1,578	942	636	128
Median earnings (dol.) [2].	35,795	36,784	27,337	35,813	23,140	21,762
HOUSEHOLD SIZE [3]						
Total households.	**112,000**	**97,840**	**14,159**	**6,567**	**7,592**	**1,606**
One person.	29,586	27,145	2,442	1,318	1,123	246
Two persons.	37,366	33,988	3,378	1,801	1,577	435
Three persons	17,968	15,278	2,690	1,177	1,513	338
Four persons	16,065	13,203	2,862	1,203	1,659	319
Five persons	7,150	5,546	1,604	633	971	175
Six persons	2,476	1,784	692	268	425	46
Seven persons or more	1,388	897	491	167	324	46
INCOME IN 2003 [3]						
Total family households	**76,217**	**65,201**	**11,016**	**5,034**	**5,983**	**1,184**
Under $15,000.	6,761	5,433	1,328	420	908	235
$15,000 to $24,999.	8,247	6,599	1,648	582	1,066	210
$25,000 to $34,999.	8,533	7,051	1,483	543	940	199
$35,000 to $49,999.	11,590	9,828	1,763	765	998	186
$50,000 to $74,999.	15,690	13,719	1,971	1,005	966	174
$75,000 and over	25,395	22,572	2,824	1,719	1,105	180
Median income (dol.) [2]	53,991	55,914	42,677	54,520	35,804	31,930
POVERTY STATUS IN 2003 [4]						
Persons at or below poverty level	35,861	29,965	5,897	1,309	4,588	1,647
Persons above poverty level.	251,838	223,513	28,325	11,819	16,506	4,392
HOUSING TENURE [3] [5]						
Owner-occupied unit	77,092	69,807	7,285	4,537	2,749	286
Renter-occupied unit	33,415	26,690	6,725	1,956	4,768	1,304

[1] Covers only year-round full-time workers. [2] For definition of median, see Guide to Tabular Presentation. [3] Based on citizenship of householder. [4] Persons for whom poverty status is determined. Excludes unrelated individuals under 15 years old. [5] Excludes occupiers who paid no cash rent.

Source: U.S. Census Bureau, "Foreign-Born Population of the United States Current Population Survey - March 2004 Detailed Tables (PPL-176)"; published 17 February 2005; <http://www.census.gov/population/www/socdemo/foreign/ppl-176.html>.

46 Population

Table 46. Population by Selected Ancestry Group and Region: 2003

In thousands (282,910 represents 282,910,000). Covers single and multiple ancestries. The American Community Survey universe is limited to the household population and excludes the population living in institutions, college dormitories, and other group quarters. Based on a sample and subject to sampling variability; see text of this section and Appendix III. For composition of regions, see map, inside front cover]

Ancestry group	Total (1,000)	Percent distribution by region				Ancestry group	Total (1,000)	Percent distribution by region			
		North-east	Mid-west	South	West			North-east	Mid-west	South	West
Total population..	282,910	19	22	36	23	Lithuanian	720	41	28	18	13
Arab	1,258	25	24	27	24	Norwegian	4,494	6	50	11	33
Austrian	790	31	24	22	23	Polish	9,304	34	38	17	11
British	1,153	17	17	38	28	Portuguese.....	1,349	47	3	12	38
Canadian	698	32	17	24	27	Russian	2,975	38	18	20	24
Czech	1,426	12	45	26	17	Scotch-Irish	5,099	14	20	45	21
Danish	1,435	8	33	15	44	Scottish	5,811	18	20	36	26
Dutch	5,059	16	37	27	21	Slovak	811	46	35	11	8
English	28,403	17	22	37	24	Subsaharan					
European.....	2,164	13	19	31	36	African [1].....	1,884	25	17	42	15
Finnish.	778	10	59	10	20	African	1,144	19	17	48	15
French (except						Swedish......	4,254	14	40	15	31
Basque)	9,678	26	24	31	19	Swiss	984	14	35	18	33
French						Ukrainian	870	44	21	17	18
Canadian	2,188	42	20	23	16	United States or					
German	47,842	16	39	25	19	American	19,677	10	20	54	16
Greek	1,229	34	22	24	20	Welsh	1,890	20	24	30	26
Hungarian	1,495	33	31	20	17	West Indian [1,2] .	2,129	50	4	42	4
Irish.	33,992	26	24	31	18	Haitian	666	43	2	53	2
Italian.	16,726	47	16	21	16	Jamaican	825	52	5	39	4

[1] Includes other groups not shown separately. [2] Excludes Hispanic origin groups.

Source: U.S. Census Bureau, American FactFinder, 2003 American Community Survey Summary Tables, PCT023 Ancestry; and PCT026 Ancestry (Total Categories Tallied) For People With One Or More Ancestry Categories Reported; <http://factfinder.census.gov/>; (accessed: 4 August 2005).

Table 47. Languages Spoken at Home by Language: 2003

[263,230 represents 263,230,000. Covers population 5 years old and over. The American Community Survey universe is limited to the household population and excludes the population living in institutions, college dormitories, and other group quarters. Based on a sample and subject to sampling variability; see text of this section and Appendix III]

Language	Number (1,000)	Language	Number (1,000)
Total population 5 years and over	263,230	Other Indic languages	524
Speak only English	214,809	Other Indo-European languages	376
Spanish or Spanish Creole	29,698	Chinese..........................	2,193
French (incl. Patois, Cajun).............	1,379	Japanese.........................	475
French Creole	483	Korean	967
Italian...........................	782	Mon-Khmer, Cambodian...............	163
Portuguese or Portuguese Creole	560	Miao, Hmong......................	175
German..........................	1,094	Thai	112
Yiddish	142	Laotian	174
Other West Germanic languages	311	Vietnamese	1,104
Scandinavian languages	136	Other Asian languages................	525
Greek...........................	333	Tagalog..........................	1,262
Russian..........................	705	Other Pacific Island languages	300
Polish...........................	601	Navajo	136
Serbo-Croatian.....................	234	Other Native North American language	166
Other Slavic languages	284	Hungarian	90
Armenian.........................	195	Arabic...........................	558
Persian..........................	360	Hebrew	168
Gujarathi.........................	280	African languages	503
Hindi............................	396	Other and unspecified languages	142
Urdu............................	335		

Source: U.S. Census Bureau, American FactFinder, 2003 American Community Survey Summary Table, P034. Language Spoken at Home for the Population 5 Years and Over; <http://factfinder.census.gov/>; (accessed: 10 July 2005).

Population   47

Table 48. Language Spoken at Home by Resident Population by State: 2003

[In thousands, except percent (263,230 represents 263,230,000). The American Community Survey universe is limited to the household population and excludes the population living in institutions, college dormitories, and other group quarters. Based on a sample and subject to sampling variability; see text of this section and Appendix III]

State	Population 5 years and over	English only	Language other than English Number	Percent of population 5 years and over	State	Population 5 years and over	English only	Language other than English Number	Percent of population 5 years and over
U.S. . . .	263,230	214,809	48,421	18.4	MO	5,160	4,886	274	5.3
AL	4,088	3,949	139	3.4	MT	840	806	35	4.1
AK	582	509	73	12.6	NE	1,569	1,445	123	7.8
AZ	5,032	3,703	1,328	26.4	NV	2,045	1,554	491	24.0
AR	2,461	2,347	113	4.6	NH	1,179	1,084	95	8.1
CA	32,116	19,013	13,102	40.8	NJ	7,887	5,815	2,072	26.3
CO	4,124	3,506	618	15.0	NM	1,708	1,093	616	36.0
CT	3,158	2,598	560	17.7	NY	17,395	12,616	4,779	27.5
DE	738	663	75	10.2	NC	7,557	6,936	621	8.2
DC	495	407	88	17.8	ND	573	540	33	5.7
FL	15,572	11,808	3,765	24.2	OH	10.396	9,815	581	5.6
GA	7,780	6,958	822	10.6	OK	3,163	2.945	218	6.9
HI	1,137	869	268	23.6	OR	3,257	2,851	406	12.5
ID	1,230	1,101	128	10.4	PA	11,218	10,305	913	8.1
IL	11,442	9,129	2,313	20.2	RI	976	788	189	19.3
IN	5,596	5,157	438	7.8	SC	3,736	3.555	181	4.8
IA	2,661	2,511	150	5.6	SD	683	650	33	4.9
KS	2,450	2,248	202	8.2	TN	5,310	5,059	250	. 4.7
KY	3,733	3,584	149	4.0	TX	19,751	13,334	6,418	32.5
LA	4,039	3,722	317	7.8	UT	2,083	1,836	247	11.9
ME	1,204	1,115	88	7.3	VT	567	538	29	5.1
MD	5,007	4,354	653	13.0	VA	6,667	5,869	798	12.0
MA	5,822	4,698	1,124	19.3	WA	5,600	4,831	769	13.7
MI	9,178	8,391	787	8.6	WV	1,664	1,629	35	2.1
MN	4,591	4,167	424	9.2	WI	4,978	4,589	389	7.8
MS	2,578	2,499	78	3.0	WY	456	433	23	5.0

Source: U.S. Census Bureau, American FactFinder, 2003 American Community Survey Summary Table, P035. Age by Language Spoken at Home by Ability to Speak English for the Population 5 Years and Over; <http://factfinder.census.gov/>; (accessed: 13 July 2005).

Table 49. Language Spoken at Home by Resident Population—25 Largest Cities: 2003

[In thousands, except percent (602 represents 602,000). The American Community Survey universe is limited to the household population and excludes the population living in institutions, college dormitories, and other group quarters. Based on a sample and subject to sampling variability; see text of this section and Appendix III]

City	Population 5 years and over	English only	Language other than English, total [1] Number	Percent of population 5 years and over	Speak English less than "very well"	Spanish	Other Indo-European languages	Asian and Pacific Island languages
Austin, TX	602	400	202	33.6	106	161	16	23
Baltimore, MD.	560	520	41	7.2	16	11	19	8
Boston, MA	506	326	180	35.5	86	78	62	33
Charlotte, NC	522	442	79	15.2	48	43	21	14
Chicago, IL	2,505	1,622	883	35.3	429	593	183	82
Columbus, OH	640	567	73	11.5	38	21	18	20
Dallas, TX	1.090	617	472	43.4	287	408	30	27
Denver, CO	495	369	127	25.6	52	102	12	9
Detroit, MI	802	725	77	9.7	45	46	19	4
El Paso, TX	517	121	397	76.7	142	385	7	3
Fort Worth, TX	506	368	137	27.2	76	117	7	10
Houston, TX. . . . [2] . . .	1,766	998	768	43.5	425	628	53	68
Indianapolis, IN [2]	701	635	66	9.4	35	41	14	6
Jacksonville, FL	689	610	79	11.4	36	29	26	17
Los Angeles, CA	3,452	1,384	2,068	59.9	1,070	1,507	216	297
Memphis, TN	554	519	36	6.4	21	19	7	12
Milwaukee, WI	514	423	92	17.8	52	65	14	12
New York, NY	7,345	3,938	3,408	46.4	1,818	1,851	900	540
Philadelphia, PA	1,325	1,075	250	18.9	119	108	68	54
Phoenix, AZ	1,206	787	419	34.8	226	364	21	21
San Antonio, TX	1,091	593	498	45.7	168	465	21	9
San Diego, CA	1,138	691	447	39.3	229	258	46	132
San Francisco, CA . . .	696	390	306	44.0	167	77	41	185
San Jose, CA.	786	350	436	55.5	212	193	45	184
Seattle, WA	503	420	83	16.5	34	13	17	47

[1] Includes other language groups not shown separately.   [2] Represents the portion of a consolidated city that is not within one or more separately incorporated places.

Source: U.S. Census Bureau, American FactFinder, 2003 American Community Survey Summary Table, P035. Age by Language Spoken at Home by Ability to Speak English for the Population 5 Years and Over; <http://factfinder.census.gov/>; (accessed: 8 August 2005).

Table 50. **Marital Status of the Population by Sex, Race, and Hispanic Origin: 1990 to 2004**

[In millions, except percent (181.8 represents 181,800,000). As of March. Persons 18 years old and over. Excludes members of Armed Forces except those living off post or with their families on post. Population controls for 2004 based on Census 2000 and an expanded sample of households. Based on Current Population Survey, see text of this section, and Appendix III]

Marital status, race, and Hispanic origin	Total				Male				Female			
	1990	1995	2000	2004	1990	1995	2000	2004	1990	1995	2000	2004
Total [1]	181.8	191.6	201.8	214.5	86.9	92.0	96.9	103.6	95.0	99.6	104.9	110.9
Never married	40.4	43.9	48.2	53.2	22.4	24.6	26.1	29.6	17.9	19.3	22.1	23.7
Married	112.6	116.7	120.1	125.8	55.8	57.7	59.6	62.5	56.7	58.9	60.4	63.3
Widowed	13.8	13.4	13.7	13.8	2.3	2.3	2.6	2.6	11.5	11.1	11.1	11.1
Divorced	15.1	17.6	19.8	21.8	6.3	7.4	8.5	9.0	8.8	10.3	11.3	12.8
Percent of total	100.0	100.0	100.0	100.0	100.0	100.0	100.0	100.0	100.0	100.0	100.0	100.0
Never married	22.2	22.9	23.9	24.8	25.8	26.8	27.0	28.5	18.9	19.4	21.1	21.3
Married	61.9	60.9	59.5	58.5	64.3	62.7	61.5	60.3	59.7	59.2	57.6	57.1
Widowed	7.6	7.0	6.8	6.4	2.7	2.5	2.7	2.5	12.1	11.1	10.5	10.0
Divorced	8.3	9.2	9.8	10.2	7.2	8.0	8.8	8.6	9.3	10.3	10.8	11.5
White [2], total	155.5	161.3	168.1	175.9	74.8	78.1	81.6	85.9	80.6	83.2	86.6	90.1
Never married	31.6	33.2	36.0	39.5	18.0	19.2	20.3	22.7	13.6	14.0	15.7	16.8
Married	99.5	102.0	104.1	107.2	49.5	50.6	51.8	53.6	49.9	51.3	52.2	53.7
Widowed	11.7	11.3	11.5	11.5	1.9	1.9	2.2	2.2	9.8	9.4	9.3	9.3
Divorced	12.6	14.8	16.5	17.8	5.4	6.3	7.2	7.5	7.3	8.4	9.3	10.3
Percent of total	100.0	100.0	100.0	100.0	100.0	100.0	100.0	100.0	100.0	100.0	100.0	100.0
Never married	20.3	20.6	21.4	22.5	24.1	24.6	24.9	26.4	16.9	16.9	18.1	18.6
Married	64.0	63.2	62.0	60.9	66.2	64.9	63.5	62.4	61.9	61.7	60.3	59.6
Widowed	7.5	7.0	6.8	6.5	2.6	2.5	2.7	2.6	12.2	11.3	10.8	10.3
Divorced	8.1	9.1	9.8	10.1	7.2	8.1	8.8	8.7	9.0	10.1	10.7	11.4
Black [2], total	20.3	22.1	24.0	24.6	9.1	9.9	10.7	11.0	11.2	12.2	13.3	13.6
Never married	7.1	8.5	9.5	9.8	3.5	4.1	4.3	4.6	3.6	4.4	5.1	5.2
Married	9.3	9.6	10.1	10.1	4.5	4.6	5.0	5.0	4.8	4.9	5.1	5.2
Widowed	1.7	1.7	1.7	1.7	0.3	0.3	0.3	0.3	1.4	1.4	1.4	1.4
Divorced	2.1	2.4	2.8	3.0	0.8	0.8	1.1	1.1	1.3	1.5	1.7	1.9
Percent of total	100.0	100.0	100.0	100.0	100.0	100.0	100.0	100.0	100.0	100.0	100.0	100.0
Never married	35.1	38.4	39.4	39.8	38.4	41.7	40.2	41.8	32.5	35.8	38.3	38.2
Married	45.8	43.2	42.1	41.1	49.2	46.7	46.7	45.5	43.0	40.4	38.3	38.2
Widowed	8.5	7.6	7.0	6.9	3.7	3.1	2.8	2.7	12.4	11.3	10.5	10.3
Divorced	10.6	10.7	11.5	12.2	8.8	8.5	10.3	10.0	12.0	12.5	12.8	13.7
Asian [2], total	(NA)	(NA)	(NA)	9.1	(NA)	(NA)	(NA)	4.4	(NA)	(NA)	(NA)	4.7
Never married	(NA)	(NA)	(NA)	2.3	(NA)	(NA)	(NA)	1.3	(NA)	(NA)	(NA)	0.9
Married	(NA)	(NA)	(NA)	6.0	(NA)	(NA)	(NA)	2.8	(NA)	(NA)	(NA)	3.2
Widowed	(NA)	(NA)	(NA)	0.4	(NA)	(NA)	(NA)	0.1	(NA)	(NA)	(NA)	0.3
Divorced	(NA)	(NA)	(NA)	0.4	(NA)	(NA)	(NA)	0.1	(NA)	(NA)	(NA)	0.3
Percent of total	100.0	100.0	100.0	100.0	100.0	100.0	100.0	100.0	100.0	100.0	100.0	100.0
Never married	(NA)	(NA)	(NA)	25.3	(NA)	(NA)	(NA)	30.8	(NA)	(NA)	(NA)	19.1
Married	(NA)	(NA)	(NA)	65.9	(NA)	(NA)	(NA)	64.5	(NA)	(NA)	(NA)	68.1
Widowed	(NA)	(NA)	(NA)	4.4	(NA)	(NA)	(NA)	1.5	(NA)	(NA)	(NA)	6.4
Divorced	(NA)	(NA)	(NA)	4.4	(NA)	(NA)	(NA)	3.2	(NA)	(NA)	(NA)	6.4
Hispanic, [3] total	13.6	17.6	21.1	26.6	6.7	8.8	10.4	13.7	6.8	8.8	10.7	12.9
Never married	3.7	5.0	5.9	8.4	2.2	3.0	3.4	5.1	1.5	2.1	2.5	3.3
Married	8.4	10.4	12.7	15.2	4.1	5.1	6.2	7.6	4.3	5.3	6.5	7.6
Widowed	0.5	0.7	0.9	1.0	0.1	0.2	0.2	0.2	0.4	0.6	0.7	0.8
Divorced	1.0	1.4	1.6	2.0	0.4	0.6	0.7	0.9	0.6	0.8	1.0	1.2
Percent of total	100.0	100.0	100.0	100.0	100.0	100.0	100.0	100.0	100.0	100.0	100.0	100.0
Never married	27.2	28.6	28.0	31.6	32.1	33.8	32.3	37.0	22.5	23.5	23.4	25.6
Married	61.7	59.3	60.2	57.1	60.9	57.9	59.7	55.3	62.4	60.7	60.7	58.9
Widowed	4.0	4.2	4.2	3.8	1.5	1.8	1.6	1.4	6.5	6.6	6.5	6.2
Divorced	7.0	7.9	7.6	7.5	5.5	6.6	6.4	6.3	8.5	9.2	9.3	9.3
Non-Hispanic White, [2][3] total	(NA)	(NA)	(NA)	151.3	(NA)	(NA)	(NA)	73.1	(NA)	(NA)	(NA)	78.2
Never married	(NA)	(NA)	(NA)	31.8	(NA)	(NA)	(NA)	18.0	(NA)	(NA)	(NA)	13.8
Married	(NA)	(NA)	(NA)	92.9	(NA)	(NA)	(NA)	46.4	(NA)	(NA)	(NA)	46.6
Widowed	(NA)	(NA)	(NA)	10.6	(NA)	(NA)	(NA)	2.0	(NA)	(NA)	(NA)	8.6
Divorced	(NA)	(NA)	(NA)	16.0	(NA)	(NA)	(NA)	6.7	(NA)	(NA)	(NA)	9.3
Percent of total	100.0	100.0	100.0	100.0	100.0	100.0	100.0	100.0	100.0	100.0	100.0	100.0
Never married	(NA)	(NA)	(NA)	21.0	(NA)	(NA)	(NA)	24.6	(NA)	(NA)	(NA)	17.6
Married	(NA)	(NA)	(NA)	61.4	(NA)	(NA)	(NA)	63.5	(NA)	(NA)	(NA)	59.5
Widowed	(NA)	(NA)	(NA)	7.0	(NA)	(NA)	(NA)	2.7	(NA)	(NA)	(NA)	11.0
Divorced	(NA)	(NA)	(NA)	10.6	(NA)	(NA)	(NA)	9.2	(NA)	(NA)	(NA)	11.9

NA Not available. [1] Includes persons of other races, not shown separately. [2] 2004 data represent persons who selected this race group only and exclude persons reporting more than one race. The CPS in prior years only allowed respondents to report one race group. See also comments on race in the text for this section. [3] Hispanic persons may be of any race.

Source: U.S. Census Bureau, *Current Population Reports*, P20-537, and earlier reports; and "America's Families and Living Arrangements: 2004 Table A1. Marital Status of People 15 Years and Over, by Age, Sex, Personal Earnings, Race, and Hispanic Origin, 2004"; published 29 June 2005; <http://www.census.gov/population/www/socdemo/hh-fam/cps2004.html>.

Population 49

Table 51. Marital Status of the Population by Sex and Age: 2004

[As of March (103,641 represents 103,641,000). See headnote, Table 50]

Sex and age	Number of persons (1,000)					Percent distribution				
	Total	Never married	Married	Widowed	Divorced	Total	Never married	Married	Widowed	Divorced
Male . . . . / . .	103,641	29,561	62,483	2,641	8,956	100.0	28.5	60.3	2.5	8.6
18 to 19 years old	3,923	3,868	49	/ -	6	100.0	98.6	1.2	-	0.2
20 to 24 years old	10,241	8,850	1,308	2	81	100.0	86.4	12.8	-	0.8
25 to 29 years old	9,535	5,395	3,812	8	320	100.0	56.6	40.0	0.1	3.4
30 to 34 years old	10,018	3,223	6,085	20	690	100.0	32.2	60.7	0.2	6.9
35 to 39 years old	10,306	2,410	6,864	30	1,002	100.0	23.4	66.6	0.3	9.7
40 to 44 years old	11,213	1,978	7,767	54	1,414	100.0	17.6	69.3	0.5	12.6
45 to 54 years old	20,070	2,437	14,715	203	2,715	100.0	12.1	73.3	1.0	13.5
55 to 64 years old	13,543	797	10,756	293	1,697	100.0	5.9	79.4	2.2	12.5
65 to 74 years old	8,352	370	6,630	626	726	100.0	4.4	79.4	7.5	8.7
75 years old and over . . .	6,440	233	4,497	1,405	305	100.0	3.6	69.8	21.8	4.7
Female	110,883	23,655	63,282	11,141	12,804	100.0	21.3	57.1	10.0	11.5
18 to 19 years old	3,552	3,391	147		14	100.0	95.5	4.1		0.4
20 to 24 years old	10,060	7,581	2,326	11	142	100.0	75.4	23.1	0.1	1.4
25 to 29 years old	9,460	3,855	5,004	42	559	100.0	40.8	52.9	0.4	5.9
30 to 34 years old	10,127	2,400	6,797	67	863	100.0	23.7	67.1	0.7	8.5
35 to 39 years old	10,477	1,534	7,408	135	1,400	100.0	14.6	70.7	1.3	13.4
40 to 44 years old	11,560	1,406	8,227	162	1,765	100.0	12.2	71.2	1.4	15.3
45 to 54 years old	20,974	1,949	14,691	633	3,701	100.0	9.3	70.0	3.0	17.6
55 to 64 years old	14,823	796	9,973	1,458	2,596	100.0	5.4	67.3	9.8	17.5
65 to 74 years old	9,880	365	5,589	2,768	1,158	100.0	3.7	56.6	28.0	11.7
75 years old and over . . .	9,970	378	3,121	5,865	606	100.0	3.8	31.3	58.8	6.1

- Represents or rounds to zero.

Source: U.S. Census Bureau, "America's Families and Living Arrangements: 2004 Table A1. Marital Status of People 15 Years and Over, by Age, Sex, Personal Earnings, Race, and Hispanic Origin, 2004"; published 29 June 2005; <http://www.census.gov/population/www/socdemo/hh-fam/cps2004.html>.

Table 52. Living Arrangements of Persons 15 Years Old and Over by Selected Characteristics: 2004

[In thousands (227,343 represents 227,343,000). As of March. See headnote, Table 50]

Living arrangement	Total	15 to 19 years old	20 to 24 years old	25 to 34 years old	35 to 44 years old	45 to 54 years old	55 to 64 years old	65 to 74 years old	75 years old and over
Total ¹	227,343	20,296	20,302	39,140	43,555	41,047	28,365	18,231	16,408
Alone	29,586	146	1,384	3,888	3,883	5,026	4,600	4,198	6,461
With spouse	118,128	195	3,251	20,123	28,270	27,601	19,731	11,732	7,226
With other persons	79,629	19,955	15,667	15,129	11,402	8,420	4,034	2,301	2,721
White ²	185,742	15,778	15,912	30,755	35,083	33,857	24,072	15,709	14,577
Alone	24,094	91	1,069	2,917	2,981	3,994	3,729	3,569	5,744
With spouse	101,812	170	2,789	16,885	23,876	23,707	17,312	10,453	6,620
With other persons	59,836	15,517	12,054	10,953	8,226	6,156	3,031	1,687	2,213
Black ²	26,665	3,048	2,825	5,035	5,397	4,710	2,777	1,602	1,271
Alone	4,137	34	229	630	680	864	675	489	535
With spouse	8,527	9	245	1,528	2,297	2,082	1,331	683	353
With other persons	14,001	3,005	2,351	2,877	2,420	1,764	771	430	383
Asian ²	9,577	746	870	2,199	2,022	1,654	1,033	640	412
Alone	781	14	54	227	120	71	94	76	125
With spouse	5,554	5	118	1,186	1,490	1,326	791	437	202
With other persons	3,242	727	698	786	412	257	148	127	85
Hispanic origin ³	28,517	3,240	3,693	7.412	6.007	3,924	2,162	1,272	808
Alone	1,753	20	120	363	280	273	261	249	186
With spouse	13,297	72	778	3,824	3,758	2,464	1,389	680	332
With other persons	13,467	3,148	2,795	3,225	1,969	1,187	512	343	290
Non-Hispanic White ² ³ . .	159,307	12,806	12,526	23,866	29,548	30,203	22,040	14,514	13,803
Alone	22,474	73	958	2,597	2,726	3,739	3,481	3,336	5,563
With spouse	89,369	102	2,080	13,307	20,395	21,385	15,992	9,806	6,301
With other persons	47,464	12,631	9,488	7,962	6,427	5,079	2,567	1,372	1,939

¹ Includes other races and persons not of Hispanic origin, not shown separately. ² See footnote 2, Table 50. ³ Persons of Hispanic origin may be of any race.

Source: U.S. Census Bureau, "America's Families and Living Arrangements: 2004 Table A2. Family Status and Household Relationship of People 15 Years and Over, by Marital Status, Age, Sex, Race, and Hispanic Origin: 2004"; published 29 June 2005; <http://www.census.gov/population/www/socdemo/hh-fam/cps2004.html>.

Table 53. Households, Families, Subfamilies, and Married Couples: 1980 to 2004

[In thousands, except as indicated (80,776 represents 80,776,000). As of March. Excludes members of Armed Forces except those living off post or with their families on post. Beginning 2002, population controls based on Census 2000 and an expanded sample of households. Based on Current Population Survey, see text of this section, and Appendix III. Minus sign (-) indicates decrease]

Type of unit	1980	1990	1995	2000	2002	2003	2004	Percent change 1980-1990	1990-2000	2000-2004
Households	80,776	93,347	98,990	104,705	109,297	111,278	112,000	16	12	7
Average size.	2.76	2.63	2.65	2.62	2.58	2.57	2.57	(X)	(X)	(X)
White [1]	70,766	80,163	83,737	87,671	90,682	91,645	91,962	13	9	(X)
Black [1]	8,586	10,486	11,655	12,849	13,315	13,465	13,629	22	23	(X)
Hispanic [2]	3,684	5,933	7,735	9,319	10,499	11,339	11,182	61	57	20
Family households	59,550	66,090	69,305	72,025	74,329	75,596	76,217	11	9	6
Married couple	49,112	52,317	53,858	55,311	56,747	57,320	57,719	7	6	4
Male householder [3]	1,733	2,884	3,226	4,028	4,438	4,656	4,716	66	40	17
Female householder [3]	8,705	10,890	12,220	12,687	13,143	13,620	13,781	25	17	9
Nonfamily households	21,226	27,257	29,686	32,680	34,969	35,682	35,783	28	20	9
Male householder	8,807	11,606	13,190	14,641	15,579	16,020	16,136	32	26	10
Female householder	12,419	15,651	16,496	18,039	19,390	19,662	19,647	26	15	6
One person	18,296	22,999	24,732	26,724	28,775	29,431	29,586	26	16	11
Families.	59,550	66,090	69,305	72,025	74,329	75,596	76,217	11	9	6
Average size.	3.29	3.17	3.19	3.17	3.15	3.13	3.13	(X)	(X)	(X)
With own children [4]	31,022	32,289	34,296	34,605	35,705	35,968	35,944	4	7	4
Without own children [4]	28,528	33,801	35,009	37,420	38,623	39,628	40,273	18	11	8
Married couple	49,112	52,317	53,858	55,311	56,747	57,320	57,719	7	6	4
With own children [4]	24,961	24,537	25,241	25,248	25,792	25,914	25,793	-2	3	2
Without own children [4] . . .	24,151	27,780	28,617	30,062	30,955	31,406	31,926	15	8	6
Male householder [3]	1,733	2,884	3,226	4,028	4,438	4,656	4,716	66	40	17
With own children [4]	616	1,153	1,440	1,786	1,903	1,915	1,931	87	55	8
Without own children [4] . . .	1,117	1,731	1,786	2,242	2,535	2,741	2,786	55	30	24
Female householder [3]	8,705	10,890	12,220	12,687	13,143	13,620	13,781	25	17	9
With own children [4]	5,445	6,599	7,615	7,571	8,010	8,139	8,221	21	15	9
Without own children [4]	3,261	4,290	4,606	5,116	5,133	5,481	5,560	32	19	9
Unrelated subfamilies	360	534	674	571	474	525	509	48	7	-11
Married couple . . . . [3] . . .	20	68	64	37	43	34	42	(B)	(B)	(B)
Male reference persons [3] . . .	36	45	59	57	59	84	61	(B)	(B)	(B)
Female reference persons [3] . . .	304	421	550	477	371	407	406	39	13	-15
Related subfamilies	1,150	2,403	2,878	2,984	2,986	3,089	3,309	109	24	11
Married couple	582	871	1,015	1,149	1,129	1,232	1,303	50	32	13
Father-child [3]	54	153	195	201	269	260	296	(B)	31	47
Mother-child [3]	512	1,378	1,668	1,634	1,588	1,596	1,710	169	19	5
Married couples	49,714	53,256	54,937	56,497	57,919	58,586	59,064	7	6	5
With own household	49,112	52,317	53,858	55,311	56,747	57,320	57,719	7	6	4
Without own household	602	939	1,079	1,186	1,172	1,266	1,345	56	26	13
Percent without	1.2	1.8	2.0	2.1	2.0	2.2	2.3	(X)	(X)	(X)

B Not shown; base less than 75,000. X Not applicable. [1] Beginning with the 2003 Current Population Survey (CPS), respondents could choose more than one race. Beginning 2003, data represent persons who selected this race group only and exclude persons reporting more than one race. The CPS in prior years only allowed respondents to report one race group. See also comments on race in the text for this section. [2] Persons of Hispanic origin may be of any race. [3] No spouse present. [4] Under 18 years old.

Source: U.S. Census Bureau, "Families and Living Arrangements"; <http://www.census.gov/population/www/socdemo/hh-fam.html>.

Table 54. Married Couples by Race and Hispanic Origin of Spouses: 1980 to 2004

[In thousands (49,714 represents 49,714,000). As of March. Persons 15 years old and over. Persons of Hispanic origin may be of any race. Based on Current Population Survey; see headnote, Table 50 and Appendix III]

Race and origin of spouses	1980	1990	2000	2004
Married couples, total [1]	49,714	53,256	56,497	59,064
Interracial married couples, total	651	964	1,464	2,157
White [2]/Black [2]	167	211	363	413
Black husband/White wife	122	150	268	287
White husband/Black wife	45	61	95	126
White [2]/other race [3]	450	720	1,051	1,622
Black [2]/other race [3]	34	33	50	122
HISPANIC ORIGIN				
Hispanic/Hispanic	1,906	3,085	4,739	5,611
Hispanic/other origin (not Hispanic)	891	1,193	1,743	2,076
All other couples (not of Hispanic origin)	46,917	48,979	50,015	51,378

[1] Includes other married couples not shown separately [2] See footnote 2, Table 50. [3] "Other race," is any race other than White or Black, such as American Indian, Japanese, Chinese, etc. This total excludes combinations of other races by other races.

Source: U.S. Census Bureau, Table MS-3. Interracial Married Couples: 1980 to 2002; published 15 September 2004; <http://www.census.gov/population/www/socdemo/hh-fam.html>; and unpublished data.

Table 55. Households and Persons Per Household by Type of Household: 1990 to 2004

[As of March (93,347 represents 93,347,000). See headnote, Table 53]

Type of household	Households						Persons per household		
	Number (1,000)			Percent distribution					
	1990	2000	2004	1990	2000	2004	1990	2000	2004
Total households	93,347	104,705	112,000	100	100	100	2.63	2.62	2.57
Family households	66,090	72,025	76,217	71	69	68	3.22	3.24	3.19
Married couple family.	52,317	55,311	57,719	56	53	52	3.25	3.26	3.21
Male householder, no spouse present. . .	2,884	4,028	4,716	3	4	4	3.04	3.16	3.14
Female householder, no spouse present	10,890	12,687	13,781	12	12	12	3.10	3.17	3.15
Nonfamily households	27,257	32,680	35,783	29	31	32	1.22	1.25	1.25
Living alone	22,999	26,724	29,586	25	26	26	1.00	1.00	1.00
Male householder	11,606	14,641	16,136	12	14	14	1.33	1.34	1.34
Living alone	9,049	11,181	12,562	10	11	11	1.00	1.00	1.00
Female householder	15,651	18,039	19,647	17	17	18	1.14	1.17	1.17
Living alone	13,950	15,543	17,024	15	15	15	1.00	1.00	1.00

Source: U.S. Census Bureau, Current Population Reports, P20-537, and earlier reports; and "America's Families and Living Arrangements: 2004"; published 29 June 2005; <http://www.census.gov/population/www/socdemo/hh-fam/cps2004.html>.

Table 56. Households by Age of Householder and Size of Household: 1990 to 2004

[In millions (93.3 represents 93,300,000). As of March. Based on Current Population Survey; see headnote, Table 53]

Age of householder and size of household	1990	1995	2000	2004					
				Total [1]	White [2]	Black [2]	Asian [2]	Hispanic [3]	Non-Hispanic White [3]
Total.	93.3	99.0	104.7	112.0	92.1	13.6	4.0	11.7	81.1
Age of householder:									
15 to 24 years old	5.1	5.4	5.9	6.6	5.0	1.1	0.3	1.2	4.0
25 to 29 years old	9.4	8.4	8.5	8.7	6.8	1.2	0.4	1.5	5.5
30 to 34 years old	11.0	11.1	10.1	10.4	8.1	1.5	0.6	1.7	6.5
35 to 44 years old	20.6	22.9	24.0	23.2	18.6	3.1	1.0	3.0	15.9
45 to 54 years old	14.5	17.6	20.9	23.1	19.0	2.9	0.8	2.0	17.1
55 to 64 years old	12.5	12.2	13.6	16.8	14.2	1.8	0.5	1.2	13.0
65 to 74 years old	11.7	11.8	11.3	11.5	9.9	1.1	0.3	0.7	9.3
75 years old and over . . .	8.4	9.6	10.4	11.6	10.3	0.9	0.2	0.4	9.9
One person	23.0	24.7	26.7	29.6	24.1	4.1	0.8	1.8	22.5
Male	9.0	10.1	11.2	12.6	10.2	1.7	0.3	0.9	9.4
Female.	14.0	14.6	15.5	17.0	13.9	2.4	0.4	0.9	13.1
Two persons.	30.1	31.8	34.7	37.4	32.0	3.7	1.1	2.6	29.5
Three persons.	16.1	16.8	17.2	18.0	14.3	2.5	0.8	2.3	12.2
Four persons	14.5	15.3	15.3	16.1	13.0	1.9	0.8	2.4	10.8
Five persons.	6.2	6.6	7.0	7.2	5.7	0.9	0.3	1.6	4.3
Six persons	2.1	2.3	2.4	2.5	1.9	0.3	0.1	0.7	1.3
Seven persons or more. . . .	1.3	1.4	1.4	1.4	1.0	0.2	0.1	0.5	0.6

[1] Includes other races, not shown separately. [2] Beginning with the 2003 Current Population Survey (CPS), respondents could choose more than one race. 2004 data represent persons who selected this race group only and exclude persons reporting more than one race. The CPS in prior years only allowed respondents to report one race group. See also comments on race in the text for this section. [3] Hispanic persons may be of any race.

Source: U.S. Census Bureau, Current Population Reports, P20-537, and earlier reports; and "America's Families and Living Arrangements: 2004"; published 29 June 2005; <http://www.census.gov/population/www/socdemo/hh-fam/cps2004.html>.

Table 57. Unmarried-Partner Households by Sex of Partners: 2003

[The American Community Survey universe is limited to the household population and excludes the population living in institutions, college dormitories, and other group quarters. Based on a sample and subject to sampling variability; see text of this section and Appendix III]

Item	Number
Total households	108,419,506
Unmarried-partner households.	5,571,436
Male householder and male partner	363,072
Male householder and female partner	2,457,557
Female householder and female partner	338,661
Female householder and male partner.	2,412,146
All other households	102,848,070

Source: U.S. Census Bureau, American FactFinder, 2003 American Community Survey Summary Tables, Table PCT008. Unmarried-Partner Households by Sex of Partner; <http://factfinder.census.gov/>; (accessed: 2 August 2005).

Table 58. Family Groups with Children Under 18 Years Old by Race and Hispanic Origin: 1990 to 2004

[In thousands. As of March (34,670 represents 34,670,000). Family groups comprise family households, related subfamilies, and unrelated subfamilies. Excludes members of Armed Forces except those living off post or with their families on post. Population controls for 2004 based on Census 2000 and an expanded sample of households. Based on Current Population Survey, see text of this section, and Appendix III]

Race and Hispanic origin of householder or reference person	1990	1995	2000	2004 Total	2004 Family households	2004 Subfamilies Total	2004 Subfamilies Related	2004 Subfamilies Unrelated
All races, total [1]	34,670	37,168	37,496	38,980	35,923	3,057	2,577	480
Two-parent family groups	24,921	25,640	25,771	26,377	25,793	584	571	13
One-parent family groups	9,749	11,528	11,725	12,603	10,130	2,473	2,006	467
Maintained by mother	8,398	9,834	9,681	10,322	8,206	2,116	1,710	406
Maintained by father	1,351	1,694	2,044	2,282	1,924	357	296	61
White, total [2]	28,294	29,846	30,079	30,459	28,400	2,057	1,695	362
Two-parent family groups	21,905	22,320	22,241	22,200	21,769	430	419	11
One-parent family groups	6,389	7,525	7,838	8,259	6,631	1,627	1,276	351
Maintained by mother	5,310	6,239	6,216	6,584	5,196	1,389	1,081	308
Maintained by father	1,079	1,286	1,622	1,674	1,435	240	196	44
Black, total [2]	5,087	5,491	5,530	5,678	4,963	715	628	87
Two-parent family groups	2,006	1,962	2,135	2,091	2,035	56	56	-
One-parent family groups	3,081	3,529	3,396	3,587	2,928	659	572	87
Maintained by mother	2,860	3,197	3,060	3,138	2,575	563	493	70
Maintained by father	221	332	335	448	353	96	79	17
Asian, total [2]	(NA)	(NA)	1,469	1,775	1,642	133	126	7
Two-parent family groups	(NA)	(NA)	1,184	1,485	1,422	62	61	1
One-parent family groups	(NA)	(NA)	285	290	220	71	65	6
Maintained by mother	(NA)	(NA)	236	242	179	63	58	5
Maintained by father	(NA)	(NA)	49	49	41	7	7	-
Hispanic, total [3]	3,429	4,527	5,503	6,568	5,833	735	655	80
Two-parent family groups	2,289	2,879	3,625	4,273	4,086	187	179	8
One-parent family groups	1,140	1,647	1,877	2,295	1,747	548	476	72
Maintained by mother	1,003	1,404	1,565	1,867	1,419	449	389	60
Maintained by father	138	243	313	428	328	100	88	12
Non-Hispanic White, total [3]	(NA)	(NA)	24,847	24,412	23,034	1,379	1,085	294
Two-parent family groups	(NA)	(NA)	18,750	18,215	17,961	254	251	3
One-parent family groups	(NA)	(NA)	6,096	6,197	5,073	1,125	834	291
Maintained by mother	(NA)	(NA)	4,766	4,901	3,922	979	721	258
Maintained by father	(NA)	(NA)	1,331	1,296	1,150	146	113	33

- Represents or rounds to zero.   NA Not available.   [1] Includes other races, not shown separately.   [2] Beginning with the 2003 Current Population Survey (CPS) respondents could choose more than one race. 2004 data represent persons who selected this race group only and exclude persons reporting more than one race. The CPS prior to 2003 allowed respondents to report only one race group. See also comments on race in the text for this section.   [3] Hispanic persons may be of any race.

Source: U.S. Census Bureau, Current Population Reports, P20-537, and earlier reports; and "America's Families and Living Arrangements: 2004"; published 29 June 2005; <http://www.census.gov/population/www/socdemo/hh-fam/cps2004.html>.

Table 59. Parents and Children in Stay-At-Home Parent Family Groups: 1995 to 2004

[In thousands (22,973 represents 22,973,000). Family groups with children include those families that maintain their own household (family households with own children); those that live in the home of a relative (related subfamilies); and those that live in the home of a nonrelative (unrelated subfamilies). Stay-at-home family groups are married-couple family groups with children under 15 where one parent is in the labor force all of the previous year and their spouse is out of the labor force for the entire year with the reason 'taking care of home and family.' Only married couples with children under 15 are included. Based on Current Population Survey; see Appendix III]

Year	Married-couple family groups Total	Married-couple family groups With stay-at-home mothers	Married-couple family groups With stay-at-home fathers	Children under 15 years old in married-couple family groups Total in married-couple family groups	Children under 15 years old in married-couple family groups With stay-at-home mothers	Children under 15 years old in married-couple family groups With stay-at-home fathers
1995	22,973	4,440	64	41,008	9,106	125
1996	22,808	4,633	49	40,739	9,693	115
1997	22,779	4,617	71	40,798	9,788	140
1998	22,881	4,555	90	41,038	9,432	196
1999	22,754	4,731	71	41,003	9,796	143
2000	22,953	4,785	93	41,860	10,087	180
2001	22,922	4,934	81	41,862	10,194	148
2002	23,339	5,206	106	41,802	10,573	189
2003	23,209	5,388	98	41,654	11,028	175
2004	23,160	5,571	147	41,409	11,205	268

Source: U.S. Census Bureau, "Families and Living Arrangements"; published 29 June 2005; <http://www.census.gov/population/www /socdemo/hh-fam.html>.

Table 60. Children Under 18 Years Old by Presence of Parents: 1980 to 2004

[As of March (63,427 represents 63,427,000). Excludes persons under 18 years old who maintained households or family groups. Based on Current Population Survey; see headnote, Table 53]

Race Hispanic origin, and year	Number (1,000)	Both parents	\multicolumn{6}{c}{Percent living with—}	Father only	Neither parent
			Total	Divorced	Married, spouse absent	Never married	Widowed		
ALL RACES [1]									
1980	63,427	76.7	18.0	7.5	5.7	2.8	2.0	1.7	3.7
1990	64,137	72.5	21.6	8.0	5.3	6.8	1.5	3.1	2.8
1995	70,254	68.7	23.5	8.6	5.6	8.3	1.0	3.5	4.3
2000	72,012	69.1	22.4	7.9	4.5	9.2	1.0	4.2	4.2
2004	73,205	67.8	23.3	8.0	4.5	9.9	1.0	4.6	4.3
WHITE [2]									
1980	52,242	82.7	13.5	(NA)	(NA)	(NA)	(NA)	1.6	2.2
1990	51,390	79.0	16.2	(NA)	(NA)	(NA)	(NA)	3.0	1.8
1995	55,327	75.8	17.8	(NA)	(NA)	(NA)	(NA)	3.4	3.0
2000	56,455	75.3	17.3	(NA)	(NA)	(NA)	(NA)	4.3	3.1
2004	55,902	74.3	18.0	7.9	3.7	5.6	0.8	4.4	3.3
BLACK [2]									
1980	9,375	42.2	43.9	(NA)	(NA)	(NA)	(NA)	1.9	12.0
1990	10,018	37.7	51.2	(NA)	(NA)	(NA)	(NA)	3.5	7.5
1995	11,301	33.1	52.0	(NA)	(NA)	(NA)	(NA)	4.1	10.8
2000	11,412	37.6	49.0	(NA)	(NA)	(NA)	(NA)	4.2	9.2
2004	11,424	34.8	50.4	9.4	8.5	31.0	1.5	5.8	9.1
HISPANIC [3]									
1980	5,459	75.4	19.6	(NA)	(NA)	(NA)	(NA)	1.5	3.5
1990	7,174	66.8	27.1	(NA)	(NA)	(NA)	(NA)	2.9	3.2
1995	9,843	62.9	28.4	(NA)	(NA)	(NA)	(NA)	4.2	4.4
2000	11,613	65.1	25.1	(NA)	(NA)	(NA)	(NA)	4.4	5.4
2004	13,752	64.6	25.4	6.1	6.9	11.5	1.0	5.3	4.7

NA Not available. [1] Includes other races not shown separately. [2] Beginning with the 2003 Current Population Survey (CPS), respondents could choose more than one race. 2004 data represent persons who selected this race group only and exclude persons reporting more than one race. The CPS prior to 2003 allowed respondents to report only one race group. See also comments on race in the text for this section. [3] Hispanic persons may be of any race.

Source: U.S. Census Bureau, "Families and Living Arrangements"; published 29 June 2005; <http://www.census.gov/population/www /socdemo/hh-fam.html>.

Table 61. Adopted Children of Householder—Summary: 2000

[In thousands (2,059 represents 2,059,000), except as indicated. As of April 1. Based on a sample from the 2000 Census of Population and Housing; see text of this section and Appendix III]

Characteristic of adopted child	\multicolumn{3}{c}{Adopted children of householder}	Characteristic	\multicolumn{3}{c}{Householder's children under 18 years old}
	Total	Under 18 years old	18 years old and over		Adopted children	Stepchil-dren	Bio-logical children
Total	2,059	1,586	473	**Total**	1,586	3,292	59,774
Place of birth:				CHARACTERISTIC OF CHILDREN			
Native	1,801	1,387	414	Under 5 years old	307	214	16,034
Foreign born	258	199	59	5 to 13 years old	892	1,940	30,999
Korea	57	48	9	14 to 17 years old	387	1,138	12,741
Mexico	28	18	10				
China	22	21	1				
Russia	20	20	1	Male	751	1,655	30,741
Philippines	10	6	4	Female	835	1,638	29,033
Colombia	10	7	3				
India	10	8	2	CHARACTERISTIC OF HOUSEHOLDER			
				Median household income	$56,138	$50,900	$48,200
Different race than householder [1]	321	271	50	Percent bachelor's degree or more	33.4	15.7	25.9
Different Hispanic origin than householder [2]	125	105	20	Percent owning home	77.8	66.8	66.8

[1] Child and householder do not report the same group, where race groups are: White alone, Black alone, American Indian and Alaska Native alone, Asian alone, Native Hawaiian or Pacific Islander alone, Some Other Race alone, or either the child or householder reports multiple race groups. [2] Child is Hispanic and householder is not Hispanic, or vice versa.

Source: U.S. Census Bureau, Adopted Children and Stepchildren: 2000, Census 2000 Special Reports (CENSR-6RV), October 2003.

54 Population

Table 62. Families by Number of Own Children Under 18 Years Old: 1990 to 2004

[As of March (66,090 represents 66,090,000). Based on Current Population Survey; see headnote, Table 58]

Race, Hispanic origin, and year	Number of families (1,000)					Percent distribution				
	Total	No children	One child	Two children	Three or more children	Total	No children	One child	Two children	Three or more children
ALL FAMILIES [1]										
1990	66,090	33,801	13,530	12,263	6,496	100	51	20	19	10
1995	69,305	35,009	14,088	13,213	6,995	100	51	20	19	10
2000	72,025	37,420	14,311	13,215	7,080	100	52	20	18	10
2004, total	76,217	40,273	14,964	13,696	7,283	100	53	20	18	10
Married couple	57,719	31,926	9,763	10,481	5,548	100	55	17	18	10
Male householder [2]	4,716	2,786	1,146	550	235	100	59	24	12	5
Female householder [2]	13,781	5,560	4,055	2,665	1,501	100	40	29	19	11
WHITE FAMILIES [3]										
1990	56,590	29,872	11,186	10,342	5,191	100	53	20	18	9
1995	58,437	30,486	11,491	10,983	5,478	100	52	20	19	9
2000	60,251	32,144	11,496	10,918	5,693	100	53	19	18	9
2004, total	62,604	34,199	11,725	11,017	5,668	100	55	19	18	9
Married couple	50,021	28,252	8,187	8,896	4,686	100	56	16	18	9
Male householder [2]	3,537	2,100	849	418	170	100	59	24	12	5
Female householder [2]	9,050	3,847	2,689	1,702	812	100	43	30	19	9
BLACK FAMILIES [3]										
1990	7,470	3,093	1,894	1,433	1,049	100	41	25	19	14
1995	8,093	3,411	1,971	1,593	1,117	100	42	24	20	14
2000	8,664	3,882	2,101	1,624	1,058	100	45	24	19	12
2004, total	8,912	3,940	2,134	1,706	1,133	100	44	24	19	13
Married couple	4,146	2,111	791	764	480	100	51	19	18	12
Male householder [2]	782	426	211	98	42	100	54	27	13	6
Female householder [2]	3,984	1,402	1,131	845	607	100	35	28	21	15
ASIAN FAMILIES [3]										
2004, total	3,064	1,422	744	648	251	100	46	24	21	8
Married couple	2,497	1,074	613	598	211	100	43	25	24	8
Male householder [2]	219	178	25	10	6	100	81	11	5	3
Female householder [2]	348	170	105	40	33	100	49	30	11	9
HISPANIC FAMILIES [4]										
1990	4,840	1,790	1,095	1,036	919	100	37	23	21	19
1995	6,200	2,216	1,408	1,406	1,171	100	36	23	23	19
2000	7,561	2,747	1,791	1,693	1,330	100	36	24	22	18
2004, total	9,272	3,434	2,112	2,098	1,627	100	37	23	23	18
Married couple	6,227	2,140	1,310	1,556	1,220	100	34	21	25	20
Male householder [2]	908	579	154	108	67	100	64	17	12	7
Female householder [2]	2,138	715	648	434	340	100	33	30	20	16
NON-HISPANIC WHITE FAMILIES [3][4]										
2004, total	54,023	30,982	9,809	9,068	4,164	100	57	18	17	8
Married couple	44,197	26,236	6,956	7,446	3,559	100	59	16	17	8
Male householder [2]	2,711	1,559	723	320	109	100	58	27	12	4
Female householder [2]	7,115	3,188	2,129	1,301	497	100	45	30	14	7

[1] Includes other races, not shown separately. [2] No spouse present. [3] Beginning with the 2003 Current Population Survey (CPS) respondents could choose more than one race. 2004 data represent persons who selected this race group only and exclude persons reporting more than one race. The CPS prior to 2003 only allowed respondents to report one race group. See also comments on race in the text for this section. [4] Hispanic persons may be of any race.

Source: U.S. Census Bureau, Current Population Reports, P20-537 and earlier reports; and "Families and Living Arrangements"; published 29 June 2005; <http://www.census.gov/population/www/socdemo/hh-fam.html>.

Table 63. Families by Size and Presence of Children: 1990 to 2004

[In thousands, except as indicated (66,090 represents 66,090,000). As of March. See headnote, Table 58]

Characteristic	Number				Percent distribution			
	1990	1995	2000	2004	1990	1995	2000	2004
Total	66,090	69,305	72,025	76,217	100	100	100	100
Size of family:								
Two persons	27,606	29,176	31,455	34,091	42	42	44	45
Three persons	15,353	15,903	16,073	16,747	23	23	22	22
Four persons	14,026	14,624	14,496	15,243	21	21	20	20
Five persons	5,938	6,283	6,526	6,662	9	9	9	9
Six persons	1,997	2,106	2,226	2,299	3	3	3	3
Seven or more persons	1,170	1,213	1,249	1,175	2	2	2	2
Own children under age 6:								
None	50,905	53,695	57,039	60,603	77	77	79	80
One	10,304	10,733	10,454	10,704	16	15	15	14
Two or more	4,882	4,876	4,533	4,911	7	7	6	6

Source: U.S. Census Bureau, Current Population Reports, P20-537 and earlier reports; and "Families and Living Arrangements"; published 29 June 2005; <http://www.census.gov/population/www/socdemo/hh-fam.html>.

Table 64. Families by Type, Race, and Hispanic Origin: 2004

[In thousands (76,217 represents 76,217,000). As of March. Excludes members of Armed Forces except those living off post or with their families on post. Population controls based on Census 2000 and an expanded sample of households. Based on Current Population Survey, see text of this section and Appendix III]

Characteristic	All families	Married couple families						Female family householder [4]						Male family householder, [4] all races
	All races [1]	White [2]	Black [2]	Asian [2]	Hispanic [3]	Non-Hispanic White [2,3]	All races [1]	White [2]	Black [2]	Asian [2]	Hispanic [3]	Non-Hispanic White [2,3]	
All families	76,217	57,719	50,021	4,146	2,497	6,227	44,197	13,781	9,050	3,984	348	2,138	7,115	4,716
Age of householder:														
Under 25 years old	3,589	1,416	1,234	109	33	364	905	1,398	807	481	46	264	570	774
25 to 34 years old	13,557	9,573	8,078	738	520	1,754	6,431	2,959	1,757	1,037	75	572	1,239	1,025
35 to 44 years old	18,323	13,584	11,542	1,074	692	1,772	9,905	3,642	2,400	1,047	96	599	1,863	1,096
45 to 54 years old	17,138	13,500	11,627	1,024	608	1,160	10,533	2,692	1,811	723	76	383	1,463	945
55 to 64 years old	11,621	9,834	8,655	661	362	700	7,986	1,357	975	325	36	180	809	430
65 to 74 years old	7,055	6,019	5,395	359	189	319	5,095	823	574	208	13	73	507	213
75 years old and over	4,933	3,793	3,490	181	93	157	3,341	910	727	165	7	66	663	231
Without own children under 18	40,273	31,926	28,252	2,111	1,074	2,140	26,236	5,560	3,847	1,402	170	715	3,188	2,786
With own children under 18	35,944	25,793	21,769	2,035	1,422	4,086	17,961	8,221	5,203	2,582	179	1,422	3,927	1,931
One own child under 18	14,964	9,763	8,187	791	613	1,310	6,956	4,055	2,689	1,131	105	648	2,129	1,146
Two own children under 18	13,696	10,481	8,896	764	598	1,556	7,446	2,665	1,702	845	40	434	1,301	550
Three or more own children under 18	7,283	5,548	4,686	480	211	1,220	3,559	1,501	812	607	33	340	497	235
Average per family with own children under 18	1.83	1.89	1.88	1.90	1.54	2.09	1.83	1.72	1.59	1.90	1.41	2.00	1.46	1.53
Age of own children:														
Of any age	46,253	31,608	26,639	2,556	1,718	4,693	21,945	11,728	7,700	3,419	259	1,835	6,040	2,918
Under 25 years	41,544	29,557	25,095	2,330	1,581	4,469	20,834	9,579	6,097	2,965	218	1,625	4,641	2,408
Under 12 years	26,118	19,077	16,095	1,448	1,087	3,353	12,970	5,727	3,506	1,900	126	1,074	2,536	1,314
Under 6 years	15,614	11,711	9,902	837	701	2,225	7,822	3,136	1,832	1,108	73	597	1,287	766
Under 3 years	8,954	6,909	5,892	428	420	1,274	4,704	1,597	917	586	25	301	640	447
Under 1 year	3,057	2,337	2,007	129	156	445	1,601	541	334	182	10	107	232	178
Members 65 and older:														
Without members 65 and older	61,287	45,952	39,558	3,433	2,045	5,517	34,402	11,458	7,341	3,483	290	1,897	5,629	3,876
With members 65 and older	14,930	11,767	10,463	713	451	710	9,795	2,323	1,709	501	59	241	1,486	840
Marital status of householder:														
Married, spouse present	57,719	57,719	50,021	4,146	2,497	6,227	44,197	(X)	(X)	(X)	(X)	(X)	(X)	(X)
Married, spouse absent	2,512	(X)	(X)	(X)	(X)	(X)	(X)	1,958	1,247	586	67	511	782	553
Separated	1,772	(X)	(X)	(X)	(X)	(X)	(X)	1,457	944	439	29	390	586	315
Other	739	(X)	(X)	(X)	(X)	(X)	(X)	501	303	147	38	121	196	238
Widowed	2,644	(X)	(X)	(X)	(X)	(X)	(X)	2,213	1,669	448	45	233	1,455	431
Divorced	6,546	(X)	(X)	(X)	(X)	(X)	(X)	4,960	3,802	924	108	575	3,271	1,587
Never married	6,796	(X)	(X)	(X)	(X)	(X)	(X)	4,651	2,333	2,026	128	818	1,607	2,145

X Not applicable. [1] Includes other races not shown separately. [2] Beginning with the 2003 Current Population Survey (CPS), respondents could choose more than one race. Data represent persons who selected this race group only and exclude persons reporting more than one race. See also comments on race in the text for this section. [3] Persons of Hispanic origin may be of any race. [4] No spouse present.

Source: U.S. Census Bureau, "Families and Living Arrangements"; published 29 June 2005; <http://www.census.gov/population/www/socdemo/hh-fam.html>.

Table 65. **Family Households With Own Children Under Age 18 by Type of Family, 1990 to 2004, and by Age of Householder, 2004**

[As of March (32,289 represents 32,289,000). Excludes members of Armed Forces except those living off post or with their families on post. Population controls for 2004 based on Census 2000 and an expanded sample of households. Based on Current Population Survey, see text of this section and Appendix III]

Family type			2004						
	1990	2000	Total	15 to 24 years old	25 to 34 years old	35 to 44 years old	45 to 54 years old	55 to 64 years old	65 years old and over
NUMBER (1,000)									
Family households with children. . .	32,289	34,605	35,944	1,980	10,246	14,656	7,772	1,128	164
Married couple	24,537	25,248	25,793	829	6,992	10,866	6,053	939	115
Male householder [1]	1,153	1,786	1,931	174	565	716	390	70	16
Female householder [1]	6,599	7,571	8,221	979	2,688	3,074	1,329	119	32
HOUSEHOLDS WITH CHILDREN, AS A PERCENT OF ALL FAMILY HOUSEHOLDS BY TYPE									
Family households with children, total	49	48	47	55	76	80	45	10	1
Married couple	47	46	45	59	73	80	45	10	1
Male householder [1]	40	44	41	22	55	65	41	16	4
Female householder [1]	61	60	60	70	91	84	49	9	2

[1] No spouse present.

Source: U.S. Census Bureau, Current Population Reports, P20-537 and earlier reports; and "Families and Living Arrangements"; published 29 June 2005; <http://www.census.gov/population/www/socdemo/hh-fam.html>.

Table 66. **Nonfamily Households by Sex and Age of Householder: 2004**

[In thousands (16,136 represents 16,136,000). As of March. See headnote, Table 65]

Item	Male householder					Female householder				
	Total	15 to 24 yrs. old	25 to 44 yrs. old	45 to 64 yrs. old	65 yrs. old and over	Total	15 to 24 yrs. old	25 to 44 yrs. old	45 to 64 yrs. old	65 yrs. old and over
Total	16,136	1,521	6,392	5,249	2,974	19,647	1,498	4,108	5,954	8,085
One person (living alone) . .	12,562	769	4,629	4,380	2,784	17,024	762	3,142	5,246	7,874
Nonrelatives present	3,574	753	1,763	869	190	2,623	736	967	708	212
Never married.	8,127	1,477	4,444	1,777	431	6,131	1,440	2,865	1,322	503
Married [1]	1,462	24	537	598	302	1,152	28	296	552	276
Widowed	1,797	-	45	252	1,500	7,169	1	95	1,051	6,022
Divorced	4,750	20	1,368	2,621	742	5,195	28	854	3,029	1,284

- Represents or rounds to zero.   [1] No spouse present.

Source: U.S. Census Bureau, "Families and Living Arrangements"; published 29 June 2005; <http://www.census.gov/population/www/socdemo/hh-fam.html>.

Table 67. **Persons Living Alone by Sex and Age: 1990 to 2004**

[As of March (22,999 represents 22,999,000). Excludes members of Armed Forces except those living off post or with their families on post. Beginning 2003, population controls based on Census 2000 and an expanded sample of households. Based on Current Population Survey, see text of this section and Appendix III]

Sex and age	Number of persons (1,000)					Percent distribution				
	1990	1995	2000	2003	2004	1990	1995	2000	2003	2004
Both sexes	22,999	24,732	26,724	29,431	29,586	100	100	100	100	100
15 to 24 years old.	1,210	1,196	1,144	1,540	1,530	5	5	4	5	5
25 to 34 years old.	3,972	3,653	3,848	3,809	3,888	17	15	14	13	13
35 to 44 years old.	3,138	3,663	4,109	4,210	3,883	14	15	15	14	13
45 to 64 years old.	5,502	6,377	7,842	9,324	9,626	24	26	29	32	33
65 to 74 years old.	4,350	4,374	4,091	4,201	4,198	19	18	15	14	14
75 years old and over	4,825	5,470	5,692	6,347	6,461	21	22	21	22	22
Male	9,049	10,140	11,181	12,511	12,562	39	41	42	43	42
15 to 24 years old.	674	623	556	722	769	3	3	2	2	3
25 to 34 years old.	2,395	2,213	2,279	2,212	2,229	10	9	9	8	8
35 to 44 years old.	1,836	2,263	2,569	2,573	2,400	8	9	10	9	8
45 to 64 years old.	2,203	2,787	3,422	4,280	4,380	10	11	13	15	15
65 to 74 years old.	1,042	1,134	1,108	1,291	1,293	5	5	4	4	4
75 years old and over	901	1,120	1,247	1,434	1,491	4	5	5	5	5
Female	13,950	14,592	15,543	16,919	17,024	61	59	58	57	58
15 to 24 years old.	536	572	588	818	762	2	2	2	3	3
25 to 34 years old.	1,578	1,440	1,568	1,597	1,660	7	6	6	5	6
35 to 44 years old.	1,303	1,399	1,540	1,638	1,482	6	6	6	6	5
45 to 64 years old.	3,300	3,589	4,420	5,044	5,246	14	15	17	17	18
65 to 74 years old.	3,309	3,240	2,983	2,911	2,904	14	13	11	10	10
75 years old and over	3,924	4,351	4,444	4,913	4,970	17	18	17	17	17

Source: U.S. Census Bureau, Current Population Reports, P20-553 and earlier reports; and "Families and Living Arrangements"; published 29 June 2005; <http://www.census.gov/population/www/socdemo/hh-fam.html>.

Population   57

Table 68. Population in Group Quarters by Sex, Age, and Group Quarters Type: 2000

[In thousands (7,779 represents 7,779,000). As of April. For definitions of group quarters, see text, this section]

Group quarters type	Total population	Male Total	Male Under 18 years	Male 18 to 64 years	Male 65 years and over	Female Total	Female Under 18 years	Female 18 to 64 years	Female 65 years and over
Total	7,779	4,502	215	3,740	548	3,276	108	1,722	1,446
Institutionalized population	4,059	2,534	122	1,968	444	1,525	36	292	1,197
Correctional institutions.	1,976	1,806	19	1,773	14	170	2	166	2
Nursing homes	1,721	488	-	88	401	1,232	-	75	1,157
Hospitals/wards and hospices for chronically ill	40	20	1	10	9	20	1	6	14
Mental (psychiatric) hospitals or wards	79	50	7	37	6	29	4	18	7
Juvenile institutions	128	101	88	13	-	27	24	2	-
Other institutions	115	68	8	47	14	47	5	25	18
Noninstitutionalized population	3,720	1,968	93	1,772	104	1,751	72	1,431	249
College dormitories [1]	2,064	958	5	952	-	1,107	5	1,101	-
Military quarters	355	307	1	306	-	48	1	47	-
Other noninstitutional group quarters	1,300	703	86	513	104	597	66	283	249

- Represents or rounds to zero. [1] Includes college quarters off campus.

Source: U.S. Census Bureau, American FactFinder, PCT17. Group Quarters Population by Sex by Age by Group Quarters Type, Census 2000 Summary File 1 (SF 1) 100-Percent Data; <http://factfinder.census.gov>.

Table 69. Self-Described Religious Identification of Adult Population: 1990 and 2001

[In thousands (175,440 represents 175,440,000). The American Religious Identification Survey (ARIS) 2001 was based on a random digit-dialed telephone survey of 50,281 American residential households in the continental U.S.A. (48 states). Respondents were asked to describe themselves in terms of religion with an open-ended question. Interviewers did not prompt or offer a suggested list of potential answers. Moreover, the self-description of respondents was not based on whether established religious bodies, institutions, churches, mosques or synagogues considered them to be members. Quite the contrary, the survey sought to determine whether the respondents themselves regarded themselves as adherents of a religious community. Subjective rather than objective standards of religious identification were tapped by the surveys]

Religious group	1990	2001	Religious group	1990	2001
Adult population, total [1]	175,440	207,980	Fundamentalist	27	61
Total Christian	151,496	159,506	Salvation Army.	27	25
Catholic	46,004	50,873	Independent Christian Church	25	71
Baptist	33,964	33,830			
Protestant–no denomination supplied. . .	17,214	4,647	Total other religions	5,853	7,740
Methodist/Wesleyan	14,174	14,150	Jewish	3,137	2,831
Lutheran	9,110	9,580	Muslim/Islamic	527	1,104
Christian–no denomination supplied. . . .	8,073	14,150	Buddhist	401	1,082
Presbyterian	4,985	5,596	Unitarian/Universalist	502	629
Pentecostal/Charismatic	3,191	4,407	Hindu	227	766
Episcopalian/Anglican	3,042	3,451	Native American.	47	103
Mormon/Latter-Day Saints	2,487	2,787	Scientologist	45	55
Churches of Christ	1,769	2,593	Baha'i	28	84
Jehovah's Witness	1,381	1,331	Taoist.	23	40
Seventh-Day Adventist	668	724	New Age.	20	68
Assemblies of God	660	1,106	Eckankar	18	26
Holiness/Holy	610	569	Rastafarian	14	11
Congregational/ United Church of Christ	599	1,378	Sikh.	13	57
Church of the Nazarene	549	544	Wiccan.	8	134
Church of God	531	944	Deity	6	49
Orthodox (Eastern)	502	645	Druid	(NA)	33
Evangelical [2]	242	1,032	Santeria	(NA)	22
Mennonite.	235	346	Pagan	(NA)	140
Christian Science	214	194	Spiritualist.	(NA)	116
Church of the Brethren	206	358	Ethical Culture	(NA)	4
Born Again [2]	204	56	Other unclassified.	837	386
Nondenominational [2].	195	2,489	No religion specified, total.	14,331	29,481
Disciples of Christ	144	492	Atheist	(NA)	902
Reformed/Dutch Reform	161	289	Agnostic	1,186	991
Apostolic/New Apostolic.	117	254	Humanist	29	49
Quaker.	67	217	Secular.	(NA)	53
Full Gospel	51	168	No religion	13,116	27,486
Christian Reform	40	79			
Foursquare Gospel	28	70	Refused to reply to question	4,031	11,246

NA Not available. [1] Refers to the total number of adults in all fifty states. All other figures are based on projections from surveys conducted in the continental United States (48 states). [2] Because of the subjective nature of replies to open-ended question, these categories are most unstable as they do not refer to clearly identifiable denominations as much as underlying feelings about religion. Thus they may be the most subject to fluctuation over time.

Source: 1990 data, Barry A. Kosmin and Seymour P. Lachman, "One Nation Under God: Religion in Contemporary American Society," 1993; 2001 data, The Graduate Center of the City University of New York, New York, NY, Barry A. Kosmin, Egon Mayer and Ariela Keysar, American Religious Identification Survey, 2001 (copyright).

Table 70. Religious Bodies—Selected Data

[Membership data: 2,500 represents 2,500,000. Includes the self-reported membership of religious bodies with 750,000 or more as reported to the Yearbook of American and Canadian Churches. Groups may be excluded if they do not supply information. The data are not standardized so comparisons between groups are difficult. The definition of "church member" is determined by the religious body]

Religious body	Year reported	Churches reported	Membership (1,000)
African Methodist Episcopal Church	1999	4,174	2,500
African Methodist Episcopal Zion Church, The	2003	3,236	1,433
American Baptist Churches in the U.S.A.	2003	5,834	1,433
Assemblies of God	2003	12,222	2,730
Baptist Bible Fellowship International	2003	4,500	1,200
Catholic Church, The	2003	19,431	67,260
Christian Church (Disciples of Christ) in the United States and Canada	2003	3,717	771
Christian Churches and Churches of Christ	1988	5,579	1,072
Christian Methodist Episcopal Church	2002	3,300	850
Church of God (Cleveland, Tennessee)	2003	6,623	961
Church of God in Christ, The	1991	15,300	5,500
Church of Jesus Christ of Latter-day Saints, The	2003	12,112	5,503
Churches of Christ	1999	15,000	1,500
Episcopal Church	2002	7,305	2,320
Evangelical Lutheran Church in America	2003	10,657	4,985
Greek Orthodox Archdiocese of America	2003	510	1,500
Jehovah's Witnesses	2003	12,054	1,041
Lutheran Church—Missouri Synod (LCMS), The	2003	6,160	2,489
National Baptist Convention of America, Inc.	2000	(NA)	3,500
National Baptist Convention, U.S.A., Inc.	(NA)	9,000	5,000
National Missionary Baptist Convention of America	1992	(NA)	2,500
Orthodox Church in America, The	2003	731	1,000
Pentecostal Assemblies of the World, Inc.	1998	1,750	1,500
Presbyterian Church (U.S.A.)	2003	11,064	3,241
Progressive National Baptist Convention, Inc.	1995	2,000	2,500
Seventh-day Adventist Church	2003	4,683	935
Southern Baptist Convention	2003	42,972	16,440
United Church of Christ	2003	5,738	1,297
United Methodist Church, The	2002	35,102	8,251

NA Not available.

Source: National Council of Churches, New York, NY, 2005 Yearbook of American & Canadian Churches, annual (copyright). (For more church-related information, visit <http://www.ncccusa.org> or call 888-870-3325).

Table 71. Christian Church Adherents, 2000, and Jewish Population, 2003—States

[133,377 represents 133,377,000. Christian church adherents were defined as "all members, including full members, their children and the estimated number of other regular participants who are not considered as communicants, confirmed or full members." The Jewish population includes Jews who define themselves as Jewish by religion as well as those who define themselves as Jewish in cultural terms. Data on Jewish population are based primarily on a compilation of individual estimates made by local Jewish federations. Additionally, most large communities have completed Jewish demographic surveys from which the Jewish population can be determined]

State	Christian adherents, 2000		Jewish population, 2003		State	Christian adherents, 2000		Jewish population, 2003	
	Number (1,000)	Percent of population [1]	Number (1,000)	Percent of population [1]		Number (1,000)	Percent of population [1]	Number (1,000)	Percent of population [1]
U.S.	133,377	47.4	6,155	2.2	MO	2,813	50.3	63	1.1
AL	2,418	54.4	9	0.2	MT	401	44.4	1	0.1
AK	210	33.6	3	0.5	NE	995	58.2	7	0.4
AZ	1,946	37.9	82	1.6	NV	604	30.2	77	3.8
AR	1,516	56.7	2	0.1	NH	571	46.2	10	0.8
CA	14,328	42.3	999	2.9	NJ	4,262	50.7	485	5.8
CO	1,604	37.3	73	1.7	NM	1,041	57.2	12	0.6
CT	1,828	53.7	111	3.3	NY	9,569	50.4	1,657	8.7
DE	299	38.2	14	1.7	NC	3,598	44.7	26	0.3
DC	331	57.8	26	4.5	ND	468	72.9	(Z)	0.1
FL	5,904	36.9	620	3.9	OH	4,912	43.3	149	1.3
GA	3,528	43.1	94	1.1	OK	2,079	60.3	5	0.1
HI	431	35.6	7	0.6	OR	1,029	30.1	32	0.9
ID	624	48.3	1	0.1	PA	6,751	55.0	282	2.3
IL	6,457	52.0	270	2.2	RI	646	61.7	16	1.5
IN	2,578	42.4	18	0.3	SC	1,874	46.7	11	0.3
IA	1,698	58.0	6	0.2	SD	510	67.6	(Z)	(Z)
KS	1,307	48.6	14	0.5	TN	2,867	50.4	18	0.3
KY	2,141	53.0	12	0.3	TX	11,316	54.3	131	0.6
LA	2,599	58.2	16	0.4	UT	1,659	74.3	5	0.2
ME	450	35.3	9	0.7	VT	230	37.8	6	0.9
MD	2,012	38.0	213	4.0	VA	2,807	39.7	66	0.9
MA	3,725	58.7	275	4.3	WA	1,872	31.8	43	0.7
MI	3,970	39.9	110	1.1	WV	646	35.7	2	0.1
MN	2,974	60.5	42	0.9	WI	3,198	59.6	28	0.5
MS	1,549	54.5	1	0.1	WY	229	46.4	(Z)	0.1

Z Fewer than 500 or .05 percent. [1] Based on U.S. Census Bureau data for resident population enumerated as of April 1, 2000, and estimated as of July 1, 2003.

Source: Christian church adherents—Dale E. Jones, Sherri Doty, Clifford Grammich, James E. Horsch, Richard Houseal, John P. Marcum, Kenneth M. Sanchagrin, and Richard H. Taylor, Religious Congregations and Membership in the United States: 2000, Glenmary Research Center, Nashville, TN, 2002 (copyright); Jewish population—American Jewish Committee, New York, NY, American Jewish Year Book (copyright).

Population 59

No. 41.—DEATHS: Number and Proportion per 1,000, Calendar Years 1900 to 1906, and Annual Average, 1901 to 1905, in the Registration Area,* by Sex and Age.

[From reports of the Bureau of the Census, Department of Commerce and Labor.]

NUMBER OF DEATHS FROM ALL CAUSES.

Sex and age.	Average, 1901–5.	1900	1901	1902	1903	1904	1905	1906
Sex:								
Male	283,962	285,999	276,020	273,585	281,041	296,252	292,912	358,286
Female	245,668	253,940	242,187	235,055	243,374	255,102	252,621	299,819
Age:								
Under 1 year	100,268	111,687	97,477	98,375	96,857	102,880	105,553	133,105
1 year	22,325	26,722	22,461	22,978	21,956	22,268	21,960	28,860
2 years	10,605	12,129	10,031	10,525	10,079	9,790	9,638	12,188
3 years	6,350	7,812	6,605	6,475	6,429	6,323	5,916	7,450
4 years	4,737	5,787	5,104	4,962	4,619	4,681	4,817	5,375
Under 5 years	143,684	164,137	141,678	143,515	139,940	145,902	147,384	186,978
5 to 9 years	13,679	15,678	13,982	13,790	14,047	13,774	12,851	15,317
10 to 14 years	8,703	9,144	8,416	8,163	8,733	9,308	8,835	10,443
15 to 19 years	14,531	14,498	13,969	13,709	14,541	15,496	14,911	17,928
20 to 24 years	22,246	22,260	21,809	21,390	22,227	23,206	22,600	26,805
25 to 29 years	24,439	24,573	24,239	23,542	24,639	25,336	24,438	28,633
30 to 34 years	24,169	23,727	23,665	23,382	24,053	25,237	24,506	28,502
35 to 39 years	25,332	24,606	24,456	24,146	25,311	26,449	26,296	30,790
40 to 44 years	24,743	23,364	24,317	23,797	24,672	25,787	25,143	29,101
45 to 49 years	24,068	22,521	22,802	22,419	23,686	25,487	25,948	30,703
50 to 54 years	25,706	24,283	24,804	24,340	25,534	27,182	26,671	31,166
55 to 59 years	26,081	25,024	25,308	24,654	26,030	27,359	27,054	31,989
60 to 64 years	29,474	27,633	28,491	27,359	29,042	31,453	31,026	36,109
65 to 69 years	30,382	29,123	29,422	28,427	30,835	31,688	32,037	38,040
70 to 74 years	30,124	29,025	29,161	28,196	29,736	32,182	31,343	37,627
75 to 79 years	26,420	25,447	25,782	24,474	26,298	27,666	27,928	33,501
80 to 84 years	19,446	18,843	19,494	18,147	19,222	20,476	19,889	24,025
85 to 89 years	9,982	9,646	9,669	8,946	9,735	10,621	10,841	13,071
90 to 94 years	3,522	3,367	3,483	3,263	3,447	3,814	3,601	4,179
95 years and over	1,118	1,113	1,108	1,072	1,124	1,127	1,158	1,393
Unknown	1,801	1,927	2,252	1,909	2,060	1,743	1,043	1,805
Aggregate	529,630	539,939	518,207	508,640	524,415	551,354	545,583	658,105

PROPORTION PER 1,000 DEATHS.

Sex and age.	Average, 1901–5.	1900	1901	1902	1903	1904	1905	1906
Sex:								
Male	536.2	529.7	532.6	537.9	535.9	537.3	536.9	544.4
Female	463.8	470.3	467.4	462.1	464.1	462.7	463.1	455.6
Age:								
Under 1 year	189.3	206.8	188.1	193.8	184.7	186.6	193.5	202.3
1 year	42.2	49.5	43.3	45.2	41.9	40.4	40.3	43.9
2 years	18.9	22.5	19.4	20.7	19.2	17.7	17.7	18.5
3 years	12.0	14.5	12.7	12.7	12.3	11.5	10.8	11.3
4 years	8.9	10.7	9.8	9.8	8.8	8.5	7.9	8.2
Under 5 years	271.3	304.0	273.4	282.2	266.8	264.6	270.2	284.1
5 to 9 years	25.8	29.0	26.9	27.1	26.8	25.0	23.5	23.3
10 to 14 years	16.4	16.9	16.2	16.0	16.7	17.0	16.2	15.9
15 to 19 years	27.4	26.9	27.0	27.0	27.7	28.1	27.4	27.2
20 to 24 years	42.0	41.2	42.1	42.1	42.4	42.1	41.4	40.7
25 to 29 years	46.1	45.5	46.8	46.3	47.0	46.0	44.8	43.5
30 to 34 years	45.6	43.9	45.7	46.0	45.9	45.8	44.9	43.3
35 to 39 years	47.8	45.6	47.2	47.5	48.3	48.0	48.2	46.8
40 to 44 years	46.7	43.3	46.9	46.8	47.0	46.8	46.1	44.2
45 to 49 years	45.4	41.7	44.0	44.1	45.2	46.2	47.6	46.7
50 to 54 years	48.5	45.0	47.9	47.9	48.7	49.3	48.9	47.4
55 to 59 years	49.2	46.3	48.8	48.5	49.6	49.6	49.6	48.6
60 to 64 years	55.7	51.2	55.0	53.8	55.4	57.0	56.9	54.9
65 to 69 years	57.4	53.9	56.8	55.9	57.8	57.5	58.7	57.8
70 to 74 years	56.9	53.8	56.3	55.4	56.7	58.4	57.5	57.2
75 to 79 years	49.9	47.1	49.7	48.1	50.1	50.2	51.2	50.9
80 to 84 years	36.7	34.9	37.6	35.7	36.7	37.1	36.5	36.5
85 to 89 years	18.8	17.9	18.7	17.6	18.6	19.3	19.9	19.9
90 to 94 years	6.6	6.2	6.7	6.4	6.6	6.9	6.6	6.4
95 years and over	2.1	2.1	2.1	2.1	2.1	2.0	2.1	2.1
Unknown	3.4	3.6	4.3	3.8	3.9	3.2	1.9	2.7
Aggregate	1,000.0	1,000.0	1,000.0	1,000.0	1,000.0	1,000.0	1,000.0	1,000.0

* See footnote on page 87.

Source: Statistical Abstract of the United States: 1908 Edition.

Section 2
Vital Statistics

This section presents vital statistics data on births, deaths, abortions, fetal deaths, fertility, life expectancy, marriages, and divorces. Vital statistics are compiled for the country as a whole by the National Center for Health Statistics (NCHS) and published in its annual report, *Vital Statistics of the United States*, in certain reports of the *Vital and Health Statistics* series, and in the *National Vital Statistics Reports* (formerly *Monthly Vital Statistics Report*). Reports in this field are also issued by the various state bureaus of vital statistics. Data on fertility, on age of persons at first marriage, and on marital status and marital history are compiled by the U.S. Census Bureau from its Current Population Survey (CPS; see text, Section 1) and published in *Current Population Reports*, P20 Series. Data on abortions are published by the Alan Guttmacher Institute, New York, NY, in selected issues of *Family Planning Perspectives* online at <www.agi-usa.org/sections/abortion.html>.

Registration of vital events—The registration of births, deaths, fetal deaths, and other vital events in the United States is primarily a state and local function. The civil laws of every state provide for a continuous and permanent birth- and death-registration system. Many states also provide for marriage- and divorce-registration systems. Vital events occurring to U.S. residents outside the United States are not included in the data.

Births and deaths—The live-birth, death, and fetal-death statistics prepared by NCHS are based on vital records filed in the registration offices of all states, New York City, and the District of Columbia. The annual collection of death statistics on a national basis began in 1900 with a national death-registration area of ten states and the District of Columbia; a similar annual collection of birth statistics for a national birth-registration area began in 1915, also with ten reporting states and the District of Columbia. Since 1933, the birth- and death-registration areas have comprised the entire United

States, including Alaska (beginning 1959) and Hawaii (beginning 1960). National statistics on fetal deaths were first compiled for 1918 and annually since 1922.

Prior to 1951, birth statistics came from a complete count of records received in the Public Health Service (now received in NCHS). From 1951 through 1971, they were based on a 50-percent sample of all registered births (except for a complete count in 1955 and a 20- to 50-percent sample in 1967). Beginning in 1972, they have been based on a complete count for states participating in the Vital Statistics Cooperative Program (VSCP) (for details, see the technical appendix in *Vital Statistics of the United States*) and on a 50-percent sample of all other areas. Beginning in 1986, all reporting areas participated in the VSCP. Mortality data have been based on a complete count of records for each area (except for a 50-percent sample in 1972). Beginning in 1970, births to and deaths of nonresident aliens of the United States and U.S. citizens outside the United States have been excluded from the data. Fetal deaths and deaths among Armed Forces abroad are excluded. Data based on samples are subject to sampling error; for details, see annual issues of *Vital Statistics of the United States*.

Mortality statistics by cause of death are compiled in accordance with World Health Organization regulations according to the *International Classification of Diseases* (ICD). The ICD is revised approximately every 10 years. The tenth revision of the ICD was employed beginning in 1999. Deaths for prior years were classified according to the revision of the ICD in use at the time. Each revision of the ICD introduces a number of discontinuities in mortality statistics; for a discussion of those between the ninth and tenth revisions of the ICD, see *National Vital Statistics Reports*, Vol. 49, Nos. 2 and 8. Preliminary mortality data are based on a percentage of death records weighted up to the total number of deaths reported for the given

U.S. Census Bureau, Statistical Abstract of the United States: 2006

year; for a discussion of preliminary data, see *National Vital Statistics Reports*, Vol. 49, No. 3. Information on tests of statistical significance, differences between death rates, and standard errors can also be found in the reports mentioned above.

Some of the tables present age-adjusted death rates in addition to crude death rates. Age-adjusted death rates shown in this section were prepared using the direct method, in which age-specific death rates for a population of interest are applied to a standard population distributed by age. Age adjustment eliminates the differences in observed rates between points in time or among compared population groups that result from age differences in population composition.

Fertility and life expectancy—The total fertility rate, defined as the number of births that 1,000 women would have in their lifetime if, at each year of age, they experienced the birth rates occurring in the specified year, is compiled and published by NCHS. Other data relating to social and medical factors that affect fertility rates, such as contraceptive use and birth expectations, are collected and made available by both NCHS and the Census Bureau. NCHS figures are based on information in birth and fetal death certificates and on the periodic National Surveys of Family Growth; Census Bureau data are based on decennial censuses and the CPS.

Data on life expectancy, the average remaining lifetime in years for persons who attain a given age, are computed and published by NCHS. For details, see *National Vital Statistics Reports*, Vol. 52, No. 3.

Marriage and divorce—The compilation of nationwide statistics on marriages and divorces in the United States began in 1887–88, when the National Office of Vital Statistics prepared estimates for the years 1867–86. Although periodic updates took place after 1888, marriage and divorce statistics were not collected and published annually until 1944 by that office. In 1957 and 1958, respectively, the same office established marriage- and divorce-registration areas. Beginning in 1957, the marriage-registration area comprised 30 states, plus Alaska, Hawaii,

Puerto Rico, and the Virgin Islands; it currently includes 42 states and the District of Columbia. The divorce-registration area, starting in 1958 with 14 states, Alaska, Hawaii, and the Virgin Islands, currently includes a total of 31 states and the Virgin Islands. Procedures for estimating the number of marriages and divorces in the registration states are discussed in *Vital Statistics of the United States*, Vol. III— Marriage and Divorce. Total counts of events for registration and nonregistration states are gathered by collecting already summarized data on marriages and divorces reported by state offices of vital statistics and by county offices of registration. The collection and publication of detailed marriage and divorce statistics (for example: by age and race) was suspended beginning in January 1996. For additional information contact the National Center for Health Statistics online at <http://www.cec.gov/nchs/releases/96facts/mardiv.htm>.

Vital statistics rates—Except as noted, vital statistics rates computed by NCHS are based on decennial census population figures as of April 1 for 1940, 1950, 1960, 1970, 1980, 1990, and 2000; and on midyear population figures for other years, as estimated by the Census Bureau (see text, Section 1).

Race—Data by race for births, deaths, marriages, and divorces from NCHS are based on information contained in the certificates of registration. The Census Bureau's Current Population Survey obtains information on race by asking respondents to classify their race as (1) White, (2) Black, (3) American Indian or Alaskan Native, Native Hawaiian or other Pacific Islander, and (4) Asian.

Beginning with the 1989 data year, NCHS is tabulating its birth data primarily by race of the mother. In 1988 and prior years, births were tabulated by race of the child, which was determined from the race of the parents as entered on the birth certificate.

Trend data by race shown in this section are by race of mother beginning with the 1980 data. Hispanic origin of the mother is reported and tabulated independently of race. Thus, persons of Hispanic origin may be any race. In 1994, 91 percent of women of Hispanic origin were reported as White.

Figure 2.1
Infant Mortality Rates by State: 2002

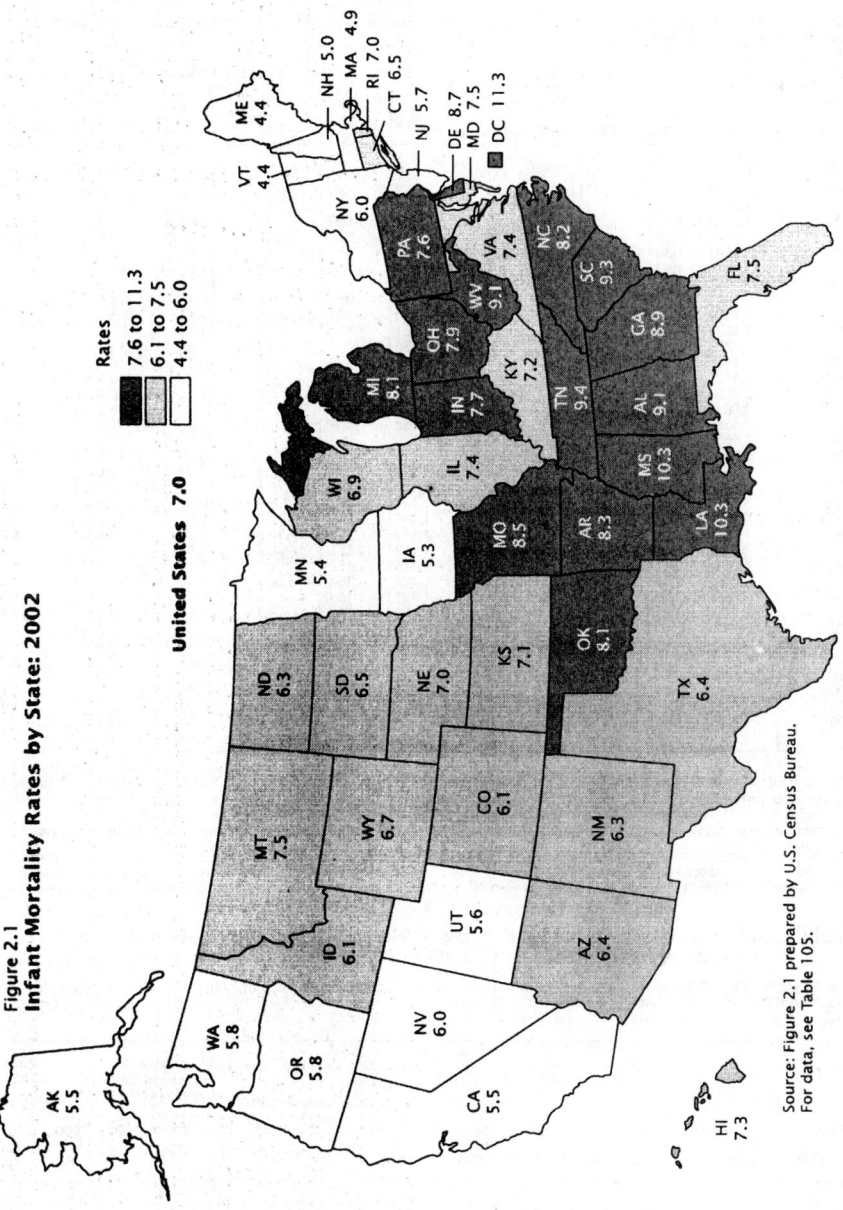

Rates

- 7.6 to 11.3
- 6.1 to 7.5
- 4.4 to 6.0

United States 7.0

State	Rate
NH	5.0
MA	4.9
RI	7.0
CT	6.5
NJ	5.7
DE	8.7
MD	7.5
DC	11.3
ME	4.4
VT	4.4
NY	6.0
PA	7.6
VA	7.4
NC	8.2
WV	9.1
SC	9.3
FL	7.5
OH	7.9
GA	8.9
KY	7.2
MI	8.1
IN	7.7
TN	9.4
AL	9.1
WI	6.9
IL	7.4
MS	10.3
MN	5.4
IA	5.3
MO	8.5
AR	8.3
LA	10.3
ND	6.3
SD	6.5
NE	7.0
KS	7.1
OK	8.1
TX	6.4
MT	7.5
WY	6.7
CO	6.1
NM	6.3
ID	6.1
UT	5.6
AZ	6.4
WA	5.8
OR	5.8
NV	6.0
CA	5.5
AK	5.5
HI	7.3

Source: Figure 2.1 prepared by U.S. Census Bureau.
For data, see Table 105.

U.S. Census Bureau, Statistical Abstract of the United States: 2006

Table 72. Live Births, Deaths, Marriages, and Divorces: 1950 to 2003

[3,632 represents 3,632,000. Prior to 1960, excludes Alaska and Hawaii. Beginning 1970, excludes births to, and deaths of nonresidents of the United States. See Appendix III]

Year	Number (1,000)					Rate per 1,000 population				
		Deaths					Deaths			
	Births [1]	Total	Infant [2]	Marriages [3]	Divorces [4]	Births [1]	Total	Infant [2]	Marriages [3]	Divorces [4]
1950	3,632	1,452	104	1,667	385	24.1	9.6	29.2	11.1	2.6
1955	4,097	1,529	107	1,531	377	25.0	9.3	26.4	9.3	2.3
1960	4,258	1,712	111	1,523	393	23.7	9.5	26.0	8.5	2.2
1965	3,760	1,828	93	1,800	479	19.4	9.4	24.7	9.3	2.5
1970	3,731	1,921	75	2,159	708	18.4	9.5	20.0	10.6	3.5
1971	3,556	1,928	68	2,190	773	17.2	9.3	19.1	10.6	3.7
1972	3,258	1,964	60	2,282	845	15.6	9.4	18.5	10.9	4.0
1973	3,137	1,973	56	2,284	915	14.8	9.3	17.7	10.8	4.3
1974	3,160	1,934	53	2,230	977	14.8	9.1	16.7	10.5	4.6
1975	3,144	1,893	51	2,153	1,036	14.6	8.8	16.1	10.0	4.8
1976	3,168	1,909	48	2,155	1,083	14.6	8.8	15.2	9.9	5.0
1977	3,327	1,900	47	2,178	1,091	15.1	8.6	14.1	9.9	5.0
1978	3,333	1,928	46	2,282	1,130	15.0	8.7	13.8	10.3	5.1
1979	3,494	1,914	46	2,331	1,181	15.6	8.5	13.1	10.4	5.3
1980	3,612	1,990	46	2,390	1,189	15.9	8.8	12.6	10.6	5.2
1981	3,629	1,978	43	2,422	1,213	15.8	8.6	11.9	10.6	5.3
1982	3,681	1,975	42	2,456	1,170	15.9	8.5	11.5	10.6	5.1
1983	3,639	2,019	41	2,446	1,158	15.6	8.6	11.2	10.5	5.0
1984	3,669	2,039	40	2,477	1,169	15.6	8.6	10.8	10.5	5.0
1985	3,761	2,086	40	2,413	1,190	15.8	8.8	10.6	10.1	5.0
1986	3,757	2,105	39	2,407	1,178	15.6	8.8	10.4	10.0	4.9
1987	·3,809	2,123	38	2,403	1,166	15.7	8.8	10.1	9.9	4.8
1988	3,910	2,168	39	2,396	1,167	16.0	8.9	10.0	9.8	4.8
1989	4,041	2,150	40	2,403	1,157	16.4	8.7	9.8	9.7	4.7
1990	4,158	2,148	38	2,443	1,182	16.7	8.6	9.2	9.8	4.7
1991	4,111	2,170	37	2,371	1,187	16.2	8.6	8.9	9.4	4.7
1992	4,065	2,176	35	2,362	1,215	15.8	8.5	8.5	9.3	4.8
1993	4,000	2,269	33	2,334	1,187	15.4	8.8	8.4	9.0	4.6
1994	3,953	2,279	31	2,362	1,191	15.0	8.8	8.0	9.1	4.6
1995	3,900	2,312	30	2,336	1,169	14.6	8.7	7.6	8.9	4.4
1996	3,891	2,315	28	2,344	1,150	14.4	8.6	7.3	8.8	4.3
1997 [5]	3,881	2,314	28	2,384	1,163	14.2	8.5	7.2	8.9	4.3
1998 [5]	3,942	2,337	28	2,244	1,135	14.3	8.5	7.2	8.4	4.2
1999 [5]	3,959	2,391	28	2,358	(NA)	14.2	8.6	7.1	8.6	4.1
2000 [5]	4,059	2,403	28	2,329	(NA)	14.4	8.5	6.9	8.3	4.1
2001 [5]	4,026	2,416	28	2,345	(NA)	14.1	8.5	6.8	8.2	4.0
2002 [5]	4,022	2,443	28	2,254	(NA)	13.9	8.5	7.0	7.8	4.0
2003 [6]	4,091	2,444	28	2,187	(NA)	14.1	8.4	6.9	7.5	3.8

NA Not available. [1] Prior to 1960, data adjusted for underregistration. [2] Infants under 1 year, excluding fetal deaths; rates per 1,000 registered live births. [3] Includes estimates for some states through 1965 and also for 1976 and 1977 and marriage licenses for some states for all years except 1973 and 1975. Beginning 1978, includes nonlicensed marriages in California. [4] Includes reported annulments and some estimated state figures for all years. [5] Divorce rate excludes data for California, Colorado, Indiana, and Louisiana; population for this rate also excludes these states. [6] Mortality and natality are based on preliminary data.

Source: U.S. National Center for Health Statistics, *Vital Statistics of the United States*, annual; and *National Vital Statistics Reports (NVSR)* (formerly *Monthly Vital Statistics Report*); and unpublished data. See also <http://www.cdc.gov/nchs>.

Table 73. Live Births by Race and Type of Hispanic Origin—Selected Characteristics: 2000 and 2002

[4,059 represents 4,059,000. Represents registered births. Excludes births to nonresidents of the United States. Data are based on Hispanic origin of mother and race of mother. Hispanic origin data are available from only 48 states and the District of Columbia.]

Race and Hispanic origin	Number of births (1,000)		Births to teenage mothers, percent of total		Births to unmarried mothers, percent of total		Prenatal care beginning first trimester, percent of total		Late or no prenatal care, percent of total		Percent of births with low birth weight [1]	
	2000	2002	2000	2002	2000	2002	2000	2002	2000	2002	2000	2002
Total.	4,059	4,022	11.8	10.8	33.2	34.0	83.2	83.7	3.9	3.6	7.6	7.8
White.	3,194	3,175	10.6	9.8	27.1	28.5	85.0	85.4	3.3	3.1	6.5	6.8
Black.	623	594	19.7	18.0	68.5	68.2	74.3	75.2	6.7	6.2	13.0	13.3
American Indian, Eskimo, Aleut . . .	42	42	19.7	18.5	58.4	59.7	69.3	69.8	8.6	8.1	6.8	7.2
Asian and Pacific Islander [2]	201	211	4.5	3.8	14.8	14.9	84.0	84.8	3.3	3.1	7.3	7.8
Filipino	32	33	5.3	4.5	20.3	20.0	84.9	85.4	3.0	2.8	8.5	8.6
Chinese	34	34	0.9	0.9	7.6	9.0	87.6	87.2	2.2	2.1	5.1	5.5
Japanese	9	9	1.9	1.7	9.5	10.3	91.0	90.5	1.8	2.1	7.1	7.6
Hawaiian.	7	7	17.4	14.6	50.0	50.4	79.9	78.1	4.2	4.7	6.8	8.1
Hispanic origin [3]	816	877	16.2	14.9	42.7	43.5	74.4	76.8	6.3	5.5	6.4	6.5
Mexican	582	628	17.0	15.9	40.7	42.1	72.9	75.7	6.9	5.8	6.0	6.2
Puerto Rican	58	57	20.0	17.8	59.6	59.1	78.5	79.9	4.5	4.1	9.3	9.7
Cuban	13	14	7.5	8.1	27.3	29.8	91.7	92.0	1.4	1.3	6.5	6.5
Central and South American. . . .	113	126	9.9	8.5	44.7	44.8	77.6	78.7	5.4	4.9	6.3	6.5
Other and unknown Hispanic . . .	49	51	18.8	16.7	46.2	44.4	75.8	76.7	5.9	5.3	7.8	7.9

[1] Births less than 2,500 grams (5 lb.-8 oz.). [2] Includes other races not shown separately. [3] Hispanic persons may be of any race. Includes other types, not shown separately.

Source: U.S. National Center for Health Statistics; *Vital Statistics of the United States*, annual; *National Vital Statistics Report (NVSR)* (formerly *Monthly Vital Statistics Report*); and unpublished data.

Table 74. **Births and Birth Rates by Race, Sex, and Age: 1980 to 2003**

[**Births in thousands. (3,612 represents 3,612,000). Births by race of mother.** Excludes births to nonresidents of the United States. For population bases used to derive these data, see text this section, and Appendix III]

Item	1980	1985	1990	1995	1997	1998	1999	2000	2001	2002	2003, prel.
Live births [1]	3,612	3,761	4,158	3,900	3,881	3,942	3,959	4,059	4,026	4,022	4,091
White..........................	2,936	3,038	3,290	3,099	3,073	3,119	3,133	3,194	3,178	3,175	3,228
Black..........................	568	582	684	603	600	610	606	623	606	594	599
American Indian, Eskimo, and Aleut.	29	34	39	37	39	40	41	42	42	42	43
Asian or Pacific Islander	74	105	142	160	170	173	182	201	200	211	221
Male	1,853	1,928	2,129	1,996	1,986	2,016	2,028	2,077	2,058	2,058	(NA)
Female.........................	1,760	1,833	2,029	1,903	1,895	1,925	1,934	1,982	1,968	1,964	(NA)
Males per 100 females.	105	105	105	105	105	105	106	105	105	105	(NA)
Age of mother:											
Under 20 years old	562	478	533	512	493	494	485	478	454	433	422
20 to 24 years old...............	1,226	1,141	1,094	966	942	965	982	1,018	1,022	1,022	1,032
25 to 29 years old...............	1,108	1,201	1,277	1,064	1,069	1,083	1,078	1,088	1,058	1,060	1,087
30 to 34 years old................	550	696	886	905	887	889	892	929	943	951	976
35 to 39 years old...............	141	214	318	384	410	425	434	452	452	454	468
40 to 44 years old	(NA)	(NA)	(NA)	(NA)	76	81	83	90	93	96	101
45 to 49 years old	(NA)	(NA)	(NA)	(NA)	3	4	4	4	5	5	6
Birth rate per 1,000 population ...	15.9	15.8	16.7	14.6	14.2	14.3	14.2	14.4	14.1	13.9	14.1
White..........................	15.1	15.0	15.8	14.1	13.7	13.8	13.7	13.9	13.7	13.5	(NA)
Black..........................	21.3	20.4	22.4	17.8	17.1	17.1	16.8	17.0	16.3	15.7	(NA)
American Indian..................	20.7	19.8	18.9	15.3	14.7	14.8	14.2	14.0	13.7	13.8	13.7
Asian or Pacific Islander	19.9	18.7	19.0	16.7	16.2	15.9	15.9	17.1	16.4	16.5	16.8
Fertility rate per 1,000 women [2] ...	68.4	66.2	70.9	64.6	63.6	64.3	64.4	65.9	65.3	64.8	66.1
White [2]..........................	65.6	64.1	68.3	63.6	62.8	63.6	64.0	65.3	65.0	64.8	66.2
Black [2].........................	84.9	78.8	84.8	71.0	69.0	69.4	68.5	70.0	67.6	65.8	66.2
American Indian [2]...............	82.7	78.6	76.2	63.0	60.8	61.3	59.0	58.7	58.1	58.0	57.9
Asian or Pacific Islander [2]	73.2	68.4	69.6	62.6	61.3	60.1	60.9	65.8	64.2	64.1	66.3
Age of mother:											
10 to 14 years old	1.1	1.2	1.4	1.3	1.1	1.0	0.9	0.9	0.8	0.7	0.6
15 to 19 years old...............	53.0	51.0	59.9	56.0	51.3	50.3	48.8	47.7	45.3	43.0	41.7
20 to 24 years old...............	115.1	108.3	116.5	107.5	107.3	108.4	107.9	109.7	106.2	103.6	102.6
25 to 29 years old...............	112.9	111.0	120.2	108.8	108.3	110.2	111.2	113.5	113.4	113.6	115.7
30 to 34 years old...............	61.9	69.1	80.8	81.1	83.0	85.2	87.1	91.2	91.9	91.5	95.2
35 to 39 years old...............	19.8	24.0	31.7	34.0	35.7	36.9	37.8	39.7	40.6	41.4	43.8
40 to 44 years old...............	3.9	4.0	5.5	6.6	7.1	7.4	7.4	8.0	8.1	8.3	8.7
45 to 49 years old...............	0.2	0.2	0.2	0.3	0.4	0.4	0.4	0.5	0.5	0.5	0.5

NA Not available.   [1] Includes other races not shown separately.   [2] Number of live births per 1,000 women, 15 to 44 years old in specified group. The rate for age of mother 45 to 49 years old computed by relating births to mothers 45 years old and over to women 45 to 49 years old.

Source: U.S. National Center for Health Statistics, *Vital Statistics of the United States*, annual; *National Vital Statistics Report (NVSR)* (formerly *Monthly Vital Statistics Report*); and unpublished data.

Table 75. **Live Births and Ratios by Plurality of Birth and Race of Mother: 1995 to 2002**

[See Appendix III]

Plurality and race of mother	1995	1998	1999	2000	2001	2002
NUMBER						
Live births, total [1]	3,899,589	3,941,553	3,959,417	4,058,814	4,025,933	4,021,726
White................................	3,098,885	3,118,727	3,132,501	3,194,005	3,177,626	3,174,760
Black	603,139	609,902	605,970	622,598	606,156	593,691
Live births in single deliveries [1]	3,797,880	3,823,258	3,837,789	3,932,573	3,897,216	3,889,191
White	3,018,184	3,024,693	3,035,757	3,094,219	3,075,683	3,069,915
Black	585,787	590,372	586,027	601,451	585,189	572,659
Live births in twin deliveries [1]	96,736	110,670	114,307	118,916	121,246	125,134
White	76,196	87,163	90,191	93,235	95,315	98,304
Black	17,000	19,001	19,374	20,626	20,414	20,423
Live births in higher-order multiple deliveries [1] . . .	4,973	7,625	7,321	7,325	7,471	7,401
White	4,505	6,871	6,553	6,551	6,628	6,541
Black	352	529	569	521	553	609
RATIO PER 1,000 LIVE BIRTHS						
All multiple births [1].....................	26.1	30.0	30.7	31.1	32.0	33.0
White	26.0	30.2	30.9	31.2	32.1	33.0
Black	28.8	32.0	32.9	34.0	34.6	35.4
Twin births [1].........................	24.8	28.1	28.9	29.3	30.1	31.1
White................................	24.6	27.9	28.8	29.2	30.0	31.0
Black................................	28.2	31.2	32.0	33.1	33.7	34.4
RATIO PER 100,000 LIVE BIRTHS						
Higher-order multiple births [1]	127.5	193.5	184.9	180.5	185.6	184.0
White	145.4	220.3	209.2	205.1	208.6	206.0
Black	58.4	86.7	93.9	83.7	91.2	102.6

[1] Includes races other than White and Black.

Source: U.S. National Center for Health Statistics. *Advance Report of Final Natality Statistics*, and *National Vital Statistics Reports (NVSR)* (formerly *Monthly Vital Statistics Report*).

Vital Statistics 65

Table 76. **Live Births by State and Island Areas: 2003**

[Number of births, except rate. Registered births. Excludes births to nonresidents of the United States. By race of mother. Data is preliminary. See Appendix III]

State	All races [1]	White	Black	Asian or Pacific Islander	American Indian, Eskimo, Aleut	Hispanic [2]	Birth rate [3]	Fertility rate [4]
United States.....	4,091,063	3,227,755	599,414	221,247	42,647	912,256	14.1	66.1
Alabama...........	59,621	40,912	17,959	606	144	2,907	13.2	62.6
Alaska	10,122	6,491	406	717	2,508	776	15.6	72.7
Arizona...........	91,005	78,966	3,279	2,699	6,060	39,798	16.3	79.3
Arkansas	38,159	30,048	7,307	544	260	3,307	14.0	68.1
California	540,995	438,035	32,676	67,603	2,681	268,867	15.2	69.9
Colorado..........	69,363	63,189	2,938	2,672	564	21,398	15.2	69.5
Connecticut........	42,848	35,372	5,184	2,031	261	7,547	12.3	59.6
Delaware	11,264	7,903	2,883	446	31	1,369	13.8	64.3
District of Columbia	7,606	2,125	5,223	253	4	954	13.5	53.8
Florida...........	212,286	158,053	47,349	5,795	1,089	54,864	12.5	63.4
Georgia	136,012	88,085	43,059	4,549	319	18,266	15.7	69.3
Hawaii	18,114	4,831	519	12,700	64	2,619	14.4	72.3
Idaho	21,802	20,972	108	353	369	2,940	16.0	76.0
Illinois	182,590	142,216	31,602	8,530	243	42,486	14.4	67.0
Indiana...........	86,600	75,688	9,387	1,389	136	6,764	14.0	66.5
Iowa	38,182	35,692	1,287	941	262	2,521	13.0	63.3
Kansas...........	39,493	35,019	2,765	1,226	483	5,443	14.5	69.5
Kentucky	55,281	49,457	4,859	867	99	1,964	13.4	63.2
Louisiana	65,298	37,459	26,328	1,106	406	1,684	14.5	66.4
Maine............	13,861	13,371	184	208	98	167	10.6	52.1
Maryland	74,856	45,780	24,776	4,052	248	6,296	13.6	62.3
Massachusetts.......	80,250	66,061	8,606	5,398	184	9,809	12.5	57.2
Michigan..........	130,937	103,042	22,574	4,682	639	7,666	13.0	61.6
Minnesota.........	70,157	59,491	5,378	3,871	1,417	4,937	13.9	64.2
Mississippi	42,362	23,575	18,367	289	131	461	14.7	67.9
Missouri	77,079	63,814	11,163	1,736	366	3,480	13.5	64.1
Montana...........	11,416	9,833	51	133	1,399	381	12.4	62.6
Nebraska	25,924	23,382	1,467	604	470	3,449	14.9	71.4
Nevada	33,644	27,693	2,905	2,528	518	12,207	15.0	72.2
New Hampshire.......	14,393	13,646	244	468	35	527	11.2	52.7
New Jersey........	116,269	85,278	20,120	10,685	186	26,504	13.5	64.5
New Mexico	27,845	23,306	533	402	3,603	14,856	14.9	71.5
New York	254,187	184,059	48,098	21,394	636	55,340	13.2	61.1
North Carolina	118,308	86,395	27,140	3,106	1,637	16,084	14.1	65.8
North Dakota........	7,975	6,893	109	115	858	168	12.6	61.6
Ohio	151,983	125,476	23,059	3,144	304	5,444	13.3	63.7
Oklahoma..........	50,484	39,578	4,568	1,076	5,263	5,654	14.4	69.2
Oregon...........	45,975	41,590	1,024	2,493	868	8,440	12.9	62.5
Pennsylvania........	140,660	114,043	21,333	4,975	311	10,494	11.4	56.0
Rhode Island........	13,192	11,208	1,260	562	161	2,514	12.3	56.5
South Carolina.......	55,658	36,266	18,345	893	154	3,587	13.4	63.0
South Dakota	11,035	8,910	122	127	1,876	340	14.4	70.8
Tennessee	78,901	60,982	16,250	1,489	180	4,934	13.5	63.1
Texas............	381,239	324,790	42,245	13,292	911	184,912	17.2	78.3
Utah	49,870	47,338	384	1,532	616	7,072	21.2	92.2
Vermont	6,591	6,413	54	119	6	59	10.6	51.1
Virginia...........	101,226	71,900	22,605	6,544	177	10,689	13.7	63.3
Washington.........	80,474	66,569	4,029	7,833	2,043	13,307	13.1	61.2
West Virginia........	20,908	20,005	722	156	25	99	11.5	58.1
Wisconsin..........	70,053	60,256	6,496	2,247	1,054	5,539	12.8	60.7
Wyoming	6,708	6,299	53	66	290	666	13.4	65.7
Puerto Rico	49,427	44,972	4,455	-	-	(NA)	(NA)	(NA)
Virgin Islands	997	227	752	17	1	232	(NA)	(NA)
Guam	3,286	277	39	2,965	5	54	(NA)	(NA)
American Samoa	1,015	-	-	1,015	-	(NA)	(NA)	(NA)
Northern Marianas ...	1,344	13	-	1,331	-	(NA)	(NA)	(NA)

- Represents zero.   NA Not available.   [1] Includes other races not shown separately.   [2] Persons of Hispanic origin may be of any race. Births by Hispanic origin of mother.   [3] Per 1,000 estimated population.   [4] Number of births per 1,000 women aged 15-44 years estimated.

Source: U.S. National Center for Health Statistics, *Vital Statistics of the United States*, annual; and *National Vital Statistics Reports (NVSR)*Vol. 53, No.9. (formerly *Monthly Vital Statistics Report*). See also: <http://www.cdc.gov/nchs/nvss.htm>.

Table 77. Total Fertility Rate by Race: 1970 to 2003

[Based on race of child and registered births only, through 1979. Beginning 1980, based on race of mother. Excludes births to non-residents of United States. The total fertility rate is the number of births that 1,000 women would have in their lifetime if, at each year of age, they experienced the birth rates occurring in the specified year. A total fertility rate of 2,110 represents "replacement-level" fertility for the total population under current mortality conditions (assuming no net immigration). See also Appendix III]

Year	Total [1]	White	Black [2]	Year	Total [1]	White	Black [2]
1970	2,480	2,385	3,067	1987	1,872	1,805	2,198
1971	2,267	2,161	2,920	1988	1,934	1,857	2,298
1972	2,010	1,907	2,628	1989	2,014	1,931	2,433
1973	1,879	1,783	2,443	1990	2,081	2,003	2,480
1974	1,835	1,749	2,339	1991	2,063	1,988	2,462
1975	1,774	1,686	2,276	1992	2,046	1,978	2,416
1976	1,738	1,652	2,223	1993	2,020	1,962	2,351
1977	1,790	1,703	2,279	1994	2,002	1,958	2,259
1978	1,760	1,668	2,265	1995	1,978	1,955	2,128
1979	1,808	1,716	2,310	1996	1,976	1,961	2,089
1980	1,840	1,773	2,177	1997	1,971	1,955	2,092
1981	1,812	1,748	2,118	1998	1,999	1,991	2,112
1982	1,828	1,767	2,107	1999	2,008	2,008	2,083
1983	1,799	1,741	2,066	2000	2,056	2,051	2,129
1984	1,807	1,749	2,071	2001	2,034	2,040	2,051
1985	1,844	1,787	2,109	2002	2,013	2,028	1,991
1986	1,838	1,776	2,136	2003³....	2,044	(NA)	(NA)

[1] Includes races, not shown separately. [2] Data for 1984 and earlier includes races other than Black. [3] Preliminary data.

Source: U.S. National Center for Health Statistics, *Vital Statistics of the United States*, annual; and unpublished data. See also: <http://www.cdc.gov/nchs>.

Table 78. Projected Fertility and Birth Rates by Race, Hispanic Origin, and Age Group: 2010

[For definition of total fertility rate, see headnote, Table 77. Birth rates represent live births per 1,000 women in age group indicated. Projections are based on middle fertility assumptions. For explanations of methodology, see text, Section 1, Population]

Age group	All races [1]	White	Black	American Indian, Eskimo, Aleut	Asian and Pacific Islanders	Hispanic [2]
Total fertility rate	2,123	2,098	2,140	2,451	2,252	2,818
Birth rates:						
10 to 14 years old.....................	1.3	0.9	3.5	2.0	0.7	2.3
15 to 19 years old.....................	60.2	54.3	95.6	93.6	29.6	95.7
20 to 24 years old.....................	115.8	112.6	137.1	159.6	83.7	175.2
25 to 29 years old.....................	115.7	118.5	95.5	118.6	134.5	146.7
30 to 34 years old.....................	87.8	90.0	63.4	77.3	128.2	91.6
35 to 39 years old.....................	36.7	36.6	28.9	33.7	59.0	41.9
40 to 44 years old.....................	7.3	7.1	6.0	7.4	13.8	9.9
	0.3	0.3	0.3	0.3	0.9	0.6

[1] Includes other races not shown separately. [2] Persons of Hispanic origin may be any race.

Source: U.S. Census Bureau, Population Division Working Paper No. 38. See also: <http://www.census.gov/population/www/techpap.html>.

Table 79. Birth Rates by Live-Birth Order and Race: 1990 to 2003

[Births per 1,000 women 15 to 44 years old in specified racial group. Live-birth order refers to number of children born alive. Figures for births of order not stated are distributed. See also headnote, Table 74. See Appendix III]

Live-birth order	All races [1]					White					Black				
	1990	1995	2000	2002	2003 [2]	1990	1995	2000	2002	2003[2]	1990	1995	2000	2002	2003 [2]
Total	70.9	64.6	65.9	64.8	66.1	68.3	63.6	65.3	64.8	66.2	86.8	71.0	70.0	65.8	66.2
First birth.....	29.0	26.9	26.5	25.8	26.7	28.4	26.6	26.3	25.7	26.7	32.4	28.2	26.2	24.8	25.4
Second birth	22.8	20.7	21.4	21.1	21.5	22.4	20.9	21.5	21.5	21.9	25.6	20.4	20.8	19.2	19.5
Third birth³.....	11.7	10.3	11.0	10.9	11.0	11.1	10.2	11.0	11.0	11.1	15.6	11.8	12.5	11.7	11.7
Fourth birth³	4.5	4.0	4.2	4.3	6.8	4.0	3.7	4.0	4.1	6.5	7.4	5.6	5.8	5.5	9.6
Fifth birth.......	1.7	1.5	1.6	1.5	(NA)	1.4	1.3	1.4	1.4	(NA)	3.2	2.6	2.5	2.4	(NA)
Sixth & seventh ..	1.0	0.9	0.9	0.9	(NA)	0.8	0.7	0.8	0.8	(NA)	2.0	1.8	1.7	1.6	(NA)
Eighth & over....	0.3	0.3	0.3	0.3	(NA)	0.2	0.2	0.2	0.2	(NA)	0.6	0.6	0.6	0.5	(NA)

NA Not available. [1] Includes other races not shown separately. [2] Preliminary data. [3] 2003 data includes fourth birth and over.

Source: U.S. National Center for Health Statistics, *Vital Statistics of the United States*, annual; and *National Vital Statistics Reports (NVSR)* (formerly *Monthly Vital Statistics Report*).

Vital Statistics 67

Table 80. **Births to Teens, Unmarried Mothers, and Prenatal Care: 1990 to 2002**

[In percent. Represents registered births. See headnote. Table 73. See Appendix III]

Characteristics	1990	1995	1998	1999	2000	2001	2002
Percent of births to teenage mothers . . .	12.8	13.1	12.5	12.3	11.8	11.3	10.8
White	10.9	11.5	11.1	10.9	10.6	10.2	9.8
Black	23.1	23.1	21.5	20.7	19.7	18.9	18.0
American Indian, Eskimo, Aleut	19.5	21.4	20.9	20.2	19.7	19.3	18.5
Asian and Pacific Islander [1]	5.7	5.6	5.4	5.1	4.5	4.3	3.8
Filipino.	6.1	6.2	6.2	5.9	5.3	5.1	4.5
Chinese	1.2	0.9	0.9	0.9	0.9	1.0	0.9
Japanese	2.9	2.5	2.4	2.1	1.9	1.7	1.7
Hawaiian	18.4	19.1	18.8	18.2	17.4	16.2	14.6
Other.	(NA)	6.3	5.8	5.5	4.8	4.6	4.0
Hispanic origin [2]	16.8	17.9	16.9	16.7	16.2	15.6	14.9
Mexican.	17.7	18.8	17.5	17.4	17.0	16.5	15.9
Puerto Rican.	21.7	23.5	21.9	21.1	20.0	19.2	17.8
Cuban	7.7	7.7	6.9	7.7	7.5	7.5	8.1
Central and South American	9.0	10.6	10.3	10.0	9.9	9.4	8.5
Other and unknown Hispanic	(NA)	20.1	20.2	19.5	18.8	17.3	16.7
Percent births to unmarried mothers . . .	26.6	32.2	32.8	33.0	33.2	33.5	34.0
White	16.9	25.3	26.3	26.8	27.1	27.7	28.5
Black	66.7	69.9	69.1	68.9	68.5	68.4	68.2
American Indian, Eskimo, Aleut	53.6	57.2	59.3	58.9	58.4	59.7	59.7
Asian and Pacific Islander [1]	13.2	16.3	15.6	15.4	14.8	14.9	14.9
Filipino.	15.9	19.5	19.7	21.1	20.3	20.4	20.0
Chinese	5.0	7.9	6.4	6.9	7.6	8.4	9.0
Japanese	9.6	10.8	9.7	9.9	9.5	9.2	10.3
Hawaiian	45.0	49.0	51.1	50.4	50.0	50.6	50.4
Hispanic origin [2]	36.7	40.8	41.6	42.2	42.7	42.5	43.5
Mexican.	33.3	38.1	39.6	40.1	40.7	40.8	42.1
Puerto Rican.	55.9	60.0	59.5	59.6	59.6	58.9	59.1
Cuban	18.2	23.8	24.8	26.4	27.3	27.2	29.8
Central and South American	41.2	44.1	42.0	43.7	44.7	44.3	44.8
Percent of mothers beginning prenatal care 1st trimester.	74.2	81.3	82.8	83.2	83.2	83.4	83.7
White	77.7	83.6	84.8	85.1	85.0	85.2	85.4
Black	60.7	70.4	73.3	74.1	74.3	74.5	75.2
American Indian, Eskimo, Aleut	57.9	66.7	68.8	69.5	69.3	69.3	69.8
Asian and Pacific Islander [1]	(NA)	79.9	83.1	83.7	84.0	84.0	84.8
Filipino.	77.1	80.9	84.2	84.2	84.9	85.0	85.4
Chinese	81.3	85.7	88.5	88.5	87.6	87.0	87.2
Japanese	87.0	89.7	90.2	90.7	91.0	90.1	90.5
Hawaiian	65.8	75.9	78.8	79.6	79.9	79.1	78.1
Hispanic origin [2]	60.2	70.8	74.3	74.4	74.4	75.7	76.8
Mexican.	57.8	69.1	72.8	73.1	72.9	74.6	75.7
Puerto Rican.	63.5	74.0	76.9	77.7	78.5	79.1	79.9
Cuban	84.8	89.2	91.8	91.4	91.7	91.8	92.0
Central and South American	61.5	73.2	78.0	77.6	77.6	77.4	78.7
Percent of mothers beginning prenatal care 3d trimester or no care . . .	6.0	4.2	3.9	3.8	3.9	3.7	3.6
White	4.9	3.5	3.3	3.2	3.3	3.2	3.1
Black	10.9	7.6	7.0	6.6	6.7	6.5	6.2
American Indian, Eskimo, Aleut	12.9	9.5	8.5	8.2	8.6	8.2	8.1
Asian and Pacific Islander [1]	(NA)	4.3	3.6	3.5	3.3	3.4	3.1
Filipino.	4.5	4.1	3.1	2.8	3.0	3.0	2.8
Chinese	3.4	3.0	2.2	2.0	2.2	2.4	2.1
Japanese	2.9	2.3	2.1	2.1	1.8	2.0	2.1
Hawaiian	8.7	5.1	4.7	4.0	4.2	4.8	4.7
Hispanic origin [2]	12.0	7.4	6.3	6.3	6.3	5.9	5.5
Mexican.	13.2	8.1	6.8	6.7	6.9	6.2	5.8
Puerto Rican.	10.6	5.5	5.1	5.0	4.5	4.6	4.1
Cuban	2.8	2.1	1.2	1.4	1.4	1.3	1.3
Central and South American	10.9	6.1	4.9	5.2	5.4	5.7	4.9
Percent of births with low birth weight [3].	7.0	7.3	7.6	7.6	7.6	7.7	7.8
White	5.7	6.2	6.5	6.6	6.5	6.7	6.8
Black	13.3	13.1	13.0	13.1	13.0	13.0	13.3
American Indian, Eskimo, Aleut	6.1	6.6	6.8	7.1	6.8	7.3	7.2
Asian and Pacific Islander [1]	(NA)	6.9	7.4	7.4	7.3	7.5	7.8
Filipino.	7.3	7.8	8.2	8.3	8.5	8.7	8.6
Chinese	4.7	5.3	5.3	5.2	5.1	5.3	5.5
Japanese	6.2	7.3	7.5	7.9	7.1	7.3	7.6
Hawaiian	7.2	6.8	7.2	7.7	6.8	7.9	8.1
Hispanic origin [2]	6.1	6.3	6.4	6.4	6.4	6.5	6.5
Mexican.	5.5	5.8	6.0	5.9	6.0	6.1	6.2
Puerto Rican.	9.0	9.4	9.7	9.3	9.3	9.3	9.7
Cuban	5.7	6.5	6.5	6.8	6.5	6.5	6.5
Central and South American	5.8	6.2	6.5	6.4	6.3	6.5	6.5

NA Not available.   [1] Includes other races not shown separately.   [2] Hispanic persons may be of any race. Includes other types, not shown separately.   [3] Births less than 2,500 grams (5 lb.-8 oz.).

Source: U.S. National Center for Health Statistics, *Vital Statistics of the United States*, annual; and *National Vital Statistics Reports (NVSR)* (formerly *Monthly Vital Statistics Report*).

Table 81. Teenagers—Births and Birth Rates by Race and Age: 1990 to 2003

[Birth rates per 1,000 women in specified group, see text, this section]

Item	1990	1995	1996	1997	1998	1999	2000	2001	2002	2003[1]
NUMBER OF BIRTHS										
All races, total[2]	521,826	499,873	494,272	489,211	484,975	476,050	468,990	445,944	425,493	414,961
15-17 years	183,327	192,508	186,762	183,324	173,252	163,588	157,209	145,324	138,731	134,617
18-19 years	338,499	307,365	307,509	305,886	311,724	312,462	311,781	300,620	286,762	280,344
White	354,482	349,635	346,509	342,029	340,894	337,888	333,013	318,563	305,988	298,821
15-17 years	114,934	127,165	124,031	121,864	116,699	111,624	106,786	99,192	95,864	92,807
18-19 years	239,548	222,470	222,477	220,164	224,195	226,264	226,227	219,371	210,124	206,014
Black	151,613	133,694	131,059	130,401	126,865	121,166	118,954	110,843	103,795	100,864
15-17 years	62,881	59,112	56,218	54,883	50,062	45,919	44,618	40,842	37,889	36,855
18-19 years	88,732	74,582	74,841	75,518	76,803	75,247	74,336	70,001	65,906	64,009
BIRTH RATE										
All races, total[2]	59.9	56.0	53.5	51.3	50.3	48.8	47.7	45.3	43.0	41.7
15-17 years	37.5	35.5	33.3	31.4	29.9	28.2	26.9	24.7	23.2	22.4
18-19 years	88.6	87.7	84.7	82.1	80.9	79.1	78.1	76.1	72.8	70.8
White	50.8	49.5	47.5	45.5	44.9	44.0	43.2	41.2	39.4	38.3
15-17 years	29.5	29.7	28.0	26.6	25.6	24.5	23.3	21.4	20.5	19.8
18-19 years	78.0	80.0	77.4	74.8	73.9	72.8	72.3	70.8	68.0	66.3
Black	112.8	94.4	89.6	86.3	83.5	79.1	77.4	71.8	66.6	63.7
15-17 years	82.3	68.6	63.4	59.4	55.5	50.7	49.0	43.9	40.0	38.2
18-19 years	152.9	134.6	130.1	127.4	124.3	120.1	118.8	114.0	107.6	103.6

[1] Preliminary data. [2] Includes races other than White and Black.

Source: U.S. National Center for Health Statistics, *Vital Statistics of the United States*, annual; *National Vital Statistics Report* (NVSR) (formerly *Monthly Vital Statistics Report*), and unpublished data. See also <http://www.cdc.gov/nchs.htm>.

Table 82. Births to Unmarried Women by Race of Child and Age of Mother: 1990 to 2003

[Excludes births to nonresidents of United States. Marital status is inferred from a comparison of the child's and parents' surnames on the birth certificate for those States that do not report on marital status. No estimates included for misstatements on birth records or failures to register births. See also Appendix III]

Race of child and age of mother	1990	1995	2000	2002	2003 prel.
NUMBER (1,000)					
Total live births[1]	1,165	1,254	1,347	1,366	1,416
White	647	785	866	904	(NA)
Black	473	421	427	405	(NA)
Under 15 years	11	11	8	7	6
15 to 19 years	350	376	369	340	337
20 to 24 years	404	432	504	528	(NA)
25 to 29 years	230	229	255	268	(NA)
30 to 34 years	118	133	130	139	(NA)
35 to 39 years	(NA)	60	65	66	(NA)
40 years and over	(NA)	13	16	17	(NA)
PERCENT DISTRIBUTION					
Total[1]	100.0	100.0	100.0	100.0	(NA)
White	55.6	62.6	64.3	66.2	(NA)
Black	40.6	33.6	31.7	29.6	(NA)
Under 15 years	0.9	0.9	0.6	0.5	0.4
15 to 19 years	30.0	30.0	27.4	24.9	23.8
20 to 24 years	34.7	34.5	37.4	38.6	(NA)
25 to 29 years	19.7	18.2	18.9	19.7	(NA)

Race of child and age of mother	1990	1995	2000	2002	2003 prel.
30 to 34 years	10.1	10.6	9.7	10.2	(NA)
35 to 39 years	(NA)	5.8	6.0	4.8	(NA)
40 years and over	(NA)	(NA)	1.2	1.3	(NA)
AS PERCENT OF ALL BIRTHS IN RACIAL GROUPS					
Total[1]	26.6	32.2	33.2	34.0	34.6
White	16.9	25.3	27.1	28.5	(NA)
Black	66.7	69.9	68.5	68.2	(NA)
BIRTH RATE[2]					
Total[1][3]	43.8	44.3	44.0	43.7	(NA)
White[3]	32.9	37.0	38.2	38.9	(NA)
Black[3]	90.5	74.5	70.5	66.2	(NA)
15 to 19 years	42.5	43.8	39.0	35.4	(NA)
20 to 24 years	65.1	68.7	72.1	70.5	(NA)
25 to 29 years	56.0	54.3	58.5	61.5	(NA)
30 to 34 years	37.6	38.9	39.3	40.8	(NA)
35 to 39 years	17.3	19.3	19.7	20.8	(NA)
40 to 44 years	3.6	4.7	5.0	5.4	(NA)

NA Not available. [1] Includes other races not shown separately. [2] Rate per 1,000 unmarried women (never-married, widowed, and divorced) estimated as of July 1. [3] Covers women aged 15 to 44 years.

Source: U.S. National Center for Health Statistics, *Vital Statistics of the United States*, annual; and *National Vital Statistics Reports (NVSR)* (formerly *Monthly Vital Statistics Report*).

Vital Statistics 69

Table 83. Low Birth Weight and Births to Teenage Mothers and to Unmarried Women—States and Island Areas: 1990 to 2002

[Represents registered births. Excludes births to nonresidents of the United States. Based on 100 percent of births in all states and the District of Columbia. See Appendix III]

State and outlying area	Percent of births with low birth weight [1]			Births to teenage mothers, percent of total [2]			Births to unmarried women, percent of total		
	1990	2000	2002	1990	2000	2002	1990	2000	2002
U.S.	7.0	7.6	7.8	12.8	11.8	10.8	26.6	33.2	34.0
Alabama.	8.4	9.7	9.9	18.2	15.7	14.6	30.1	34.3	34.8
Alaska	4.8	5.6	5.8	9.7	11.8	10.9	26.2	33.0	34.0
Arizona.	6.4	7.0	6.8	14.2	14.3	13.2	32.7	39.3	40.4
Arkansas	8.2	8.6	8.6	19.7	17.3	15.5	29.4	35.7	37.1
California	5.8	6.2	6.4	11.6	10.6	9.6	31.6	32.7	33.0
Colorado.	8.0	8.4	8.9	11.3	11.7	10.7	21.2	25.0	26.8
Connecticut.	6.6	7.4	7.8	8.2	7.8	7.0	26.6	29.3	29.1
Delaware	7.6	8.6	9.9	11.9	12.3	11.1	29.0	37.9	40.6
District of Columbia	15.1	11.9	11.6	17.8	14.2	12.8	64.9	60.3	56.5
Florida	7.4	8.0	8.4	13.9	12.6	11.5	31.7	38.2	39.3
Georgia	8.7	8.6	8.9	16.7	13.9	12.4	32.8	37.0	37.8
Hawaii	7.1	7.5	8.3	10.5	10.3	8.9	24.8	32.2	33.6
Idaho	5.7	6.7	6.1	12.3	11.6	10.0	16.7	21.6	21.9
Illinois	7.6	7.9	8.2	13.1	11.4	10.3	31.7	34.5	34.8
Indiana.	6.6	7.4	7.6	14.5	12.5	11.4	26.2	34.7	36.4
Iowa	5.4	6.1	6.6	10.2	10.0	9.1	21.0	28.0	29.3
Kansas.	6.2	6.9	7.0	12.3	12.0	11.1	21.5	29.0	31.1
Kentucky	7.1	8.2	8.6	17.5	14.1	12.9	23.6	31.0	33.2
Louisiana	9.2	10.3	10.4	17.6	17.0	15.9	36.8	45.6	47.0
Maine.	5.1	6.0	6.3	10.8	9.4	8.5	22.6	31.0	32.6
Maryland	7.8	8.6	9.0	10.5	9.9	9.1	29.6	34.6	34.8
Massachusetts.	5.9	7.1	7.5	8.0	6.6	5.8	24.7	26.5	26.8
Michigan.	7.6	7.9	8.0	13.5	10.5	9.6	26.2	33.3	34.1
Minnesota.	5.1	6.1	6.3	8.0	8.3	7.6	20.9	25.8	27.4
Mississippi	9.6	10.7	11.2	21.3	18.8	17.2	40.5	46.0	47.1
Missouri	7.1	7.6	8.0	14.4	13.1	11.9	28.6	34.6	35.2
Montana.	6.2	6.2	6.8	11.5	11.6	11.5	23.7	30.8	32.8
Nebraska	5.3	6.8	7.2	9.8	10.2	9.5	20.7	27.2	28.6
Nevada	7.2	7.2	7.5	12.6	12.7	11.4	25.4	36.4	37.4
New Hampshire	4.9	6.3	6.3	7.2	6.8	6.1	16.9	24.7	24.6
New Jersey.	7.0	7.7	8.0	8.4	7.1	6.5	24.3	28.9	29.3
New Mexico	7.4	8.0	8.0	16.3	17.4	16.6	35.4	45.6	46.9
New York	7.6	7.7	7.9	9.1	8.2	7.4	33.0	36.6	35.7
North Carolina	8.0	8.8	9.0	16.2	13.0	12.0	29.4	33.3	34.7
North Dakota.	5.5	6.4	6.3	8.6	9.2	8.5	18.4	28.3	29.0
Ohio	7.1	7.9	8.3	13.8	12.1	10.7	28.9	34.6	35.4
Oklahoma.	6.6	7.5	8.0	16.2	15.9	14.8	25.2	34.3	36.4
Oregon.	5.0	5.6	5.8	12.0	11.3	9.9	25.7	30.1	30.9
Pennsylvania.	7.1	7.7	8.2	10.9	9.9	9.2	28.6	32.7	33.4
Rhode Island.	6.2	7.2	7.9	10.5	10.2	9.4	26.3	35.5	35.7
South Carolina.	8.7	9.7	10.0	17.1	15.3	13.7	32.7	39.8	40.4
South Dakota	5.1	6.2	7.2	10.8	11.6	10.7	22.9	33.5	35.0
Tennessee	8.2	9.2	9.2	17.6	14.7	13.5	30.2	34.5	36.2
Texas	6.9	7.4	7.7	15.6	15.3	14.3	17.5	30.5	32.4
Utah	5.7	6.6	6.4	10.3	8.9	7.3	13.5	17.3	17.2
Vermont	5.3	6.1	6.4	8.5	8.0	8.4	20.1	28.1	31.9
Virginia.	7.2	7.9	7.9	11.7	9.9	9.2	26.0	29.9	30.3
Washington.	5.3	5.6	5.9	10.8	10.2	9.0	23.7	28.2	28.8
West Virginia.	7.1	8.3	9.0	17.8	15.9	12.8	25.4	31.7	32.9
Wisconsin	5.9	6.5	6.6	10.2	10.2	9.5	24.2	29.3	30.0
Wyoming	7.4	8.3	8.4	13.6	13.5	12.4	19.8	28.8	30.3
Puerto Rico	(NA)	10.8	11.5	(NA)	(NA)	(NA)	(NA)	49.7	52.0
Virgin Islands	(NA)	9.1	11.8	(NA)	(NA)	(NA)	(NA)	66.7	67.3
Guam.	(NA)	7.6	8.0	(NA)	(NA)	(NA)	(NA)	54.8	55.4
American Samoa	(NA)	2.7	3.9	(NA)	(NA)	(NA)	(NA)	35.5	32.0
Northern Marianas	(NA)	8.9	6.9	(NA)	(NA)	(NA)	(NA)	(NA)	59.7

NA Not available. [1] Less than 2,500 grams (5 pounds-8 ounces). [2] Defined as mothers who are 19 years of age or younger.

Source: U.S. National Center for Health Statistics, *Vital Statistics of the United States*, annual; and *National Vital Statistics Reports (NVSR)* (formerly *Monthly Vital Statistics Report*). See also: <http://www.cdc.gov/nchs>.

70   Vital Statistics

Table 84. Live Births by Place of Delivery, Median and Low Birth Weight, and Prenatal Care: 1990 to 2002

[4,110 represents 4,110,000. Represents registered births. Excludes births to nonresidents of the United States. For total number of births, see Table 74. See Appendix III]

Item	1990	1995	1997	1998	1999	2000	2001	2002
Births attended (1,000):								
In hospital [1]	4,110	3,861	3,881	3,904	3,923	4,021	3,990	3,986
By physician, not in hospital	14	6	5	6	5	5	4	4
By midwife and other, not in hospital [2]	21	21	20	21	21	21	22	22
Median birth weight [3]	7 lb.-7 oz.	(NA)	7 lb.-7 oz.	7 lb.-7 oz.	(NA)	7 lb.-7 oz.	7 lb.-6 oz.	7 lb.-6oz.
Percent of births with low birth weight	7.0	7.3	7.5	7.6	7.6	7.6	7.7	7.8
White	5.7	6.2	6.5	6.5	6.6	6.5	6.7	6.8
Black	13.3	13.1	13.0	13.0	13.1	13.0	13.0	13.3
Hispanic [3]	6.1	6.3	6.4	6.4	6.4	6.4	6.5	6.5
Percent of births by period in which prenatal care began:								
1st trimester	74.2	81.3	82.5	82.8	83.2	83.2	83.4	83.7
3d trimester or no prenatal care	6.0	4.2	3.9	3.9	3.8	3.9	3.7	3.6

NA Not available. [1] Includes all births in hospitals or institutions and in clinics. [2] Includes births with attendant not specified. [3] Hispanic persons may be any race.

Source: U.S. National Center for Health Statistics of the United States, *Vital Statistics of the United States,* annual; and *National Vital Statistics Reports* (NVSR) formerly *Monthly Vital Statistics Report*), and unpublished data. See also <http://www.cdc.gov/nchs/births.htm>

Table 85. Method of Delivery by Race: 1990 to 2002

[In thousands (4,111 represents 4,111,000), except rate. 1990 excludes data for Oklahoma, which did not report method of delivery on the birth certificate. See Appendix III]

Age of mother	1990	2000	2002	Age of mother	1990	2000	2002
Births, total	4,111	4,059	4,022	Not stated	16	4	3
Vaginal	3,111	3,108	2,958				
After previous Cesarean	84	90	59	Hispanic births	595	816	877
Cesarean deliveries	914	924	1,044	Vaginal	458	633	654
Primary	575	578	634	After previous Cesarean	10	17	13
Repeat	339	346	409	Cesarean deliveries	123	130	220
Not stated	85	27	19	Primary	76	105	123
White births	3,252	3,194	3,175	Repeat	47	75	97
Vaginal	2,454	2,449	2,341	Not stated	14	3	3
After previous Cesarean	67	70	46				
Cesarean deliveries	733	723	818	Cesarean delivery rate [1]	22.7	22.9	26.1
Primary	459	449	493	White	23.0	22.8	25.9
Repeat	274	274	325	Black	22.1	24.3	27.6
Not stated	66	22	16	Primary [2]	16.0	16.1	18.0
Black births	679	623	594	White	16.1	15.9	17.7
Vaginal	517	468	428	Black	15.7	17.3	19.4
After previous Cesarean	13	14	10	Rate of vaginal birth			
Cesarean deliveries	146	150	163	after previous Cesarean [3]	19.9	20.6	12.6
Primary	93	95	101	White	19.7	20.4	12.4
Repeat	53	56	63	Black	20.3	20.5	13.2

[1] Cesarean rates are the number of Cesarean deliveries per 100 total deliveries for specified category. [2] Number of primary Cesareans per 100 live births to women who have not had a previous Cesarean. [3] Number of vaginal births after previous Cesarean delivery per 100 live births to women with a previous Cesarean delivery.

Source: U.S. National Center for Health Statistics, *Vital Statistics of the United States,* annual.

Table 86. Percent Low Birthweight by Smoking Status, Age, and Race of Mother: 2002

[Low birthweight is defined as weight of less than 2,500 grams (5 lb.-8 oz.). Excludes California, Indiana, New York State (but includes New York City), and South Dakota, which did not require reporting of tobacco use during pregnancy]

Smoking status and race of mother	All ages	Under 15 years	15-19 years Total	15-17 years	18-19 years	20-24 years	25-29 years	30-34 years	35-39 years
All races [1]	8.0	13.8	9.9	10.7	9.5	8.2	7.1	7.4	8.8
Smoker	12.2	12.9	11.5	12.2	11.2	11.0	11.4	13.7	16.7
Nonsmoker	7.5	13.7	9.5	10.5	9.1	7.6	6.6	6.9	8.1
White	7.0	12.5	8.4	9.1	8.0	6.9	6.2	6.6	7.8
Smoker	11.0	13.3	10.9	11.6	10.6	10.2	10.4	12.0	14.6
Nonsmoker	6.4	12.3	7.7	8.6	7.3	6.1	5.7	6.1	7.2
Black	13.4	15.2	14.0	14.5	13.7	13.0	12.5	13.4	15.3
Smoker	20.1	(B)	16.9	17.8	16.5	17.1	18.8	25.7	28.7
Nonsmoker	12.7	15.2	13.8	14.3	13.4	12.5	11.8	12.4	13.8

B Base figure too small to meet statistical standards for reliability of a derived figure. [1] Includes races other than White and Black.

Source: U.S. National Center for Health Statistics, *National Vital Statistics Reports (NVSR)Vol. 52, No.10* (formerly *Monthly Vital Statistics Report).* See also: <http://www.cdc.gov/nchs/nvss.htm>.

Table 87. Women Who Have Had a Child in the Last Year by Age: 1990 to 2004

[**3,913 represents 3,913,000.** As of June. Excludes births to nonresidents of the United States. Data are by place of residence. See headnote, Table 88.]

Age of mother	Women who had a child in last year (1,000)			Total births per 1,000 women			First births per 1,000 women		
	1990	2000	2004	1990	2000	2004	1990	2000	2004
Total	3,913	3,934	3,746	67.0	64.6	60.8	26.4	26.7	23.9
15 to 29 years old	2,568	2,432	2,205	90.8	85.9	74.7	43.2	43.1	35.1
15 to 19 years old . .	338	586	385	39.8	59.7	38.7	30.1	38.7	22.1
20 to 24 years old . .	1,038	850	882	113.4	91.8	87.6	51.8	47.1	43.0
25 to 29 years old . .	1,192	996	938	112.1	107.9	98.4	46.2	43.7	40.2
30 to 44 years old	1,346	1,502	1,542	44.7	46.1	48.1	10.6	12.5	13.7
30 to 34 years old . .	892	871	946	80.4	87.9	93.8	21.9	27.5	28.4
35 to 39 years old . .	377	506	443	37.3	45.1	42.4	6.5	9.6	11.5
40 to 44 years old . .	77	125	153	8.6	10.9	13.2	1.2	2.3	2.8

Source: U.S. Census Bureau, *Current Population Reports*, P20-548.

Table 88. Characteristics of Women Who Have Had a Child in the Last Year: 2000 and 2004

[**As of June.** Covers civilian noninstitutional population. Since the number of women who had a birth during the 12-month period was tabulated and not the actual numbers of births, some small underestimation of fertility for this period may exist due to the omission of: (1) multiple births, (2) two or more live births spaced within the 12-month period (the woman is counted only once), (3) women who had births in the period and who did not survive to the survey date, (4) women who were in institutions and therefore not in the survey universe. These losses may be somewhat offset by the inclusion in the CPS of births to immigrants who did not have their children born in the United States and births to nonresident women. These births would not have been recorded in the vital registration system. Based on Current Population Survey (CPS). The 2003 Current Population Survey(CPS) allowed respondents to choose more than one race. Beginning 2003, data represent persons who selected this race group only and exclude persons reporting more than one race. The CPS in prior years allowed respondents to report only one race group. See also comments on race in the text for Section 1, Population, and Appendix III]

Characteristic	2000			2004		
		Women who have had a child in the last year			Women who have had a child in the last year	
	Number of women (1,000)	Total births per 1,000 women	First births per 1,000 women	Number of women (1,000)	Total births per 1,000 women	First births per 1,000 women
Total [1]	60,873	64.6	26.7	61,588	60.8	23.9
White	48,506	65.4	27.2	47,984	60.0	23.2
Black	8,939	63.2	21.9	8,798	58.5	21.8
Hispanic [2]	8,002	95.1	38.6	9,618	85.0	28.0
Currently married	30,497	88.8	35.5	29,909	85.5	31.0
Married, spouse present . .	28,215	90.8	37.0	27,586	87.6	32.4
Married, spouse absent [3]	2,282	64.5	16.6	2,323	61.1	14.2
Widowed or divorced.	5,281	31.0	6.8	5,294	27.3	7.0
Never married	25,095	42.3	20.2	26,385	39.6	19.3
Educational attainment:						
Less than high school	13,006	70.7	29.5	12,965	57.7	18.1
High school, 4 years	17,205	70.0	29.5	16,137	67.3	24.6
College: 1 or more years	30,662	59.0	24.0	32,486	58.9	25.9
No degree	12,603	51.6	19.2	12,667	53.0	19.1
Associate's degree.	4,955	60.6	23.6	5,335	55.3	26.8
Bachelor's degree	9,926	61.7	27.7	10,807	63.0	30.7
Graduate or professional degree. . .	3,178	77.7	32.0	3,678	72.5	33.9
Labor force status:						
Employed	41,369	47.7	20.7	39,441	46.2	20.2
Unemployed	2,493	79.4	31.1	3,180	70.0	26.3
Not in labor force.	17,011	103.7	40.6	18,967	89.6	31.3
Occupation of employed women:						
Managerial-professional	12,481	52.2	22.9	(NA)	(NA)	(NA)
Technical, sales, admin. support.	16,561	44.0	20.3	(NA)	(NA)	(NA)
Service workers	8,102	51.0	20.1	(NA)	(NA)	(NA)
Farming, forestry, and fishing.	473	69.6	21.8	(NA)	(NA)	(NA)
Precision prod., craft, repair.	880	42.3	15.1	(NA)	(NA)	(NA)
Operators, fabricators, laborers	2,872	38.1	17.2	(NA)	(NA)	(NA)
Family income:						
Under $10,000	4,249	86.8	32.5	3,979	95.8	27.7
$10,000 to $19,999	6,203	74.8	25.3	5,098	78.7	27.0
$20,000 to $24,999	3,439	76.2	37.3	2,931	75.6	22.6
$25,000 to $29,999	3,761	78.9	34.0	3,242	59.6	24.9
$30,000 to $34,999	3,572	62.4	27.3	3,468	65.3	24.3
$35,000 to $49,999	8,864	64.9	25.3	8,149	57.1	24.3
$50,000 to $74,999	10,646	61.2	26.8	10,659	55.2	23.3
$75,000 and over	12,506	60.1	24.3	13,812	54.3	22.9

[1] Includes women of other races and women with family income not reported, not shown separately.   [2] Persons of Hispanic origin may be any race.   [3] Includes separated women.

Source: U.S. Census Bureau, *Current Population Reports*, P20-548 and unpublished data.

Table 89. **Women Who Have Had a Child in the Last Year by Age and Labor Force Status: 1980 to 2004**

[3,247 represents 3,247,000. See headnote, Table 88. See Appendix III]

Year	Total, 18 to 44 years old			18 to 29 years old			30 to 44 years old		
		In the labor force			In the labor force			In the labor force	
	Number (1,000)	Number (1,000)	Percent	Number (1,000)	Number (1,000)	Percent	Number (1,000)	Number (1,000)	Percent
1980	3,247	1,233	38	2,476	947	38	770	287	37
1985 [1]	3,497	1,691	48	2,512	1,204	48	984	488	50
1990 [1]	3,913	2,068	53	2,568	1,275	50	1,346	793	59
1995 [1]	3,696	2,034	55	2,252	1,150	51	1,444	884	61
2000 [1]	3,934	2,170	55	2,432	1,304	54	1,502	866	58
2002 [1]	3,766	2,056	55	2,318	1,175	51	1,448	881	61
2004 [1]	3,746	2,046	55	2,205	(NA)	(NA)	1,542	(NA)	(NA)

NA Not available. [1] Lower age limit is 15 years old.
Source: U.S. Census Bureau, *Current Population* Reports, P20-548; and unpublished data.

Table 90. **Contraceptive Use by Women, 15 to 44 Years of Age: 1982 to 2002**

[46,684 represents 46,684,000. Based on samples of the female population of the United States; see source for details]

Contraceptive status and method	1982	1995	2002			
				Non-Hispanic		
			Total[1]	White	Black	Hispanic
All women (1,000)......................	46,684	53,800	54,190	35,789	·7,693	7,887
PERCENT DISTRIBUTION						
Any method........................	94.8	98.2	98.2	98.8	97.3	96.5
Female sterilization....................	22.3	23.4	20.7	19.4	26.6	24.1
Male sterilization	10.1	14.6	13.0	16.7	4.9	4.4
Pill................................	76.3	82.2	82.3	87.1	79.2	68.5
Norplant implant.....................	(X)	2.1	2.1	1.4	3.2	4.0
1-month injectable (Lunelle ™).........	(X)	(X)	0.9	0.5	0.9	3.1
3-month injectable (Depo-Provera ™)	(X)	4.5	16.8	13.7	23.9	24.3
Emergency contraception	(X)	0.8	4.2	4.3	4.0	3.8
Contraceptive Patch	(X)	(X)	0.9	0.7	1.3	1.1
Today™	(X)	12.0	7.3	8.8	6.2	2.7
Intrauterine device	18.4	10.0	5.8	4.7	5.5	10.0
Diaphragm	17.1	15.2	8.5	10.3	6.9	3.4
Condom............................	51.8	82.0	89.7	92.2	92.0	78.2
Female condom......................	(X)	1.2	1.9	1.2	5.3	1.4
Periodic abstinence-calender rhythm	17.0	24.3	16.2	16.6	13.9	16.2
Periodic abstinence-natural family planning.......	2.3	4.9	3.5	3.6	1.9	4.7
Withdrawal..........................	24.5	40.6	56.1	59.7	50.6	47.2
Foam alone..........................	24.9	18.3	12.1	12.7	15.4	8.2
Jelly/cream alone	5.8	9.1	7.3	7.8	9.7	3.4
Suppository/insert.....................	9.7	10.6	7.5	8.1	8.6	4.5
Other methods.......................	9.3	0.3	1.0	0.8	1.3	1.3

X Not applicable. [1] Includes other races, not shown separately.
Source: U.S. National Center for Health Statistics, *Use of Contraception and Use of Family Planning Services in the United States: 1982-2002.*

Table 91. **Select Family Planning and Medical Service Use by Women, 15 to 44 Years of Age: 2002**

[61,561 represents 61,561,000. Based on samples of the female population of the United States; see source for details]

Characteristic		Percent using-							
		Family planning services			Medical services				
	Number (1,000)	At least one family planning service	Birth control method	Birth control checkup or test	At least one medical service	Pregnancy test	Pap smear	Pelvic exam	Counseling/test/treatment for STD[1]
All women [2]	61,561	41.7	33.9	23.6	69.1	19.7	64.4	59.7	12.6
15-19 years.............	9,834	39.9	31.1	22.0	40.6	18.3	34.6	27.0	15.2
15-17 years...........	5,819	31.8	22.2	15.8	28.0	11.4	23.2	17.9	11.1
18-19 years...........	4,016	51.6	43.9	31.0	58.9	28.2	51.2	40.2	21.1
20-24 years.............	9,840	63.3	54.0	35.7	75.7	31.5	69.7	60.6	22.3
25-29 years.............	9,249	55.4	46.3	30.2	75.9	30.2	70.7	66.0	16.6
30-34 years.............	10,272	47.0	39.1	27.2	78.1	22.2	72.7	69.7	12.2
35-39 years.............	10,853	30.5	23.9	18.6	71.5	13.6	68.3	65.9	6.9
40-44 years.............	11,512	19.5	14.0	10.8	71.8	5.9	69.4	67.0	4.4
Currently married	28,327	39.5	31.5	21.3	77.2	21.1	73.1	69.8	8.1
Currently cohabiting	5,570	50.4	43.2	30.2	77.2	31.0	72.2	64.7	20.3
Never married, not cohabiting....	21,568	44.4	36.4	25.4	55.8	16.5	50.7	43.9	15.9
Formerly married, not cohabiting..	6,096	34.5	28.0	22.0	71.0	14.1	66.0	64.0	14.4
Non-Hispanic White	40,420	43.2	36.4	25.4	70.0	17.5	64.9	63.1	12.0
Non-Hispanic Black	8,587	39.6	30.6	21.5	74.5	23.7	69.2	58.9	16.1
Hispanic[3]	9,107	39.7	28.9	20.6	63.4	24.3	57.1	48.5	12.5

[1] STD stands for sexually transmitted disease. [2] Includes other races, not shown separately. [3] Persons of Hispanic origin may be any race.
Source: U.S. National Center for Health Statistics, *Use of Contraception and Use of Family Planning Services in the United States: 1982-2002.*

Vital Statistics 73

Table 92. Contraceptive Use by Women, 15 to 44 Years of Age: 1995 and 2002

[In percent, except total. 60,201 represents 60,201,000. Based on samples of the female population of the United States; see source for details]

Contraceptive status and method	1995 — All women	1995 — Never married	1995 — Currently married	1995 — Formerly married	2002 — All women[1]	Age 15-19 years	Age 20-24 years	Age 25-29 years	Age 30-34 years	Age 35-39 years	Age 40-44 years	NH White	NH Black	Hispanic	Never married, not cohabiting	Currently married	Formerly married, not cohabiting
All women (1,000)	60,201	22,679	29,673	7,849	61,561	9,834	9,840	9,249	10,272	10,853	11,512	40,420	8,587	9,107	21,568	28,327	6,096
PERCENT DISTRIBUTION																	
Using contraception (contraceptors)[2]	64.2	37.2	63.6	71.5	61.9	31.5	60.7	68.0	69.2	70.8	69.1	64.5	57.4	59.0	44.0	72.9	64.4
Female sterilization	17.8	(NA)	(NA)	(NA)	16.7	-	2.2	10.3	19.0	29.2	34.7	15.5	22.3	19.9	4.4	21.7	35.3
Male sterilization	7.0	(NA)	(NA)	(NA)	5.7	-	0.5	2.8	6.4	10.0	12.7	7.5	1.4	2.6	0.4	11.2	2.2
Pill	18.1	(NA)	(NA)	(NA)	19.6	17.1	32.6	29.5	22.7	13.7	7.7	22.8	13.4	14.7	22.3	18.3	12.8
3-month injectable (Depo-Provera)	1.9	(X)	(X)	(X)	3.3	4.4	6.1	4.4	2.9	1.5	1.1	2.7	5.6	4.3	4.2	2.2	1.7
Intrauterine device	0.5	0.3	0.7	0.4	1.3	0.1	1.1	0.3	2.2	1.0	0.8	0.9	0.8	3.2	0.2	1.9	1.9
Diaphragm	1.2	0.5	1.8	0.9	0.2	-	0.1	0.3	0.1	-	0.4	0.2	0.1	-	0.2	0.2	-
Condom	13.1	13.9	13.3	10.1	11.1	8.5	14.0	14.0	11.8	11.1	8.0	10.7	11.4	10.9	10.3	12.0	8.0
Periodic abstinence-calendar rhythm	1.3	0.6	2.3	0.7	0.7	-	0.8	0.3	0.9	1.1	1.2	0.8	0.3	0.6	0.2	1.3	0.3
Periodic abstinence-natural family planning	0.2	-	-	-	0.2	-	-	0.4	0.2	0.3	0.4	0.2	0.1	0.3	0.0	0.4	-
Withdrawal	2.0	1.5	2.3	1.8	2.5	0.8	3.1	5.3	2.6	2.4	1.0	2.5	1.5	2.2	1.6	3.0	1.3
Other methods[3]	1.1	(NA)	(NA)	(NA)	0.6	0.6	0.2	0.4	0.4	0.5	1.1	0.7	0.5	0.3	0.2	0.7	0.9
Not using contraception (noncontraceptive)	35.8	62.8	36.4	28.5	38.1	68.5	39.3	32.0	30.8	29.2	30.9	35.5	42.6	41.0	56.0	27.1	35.6
Surgically sterile-female	3.0	(NA)	(NA)	(NA)	1.5	-	-	0.4	0.9	2.1	4.9	1.7	1.5	0.9	0.4	2.1	3.0
Nonsurgically sterile-female or male[4]	1.7	1.1	2.0	(NA)	1.6	0.7	0.7	0.9	1.4	1.2	4.4	1.7	1.5	1.7	1.0	2.0	2.5
Pregnant or postpartum	4.6	3.1	6.4	2.2	5.3	3.5	9.5	8.4	6.9	3.8	0.8	4.6	5.9	6.9	2.3	7.5	2.2
Seeking pregnancy	4.0	1.5	6.4	1.9	4.2	1.2	2.8	5.5	7.0	5.1	3.3	3.9	4.2	5.2	0.8	6.9	2.0
Other nonuse	22.5	46.8	4.7	18.4	25.5	63.1	26.3	16.9	14.6	16.9	17.6	23.7	29.7	26.4	51.4	8.6	26.0
Never had intercourse or no intercourse in 3 months before interview	17.1	40.4	0.5	12.7	18.1	56.2	17.9	8.9	7.6	9.1	10.8	17.0	19.4	18.7	42.9	2.3	17.7
Had intercourse in 3 months before interview	5.2	6.4	4.2	5.7	7.4	6.9	8.4	8.0	7.0	7.7	6.7	6.7	10.2	7.7	8.5	6.3	8.2
All other nonusers	0.2	(NA)	(NA)	(NA)	-	-	-	-	-	0.1	0.1	-	0.1	-	-	-	0.1

- Represents or rounds to zero. X Not applicable. NA Not available.
[1] Includes other races, not shown separately. [2] Percents may not add to the total who were using contraception because more than one method could have been used in the month of interview. [3] Includes implants, injectables, morning-after-pill, suppository, Today(TM) sponge and less frequently used methods. [4] Persons sterile from illness, accident, or congenital conditions.

Source: U.S. National Center for Health Statistics, *Use of Contraception and Use of Family Planning Services in the United States: 1982-2002*.

Table 93. Abortions—Number, Rate, and Ratio by Race: 1975 to 2002

	All races				White				Black and other			
		Abortions				Abortions				Abortions		
Year	Women 15-44 years old (1,000)	Num-ber (1,000)	Rate per 1,000 women	Ratio per 1,000 live births[1]	Women 15-44 years old (1,000)	Num-ber (1,000)	Rate per 1,000 women	Ratio per 1,000 live births[1]	Women 15-44 years old (1,000)	Num-ber (1,000)	Rate per 1,000 women	Ratio per 1,000 live births[1]
1975...	47,606	1,034	21.7	331	40,857	701	17.2	276	6,749	333	49.3	565
1980...	53,048	1,554	29.3	428	44,942	1,094	24.3	376	8,106	460	56.5	642
1981...	53,901	1,577	29.3	430	45,494	1,108	24.3	377	8,407	470	55.9	645
1982...	54,679	1,574	28.8	428	46,049	1,095	23.8	373	8,630	479	55.5	646
1983[2]..	55,340	1,575	28.5	436	46,506	1,084	23.3	376	8,834	491	55.5	670
1984...	56,061	1,577	28.1	423	47,023	1,087	23.1	366	9,038	491	54.3	646
1985...	56,754	1,589	28.0	422	47,512	1,076	22.6	360	9,242	513	55.5	659
1986[2]..	57,483	1,574	27.4	416	48,010	1,045	21.8	350	9,473	529	55.9	661
1987...	57,964	1,559	27.1	405	48,288	1,017	21.1	338	9,676	542	56.0	648
1988...	58,192	1,591	27.3	401	48,325	1,026	21.2	333	9,867	565	57.3	638
1989[2]..	58,365	1,567	26.8	380	48,104	1,006	20.9	309	10,261	561	54.7	650
1990[2]..	58,700	1,609	27.4	389	48,224	1,039	21.5	318	10,476	570	54.4	655
1991...	59,305	1,557	26.2	379	48,560	982	20.2	303	10,745	574	53.5	661
1992...	59,417	1,529	25.7	380	48,435	943	19.5	298	10,982	585	53.3	681
1993[2]..	59,712	1,495	25.0	376	48,497	908	18.7	290	11,215	587	52.4	698
1994[2]..	60,020	1,423	23.7	362	48,592	856	17.6	275	11,429	567	49.6	696
1995...	60,368	1,359	22.5	350	48,719	817	16.8	265	11,648	542	46.6	684
1996...	60,704	1,360	22.4	349	48,837	797	16.3	258	11,867	563	47.5	699
1997...	61,041	1,335	21.9	341	48,942	777	15.9	251	12,099	558	46.1	684
1998...	61,326	1,319	21.5	334	49,012	762	15.5	244	12,313	557	45.2	678
1999...	61,475	1,315	21.4	327	48,974	743	15.2	234	12,501	572	45.8	674
2000...	61,631	1,313	21.3	324	48,936	733	15.0	230	12,695	580	45.7	676
2001...	61,673	1,303	21.1	325	48,868	723	14.8	229	12,805	579	45.3	686
2002...	62,044	1,293	20.8	319	(NA)	(NA)	(NA)	(NA)	(NA)	(NA)	(NA)	(NA)

NA Not available.   [1] Live births are those which occurred from July 1 of year shown through June 30 of the following year (to match time of conception with abortions). Births are classified by race of child 1975-1988, and by race of mother after 1988.   [2] Total numbers of abortions in 1983 and 1986 have been estimated by interpolation; 1989, 1990, 1993, and 1994 have been estimated using trends in CDC data.

Source: S. K. Henshaw and J. Van Vort, eds., *Abortion Factbook, 1992 Edition: Readings, Trends, and State and Local Data to 1988*, The Alan Guttmacher Institute, New York, NY, 1992 (copyright); S. K. Henshaw and J. Van Vort, *Abortion Services in the United States, 1991 and 1992. Family Planning Perspectives*, 26:100, 1994; L. B. Finer and S. K. Henshaw, Abortion Incidence and Services in the United States, 2000, *Perspectives on Sexual and Reproductive Health*, 356, 2003; and unpublished data.

Table 94. Abortions by Selected Characteristics: 1990 to 2001

[Number of abortions from surveys conducted by source; characteristics from the U.S. Centers for Disease Control's (CDC) annual abortion surveillance summaries, with adjustments for changes in states reporting data to the CDC each year. Total number of abortions in 1990 have been estimated using trends in CDC data]

Characteristic	Number (1,000)			Percent distribution			Abortion ratio[1]		
	1990	2000	2001	1990	2000	2001	1990	2000	2001
Total abortions..........	1,609	1,313	1,303	100	100	100	280	245	245
Age of woman:									
Less than 15 years old.......	13	9	8	1	1	1	515	512	519
15 to 19 years old.........	351	235	225	22	18	17	403	339	341
20 to 24 years old.........	532	430	434	33	33	33	328	296	298
25 to 29 years old.........	360	303	295	22	23	23	224	220	219
30 to 34 years old.........	216	190	194	13	15	15	196	169	171
35 to 39 years old.........	108	110	109	7	8	8	249	195	195
40 years old and over........	29	37	38	2	3	3	354	276	276
Race of woman:									
White.................	1,039	733	723	65	56	56	241	187	186
Black and other..........	570	580	579	35	44	44	396	403	407
Marital status of woman: [2]									
Married...............	341	246	238	21	19	18	104	84	80
Unmarried.............	1,268	1,067	1,065	79	81	82	516	443	456
Number of prior live births:									
None................	780	533	521	49	41	40	316	248	247
One.................	396	361	360	25	28	28	230	216	216
Two.................	280	260	261	17	20	20	292	278	279
Three...............	102	104	105	6	8	8	279	285	285
Four or more...........	50	56	56	3	4	4	223	250	248
Number of prior induced abortions:									
None................	891	699	700	55	53	54	(NA)	(NA)	(NA)
One.................	443	355	349	28	27	27	(NA)	(NA)	(NA)
Two or more...........	275	259	254	17	20	19	(NA)	(NA)	(NA)
Weeks of gestation:									
Less than 9 weeks..........	825	757	772	51	58	59	(NA)	(NA)	(NA)
9 to 10 weeks...........	416	266	251	26	20	19	(NA)	(NA)	(NA)
11 to 12 weeks..........	195	138	132	12	11	10	(NA)	(NA)	(NA)
13 weeks or more.........	173	153	147	11	12	11	(NA)	(NA)	(NA)

NA Not available.   [1] Number of abortions per 1,000 abortions and live births. Live births are those which occurred from July 1 of year shown through June 30 of the following year (to match time of conception with abortions).   [2] Separated women included with unmarried.

Source: S. K. Henshaw and J. Van Vort, eds., *Abortion Factbook, 1992 Edition: Readings, Trends, and State and Local Data to 1988*, The Alan Guttmacher Institute, New York, NY, 1992 (copyright); S. K. Henshaw and J. Van Vort, *Abortion Services in the United States, 1991 and 1992. Family Planning Perspectives*, 26:100, 1994; L. B. Finer and S. K. Henshaw, Abortion Incidence and Services in the United States, 2000, *Perspectives on Sexual and Reproductive Health*, 356, 2003; and unpublished data.

Vital Statistics 75

Table 95. Abortions—Number and Rate by State: 1992 and 2000

[Number of abortions from surveys of hospitals, clinics, and physicians identified as providers of abortion services conducted by The Alan Guttmacher Institute. Abortion rates are computed per 1,000 women, 15 to 44 years of age, on July 1 of specified year]

State	Number (1,000) 1992	Number (1,000) 2000	Rate [1] 1992	Rate [1] 2000	State	Number (1,000) 1992	Number (1,000) 2000	Rate [1] 1992	Rate [1] 2000
U.S.	1,529	1,313	25.7	21.3	MO	14	8	11.5	6.6
AL	17	14	18.1	14.3	MT	3	3	18.4	13.5
AK	2	2	16.5	11.7	NE	6	4	15.6	11.6
AZ	21	18	23.5	16.5	NV	13	14	43.3	32.2
AR	7	6	13.5	9.8	NH	4	3	14.6	11.2
CA	304	236	41.8	31.2	NJ	55	66	30.4	36.3
CO	20	16	23.6	15.9	NM	6	6	17.6	14.7
CT	20	15	26.0	21.1	NY	195	165	45.6	39.1
DE	6	5	34.9	31.3	NC	36	38	22.2	21.0
DC	21	10	133.1	68.1	ND	1	1	10.7	9.9
FL	85	103	29.3	31.9	OH	50	40	19.5	16.5
GA	40	32	23.7	16.9	OK	9	7	12.5	10.1
HI	12	6	46.0	22.1	OR	16	17	23.9	23.5
ID	2	2	7.2	7.0	PA	50	37	18.6	14.3
IL	68	64	25.2	23.2	RI	7	6	29.5	24.1
IN	16	12	12.0	9.4	SC	12	8	14.2	9.3
IA	7	6	11.3	9.8	SD	1	1	6.9	5.5
KS	13	12	22.4	21.4	TN	19	19	16.1	15.2
KY	10	5	11.4	5.3	TX	97	89	23.1	18.8
LA	14	13	13.4	13.0	UT	4	4	9.2	6.6
ME	4	3	14.9	9.9	VT	3	2	21.5	12.7
MD	31	35	26.2	29.0	VA	35	29	22.6	18.1
MA	41	30	28.1	21.4	WA	33	26	27.7	20.3
MI	56	46	25.1	21.6	WV	3	3	7.8	6.8
MN	16	15	15.6	13.5	WI	15	11	13.5	9.6
MS	8	4	12.4	5.9	WY	(Z)	(Z)	4.4	0.9

Z Represents less than 500.   [1] Rate per 1,000 women, 15 to 44 years old.

Source: S. K. Henshaw and J. Van Vort, *Abortion Services in the United States, 1991 and 1992, Family Planning Perspectives,* 26:100, 1994; and, L. B. Finer and S. K. Henshaw, *Abortion Incidence and Services in the United States in 2000, Perspectives on Sexual and Reproductive Health,* 35:6, 2003; and unpublished data.

Table 96. Expectation of Life at Birth, 1970 to 2003, and Projections, 2005 and 2010

[In years. Excludes deaths of nonresidents of the United States. See Appendix III]

Year	Total — Total	Total — Male	Total — Female	White — Total	White — Male	White — Female	Black — Total	Black — Male	Black — Female
1970	70.8	67.1	74.7	71.7	68.0	75.6	64.1	60.0	68.3
1975	72.6	68.8	76.6	73.4	69.5	77.3	66.8	62.4	71.3
1980	73.7	70.0	77.4	74.4	70.7	78.1	68.1	63.8	72.5
1982	74.5	70.8	78.1	75.1	71.5	78.7	69.4	65.1	73.6
1983	74.6	71.0	78.1	75.2	71.6	78.7	69.4	65.2	73.5
1984	74.7	71.1	78.2	75.3	71.8	78.7	69.5	65.3	73.6
1985	74.7	71.1	78.2	75.3	71.8	78.7	69.3	65.0	73.4
1986	74.7	71.2	78.2	75.4	71.9	78.8	69.1	64.8	73.4
1987	74.9	71.4	78.3	75.6	72.1	78.9	69.1	64.7	73.4
1988	74.9	71.4	78.3	75.6	72.2	78.9	68.9	64.4	73.2
1989	75.1	71.7	78.5	75.9	72.5	79.2	68.8	64.3	73.3
1990	75.4	71.8	78.8	76.1	72.7	79.4	69.1	64.5	73.6
1991	75.5	72.0	78.9	76.3	72.9	79.6	69.3	64.6	73.8
1992	75.8	72.3	79.1	76.5	73.2	79.8	69.6	65.0	73.9
1993	75.5	72.2	78.8	76.3	73.1	79.5	69.2	64.6	73.7
1994	75.7	72.3	79.0	76.4	73.2	79.6	69.6	64.9	74.1
1995	75.8	72.5	78.9	76.5	73.4	79.6	69.6	65.4	74.0
1996	76.1	73.0	79.0	76.8	73.8	79.6	70.3	66.1	74.2
1997	76.5	73.6	79.4	77.1	74.3	79.9	71.1	67.2	74.7
1998 [1]	76.7	73.8	79.5	77.3	74.5	80.0	71.3	67.6	74.8
1999	76.7	73.9	79.4	77.3	74.6	79.9	71.4	67.8	74.7
2000	77.0	74.3	79.7	77.6	74.9	80.1	71.7	68.3	75.2
2001	77.2	74.4	79.8	77.7	75.0	80.2	72.2	68.6	75.5
2002 [2]	77.3	74.5	79.9	77.7	75.1	80.3	72.3	68.8	75.6
2003 [2]	77.6	74.8	80.1	78.0	75.4	80.5	72.8	69.2	76.1
Projections [3]:									
2005	77.8	74.9	80.7	78.3	75.4	81.1	73.5	69.9	76.8
2010	78.5	75.6	81.4	79.0	76.1	81.8	74.5	70.9	77.8

[1] The 1998 life table values are based upon an 85-percent sample of deaths.   [2] Preliminary data.   [3] Based on middle mortality assumptions; for details, see source. Source: U.S. Census Bureau, Population Division Working Paper No. 38.

Source: Except as noted, U.S. National Center for Health Statistics, *Vital Statistics of the United States,* annual, and *National Vital Statistics Reports (NVSR)* (formerly *Monthly Vital Statistics Reports*).

Table 97. Selected Life Table Values: 1979 to 2002

[See Appendix III]

Age and sex	Total[1]								White								Black							
	1979-1981	1985	1990	1995	1999	2000	2001	2002	1979-1981	1985	1990	1995	1999	2000	2001	2002	1979-1981	1985	1990	1995	1999	2000	2001	2002
AVERAGE EXPECTATION OF LIFE IN YEARS																								
At birth: Male	70.1	71.1	71.8	72.5	73.9	74.3	74.4	74.5	70.8	71.8	72.7	73.4	74.6	74.9	75.0	75.1	64.1	65.0	64.5	65.4	67.8	68.3	68.6	68.8
Female	77.6	78.2	78.8	78.9	79.4	79.7	79.8	79.9	78.2	78.7	79.4	79.6	79.9	80.1	80.2	80.3	72.9	73.4	73.6	74.0	74.7	75.2	75.5	75.6
Age 20: Male	51.9	52.6	53.3	53.8	55.0	55.3	55.5	55.6	52.5	53.2	54.0	54.5	55.6	55.8	56.0	56.1	46.4	47.1	46.7	47.3	49.6	50.0	50.3	50.5
Female	59.0	59.3	59.8	59.9	60.2	60.5	60.6	60.7	59.4	59.8	60.3	60.3	60.7	60.9	60.9	61.0	54.9	55.3	55.5	55.5	56.2	56.6	56.8	57.0
Age 40: Male	33.6	34.2	35.0	35.6	36.5	36.7	37.0	37.0	34.0	34.7	35.6	36.1	36.9	37.1	37.3	37.4	29.5	29.8	30.1	30.6	31.9	32.3	32.6	32.8
Female	39.8	40.0	40.6	40.7	41.2	41.3	41.3	41.4	40.2	40.4	41.0	41.0	41.3	41.5	41.6	41.6	36.3	36.8	37.0	37.0	37.4	37.8	38.0	38.1
Age 50: Male	25.0	25.5	26.4	27.0	27.8	28.0	28.1	28.3	25.3	25.8	26.7	27.3	28.0	28.2	28.4	28.5	22.0	22.1	23.1	23.1	24.0	24.2	24.5	24.6
Female	30.7	30.8	31.3	31.4	31.7	32.0	32.1	32.2	31.0	31.1	31.6	31.7	32.0	32.2	32.3	32.4	27.8	27.8	28.2	28.5	28.7	29.1	29.4	29.5
Age 65: Male	14.2	14.5	15.1	15.6	16.1	16.2	16.4	16.6	14.3	14.5	15.2	15.7	16.1	16.3	16.5	16.6	13.3	13.0	13.2	13.7	14.3	14.2	14.4	14.6
Female	18.4	18.5	18.9	18.9	19.1	19.3	19.4	19.5	18.6	18.7	19.1	19.0	19.2	19.4	19.5	19.5	17.1	16.9	17.2	17.2	17.3	17.7	17.9	18.0
EXPECTED DEATHS PER 1,000 ALIVE AT SPECIFIED AGE[2]																								
At birth: Male	13.9	12.0	10.3	8.3	7.7	7.5	7.5	7.6	12.3	10.6	8.6	7.0	6.4	6.2	6.2	6.4	23.0	19.9	19.7	16.2	15.9	15.6	15.4	15.4
Female	11.2	9.4	8.2	6.8	6.4	6.2	6.1	6.3	9.7	8.0	6.6	5.6	5.2	5.1	5.1	5.1	19.3	16.5	16.3	13.8	13.2	12.7	12.5	13.2
Age 20: Male	1.8	1.5	1.6	(NA)	1.3	1.3	1.4	1.4	1.8	1.4	1.4	(NA)	1.2	1.2	1.2	1.3	2.2	1.9	2.7	(NA)	2.1	2.0	2.1	2.6
Female	0.6	0.5	0.5	(NA)	0.5	0.5	0.5	0.5	0.6	0.5	0.5	(NA)	0.4	0.4	0.4	0.4	0.7	0.7	0.7	(NA)	0.6	0.6	0.6	0.6
Age 40: Male	3.0	2.8	3.1	(NA)	2.6	2.5	2.6	2.7	3.0	2.5	2.7	(NA)	2.3	2.4	2.4	2.5	6.9	6.5	6.9	(NA)	4.8	4.6	4.3	4.3
Female	1.6	1.4	1.4	(NA)	1.4	1.4	1.5	1.5	1.4	1.3	1.2	(NA)	1.2	1.3	1.3	1.4	3.2	2.9	3.1	(NA)	2.9	2.8	2.9	2.6
Age 50: Male	7.8	6.8	6.2	(NA)	5.6	5.2	5.7	5.7	7.1	6.2	5.6	(NA)	5.1	5.2	5.2	5.7	14.9	13.3	13.8	(NA)	11.3	11.2	10.6	10.4
Female	4.2	3.8	3.5	(NA)	3.2	3.1	3.2	3.2	3.8	3.5	3.2	(NA)	2.9	2.9	2.9	2.8	7.7	6.8	6.8	(NA)	6.0	6.2	6.2	6.0
Age 65: Male	28.2	26.1	25.2	(NA)	20.5	19.8	19.3	18.9	27.4	25.2	23.0	(NA)	19.8	19.2	18.5	18.2	38.5	28.5	36.8	(NA)	30.5	29.6	30.0	29.3
Female	14.3	14.1	13.5	(NA)	12.8	12.8	12.3	12.1	13.6	13.5	12.8	(NA)	12.3	12.2	11.8	11.7	21.6	21.4	21.4	(NA)	18.3	18.2	18.0	17.8
NUMBER SURVIVING TO SPECIFIED AGE PER 1,000 BORN ALIVE																								
Age 20: Male	973	977	979	981	984	984	984	984	975	979	979	981	986	986	986	986	961	966	963	967	971	973	973	974
Female	982	985	986	987	989	989	989	989	984	986	988	987	990	990	991	991	972	976	976	978	980	981	982	981
Age 40: Male	933	941	938	940	952	953	953	954	940	946	946	940	953	954	954	958	885	897	880	885	917	918	920	920
Female	965	970	971	971	974	975	975	975	969	973	975	975	977	978	978	978	941	948	944	944	954	955	957	957
Age 50: Male	890	902	899	899	912	917	918	918	901	911	912	912	925	925	925	925	801	820	801	803	850	855	859	862
Female	941	948	950	950	954	954	954	954	947	953	957	957	960	960	959	959	896	908	904	902	915	915	918	918
Age 65: Male	706	727	741	750	777	779	785	786	724	744	760	750	793	794	799	786	551	571	571	581	633	640	656	657
Female	835	844	855	855	863	863	866	867	848	855	864	855	874	874	875	876	733	746	751	758	777	780	796	785

NA Not available. [1] Includes other races not shown separately. [2] See footnote 1, Table 98.

Source: U.S. National Center for Health Statistics, *U.S. Life Tables* and *Actuarial Tables, 1979-81*; *Vital Statistics of the United States*, annual; and unpublished data.

Table 98. Expectation of Life and Expected Deaths by Race, Sex, and Age: 2002

[See Appendix III]

Age (years)	Expectation of life in years					Expected deaths per 1,000 alive at specified age [1]				
	Total	White Male	White Female	Black Male	Black Female	Total	White Male	White Female	Black Male	Black Female
At birth	77.3	75.1	80.3	68.8	75.6	6.97	6.42	5.12	15.40	13.22
1	76.8	74.6	79.7	68.8	75.6	0.47	0.47	0.38	0.82	0.61
2	75.8	73.6	78.7	67.9	74.6	0.32	0.33	0.26	0.54	0.41
3	74.9	72.6	77.7	66.9	73.7	0.24	0.25	0.18	0.43	0.27
4	73.9	71.7	76.8	66.0	72.7	0.20	0.21	0.15	0.37	0.27
5	72.9	70.7	75.8	65.0	71.7	0.18	0.17	0.15	0.26	0.21
6	71.9	69.7	74.8	64.0	70.7	0.14	0.16	0.12	0.20	0.19
7	70.9	68.7	73.8	63.0	69.7	0.14	0.15	0.11	0.19	0.18
8	69.9	67.7	72.8	62.0	68.7	0.15	0.15	0.13	0.27	0.17
9	68.9	66.7	71.8	61.0	67.8	0.15	0.14	0.12	0.28	0.19
10	67.9	65.7	70.8	60.1	66.8	0.15	0.16	0.11	0.25	0.20
11	67.0	64.7	69.8	59.1	65.8	0.15	0.16	0.12	0.27	0.19
12	66.0	63.8	68.8	58.1	64.8	0.19	0.20	0.13	0.35	0.22
13	65.0	62.8	67.8	57.1	63.8	0.23	0.24	0.18	0.35	0.21
14	64.0	61.8	66.8	56.1	62.8	0.27	0.30	0.20	0.46	0.25
15	63.0	60.8	65.9	55.2	61.8	0.35	0.43	0.25	0.52	0.28
16	62.0	59.8	64.9	54.2	60.9	0.57	0.73	0.41	0.91	0.33
17	61.1	58.9	63.9	53.2	59.9	0.68	0.89	0.45	1.13	0.42
18	60.1	57.9	62.9	52.3	58.9	0.85	1.15	0.46	1.65	0.51
19	59.2	57.0	62.0	51.4	57.9	0.94	1.33	0.46	1.91	0.51
20	58.2	56.1	61.0	50.5	57.0	0.93	1.29	0.44	2.06	0.60
21	57.3	55.1	60.0	49.6	56.0	0.99	1.34	0.49	2.26	0.66
22	56.3	54.2	59.0	48.7	55.0	0.94	1.25	0.42	2.31	0.71
23	55.4	53.3	58.1	47.8	54.1	0.95	1.30	0.42	2.34	0.72
24	54.4	52.3	57.1	46.9	53.1	0.95	1.26	0.46	2.44	0.70
25	53.5	51.4	56.1	46.0	52.1	0.93	1.20	0.46	2.48	0.81
26	52.5	50.5	55.1	45.1	51.2	0.95	1.23	0.46	2.58	0.89
27	51.6	49.5	54.2	44.3	50.2	0.91	1.15	0.44	2.59	0.93
28	50.6	48.6	53.2	43.4	49.3	0.94	1.17	0.53	2.44	0.93
29	49.7	47.6	52.2	42.5	48.3	0.99	1.23	0.52	2.67	1.23
30	48.7	46.7	51.2	41.6	47.4	1.02	1.29	0.56	2.56	1.15
31	47.8	45.8	50.3	40.7	46.4	1.06	1.32	0.59	2.72	1.21
32	46.8	44.8	49.3	39.8	45.5	1.06	1.25	0.63	2.55	1.37
33	45.9	43.9	48.3	38.9	44.6	1.19	1.47	0.70	2.70	1.49
34	44.9	42.9	47.4	38.0	43.6	1.25	1.48	0.76	3.12	1.58
35	44.0	42.0	46.4	37.1	42.7	1.37	1.58	0.86	3.46	1.75
36	43.0	41.1	45.4	36.2	41.8	1.45	1.68	0.93	3.52	1.85
37	42.1	40.1	44.5	35.4	40.8	1.57	1.87	1.00	3.36	1.99
38	41.2	39.2	43.5	34.5	39.9	1.72	2.03	1.08	3.93	2.28
39	40.2	38.3	42.6	33.6	39.0	1.91	2.23	1.29	4.02	2.62
40	39.3	37.4	41.6	32.8	38.1	2.07	2.51	1.36	4.25	2.62
41	38.4	36.5	40.7	31.9	37.2	2.24	2.65	1.47	4.68	3.13
42	37.5	35.6	39.7	31.0	36.3	2.36	2.77	1.57	4.92	3.11
43	36.6	34.7	38.8	30.2	35.4	2.63	3.07	1.77	5.41	3.82
44	35.7	33.8	37.9	29.4	34.6	2.83	3.35	1.85	5.87	4.03
45	34.8	32.9	36.9	28.5	33.7	3.06	3.56	2.07	6.65	4.25
46	33.9	32.0	36.0	27.7	32.8	3.30	3.96	2.13	7.21	4.41
47	33.0	31.1	35.1	26.9	32.0	3.51	4.14	2.31	7.74	4.78
48	32.1	30.2	34.2	26.1	31.1	3.89	4.53	2.55	9.07	5.42
49	31.2	29.4	33.3	25.4	30.3	4.13	4.87	2.73	9.61	5.69
50	30.3	28.5	32.4	24.6	29.5	4.42	5.23	2.84	10.43	6.19
51	29.5	27.7	31.4	23.8	28.7	4.82	5.66	3.18	11.47	6.63
52	28.6	26.8	30.5	23.1	27.8	5.00	5.91	3.29	11.74	6.59
53	27.8	26.0	29.6	22.4	27.0	5.55	6.47	3.83	12.88	7.14
54	26.9	25.1	28.8	21.7	26.2	5.85	6.76	4.08	13.82	7.91
55	26.1	24.3	27.9	21.0	25.4	6.72	7.87	4.74	15.55	9.02
56	25.2	23.5	27.0	20.3	24.7	6.62	7.77	4.65	15.06	8.61
57	24.4	22.7	26.1	19.6	23.9	7.62	8.87	5.54	16.68	9.68
58	23.6	21.9	25.3	18.9	23.1	8.34	9.72	6.04	18.48	10.77
59	22.8	21.1	24.4	18.3	22.3	9.43	11.12	6.86	20.25	11.83
60	22.0	20.3	23.6	17.6	21.6	9.75	11.38	7.22	21.16	11.82
61	21.2	19.6	22.7	17.0	20.8	10.88	12.84	8.02	22.43	13.52
62	20.4	18.8	21.9	16.4	20.1	11.91	14.14	8.79	24.84	14.02
63	19.7	18.1	21.1	15.8	19.4	12.96	15.41	9.67	26.03	15.43
64	18.9	17.3	20.3	15.2	18.7	14.10	16.62	10.71	28.17	16.37
65	18.2	16.6	19.5	14.6	18.0	15.31	18.18	11.65	29.34	17.78
70	14.7	13.3	15.8	11.8	14.7	23.64	28.63	18.56	40.82	25.78
75	11.5	10.3	12.3	9.5	11.7	36.58	44.65	29.54	59.17	39.44
80	8.8	7.7	9.8	7.5	9.2	57.60	69.81	49.14	87.34	56.93

[1] Based on the proportion of the cohort who are alive at the beginning of an indicated age interval who will die before reaching the end of that interval. For example, out of every 1,000 people alive and exactly 50 years old at the beginning of the period, between 4 and 5 (4.42) will die before reaching their 51st birthdays.

Source: U.S. National Center for Health Statistics, *Vital Statistics of the United States*, annual; and *National Vital Statistics Report*, Vol. 53, No. 5, and unpublished data.

78   Vital Statistics

Table 99. **Deaths and Death Rates by Sex and Race: 1970 to 2002**

[1,921 represents 1,921,000. Rates are per 1,000 population for specified groups. Excludes deaths of nonresidents of the United States and fetal deaths. For explanation of age-adjustment, see text, this section. The standard population for age-adjustment is the projected year 2000 population of the United States. See Appendix III. Data for Hispanic origin and specified races other than White and Black should be interpreted with caution because of inconsistencies between reporting Hispanic origin and race on death certificates and censuses and surveys]

Sex and race	1970	1980	1990	1995	1996	1997	1998	1999	2000	2001	2002
Deaths [1] (1,000)......	1,921	1,990	2,148	2,312	2,315	2,314	2,337	2,391	2,403	2,416	2,443
Male [1] (1,000).........	1,078	1,075	1,113	1.173	1,164	1.154	1,157	1,175	1,178	1,183	1,199
Female [1] (1,000)........	843	915	1,035	1,139	1,151	1,160	1,180	1,216	1,226	1,233	1,244
White (1,000).........	1,682	1,739	1,853	1,987	1,993	1,996	2,016	2,061	2,071	2,080	2,103
Male (1,000).........	942	934	951	997	992	987	990	1,005	1,007	1,011	1,025
Female (1,000)........	740	805	902	990	1,001	1,010	1,026	1,056	1,064	1,068	1,077
Black (1,000)...........	226	233	265	286	282	277	278	285	286	288	290
Male (1,000).........	128	130	145	154	149	144	143	146	145	146	147
Female (1,000)........	98	103	120	132	133	132	135	139	141	142	143
American Indian, Eskimo,											
Aleut (1,000).........	6	7	8	10	10	11	11	11	11	12	12
Male (1,000).........	3	4	5	6	6	6	6	6	6	6	7
Female (1,000)........	2	3	3	4	5	5	5	5	5	6	6
Asian and Pacific Islander											
(1,000)...............	(NA)	11	21	28	30	31	32	34	35	37	38
Male (1,000).........	(NA)	7	12	16	17	17	18	18	19	20	20
Female (1,000)........	(NA)	4	9	12	13	14	14	15	16	17	18
Hispanic origin (1,000).....	(NA)	(NA)	(NA)	(NA)	(NA)	95	98	104	107	113	117
Male (1,000).........	(NA)	(NA)	(NA)	(NA)	(NA)	54	56	58	60	63	66
Female (1,000)........	(NA)	(NA)	(NA)	(NA)	(NA)	41	43	46	47	50	51
Non-Hispanic White origin											
(1,000)...............	(NA)	(NA)	(NA)	(NA)	(NA)	1,895	1,913	1,953	1,960	1,963	1,982
Male (1,000).........	(NA)	(NA)	(NA)	(NA)	(NA)	930	932	945	945	946	958
Female (1,000)........	(NA)	(NA)	(NA)	(NA)	(NA)	966	981	1,008	1,015	1,017	1,024
Death rates [1]........	9.5	8.8	8.6	8.7	8.6	8.5	8.5	8.6	8.5	8.5	8.5
Male [1]..............	10.9	9.8	9.2	9.0	8.8	8.6	8.6	8.6	8.5	8.5	8.5
Female [1].............	8.1	7.9	8.1	8.4	8.4	8.3	8.4	8.5	8.6	8.5	8.5
White...............	9.5	8.9	8.9	9.0	9.0	8.9	8.9	9.0	9.0	9.0	9.0
Male...............	10.9	9.8	9.3	9.3	9.1	8.9	8.9	9.1	8.9	8.8	8.8
Female..............	8.1	8.1	8.5	8.9	8.9	8.9	8.9	9.2	9.1	9.1	9.1
Black...............	10.0	8.8	8.7	8.5	8.2	7.9	7.8	7.9	7.8	7.7	7.7
Male...............	11.9	10.3	10.1	9.8	9.2	8.7	8.5	8.8	8.3	8.2	8.2
Female..............	8.3	7.3	7.5	7.6	7.3	7.2	7.2	7.6	7.3	7.3	7.2
American Indian, Eskimo,											
Aleut...............	(NA)	4.9	4.0	4.1	4.0	4.0	4.0	4.0	3.8	3.9	4.0
Male...............	(NA)	6.0	4.8	4.6	4.4	4.6	4.4	4.3	4.2	4.2	4.4
Female..............	(NA)	3.8	3.3	3.6	3.6	3.5	3.5	3.7	3.5	3.6	3.7
Asian and Pacific Islander ...	(NA)	3.0	2.8	2.9	2.9	2.9	2.9	3.0	3.0	3.0	3.0
Male...............	(NA)	3.8	3.3	3.4	3.4	3.4	3.4	3.3	3.3	3.4	3.3
Female..............	(NA)	2.2	2.3	2.5	2.5	2.5	2.5	2.6	2.6	2.7	2.7
Hispanic origin..........	(NA)	(NA)	(NA)	(NA)	(NA)	3.1	3.0	3.1	3.0	3.1	3.0
Male...............	(NA)	(NA)	4.1	(NA)	(NA)	3.4	3.3	3.7	3.3	3.3	3.3
Female..............	(NA)	(NA)	2.9	(NA)	(NA)	2.7	2.7	2.9	2.7	2.8	2.7
Non-Hispanic White	(NA)	(NA)	(NA)	(NA)	(NA)	9.7	9.7	9.9	9.9	9.9	10.0
Male...............	(NA)	(NA)	(NA)	(NA)	(NA)	9.7	9.7	9.8	9.8	9.8	9.8
Female..............	(NA)	(NA)	(NA)	(NA)	(NA)	9.6	9.8	10.0	10.1	10.1	10.1
Age-adjusted death rates [1]...........	12.2	10.4	9.4	9.2	8.9	8.8	8.7	8.8	8.7	8.5	8.5
Male [1]..............	15.4	13.5	12.0	11.5	11.2	10.9	10.7	10.7	10.5	10.3	10.1
Female [1].............	9.7	8.2	7.5	7.5	7.3	7.3	7.2	7.3	7.3	7.2	7.2
White...............	11.9	10.1	9.1	8.9	8.7	8.6	8.5	8.5	8.5	8.4	8.3
Male...............	15.1	13.2	11.7	11.1	10.8	10.6	10.4	10.4	10.3	10.1	9.9
Female..............	9.4	8.0	7.3	7.3	7.1	7.1	7.1	7.2	7.2	7.1	7.0
Black...............	15.2	13.1	12.5	12.2	11.8	11.4	11.3	11.4	11.2	11.0	10.8
Male...............	18.7	17.0	16.4	15.8	15.2	14.6	14.3	14.3	14.0	13.8	13.4
Female..............	12.3	10.3	9.8	9.7	9.4	9.2	9.2	9.3	9.3	9.1	9.0
American Indian, Eskimo,											
Aleut...............	(NA)	8.7	7.2	7.2	7.6	7.7	7.7	7.8	7.1	6.9	6.8
Male...............	(NA)	11.1	9.2	8.6	9.2	9.7	9.4	9.3	8.4	8.0	7.9
Female..............	(NA)	6.6	5.6	5.9	6.4	6.3	6.4	6.7	6.0	5.9	5.8
Asian and Pacific Islander ...	(NA)	5.9	5.8	6.2	5.4	5.3	5.2	5.2	5.1	4.9	4.7
Male...............	(NA)	7.9	7.2	7.9	6.8	6.6	6.5	6.4	6.2	6.0	5.8
Female..............	(NA)	4.3	4.7	4.9	4.4	4.3	4.3	4.3	4.2	4.1	4.0
Hispanic origin..........	(NA)	(NA)	(NA)	(NA)	(NA)	6.7	6.7	6.8	6.7	6.6	6.3
Male...............	(NA)	(NA)	8.9	(NA)	(NA)	8.4	8.3	7.4	8.2	8.0	7.7
Female..............	(NA)	(NA)	5.4	(NA)	(NA)	5.4	5.4	4.9	5.5	5.4	5.2
Non-Hispanic White	(NA)	(NA)	(NA)	(NA)	(NA)	8.6	8.5	8.6	8.6	8.4	8.4
Male...............	(NA)	(NA)	(NA)	(NA)	(NA)	10.6	10.5	10.5	10.4	10.1	10.0
Female..............	(NA)	(NA)	(NA)	(NA)	(NA)	7.1	7.1	7.2	7.2	7.1	7.1

NA Not available. [1] Includes other races, not shown separately.

Source: U.S. National Center for Health Statistics, Vital Statistics of the United States, annual; and National Vital Statistics Reports (NVSR) (formerly Monthly Vital Statistics Report).

Vital Statistics 79

Table 100. **Death Rates by Age: 1940 to 2003**

[Rates per 100,000 population. See Appendix III]

Characteristic	All ages[1]	Under 1 year	1-4 years	5-14 years	15-24 years	25-34 years	35-44 years	45-54 years	55-64 years	65-74 years	75-84 years	85 years and older
MALE:												
1940	1,197.4	6,189.8	311.5	117.8	228.9	338.4	588.1	1,248.8	2,612.0	5,462.3	12,126.4	24,639.0
1950	1,106.1	3,728.0	151.7	70.9	167.9	216.5	428.8	1,067.1	2,395.3	4,931.4	10,426.0	21,636.0
1960	1,104.5	3,059.3	119.5	55.7	152.1	187.9	372.8	992.2	2,309.5	4,914.4	10,178.4	21,186.3
1970	1,090.3	2,410.0	93.2	50.5	188.5	215.3	402.6	958.5	2,282.7	4,873.8	10,010.2	17,821.5
1980	976.9	1,428.5	72.6	36.7	172.3	196.1	299.2	767.3	1,815.1	4,105.2	8,816.7	18,801.1
1990	918.4	1,082.8	52.4	28.5	147.4	204.3	310.4	610.3	1,553.4	3,491.5	7,888.6	18,056.6
2000[2]	853.0	806.5	35.9	20.9	114.9	138.6	255.2	542.8	1,230.7	2,979.6	6,972.6	17,501.4
2003[2]	837.9	788.6	34.8	19.6	114.4	139.5	252.3	548.0	1,160.2	2,771.2	6,632.9	15,774.7
White:												
1980	983.3	1,230.3	66.1	35.0	167.0	171.3	257.4	698.9	1,728.5	4,035.7	8,829.8	19,097.3
1985	963.6	1,056.5	52.8	30.1	134.2	158.8	243.1	611.7	1,625.8	3,770.7	8,486.1	18,980.1
1990	930.9	896.1	45.9	26.4	131.3	176.1	268.2	548.7	1,467.2	3,397.7	7,844.9	18,268.3
1995	932.1	717.5	38.8	24.5	122.3	177.7	287.7	534.6	1,330.8	3,199.0	7,320.6	18,152.9
2000[2]	887.8	667.6	32.6	19.8	105.8	124.1	233.6	496.9	1,163.3	2,905.7	6,933.1	17,716.4
2003[2]	875.8	669.4	31.2	18.3	107.0	127.1	235.1	505.9	1,098.4	2,708.5	6,618.7	16,026.4
Black:												
1980	1,034.1	2,586.7	110.5	47.4	209.1	407.3	689.8	1,479.9	2,873.0	5,131.1	9,231.6	16,098.8
1985	989.3	2,219.9	90.1	42.3	173.6	351.9	630.2	1,292.9	2,779.8	5,172.4	9,262.3	15,774.2
1990	1,008.0	2,112.4	85.8	41.2	252.2	430.8	699.6	1,261.0	2,618.4	4,946.1	9,129.5	16,954.9
1995	980.7	1,590.8	77.5	40.2	249.2	416.5	721.2	1,273.0	2,437.5	4,610.5	8,778.8	16,728.7
2000[2]	834.1	1,567.6	54.5	28.2	181.4	261.0	453.0	1,017.7	2,080.1	4,253.5	8,486.0	16,791.0
2003[2]	807.1	1,419.5	53.1	26.3	168.3	252.7	422.3	980.5	1,997.8	3,961.6	7,976.1	14,825.2
Hispanic[3]:												
1985	374.6	1,044.6	53.8	23.0	147.5	202.1	290.1	495.7	1,129.4	2,484.9	5,696.1	12,156.2
1990	411.6	921.8	53.8	26.0	159.3	234.0	341.8	533.9	1,123.7	2,368.2	5,369.1	12,272.1
2000[2]	331.3	637.1	31.5	17.9	107.7	120.2	211.0	439.0	965.7	2,287.9	5,395.3	13,086.2
2003[2]	324.2	679.5	32.1	18.3	107.9	114.1	184.0	422.7	912.6	2,090.4	4,865.6	10,816.8
Non-Hispanic White[3]:												
2003[2]	978.4	657.0	30.4	18.0	104.9	129.0	242.0	511.1	1,107.1	2,742.1	6,694.8	16,232.3
Asian or Pacific Islander[3]:												
2003[2]	326.4	521.4	26.1	14.9	54.0	53.0	95.4	237.5	545.7	1,476.4	4,007.7	10,242.6
American Indian[3]:												
2003[2]	455.6	930.2	54.2	28.3	151.4	182.8	337.2	576.1	1,058.3	2,237.3	4,635.5	9,567.2
FEMALE:												
1940	954.6	4,774.3	267.0	89.1	181.1	274.3	452.2	860.7	1,800.4	4,222.2	10,368.6	22,759.1
1950	823.5	2,854.6	126.7	48.9	89.1	142.7	290.3	641.5	1,404.8	3,333.2	8,399.6	19,194.7
1960	809.2	2,321.3	98.4	37.3	61.3	106.6	229.4	526.7	1,196.4	2,871.8	7,633.1	19,008.4
1970	807.8	1,863.7	75.4	31.8	68.1	101.6	231.1	517.2	1,098.9	2,579.7	6,677.6	15,518.0
1980	785.3	1,141.7	54.7	24.2	57.5	75.9	159.3	412.9	934.3	2,144.7	5,440.1	14,746.9
1990	812.0	855.7	41.0	19.3	49.0	74.2	137.9	342.7	878.8	1,991.2	4,883.1	14,274.3
2000[2]	855.0	663.4	28.7	15.0	43.1	63.5	143.2	312.5	772.2	1,921.2	4,814.7	14,719.2
2003[2]	842.8	628.0	27.2	13.9	44.0	63.7	146.6	316.8	730.6	1,820.8	4,676.5	14,074.4
White:												
1980	806.1	962.5	49.3	22.9	55.5	65.4	138.2	372.7	876.2	2,066.6	5,401.7	14,979.6
1985	840.1	799.3	40.0	19.5	48.1	59.4	121.9	341.7	869.1	2,027.1	5,111.6	14,745.4
1990	846.9	690.0	36.1	17.9	45.9	61.5	117.4	309.3	822.7	1,923.5	4,839.1	14,400.6
1995	891.3	571.6	31.2	16.6	44.3	64.3	125.8	298.6	788.4	1,924.5	4,831.1	14,639.1
2000[2]	912.3	550.5	25.5	14.1	41.1	55.1	125.7	281.4	730.9	1,868.3	4,785.3	14,890.7
2003[2]	902.5	531.1	24.9	12.8	42.7	57.2	131.0	285.7	692.7	1,780.1	4,674.9	14,266.1
Black:												
1980	733.3	2,123.7	84.4	30.5	70.5	150.0	333.9	768.2	1,561.0	3,057.4	6,212.1	12,367.2
1985	734.2	1,821.4	71.1	28.6	59.6	137.6	276.5	667.6	1,532.5	2,967.8	6,078.0	12,703.0
1990	747.9	1,735.5	67.6	27.5	68.7	159.5	298.6	639.4	1,452.6	2,865.7	5,688.3	13,309.5
1995	759.0	1,342.0	62.9	26.5	70.3	166.6	327.7	619.0	1,350.3	2,823.7	5,840.3	13,472.2
2000[2]	733.0	1,279.8	45.3	20.0	58.3	121.8	271.9	588.3	1,227.2	2,689.6	5,696.5	13,941.3
2003[2]	713.4	1,133.1	39.2	19.3	54.5	111.4	267.3	579.7	1,168.1	2,468.1	5,366.0	13,500.8
Hispanic[3]:												
1985	251.9	791.4	42.3	16.0	36.2	56.3	100.0	251.3	619.7	1,449.5	3,551.8	10,228.6
1990	285.4	746.6	42.1	17.3	40.6	62.9	109.3	253.3	607.5	1,453.8	3,351.3	10,098.7
2000[2]	274.6	553.6	27.5	13.4	31.7	43.4	100.5	223.8	548.4	1,423.2	3,624.5	11,202.8
2003[2]	275.5	563.2	24.8	12.0	35.4	41.2	92.9	216.4	524.6	1,322.6	3,478.2	9,931.3
Non-Hispanic White[3]:												
2003[2]	1,008.5	512.6	24.6	12.8	43.8	60.7	136.2	291.8	704.2	1,809.0	4,725.5	14,412.3
Asian or Pacific Islander[3]:												
2003[2]	276.9	444.3	20.6	12.1	26.4	29.3	57.6	149.2	355.5	991.9	2,657.8	8,211.7
American Indian[3]:												
2003[2]	387.5	661.7	44.1	17.5	61.1	87.8	190.9	363.8	787.6	1,721.9	3,870.5	7,842.2

[1] Figures for age not stated are included in "All ages" but not distributed among age groups. [2] Preliminary data. [3] The death rates for Hispanic origin and specified races other than White and Black should be interpreted with caution because of inconsistencies between reporting Hispanic origin and race on death certificates and censuses and surveys.

Source: U.S. National Center for Health Statistics, Vital Statistics of the United States, annual.

Table 101. Age-Adjusted Death Rates by Race and Sex: 1940 to 2002

[Age adjusted rates per 100,000 population; see headnote, Table 99. Populations enumerated as of April 1 for census years and estimated as of July 1 for all other years. Beginning 1970, excludes deaths of nonresidents of the United States. Data for specified races other than White and Black should be interpreted with caution because of inconsistencies reporting race on death certificates and on censuses and surveys. See Appendix III]

Sex and Race	1940	1950	1960	1970	1980	1990	1995	2000	2001	2002
ALL RACES [1]										
Total	1,785.0	1,446.0	1,339.2	1,222.6	1,039.1	938.7	918.5	869.0	854.5	845.3
Male	1,976.0	1,674.2	1,609.0	1,542.1	1,348.1	1,202.8	1,150.3	1,053.8	1,029.1	1,013.7
Female	1,599.4	1,236.0	1,105.3	971.4	817.9	750.9	748.2	731.4	721.8	715.2
WHITE										
Total	1,735.3	1,410.8	1,311.3	1,193.3	1,012.7	909.8	890.0	849.8	836.5	829.0
Male	1,925.2	1,642.5	1,586.0	1,513.7	1,317.6	1,165.9	1,112.7	1,029.4	1,006.1	992.9
Female	1,550.4	1,198.0	1,074.4	944.0	796.1	728.8	726.6	715.3	706.7	701.3
BLACK										
Total	(NA)	(NA)	1,577.5	1,518.1	1,314.8	1,250.3	1,224.5	1,121.4	1,101.2	1,083.3
Male	(NA)	(NA)	1,811.1	1,873.9	1,697.8	1,644.5	1,582.3	1,403.5	1,375.0	1,341.4
Female	(NA)	(NA)	1,369.7	1,228.7	1,033.3	975.1	970.1	927.6	912.5	901.8
AMERICAN INDIAN [2]										
Total	(NA)	(NA)	(NA)	(NA)	867.0	716.3	716.5	709.3	686.7	677.4
Male	(NA)	(NA)	(NA)	(NA)	1,111.5	916.2	864.2	841.5	798.9	794.2
Female	(NA)	(NA)	(NA)	(NA)	662.4	561.8	592.8	604.5	594.0	581.1
ASIAN OR PACIFIC ISLANDER [3]										
Total	(NA)	(NA)	(NA)	(NA)	589.9	582.0	616.0	506.4	492.1	474.4
Male	(NA)	(NA)	(NA)	(NA)	786.5	716.4	788.1	624.2	597.4	578.4
Female	(NA)	(NA)	(NA)	(NA)	425.9	469.3	488.4	416.8	412.0	395.9
NON-HISPANIC WHITE										
Total	(NA)	(NA)	(NA)	(NA)	(NA)	(NA)	(NA)	855.5	842.9	837.5
Male	(NA)	(NA)	(NA)	(NA)	(NA)	(NA)	(NA)	1,035.4	1,012.8	1,002.2
Female	(NA)	(NA)	(NA)	(NA)	(NA)	(NA)	(NA)	721.5	713.5	709.9

NA Not available. [1] For 1940-91 includes deaths among races not shown separately; see Other races and Race not stated in the technical notes for information for 1992 to present. [2] Includes Aleuts and Eskimos. [3] Includes Chinese, Filipino, Hawaiian, Japanese, and Other Asian or Pacific Islander.

Source: U.S. National Center for Health Statistics, *Vital Statistics of the United States*, annual.

Table 102. Death Rates by Hispanic Origin, Age and Sex: 1990 to 2003

[Rates per 100,000 population. Rates are based on populations enumerated as of April 1 for census years and estimated as of July 1 for all other years. Excludes deaths of nonresidents of the United States. Data for Hispanic origin should be interpreted with caution because of inconsistencies between reporting Hispanic origin and race on death certificates and censuses and surveys]

Year	Hispanic male				Hispanic female				Non-Hispanic White male		Non-Hispanic White female	
	1990	2000	2002	2003 [1]	1990	2000	2002	2003 [1]	2002	2003[1]	2002	2003 [1]
Age adjusted [2]	886.4	818.1	766.7	734.8	537.1	546.0	518.3	508.8	1,002.2	983.3	709.9	702.4
Crude	411.6	331.3	328.7	324.2	285.4	274.6	274.0	275.5	983.9	978.4	1,010.6	1,008.5
Under 1	921.8	637.1	644.0	679.5	746.6	553.6	539.1	563.2	643.5	657.0	504.8	512.6
1-4 years	53.8	31.5	34.2	32.1	42.1	27.5	25.3	24.8	30.3	30.4	23.8	24.6
5-14 years	26.0	17.9	17.4	18.3	17.3	13.4	13.5	12.0	18.3	18.0	13.6	12.8
15-24 years	159.3	107.7	114.4	107.9	40.6	31.7	34.1	35.4	106.7	104.9	43.8	43.8
25-34 years	234.0	120.2	112.5	114.1	62.9	43.4	40.0	41.2	130.9	129.0	60.3	60.7
35-44 years	341.8	211.0	192.5	184.0	109.3	100.5	94.9	92.9	244.9	242.0	138.3	136.2
45-54 years	533.9	439.0	423.4	422.7	253.3	223.8	219.8	216.4	509.9	511.1	292.1	291.8
55-64 years	1,123.7	965.7	937.4	912.6	607.5	548.4	524.3	524.6	1,126.5	1,107.1	710.5	704.2
65-74 years	2,368.2	2,287.9	2,193.4	2,090.4	1,453.8	1,423.2	1,368.7	1,322.6	2,824.1	2,742.1	1,846.0	1,809.0
75-84 years	5,369.1	5,395.3	5,043.5	4,865.6	3,351.3	3,624.5	3,526.4	3,478.2	6,801.7	6,694.8	4,787.9	4,725.5
85 years and over	12,272.1	13,086.2	11,674.1	10,816.8	10,098.7	11,202.8	10,186.0	9,931.3	16,641.9	16,232.3	14,504.3	14,412.3

[1] Preliminary data. [2] See headnote, Table 99.

Source: U.S. National Center for Health Statistics, *Vital Statistics of the United States*, annual.

Vital Statistics 81

Table 103. Deaths and Death Rates by State and Outlying Areas: 1990 to 2003

[2,148 represents 2,148,000. By state of residence. Excludes deaths of nonresidents of the United States, except as noted. Caution should be used in comparing death rates by state; rates are affected by the population composition of the area. For explanation of age adjustment, see table 99. See also Appendix III]

State	Number of deaths (1,000)						Crude rate per 1,000 population [1]						Age adjuted rate, 2003
	1990	1995	2000	2001	2002	2003 [2]	1990	1995	2000	2001	2002	2003	
United States ...	2,148	2,312	2,403	2,416	2,443	2,443	8.6	8.7	8.5	8.5	8.5	8.4	8.3
Alabama.........	39	42	45	45	46	47	9.7	10.0	10.1	10.1	10.3	10.4	10.0
Alaska	2	3	3	3	3	3	4.0	4.2	4.6	4.7	4.7	4.9	8.3
Arizona.........	29	35	41	41	43	43	7.9	8.4	7.9	7.7	7.8	7.8	7.9
Arkansas	25	27	28	28	29	28	10.5	10.8	10.6	10.3	10.5	10.2	9.4
California	214	224	230	234	235	(NA)	7.2	7.1	6.8	6.8	6.7	(NA)	(NA)
Colorado.........	22	25	27	28	29	30	6.6	6.7	6.3	6.4	6.5	6.5	7.9
Connecticut.......	28	29	30	30	30	29	8.4	9.0	8.8	8.7	8.7	8.4	7.3
Delaware	6	6	7	7	7	7	8.7	8.8	8.8	8.9	8.5	8.6	8.4
Dist. of Columbia ...	7	7	6	6	6	6	12.0	12.4	10.5	10.4	10.2	9.8	9.7
Florida.........	134	153	164	167	168	169	10.4	10.8	10.3	10.2	10.0	9.9	7.8
Georgia	52	58	64	64	65	66	8.0	8.1	7.8	7.7	7.6	7.7	9.5
Hawaii	7	8	8	8	9	9	6.1	6.4	6.8	6.8	7.1	7.1	6.5
Idaho...........	7	9	10	10	10	10	7.4	7.3	7.4	7.4	7.4	7.6	8.0
Illinois	103	108	107	105	107	(NA)	9.0	9.2	8.6	8.4	8.5	(NA)	(NA)
Indiana.........	50	53	55	55	55	56	8.9	9.2	9.1	9.0	9.0	9.1	9.0
Iowa	27	28	28	28	28	28	9.7	9.9	9.6	9.5	9.5	9.5	7.7
Kansas.........	22	24	25	25	25	25	9.0	9.3	9.2	9.1	9.2	9.0	8.2
Kentucky	35	37	40	40	41	40	9.5	9.6	9.8	9.8	9.9	9.8	9.8
Louisiana	38	40	41	42	42	43	8.9	9.1	9.2	9.3	9.4	9.5	10.1
Maine...........	11	12	12	12	13	13	9.0	9.5	9.7	9.7	9.8	9.6	8.2
Maryland	38	42	44	44	44	45	8.0	8.3	8.3	8.1	8.1	8.1	8.5
Massachusetts.....	53	55	57	57	57	56	8.8	9.1	8.9	8.9	8.9	8.8	7.8
Michigan.........	79	84	87	86	88	87	8.5	8.8	8.7	8.6	8.7	8.6	8.5
Minnesota........	35	38	38	38	39	38	7.9	8.1	7.7	7.6	7.7	7.4	7.1
Mississippi	25	27	29	28	29	29	9.8	10.0	10.1	9.9	10.0	9.9	10.2
Missouri	50	54	55	55	56	56	9.8	10.2	9.8	9.8	9.9	9.7	9.0
Montana.........	7	8	8	8	9	8	8.6	8.8	9.0	9.1	9.4	9.2	8.3
Nebraska........	15	15	15	15	16	15	9.4	9.3	8.8	8.8	9.1	8.9	7.9
Nevada	9	13	15	16	17	18	7.8	8.2	7.6	7.8	7.8	8.0	9.3
New Hampshire....	8	9	10	10	10	10	7.7	8.0	7.8	7.8	7.7	7.5	7.5
New Jersey.......	70	74	75	75	74	74	9.1	9.3	8.9	8.8	8.6	8.5	7.9
New Mexico	11	13	13	14	14	15	7.0	7.4	7.4	7.7	7.7	7.9	8.3
New York.........	169	168	158	159	158	156	9.4	9.3	8.3	8.3	8.3	8.1	7.6
North Carolina....	57	65	72	71	72	74	8.6	9.0	8.9	8.6	8.7	8.7	9.1
North Dakota.....	6	6	6	6	6	6	8.9	9.3	9.1	9.5	9.3	9.6	7.7
Ohio	99	106	108	108.	110	109	9.1	9.5	9.5	9.5	9.6	9.5	8.9
Oklahoma........	30	33	35	35	36	36	9.7	10.0	10.2	10.0	10.2	10.2	9.7
Oregon..........	25	28	30	30	31	31	8.8	9.0	8.6	8.7	8.8	8.7	8.1
Pennsylvania.....	122	128	131	130	130	130	10.3	10.6	10.7	10.5	10.6	10.5	8.5
Rhode Island.....	10	10	10	10	10	10	9.5	9.8	9.6	9.5	9.6	9.3	7.9
South Carolina....	30	34	37	37	38	38	8.5	9.1	9.2	9.0	9.2	9.2	9.3
South Dakota	6	7	7	7	7	7	9.1	9.5	9.3	9.1	9.1	9.3	7.9
Tennessee	46	51	55	55	57	57	9.5	9.8	9.7	9.6	9.8	9.8	9.8
Texas...........	125	138	150	153	156	155	7.4	7.4	7.2	7.1	7.1	7.0	8.6
Utah	9	11	12	13	13	13	5.3	5.6	5.5	5.6	5.7	5.7	7.8
Vermont	5	5	5	5	5	5	8.2	8.5	8.4	8.5	8.2	8.3	7.6
Virginia..........	48	53	56	56	57	58	7.8	8.0	8.0	7.8	7.8	7.9	8.5
Washington.......	37	41	44	45	45	46	7.6	7.5	7.5	7.4	7.5	7.5	7.8
West Virginia.....	19	20	21	21	21	21	10.8	11.1	11.7	11.6	11.7	11.8	9.9
Wisconsin........	43	45	46	47	47	46	8.7	8.8	8.7	8.6	8.6	8.4	7.7
Wyoming........	3	4	4	4	4	4	7.1	7.7	7.9	8.2	8.4	8.3	8.5
Puerto Rico	26	30	28	29	28	28	7.3	8.1	7.2	7.6	7.2	7.3	7.8
Virgin Islands....	(NA)	1	1	1	1	1	4.6	5.8	5.3	5.6	5.7	5.8	7.1
Guam...........	1	1	1	1	1	1	3.9	4.1	4.2	4.2	4.0	4.1	7.5
American Samoa .	(NA)	(NA)	(Z)	(Z)	(Z)	(Z)	(NA)	(NA)	3.3	4.2	5.0	(NA)	(NA)
Northern Marianas......	(NA)	(NA)	(Z)	(Z)	(Z)	(Z)	(NA)	(NA)	1.9	2.1	2.2	1.9	8.1

NA Not available.   Z Less than half the unit of measure.   [1] Rates based on enumerated resident population as of April 1 for 1990 and 2000; estimated resident population as of July 1 for all other years.   [2] Preliminary data.

Source: U.S. National Center for Health Statistics, *Vital Statistics of the United States*, annual; *National Vital Statistics Reports (NVSR)* (formerly *Monthly Vital Statistics Report*).

Table 104. Infant, Maternal, and Neonatal Mortality Rates by Race: 1980 to 2002

[Deaths per 1,000 live births, except as noted. Excludes deaths of nonresidents of the United States. Beginning 1990, race for live births tabulated according to race of mother. Infant deaths based on race of child as stated on death certificate. See also Appendix III]

Item	1980	1990	1995	1998	1999 [1]	2000	2001	2002
Infant deaths [2]	12.6	9.2	7.6	7.2	7.1	6.9	6.8	7.0
White	10.9	7.6	6.3	6.0	5.8	5.7	5.7	5.8
Black and other	20.2	15.5	12.6	11.9	11.9	11.4	11.3	11.4
Black	22.2	18.0	15.1	14.3	14.6	14.1	14.0	14.4
Maternal deaths [3]	9.2	8.2	7.1	7.1	9.9	9.8	9.9	8.9
White	6.7	5.4	4.2	5.1	6.8	7.5	7.2	6.0
Black and other	19.8	19.1	18.5	14.9	21.4	18.0	20.2	19.7
Black	21.5	22.4	22.1	17.1	25.4	22.0	24.7	24.9
Neonatal deaths [4]	8.5	5.8	4.9	4.8	4.7	4.6	4.5	4.7
White	7.4	4.8	4.1	4.0	3.9	3.8	3.8	3.9
Black and other	13.2	9.9	8.1	7.9	7.9	7.6	7.4	7.5
Black	14.6	11.6	9.8	9.5	9.8	9.4	9.2	9.5

[1] Beginning 1999, deaths are classified according to the tenth revision of the *International Classification of Diseases*; earlier years classified according to the revision in use at the time; see text, this section. [2] Represents deaths of infants under 1 year old, exclusive of fetal deaths. [3] Per 100,000 live births from deliveries and complications of pregnancy, childbirth, and the puerperium. Deaths are classified according to the tenth revision of the *International Classification of Diseases*; earlier years classified according to the revision in use at the time; see text, this section 2. [4] Represents deaths of infants under 28 days old, exclusive of fetal deaths.

Source: U.S. National Center for Health Statistics, *Vital Statistics of the United States*, annual; and *National Vital Statistics Reports (NVSR)* (formerly *Monthly Vital Statistics Report*).

Table 105. Infant Mortality Rates by Race—States: 1980 to 2002

[Deaths per 1,000 live births, by place of residence. Represents deaths of infants under 1 year old, exclusive of fetal deaths. Excludes deaths of nonresidents of the United States. See Appendix III]

State	Total [1]				White				Black			
	1980	1990	2000	2002	1980	1990	2000	2002	1980	1990	2000	2002
U.S.	12.6	9.2	6.9	7.0	10.9	7.6	5.7	5.8	22.2	18.0	14.1	14.4
Alabama	15.1	10.8	9.4	9.1	11.6	8.1	6.6	7.1	21.6	16.0	15.4	13.9
Alaska	12.3	10.5	6.8	5.5	9.4	7.6	5.8	4.2	19.5	(B)	(B)	(B)
Arizona	12.4	8.8	6.7	6.4	11.8	7.8	6.2	6.2	18.4	20.6	17.6	13.0
Arkansas	12.7	9.2	8.4	8.3	10.3	8.4	7.0	6.9	20.0	13.9	13.7	13.9
California	11.1	7.9	5.4	5.5	10.6	7.0	5.1	5.2	18.0	16.8	12.9	12.9
Colorado	10.1	8.8	6.2	6.1	9.8	7.8	5.6	5.5	19.1	19.4	19.5	21.1
Connecticut	11.2	7.9	6.6	6.5	10.2	6.3	5.6	5.5	19.1	17.6	14.4	14.2
Delaware	13.9	10.1	9.2	8.7	9.8	9.7	7.9	7.3	27.9	20.1	14.8	12.9
District of Columbia	25.0	20.7	12.0	11.3	17.8	(B)	(B)	(B)	26.7	24.6	16.1	14.5
Florida	14.6	9.6	7.0	7.5	11.8	6.7	5.4	5.8	22.8	16.8	12.6	13.6
Georgia	14.5	12.4	8.5	8.9	10.8	7.4	5.9	6.6	21.0	18.3	13.9	13.7
Hawaii	10.3	6.7	8.1	7.3	11.6	6.1	6.5	(B)	(B)	(B)	(B)	(B)
Idaho	10.7	8.7	7.5	6.1	10.7	8.6	7.5	6.1	(NA)	(B)	(B)	(B)
Illinois	14.8	10.7	8.5	7.4	11.7	7.9	6.6	5.6	26.3	22.4	17.1	16.3
Indiana	11.9	9.6	7.8	7.7	10.5	7.9	6.9	6.8	23.4	17.4	15.8	15.3
Iowa	11.8	8.1	6.5	5.3	11.5	7.9	6.0	5.1	27.2	21.9	21.1	(B)
Kansas	10.4	8.4	6.8	7.1	9.5	8.0	6.4	6.5	20.6	17.7	12.2	15.2
Kentucky	12.9	8.5	7.2	7.2	12.0	8.2	6.7	6.6	22.0	14.3	12.7	14.2
Louisiana	14.3	11.1	9.0	10.3	10.5	8.1	5.9	6.9	20.6	16.7	13.3	15.0
Maine	9.2	6.2	4.9	4.4	9.4	6.7	4.8	4.3	(B)	(B)	(B)	(B)
Maryland	14.0	9.5	7.6	7.5	11.6	6.8	4.8	5.3	20.4	17.1	13.2	12.3
Massachusetts	10.5	7.0	4.6	4.9	10.1	6.1	4.0	4.5	16.8	11.9	9.9	9.1
Michigan	12.8	10.7	8.2	8.1	10.6	7.4	6.0	6.0	24.2	21.6	18.2	18.5
Minnesota	10.0	7.3	5.6	5.4	9.6	6.7	4.8	5.0	20.0	23.7	14.6	10.3
Mississippi	17.0	12.1	10.7	10.3	11.1	7.4	6.8	6.9	23.7	16.2	15.3	14.8
Missouri	12.4	9.4	7.2	8.5	11.1	7.9	5.9	7.1	20.7	18.2	14.7	17.1
Montana	12.4	9.0	6.1	7.5	11.8	6.0	5.5	7.1	(NA)	(B)	(B)	(B)
Nebraska	11.5	8.3	7.3	7.0	10.7	6.9	6.4	6.1	25.2	18.9	20.3	20.8
Nevada	10.7	8.4	6.5	6.0	10.0	8.2	6.0	5.1	20.6	14.2	12.7	18.4
New Hampshire	9.9	7.1	5.7	5.0	9.9	6.0	5.5	5.3	22.5	(B)	(B)	(B)
New Jersey	12.5	9.0	6.3	5.7	10.3	6.4	5.0	4.5	21.9	18.4	13.6	12.8
New Mexico	11.5	9.0	6.6	6.3	11.3	7.6	6.3	5.7	23.1	(B)	(B)	(B)
New York	12.5	9.6	6.4	6.0	10.8	7.4	5.4	5.4	20.0	18.1	10.9	9.9
North Carolina	14.5	10.6	8.6	8.2	12.1	8.0	6.3	5.9	20.0	16.5	15.7	15.6
North Dakota	12.1	8.0	8.1	6.3	11.7	7.2	7.5	5.6	27.5	(B)	(B)	(B)
Ohio	12.8	9.8	7.6	7.9	11.2	7.8	6.3	6.2	23.0	19.5	15.4	17.7
Oklahoma	12.7	9.2	8.5	8.1	12.1	9.1	7.9	7.1	21.8	14.3	16.9	17.2
Oregon	12.2	8.3	5.6	5.8	12.2	7.0	5.5	5.6	15.9	(B)	(B)	(B)
Pennsylvania	13.2	9.6	7.1	7.6	11.9	7.4	5.8	6.6	23.1	20.5	15.7	15.1
Rhode Island	11.0	8.1	6.3	7.0	10.9	7.0	5.9	6.4	(B)	(B)	(B)	(B)
South Carolina	15.6	11.7	8.7	9.3	10.8	8.1	5.4	6.0	22.9	17.3	14.8	15.8
South Dakota	10.9	10.1	5.5	6.5	9.0	8.0	4.3	4.9	(NA)	(B)	(B)	(B)
Tennessee	13.5	10.3	9.1	9.4	11.9	7.3	6.8	7.0	19.3	17.9	18.0	18.3
Texas	12.2	8.1	5.7	6.4	11.2	6.7	5.1	5.6	18.8	14.7	11.4	13.5
Utah	10.4	7.5	5.2	5.6	10.5	6.0	5.1	5.5	27.3	(B)	(B)	(B)
Vermont	10.7	6.4	6.0	4.4	10.7	5.9	6.1	4.5	(B)	(B)	(B)	(B)
Virginia	13.6	10.2	6.9	7.4	11.9	7.4	5.4	5.5	19.8	19.5	12.4	14.6
Washington	11.8	7.8	5.2	5.8	11.5	7.3	4.9	5.5	16.4	20.6	9.4	12.7
West Virginia	11.8	9.9	7.6	9.1	11.4	8.1	7.4	8.5	21.5	(B)	(B)	(B)
Wisconsin	10.3	8.2	6.6	6.9	9.7	7.7	5.5	5.6	18.5	19.0	17.2	18.9
Wyoming	9.8	8.6	6.7	6.7	9.3	7.5	6.5	6.8	25.9	(B)	(B)	(B)

B Base figure too small to meet statistical standards for reliability.   NA Not available.   [1] Includes other races, not shown separately.

Source: U.S. National Center for Health Statistics, *Vital Statistics of the United States*, annual; and unpublished data.

Table 106. Age-Adjusted Death Rates by Major Causes: 1960 to 2003

[Rates per 100,000 population; see headnote, Table 99. See Appendix III]

Year	Heart disease	Cancer	Cerebro-vascular diseases	Chronic lower respira-tory diseases	Accidents	Diabetes mellitus	Influenza and pneu-monia	Inten-tional self-harm (suicide)	Chronic liver disease and cirrhosis	Assault (homicide)
1960	559.0	193.9	177.9	12.5	63.1	22.5	53.7	12.5	13.3	5.2
1961	545.3	193.4	173.1	12.6	60.6	22.1	43.4	12.2	13.3	5.2
1962	556.9	193.3	174.0	14.2	62.9	22.6	47.1	12.8	13.8	5.4
1963	563.4	194.7	173.9	16.5	64.0	23.1	55.6	13.0	14.0	5.4
1964	543.3	193.6	167.0	16.3	64.1	22.5	45.4	12.7	14.2	5.7
1965	542.5	195.6	166.4	18.3	65.8	22.9	46.8	13.0	14.9	6.1
1966	541.2	196.5	165.8	19.2	67.6	23.6	47.9	12.7	15.9	6.5
1967	524.7	197.3	159.3	19.2	66.2	23.4	42.2	12.5	16.3	7.5
1968	531.0	198.8	162.5	20.7	65.5	25.3	52.8	12.4	16.9	8.1
1969	516.8	198.5	155.4	20.9	64.9	25.1	47.9	12.7	17.1	8.3
1970	492.7	198.6	147.7	21.3	62.2	24.3	41.7	13.1	17.8	9.0
1971	492.9	199.3	147.6	21.8	60.3	23.9	38.4	13.1	17.8	9.8
1972	490.2	200.3	147.3	22.8	60.2	23.7	41.3	13.3	18.0	10.0
1973	482.0	200.0	145.2	23.6	59.3	23.0	41.2	13.1	18.1	10.2
1974	458.8	201.5	136.8	23.2	52.7	22.1	35.5	13.2	17.9	10.5
1975	431.2	200.1	123.5	23.7	50.8	20.3	34.9	13.6	16.7	10.2
1976	426.9	202.5	117.4	24.9	48.7	19.5	38.8	13.2	16.4	9.2
1977	413.7	203.5	110.4	24.7	48.8	18.2	31.0	13.7	15.8	9.2
1978	409.9	204.9	103.7	26.3	48.9	18.3	34.5	12.9	15.2	9.2
1979	401.6	204.0	97.1	25.5	46.5	17.5	26.1	12.6	14.8	9.9
1980	412.1	207.9	96.4	28.3	46.4	18.1	31.4	12.2	15.1	10.5
1981	397.0	206.4	89.5	29.0	43.4	17.6	30.0	12.3	14.2	10.1
1982	389.0	208.3	84.2	29.1	40.1	17.2	26.5	12.5	13.2	9.4
1983	388.9	209.1	81.2	31.6	39.1	17.6	29.8	12.4	12.8	8.4
1984	378.8	210.8	78.7	32.4	38.8	17.2	30.6	12.6	12.7	8.1
1985	375.0	211.3	76.6	34.5	38.5	17.4	34.5	12.5	12.3	8.0
1986	365.1	211.5	73.1	34.8	38.6	17.2	34.8	13.0	11.8	8.6
1987	355.9	211.7	71.6	35.0	38.2	17.4	33.8	12.8	11.7	8.3
1988	352.5	212.5	70.6	36.5	38.9	18.0	37.3	12.5	11.6	8.5
1989	332.0	214.2	66.9	36.6	37.7	20.5	35.9	12.3	11.6	8.8
1990	321.8	216.0	65.5	37.2	36.3	20.7	36.8	12.5	11.1	9.5
1991	313.8	215.8	63.2	38.0	34.9	20.7	34.9	12.3	10.7	10.1
1992	306.1	214.3	62.0	37.9	33.4	20.8	33.1	12.1	10.5	9.6
1993	309.9	214.6	63.1	40.9	34.5	22.0	35.2	12.2	10.3	9.8
1994	299.7	213.1	63.1	40.6	34.6	22.7	33.9	12.1	10.2	9.4
1995	296.3	211.7	63.9	40.5	34.9	23.4	33.8	12.0	10.0	8.6
1996	288.3	208.7	63.2	41.0	34.9	24.0	33.2	11.7	9.8	7.8
1997	280.4	205.7	61.8	41.5	34.8	24.0	33.6	11.4	9.6	7.3
1998	272.4	202.4	59.6	42.0	35.0	24.2	34.6	11.3	9.5	6.7
1999	267.8	202.7	61.8	45.8	35.9	25.2	23.6	10.7	9.7	6.2
2000	257.6	199.6	60.9	44.2	34.9	25.0	23.7	10.4	9.5	5.9
2001	247.8	196.0	57.9	43.7	35.7	25.3	22.0	10.7	9.5	7.1
2002 ¹	240.8	193.5	56.2	43.5	36.9	25.4	22.6	10.9	9.4	6.1
2003 ¹	232.1	189.3	53.6	43.2	36.1	25.2	21.9	10.5	9.2	5.8

¹ Preliminary data.

Source: U.S. National Center for Health Statistics, *Vital Statistics of the United States*, annual.

U.S. Census Bureau, Statistical Abstract of the United States: 2006

Table 107. **Deaths and Death Rates by Selected Causes: 2002 and 2003**

[Rates per 100,000 population. Figures are weighted data rounded to the nearest individual, so categories may not add to total or subtotal. Excludes deaths of nonresidents of the United States, except as noted. Deaths classified according to tenth revision of International Classification of Diseases; See also Appendix III]

Cause of death	2002 Number	2002 Rate	2002 Age-adjusted rate [1]	2003 [2] Number	2003 Rate	2003 Age-adjusted rate [1]
All causes..........................	2,443,387	847.3	845.3	2,443,930	840.4	831.2
Major cardiovascular diseases [3]	918,628	318.6	317.4	901,753	310.1	305.8
Diseases of heart......................	696,947	241.7	240.8	684,462	235.4	232.1
Acute rheumatic fever and chronic rheumatic heart disease	3,579	1.2	1.2	3,554	1.2	1.2
Hypertensive heart disease	26,551	9.2	9.1	27,653	9.5	9.3
Hypertensive heart and renal disease	2,895	1.0	1.0	3,110	1.1	1.1
Ischemic heart disease.................	494,382	171.4	170.8	479,304	164.8	162.6
Other heart diseases	169,540	58.8	58.5	170,841	58.7	57.9
Essential (primary) hypertension and hypertensive renal disease	20,261	7.0	7.0	21,841	7.5	7.4
Cerebrovascular diseases	162,672	56.4	56.2	157,803	54.3	53.6
Atherosclerosis......................	13,821	4.8	4.7	13,030	4.5	4.4
Other disorders of circulatory system	4,711	1.6	1.6	4,683	1.6	1.6
Malignant neoplasms [3]	557,271	193.2	193.5	554,643	190.7	189.3
Malignant neoplasms of lip, oral cavity, and pharynx..........................	7,737	2.7	2.7	7,712	2.7	2.6
Malignant neoplasms of colon, rectum and anus..	56,741	19.7	19.7	55,616	19.1	18.9
Malignant neoplasms of trachea, bronchus and lung..............................	157,713	54.7	54.9	157,521	54.2	53.9
Malignant neoplasm of breast	41,883	14.5	14.5	41,941	14.4	14.2
Malignant neoplasms of kidney and renal pelvis..	12,165	4.2	4.2	12,179	4.2	4.1
Malignant neoplasms of lymphoid, hematopoietic and related tissue	56,225	19.5	19.5	55,571	19.1	19.0
Leukemia	21,498	7.5	7.5	21,446	7.4	7.3
Accidents (unintentional injuries) [3]	106,742	37.0	36.9	105,695	36.3	36.1
Motor vehicle accidents	45,380	15.7	15.7	44,059	15.2	15.0
Accidental discharge of firearms	762	0.3	0.3	752	0.3	0.2
Accidental drowning and submersion	3,447	1.2	1.2	3,222	1.1	1.1
Accidental exposure to smoke, fire and flames...	3,159	1.1	1.1	3,363	1.2	1.1
Accidental poisoning and exposure to noxious substances	17,550	6.1	6.1	16,969	5.8	5.8
Other acute lower respiratory infections	386	0.1	0.1	406	0.1	0.1
Chronic lower respiratory diseases	124,816	43.3	43.5	126,128	43.4	43.2
Bronchitis, chronic and unspecified	955	0.3	0.3	851	0.3	0.3
Emphysema........................	15,489	5.4	5.4	14,793	5.1	5.1
Asthma...........................	4,261	1.5	1.5	3,964	1.4	1.3
Other chronic lower respiratory diseases......	104,111	36.1	36.2	106,520	36.6	36.5
Influenza and pneumonia.................	65,681	22.8	22.6	64,847	22.3	21.9
Influenza	727	0.3	0.2	1,605	0.6	0.5
Pneumonia	64,954	22.5	22.4	63,241	21.7	21.4
Tuberculosis	784	0.3	0.3	704	0.2	0.2
Septicemia..........................	33,865	11.7	11.7	34,243	11.8	11.7
Human immunodeficiency virus (HIV) disease	14,095	4.9	4.9	13,544	4.7	4.7
Anemias............................	4,614	1.6	1.6	4,599	1.6	1.6
Diabetes mellitus......................	73,249	25.4	25.4	73,965	25.4	25.2
Nutritional deficiencies..................	3,779	1.3	1.3	3,358	1.2	1.1
Meningitis..........................	700	0.2	0.2	708	0.2	0.2
Parkinsons disease	16,959	5.9	5.9	17,898	6.2	6.1
Alzheimers disease.....................	58,866	20.4	20.2	63,343	21.8	21.4
Chronic liver disease and cirrhosis	27,257	9.5	9.4	27,201	9.4	9.2
Alcoholic liver disease	12,121	4.2	4.2	12,064	4.1	4.1
Other chronic liver disease and cirrhosis	15,136	5.2	5.2	15,137	5.2	5.1
Nephritis, nephrotic syndrome and nephrosis [3]	40,974	14.2	14.2	42,536	14.6	14.5
Renal failure	40,222	13.9	13.9	41,818	14.4	14.2
Other disorders of kidney................	33	(Z)	(Z)	27	(Z)	(Z)
Infections of kidney....................	788	0.3	0.3	821	0.3	0.3
Pregnancy, childbirth and the puerperium	379	0.1	0.1	515	0.2	0.2
Congenital malformations, deformations and chromosomal abnormalities	10,687	3.7	3.7	10,430	3.6	3.6
All other diseases (Residual)	194,591	67.5	67.1	200,322	68.9	67.9
Intentional self-harm (suicide)...............	31,655	11.0	10.9	30,642	10.5	10.5
Assault (homicide)	17,638	6.1	6.1	17,096	5.9	5.8
Legal intervention......................	384	0.1	0.1	394	0.1	0.1
Events of undetermined intent	4,830	1.7	1.7	4,602	1.6	1.6
Operations of war and their sequelae..........	20	(Z)	(Z)	16	(B)	(B)
Complications of medical and surgical care.......	2,843	1.0	1.0	2,766	1.0	0.9
Injury by firearms [4]	30,242	10.5	10.4	29,730	10.2	10.1
Drug-induced deaths [4]	26,018	9.0	9.0	25,162	8.7	8.7
Alcohol-induced deaths [4]	19,928	6.9	6.9	19,699	6.8	6.6
Injury at work........................	5,305	2.3	2.3	4,735	2.1	2.0

B Base figure too small to meet statistical standards for reliability; see text, this section.   Z Less than 0.05.   [1] See headnote, Table 99.   [2] Preliminary data.   [3] Includes other causes not shown separately.   [4] Included in selected categories.

Source: U.S. National Center for Health Statistics , Vital Statistics of the United States,

Table 108. Deaths by Selected Causes: 2000 and 2002

[Deaths in thousands (2,403 represents 2,403,000). Deaths are classified according to the Tenth Revision of the International Classification of Diseases. See Appendix III]

Cause of Death	2000 All ages	Under 1 year	1-4 years	5-14 years	15-24 years	25-34 years	35-44 years	45-54 years	55-64 years	65-74 years	75-84 years	85 yrs. & over	2002 All ages	Under 1 year	1-4 years	5-14 years	15-24 years	25-34 years	35-44 years	45-54 years	55-64 years	65-74 years	75-84 years	85 yrs. & over
All causes	2,403	28	5	7	31	40	90	160	241	441	700	658	2,443	28	5	7	33	41	91	172	253	423	708	681
Tuberculosis	1	-	-	-	-	-	-	-	-	-	-	-	1	-	-	-	-	-	-	-	-	-	-	-
Vital hepatitis	5	-	-	-	-	-	-	2	1	1	1	-	6	-	-	-	-	-	1	2	1	1	1	-
Human immunodeficiency virus (HIV) disease	14	-	-	-	-	2	4	4	2	1	1	-	14	-	-	-	-	2	4	4	2	1	1	-
Malignant neoplasms	553	-	-	1	2	4	17	48	89	150	165	77	557	-	-	1	2	4	16	50	93	145	167	79
Malignant neoplasms of colon, rectum and anus	57	-	-	-	-	-	1	4	8	14	18	11	57	-	-	-	-	-	1	5	8	13	17	11
Malignant neoplasms of trachea, bronchus and lung	156	-	-	-	-	-	3	12	30	52	46	13	158	-	-	-	-	-	3	12	31	50	48	14
Malignant neoplasm of breast	42	-	-	-	-	-	3	6	8	9	10	6	42	-	-	-	-	-	3	6	8	9	10	6
Leukemia	21	-	-	-	1	-	1	1	2	5	7	4	21	-	-	-	1	-	1	1	2	5	7	4
Diabetes mellitus	69	-	-	-	-	-	2	5	9	17	22	14	73	-	-	-	-	-	2	5	10	17	23	15
Nutritional deficiencies	4	-	-	-	-	-	-	-	-	1	1	2	4	-	-	-	-	-	-	-	-	1	1	2
Alzheimer's disease	50	-	-	-	-	-	-	-	1	4	17	28	59	-	-	-	-	-	-	-	-	4	20	35
Major cardiovascular diseases	937	1	-	-	1	4	17	44	77	156	296	340	919	1	-	-	1	4	17	46	78	144	287	339
Diseases of heart	711	1	-	-	1	3	13	35	63	122	220	251	697	1	-	-	1	3	14	38	64	113	214	250
Hypertensive heart disease	24	-	-	-	-	-	1	2	3	4	6	8	27	-	-	-	-	-	1	3	3	4	6	9
Ischemic heart diseases	515	-	-	-	-	-	8	25	48	93	164	177	494	-	-	-	-	-	8	26	47	84	155	173
Acute myocardial infarction	193	-	-	-	-	-	3	11	21	38	62	57	180	-	-	-	-	-	3	11	20	34	57	55
Influenza and pneumonia	65	-	-	-	-	-	1	2	3	7	20	32	66	-	-	-	-	-	1	2	3	7	20	32
Chronic lower respiratory diseases	122	-	-	-	-	-	1	3	11	31	48	27	125	-	-	-	-	-	1	3	11	30	49	29
Chronic liver disease and cirrhosis	27	-	-	-	-	-	3	7	6	5	4	1	27	-	-	-	-	-	3	7	6	5	4	1
Accidents (unintentional injuries)	98	1	2	3	14	12	15	12	8	8	12	12	107	1	2	3	15	13	17	15	8	8	13	13
Transport accidents	47	-	1	2	11	7	8	6	4	3	3	2	48	-	1	2	12	7	8	7	4	3	3	1
Motor vehicle accidents	43	-	1	2	11	7	7	5	4	3	2	1	45	-	1	2	11	7	7	6	4	3	3	1
Intentional self-harm (suicide)	29	(X)	-	-	4	5	7	5	3	2	2	1	32	(X)	-	-	4	5	7	6	4	2	2	1
Assault (homicide)	17	-	1	-	5	4	3	2	1	-	-	-	18	-	1	-	5	4	3	2	1	-	-	-
Complications of medical & surgical care	3	-	-	-	-	-	-	-	-	1	1	1	3	-	-	-	-	-	-	-	-	1	1	1

- Represents or rounds to zero.   X Not applicable.

Source: U.S. National Center for Health Statistics, Vital Statistics of the United States, annual; National Vital Statistics Reports (NVSR) (formerly Monthly Vital Statistics Report).

Table 109. Deaths and Death Rates by Leading Causes of Death and Age: 2002

[Data are based on the tenth revision of the *International Classification of Diseases* (ICD). Rates per 100,000 population in specified group. Numbers are based on weighted data rounded to the nearest individual, so categories may not add to totals. See Appendix III]

Age	Number	Rate	Age	Number	Rate
ALL AGES [1]			Malignant neoplasms	16,085	35.8
			Diseases of heart	13,688	30.5
All causes	**2,443,387**	**847.3**	Intentional self-harm (suicide)	6,851	15.3
Diseases of heart	696,947	241.7	Human immunodeficiency virus (HIV)		
Malignant neoplasms	557,271	193.2	disease	5,707	12.7
Cerebrovascular diseases	162,672	56.4			
Chronic lower respiratory diseases . . .	124,816	43.3	**45–54 YEARS**		
Accidents (unintentional injuries)	106,742	37.0			
			All causes	**172,385**	**430.1**
1–4 Years			Malignant neoplasms	49,637	123.8
			Diseases of heart	37,570	93.7
All causes	**4,858**	**31.2**	Accidents	14,675	36.6
Accidents (unintentional injuries)	1,641	10.5	Chronic liver disease and cirrhosis . . .	7,216	18.0
Congenital malformations.	530	3.4	Intentional self-harm (suicide)	6,308	15.7
Assault (homicide)	423	2.7			
Malignant neoplasms	402	2.6	**55–64 YEARS**		
Diseases of heart	165	1.1			
			All causes	**253,342**	**952.4**
5–14 years			Malignant neoplasms	93,391	351.1
			Diseases of heart	64,234	241.5
All causes	**7,150**	**17.4**	Chronic lower respiratory diseases . . .	11,280	42.4
Accidents (unintentional injuries)	2,718	6.6	Diabetes mellitus	10,022	37.7
Malignant neoplasms	1,072	2.6	Cerebrovascular diseases	9,897	37.2
Congenital malformations.	417	1.0			
Assault (homicide)	356	0.9	**65–74 YEARS**		
Diseases of heart	255	0.6			
Intentional self-harm (suicide)	264	0.6	All causes	**422,990**	**2,314.7**
			Malignant neoplasms	144,757	792.1
15–24 years			Diseases of heart	112,547	615.9
			Chronic lower respiratory diseases . . .	29,788	163.0
All causes	**33,046**	**81.4**	Cerebrovascular diseases	21,992	120.3
Accidents (unintentional injuries)	15,412	38.0	Diabetes mellitus	16,709	91.4
Assault (homicide)	5,219	12.9			
Intentional self-harm (suicide)	4,010	9.9	**75–84 YEARS**		
Malignant neoplasms	1,730	4.3			
Diseases of heart	1,022	2.5	All causes	**707,654**	**5,556.9**
			Diseases of heart	213,581	1,677.2
25–34 YEARS			Malignant neoplasms	167,062	1,311.9
			Cerebrovascular diseases	54,889	431.0
All causes	**41,355**	**103.6**	Chronic lower respiratory diseases . . .	49,241	386.7
Accidents	12,569	31.5	Diabetes mellitus	23,282	182.8
Intentional self-harm (suicide)	5,046	12.6			
Assault (homicide)	4,489	11.2	**85 YEARS AND OVER**		
Malignant neoplasms	3,872	9.7			
Diseases of heart	3,165	7.9	All causes	**681,076**	**14,828.3**
			Diseases of heart	250,173	5,446.8
35–44 YEARS			Malignant neoplasms	79,182	1,723.9
			Cerebrovascular diseases	66,412	1,445.9
All causes	**91,140**	**202.9**	Alzheimer's disease	34,552	752.3
Accidents	16,710	37.2	Influenza and pneumonia.	31,995	696.6

[1] Includes deaths under 1 year of age.

Source: U.S. National Center for Health Statistics, Vital Statistics of the United States, annual; and National Vital Statistics Reports (NVSR), Vol. 53, No. 17. See also <http://www.cdc.gov/nchs/data/nvsr/nvsr53/nvsr5317.pdf> (released 7 March 2005).

Table 110. Death Rates for Major Causes of Death—States and Outlying Areas: 2002

[Deaths per 100,000 resident population estimated as of July 1. By place of residence. Excludes nonresidents of the United States. Causes of death classified according to tenth revisions of International Classification of Diseases. See Appendix III]

State and outlying areas	Total	Heart disease	Cancer	Cerebro-vascular diseases	Acci-dents	Motor vehicle acci-dents	Chronic lower respira-tory diseases	Diabe-tes mellitus	HIV [1]	Inten-tional self-harm (suicide)	Assault (homi-cide)
United States. . .	847.3	241.7	193.2	56.4	37.0	15.7	43.3	25.4	4.9	11.0	6.1
AL.	1,026.8	294.1	216.2	71.3	49.7	24.9	51.9	33.1	4.2	11.5	9.3
AK.	470.7	88.1	111.1	24.5	53.7	17.4	22.1	13.4	(S)	20.5	6.2
AZ.	784.7	198.9	171.5	46.5	47.2	20.3	47.2	22.6	3.0	16.2	9.2
AR.	1,052.1	307.4	231.8	82.4	48.4	25.6	53.2	29.3	3.0	13.9	7.2
CA.	668.0	195.9	154.2	50.2	28.8	12.1	36.1	19.4	4.1	9.2	7.1
CO	648.2	142.6	141.7	42.5	40.2	17.3	41.0	14.6	2.3	16.1	4.1
CT.	870.5	254.7	207.0	53.8	34.2	10.1	42.0	19.5	5.4	7.5	2.8
DE.	849.8	237.6	200.8	50.2	36.2	15.0	43.3	26.6	8.7	9.2	4.7
DC	1,024.9	291.8	227.4	48.9	35.0	10.2	23.3	33.5	40.8	5.4	40.1
FL.	1,004.1	294.6	234.2	61.4	44.3	19.1	54.2	27.4	10.3	14.0	6.0
GA	764.6	204.8	163.3	49.8	38.9	17.8	36.9	18.4	8.3	10.6	7.9
HI	707.0	201.8	156.2	65.2	31.6	9.7	21.3	16.4	2.1	9.6	3.1
ID	739.9	188.8	159.4	54.9	45.6	22.1	44.4	24.0	(S)	15.1	2.4
IL	846.5	244.6	196.3	57.0	33.5	12.5	38.3	23.9	3.9	9.1	8.1
IN	899.4	248.8	208.9	60.4	34.9	15.6	50.9	27.4	1.9	12.1	6.3
IA	952.7	278.6	220.4	75.8	37.2	14.5	53.8	25.0	1.0	10.7	1.9
KS.	921.3	246.0	197.4	67.9	41.9	20.7	50.3	28.2	1.4	12.7	4.7
KY.	994.3	285.8	230.6	62.4	51.1	22.6	58.7	30.9	2.4	13.2	4.8
LA.	936.6	249.5	210.6	57.9	47.2	21.4	37.8	39.6	8.1	11.1	13.5
ME	980.6	244.9	247.7	63.6	39.5	16.6	61.1	31.2	(S)	12.8	(S)
MD	805.6	220.0	190.4	51.5	24.4	13.2	35.6	27.8	11.2	8.7	9.9
MA	885.7	229.3	216.5	55.4	22.0	8.8	42.7	22.1	3.6	6.8	2.9
MI	873.5	265.3	198.8	57.8	32.7	13.8	44.1	27.7	2.4	11.0	6.9
MN	767.2	171.4	183.5	53.9	38.4	14.8	39.3	26.2	1.1	9.9	2.5
MS	1,004.7	315.5	211.3	67.1	57.2	30.6	48.0	23.4	6.4	11.9	10.6
MO	986.1	294.5	217.2	68.5	46.6	21.4	50.5	28.6	2.2	12.2	6.5
MT	935.3	213.8	210.1	70.3	57.6	28.0	63.3	23.1	(S)	20.2	2.5
NE.	910.1	245.3	198.5	63.8	44.1	19.5	54.0	22.7	1.2	11.6	2.9
NV.	778.8	203.4	181.1	44.9	39.6	17.8	54.0	15.8	3.5	19.5	8.1
NH	772.8	217.7	198.3	49.2	28.0	9.8	45.3	24.4	(S)	10.4	(S)
NJ.	861.5	262.0	207.5	46.8	30.3	9.1	33.6	29.5	8.9	6.4	3.9
NM	773.2	181.1	165.3	38.5	59.6	22.8	46.2	31.4	1.9	18.8	8.7
NY.	825.4	295.8	191.4	39.8	24.3	8.8	36.4	20.5	10.3	6.4	4.8
NC	865.7	222.6	194.8	63.2	44.5	20.3	44.2	26.5	5.8	11.9	7.7
ND	929.2	255.9	203.9	74.0	38.8	17.5	50.8	33.7	(S)	14.4	(S)
OH	961.1	274.8	220.4	63.5	36.3	14.0	53.1	33.7	2.1	11.3	4.8
OK.	1,016.2	321.4	213.9	69.5	45.2	21.9	56.9	30.5	2.6	14.3	5.6
OR.	883.7	206.2	205.8	75.1	39.7	13.1	52.4	29.6	2.6	14.7	3.0
PA.	1,055.7	315.0	242.0	69.5	38.3	14.1	48.8	30.1	4.0	10.9	5.2
RI.	957.8	290.6	224.7	56.6	25.9	8.9	48.7	24.6	2.2	8.0	4.0
SC.	918.8	235.2	202.9	68.7	48.0	24.9	46.0	27.1	7.3	10.7	7.9
SD.	906.4	254.5	205.2	68.1	45.7	24.4	50.3	25.6	(S)	12.4	2.9
TN.	976.4	279.9	215.9	68.7	47.3	21.6	51.9	30.2	6.0	13.4	8.1
TX.	714.1	199.5	156.9	48.4	37.8	18.5	35.4	26.0	4.9	10.6	6.5
UT.	566.3	128.5	102.6	39.0	30.8	14.2	26.0	22.2	(S)	14.7	2.3
VT.	823.1	222.2	198.5	54.3	38.9	12.7	44.8	28.2	(S)	14.9	(S)
VA.	784.2	205.0	186.5	54.3	34.0	13.2	37.7	21.4	3.6	11.0	5.4
WA	747.0	183.6	178.9	61.8	36.3	12.5	44.8	24.6	2.0	13.4	3.5
WV	1,166.3	343.5	258.2	69.9	53.1	23.0	68.2	47.0	1.1	15.3	5.3
WI.	863.4	237.5	199.0	63.9	41.8	16.0	42.9	24.9	1.4	11.5	3.5
WY	837.0	201.5	172.2	48.7	58.0	31.5	65.0	29.1	(S)	21.1	4.6
PR	723.6	154.2	120.9	40.8	29.1	13.8	27.9	63.9	15.0	6.2	19.0
VI	567.0	174.6	118.6	37.7	23.9	(S)	(S)	23.9	(S)	(S)	37.7
GU.	396.1	124.8	73.3	30.4	19.2	(S)	16.8	(S)	(S)	(S)	(S)
AS	502.5	93.6	58.9	36.4	(S)	(S)	(S)	53.7	(S)	13.0	(S)
MP.	217.6	36.5	(S)	(S)	(S)	(S)	(S)	(S)	(S)	(S)	(S)

S Figure does not meet standards of reliability or precision.   [1] Human immunodeficiency virus.

Source: U.S. National Center for Health Statistics, National Vital Statistics Report (NVSR).

88   Vital Statistics

Table 111. **Death Rates from Heart Disease by Sex and Age: 1990 to 2002**

[Rates per 100,000 population. Starting with 1999 data, cause of death is coded according to ICD-10. For explanation, see text, this section. For explanation of age-adjustment, see headnote, Table 99. See Appendix III.]

Characteristic	Male						Female					
	1990	1995	1999	2000	2001	2002	1990	1995	1999	2000	2001	2002
All ages, age adjusted	412.4	372.7	328.1	315.0	305.4	297.4	257.0	239.7	220.9	213.0	203.9	197.2
All ages, crude . .	297.6	282.7	263.8	256.1	242.5	240.7	281.8	278.8	268.0	260.2	249.0	242.7
Under 1 year.	21.9	17.5	13.8	13.2	11.8	12.9	18.3	16.7	13.6	12.4	12.0	11.8
1-4 years	1.9	1.7	1.3	1.4	1.5	1.1	1.9	1.5	1.1	1.0	1.4	1.0
5-14 years	0.9	0.8	0.8	0.8	0.7	0.7	0.8	0.7	0.6	0.6	0.7	0.6
15-24 years.	3.1	3.6	3.4	3.2	3.2	3.3	1.8	2.2	2.2	2.1	1.8	1.7
25-34 years.	10.3	11.4	10.6	10.3	10.5	10.5	5.0	5.6	5.6	5.5	5.6	5.2
35-44 years.	48.1	47.2	43.3	41.6	41.7	43.1	15.1	17.1	17.6	17.2	17.6	18.0
45-54 years.	183.0	168.6	145.7	142.7	136.6	138.4	61.0	56.0	51.9	50.3	50.7	50.6
55-64 years.	537.3	465.4	391.6	378.6	349.8	343.4	215.7	193.9	167.5	160.4	151.8	147.2
65-74 years.	1,250.0	1,102.3	961.6	909.2	(NA)	827.1	616.8	557.8	503.2	479.9	(NA)	440.1
75-84 years.	2,968.2	2,615.0	2,308.9	2,210.1	(NA)	2,110.1	1,893.8	1,715.2	1,562.5	1,501.5	(NA)	1,389.7
85 years and over . .	7,418.4	7,039.6	6,313.3	6,100.8	(NA)	5,283.5	6,478.1	6,267.8	5,913.8	5,740.1	(NA)	5,283.3

Source: U.S. National Center for Health Statistics , *Vital Statistics of the United States*, annual; National Vital Statistics Reports (NVSR) (formerly *Monthly Statistics Report*); and unpublished data.

Table 112. **Death Rates from Cerebrovascular Diseases by Race, Sex, and Age: 1950 to 2002**

Rates per 100,000 population. Starting with 1999 data, cause of death is coded according to ICD-10. For explanation, see text, this section. For explanation of age-adjustment, see headnote, Table 99. See Appendix III]

Characteristic	1950 [1]	1960 [1]	1970	1980	1985	1990	1995	1999	2000	2001	2002
All ages, age adjusted	180.7	177.9	147.7	96.4	76.6	65.5	63.9	61.8	60.9	57.9	56.2
Under 1 year	5.1	4.1	5.0	4.4	3.7	3.8	5.8	2.7	3.3	2.7	2.9
1-4 years.	0.9	0.8	1.0	0.5	0.3	0.3	0.4	0.3	0.3	0.4	0.3
5-14 years.	0.5	0.7	0.7	0.3	0.2	0.2	0.2	0.2	0.2	0.2	0.2
15-24 years.	1.6	1.8	1.6	1.0	0.8	0.6	0.5	0.5	0.5	0.5	0.4
25-34 years	4.2	4.7	4.5	2.6	2.2	2.2	1.8	1.4	1.5	1.5	1.4
35-44 years	18.7	14.7	15.6	8.5	7.2	6.5	6.5	5.7	5.8	5.5	5.4
45-54 years	70.4	49.2	41.6	25.2	21.3	18.7	17.6	15.2	16.0	15.1	15.1
55-64 years	194.2	147.3	115.8	65.2	54.8	48.0	46.1	40.6	41.0	38.0	37.2
65-74 years	554.7	469.2	384.1	219.5	172.8	144.4	137.2	130.8	128.6	123.4	120.3
75-84 years	1,499.6	1,491.3	1,254.2	788.6	601.5	499.3	481.4	469.8	461.3	443.9	431.0
85 years and over.	2,990.1	3,680.5	3,014.3	2,288.9	1,865.1	1,633.9	1,636.5	1,614.8	1,589.2	1,500.2	1,445.9
Male, all ages, age adjusted	186.4	186.1	157.4	102.4	80.2	68.7	66.3	62.4	62.4	59.0	56.5
Under 1 year	6.4	5.0	5.8	5.0	4.6	4.4	6.3	3.3	3.8	3.1	3.2
1-4 years.	1.1	0.9	1.2	0.4	0.4	0.3	0.4	0.3	(B)	0.3	0.4
5-14 years.	0.5	0.7	0.8	0.3	0.2	0.2	0.2	0.2	0.2	0.2	0.2
15-24 years.	1.8	1.9	1.8	1.1	0.7	0.7	0.5	0.5	0.5	0.5	0.5
25-34 years	4.2	4.5	4.4	2.6	2.2	2.1	1.9	1.5	1.5	1.6	1.4
35-44 years	17.5	14.6	15.7	8.7	7.4	6.8	7.1	5.8	5.8	5.7	5.3
45-54 years	67.9	52.2	44.4	27.3	23.2	20.5	19.8	16.7	17.5	16.7	16.7
55-64 years	205.2	163.8	138.7	74.7	63.5	54.4	53.4	46.5	47.2	43.4	42.7
65-74 years	589.6	530.7	449.5	259.2	201.4	166.8	155.9	147.3	145.0	140.4	135.0
75-84 years	1,543.6	1,555.9	1,361.6	868.3	661.2	552.7	517.1	500.4	490.8	467.3	445.9
85 years and over.	3,048.6	3,643.1	2,895.2	2,199.2	1,730.1	1,533.2	1,537.7	1,512.8	1,484.3	1,380.2	1,317.9
Female, all ages, age adjusted	175.8	170.7	140.0	91.9	73.5	62.7	61.5	60.5	59.1	56.4	55.2
Under 1 year	3.7	3.2	4.0	3.8	2.7	3.1	5.2	2.1	2.7	2.3	2.5
1-4 years.	0.7	0.7	0.7	0.5	0.3	0.3	0.3	0.3	0.4	0.4	0.3
5-14 years.	0.4	0.6	0.6	0.3	0.3	0.2	0.2	0.2	0.2	0.2	0.2
15-24 years	1.5	1.6	1.4	0.8	0.8	0.6	0.4	0.5	0.5	0.5	0.3
25-34 years	4.3	4.9	4.7	2.6	2.1	2.2	1.7	1.4	1.5	1.5	1.4
35-44 years	19.9	14.8	15.6	8.4	6.9	6.1	6.0	5.6	5.7	5.4	5.5
45-54 years	72.9	46.3	39.0	23.3	19.4	17.0	15.5	13.8	14.5	13.6	13.6
55-64 years	183.1	131.8	95.3	56.9	47.2	42.2	39.4	35.1	35.3	32.9	32.1
65-74 years	522.1	415.7	333.3	189.0	150.7	126.9	122.2	117.2	115.1	109.3	108.1
75-84 years	1,462.2	1,441.1	1,183.1	741.6	566.3	467.4	458.7	449.8	442.1	428.6	421.2
85 years and over.	2,949.4	3,704.4	3,081.0	2,328.2	1,918.9	1,672.7	1,675.0	1,656.0	1,632.0	1,550.4	1,501.5
White male, age adjusted. . .	182.1	181.6	153.7	99.0	77.4	65.7	63.2	60.0	59.8	56.5	54.2
Black male, age adjusted . . .	228.8	238.5	206.4	142.1	112.7	102.5	96.7	87.4	89.6	85.4	81.7
White female, age adjusted .	169.7	165.0	135.5	89.2	70.9	60.5	59.5	58.7	57.3	54.5	53.4
Black female, age adjusted. .	238.4	232.5	189.3	119.8	99.4	84.0	81.0	78.1	76.2	73.7	71.8

[1] Includes deaths of persons who were not residents of the 50 States and the District of Columbia.

Source: U.S. National Center for Health Statistics. *Vital Statistics of the United States*, annual; National Vital Statistics Reports (NVSR); and unpublished data.

Vital Statistics 89

Table 113. **Death Rates from Malignant Neoplasms, by Race, Sex and Age: 1990 to 2002**

[Rates per 100,000 population. Starting with 1999 data, cause of death is coded according to ICD-10. For explanation, see text, this section. For explanation of age-adjustment, see headnote, Table 99. See Appendix III]

Characteristic	1990	1995	1999	2000	2001	2002
Total, age adjusted	**216.0**	**211.7**	**202.7**	**199.6**	**196.0**	**193.5**
Under 1 year.	2.3	1.8	1.8	2.4	1.6	1.8
1-4 years	3.5	3.1	2.7	2.7	2.7	2.6
5-14 years	3.1	2.7	2.5	2.5	2.5	2.6
15-24 years	4.9	4.6	4.5	4.4	4.3	4.3
25-34 years	12.6	11.9	10.0	9.8	10.1	9.7
35-44 years	43.3	40.3	37.1	36.6	36.8	35.8
45-54 years	158.9	142.2	127.6	127.5	126.5	123.8
55-64 years	449.6	416.0	374.6	366.7	356.5	351.1
65-74 years	872.3	868.2	827.1	816.3	802.8	792.1
75-84 years	1,348.5	1,364.8	1,331.5	1,335.6	1,315.8	1,311.9
85 years and over	1,752.9	1,823.8	1,805.8	1,819.4	1,765.6	1,723.9
Male, age adjusted	280.4	268.8	251.6	247.4	243.7	238.9
Female, age adjusted.	175.7	175.4	169.9	205.9	164.7	163.1
White male, age adjusted	272.2	261.8	246.5	242.5	239.2	235.2
Black male, age adjusted	397.9	372.8	340.5	333.2	330.9	319.6
Hispanic male, age adjusted [1]	174.7	172.5	151.4	150.1	168.2	161.4
White, non-Hispanic male, age adjusted [1]	276.7	264.9	251.3	253.0	243.1	239.6
White female, age adjusted	174.0	173.7	168.6	168.7	163.9	162.4
Black female, age adjusted	205.9	206.0	200.0	196.6	191.3	190.3
Hispanic female, age adjusted [1] . . .	111.9	106.1	101.4	100.6	108.6	106.1
White, non-Hispanic female, age adjusted [1]	177.5	176.6	172.1	172.5	167.2	165.9
DEATH RATES FOR MALIGNANT NEOPLASM OF BREASTS FOR FEMALES						
All ages, age adjusted	33.3	30.8	27.0	27.1	26.0	25.6
All ages, crude	34.0	32.6	29.5	29.8	(NA)	(NA)
Under 25 years	(B)	(B)	(B)	(B)	(B)	(B)
25-34 years	2.9	2.7	2.2	2.3	2.4	2.1
35-44 years	17.8	15.0	12.0	12.4	12.4	12.0
45-54 years	45.4	41.4	32.9	33.0	32.8	31.4
55-64 years	78.6	69.8	59.2	59.3	57.5	56.2
65-74 years	111.7	103.3	88.9	88.3	85.8	84.4
75-84 years	146.3	142.0	128.9	128.9	125.8	125.9
85 years and over	196.8	203.7	200.8	205.7	188.9	191.5
DEATH RATES FOR MALIGNANT NEOPLASM OF TRACHEA, BRONCHUS, AND LUNG						
All ages, age adjusted	59.3	58.9	56.0	56.5	55.3	54.9
All ages, crude	56.8	57.5	55.8	55.6	54.8	57.7
Under 25 years	-	-	-	-	-	-
25-34 years	0.7	0.7	0.4	0.5	0.4	0.4
35-44 years	6.8	6.0	6.0	6.1	6.2	6.0
45-54 years	46.8	38.0	31.3	31.6	30.7	30.3
55-64 years	160.6	142.9	123.4	122.4	117.7	115.3
65-74 years	288.4	297.1	281.5	284.2	279.7	275.0
75-84 years	333.3	361.4	362.1	370.8	371.4	377.6
85 years and over	242.5	284.0	297.0	302.1	302.7	297.2

- Represents zero or rounds to less than half the unit of measurement shown.   B Base figure too small to meet statistical standards for reliability of a derived figure.   NA Not available.   [1] Excludes data from States lacking an Hispanic-origin item on their death certificates. See text, this section.

90   Vital Statistics

Table 114. **Death Rates From Suicide, by Sex and Race: 1990 to 2002**

[Rates per 100,000 population. Starting with 1999 data, cause of death is coded according to ICD 10. For explanation of age-adjustment, see headnote, Table 99. See Appendix III]

Characteristic	1990	1995	1999	2000	2001	2002
All ages, age adjusted	**12.5**	**12.0**	**10.7**	**10.4**	**10.7**	**10.9**
All ages, crude.	**12.4**	**11.9**	**10.5**	**10.4**	**10.8**	**11.0**
Under 1 year	(X)	(X)	(X)	(X)	(X)	(X)
1-4 years.	(X)	(X)	(X)	(X)	(X)	(X)
5-14 years	0.8	0.9	0.6	0.7	0.7	0.6
15-24 years	13.2	13.3	10.1	10.2	9.9	9.9
25-34 years	15.2	15.4	12.7	12.0	12.8	12.6
35-44 years	15.3	15.2	14.3	14.5	14.7	15.3
45-54 years	14.8	14.6	13.9	14.4	15.2	15.7
55-64 years	16.0	13.3	12.2	12.1	13.1	13.6
65-74 years	17.9	15.8	13.4	12.5	13.3	13.5
75-84 years	24.9	20.7	18.1	17.6	17.4	17.7
85 years and over	22.2	21.6	19.3	19.6	17.5	18.0
White male, age adjusted	22.8	21.9	19.4	19.1	19.6	20.0
Black male, age adjusted	12.8	12.5	10.4	10.0	9.8	9.8
White female, age adjusted. . . .	5.2	4.7	4.4	4.3	4.5	4.7
Black female, age adjusted	2.4	2.1	1.6	1.8	1.8	1.6

X Not applicable.

Source: U.S. National Center for Health Statistics , *Vital Statistics of the United States,* annual; National Vital Statistics Reports (NVSR) (formerly *Monthly Vital Statistics Report*); and unpublished data.

Table 115. **Death Rates from Human Immunodeficiency Virus (HIV) Disease by Age, Sex, and Race: 1990 to 2002**

[Rates per 100,000 population. Starting with 1999 data, cause of death is coded according to ICD-10, for explanation, see text, this section. For explanation of age-adjustment, see headnote, Table 99. See Appendix III]

Characteristic	1990	1995	1999	2000	2001	2002
All ages, age adjusted. . .	**10.2**	**16.3**	**5.4**	**5.2**	**5.0**	**4.9**
Under 1 year	2.7	1.5	(B)	(B)	(B)	(B)
1-4 years.	0.8	1.3	0.2	(B)	(B)	(B)
5-14 years	0.2	0.5	0.2	0.1	0.1	0.1
15-24 years	1.5	1.7	0.5	0.5	0.6	0.4
25-34 years	19.7	29.1	6.8	6.1	5.3	4.6
35-44 years	27.4	44.4	13.8	13.1	13.0	12.7
45-54 years	15.2	26.3	10.7	11.0	10.5	11.2
55-64 years	6.2	11.0	4.8	5.1	5.2	5.1
65-74 years	2.0	3.6	2.2	2.2	2.1	2.2
75-84 years	0.7	0.7	0.6	0.7	0.7	0.8
85 years and over	(B)	(B)	(B)	(B)	(B)	(B)
Male, age adjusted.	**18.5**	**27.7**	**8.4**	**7.9**	**7.5**	**7.4**
Under 1 year	2.4	1.7	(B)	(B)	(B)	(B)
1-4 years.	0.8	1.2	(B)	(B)	(B)	(B)
5-14 years	0.3	0.5	0.2	0.1	0.1	(B)
15-24 years	2.2	2.1	0.5	0.5	0.5	0.4
25-34 years	34.5	47.1	9.5	8.0	7.1	5.9
35-44 years	50.2	75.9	21.0	19.8	19.5	18.8
45-54 years	29.1	46.9	17.5	17.8	16.8	17.7
55-64 years	12.0	19.9	8.3	8.7	8.6	8.5
65-74 years	3.7	6.4	3.8	3.8	3.5	3.9
75-84 years	1.1	1.3	1.0	1.3	1.5	1.4
85 years and over	(B)	(B)	(B)	(B)	(B)	(B)
Female, age adjusted	**2.2**	**5.3**	**2.6**	**2.5**	**2.5**	**2.5**
Under 1 year	3.0	1.2	(B)	(B)	(B)	(B)
1-4 years.	0.8	1.5	(B)	(B)	(B)	(B)
5-14 years	0.2	0.5	0.2	0.1	(B)	(B)
15-24 years	0.7	1.4	0.5	0.4	0.6	0.4
25-34 years	4.9	11.1	4.1	4.2	3.5	3.3
35-45 years	5.2	13.4	6.7	6.5	6.7	6.7
45-54 years	1.9	6.7	4.1	4.4	4.4	4.8
55-64 years	1.1	2.9	1.6	1.8	2.0	1.9
65-74 years	0.8	1.4	0.8	0.8	0.9	0.8
75-84 years	0.4	0.3	0.3	0.3	(B)	0.3
85 years and over	(B)	(B)	(B)	(B)	(B)	(B)
Race, age adjusted						
White male.	15.7	20.7	5.0	4.6	4.4	4.3
Black male.	46.3	90.4	37.1	35.1	33.8	33.3
White female	1.1	2.5	1.0	1.0	0.9	0.9
Black female	10.1	24.7	13.4	13.2	13.4	13.4

B Base figure too small to meet statistical standards for reliability of a derived figure.

Source: U.S. National Center for Health Statistics. *Vital Statistics of the United States,* annual; *National Vital Statistics Reports* (NVSR); and unpublished data.

U.S. Census Bureau, Statistical Abstract of the United States: 2006

Table 116. **Deaths—Life Years Lost and Mortality Costs by Age, Sex, and Cause: 2000 and 2002**

[Life years lost: Number of years person would have lived in absence of death. **Mortality cost:** value of lifetime earnings lost by persons who die prematurely, discounted at 6 percent]

Characteristic	Number of deaths (1,000)	Life years lost [1]		Mortality cost [2]	
		Total (1,000)	Per death	Total (mil. dol.)	Per death (dol.)
Total, 2000.	2,403	38,843	16.2	431,992	179,772
Under 5 yrs. old.	33	2,522	76.4	30,421	921,471
5 to 14 yrs. old	7	513	69.2	8,331	1,123,778
15 to 24 yrs. old.	31	1,835	58.6	43,039	1,374,751
25 to 44 yrs. old.	130	5,604	43.1	144,409	1,108,713
45 to 64 yrs. old.	346	10,555	30.5	168,201	486,146
65 yrs. old and over	1,855	17,815	9.6	37,591	20,265
Heart disease	711	8,917	12.5	72,224	101,623
Cancer.	553	10,028	18.1	107,501	194,367
Cerebrovascular diseases	168	1,934	11.5	12,103	72,187
Accidents and adverse effects . . .	98	3,303	33.8	69,429	709,801
Other	874	14,661	16.8	170,736	195,408
Male.	1,177	20,415	17.3	316,850	269,135
Under 5 yrs. old.	19	1,373	74.0	19,287	1,040,197
5 to 14 yrs. old	4	295	67.0	5,540	1,258,796
15 to 24 yrs. old.	23	1,319	57.2	34,230	1,483,692
25 to 44 yrs. old.	85	3,549	41.7	107,638	1,263,555
45 to 64 yrs. old.	244	6,098	25.0	123,301	505,917
65 yrs. old and over	802	7,781	9.7	26,853	33,467
Heart disease	345	4,709	13.7	56,883	164,989
Cancer.	286	5,333	18.6	75,819	265,036
Cerebrovascular diseases	65	777	12.0	7,861	121,377
Accidents and adverse effects . . .	64	2,259	35.4	55,756	874,831
Other	418	7,336	17.6	120,531	288,386
Female.	1,226	18,428	15.0	115,142	93,939
Under 5 yrs. old.	14	1,149	79.4	11,134	769,356
5 to 14 yrs. old	3	218	72.4	2,791	926,495
15 to 24 yrs. old.	8	516	62.6	8,809	1,069,584
25 to 44 yrs. old.	45	2,054	45.6	36,770	815,994
45 to 64 yrs. old.	102	4,457	43.6	44,899	439,031
65 yrs. old and over	1,053	10,034	9.5	10,738	10,201
Heart disease	366	4,208	11.5	15,341	41,923
Cancer.	267	4,695	17.6	31,681	118,653
Cerebrovascular diseases	103	1,157	11.2	4,241	41,223
Accidents and adverse effects . . .	34	1,044	30.6	13,673	401,183
Other	456	7,325	16.1	50,205	110,150
Total, 2002.	2,443	40,216	16.5	475,101	194,472
Under 5 yrs. old.	33	2,526	76.8	31,176	947,825
5 to 14 yrs. old	7	497	69.5	8,247	1,153,363
15 to 24 yrs. old.	33	1,947	58.9	46,412	1,404,461
25 to 44 yrs. old.	132	5,743	43.3	153,188	1,156,179
45 to 64 yrs. old.	369	11,381	30.8	195,403	529,031
65 yrs. old and over	1,868	18,123	9.7	40,677	21,774
Heart disease	697	8,965	12.9	79,541	114,136
Cancer.	557	10,288	18.5	118,618	212,858
Cerebrovascular diseases	163	1,909	11.7	12,771	78,511
Accidents and adverse effects . . .	107	3,594	33.7	77,859	729,992
Other	920	15,460	16.8	186,312	202,614
Male.	1,199	21,137	17.6	340,827	284,264
Under 5 yrs. old.	19	1,379	74.4	19,341	1,044,188
5 to 14 yrs. old	4	282	67.3	5,312	1,265,460
15 to 24 yrs. old.	24	1,404	57.5	36,464	1,493,433
25 to 44 yrs. old.	86	3,626	42.0	111,931	1,296,567
45 to 64 yrs. old.	259	6,584	25.4	140,248	541,322
65 yrs. old and over	806	7,862	9.7	27,530	34,138
Heart disease	341	4,762	14.0	61,487	180,367
Cancer.	289	5,481	19.0	81,952	283,805
Cerebrovascular diseases	63	763	12.2	8,041	128,410
Accidents and adverse effects . . .	69	2,444	35.3	61,311	886,215
Other	438	7,687	17.6	128,036	292,642
Female.	1,244	19,080	15.3	134,274	107,933
Under 5 yrs. old.	14	1,147	79.8	11,834	823,603
5 to 14 yrs. old	3	215	72.7	2,934	993,950
15 to 24 yrs. old.	9	543	62.9	9,948	1,152,744
25 to 44 yrs. old.	46	2,116	45.8	41,257	893,658
45 to 64 yrs. old.	110	4,798	43.5	55,154	500,156
65 yrs. old and over	1,062	10,261	9.7	13,147	12,383
Heart disease	356	4,203	11.8	18,055	50,715
Cancer.	269	4,807	17.9	36,666	136,557
Cerebrovascular diseases	100	1,146	11.5	4,730	47,279
Accidents and adverse effects . . .	37	1,150	30.7	16,548	441,578
Other	482	7,774	16.1	58,276	120,899

[1] Based on life expectancy at year of death. [2] Cost estimates based on the person's age, sex, life expectancy at the time of death, labor force participation rates, annual earnings, value of homemaking services, and a 4-percent discount rate by which to convert to present worth the potential aggregate earnings lost over the years.

Source: Institute for Health and Aging, University of California, San Francisco, CA, unpublished data.

92 Vital Statistics

Table 117. **Marriages and Divorces—Number and Rate by State: 1990 to 2004**

[2,443.0 represents 2,443,000. By place of occurence. See Appendix III]

State	Marriages [1]						Divorces [3]					
	Number (1,000)			Rate per 1,000 population [2]			Number (1,000)			Rate per 1,000 population [2]		
	1990	2000	2004	1990	2000	2004	1990	2000	2004	1990	2000	2004
U.S. [4]	2,443.0	2,329.0	2,178.4	9.8	8.3	7.4	1,182.0	(NA)	(NA)	4.7	4.2	3.7
Alabama	43.3	45.0	40.6	10.6	10.3	9.0	25.3	23.5	21.5	6.1	5.4	4.7
Alaska	5.7	5.6	5.4	10.2	8.9	8.3	2.9	2.7	3.1	5.5	4.4	4.8
Arizona	37.0	38.7	37.9	10.0	7.9	6.6	25.1	21.6	24.4	6.9	4.4	4.2
Arkansas	35.7	41.1	35.7	15.3	16.0	13.0	16.8	17.9	17.4	6.9	6.9	6.3
California [5]	236.7	196.9	172.3	7.9	5.9	4.8	128.0	(NA)	(NA)	4.3	(NA)	(NA)
Colorado	31.5	35.6	34.5	9.8	8.6	7.5	18.4	(NA)	20.2	5.5	(NA)	4.4
Connecticut	27.8	19.4	16.5	7.9	5.9	4.7	10.3	6.5	10.3	3.2	2.0	2.9
Delaware	5.6	5.1	5.1	8.4	6.7	6.1	3.0	3.2	3.1	4.4	4.2	3.7
District of Columbia	4.7	2.8	2.9	8.2	5.4	5.3	2.7	1.5	0.9	4.5	3.0	1.7
Florida	142.3	141.9	156.4	10.9	9.3	9.0	81.7	81.9	82.7	6.3	5.3	4.8
Georgia	64.4	56.0	64.5	10.3	7.1	7.3	35.7	30.7	(NA)	5.5	3.9	(NA)
Hawaii	18.1	25.0	28.4	16.4	21.2	22.5	5.2	4.6	(NA)	4.6	3.9	(NA)
Idaho	15.0	14.0	15.2	13.9	11.0	10.9	6.6	6.9	7.1	6.5	5.4	5.1
Illinois	97.1	85.5	77.8	8.8	7.0	6.1	44.3	39.1	33.1	3.8	3.2	2.6
Indiana	54.3	34.5	48.4	9.6	5.8	7.8	(NA)	(NA)	(NA)	(NA)	(NA)	(NA)
Iowa	24.8	20.3	20.5	9.0	*7.0	6.9	11.1	9.4	8.3	3.9	3.3	2.8
Kansas	23.4	22.2	19.1	9.2	8.3	7.0	12.6	10.6	9.1	5.0	4.0	3.3
Kentucky	51.3	39.7	36.8	13.5	10.0	8.9	21.8	21.6	20.5	5.8	5.4	4.9
Louisiana	41.2	40.5	30.2	9.6	9.3	6.7	(NA)	(NA)	(NA)	(NA)	(NA)	(NA)
Maine	11.8	10.5	10.9	9.7	8.3	8.3	5.3	5.8	4.7	4.3	4.6	3.6
Maryland	46.1	40.0	37.7	9.7	7.7	6.8	16.1	17.0	17.1	3.4	3.3	3.1
Massachusetts . . .	47.8	37.0	41.2	7.9	6.0	6.4	16.8	18.6	14.1	2.8	3.0	2.2
Michigan	76.1	66.4	62.6	8.2	6.7	6.2	40.2	39.4	35.0	4.3	4.0	3.5
Minnesota	33.7	33.4	30.1	7.7	6.9	5.9	15.4	14.8	14.2	3.5	3.1	2.8
Mississippi	24.3	19.7	17.8	9.4	7.1	6.1	14.4	14.4	13.1	5.5	5.2	4.5
Missouri	49.3	43.7	36.5	9.6	7.9	6.3	26.4	26.5	21.9	5.1	4.8	3.8
Montana	7.0	6.6	6.8	8.6	7.4	7.4	4.1	2.1	3.5	5.1	2.4	3.8
Nebraska	12.5	13.0	12.9	8.0	7.8	7.4	6.5	6.4	6.4	4.0	3.8	3.6
Nevada	123.4	144.3	145.8	99.0	76.7	62.4	13.3	18.1	14.8	11.4	9.6	6.4
New Hampshire . .	10.6	11.6	9.8	9.5	9.5	7.6	5.3	7.1	5.0	4.7	5.8	3.9
New Jersey	58.0	50.4	50.1	7.6	6.1	5.8	23.6	25.6	26.0	3.0	3.1	3.0
New Mexico	13.2	14.5	14.1	8.8	8.3	7.4	7.7	9.2	8.8	4.9	5.3	4.6
New York	169.3	162.0	124.4	8.6	8.9	6.5	57.9	62.8	57.8	3.2	3.4	3.0
North Carolina . . .	52.1	65.6	65.9	7.8	8.5	7.7	34.0	36.9	37.7	5.1	4.8	4.4
North Dakota	4.8	4.6	4.1	7.5	7.3	6.5	2.3	2.0	1.8	3.6	3.2	2.8
Ohio	95.8	88.5	75.9	9.0	7.9	6.6	51.0	49.3	42.4	4.7	4.4	3.7
Oklahoma	33.2	15.6	22.8	10.6	4.6	6.5	24.9	12.4	(NA)	7.7	3.7	(NA)
Oregon	25.2	26.0	29.0	8.9	7.8	8.1	15.9	16.7	14.8	5.5	5.0	4.1
Pennsylvania	86.8	73.2	65.1	7.1	6.1	5.3	40.1	37.9	30.7	3.3	3.2	2.5
Rhode Island	8.1	8.0	8.2	8.1	8.0	7.6	3.8	3.1	3.3	3.7	3.1	3.0
South Carolina . . .	55.8	42.7	34.5	15.9	10.9	8.2	16.1	14.4	13.4	4.5	3.7	3.2
South Dakota	7.7	7.1	6.5	11.1	9.6	8.4	2.6	2.7	2.5	3.7	3.6	3.2
Tennessee	66.6	88.2	67.5	13.9	15.9	11.4	32.3	33.8	29.8	6.5	6.1	5.0
Texas	182.8	196.4	176.3	10.5	9.6	7.8	94.0	85.2	81.9	5.5	4.2	3.6
Utah	19.0	24.1	13.2	11.2	11.1	5.5	8.8	9.7	9.3	5.1	4.5	3.9
Vermont	6.1	6.1	6.0	10.9	10.2	9.6	2.6	5.1	2.4	4.5	8.6	3.9
Virginia	71.3	62.4	62.5	11.4	9.0	8.4	27.3	30.2	30.1	4.4	4.3	4.0
Washington	48.6	40.9	40.1	9.5	7.0	6.5	28.8	27.2	25.2	5.9	4.7	4.1
West Virginia	13.2	15.7	13.2	7.2	8.7	7.3	9.7	9.3	8.6	5.3	5.2	4.7
Wisconsin	41.2	36.1	34.1	7.9	6.8	6.2	17.8	17.6	17.0	3.6	3.3	3.1
Wyoming	4.8	4.9	4.8	10.7	10.3	9.4	3.1	2.8	2.7	6.6	5.9	5.3

NA Not available. [1] Data are counts of marriages performed, except as noted. [2] Based on total population residing in area; population enumerated as of April 1 for 1990 and 2000; estimated as of July 1 for all other years. [3] Includes annulments. [4] U.S. totals for the number of divorces is an estimate which includes states not reporting (CA, CO, IN, and LA). [5] Marriage data include nonlicensed marriages registered.

Source: U.S. National Center for Health Statistics, *Vital Statistics of the United States*, annual; *National Vital Statistics Reports* (NVSR) (formerly *Monthly Vital Statistical Report*).

Vital Statistics 93

No. 43.—INSANE ENUMERATED IN HOSPITALS: NUMBER AND RATIO PER 100,000 OF POPULATION IN 1890, 1903, AND 1910, BY STATES, BY GEOGRAPHIC DIVISIONS, AND (FOR 1903) BY NATIVITY AND COLOR.

[Source: Reports of the Bureau of the Census, Department of Commerce and Labor.]

State.	June 1, 1890.		Dec. 31, 1903.						Jan. 1, 1910.[1]	
	Number.	Number per 100,000 of population.	Number.	Number per 100,000 of population.[2]	Native white.	Foreign-born white.	White, nativity unknown.	Colored.	Number.	Number per 100,000 of population.
Alabama	1,014	67.0	1,603	82.6	1,085	41	30	447	2,039	95.4
Arizona	65	109.0	224	165.5	100	95	19	10	337	164.9
Arkansas	390	34.6	867	48.4	537	21	1	108	1,092	60.4
California	3,289	272.2	5,717	361.3	2,556	2,795	88	278	6,653	277.7
Colorado	239	58.0	754	128.9	441	267	23	23	1,199	150.1
Connecticut	1,544	206.9	2,831	292.0	1,786	980	8	57	3,574	320.6
Delaware	142	84.2	353	185.2	193	78	4	78	441	218.0
Dist. of Columbia	1,496	649.3	2,453	828.6	1,255	728	7	463	2,890	872.9
Florida	202	51.6	713	123.4	308	73	55	277	849	112.8
Georgia	1,491	81.1	2,839	120.7	1,907	34	2	896	3,132	130.0
Idaho	63	74.7	255	135.6	137	104	9	5	388	110.2
Illinois	4,767	124.6	9,607	185.5	5,138	3,667	562	240	12,838	227.7
Indiana	1,798	82.0	4,358	165.5	3,559	580	111	108	4,529	167.7
Iowa	2,630	106.2	4,385	186.9	2,935	1,320	72	58	5,377	241.7
Kansas	1,261	88.4	2,460	165.6	1,802	549	13	96	2,912	172.2
Kentucky	1,991	107.1	3,058	135.9	2,362	174	46	476	3,538	154.5
Louisiana	608	54.4	1,585	107.4	936	167	16	466	2,158	130.3
Maine	612	92.6	885	125.3	742	129	6	8	1,258	169.5
Maryland	1,416	135.8	2,505	202.0	1,740	413	25	327	3,230	248.6
Massachusetts	4,054	181.1	8,679	288.5	4,917	3,558	77	127	11,602	344.6
Michigan	2,771	132.3	5,430	215.6	2,929	2,253	173	75	6,699	238.4
Minnesota	1,859	142.8	4,070	213.1	1,463	2,547	49	11	4,744	228.5
Mississippi	682	52.9	1,493	90.8	896	36	3	558	1,978	110.5
Missouri	2,417	90.2	5,103	156.5	3,474	997	383	249	6,170	187.3
Montana	172	130.1	543	194.4	221	303	1	18	697	185.3
Nebraska	642	60.6	1,536	143.9	873	639	8	16	1,991	167.0
Nevada	172	375.9	200	472.4	65	111	11	13	231	282.1
New Hampshire	342	90.8	496	116.9	374	113	8	1	909	211.1
New Jersey	1,744	120.7	4,865	238.4	2,756	1,803	109	197	6,044	238.2
New Mexico			113	54.4	93	12	7	1	219	66.9
New York	13,434	224.0	26,176	339.0	13,452	11,858	336	530	31,279	343.2
North Carolina	972	60.1	1,883	94.5	1,349	13		521	2,522	114.3
North Dakota	200	109.5	446	122.2	140	303	1	2	628	108.8
Ohio	4,960	135.1	8,621	190.0	6,542	1,688	146	245	10,594	222.2
Oklahoma			413	80.5	366	36		11	1,110	67.0
Oregon	554	176.6	1,285	286.9	739	487	15	44	1,565	232.2
Pennsylvania	6,257	119.0	11,521	172.6	7,516	3,367	229	409	15,040	196.5
Rhode Island	660	191.0	1,077	235.0	681	358	11	27	1,243	229.1
South Carolina	664	57.7	1,156	82.1	681	6		469	1,541	101.7
South Dakota	232	70.6	595	141.5	286	285	3	21	864	148.0
Tennessee	806	45.6	1,713	81.1	1,356	33	13	311	2,205	100.9
Texas	1,045	46.7	3,345	100.1	2,364	426	144	411	4,053	104.0
Utah	124	59.6	344	114.5	189	149	4	2	342	91.6
Vermont	481	144.7	887	255.1	712	152	21	2	990	278.1
Virginia	1,764	106.5	3,137	162.9	2,045	64	3	1,025	3,636	176.4
Washington	341	97.6	1,178	204.6	561	588	14	15	1,988	174.1
West Virginia	860	112.7	1,475	143.3	1,262	123	8	82	1,722	141.0
Wisconsin	1,378	81.7	5,023	227.9	2,426	2,512	63	22	6,586	282.2
Wyoming	23	37.9	96	93.0	50	43		3	162	111.0
Total	74,028	118.2	150,151	186.2	90,297	47,078	2,937	9,839	187,798	204.2
Geographic divisions.[3]										
New England	7,603	163.7	14,855	251.3	9,212	5,290	131	222	19,576	298.7
Middle Atlantic	21,435	168.8	42,562	258.9	23,724	17,028	674	1,136	52,383	271.2
East North Central	15,674	116.3	33,039	195.9	20,504	10,700	1,055	690	41,246	226.0
West North Central	8,641	97.2	18,595	171.3	10,973	6,640	529	453	22,686	194.9
South Atlantic	9,007	101.7	16,514	150.0	10,740	1,532	104	4,138	19,953	163.6
East South Central	4,493	69.9	7,867	99.0	5,699	284	92	1,792	9,760	116.1
West South Central	2,043	45.0	6,010	83.8	4,203	650	161	996	8,413	95.8
Mountain	858	74.2	2,529	137.3	1,296	1,084	74	75	3,575	135.8
Pacific	4,184	223.6	8,180	313.9	3,856	3,870	117	337	10,206	243.4

[1] Provisional figures subject to correction.
[2] Figures based on estimated population, Dec. 31, 1903.
[3] For States included in each division see note 5, p. 38.

Source: Statistical Abstract of the United States: 1912 Edition.

Health and Nutrition

This section presents statistics on health expenditures and insurance coverage, including Medicare and Medicaid, medical personnel, hospitals, nursing homes and other care facilities, injuries, diseases, disability status, nutritional intake of the population, and food consumption. Summary statistics showing recent trends on health care and discussions of selected health issues are published annually by the U.S. National Center for Health Statistics (NCHS) in *Health, United States*. Data on national health expenditures, medical costs, and insurance coverage are compiled by the U.S. Centers for Medicare & Medicaid Services (CMS) (formerly Health Care Financing Administration), and appear on the CMS Web site at <http://www.cms.hhs.gov/statistics/nhe> and in the annual *Medicare and Medicaid Statistical Supplement* to the *Health Care Financing Review*. Statistics on health insurance are also collected by NCHS and are published in Series 10 of *Vital and Health Statistics*. U.S. Census Bureau also publishes data on utilization of insurance coverage. Statistics on hospitals are published annually by the Health Forum, L.L.C., an American Hospital Association Company, in *Hospital Statistics*. Primary source for data on nutrition is the annual *Food Consumption, Prices, and Expenditures*, issued by the U.S. Department of Agriculture. NCHS also conducts periodic surveys of nutrient levels in the population, including estimates of food and nutrient intake, overweight and obesity, hypercholesterolemia, hypertension, and clinical signs of malnutrition.

National health expenditures—CMS compiles estimates of national health expenditures (NHE) to measure spending for health care in the United States. The NHE accounts are structured to show spending by type of expenditure (i.e., hospital care, physician and clinical care, dental care, and other professional care; home health care; retail sales of prescription drugs; other medical nondurables; vision products and other medical durables; nursing home care and other personal health expenditures; plus non-personal health expenditures for such items as public health, research, construction of medical facilities, administration, and the net cost of private health insurance) and by source of funding (e.g., private health insurance, out-of-pocket payments, and a range of public programs including Medicare, Medicaid, and those operated by the Department of Veterans Affairs (VA)).

Data used to estimate health expenditures come from existing sources, which are tabulated for other purposes. The type of expenditure estimates rely upon statistics produced by such groups as the American Hospital Association, the Census Bureau, and the Department of Health and Human Services (HHS). Source of funding estimates are constructed using administrative and statistical records from the Medicare and Medicaid programs, the Department of Defense and VA medical programs, the Social Security Administration, Census Bureau's *Governmental Finances*, state and local governments, other HHS agencies, and other nongovernment sources. More information and detailed descriptions of sources and methods are available on the CMS home page at <http://cms.hhs.gov/statistics/nhe/default.asp>.

Medicare, Medicaid and SCHIP—Since July 1966, the federal Medicare program has provided two coordinated plans for nearly all people age 65 and over: (1) A hospital insurance plan, which covers hospital and related services and (2) a voluntary supplementary medical insurance plan, financed partially by monthly premiums paid by participants, which partly covers physicians' and related medical services. Such insurance also applies, since July 1973, to disabled beneficiaries of any age after 24 months of entitlement to cash benefits under the social security or railroad retirement programs and to persons with end stage renal disease.

Medicaid is a health insurance program for certain low-income people. These include: certain low-income families with children; aged, blind, or disabled people on supplemental security income; certain low-income pregnant women and children; and people who have very high medical bills. Medicaid is funded and administered through a state-federal partnership. Although there are broad federal requirements for Medicaid, states have a wide degree of flexibility to design their program. States have authority to establish eligibility standards, determine what benefits and services to cover, and set payment rates. Congress created the State Children's Health Insurance Program (SCHIP) to address the growing problem of children without health insurance.· SCHIP was designed as a federal/state partnership, similar to Medicaid, with the goal of expanding health insurance to children whose families earn too much money to be eligible for Medicaid, but not enough money to purchase private insurance.

Health resources—Hospital statistics based on data from the American Hospital Association's yearly survey are published annually in *Hospital Statistics* and cover all hospitals accepted for registration by the Association. To be accepted for registration, a hospital must meet certain requirements relating to number of beds, construction, equipment, medical and nursing staff, patient care, clinical records, surgical and obstetrical facilities, diagnostic and treatment facilities, laboratory services, etc. Data obtained from NCHS cover all U.S. hospitals that meet certain criteria for inclusion. The criteria are published in *Vital and Health Statistics* reports, Series 13. NCHS defines a hospital as a nonfederal short-term general or special facility with six or more inpatient beds with an average stay of less than 30 days.

Statistics on the demographic characteristics of persons employed in the health occupations are compiled by the U.S. Bureau of Labor Statistics and reported in *Employment and Earnings* (monthly) (see Table 604, Section 12, Labor Force, Employment, and Earnings). Data based on surveys of health personnel and utilization of health facilities providing long-term care, ambulatory care, and hospital care are presented in NCHS Series 13, *Data on Health Resources Utilization and Advance Data from Vital and Health Statistics*. Statistics on patient visits to health care providers, as reported in health interviews, appear in NCHS Series 10, *National Health Interview Survey Data*.

The CMS's *Health Care Financing Review* and its annual *Medicare and Medicaid Statistical Supplement* present data for hospitals and nursing homes as well as extended care facilities and home health agencies. These data are based on records of the Medicare program and differ from those of other sources because they are limited to facilities meeting federal eligibility standards for participation in Medicare.

Disability and illness—General health statistics, including morbidity, disability, injuries, preventive care, and findings from physiological testing are collected by NCHS in its National Health Interview Survey and its National Health and Nutrition Examination Surveys and appear in *Vital and Health Statistics*, Series 10 and 11, respectively. The Department of Labor compiles statistics on occupational injuries (see Section 12, Labor Force, Employment, and Earnings). Annual incidence data on notifiable diseases are compiled by the Public Health Service (PHS) at its Centers for Disease Control and Prevention in Atlanta, Georgia, and are published as a supplement to its *Morbidity and Mortality Weekly Report*. The list of diseases is revised annually and includes those which, by mutual agreement of the states and PHS, are communicable diseases of national importance.

Nutrition—Statistics on annual per capita consumption of food and its nutrient value are estimated by the U.S. Department of Agriculture. Data are available online at <http://www.ers .usda.gov /data/foodconsumption>. Statistics on food insufficiency and food and nutrient intake are collected by NCHS to estimate the diet of the nation's population. NCHS also collects physical examination data to assess the population's nutritional status, including growth, overweight/obesity, nutritional deficiencies, and prevalence of nutrition-related conditions, such as hypertension, hypercholesterolemia, and diabetes.

Statistical reliability—For discussion of statistical collection, estimation, and sampling procedures and measures of reliability applicable to data from NCHS and CMS, see Appendix III.

Figure 3.1
Number of retail drug prescriptions:
1995 to 2004

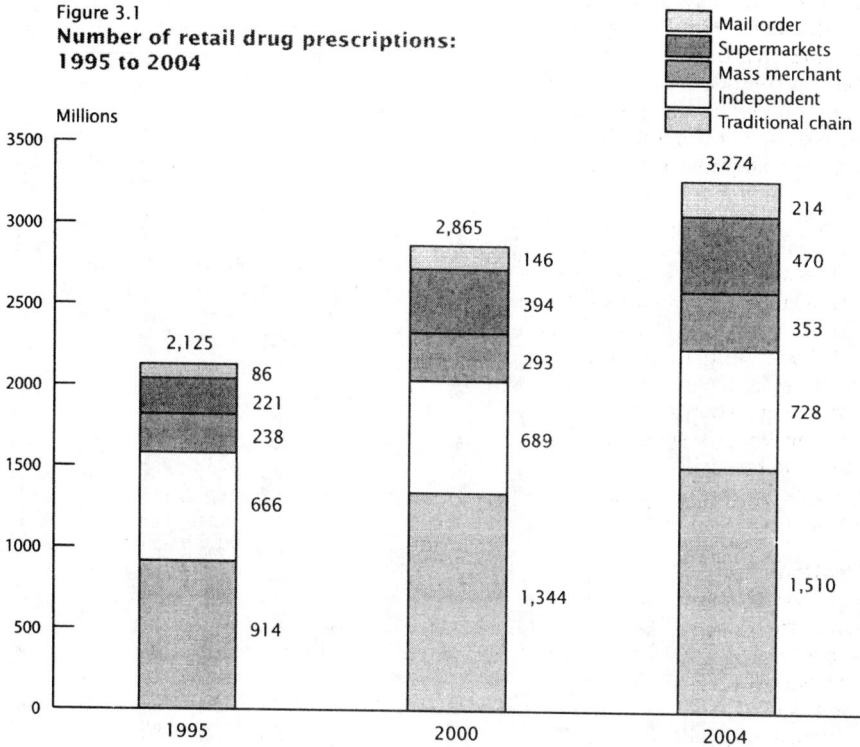

Source: Figure 3.1 prepared by U.S. Census Bureau. For data, see Table 126.

U.S. Census Bureau, Statistical Abstract of the United States: 2006

Table 118. **National Health Expenditures—Summary, 1960 to 2003, and Projections, 2004 to 2014**

[In billions of dollars (27 represents $27,000,000,000). Excludes Puerto Rico and island areas]

Year	Private expenditures			Public expenditures			Health services and supplies				
	Total expendi-tures [1]	Total [2]	Out-of-pocket	Insur-ance	Total	Federal	State and local	Total [3]	Hospi-tal care	Physi-cian and clinical ser-vices	Pre-scrip-tion drugs	Nursing home care
1960	27	20	13	6	7	3	4	25	9	5	3	1
1961	29	21	13	7	7	3	4	27	10	6	3	1
1962	31	23	14	7	8	4	4	29	11	6	3	1
1963	34	25	15	8	9	4	5	31	12	7	3	1
1964	38	28	17	9	9	4	5	34	13	8	3	1
1965	41	31	18	10	10	5	6	37	14	8	4	2
1966	45	32	19	10	14	7	6	41	16	9	4	2
1967	51	32	19	11	19	12	7	47	18	10	4	2
1968	58	36	21	12	22	14	8	53	21	11	5	3
1969	65	40	23	13	24	16	9	59	24	12	5	4
1970	73	45	25	16	28	18	10	67	28	14	6	4
1971	81	50	26	18	31	20	11	75	31	16	6	5
1972	91	56	29	21	35	23	12	84	34	17	6	6
1973	101	61	32	23	39	25	14	93	39	19	7	6
1974	114	67	35	26	46	30	16	106	45	22	7	7
1975	130	75	37	30	55	36	19	121	52	25	8	9
1976	149	87	41	37	62	43	20	139	60	28	9	10
1977	169	99	45	45	70	47	23	160	68	33	9	12
1978	189	110	48	52	80	54	26	179	76	35	10	13
1979	214	124	53	60	90	61	29	203	87	41	11	15
1980	246	141	58	68	105	71	34	234	102	47	12	18
1981	285	164	66	81	121	83	39	271	119	55	13	20
1982	321	187	72	94	134	92	42	305	135	61	15	23
1983	354	206	79	104	148	102	46	336	146	68	17	26
1984	390	229	86	118	161	113	48	372	156	77	20	28
1985	427	252	96	130	175	122	52	409	167	90	22	31
1986	457	267	103	135	190	132	59	439	178	100	24	34
1987	498	289	109	148	209	143	66	478	192	112	27	36
1988	558	332	119	175	226	154	72	535	209	127	31	41
1989	623	371	126	205	252	172	79	599	229	142	35	46
1990	696	414	137	234	283	193	90	670	254	158	40	53
1991	762	441	142	254	321	222	99	735	280	175	45	58
1992	827	469	146	274	359	251	107	797	302	190	48	62
1993	888	498	147	298	390	274	116	856	320	201	51	66
1994	937	510	144	312	427	299	129	905	332	211	55	68
1995	990	533	146	330	457	323	134	958	344	221	61	75
1996	1,040	557	152	344	483	345	138	1,006	355	229	67	80
1997	1,093	590	162	361	503	360	143	1,056	368	241	76	85
1998	1,151	631	176	385	520	367	153	1,113	379	257	87	90
1999	1,222	672	185	414	550	386	164	1,180	393	271	104	91
2000	1,310	718	193	451	592	416	176	1,261	413	290	122	95
2001	1,426	772	202	497	655	464	191	1,374	446	315	141	101
2002	1,559	841	214	550	718	509	209	1,500	484	341	162	107
2003	1,679	913	231	601	766	542	224	1,614	516	370	179	111
2004, proj...	1,805	981	246	647	824	584	241	1,736	552	397	201	115
2005, proj...	1,937	1,045	262	691	891	627	264	1,863	589	426	224	121
2006, proj...	2,078	1,078	258	722	1,000	731	275	1,998	624	454	249	127
2007, proj...	2,233	1,156	276	775	1,077	787	297	2,147	663	487	276	134
2008, proj...	2,399	1,241	296	834	1,158	846	320	2,307	704	522	305	141
2009, proj...	2,573	1,330	316	896	1,243	907	344	2,475	749	560	336	149
2010, proj...	2,754	1,421	338	957	1,333	972	370	2,649	795	599	369	157
2011, proj...	2,944	1,517	361	1,023	1,427	1,039	397	2,832	844	640	404	166
2012, proj...	3,146	1,615	385	1,089	1,532	1,116	426	3,027	895	685	441	175
2013, proj...	3,361	1,714	408	1,157	1,647	1,201	457	3,234	950	732	480	184
2014, proj...	3,586	1,813	431	1,225	1,773	1,295	490	3,451	1,007	783	521	195

[1] Includes medical research and medical facilities construction, not shown separately. [2] Includes other private expenditures, not shown separately. [3] Includes other objects of expenditure, not shown separately.

Source: U. S. Centers for Medicare & Medicaid Services, Office of the Actuary, "Health Accounts"; <http://www.cms.hhs.gov/statistics/nhe/default.asp>.

98 Health and Nutrition

Table 119. National Health Expenditures by Type: 1990 to 2003

[In billions of dollars (696.0 represents $696,000,000,000), except percent. Excludes Puerto Rico and island areas]

Type of expenditure	1990	1995	1998	1999	2000	2001	2002	2003
Total	696.0	990.2	1,150.9	1,222.2	1,309.9	1,426.4	1,559.0	1,678.9
Annual percent change [1]	11.8	5.7	5.3	6.2	7.2	8.9	9.3	7.7
Percent of gross domestic product	12.0	13.4	13.2	13.2	13.3	14.1	14.9	15.3
Private expenditures..........	413.5	533.4	631.1	671.9	717.5	771.8	841.0	913.2
Health services and supplies..........	401.9	520.9	615.5	655.8	699.2	754.2	821.3	892.6
Out-of-pocket payments	137.3	146.5	175.6	184.7	193.1	202.0	214.2	230.5
Insurance premiums [2]	233.5	329.7	384.7	413.7	450.6	496.6	549.5	600.6
Other	31.1	44.9	55.3	57.3	55.5	55.6	57.6	61.5
Medical research	1.0	1.4	2.0	2.1	3.4	2.6	2.6	2.5
Medical facilities construction	10.7	11.1	13.6	14.1	14.9	14.9	17.2	18.1
Public expenditures	282.5	456.6	519.8	550.3	592.4	654.6	718.0	765.7
Percent federal of public	68.2	70.6	70.6	70.2	70.2	70.8	70.8	70.7
Health services and supplies.........	267.7	436.7	497.1	524.4	561.7	619.6	678.5	721.7
Medicare [3]	110.2	183.3	208.8	213.0	224.5	248.8	267.7	283.1
Public assistance medical payments [4] ...	78.7	149.5	176.6	191.7	209.3	231.6	259.9	279.0
Temporary disability insurance [5]	0.1	0.1	0.1	-	-	-	-	-
Workers' compensation (medical) [5].....	17.5	21.9	20.7	22.8	25.3	27.7	31.0	34.0
Defense Dept. hospital, medical.......	10.4	12.1	12.2	12.9	14.0	15.2	17.6	17.2
Maternal, child health programs	1.8	2.2	2.4	2.6	2.7	2.7	2.7	2.7
Public health activities	20.2	31.4	37.9	41.2	43.9	47.4	51.2	53.8
Veterans' hospital, medical care.......	11.3	15.4	16.9	17.7	19.1	21.5	22.2	24.5
Medical vocational rehabilitation.......	0.5	0.7	0.8	0.8	0.8	0.8	0.9	0.9
State and local hospitals [6]	13.1	14.1	13.8	13.7	13.4	14.0	14.7	15.5
Other [7]	3.8	6.0	6.9	8.0	8.8	9.8	10.5	15.5
Medical research .... : ..	11.7	15.7	18.6	21.6	25.7	30.3	33.9	37.6
Medical facilities construction	3.1	4.4	4.2	4.3	5.0	4.8	5.6	6.4

- Represents zero or rounds to zero.

[1] Change from immediate prior year. For explanation of average annual percent change, see Guide to Tabular Presentation. [2] Covers insurance benefits and amount retained by insurance companies for expenses, additions to reserves, and profits (net cost of insurance). [3] Represents expenditures for benefits and administrative cost from Federal hospital and medical insurance trust funds under old-age, survivors, disability, and health insurance programs; see text, this section. [4] Payments made directly to suppliers of medical care (primarily medicaid). [5] Includes medical benefits paid under public law by private insurance carriers, state governments, and self-insurers. [6] Expenditures not offset by other revenues. [7] Covers expenditures for Substance Abuse and Mental Health Services Administration, Indian Health Service; school health and other programs.

Source: U. S. Centers for Medicare & Medicaid Services, Office of the Actuary, "Health Accounts"; <http://www.cms.hhs.gov/statistics/nhe/default.asp>.

Table 120. National Health Expenditures by Object, 1990 to 2003, and Projections, 2004

[In billions of dollars (696.0 represents $696,000,000,000). Excludes Puerto Rico and outlying areas]

Object of expenditure	1990	1995	1998	1999	2000	2001	2002	2003	2004, proj.
Total........................	696.0	990.2	1,150.9	1,222.2	1,309.9	1,426.4	1,559.0	1,678.9	1,804.7
Spent by—									
Consumers	370.8	476.2	560.3	598.5	643.7	698.6	763.7	831.1	892.7
Out-of-pocket	137.3	146.5	175.6	184.7	193.1	202.0	214.2	230.5	245.9
Private insurance...............	233.5	329.7	384.7	413.7	450.6	496.6	549.5	600.6	646.9
Public	282.5	456.6	519.8	550.3	592.4	654.6	718.0	765.7	824.2
Other [1]	42.8	57.4	70.8	73.4	73.8	73.1	77.4	82.1	87.7
Spent for—									
Health services and supplies..........	669.6	957.6	1,112.6	1,180.2	1,260.9	1,373.8	1,499.8	1,614.2	1,735.5
Personal health care expenses	609.4	865.7	1,009.8	1,065.6	1,136.1	1,235.5	1,342.9	1,440.8	1,549.0
Hospital care	253.9	343.6	378.5	393.4	413.1	446.4	484.2	515.9	551.8
Physician and clinical services	157.5	220.5	256.8	270.9	290.2	315.1	340.8	369.7	397.2
Dental services	31.5	44.5	53.2	56.4	60.7	65.6	70.9	74.3	79.1
Other professional services [2]	18.2	28.6	35.5	36.7	38.8	42.6	46.1	48.5	52.2
Home health care..............	12.6	30.5	33.6	32.3	31.6	36.5	40.0	45.2	
Prescription drugs	40.3	60.8	87.3	104.4	121.5	140.8	161.8	179.2	200.5
Other nondurable medical products ...	22.5	25.6	28.4	30.0	30.4	30.5	31.1	32.5	33.7
Durable medical equipment [3]	10.6	14.2	16.9	17.2	17.7	18.4	19.6	20.4	21.2
Nursing home care.............	52.7	74.6	89.5	90.7	95.3	101.2	106.6	110.8	115.4
Other personal health care........	9.6	22.9	30.2	33.7	36.7	41.1	45.3	49.5	52.8
Public administration and net cost of private health insurance [4]	40.0	60.5	64.9	73.3	81.0	90.9	105.7	119.7	128.2
Public health activities	20.2	31.4	37.9	41.2	43.9	47.4	51.2	53.8	58.3
Medical research [5]	12.7	17.1	20.5	23.7	29.1	32.9	36.5	40.2	43.1
Medical facilities construction	13.7	15.5	17.7	18.3	19.8	19.7	22.7	24.5	26.1

[1] Includes nonpatient revenues, privately-funded construction, and industrial inplant. [2] Includes services of registered and practical nurses in private duty, podiatrists, optometrists, physical therapists, clinical psychologists, chiropractors, naturopaths, and Christian Science practitioners. [3] Includes expenditures for eyeglasses, hearing aids, orthopedic appliances, artificial limbs, crutches, wheelchairs, etc. [4] Includes administrative expenses of federally-financed health programs. [5] Research and development expenditures of drug companies and other manufacturers and providers of medical equipment and supplies are excluded from research expenditures, but are included in the expenditure class in which the product falls.

Source: U. S. Centers for Medicare & Medicaid Services, Office of the Actuary, "Health Accounts"; <http://www.cms.hhs.gov/statistics/nhe/default.asp>.

Health and Nutrition 99

Table 121. **Health Services and Supplies—Per Capita Consumer Expenditures by Object: 1990 to 2003**

[In dollars, **except percent.** Based on Social Security Administration estimates of total U.S. population as of July 1, excluding Armed Forces and Federal employees abroad and civilian population of Puerto Rico and island areas. Excludes medical research and construction]

Object of expenditure	1990	1995	1998	1999	2000	2001	2002	2003
Total, national	2,633	3,530	3,962	4,154	4,389	4,733	5,115	5,452
Annual percent change [1]	10.5	4.6	4.2	4.9	5.7	7.8	8.1	6.6
Hospital care	998	1,267	1,348	1,385	1,438	1,538	1,652	1,742
Physician and clinical services	619	813	914	954	1,010	1,085	1,162	1,249
Dental services	124	164	189	198	211	226	242	251
Other professional services [2]	71	105	126	129	135	147	157	164
Home health care	49	113	120	114	110	116	125	135
Prescription drugs	158	224	311	368	423	485	552	605
Other nondurable medical products	88	94	101	106	106	105	106	110
Durable medical equipment [2]	42	52	60	61	62	64	67	69
Nursing home care	207	275	319	319	332	349	363	374
Other personal health care	38	84	107	119	128	142	155	167
Public administration and net cost of private health insurance	157	223	231	258	282	313	361	404
Public health activities	80	116	135	145	153	163	174	182
Total, private consumer [3]	1,458	1,755	1,995	2,107	2,241	2,407	2,605	2,807
Hospital care	426	450	474	494	524	562	609	654
Physician and clinical services	386	491	553	567	602	641	689	747
Dental services	120	156	180	189	200	212	226	234
Other professional services [2]	47	68	86	88	92	99	103	108
Home health care	20	37	53	52	48	44	44	47
Prescription drugs	132	179	245	290	330	377	426	459
Other nondurable medical products	86	90	97	101	101	100	101	104
Durable medical equipment [2]	33	38	43	43	43	43	43	43
Nursing home care	90	95	116	118	122	125	124	133
Net cost of private health insurance	117	151	147	164	178	203	240	276

[1] Change from immediate prior year. [2] See footnotes for corresponding objects in Table 120. [3] Represents out-of-pocket payments and private health insurance.

Source: U. S. Centers for Medicare and Medicaid Services, Office of the Actuary, "Health Accounts"; <http://www.cms.hhs.gov /statistics/nhe/default.asp>.

Table 122. **Government Expenditures for Health Services and Supplies: 2003**

[In millions of dollars (721,658 represents $721,658,000,000). Excludes Puerto Rico and island areas. Excludes medical research and construction]

Type of service	Total [1]	Federal	State and local	Medicare [2] (OASDHI)	Public assistance [3]	Other health services Veterans	Other health services Defense Dept. [4]	Other health services Workers' compensation [5]
Total [1]	721,658	507,480	214,178	283,104	279,019	24,549	17,223	33,975
Hospital care	300,770	242,051	58,720	156,427	90,724	18,146	10,567	11,178
Physician and clinical services	122,988	101,253	21,735	73,751	28,185	1,478	3,340	10,290
Prescription drugs	43,162	25,206	17,957	2,841	37,491	126	1,338	1,170
Nursing home care	67,264	45,511	21,753	13,729	51,230	2,305	-	-
Public administration	36,394	20,218	16,175	8,188	19,328	106	757	7,686
Public health activities	53,752	7,432	46,319	-	-	-	-	-

- Represents zero. [1] Includes other items not shown separately. [2] Covers hospital and medical insurance payments and administrative costs under old-age, survivors, disability, and health insurance program. [3] Covers medicaid and other medical public assistance. Excludes funds paid into medicare trust fund by states to cover premiums for public assistance recipients and medically indigent persons. [4] Includes care for retirees and military dependents. [5] Medical benefits.

Source: U. S. Centers for Medicare and Medicaid Services, Office of the Actuary, "Health Accounts"; <http://www.cms.hhs.gov /statistics/nhe/default.asp>.

Table 123. **Personal Health Care—Third Party Payments and Private Consumer Expenditures, 1990 to 2003, and Projections, 2004**

[In billions of dollars (609.4 represents $609,400,000,000), except percent. See headnote, Table 124]

Item	1990	1995	1998	1999	2000	2001	2002	2003	2004, proj
Personal health care expenditures	609.4	865.7	1,009.8	1,065.6	1,136.1	1,235.5	1,342.9	1,440.8	1,549.0
Third party payments, total	472.1	719.3	834.2	880.9	943.0	1,033.5	1,128.7	1,210.3	1,303.1
Percent of personal health care	77.5	83.1	82.6	82.7	83.0	83.7	84.0	84.0	84.1
Private insurance payments	203.6	288.7	343.4	367.0	399.3	437.6	479.1	518.7	558.8
Public expenditures	237.9	386.4	436.4	457.6	489.2	541.6	593.3	631.5	680.2
Other [1]	30.6	44.2	54.4	56.3	54.4	54.3	56.2	60.0	64.2
Private consumer expenditures [2]	340.9	435.1	519.0	551.8	592.4	639.6	693.3	749.2	804.6
Percent met by private insurance	59.7	66.3	66.2	66.5	67.4	68.4	69.1	69.2	69.4
Hospital care	108.4	122.1	133.0	140.2	150.6	163.3	178.4	193.7	206.0
Percent met by private insurance	89.6	91.4	91.0	91.1	91.6	91.8	91.7	91.6	91.5
Physician and clinical services	98.1	133.2	155.3	161.1	172.9	186.2	202.0	221.2	236.5
Percent met by private insurance	69.0	80.3	80.0	80.2	81.4	82.2	82.8	83.0	83.1
Prescription drugs	33.6	48.5	68.9	82.3	94.9	109.4	124.8	136.0	153.4
Percent met by private insurance	29.2	46.5	55.7	58.2	59.6	61.1	61.8	60.9	61.5

[1] Includes nonpatient revenues and industrial inplant health services. [2] Includes expenditures not shown separately. Represents out-of-pocket payments and private health insurance benefits. Excludes net cost of insurance.

Source: U. S. Centers for Medicare and Medicaid Services, Office of the Actuary, "Health Accounts"; <http://cms.hhs.gov/statistics/nhe /default.asp>.

100 Health and Nutrition

Table 124. **Personal Health Care Expenditures by Object and Source of Payment: 2003**

[In millions of dollars (1,440,759 represents $1,440,759,000,000). Excludes Puerto Rico and island areas. Covers all expenditures for health services and supplies, except net cost of insurance and administration, government public health activities, and expenditures of philanthropic agencies for fund raising activities]

| Object of expenditure | Total | Private payments | | | | | Govern- ment | Third party pay- ments [2] |
| | | Total | Consumer | | | | | |
			Total	Out of pocket pay- ments	Private health insur- ance	Other [1]		
Total	1,440,759	809,246	749,220	230,483	518,737	60,026	631,513	1,210,276
Hospital care	515,866	215,096	193,746	16,309	177,437	21,350	300,770	499,557
Physician and clinical services	369,746	246,759	221,238	37,649	183,589	25,521	122,988	332,097
Dental services	74,270	69,396	69,359	32,864	36,495	37	4,874	41,406
Other professional services [3]	48,507	34,892	32,054	13,272	18,782	2,837	13,615	35,234
Home health care	40,009	15,095	13,884	6,595	7,289	1,211	24,914	33,414
Prescription drugs	179,204	136,042	136,042	53,151	82,891	-	43,162	126,053
Other nondurable medical products	32,468	30,739	30,739	30,739	-	-	1,729	1,729
Durable medical equipment [3]	20,393	12,791	12,791	8,996	3,795	-	7,602	11,397
Nursing home care	110,797	43,533	39,368	30,908	8,459	4,165	67,264	79,889
Other personal health care	49,499	4,906	-	-	-	-	44,594	49,499

- Represents zero or rounds to zero.   [1] Includes nonpatient revenues and industrial plant.   [2] Covers private health insurance, other private payments, and government.   [3] See footnotes for corresponding items on Table 120.

Source: U. S. Centers for Medicare and Medicaid Services, Office of the Actuary "Health Accounts"; <http://cms.hhs.gov/statistics /nhe/default.asp>.

Table 125. **Hospital Care, Physician and Clinical Services, and Nursing Home Care Expenditures by Source of Payment: 1990 to 2003**

[In billions of dollars (253.9 represents $253,900,000,000)]

Source of payment	1990	1995	1997	1998	1999	2000	2001	2002	2003
Hospital care, total	253.9	343.6	367.6	378.5	393.4	413.1	446.4	484.2	515.9
Out-of-pocket payments	11.2	10.5	11.1	11.9	12.4	12.7	13.4	14.8	16.3
Third-party payments	242.7	333.1	356.5	366.6	381.0	400.4	433.1	469.4	499.6
Private health insurance	97.1	111.5	114.7	121.0	127.8	137.9	149.9	163.6	177.4
Other private funds	10.3	14.7	18.0	19.8	20.5	20.2	19.5	20.1	21.3
Government	135.2	206.8	223.8	225.8	232.7	242.3	263.7	285.7	300.8
Federal	102.7	166.6	182.3	181.0	186.0	193.6	212.7	229.8	242.1
State and local	32.4	40.2	41.5	44.7	46.7	48.7	50.9	55.9	58.7
Medicare [1]	67.8	107.4	122.7	121.1	122.6	126.4	138.9	148.6	156.4
Medicaid [2]	27.6	54.5	58.1	61.0	66.3	69.9	74.2	83.0	87.0
Physician and clinical services, total	157.5	220.5	241.0	256.8	270.9	290.2	315.1	340.8	369.7
Out-of-pocket payments	30.4	26.2	28.8	31.1	31.8	32.1	33.1	34.8	37.6
Third-party payments	127.1	194.3	212.2	225.8	239.1	258.1	282.0	306.0	332.1
Private health insurance	67.7	107.0	116.4	124.2	129.2	140.8	153.1	167.2	183.6
Other private funds	11.3	17.6	20.1	21.6	22.4	21.3	22.3	23.6	25.5
Government	48.2	69.8	75.7	80.0	87.4	96.0	106.6	115.2	123.0
Federal	38.7	56.4	62.2	66.0	72.4	79.6	88.2	95.0	101.3
State and local	9.4	13.3	13.5	14.0	15.0	16.4	18.3	20.3	21.7
Medicare [1]	30.2	41.9	47.0	49.8	54.1	59.3	65.3	69.0	73.8
Medicaid [2]	7.0	14.8	16.3	16.7	17.6	19.1	21.6	24.4	26.1
Nursing home care, total	52.7	74.6	85.1	89.5	90.7	95.3	101.2	106.6	110.8
Out-of-pocket payments	19.8	20.1	21.6	25.1	25.9	27.4	28.3	28.3	30.9
Third-party payments	32.9	54.5	63.5	64.4	64.7	67.9	72.9	78.2	79.9
Private health insurance	3.1	5.6	7.0	7.4	7.7	7.5	7.9	8.1	8.5
Other private funds	3.9	4.8	5.2	4.6	4.6	4.3	3.9	3.8	4.2
Government	25.9	44.1	51.2	52.3	52.4	56.1	61.1	66.4	67.3
Federal	15.8	28.5	34.3	35.1	34.5	37.7	42.4	46.2	45.5
State and local	10.2	15.5	17.0	17.2	17.9	18.4	18.7	20.1	21.8
Medicare [1]	1.7	6.9	9.8	10.3	8.6	9.5	12.2	13.6	13.7
Medicaid [2]	23.2	35.4	39.6	40.1	41.8	44.5	46.7	50.5	51.0

[1] Medicare expenditures come from federal funds.   [2] Medicaid expenditures come from federal and state and local funds.

Source: U. S. Centers for Medicare and Medicaid Services, Office of the Actuary, "Health Accounts"; <http://cms.hhs.gov/statistics /nhe/default.asp>.

Health and Nutrition   101

Table 126. Retail Prescription Drug Sales: 1995 to 2004

[2,125 represents 2,125,000,000]

Sales outlet	Unit	1995	1997	1998	1999	2000	2001	2002	2003	2004
Number of prescriptions...	Mil......	2,125	2,316	2,481	2,707	2,865	3,009	3,139	3,215	3,274
Traditional chain...........	Mil......	914	1,038	1,129	1,246	1,344	1,415	1,474	1,494	1,510
Independent	Mil......	666	646	651	680	689	700	708	726	728
Mass merchant..........	Mil......	238	254	272	289	293	314	339	345	353
Supermarkets	Mil......	221	269	306	357	394	418	444	462	470
Mail order	Mil......	86	109	123	134	146	161	174	189	214
Retail sales............	Bil. dol....	72.2	93.8	108.7	125.8	145.6	164.1	182.7	203.1	221.0
Traditional chain..........	Bil. dol. ...	28.8	38.2	45.5	53.8	61.2	67.7	75.9	85.4	90.6
Independent	Bil. dol. ...	21.1	23.7	26.1	28.9	31.4	33.9	35.4	38.3	40.5
Mass merchant...........	Bil. dol. ...	7.7	9.6	10.9	11.8	13.5	15.2	18.0	19.5	21.5
Supermarkets	Bil. dol. ...	7.4	10.3	12.0	13.8	17.4	19.8	23.1	25.1	27.0
Mail order	Bil. dol. ...	7.4	11.9	14.3	17.4	22.1	27.6	30.2	34.9	41.3
Average Prices[1]										
All prescriptions	Dollars ...	30.01	35.72	38.43	42.42	45.79	50.06	55.37	59.52	63.59
Brand drugs..............	Dollars ...	40.22	49.55	53.51	60.66	65.29	69.75	77.49	85.57	95.86
Generic drugs	Dollars ...	14.84	16.95	17.33	18.16	19.33	21.72	24.89	27.69	28.71
Percentage of Number of Drug Prescriptions by Brand/Generic Mix										
Brand drugs.............	Percent...	59.8	57.6	58.3	57.1	57.6	59.0	57.9	55.0	51.9
Generic drugs	Percent...	40.2	42.4	41.7	42.9	42.4	41.0	42.1	45.0	48.1

[1] Excludes mail order.
Source: National Association of Chain Drug Stores, Alexandria, VA, *NACDS Foundation Chain Pharmacy Industry Profile, 2005* (copyright); <http://www.nacds.org>.

Table 127. Prescription Drug Use in the Past Month by Sex, Age, Race, and Hispanic Origin: 1988–1994 and 1999–2002

[Data are based on National Health and Nutrition Examination Survey, a sample of the civilian noninstitutionalized population]

Sex and age	Percent of population using at least one prescription drug in past month							
	All persons [1]		Not Hispanic or Latino[2]				Mexican [3]	
			White		Black or African American			
	1988–1994	1999–2002	1988–1994	1999–2002	1988–1994	1999–2002	1988–1994	1999–2002
Both sexes, age adjusted [4]..	39.1	45.3	41.1	48.9	36.9	40.1	31.7	31.7
Male	32.7	39.9	34.2	43.1	31.1	35.4	27.5	25.8
Female.................	45.0	50.4	47.6	54.5	41.4	43.8	36.0	37.8
Both sexes, crude.........	37.8	45.1	41.4	50.9	31.2	36.0	24.0	23.7
Male	30.6	38.7	33.5	43.9	25.5	30.8	20.1	18.8
Female.................	44.6	51.2	48.9	57.6	36.2	40.6	28.1	28.9
Under 18 years old..........	20.5	24.2	22.9	27.6	14.8	18.6	16.1	15.9
18 to 44 years old........	31.3	35.9	34.3	41.3	27.8	28.5	21.1	19.2
45 to 64 years old	54.8	64.1	55.5	66.1	57.5	62.3	48.1	49.3
65 years old and over........	73.6	84.7	74.0	85.4	74.5	81.1	67.7	72.0
Male:								
Under 18 years old	20.4	26.2	22.3	30.6	15.5	19.8	16.3	16.2
18 to 44 years old........	21.5	27.1	23.5	31.2	21.1	21.5	14.9	13.0
45 to 64 years old........	47.2	55.6	48.1	57.4	48.2	54.0	43.8	36.4
65 years old and over	67.2	80.1	67.4	81.0	64.4	78.1	61.3	66.8
Female:								
Under 18 years old	20.6	22.0	23.6	24.4	14.2	17.3	16.0	15.6
18 to 44 years old........	40.7	44.6	44.7	51.7	33.4	34.2	28.1	26.2
45 to 64 years old........	62.0	72.0	62.6	74.7	64.4	69.0	52.2	62.4
65 years old and over	78.3	88.1	78.8	88.8	81.3	83.1	73.0	76.3

[1] Includes persons of other races and Hispanic origins, not shown separately. [2] Starting with data year 1999 race-specific estimates are not comparable with estimates for earlier years, see footnote 2, Table 156. [3] Persons of Mexican origin may be of any race. [4] Age adjusted to the 2000 standard population using four age groups: Under 18, 18 to 44, 45 to 64, and 65 years and over. See text Section 2.

Source: National Center for Health Statistics *Health, United States, 2005.* <http://www.cdc.gov/nchs/hus.htm>.

Table 128. **Consumer Price Indexes of Medical Care Prices: 1980 to 2004**

[1982–1984 = 100. Indexes are annual averages of monthly data based on components of consumer price index for all urban consumers; for explanation, see text, Section 14, Prices. See Appendix III]

Year	Medical care services						Medical care commodities			Annual percent change [3]		
	Medical care, total	Total [1]	Professional services			Hospital and related services	Total [2]	Prescription drugs and medical supplies		Medical care, total	Medical care services	Medical care commodities
			Total [1]	Physicians	Dental							
1980....	74.9	74.8	77.9	76.5	78.9	69.2	75.4	72.5		11.0	11.3	9.3
1985....	113.5	113.2	113.5	113.3	114.2	116.1	115.2	120.1		6.3	6.1	7.2
1990....	162.8	162.7	156.1	160.8	155.8	178.0	163.4	181.7		9.0	9.3	8.4
1995....	220.5	224.2	201.0	208.8	206.8	257.8	204.5	235.0		4.5	5.1	1.9
1997....	234.6	239.1	215.4	222.9	226.6	278.4	215.3	249.3		2.8	2.9	2.3
1998....	242.1	246.8	222.2	229.5	236.2	287.5	221.8	258.6		3.2	3.2	3.0
1999....	250.6	255.1	229.2	236.0	247.2	299.5	230.7	273.4		3.5	3.4	4.0
2000....	260.8	266.0	237.7	244.7	258.5	317.3	238.1	285.4		4.1	4.3	3.2
2001....	272.8	278.8	246.5	253.6	269.0	338.3	247.6	300.9		4.6	4.8	4.0
2002....	285.6	292.9	253.9	260.6	281.0	367.8	256.4	316.5		4.7	5.1	3.6
2003....	297.1	306.0	261.2	267.7	292.5	394.8	262.8	326.3		4.0	4.5	2.5
2004....	310.1	321.3	271.5	278.3	306.9	417.9	269.3	337.1		4.4	5.0	2.5

[1] Includes other services not shown separately. [2] Includes other commodities not shown separately. [3] Percent change from the immediate prior year.

Source: U.S. Bureau of Labor Statistics, *CPI Detailed Report*, January 2005.

Table 129. **Average Annual Expenditures Per Consumer Unit for Health Care: 1990 to 2003**

[In dollars, except percent. See text, Section 13, Income, Expenditures and Wealth and headnote, Table 669. For composition of regions, see map, inside front cover]

Item	Health care, total		Health insurance	Medical services	Drugs and medical supplies [1]	Percent distribution		
	Amount	Percent of total expenditures				Health insurance	Medical services	Drugs and medical supplies [1]
1990	1,480	5.2	581	562	337	39.3	38.0	22.8
1995	1,732	5.4	860	512	360	49.7	29.6	20.8
1999	1,959	5.3	923	558	479	47.1	28.5	24.5
2000	2,066	5.4	983	568	515	47.6	27.5	24.9
2001	2,182	5.5	1,061	573	549	48.6	26.3	25.2
2002	2,350	5.8	1,168	590	592	49.7	25.1	25.2
2003	**2,416**	**5.9**	**1,252**	**591**	**574**	**51.8**	**24.5**	**23.8**
Age of reference person:								
Under 25 years old..........	546	2.4	281	129	137	51.5	23.6	25.1
25 to 34 years old	1,468	3.6	810	394	264	55.2	26.8	18.0
35 to 44 years old	2,105	4.5	1,109	598	398	52.7	28.4	18.9
45 to 54 years old	2,479	4.9	1,166	718	596	47.0	29.0	24.0
55 to 64 years old	3,059	6.9	1,572	742	745	51.4	24.3	24.4
65 to 74 years old	3,626	10.8	1,974	681	971	54.4	18.8	26.8
75 years old and over........	3,856	15.4	2,031	695	1,130	52.7	18.0	29.3
Race of reference person:								
White and other.............	2,566	6.0	1,316	640	610	51.3	24.9	23.8
Black	1,309	4.6	774	229	306	59.1	17.5	23.4
Origin of reference person:								
Hispanic....................	1,439	4.2	747	365	328	51.9	25.4	22.8
Non-Hispanic...............	2,527	6.1	1,309	616	602	51.8	24.4	23.8
Region of residence:								
Northeast	2,127	5.0	1,237	448	442	58.2	21.1	20.8
Midwest	2,586	6.4	1,332	621	632	51.5	24.0	24.4
South......................	2,396	6.4	1,223	563	610	51.0	23.5	25.5
West	2,525	5.6	1,227	729	569	48.6	28.9	22.5
Size of consumer unit:								
One person.................	1,558	6.6	779	360	419	50.0	23.1	26.9
Two or more persons	2,774	5.8	1,449	687	637	52.2	24.8	23.0
Two persons	3,093	7.1	1,597	700	795	51.6	22.6	25.7
Three persons	2,532	5.3	1,326	642	564	52.4	25.4	22.3
Four persons	2,581	4.7	1,402	694	485	54.3	26.9	18.8
Five persons or more........	2,379	4.5	1,224	705	450	51.5	29.6	18.9
Income before taxes:								
Complete income reporters [2]	2,495	5.8	1,267	612	616	50.8	24.5	24.7
Quintiles of income:								
Lowest 20 percent	1,439	7.8	742	262	435	51.6	18.2	30.2
Second 20 percent........	2,132	8.0	1,124	378	631	52.7	17.7	29.6
Third 20 percent	2,553	7.0	1,306	636	611	51.2	24.9	23.9
Fourth 20 percent	2,745	5.4	1,440	695	610	52.5	25.3	22.2
Highest 20 percent........	3,606	4.4	1,723	1,087	796	47.8	30.1	22.1
Incomplete reporters of income...	2,055	6.4	1,167	480	409	56.8	23.4	19.9

[1] Includes prescription and nonprescription drugs. [2] A complete reporter is a consumer unit providing values for at least one of the major sources of income.

Source: U.S. Bureau of Labor Statistics, *Consumer Expenditure Survey*, annual; <http://www.bls.gov/cex/>.

Health and Nutrition 103

Table 130. Medicare Benefits by Type of Provider: 1990 to 2004

[In millions of dollars (65,721 represents $65,721,000,000). For years ending Sept. 30. Distribution of benefits by type is estimated and subject to change]

Type of provider	1990	1995	1999	2000	2001	2002	2003	2004
Hospital insurance benefits, total. . .	**65,721**	**113,395**	**129,107**	**125,992**	**135,979**	**144,140**	**153,144**	**163,764**
Inpatient hospital.	57,012	81,095	86,334	86,858	93,237	101,713	108,255	113,634
Skilled nursing facility.	2,761	8,684	11,230	10,357	12,745	15,168	14,764	16,464
Home health agency	3,295	15,715	8,615	4,496	3,696	4,879	4,979	5,496
Hospice.	318	1,854	2,494	2,818	3,464	4,516	5,879	7,238
Managed care	2,335	6,047	20,435	21,463	22,837	17,865	19,267	20,932
Supplementary medical insurance benefits, total	**41,498**	**63,490**	**79,151**	**88,876**	**100,514**	**108,068**	**119,455**	**131,378**
Physician fee schedule.	(NA)	31,110	33,389	35,958	40,447	44,216	47,384	52,022
Durable medical equipment.	(NA)	3,576	4,270	4,577	5,222	6,134	7,557	7,868
Carrier lab [1]	(NA)	2,819	2,086	2,194	2,361	2,692	2,941	3,202
Other carrier [2]	(NA)	4,513	6,398	7,154	8,396	10,304	12,412	13,821
Hospital [3].	(NA)	8,448	8,453	8,516	11,774	13,456	14,727	16,885
Home health.	(NA)	223	344	4,281	4,192	4,824	5,174	5,684
Intermediary lab [4]	(NA)	1,437	1,597	1,748	1,928	2,149	2,412	2,652
Other intermediary [5]	(NA)	5,110	5,644	6,099	6,945	8,241	9,645	10,415
Managed care	(NA)	6,253	16,970	18,348	19,249	16,052	17,203	18,830

NA Not available. [1] Lab services paid under the lab fee schedule performed in a physician's office lab or an independent lab. [2] Includes free-standing ambulatory surgical centers facility costs, ambulance, and supplies. [3] Includes the hospital facility costs for Medicare Part B services which are predominantly in the outpatient department. The physician reimbursement associated with these services is included on the "Physician Fee Schedule" line. [4] Lab fee services paid under the lab fee schedule performed in a hospital outpatient department. [5] Includes ESRD free-standing dialysis facility payments and payments to rural health clinics, outpatient rehabilitation facilities, psychiatric hospitals, and federally qualified health centers.

Source: U.S. Centers for Medicare and Medicaid Services, unpublished data. <http://www.cms.hhs.gov/publications /trusteesreport/2005/>

Table 131. Medicare—Enrollment by State and Other Areas: 1995 to 2003

[(37,535 represents 37,535,000) Hospital and/or medical insurance enrollment as July 1]

State and area	1995	2000	2002	2003	State and area	1995	2000	2002	2003
All areas. . .	**37,535**	**39,620**	**40,489**	**41,087**	MO	833	861	874	884
					MT.	130	137	140	142
U.S.	**36,758**	**38,762**	**39,594**	**40,173**	NE.	249	254	256	257
					NV.	194	240	261	274
AL	642	685	706	719	NH.	156	170	176	180
AK	34	42	46	48	NJ	1,168	1,203	1,213	1,220
AZ	602	675	708	729	NM	211	234	244	250
AR	423	439	446	453	NY	2,630	2,715	2,747	2,763
CA	3,633	3,901	4,009	4,078	NC	1,027	1,133	1,178	1,205
CO	421	467	484	493	ND	103	103	103	103
CT	502	515	518	522	OH	1,666	1,701	1,713	1,727
DE	101	112	116	119	OK.	488	508	515	521
DC	78	75	74	74	OR.	469	489	504	513
FL	2,628	2,804	2,876	2,921	PA	2,071	2,095	2,101	2,110
GA	833	916	951	974	RI	168	172	172	172
HI	149	165	171	175	SC.	509	568	592	606
ID	150	165	173	178	SD	117	119	121	122
IL	1,617	1,635	1,646	1,661	TN	771	829	855	872
IN	823	852	865	878	TX	2,080	2,265	2,338	2,390
IA	474	477	479	482	UT	187	206	215	220
KS	383	390	392	394	VT	83	89	91	93
KY	586	623	637	648	VA	818	893	927	946
LA	581	602	612	620	WA	688	736	759	775
ME.	201	216	223	227	WV	330	338	343	347
MD	602	645	664	674	WI	762	783	794	804
MA	933	961	963	966	WY	60	65	67	69
MI	1,347	1,403	1,426	1,445					
MN	631	654	667	676	PR	477	537	562	575
MS	397	419	429	437	Other areas . . .	300	321	333	340

Source: U.S. Centers for Medicare and Medicaid Services, "Medicare Beneficiaries enrolled as of July 1 of each year, 1995-1998," published July 1999. "Medicare Beneficiaries Enrolled by State as of July 1, 1999-2003"; published September 2004. <http://www.cms.hhs.gov/statistics/enrollment/default.asp>.

Table 132. Medicare Enrollees: 1980 to 2004

[In millions (28.4 represents 28,400,000). As of July 1. Includes Puerto Rico and island areas and enrollees in foreign countries and unknown place of residence]

Item	1980	1990	1995	2000	2001	2002	2003	2004
Total	28.4	34.3	37.6	39.7	40.1	40.5	41.1	41.7
Aged	25.5	31.0	33.2	34.3	34.5	34.7	35.0	35.4
Disabled	3.0	3.3	4.4	5.4	5.6	5.8	6.1	6.3
Hospital insurance	28.0	33.7	37.2	39.3	39.7	40.1	40.6	41.2
Aged	25.0	30.5	32.7	33.8	34.0	34.2	34.6	34.9
Disabled	3.0	3.3	4.4	5.4	5.6	5.8	6.1	6.3
Supplementary medical insurance	27.3	32.6	35.6	37.3	37.7	38.0	38.4	38.8
Aged	24.6	29.6	31.7	32.6	32.7	32.9	33.1	33.3
Disabled	2.7	2.9	3.9	4.8	4.9	5.1	5.3	5.5

Source: U.S. Centers for Medicare and Medicaid Services, Office of the Actuary. CMS Statistics Medicare Enrollment. <http://www.cms.hhs.gov/statistics/enrollment/default.ASP>.

Table 133. Medicare Disbursements by Type of Beneficiary: 1990 to 2004

[In millions of dollars (109,709 represents $109,709,000,000). For years ending September 30. Distribution of benefits by type is estimated and subject to change]

Type of beneficiary	1990	1995	1999	2000	2001	2002	2003	2004
Total disbursements	109,709	180,096	211,959	219,276	241,175	256,856	277,846	301,488
Hospital insurance disbursements. . .	66,687	114,883	131,441	130,284	141,723	148,031	153,792	166,998
Benefits	65,722	113,394	129,107	125,992	135,979	144,140	153,144	163,764
Aged . . :	58,503	100,107	113,289	110,261	118,816	125,248	132,415	141,277
Disabled	7,218	13,288	15,818	15,731	17,163	18,892	20,729	22,487
ESRD [1]	6,467	12,300	14,794	14,705	16,029	17,627	19,341	20,954
Home health transfer [2]	751	988	1,024	1,026	1,134	1,265	1,388	1,533
Quality improvement activity [3]	-	-	179	1,706	3,103	1,168	-2,174	-
Administrative expenses [4]	191	189	177	236	274	259	280	314
	774	1,300	1,978	2,350	2,368	2,464	2,542	2,920
Supplementary medical insurance disbursements.	43,022	65,213	80,518	88,992	99,452	108,825	124,055	134,490
Benefits	41,498	63,489	79,151	88,875	100,514	108,068	119,455	131,378
Aged	36,837	54,830	67,965	76,340	86,108	91,667	100,505	109,936
Disabled	4,661	8,660	11,187	12,535	14,406	16,400	18,950	21,442
Disabled	3,758	7,363	9,838	11,683	13,657	15,523	17,981	20,448
ESRD [1]	903	1,297	1,349	852	749	877	969	994
Home health transfer [2]	-	-	-179	-1,706	-3,103	-1,168	2,174	-
Quality improvement activity [3]	-	2	36	43	55	95	70	79
Administrative expenses	1,524	1,722	1,510	1,780	1,986	1,830	2,356	3,033

- Represents zero. [1] Represents persons entitled because of End Stage Renal Disease only. Benefits for those who have ESRD, but would be entitled due to their aged or disabled status are included in aged and disabled benefits. [2] Beginning 1998, home health agency transfers are excluded from total supplementary medical insurance disbursements and included in total hospital insurance disbursements. [3] Beginning in 2002, Peer Review Organizations were renamed Quality Improvement Organizations. [4] Includes costs of experiments and demonstration projects. Includes costs of the health care fraud and abuse control program.

Source: U.S. Centers for Medicare and Medicaid Services, Annual Report of the Boards of Trustees <http://www.cms.hhs.gov/publications /trusteesreport/tr2005.pdf> (accessed 26 September 2005).

Table 134. Medicare Trust Funds: 1990 to 2004

[In billions of dollars (126.3 represents $126,300,000,000)]

Type of trust fund	1990	1995	1998	1999	2000	2001	2002	2003	2004
TOTAL MEDICARE									
Total income	126.3	175.3	228.3	232.5	257.1	273.3	284.8	291.6	317.7
Total expenditures.	111.0	184.2	213.4	213.0	221.8	244.8	265.7	280.8	308.9
Assets, end of year.	114.4	143.4	166.6	186.2	221.5	250.0	269.1	280.0	288.8
Net change in assets.	15.3	-8.9	14.9	19.5	35.3	28.5	19.1	10.8	8.8
HOSPITAL INSURANCE (HI)									
Net contribution income [1]	72.1	103.3	130.7	140.3	154.5	160.9	162.7	159.2	167.1
Interest received [2]	8.5	10.8	9.3	10.1	11.7	14.0	15.1	15.8	16.0
Benefit payments [3]	66.2	116.4	134.0	128.8	128.5	141.2	149.9	152.1	167.6
Assets, end of year.	98.9	130.3	120.4	141.4	177.5	208.7	234.8	256.0	269.3
SUPPLEMENTARY MEDICAL INSURANCE (SMI)									
Net premium income	11.3	19.7	[4]20.9	[4]19.0	20.6	22.8	25.1	27.4	31.4
Transfers from general revenue.	33.0	39.0	[4]64.1	[4]59.1	65.9	72.8	78.3	86.4	100.4
Interest received [2]	1.6	1.6	2.7	2.8	3.5	3.1	2.8	2.0	1.5
Benefit payments [3]	42.5	65.0	76.1	80.7	88.9	99.7	111.0	123.8	135.0
Assets, end of year.	15.5	13.1	46.2	44.8	44.0	41.3	34.3	24.0	19.4

[1] Includes income from taxation of benefits beginning in 1994. Includes premiums from aged ineligibles enrolled in HI. [2] Includes recoveries of amounts reimbursed from the trust fund. [3] Beginning 1998, monies transferred to the SMI trust fund for home health agency costs, as provided for by P.L. 105-33, are included in HI benefit payments, but excluded from SMI benefit payments. [4] Premiums withheld from check and associated general revenue contributions that were to occur on January 3, 1999, actually occurred on December 31, 1998. These amounts are therefore excluded from 1999 data.

Source: U.S. Centers for Medicare and Medicaid Services, Annual Report of the Board of Trustees of the Annual Report of the Federal Hospital Insurance and Supplementary Medical Insurance Trust Funds; <http://www.cms.hhs.gov/publications/trusteesreport/2005.pdf> (accessed 26 September 2005).

Health and Nutrition 105

Table 135. Medicaid—Selected Characteristics of Persons Covered: 2003

[In thousands, except percent (35,394 represents 35,394,000). Represents number of persons as of March of following year who were enrolled at any time in year shown. Excludes unrelated individuals under age 15. Person did not have to receive medical care paid for by medicaid in order to be counted. See headnote, Table 557]

Poverty status	Total [1]	White alone [2]	Black alone [3]	Hispanic [4]	Under 18 years old	18-44 years old	45-64 years old	65 years old and over
Persons covered, total . . .	35,394	23,792	8,736	8,453	19,140	8,949	4,116	3,190
Below poverty level	15,103	9,305	4,702	4,093	8,497	3,976	1,734	895
Above poverty level	20,291	14,487	4,034	4,360	10,643	4,973	2,382	2,295
Percent of population								
covered	12.3	10.3	24.3	21.0	26.2	8.1	5.9	9.2
Below poverty level	42.1	38.3	53.5	45.2	66.0	28.8	30.7	25.2
Above poverty level	8.1	7.0	14.8	14.0	17.7	5.1	3.7	7.4

[1] Includes other races not shown separately. [2] White alone refers to people who reported White and did not report any other race category. [3] Black alone refers to people who reported Black and did not report any other race category. [4] Persons of Hispanic origin may be of any race.

Source: U.S. Census Bureau, "Table HI02. Health Insurance Coverage Status and Type of Coverage by Selected Characteristics for People in the Poverty Universe: 2003"; published August 2004; <http://pubdb3.census.gov/macro/032004/health/toc.htm>; and "Table HI03. Health Insurance Coverage Status and Type of Coverage by Selected Characteristics for Poor People in the Poverty Universe: 2003"; published August 2004; <http://pubdb3.census.gov/macro/032004/health/toc.htm>.

Table 136. Medicaid—Beneficiaries and Payments: 1999 to 2002

[For year ending September 30 (40,300 represents 40,300,000). Starting in 1999, states were required to submit all their eligibility and claims data to the Centers for Medicare & Medicaid Services (CMS) on a quarterly basis through the Medicaid Statistical Information System (MSIS). The Federal requirement for the HCFA-Form 2082 (used for 1998 and preceding years) was eliminated.]

Basis of eligibility and type of service	Beneficiaries (1,000) [1]				Payments (mil. dol.)			
	1999	2000	2001	2002	1999	2000	2001	2002
Total	40,300	42,887	46,164	49,755	147,373	168,443	186,914	213,491
Age 65 and over	3,698	3,730	3,812	3,886	40,471	44,560	48,431	51,733
Blind/Disabled	6,692	6,890	7,118	7,414	63,028	72,772	80,494	91,889
Children	18,045	19,018	20,340	22,369	20,765	23,490	26,771	31,247
Adults	7,449	8,671	9,769	11,238	15,142	17,671	20,097	23,460
Foster Care Children.	734	761	775	816	2,806	3,309	3,773	4,282
Unknown . . . . . ., ...	3,682	3,817	4,349	4,027	5,161	6,639	7,347	10,848
BCCA WOMEN [2]	(NA)	(NA)	(Z)	5	(NA)	(NA)	1	33
Capitated care [3]	20,679	21,292	23,356	25,864	21,225	25,026	29,368	33,634
Clinic services	6,661	7,678	8,464	9,499	5,439	6,138	5,603	6,694
Dental services	5,577	5,922	7,019	7,886	1,156	1,413	1,897	2,309
Home health services	809	1,007	1,014	1,065	2,714	3,133	3,521	3,925
ICF/MR services [4]	121	119	117	117	8,757	9,376	9,701	10,681
Inpatient hospital services	4,479	4,913	4,879	5,051	21,341	24,131	25,943	29,127
Lab and X-ray services . . . , . . .	10,104	11,439	12,339	14,067	1,144	1,292	1,623	2,157
Mental health facility services [5] . . .	97	100	91	99	1,639	1,769	1,959	2,122
Nursing facility services	1,624	1,706	1,702	1,766	31,976	34,528	37,323	39,282
Other care [6]	8,482	9,022	9,709	10,959	12,401	14,755	16,617	19,877
Outpatient hospital services	12,324	13,170	13,731	14,861	5,895	7,082	7,496	8,471
Other practitioner services	3,946	4,758	5,103	5,571	464	664	762	842
PCCM services [7]	3,963	5,649	6,378	7,178	445	177	187	200
Prescribed drugs	19,428	20,325	21,911	24,424	15,934	19,898	23,764	28,408
Physician services . . . ., . .	18,053	18,965	20,021	22,103	6,421	6,809	7,439	8,355
Personal support services [8]	4,062	4,559	4,978	5,688	9,845	11,629	13,135	15,363
Sterilizations	133	137	144	164	119	128	140	166
Unknown	166	74	45	73	458	496	438	1,879

NA Not available. Z Less than 500. [1] Beneficiaries data do not add due to number of beneficiaries that are reported in more than one category. [2] Women-Breast and Cervical Cancer Assistance. [3] HMO payments and prepaid health plans. [4] Intermediate care facilities for mentally retarded. [5] Inpatient mental health-aged and inpatient mental health-under 21. [6] Includes beneficiaries of, and payments for, other care not shown separately. [7] Primary Care Case Management Services. [8] Includes personal care services, rehabilitative services, physical occupational targeted case management services, speech therapies, hospice services, nurse midwife services, nurse practitioner services, private duty nursing services, and religious non-medical health care institutions.

Source: U.S. Centers for Medicare and Medicaid Services, "Medicaid Program Statistics, Medicaid Statistical Information System"; <http://www.cms.hhs.gov/medicaid/msis/mstats.asp>.

106   Health and Nutrition

Table 137. Medicaid—Summary by State: 2000 and 2002

[In the thousands (42,887 represents 42,887,000). For year ending September 30. See headnote, Table 136.]

State	Beneficiaries [1] (1,000)		Payments [2] (mil. dol)		State	Beneficiaries [1] (1,000)		Payments [2] (mil. dol)	
	2000	2002	2000	2002		2000	2002	2000	2002
U.S.	42,887	49,755	168,443	213,491	MO	890	1,036	3,274	4,072
AL	619	765	2,393	3,204	MT	104	104	422	533
AK	96	110	473	687	NE	229	256	960	1,255
AZ	681	878	2,112	2,882	NV	138	202	516	724
AR	489	579	1,543	2,015	NH	97	104	651	746
CA	7,918	9,301	17,105	23,636	NJ	822	954	4,714	5,497
CO	381	426	1,809	2,166	NM	376	799	1,249	1,797
CT	420	479	2,839	3,245	NY	3,420	3,921	26,148	31,489
DE	115	167	529	651	NC	1,214	1,355	4,834	6,041
DC	139	193	793	1,027	ND	63	70	358	423
FL	2,373	2,676	7,433	9,827	OH	1,305	1,656	7,115	9,186
GA	1,369	1,637	3,624	4,796	OK	507	631	1,604	2,238
HI	194	200	600	695	OR	558	621	1,714	2,136
ID	131	176	594	792	PA	1,492	1,627	6,366	8,524
IL	1,519	1,731	7,807	9,122	RI	179	199	1,070	1,251
IN	706	849	2,977	3,725	SC	689	809	2,765	3,383
IA	314	353	1,477	1,856	SD	102	118	402	504
KS	263	289	1,227	1,501	TN	1,568	1,732	3,491	4,748
KY	764	808	2,921	3,459	TX	2,633	2,953	9,277	11,121
LA	761	899	2,632	3,234	UT	225	275	960	1,216
ME	194	276	1,310	1,717	VT	139	154	480	607
MD	626	693	3,003	3,662	VA	627	665	2,479	3,018
MA	1,060	1,066	5,413	6,387	WA	896	1,039	2,435	4,373
MI	1,352	1,450	4,881	5,919	WV	342	362	1,394	1,578
MN	558	621	3,280	4,439	WI	577	716	2,968	3,606
MS	605	712	1,808	2,500	WY	46	59	215	280

[1] Persons who had payments made on their behalf at any time during the fiscal year. [2] Payments are for fiscal year and reflect federal and state contribution payments. Data exclude disproportionate share hospital payments. Disproportionate share hospitals receive higher medicaid reimbursement than other hospitals because they treat a disproportionate share of Medicaid patients.

Source: U.S. Centers for Medicare and Medicaid Services, "Medicaid Program Statistics, Medicaid Statistical Information System"; <http://www.cms.hhs.gov/medicaid/msis/mstats.asp>.

Table 138. State Children's Health Insurance Program (SCHIP)—Enrollment and Expenditures by State: 2000 and 2004

[(3,357.4 represents 3,357,400). For year ending September 30. This program provides health benefits coverage to children living in families whose incomes exceed the eligibility limits for medicaid. Although it is generally targeted to families with incomes at or below 200 percent of the federal poverty level, each state may set its own income eligibility limits, within certain guidelines. States have three options: they may expand their medicaid programs, develop a separate child health program that functions independently of medicaid, or do a combination of both]

State	Enrollment [1] (1,000)		Expenditures [2] (mil. dol.)		State	Enrollment [1] (1,000)		Expenditures [2] (mil. dol.)	
	2000	2004	2000	2004		2000	2004	2000	2004
US	3,357.4	6,058.9	1,928.8	4,600.7	MO	72.8	176.0	41.2	80.2
AL	37.6	79.4	31.9	19.4	MT	8.3	15.3	4.3	14.3
AK	13.4	18.9	18.1	72.8	NE	11.4	33.3	6.1	35.3
AZ	59.6	87.7	29.4	258.9	NV	15.9	38.5	9.0	20.6
AR	1.9	(NA)	1.5	28.5	NH	4.3	11.0	1.6	7.3
CA	484.4	1,035.8	187.3	661.6	NJ	89.0	127.2	46.9	221.9
CO	34.9	57.2	13.9	37.6	NM	8.0	20.8	3.4	21.4
CT	19.9	21.4	12.8	17.2	NY	769.5	826.6	401.0	296.9
DE	4.5	10.3	1.5	5.3	NC	103.6	174.3	65.5	166.2
DC	2.3	6.1	5.8	7.2	ND	2.6	5.1	1.8	6.9
FL	227.5	419.7	125.7	176.5	OH	118.3	220.2	53.1	167.1
GA	120.6	280.1	48.7	215.0	OK	57.7	100.8	51.3	46.1
HI	(z)	19.2	0.4	10.5	OR	37.1	46.7	12.5	25.3
ID	12.4	17.4	7.5	14.4	PA	119.7	177.4	70.7	126.6
IL	62.5	234.0	32.7	309.8	RI	11.5	25.6	10.4	25.2
IN	44.4	80.7	53.7	65.4	SC	60.4	75.6	46.6	50.8
IA	20.0	40.8	15.5	37.3	SD	5.9	13.4	3.1	10.9
KS	26.3	44.4	12.8	39.6	TN	14.9	(NA)	41.7	4.5
KY	55.6	94.5	60.0	71.5	TX	131.1	650.9	41.4	282.5
LA	50.0	105.6	25.3	94.4	UT	25.3	38.7	12.8	28.0
ME	22.7	29.2	11.4	25.2	VT	4.1	6.7	1.4	3.2
MD	93.1	111.5	92.2	106.4	VA	37.7	99.6	18.6	63.0
MA	113.0	166.5	44.2	119.1	WA	2.6	17.0	0.6	39.7
MI	55.4	(NA)	36.2	159.5	WV	21.7	36.9	9.7	30.8
MN	(Z)	4.8	(Z)	72.7	WI	47.1	67.9	21.4	93.7
MS	12.2	82.9	21.1	101.9	WY	2.5	5.5	1.0	5.2

NA Not available.   Z Less than 50 or $50,000.   [1] Number of children ever enrolled during the year in SCHIP.
[2] Expenditures for which states are entitled to federal reimbursement under Title XXI and which reconcile any advance of Title XXI Federal funds made on the basis of estimates.

Source: U.S. Centers for Medicare & Medicaid Services, The State Children's Health Insurance Program, Annual Enrollment Report and the Statement of Expenditures for the SCHIP Program (CMS-21). See <http://www.cms.hhs.gov/schip/enrollment/>.

Health and Nutrition 107

Table 139. **Medicaid Managed Care Enrollment by State and Other Areas: 1995 to 2004**

[For year ending June 30. (33,373 represents 33,373,000)]

State and area	Total enroll-ment [1] (1,000)	Managed care enrollment [2] Number (1,000)	Managed care enrollment [2] Percent of total	State and area	Total enroll-ment [1] (1,000)	Managed care enrollment [2] Number (1,000)	Managed care enrollment [2] Percent of total	State and area	Total enroll-ment [1] (1,000)	Managed care enrollment [2] Number (1,000)	Managed care enrollment [2] Percent of total
1995	33,373	9,800	29.4	IL.	1,740	159	9.1	NC.	1,112	789	70.9
2000	33,690	18,786	55.8	IN	804	510	63.4	ND......	52	33	63.0
2003	42,741	24,406	58.4	IA	285	262	92.1	OH......	1,645	507	30.8
2004,				KS	269	153	57.0	OK......	519	354	68.2
total ..	44,356	26,914	60.7	KY	679	626	92.2	OR......	427	345	80.9
U.S....	43,472	26,071	60.0	LA	919	724	78.8	PA	1,600	1,266	79.1
AL......	801	440	54.9	ME......	259	155	59.8	RI	181	125	69.2
AK......	97	-	-	MD......	696	470	67.5	SC......	846	70	8.3
AZ......	905	806	89.1	MA......	947	582	61.4	SD......	98	96	97.8
AR......	594	386	65.0	MI	1,410	1,255	89.0	TN	1,345	1,345	100.0
CA......	6,471	3,259	50.4	MN......	569	361	63.5	TX	2,692	1,151	42.7
CO......	378	369	97.6	MS......	638	73	11.5	UT	189	167	88.6
CT......	402	303	75.4	MO......	974	432	44.4	VT	131	86	66.0
DE......	135	100	73.7	MT......	86	58	67.1	VA	607	399	65.7
DC......	139	88	63.8	NE......	207	149	72.3	WA	1,081	835	77.3
FL......	2,207	1,450	65.7	NV......	169	90	53.1	WV	298	156	52.5
GA......	1,323	1,273	96.2	NH......	96	-	-	WI	792	374	47.2
HI	190	149	78.0	NJ......	798	542	67.9	WY	59	-	-
ID	166	132	79.3	NM......	421	273	64.9	PR	873	843	96.5
				NY......	4,023	2,342	58.2	VI.....	11	-	-

- Represents zero. [1] The unduplicated Medicaid enrollment figures include individuals in state health care reform programs that expand eligiblity beyond traditional Medicaid eligibility standards. [2] The unduplicated managed care enrollment figures include enrollees receiving comprehensive and limited benefits.

Source: U.S. Centers for Medicare and Medicaid Services, "2004 Medicaid Managed Care Enrollment Report";<http://www.cms.hhs.gov/medicaid/managedcare/enrolstats.asp>.

Table 140. **Health Maintenance Organizations (HMOs): 1990 to 2003**

[As of January 1 (33.0 represents 33,000,000). An HMO is a prepaid health plan delivering comprehensive care to members through designated providers, having a fixed periodic payment for health care services, and requiring members to be in a plan for a specified period of time (usually 1 year). A group HMO delivers health services through a physician group that is controlled by the HMO unit or contracts with one or more independent group practices to provide health services. An individual practice association (IPA) HMO contracts directly with physicians in independent practice, and/or contracts with one or more associations of physicians in independent practice, and/or contracts with one or more multispecialty group practices. Data are based on a census of HMOs]

Model type	Number of plans 1990	1995	2000	2001	2002	2003	Enrollment [1] (mil.) 1990	1995	2000	2001	2002	2003
Total	572	550	568	541	500	454	33.0	46.2	80.9	79.5	76.1	71.8
IPA	360	323	278	257	229	203	13.7	17.4	33.4	33.1	31.6	28.0
Group	212	107	102	104	100	105	19.3	12.9	15.2	15.6	14.9	16.1
Mixed.......	(NA)	120	188	180	171	146	(NA)	15.9	32.3	30.8	29.5	27.7

NA Not available. [1] 1990–1995 exclude enrollees participating in open-ended plans; beginning 1999, includes open-ended enrollment.

Source: HealthLeaders-InterStudy, Nashville, TN, The InterStudy Competitive Edge, annual (copyright).

Table 141. **Persons Enrolled in Health Maintenance Organizations (HMOs) by State: 2000 and 2003**

[71,673 represents 71,673,000. Data are based on a census of health maintenance organizations. Pure and open-ended enrollment as of January 1]

State	Number 2003 (1,000)	Percent of population 2000	2003	State	Number 2003 (1,000)	Percent of population 2000	2003	State	Number 2003 (1,000)	Percent of population 2000	2003
US [1]..	71,673	29.7	24.9	KS	211	17.9	7.8	ND.....	2	2.5	0.4
AL.....	171	7.2	3.8	KY	1,278	31.5	31.2	OH.....	2,123	25.1	18.6
AK.....	-			LA	547	17.0	12.2	OK.....	486	14.7	13.9
AZ.....	1,161	30.9	21.3	ME	274	22.3	21.1	OR.....	851	41.1	24.2
AR.....	192	10.4	7.1	MD.....	1,340	43.9	30.6	PA	3,911	33.9	31.7
CA.....	17,026	53.5	48.5	MA.....	2,489	53.0	38.7	RI	339	38.1	31.7
CO.....	1,366	39.5	30.3	MI	2,613	27.1	26.0	SC.....	266	9.9	6.5
CT.....	1,306	44.6	37.8	MN....	1,386	29.9	27.6	SD.....	81	6.7	10.6
DE.....	123	22.0	15.3	MS....	24	1.1	0.8	TN	1,046	33.0	18.0
DC.....	858	35.2	27.8	MO	1,830	35.2	32.3	TX	2,789	18.5	12.8
FL.....	4,339	31.4	26.0	MT	47	7.0	5.2	UT	600	35.3	25.9
GA.....	1,151	17.4	13.4	NE	152	11.2	8.8	VT	61	4.6	9.9
HI	374	30.0	30.0	NV....	459	23.5	21.1	VA	852	18.5	16.5
ID	38	7.9	2.8	NH....	331	33.7	25.9	WA	917	15.2	15.1
IL.....	1,852	21.0	14.7	NJ.....	2,323	30.9	27.0	WV	163	10.3	10.1
IN	731	12.4	11.9	NM....	562	37.7	30.3	WI	1,582	30.2	29.1
IA	279	7.4	9.5	NC....	963	17.8	11.6	WY	12	1.4	2.4

- Represents zero. [1] Includes Guam and Puerto Rico not shown separately.

Source: HealthLeaders-InterStudy, Nashville, TN, The InterStudy Competitive Edge, annual (copyright).

Table 142. **Health Insurance Coverage Status by Selected Characteristics: 1990 to 2003**

[Persons as of following year for coverage in the year shown (248.9 represents 248,900,000). Government health insurance includes medicare, medicaid, and military plans. Based on Current Population Survey; see text, Section 1, Population, and Appendix III]

Characteristic	Number (mil.)							Percent			
		Covered by private or government health insurance					Not covered by health insurance	Covered by private or government health insurance			Not covered by health insurance
	Total persons	Total [1]	Private					Total [1]	Private	Medicaid [3]	
			Total	Group health [2]	Medicare	Medicaid [3]					
1990	248.9	214.2	182.1	150.2	32.3	24.3	34.7	86.1	73.2	9.7	13.9
1995 [4]	264.3	223.7	185.9	161.5	34.7	31.9	40.6	84.6	70.3	12.1	15.4
2000 [4, 5]	279.5	239.7	201.1	177.8	37.7	29.5	39.8	85.8	71.9	10.6	14.2
2002 [4, 5]	285.9	242.4	199.0	175.3	38.4	33.2	43.6	84.8	69.6	11.6	15.2
2003, total [4, 5]	288.3	243.3	197.9	174.0	39.5	35.6	45.0	84.4	68.6	12.4	15.6
Age:											
Under 18 years	73.6	65.2	48.5	45.0	0.5	19.4	8.4	88.6	65.9	26.4	11.4
Under 6 years	23.8	21.4	14.8	14.0	0.2	7.5	2.5	89.7	62.0	31.4	10.3
6 to 11 years	23.9	21.3	15.8	14.9	0.1	6.3	2.6	89.0	66.3	26.3	11.0
12 to 17 years	25.8	22.5	17.8	16.1	0.1	5.6	3.3	87.3	69.1	21.8	12.7
18 to 24 years	27.8	19.4	16.5	13.4	0.2	3.0	8.4	69.8	59.4	10.8	30.2
25 to 34 years	39.2	28.9	25.6	23.9	0.5	3.1	10.3	73.6	65.3	7.8	26.4
35 to 44 years	43.6	35.7	32.5	30.4	0.9	2.9	7.9	81.9	74.7	6.6	18.1
45 to 54 years	41.1	35.1	32.0	29.7	1.6	2.4	6.0	85.5	77.9	5.7	14.5
55 to 64 years	28.4	24.7	21.6	19.3	2.5	1.8	3.7	87.0	76.0	6.2	13.0
65 years and over	34.7	34.4	21.2	12.2	33.3	3.2	0.3	99.2	61.1	9.2	0.8
Sex: Male	141.2	117.4	97.0	86.5	17.3	15.9	23.8	83.2	68.7	11.3	16.8
Female	147.1	125.9	100.9	87.5	22.1	19.7	21.2	85.6	68.6	13.4	14.4
Race: White alone	232.3	198.3	165.9	144.8	33.8	24.0	34.0	85.4	71.4	10.3	14.6
Black alone	36.1	29.0	19.3	17.9	4.0	8.8	7.1	80.4	53.5	24.4	19.6
Asian alone	11.9	9.6	8.1	7.2	1.1	1.2	2.2	81.2	68.6	10.4	18.8
Hispanic origin [6]	40.4	27.2	18.2	16.8	2.5	8.5	13.2	67.3	45.0	21.0	32.7
Household income:											
Less than $25,000	63.4	48.0	22.8	14.6	18.0	19.7	15.3	75.8	35.9	31.1	24.2
$25,000-$49,999	74.7	59.9	47.7	41.0	11.7	9.8	14.8	80.2	63.8	13.2	19.9
$50,000-$74,999	57.7	50.5	46.0	42.3	4.7	3.5	7.2	87.5	79.8	6.1	12.5
$75,000 or more	92.6	85.0	81.4	76.1	5.1	2.5	7.6	91.8	88.0	2.7	8.2
Persons below poverty	35.9	24.9	8.6	5.6	5.0	15.1	11.0	69.3	23.9	42.1	30.7

[1] Includes other government insurance, not shown separately. Persons with coverage counted only once in total, even though they may have been covered by more than one type of policy. [2] Related to employment of self or other family members. [3] Beginning 1997 persons with no coverage other than access to Indian Health Service are no longer considered covered by health insurance; instead they are considered to be uninsured. The effect of this change on the overall estimates of health insurance coverage is negligible; however, the decrease in the number of people covered by Medicaid may be partially due to this change. [4] Estimates reflect results of follow-up verification questions. [5] Implementation of Census-2000-based population controls. Sample expanded by 28,000 households. [6] Persons of Hispanic origin may be any race.
Source: U.S. Census Bureau, Current Population Reports, P60-226, and unpublished data. See also <http://www.census.gov /hhes/www/hlthins/hlthin03.html>.

Table 143. **Persons With and Without Health Insurance Coverage by State: 2003**

[243,320 represents 243,320,000. Based on the Current Population Survey and subject to sampling error; see text, Section 1, Population, and Appendix III]

State	Total persons covered (1,000)	Total persons not covered		Children not covered		State	Total persons covered (1,000)	Total persons not covered		Children not covered	
		Number (1,000)	Percent of total	Number (1,000)	Percent of total			Number (1,000)	Percent of total	Number (1,000)	Percent of total
U.S.	243,320	44,961	15.6	8,373	11.4	MO	5,004	620	11.0	103	7.3
AL	3,798	629	14.2	95	8.7	MT	739	177	19.4	38	17.7
AK	523	122	18.9	24	12.3	NE	1,532	195	11.3	31	7.0
AZ	4,626	951	17.0	223	14.6	NV	1,824	426	18.9	103	17.4
AR	2,206	465	17.4	71	10.5	NH	1,133	131	10.3	17	5.5
CA	28,895	6,499	18.4	1,196	12.5	NJ	7,378	1,201	14.0	237	11.0
CO	3,708	772	17.2	159	13.7	NM	1,457	414	22.1	65	13.2
CT	3,065	357	10.4	71	8.3	NY	16,104	2,866	15.1	432	9.4
DE	729	91	11.1	17	8.5	NC	6,829	1,424	17.3	249	11.9
DC	475	79	14.3	12	11.4	ND	563	69	10.9	11	7.5
FL	13,849	3,071	18.2	616	15.5	OH	9,885	1,362	12.1	236	8.3
GA	7,162	1,409	16.4	314	13.7	OK	2,737	701	20.4	154	17.9
HI	1,126	127	10.1	23	7.4	OR	2,957	613	17.2	113	13.5
ID	1,107	253	18.6	51	13.7	PA	10,771	1,384	11.4	239	8.4
IL	10,810	1,818	14.4	320	10.0	RI	946	108	10.2	13	5.2
IN	5,296	853	13.9	143	9.0	SC	3,481	584	14.4	92	8.9
IA	2,593	329	11.3	60	8.6	SD	659	91	12.2	16	8.4
KS	2,389	294	11.0	45	6.4	TN	5,131	778	13.2	150	10.8
KY	3,537	574	14.0	107	10.5	TX	16,484	5,374	24.6	1,264	20.0
LA	3,517	912	20.6	182	15.2	UT	2,055	298	12.7	69	9.0
ME	1,150	133	10.4	17	6.0	VT	553	58	9.5	5	3.9
MD	4,731	762	13.9	114	8.1	VA	6,424	962	13.0	162	8.9
MA	5,685	682	10.7	118	7.9	WA	5,147	944	15.5	125	8.4
MI	8,838	1,080	10.9	147	5.8	WV	1,491	296	16.6	34	8.4
MN	4,633	444	8.7	77	6.2	WI	4,836	593	10.9	104	7.7
MS	2,343	511	17.9	92	12.1	WY	411	78	15.9	15	12.5

Source: U.S. Census Bureau, Current Population Reports, P60-226, and unpublished data. See also <http://www.census.gov /hhes/www/hlthins/hlthin03.html>.

Table 144. People Without Health Insurance for the Entire Year by Selected Characteristics: 2000 and 2003

[In thousands, except as noted (279,517 represents 279,517,000). Based on the Current Population Survey; Annual Demographic Survey and subject to sampling error; see text, Section 1 and Appendix III]

Characteristic	2000			2003		
		Uninsured persons			Uninsured persons	
	Total persons	Number	Percent distribution	Total persons	Number	Percent distribution
Total [1].............	279,517	39,804	100.0	288,280	44,961	100.0
Under 18 years	72,314	8,617	21.6	73,580	8,373	18.6
18 to 24 years	26,815	7,406	18.6	27,824	8,414	18.7
25 to 34 years	38,865	8,507	21.4	39,201	10,345	23.0
35 to 44 years	44,566	6,898	17.3	43,573	7,885	17.5
45 to 64 years	63,391	8,124	20.4	69,443	9,657	21.5
65 years and over	33,566	251	0.6	34,659	286	0.6
Male	136,559	20,791	52.2	141,227	23,788	52.9
Female.................	142,958	19,013	47.8	147,053	21,173	47.1
White..................	228,208	30,075	75.6	(NA)	(NA)	(NA)
Non-Hispanic	193,931	18,683	46.9	(NA)	(NA)	(NA)
Black..................	35,597	6,683	16.8	(NA)	(NA)	(NA)
Asian and Pacific Islander	12,693	2,287	5.7	(NA)	(NA)	(NA)
White alone [2]	(NA)	(NA)	(NA)	232,254	33,983	75.6
Black alone [2].	(NA)	(NA)	(NA)	36,121	7,080	15.7
Asian alone [2].	(NA)	(NA)	(NA)	11,869	2,228	5.0
Hispanic [3]..............	35,093	11,883	29.9	40,425	13,237	29.4

NA Not available.   [1] Includes other races not shown separately.   [2] Refers to people who reported specified race and did not report any other race category.   [3] Persons of Hispanic origin may be of any race.

Source: U.S. Census Bureau, "Table H101. Health Insurance Coverage Status and Type of Coverage by Selected Characteristics: 2003;" <http://pubdb3.census.gov/macro/032004/health/toc.htm>.

Table 145. Percent of Workers Participating in Health Care Benefit Programs and Percent of Participants Required to Contribute: 2004

[Based on National Compensation Survey, a sample survey of 4,703 private industry establishments of all sizes, representing over 102 million workers; see Appendix III. See also Table 639]

Characteristic	Percent of workers participating—			Single coverage medical care			Family coverage medical care		
	Medical care	Dental care	Vision care	Employee contributions not required (percent)	Employee contributions required (percent)	Average monthly contribution [1] (dol.)	Employee contributions not required (percent)	Employee contributions required (percent)	Average monthly contribution [1] (dol.)
Total	53	37	22	24	76	67.57	11	89	264.59
White-collar occupations...	59	43	25	22	78	69.07	9	91	271.60
Blue-collar occupations....	60	40	25	30	70	63.15	16	84	242.81
Service occupations......	24	16	11	19	81	72.40	9	91	294.58
Full-time [2]	66	46	27	24	76	67.05	11	89	263.65
Part-time [2].	11	8	6	29	71	78.61	17	83	284.66
Union [3]	81	68	50	43	57	56.53	33	67	195.12
Nonunion.............	50	33	19	21	79	68.98	7	93	273.51

[1] The average is presented for all covered workers and excludes workers without the plan provision. Averages are for plans stating a flat monthly cost.   [2] Employees are classified as working either a full-time or part-time schedule based on the definition used by each establishment.   [3] Union workers are those whose wages are determined through collective bargaining.

Source: U.S. Bureau of Labor Statistics, National Compensation Survey: Employee Benefits in Private Industry in the United States, 2004. See also <http://www.bls.gov/ncs/ebs/sp/ebsm0002.pdf> (accessed: 9 July 2005).

Table 146. Outpatient Prescription Drug Benefits: 2002

[In percent. Based on National Compensation Survey, a sample survey of 2,924 private industry establishments of all sizes, representing over 103 million workers; Summary of coverage, all private industry workers. see Appendix III. See also Table 639]

Characteristic	All workers	White collar	Blue collar	Service
Total with outpatient prescription [1]	100	100	100	100
Coverage for brand name drugs.	99	99	99	99
Higher reimbursement for generic drugs.	83	84	78	90
Coverage for mail order drugs [2]	70	73	65	75
Prescription card plan.	9	8	12	6
Higher reimbursement for formulary drugs	27	30	22	22
Not determinable	6	5	7	7

[1] Sum of individual items is greater than the total because some participants were in plans with more than one type of coverage.   [2] Programs that provide drugs for maintenance purposes, that is, drugs required on a continuous basis.

Source: U.S. Bureau of Labor Statistics, National Compensation Survey: Employee Benefits in Private Industry in the United States, 2002-2003, <http://www.bls.gov/ncs/ebs/sp/ebbl0020.pdf> (accessed: 8 July 2005).

110   Health and Nutrition

Table 147. Medical Care Benefits of Workers by Type and Amount of Employee Contribution: 2004

[In percent. See headnote, Table 145]

Type and amount of contribution	Individual coverage				Type and amount of contribution	Family coverage			
	All employees	White-collar occupations	Blue-collar occupations	Service occupations		All employees	White-collar occupations	Blue-collar occupations	Service occupations
Total with contributory coverage	100	100	100	100	Total with contributory coverage	100	100	100	100
Flat monthly amount	73	74	73	74	Flat monthly amount	74	73	76	73
Less than $5.00	(Z)	(Z)	(Z)	(Z)	Less than $25.00	1	1	2	(Z)
$5.00-$9.99	1	1	(Z)	(Z)	$25.00-$49.99	2	1	5	1
$10.00-$14.99	2	2	3	1	$50.00-$74.99	3	3	4	2
$15.00-$19.99	2	2	3	2	$75.00-$99.99	3	3	4	2
$20.00-$29.99	6	6	5	6	$100.00-$124.99	5	4	7	4
$30.00-$39.99	8	8	9	5	$125.00-$149.99	5	6	5	2
$40.00-$49.99	9	9	8	8	$150.00-$174.99	6	6	5	5
$50.00-$59.99	10	10	9	9	$175.00-$199.99	6	5	6	5
$60.00-$69.99	8	7	7	11	$200.00-$224.99	5	5	6	7
$70.00-$79.99	7	6	7	8	$225.00-$249.99	5	4	5	2
$80.00-$89.99	6	6	6	4	$250.00-$274.99	4	5	3	2
$90.00-$99.99	3	3	2	3	$275.00-$299.99	3	3	3	5
$100.00-$124.99	6	7	4	7	$300.00-$324.99	3	3	4	2
$125.00 or more	7	7	6	8	$325.00-$349.99	3	2	1	11
Dollar amount not specified	-	-	-	-	$350.00 or more	26	26	23	29
Composite rate [1]	1	1	(Z)	1	Composite rate [1]	1	1	(Z)	1
Varies [2]	4	4	3	4	Varies [2]	3	3	2	3
Flexible benefits [3]	2	2	1	1	Flexible benefits [3]	1	2	1	1
Percent of earnings	(Z)	(Z)	(Z)	1	Percent of earnings	(Z)	(Z)	(Z)	(Z)
Exists, but unknown	17	16	17	(Z)	Exists, but unknown	18	19	16	20
Other	3	2	5	2	Other	3	2	4	3

- Represents zero. Z Less than 0.5 percent. [1] A composite rate is a set contribution covering more than one benefit area; for example, health care and life insurance. Cost data for individual plans cannot be determined. [2] Based on worker attributes. For example, employee contributions may vary based on earnings, length of service, or age. [3] Amount varies by options selected under a "cafeteria plan" or employer-sponsored reimbursement account.

Source: U.S. Bureau of Labor Statistics, "National Compensation Survey, Employee Benefits in Private Industry, March 2004"; <http://www.bls.gov/ncs/ebs/sp/ebsm0002.pdf> (accessed 9 July 2005).

Table 148. Annual Receipts/Revenue for Health Care Industries: 1998 to 2003

[In millions of dollars (374,348 represents $374,348,000,000). Based on the North American Industry Classification System, 1997 (NAICS); see text, Section 15. All firms in NAICS 6211, 6212, 6213, and 6215 are defined as taxable. Estimates for the non-employer portion are derived from administrative records data provided by other federal agencies. These data are available only at the total revenue level. See Appendix III]

Kind of business	NAICS code	Total, all firms [1]			Employer firms		
		1998	2000	2003	1998	2000	2003
Ambulatory health care services	621	374,348	415,962	525,594	328,083	364,769	460,203
Offices of physicians	6211	181,579	202,913	256,391	181,579	202,913	256,391
Offices of dentists	6212	51,476	58,812	70,820	51,476	58,812	70,820
Offices of other health practitioners [2]	6213	30,018	32,512	40,321	30,018	32,512	40,321
Offices of chiropractors	62131	6,946	7,576	9,370	6,946	7,576	9,370
Offices of optometrists	62132	6,885	7,941	8,948	6,885	7,941	8,948
Offices of PT/OT/speech therapy & audiology [3]	62134	9,003	8,531	11,868	9,003	8,531	11,868
Outpatient care centers	6214	51,851	59,571	78,429	19,884	23,606	31,513
Medical & diagnostic laboratories	6215	18,501	22,261	29,105	18,501	22,261	29,105
Home health care services	6216	30,579	28,285	35,952	20,630	18,474	24,135
Other ambulatory health care services	6219	10,345	11,568	14,575	5,996	6,191	7,918
Hospitals	622	397,373	430,329	536,268	42,054	44,847	64,256
General medical & surgical hospitals	6221	370,862	402,578	502,289	35,193	37,256	53,602
Psychiatric & substance abuse hospitals	6222	14,686	14,944	15,208	3,813	4,406	4,611
Other specialty hospitals	6223	11,825	12,807	18,771	3,048	3,185	6,043
Nursing and residential care facilities	623	98,984	107,421	126,785	58,935	63,433	74,148
Nursing care facilities	6231	63,085	65,774	75,786	46,721	48,182	54,693
Residential mental retardation/health facilities [2]	6232	12,479	14,353	17,750	3,721	4,203	5,291
Residential mental retardation facilities	62321	8,287	9,301	11,344	2,536	2,834	3,639
Community care facilities for the elderly	6233	18,041	21,504	26,318	7,893	10,354	13,307

[1] Includes taxable nonemployer firms, not shown separately. [2] Includes other kinds of business not shown separately. [3] Offices of physical, occupational and speech therapists, and audiologists.

Source: U.S. Census Bureau, Service Annual Survey, 2003. <www.census.gov/svsd/www/sas62rpt.pdf> (accessed 19 June 2005).

Table 149. Receipts for Selected Health Service Industries by Source of Revenue: 2000 and 2003

[In millions of dollars (202,913 represents $202,913,000,000). Based on the 1997 North American Industry Classification System (NAICS), see text, Section 15. Based on a sample of employer firms only and does not include nonemployer revenue. See Appendix III]

Source of revenue	Offices of physicians (NAICS 6211)		Offices of dentists (NAICS 6212)		Hospitals (NAICS 622)		Nursing and residential care facilities (NAICS 623)	
	2000	2003	2000	2003	2000	2003	2000	2003
Total	202,913	256,391	57,395	69,559	430,329	536,270	107,150	119,640
Medicare	48,370	62,907	(S)	(S)	138,843	166,627	12,699	17,228
Medicaid	13,896	18,209	1,416	2,476	52,305	64,914	43,834	51,762
Other government [1]	2,025	2,761	(S)	(S)	22,687	28,844	7,157	9,281
Worker's compensation	7,419	8,222	(S)	(S)	4,720	5,849	(S)	(S)
Private insurance	97,193	124,144	30,232	36,148	155,206	203,567	6,231	6,280
Patient (out-of-pocket)	22,865	26,096	25,747	30,935	22,928	29,219	[2]27,019	[2]28,812
Other patient care sources, n.e.c [3]	7,299	9,165	(S)	(S)	10,622	10,667	3,300	2,777
Non-patient care revenue	3,846	4,887	(S)	(S)	23,019	26,583	6,910	3,500

S Figure does not meet publication standards. [1] Veterans, National Institute of Health, Indian Affairs, etc. [2] Represents payment from patients and their families plus patients' assigned social security benefits. [3] Not elsewhere classified.

Source: U.S. Census Bureau, Current Business Reports, Service Annual Survey: 2003. <http://www.census.gov/svsd/www/sas62.html>.

Table 150. Employment in the Health Service Industries: 1990 to 2004

[In thousands (2,842 represents 2,842,000). See head note Table 620]

Industry	NAICS code [1]	1990	1995	2000	2002	2003	2004
Ambulatory health care services [2]	621	2,842	3,768	4,320	4,633	4,786	4,946
Offices of physicians	6211	1,278	1,540	1,840	1,968	2,003	2,054
Offices of dentists	6212	513	592	688	725	744	760
Offices of other health practitioners	6213	276	395	438	486	503	523
Medical and diagnostic laboratories	6215	129	146	162	175	182	189
Home health care services	6216	288	622	633	680	733	773
Hospitals	622	3,513	3,734	3,954	4,160	4,245	4,294
General medical and surgical hospitals	6221	3,305	3,520	3,745	3,930	4,005	4,051
Psychiatric and substance abuse hospitals	6222	113	101	86	90	92	92
Other hospitals	6223	95	112	123	140	148	151
Nursing and residential care facilities [2]	623	1,856	2,308	2,583	2,743	2,786	2,815
Nursing care facilities	6231	1,170	1,413	1,514	1,573	1,580	1,575

[1] Based on the North American Industry Classification System 2002 code; see text, Section 15. [2] Includes other industries not shown separately.

Source: U.S. Bureau of Labor Statistics, Employment and Earnings, March issues. See also <http://stats.bls.gov/ces/home.htm>

Table 151. Registered Nurses by Employment Status: 1996 and 2000

[As of March (2,559 represents 2,559,000). Based on a sample and subject to sampling variability; see source for details]

Age, race and Hispanic origin status	Total (1,000)	Employed in nursing			Not employed in nursing (1,000)
		Number (1,000)	Percent distribution		
1996	2,559	2,116	100.0		443
2000	2,697	2,202	100.0		495
Less than 25 years	66	65	2.9		2
25 to 29 years	177	166	7.5		11
30 to 34 years	248	225	10.2		24
35 to 39 years	360	316	14.4		44
40 to 44 years	464	409	18.6		55
45 to 49 years	465	406	18.5		58
50 to 54 years	342	288	13.1		55
55 to 59 years	238	180	8.2		58
60 to 64 years	156	87	4.0		69
65 years and over	154	41	1.9		113
Unknown age	25	19	0.8		6
White non-Hispanic	2,334	1,891	85.9		443
Black non-Hispanic	133	113	5.1		20
Asian non-Hispanic	93	83	3.8		11
Native Hawaiian/Pacific Islander	6	6	0.3		1
American Indian/Alaska Native	13	11	0.5		2
Hispanic [1]	55	48	2.2		7
Two or more races non-Hispanic	33	27	1.2		6
Unknown race/ethnic	29	23	1.1		6

[1] Persons of Hispanic origin may be of any race.

Source: U.S. Department of Health and Human Services, Health Resources and Services Administration, The Registered Nurse Population, March 2000, September 2001. See also <http://bhpr.hrsa.gov/>.

Table 152. **Physicians by Sex and Specialty: 1980 to 2003**

[In thousands (467.7 represents 467,700). As of Dec. 31, except 1990 as of Jan. 1, and as noted. Includes Puerto Rico and island areas]

Activity	1980[1] Total	1980[1] Office-based	1990[1] Total	1990[1] Office-based	2000[1] Total	2000[1] Office-based	2003[1] Total	2003[1] Office-based
Doctors of medicine, total........	467.7	272.0	615.4	361.0	813.8	490.4	871.5	529.8
Place of medical education:								
U.S. medical graduates	370.0	226.2	483.7	286.2	616.8	376.5	654.3	407.8
International medical graduates [2].....	97.7	45.8	131.8	74.8	197.0	113.9	217.2	122.0
Sex: Male...................	413.4	251.4	511.2	311.7	618.2	382.3	646.5	400.3
Female	54.3	20.6	104.2	49.2	195.5	108.1	225.0	129.5
Allergy/immunology.............	1.5	1.4	3.4	2.5	4.0	3.1	4.2	3.2
Anesthesiology................	16.0	11.3	26.0	17.8	35.7	27.6	38.5	29.3
Cardiovascular diseases	9.8	6.7	15.9	10.7	21.0	16.3	22.3	17.3
Child psychiatry...............	3.3	2.0	4.3	2.6	6.2	4.3	6.7	4.8
Dermatology..................	5.7	4.4	7.6	6.0	9.7	8.0	10.3	8.5
Diagnostic radiology.............	7.0	4.2	15.4	9.8	21.1	14.6	23.3	16.4
Emergency medicine.............	5.7	3.4	14.2	8.4	23.1	14.5	26.6	17.7
Family practice	27.5	18.4	47.6	37.5	71.6	54.2	79.1	62.3
Gastroenterology..............	4.0	2.7	7.5	5.2	10.6	8.5	11.7	9.3
General practice................	32.5	29.6	22.8	20.5	15.2	13.0	13.2	11.2
General surgery................	34.0	22.4	38.4	24.5	36.7	24.5	37.8	25.3
Internal medicine..............	71.5	40.6	98.3	58.0	134.5	89.7	147.6	99.7
Neurology...................	5.7	3.3	9.2	5.6	12.3	8.6	13.3	9.3
Neurological surgery.............	3.3	2.5	4.4	3.1	5.0	3.7	5.1	3.9
Obstetrics and gynecology.........	26.3	19.5	33.7	25.5	40.2	31.7	41.9	33.6
Ophthalmology................	13.0	10.6	16.1	13.1	18.1	15.6	18.7	16.2
Orthopedic surgery.............	14.0	10.7	19.1	14.2	22.3	17.4	23.5	18.4
Otolaryngology	6.6	5.3	8.1	6.4	9.4	7.6	9.9	8.1
Pathology...................	13.6	6.1	16.6	7.5	18.8	10.6	18.9	10.6
Pediatrics...................	29.5	18.2	41.9	27.1	63.9	43.2	70.5	49.2
Physical med./rehab.............	2.1	1.0	4.1	2.2	6.5	4.3	7.1	4.9
Plastic surgery................	3.0	2.4	4.6	3.8	6.2	5.3	6.7	5.7
Psychiatry...................	27.5	16.0	35.2	20.1	39.5	25.0	40.3	25.7
Pulmonary diseases	3.7	2.0	6.1	3.7	8.7	5.9	9.7	6.9
Radiology...................	11.7	7.8	8.5	6.1	8.7	6.7	4.3	3.3
Radiation oncology.............	1.6	1.0	2.8	2.0	3.9	3.0	8.9	7.0
Urological surgery.............	7.7	6.2	9.4	7.4	10.3	8.5	10.6	8.8
Other specialty................	5.8	2.4	7.3	2.7	5.8	2.3	5.6	2.3
Other surgical specialty [3].......	2.9	2.3	2.9	2.4	6.1	5.1	6.3	5.3
Other remaining specialty [4]	6.1	2.5	7.8	3.3	8.8	4.2	8.9	4.2
Not classified...............	20.6	(X)	12.7	(X)	45.1	(X)	50.4	(X)
Other categories [5]..........	32.1	(X)	55.4	(X)	75.2	(X)	84.9	(X)
Doctors of Osteopathy [6].........	18.8	(X)	30.9	(X)	44.9	(X)	51.7	(X)

X Not applicable. [1] Includes unspecified physicians. [2] International medical graduates received their medical education in schools outside the United States and Canada. [3] Includes colon and rectal surgery and thoracic surgery. [4] Includes aerospace medicine, general preventive medicine, nuclear medicine, occupational medicine, medical genetics, and public health. [5] Includes inactive and address unknown. [6] Total number of DOs as of June 1. Data from American Osteopathic Association Fact Sheet, American Osteopathic Association, Chicago, IL. <http://www.osteopathic.org/index.cfm?PageID=aoaannualrprt>

Source: Except as noted, American Medical Association, Chicago, IL, *Physician Characteristics and Distribution in the U.S.* annual (copyright).

Table 153. **Active Physicians, 2003, and Nurses, 2001, By State**

[As of December. Excludes doctors of osteopathy, and physicians with addresses unknown. Includes all physicians not classified according to activity status]

State	Physicians [1] Total	Physicians [1] Rate [2]	Nurses Total	Nurses Rate [2]	State	Physicians [1] Total	Physicians [1] Rate [2]	Nurses Total	Nurses Rate [2]
United States ...	774,849	266	2,262,020	793	Missouri	13,732	241	52,970	940
Alabama.........	9,547	212	36,400	814	Montana.........	2,079	227	7,620	842
Alaska..........	1,439	222	4,930	778	Nebraska........	4,216	242	15,970	928
Arizona.........	11,679	209	34,880	657	Nevada	4,152	185	10,840	517
Arkansas	5,516	202	19,860	737	New Hampshire	3,392	263	11,190	889
California	92,470	261	185,550	536	New Jersey......	26,804	310	71,500	840
Colorado........	11,600	255	33,510	756	New Mexico	4,473	239	11,630	635
Connecticut......	12,603	362	32,740	953	New York	75,048	391	165,580	868
Delaware	2,069	253	7,280	913	North Carolina.....	21,287	253	72,050	878
Dist. of Columbia ...	4,329	768	8,600	1,498	North Dakota.....	1,529	241	6,460	1,014
Florida	42,213	248	129,610	792	Ohio	29,153	255	103,870	912
Georgia	19,222	221	58,600	697	Oklahoma	6,034	172	22,890	660
Hawaii	3,901	310	8,680	707	Oregon	9,342	262	26,040	750
Idaho..........	2,324	170	8,400	636	Pennsylvania	36,421	295	132,120	1,074
Illinois	34,461	272	104,830	837	Rhode Island......	3,770	350	11,160	1,053
Indiana.........	13,346	215	49,590	809	South Carolina....	9,521	230	28,130	693
Iowa	5,544	188	30,190	1,030	South Dakota	1,640	215	8,440	1,114
Kansas.........	5,947	218	24,680	913	Tennessee	15,178	260	48,880	850
Kentucky	9,348	227	34,920	858	Texas	46,802	212	129,710	607
Louisiana	11,904	265	36,690	821	Utah	4,987	212	13,830	607
Maine..........	3,485	267	13,390	1,043	Vermont.........	2,250	363	5,820	949
Maryland	22,819	414	43,340	805	Virginia.........	20,220	274	55,440	770
Massachusetts....	28,474	443	75,580	1,181	Washington	16,347	267	45,170	754
Michigan........	24,004	238	83,950	839	West Virginia	4,168	230	15,850	880
Minnesota.......	14,088	278	46,990	943	Wisconsin........	13,769	252	49,610	918
Mississippi	5,240	182	22,290	779	Wyoming	963	192	3,780	765

[1] 2002 and earlier data excludes federally-employed persons. [2] Per 100,000 resident population. Based on U.S. Census Bureau estimates as of July 1.

Source: Physicians: American Medical Association, Chicago, IL, *Physician Characteristics and Distribution in the U.S.*, annual (copyright); Nurses: U.S. Dept. of Health and Human Services, Health Resources and Services Administration, unpublished data.

Health and Nutrition 113

Table 154. **Health Professions—Practitioners and Schools: 1990 to 2002**

[(573 represents 573,000). Data on the number of schools and total enrollment are reported as of the beginning of the academic year; all other school data are reported as of the end of the academic year. Data are based on reporting by health professions' schools]

Year	Medi-cine	Osteo-pathy	Registered nursing				Licensed practical nursing	Den-tistry [1]	Optom-etry	Phar-macy
			Total	Bacca-laure-ate	Associ-ate's degree	Diploma				
ACTIVE PERSONNEL (1,000)										
1990	573	28	[2]1,790	682	1,107	[3]	441	148	26	168
1995	646	36	[2]2,116	881	1,235	[3]	399	159	29	181
2000	738	45	[2]2,249	983	1,267	[3]	374	168	32	196
2001	752	42	[2]2,262	1,000	1,262	[3]	(NA)	(NA)	(NA)	(NA)
NUMBER OF SCHOOLS [4]										
1990	126	15	1,470	489	829	152	1,154	56	17	74
1995	125	16	1,516	521	876	119	1,210	54	17	75
2000	125	19	(NA)	(NA)	(NA)	(NA)	(NA)	55	17	81
2001	125	19	(NA)	(NA)	(NA)	(NA)	(NA)	54	17	83
2002	125	19	(NA)	(NA)	(NA)	(NA)	(NA)	54	(NA)	83
TOTAL ENROLLMENT										
1990	65,016	6,615	201,458	74,865	106,175	20,418	46,720	16,412	4,723	23,013
1995	66,788	8,146	268,350	112,659	135,895	19,796	59,428	16,353	5,201	27,667
2000	66,377	10,388	192,202	89,508	95,598	7,096	(NA)	17,242	5,464	29,586
2001	66,160	10,817	(NA)	(NA)	(NA)	(NA)	(NA)	17,349	5,428	30,301
2002	66,253	11,101	(NA)	(NA)	(NA)	(NA)	(NA)	17,487	(NA)	31,769
GRADUATES										
1990	15,398	1,529	66,088	18,571	42,318	5,199	35,417	4,233	1,115	6,956
1995	15,883	1,843	97,052	31,254	58,749	7,049	44,234	3,908	1,219	7,837
2000	15,714	2,279	(NA)	(NA)	(NA)	(NA)	(NA)	4,171	1,315	7,260
2001	15,785	2,510	(NA)	(NA)	(NA)	(NA)	(NA)	4,367	1,310	7,000
2002	15,652	2,534	(NA)	(NA)	(NA)	(NA)	(NA)	4,349	(NA)	7,573

NA Not available. [1] Personnel data exclude dentists in military service, U.S. Public Health Service, and U.S. Dept. of Veterans Affairs. [2] Includes nurses with advanced degrees. [3] Diploma nurses included with associate's degree nurses. [4] Some nursing schools offer more than one type of program. Numbers shown for nursing are number of nursing programs.

Source: U.S. Department of Health and Human Services, Bureau of Health Professions, unpublished data; American Medical Association, Chicago, IL, *Physician Characteristics and Distribution in the U.S.*, annual; and American Association of Colleges of Osteopathic Medicine, Rockville, MD, *Annual Statistical Report*.

Table 155. **Adults 18 Years and Over Who Used Complementary and Alternative Medicine (CAM), by Type of Therapy: 2002**

[In thousands (149,271 represents 149,721,000) The denominators for statistics shown exclude persons with unknown CAM information. Estimates were age adjusted to the year 2000 U.S. standard population using four age groups: 18 to 24 years, 25 to 44 years, 45 to 64 years, and 65 years and over]

Therapy	Ever used	Used during past 12 months	Therapy	Ever used	Used during past 12 months
Any CAM [1] use	**149,271**	**123,606**	Manipulative and body-based therapies:		
Alternative medical systems:			Chiropractic care	40,242	15,226
Acupuncture	8,188	2,136	Massage	18,899	10,052
Ayurveda	751	154	Mind-body therapies:		
Homeopathic treatment	7,379	3,433	Biofeedback	1,986	278
Naturopathy	1,795	498	Meditation	20,698	15,336
			Guided imagery	6,067	4,194
Biologically-based therapies:			Progressive relaxation	8,518	6,185
Chelation therapy	270	(B)	Deep breathing exercises	29,658	23,457
Folk medicine	1,393	233	Hypnosis	3,733	505
Nonvitamin, nonmineral, natural			Yoga	15,232	10,386
products	50,613	38,183	Tai chi.	5,056	2,565
Diet-based therapies [2]	13,799	7,099	Qi gong	950	527
Vegetarian diet	5,324	3,184	Prayer for health reasons [3]	110,012	89,624
Macrobiotic diet.	1,368	317	Prayed for own health	103,662	85,432
Atkins diet	7,312	3,417	Others ever prayed for your		
Pritikin diet.	580	137	health	62,348	48,467
Ornish diet.	290	(B)	Participate in prayer group	25,167	18,984
Zone diet	1,062	430	Healing ritual for own health	9,230	4,045
Megavitamin therapy	7,935	5,739	Energy healing therapy/Reiki.	2,264	1,080

B Base figure too small to meet statistical standards for reliability of derived figures. [1] Respondents may have reported using more than one type of therapy. [2] The sum of the categories listed under "Diet-based therapies" are greater than the total number of "Diet-based therapies" because respondents could choose more than one diet-based therapy. [3] The sum of the categories listed under "Prayer for health reasons" are greater than the total number of "Prayer for health reasons" because respondents could choose more than one method of prayer.

Source: U.S. National Center for Health Statistics, Advance Data, No. 343. May 27, 2004. <http://www.cdc.gov/nchs/data/ad/ad343.pdf>.

Table 156. **Percent Distribution of Number of Visits to Health Care Professionals by Selected Characteristics: 2002 and 2003**

[Covers ambulatory visits to doctor's offices and emergency departments, and home health care visits during a 12-month period. Based on the redesigned National Health Interview Survey, a sample survey of the civilian noninstitutionalized population. See Appendix III]

Characteristic	None		1-3 visits		4-9 visits		10 or more visits	
	2002	2003	2002	2003	2002	2003	2002	2003
All persons [1]	15.9	15.8	45.5	45.8	25.2	24.8	13.4	13.6
Age:								
Under 6 years	5.6	5.5	47.0	46.0	37.1	39.0	10.4	9.4
6-17 years	13.0	14.0	59.0	58.7	22.3	20.8	5.7	6.6
18-44 years	22.6	22.4	45.7	46.7	19.4	19.1	12.4	11.8
45-64 years	14.8	14.7	41.9	42.2	26.9	26.6	16.4	16.5
65-74 years	9.1	7.1	33.7	34.0	36.8	35.7	20.5	23.3
75 years and over	7.3	5.4	28.6	28.6	35.8	36.0	28.3	30.0
Sex: [1]								
Male	20.6	20.6	46.5	46.8	22.2	21.9	10.7	10.7
Female	11.4	11.1	44.5	44.9	28.0	27.7	16.1	16.3
Race: [1, 2]								
White only	15.6	15.7	45.1	45.6	25.4	25.1	13.8	13.6
Black only	15.3	14.7	45.8	45.8	26.0	25.2	13.0	14.3
American Indian or Alaska Native only	18.1	23.3	43.7	41.4	21.7	20.6	16.6	14.7
Asian only	21.2	22.6	49.7	47.8	20.3	20.7	8.8	8.9
Two or more races	13.5	11.1	43.7	44.9	27.3	23.0	15.4	21.0
Race and Hispanic origin: [1]								
Hispanic	25.7	25.3	41.5	42.9	21.1	20.3	11.7	11.5
White, non-Hispanic	14.0	13.5	45.8	46.2	26.1	26.1	14.2	14.2
Black, non-Hispanic	15.3	14.6	45.7	45.9	26.0	25.3	13.1	14.2

[1] Estimates are age adjusted to the year 2000 standard using six age groups: Under 18 years, 18-44 years, 45-54 years, 55-64 years, 65-74 years, and 75 years and over. [2] Estimates by race and Hispanic origin are tabulated using the 1997 Standards for Federal data on race and ethnicity. Estimates for specific race groups are shown when they meet requirements for statistical reliability and confidentiality. The categories "White only," "Black or African American only," "American Indian and Alaska Native (AI/AN) only," and "Asian only" include persons who reported only one racial group; and the category "2 or more races" includes persons who reported more than one of the five racial groups in the 1997 Standards or one of the five racial groups and "Some other race."

Source: U.S. National Center for Health Statistics, Health, United States, 2005. See also <www.cdc.gov/nchs/hus/htm>

Table 157. **Ambulatory Care Visits to Physicians' Offices and Hospital Outpatient and Emergency Departments: 2003**

[1,114.5 represents 1,114,500,000. Based on the annual National Ambulatory Medical Care Survey and National Hospital Ambulatory Medical Care Survey and subject to sampling error; see source for details. For composition of regions, see map inside front cover]

Characteristic	Number of visits (mil.)				Visits per 100 persons			
	Total	Physician offices	Outpatient dept.	Emergency dept.	Total	Physician offices	Outpatient dept.	Emergency dept.
Total	1,114.5	906.0	94.6	113.9	390.3	317.3	33.1	39.9
Age:								
Under 15 years old	192.0	145.2	22.1	24.7	316.4	239.3	36.3	40.8
15 to 24 years old	101.4	72.4	11.2	17.7	252.8	180.6	28.0	44.2
25 to 44 years old	261.2	203.6	24.8	32.9	317.7	247.5	30.1	40.0
45 to 64 years old	301.5	257.3	23.2	21.0	442.0	377.2	34.1	30.8
65 to 74 years old	120.8	106.4	7.2	7.2	667.8	588.2	40.0	39.5
75 years old and over	137.6	121.1	6.1	10.4	849.9	748.2	37.5	64.2
Sex:								
Male	458.5	368.7	36.8	52.9	328.8	264.4	26.4	37.9
Female	656.1	537.3	57.8	61.0	449.1	367.8	39.5	41.8
Race:								
White	932.5	777.1	69.6	85.8	404.6	337.2	30.2	37.2
Black/African-American	129.7	84.3	20.7	24.7	363.1	235.9	58.0	69.3
Asian	41.9	37.1	2.7	2.0	353.2	313.2	22.9	17.1
Native Hawaiian/Other Pacific Islander	[1]3.7	[1]2.9	0.3	[1]0.5	[1]761.3	[1]599.3	68.0	[1]94.0
American Indian/Alaska Native	3.1	[1]2.1	[1]0.4	0.7	115.0	[1]75.8	[1]14.3	24.9
More than one race reported	3.5	2.5	[1]0.8	0.2	83.0	59.6	[1]19.6	3.8
Region:								
Northeast	239.4	189.4	26.2	23.8	446.7	353.5	48.8	44.5
Midwest	232.7	182.1	25.4	25.2	361.5	282.9	39.5	39.2
South	415.8	339.0	31.9	45.0	406.8	331.6	39.5	44.0
West	226.6	195.5	[1]11.1	19.9	346.7	299.2	[1]17.0	30.5
Primary source of payment:								
Private insurance	588.1	508.9	37.7	41.5	(X)	(X)	(X)	(X)
Medicare	237.9	206.3	13.0	18.5	(X)	(X)	(X)	(X)
Medicaid	142.3	92.2	25.7	24.4	(X)	(X)	(X)	(X)
Worker's compensation	13.2	10.4	0.6	2.1	(X)	(X)	(X)	(X)
Self pay	64.9	41.5	7.3	16.1	(X)	(X)	(X)	(X)
No charge	7.1	2.7	[1]3.3	[1]1.1	(X)	(X)	(X)	(X)
Other	26.4	20.5	3.1	2.8	(X)	(X)	(X)	(X)
Unknown	34.6	23.5	3.8	7.4	(X)	(X)	(X)	(X)

X Not applicable   [1] Figures do not meet standard of reliability or precision.

Source: U.S. National Center for Health Statistics, Advance Data, No. 358, May 26, 2005; and unpublished data. <http://www.cdc.gov/nchs/about/major/ahcd/adata.htm>

Health and Nutrition 115

Table 158. **Visits to Office-Based Physicians and Hospital Outpatient Departments by Diagnosis: 2000 and 2003**

[369.0 represents 369,000,000. See headnote, Table 157]

Leading diagnoses [1]	Number (mil.) 2000	Number (mil.) 2003	Rate per 1,000 persons [2] 2000	Rate per 1,000 persons [2] 2003	Leading diagnoses [1]	Number (mil.) 2000	Number (mil.) 2003	Rate per 1,000 persons [2] 2000	Rate per 1,000 persons [2] 2003
MALE					**FEMALE**				
All ages	**369.0**	**405.5**	**2,760**	**2,908**	**All ages**	**537.8**	**595.1**	**3,829**	**4,074**
Under 15 years old [3]	85.3	89.2	2,765	2,873	Under 15 years old [3]	75.4	78.1	2,556	2,635
Routine infant or child health check	17.9	16.8	580	541	Routine infant or child health check	17.5	14.0	593	472
Otitis media and Eustachian tube disorders	7.1	8.3	231	269	Acute respiratory infections [4]	8.1	7.8	276	263
Acute respiratory infections [4]	8.5	7.9	276	253	Otitis media and Eustachian tube disorders	6.6	6.5	222	218
Asthma	3.1	3.4	101	111	Acute pharyngitis	2.3	3.3	78	112
Attention deficit disorder	3.4	3.3	110	106	Asthma	1.2	2.1	40	71
15 to 44 years old [3]	98.9	103.8	1,660	1,707	15 to 44 years old [3]	194.8	208.1	3,199	3,383
General medical examination	3.9	4.3	66	71	Normal pregnancy	24.5	25.7	402	417
Acute respiratory infections [4]	3.6	4.0	60	65	Gynecological examination	6.1	9.8	100	160
Spinal disorders	3.0	3.4	50	56	Acute respiratory infections [4]	6.0	7.6	98	124
Chronic sinusitis	1.4	2.6	24	43	Complications of pregnancy, childbirth and the puerperium	6.2	7.4	102	121
Arthropathies and related disorders	2.8	2.4	47	39	General medical examination	6.6	5.5	108	89
45 to 64 years old [3]	96.5	112.6	3,294	3,404	45 to 64 years old [3]	141.0	167.9	4,511	4,779
Essential hypertension	6.8	7.6	233	231	Essential hypertension	8.3	8.2	264	232
Diabetes mellitus	5.8	5.1	199	155	Arthropathies and related disorders	6.6	8.1	212	232
Spinal disorders	3.1	4.7	106	143	Diabetes mellitus	5.6	6.0	181	170
Arthropathies and related disorders	2.9	4.5	99	135	Rheumatism, excluding back	4.6	5.9	146	169
General medical examination	2.3	3.8	79	114	Gynecological examination	3.1	5.9	100	167
65 years old and over [3]	88.2	99.9	6,340	6,886	65 years old and over [3]	126.6	141.0	6,736	7,128
Essential hypertension	6.6	7.2	478	498	Essential hypertension	11.8	11.2	628	566
Malignant neoplasms	7.1	6.3	507	435	Arthropathies and related disorders	6.3	8.1	333	409
Diabetes mellitus	4.8	5.5	344	379	Diabetes mellitus	6.0	5.3	318	269
Heart disease, excluding ischemic	4.1	3.7	296	257	Cataract	4.0	4.3	212	219
Ischemic heart disease	4.9	3.6	349	251	Heart disease, excluding ischemic	3.6	4.3	194	217

[1] Based on the International Classification of Diseases, 9th Revision, Clinical Modification, (ICD-9-CM). [2] Based on U.S. Census Bureau estimated civilian population as of July 1. [3] Includes other first-listed diagnoses, not shown separately. [4] Excluding pharyngitis.

Source: U.S. National Center for Health Statistics, unpublished data. <http://www.cdc.gov/nchs/about/major/ahcd/adata.htm>

Table 159. **Visits to Hospital Emergency Departments by Diagnosis: 2003**

[52,908 represents 52,908,000. See headnote, Table 157]

Leading diagnoses [1]	Number (1,000)	Rate per 1,000 persons [2]	Leading diagnoses [1]	Number (1,000)	Rate per 1,000 persons [2]
MALE			**FEMALE**		
All ages	**52,908**	**379**	**All ages**	**60,995**	**418**
Under 15 years old [3]	13,524	436	Under 15 years old [3]	11,209	378
Acute upper respiratory infections [4]	1,469	47	Acute respiratory infections [4]	1,163	39
Otitis media and Eustachian tube disorders	1,070	34	Otitis media and Eustachian tube disorders	971	33
Contusions with intact skin surfaces	656	21	Pyrexia of unknown origin	618	21
Pyrexia of unknown origin	643	21	Contusions with intact skin surfaces	479	16
15 to 44 years old [3]	22,102	363	15 to 44 years old [3]	28,535	464
Open wound, excluding head	1,500	25	Abdominal pain	1,660	27
Contusions with intact skin surfaces	1,101	18	Complications of pregnancy, childbirth, and the puerperium	1,494	24
Abdominal pain	788	13	Contusions with intact skin surfaces	1,118	18
Chest pain	758	12	Sprains and strains of neck and back	889	14
Strains and sprains, excluding ankle and back	743	12	Spinal disorders	886	14
45 to 64 years old [3]	9,772	295	45 to 64 years old [3]	11,220	319
Chest pain	673	20	Chest pain	789	22
Open wound, excluding head	420	13	Abdominal pain	533	15
Contusions with intact skin surfaces	412	12	Contusions with intact skin surfaces	468	13
Spinal disorders	362	11	Spinal disorders	461	13
65 years old and over [3]	7,511	518	65 years old and over [3]	10,031	507
Chest pain	431	30	Heart disease, excluding ischemic	619	31
Heart disease, excluding ischemic	416	29	Chest pain	601	30
Pneumonia	303	21	Contusions with intact skin surfaces	409	21
Abdominal pain	240	17	Abdominal pain	375	19
Chronic and unspecified bronchitis	234	16	Pneumonia	359	18

[1] Based on the International Classification of Diseases, 9th Revision, Clinical Modification, (ICD-9-CM). [2] Based on U.S. Census Bureau estimated civilian population as of July 1. [3] Includes other first-listed diagnoses, not shown separately. [4] Excluding pharyngitis.

Source: U.S. National Center for Health Statistics, *Advance Data*, No. 358; May 26, 2005.

Table 160. Hospitals—Summary Characteristics: 1980 to 2003

[For beds, (1,365 represents 1,365,000). Covers hospitals accepted for registration by the American Hospital Association; see text, this section. Short-term hospitals have an average patient stay of less than 30 days; long-term, an average stay of longer duration. Special hospitals include obstetrics and gynecology; eye, ear, nose, and throat; rehabilitation; orthopedic; and chronic and other special hospitals except psychiatric, tuberculosis, alcoholism, and chemical dependency hospitals]

Item	1980	1990	1995	1998	1999	2000	2001	2002	2003
Number:									
All hospitals	6,965	6,649	6,291	6,021	5,890	5,810	5,801	5,794	5,764
With 100 beds or more	3,755	3,620	3,376	3,216	3,140	3,102	3,084	3,032	3,007
Nonfederal [1]	6,606	6,312	5,992	5,746	5,626	5,565	5,558	5,554	5,525
Community hospitals [2]	5,830	5,384	5,194	5,015	4,956	4,915	4,908	4,927	4,895
Nongovernmental nonprofit	3,322	3.191	3,092	3,026	3,012	3,003	2,998	3,025	2,984
For profit	730	749	752	771	747	749	754	766	790
State and local government	1,778	1,444	1,350	1,218	1,197	1,163	1,156	1,136	1,121
Long-term general and special	157	131	112	125	129	131	136	124	126
Psychiatric	534	757	657	579	516	496	491	477	477
Tuberculosis	11	4	3	3	4	4	4	4	4
Federal	359	337	299	275	264	245	243	240	239
Beds (1,000) [3]:									
All hospitals	1,365	1,213	1,081	1,013	994	984	987	976	965
Rate per 1,000 population [4]	6.0	4.9	4.1	3.7	3.6	3.5	3.5	3.4	3.3
Beds per hospital	196	182	172	168	169	169	170	168	167
Nonfederal [1]	1,248	1,113	1,004	956	939	931	936	926	917
Community hospitals [2]	988	927	873	840	830	824	826	821	813
Rate per 1,000 population [4]	4.3	3.7	3.3	3.0	3.0	2.9	2.9	2.8	2.8
Nongovernmental nonprofit	692	657	610	588	587	583	585	582	575
For profit	87	102	106	113	107	110	109	108	110
State and local government	209	169	157	139	136	131	132	130	120
Long-term general and special	39	25	19	18	20*	18	19	18	18
Psychiatric	215	158	110	95	87	87	89	85	85
Tuberculosis	2	(Z)	(Z)	(Z)	(Z)	(Z)	(Z)	(Z)	(Z)
Federal	117	98	78	57	55	53	53	50	47
Average daily census (1,000):									
All hospitals	1,060	844	710	662	657	650	658	662	657
Community hospitals [2]	747	619	548	525	526	526	533	540	539
Nongovernmental nonprofit	542	455	393	377	381	382	385	391	389
For profit	57	54	55	60	58	61	63	64	65
State and local government	149	111	100	87	86	83	85	84	84
Expenses (bil. dol.): [5]									
All hospitals	91.9	234.9	320.3	355.5	372.9	395.4	426.8	462.2	498.1
Nonfederal [1]	84.0	219.6	300.0	332.9	349.2	371.5	399.3	432.5	467.2
Community hospitals [2]	76.9	203.7	285.6	318.8	335.2	356.6	383.7	416.6	450.1
Nongovernmental nonprofit	55.8	150.7	209.6	238.0	251.5	267.1	287.3	312.7	337.7
For profit	5.8	18.8	26.7	31.7	31.2	35.0	37.3	40.1	44.0
State and local government	15.2	34.2	49.3	49.1	52.5	54.5	59.1	63.8	68.4
Long-term general and special	1.2	2.7	2.2	2.6	2.8	2.8	3.3	3.6	3.6
Psychiatric	5.8	12.9	11.7	11.2	11.0	11.9	13.2	12.1	13.1
Tuberculosis	0.1	0.1	0.4	(Z)	(Z)	(Z)	(Z)	(Z)	(Z)
Federal	7.9	15.2	20.2	22.6	23.7	23.9	27.5	29.7	30.9
Personnel (1,000): [6]									
All hospitals	3,492	4,063	4,273	4,407	4,369	4,454	4,535	4,610	4,650
Nonfederal [1]	3,213	3,760	3,971	4,071	4,074	4,157	4,236	4,312	4,350
Community hospitals [2]	2,873	3,420	3,714	3,831	3,838	3,911	3,987	4,069	4,108
Nongovernmental nonprofit	2,086	2,533	2,702	2,834	2,862	2,919	2,971	3,039	3,058
For profit	189	273	343	383	362	378	379	380	391
State and local government	598	614	670	614	614	614	637	651	658
Long-term general and special	56	55	38	37	42	41	44	46	45
Psychiatric	275	280	215	198	191	200	201	193	194
Tuberculosis	3	1	1	1	1	1	1	1	1
Federal	279	303	301	336	295	297	299	299	300
Outpatient visits (mil.)	263.0	368.2	483.2	545.5	573.5	592.7	612.0	640.5	648.6
Emergency	82.0	92.8	99.9	99.0	99.0	103.8	106.9	109.8	114.2	115.1

Z Less than 500 beds or $50 million.   [1] Includes hospital units of institutions.   [2] Short term (average length of stay less than 30 days) general and special (e.g., obstetrics and gynecology; eye, ear, nose and throat; rehabilitation etc. except psychiatric, tuberculosis, alcoholism and chemical dependency). Excludes hospital units of institutions.   [3] Beginning 1990, number of beds at end of reporting period; prior years, average number in 12-month period.   [4] Based on Census Bureau estimated resident population as of July 1. Estimates reflect revisions based on the 2000 Census of Population.   [5] Excludes new construction.   [6] Includes full-time equivalents of part-time personnel.

Source: Health Forum, An American Hospital Association Company, Chicago, IL, *Hospital Statistics 2005 Edition*, and prior years (copyright). <http://www.healthforum.com/>.

Health and Nutrition   117

Table 161. Average Cost to Community Hospitals Per Patient: 1980 to 2003

[In dollars, except percent. Covers non-federal short-term general or special hospitals (excluding psychiatric or tuberculosis hospitals and hospital units of institutions). Total cost per patient based on total hospital expenses (payroll, employee benefits, professional fees, supplies, etc.). Data have been adjusted for outpatient visits]

Type of expense and hospital	1980	1990	1995	1997	1998	1999	2000	2001	2002	2003
Average cost per day, total	245	687	968	1,033	1,067	1,103	1,149	1,217	1,290	1,379
Annual percent change [1]	12.9	7.8	4.0	2.6	3.3	3.3	4.2	5.9	6.0	6.9
Nongovernmental nonprofit	246	692	994	1,074	1,111	1,140	1,182	1,255	1,329	1,429
For profit	257	752	947	962	968	999	1,057	1,121	1,181	1,264
State and local government	239	635	878	914	949	1,007	1,064	1,114	1,188	1,238
Average cost per stay, total	1,851	4,947	6,216	6,262	6,386	6,512	6,649	6,980	7,346	7,796
Nongovernmental nonprofit	1,902	5,001	6,279	6,393	6,526	6,608	6,717	7,052	7,458	7,905
For profit	1,676	4,727	5,425	5,219	5,262	5,350	5,642	5,972	6,161	6,590
State and local government	1,750	4,838	6,445	6,475	6,612	6,923	7,106	7,400	7,773	8,205

[1] Change from immediate prior year.

Source: Health Forum, An American Hospital Association Company, Chicago, IL, *Hospital Statistics 2005 Edition*, and prior years (copyright). <http://www.healthforum.com/>.

Table 162. Community Hospitals—States: 2000 and 2003

[For beds, 823.6 represents 823,600. For definition of community hospitals see footnote 2, Table 160]

State	Number of hospitals		Beds (1,000)		Patients admitted (1,000)		Average daily census [1] (1,000)		Outpatient visits (mil.)		Average cost per day (dol.)	
	2000	2003	2000	2003	2000	2003	2000	2003	2000	2003	2000	2003
United States . . .	4,915	4,895	823.6	813.3	33,089	34,783	525.7	538.8	521.4	563.1	1,149	1,379
Alabama	108	107	16.4	15.6	680	709	9.8	9.7	8.0	8.9	980	1,166
Alaska	18	19	1.4	1.5	47	46	0.8	0.8	1.3	1.4	1,495	1,952
Arizona.	61	61	10.9	10.8	539	603	6.8	7.3	5.3	6.7	1,311	1,570
Arkansas	83	88	9.8	9.9	368	388	5.7	5.7	4.4	4.6	908	1,130
California	389	370	72.7	74.3	3,315	3,474	47.8	51.5	44.9	48.0	1,438	1,763
Colorado.	69	68	9.4	9.5	397	444	5.4	6.2	6.7	7.0	1,280	1,551
Connecticut.	35	34	7.7	7.2	349	372	5.8	5.6	6.7	6.8	1,373	1,684
Delaware	5	6	1.8	2.0	83	97	1.4	1.7	1.5	2.0	1,311	1,508
District of Columbia.	11	10	3.3	3.4	129	135	2.5	2.5	1.3	1.6	1,512	1,824
Florida	202	203	51.2	50.7	2,119	2,296	31.0	32.8	21.8	22.0	1,161	1,387
Georgia	151	146	23.9	24.6	863	926	15.0	16.5	11.2	12.8	978	1,044
Hawaii	21	24	3.1	3.1	100	112	2.3	2.2	2.5	1.9	1,088	1,350
Idaho	42	39	3.5	3.4	123	136	1.8	1.9	2.2	2.8	1,003	1,235
Illinois	196	192	37.3	35.0	1,531	1,594	22.4	22.4	25.1	27.0	1,278	1,497
Indiana.	109	112	19.2	18.9	700	712	10.8	11.0	14.1	15.0	1,132	1,352
Iowa	115	116	11.8	11.0	360	363	6.8	6.5	9.2	9.7	740	952
Kansas.	129	134	10.8	10.6	310	331	5.7	5.9	5.3	6.0	837	952
Kentucky.	105	103	14.8	14.9	582	600	9.1	9.3	8.7	8.5	929	1,106
Louisiana	123	127	17.5	17.8	654	690	9.8	10.6	10.0	10.8	1,075	1,177
Maine.	37	37	3.7	3.7	147	149	2.4	2.2	3.2	3.9	1,148	1,416
Maryland	49	51	11.2	11.6	587	645	8.2	8.7	6.0	6.5	1,315	1,571
Massachusetts.	80	79	16.6	16.0	740	785	11.7	11.9	16.7	19.6	1,467	1,631
Michigan.	146	144	26.1	25.8	1,106	1,168	16.9	17.1	24.9	27.0	1,211	1,382
Minnesota.	135	131	16.7	16.4	571	615	11.2	11.3	7.3	9.1	932	1,109
Mississippi	95	92	13.6	13.0	425	416	8.0	7.4	3.7	4.0	719	882
Missouri	119	119	20.1	19.3	773	831	11.7	11.9	14.8	15.7	1,185	1,403
Montana	52	53	4.3	4.3	99	107	2.9	2.9	2.6	2.7	579	733
Nebraska	85	85	8.2	7.5	209	212	4.8	4.4	3.4	3.7	743	1,043
Nevada	22	25	3.8	4.3	199	213	2.7	3.0	2.2	2.3	1,285	1,608
New Hampshire. . . .	28	28	2.9	2.8	111	118	1.7	1.7	2.8	3.1	1,201	1,389
New Jersey.	80	78	25.3	22.8	1,074	1,108	17.3	16.9	16.3	14.7	1,299	1,411
New Mexico	35	37	3.5	3.7	174	166	2.0	2.1	3.1	4.5	1,388	1,563
New York	215	207	66.4	64.7	2,416	2,499	52.1	50.6	46.4	48.0	1,118	1,402
North Carolina.	113	113	23.1	23.3	971	987	16.0	16.6	12.4	14.5	1,061	1,200
North Dakota.	42	40	3.9	3.6	89	88	2.3	2.1	1.7	1.8	747	859
Ohio	163	163	33.8	33.0	1,404	1,458	20.6	20.6	26.9	30.0	1,198	1,504
Oklahoma.	108	108	11.1	11.0	429	450	6.2	6.5	4.7	5.5	1,031	1,177
Oregon.	59	58	6.6	6.8	330	342	3.9	4.0	7.3	8.2	1,461	1,842
Pennsylvania.	207	201	42.3	40.9	1,796	1,824	28.8	28.2	31.8	33.0	1,080	1,326
Rhode Island.	11	11	2.4	2.4	119	122	1.7	1.8	2.1	2.0	1,313	1,591
South Carolina. . . .	63	61	11.5	11.1	495	506	8.0	8.1	7.8	7.4	1,101	1,355
South Dakota	48	50	4.3	4.4	99	103	2.8	2.7	1.7	1.5	476	747
Tennessee	121	125	20.6	20.3	737	813	11.5	12.4	10.3	10.0	1,078	1,187
Texas.	403	414	55.9	57.3	2,367	2,550	33.1	36.4	29.4	32.3	1,274	1,482
Utah	42	42	4.3	4.4	194	215	2.4	2.5	4.5	4.5	1,375	1,654
Vermont	14	14	1.7	1.5	52	52	1.1	0.9	1.2	2.2	888	1,148
Virginia.	88	84	16.9	17.2	727	758	11.4	12.0	9.5	11.2	1,057	1,277
Washington.	84	85	11.1	11.2	505	516	6.6	6.8	9.6	10.3	1,511	1,827
West Virginia.	57	57	8.0	7.8	288	296	4.8	4.8	5.2	5.8	844	993
Wisconsin.	118	121	15.3	14.8	558	588	9.1	9.2	10.9	11.8	1,055	1,282
Wyoming	24	23	1.9	1.8	48	53	1.1	0.9	0.9	0.9	677	943

[1] Inpatients receiving treatment each day; excludes newborn.

Source: Health Forum, An American Hospital Association Company, Chicago, IL, *Hospital Statistics 2005 Edition*, and prior years (copyright). <http://www.healthforum.com/>.

118 Health and Nutrition

Table 163. **Hospital Use Rates by Type of Hospital: 1980 to 2003**

Type of hospital	1980	1990	1995	1999	2000	2001	2002	2003
Community hospitals: [1]								
Admissions per 1,000 population [2]	159	125	116	116	117	118	120	120
Admissions per bed	37	34	35	39	40	40	42	43
Average length of stay [3] (days)	7.6	7.2	6.5	5.9	5.8	5.7	5.7	5.7
Outpatient visits per admission	5.6	9.7	13.4	15.3	15.8	15.9	16.1	16.2
Outpatient visits per 1,000 population [2]	890	1,207	1,556	1,816	1,852	1,890	1,932	1,937
Surgical operations (million [4])	18.8	21.9	23.2	26.3	26.1	26.5	27.6	27.1
Number per admission	0.5	0.7	0.7	0.8	0.8	0.8	0.8	0.8
Nonfederal psychiatric:								
Admissions per 1,000 population [2]	2.5	2.9	2.7	2.4	2.4	2.6	2.5	2.6
Days in hospital per 1,000 population [2]	295	190	122	94	93	94	92	91

[1] For definition of community hospitals, see footnote 2, Table 160. [2] Based on U.S. Census Bureau estimated resident population as of July 1. Estimates reflect revisions based on the 2000 Census of Population. [3] Number of inpatient days divided by number of admissions. [4] 18.8 represents 18,800,000.

Source: Health Forum, An American Hospital Association Company, Chicago, IL, *Hospital Statistics 2005 Edition*, and prior years (copyright); <http://www.healthforum.com/>.

Table 164. **Hospital Utilization Rates by Sex: 1990 to 2003**

[30,788 represents 30,788,000. Represents estimates of inpatients discharged from noninstitutional, short-stay hospitals, exclusive of federal hospitals. Excludes newborn infants. Based on sample data collected from the National Hospital Discharge Survey, a sample survey of hospital records of patients discharged in year shown; subject to sampling variability]

Item and Sex	1990	1995	1997	1998	1999	2000	2001	2002	2003.
Patients discharged (1,000)	30,788	30,722	30,914	31,827	32,132	31,706	32,653	33,727	34,738
Patients discharged per 1,000 persons, total [1]	122	116	114	117	117	114	115	118	120
Male	100	94	93	93	95	92	93	95	98
Female	143	136	135	139	138	135	137	139	141
Days of care per 1,000 persons, total [1]	784	620	582	589	581	560	562	572	578
Male	694	551	508	517	510	491	490	506	507
Female	869	686	653	658	649	627	631	635	646
Average stay (days)	6.4	5.4	5.1	5.1	5.0	4.9	4.9	4.9	4.8
Male	6.9	5.8	5.5	5.5	5.4	5.3	5.3	5.3	5.2
Female	6.1	5.0	4.8	4.7	4.7	4.6	4.6	4.6	4.6

[1] Rates are computed using Census Bureau estimates of the civilian population as of July 1, based on the 2000 census. Population estimates used to calculate rates for 2001-2003 were based on the 2000 census. Rates for 1991-2000 data were computed using postcensual estimates of the civilian population based on the 1990 census.

Source: U.S. National Center for Health Statistics, *Vital and Health Statistics*, Series 13; and unpublished data. <http://www.cdc.gov/nchs/products/pubs/pubd/series/ser.htm>

Table 165. **Hospital Discharges and Days of Care: 2002 and 2003**

[32,727 represents 32,727,000. See headnote, Table 164. For composition of regions, see map, inside front cover]

Age, race and region	Discharges				Days of care per 1,000 persons [1]		Average stay (days)	
	Number (1,000)		Per 1,000 persons [1]					
	2002	2003	2002	2003	2002	2003	2002	2003
Total	33,727	34,738	118	120	572	578	4.9	4.8
Age:								
Under 1 year old	810	833	201	208	1,134	1,218	5.6	5.9
1 to 4 years old	713	751	46	48	159	149	3.5	3.1
5 to 14 years old	1,016	986	25	24	109	108	4.4	4.5
15 to 24 years old	3,083	3,138	77	77	266	268	3.5	3.5
25 to 34 years old	3,897	4,011	99	102	328	353	3.3	3.5
35 to 44 years old	3,757	3,683	84	83	368	359	4.4	4.3
45 to 64 years old	7,723	8,120	116	118	575	582	5.0	4.9
65 to 74 years old	4,642	4,861	254	265	1,412	1,429	5.6	5.4
75 years old and over	8,085	8,356	467	475	2,795	2,776	6.0	5.8
Race:								
White	20,806	21,292	90	91	436	437	4.9	4.8
Black	3,995	4,102	109	111	584	611	5.3	5.5
Asian/Pacific Islander	538	550	45	44	243	231	5.4	5.2
American Indian/ Eskimo/Aleut	173	120	63	43	330	224	5.2	5.2
Region:								
Northeast	6,990	7,267	129	134	727	735	5.6	5.5
Midwest	7,503	7,786	115	119	512	520	4.4	4.4
South	12,994	13,055	127	126	618	610	4.9	4.9
West	6,239	6,631	96	100	430	455	4.5	4.5

[1] Based on U.S. Census Bureau estimated civilian population as of July 1. Population estimates based on the 2000 Census were used to calculate rates.

Source: U.S. National Center for Health Statistics, *Vital and Health Statistics*, Series 13; and unpublished data. <http://www.cdc.gov/nchs/products/pubs/pubd/series/ser.htm>.

Health and Nutrition 119

Table 166. Hospital Discharges and Days of Care by Sex: 2003

[**13,874 represents** 13,874,000. Represents estimates of inpatients discharged from noninstitutional, short-stay hospitals, exclusive of federal hospitals. Diagnostic categories are based on the International Classification of Diseases, Ninth Revision, Clinical Modification. See headnote, Table 164]

Age and first-listed diagnosis	Discharges Number (1,000)	Discharges Per 1,000 persons [1]	Days of care per 1,000 persons [1]	Average stay (days)	Age and first-listed diagnosis	Discharges Number (1,000)	Discharges Per 1,000 persons [1]	Days of care per 1,000 persons [1]	Average stay (days)
MALE					**FEMALE**				
All ages [2]	**13,874**	**104.4**	**546.7**	**5.2**	**All ages [2]**	**20,864**	**135.1**	**605.2**	**4.5**
Under 18 years [3]	1,679	44.9	200.0	4.5	Under 18 years [3]	1,504	42.2	190.9	4.5
Pneumonia	221	5.9	19.1	3.2	Pneumonia	159	4.5	15.4	3.1
Injuries and poisoning	207	5.5	21.6	3.9	Injuries and poisoning	128	3.6	[6]15.4	[6]4.3
Fracture, all sites	77	2.0	6.1	3.0	Asthma	46	1.3	[6]3.1	[6]2.4
18 to 44 years [3]	2,683	47.7	236.0	4.9	18 to 44 years [3]	7,537	135.2	444.2	3.3
Injuries and poisoning	470	8.4	40.8	4.9	Delivery	3,874	69.5	179.6	2.6
Serious mental illness [4]	323	5.8	46.2	8.0	Serious mental illness [4]	333	6.0	48.2	8.1
Alcohol and drug [4][5]	203	3.6	14.9	4.1	Injuries and poisoning	268	4.8	18.9	3.9
Fracture, all sites	171	3.0	15.5	5.1					
45 to 64 years [3]	4,016	120.1	605.0	5.0	45 to 64 years [3]	4,104	116.5	560.9	4.8
Diseases of heart	827	24.7	99.0	4.0	Diseases of heart	498	14.1	59.7	4.2
Ischemic heart disease	494	14.8	56.1	3.8	Injuries and poisoning	310	8.8	48.8	5.5
Injuries and poisoning	369	11.0	60.9	5.5	Ischemic heart disease	242	6.9	25.0	3.6
Malignant neoplasms	221	6.6	44.7	6.7	Malignant neoplasms	226	6.4	37.9	5.9
Acute myocardial infarction	161	4.8	25.0	5.2					
Serious mental illness [4]	147	4.4	39.9	9.1	65 to 74 years [3]	2,552	255.5	1,398.4	5.5
65 to 74 years [3]	2,309	276.5	1,465.3	5.3	Diseases of heart	480	48.0	229.6	4.8
Diseases of heart	553	66.3	290.0	4.4	Ischemic heart disease	205	20.5	86.8	4.2
Ischemic heart disease	294	35.2	147.4	4.2	Injuries and poisoning	184	18.5	103.2	5.6
Malignant neoplasms	161	19.3	124.7	6.5	Malignant neoplasms	144	14.5	98.5	6.8
					Osteoarthritis	132	13.2	54.7	4.1
75 years old and over [3]	3,188	483.1	2,844.9	5.9					
Diseases of heart	728	110.3	560.2	5.1	75 years old and over [3]	5,168	470.5	2,734.8	5.8
Ischemic heart disease	311	47.2	238.8	5.1	Diseases of heart	1,067	97.2	480.1	4.9
Pneumonia	262	39.7	245.2	6.2	Injuries and poisoning	507	46.2	271.0	5.9
Injuries and poisoning	228	34.6	226.1	6.5	Ischemic heart disease	352	32.1	150.8	4.7
Congestive heart failure	205	31.1	170.6	5.5	Pneumonia	327	29.7	189.9	6.4
Cerebrovascular diseases	192	29.1	142.2	4.9	Congestive heart failure	325	29.6	159.4	5.4

[1] Based on Census Bureau estimated civilian population as of July 1. [2] Average length of stay and rates per 1,000 population are age-adjusted to the year 2000 standard using five age groups; Under 18 years, 18-44 years, 45-64 years, 65-74 years, and 75 years and over. [3] Includes other first-listed diagnoses not shown separately. [4] Excludes discharges from facilities such as the Department of Veterans Affairs or long-term hospitals. [5] Includes abuse, dependence, and withdrawal. [6] Estimates are considered unreliable. Data has a relative standard error of 20 to 30 percent.

Source: U.S. National Center for Health Statistics, *Health, United States 2005*. See also <www.cdc.gov/nchs/hus.htm>.

Table 167. Organ Transplants and Grafts: 1990 to 2004

[**As of end of year.** Based on reports of procurement programs and transplant centers in the United States, except as noted]

Procedure	Number of procedures 1990	1995	2000	2002	2003	2004	Number of centers 1990	2004	Number of people waiting, 2004	1-year patient survival rates, 2003 (percent)
Transplant: [1]										
Heart	2,095	2,342	2,172	2,153	2,057	2,016	148	134	3,133	87.7
Heart-lung	52	69	47	33	29	39	79	60	164	56.4
Lung	203	869	955	1,042	1,085	1,173	70	68	3,521	82.8
Liver	2,631	3,818	4,816	5,326	5,671	6,168	85	123	17,409	86.3
Kidney	9,358	10,957	13,258	14,741	15,129	16,000	232	246	62,454	98
Kidney-pancreas	459	915	910	903	871	880	(NA)	(NA)	2,461	95.5
Pancreas	60	103	420	546	502	604	84	138	1,685	94.2
Intestine	1	21	29	107	116	152	(NA)	46	189	82.4
Multi-organ	71	124	213	320	350	438	(NA)	(NA)	(NA)	(NA)
Cornea grafts [2]	40,631	44,652	46,949	46,625	46,436	46,841	[3]107	[3]88	(NA)	(NA)
Bone grafts(1,000)	350	450	800	1,050	1,200	1,500	30	61	(X)	(NA)
Skin grafts [4][5]	5,500	5,500	13,000	15,000	16,000	19,000	25	44	(X)	(NA)

NA Not available. X Not applicable. [1] Kidney-pancreas and heart-lung transplants are each counted as one organ. All other multi-organ transplants, excluding kidney-pancreas and heart-lung, are included in the multi-organ row. Based on the Organ Procurement and Transplant Network (OPTN) as of July 18, 2005. The data have been supplied by UNOS under contract with HHS. This work was supported in part by Health Resources and Services Administration contract 231-00-0015. The authors alone are responsible for the reporting and interpretation of these data. Data subject to change based on future data submission or correction. [2] 1990-1992, number of procedures and eye banks include Canada. From 1993 on, the data is for the U.S. only. [3] Eye banks. [4] Procedure data are shown in terms of square feet. [5] Data for 2000-2003 has been revised.

Source: U.S. Department of Health and Human Services, Health Resources and Services Administration, Office of Special Programs, Division of Transplantation, Rockville, MD; United Network for Organ Sharing (UNOS), Richmond, VA; University Renal Research and Education Association, Ann Arbor, MI; American Association of Tissue Banks, McLean, VA; and Eye Bank and Eye Bank Association of America, Washington, DC; and unpublished data. See also <www.optn.org/latestdata/rptData>.

Table 168. Procedures for Inpatients Discharged From Short-Stay Hospitals: 1990 to 2003

[23,051 represents 23,051,000. Procedure categories are based on the International Classification of Diseases, Ninth Revision, Clinical Modification.See headnote, Table 164]

Sex and type of procedure	Number of procedures (1,000)				Rate per 1,000 population [1]			
	1990	1995	2000	2003	1990	1995	2000	2003
Surgical procedures, total [2]	**23,051**	**22,530**	**23,244**	**25,826**	**92.4**	**86.2**	**83.6**	**89.2**
Cardiac catheterization	995	1,068	1,221	1,257	4.0	4.1	4.4	4.3
Removal of coronary artery obstruction [3]	285	434	1,025	1,244	1.2	1.7	3.7	4.3
Repair of current obstetric laceration	795	964	1,136	1,198	3.2	3.7	4.1	4.1
Cesarean section	945	785	855	1,130	3.8	3.0	3.1	3.9
Reduction of fracture [4]	609	577	628	643	2.4	2.2	2.3	2.2
Male, total [2]	**8,538**	**8,388**	**8,689**	**9,878**	**70.6**	**65.9**	**63.9**	**69.6**
Removal of coronary artery obstruction [3]	200	285	655	812	1.7	2.2	4.8	5.7
Cardiac catheterization	620	660	732	763	5.1	5.2	5.4	5.4
Coronary artery bypass graft	286	423	371	346	2.4	3.3	2.7	2.4
Female, total [2]	**14,513**	**14,142**	**14,556**	**15,948**	**113.0**	**105.3**	**102.4**	**108.1**
Repair of current obstetric laceration	795	964	1,136	1,198	6.2	7.2	8.0	8.1
Cesarean section	945	785	855	1,130	7.4	5.8	6.0	7.7
Hysterectomy	591	583	633	615	4.6	4.3	4.5	4.2
Diagnostic and other nonsurgical procedures [5]	**17,455**	**17,278**	**16,737**	**18,063**	**70.0**	**66.1**	**60.2**	**62.4**
Angiocardiography and arteriography [6]	1,735	1,834	2,005	1,984	7.0	7.0	7.2	6.9
Respiratory therapy	1,164	1,127	991	1,154	4.7	4.3	3.6	4.0
Manual assisted delivery	750	866	898	977	3.0	3.3	3.2	3.4
CAT scan [7]	1,506	967	754	867	6.0	3.7	2.7	3.0
Diagnostic ultrasound	1,608	1,181	886	866	6.4	4.5	3.2	3.0
Male, total [5]	**7,378**	**7,261**	**6,965**	**7,560**	**61.0**	**57.1**	**51.2**	**53.3**
Angiocardiography and arteriography [6]	1,051	1,076	1,157	1,120	8.7	8.5	8.5	7.9
Respiratory therapy	586	572	507	592	4.9	4.5	3.7	4.2
CAT scan [7]	736	473	345	442	6.1	3.7	2.5	2.8
Female, total [5]	**10,077**	**10,016**	**9,772**	**10,503**	**78.5**	**74.6**	**68.8**	**71.2**
Manual assisted delivery	750	866	898	977	5.9	6.5	6.3	6.6
Fetal EKG and fetal monitoring	1,377	935	750	829	10.8	7.0	5.5	5.6
Diagnostic ultrasound	941	682	501	464	7.3	5.1	3.5	3.1

[1] Based on Census Bureau estimated civilian population as of July 1. Population estimates based on the 1990 Census were used to calculate rates for 1990 and 1995. Population estimates based on the 2000 census were used to calculate rates for 2000 and 2003.   [2] Includes other types of surgical procedures not shown separately.   [3] Beginning 1996, includes separately coded "insertion of stent."   [4] Excluding skull, nose, and jaw.   [5] Includes other nonsurgical procedures not shown separately.   [6] Using contrast material.   [7] Computerized axial tomography.

Source: U.S. National Center for Health Statistics, *Vital and Health Statistics*, series 13; and unpublished data; <http://www.cdc.gov /nchs/products/pubs/pubd/series/ser.htm>

Table 169. Hospital Utilization Measures for HIV Patients: 1990 to 2003

[HIV represents human immunodeficiency virus. See headnote, Table 164]

Measure of utilization	Unit	1990	1995	2000	2001	2002	2003
Number of patients discharged	1,000....	146	249	173	185	189	207
Rate of patient discharges [1]	Rate....	5.8	9.4	6.2	6.5	6.6	7.2
Number of days of care	1,000....	2,188	2,326	1,257	1,435	1,322	1,696
Rate of days of care [1]	Rate....	86.9	87.6	45.2	50.6	46.0	58.6
Average length of stay	Days....	14.9	9.3	7.3	7.8	7.0	8.2

[1] Per 10,000 population. Based on Census Bureau estimated civilian population as of July 1. Beginning in 1997, rates are based on civilian population estimates that have been adjusted for net underenumeration in the 1990 census. Population estimates for the 2000 census were first used to calculate rates in 2001. The 2000 population estimates were based on the 1990 census.

Source: National Center for Health Statistics, *Vital and Health Statistics*, Series 13; and unpublished data. <http://www.cdc.gov /nchs/products/pubs/pubd/series/ser.htm>

Table 170. Skilled Nursing Facilities: 1980 to 2003

[(436 represents 436,000). Covers facilities and beds certified for participation under Medicare and are deemed to meet Medicaid standards. Includes facilities which have transfer agreements with one or more participating hospitals, and are engaged primarily in providing skilled nursing care and related services for the rehabilitation of injured, disabled, or sick persons]

Item	Unit	1980 [1]	1990 [1]	1995	1999	2000	2001	2002 [2]	2003 [2]
Skilled nursing facilities	Number.	5,052	8,937	13,122	14,913	14,913	14,841	14,755	14,838
Beds	1,000...	436	509	652	837	837	939	1,050	1,261
Per 1,000 Medicare enrollees [3]	Rate ...	20.0	15.2	17.7	21.6	21.3	23.7	26.2	31.1

[1] Facility data are as of July 1.   [2] Facility data are as of December 31.   [3] Based on total number of beneficiaries enrolled in the medicare hospital insurance program as of July 1 of year stated.

Source: U.S. Centers for Medicare and Medicaid Services, Data Compendium 2003, Other Medicare Providers and Suppliers. <http://www.cms.hhs.gov/researchers/pubs/datacompendium/2003/03pg56b.pdf>

Table 171. **Home Health and Hospice Care Patients by Selected Characteristics: 2000**

[In percent, except as indicated (1,460.8 represents 1,460,800). Based on the National Home and Hospice Care Survey. Home health care is provided to individuals and families in their place of residence. Hospice care is available in both the home and inpatient settings.]

Item	Current patients [1]			Discharges [2]		
	Total	Home health care	Hospice care	Total	Home health care	Hospice care
Total (1,000)	1,460.8	1,355.3	105.5	7,800.1	7,179.0	621.1
PERCENT DISTRIBUTION						
Age: [3]						
Under 45 years old	13.2	13.9	4.5	13.7	14.5	3.9
45-54 years old	6.5	6.7	5.1	6.2	6.3	5.0
55-64 years old	8.9	8.9	8.9	10.2	10.0	11.5
65 years old and over	71.3	70.5	81.4	70.0	69.1	79.6
65-69 years old	7.1	7.1	7.3	9.4	9.4	10.1
70-74 years old	10.2	10.2	9.9	11.1	10.8	14.5
75-79 years old	17.1	16.8	20.9	15.5	15.8	12.5
80-84 years old	14.6	14.5	16.1	16.2	16.2	15.9
85 years old and over	22.3	21.9	27.2	17.8	17.0	26.5
Sex:						
Male	35.8	35.2	42.6	37.3	36.2	49.8
Female	64.2	64.8	57.4	62.7	63.8	50.2
Race:						
White.	76.3	76.0	82.8	79.5	79.1	84.1
Black.	12.4	12.6	10.6	9.8	10.0	8.1
Unknown	9.0	9.4	5.0	8.3	8.5	5.5

[1] Patients on the rolls of the agency as of midnight the day prior to the survey. [2] Patients removed from the rolls of the agency during the 12 months prior to the day of the survey. A patient could be included more than once if the individual had more than one episode of care during the year. [3] For current patients, current age for discharged patients, age at time of discharge. Source: U.S. National Center for Health Statistics, *Health, U.S., 2002* <http://www.cdc.gov/nchs/hus.htm>.

Table 172. **Nursing Homes—Selected Characteristics: 1999**

[Beds: 1,624 represents 1,624,000. Covers licensed and/or certified nursing homes in the conterminous United States that had three or more beds. Based on the 1999 National Nursing Home Survey, a two-stage survey sample of nursing homes and their residents. Subject to sampling variability.]

Characteristic		Beds		Current residents		Full-time equivalent employment			
						Administrative, medical, and therapeutic		Nursing	
	Nursing homes	Number (1,000)	Per nursing home	Number (1,000)	Occu-pancy rate [1]	Number (1,000)	Rate per 100 beds	Number (1,000)	Rate per 100 beds
Total.	18,000	1,965	109	1,627	82.8	96.6	4.9	961	48.9
Certification:									
Medicare and medicaid certified.	14,700	1,698	116	1,414	83.3	83.2	4.9	842	49.6
Medicare only	[2]600	49	82	37	75.5	2.8	5.7	26	53.1
Medicaid only	2,100	177	89	143	80.8	9.0	5.1	75	42.4
Not certified.	[2]500	40	80	33	82.5	1.6	4.0	18	45.0
Bed size:									
Less than 50 beds	2,000	72	36	59	81.9	7.1	9.9	43	59.7
50-99 beds	7,000	503	72	414	82.3	28.8	5.7	252	50.1
100-199 beds	7,500	998	133	826	82.8	45.0	4.5	476	47.7
200 beds or more.	1,400	392	280	328	83.7	15.7	4.0	190	48.5

[1] Number of residents divided by number of available beds multiplied by 100. [2] Figure does not meet standards of reliability or precision.

Source: U.S. National Center for Health Statistics, Vital and Health Statistics, *Series 13, No. 152, The National Nursing Home Survey: 1999 Summary.* See also <http://www.cdc.gov/nchs/fastats/nursingh.htm>.

Table 173. **Mental Health Facilities—Summary by Type of Facility: 2002**

[Beds: 211.2 represents 211,200. Facilities, beds and inpatients as of year-end. Excludes private psychiatric office practice and psychiatric service modes of all types in hospitals or outpatient clinics of federal agencies other than U.S. Dept. of Veterans Affairs. Excludes data from Puerto Rico, Virgin Islands, Guam, and other territories]

Type of facility	Number of facilities	Inpatient beds		Inpatients		Inpatient care episodes [2] (1,000)
		Total (1,000)	Rate [1]	Total (1,000)	Rate [1]	
Total	4,301	211.2	73.3	180.5	62.7	2,443
Mental hospitals:						
State and county	222	57.2	19.9	52.6	18.3	294
Private [3]	761	64.1	22.3	53.6	18.6	506
General hospitals [4]	1,285	40.2	14.0	28.5	9.9	1,123
Veterans Administration [5] . . .	140	9.7	3.4	8.4	2.9	198
Other [6]	1,893	39.9	13.9	37.5	13.0	178

[1] Rate per 100,000 population. Based on U.S. Census Bureau estimated civilian population as of July 1. [2] "Inpatient care episodes" is defined as the number of residents in inpatient facilities at the beginning of the year plus the total additions to inpatient facilities during the year. [3] Includes residential treatment centers for emotionally disturbed children. [4] Non-federal hospitals with separate psychiatric services. [5] Includes U.S. Department of Veterans Affairs (VA) neuropsychiatric hospitals, VA general hospitals with separate psychiatric settings and VA freestanding psychiatric outpatient clinics. [6] Includes other multiservice mental health facilities with two or more settings, which are not elsewhere classified, as well as freestanding partial care facilities which only provide psychiatric partial care services. Number of facilities, expenditures, and staff data also include freestanding psychiatric partial care facilities.

Source: U.S. Substance Abuse and Mental Health Services Administration, Center for Mental Health Services, unpublished data. See also <http://www.mentalhealth.samhsa.gov/cmhs/MentalHealthStatistics/>.

Table 174. Injury and Poisoning Episodes and Conditions by Age and Sex: 2003

[23,782 represents 23,782,000. Covers all medically attended injuries and poisonings occurring during the 3-month period prior to the survey interview. Age adjustment is used to adjust for differences in the age distribution of populations being compared. There may be more than one condition per episode. Based on the redesigned National Health Interview Survey, a sample survey of the civilian noninstitutionalized population; see Appendix III]

External cause and nature of injury	Total	Both sexes						Male, total	Female, total
		Total, age-ad-justed [1]	Under 12 years old	12 to 21 years old	22 to 44 years old	45 to 64 years old	65 years old and over		
EPISODES									
Number (1,000)	23,782	(X)	3,473	4,493	8,229	4,725	2,862	12,739	11,043
Annual rate per 1,000									
population, total [2]	83.2	82.1	72.3	110.1	86.9	69.2	83.5	91.3	75.4
Fall.	28.0	27.4	27.6	33.1	19.1	22.5	58.0	26.2	29.7
Struck by or against a person									
or an object	10.5	9.7	12.8	22.8	9.0	7.3	[4]2.7	14.1	7.0
Transportation [3]	13.2	12.9	8.3	22.7	17.4	8.2	7.3	14.6	11.9
Overexertion	11.8	12.0	4.0	12.0	17.2	13.0	5.0	13.3	10.3
Cutting, piercing instruments. . .	6.6	6.8	[4]5.34	5.7	9.2	6.1	[4]3.0	8.6	4.6
Poisoning[5]	2.5	2.4	[4]4.24	[4]3.6	2.2	[4]1.94	[4]1.1	2.6	2.5
CONDITIONS									
Annual rate per 1,000									
population, total [2]	105.7	104.6	81.7	137.9	113.3	89.1	113.1	112.3	99.4
Sprains/strains	22.0	21.9	6.8	33.7	31.4	18.6	10.5	23.1	21.0
Open wounds.	13.6	13.6	20.6	14.0	13.7	11.6	7.4	17.5	9.9
Fractures.	15.8	15.4	14.1	20.5	12.6	12.0	28.7	16.7	14.9
Contusions	8.1	7.8	4.7	11.6	6.3	7.7	14.4	7.5	8.7

X Not applicable.   [1] Data were age-adjusted using the 2000 standard population.   [2] Includes other items not shown separately.   [3] Includes the categories "Motor vehicle traffic"; "Pedal cycle, other"; "Pedestrian, other"; and "Transport, other".   [4] Figure does not meet standard of reliability or precision.   [5] Poisoning episodes are assumed to have a single condition resulting from the episode.

Source: U.S. National Center for Health Statistics, unpublished data. See also <http://www.cdc.gov/nchs/injury.htm>.

Table 175. Injuries Associated With Consumer Products: 2002

[Estimates calculated from a representative sample of hospitals with emergency treatment departments in the United States. Data are estimates of the number of emergency room treated cases nationwide associated with various products. Product involvement does not necessarily mean the product caused the accident. Products were selected from the U.S. Consumer Product Safety Commission's National Electronic Injury Surveillance System]

Product	Number	Product	Number
Home workshop equipment:		Sofas, couches, davenports, etc.	135,190
Saws (hand or power)	92,384	Home entertainment equipment:	
Hammers.	36,894	Televisions	42,811
Household packaging and containers:		Personal use items:	
Household containers and packaging	216,498	Footwear	114,454
Bottles and jars.	76,487	Wheelchairs	95,228
Housewares:		Jewelry	73,943
Knives.	441,250	Yard and garden equipment:	
Tableware and flatware.	106,852	Lawn mowers.	72,480
Drinking glasses	86,909		
Home furnishings:		Sports and recreation equipment:	
Beds.	495,050	Bicycles.	521,328
Tables [1]	307,843	All-terrain vehicles	113,900
Chairs.	298,234	Skateboards	113,192
Household cabinets, racks, and shelves . .	261,622	Trampolines	89,393
Bathtubs and showers	216,221	Swimming pools	82,304
Ladders.	163,417	Playground climbing equipment	81,745

[1] Excludes baby changing and television tables or stands.

Source: National Safety Council, Itasca, IL, Injury Facts, Annual(copyright). <http://www.nsc.org/lrs/statstop.htm>

Table 176. Costs of Unintentional Injuries: 2003

[607.7 represents $607,700,000,000. Covers costs of deaths or disabling injuries together with vehicle accidents and fires]

Cost	Amount (bil. dol.)					Percent distribution				
	Total [1]	Motor vehicle	Work	Home	Other	Total [1]	Motor vehicle	Work	Home	Other
Total	607.7	240.7	156.2	135.1	95.4	100.0	100.0	100.0	100.0	100.0
Wage and productivity losses [2]	301.5	82.4	78.3	84.3	60.5	49.6	34.2	50.1	62.4	63.4
Medical expense	118.7	31.5	30.9	33.5	24.4	19.5	13.1	19.8	24.8	25.6
Administrative expenses [3]	103.7	75.8	28.7	6.0	4.9	17.1	31.5	18.4	4.4	5.1
Motor vehicle damage	48.8	48.8	2.0	(NA)	(NA)	8.0	20.3	1.3	(NA)	(NA)
Employer uninsured cost [4]	24.5	2.2	13.7	5.0	4.0	4.0	0.9	8.8	3.7	4.2
Fire loss	10.5	(NA)	2.6	6.3	1.6	1.7	(NA)	1.7	4.7	1.7

NA Not available.   [1] Excludes duplication between work and motor vehicle ($19.7 billion in 2003).   [2] Actual loss of wages and household production, and the present value of future earnings lost.   [3] Home and other costs may include costs of administering medical treatment claims for some motor-vehicle injuries filed through health insurance plans.   [4] Estimate of the uninsured costs incurred by employers, representing the money value of time lost by noninjured workers.

Source: National Safety Council, Itasca, IL, Injury Facts, Annual(copyright). <http://www.nsc.org/lrs/statstop.htm>

Table 177. Specified Reportable Diseases—Cases Reported: 1980 to 2003

[190.9 represents 190,900. Figures should be interpreted with caution. Although reporting of some of these diseases is incomplete, the figures are of value in indicating trends of disease incidence. Includes cases imported from outside the United States]

Disease	1980	1985	1990	1995	1999	2000	2001	2002	2003
AIDS [1]	(2)	8,249	41,595	71,547	45,104	40,758	41,868	42,745	44,232
Botulism [3]	89	122	92	97	154	138	155	118	129
Brucellosis (undulant fever)	183	153	85	98	82	87	136	125	104
Chickenpox (Varicella) [4] (1,000)	190.9	178.2	173.1	120.6	46.0	27.4	22.5	22.8	20.9
Coccidoidomycosis	(2)	(2)	(2)	(2)	2,826	2,867	3,922	4,968	4,870
Cholera	9	4	6	23	6	5	3	2	2
Cryptosporidiosis	(2)	(2)	(2)	(NA)	2,361	3,128	3,785	3,016	3,506
Diphtheria	3	3	4	-	1	1	2	1	1
Encephalitis/menigitis, arboviral West Nile	(2)	(2)	(2)	(2)	(2)	(2)	(2)	2,840	2,866
Enterohemorrhagic Escherichia coli 0157:H7	(2)	(2)	(2)	2,139	4,513	4,528	3,287	3,840	2,671
Haemophilus influenza	(2)	(2)	(2)	1,180	1,309	1,398	1,597	1,743	2,013
Hansen disease (Leprosy)	223	361	198	144	108	91	79	96	95
Hepatitis: B (serum) (1,000)	19.0	26.6	21.1	10.8	7.7	8.0	7.8	8.0	7.5
A (infectious) (1,000)	29.1	23.2	31.4	31.6	17.0	13.4	10.6	8.8	7.7
C/Non-A, non-B (1,000) [5]	(2)	4.2	2.6	4.6	3.1	3.2	4.0	1.8	1.1
Legionellosis	(2)	830	1,370	1,241	1,108	1,127	1,168	1,321	2,232
Lyme disease	(2)	(2)	(2)	11,700	16,273	17,730	17,029	23,763	21,273
Malaria	2,062	1,049	1,292	1,419	1,666	1,560	1,544	1,430	1,402
Measles (1,000)	13.5	2.8	27.8	0.3	0.1	0.1	0.1	-	0.1
Meningococcal infections	2,840	2,479	2,451	3,243	2,501	2,256	2,333	1,814	1,756
Mumps (1,000)	8.6	3.0	5.3	0.9	0.4	0.3	0.3	0.3	0.2
Pertussis [6] (1,000)	1.7	3.6	4.6	5.1	7.3	7.9	7.6	9.8	11.6
Plague	18	17	2	9	9	6	2	2	1
Poliomyelitis, acute [7]	9	7	6	7	2	-	-	-	-
Psittacosis	124	119	113	64	16	17	25	18	12
Rabies, animal	6,421	5,565	4,826	7,811	6,730	6,934	7,150	7,609	6,846
Rabies, human	-	1	-	5	-	4	1	3	2
Rocky Mountain spotted fever	1,163	714	651	590	579	495	695	1,104	1,091
Rubella [8]	3,904	630	1,125	128	267	176	23	18	7
Salmonellosis [9] (1,000)	33.7	65.3	48.6	46.0	40.6	39.6	40.5	44.3	43.7
Shigellosis [10] (1,000)	19.0	17.1	27.1	32.1	17.5	22.9	20.2	23.5	23.6
Streptococcal disease, invasive, Group A	(2)	(2)	(2)	(2)	2,667	3,144	3,750	4,720	5,872
Streptococcus pneumoniae, invasive:									
Drug-resistant	(2)	(2)	(2)	(2)	(2)	(2)	498	513	845
Age less than 5 years	(2)	(2)	(2)	(2)	4,625	4,533	2,896	2,546	2,356
Tetanus	95	83	64	41	40	35	37	25	20
Toxic-shock syndrome	(2)	384	322	191	113	135	127	109	133
Trichinosis	131	61	129	29	12	16	22	14	6
Tuberculosis [11] (1,000)	27.7	22.2	25.7	22.9	17.5	16.4	16.0	15.1	14.9
Typhoid fever	510	402	552	369	346	377	368	321	356
Sexually transmitted diseases:									
Gonorrhea (1,000)	1,004	911	690	393	360	359	362	352	335
Syphilis (1,000)	69	68	134	69	36	32	32	34	34
Chlamydia (1,000)	(2)	(2)	(2)	478	657	702	783	835	877
Chancroid	788	2,067	4,212	606	143	78	38	67	54

- Represents zero or rounds to zero.   [1] Acquired immunodeficiency syndrome was not a notifiable disease until 1984. Figures are shown for years in which cases were reported to the CDC. Beginning 1995, based on revised classification system and expanded surveillance case definition.   [2] Disease was not notifiable.   [3] Includes foodborne, infant, wound, and unspecified cases.   [4] Chickenpox was taken off the nationally notifiable list in 1991, but many states continue to report.   [5] Includes some persons positive for antibody to hepatitis C virus who do not have hepatitis.   [6] Whooping cough.   [7] Revised. Data subject to annual revisions.   [8] German measles. Excludes rubella, congenital syndrome.   [9] Excludes typhoid fever.   [10] Bacillary dysentery.   [11] Newly reported active cases.

Source: U.S. Centers for Disease Control and Prevention, Atlanta, GA, *Summary of Notifiable Diseases, United States, 2003, Morbidity and Mortality Weekly Report*, Vol. 52, No. 54, April 22, 2005.

Table 178. Children Immunized Against Specified Diseases: 1995 to 2003

[In percent. Covers civilian noninstitutionalized population ages 19 months to 35 months. Based on estimates from the National Immunization Survey. The health care providers of the children are contacted to verify and/or complete vaccination information. Results are based on race/ethnic status of the child]

Vaccination	1995, total	2000, total	2003 Total	White non-Hispanic	Black non-Hispanic	Hispanic	American Indian/Alaska Native [1]	Asian [1]
Diphtheria-tetanus-pertussis (DTP) diphtheria-tetanus:								
3+ doses	95	94	96.0	96.8	95.2	94.8	93.6	97.0
4+ doses	79	82	84.8	87.5	79.9	81.9	80.1	88.5
Polio: 3+ doses	88	90	91.6	93.0	89.2	90.1	91.3	91.3
Hib [2]: 3+ doses	92	93	93.9	95.1	92.4	93.1	88.8	91.1
Measles, mumps, rubella vaccine	90	91	93.0	93.2	92.1	92.7	91.8	96.0
Hepatitis B: 3+ doses	68	90	92.4	93.2	91.6	91.2	90.3	93.6
Varicella [3]	(NA)	68	84.8	83.8	85.4	85.7	81.4	91.1
4+ DTP/3+ polio/1+ MCV [4]	76	78	82.2	85.0	76.7	79.3	78.5	83.8
4+ DTP/3+ polio/1+ MCV/3+ Hib	74	76	81.3	84.3	75.2	78.7	76.9	80.7

NA Not available.   [1] Non-Hispanic.   [2] Haemophilus B.   [3] Data collection for varicella (chicken pox) began in July 1996.   [4] MCV = Measles containing vaccine.

Source: U.S. Centers for Disease Control and Prevention, Atlanta, GA, National Immunization Program, Data and Statistics, "Immunization Coverage in the U.S."; <http://www.cdc.gov/nip/coverage/default.htm>.

Table 179. **Reported AIDS Cases for Adults and Adolescents, by Transmission Category and Sex: Cumulative Through 2003**

[Provisional. For cases reported in the year shown. Includes Puerto Rico, Virgin Islands, Guam, and U.S. Pacific Islands. Acquired immunodeficiency syndrome (AIDS) is a specific group of diseases or conditions which are indicative of severe immunosuppression related to infection with the human immunodeficiency virus (HIV). Data are subject to retrospective changes and may differ from those data in Table 177]

	2003			Cumulative through 2003[1]		
	Total	Male	Female	Total	Male	Female
Persons 13 years old and over, total	44,811	33,250	11,561	892,875	729,478	163,396
Male-to-male sexual contact.	15,859	15,859	(X)	401,392	401,392	(X)
Injection drug use.	7,128	4,866	2,262	218,196	156,575	61,621
Men who have sex with men and injecting drug use.	1,695	1,695	(X)	57,998	57,998	(X)
Hemophilia/coagulation disorder	85	74	11	5,448	5,130	318
Heterosexual contact	8,605	3,371	5,234	111,147	40,947	70,200
Sex with injuction drug user	1,462	477	985	35,078	10,930	24,148
Sex with bisexual male	223	(X)	223	4,402	(X)	4,402
Sex with person with hemophilia	23	7	16	545	80	465
Sex with HIV-infected transfusion recipient	61	24	37	1,210	505	705
Sex with HIV-infected person, risk not specified.	6,836	2,863	3,973	69,912	29,432	40,480
Receipt of blood transfusion, blood components, or tissue.	219	111	108	9,295	5,219	4,076
Other/risk not reported or identified	11,220	7,274	3,946	89,399	62,217	27,181

X Not applicable.   [1] Includes persons with characteristics unknown.

Source: U.S. Centers for Disease Control and Prevention, Atlanta, GA, *HIV/AIDS Surveillance Report*, Volume 15. <http://www.cdc.gov/hiv/stats/hasrlink.htm>.

Table 180. **Estimated Persons Living With Acquired Immunodeficiency Syndrome (AIDS) by Year and Selected Characteristics: 1999 to 2003**

[These numbers do not represent actual cases of persons living with AIDS. Rather, these numbers are point estimates of persons living with AIDS that have been adjusted for reporting delays and for redistribution of cases in persons initially reported without an identified risk. The estimates have not been adjusted for incomplete reporting.]

Age and characteristic	1999	2000	2001	2002	2003
Total [1]	311,205	334,731	357,040	380,771	405,926
AGE AS OF END OF YEAR					
Less than 13 years old	3,034	2,843	2,605	2,335	1,998
13 and 14 years old	440	517	645	728	768
15 to 24 years.	4,719	4,991	5,229	5,668	6,313
25 to 34 years.	60,184	56,686	53,687	51,410	49,906
35 to 44 years.	141,295	151,180	158,173	163,732	168,322
45 to 54 years.	77,216	89,461	102,252	115,613	129,311
55 to 64 years.	19,258	22,922	27,197	32,703	38,997
65 years old and over.	5,058	6,132	7,251	8,583	10,310
RACE/ETHNICITY					
White, not Hispanic.	119,674	126,162	132,258	139,089	146,544
Black, not Hispanic.	126,044	137,524	148,469	160,022	172,278
Hispanic.	61,194	66,266	71,034	75,782	80,623
Asian/Pacific Islander	2,484	2,755	3,056	3,414	3,826
American Indian/Alaska Native	1,047	1,166	1,262	1,380	1,498
MALE ADULT/ADOLESCENT TRANSMISSION CATEGORY					
Males 13 years old and over, total	244,291	261,223	277,366	294,767	313,183
Male-to-male sexual contact.	140,216	150,172	160,076	171,035	182,989
Injection drug use.	58,006	61,249	63,723	66,003	68,191
Male-to-male sexual contact and injection drug use . . .	21,667	22,403	23,033	23,690	24,334
Heterosexual contact	20,595	23,478	26,471	29,835	33,324
Other [2]	3,807	3,922	4,062	4,204	4,345
FEMALE ADULT/ADOLESCENT TRANSMISSION CATEGORY					
Females 13 years old and over, total	63,093	69,647	75,765	82,052	88,815
Injection drug use.	25,744	27,317	28,602	29,670	30,710
Heterosexual contact	35,603	40,422	45,097	50,144	55,685
Other [2]	1,746	1,908	2,067	2,239	2,420

[1] Includes persons of unknown or multiple race and of unknown sex.   [2] Includes hemophilia, blood transfusion, perinatal, and risk not reported or not identified.

Source: U.S. Centers for Disease Control and Prevention, Atlanta, GA, *HIV/AIDS Surveillance Report*, Volume 15. See also <http://www.cdc.gov/hiv/stats/hasrlink.htm>.

State	AIDS	Syphilis	Tuber-culosis	State	AIDS	Syphilis	Tuber-culosis	State	AIDS	Syphilis	Tuber-culosis
U.S. ...	[1]44,232	34,270	14,874	KS......	111	77	75	ND......	2	2	6
				KY......	220	160	138	OH......	775	481	229
AL......	471	566	258	LA......	1,048	1,576	260	OK......	214	353	163
AK......	17	8	57	ME......	52	21	25	OR......	242	118	106
AZ......	628	1,106	295	MD......	1,572	974	268	PA......	1,906	705	336
AR......	189	296	127	MA......	757	644	261	RI......	102	90	46
CA......	5,967	4,202	3,227	MI......	676	860	243	SC......	778	548	254
CO......	368	144	111	MN......	179	195	214	SD......	13	5	20
CT......	733	207	111	MS......	509	435	128	TN......	835	876	285
DE......	216	47	33	MO......	404	207	131	TX......	3,413	3,996	1,594
DC......	961	330	79	MT......	7	-	7	UT......	75	72	39
FL......	4,774	3,282	1,046	NE......	60	27	28	VT......	16	1	9
GA......	1,907	2,152	526	NV......	279	149	107	VA......	786	552	332
HI......	110	59	117	NH......	37	37	15	WA......	527	239	250
ID......	25	45	13	NJ......	1,514	1,089	495	WV......	95	11	21
IL......	1,734	1,376	633	NM......	111	205	49	WI......	184	111	66
IN......	506	375	143	NY......	5,133	3,825	1,140	WY......	8	4	4
IA......	75	46	40	NC......	1,102	848	374				

- Represents zero.   [1] Includes cases among persons with unknown state of residence.

Source: U.S. Centers for Disease Control and Prevention, Atlanta, GA, *Summary of Notifiable Diseases, United States, 2003, Morbidity and Mortality Weekly Report*, Vol. 52, No. 54, April 22, 2005.

Table 182. Persons with Limitation of Activity Caused by Chronic Conditions: 2000 to 2003

[In percent. Limitation of activity is assessed by asking respondents a series of questions about limitations in their ability to perform activities usual for their age group because of a physical, mental, or emotional problem. Respondents are asked about limitations in activities of daily living, or instrumental activities of daily living, play, school, work, difficulty walking or remembering, and any other activity limitations. For reported limitations the causal health conditions are determined and respondents are considered limited if one or more of these conditions is chronic. Based on the National Health Interview Survey, a sample survey of the civilian noninstitutionalized population; see Appendix III]

Characteristic	2000	2001	2002	2003	Characteristic	2000	2001	2002	2003
Total [1, 2]...........	11.7	12.1	12.4	12.1	Male [2]...............	11.7	12.2	12.3	11.9
Under 18 years	6.0	6.7	7.1	6.9	Female [2].............	11.5	11.9	12.3	12.2
18 to 44 years	5.8	6.1	6.3	6.0					
45 to 54 years	12.4	13.1	13.7	13.0	White, non-Hispanic [2]......	11.5	11.8	12.1	11.8
55 to 64 years	19.7	20.7	21.1	21.1	Black, non-Hispanic [2]......	14.3	15.6	14.9	15.3
65 to 74 years	26.1	26.0	25.2	26.3	Hispanic [2, 3]...........	10.3	10.6	10.7	10.2
75 years and over	45.1	44.7	45.1	44.0	Mexican.............	10.4	10.3	10.8	9.7

[1] Includes all other races not shown separately.   [2] Estimates for all persons are age adjusted to the year 2000 standard using six age groups: Under 18 years, 18-44 years, 45-54 years, 55-64 years. 65-74 years, and 75 years and over.   [3] Persons of Hispanic origin may be of any race.

Source: U.S. National Center for Health Statistics, *Health, United States, 2005.* <http://www.cdc.gov/nchs/hus.htm>.

Table 183. Persons 65 Years Old and Over With Limitation of Activity Caused by Chronic Conditions: 2000 to 2003

[In percent. Covers noninstitutionalized persons 65 years old and over. To determine activities of daily living (ADL) limitations respondents were asked "Because of a physical, mental, or emotional problem, does (this person) need the help of other persons with personal care needs, such as eating, bathing, dressing, or getting around inside this home?" Instrumental activities of daily living (IADL) were determined by asking respondents "Because of a physical, mental, or emotional problem, does (this person) need the help of other persons in handling routine needs, such as everyday household chores, doing necessary business, shopping, or getting around for other purposes?" See also headnote, Table 182]

Characteristic	Percent with ADL limitation				Percent with IADL limitation			
	2000	2001	2002	2003	2000	2001	2002	2003
Total [1] [2]..................	6.3	6.4	6.1	6.4	12.7	12.6	12.2	12.2
65 to 74 years	3.3	3.4	2.7	3.1	6.6	6.7	6.0	6.5
75 years and over.............	9.5	9.6	9.8	9.9	19.3	18.9	18.9	18.4
Male [2].....................	5.1	6.1	4.7	5.2	9.2	9.6	7.8	8.6
Female [2]...................	7.0	6.6	7.0	7.2	15.1	14.6	15.2	14.6
Not Hispanic or Latino [2]......	6.1	6.1	5.9	6.1	12.6	12.3	12.1	12.1
White......................	5.7	5.5	5.5	5.7	12.1	11.6	11.5	11.4
Black or African American	10.1	11.8	9.9	10.4	19.1	18.7	18.4	19.0
Hispanic or Latino [2] [3].............	8.6	11.2	9.2	10.3	13.4	17.0	13.1	13.8
Mexican....................	9.4	10.6	10.1	9.8	16.3	17.0	13.9	15.1

[1] Includes other races not shown separately.   [2] Estimates are age adjusted to the year 2000 standard using two age groups: 65-74 years and 75 years and over.   [3] Persons of Hispanic origin may be of any race.

Source: U.S. National Center for Health Statistics, *Health, United States, 2005.*

Table 184. **Persons 18 Years and Over With Selected Diseases and Conditions, by Selected Characteristics: 2003**

[In thousands (213,042 represents 213,042,000). Based on the National Health Interview Survey, a sample survey of the civilian noninstitutionalized population; see Appendix III]

Selected characteristics	Total persons	Persons with selected diseases and conditions					
		Diabetes[1,2]	Ulcers[1]	Kidney disease[3,4]	Liver disease[3]	Arthritis diagnosis[5]	Chronic joint symptoms[5,6]
Total[7]	213,042	14,012	14,456	3,017	2,511	45,793	57,242
Male	102,298	6,990	6,480	1,489	1,253	17,692	24,776
Female	110,744	7,022	7,976	1,528	1,258	28,102	32,466
Age:							
18 to 44 years old	110,538	2,101	4,757	617	766	8,633	18,201
45 to 64 years old	68,248	6,239	5,697	1,162	1,297	20,539	23,797
65 to 74 years old	18,097	3,180	2,098	540	223	8,322	7,947
75 years old and over	16,159	2,491	1,903	697	226	8,299	7,298
Race alone:[8]	210,869	13.833	14,245	2,964	2,447	45,268	56,619
White	177,830	11,199	12,513	2,420	2,025	39,606	49,561
Black or African American	24,111	2,120	1,319	427	306	4,679	5,567
American Indian or Alaska Native	1,285	146	[9]144	[9]38	[9]38	332	453
Asian	7,361	355	256	[9]72	[9]78	633	1,004
Native Hawaiian or other Pacific Islander	282	[9]12	[9]13	[9]7	-	[9]18	[9]33
2 or more races[10]	2,173	179	211	[9]53	[9]64	525	624
Hispanic or Latino origin[11]	26,272	1,556	1,285	402	310	2,896	4,218
Mexican or Mexican American	16,661	964	735	234	194	1,566	2,419

- Represents zero. [1] Respondents were asked if they had ever been told by a health professional that they had an ulcer or diabetes. A person may be represented in more than one column. [2] Excludes borderline diabetes. [3] Respondents were asked if they had been told in the last 12 months by a health professional that they had weak or failing kidneys or any kind of liver condition. [4] Excludes kidney stones, bladder infections, or incontinence. [5] Respondents were asked if they had ever been told by a health professional that they had some form of arthritis, rheumatoid arthritis, gout,lupus or fibromyalgia. [6] Respondents with joint symptoms that began more than 3 months ago prior to interview. Excludes back and neck. [7] Total includes other races not shown separately. [8] Refers to persons who indicated only a single race group. [9] Figures do not meet standard of reliability or precision. [10] Refers to all persons who indicated more than one race group. [11] Persons of Hispanic or Latino origin may be any race or combination of races.

Source: National Center for Health Statistics, Health, United States, 2005 <http://www.cdc.gov/nchs/hus.htm>

Table 185. **Disabilities Tallied by Age Group and by State: 2003**

[In thousands (3,668 represents 3,668,000). Data are limited to the household population and exclude the population living in institutions, college dormitories, and other group quarters. A disability is a long-lasting physical, mental, or emotional condition. This condition can make it difficult for a person to do activities such as walking, climbing stairs, dressing, bathing, learning, or remembering. This condition can also impede a person from being able to go outside the home alone or to work at a job or business. Based on data from the 2003 American Community Survey (ACS). See text, Section 1 and Appendix III]

State	Total disabilities tallied			State	Total disabilities tallied		
	5 to 15 years[1]	16 to 64 years[2]	65 years and over[3]		5 to 15 years[1]	16 to 64 years[2]	65 years and over[3]
U.S.	3,668	45,531	28,231	MO	74	924	602
AL	69	1,024	596	MT	7	164	91
AK	12	122	38	NE	20	266	158
AZ	74	800	482	NV	17	308	172
AR	49	662	403	NH	14	177	100
CA	381	4,945	3,107	NJ	92	1,016	814
CO	53	530	305	NM	24	347	218
CT	27	405	298	NY	209	2,766	1,885
DE	11	113	80	NC	133	1,587	891
DC	6	83	45	ND	5	79	62
FL	207	2,598	2,038	OH	190	1,990	1,160
GA	94	1,412	751	OK	46	702	396
HI	10	158	114	OR	39	626	353
ID	23	242	136	PA	165	1,952	1,346
IL	142	1,501	1,171	RI	16	164	111
IN	81	1,072	607	SC	53	785	403
IA	36	442	287	SD	7	78	69
KS	27	379	263	TN	85	1,219	678
KY	68	1,051	494	TX	282	3,103	1,878
LA	69	899	501	UT	31	241	152
ME	16	289	143	VT	7	110	60
MD	70	784	475	VA	91	1,108	650
MA	81	827	567	WA	77	1,021	522
MI	166	1,695	969	WV	22	545	284
MN	61	593	377	WI	69	791	478
MS	54	755	410	WY	5	77	43

[1] Persons aged 5-15 were classified as having a disability if they reported any one of the four conditions; sensory, physical, mental or self-care disability. [2] Persons aged 16-64 were classified as having a disability if they reported any one of the six conditions; sensory, physical, mental, self-care disability, go-outside-home or employment disability. [3] Persons 65 years and over were classified as having a disability if they reported any one of the five conditions; sensory, physical, mental, self-care disability or go-outside-home disability.

Source: U.S. Census Bureau, "American Factfinder, 2003 American Community Survey, Summary Table, Total Disabilities Tallied for The Civilian Noninstitutional Population." <http://factfinder.census.gov/>; (accessed: 10 July 2005).

Health and Nutrition 127

Table 186. **Selected Respiratory Diseases Among Persons 18 Years of Age and Over, by Selected Characteristics: 2003**

[In thousands (213,042 represents 213,042,000). Respondents were asked in two separate questions if they had ever been told by a doctor or other health professional that they had emphysema or asthma. Respondents who had been told they had asthma were asked if they still had asthma. Respondents were asked in three separate questions if they had been told by a doctor or other health professional in the past 12 months that they had hay fever, sinusitis, or bronchitis. Based on the National Health Interview Survey, a sample survey of the civilian noninstitutionalized population; see Appendix III]

Selected characteristic	Total persons	Emphy-sema	Asthma Ever	Asthma Still	Hay fever	Sinusitis	Chronic bronchitis
Total [2].	213,042	3,115	20,697	13,623	18,356	29,673	8,560
Male	102,298	1,701	8,253	4,665	7,880	10,225	2,741
Female.	110,744	1,414	12,444	8,958	10,476	19,447	5,820
Age:							
18 to 44 years old.	110,538	155	11,204	6,972	9,407	13,183	3,254
45 to 64 years old.	68,248	1,261	6,722	4,678	6,710	11,755	3,311
65 to 74 years old.	18,097	928	1,602	1,129	1,381	2,776	1,131
75 years old and over	16,159	771	1,169	844	858	1,958	865
Race alone: [3]	210,869	3,086	20,342	13,393	18,091	29,392	8,423
White	177,830	2,854	17,127	11,348	15,838	25,355	7,365
Black or African American.	24,111	194	2,610	1,765	1,654	3,421	910
American Indian or Alaska Native.	1,285	[4]14	161	109	112	177	[4]72
Asian	7,361	[4]24	436	172	469	427	[4]77
Native Hawaiian or Other Pacific Islander . . .	282	-	[4]8	-	[4]17	[4]12	-
2 or more races [5].	2,173	[4]29	354	230	265	280	137
Hispanic or Latino origin [6]	26,272	80	1,904	[*]1,207	1,529	2,030	604
Mexican or Mexican American.	16,661	[4]50	926	588	893	1,122	327

- Represents zero. [1] A person may be represented in more than one column. [2] Total includes other races not shown separately. [3] Refers to persons who indicated only a single race group. [4] Figures do not meet standard of reliability or precision. [5] Refers to all persons who indicated more than one race group. [6] Persons of Hispanic or Latino origin may be any race or combination of races.

Source: National Center for Health Statistics, *Health, United States, 2005* <http://www.cdc.gov/nchs/hus.htm>

Table 187. **Asthma Incidence Among Children Under 18 Years of Age, by Selected Characteristics: 2003**

[In thousands, except percent (72,973 represents 72,973,000) Based on the National Health Interview Survey, a sample survey of the civilian noninstitutionalized population; see Appendix III]

Selected characteristic	Total	Ever told had asthma Number	Ever told had asthma Percent	Had asthma attack in past 12 months Number	Had asthma attack in past 12 months Percent
Total [1] (age-adjusted)	72,973	9,071	12.5	3,975	5.5
Total [1] (crude)	72,973	9,071	12.5	3,975	5.4
Male	37,303	5,251	14.1	2,329	6.3
Female.	35,670	3,820	10.7	1,646	4.6
Age: [2]					
0 to 4 years old	19,856	1,491	7.5	838	4.2
5 to 11 years old.	28,340	3,954	14	1,684	5.9
12 to 17 years old.	24,776	3,626	14.7	1,452	5.9
Race alone: [3]	70,797	8,624	12.2	3,719	5.3
White	56,545	6,389	11.3	2,663	4.7
Black or African American.	11,061	1,893	17.2	877	8
American Indian or Alaska Native.	734	148	20.7	[4]64	[4]8.9
Asian	2,343	153	6.8	[4]87	[4]4
Native Hawaiian or Other Pacific Islander	113	[4]41	[4]29.7	[4]29	[4]21.2
2 or more races [5].	2,176	447	20.8	255	12.2
Hispanic or Latino Origin [5]	13,464	1,575	12.0	597	4.5
Mexican or Mexican American.	9,391	823	9.0	254	2.7

[1] Includes other races not shown separately. [2] Estimates for age groups are not age adjusted. [3] Refers to persons who indicated only a single race group. [4] Figures do not meet standard of reliability or precision. [5] Refers to all persons who indicated more than one race group. [6] Persons of Hispanic or Latino origin may be any race or combination of races.

Source: National Center for Health Statistics, *Health, United States, 2005* <http://www.cdc.gov/nchs/hus.htm>

Table 188. Cancer—Estimated New Cases, 2005, and Survival Rates, 1980–1982 to 1995–2001

[1,373 represents 1,373,000. The 5-year relative survival rate, which is derived by adjusting the observed survival rate for expected mortality, represents the likelihood that a person will not die from causes directly related to their cancer within 5 years. Survival data shown are based on those patients diagnosed while residents of an area listed below during the time periods shown. Data are based on information collected as part of the National Cancer Institute's Surveillance, Epidemiology and End Results (SEER) program, a collection of population-based registries in Connecticut, New Mexico, Utah, Iowa, Hawaii, Atlanta, Detroit, Seattle-Puget Sound, and San Francisco-Oakland]

Site	Estimated new cases,[1] 2005 (1,000) Total	Male	Female	White 1980-1982	1989-1991	1992-1994	1995-2001	Black 1980-1982	1989-1991	1992-1994	1995-2001
All sites[2]	1,373	710	663	52.1	60.3	63.9	66.4	39.8	46.2	52.1	56.0
Lung	173	93	80	13.5	14.4	15.0	15.5	12.1	10.8	11.9	13.2
Breast[3]	213	2	211	77.1	86.2	87.6	89.5	65.8	71.2	72.6	75.9
Colon and rectum	145	72	73	54.9	62.4	62.8	65.0	46.7	54.1	52.2	55.0
Colon	105	48	57	55.6	63.2	63.1	64.9	49.4	53.9	51.9	54.7
Rectum	40	24	17	53.1	60.5	62.1	65.1	38.3	54.5	53.0	55.9
Prostate	232	232	(X)	74.5	92.0	98.2	99.9	64.8	80.8	92.4	96.7
Bladder	63	47	16	78.9	82.2	82.4	82.8	58.5	62.0	64.0	64.3
Corpus uteri	41	(X)	41	82.8	85.7	86.3	86.2	55.2	57.8	55.9	61.8
Non-Hodgkin's lymphoma[4]	56	29	27	51.9	52.1	54.5	61.2	50.5	43.7	42.5	52.3
Oral cavity and pharynx	29	19	10	55.7	55.6	58.5	61.6	31.1	33.3	34.7	39.0
Leukemia[4]	35	20	15	39.5	46.4	49.5	49.1	32.9	34.9	39.9	38.1
Melanoma of skin	60	34	26	83.3	89.0	89.4	91.8	58.3	78.8	59.4	77.5
Pancreas	32	16	16	2.8	4.1	4.7	4.4	4.5	3.9	3.8	4.4
Kidney	36	22	14	51.1	60.8	63.0	64.7	56.3	58.1	60.4	63.6
Stomach	22	14	8	16.5	18.4	20.9	21.4	19.1	24.8	19.1	22.8
Ovary	22	(X)	22	38.7	41.2	42.1	44.5	39.3	30.7	45.9	37.7
Cervix uteri[5]	10	(X)	10	68.2	72.5	72.7	74.6	61.5	62.6	57.8	66.1

X Not applicable.   [1] Estimates provided by American Cancer Society are based on rates from the National Cancer Institute's SEER program.   [2] Includes other sites not shown separately.   [3] Survival rates for female only.   [4] All types combined.   [5] Invasive cancer only.

Source: U.S. National Institutes of Health, National Cancer Institute, <http://seer.cancer.gov/csr/1975_2002/>.

Table 189. Cancer—Estimated New Cases and Deaths by State: 2005

[In thousands (1,372.9 represents 1,372,900). Excludes basal and squamous cell skin cancers and in situ carcinomas except urinary bladder]

State	New cases[1] Total[2]	Lung	Female breast	Deaths Total[2]	Lung	Female breast	State	New cases[1] Total[2]	Lung	Female breast	Deaths Total[2]	Lung	Female breast
U.S.	1,372.9	172.6	211.2	570.3	163.5	40.4	MO	30.2	4.1	4.6	12.6	3.9	0.9
AL	24.3	3.3	3.8	10.1	3.2	0.7	MT	4.9	0.6	0.7	2.0	0.6	0.1
AK	1.9	0.2	0.3	0.8	0.2	0.1	NE	8.3	1.0	1.2	3.5	1.0	0.2
AZ	23.9	2.9	3.8	9.9	2.7	0.7	NV	11.1	1.5	1.6	4.6	1.5	0.3
AR	15.0	2.5	2.1	6.2	2.4	0.4	NH	6.3	0.8	0.9	2.6	0.8	0.2
CA	135.0	15.2	21.2	56.1	14.4	4.1							
							NJ	43.0	4.8	7.7	17.9	4.6	1.5
CO	16.1	1.8	2.6	6.7	1.7	0.5	NM	7.8	0.8	1.0	3.2	0.7	0.2
CT	16.9	2.0	2.7	7.0	1.9	0.5	NY	87.1	9.9	14.4	36.2	9.4	2.8
DE	3.8	0.5	0.6	1.6	0.5	0.1	NC	40.5	5.5	6.3	16.8	5.2	1.2
DC	2.8	0.3	0.5	1.2	0.3	0.1	ND	3.1	0.3	0.5	1.3	0.3	0.1
FL	96.2	13.1	13.4	40.0	12.4	2.6							
							OH	59.7	7.8	9.7	24.8	7.4	1.9
GA	35.7	4.8	5.9	14.8	4.6	1.1	OK	18.5	2.6	2.8	7.7	2.4	0.5
HI	4.8	0.5	0.7	2.0	0.5	0.1	OR	17.7	2.2	2.6	7.4	2.1	0.5
ID	5.5	0.6	0.9	2.3	0.6	0.2	PA	71.8	8.5	11.3	29.8	8.0	2.2
IL	59.7	7.2	9.3	24.8	6.8	1.8	RI	5.9	0.7	0.8	2.4	0.7	0.2
IN	31.9	4.4	4.6	13.3	4.2	0.9							
							SC	21.9	2.9	3.3	9.1	2.7	0.6
IA	15.9	1.8	2.3	6.6	1.7	0.4	SD	3.9	0.4	0.5	1.6	0.4	0.1
KS	12.9	1.6	2.0	5.4	1.5	0.4	TN	31.1	4.6	4.2	12.9	4.4	0.8
KY	23.0	3.7	3.3	9.6	3.5	0.6	TX	86.9	11.2	12.9	36.1	10.6	2.5
LA	23.3	3.1	3.9	9.7	2.9	0.7	UT	6.4	0.5	1.2	2.7	0.4	0.2
ME	7.8	1.0	0.9	3.2	0.9	0.2							
							VT	3.0	0.4	0.5	1.3	0.4	0.1
MD	25.5	3.2	4.4	10.6	3.0	0.8	VA	33.7	4.4	6.0	14.0	4.2	1.2
MA	33.0	4.0	4.9	13.7	3.8	0.9	WA	27.4	3.4	3.9	11.4	3.3	0.8
MI	50.2	6.1	7.2	20.9	5.8	1.4	WV	11.2	1.7	1.4	4.7	1.6	0.3
MN	22.9	2.6	3.2	9.5	2.5	0.6	WI	26.3	3.1	4.1	10.9	2.9	0.8
MS	15.0	2.2	2.4	6.2	2.1	0.5	WY	2.4	0.3	0.3	1.0	0.3	0.1

[1] Estimates are offered as a rough guide and should be interpreted with caution. They are calculated according to the distribution of estimated 2004 cancer deaths by state.   [2] Includes other types of cancer, not shown separately.

Source: American Cancer Society, Inc., Atlanta, Georgia, Cancer Facts and Figures—2005 (copyright). <http://www.cancer.org/docroot/STT/stt0.asp>.

Health and Nutrition   129

Table 190. Current Cigarette Smoking: 1990 to 2003

[In percent. Prior to 1995, a current smoker is a person who has smoked at least 100 cigarettes and who now smokes. Beginning 1995, definition includes persons who smoke only "some days." Excludes unknown smoking status. Based on the National Health Interview Survey; for details, see Appendix III]

Sex, age, and race	1990[1]	1995[1]	2000	2003	Sex, age, and race	1990[1]	1995[1]	2000	2003
Total smokers, age-adjusted [2]	25.3	24.6	23.1	21.5	Black, total	32.5	28.5	26.1	25.7
					18 to 24 years	21.3	[3]14.6	20.8	18.6
Male	28.0	26.5	25.2	23.7	25 to 34 years	33.8	25.1	23.3	31.0
Female	22.9	22.7	21.1	19.4	35 to 44 years	42.0	36.3	30.8	23.6
White male	27.6	26.2	25.5.	23.8	45 to 64 years	36.7	33.9	32.2	30.1
Black male	32.8	29.4	25.7	25.3	65 years and over	21.5	28.5	14.2	18.0
White female	23.5	23.4	22.0	20.1	Female, total	22.8	22.6	21.0	19.2
Black female	20.8	23.5	20.7	17.9	18 to 24 years	22.5	21.8	25.1	21.5
					25 to 34 years	28.2	26.4	22.5	21.3
Total smokers	25.5	24.7	23.3	21.6	35 to 44 years	24.8	27.1	26.2	24.2
					45 to 64 years	24.8	24.0	21.6	20.2
Male, total	28.4	27.0	25.7	24.1	65 years and over	11.5	11.5	9.3	8.3
18 to 24 years	26.6	27.8	28.5	26.3	White, total	23.4	23.1	21.6	19.7
25 to 34 years	31.6	29.5	29.0	28.7	18 to 24 years	25.4	24.9	28.7	23.6
35 to 44 years	34.5	31.5	30.2	28.1	25 to 34 years	28.5	27.3	25.1	22.5
45 to 64 years	29.3	27.1	26.4	23.9	35 to 44 years	25.0	27.0	26.6	25.2
65 years and over	14.6	14.9	10.2	10.1	45 to 64 years	25.4	24.3	21.4	20.1
					65 years and over	11.5	11.7	9.1	8.4
White, total	28.0	26.6	25.8	24.0	Black, total	21.2	23.5	20.8	18.1
18 to 24 years	27.4	28.4	30.9	27.7	18 to 24 years	[3]10.0	8.8	14.2	10.8
25 to 34 years	31.6	29.9	29.9	28.8	25 to 34 years	29.1	26.7	15.5	17.0
35 to 44 years	33.5	31.2	30.6	28.8	35 to 44 years	25.5	31.9	30.2	23.2
45 to 64 years	28.7	26.3	25.8	23.3	45 to 64 years	22.6	27.5	25.6	23.3
65 years and over	13.7	14.1	9.8	9.6	65 years and over	11.1	13.3	10.2	8.0

[1] Data prior to 1997 are not strictly comparable with data for later years due to the 1997 questionnaire redesign. [2] Estimates are age adjusted to the year 2000 standard using five age groups: 18-24 years, 25-34 years, 35-44 years, 45-64 years, 65 years and over. [3] Data have a relative standard error of 20-30 percent.

Source: U.S. National Center for Health Statistics, Health, United States, annual. See also <www.cdc.gov/nchs/hus.htm>.

Table 191. Current Cigarette Smoking by Sex and State: 2003

[In percent. Current cigarette smoking is defined as persons who reported having smoked 100 or more cigarettes during their lifetime and who currently smoke every day or some days. Based on the Behavioral Risk Factor Surveillance System, a telephone survey of health behaviors of the civilian, noninstitutionalized U.S. population, 18 years old and over; for details, see source]

State	Total	Male	Female	State	Total	Male	Female	State	Total	Male	Female
U.S.[1]	22.1	24.8	20.3	KS	20.4	21.0	19.7	ND	20.5	22.0	19.0
				KY	30.8	33.8	28.1	OH	25.4	26.9	24.0
AL	25.3	28.5	22.4	LA	26.6	30.3	23.2	OK	25.2	27.8	22.7
AK	26.3	30.3	21.9	ME	23.6	23.1	24.0	OR	21.0	23.1	18.9
AZ	21.0	23.8	18.2	MD	20.2	23.0	17.7	PA	25.5	27.1	24.1
AR	24.8	27.6	22.3	MA	19.2	20.0	18.4	RI	22.4	23.8	21.1
CA	16.8	20.5	13.2	MI	26.2	30.2	22.3	SC	25.5	28.5	22.8
CO	18.5	19.6	17.5	MN	21.1	22.4	19.9	SD	22.7	24.7	20.7
CT	18.7	19.7	17.9	MS	25.6	31.1	20.7	TN	25.7	27.3	24.2
DE	21.9	26.0	18.2	MO	27.3	31.2	23.8	TX	22.1	26.7	17.6
DC	22.3	26.2	19.0	MT	19.9	19.5	20.3	UT	12.0	14.0	9.9
FL	23.9	26.0	22.1	NE	21.3	23.6	19.0	VT	19.6	19.8	19.4
GA	22.8	25.8	20.0	NV	25.2	29.0	21.3	VA	22.1	26.4	18.0
HI	17.3	20.1	14.4	NH	21.2	22.4	20.2	WA	19.5	20.9	18.2
ID	19.0	19.5	18.5	NJ	19.5	21.2	17.9	WV	27.4	27.6	27.2
IL	24.3	28.3	20.5	NM	22.0	23.6	20.5	WI	22.1	24.0	20.3
IN	26.1	28.6	23.8	NY	21.6	24.8	18.8	WY	24.6	25.2	24.1
IA	21.7	22.8	20.7	NC	24.8	28.0	21.9				

[1] Represents median value among the states and DC. For definition of median, see Guide to Tabular Presentations

Source: U.S. Centers for Disease Control and Prevention, Atlanta, GA, Morbidity and Mortality Weekly Report, Vol. 53, No. 44, November 12, 2004. <http://www.cdc.gov/mmwr>.

Table 192. Use of Mammography for Women 40 Years Old and Over by Patient Characteristics: 1990 to 2003

[Percent of women having a mammogram within the past 2 years. Covers civilian noninstitutional population. Based on National Health Interview Survey; see Appendix III] Data years 2001 and 2002 are not available.

Characteristic	1990	2000[1]	2003[2]	Characteristic	1990	2000[1]	2003[2]
Total [3]	51.4	70.4	69.7	Years of school completed:			
40 to 49 years old	55.1	64.3	64.4	Less than 12 years	36.4	57.7	58.1
50 years old and over	49.7	73.6	72.4	12 years	52.7	69.7	67.8
50 to 64 years old	56.0	78.7	76.2	13 years or more	62.8	76.2	75.1
65 years old and over	43.4	67.9	67.7				
White, non-Hispanic	52.7	72.2	70.5	Poverty status: [5]			
Black, non-Hispanic	46.0	67.9	70.5	Below poverty	28.7	54.8	55.3
Hispanic origin [4]	45.2	61.2	65.0	At or above poverty	54.8	72.1	71.5

[1] Adjusted data—data for 2000 have been reweighted using the 2000 census population controls. [2] Data for 2003 are weighted using the 2000 census population controls. [3] Includes all other races not shown separately and unknown education level and poverty status. [4] Persons of Hispanic origin may be of any race. [5] For explanation of poverty level, see text, Section 13, Income, Expenditures and Wealth.

Source: U.S. National Center for Health Statistics, Health, United States, annual. See also <http://www.cdc.gov/nchs/hus.htm>.

130   Health and Nutrition

Table 193. **Substance Abuse Treatment Facilities and Clients: 1995 to 2004**

[As of October 2 (1995); as of October 1 (1996–2000); as of March 29 (2002); and as of March 31 (2003–2004). Based on the Uniform Facility Data Set (UFDS)/National Survey of Substance Abuse Treatment Services (N-SSATS) survey, a census of all known facilities that provide substance abuse treatment in the United States and associated jurisdictions. Selected missing data for responding facilities were imputed]

Primary focus	Number	Primary focus	Number	Type of care and type of problem	Number of clients
FACILITIES		CLIENTS		2004, total [1]	1,066,351
1995	10,746	1995	1,009,127	Outpatient rehab	937,626
1996	10,641	1996	940,141	Outpatient detoxification ...	11,961
1997	10,860	1997	929,086	24 hour rehab	103,818
1998	13,455	1998	1,038,378	24 hour detoxification	12,946
1999	15,239	2000	1,000,896		
2000	13,428	2003	1,092,546		
2002	13,720				
2003	13,623			Drug only	362,103
2004 total	13,454	2004 total	1,072,251	Alcohol only	210,696
Substance abuse		Substance abuse		Both alcohol & drug	493,552
treatment services ...	8,340	treatment services ...	733,905		
Mental health services. ..	1,104	Mental health services. ..	50,922	Total with a drug problem [2]	855,655
General health care	219	General health care ...	16,744	Total with an	
Both substance abuse		Both substance abuse...		alcohol problem [3]	704,248
and mental health.....	3,558	and mental health.....	251,687		
Other..............	233	Other.............	18,993		

[1] Excludes clients at facilities that did not provide data on type of substance abuse problem treated.   [2] The sum of clients with a drug problem and clients with both diagnoses.   [3] The sum of clients with an alcohol problem and clients with both diagnoses.

Source: U.S. Substance Abuse and Mental Health Services Administration, *Uniform Facility Data Set (UFDS): Annual surveys for 1995–1999* and National Survey of Substance Abuse Treatment Services (N-SSATS) 2000, 2002, 2003, and 2004; <http://oas.samhsa.gov/oasftp.cfm#Data>.

Table 194. **Drug Use by Type of Drug and Age Group: 2002 and 2003**

[In percent.The 2002 Survey changed names from the National Household Survey on Drug Abuse to National Household Survey on Drug Use and Health (NSDUH). Current users are those who used drugs at least once within month prior to this study. Based on a representative sample of the U.S. population age 12 and older, including persons living in households and in some group quarters such as dormitories and homeless shelters. Estimates are based on computer-assisted interviews of about 68,000 respondents. Subject to sampling variability; see source]

Age and type of drug	Ever used		Current user		Age and type of drug	Ever used		Current user	
	2002	2003	2002	2003		2002	2003	2002	2003
12 YEARS OLD AND OVER					18 TO 25 YEARS OLD				
Any illicit drug...........	46.0	46.4	8.3	8.2	Any illicit drug...........	59.8	60.5	20.2	20.3
Marijuana and hashish	40.4	40.6	6.2	6.2	Marijuana and hashish	53.8	53.9	17.3	17.0
Cocaine..............	14.4	14.7	0.9	1.0	Cocaine	15.4	15.0	2.0	2.2
Crack..............	3.6	3.3	0.2	0.3	Hallucinogens	24.2	23.3	1.9	1.7
Heroin	1.6	1.6	0.1	0.1	Inhalants	15.7	14.9	0.5	0.4
Hallucinogens	14.6	14.5	0.5	0.4	Any psychotherapeutic [1] ...	27.7	29.0	5.4	6.0
LSD	10.4	10.3	-	0.1	Alcohol	86.7	87.1	60.5	61.4
PCP.............	3.2	3.0	-	-	"Binge" alcohol use [2]	(NA)	(NA)	40.9	41.6
Inhalants	9.7	9.7	0.3	0.2	Cigarettes	71.2	70.2	40.8	40.2
Any psychotherapeutic [1] ...	19.8	20.1	2.6	2.7	Smokeless tobacco	23.7	22.0	4.8	4.7
Pain relievers [1]	12.6	13.1	1.9	2.0	Cigars	45.6	45.2	11.0	11.4
Tranquilizers [1]	8.2	8.5	0.8	0.8	26 TO 34 YEARS OLD				
Stimulants [1]...........	9.0	8.8	0.5	0.5	Any illicit drug...........	58.3	57.3	10.5	10.7
Methamphetamine [1]...	5.3	5.2	0.3	0.3	Marijuana and hashish	52.2	51.0	7.7	8.4
Sedatives [1]	4.2	4.0	0.2	0.1	Cocaine	17.6	18.1	1.2	1.5
Alcohol	83.1	83.1	51.0	50.1	Hallucinogens	20.6	20.3	0.5	0.5
"Binge" alcohol use [2]	(NA)	(NA)	22.9	22.6	Inhalants	14.1	13.6	0.1	-
Cigarettes	69.1	68.7	26.0	25.4	Any psychotherapeutic [1] ...	24.4	24.7	3.6	3.4
Smokeless tobacco	19.9	19.4	3.3	3.3	35 YEARS OLD AND OVER				
Cigars..............	37.4	37.1	5.4	5.4	Any illicit drug............	42.7	43.4	4.6	4.4
Pipes	17.0	16.9	0.8	0.7	Marijuana and hashish	38.0	38.9	3.1	3.0
12 to 17 YEARS OLD					Cocaine	15.4	15.9	0.6	0.6
Any illicit drug...........	30.9	30.5	11.6	11.2	Hallucinogens	12.6	12.8	0.1	0.1
Marijuana and hashish	20.6	19.6	8.2	7.9	Inhalants	7.2	7.4	0.1	0.1
Cocaine	2.7	2.6	0.6	0.6	Any psychotherapeutic [1] ...	18.0	18.3	1.6	1.5
Hallucinogens	5.7	5.0	1.0	1.0					
Inhalants .... [1]	10.5	10.7	1.2	1.3	26 YEARS OLD AND OVER				
Any psychotherapeutic [1] ...	13.7	13.4	4.0	4.0	Alcohol	88.0	88.0	53.9	52.5
Alcohol	43.4	42.9	17.6	17.7	"Binge" alcohol use [2]	(NA)	(NA)	21.4	21.0
"Binge" alcohol use [2]	(NA)	(NA)	10.7	10.6	Cigarettes	73.7	73.6	25.2	24.7
Cigarettes	33.3	31.0	13.0	12.2	Smokeless tobacco	20.9	20.6	3.2	3.2
Smokeless tobacco	8.0	7.6	2.0	2.0	Cigars..............	39.0	38.7	4.6	4.5
Cigars..............	16.3	15.1	4.5	4.5					

- Represents or rounds to zero.   NA Not available.   [1] Nonmedical use of any prescription-type pain reliever, tranquilizer, stimulant, or sedative; does not include over-the-counter drugs.   [2] Binge use is defined as drinking five or more drinks on the same occasion on at least one day in the past 30 days.

Source: U.S. Substance Abuse and Mental Health Services Administration, *Summary of Findings from the 2003 National Household Survey on Drug Use and Health.* <http://www.oas.samhsa.gov/nhsda.htm#Reports>.

Health and Nutrition   131

Table 195. Estimated Use of Selected Drugs by State: 2002–2003

[19,497 represents 19,497,000. Data in this table cover a two-year period. The 2002 survey changed names from the National Household Survey on Drug Abuse to National Household Survey on Drug Use and Health (NSDUH). Due to the impact of survey improvements, 2002 data should not be compared with data collected in 2001 or earlier years. Current users are those persons 12 years old and over who used drugs at least once within month prior to this study. Based on national sample of respondents (see also headnote, Table 194). The state estimates were produced by combining the prevalence rate based on the state sample data and the prevalence rate based on a national regression model applied to local-area county and census block group/tract-level estimates from the state. The parameters of the regression model are estimated from the entire national sample. For comparison purposes, the data shown here display estimates for all 50 States and the District of Columbia utilizing the modeled estimates for all 51 areas]

State	Estimated current users (1,000)					Current users as percent of population				
	Any illicit drug [1]	Marijuana	Any illicit drug other than marijuana [1]	Cigarettes	Binge alcohol [2]	Any illicit drug [1]	Marijuana	Any illicit drug other than marijuana [1]	Cigarettes	Binge alcohol [2]
U.S.	19,497	14,612	8,813	60,777	53,782	8.2	6.2	3.7	25.7	22.7
AL	245	160	137	976	669	6.6	4.3	3.7	26.4	18.1
AK	60	49	20	129	116	12.0	9.8	4.0	25.7	23.1
AZ	392	251	206	1,215	1,075	8.9	5.7	4.7	27.5	24.3
AR	173	126	87	730	484	7.8	5.6	3.9	32.8	21.8
CA	2,564	1,850	1,122	5,508	6,047	9.0	6.5	3.9	19.4	21.3
CO	410	313	172	985	948	11.1	8.5	4.7	26.8	25.8
CT	249	198	93	678	659	8.7	6.9	3.3	23.8	23.1
DE	58	46	26	174	159	8.7	6.9	3.9	26.1	23.7
DC	56	46	20	125	122	11.6	9.6	4.1	26.1	25.3
FL	1,218	919	518	3,355	3,040	8.7	6.6	3.7	24.0	21.7
GA	520	340	274	1,779	1,430	7.5	4.9	4.0	25.8	20.7
HI	88	69	34	217	234	8.9	6.9	3.5	22.0	23.7
ID	79	55	41	260	229	7.2	5.1	3.7	23.9	21.1
IL	772	576	339	2,754	2,590	7.5	5.6	3.3	26.8	25.2
IN	407	309	180	1,427	1,122	8.1	6.1	3.6	28.3	22.3
IA	158	120	77	647	644	6.5	4.9	3.2	26.5	26.3
KS	149	108	68	573	479	6.7	4.9	3.1	26.0	21.7
KY	282	191	148	1,178	652	8.3	5.6	4.4	34.8	19.2
LA	292	209	153	1,021	859	8.1	5.8	4.2	28.3	23.8
ME	103	88	42	297	241	9.3	7.9	3.8	26.8	21.7
MD	338	255	154	1,039	968	7.6	5.7	3.4	23.2	21.7
MA	500	420	196	1,207	1,465	9.3	7.8	3.6	22.4	27.2
MI	750	596	300	2,336	2,026	9.1	7.2	3.6	28.2	24.5
MN	317	266	134	1,122	1,172	7.6	6.4	3.2	26.9	28.1
MS	152	107	83	680	455	6.6	4.6	3.6	29.4	19.7
MO	429	316	194	1,472	1,147	9.2	6.8	4.2	31.5	24.6
MT	81	70	29	212	209	10.6	9.2	3.8	27.7	27.4
NE	109	85	49	367	372	7.7	6.0	3.4	25.9	26.3
NV	183	136	80	543	371	10.3	7.6	4.5	30.5	20.9
NH	120	110	44	281	258	11.2	10.2	4.1	26.2	24.0
NJ.	494	358	241	1,662	1,542	7.0	5.1	3.4	23.4	21.7
NM	151	111	69	363	363	10.0	7.4	4.6	24.0	24.0
NY	1,416	1,167	492	4,052	3,861	8.9	7.3	3.1	25.5	24.3
NC	536	399	268	2,010	1,307	7.9	5.9	4.0	29.7	19.3
ND	38	28	17	145	165	7.2	5.3	3.3	27.5	31.4
OH	756	610	323	2,865	2,294	8.0	6.5	3.4	30.5	24.4
OK	243	158	125	858	539	8.6	5.6	4.4	30.3	19.0
OR	319	262	126	735	604	10.8	8.9	4.3	25.0	20.5
PA	774	582	355	2,858	2,357	7.5	5.6	3.4	27.7	22.8
RI.	99	86	42	246	243	10.9	9.6	4.6	27.3	27.0
SC	245	191	121	907	762	7.2	5.7	3.6	26.8	22.5
SD	45	33	21	188	175	7.2	5.2	3.3	30.3	28.1
TN	321	220	175	1,343	793	6.7	4.6	3.6	28.0	16.6
TX	1,208	829	674	4,428	4,140	7.0	4.8	3.9	25.6	23.9
UT	115	73	68	304	288	6.3	4.0	3.7	16.7	15.9
VT	58	52	20	134	135	11.0	9.8	3.9	25.4	25.5
VA	453	352	209	1,487	1,211	7.7	6.0	3.5	25.2	20.5
WA	499	371	211	1,172	1,049	10.0	7.4	4.2	23.4	20.9
WV	101	79	54	452	296	6.6	5.1	3.5	29.5	19.3
WI.	339	245	165	1,167	1,313	7.5	5.4	3.6	25.8	29.0
WY	31	23	15	151	103	7.5	5.4	3.7	26.8	24.9

[1] Any illicit drug indicates use at least once of marijuana/hashish, cocaine (including crack), inhalants, hallucinogens (including PCP and LSD), heroin, or any prescription-type psychotherapeutic used nonmedically. Any illicit drug other than marijuana indicates use at least once of any of these listed drugs, regardless of marijuana/hashish use; marijuana/hashish users who also have used any of the other listed drugs are included.   [2] Binge use is defined as drinking five or more drinks on the same occasion on at least one day in the past 30 days. By "occasion" means at the same time or within a couple hours of each other.

Source: U.S. Substance Abuse and Mental Health Services Administration, National Household Survey on Drug Use and Health, 2003. <http://www.oas.samhsa.gov/nhsda.htm#Reports>.

Table 196. Cumulative Percent Distribution of Population by Height and Sex: 1998-2002

[Data are based on National Health and Nutrition Examination Survey. Height was measured without shoes. Based on sample and subject to sampling variability; see source]

Height	Males 20-29 years	30-39 years	40-49 years	50-59 years	60-69 years	70-79 years	Females 20-29 years	30-39 years	40-49 years	50-59 years	60-69 years	70-79 years
Percent under—												
4'8"	-	-	-	-	-	-	0.4	0.0	-	-	0.6	0.9
4'9"	-	-	-	-	-	-	0.5	0.2	0.1	0.4	1.1	1.1
4'10"	-	-	-	-	-	-	1.8	0.9	0.4	1.7	2.3	1.8
4'11"	-	-	-	0.3	-	-	2.8	2.1	1.5	2.5	5.0	8.9
5'	-	-	-	0.4	0.3	-	5.1	5.3	5.0	6.7	10.0	16.1
5'1"	0.4	0.1	0.3	0.7	0.3	0.6	12.2	11.0	10.8	11.3	17.7	23.5
5'2"	1.0	0.6	0.5	1.1	0.8	1.2	21.4	19.4	18.1	22.4	29.9	39.7
5'3"	2.4	1.6	0.8	1.7	1.7	4.5	31.9	29.9	28.8	34.2	45.9	54.6
5'4"	4.1	4.1	2.7	4.6	3.4	8.5	46.3	45.1	44.5	50.2	58.9	70.8
5'5"	7.2	7.4	4.3	8.2	8.6	15.6	61.1	61.9	58.1	66.4	75.4	82.4
5'6"	11.1	11.4	9.0	12.9	16.5	25.0	76.3	75.2	72.7	79.8	85.7	90.5
5'7"	18.0	19.5	16.0	21.1	24.7	35.6	84.7	85.4	84.6	88.2	93.6	96.0
5'8"	28.2	29.3	27.0	32.7	35.5	48.6	93.5	91.6	91.6	93.0	97.7	98.6
5'9"	39.1	44.4	39.5	44.9	50.4	62.2	97.4	96.9	96.0	98.0	99.8	99.3
5'10"	55.1	56.1	52.7	58.8	64.8	72.7	98.8	98.3	98.6	99.1	100.0	100.0
5'11"	70.5	69.3	66.4	70.2	77.5	84.6	99.8	99.3	99.6	99.7	100.0	100.0
6'	79.8	78.9	76.4	80.8	86.8	92.2	99.8	99.5	100.0	99.8	100.0	100.0
6'1"	87.1	87.5	87.8	88.8	93.2	95.6	100.0	99.8	100.0	100.0	100.0	100.0
6'2"	91.9	92.7	92.8	95.5	97.7	99.2	100.0	100.0	100.0	100.0*	100.0	100.0
6'3"	95.8	96.7	96.3	98.1	99.9	100.0	100.0	100.0	100.0	100.0	100.0	100.0

- Represents or rounds to zero.

Source: U.S. National Center for Health Statistics, unpublished data. See also <http://www.cdc.gov/nchs/nhanes.htm>.

Table 197. Age-adjusted Percent Distributions of Body Mass Index (BMI) Among Persons 18 Years Old and Over, by Selected Characteristics: 2003

[Body Mass Index (BMI) is a measure that adjusts body weight for height. It is calculated as weight in kilograms divided by height in meters squared. For both men and women, underweight is indicated by a BMI under 18.5; healthy weight is indicated by a BMI greater than or equal to 18.5 and less than 25; overweight is indicated by those who have a BMI equal to 25 and less than 30. Percent who are obese represent those who have a BMI equal to or above 30. BMI is calculated from the information respondents supplied in response to the questions in the survey regarding height and weight. Based on the National Health Interview Survey; for details, see Appendix III]

Selected characteristic	Underweight	Healthy weight	Above healthy weight Total	Overweight	Obese
Total [1] (age-adjusted)	2.0	39.2	58.7	35.7	23.0
Total [1] (crude)	2.0	39.0	59.0	35.8	23.2
Age: [2]					
18 to 44 years	2.5	43.6	53.9	33.2	20.7
45 to 64 years	0.9	31.8	67.2	38.5	28.7
65 to 74 years	1.6	33.3	65.1	39.9	25.2
75 years and over	3.7	43.7	52.6	37.3	15.3
Sex:					
Male	0.9	32.2	66.8	44.1	22.7
Female	3.0	46.1	50.9	27.6	23.3
Race:					
White alone [3]	2.0	39.5	58.5	36.3	22.2
Black or African American alone [3]	1.1	30.2	68.7	35.1	33.6
American Indian or Alaska Native alone [3]	[4]2.9	31.9	65.2	33.8	31.4
Asian alone [3]	6.2	63.2	30.7	24.8	5.9
Native Hawaiian or other Pacific Islander alone [3]	-	[4]32.1	67.9	42.2	[4]25.7
2 or more races [5]	[4]2.1	39.6	58.3	31.4	26.9
Hispanic or Latino origin status [6]:					
Hispanic or Latino	1.1	33.9	65.0	39.8	25.2
Not Hispanic or Latino	2.2	39.9	57.9	35.2	22.7
Education: [7]					
Less than a high school diploma	1.8	32.3	65.9	37.7	28.2
High school diploma or GED	1.5	33.6	64.9	37.9	27.0
Some college	1.8	34.6	63.6	36.3	27.3
Bachelor's degree or higher	1.6	44.4	54.0	37.1	16.9

- Represents zero. [1] Total includes other races not shown separately and persons with unknown characteristics. [2] Estimates for age groups are not age adjusted. [3] Refers to persons who indicated only a single race group. [4] Base figure too small to meet statistical standards for reliability of a derived figure. [5] The "two or more races" refers to all persons who indicated more than one race group. [6] Persons of Hispanic origin may be of any race. [7] Education is shown only for persons 25 years old and over.

Source: U.S. National Center for Health Statistics, Vital and Health Statistics, Series 10, Number 225, Summary Health Statistics for U.S. Adults: National Health Interview Survey, 2003; <http://www.cdc.gov/nchs/products/pubs/pubd/series/ser.htm>

Health and Nutrition 133

Table 198. Percentage of Adults Engaging in Leisure-Time, Transportation-Related and Household-Related Physical Activity: 2003

[In percent. Covers persons 18 years old and over. Based on responses to questions about physical activity in prior month from the Behavioral Risk Factor Surveillance System. Estimates are age-adjusted to the year 2000 standard population. Based on a survey sample of approximately 257,000 persons in 50 states and the District of Columbia in 2003]

Characteristic	Persons who meet recom-mended activity [1]	Persons not meeting recom-mended activity [2]	Persons who are physically inactive [3]	Characteristic	Persons who meet recom-mended activity [1]	Persons not meeting recom-mended activity [2]	Persons who are physically inactive [3]
Total.	46.0	54.0	24.3				
				45 to 64 years old	42.6	57.4	26.7
Male.	48.2	51.8	22.0	65 to 74 years old	37.1	62.9	31.2
Female.	44.0	56.0	26.3	75 years old and			
				over	27.6	72.4	42.0
White, non-Hispanic	49.0	51.0	20.9				
Black, non-Hispanic.	36.3	63.7	32.7	School years			
Hispanic	37.5	62.5	36.0	completed:			
Other	43.5	56.5	25.2	Less than 12 years . . .	33.8	66.2	45.7
				12 years	43.1	56.9	30.5
Males:				Some college			
18 to 29 years old	57.8	42.2	17.1	(13 to 15 years).	47.5	52.5	21.0
30 to 44 years old	48.7	51.3	20.7	College			
45 to 64 years old	43.2	56.8	24.4	(16 or more years). . . .	51.9	48.1	13.1
65 to 74 years old	45.7	54.3	24.9				
75 years old and				Household income:			
over	36.7	63.3	31.0	Less than $10,000. . . .	34.7	65.3	42.2
Females:				$10,000 to $19,999 . . .	37.0	63.0	38.9
18 to 29 years old	50.1	49.9	21.9	$20,000 to $34,999 . . .	43.6	56.4	29.4
30 to 44 years old	47.7	52.3	23.4	$35,000 to $49,999 . . .	47.3	52.7	21.9
				$50,000 and over	53.6	46.4	13.6

[1] Recommended activity is physical activity at least 5 times/week x 30 minutes/week or vigorous physical activity for 20 minutes at a time at least 3 times/week.   [2] Persons whose reported physical activity does not meet recommended level or report no leisure-time, transportation-related, or household-related physical activity.   [3] Persons with no reported physical activity.

Source: U.S. National Center for Chronic Disease Prevention and Health Promotion, "Nutrition and Physical Activity"; and unpublished data; <http://www.cdc.gov/nccdphp/dnpa>.

Table 199. Households and Persons Having Problems With Access to Food: 2000 to 2003

[106,043 represents 106,043,000. Food secure means that a household had access at all times to enough food for an active healthy life for all household members, with no need for recourse to socially unacceptable food sources or extraordinary coping behaviors to meet their basic food needs. Food insecure households had limited or uncertain ability to acquire acceptable foods in socially acceptable ways. Food insecure households with hunger were those with one or more household members who were hungry at least sometime during the period due to inadequate resources for food. The omission of homeless persons may be a cause of underreporting. The severity of food insecurity and hunger in households is measured through a series of questions about experiences and behaviors known to characterize households that are having difficulty meeting basic food needs. These experiences and behaviors generally occur in an ordered sequence as the severity of food insecurity increases. As resources become more constrained, adults in typical households first worry about having enough food, then they stretch household resources and juggle other necessities, then decrease the quality and variety of household members' diets, then decrease the frequency and quantity of adults' food intake, and finally decrease the frequency and quantity of children's food intake. All questions refer to the previous 12 months and include a qualifying phrase reminding respondents to report only those occurrences that resulted from inadequate financial resources. Restrictions to food intake due to dieting or busy schedules are excluded. Data are from the Food Security Supplement to the Current Population Survey (CPS); for details about the CPS, see text, Section 1 and Appendix III]

Household food security level	Number (1,000)				Percent distribution			
	2000	2001	2002	2003	2000	2001	2002	2003
Households, total	106,043	107,824	108,601	112,214	100.0	100.0	100.0	100.0
Food secure	94,942	96,303	96,543	99,631	89.5	89.3	88.9	88.8
Food insecure.	11,101	11,521	12,058	12,583	10.5	10.7	11.1	11.2
Without hunger	7,786	8,010	8,259	8,663	7.3	7.4	7.6	7.7
With hunger	3,315	3,511	3,799	3,920	3.1	3.3	3.5	3.5
With hunger among children [1] . .	255	211	265	207	0.7	0.6	0.7	0.5
Adult members	201,922	204,340	206,493	213,441	100.0	100.0	100.0	100.0
In food secure households	181,586	183,398	184,718	190,451	89.9	89.8	89.5	89.2
In food insecure households	20,336	20,942	21,775	22,990	10.1	10.2	10.5	10.8
Without hunger	14,763	14,879	15,486	16,358	7.3	7.3	7.5	7.7
With hunger [2]	5,573	6,063	6,289	6,632	2.8	3.0	3.0	3.1
Child members	71,763	72,321	72,542	72,969	100.0	100.0	100.0	100.0
In food secure households	58,868	59,620	59,415	59,704	82.0	82.4	81.9	81.8
In food insecure households	12,895	12,701	13,127	13,265	18.0	17.6	18.1	18.2
Without hunger	12,334	12,234	12,560	12,845	17.2	16.9	17.3	17.6
With hunger among children [1] . .	562	467	567	420	0.8	0.6	0.8	0.6

[1] One or more children in these households was hungry at some time during the year because of the household's food insecurity. Percent distribution of households with hunger among children excludes households with no child from the denominator.   [2] One or more adults in these households was hungry at some time during the year because of the household's food insecurity.

Source: U.S. Department of Agriculture, Economic Research Service, Household Food Security in the United States, 2003, Food Assistance and Nutrition Research Report No. 42; October 2004; <http://www.ers.usda.gov/briefing/foodsecurity/>.

Table 200. **Nutrition—Nutrients in Foods Available for Civilian Consumption Per Capita Per Day: 1970 to 2000**

[Computed by the Center for Nutrition Policy and Promotion (CNPP). Based on Economic Research Service (ERS) estimates of per capita quantities of food available for consumption from "Food Consumption, Prices, and, Expenditures," on imputed consumption data for foods no longer reported by ERS, and on CNPP estimates of quantities of produce from home gardens. Food supply estimates do not reflect loss of food or nutrients from further marketing or home processing. Enrichment and fortification levels of iron, zinc, thiamin, riboflavin, niacin, folate, vitamin A, vitamin B6, vitamin B12, and Vitamin C are included]

Nutrient	Unit	1970–79	1980–89	1990–99	1995	2000
Food energy	Kilocalories	3,200	3,400	3,700	3,700	3,900
Carbohydrate	Grams	388	411	472	473	490
Dietary fiber	Grams	19	20	23	23	24
Protein	Grams	95	98	107	106	110
Total fat [1]	Grams	149	156	157	156	170
Saturated	Grams	51	52	50	50	54
Monounsaturated	Grams	60	63	67	66	72
Polyunsaturated	Grams	28	31	33	32	36
Cholesterol	Milligrams	440	420	410	400	430
Vitamin A	Micrograms RAE [2]	1,240	1,210	1,250	1,260	1,260
Carotenes	Micrograms RE [3]	550	590	720	720	720
Vitamin E	Milligrams α-TE [4]	13.9	15.6	17.1	16.8	19.2
Vitamin C	Milligrams	110	117	126	126	126
Thiamin	Milligrams	2.2	2.5	2.9	2.9	2.9
Riboflavin	Milligrams	2.5	2.7	2.9	2.8	2.9
Niacin	Milligrams	24.0	28.0	31.0	31.0	32.0
Vitamin B6	Milligrams	2.0	2.2	2.4	2.4	2.4
Total Folate	Micrograms	317	346	439	375	691
Folate [5, 6]	Micrograms DFE	332	375	505	401	907
Vitamin B12	Micrograms	8.9	8.2	7.9	8.0	8.3
Calcium	Milligrams	910	920	960	960	960
Phosphorus	Milligrams	1,490	1,530	1,640	1,630	1,670
Magnesium	Milligrams	330	350	380	370	380
Iron	Milligrams	16.3	19.4	22.5	22.3	23.1
Zinc	Milligrams	12.9	13.9	14.8	14.7	14.9
Copper	Milligrams	1.6	1.7	1.9	1.8	1.9
Potassium	Milligrams	3,430	3,470	3,690	3,650	3,740
Selenium	Milligrams	130	139	160	156	176
Sodium [7]	Milligrams	1,350	1,340	1,350	1,340	1,330

[1] Includes other types of fat not shown separately. [2] Retinol activity equivalents. [3] Retinol equivalents. [4] Alpha-Tocopherol equivalents. [5] Dietary Folate Equivalents. [6] Reflects new terminology from Institute of Medicine's Dietary Reference Intakes reports. [7] Does not include amount from processed foods; underestimates actual availability.

Source: U.S. Department of Agriculture, Center for Nutrition Policy and Promotion, *Nutrient Content of the U.S. Food Supply, 1909–2000*, in press. Data also published by Economic Research Service in *Food Consumption, Prices, and Expenditures,* annual; <www.usda.gov/cnpp/>.

Table 201. **Per Capita Consumption of Selected Beverages by Type: 1980 to 2003**

[In gallons. See headnote, Table 202. Per capita consumption uses U.S. resident population, July 1, for all beverages except coffee, tea, and fruit juices which use U.S. total population, July 1]

Commodity	1980	1985	1990	1995	1999	2000	2001	2002	2003
Nonalcoholic	(NA)	(NA)	128.3	128.2	141.3	(NA)	(NA)	(NA)	(NA)
Milk (plain and flavored)	27.6	26.7	25.7	23.9	22.9	22.5	22.0	21.9	21.6
Whole	17.0	14.3	10.5	8.6	8.2	8.1	7.8	7.7	7.6
Reduced-fat, light, and skim	10.5	12.3	15.2	15.3	14.8	14.4	14.2	14.2	13.9
Tea	7.3	7.1	6.9	7.9	8.2	7.8	8.2	7.8	7.6
Coffee	26.7	27.4	26.8	20.2	25.1	26.3	24.2	23.6	24.3
Bottled water	2.4	4.5	8.0	12.1	16.4	17.4	18.8	20.7	22.0
Carbonated soft drinks	35.1	35.7	46.2	47.4	49.7	49.3	46.7	46.6	46.4
Diet	5.1	7.1	10.7	10.9	11.4	11.6	11.2	11.2	11.1
Regular	29.9	28.7	35.6	36.5	38.2	37.7	35.5	35.4	35.3
Fruit juices	7.4	7.8	7.0	8.1	9.0	8.9	9.1	8.4	8.4
Fruit drinks, cocktails, and ades	(NA)	(NA)	6.3	7.7	7.7	(NA)	(NA)	(NA)	(NA)
Canned iced tea	(NA)	(NA)	0.1	0.7	0.7	(NA)	(NA)	(NA)	(NA)
Vegetable juices	(NA)	(NA)	0.3	0.3	0.3	(NA)	(NA)	(NA)	(NA)
Alcoholic	28.3	28.0	27.5	24.7	25.0	24.9	25.0	25.2	25.1
Beer	24.3	23.8	23.9	21.8	21.8	21.7	21.8	21.8	21.6
Wine [1]	2.1	2.4	2.0	1.7	2.0	2.0	2.0	2.1	2.2
Distilled spirits	2.0	1.8	1.5	1.2	1.2	1.3	1.3	1.3	1.3

NA Not available. [1] Beginning 1985, includes wine coolers.

Source: U.S. Department of Agriculture, Economic Research Service, *Food Consumption, Prices, and Expenditures,* 1970-1997; online at <http://www.ers.usda.gov/data/foodconsumption/>.

Health and Nutrition 135

Table 202. Per Capita Consumption of Major Food Commodities: 1980 to 2003

[In pounds, retail weight, except as indicated. Consumption represents the residual after exports, nonfood use and ending stocks are subtracted from the sum of beginning stocks, domestic production, and imports. Based on Census Bureau estimated population]

Commodity	Unit	1980	1985	1990	1995	2000	2002	2003
Red meat, total (boneless, trimmed weight) [1] [2]	Pounds	126.4	124.9	112.2	113.6	113.7	114.0	111.9
Beef	Pounds	72.1	74.6	63.9	63.5	64.5	64.5	62.0
Veal	Pounds	1.3	1.5	0.9	0.8	0.5	0.5	0.5
Lamb and mutton	Pounds	1.0	1.1	1.0	0.9	0.8	0.9	0.8
Pork	Pounds	52.1	47.7	46.4	48.4	47.8	48.2	48.5
Poultry (boneless, trimmed weight) [2]	Pounds	40.8	45.6	56.2	62.1	67.9	70.7	71.2
Chicken	Pounds	32.7	36.4	42.4	48.2	54.2	56.8	57.5
Turkey	Pounds	8.1	9.1	13.8	13.9	13.7	14.0	13.7
Fish and shellfish (boneless, trimmed weight)	Pounds	12.4	15.0	15	14.8	15.2	15.6	16.3
Eggs	Number	271	255	234	232	251	254	253
Shell	Number	236	216	186	172	178	180	181
Processed	Number	35	39	48	60	73	74	72
Dairy products, total [3]	Pounds	543.1	593.6	568.0	576.2	592.3	585.3	593.9
Fluid milk products [4]	Gallons	27.9	27.1	26.2	24.6	23.2	22.7	22.5
Beverage milks	Gallons	27.6	26.7	25.7	23.9	22.5	21.9	21.6
Plain whole milk	Gallons	16.5	13.9	10.2	8.3	7.7	7.3	7.2
Plain reduced-fat milk (2%)	Gallons	6.3	7.9	9.1	8.0	7.1	7.0	6.9
Plain light and skim milks	Gallons	3.1	3.2	4.9	6.1	6.1	5.8	5.6
Flavored whole milk	Gallons	0.6	0.4	0.3	0.3	0.4	0.4	0.4
Flavored milks other than whole	Gallons	0.6	0.7	0.8	0.8	1.0	1.2	1.2
Buttermilk	Gallons	0.5	0.5	0.4	0.3	0.3	0.2	0.2
Yogurt (excludes frozen)	1/2 pints	4.6	7.3	7.8	11.4	12.0	13.7	15.2
Fluid cream products [5]	1/2 pints	10.5	13.5	14.3	15.6	18.3	19.7	22.2
Cream [6]	1/2 pints	6.3	8.2	8.7	9.4	11.6	12.1	13.9
Sour cream and dips	1/2 pints	3.4	4.3	4.7	5.4	6.1	6.7	7.5
Condensed and evaporated milks	Pounds	7.0	7.5	7.9	6.8	5.8	6.0	5.6
Whole milk	Pounds	3.8	3.7	3.1	2.3	2.0	2.3	2.5
Skim milk	Pounds	3.3	3.8	4.8	4.5	3.8	3.7	3.1
Cheese [7]	Pounds	17.5	22.5	24.6	26.9	29.8	30.5	30.6
American [8]	Pounds	9.6	12.2	11.1	11.7	12.7	12.8	12.7
Cheddar	Pounds	6.8	9.8	9.0	9.0	9.7	9.6	9.5
Italian [8]	Pounds	4.4	6.5	9.0	10.3	12.0	12.4	12.3
Mozzarella	Pounds	3.0	4.6	6.9	8.0	9.3	9.7	9.6
Other [8]	Pounds	3.4	3.9	4.5	5.0	5.1	5.2	5.2
Swiss	Pounds	1.3	1.3	1.4	1.1	1.0	1.1	1.1
Cream and Neufchatel	Pounds	1.0	1.2	1.7	2.0	2.4	2.4	2.4
Cottage cheese, total	Pounds	4.5	4.1	3.4	2.7	2.6	2.6	2.7
Lowfat	Pounds	0.8	1.0	1.2	1.2	1.3	1.3	1.3
Frozen dairy products	Pounds	26.4	27.9	28.5	29.0	28.0	26.6	26.7
Ice cream	Pounds	17.5	18.1	15.8	15.5	16.7	16.7	16.7
Lowfat ice cream	Pounds	7.1	6.9	7.7	7.4	7.3	6.5	6.7
Sherbet	Pounds	1.2	1.3	1.2	1.3	1.2	1.3	1.3
Frozen yogurt	Pounds	(NA)	(NA)	2.8	3.4	2.0	1.5	1.4
Fats and oils:								
Total, fat content only	Pounds	56.9	64.1	63.0	65.4	82.1	87.9	85.8
Butter (product weight)	Pounds	4.5	4.9	4.4	4.5	4.5	4.5	4.2
Margarine (product weight)	Pounds	11.3	10.8	10.9	9.1	7.5	6.5	6.2
Lard (direct use)	Pounds	2.3	1.6	1.6	1.6	1.9	2.4	2.4
Edible beef tallow (direct use)	Pounds	1.1	2.0	0.6	2.7	4.0	3.4	3.8
Shortening	Pounds	18.2	22.9	22.2	22.2	31.3	34.1	32.5
Salad and cooking oils	Pounds	21.2	23.5	25.2	26.5	33.7	37.7	37.3
Other edible fats and oils	Pounds	1.5	1.6	1.2	1.6	1.5	1.5	1.5
Flour and cereal products [9]	Pounds	144.7	156.5	180.7	188.5	198.9	191.4	194.0
Wheat flour	Pounds	116.9	124.6	135.9	140.0	146.3	136.7	137.9
Rice, milled	Pounds	9.4	9.1	15.6	16.9	18.6	19.3	20.1
Corn products	Pounds	12.9	17.2	21.4	24.9	28.4	29.7	30.3
Oat products	Pounds	3.9	4.0	6.5	5.4	4.3	4.5	4.6
Caloric sweeteners, total [10]	Pounds	120.2	126.2	132.4	144.1	148.8	146.1	141.7
Sugar, refined cane and beet	Pounds	83.6	62.7	64.4	64.9	65.5	63.2	61.1
Corn sweeteners [11]	Pounds	35.3	62.2	66.8	77.9	81.8	81.5	79.2
High-fructose corn syrup	Pounds	19.0	45.2	49.6	57.6	62.6	62.8	60.9
Other:								
Cocoa beans	Pounds	3.4	4.6	5.4	4.5	5.9	4.9	5.7
Coffee (green beans)	Pounds	10.3	10.5	10.3	7.9	10.3	9.2	9.5
Peanuts (shelled)	Pounds	5.0	6.4	6.1	5.6	5.8	5.8	6.3
Tree nuts (shelled)	Pounds	1.79	2.45	2.42	1.92	2.54	2.86	2.93

NA Not available. [1] Excludes edible offals. [2] Excludes shipments to Puerto Rico and the other U.S. possessions. [3] Milk-equivalent, milkfat basis. Includes butter. [4] Fluid milk figures are aggregates of commercial sales and milk produced and consumed on farms. [5] Includes eggnog, not shown separately. [6] Heavy cream, light cream, and half-and-half. [7] Excludes full-skim American, cottage, pot, and baker's cheese. [8] Includes other cheeses not shown separately. [9] Includes rye flour and barley products not shown separately. Excludes quantities used in alcoholic beverages. [10] Dry weight. Includes edible syrups (maple, molasses, etc.) and honey not shown separately. [11] Includes glucose and dextrose not shown separately.

Source: U.S. Department of Agriculture, Economic Research Service, *Food Consumption, Prices, and Expenditures,* 1970–1997; and online at <http://www.ers.usda.gov/data/foodconsumption/>.

136 Health and Nutrition

Table 203. **Per Capita Utilization of Commercially-Produced Fruits and Vegetables: 1980 to 2003**

[In pounds, farm weight. Domestic food use of fresh fruits and vegetables reflects the fresh-market share of commodity production plus imports and minus exports]

Commodity	1980	1985	1990	1995	1999	2000	2001	2002	2003
Fruits and vegetables, total [1]	606.3	631.5	659.2	691.5	712.0	709.4	686.3	681.5	691.5
Fruits, total	267.9	271.5	273.2	283.7	291.7	286.9	275.5	271.1	274.9
Fresh fruits	105.1	110.8	116.6	122.9	129.8	128.0	125.7	126.9	126.7
Noncitrus	79.0	89.4	95.3	99.1	109.4	104.5	101.8	103.6	102.8
Apples	19.4	17.4	19.8	18.9	18.7	17.6	15.8	16.2	16.7
Bananas	20.8	23.5	24.3	27.1	30.7	28.4	26.6	26.8	26.2
Cantaloupes	5.8	8.5	9.2	9.0	11.4	11.1	11.2	11.1	10.8
Grapes	4.0	6.9	8.0	7.5	8.1	7.4	7.7	8.7	7.5
Peaches and nectarines	7.1	5.5	5.5	5.3	5.3	5.3	5.2	5.2	5.2
Pears	2.6	2.8	3.3	3.4	3.6	3.4	3.3	3.1	3.1
Pineapples	1.5	1.5	2.0	1.9	3.0	3.2	3.2	3.8	4.4
Plums and prunes	1.5	1.4	1.5	0.9	1.3	1.2	1.3	1.3	1.2
Strawberries	2.0	3.0	3.2	4.1	4.6	4.9	4.2	4.6	5.0
Watermelons	10.7	13.5	13.3	15.2	15.2	13.8	15.0	14.0	13.8
Other [2]	3.6	5.4	5.0	5.8	7.6	8.1	8.3	8.8	9.0
Fresh citrus	26.1	21.5	21.4	23.8	20.4	23.5	23.9	23.4	23.9
Oranges	14.3	11.6	12.4	11.8	8.4	11.7	11.9	11.7	11.9
Grapefruit	7.3	5.5	4.4	6.0	5.7	5.1	4.8	4.6	4.1
Other [3]	4.5	4.4	4.6	6.0	6.2	6.7	7.2	7.0	8.0
Processed fruits	162.8	160.7	156.6	160.9	161.9	158.9	149.8	144.1	148.2
Frozen fruits [4]	3.1	3.3	3.8	4.8	4.7	4.3	7.0	4.7	4.5
Dried fruits [5]	11.2	12.8	12.1	12.6	10.1	10.4	10.2	10.4	10.0
Canned fruits [6]	24.6	20.9	21.0	17.3	19.2	17.5	17.6	16.7	17.1
Fruit juices [7]	123.2	123.4	119.4	125.8	127.4	126.2	114.4	111.8	116.0
Vegetables, total	338.4	360.0	386.1	407.8	420.3	422.5	410.8	410.4	416.6
Fresh vegetables	151.4	158.6	170.7	181.5	197.7	198.0	194.5	193.5	195.6
Asparagus (all uses)	0.3	0.5	0.6	0.6	0.9	1.0	0.9	1.0	1.1
Broccoli	1.4	2.6	3.4	4.3	6.2	5.9	5.4	5.3	5.7
Cabbage	8.0	8.7	8.3	8.1	7.6	8.9	8.8	8.3	7.5
Carrots	6.2	6.5	8.3	11.2	9.3	9.2	9.4	8.4	8.8
Cauliflower	1.1	1.8	2.2	1.6	1.8	1.7	1.5	1.4	1.7
Celery (all uses)	7.4	6.9	7.2	6.9	6.5	6.2	6.4	6.3	6.1
Corn	6.5	6.4	6.7	7.8	9.1	9.0	9.2	9.0	9.7
Cucumbers	3.9	4.4	4.7	5.6	6.7	6.4	6.3	6.5	6.1
Head lettuce	25.6	23.7	27.7	22.2	24.9	23.5	23.0	22.5	21.4
Mushrooms	1.2	1.8	2.0	2.0	2.5	2.6	2.6	2.6	2.6
Onions	11.4	13.6	15.1	17.8	18.5	18.9	18.5	19.3	19.2
Snap beans	1.3	1.3	1.1	1.6	1.9	2.0	2.2	2.1	2.0
Bell peppers (all uses)	2.9	3.8	4.5	6.2	6.7	7.0	6.9	6.8	7.0
Potatoes	51.1	46.3	46.7	49.2	47.9	47.4	46.4	44.3	46.6
Sweet potatoes (all uses)	4.4	5.3	4.4	4.2	3.7	4.2	4.4	3.8	4.7
Tomatoes	12.8	14.9	15.5	16.8	18.0	18.0	18.2	19.2	18.1
Other fresh vegetables [8]	5.8	10.1	11.6	14.2	18.1	19.0	18.3	20.5	21.1
Processed vegetables	187.0	201.4	215.4	226.2	222.6	224.5	216.3	216.9	221.0
Selected vegetables for freezing	51.5	64.5	66.8	78.8	80.9	79.6	78.3	76.5	78.9
Selected vegetables for canning	102.5	99.0	110.4	108.0	102.8	103.1	97.2	100.6	100.6
Vegetables for dehydrating [9]	10.5	12.8	14.6	14.5	14.6	17.4	15.6	15.9	16.9
Potatoes for chips	16.5	17.6	16.4	16.4	15.9	16.0	17.6	16.4	17.2
Pulses [10]	5.9	7.6	7.2	8.4	8.3	8.4	7.5	7.5	7.3

[1] Excludes wine grapes. [2] Apricots, avocados, cherries, cranberries, kiwifruit, mangoes, papayas, and honeydew melons. [3] Lemons, limes, tangerines, and tangelos. [4] Apples, apricots, blackberries, blueberries, boysenberries, cherries, loganberries, peaches, plums, prunes, raspberries, and strawberries. [5] Apples, apricots, dates, figs, peaches, pears, prunes, and raisins. [6] Apples, apricots, cherries, olives, peaches, pears, pineapples, plums, and prunes. [7] Apple, cranberry, grape, grapefruit, lemon, lime, orange, pineapple, and prunes. [8] Artichokes, brussels sprouts, eggplant, escarole, endive, garlic, romaine, leaf lettuce, radishes, spinach, and squash. Beginning 2000, includes collard greens, kale, mustard greens, okra, pumpkin, and turnip greens. [9] Onions and potatoes. [10] Dry peas, lentils, and dry edible beans.

Source: U.S. Department of Agriculture, Economic Research Service, *Food Consumption, Prices, and Expenditures, 1970-1997*; online at <http://www.ers.usda.gov/data/foodconsumption/>.

No. 150.—PUBLIC SCHOOL STATISTICS of the UNITED STATES in 1879.

[From Report of the Commissioner of Education.]

STATES AND TERRITORIES.	School age.	School population.	Number between 6 and 16 years of age.	Number enrolled in public schools.	Average daily attendance.	Average duration of school in days.
Alabama	7–21	376, 649		174, 585	112, 374	84
Arkansas	6–21	236, 601		53, 049		
California	5–17	216, 404		156, 769	98, 468	149
Colorado	6–21	29, 738		14, 111	10, 899	89
Connecticut	4–16	138, 428	a115, 000	119, 382	72, 643	178. 6
Delaware	5–21	35, 649		26, 672		148
Florida	b4–21	c72, 985		b36, 964	b23, 933	b105. 8
Georgia	6–18	433, 444		226, 627	a132, 000	
Illinois	6–21	1, 000, 694		693, 334	404, 479	150
Indiana	6–21	708, 101	530, 839	503, 892	312, 143	132
Iowa	5–21	577, 353	369, 447	431, 317	264, 702	147
Kansas	5–21	312, 231	197, 342	208, 434	123, 715	124
Kentucky	d6–20	539, 843		d227, 607	e160, 000	e119
Louisiana	6–21	330, 930		78, 528	a50, 248	
Maine	4–21	215, 724		151, 948	103, 737	121
Maryland	5–20	f276, 120		165, 486	84, 245	189
Massachusetts	5–15	303, 836		311, 528	234, 249	175
Michigan	5–20	486, 993		342, 138	a201, 179	150
Minnesota	5–21	b271, 428		171, 945	a111, 764	92
Mississippi	5–21	382, 370		217, 753	139, 973	g77. 5
Missouri	6–20	702, 153		450, 000	a207, 422	100
Nebraska	5–21	123, 411		76, 956		107
Nevada	6–18	10, 295		7, 590	5, 108	161
New Hampshire	5–21	a72, 102		65, 048	48, 910	101. 5
New Jersey	5–18	327, 818	278, 646	203, 568	112, 070	194
New York	5–21	1, 628, 727		1, 030, 041	570, 382	179
North Carolina	6–21	426, 189		238, 749	150, 788	46
Ohio	6–21	1, 043, 320	770, 070	734, 651	459, 990	150
Oregon	4–20	56, 464		32, 718	20, 840	88
Pennsylvania	6–21	A1, 200, 000		935, 740	587, 672	149
Rhode Island	5–15	49, 562		45, 700	28, 735	182
South Carolina	6–16	228, 128	228. 128	122, 463		73. 23
Tennessee	6–21	514, 643		264, 687	186, 162	69
Texas	8–14	208, 324		192, 616		80
Vermont	5–20	92, 831		77, 521	49, 231	125. 5
Virginia	5–21	483, 701	307, 742	108, 074	65, 771	107
West Virginia	6–21	206, 123		135, 526	90, 268	100. 76
Wisconsin	4–20	483, 453		266, 286		i153. 7
Total		14, 782, 765	2, 797, 214	9, 327, 003	5, 223, 100	
Arizona	6–21	5, 291		3, 143	1, 992	165
Dakota	5–21	18, 525		9, 822	4, 618	97
District of Columbia	6–17	b38, 800	35, 948	25, 130	19, 488	189
Idaho	5–21	5, 596		3, 482		
Montana	4–21	5, 885		3, 909	2, 804	105
New Mexico	j7–18	f29, 312		j5, 151		j132
Utah	6–16	34, 929	34, 929	23, 124	16, 076	139
Washington	5–21	24, 223		14, 032	9, 585	
Wyoming	e7–21			e1, 690		
Indian : Cherokees				3, 200	a1, 714	
Chickasaws				650		
Choctaws	5–20	b17, 000		1, 400	a921	
Creeks				860	a582	
Seminoles				200	170	
Total		179, 571	70, 877	95, 683	57, 950	
Grand total		14, 962, 336	2, 868, 091	9, 422, 686	5, 281, 050	

a Estimated. b In 1878. c In 1876. d For colored population the school age is from 6 to 16. e In 1877– f Census of 1870. g In the country; 130 in towns. h In 1873. i In the counties. j In 1875.

Source: Statistical Abstract of the United States: 1880 Edition.

Section 4
Education

This section presents data primarily concerning formal education as a whole, at various levels, and for public and private schools. Data shown relate to the school-age population and school enrollment, educational attainment, education personnel, and financial aspects of education. In addition, data are shown for charter schools, computer usage in schools, distance education, and adult education. The chief sources are the decennial census of population and the Current Population Survey (CPS), both conducted by the U.S. Census Bureau (see text, Section 1, Population); annual, biennial, and other periodic surveys conducted by the National Center for Education Statistics (NCES), a part of the U.S. Department of Education; and surveys conducted by the National Education Association.

The censuses of population have included data on school enrollment since 1840 and on educational attainment since 1940. The CPS has reported on school enrollment annually since 1945 and on educational attainment periodically since 1947.

The NCES is continuing the pattern of statistical studies and surveys conducted by the U.S. Office of Education since 1870. The annual *Digest of Education Statistics* provides summary data on pupils, staff, finances, including government expenditures, and organization at the elementary, secondary, and higher education levels. It is also a primary source for detailed information on federal funds for education, projections of enrollment, graduates, and teachers. *The Condition of Education*, issued annually, presents a summary of information on education of particular interest to policymakers. NCES also conducts special studies periodically.

The census of governments, conducted by the Census Bureau every 5 years (for the years ending in "2" and "7"), provides data on school district finances and state and local government expenditures for education. Reports published by the

Bureau of Labor Statistics contain data relating civilian labor force experience to educational attainment (see also Tables 580, 607, and 615 in Section 12, Labor Force, Employment, and Earnings).

Types and sources of data—The statistics in this section are of two general types. One type, exemplified by data from the Census Bureau, is based on direct interviews with individuals to obtain information about their own and their family members' education. Data of this type relate to school enrollment and level of education attained, classified by age, sex, and other characteristics of the population. The school enrollment statistics reflect attendance or enrollment in any regular school within a given period; educational attainment statistics reflect the highest grade completed by an individual, or beginning 1992, the highest diploma or degree received.

Beginning in 2001, the CPS used Census 2000 population controls. From 1994 to 2000, the CPS used 1990 census population controls plus adjustment for under-count. Also the survey changed from paper to computer-assisted technology. For years 1981 through 1993, 1980 census population controls were used; 1971 through 1980, 1970 census population controls had been used. These changes had little impact on summary measures (e.g., medians) and proportional measures (e.g., enrollment rates); however, use of the controls may have significant impact on absolute numbers.

The second type, generally exemplified by data from the NCES and the National Education Association, is based on reports from administrators of educational institutions and of state and local agencies having jurisdiction over education. Data of this type relate to enrollment, attendance, staff, and finances for the nation, individual states, and local areas.

Unlike the NCES, the Census Bureau does not regularly include specialized vocational, trade, business, or correspondence schools in its surveys. The NCES includes nursery schools and kindergartens that are part of regular grade schools in their enrollment figures. The Census Bureau includes all nursery schools and kindergartens. At the higher education level, the statistics of both agencies are concerned with institutions granting degrees or offering work acceptable for degree-credit, such as junior colleges.

School attendance—All states require that children attend school. While state laws vary as to the ages and circumstances of compulsory attendance, generally they require that formal schooling begin by age 6 and continue to age 16.

Schools—The NCES defines a school as "a division of the school system consisting of students composing one or more grade groups or other identifiable groups, organized as one unit with one or more teachers to give instruction of a defined type, and housed in a school plant of one or more buildings. More than one school may be housed in one school plant, as is the case when the elementary and secondary programs are housed in the same school plant."

Regular schools are those which advance a person toward a diploma or degree. They include public and private nursery schools, kindergartens, graded schools, colleges, universities, and professional schools.

Public schools are schools controlled and supported by local, state, or federal governmental agencies; private schools are those controlled and supported mainly by religious organizations or by private persons or organizations.

The Census Bureau defines *elementary* schools as including grades 1 through 8; *high* schools as including grades 9 through 12; and *colleges* as including junior or community colleges, regular 4-year colleges, and universities and graduate or professional schools. Statistics reported by the NCES and the National Education Association by type of organization, such as elementary level and secondary level, may not be strictly comparable with those from the Census Bureau because the grades included at the two levels vary, depending on the level assigned to the middle or junior high school by the local school systems.

School year—Except as otherwise indicated in the tables, data refer to the school year which, for elementary and secondary schools, generally begins in September of the preceding year and ends in June of the year stated. For the most part, statistics concerning school finances are for a 12-month period, usually July 1 to June 30. Enrollment data generally refer to a specific point in time, such as fall, as indicated in the tables.

Statistical reliability—For a discussion of statistical collection, estimation, and sampling procedures and measures of statistical reliability applicable to the Census Bureau and the NCES data, see Appendix III.

U.S. Census Bureau, Statistical Abstract of the United States: 2006

Table 204. **School Enrollment: 1970 to 2013**

[In thousands (59,838 represents 59,838,000). As of fall. Based on survey of state education agencies; see source for details]

Year	Total	All levels		Pre-K through grade 8		Grades 9 through 12		College [1]	
		Public	Private	Public	Private	Public	Private	Public	Private
1970	59,838	52,322	7,516	32,558	4,052	13,336	1,311	6,428	2,153
1975	61,004	53,654	7,350	30,515	3,700	14,304	1,300	8,835	2,350
1980	58,305	50,335	7,971	27,647	3,992	13,231	1,339	9,457	2,640
1981	57,916	49,691	8,225	27,280	4,100	12,764	1,400	9,647	2,725
1982	57,591	49,262	8,330	27,161	4,200	12,405	1,400	9,696	2,730
1983	57,432	48,935	8,497	26,981	4,315	12,271	1,400	9,683	2,782
1984	57,150	48,686	8,465	26,905	4,300	12,304	1,400	9,477	2,765
1985	57,226	48,901	8,325	27,034	4,195	12,388	1,362	9,479	2,768
1986	57,709	49,467	8,242	27,420	4,116	12,333	1,336	9,714	2,790
1987	58,253	49,982	8,272	27,933	4,232	12,076	1,247	9,973	2,793
1988	58,485	50,349	8,136	28,501	4,036	11,687	1,206	10,161	2,894
1989	59,279	51,120	8,159	29,152	4,035	11,390	1,163	10,578	2,961
1990	60,269	52,061	8,208	29,878	4,084	11,338	1,150	10,845	2,974
1991	61,681	53,357	8,324	30,506	4,113	11,541	1,162	11,310	3,049
1992	62,633	54,208	8,425	31,088	4,175	11,735	1,147	11,385	3,103
1993	63,118	54,654	8,464	31,504	4,215	11,961	1,132	11,189	3,116
1994	63,888	55,245	8,643	31,898	4,335	12,213	1,163	11,134	3,145
1995	64,764	55,933	8,831	32,341	4,465	12,500	1,197	11,092	3,169
1996	65,744	56,733	9,011	32,764	4,551	12,847	1,213	11,121	3,247
1997	66,470	57,323	9,147	33,073	4,623	13,054	1,218	11,196	3,306
1998	66,983	57,677	9,306	33,346	4,702	13,193	1,235	11,138	3,369
1999	67,667	58,166	9,501	33,488	4,765	13,369	1,254	11,309	3,482
2000	68,671	58,956	9,714	33,688	4,868	13,515	1,287	11,753	3,560
2001	69,936	59,921	10,014	33,952	4,993	13,736	1,326	12,233	3,695
2002 [2]	71,215	60,954	10,261	34,135	5,042	14,067	1,359	12,752	3,860
2003, proj. . . .	71,442	61,165	10,277	33,917	4,935	14,296	1,384	12,952	3,958
2004, proj. . . .	71,688	61,362	10,326	33,686	4,910	14,584	1,414	13,092	4,003
2005, proj. . . .	72,075	61,658	10,417	33,528	4,910	14,847	1,439	13,283	4,068
2006, proj. . . .	72,657	62,093	10,564	33,565	4,963	15,010	1,456	13,518	4,146
2007, proj. . . .	73,078	62,416	10,662	33,603	4,978	15,060	1,461	13,752	4,223
2008, proj. . . .	73,505	62,731	10,775	33,702	5,002	14,994	1,457	14,034	4,316
2009, proj. . . .	73,861	62,991	10,870	33,870	5,030	14,871	1,450	14,251	4,389
2010, proj. . . .	74,168	63,222	10,946	34,097	5,064	14,745	1,446	14,380	4,436
2011, proj. . . .	74,523	63,498	11,025	34,439	5,114	14,565	1,433	14,494	4,478
2012, proj. . . .	74,971	63,860	11,111	34,846	5,171	14,402	1,419	14,612	4,520
2013, proj. . . .	75,514	64,313	11,201	35,268	5,231	14,315	1,410	14,730	4,560

[1] Data beginning 1996 based on new classification system. See footnote 1, Table 265.   [2] Public Pre-K to 8 and 9 to 12 data preliminary.

Source: U.S. National Center for Education Statistics, *Digest of Education Statistics,* annual, and *Projections of Education Statistics,* annual.

Table 205. **School Expenditures by Type of Control and Level of Instruction in Constant (2001–2002) Dollars: 1960 to 2002**

[In millions of dollars (144,699 represents $144,699,000,000). For school years ending in year shown. Total expenditures for public elementary and secondary schools include current expenditures, interest on school debt and capital outlay. Data deflated by the Consumer Price Index, wage earners, and clerical workers through 1975; thereafter, all urban consumers, on a school-year basis (supplied by the National Center for Education Statistics). See also Appendix III. Based on survey of state education agencies; see source for details]

Year	Total	Elementary and secondary schools			Colleges and universities [2]		
		Total	Public	Private [1]	Total	Public	Private
1960	144,699	101,356	94,685	6,671	43,343	23,673	19,670
1970	322,934	203,704	191,911	11,793	119,230	76,580	42,650
1975	373,863	236,867	223,105	13,762	136,996	92,779	44,217
1980	380,163	236,787	220,260	16,526	143,376	95,103	48,273
1985	417,243	251,703	230,812	20,891	165,539	107,328	58,213
1986	441,293	264,954	243,338	21,616	176,339	114,741	61,598
1987	467,731	280,664	257,756	22,908	187,068	119,430	67,638
1988	482,044	289,186	265,651	23,535	192,858	122,842	70,014
1989	510,033	307,854	283,740	24,113	202,179	128,076	74,102
1990	535,416	324,134	298,592	25,541	211,283	135,266	76,019
1991	549,081	331,230	305,283	25,947	217,851	138,960	78,890
1992	558,249	336,835	310,791	26,044	221,414	140,104	81,310
1993	570,201	342,987	316,231	26,755	227,214	143,990	83,224
1994	581,600	350,379	323,325	27,055	231,221	145,722	85,499
1995	597,010	358,260	330,537	27,722	238,751	151,163	87,586
1996	610,807	367,048	338,675	28,372	243,759	153,109	90,649
1997	631,063	380,307	351,152	29,155	250,756	156,563	94,193
1998	655,348	398,173	368,317	29,856	257,175	161,988	95,187
1999	686,846	415,897	385,357	30,539	270,950	168,177	102,773
2000	718,736	433,174	401,912	31,261	285,563	177,148	108,415
2001	750,983	450,455	418,804	31,651	300,528	190,209	110,319
2002	780,100	462,700	430,600	32,100	317,400	198,600	118,800

[1] Estimated.   [2] Data beginning 1996 based on new classification system. See footnote 1, Table 265.

Source: U.S. National Center for Education Statistics, *Digest of Education Statistics,* annual.

Education 141

Table 206. **School Enrollment, Faculty, Graduates, and Finances—Projections 2004 to 2010**

[As of fall, except as indicated (54,593 represents 54,593,000)]

Item	Unit	2004	2005	2006	2007	2008	2009	2010
ELEMENTARY AND SECONDARY SCHOOLS								
School enrollment, total..........	1,000 ...	54,593	54,725	54,993	55,102	55,154	55,221	55,352
Pre-kindergarten through grade 8 ..	1,000 ...	38,596	38,439	38,528	38,581	38,704	38,900	39,160
Grades 9 through 12..........	1,000 ...	15,998	16,286	16,465	16,521	16,450	16,321	16,192
Public...................	1,000 ...	48,270	48,375	48,574	48,664	48,696	48,740	48,842
Pre-kindergarten through grade 8.	1,000 ...	33,686	33,528	33,565	33,603	33,702	33,870	34,097
Grades 9 through 12	1,000 ...	14,584	14,847	15,010	15,060	14,994	14,871	14,745
Private..................	1,000 ...	6,323	6,349	6,419	6,439	6,458	6,481	6,510
Pre-kindergarten through grade 8.	1,000 ...	4,910	4,910	4,963	4,978	5,002	5,030	5,064
Grades 9 through 12	1,000 ...	1,414	1,439	1,456	1,461	1,457	1,450	1,446
Classroom teachers, total FTE [1]	1,000 ...	3,501	3,526	3,570	3,601	3,625	3,650	3,680
Public...................	1,000 ...	3,100	3,122	3,161	3,188	3,209	3,230	3,256
Private..................	1,000 ...	401	404	409	413	416	420	424
High school graduates, total [2].......	1,000 ...	3,062	3,089	3,152	3,227	3,309	3,328	3,311
Public...................	1,000 ...	2,758	2,780	2,836	2,904	2,978	2,995	2,980
Public schools: [2]								
Average daily attendance (ADA) ...	1,000 ...	44,754	44,807	44,904	45,089	45,172	45,202	45,243
Current dollars: [3]								
Teachers' average salary	Dol.	46,826	47,423	48,412	50,050	51,220	(NA)	(NA)
Current school expenditure	Bil. dol.	403.1	418.4	433.9	456.8	476.6	(NA)	(NA)
Per pupil in fall enrollment	Dol. ...	8,361	8,667	8,970	9,404	9,794	(NA)	(NA)
Constant (2002-2003) dollars: [3][4]								
Teachers' average salary	Dol.	45,008	45,041	45,345	46,107	46,222	(NA)	(NA)
Current school expenditure	Bil. dol..	395.9	406.1	415.3	430.0	439.5	(NA)	(NA)
Per pupil in fall enrollment	Dol. ...	8,211	8,412	8,586	8,852	9,031	(NA)	(NA)
HIGHER EDUCATION								
Enrollment, total...............	1,000 ...	17,095	17,350	17,664	17,975	18,351	18,640	18,816
Male....................	1,000 ...	7,268	7,356	7,461	7,568	7,695	7,802	7,872
Full-time.................	1,000 ...	4,527	4,584	4,656	4,733	4,827	4,906	4,955
Part-time................	1,000 ...	2,741	2,772	2,805	2,835	2,868	2,896	2,917
Female..................	1,000 ...	9,826	9,995	10,203	10,407	10,655	10,838	10,944
Full-time.................	1,000 ...	5,776	5,899	6,050	6,201	6,384	6,525	6,608
Part-time................	1,000 ...	4,050	4,096	4,153	4,206	4,271	4,313	4,336
Public...................	1,000 ...	13,092	13,283	13,518	13,752	14,034	14,251	14,380
Four-year institutions	1,000 ...	6,785	6,893	7,024	7,153	7,310	7,435	7,516
Two-year institutions	1,000 ...	6,307	6,389	6,494	6,599	6,724	6,817	6,864
Private..................	1,000 ...	4,003	4,068	4,146	4,223	4,316	4,389	4,436
Four-year institutions	1,000 ...	3,727	3,788	3,860	3,931	4,018	4,085	4,130
Two-year institutions	1,000 ...	276	280	286	292	299	304	307
Undergraduate..............	1,000 ...	14,628	14,845	15,115	15,385	15,715	15,973	16,125
Graduate.................	1,000 ...	2,114	2,146	2,183	2,216	2,254	2,280	2,299
First-time professional	1,000 ...	352	359	366	374	382	388	392
Full-time equivalent	1,000 ...	12,737	12,943	13,198	13,456	13,769	14,013	14,161
Public...................	1,000 ...	9,343	9,491	9,676	9,863	10,091	10,268	10,372
Private..................	1,000 ...	3,394	3,452	3,522	3,593	3,678	3,745	3,789
Degrees conferred, total [2]	1,000 ...	2,727	2,778	2,815	2,860	2,921	2,990	3,054
Associate's	1,000 ...	667	668	668	676	689	705	719
Bachelor's................	1,000 ...	1,401	1,416	1,431	1,449	1,475	1,507	1,538
Master's.................	1,000 ...	531	562	580	596	615	634	650
Doctorate	1,000 ...	46	47	49	50	50	51	51
First-professional	1,000 ...	82	85	88	90	92	94	96
Public 4-year colleges: [2]								
FTE enrollment [1]	1,000 ...	5,670	5,766	5,882	5,998	6,141	6,255	6,328
Current dollars: [3]								
Current fund expenditures.....	Bil. dol...	168.2	178.0	187.2	196.4	206.7	(NA)	(NA)
Per FTE	Dol.	30,039	31,400	32,459	33,390	34,466	(NA)	(NA)
Constant (2002-03) dollars: [3][4]								
Current fund expenditures.....	Bil. dol...	165.2	172.8	179.1	184.9	190.6	(NA)	(NA)
Per FTE	Dol.	29,500	30,475	31,068	31,434	31,783	(NA)	(NA)
Public 2-year colleges: [2]								
FTE enrollment [1]	1,000 ...	3,673	3,725	3,794	3,865	3,950	4,014	4,044
Current dollars: [3]								
Current fund expenditures.....	Bil. dol...	36.4	39.8	42.2	44.4	46.7	(NA)	(NA)
Per FTE	Dol.	10,039	10,834	11,337	11,696	12,093	(NA)	(NA)
Constant (2002-03) dollars: [3][4]								
Current fund expenditures.....	Bil. dol...	35.7	38.6	40.4	41.8	43.1	(NA)	(NA)
Per FTE	Dol.	9,859	10,515	10,852	11,011	11,152	(NA)	(NA)

NA Not available. [1] Full-time equivalent. [2] For school year ending in June the following year. [3] Limited financial projections are shown due to the uncertain behavior of inflation over the long term. [4] Based on the Consumer Price Index (CPI) for all urban consumers, U.S. Bureau of Labor Statistics. CPI adjusted to a school year basis by NCES.

Source: U.S. National Center for Education Statistics, *Projections of Education Statistics to 2014*, NCES 2005-074, See Internet site <http://www.nces.ed.gov/surveys/AnnualReports/>.

Table 207. Federal Funds for Education and Related Programs: 2002 to 2004

[In millions of dollars (109,619.9 represents $109,619,900,000), except percent. For fiscal years ending in September. Figures represent on-budget funds]

Level, agency, and program	2002	2003	2004 [1]
Total, all programs	**109,619.9**	**125,702.0**	**132,458.9**
Percent of Federal budget outlays	5.4	5.8	5.7
Elementary/secondary education programs	**53,162.5**	**59,719.5**	**66,736.7**
Department of Education [2]	25,246.2	30,749.3	36,925.2
Grants for the disadvantaged	9,247.7	11,253.0	14,150.9
School improvement programs	3,810.0	6,752.9	9,217.1
Indian education	103.9	115.9	126.2
Special education	7,000.1	8,490.7	9,101.4
Vocational and adult education	1,777.7	1,942.7	1,931.8
Education reform—Goals 2000	1,767.6	531.9	225.9
Department of Agriculture [2]	10,836.4	11,215.3	12,059.6
Child nutrition programs	10,253.9	10,828.3	11,455.4
Agricultural Marketing Service—commodities [3]	399.9	200.0	400.0
Special milk program [4]	(³)	(³)	(³)
Department of Defense [2]	1,439.8	1,684.3	1,781.3
Overseas dependents schools	834.0	1,056.1	1,123.9
Section VI schools [5]	366.8	376.1	372.7
Department of Health and Human Services	7,365.8	7,571.0	7,682.6
Head Start	6,537.0	6,666.8	6,774.8
Social security student benefits [2]	812.3	904.2	907.7
Department of the Interior [2]	945.3	963.0	1,000.6
Mineral Leasing Act and other funds	130.8	138.7	167.4
Indian Education	813.4	823.3	832.2
Department of Justice	408.4	445.4	491.5
Inmate programs	401.4	437.4	484.5
Department of Labor	5,859.0	5,972.0	5,600.0
Job Corps	1,467.0	1,423.0	1,551.0
Department of Veterans Affairs	487.5	514.6	550.0
Vocational rehab for disabled veterans	487.5	514.6	550.0
Other agencies and programs	574.2	604.7	645.9
Higher education programs [2]	**22,964.2**	**29,498.3**	**28,717.7**
Department of Education [2]	17,056.2	22,706.4	21,589.5
Student financial assistance	12,577.9	14,092.4	14,478.8
Federal Family Education Loans [2]	2,342.8	1,216.0	1,290.7
Department of Agriculture	88.8	93.6	93.8
Department of Commerce	4.2	4.0	4.0
Department of Defense	1,485.6	1,673.4	1,732.1
Tuition assistance for military personnel	401.5	548.6	553.1
Service academies [6]	245.8	268.7	275.2
Senior ROTC	471.9	521.2	548.3
Professional development education	366.4	334.9	355.5
Department of Health and Human Services [2]	1,567.4	1,692.8	1,749.6
Health professions training programs	818.1	882.4	909.2
National Health Service Corps scholarships	46.2	46.3	46.0
National Institutes of Health training grants [7]	650.7	711.4	741.7
Department of the Interior	185.8	234.2	259.3
Shared revenues, Mineral Leasing Act and other receipts—estimated education share	89.6	135.1	155.6
Indian programs	96.2	99.1	103.7
Department of State	385.0	387.0	345.0
Department of Transportation [2]	78.7	65.0	66.0
Department of Veterans Affairs [2]	1,634.8	2,005.3	2,247.8
Post-Vietnam veterans	.2	1.2	2.0
All-volunteer force educational assistance	1,385.1	1,712.6	1,907.7
Other agencies and programs [2]	477.8	636.2	630.7
National Endowment for the Humanities	30.0	34.1	36.0
National Science Foundation	415.0	535.0	524.0
Other education programs [2]	**6,297.7**	**6,532.5**	**6,841.8**
Department of Education [2]	3,396.8	3,435.2	3,751.7
Administration	531.3	548.3	522.5
Rehabilitative services and handicapped research	2,852.2	2,871.8	3,206.8
Department of Agriculture	469.4	473.6	460.2
Department of Health and Human Services	276.2	300.0	309.0
Department of Justice	23.4	19.6	20.7
Department of State	102.1	107.7	111.9
Department of the Treasury [2]	163.0		
Other agencies and programs [2]	1,866.8	2,196.4	2,188.1
Agency for International Development	480.0	489.2	600.4
Library of Congress	397.0	389.0	406.0
National Endowment for the Arts	5.3	2.5	2.4
National Endowment for the Humanities	67.2	66.7	67.0
Research programs at universities and related institutions [2]	**27,195.5**	**29,951.7**	**30,162.7**
Department of Agriculture	591.9	665.1	519.9
Department of Defense	2,537.8	2,730.8	2,039.0
Department of Energy	3,964.4	4,045.5	4,116.9
Department of Health and Human Services	13,484.0	15,729.0	16,225.8
National Aeronautics and Space Administration	2,405.2	2,515.2	2,628.4
National Science Foundation	3,074.8	3,205.4	3,543.9

- Represents or rounds to zero. [1] Estimated. [2] Includes other programs and agencies, not shown separately. [3] The Special Milk Program is included in the Child Nutrition Program. [4] Purchased under Section 32 of the Act of August 1935 for use in child nutrition programs. [5] Program provides for the education of dependents of Federal employees residing on federal property where free public education is unavailable in the nearby community. [6] Instructional costs only including academics, audiovisual, academic computer center, faculty training, military training, physical education, and libraries. [7] Includes alcohol, drug abuse, and mental health.

Source: U.S. National Center for Education Statistics, *Digest of Education Statistics,* annual.

Education 143

Table 208. **School Enrollment by Age: 1970 to 2003**

[As of October (60,357 represents 60,357,000). Covers civilian noninstitutional population enrolled in nursery school and above. Based on Current Population Survey, see text, Section 1, and Appendix III]

Age	1970	1980	1985	1990	1995	1999	2000	2001	2002	2003
ENROLLMENT (1,000)										
Total 3 to 34 years old	**60,357**	**57,348**	**58,013**	**60,588**	**66,939**	**69,601**	**69,560**	**70,271**	**71,003**	**72,116**
3 and 4 years old	1,461	2,280	2,801	3,292	4,042	4,273	4,097	4,030	4,187	4,590
5 and 6 years old	7,000	5,853	6,697	7,207	7,901	7,774	7,648	7,526	7,353	7,309
7 to 13 years old.	28,943	23,751	22,849	25,016	27,003	28,209	28,296	28,570	28,525	28,184
14 and 15 years old.	7,869	7,282	7,362	6,555	7,651	7,741	7,885	7,914	8,022	8,329
16 and 17 years old.	6,927	7,129	6,654	6,098	6,997	7,611	7,341	7,483	7,669	8,177
18 and 19 years old.	3,322	3,788	3,716	4,044	4,274	4,840	4,871	4,926	5,007	4,856
20 and 21 years old.	1,949	2,515	2,708	2,852	3,025	3,256	3,314	3,570	3,696	3,684
22 to 24 years old	1,410	1,931	2,068	2,231	2,545	2,664	2,731	2,798	3,003	3,397
25 to 29 years old	1,011	1,714	1,942	2,013	2,216	2,018	2,030	2,140	2,196	2,212
30 to 34 years old	466	1,105	1,218	1,281	1,284	1,215	1,292	1,370	1,345	1,378
35 years old and over	(NA)	1,290	1,766	2,439	2,830	2,794	2,653	2,852	3,043	2,797
ENROLLMENT RATE										
Total 3 to 34 years old	**56.4**	**49.7**	**48.3**	**50.2**	**53.7**	**56.0**	**55.8**	**55.7**	**56.1**	**56.2**
3 and 4 years old	20.5	36.7	38.9	44.4	48.7	54.2	52.1	52.2	54.5	55.1
5 and 6 years old	89.5	95.7	96.1	96.5	96.0	96.0	95.6	95.3	95.2	94.5
7 to 13 years old.	99.2	99.3	99.2	99.6	98.9	98.7	98.2	98.3	98.3	98.3
14 and 15 years old.	98.1	98.2	98.1	99.0	98.9	98.2	98.7	98.1	98.4	97.5
16 and 17 years old.	90.0	89.0	91.7	92.5	93.6	93.6	92.8	93.4	94.3	94.9
18 and 19 years old.	47.7	46.4	51.6	57.3	59.4	60.6	61.2	61.0	63.3	64.5
20 and 21 years old.	31.9	31.0	35.3	39.7	44.9	45.3	44.1	45.5	47.8	48.3
22 to 24 years old	14.9	16.3	16.9	21.0	23.2	24.5	24.6	25.1	25.6	27.8
25 to 29 years old	7.5	9.3	9.2	9.7	11.6	11.1	11.4	11.7	12.1	11.8
30 to 34 years old	4.2	6.4	6.1	5.8	6.0	6.2	6.7	6.8	6.6	6.8
35 years old and over	(NA)	1.4	1.6	2.1	2.2	1.8	1.9	2.0	2.1	1.9

NA Not available.

Source: U.S. Census Bureau, Current Population Reports, PPL-148; and earlier PPL and P-20 reports; and data published on the Internet. See Internet site <http://www.census.gov/population/www/socdemo/school.html>.

Table 209. **School Enrollment by Race, Hispanic Origin, and Age: 1980 to 2003**

[(47,673 represents 47,673,000). See headnote, Table 208]

Age	White [1]			Black [1]			Hispanic origin [2]		
	1980	1990	2003	1980	1990	2003	1980	1990	2003
ENROLLMENT (1,000)									
Total 3 to 34 years old	**47,673**	**48,899**	**55,218**	**8,251**	**8,854**	**10,971**	**4,263**	**6,073**	**11,679**
3 and 4 years old	1,844	2,700	3,550	371	452	714	172	249	728
5 and 6 years old	4,781	5,750	5,670	904	1,129	1,049	491	835	1,386
7 to 13 years old	19,585	20,076	21,377	3,598	3,832	4,541	2,009	2,794	5,073
14 and 15 years old	6,038	5,265	6,427	1,088	1,023	1,315	568	739	1,415
16 and 17 years old	5,937	4,858	6,311	1,047	962	1,267	454	592	1,242
18 and 19 years old	3,199	3,271	3,812	494	596	651	226	329	614
20 and 21 years old	2,206	2,402	2,890	242	305	458	111	213	454
22 to 24 years old.	1,669	1,781	2,559	196	274	459	93	121	353
25 to 29 years old.	1,473	1,706	1,621	187	162	297	84	130	240
30 to 34 years old.	942	1,090	1,001	124	119	220	54	72	174
35 years old and over	1,104	2,096	2,173	186	238	438	(NA)	145	250
ENROLLMENT RATE									
Total 3 to 34 years old	**48.9**	**49.5**	**55.4**	**53.9**	**51.9**	**59.2**	**49.8**	**47.4**	**49.6**
3 and 4 years old	36.3	44.9	55.3	38.2	41.6	55.6	28.5	29.8	43.7
5 and 6 years old	95.8	96.5	94.7	95.4	96.3	94.4	94.5	94.8	91.6
7 to 13 years old	99.2	99.6	98.3	99.4	99.8	98.3	99.2	99.4	98.0
14 and 15 years old	98.3	99.1	97.3	97.9	99.2	97.9	94.3	99.0	96.7
16 and 17 years old	88.6	92.5	95.0	90.6	91.7	94.3	81.8	85.4	92.1
18 and 19 years old	46.3	57.1	64.4	45.7	55.2	61.9	37.8	44.1	50.5
20 and 21 years old	31.9	41.0	48.2	23.4	28.4	41.3	19.5	27.2	33.7
22 to 24 years old.	16.4	20.2	26.7	13.6	20.0	27.4	11.7	9.9	16.1
25 to 29 years old.	9.2	9.9	11.0	8.8	6.1	12.2	6.9	6.3	6.2
30 to 34 years old.	6.3	5.9	6.2	6.8	4.4	8.6	5.1	3.6	4.6
35 years old and over	1.3	2.1	1.8	1.8	2.1	2.8	(NA)	2.1	1.8

NA Not available. [1] Beginning 2003 for persons who selected this race group only. See footnote 2, Table 214. [2] Persons of Hispanic origin may be of any race.

Source: U.S. Census Bureau, Current Population Reports, PPL-148; and earlier PPL and P-20 reports; and data published on the Internet. See Internet site <http://www.census.gov/population/www/socdemo/school.html>.

Table 210. Enrollment in Public and Private Schools: 1970 to 2003

[In millions (52.2 represents 52,200,000), except percent. As of October. For civilian noninstitutional population. For 1970 to 1985, persons 3 to 34 years old; beginning 1986, for 3 years old and over. For college enrollment 35 years old and over, see Table 268. See also headnote, Table 208]

Year	Public Total	Public Nursery	Public Kindergarten	Public Elementary	Public High school	Public College	Private Total	Private Nursery	Private Kindergarten	Private Elementary	Private High school	Private College
1970	52.2	0.3	2.6	30.0	13.5	5.7	8.1	0.8	0.5	3.9	1.2	1.7
1975	52.8	0.6	2.9	27.2	14.5	7.7	8.2	1.2	0.5	3.3	1.2	2.0
1980	(NA)	0.6	2.7	24.4	(NA)	(NA)	(NA)	1.4	0.5	3.1	(NA)	(NA)
1985	49.0	0.9	3.2	23.8	12.8	8.4	9.0	1.6	0.6	3.1	1.2	2.5
1986 [1]	51.2	0.8	3.4	24.2	13.0	9.8	9.4	1.7	0.6	3.0	1.2	2.9
1987	51.7	0.8	3.4	24.8	12.7	10.0	8.9	1.7	0.6	2.8	1.1	2.8
1988	52.2	0.9	3.4	25.5	12.2	10.3	8.9	1.8	0.5	2.8	1.0	2.8
1989	52.5	0.9	3.3	25.9	12.1	10.3	8.9	1.9	0.6	2.7	0.8	2.9
1990	53.8	1.2	3.3	26.6	11.9	10.7	9.2	2.2	0.6	2.7	0.9	2.9
1991	54.5	1.1	3.5	26.6	12.2	11.1	9.4	1.8	0.6	3.0	1.0	3.0
1992	55.0	1.1	3.5	27.1	12.3	11.1	9.4	1.8	0.6	3.1	1.0	3.0
1993	56.0	1.2	3.5	27.7	12.6	10.9	9.4	1.8	0.7	2.9	1.0	3.0
1994	58.6	1.9	3.3	28.1	13.5	11.7	9.4	2.3	0.6	3.4	1.1	3.3
1995	58.7	2.0	3.2	28.4	13.7	11.4	11.1	2.4	0.7	3.4	1.2	3.3
1996	59.5	1.9	3.4	28.1	14.1	12.0	10.8	2.3	0.7	3.4	1.2	3.2
1997	61.6	2.3	3.3	29.3	14.6	12.1	10.5	2.2	0.7	3.1	1.2	3.3
1998	60.8	2.3	3.1	29.1	14.3	12.0	11.3	2.3	0.7	3.4	1.2	3.6
1999	60.8	2.3	3.2	29.2	14.4	11.7	11.4	2.3	0.7	3.6	1.3	3.5
2000	61.2	2.2	3.2	29.4	14.4	12.0	11.0	2.2	0.7	3.5	1.3	3.3
2001	62.4	2.2	3.1	29.8	14.8	12.4	10.8	2.1	0.6	3.4	1.2	3.5
2002	62.8	2.2	3.0	29.7	15.1	12.8	11.3	2.2	0.6	3.5	1.3	3.5
2003	63.8	2.6	3.1	29.2	15.8	13.1	11.1	2.4	0.6	3.4	1.3	3.5
Percent White:												
1970	84.5	59.5	84.4	83.1	85.6	90.7	93.4	91.1	88.2	94.1	96.1	92.8
1980	(NA)	68.2	80.7	80.9	(NA)	(NA)	(NA)	89.0	87.0	90.7	(NA)	(NA)
1990	79.8	71.7	78.3	78.9	79.2	84.1	87.4	89.6	83.2	88.2	89.4	85.0
2000	77.0	69.4	77.3	76.7	78.0	78.0	83.5	84.9	82.8	85.9	84.6	79.8
2001	76.5	68.7	76.1	76.7	77.4	76.5	83.1	84.3	84.4	85.6	86.7	78.4
2002	76.6	71.8	75.3	76.5	77.9	76.2	83.8	83.6	87.5	84.1	86.4	82.1
2003 [2]	75.6	74.7	76.4	75.0	75.6	77.1	82.3	84.3	80.3	83.8	86.0	79.0

NA Not available. [1] Beginning 1986, based on a revised edit and tabulation package. [2] Beginning 2003, for persons who selected this race group only. See footnote 2, Table 214.

Source: U.S. Census Bureau, Current Population Reports, PPL-148; and earlier PPL and P-20 reports; and data published on the Internet. See Internet site <http://www.census.gov/population/www/socdemo/school.html>.

Table 211. School Enrollment by Sex and Level: 1970 to 2003

[In millions (60.4 represents 60,400,000). As of October. For the civilian noninstitutional population. 1970–1979, for persons 3 to 34 years old; beginning 1980, 3 years old and over. Elementary includes kindergarten and grades 1-8; high school, grades 9-12; and college, 2-year and 4-year colleges, universities, and graduate and professional schools. Data for college represent degree-credit enrollment. See headnote, Table 208]

Year	All levels [1] Total	Male	Female	Elementary Total	Male	Female	High school Total	Male	Female	College Total	Male	Female
1970	60.4	31.4	28.9	37.1	19.0	18.1	14.7	7.4	7.3	7.4	4.4	3.0
1975	61.0	31.6	29.4	33.8	17.3	16.5	15.7	8.0	7.7	9.7	5.3	4.4
1980	58.6	29.6	29.1	30.6	15.8	14.9	14.6	7.3	7.3	11.4	5.4	6.0
1984	58.9	29.9	29.0	30.3	15.6	14.7	13.9	7.1	6.8	12.3	6.0	6.3
1985 [2]	59.8	30.0	29.7	30.7	15.7	15.0	14.1	7.2	6.9	12.5	5.9	6.6
1986	60.5	30.6	30.0	31.1	16.1	15.0	14.2	7.2	7.0	12.7	6.0	6.7
1987	60.6	30.7	29.9	31.6	16.3	15.3	13.8	7.0	6.8	12.7	6.0	6.7
1988	61.1	30.7	30.5	32.2	16.6	15.6	13.2	6.7	6.4	12.7	6.0	6.7
1989	61.5	30.8	30.7	32.5	16.7	15.8	12.9	6.6	6.3	13.2	5.9	7.2
1990	63.0	31.5	31.5	33.2	17.1	16.0	12.8	6.5	6.4	13.2	6.0	7.2
1991	63.9	32.1	31.8	33.8	17.3	16.4	13.1	6.8	6.4	14.1	6.2	7.4
1992	64.6	32.2	32.3	34.3	17.7	16.6	13.3	6.8	6.5	14.1	6.4	7.6
1993	65.4	32.9	32.5	34.8	17.9	16.9	13.6	7.0	6.6	14.0	6.2	7.8
1994	69.3	34.6	34.6	35.4	18.2	17.2	14.6	7.4	7.2	13.9	6.3	7.6
1995	69.8	35.0	34.8	35.7	18.3	17.4	15.0	7.7	7.3	14.7	6.7	8.0
1996	70.3	35.1	35.2	35.5	18.3	17.3	15.3	7.9	7.4	15.2	6.8	8.4
1997	72.0	35.9	36.2	36.3	18.7	17.6	15.8	8.0	7.7	15.4	6.8	8.6
1998	72.1	36.0	36.1	36.4	18.7	17.7	15.6	7.9	7.6	15.5	6.9	8.6
1999	72.4	36.3	36.1	36.7	18.8	17.9	15.9	8.2	7.7	15.2	7.0	8.2
2000	72.2	35.8	36.4	36.7	18.9	17.9	15.8	8.1	7.7	15.3	6.7	8.6
2001	73.1	36.3	36.9	36.9	19.0	17.9	16.1	8.2	7.8	15.9	6.9	9.0
2002	74.0	36.8	37.3	36.7	18.9	17.8	16.4	8.3	8.0	15.9	6.9	9.0
2003	74.9	37.3	37.6	36.3	18.7	17.6	17.1	8.6	8.4	16.6	7.3	9.3

[1] Includes nursery schools, not shown separately. [2] Revised. Data beginning 1986, based on a revised edit and tabulation package.

Source: U.S. Census Bureau, Current Population Reports, PPL-148; and earlier PPL and P-20 reports; and data published on the Internet. See Internet site <http://www.census.gov/population/www/socdemo/school.html>.

Education 145

Table 212. **School Enrollment by Control and Level: 1980 to 2003**

[In thousands (58,305 represents 58,305,000). As of fall. Data below college level are for regular day schools and exclude subcollegiate departments of colleges, federal schools and home-schooled children. College data include degree-credit and nondegree-credit enrollment. Based on survey of state education agencies; see source for details. For projections, see Table 206]

Control of school and level	1980	1990	1995	1997	1998	1999	2000	2001	2002 [1]	2003, proj.
Total..............	58,305	60,269	64,764	66,470	66,982	67,667	68,671	69,935	71,215	71,442
Public...............	50,335	52,061	55,933	57,323	57,677	58,166	58,956	59,921	60,954	61,165
Private	7,971	8,208	8,831	9,147	9,306	9,501	9,715	10,014	10,261	10,277
Pre-kindergarten through 8 ..	31,639	33,962	36,806	37,696	38,048	38,253	38,556	38,945	39,177	38,852
Public..............	27,647	29,878	32,341	33,073	33,346	33,488	33,688	33,952	34,135	33,917
Private	3,992	4,084	4,465	4,623	4,702	4,765	4,868	4,993	5,042	4,935
Grades 9 through 12.......	14,570	12,488	13,697	14,272	14,427	14,623	14,802	15,062	15,426	15,680
Public..............	13,231	11,338	12,500	13,054	13,193	13,369	13,515	13,736	14,067	14,296
Private	1,339	1,150	1,197	1,218	1,235	1,254	1,287	1,326	1,359	1,384
College [2]	12,097	13,819	14,262	14,502	14,507	14,791	15,313	15,928	16,612	16,910
Public..............	9,457	10,845	11,092	11,196	11,138	11,309	11,753	12,233	12,752	12,952
Private	2,640	2,974	3,169	3,306	3,369	3,482	3,560	3,695	3,860	3,958

[1] Public Prekindergarten to 8, and 9 to 12 data preliminary.   [2] Data beginning 1996, reflects new classification system. See footnote 1, Table 265.

Source: U.S. National Center for Education Statistics, *Digest of Education Statistics,* annual.

Table 213. **Students Who Are Foreign-Born or Who Have Foreign-Born Parents: 2003**

[In thousands (49,626 represents 49,626,000), except percent. As of October. Covers civilian noninstitutional population enrolled in elementary school and above. Based on Current Population Survey, see text, Section 1 and Appendix III]

Characteristic	All students	Students with at least one foreign-born parent					
		Total		Foreign-born student		Native student	
		Number	Percent	Number	Percent	Number	Percent
ELEMENTARY AND HIGH SCHOOL							
Total [1]..............	49,626	10,860	21.9	2,771	5.6	8,089	16.3
White [2].................	37,747	7,542	20.0	1,954	5.2	5,588	14.8
White, non-Hispanic	29,716	2,153	7.2	453	1.5	1,700	5.7
Black [2]	8,010	1,090	13.6	284	3.5	806	10.1
Asian [2][3]...............	1,890	1,720	91.0	434	23.0	1,286	68.0
Hispanic [4].............	8,753	5,739	65.6	1,588	18.1	4,151	47.4
COLLEGE, 1 TO 4 YEARS							
Total [1]..............	13,370	2,930	21.9	1,381	10.3	1,549	11.6
White [2].................	10,389	1,722	16.6	673	6.5	1,048	10.1
White, non-Hispanic	8,964	831	9.3	334	3.7	497	5.5
Black [2]	1,810	401	22.2	275	15.2	126	7.0
Asian [2][3]...............	754	697	92.4	399	52.9	298	39.5
Hispanic [4].............	1,544	953	61.7	367	23.8	586	38.0
GRADUATE SCHOOL							
Total [1]..............	3,268	878	26.9	585	17.9	293	9.0
White [2].................	2,481	396	16.0	225	9.1	171	6.9
White, non-Hispanic	2,331	307	13.2	177	7.6	130	5.6
Black [2]	334	76	22.8	55	16.5	21	6.3
Asian [2][3]...............	408	388	95.1	302	74.0	87	21.3
Hispanic [4].............	170	100	58.8	49	28.8	51	30.0

[1] Includes other races, not shown separately.   [2] For persons who selected this race group only. See footnote 2, Table 214.   [3] Data are for Asians only; excludes Pacific Islanders.   [4] Persons of Hispanic origin may be of any race.

Source: U.S. Census Bureau, Current Population Survey, unpublished data. See Internet site <http://www.census.gov/population/www/socdemo/school.html>.

Table 214. Educational Attainment by Race and Hispanic Origin: 1960 to 2004

[In percent. For persons 25 years old and over. 1960, 1970, and 1980 as of April 1 and based on sample data from the censuses of population. **Other years as of March**, and based on the Current Population Survey; see text, Section 1, Population, and Appendix III. See Table 215 for data by sex]

Year	Total [1]	White [2]	Black [2]	Asian and Pacific Islander [2]	Hispanic [3] Total [4]	Mexican	Puerto Rican	Cuban
HIGH SCHOOL GRADUATE OR MORE [5]								
1960	41.1	43.2	20.1	(NA)	(NA)	(NA)	(NA)	(NA)
1970	52.3	54.5	31.4	(NA)	32.1	24.2	23.4	43.9
1980	66.5	68.8	51.2	(NA)	44.0	37.6	40.1	55.3
1990	77.6	79.1	66.2	80.4	50.8	44.1	55.5	63.5
1995	81.7	83.0	73.8	(NA)	53.4	46.5	61.3	64.7
2000	84.1	84.9	78.5	85.7	57.0	51.0	64.3	73.0
2001	84.1	84.8	78.8	87.6	56.8	50.7	64.6	72.2
2002	84.1	84.8	78.7	87.4	57.0	50.6	66.8	70.8
2003	84.6	85.1	80.0	[6]87.6	57.0	50.9	69.7	70.8
2004	85.2	85.8	80.6	86.8	58.4	51.9	71.8	72.1
COLLEGE GRADUATE OR MORE [5]								
1960	7.7	8.1	3.1	(NA)	(NA)	(NA)	(NA)	(NA)
1970	10.7	11.3	4.4	(NA)	4.5	2.5	2.2	11.1
1980	16.2	17.1	8.4	(NA)	7.6	4.9	5.6	16.2
1990	21.3	22.0	11.3	39.9	9.2	5.4	9.7	20.2
1995	23.0	24.0	13.2	(NA)	9.3	6.5	10.7	19.4
2000	25.6	26.1	16.5	43.9	10.6	6.9	13.0	23.0
2001	26.2	26.6	15.7	47.5	11.1	7.8	12.9	19.3
2002	26.7	27.2	17.0	47.2	11.1	7.6	14.0	18.6
2003	27.2	27.6	17.3	[6]49.8	11.4	7.8	12.3	21.6
2004	27.7	28.2	17.6	49.4	12.1	7.9	14.0	24.0

NA Not available. [1] Includes other races, not shown separately. [2] The 2003 Current Population Survey (CPS) allowed respondents to choose more than one race. Beginning 2003 data represent persons who selected this race group only and exclude persons reporting more than one race. In prior years only allowed respondents to report one race group. See also comments on race in the text for Section 1. [3] Persons of Hispanic origin may be of any race. [4] Includes persons of other Hispanic origin, not shown separately. [5] Through 1990, completed 4 years of high school or more and 4 years of college or more. [6] Starting in 2003, data are for Asians only, excludes Pacific Islanders.

Source: U.S. Census Bureau, U.S. Census of Population, *U.S. Summary*, PC80-1-C1 and Current Population Report P20-550, and earlier reports, unpublished data, and data published on the Internet. See Internet site <http://www.census.gov/population/www/socdemo/educ-attn.html>.

Table 215. Educational Attainment by Race, Hispanic Origin, and Sex: 1960 to 2004

[In percent. See Table 214 for headnote and totals for both sexes]

Year	All races [1] Male	Female	White [2] Male	Female	Black [2] Male	Female	Asian and Pacific Islander [2] Male	Female	Hispanic [3] Male	Female
HIGH SCHOOL GRADUATE OR MORE [4]											
1960	39.5	42.5	41.6	44.7	18.2	21.8	(NA)	(NA)	(NA)	(NA)
1970	51.9	52.8	54.0	55.0	30.1	32.5	(NA)	(NA)	37.9	34.2
1980	67.3	65.8	69.6	68.1	50.8	51.5	(NA)	(NA)	67.3	65.8
1990	77.7	77.5	79.1	79.0	65.8	66.5	84.0	77.2	50.3	51.3
1995	81.7	81.6	83.0	83.0	73.4	74.1	(NA)	(NA)	52.9	53.8
2000	84.2	84.0	84.8	85.0	78.7	78.3	88.2	83.4	56.6	57.5
2001	84.1	84.2	84.8	85.1	79.2	78.5	90.3	85.1	55.5	58.0
2002	83.8	84.4	84.3	85.2	78.5	78.9	89.5	85.5	56.1	57.9
2003	84.1	85.0	84.5	85.7	79.6	80.3	[5]89.5	[5]86.0	56.3	57.8
2004	84.8	85.4	85.3	86.3	80.4	80.8	88.7	85.0	57.3	59.5
COLLEGE GRADUATE OR MORE [4]											
1960	9.7	5.8	10.3	6.0	2.8	3.3	(NA)	(NA)	(NA)	(NA)
1970	13.5	8.1	14.4	8.4	4.2	4.6	(NA)	(NA)	7.8	4.3
1980	20.1	12.8	21.3	13.3	8.4	8.3	(NA)	(NA)	9.4	6.0
1990	24.4	18.4	25.3	19.0	11.9	10.8	44.9	35.4	9.8	8.7
1995	26.0	20.2	27.2	21.0	13.6	12.9	(NA)	(NA)	10.1	8.4
2000	27.8	23.6	28.5	23.9	16.3	16.7	47.6	40.7	10.7	10.6
2001	28.2	24.3	28.7	24.0	15.3	16.1	52.3	43.2	10.8	11.4
2002	28.5	25.1	29.1	25.4	16.4	17.5	50.9	43.8	11.0	11.2
2003	28.9	25.7	29.5	25.9	16.7	17.8	[5]53.9	[5]46.1	11.2	11.6
2004	29.4	26.1	30.0	26.4	16.6	18.5	53.7	45.6	11.8	12.3

NA Not available. [1] Includes other races, not shown separately. [2] Beginning 2003, for persons who selected this race group only. See footnote 2, Table 214. [3] Persons of Hispanic origin may be of any race. [4] Through 1990, completed 4 years of high school or more and 4 years of college or more. [5] Starting in 2003, data are for Asians only, excludes Pacific Islanders.

Source: U.S. Census Bureau, U.S. Census of Population, 1960, 1970, and 1980, Vol. 1; and Current Population Reports P20-550 and earlier reports; and data published on the Internet. See Internet site <http://www.census.gov/population/www/socdemo/educ-attn.html>.

Education 147

Table 216. Educational Attainment by Selected Characteristic: 2004

[For persons 25 years old and over (186,877 represents 186,877,000). As of March. Based on the Current Population Survey; see text, Section 1, and Appendix III. For composition of regions, see map inside front cover]

Characteristic	Population (1,000)	Percent of population—highest level					
		Not a high school graduate	High school graduate	Some college, but no degree	Associate's degree[1]	Bachelor's degree	Advanced degree
Total persons	186,877	14.8	32.0	17.0	8.4	18.1	9.6
Age:							
25 to 34 years old	39,201	12.9	28.7	19.3	8.8	22.3	7.9
35 to 44 years old	43,573	12.0	31.5	17.0	9.9	20.2	9.3
45 to 54 years old	41,068	10.3	31.4	17.6	10.1	19.1	11.5
55 to 64 years old	28,375	13.6	33.3	17.0	7.9	16.1	12.2
65 to 74 years old	18,238	23.6	36.3	14.6	5.0	11.6	8.8
75 years old or over	16,421	30.6	35.7	12.8	4.2	10.2	6.5
Sex:							
Male	89,558	15.2	31.1	16.8	7.5	18.6	10.8
Female	97,319	14.6	32.8	17.3	9.3	17.6	8.5
Race:							
White [2]	154,150	14.2	32.2	17.0	8.5	18.4	9.8
Black [2]	20,812	19.4	36.0	19.2	7.8	12.3	5.3
Other	11,914	15.6	23.0	14.0	8.2	24.2	15.1
Hispanic origin:							
Hispanic	21,596	41.6	27.7	13.2	5.4	8.8	3.3
Non-Hispanic	165,280	11.3	32.6	17.5	8.8	19.3	10.4
Region:							
Northeast	35,869	13.5	35.2	12.7	7.8	19.1	11.8
Midwest	42,097	11.7	35.3	17.8	9.3	17.0	9.0
South	67,053	17.0	32.5	17.0	7.9	16.9	8.5
West	41,859	15.7	25.2	20.0	8.9	20.1	10.1
Marital status:							
Never married	29,585	15.0	31.1	17.4	7.4	20.4	8.8
Married spouse present	114,690	12.4	31.1	16.8	8.9	19.9	11.0
Married spouse absent [3]	3,005	29.3	29.5	12.3	6.0	13.7	9.1
Separated	4,268	25.5	34.5	17.2	8.2	10.5	4.2
Widowed	13,790	31.6	36.8	13.5	5.2	8.7	4.3
Divorced	21,538	12.8	35.2	20.7	10.1	13.5	7.8
Civilian labor force status:							
Employed	118,226	9.4	29.9	18.0	9.7	21.4	11.6
Unemployed	6,295	20.2	35.1	17.9	8.4	12.6	5.8
Not in the labor force	61,651	24.8	35.9	15.0	6.0	12.2	6.1

[1] Includes vocational degrees. [2] For persons who selected this race group only. See footnote 2, Table 214. [3] Excludes those separated.

Source: U.S. Census Bureau, Current Population Report P20-550; and data published on the Internet. See Internet site <http://www.census.gov/population/www/socdemo/educ-attn.html>.

Table 217. Mean Earnings by Highest Degree Earned: 2003

[In dollars. For persons 18 years old and over with earnings. Persons as of March the following year. Based on Current Population Survey; see text, Section 1, and Appendix III. For definition of mean, see Guide to Tabular Presentation]

Characteristic	Total persons	Level of highest degree							
		Not a high school graduate	High school graduate only	Some college, no degree	Associate's	Bachelor's	Master's	Professional	Doctorate
All persons [1]	37,046	18,734	27,915	29,533	35,958	51,206	62,514	115,212	88,471
Age:									
25 to 34 years old	33,212	18,920	26,073	28,954	32,276	43,794	51,040	74,120	62,109
35 to 44 years old	42,475	22,123	31,479	36,038	38,442	57,438	66,264	126,165	101,382
45 to 54 years old	45,908	23,185	32,978	40,291	41,511	59,208	68,344	132,180	92,229
55 to 64 years old	45,154	23,602	31,742	38,131	39,147	57,423	66,760	138,845	98,433
65 years old and over	28,918	17,123	20,618	28,017	23,080	41,323	42,194	77,312	56,724
Sex:									
Male	44,726	21,447	33,266	36,419	43,462	63,084	76,896	136,128	95,894
Female	28,367	14,214	21,659	22,615	29,537	38,447	48,205	72,445	73,516
White [2]	38,053	19,110	28,708	30,316	36,881	52,259	62,981	119,712	89,640
Male	46,114	21,791	34,224	37,550	44,557	65,264	77,845	140,419	99,015
Female	28,591	14,149	22,028	22,790	30,099	37,739	48,388	72,184	70,536
Black [2]	28,838	16,201	23,777	25,616	31,415	42,968	57,449	87,713	81,457
Male	32,545	17,915	28,102	29,320	38,234	45,635	69,557	103,155	(B)
Female	25,735	14,513	19,623	22,790	27,054	41,066	49,344	(B)	(B)
Hispanic [3]	25,810	18,349	23,472	27,586	31,032	43,676	56,486	78,190	(B)
Male	28,806	20,637	26,652	33,595	35,896	49,298	63,026	(B)	(B)
Female	21,391	13,632	18,967	20,776	26,535	37,550	48,433	(B)	(B)

B Base figure too small to meet statistical standards for reliability of a derived figure. [1] Includes other races, not shown separately. [2] For persons who selected this race group only. See footnote 2, Table 214. [3] Persons of Hispanic origin may be of any race.

Source: U.S. Census Bureau, Current Population Report P20-550 and data published on the Internet. See Internet site <http://www.census.gov/population/www/socdemo/educ-attn.html>.

Table 218. Educational Attainment by State: 1990 to 2004

[In percent. As of March, except 1990 as of April. For persons 25 years old and over. Based on the 1990 Census of Population and the Current Population Survey; see text, Section 1, and Appendix III]

State	1990 High school graduate or more	1990 Bachelor's degree or more	1998 High school graduate or more	1998 Bachelor's degree or more	2000 High school graduate or more	2000 Bachelor's degree or more	2004 High school graduate or more	2004 Bachelor's degree or more
United States.....	75.2	20.3	82.8	24.4	84.1	25.6	85.2	27.7
Alabama............	66.9	15.7	78.8	20.6	77.5	20.4	82.4	22.3
Alaska.............	86.6	23.0	90.6	24.2	90.4	28.1	90.2	25.5
Arizona............	78.7	20.3	81.9	21.9	85.1	24.6	84.4	28.0
Arkansas..........	66.3	13.3	76.8	16.2	81.7	18.4	79.2	18.8
California..........	76.2	23.4	80.1	26.4	81.2	27.5	81.3	31.7
Colorado...........	84.4	27.0	89.6	34.0	89.7	34.6	88.3	35.5
Connecticut........	79.2	27.2	83.7	31.4	88.2	31.6	88.8	34.5
Delaware..........	77.5	21.4	85.2	25.1	86.1	24.0	86.5	26.9
District of Columbia	73.1	33.3	83.8	36.5	83.2	38.3	86.4	45.7
Florida............	74.4	18.3	81.9	22.5	84.0	22.8	85.9	26.0
Georgia...........	70.9	19.3	80.0	20.7	82.6	23.1	85.2	27.6
Hawaii............	80.1	22.9	84.6	24.0	87.4	26.3	88.0	26.6
Idaho.............	79.7	17.7	82.7	20.3	86.2	20.0	87.9	23.8
Illinois............	76.2	21.0	84.2	25.8	85.5	27.1	86.8	27.4
Indiana............	75.6	15.6	83.5	17.7	84.6	17.1	87.2	21.1
Iowa..............	80.1	16.9	87.7	20.3	89.7	25.5	89.8	24.3
Kansas............	81.3	21.1	89.2	28.5	88.1	27.3	89.6	30.0
Kentucky..........	64.6	13.6	77.9	20.1	78.7	20.5	81.8	21.0
Louisiana..........	68.3	16.1	78.6	19.5	80.8	22.5	78.7	22.4
Maine.............	78.8	18.8	86.7	19.2	89.3	24.1	87.1	24.2
Maryland...........	78.4	26.5	84.7	31.8	85.7	32.3	87.4	35.2
Massachusetts........	80.0	27.2	85.6	31.0	85.1	32.7	86.9	36.7
Michigan...........	76.8	17.4	85.4	22.1	86.2	23.0	87.9	24.4
Minnesota..........	82.4	21.8	89.4	31.0	90.8	31.2	92.3	32.5
Mississippi	64.3	14.7	77.3	19.5	80.3	18.7	83.0	20.1
Missouri...........	73.9	17.8	82.9	22.4	86.6	26.2	87.9	28.1
Montana...........	81.0	19.8	89.1	23.9	89.6	23.8	91.9	25.5
Nebraska..........	81.8	18.9	87.7	20.9	90.4	24.6	91.3	24.8
Nevada	78.8	15.3	89.1	20.6	82.8	19.3	86.3	24.5
New Hampshire........	82.2	24.4	84.0	26.6	88.1	30.1	90.8	35.4
New Jersey.........	76.7	24.9	86.5	30.1	87.3	30.1	87.6	34.6
New Mexico	75.1	20.4	79.6	23.1	82.2	23.6	82.9	25.1
New York	74.8	23.1	81.5	26.8	82.5	28.7	85.4	30.6
North Carolina.......	70.0	17.4	81.4	23.3	79.2	23.2	80.9	23.4
North Dakota........	76.7	18.1	84.3	22.5	85.5	22.6	89.5	25.2
Ohio	75.7	17.0	86.2	21.5	87.0	24.6	88.1	24.6
Oklahoma..........	74.6	17.8	84.6	20.5	86.1	22.5	85.2	22.9
Oregon............	81.5	20.6	85.5	27.7	88.1	27.2	87.4	25.9
Pennsylvania........	74.7	17.9	84.1	22.1	85.7	24.3	86.5	25.3
Rhode Island........	72.0	21.3	80.7	27.8	81.3	26.4	81.1	27.2
South Carolina........	68.3	16.6	78.6	21.3	83.0	19.0	83.6	24.9
South Dakota	77.1	17.2	86.3	21.8	91.8	25.7	87.5	25.5
Tennessee	67.1	16.0	76.9	16.9	79.9	22.0	82.9	24.3
Texas.............	72.1	20.3	78.3	23.3	79.2	23.9	78.3	24.5
Utah	85.1	22.3	89.3	27.6	90.7	26.4	91.0	30.8
Vermont...........	80.8	24.3	86.7	27.1	90.0	28.8	90.8	34.2
Virginia............	75.2	24.5	82.6	30.3	86.6	31.9	88.4	33.1
Washington.........	83.8	22.9	92.0	28.1	91.8	28.6	89.7	29.9
West Virginia........	66.0	12.3	76.4	16.3	77.1	15.3	80.9	15.3
Wisconsin..........	78.6	17.7	88.0	22.3	86.7	23.8	88.8	25.6
Wyoming..........	83.0	18.8	90.0	19.8	90.0	20.6	91.9	22.5

Source: U.S. Census Bureau, 1990 Census of Population, CPH-L-96, and Current Population Reports, P20-550, and earlier reports; and data published on the Internet. See Internet site <http://www.census.gov/population/www/socdemo/educ-attn.html>.

Table 219. **Nonfatal Crimes Against Students: 2001 and 2002**

[For students aged 12 through 18 (2,001.3 represents 2,001,300). For crimes occurring at school or going to or from school. Based on the National Crime Victimization Survey; see Appendix III]

Student characteristic	2001				2002			
	Total	Theft	Violent		Total	Theft	Violent	
			Total	Serious [1]			Total	Serious [1]
Total (1,000)..............	2,001.3	1,237.6	763.7	160.9	1,753.6	1,095.0	658.6	88.1
RATE PER 1,000 STUDENTS								
Total [2]...............	73	45	28	6	64	40	24	3
Sex:								
Male..................	78	48	30	6	66	39	27	4
Female................	67	42	26	5	62	41	21	[3]2
Age:								
12 to 14 years old.........	82	47	35	7	73	41	31	4
15 to 18 years old..........	66	43	22	5	56	39	18	2
Race/ethnicity:								
White, non-Hispanic........	79	50	29	5	72	44	28	3
Black, non-Hispanic.........	63	38	25	[3]7	52	34	18	[3]4
Hispanic................	64	31	33	9	53	30	22	[3]5
Other, non-Hispanic........	51	46	[3]4	[3]2	42	42	-	-
Urbanicity: [4]								
Urban.................	73	44	29	7	70	41	29	5
Suburban	76	48	28	6	67	44	24	3
Rural	66	41	25	[3]5	46	27	18	[3]1
Household income:								
Less than $7,500	57	29	[3]28	[3]10	44	[3]23	[3]22	[3]7
$7,500 to $14,999..........	55	33	22	[3]3	49	21	28	[3]4
$15,000 to $24,999.........	79	38	41	[3]9	53	34	19	[3]5
$25,000 to $34,999.........	68	40	28	[3]4	59	32	27	[3]3
$35,000 to $49,999.........	80	45	36	11	76	45	31	[3]3
$50,000 to $74,999.........	80	59	21	[3]5	68	41	27	[3]2
$75,000 and over	88	59	29	[3]4	81	57	24	[3]4

- Represents or rounds to zero. [1] Includes rape, sexual assault, robbery and aggravated assault. [2] Includes those whose incomes are unknown. [3] Estimate based on fewer than 10 cases. [4] Urban: The largest city (or groupings of cities) of an MSA; suburban: those portions of metro areas outside central cities; rural: places outside MSAs.

Source: U.S. National Center for Education Statistics and U.S. Bureau of Justice "Statistics, *Indicators of School Crime and Safety: 2004*, November 2004, NCES 2005–002."

Table 220. **Students Who Reported Carrying a Weapon: 1993 to 2003**

[In percent. For students in grades 9 to 12. Percentages are based on students who reported carrying a weapon at least one day during the previous thirty days. Weapons are such things as guns, knives, and clubs. Based on the Youth Risk Behavior Surveillance System. See source for details. See also <http://www.cdc.gov/HealthyYouth/yrbs/index.htm>.]

Student characteristic	Anywhere					On school property				
	1993	1995	1999	2001	2003	1993	1995	1999	2001	2003
Total	22.1	20.0	17.3	17.4	17.1	11.8	9.8	6.9	6.4	6.1
Sex:										
Male...............	34.3	31.1	28.6	29.3	26.9	17.9	14.3	11.0	10.2	8.9
Female..............	9.2	8.3	6.0	6.2	6.7	5.1	4.9	2.8	2.9	3.1
Race/ethnicity:										
White, non-Hispanic	(1)	(1)	16.4	17.9	16.7	(1)	(1)	6.4	6.1	5.5
Black, non-Hispanic......	(1)	(1)	17.2	15.2	17.3	(1)	(1)	5.0	6.3	6.9
Hispanic [2]	(1)	(1)	18.7	16.5	16.5	(1)	(1)	7.9	6.4	6.0
Asian	(1)	(1)	13.0	10.6	11.6	(1)	(1)	6.5	7.2	6.6
American Indian	(1)	(1)	21.8	31.2	29.3	(1)	(1)	11.6	16.4	12.9
Pacific Islander.........	(1)	(1)	25.3	17.4	16.3	(1)	(1)	9.3	10.0	4.9
More than one race......	(1)	(1)	22.2	25.2	29.8	(1)	(1)	11.4	13.2	13.3
Grade:										
9th.................	25.5	22.6	17.6	19.8	18.0	12.6	10.7	7.2	6.7	5.3
10th................	21.4	21.1	18.7	16.7	15.9	11.5	10.4	6.6	6.7	6.0
11th................	21.5	20.3	16.1	16.8	18.2	11.9	10.2	7.0	6.1	6.6
12th................	19.9	16.1	15.9	15.1	15.5	10.8	7.6	6.2	6.1	6.4

[1] The response categories for race/ethnicity changed in 1999 making comparisons of some categories with earlier years problematic. [2] Persons of Hispanic origin may be of any race.

Source: U.S. National Center for Education Statistics and U.S. Bureau of Justice "Statistics, *Indicators of School Crime and Safety: 2004*, November 2004, NCES 2005-002."

150 Education

Table 221. **Children's Involvement in Home Literacy Activities: 1993 and 2001**

[In percent, except number of children (8,579 represents 8,579,000). For children 3 to 5 years old not yet enrolled in kindergarten who participated in activities with a family member. Based on the School Readiness Survey of the National Household Education Survey Program; see source and Appendix III. See also Table 224]

Characteristic	Children (1,000)		Read to [1]		Told a story [1]		Taught letters, words, or numbers [1]		Visited a library [2]	
	1993	2001	1993	2001	1993	2001	1993	2001	1993	2001
Total	8,579	8,551	78	84	43	54	58	74	38	36
Age:										
3 years old	3,889	3,795	79	84	46	54	57	71	34	35
4 years old	3,713	3,861	78	85	41	55	58	77	41	37
5 years old	976	896	76	81	36	52	58	75	38	37
Race/ethnicity:										
White, non-Hispanic	5,902	5,313	85	89	44	58	58	75	42	39
Black, non-Hispanic	1,271	1,251	66	77	39	51	63	78	29	31
Hispanic	1,026	1,506	58	71	38	42	54	68	26	30
Other	381	482	73	87	50	60	59	78	43	38
Mother's home language: [3]										
English	7,805	7,368	81	88	44	56	58	76	39	38
Not English	603	984	42	60	36	38	52	61	26	25
Mother's highest education: [3]										
Less than high school	1,036	996	60	69	37	43	56	67	22	21
High school	3,268	2,712	76	81	41	53	56	73	31	30
Vocational ed or some college . . .	2,624	2,406	83	86	45	53	60	76	44	39
College degree	912	1,418	90	93	48	59	56	75	55	45
Graduate/professional training or degree	569	820	90	96	50	63	60	80	59	55

[1] Three or more times in the past week. [2] At least once in the past month. [3] Excludes children with no mother in the household and no female guardian.

Source: U.S. National Center for Education Statistics, *Statistical Brief*, NCES 2000-026, November 1999; and unpublished data. See Internet site <http://nces.ed.gov/pubsearch/getpubcats.asp?sid=004>.

Table 222. **Children Who Speak a Language Other Than English at Home: 2000 to 2003**

[In percent, except as indicated. For children 5 to 17 years old (9.5 represents 9,500,000). Based on the American Community Survey; see text Section 1, and Appendix III]

Characteristic	2000	2001	2002	2003
Children who speak another language at home (mil.)	9.5	9.8	9.8	9.9
Percent of children 5 to 17 years old	18.1	18.5	18.5	18.6
Race and Hispanic origin:				
White alone, non-Hispanic	5.7	5.7	5.6	5.1
Black alone, non-Hispanic	4.4	4.5	4.5	5.0
American Indian and Alaska Native alone	20.5	24.2	22.3	20.7
Asian alone	67.1	66.6	64.4	63.5
Native Hawaiian and Other Pacific Islander alone	29.8	36.9	31.5	26.0
Hispanic [1]	68.6	68.7	67.8	67.6
Region: [2]				
Northeast	19.1	18.7	18.4	19.0
Midwest	9.5	9.9	10.0	9.9
South	14.6	15.1	15.4	15.7
West	31.0	31.1	31.3	31.0
Living in linguistically isolated household [3] (mil.)	2.4	2.6	2.6	2.8
Percent of children 5 to 17 years old	4.6	4.9	4.9	5.3
Children who speak another language at home and have difficulty speaking English (mil) [4]	2.9	2.8	2.8	2.9
Percent of children 5 to 17 years old	5.5	5.4	5.3	5.4
Race and Hispanic origin:				
White alone, non-Hispanic	1.3	1.4	1.3	1.4
Black alone, non-Hispanic	1.2	1.0	1.2	1.3
American Indian and Alaska Native alone	4.6	4.4	4.4	3.8
Asian alone	19.8	20.5	18.7	17.5
Native Hawaiian and Other Pacific Islander alone	10.3	8.4	6.3	6.2
Hispanic [1]	22.8	21.3	20.5	20.9
Region: [2]				
Northeast	5.0	5.1	5.0	5.5
Midwest	2.8	2.9	3.0	3.2
South	4.4	4.1	4.3	4.7
West	10.0	9.7	9.0	8.7

[1] Persons of Hispanic origin may be of any race. [2] For composition of regions, see map, inside front cover. [3] No person in the household aged 14 or over speaks English at least "very well." [4] Children who speak English less than "very well".

Source: Federal Interagency Forum on Child and Family Statistics, *America's Children: Key National Indicators of Well-Being*, 2005. See Internet site <http://www.childstats.gov/americaschildren/>.

Education 151

Table 223. Preprimary School Enrollment—Summary: 1970 to 2003

[As of October. Civilian noninstitutional population (10,949 represents 10,949,000). Includes public and nonpublic nursery school and kindergarten programs. Excludes 5-year olds enrolled in elementary school. Based on Current Population Survey; see text, Section 1, and Appendix III]

Item	1970	1975	1980	1985	1990	1995	2000	2002	2003
NUMBER OF CHILDREN (1,000)									
Population, 3 to 5 years old.......	10,949	10,183	9,284	10,733	11,207	12,518	11,858	11,481	12,204
Total enrolled [1].............	4,104	4,954	4,878	5,865	6,659	7,739	7,592	7,504	7,921
Nursery....................	1,094	1,745	1,981	2,477	3,378	4,331	4,326	4,423	4,859
Public...................	332	570	628	846	1,202	1,950	2,146	2,205	2,512
Private.................	762	1,174	1,353	1,631	2,177	2,381	2,180	2,218	2,347
Kindergarten.............	3,010	3,211	2,897	3,388	3,281	3,408	3,266	3,081	3,062
Public.................	2,498	2,682	2,438	2,847	2,767	2,799	2,701	2,551	2,539
Private................	511	528	459	541	513	608	565	530	523
White [2]...................	3,443	4,105	3,994	4,757	5,389	6,144	5,861	5,799	6,204
Black [2]...................	586	731	725	919	964	1,236	1,265	1,239	1,156
Hispanic [3].................	(NA)	(NA)	370	496	642	1,040	1,155	1,263	1,320
3 years old................	454	683	857	1,035	1,205	1,489	1,540	1,619	1,806
4 years old................	1,007	1,418	1,423	1,765	2,086	2,553	2,556	2,568	2,785
5 years old................	2,643	2,852	2,598	3,065	3,367	3,697	3,496	3,317	3,331
ENROLLMENT RATE									
Total enrolled [1].............	37.5	48.6	52.5	54.6	59.4	61.8	64.0	65.4	64.9
White [2]...................	37.8	48.6	52.7	54.7	59.7	63.0	63.2	65.0	65.8
Black [2]...................	34.9	48.1	51.8	55.8	57.8	58.9	68.5	67.7	62.7
Hispanic [3].................	(NA)	(NA)	43.3	43.3	49.0	51.1	52.6	56.1	54.2
3 years old................	12.9	21.5	27.3	28.8	32.6	35.9	39.2	42.4	42.4
4 years old................	27.8	40.5	46.3	49.1	56.0	61.6	64.9	66.6	68.3
5 years old................	69.3	81.3	84.7	86.5	88.8	87.5	87.6	87.2	86.1

NA Not available.   [1] Includes races not shown separately.   [2] Beginning 2003 for persons who selected this race group only. See footnote 2, Table 214.   [3] Persons of Hispanic origin may be of any race. The method of identifying Hispanic children was changed in 1980 from allocation based on status of mother to status reported for each child. The number of Hispanic children using the new method is larger.

Source: U.S. Census Bureau, Current Population Reports, PPL-148; and earlier PPL and P-20 reports; and data published on the Internet. See Internet site <http://www.census.gov/population/www/socdemo/school.html>.

Table 224. Children's School Readiness Skills: 1993 and 2001

[In percent. For children 3 to 5 years old not yet enrolled in kindergarden. Based on the School Readiness Surey of the National Household Education Survey Program; see source for details. See also Table 221]

Characteristic	Recognizes all letters		Counts to 20 or higher		Writes name		Reads or pretends to read storybooks		Has 3 to 4 skills	
	1993	2001	1993	2001	1993	2001	1993	2001	1993	2001
Total..............	21	23	52	57	50	53	72	71	35	39
Age:										
3 years old	11	12	37	39	22	23	66	64	15	16
4 years old	28	29	62	68	70	73	75	76	49	53
5 years old	36	38	78	82	84	89	81	80	65	71
Sex:										
Male...............	19	19	49	52	47	47	68	68	32	34
Female.............	23	27	56	61	53	58	76	74	39	43
Race/ethnicity:										
White, non-Hispanic	23	24	56	61	52	55	76	78	39	43
Black, non-Hispanic......	18	23	53	57	45	52	63	64	31	35
Hispanic	10	14	32	39	42	43	59	52	22	22
Other	22	35	49	61	52	57	70	64	36	48
Mother's employment status:										
Employed	23	23	57	60	52	56	75	74	39	42
Unemployed	17	17	41	47	46	47	67	55	29	28
Not in the labor force.....	18	22	49	52	47	48	68	67	32	34
Family type:										
Two parents..........	22	24	54	58	51	54	74	74	37	41
None or one parent......	18	17	49	51	47	48	65	61	31	31
Poverty status:										
Above threshold	24	25	57	61	53	55	74	75	40	44
Below threshold	12	14	41	43	41	45	64	57	23	23

Source: U.S. National Center for Education Statistics, Home Literacy Activities and Signs of Children's Emerging Literacy, 1993 and 1999, NCES 2000-026, November 1999; and unpublished data. See Internet site <http://nces.ed.gov/pubsearch /getpubcats.asp?sid=004>.

Table 225. **Type of School Attended By Student and Household Characteristics: 1993 and 2003**

[In percent, except total in thousands (33,900 represent 33,900,000. For students in grades 1 to 12. Includes homeschooled students enrolled in public or private school, 9 or more hours per week. Based on the Parent and Family Involvement Survey of the National Household Education Survey Program; see source and Appendix III for details]

Characteristic	Public				Private			
	Assigned		Chosen		Church-related		Not church-related	
	1993	2003	1993	2003	1993	2003	1993	2003
Total students (1,000)	33,900	35,300	4,700	7,400	3,200	4,000	700	1,100
Percent distribution	79.9	73.9	11.0	15.4	7.5	8.4	1.6	2.4
Grade level:								
1 to 5	78.6	71.6	11.6	16.6	8.3	9.7	1.5	2.1
6 to 8	81.3	75.0	9.9	14.5	7.4	7.9	1.5	2.5
9 to 12.	80.6	76.0	11.2	14.4	6.5	6.9	1.8	2.6
Race/ethnicity:								
White, non-Hispanic	81.0	74.7	8.6	12.9	8.6	9.7	1.8	2.7
Black, non-Hospanic.	77.2	68.1	18.6	24.0	3.4	5.7	0.8	2.2
Other, non-Hospanic	73.0	70.1	14.9	19.3	9.0	7.2	3.1	3.4
Hispanic [1].	79.2	77.9	13.7	15.1	6.4	6.2	0.7	0.8
Family type:								
Two-parent household	80.1	73.6	9.3	14.1	8.8	9.7	1.8	2.6
One-parent household	78.9	74.5	15.2	18.3	4.8	5.3	1.1	1.9
Nonparent guardians	83.7	74.7	13.5	20.0	2.1	3.7	0.7	1.5
Parents' education:								
Less than high school.	83.6	77.6	13.7	19.7	2.4	2.1	0.2	0.6
High school diploma								
or equivalent	83.5	79.3	11.4	15.8	4.6	3.7	0.5	.1.2
Some college, including								
vocational/technical	79.8	75.8	11.1	15.8	7.7	6.7	1.4	1.7
Bachelor's degree	75.8	69.0	9.2	13.7	12.5	14.5	2.6	2.8
Graduate/professional degree	72.7	66.2	9.8	14.1	13.1	14.1	4.4	5.6
Region: [2]								
Northeast	77.8	73.5	9.3	11.6	10.5	11.0	2.4	3.9
South	82.0	75.9	10.9	15.8	5.4	6.1	1.7	2.1
Midwest	79.6	71.6	10.4	14.4	9.2	12.1	·0.8	1.9
West	78.7	73.6	13.4	18.6	6.5	5.8	1.5	2.0

[1] Persons of Hispanic origin may be of any race.   [2] For composition of regions see map, inside front cover.

Source: U.S. National Center for Education Statistics, *Condition of Education, 2004*, NCES 2004-077, June 2004.

Table 226. **Public Charter and Traditional Schools—Selected Characteristics: 1999-2000**

[45,100 represents 45,100,000. A public charter school is a public school that, in accordance with an enabling state statute, has been granted a charter exempting it from selected state and local rules and regulations. All schools open as public charter schools during 1998-99 and still open in the 1999-2000 school year were surveyed. Based in the School and Staffing Survey; see source for details]

Characteristic	All schools		Elementary		Secondary		Combined	
	Tradi-tional	Public charter	Tradi-tional	Public charter	Tradi-tional	Public charter	Tradi-tional	Public charter
Number of schools	83,725	1,010	59,900	586	20,651	235	3,174	190
Enrollment (1,000)	45,100	267	29,050	159	15,201	58	848	50
PERCENT DISTRIBUTION OF STUDENTS								
Race/ethnicity	100.0	100.0	100.0	100.0	100.0	100.0	100.0	100.0
White, non-Hispanic	63.2	46.4	61.4	44.7	66.4	42.0	68.6	57.0
Black, non-Hispanic.	16.9	27.3	18.0	31.0	14.9	23.4	17.1	19.9
Hispanic [1]	14.9	20.8	15.8	19.5	13.6	28.9	9.1	15.5
Asian/Pacific Islander.	3.7	3.2	3.6	3.3	4.1	2.8	1.7	3.5
American Indian/Alaskan Native. . . .	1.2	2.3	1.2	1.5	1.1	3.0	3.4	4.1
PERCENT DISTRIBUTION OF SCHOOLS								
Size of enrollment	100.0	100.0	100.0	100.0	100.0	100.0	100.0	100.0
Less than 300	28.5	72.2	25.5	69.3	31.1	80.2	69.9	71.4
300 to 599.	39.4	16.5	46.4	18.6	22.6	10.9	16.5	16.9
600 to 999.	21.8	8.4	23.4	9.9	19.2	3.9	10.3	9.2
1,000 or more	10.2	2.9	4.8	2.1	27.1	4.9	3.4	2.5
Percent minority enrollment	100.0	100.0	100.0	100.0	100.0	100.0	100.0	100.0
Less than 10.0	38.2	17.8	36.8	18.5	43.3	14.3	32.0	20.1
10.0 to 24.9	17.4	19.5	17.1	19.0	19.0	18.2	12.2	22.9
25.0 to 49.9	16.5	14.6	16.9	13.7	15.5	14.3	15.4	17.5
50.0 to 74.9	11.6	13.0	12.1	11.9	9.9	17.8	15.0	10.4
75.0 or more	16.3	35.1	17.1	36.9	12.4	35.3	25.4	29.1
Percent of students eligible for free or reduced-price lunch	100.0	100.0	100.0	100.0	100.0	100.0	100.0	100.0
Less than 15.0	23.4	29.8	20.4	30.2	32.9	28.4	17.4	30.3
15.0 to 29.9	19.7	11.4	19.2	11.6	23.0	11.9	8.4	10.5
30.0 to 49.9	21.5	16.7	22.0	16.7	19.7	17.1	23.6	16.5
50.0 to 74.9	18.6	16.7	20.2	14.8	14.1	19.8	19.4	19.0
75.0 or more	16.7	25.3	18.2	26.8	10.3	22.8	31.3	23.7

[1] Persons of Hispanic origin maybe of any race.

Source: U.S. National Center for Education Statistics, *Digest Education Statistics, 2002*.

Education 153

Table 227. **Students Who Are Homeschooled by Selected Characteristics: 2003**

[As of spring. (50,707 represents 50,707,000). For students 5 to 17 with a grade equivalent of K-12. Homeschoolers are students whose parents reported them to be schooled at home instead of a public or private school. Excludes students who were enrolled in school for more than 25 hours a week or were homeschooled due to a temporary illness. Based on the Parent and Family Involvement Survey of the National Household Education Surveys Program; see source and Appendix III for details]

Characteristic	Number of students			Percent distribution		
	Total (1,000)	Home-schooled (1,000)	Percent home-schooled	All students	Home-schooled	Non-home-schooled
Total	50,707	1,096	2.2	100.0	100.0	100.0
Grade equivalent: [1]						
K-5.	24,269	472	1.9	47.9	43.3	48.0
Kindergarten.	3,643	98	2.7	7.2	9.0	7.2
Grades 1 to 3	12,098	214	1.8	23.9	19.7	24.0
Grades 4 to 5	8,528	160	1.9	16.8	14.7	16.9
Grades 6 to 8.	12,472	302	2.4	24.6	27.8	24.5
Grades 9 to 12	13,958	315	2.3	27.5	28.9	27.5
Sex:						
Male.	25,819	569	2.2	50.9	51.9	50.9
Female	24,888	527	2.1	49.1	48.1	49.1
Race/ethnicity:						
White, non-Hispanic.	31,584	843	2.7	62.3	77.0	62.0
Black, non-Hispanic.	7,985	103	1.3	15.7	9.4	15.9
Hispanic [2]	8,075	59	0.7	15.9	5.3	16.2
Other [2]	3,063	91	3.0	6.0	8.3	6.0
Number of children in the household:						
One child.	8,005	110	1.4	15.8	10.1	16.0
Two children.	20,510	306	1.5	40.4	28.0	40.8
Three or more children.	22,192	679	3.1	43.8	62.0	43.3
Number of parents in the household:						
Two parents	35,936	886	2.5	70.9	80.8	70.7
One parent.	13,260	196	1.5	26.2	17.9	26.3
Nonparental guardians	1,511	14	0.9	3.0	1.3	3.0
Parents' participation in the labor force:						
Two parents-one in labor force.	10,545	594	5.6	20.8	54.2	20.1
Two parents-both in labor force	25,108	274	1.1	49.5	25.0	50.1
One parent in labor force	12,045	174	1.4	23.8	15.9	23.9
No parent in labor force	3,008	54	1.8	5.9	4.9	6.0
Household income:						
$25,000 or less.	12,375	283	2.3	24.4	25.8	24.4
$25,001 to 50,000	13,220	311	2.4	26.1	28.4	26.0
$50,001 to 75,000	10,944	264	2.4	21.6	24.1	21.6
$75,001 or more	14,167	238	1.7	27.9	21.7	28.0
Parents' highest educational attainment:						
High school diploma or less	16,106	269	1.7	31.8	24.5	31.9
Voc/tech degree or some college	16,068	338	2.1	31.7	30.8	31.7
Bachelor's degree	9,798	274	2.8	19.3	25.0	19.2
Graduate/professional school.	8,734	215	2.5	17.2	19.6	17.2

[1] Excludes those ungraded. [2] Persons of Hispanic origin maybe of any race.

Source: U.S. National Center for Education Statistics, Parent and Family Involvement in Education Survey of the 2003 National Household Education Surveys Porgram, unpublished data.

Table 228. **Public Elementary and Secondary Schools by Type and Size of School: 2002–2003**

[Enrollment in thousands (47,965 represents 47,965,000). Data reported by schools, rather than school districts. Based on the Common Core of Data Survey; see source for details]

Enrollment size of school	Number of schools					Enrollment [1]				
	Total	Elemen-tary [2]	Second-ary [3]	Com-bined [4]	Other [5]	Total	Elemen-tary [2]	Second-ary [3]	Com-bined [4]	Other [5]
Total	95,615	66,901	22,398	5,552	764	47,965	31,082	15,504	1,291	88
PERCENT										
Total	100.00	100.00	100.00	100.00	100.00	100.00	100.00	100.00	100.00	100.00
Under 100 students.	14.11	8.59	19.42	52.29	63.87	0.96	0.66	1.03	6.52	16.42
100 to 199 students	9.36	8.42	10.68	14.27	17.80	2.79	2.75	2.25	8.97	21.60
200 to 299 students	11.21	12.61	7.94	7.78	8.77	5.63	6.87	2.85	8.18	19.22
300 to 399 students	12.95	15.41	7.53	6.48	3.27	9.02	11.61	3.79	9.58	9.86
400 to 499 students	12.58	15.55	6.05	4.45	3.40	11.25	15.02	3.91	8.55	13.08
500 to 599 students	10.49	12.81	5.67	3.35	1.18	11.45	15.08	4.49	7.85	5.58
600 to 699 students	7.83	9.15	5.30	3.15	0.39	10.10	12.74	4.96	8.73	2.23
700 to 799 students	5.34	5.99	4.40	1.96	0.52	7.94	9.62	4.75	6.28	3.53
800 to 999 students	6.64	6.73	7.62	2.54	0.26	11.76	12.81	9.86	9.70	1.99
1,000 to 1,499 students . . .	5.82	4.08	12.07	2.32	0.39	13.86	10.25	21.29	12.06	4.17
1,500 to 1,999 students . . .	2.12	0.54	7.21	0.88	-	7.25	1.93	18.00	6.42	-
2,000 to 2,999 students . . .	1.26	0.12	4.94	0.31	0.13	5.90	0.58	16.80	3.08	2.33
3,000 or more students . . .	0.29	0.01	1.17	0.22	-	2.10	0.08	6.01	4.07	-
Average enrollment	(X)	(X)	(X)	(X)	(X)	502	465	692	233	115

- Represents zero. X Not applicable. [1] Data are approximations only and are for those schools reporting enrollment. [2] Includes schools beginning with grade 6 or below and with no grade higher than 8. [3] Includes schools with no grade lower than 7. [4] Includes schools with both elementary and secondary grades. [5] Includes special education, alternative, and other schools not classified by grade span.

Source: U.S. National Center for Education Statistics, *Digest of Education Statistics*, annual.

154 Education

Table 229. Public Elementary and Secondary Schools—Summary: 1980 to 2004

[For school year ending in year shown, except as indicated (48,041 represents 48,041,000). Data are estimates]

Item	Unit	1980	1985	1990	1995	2000	2003	2004
School districts, total.	Number. . .	16,044	15,812	15,552	14,947	15,403	15,732	15,695
ENROLLMENT								
Population 5-17 years old [1]	1,000	48,041	44,787	44,949	48,855	52,811	53,316	53,259
Percent of resident population. . . .	Percent . . .	21.4	19.0	18.2	18.6	18.9	18.5	18.3
Fall enrollment [2].	1,000	41,778	39,354	40,527	43,898	46,581	47,804	48,133
Percent of population 5-17 years old	Percent . . .	87.0	87.9	90.2	89.9	88.2	89.7	90.4
Elementary [3]	1,000	24,397	23,830	26,253	28,148	29,245	29,590	29,628
Secondary [4].	1,000	17,381	15,524	14,274	15,750	17,336	18,215	18,505
Average daily attendance (ADA)	1,000	38,411	36,530	37,573	40,792	43,269	44,674	45,082
High school graduates	1,000	2,762	2,424	2,327	2,282	2,540	2,706	2,772
INSTRUCTIONAL STAFF								
Total [5]	1,000	2,521	2,473	2,685	2,919	3,273	3,448	3,469
Classroom teachers.	1,000	2,211	2,175	2,362	2,565	2,891	3,030	3,044
Average salaries:								
Instructional staff.	Dollar	16,715	24,666	32,638	38,349	43,837	47,462	48,402
Classroom teachers.	Dollar	15,970	23,600	31,367	36,675	41,807	45,776	46,752
REVENUES								
Revenue receipts	Mil. dol. . . .	97,635	141,013	208,656	273,255	369,754	433,904	452,795
Federal	Mil. dol. . . .	9,020	9,533	13,184	18,764	26,346	35,598	38,856
State	Mil. dol. . . .	47,929	69,107	100,787	129,958	183,986	212,965	217,140
Local	Mil. dol. . . .	40,686	62,373	94,685	124,533	159,421	185,340	196,798
Percent of total:								
Federal	Percent . . .	9.2	6.8	6.3	6.9	7.1	8.2	8.6
State	Percent . . .	49.1	49.0	48.3	47.6	49.8	49.1	48.0
Local	Percent . . .	41.7	44.2	45.4	45.6	43.1	42.7	43.5
EXPENDITURES								
Total	Mil. dol. . . .	96,105	139,382	209,698	276,584	374,782	451,706	471,965
Current expenditures								
(day schools)	Mil. dol. . . .	85,661	127,230	186,583	242,995	320,954	385,557	397,015
Other current expenditures [6]	Mil. dol. . . .	1,859	2,109	3,341	5,564	6,618	8,273	8,309
Capital outlay	Mil. dol. . . .	6,504	7,529	16,012	21,646	37,552	44,577	47,707
Interest on school debt	Mil. dol. . . .	2,081	2,514	3,762	6,379	9,659	13,299	18,934
Percent of total:								
Current expenditures								
(day schools)	Percent . . .	89.1	91.3	89.0	87.9	85.6	85.4	84.1
Other current expenditures [6]	Percent . . .	1.9	1.5	1.6	2.0	1.8	1.8	1.8
Capital outlay	Percent . . .	6.8	5.4	7.6	7.8	10.0	9.9	10.1
Interest on school debt	Percent . . .	2.2	1.8	1.8	2.3	2.6	2.9	4.0
In current dollars:								
Revenue receipts per pupil enrolled	Dollar	2,337	3,583	5,149	6,225	7,938	9,077	9,407
Current expenditures per pupil enrolled	Dollar	2,050	3,233	4,604	5,535	6,890	8.065	8,248
In constant (2004) dollars: [7]								
Revenue receipts per pupil enrolled	Dollar	5,605	6,303	7,544	7,702	8,726	9,276	9,407
Current expenditures per pupil enrolled	Dollar	4,917	5,687	6,746	6,849	7,574	8,242	8,248

[1] Estimated resident population as of July 1 of the previous year, except 1980, 1990, and 2000 population enumerated as of April 1. Estimates reflect revisions based on the 2000 Census of Population. [2] Fall enrollment of the previous year. [3] Kindergarten through grade 6. [4] Grades 7 through 12. [5] Full-time equivalent. [6] Current expenses for summer schools, adult education, post-high school vocational education, personnel retraining, etc., when operated by local school districts and not part of regular public elementary and secondary day-school program. [7] Compiled by U.S. Census Bureau. Deflated by the Consumer Price Index, all urban consumers (for school year July through June) supplied by U.S. National Center for Education Statistics.

Source: Except as noted, National Education Association, Washington, DC, Estimates of School Statistics Database (copyright).

Education 155

Table 230. **Public Elementary and Secondary Schools and Enrollment—States: 2002–2003**

[For schools with membership (48,202 represents 48,202,000). Based on the Common Core of Data Program; see source for details]

State	Total number of schools with member- ship	Total number of students (1,000)	Type of school										
			Regular		Special education [1]		Vocational education [2]		Alternative education [3]			
			Number of schools	Percent of students	Number of schools	Percent of students	Number of schools	Percent of students	Number of schools	Percent of students
Total.......	92,330	48,202	85,447	98	1,798	0.4	320	0.3	4,765	1.1
Alabama.......	1,391	740	1,344	100	18	0.1	1	(Z)	28	0.3
Alaska	500	134	470	98	2	0.2	1	(Z)	27	1.8
Arizona........	1,801	938	1,694	96	10	(Z)	45	2.9	52	1.3
Arkansas	1,129	451	1,120	100	4	0.1	1	(Z)	4	(Z)
California	9,087	6,356	7,783	97	126	0.5	-	-	1,178	2.7
Colorado........	1,662	752	1,562	98	15	0.1	2	(Z)	83	1.4
Connecticut.....	1,087	570	996	97	22	0.6	17	2.0	52	0.6
Delaware	201	116	172	93	15	1.3	5	4.8	9	1.3
District of Columbia.....	203	76	181	93	13	4.3	2	1.3	7	1.8
Florida	3,382	2,540	3,048	98	121	0.6	25	0.1	188	0.9
Georgia	2,003	1,496	1,972	100	2	(Z)	-	-	29	0.5
Hawaii.........	283	184	279	100	3	0.1	-	-	1	0.1
Idaho.........	660	249	593	98	5	0.1	-	-	62	1.8
Illinois	4,271	2,084	3,918	98	241	1.2	-	-	112	0.7
Indiana........	1,909	1,004	1,845	99	17	0.2	4	0.1	43	0.4
Iowa	1,500	482	1,452	99	11	0.2	-	-	37	0.9
Kansas........	1,431	471	1,421	100	5	(Z)	-	-	5	0.1
Kentucky	1,381	661	1,230	99	9	0.1	1	(Z)	141	1.2
Louisiana	1,522	730	1,387	98	35	0.2	-	-	100	1.7
Maine.........	672	204	670	100	2	(Z)	-	-	-	-
Maryland	1,359	867	1,250	97	50	0.9	11	1.0	48	1.1
Massachusetts....	1,894	983	1,823	96	1	(Z)	41	3.3	29	0.3
Michigan........	3,871	1,785	3,490	97	155	1.4	16	0.1	210	1.4
Minnesota.......	2,182	847	1,611	97	232	1.3	-	-	339	2.0
Mississippi	887	493	887	100	-	-	-	-	-	-
Missouri	2,286	924	2,167	99	55	0.4	-	-	64	0.3
Montana.......	865	150	860	100	2	(Z)	-	-	3	0.1
Nebraska.......	1,250	285	1,205	99	45	0.6	-	-	-	-
Nevada	527	369	484	98	10	0.3	2	0.5	31	0.9
New Hampshire...	473	208	473	100	-	-	-	-	-	-
New Jersey......	2,414	1,367	2,278	98	80	0.7	39	1.2	17	0.4
New Mexico......	801	320	732	97	16	0.7	-	-	53	1.9
New York	4,470	2,888	4,173	97	76	0.7	25	1.2	196	1.1
North Carolina ...	2,245	1,336	2,151	99	19	0.2	1	(Z)	74	0.4
North Dakota....	528	104	528	100	-	-	-	-	-	-
Ohio	3,815	1,838	3,763	100	32	0.2	10	0.1	10	0.1
Oklahoma.......	1,806	625	1,806	100	-	-	-	-	-	-
Oregon........	1,262	554	1,181	98	10	0.1	-	-	71	1.4
Pennsylvania.....	3,186	1,817	3,145	98	12	0.9	16	0.7	13	0.1
Rhode Island.....	326	159	312	98	4	0.1	5	0.9	5	0.7
South Carolina ...	1,081	695	1,055	100	6	0.1	-	-	20	0.3
South Dakota	738	128	716	99	6	0.1	-	-	16	0.7
Tennessee	1,628	928	1,589	100	13	0.1	5	0.1	21	0.1
Texas.........	7,757	4,260	6,784	98	125	0.1	29	(Z)	819	1.6
Utah	803	489	726	98	21	0.4	-	-	56	1.5
Vermont........	359	100	315	98	42	1.5	-	-	2	0.1
Virginia........	1,846	1,177	1,805	99	10	0.1	-	-	31	0.5
Washington......	2,207	1,015	1,863	96	82	0.3	10	0.1	252	3.1
West Virginia.....	768	282	737	100	7	0.1	5	(Z)	19	0.3
Wisconsin.......	2,232	881	2,039	97	11	0.1	1	(Z)	181	2.6
Wyoming	389	88	362	98	-	-	-	-	27	2.1

- Represents zero. Z Less than 0.05 percent. [1] Focuses on special education with materials and instructional approaches adapted to meet the students' needs. [2] Focuses on vocational, technical, or career education and provides education and training in at least one semi-skilled or technical occupation. [3] Addresses the needs of students that typically cannot be met in the regular school setting, and provides nontraditional education.

Source: U.S. National Center for Education Statistics, *Public Elementary and Secondary Staff, Schools and School Districts: School Year 2002–03*, NCES 2005-314, February 2005.

Table 231. **Selected Statistics for the Largest Public School Districts: 2002-2003**

[For the 50 largest districts by enrollment size. Based on reports from state educatuion agencies in the spring 2003. Data from the Common Core Data Program; see source for details. School district boundaries are not necessarily the same as city or county boundaries]

School district	City	County	Number of students [1]	Number of full-time equivalent (FTE) teachers	Number of 2001-02 com- pleters [2]	Num- ber of schools
New York City Public Schools, NY.........	Brooklyn	Kings	1,077,381	65,803	39,539	1,429
Los Angeles Unified, CA	Los Angeles	Los Angeles	746,852	35,483	27,720	677
Puerto Rico Department of Education, PR ...	San Juan	San Juan	596,502	42,369	32,895	1,532
City of Chicago School District, IL.........	Chicago	Cook	436,048	24,584	15,653	608
Dade County School District, FL...........	Miami	Miami-Dade	373,395	18,656	18,117	370
Broward County School District, FL........	Fort Lauderdale	Broward	267,925	13,264	12,192	259
Clark County School District, NV..........	Las Vegas	Clark	256,574	13,070	10,734	282
Houston Independent School District, TX	Houston	Harris	212,099	12,386	7,945	308
Philadelphia City School District, PA	Philadelphia	Philadelphia	192,683	9,866	8,559	262
Hawaii Department of Education, HI	Honolulu	Honolulu	183,829	10,973	10,669	284
Hillsborough County School District, FL	Tampa	Hillsborough	175,454	10,499	8,118	229
Detroit City School District, MI	Detroit	Wayne	173,742	5,683	5,540	273
Palm Beach County School District, FL	West Palm Beach	Palm Beach	164,896	8,826	8,282	208
Dallas Independent School District, TX......	Dallas	Dallas	163,347	10,941	6,532	228
Fairfax County Public Schools, VA.........	Fairfax	Fairfax	162,585	13,947	10,649	202
Orange County School District, FL.........	Orlando	Orange	158,718	9,128	7,686	188
San Diego Unified, CA	San Diego	San Diego	140,753	7,495	6,504	185
Montgomery County Public Schools, MD	Rockville	Montgomery	138,983	9,015	8,373	194
Prince George's County Pub Schools, MD ...	Upper Marlboro	Prince George's	135,439	8,365	7,661	204
Duval County School District, FL........	Jacksonville	Duval	128,126	6,620	5,295	181
Gwinnett School District County, GA	Lawrenceville	Gwinnett	122,570	8,048	6,390	89
Memphis City School District, TN	Memphis	Shelby	118,039	7,204	4,017	178
Pinellas County School District, FL	Largo	Pinellas	114,772	6,516	5,647	172
Charlotte-Mecklenburg Schools, NC........	Charlotte	Mecklenburg	109,767	7,262	5,195	134
Baltimore County Public Schools, MD	Towson	Baltimore	108,297	7,078	6,917	170
Wake County Schools, NC...............	Raleigh	Wake	104,836	6,789	5,443	123
Cobb County School District, GA..........	Marietta	Cobb	100,389	6,807	5,570	102
DeKalb County School District, GA	Decatur	DeKalb	97,967	6,595	4,777	139
Milwaukee School District, WI............	Milwaukee	Milwaukee	97,293	6,495	3,912	218
Long Beach Unified, CA	Long Beach	Los Angeles	97,212	4,521	4,664	89
Baltimore City Public School System, MD....	Baltimore	Baltimore City	96,230	6,530	4,529	184
Jefferson County, KY	Louisville	Jefferson	95,651	5,329	4,998	175
Albuquerque Public Schools, NM	Albuquerque	Bernalillo	88,120	5,968	4,708	144
Jefferson County, CO	Golden	Jefferson	87,925	4,857	5,411	169
Polk County School District, FL...........	Bartow	Polk	82,179	4,801	4,096	148
Fresno Unified, CA...................	Fresno	Fresno	81,222	3,938	3,721	103
Fort Worth Independent School District, TX..	Fort Worth	Tarrant	81,081	4,967	3,222	146
Austin Independent School District, TX.....	Austin	Travis	78,608	5,382	3,705	111
Virginia Beach City Public Schools, VA......	Virginia Beach	Virginia Beach	75,902	5,339	4,558	85
Mesa Unified District, AZ...............	Mesa	Maricopa	75,269	3,682	4,053	91
Anne Arundel County Public Schools, MD....	Annapolis	Anne Arundel	74,787	4,511	4,466	119
Jordan School District, UT..............	Sandy	Salt Lake	73,808	3,120	4,916	80
Brevard County School District, FL	Viera	Brevard	72,601	4,079	3,671	110
Denver County, CO	Denver	Denver	71,972	4,472	2,612	144
Cleveland Municipal School District, OH.....	Cleveland	Cuyahoga	71,616	6,671	2,443	129
Fulton County School District, GA.........	Atlanta	Fulton	71,372	4,861	3,559	81
Granite School District, UT..............	Salt Lake City	Salt Lake	71,181	3,438	4,188	96
Cypress-Fairbanks Independent School District, TX	Houston	Harris	71,165	4,603	3,938	59
Orleans Parish School Board, LA	New Orleans	Orleans	70,246	4,236	3,648	128
North Side Independent School District, TX...	San Antonio	Bexar	69,409	4,574	3,928	89

[1] Number of students receiving educational services from the school district. [2] Includes high school diploma recipients and other completers (for example certificates of attendance) but does not include high school equivalents (GEDs).

Source: U.S. National Center for Education Statistics, Common Core of Data (CCD) Local Education Agency Universe, 2002-03, special tabulation.

Education 157

Table 232. **Public Elementary and Secondary School Enrollment by State: 1980 to 2002**

[In thousands (27,647 represents 27,647,000), except rate. As of fall. Includes unclassified students. Based on survey of state education agencies; see source for details]

State	Enrollment								Enrollment rate [1]			
	Prekindergarten through grade 8				Grades 9 through 12							
	1980	1990	2000	2002, prel.	1980	1990	2000	2002, prel.	1980	1990	2000	2002, prel.
United States. . .	27,647	29,878	33,688	34,135	13,231	11,338	13,515	14,067	86.2	91.2	88.8	90.4
Alabama	528	527	539	534	231	195	201	206	87.6	93.2	89.6	90.8
Alaska	60	85	94	94	26	29	39	40	94.0	97.4	93.4	94.9
Arizona	357	479	641	660	157	161	237	277	88.9	93.3	88.4	88.6
Arkansas.	310	314	318	319	138	123	132	132	90.3	95.8	90.2	90.6
California.	2,730	3,615	4,408	4,529	1,347	1,336	1,733	1,828	87.1	92.6	90.5	92.6
Colorado.	374	420	517	534	172	154	208	217	92.2	94.6	89.7	91.0
Connecticut	364	347	406	406	168	122	156	164	83.3	90.2	90.7	91.3
Delaware.	62	73	81	82	37	27	34	34	79.5	87.2	80.3	81.6
District of Columbia.	71	61	54	59	29	19	15	17	91.8	100.6	84.0	99.2
Florida	1,042	1,370	1,760	1,809	468	492	675	731	84.4	92.6	89.7	89.7
Georgia	742	849	1,060	1,089	327	303	385	407	86.8	93.7	91.4	92.1
Hawaii	110	123	132	131	55	49	52	53	83.4	87.4	84.8	86.3
Idaho	144	160	170	173	59	61	75	75	95.4	96.9	90.3	91.5
Illinois.	1,335	1,310	1,474	1,488	649	512	575	597	82.6	86.9	86.4	88.5
Indiana	708	676	703	714	347	279	286	290	88.0	90.4	85.8	85.9
Iowa.	351	345	334	326	183	139	161	156	88.4	92.1	91.3	92.6
Kansas.	283	320	323	322	133	117	147	149	88.7	92.5	90.0	92.2
Kentucky.	464	459	471	477	206	177	194	184	83.7	90.5	91.4	91.4
Louisiana	544	586	547	537	234	199	197	194	80.2	88.1	82.6	84.2
Maine.	153	155	146	142	70	60	61	63	91.6	96.5	90.3	91.6
Maryland.	493	527	609	610	258	188	244	256	83.9	89.1	84.9	85.6
Massachusetts	676	604	703	701	346	230	273	282	88.6	88.8	88.5	90.2
Michigan	1,227	1,145	1,222	1,254	570	440	498	531	86.9	90.3	89.5	93.7
Minnesota	482	546	578	568	272	211	277	279	87.2	91.3	89.5	90.6
Mississippi.	330	372	364	360	147	131	134	132	79.6	91.3	87.5	88.9
Missouri	567	588	645	653	277	228	268	272	83.8	86.5	86.5	88.9
Montana	106	111	105	101	50	42	50	49	92.9	94.1	89.1	90.6
Nebraska	189	198	195	195	91	76	91	90	86.6	88.7	86.2	88.1
Nevada	101	150	251	271	49	51	90	99	93.4	98.6	91.8	90.8
New Hampshire . . .	112	126	147	144	55	46	61	64	85.3	89.1	89.1	88.7
New Jersey	820	784	968	979	426	306	346	389	81.5	85.9	85.9	87.9
New Mexico.	186	208	225	224	85	94	95	96	89.5	94.4	85.0	86.5
New York	1,838	1,828	2,029	2,017	1,033	770	853	871	80.8	86.6	83.6	85.8
North Carolina	786	783	945	964	343	304	348	372	90.1	94.8	90.4	90.3
North Dakota	77	85	72	69	40	33	37	35	85.9	92.6	90.9	92.9
Ohio.	1,312	1,258	1,294	1,284	645	514	541	554	84.8	88.0	86.1	87.8
Oklahoma	399	425	445	449	179	154	178	176	92.9	95.1	95.4	97.8
Oregon	319	340	379	382	145	132	167	172	88.5	90.6	87.5	88.2
Pennsylvania	1,231	1,172	1,258	1,242	678	496	556	575	80.4	83.5	82.8	84.6
Rhode Island	98	102	114	113	51	37	44	47	80.1	87.5	85.6	87.2
South Carolina	426	452	493	501	193	170	184	194	88.1	93.9	90.9	93.2
South Dakota	86	95	88	87	42	34	41	41	87.4	89.9	85.3	87.7
Tennessee.	602	598	668	674	252	226	241	254	87.8	93.5	88.8	91.4
Texas	2,049	2,511	2,943	3,080	851	872	1,117	1,180	92.4	98.4	94.9	97.0
Utah.	250	325	333	343	93	122	148	147	98.2	97.8	94.5	95.5
Vermont	66	71	70	68	29	25	32	32	87.9	94.3	90.5	92.5
Virginia	703	728	816	832	307	270	329	346	90.7	94.2	89.5	90.6
Washington	515	613	694	697	242	227	310	318	91.7	94.1	89.8	91.1
West Virginia	270	224	201	200	113	98	85	82	92.6	95.7	95.6	96.5
Wisconsin	528	566	595	592	303	232	285	290	82.1	86.1	86.0	87.9
Wyoming.	70	71	60	60	28	27	30	28	97.3	97.7	92.7	95.4

[1] Percent of persons 5-17 years old. Based on enumerated resident population as of April 1, 1980 and 1990, and estimated resident population as of July 1 for 2000 and 2002.

Source: U.S. National Center for Education Statistics, *Digest of Education Statistics*, annual.

Table 233. Public School Districts With Alternative Schools or Programs for at-Risk Students: 2000–2001

[For the school year. Alternative schools and programs are designed to address the needs of students that typically cannot be met in regular schools. The schools and programs in data shown here serve students who are typically at risk for educational failure (as indicated by poor grades or truancy, for example). Alternative schools are usually housed in a separate facility where students are removed from regular schools. Alternative programs are usually housed within regular schools. Based on the Fast Response Survey System; see source for details]

District characteristic	Percent of districts with schools or programs	Number of schools or programs			Percent of district students enrolled			
		One	Two	Three or more	Less than 1 percent	1 to 1.99 percent	2 to 2.99 percent	3 percent or more
Total	39	65	18	17	43	27	14	16
Metropolitan status: [1]								
Urban	66	33	15	52	36	30	17	16
Suburban.	41	63	19	18	49	26	12	13
Rural.	35	74	17	8	38	28	16	18
Enrollment size:								
Less that 2,500.	26	82	11	7	39	26	15	20
2,500 to 9,999	69	58	26	16	46	29	13	12
10,000 or more.	95	27	17	56	46	25	17	12
Percent minority enrollment:								
5 percent or less	26	75	15	10	49	26	11	14
6 to 20 percent	43	63	20	17	48	22	14	16
21 to 50 percent	51	63	16	22	38	32	18	12
More than 50 percent. . .	62	58	20	22	34	28	16	22
Poverty concentration:								
10 percent or less	31	68	15	16	56	24	10	10
11 to 20 percent	43	59	22	20	40	27	17	16
More than 20 percent. . .	45	71	15	14	38	29	15	18

[1] Urban: Primarily serves the central city of a Metropolitan Statistical Area (MSA); suburban: serves an MSA, but not primarily the central city; rural: does not serve an MSA.

Source: U.S. National Center for Education Statistics, *Public School Alternative Schools and Programs for Students At Risk of Education Failure 2000-01*, September 2002, NCES 2002-004.

Table 234. Public Elementary and Secondary School Enrollment by Grade: 1980 to 2002

[In thousands (40,877 represents 40,877,000). As of fall of year. Based on survey of state education agencies; see source for details]

Grade	1980	1985	1990	1994	1995	1996	1997	1998	1999	2000	2001	2002, prel.
Pupils enrolled.	40,877	39,422	41,217	44,111	44,840	45,611	46,127	46,539	46,857	47,204	47,688	48,202
Pre-kindergarten to 8.	27,647	27,034	29,878	31,898	32,341	32,764	33,073	33,346	33,488	33,688	33,952	34,135
Pre-K and Kindergarten .	2,689	3,192	3,610	4,047	4,173	4,202	4,198	4,172	4,148	4,158	4,258	4,368
First	2,894	3,239	3,499	3,593	3,671	3,770	3,755	3,727	3,684	3,636	3,614	3,594
Second	2,800	2,941	3,327	3,440	3,507	3,600	3,689	3,681	3,656	3,634	3,593	3,565
Third	2,893	2,895	3,297	3,439	3,445	3,524	3,597	3,696	3,691	3,676	3,653	3,623
Fourth	3,107	2,771	3,248	3,426	3,431	3,454	3,507	3,592	3,686	3,711	3,695	3,669
Fifth	3,130	2,776	3,197	3,372	3,438	3,453	3,458	3,520	3,604	3,707	3,727	3,711
Sixth	3,038	2,789	3,110	3,381	3,395	3,494	3,492	3,497	3,564	3,663	3,769	3,788
Seventh.	3,085	2,938	3,067	3,404	3,422	3,464	3,520	3,530	3,541	3,629	3,720	3,821
Eighth	3,086	2,982	2,979	3,302	3,356	3,403	3,415	3,480	3,497	3,538	3,616	3,709
Unclassified [1]	924	511	543	494	502	401	442	451	417	336	306	287
Grades 9 to 12.	13,231	12,388	11,338	12,213	12,500	12,847	13,054	13,193	13,369	13,515	13,734	14,067
Ninth.	3,377	3,439	3,169	3,604	3,704	3,801	3,819	3,856	3,935	3,963	4,012	4,105
Tenth	3,368	3,230	2,896	3,131	3,237	3,323	3,376	3,382	3,415	3,491	3,528	3,584
Eleventh	3,195	2,866	2,612	2,748	2,826	2,930	2,972	3,021	3,034	3,083	3,174	3,229
Twelfth	2,925	2,550	2,381	2,488	2,487	2,586	2,673	2,722	2,782	2,803	2,863	2,990
Unclassified [1]	366	303	282	242	245	206	214	212	203	175	157	160

[1] Includes ungraded and special education.

Source: U.S. National Center for Education Statistics, *Digest of Education Statistics*, annual.

Education 159

Table 235. **School Enrollment Below Postsecondary—Summary by Sex, Race, and Hispanic Origin: 2003**

[In thousands (58,273 represents 58,273,000), except percent and rate. As of October. Covers civilian noninstitutional population enrolled in nursery school through high school. Based on Current Population Survey, see text, Section 1, and Appendix III]

Characteristic	Total [1]	Sex		Race and Hispanic origin				
		Male	Female	White [2]		Black [2]	Asian [2]	Hispanic [3]
				Total	Non-Hispanic			
All students	58,273	30,005	28,269	44,522	35,145	9,264	2,151	10,215
Nursery	4,928	2,637	2,291	3,909	3,184	697	138	768
Full day	2,533	1,343	1,189	1,840	1,419	525	83	445
Part day	2,395	1,294	1,101	2,069	1,765	172	55	323
Kindergarten	3,719	1,887	1,832	2,866	2,245	558	122	694
Elementary	32,565	16,845	15,719	24,711	19,252	5,245	1,258	5,974
High school	17,062	8,635	8,427	13,036	10,463	2,765	632	2,779
Students in public schools	50,653	26,132	24,522	38,117	29,395	8,613	1,856	9,513
Nursery	2,567	1,387	1,180	1,918	1,382	484	56	561
Full day	1,339	694	645	936	621	336	31	323
Part day	1,228	694	534	982	761	148	25	238
Kindergarten	3,098	1,577	1,521	2,367	1,804	495	93	633
Elementary	29,204	15,166	14,038	21,893	16,735	4,942	1,122	5,651
High school	15,785	8,002	7,784	11,939	9,473	2,691	585	2,667
Population 15 to 17 years old:	12,753	6,569	6,184	9,889	7,980	1,950	458	2,063
Percent below modal grade [4] . . .	30.6	35.1	25.8	29.4	28.7	37.4	24.5	32.7
Students, 10th to 12th grade:	12,605	6,451	6,154	9,665	7,758	2,018	466	2,061
Annual dropout rate	3.8	4.0	3.6	3.7	3.0	4.5	2.4	6.5
Population 18 to 24 years old	27,404	13,681	13,724	21,502	17,158	3,837	1,144	4,754
Dropouts	3,228	1,875	1,354	2,489	1,267	545	56	1,353
High school graduates	22,603	10,919	11,684	17,901	15,070	2,948	1,030	3,096
Enrolled in college	10,364	4,697	5,667	8,150	7,129	1,225	693	1,115

[1] Includes other races, not shown separately. [2] For persons who selected this race group only. See footnote 2, Table 214.
[3] Persons of Hispanic origin may be of any race. [4] The modal grade is the grade most common for a given age.

Source: U.S. Census Bureau, Current Population Survey, unpublished data. See Internet site <http://www.census.gov/population/www/socdemo/school.html>.

Table 236. **Elementary and Secondary Schools—Teachers, Enrollment, and Pupil-Teacher Ratio: 1960 to 2002**

[In thousands (1,600 represents 1,600,000), except ratios. As of fall. Data are for full-time equivalent teachers. Based on survey of state education agencies; see source for details]

Year	Teachers			Enrollment			Pupil-teacher ratio		
	Total	Public	Private	Total	Public	Private	Total	Public	Private
1960	1,600	1,408	192	42,181	36,281	5,900	26.4	25.8	30.7
1965	1,933	1,710	223	48,473	42,173	6,300	25.1	24.7	28.3
1970	2,292	2,059	233	51,257	45,894	5,363	22.4	22.3	23.0
1975	2,453	2,198	255	49,819	44,819	5,000	20.3	20.4	19.6
1977	2,488	2,209	279	48,717	43,577	5,140	19.6	19.7	18.4
1978	2,479	2,207	272	47,635	42,550	5,085	19.2	19.3	18.7
1979	2,461	2,185	276	46,651	41,651	5,000	19.0	19.1	18.1
1980	2,485	2,184	301	46,208	40,877	5,331	18.6	18.7	17.7
1981	2,440	2,127	313	45,544	40,044	5,500	18.7	18.8	17.6
1982	2,458	2,133	325	45,165	39,566	5,600	18.4	18.6	17.2
1983	2,476	2,139	337	44,967	39,252	5,715	18.2	18.4	17.0
1984	2,508	2,168	340	44,908	39,208	5,700	17.9	18.1	16.8
1985	2,549	2,206	343	44,979	39,422	5,557	17.6	17.9	16.2
1986	2,592	2,244	348	45,205	39,753	5,452	17.4	17.7	15.7
1987	2,631	2,279	352	45,487	40,008	5,479	17.3	17.6	15.6
1988	2,668	2,323	345	45,430	40,189	5,242	17.0	17.3	15.2
1989	2,734	2,357	377	45,741	40,543	5,198	16.7	17.2	13.8
1990	2,753	2,398	355	46,451	41,217	5,234	16.9	17.2	14.7
1991	2,787	2,432	355	47,322	42,047	5,275	17.0	17.3	14.9
1992	2,822	2,459	363	48,145	42,823	5,322	17.1	17.4	14.7
1993	2,870	2,504	366	48,813	43,465	5,348	17.0	17.4	14.6
1994	2,926	2,552	374	49,609	44,111	5,498	17.0	17.3	14.7
1995	2,978	2,598	380	50,502	44,840	5,662	17.0	17.3	14.9
1996	3,054	2,667	387	51,375	45,611	5,764	16.8	17.1	14.9
1997	3,134	2,746	388	51,968	46,127	5,841	16.6	16.8	15.1
1998	3,221	2,830	391	52,475	46,539	5,937	16.3	16.4	15.2
1999	3,306	2,911	395	52,876	46,857	6,018	16.0	16.1	15.2
2000 [1]	3,332	2,941	390	53,385	47,223	6,162	16.0	16.0	15.8
2001 [1]	3,388	2,998	390	53,890	47,688	6,202	15.9	15.9	15.9
2002, proj.	3,369	2,983	385	54,158	47,918	6,241	16.1	16.1	16.2

[1] Public school enrollment data preliminary. Data not revised and may not agree with data in other tables.

Source: U.S. National Center for Education Statistics, *Digest of Education Statistics*, annual.

160   Education

Table 237. Public Elementary and Secondary School Teachers—Selected Characteristics: 1999–2000

[For school year. (509 represents 509,000) Based on School and Staffing Survey and subject to sampling error; for details, see source Web site at <http://nces.ed.gov/surveys/sass/>. Excludes prekindergarten teachers. See Table 251 for similar data on private school teachers]

Characteristic	Unit	Age				Sex		Race/ethnicity		
		Under 30 years old	30 to 39 years old	40 to 49 years old	Over 50 years old	Male	Female	White [1]	Black [1]	Hispanic
Total teachers [2]	1,000	509	661	953	879	754	2,248	2,532	228	169
Highest degree held:										
Bachelor's	Percent	77.9	56.7	46.8	39.0	49.7	52.8	51.2	51.1	65.5
Master's	Percent	20.4	38.5	46.9	51.4	42.7	41.6	43.0	40.3	28.5
Education specialist	Percent	1.2	3.8	4.9	7.3	4.7	4.8	4.6	6.2	4.1
Doctorate	Percent	(Z)	0.4	0.7	1.5	1.4	0.5	0.6	1.6	1.2
Full-time teaching experience:										
Less than 3 years	Percent	46.1	11.5	5.9	2.3	13.0	12.9	12.2	15.2	18.7
3 to 9 years	Percent	53.9	51.5	19.3	7.5	28.1	29.1	28.1	27.6	39.1
10 to 20 years	Percent	(X)	37.0	41.4	24.5	23.4	30.2	29.1	24.5	24.6
20 years or more	Percent	(X)	(X)	33.4	65.7	35.6	27.9	30.6	32.7	17.7
Full-time teachers	1,000	475	600	863	805	700	2,042	2,303	214	157
Earned income	Dollars	33,583	38,468	44,375	50,278	46,891	41,596	43,032	43,150	41,241
Salary	Dollars	30,386	35,502	41,407	47,138	41,104	39,475	40,022	39,377	38,488

X Not applicable. Z Less than 0.05 percent. [1] Non-Hispanic. [2] Includes teachers with no degrees and associate's degrees, not shown separately.

Source: U.S. National Center for Education Statistics, *Digest of Education Statistics, 2002*.

Table 238. Public Elementary and Secondary Schools—Number and Average Salary of Classroom Teachers, 1990 to 2004, and by State, 2004

[Estimates for school year ending in **June of year shown (2,362 represents 2,362,000)**. Schools classified by type of organization rather than by grade-group; elementary includes kindergarten]

Year and state	Teachers [1] (1,000)			Avg. salary ($1,000)			Year and state	Teachers [1] (1,000)			Avg. salary ($1,000)		
	Total	Elementary	Secondary	All teachers	Elementary	Secondary		Total	Elementary	Secondary	All teachers	Elementary	Secondary
1990	2,362	1,390	972	31.4	30.8	32.0	ME	15.7	10.7	5.0	39.9	39.8	40.0
1995	2,565	1,517	1,048	36.7	36.1	37.5	MD	55.2	32.7	22.5	50.3	50.2	48.5
1996	2,605	1,543	1,062	37.6	37.1	38.4	MA	65.2	28.0	37.2	53.2	53.2	53.2
1997	2,671	1,586	1,086	38.4	38.0	39.2	MI	95.2	49.2	45.9	54.4	54.4	54.4
1998	2,746	1,630	1,116	39.4	39.0	39.9	MN	52.2	26.6	25.7	45.4	44.8	44.3
1999	2,814	1,650	1,164	40.5	40.1	41.3	MS	30.7	18.3	12.4	35.7	35.7	35.7
2000	2,891	1,696	1,195	41.8	41.3	42.5	MO	65.0	33.2	31.8	38.0	38.1	37.9
2001 [2]	2,947	1,739	1,211	43.4	42.9	44.0	MT	10.3	6.9	3.4	37.2	37.2	37.2
2002 [2]	2,992	1,759	1,236	44.7	44.2	45.3	NE	20.7	13.5	7.1	38.4	38.4	38.4
2003 [2]	3,030	1,779	1,254	45.8	45.5	46.1	NV	20.0	11.8	8.2	42.3	41.9	42.7
2004, U.S. [2]	3,044	1,782	1,265	46.8	46.4	47.1	NH	15.1	10.5	4.6	42.7	42.7	42.7
							NJ	107.5	39.7	67.8	55.6	54.4	56.3
AL [2]	45.9	28.0	20.5	38.3	37.9	38.7	NM	21.5	15.3	6.2	38.1	37.7	38.9
AK	7.8	5.1	2.7	51.7	51.5	52.2	NY	224.0	111.0	113.0	55.2	54.7	55.8
AZ	45.5	30.8	14.7	41.8	41.8	41.8	NC	87.9	61.7	26.3	43.2	43.2	43.2
AR	32.0	15.6	16.4	39.3	37.4	41.1	ND	7.7	5.2	2.5	35.4	35.8	34.8
CA	305.9	220.7	85.2	56.4	56.4	56.4	OH	117.8	80.6	37.2	47.5	47.5	47.4
CO	44.9	22.4	22.5	43.3	43.3	43.2	OK	39.2	20.4	18.8	35.1	34.8	35.3
CT	43.0	30.3	12.7	57.3	56.9	58.1	OR	27.7	17.8	9.9	49.2	49.2	49.2
DE	7.8	3.8	3.9	49.4	49.0	49.7	PA	118.3	61.9	56.5	51.8	51.9	51.8
DC	5.7	4.1	1.6	57.0	57.0	57.0	RI	13.7	8.3	5.3	52.3	52.3	52.3
FL	148.2	74.6	73.6	40.6	40.6	40.6	SC	45.2	31.8	13.3	41.2	39.3	40.0
GA	103.6	62.5	41.1	46.0	45.4	46.9	SD	9.0	6.3	2.7	33.2	33.3	33.1
HI	11.3	6.0	5.3	45.5	45.5	45.5	TN	58.6	42.4	16.2	40.3	40.0	41.1
ID	14.1	7.2	6.9	41.1	41.1	41.1	TX	289.5	148.9	140.6	40.5	40.0	40.9
IL	130.0	89.9	40.1	54.2	50.9	61.8	UT	21.7	11.7	9.9	39.0	39.0	39.0
IN	59.8	32.1	27.7	45.8	45.8	45.8	VT	9.0	4.7	4.3	42.0	41.7	42.3
IA	34.8	16.5	18.3	39.4	38.6	40.2	VA	98.7	56.9	41.7	43.7	42.8	44.9
KS	32.6	16.0	16.6	38.6	38.6	38.6	WA	52.9	29.3	23.6	45.4	45.5	45.4
KY	39.3	27.7	11.6	40.2	40.0	40.8	WV	19.9	13.7	6.1	38.5	38.2	39.0
LA	50.4	35.3	15.1	37.9	37.9	37.9	WI	60.0	41.3	18.8	42.9	42.7	43.3
							WY	6.5	3.2	3.4	39.5	39.6	39.5

[1] Full-time equivalent. [2] Total number of teachers excludes some duplication in elementary and secondary levels.

Source: National Education Association, Washington, DC, Estimates of School Statistics Database (copyright).

Education 161

Table 239. **Average Salary and Wages Paid in Public School Systems: 1985 to 2004**

[In dollars. For school year ending in year shown. Data reported by a stratified sample of school systems enrolling 300 or more pupils. Data represent unweighted means of average salaries paid school personnel reported by each school system]

Position	1985	1990	1995	1999	2000	2001	2002	2003	2004
ANNUAL SALARY									
Central-office administrators:									
Superintendent (contract salary). . .	56,954	75,425	90,198	106,122	112,158	118,496	121,794	126,268	125,609
Deputy/assoc. superintendent	52,877	69,623	81,266	92,936	97,251	104,048	107,458	112,104	113,790
Assistant superintendent.	48,003	62,698	75,236	86,005	88,913	94,137	96,627	98,623	100,808
Administrators for—									
Finance and business	40,344	52,354	61,323	71,387	73,499	77,768	80,132	81,451	82,269
Instructional services	43,452	56,359	66,767	75,680	79,023	82,725	82,418	84,640	84,866
Public relations/information	35,287	44,926	53,263	59,214	60,655	65,505	67,170	67,298	70,291
Staff personnel services	44,182	56,344	65,819	73,850	76,608	80,969	83,035	85,041	86,333
Technology	(X)	(X)	(X)	(X)	(X)	(X)	72,962	73,931	76,139
Subject area supervisors.	34,422	45,929	54,534	61,083	63,103	64,659	66,351	66,582	67,098
School building administrators:									
Principals:									
Elementary	36,452	48,431	58,589	67,348	69,407	72,587	73,114	75,291	75,144
Junior high/middle	39,650	52,163	62,311	71,499	73,877	77,382	78,176	80,708	80,060
Senior high	42,094	55,722	66,596	76,768	79,839	83,367	83,944	86,452	86,160
Assistant principals:									
Elementary	30,496	40,916	48,491	54,306	56,419	59,080	60,672	62,230	62,213
Junior high/middle	33,793	44,570	52,942	59,238	60,842	63,709	64,375	67,288	66,360
Senior high	35,491	46,486	55,556	62,691	64,811	67,593	67,822	70,847	70,495
Classroom teachers	23,587	31,278	37,264	41,351	42,213	43,658	43,802	45,026	45,646
Auxiliary professional personnel:									
Counselors.	27,593	35,979	42,486	47,287	48,195	50,003	50,022	51,706	52,303
Librarians.	24,981	33,469	40,418	45,680	46,732	49,007	48,741	49,611	50,403
School nurses.	19,944	26,090	31,066	35,520	35,540	37,188	38,221	39,165	40,201
Secretarial/clerical personnel:									
Central office:									
Secretaries	15,343	20,238	23,935	27,540	28,405	29,514	30,039	31,295	31,830
Accounting/payroll clerks	15,421	20,088	24,042	27,630	28,498	29,898	30,551	32,154	32,632
Typists/data entry clerks	12,481	16,125	18,674	22,474	22,853	24,232	24,840	25,793	25,318
School building level:									
Secretaries	12,504	16,184	19,170	21,831	22,630	23,630	24,041	24,853	24,964
Library clerks.	9,911	12,152	14,381	16,033	16,509	17,052	18,104	18,170	18,427
HOURLY WAGE RATE									
Other support personnel:									
Teacher aides:									
Instructional	5.89	7.43	8.77	9.80	10.00	10.41	10.68	10.93	11.22
Noninstructional.	5.60	7.08	8.29	9.31	9.77	10.15	10.42	10.98	11.08
Custodians.	6.90	8.54	10.05	11.22	11.35	11.85	11.96	12.40	12.47
Cafeteria workers	5.42	6.77	7.89	8.82	9.02	9.41	9.71	9.98	10.18
Bus drivers.	7.27	9.21	10.69	12.04	12.48	12.99	13.49	13.85	13.79

X Not applicable.

Source: Educational Research Service, Arlington, VA, *National Survey of Salaries and Wages in Public Schools*, annual. (All rights reserved. Copyright.)

Table 240. **Public School Employment: 1982 and 2004**

[In thousands (3,082 represents 3,082,000). Covers a sample of all public elementary-secondary school districts with 15 or more full-time employees in 1982, and covers all public elementary-secondary school districts with 100 or more full-time employees in 2004]

Occupation	1982					2004				
	Total	Male	Female	White [1]	Black [1]	Total	Male	Female	White [1]	Black [1]
All occupations	3,082	1,063	2,019	2,498	432	4,499	1,170	3,329	3,424	582
Officials, administrators	41	31	10	36	3	61	30	31	50	7
Principals and assistant										
principals.	90	72	19	76	11	122	57	65	91	20
Classroom teachers [2]	1,680	534	1,146	1,435	186	2,467	608	1,859	2,033	230
Elementary schools	798	129	669	667	98	1,246	173	1,073	1,019	109
Secondary schools	706	363	343	619	67	921	374	547	769	85
Other professional staff	235	91	144	193	35	373	76	297	300	42
Teachers' aides [3]	215	14	200	146	45	472	58	414	308	90
Clerical, secretarial staff.	210	4	206	177	19	298	10	288	217	35
Service workers [4]	611	316	295	434	132	707	331	376	425	158

[1] Excludes individuals of Hispanic origin. [2] Includes other classroom teachers, not shown separately. [3] Includes technicians. [4] Includes craftworkers and laborers.

Source: U.S. Equal Employment Opportunity Commission, *Elementary-Secondary Staff Information (EEO-5)*, biennial.

Table 241. Public Elementary and Secondary School Price Indexes: 1975 to 2001

[1983 = 100. For years ending June 30. Reflects prices paid by public elementary-secondary schools. For explanation of average annual percent change, see Guide to Tabular Presentation]

Year	Index, total	Personnel compensation				Contracted services, supplies and equipment						
		Total	Profes-sional salaries	Nonpro-fessional salaries	Fringe benefits	Total	Ser-vices	Sup-plies and materi-als	Equip-ment replace-ment	Library materi-als and text-books	Utilities	Fixed costs
1975...	52.7	53.4	56.0	55.6	40.9	50.4	55.7	58.0	53.7	53.8	34.5	45.2
1980...	76.6	75.9	76.7	77.8	71.0	79.2	77.4	85.9	79.6	82.1	71.1	77.9
1985...	112.1	113.7	113.4	111.3	117.1	106.0	112.4	103.2	107.2	111.0	96.1	110.8
1986...	118.5	121.1	121.4	117.6	123.3	108.3	117.4	103.0	109.3	120.8	93.7	116.2
1987...	123.3	127.4	128.4	121.9	128.8	107.5	123.7	101.5	112.9	126.5	75.3	122.7
1988...	129.8	134.5	135.5	127.5	137.0	111.7	126.1	105.9	113.4	140.0	78.1	128.4
1989...	136.3	141.6	142.2	133.3	147.0	116.1	131.8	112.0	116.0	149.4	75.1	134.6
1990...	144.5	150.0	150.1	139.4	159.3	123.5	137.7	119.2	121.2	171.7	82.1	140.3
1991...	152.3	158.3	158.1	146.5	169.8	129.6	142.5	122.7	125.7	189.5	92.6	144.9
1992...	158.5	165.5	165.9	152.4	175.8	131.9	148.0	122.5	128.5	199.8	90.8	148.9
1993...	162.2	169.6	169.3	155.1	184.5	133.9	151.5	121.9	131.8	205.6	90.4	153.8
1994...	167.1	175.2	175.1	159.3	190.2	136.5	154.0	122.7	135.4	218.6	90.6	158.8
1995...	170.9	179.2	178.9	163.7	194.9	139.3	157.2	124.4	138.7	230.4	89.7	163.9
1996...	177.5	185.6	185.7	169.2	200.3	146.6	161.8	138.1	143.2	243.0	91.0	169.1
1997...	182.0	190.2	190.2	174.5	204.2	150.8	165.2	137.2	145.2	263.7	100.1	172.9
1998...	184.9	193.3	193.3	177.9	207.6	152.7	168.0	137.6	144.2	278.7	98.1	177.0
1999...	189.5	199.2	199.1	184.5	213.4	152.3	172.1	135.2	145.6	295.8	87.5	178.3
2000...	194.2	204.1	203.5	189.3	220.2	156.1	175.5	136.4	147.9	312.5	92.6	182.1
2001...	201.8	211.4	210.8	197.6	226.3	165.6	177.4	143.2	149.4	334.0	118.4	186.7

Source: Research Associates of Washington, Arlington, VA, *Inflation Measures for Schools, Colleges, and Libraries*, periodic (copyright). Series discontinued by Research Associates of Washington.

Table 242. Finances of Public Elementary and Secondary School Systems by Enrollment-Size Group: 2002–2003

[In millions of dollars (440,316 represents $440,316,000,000), except as indicated. Data are based on annual survey. For details, see source. See also Appendix III]

Item	All school systems	School systems with enrollment of—						
		50,000 or more	25,000 to 49,999	15,000 to 24,999	7,500 to 14,999	5,000 to 7,499	3,000 to 4.999	Under 3,000
Fall enrollment (1,000)	47,633	10,177	5,548	4,986	7,011	4,348	5,485	10,077
General revenue	440,316	92,539	48,040	42,321	63,250	40,027	51,356	102,783
From federal sources.	36,806	9,287	4,083	3,172	4,794	2,683	3,483	9,304
Through state	33,333	8,650	3,764	2,931	4,221	2,445	3,181	8,142
Child nutrition programs.	7,436	2,041	948	742	997	586	732	1,390
Direct	3,472	638	318	242	573	238	302	1,162
From state sources [1]	215,551	43,177	24,658	22,554	31,764	18,641	23,526	51,232
General formula assistance	145,685	27,064	16,394	15,630	21,881	12,804	16,299	35,613
Compensatory programs.	4,585	866	1,035	529	766	399	360	630
Special education	13,736	3,519	1,387	1,029	1,715	1,087	1,569	3,431
From local sources	187,959	40,074	19,300	16,595	26,692	18,703	24,347	42,247
Taxes	126,857	21,780	13,441	11,420	19,095	13,539	17,421	30,161
Contributions from parent government	32,513	13,665	2,822	2,347	3,571	2,651	3,488	3,970
From other local governments . . .	4,256	526	459	282	383	356	633	1,618
Current charges	11,270	1,811	1,134	1,129	1,697	1,034	1,362	3,103
School lunch	6,089	910	628	650	985	629	813	1,474
Other	13,063	2,292	1,445	1,417	1,947	1,123	1,444	3,395
General expenditure	453,558	97,006	49,245	42,932	64,863	41,199	52,546	105,768
Current spending	389,867	83,396	42,181	36,755	55,531	35,449	45,244	91,311
By function:								
Instruction.	236,038	51,333	25,538	22,362	33,915	21,764	27,580	53,545
Support services	132,933	27,424	14,288	12,341	18,643	11,945	15,400	32,894
Other current spending	20,895	4,639	2,355	2,052	2,974	1,739	2,264	4,872
By object:								
Total salaries and wages	246,824	52,940	27,447	23,914	35,671	22,668	28,619	55,565
Total employee benefits.	68,480	14,384	7,101	6,492	10,053	6,357	8,114	15,979
Other.	74,564	16,072	7,633	6,349	9,806	6,423	8,511	19,768
Capital outlay.	50,509	11,039	5,673	5,013	7,346	4,379	5,561	11,499
Interest on debt	11,206	2,280	1,261	1,122	1,653	1,072	1,444	2,375
Payments to other governments . . .	1,975	290	130	43	333	300	297	583
Debt outstanding	251,826	55,923	27,261	24,355	35,977	23,731	31,602	52,977
Long-term	241,816	55,167	26,410	23,540	34,391	22,709	30,221	49,377
Short-term	10,010	756	851	815	1,586	1,022	1,380	3,600
Long-term debt issued	48,075	11,444	5,383	4,719	6,596	4,090	5,551	10,291
Long-term debt retired.	26,036	3,391	3,005	2,528	3,844	2,543	3,708	7,016

[1] Includes other sources, not shown separately.

Source: U.S. Census Bureau, *Public Education Finances, 2003*, March 2005. See Internet site <http://www.census.gov/govs/www/school.html>

Table 243. **Public Elementary and Secondary Estimated Finances, 1980 to 2004, and by State, 2004**

[In millions of dollars (101,724 represents $101,724,000,000), except as noted. For school years ending in June of year shown]

Year and state	Receipts						Expenditures				
	Revenue receipts							Current expenditures			
		Source			Non-revenue re-ceipts[1]	Total[2]	Per capita[3] (dol.)	Ele-mentary and second-ary day schools	Average per pupil in ADA[4]	
	Total	Total	Federal	State	Local					Amount (dol.)	Rank
1980	101,724	97,635	9,020	47,929	40,686	4,089	96,105	427	85,661	2,230	(X)
1985	146,976	141,013	9,533	69,107	62,373	5,963	139,382	591	127,230	3,483	(X)
1990	218,126	208,656	13,184	100,787	94,685	9,469	209,698	850	186,583	4,966	(X)
1995	288,501	273,255	18,764	129,958	124,533	15,246	276,584	1,051	242,995	5,957	(X)
1997	325,007	303,400	19,965	148,184	135,251	21,607	310,719	1,153	269,824	6,401	(X)
1998	349,787	324,429	21,668	159,596	143,164	25,359	330,952	1,214	285,213	6,666	(X)
1999	370,735	345,901	23,583	170,606	151,711	24,835	350,539	1,271	301,380	7,011	(X)
2000	390,861	369,754	26,346	183,986	159,421	21,106	374,782	1,343	320,954	7,418	(X)
2001	425,283	396,395	28,009	198,310	170,076	28,888	402,809	1,431	342,911	7,841	(X)
2002	448,945	416,754	32,101	206,139	178,514	32,191	426,340	1,495	361,814	8,183	(X)
2003	469,785	433,904	35,598	212,965	185,340	35,882	451,706	1,569	385,557	8,630	(X)
2004, total	**488,447**	**452,795**	**38,856**	**217,140**	**196,798**	**35,653**	**471,965**	**1,623**	**397,015**	**8,807**	**(X)**
Alabama	5,613	5,328	639	2,977	1,711	285	5,499	1,221	4,887	6,953	43
Alaska	1,443	1,285	161	817	308	157	1,418	2,187	1,314	11,432	6
Arizona	7,145	7,049	552	3,589	2,907	96	6,346	1,137	5,154	5,595	49
Arkansas	3,596	3,535	391	1,851	1,293	61	3,160	1,158	2,715	6,663	45
California	70,408	60,595	6,501	35,401	18,692	9,813	58,752	1,657	47,771	7,860	32
Colorado	7,557	6,489	426	2,797	3,267	1,067	7,272	1,599	6,079	8,651	25
Connecticut	7,469	7,457	436	2,967	4,055	12	7,469	2,142	6,784	12,394	2
Delaware	1,429	1,254	82	804	369	175	1,380	1,687	1,161	10,347	11
District of Columbia . . .	827	827	115	-	712	-	1,042	1,869	867	14,621	(X)
Florida	22,752	21,161	2,220	9,195	9,746	1,591	21,869	1,286	17,380	7,181	40
Georgia	14,299	13,883	1,227	6,335	6,320	416	14,299	1,648	12,347	8,671	24
Hawaii	2,138	2,106	173	1,901	32	32	1,683	1,347	1,510	9,019	22
Idaho	1,700	1,650	150	1,000	500	50	1,700	1,244	1,585	6,779	44
Illinois	20,325	18,240	1,408	5,546	11,286	2,085	29,528	2,334	20,299	10,866	9
Indiana	10,471	9,763	642	4,908	4,212	709	10,191	1,644	8,502	9,138	21
Iowa	4,535	4,251	312	1,965	1,974	285	4,139	1,407	3,503	7,696	35
Kansas	4,760	4,274	345	2,138	1,791	486	3,863	1,418	3,435	8,189	29
Kentucky	5,205	5,196	620	3,031	1,545	10	5,203	1,263	4,736	8,298	28
Louisiana	6,442	5,779	782	2,811	2,185	664	6,144	1,367	5,282	7,840	33
Maine	2,247	2,132	201	891	1,039	115	2,247	1,716	2,051	10,961	8
Maryland	9,278	9,074	663	3,458	4,953	205	8,971	1,627	7,983	9,824	16
Massachusetts . .	12,228	12,227	838	4,722	6,667	1	11,602	1,807	10,562	11,445	5
Michigan	17,055	16,713	944	11,204	4,566	342	18,954	1,880	14,857	9,416	19
Minnesota	9,716	8,612	543	6,138	1,931	1,105	9,417	1,860	7,469	9,513	17
Mississippi	3,586	3,436	513	1,869	1,053	150	3,394	1,178	2,994	6,556	46
Missouri	8,609	7,972	697	2,577	4,698	637	7,366	1,288	6,203	7,548	37
Montana	1,279	1,251	148	590	512	28	1,205	1,312	1,141	8,631	26
Nebraska	2,230	2,209	157	892	1,159	21	2,385	1,373	2,089	7,947	30
Nevada	3,617	3,025	216	965	1,844	592	3,399	1,516	2,552	6,177	48
New Hampshire. . .	2,309	2,075	121	961	993	234	2,103	1,632	1,878	9,902	15
New Jersey	18,297	18,143	520	6,892	10,731	154	16,449	1,903	15,728	11,847	4
New Mexico	2,998	2,901	512	2,002	387	97	3,022	1,608	2,547	8,772	23
New York	39,242	38,500	2,400	17,500	18,600	742	39,309	2,046	34,832	12,408	1
North Carolina . . .	10,268	9,422	1,015	6,035	2,371	846	10,382	1,233	9,344	7,511	38
North Dakota . . .	938	847	111	307	429	91	833	1,316	676	7,112	41
Ohio	21,487	18,546	1,167	8,472	8,908	2,941	19,065	1,667	16,673	10,102	13
Oklahoma	4,600	4,343	553	2,358	1,432	257	4,078	1,163	3,740	6,405	47
Oregon	4,776	4,402	468	2,354	1,580	374	4,934	1,384	4,217	8,575	27
Pennsylvania	19,552	19,374	1,529	7,007	10,839	178	20,008	1,617	16,866	9,949	14
Rhode Island . . .	1,496	1,496	55	553	888	-	1,715	1,594	1,640	10,976	7
South Carolina . . .	6,809	6,004	640	2,769	2,595	804	5,899	1,422	4,767	7,395	39
South Dakota . . .	1,092	1,006	159	339	507	86	1,017	1,329	887	7,611	36
Tennessee	6,523	6,191	709	2,804	2,679	332	6,309	1,079	5,980	6,983	42
Texas	39,680	35,387	3,882	13,644	17,862	4,292	37,498	1,696	30,905	7,698	34
Utah	3,023	3,022	279	1,756	987	1	3,103	1,319	2,479	5,556	50
Vermont	1,232	1,182	95	801	286	50	1,206	1,948	1,055	12,157	3
Virginia	12,110	11,310	770	4,588	5,951	800	12,012	1,631	10,381	9,401	20
Washington	9,553	8,758	829	5,457	2,473	795	9,574	1,561	7,511	7,904	31
West Virginia	2,837	2,728	321	1,641	765	110	2,785	1,538	2,530	9,509	18
Wisconsin	10,675	9,413	522	5,052	3,838	1,262	9,813	1,792	8,345	10,293	12
Wyoming	991	970	94	506	370	20	952	1,896	820	10,413	10

- Represents or rounds to zero.   X Not applicable.   [1] Amount received by local education agencies from the sales of bonds and real property and equipment, loans, and proceeds from insurance adjustments.   [2] Includes interest on school debt and other current expenditures not shown separately.   [3] Based on U.S. Census Bureau estimated resident population, as of July 1, the previous year, except 1980, 1990, and 2000 population enumerated as of April 1.   [4] Average daily attendance.

Source: National Education Association, Washington, DC, Estimates of School Statistics Database (copyright).

164 Education

Table 244. Public Schools With Internet Access: 1995 to 2003

[In percent. As of fall. Excludes special education, vocational education, and alternative schools. Based on the Fast Response Survey System and subject to sampling error; see source for details]

School characteristic	Percent of schools with Internet access				Percent of instructional classrooms with Internet access				Students per instructional computer with Internet access, 2003	Schools with Internet available to students outside of regular school hours, 2003
	1995	2000	2002	2003	1995	2000	2002	2003		
Total [1]	50	98	99	100	8	77	92	93	4.4	48
Instructional level:										
Elementary	46	97	99	100	8	76	92	93	4.9	41
Secondary	65	100	100	100	8	79	91	94	3.8	69
Size of enrollment:										
Less than 300	39	96	96	100	9	83	91	93	3.2	39
300 to 999	52	98	100	100	8	78	93	93	4.7	47
1,000 or more	69	99	100	100	4	70	89	94	4.3	74
Percent minority enrollment:										
Less than 6 percent	52	98	97	100	9	85	93	93	4.1	45
6 to 20 percent	58	100	100	100	10	83	94	95	4.1	50
21 to 49 percent	55	98	99	99	9	79	91	95	4.1	46
50 percent or more	39	96	99	100	3	64	89	92	5.1	51
Percent of students eligible for free or reduced-price lunch:										
Less than 35 percent	60	99	98	100	10	82	93	95	4.2	47
35 to 49 percent	48	99	100	100	6	81	90	93	4.4	48
50 to 74 percent	41	97	100	100	6	77	91	94	4.4	46
75 percent or more	31	94	99	99	3	60	89	90	5.1	53

[1] Includes combined schools.

Source: U.S. National Center for Education Statistics, Internet Access in U.S. Public Schools and Classrooms: 1994-2003, NCES 2005-015, February 2005.

Table 245. Public Schools With Broadband and Wireless Connections: 2000 to 2003

[In percent. As of fall. Excludes special education, vocational education, and alternative schools. Broadband connections include T3/DS3, fractional T3, T1/DS1, fractional T1, and cable modem connections. Beginning 2001 they also included DSL connections, not asked in 2000. Based on the Fast Response Survey System and subject to sampling error; see source for details]

School characteristic	Percent of schools with Internet access using broadband connections				Percent of schools with Internet access using any type of wireless Internet connection		Percent of instructional rooms with wireless Internet connections	
	2000	2001	2002	2003	2002	2003	2002	2003
Total [1]	80	85	94	95	23	32	15	11
Instructional level:								
Elementary	77	83	93	94	20	29	13	11
Secondary	89	94	98	97	33	42	19	11
Size of enrollment:								
Less than 300	67	72	90	90	17	28	12	15
300 to 999	83	89	94	96	23	30	14	10
1,000 or more	90	96	100	100	37	51	19	11
Percent minority enrollment:								
Less than 6 percent	76	81	92	90	21	31	14	14
6 to 20 percent	82	85	91	96	23	36	13	12
21 to 49 percent	84	85	96	98	25	35	15	10
50 percent or more	81	93	95	97	23	28	16	9
Percent of students eligible for free or reduced-price lunch:								
Less than 35 percent	81	84	93	95	24	36	15	13
35 to 49 percent	82	86	96	96	25	33	15	12
50 to 74 percent	79	84	93	96	23	28	17	9
75 percent or more	75	90	95	93	20	25	11	9

[1] Includes combined schools.

Source: U.S. National Center for Education Statistics, Internet Access in U.S. Public Schools and Classrooms: 1994-2003, NCES 2005-015, February 2005.

Education 165

Table 246. **Computers for Student Instruction in Elementary and Secondary Schools: 2004–2005**

[54,699 represents 54,699,000. Market Data Retrieval collects student use computer information in elementary and secondary schools nationwide through a comprehensive annual technology survey that utilizes both mail, telephone, and Internet data methods]

Level	Total schools	Total enroll-ment (1,000)	Number of com puters [1] (1,000)	Students per com-puter	Schools with wireless network (percent)	Schools with distance learning programs for students (percent) [2]	Schools with laptop com-puters (percent) [3]	Schools with high speed Internet access (percent) [4]	Schools with video-streaming (percent)
U.S. total	114,315	54,699	13,589	4.0	43.6	17.5	51.7	82.4	27.6
Public schools, total. . .	91,314	49,392	12,445	4.0	45.1	19.1	54.2	84.3	29.8
Elementary	53,012	23,868	5,412	4.4	40.3	10.3	49.4	83.1	25.8
Middle/junior high. . .	14,197	9,445	2,378	4.0	51.3	13.0	59.7	85.1	34.8
Senior high	16,921	13,704	3,948	3.5	54.1	41.3	62.5	86.1	37.7
K to 12/other.	7,184	2,376	708	3.4	44.1	42.7	57.5	87.3	29.0
Catholic schools, total	7,863	2,518	528	4.8	36.9	6.8	41.2	83.5	16.3
Elementary	6,495	1,830	354	5.2	32.9	4.6	38.1	82.1	14.8
Secondary	1,195	623	162	3.8	55.7	16.7	55.7	90.7	22.0
K to 12/other.	173	65	13	5.1	48.0	16.0	48.0	84.0	32.0
Other private schools, total	15,138	2,789	616	4.5	38.8	8.4	34.4	69.2	10.9
Elementary . . . : . . .	7,449	1,167	227	5.1	36.1	3.9	33.7	68.7	9.1
Secondary	1,279	260	75	3.5	61.2	23.1	43.8	77.7	20.7
K to 12/other.	6,410	1,363	314	4.3	37.8	11.2	33.4	68.3	11.2

[1] Includes estimates for schools not reporting number of computers. [2] Distance learning programs as determined by respondents. [3] For student instruction. [4] Statistics based on responses to those indicating type of Internet connection. High speed includes Internet connection types: T1, T3, and cable modem.

Source: Market Data Retrieval, Shelton, CT, unpublished data (copyright).

Table 247. **Computer and Internet Use by Children and Adolescents: 2003**

[For persons 5 to 17 years old (53,561 represents 53,561,000). As of September. Based on the Current Population Survey; see source and Appendix III for details]

User characteristics	Number of chil-dren (1,000)	Percent using comput-ers at school	Percent using comput-ers at home [1]	Home use activity (percent)					
				Word process-ing	Connect to the Internet	E-mail	Complete school assign-ments	Play games
Total	53,561	84.5	68.6	33.4	46.6	32.9	49.2	56.9
Age: 5 to 7 years old	11,785	72.2	59.3	9.6	23.3	7.7	16.6	51.7
8 to 10 years old	11,849	86.3	66.1	23.5	38.2	19.5	42.7	58.0
11 to 14 years old	17,173	89.0	72.0	42.7	54.8	40.9	61.8	61.0
15 to 17 years old	12,753	87.9	75.0	51.9	64.7	57.7	68.1	55.4
Sex: Male	27,422	84.2	68.0	31.2	45.5	30.2	47.5	57.8
Female	26,139	84.7	69.3	35.6	47.7	35.7	50.9	56.0
Race/ethnicity: White alone, non-Hispanic	32,279	86.6	79.6	40.1	56.9	41.1	56.6	67.3
Black alone, non-Hispanic	8,048	82.6	47.2	20.5	28.0	18.6	35.9	39.1
Hispanic	9,503	79.7	48.3	20.2	27.2	17.1	34.4	37.8
Other	3,731	82.1	71.4	35.9	46.4	32.6	50.8	54.7
Parent educational attainment: Less than high school credential.	10,001	77.9	43.7	17.7	24.2	16.3	29.5	34.6
High school credential	15,270	84.1	61.4	26.9	39.9	28.2	43.7	50.6
Some college	14,384	86.8	75.4	35.5	51.9	35.7	54.1	63.4
Bachelor's degree	9,410	86.9	86.5	47.4	62.9	45.2	63.2	73.0
Graduate education.	4,495	87.6	89.5	53.8	67.9	50.5	66.0	73.6
Household language: Spanish-only	2,680	75.3	33.6	12.7	14.3	9.0	24.1	26.7
Not Spanish-only	50,881	84.9	70.5	34.4	48.3	34.1	50.5	58.5
Family income: Under $20,000	16,459	81.3	51.7	23.1	30.7	21.7	36.2	41.2
20,000 to 34,999	8,615	81.9	55.7	22.9	33.3	23.2	38.2	45.4
35,000 to 49,999	6,993	85.9	72.2	33.2	46.7	32.3	50.5	60.5
50,000 to 74,999	9,053	86.0	80.5	38.6	56.7	39.2	57.6	67.1
75,000 or more.	12,441	88.5	89.3	50.5	69.3	50.1	67.0	76.4

[1] Includes other home activities, not shown separately.

Source: U.S. National Center for Education Statistics, CPS October (Education) Supplement, October 2003, special tabulation.

Table 248. **Distance Education in Public Elementary and Secondary Schools: 2002–03**

[For the school year. Distance education courses are for-credit classes offered to students enrolled in the district where the teacher and student were in different locations. They could be delivered via audio, video, Internet or other computer technologies. Reasons for districts providing these courses include providing courses not otherwise available, offering Advanced Placement courses, addressing growing populations and space limitations, reducing scheduling conflicts for students, and permitting students who failed a course to take the course again. Excludes such things as virtual field trips, online homework, or a course delivered mainly by written correspondence. Based on the Fast Response Survey System and subject to sampling error; see source for details]

District characteristic	Number of districts — Total	With students enrolled in distance education courses	Enrollments in distance education courses — Total[1]	Curriculum — English/language arts	Social studies/social sciences	Computer sciences	Natural/physical sciences	Math	Foreign language	High school level
All public school districts[2] . . .	15,040	5,480	327,670	61,590	74,570	11,660	38,920	49,210	39,090	222,090
District enrollment size:										
Less than 2,500.	11,080	4,060	117,730	21,480	25,550	3,060	12,900	15,060	22,300	74,160
2,500 to 9,999.	3,100	1,010	85,640	15,810	18,950	1,970	11,090	13,480	9,290	44,780
10,000 or more	820	410	124,300	24,300	30,070	6,630	14,930	20,670	7,500	103,150
Region:[3]										
Northeast	3,040	640	42,070	6,060	8,280	3,020	4,830	4,730	5,300	17,420
South.	1,750	790	59,010	10,240	12,490	1,420	5,400	8,920	11,120	50,410
Midwest	5,390	2,500	108,140	21,250	21,500	2,750	14,270	17,040	14,250	60,560
West	4,850	1,540	118,450	24,040	32,290	4,470	14,420	18,520	8,410	93,700
Poverty concentration:[4]										
Less than 10 percent	4,850	1,620	77,380	15,300	17,350	2,140	6,900	10,590	9,600	57,320
10 to 19 percent	5,330	2,220	97,300	18,370	23,820	3,000	10,720	15,030	10,600	77,810
20 percent or more.	3,690	1,560	93,280	17,800	22,770	6,290	11,800	14,150	15,330	83,100

[1] Includes other curriculum not shown separately.   [2] Includes districts and enrollments where enrollment size and poverty concentration were not known.   [3] For composition or regions, see map inside front cover.   [4] Percentage of children in the district ages 5 to 17 in families living below the poverty level.

Source: U.S. National Center for Education Statistics, *Distance Education Courses for Public Elementary and Secondary School Students: 2002–03* NCES 2005-010, March 2005.

Table 249. **Children and Youth With Disabilities Served by Selected Programs: 1995 to 2004**

[In thousands (4,907.4 represents 4,907,400). For school year ending in year shown. Excludes outlying areas. For individuals with Disabilities Act (IDEA), Parts B and C]

Disability	1995	1998	1999	2000	2001	2002	2003	2004
Total	4,907.4	5,396.9	5,539.7	5,677.9	5,773.9	5,861.4	5,959.1	6,046.1
Specific learning disabilities.	2,510.1	2,754.4	2,815.5	2,867.7	2,881.6	2,878.3	2,878.6	2,866.9
Speech impairments	1,020.3	1,063.6	1,074.1	1,087.8	1,093.4	1,093.2	1,110.9	1,129.3
Mental retardation	570.5	603.3	610.7	614.3	613.4	605.0	591.7	582.7
Emotional disturbance	428.0	454.4	462.8	469.8	474.3	477.8	482.0	484.5
Multiple disabilities.	89.6	107.3	107.8	113.0	122.9	128.7	130.8	132.6
Hearing impairments	65.2	69.8	70.9	71.4	70.8	71.2	72.0	72.0
Orthopedic impairments	60.5	67.4	69.4	71.4	73.0	73.7	74.0	68.2
Other health impairments	107.1	191.1	221.8	255.3	294.0	341.3	393.0	452.4
Visually impaired.	24.7	26.0	26.1	26.4	26.0	25.8	26.1	25.9
Autism	22.7	42.5	54.1	66.0	79.6	98.6	118.8	141.0
Deaf-blind	1.3	1.3	1.6	1.7	1.3	1.6	1.6	1.7
Traumatic brain injury	7.3	11.9	13.0	13.9	14.9	20.8	21.5	22.5
Developmental delay[1]	(X)	3.8	11.9	19.3	28.6	45.3	58.3	66.3

X Not applicable.   [1] States had the option of reporting children ages 3 to 9 under developmental delay beginning 1997-98.

Source: U.S. Department of Education, Office of Special Education Programs, Data Analysis System (DANS).

Table 250. **Private Schools: 2001-2002**

[5,342 represents 5,342,000. Based on the Private School Survey, conducted every 2 years; see source for details. For composition of regions, see map, inside front cover]

Characteristic	Schools				Students (1,000)				Teachers (1,000) [1]			
	Number	Elementary	Secondary	Combined	Total	Elementary	Secondary	Combined	Total	Elementary	Secondary	Combined
Total........	29,273	17,427	2,704	9,142	5,342	2,883	835	1,623	425	202	67	156
School type:												
Catholic........	8,207	6,763	1,110	335	2,516	1,794	616	106	156	104	43	9
Parochial.....	4,347	4,087	200	61	1,222	1,118	81	23	71	63	6	2
Diocesan.....	2,933	2,351	496	86	925	607	290	28	56	35	19	2
Private.......	927	325	414	188	369	68	245	55	28	5	18	5
Other religious ...	14,388	7,367	747	6,275	1,925	784	124	1,017	166	65	12	89
Conservative Christian	5,527	2,005	203	3,319	823	245	34	544	67	19	3	45
Affiliated......	3,406	2,156	284	966	563	268	53	241	51	23	5	23
Unaffiliated....	5,455	3,206	260	1,989	539	270	36	232	48	22	4	22
Nonsectarian ...	6,678	3,297	847	2,533	901	306	96	500	104	34	13	58
Regular......	2,939	1,573	340	1,027	623	193	66	363	67	20	9	39
Special emphasis....	2,381	1,550	299	533	177	101	19	57	20	12	2	6
Special education....	1,358	175	209	973	101	11	10	80	16	2	2	12
Program emphasis:												
Regular el/sec ...	23,991	15,082	2,050	6,858	4,933	2,724	778	1,431	375	183	61	131
Montessori.....	1,377	1,124	-	252	85	69	-	15	10	8	-	2
Special program emphasis.....	1,076	465	156	455	127	46	26	55	13	5	3	6
Special educ.....	1,552	233	223	1,096	115	15	11	89	18	3	2	14
Vocational/tech...	(B)	(B)	(B)	(B)	(B)	(B)	(B)	(B)	(B)	(B)	(B)	(B)
Alternative.....	1,148	421	266	460	75	24	17	33	9	3	2	4
Early childhood...	120	101	(X)	(B)	5	4	(X)	(B)	1	(Z)	(X)	(B)
Size:												
Less than 50	8,955	4,770	682	3,503	232	126	17	89	32	15	3	14
50 to 149	8,336	5,127	553	2,656	765	481	49	234	80	46	6	29
150 to 299......	6,554	4,765	449	1,341	1,408	1,022	98	288	105	68	10	27
300 to 499......	3,199	2,005	410	784	1,223	764	161	298	87	47	14	26
500 to 749......	1,392	642	285	465	830	375	173	282	57	20	13	25
750 or more.....	836	118	325	393	883	115	338	431	63	6	22	36
Region:												
Northeast	6,556	4,052	819	1,685	1,337	754	278	305	111	52	24	35
Midwest........	7,455	5,239	639	1,576	1,355	875	238	241	96	57	17	21
South........	9,171	4,563	559	4,049	1,641	686	162	793	143	55	13	75
West.........	6,092	3,573	686	1,833	1,008	568	157	284	76	38	13	25

- Represents zero.   B Does not meet standard of reliability or precision.   X Not applicable.   Z Less than 500.   [1] Full time equivalents.

Source: U.S. National Center for Education Statistics, *Private School Universe Survey,* NCES 2005-305, October 2004. See Internet site <http://nces.ed.gov/surveys/pss/>.

Table 251. **Private Elementary and Secondary School Teachers— Selected Characteristics: 1999-2000**

[For school year (87 represents 87,000). Based on School and Staffing Survey and subject to sampling error; for details, see source Web site at <http://nces.ed.gov/surveys/sass/>. Data revised since originally published. See Table 237 for similar data on public school teachers]

Characteristic	Unit	Age				Sex		Race/ethnicity		
		Under 30 years old	30 to 39 years old	40 to 49 years old	50 years old and over	Male	Female	White [1]	Black [1]	Hispanic
Total teachers [2] ...	1,000...	87	101	131	131	107	342	402	17	21
Highest degree held:										
Bachelor's	Percent .	75.7	58.9	56.0	45.8	48.2	60.4	57.8	58.9	54.6
Master's.........	Percent .	13.9	28.0	32.4	40.9	38.5	27.8	31.0	18.4	26.4
Educ. specialist	Percent .	0.6	2.2	3.4	5.1	3.7	2.9	3.0	2.5	3.9
Doctorate	Percent .	0.3	1.6	1.3	3.4	4.9	0.8	1.8	0.7	1.5
Full-time teaching experience:										
Less than 3 years ..	Percent .	57.6	24.4	17.3	8.1	25.3	23.5	23.2	32.3	29.7
3 to 9 years	Percent .	42.1	46.5	30.6	12.3	28.2	31.9	31.0	30.1	33.0
10 to 20 years.....	Percent .	(NA)	29.2	36.7	34.1	22.7	28.6	27.4	22.5	28.7
20 years or more....	Percent .	(NA)	(NA)	15.4	46.2	23.8	15.9	18.5	15.1	8.7
Full-time teachers	1,000...	76	81	104	105	86	280	327	14	17
Earned income	Dollars .	25,289	29,841	29,638	33,278	36,524	27,771	29,942	27,593	29,508
Salary	Dollars ..	22,299	26,828	27,229	31,063	31,438	25,922	27,340	24,374	27,162

NA Not available.   [1] Non-Hispanic.   [2] Includes teachers with no degrees and associate's degrees, not shown separately.

Source: U.S. National Center for Education Statistics, *Digest of Education Statistics, 2002;* and unpublished data.

168   Education

Table 252. SAT Scores and Characteristics of College-Bound Seniors: 1967 to 2004

[For school year ending in year shown. Data are for the SAT I: Reasoning Tests. SAT I: Reasoning Test replaced the SAT in March 1994. Scores between the two tests have been equated to the same 200-800 scale and are thus comparable. Scores for 1995 and prior years have been recentered and revised]

Type of test and characteristic	Unit	1967	1970	1975	1980	1985	1990	1995	2000	2003	2004
AVERAGE TEST SCORES [1]											
Verbal, total [2]	Point	543	537	512	502	509	500	504	505	507	508
Male	Point	540	536	515	506	514	505	505	507	512	512
Female	Point	545	538	509	498	503	496	502	504	503	504
Math, total [2]	Point	516	512	498	492	500	501	506	514	519	518
Male	Point	535	531	518	515	522	521	525	533	537	537
Female	Point	495	493	479	473	480	483	490	498	503	501
PARTICIPANTS											
Total [3]	1,000	(NA)	(NA)	996	922	977	1,026	1,068	1,260	1,406	1,419
Male	Percent	(NA)	(NA)	49.9	48.2	48.3	47.8	46.4	46.2	46.4	46.5
White	Percent	(NA)	(NA)	86.0	82.1	81.0	73.0	69.2	66.4	63.8	62.7
Black	Percent	(NA)	(NA)	7.9	9.1	7.5	10.0	10.7	11.2	12.0	12.0
Obtaining scores [1] of—											
600 or above:											
Verbal	Percent	(NA)	(NA)	(NA)	(NA)	(NA)	20.3	21.9	21.1	21.9	22.2
Math	Percent	(NA)	(NA)	(NA)	(NA)	(NA)	20.4	23.4	24.2	26.2	25.5
Below 400:											
Verbal	Percent	(NA)	(NA)	(NA)	(NA)	(NA)	17.3	16.4	15.9	15.3	15.2
Math	Percent	(NA)	(NA)	(NA)	(NA)	(NA)	15.8	16.0	14.7	14.2	13.9
Selected intended area of study:											
Business and commerce	Percent	(NA)	(NA)	11.5	18.6	21.0	20.9	13.3	13.6	13.4	13.5
Engineering	Percent	(NA)	(NA)	6.7	11.1	11.7	10.2	8.8	8.5	9.3	9.1
Social science	Percent	(NA)	(NA)	7.7	7.8	7.5	12.6	11.6	10.6	10.1	9.6
Education	Percent	(NA)	(NA)	9.1	6.1	4.7	7.5	8.1	8.8	8.6	8.2

NA Not available. [1] Minimum score 200; maximum score, 800. [2] 1967 and 1970 are estimates based on total number of persons taking SAT. [3] 996 represents 996,000.

Source: The College Board, New York, NY, *College Bound Seniors*. Copyright 1967 to 2004. Reproduced with permission. All rights reserved. See Internet site <http://www.collegeboard.com/>.

Table 253. ACT Program Scores and Characteristics of College-Bound Students: 1970 to 2004

[For academic year ending in year shown. Except as indicated, test scores and characteristics of college-bound students. Through 1980, data based on 10 percent sample; thereafter, based on all ACT tested graduating seniors]

Type of test and characteristic	Unit	1970	1975	1980	1985	1990 [1]	1995 [1]	2000 [1]	2002 [1]	2003 [1]	2004 [1]
TEST SCORES [2]											
Composite	Point	19.9	18.6	18.5	18.6	20.6	20.8	21.0	20.8	20.8	20.9
Male	Point	20.3	19.5	19.3	19.4	21.0	21.0	21.2	20.9	21.0	21.0
Female	Point	19.4	17.8	17.9	17.9	20.3	20.7	20.9	20.7	20.8	20.9
English	Point	18.5	17.7	17.9	18.1	20.5	20.2	20.5	20.2	20.3	20.4
Male	Point	17.6	17.1	17.3	17.6	20.1	19.8	20.0	19.7	19.8	19.9
Female	Point	19.4	18.3	18.3	18.6	20.9	20.6	20.9	20.6	20.7	20.8
Math	Point	20.0	17.6	17.4	17.2	19.9	20.2	20.7	20.6	20.6	20.7
Male	Point	21.1	19.3	18.9	18.6	20.7	20.9	21.4	21.2	21.2	21.3
Female	Point	18.8	16.2	16.2	16.0	19.3	19.7	20.2	20.4	20.1	20.2
Reading [3]	Point	19.7	17.4	17.2	17.4	(NA)	21.3	21.4	21.1	21.2	21.3
Male	Point	20.3	18.7	18.2	18.3	(NA)	21.1	21.2	20.9	21.0	21.1
Female	Point	19.0	16.4	16.4	16.6	(NA)	21.4	21.5	21.3	21.4	21.5
Science reasoning [4]	Point	20.8	21.1	21.1	21.2	(NA)	21.0	21.0	20.8	20.8	20.9
Male	Point	21.6	22.4	22.4	22.6	(NA)	21.6	21.6	21.3	21.3	21.3
Female	Point	20.0	20.0	20.0	20.0	(NA)	20.5	20.6	20.4	20.4	20.5
PARTICIPANTS [5]											
Total [6]	1,000	788	714	822	739	817	945	1,065	1,116	1,175	1,171
Male	Percent	52	46	45	46	46	44	43	44	44	44
White	Percent	(NA)	77	83	82	79	75	76	74	73	72
Black	Percent	4	7	8	8	9	10	11	12	12	12
Obtaining composite scores of—											
27 or above	Percent	14	14	13	14	12	13	14	13	13	14
18 or below	Percent	21	33	33	32	35	34	32	35	35	34
Planned educational major:											
Business [8]	Percent	18	21	20	21	20	14	11	11	11	11
Engineering	Percent	8	6	8	9	9	9	6	6	6	5
Social science [9]	Percent	10	9	6	7	10	9	8	9	9	8
Education	Percent	16	12	9	6	8	9	9	9	9	8

NA Not available. [1] Beginning 1990, not comparable with previous years because a new version of the ACT was introduced. Estimated average composite scores for prior years: 1989, 20.6; 1988, 1987, and 1986, 20.8. [2] Minimum score, 1; maximum score, 36. [3] Prior to 1990, social studies; data not comparable with previous years. [4] Prior to 1990, natural sciences; data not comparable with previous years. [5] Beginning 1985, data are for seniors who graduated in year shown and had taken the ACT in their junior or senior years. Data by race are for those responding to the race question. [6] 788 represents 788,000. [7] Prior to 1990, 26 or above and 15 or below. [8] Includes political and persuasive (e.g. sales) fields through 1975; 1980 and 1985 business and commerce; thereafter, business and management and business and office. [9] Includes religion through 1975.

Source: ACT, Inc., Iowa City, IA, *High School Profile Report*, annual.

Table 254. Proficiency Test Scores for Selected Subjects by Characteristic: 1977 to 2001

[Based on The National Assessment of Educational Progress (NAEP) Tests which are administered to a representative sample of students in public and private schools. Reading, writing, mathematics. and social science based on NAEP Long-Term Assessments. Test scores can range from 0 to 500, except as indicated. For details, see source]

Test and year	Sex			Race		His-panic origin	Parental education				
	Total	Male	Female	White [1]	Black [1]		Less than high school	High school	More than high school		
									Total	Some college	College graduate
READING											
9 year olds:											
1979-80	215	210	220	221	189	190	194	213	226	(NA)	(NA)
1987-88	212	208	216	218	189	194	193	211	220	(NA)	(NA)
1998-99	212	209	215	221	186	193	199	206	220	(NA)	(NA)
13 year olds:											
1979-80	259	254	263	264	233	237	239	254	271	(NA)	(NA)
1987-88	258	252	263	261	243	240	247	253	265	(NA)	(NA)
1998-99	259	254	265	267	238	244	238	251	270	(NA)	(NA)
17 year olds:											
1979-80	286	282	289	293	243	261	262	278	299	(NA)	(NA)
1987-88	290	286	294	295	274	271	267	282	300	(NA)	(NA)
1998-99	288	282	295	295	264	271	265	274	298	(NA)	(NA)
WRITING [2]											
4th graders:											
1983-84	204	201	208	211	182	189	179	192	217	208	218
1987-88	206	199	213	215	173	190	194	199	212	211	212
1995-96	207	200	214	216	182	191	190	203	(NA)	205	214
8th graders:											
1983-84	267	258	276	272	247	247	258	261	276	271	278
1987-88	264	254	274	269	246	250	254	258	271	275	271
1995-96	264	251	276	271	242	246	245	258	(NA)	270	274
11th graders:											
1983-84	290	281	299	297	270	259	274	284	299	298	300
1987-88	291	282	299	296	275	274	276	285	298	296	299
1995-96	283	275	292	289	267	269	260	275	(NA)	287	291
MATHEMATICS											
9 year olds:											
1977-78	219	217	220	224	192	203	200	219	231	230	231
1985-86	222	222	222	227	202	205	201	218	231	229	231
1998-99	232	233	231	239	211	213	214	224	(NA)	237	240
13 year olds:											
1977-78	264	264	265	272	230	238	245	263	280	273	284
1985-86	269	270	268	274	249	254	252	263	278	274	280
1998-99	276	277	275	283	251	259	256	264	(NA)	279	286
17 year olds:											
1977-78	300	304	297	306	268	276	280	294	313	305	317
1985-86	302	305	299	308	279	283	279	293	310	305	314
1998-99	308	310	307	315	283	293	289	299	(NA)	308	317
SCIENCE											
9 year olds:											
1976-77	220	222	218	230	175	192	199	223	233	237	232
1985-86	224	227	221	232	196	199	204	220	235	236	235
1998-99	229	231	228	240	199	206	213	218	(NA)	234	237
13 year olds:											
1976-77	247	251	244	256	208	213	224	245	264	260	266
1985-86	251	256	247	259	222	226	229	245	262	258	264
1998-99	256	259	253	266	227	227	229	243	(NA)	261	268
17 year olds:											
1976-77	290	297	282	298	240	262	265	284	304	296	309
1985-86	289	295	282	298	253	259	258	277	300	295	304
1998-99	295	300	291	306	254	276	264	281	(NA)	297	307
HISTORY, 2001											
4th graders	209	209	209	220	188	186	177	197	(NA)	214	216
8th graders	262	264	261	271	243	243	241	251	(NA)	264	270
12th graders	287	288	286	292	269	274	263	276	(NA)	287	296
GEOGRAPHY, 2001											
4th graders	209	212	207	222	181	184	186	197	(NA)	216	216
8th graders	262	264	260	273	234	240	238	250	(NA)	265	272
12th graders	285	287	282	291	260	270	263	274	(NA)	286	294
CIVICS, 1997-98 [3]											
4th graders	150	149	151	159	132	126	124	153	(NA)	150	153
8th graders	150	148	152	159	133	127	123	144	(NA)	143	160
12th graders	150	148	152	158	131	130	124	140	(NA)	145	160

NA Not available. [1] Non-Hispanic. [2] Writing scores revised from previous years; previous writing scores were recorded on a 0 to 400 rather than 0 to 500 scale. [3] Civics uses a scale of 0 to 300.

Source: U.S. National Center for Education Statistics, *Digest of Education Statistics*, annual, and *NAEP 1998 Civics Report Card for the Nation* ; and *NAEP 2001 Geography and History Report Card for the Nation.*

Table 255. Advanced Placement Program—Summary: 2003 and 2004

[Includes exams taken by candidates abroad. In 2004, this represents 35,070 examinations taken by 20,700 students in 760 schools abroad. Minus sign (-)indicates decrease]

Item	Schools repre- sented, 2004	Exams taken 2003	Exams taken 2004	Percent change, 2003-04	10th grade	11th grade	12th grade	Male	Female
Exams taken, total [1] . .	(X)	1,737,231	1,887,770	9	143,690	662,123	994,220	856,010	1,031,760
By subject area:									
Art History.	1,056	13,720	13,753	-	1,301	4,018	7,773	4,615	9,138
Biology.	7,307	103,944	111,104	7	9,223	40,517	55,815	46,165	64,939
Calculus AB.	10,865	166,821	175,094	5	2,077	27,773	138,525	91,520	83,574
Calculus BC	3,982	45,973	50,134	9	884	9,717	37,884	30,087	20,047
Chemistry	5,788	65,698	71,070	8	4,006	35,756	28,662	38,367	32,703
Computer Science—A. . .	2,067	14,674	14,337	-2	1,972	5,383	6,330	12,004	2,333
Computer Science—AB . .	1,166	7,071	6,077	-14	628	2,266	2,965	5,431	646
Economics—Macro.	2,351	38,177	41,265	8	401	3,930	35,219	22,792	18,473
Economics—Micro	1,959	25,667	27,674	8	401	3,338	22,804	16,037	11,637
English Language/ Composition	7,071	175,860	198,514	13	2,271	151,061	37,289	73,790	124,724
English Literature/ Composition	11,134	229,367	239,493	4	354	15,247	214,457	87,216	152,277
Environmental Science . .	1,715	29,906	32,635	9	951	10,904	19,067	14,354	18,281
European History	3,878	73,807	79,169	7	38,795	11,639	25,224	36,994	42,175
French Language	3,238	18,496	19,016	3	951	5,065	11,983	5,735	13,281
French Literature	416	1,862	1,821	-2	71	419	1,245	533	1,288
German Language	1,213	3,973	4,500	13	277	899	2,998	2,203	2,297
Government and Politics—Comparative . .	1,173	12,001	12,980	8	1,007	1,912	9,518	6,788	6,192
Government and Politics—U.S.	5,254	104,636	112,894	8	4,901	10,356	92,575	53,440	59,454
Human Geography	561	7,329	10,471	43	2,551	1,850	3,180	4,857	5,614
Latin—Literature.	488	2,703	3,132	16	156	1,345	1,524	1,493	1,639
Latin—Vergil	632	3,942	4,061	3	304	1,682	1,918	2,102	1,959
Music Theory.	1,773	7,894	9,077	15	805	2,799	5,041	4,913	4,164
Physics B	3,706	40,926	43,295	6	961	15,180	25,389	28,210	15,085
Physics—Electricity and Magnetism	1,415	10,019	10,772	8	99	1,054	9,230	8,394	2,378
Physics—Mechanics. . . .	2,370	20,491	21,903	7	163	2,756	18,185	16,269	5,634
Psychology.	3,105	62,666	72,287	15	1,822	21,278	45,839	24,844	47,443
Spanish Language	5,825	83,811	90,828	8	10,184	31,164	41,562	31,932	58,896
Spanish Literature	1,254	10,848	12,303	13	848	3,597	7,023	3,920	8,383
Statistics.	3,611	58,230	65,878	13	2,417	12,619	48,319	32,963	32,915
Studio Art, Drawing.	2,586	10,642	11,707	10	193	2,056	8,814	3,873	7,834
Studio Art, 2D Design . . .	1,981	7,601	8,355	10	148	1,366	6,404	2,619	5,736
Studio Art, 3D Design . . .	746	1,491	1,707	14	21	227	1,352	662	1,045
U.S. History.	9,592	242,699	262,906	8	17,076	218,165	16,658	119,373	143,533
World History.	1,932	34,286	47,558	39	35,471	4,785	3,424	21,515	26,043
Candidates taking exams [1] .	(X)	1,017,396	1,101,802	8	128,544	412,300	502,579	482,950	618,852

- Represents or rounds to zero.   X Not applicable.   [1] Includes candidates and exams taken in other grades not shown separately.

Source: The College Entrance Examination Board, New York, NY, *National Summary Report, 2004* (copyright). All rights reserved. See Internet site <http://www.collegeboard.com>.

Table 256. Foreign Language Enrollment in Public High Schools: 1970 to 2000

[In thousands (13,301.9 represents 13,301,900), except percent. As of fall, for grades 9 through 12]

Language	1970	1974	1978	1982	1985	1990	1994	2000
Total enrollment	13,301.9	13,648.9	13,941.4	12,879.3	12,466.5	11,099.6	11,847.5	13,457.8
Enrolled in all foreign languages. . . .	3,779.3	3,294.5	3,200.1	2,909.8	4,028.9	4,256.9	5,001.9	5,899.4
Percent of all students	28.4	24.1	23.0	22.6	32.3	38.4	42.2	43.8
Enrolled in modern foreign languages [1] . . .	3,514.1	3,127.3	3,048.3	2,740.2	3,852.0	4,093.0	4,813.0	5,721.9
Spanish	1,810.8	1,678.1	1,631.4	1,562.8	2,334.4	2,611.4	3,219.8	4,057.6
French	1,230.7	977.9	856.0	858.0	1,133.7	1,089.4	1,105.9	1,075.4
German	410.5	393.0	330.6	266.9	312.2	295.4	326.0	283.3
Italian	27.3	40.2	45.5	44.1	47.3	40.4	43.8	64.1
Japanese	(NA)	(NA)	(NA)	6.2	8.6	24.1	42.3	50.9
Russian	20.2	15.1	8.8	5.7	6.4	16.5	16.4	10.6
Percent of all students [1]	26.4	22.9	21.9	21.3	30.9	36.9	40.6	42.5
Spanish	13.6	12.3	11.7	12.1	18.7	23.5	27.2	30.2
French.	9.3	7.2	6.1	6.7	9.1	9.8	9.3	8.0
German	3.1	2.9	2.4	2.1	2.5	2.7	2.8	2.1
Italian	0.2	0.3	0.3	0.3	0.4	0.4	0.4	0.5
Japanese	(NA)	(NA)	(NA)	0.1	0.1	0.2	0.4	0.4
Russian	0.2	0.1	0.1	(Z)	0.1	0.2	0.1	0.1

NA Not available.   Z Less than 0.05 percent.   [1] Includes other foreign languages, not shown separately.

Source: The American Council on the Teaching of Foreign Languages, Yonkers, NY, *Foreign Language Enrollments in Public Secondary Schools, fall 1994* and *fall 2000.*

Education 171

Table 257. Public High School Graduates by State: 1980 to 2004

[In thousands (2,747.7 represents 2,747,700). For school year ending in year shown]

State	1980	1990	2000	2004. est.	State	1980	1990	2000	2004. est.
United States ...	2,747.7	2,320.3	2,553.8	2,757.5	Missouri.	62.3	49.0	52.8	57.0
Alabama	45.2	40.5	37.8	37.6	Montana	12.1	9.4	10.9	10.5
Alaska.	5.2	5.4	6.6	7.1	Nebraska.	22.4	17.7	20.1	20.0
Arizona	28.6	32.1	38.3	57.0	Nevada	8.5	9.5	14.6	16.2
Arkansas	29.1	26.5	27.3	26.9	New Hampshire	11.7	10.8	11.8	13.3
California	249.2	236.3	309.9	342.6					
					New Jersey	94.6	69.8	74.4	88.3
Colorado	36.8	33.0	38.9	42.9	New Mexico	18.4	14.9	18.0	18.1
Connecticut	37.7	27.9	31.6	34.4	New York.	204.1	143.3	141.7	150.9
Delaware	7.6	5.6	6.1	6.8	North Carolina	70.9	64.8	62.1	71.4
District of Columbia . . .	5.0	3.6	2.7	3.2	North Dakota	9.9	7.7	8.6	7.8
Florida.	87.3	88.9	106.7	129.0					
					Ohio	144.2	114.5	111.7	116.3
Georgia	61.6	56.6	62.6	69.7	Oklahoma	39.3	35.6	37.6	36.7
Hawaii.	11.5	10.3	10.4	10.3	Oregon	29.9	25.5	30.2	32.5
Idaho	13.2	12.0	16.2	15.5	Pennsylvania	146.5	110.5	114.0	121.6
Illinois	135.6	108.1	111.8	121.3	Rhode Island	10.9	7.8	8.5	9.3
Indiana	73.1	60.0	57.0	57.6					
					South Carolina	38.7	32.5	31.6	32.1
Iowa	43.4	31.8	33.9	33.8	South Dakota	10.7	7.7	9.3	9.1
Kansas	30.9	25.4	29.1	30.0	Tennessee	49.8	46.1	41.6	43.6
Kentucky	41.2	38.0	36.8	36.2	Texas	171.4	172.5	212.9	236.7
Louisiana	46.3	36.1	38.4	36.2	Utah	20.0	21.2	32.5	29.9
Maine	15.4	13.8	12.2	13.4					
					Vermont	6.7	6.1	6.7	7.0
Maryland	54.3	41.6	47.8	53.0	Virginia	66.6	60.6	65.6	71.7
Massachusetts	73.8	55.9	53.0	57.9	Washington	50.4	45.9	57.6	60.4
Michigan	124.3	93.8	97.7	106.3	West Virginia	23.4	21.9	19.4	17.1
Minnesota	64.9	49.1	57.4	59.8	Wisconsin	69.3	52.0	58.5	62.3
Mississippi.	27.6	25.2	24.2	23.6	Wyoming	6.1	5.8	6.5	5.7

Source: U.S. National Center for Education Statistics, Digest of Education Statistics, annual.

Table 258. High School Dropouts by Race and Hispanic Origin: 1975 to 2003

[In percent. As of October]

Item	1975	1980	1985	1990[1]	1995	1997	1998	1999	2000	2001	2002	2003
EVENT DROPOUTS[2]												
Total[3]	5.8	6.0	5.2	4.5	5.4	4.3	4.4	4.7	4.5	4.7	3.3	3.8
White[4].	5.4	5.6	4.8	3.9	5.1	4.2	4.4	4.4	4.3	4.6	3.0	3.7
Male.	5.0	6.4	4.9	4.1	5.4	4.9	4.4	4.1	4.7	5.3	3.0	3.9
Female	5.8	4.9	4.7	3.8	4.8	3.5	4.4	4.7	4.0	3.8	3.0	3.4
Black[4].	8.7	8.3	7.7	7.7	6.1	4.8	5.0	6.0	5.6	5.7	4.4	4.5
Male.	8.3	8.0	8.3	6.9	7.9	4.1	4.6	5.2	7.6	6.1	5.1	4.1
Female	9.0	8.5	7.2	8.6	4.4	5.7	5.5	6.8	3.8	5.4	3.8	4.9
Hispanic[5]	10.9	11.5	9.7	7.7	11.6	8.6	8.4	7.1	6.8	8.1	5.3	6.5
Male.	10.1	16.9	9.3	7.6	10.9	10.4	8.6	6.9	7.1	7.6	6.2	7.7
Female	11.6	6.9	9.8	7.7	12.5	6.7	8.2	7.3	6.5	8.7	4.4	5.4
STATUS DROPOUTS[6]												
Total[3]	15.6	15.6	13.9	14.4	13.9	13.0	13.9	13.1	12.4	13.0	12.3	11.8
White[4].	13.9	14.4	13.5	14.1	13.6	12.4	13.7	12.8	12.2	13.4	12.2	11.6
Male.	13.5	15.7	14.7	15.4	14.3	13.8	15.7	13.9	13.5	15.3	13.7	13.3
Female	14.2	13.2	12.3	12.8	13.0	10.9	11.7	11.8	10.9	11.4	10.6	9.8
Black[4].	27.3	23.5	17.6	16.4	14.4	16.7	17.1	16.0	15.3	13.8	14.6	14.2
Male.	27.8	26.0	18.8	18.6	14.2	18.3	17.4	16.3	17.4	16.9	16.9	16.7
Female	26.9	21.5	16.6	14.5	14.6	16.1	14.3	15.7	13.5	11.0	12.5	12.0
Hispanic[5]	34.9	40.3	31.5	37.7	34.7	30.6	34.4	33.9	32.3	31.7	30.1	28.4
Male.	32.6	42.6	35.8	40.3	34.2	33.2	39.7	36.4	36.8	37.1	33.8	31.7
Female	36.8	38.1	27.0	35.0	35.4	27.6	28.6	31.1	27.3	25.5	25.6	24.7

[1] Beginning 1990, reflects new editing procedures for cases with missing data on school enrollment. [2] Percent of students who drop out in a single year without completing high school. For grades 10 to 12. [3] Includes other races, not shown separately. [4] Beginning 2003, for persons who selected this race group only. See footnote 2, Table 214. [5] Persons of Hispanic origin may be of any race. [6] Percent of the population who have not completed high school and are not enrolled, regardless of when they dropped out. For persons 18 to 24 years old.

Source: U.S. Census Bureau, Current Population Reports, PPL-148; and earlier PPL and P-20 reports; and data published on the Internet. See Internet site <http://www.census.gov/population/www/socdemo/school.html>.

Table 259. **High School Dropouts by Age, Race, and Hispanic Origin: 1980 to 2003**

[As of October (5,212 represents 5,212,000). For persons 14 to 24 years old. See Table 261 for definition of dropouts]

Age and race	Number of dropouts (1,000)					Percent of population				
	1980	1990	1995	2000	2003	1980	1990	1995	2000	2003
Total dropouts [1][2]	5,212	3,854	3,963	3,883	3,734	12.0	10.1	9.9	9.1	8.4
16 to 17 years	709	418	406	460	323	8.8	6.3	5.4	5.8	3.8
18 to 21 years	2,578	1,921	1,980	2,005	1,735	15.8	13.4	14.2	12.9	11.4
22 to 24 years	1,798	1,458	1,491	1,310	1,493	15.2	13.8	13.6	11.8	12.2
White [2][3]	4,169	3,127	3,098	3,065	2,875	11.3	10.1	9.7	9.1	8.3
16 to 17 years	619	334	314	366	233	9.2	6.4	5.4	5.8	3.5
18 to 21 years	2,032	1,516	1,530	1,558	1,363	14.7	13.1	13.8	12.6	11.4
22 to 24 years	1,416	1,235	1,181	1,040	1,126	14.0	14.0	13.4	11.7	11.8
Black [2][3]	934	611	605	705	629	16.0	10.9	10.0	10.9	9.7
16 to 17 years	80	73	70	84	63	6.9	6.9	5.8	7.0	4.7
18 to 21 years	486	345	328	383	276	23.0	16.0	15.8	16.0	12.8
22 to 24 years	346	185	194	232	269	24.0	13.5	12.5	14.3	16.0
Hispanic [2][4]	919	1,122	1,355	1,499	1,480	29.5	26.8	24.7	23.5	19.6
16 to 17 years	92	89	94	121	84	16.6	12.9	10.7	11.0	6.3
18 to 21 years	470	502	652	733	627	40.3	32.9	29.9	30.0	24.4
22 to 24 years	323	523	598	602	726	40.6	42.8	37.4	35.5	33.1

[1] Includes other groups not shown separately. [2] Includes persons 14 to 15 years, not shown separately. [3] Beginning 2003, for persons who selected this race group only. See footnote 2, Table 214. [4] Persons of Hispanic origin may be of any race.

Source: U.S. Census Bureau, Current Population Reports, PPL-148; and earlier PPL and P-20 reports; and data published on the Internet. See Internet site <http://www.census.gov/population/www/socdemo/school.html>.

Table 260. **Enrollment Status by Race, Hispanic Origin, and Sex: 1975 and 2003**

[As of October (15,693 represents 15,693,000). For persons 18 to 21 years old. For the civilian noninstitutional population. Based on the Current Population Survey; see text, Section 1, and Appendix III]

Characteristic	Total persons 18 to 21 years old (1,000)		Percent distribution							
			Enrolled in high school		High school graduates				Not high school graduates	
					Total		In college			
	1975	2003	1975	2003	1975	2003	1975	2003	1975	2003
Total [1]	15,693	15,167	5.7	9.7	78.0	78.6	33.5	45.2	16.3	11.7
White [2]	13,448	11,917	4.7	8.8	80.6	79.5	34.6	46.0	14.7	11.7
Black [2]	1,997	2,159	12.5	14.8	60.4	72.5	24.9	35.0	27.0	12.7
Hispanic [3]	899	2,564	12.0	10.5	57.2	64.7	24.4	29.7	30.8	24.8
Male [1]	7,584	7,505	7.4	11.2	76.6	75.2	35.4	40.7	15.9	13.6
White [2]	6,545	5,984	6.2	10.5	79.7	76.0	36.9	40.9	14.1	13.5
Black [2]	911	1,013	15.9	16.3	55.0	68.3	23.9	30.4	29.0	15.4
Hispanic [3]	416	1,358	17.3	12.2	54.6	60.5	25.2	22.8	27.9	27.3
Female [1]	8,109	7,662	4.2	8.3	79.2	82.0	31.8	49.5	16.6	9.7
White [2]	6,903	5,933	3.2	7.1	81.4	83.0	32.4	51.1	15.3	9.9
Black [2]	1,085	1,147	9.7	13.5	65.0	76.1	25.8	39.1	25.4	10.4
Hispanic [3]	484	1,205	7.6	8.6	59.3	69.5	23.6	37.4	33.1	21.9

[1] Includes other races not shown separately. [2] Beginning 2003, for persons who selected this race group only. See footnote 2, Table 214. [3] Persons of Hispanic origin may be of any race.

Source: U.S. Census Bureau, Current Population Reports, PPL-148; and earlier PPL and P-20 reports; and data published on the Internet. See Internet site <http://www.census.gov/population/www/socdemo/school.html>.

Table 261. **Employment Status of High School Graduates and School Dropouts: 1980 to 2004**

[In thousands (11,622 represents 11,622,000), except percent. As of October. For civilian noninstitutional population 16 to 24 years old. Based on Current Population Survey; see text, Section 1, and Appendix III]

Employment status, sex, and race	Graduates [1]				Dropouts [3]			
	1980	1990	2000 [2]	2004 [2]	1980	1990	2000 [2]	2004 [2]
Civilian population	11,622	8,370	7,351	7,243	5,254	3,800	3,776	3,766
In labor force	9,795	7,107	6,195	5,924	3,549	2,506	2,612	2,534
Percent of population	84.3	84.9	84.3	81.8	67.5	66.0	69.2	67.3
Employed	8,567	6,279	5,632	5,160	2,651	1,993	2,150	1,996
Percent of labor force	87.5	88.3	90.9	87.1	74.7	79.5	82.3	78.7
Unemployed	1,228	828	563	763	898	513	463	539
Unemployment rate, total [4]	12.5	11.7	9.1	12.9	25.3	20.5	17.7	21.3
Male	13.5	11.1	9.3	12.1	23.5	18.8	16.3	20.0
Female	11.5	12.3	8.8	14.0	28.7	23.5	20.3	23.6
White [5]	10.8	9.0	7.2	10.7	21.6	17.0	15.0	16.2
Black [5]	26.1	26.0	18.1	21.9	43.9	43.3	33.2	44.3
Not in labor force	1,827	1,262	1,156	1,319	1,705	1,294	1,163	1,231
Percent of population	15.7	15.1	15.7	18.2	32.5	34.1	30.8	32.7

[1] For persons not enrolled in college who have completed 4 years of high school only. See text, this section, and February 2000, 2003 and 2004 issues of Employment and Earnings. [2] Data not strictly comparable with data for earlier years. See text, this section, and February 2000, 2003 and 2004 issues of Employment and Earnings. [3] For persons not in regular school and who have not completed the 12th grade nor received a general equivalency degree. [4] Includes other races not shown separately. [5] For 2004, for persons who selected this race group only. See footnote 2, Table 214.

Source: U.S. Bureau of Labor Statistics, Bulletin 2307; News, USDL 05-487, March 25, 2005; and unpublished data. See Internet site <http://www.bls.gov/news.release/hsgec.toc.htm>.

Table 262. **General Educational Development (GED) Credentials Issued: 1975 to 2001**

[GEDs issued in thousands (340 represents 340,000). For the 50 states and DC]

Year	GEDs issued	Percent distribution by age of test taker				
		19 years old or under	20 to 24 years old	25 to 29 years old	30 to 34 years old	35 years old and over
1975	340	33	26	14	9	18
1980	479	37	27	13	8	15
1985	413	32	26	15	10	16
1990	410	36	25	13	10	15
1995	504	38	25	13	9	15
1997	460	43	24	12	8	13
1998	481	44	24	11	7	13
1999	498	44	25	11	7	13
2000	487	45	25	11	7	13
2001	648	41	26	11	8	14

Source: U.S. National Center for Education Statistics, *Digest of Education Statistics*, 2003.

Table 263. **College Enrollment of Recent High School Graduates: 1970 to 2003**

[2,758 represents 2,758,000. For persons 16 to 24 who graduated from high school in the preceeding 12 months. Includes persons receiving GEDs. Based on surveys and subject to sampling error]

Year	Number of high school graduates (1,000)						Percent enrolled in college [3]					
	Total [1]	Male	Female	White	Black	Hispanic [2]	Total [1]	Male	Female	White	Black	Hispanic [2]
1970 . . .	2,758	1,343	1,415	2,461	(NA)	(NA)	51.7	55.2	48.5	52.0	(NA)	(NA)
1975 . . .	3,185	1,513	1,672	2,701	302	(NA)	50.7	52.6	49.0	51.1	41.7	58.0
1980 . . .	3,088	1,498	1,589	2,554	350	129	49.3	46.7	51.8	49.8	42.7	52.3
1985 . . .	2,668	1,287	1,381	2,104	332	141	57.7	58.6	56.8	60.1	42.2	51.0
1986 . . .	2,786	1,332	1,454	2,146	378	169	53.8	55.8	51.9	56.8	36.9	44.0
1987 . . .	2,647	1,278	1,369	2,040	333	176	56.8	58.3	55.3	58.6	52.2	33.5
1988 . . .	2,673	1,334	1,339	2,013	378	179	58.9	57.1	60.7	61.1	44.4	57.1
1989 . . .	2,450	1,204	1,246	1,889	332	168	59.6	57.6	61.6	60.7	53.4	55.1
1990 . . .	2,362	1,173	1,189	1,819	331	112	60.1	58.0	62.2	63.0	46.8	42.7
1991 . . .	2,276	1,140	1,136	1,727	310	154	62.5	57.9	67.1	65.4	46.4	57.2
1992 . . .	2,397	1,216	1,180	1,724	354	199	61.9	60.0	63.8	64.3	48.2	55.0
1993 . . .	2,342	1,120	1,223	1,719	304	200	62.6	59.9	65.2	62.9	55.6	62.2
1994 . . .	2,517	1,244	1,273	1,915	316	178	61.9	60.6	63.2	64.5	50.8	49.1
1995 . . .	2,599	1,238	1,361	1,861	349	288	61.9	62.6	61.3	64.3	51.2	53.7
1996 . . .	2,660	1,297	1,363	1,875	406	227	65.0	60.1	69.7	67.4	56.0	50.8
1997 . . .	2,769	1,354	1,415	1,909	384	336	67.0	63.6	70.3	68.2	58.5	65.6
1998 . . .	2,810	1,452	1,358	1,980	386	314	65.6	62.4	69.1	68.5	61.9	47.4
1999 . . .	2,897	1,474	1,423	1,978	436	329	62.9	61.4	64.4	66.3	58.9	42.3
2000 . . .	2,756	1,251	1,505	1,938	393	300	63.3	59.9	66.2	65.7	54.9	52.9
2001 . . .	2,545	1,275	1,270	1,832	379	241	61.7	59.7	63.6	64.2	54.6	51.7
2002 . . .	2,796	1,412	1,384	1,903	382	344	65.2	62.1	68.4	67.0	55.3	45.4
2003 . . .	2,677	1,306	1,372	1,832	327	314	63.9	61.2	66.5	66.2	57.5	58.6

NA Not available. [1] Includes other races, not shown separately. [2] Persons of Hispanic origin may be of any race. Due to small sample size data should be used with caution. [3] As of October.

Source: U.S. National Center for Education Statistics, *Digest of Education Statistics*, annual.

Table 264. **College Enrollment by Sex and Attendance Status: 1983 to 2003**

[As of fall. In thousands (12,465 represents 12,465,000)]

Sex and age	1983		1988		1993		1998 [1]		2003, proj. [1]	
	Total	Part-time	Total	Part-time	Total	Part-time	Total	Part-time	Total	Part-time
Total	12,465	5,204	13,055	5,619	14,305	6,177	14,507	5,944	16,910	6,755
Male	6,024	2,264	6,002	2,340	6,427	2,537	6,369	2,436	7,259	2,742
14 to 17 years old	102	16	55	5	83	10	45	5	79	18
18 to 19 years old	1,256	158	1,290	132	1,224	138	1,535	296	1,575	298
20 to 21 years old	1,241	205	1,243	216	1,294	209	1,374	245	1,401	291
22 to 24 years old	1,158	382	1,106	378	1,260	392	1,127	350	1,401	424
25 to 29 years old	1,115	624	875	485	950	564	908	485	909	431
30 to 34 years old	570	384	617	456	661	484	463	322	546	363
35 years old and over	583	494	816	668	955	739	917	733	1,164	917
Female	6,441	2,940	7,053	3,278	7,877	3,640	8,138	3,508	9,652	4,013
14 to 17 years old	142	16	115	17	93	6	74	21	112	20
18 to 19 years old	1,496	179	1,536	195	1,416	172	1,847	292	1,976	343
20 to 21 years old	1,125	204	1,278	218	1,414	279	1,437	295	1,809	319
22 to 24 years old	884	378	932	403	1,263	493	1,250	463	1,661	630
25 to 29 years old	947	658	932	633	1,058	689	1,083	617	1,335	677
30 to 34 years old	721	553	698	499	811	575	732	506	764	476
35 years old and over	1,126	953	1,563	1,313	1,824	1,427	1,715	1,315	1,994	1,550

[1] In this table, data beginning in 1998 reflect the new classification of institutions. See footnote 1, Table 265.

Source: U.S. National Center for Education Statistics, *Digest of Education Statistics*, annual.

Table 265. Higher Education—Summary: 1980 to 2002

[Institutions, staff, and enrollment as of fall (686 represents 686,000). Finances for fiscal year ending in the following year. Covers universities, colleges, professional schools, junior and teachers colleges, both publicly and privately controlled, regular session. Includes estimates for institutions not reporting. See also Appendix III]

Item	Unit	1980	1985	1990	1995	1998	1999	2000	2001	2002
ALL INSTITUTIONS										
Number of institutions [1]	Number...	3,231	3,340	3,559	3,706	4,048	4,084	4,182	4,197	4,168
4-year	Number...	1,957	2,029	2,141	2,244	2,335	2,363	2,450	2,364	2,324
2-year	Number...	1,274	1,311	1,418	1,462	1,713	1,721	1,732	1,833	1,844
Instructional staff—										
(Lecturer or above) [2]	1,000....	686	715	817	932	999	1,028	(NA)	1,113	1,175
Percent full-time	Percent...	66	64	61	59	(NA)	57	(NA)	58	54
Total enrollment [3][4]	1,000.....	12,097	12,247	13,819	14,262	14,507	14,791	15,312	15,928	16,612
Male	1,000.....	5,874	5,818	6,284	6,343	6,369	6,491	6,722	6,961	7,202
Female	1,000.....	6,223	6,429	7,535	7,919	8,138	8,301	8,591	8,967	9,410
4-year institutions	1,000.....	7,571	7,716	8,579	8,769	9,018	9,199	9,364	9,677	10,082
2-year institutions	1,000.....	4,526	4,531	5,240	5,493	5,489	5,593	5,948	6,251	6,529
Full-time	1,000.....	7,098	7,075	7,821	8,129	8,563	8,786	9,010	9,448	9,946
Part-time	1,000.....	4,999	5,172	5,998	6,133	5,944	6,005	6,303	6,480	6,665
Public	1,000.....	9,457	9,479	10,845	11,092	11,138	11,309	11,753	12,233	12,752
Private	1,000.....	2,640	2,768	2,974	3,169	3,369	3,482	3,560	3,695	3,860
Not-for-profit	1,000.....	2,528	2,572	2,760	2,929	3,005	3,052	3,109	3,167	3,265
For profit	1,000.....	112	196	213	240	364	430	450	528	594
Undergraduate [4]	1,000.....	10,475	10,597	11,959	12,232	12,437	12,681	13,155	13,716	14,257
Men	1,000.....	5,000	4,962	5,380	5,401	5,446	5,559	5,778	6,004	6,192
Women	1,000.....	5,475	5,635	6,579	6,831	6,991	7,122	7,377	7,711	8,065
First-time freshmen	1,000.....	2,588	2,292	2,257	2,169	2,213	2,352	2,428	2,497	2,571
First professional	1,000.....	278	274	273	298	302	303	307	309	319
Men	1,000.....	199	180	167	174	169	165	164	161	163
Women	1,000.....	78	94	107	124	134	138	143	148	156
Graduate [4]	1,000.....	1,343	1,376	1,586	1,732	1,768	1,807	1,850	1,904	2,035
Men	1,000.....	675	677	737	768	754	766	780	796	847
Women	1,000.....	670	700	849	965	1,013	1,041	1,071	1,108	1,189
Public institutions:										
Current funds revenues [5]	Mil. dol...	43,196	65,005	94,905	123,501	144,970	157,314	176,645	174,503	(NA)
Tuition and fees	Mil. dol...	5,570	9,439	15,258	23,257	27,428	29,126	31,919	31,464	(NA)
Federal government	Mil. dol...	5,540	6,852	9,763	13,672	15,554	16,952	19,744	18,668	(NA)
State government	Mil. dol...	19,676	29,221	38,240	44,243	52,132	56,370	62,895	62,543	(NA)
Auxiliary enterprises	Mil. dol...	4,615	6,685	9,059	11,595	13,776	15,174	16,501	16,379	(NA)
Public institutions:										
Current funds expenditures [5]	Mil. dol...	42,280	63,194	92,961	119,525	140,539	152,325	170,345	168,296	(NA)
Educational and general	Mil. dol...	34,173	50,873	74,395	96,086	113,594	122,709	136,613	135,549	(NA)
Auxiliary enterprises	Mil. dol...	4,658	6,830	9,050	11,309	13,567	14,448	16,377	16,245	(NA)
2-YEAR INSTITUTIONS										
Number of institutions [1][6]	Number...	1,274	1,311	1,418	1,462	1,713	1,721	1,732	1,833	1,844
Public	Number...	945	932	972	1,047	1,069	1,068	1,076	1,101	1,101
Private	Number...	329	379	446	415	644	653	656	732	743
Instructional staff—										
(Lecturer or above) [2]	1,000.....	192	211	(NA)	285	(NA)	314	(NA)	349	359
Enrollment [3][4]	1,000.....	4,526	4,531	5,240	5,493	5,489	5,593	5,948	6,251	6,529
Public	1,000.....	4,329	4,270	4,996	5,278	5,246	5,339	5,697	5,997	6,270
Private	1,000.....	198	261	244	215	243	253	251	254	259
Male	1,000.....	2,047	2,002	2,233	2,329	2,333	2,387	2,559	2,675	2,753
Female	1,000.....	2,479	2,529	3,007	3,164	3,156	3,205	3,390	3,575	3,776

NA Not available. [1] Number of institutions includes count of branch campuses. Due to revised survey procedures, data beginning 1998 reflect a new classification of institutions; this classification includes some additional, primarily 2-year, colleges and excludes a few institutions that did not award degrees. Includes institutions that were eligible to participate in Title IV federal financial aid programs. [2] Due to revised survey methods, data beginning 1990 not comparable with previous years. [3] Branch campuses counted according to actual status, e.g., 2-year branch in 2-year category. [4] Includes unclassified students. (Students taking courses for credit, but are not candidates for degrees.) [5] Includes items not shown separately. [6] Includes schools accredited by the National Association of Trade and Technical Schools. See footnote 1 for information pertaining to data beginning 1998.

Source: U.S. National Center for Education Statistics, *Digest of Education Statistics*, annual; and unpublished data.

Education 175

Table 266. **College Enrollment by Selected Characteristics: 1990 to 2002**

[In thousands (13,818.6 represents 13,818,600). As of fall. Nonresident alien students are not distributed among racial/ethnic groups]

Characteristic	1990	1995	1997 [1]	1998 [1]	1999 [1]	2000 [1]	2001 [1]	2002 [1]
Total.........	13,818.6	14,261.8	14,502.3	14,507.0	14,791.2	15,312.3	15,928.0	16,612.0
Male............	6,283.9	6,342.5	6,396.0	6,369.3	6,490.6	6,721.8	6,960.8	7,202.0
Female...........	7,534.7	7,919.2	8,106.3	8,137.7	8,300.6	8,590.5	8,967.2	9,410.0
Public...........	10,844.7	11,092.4	11,196.1	11,137.8	11,309.4	11,752.8	12,233.2	12,752.0
Private...........	2,973.9	3,169.4	3,306.2	3,369.2	3,481.8	3,559.5	3,694.8	3,860.0
2-year...........	5,240.1	5,492.5	5,605.6	5,489.3	5,592.7	5,948.4	6,250.6	6,529.0
4-year...........	8,578.6	8,769.3	8,896.8	9,017.7	9,198.5	9,363.9	9,677.4	10,082.0
Undergraduate.......	11,959.2	12,232.0	12,450.6	12,436.9	12,681.2	13,155.4	13,715.6	14,257.0
Graduate	1,586.2	1,732.0	1,753.5	1,767.6	1,806.8	1,850.3	1,903.7	2,036.0
First professional	273.4	297.6	298.3	302.5	303.2	306.6	308.6	319.0
White [2]	10,722.5	10,311.2	10,266.1	10,178.8	10,282.1	10,462.1	10,774.5	11,140.2
Male	4,861.0	4,594.1	4,548.8	4,499.4	4,551.1	4,634.6	4,762.3	4,897.9
Female...........	5,861.5	5,717.2	5,717.4	5,679.4	5,731.0	5,827.5	6,012.2	6,242.3
Public...........	8,385.4	7,945.4	7,857.8	7,750.6	7,803.2	7,963.4	8,214.0	8,490.5
Private...........	2,337.0	2,365.9	2,408.3	2,428.3	2,478.8	2,498.7	2,560.5	2,649.8
2-year...........	3,954.3	3,794.0	3,770.0	3,641.3	3,672.0	3,804.1	3,955.7	4,086.5
4-year...........	6,768.1	6,517.2	6,496.1	6,537.5	6,610.1	6,658.0	6,818.8	7,053.8
Undergraduate.......	9,272.6	8,805.6	8,783.9	8,703.6	8,805.7	8,983.5	9,278.7	9,564.9
Graduate	1,228.4	1,282.3	1,261.8	1,254.3	1,256.5	1,258.5	1,275.1	1,348.0
First professional	221.5	223.3	220.4	220.9	219.9	220.1	220.8	227.4
Black [2]	1,247.0	1,473.7	1,551.0	1,582.9	1,643.2	1,730.3	1,850.4	1,978.7
Male	484.7	555.9	579.8	584.0	604.2	635.3	672.4	708.6
Female...........	762.3	917.8	971.3	999.0	1,038.9	1,095.0	1,178.0	1,270.2
Public...........	976.4	1,160.6	1,205.3	1,218.8	1,253.4	1,319.2	1,397.1	1,487.2
Private...........	270.6	313.0	345.8	364.2	389.8	411.1	453.3	491.6
2-year...........	524.3	621.5	654.6	655.4	679.1	734.9	795.7	859.1
4-year...........	722.8	852.2	896.4	927.6	964.1	995.4	1,054.7	1,119.7
Undergraduate.......	1,147.2	1,333.6	1,398.1	1,421.7	1,471.9	1,548.9	1,657.1	1,763.9
Graduate	83.9	118.6	131.6	138.7	148.7	157.9	169.4	189.6
First professional	15.9	21.4	21.4	22.5	22.5	23.5	23.9	25.3
Hispanic	782.4	1,093.8	1,218.5	1,257.1	1,319.1	1,461.8	1,560.6	1,661.7
Male	353.9	480.2	525.8	538.6	563.6	627.1	664.2	699.0
Female...........	428.5	613.7	692.7	718.5	755.5	834.7	896.4	962.7
Public...........	671.4	937.1	1,031.6	1,057.8	1,099.1	1,229.3	1,308.8	1,388.7
Private...........	111.0	156.8	186.9	199.3	220.0	232.5	251.8	273.1
2-year...........	424.2	608.4	688.5	704.2	735.7	843.9	904.3	958.9
4-year...........	358.2	485.5	530.0	552.9	583.4	617.9	656.3	702.9
Undergraduate.......	724.6	1,012.0	1,125.9	1,159.8	1,214.0	1,351.0	1,444.4	1,533.3
Graduate	47.2	68.0	78.7	82.9	90.4	95.4	100.5	112.3
First professional	10.7	13.8	13.9	14.4	14.7	15.4	15.6	16.1
American Indian/ Alaska Native	102.8	131.3	142.5	144.2	145.5	151.2	158.2	165.9
Male	43.1	54.8	59.0	59.0	58.6	61.4	63.6	65.7
Female...........	59.7	76.5	83.4	85.1	86.8	89.7	94.5	100.2
Public...........	90.4	113.8	123.6	122.6	124.2	127.3	133.6	140.0
Private...........	12.4	17.5	18.8	21.5	21.3	23.9	24.6	25.9
2-year...........	54.9	65.6	71.0	71.5	72.1	74.7	78.2	81.3
4-year...........	47.9	65.7	71.5	72.6	73.4	76.5	80.0	84.6
Undergraduate.......	95.5	120.7	130.8	132.2	133.4	138.5	144.8	151.7
Graduate	6.2	8.5	9.4	9.8	10.0	10.3	11.2	11.9
First professional	1.1	2.1	2.3	2.2	2.1	2.3	2.1	2.2
Asian/ Pacific Islander ...	572.4	797.4	859.2	900.5	913.0	978.2	1,019.0	1,074.2
Male	294.9	393.3	417.7	433.6	437.1	465.9	480.8	503.9
Female...........	277.5	404.1	441.5	466.9	475.8	512.3	538.3	570.2
Public...........	461.0	638.0	680.4	713.2	716.1	770.5	806.1	851.6
Private...........	111.5	159.4	178.8	187.3	196.9	207.7	213.0	222.6
2-year...........	215.2	314.9	340.7	361.9	356.2	401.9	417.5	441.0
4-year...........	357.2	482.4	518.5	538.5	556.8	576.3	601.6	633.1
Undergraduate.......	500.5	692.2	743.7	778.3	786.0	845.5	883.9	927.4
Graduate	53.2	75.6	82.6	87.0	90.7	95.8	97.4	107.1
First professional	18.7	29.6	32.9	35.1	36.3	36.8	37.7	39.6
Nonresident alien ...	391.5	454.4	465.0	443.5	488.5	528.7	565.3	590.9
Male	246.3	264.3	264.9	254.6	276.0	297.3	317.4	327.0
Female...........	145.2	190.1	200.1	188.9	212.4	231.4	247.8	263.9
Public...........	260.0	297.5	297.3	274.9	313.3	343.1	373.6	394.1
Private...........	131.4	156.9	167.7	168.7	175.1	185.6	191.6	196.8
2-year...........	67.1	88.1	80.7	55.0	77.6	89.0	99.2	102.6
4-year...........	324.3	366.2	384.3	388.5	410.8	439.7	466.1	488.3
Undergraduate.......	218.7	267.6	268.2	241.3	270.3	288.0	306.7	316.0
Graduate	167.3	179.5	189.4	194.8	210.6	232.3	250.1	266.6
First professional	5.4	7.3	7.5	7.4	7.6	8.4	8.4	8.3

[1] In this table, data beginning 1997 reflect a new classification of institutions; for more on this classification, see footnote 1, table 265. [2] Non-Hispanic.

Source: U.S. National Center for Education Statistics, *Digest of Education Statistics*, annual.

Table 267. Degree-Granting Institutions, Number and Enrollment by State: 2002

[16,612 represents 16,612,000. Number of institutions beginning in academic year. Opening fall enrollment of resident and extension students attending full-time or part-time. Excludes students taking courses for credit by mail, radio, or TV, and students in branches of U.S. institutions operated in foreign countries. See Appendix III]

State	Number of institutions [1]	Enrollment (1,000)							Minority enrollment			Nonresident alien
		Total	Male	Female	Public	Private	Full time	White [2]	Total [3]	Black [2]	Hispanic	
United States ...	4,168	16,612	7,202	9,410	12,752	3,860	9,946	11,140	4,881	1,979	1,662	591
Alabama.........	75	246	105	142	218	29	165	163	78	70	3	6
Alaska..........	8	30	12	18	28	1	12	22	7	1	1	1
Arizona.........	71	402	179	223	307	94	215	274	116	20	66	12
Arkansas........	46	127	52	75	114	14	85	97	27	22	2	3
California.......	400	2,474	1,098	1,376	2,121	353	1,186	1,128	1,267	187	602	79
Colorado........	76	282	125	157	234	49	156	220	56	12	30	7
Connecticut......	45	171	72	98	109	62	102	126	37	17	12	7
Delaware	10	49	20	30	37	12	31	36	12	9	1	1
District of Columbia.....	16	91	38	53	6	85	58	44	39	28	4	8
Florida	161	792	333	459	618	174	426	466	296	135	131	30
Georgia	124	398	167	231	317	80	258	244	141	119	8	12
Hawaii	20	65	28	37	48	17	40	17	43	2	2	6
Idaho..........	14	72	32	40	58	14	49	65	5	1	3	2
Illinois ....•.....	175	777	334	443	554	223	427	510	240	105	87	26
Indiana.........	99	342	154	188	259	83	232	286	43	27	9	13
Iowa...........	62	203	91	112	146	57	142	178	17	7	4	8
Kansas.........	60	188	84	104	168	20	110	156	25	10	7	7
Kentucky	79	225	97	128	189	37	141	197	24	19	2	4
Louisiana	87	232	93	139	198	35	169	145	80	69	5	7
Maine..........	32	63	25	38	45	18	37	59	3	1	1	1
Maryland	63	300	123	177	247	53	157	179	108	78	10	13
Massachusetts.....	119	431	185	246	188	243	287	314	88	31	24	29
Michigan........	109	606	261	345	496	110	340	467	114	74	15	24
Minnesota.......	113	324	142	182	236	88	206	276	38	16	5	10
Mississippi	41	147	59	88	134	13	111	88	57	55	1	2
Missouri	119	348	149	199	214	134	207	279	58	39	8	11
Montana........	22	45	21	25	41	4	34	39	5	(Z)	1	1
Nebraska	38	117	52	64	92	25	76	102	11	5	1	3
Nevada	14	96	41	55	90	6	42	64	29	7	11	2
New Hampshire....	25	69	29	39	41	28	45	62	5	1	2	2
New Jersey......	57	362	155	207	289	72	213	222	124	49	45	16
New Mexico......	43	121	50	71	112	9	64	54	65	4	48	2
New York	310	1,107	466	641	611	497	763	686	359	155	118	62
North Carolina....	126	447	184	264	368	79	284	308	127	103	9	11
North Dakota.....	22	46	22	23	41	5	36	40	4	1	(Z)	1
Ohio	179	588	256	332	442	146	387	480	89	64	11	19
Oklahoma........	53	198	88	110	171	27	128	141	47	17	6	10
Oregon.........	57	205	93	111	174	31	118	168	30	4	9	6
Pennsylvania.....	257	655	290	365	370	284	466	525	107	62	17	23
Rhode Island.....	13	77	34	44	39	39	53	62	13	5	5	3
South Carolina....	63	202	80	122	168	34	134	136	62	56	3	4
South Dakota	27	48	21	27	38	10	32	41	5	1	(Z)	1
Tennessee	89	262	111	151	194	68	186	200	56	47	4	6
Texas..........	200	1,152	509	643	1,007	146	643	629	476	135	278	48
Utah	25	179	92	87	136	43	114	159	14	1	6	6
Vermont........	27	37	16	20	21	15	26	33	2	1	1	1
Virginia.........	100	405	174	231	337	68	238	281	112	76	13	12
Washington......	78	339	149	190	293	46	210	260	68	14	16	10
West Virginia.....	37	94	41	52	80	14	69	85	7	5	1	2
Wisconsin.......	68	329	142	187	268	61	207	286	36	16	8	7
Wyoming	9	33	14	18	31	2	18	30	3	(Z)	1	(Z)
U.S. military [4]....	5	14	12	2	14	-	14	12	3	1	1	(Z)

- Represents zero. Z Fewer than 500. [1] Branch campuses counted as separate institutions. [2] Non-Hispanic. [3] Includes other races not shown separately. [4] Service schools.

Source: U.S. National Center for Education Statistics, *Digest of Education Statistics*, annual.

U.S. Census Bureau, Statistical Abstract of the United States: 2006

Table 268. College Enrollment by Sex, Age, Race, and Hispanic Origin: 1980 to 2003

[In thousands (11,387 represents 11,387,000). As of October for the civilian noninstitutional population, 14 years old and over. Based on the Current Population Survey; see text, Section 1, and Appendix III]

Characteristic	1980	1985	1990 [1]	1995	1997	1998	1999	2000	2001	2002	2003
Total [2]	11,387	12,524	13,621	14,715	15,436	15,546	15,203	15,314	15,873	16,497	16,638
Male [3]	5,430	5,906	6,192	6,703	6,843	6,905	6,956	6,682	6,875	7,240	7,318
18 to 24 years	3,604	3,749	3,922	4,089	4,374	4,403	4,397	4,342	4,437	4,629	4,697
25 to 34 years	1,325	1,464	1,412	1,561	1,509	1,500	1,458	1,361	1,476	1,460	1,590
35 years old and over . . .	405	561	772	985	899	953	1,024	918	908	1,071	970
Female [3]	5,957	6,618	7,429	8,013	8,593	8,641	8,247	8,631	8,998	9,258	9,319
18 to 24 years	3,625	3,788	4,042	4,452	4,829	4,919	4,863	5,109	5,192	5,404	5,667
25 to 34 years	1,378	1,599	1,749	1,788	1,760	1,915	1,637	1,846	1,946	1,941	1,904
35 years old and over . . .	802	1,100	1,546	1,684	1,892	1,732	1,675	1,589	1,776	1,797	1,660
White [3, 4]	9,925	10,781	11,488	12,021	12,442	12,401	12,053	11,999	12,208	12,781	12,870
18 to 24 years	6,334	6,500	6,635	7,011	7,495	7,541	7,446	7,566	7,548	7,921	8,150
25 to 34 years	2,328	2,604	2,698	2,686	2,522	2,568	2,345	2,339	2,469	2,515	2,545
35 years old and over . . .	1,051	1,448	2,023	2,208	2,297	2,199	2,174	1,978	2,103	2,236	2,075
Male	4,804	5,103	5,235	5,535	5,552	5,602	5,562	5,311	5,383	5,719	5,714
Female	5,121	5,679	6,253	6,486	6,890	6,799	6,491	6,689	6,826	7,062	7,155
Black [3, 4]	1,163	1,263	1,393	1,772	1,903	2,016	1,998	2,064	2,230	2,278	2,144
18 to 24 years	688	734	894	988	1,085	1,115	1,146	1,216	1,206	1,227	1,225
25 to 34 years	289	295	258	426	423	539	453	567	562	542	503
35 years old and over . . .	156	213	207	334	372	340	354	361	429	454	388
Male	476	552	587	710	723	770	833	815	781	802	798
Female	686	712	807	1,062	1,180	1,247	1,164	1,349	1,449	1,476	1,346
Hispanic origin [3, 5]	443	580	748	1,207	1,260	1,363	1,302	1,426	1,700	1,656	1,714
18 to 24 years	315	375	435	745	806	820	740	899	1,035	979	1,115
25 to 34 years	118	189	168	250	254	336	334	309	392	414	380
35 years old and over . . .	(NA)	(NA)	130	193	151	198	226	195	260	249	207
Male	222	279	364	568	555	550	568	619	731	705	703
Female	221	299	384	639	704	814	739	807	969	951	1,011

NA Not available. [1] Beginning 1990, based on a revised edit and tabulation package. [2] Includes other races not shown separately. [3] Includes persons 14 to 17 years old, not shown separately. [4] Beginning 2003, for persons who selected this race group only. See footnote 2, Table 214. [5] Persons of Hispanic origin may be of any race.

Source: U.S. Census Bureau, Current Population Reports, PPL-148; and earlier PPL and P-20 reports. See Internet site <http://www.census.gov/population/www/socdemo/school.html>.

Table 269. Foreign (Nonimmigrant) Student Enrollment in College: 1976 to 2004

[In thousands (179 represents 179,000). For fall of the previous year]

Region of origin	1976	1980	1985	1990	1994	1995	1996	1997	1998	1999	2000	2001	2002	2003	2004
All regions . . .	179	286	342	387	449	453	454	458	481	491	515	548	583	586	573
Africa	25	36	40	25	21	21	21	22	23	26	30	34	38	40	38
Nigeria	11	16	18	4	2	2	2	2	2	3	4	4	4	6	6
Asia [1]	97	165	200	245	294	292	290	291	308	308	315	339	363	367	356
China: Taiwan . . .	11	18	23	31	37	36	33	30	31	31	29	29	29	28	26
Hong Kong	12	10	10	11	14	13	12	11	10	9	8	8	8	8	7
India	10	9	15	26	35	34	32	31	34	37	42	55	67	75	80
Indonesia	1	2	7	9	11	12	13	12	13	12	11	12	12	10	9
Iran	20	51	17	7	4	3	3	2	2	2	2	2	2	2	2
Japan	7	12	13	30	44	45	46	46	47	46	47	46	47	46	41
Malaysia	2	4	22	14	14	14	14	15	15	12	9	8	7	7	6
Saudi Arabia	3	10	8	4	4	4	4	4	5	5	5	5	6	4	4
South Korea	3	5	16	22	31	34	36	37	43	39	41	46	49	52	52
Thailand	7	7	7	7	9	11	12	13	15	12	11	11	12	10	9
Europe	14	23	33	46	62	65	67	68	72	74	78	81	82	78	74
Latin America [2]	30	42	49	48	45	47	47	50	51	55	62	64	68	69	70
Mexico	5	6	6	7	8	9	9	9	10	10	11	11	13	13	13
Venezuela	5	10	10	3	4	4	4	5	5	5	5	5	6	5	5
North America	10	16	16	19	23	23	24	24	23	23	24	26	27	27	28
Canada	10	15	15	18	22	23	23	23	22	23	24	25	27	27	27
Oceania	3	4	4	4	4	4	4	4	4	4	5	5	5	5	5

[1] Includes countries not shown separately. [2] Includes Central America, Caribbean, and South America.

Source: Institute of International Education, New York, NY, Open Doors Report on International Educational Exchange, annual (copyright).

Table 270. College Enrollment—Summary by Sex, Race and Hispanic Origin: 2003

[In thousands (16,638 represents 16,638,000), except percent. As of October. Covers civilian noninstitutional population 15 years old and over enrolled in colleges and graduate schools. Based on Current Population Survey, see text, Section 1, Population and Appendix III]

Characteristic	Total [1]	Sex		Race and Hispanic origin				
		Male	Female	White [2]		Black [2]	Asian [2]	Hispanic [3]
				Total	Non-Hispanic			
Total enrollment	16,638	7,318	9,319	12,870	11,295	2,144	1,162	1,714
15 to 17 years old.	150	61	89	100	90	28	16	12
18 to 19 years old.	3,512	1,568	1,944	2,833	2,486	374	209	379
20 to 21 years old.	3,533	1,551	1,982	2,796	2,419	415	219	407
22 to 24 years old.	3,320	1,578	1,742	2,521	2,225	435	264	329
25 to 29 years old.	2,164	982	1,181	1,585	1,371	289	228	224
30 to 34 years old.	1,330	607	723	960	832	214	108	156
35 years old and over	2,630	970	1,660	2,075	1,872	388	116	207
Type of school:								
2-year.	4,384	1,782	2,603	3,320	2,741	654	221	626
15 to 19 years old	1,178	544	634	910	763	143	74	171
20 to 24 years old	1,589	700	889	1,193	959	237	87	244
25 years old and over . .	1,618	538	1,080	1,217	1,019	274	61	211
4-year.	8,985	4,120	4,865	7,069	6,224	1,156	533	918
15 to 19 years old	2,455	1,079	1,376	2,003	1,795	250	152	217
20 to 24 years old	4,547	2,133	2,415	3,577	3,158	541	312	461
25 years old and over . .	1,983	908	1,075	1,488	1,271	365	69	240
Graduate school	3,268	1,416	1,852	2,481	2,331	334	408	170
15 to 24 years old	745	302	443	566	545	81	85	33
25 to 34 years old	1,399	685	714	1,025	957	122	234	75
35 years old and over . .	1,123	429	694	889	829	131	90	61
Public	13,109	5,711	7,399	10,102	8,743	1,773	833	1,480
2-year	3,999	1,619	2,381	3,032	2,499	601	194	578
4-year	6,981	3,173	3,808	5,468	4,739	942	377	790
Graduate	2,129	919	1,210	1,602	1,505	230	262	112
Percent of students:								
Employed full-time.	31.7	34.1	29.8	32.2	32.4	34.7	20.6	30.9
Employed part-time	45.7	46.5	45.1	49.2	49.9	29.8	32.4	44.7

[1] Includes other races, not shown separately. [2] For persons who selected this race group only. See footnote 2, Table 214.
[3] Persons of Hispanic origin may be of any race.

Source: U.S. Census Bureau, unpublished data. See Internet site <http://www.census.gov/population/www/socdemo/school.html>.

Table 271. Higher Education Enrollments in Foreign Languages: 1970 to 2002

[As of fall (1,111.5 represents 1,111,500). For credit enrollment]

Enrollment	1970	1977	1980	1983	1986	1990	1995	1998	2002
Registrations [1] (1,000).	1,111.5	933.5	924.8	966.0	1,003.2	1,184.1	1,138.8	1,193.8	1,397.3
By selected language (1,000):									
Spanish	389.2	376.7	379.4	386.2	411.3	533.9	606.3	656.6	746.3
French	359.3	246.1	248.4	270.1	275.3	272.5	205.4	199.1	202.0
German	202.6	135.4	126.9	128.2	121.0	133.3	96.3	89.0	91.1
Italian	34.2	33.3	34.8	38.7	40.9	49.7	43.8	49.3	63.9
American Sign Language	(X)	(X)	(X)	(X)	(X)	1.6	4.3	11.4	60.8
Japanese	6.6	10.7	11.5	16.1	23.5	45.7	44.7	43.1	52.2
Chinese	6.2	9.8	11.4	13.2	16.9	19.5	26.5	28.5	34.2
Latin	27.6	24.4	25.0	24.2	25.0	28.2	25.9	26.1	29.8
Russian	36.2	27.8	24.0	30.4	34.0	44.6	24.7	23.8	23.9
Hebrew	16.6	19.4	19.4	18.2	15.6	13.0	13.1	15.8	22.8
Ancient Greek.	16.7	25.8	22.1	19.4	17.6	16.4	16.3	16.4	20.4
Arabic	1.3	3.1	3.5	3.4	3.4	3.5	4.4	5.5	10.6
Portuguese	5.1	5.0	4.9	4.4	5.1	6.2	6.5	6.9	8.4
Korean	0.1	0.2	0.4	0.7	0.9	2.3	3.3	4.5	5.2
Index (1960 = 100)	171.8	144.3	142.9	149.3	155.0	183.0	176.0	184.5	215.9

X Not applicable. [1] Includes other foreign languages, not shown separately.

Source: Association of Departments of Foreign Languages, New York, NY, ADFL Bulletin, Vol. 35, No. 2, Winter 2004; and earlier issues (copyright).

Education 179

Table 272. College Freshmen—Summary Characteristics: 1970 to 2004

[In percent, except as indicated (12.8 represents $12,800). As of fall for first-time full-time freshmen in 4-year colleges and universities. Based on sample survey and subject to sampling error; see source]

Characteristic	1970	1980	1985	1990	1995	2000	2002	2003	2004
Sex: Male	52.1	48.8	48.9	46.9	45.6	45.2	45.0	45.1	44.9
Female	47.9	51.2	51.1	53.1	54.4	54.8	55.0	55.0	55.1
Applied to three or more colleges	(NA)	31.5	35.4	42.9	44.4	50.5	50.8	54.2	52.8
Average grade in high school:									
A- to A+	19.6	26.6	28.7	29.4	36.1	42.9	45.7	46.6	47.5
B- to B+	62.5	58.2	57.1	57.0	54.2	50.5	49.0	48.3	47.6
C to C+	17.7	14.9	14.0	13.4	9.6	6.5	5.2	5.0	5.0
D	0.3	0.2	0.2	0.2	0.1	0.1	0.1	0.1	0.1
Political orientation:									
Liberal	35.7	21.0	22.4	24.6	22.9	24.8	25.3	24.2	26.1
Middle of the road	43.4	57.0	53.1	51.7	51.3	51.9	50.8	50.3	46.4
Conservative	17.3	19.0	21.3	20.6	21.8	18.9	20.0	21.1	21.9
Probable field of study:									
Arts and humanities	(NA)	10.5	10.1	10.5	11.2	12.1	12.6	12.3	12.0
Biological sciences	(NA)	4.5	4.5	4.9	8.3	6.6	7.2	7.3	7.7
Business	(NA)	21.2	24.6	21.1	15.4	16.7	16.2	15.9	16.0
Education	(NA)	8.4	6.9	10.3	10.1	11.0	10.6	10.1	9.6
Engineering	(NA)	11.2	11.0	9.7	8.1	8.7	9.5	9.3	9.6
Physical science	(NA)	3.2	3.2	2.8	3.1	2.6	2.7	2.7	3.0
Social science	(NA)	8.2	9.4	11.0	9.9	10.0	10.4	10.5	10.3
Professional	(NA)	15.5	13.1	13.0	16.5	11.6	12.3	14.3	15.1
Technical	(NA)	3.1	2.4	1.1	1.2	2.1	1.4	1.5	1.5
Data processing/computer programming	(NA)	1.7	1.7	0.7	0.8	1.5	0.9	0.7	0.6
Other [1]	(NA)	14.0	15.1	15.8	16.0	17.9	16.9	16.0	15.0
Communications	(NA)	2.4	2.8	2.9	1.8	2.7	2.5	2.4	1.9
Computer science	(NA)	2.6	2.4	1.7	2.2	3.7	2.2	1.7	1.4
Personal objectives—very important or essential:									
Being very well off financially	36.2	62.5	69.2	72.3	72.8	73.4	73.2	73.8	73.6
Developing a meaningful philosophy of life	79.1	62.5	46.9	45.9	45.4	42.4	40.6	39.3	42.1
Keeping up to date with political affairs	57.2	45.2	(NA)	46.6	32.3	28.1	32.9	33.9	34.3
Attitudes—agree or strongly agree:									
Capital punishment should be abolished	59.4	34.8	27.6	23.1	22.0	31.2	32.1	32.6	33.2
Legalize marijuana	40.6	37.1	21.4	18.8	33.4	34.2	39.7	38.8	37.2
There is too much concern for the rights of criminals	50.7	65.0	(NA)	65.1	73.2	66.5	64.0	61.1	58.1
Abortion should be legalized	85.7	53.7	56.4	65.5	59.9	53.9	53.6	54.5	53.9
Median family income ($1,000)	12.8	24.5	37.3	46.6	54.8	64.4	69.5	71.3	71.9

NA Not available. [1] Includes other fields, not shown separately.

Source: The Higher Education Research Institute, University of California, Los Angeles, CA, *The American Freshman: National Norms,* annual.

Table 273. Undergraduates Reported Disability Status by Selected Characteristic: 1999–2000

[In percent. Persons with any disability or difficulty include those who indicated they had a long-lasting condition, such as blindness or deafness; or a condition substantially limiting a basic physical activity, such as walking or lifting; or a physical, emotional, or mental condition lasting six months or more which made it difficult to do any one of the following: get to school, get around campus, learn, dress, or work at a job. Based on the 1999-2000 National Postsecondary Student Aid Survey; see source and Appendix III for details]

Student characteristic	Any disability or difficulty reported [1]	None reported	Consider self with disability	Don't consider self with disability
Total	9.3	90.7	3.6	96.4
PERCENT DISTRIBUTION				
Total	100.0	100.0	100.0	100.0
Age: [1]				
18 years or younger	5.8	9.9	3.1	9.8
19 to 23 years old	36.3	49.3	24.5	49.1
24 to 29 years old	15.5	16.1	15.3	16.1
30 to 39 years old	19.2	13.5	23.7	13.7
40 years or older	23.3	11.1	33.4	11.5
Sex: Male	39.6	42.4	46.2	42.0
Female	60.4	57.6	53.8	58.0
Race:				
White, non-Hispanic	70.8	66.7	70.8	67.1
Black, non-Hispanic	10.9	11.8	13.0	11.7
Hispanic	9.9	11.6	8.0	11.4
Asian	2.1	4.9	1.1	4.8
American Indian/Alaska Native	1.9	0.7	2.5	0.8
Native Hawaiian/Other Pacific Islander	0.8	0.8	1.4	0.7
Other race	1.4	1.5	0.8	1.6
More than one race	2.3	1.9	2.5	1.9
Parents' highest education level:				
High school or less	40.7	36.4	45.1	36.4
Some postsecondary education	24.1	22.8	21.6	23.0
Bachelor's degree or equivalent	35.2	40.9	33.3	40.7

Source: U.S. National Center for Education Statistics, *Profile of Undergraduates in U.S. Postsecondary Education Institutions, 1999-2000,* NCES 2002-168, July 2002.

Table 274. **Distance Education in Degree-Granting Postsecondary Institutions: 2000–01**

[For the school year (3,077 represents 3,077,000). Distance education is education or training courses delivered to off-campus sites via audio, video (live or prerecorded), or computer technologies (simultaneous or not simultaneous). Based on the Postsecondary Education Quick Information System; see source for details]

Institution type and size	Institutions offering distance education courses			Enrollments in distance education courses (1,000)	Enrollments in college-level courses		
	Number of institu- tions	Number	Percent	Total [1]	Total [2]	Under- graduate enroll- ments	Graduate enroll- ments [3]
All institutions [4]	4,130	2,320	56	3,077	2,876	2,350	510
Type:							
Public 2-year	1.070	960	90	1,472	1,436	1,435	(B)
Private 2-year	640	100	16	(B)	(B)	(B)	(B)
Public 4-year	620	550	89	945	888	566	308
Private 4-year	1,800	710	40	589	480	278	202
Enrollment size:							
Less than 3,000	2,840	1,160	41	486	460	368	91
3,000 to 9,999	870	770	88	1,171	1,132	932	197
10,000 or more	420	400	95	1,420	1,284	1,049	222

B Base figure too small to meet statistical standards of reliability for a derived figure. [1] Includes all levels and audiences (for example, adult education and continuing education). [2] Includes duplication for students enrolled in more than one course. [3] Includes first-professional. [4] Includes data for private 2-year institutions.

Source: U.S. National Center for Education Statistics, *Distance Education at Degree-Granting Postsecondary Institutions: 2000–2001*, NCES 2003–017, July 2003.

Table 275. **Average Total Price of Attendance of Undergraduate Education: 1999–2000**

[In dollars. Excludes students attending more than one institution. Price of attendance includes tuition and fees, books and supplies, room and board, transportation, and personal and other expenses allowed for federal cost of attendance budgets. Based on the 1999-2000 National Postsecondary Student-Aid Study; see source for details. See also Appendix III]

Student characteristic	Type of institution						
			Public 4-year		Private not-for-profit 4-year		
	Total [1]	Public 2-year	Non- doctorate	Doctor- ate	Non- doctorate	Doctor- ate	Private for-profit
Total	9,283	4,997	8,839	10,915	16,242	22,212	14,294
Age: [2]							
18 years or younger	11,077	5,674	9,127	12,006	19,170	25,991	14,289
19 to 23 years	11,150	5,688	9,461	11,563	19,551	24,529	14,112
24 to 29 years	7,962	5,038	8,397	9,571	12,474	14,190	14,517
30 to 39 years	6,696	4,555	7,817	8,624	10,327	11,050	14,452
40 years or older	5,341	3,667	6,691	7,117	9,641	9,597	14,068
Sex:							
Male	9,298	4,943	8,852	10,895	16,288	22,196	14,972
Female	9,271	5,039	8,829	10,933	16,209	22,225	13,846
Race:							
One race:							
White	9,410	4,940	8,834	10,878	16,855	22,361	14,585
Black or African American	8,559	5,041	8,826	10,655	13,647	19,489	13,270
Asian	10,132	5,200	9,166	11,890	18,513	25,991	15,688
American Indian/Alaska Native	7,369	5,132	7,381	9,381	12,225	(B)	12,292
Native Hawaiian or other Pacific Islander	8,345	5,431	9,698	9,645	(B)	(B)	13,691
Other race	8,897	5,309	8,505	10,825	12,827	20,746	14,310
More than one race	9,488	4,919	9,545	11,436	12,792	20,921	13,308
Hispanic or Latino (any race):							
Not Hispanic or Latino	9,428	5,001	8,961	10,989	17,053	22,678	14,468
Hispanic or Latino	8,235	4,974	7,922	10,119	11,090	18,279	13,639
Attendance pattern:							
Full-time, full-year	14,710	9,083	11,238	13,278	21,131	26,790	18,360
Full-time, part-year	7,991	4,978	6,537	7,394	11,584	14,865	12,875
Part-time, full-year	8,109	6,209	8,605	10,089	12,725	15,431	14,076
Part-time, part-year	2,968	2,325	3,414	4,323	5,492	5,691	7,842
Local residence:							
On campus	15,713	5,261	10,492	12,694	22,138	26,984	17,222
Off campus	8,180	4,828	8,802	10,626	12,740	18,212	14,373
With parents/other relatives	7,915	5,347	7,758	9,361	14,312	19,722	13,676

B Base too small to meet statistical standards for reliability of a derived figure. [1] Includes public less-than-2-year and private not-for-profit, less-than-4-year. [2] As of December 31, 1999.

Source: U.S. National Center for Education Statistics, *Student Financing of Undergraduate Education 1999-2000*, July 2002, NCES 2002-167.

Table 276. **Higher Education Price Indexes: 1970 to 2004**

[1983 = 100. **For years ending June 30.** Reflects prices paid by colleges and universities]

Year	Index, total	Personnel compensation				Contracted services, supplies, and equipment					
		Total	Profes-sional salaries	Nonpro-fessional salaries	Fringe benefits	Total	Serv-ices	Supplies and materials	Equip-ment	Library acquisi-tions	Utilities
1970 . . .	39.5	42.1	47.7	38.8	24.7	31.9	42.8	37.6	41.9	25.7	16.3
1975 . . .	54.3	56.3	60.3	54.6	42.9	48.5	56.8	58.0	58.3	46.7	31.8
1980 . . .	77.5	78.4	79.4	80.2	72.6	75.0	77.0	84.6	81.6	77.8	64.1
1981 . . .	85.8	85.8	86.3	87.7	81.8	85.9	85.2	95.6	89.6	85.9	79.7
1982 . . .	93.9	93.5	93.7	94.6	91.5	94.9	94.2	100.4	96.4	93.5	92.4
1983 . . .	100.0	100.0	100.0	100.0	100.0	100.0	100.0	100.0	100.0	100.0	100.0
1984 . . .	104.8	105.4	104.7	105.1	108.3	103.0	104.9	99.7	102.3	105.3	102.5
1985 . . .	110.8	112.0	111.4	109.2	117.7	107.1	110.8	103.0	104.8	111.3	105.3
1986 . . .	116.3	118.8	118.2	112.8	127.7	109.0	115.1	102.6	107.2	121.2	103.1
1987 . . .	120.9	125.4	125.0	116.3	137.4	107.4	119.7	99.0	108.9	132.9	91.0
1988 . . .	126.2	131.7	130.9	120.6	147.2	109.8	123.0	101.1	120.5	140.5	87.7
1989 . . .	132.8	139.6	138.8	125.3	158.8	112.8	128.8	108.3	115.1	153.5	85.3
1990 . . .	140.8	148.3	147.6	130.3	171.4	118.7	134.0	114.3	119.6	167.0	90.1
1991 . . .	148.2	156.5	155.6	135.4	184.3	123.3	139.8	116.4	123.3	179.8	92.4
1992 . . .	153.5	162.4	160.8	140.2	194.3	126.9	145.7	115.2	126.3	193.9	93.3
1993 . . .	158.0	167.6	165.0	144.2	204.3	129.4	149.5	113.2	128.6	203.4	94.7
1994 . . .	163.3	173.3	170.3	148.2	213.6	133.6	154.8	114.3	130.8	213.6	98.7
1995 . . .	168.1	179.1	176.1	152.5	221.4	135.3	158.0	115.7	133.5	220.2	96.8
1996 . . .	173.0	184.1	181.7	157.3	224.5	139.9	163.8	130.1	137.0	230.9	93.3
1997 . . .	178.4	189.0	,187.2	162.1	226.7	147.2	167.3	128.6	139.3	253.4	106.1
1998 . . .	184.7	195.8	193.5	168.0	236.7	151.6	172.8	126.2	141.3	266.5	111.1
1999 . . .	189.1	202.0	200.7	174.1	239.2	150.8	177.0	123.2	143.3	282.1	100.5
2000 . . .	196.9	210.8	208.4	180.4	254.8	155.8	182.9	123.1	145.0	298.6	104.9
2001 . . .	206.5	218.1	215.8	187.9	261.7	172.2	189.2	130.5	147.3	317.4	140.7
2002 . . .	215.0	(NA)	(NA)	(NA)	(NA)	(NA)	(NA)	(NA)	(NA)	(NA)	(NA)
2003 . . .	221.2	(NA)	(NA)	(NA)	(NA)	(NA)	(NA)	(NA)	(NA)	(NA)	(NA)
2004 . . .	231.5	(NA)	(NA)	(NA)	(NA)	(NA)	(NA)	(NA)	(NA)	(NA)	(NA)

NA Not available.

Source: The Commonfund Institute, Wilton, CT, (data under copyright). See Internet site <http://www.commonfund.org>.

Table 277. **Federal Student Financial Assistance: 1995 to 2005**

[**For award years July 1 of year shown to the following June 30 (35,477 represents ($35,477,000,000).** Funds utilized exclude operating costs, etc., and represent funds given to students]

Type of assistance	1995	2000	2001	2002	2003	2004	2005, est.
FUNDS UTILIZED (mil. dol.)							
Total	35,477	44,007	48,582	55,525	62,249	68,629	73,020
Federal Pell Grants	5,472	7,956	9,975	11,640	12,681	13,091	12,901
Federal Supplemental Educational Opportunity Grant	764	907	1,007	1,033	1,064	975	985
Federal Work-Study	764	939	1,032	1,097	1,106	1,194	1,184
Federal Perkins Loan	1,029	1,144	1,239	1,460	1,638	1,263	1,137
Federal Direct Student Loan (FDSL)	8,296	10,348	10,635	11,689	11,969	12,840	13,860
Federal Family Education Loans (FFEL)	19,152	22,712	24,694	28,606	33,791	39,266	42,953
NUMBER OF AWARDS (1,000)							
Total	13,667	15,043	16,154	17,976	19,616	20,630	21,454
Federal Pell Grants	3,612	3,899	4,341	4,953	5,341	5,302	5,330
Federal Supplemental Educational Opportunity Grant	1,083	1,175	1,295	1,354	1,389	1,278	1,292
Federal Work-Study	702	713	740	759	764	826	819
Federal Perkins Loan	688	639	660	728	756	673	606
Federal Direct Student Loan (FDSL)	2,339	2,739	2,763	2,908	2,937	3,001	3,128
Federal Family Education Loans (FFEL)	5,243	5,878	6,355	7,274	8,429	9,550	10,279
AVERAGE AWARD (dol.)							
Total	2,596	2,925	3,007	3,089	3,173	3,327	3,404
Federal Pell Grants	1,515	2,041	2,298	2,350	2,374	2,469	2,420
Federal Supplemental Educational Opportunity Grant	705	772	778	763	766	763	763
Federal Work-Study	1,088	1,318	1,395	1,446	1,447	1,446	1,446
Federal Perkins Loan	1,496	1,790	1,877	2,003	2,166	1,875	1,875
Federal Direct Student Loan (FDSL)	3,547	3,778	3,849	4,020	4,075	4,279	4,431
Federal Family Education Loans (FFEL)	3,653	3,864	3,886	3,933	4,009	4,112	4,179
COHORT DEFAULT RATE [1]							
Federal Perkins Loan	12.6	9.9	9.5	8.8	8.3	(NA)	(NA)
FFEL/FDSL Combined Rates	10.4	5.9	5.4	5.2	(NA)	(NA)	(NA)

NA Not available.   [1] As of June 30. Represents the percent of borrowers entering repayment status in year shown who defaulted in the following year.

Source: U.S. Dept. of Education, Office of Postsecondary Education, unpublished data.

Table 278. State and Local Financial Support for Higher Education by State: 2003–2004

[For 2003–2004 academic year, except as indicated (9,916.6 represents 9,916,600). Data for the 50 states]

State	FTE enrollment [1] (1,000)	Educational appropriations per FTE [2] (dol.)	Appropriations for higher ed. as a percent of state and local tax revenue 2002-2003 [3]	State	FTE enrollment [1] (1,000)	Educational appropriations per FTE [2] (dol.)	Appropriations for higher ed. as a percent of state and local tax revenue 2002-2003 [3]
Total . . .	9,916.6	5,716	7.7	MO	138.1	7,031	7.0
AL.	183.3	4,693	12.0	MT	35.8	3,915	7.0
AK.	37.6	5,269	10.2	NE.	71.3	5,475	11.1
AZ.	211.2	5,699	8.5	NV.	57.2	7,834	5.6
AR.	97.7	5,233	9.6	NH	30.5	3,316	3.0
CA.	1,623.5	6,103	9.7	NJ	195.5	8,326	5.7
CO	161.2	3,202	4.6	NM	79.6	5,586	14.5
CT	70.0	8,916	5.0	NY	487.3	6,663	5.1
DE.	31.0	10,907	6.8	NC	315.2	6,699	11.4
FL	526.7	4,293	5.8	ND	36.2	4,345	11.8
GA	210.0	8,231	8.6	OH	378.7	4,680	6.0
HI	35.4	9,566	8.7	OK	133.4	4,872	9.9
ID	49.8	6,050	10.1	OR	124.4	4,772	6.8
IL	378.1	6,777	8.1	PA.	322.7	5,355	5.6
IN	218.4	5,103	7.8	RI	27.8	6,180	4.7
IA	117.7	5,255	9.8	SC.	137.1	5,053	7.0
KS.	110.2	5,940	10.1	SD.	28.1	4,408	8.2
KY.	144.7	6,360	9.9	TN.	169.4	5,053	8.9
LA	183.3	5,037	8.7	TX.	812.9	5,282	9.5
ME	34.5	5,900	5.2	UT.	108.6	5,048	10.2
MD	165.5	5,378	7.2	VT.	17.8	2,575	3.0
MA	137.5	7,021	4.8	VA.	257.7	4,571	6.5
MI	357.6	5,950	8.5	WA	220.0	5,509	7.0
MN	189.8	5,564	7.2	WV	69.5	4,135	9.3
MS	145.9	3,980	11.9	WI	218.9	5,941	8.2
				WY	22.2	11,358	14.7

[1] Full-time equivalent. Includes degree enrollment and enrollment in public postsecondary programs resulting in a certificate or other formal recognition. Includes summer sessions. Excludes medical enrollments. [2] State and local appropriations for public postsecondary education. Includes state-funded financial aid to students attending in-state public institutions. Excludes sums for research, agriculture experiment stations and cooperative extension, and teaching hospitals and medical schools. [3] Includes state and local appropriations for public and independent postsecondary education (including sums for research, agriculture experiment stations and cooperative extension, and teaching hospitals and medical schools).

Source: State Higher Education Executive Officers, Denver, CO, (copyright). See Internet site <http://www.sheeo.org/>.

Table 279. Average Amount of Aid Received by Undergraduates Receiving Aid: 1999-2000

[Average amount in dollars. Based on the Student Postsecondary Aid Study and subject to sampling error; see source for details. See also Appendix III]

Characteristic	Total aid [1]		Total grants		Total loans [2]	
	Percent receiving aid	Average amount	Percent receiving grants	Average amount	Percent receiving loans	Average amount
Total	55.3	6,206	44.4	3,476	28.8	5,131
Attendance pattern:						
Full-time, full-year	72.5	8,474	58.7	4,949	45.4	5,437
Part-time or part-year.	44.6	3,902	35.4	1,952	18.4	4,660
Institution type: [3]						
Public 2-year	37.8	2,311	32.7	1,571	7.4	3,319
Public 4-year	62.1	6,188	46.3	3,203	39.6	4,834
Private not-for-profit 4-year	76.1	11,577	66.4	7,008	49.8	6,226
Private for-profit	84.9	7,218	59.7	2,654	66.5	5,772
Price of attendance: [3]						
Less than $4,000	24.8	763	22.1	673	1.4	1,635
$4,000 to 7,999	50.6	2,581	42.1	1,843	14.8	2,762
$8,000 to 11,999.	64.2	4,948	49.7	2,692	35.4	4,268
$12,000 or more.	78.4	11,035	62.1	6,145	59.5	6,222
Dependency status: [4]						
Dependent.	58.9	7,367	46.1	4,574	34.9	4,612
Independent.	51.9	4,932	42.7	2,331	23.0	5,893

[1] Includes other aid not shown separately. [2] Includes only loans to students. [3] Excludes students attending more than one institution. [4] Dependent or independent for federal aid purposes.

Source: U.S. National Center for Education Statistics, *Student Financing of Undergraduate Education 1999-2000*, July 2002, NCES 2002-167.

Education 183

Table 280. Institutions of Higher Education—Charges: 1985 to 2004

[In dollars. Estimated. **For the entire academic year ending in year shown.** Figures are average charges per full-time equivalent student. Room and board are based on full-time students]

Academic control and year	Tuition and required fees [1]				Board rates [2]				Dormitory charges			
	All institutions	2-yr. colleges	4-yr. colleges	Other 4-yr. schools	All institutions	2-yr. colleges	4-yr. colleges	Other 4-yr. schools	All institutions	2-yr. colleges	4-yr. colleges	Other 4-yr. schools
Public:												
1985......	971	584	1,386	1,117	1,241	1,302	1,276	1,201	1,196	921	1,237	1,200
1990......	1,356	756	2,035	1,608	1,635	1,581	1,728	1,561	1,513	962	1,561	1,554
1995......	2,057	1,192	2,977	2,499	1,949	1,712	2,108	1,866	1,959	1,232	1,992	2,044
1999......	2,430	1,327	3,640	2,974	2,347	1,828	2,576	2,247	2,330	1,450	2,408	2,410
2000......	2,506	1,338	3,768	3,091	2,364	1,834	2,628	2,239	2,440	1,549	2,516	2,521
2001......	2,562	1,333	3,979	3,208	2,455	1,906	2,686	2,358	2,569	1,600	2,657	2,652
2002......	2,700	1,380	4,273	3,409	2,597	2,036	2,835	2,498	2,721	1,722	2,837	2,793
2003......	2,903	1,483	4,686	3,668	2,702	2,174	2,939	2,605	2,925	1,943	3,023	3,022
2004, prel....	3,313	1,670	5,368	4,193	2,825	2,224	3,086	2,724	3,108	2,092	3,229	3,200
Private:												
1985......	5,315	3,485	6,843	5,135	1,462	1,294	1,647	1,405	1,426	1,424	1,753	1,309
1990......	8,174	5,196	10,348	7,778	1,948	1,811	2,339	1,823	1,923	1,663	2,411	1,774
1995......	11,111	6,914	14,537	10,653	2,509	2,023	3,035	2,362	2,587	2,233	3,469	2,347
1999......	13,428	7,854	18,340	12,815	2,865	2,884	3,188	2,765	3,075	2,581	3,914	2,850
2000......	14,081	8,235	19,307	13,361	2,882	2,922	3,157	2,790	3,224	2,808	4,070	2,976
2001......	15,000	9,067	20,106	14,233	2,993	3,000	3,300	2,893	3,374	2,722	4,270	3,121
2002......	15,742	10,076	21,176	14,923	3,104	2,633	3,462	2,996	3,567	3,116	4,478	3,301
2003......	16,383	10,651	22,716	15,416	3,206	3,870	3,602	3,071	3,752	3,232	4,724	3,478
2004, prel....	17,442	11,635	24,105	16,419	3,365	4,353	3,783	3,222	3,941	3,622	4,970	3,642

[1] For in-state students. [2] Beginning 1990, rates reflect 20 meals per week, rather than meals served 7 days a week.

Source: U.S. National Center for Education Statistics, *Digest of Education Statistics,* annual.

Table 281. Voluntary Financial Support of Higher Education: 1990 to 2004

[**For school years ending in years shown (9,800 represents $9,800,000,000); enrollment as of fall of preceding year.** Voluntary support, as defined in Gift Reporting Standards, excludes income from endowment and other invested funds as well as all support received from Federal, state, and local governments and their agencies and contract research]

Item	Unit	1990	1995	1999	2000	2001	2002	2003	2004
Estimated support, total	Mil. dol ...	9,800	12,750	20,400	23,200	24,200	23,900	23,900	24,400
Individuals..............	Mil. dol ...	4,770	6,540	10,740	12,220	12,030	11,300	11,150	11,900
Alumni...............	Mil. dol ...	2,540	3,600	5,930	6,800	6,830	5,900	6,600	6,700
Business corporations	Mil. dol ...	2,170	2,560	3,610	4,150	4,350	4,370	4,250	4,400
Foundations...........	Mil. dol ...	1,920	2,460	4,530	5,080	6,000	6,300	6,600	6,200
Fundraising consortia and other organizations	Mil. dol ...	700	940	1,190	1,380	1,450	1,570	1,540	1,550
Religious organizations	Mil. dol ...	240	250	330	370	370	360	360	350
Current operations	Mil. dol ...	5,440	7,230	9,900	11,270	12,200	12,400	12,900	13,600
Capital purposes..........	Mil. dol ...	4,360	5,520	10,500	11,930	12,000	11,500	11,000	10,800
Enrollment, higher education [1]........	1,000	13,819	14,262	14,791	15,312	15,442	15,608	15,756	15,947
Support per student........	Dollars ..	709	894	1,379	1,515	1,567	1,531	1,517	1,530
In 2003-2004 dollars	Dollars ..	1,025	1,108	1,564	1,662	1,672	1,608	1,557	1,530
Expenditures, higher education	Bil. dol ...	164	211	267	284	295	313	339	346
Expenditures per student	Dollars ..	11,848	14,819	18,049	18,534	19,103	20,064	21,506	21,694
In 2003-2004 dollars	Dollars ..	17,123	18,368	20,465	20,332	20,376	21,068	22,078	21,694
Institutions reporting support ...	Number..	1,056	1,086	938	945	960	955	954	971
Total support reported	Mil. dol ...	8,214	10,992	17,229	19,419	20,569	19,824	19,823	19,630
Private 4-year institutions....	Mil. dol ...	5,072	6,500	9,848	11,047	11,391	10,953	10,318	10,695
Public 4-year institutions....	Mil. dol ...	3,056	4,382	7,252	8,254	9,026	8,754	9,400	8,802
2-year colleges...........	Mil. dol ...	85	110	129	117	152	117	105	133

[1] Excludes proprietary schools.

Source: Council for Aid to Education, New York, NY, *Voluntary Support of Education,* annual.

Table 282. Average Salaries for College Faculty Members: 2003 to 2005

[**In thousands of dollars (64.0 represents $64,000). For academic year ending in year shown.** Figures are for 9 months teaching for full-time faculty members in 2-year and 4-year institutions with ranks. Fringe benefits averaged in 2003, $16,208 in public institutions and $19,261 in private institutions; in 2004, $17,090 in public institutions and $20,565 in private institutions and in 2005, $17,966 in public institutions and $21,332 in private institutions]

Type of control and academic rank	2003	2004	2005	Type of control and academic rank	2003	2004	2005
Public: All ranks..........	64.0	65.0	66.9	**Private: [1] All ranks..........**	74.4	76.6	79.3
Professor	84.1	85.8	88.5	Professor	101.2	104.0	108.2
Associate professor	61.5	62.4	64.4	Associate professor	66.3	68.5	71.0
Assistant professor........	51.5	52.5	54.3	Assistant professor........	55.6	57.5	59.4
Instructor	37.2	37.9	39.4	Instructor	41.1	41.8	42.2

[1] Excludes church-related colleges and universities.

Source: American Association of University Professors, Washington, DC, *AAUP Annual Report on the Economic Status of the Profession.*

Table 283. Employees in Higher Education Institutions by Sex and Occupation: 1976 to 2003

[In thousands (1,863.8 represents 1,863,800). As of fall. Based on survey and subject to sampling error; see source]

Year and status	Total	Professional staff									Nonpro-fessional staff, total
		Total	Executive, administrative, and managerial		Faculty [1]		Research/ instruction assistants		Other		
			Male	Female	Male	Female	Male	Female	Male	Female	
1976, total	1,863.8	1,073.1	74.6	26.6	460.6	172.7	106.5	53.6	87.5	91.0	790.7
Full-time	1,339.9	709.4	72.0	25.0	326.8	107.2	18.6	9.4	76.2	74.1	630.5
Part-time	523.9	363.7	2.6	1.7	133.7	65.4	87.9	44.2	11.3	16.9	160.2
1991, total	2,545.2	1,595.5	85.4	59.3	525.6	300.7	119.1	78.6	165.4	261.3	949.8
Full-time	1,812.9	1,031.8	82.9	56.2	366.2	169.4	-	-	142.6	214.8	781.1
Part-time	732.3	563.7	2.5	3.1	159.4	131.2	119.1	78.6	23.2	46.4	168.7
2003, total [2]	3,194.2	2,272.6	91.8	94.7	664.8	510.1	157.4	135.7	248.4	369.8	921.6
Full-time	2,085.9	1,340.4	89.3	90.9	382.8	248.8	-	-	216.1	312.5	745.5
Part-time	1,108.2	932.2	2.5	3.8	282.0	261.3	157.4	135.7	32.3	57.3	176.1

- Represents zero.   [1] Instruction and research.   [2] In this table, 2003 data reflect the new classification of institutions. See footnote 1, Table 265.

Source: U.S. National Center for Education Statistics, *Fall Staff in Postsecondary Institutions, 2001*, NCES 2004-159, November 2003, and earlier issues; and *Digest of Education Statistics, annual.*

Table 284. Faculty in Institutions of Higher Education: 1975 to 2003

[In thousands (628 represents 628,000), except percent. As of fall. Based on survey and subject to sampling error; see source]

Year	Employment status			Control		Level		Percent		
	Total	Full-time	Part-time	Public	Private	4-Year	2-Year or less	Part-time	Public	2-Year or less
1975 [1]	628	440	188	443	185	467	161	30	71	26
1980 [1]	686	450	236	495	191	494	192	34	72	28
1985 [1]	715	459	256	503	212	504	211	36	70	30
1991 [2]	826	536	291	581	245	591	235	35	70	28
1993	915	546	370	650	265	626	289	40	71	32
1995	932	551	381	657	275	647	285	41	70	31
1997 [3]	990	569	421	695	295	683	307	43	70	31
1999	1,028	591	437	713	315	714	314	43	69	31
2001	1,113	618	495	771	342	764	349	44	69	31
2003	1,175	632	543	793	382	816	359	46	67	31

[1] Estimated on the basis of enrollment.   [2] Data beginning 1991 not comparable to prior years.   [3] In this table, data beginning in 1997 reflect the new classification of institutions. See footnote 1, Table 265.

Source: U.S. National Center for Education Statistics, *Digest of Education Statistics, annual.*

Table 285. Salary Offers to Candidates for Degrees: 2002 to 2004

[In dollars. Data are average beginning salaries based on offers made by business, industrial, government, nonprofit, and educational employers to graduating students. Data from representative colleges throughout the United States]

Field of study	Bachelor's			Master's [1]			Doctorate		
	2002	2003	2004	2002	2003	2004	2002	2003	2004
Accounting.	39,494	40,647	41,058	43,625	42,241	43,042	(NA)	(NA)	(NA)
Business administration/ management [2]	36,378	36,012	38,254	52,241	[3]50,835	[3]44,807	[3]81,357	[3]87,000	[3]75,125
Marketing.	33,690	34,038	34,712	[3]56,000	[3]35,000	[3]65,000	(NA)	(NA)	(NA)
Engineering:									
Civil.	41,193	41,669	42,056	47,756	47,245	48,852	[3]56,228	[3]69,079	[3]53,067
Chemical	51,137	52,384	52,539	[3]55,812	[3]57,857	[3]53,920	75,552	[3]70,729	[3]72,613
Computer	51,135	51,343	51,297	[3]64,268	[3]64,200	[3]63,563	[3]59,211	(NA)	(NA)
Electrical	50,391	49,794	51,124	62,194	64,556	63,413	77,316	74,283	73,674
Mechanical	48,282	48,585	48,578	55,013	59,098	58,298	63,161	[3]69,904	[3]68,003
Nuclear [4]	[3]48,583	[3]50,104	[3]47,914	[3]51,500	(NA)	[3]66,350	(NA)	(NA)	(NA)
Petroleum.	56,622	55,987	[3]58,518	(NA)	[3]67,500	[3]71,332	(NA)	(NA)	(NA)
Engineering technology. .	45,059	44,930	43,425	(NA)	(NA)	(NA)	(NA)	(NA)	(NA)
Chemistry	34,566	37,733	37,618	[3]59,836	[3]52,583	[3]59,043	63,168	58,481	60,986
Mathematics.	41,543	40,512	43,567	[3]82,000	[3]42,348	[3]37,805	[3]54,219	[3]58,778	[3]49,254
Physics	[3]47,471	[3]42,365	[3]38,945	[3]41,333	(NA)	[3]37,440	[3]51,936	[3]55,485	[3]54,729
Humanities	[3]31,087	[3]29,694	30,626	[3]29,944	[3]32,465	[3]33,049	[3]41,750	[3]41,100	[3]47,500
Social sciences [5]	28,835	29,098	31,698	[3]38,109	[3]36,992	[3]35,174	[3]47,434	[3]43,603	[3]42,727
Computer science	49,413	47,109	49,036	65,001	62,806	60,457	[3]74,453	[3]64,640	[3]74,598

NA Not available.   [1] Candidates with 1 year or less of full-time nonmilitary employment.   [2] For master's degree, offers are after nontechnical undergraduate degree.   [3] Fewer than 50 offers reported.   [4] Includes engineering physics.   [5] Excludes economics.

Source: National Association of Colleges and Employers, Bethlehem, PA (copyright holder). Reprinted with permission from Fall 2002, 2003, and 2004 Salary Survey. All rights reserved.

Education   185

Table 286. Earned Degrees Conferred by Level and Sex: 1960 to 2003

[In thousands (477 represents 477,000), except percent. Based on survey; see Appendix III]

Year ending	All degrees Total	All degrees Percent male	Associate's Male	Associate's Female	Bachelor's Male	Bachelor's Female	Master's Male	Master's Female	First professional Male	First professional Female	Doctor's Male	Doctor's Female
1960 [1]	477	65.8	(NA)	(NA)	254	138	51	24	(NA)	(NA)	9	1
1965 [1]	660	61.5	(NA)	(NA)	282	212	81	40	27	1	15	2
1970	1,271	59.2	117	89	451	341	126	83	33	2	26	4
1975	1,666	56.0	191	169	505	418	162	131	49	7	27	7
1980	1,731	51.1	184	217	474	456	151	147	53	17	23	10
1985	1,828	49.3	203	252	483	497	143	143	50	25	22	11
1987	1,823	48.4	191	245	481	510	141	148	47	25	22	12
1988	1,835	48.0	190	245	477	518	145	154	45	25	23	12
1989	1,873	47.3	186	250	483	535	149	161	45	26	23	13
1990	1,940	46.6	191	264	492	560	154	171	44	27	24	14
1991	2,025	45.8	199	283	504	590	156	181	44	28	25	15
1992	2,108	45.6	207	297	521	616	162	191	45	29	26	15
1993	2,167	45.5	212	303	533	632	169	200	45	30	26	16
1994	2,206	45.1	215	315	532	637	176	211	45	31	27	17
1995 [2]	2,218	44.9	218	321	526	634	179	219	45	31	27	18
1996 [2]	2,248	44.2	220	336	522	642	179	227	45	32	27	18
1997 [2]	2,288	43.6	224	347	521	652	181	238	46	33	27	19
1998 [2]	2,298	43.2	218	341	520	664	184	246	45	34	27	19
1999 [2]	2,323	42.7	218	342	519	682	186	254	44	34	25	19
2000 [2]	2,385	42.6	225	340	530	708	192	265	44	36	25	20
2001 [2]	2,416	42.4	232	347	532	712	194	274	43	37	25	20
2002 [2]	2,494	42.2	238	357	550	742	199	283	43	38	24	20
2003 [2]	2,621	42.1	253	380	573	775	211	301	42	39	24	22

NA Not available. [1] First-professional degrees are included with bachelor's degrees. [2] Data beginning in 1996 reflect the new classification of institutions. See footnote 1, Table 265.

Source: U.S. National Center for Education Statistics, *Digest of Education Statistics*, annual.

Table 287. Degrees Earned by Level and Race/Ethnicity: 1981 to 2003

[For school year ending in year shown. Based on survey; see Appendix III]

Level of degree and race/ethnicity	Total 1981 [1]	Total 1985 [1]	Total 1990	Total 1995	Total 2000 [2]	Total 2003 [2]	Percent distribution 1981	Percent distribution 2003 [2]
Associate's degrees, total	410,174	429,815	455,102	539,691	564,933	632,912	100.0	100.0
White, non-Hispanic	339,167	355,343	376,816	420,656	408,772	437,794	82.7	69.2
Black, non-Hispanic	35,330	35,791	34,326	47,067	60,221	75,430	8.6	11.9
Hispanic	17,800	19,407	21,504	35,962	51,573	66,175	4.3	10.5
Asian or Pacific Islander	8,650	9,914	13,066	20,677	27,782	32,610	2.1	5.2
American Indian/Alaskan Native	2,584	2,953	3,430	5,482	6,497	7,462	0.6	1.2
Nonresident alien	6,643	6,407	5,960	9,847	10,088	13,441	1.6	2.1
Bachelor's degrees, total	934,800	968,311	1,051,344	1,160,134	1,237,875	1,348,503	100.0	100.0
White, non-Hispanic	807,319	826,106	887,151	914,610	929,106	994,234	86.4	73.7
Black, non-Hispanic	60,673	57,473	61,046	87,236	108,013	124,241	6.5	9.2
Hispanic	21,832	25,874	32,829	54,230	75,059	89,030	2.3	6.6
Asian or Pacific Islander	18,794	25,395	39,230	60,502	77,912	87,943	2.0	6.5
American Indian/Alaskan Native	3,593	4,246	4,390	6,610	8,719	9,816	0.4	0.7
Nonresident alien	22,589	29,217	26,698	36,946	39,066	43,239	2.4	3.2
Master's degrees, total	294,183	280,421	324,301	397,629	457,056	512,645	100.0	100.0
White, non-Hispanic	241,216	223,628	254,299	293,345	320,485	341,735	82.0	66.7
Black, non-Hispanic	17,133	13,939	15,336	24,166	35,874	44,272	5.8	8.6
Hispanic	6,461	6,864	7,892	12,905	19,253	24,974	2.2	4.9
Asian or Pacific Islander	6,282	7,782	10,439	16,847	23,218	27,245	2.1	5.3
American Indian/Alaskan Native	1,034	1,256	1,090	1,621	2,246	2,837	0.4	0.6
Nonresident alien	22,057	26,952	35,245	48,745	55,980	71,582	7.5	14.0
Doctor's degrees, total	32,839	32,307	38,371	44,446	44,808	46,024	100.0	100.0
White, non-Hispanic	25,908	23,934	26,221	27,846	27,843	27,698	78.9	60.2
Black, non-Hispanic	1,265	1,154	1,149	1,667	2,246	2,517	3.9	5.5
Hispanic	456	677	780	984	1,305	1,561	1.4	3.4
Asian or Pacific Islander	877	1,106	1,225	2,689	2,420	2,426	2.7	5.3
American Indian/Alaskan Native	130	119	98	130	160	196	0.4	0.4
Nonresident alien	4,203	5,317	8,898	11,130	10,834	11,626	12.8	25.3
First-professional degrees, total	71,340	71,057	70,988	75,800	80,057	80,810	100.0	100.0
White, non-Hispanic	64,551	63,219	60,487	59,402	59,637	58,678	90.5	72.6
Black, non-Hispanic	2,931	3,029	3,409	4,747	5,555	5,715	4.1	7.1
Hispanic	1,541	1,884	2,425	3,231	3,865	4,086	2.2	5.1
Asian or Pacific Islander	1,456	1,816	3,362	6,396	8,584	9,790	2.0	12.1
American Indian/Alaskan Native	192	248	257	413	564	586	0.3	0.7
Nonresident alien	669	861	1,048	1,611	1,852	1,955	0.9	2.4

[1] Excludes some persons whose race/ethnicity was unknown and are slight undercounts of degrees awarded. [2] In this table, data beginning in 2000 reflect the new classification of institutions. See footnote 1, Table 265.

Source: U.S. National Center for Education Statistics, *Digest of Education Statistics*, annual.

Table 288. Degrees and Awards Earned Below Bachelor's by Field: 2002

[Covers associate's degrees and other awards based on postsecondary curriculums of less than 4 years in institutions of higher education. Field of degree classifications not revised as in other tables. Based on survey; see Appendix III]

Field of study	Less than 1-year awards		1- to less than 4-year awards		Associate's degrees	
	Total	Women	Total	Women	Total	Women
Total	**163,977**	**83,563**	**145,254**	**83,339**	**595,133**	**357,024**
Agriculture and natural resources	2,994	549	2,272	746	6,494	2,299
Architecture and related programs	31	20	114	99	443	342
Area, ethnic, and cultural studies	263	198	96	82	1,517	1,039
Biological/life sciences	82	38	29	17	319	256
Business management and administrative services [1]	34,339	21,134	25,094	18,409	98,796	67,585
Communications and communications technologies	785	392	683	284	4,840	2,198
Computer and information sciences	9,014	2,838	8,634	3,171	30,965	11,150
Construction trades	3,916	217	5,440	207	2,639	139
Consumer and personal services	5,881	4,514	8,945	6,624	10,115	4,808
Education	2,056	1,616	893	770	9,267	7,397
Engineering and engineering technologies	5,080	918	6,110	786	34,619	4,803
English language and literature/letters	324	212	121	80	864	569
Foreign languages and literatures	280	199	41	39	517	297
Health professions and related sciences	44,405	34,703	43,942	38,274	79,888	69,703
Home economics and vocational home economics	9,025	6,787	4,443	3,987	9,480	8,739
Law and legal studies	768	663	1,390	1,221	6,825	6,048
Liberal/general studies and humanities	268	182	3,408	2,246	207,163	130,987
Library science	150	136	49	39	96	84
Mathematics	2	-	5	3	685	240
Mechanics and repairers	9,419	944	15,180	824	12,086	767
Multi/interdisciplinary studies	436	224	193	143	13,204	7,434
Parks, recreation, leisure, and fitness	250	124	411	278	830	367
Physical sciences	167	76	130	63	2,308	1,062
Precision production trades	5,454	804	7,823	1,172	10,818	2,427
Protective services	13,740	3,182	4,104	987	16,689	6,397
Psychology	50	42	34	30	1,705	1,334
Public administration and services	489	410	376	309	3,323	2,855
R.O.T.C. and military technologies	-	-	-	-	62	8
Social sciences and history	291	135	48	25	5,593	3,747
Theological studies, religion and philosophy	81	49	470	226	548	300
Transportation and material moving	12,275	1,482	842	66	1,159	161
Visual and performing arts	1,659	774	3,854	2,073	20,911	11,298
Undistributed and unclassified	3	1	80	59	365	184

- Represents zero.   [1] Includes marketing.

Source: U.S. National Center for Education Statistics, *Digest of Education Statistics*, annual.

Table 289. Bachelor's Degrees Earned by Field: 1980 to 2003

[The new Classification of Instructional Programs was introduced in 2002–03. Data for previous years has been reclassified where necessary to conform to the new classifications. Based on survey; see Appendix III]

Field of study	1980	1990	2000	2001	2002	2003
Total	**929,417**	**1,051,344**	**1,237,875**	**1,244,171**	**1,291,900**	**1,348,503**
Agriculture and natural resources	22,802	12,900	24,238	23,370	23,331	23,294
Architecture and related services	9,132	9,364	8,462	8,480	8,808	9,054
Area, ethnic, cultural, and gender studies	2,840	4,447	6,212	6,160	6,390	6,629
Biological and biomedical sciences	46,190	37,204	63,005	59,865	59,415	60,072
Business	186,264	248,568	256,070	263,515	278,217	293,545
Communication, journalism, and related programs [1]	28,616	51,572	57,058	59,191	64,036	69,792
Computer and information sciences	11,154	27,347	37,788	44,142	50,365	57,439
Education	118,038	105,112	108,034	105,458	106,295	105,790
Engineering and engineering technologies	69,387	82,480	73,419	72,975	74,679	77,267
English language and literature/letters	32,187	46,803	50,106	50,569	52,375	53,670
Family and consumer sciences/human sciences	18,411	13,514	16,321	16,421	16,938	18,166
Foreign languages, literatures, and linguistics	12,480	13,133	15,886	16,128	16,258	16,901
Health professions and related clinical sciences	63,848	58,983	80,863	75,933	72,887	71,223
Legal professions and studies	683	1,632	1,969	1,991	2,003	2,466
Liberal arts and sciences, general studies, and humanities	23,196	27,985	36,104	37,962	39,333	40,221
Mathematics and statistics	11,378	14,276	11,418	11,171	11,950	12,493
Multi/interdisciplinary studies	11,457	16,557	28,561	27,189	28,943	28,757
Parks, recreation, leisure and fitness studies	5,753	4,582	17,571	17,948	18,885	21,428
Philosophy and religious studies	7,069	7,034	8,535	8,717	9,473	10,344
Physical sciences and science technologies	23,407	16,056	18,331	17,919	17,799	17,940
Psychology	42,093	53,952	74,194	73,645	76,775	78,613
Public administration and social services	16,644	13,908	20,185	19,447	19,392	19,878
Security and protective services	15,015	15,354	24,877	25,211	25,536	26,189
Social sciences and history	103,662	118,083	127,101	128,036	132,874	143,218
Theology and religious vocations	6,170	5,185	6,789	6,945	7,762	7,926
Transportation and materials moving	213	2,387	3,395	3,748	4,020	4,567
Visual and performing arts	40,892	39,934	58,791	61,148	66,773	71,474
Other and unclassified	436	2,992	2,592	887	388	147

[1] Includes technologies.

Source: U.S. National Center for Education Statistics, *Digest of Education Statistics*, annual; and unpublished data.

Table 290. **Master's and Doctorate's Degrees Earned by Field: 1980 to 2003**

[The new Classification of Instructional Programs was introduced in 2002–03. Data for previous years has been reclassified where necessary to conform to the new classifications. Based on survey; see Appendix III]

Field of study	1980	1990	2000	2001	2002	2003
MASTER'S DEGREES						
Total...........................	298,081	324,301	457,056	468,476	482,118	512,645
Agriculture and natural resources	3,976	3,382	4,360	4,272	4,503	4,492
Architecture and related services.............	3,139	3,499	4,268	4,302	4,566	4,925
Area, ethnic, cultural, and gender studies	852	1,191	1,544	1,555	1,541	1,509
Biological and biomedical sciences	6,322	4,906	6,781	6,955	6,937	6,990
Business	55,008	76,676	111,532	115,602	119,725	127,545
Communication, journalism, and related programs [1]	3,082	4,353	5,525	5,645	5,980	6,495
Computer and information sciences.............	3,647	9,677	14,990	16,911	17,173	19,503
Education	101,819	84,890	123,045	127,829	135,189	147,448
Engineering and engineering technologies	16,765	25,294	26,726	27,272	27,057	30,669
English language and literature/letters	6,026	6,317	7,022	6,763	7,097	7,413
Family and consumer sciences/human sciences ...	2,690	1,679	1,882	1,838	1,683	1,610
Foreign languages, literatures, and linguistics	3,067	3,018	3,037	3,035	3,075	3,049
Health professions and related clinical sciences....	15,374	20,406	42,593	43,623	43,560	42,715
Legal professions and studies	1,817	1,888	3,750	3,829	4,053	4,126
Liberal arts and sciences, general studies, and humanities	2,646	1,999	3,256	3,193	2,754	3,312
Library science	5,374	4,341	4,577	4,727	5,113	5,314
Mathematics and statistics....................	2,860	3,624	3,208	3,209	3,350	3,626
Multi/interdisciplinary studies	2,494	3,182	3,487	3,475	3,708	3,780
Parks, recreation, leisure and fitness studies......	647	529	2,322	2,354	2,580	2,978
Philosophy and religious studies	1,204	1,327	1,376	1,386	1,371	1,578
Physical sciences and science technologies	5,167	5,410	4,810	5,049	5,012	5,109
Psychology	9,938	10,730	15,740	16,539	16,357	17,123
Public administration and social services	17,560	17,399	25,594	25,268	25,448	25,894
Security and protective services	1,805	1,151	2,609	2,514	2,935	2,955
Social sciences and history	12,176	11,634	14,066	13,791	14,112	14,634
Theology and religious vocations.	3,872	4,941	5,534	4,850	4,909	5,099
Visual and performing arts....................	8,708	8,481	10,918	11,404	11,595	11,986
Other and unclassified	46	2,377	2,504	1,286	735	768
DOCTORATE'S DEGREES						
Total...........................	32,615	38,371	44,808	44,904	44,160	46,024
Agriculture and natural resources	991	1,295	1,168	1,127	1,148	1,229
Architecture and related services.............	79	103	129	153	183	152
Area, ethnic, cultural, and gender studies	151	125	205	216	212	186
Biological and biomedical sciences	3,527	3,837	5,180	4,953	4,823	5,003
Business	767	1,093	1,194	1,180	1,156	1,251
Communication, journalism, and related programs [1]	193	272	357	370	383	398
Computer and information sciences.............	240	627	779	768	752	816
Education	7,314	6,503	6,409	6,284	6,549	6,835
Engineering and engineering technologies	2,546	5,030	5,421	5,604	5,245	5,333
English language and literature/letters	1,196	986	1,470	1,330	1,291	1,246
Family and consumer sciences/human sciences ...	192	273	327	354	311	372
Foreign languages, literatures, and linguistics	857	816	1,086	1,078	1,003	1,042
Health professions and related clinical sciences....	821	1,449	2,053	2,242	2,913	3,328
Legal professions and studies	40	111	74	286	79	105
Liberal arts and sciences, general studies, and humanities	192	63	83	102	113	78
Mathematics and statistics....................	724	917	1,075	997	923	1,007
Multi/interdisciplinary studies	318	442	792	784	765	899
Parks, recreation, leisure and fitness studies......	21	35	134	177	151	199
Philosophy and religious studies	374	445	598	600	610	662
Physical sciences and science technologies	3,044	4,116	3,963	3,911	3,760	3,858
Psychology	3,395	3,811	4,731	5,091	4,759	4,831
Public administration and social services	342	508	537	574	571	596
Security and protective services	18	38	52	44	49	72
Social sciences and history	3,230	3,010	4,095	3,930	3,902	3,850
Theology and religious vocations.	1,315	1,317	1,630	1,461	1,350	1,321
Visual and performing arts....................	655	849	1,127	1,167	1,114	1,293
Other and unclassified	73	300	139	121	45	62

[1] Includes technologies.

Source: U.S. National Center for Education Statistics, *Digest of Education Statistics*, annual; and unpublished data.

U.S. Census Bureau, Statistical Abstract of the United States: 2006

Table 291. **First Professional Degrees Earned in Selected Professions: 1970 to 2002**

[First professional degrees include degrees which require at least 6 years of college work for completion (including at least 2 years of preprofessional training). Based on survey; see Appendix III]

Type of degree and sex of recipient	1970	1975	1980	1985	1990	1995	1999	2000	2001	2002
Medicine (M.D.):										
Institutions conferring degrees.....	86	104	112	120	124	119	118	118	118	118
Degrees conferred, total.........	8,314	12,447	14,902	16,041	15,075	15,537	15,562	15,286	15,403	15,237
Percent to women..........	8.4	13.1	23.4	30.4	34.2	38.8	42.5	42.7	43.3	44.4
Dentistry (D.D.S. or D.M.D.):										
Institutions conferring degrees.....	48	52	58	59	57	53	53	54	54	53
Degrees conferred, total.........	3,718	4,773	5,258	5,339	4,100	3,897	4,144	4,250	4,391	4,239
Percent to women..........	0.9	3.1	13.3	20.7	30.9	36.4	35.5	40.1	38.6	38.5
Law (LL.B. or J.D.):										
Institutions conferring degrees.....	145	154	179	181	182	183	188	190	192	192
Degrees conferred, total.........	14,916	29,296	35,647	37,491	36,485	39,349	39,167	38,152	37,904	38,981
Percent to women..........	5.4	15.1	30.2	38.5	42.2	42.6	44.8	45.9	47.3	48.0
Theological (B.D., M.Div., M.H.L.):										
Institutions conferring degrees.....	(NA)	(NA)	(NA)	(NA)	(NA)	192	193	198	191	191
Degrees conferred, total.........	5,298	5,095	7,115	7,221	5,851	5,978	5,558	6,129	5,026	5,195
Percent to women..........	2.3	6.8	13.8	18.5	24.8	25.7	28.3	29.2	32.0	32.9

NA Not available.

Source: U.S. National Center for Education Statistics, *Digest of Education Statistics*, annual.

Table 292. **Participation in Adult Education: 2000–2001**

[In thousands (198,803 represents 198,803,000), except percent. For the civilian noninstitutional population 16 years old. Adult education includes enrollment in formal education activities in the previous 12 months. Excludes participants in only postsecondary degree, certificate or diploma programs as full-time students. Based on the Adult Education Survey of the National Household Education Survey Program and subject to sampling error; see source and Appendix III for details]

Characteristic	Adult population (1,000)	Number taking adult education courses (1,000)	Percent of total	Reason for taking course (percent) College or university degree program	Reason for taking course (percent) Work-related course	Reason for taking course (percent) Personal interest course
Total......................	198,803	92,278	46	4	30	21
Age:						
16 to 30 years old.................	46,905	25,030	53	10	28	24
31 to 40 years old.................	41,778	22,200	53	4	39	20
41 to 50 years old.................	41,255	22,525	55	4	42	21
51 to 65 years old.................	39,523	16,218	41	1	28	21
66 years old and over	29,342	6,304	21	-	4	19
Sex:						
Male........................	94,955	40,897	43	4	29	16
Female......................	103,848	51,382	49	5	30	26
Race/ethnicity:						
White, Non-Hispanic	144,147	68,335	47	4	32	22
Black, Non-Hispanic	22,186	9,605	43	5	23	26
Hispanic	21,537	8,984	42	4	22	16
Other	10,932	5,355	49	6	32	18
Educational attainment:						
Less than high school	31,343	6,957	22	-	6	11
High school diploma or GED............	64,606	21,692	34	2	20	15
Some college...................	52,559	30,273	58	8	36	26
Bachelor's degree or higher	50,295	33,357	66	6	51	30
Marital status:						
Married......................	121,455	57,644	47	3	33	21
Living with partner, unmarried	14,009	6,026	43	5	27	15
Separated/divorced/widowed...........	30,503	11,512	38	2	23	20
Never married	32,836	17,096	52	10	26	26
Employment/occupation:						
Employed	145,249	78,883	54	6	39	22
Professional or managerial	42,230	30,087	71	8	59	29
Services, sales, or support	65,298	35,883	55	6	36	23
Trades	37,722	12,914	34	2	21	12
Unemployed	53,553	13,395	25	1	5	19
Continuing ed requirements:						
Yes	50,549	32,286	64	4	49	25
No.........................	148,253	59,993	40	4	23	20
Household income:						
$20,000 or less	40,246	11,451	28	3	12	15
$20,001 to $35,000................	38,876	14,969	39	4	20	18
$35,001 to $50,000................	33,035	15,857	48	4	31	22
$50,001 to $75,000................	40,725	22,699	56	6	39	24
$75,001 or more..................	45,922	27,302	59	5	45	26
Children under 10 in household:						
Yes	55,333	28,643	52	5	35	21
No.........................	143,469	63,635	44	4	28	21

- Represents or rounds to zero.   [1] Includes English as a Second Language, basic education skills, vocational or technical diploma programs, and apprenticeship programs each with a total participation rate of about 1 percent.

Source: U.S. National Center for Education Statistics, *Participation in Adult Education and Lifelong Learning: 2000–01*, NCES 2004-050, September 2004.

Education 189

No. 23.—JUVENILE DELINQUENTS IN 1890 AND 1904: Total Number and Ratio per 100,000 of Population, by Color and by States and Territories.

[From reports of the Bureau of the Census, Department of Commerce and Labor.]

State or Territory.	Juvenile delinquents.				Number of juvenile delinquents per 100,000 of population.			
	June 1, 1890.		June 30, 1904.		June 1, 1890.		June 30, 1904 (based on population of 1900).	
	Number.	Number per 100,000 of population.	Number.	Number per 100,000 of population.*	White.	Colored.	White.	Colored.
North Atlantic division:								
Maine............	169	25.6	226	81.9	25.2	164.6	82.2	133.9
New Hampshire.........	102	27.1	181	42.5	26.1	579.7	44.1	....
Vermont............	86	25.9	137	39.3	24.1	597.6	39.7	114.9
Massachusetts	698	31.2	1,107	36.5	30.3	114.6	37.9	163.0
Rhode Island	270	78.1	356	77.0	72.2	340.0	76.6	368.2
Connecticut..........	625	83.9	702	72.0	75.5	561.6	67.8	606.4
New York...........	3,675	61.3	5,826	74.8	59.4	211.1	77.8	232.1
New Jersey..........	608	42.1	650	31.5	38.6	142.7	28.4	189.2
Pennsylvania...........	1,154	21.9	1,692	25.1	17.7	220.5	23.2	165.2
Total..........	7,388	42.5	10,877	48.3	39.6	216.4	48.6	208.9
South Atlantic division:								
Delaware	45	26.7	98	51.2	15.0	84.4	37.0	133.3
Maryland	1,061	101.8	1,070	85.8	83.6	171.4	79.8	181.6
District of Columbia	187	81.2	405	135.7	44.0	197.2	55.9	341.8
Virginia	(b)	(b)	279	14.4	....	....	12.8	19.1
West Virginia..........	(b)	(b)	314	30.2	....	....	30.0	89.5
Georgia	(b)	(b)	99	4.2	....	...l....	3.8	5.2
Florida............	(b)	(b)	31	5.3	....	...z...	1.3	11.7
Total..................	1,293	14.6	2,296	20.7	13.9	15.7	20.9	23.9
North Central division:								
Ohio..................	1,529	41.6	1,741	40.0	36.0	273.1	35.6	301.1
Indiana..............	636	29.0	872	32.9	24.6	236.5	28.5	295.0
Illinois..............	383	10.0	1,386	26.5	8.7	93.2	24.5	261.9
Michigan	696	33.2	1,114	44.0	31.4	214.2	43.9	276.6
Wisconsin.............	591	35.0	543	24.4	34.5	171.7	25.7	134.8
Minnesota ,..........	284	21.8	360	18.6	21.1	176.5	19.9	104.5
Iowa............	527	27.6	714	30.2	24.2	619.8	29.3	477.8
Missouri	360	13.4	670	20.4	10.8	58.4	17.5	95.8
North Dakota..........	(b)	(b)	39	10.5	....	....	12.5	....
South Dakota..........	(b)	(b)	65	15.4	....	....	16.3	14.4
Nebraska...........	237	22.4	164	15.4	21.6	91.5	15.0	61.4
Kansas................	208	14.6	372	25.0	12.7	65.3	18.9	193.8
Total.....	5,451	24.4	8,040	28.8	21.8	147.9	26.9	200.7*
South Central division:								
Kentucky................	273	14.7	301	13.3	11.9	31.0	9.4	44.2
Tennessee............	(b)	(b)	246	11.6	....	....	12.3	11.7
Alabama............	(b)	(b)	37	1.9	....	....	3.7	....
Louisiana ,..........	86	7.7	36	2.4	3.4	12.0	3.2	2.0
Total................	359	3.3	620	4.1	2.8	4.3	4.3	4.6
Western division:								
Montana..............	(a)	(b)	78	27.4	....	....	29.6	61.5
Colorado	149	36.1	288	48.7	35.4	77.6	46.7	384.8
Arizona..............	(b)	(b)	31	22.6	....	....	32.3	3.3
Utah	(b)	(b)	79	26.0	....	....	27.9	70.0
Washington.............	(b)	(b)	158	27.1	....	....	30.8	22.9
Oregon.............	(b)	(b)	93	20.5	....	....	23.6	....
California..............	206	17.1	474	29.7	18.3	3.1	31.0	47.4
Total.................	355	11.7	1,201	26.7	12.1	5.7	28.4	46.9
Continental U. S........	14,846	23.7	23,034	28.3	23.5	25.4	29.7	84.4

a Estimated, July 1, 1904.   b No returns.

Source: Statistical Abstract of the United States: 1907 Edition.

Section 5
Law Enforcement, Courts, and Prisons

This section presents data on crimes committed, victims of crimes, arrests, and data related to criminal violations and the criminal justice system. The major sources of these data are the Bureau of Justice Statistics (BJS), the Federal Bureau of Investigation (FBI), and the Administrative Office of the U.S. Courts. BJS issues several reports, including *Sourcebook of Criminal Justice Statistics, Criminal Victimization in the United States, Prisoners in State and Federal Institutions, Census of State Correctional Facilities and Survey of Prison Inmates, Census of Jails and Survey of Jail Inmates, Parole in the United States, Capital Punishment,* and the annual *Expenditure and Employment Data for the Criminal Justice System.* The Federal Bureau of Investigation's major annual reports are *Crime in the United States, Law Enforcement Officers Killed and Assaulted,* annual, and *Hate Crimes,* annual. which presents data on reported crimes as gathered from state and local law enforcement agencies.

Legal jurisdiction and law enforcement—Law enforcement is, for the most part, a function of state and local officers and agencies. The U.S. Constitution reserves general police powers to the states. By act of Congress, federal offenses include only offenses against the U.S. government and against or by its employees while engaged in their official duties and offenses which involve the crossing of state lines or an interference with interstate commerce. Excluding the military, there are 52 separate criminal law jurisdictions in the United States: 1 in each of the 50 states, 1 in the District of Columbia, and the federal jurisdiction. Each of these has its own criminal law and procedure and its own law enforcement agencies. While the systems of law enforcement are quite similar among the states, there are often substantial differences in the penalties for like offenses.

Law enforcement can be divided into three parts: Investigation of crimes and

arrests of persons suspected of committing them; prosecution of those charged with crime; and the punishment or treatment of persons convicted of crime.

Crime—There are two major approaches taken in determining the extent of crime. One perspective is provided by the FBI through its Uniform Crime Reporting Program (UCR). The FBI receives monthly and annual reports from law enforcement agencies throughout the country, currently representing 93 percent of the national population. Each month, city police, sheriffs, and state police file reports on the number of index offenses, hate crimes and law enforcement assaults that become known to them. Additionally, data are collected for officers killed in the line of duty.

The FBI Crime Index offenses are as follows: *Murder and nonnegligent manslaughter* is based on police investigations, as opposed to the determination of a medical examiner or judicial body, includes willful felonious homicides and excludes attempts and assaults to kill, suicides, accidental deaths, justifiable homicides, and deaths caused by negligence; *forcible rape* includes forcible rapes and attempts; *robbery* includes stealing or taking anything of value by force or violence or threat of force or violence and includes attempted robbery; *aggravated assault* includes assault with intent to kill; *burglary* includes any unlawful entry to commit a felony or a theft and includes attempted burglary and burglary followed by larceny; *larceny* includes theft of property or articles of value without use of force and violence or fraud and excludes embezzlement, "con games," forgery, etc.; *motor vehicle theft* includes all cases where vehicles are driven away and abandoned but excludes vehicles taken for temporary use and returned by the taker. Arson was added as the eighth Index offense in April 1979 following a Congressional mandate. *Arson* includes any willful or malicious burning

U.S. Census Bureau, Statistical Abstract of the United States: 2006

or attempt to burn, with or without intent to defraud, a dwelling house, public building, motor vehicle or aircraft, personal property of another, etc.

The monthly Uniform Crime Reports also contain data on crimes cleared by arrest and on characteristics of persons arrested for all criminal offenses. In summarizing and publishing crime data, the FBI depends primarily on the adherence to the established standards of reporting for statistical accuracy, presenting the data as information useful to persons concerned with the problem of crime and criminal law enforcement.

National Crime Victimization Survey (NCVS)—A second perspective on crime is provided by this survey of the Bureau of Justice Statistics. Details about the crimes come directly from the victims. No attempt is made to validate the information against police records or any other source.

The NCVS measures rape, robbery, assault, household and personal larceny, burglary, and motor vehicle theft. The NCVS includes offenses reported to the police, as well as those not reported.

Police reporting rates (percent of victimizations) varied by type of crime. In 2003, for instance, 33 percent of rapes/ sexual assaults were reported; 61 percent of robberies; 46 percent of assaults; 32 percent of personal thefts; 54 percent of household burglaries; and 77 percent of motor vehicle thefts.

Murder and kidnaping are not covered. Commercial burglary and robbery were dropped from the program during 1977. The so-called victimless crimes, such as drunkenness, drug abuse, and prostitution, also are excluded, as are crimes for which it is difficult to identify knowledgeable respondents or to locate data records.

Crimes of which the victim may not be aware also cannot be measured effectively. Buying stolen property may fall into this category, as may some instances of embezzlement. Attempted crimes of many types probably are under recorded

for this reason. Events in which the victim has shown a willingness to participate in illegal activity also are excluded.

In any encounter involving a personal crime, more than one criminal act can be committed against an individual. For example, a rape may be associated with a robbery, or a household offense, such as a burglary, can escalate into something more serious in the event of a personal confrontation. In classifying the survey-measured crimes, each criminal incident has been counted only once–by the most serious act that took place during the incident and ranked in accordance with the seriousness classification system used by the Federal Bureau of Investigation. The order of seriousness for crimes against persons is as follows: Rape, robbery, assault, and larceny. Personal crimes take precedence over household offenses.

A *victimization*, basic measure of the occurrence of crime, is a specific criminal act as it affects a single victim. The number of victimizations is determined by the number of victims of such acts. Victimization counts serve as key elements in computing rates of victimization. For crimes against persons, the rates are based on the total number of individuals age 12 and over or on a portion of that population sharing a particular characteristic or set of traits. As general indicators of the danger of having been victimized during the reference period, the rates are not sufficiently refined to represent true measures of risk for specific individuals or households.

An *incident* is a specific criminal act involving one or more victims; therefore the number of incidents of personal crimes is lower than that of victimizations.

Courts—Statistics on criminal offenses and the outcome of prosecutions are incomplete for the country as a whole, although data are available for many states individually. The only national compilations of such statistics were made by the Census Bureau for 1932 to 1945 covering a maximum of 32 states and by the Bureau of Justice Statistics for 1986, 1988, 1990, and 1992 based on a nationally representative sample survey.

The bulk of civil and criminal litigation in the country is commenced and determined in the various state courts. Only when the U.S. Constitution and acts of Congress specifically confer jurisdiction upon the federal courts may civil or criminal litigation be heard and decided by them. Generally, the federal courts have jurisdiction over the following types of cases: Suits or proceedings by or against the United States; civil actions between private parties arising under the Constitution, laws, or treaties of the United States; civil actions between private litigants who are citizens of different states; civil cases involving admiralty, maritime, or prize jurisdiction; and all matters in bankruptcy. The Administrative Office of the United States Courts has compiled statistics on the caseload of the federal courts annually since 1940.

There are several types of courts with varying degrees of legal jurisdiction. These jurisdictions include original, appellate, general, and limited or special. A court of original jurisdiction is one having the authority initially to try a case and pass judgment on the law and the facts; a court of appellate jurisdiction is one with the legal authority to review cases and hear appeals; a court of general jurisdiction is a trial court of unlimited original jurisdiction in civil and/or criminal cases, also called a "major trial court"; a court of limited or special jurisdiction is a trial court with legal authority over only a particular class of cases, such as probate, juvenile, or traffic cases.

The 94 federal courts of original jurisdiction are known as the U.S. district courts. One or more of these courts is established in every state and one each in the District of Columbia, Puerto Rico, the Virgin Islands, the Northern Mariana Islands, and Guam. Appeals from the district courts are taken to intermediate appellate courts of which there are 13, known as U.S. courts of appeals and the United States Court of Appeals for the Federal Circuit. The Supreme Court of the United States is the final and highest appellate court in the federal system of courts.

Juvenile offenders—For statistical purposes, the FBI and most states classify as juvenile offenders persons under the age of 18 years who have committed a crime or crimes.

Delinquency cases are all cases of youths referred to a juvenile court for violation of a law or ordinance or for seriously "antisocial" conduct. Several types of facilities are available for those adjudicated delinquents, ranging from the short-term physically unrestricted environment to the long-term very restrictive atmosphere.

Prisoners—Data on prisoners in federal and state prisons and reformatories were collected annually by the Census Bureau until 1950, by the Federal Bureau of Prisons until 1971, transferred then to the Law Enforcement Assistance Administration, and, in 1979, to the Bureau of Justice Statistics. Adults convicted of criminal activity may be given a prison or jail sentence. A *prison* is a confinement facility having custodial authority over adults sentenced to confinement of more than 1 year. A *jail* is a facility, usually operated by a local law enforcement agency, holding persons detained pending adjudication and/or persons committed after adjudication to 1 year or less. Nearly every state publishes annual data either for its whole prison system or for each separate state institution.

Statistical reliability—For discussion of statistical collection, estimation and sampling procedures, and measures of statistical reliability pertaining to the National Crime Victimization Survey and Uniform Crime Reporting Program, see Appendix III.

Table 293. Crimes and Crime Rates by Type of Offense: 1980 to 2003

[1,345 represents 1,345,000. Data refer to offenses known to the police. Rates are based on Census Bureau estimated resident population as of July 1; 1980, 1990 and 2000, enumerated as of April 1. See source for details. For definitions of crimes, see text, this section.]

Item and year	Violent crime					Property crime			
	Total	Murder [1,2]	Forcible rape	Robbery	Aggravated assault	Total	Burglary	Larceny/ theft	Motor vehicle theft
Number of offenses (1,000):									
1980	1,345	23	83	566	673	12,064	3,795	7,137	1,132
1985	1,328	19	88	498	723	11,103	3,073	6,926	1,103
1988	1,566	21	92	543	910	12,357	3,218	7,706	1,433
1989	1,646	22	95	578	952	12,605	3,168	7,872	1,565
1990	1,820	23	103	639	1,055	12,655	3,074	7,946	1,636
1991	1,912	25	107	688	1,093	12,961	3,157	8,142	1,662
1992	1,932	24	109	672	1,127	12,506	2,980	7,915	1,611
1993	1,926	25	106	660	1,136	12,219	2,835	7,821	1,563
1994	1,858	23	102	619	1,113	12,132	2,713	7,880	1,539
1995	1,799	22	97	581	1,099	12,064	2,594	7,998	1,472
1996	1,689	20	96	536	1,037	11,805	2,506	7,905	1,394
1997	1,636	18	96	499	1,023	11,558	2,461	7,744	1,354
1998	1,534	17	93	447	977	10,952	2,333	7,376	1,243
1999	1,426	16	89	409	912	10,208	2,101	6,956	1,152
2000	1,425	16.	90	408	912	10,183	2,051	6,972	1,160
2001	1,439	16	91	424	909	10,437	2,117	7,092	1,228
2002	1,424	16	95	421	891	10,455	2,151	7,057	1,247
2003	1,381	17	93	413	858	10,436	2,153	7,022	1,260
Rate per 100,000 population:									
1980	597	10.2	36.8	251	299	5,353	1,684	3,167	502
1985	558	8.0	36.8	209	304	4,666	1,292	2,911	464
1988	641	3.5	37.8	222	372	5,054	1,316	3,152	586
1989	667	8.7	38.3	234	386	5,107	1,284	3,190	634
1990	730	9.4	41.1	256	423	5,073	1,232	3,185	656
1991	758	9.8	42.3	273	433	5,140	1,252	3,229	659
1992	758	9.3	42.8	264	442	4,904	1,168	3,104	632
1993	747	9.5	41.1	256	441	4,740	1,100	3,034	606
1994	714	9.0	39.3	238	428	4,660	1,042	3,027	591
1995	685	8.2	37.1	221	418	4,591	987	3,043	560
1996	637	7.4	36.3	202	391	4,451	945	2,980	526
1997	611	6.8	35.9	186	382	4,316	919	2,892	506
1998	568	6.3	34.5	166	361	4,053	863	2,730	460
1999	523	5.7	32.8	150	334	3,744	770	2,551	423
2000	507	5.5	32.0	145	324	3,618	729	2,477	412
2001	505	5.6	31.8	149	319	3,658	742	2,486	431
2002	494	5.6	33.1	146	310	3,631	747	2,451	433
2003	475	5.7	32.1	142	295	3,588	741	2,415	433

[1] Includes nonnegligent manslaughter. [2] The murder and nonnegligent homicides that occurred as a result of the events of September 11, 2001, were not included in this table.

Source: U.S. Federal Bureau of Investigation, *Crime in the United States*, annual. See also /<http://www.fbi.gov/ucr/cius_03/pdf/toc03.pdf> (released November 2004)

Table 294. Crimes and Crime Rates by Type and Area: 2003

[In thousands (1,381 represents 1,381,000), except rate. Rate per 100,000 population; see headnote, Table 293. Estimated totals based on reports from city and rural law enforcement agencies representing 96 percent of the national population. For definitions of crimes, see text, this section]

Type of crime	United States		Metropolitan areas [1]		Other cities		Rural areas	
	Total	Rate	Total	Rate	Total	Rate	Total	Rate
Violent crime	1,381	475	1,244	517	76	385	61	202
Murder and nonnegligent manslaughter	17	6	15	6	1	4	1	4
Forcible rape	93	32	79	33	8	38	7	23
Robbery	413	142	397	165	12	60	5	16
Aggravated assault	858	295	754	313	56	283	48	159
Property crime	10,436	3,588	9,108	3,783	819	4,148	508	1,677
Burglary	2,153	741	1,824	758	161	816	168	555
Larceny-theft	7,022	2,415	6,102	2,534	619	3,132	301	994
Motor vehicle theft	1,260	433	1,182	491	39	200	39	129

[1] For definition, see Appendix II.

Source: U.S. Federal Bureau of Investigation, <http://www.fbi.gov/ucr/cius_03/pdf/toc03.pdf (released November 2004)

Table 295. Crime Rates by State, 2002 and 2003, and by Type, 2003

[Offenses known to the police per 100,000 population. Based on Census Bureau estimated resident population as of July 1; 2000 enumerated as of April 1. For definitions of crimes, see text, this section]

State	Violent crime						Property crime				
	2002 ,total	2003					2002 ,total	2003			
		Total	Mur-der [1]	Forc-ible rape	Rob-bery	Aggra-vated assault		Total	Bur-glary	Lar-ceny/ theft	Motor vehicle theft
United States.....	494	475	6	32	142	295	3,631	3,588	741	2,415	433
Alabama.........	445	430	7	37	134	252	4,028	4,049	961	2,756	332
Alaska...........	565	593	6	93	68	427	3,760	3,742	594	2,771	377
Arizona..........	555	513	8	33	137	336	5,850	5,632	1,050	3,561	1,021
Arkansas.........	425	456	6	33	82	335	3,738	3,621	914	2,487	221
California.........	595	579	7	28	180	365	3,361	3,424	683	2,061	680
Colorado.........	353	345	4	42	82	218	4,000	3,941	711	2,731	499
Connecticut.......	313	308	3	19	119	168	2,701	2,607	448	1,842	317
Delaware [2].......	600	658	3	43	170	442	3,346	3,384	730	2,302	352
District of Columbia [3]........	1,638	1,608	44	49	700	816	6,409	5,800	829	3,213	1,758
Florida..........	771	730	5	40	185	500	4,656	4,452	1,003	2,970	479
Georgia..........	460	454	8	26	162	259	4,056	4,255	909	2,846	499
Hawaii...........	263	270	2	29	93	147	5,801	5,238	907	3,563	767
Idaho...........	255	243	2	37	18	186	2,913	2,909	570	2,148	191
Illinois [4]........	602	557	7	33	188	329	3,420	3,284	619	2,336	330
Indiana	357	353	6	28	103	216	3,394	3,358	671	2,351	335
Iowa	286	272	2	26	38	207	3,164	2,961	596	2,175	190
Kansas [4]........	377	396	5	38	83	270	3,716	3,994	804	2,905	286
Kentucky [4]........	271	262	5	26	78	154	2,655	2,682	672	1,782	228
Louisiana.........	663	646	13	41	157	435	4,442	4,350	998	2,909	442
Maine...........	108	109	1	27	22	58	2,547	2,457	504	1,841	112
Maryland.........	771	704	10	25	242	428	3,983	3,801	701	2,439	661
Massachusetts	485	469	2	28	124	315	2,612	2,550	540	1,613	397
Michigan.........	541	511	6	54	112	339	3,336	3,277	677	2,067	533
Minnesota	267	263	3	41	77	142	3,264	3,117	547	2,297	272
Mississippi........	344	326	9	37	105	174	3,823	3,720	1,036	2,374	311
Missouri..........	539	473	5	24	109	335	4,066	4,015	717	2,795	502
Montana [4]	351	365	3	27	33	303	3,158	3,098	406	2,485	208
Nebraska.........	314	289	3	29	67	191	3,947	3,711	579	2,780	352
Nevada	639	614	9	39	230	336	3,871	4,288	981	2,378	930
New Hampshire	161	149	1	33	37	77	2,060	2,054	354	1,552	149
New Jersey	376	366	5	15	155	191	2,656	2,544	503	1,641	400
New Mexico.......	741	665	6	50	104	505	4,345	4,124	1,025	2,711	387
New York.........	497	465	5	20	186	254	2,311	2,248	393	1,619	236
North Carolina	471	455	6	25	146	278	4,259	4,278	1,198	2,761	320
North Dakota	78	78	2	24	8	44	2,329	2,096	306	1,620	170
Ohio............	352	333	5	40	148	141	3,760	3,641	830	2,452	359
Oklahoma	504	506	6	43	92	365	4,245	4,306	992	2,945	369
Oregon	293	296	2	34	80	179	4,578	4,782	804	3,445	534
Pennsylvania	402	398	5	29	145	219	2,440	2,431	436	1,725	270
Rhode Island	286	286	2	47	77	159	3,308	2,995	513	2,074	408
South Carolina	823	794	7	44	137	605	4,479	4,477	1,051	3,046	380
South Dakota	178	173	1	46	14	112	2,103	2,002	376	1,511	114
Tennessee........	718	688	7	36	160	485	4,308	4,379	1,082	2,845	452
Texas...........	580	553	6	36	167	343	4,620	4,595	994	3,158	444
Utah............	237	249	2	38	53	155	4,211	4,226	713	3,182	330
Vermont	107	110	2	20	10	79	2,424	2,200	478	1,618	104
Virginia..........	292	276	6	24	90	156	2,851	2,704	392	2,070	243
Washington	346	347	3	47	93	204	4,763	4,755	950	3,142	663
West Virginia	234	258	4	16	40	197	2,277	2,359	562	1,603	195
Wisconsin	225	221	3	22	80	116	3,029	2,883	485	2,172	225
Wyoming.........	273	262	3	27	17	216	3,307	3,321	521	2,641	159

[1] Includes nonnegligent manslaughter. [2] Forcible rape figures furnished by the state-level uniform crime reporting (UCR) program administered by the Delaware State Bureau of Investigation were not in accordance with the national UCR guidelines; therefore, it was necessary that the forcible rape count be estimated. [3] Includes offenses reported by the police at the National Zoo. [4] Complete data were not available; therefore, it was necessary for the crime counts to be estimated for Illinois, Kansas, Kentucky, and Montana for all years shown.

Source: U.S. Federal Bureau of Investigation, *Crime in the United States*, annual. See also <http://www.fbi.gov/ucr/cius_03 /pdf/toc03.pdf> (released November 2004).

U.S. Census Bureau, Statistical Abstract of the United States: 2006

Table 296. Crime Rates by Type—Selected Large Cities: 2003

[Offenses known to the police per 100,000 population. Based on U.S. Census Bureau estimated resident population as of July 1. For definitions of crimes, see text, this section]

City ranked by population size, 2003	Violent crime					Property crime			
	Total	Murder	Forcible rape	Robbery	Aggra-vated assault	Total	Burglary	Larceny-theft	Motor vehicle theft
New York, NY	734	7.4	19.9	321	386	2,183	349	1,542	292
Los Angeles, CA	1,272	13.4	31.9	432	795	3,537	654	2,009	874
Chicago, IL [1]	(NA)	20.6	(NA)	597	683	4,990	865	3,339	786
Houston, TX.	1,175	13.6	37.6	538	586	5,879	1,299	3,529	1,051
Philadelphia, PA.	1,378	23.3	67.1	643	645	4,175	712	2,531	931
Phoenix, AZ	693	17.2	37.5	262	376	6,971	1,219	3,924	1,828
San Diego, CA.	579	5.1	31.9	128	414	3,644	635	2,022	987
Dallas, TX	1,371	18.4	48.8	647	656	7,957	1,782	4,759	1,416
San Antonio, TX	598	7.0	44.3	170	377	6,844	1,205	5,127	511
Las Vegas MPD Jurisdiction, NV	770	11.9	43.0	333	383	4,839	1,075	2,527	1,237
Detroit, MI.	[2]2,018	39.4	87.7	627	1,264	6,985	1,520	2,733	2,733
San Jose, CA	371	3.2	30.7	90	248	2,280	364	1,513	403
Honolulu, HI	288	1.7	29.4	109	148	5,336	880	3,544	912
Indianapolis, IN	883	13.1	52.5	353	464	5,672	1,257	3,486	929
Jacksonville, FL	867	11.8	27.4	302	525	5,640	1,148	3,869	623
San Francisco, CA	742	8.9	27.8	397	308	4,943	749	3,288	905
Columbus, OH.	856	15.0	84.7	459	297	7,758	2,017	4,592	1,149
Austin, TX	462	4.0	33.1	183	242	6,195	1,061	4,728	406
Charlotte-Mecklenburg PD, NC.	1,077	9.9	45.8	402	619	6,667	1,657	3,986	1,024
Memphis, TN	1,577	19.3	68.7	657	832	8,494	2,586	4,603	1,305
Baltimore, MD	1,735	41.9	31.6	988	673	5,813	1,208	3,541	1,064
Louisville Metro, KY	522	6.7	13.3	233	268	4,011	1,027	2,479	506
Milwaukee, WI.	890	18.5	41.4	483	348	6,360	1,017	4,295	1,049
Boston, MA.	1,216	6.6	44.4	468	697	4,726	737	2,894	1,096
El Paso, TX	597	3.6	37.3	99	457	3,714	373	3,024	317
Fort Worth, TX	651	9.9	42.2	254	345	6,512	1,525	4,354	633
Seattle, WA.	684	5.6	30.2	262	387	8,035	1,481	4,983	1,571
Denver, CO.	624	11.1	53.7	251	308	5,136	1,254	2,622	1,260
Washington, DC.	1,569	44.0	48.5	681	796	5,606	829	3,082	1,695
Nashville, TN	1,502	13.0	60.4	396	1,032	6,965	1,328	4,800	838
Portland, OR.	814	5.0	56.9	251	501	7,694	1,189	5,428	1,076
Oklahoma City, OK.	890	9.4	70.0	265	546	9,123	1,591	6,779	753
Tucson, AZ	915	9.1	64.1	287	555	9,191	1,243	6,712	1,236
Long Beach, CA	750	10.3	28.5	296	415	3,105	629	1,691	785
New Orleans, LA	967	57.7	44.8	436	429	5,152	1,027	2,678	1,446
Albuquerque, NM	947	10.9	56.1	230	650	6,249	1,182	4,195	872
Cleveland, OH.	1,324	15.6	137.9	676	494	5,567	1,718	2,739	1,110
Fresno, CA	779	8.2	36.5	270	464	6,045	873	3,914	1,258
Kansas City, MO	1,379	18.4	69.1	424	868	7,953	1,546	5,151	1,256
Sacramento, CA.	778	9.8	42.5	371	355	6,427	1,275	3,496	1,657
Virginia Beach, VA	212	5.5	27.5	93	86	3,321	487	2,650	184
Mesa, AZ	537	3.2	26.6	99	409	5,985	942	3,998	1,045
Atlanta, GA.	1,970	34.3	65.2	859	1,012	8,869	1,871	5,320	1,678
Oakland, CA	1,379	26.8	65.8	608	679	5,560	1,122	3,084	1,354
Omaha, NB.	654	8.7	44.6	223	378	6,102	859	4,199	1,044
Tulsa, OK	1,093	15.5	69.1	226	782	6,919	1,626	4,403	890
Miami, FL.	1,875	19.4	28.0	767	1,061	6,909	1,540	4,036	1,333
Minneapolis, MN	1,193	12.1	101.4	579	501	5,390	1,184	3,276	929
Colorado Springs, CO. . .	462	4.5	64.0	113	281	4,945	898	3,563	485
Wichita, KS.	[2]610	4.9	60.3	152	393	5,382	1,053	3,933	396

NA Not available. [1] The rates for forcible rape, violent crime, and crime index are not shown because the forcible rape figures were not in accordance with national Uniform Crime Reporting guidelines. [2] Due to reporting changes or annexations, figures are not comparable to previous years

Source: U.S. Federal Bureau of Investigation, *Crime in the United States*, annual. See also <http://www.fbi.gov/ucr/cius_03 /pdf/toc03.pdf> (released November 2004).

U.S. Census Bureau, Statistical Abstract of the United States: 2006

Table 297. Murder Victims—Circumstances and Weapons Used or Cause of Death: 1990 to 2003

[Based solely on police investigation. For definition of murder, see text, this section]

Characteristic	1990	2000	2002	2003	Characteristic	1990	2000	2002	2003
Murders, total					Other motives	19.4	20.2	21.4	20.5
(1,000)	20,273	13,230	14,274	14,493	Unknown.	24.8	30.8	32.7	33.6
Percent distribution....	100.0	100.0	100.0	100.0					
CIRCUMSTANCES					TYPE OF WEAPON OR CAUSE OF DEATH				
Felonies, total	20.8	16.8	16.4	16.5					
Robbery	9.2	8.1	7.8	7.3	Guns	64.3	65.5	66.8	66.8
Narcotics	6.7	4.5	4.7	4.7	Handguns	49.8	51.2	51.1	53.5
Sex offenses	1.1	0.6	0.4	0.5	Cutting or stabbing	17.4	13.5	12.5	12.6
Other felonies......	3.7	3.7	3.5	4.0	Blunt objects [1]	5.4	4.7	4.8	4.5
Suspected felonies	0.7	0.5	0.5	0.6	Personal weapons [2] ...	5.5	7.0	6.7	6.6
Argument, total.......	34.4	31.8	29.1	28.8	Strangulations,				
Property or money...	2.5	1.6	1.4	1.5	asphyxiations	2.0	2.0	1.7	2.2
Romantic triangle ...	2.0	0.9	0.9	0.7	Fire	1.4	1.0	0.7	1.2
Other arguments....	29.8	29.3	26.7	26.6	All other [3]	4.0	6.4	6.8	6.1

[1] Refers to club, hammer, etc. [2] Hands, fists, feet, etc. [3] Includes poison, drowning, explosives, narcotics, and unknown.

Source: U.S. Federal Bureau of Investigation, *Crime in the United States,* annual. See also <http://www.fbi.gov/ucr/cius_03/pdf/toc03.pdf> (released November 2004).

Table 298. Murder Victims by Age, Sex, and Race: 2003

[Based solely on police investigation. For definition of murder, see text, this section]

| Age | Total | Sex | | | Race | | | |
		Male	Female	Unknown	White	Black	Other	Unknown
Total	14,493	11,217	3,251	25	6,966	6,912	411	204
Percent of total	100	77	22	-	48	48	3	1
Under 18 yrs. old...........	1,353	914	436	3	675	621	41	16
18 yrs. old and over	12,878	10,124	2,747	7	6,172	6,211	360	135
Infant (under 1 year old)	231	135	93	3	144	73	7	7
1 to 4 years old	312	165	147	-	171	131	6	4
5 to 8 years old	84	42	42	-	46	34	3	1
9 to 12 years old	71	37	34	-	34	35	1	1
13 to 16 years old	371	293	78	-	151	202	15	3
17 to 19 years old	1,290	1,117	172	1	548	695	34	13
20 to 24 years old	2,865	2,439	423	3	1,171	1,589	74	31
25 to 29 years old	2,167	1,840	327	-	852	1,239	54	22
30 to 34 years old	1,600	1,253	346	1	695	843	45	17
35 to 39 years old	1,293	975	318	-	641	607	36	9
40 to 44 years old	1,118	787	330	1	592	485	31	10
45 to 49 years old	960	698	261	1	557	365	27	11
50 to 54 years old	632	465	167	-	384	226	19	3
55 to 59 years old	366	257	109	-	236	114	12	4
60 to 64 years old	228	161	67	-	150	57	16	5
65 to 69 years old	165	114	51	-	122	33	8	2
70 to 74 years old	153	90	63	-	105	42	4	2
75 years old and over........	325	170	155	-	248	62	9	6
Age unknown	262	179	68	15	119	80	10	53

- Represents zero.

Source: U.S. Federal Bureau of Investigation, *Crime in the United States,* annual. See also <http://www.fbi.gov/ucr/cius_03/pdf/toc03.pdf> (released November 2004).

Table 299. Murder Victims of September 11, 2001 Terrorist Attacks, by Race, Sex, and Location

| Race | Total | Sex | | | Race | Total | Sex | | |
		Male	Female	Unknown			Male	Female	Unknown
All locations					**Pentagon**				
Total	2,973	2,256	712	5	Total	184	108	71	5
White.	2,401	1,879	522	-	White.	120	79	41	-
Black.	265	162	103	-	Black.	49	21	28	-
Other.	173	117	56	-	Other.	2	2	-	-
Unknown	134	98	31	5	Unknown	13	6	2	5
World Trade Center					**Somerset County, Pennsylvania**				
Total	2,749	2,128	621	-	Total	40	20	20	-
White.	2,245	1,782	463	-	White.	36	18	18	-
Black.	213	140	73	-	Black.	3	1	2	-
Other.	170	114	56	-	Other.	1	1	-	-
Unknown	121	92	29	-	Unknown	-	-	-	-

- Represents zero.

Source: US Federal Bureau of Investigation, *Crime in the United States,* annual. See also/<http://www.fbi.gov/ucr/cius_01/01crime.pdf> (Released 28 October 2002).

Law Enforcement, Courts, and Prisons 197

Table 300. Homicide Trends: 1976 to 2002

[Rate per 100,000 inhabitants. Not all agencies which report offense information to the FBI also submit supplemental data on homicides. To account for the total number of homicide victims, the data was weighted to match national and state estimates prepared by the FBI; hence, columns may not equal total]

Year	Number of victims						Rate					
	Total	Male	Female	White	Black	Other	Total	Male	Female	White	Black	Other
1976	18,780	14,171	4,590	9,585	8,745	238	8.8	13.6	4.2	5.1	37.1	4.9
1977	19,120	14,397	4,710	10,041	8,669	236	8.8	13.7	4.2	5.4	36.2	4.7
1978	19,560	14,895	4,642	10,568	8,572	207	9.0	14.0	4.1	5.6	35.1	4.0
1979	21,460	16,428	5,017	11,625	9,311	215	9.7	15.4	4.4	6.1	37.5	4.1
1980	23,040	17,788	5,232	12,275	9,767	327	10.2	16.2	4.5	6.3	37.7	5.7
1981	22,520	17,405	5,096	12,163	9,862	348	9.8	15.6	4.3	6.2	36.4	6.1
1982	21,010	15,902	5,093	11,644	8,880	399	9.1	14.1	4.3	5.9	32.3	6.5
1983	19,308	14,588	4,703	10,604	8,201	417	8.3	12.8	3.9	5.3	29.4	6.4
1984	18,692	13,910	4,741	10,490	7,678	377	7.9	12.1	3.9	5.2	27.2	5.5
1985	18,976	14,079	4,880	10,590	7,891	399	8.0	12.2	4.0	5.2	27.6	5.5
1986	20,613	15,471	5,109	10,916	9,107	484	8.6	13.2	4.1	5.4	31.5	6.2
1987	20,096	14,811	5,268	10,526	9,000	424	8.3	12.6	4.2	5.1	30.7	5.2
1988	20,675	15,414	5,238	10,184	9,959	344	8.5	12.9	4.2	4.9	33.5	4.0
1989	21,500	16,407	5,085	10,325	10,566	390	8.7	13.6	4.0	5.0	35.1	4.3
1990	23,438	18,304	5,115	11,279	11,488	400	9.4	15.0	4.0	5.4	37.6	4.2
1991	24,703	19,270	5,394	11,661	12,226	608	9.8	15.7	4.2	5.5	39.3	6.0
1992	23,760	18,513	5,217	11,229	11,777	573	9.3	14.9	4.0	5.3	37.2	5.4
1993	24,526	18,937	5,550	11,278	12,435	601	9.5	15.0	4.2	5.3	38.7	5.5
1994	23,326	18,294	5,007	10,773	11,856	526	9.0	14.4	3.8	5.0	36.4	4.6
1995	21,606	16,552	5,022	10,376	10,444	581	8.2	12.9	3.7	4.8	31.6	4.9
1996	19,645	15,153	4,469	9,483	9,476	512	7.4	11.7	3.3	4.3	28.3	4.1
1997	18,208	14,057	4,125	8,620	8,842	524	6.8	10.7	3.0	3.9	26.0	4.1
1998	16,974	12,753	4,139	8,389	7,931	393	6.3	9.7	3.0	3.8	23.0	2.9
1999	15,522	11,704	3,800	7,777	7,139	458	5.7	8.8	2.7	3.5	20.5	3.3
2000	15,586	11,818	3,733	7,560	7,425	399	5.5	8.6	2.6	3.3	20.5	2.7
2001	16,037	12,232	3,775	7,884	7,522	424	5.6	8.8	2.6	3.4	20.4	2.8
2002	16,204	12,410	3,764	7,784	7,758	437	5.6	8.8	2.6	3.3	20.8	2.7

Source: U.S. Bureau of Justice Statistics, Homicide Trends in the United States, 1976-2002. See also: <http://www.ojp.usdoj.gov/bjs/pub/pdf/htius.pdf>

Table 301. Homicide Victims by Race and Sex: 1980 to 2002

[Rates per 100,000 resident population in specified group. Excludes deaths to nonresidents of United States. Begining 1999, deaths classified according to the tenth revision of the International Classification of Diseases; see text, Section 2, and footnote 3]

Year	Homicide victims					Homicide rate [2]				
		White		Black			White		Black	
	Total [1]	Male	Female	Male	Female	Total [1]	Male	Female	Male	Female
1980	24,278	10,381	3,177	8,385	1,898	10.7	10.9	3.2	66.6	13.5
1985	19,893	8,122	3,041	6,616	1,666	8.3	8.2	2.9	48.4	11.0
1988	22,032	7,994	3,072	8,314	2,089	9.0	7.9	2.9	58.0	13.2
1989	22,909	8,337	2,971	8,888	2,074	9.2	8.2	2.8	61.1	12.9
1990	24,932	9,147	3,006	9,981	2,163	10.0	9.0	2.8	69.2	13.5
1991	26,513	9,581	3,201	10,628	2,330	10.5	9.3	3.0	72.0	14.2
1992	25,488	9,456	3,012	10,131	2,187	10.0	9.1	2.8	67.5	13.1
1993	26,009	9,054	3,232	10,640	2,297	10.1	8.6	3.0	69.7	13.6
1994	24,926	9,055	2,921	10,083	2,124	9.6	8.5	2.6	65.1	12.4
1995	22,895	8,336	3,028	8,847	1,936	8.7	7.8	2.7	56.3	11.1
1996	20,971	7,570	2,747	8,183	1,800	7.9	7.0	2.5	51.5	10.2
1997	19,846	7,343	2,570	7,601	1,652	7.4	6.7	2.3	47.1	9.3
1998	18,272	6,707	2,534	6,873	1,547	6.8	6.1	2.2	42.1	8.6
1999 [3]	16,889	6,162	2,466	6,214	1,434	6.2	5.6	2.2	37.5	7.8
2000	16,765	5,925	2,414	6,482	1,385	6.1	5.3	2.1	38.6	7.5
2001	20,308	8,254	3,074	6,780	1,446	7.1	7.2	2.6	38.3	7.4
2002	17,638	6,282	2,403	6,896	1,391	6.1	5.4	2.0	38.4	7.0

[1] Includes races not shown separately. [2] Rate based on enumerated population figures as of April 1 for 1980, 1990 and 2000; July 1 estimates for other years. [3] Effective with data for 1999, causes of death are classified by The Tenth Revision International Classification of Diseases (ICD-10), replacing the Ninth Revision (ICD-9) used for 1979-98 data. Breaks in the comparability of some cause of death statistics result from changes in category titles, changes in the structure and content of the classification, and changes in coding rules used to select the underlying cause of death. In ICD-9, the category Homicide also inludes death as a result of legal intervention. ICD-10 has two separate categories for these two causes of death. Some caution should be used in comparing data between 1998 and 1999.

Source: U.S. National Center for Health Statistics, Vital Statistics of the United States, annual; and National Vital Statistics Reports (NVSR) (formerly Monthly Vital Statistics Report); and unpublished data.

Table 302. Forcible Rape—Number and Rate: 1980 to 2003

[Minus sign (-) indicates decrease. For definition of rape, see text, this section]

Item	1980	1990	1995	1997	1998	1999	2000	2001	2002	2003
NUMBER										
Total.	82,990	102,560	97,460	96,153	93,144	89,411	90,186	90,863	95,136	93,433
By force	63,599	86,541	85,249	84,931	82,823	79,697	81,111	82,004	86,564	85,426
Attempt	19,391	16,019	12,211	11,222	10,321	9,714	9,075	8,859	8,572	8,007
RATE										
Per 100,000 population	36.8	41.1	37.1	35.9	34.5	32.8	32.0	31.8	33.1	32.1
Per 100,000 females	71.6	80.5	72.5	70.4	67.4	64.1	62.7	62.6	65.0	63.2
AVERAGE ANNUAL PERCENT CHANGE IN RATE [1]										
Per 100,000 population	6.1	8.1	-5.6	-1.1	-3.9	-4.9	-2.4	-0.6	4.1	-3.0

[1] Represents annual average from immediate prior year.

Source: U.S. Federal Bureau of Investigation, *Population-at-Risk Rates and Selected Crime Indicators*, annual.

Table 303. Rape and Sexual Assault—Reports to Police and Medical Attention: 1992-2000

[Data are annual averages for period 1992 to 2000]

Injury status and police report	Completed Rape		Attempted Rape		Sexual Assault	
	Number	Percent	Number	Percent	Number	Percent
Total victimizations.	131,950	100	98,970	100	135,540	100
Not injured	-	-	60,010	61	112,520	83
Injured	131,950	100	38,960	39	23,020	17
Serious injury	7,180	5	(B)	(B)	(B)	(B)
Minor injury	42,630	33	25,450	26	12,390	9
Undetermined injury.	81,140	61	10,730	11	8,590	6
Reported to police	47,960	36	33,560	34	34,830	26
By victim	23,890	18	24,040	24	21,560	16
By other household member	10,080	8	(B)	(B)	4,970	4
By someone else	13,990	11	6,010	6	8,310	6
Not reported	83,700	63	64,600	65	99,840	74
Medical treatment received:						
Total injured	131,950	100	38,960	100	23,020	100
Treated	42,230	32	12,490	32	6,250	27

- Represents zero.   B Base figure too small to meet statistical standards for reliablity of a derived figure.

Source: U.S. Bureau of Justice Statistics, *Rape and Sexual Assault: Reporting to Police and Medical Attention, 1992-2000,* Serices NCJ 194530, August 2002.

Table 304. Violence by Intimate Partners by Sex, 1993 to 2003, and by Type of Crime, 2003

[Violent acts covered include murder, rape, sexual assault, robbery, and aggravated and simple assault. Intimate partners involve current spouses, former spouses, current boy/girlfriends, and former boy/girlfriends. Based on the National Criminal Victimization Survey; see text, this section, and Appendix III.]

Year and type of crime	All persons		Female victims		Male victims	
	Number	Rate per 100,000 [1]	Number	Rate per 100,000 [1]	Number	Rate per 100,000 [1]
1993	1,228,760	580.9	1,072,090	982.0	156,670	153.1
1994	1,148,210	537.2	1,003,190	908.9	145,020	140.3
1995	1,063,520	493.0	953,700	855.8	109,820	105.3
1996	1,008,860	462.8	879,290	781.7	129,570	122.8
1997	953,780	432.7	848,480	747.3	105,300	98.5
1998	1,054,260	475.7	896,030	780.9	158,230	146.7
1999	783,120	347.7	672,330	578.4	110,790	101.6
2000	630,530	277.2	547,310	466.5	83,220	75.5
2001	693,321	301.4	589,692	497.1	103,629	92.8
2002	568,690	245.4	495,772	214.0	72,918	31.5
2003, total	521,760	218.0	437,990	183.0	83,750	35.0
Rape or sexual assault	27,380	11.4	(B)	(B)	(B)	(B)
Robbery	37,120	15.5	(B)	(B)	(B)	(B)
Aggravated assault.	123,310	51.5	101,400	42.4	(B)	(B)
Simple assault.	333,950	139.5	284,170	118.7	49,780	20.8

B Base figure too small to meet statistical standards for reliability of derived figure. In this case, 10 or fewer sample cases.
[1] Rates are the number of victimizations per 100,000 persons.

Source: U.S. Bureau of Justice Statistics, *Intimate Partner Violence,* and unpublished data.

Law Enforcement, Courts, and Prisons   199

Table 305. **Hate Crimes—Number of Incidents, Offenses, Victims, and Known Offenders by Bias Motivation: 2000 to 2003**

[The FBI collected statistics on hate crimes from 11,993 law enforcement agencies representing over 242 million inhabitants in 2003. Hate crime offenses cover incidents motivated by race, religion, sexual orientation, ethnicity/national origin, and disability]

Bias motivation	Incidents reported	Offenses	Victims[1]	Known offenders[2]
2000, Total.	8,213	9,619	10,117	7,690
2001, Total.	9,878	11,628	12,218	9,442
2002, Total.	7,462	8,832	9,222	7,314
2003, Total.	7,531	8,775	9,166	6,978
Race, total	3,859	4,601	4,786	3,908
Anti-White	829	976	1,017	1,020
Anti-Black	2,568	3,050	3,170	2,475
Anti-AmericanIndian/Alaskan native	69	76	77	76
Anti-Asian/Pacific Islander	232	279	291	198
Anti-multi-racial group	161	220	231	139
Ethnicity/national origin, total	1,033	1,245	1,335	1,128
Anti-Hispanic	431	535	601	584
Anti-other ethnicity/national origin	602	710	734	544
Religion, total.	1,343	1,428	1,492	573
Anti-Jewish	930	991	1,029	335
Anti-Catholic	75	77	80	32
Anti-Protestant	49	50	54	20
Anti-Islamic	149	157	173	92
Anti-other religious group	108	116	118	67
Anti-multi religious group	23	24	25	17
Anti-atheism/agnosticism/etc.	9	13	13	10
Sexual orientation, total	1,246	1,439	1,488	1,318
Anti-male homosexual.	788	887	916	868
Anti-female homosexual.	185	218	228	167
Anti-homosexual.	249	308	317	256
Anti-heterosexual	16	17	17	11
Anti-bisexual	8	9	10	16
Disability, total	46	53	56	44
Anti-physical	36	42	44	32
Anti-mental	10	11	12	12
Multiple bias	4	9	9	7

[1] The term "victim" may refer to a person, business, institution, or a society as a whole.   [2] The term "known offender" does not imply that the identity of the suspect is known, but only that an attribute of the suspect is identified which distinquishes him/her from an unknown offender.

Source: U.S. Federal Bureau of Investigation, *Hate Crime Statistics,* annual.   See also <http://www.fbi.gov/ucr/03hc.pdf> (released November 2004) and subsequent updates because of late data submissions.

Table 306. **Hate Crimes Reported, by State: 2003**

[See headnote, Table 305]

State	Number of participating agencies	Population covered (1,000)	Agencies submitting incidents	Incidents reported	State	Number of participating agencies	Population covered (1,000)	Agencies submitting incidents	Incidents reported
United States . . .	11,993	242,061	1,982	7,531	Missouri	186	3,037	21	55
					Montana	82	853	5	5
Alabama	36	234	1	1	Nebraska	202	1,369	16	44
Alaska	1	271	1	13	Nevada	35	2,241	9	97
Arizona	89	5,411	26	247	New Hampshire	125	832	29	36
Arkansas	128	1,167	43	173	New Jersey	555	8,638	236	594
California	727	35,484	235	1,472	New Mexico	50	1,197	2	11
Colorado	185	4,154	35	86					
Connecticut	97	3,304	54	147	New York	520	19,162	61	602
Delaware	53	817	8	20	North Carolina	461	8,337	22	77
District of Columbia. . .	2	563	2	31	North Dakota	65	550	7	10
Florida	489	16,973	86	231	Ohio	388	8,549	66	244
Georgia	83	1,617	7	23	Oklahoma	298	3,512	23	38
Hawaii	(1)	(1)	(1)	(1)	Oregon	6	829	6	103
Idaho	119	1,357	12	20	Pennsylvania	859	11,292	31	119
Illinois	73	5,140	61	208	Rhode Island	48	1,076	10	45
Indiana	139	3,086	19	48	South Carolina	419	4,145	31	64
Iowa	221	2,870	27	38					
Kansas	341	2,380	19	49	South Dakota	149	764	6	10
Kentucky	435	3,750	42	81	Tennessee	456	5,842	62	161
Louisiana	140	3,422	6	6	Texas	983	22,101	85	290
Maine	149	1,306	25	77	Utah	57	1,775	22	60
Maryland	149	5,509	31	248	Vermont	59	562	11	27
					Virginia	393	7,312	68	285
Massachusetts	247	5,209	97	401	Washington	253	6,071	56	223
Michigan	612	8,786	163	421	West Virginia	393	1,713	16	31
Minnesota	327	5,029	60	215	Wisconsin	16	1,338	16	31
Mississippi	57	826	1	1	Wyoming	36	295	4	12

[1] Did not report.

Source: U.S. Federal Bureau of Investigation, *Hate Crime Statistics,* annual. See also <http://www.fbi.gov/ucr/03hc.pdf> (released November 2004) and subsequent updates because of late data submissions.

Table 307. Robbery and Property Crimes by Type and Selected Characteristic: 1990 to 2003

[For definition of crime, see text, this section]

Characteristic of offenses	Number of offenses (1,000)				Rate per 100,000 inhabitants				Average value lost (dol.)	
	1990	2000	2002	2003	1990	2000	2002	2003	2002	2003
Robbery, total [1]	639	408	421	413	256.3	144.9	146.1	142.2	1,291	1,244
Type of crime:										
Street or highway	359	188	180	179	144.2	66.7	62.5	61.7	1,040	898
Commercial house	73	57	61	60	29.5	20.1	21.3	20.8	1,641	1,778
Gas station	18	12	11	11	7.1	4.1	3.9	3.9	1,821	690
Convenience store	39	26	27	26	15.6	9.3	9.4	8.9	682	662
Residence	62	50	57	57	25.1	17.7	19.7	19.5	662	813
Bank	9	9	10	10	3.8	3.1	3.4	3.3	4,825	4,767
Weapon used:										
Firearm	234	161	173	174	94.1	57.0	60.1	59.7	(NA)	(NA)
Knife or cutting instrument	76	36	37	36	30.7	12.8	12.8	12.5	(NA)	(NA)
Other dangerous weapon	61	53	44	39	24.5	18.9	15.2	13.4	(NA)	(NA)
Strongarm	268	159	167	164	107.7	56.4	57.9	56.5	(NA)	(NA)
Burglary, total	3,074	2,050	2,151	2,153	1,232.2	728.4	747.0	740.5	1,549	1626
Forcible entry	2,150	1,297	1,346	1,339	864.5	460.7	467.3	460.6	(NA)	(NA)
Unlawful entry	678	615	662	677	272.8	218.7	229.7	232.7	(NA)	(NA)
Attempted forcible entry	245	138	144	137	98.7	49.0	50.1	47.2	(NA)	(NA)
Residence	2,033	1,335	1,416	1,418	817.4	474.3	491.6	487.4	1,487	1,600
Nonresidence	1,041	715	736	736	418.5	254.1	255.5	253.1	1,669	1,676
Occurred during the night	1,135	699	731	719	456.4	248.3	253.7	247.2	(NA)	(NA)
Occurred during the day	1,151	836	902	889	462.8	297.2	313.4	305.8	(NA)	(NA)
Larceny-theft, total	7,946	6,972	7,057	7,022	3,185.1	2,477.3	2,450.7	2,414.5	698	698
Pocket picking	81	36	32	32	32.4	12.7	11.3	11.0	329	293
Purse snatching	82	37	39	42	32.8	13.2	13.5	14.5	331	367
Shoplifting	1,291	959	986	1,013	519.1	340.7	342.5	348.2	165	163
From motor vehicles	1,744	1,754	1,867	1,856	701.3	623.3	648.3	638.3	680	680
Motor vehicle accessories	1,185	677	756	781	476.3	240.6	262.6	268.5	428	442
Bicycles	443	312	277	272	178.2	110.9	96.2	93.4	256	247
From buildings	1,118	914	884	868	449.4	324.6	306.9	298.5	1,022	1,030
From coin-operated machines	63	46	52	52	25.4	16.2	18.2	18.0	249	262
Other	1,940	2,232	2,163	2,106	780.0	793.0	751.2	724.2	978	1,012
Motor vehicles, total [2]	1,636	1,160	1,247	1,260	655.8	412.2	432.9	433.4	6,701	5,797
Automobiles	1,304	877	920	927	524.3	311.5	319.4	318.7	(NA)	(NA)
Trucks and buses	238	209	230	229	95.5	74.1	79.9	78.9	(NA)	(NA)

NA Not available. [1] Includes other crimes not shown separately. [2] Includes other types of motor vehicles not shown separately.

Source: U.S. Federal Bureau of Investigation, *Population-at-Risk Rates and Selected Crime Indicators*, annual.

Table 308. Victimization Rates by Type of Violent Crime and Characteristic of the Victim: 2003

[Rate per 1,000 persons age 12 years or older. Based on National Crime Victimization Survey; see text, this section, and Appendix III]

Characteristic of the victim	All crimes	Crimes of violence						Personal theft
		Total	Rape/ sexual assault	Robbery	Assault			
					Total	Aggra-vated	Simple	
Total	23.3	22.6	0.8	2.5	19.3	4.6	14.6	0.8
Male	26.7	26.3	0.2	[1]3.2	23.0	5.9	17.1	0.4
Female	20.2	19.0	1.5	1.9	15.7	3.3	12.4	1.1
12 to 15 years old	53.1	51.6	1.2	[1]5.2	45.3	8.9	36.4	[1]1.5
16 to 19 years old	54.4	53.0	1.3	[1]5.1	46.6	11.9	34.7	[1]1.4
20 to 24 years old	45.0	43.3	1.7	6.4	35.3	9.8	25.5	1.6
25 to 34 years old	27.4	26.4	1.6	2.5	22.3	6.0	16.3	1.0
35 to 49 years old	19.0	18.5	0.6	1.7	16.1	3.8	12.3	0.5
50 to 64 years old	10.5	10.3	0.4	[1]1.4	8.5	1.6	7.0	[1]0.3
65 years old and over	2.5	2.0	0.1	[1]0.7	[1]1.2	0.1	[1]1.1	[1]0.5
White	22.1	21.5	0.8	1.9	18.8	4.2	14.7	0.6
Black	30.7	29.1	0.8	[1]5.9	22.3	6.0	16.3	1.7
Other	16.9	16.0	0.2	[1]3.4	12.4	5.4	7.0	[1]0.9
Hispanic	25.3	24.2	0.4	[1]3.1	20.8	4.6	16.1	[1]1.1
Non-Hispanic	23.0	22.3	0.9	2.4	19.0	4.6	14.4	0.7
Household income:								
Less than $7,500	51.1	49.9	1.6	[1]9.0	39.3	10.8	28.5	[1]1.2
$7,500-$14,999	31.9	30.8	1.8	[1]4.0	25.0	7.9	17.0	[1]1.1
$15,000-$24,999	27.0	26.3	0.8	[1]4.0	21.5	4.5	17.0	[1]0.7
$25,000-$34,999	25.8	24.9	0.9	[1]2.2	21.8	5.0	16.9	[1]0.8
$35,000-$49,999	22.0	21.4	0.9	[1]2.1	18.3	4.8	13.5	[1]0.7
$50,000-$74,999	23.3	22.9	0.5	[1]2.0	20.4	5.2	15.2	[1]0.5
$75,000 or more	18.5	17.5	0.5	[1]1.7	15.4	2.7	12.6	1.0

[1] Based on 10 or fewer sample cases.

Source: U.S. Bureau of Justice Statistics, *Criminal Victimization*, annual; and series NCJ-199994. See also <http://www.ojp.usdoj.gov/bjs/pub/pdf/cv03.pdf>.

Table 309. **Criminal Victimizations and Victimization Rates: 1995 to 2003**

[Based on National Crime Victimization Survey; see text, this section and Appendix III]

Type of crime	Number of victimizations (1,000)				Victimization rates [1]			
	1995	2000	2002	2003	1995	2000	2002	2003
All crimes, total	39,926	25,893	23,036	24,213	(X)	(X)	(X)	(X)
Personal crimes [2]	10,436	6,597	5,497	5,586	46.2	29.1	23.7	23.3
Crimes of violence	10,022	6,323	5,341	5,402	44.5	27.9	23.1	22.6
Completed violence	2,960	2,044	1,753	1,655	12.9	9.0	7.6	6.9
Attempted/threatened violence . . .	7,061	4,279	3,588	3,747	31.6	18.9	15.5	15.7
Rape/sexual assault	363	261	248	199	1.6	1.2	1.1	0.8
Rape/attempted rape	252	147	168	117	1.1	0.6	0.7	0.5
Rape	153	92	90	72	0.7	0.4	0.4	0.3
Attempted rape	99	55	78	45	0.4	0.2	0.3	0.2
Sexual assault	112	114	80	82	0.5	0.5	0.3	0.3
Robbery	1,171	732	513	596	5.3	3.2	2.2	2.5
Completed/property taken	753	520	386	378	3.5	2.3	1.7	1.6
With injury	224	160	170	160	1.0	0.7	0.7	0.7
Without injury	529	360	216	218	2.4	1.6	0.9	0.9
Attempted to take property	418	212	127	218	1.8	0.9	0.5	0.9
With injury	84	66	43	54	0.4	0.3	0.2	0.2
Without injury	335	146	84	165	1.4	0.6	0.4	0.7
Assault	8,487	5,330	4,581	4,607	37.6	23.5	19.8	19.3
Aggravated	2,050	1,293	990	1,101	8.8	5.7	4.3	4.6
With injury	533	346	316	362	2.4	1.5	1.4	1.5
Threatened with weapon	1,517	946	674	740	6.4	4.2	2.9	3.1
Simple	6,437	4,038	3,591	3,506	28.9	17.8	15.5	14.6
With minor injury	1,426	989	907	769	6.0	4.4	3.9	3.2
Without injury	5,012	3,048	2,684	2,737	22.9	13.4	11.6	11.4
Personal theft [3]	414	274	155	185	1.7	1.2	0.7	0.8
Property crimes	29,490	19,297	17,539	18,626	279.5	178.1	159.0	163.2
Household burglary	5,004	3,444	3,056	3,396	47.4	31.8	27.7	29.8
Completed	4,232	2,909	2,597	2,811	40.0	26.9	23.5	24.6
Attempted forcible entry	773	534	458	585	7.4	4.9	9.2	5.1
Motor vehicle theft	1,717	937	989	1,032	16.2	8.6	9.0	9.0
Completed	1,163	642	781	764	10.8	5.9	7.1	6.7
Attempted	554	295	208	269	5.5	2.7	1.9	2.4
Theft	22,769	14,916	13,495	14,198	215.9	137.7	122.3	124.4
Completed [4]	21,857	14,300	13,040	13,719	207.6	132.0	118.2	120.2
Attempted	911	616	455	479	8.4	5.7	4.1	4.2

X Not applicable.   [1] Per 1,000 persons age 12 or older or per 1,000 households.   [2] The victimization survey cannot measure murder because of the inability to question the victim.   [3] Includes pocket picking, purse snatching, and attempted purse snatching.   [4] Includes thefts in which the amount taken was not ascertained.

Source: U.S. Bureau of Justice Statistics, *Criminal Victimization*, annual; and *Criminal Victimization 2003, Changes 2002-03 with Trends 1993-2003*, Series NCJ-194610. See also <http://www.ojp.usdoj.gov/bjs/pub/pdf/cv03.pdf>.

Table 310. **Criminal Victimizations by Age of Victim: 1993–2002**

[In percent. Covers period 1993 to 2002. Offender characteristics are based on victim's perception. See source for details. For definitions of crimes, see text, this section.]

Characteristic	Age of victim		Characteristic	Age of victim	
	12-64 years old	65 years old or older		12-64 years old	65 years old or older
NONFATAL VIOLENT VICTIMIZATIONS			Boyfriend/girlfriend	5.9	[1]0.6
			Own child	0.9	2.6
Victims facing weapons	25.7	30.2	Other relatives	4.0	4.1
Firearm	9.4	12.7	Well-known person	15.8	13.9
Knife	6.3	6.4	Casual acquaintance	18.2	15.7
Other type	8.7	9.3	Stranger	46.3	52.5
Don't know type	1.2	1.8	Don't know relationship	3.7	8.2
Victims resisting	71.0	55.5	Age 30 or older	30.2	48.3
Threatened/attacked with weapon	2.2	2.5	Male	78.8	75.6
Threatened/attacked without weapon . . .	27.9	15.3	**CHARACTERISTICS OF CRIMES**		
Nonconfrontational resistance	29.5	24.9	Occurring at night:		
Other or unknown type	11.3	12.9	Violence	45.8	27.2
Victims not resisting	29.0	44.5	Personal theft	34.4	[1]14.8
Victims injured	25.9	21.8	Property crimes	29.2	20.9
Serious injury	3.3	2.8	Occurring at/near home:		
Minor injury	21.2	18.7	Violence	27.0	45.5
Rape without injury	1.2	[1]0.3	Personal theft	5.4	[1]5.8
			Property crimes	54.3	67.0
CHARACTERISTIC OF OFFENDER			Crime reported to police:		
Relationship to victim:			Violence	43.9	53.0
Known to victim	31.7	23.6	Personal theft	32.1	42.3
Spouse/exspouse	5.1	2.4	Property crimes	34.7	35.5

[1] Based on 10 or fewer sample cases.

Source: U.S. Bureau of Justice Statistics, *Crimes Against Persons Age 65 or Older 1993-2002*: Series NCJ 206154, January 2005.

Table 311.

Table 311. Victim-Offender Relationship in Crimes of Violence, by Characteristics of the Criminal Incident: 2003

[In percent. Covers only crimes of violence. Based on National Crime Victimization Survey: see text, this section, and Appendix III]

Characteristics of incident	Total	Rape/ sexual assault	Robbery	Assault Total	Aggravated[1]	Simple
Total......................	100.0	100.0	100.0	100.0	100.0	100.0
Victim/offender relationship:[2]						
Relatives...................	9.8	9.9	7.2	10.1	8.2	10.7
Well-known..............	24.4	38.8	14.6	25.0	23.8	25.4
Casual acquaintance..........	13.9	20.0	5.6	14.7	11.3	15.8
Stranger................	44.5	29.7	55.3	43.7	48.2	42.3
Time of day:[3]						
6 a.m. to 6 p.m............	53.4	35.1	41.1	55.9	47.6	58.3
6 p.m. to midnight..........	31.2	30.4	38.4	30.3	37.7	28.2
Midnight to 6 a.m...........	11.8	28.4	17.0	10.4	10.7	10.3
Location of crime:						
At or near victim's home or lodging	29.8	37.0	33.5	29.1	26.7	29.8
Friend's/relative's/neighbor's home.....	8.6	35.6	4.0	8.0	10.1	7.3
Commercial places..............	11.3	10.5	7.0	12.0	11.0	12.3
Parking lots/garages	7.6	-	14.3	7.1	9.4	6.4
School...................	14.1	2.1	7.4	15.5	8.6	17.5
Streets other than near victim's home...	16.9	5.1	25.5	16.3	21.6	14.8
Other[4]................	11.6	9.8	8.3	12.0	12.6	11.8
Victim's activity:[5]						
At work·or traveling to or from work	18.8	9.1	12.0	(NA)	20.6	19.9
School.................	12.7	1.6	8.4	(NA)	7.9	15.4
Activities at home.............	25.5	39.9	23.7	(NA)	22.0	25.9
Shopping/errands..............	4.6	2.3	9.1	(NA)	4.0	4.1
Leisure activities away from home	21.7	32.0	26.8	(NA)	23.7	19.6
Traveling.................	7.8	1.2	10.2	(NA)	10.6	7.0
Other[6]................	8.6	13.7	9.6	(NA)	10.5	7.6
Distance from victim's home:[7]						
Inside home or lodging	16.8	33.6	19.7	15.7	13.6	16.3
Near victim's home..............	15.2	8.6	15.9	15.5	17.1	15.0
1 mile or less................	20.4	15.4	21.4	20.5	26.5	18.8
5 miles or less	23.7	18.5	24.3	23.8	16.1	26.0
50 miles or less	19.1	19.4	13.4	19.8	21.3	19.4
More than 50 miles	3.7	4.6	3.8	3.6	5.0	3.3
Weapons:						
No weapons present	68.7	84.1	40.5	71.7	5.1	91.0
Weapons present	23.6	10.8	44.6	21.4	94.9	-
Firearm ....`..........	7.4	3.1	25.0	5.3	23.5	-
Other type of weapon[8]...........	16.1	7.7	19.6	16.0	71.3	-

NA Not available. - Represents zero. [1] An aggravated assault is any assault in which an offender possesses or uses a weapon or inflicts serious injury. [2] Excludes "don't know" relationships. [3] Excludes "not known and not available" time of day. [4] Includes areas on public transportation or inside station, in apartment yard, park, field, playground, or other areas. [5] Excludes "don't know" and "not available" victim activity. [6] Includes sleeping. [7] Excludes "don't know" and "not available" distance from victim's home. [8] Includes knives, other sharp objects, blunt objects, and other types of weapons.

Source: U.S. Bureau of Justice Statistics, *Criminal Victimization*, annual; and series NCJ-205455, September 2004. See also <http://www.ojp.usdoj.gov/bjs/pub/pdf/cv03.pdf>.

Table 312. Property Victimization Rates by Selected Household Characteristic: 2003

[Victimizations per 1,000 households. Based on National Crime Victimization Survey; see text, this section, and Appendix III]

Characteristic	Total	Burglary	Motor vehicle theft	Theft
Total.................................	163.2	29.8	9.0	124.4
Race:				
White...............................	159.1	28.4	7.8	122.9
Black...............................	190.2	38.8	15.3	136.2
Other...............................	141.7	28.5	13.3	99.8
Ethnicity:				
Hispanic...........................	207.8	34.0	14.0	159.8
Non-Hispanic.......................	158.2	29.1	8.4	120.7
Household income:				
Less than $7,500.................	204.6	58.0	6.3	140.3
$7,500-$14,999	167.7	42.2	7.3	118.3
$15,000-$24,999	179.2	38.4	8.9	131.9
$25,000-$34,999	180.7	35.3	12.3	133.1
$35,000-$49,999	177.1	27.6	9.5	140.0
$50,000-$74,999	168.1	24.9	8.4	134.7
$75,000 or more	176.4	20.8	11.9	143.7
Residence:				
Urban..............................	216.3	38.7	13.0	164.7
Suburban...........................	144.8	24.0	9.3	111.6
Rural..............................	136.6	30.5	4.0	102.1
Form of tenure:				
Home owned.........................	143.5	24.5	7.3	111.7
Home rented........................	206.4	41.2	13.0	152.2

Source: U.S. Bureau of Justice Statistics, *Criminal Victimization*, annual; and series NCJ-205455. See also <http://www.ojp.usdoj.gov/bjs/pub/pdf/cv03.pdf>.

Table 313. **Persons Arrested by Charge and Selected Characteristics: 2003**

[(In thousands) 10,324.5 represents 10,324,500). Represents arrests (not charges) reported by approximately 11,368 agencies with a total 2003 population of approximately 220 million as estimated by FBI. Age and sex data are mandatory, while race data are optional and not always reported with arrest data; hence, two different total number of arrests]

Offense charged	Total arrests	Male	Female	Total arrests	White	Black	American Indian or Alaska Native	Asian or Pacific Islander
Total	10,324.5	7,913.9	2,410.6	10,268.7	7,189.8	2,827.3	133.5	118.1
Serious crimes [1]:	1,677.1	1,219.6	457.5	1,668.9	1,095.5	531.7	18.7	23.0
Murder and nonnegligent manslaughter . . .	10.1	9.0	1.1	10.1	4.8	5.0	(Z)	(Z)
Forcible rape	20.1	19.9	0.3	20.1	12.7	6.8	(Z)	(Z)
Robbery	81.0	72.6	8.4	80.7	35.1	44.2	0.5	1.0
Aggravated assault	339.2	268.9	70.3	337.5	214.7	115.0	3.7	4.1
Burglary.	220.2	189.9	30.4	219.5	153.9	61.0	2.2	2.3
Larceny/theft	883.0	556.3	326.6	878.1	596.6	257.5	10.7	13.2
Motor vehicle theft.	111.5	92.9	18.6	111.1	68.4	39.6	1.1	2.0
Arson	12.0	10.1	1.9	12.0	9.2	2.5	(Z)	(Z)
All other nonserious crimes:								
Other assaults	961.3	728.3	233.1	956.8	626.0	307.7	12.2	11.0
Forgery and counterfeiting	85.5	50.9	34.6	85.1	58.7	25.0	(Z)	1.0
Fraud	246.2	133.9	112.3	245.0	167.2	75.0	1.3	1.5
Embezzlement	13.4	6.6	6.7	13.3	9.0	4.0	(Z)	(Z)
Stolen property—buying, receiving, possessing.	96.7	79.3	17.4	96.1	57.5	36.9	0.7	1.0
Vandalism	208.1	173.5	34.5	207.3	156.3	45.8	2.8	2.4
Weapons; carrying, possessing etc.	127.0	116.5	10.5	126.5	77.4	46.8	0.9	1.4
Prostitution and commercialized vice.	59.8	20.3	39.5	59.5	34.7	23.2	(Z)	1.3
Sex offenses (except forcible rape and prostitution)	68.2	62.3	5.9	68.0	49.7	16.6	0.7	0.9
Drug abuse violations.	124.4	101.6	22.7	1,239.3	811.6	410.5	7.7	9.5
Gambling.	8.0	7.2	0.9	8.0	2.1	5.6	(Z)	(Z)
Offenses against family and children.	100.6	76.8	23.7	100.2	67.0	30.8	1.3	1.2
Driving under the influence	1,048.0	857.3	190.7	1,039.9	914.2	100.7	14.6	10.3
Liquor laws.	464.3	345.5	118.8	461.2	400.2	43.7	12.7	4.5
Drunkenness	411.8	352.1	59.7	410.5	343.2	54.8	10.3	2.3
Disorderly conduct.	506.8	380.0	126.9	504.7	331.4	161.9	7.5	3.9
Vagrancy.	22.1	17.6	4.5	22.1	12.6	9.0	(Z)	(Z)
Suspicion.	1.9	1.6	0.3	1.8	1.2	0.6	(Z)	(Z)
Curfew and loitering law violations	102.4	71.2	31.3	102.2	69.1	30.9	0.8	1.4
Runaways	91.4	37.7	53.8	91.2	67.0	18.4	1.5	4.2
All other offenses (except traffic)	2,780.2	2,159.4	620.8	2,761.0	1,838.1	847.8	38.4	36.7

Z Less than 500. [1] Includes arson.

Source: U.S. Federal Bureau of Investigation, Crime in the United States, annual. See also <http://www.fbi.gov/ucr/03Cius.htm> (released 27 October 2004).

Table 314. **Violent Victimizations of Persons 18 to 24 years old: 1995–2002**

[Average annual rates per 1,000 persons ages 18-24. Covers period 1992 to 2002. Based on National Crime Victimization Survey; see text, this section, and Appendix III]

Victims	Population	Violent crime	Rape/ sexual assault	Robbery	Aggravated assault	Simple assault	Serious violent crime
College students, total	7,894,930	60.7	3.8	5.0	13.5	38.4	22.3
Sex:							
Male.	3,796,380	80.2	1.4	7.4	21.4	49.9	30.2
Female	4,098,550	42.7	6.0	2.7	6.2	27.7	15.0
Race/ethnicity: [1]							
White	5,592,920	64.9	4.0	4.4	13.2	43.3	21.6
Black	934,160	52.4	(B)	8.7	15.6	24.9	27.5
Other	580,700	37.2	(B)	7.0	9.8	18.4	18.8
Hispanic	811,370	56.1	(B)	(B)	15.4	33.4	22.8
Non-Students, total	17,947,440	75.3	4.1	9.5	17.7	44.1	31.3
Sex:							
Male.	9,143,340	79.2	(B)	12.4	22.4	44.0	35.2
Female	8,804,110	71.3	7.9	6.4	12.9	44.1	27.2
Race/ethnicity: [1]							
White	11,237,850	81.2	4.5	7.5	17.6	51.6	29.6
Black	2,656,380	83.2	4.9	16.7	22.5	39.1	44.1
Other	662,970	43.1	(B)	7.5	12.1	20.0	23.1
Hispanic	3,390,240	55.9	1.9	10.8	15.7	27.5	28.4

B Base figure too small to meet statistical standards for reliability. In this case, 10 or fewer sample cases. [1] All racial categories do not include Hispanics. "Other" includes Asian, Pacific Islanders, and Native Americans.

Source: U.S. Bureau of Justice Statistics, Violent Victimizations of College Students, 1995-2002, Series NCJ 206836, January 2005.

Table 315. **Number of School-Associated Violent Deaths Occuring at and Away From School: 1992 to 2002**

[At school includes on school property, on the way to or from school, and while attending or traveling to or from a school-sponsored event]

School year	Total student, staff, and nonstudent school-associated violent deaths	Homicides of youth ages 5-19	
		Homicides at school	Homicides away from school
Total 1992-2000	390	234	24,406
1992-93	57	34	3,583
1993-94	48	29	3,806
1994-95	48	28	3,546
1995-96	53	32	3,303
1996-97	48	28	2,950
1997-98	57	34	2,728
1998-99	47	33	2,366
1999-2000	32	16	2,124
2000-01	27	10	2,045
2001-02	31	14	(NA)

NA Not available.
Source: National Center for Education Statistics, *Indicators of School Crime and Safety, 2003.*

Table 316. **Juvenile Arrests for Selected Offenses: 1980 to 2003**

[169,439 represents 169,439,000. Juveniles are persons under 18 years of age]

Offense	1980	1990	1995	1997	1998	1999	2000	2001	2002	2003
Number of contributing agencies	8,178	10,765	10,037	9,472	9,589	9,502	9,904	10,281	10,946	11,368
Population covered (1,000) . . .	169,439	204,543	206,762	194,925	194,612	195,324	204,965	215,380	220,157	219,562
NUMBER										
Violent crime, total	77,220	97,103	123,131	100,273	90,201	81,715	78,450	78,443	71,059	69,060
Murder	1,475	2,661	2,812	1,887	1,587	1,131	1,027	1,069	1,014	960
Forcible rape	3,668	4,971	4,556	4,127	3,988	3,544	3,402	3,504	3,553	3,195
Robbery	38,529	34,944	47,240	36,419	29,989	26,125	24,206	23,408	19,491	18,950
Aggravated assault	33,548	54,527	68,523	57,840	54,637	50,915	49,815	50,462	47,001	45,955
Weapon law violations	21,203	33,123	46,506	39,358	34,122	31,307	28,514	29,290	26,786	29,512
Drug abuse, total	86,685	66,300	149,236	155,444	148,066	138,774	146,594	146,758	133,557	134,746
Sale and manufacturing. . . .	13,004	24,575	34,077	30,761	29,312	26,134	26,432	24,649	22,086	21,987
Heroin/cocaine	1,318	17,511	19,187	15,855	15,094	12,686	11,000	10,535	8,832	7,848
Marijuana	8,876	4,372	10,682	11,208	10,808	10,770	11,792	10,552	9,962	10,463
Synthetic narcotics	465	346	701	671	813	722	945	911	974	1,043
Dangerous nonnarcotic drugs	2,345	2,346	3,507	3,027	2,597	1,956	2,695	2,651	2,318	2,633
Possession	73,681	41,725	115,159	124,683	118,754	112,640	120,432	122,109	111,471	112,759
Heroin/cocaine	2,614	15,194	21,253	18,328	16,278	13,445	12,586	11,734	10,969	9,932
Marijuana	64,465	20,940	82,015	94,046	91,467	89,523	95,962	97,088	85,769	87,909
Synthetic narcotics	1,524	1,155	2,047	1,987	1,916	1,581	2,052	2,237	2,805	2,872
Dangerous nonnarcotic drugs	5,078	4,436	9,844	10,322	9,093	8,091	9,832	11,050	11,928	12,046

Source: U.S. Federal Bureau of Investigation, *Crime in the United States,* annual. See also <http://www.fbi.gov/ucr/03Cius.htm>(released October 2004).

Table 317. **Drug Use by Arrestees in Major U.S. Cities by Type of Drug and Sex: 2003**

[Percent testing positive. Based on data from the Arrestee Drug Abuse Monitoring Program]

City	Male				Female			
	Any drug [1]	Marijuana	Cocaine	Opiates	Any drug [1]	Marijuana	Cocaine	Opiates
Albuquerque, NM	70.3	41.6	35.0	11.2	70.0	29.4	38.1	13.8
Atlanta, GA	73.5	41.8	49.8	3.0	(NA)	(NA)	(NA)	(NA)
Chicago, IL	86.0	53.2	50.6	24.9	66.7	38.9	33.3	22.2
Cleveland, OH	74.9	48.9	39.0	5.4	72.4	27.2	52.7	6.7
Dallas, TX	63.8	39.1	32.7	6.9	(NA)	(NA)	(NA)	(NA)
Denver, CO	72.6	42.3	38.3	6.8	75.1	34.3	52.5	6.1
Indianapolis, IN	66.4	44.8	35.3	5.1	79.9	42.0	55.7	5.7
Las Vegas, NV	70.0	34.4	21.9	6.4	(NA)	(NA)	(NA)	(NA)
Los Angeles, CA.	68.9	40.7	23.5	2.0	63.0	29.6	25.9	0.0
New Orleans, LA	79.6	50.8	47.6	14.0	62.2	30.3	37.3	13.3
New York, NY	72.7	43.1	35.7	15.0	73.3	36.7	50.0	23.3
Oklahoma City, OK	73.5	54.9	24.6	3.0	78.4	43.3	35.3	5.6
Philadelphia, PA	68.8	45.8	30.3	11.5	(NA)	(NA)	(NA)	(NA)
Phoenix, AZ.	76.8	40.9	23.4	4.4	78.5	31.6	28.1	6.1
Portland, OR	72.7	38.4	29.7	15.0	84.4	35.2	39.6	22.0
Sacramento, CA.	81.1	49.2	21.6	6.9	(NA)	(NA)	(NA)	(NA)
San Antonio, TX	65.2	41.9	30.5	9.1	(NA)	(NA)	(NA)	(NA)
San Diego, CA.	71.2	41.0	10.3	5.1	72.6	29.1	15.2	8.7
San Jose, CA.	63.7	35.4	12.9	3.1	72.8	29.1	10.1	3.4
Seattle, WA	69.4	37.2	36.6	6.8	(NA)	(NA)	(NA)	(NA)
Tucson, AZ	76.4	44.1	42.5	4.2	73.2	29.0	40.0	9.7
Washington, DC	65.8	37.4	26.5	9.8	66.7	29.1	30.9	10.9

NA Not available.   [1] Includes other drugs not shown separately.

Source: U.S. National Institute of Justice, *ADAM 2003 Annual Report on Drug Use Among Adult and Juvenile Arrestees,* June 2004. See also <http://www.ncjrs.org/drgswww.html#top>.

Law Enforcement, Courts, and Prisons **205**

Table 318. Drug Arrest Rates for Drug Abuse Violations, 1990 to 2003, and by Region, 2003

[Rate per 100,000 inhabitants. Based on Census Bureau estimated resident population as of July 1, except 1990 and 2000, enumerated as of April 1. For composition of regions, see map, inside front cover]

Offense	1990	1995	2000	2003 Total	North-east	Midwest	South	West
Drug arrest rate, total	435.3	564.7	587.1	526.9	458.2	397.6	550.9	640.4
Sale and/or manufacture	139.0	140.7	122.7	103.7	116.3	78.0	115.0	102.2
Heroin or cocaine [1]	93.7	83.7	60.8	46.9	77.2	19.4	56.5	37.5
Marijuana....................	26.4	32.7	34.2	29.0	29.0	29.3	30.7	26.8
Synthetic or manufactured drugs	2.7	3.9	6.4	8.0	4.5	5.4	14.3	4.9
Other dangerous nonnarcotic drugs...	16.2	20.3	21.3	19.9	5.7	23.9	13.6	33.0
Possession	296.3	423.9	464.4	423.2	341.9	319.7	435.9	538.2
Heroin or cocaine [1]	144.4	157.4	138.7	111.1	112.6	46.5	119.3	149.6
Marijuana....................	104.9	192.7	244.4	209.7	195.0	200.0	256.9	171.6
Synthetic or manufactured drugs	6.6	8.5	12.0	16.6	8.3	11.7	22.3	18.9
Other dangerous nonnarcotic drugs...	40.4	65.4	69.4	85.8	26.0	61.5	37.4	198.1

[1] Includes other derivatives such as morphine, heroin, and codeine.

Source: U.S. Federal Bureau of Investigation, Crime in the United States, annual. See also <http://www.fbi.gov/ucr/cius_03/03crime.pdf> (released October 2004).

Table 319. Federal Drug Seizures by Type of Drug: 1990 to 2004

[In pounds. For fiscal years ending in year shown. Reflects the combined drug seizure effort of the Drug Enforcement Administration, the Federal Bureau of Investigation, the U.S. Customs Services, and beginning October 1993, the U.S. Border Patrol within the jurisdiction of the United States as well as maritime seizures by the U.S. Coast Guard. Based on reports to the Federal-wide Drug Seizure System, which eliminates duplicate reporting of a seizure involving more than one federal agency]

Drug	1990	1995	1998	1999	2000	2001	2002	2003	2004
Total	745,003	1,662,592	2,084,480	2,659,945	2,986,002	2,915,081	2,661,706	2,975,368	2,813,378
Heroin......	1,515	3,406	3,212	2,539	3,694	5,503	6,113	5,282	4,065
Cocaine.......	211,828	244,888	259,896	288,952	235,053	232,885	225,962	258,013	365,330
Cannabis.......	531,660	1,414,298	1,821,372	2,368,454	2,747,256	2,676,693	2,429,631	2,712,073	2,443,984
Marijuana.....	514,723	1,382,396	1,820,840	2,366,696	2,723,274	2,676,339	2,428,262	2,711,731	2,440,367
Hashish......	16,937	31,902	532	1,758	23,982	354	1,369	342	3,617

Source: U.S. Drug Enforcement Administration, unpublished data from Federal-wide Drug Seizure System.

Table 320. Authorized Intercepts of Communication—Summary: 1980 to 2004

[Data for jurisdictions with statutes authorizing or approving interception of wire or oral communication]

Item	1980	1985	1990	1995	1997	1998	1999	2000	2001	2002	2003	2004
Jurisdictions: [1]												
With wiretap statutes........	28	32	40	41	45	45	45	45	46	47	47	47
Reporting interceptions	22	22	25	19	24	26	28	26	25	20	24	20
Intercept applications authorized	564	784	872	1,156	1,279	1,482	1,489	1,266	1,561	1,358	1,442	1,710
Intercept installations........	524	722	812	1,024	1,094	1,245	1,277	1,139	1,405	1,273	1,367	1,633
Federal.................	79	235	321	527	563	562	595	472	481	490	576	723
State..................	445	487	491	497	531	683	682	667	924	783	791	910
Intercepted communications, average [2]	1,058	1,320	1,487	2,028	2,081	1,858	1,921	1,769	1,565	1,708	3,004	3,017
Incriminating	315	275	321	459	418	350	390	402	333	403	993	619
Persons arrested [3]	1,871	2,469	2,057	2,577	3,086	3,450	4,372	3,411	3,683	3,060	3,674	4,056
Convictions [3]	259	660	420	494	542	911	654	736	732	493	843	634
Major offense specified:												
Gambling	199	206	116	95	98	93	60	49	82	82	49	90
Drugs..................	282	434	520	732	870	955	978	894	1,167	1,052	1,104	1,308
Homicide and assault	13	25	21	30	31	55	62	72	52	58	80	48
Racketeering	(NA)	(NA)	(NA)	98	93	153	139	76	70	72	96	138
Other	70	119	215	201	187	228	250	175	190	94	113	126

NA Not available. [1] Jurisdictions include federal government, states, and District of Columbia. [2] Average per authorized installation. [3] Based on information received from intercepts installed in year shown; additional arrests/convictions will occur in subsequent years but are not shown here.

Source: Administrative Office of the U.S. Courts, Report on Applications for Orders Authorizing or Approving the Interception of Wire, Oral or Electronic Communications (Wiretap Report), annual. See also <http://www.uscourts.gov/wiretap04/contents.html> (issued April 2005).

Table 321. **Background Checks for Firearm Transfers: 1994 to 2003**

[In thousands (53,548 represents 53,548,000), except rates. For "Interim period" of 1994 to November 29, 1998, covered handgun purchases from licensed firearm dealers; beginning November 29, 1998, (effective date for the Brady Handgun Violence Prevention Act, P.L. 103-159,1993) covers the transfer of both handguns and long guns from a federal firearms licensee, as well as purchases from pawnshops and retail gun shops]

Inquiries and rejections	1994-2003, period [1]	Interim period			Permanent Brady				
		1995	1997	1998 [2]	1999	2000	2001	2002	2003
Applications and rejections:									
Applications received.....	53,548	2,706	2,574	3,277	8,621	7,699	7,958	7,806	7,831
Applications rejected	1,102	41	69	90	204	153	151	136	126
Rejection rate	2.1	1.5	2.7	2.9	2.4	2.0	1.9	1.7	1.6

[1] Represents from the inception of the Brady Act on March 1, 1994, to 2003. [2] For period January 1 to November 29, 1998. Counts are from the National Instant Criminal Background Check System and may include multiple transactions for the same application.

Source: U.S. Bureau of Justice Statistics, *Background Checks for Firearm Transfers, 2003*, Series NCJ 204428, September 2004. See also <http://www.ojp.usdoj.gov/bjs/pub/pdf/bcft03.pdf>.

Table 322. **Requests for Forensic Services: 2002**

Type of function	Back-logged request [1]	New requests	Requests completed [2]	Type of function	Back-logged request [1]	New requests	Requests completed [2]
Total	**289,938**	**2,706,785**	**2,495,313**	Trace	9,997	41,531	36,878
Controlled substances ...	95,404	1,291,488	1,154,221	DNA analysis ...,....	29,516	60,887	41,592
Biology screening	18,456	88,857	76,332	Toxicology	17,523	467,752	455,624
Firearms/toolmarks	22,636	104,068	88,997	Questioned documents...	3,391	16,683	15,562
Crime scene.........	1,579	166,588	165,461	Computer crimes.......	952	2,839	2,757
Latent prints.........	50,245	274,225	238,135	Other functions	40,239	191,867	219,754

[1] As of January 2, 2002. [2] As of December 31, 2002.

Source: US Bureau of Justice Statistics, *Census of Publicly Funded Forensic Crime Laboratories, 2003* Series NCJ 207205, February 2005.

Table 323. **Law Enforcement Officers Killed and Assaulted: 1990 to 2003**

[Covers officers killed feloniously and accidentally in line of duty; includes federal officers. For composition of regions, see map, inside front cover]

Item	1990	1995	1997	1998	1999	2000	2001 [1]	2002	2003
OFFICERS KILLED									
Total killed	**132**	**133**	**133**	**142**	**107**	**134**	**218**	**132**	**133**
Northeast	13	16	16	6	11	13	79	10	13
Midwest	20	19	25	19	17	32	26	22	20
South.................	68	63	55	70	56	67	68	65	66
West	23	32	30	36	22	19	38	28	31
Puerto Rico............	8	2	7	9	1	3	7	7	3
Outlying areas, foreign countries.............	-	1	-	2	-	-	-	-	-
Feloniously killed	65	74	70	61	42	51	142	56	52
Firearms	56	62	68	58	41	47	61	51	45
Handgun	47	43	50	40	25	33	46	38	34
Rifle	8	14	12	17	11	10	11	10	10
Shotgun..........	1	5	6	1	5	4	4	3	1
Knife	3	2	1	1	-	1	-	1	
Bomb	-	8	-	1	-	-	-		
Personal weapons	2	-	1	-	-	-	1	-	
Other	4	2	-	1	1	3	80	4	7
Accidentally killed........	67	59	63	81	65	83	76	76	81
ASSAULTS									
Population (1,000) [2]	197,426	191,759	184,825	193,098	207,124	204,599	213,645	219,425	216,103
Number of—									
Agencies represented	9,343	8,503	8,120	8,153	9,832	8,940	9,773	10,164	10,141
Police officers..........	410,131	428,379	411,015	452,361	462,782	452,531	471,096	491,009	482,985
Total assaulted	**72,091**	**57,762**	**52,149**	**60,673**	**55,971**	**58,398**	**57,463**	**59,526**	**57,841**
Firearm	3,651	2,354	2,110	2,126	1,772	1,749	1,841	1,927	1,866
Knife or cutting instrument ...	1,647	1,356	971	1,098	999	1,015	1,168	1,061	1,074
Other dangerous weapon ...	7,423	6,414	5,800	7,415	7,560	8,132	8,233	8,526	8,059
Hands, fists, feet, etc	59,370	47,638	43,268	50,034	45,640	47,502	46,221	48,012	46,842

- Represents zero. [1] The 72 officers feloniously slain during the events of September 11, 2001, are included in data for 2001. [2] Represents the number of persons covered by agencies shown.

Source: U.S. Federal Bureau of Investigation, *Law Enforcement Officers Killed and Assaulted*, annual.

Table 324. U.S. Supreme Court—Cases Filed and Disposition: 1980 to 2003

[Statutory term of court begins first Monday in **October**]

Action	1980	1990	1995	1998	1999	2000	2001	2002	2003
Total cases on docket	**5,144**	**6,316**	**7,565**	**8,083**	**8,445**	**8,965**	**9,176**	**9,406**	**8,882**
Appellate cases on docket	2,749	2,351	2,456	2,387	2,413	2,305	2,210	2,190	2,058
From prior term	527	365	361	326	321	351	324	321	336
Docketed during present term	2,222	1,986	2,095	2,061	2,092	1,954	1,886	1,869	1,722
Cases acted upon [1]	2,324	2,042	2,130	2,092	2,096	2,024	1,932	1,899	1,798
Granted review	167	114	92	72	78	85	82	83	74
Denied, dismissed, or withdrawn	1,999	1,802	1,945	1,940	1,958	1,842	1,751	1,727	1,641
Summarily decided	90	81	62	44	34	63	57	46	37
Cases not acted upon	425	309	326	295	317	281	278	291	260
Pauper cases on docket	2,371	3,951	5,098	5,689	6,024	6,651	6,958	7,209	6,818
Cases acted upon	2,027	3,436	4,514	4,951	5,273	5,736	6,139	6,488	6,036
Granted review	17	27	13	9	14	14	6	8	13
Denied, dismissed, or withdrawn	1,968	3,369	4,439	4,926	5,239	5,658	6,114	6,459	6,005
Summarily decided	32	28	55	11	16	61	19	17	13
Cases not acted upon	344	515	584	738	751	915	819	721	782
Original cases on docket	24	14	11	7	8	9	8	7	6
Cases disposed of during term	7	3	5	2	-	2	1	1	2
Total cases available for argument	**264**	**201**	**145**	**124**	**124**	**138**	**137**	**139**	**140**
Cases disposed of	162	131	93	94	87	89	90	87	93
Cases argued	154	125	90	90	83	86	88	84	91
Cases dismissed or remanded without argument	8	6	3	4	4	3	2	3	2
Cases remaining	102	70	52	30	37	49	47	52	47
Cases decided by signed opinion	144	121	87	84	79	83	85	79	89
Cases decided by per curiam opinion. . . .	8	4	3	4	2	4	3	5	2
Number of signed opinions.	123	112	75	75	74	77	76	71	73

- Represents zero. [1] Includes cases granted review and carried over to next term, not shown separately.

Source: Office of the Clerk, Supreme Court of the United States, unpublished data.

Table 325. U.S. District Courts—Civil Cases Commenced and Pending: 2000 to 2004

[For years ending **June 30**]

Type of case	Cases commenced				Cases pending			
	2000	2002	2003	2004	2000	2002	2003	2004
Cases total [1]	**263,049**	**268,071**	**254,499**	**258,117**	**249,692**	**270,667**	**261,608**	**267,881**
Contract actions [1]	54,494	36,845	32,356	29,687	38,262	33,237	30,789	28,413
Recovery of overpayments [2] . . .	25,636	6,737	3,466	2,914	12,107	5,342	2,713	2,146
Real property actions	6,481	7,731	7,503	6,341	4,249	6,485	6,302	5,651
Tort actions	40,877	56,565	46,295	51,881	63,116	76,907	65,562	74,589
Personal injury	36,867	52,654	42,233	45,948	59,232	72,962	61,496	68,928
Personal injury product liability [1]	15,349	35,074	24,255	29,089	31,772	46,264	34,655	42,886
Asbestos	7,893	24,844	3,718	1,208	4,949	21,045	5,606	2,528
Other personal injury	21,518	17,580	17,978	16,859	27,460	26,698	26,841	26,042
Personal property damage	4,010	3,911	4,062	5,933	3,884	3,945	4,066	5,661
Actions under statutes [1]	161,187	166,920	168,332	170,168	144,053	154,027	158,943	159,200
Civil rights [1]	41,226	40,172	40,567	40,118	44,259	43,589	43,981	43,431
Employment	21,404	20,881	20,777	19,670	24,456	23,778	23,618	22,964
Bankruptcy suits	3,378	3,792	3,342	3,982	2,555	2,921	2,522	2,684
Commerce (ICC rates, etc.) . . .	1,007	578	574	483	444	453	455	427
Environmental matters	894	848	935	999	1,355	2,134	2,296	2,282
Prisoner petitions	57,706	55,596	55,112	53,132	43,560	44,210	44,306	44,317
Forfeiture and penalty	2,246	2,062	2,120	2,112	1,772	1,787	1,932	2,017
Labor laws	14,229	17,706	17,290	18,189	11,267	14,084	14,621	15,131
Protected property rights [3]	8,745	8,500	8,613	9.289	7,858	8,094	8,654	8,992
Securities commodities and exchanges.	2,500	3,559	3,449	3,081	3,578	4,659	5,227	5,325
Social Security laws	14,365	17,868	17,483	15,935	13,667	17,489	17,526	14,853
Tax suits	938	1,147	1,232	1,291	1,068	1,115	1,106	1,158
Freedom of information	335	284	266	300	380	348	347	360

[1] Includes other types not shown separately. [2] Includes enforcement of judgments in student loan cases, and overpayments of veterans' benefits. [3] Includes copyright, patent, and trademark rights.

Source: Administrative Office of the U.S. Courts, *Statistical Tables for the Federal Judiciary*, annual.

Table 326. **U.S. District Courts—Offenders Convicted and Sentenced to Prison and Length of Sentence: 2002**

Most serious offense of conviction	Offenders convicted	Convicted offenders sentenced to prison	Mean length of sentence (mo.) [1]	Most serious offense of conviction	Offenders convicted	Convicted offenders sentenced to prison	Mean length of sentence (mo.) [1]
Total [2]	71,798	55,682	57.1	Possession	2,060	1,844	19.4
Violent offenses	2,578	2,408	88.5	Trafficking and			
Property offenses	13,101	7,746	25.0	manufacturing	24,174	22,107	75.7
Fraudulent offenses [3]	11,107	6,654	23.4	Public-order offenses	4,630	3,053	38.5
Embezzlement	763	381	15.3	Regulatory offenses	1,403	641	25.9
Fraud [4]	8,926	5,426	24.4	Other offenses [5]	3,227	2,412	41.9
Forgery	90	43	14.8	Tax law violations [5]	517	294	22.2
Other offenses [3]	1,994	1,092	34.7	Weapons	5,563	5,134	83.9
Larceny	1,431	686	29.1	Immigration	11,132	9,954	27.9
Drug offenses [3]	26,234	23,951	76.0	Misdemeanors	8,499	1,408	9.8

[1] Excludes sentences of life, death, and indeterminate sentences. [2] Total may include offenders for whom offense category could not be determined. [3] Includes offenses not shown separately. [4] Excludes tax fraud. [5] Includes tax fraud.

Source: U.S. Bureau of Justice Statistics, Compendium of Federal Justice Statistics, 2002, Series NCJ 205368, September 2004.

Table 327. **Federal Prosecutions of Public Corruption: 1980 to 2003**

[As of December 31. Prosecution of persons who have corrupted public office in violation of Federal Criminal Statutes]

Prosecution status	1980	1985	1990	1995	1996	1997	1998	1999	2000	2001	2002	2003
Total: [1] Indicted	727	1,157	1,176	1,051	984	1,057	1,174	1,134	1,000	1,087	1,136	1,150
Convicted	602	997	1,084	878	902	853	1,014	1,065	938	920	1,011	868
Awaiting trial	213	256	300	323	244	327	340	329	327	437	413	412
Federal officials: Indicted	123	563	615	527	456	459	442	480	441	502	478	479
Convicted	131	470	583	438	459	392	414	460	422	414	429	421
Awaiting trial	16	90	103	120	64	83	85	101	92	131	119	129
State officials: Indicted	72	79	96	61	109	51	91	115	92	95	110	94
Convicted	51	66	79	61	83	49	58	80	91	61	132	87
Awaiting trial	28	20	28	23	40	20	37	44	37	75	50	38
Local officials: Indicted	247	248	257	236	219	255	277	237	211	224	299	259
Convicted	168	221	225	191	190	169	264	219	183	184	262	119
Awaiting trial	82	49	98	89	60	118	90	95	89	110	118	106

[1] Includes individuals who are neither public officials nor employees, but who were involved with public officials or employees in violating the law, not shown separately.

Source: U.S. Department of Justice, Federal Prosecutions of Corrupt Public Officials, 1970-1980 and Report to Congress on the Activities and Operations of the Public Integrity Section, annual.

Table 328. **Percent of Prosecutors' Offices Prosecuting Computer Related Crimes : 2001**

[In percent]

Type of computer crime prosecuted	All offices	Full-time offices (population served)			Part-time
		Large (1,000,000 or more)	Medium (250,000 to 999,999)	Small (under 250,000)	
Any computer-related crime	41.5	97.0	72.9	44.2	16.8
Credit card fraud [1]	27.4	93.5	61.2	28.2	7.4
Bank card fraud [1]	22.3	83.3	50.9	22.6	6.9
Computer forgery [2]	13.3	63.0	39.2	12.8	2.7
Computer sabotage [3]	4.6	53.6	14.4	3.8	0.5
Unauthorized access to computer [4]	9.6	60.7	28.8	8.8	2.3
Unauthorized copying or distribution of computer programs [5]	2.7	53.8	9.0	1.8	0.2
Cyberstalking [6]	16.3	76.7	47.8	15.1	4.5
Theft of intellectual property	3.2	40.7	13.4	2.3	0.5
Transmitting child pornography	30.0	87.1	67.1	30.4	10.8
Identity theft	18.2	80.0	51.9	17.2	4.5

[1] ATM or debit. [2] Alteration of computerized documents. [3] To hinder the normal function of a computer system through the introduction of worms, viruses, or logic bombs. [4] Hacking. [5] Software copyright infringement. [6] The activity of users sending harassing or threatening e-mail to other users.

Source: U.S. Bureau of Justice Statistics, Prosecutors in State Courts, 2001. See also <http://www.ojp.usdoj.gov/bjs> (Released May 2002).

Law Enforcement, Courts, and Prisons 209

Table 329. State Trends in Identity Theft: 2004

[Rate per 100,000 population. As of December 31. Based on Census Bureau population estimates]

Consumer State	Fraud complaints		Identity theft victims	
	Number	Rate	Number	Rate
United States	338,509	(NA)	239,531	(NA)
Alabama........................	4,143	91.5	2,216	48.9
Alaska.........................	1,143	174.4	433	66.1
Arizona........................	10,366	180.5	8,186	142.5
Arkansas	2,085	75.7	1,397	50.8
California	46,867	130.6	43,839	122.1
Colorado.......................	6,558	142.5	4,409	95.8
Connecticut.....................	4,170	119.0	2,000	57.1
Delaware	1,051	126.6	553	66.6
District of Columbia	1,196	216.1	922	166.6
Florida	22,263	128.0	16,062	92.3
Georgia	8,549	96.8	7,440	84.3
Hawaii	1,807	143.1	640	50.7
Idaho..........................	1,565	112.3	600	43.1
Illinois	14,766	116.1	11,138	87.6
Indiana........................	7,168	114.9	4,274	68.5
Iowa	2,645	89.5	1,028	34.8
Kansas........................	3,059	111.8	1,677	61.3
Kentucky	3,667	88.4	1,662	40.1
Louisiana	3,625	80.3	2,254	49.9
Maine....	1,345	102.1	424	32.2
Maryland	7,298	131.3	4,612	83.0
Massachusetts..................	6,976	108.7	3,921	61.1
Michigan.......................	10,998	108.8	7,307	72.3
Minnesota......................	5,284	103.6	2,905	57.0
Mississippi	1,939	66.8	1,350	46.5
Missouri	6,398	111.2	3,905	67.9
Montana.......................	1,101	118.8	364	39.3
Nebraska......................	2,002	114.6	788	45.1
Nevada	3,532	151.3	2,935	125.7
New Hampshire.................	1,734	133.4	543	41.8
New Jersey.....................	9,917	114.0	6,530	75.1
New Mexico	2,365	124.3	1,588	83.4
New York	20,699	107.7	17,680	92.0
North Carolina..................	8,291	97.1	5,623	65.8
North Dakota....................	571	90.0	188	29.6
Ohio	13,066	114.0	6,956	60.7
Oklahoma......................	3,444	97.7	1,973	56.0
Oregon........................	4,756	132.3	3,156	87.8
Pennsylvania...................	14,786	119.2	7,563	61.0
Rhode Island...................	1,089	100.8	547	50.6
South Carolina..................	4,588	109.3	2,148	51.2
South Dakota	663	86.0	179	23.2
Tennessee	5,406	91.6	3,246	55.0
Texas.........................	21,435	95.3	26,454	117.6
Utah	2,927	122.5	1,831	76.6
Vermont	679	109.3	208	33.5
Virginia........................	10,023	134.4	4,742	63.6
Washington.....................	9,378	151.2	5,654	91.1
West Virginia...................	1,835	101.1	621	34.2
Wisconsin......................	6,643	120.6	2,646	48.0
Wyoming	648	127.9	214	42.2

NA Not available.

Source: U.S. Federal Trade Commission, *National and State Trends in Fraud and Identity Theft*, 2004, February 2005 See also
<http://www.consumer.gov/sentinel/pubs/Top10Fraud2004.pdf>.

Table 330. Delinquency Cases Disposed by Juvenile Courts by Reason for Referral: 1990 to 2000

[In thousands (1,317 represents 1,317,000), except rate. A delinquency offense is an act committed by a juvenile for which an adult could be prosecuted in a criminal court. Disposition of a case involves taking a definite action such as waiving the case to criminal court, dismissing the case, placing the youth on probation, placing the youth in a facility for delinquents, or such actions as fines, restitution, and community service]

Reason for referral	1990	1991	1992	1993	1994	1995	1996	1997	1998	1999	2000
All delinquency offenses . . .	1,317	1,414	1,482	1,522	1,666	1,768	1,796	1,811	1,743	1,667	1,612
Case rate [1]	51.4	54.0	55.2	55.3	59.4	61.9	62	61.7	58.8	55.5	52.5
Violent offenses	94	106.	114	118	132	137	128	109	100	86	81
Criminal homicide	2	2	2	3	3	3	3	2	2	2	2
Forcible rape	5	6	6	7	7	7	6	6	5	4	5
Robbery	28	32	33	35	38	40	38	34	29	25	22
Aggravated assault	59	66	72	73	84	87	81	67	64	55	52
Property offenses	773	849	862	834	868	888	874	846	779	703	661
Burglary	564	615	619	594	609	630	621	601	539	481	452
Larceny	145	155	160	151	146	142	145	142	131	113	109
Motor vehicle theft	341	382	382	372	392	424	413	398	355	321	299
Arson	70	71	70	62	62	54	54	52	45	38	37
Delinquency offenses	660	692	749	810	925	1,001	1,048	1,101	1,103	1,100	1,079
Simple assault	132	143	162	177	198	219	223	248	254	255	248
Vandalism	99	113	119	119	130	127	123	118	117	111	107
Drug law violations	71	65	73	92	131	166	185	194	194	191	193
Obstruction of justice	80	74	78	94	110	122	150	166	169	191	193
Other [2]	278	297	317	328	356	368	367	375	370	371	352

[1] Number of cases disposed per 1,000 youth (ages 10 to 17) at risk. [2] Includes such offenses as stolen property offenses, trespassing, weapons offenses, other sex offenses, liquor law violations, disorderly conduct, and miscellaneous offenses.

Source: National Center for Juvenile Justice, Pittsburgh, PA, *Juvenile Court Statistics*, annual. See also <http://www.ojjdp.ncjrs.org/ojstatbb/index.html>.

Table 331. Delinquency Cases and Case Rates by Sex and Race: 1992 to 2000

[A delinquency offense is an act committed by a juvenile for which an adult could be prosecuted in a criminal court. Disposition of a case involves taking a definite action such as waiving the case to criminal court, dismissing the case, placing the youth on probation, placing the youth in a facility for delinquents, or such actions as fines, restitution, and community service. Offenses may not add to total sex and race categories due to rounding]

Sex, race, and offense	Number of cases disposed			Case rate [1]		
	1992	1999	2000	1992	1999	2000
Male, total	1,195,200	1,270,000	1,216,500	86.6	82.4	77.2
Person	243,800	281,600	267,700	17.7	18.3	17.0
Property	694,500	535,400	499,400	50.3	34.8	31.7
Drugs	64,000	160,900	160,700	4.6	10.4	10.2
Public order	193,000	292,100	288,700	14.0	19.0	18.3
Female, total	286,900	397,100	396,000	21.9	27.2	26.5
Person	64,900	103,800	101,300	5.0	7.1	6.8
Property	167,800	167,700	162,000	12.8	11.5	10.8
Drugs	8,700	30,400	32,400	0.7	2.1	2.2
Public order	45,600	95,300	100,300	3.5	6.5	6.7
White, total	975,600	1,137,400	1,111,100	45.3	47.9	46.0
Person	177,300	241,700	229,500	8.2	10.2	9.5
Property	607,000	492,800	462,700	28.2	20.8	19.2
Drugs	37,500	135,600	145,800	1.7	5.7	6.0
Public order	153,800	267,300	273,200	7.1	11.3	11.3
Black, total	453,500	473,600	445,000	112.1	102.2	92.5
Person	121,700	132,400	128,100	30.1	28.6	26.6
Property	221,300	181,400	171,200	54.7	39.2	35.6
Drugs	33,500	51,300	42,600	8.3	11.1	8.9
Public order	77,100	108,500	103,100	19.1	23.4	21.4
Other races, total	53,000	56,100	56,400	40.5	33.9	32.3
Person	9,700	11,200	11,500	7.4	6.8	6.6
Property	34,000	28,900	27,500	26.0	17.4	15.8
Drugs	1,600	4,400	4,800	1.2	2.6	2.7
Public order	7,600	11,600	12,700	5.8	7.0	7.3

[1] Cases per 1,000 youth (ages 10 to 17) at risk.

Source: National Center for Juvenile Justice, Pittsburgh, PA, *Juvenile Court Statistics*, annual. See also <http://www.ojjdp.ncjrs.org/ojstatbb/index.html>.

Table 332. **Child Abuse and Neglect Cases Substantiated and Indicated—Victim Characteristics: 1990 to 2003**

[Based on reports alleging child abuse and neglect that were referred for investigation/assessment by the respective child protective services agency in each state. The reporting period may be either calendar or fiscal year. Children are counted each time they were subjects of an investigation report. Victims are children whose alleged maltreatments have been substantiated, indicated, or assessed as maltreatments. A substantiated case represents a type of investigation disposition that determines that there is sufficient evidence under state law to conclude that maltreatment occurred or that the child is at risk of maltreatment. An indicated case represents a type of disposition that concludes that there was a reason to suspect maltreatment had occurred. An alternative response-victim case represents a type of disposition that identifies a child as a victim within the alternative response system]

ITEM	1990		2000		2002		2003	
	Number	Percent	Number	Percent	Number	Percent	Number	Percent
TYPES OF SUBSTANTIATED MALTREATMENT								
Victims, total [1]	690,658	(X)	864,837	(X)	897,168	(X)	787,156	(X)
Neglect	338,770	49.1	517,118	59.8	525,131	58.5	479,567	60.9
Physical abuse	186,801	27.0	167,713	19.4	167,168	18.6	148,877	18.9
Sexual abuse	119,506	17.3	87,770	10.2	88,688	9.9	78,188	9.9
Emotional maltreatment	45,621	6.6	66,965	7.7	58,029	6.5	38,603	4.9
Medical neglect	(NA)	(NA)	25,498	3.0	18,128	2.0	17,945	2.3
SEX OF VICTIM								
Victims, total	742,519	100.0	864,837	100.0	897,168	100.0	787,156	100.0
Male	323,339	43.5	413,744	47.8	429,637	47.9	378,374	48.1
Female	369,919	49.8	446,230	51.6	463,675	51.7	405,505	51.5
AGE OF VICTIM								
Victims, total	731,282	100.0	864,837	100.0	897,168	100.0	787,156	100.0
1 year and younger	97,101	13.3	133,094	15.4	142,189	15.9	127,618	16.2
2 to 5 years old	172,791	23.6	205,790	23.8	218,000	24.3	196,150	24.9
6 to 9 years old	157,681	21.6	212,186	24.5	207,862	23.2	176,951	22.5
10 to 13 years old	135,130	18.5	176,071	20.4	188,492	21.0	162,838	20.7
14 to 17 years old	103,383	14.1	126,207	14.6	135,070	15.1	118,698	15.1
18 and over	4,880	0.7	992	0.1	994	0.1	493	0.1

NA Not available.   X Not applicable.   [1] A child may be a victim of more than one maltreatment. Therefore, the total for this item adds up to more than 100%.

Source: U.S. Department of Health and Human Services, Administration on Children, Youth and Families. *Child Maltreatment 2003*, (Washington, DC: U. S. Government Printing Office, 2005).

Table 333. **Child Abuse and Neglect Cases Reported and Investigated by State: 2003**

[See headnote, Table 332]

State	Population under 18 years old	Number of reports [1]	Number of children subject of an investigation [2]	Number of child victims [3]
U.S. [4]	73,043,506	1,576,390	2,856,284	787,156
AL	1,107,973	18,015	29,679	9,290
AK	189,289	10,575	10,575	7,996
AZ	1,519,312	33,649	76,269	4,838
AR	682,013	19,747	44,666	7,232
CA	9,419,970	(NA)	(NA)	(NA)
CO	1,152,751	29,362	43,217	8,137
CT	835,375	32,802	50,115	12,256
DE	198,842	5,469	12,497	1,236
DC	108,403	4,673	11,000	2,518
FL	3,924,123	157,474	351,499	138,499
GA	2,296,759	71,501	121,269	43,923
HI	297,142	3,894	8,230	4,046
ID	372,027	6,264	9,458	1,527
IL	3,230,606	59,280	134,919	28,344
IN	1,603,901	34,388	52,195	21,205
IA	693,428	24,172	36,544	13,303
KS	695,081	15,840	24,250	5,682
KY	994,182	45,348	69,201	18,178
LA	1,177,555	25,480	41,726	11,432
ME	286,746	5,152	9,425	4,719
MD	1,378,092	(NA)	(NA)	16,688
MA	1,487,118	39,692	83,270	36,558
MI	2,538,920	74,675	195,583	28,690
MN	1,248,770	17,587	25,878	9,230
MS	761,268	15,998	24,503	5,940
MO	1,407,342	55,580	84,383	10,183
MT	215,774	9,023	14,966	1,951
NE	440,840	7,160	14,767	3,875
NV	581,397	13,641	28,148	4,578
NH	306,231	6,878	9,697	1,043
NJ	2,131,617	42,762	77,915	8,123
NM	502,034	15,278	25,259	6,238
NY	4,532,748	149,847	253,866	75,784
NC	2,087,443	60,466	120,194	32,847
ND	146,827	3,899	5,900	1,494
OH	2,815,289	68,399	163,816	47,444
OK	878,243	36,641	63,935	12,529
OR	849,172	20,552	32,694	10,368
PA	2,830,694	23,601	23,601	4,571
RI	244,049	7,012	10,362	3,290
SC	1,023,504	18,449	39,396	11,143
SD	195,426	5,534	9,925	4,346
TN	1,394,479	(NA)	46,522	9,421
TX	6,240,162	133,827	215,602	50,522
UT	742,927	20,113	31,679	12,366
VT	137,446	2,936	3,632	1,233
VA	1,798,767	15,975	31,915	6,485
WA	1,496,581	30,222	47,713	6,020
WV	390,901	19,604	43,523	8,875
WI	1,332,894	55,573	41,377	10,174
WY	121,073	2,381	4,529	786

NA Not available.   [1] The number of investigations includes assessments. The number of investigations is based on the total number of investigations that received a disposition in 2001. [2] The number of Children Subject of an Investigation of Assessment is based on the total number of children for whom an alleged maltreatment was substantiated, indicated, or assessed to have occurred or the child was at risk of occurrence. [3] Victims are defined as children subject of a substantiated, indicated, or alternative response-victim maltreatment. [4] Includes estimates for states that did not report.

Source: U.S. Department of Health and Human Services, Administration on Children, Youth and Families. *Child Maltreatment 2003*, (Washington, DC: U. S. Government Printing Office, 2005).

Table 334. Characteristics of Missing Children: 1999

Characteristic	Estimated number of children	Percent	Characteristic	Estimated number of children	Percent
RUNAWAY CHILDREN			FAMILY ABDUCTED CHILDREN		
Characteristic of episode:					
Season:			Characteristic of child:		
Winter	335,400	20	Age:		
Spring	333,600	20	0 to 3 years old	43,400	21
Summer	655,100	39	3 to 5 years old	47,100	23
Fall	343,300	20	6 to 11 years old	71,000	35
Number of miles traveled from home:			12 to 14 years old	35,200	17
2 or less	139,900	8	15 to 17 years old	7,200	4
3 to 10	503,100	30			
12 to 50	521,900	31	Gender:		
52 to 100	160,100	10	Male	100,300	49
More than 101	210,600	13	Female	103,500	51
No information	147,300	9			
Child left the State			Race/Ethnicity:		
Yes	147,600	9	White	119,400	59
No	1,393,000	83	Black	23,900	12
No information	142,300	8	Hispanic	40,600	20
Duration 8 hours to 23 hours	307,400	18	Other	16,200	8
25 hours to 6 days	975,700	58			
1 week to less than 1 month	248,000	15	Family Structure:		
Episode outcome:			Single parent	85,500	42
Child returned	1,676,200	99	One parent and partner	35,300	17
			Relative or foster parent	30,300	15

Source: Office of Justice Programs, Office of Juvenile Justice and Delinquency Prevention, *National Incidence Studies of Missing, Abducted, Runaway and Thrownaway Children*, Octber 2002. See also <http://www.missingkids.com/enUS/documents /nismart2overview.pdf> (issued October 2002).

Table 335. Jail Inmates by Sex, Race, and Hispanic Origin: 1990 to 2003

[As of June 30. Excludes Federal and state prisons or other correctional institutions; institutions exclusively for juveniles; state-operated jails in Alaska, Connecticut, Delaware, Hawaii, Rhode Island, and Vermont; and other facilities which retain persons for less than 72 hours. Data based on the Annual Survey of Jails, which is a sample survey and subject to sampling variability. Due to rounding, inmates may not add to total.]

Characteristic	1990	1995	1998	1999	2000	2001	2002	2003
Total inmates	405,320	507,044	592,462	605,943	621,149	631,240	665,475	691,301
Male	365,821	448,000	520,581	528,998	543,120	551,007	581,411	602,781
Female	37,198	51,300	63,791	67,487	70,414	72,621	76,817	81,650
Juveniles	2,301	7,800	8,090	9,458	7,613	7,613	7,248	6,869
White non-Hispanic	169,600	203,300	244,900	249,900	260,500	271,700	291,800	301,200
Black non-Hispanic	172,300	220,600	244,000	251,800	256,300	256,200	264,900	271,000
Hispanic	58,100	74,400	91,800	93,800	94,100	93,000	98,000	106,600
Other [1]	5,400	8,800	11,800	10,400	10,200	10,300	10,800	12,500

[1] Includes American Indians, Alaska Natives, Asians, and Pacific Islanders.

Source: U.S. Bureau of Justice Statistics, through 1994, Jail Inmates, annual; beginning 1995, *Prison and Jail Inmates at Midyear*, annual.

Table 336. State and Federal Correctional Facilities—Inmates and Staff: 1990 to 2000

[Covers all state and Federal correctional institutions or places of confinement such as prisons, prison farms, boot camps, and community based halfway houses and work release centers. Excludes jails and other regional detention centers, private facilities, facilities for the military, Immigration and Naturalization Service, Bureau of Indian Affairs, U.S. Marshall Service, and correctional hospital wards not operated by correctional authorities]

Characteristic	1990	1995	2000	Characteristic	1990	1995	2000
FACILITIES				INMATES			
Total	1,287	1,464	1,668	Total	715,649	1,023,572	1,305,253
Type of facility:				Male	675,624	961,210	1,219,225
Confinement	1,037	1,160	1,208	Female	40,025	62,362	86,028
Community	250	304	460	Type of facility:			
Federal	80	77	84	Confinement	698,570	992,333	1,244,574
State	1,207	1,387	1,584	Community	17,079	31,239	60,679
Size of facility:				Federal	56,821	80,960	110,974
Fewer than 500 inmates	816	817	860	State	658,828	942,612	1,194,279
500-999 inmates	260	283	305	Custody level:			
1,000-2,499 inmates	185	309	438	Maximum/close/high	150,205	202,174	244,797
2,500 or more inmates	26	55	65	Medium	292,372	415,688	509,558
Age of facility:				Minimum/low	219,907	366,227	474,353
Less than 10 years	314	497	444	Not classified	53,165	39,483	76,545
10-19 years old	163	273	398				
20-49 years old	373	366	380	STAFF			
50-99 years old	379	310	290	Total	264,201	347,320	430,033
100 years old or more	58	45	81	Federal	18,451	25,379	32,700
Not reported	-	9	75	State	245,750	321,941	397,333

- Represents zero.

Source: U.S. Bureau of Justice Statistics, *Census of State and Federal Correctional Facilities, 2000.*

Law Enforcement, Courts, and Prisons   213

Table 337. **Prisoners Under Jurisdiction of State and Federal Correctional Authorities—Summary by State: 1990 to 2003**

[For years ending December 31. Minus sign (-) indicates decrease]

State	1990	2000	2002	2003, advance Total	2003, advance Percent change, 2002-2003	State	1990	2000	2002	2003, advance Total	2003, advance Percent change, 2002-2003
U.S.[1]	773,919	1,391,261	1,440,144	1,470,045	2.1	MO	14,943	27,543	30,099	30,303	0.7
AL	15,665	26,332	27,947	29,253	4.7	MT	1,425	3,105	3,323	3,620	8.9
AK[2]	2,622	4,173	4,398	4,527	2.9	NE	2,403	3,895	4,058	4,040	-0.4
AZ[3]	14,261	26,510	29,359	31,170	6.2	NV	5,322	10,063	10,478	10,543	0.6
AR	7,322	11,915	13,091	13,084	-0.1	NH	1,342	2,257	2,451	2,434	-0.7
CA	97,309	163,001	161,361	164,487	1.9	NJ	21,128	29,784	27,891	27,246	-2.3
CO	7,671	16,833	18,833	19,671	4.4	NM	3,187	5,342	5,991	6,223	3.9
CT[2]	10,500	18,355	20,720	19,846	-4.2	NY	54,895	70,199	67,065	65,198	-2.8
DE[2]	3,471	6,921	6,778	6,794	0.2	NC	18,411	31,266	32,832	33,560	2.2
DC[2,4]	9,947	7,456	(NA)	(NA)	(NA)	ND	483	1,076	1,112	1,239	11.4
FL[3]	44,387	71,319	75,210	79,594	5.8	OH	31,822	45,833	45,646	44,778	-1.9
GA[3]	22,411	44,232	47,445	47,208	-0.5	OK	12,285	23,181	22,802	22,821	0.1
HI[2]	2,533	5,053	5,423	5,828	7.5	OR	6,492	10,580	12,085	12,715	5.2
ID	1,961	5,535	5,746	5,887	2.5	PA	22,290	36,847	40,168	40,890	1.8
IL[3]	27,516	45,281	42,693	43,418	1.7	RI[2]	2,392	3,286	3,520	3,527	0.2
IN	12,736	20,125	21,611	23,069	6.7	SC	17,319	21,778	23,715	23,719	0.0
IA[3]	3,967	7,955	8,398	8,546	1.8	SD	1,341	2,616	2,918	3,026	3.7
KS	5,775	8,344	8,935	9,132	2.2	TN	10,388	22,166	24,989	25,403	1.7
KY:	9,023	14,919	15,820	16,622	5.1	TX	50,042	166,719	162,003	166,911	3.0
LA	18,599	35,207	36,032	36,047	-	UT[2]	2,496	5,637	5,562	5,763	3.6
ME	1,523	1,679	1,900	2,013	5.9	VT[2]	1,049	1,697	1,863	1,944	4.3
MD	17,848	23,538	24,162	23,791	-1.5	VA	17,593	30,168	34,973	35,067	0.3
MA[3,5]	8,345	10,722	10,329	10,232	-0.9	WA	7,995	14,915	16,062	16,148	0.5
MI[3,5]	34,267	47,718	50,591	49,358	-2.4	WV	1,565	3,856	4,544	4,758	4.7
MN	3,176	6,238	7,129	7,865	10.3	WI	7,465	20,754	22,113	22,614	2.3
MS	8,375	20,241	22,705	23,182	2.1	WY	1,110	1,680	1,737	1,872	7.8

- Represents or rounds to zero. NA Not available. [1] State-level data excludes Federal inmates. [2] Includes both jail and prison inmates (State has combined jail and prison system). [3] Numbers are for custody rather than jurisdiction counts. [4] The transfer of responsibility for sentenced felons from the District of Columbia to the Federal System was completed by year-end 2001. Since June 30, 2000, the inmate population in the District of Columbia has dropped by 5825 inmates. Approximately 58% of the growth in the Federal System in the last 6 months of 2001 was the result of this transfer of responsibility. [5] 1990, data are for custody counts; thereafter, jurisdiction counts are reported.

Source: U.S. Bureau of Justice Statistics, *Prisoners in 2003,* Series NCJ 205335; and earlier reports.

Table 338. **Adults on Probation, in Jail or Prison, or on Parole: 1980 to 2003**

[As of December 31, except jail counts as of June 30]

Year	Total[1]	Percent of adult population	Probation	Jail	Prison	Parole	Male	Female
1980	1,840,400	(NA)	1,118,097	[2]182,288	319,598	220,438	(NA)	(NA)
1981	2,006,600	(NA)	1,225,934	[2]195,085	360,029	225,539	(NA)	(NA)
1982	2,192,600	(NA)	1,357,264	207,853	402,914	224,604	(NA)	(NA)
1983	2,475,100	(NA)	1,582,947	221,815	423,898	246,440	(NA)	(NA)
1984	2,689,200	(NA)	1,740,948	233,018	448,264	266,992	(NA)	(NA)
1985	3,011,500	1.7	1,968,712	254,986	487,593	300,203	2,606,000	405,500
1986	3,239,400	1.8	2,114,621	272,735	526,436	325,638	2,829,100	410,300
1987	3,459,600	1.9	2,247,158	294,092	562,814	355,505	3,021,000	438,600
1988	3,714,100	2.0	2,356,483	341,893	607,766	407,977	3,223,000	491,100
1989	4,055,600	2.2	2,522,125	393,303	683,367	456,803	3,501,600	554,000
1990	4,348,000	2.3	2,670,234	403,019	743,382	531,407	3,746,300	601,700
1991	4,535,600	2.4	2,728,472	424,129	792,535	590,442	3,913,000	622,600
1992	4,762,600	2.5	2,811,611	441,781	850,566	658,601	4,050,300	712,300
1993	4,944,000	2.6	2,903,061	455,500	909,381	676,100	4,215,800	728,200
1994	5,141,300	2.7	2,981,022	479,800	990,147	690,371	4,377,400	763,900
1995	5,335,100	2.8	3,077,861	499,300	1,078,542	679,421	4,513,000	822,100
1996	5,482,700	2.8	3,164,996	510,400	1,127,528	679,733	4,629,900	852,800
1997	5,725,800	2.9	3,296,513	557,974	1,176,564	694,787	4,825,300	900,500
1998	6,126,100	3.1	3,670,441	584,372	1,224,469	696,385	(NA)	(NA)
1999	6,331,400	3.1	3,779,922	596,485	1,287,172	714,457	(NA)	(NA)
2000	6,437,400	3.1	3,826,209	613,534	1,316,333	723,898	(NA)	(NA)
2001	6,584,400	3.1	3,931,731	623,627	1,330,007	732,333	(NA)	(NA)
2002	6,750,500	3.1	4,024,067	658,227	1,367,547	750,934	(NA)	(NA)
2003, advance	6,900,000	3.2	4,073,987	684,432	1,394,319	774,588	(NA)	(NA)

NA Not available. [1] Totals may not add due to individuals having multiple correctional statuses. [2] Estimated.

Source: U.S. Bureau of Justice Statistics, *Correctional Populations in the United States,* annual.

Table 339. **Federal and State Prisoners by Sex: 1980 to 2003**

[Prisoners, as of **December 31**. Includes all persons under jurisdiction of Federal and State authorities rather than those in the custody of such authorities. Represents inmates sentenced to maximum term of more than a year]

Year	Total [1]	Rate [2]	State	Male	Female	Year	Total [1]	Rate [2]	State	Male	Female
1980	315,974	139	295,363	303,643	12,331	1992	846,277	332	780,571	799,776	46,501
1981	353,673	154	331,504	339,375	14,298	1993	932,074	359	857,675	878,037	54,037
1982	395,516	171	371,864	379,075	16,441	1994	1,016,691	389	936,896	956,566	60,125
1983	419,346	179	393,015	401,870	17,476	1995	1,085,022	411	1,001,359	1,021,059	63,963
1984	443,398	188	415,796	424,193	19,205	1996	1,137,722	427	1,048,907	1,068,123	69,599
1985	480,568	202	447,873	459,223	21,345	1997	1,195,498	445	1,100,511	1,121,663	73,835
1986	522,084	217	485,553	497,540	24,544	1998	1,245,402	461	1,141,720	1,167,802	77,600
1987	560,812	231	521,289	533,990	26,822	1999	1,304,074	476	1,189,799	1,221,611	82,463
1988	603,732	247	560,994	573,587	30,145	2000	1,331,278	[3]470	1,204,323	1,246,234	85,044
1989	680,907	276	633,739	643,643	37,264	2001	1,345,217	470	1,208,708	1,260,033	85,184
1990	739,980	297	689,577	699,416	40,564	2002	1,380,516	476	1,237,476	1,291,450	89,066
1991	789,610	313	732,914	745,808	43,802	2003	1,409,280	482	1,257,361	1,316,495	92,785

[1] Includes federal. [2] Rate per 100,000 estimated population. Based on U.S. Census Bureau estimated resident population. [3] Decrease in incarceration rate from 1999 to 2000 due to use of new Census numbers.

Source: U.S. Bureau of Justice Statistics, *Prisoners in State and Federal Institutions on December 31*, annual.

Table 340. **Prisoners Under Sentence of Death by Characteristic: 1980 to 2003**

[**As of December 31**. Excludes prisoners under sentence of death who remained within local correctional systems pending exhaustion of appellate process or who had not been committed to prison]

Characteristic	1980	1990	1994	1995	1996	1997	1998	1999	2000	2001	2002	2003
Total [1, 2]	688	2,346	2,905	3,064	3,242	3,328	3,465	3,540	3,601	3,577	3,562	3,374
White	418	1,368	1,653	1,732	1,833	1,864	1,917	1,960	1,989	1,968	1,939	1,878
Black and other	270	978	1,252	1,332	1,409	1,464	1,548	1,580	1,612	1,609	1,623	1,496
Under 20 years	11	8	19	20	17	16	16	16	16	11	4	1
20 to 24 years	173	168	231	264	288	275	273	251	237	192	153	133
25 to 34 years	334	1,110	1,088	1,068	1,088	1,077	1,108	1,108	1,103	1,099	1,058	965
35 to 54 years	186	1,006	1,449	1,583	1,711	1,809	1,897	1,958	2,019	2,043	2,069	1,969
55 years and over	10	64	103	119	138	151	171	194	223	243	273	306
Years of school completed:												
7 years or less	68	178	186	191	196	205	208	201	214	212	215	213
8 years	74	186	198	195	201	206	218	221	233	236	234	227
9 to 11 years	204	775	930	979	1,040	1,069	1,122	1,142	1,157	1,145	1,130	1,073
12 years	162	729	939	995	1,037	1,084	1,128	1,157	1,184	1,183	1,173	1,108
More than 12 years	43	209	255	272	282	288	301	307	315	304	294	270
Unknown	163	279	382	422	486	476	488	499	490	501	511	483
Marital status:												
Never married	268	998	1,320	1,412	1,507	1,555	1,645	1,689	1,749	1,763	1,746	1,641
Married	229	632	707	718	739	740	752	731	739	716	709	684
Divorced [3]	217	726	863	924	996	1,033	1,068	1,107	1,105	1,102	1,102	1,049
Time elapsed since sentencing:												
Less than 12 months	185	231	280	287	306	262	293	259	208	151	147	137
12 to 47 months	389	753	755	784	816	844	816	800	786	734	609	495
48 to 71 months	102	438	379	423	447	456	482	499	507	476	468	451
72 months and over	38	934	1,476	1,560	1,673	1,766	1,874	1,969	2,092	2,220	2,333	2,291
Legal status at arrest:												
Not under sentence	384	1,345	1,662	1,764	1,881	1,957	2,036	2,088	2,202	2,189	2,165	2,048
Parole or probation [4]	115	578	800	866	894	880	879	886	921	918	909	845
Prison or escaped	45	128	103	110	112	116	127	125	126	135	141	137
Unknown	170	305	325	314	355	375	423	428	344	339	342	344

[1] Revisions to the total number of prisoners were not carried to the characteristics except for race. [2] Includes races not shown separately. [3] Includes persons married but separated, widows, widowers, and unknown. [4] Includes prisoners on mandatory conditional release, work release, leave, AWOL, or bail. Covers 28 prisoners in 1990, and 29 in 1991 and 1992, 33 in 1993 and 1995, 31 in 1994 and 1996, 30 in 1997, 26 in 1998, 21 in 1999 and 2000, and 17 in 2001 2002 and 2003.

Source: U.S. Bureau of Justice Statistics, *Capital Punishment*, annual. See also <http://www.ojp.usdoj.gov/bjs/pub/pdf/cp03.pdf> (Released November 2003).

U.S. Census Bureau, *Statistical Abstract of the United States: 2006*

Table 341. **Movement of Prisoners Under Sentence of Death: 1980 to 2003**

[Prisoners reported under sentence of death by civil authorities. The term "under sentence of death" begins when the court pronounces the first sentence of death for a capital offense]

Status	1980	1990	1994	1995	1996	1997	1998	1999	2000	2001	2002	2003
Under sentence of death, Jan. 1	595	2,243	2,727	2,905	3,064	3,242	3,328	3,465	3,540	3,601	3,577	3,562
Received death sentence [1]	203	244	306	310	299	256	285	272	214	155	159	144
White	125	147	162	168	174	146	145	157	122	89	83	92
Black	77	94	136	138	119	106	132	104	86	61	73	44
Dispositions other than executions	101	108	112	105	99	89	93	112	76	109	108	267
Executions	-	23	31	56	45	74	68	98	85	66	71	65
Under sentence of death, Dec. 31 [1,2]	688	2,346	2,890	3,054	3,242	3,335	3,452	3,527	3,593	3,581	3,557	3,374
White	418	1,368	1,653	1,732	1,833	1,864	1,977	1,960	1,989	1,968	1,939	1,878
Black	268	940	1,197	1,275	1,358	1,406	1,486	1,514	1,535	1,538	1,554	1,418

- Represents zero. [1] Includes races other than White or Black. [2] Revisions to total number of prisoners under death sentence not carried to this category.

Source: U.S. Bureau of Justice Statistics, *Capital Punishment,* annual. See also <http://www.ojp.usdoj.gov/bjs/pub/pdf/cp03.pdf>.

Table 342. **Prisoners Executed Under Civil Authority by Sex and Race: 1930 to 2004**

[Excludes executions by military authorities. The Army (including the Air Force) carried out 160 (148 between 1942 and 1950; 3 each in 1954, 1955, and 1957; and 1 each in 1958, 1959, and 1961). Of the total, 106 were executed for murder (including 21 involving rape), 53 for rape, and 1 for desertion. The Navy carried out no executions during the period]

Year or period	Total [1]	Male	Female	White	Black	Executed for murder Total [1]	White	Black
All years, 1930-2004 ...	4,803	4,761	42	2,358	2,388	4,278	2,271	1,952
1930 to 1939	1,667	1,656	11	827	816	1,514	803	687
1940 to 1949 [2]	1,284	1,272	12	490	781	1,064	458	595
1950 to 1959 [2]	717	709	8	336	376	601	316	280
1960 to 1967	191	190	1	98	93	155	87	68
1968 to 1976	-	-	-	-	-	-	-	-
1977 to 2004	944	934	10	607	322	944	607	322
1985	18	18	-	11	7	18	11	7
1986	18	18	-	11	7	18	11	7
1987	25	25	-	13	12	25	13	12
1988	11	11	-	6	5	11	6	5
1989	16	16	-	8	8	16	8	8
1990	23	23	-	16	7	23	16	7
1991	14	14	-	7	7	14	7	7
1992	31	31	-	19	11	31	19	11
1993	38	38	-	23	14	38	23	14
1994	31	31	-	20	11	31	20	11
1995	56	56	-	33	22	56	33	22
1996	45	45	-	31	14	45	31	14
1997	74	74	-	45	27	74	45	27
1998	68	66	2	48	18	68	48	18
1999	98	98	-	61	33	98	61	33
2000	85	83	2	49	35	85	49	35
2001	66	63	3	48	17	66	48	17
2002	71	69	2	53	18	71	53	18
2003	65	65	-	44	20	65	44	20
2004	59	59	-	39	19	59	39	19

- Represents zero. [1] Includes races other than White or Black. [2] Includes 25 armed robbery, 20 kidnapping, 11 burglary, 8 espionage (6 in 1942 and 2 in 1953), and 6 aggravated assault.

Source: Through 1978, U.S. Law Enforcement Assistance Administration; thereafter, U.S. Bureau of Justice Statistics, *Correctional Populations in the United States,* annual; and *Capital Punishment,* annual.

Table 343. **Prisoners Under Sentence of Death and Executed Under Civil Authority by State: 1977 to 2004**

[Alaska, District of Columbia, Hawaii, Iowa, Maine, Massachusetts, Michigan, Minnesota, New York, North Dakota, Rhode Island, Vermont, West Virginia, and Wisconsin are jurisdictions without a death penalty]

State	1977 to 2004	2000	2002	2003	2004	State	1977 to 2004	2000	2002	2003	2004	State	1977 to 2004	2000	2002	2003	2004
U.S..	944	85	71	65	59	IL	12	-	-	-	-	OK ...	75	11	7	14	6
						IN	11	-	-	2	-	OR ...	2	-	-	-	-
AL ...	30	4	2	3	2	KY ...	2	-	-	-	-	PA ...	3	-	-	-	-
AZ ...	22	3	-	-	-	LA ...	27	1	1	-	-	SC ...	32	1	3	-	4
AR ...	26	2	-	1	1	MD ...	4	-	-	-	1	TN ...	1	1	-	-	-
CA ...	10	1	1	-	-	MS ...	6	-	2	-	-	TX ...	336	40	33	24	23
DE ...	13	1	-	-	-	MO ...	61	5	6	2	-	UT ...	6	-	-	-	-
FL ...	59	6	3	3	2	NE ...	3	-	-	-	-	VA ...	94	8	4	2	5
GA ...	36	-	4	3	2	NV ...	11	-	-	-	2	WA ...	4	-	-	-	-
ID	1	-	-	-	-	NC ...	34	1	2	7	4	WY ...	1	-	-	-	-

- Represents zero.

Source: Through 1978, U.S. Law Enforcement Assistance Administration; thereafter, U.S. Bureau of Justice Statistics, *Capital Punishment,* annual.

Table 344. **Fire Losses—Total and Percent Change: 1980 to 2003**

[5,579 represents $5,579,000,000. Includes allowance for uninsured and unreported losses]

Year	Total (mil. dol.)	Per capita [1] (dol.)	Year	Total (mil. dol.)	Per capita [1] (dol.)	Year	Total (mil. dol.)	Per capita [1] (dol.)
1980	5,579	24.56	1988	9,626	39.11	1996	12,544	47.29
1981	5,625	24.53	1989	9,514	38.33	1997	12,940	48.32
1982	5,894	25.61	1990	9,495	38.07	1998	11,510	45.59
1983	6,320	27.20	1991	11,302	44.82	1999	12,428	45.58
1984	7,602	32.35	1992	13,588	53.28	2000	13,457	47.68
1985	7,753	32.70	1993	11,331	43.96	2001 [2]	17,118	60.00
1986	8,488	35.21	1994	12,778	49.08	2002	17,586	61.07
1987	8,504	34.96	1995	11,887	45.23	2003	19,487	67.01

[1] Based on U.S. Census Bureau resident population as of July 1. [2] Excludes fire losses related to 9/11 terrorist attack.

Source: Insurance Information Institute, New York, NY, *The Fact Book, Property/Casualty Insurance Facts*, annual (copyright).

Table 345. **Fires—Number and Loss, by Type and Property Use: 2000 to 2003**

[Number of **1,708** represents 1,708,000 and property loss of **10,024** represents $10,024,000,000. Based on annual sample survey of fire departments. No adjustments were made for unreported fires and losses. Property loss includes direct property loss only]

Type and property use	Number (1,000)				Property loss (mil. dol.)			
	2000	2001	2002	2003	2000	2001	2002	2003
Fires, total	**1,708**	**1,734**	**1,688**	**1,584**	[1, 2]**10,207**	**44,023**	**10,337**	**12,367**
Structure	506	521	519	520	[2]8,501	42,314	8,742	8,678
Outside of structure [3]	69	75	71	66	214	86	121	162
Brush and rubbish	670	623	603	550	-	-	-	-
Vehicle	349	351	330	312	1,381	1,512	1,392	1,356
Other	114	164	165	136	111	111	82	[4]2,171
Structure by property use:								
Public assembly	15	15	14	14	365	336	342	302
Educational	7	7	7	7	108	170	92	69
Institutional	7	7	7	7	20	27	26	28
Stores and offices	24	26	24	25	[2]587	34,155	604	721
Residential	380	396	401	402	5,674	5,643	6,055	6,074
1-2 family units [5]	284	295	301	297	4,639	4,652	5,005	5,052
Apartments	85	88	88	92	886	864	926	897
Other residential [6]	11	13	12	13	149	127	124	125
Storage [7]	33	34	32	32	694	930	627	675
Industry, utility, defense [7]	15	13	12	11	778	858	658	625
Special structures	25	23	22	22	275	195	338	184

- Represents zero. [1] Includes $1 billion in property damage in the Cerro Grande, New Mexico Wildland Fire. Property loss by specific property type was not available. [2] Includes $33.4 billion in property loss that occured due to the events of September 11, 2001. [3] Includes outside storage, crops, timber, etc. 1998 property loss data include $390 million loss in timber from Florida wildfires. [4] Includes Southern California wildfires where there was an estimated $2.044 billion in property loss. [5] Includes mobile homes. [6] Includes hotels and motels, college dormitories, boarding houses, etc. [7] Data underreported as some incidents were handled by private fire brigades or fixed suppression systems which do not report.

Source: National Fire Protection Association, Quincy, MA, "2003 U.S. Fire Loss," *NFPA Journal*, November 2004, and prior issues (copyright 2004).

Table 346. **Fires and Property Loss for Incendiary and Suspicious Fires and Civilian Fire Deaths and Injuries, by Selected Property Type: 2000 to 2003**

[506 represents 506,000. Based on sample survey of fire departments]

Characteristic	2000	2001	2002	2003	Characteristic	2000	2001	2002	2003
NUMBER (1,000)					CIVILIAN FIRE DEATHS				
Structure fires, total	**506**	**521**	**519**	**520**	**Deaths, total [3]**	**4,045**	[4]**6,196**	**3,380**	**3,925**
Structure fires of incendiary or suspicious origin	75	-	-	-	Residential property	3,445	3,140	2,695	3,165
Fires of incendiary origin	46	46	45	38	One- and two-family dwellings	2,920	2,650	2,280	2,735
Fires of suspicious origin	29	-	-	-	Apartments	500	460	390	410
					Vehicles	465	485	565	475
PROPERTY LOSS [1] (mil. dol.)					CIVILIAN FIRE INJURIES				
Structure fires, total	**8,501**	[2]**42,314**	**8,742**	**8,678**	**Injuries, total [3]**	**22,350**	[5]**21,100**	**18,425**	**18,125**
Structure fires of incendiary or suspicious origin	1,340	-	-	-	Residential property	17,400	15,575	14,050	14,075
Fires of incendiary origin	792	[2]34,453	919	692	One- and two-family dwellings	12,575	11,400	9,950	10,000
Fires of suspicious origin	548	-	-	-	Apartments	4,400	3,800	3,700	3,650
					Vehicles	1,600	1,875	1,125	1,600

- Represents zero. [1] Direct property loss only. [2] Includes $33.44 billion in property loss due to the events of September 11, 2001. [3] Includes other not shown separately. [4] Includes 2,451 civilian deaths due to the events of September 11, 2001. [5] Includes 800 civilian fire injuries due to the events of September 11, 2001.

Source: National Fire Protection Association, Quincy, MA, "2003 U.S. Fire Loss," *NFPA Journal*, November 2004, and prior issues (copyright 2004).

Law Enforcement, Courts, and Prisons 217

No. 168.—AREA IN ACRES OF ORIGINAL HOMESTEAD ENTRIES IN EACH STATE AND TERRITORY OF THE UNITED STATES DURING EACH YEAR ENDING JUNE 30, FROM 1880 to 1889, INCLUSIVE.

[From the Annual Report of the Commissioner of the General Office.]

States and Territories.	1880.	1881.	1882.	1883.	1884.	1885.	1886.	1887.	1888.	1889.
	Acres.	Acres.	Acres.	Acres.	Acres.	Acres.	Acres.	Acres.	Acres.	Acres.
Alabama	310,885.72	300,872.88	256,123.44	256,733.09	284,996.52	165,821.27	197,687.66	338,722.87	348,007.54	231,287.07
Arizona	7,056.69	8,037.43	8,402.84	10,422.81	14,762.85	48,678.60	28,027.36	24,337.90	53,456.18	31,085.73
Arkansas	372,437.52	408,511.41	365,913.98	353,824.00	275,187.10	218,055.17	240,881.44	337,769.45	329,136.76	306,191.40
California	229,784.18	247,546.62	285,651.96	299,800.12	427,761.65	434,209.26	472,116.67	601,574.79	677,050.37	408,124.84
Colorado	98,092.28	116,550.99	136,406.88	210,600.43	198,894.92	176,214.39	281,801.14	601,574.79	1,007,554.68	526,777.64
Dakota	1,328,945.66	1,366,572.18	2,208,268.04	2,497,266.68	2,161,297.68	1,218,478.12	1,185,138.37	746,203.70	597,368.53	583,052.08
Florida	86,213.82	104,201.17	191,053.22	212,805.66	266,013.01	175,553.45	130,274.96	107,928.88	132,812.40	78,530.12
Idaho	63,941.12	64,555.01	90,632.00	90,907.61	118,871.56	110,493.73	102,332.58	85,181.22	111,229.95	105,583.50
Illinois										120.00
Indiana		40.00	40.00	56.70	184.40					161.25
Indian Territory					40.00			122.53		905,062.10
Iowa	3,131.78	1,683.82	3,124.14	1,992.61	2,293.23	1,434.76	067.69	1,079.84	20,755.14	2,679.64
Kansas	1,061,512.77	447,347.04	537,349.07	508,780.19	514,726.34	1,590,972.17	2,324,214.59	1,974,549.98	876,484.89	844,800.84
Louisiana	81,525.24	96,628.77	116,703.70	124,660.19	145,610.39	92,810.28	81,647.38	48,904.83	161,411.36	151,809.57
Michigan	118,387.66	87,572.70	103,465.57	70,173.12	71,656.30	55,981.12	56,550.35	49,383.73	60,667.00	113,960.00
Minnesota	682,408.06	588,343.01	138,486.30	431,672.75	444,358.50	280,211.91	225,810.06	288,052.90	262,672.15	181,099.43
Mississippi	55,901.26	109,517.66	134,222.68	167,079.80	145,896.92	97,619.23	95,874.39	90,047.63	124,919.93	131,338.92
Missouri	92,046.17	105,266.65	471,939.05	206,233.16	320,649.41	260,361.84	244,155.38	206,946.88	181,185.88	168,957.49
Montana	40,514.90	56,361.46	64,682.59	81,213.01	81,821.82	70,561.72	68,633.37	66,461.58	77,697.05	85,407.86
Nebraska	830,441.10	365,922.00		716,509.90	1,362,106.23	1,748,841.54	1,590,410.71	1,068,656.01	830,676.77	622,626.90
Nevada	8,015.61	6,064.01	4,540.06	3,887.30	2,079.37	1,781.94	2,117.96	1,576.69	2,087.19	640.00
New Mexico	10,189.15	73,852.50	86,706.77	151,800.87	78,523.56	68,075.81	67,894.29	57,909.48	64,730.39	59,397.35
Ohio			91.00	40.00					240.00	
Oregon	138,653.72	112,094.46	153,532.46	226,362.04	233,148.55	191,444.04	287,231.28	225,278.54	240,965.04	257,080.36
Utah	68,600.55	54,442.57	54,745.43	88,639.00	50,691.46	65,838.81	76,975.37	45,513.08	49,355.44	41,809.33
Washington	240,820.14	227,902.56	231,132.06	375,735.94	419,365.13	259,264.34	290,513.13	269,499.75	323,070.88	480,635.79
Wisconsin	114,742.14	98,463.27	98,478.05	113,567.04	133,241.72	109,517.66	105,700.52	101,576.22	80,116.91	75,927.73
Wyoming	8,337.08	9,216.51	17,387.56	27,746.98	44,153.73	46,196.28	59,477.62	62,334.81	63,959.98	74,712.29
Total	6,045,570.60	5,025,100.69	6,348,045.05	8,171,914.58	7,831,509.88	7,415,885.58	9,145,185.76	7,594,350.16	8,676,615.93	6,029,220.26

Section 6
Geography and Environment

This section presents a variety of information on the physical environment of the United States, starting with basic area measurement data and ending with climatic data for selected weather stations around the country. The subjects covered between those points are mostly concerned with environmental trends but include related subjects such as land use, water consumption, air pollutant emissions, toxic releases, oil spills, hazardous waste sites, municipal waste and recycling, threatened and endangered wildlife, and the environmental industry.

The information in this section is selected from a wide range of federal agencies that compile the data for various administrative or regulatory purposes, such as the Environmental Protection Agency (EPA), U.S. Geological Survey (USGS), National Oceanic and Atmospheric Administration (NOAA), Natural Resources Conservation Service (NRCS), and General Services Administration (GSA). New information on hazardous waste generation and shipment by state and federal funding for several environmental programs may be found in Tables 370 and 371.

Area—For the 2000 census, area measurements were calculated by computer based on the information contained in a single, consistent geographic database, the Topologically Integrated Geographic Encoding & Referencing system (TIGER®) database, rather than relying on historical, local, and manually calculated information. Information from the 2000 census may be found in Table 346.

Geography—The USGS conducts investigations, surveys, and research in the fields of geography, geology, topography, geographic information systems, mineralogy, hydrology, and geothermal energy resources as well as natural hazards. The USGS provides United States cartographic

data through the Earth Sciences Information Center, water resources data through the National Water Data Exchange (NAWDEX), and a variety of research and Open-File reports which are announced monthly in *New Publications of the USGS*.

In a joint project with the U.S. Census Bureau, during the 1980s, the USGS provided the basic information on geographic features for input into a national geographic and cartographic database prepared by the Census Bureau, called TIGER® database. Since then, using a variety of sources, the Census Bureau has updated these features and their related attributes (names, descriptions, etc.) and inserted current information on the boundaries, names, and codes of legal and statistical geographic entities; very few of these updates added aerial water features. Maps prepared by the Census Bureau using the TIGER® database show the names and boundaries of entities and are available on a current basis.

The U.S. Census Bureau uses the Boundary and Annexation Survey to maintain a current inventory of government units and their legal boundaries. The information is available to the public online. There are also several series of maps for Census 2000: P.L. County Block Maps, Census Tract Outline Maps, and Voting District/State Legislative District Outline Maps. These maps can be obtained online via the American Fact-Finder®.

An inventory of the nation's land resources by type of use/cover was conducted by the National Resources Inventory Conservation Service every 5 years beginning in 1977. The most recent survey results, which were published in the 1997 National Resources Inventory, cover

U.S. Census Bureau, Statistical Abstract of the United States: 2006

all nonfederal land in Puerto Rico, the Virgin Islands, and the United States except Alaska. Tables 349 to 351 provide results from the survey. Beginning with the release of the 2001 estimates, this program will shift to become an annual release of land use data.

Environment —The principal federal agency responsible for pollution abatement and control activities is the Environmental Protection Agency (EPA). It is responsible for establishing and monitoring national air quality standards, water quality activities, solid and hazardous waste disposal, and control of toxic substances. Many of these series now appear in the Envirofacts portion of the EPA Web site at <http://www.epa.gov/enviro/>. In 2003, EPA released a major compilation of environmental indicators, entitled *Draft Report on the Environment: 2003*, found at <http://www.epa.govindicators/roe/htm/roeTOC.htm>. A new series of reports (technical, public, and electronic) are planned for 2006.

National Ambient Air Quality Standards (NAAQS) for suspended particulate matter, sulfur dioxide, photochemical oxidants, carbon monoxide, and nitrogen dioxide were originally set by the EPA in April 1971. Every 5 years, each of the NAAQS is reviewed and revised to include any additional or new health or welfare data. The standard for photochemical oxidants, now called ozone, was revised in February 1979. Also, a new NAAQS for confining lead was promulgated in October 1978 and for suspended particulate matter in 1987. Table 359 gives some of the health-related standards for the six air pollutants having NAAQS. Data gathered from state networks are periodically submitted to EPA's National Aerometric Information Retrieval System (AIRS) for summarization in annual reports on the nationwide status and trends in air quality. For details, see *National Air Quality and Emissions Trends Report*. More current information on emissions may be found on the EPA Web site at <http://www.epa.gov/airtrends>.

The Toxics Release Inventory (TRI), published by the EPA, is a valuable source of information on nearly 650 chemicals that are being used, manufactured, treated, transported, or released into the environment. Sections 313 of the Emergency Planning and Community Right-To-Know Act (EPCRA) and 6607 of the Pollution Prevention Act (PPA), mandate that a publicly-accessible toxic chemical database be developed and maintained by EPA. This database, known as the TRI, contains information concerning waste management activities and the release of toxic chemicals by facilities that manufacture, process, or otherwise use said materials. Data on the release of these chemicals are collected from over 23,000 facilities and facilities added in 1998 that have the equivalent of 10 or more full-time employees and meet the established thresholds for manufacturing, processing, or "other use" of listed chemicals. Facilities must report their releases and other waste management quantities. Since 1994 federal facilities have been required to report their data regardless of industry classification. In May 1997, EPA added seven new industry sectors that reported to the TRI for the first time in July 1999 for the 1998 reporting year.

Climate—NOAA, through the National Weather Service and the National Environmental Satellite, Data, and Information Service, is responsible for climate data. NOAA maintains about 11,600 weather stations, of which over 3,000 produce autographic precipitation records, about 600 take hourly readings of a series of weather elements, and the remainder record data once a day. These data are reported monthly in the Climatological Data and Storm Data, published monthly and annually in the Local Climatological Data (published by location for major cities).

The normal climatological temperatures, precipitation, and degree days listed in this publication are derived for comparative purposes and are averages for the 30-year period, 1971–2000. For stations that did not have continuous records for the entire 30 years from the same instrument site, the normals have been adjusted to provide representative values for the current location. The information in all other tables is based on data from the beginning of the record at that location through 2003.

Table 347. Land and Water Area of States and Other Entities: 2000

[One square mile = 2.59 square kilometers. Area is calculated from the specific boundary recorded for each entity in the U.S. Census Bureau's geographic TIGER database]

State and other area	Total area Sq. mi.	Sq. km.	Land area Sq. mi.	Sq. km.	Water area Total Sq. mi.	Sq. km.	Inland (sq. mi.)	Coastal (sq. mi.)	Great Lakes (sq. mi.)	Territorial (sq. mi.)
Total	3,800,286	9,842,696	3,540,999	9,171,146	259,287	671,550	79,018	42,241	60,251	77,777
United States	3,794,083	9,826,630	3,537,438	9,161,923	256,645	664,707	78,797	42,225	60,251	75,372
Alabama	52,419	135,765	50,744	131,426	1,675	4,338	956	519	-	200
Alaska	663,267	1,717,854	571,951	1,481,347	91,316	236,507	17,243	27,049	-	47,024
Arizona	113,998	295,254	113,635	294,312	364	942	364	-	-	-
Arkansas	53,179	137,732	52,068	134,856	1,110	2,876	1,110	-	-	-
California	163,696	423,970	155,959	403,933	7,736	20,037	2,674	222	-	4,841
Colorado	104,094	269,601	103,718	268,627	376	974	376	-	-	-
Connecticut	5,543	14,357	4,845	12,548	699	1,809	161	538	-	-
Delaware	2,489	6,447	1,954	5,060	536	1,388	72	371	-	93
District of Columbia	68	177	61	159	7	18	7	-	-	-
Florida	65,755	170,304	53,927	139,670	11,828	30,634	4,672	1,311	-	5,845
Georgia	59,425	153,909	57,906	149,976	1,519	3,933	1,016	48	-	455
Hawaii	10,931	28,311	6,423	16,635	4,508	11,677	38	-	-	4,470
Idaho	83,570	216,446	82,747	214,314	823	2,131	823	-	-	-
Illinois	57,914	149,998	55,584	143,961	2,331	6,037	756	-	1,575	-
Indiana	36,418	94,321	35,867	92,895	551	1,427	316	-	235	-
Iowa	56,272	145,743	55,869	144,701	402	1,042	402	-	-	-
Kansas	82,277	213,096	81,815	211,900	462	1,197	462	-	-	-
Kentucky	40,409	104,659	39,728	102,896	681	1,763	681	-	-	-
Louisiana	51,840	134,264	43,562	112,825	8,278	21,440	4,154	1,935	-	2,189
Maine	35,385	91,646	30,862	79,931	4,523	11,715	2,264	613	-	1,647
Maryland	12,407	32,133	9,774	25,314	2,633	6,819	680	1,843	-	110
Massachusetts	10,555	27,336	7,840	20,306	2,715	7,031	423	977	-	1,314
Michigan	96,716	250,494	56,804	147,121	39,912	103,372	1,611	-	38,301	-
Minnesota	86,939	225,171	79,610	206,189	7,329	18,982	4,783	-	2,546	-
Mississippi	48,430	125,434	46,907	121,489	1,523	3,945	785	590	-	148
Missouri	69,704	180,533	68,886	178,414	818	2,120	818	-	-	-
Montana	147,042	380,838	145,552	376,979	1,490	3,859	1,490	-	-	-
Nebraska	77,354	200,345	76,872	199,099	481	1,247	481	-	-	-
Nevada	110,561	286,351	109,826	284,448	735	1,903	735	-	-	-
New Hampshire	9,350	24,216	8,968	23,227	382	989	314	-	-	68
New Jersey	8,721	22,588	7,417	19,211	1,304	3,377	396	401	-	507
New Mexico	121,590	314,915	121,356	314,309	234	606	234	-	-	-
New York	54,556	141,299	47,214	122,283	7,342	19,016	1,895	981	3,988	479
North Carolina	53,819	139,389	48,711	126,161	5,108	13,229	3,960	-	-	1,148
North Dakota	70,700	183,112	68,976	178,647	1,724	4,465	1,724	-	-	-
Ohio	44,825	116,096	40,948	106,056	3,877	10,040	378	-	3,499	-
Oklahoma	69,898	181,036	68,667	177,847	1,231	3,189	1,231	-	-	-
Oregon	98,381	254,805	95,997	248,631	2,384	6,174	1,050	80	-	1,254
Pennsylvania	46,055	119,283	44,817	116,075	1,239	3,208	490	-	749	-
Rhode Island	1,545	4,002	1,045	2,706	500	1,295	178	9	-	314
South Carolina	32,020	82,932	30,110	77,983	1,911	4,949	1,008	72	-	831
South Dakota	77,117	199,731	75,885	196,540	1,232	3,191	1,232	-	-	-
Tennessee	42,143	109,151	41,217	106,752	926	2,399	926	-	-	-
Texas	268,581	695,621	261,797	678,051	6,784	17,570	5,056	404	-	1,324
Utah	84,899	219,887	82,144	212,751	2,755	7,136	2,755	-	-	-
Vermont	9,614	24,901	9,250	23,956	365	945	365	-	-	-
Virginia	42,774	110,785	39,594	102,548	3,180	8,237	1,006	1,728	-	446
Washington	71,300	184,665	66,544	172,348	4,756	12,317	1,553	2,537	-	666
West Virginia	24,230	62,755	24,078	62,361	152	394	152	-	-	-
Wisconsin	65,498	169,639	54,310	140,663	11,188	28,976	1,830	-	9,358	-
Wyoming	97,814	253,336	97,100	251,489	713	1,847	713	-	-	-
Other areas:										
Puerto Rico	5,325	13,790	3,425	8,870	1,900	4,921	67	16	-	1,817
U.S. Minor Outlying Islands	141	365	3	7	138	359	138	-	-	-
Virgin Islands of the U.S.	737	1,910	134	346	604	1,564	16	-	-	588

- Represents or rounds to zero.

Source: U.S. Census Bureau, 2000 Census of Population and Housing, *Summary Population and Housing Characteristics,* Series PHC-1; and unpublished data from the Census TIGER™ data base.

Geography and Environment 221

Table 348. **Total and Federally Owned Land by State: 2003**

[(2,271,343 represents 2,271,343,000). As of September 30. Total land area figures are not comparable with those in Table 347]

State	Total (1,000 acres)	Not owned by federal government (1,000 acres)	Owned by federal government [1] Acres (1,000)	Owned by federal government [1] Per- cent	State	Total (1,000 acres)	Not owned by federal govern- ment (1,000 acres)	Owned by federal government [1] Acres (1,000)	Owned by federal government [1] Per- cent
United States...	2,271,343	1,599,584	671,759	29.6	Mississippi......	30,223	28,122	2,101	7.0
					Missouri	44,248	42,010	2,238	5.1
Alabama........	32,678	31,476	1,203	3.7	Montana	93,271	64,032	29,239	31.3
Alaska	365,482	121,635	243,847	66.7	Nebraska	49,032	47,573	1,459	3.0
Arizona........	72,688	36,193	36,495	50.2	Nevada.........	70,264	5,675	64,589	91.9
Arkansas.......	33,599	29,643	3,956	11.8	New Hampshire ...	5,769	4,939	830	14.4
California.......	100,207	53,227	46,980	46.9	New Jersey......	4,813	4,633	180	3.7
Colorado........	66,486	43,311	23,174	34.9	New Mexico......	77,766	51,248	26,518	34.1
Connecticut	3,135	3,120	15	0.5	New York	30,681	30,439	242	0.8
Delaware........	1,266	1,236	29	2.3	North Carolina	31,403	27,801	3,602	11.5
District					North Dakota	44,452	43,119	1,333	3.0
of Columbia	39	29	10	26.3	Ohio...........	26,222	25,764	458	1.7
Florida	34,721	30,116	4,606	13.3	Oklahoma.......	44,088	42,756	1,331	3.0
Georgia	37,295	34,981	2,314	6.2	Oregon.........	61,599	30,960	30,639	49.7
Hawaii	4,106	3,434	672	16.4	Pennsylvania	28,804	28,080	725	2.5
Idaho..........	52,933	17,797	35,136	66.4	Rhode Island	677	672	5	0.8
Illinois.........	35,795	35,144	652	1.8	South Carolina	19,374	18,138	1,236	6.4
Indiana	23,158	22,624	534	2.3	South Dakota.....	48,882	46,568	2,314	4.7
Iowa...........	35,860	35,558	303	0.8	Tennessee......	26,728	24,712	2,016	7.5
Kansas.........	52,511	51,869	642	1.2	Texas..........	168,218	165,046	3,172	1.9
Kentucky........	25,512	23,806	1,707	6.7	Utah...........	52,697	17,672	35,025	66.5
Louisiana	28,868	27,366	1,502	5.2	Vermont	5,937	5,487	450	7.6
Maine..........	19,848	19,684	164	0.8	Virginia........	25,496	22,879	2,617	10.3
Maryland........	6,319	6,127	193	3.0	Washington	42,694	29,447	13,247	31.0
Massachusetts....	5,035	4,929	106	2.1	West Virginia	15,411	14,144	1,266	8.2
Michigan	36,492	32,854	3,639	10.0	Wisconsin	35,011	33,029	1,982	5.7
Minnesota	51,206	47,671	3,535	6.9	Wyoming........	62,343	30,812	31,532	50.6

[1] Excludes trust properties.

Source: U.S. General Services Administration, *Federal Real Property Profile*, annual. For most recent report, see <http://www.gsa.gov/gsa/cmattachments/GSADOCUMENT/Annual%20Report%20%20FY2003-R4R2M-n110Z5RDZ-i34K-pR.pdf>.

Table 349. **Land Cover/Use by Type: 1982 to 2002**

[In millions of acres (1,937.7 represents 1,937,700,000), except percent. Excludes Alaska and District of Columbia]

Year	Total surface area	Nonfederal rural land Rural land, total [1]	Nonfederal rural land Crop- land	Nonfederal rural land Pasture land	Nonfederal rural land Range- land	Nonfederal rural land Forest land	Nonfederal rural land Other rural land	Devel- oped land	Water areas	Fed- eral land
Land										
1982	1,937.7	1,417.2	420.4	131.4	414.5	402.6	48.3	72.8	48.6	399.1
1992	1,937.6	1,400.2	381.2	125.1	406.6	404.0	49.3	86.5	49.4	401.5
2002	1,937.7	1,378.1	368.4	117.3	405.3	404.9	50.6	107.3	50.4	401.9
Percent of total land										
1982	100.0	73.1	21.7	6.8	21.4	20.8	2.5	3.8	2.5	20.6
1992	100.0	72.3	19.7	6.5	21.0	20.9	2.5	4.5	2.5	20.7
2002	100.0	71.1	19.0	6.1	20.9	20.9	2.6	5.5	2.6	20.7

[1] Includes Conservation Reserve Program land not shown separately.

Source: U.S. Department of Agriculture, Natural Resources and Conservation Service, *National Resources Inventory 2002 Annual NRI, Land Use*, April 2004. See also <http://www.nrcs.usda.gov/technical/land/nri02/landuse.pdf>.

Table 350. **Developed Land by Type: 1982 to 2001**

[In millions of acres (1,937.7 represents 1,937,700,000) except percent. Excludes Alaska and District of Columbia]

Year	Total surface area	Developed land Developed land, total	Developed land Large urban and built-up areas	Developed land Small built-up areas	Developed land Rural trans- portation land
Land					
1982	1,937.7	72.8	46.9	4.7	21.2
1992	1,937.7	86.5	59.6	5.4	21.5
2001	1,937.7	106.3	77.6	6.7	22.0
Percent of total land					
1982	100.0	3.8	2.4	0.2	1.1
1992	100.0	4.5	3.1	0.3	1.1
2001	100.0	5.5	4.0	0.3	1.1

Source: U.S. Department of Agriculture, Natural Resources and Conservation Service, *National Resources Inventory 2001 Annual NRI, Urbanization and Development of Rural Land*, July 2003. See also <http://www.nrcs.usda.gov/technical/land/nri01/urban.pdf> (released July 2003).

Table 351. Land Cover/Use by State: 1997

[In thousands of acres (1,944,130 represents 1,944,130,000), except percent. Excludes Alaska and District of Columbia]

State	Total surface area	Rural land, total	Percent of total	Nonfederal rural land Crop-land	CRP land [1]	Pasture-land	Range-land	Forest-land	Other rural land
Total........	1,944,130	1,393,760	71.7	376,998	32,696	119,992	405,977	406,955	51,142
United States ...	1,941,823	1,392,098	71.7	376,630	32,696	119,549	405,832	406,315	51,077
Alabama.........	33,424	28,950	86.6	2,954	522	3,528	74	21,261	612
Arizona.........	72,964	40,858	56.0	1,212	-	73	32,323	4,216	3,035
Arkansas	34,037	28,638	84.1	7,625	230	5,351	38	15,011	384
California.......	101,510	47,555	46.8	9,635	173	1,049	18,269	13,936	4,494
Colorado........	66,625	40,850	61.3	8,770	1,890	1,211	24,574	3,442	964
Connecticut......	3,195	2,178	68.2	204	-	112	-	1,759	103
Delaware	1,534	988	64.4	485	1	24	-	352	128
Florida..........	37,534	25,498	67.9	2,752	120	4,231	3,229	12,536	2,630
Georgia	37,741	30,648	81.2	4,757	595	2,865	-	21,560	872
Hawaii	4,158	3,565	85.7	246	-	36	1,009	1,635	639
Idaho...........	53,488	18,618	34.8	5,517	785	1,315	6,501	3,948	553
Illinois	36,059	31,675	87.8	24,011	726	2,502	-	3,784	652
Indiana.........	23,158	20,069	86.7	13,407	378	1,830	-	3,781	674
Iowa	36,017	33,673	93.5	25,310	1,739	3,572	-	2,182	870
Kansas.........	52,661	49,685	94.3	26,524	2,849	2,322	15,728	1,546	716
Kentucky	25,863	22,327	86.3	5,178	332	5,686	-	10,667	465
Louisiana	31,377	24,664	78.6	5,659	140	2,385	277	13,226	2,976
Maine...........	20,966	18,794	89.6	413	30	123	-	17,691	537
Maryland	7,870	4,808	61.1	1,616	19	478	-	2,373	321
Massachusetts.....	5,339	3,394	63.6	277	-	119	-	2,744	254
Michigan........	37,349	29,426	78.8	8,540	321	2,032	-	16,354	2,178
Minnesota.......	54,010	45,356	84.0	21,414	1,544	3,434	-	16,248	2,716
Mississippi	30,527	26,429	86.6	5,352	799	3,679	-	16,209	389
Missouri	44,614	39,358	88.2	13,751	1,606	10,849	88	12,431	634
Montana........	94,110	64,958	69.0	15,171	2,721	3,443	36,751	5,431	1,443
Nebraska.......	49,510	47,187	95.3	19,469	1,245	1,801	23,089	826	757
Nevada	70,763	10,079	14.2	701	2	279	8,372	305	420
New Hampshire....	5,941	4,353	73.3	134	-	94	-	3,932	193
New Jersey......	5,216	2,766	53.0	589	1	111	-	1,698	367
New Mexico	77,823	50,071	64.3	1,875	467	231	39,990	5,467	2,041
New York	31,361	26,702	85.1	5,417	54	2,722	-	17,702	808
North Carolina....	33,709	24,592	73.0	5,639	131	2,039	-	15,959	824
North Dakota.....	45,251	41,442	91.6	25,004	2,802	1,129	10,689	454	1,363
Ohio	26,445	22,070	83.5	11,627	324	2,006	-	7,081	1,032
Oklahoma.......	44,738	40,610	90.8	9,737	1,138	7,963	14,033	7,281	459
Oregon.........	62,161	28,858	46.4	3,762	483	1,961	9,286	12,643	724
Pennsylvania.....	28,995	23,816	82.1	5,471	90	1,845	-	15,478	932
Rhode Island.....	813	458	56.3	22	-	25	-	387	24
South Carolina....	19,939	16,018	80.3	2,574	263	1,197	-	11,188	797
South Dakota	49,358	44,411	90.0	16,738	1,686	2,108	21,876	518	1,484
Tennessee	26,974	22,597	83.8	4,644	374	4,990	-	12,042	547
Texas..........	171,052	155,530	90.9	26,938	3,906	15,914	95,745	10,816	2,211
Utah	54,339	17,599	32.4	1,679	216	695	10,733	1,883	2,392
Vermont........	6,154	5,183	84.2	607	-	338	-	4,150	88
Virginia.........	27,087	19,886	73.4	2,918	71	2,995	-	13,316	587
Washington......	44,035	28,508	64.7	6,656	1,017	1,193	5,857	12,835	951
West Virginia.....	15,508	13,252	85.5	864	-	1,527	-	10,582	279
Wisconsin.......	35,920	30,374	84.6	10,613	661	2,994	-	14,448	1,658
Wyoming	62,603	32,773	52.4	2,174	247	1,146	27,302	1,004	900
Caribbean	2,307	1,662	72.0	368	-	443	145	640	65

- Represents or rounds to zero.   [1] Conservation Reserve Program (CRP). A federal program established under the Food Security Act of 1985 to assist private landowners to convert highly erodible cropland to vegetative cover for 10 years.

Source: U.S. Department of Agriculture, Natural Resources and Conservation Service, and Iowa State University, Statistical Laboratory, *Summary Report, 1997 National Resources Inventory*, revised December 2000. See also <http://www.nrcs.usda.gov /technical/NRI/1997/summaryreport/> (revised December 2000).

Geography and Environment 223

Table 352. **Extreme and Mean Elevations by State and Other Area**

[One foot = .305 meter]

State and other areas	Highest point			Lowest point			Approximate mean elevation	
	Name	Elevation		Name	Elevation			
		Feet	Meters		Feet	Meters	Feet	Meters
United States...	Mt. McKinley (AK).......	20,320	6,198	Death Valley (CA)....	-282	-86	2,500	763
AL........	Cheaha Mountain.........	2,405	733	Gulf of Mexico......	(¹)	(¹)	500	153
AK........	Mount McKinley..........	20,320	6,198	Pacific Ocean.......	(¹)	(¹)	1,900	580
AZ........	Humphreys Peak.........	12,633	3,853	Colorado River.....	70	21	4,100	1,251
AR........	Magazine Mountain.......	2,753	840	Ouachita River......	55	17	650	198
CA........	Mount Whitney...........	14,494	4,419	Death Valley........	-282	-86	2,900	885
CO........	Mt. Elbert..............	14,433	4,402	Arkansas River......	3,350	1,022	6,800	2,074
CT........	Mt. Frissell on South slope...	2,380	726	Long Island Sound...	(¹)	(¹)	500	153
DE........	Ebright Road, [2] New Castle County	448	137	Atlantic Ocean......	(¹)	(¹)	60	18
DC........	Tenleytown at Reno Reservoir.	410	125	Potomac River......	1	(Z)	150	46
FL........	Sec. 30, T6N, R20W, Walton County	345	105	Atlantic Ocean.....	(¹)	(¹)	100	31
GA........	Brasstown Bald..........	4,784	1,459	Atlantic Ocean......	(¹)	(¹)	600	183
HI........	Puu Wekiu..............	13,796	4,208	Pacific Ocean......	(¹)	(¹)	3,030	924
ID........	Borah Peak.............	12,662	3,862	Snake River........	710	217	5,000	1,525
IL........	Charles Mound...........	1,235	377	Mississippi River.....	279	85	600	183
IN........	Franklin Twp., Wayne Co....	1,257	383	Ohio River........	320	98	700	214
IA........	Sec. 29, T100N, R41W, Osceola County [3]	1,670	509	Mississippi River....	480	146	1,100	336
KS........	Mount Sunflower..........	4,039	1,232	Verdigris River.....	679	207	2,000	610
KY........	Black Mountain..........	4,139	2,162	Mississippi River.....	257	78	750	229
LA........	Driskill Mountain..........	535	163	New Orleans......	-8	-2	100	31
ME........	Mount Katahdin.........	5,267	1,606	Atlantic Ocean......	(¹)	(¹)	600	183
MD........	Backbone Mountain......	3,360	1,025	Atlantic Ocean......	(¹)	(¹)	350	107
MA........	Mount Greylock.........	3,487	1,064	Atlantic Ocean......	(¹)	(¹)	500	153
MI........	Mount Arvon...........	1,979	604	Lake Erie.........	571	174	900	275
MN........	Eagle Mountain, Cook Co....	2,301	702	Lake Superior......	601	183	1,200	366
MS........	Woodall Mountain.........	806	246	Gulf of Mexico......	(¹)	(¹)	300	92
MO........	Taum Sauk Mountain......	1,772	540	St. Francis River....	230	70	800	244
MT........	Granite Peak...........	12,799	3,904	Kootenai River.....	1,800	549	3,400	1,037
NE........	Johnson Twp., Kimball Co...	5,424	1,654	Missouri River.....	840	256	2,600	793
NV........	Boundary Peak.........	13,140	4,007	Colorado River.....	479	146	5,500	1,678
NH........	Mount Washington........	6,288	1,918	Atlantic Ocean......	(¹)	(¹)	1,000	305
NJ........	High Point..............	1,803	550	Atlantic Ocean......	(¹)	(¹)	250	76
NM........	Wheeler Peak...........	13,161	4,014	Red Bluff Reservoir...	2,842	867	5,700	1,739
NY........	Mount Marcy...........	5,344	1,630	Atlantic Ocean......	(¹)	(¹)	1,000	305
NC........	Mount Mitchell..........	6,684	2,039	Atlantic Ocean......	(¹)	(¹)	700	214
ND........	White Butte, Slope Co.....	3,506	1,069	Red River........	750	229	1,900	580
OH........	Campbell Hill...........	1,549	472	Ohio River........	455	139	850	259
OK........	Black Mesa............	4,973	1,517	Little River........	289	88	1,300	397
OR........	Mount Hood............	11,239	3,428	Pacific Ocean......	(¹)	(¹)	3,300	1,007
PA........	Mount Davis............	3,213	980	Delaware River.....	(¹)	(¹)	1,100	336
RI........	Jerimoth Hill............	812	248	Atlantic Ocean.....	(¹)	(¹)	200	61
SC........	Sassafras Mountain.......	3,560	1,086	Atlantic Ocean......	(¹)	(¹)	350	107
SD........	Harney Peak...........	7,242	2,209	Big Stone Lake....	966	295	2,200	671
TN........	Clingmans Dome.........	6,643	2,026	Mississippi River.....	178	54	900	275
TX........	Guadalupe Peak.........	8,749	2,668	Gulf of Mexico.....	(¹)	(¹)	1,700	519
UT........	Kings Peak............	13,528	4,126	Beaver Dam Wash...	2,000	610	6,100	1,861
VT........	Mount Mansfield.........	4,393	1,340	Lake Champlain.....	95	29	1,000	305
VA........	Mount Rogers..........	5,729	1,747	Atlantic Ocean.....	(¹)	(¹)	950	290
WA........	Mount Rainier..........	14,410	4,395	Pacific Ocean......	(¹)	(¹)	1,700	519
WV........	Spruce Knob...........	4,861	1,483	Potomac River.....	240	73	1,500	458
WI........	Timms Hill.............	1,951	595	Lake Michigan.....	579	177	1,050	320
WY........	Gannett Peak..........	13,804	4,210	Belle Fourche River...	3,099	945	6,700	2,044
Other areas:								
Puerto Rico....	Cerro de Punta..........	4,390	1,339	Atlantic Ocean......	(¹)	(¹)	1,800	549
American Samoa...	Lata Mountain..........	3,160	964	Pacific Ocean......	(¹)	(¹)	1,300	397
Guam....	Mount Lamlam.........	1,332	406	Pacific Ocean......	(¹)	(¹)	330	101
Virgin Is....	Crown Mountain.........	1,556	475	Atlantic Ocean.....	(¹)	(¹)	750	229

Z Less than 0.5 meter.   [1] Sea level.   [2] At DE-PA state line.   [3] "Sec." denotes section; "T," township; "R," range; "N," north; and "W," west.

Source: U.S. Geological Survey, for highest and lowest points, *Elevations and Distances in the United States, 1990;* for mean elevations, 1983 edition. See also "Elevations and Distances in the United States;" (published 23 February 2005); <http://erg.usgs.gov/isb/pubs/booklets/elvadist/elvadist.html>.

224   Geography and Environment

Table 353. U.S. Wetland Resources and Deepwater Habitats by Type: 1986 and 1997

[In thousands of acres (144,673.3 represents 144,677,300). Wetlands and deepwater habitats are defined separately because the term wetland does not include permanent water bodies. Deepwater habitats are permanently flooded land lying below the deepwater boundary of wetlands. Deepwater habitats include environments where surface water is permanent and often deep, so that water, rather than air, is the principal medium within which the dominant organisms live, whether or not they are attached to the substrate. As in wetlands, the dominant plants are hydrophytes; however, the substrates are considered nonsoil because the water is too deep to support emergent vegetation. In general terms, wetlands are lands where saturation with water is the dominant factor determining the nature of soil development and the types of plant and animal communities living in the soil and on its surface. The single feature that most wetlands share is soil or substrate that is at least periodically saturated with or covered by water. Wetlands are lands transitional between terrestrial and aquatic systems where the water table is usually at or near the surface or the land is covered by shallow water]

Wetland or deepwater category	1986	1997	Change, 1986 to 1997
All wetlands and deepwater habitates, total	**144,673.3**	**144,136.8**	**-536.5**
All deepwater habitats, total	38,537.6	38,645.1	107.5
Lacustrine [1]	14,608.9	14,725.3	116.4
Riverine [2]	6,291.1	6,255.9	-35.2
Estuarine Subtidal [3]	17,637.6	17,663.9	26.3
All wetlands, total	106,135.7	105,491.7	-644.0
Intertidal wetlands [4]	5,336.6	5,326.2	-10.4
Marine intertidal	133.1	130.9	-2.2
Estuarine intertidal nonvegetated	580.4	580.1	-0.3
Estuarine intertidal vegetated	4,623.1	4,615.2	-7.9
Freshwater wetlands	100,799.1	100,165.5	-633.6
Freshwater nonvegetated	5,251.0	5,914.3	663.3
Freshwater vegetated	95,548.1	94,251.2	-1,296.9
Freshwater emergent [5]	26,383.3	25,157.1	-1,226.2
Freshwater forested [6]	51,929.6	50,728.5	-1,201.1
Freshwater shrub [7]	17,235.2	18,365.6	1,130.4

[1] The lacustrine system includes deepwater habitats with all of the following characteristics: (1) situated in a topographic depression or a dammed river channel; (2) lacking trees, shrubs, persistent emergents, emergent mosses or lichens with greater than 30 percent coverage; (3) total area exceeds 20 acres. [2] The riverine system includes deepwater habitats contained within a channel, with the exception of habitats with water containing ocean derived salts in excess of 0.5 parts per thousand. [3] The estuarine system consists of deepwater tidal habitats and adjacent tidal wetland that are usually semi-enclosed by land but have open, partly obstructed, or sporadic access to the open ocean, and in which ocean water is at least occasionally diluted by freshwater runoff from the land. Subtidal is where the substrate is continuously submerged by marine or estuarine waters. [4] Intertidal is where the substrate is exposed and flooded by tides. Intertidal includes the splash zone of coastal waters. [5] Emergent wetlands are characterized by erect, rooted, herbaceous hydrophytes, excluding mosses and lichens. This vegetation is present for most of the growing season in most years. These wetlands are usually dominated by perennial plants. [6] Forested wetlands are characterized by woody vegetation that is 20 feet tall or taller. [7] Shrub wetlands include areas dominated by woody vegetation less than 20 feet tall. The species include true shrubs, young trees, and trees or shrubs that are small or stunted because of environmental conditions.

Source: U.S. Fish and Wildlife Service, *Status and Trends of Wetlands in the Conterminous United States, 1986 to 1997,* January 2001. See also <ftp://wetlands.fws.gov/status-trends/SandT2000Reportlowres.pdf>.

Table 354. Flows of Largest U.S. Rivers—Length, Discharge, and Drainage Area

River	Location of mouth	Source stream (name and location)	Length (miles) [1]	Average discharge at mouth (1,000 cubic ft. per second)	Drainage area (1,000 sq. mi.)
Missouri	Missouri	Red Rock Creek, MT	2,540	76.2	[2]529
Mississippi	Louisiana	Mississippi River, MN	[3]2,340	[4]593	[2][5]1,150
Yukon	Alaska	McNeil River, Canada	1,980	225	[2]328
St. Lawrence	Canada	North River, MN	1,900	348	[2]396
Rio Grande	Mexico-Texas	Rio Grande, CO	1,900	-	336
Arkansas	Arkansas	East Fork Arkansas River, CO	1,460	41	161
Colorado	Mexico	Colorado River, CO	1,450	-	246
Atchafalaya [6]	Louisiana	Tierra Blanca Creek, NM	1,420	58	95.1
Ohio	Illinois-Kentucky	Allegheny River, PA	1,310	281	203
Red	Louisiana	Tierra Blanca Creek, NM	1,290	56	93.2
Brazos	Texas	Blackwater Draw, NM	1,280	-	45.6
Columbia	Oregon-Washington	Columbia River, Canada	1,240	265	[2]258
Snake	Washington	Snake River, WY	1,040	56.9	108
Platte	Nebraska	Grizzly Creek, CO	990	-	84.9
Pecos	Texas	Pecos River, NM	926	-	44.3
Canadian	Oklahoma	Canadian River, CO	906	-	46.9
Tennessee	Kentucky	Courthouse Creek, NC	886	68	40.9
Colorado (of Texas)	Texas	Colorado River, TX	862	-	42.3
North Canadian	Oklahoma	Corrumpa Creek, NM	800	-	17.6
Mobile	Alabama	Tickanetley Creek, GA	774	67.2	44.6
Kansas	Kansas	Arikaree River, CO	743	-	59.5
Kuskokwim	Alaska	South Fork Kuskokwim River, AK	724	67	48
Yellowstone	North Dakota	North Folk Yellowstone River, WY	692	-	70
Tanana	Alaska	Nabesna River, AK	659	41	44.5
Gila	Arizona	Middle Fork Gila River, NM	649	-	58.2
Porcupine	Alaska	Porcupine River, Canada	569	23	45.1
Susquehanna	Maryland	Hayden Creek, NY	447	38.2	27.2

- Represents zero. [1] From source to mouth. [2] Drainage area includes both the United States and Canada. [3] The length from the source of the Missouri River to the Mississippi River and thence to the Gulf of Mexico is about 3,710 miles. [4] Includes about 167,000 cubic ft. per second diverted from the Mississippi into the Atchafalaya River but excludes the flow of the Red River. [5] Excludes the drainage areas of the Red and Atchafalaya Rivers. [6] In east-central Louisiana, the Red River flows into the Atchafalaya River, a distributary of the Mississippi River. Data on average discharge, length, and drainage area include the Red River, but exclude all water diverted into the Atchafalaya from the Mississippi River.

Source: U.S. Geological Survey, *Largest Rivers in the United States,* Open File Report 87-242, May 1990.

Geography and Environment 225

Table 355. **U.S. Water Withdrawals and Consumptive Use Per Day by End Use: 1940 to 2000**

[In billions of gallons, except as indicated. (140 represents 140,000,000,000). Includes Puerto Rico. Withdrawal signifies water physically withdrawn from a source. Includes fresh and saline water; excludes water used for hydroelectric power]

Year	Total (bil. gal.)	Per capita [1] (gal.)	Irrigation (bil. gal.)	Public supply [2] (bil. gal.)	Rural [3] (bil. gal.)	Industrial and misc. [4] (bil. gal.)	Steam electric utilities (bil. gal.)
WITHDRAWALS							
1940	140	1,027	71	10	3.1	29	23
1950	180	1,185	89	14	3.6	37	40
1955	240	1,454	110	17	3.6	39	72
1960	270	1,500	110	21	3.6	38	100
1965	310	1,602	120	24	4.0	46	130
1970	370	1,815	130	27	4.5	47	170
1975	420	1,972	140	29	4.9	45	200
1980	440	1,953	150	34	5.6	45	210
1985	399	1,650	137	38	7.8	31	187
1990	408	1,620	137	41	7.9	30	195
1995	402	1,500	134	40	8.9	29	190
2000	408	1,430	137	43	9.2	23	196
CONSUMPTIVE USE							
1960	61	339	52	3.5	2.8	3.0	0.2
1965	77	403	66	5.2	3.2	3.4	0.4
1970	87	427	73	5.9	3.4	4.1	0.8
1975	96	451	80	6.7	3.4	4.2	1.9
1980	100	440	83	7.1	3.9	5.0	3.2
1985	92	380	74	(5)	9.2	6.1	6.2
1990	94	370	76	(5)	8.9	6.7	4.0
1995	100	374	81	(5)	9.9	4.8	3.7
2000	(NA)	(NA)	(NA)	(NA)	(NA)	(NA)	(NA)

[1] Based on U.S. Census Bureau resident population as of July 1. [2] Includes commercial water withdrawals. [3] Rural farm and nonfarm household and garden use, and water for farm stock and dairies. [4] For 1940 to 1960, includes manufacturing and mineral industries, rural commercial industries, air-conditioning, resorts, hotels, motels, military and other state and Federal agencies, and miscellaneous; thereafter, includes manufacturing, mining and mineral processing, ordnance, construction, and miscellaneous. [5] Public supply consumptive use included in end-use categories.

Source: 1940-1960, U.S. Bureau of Domestic Business Development, based principally on committee prints, *Water Resources Activities in the United States*, for the Senate Committee on National Water Resources, U.S. Senate, thereafter, U.S. Geological Survey, *Estimated Use of Water in the United States in 2000*, circular 1268. See also <http://water.usgs.gov/pubs/circ/2004/circ1268/> (released 12 March 2004).

Table 356. **Water Withdrawals by Source, Type, and Use—State and Other Areas: 2000**

[In millions of gallons per day(408,000 represents 408,000,000,000). Figures may not add due to rounding. Withdrawal signifies water physically withdrawn from a source. Includes fresh and saline water. For information on methodology and differences with prior surveys, see <http://water.usgs.gov/pubs/circ/2004/circ1268/htdocs/text-intro.html>]

State and other area	Water with-drawals, total (mil. gal. per day)	Source, percent — Ground water	Source, percent — Surface water	Selected major uses, percent — Public supply	Selected major uses, percent — Irriga-tion	State and other area	Water with-drawals, total (mil. gal. per day)	Source, percent — Ground water	Source, percent — Surface water	Selected major uses, percent — Public supply	Selected major uses, percent — Irriga-tion
Total [1]	408,000	20.7	79.2	10.6	33.6	MT	8,290	2.3	97.7	1.8	95.9
AL	9,990	4.4	95.6	8.3	0.4	NE	12,300	63.9	35.7	2.7	71.5
AK	305	46.2	53.8	26.2	0.3	NV	2,810	26.9	73.0	22.4	75.1
AZ	6,730	51.0	49.0	16.0	80.2	NH	1,210	7.0	92.6	8.0	0.4
AR	10,900	63.5	36.2	3.9	72.6	NJ	5,560	10.5	89.6	18.9	2.5
CA	51,200	30.1	69.9	12.0	59.6	NM	3,260	47.2	52.5	9.1	87.7
CO	12,600	18.4	81.7	7.1	90.5	NY	12,100	7.4	92.6	21.2	0.3
CT	4,150	3.4	96.6	10.2	0.7	NC	11,400	5.1	94.7	8.3	2.5
DE	1,320	8.7	91.7	7.2	3.3	ND	1,140	10.8	89.5	5.6	12.7
DC	10	0.0	100.0	0.0	1.8	OH	11,100	7.9	92.8	13.2	0.3
FL	20,100	25.0	75.1	12.1	21.3	OK	2,020	51.0	49.0	33.4	35.5
GA	6,500	22.3	77.8	19.2	17.5	OR	6,930	14.3	85.7	8.2	87.7
HI	641	67.7	32.4	39.0	56.8	PA	9,950	6.7	93.4	14.7	0.1
ID	19,500	21.2	78.5	1.3	87.7	RI	429	6.7	93.2	27.7	0.8
IL	13,700	5.9	94.2	12.8	1.1	SC	7,170	4.6	95.4	7.9	3.7
IN	10,100	6.5	93.7	6.6	1.0	SD	528	42.0	58.0	17.7	70.6
IA	3,360	20.2	79.8	11.4	0.6	TN	10,800	3.9	96.3	8.2	0.2
KS	6,610	57.3	42.7	6.3	56.1	TX	29,600	30.3	69.9	14.3	29.2
KY	4,160	4.5	95.4	12.6	0.7	UT	4,970	21.1	78.9	12.8	77.7
LA	10,400	15.7	83.9	7.2	9.8	VT	447	9.7	90.4	13.4	0.8
ME	799	10.1	89.9	12.8	0.7	VA	8,830	3.6	96.5	8.2	0.3
MD	7,910	2.8	97.2	10.4	0.5	WA	5,310	27.7	72.3	19.2	57.3
MA	4,660	5.8	94.2	15.9	2.7	WV	5,150	1.8	98.3	3.7	0.0
MI	10,000	7.3	92.6	11.4	2.0	WI	7,590	10.7	89.3	8.2	2.6
MN	3,870	18.6	81.4	12.9	5.9	WY	5,170	14.8	85.1	2.1	87.0
MS	2,960	73.6	26.4	12.1	47.6	PR	2,810	4.9	95.0	18.3	3.4
MO	8,230	21.6	78.4	10.6	17.4	VI	148	0.7	99.3	4.1	0.3

[1] Represents both fresh and saline water.

Source: U.S. Geological Survey, *Estimated Use of Water in the United States in 2000*, circular 1268. See also <http://water.usgs.gov/pubs/circ/2004/circ1268/#availability> (released 12 March 2004).

Table 357. U.S. Water Quality Conditions by Type of Waterbody: 2000

[Section 305(b) of the Clean Water Act requires states and other jurisdictions to assess the health of their waters and the extent to which their waters support water quality standards. Section 305(b) requires that states submit reports describing water quality conditions to the Environmental Protection Agency every two years. Water quality standards have three elements (designated uses, criteria developed to protect each use, and an antidegradation policy). For information on survey methodology and assessment criteria, see report]

Item	Rivers and streams (miles)	Lakes, reservoirs, and ponds (acres)	· Estuaries (sq. miles)	Great Lakes shoreline (miles)	Ocean shoreline (miles)
Total size	3,692,830	40,603,893	87,369	5,521	58,618
Amount accessed [1]	699,946	17,339,080	31,072	5,066	3,221
Percent of total size	19	43	36	92	6
Amount accessed as—					
Good [2]	463,441	8,026,988	13,850	-	2,176
Good but threatened [3]	85,544	1,343,903	1,023	1,095	193
Polluted [4]	291,264	7,702,370	15,676	3,955	434
Percent of accessed as—					
Good [2]	53	47	45	-	79
Good but threatened [3]	8	8	4	22	7
Polluted [4]	39	45	51	78	14
Amount impaired by leading sources of pollution: [5]					
Agriculture	128,859	3,158,393	2,811	75	(NA)
Atmospheric deposition	(NA)	983,936	3,692	71	(NA)
Construction	(NA)	(NA)	(NA)	(NA)	29
Contaminated sediments	(NA)	(NA)	(NA)	519	(NA)
Forestry	28,156	(NA)	(NA)	(NA)	(NA)
Habitat modification	37,654	(NA)	(NA)	62	(NA)
Hydrologic modification	53,850	1,413,624	2,171	(NA)	(NA)
Industrial discharges/point sources. . .	(NA)	(NA)	4,116	(NA)	76
Land disposal of wastes	(NA)	856,586	(NA)	(NA)	123
Municipal point sources	27,988	943,715	5,779	61	89
Nonpoint sources	(NA)	1,045,036	(NA)	(NA)	142
Resource extraction	27,695	(NA)	1,913	(NA)	(NA)
Septic tanks	(NA)	(NA)	(NA)	61	103
Urban runoff and storm sewers	34,871	13,699,327	5,045	152	241

- Represents zero.   NA Not available.   [1] Includes waterbodies assessed as not attainable for one or more uses. Most states do not assess all their waterbodies during the 2-year reporting cycle, but use a "rotating basin approach" whereby all waters are monitored over a set period of time.   [2] Based on accessment of available data, water quality supports all designated uses. Water quality meets narrative and/or numeric criteria adopted to protect and support a designated use.   [3] Although all assessed uses are currently met, data show a declining trend in water quality. Projections based on this trend indicate water quality will be impaired in the future, unless action is taken to prevent further degradation.   [4] Impaired or not attainable. The reporting state or jurisdiction has performed a "use-attainability analysis" and demonstrated that support of one or more designated beneficial uses is not attainable due to specific biological, chemical, physical, or economic/social conditions.   [5] Excludes unknown and natural sources.

Source: U.S. Environmental Protection Agency, National Water Quality Inventory: 2000 Report, EPA-841-R-02-001, August 2002. See also <http://www.epa.gov/305b/2000report>.

Table 358. Oil Spills in U.S. Water—Number and Volume: 1998 to 2001

[Based on reported discharges into U.S. navigable waters, including territorial waters (extending 3 to 12 miles from the coastline), tributaries, the contiguous zone, onto shoreline, or into other waters that threaten the marine environment. Data found in Marine Safety Management System]

Spill characteristic	Number of spills				Spill volume (gallons)			
	1998	1999	2000	2001	1998	1999	2000	2001
Total	8,315	8,539	8,354	7,559	885,303	1,172,449	1,431,370	854,520
Size of spill (gallons):								
1-100	7,962	8,212	8,058	7,256	38,093	39,119	39,355	33,276
101-1,000	259	240	219	216	86,606	86,530	78,779	86,955
1,001-3,000	54	42	37	45	96,743	74,582	67,529	77,447
3,001-5,000	15	18	12	16	64,609	73,798	45,512	67,241
5,001-10,000	15	10	16	11	108,148	66,274	112,415	89,224
10,001-50,000	8	12	6	14	216,335	301,510	108,400	376,057
50,001-100,000	-	4	4	-	-	245,406	266,380	-
100,001-1,000,000	2	1	2	1	274,769	285,230	713,000	124,320
1,000,000 and over	-	-	-	-	-	-	-	-
Waterbody:								
Atlantic ocean	109	148	150	83	6,674	29,440	135,010	7,168
Pacific ocean	644	758	623	493	192,775	150,694	36,301	53,295
Gulf of Mexico	2,190	1,756	1,838	1,728	181,372	45,786	112,069	133,872
Great Lakes	119	129	96	109	3,006	906	4,535	1,600
Lakes	25	31	32	35	63	624	349	244
Rivers and canals	1,944	1,924	1,816	1,682	280,651	504,264	663,404	237,980
Bays and sounds	891	1,299	1,248	1,140	24,234	136,650	49,783	139,300
Harbors	790	907	801	893	97,223	105,213	273,095	158,667
Other	1,603	1,587	1,750	1,396	99,305	198,872	156,824	122,394
Source:								
Tankship	104	92	111	95	56,673	8,414	608,176	125,217
Tankbarge	220	227	229	246	248,089	158,977	133,540	212,298
All other vessels	4,848	5,361	5,220	4,680	316,473	409,084	291,927	232,341
Facilities	937	1,019	1,054	995	166,269	367,537	311,604	201,025
Pipelines	45	25	25	34	47,863	36,140	17,021	13,577
All other nonvessels	571	571	566	436	32,584	147,704	45,136	55,921
Unknown	1,590	1,244	1,149	1,073	17,352	44,593	23,966	14,141

- Represents or rounds to zero.

Source: U.S. Coast Guard, <http://www.uscg.mil/hq/g-m/nmc/response/stats/Summary.htm> and <http://www.uscg.mil/hq/g-m/nmc/response/stats/chpt2001.pdf> (released August 2003).

Geography and Environment   227

Table 359. National Ambient Air Pollutant Concentrations: 1990 to 2003

[Data represent annual composite averages of pollutant based on daily 24-hour averages of monitoring stations, except carbon monoxide is based on the second-highest, nonoverlapping, 8-hour average; ozone, the second-highest daily maximum 1-hour value or the fourth-highest maximum 8-hour value; and lead, the maximum quarterly average of ambient lead levels. Based on data from the Air Quality System. µg/m³ = micrograms of pollutant per cubic meter of air; ppm = parts per million]

Pollutant	Unit	Monitoring stations, number	Air quality standard [1]	1990	1995	1999	2000	2001	2002	2003
Carbon monoxide	ppm....	387	[2]9	6.0	4.7	3.9	3.4	3.2	3.0	2.8
Ozone............	ppm....	785	[3].12	0.111	0.112	0.108	0.101	0.101	0.105	0.101
Ozone............	ppm....	785	[4]0.08	0.085	0.088	0.086	0.080	0.081	0.085	0.080
Sulfur dioxide	ppm.,..	449	.03	0.0384	0.0261	0.0237	0.0230	0.0216	0.0198	0.0210
Particulates (PM-10). . .	µg/m³. . .	770	[5]50	30.9	26.1	25.2	24.8	24.1	23.4	23.5
Nitrogen dioxide ....:	ppm.,..	250	.053	(NA)	(NA)	13.4	13.2	12.9	12.3	12.0
Lead............	µg/m³. . .	96	[6]1.5	0.019	0.018	0.018	0.017	0.017	0.016	0.016

[1] Refers to the primary National Ambient Air Quality Standard that protects the public health. [2] Based on 8-hour standard of 9 ppm. [3] Based on 1-hour standard of .12 ppm. [4] Based on 8-hour standard of .08 ppm. [5] The particulates (PM-10) standard replaced the previous standard for total suspended particulates in 1987. [6] Based on 3-month standard of 1.5 µg/m³.

Table 360. National Air Pollutant Emissions: 1970 to 2002

[In thousands of tons (13,042 represents 13,042,000), except as indicated. PM-10 = Particulate matter of less than ten microns; PM-2.5 = particulate matter of less than 2.5 microns effective diameter. Methodologies to estimate data for 1970 to 1980 period and 1985 to present emissions differ. Beginning with 1985, the methodology for more recent years is described in the document available at <http://www.epa.gov/ttn/chief/trends/trends99/neiproc99.pdf>.]

Year	PM-10	PM-10, fugitive dust[1]	PM-2.5	Sulfur dioxide	Nitrogen dioxides	Volatile organic compounds	Carbon monoxide	Lead (tons)[2]
1970	13,042	(NA)	(NA)	31,218	26,883	34,659	204,043	220,869
1975	7,671	(NA)	(NA)	28,043	26,337	30,765	188,398	159,659
1980	7,013	(NA)	(NA)	25,925	27,079	31,106	185,407	74,153
1985	11,590	29,734	(NA)	23,307	25,757	27,404	176,844	22.890
1990	9,689	18,063	7,559	23,076	25,529	24,108	154,186	4,975
1991	9,270	18,075	7,320	22,375	25,179	23,577	147,128	4,169
1992	8,927	18,170	7,198	22,082	25,260	23,066	140,896	3,810
1993	8,411	18,953	7,150	21,772	25,357	22,730	135,901	3,916
1994	8,888	19,722	7,541	21,346	25,349	22,569	133,559	4,047
1995	8,807	17,012	6,929	18,619	24,956	22,041	126,777	3,929
1996	9,014	13,844	6,725	18,385	24,787	20,871	128,858	2,627
1997	8,393	14,516	6,256	18,840	24,705	19,530	117,910	(NA)
1998	8,343	14,550	6,261	18,944	24,348	18,782	115,380	(NA)
1999	9,391	14,112	7,333	17,545	22,845	18,776	114,541	(NA)
2000	9,440	14,307	7,288	16,347	22,598	17,512	114,467	(NA)
2001	9,118	13,769	6,632	15,932	21,547	17,118	106,295	(NA)
2002	8,882	13,272	6,803	15,353	21,102	16,544	112,049	(NA)

NA Not available. [1] Sources such as agricultural tilling, construction, mining and quarrying, paved roads, unpaved roads, and wind erosion. [2] Beginning 1996, lead and lead compounds are inventoried through the hazardous air pollutants (HAPs) portion of the National Emission Inventory (NEI) every three years; data for 1997 forward are currently not available.

Table 361. Air Pollutant Emissions by Pollutant and Source: 2002

[In thousands of tons, except as indicated. See headnote, Table 360]

Source	PM-10 [1]	PM-2.5	Sulfur dioxide	Nitrogen dioxides	Volatile organic compounds	Carbon monoxide
Total emissions	**22,153**	**6,802**	**15,351**	**21,103**	**16,544**	**112,049**
Fuel combustion, stationary sources.	1,369	1,157	13,167	8,294	1,012	4,433
Electric utilities	695	582	10,293	4,699	52	499
Industrial	269	191	2,299	2,870	170	1,436
Other fuel combustion	405	384	575	725	790	2,498
Residential	177	319	150	360	765	2,331
Industrial processes	586	368	1,363	825	1,064	2,394
Chemical and allied product manufacture.	36	27	328	105	214	337
Metals processing	118	81	271	84	69	1,294
Petroleum and related industries	34	20	348	149	375	128
Other	398	240	416	487	406	635
Solvent utilization	16	14	2	8	4,692	51
Storage and transport	82	33	5	16	1,205	215
Waste disposal and recycling	443	419	28	152	457	1,847
Highway vehicles	204	149	275	7,366	4,543	62,161
Light-duty gas vehicles and motorcycles	52	27	93	2,166	2,496	34,400
Light-duty gas trucks	30	16	65	1,401	1,638	24,191
Heavy-duty gas vehicles.	9	7	12	404	201	2,554
Diesels .,........................	113	99	105	3,395	208	1,016
Off-highway [2] .,....................	311	285	420	4,086	2,688	24,450
Miscellaneous [3]	19,142	4,377	91	356	883	16,498

[1] Represents both PM-10 and PM-10 fugitive dust; see Table 360. [2] Includes emissions from farm tractors and other farm machinery, construction equipment, industrial machinery, recreational marine vessels, and small general utility engines such as lawn mowers. [3] Includes emissions such as from forest fires and other kinds of burning, various agricultural activities, fugitive dust from paved and unpaved roads, and other construction and mining activities, and natural sources.

Source of Tables 359-361: U.S. Environmental Protection Agency, "Air Pollutant Emission Trends, 1970-2002"; published 7 January 2005; <http://www.epa.gov/ttn/chief/trends/index.html#tables>.

Table 362. Emissions of Greenhouse Gases by Type and Source: 1990 to 2002

[6,156.0 represents 6,156,000,000 tons. Emission estimates were mandated by Congress through Section 1605(a) of the Energy Policy Act of 1992 (Title XVI). Gases that contain carbon can be measured either in terms of the full molecular weight of the gas or just in terms of their carbon dioxide equivalent. Both measures are utilized below]

Type and source	Unit	1990	1995	1999	2000	2001	2002
CARBON DIOXIDE EQUIVALENT							
Total emissions	Mil. metric tons ...	6,156.0	6,470.0	6,795.0	6,957.0	6,829.0	6,862.0
Carbon dioxide, total	Mil. metric tons ...	5,006.1	5,318.5	5,686.1	5,854.0	5,748.3	5,795.6
Energy sources	Mil. metric tons ...	4,988.6	5,255.8	5,630.5	5,798.6	5,691.7	5,729.3
CO$_2$ in natural gas	Mil. metric tons	14.0	16.7	17.8	18.2	18.6	18.1
Cement production	Mil. metric tons	33.3	36.9	40.1	41.3	41.4	43.3
Gas flaring	Mil. metric tons	9.1	17.2	6.7	5.5	5.2	5.1
Other industrial	Mil. metric tons	26.8	28.4	29.3	29.6	27.7	27.4
Waste combustion	Mil. metric tons	17.0	22.2	25.2	19.9	19.8	19.8
Other, adjustments	Mil. metric tons	-82.7	-58.6	-63.5	-59.1	-56.2	-47.3
Methane	Mil. metric tons	719.1	701.8	639.7	638.8	630.2	612.8
Nitrous oxide	Mil. metric tons	333.8	355.3	347.2	341.2	336.8	333.1
HFCs, PFCs, and SF6 [1]	Mil. metric tons	96.8	94.6	122.1	123.2	113.6	120.6
GAS							
Carbon dioxide	Mil. metric tons	5,006.1	5,318.5	5,686.1	5,854.0	5,748.3	5,795.6
Methane, total	Mil. metric tons	31.27	30.51	27.81	27.77	27.40	26.65
Nitrous oxide, total	Mil. metric tons	1.128	1.200	1.173	1.153	1.138	1.125
HFCs, PFCs, and SF6 [1]	Mil. metric tons	(2)	(2)	(2)	(2)	(2)	(2)

[1] Hydrofluorocarbons, perfluorocarbons, and sulfur hexafluoride.   [2] Mixture of gases.

Source: U.S. Energy Information Administration, *Emissions of Greenhouse Gases in the United States*, Series DOE/EIA-0573(2003), annual. See also <http://tonto.eia.doe.gov/FTPROOT/environment/057303.pdf> (released 01 December 2004).

Table 363. Municipal Solid Waste Generation, Recovery, and Disposal: 1980 to 2003

[In millions of tons (151.6 represents 151,600,000), except as indicated. Covers post-consumer residential and commercial solid wastes which comprise the major portion of typical municipal collections. Excludes mining, agricultural and industrial processing, demolition and construction wastes, sewage sludge, and junked autos and obsolete equipment wastes. Based on material-flows estimating procedure and wet weight as generated]

Item and material	1980	1990	1995	2000	2001	2002	2003
Waste generated	151.6	205.2	211.4	234.0	231.2	235.5	236.2
Per person per day (lb.)	3.7	4.5	4.4	4.5	4.4	4.5	4.4
Materials recovered	14.5	33.2	54.9	68.9	69.3	70.5	72.3
Per person per day (lb.)	0.35	0.7	1.1	1.3	1.3	1.3	1.4
Combustion for energy recovery	2.7	31.9	35.5	33.7	33.6	33.4	33.1
Per person per day (lb.)	0.06	0.7	0.7	0.7	0.7	0.6	0.6
Combustion without energy recovery	11.0	(1)	(1)	(1)	(1)	(1)	(1)
Per person per day (lb.)	0.27	(1)	(1)	(1)	(1)	(1)	(1)
Landfill, other disposal	123.4	140.1	120.9	131.4	128.3	131.7	130.8
Per person per day (lb.)	3.0	3.1	2.5	2.6	2.5	2.5	2.5
Percent distribution of generation:							
Paper and paperboard	36.4	35.4	38.6	37.5	35.7	35.8	35.2
Glass	10.0	6.4	6.1	5.4	5.4	5.4	5.3
Metals	10.2	8.1	7.5	7.8	7.9	7.8	8.0
Plastics	4.5	8.3	8.9	10.5	10.9	11.2	11.3
Rubber and leather	2.8	2.8	2.9	2.8	2.9	2.8	2.9
Textiles	1.7	2.8	3.5	4.0	4.2	4.4	4.5
Wood	4.6	6.0	4.9	5.5	5.7	5.7	5.8
Food wastes	8.6	10.1	10.3	11.3	11.7	11.6	11.7
Yard wastes	18.1	17.1	14.0	11.8	12.1	12.0	12.1
Other wastes	3.2	3.0	3.3	3.2	3.4	3.3	3.2

[1] Combustion without energy recovery is no longer available separately.

Source: Franklin Associates, a Division of ERG, Prairie Village, KS, *Municipal Solid Waste Generation, Recycling, and Disposal in the United States: Facts and Figures for 2003*. Prepared for the U.S. Environmental Protection Agency. Prepared for the U.S. Environmental Protection Agency. See also <http://www.epa.gov/epaoswer/non-hw/muncpl/>.

Table 364. **Generation and Recovery of Selected Materials in Municipal Solid Waste: 1980 to 2003**

[In millions of tons (151.6 represents 151,600,000), except as indicated. Covers post-consumer residential and commercial solid wastes which comprise the major portion of typical municipal collections. Excludes mining, agricultural and industrial processing, demolition and construction wastes, sewage sludge, and junked autos and obsolete equipment wastes. Based on material-flows estimating procedure and wet weight as generated]

Item and material	1980	1990	1995	2000	2001	2002	2003
Waste generated, total	151.6	205.2	211.4	234.0	231.2	235.5	236.2
Paper and paperboard.	55.2	72.7	81.7	87.7	82.7	84.2	83.1
Ferrous metals.	12.6	12.6	11.6	13.5	13.5	13.6	14.0
Aluminum	1.7	2.8	3.0	3.1	3.2	3.2	3.2
Other nonferrous metals	1.2	1.1	1.3	1.6	1.6	1.6	1.6
Glass.	15.1	13.1	12.8	12.6	12.6	12.8	12.5
Plastics.	6.8	17.1	18.9	24.7	25.3	26.3	26.7
Yard waste	27.5	35.0	29.7	27.7	28.0	28.3	28.6
Other wastes.	31.5	50.7	52.4	63.1	64.4	65.5	66.5
Materials recovered, total	14.5	33.2	54.9	68.9	69.3	70.5	72.3
Paper and paperboard.	11.9	20.2	32.7	37.6	37.7	38.3	40.0
Ferrous metals.	0.4	2.2	4.1	4.6	4.6	4.9	5.1
Aluminum	0.3	1.0	0.9	0.9	0.8	0.8	0.7
Other nonferrous metals	0.5	0.7	0.8	1.1	1.1	1.1	1.1
Glass.	0.8	2.6	3.1	2.7	2.4	2.5	2.4
Plastics.	-	0.4	1.0	1.4	1.4	1.4	1.4
Yard waste	-	4.2	9.0	15.8	15.8	16.0	16.1
Other wastes.	0.6	1.8	3.2	4.9	5.6	· 5.6	5.6
Percent of generation recovered, total	9.6	16.2	26.0	29.4	30.0	29.9	30.6
Paper and paperboard.	21.6	27.8	40.0	42.8	45.6	45.5	48.1
Ferrous metals.	3.2	17.5	35.3	34.1	34.1	36.0	36.4
Aluminum	17.6	35.7	30.0	28.7	25.0	23.8	21.4
Other nonferrous metals	41.7	63.6	61.5	67.9	67.5	67.5	66.7
Glass.	5.3	19.8	24.2	21.4	19.0	19.1	18.8
Plastics.	-	2.3	5.3	5.5	5.5	5.2	5.2
Yard waste	-	12.0	30.3	57.0	56.4	56.5	56.3
Other wastes.	1.9	3.6	6.1	7.8	8.6	8.6	8.5

- Represents zero.

Source: Franklin Associates, a Division of ERG, Prairie Village, KS, *Municipal Solid Waste Generation, Recycling, and Disposal in the United States: Facts and Figures for 2003.* Prepared for the U.S. Environmental Protection Agency. See also <http://www.epa.gov/epaoswer/non-hw/muncpl/>.

Table 365. **Curbside Recycling Programs—Number and Population Served by Region: 1995 to 2001**

[(121,335 represents 121,335,000).] Data for 1998 are not available. For composition of regions, see map, inside front cover]

Region	Number of programs					Population served [1] (1,000)				
	1995	1997	1999	2000	2001	1995	1997	1999	2000	2001
Total	7,375	8,969	9,349	9,247	9,704	121,335	136,229	139,826	133,165	139,366
Northeast.	2,210	3,406	3,414	3,459	3,421	37,256	43,200	43,162	43,482	43,981
South	1,281	1,344	1,581	1,427	1,677	31,521	36,952	37,914	37,510	26,496
Midwest.	2,985	3,357	3,477	3,582	3,572	25,487	26,970	30,106	22,618	25,851
West.	899	862	877	779	1,034	27,071	29,107	28,644	29,555	43,038

[1] Calculated using population of states reporting data.

Source: Franklin Associates, a Division of ERG, Prairie Village, KS, *Municipal Solid Waste in the United States: 2001 Facts and Figures.* Prepared for the U.S. Environmental Protection Agency. Also in *Biocycle Magazine.*

Table 366. Toxic Chemical Releases and Transfers by Media: 1998 to 2003

[In millions of pounds (6,789.8 represents 6,789,800,000), except as indicated. Based on reports filed as required by section 313 of the Emergency Planning and Community Right-to-Know Act (EPCRA, or Title III of the Superfund Amendments and Reauthorization Act of 1986). Public Law 99-499. Owners and operators of facilities that are classified within Standard Classification Code groups 20 through 39, have 10 or more full-time employees, and that manufacture, process, or otherwise use any listed toxic chemical in quantities greater than the established threshold in the course of a calendar year are covered and required to report]

Media	1998	2000	2001	2002	2003
Total facilities reporting	23,549	23,095	22,296	21,522	20,681
Total releases	6,789.8	6,215.6	5,067.9	4,279.5	3,919.8
On-site releases	6,382.5	5,737.8	4,587.6	3,812.5	3,438.3
Air emissions	2,088.0	1,914.5	1,650.7	1,631.1	1,583.0
Surface water discharges	254.1	267.0	230.3	231.5	221.6
Underground injection class I wells	232.4	239.6	192.3	201.5	199.0
Underground injection class II-V wells	26.1	29.7	16.0	13.6	14.7
RCRA subtitle C landfills	190.7	199.8	117.1	105.3	121.3
Other landfills	260.3	274.8	273.7	229.6	219.9
Land treatment/application farming	9.7	13.8	13.5	20.3	15.1
Surface impoundments	1,289.5	963.0	801.8	631.4	666.1
Other land disposal	2,031.7	1,835.7	1,292.3	748.3	397.6
Off-site releases	407.3	477.7	480.2	467.0	481.6
Total transfers offsite for further waste management	3,859.5	3,898.3	3,758.7	3,618.0	3,434.3
Tranfers to recycling	1,774.9	1,893.6	1,737.5	1,695.9	1,622.3
Transfers to energy recovery	910.3	812.7	835.6	802.4	705.3
Transfers to treatment	327.1	279.0	281.6	274.6	285.8
Transfers to POTWs [2]	333.1	341.0	343.0	303.3	269.2
Transfers to POTWs metal and metal compounds [1]	3.6	2.9	2.2	1.9	1.8
Other off-site transfers	0.7	1.1	1.4	0.8	0.5
Transfers off-site for disposal or other releases	509.9	568.0	557.5	539.0	549.4
Total production-related waste managed	28,038.9	32,040.2	25,856.3	24,907.1	24,473.9
Recycled on-site	7,385.1	7,585.0	7,058.0	7,249.1	6,881.2
Recycled off-site	1,833.6	1,959.2	1,768.9	1,688.8	1,630.3
Energy recovery on-site	2,717.3	2,777.8	2,638.5	2,865.5	2,727.2
Energy recovery off-site	903.1	827.0	822.7	803.5	705.1
Treated on-site	7,635.7	12,194.3	7,789.8	7,349.8	7,985.2
Treated off-site	686.0	612.1	620.9	562.7	524.4
Quantity disposed or otherwise release of on- and off-site	6,876.2	6,084.7	5,157.4	4,387.7	4,020.5
Non-production-related waste managed	25.9	243.0	37.1	20.5	28.0

[1] POTW (Publicly-Owned Treatment Work) is a wastewater treatment facility that is owned by a state or municipality.

Table 367. Toxic Chemical Releases by Industry: 2003

[In millions of pounds (4,438.7 represents 4,438,700,000), except as indicated. "Original Industries" include owners and operators. Covers facilities that are classified within Standard Classification Code groups 20 through 39, 10, 12, 49, 5169, 5171, and 4953/7169 that have 10 or more full-time employees, and that manufacture, process, or otherwise use any listed toxic chemical in quantities greater than the established threshold in the course of a calendar year and required to report]

Industry	1987 SIC[1] code	Total on- and off-site releases	On-site release Total [2]	On-site release Point source air emissions	On-site release Surface water discharges	Off-site releases/ transfers to disposal
Total [3]	(X)	4,438.7	3,920.7	1,381.3	222.6	518.0
Metal mining	10	1,245.7	1,244.7	1.8	0.7	1.0
Coal mining	12	12.9	12.9	0.1	0.2	-
Food and kindred products	20	153.2	145.8	35.1	83.1	7.3
Tobacco products	21	3.2	2.8	2.4	0.1	0.4
Textile mill products	22	7.4	6.5	4.8	0.3	0.9
Apparel and other textile products	23	0.7	0.5	0.4		0.2
Lumber and wood products	24	33.0	31.0	27.0	0.1	2.0
Furniture and fixtures	25	6.2	6.1	5.4	0.0	0.1
Paper and allied products	26	215.0	209.6	146.2	18.7	5.3
Printing and publishing	27	15.0	14.7	7.4	-	0.3
Chemical and allied products	28	544.7	500.3	168.6	44.5	44.4
Petroleum and coal products	29	75.0	71.9	34.6	17.1	3.1
Rubber and miscellaneous plastic products	30	75.3	65.8	51.3	0.1	9.5
Leather and leather products	31	2.1	1.0	0.7	0.0	1.1
Stone, clay, glass products	32	51.2	45.8	38.1	2.1	5.5
Primary metal industries	33	477.5	198.1	35.9	39.4	279.4
Fabricated metals products	34	58.6	38.8	23.7	2.3	19.8
Industrial machinery and equipment	35	14.3	10.7	4.1	0.2	3.6
Electronic, electric equipment	36	20.3	13.8	6.5	3.6	6.4
Transportation equipment	37	74.8	63.5	51.1	0.2	11.2
Instruments and related products	38	8.7	7.9	5.1	1.0	0.8
Miscellaneous	39	7.1	4.9	3.9	0.1	2.2
Electric utilities	49	3.2	2.8	1.8	-	0.3
Chemical wholesalers	5169	227.1	194.1	0.5	0.3	33.0
Petroleum bulk terminals	5171	22.4	21.2	2.9	4.9	1.3

- Represents or rounds to zero.   X Not applicable.   [1] Standard Industrial Classification, see text, Section 12, Labor Force.
[2] Includes on-site disposal to underground injection for Class I wells, Class II to V wells, other surface impoundments, land releases, and other releases, not shown separately.   [3] Includes industries with no specific industry identified, not shown separately.

Source of Tables 366 and 367: U.S. Environmental Protection Agency, *2003 TRI Public Data Release eReport,* See also <http://www.epa.gov/tri/tridata/tri03/2003eReport.pdf> (released May 2005).

Geography and Environment 231

Table 368. Toxic Chemical Releases by State: 2003

[In millions of pounds (4,438.7 represents 4,438,700,000). Excludes delisted chemicals, chemicals added in 1990, 1994, and 1995, and aluminum oxide, ammonia, hydrochloric acid, PBT chemicals, sulfuric acid, vanadium, and vanadium compounds. See headnote, Table 366]

State and Outlying areas	Total on- and off-site releases	On-site release Total[1]	On-site release Point source air emissions	On-site release Surface water discharges	Off-site releases/transfers to disposal	State and Outlying areas	Total on- and off-site releases	On-site release Total[1]	On-site release Point source air emissions	On-site release Surface water discharges	Off-site releases/transfers to disposal
Total	4,438.7	3,920.7	1,381.3	222.6	518.0	NV	409.1	408.3	1.3	0.1	0.8
U.S. total	4,428.3	3,911.0	1,373.2	222.2	517.3	NH	5.9	5.5	5.2	0.1	0.5
AL	118.4	99.5	48.0	7.8	19.0	NJ	23.1	16.8	10.5	4.1	6.3
AK	539.6	539.4	1.7	0.5	0.2	NM	17.9	17.8	0.6	0.1	0.1
AZ	48.2	47.6	3.6	0.0	0.6	NY	44.0	39.5	24.3	7.9	4.5
AR	40.6	34.4	14.0	5.4	6.2	NC	129.1	119.1	93.4	8.6	10.0
CA	57.9	50.2	14.2	4.6	7.7	ND	23.6	14.4	4.6	0.2	9.2
CO	22.5	18.0	2.2	3.0	4.5	OH	251.6	206.4	123.3	6.7	45.2
CT	5.4	3.7	2.2	0.7	1.7	OK	30.0	25.3	13.5	3.5	4.6
DE	13.6	9.5	7.0	0.9	4.1	OR	42.1	40.9	10.8	2.5	1.2
DC	(Z)	(Z)	(Z)	(Z)	(Z)	PA	166.9	114.0	85.1	9.7	52.9
FL	126.5	123.0	71.7	2.5	3.4	RI	0.9	0.6	0.4	(Z)	0.3
GA	126.7	124.3	90.2	9.6	2.4	SC	83.7	61.4	45.4	3.5	22.3
HI	3.1	2.7	1.9	0.4	0.4	SD	10.3	10.2	0.8	3.2	0.1
ID	61.3	60.7	3.0	4.6	0.6	TN	142.5	135.4	77.7	2.4	7.2
IL	132.4	100.9	47.4	7.2	31.5	TX	261.9	235.4	56.5	21.7	26.5
IN	234.8	134.9	65.0	23.3	99.9	UT	242.0	238.9	7.3	0.1	3.1
IA	37.4	29.9	18.3	3.3	7.5	VT	0.3	0.2	(Z)	0.1	0.1
KS	28.9	25.6	10.6	4.0	3.3	VA	74.2	64.8	45.7	8.2	9.4
KY	90.6	82.8	51.7	3.0	7.8	WA	22.9	21.1	11.8	1.4	1.7
LA	126.8	121.1	42.7	11.3	5.8	WV	102.2	96.7	75.1	4.2	5.4
ME	9.3	8.5	3.6	3.3	0.8	WI	50.8	31.1	21.8	4.6	19.7
MD	45.5	40.8	35.3	2.7	4.7	WY	19.3	18.2	1.6	(Z)	1.0
MA	9.0	6.9	5.3	0.1	2.1	American Samoa	(Z)	(Z)	(Z)	-	-
MI	101.6	64.7	46.3	1.2	36.9	Guam	0.2	0.2	0.2	0.1	(Z)
MN	31.4	25.8	10.5	1.2	5.6	Northern Marianas	(Z)	(Z)	(Z)	(Z)	(Z)
MS	63.1	61.6	26.0	7.8	1.5	Puerto Rico	8.8	8.1	7.1	-	0.7
MO	102.5	94.4	24.9	2.6	8.1	Virgin Islands	1.3	1.3	0.8	0.4	(Z)
MT	45.2	44.2	3.5	(Z)	1.0						
NE	51.5	33.7	6.0	18.2	17.7						

- Represents zero.   Z Less than 50,000.   [1] Includes other types of release not shown separately.
Source: U.S. Environmental Protection Agency, 2003 TRI Public Data Release eReport, (released May 2005). See also <http://www.epa.gov/tri/tridata/tri03/2003eReport.pdf> (released May 2005).

Table 369. Hazardous Waste Sites on the National Priority List by State and Outlying Area: 2004

[As of December 31. Includes both proposed and final sites listed on the National Priorities List for the Superfund program as authorized by the Comprehensive Environmental Response, Compensation, and Liability Act of 1980, and the Superfund Amendments and Reauthorization Act of 1986]

State and outlying area	Total sites	Rank	Percent distribution	Federal	Non-federal	State and outlying area	Total sites	Rank	Percent distribution	Federal	Non-federal
Total	1,302	(X)	(X)	164	1,138	Montana	15	27	1.2	-	15
United States	1,286	(X)	100.0	162	1,124	Nebraska	12	35	0.9	1	11
Alabama	15	25	1.2	3	12	Nevada	1	49	0.1	-	1
Alaska	6	44	0.5	5	1	New Hampshire	20	20	1.6	1	19
Arizona	9	41	0.7	2	7	New Jersey	114	1	8.9	8	106
Arkansas	10	40	0.8	-	10	New Mexico	13	32	1.0	1	12
California	95	3	7.4	23	72	New York	91	4	7.1	4	87
Colorado	18	21	1.4	3	15	North Carolina	30	14	2.3	2	28
Connecticut	16	23	1.2	1	15	North Dakota	-	50	0.0	-	-
Delaware	14	28	1.1	1	13	Ohio	37	11	2.9	5	32
District of Columbia	1	(X)	0.1	1	-	Oklahoma	11	37	0.9	1	10
Florida	52	6	4.0	6	46	Oregon	11	38	0.9	2	9
Georgia	15	26	1.2	2	13	Pennsylvania	96	2	7.5	6	90
Hawaii	3	46	0.2	2	1	Rhode Island	12	36	0.9	2	10
Idaho	9	42	0.7	2	7	South Carolina	26	17	2.0	2	24
Illinois	47	7	3.7	5	42	South Dakota	2	47	0.2	1	1
Indiana	30	13	2.3	-	30	Tennessee	14	30	1.1	4	10
Iowa	13	31	1.0	1	12	Texas	43	9	3.3	4	39
Kansas	12	33	0.9	2	10	Utah	17	22	1.3	4	13
Kentucky	14	29	1.1	1	13	Vermont	11	39	0.9	-	11
Louisiana	16	24	1.2	1	15	Virginia	30	15	2.3	11	19
Maine	12	34	0.9	3	9	Washington	47	8	3.7	14	33
Maryland	20	19	1.6	9	11	West Virginia	9	43	0.7	2	7
Massachusetts	32	12	2.5	7	25	Wisconsin	39	10	3.0	-	39
Michigan	69	5	5.4	1	68	Wyoming	2	48	0.2	1	1
Minnesota	24	18	1.9	2	22	Guam	2	(X)	(X)	1	1
Mississippi	5	45	0.4	-	5	Puerto Rico	12	(X)	(X)	1	11
Missouri	26	16	2.0	3	23	Virgin Islands	2	(X)	(X)	-	2

X Not applicable.   - Represents zero.
Source: U.S. Environmental Protection Agency, Supplementary Materials: CERCLIS3/WasteLan Database (25 April 2005).

232   Geography and Environmental

Table 370. **Federal Funding for the Superfund, Brownfields, and Related Programs: 1995 to 2005**

[In millions of dollars (1,354 represents $1,354,000,000). For fiscal years ending in year shown; see text, Section 8, State and Local Government Finances and Employment. Represents either outlays or obligations; see footnotes below for further explanation]

Program	1995	1996	1997	1998	1999	2000	2001	2002	2003	2004	2005
Current dollars											
Total	1,354	1,314	1,394	1,503	1,503	1,403	1,408	1,418	1,590	1,579	1,567
Superfund [1]	1,224	1,195	1,239	1,279	1,273	1,178	1,179	1,175	1,265	1,258	1,247
Brownfields [3]	2	8	37	89	91	92	91	95	167	170	164
ATSDR [4]	69	59	64	74	76	70	75	78	82	73	76
NIEHS [5]	59	52	54	61	63	63	63	70	76	78	80
Constant (2004) dollars [6]											
Total	1,589	1,514	1,578	1,682	1,660	1,519	1,489	1,473	1,622	1,579	1,537
Superfund [2]	1,437	1,377	1,403	1,431	1,406	1,275	1,247	1,220	1,290	1,258	1,223
Brownfields [3]	2	9	42	100	100	100	96	99	170	170	161
ATSDR [4]	81	68	72	83	84	76	79	81	84	73	75
NIEHS [5]	69	60	61	68	70	68	67	73	78	78	78

[1] For purposes of this analysis, excludes all emergency supplemental appropriations designated specifically for homeland security purposes. [2] Superfund program funding is the enacted appropriations excluding amounts designated for the Brownfields, ATSDR, and NIEHS programs. [3] Brownfields funding includes amounts received through the Superfund appropriations for fiscal years 1995 through 2002 and direct appropriations for fiscal years 2003 through 2005. [4] Agency for Toxic Substances and Disease Registry (ATSDR) and National Institute for Environmental Health Sciences (NIEHS) funding includes amounts received through the Superfund appropriations for fiscal years 1995 through 2000 and direct appropriations for fiscal years 2001 through 2005. [5] The amount designated for the Brownfields program in fiscal year 1993 was 0.15 million in current year dollars and 0.18 in constant year 2004 dollars. [6] The current years dollars adjusted for inflation using the Gross Domestic Product (Chained) Price Index, with 2004 as the reference year.

Source: U.S. Government Accountability Office, *Hazardous Waste Programs: Information on Appropriations and Expenditures for Superfund, Brownfields, and Related Programs*, series GAO-05-746R, June 30, 2005. See also <http://www.gao.gov/new.items/d05746r.pdf> (released 30 June 2005).

Table 371. **Hazardous Waste Generated, Shipped, and Received by State and Outlying Area: 2001**

[In thousands of tons (40,821 represents 40,821,000). Covers hazardous wastes regulated under the Resource Conservation and Recovery Act (RCRA) of 1976 as amended. For generation, based on reports from any large quantity generator while for shipments based on large quantity generators and facilities which treated, stored, or disposed on RCRA hazardous wastes on site. For further information on coverage, see report]

State and outlying area	Generated	Shipped	Received	State and outlying area	Generated	Shipped	Received
Total	40,821.5	6,831.8	8,094.7	Montana	6.9	6.5	-
				Nebraska	31.4	26.3	580.1
United States.	40,633.4	6,730.6	8,050.2	Nevada	277.3	5.6	54.7
				New Hampshire	12.3	12.3	-
Alabama	1,569.7	276.7	149.8	New Jersey	586.2	389.6	540.1
Alaska	5.1	4.0	-	New Mexico.	962.8	7.4	1.5
Arizona	96.5	59.3	50.6				
Arkansas.	857.9	290.1	262.3	New York	3,534.3	181.7	585.3
California.	807.3	716.7	269.3	North Carolina	329.7	85.8	24.6
Colorado.	66.8	29.9	14.5	North Dakota	574.6	3.5	0.5
Connecticut	62.5	74.9	52.1	Ohio.	1,889.1	703.7	885.6
Delaware.	17.5	16.9	3.3	Oklahoma	887.6	35.4	72.6
District of Columbia. . . .	2.1	2.1	-	Oregon	49.9	48.5	40.8
Florida	400.1	58.3	14.9	Pennsylvania	398.4	313.7	417.4
Georgia	760.0	110.7	19.4	Rhode Island	9.4	9.3	6.8
Hawaii	464.9	0.8	0.1	South Carolina	142.5	155.6	268.8
Idaho	214.4	5.1	90.4	South Dakota	1.0	1.3	0.2
Illinois.	1,412.1	370.8	354.3	Tennessee	629.8	54.4	40.6
Indiana	1,127.5	426.6	501.3	Texas	7,555.4	663.5	762.0
Iowa	47.1	44.9	1.0	Utah.	88.7	88.6	83.3
Kansas.	1,571.6	46.9	169.6	Vermont	4.1	4.4	0.3
Kentucky.	2,686.6	205.2	96.5	Virginia	209.4	89.4	75.7
Louisiana	3,883.6	150.2	258.3	Washington	240.8	77.5	41.0
Maine	6.2	5.4	1.4	West Virginia	101.2	43.1	8.4
Maryland.	17.6	10.6	53.6	Wisconsin	294.8	163.0	112.2
Massachusetts	1,121.8	61.9	26.9	Wyoming.	37.6	1.8	-
Michigan	649.2	426.6	568.5				
Minnesota	1,662.6	62.2	182.3	Guam	0.4	0.4	0.1
Mississippi.	2,165.7	36.5	68.1	Puerto Rico	176.6	98.1	44.4
Missouri	101.8	65.5	239.4	Virgin Islands	2.0	2.0	-

- Represents zero.

Source: U.S. Environmental Protection Agency, *The National Biennial RCRA Hazardous Waste Report (Based on 2001 Data)*, series EPA530-R-03-007. See also <http://www.epa.gov/epaoswer/hazwaste/data/brs01/national.pdf> (released 15 July 2003).

Geography and Environment   **233**

Table 372. **Environmental Industry—Revenues and Employment, by Industry Segment: 1990 to 2004**

[148.8 represents $148,800,000,000. Covers approximately 59,000 private and public companies engaged in environmental activities]

Industry segment	Revenue (bil. dol.)				Employment			
	1990	1995	2000	2004	1990	1995	2000	2004
Industry total.............	**148.8**	**186.3**	**214.2**	**240.8**	**1,171,700**	**1,358,600**	**1,451,400**	**1,501,600**
Analytical services [1].......	2.1	1.8	1.8	1.8	24,100	21,200	20,200	19,800
Wastewater treatment works [2]	18.4	25.1	28.7	32.6	82,600	108,500	118,800	128,000
Solid waste management [3]	26.1	32.5	39.4	44.1	205,500	243,400	266,300	279,300
Hazardous waste management [4].....	7.1	8.4	8.5	8.5	60,300	70,800	70,000	66,800
Remediation/industrial services.....	9.9	9.9	10.1	10.5	118,900	112,000	100,200	93,300
Consulting and engineering	12.5	15.5	17.4	20.0	147,100	180,300	184,000	195,900
Water equipment and chemicals	13.4	16.6	19.8	23.6	91,800	110,300	130,500	142,000
Instrument manufacturing	2.0	3.0	3.8	4.1	18,000	26,200	30,300	31,200
Air pollution control equipment [5].....	11.1	15.3	19.1	19.4	81,500	109,100	129,600	127,300
Waste management equipment [6]....	8.7	9.8	10.0	9.5	69,600	75,500	75,500	68,200
Process and prevention technology ...	0.4	0.8	1.2	1.5	9,300	19,500	29,000	27,600
Water utilities [7]	19.8	25.3	29.9	33.8	98,500	118,200	130,000	138,100
Resource recovery [8].............	13.1	16.9	16.0	17.1	142,900	136,000	127,000	128,500
Clean energy systems and power	4.3	5.6	8.6	14.3	21,600	27,600	40,000	55,600

[1] Covers environmental laboratory testing and services. [2] Mostly revenues collected by municipal entities. [3] Covers such activities as collection, transportation, transfer stations, disposal, landfill ownership and management for solid waste. [4] Transportation and disposal of hazardous, medical and nuclear waste. [5] Includes stationary and mobile sources. [6] Includes vehicles, containers, liners, processing and remediation equipment. [7] Revenues generated from the sale of water. [8] Revenues generated from the sale of recovered metals, paper, plastic, etc.

Source: Environmental Business International, Inc., San Diego, CA, *Environmental Business Journal*, monthly (copyright).

Table 373. **Threatened and Endangered Wildlife and Plant Species—Number: 2005**

[As of **April**. Endangered species: One in danger of becoming extinct throughout all or a significant part of its natural range. Threatened species: One likely to become endangered in the foreseeable future]

Item	Mammals	Birds	Reptiles	Amphibians	Fish	Snails	Clams	Crustaceans	Insects	Arachnids	Plants
Total listings	**349**	**271**	**116**	**30**	**125**	**33**	**72**	**21**	**48**	**12**	**749**
Endangered species, total..............	**319**	**252**	**78**	**19**	**81**	**22**	**64**	**18**	**39**	**12**	**600**
United States.......	68	77	14	11	70	21	62	18	35	12	599
Foreign...........	251	175	64	8	11	1	2	-	4	-	1
Threatened species, total..............	**30**	**19**	**38**	**11**	**44**	**11**	**8**	**3**	**9**	**-**	**149**
United States.......	10	13	22	10	43	11	8	3	9	-	147
Foreign...........	20	6	16	1	1	-	-	-	-	-	2

Source: U.S. Fish and Wildlife Service, *Endangered Species Bulletin*, bimonthly; and <http://ecos.fws.gov/tesspublic/TESSBoxscore> (released 05 April 2005).

Table 374. **Tornadoes, Floods, Tropical Storms, and Lightning: 1993 to 2003**

Weather type	1993	1994	1995	1996	1997	1998	1999	2000	2001	2002	2003, prel.
Tornadoes: [1]											
Lives lost	33	69	30	26	67	130	94	41	40	55	54
Injuries	(NA)	(NA)	650	705	1,033	1,868	1,842	882	743	968	1,087
Property loss (mil. dol.)	(NA)	(NA)	410.8	719.6	730.7	1,714.2	1,989.9	423.6	630.1	801.3	1,263.2
Floods and flash floods:											
Lives lost	103	91	80	131	118	136	68	38	48	49	85
Injuries	(NA)	(NA)	57	95	525	6,440	301	47	277	88	65
Property loss (mil. dol.)	(NA)	(NA)	1,250.5	2,120.7	6,910.6	2,324.8	1,420.7	1,255.1	1,220.3	655.0	2,540.9
North Atlantic tropical storms and hurricanes [2]	8	7	19	13	7	14	12	15	15	12	(NA)
Number of hurricanes reaching U.S. mainland ...	1	-	2	2	1	3	3	-	-	1	(NA)
Direct deaths on U.S mainland............	2	9	17	37	1	9	19	-	24	51	14
Property loss in U.S. mil.dol.).............	57.0	973.0	5,932.3	1,436.1	667.6	3,546.6	4,190.1	8.1	5,187.8	1,104.4	1,879.5
Lightning:											
Deaths	43	69	85	52	42	44	46	51	44	51	44
Injuries	295	577	433	309	306	283	243	364	371	256	237

- Represents zero. NA Not available. [1] Source: U.S. National Weather Service, Internet site <http://www.spc .noaa.gov/climo/torn/monthlytornstats.html> (accessed 14 April 2004). A violent, rotating column of air descending from a cumulonimbus cloud in the form of a tubular- or funnel-shaped cloud, usually characterized by movements along a narrow path and wind speeds from 100 to over 300 miles per hour. Also known as a "twister" or "waterspout." [2] Source: National Hurricane Center (NHC), Coral Gables, FL, unpublished data. For data on individual hurricanes, see the NHC Web site at <http://www.nhc.noaa.gov/>. Tropical storms have winds of 39 to 73 miles per hour; hurricanes have winds of 74 miles per hour or higher.

Source: Except as noted, U.S. National Oceanic and Atmospheric Administration (NOAA), *Storm Data*, monthly. See also NOAA Web site at <http://www.nws.noaa.gov/om/hazstats.shtml> and <http://www.nws.noaa.gov/om/severeweather/sum03.pdf> (released 03 March 2004).

Table 375. Major U.S. Weather Disasters: 1995 to 2004

[6.5 represents $6,500,000,000. Covers only weather related disasters costing $1 billion or more]

Event	Description	Time period	Estimated cost (bil.dol.)	Deaths
Hurricane Jeanne	Category 3 hurricane makes landfall in east-central Florida, causing considerable damage in Florida and some flood damage in GA, SC, NC, VA, MD, DE, NJ, PA, and NY.	September 2004	over 6.5	28
Hurricane Ivan	Category 3 hurricane makes landfall on Gulf coast of Alabama causing significant damage in AL and FL and wind/flood damage in GA, SC, NC, LA, MS, WV, MD, TN, KY, OH, DE, NJ, PA, and NY.	September 2004	over 12	52
Hurricane Jeanne	Category 2 hurricane makes landfall in east-central Florida causing significant damage in FL and considerable flood damage in GA, SC, NC, and NY.	September 2004	over 9	38
Hurricane Charly	Category 4 hurricane makes landfall in southwest FL resulting in major damage in FL and some damage in SC and NC.	September 2004	over 14	34
Southern California wildfires	Dry weather, high winds, and resulting wildfires in southern CA burned 743,000 acres and destroyed 3700 homes.	Oct.–early Nov. 2003	2.5	22
Hurricane Isabel	Category 2 hurricane makes landfall in eastern NC, causing damage along coasts of NC, VA, and MD with wind damage and flooding in NC, VA, MD, DE, WV, NJ, NY and PA.	September 2003	over 4	47
Midwest severe storms and tornadoes	Numerous tornadoes over the midwest, MS River valley, and OH/TN River valleys with record 400 tornadoes in one week.	Early May 2003	over 3.1	41
Storms and hail	Severe storms and large hail over southern plains, lower MS River valley, and TX.	Early April 2003	over 1.6	21
Widespread drought	Moderate to extreme drought over large portions of 30 states.	Spring to fall 2002	over 10	43
Western fire season	Major fires over 11 western states from Rockies to west coast.	Spring to fall 2002	over 2	3
Tropical Storm Allison	Tropical storm produced rainfall and severe flooding in coastal portions of TX and LA and damage in MS, FL, VA, and PA.	June 2001	5.0	140
Midwest and Ohio Valley hail and tornadoes	Storms, tornadoes, and hail in TX, OK, KS, NE, IA, MO, IL, IN, WI, MI, OH, KY, and PA.	April 2001	1.7	75
Southern drought/heat wave	Severe drought and heat over south-central and southeastern states cause significant losses in agriculture and related industries.	Spring–summer 2000	over 4.0	256
Western fire season	Severe fire season in western states.	Spring–summer 2000	over 2.0	55
Hurricane Floyd	Category 2 hurricane in NC, causing severe flooding in NC and some flooding in SC, VA, MD, PA, NY, NJ, DE, RI, CT, MA, and VT.	September 1999	6.0	31
Drought/heat wave	Drought/heatwave over eastern U.S.	Summer 1999	1.0	40
Oklahoma-Kansas tornadoes	Category F4-F5 tornadoes hit OK, KS, TX, and TN.	May 1999	1.0	75
Arkansas-Tennessee tornadoes	Two outbreaks of tornadoes in 6-day period.	January 1999	1.3	256
Texas flooding	Severe flooding in southeast Texas from 2 heavy rain events with 10–20 in. totals.	Oct.–Nov. 1998	1.0	55
Hurricane Georges	Category 2 hurricane in Puerto Rico, Florida Keys, and Gulf coasts of LA, MS, AL, and FL.	September 1998	3-4	31
Hurricane Bonnie	Category 3 hurricane in eastern NC and VA.	August 1998	1.0	31
Southern drought/ heat wave	Severe drought and heat wave from TX/OK to the Carolinas.	Summer 1998	6.0	16
Minnesota severe storms/hail	Very damaging severe thunderstorms with large hail over wide areas of Minnesota.	May 1998	1.5	2
Southeast severe weather	Tornadoes and flooding related to strong El Nino in the southeast.	Winter/Spring 1998	1.0	200
Northeast ice storm	Intense ice storm hits ME, NH, VT, and NY.	January 1998	1.4	16
Northern plains flooding	Severe flooding in Dakotas and Minnesota due to heavy spring snowmelt.	April–May 1997	2.0	11
MS and OH valleys flooding	Tornadoes and severe flooding hit the states of AR, MO, MS, TN, IL, IN, KY, OH, and WV.	March 1997	1.0	67
West Coast flooding	Flooding from rains and snowmelt in CA, WA, OR, ID, NV, and MT	Dec. 1996–Jan. 1999	2-3	36
Hurricane Fran	Category 3 hurricane in NC and VA.	Sept. 1996	5.0	(NA)
Southern Plains severe drought	Drought in agricultural areas of TX and OK.	Fall 1995– summer 1996	Over 4	9
Pacific Northwest severe flooding	Flooding from heavy rain and snowmelt in OR, WA, ID, and MT.	Feb. 1996	1.0	187
Blizzard of '96 followed by flooding	Heavy snowstorm followed by severe flooding in Appalachians, Mid-Atlantic, and Northeast.	Jan. 1996	3.0	27

- Represents zero. NA Not available or not reported.

Source: U.S. National Oceanic and Atmospheric Administration, National Climatic Data Center, *"Billion Dollar U.S. Weather Disasters, 1980-2003"* (release date: March 2, 2004) and also <http://www.ncdc.noaa.gov/oa/reports/billionz.html#TOP> (released 12 January 2005).

Geography and Environment **235**

Table 376. Highest and Lowest Temperatures by State Through 2000

State	Highest temperatures			Lowest temperatures		
	Station	Tempera-ture (F)	Date	Station	Tempera-ture (F)	Date
U.S. . . .	Greenland Ranch, CA. .	134	Jul. 10, 1913	Prospect Creek, AK . . .	-80	Jan. 23, 1971
AL.	Centerville	112	Sep. 5, 1925	New Market	-27	Jan. 30, 1966
AK.	Fort Yukon	100	[1]Jun. 27, 1915	Prospect Creek Camp . .	-80	Jan. 23, 1971
AZ.	Lake Havasu City	128	Jun. 29, 1994	Hawley Lake	-40	Jan. 7, 1971
AR.	Ozark	120	Aug. 10, 1936	Pond.	-29	Feb. 13, 1905
CA.	Greenland Ranch	134	Jul. 10, 1913	Boca	-45	Jan. 20, 1937
CO	Bennett	118	Jul. 11, 1888	Maybell	-61	Feb. 1, 1985
CT.	Danbury	106	Jul. 15, 1995	Falls Village	-32	Feb. 16, 1943
DE.	Millsboro	110	Jul. 21, 1930	Millsboro	-17	Jan. 17, 1893
FL.	Monticello	109	Jun. 29, 1931	Tallahassee	-2	Feb. 13, 1899
GA	Greenville	112	Aug. 20, 1983	CCC Camp F-16.	-17	[1]Jan. 27, 1940
HI	Pahala	100	Apr. 27, 1931	Mauna Kea Obs. 111.2. .	12	May 17, 1979
ID	Orofino	118	Jul. 28, 1934	Island Park Dam	-60	Jan. 18, 1943
IL	East St. Louis.	117	Jul. 14, 1954	Congerville.	-36	Jan. 5, 1999
IN	Collegeville	116	Jul. 14, 1936	New Whiteland	-36	Jan. 19, 1994
IA	Keokuk	118	Jul. 20, 1934	Elkader	-47	[2]Feb. 3, 1996
KS.	Alton (near)	121	[2]Jul. 24, 1936	Lebanon	-40	Feb. 13, 1905
KY.	Greensburg	114	Jul. 28, 1930	Shelbyville	-37	Jan. 19, 1994
LA	Plain Dealing	114	Aug. 10, 1936	Minden	-16	Feb. 13, 1899
ME	North Bridgton	105	[2]Jul. 10, 1911	Van Buren	-48	Jan. 19, 1925
MD	Cumberland & Frederick .	109	[2]Jul. 10, 1936	Oakland . . , ...	-40	Jan. 13, 1912
MA	New Bedford & Chester .	107	Aug. 2, 1975	Chester.	-35	Jan. 12, 1981
MI.	Mio.	112	Jul. 13, 1936	Vanderbilt	-51	Feb. 9, 1934
MN	Moorhead	114	[2]Jul. 6, 1936	Tower	-60	Feb. 2, 1996
MS	Holly Springs	115	Jul. 29, 1930	Corinth	-19	Jan. 30, 1966
MO	Warsaw & Union	118	[2]Jul. 14, 1954	Warsaw.	-40	Feb. 13, 1905
MT	Medicine Lake	117	Jul. 5, 1937	Rogers Pass	-70	Jan. 20, 1954
NE.	Minden	118	[2]Jul. 24, 1936	Camp Clarke	-47	Feb. 12, 1899
NV.	Laughlin	125	Jun. 29, 1994	San Jacinto	-50	Jan. 8, 1937
NH	Nashua	106	Jul. 4, 1911	Mt. Washington.	-47	Jan. 29, 1934
NJ	Runyon	110	Jul. 10, 1936	River Vale	-34	Jan. 5, 1904
NM	Waste Isolat Pilot Plt . . .	122	Jun. 27, 1994	Gavilan	-50	Feb. 1, 1951
NY.	Troy	108	Jul. 22, 1926	Old Forge	-52	[2]Feb. 18, 1979
NC	Fayetteville.	110	Aug. 21, 1983	Mt. Mitchell	-34	Jan. 21, 1985
ND	Steele.	121	Jul. 6, 1936	Parshall.	-60	Feb. 15, 1936
OH	Gallipolis (near).	113	[2]Jul. 21, 1934	Milligan	-39	Feb. 10, 1899
OK	Tipton	120	[2]Jun. 27, 1994	Watts	-27	Jan. 18, 1930
OR	Pendleton	119	Aug. 10, 1898	Seneca	-54	[2]Feb. 10, 1933
PA	Phoenixville	111	[2]Jul. 10, 1936	Smethport	-42	[1]Jan. 5, 1904
RI	Providence	104	Aug. 2, 1975	Kingston	-23	Jan. 11, 1942
SC.	Camden	111	[2]Jun. 28, 1954	Caesars Head	-19	Jan. 21, 1985
SD.	Gannvalley.	120	Jul. 5, 1936	McIntosh	-58	Feb. 17, 1936
TN.	Perryville	113	[2]Aug. 9, 1930	Mountain City	-32	Dec. 30, 1917
TX.	Seymour	120	Aug. 12, 1936	Seminole	-23	[2]Feb. 8, 1933
UT.	Saint George	117	Jul. 5, 1985	Peter's Sink	-69	Feb. 1, 1985
VT.	Vernon	105	Jul. 4, 1911	Bloomfield	-50	Dec. 30, 1933
VA	Balcony Falls	110	Jul. 15, 1954	Mtn. Lake Bio. Stn. . . .	-30	Jan. 22, 1985
WA	Ice Harbor Dam	118	[2]Aug. 5, 1961	Mazama & Winthrop . . .	-48	Dec. 30, 1968
WV	Martinsburg	112	[2]Jul. 10, 1936	Lewisburg	-37	Dec. 30, 1917
WI	Wisconsin Dells	114	Jul. 13, 1936	Couderay.	-55	Feb. 4, 1996
WY	Basin	114	Jul. 12, 1900	Riverside R.S.	-66	Feb. 9, 1933

[1] Estimated. [2] Also on earlier dates at the same or other places.

Source: U.S. National Oceanic and Atmospheric Administration, <http://www.lwf.ncdc.noaa.gov/oa/climate/severeweather/temperatures.html> (released 25 April 2002).

Table 377. Normal Daily Mean, Maximum, and Minimum Temperatures— Selected Cities

[In Fahrenheit degrees. Airport data except as noted. Based on standard 30-year period, 1971 through 2000]

State	Station	Daily mean temperature			Daily maximum temperature			Daily minimum temperature		
		Jan.	July	Annual average	Jan.	July	Annual average	Jan.	July	Annual average
AL	Mobile	50.1	81.5	66.8	60.7	91.2	77.4	39.5	71.8	56.2
AK	Juneau	25.7	56.8	41.5	30.6	64.3	47.6	20.7	49.2	35.3
AZ	Phoenix	54.2	92.8	72.9	65.0	104.2	84.5	43.4	81.4	61.1
AR	Little Rock	40.1	82.4	62.1	49.5	92.8	72.7	30.8	72.0	51.5
CA	Los Angeles	57.1	69.3	63.3	65.6	75.3	70.6	48.6	63.3	56.1
	Sacramento	46.3	75.4	61.1	53.8	92.4	73.7	38.8	58.3	48.4
	San Diego	57.8	70.9	64.4	65.8	75.8	70.8	49.7	65.9	58.1
	San Francisco	49.4	62.8	57.3	55.9	71.1	65.1	42.9	54.5	49.6
CO	Denver	29.2	73.4	50.1	43.2	88.0	64.2	15.2	58.7	35.8
CT	Hartford	25.7	73.7	50.2	34.1	84.9	60.5	17.2	62.4	40.0
DE	Wilmington	31.5	76.6	54.4	39.3	86.0	63.6	23.7	67.3	45.1
DC	Washington	34.9	79.2	57.5	42.5	88.3	66.4	27.3	70.1	48.6
FL	Jacksonville	53.1	81.6	68.0	64.2	90.8	78.4	41.9	72.4	57.6
	Miami	68.1	83.7	76.7	76.5	90.9	84.2	59.6	76.5	69.1
GA	Atlanta	42.7	80.0	62.2	51.9	89.4	72.0	33.5	70.6	52.3
HI	Honolulu	73.0	80.8	77.5	80.4	87.8	84.7	65.7	73.8	70.2
ID	Boise	30.2	74.7	52.0	36.7	89.2	62.6	23.6	60.3	41.3
IL	Chicago	22.0	73.3	49.1	29.6	83.5	58.3	14.3	63.2	39.8
	Peoria	22.5	75.1	50.8	30.7	85.7	60.7	14.3	64.6	40.9
IN	Indianapolis	26.5	75.4	52.5	34.5	85.6	62.3	18.5	65.2	42.7
IA	Des Moines	20.4	76.1	50.0	29.1	86.0	59.8	11.7	66.1	40.2
KS	Wichita	30.2	81.0	56.4	40.1	92.9	67.4	20.3	69.1	45.2
KY	Louisville	33.0	78.4	57.0	41.0	87.0	66.0	24.9	69.8	47.9
LA	New Orleans	52.6	82.7	68.8	61.8	91.1	78.0	43.4	74.2	59.6
ME	Portland	21.7	68.7	45.8	30.9	78.8	55.2	12.5	58.6	36.3
MD	Baltimore	32.3	76.5	54.6	41.2	87.2	65.1	23.5	65.8	44.2
MA	Boston	29.3	73.9	51.6	36.5	82.2	59.3	22.1	65.5	43.9
MI	Detroit	24.5	73.5	49.8	31.1	83.4	58.4	17.8	63.6	41.0
	Sault Ste. Marie	13.2	63.9	40.1	21.5	75.7	49.6	4.9	52.0	30.5
MN	Duluth	8.4	65.5	39.1	17.9	76.3	48.7	-1.2	54.6	29.3
	Minneapolis-St. Paul	13.1	73.2	45.4	21.9	83.3	54.7	4.3	63.0	35.9
MS	Jackson	45.0	81.4	64.1	55.1	91.4	75.0	35.0	71.4	53.2
MO	Kansas City	26.9	78.5	54.2	36.0	88.8	64.3	17.8	68.2	44.0
	St. Louis	29.6	80.2	56.3	37.9	89.8	65.7	21.2	70.6	46.9
MT	Great Falls	21.7	66.2	43.8	32.1	82.0	56.4	11.3	50.4	31.1
NE	Omaha	21.7	76.7	50.7	31.7	87.4	61.5	11.6	65.9	39.8
NV	Reno	33.6	71.3	51.3	45.5	91.2	67.4	21.8	51.4	35.2
NH	Concord	20.1	70.0	45.9	30.6	82.9	57.7	9.7	57.1	34.1
NJ	Atlantic City	32.1	75.3	53.5	41.4	85.1	63.6	22.8	65.4	43.3
NM	Albuquerque	35.7	78.5	56.8	47.6	92.3	70.4	23.8	64.7	43.2
NY	Albany	22.2	71.1	47.6	31.1	82.2	57.6	13.3	60.0	37.5
	Buffalo	24.5	70.8	48.0	31.1	79.6	55.9	17.8	62.1	39.9
	New York [1]	32.1	76.5	54.6	38.0	84.2	61.7	26.2	68.8	47.5
NC	Charlotte	41.7	80.3	61.4	51.3	90.1	71.7	32.1	70.6	51.0
	Raleigh	39.7	78.8	59.6	49.8	89.1	70.6	29.6	68.5	48.6
ND	Bismarck	10.2	70.4	42.3	21.1	84.5	54.5	-0.6	56.4	30.1
OH	Cincinnati	29.7	76.3	54.2	38.0	86.4	64.0	21.3	66.1	44.3
	Cleveland	25.7	71.9	49.7	32.6	81.4	58.1	18.8	62.3	41.2
	Columbus	28.3	75.1	52.9	36.2	85.3	62.6	20.3	64.9	43.2
OK	Oklahoma City	36.7	82.0	60.1	47.1	93.1	71.1	26.2	70.8	49.2
OR	Portland	39.9	68.1	53.5	45.6	79.3	62.1	34.2	56.9	44.8
PA	Philadelphia	32.3	77.6	55.3	39.0	85.5	63.2	25.5	69.7	47.4
	Pittsburgh	27.5	72.6	51.0	35.1	82.7	60.4	19.9	62.4	41.5
RI	Providence	28.7	73.3	51.1	37.1	82.6	60.2	20.3	64.1	42.0
SC	Columbia	44.6	82.0	63.6	55.1	92.1	74.8	34.0	71.8	52.5
SD	Sioux Falls	14.0	73.0	45.1	25.2	85.6	57.2	2.9	60.3	33.0
TN	Memphis	39.9	82.5	62.4	48.6	92.1	72.1	31.3	72.9	52.5
	Nashville	36.8	79.1	58.9	45.6	88.7	69.0	27.9	69.5	48.8
TX	Dallas-Fort Worth	44.1	85.0	65.5	54.1	95.4	75.8	34.0	74.6	55.1
	El Paso	45.1	83.3	64.7	57.2	94.5	77.1	32.9	72.0	52.1
	Houston	51.8	83.6	68.8	62.3	93.6	79.4	41.2	73.5	58.2
UT	Salt Lake City	29.2	77.0	52.0	37.0	90.6	62.9	21.3	63.4	41.2
VT	Burlington	18.0	70.6	45.2	26.7	81.4	54.5	9.3	59.8	35.8
VA	Norfolk	40.1	79.1	59.6	47.8	86.8	67.8	32.3	71.4	51.4
	Richmond	36.4	77.9	57.6	45.3	87.5	67.8	27.6	68.3	47.4
WA	Seattle-Tacoma	40.9	65.3	52.3	45.8	75.3	59.8	35.9	55.3	44.8
	Spokane	27.3	68.6	47.3	32.8	82.5	57.4	21.7	54.6	37.2
WV	Charleston	33.4	73.9	54.5	42.6	84.9	65.4	24.2	62.9	43.5
WI	Milwaukee	20.7	72.0	47.5	28.0	81.1	55.9	13.4	62.9	39.2
WY	Cheyenne	25.9	67.7	45.0	37.1	81.9	57.6	14.8	53.4	32.3
PR	San Juan	76.6	82.2	79.9	82.4	87.4	85.5	70.8	76.9	74.2

[1] City office data.

Source: U.S. National Oceanic and Atmospheric Administration, Climatography of the United States, No. 81.

Geography and Environment 237

Table 378. **Highest Temperature of Record—Selected Cities**

[In Fahrenheit degrees. Airport data, except as noted. For period of record through 2003]

State	Station	Length of record (years)	Jan.	Feb.	Mar.	Apr.	May	June	July	Aug.	Sept.	Oct.	Nov.	Dec.	Annual
AL	Mobile	62	84	82	90	94	100	102	104	105	99	93	87	81	105
AK	Juneau	59	57	57	61	74	82	86	90	83	73	61	56	54	90
AZ	Phoenix	66	88	92	100	105	113	122	121	116	118	107	95	88	122
AR	Little Rock	62	83	85	91	95	98	105	112	109	106	97	86	80	112
CA	Los Angeles	68	91	92	95	102	97	104	97	98	110	106	101	94	110
	Sacramento	53	70	76	88	95	105	115	114	110	108	104	87	72	115
	San Diego	63	88	90	93	98	96	101	95	98	111	107	97	88	111
	San Francisco.	76	72	78	85	92	97	106	105	100	103	99	85	75	106
CO	Denver.	61	73	76	84	90	96	104	104	101	97	89	79	75	104
CT	Hartford	49	66	73	89	96	99	100	102	102	99	91	81	76	102
DE	Wilmington	56	75	78	86	94	96	100	102	101	100	91	85	75	102
DC	Washington	62	79	82	89	95	99	101	104	105	101	94	86	79	105
FL	Jacksonville	62	85	88	91	95	100	103	105	102	100	96	88	84	105
	Miami	61	88	89	93	96	96	98	98	98	97	95	91	87	98
GA	Atlanta	55	79	80	89	93	95	101	105	102	98	95	84	79	105
HI	Honolulu	34	88	88	88	91	93	92	94	93	95	94	93	89	95
ID	Boise.	64	63	71	81	92	99	109	111	110	102	94	78	65	111
IL	Chicago	45	65	72	88	91	93	104	104	101	99	91	78	71	104
	Peoria	64	70	72	86	92	93	105	103	103	100	90	81	71	105
IN	Indianapolis	64	71	76	85	89	93	102	104	102	100	90	81	74	104
IA	Des Moines	64	67	73	91	93	98	103	105	108	101	95	81	69	108
KS	Wichita	51	75	87	89	96	100	110	113	110	108	95	85	83	113
KY	Louisville	56	77	77	86	91	95	102	106	101	104	92	84	76	106
LA	New Orleans.	57	83	85	89	92	96	100	101	102	101	94	87	84	102
ME	Portland	63	64	64	88	85	94	98	99	103	95	88	74	71	103
MD	Baltimore	53	75	79	89	94	98	101	104	105	100	92	83	77	105
MA	Boston.	52	66	70	89	94	95	100	102	102	100	90	79	76	102
MI	Detroit	45	62	70	81	89	93	104	102	100	98	91	77	69	104
	Sault Ste. Marie.	63	45	49	75	85	89	93	97	98	95	80	67	62	98
MN	Duluth	62	52	55	78	88	90	94	97	97	95	86	71	55	97
	Minneapolis-St. Paul. . .	65	58	61	83	95	96	102	105	102	98	90	77	68	105
MS	Jackson	40	83	85	89	94	99	105	106	107	104	95	88	84	107
MO	Kansas City	31	71	77	86	93	95	105	107	109	106	92	82	74	109
	St. Louis	46	76	85	89	93	94	102	107	107	104	94	85	76	107
MT	Great Falls	66	67	70	78	89	93	101	105	106	98	91	76	69	106
NE	Omaha	67	69	78	89	97	99	105	114	110	104	96	83	72	114
NV	Reno.	62	71	75	83	89	97	103	108	105	101	91	77	70	108
NH	Concord.	62	68	67	89	95	97	98	102	101	98	90	80	73	102
NJ	Atlantic City	60	78	75	87	94	99	106	104	103	99	90	84	77	106
NM	Albuquerque	64	69	76	85	89	98	107	105	101	100	91	77	72	107
NY	Albany.	57	65	68	89	92	94	99	100	99	100	89	82	71	100
	Buffalo	60	72	71	81	94	90	96	97	99	98	87	80	74	99
	New York [1]	135	72	75	86	96	99	101	106	104	102	94	84	75	106
NC	Charlotte	64	79	81	90	93	100	103	103	103	104	98	85	78	104
	Raleigh	59	80	84	92	95	97	104	105	105	104	98	88	80	105
ND	Bismarck	64	63	69	81	93	98	111	109	109	105	95	79	65	111
OH	Cincinnati	42	69	75	84	89	93	102	103	102	98	88	81	75	103
	Cleveland.	62	73	74	83	88	92	104	103	102	101	90	82	77	104
	Columbus.	64	74	75	85	89	94	102	100	101	100	90	80	76	102
OK	Oklahoma City	50	80	92	93	100	104	105	110	110	108	96	87	86	110
OR	Portland	63	63	71	80	90	100	100	107	107	105	92	73	65	107
PA	Philadelphia	62	74	74	87	95	97	100	104	101	100	96	81	73	104
	Pittsburgh	51	72	76	82	89	91	98	103	100	97	87	82	74	103
RI	Providence	50	69	72	85	98	95	97	102	104	100	86	78	77	104
SC	Columbia	56	84	84	91	94	101	107	107	107	101	101	90	83	107
SD	Sioux Falls	58	66	70	87	94	100	110	108	108	104	94	81	63	110
TN	Memphis	62	79	81	85	94	99	104	108	107	103	95	86	81	108
	Nashville	64	78	84	86	91	97	106	107	104	105	94	84	79	107
TX	Dallas-Fort Worth.	50	88	95	96	95	103	113	110	109	111	102	89	88	113
	El Paso	64	80	83	89	98	104	114	112	108	104	96	87	80	114
	Houston.	34	84	91	91	95	99	103	104	107	109	96	89	85	109
UT	Salt Lake City	75	63	69	78	86	99	104	107	106	100	89	75	69	107
VT	Burlington.	60	66	62	84	91	93	100	100	101	98	85	75	67	101
VA	Norfolk.	55	80	82	88	97	100	101	103	104	99	95	86	80	104
	Richmond.	74	81	83	93	96	100	104	105	102	103	99	86	81	105
WA	Seattle-Tacoma	59	64	70	75	85	93	96	100	99	98	89	74	64	100
	Spokane	56	59	63	71	90	96	101	103	108	98	86	67	56	108
WV	Charleston	56	79	79	89	94	93	98	104	101	102	92	85	80	104
WI	Milwaukee	63	62	68	82	91	93	101	103	103	98	89	77	68	103
WY	Cheyenne	68	66	71	74	83	91	100	100	96	95	83	75	69	100
PR	San Juan	49	92	96	96	97	96	97	95	97	97	98	96	94	98

[1] City office data.

Source: U.S. National Oceanic and Atmospheric Administration, *Comparative Climatic Data*, annual.

Table 379. Lowest Temperature of Record—Selected Cities

[In Fahrenheit degrees. Airport data, except as noted. For period of record through 2003]

State	Station	Length of record (years)	Jan.	Feb.	Mar.	Apr.	May	June	July	Aug.	Sept.	Oct.	Nov.	Dec.	Annual
AL	Mobile	62	3	11	21	32	43	49	60	59	42	30	22	8	3
AK	Juneau	59	-22	-22	-15	6	25	31	36	27	23	11	-5	-21	-22
AZ	Phoenix	66	17	22	25	32	40	50	61	60	47	34	25	22	17
AR	Little Rock	62	-4	-5	11	28	40	46	54	52	37	29	17	-1	-5
CA	Los Angeles	68	23	32	34	39	43	48	49	51	47	16	34	32	16
	Sacramento	53	23	23	26	31	36	41	48	49	43	36	26	18	18
	San Diego	63	29	36	39	41	48	51	55	57	51	43	38	34	29
	San Francisco	76	24	25	30	31	36	41	43	42	38	34	25	20	20
CO	Denver [1]	61	-25	-30	-11	-2	22	30	43	41	17	3	-8	-25	-30
CT	Hartford	49	-26	-21	-6	9	28	35	44	36	30	17	1	-14	-26
DE	Wilmington	56	-14	-6	2	18	30	41	48	43	36	24	14	-7	-14
DC	Washington	62	-5	4	11	24	34	47	54	49	39	29	16	1	-5
FL	Jacksonville	62	7	19	23	34	45	47	47	59	48	36	21	11	7
	Miami	61	30	32	32	46	53	60	69	68	68	51	39	30	30
GA	Atlanta	55	-8	5	10	26	37	46	53	55	36	28	3	-	-8
HI	Honolulu	34	53	53	55	57	60	65	66	67	66	61	57	54	53
ID	Boise	64	-17	-15	6	19	22	31	35	34	23	11	-3	-25	-25
IL	Chicago	45	-27	-19	-8	7	24	36	40	41	28	17	1	-25	-27
	Peoria	64	-25	-19	-10	14	25	39	47	41	26	19	-2	-23	-25
IN	Indianapolis	64	-27	-21	-7	16	28	37	44	41	28	17	-2	-23	-27
IA	Des Moines	64	-24	-26	-22	9	30	38	47	40	26	14	-4	-22	-26
KS	Wichita	51	-12	-21	-2	15	31	43	51	48	31	18	1	-16	-21
KY	Louisville	56	-22	-19	-1	22	31	42	50	46	33	23	-1	-15	-22
LA	New Orleans	57	14	16	25	32	41	50	60	60	42	35	24	11	11
ME	Portland	63	-26	-39	-21	8	23	33	40	33	23	15	3	-21	-39
MD	Baltimore	53	-7	-3	6	20	32	40	50	45	35	25	13	-	-7
MA	Boston	52	-12	-4	6	16	34	45	50	47	38	28	15	-7	-12
MI	Detroit	45	-21	-15	-4	10	25	36	41	38	29	17	9	-10	-21
	Sault Ste. Marie	63	-36	-35	-24	-2	18	26	36	29	25	16	-10	-31	-36
MN	Duluth	62	-39	-39	-29	-5	17	27	35	32	22	8	-23	-34	-39
	Minneapolis-St. Paul	65	-34	-32	-32	2	18	34	43	39	26	13	-17	-29	-34
MS	Jackson	40	2	10	15	27	38	47	51	55	35	26	17	4	2
MO	Kansas City	31	-17	-19	-10	12	30	42	51	43	31	17	1	-23	-23
	St. Louis	46	-18	-12	-5	22	31	43	51	47	36	23	1	-16	-18
MT	Great Falls	66	-37	-35	-29	-6	15	31	36	30	16	-11	-25	-43	-43
NE	Omaha	67	-23	-21	-16	5	27	38	44	43	25	13	-9	-23	-23
NV	Reno	62	-16	-16	-2	13	18	25	33	24	20	8	1	-16	-16
NH	Concord	62	-33	-37	-16	8	21	30	35	29	21	10	-5	-22	-37
NJ	Atlantic City	60	-10	-11	5	12	25	37	42	40	32	20	10	-7	-11
NM	Albuquerque	64	-17	-5	8	19	16	40	52	50	37	21	-7	-7	-17
NY	Albany	57	-28	-21	-21	10	26	36	40	34	24	16	5	-22	-28
	Buffalo [2]	60	-16	-20	-7	12	26	35	43	38	32	20	9	-10	-20
	New York [2]	135	-6	-15	3	12	32	44	52	50	39	28	5	-13	-15
NC	Charlotte	64	-5	5	4	24	32	45	53	53	39	24	11	2	-5
	Raleigh	59	-9	-	11	23	31	38	48	46	37	19	11	4	-9
ND	Bismarck	64	-44	-43	-31	-12	15	30	35	33	11	-10	-30	-43	-44
OH	Cincinnati	42	-25	-11	-11	15	27	39	47	43	31	16	1	-20	-25
	Cleveland	62	-20	-15	-5	10	25	31	41	38	32	19	3	-15	-20
	Columbus	64	-22	-13	-6	14	25	35	43	39	31	20	5	-17	-22
OK	Oklahoma City	50	-4	-3	3	20	37	47	53	51	36	16	11	-8	-8
OR	Portland	63	-2	-3	19	29	29	39	43	44	34	26	13	6	-3
PA	Philadelphia	62	-7	-4	7	19	28	44	51	44	35	25	15	1	-7
	Pittsburgh	51	-22	-12	-1	14	26	34	42	39	31	16	-1	-12	-22
RI	Providence	50	-13	-7	1	14	29	41	48	40	33	20	6	-10	-13
SC	Columbia	56	-1	5	4	26	34	44	54	53	40	23	12	4	-1
SD	Sioux Falls	58	-36	-31	-23	5	17	33	38	34	22	9	-17	-28	-36
TN	Memphis	62	-4	-11	12	29	38	48	52	48	36	25	9	-13	-13
	Nashville	64	-17	-13	2	23	34	42	51	47	36	26	-1	-10	-17
TX	Dallas-Fort Worth	50	4	7	15	29	41	51	59	56	43	29	20	-1	-1
	El Paso	64	-8	8	14	23	31	46	57	56	41	25	1	5	-8
	Houston	34	12	20	22	31	44	52	62	60	48	29	19	7	7
UT	Salt Lake City	75	-22	-30	2	14	25	35	40	37	27	16	-14	-21	-30
VT	Burlington	60	-30	-30	-20	2	24	33	39	35	25	15	-2	-26	-30
VA	Norfolk	55	-3	8	18	28	36	45	54	49	45	27	20	7	-3
	Richmond	74	-12	-10	11	23	31	40	51	46	35	21	10	-1	-12
WA	Seattle-Tacoma	59	-	1	11	29	28	38	43	44	35	28	6	6	-
	Spokane	56	-22	-24	-7	17	24	33	37	35	22	7	-21	-25	-25
WV	Charleston	56	-16	-12	-	19	26	33	46	41	34	17	6	-12	-16
WI	Milwaukee	63	-26	-26	-10	12	21	33	40	44	28	18	-5	-20	-26
WY	Cheyenne	68	-29	-34	-21	-8	16	25	38	36	8	-1	-16	-28	-34
PR	San Juan	49	61	62	60	64	66	69	69	70	69	46	66	59	46

- Represents zero. [1] Period of record through 2000. [2] City office data.

Source: U.S. National Oceanic and Atmospheric Administration, *Comparative Climatic Data*, annual.

Geography and Environment 239

Table 380. **Normal Monthly and Annual Precipitation—Selected Cities**

[**In inches.** Airport data, except as noted. Based on standard 30-year period, 1971 through 2000]

State	Station	Jan.	Feb.	Mar.	Apr.	May	June	July	Aug.	Sept.	Oct.	Nov.	Dec.	Annual
AL	Mobile	5.75	5.10	7.20	5.06	6.10	5.01	6.54	6.20	6.01	3.25	5.41	4.66	66.29
AK	Juneau	4.81	4.02	3.51	2.96	3.48	3.36	4.14	5.37	7.54	8.30	5.43	5.41	58.33
AZ	Phoenix	0.83	0.77	1.07	0.25	0.16	0.09	0.99	0.94	0.75	0.79	0.73	0.92	8.29
AR	Little Rock	3.61	3.33	4.88	5.47	5.05	3.95	3.31	2.93	3.71	4.25	5.73	4.71	50.93
CA	Los Angeles	2.98	3.11	2.40	0.63	0.24	0.08	0.03	0.14	0.26	0.36	1.13	1.79	13.15
	Sacramento	3.84	3.54	2.80	1.02	0.53	0.20	0.05	0.06	0.36	0.89	2.19	2.45	17.93
	San Diego	2.28	2.04	2.26	0.75	0.20	0.09	0.03	0.09	0.21	0.44	1.07	1.31	10.77
	San Francisco	4.45	4.01	3.26	1.17	0.38	0.11	0.03	0.07	0.20	1.04	2.49	2.89	20.11
CO	Denver	0.51	0.49	1.28	1.93	2.32	1.56	2.16	1.82	1.14	0.99	0.98	0.63	15.81
CT	Hartford	3.84	2.96	3.88	3.86	4.39	3.85	3.67	3.98	4.13	3.94	4.06	3.60	46.16
DE	Wilmington	3.43	2.81	3.97	3.39	4.15	3.59	4.28	3.51	4.01	3.08	3.19	3.40	42.81
DC	Washington	3.21	2.63	3.60	2.77	3.82	3.13	3.66	3.44	3.79	3.22	3.03	3.05	39.35
FL	Jacksonville	3.69	3.15	3.93	3.14	3.48	5.37	5.97	6.87	7.90	3.86	2.34	2.64	52.34
	Miami	1.88	2.07	2.56	3.36	5.52	8.54	5.79	8.63	8.38	6.19	3.43	2.18	58.53
GA	Atlanta	5.02	4.68	5.38	3.62	3.95	3.63	5.12	3.67	4.09	3.11	4.10	3.82	50.20
HI	Honolulu	2.73	2.35	1.89	1.11	0.78	0.43	0.50	0.46	0.74	2.18	2.26	2.85	18.29
ID	Boise	1.39	1.14	1.41	1.27	1.27	0.74	0.39	0.30	0.76	0.76	1.38	1.38	12.19
IL	Chicago	1.75	1.63	2.65	3.68	3.38	3.63	3.51	4.62	3.27	2.71	3.01	2.43	36.27
	Peoria	1.50	1.67	2.83	3.56	4.17	3.84	4.02	3.16	3.12	2.76	2.99	2.40	36.03
IN	Indianapolis	2.48	2.41	3.44	3.61	4.35	4.13	4.42	3.82	2.88	2.76	3.61	3.03	40.95
IA	Des Moines	1.03	1.19	2.21	3.58	4.25	4.57	4.18	4.51	3.15	2.62	2.10	1.33	34.72
KS	Wichita	0.84	1.02	2.71	2.57	4.16	4.25	3.31	2.94	2.96	2.45	1.82	1.35	30.38
KY	Louisville	3.28	3.25	4.41	3.91	4.88	3.76	4.30	3.41	3.05	2.79	3.80	3.69	44.54
LA	New Orleans	5.87	5.47	5.24	5.02	4.62	6.83	6.20	6.15	5.55	3.05	5.09	5.07	64.16
ME	Portland	4.09	3.14	4.14	4.26	3.82	3.28	3.32	3.05	3.37	4.40	4.72	4.24	45.83
MD	Baltimore	3.47	3.02	3.93	3.00	3.89	3.43	3.85	3.74	3.98	3.16	3.12	3.35	41.94
MA	Boston	3.92	3.30	3.85	3.60	3.24	3.22	3.06	3.37	3.47	3.79	3.98	3.73	42.53
MI	Detroit	1.91	1.88	2.52	3.05	3.05	3.55	3.16	3.10	3.27	2.23	2.66	2.51	32.89
	Sault Ste. Marie	2.64	1.60	2.41	2.57	2.50	3.00	3.14	3.47	3.71	3.32	3.40	2.91	34.67
MN	Duluth	1.12	0.83	1.69	2.09	2.95	4.25	4.20	4.22	4.13	2.46	2.12	0.94	31.00
	Minneapolis-St. Paul	1.04	0.79	1.86	2.31	3.24	4.34	4.04	4.05	2.69	2.11	1.94	1.00	29.41
MS	Jackson	5.67	4.50	5.74	5.98	4.86	3.82	4.69	3.66	3.23	3.42	5.04	5.34	55.95
MO	Kansas City	1.15	1.31	2.44	3.38	5.39	4.44	4.42	3.54	4.64	3.33	2.30	1.64	37.98
	St. Louis	2.14	2.28	3.60	3.69	4.11	3.76	3.90	2.98	2.96	2.76	3.71	2.86	38.75
MT	Great Falls	0.68	0.51	1.01	1.40	2.53	2.24	1.45	1.65	1.23	0.93	0.59	0.67	14.89
NE	Omaha	0.77	0.80	2.13	2.94	4.44	3.95	3.86	3.21	3.17	2.21	1.82	0.92	30.22
NV	Reno	1.06	1.06	0.86	0.35	0.62	0.47	0.24	0.27	0.45	0.42	0.80	0.88	7.48
NH	Concord	2.97	2.36	3.04	3.07	3.33	3.10	3.37	3.21	3.16	3.46	3.57	2.96	37.60
NJ	Atlantic City	3.60	2.85	4.06	3.45	3.38	2.66	3.86	4.32	3.14	2.86	3.26	3.15	40.59
NM	Albuquerque	0.49	0.44	0.61	0.50	0.60	0.65	1.27	1.73	1.07	1.00	0.62	0.49	9.47
NY	Albany	2.71	2.27	3.17	3.25	3.67	3.74	3.50	3.68	3.31	3.23	3.31	2.76	38.60
	Buffalo	3.16	2.42	2.99	3.04	3.35	3.82	3.14	3.87	3.84	3.19	3.92	3.80	40.54
	New York [1]	4.13	3.15	4.37	4.28	4.69	3.84	4.62	4.22	4.23	3.85	4.36	3.95	49.69
NC	Charlotte	4.00	3.55	4.39	2.95	3.66	3.42	3.79	3.72	3.83	3.66	3.36	3.18	43.51
	Raleigh	4.02	3.47	4.03	2.80	3.79	3.42	4.29	3.78	4.26	3.18	2.97	3.04	43.05
ND	Bismarck	0.45	0.51	0.85	1.46	2.22	2.59	2.58	2.15	1.61	1.28	0.70	0.44	16.84
OH	Cincinnati	2.92	2.75	3.90	3.96	4.59	4.42	3.75	3.79	2.82	2.96	3.46	3.28	42.60
	Cleveland	2.48	2.29	2.94	3.37	3.50	3.89	3.52	3.69	3.77	2.73	3.38	3.14	38.71
	Columbus	2.53	2.20	2.89	3.25	3.88	4.07	4.61	3.72	2.92	2.31	3.19	2.93	38.52
OK	Oklahoma City	1.28	1.56	2.90	3.00	5.44	4.63	2.94	2.48	3.98	3.64	2.11	1.89	35.85
OR	Portland	5.07	4.18	3.71	2.64	2.38	1.59	0.72	0.93	1.65	2.88	5.61	5.71	37.07
PA	Philadelphia	3.52	2.74	3.81	3.49	3.88	3.29	4.39	3.82	3.88	2.75	3.16	3.31	42.05
	Pittsburgh	2.70	2.37	3.17	3.01	3.80	4.12	3.96	3.38	3.21	2.25	3.02	2.86	37.85
RI	Providence	4.37	3.45	4.43	4.16	3.66	3.38	3.17	3.90	3.70	3.69	4.40	4.14	46.45
SC	Columbia	4.66	3.84	4.59	2.98	3.17	4.99	5.54	5.41	3.94	2.89	2.88	3.38	48.27
SD	Sioux Falls	0.51	0.51	1.81	2.65	3.39	3.49	2.93	3.01	2.58	1.93	1.36	0.52	24.69
TN	Memphis	4.24	4.31	5.58	5.79	5.15	4.30	4.22	3.00	3.31	3.31	5.76	5.68	54.65
	Nashville	3.97	3.69	4.87	3.93	5.07	4.08	3.77	3.28	3.59	2.87	4.45	4.54	48.11
TX	Dallas-Fort Worth	1.90	2.37	3.06	3.20	5.15	3.23	2.12	2.03	2.42	4.11	2.57	2.57	34.73
	El Paso	0.45	0.39	0.26	0.23	0.38	0.87	1.49	1.75	1.61	0.81	0.42	0.77	9.43
	Houston	3.68	2.98	3.36	3.60	5.15	5.35	3.18	3.83	4.33	4.50	4.19	3.69	47.84
UT	Salt Lake City	1.37	1.33	1.91	2.02	2.09	0.77	0.72	0.76	1.33	1.57	1.40	1.23	16.50
VT	Burlington	2.22	1.67	2.32	2.88	3.32	3.43	3.97	4.01	3.83	3.12	3.06	2.22	36.05
VA	Norfolk	3.93	3.34	4.08	3.38	3.74	3.77	5.17	4.79	4.06	3.47	2.98	3.03	45.74
	Richmond	3.55	2.98	4.09	3.18	3.95	3.54	4.67	4.18	3.98	3.60	3.06	3.12	43.91
WA	Seattle-Tacoma	5.13	4.18	3.75	2.59	1.77	1.49	0.79	1.02	1.63	3.19	5.90	5.62	37.07
	Spokane	1.82	1.51	1.53	1.28	1.60	1.18	0.76	0.68	0.76	1.06	2.24	2.25	16.67
WV	Charleston	3.25	3.19	3.90	3.25	4.30	4.09	4.86	4.11	3.45	2.67	3.66	3.32	44.05
WI	Milwaukee	1.85	1.65	2.59	3.78	3.06	3.56	3.58	4.03	3.30	2.49	2.70	2.22	34.81
WY	Cheyenne	0.45	0.44	1.05	1.55	2.48	2.12	2.26	1.82	1.43	0.75	0.64	0.46	15.45
PR	San Juan	3.02	2.30	2.14	3.71	5.29	3.52	4.16	5.22	5.60	5.06	6.17	4.57	50.76

[1] City office data.

Source: U.S. National Oceanic and Atmospheric Administration, *Climatography of the United States*, No. 81.

Table 381. Average Number of Days With Precipitation of 0.01 Inch or More—Selected Cities

[Airport data, except as noted. For period of record through 2003]

State	Station	Length of record (years)	Jan.	Feb.	Mar.	Apr.	May	June	July	Aug.	Sept.	Oct.	Nov.	Dec.	Annual
AL	Mobile	61	11	9	10	7	8	11	14	10	10	6	8	10	121
AK	Juneau	58	19	17	18	17	17	16	17	18	21	24	20	21	223
AZ	Phoenix	63	4	4	4	2	1	1	4	5	3	3	2	4	36
AR	Little Rock	60	10	9	10	10	10	8	8	7	7	7	8	9	104
CA	Los Angeles	67	6	6	6	3	1	1	1	(Z)	1	2	3	5	35
	Sacramento	63	10	9	9	5	3	1	(Z)	(Z)	1	3	7	9	58
	San Diego	62	7	6	7	5	2	1	(Z)	(Z)	1	2	4	6	42
	San Francisco [1]	75	11	10	10	6	3	1	(Z)	-	1	4	7	10	63
CO	Denver	61	6	6	9	9	11	9	9	9	6	5	6	5	89
CT	Hartford	48	11	10	12	11	12	11	10	10	10	9	11	12	127
DE	Wilmington	55	11	9	11	11	11	10	9	9	8	8	9	10	117
DC	Washington	61	10	9	11	10	11	10	10	9	8	7	8	9	112
FL	Jacksonville	61	8	8	8	6	8	13	14	15	13	9	6	8	116
	Miami	60	7	6	6	6	10	15	16	18	17	14	8	7	131
GA	Atlanta	68	12	10	11	9	9	10	12	9	8	7	9	10	115
HI	Honolulu	53	9	9	9	9	7	6	7	6	7	8	9	10	96
ID	Boise	63	12	10	10	8	8	6	2	2	4	6	10	11	89
IL	Chicago	44	11	9	12	13	11	10	10	9	9	9	11	11	125
	Peoria	63	9	8	11	12	12	10	9	8	8	9	11	11	114
IN	Indianapolis	63	12	10	13	12	12	10	10	9	8	8	9	10	126
IA	Des Moines	63	7	7	10	10	12	11	10	9	8	8	10	12	108
KS	Wichita	49	5	5	8	8	11	9	8	7	8	8	6	5	86
KY	Louisville	55	11	10	13	12	12	10	10	8	7	8	7	12	124
LA	New Orleans	54	10	9	9	7	8	11	14	13	10	6	8	10	114
ME	Portland	62	11	10	11	12	12	11	10	9	9	9	12	11	129
MD	Baltimore	52	10	9	11	11	11	10	9	9	8	7	9	9	114
MA	Boston	51	12	10	12	11	12	11	9	9	8	7	9	9	126
MI	Detroit	44	13	11	13	13	13	11	10	10	9	9	11	12	135
	Sault Ste. Marie	61	19	14	13	11	11	11	10	11	13	14	17	19	165
MN	Duluth	61	12	9	11	11	11	11	10	10	10	10	12	13	134
	Minneapolis-St. Paul	64	9	7	10	10	11	12	10	10	10	10	11	11	116
MS	Jackson	39	11	9	10	10	10	8	10	9	8	6	8	9	110
MO	Kansas City	30	9	7	10	8	11	11	10	9	9	8	7	10	105
	St. Louis	45	9	8	11	11	11	9	9	8	8	8	9	9	111
MT	Great Falls	65	9	8	9	9	11	12	8	8	7	6	7	7	100
NE	Omaha	66	6	7	8	10	12	10	9	9	8	6	6	6	99
NV	Reno	60	6	6	6	4	4	3	2	2	3	3	5	6	51
NH	Concord	61	11	9	11	11	12	11	10	10	9	9	11	11	127
NJ	Atlantic City	59	11	10	11	11	10	9	9	9	8	7	9	10	113
NM	Albuquerque	63	4	4	5	3	4	4	9	9	6	5	4	4	61
NY	Albany	56	13	11	12	12	13	11	11	10	10	10	12	12	135
	Buffalo	59	20	17	16	14	13	11	10	10	11	12	16	19	168
	New York [2]	133	11	10	11	11	11	11	10	10	11	12	16	19	121
NC	Charlotte	63	10	9	11	9	9	9	10	10	8	8	9	10	111
	Raleigh	58	10	10	10	9	9	10	11	10	7	7	8	10	113
ND	Bismarck	63	8	7	8	8	10	12	9	8	7	6	6	7	96
OH	Cincinnati	55	12	11	13	13	12	11	10	9	8	8	11	12	130
	Cleveland	61	16	14	15	15	13	11	10	10	9	8	11	14	155
	Columbus	63	13	11	13	13	13	11	11	9	8	8	10	13	137
OK	Oklahoma City	63	5	6	7	7	8	10	6	6	7	7	5	6	83
OR	Portland	62	18	16	17	15	12	9	4	5	7	12	18	19	152
PA	Philadelphia	62	11	9	11	11	11	10	9	9	8	7	12	18	117
	Pittsburgh	50	16	14	15	14	13	11	10	9	8	9	12	16	152
RI	Providence	49	11	10	12	11	11	11	9	9	9	9	10	12	124
SC	Columbia	55	10	9	10	8	8	10	12	11	8	6	7	9	109
SD	Sioux Falls	57	6	7	9	10	11	11	10	9	7	6	7	6	98
TN	Memphis	52	10	9	11	10	9	9	9	7	7	6	9	10	107
	Nashville	61	11	10	11	11	11	10	10	9	8	7	9	11	119
TX	Dallas-Fort Worth	49	7	7	8	8	9	7	5	5	6	6	6	7	79
	El Paso	63	4	3	2	2	2	3	8	8	5	4	3	4	49
	Houston	33	10	8	9	7	8	10	9	9	9	8	8	9	105
UT	Salt Lake City	74	10	9	10	10	8	5	4	6	6	8	8	9	91
VT	Burlington	59	15	11	13	12	14	13	12	12	12	12	14	15	154
VA	Norfolk	54	11	10	11	10	10	9	11	10	8	7	8	9	116
	Richmond	65	10	9	11	9	11	9	11	9	8	7	8	9	113
WA	Seattle-Tacoma	58	19	16	17	14	11	9	5	6	8	13	18	19	155
	Spokane	55	14	11	11	9	9	8	5	6	8	9	13	14	112
WV	Charleston	55	15	14	15	14	13	12	13	11	9	9	12	14	151
WI	Milwaukee	62	11	10	12	12	12	11	10	9	9	9	12	11	125
WY	Cheyenne	67	6	6	9	10	12	11	11	10	8	6	6	6	100
PR	San Juan	47	17	13	12	13	16	15	19	19	18	17	19	19	197

- Represents zero.   Z Less than 1/2 day.   [1] Period of record through 2000.   [2] City office data.

Source: U.S. National Oceanic and Atmospheric Administration, *Comparative Climatic Data*, annual.

Table 382. Snow and Ice Pellets—Selected Cities

[In inches. Airport data, except as noted. For period of record through 2003. T denotes trace]

State	Station	Length of record (years)	Jan.	Feb.	Mar.	Apr.	May	June	July	Aug.	Sept.	Oct.	Nov.	Dec.	Annual
AL	Mobile	61	0.1	0.1	0.1	T	T	-	T	-	-	-	T	0.1	0.4
AK	Juneau	59	25.4	18.9	14.7	3.3	T	T	-	-	T	1.0	12.0	21.7	97.0
AZ	Phoenix [2]	62	T	-	T	T	T	-	-	-	-	T	-	T	T
AR	Little Rock [2]	56	2.4	1.5	0.5	T	T	T	-	-	-	T	0.2	0.6	5.2
CA	Los Angeles [2]	62	T	T	T	-	-	-	-	-	-	-	-	T	T
	Sacramento [2]	50	T	T	T	-	T	-	-	-	-	-	-	T	T
	San Diego [2]	60	T	-	T	T	-	-	-	-	-	-	T	T	T
	San Francisco [2]	69	-	T	T	-	-	-	-	-	-	-	-	-	T
CO	Denver [2]	61	8.1	7.5	12.5	8.9	1.6	-	T	T	1.6	3.7	9.1	7.3	60.3
CT	Hartford	46	13.0	12.4	10.1	1.5	-	T	-	-	-	0.1	2.1	10.4	49.6
DE	Wilmington	53	6.7	6.6	3.2	0.2	T	T	T	-	-	0.1	0.9	3.4	21.1
DC	Washington	60	5.5	5.5	2.3	T	T	T	T	T	-	-	0.8	3.0	17.1
FL	Jacksonville [2]	60	T	-	-	T	-	T	T	-	-	-	-	-	T
	Miami [2]	59	-	-	-	-	T	-	-	-	-	-	-	-	T
GA	Atlanta	65	1.0	0.5	0.4	T	-	-	-	-	-	T	T	0.2	2.1
HI	Honolulu [2]	52	-	-	-	-	-	-	-	-	-	-	-	-	-
ID	Boise	64	6.5	3.6	1.7	0.6	0.1	T	T	T	T	0.1	2.3	5.7	20.6
IL	Chicago	44	11.0	7.8	6.9	1.6	0.1	T	T	T	T	0.4	2.0	8.2	38.0
	Peoria	60	6.7	5.0	4.2	0.8	T	T	T	-	T	0.1	2.0	6.1	24.9
IN	Indianapolis	72	6.9	5.6	3.5	0.5	T	T	T	-	T	0.2	1.9	5.3	23.9
IA	Des Moines	60	8.2	7.2	6.0	1.9	-	T	T	-	T	0.3	3.1	6.6	33.3
KS	Wichita	50	4.1	4.1	2.8	0.2	T	T	T	T	T	-	1.3	3.4	15.9
KY	Louisville	56	5.4	4.3	3.1	0.1	T	T	T	T	-	0.1	1.0	2.4	16.4
LA	New Orleans [2]	51	T	0.1	T	T	T	-	-	-	-	-	T	0.1	0.2
ME	Portland	63	19.3	16.5	13.3	2.9	0.2	-	T	-	T	0.2	3.3	14.7	70.4
MD	Baltimore	53	6.3	7.1	3.8	0.1	T	T	T	-	-	T	1.0	3.2	21.5
MA	Boston	66	12.7	12.0	8.1	0.9	-	-	T	-	T	T	1.3	7.8	42.8
MI	Detroit	45	10.7	9.2	6.9	1.8	T	-	-	-	T	0.2	2.6	9.9	41.3
	Sault Ste. Marie [2]	57	29.2	18.2	14.6	5.8	0.5	T	T	T	0.1	2.4	15.6	31.0	117.4
MN	Duluth	60	17.5	11.8	13.9	6.9	0.7	T	T	T	0.1	1.6	13.0	15.1	80.6
	Minneapolis-St. Paul [2]	62	10.7	8.1	10.5	2.8	0.1	T	T	T	T	0.5	7.8	9.4	49.9
MS	Jackson [2]	38	0.5	0.2	0.2	T	-	-	T	-	T	-	T	0.1	1.0
MO	Kansas City	69	5.6	4.4	3.4	0.8	T	T	T	T	T	0.1	1.2	4.4	19.9
	St. Louis	67	5.4	4.5	3.8	0.5	-	T	T	-	-	T	1.4	4.0	19.6
MT	Great Falls	66	9.4	8.6	10.6	7.0	1.9	0.3	T	0.1	1.5	3.4	7.3	8.1	58.2
NE	Omaha	68	7.2	6.8	6.3	1.1	0.1	T	T	T	T	0.3	2.6	5.7	30.1
NV	Reno [2]	54	5.8	5.2	4.3	1.2	0.8	-	-	-	-	0.3	2.4	4.3	24.3
NH	Concord	62	18.0	14.2	11.5	2.7	0.1	T	T	-	T	0.1	3.9	14.0	64.5
NJ	Atlantic City	54	4.9	5.8	2.5	0.3	T	T	T	-	-	T	0.4	2.3	16.2
NM	Albuquerque	64	2.5	2.1	1.8	0.6	T	T	T	T	T	0.1	1.2	2.7	11.0
NY	Albany	57	17.0	13.8	11.5	2.8	0.1	T	T	-	T	0.2	4.2	14.8	64.4
	Buffalo	60	24.2	17.7	12.4	3.2	0.2	T	T	T	T	0.3	11.3	24.3	93.6
	New York [1]	135	7.5	8.6	5.1	0.9	T	-	T	-	-	T	0.9	5.6	28.6
NC	Charlotte	64	2.2	1.6	1.2	T	T	T	-	-	-	-	0.1	0.5	5.6
	Raleigh	59	2.8	2.5	1.3	T	T	T	-	-	-	-	0.1	0.8	7.5
ND	Bismarck	64	7.8	7.0	8.5	4.0	0.9	T	T	T	0.2	1.9	7.1	6.9	44.3
OH	Cincinnati	56	7.2	5.6	4.2	0.5	-	T	T	T	-	0.3	2.0	3.7	23.5
	Cleveland	62	13.8	12.3	10.8	2.4	0.1	T	T	-	T	0.6	5.3	12.3	57.6
	Columbus	56	8.9	6.3	4.4	0.9	T	T	T	-	T	0.1	2.2	5.4	28.2
OK	Oklahoma City	64	3.2	2.4	1.5	T	T	T	T	T	T	-	0.4	1.4	9.5
OR	Portland [2]	55	3.2	1.1	0.4	T	-	T	-	T	T	-	0.4	1.4	6.5
PA	Philadelphia	61	6.1	7.0	3.4	0.3	T	T	-	-	-	T	0.7	3.3	20.8
	Pittsburgh	51	11.9	9.2	8.4	1.7	0.1	T	T	T	T	0.4	3.5	8.4	43.6
RI	Providence	50	9.5	9.9	7.3	0.7	0.2	-	-	-	-	0.1	1.2	7.1	36.0
SC	Columbia [2]	55	0.6	0.8	0.2	T	-	-	T	-	-	-	T	0.3	1.9
SD	Sioux Falls	58	6.9	8.0	9.2	3.0	T	T	T	T	T	0.9	6.1	7.1	41.2
TN	Memphis [2]	49	2.2	1.4	0.8	T	T	T	-	-	-	-	0.1	0.6	5.1
	Nashville [2]	58	3.8	3.0	1.5	-	-	T	-	T	-	-	0.4	1.4	10.1
TX	Dallas-Fort Worth	45	1.1	1.0	0.2	T	T	-	-	-	-	T	0.1	0.2	2.6
	El Paso [2]	57	1.3	0.8	0.4	0.3	T	-	T	-	T	-	0.9	1.6	5.3
	Houston	69	0.2	0.2	T	T	T	-	-	-	-	-	T	T	0.4
UT	Salt Lake City	75	13.6	9.8	9.2	5.0	0.6	T	T	T	0.1	1.3	7.0	12.1	58.7
VT	Burlington	60	19.5	16.4	13.8	4.2	0.2	-	T	T	T	0.2	6.7	18.3	79.3
VA	Norfolk	53	3.0	2.9	1.0	-	T	T	T	-	-	-	-	0.9	7.8
	Richmond	64	5.0	3.9	2.4	0.1	T	-	T	-	-	T	0.4	2.0	13.8
WA	Seattle-Tacoma [2]	52	4.9	1.6	1.3	0.1	T	-	T	-	T	-	1.1	2.4	11.4
	Spokane	56	15.2	7.5	3.9	0.6	0.1	T	-	-	T	0.4	6.5	14.4	48.6
WV	Charleston [2]	49	11.1	8.7	5.4	0.9	-	T	T	T	T	0.2	2.4	5.3	34.0
WI	Milwaukee	63	13.7	9.2	8.4	1.9	0.1	T	T	T	T	0.2	3.0	10.5	47.0
WY	Cheyenne	68	6.3	6.4	12.0	9.3	3.4	0.2	T	T	1.1	3.8	7.1	6.2	55.8
PR	San Juan	48	-	-	-	-	-	-	-	-	T	-	-	-	T

- Represents zero or rounds to zero.   [1] City office data.   [2] Period of record through 2000.

Source: U.S. National Oceanic and Atmospheric Administration, *Comparative Climatic Data*, annual.

Table 383. Sunshine, Average Wind Speed, Heating and Cooling Degree Days, and Average Relative Humidity—Selected Cities

[Airport data, except as noted. For period of record through 2003, except heating and cooling normals for period 1971–2000. M = morning. A = afternoon]

State	Station	Avg % possible sunshine — Length of record (yr.)	Avg % possible sunshine — Annual	Avg wind speed (m.p.h.) — Length of record (yr.)	Annual	Jan.	July	Heating degree days	Cooling degree days	Humidity — Length of record (yr.)	Annual M	Annual A	Jan. M	Jan. A	July M	July A
AL	Mobile	47	60	55	8.8	10.1	6.9	1,667	2,548	41	87	63	83	65	90	66
AK	Juneau	47	23	58	8.2	8.1	7.5	8,574	-	37	80	70	78	75	79	67
AZ	Phoenix	57	81	58	6.2	5.3	7.1	1,040	4,355	43	50	23	64	32	43	20
AR	Little Rock	35	60	61	7.8	8.4	6.7	3,084	2,086	39	83	61	80	65	86	59
CA	Los Angeles	60	72	55	7.5	6.7	7.9	1,286	682	44	79	65	71	61	86	69
	Sacramento	49	73	53	7.8	7.0	8.9	2,666	1,248	17	83	46	91	70	77	30
	San Diego	55	72	63	7.0	6.0	7.5	1,063	866	43	77	63	72	58	83	67
	San Francisco	68	71	76	10.6	7.2	13.6	2,862	142	44	84	62	87	68	86	60
CO	Denver	61	67	47	8.6	8.6	8.3	6,128	695	35	67	40	63	49	68	34
CT	Hartford	41	52	49	8.4	8.9	7.3	6,104	759	44	77	53	72	57	79	51
DE	Wilmington	47	55	55	9.0	9.8	7.8	4,887	1,125	56	79	55	76	60	79	54
DC	Washington	48	55	55	9.4	10.0	8.3	3,999	1,560	43	75	54	71	56	77	53
FL	Jacksonville	47	61	54	7.8	8.1	7.0	1,353	2,636	67	89	56	88	58	89	59
	Miami	46	68	54	9.2	9.5	7.9	155	4,383	39	83	61	84	59	83	63
GA	Atlanta	61	59	65	9.1	10.4	7.7	2,827	1,810	43	82	56	78	59	88	59
HI	Honolulu	47	74	54	11.3	9.4	13.1	-	4,561	34	72	56	81	61	68	52
ID	Boise	56	58	64	8.7	7.9	8.4	5,809	769	64	69	43	81	71	54	21
IL	Chicago	37	52	45	10.3	11.6	8.4	6,493	835	45	80	63	78	70	82	60
	Peoria	52	53	60	9.8	10.9	7.8	6,095	998	44	83	65	80	71	86	64
IN	Indianapolis	64	51	55	9.6	10.9	7.5	5,521	1,042	44	84	62	81	71	87	60
IA	Des Moines	46	55	54	10.7	11.4	8.9	6,432	1,052	42	80	64	77	70	83	62
KS	Wichita	46	58	50	12.2	12.0	11.3	4,765	1,658	50	80	59	79	65	79	54
KY	Louisville	47	53	56	8.3	9.5	6.8	4,352	1,443	43	81	59	78	65	85	58
LA	New Orleans	47	60	55	8.2	9.3	6.1	1,417	2,776	55	87	66	84	69	91	68
ME	Portland	54	55	63	8.7	9.0	7.6	7,325	347	63	79	59	76	61	80	59
MD	Baltimore	45	58	53	8.8	9.4	7.6	4,634	1,220	50	78	54	73	57	80	53
MA	Boston	60	55	46	12.4	13.7	11.0	5,630	777	39	73	58	69	58	74	57
MI	Detroit	37	49	45	10.2	11.9	8.5	6,449	727	45	81	60	80	70	82	54
	Sault Ste. Marie	54	43	62	9.2	9.6	7.8	9,230	145	62	85	66	81	74	88	62
MN	Duluth	47	49	54	11.0	11.6	9.4	9,742	189	42	81	66	78	72	85	63
	Minneapolis-St. Paul	57	54	65	10.5	10.5	9.4	7,882	699	44	78	63	75	69	81	59
MS	Jackson	30	59	40	7.0	8.2	5.2	2,368	2,290	40	90	63	86	68	93	65
MO	Kansas City	23	59	31	10.6	11.1	9.2	5,249	1,325	31	81	65	77	68	84	64
	St. Louis	47	55	54	9.6	10.6	8.0	4,757	1,561	43	81	63	80	68	83	60
MT	Great Falls	57	51	62	12.5	14.9	10.0	7,675	326	42	68	45	67	61	68	31
NE	Omaha	49	59	67	10.5	10.9	8.8	6,312	1,095	39	81	63	78	68	84	63
NV	Reno	53	69	61	6.6	5.6	7.2	5,601	493	40	68	31	79	50	59	19
NH	Concord	54	55	61	6.7	7.2	5.7	7,485	442	38	81	53	76	59	83	51
NJ	Atlantic City	37	56	45	9.8	10.7	8.3	5,113	935	39	82	57	79	59	83	57
NM	Albuquerque	56	76	64	8.9	8.0	8.9	4,281	1,290	43	59	29	68	39	59	27
NY	Albany	57	49	65	8.9	9.8	7.5	6,861	544	38	80	58	78	64	81	55
	Buffalo	52	43	64	11.8	14.0	10.2	6,693	548	43	80	63	79	73	79	56
	New York[2]	42	64	66	9.3	10.6	7.6	4,744	1,160	69	72	56	68	60	75	55
NC	Charlotte	49	59	54	7.4	7.8	6.6	3,208	1,644	43	82	54	78	55	86	57
	Raleigh	47	59	54	7.6	8.2	6.7	3,465	1,521	39	85	54	79	55	89	58
ND	Bismarck	56	55	64	10.2	10.0	9.2	8,809	471	44	80	61	76	71	84	53
OH	Cincinnati	44	49	56	9.0	10.4	7.2	5,200	1,053	41	82	60	80	68	86	58
	Cleveland	54	45	62	10.5	12.2	8.6	6,097	712	43	80	62	79	70	82	57
	Columbus	46	48	54	8.3	9.8	6.5	5,546	925	44	81	59	78	68	84	56
OK	Oklahoma City	44	64	55	12.2	12.5	10.9	3,663	1,907	38	80	59	78	63	80	55
OR	Portland	47	39	55	7.9	9.9	7.6	4,366	398	63	85	59	85	76	82	45
PA	Philadelphia	55	56	63	9.5	10.3	8.2	4,759	1,235	44	77	55	74	59	79	54
	Pittsburgh	43	44	51	9.0	10.4	7.3	5,829	726	43	80	58	77	66	83	54
RI	Providence	42	55	50	10.4	10.9	9.4	5,754	714	40	75	55	72	57	77	56
SC	Columbia	48	60	55	6.8	7.2	6.3	2,595	2,063	37	86	51	82	54	88	54
SD	Sioux Falls	50	57	55	11.0	10.9	9.8	7,746	757	40	82	65	78	71	84	60
TN	Memphis	43	59	55	8.8	10.0	7.5	3,033	2,190	64	80	59	78	65	84	60
	Nashville	54	57	62	8.0	9.1	6.5	3,658	1,656	38	83	62	79	67	88	62
TX	Dallas-Ft. Worth	42	64	50	10.7	11.0	9.8	2,370	2,571	40	81	60	79	64	79	54
	El Paso	53	80	61	8.8	8.3	8.3	2,604	2,165	43	56	27	64	34	61	29
	Houston	26	56	34	7.6	8.1	6.6	1,525	2,893	34	89	65	85	69	92	64
UT	Salt Lake City	69	62	74	8.8	7.5	9.5	5,607	1,089	43	67	43	79	69	52	22
VT	Burlington	52	44	60	9.0	9.7	8.0	7,665	489	38	77	59	73	64	78	53
VA	Norfolk	47	58	55	10.5	11.4	8.9	3,342	1,630	65	78	58	75	59	81	55
	Richmond	50	56	55	7.7	8.1	6.9	3,878	1,466	69	83	53	80	57	85	56
WA	Seattle-Tacoma[3]	51	38	55	8.8	9.5	8.1	4,797	173	44	84	62	82	75	82	49
	Spokane	48	48	56	8.9	8.7	8.6	6,820	394	44	78	52	86	80	65	27
WV	Charleston	47	48	56	5.8	6.9	4.8	4,589	1,064	56	84	57	78	63	91	60
WI	Milwaukee	55	52	63	11.5	12.6	9.7	7,096	616	43	80	66	76	70	81	64
WY	Cheyenne	60	64	46	12.9	15.2	10.4	7,289	280	44	66	45	58	50	70	38
PR	San Juan	40	76	55	8.4	8.3	9.7	-	5,426	48	79	65	82	65	79	67

- Represents zero. [1] Percent of days that are either clear or partly cloudy. [2] Airport data for sunshine. [3] Does not represent airport data.

Source: U.S. National Oceanic and Atmospheric Administration, Comparative Climatic Data, annual.

Geography and Environment 243

No. 18.—APPORTIONMENT OF CONGRESSIONAL REPRESENTATION: Ratios under the Constitution and at Each Census, 1790 to 1900, by States.

[From reports of the Bureau of the Census, Department of Commerce and Labor.]

State	Constitution.	1790	1800	1810	1820	1830	1840	1850	1860	1870	1880	1890	1900
(Ratios)	30,000	33,000	33,000	35,000	40,000	47,700	70,680	93,423	127,381	131,425	151,911	173,901	194,182
							Representation.						
Alabama				1	3	5	7	7	6	8	8	9	9
Arkansas						1	1	2	2	3	4	6	7
California										1	1	2	3
Colorado										1	1	2	3
Connecticut	5	7	7	7	6	6	4	4	4	4	4	4	5
Delaware	1	1	1	2	1	1	1	1	1	1	1	1	1
Florida						1	1	1	1	1	2	2	3
Georgia	3	2	4	6	7	9	8	8	7	9	10	11	11
Idaho											1	1	1
Illinois				1	1	3	7	9	14	19	20	22	25
Indiana				1	3	7	10	11	11	13	13	13	13
Iowa							2	2	6	9	11	11	11
Kansas									1	3	7	8	8
Kentucky		2	6	10	12	13	10	10	9	10	11	11	11
Louisiana				1	3	3	4	4	5	6	6	6	7
Maine					*7	7	8	7	5	5	4	4	4
Maryland	6	8	9	9	9	8	6	6	5	6	6	6	6
Massachusetts	8	14	17	13	13	12	10	11	10	11	12	13	14
Michigan						3	4	6	9	11	12	12	12
Minnesota								2	2	3	5	7	9
Mississippi				1	1	2	4	5	5	6	7	7	8
Missouri					1	2	5	7	9	13	14	15	16
Montana											1	1	1
Nebraska										1	3	6	6
Nevada										1	1	1	1
New Hampshire	3	4	5	6	6	5	4	3	3	3	2	2	2
New Jersey	4	5	6	6	6	6	5	5	5	7	7	8	10
New York	6	10	17	27	34	40	34	33	31	33	34	34	37
North Carolina	5	10	12	13	13	13	9	8	7	8	9	9	10
North Dakota											1	1	2
Ohio				1	6	14	19	21	21	19	20	21	21
Oklahoma													5
Oregon									1	1	1	2	2
Pennsylvania	8	13	18	23	26	28	24	25	24	27	28	30	32
Rhode Island	1	2	2	2	2	2	2	2	2	2	2	2	2
South Carolina	5	6	8	9	9	9	7	6	4	5	7	7	7
South Dakota											2	2	2
Tennessee			1	3	6	9	13	11	10	8	10	10	10
Texas								2	4	6	11	13	16
Utah												1	1
Vermont		2	4	6	5	5	4	3	3	3	2	2	2
Virginia	10	19	22	23	22	21	15	13	11	9	10	10	10
Washington											2	2	3
West Virginia										3	4	4	5
Wisconsin								2	3	6	8	9	10
Wyoming											1	1	1
Total	65	106	142	186	213	242	232	237	243	293	332	357	391

* Included in the 20 members originally assigned to Massachusetts, but credited to Maine after its admission as a State March 15, 1820.

NOTE.—The following representation included in the table was added after the several census apportionments indicated: First—Tennessee, 1. Second—Ohio, 1. Third—Alabama, 1; Illinois, 1; Indiana, 1; Louisiana, 1; Maine, 7; Mississippi, 1. Fifth—Arkansas, 1; Michigan, 1. Sixth—California, 2; Florida, 1; Iowa, 2; Texas, 2; Wisconsin, 2. Seventh—Massachusetts, 1; Minnesota, 2; Oregon, 1. Eighth—Illinois, 1; Iowa, 1; Kentucky, 1; Minnesota, 1; Nebraska, 1; Nevada, 1; Ohio, 1; Pennsylvania, 1; Rhode Island, 1; Vermont, 1. Ninth—Colorado, 1. Tenth—Idaho, 1; Montana, 1; North Dakota, 1; South Dakota, 2; Washington, 1; Wyoming, 1. Eleventh—Utah, 1.

Source: Statistical Abstract of the United States: 1908 Edition.

Elections

This section relates primarily to presidential, congressional, and gubernatorial elections. Also presented are summary tables on congressional legislation; state legislatures; Black, Hispanic, and female officeholders; population of voting age; voter participation; and campaign finances.

Official statistics on federal elections, collected by the Clerk of the House, are published biennially in *Statistics of the Presidential and Congressional Election* and *Statistics of the Congressional Election*. Federal and state elections data appear also in *America Votes*, a biennial volume published by CQ Press (a division of Congressional Quarterly, Inc.), Washington, DC. Federal elections data also appear in the U.S. Congress, *Congressional Directory*, and in official state documents. Data on reported registration and voting for social and economic groups are obtained by the U.S. Census Bureau as part of the Current Population Survey (CPS) and are published in Current Population Reports, Series P20 (see text, Section 1).

Almost all federal, state, and local governmental units in the United States conduct elections for political offices and other purposes. The conduct of elections is regulated by state laws or, in some cities and counties, by local charter. An exception is that the U.S. Constitution prescribes the basis of representation in Congress and the manner of electing the President and grants to Congress the right to regulate the times, places, and manner of electing federal officers. Amendments to the Constitution have prescribed national criteria for voting eligibility. The 15th Amendment, adopted in 1870, gave all citizens the right to vote regardless of race, color, or previous condition of servitude. The 19th Amendment, adopted in 1919, further extended the right to vote to all citizens regardless of sex. The payment of poll taxes as a prerequisite to voting in federal elections was banned by the 24th Amendment in 1964. In 1971, as a result of the 26th Amendment, eligibility to vote in national elections was extended to all citizens, 18 years old and over.

Presidential election—The Constitution specifies how the President and Vice President are selected. Each state elects, by popular vote, a group of electors equal in number to its total of members of Congress. The 23d Amendment, adopted in 1961, grants the District of Columbia three presidential electors, a number equal to that of the least populous state. Subsequent to the election, the electors meet in their respective states to vote for President and Vice President. Usually, each elector votes for the candidate receiving the most popular votes in his or her state. A majority vote of all electors is necessary to elect the President and Vice President. If no candidate receives a majority, the House of Representatives, with each state having one vote, is empowered to elect the President and Vice President, again, with a majority of votes required.

The 22nd Amendment to the Constitution, adopted in 1951, limits presidential tenure to two elective terms of 4 years each or to one elective term for any person who, upon succession to the Presidency, has held the office or acted as President for more than 2 years.

Congressional election—The Constitution provides that Representatives be apportioned among the states according to their population, that a census of population be taken every 10 years as a basis for apportionment, and that each state have at least one Representative. At the time of each apportionment, Congress decides what the total number of Representatives will be. Since 1912, the total has been 435, except during 1960 to 1962 when it increased to 437, adding one Representative each for Alaska and Hawaii. The total reverted to 435 after

U.S. Census Bureau, Statistical Abstract of the United States: 2006

reapportionment following the 1960 census. Members are elected for 2-year terms, all terms covering the same period. The District of Columbia, American Samoa, Guam, and the Virgin Islands each elect one nonvoting Delegate, and Puerto Rico elects a nonvoting Resident Commissioner.

The Senate is composed of 100 members, 2 from each state, who are elected to serve for a term of 6 years. One-third of the Senate is elected every 2 years. Senators were originally chosen by the state legislatures. The 17th Amendment to the Constitution, adopted in 1913, prescribed that Senators be elected by popular vote.

Voter eligibility and participation— The Census Bureau publishes estimates of the population of voting age and the percent casting votes in each state for Presidential and congressional election years. These voting-age estimates include a number of persons who meet the age requirement but are not eligible to vote, (e.g. aliens and some institutionalized persons). In addition, since 1964, voter participation and voter characteristics data have been collected during November of election years as part of the CPS. These survey data include noncitizens in the voting age population estimates, but exclude members of the Armed Forces and the institutional population.

Statistical reliability— For a discussion of statistical collection and estimation, sampling procedures, and measures of statistical reliability applicable to Census Bureau data, see Appendix III.

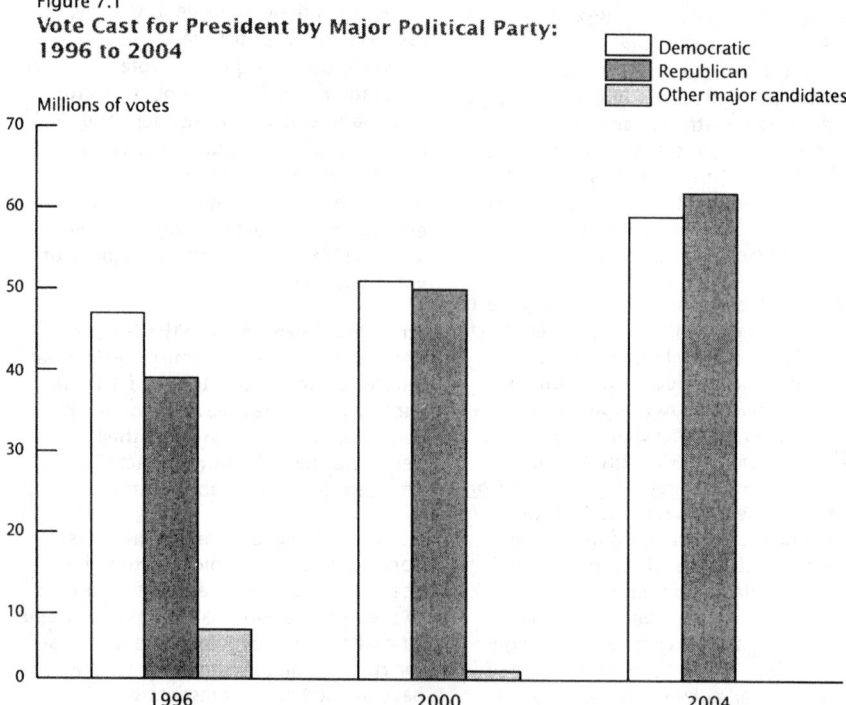

Figure 7.1
Vote Cast for President by Major Political Party: 1996 to 2004

☐ Democratic
▨ Republican
▨ Other major candidates[1]

Millions of votes

¹Candidates with 1 million or more votes: 1996—Reform, Ross Perot; 2000—Green, Ralph Nader.

Source: Figure 7.1 prepared by U.S. Census Bureau. For data, see Tables 384 and 385.

U.S. Census Bureau, Statistical Abstract of the United States: 2006

Table 384. **Votes Cast for President by Major Political Party: 1948 to 2004**

[48,794 represents 48,794,000. Prior to 1960, excludes Alaska and Hawaii; prior to 1964, excludes DC. Votes cast for major party candidates include the votes of minor parties cast for those candidates]

Year	Candidates for President Democratic	Candidates for President Republican	Total popular vote [1] (1,000)	Vote cast for President Democratic Popular vote Number (1,000)	Vote cast for President Democratic Popular vote Per- cent	Vote cast for President Democratic Electoral vote	Vote cast for President Republican Popular vote Number (1,000)	Vote cast for President Republican Popular vote Per- cent	Vote cast for President Republican Electoral vote
1948....	Truman......	Dewey.......	48,794	24,179	49.6	303	21,991	45.1	189
1952....	Stevenson....	Eisenhower...	61,551	27,315	44.4	89	33,936	55.1	442
1956....	Stevenson....	Eisenhower...	62,027	26,023	42.0	73	35,590	57.4	457
1960....	Kennedy.....	Nixon.......	68,838	34,227	49.7	303	34,108	49.5	219
1964....	Johnson.....	Goldwater....	70,645	43,130	61.1	486	27,178	38.5	52
1968....	Humphrey....	Nixon.......	73,212	31,275	42.7	191	31,785	43.4	301
1972....	McGovern....	Nixon.......	77,719	29,170	37.5	17	47,170	60.7	520
1976....	Carter.......	Ford........	81,556	40,831	50.1	297	39,148	48.0	240
1980....	Carter.......	Reagan......	86,515	35,484	41.0	49	43,904	50.7	489
1984....	Mondale.....	Reagan......	92,653	37,577	40.6	13	54,455	58.8	525
1988....	Dukakis......	Bush........	91,595	41,809	45.6	111	48,886	53.4	426
1992....	Clinton......	Bush........	104,425	44,909	43.0	370	39,104	37.4	168
1996....	Clinton......	Dole........	96,278	47,402	49.2	379	39,199	40.7	159
2000....	Gore........	Bush........	105,397	50,992	48.4	266	50,455	47.9	271
2004....	Kerry.......	Bush........	122,349	58,895	48.1	251	61,873	50.6	286

[1] Include votes for minor party candidates, independents, unpledged electors, and scattered write-in votes.

Source: Through 2000, CQ Press (a division of Congressional Quarterly, Inc.), Washington, D.C., *America at the Polls 2*, 1965, and *America Votes*, biennial, (copyright). Thereafter, Office of the Clerk, *Statistics of the Presidential and Congressional Election*, June 7, 2005. See also <http://clerk.house.gov/members/electionInfo/2004election.pdf>.

Table 385. **Votes Cast for Leading Minority Party Candidates for President: 1948 to 2004**

[1,176 represents 1,176,000. See headnote, Table 384]

Year	Candidate	Party	Popular vote (1,000)	Candidate	Party	Popular vote (1,000)
1948..	Strom Thurmond...	States' Rights.......	1,176	Henry Wallace.....	Progressive......	1,157
1952..	Vincent Hallinan....	Progressive........	140	Stuart Hamblen....	Prohibition.......	73
1956..	T. Coleman Andrews.	States' Rights......	111	Eric Hass........	Socialist Labor....	44
1960..	Eric Hass........	Socialist Labor.....	48	Rutherford Decker..	Prohibition.......	46
1964..	Eric Hass........	Socialist Labor.....	45	Clifton DeBerry....	Socialist Workers..	33
1968..	George Wallace....	American Independent.	9,906	Henning Blomen....	Socialist Labor....	53
1972..	John Schmitz......	American.........	1,099	Benjamin Spock....	People's........	79
1976..	Eugene McCarthy..	Independent.......	757	Roger McBride.....	Libertarian.......	173
1980..	John Anderson....	Independent.......	5,720	Ed Clark........	Libertarian.......	921
1984..	David Bergland....	Libertarian........	228	Lyndon H. LaRouche.	Independent......	79
1988..	Ron Paul........	Libertarian........	432	Lenora B. Fulani....	New Alliance.....	217
1992..	H. Ross Perot.....	Independent.......	19,742	Andre Marrou.....	Libertarian.......	292
1996..	H. Ross Perot.....	Reform..........	8,085	Ralph Nader......	Green..........	685
2000..	Ralph Nader......	Green...........	2,883	Pat Buchanan.....	Reform.........	449
2004..	Ralph Nader......	Green...........	464	Michael Badnarik...	Libertarian.......	397

Source: Through 2000, CQ Press (a division of Congressional Quarterly, Inc.), Washington, DC, *America at the Polls 1920-1996, 1997*; and *America Votes*, biennial (copyright). Thereafter, U.S. Federal Elections Commission, *Federal Elections 2004*, May 2005. See also <http://www.fec.gov/pubrec/fe2004/federalelections2004.pdf>.

Table 386. **Democratic and Republican Percentages of Two-Party Presidential Vote by Selected Characteristics of Voters: 2000 and 2004**

[In percent. Covers citizens of voting age living in private housing units in the contiguous United States. Percentages for Democratic Presidential vote are computed by subtracting the percentage Republican vote from 100 percent; third-party or independent votes are not included as valid data. Data are from the National Election Studies and are based on a sample and subject to sampling variability; for details, see source]

Characteristic	2000 Demo-cratic	2000 Repub-lican	2004 Demo-cratic	2004 Repub-lican	Characteristic	2000 Demo-cratic	2000 Repub-lican	2004 Demo-cratic	2004 Repub-lican
Total [1]	52	48	50	50	Race:				
Year of birth:					White............	46	54	42	58
1975 or later.......	63	37	66	34	Black............	92	8	90	10
1959 to 1974	46	54	45	55	Education:				
1943 to 1958	53	47	44	56	Grade school......	74	26	69	31
1927 to 1942	48	52	51	49	High school.......	54	46	45	54
1911 to 1926......	64	36	52	48	Some college, no				
1895 to 1910	-	100	-	-	degree..........	50	50	47	53
Sex:					College	50	50	50	50
Male	47	53	46	54	Union household......	61	39	64	36
Female	56	44	53	47	Non-union household...	50	50	46	54

- Represents zero.   [1] Includes other characteristics, not shown separately.

Source: Center for Political Studies, University of Michigan, Ann Arbor, MI, National Election Studies (NES); "The NES Guide to Public Opinion and Electoral Behavior;" accessed 19 July 2005; (copyright) and The NES 2004 Election Study; <http://www.umich.edu/nes/studyres/download/newdatacenter.htm>.

Table 387. **Electoral Vote Cast for President, by Major Political Party—States: 1964 to 2004**

[D = Democratic, R = Republican. For composition of regions, see map, inside front cover]

State	1964	1968[1]	1972[2]	1976[3]	1980	1984	1988[4]	1992	1996	2000[5]	2004[6]
Democratic ...	486	191	17	297	49	13	111	370	379	266	251
Republican ...	52	301	520	240	489	525	426	168	159	271	286
Northeast:											
Democratic	126	102	14	86	4	-	53	106	106	102	101
Republican	-	24	108	36	118	113	60	-	-	4	-
Midwest:											
Democratic	149	31	-	58	10	10	29	100	100	68	57
Republican	-	118	145	87	135	127	108	29	29	61	66
South:											
Democratic	121	45	3	149	31	3	8	68	80	15	16
Republican	47	77	165	20	138	174	168	116	104	168	173
West:											
Democratic	90	13	-	4	4	-	21	96	93	81	77
Republican	5	82	102	97	98	111	90	23	26	38	47
AL..............	R-10	(1)	R-9	D-9	R-9	R-9	R-9	R-9	R-9	R-9	R-9
AK..............	D-3	R-3	R-3	R-3	R-3	R-3	R-3	R-3	R-3	R-3	R-3
AZ..............	R-5	R-5	R-6	R-6	R-6	R-7	R-7	R-8	D-8	R-8	R-10
AR..............	D-6	(1)	R-6	D-6	R-6	R-6	R-6	D-6	D-6	R-6	R-6
CA..............	D-40	R-40	R-45	R-45	R-45	R-47	R-47	D-54	D-54	D-54	D-55
CO..............	D-6	R-6	R-7	R-7	R-7	R-8	R-8	D-8	R-8	R-8	R-9
CT..............	D-8	D-8	R-8	R-8	R-8	R-8	R-8	D-8	D-8	D-8	D-7
DE..............	D-3	R-3	R-3	D-3	R-3	R-3	R-3	D-3	D-3	D-3	D-3
DC..............	D-3	D-3	D-3	D-3	D-3	D-3	D-3	D-3	D-3	[5]D-2	D-3
FL..............	D-14	R-14	R-17	D-17	R-17	R-21	R-21	R-25	D-25	R-25	R-27
GA	R-12	(1)	R-12	D-12	D-12	R-12	R-12	D-13	R-13	R-13	R-15
HI..............	D-4	D-4	R-4	D-4	D-4	R-4	D-4	D-4	D-4	D-4	D-4
ID..............	D-4	R-4	R-4	R-4	R-4	R-4	R-4	R-4	R-4	R-4	R-4
IL..............	D-26	R-26	R-26	R-26	R-26	R-24	R-24	D-22	D-22	D-22	D-21
IN..............	D-13	R-13	R-13	R-13	R-13	R-12	R-12	R-12	R-12	R-12	R-11
IA..............	D-9	R-9	R-8	R-8	R-8	R-8	D-8	D-7	D-7	D-7	R-7
KS..............	D-7	R-7	R-7	R-7	R-7	R-7	R-7	R-6	R-6	R-6	R-6
KY..............	D-9	R-9	R-9	D-9	R-9	R-9	R-9	D-8	D-8	R-8	R-8
LA..............	R-10	(1)	R-10	D-10	R-10	R-10	R-10	D-9	D-9	R-9	R-9
ME	D-4	D-4	R-4	R-4	R-4	R-4	R-4	D-4	D-4	D-4	D-4
MD	D-10	D-10	R-10	D-10	D-10	R-10	R-10	D-10	D-10	D-10	D-10
MA	D-14	D-14	D-14	D-14	D-14	R-13	D-13	D-12	D-12	D-12	D-12
MI	D-21	D-21	R-21	R-21	R-21	R-20	R-20	D-18	D-18	D-18	D-17
MN	D-10	D-10	R-10	D-10	D-10	D-10	D-10	D-10	D-10	D-10	D-9
MS	R-7	(1)	R-7	D-7	R-7	R-7	R-7	R-7	R-7	R-7	R-6
MO	D-12	R-12	R-12	D-12	R-12	R-11	R-11	D-11	D-11	R-11	R-11
MT	D-4	R-4	R-4	R-4	R-4	R-4	R-4	D-3	R-3	R-3	R-3
NE..............	D-5	R-5	R-5	R-5	R-5	R-5	R-5	R-5	R-5	R-5	R-5
NV..............	D-3	R-3	R-3	R-3	R-3	R-4	R-4	D-4	D-4	R-4	R-5
NH..............	D-4	R-4	R-4	R-4	R-4	R-4	R-4	D-4	D-4	R-4	D-4
NJ..............	D-17	R-17	R-17	R-17	R-17	R-16	R-16	D-15	D-15	D-15	D-15
NM	D-4	R-4	R-4	R-4	R-4	R-5	R-5	D-5	D-5	D-5	R-5
NY..............	D-43	D-43	R-41	R-41	R-41	R-36	R-36	D-33	D-33	D-33	D-31
NC..............	D-13	[1]R-12	R-13	D-13	R-13	R-13	R-13	R-14	R-14	R-14	R-15
ND	D-4	R-4	R-3	R-3	R-3	R-3	R-3	R-3	R-3	R-3	R-3
OH	D-26	R-26	R-25	D-25	R-25	R-23	R-23	D-21	D-21	R-21	R-20
OK	D-8	R-8	R-8	R-8	R-8	R-8	R-8	R-8	R-8	R-8	R-7
OR	D-6	R-6	R-6	R-6	R-6	R-7	D-7	D-7	D-7	D-7	D-7
PA..............	D-29	D-29	R-27	D-27	R-27	R-25	R-25	D-23	D-23	D-23	D-21
RI..............	D-4	D-4	R-4	D-4	D-4	R-4	D-4	D-4	D-4	D-4	D-4
SC..............	R-8	R-8	R-8	D-8	R-8	R-8	R-8	R-8	R-8	R-8	R-8
SD..............	D-4	R-4	R-4	R-4	R-4	R-3	R-3	R-3	R-3	R-3	R-3
TN..............	D-11	R-11	R-10	D-10	R-10	R-11	R-11	D-11	D-11	R-11	R-11
TX..............	D-25	D-25	R-26	D-26	R-26	R-29	R-29	R-32	R-32	R-32	R-34
UT..............	D-4	R-4	R-4	R-4	R-4	R-5	R-5	R-5	R-5	R-5	R-5
VT..............	D-3	R-3	R-3	R-3	R-3	R-3	R-3	D-3	D-3	D-3	D-3
VA..............	D-12	R-12	[2]R-11	R-12	R-12	R-12	R-12	R-13	R-13	R-13	R-13
WA	D-9	D-9	R-9	[3]R-8	R-9	R-10	D-10	D-11	D-11	D-11	D-11
WV	D-7	D-7	R-6	D-6	D-6	R-6	[4]D-5	D-5	D-5	R-5	R-5
WI	D-12	R-12	R-11	D-11	R-11	R-11	D-11	D-11	D-11	D-11	D-10
WY	D-3	R-3	R-3	R-3	R-3	R-3	R-3	R-3	R-3	R-3	R-3

- Represents zero. [1] Excludes 46 electoral votes cast for American Independent George C. Wallace as follows: AL 10, AR 6, GA 12, LA 10, MS 7, and NC 1. [2] Excludes one electoral vote cast for Libertarian John Hospers in Virginia. [3] Excludes one electoral vote cast for Ronald Reagan in Washington. [4] Excludes one electoral vote cast for Lloyd Bentsen for President in West Virginia. [5] Excludes one electoral vote left blank by a Democratic elector in the District of Columbia. [6] Excludes one electoral vote cast for Democratic vice presential nominee John Edwards.

Source: Office of the Clerk, *Statistics of the Presidential and Congressional Election,* biennial. See also <http://clerk.house.gov/members/electionInfo/elections.html>.

Table 388. Popular Vote Cast for President by Political Party—States: 2000 and 2004

[In thousands (105,594 represents 105,594,000), except percent]

State	2000					2004				
				Percent of total vote					Percent of total vote	
	Total [1]	Demo-cratic Party	Repub-lican Party	Demo-cratic Party	Repub-lican Party	Total [1]	Demo-cratic Party	Repub-lican Party	Demo-cratic Party	Repub-lican Party
United States ...	105,594	50,996	50,465	48.3	47.8	122,349	58,895	61,873	48.1	50.6
Alabama	1,666	693	941	41.6	56.5	1,883	694	1,176	36.8	62.5
Alaska	286	79	167	27.7	58.6	313	111	191	35.5	61.1
Arizona	1,532	685	782	44.7	51.0	2,013	894	1,104	44.4	54.9
Arkansas	922	423	473	45.9	51.3	1,055	470	573	44.5	54.3
California	10,966	5,861	4,567	53.4	41.7	12,421	6,745	5,510	54.3	44.4
Colorado	1,741	738	884	42.4	50.8	2,130	1,002	1,101	47.0	51.7
Connecticut	1,460	816	561	55.9	38.4	1,579	857	694	54.3	43.9
Delaware	328	180	137	55.0	41.9	375	200	172	53.3	45.8
District of Columbia	202	172	18	85.2	9.0	228	203	21	89.2	9.3
Florida	5,963	2,912	2,913	48.8	48.8	7,610	3,584	3,965	47.1	52.1
Georgia	2,583	1,116	1,420	43.2	55.0	3,302	1,366	1,914	41.4	58.0
Hawaii	368	205	138	55.8	37.5	429	232	194	54.0	45.3
Idaho	502	139	337	27.6	67.2	598	181	409	30.3	68.4
Illinois	4,742	2,589	2,019	54.6	42.6	5,274	2,892	2,346	54.8	44.5
Indiana	2,199	902	1,246	41.0	56.6	2,468	969	1,479	39.3	59.9
Iowa	1,353	639	634	47.2	46.9	1,507	742	752	49.2	49.9
Kansas	1,072	399	622	37.2	58.0	1,188	435	736	36.6	62.0
Kentucky	1,544	639	873	41.4	56.5	1,796	713	1,069	39.7	59.5
Louisiana	1,766	792	928	44.9	52.6	1,943	820	1,102	42.2	56.7
Maine	652	320	287	49.1	44.0	741	397	330	53.6	44.6
Maryland	2,025	1,144	814	56.5	40.2	2,384	1,334	1,025	56.0	43.0
Massachusetts	2,734	1,616	879	59.1	32.1	2,927	1,804	1,071	61.6	36.6
Michigan	4,233	2,170	1,953	51.3	46.1	4,839	2,479	2,314	51.2	47.8
Minnesota	2,439	1,168	1,110	47.9	45.5	2,828	1,445	1,347	51.1	47.6
Mississippi	994	405	573	40.7	57.6	1,140	458	673	40.2	59.0
Missouri	2,360	1,111	1,190	47.1	50.4	2,731	1,259	1,456	46.1	53.3
Montana	411	137	240	33.4	58.4	450	174	266	38.6	59.1
Nebraska	697	232	434	33.3	62.2	778	254	513	32.7	65.9
Nevada	609	280	302	45.9	49.5	830	397	419	47.9	50.5
New Hampshire	569	266	274	46.8	48.1	678	341	331	50.2	48.8
New Jersey	3,187	1,789	1,284	56.1	40.3	3,612	1,911	1,670	52.9	46.2
New Mexico	599	287	286	47.9	47.8	756	371	377	49.0	49.8
New York	6,960	4,108	2,403	59.0	34.5	7,448	4,181	2,807	56.1	37.7
North Carolina	2,915	1,258	1,631	43.1	56.0	3,501	1,526	1,961	43.6	56.0
North Dakota	288	95	175	33.1	60.7	313	111	197	35.5	62.9
Ohio	4,702	2,184	2,350	46.4	50.0	5,628	2,741	2,860	48.7	50.8
Oklahoma	1,234	474	744	38.4	60.3	1,464	504	960	34.4	65.6
Oregon	1,534	720	714	47.0	46.5	1,837	943	867	51.3	47.2
Pennsylvania	4,912	2,486	2,281	50.6	46.4	5,770	2,938	2,794	50.9	48.4
Rhode Island	409	250	131	61.0	31.9	437	260	169	59.4	38.7
South Carolina	1,384	566	787	40.9	56.9	1,618	662	938	40.9	58.0
South Dakota	316	119	191	37.6	60.3	388	149	233	38.4	59.9
Tennessee	2,076	982	1,062	47.3	51.1	2,437	1,036	1,384	42.5	56.8
Texas	6,408	2,434	3,800	38.0	59.3	7,411	2,833	4,527	38.2	61.1
Utah	771	203	515	26.3	66.8	928	241	664	26.0	71.5
Vermont	294	149	120	50.6	40.7	312	184	121	58.9	38.8
Virginia	2,739	1,217	1,437	44.4	52.5	3,195	1,455	1,717	45.5	53.7
Washington	2,487	1,248	1,109	50.2	44.6	2,859	1,510	1,305	52.8	45.6
West Virginia	648	295	336	45.6	51.9	756	327	424	43.2	56.1
Wisconsin	2,599	1,243	1,237	47.8	47.6	2,997	1,490	1,478	49.7	49.3
Wyoming	214	60	148	28.3	69.2	244	71	168	29.0	68.7

[1] Includes other parties.

Source: Office of the Clerk, *Statistics of the Presidential and Congressional Election*, biennial. See also <http://clerk.house.gov/members/electionInfo/elections.html>.

Elections 249

Table 389. Vote Cast for United States Senators, 2002 and 2004, and Incumbent Senators, 2004—States

[1,353 represents 1,353,000. D = Democrat; R = Republican]

State	2002 Total (1,000)[1]	2002 Percent for leading party	2004 Total (1,000)[1]	2004 Percent for leading party	Incumbent senators and year term expires — Name, party, and year	Incumbent senators and year term expires — Name, party, and year
Alabama	1,353	R-58.6	1,839	R-67.5	Jeffrey Sessions (R) 2009	Richard Shelby (R) 2011
Alaska	230	R-78.2	308	R-48.6	Lisa Murkowski (R) 2011	Ted Stevens (R) 2009
Arizona	(X)	(X)	1,962	R-76.7	Jon Kyl (R) 2007	John McCain (R) 2011
Arkansas	804	D-53.9	1,039	D-55.9	Blanche Lincoln (D) 2011	Mark Pryor (D) 2009
California	(X)	(X)	12,053	D-57.7	Barbara Boxer (D) 2011	Dianne Feinstein (D) 2007
Colorado	1,416	R-50.7	2,107	D-51.3	Wayne Allard (R) 2009	Ken Salazar (D) 2011
Connecticut	(X)	(X)	1,425	D-66.4	Christopher Dodd (D) 2011	Joseph Lieberman (D) 2007
Delaware	232	D-58.2	(X)	(X)	Joseph Biden (D) 2009	Thomas Carper (D) 2007
Florida	(X)	(X)	7,430	R-49.4	Mel Martinez (R) 2011	Bill Nelson (D) 2007
Georgia	2,032	R-52.7	3,221	R-57.8	Saxby Chambliss (R) 2009	Johnny Isakson (R) 2011
Hawaii	(X)	(X)	415	D-75.5	Daniel Akaka (D) 2007	Daniel Inouye (D) 2011
Idaho	409	R-65.2	504	R-99.2	Larry Craig (R) 2009	Michael Crapo (R) 2011
Illinois	3,487	D-60.3	5,142	D-70.0	Richard Durbin (D) 2009	Barack Obama (D) 2011
Indiana	(X)	(X)	2,428	D-61.6	Evan Bayh (D) 2011	Richard Lugar (R) 2007
Iowa	1,023	D-54.2	1,479	R-70.2	Chuck Grassley (R) 2011	Tom Harkin (D) 2009
Kansas	767	R-83.6	1,129	R-69.2	Sam Brownback (R) 2011	Pat Roberts (R) 2009
Kentucky	1,131	R-64.7	1,724	R-50.7	Jim Bunning (R) 2011	Mitch McConnell (R) 2009
Louisiana [2]	1,235	D-51.7	1,848	R-51.0	Mary Landrieu (D) 2009	David Vitter (R) 2011
Maine	505	R-58.4	(X)	(X)	Susan Collins (R) 2009	Olympia Snowe (R) 2007
Maryland	(X)	(X)	2,322	D-64.8	Barbara Mikulski (D) 2011	Paul Sarbanes (D) 2007
Massachusetts	2,220	D-72.3	(X)	(X)	Edward Kennedy (D) 2007	John Kerry (D) 2009
Michigan	3,129	D-60.6	(X)	(X)	Carl Levin (D) 2009	Debbie Stabenow (D) 2007
Minnesota	2,255	R-49.5	(X)	(X)	Norm Coleman (R) 2009	Mark Dayton (D) 2007
Mississippi	630	R-84.6	(X)	(X)	Thad Cockran (R) 2009	Trent Lott (R) 2007
Missouri	(X)	(X)	2,706	R-56.1	Christopher Bond (R) 2011	James Talent (R) 2007
Montana	327	D-62.7	(X)	(X)	Max Baucus (D) 2009	Conrad Burns (R) 2007
Nebraska	480	R-82.8	(X)	(X)	Chuck Hagel (R) 2009	Ben Nelson (D) 2007
Nevada	(X)	(X)	810	D-61.1	John Ensign (R) 2007	Harry Reid (D) 2011
New Hampshire	447	R-50.8	657	R-66.2	Judd Gregg (R) 2011	John Sununu (R) 2009
New Jersey	2,113	D-53.9	(X)	(X)	Jon Corzine (D) 2007	Frank Lautenberg (D) 2009
New Mexico	483	R-65.0	(X)	(X)	Jeff Bingaman (D) 2007	Pete Domenici (R) 2009
New York	(X)	(X)	7,448	D-58.9	Hillary Clinton (D) 2007	Charles Schumer (D) 2011
North Carolina	2,331	R-53.6	3,472	R-51.6	Richard Burr (R) 2011	Elizabeth Dole (R) 2009
North Dakota	(X)	(X)	311	D-68.3	Kent Conrad (D) 2007	Byron Dorgan (D) 2011
Ohio	(X)	(X)	5,426	R-63.8	Mike DeWine (R) 2007	George Voinovich (R) 2011
Oklahoma	1,018	R-57.3	1,447	R-52.8	Tom Coburn (R) 2011	James Inhofe (R) 2009
Oregon	1,267	R-56.2	1,781	D-63.4	Gordon Smith (R) 2009	Ron Wyden (D) 2011
Pennsylvania	(X)	(X)	5,559	R-52.6	Rick Santorum (R) 2007	Arlen Specter (R) 2011
Rhode Island	324	D-78.4	(X)	(X)	Lincoln Chafee (R) 2007	Jack Reed (D) 2009
South Carolina	1,103	R-54.4	1,597	R-53.7	Jim DeMint (R) 2011	Lindsey Graham (R) 2009
South Dakota	338	D-49.6	391	R-50.6	Tim Johnson (D) 2009	John Thune (R) 2011
Tennessee	1,642	R-54.3	(X)	(X)	Lamar Alexander (R) 2009	Bill Frist (R) 2007
Texas	4,514	R-55.3	(X)	(X)	John Cornyn (R) 2009	Kay Hutchison (R) 2007
Utah	(X)	(X)	912	R-68.7	Robert Bennett (R) 2011	Orrin Hatch (R) 2007
Vermont	(X)	(X)	307	D-70.6	James Jeffords (I) 2007	Patrick Leahy (D) 2011
Virginia	1,489	R-82.6	(X)	(X)	George Allen (R) 2007	John Warner (R) 2009
Washington	(X)	(X)	2,819	D-55.0	Maria Cantwell (D) 2007	Patty Murray (D) 2011
West Virginia	436	D-63.1	(X)	(X)	Robert Byrd (D) 2007	John Rockefeller (D) 2009
Wisconsin	(X)	(X)	2,950	D-55.4	Russell Feingold (D) 2011	Herb Kohl (D) 2007
Wyoming	183	R-73.0	(X)	(X)	Michael Enzi (R) 2009	Craig Thomas (R) 2007

X Not applicable.   [1] Includes vote cast for minor parties.   [2] Louisiana holds an open-primary election with candidates from all parties running on the same ballot. Any candidate who receives a majority is elected.

Source: Office of the Clerk, *Statistics of the Presidential and Congressional Election*, biennial. See also <http://clerk.house .gov/members/electionInfo/elections.html>.

U.S. Census Bureau, *Statistical Abstract of the United States: 2006*

Table 390. **Vote Cast for United States Representatives by Major Political Party—States: 2000 to 2004**

[In thousands (98,800 represents 98,800,000), except percent. R = Republican,D = Democrat, and I = Independent. In each state, totals represent the sum of votes cast in each Congressional District or votes cast for Representative-at-Large in states where only one member is elected. In all years there are numerous districts within the state where either the Republican or Democratic party had no candidate. In some states the Republican and Democratic vote includes votes cast for the party candidate by endorsing parties]

State	2000				2002				2004			
	Total[1]	Demo-cratic	Repub-lican	Percent for leading party	Total[1]	Demo-cratic	Repub-lican	Percent for leading party	Total[1]	Demo-cratic	Repub-lican	Percent for leading party
U.S....	98,800	46,412	46,750	R-47.3	74,707	33,642	37,091	R-49.6	113,192	52,745	55,713	R-49.2
AL	1,439	486	849	R-59.0	1,269	507	695	R-54.7	1,793	708	1,080	R-60.2
AK	274	45	191	R-69.6	228	39	170	R-74.5	300	67	213	R-71.1
AZ	1,466	558	855	R-58.3	1,194	472	682	R-57.1	1,871	598	1,128	R-60.3
AR [2]	633	355	277	D-56.2	688	392	284	D-57.0	791	426	358	D-53.9
CA	10,437	5,407	4,446	D-51.8	7,258	3,731	3,226	D-51.4	11,624	6,224	5,031	D-53.5
CO	1,624	496	969	R-59.7	1,397	589	753	R-53.9	2,039	995	992	D-48.8
CT	1,313	699	591	D-53.2	989	509	466	D-51.5	1,429	786	630	D-55.0
DE	313	96	212	R-67.6	228	61	165	R-72.1	356	106	246	R-69.1
FL [2]	5,011	1,976	2,852	R-56.9	3,767	1,537	2,161	R-57.4	5,627	2,212	3,319	R-59.0
GA	2,417	918	1,498	R-62.0	1,919	814	1,105	R-57.6	2,961	1,141	1,820	R-61.5
HI.	340	221	111	D-65.0	360	232	117	D-64.5	417	262	148	D-62.9
ID.	493	142	333	R-67.5	405	138	256	R-63.3	572	171	401	R-70.1
IL.	4,393	2,454	1,907	D-55.9	3,429	1,741	1,657	D-50.8	4,989	2,675	2,272	D-53.6
IN.	2,157	953	1,141	R-52.9	1,521	641	841	R-55.3	2,416	999	1,382	R-57.2
IA.	1,276	532	717	R-56.2	1,013	454	546	R-54.0	1,458	625	823	R-56.4
KS	1,036	328	656	R-63.3	830	260	536	R-64.6	1,156	387	724	R-62.6
KY	1,435	562	825	R-57.5	1,094	351	694	R-63.4	1,635	602	1,017	R-62.2
LA [2]	1,202	360	747	R-62.1	1,140	391	668	R-58.6	1,259	478	780	R-62.0
ME	638	423	203	D-66.2	495	290	206	D-58.5	710	418	283	D-58.9
MD	1,927	1,061	856	D-55.1	1,659	904	753	D-54.5	2,254	1,311	896	D-58.2
MA	2,734	1,968	343	D-72.0	2,220	1,529	290	D-68.8	2,927	2,060	435	D-70.4
MI	4,070	2,178	1,787	D-53.5	3,056	1,507	1,474	D-49.3	4,631	2,242	2,289	R-49.4
MN	2,364	1,234	993	D-52.2	2,202	1,098	1,030	D-49.9	2,722	1,400	1,236	D-51.4
MS	986	496	468	D-50.3	678	320	339	R-50.0	1,116	335	659	R-59.0
MO	2,326	1,136	1,136	D-48.8	1,854	829	986	R-53.2	2,667	1,193	1,430	R-53.6
MT	411	190	211	R-51.5	331	108	214	R-64.6	444	146	286	R-64.4
NE	683	178	487	R-71.2	474	47	387	R-81.6	765	231	515	R-67.3
NV	587	225	331	R-56.4	502	171	301	R-60.0	791	334	421	R-53.2
NH	556	239	303	R-54.5	443	176	255	R-57.5	652	244	396	R-60.8
NJ	2,988	1,532	1,384	D-51.3	2,006	1,030	934	D-51.4	3,285	1,721	1,515	D-52.4
NM	588	300	274	D-51.0	437	262	175	D-59.9	743	385	358	D-51.8
NY	6,949	3,052	2,235	D-43.9	4,701	1,778	1,526	D-37.8	7,448	3,457	2,209	D-46.4
NC	2,780	1,194	1,515	R-54.5	2,244	971	1,209	R-53.9	3,413	1,670	1,743	R-51.1
ND	286	151	127	D-52.9	231	121	110	D-52.4	311	185	126	D-59.6
OH	4,585	2,099	2,235	R-48.8	3,158	1,332	1,776	R-56.2	5,184	2,515	2,650	R-51.1
OK	1,088	337	702	R-64.5	1,002	392	547	R-54.6	1,375	389	875	R-63.7
OR	1,440	790	607	D-54.9	1,240	677	529	D-54.6	1,772	952	762	D-53.7
PA	4,552	2,279	2,229	D-50.1	3,310	1,349	1,859	R-56.2	5,151	2,478	2,565	R-49.8
RI.	384	247	89	D-64.3	329	225	97	D-68.3	402	279	113	D-69.5
SC	1,321	523	730	R-55.2	984	345	569	R-57.8	1,439	486	913	R-63.5
SD	315	78	231	R-73.4	337	154	180	R-53.5	389	208	179	D-53.4
TN	1,854	819	992	R-53.5	1,529	708	771	R-50.4	2,219	1,032	1,161	R-52.3
TX	5,986	2,799	2,932	R-49.0	4,295	1,885	2,291	R-53.3	6,959	2,714	4,013	R-57.7
UT	759	305	427	R-56.2	557	221	322	R-57.8	909	362	520	R-57.3
VT	283	15	52	I-73.4	225	(X)	73	I-64.3	305	22	74	I-67.5
VA	2,422	1,060	1,132	R-46.7	1,516	440	956	R-63.0	3,004	1,023	1,817	R-60.5
WA	2,382	1,246	998	D-52.3	1,739	907	779	D-52.2	2,730	1,609	1,095	D-58.9
WV	580	421	109	D-72.6	400	264	136	D-66.0	722	415	303	D-57.6
WI	2,506	1,188	1,311	R-52.3	1,638	677	889	R-54.3	2,822	1,369	1,381	R-48.9
WY	212	61	142	R-66.8	182	66	110	R-60.5	239	100	132	R-55.2

X Not applicable.   [1] Includes vote cast for minor parties.   [2] State law does not require tabulation of votes for unopposed candidates.

Source: Office of the Clerk, *Statistics of the Presidential and Congressional Election*, biennial. See also <http://clerk.house.gov/members/electionInfo/elections.html>.

Elections 251

Table 391. Vote Cast for United States Representatives by Major Political Party—Congressional Districts: 2004

[In some states the Democratic and Republican vote includes votes cast for the party candidate by endorsing parties]

State and district	Democratic candidate — Name	Percent of total	Republican candidate — Name	Percent of total
AL....	(X)	(X)	(X)	(X)
1st...	Belk	36.81	Bonner	63.12
2d...	James	28.46	Everett	71.42
3d...	Fuller	38.75	Rogers	61.20
4th..	Cole	25.14	Aderholt	74.73
5th...	Cramer, Jr.	72.97	Wallace	26.92
6th...	[1]	[1]	Bachus	98.80
7th...	Davis	74.97	Cameron	24.94
AK....	Higgins	22.36	Young	71.08
AZ....	(X)	(X)	(X)	(X)
1st...	Babbitt	36.22	Renzi	58.54
2d...	Camacho	38.46	Franks	59.17
3d...	[1]	[1]	Shadegg	80.10
4th...	Pastor	70.12	Hayworth	25.66
5th...	Rogers	38.19	Hayworth	59.50
6th...	[1]	[1]	Flake	79.38
7th...	Grijalva	62.06	Sweeney	33.67
8th...	Bacal	36.20	Kolbe	60.36
AR....	(X)	(X)	(X)	(X)
1st...	Berry	66.57	Humphrey	33.43
2d...	Snyder	58.17	Parks	41.83
3d...	Judy	38.09	Boozman	59.32
4th...	Ross	[2]	[1]	[1]
CA....	(X)	(X)	(X)	(X)
1st...	Thompson	66.92	Wiesner	28.26
2d...	Johnson	33.15	Herger	66.85
3d...	Castillo	34.84	Lungren	61.91
4th...	Winters	34.61	Doolittle	65.39
5th...	Matsui	71.36	Dugas	23.33
6th...	Woolsey	72.65	Erickson	27.35
7th...	Miller	76.08	Hargrave	23.92
8th...	Pelosi	82.95	DePalma	11.51
9th...	Lee	84.55	Bermudez	12.26
10th..	Tauscher	65.71	Ketelson	34.29
11th..	McNerney	38.77	Pombo	61.23
12th..	Lantos	68.03	Garza	20.82
13th..	Stark	71.61	Bruno	23.99
14th..	Eshoo	69.77	Haugen	26.56
15th..	Honda	72.03	Chukwu	27.97
16th..	Lofgren	70.89	McNea	26.33
17th..	Farr	66.73	Risley	29.17
18th..	Cardoza	67.49	Pringle	32.51
19th..	Bufford	27.22	Radanovich	66.03
20th..	Costa	53.40	Ashburn	46.60
21st..	Davis	26.83	Nunes	73.17
22d...	[1]	[1]	Thomas	100.00
23d...	Capps	63.03	Regan	34.35
24th..	Wagner	33.90	Gallegly	62.82
25th..	Willoughby	35.58	McKeon	64.42
26th..	Matthews	42.80	Dreier	53.58
27th..	Sherman	62.27	Levy	33.27
28th..	Berman	70.95	Hernandez	23.30
29th..	Schiff	64.63	Scolinos	30.40
30th..	Waxman	71.24	Elizalde	28.76
31st..	Becerra	80.21	Vega	19.79
32d...	Solis	85.01	[1]	[1]
33d...	Watson	88.58	[1]	[1]
34th..	Roybal-Allard	74.49	Miller	25.51
35th..	Waters	80.53	Moen	15.08
36th..	Harman	61.96	Whitehead	33.46
37th..	Millender-McDonald	75.05	Van	20.19
38th..	Napolitano	100.00	[1]	[1]
39th..	Sanchez	60.70	Escobar	39.30
40th..	Williams	32.07	Royce	67.93
41st..	[1]	[1]	Lewis	82.95
42d...	Myers	31.86	Miller	68.14
43d...	Baca	66.37	Laning	33.63
44th..	Vandenberg	35.00	Calvert	61.64
45th..	Meyer	33.39	Bono	66.61
46th..	Brandt	32.57	Rohrabacher	61.92
47th..	Sanchez	60.38	Coronado	44.22
48th..	Graham	32.15	Cox	64.98
49th..	Byron	34.91	Issa	62.55
50th..	Busby	36.49	Cunningham	58.42
51st..	Filner	61.61	Giorgino	35.12
52d...	Keliher	27.58	Hunter	69.19
53d...	Davis	66.14	Hunzeker	28.86
CO....	(X)	(X)	(X)	(X)
1st...	DeGette	73.50	Chicas	24.35
2d...	Udall	67.20	Hackman	30.44
3d...	Salazar	50.55	Walcher	46.56
4th...	Matsunaka	44.78	Musgrave	51.05
5th...	Hardee	27.04	Hefley	70.54
6th...	Conti	39.10	Tancredo	59.48
7th...	Thomas	42.79	Beauprez	54.72
CT....	(X)	(X)	(X)	(X)
1st...	Larson	72.98	Halstead	27.02
2d...	Sullivan	45.77	Simmons	54.19
3d...	DeLauro	72.44	Elser	24.97
4th...	Farrell	47.56	Shays	52.43
5th...	Gerratana	38.17	Johnson	59.79
DE....	Donnelly	29.69	Castle	69.09
FL....	(X)	(X)	(X)	(X)
1st...	Coutu	23.46	Miller	76.54
2d...	Boyd	61.65	Kilmer	38.35
3d...	Brown	99.24	[1]	[1]
4th...	[1]	[1]	Crenshaw	99.55
5th...	Whittel	34.06	Brown-Waite	65.93
6th...	Bruderly	35.59	Stearns	64.40
7th...	[1]	[1]	Mica	[2]
8th...	Murray	39.48	Keller	60.52
9th...	[1]	[1]	Bilirakis	99.91
10th..	Derry	30.67	Young	69.33
11th..	Davis	85.81	[1]	[1]
12th..	Hagenmaier	35.11	Putnam	64.89
13th..	Schneider	44.70	Harris	55.30
14th..	Neeld	32.41	Mack	67.59
15th..	Pristoop	34.65	Weldon	65.35
16th..	Fisher	31.96	Foley	68.04
17th..	Meek	99.59	[1]	[1]
18th..	Sheldon	35.27	Ros-Lehtinen	64.73
19th..	Wexler	[2]	[1]	[1]
20th..	Schultz	70.19	Hostetter	29.81
21st..	[1]	[1]	Balart	72.80
22d...	Rorapaugh	35.29	Shaw	62.79
23d...	Hastings	[2]	[1]	[1]
24th..	[1]	[1]	Feeney	[2]
25th..	[1]	[1]	Diaz-Balart	[2]
GA....	(X)	(X)	(X)	(X)
1st...	[1]	[1]	Kingston	100.00
2d...	Bishop, Jr.	66.79	Eversman	33.21
3d...	Marshall	62.88	Clay	37.12
4th...	McKinney	63.76	Davis	36.24
5th...	Lewis	100.00	[1]	[1]
6th...	[1]	[1]	Price	99.97
7th...	[1]	[1]	Linder	100.00
8th...	Delamar	24.45	Westmoreland	75.55
9th...	Ellis	25.71	Norwood	74.29
10th..	[1]	[1]	Deal	100.00
11th..	Crawford	42.60	Gingrey	57.40
12th..	Barrow	51.81	Burns	48.19
13th..	Scott	100.00	[1]	[1]
HI....	(X)	(X)	(X)	(X)
1st...	Abercrombie	62.97	Tanonaka	33.98
2d...	Case	62.77	Gabbard	37.23
ID....	(X)	(X)	(X)	(X)
1st...	Preston	30.45	Otter	69.55
2d...	Whitworth	29.26	Simpson	70.74

See footnotes at end of table.

252 Elections

Table 391. Vote Cast for United States Representatives by Major Political Party—Congressional Districts: 2004—Con.

[See headnote, p. 252]

State and district	Democratic candidate Name	Percent of total	Republican candidate Name	Percent of total
IL.....	(X)	(X)	(X)......	(X)
1st...	Rush	84.86	Wardingley	15.14
2d...	Jackson	88.49	(¹)......	(¹)
3d...	Lipinski	72.64	Chlada	25.15
4th...	Gutierrez	83.71	Cisneros	12.41
5th...	Emanuel	76.18	Best	23.82
6th...	Cegelis	44.17	Hyde	55.83
7th...	Davis	86.13	Davis-Fairman	13.87
8th...	Bean	51.70	Crane	48.30
9th...	Schakowsky	75.74	Eckhardt	24.26
10th...	Goodman	35.86	Kirk	64.14
11th...	Renner	41.33	Weller	58.67
12th...	Costello	69.46	Zweigart	28.86
13th...	Andersen	34.98	Biggert	65.02
14th...	Zamora	31.37	Hastert	68.63
15th...	Gill	38.95	Johnson	61.05
16th...	Kutsch	58.25	Manzullo	69.08
17th...	Evans	32.20	Zinga	39.32
18th...	Waterworth	29.76	LaHood	70.24
19th...	Bagwell	30.64	Shimkus	69.36
IN.....	(X)	(X)	(X)......	(X)
1st...	Visclosky	68.29	Leyva	31.71
2d...	Donnelly	44.54	Chocola	54.17
3d...	Parra	30.79	Souder	69.21
4th...	Sanders	28.30	Buyer	69.47
5th...	Carr	25.96	Burton	71.84
6th...	Fox	31.29	Pence	67.09
7th...	Carson	54.35	Horning	43.68
8th...	Jennings	44.55	Hostettler	53.37
9th...	Hill	48.96	Sodrel	49.46
IA.....	(X)	(X)	(X)......	(X)
1st...	Gluba	43.26	Nussle	55.16
2d...	Franker	39.15	Leach	58.92
3d...	Boswell	55.21	Thompson	44.72
4th...	Johnson	39.02	Latham	60.93
5th...	Schulte	36.64	King	63.30
KS.....	(X)	(X)	(X)......	(X)
1st...	(¹)	(¹)	Moran	90.72
2d...	Boyda	41.28	Ryun	56.15
3d...	Moore	54.82	Kobach	43.35
4th...	Kinard	31.07	Tiahrt	66.11
KY.....	(X)	(X)	(X)......	(X)
1st...	Cartwright	32.61	Whitfield	67.32
2d...	Smith	32.08	Lewis	67.92
3d...	Miller	37.80	Northup	60.26
4th...	Clooney	43.89	Davis	54.40
5th...	(¹)	(¹)	Rogers	100.00
6th...	Chandler	58.60	Buford	40.01
LA³....	(X)	(X)	(X)......	(X)
1st...	Armstrong	6.69	Jindal	78.40
2d...	Jefferson	79.01	Schwertz	20.99
3d...	Melancon	50.25	Tauzin III	49.75
4th...	(¹)	(¹)	McCrery	(²)
5th...	Blakes	24.61	Alexander	59.44
6th...	Craig, Jr.	19.37	Baker	72.21
7th...	Mount	45.04	Boustany, Jr.	54.96
ME.....	(X)	(X)	(X)......	(X)
1st...	Allen	59.74	Summers, Jr.	40.26
2d...	Michaud	58.03	Hamel	39.47
MD.....	(X)	(X)	(X)......	(X)
1st...	Alexakis	24.11	Gilchrest	75.89
2d...	Ruppersberger	66.68	Brooks	30.68
3d...	Cardin	63.44	Duckworth	33.80
4th...	Wynn	75.23	McKinnis	20.22
5th...	Hoyer	68.72	Jewitt	29.25
6th...	Bosley	29.49	Bartlett	67.45
7th...	Cummings	73.43	Salazar	24.63
8th...	Van Hollen	74.91	Floyd	25.07
MA.....	(X)	(X)	(X)......	(X)
1st...	Olver	77.73	(¹)......	(¹)
2d...	Neal	75.62	(¹)......	(¹)
3d...	McGovern	67.15	Crews	28.04
4th...	Frank	73.14	(¹)......	(¹)

State and district	Democratic candidate Name	Percent of total	Republican candidate Name	Percent of total
5th...	Meehan	64.09	Tierney	31.48
6th...	Tierney	66.35	O'Malley, Jr.	28.47
7th...	Markey	69.27	Chase	20.65
8th...	Capuano	76.85	(¹)......	(¹)
9th...	Lynch	73.25	(¹)......	(¹)
10th...	Delahunt	63.30	Jones	32.75
MI.....	(X)	(X)	(X)......	(X)
1st...	Stupak	65.57	Hooper	32.76
2d...	Kotos	28.93	Hoekstra	69.34
3d...	Hickey	31.48	Ehlers	66.58
4th...	Huckleberry	34.77	Camp	64.36
5th...	Kildee	67.17	Kirkwood	31.28
6th...	Elliott	32.43	Upton	65.34
7th...	Renier	36.31	Schwarz	58.36
8th...	Alexander	36.87	Rogers	61.03
9th...	Reifman	39.54	Knollenberg	58.45
10th...	Casey	29.54	Miller	68.62
11th...	Truran	41.04	McCotter	56.97
12th...	Levin	69.32	Shafer	29.02
13th...	Kilpatrick	78.16	Cassell	18.47
14th...	Conyers	83.93	Pedraza	33.42
15th...	Dingell	70.92	Reamer	26.57
MN.....	(X)	(X)	(X)......	(X)
1st...	Pomeroy	35.51	Gutknecht	59.60
2d...	Daley	40.31	Kline	56.38
3d...	Watts	35.29	Ramstad	64.61
4th...	McCollum	57.48	Bataglia	33.24
5th...	Sabo	69.67	Mathias	24.43
6th...	Wetterling	45.94	Kennedy	53.99
7th...	Peterson	66.07	Sturrock	33.84
8th...	Oberstar	65.22	Groettum	32.15
MS.....	(X)	(X)	(X)......	(X)
1st...	(¹)	(¹)	Wicker	79.01
2d...	Thompson	58.38	LeSueur	40.64
3d...	(¹)	(¹)	Pickering	80.06
4th...	Taylor	64.19	Lott	34.50
MO.....	(X)	(X)	(X)......	(X)
1st...	Clay	75.29	Farr, II	22.83
2d...	Weber	32.97	Akin	65.37
3d...	Carnahan	52.86	Federer	45.13
4th...	Skelton	66.20	Noland	32.38
5th...	Cleaver, II	55.19	Patterson	42.12
6th...	Broomfield	34.75	Graves	63.83
7th...	Newberry	28.29	Blunt	70.45
8th...	Henderson	26.62	Emerson	72.21
9th...	Jacobsen	33.84	Hulshof	64.60
MT.....	Velazquez	32.78	Rehberg	64.40
NE.....	(X)	(X)	(X)......	(X)
1st...	Connealy	43.00	Fortenberry	54.23
2d...	Thompson	36.15	Terry	61.10
3d...	Anderson	10.57	Osborne	87.45
NV.....	(X)	(X)	(X)......	(X)
1st...	Berkley	65.98	Mickelson	31.12
2d...	Cochran	27.48	Gibbons	67.15
3d...	Gallagher	40.40	Porter	54.46
NH.....	(X)	(X)	(X)......	(X)
1st...	Nadeau	36.56	Bradley	63.34
2d...	Hodes	38.17	Bass	58.25
NJ.....	(X)	(X)	(X)......	(X)
1st...	Andrews	75.00	Hutchison	24.65
2d...	Robb	32.70	LoBiondo	65.09
3d...	Conaway	34.65	Saxton	63.44
4th...	Vasquez	32.28	Smith	67.00
5th...	Wolfe	41.11	Garrett	57.57
6th...	Pallone, Jr.	66.90	Fernandez	30.82
7th...	Brozak	41.66	Ferguson	56.88
8th...	Pascrell, Jr.	69.46	Ajjan	28.68
9th...	Rothman	67.53	Trawinski	31.71
10th...	Payne	96.88	(¹)......	(¹)
11th...	Buell	31.02	Frelinghuysen	67.88
12th...	Holt	59.25	Spadea	39.69
13th...	Menendez	75.85	Piatkowski	22.12

See footnotes at end of table.

Elections 253

Table 391. **Vote Cast for United States Representatives by Major Political Party—Congressional Districts: 2004—Con.**

[See headnote, p. 252]

State and district	Democratic candidate Name	Percent of total	Republican candidate Name	Percent of total	State and district	Democratic candidate Name	Percent of total	Republican candidate Name	Percent of total
NM....	(X).......	(X)	(X).......	(X)	12th..	Brown	38.03	Tiberi......	61.96
1st...	Romero	45.53	Wilson.....	54.40	13th..	Brown	67.43	Lucas......	67.65
2d...	King......	39.80	Pearce.....	60.20	14th..	Cafaro	40.16	LaTourette ..	51.82
3d...	Udall...	68.68	Tucker.....	31.32	15th..	Brown	34.51	Pryce......	73.01
NY....	(X).......	(X)	(X).......	(X)	16th..	Seemann ...	33.45	Regula.....	66.55
1st...	Bishop.....	44.87	Manger	35.29	17th..	Ryan	77.19	Cusimano ..	22.81
2d...	Israel......	51.93	Hoffmann ...	25.73	18th..	Thomas	33.84	Ney	66.16
3d...	Mathies	31.87	King.......	47.87	OK	(X).......	(X)	(X)........	(X)
4th...	McCarthy ...	52.23	Gamer......	30.05	1st...	Dodd	37.54	Sullivan	60.19
5th...	Ackerman...	55.26	Graves.....	20.82	2d ...	Boren......	65.89	Smalley	34.11
6th...	Meeks.....	67.65	(¹)	(¹)	3d ...	(¹)........	(¹)	Lucas......	82.21
7th...	Crowley	56.57	Cinquemani.	12.31	4th...	(¹)........	(¹)	Cole.......	77.77
8th...	Nadler.....	61.24	Hort.......	13.98	5th...	Smith......	33.94	Istook, Jr. ...	66.06
9th...	Weiner.....	53.60	Cronin	19.57	OR	(X).......	(X)	(X)........	(X)
10th:.	Towns	66.72	Clarke	5.68	1st...	Wu	57.51	Ameri......	38.15
11th..	Owens.....	66.41	(¹)........	(¹)	2d ...	McColgan...	25.63	Walden.....	71.63
12th..	Velazquez...	61.47	Rodriguez...	9.61	3d ...	Blumenauer .	70.86	Mars	23.67
13th..	Barbaro	33.13	Fossella	47.14	4th...	DeFazio	60.98	Feldkamp...	37.58
14th..	Maloney	64.18	Srdanovic ...	15.30	5th...	Hooley	52.86	Zupancic ..	44.33
15th..	Rangel.....	70.03	Jefferson, Jr..	5.65	PA	(X)........	(X)	(X)........	(X)
16th..	Serrano	72.06	Mohamed ...	3.32	1st...	Brady......	86.27	Williams	13.38
17th..	Engel.....•	58.78	Brennan	17.60	2d ...	Fattah	88.04	Bolno......	11.96
18th..	Lowey	54.81	Hoffman	25.49	3d ...	Porter......	39.92	English.....	60.08
19th..	Jaliman	28.50	Kelly	49.57	4th...	Drobac, Jr. ..	35.91	Hart.......	63.08
20th..	Kelly	29.81	Sweeney ...	50.39	5th...	(¹)........	(¹)	Peterson....	88.02
21st..	McNulty	53.63	Redlich.....	25.69	6th...	Murphy.....	48.99	Gerlach	51.01
22d ..	Hinchey	51.70	Brenner	28.49	7th...	Scoles	40.34	Weldon.....	58.76
23d ..	Johnson....	25.07	McHugh	51.40	8th...	Schrader ...	43.30	Fitzpatrick...	55.31
24th..	Miller	29.70	Boehlert	44.82	9th...	Politis......	30.47	Shuster	69.53
25th..	(¹)........	(¹)	Walsh	49.12	10th..	(¹)........	(¹)	Sherwood ...	92.84
26th..	Davis	36.28	Reynolds ...	42.80	11th..	Kanjorski ...	94.42	(¹)........	(¹)
27th..	Higgins.....	42.46	Naples	41.80	12th..	Murtha	100.00	(¹)........	(¹)
28th..	Slaughter ...	57.37	Laba	18.68	13th..	Schwartz ...	55.74	Brown	41.28
29th..	Barend.....	34.16	Kuhl, Jr.	44.72	14th..	Doyle......	100.00	(¹)........	(¹)
NC	(X).......	(X)	(X).......	(X)	15th..	Driscoll.....	39.38	Dent	58.61
1st...	Butterfield ...	63.98	Dority......	36.02	16th..	Herr.......	34.49	Pitts.......	64.36
2d ...	Etheridge ...	62.30	Creech.....	37.70	17th..	Holden	59.09	Paterno	38.93
3d ...	Eaton......	29.30	Jones......	70.70	18th..	Boles	37.24	Murphy.....	62.76
4th...	Price	64.10	Batchelor ...	35.88	19th..	(¹)........	(¹)	Platts......	91.51
5th...	Harrell, Jr...	41.17	Foxx	58.83	RI	(X)........	(X)	(X)........	(X)
6th...	Jordan.....	26.85	Coble......	73.15	1st...	Kennedy....	64.06	Rogers.....	35.80
7th...	McIntyre	73.19	Plonk.....	26.81	2d ...	Langevin ..	74.53	Barton, III ..	20.82
8th...	Troutman ...	44.46	Hayes	55.54	SC	(X)........	(X)	(X)........	(X)
9th...	Flynn	29.76	Myrick	70.24	1st...	(¹)........	(¹)	Brown, Jr....	87.82
10th..	Fischer.....	35.86	McHenry....	64.15	2d ...	Ellisor......	33.32	Wilson	64.98
11th..	Keever.....	45.10	Taylor.....	54.90	3d ...	(¹)........	(¹)	Barrett	99.51
12th..	Watt.......	66.83	Fisher	33.17	4th...	Brown	28.96	Inglis......	69.77
13th..	Miller	58.79	Johnson	41.21	5th...	Spratt, Jr. ...	63.03	Spencer	36.93
ND	Pomeroy....	59.56	Sand	40.44	6th...	Clyburn	66.98	McLeod	31.20
OH	(X).......	(X)	(X).......	(X)	SD	Daschle	53.36	Diedrich....	45.91
1st...	Harris......	40.10	Chabot.....	59.83	TN	(X)........	(X)	(X)........	(X)
2d ...	Sanders	28.29	Portman	71.70	1st...	Leonard	24.13	Jenkins ...	73.88
3d ...	Mitakides ...	37.71	Turner	62.29	2d ...	Greene.....	19.11	Duncan, Jr...	79.07
4th...	Konop	41.40	Oxley......	58.60	3d ...	Wolfe......	32.85	Wamp	64.74
5th...	Weirauch ...	32.95	Gillmor.....	67.05	4th...	Davis	54.80	Bowling	43.54
6th...	Strickland ...	99.94	(¹)........	(¹)	5th...	Cooper.....	69.26	Knapp	30.73
7th...	Anastasio ...	35.04	Hobson	64.96	6th...	Gordon.....	64.24	Demas.....	33.58
8th...	Hardenbrook.	30.99	Boehner	69.01	7th...	(¹)........	(¹)	Blackburn ...	100.00
9th...	Kaptur.....	68.13	Kaczala	31.87	8th...	Tanner	74.34	Hart.......	25.63
10th..	Kucinich	60.03	Herman	33.59	9th...	Ford, Jr.	82.04	Fort	17.89
11th..	Jones......	100.00	(¹)........	(¹)					

See footnotes at end of table.

U.S. Census Bureau, Statistical Abstract of the United States: 2006

Table 391. Vote Cast for United States Representatives by Major Political Party—Congressional Districts: 2004—Con.

[See headnote, p. 252]

State and district	Democratic candidate Name	Percent of total	Republican candidate Name	Percent of total
TX	(X)		(X)	
1st...	Sandlin	37.68	Gohmert	61.47
2d...	Lampson	42.91	Poe	55.53
3d...	[1]		Johnson	85.62
4th..	Nickerson	30.45	Hall	68.25
5th...	Bernstein	32.88	Hensarling	64.47
6th...	Meyer	32.71	Barton	66.02
7th...	Martinez	33.30	Culberson	64.11
8th...	Wright	29.67	Brady	68.91
9th...	Green	72.19	Molina	26.57
10th..	[1]		McCaul	78.62
11th..	Raasch	21.79	Conaway	76.76
12th..	Alvarado	27.68	Granger	72.32
13th..	[1]		Thornberry	92.31
14th..	[1]		Paul	100.00
15th..	Hinojosa	57.76	Thamm	40.83
16th..	Reyes	67.53	Brigham	31.08
17th..	Edwards	51.20	Wohlgemuth	47.42
18th..	Jackson-Lee	88.91	[1]	
19th..	Stenholm	40.05	Neugebauer	58.44
20th..	Gonzalez	65.47	Scott	32.00
21st..	Smith	35.51	Smith	61.50
22d..	Morrison	41.10	DeLay	55.16
23d..	Sullivan	29.40	Bonilla	69.26
24th..	Page	34.22	Marchant	63.98
25th..	Doggett	67.60	Klein	30.74
26th..	Reyes	32.71	Burgess	65.75
27th..	Ortiz	63.13	Vaden	34.90
28th..	Cuellar	59.01	Hopson	38.60
29th..	Green	94.14	[1]	
30th..	Johnson	93.03	[1]	
31st..	Porter	32.45	Carter	64.77
32d..	Frost	44.02	Sessions	54.32
UT	(X)		(X)	
1st...	Thompson	29.13	Bishop	67.91
2d...	Matheson	54.76	Swallow	43.21
3d...	Babka	32.52	Cannon	63.39
VT[4]	Drown	7.11	Parke	24.35

State and district	Democratic candidate Name	Percent of total	Republican candidate Name	Percent of total
VA	(X)		(X)	
1st...	[1]		Davis	78.55
2d...	Ashe	44.82	Drake	55.08
3d...	Scott	69.33	Sears	30.53
4th...	Menefee	35.48	Forbes	64.46
5th...	Weed, III.	36.28	Goode, Jr.	63.68
6th...	[1]		Goodlatte	96.68
7th...	[1]		Cantor	75.50
8th...	Moran	59.73	Cheney	36.90
9th...	Boucher	59.32	Triplett	38.94
10th..	Socas	36.11	Wolf	63.77
11th..	Longmyer	38.26	Davis	60.25
WA	(X)		(X)	
1st...	Inslee	62.28	Eastwood	35.96
2d...	Larsen	63.91	Sinclair	33.58
3d...	Baird	61.93	Crowson	38.07
4th...	Matheson	37.43	Hastings	62.57
5th...	Barbieri	40.32	McMorris	59.68
6th...	Dicks	68.99	Cloud	31.01
7th...	McDermott	80.68	Cassady	19.32
8th...	Ross	46.70	Reichert*	51.50
9th...	Smith	63.28	Lord	34.40
WV	(X)		(X)	
1st...	Mollohan	67.78	Parks	32.22
2d...	Wells	41.29	Capito	57.46
3d...	Rahall, II.	65.20	Snuffer	34.80
WI	(X)		(X)	
1st...	Thomas	32.57	Ryan	65.37
2d...	Baldwin	63.27	Magnum	36.66
3d...	Kind	56.43	Schultz	43.49
4th...	Moore	69.60	Boyle	28.16
5th...	Kennedy	31.77	Sensenbrenner, Jr.	66.57
6th...	Hall	30.12	Petri	67.03
7th...	Obey	85.64	[1]	
8th...	Le Clair	29.83	Green	70.13
WY	Ladd	41.81	Cubin	55.24

X Not applicable. [1] No candidate. [2] According to state law, it is not required to tabulate votes for unopposed candidates. [3] Louisiana holds an open-primary election with candidates from all parties running on the same ballot. Any candidate who receives a majority is elected; if no candidate receives 50 percent, there is a run-off election in November between the top two finishers. [4] Sanders, an Independent, was elected with 67.5 percent of the vote in 2004.

Source: Office of the Clerk, Statistics of the Presidential and Congressional Election, June 7, 2005. See also <http://clerk.house.gov/members/electionInfo/elections.html>.

Table 392. Composition of Congress by Political Party: 1975 to 2005

[D = Democratic, R = Republican. Data reflect immediate result of elections. Vacancies at beginning of sessions are noted]

Year	Party and President	Congress	House Majority party	Minority party	Other	Senate Majority party	Minority party	Other
1975 [1]	R (Ford)	94th	D-291	R-144	-	D-61	R-37	2
1977 [2]	D (Carter)	95th	D-292	R-143	-	D-61	R-38	1
1979 [2]	D (Carter)	96th	D-277	R-158	-	D-58	R-41	1
1981 [2]	R (Reagan)	97th	D-242	R-192	1	R-53	D-46	1
1983	R (Reagan)	98th	D-269	R-166	-	R-54	D-46	-
1985	R (Reagan)	99th	D-253	R-182	-	R-53	D-47	-
1987	R (Reagan)	100th	D-258	R-177	-	D-55	R-45	-
1989 [3]	R (Bush)	101st	D-260	R-175	-	D-55	R-45	-
1991 [3]	R (Bush)	102d	D-267	R-167	1	D-56	R-44	-
1993 [3]	D (Clinton)	103d	D-258	R-176	1	D-57	R-43	-
1995 [3]	D (Clinton)	104th	R-230	D-204	1	R-52	D-48	-
1997 [3]	D (Clinton)	105th	R-226	D-207	2	R-55	D-45	-
1999 [3]	D (Clinton)	106th	R-223	D-211	1	R-55	D-45	-
2001 [5]	R (Bush)	107th	R-221	D-212	2	D-50	R-50	-
2003 [5]	R (Bush)	108th	R-229	D-204	1	R-51	D-48	1
2005 [5]	R (Bush)	109th	R-232	D-202	1	R-55	D-44	1

- Represents zero. [1] Senate had one Independent, one Conservative-Republican, and one undecided (New Hampshire). [2] Senate had one Independent. [3] House had one Independent-Socialist. [4] House had one Independent-Socialist and one Independent. [5] House and Senate each had one Independent.

Source: U.S. House of Representatives, Office of the Clerk, Official List of Members, annual. See also <http://clerk.house.gov/members/olm109.pdf>.

Table 393. Composition of Congress by Political Party Affiliation—States: 1999 to 2005

[Figures are for the beginning of the first session (as of January 3), except as noted. Dem. = Democratic; Rep. = Republican]

State	| Representatives								| Senators							
	106th Cong.,[1] 1999		107th Cong.,[1,2,3] 2001		108th Cong.,[1] 2003		109th Cong.,[1,4,5] 2005		106th Cong., 1999		107th Cong.,[6] 2001		108th Cong.,[6] 2003		109th Cong.,[5,6] 2005	
	Dem.	Rep.	Dem.	Rep.	Dem.	Rep.	Dem.	Rep.	Dem.	Rep.	Dem.	Rep.	Dem.	Rep.	Dem.	Rep.
U.S. . . .	212	222	211	221	205	229	202	231	45	55	50	50	48	51	44	55
AL.	2	5	2	5	2	5	2	5	-	2	-	2	-	2	-	2
AK.	-	1	-	1	-	1	-	1	-	2	-	2	-	2	-	2
AZ.	1	5	1	5	2	6	2	6	-	2	-	2	-	2	-	2
AR.	2	2	3	1	3	1	3	1	1	1	1	1	2	-	2	-
CA.	28	24	31	20	33	20	33	20	2	-	2	-	2	-	2	-
CO	2	4	2	4	2	5	3	4	-	2	-	2	-	2	1	1
CT.	4	2	3	3	2	3	2	3	2	-	2	-	2	-	2	-
DE.	-	1	-	1	-	1	-	1	1	1	2	-	2	-	2	-
FL.	8	15	8	15	7	18	7	18	1	1	2	-	2	-	1	1
GA.	3	8	3	8	5	8	6	7	1	1	2	-	1	1	-	2
HI.	2	-	2	-	2	-	2	-	2	-	2	-	2	-	2	-
ID	-	2	-	2	-	2	-	2	-	2	-	2	-	2	-	2
IL	10	10	10	10	9	10	10	9	1	1	1	1	1	1	2	-
IN	4	6	4	6	3	6	2	7	1	1	1	1	1	1	1	1
IA	1	4	1	4	1	4	1	4	1	1	1	1	1	1	1	1
KS.	1	3	1	3	1	3	1	3	-	2	-	2	-	2	-	2
KY.	1	5	1	5	1	5	1	5	-	2	-	2	-	2	-	2
LA.	2	5	2	5	3	4	2	5	2	-	2	-	2	-	1	1
ME	2	-	2	-	2	-	2	-	-	2	-	2	-	2	-	2
MD	4	4	4	4	6	2	6	2	2	-	2	-	2	-	2	-
MA	10	-	10	-	10	-	10	-	2	-	2	-	2	-	2	-
MI	10	6	9	7	6	9	6	9	1	1	2	-	2	-	2	-
MN	6	2	5	3	4	4	4	4	1	1	2	-	1	1	1	1
MS	3	2	3	2	2	2	2	2	-	2	-	2	-	2	-	2
MO	5	4	4	5	4	5	4	5	-	2	1	1	-	2	-	2
MT	-	1	-	1	-	1	-	1	1	1	1	1	1	1	1	1
NE.	-	3	-	3	-	3	-	3	1	1	1	1	1	1	1	1
NV.	1	1	1	1	1	2	1	2	2	-	1	1	1	1	1	1
NH.	-	2	-	2	-	2	-	2	-	2	-	2	-	2	-	2
NJ.	7	6	7	6	7	6	7	6	2	-	2	-	2	-	2	-
NM	1	2	1	2	1	2	1	2	1	1	1	1	1	1	1	1
NY	19	12	19	12	19	10	20	9	2	-	2	-	2	-	2	-
NC	5	7	5	7	6	7	6	7	1	1	1	1	1	1	-	2
ND	1	-	1	-	1	-	1	-	2	-	2	-	2	-	2	-
OH	8	11	8	11	6	12	6	11	-	2	-	2	-	2	-	2
OK	-	6	1	5	1	4	1	4	-	2	-	2	-	2	-	2
OR	4	1	4	1	4	1	4	1	1	1	1	1	1	1	1	1
PA.	11	10	10	11	7	12	7	12	-	2	-	2	-	2	-	2
RI	2	-	2	-	2	-	2	-	1	1	1	1	1	1	1	1
SC.	2	4	2	4	2	4	2	4	1	1	1	1	1	1	-	2
SD.	-	1	-	1	-	1	1	-	2	-	2	-	2	-	1	1
TN.	4	5	4	5	5	4	5	4	-	2	-	2	-	2	-	2
TX.	17	13	17	13	17	15	11	21	-	2	-	2	-	2	-	2
UT.	-	3	1	2	1	2	1	2	-	2	-	2	-	2	-	2
VT.	-	-	-	-	-	-	-	-	1	1	1	1	1	-	1	-
VA.	6	5	4	6	3	8	3	8	1	1	-	2	-	2	-	2
WA	5	4	6	3	6	3	6	3	1	1	2	-	2	-	2	-
WV	3	-	2	1	2	1	2	1	2	-	2	-	2	-	2	-
WI	5	4	5	4	4	4	4	4	2	-	2	-	2	-	2	-
WY	-	1	-	1	-	1	-	1	-	2	-	2	-	2	-	2

- Represents zero.   [1] Vermont had one Independent Representative.   [2] California had one vacancy.   [3] Virginia had one Independent Representative.   [4] Vacancy due to the resignation of Rob Portman (OH) April 29, 2005.   [5] As of June 28, 2005.   [6] Vermont had one Independent Senator. (Jeffords was reelected in Vermont in 2000 as a Republican, but subsequently switched to Independent status in June 2001.)

Source: U.S. Congress, Joint Committee on Printing, *Congressional Directory*, biennial through 2001; Starting in 2003. Office of the Clerk, *Official List of Members by State*, annual. See also <http://clerk.house.gov/members/olm109.pdf>.

Table 394. Members of Congress—Incumbents Reelected: 1966 to 2004

	Representatives						Senators					
		Incumbent candidates						Incumbent candidates				
			Re-elected		Defeated in—				Re-elected		Defeated in—	
Year	Retirements[1]	Total	Number	Per-cent of candidates	Pri-mary	General election	Retirements[1]	Total	Number	Per-cent of candidates	Pri-mary	General election
PRESIDENTIAL-YEAR ELECTIONS												
1968	23	409	396	96.8	4	9	6	28	20	71.4	4	4
1972	40	390	365	93.6	12	13	6	27	20	74.1	2	5
1976	47	384	368	95.8	3	13	8	25	16	64.0	-	9
1980	34	398	361	90.7	6	31	5	29	16	55.2	4	9
1984	22	411	392	95.4	3	16	4	29	26	89.7	-	3
1988	23	409	402	98.3	1	6	6	27	23	85.2	-	4
1992	65	368	325	88.3	[2]19	[3]24	7	28	23	82.1	1	4
1996	45	384	361	94.0	2	21	13	21	19	90.5	1	1
2000	30	403	394	97.8	3	6	5	29	23	79.3	-	6
2004	29	404	395	97.8	2	7	8	26	25	96.2	-	1
MIDTERM ELECTIONS												
1966	22	411	362	88.1	8	41	3	32	28	87.5	3	1
1970	29	401	379	94.5	10	12	4	31	24	77.4	1	6
1974	43	391	343	87.7	8	40	7	27	23	85.2	2	2
1978	49	382	358	93.7	5	19	10	25	15	60.0	3	7
1982	40	393	354	90.1	[2]10	[3]29	3	30	28	93.3	-	2
1986	40	394	385	97.7	3	6	6	28	21	75.0	-	7
1990	27	406	391	96.3	1	15	3	32	31	96.9	-	1
1994	48	387	349	90.2	4	34	8	26	24	92.3	-	2
1998	31	403	395	98.3	2	7	5	29	26	89.7	-	3
2002	35	398	382	96.0	[2]8	[3]8	6	28	24	85.7	1	3

- Represents zero. [1] Does not include persons who died or resigned before the election. [2] Number of incumbents defeated in primaries by other incumbents due to redistricting: six in 1982 and four each in 1992 and 2002. [3] Number of incumbents defeated in general election by other incumbents due to redistricting: six in 1982, five in 1992, and four in 2002.

Source: 1966-1996: Ornstein, Norman J., et al., eds., *Vital Statistics on Congress, 1997-1998* (Congressional Quarterly, Washington, DC, 1998) 1998-2004: CQ Weekly (1998, 2000, 2002, 2004).

Table 395. Members of Congress—Selected Characteristics: 1985 to 2003

[As of beginning of first session of each Congress, (January 3). Figures for Representatives exclude vacancies]

Members of Congress and year	Male	Fe-male	Black[1]	API[2]	His-panic[3]	Age[4] (in years)					Seniority[5,6]				
						Under 40	40 to 49	50 to 59	60 to 69	70 and over	Less than 2 yrs.	2 to 9 yrs.	10 to 19 yrs.	20 to 29 yrs.	30 yrs. or more
REPRESENTATIVES															
99th Cong., 1985	412	22[7]	21	5	10	71	154	131	59	19	49	237	104	34	10
100th Cong., 1987	412	23[7]	23	6	11	63	153	137	56	26	51	221	114	37	12
101st Cong., 1989	408	25[7]	24	6	10	41	163	133	74	22	39	207	139	35	13
102d Cong., 1991	407	28[7]	26	5	11	39	152	134	86	24	55	178	147	44	11
103d Cong., 1993[8]	388	47[7]	38	7	17	47	151	128	89	15	118	141	132	32	12
104th Cong., 1995	388	47[9]	40	7	17	53	155	135	79	13	92	188	110	36	9
106th Cong., 1999	379	56[9]	39	6	19	23	116	173	87	35	41	236	104	46	7
107th Cong., 2001	376	59[9]	39	7	19	14	97	167	117	35	44	155	158	63	14
108th Cong., 2003	376	59[9]	39	5	22	19	86	174	121	32	54	178	140	48	13
SENATORS															
99th Cong., 1985	98	2	-	2	-	4	27	38	25	6	8	56	27	7	4
100th Cong., 1987	98	2	-	2	-	5	30	36	22	7	14	41	36	7	2
101st Cong., 1989	98	2	-	3	-	-	30	40	22	8	23	22	43	10	2
102d Cong., 1991	98	2	-	2	-	-	23	46	24	7	5	34	47	10	4
103d Cong., 1993[8]	93	7	1	2	-	1	16	48	22	12	15	30	39	11	5
104th Cong., 1995	92	8	1	2	-	1	14	41	27	17	12	38	30	15	5
106th Cong., 1999	91	9	-	2	-	-	14	38	35	13	8	39	33	14	6
107th Cong., 2001	87	13	-	2	-	-	8	39	39	18	11	34	30	14	9
108th Cong., 2003	86	14	-	2	-	1	12	29	34	24	9	42	29	13	7

- Represents zero. [1] Source: Joint Center for Political and Economic Studies, Washington, DC, *Black Elected Officials: Statistical Summary*, annual (copyright). [2] Asian and Pacific Islanders. Source: Library of Congress, Congressional Research Service, "Asian Pacific Americans in the United States Congress," Report 94-767 GOV. [3] Source: National Association of Latino Elected and Appointed Officials, Washington, DC, *National Roster of Hispanic Elected Officials*, annual. [4] Some members do not provide date of birth. [5] Represents consecutive years of service. [6] Some members do not provide years of service. [7] Includes District of Columbia delegate but not Virgin Islands Delegate. [8] Includes members elected to fill vacant seats through June 14, 1993. [9] Includes District of Columbia and Virgin Islands delegate.

Source: Except as noted, compiled by U.S. Census Bureau from data published in *Congressional Directory*, biennial.

Elections 257

Table 396. **U.S. Congress—Measures Introduced and Enacted and Time in Session: 1987 to 2004**

[Excludes simple and concurrent resolutions]

Item	100th Cong., 1987-88	101st Cong., 1989-90	102d Cong., 1991-92	103d Cong., 1993-94	104th Cong., 1995-96	105th Cong., 1997-98	106th Cong., 1999-00	107th Cong., 2001-02	108th Cong., 2003-04
Measures introduced	9,588	6,664	6,775	8,544	6,808	7,732	9,158	9,130	8,625
Bills	8,515	5,977	6,212	7,883	6,545	7,532	8,968	8,953	8,468
Joint resolutions	1,073	687	563	661	263	200	190	177	157
Measures enacted	761	666	609	473	337	404	604	337	504
Public	713	650	589	465	333	394	580	331	498
Private	48	16	20	8	4	10	24	6	6
HOUSE OF REPRESENTATIVES									
Number of days	298	281	280	265	290	251	272	265	243
Number of hours	1,659	1,688	1,796	1,887	2,445	2,001	2,179	1,694	1,894
Number of hours per day...	5.6	6.0	6.4	7.1	8.4	8.0	8.0	6.4	7.8
SENATE									
Number of days	307	274	287	291	343	296	303	322	300
Number of hours	2,341	2,254	2,292	2,514	2,876	2,188	2,200	2,279	2,486
Number of hours per day...	7.6	8.2	8.0	8.6	8.4	7.4	7.3	7.1	8.3

Source: U.S. Congress, *Congressional Record* and *Daily Calendar*, selected issues. See also <http://www.senate.gov /pagelayout/reference/twocolumntable/Resumes.htm>.

Table 397. **Congressional Bills Vetoed: 1961 to 2005**

Period	President	Total vetoes	Regular vetoes	Pocket vetoes	Vetoes sustained	Bills passed over veto
1961-63	John F. Kennedy	21	12	9	21	-
1963-69	Lyndon B. Johnson	30	16	14	30	-
1969-74	Richard M. Nixon	43	26	17	36	7
1974-77	Gerald R. Ford	66	48	18	54	12
1977-81	Jimmy Carter	31	13	18	29	2
1981-89	Ronald W. Reagan	78	39	39	69	9
1989-93	George Bush	44	29	15	43	1
1993-2001	William J. Clinton	38	37	1	36	2
2001-2005 [1]	George W. Bush	-	-	-	-	-

- Represents zero. [1] Through May 13, 2005.

Source: U.S. Congress, Senate Library, *Presidential Vetoes ... 1789-1968*; U.S. Congress, *Calendars of the U.S. House of Representatives and History of Legislation*, annual. See also <http://clerk.house.gov/>.

Table 398. **Number of Governors by Political Party Affiliation: 1975 to 2004**

[Reflects figures after inaugurations for each year]

Year	Demo-cratic	Repub-lican	Indepen-dent/other	Year	Demo-cratic	Repub-lican	Indepen-dent/other	Year	Demo-cratic	Repub-lican	Indepen-dent/other
1975	36	13	1	1993	30	18	2	1999	17	31	2
1980	31	19	-	1994	29	19	2	2000	17	31	2
1985	34	16	-	1995	19	30	1	2001	21	27	2
1990	29	21	-	1996	18	31	1	2002	21	27	2
1991[1] ...	29	19	2	1997	17	32	1	2003	24	26	-
1992	28	20	2	1998	17	32	1	2004	22	28	-

- Represents zero. [1] Reflects result of runoff election in Arizona in February 1991.

Source: National Governors Association, Washington, DC, 1970-87 and 1991-2004, *Directory of Governors of the American States, Commonwealths & Territories*, annual; and 1988-90, *Directory of Governors*, annual. (copyright).

U.S. Census Bureau, Statistical Abstract of the United States: 2006

Table 399. Vote Cast for and Governor Elected by State: 1990 to 2004

[In thousands (1,216 represents 1,216,000), except percent. D = Democratic, R = Republican, I = Independent]

State	1990 Total vote [1]	1990 Percent leading party	2000 Total vote [1]	2000 Percent leading party	2002 Total vote [1]	2002 Percent leading party	2004 Total vote [1]	2004 Percent leading party	Candidate elected at most recent election
AL......	1,216	R-52.1	(X)	(X)	1,367	R-49.2	(X)	(X)	Bob Riley
AK......	195	I-38.9	(X)	(X)	231	R-55.8	(X)	(X)	Frank H. Murkowski
AZ......	[2]941	[2]R-52.4	(X)	(X)	1,226	D-46.2	(X)	(X)	Janet Napolitano
AR......	696	D-57.5	(X)	(X)	806	R-53.0	(X)	(X)	Mike Huckabee
CA......	7,699	R-49.2	(X)	(X)	7,476	D-47.3	8,658	R-48.6	Arnold Schwarzenegger [3]
CO......	1,011	D-61.9	(X)	(X)	1,413	R-62.6	(X)	(X)	Bill Owens
CT......	1,141	I-40.4	(X)	(X)	1,023	R-56.1	(X)	(X)	John G. Rowland
DE......	(X)	(X)	324	D-59.2	(X)	(X)	365	D-50.9	Ruth Ann Minner
FL......	3,531	D-56.5	(X)	(X)	5,101	R-56.0	(X)	(X)	Jeb Bush
GA......	1,450	D-52.9	(X)	(X)	2,027	R-51.4	(X)	(X)	Sonny Perdue
HI......	340	D-59.8	(X)	(X)	382	R-51.6	(X)	(X)	Linda Lingle
ID......	321	D-68.2	(X)	(X)	411	R-56.3	(X)	(X)	Dirk Kempthorne
IL......	3,257	R-50.7	(X)	(X)	3,539	D-52.2	(X)	(X)	Rod R. Blagojevich
IN......	(X)	(X)	2,179	D-56.6	(X)	(X)	2,448	R-53.2	Mitch Daniels
IA......	976	R-60.6	(X)	(X)	1,026	D-52.7	(X)	(X)	Tom Vilsack
KS......	783	D-48.6	(X)	(X)	836	D-52.9	(X)	(X)	Kathleen Sebelius
KY [4]...	(X)	(X)	580	D-60.7	1,083	R-55.0	1,083	R-55.0	Ernie Fletcher
LA [4]...	(X)	(X)	1,295	R-62.2	1,407	D-51.9	1,408	D-51.9	Kathleen Babineaux Blanco
ME......	522	R-46.7	(X)	(X)	505	D-47.1	(X)	(X)	John Baldacci
MD......	1,111	D-59.8	(X)	(X)	1,706	R-51.6	(X)	(X)	Robert L. Erlich Jr.
MA......	2,343	R-50.2	(X)	(X)	2,194	R-49.8	(X)	(X)	Mitt Romney
MI......	2,565	R-49.8	(X)	(X)	3,178	D-51.4	(X)	(X)	Jennifer M. Granholm
MN......	1,807	R-49.6	(X)	(X)	2,252	R-44.4	(X)	(X)	Tim Pawlenty
MS [4]...	(X)	(X)	764	D-49.6	894	D-52.6	894	R-52.6	Haley Barbour
MO......	(X)	(X)	2,347	D-49.1	(X)	(X)	2,720	R-50.8	Matt Blunt
MT......	(X)	(X)	410	R-51.0	(X)	(X)	446	D-50.4	Brian Schweitzer
NE......	587	D-49.9	(X)	(X)	481	R-68.7	(X)	(X)	Mike Johanns
NV......	321	D-64.8	(X)	(X)	504	R-68.2	(X)	(X)	Kenny Guinn
NH......	295	R-60.3	565	D-48.7	443	R-58.6	667	D-51.0	John Lynch
NJ [5]...	2,254	D-61.2	(X)	(X)	2,227	D-56.4	(X)	(X)	James E. McGreevey
NM......	411	D-54.6	(X)	(X)	484	D-55.5	(X)	(X)	Bill Richardson
NY......	4,057	D-53.2	(X)	(X)	4,579	R-49.4	(X)	(X)	George E. Pataki
NC......	(X)	(X)	2,942	D-52.0	(X)	(X)	3,487	D-55.6	Michael F. Easley
ND......	(X)	(X)	289	R-55.0	(X)	(X)	310	R-71.3	John Hoeven
OH......	3,478	R-55.7	(X)	(X)	3,229	R-57.8	(X)	(X)	Bob Taft
OK......	911	D-57.4	(X)	(X)	1,036	D-43.3	(X)	(X)	Brad Henry
OR......	1,113	D-45.7	(X)	(X)	1,260	D-49.0	(X)	(X)	Theodore R. Kulongoski
PA......	3,053	D-67.7	(X)	(X)	3,583	D-53.4	(X)	(X)	Edward G. Rendell
RI......	357	D-74.1	(X)	(X)	333	R-54.7	(X)	(X)	Donald L. Carcieri
SC......	761	R-69.5	(X)	(X)	1,108	R-52.8	(X)	(X)	Mark Sanford
SD......	257	R-58.9	(X)	(X)	335	R-56.8	(X)	(X)	Mike Rounds
TN......	790	D-60.8	(X)	(X)	1,653	D-50.6	(X)	(X)	Phil Bredesen
TX......	3,893	D-49.5	(X)	(X)	4,554	R-57.8	(X)	(X)	Rick Perry
UT......	(X)	(X)	762	R-55.8	(X)	(X)	920	R-57.7	Jon Huntsman, Jr.
VT......	211	R-51.8	293	D-50.5	230	R-44.9	309	R-58.7	Jim Douglas
VA [5]...	1,789	D-50.1	(X)	(X)	1,887	D-52.2	(X)	(X)	Mark Warner
WA......	(X)	(X)	2,470	D-58.4	(X)	(X)	2,810	D-48.9	Christine Gregoire
WV......	(X)	(X)	648	D-50.1	(X)	(X)	744	D-63.5	Joe Manchin III
WI......	1,380	R-58.2	(X)	(X)	1,775	D-45.1	(X)	(X)	James E. Doyle
WY......	160	D-65.4	(X)	(X)	185	(X)	(X)	(X)	Dave Freudenthal

X Not applicable. [1] Includes minor party and scattered votes. [2] Runoff election in 1991. [3] Recall election in 2003; Arnold Schwarzenegger (Republican) was elected governor. [4] Voting years 1991, 1999 and 2003. [5] Voting years 1989 and 2001.

Source: CQ Press (a division of Congressional Quarterly, Inc.), Washington, DC, *America Votes*, biennial; and unpublished data (copyright).

U.S. Census Bureau, Statistical Abstract of the United States: 2006

Table 400. Composition of State Legislatures by Political Party Affiliation: 2003 and 2005

[Data reflect election results in year shown for most states; and except as noted, results in previous year for other states. Figures reflect immediate results of elections, including holdover members in state houses which do not have all of their members running for re-election. Dem. = Democrat, Rep. = Republican, Vac. = Vacancies. In general, Lower House refers to body consisting of state Representatives; Upper House, of state Senators]

State	Lower House 2003 Dem.	Rep.	Other	Vac.	Lower House 2005[1] Dem.	Rep.	Other	Vac.	Upper House 2003 Dem.	Rep.	Other	Vac.	Upper House 2005[1] Dem.	Rep.	Other	Vac.
U.S.	2,700	2,693	16	2	2,704	2,683	15	9	941	977	2	2	951	963	3	5
AL[2]	63	42	-	-	62	40	-	3	25	10	-	-	25	10	-	-
AK[3]	13	27	-	-	14	26	-	-	8	12	-	-	8	12	-	-
AZ[4]	21	39	-	-	22	38	-	-	13	17	-	-	12	18	-	-
AR[3]	70	30	-	-	72	28	-	-	27	8	-	-	27	8	-	-
CA[3]	48	32	-	-	48	32	-	-	25	15	-	-	25	15	-	-
CO[3]	28	37	-	-	35	30	-	-	17	18	-	-	18	17	-	-
CT[4]	95	56	-	-	99	52	-	-	21	15	-	-	24	12	-	-
DE[3]	12	29	-	-	15	25	1	-	13	8	-	-	13	8	-	-
FL[3]	39	81	-	-	36	84	-	-	14	26	-	-	14	26	-	-
GA[4]	107	72	1	-	80	99	1	-	26	30	-	-	22	34	-	-
HI[3]	36	15	-	-	41	10	-	-	20	5	-	-	20	5	-	-
ID[4]	16	54	-	-	13	57	-	-	7	28	-	-	7	28	-	-
IL[5]	66	52	-	-	65	53	-	-	26	32	1	-	31	27	1	-
IN[3]	51	49	-	-	48	52	-	-	18	32	-	-	17	33	-	-
IA[3]	47	53	-	-	49	51	-	-	21	29	-	-	25	25	-	-
KS[3]	45	80	-	-	42	83	-	-	10	30	-	-	10	30	-	-
KY[3]	63	36	-	1	57	43	-	-	16	22	-	-	15	22	1	-
LA[2]	68	37	-	-	67	37	1	-	24	15	-	-	24	15	-	-
ME[4]	80	67	4	-	76	73	2	-	18	17	-	-	19	16	-	-
MD[2]	98	43	-	-	98	43	-	-	33	14	-	-	33	14	-	-
MA[4]	136	23	1	-	136	21	-	3	34	6	-	-	34	6	-	-
MI[3]	63	47	-	-	52	58	-	-	16	22	-	-	16	22	-	-
MN[3]	53	81	-	-	66	68	-	-	35	31	1	-	35	31	1	-
MS[2]	80	42	-	-	75	47	-	-	30	22	-	-	28	24	-	-
MO[3]	73	90	-	-	66	97	-	-	14	20	-	-	10	22	-	2
MT[3]	47	53	-	-	49	50	1	-	21	29	-	-	27	23	-	-
NE[6]	(5)	(5)	(5)	(5)	(5)	(5)	(5)	(5)	(5)	(5)	(5)	(5)	(5)	(5)	(5)	(5)
NV[3]	23	19	-	-	26	16	-	-	8	13	-	-	9	12	-	-
NH[4]	119	281	-	-	147	250	-	3	6	18	-	-	8	16	-	-
NJ[3]	47	33	-	-	47	33	-	-	22	18	-	-	22	18	-	-
NM[3]	43	27	-	-	42	28	-	-	24	18	-	-	24	18	-	-
NY[4]	103	47	-	-	104	46	-	-	25	37	-	-	28	34	-	-
NC[4]	59	61	-	-	63	57	-	-	28	22	-	-	29	21	-	-
ND[2]	28	66	-	-	27	67	-	-	16	31	-	-	15	32	-	-
OH[3]	37	62	-	-	40	59	-	-	11	22	-	-	11	22	-	-
OK[3]	53	48	-	-	44	57	-	-	28	20	-	-	26	22	-	-
OR[3]	25	35	-	-	27	33	-	-	14	15	-	1	18	12	-	-
PA[3]	94	108	-	1	93	110	-	-	21	29	-	-	18	29	-	3
RI[4]	63	11	1	-	60	15	-	-	32	6	-	-	33	5	-	-
SC[3]	51	73	-	-	50	74	-	-	20	25	-	1	20	26	-	-
SD[4]	21	49	-	-	19	51	-	-	9	26	-	-	10	25	-	-
TN[5]	54	45	-	-	53	46	-	-	18	15	-	-	16	17	-	-
TX[3]	62	88	-	-	63	87	-	-	12	19	-	-	12	19	-	-
UT[3]	19	56	-	-	19	56	-	-	7	22	-	-	8	21	-	-
VT[3]	69	74	7	-	83	60	7	-	19	11	-	-	21	9	-	-
VA[3]	37	61	2	-	38	60	2	-	16	24	-	-	16	24	-	-
WA[3]	52	46	-	-	55	43	-	-	24	25	-	-	26	23	-	-
WV[3]	68	32	-	-	68	32	-	-	24	10	-	-	21	13	-	-
WI[3]	40	59	-	-	39	60	-	-	15	18	-	-	14	19	-	-
WY[3]	15	45	-	-	14	46	-	-	10	20	-	-	7	23	-	-

- Represents zero. [1] As of February, 2005. [2] Members of both houses serve 4-year terms. [3] Upper House members serve 4-year terms and Lower House members serve 2-year terms. [4] Members of both houses serve 2-year terms. [5] Illinois—4- and 2-year term depending on district. [6] Nebraska—4-year term and only state to have a nonpartisan legislature.

Source: The Council of State Governments, Lexington, KY, The Book of States 2005, biennial (copyright).

Table 401. Political Party Control of State Legislatures by Party: 1983 to 2005

[As of beginning of year. Nebraska has a nonpartisan legislature]

Year	Legislatures under— Democratic control	Split control or tie	Republican control	Year	Legislatures under— Democratic control	Split control or tie	Republican control	Year	Legislatures under— Democratic control	Split control or tie	Republican control
1983 [1] ...	34	4	11	1993	25	16	8	2000	16	15	18
1985	27	11	11	1994	24	17	8	2001	16	15	18
1987	28	12	9	1995	18	12	19	2002	17	15	17
1989 [2] ...	28	13	8	1996	16	15	18	2003	16	12	21
1990	29	11	9	1997	20	11	18	2004	17	11	21
1992	29	14	6	1999	20	12	17	2005	19	10	20

[1] Two 1984 midterm recall elections resulted in a change in control of the Michigan State Senate. At the time of the 1984 election, therefore, Democrats controlled 33 legislatures. [2] A party change during the year by a Democratic representative broke the tie in the Indiana House of Representatives, giving the Republicans control of both chambers.

Source: National Conference of State Legislatures, Denver, CO, *State Legislatures*, periodic.

Table 402. Women Holding State Public Offices by Office and State: 2004

[As of January. For data on women in U.S. Congress, see Table 395]

State	Statewide elective executive office [1]	State legislature	State	Statewide elective executive office [1]	State legislature	State	Statewide elective executive office [1]	State legislature
United States...	81	1,659	Kentucky........	1	15	North Dakota.....	2	23
Alabama........	5	14	Louisiana	1	24	Ohio............	2	28
Alaska.........	-	12	Maine..........	-	50	Oklahoma	4	19
Arizona........	3	25	Maryland........	-	64	Oregon.........	1	26
Arkansas.......	-	22	Massachusetts....	1	50	Pennsylvania.....	2	36
California.......	-	36	Michigan........	2	35	Rhode Island.....	-	23
Colorado........	2	34	Minnesota.......	3	55	South Carolina....	1	16
Connecticut.....	4	55	Mississippi.......	1	22	South Dakota.....	-	17
Delaware.......	3	18	Missouri	2	42	Tennessee.......	-	23
Florida........	1	40	Montana	2	37	Texas..........	2	35
Georgia	3	51	Nebraska	2	9	Utah...........	1	22
Hawaii	1	21	Nevada........	2	18	Vermont	2	56
Idaho	1	27	New Hampshire ...	-	117	Virginia	-	20
Illinois.........	2	50	New Jersey......	-	19	Washington	2	52
Indiana	3	27	New Mexico......	3	34	West Virginia	-	25
Iowa..........	2	32	New York	1	48	Wisconsin	3	37
Kansas........	3	46	North Carolina ...	4	36	Wyoming.......	1	16

- Represents zero. [1] Excludes women elected to the judiciary, women appointed to State cabinet-level positions, women elected to executive posts by the legislature, and elected members of university Board of Trustees or Board of Education.

Source: Center for the American Woman and Politics, Eagleton Institute of Politics, Rutgers University, New Brunswick, NJ, information releases, (copyright).

U.S. Census Bureau, Statistical Abstract of the United States: 2006

Table 403. Black Elected Officials by Office, 1970 to 2001, and State, 2001

[As of January 2001, no Black elected officials had been identified in Hawaii, Montana, North Dakota, or South Dakota]

State	Total	U.S. and state legisla- tures[1]	City and county offices[2]	Law enforce- ment[3]	Educa- tion[4]
1970 (Feb.) .	1,469	179	715	213	362
1980 (July)..	4,890	326	2,832	526	1,206
1990 (Jan.)..	7,335	436	4,485	769	1,645
1995 (Jan.)..	8,385	604	4,954	987	1,840
1998 (Jan.)..	8,830	614	5,210	998	2,008
1999 (Jan.)..	8,896	618	5,354	997	1,927
2000 (Jan.)..	9,001	621	5,420	1,037	1,923
2001 (Jan.) .	9,061	633	5,456	1,044	1,928
AL	756	36	569	57	94
AK	3	1	2	-	-
AZ	12	1	1	5	5
AR	502	15	298	67	122
CA	224	10	70	67	77
CO	18	4	4	9	1
CT	72	14	47	3	8
DE	24	4	16	1	3
DC	176	2[5]	171	-	3
FL	243	25	163	39	16
GA	611	53	395	43	120
ID	2	-	2	-	-
IL	624	28 .	318	55	223
IN	86	13	52	13	8
IA	13	1	8	1	3
KS	17	7	4	3	3
KY	60	5	44	5	6
LA	705	32	388	122	163
ME	1	-	-	-	1
MD	175	40	93	33	9
MA	60	6	44	2	8
MI	346	25	147	55	119
MN	20	2	4	9	5
MS	892	46	607	109	130
MO	201	19	142	16	24
NE	8	1	4	-	3
NV	14	5	5	2	2
NH	5	5	-	-	-
NJ	249	16	139	1	93
NM	4	1	-	2	1
NY	325	34	83	83	125
NC	491	28	349	29	85
OH	313	20	217	28	48
OK	105	6	75	3	21
OR	6	3	1	2	-
PA	185	19	74	65	27
RI	8	7	1	-	-
SC	534	32	335	9	158
TN	180	18	108	27	27
TX	460	19	302	44	95
UT	5	1	3	1	-
VT	1	1	-	-	-
VA	246	16	130	15	85
WA	26	2	12	11	1
WV	19	2	13	3	1
WI	33	8	15	5	5
WY	1	-	1	-	-

- Represents zero. [1] Includes elected State administrators. [2] County commissioners and councilmen, mayors, vice mayors, aldermen, regional officials, and other. [3] Judges, magistrates, constables, marshals, sheriffs, justices of the peace, and other. [4] Members of State education agencies, college boards, school boards, and other. [5] Includes one shadow senator.

Source: Joint Center for Political and Economic Studies, Washington, DC, *Black Elected Officials: A Statistical Summary*, annual (copyright) and (accessed 17 April 2003).

Table 404. Hispanic Public Elected Officials by Office, 1985 to 2004, and State, 2004

[For states not shown, no Hispanic public officials had been identified]

State	Total	State execu- tives and legisla- tors[1]	County and munici- pal officials	Judicial and law enforce- ment	Educa- tion and school boards
1985 (Sept.)..	3,147	129	1,316	517	1,185
1990 (Sept.)..	4,004	144	1,819	583	1,458
1991 (Sept.)..	4,202	151	1,867	596	1,588
1992 (Sept.)..	4,994	150	1,908	628	2,308
1993 (Sept.)..	5,170	182	2,023	633	2,332
2000 (Sept.)..	5,205	223	1,846	454	2,682
2001 (Sept.)..	5,205	223	1,846	454	2,682
2002 (Jan.)..	4,303	208	1,960	532	1,603
2003 (Jan.)..	4,432	231	1,958	549	1,694
2004 (Jan.)..	4,651	231	2,059	638	1,723
AZ	354	15	135	41	163
CA	981	28	379	39	535
CO	134	8	92	9	25
CT	28	5	19	-	4
DE	2	1	1	-	-
FL	109	16	59	28	6
GA	7	3	2	2	-
HI	1	1	-	-	-
ID	1	1	-	-	-
IL	70	11	46	5	8
IN	12	1	7	3	1
KS	8	2	6	-	-
LA	2	-	-	2	-
MD	6	4	1	-	1
MA	18	4	11	-	3
MI	15	1	5	3	6
MN	4	1	1	1	1
MO	1	-	1	-	-
MT	1	-	-	1	-
NE	2	1	1	-	-
NV	7	3	2	1	1
NH	2	1	-	-	1
NJ	100	5	55	40	-
NM	627	50	326	100	151
NY	61	15	26	15	5
NC	4	2	2	-	-
ND	1	-	1	-	-
OH	5	-	4	1	-
OK	1	-	-	-	1
OR	14	3	5	5	1
PA	17	1	10	3	3
RI	6	3	3	-	-
SC	1	1	-	-	-
TN	2	1	1	-	-
TX	2,013	38	841	375	759
UT	3	-	3	-	-
VA	1	-	1	-	-
WA	14	3	6	-	5
WI	13	1	5	4	3
WY	3	1	2	-	-

- Represents zero. [1] Includes U.S. Representatives, not shown separately.

Source: National Association of Latino Elected and Appointed Officials, Washington, DC, *National Roster of Hispanic Elected Officials*, annual.

Table 405. Voting-Age Population, Percent Reporting Registered, and Voted: 1992 to 2004

[185.7 represents 185,700,000. As of November. Covers civilian noninstitutional population 18 years old and over. Includes aliens. Figures are based on Current Population Survey (see text, Section 1, Population, and Appendix III) and differ from those in Table 407 based on population estimates and official vote counts]

| | Voting-age population (mil.) | | | | | | | Percent reporting they registered | | | | | | | Percent reporting they voted | | | | | | |
| | | | | | | | | Presidential election years | | | | Congressional election years | | | Presidential election years | | | | Congressional election years | | |
Characteristic	1992	1994	1996	1998	2000	2002	2004	1992	1996	2000	2004	1994	1998	2002	1992	1996	2000	2004	1994	1998	2002
Total [1]	185.7	190.3	193.7	198.2	202.6	210.4	215.7	68.2	65.9	63.9	65.9	62.0	62.1	60.9	61.3	54.2	54.7	58.3	44.6	41.9	42.3
18 to 20 years old	9.7	10.3	10.8	11.4	11.9	11.7	11.5	48.3	45.6	40.5	50.7	37.2	32.1	32.6	38.5	31.2	28.4	41.0	16.5	13.5	15.1
21 to 24 years old	14.6	14.9	13.9	14.1	14.9	15.6	16.4	55.3	51.2	49.3	52.1	45.5	35.0	42.5	45.7	33.4	35.4	42.5	22.3	19.2	18.7
25 to 34 years old	41.6	41.1	40.1	38.6	37.3	38.5	39.0	60.6	56.9	54.7	55.6	51.5	52.4	50.2	53.2	43.1	43.7	46.9	32.2	28.0	27.1
35 to 44 years old	39.7	41.9	43.3	44.4	44.5	43.7	43.1	69.2	66.5	63.8	64.2	63.3	62.4	60.0	63.6	54.9	55.0	56.9	46.0	40.7	40.2
45 to 64 years old	49.1	50.9	53.7	57.4	61.4	66.9	71.0	75.3	73.5	71.2	72.7	71.0	71.1	69.4	70.0	64.4	64.1	66.6	56.0	53.6	53.1
65 years old and over	30.8	31.1	31.9	32.3	32.8	33.9	34.7	78.0	77.0	76.1	76.9	75.6	75.4	75.8	70.1	67.0	67.6	68.9	60.7	59.5	61.0
Male	88.6	91.0	92.6	95.2	97.1	100.9	103.8	66.9	64.4	62.2	64.0	60.8	60.6	58.9	60.2	52.8	54.1	56.3	44.4	41.4	41.4
Female	97.1	99.3	101.0	103.0	105.5	109.5	111.9	69.3	67.3	65.6	67.6	63.2	63.5	62.8	62.3	55.5	56.2	60.1	44.9	42.4	43.0
White [2]	157.8	160.3	162.8	165.8	168.7	174.1	176.6	70.1	67.7	65.6	67.9	64.2	63.9	63.1	63.6	56.0	56.4	60.3	46.9	43.3	44.1
Black [2]	21.0	21.8	22.5	23.3	24.1	24.4	24.9	63.9	63.5	63.6	64.4	58.3	60.2	58.8	54.0	50.6	53.5	56.3	37.0	39.6	39.7
Hispanic [3]	14.7	17.5	18.4	20.3	21.6	25.2	27.1	35.0	35.7	34.9	34.3	30.0	33.7	32.6	28.9	26.7	27.5	28.0	19.1	20.0	18.9
Region: [4]																					
Northeast	38.3	38.4	38.3	38.5	38.9	41.1	41.0	67.0	64.7	63.7	65.3	60.9	60.8	60.8	61.2	54.5	55.2	58.6	45.2	41.2	41.4
Midwest	44.4	44.5	45.2	45.9	46.4	44.8	48.4	74.6	71.6	70.2	72.8	68.7	68.2	66.5	67.2	59.3	60.9	65.0	48.8	47.3	47.1
South	63.7	66.4	68.1	70.1	71.8	74.2	77.2	67.2	65.9	66.9	65.5	60.7	62.7	61.6	59.0	52.2	53.5	56.4	40.5	38.6	41.6
West	39.3	41.0	42.1	43.7	45.5	46.3	49.1	63.6	60.8	56.9	60.1	58.1	56.0	54.0	58.5	51.8	49.9	54.4	46.4	42.3	39.0
School years completed:																					
8 years or less	15.4	14.7	14.1	13.3	12.9	12.3	12.6	43.9	40.7	36.1	32.5	40.1	40.2	32.4	35.1	28.1	26.8	23.6	23.2	24.6	19.4
High school: 1 to 3 years [5]	21.0	20.7	21.0	21.0	20.1	20.9	20.7	50.4	47.9	45.9	45.8	44.7	43.4	41.6	41.2	33.8	33.6	34.6	27.0	25.0	23.3
4 years [6]	65.3	64.9	65.2	65.6	66.3	68.9	68.5	64.9	62.2	60.1	61.5	58.9	58.6	57.1	57.5	49.1	49.4	52.4	40.5	37.1	37.1
College: 1 to 3 years [7]	46.7	50.4	50.9	52.9	55.3	57.3	58.9	75.4	72.9	70.0	73.7	68.4	68.3	66.7	68.7	60.5	60.3	66.1	49.1	46.2	45.8
4 years or more [8]	37.4	39.4	42.5	45.4	48.0	51.0	54.9	84.8	80.4	77.3	78.1	76.3	75.1	74.4	81.0	73.0	72.0	74.2	63.1	57.2	58.5
Employed	116.3	122.6	125.6	130.5	133.4	142.6	138.8	69.9	67.0	64.7	67.1	62.9	62.6	61.7	63.8	55.2	55.5	60.0	45.2	41.2	42.1
Unemployed	8.3	6.5	6.4	5.2	4.9	7.7	7.3	53.7	62.5	46.1	56.3	46.4	48.5	48.1	46.2	37.2	35.1	46.4	28.3	28.4	27.2
Not in labor force	61.1	61.2	61.6	62.5	64.2	67.8	69.6	66.8	65.1	63.8	64.4	61.9	62.1	60.9	58.7	54.1	54.5	56.2	45.3	44.5	44.2

[1] Includes other races not shown separately. [2] Beginning with the 2003 Current Population Survey (CPS), respondents could choose more than one race group. 2004 data represent persons who selected this race group only and exclude persons reporting more than one race. The CPS in prior years only allowed respondents to report one race group. See also comments on race in the text for Section 1. [3] Hispanic persons may be any race. [4] For composition of regions, see map, inside cover. [5] Represents those who completed 9th to 12th grade, but have no high school diploma. [6] High school graduates. [7] Some college or associate's degree. [8] Bachelor's or advanced degree.

Source: U.S. Census Bureau, Current Population Reports, P20-552, and earlier reports.

Elections   263

Table 406. Persons Reported Registered and Voted by State: 2004

[215,694 represents 215,694,000. See headnote, Table 405]

State	Voting-age population (1,000)	Percent of voting-age population Registered	Voted	State	Voting-age population (1,000)	Percent of voting-age population Registered	Voted
U.S.....	215,694	65.9	58.3	MO	4,243	78.6	66.3
AL	3,332	72.6	61.8	MT	690	75.2	69.9
AK	451	74.1	65.0	NE	1,294	70.9	61.3
AZ	4,122	60.3	54.3	NV	1,699	56.8	51.3
AR	2,010	66.1	56.7	NH	982	72.9	68.9
CA	26,085	54.4	49.1	NJ	6,413	63.7	57.6
CO	3,398	67.9	61.7	NM	1,375	68.1	60.9
CT	2,606	65.0	58.5	NY	14,492	59.5	53.1
DE	612	67.8	62.9	NC	6,250	68.7	58.2
DC	435	67.4	62.1	ND	466	88.4	70.8
FL	13,133	62.6	56.1	OH	8,469	70.9	64.8
GA	6,338	62.3	52.6	OK	2,602	68.4	59.2
HI	938	53.0	46.2	OR	2,727	75.1	70.6
ID	996	66.6	58.7	PA	9,356	69.3	62.5
IL	9,303	69.2	61.0	RI	813	64.2	57.4
IN	4,536	66.8	57.3	SC	3,061	73.1	62.0
IA	2,212	75.7	68.8	SD	564	75.4	67.0
KS	1,990	67.2	59.7	TN	4,402	62.2	52.7
KY	3,042	73.3	63.4	TX	15,813	61.2	50.3
LA	3,277	73.6	63.1	UT	1,629	70.0	62.7
ME	1,022	80.6	72.0	VT	482	73.4	65.6
MD	4,043	66.2	59.7	VA	5,364	64.1	58.4
MA	4,840	72.0	63.7	WA	4,596	68.2	62.0
MI	7,452	72.0	64.7	WV	1,395	67.0	57.2
MN	3,766	81.8	76.7	WI	4,126	78.2	73.0
MS	2,081	72.6	60.7	WY	373	71.0	66.2

Source: U.S. Census Bureau, *Current Population Reports*, P20-552, and earlier reports; and "Voting and Registration in the Election of November 2004"; published 25 May 2005; <http://www.census.gov/population/www/socdemo/voting.html>.

Table 407. Participation in Elections for President and U.S. Representatives: 1932 to 2004

[75,768 represents 75,768,000. As of November, except as noted. Estimated resident population 21 years old and over, 1932-70, except as noted, and 18 years old and over thereafter; includes Armed Forces. Prior to 1958, excludes Alaska; prior to 1960, excludes Hawaii. District of Columbia is included in votes cast for President beginning 1964]

Year	Resident population (incl. aliens) of voting age (1,000)	Votes cast For President (1,000)	Per-cent of voting-age popu-lation	For U.S. Repre-senta-tives (1,000)	Per-cent of voting-age popu-lation	Year	Resident population (incl. aliens) of voting age (1,000)	Votes cast For President (1,000)	Per-cent of voting-age popu-lation	For U.S. Repre-senta-tives (1,000)	Per-cent of voting-age popu-lation
1932...	75,768	39,817	52.5	(NA)	(NA)	1968...	120,285	73,027	60.7	66,109	55.0
1934...	77,997	(X)	(X)	32,804	42.1	1970...	124,498	(X)	(X)	54,259	43.6
1936...	80,174	45,647	56.9	(NA)	(NA)	1972...	140,777	77,625	55.1	71,188	50.6
1938...	82,354	(X)	(X)	(NA)	(NA)	1974...	146,338	(X)	(X)	52,313	35.7
1940...	84,728	49,815	58.8	(NA)	(NA)	1976...	152,308	81,603	53.6	74,259	48.8
1942...	86,465	(X)	(X)	28,074	32.5	1978...	158,369	(X)	(X)	54,584	34.5
1944...	85,654	48,026	56.1	45,110	52.7	1980...	163,945	86,497	52.8	77,874	47.5
1946...	92,659	(X)	(X)	34,410	37.1	1982...	169,643	(X)	(X)	63,881	37.7
1948...	95,573	48,834	51.1	46,220	48.4	1984...	173,995	92,655	53.3	82,422	47.4
1950...	98,134	(X)	(X)	40,430	41.2	1986...	177,922	(X)	(X)	59,758	33.6
1952...	99,929	61,552	61.6	57,571	57.6	1988...	181,956	91,587	50.3	81,682	44.9
1954...	102,075	(X)	(X)	42,583	41.7	1990...	185,812	(X)	(X)	62,355	33.6
1956...	104,515	62,027	59.3	58,886	56.3	1992...	189,493	104,600	55.2	97,198	51.3
1958...	106,447	(X)	(X)	45,719	43.0	1994...	193,010	(X)	(X)	70,494	36.5
1960...	109,672	68,836	62.8	64,124	58.5	1996...	196,789	96,390	49.0	90,233	45.9
1962...	112,952	(X)	(X)	51,242	45.4	1998...	201,270	(X)	(X)	66,605	33.1
1964...	114,090	70,098	61.4	65,879	57.7	2000 ..	[2]209,831	105,594	50.3	98,800	47.1
1966...	116,638	(X)	(X)	52,902	45.4	2002 ..	[2]215,077	(X)	(X)	74,707	34.7
						2004 ..	[2]220,377	122,349	55.5	113,192	51.4

NA Not available. X Not applicable. [1] Population 18 and over in Georgia, 1944-70, and in Kentucky, 1956-70; 20 and over in Alaska and 20 and over in Hawaii, 1960-70. Source: Through 1992, U.S. Census Bureau, *Current Population Reports*, P25-1059, and earlier reports; also see <http://www.census.gov/population/www/socdemo/voting/past-voting.html#p25> (released July 31, 2000). For 1992-1998, "Projections of the Voting-Age Population for States: November 2000"; published 31 July 2000; also see <http://www.census.gov/population/socdemo/voting/proj00/tab03.txt>. Starting 2000, "Annual Estimates of the Population by Selected Age Groups and Sex for the United States: April 1, 2000 to July 1, 2004" (NC-EST2004-02); also see <http://www.census.gov/popest /states/asrh/>. [2] As of July 1.

Source: Office of the Clerk, *Statistics of the Presidential and Congressional Election*, biennial. See also <http://clerk.house .gov/members/electionInfo/elections.html>.

Table 408. Resident Population of Voting Age and Percent Casting Votes— States: 2000 to 2004

[209,831 represents 209,831,000. Estimated population, 18 years old and over. Voting-age population excluding states without registration (210,007,000). Includes Armed Forces stationed in each state, aliens, and institutional population]

| State | Voting-age population (1,000) [1] | | | Percent casting votes for— | | | | |
| | | | | Presidential electors | | U.S. Representatives | | |
	2000	2002	2004	2000	2004	2000	2002	2004
U.S.	209,831	215,077	220,377	50.3	55.5	47.1	34.7	51.4
AL	3,330	3,370	3,436	50.0	54.8	43.2	37.7	52.2
AK	437	451	467	65.3	66.9	62.8	50.5	64.2
AZ	3,788	3,959	4,197	40.4	48.0	38.7	30.2	44.6
AR	1,998	2,025	2,076	46.1	50.8	31.7	34.0	38.1
CA	24,728	25,611	26,297	44.3	47.2	42.2	28.3	44.2
CO	3,219	3,351	3,423	54.1	62.2	50.4	41.7	59.6
CT	2,570	2,620	2,665	56.8	59.2	51.1	37.8	53.6
DE	592	611	637	55.3	58.9	52.9	37.4	55.9
DC	456	455	444	44.2	51.3	(NA)	(NA)	(NA)
FL	12,383	12,824	13,394	48.2	56.8	40.5	29.4	42.0
GA	6,050	6,273	6,497	42.7	50.8	39.9	30.6	45.6
HI	917	939	964	40.1	44.5	37.1	38.3	43.2
ID	930	970	1,021	53.9	58.6	53.0	41.7	56.1
IL	9,192	9,353	9,475	51.6	55.7	47.8	36.7	52.6
IN	4,515	4,560	4,637	48.7	53.2	47.8	33.4	52.1
IA	2,198	2,232	2,274	61.5	66.3	58.0	45.4	64.1
KS	1,981	2,013	2,052	54.1	57.9	52.3	41.2	56.4
KY	3,055	3,100	3,166	50.5	56.7	47.0	35.3	51.7
LA	3,253	3,291	3,351	54.3	58.0	37.0	34.6	37.6
ME	978	1,007	1,035	66.7	71.6	65.3	49.2	68.6
MD	3,953	4,069	4,163	51.2	57.3	48.7	40.8	54.1
MA	4,864	4,929	4,952	56.2	59.1	56.2	45.0	59.1
MI	7,362	7,482	7,579	57.5	63.8	55.3	40.8	61.1
MN	3,650	3,763	3,861	66.8	73.3	64.8	58.5	70.5
MS	2,076	2,107	2,153	47.9	52.9	47.5	32.2	51.8
MO	4,182	4,271	4,370	56.4	62.5	55.6	43.4	61.0
MT	675	692	719	60.9	62.7	60.8	47.9	61.8
NE	1,264	1,284	1,313	55.1	59.3	54.0	36.9	58.3
NV	1,500	1,602	1,731	40.6	47.9	39.1	31.3	45.7
NH	931	968	995	61.1	68.2	59.7	45.8	65.5
NJ	6,342	6,458	6,543	50.3	55.2	47.1	31.1	50.2
NM	1,315	1,352	1,411	45.5	53.6	44.7	32.4	52.7
NY	14,314	14,572	14,655	48.6	50.8	48.5	32.3	50.8
NC	6,104	6,254	6,423	47.8	54.5	45.5	35.9	53.1
ND	482	484	495	59.8	63.1	59.3	47.7	62.7
OH	8,480	8,580	8,680	55.4	64.8	54.1	36.8	59.7
OK	2,565	2,608	2,664	48.1	55.0	42.4	38.4	51.6
OR	2,583	2,670	2,742	59.4	67.0	55.7	46.4	64.6
PA	9,371	9,472	9,569	52.4	60.3	48.6	34.9	53.8
RI	803	824	837	50.9	52.2	47.8	39.9	48.1
SC	3,014	3,087	3,173	45.9	51.0	43.8	31.9	45.3
SD	554	563	580	57.1	66.9	56.8	59.8	67.1
TN	4,305	4,398	4,510	48.2	54.0	43.1	34.8	49.2
TX	15,040	15,576	16,223	42.6	45.7	39.8	27.6	42.9
UT	1,522	1,581	1,649	50.6	56.3	49.9	35.2	55.1
VT	464	476	487	63.5	64.2	61.1	47.3	62.7
VA	5,361	5,491	5,655	51.1	56.5	45.2	27.6	53.1
WA	4,398	4,561	4,718	56.6	60.6	54.2	38.1	57.9
WV	1,407	1,411	1,431	46.1	52.8	41.2	28.3	50.4
WI	4,010	4,099	4,201	64.8	71.3	62.5	39.9	67.2
WY	366	376	390	58.3	62.6	58.0	48.4	61.4

NA Not available. [1] As of July 1. Source: U.S. Census Bureau, "Annual Estimates of the Population by Selected Age Groups and Sex for the United States: April 1, 2000 to July 1, 2004," (NC-EST2004-02); also see <http://www.census.gov/popest/states/asrh/>.

Source: Office of the Clerk, *Statistics of the Presidential and Congressional Election*, biennial. See also <http://clerk.house .gov/members/electionInfo/elections.html>.

Table 409. **Political Action Committees—Number by Committee Type: 1980 to 2004**

[As of December 31]

Committee type	1980	1985	1990	1995	2000	2001	2002	2003	2004
Total	2,551	3,992	4,172	4,016	3,706	3,907	4,027	4,023	4,867
Corporate	1,206	1,710	1,795	1,674	1,523	1,545	1,528	1,552	1,756
Labor	297	388	346	334	316	317	320	308	328
Trade/membership/health	576	695	774	815	812	860	975	877	986
Nonconnected	374	1,003	1,062	1,020	902	1,026	1,055	1,147	1,650
Cooperative	42	54	59	44	39	41	39	36	38
Corporation without stock	56	142	136	129	114	118	110	103	109

Source: U.S. Federal Election Commission, press release of January 2005.

Table 410. **Political Action Committees—Financial Activity Summary by Committee Type: 1999 to 2004**

[In millions of dollars (604.9 represents $604,900,000). Covers financial activity during 2-year calendar period indicated]

Committee type	Receipts			Disbursements [1]			Contributions to candidates		
	1999-00	2001-02	2003-04	1999-00	2001-02	2003-04	1999-00	2001-02	2003-04
Total	604.9	685.3	915.7	579.4	656.5	842.9	259.8	282.0	310.5
Corporate	164.5	191.7	239.0	158.3	178.3	221.6	91.5	99.6	115.6
Labor	136.0	167.8	191.7	128.7	158.0	182.9	51.6	53.9	52.1
Trade/membership/health	142.9	166.7	181.8	137.2	165.7	170.1	71.8	46.3	83.2
Nonconnected	144.3	145.8	289.4	139.7	141.3	255.2	37.3	75.1	52.5
Cooperative	3.7	3.7	4.2	3.3	3.6	3.9	2.4	2.7	2.9
Corporation without stock	13.6	9.7	9.6	12.2	9.6	9.2	5.3	4.4	4.2

[1] Comprises contributions to candidates, independent expenditures, and other disbursements.

Source: U.S. Federal Election Commission, FEC Reports on Financial Activity, Final Report, Party and Non-party Political Committees, biennial.

Table 411. **Presidential Campaign Finances—Federal Funds for General Election: 1992 to 2004**

[In millions of dollars (110.4 represents $110,400,000). Based on FEC certifications, audit reports, and Dept. of Treasury reports]

1992		1996		2000		2004	
Candidate	Amount	Candidate	Amount	Candidate	Amount	Candidate	Amount
Total	110.4	Total	152.6	Total	147.7	Total	150.1
Bush	55.2	Clinton	61.8	Bush	67.6	Bush	74.6
Clinton	55.2	Dole	61.8	Gore	67.6	Kerry	74.6
Perot	-	Perot	29.0	Buchanan	12.6	Nader	0.9

- Represents zero.

Source: U.S. Federal Election Commission, periodic press releases.

Table 412. **Presidential Campaign Finances—Primary Campaign Receipts and Disbursements: 1995 to 2004**

[In millions of dollars (243.9 represents $243,900,000). Covers campaign finance activity during 2-year calendar period indicated. Covers candidates who received Federal matching funds or who had significant financial activity]

Item	Total [1]			Democratic			Republican		
	1995-96	1999-00	2003-04	1995-96	1999-00	2003-04	1995-96	1999-00	2003-04
Receipts, total [2]	243.9	351.6	673.9	46.2	96.6	401.8	187.0	236.7	269.6
Individual contributions	126.4	238.2	611.4	31.3	66.7	351.0	93.1	159.1	258.9
Federal matching funds	56.0	61.6	28.0	14.0	29.3	27.2	41.6	26.5	
Disbursements	234.1	343.5	661.1	41.8	92.2	389.7	182.1	233.2	268.9

[1] Includes other parties, not shown separately. [2] Includes other types of receipts, not shown separately.

Source: U.S. Federal Election Commission, FEC Reports on Financial Activity, Final Report, Presidential Pre-Nomination Campaigns, quadrennial.

Table 413. Congressional Campaign Finances—Receipts and Disbursements: 1999 to 2004

[610.4 represents $610,400,000. Covers all campaign finance activity during 2-year calendar period indicated for primary, general, run-off, and special elections. Data have been adjusted to eliminate transfers between all committees within a campaign. For further information on legal limits of contributions, see Federal Election campaign act of 1971, as amended]

Item	House of Representatives						Senate					
	Amount (mil. dol.)			Percent distribution			Amount (mil. dol.)			Percent distribution		
	1999-00	2001-02	2003-04	1999-00	2001-02	2003-04	1999-00	2001-02	2003-04	1999-00	2001-02	2003-04
Total receipts [1]	610.4	643.3	708.5	100	100	100	437.0	326.1	497.6	100	100	100
Individual contributions	315.6	322.5	396.7	52	50	56	252.1	214.3	324.1	58	66	65
Other committees	193.4	214.1	225.4	32	33	32	52.0	60.2	63.7	12	18	13
Candidate loans	61.9	72.0	47.4	10	11	7	89.0	28.1	39.8	20	9	8
Candidate contributions	6.3	9.2	7.8	1	1	1	18.7	0.8	38.2	4	(Z)	8
Democrats	286.7	314.2	307.4	47	49	43	230.4	162.9	250.6	53	50	50
Republicans	317.7	326.3	399.2	52	51	56	203.8	162.7	246.1	47	50	49
Others	6.0	2.8	1.9	1	(Z)	(Z)	2.8	0.6	0.9	1	(Z)	(Z)
Incumbents	361.8	369.8	452.6	59	57	64	130.6	145.0	171.7	30	44	35
Challengers [2]	127.4	107.0	118.2	21	17	17	99.6	109.7	79.5	23	34	16
Open seats [2]	121.1	166.5	137.8	20	26	19	206.7	71.4	246.4	47	22	50
Total disbursements	572.3	613.9	660.3	100	100	100	434.7	322.4	496.4	100	100	100
Democrats	266.8	301.1	288.5	47	49	44	226.3	162.9	254.6	52	51	51
Republicans	299.7	310.0	370.0	52	50	56	205.7	158.9	241.0	47	49	49
Others	5.7	2.9	1.8	1	(Z)	(Z)	2.7	0.6	0.8	1	(Z)	(Z)
Incumbents	327.0	343.9	410.1	57	56	62	130.2	145.6	171.7	30	45	35
Challengers [2]	125.6	103.9	116.6	22	17	18	99.3	108.4	76.6	23	34	15
Open seats [2]	119.7	166.1	133.6	21	27	20	205.1	68.5	248.1	47	21	50

Z Less than $50,000 or 0.5 percent. [1] Includes other types of receipts, not shown separately. [2] Elections in which an incumbent did not seek re-election.

Source: U.S. Federal Election Commission, *FEC Reports on Financial Activity, Final Report, U.S. Senate and House Campaigns*, biennial.

Table 414. Contributions to Congressional Campaigns by Political Action Committees (PAC) by Type of Committee: 1995 to 2004

[In millions of dollars. (155.8 represents $155,800,000). Covers amounts given to candidates in primary, general, run-off, and special elections during the 2-year calendar period indicated. For number of political action committees, see Table 409]

Type of committee	Total [1]	Democrats	Republicans	Incumbents	Challengers	Open seats [2]
HOUSE OF REPRESENTATIVES						
1995-96	155.8	77.3	77.7	113.9	21.4	20.5
1997-98	158.7	77.6	80.9	124.0	14.9	19.8
1999-00	193.4	98.2	94.7	150.5	19.9	23.0
2001-02	206.9	102.6	104.2	161.0	13.8	32.1
2003-04, total [3]	225.4	98.6	126.6	187.3	15.6	22.5
Corporate	79.1	24.8	54.3	72.6	1.9	4.6
Trade association [4]	63.2	23.0	40.1	55.5	2.3	5.4
Labor	42.8	37.3	5.4	33.0	5.2	4.6
Nonconnected [5]	35.2	11.4	23.8	21.6	6.0	7.6
SENATE						
1995-96	45.6	16.6	29.0	19.4	6.9	19.3
1997-98	48.1	20.7	27.3	34.3	6.6	7.2
1999-00	51.9	18.7	33.2	33.5	7.1	11.3
2001-02	59.2	25.4	33.8	37.0	14.2	8.1
2003-04, total [3]	63.7	28.4	35.3	39.3	5.6	18.8
Corporate	25.2	8.9	16.3	17.2	1.2	6.7
Trade association [4]	15.0	5.7	9.3	9.9	1.1	4.0
Labor	7.6	6.8	0.8	4.3	0.9	2.3
Nonconnected [5]	14.6	6.3	8.3	6.9	2.2	5.4

[1] Includes other parties, not shown separately. [2] Elections in which an incumbent did not seek re-election. [3] Includes other types of political action committees not shown separately. [4] Includes membership organizations and health organizations. [5] Represents "ideological" groups as well as other issue groups not necessarily ideological in nature.

Source: U.S. Federal Election Commission, *FEC Reports on Financial Activity, Party and Non-Party Political Committees*, Final Report, biennial.

DEBTS OF STATES AND TERRITORIES.

No. 7.—STATE, COUNTY, AND MUNICIPAL DEBTS IN EACH STATE AND TERRITORY OF THE UNITED STATES IN 1870 AND 1880, AND THE TOTAL DEBT PER CAPITA OF POPULATION IN 1880.

[From the returns of the Tenth Census, 1880.]

States and Territories.	1870. Total debt.	1880. Net State debt.	Net county debt. a	Net municipal debt. b	Total debt. a	Total debt per capita of population, 1880.
States.	*Dollars.*	*Dollars.*	*Dollars.*	*Dollars.*	*Dollars.*	*Dollars.*
Alabama	13, 277, 154	9, 071, 765	1, 703, 266	3, 953, 514	14, 728, 545	11. 67
Arkansas	4, 151, 152	4, 039, 737	3, 135, 749	763, 298	7, 938, 784	9. 89
California	18, 089, 082	3, 306, 614	7, 312, 489	6, 136, 585	16, 755, 688	19. 38
Colorado	681, 158	212, 814	2, 492, 441	889, 041	3, 594, 296	18. 49
Connecticut	17, 088, 906	4, 967, 608	191, 409	16, 932, 661	22, 001, 661	35. 33
Delaware	526, 125	889, 750	44, 000	1, 421, 835	2, 346, 585	16. 01
Florida	2, 185, 838	1, 134, 880	435, 993	1, 055, 636	2, 626, 509	9. 75
Georgia	21, 753, 712	9, 951, 500	181, 790	9, 548, 613	19, 681, 903	12. 76
Illinois	42, 191, 869	No debt.	14, 181, 134	30 999, 788	45, 189, 922	14. 68
Indiana	7, 818, 710	4, 996, 178	4, 048, 054	9, 307, 505	18, 353, 737	9. 28
Iowa	8, 043, 133	370, 435	2, 992, 573	4, 599, 759	7, 962, 787	4. 90
Kansas	6, 442, 282	1, 087, 700	7, 959, 921	6, 967, 232	16, 005, 853	16. 07
Kentucky	18, 953, 484	1, 089, 856	5, 877, 043	8, 010, 982	14, 977, 881	9. 98
Louisiana	53, 087, 441	23, 437, 640	1, 107, 951	18, 320, 361	42, 865, 952	45. 66
Maine	16, 624, 624	4, 682, 741	451, 809	17, 272, 300	22, 406, 850	34. 53
Maryland	29, 032, 577	7, 627, 668	1, 377, 325	1, 891, 013	10, 890, 006	11. 65
Massachusetts	69, 211, 538	20, 159, 478	1, 371, 219	69, 753, 222	91, 283, 913	51. 19
Michigan	6, 725, 231	No debt.	896, 700	7, 936, 444	8, 803, 144	5. 38
Minnesota	2, 788, 797	2, 565, 000	901, 412	5, 009, 652	8, 476, 064	10. 86
Mississippi	2, 504, 415	379, 485	1, 134, 763	498, 942	2, 013, 190	1. 78
Missouri	46, 909, 865	16, 259, 000	11, 923, 312	29, 249, 010	57, 431, 322	26. 48
Nebraska	2, 089, 264	375, 582	5, 120, 362	1, 929, 813	7, 425, 757	16. 41
Nevada	1, 986, 063		891, 017	133, 506	1, 024, 523	16. 45
New Hampshire	11, 153, 373	3, 561, 200	779, 634	6, 383, 936	10, 724, 170	30. 91
New Jersey	22, 854, 304	813, 675	6, 668, 463	42, 064, 964	49, 547, 102	43. 80
New York	159, 808, 234	7, 536, 732	12, 590, 308	198, 787, 274	218, 723, 314	43. 03
North Carolina	32, 474, 036	5, 766, 616	1, 524, 654	963, 336	8, 194, 606	5. 85
Ohio	22, 241, 988	5, 732, 500	2, 962, 649	40, 058, 805	48, 753, 954	15. 24
Oregon	218, 486	511, 376	211, 767	125, 359	848, 502	4. 86
Pennsylvania	89, 027, 131	20, 716, 285	9, 781, 384	83, 537, 690	114, 034, 759	26. 63
Rhode Island	5, 038, 642	1, 832, 463		11, 270, 327	13, 102, 790	47. 38
South Carolina	13, 075, 229	6, 639, 171	1, 573, 859	5, 132, 908	13, 345, 938	13. 41
Tennessee	48, 827, 191	27, 440, 431	3, 060, 545	6, 886, 924	37, 387, 900	24. 25
Texas	1, 613, 907	5, 566, 928	2, 499, 287	3, 538, 698	11, 604, 913	7. 29
Vermont	3, 594, 700	4, 000	28, 421	4, 324, 747	4, 352, 168	13. 10
Virginia	55, 921, 255	29, 345, 226	1, 283, 574	11, 471, 002	42, 099, 802	27. 83
West Virginia	561, 767	No debt.	592, 780	920, 644	1, 513, 424	2. 45
Wisconsin	5, 903, 532	2, 252, 057	2, 292, 254	7, 331, 681	11, 875, 992	9. 03
The States	865, 466, 225	234, 257, 083	121, 285, 696	675, 348, 407	1, 030, 891, 186	
Territories.						
Arizona	10, 500		353, 217	24, 284	377, 501	9. 33
Dakota	5, 761		961, 570	37, 290	998, 860	7. 39
District of Columbia	2, 596, 545			22, 675, 459	22, 675, 459	127. 66
Idaho	222, 621	88, 381	143, 742	3, 196	235, 319	7. 22
Montana	278, 719	64, 677	659, 696	35, 552	759, 925	19. 41
New Mexico	7, 560		84, 872		84, 872	. 71
Utah		9, 120	15, 132	91, 999	116, 251	. 81
Washington	88, 827		204, 384	34, 927	239, 311	3. 19
Wyoming		17, 000	169, 377	19, 085	205, 462	9. 88
The Territories	3, 210, 533	179, 178	2, 591, 990	22, 921, 792	25, 692, 960	
The United States	868, 676, 758	234, 436, 261	123, 877, 686	698, 270, 199	1, 056, 584, 146	21. 07

a The aggregate of debt after deducting sinking fund.
b Including township and school district debt.
c Old debt (1814) now being refunded.

Source: Statistical Abstract of the United States: 1887 Edition.

Section 8
State and Local Government Finances and Employment

This section presents data on revenues, expenditures, debt, and employment of state and local governments. Nationwide statistics relating to state and local governments, their numbers, finances, and employment are compiled primarily by the U.S. Census Bureau through a program of censuses and surveys. Every fifth year (for years ending in "2" and "7"), the Census Bureau conducts a census of governments involving collection of data for all governmental units in the United States. In addition, the Census Bureau conducts annual surveys which cover all the state governments and a sample of local governments.

Annually, the Census Bureau releases information on the Internet which presents financial data for the federal government, nationwide totals for state and local governments, and state-local data by states. Also released annually is a series on state, city, county, and school finances and on state and local public employment. There is also a series of quarterly data releases covering tax revenue and finances of major public employee retirement systems.

Basic information for Census Bureau statistics on governments is obtained by mail canvass from state and local officials; however, financial data for each of the state governments and for many of the large local governments are compiled from their official records and reports by Census Bureau personnel. In over two-thirds of the states, all or part of local government financial data are obtained through central collection arrangements with state governments. Financial data on the federal government are primarily based on the *Budget* published by the Office of Management and Budget (see text, Section 9, Federal Government Finances and Employment).

Governmental units—The governmental structure of the United States includes, in addition to the federal government and the states, thousands of local governments—counties, municipalities, townships, school districts, and many "special districts." In 2002, 87,525 local governments were identified by the census of governments (see Tables 415-417). As defined by the census, governmental units include all agencies or bodies having an organized existence, governmental character, and substantial autonomy. While most of these governments can impose taxes, many of the special districts—such as independent public housing authorities and numerous local irrigation, power, and other types of districts—are financed from rentals, charges for services, benefit assessments, grants from other governments, and other nontax sources. The count of governments excludes semi-autonomous agencies through which states, cities, and counties sometimes provide for certain functions—for example, "dependent" school systems, state institutions of higher education, and certain other "authorities" and special agencies which are under the administrative or fiscal control of an established governmental unit.

Finances—The financial statistics relate to government fiscal years ending June 30 or at some date within the 12 previous months. The following governments are exceptions and are included as though they were part of the June 30 group; ending September 30, the state governments of Alabama and Michigan, the District of Columbia, and Alabama school districts; and ending August 31, the state government of Texas and Texas school districts. New York State ends its fiscal year on March 31. The federal government ended the fiscal year June 30 until 1976 when its fiscal year, by an act of Congress, was revised to extend from Oct. 1 to Sept. 30. A 3-month quarter (July 1 to Sept. 30, 1976) bridged the transition.

Nationwide government finance statistics have been classified and presented in terms of uniform concepts and categories, rather than according to the highly diverse terminology, organization, and fund structure utilized by individual governments.

Statistics on governmental finances distinguish among general government, utilities, liquor stores, and insurance trusts. *General government* comprises all activities except utilities, liquor stores, and insurance trusts. Utilities include government water supply, electric light and power, gas supply, and transit systems. Liquor stores are operated by 17 states and by local governments in 6 states. Insurance trusts relate to employee retirement, unemployment compensation, and other social insurance systems administered by the federal, state, and local governments.

Data for cities or counties relate only to municipal or county and their dependent agencies and do not include amounts for other local governments in the same geographic location. Therefore, expenditure figures for "education" do not include spending by the separate school districts which administer public schools within most municipal or county areas. Variations in the assignment of governmental responsibility for public assistance, health, hospitals, public housing, and other functions to a lesser degree also have an important effect upon reported amounts of city or county expenditure, revenue, and debt.

Employment and payrolls—These data are based mainly on mail canvassing of state and local governments. Payroll includes all salaries, wages, and individual fee payments for the month specified, and employment relates to all persons on governmental payrolls during a pay period of the month covered—including paid officials, temporary help, and (unless otherwise specified) part-time as well as full-time personnel. Beginning 1986, statistics for full-time equivalent employment have been computed with a formula using hours worked by part-time employees. A payroll-based formula was used prior to 1985. Full-time equivalent employment statistics were not computed for 1985. Figures shown for individual governments cover major dependent agencies such as institutions of higher education, as well as the basic central departments and agencies of the government.

Statistical reliability—For a discussion of statistical collection and estimation, sampling procedures, and measures of statistical reliability applicable to Census Bureau data, see Appendix III.

U.S. Census Bureau, Statistical Abstract of the United States: 2006

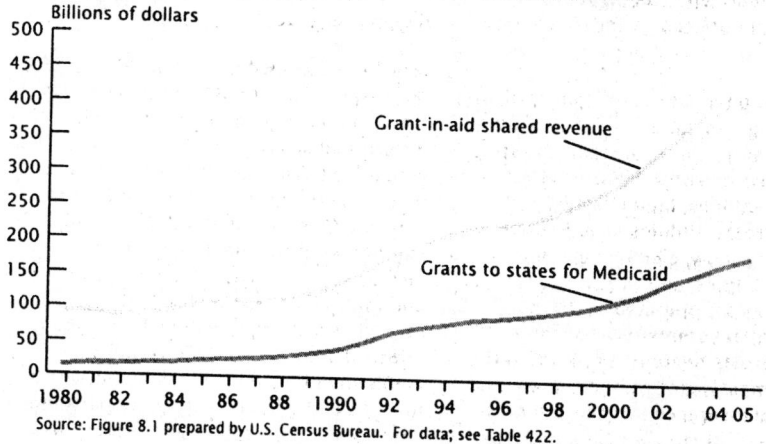

Figure 8.1
Federal Aid to State and Local Governments: 1980 to 2005

Billions of dollars

Grant-in-aid shared revenue

Grants to states for Medicaid

Source: Figure 8.1 prepared by U.S. Census Bureau. For data; see Table 422.

Figure 8.2
Government Employment: 1990 to 2003

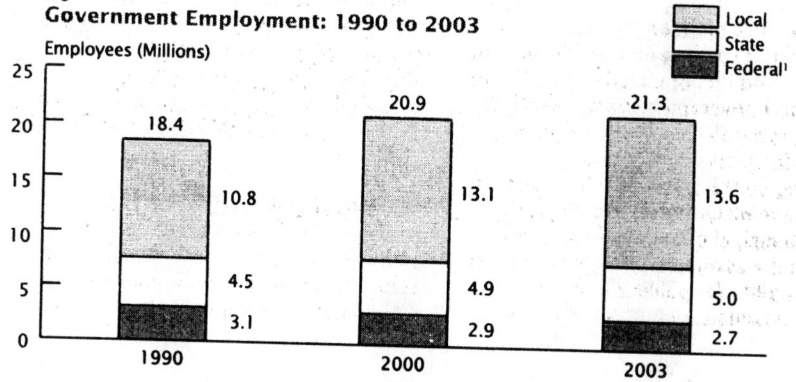

Employees (Millions)

Legend: Local / State / Federal[1]

- 1990: 18.4 total — 10.8, 4.5, 3.1
- 2000: 20.9 total — 13.1, 4.9, 2.9
- 2003: 21.3 total — 13.6, 5.0, 2.7

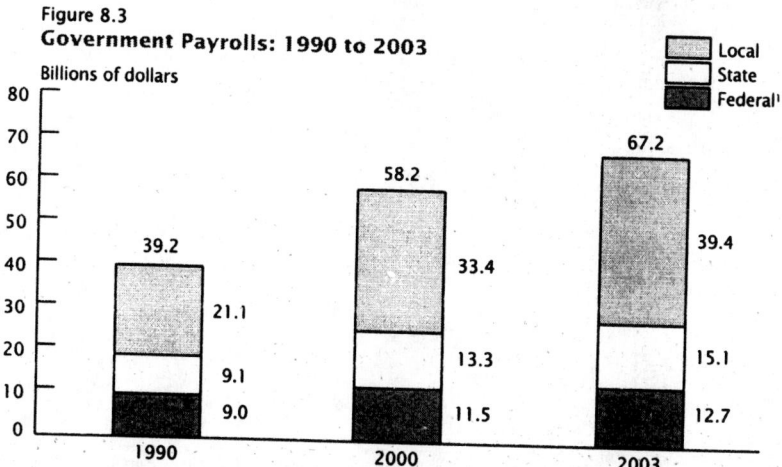

Figure 8.3
Government Payrolls: 1990 to 2003

Billions of dollars

Legend: Local / State / Federal[1]

- 1990: 39.2 total — 21.1, 9.1, 9.0
- 2000: 58.2 total — 33.4, 13.3, 11.5
- 2003: 67.2 total — 39.4, 15.1, 12.7

[1]Civilian employees only. Includes employees outside the United States.
Source: Figure 8.2 and 8.3 prepared by U.S. Census Bureau. For data, see Table 451.

U.S. Census Bureau, Statistical Abstract of the United States: 2006

Table 415. Number of Governmental Units by Type: 1952 to 2002

Type of government	1952 [1]	1962	1967	1972	1977	1982	1987	1992	1997	2002
Total units	116,807	91,237	81,299	78,269	79,913	81,831	83,237	85,006	87,504	87,576
U.S. government.	1	1	1	1	1	1	1	1	1	1
State government	50	50	50	50	50	50	50	50	50	50
Local governments	116,756	91,186	81,248	78,218	79,862	81,780	83,186	84,955	87,453	87,525
County	3,052	3,043	3,049	3,044	3,042	3,041	3,042	3,043	3,043	3,034
Municipal	16,807	18,000	18,048	18,517	18,862	19,076	19,200	19,279	19,372	19,429
Township and town	17,202	17,142	17,105	16,991	16,822	16,734	16,691	16,656	16,629	16,504
School district	67,355	34,678	21,782	15,781	15,174	14,851	14,721	14,422	13,726	13,506
Special district	12,340	18,323	21,264	23,885	25,962	28,078	29,532	31,555	34,683	35,052

[1] Adjusted to include units in Alaska and Hawaii which adopted statehood in 1959.

Source: U.S. Census Bureau, 2002 Census of Governments, Preliminary Report No. 1, Series GC02-1(P). See also <http://www.census.gov>govs/www/cog2002.html>.

Table 416. Number of Local Governments by Type—States: 2002

[Governments in existence in January. Limited to governments actually in existence. Excludes, therefore, a few counties and numerous townships and "incorporated places" existing as areas for which statistics can be presented as to population and other subjects, but lacking any separate organized county, township, or municipal government. See Appendix III]

State	All governmental units [1]	County	Municipal	Township [1]	School district	Special district [2] Total [3]	Natural resources	Fire protection	Housing & community development
United States. . .	87,525	3,034	19,429	16,504	13,506	35,052	6,979	5,725	3,399
Alabama	1,171	67	451	-	128	525	68	12	152
Alaska	175	12	149	-	-	14	-	-	13
Arizona	638	15	87	-	231	305	83	151	-
Arkansas	1,588	75	499	-	310	704	258	80	122
California	4,409	57	475	-	1,047	2,830	484	368	71
Colorado	1,928	62	270	-	182	1,414	178	250	91
Connecticut	580	-	30	149	17	384	1	64	93
Delaware	339	3	57	-	19	260	239	-	3
District of Columbia	2	-	1	-	-	1	-	-	-
Florida	1,191	66	404	-	95	626	124	57	105
Georgia	1,448	156	531	-	180	581	38	2	201
Hawaii	19	3	1	-	-	15	14	-	-
Idaho	1,158	44	200	-	116	798	176	142	10
Illinois	6,903	102	1,291	1,431	934	3,145	979	823	112
Indiana	3,085	91	567	1,008	294	1,125	141	1	63
Iowa	1,975	99	948	-	386	542	251	67	23
Kansas	3,887	104	627	1,299	324	1,533	261	-	199
Kentucky	1,439	119	424	-	176	720	166	163	17
Louisiana	473	60	302	-	66	45	4	-	-
Maine	826	16	22	467	99	222	15	-	23
Maryland	265	23	157	-	-	85	44	-	21
Massachusetts	841	5	45	306	82	403	16	16	250
Michigan	2,804	83	533	1,242	580	366	80	4	-
Minnesota	3,482	87	854	1,793	345	403	114	-	167
Mississippi.	1,000	82	296	-	164	458	242	34	57
Missouri	3,422	114	946	312	536	1,514	183	317	136
Montana	1,127	54	129	-	352	592	125	155	12
Nebraska	2,791	93	531	446	575	1,146	80	421	125
Nevada	210	16	19	-	17	158	33	19	5
New Hampshire . . .	559	10	13	221	167	148	10	14	21
New Jersey	1,412	21	324	242	549	276	16	196	2
New Mexico.	858	33	101	-	96	628	583	-	6
New York	3,420	57	616	929	683	1,135	3	911	-
North Carolina	960	100	541	-	-	319	155	-	91
North Dakota	2,735	53	360	1,332	226	764	79	281	39
Ohio.	3,636	88	942	1,308	667	631	98	73	77
Oklahoma	1,798	77	590	-	571	560	97	26	105
Oregon	1,439	36	240	-	236	927	179	256	20
Pennsylvania	5,031	66	1,018	1,546	516	1,885	7	-	90
Rhode Island	118	-	8	31	4	75	3	34	25
South Carolina	701	46	269	-	85	301	48	86	46
South Dakota	1,866	66	308	940	176	376	102	72	40
Tennessee.	930	92	349	-	14	475	108	-	98
Texas.	4,784	254	1,196	-	1,089	2,245	442	141	398
Utah.	605	29	236	-	40	300	81	19	16
Vermont	733	14	47	237	283	152	14	19	10
Virginia	521	95	229	-	1	196	47	-	-
Washington	1,787	39	279	-	296	1,173	170	387	41
West Virginia	686	55	234	-	55	342	15	-	39
Wisconsin	3,048	72	585	1,265	442	684	191	-	164
Wyoming	722	23	98	-	55	546	134	64	-

- Represents zero. [1] Includes "town" governments in the six New England states and in Minnesota, New York, and Wisconsin. [2] Single function districts. [3] Includes other special districts not shown separately.

Source: U.S. Census Bureau, Census of Governments, Volume 1, Number 1, Government Organization, Series GC02(1)-1), quinquennial. <http://www.census.gov/govs/www/cog2002.html>.

Table 417. County, Municipal, and Township Governments by Population Size: 2002

[Number of governments as of January 2002. Population enumerated as of April 1, 2000. (252,051 represents 252,051,000). Consolidated city-county governments are classified as municipal rather than county governments. Township governments include "towns" in the six New England states, Minnesota, New York, and Wisconsin. See Appendix III]

Population-size group	County governments			Municipal governments			Township governments		
	Number, 2002	Population, 2000		Number, 2002	Population, 2000		Number, 2002	Population, 2000	
		Number (1,000)	Percent		Number (1,000)	Percent		Number (1,000)	Percent
Total	3,034	252,051	100	19,429	174,882	100	16,504	57,365	100
300,000 or more.	161	131,575	52	58	47,768	27	3	1,527	3
200,000 to 299,999. . .	84	20,606	8	30	7,163	4	3	728	1
100,000 to 199,999. . .	228	31,576	13	153	21,076	12	30	3,974	7
50,000 to 99,999	383	27,160	11	364	24,960	14	97	6,588	11
25,000 to 49,999	638	22,913	9	643	22,576	13	273	9,275	16
10,000 to 24,999	869	14,488	6	1,436	22,589	13	773	12,067	21
5,000 to 9,999	385	2,911	1	1,637	11,644	7	1,085	7,560	13
2,500 to 4,999	173	643	(Z)	2,070	7,352	4	1,909	6,732	12
1,000 to 2,499	84	158	(Z)	3,677	5,951	3	3,679	5,905	10
Less than 1,000	29	21	(Z)	9,361	3,803	2	8,652	3,008	5

Z less than 0.5 percent.

Source: U.S. Census Bureau, Census of Governments, Volume 1, Number 1, Government Organization, Series GC02(1)-1), quinquennial. <http://www.census.gov/govs/www/cog2002.html>.

Table 418. Government Current Receipts and Expenditures by Type: 1990 to 2004

[In billions of dollars (1,707.8 represents $1,707,800,000,000). For explanation of national income, see text, Section 13. A comprehensive National Income and Product Accounts (NIPA) revision was released on December 10, 2003; for more information on this revision of NIPA, go to <www.bea.doc.gov/bea/dn/2003benchmark/CR2003content.htm>. Minus sign (-) indicates a deficit.]

Item	1990	1995	1999	2000	2001	2002	2003	2004
Current receipts	1,707.8	2,212.6	2,895.0	3,125.9	3,113.1	2,954.7	3,032.0	3,200.6
Current tax receipts	1,161.9	1,517.2	2,036.2	2,206.8	2,168.0	1,995.5	2,033.8	2,147.2
Personal current taxes	592.8	744.1	1,107.5	1,235.7	1,237.3	1,051.2	1,001.9	1,038.9
Taxes on production and imports	425.5	558.2	674.0	708.9	728.6	762.6	798.1	841.1
Taxes on corporate income	140.6	211.0	248.8	255.0	194.9	174.6	225.8	258.3
Taxes from the rest of the world	3.0	3.9	5.9	7.3	7.1	7.1	8.1	8.9
Contributions for government social insurance.	410.1	532.8	661.4	702.7	731.1	748.3	773.2	820.2
Income receipts on assets	98.7	92.1	106.8	117.4	113.7	101.9	104.0	106.1
Interest and miscellaneous receipts. . .	98.4	91.1	105.0	115.6	111.7	99.8	101.4	103.3
Dividends	0.2	1.0	1.8	1.9	2.0	2.1	2.5	2.8
Current transfer receipts	35.6	59.1	80.6	93.7	101.8	106.3	111.5	120.2
From business (net)	17.2	26.5	35.9	43.7	47.5	46.7	46.6	49.2
From persons	18.4	32.6	44.7	50.0	54.2	59.5	64.9	71.0
Current surplus of government enterprises	1.6	11.4	10.1	5.3	-1.4	2.8	9.5	6.9
Current expenditures	1,872.6	2,397.6	2,741.0	2,886.5	3,061.6	3,234.3	3,399.7	3,558.6
Consumption expenditures	964.4	1,136.5	1,334.0	1,417.1	1,501.6	1,609.2	1,717.1	1,804.2
Current transfer payments.	586.1	872.5	1,005.5	1,062.4	1,160.6	1,270.5	1,332.9	1,402.4
Government social benefits	574.8	860.3	990.4	1,044.1	1,146.6	1,251.6	1,309.3	1,376.2
To persons	573.1	858.4	988.0	1,041.6	1,143.9	1,248.9	1,306.4	1,373.2
To the rest of the world	1.8	1.9	2.4	2.5	2.7	2.7	2.8	3.0
Other current transfer payments to the rest of the world	11.3	12.1	15.1	18.3	18.9	18.8	23.7	26.2
Interest payments	295.3	354.6	357.3	362.8	344.1	316.4	303.0	311.6
To persons and business.	254.6	300.8	282.7	279.8	261.7	240.3	231.0	227.3
To the rest of the world.	40.8	53.8	74.5	83.0	82.4	76.1	72.0	84.4
Subsidies	26.8	34.0	44.2	44.3	55.3	38.2	46.7	40.4
Less: Wage accruals less disbursements	0.1	-	-	-	-	-	-	-
Net government saving	-164.8	-184.9	154.0	239.4	51.5	-279.5	-367.8	-358.0
Social insurance funds	45.0	23.0	95.8	114.4	89.6	49.2	46.6	67.4
Other	-209.8	-208.0	58.2	125.1	-38.1	-328.8	-414.4	-425.4

- Represents zero.

Source: U.S. Bureau of Economic Analysis, National Income and Product Accounts, 1929-2004; and Survey of Current Business, May 2005. See also <http://www.bea.doc.gov/bea/dn/nipaweb/selecttable.asp?selected=N> (released 28 April, 2005).

Table 419. Government Consumption Expenditures and Gross Investment by Level of Government and Type: 1990 to 2004

[In billions of dollars (1,180.2 represents $1,180,200,000,000). For explanation of national income, see text, Section 13. A comprehensive National Income and Product Accounts (NIPA) revision was released on December 10, 2003; for more information on this revision of NIPA, go to <http://www.bea.doc.gov/bea/dn/2003benchmark/CR2003content.htm>]

Level of government and type	1990	1995	1999	2000	2001	2002	2003	2004
Consumption expenditures & gross investment, total	1,180.2	1,369.2	1,620.8	1,721.6	1,825.6	1,956.6	2,075.5	2,183.9
Consumption expenditures [1]	964.4	1,136.5	1,334.0	1,417.1	1,501.6	1,609.2	1,717.1	1,804.2
Gross investment [2]	215.7	232.7	286.8	304.5	324.0	347.4	358.5	379.7
Structures	112.6	134.4	175.3	189.3	205.3	222.6	228.9	237.3
Equipment and software.......	103.1	98.4	111.5	115.2	118.7	124.9	129.6	142.3
Federal	508.3	519.2	555.8	578.8	612.9	680.8	752.2	809.9
Consumption expenditures	419.8	440.5	475.1	499.3	531.9	592.7	658.6	704.5
Gross investment	88.5	78.8	80.7	79.5	81.0	88.1	93.6	105.4
Structures	14.1	17.1	15.6	13.3	12.9	14.3	15.5	15.5
Equipment and software.......	74.4	61.7	65.1	66.2	68.1	73.8	78.1	89.9
National defense	374.0	348.7	360.6	370.3	392.6	437.4	496.4	547.9
Consumption expenditures	308.1	297.3	312.9	321.5	342.4	382.0	436.1	477.5
Gross investment	65.9	51.4	47.7	48.8	50.2	55.4	60.4	70.4
Structures	6.1	6.3	5.0	5.0	4.6	4.4	5.3	5.4
Equipment and software.......	59.8	45.1	42.8	43.8	45.6	51.0	55.1	65.0
Nondefense	134.3	170.5	195.2	208.5	220.3	243.4	255.7	262.0
Consumption expenditures	111.7	143.2	162.2	177.8	189.5	210.7	222.5	227.0
Gross investment	22.6	27.3	33.0	30.7	30.8	32.7	33.2	35.0
Structures	8.0	10.8	10.6	8.3	8.3	9.9	10.2	10.1
Equipment and software.......	14.6'	16.5	22.4	22.3	22.5	22.9	23.0	24.9
State and local	671.9	850.0	1,065.0	1,142.8	1,212.8	1,275.8	1,323.3	1,373.9
Consumption expenditures	544.6	696.1	858.9	917.8	969.8	1,016.5	1,058.5	1,099.7
Gross investment	127.2	154.0	206.0	225.0	243.0	259.3	264.9	274.3
Structures	98.5	117.3	159.7	176.0	192.4	208.2	213.4	221.8
Equipment and software.......	28.7	36.7	46.4	49.0	50.6	51.0	51.5	52.4

[1] Government consumption expenditures are services (such as education and national defense) produced by government that are valued at their cost of production. Excludes government sales to other sectors and government own-account investment (construction and software). [2] Gross government investment consists of general government and government enterprise expenditures for fixed assets; inventory investment is included in government consumption expenditures.

Source: U.S. Bureau of Economic Analysis, *National Income and Product Accounts, 1929-2004*; and *Survey of Current Business*, May 2005. See also <http://www.bea.doc.gov/bea/dn/nipaweb/selecttable.asp?selected=N>; (released 28 April 2005).

Table 420. Real Government Consumption Expenditures and Gross Investment in Chained (2000) Dollars by Level of Government and Type: 1990 to 2004

[In billions of dollars (1,530.0 represents $1,530,000,000,000). For explanation of national income, see text, Section 13. A comprehensive National Income and Product Accounts (NIPA) revision was released on December 10, 2003; for more information on this revision of NIPA, go to <http://www.bea.doc.gov/bea/dn/2003benchmark/CR2003content.htm>]

Item	1990	1995	1999	2000	2001	2002	2003	2004
Government consumption expenditures and gross investment, total	1,530.0	1,549.7	1,686.9	1,721.6	1,780.3	1,857.9	1,909.4	1,946.5
Consumption expenditures [1]	1,277.2	1,301.9	1,393.1	1,417.1	1,461.0	1,519.4	1,563.7	1,590.9
Gross investment [2]	253.0	248.8	294.0	304.5	319.3	338.6	345.7	355.9
Structures	151.2	159.5	183.3	189.3	198.5	209.2	210.4	208.7
Equipment and software	99.1	89.5	110.7	115.2	120.9	129.5	135.8	149.0
Federal	659.1	580.3	573.7	578.8	601.4	646.6	689.6	721.7
Consumption expenditures	562.5	502.9	492.8	499.3	519.8	557.2	594.5	616.8
Gross investment	95.4	77.6	81.0	79.5	81.5	89.5	95.1	105.7
Structures	19.0	20.0	16.3	13.3	12.4	13.5	14.2	13.5
Equipment and software	75.8	58.1	64.8	66.2	69.1	76.0	80.9	92.5
National defense	479.4	389.2	372.2	370.3	384.9	414.6	451.8	484.9
Consumption expenditures	404.9	338.1	324.6	321.5	334.1	358.2	390.3	415.0
Gross investment	72.9	50.9	47.6	48.8	50.8	56.6	61.6	70.6
Structures	8.6	7.4	5.2	5.0	4.4	4.2	4.8	4.7
Equipment and software	64.2	43.7	42.5	43.8	46.4	52.5	56.8	66.1
Nondefense	178.6	191.0	201.5	208.5	216.5	232.0	237.6	236.4
Consumption expenditures	156.5	164.7	168.1	177.8	185.8	199.0	204.0	201.4
Gross investment	23.1	26.7	33.4	30.7	30.7	32.9	33.5	35.2
Structures	10.6	12.6	11.1	8.3	8.0	9.3	9.4	8.8
Equipment and software	12.9	14.7	22.3	22.3	22.7	23.6	24.1	26.5
State and local	868.4	968.3	1,113.2	1,142.8	1,179.0	1,211.4	1,219.8	1,224.8
Consumption expenditures	714.2	798.4	900.3	917.8	941.2	962.2	969.0	973.7
Gross investment	154.6	170.4	212.9	225.0	237.8	249.2	250.9	251.1
Structures	132.1	139.5	167.0	176.0	186.0	195.7	196.1	195.1
Equipment and software	25.0	31.7	45.9	49.0	51.7	53.5	54.8	56.3
Residual........................	1.0	-1.1	-0.1	0.1	-	-0.3	0.1	-1.1

- Represents zero. [1] Government consumption expenditures are services (such as education and national defense) produced by government that are valued at their cost of production. Excludes government sales to other sectors and government own-account investment (construction and software). [2] Gross government investment consists of general government and government enterprise expenditures for fixed assets; inventory investment is included in government consumption expenditures.

Source: U.S. Bureau of Economic Analysis, *National Income and Product Accounts, 1929-2004*; and *Survey of Current Business*, May 2005. See also <http://www.bea.doc.gov/bea/dn/nipaweb/selecttable.asp?selected=N>; (released 28 April 2005).

Table 421. Federal Grants-in-Aid to State and Local Governments: 1980 to 2005

[91,385 represents $91,385,000,000, except as indicated. For year ending Sept. 30. Minus sign (-) indicates decrease]

Year	Current dollars							Constant (2000) dollars	
	Total grants (mil. dol.)	Annual percent change¹	Grants to individuals		Grants as percent of—			Total grants (bil. dol.)	Annual percent change¹
			Total (mil. dol.)	Percent of total grants	State/local govt. expenditures²	Federal outlays	Gross domestic product		
1980	91,385	9.6	32,619	35.7	39.9	15.5	3.3	192.6	-1.6
1990	135,325	11.0	77,264	57.1	25.2	10.8	2.4	172.1	6.3
1993	193,612	8.7	124,155	64.1	29.6	13.7	3.0	223.9	5.9
1994	210,596	8.8	134,153	63.7	30.9	14.4	3.0	238.1	6.3
1995	224,991	6.8	144,427	64.2	31.5	14.8	3.1	247.9	4.1
1996	227,811	1.3	146,493	64.3	30.8	14.6	3.0	245.5	-1.0
1997	234,160	2.8	148,236	63.3	30.2	14.6	2.9	247.7	0.9
1998	246,128	5.1	160,305	65.1	30.3	14.9	2.9	257.3	3.9
1999	267,081	8.5	172,384	64.5	31.2	15.7	2.9	274.7	6.8
2000	284,659	6.6	182,592	64.1	27.2	15.9	2.9	284.7	3.6
2001	317,211	11.4	203,920	64.3	28.2	17.0	3.2	309.4	8.7
2002	351,550	10.8	227,373	64.7	29.4	17.5	3.4	337.2	9.0
2003	387,366	10.2	246,570	63.7	31.4	17.9	3.6	362.9	7.6
2004	406,330	4.9	262,177	64.5	31.9	17.7	3.5	371.7	2.4
2005, est	425,793	4.8	278,294	65.4	(NA)	17.2	3.5	377.9	1.7

NA Not available. ¹ Average annual percent change from prior year shown. For explanation, see Guide to Tabular Presentation. For 1980, change from 1979, and 1990, from 1989. ² Expenditures from own sources as defined in the national income and product accounts.

Source: U. S. Office of Management and Budget, based on *Historical Tables, Budget of the United States Government*, annual.

Table 422. Federal Aid to State and Local Governments—Selected Programs: 1980 to 2005

[In millions of dollars (91,385 represents $91,385,000,000). For year ending Sept 30. Includes trust funds.]

Program	1980	1990	1995	2000	2002	2003	2004	2005 est.
Grant-in-aid shared revenue¹	91,385	135,325	224,991	284,659	351,550	387,366	406,330	425,793
Energy	499	461	492	433	528	589	608	608
Natural resources and environment	5,363	3,745	4,148	4,595	5,085	5,593	6,009	6,121
Environmental Protection Agency²	4,603	2,874	2,912	3,490	3,588	3,917	4,018	3,691
Agriculture	569	1,285	780	724	750	800	995	961
Transportation	13,022	19,174	25,787	32,222	40,998	41,029	41,471	43,870
Grants for airports²	590	1,220	1,826	1,624	2,860	2,681	2,958	3,041
Federal-aid highways³	9,208	14,171	19,475	24,711	29,833	29,960	29,791	31,457
Urban mass transportation²	3,129	3,730	4,353	5,262	7,462	7,448	7,777	8,283
Community and regional development	6,486	4,965	7,230	8,665	10,501	15,082	12,604	14,941
Rural community advance program	325	139	333	479	740	800	797	792
Homeland Security	380	1,184	1,772	2,439	3,456	7,861	5,490	7,929
Community development fund	3,902	2,818	4,333	4,955	5,429	5,569	5,388	5,373
Education, training, employment, social services	21,862	23,359	34,125	42,125	44,827	51,543	54,201	58,104
Education for the disadvantaged⁴	3,370	4,437	6,785	8,511	9,211	11,204	12,417	14,524
School improvement programs⁴	523	1,080	1,288	2,394	3,401	5,964	6,542	6,636
Vocational and adult education	854	1,287	1,449	1,448	1,742	1,908	1,909	1,963
Special education	810	1,485	2,938	4,696	6,730	8,216	9,465	9,884
Social services-block grant	2,763	2,749	2,797	1,827	1,780	1,740	1,752	1,764
Children and family services programs	1,548	2,618	4,463	5,843	7,749	8,161	8,326	8,519
Training and employment services	6,191	3,042	3,620	2,957	4,206	4,291	3,883	3,372
Health	15,758	43,890	93,587	124,843	158,677	173,814	189,883	203,253
Substance abuse, and mental health services	679	1,241	2,444	1,931	2,193	2,171	2,241	2,297
Grants to states for medicaid⁴	13,957	41,103	89,070	117,921	147,650	160,805	176,231	188,497
State children's health insurance fund⁴	(NA)	(NA)	(NA)	1,220	3,682	4,355	4,607	5,343
Income security	18,495	35,189	55,122	63,200	81,506	86,476	85,983	89,317
Food stamp program⁴	412	2,130	2,740	3,508	3,949	4,162	4,204	4,410
Child nutrition programs⁴	3,388	4,871	7,387	9,060	10,100	10,664	11,035	11,990
Temporary assistance for needy families⁴	(NA)	(NA)	(NA)	15,464	18,749	19,352	17,725	18,099
Veterans benefits and services⁴	90	134	253	434	360	403	454	505
Administration of justice	529	574	1,222	5,120	5,826	4,498	5,084	3,641

NA Not available. ¹ Includes items not shown separately. ² Grants includes trust funds. ³ Trust funds. ⁴ Includes grants for payments to individuals.

Source: U.S. Office of Management and Budget, *Historical Tables, Budget of the United States Government*, annual.

U.S. Census Bureau, Statistical Abstract of the United States: 2006

[In millions of dollars (386,707 represents $386,707,000,000). For fiscal year ending September 30.]

State and island areas	Federal aid total [1]	Department of Agriculture					Department of Education				
		Food and nutrition service						Office of Elementary and Secondary Education			
		Total	Child nutrition programs [2]	Food stamp program [3]	Special supplemental food program (WIC)	Other	Total	Special education programs	No child left behind act	Title 1 Programs	Other
United States total	386,707	22,102	10,424	4,013	4,547	3,117	29,195	6,931	3,629	8,469	10,166
Alabama	5,896	377	203	34	76	65	468	123	67	147	131
Alaska	2,407	106	30	8	19	49	141	-	13	-	128
Arizona	7,028	395	213	33	93	56	696	140	76	163	318
Arkansas	3,851	243	123	23	46	51	322	79	64	102	76
California	46,211	2,753	1,330	347	827	249	4,311	707	560	1,413	1,630
Colorado	4,232	232	95	27	47	63	423	107	48	95	173
Connecticut	4,483	155	76	26	32	21	326	94	49	102	81
Delaware	1,025	57	27	8	10	12	105	24	16	28	38
District of Columbia	3,633	54	25	10	11	8	112	19	16	35	43
Florida	17,256	973	588	88	202	95	1,646	478	194	473	501
Georgia	8,949	692	403	74	142	73	89	2	15	-	72
Hawaii	1,515	110	42	13	26	29	178	34	10	27	108
Idaho	1,651	109	43	9	18	39	146	40	21	32	53
Illinois	14,014	770	413	94	177	87	1,391	375	184	399	433
Indiana	6,283	325	173	41	62	49	510	190	57	160	104
Iowa	3,383	199	89	20	34	57	308	94	50	54	111
Kansas	2,759	182	103	14	31	34	125	14	20	-	91
Kentucky	5,968	338	178	31	66	63	508	129	66	142	171
Louisiana	6,486	452	252	48	85	66	42	1	9	-	32
Maine	2,404	84	36	8	11	29	168	43	23	38	64
Maryland	6,330	271	142	36	56	36	528	144	54	173	158
Massachusetts	9,841	291	166	32	63	30	770	267	95	228	180
Michigan	11,514	565	263	89	122	91	1,162	286	141	376	357
Minnesota	5,710	341	161	57	62	62	101	6	11	-	84
Mississippi	4,927	359	179	34	64	82	403	87	67	137	111
Missouri	7,140	384	191	48	67	77	89	2	16	-	71
Montana	1,435	102	32	12	13	45	187	30	30	34	94
Nebraska	2,079	135	66	15	21	32	202	75	15	37	75
Nevada	1,911	98	49	11	25	13	155	47	21	40	47
New Hampshire	1,425	53	20	5	10	18	120	37	13	26	44
New Jersey	10,169	400	198	94	77	31	850	261	101	273	215
New Mexico	3,766	209	115	18	36	40	356	72	39	82	164
New York	43,463	1,410	725	265	295	126	2,576	611	291	991	683
North Carolina	10,067	617	334	75	116	93	816	218	110	206	283
North Dakota	1,203	69	25	8	10	27	133	20	21	25	67
Ohio	13,233	628	300	122	136	70	97	4	18	-	75
Oklahoma	4,726	337	169	45	60	64	514	109	66	118	221
Oregon	4,716	405	108	45	58	193	359	98	53	76	131
Pennsylvania	16,655	665	300	161	120	84	1,240	340	160	436	304
Rhode Island	1,855	61	31	7	14	9	20	1	2	-	18
South Carolina	4,914	330	189	32	57	52	109	5	26	-	78
South Dakota	1,376	83	31	11	14	28	71	1	3	-	67
Tennessee	8,153	413	219	39	91	64	548	173	59	139	177
Texas	24,353	1,877	1,103	190	449	135	2,685	599	307	831	948
Utah	2,337	164	80	20	31	33	247	74	34	41	98
Vermont	1,185	59	18	12	11	19	119	23	22	25	49
Virginia	6,200	280	142	4	69	65	679	175	49	153	302
Washington	7,474	428	190	40	99	100	529	144	83	123	179
West Virginia	3,301	160	74	12	29	44	217	56	26	83	53
Wisconsin	6,773	316	139	46	58	74	620	156	81	147	236
Wyoming	1,420	42	15	6	7	13	104	20	22	23	39
Island areas:	5,715	1,916	209	1,467	193	47	572	98	39	236	199
American Samoa	131	22	9	6	6	-	19	5	1	-	13
Micronesia	122	2	-	-	-	2	8	4	1	-	3
Guam	230	19	6	3	7	-	34	15	1	-	18
Marshall Islands	58	-	-	-	-	-	3	1	1	-	1
Northern Marianas	87	14	4	8	-	2	16	4	-	-	12
Palau	47	-	-	-	-	-	3	1	-	-	2
Puerto Rico	4,695	1,744	176	1,360	175	34	484	68	35	236	145
Virgin Islands	345	115	14	90	5	6	5	-	-	-	5
Undistributed amounts	907	24	-	-	-	-	-	-	-	-	-

See footnote at end of table.

[In millions of dollars (4,623 represents $4,623,000,000). For fiscal year ending September 30]

State and island area	FEMA total [4]	Department of Housing and Urban Development						Department of Labor			
		Total	Community development block grants	Public housing programs				State unemployment insurance and employment Total	Workforce service	investment	Other
				Low rent housing assistance	Housing certificate program	Capital program	Other				
United States total. . . .	4,623	39,379	5,575	3,461	20,950	3,654	5,740	8,018	2,709	3,417	1,892
Alabama	50	512	72	112	191	82	54	124	34	64	27
Alaska	5	212	19	8	34	5	145	66	24	27	16
Arizona	11	499	79	15	174	10	221	118	34	55	30
Arkansas.	36	260	35	25	144	28	28	72	24	32	16
California.	530	4,467	582	114	3,017	115	639	1,126	390	572	164
Colorado	15	476	51	14	342	13	55	89	42	27	20
Connecticut	9	665	52	55	440	47	72	97	51	27	19
Delaware.	4	105	10	9	57	8	20	20	9	8	4
District of Columbia. . . .	3	739	57	-91	186	501	87	275	129	27	118
Florida	164	1,441	208	95	808	81	249	245	78	119	48
Georgia	23	916	119	112	479	100	105	158	48	85	25
Hawaii	3	183	27	11	98	29	18	51	15	18	18
Idaho	2	88	18	1	52	1	17	40	20	10	10
Illinois.	14	2,009	199	253	1,050	250	257	348	130	172	46
Indiana	15	572	88	40	339	35	70	99	38	37	24
Iowa.	12	243	51	5	140	11	36	58	24	12	22
Kansas	14	220	48	14	113	18	28	55	19	17	20
Kentucky	34	485	67	46	252	60	61	105	27	43	34
Louisiana	153	572	91	63	253	85	80	120	29	78	13
Maine	5	205	25	8	132	9	31	42	14	13	15
Maryland	20	772	80	74	434	50	134	192	56	55	81
Massachusetts	27	1,807	153	100	1,289	88	177	155	82	45	28
Michigan	10	952	158	47	534	53	159	278	106	109	63
Minnesota	35	621	79	38	363	46	94	113	48	31	34
Mississippi.	24	308	61	27	155	30	36	81	19	50	12
Missouri	35	719	117	39	323	132	108	110	38	45	27
Montana	3	110	15	4	45	4	41	28	9	12	7
Nebraska	7	161	31	10	80	13	27	25	12	6	7
Nevada	2	185	22	16	111	7	29	48	26	15	7
New Hampshire	6	166	15	6	124	7	14	28	14	9	5
New Jersey	37	1,502	132	155	913	127	175	158	101	38	19
New Mexico.	10	192	39	9	90	11	43	64	16	32	16
New York	2,443	5,392	1,155	819	2,274	521	622	561	165	236	160
North Carolina	116	792	82	96	411	78	125	193	68	46	80
North Dakota	15	89	12	3	44	2	27	19	7	9	3
Ohio.	31	1,552	227	157	816	129	223	286	89	149	49
Oklahoma	34	463	51	24	188	23	177	72	21	33	18
Oregon	30	351	40	15	221	14	62	125	42	56	28
Pennsylvania	22	1,803	268	244	818	225	248	348	137	133	79
Rhode Island	4	295	28	21	191	20	35	33	16	11	5
South Carolina	9	368	51	31	206	29	52	90	32	37	21
South Dakota	6	124	24	2	53	2	42	29	6	11	12
Tennessee	13	614	59	92	282	81	100	136	36	62	38
Texas	228	1,821	306	113	1,048	137	218	465	122	248	94
Utah.	7	132	25	4	78	4	21	55	31	11	13
Vermont	3	104	17	3	66	3	15	23	8	9	7
Virginia	16	683	78	62	402	39	102	257	37	50	170
Washington	30	687	66	35	367	49	170	248	81	116	50
West Virginia	21	222	50	15	116	13	26	60	15	38	7
Wisconsin	13	508	98	17	278	23	92	147	65	40	42
Wyoming	6	40	5	1	23	1	9	19	7	9	3
Island areas:	100	744	134	119	302	129	59	261	20	223	17
American Samoa. . . .	-	1	1	-	-	-	-	1	-	-	1
Micronesia	6	-	-	-	-	-	-	1	-	-	-
Guam	28	37	3	3	28	2	1	3	-	1	-
Marshall Islands	-	-	-	-	-	-	-	1	-	1	-
Northern Marianas. . .	2	2	-	-	2	-	-	2	-	-	2
Palau	-	-	-	-	-	-	-	-	-	-	-
Puerto Rico	55	654	128	95	256	119	56	247	18	217	11
Virgin Islands	9	51	3	21	16	9	2	6	2	2	2
Undistributed amounts	158	233	-	155	1	78	-	2	-	-	2

See footnote at end of table.

[In millions of dollars (221,042 represents $221,042,000,000). For fiscal year ending September 30]

State and island area	Department of Health and Human Services						Department of Transportation				Other [5] federal aid
		Administration for children			Centers for Medicare and Medicaid Services						
	Total	Tempo-rary assis-tance to needy families	Chil-dren & family ser-vices (Head Start)	Foster care and adop-tion assis-tance		Other	Total	High-way trust fund	Federal transit admin-istration	Other	
United States total. . . .	221,042	19,137	8,121	6,118	164,297	23,369	38,914	28,614	5,841	4,459	22,280
Alabama	3,332	149	131	34	2,682	335	693	530	39	124	338
Alaska	833	71	55	15	535	157	643	381	35	227	401
Arizona.	4,230	324	171	71	3,258	406	604	469	41	94	474
Arkansas.	2,254	27	85	37	1,903	202	506	392	22	93	157
California.	26,780	4,131	988	1,421	17,643	2,597	4,350	2,727	1,276	348	1,891
Colorado.	2,122	156	132	78	1,417	339	511	401	38	72	365
Connecticut	2,549	260	66	48	1,908	267	482	387	80	15	199
Delaware.	530	30	16	11	401	72	127	97	16	14	76
District of Columbia. . . .	1,456	122	99	69	833	335	407	152	189	66	587
Florida	9,969	718	320	153	7,475	1,303	2,030	1,650	199	181	784
Georgia	5,652	320	212	70	4,401	649	962	778	113	71	457
Hawaii	730	77	36	25	495	96	154	115	6	33	105
Idaho	826	38	40	10	635	104	276	209	7	61	163
Illinois.	7,400	506	332	406	5,216	940	1,367	869	406	93	713
Indiana	3,709	215	120	74	2,923	376	736	615	53	68	317
Iowa.	1,912	125	70	45	1,473	200	421	345	21	55	229
Kansas	1,577	97	83	38	1,184	174	401	358	13	30	185
Kentucky.	3,553	153	145	79	2,857	320	642	509	39	95	302
Louisiana	4,222	283	166	67	3,344	361	645	514	71	59	280
Maine.	1,519	77	41	39	1,259	104	213	181	13	20	166
Maryland.	3,497	229	100	158	2,560	450	678	425	147	105	371
Massachusetts	5,579	484	151	116	4,222	607	739	497	164	78	472
Michigan	6,994	685	292	241	4,850	925	950	776	65	108	601
Minnesota	3,567	355	112	97	2,589	415	558	367	105	85	373
Mississippi.	3,021	131	187	15	2,443	245	466	364	22	80	262
Missouri	4,521	212	152	83	3,645	429	886	725	75	86	394
Montana	675	52	44	18	459	102	66	1	7	58	263
Nebraska	1,160	53	49	27	892	139	257	222	8	27	132
Nevada.	878	57	36	23	629	134	286	180	26	80	259
New Hampshire	715	41	21	17	542	94	185	140	6	39	151
New Jersey	5,711	544	160	84	4,228	695	978	720	212	46	531
New Mexico.	2,004	104	81	26	1,599	193	311	261	16	33	619
New York	27,695	3,491	517	757	20,831	2,099	2,199	1,250	787	161	1,185
North Carolina	6,054	331	203	71	4,824	625	988	815	79	94	489
North Dakota	491	26	35	14	343	73	213	182	6	24	174
Ohio.	8,872	805	304	378	6,551	835	1,186	918	171	97	579
Oklahoma	2,502	199	124	53	1,828	297	493	398	20	75	310
Oregon	2,431	174	108	59	1,808	282	628	378	55	195	386
Pennsylvania	10,046	837	282	394	7,561	972	1,824	1,347	329	148	705
Rhode Island	1,147	104	33	21	894	95	175	142	13	21	120
South Carolina	3,228	109	106	43	2,667	303	508	438	29	40	271
South Dakota.	557	22	43	9	391	93	252	204	4	44	253
Tennessee.	5,256	209	144	40	4,450	413	672	532	53	87	500
Texas	13,198	631	614	209	10,306	1,439	3,076	2,595	264	216	1,002
Utah.	1,193	103	56	27	853	154	287	215	39	33	251
Vermont	655	50	24	19	495	67	124	108	11	6	97
Virginia	2,957	188	187	107	2,020	455	850	697	83	71	477
Washington	4,124	440	165	87	2,953	479	854	554	179	121	572
West Virginia	1,919	128	67	38	1,510	176	462	328	23	111	240
Wisconsin	4,072	364	127	96	3,032	453	686	579	42	65	410
Wyoming	328	29	24	3	223	49	282	233	3	45	600
Island areas:	830	70	260	-	256	243	272	92	121	59	932
American Samoa. . . .	15	-	4	-	4	7	25	6	-	19	48
Micronesia	1	-	-	-	-	1	-	-	-	-	104
Guam	29	4	4	-	10	11	21	14	-	7	59
Marshall Islands	-	-	-	-	-	-	-	-	-	-	54
Northern Marianas. . .	6	-	-	-	3	3	12	2	-	11	32
Palau	-	-	-	-	-	-	-	-	-	-	43
Puerto Rico	735	64	240	-	231	201	192	59	120	13	499
Virgin Islands	43	3	12	-	8	20	22	12	1	10	93
Undistributed amounts	11	-	5	-	-	7	353	249	-	104	112

- Represents or rounds to zero   [1] Includes programs not shown separately.   [2] Includes "special milk program."   [3] For Puerto Rico, amount shown is for nutritional assistance grant program, all other amounts are grant payments for food stamp administration.   [4] FEMA = Federal Emergency Management Agency. FEMA is part of Department of Homeland Security.   [5] Represents aid for other programs not shown.

Source: U.S. Census Bureau, Federal Aid to States for Fiscal Year 2003 (issued September 2004). See also <http://www.census.gov/prod/2004pubs/fas03.pdf>.

Table 424. **State and Local Government Current Receipts and Expenditures in the National Income and Product Accounts: 1990 to 2004**

[In billions of dollars (737.8 represents $737,800,000,000). For explanation of national income, see text, Section 13. A comprehensive National Income and Product Accounts (NIPA) revision released on December 10, 2003. For more information on this revision of the National Income and Product Accounts, go to <http://www.bea.doc.gov/bea/dn/2003benchmark/CR2003content.html>. Minus sign(-) indicates a deficit.]

Item	1990	1995	1998	1999	2000	2001	2002	2003	2004
Current receipts............	737.8	990.2	1,163.2	1,236.7	1,319.5	1,373.0	1,411.9	1,494.9	1,585.3
Current tax receipts	519.1	672.1	794.9	840.4	893.2	915.8	926.5	969.2	1,039.2
Personal current taxes.........	122.6	158.1	201.2	214.5	236.6	242.7	220.1	226.1	248.0
Income taxes	109.6	141.7	183.0	195.5	217.3	223.1	199.6	204.6	225.1
Other	13.0	16.4	18.2	19.0	19.4	19.6	20.5	21.6	22.9
Taxes on production and imports . . .	374.1	482.4	558.8	590.2	621.1	642.8	675.3	708.7	751.0
Sales taxes	184.3	242.7	283.9	301.6	316.6	321.1	329.1	343.9	364.4
Property taxes	161.5	202.6	231.0	242.8	254.6	269.3	291.5	305.0	321.6
Other	28.3	37.0	43.9	45.8	49.9	52.4	54.7	59.7	65.0
Taxes on corporate income......	22.5	31.7	34.9	35.8	35.5	30.2	31.2	34.4	40.2
Contributions for government social insurance	10.0	13.6	10.4	9.8	11.0	13.6	14.5	15.0	16.5
Income receipts on assets	68.4	68.4	80.9	85.3	92.2	88.8	81.6	81.0	83.2
Interest receipts	64.1	62.9	74.6	78.4	84.0	80.3	73.2	71.3	72.3
Dividends	0.2	1.0	1.7	1.8	1.9	2.0	2.1	2.5	2.8
Rents and royalties	4.2	4.5	4.6	5.1	6.3	6.5	6.2	7.1	8.1
Current transfer receipts	133.5	224.1	266.8	290.8	315.4	350.8	385.9	425.9	443.8
Federal grants-in-aid	111.4	184.1	212.8	232.9	247.3	276.1	304.4	339.9	350.4
From business (net)	7.1	13.5	22.1	23.0	28.8	31.4	32.8	32.2	33.9
From persons.	14.9	26.5	31.9	34.9	39.2	43.3	48.7	53.8	59.6
Current surplus of government enterprises	6.7	12.0	10.2	†0.4	7.7	4.0	3.3	3.7	2.6
Current expenditures	730.5	978.2	1,111.2	1,186.3	1,269.5	1,368.2	1,436.9	1,498.1	1,567.8
Consumption expenditures.........	544.6	696.1	801.4	858.9	917.8	969.8	1,016.5	1,058.5	1,099.7
Government social benefit payments to persons.	127.7	217.6	235.8	252.4	271.7	305.2	331.9	350.3	374.7
Interest payments.	57.9	64.2	73.6	74.6	79.5	85.5	87.4	88.9	92.6
Subsidies	0.4	0.3	0.4	0.4	0.5	7.7	1.0	0.3	0.7
Net state and local government	7.2	12.0	52.0	50.4	50.0	4.8	-25.0	-3.2	17.6
Social insurance funds	2.0	4.0	1.7	1.7	2.0	2.6	1.6	1.1	1.4
Other....................	5.3	8.0	50.3	48.7	47.9	2.2	-26.6	-4.3	16.2

Source: U.S. Bureau of Economic Analysis, *National Income and Product Accounts, 1929-2004*; and *Survey of Current Business*, May 2005. See also <http://www.bea.doc.gov/bea/dn/nipaweb/selecttable.asp>released 28 April 2005).

Table 425. **State and Local Government Consumption Expenditures and Social Benefits in the National Income and Product Accounts: 1990 to 2004**

[In billions of dollars (671.9 represents $671,900,000,000). For explanation of national income, see text, Section 13. A comprehensive National Income and Product Accounts (NIPA) revision released on December 10, 2003. For more information on this revision of the National Income and Product Accounts, go to <http://www.bea.doc.gov/bea/dn/2003benchmark/CR2003content.htm>.]

Expenditure	1990	1995	1998	1999	2000	2001	2002	2003	2004
Consumption expenditures	671.9	850.0	987.9	1,065.0	1,142.8	1,212.8	1,275.8	1,323.3	1,373.9
Consumption expenditures [1].......	544.6	696.1	801.4	858.9	917.8	969.8	1,016.5	1,058.5	1,099.7
Gross investment [2]	127.2	154.0	186.5	206.0	225.0	243.0	259.3	264.9	274.3
Structures	98.5	117.3	143.6	159.7	176.0	192.4	208.2	213.4	221.8
Equipment and software	28.7	36.7	43.0	46.4	49.0	50.6	51.0	51.5	52.4
Government social benefit payments to persons	127.7	217.6	235.8	252.4	271.7	305.2	331.9	350.3	(NA)
Benefits from social insurance funds .	9.2	10.7	10.4	10.6	11.5	12.7	13.9	14.9	(NA)
Temporary disability insurance	2.2	2.1	2.1	2.2	2.8	3.3	3.6	3.9	(NA)
Workers' compensation.	7.0	8.6	8.3	8.4	8.7	9.4	10.3	11.0	(NA)
Public assistance	111.1	195.8	212.9	228.3	245.4	275.9	300.1	317.0	(NA)
Medical care	78.2	155.0	175.3	189.3	205.0	234.6	258.7	274.0	(NA)
Medicaid.	73.1	149.6	170.2	184.6	199.5	227.3	250.1	264.6	(NA)
Other medical care [3].........	5.0	5.4	5.1	4.7	5.5	7.4	8.6	9.5	(NA)
Family assistance [4]	19.2	22.6	17.4	17.9	18.4	18.1	17.7	18.3	(NA)
Supplemental security income	3.8	3.8	3.9	4.2	4.4	4.5	4.8	5.0	(NA)
General assistance	2.9	3.6	3.5	3.6	3.6	3.0	3.5	3.4	(NA)
Energy assistance	1.6	1.4	1.2	1.4	1.7	2.5	1.9	2.3	(NA)
Other [5]	5.4	9.4	11.4	11.9	12.3	13.2	13.6	13.9	(NA)
Education	5.3	8.7	9.8	10.5	11.6	13.1	14.1	14.8	(NA)
Employment and training	0.9	1.1	1.1	1.1	1.0	1.4	1.7	1.8	(NA)
Other [6]	1.1	1.3	1.6	1.8	2.1	2.1	2.1	1.9	(NA)

NA Not available. [1] Government consumption expenditures are services (such as education and national defense) produced by government that are valued at their cost of production. Excludes government sales to other sectors and government own-account investment (construction and software). [2] Gross government investment consists of general government and government enterprise expenditures for fixed assets; inventory investment is included in in government consumption expenditures. [3] Consists of general medical assistance and state child health care programs. [4] Consists of aid to families with dependent children and, beginning with 1996, assistance programs operating under the Personal Responsibility and Work Opportunity Reconciliation Act of 1996. [5] Consists of expenditures for food under the supplemental program for women, infants,and children; foster care; adoption assistance; and payments to nonprofit welfare institutions. [6] Consists largely of veterans benefits, Alaska dividends, and crime-victim payments.

Source: U.S. Bureau of Economic Analysis, *National Income and Product Accounts 1929-2004; and Survey of Current Business*, May 2005 <http://www.bea.gov/bea/dn/nipaweb/selecttable.asp?selected=N.> (released April 8, 2005).

State and Local Government Finances and Employment **279**

Table 426. State and Local Governments—Summary of Finances: 1990 to 2002

[In millions of dollars (1,032,115 represents $1,032,115,000,000), except as indicated. For fiscal year ending in year shown; see text, this section. Local government amounts are estimates subject to sampling variation; see Appendix III and source. Minus sign (-) indicates net loss]

Item	Total (mil. dol.)				Per capita [1] (dol.)			
	1990	2000	2001	2002	1990	2000	2001	2002
Revenue [2]	1,032,115	1,942,328	1,890,891	1,807,573	4,150	6,902	6,627	6,277
From federal government	136,802	291,950	324,033	360,534	550	1,037	1,136	1,252
Public welfare	59,961	148,549	167,823	183,868	241	528	588	638
Highways	14,368	24,414	28,702	30,382	58	87	101	106
Education	23,233	45,873	49,945	55,997	93	163	175	194
Health and hospitals	5,904	15,611	17,839	19,678	24	55	63	68
Housing and community development	9,655	17,690	18,541	22,628	39	63	65	79
Other and unallocable	23,683	39,812	41,184	47,981	95	141	144	167
From state and local sources	895,313	1,650,379	1,566,858	1,447,039	3,600	5,864	5,492	5,025
General, net intergovernmental	712,700	1,249,373	1,323,128	1,324,241	2,865	4,439	4,637	4,598
Taxes	501,619	872,351	914,119	904,971	2,017	3,100	3,204	3,143
Property	155,613	249,178	263,689	279,122	626	885	924	969
Sales and gross receipts	177,885	309,290	320,217	324,040	715	1,099	1,122	1,125
Individual income	105,640	211,661	226,334	202,858	425	752	793	704
Corporation income	23,566	36,059	35,296	28,152	95	128	124	98
Other	38,915	66,164	68,583	70,800	156	235	240	246
Charges and miscellaneous	211,081	377,022	409,009	419,270	849	1,340	1,434	1,456
Utility and liquor stores	58,642	89,546	100,460	107,387	236	318	352	373
Water supply system	17,674	30,515	30,794	33,207	71	108	108	115
Electric power system	29,268	42,436	50,952	54,404	118	151	179	189
Gas supply system	5,216	8,049	8,764	8,950	21	29	31	31
Transit system	3,043	3,954	5,096	5,762	12	14	18	20
Liquor stores	3,441	4,592	4,854	5,065	14	16	17	18
Insurance trust revenue [3]	123,970	311,460	143,271	15,410	498	1,107	502	54
Employee retirement	94,268	273,881	102,692	-29,261	379	973	360	-102
Unemployment compensation	18,441	23,366	23,341	27,086	74	83	82	94
Direct expenditure	972,695	1,742,914	1,894,847	2,044,331	3,911	6,193	6,641	7,099
By function:								
Direct general expenditure [3]	831,573	1,502,768	1,621,760	1,730,809	3,356	5,340	5,684	6,010
Education [3]	288,148	521,612	563,575	594,591	1,159	1,853	1,975	2,065
Elementary and secondary	202,009	365,181	392,278	411,073	812	1,298	1,375	1,427
Higher education	73,418	134,352	146,158	156,810	295	477	512	545
Highways	61,057	101,336	107,235	115,467	245	360	376	401
Public welfare	107,287	233,350	257,380	279,598	444	829	902	971
Health	24,223	51,366	53,465	59,132	97	183	187	205
Hospitals	50,412	75,976	80,545	87,247	203	270	282	303
Police protection	30,577	56,798	59,584	64,492	123	202	209	224
Fire protection	13,186	23,102	24,970	25,978	53	82	88	90
Correction	24,635	48,805	52,370	54,687	100	173	184	190
Natural resources	12,330	20,235	22,163	22,000	50	72	78	76
Sanitation and sewerage	28,453	45,261	46,718	50,286	114	161	164	175
Housing and community development	15,479	26,590	27,402	31,610	62	94	96	110
Parks and recreation	14,326	25,038	27,920	30,096	58	89	98	105
Financial administration	16,217	29,300	30,007	32,653	65	104	105	113
Interest on general debt [4]	49,739	69,814	73,836	75,233	200	248	259	261
Utility and liquor stores [4]	77,801	114,916	133,544	143,851	313	408	468	500
Water supply system	22,101	35,789	36,757	40,527	89	127	129	141
Electric power system	30,997	39,719	54,921	55,952	125	141	192	194
Gas supply system	2,989	3,724	5,023	5,720	12	13	18	20
Transit system	18,788	31,883	32,875	37,468	76	113	115	130
Liquor stores	2,926	3,801	3,968	4,183	12	14	14	15
Insurance trust expenditure [3]	63,321	125,230	139,543	169,672	255	445	489	589
Employee retirement	38,355	95,679	104,414	114,208	154	340	366	397
Unemployment compensation	16,499	18,648	22,986	42,166	66	66	81	146
By character and object:								
Current operation	700,131	1,288,746	1,405,033	1,497,216	2,815	4,579	4,924	5,199
Capital outlay	123,102	217,063	233,258	257,214	495	771	818	893
Construction	89,144	161,694	177,094	197,629	358	575	621	686
Equipment, land, and existing structures	33,958	55,369	56,164	59,585	137	197	197	207
Assistance and subsidies	27,227	31,375	32,583	33,282	109	111	114	116
Interest on debt (general and utility)	58,914	80,499	84,431	86,948	237	286	296	302
Insurance benefits and repayments	63,321	125,230	139,543	169,672	255	445	489	589
Expenditure for salaries and wages [5]	*340,654*	*548,796*	*587,124*	*610,879*	*1,372*	*1,950*	*2,058*	*2,121*
Debt outstanding, year end	858,006	1,451,815	1,554,018	1,686,106	3,460	5,159	5,447	5,855
Long-term	838,700	1,427,524	1,531,897	1,642,864	3,382	5,073	5,369	5,705
Short-term	19,306	24,291	22,121	43,242	78	86	78	150
Long-term debt:								
Issued	108,468	184,831	199,576	262,339	436	657	699	911
Retired	64,831	121,897	130,574	162,463	261	433	458	564

[1] 1990 and 2000 based on enumerated resident population as of April 1. Other years based on estimated resident population as of July 1; see Table 17. [2] Aggregates exclude duplicative transactions between state and local governments; see source. [3] Includes amounts not shown separately. [4] Interest on utility debt included in "utility expenditure." For total interest on debt, see "Interest on debt (general and utility)." [5] Included in items above.

Source: U.S. Census Bureau, *Government Finances,* 2001-02. See also <http://www.census.gov/govs/www/estimate02.html> (accessed 8 April 2005).

Table 427. **State and Local Governments—Revenue and Expenditures by Function: 2002**

[In millions of dollars (1,807,573 represents $1,807,573,000,000) except as indicated. For fiscal year ending in year shown; see text, this section. Local government amounts are estimates subject to sampling variation; see Appendix III and source. Minsus sign (-) indicated net loss]

Item	Amount (mil. dol.)			Per capita [1] (dol.)		
	State and local	State	Local	State and local	State	Local
Revenue [2]	1,807,573	1,097,829	1,083,129	6,277	3,820	3,761
Intergovernmental revenue [2]	360,534	335,423	398,497	1,252	1,167	1,384
Total revenue from own sources [2]	1,447,039	762,406	684,632	5,025	2,653	2,377
General revenue from own sources	1,324,241	726,882	597,359	4,598	2,529	2,074
Taxes [3]	904,971	535,241	369,730	3,143	1,862	1,284
Property	279,122	9,702	269,419	969	34	936
Individual income	202,858	185,697	17,162	704	646	60
Corporation income..............	28,152	25,123	3,029	98	87	11
Sales and gross receipts	324,040	262,361	61,679	1,125	913	214
General	222,987	179,665	43,321	774	625	150
Selective [3]	101,053	82,695	18,358	351	288	64
Motor fuel.................	33,044	31,968	1,076	115	111	4
Alcoholic beverages	4,600	4,249	351	16	15	1
Tobacco products.............	9,093	8,902	191	32	31	1
Public utilities	20,294	10,288	10,006	70	36	35
Motor vehicle and operators' licenses...	18,364	17,060	1,304	64	59	5
Death and gift	7,510	7,384	126	26	26	-
Charges and miscellaneous [3]	419,270	191,641	227,629	1,456	667	790
Current charges [3]	253,193	99,811	153,382	879	347	533
Education [3]	72,401	55,166	17,235	251	192	60
School lunch sales...........	5,956	19	5,937	21	-	21
Higher education	61,429	54,552	6,877	213	190	24
Natural resources	2,966	2,115	850	10	7	3
Hospitals	65,645	24,144	41,502	228	84	144
Sewerage	27,089	34	27,056	94	-	94
Solid waste management	11,190	370	10,820	39	1	38
Parks and recreation	7,019	1,199	5,820	24	4	20
Housing and community development................	4,296	529	3,766	2	13	13
Airports...................	12,331	792	11,539	43	3	40
Sea and inland port facilities	2,685	736	1,949	9	3	7
Highways.................	8,369	5,262	3,106	29	18	11
Interest earnings...............	67,078	31,867	35,211	233	111	122
Special assessments.............	4,779	119	4,661	17	-	16
Sale of property	2,350	1,002	1,348	8	3	5
Utility and liquor store revenue...........	107,387	16,223	91,164	373	56	317
Insurance trust revenue	15,410	19,301	-3,891	54	67	-14
Expenditure [2]..................	**2,048,719**	**1,280,290**	**1,140,082**	**7,114**	**4,455**	**3,959**
Intergovernmental expenditure [2]	4,387	364,789	11,252	15	1,269	39
Direct expenditure [2]	2,044,331	915,501	1,128,830	7,099	3,185	3,920
General expenditure [3]	1,730,809	744,438	986,371	6,010	2,590	3,425
Education [3]	594,591	162,054	432,537	2,065	564	1,502
Elementary and secondary education...	411,073	4,065	407,008	1,427	14	1,413
Higher education	156,810	131,282	25,529	545	457	89
Public welfare	279,598	239,903	39,695	971	835	138
Hospitals	87,247	36,965	50,282	303	129	175
Health	59,132	29,837	29,295	205	104	102
Highways....................	115,467	71,248	44,219	401	248	154
Police protection	64,492	9,408	55,084	224	33	191
Fire protection	25,978	-	25,978	90	-	90
Corrections....................	54,687	36,472	18,215	190	127	63
Natural resources................	22,000	16,588	5,412	76	58	19
Sewerage....................	31,238	1,050	30,189	108	4	105
Solid waste management	19,047	2,736	16,311	66	10	57
Housing and community development	31,610	3,783	27,827	110	13	97
Governmental administration	92,789	39,912	52,878	322	139	184
Parks and recreation	30,096	4,953	25,143	105	17	87
Interest on general debt	75,303	31,426	43,876	261	109	152
Utility......................	139,668	20,279	119,389	485	71	415
Liquor store expenditure............	4,183	3,498	685	15	12	2
Insurance trust expenditure	169,672	147,286	22,386	589	512	78
By character and object:						
Current operation.................	1,497,216	620,763	876,454	5,199	2,160	3,044
Capital outlay	257,214	89,919	167,295	893	313	581
Construction	197,629	71,035	126,594	686	247	440
Equip., land, and existing structures....	59,585	18,884	40,700	207	66	141
Assistance and subsidies	33,282	24,313	8,968	116	85	31
Interest on debt (general and utility)	86,948	33,220	53,728	302	116	187
Insurance benefits and repayments......	169,672	147,286	22,386	589	512	78
Expenditure for salaries and wages [4]	610,879	169,046	441,833	2,121	588	1,534

- Represents or rounds to zero. [1] Based on estimated resident population as of July 1. [2] Aggregates exclude duplicative transactions between levels of government; see source. [3] Includes amounts not shown separately. [4] Included in items shown above.

Source: U.S. Census Bureau, *Government Finances*, 2001-02. See also <http://www.census.gov/govs/www/estimate02.html> (accessed 28 April 2005).

Table 428. **State and Local Governments—Capital Outlays: 1990 to 2002**

[In millions of dollars (123,102 represents $123,102,000,000), except percent. For fiscal year ending in year shown; see text, this section. Local government amounts are subject to sampling variation; see Appendix III and source]

Level and function	1990	1995	1997	1998	1999	2000	2001	2002
State & local governments: Total	123,102	151,440	171,414	181,871	198,483	217,063	233,258	257,214
Annual percent change [1]	4.9	10.1	7.9	6.1	9.1	9.4	7.5	10.3
Percent of direct expenditure	12.7	11.2	11.8	11.9	12.2	12.5	12.3	12.6
Direct expenditure	972,695	1,347,763	1,456,698	1,525,762	1,622,103	1,742,914	1,894,847	2,044,331
By function:								
Education [2]	25,997	35,708	44,077	49,332	54,418	60,968	65,116	71,533
Elementary and secondary	18,057	24,808	32,210	36,198	40,768	45,150	48,404	53,151
Higher education	7,441	10,461	11,279	12,590	13,114	15,257	15,911	17,648
Highways	33,867	42,561	44,962	48,067	51,906	56,439	60,108	66,170
Health and hospitals	3,848	4,883	5,065	5,692	5,699	5,502	5,630	6,136
Natural resources	2,545	2,891	3,041	3,206	3,359	4,347	4,908	4,247
Housing [3]	3,997	4,527	5,490	5,544	5,615	6,184	5,888	6,939
Air transportation	3,434	3,802	4,877	5,004	6,666	6,717	8,420	8,551
Water transportation [4]	924	1,101	1,376	1,252	1,487	1,618	4,306	1,691
Sewerage	8,356	8,894	9,589	9,061	9,718	10,093	9,224	11,574
Parks and recreation	3,877	4,085	5,577	6,154	6,486	6,916	8,540	9,093
Utilities	16,601	19,028	20,107	20,357	21,861	24,847	24,553	30,228
Water	6,873	7,466	8,721	8,644	10,325	10,542	10,742	11,818
Electric	3,976	3,715	3,459	3,026	3,613	4,177	4,812	6,538
Transit	310	340	399	986	389	400	453	358
Gas	5,443	7,507	7,528	7,701	7,533	9,728	8,545	11,514
Other	19,657	23,961	27,254	28,202	31,268	33,431	36,566	41,053
State governments: Total	45,524	57,829	59,599	64,441	68,509	76,233	81,881	89,919
Annual percent change [1]	5.6	9.3	1.1	8.1	6.3	11.3	7.4	9.8
Direct expenditure	397,291	596,325	629,049	651,098	693,432	757,027	835,782	915,501
Percent of direct expenditure	11.5	9.7	9.5	9.9	9.9	10.1	9.8	9.8
By function:								
Education [2]	7,253	10,042	10,915	11,970	12,294	14,077	14,936	16,589
Highways	24,850	31,687	32,726	35,008	37,986	41,651	44,761	49,272
Health and hospitals	1,531	2,402	2,253	2,274	2,276	2,228	2,390	2,240
Natural resources	1,593	1,956	2,058	2,199	2,349	2,758	3,105	2,766
Housing [3]	119	187	225	202	202	860	600	582
Air transportation	339	356	446	339	536	561	667	525
Water transportation [4]	202	223	269	305	270	310	362	346
Sewerage	333	853	474	639	627	403	393	405
Parks and recreation	601	650	938	1,293	1,023	1,044	1,185	1,483
Utilities	2,605	2,226	2,361	2,758	3,034	4,232	3,641	5,145
Other	6,098	7,246	6,934	7,454	7,912	8,108	9,840	10,567
Local governments: Total	77,578	93,611	111,814	117,430	129,974	140,830	151,377	167,295
Annual percent change [1]	4.5	10.6	11.8	5.0	10.7	8.4	7.5	10.5
Direct expenditure	575,404	751,438	827,648	874,664	928,671	985,886	1,059,065	1,128,830
Percent of direct expenditure	13.5	12.5	13.5	13.4	14.0	14.3	14.3	14.8
By function:								
Education [2]	18,744	29,858	33,162	37,362	42,124	46,890	50,180	54,944
Elementary and secondary	17,669	28,402	31,670	35,763	40,160	44,629	47,808	52,661
Higher education	1,076	1,456	1,492	1,600	1,964	2,261	2,372	2,283
Highways	9,017	10,874	12,235	13,059	13,920	14,789	15,347	16,898
Health and hospitals	2,316	2,481	2,811	3,418	3,423	3,274	3,239	3,895
Natural resources	952	935	983	1,007	1,010	1,589	1,803	1,481
Housing [3]	3,878	4,340	5,265	5,342	5,413	5,324	5,288	6,357
Air transportation	3,095	3,446	4,431	4,665	6,129	6,156	7,753	8,026
Water transportation [4]	722	877	1,107	947	1,217	1,308	3,944	1,345
Sewerage	8,023	8,040	9,116	8,422	9,091	9,690	8,831	11,169
Parks and recreation	3,276	3,435	4,639	4,861	5,463	5,872	7,355	7,611
Utilities	13,996	16,801	17,746	17,599	18,827	20,615	20,912	25,083
Other	13,559	16,715	20,320	20,748	23,356	25,323	26,726	30,486

[1] Change from immediate/prior year except 1990, change from 1989.   [2] Includes other education.   [3] Includes community development.   [4] Includes terminals.

Source: U.S. Census Bureau, 1990, *Government Finances*, Series GF, No. 5, annual; thereafter, <http://www.census.gov/govs/www /estimate02.html> (accessed 8 April 2005).

Table 429. **State and Local Governments—Expenditure for Public Works: 1995 to 2002**

[In millions of dollars (180,148 represents $180,148,000,000), except as noted. Public works includes expenditures on highways, airports, water transport terminals, and sewerage, solid waste management, water supply, and mass transit systems. Represents direct expenditures excluding intergovernmental grants]

Item	Total	High- ways	Airport transpor- tation	Water transport and ter- minals	Sewer- age	Solid waste manage- ment	Water supply	Mass transit
1995, Total	180,148	77,109	8,397	2,309	23,583	14,990	28,041	25,719
State	56,392	46,893	783	604	1,462	1,658	178	4,814
Local	123,756	30,216	7,614	1,706	22,121	13,331	27,863	20,904
Capital expenditures (percent)	40.7	55.2	45.3	47.7	37.7	13.2	26.6	29.2
2000, Total	230,569	101,336	13,160	3,141	28,052	17,208	35,789	31,883
State	74,974	61,942	1,106	863	955	2,347	354	7,407
Local	155,595	39,394	12,054	2,277	27,098	14,861	35,435	24,476
Capital expenditures (percent)	41.9	55.7	51.0	51.5	36.0	8.9	29.5	30.5
2002, Total	263,529	115,467	16,209	3,571	31,238	19,047	40,527	37,468
State	85,801	71,248	1,170	1,015	1,050	2,736	386	8,195
Local	177,728	44,219	15,039	2,556	30,189	16,311	40,141	29,273
Capital expenditures (percent)	42.9	57.3	52.8	47.3	37.1	8.4	29.2	30.7

Source: U.S. Census Bureau; *State and Local Government Finance Estimates by State*, annual, and unpublished data. <http://www.census.gov/govs/estimate/02.html>; (accessed 8 April 2005).

Table 430. **State and Local Governments—Revenue by State: 2002**

[In millions of dollars (1,807,573 represents $1,807,573,000,000). For fiscal year ending in year shown;see text, this section]

State	Total revenue [1]	General revenue Total	Intergov- ernmental from federal Govern- ment	General revenue own sources	Taxes Total [1]	Prop- erty	Sales and gross receipts	Indi- vidual in- come [2]	Motor vehicle	Other taxes
United States. .	1,807,573	1,684,776	360,534	1,324,241	904,971	279,122	324,040	231,010	16,944	53,856
Alabama.	24,740	23,741	6,263	17,478	9,719	1,474	4,800	2,449	207	789
Alaska	6,993	7,209	1,789	5,420	2,070	830	311	269	47	613
Arizona.	30,083	25,524	5,719	19,805	14,420	4,254	7,081	2,437	153	495
Arkansas	13,616	13,260	3,645	9,614	6,461	1,004	3,340	1,743	107	267
California	250,725	226,644	48,250	178,394	120,424	30,243	41,560	38,380	1,740	8,502
Colorado.	25,657	26,041	4,269	21,772	13,900	4,162	5,302	3,681	184	571
Connecticut.	24,831	22,805	4,039	18,766	15,125	5,995	4,516	3,835	241	538
Delaware	5,972	5,600	959	4,641	2,687	400	326	1,015	32	914
District of Columbia .	7,352	6,922	2,840	4,082	3,228	803	936	1,160	19	309
Florida	92,631	86,663	14,956	71,707	44,840	15,754	22,936	1,219	957	3,974
Georgia	46,166	44,360	9,357	35,002	24,058	6,640	9,395	7,056	269	699
Hawaii	7,452	7,429	1,547	5,881	4,240	615	2,244	1,164	133	83
Idaho	6,873	6,620	1,415	5,204	3,291	959	1,135	919	116	162
Illinois	73,588	69,098	12,717	56,382	41,570	15,873	13,876	8,855	1,458	1,508
Indiana. . . ,.	34,221	32,363	6,283	26,080	16,987	5,976	5,522	4,831	301	357
Iowa	17,601	16,871	3,626	13,245	8,330	2,878	2,886	1,903	378	285
Kansas.	15,985	14,635	3,098	11,537	7,975	2,525	3,066	1,977	145	262
Kentucky	22,475	21,231	5,414	15,817	10,781	1,977	3,942	3,798	214	849
Louisiana	27,373	26,048	6,485	19,563	12,182	1,940	6,949	2,053	118	1,121
Maine.	8,019	8,077	1,901	6,176	4,541	1,912	1,242	1,150	105	132
Maryland	33,468	32,319	5,927	26,391	19,874	5,412	4,974	8,004	200	1,285
Massachusetts.	41,925	39,002	6,176	32,826	23,895	8,722	5,363	8,725	270	815
Michigan.	63,099	57,942	12,543	45,398	30,644	9,793	10,238	8,663	891	1,059
Minnesota.	35,131	33,193	6,088	27,105	18,456	5,215	5,918	5,977	497	850
Mississippi	15,905	15,293	4,625	10,667	6,524	1,647	3,255	1,181	112	329
Missouri	30,621	29,062	7,329	21,733	15,123	3,880	6,044	4,229	249	721
Montana	5,511	5,122	1,590	3,532	2,135	852	374	586	127	196
Nebraska	12,031	9,821	1,973	7,848	5,316	1,749	1,819	1,261	104	383
Nevada	12,809	11,417	1,632	9,785	6,433	1,702	3,840	-	130	761
New Hampshire	6,729	6,406	1,296	5,110	3,599	2,169	605	449	77	299
New Jersey.	54,835	55,256	8,949	46,307	34,629	16,050	8,804	7,969	372	1,435
New Mexico	11,503	10,868	3,124	7,744	4,878	756	2,319	1,107	119	576
New York	170,982	155,541	36,186	119,356	88,878	26,826	22,491	35,283	808	3,471
North Carolina	48,597	44,165	10,241	33,924	22,576	5,422	7,852	7,933	437	932
North Dakota.	4,227	3,994	1,156	2,838	1,729	532	689	250	52	206
Ohio	72,627	65,568	13,863	51,704	36,165	10,643	10,766	12,555	718	1,483
Oklahoma	19,161	18,061	4,413	13,648	8,782	1,482	3,446	2,460	570	824
Oregon.	23,201	21,625	6,438	15,187	9,003	3,139	889	3,871	275	829
Pennsylvania.	73,694	71,961	16,026	55,935	37,627	10,911	11,291	10,708	771	3,945
Rhode Island.	6,862	6,636	1,766	4,870	3,622	1,462	1,164	852	53	91
South Carolina. . . .	24,985	21,239	5,333	15,907	9,752	3,096	3,425	2,509	110	611
South Dakota	3,964	3,902	1,150	2,752	1,841	668	930	41	66	137
Tennessee	33,483	27,484	7,604	19,880	12,974	3,453	7,461	649	342	1,069
Texas.	114,018	109,128	22,915	86,214	58,981	24,521	28,639	-	1,292	4,528
Utah	13,789	12,499	2,613	9,886	6,026	1,420	2,619	1,716	86	186
Vermont	4,046	3,857	1,087	2,770	1,965	824	573	445	41	83
Virginia.	38,780	39,026	6,235	32,791	22,131	6,711	6,542	7,020	447	1,411
Washington.	42,124	36,345	7,042	29,303	19,514	5,791	11,976	-	338	1,410
West Virginia.	11,345	10,111	2,999	7,112	4,641	901	1,980	1,255	88	418
Wisconsin.	31,424	32,555	6,456	26,100	18,610	6,466	5,698	5,419	314	713
Wyoming	4,346	4,237	1,187	3,050	1,818	692	691	-	63	372

See footnote at end of table.

U.S. Census Bureau, Statistical Abstract of the United States: 2006

Table 430. State and Local Governments—Revenue by State: 2002—Con.

[In millions of dollars (419,270 represents $419,270,000,000). For fiscal year ending in year shown; see text, this section. Minsus sign (-) indicates net loss.]

State		General revenue							Utility and liquor stores	Insurance trust revenue
		Current charges and miscellaneous revenue								
		Current charges				Miscellaneous revenue				
	Total	Total ¹	Education	Hospitals	Sewerage	Total ¹	Interest earnings	Special assessments		
United States . . .	419,270	253,193	72,401	65,645	27,089	166,077	67,078	4,779	107,387	15,410
Alabama	7,759	5,992	1,457	3,519	257	1,767	678	3	2,138	-1,140
Alaska.	3,350	696	146	65	53	2,654	1,226	8	225	-441
Arizona	5,385	2,893	1,099	265	386	2,492	1,064	73	3,193	1,367
Arkansas	3,153	1,960	707	640	171	1,194	493	8	595	-238
California	57,970	36,003	7,950	7,952	3,585	21,967	9,107	1,205	21,061	3,020
Colorado	7,872	4,603	1,618	834	488	3,269	1,323	142	1,755	-2,140
Connecticut	3,641	1,763	558	342	189	1,878	737	25	508	1,518
Delaware	1,954	908	313	33	113	1,046	364	1	170	202
District of Columbia . . .	854	302	18	-	92	553	132	1	499	-69
Florida.	26,867	15,022	2,741	3,635	1,614	11,844	4,333	1,207	5,689	278
Georgia	10,944	6,963	1,468	2,978	650	3,981	1,466	21	3,109	-1,303
Hawaii.	1,642	1,037	224	180	145	605	291	17	197	-174
Idaho	1,913	1,299	280	516	104	614	318	28	206	47
Illinois	14,812	7,886	2,868	912	831	6,926	3,089 *	145	2,781	1,708
Indiana	9,093	5,763	2,263	1,774	750	3,331	1,000	26	1,720	138
Iowa	4,915	3,288	1,271	1,295	255	1,626	479	17	731	-1
Kansas	3,562	2,084	757	546	190	1,478	683	82	864	486
Kentucky	5,037	2,824	998	586	282	2,213	1,304	34	951	292
Louisiana	7,381	4,441	995	2,308	235	2,940	1,114	5	900	425
Maine	1,635	802	311	64	116	833	308	2	174	-231
Maryland	6,517	3,920	1,800	86	590	2,597	868	108	701	448
Massachusetts	8,930	3,823	1,198	323	682	5,107	2,006	32	2,288	636
Michigan	14,754	9,324	3,644	1,912	1,118	5,430	2,194	182	2,241	2,916
Minnesota	8,649	4,874	1,429	1,034	613	3,775	1,393	276	1,581	356
Mississippi	4,144	3,066	777	1,605	139	1,077	399	8	780	-168
Missouri.	6,610	3,882	1,423	1,133	395	2,728	1,309	18	1,240	319
Montana	1,397	748	325	41	50	649	315	45	122	266
Nebraska.	2,532	1,435	563	353	102	1,097	419	37	2,348	-139
Nevada	3,352	2,196	392	496	235	1,156	586	47	835	557
New Hampshire	1,511	805	388	6	76	706	388	1	404	-81
New Jersey	11,678	6,802	1,948	783	1,135	4,876	1,574	21	1,314	-1,734
New Mexico	2,867	1,230	393	385	114	1,636	722	20	367	268
New York.	30,477	18,180	2,846	5,137	1,456	12,297	4,516	97	9,446	5,994
North Carolina	11,348	8,543	2,075	3,787	962	2,804	1,341	14	2,891	1,541
North Dakota	1,109	706	285	5	30	403	150	46	76	156
Ohio	15,539	9,107	3,653	1,793	1,362	6,432	2,604	157	2,478	4,581
Oklahoma	4,866	3,265	1,344	791	231	1,601	610	5	1,048	52
Oregon	6,184	3,894	1,073	745	525	2,290	652	58	1,319	257
Pennsylvania	18,308	11,080	3,355	2,938	1,489	7,229	3,190	83	3,184	-1,451
Rhode Island	1,248	555	252	4	59	693	289	4	135	90
South Carolina	6,155	4,579	1,202	2,215	262	1,576	681	27	2,212	1,533
South Dakota	910	424	190	29	45	486	253	4	176	-113
Tennessee	6,906	5,141	1,451	1,959	417	1,765	662	17	5,670	330
Texas	27,233	16,160	5,025	4,448	1,959	11,073	4,818	93	7,220	-2,330
Utah	3,860	2,504	955	629	163	1,356	480	22	1,577	-288
Vermont	805	437	294	-	36	368	169	3	200	-12
Virginia	10,660	6,520	2,063	1,602	741	4,140	1,604	73	1,596	-1,842
Washington	9,790	6,599	1,799	1,534	907	3,191	1,340	104	5,163	616
West Virginia	2,471	1,310	450	260	123	1,160	467	10	195	1,039
Wisconsin	7,490	4,857	1,635	752	532	2,632	1,180	110	957	-2,088
Wyoming	1,231	696	132	413	33	535	391	11	156	-46

- Represents or rounds to zero.   ¹ Includes items not shown separately.   ² Includes individual and corporate income taxes.

Source: U.S. Census Bureau; *State and Local Government Finance Estimates by State*, annual, and unpublished data. See also <http://www.census.gov/govs/estimate/02.html>; (accessed 8 April 2005).

U.S. Census Bureau, Statistical Abstract of the United States: 2006

[In millions of dollars (2,048,719 represents $2,048,719,000,000), except as indicated. For fiscal year ending in year shown; see text, this section]

State	Total expenditure [1]	Total Amount	Per capita [2] (dol.)	General expenditure — Direct general expenditures, total	Education and social services — Education	Public welfare	Health and hospitals	Highways	Public safety — Police protection	Fire protection	Corrections
United States...	2,048,719	1,735,196	6,026	1,730,809	594,591	279,598	146,380	115,467	64,492	25,978	54,687
Alabama	28,531	24,605	5,493	24,605	8,320	4,162	4,082	1,668	710	279	460
Alaska	9,397	8,443	13,172	8,443	2,107	1,035	263	916	264	85	175
Arizona	31,308	25,252	4,641	25,252	8,796	3,286	1,209	1,913	1,259	485	1,122
Arkansas	14,570	13,068	4,829	13,068	4,783	2,593	915	1,307	403	148	369
California	293,424	238,503	6,814	235,627	76,827	35,559	20,961	11,467	10,147	4,170	9,012
Colorado	31,891	27,102	6,021	27,099	9,011	2,823	2,040	2,836	1,072	424	856
Connecticut	27,592	24,199	6,996	24,199	7,852	3,472	1,903	1,224	781	391	638
Delaware	5,947	5,358	6,647	5,357	1,937	659	327	464	191	24	245
District of Columbia	7,832	6,180	10,860	6,180	1,175	1,462	555	69	385	136	174
Florida	99,307	87,082	5,217	87,082	25,795	12,500	7,491	6,720	4,393	1,856	3,365
Georgia	52,310	44,951	5,261	44,951	17,366	6,159	4,832	2,939	1,555	636	1,765
Hawaii	9,402	8,304	6,691	8,289	2,257	1,141	652	419	255	104	157
Idaho	7,565	6,804	5,066	6,804	2,423	1,035	605	618	241	82	229
Illinois	87,401	73,822	5,865	73,819	25,953	9,861	5,199	5,676	3,226	1,358	1,879
Indiana	36,302	32,796	5,327	32,796	12,193	5,313	2,876	2,031	895	503	841
Iowa	19,294	17,229	5,868	17,186	6,467	2,682	1,886	1,762	458	161	330
Kansas	16,718	14,876	5,485	14,876	5,501	2,003	1,231	1,528	478	189	361
Kentucky	24,839	21,592	5,279	21,592	6,878	4,816	1,445	1,952	543	266	599
Louisiana	27,668	24,321	5,434	24,321	7,994	3,362	3,621	1,531	889	359	774
Maine	8,677	7,984	6,166	7,948	2,491	1,792	500	618	181	84	146
Maryland	35,577	31,796	5,833	31,796	12,142	4,737	1,490	1,855	1,335	523	1,257
Massachusetts	51,146	42,527	6,622	42,347	13,443	5,731	3,174	3,257	1,441	848	1,125
Michigan	69,533	60,783	6,052	60,723	23,745	9,837	5,347	3,219	1,976	681	2,109
Minnesota	40,516	34,933	6,952	34,933	11,266	7,473	1,965	2,681	1,019	265	649
Mississippi	17,285	15,384	5,366	15,384	5,101	3,246	2,140	1,236	461	173	323
Missouri	33,036	29,048	5,123	29,045	10,556	5,520	2,433	2,473	1,018	476	816
Montana	5,616	5,052	5,552	5,051	1,792	671	378	542	170	42	122
Nebraska	12,492	9,759	5,648	9,745	3,797	1,703	607	924	268	126	258
Nevada	13,971	11,774	5,433	11,766	3,679	1,120	923	1,271	650	285	503
New Hampshire	7,066	6,343	4,979	6,343	2,439	1,030	184	504	212	119	115
New Jersey	64,289	54,467	6,352	54,387	20,544	6,608	2,736	2,963	2,419	700	1,607
New Mexico	12,689	11,436	6,175	11,436	4,176	2,077	829	1,143	410	146	371
New York	198,536	161,740	8,453	161,130	47,723	32,503	13,008	7,078	6,719	2,452	4,663
North Carolina	51,839	44,540	5,362	44,540	15,262	7,657	6,087	3,017	1,504	573	1,172
North Dakota	4,190	3,886	6,130	3,886	1,311	664	104	461	77	26	60
Ohio	79,972	67,050	5,877	67,047	23,623	12,278	5,454	4,092	2,414	1,202	1,814
Oklahoma	20,776	18,196	5,214	18,154	6,904	3,192	1,305	1,544	569	295	560
Oregon	27,731	22,990	6,531	22,990	7,543	4,045	2,194	1,197	772	376	828
Pennsylvania	86,262	73,670	5,975	73,312	24,296	14,486	5,153	5,290	2,448	482	2,451
Rhode Island	7,939	6,784	6,352	6,756	2,180	1,667	299	331	239	189	158
South Carolina	28,106	23,820	5,804	23,820	8,380	4,374	3,143	1,491	722	232	570
South Dakota	4,276	3,885	5,111	3,885	1,360	605	171	580	105	36	93
Tennessee	36,638	28,952	5,000	28,952	9,745	6,458	3,300	1,773	977	423	690
Texas	129,874	111,604	5,134	111,604	45,703	14,903	10,104	7,527	3,728	1,496	4,401
Utah	15,523	12,861	5,546	12,861	5,196	1,595	858	1,017	441	147	375
Vermont	4,218	3,815	6,193	3,805	1,460	757	88	362	92	35	80
Virginia	43,688	39,269	5,388	39,267	15,149	4,674	3,184	3,102	1,309	623	1,388
Washington	50,431	38,657	6,372	38,646	12,866	6,198	4,013	2,376	1,092	663	1,146
West Virginia	11,930	9,848	5,456	9,848	3,519	2,139	516	1,041	187	66	202
Wisconsin	39,262	34,003	6,251	34,003	12,565	5,560	2,082	2,986	1,272	490	1,176
Wyoming	4,337	3,853	7,722	3,853	1,277	381	516	477	121	42	110

See footnote at end of table.

Table 431. **State and Local Governments—Expenditures and Debt by State: 2002-Con.**

[See headnote page 285]

State	General expenditure							Utility and liquor store expenditures	Employee retirement expenditures	Debt outstanding
	Environment and housing				Governmental administration	Interest on general debt	Other general expenditure			
	Sewerage	Solid waste management	Parks and recreation	Housing[3]						
United States...	31,238	19,047	30,096	31,610	92,789	75,303	169,532	143,851	114,208	1,686,106
Alabama	612	234	340	404	955	819	1,558	2,160	1,429	19,057
Alaska	53	49	100	175	523	427	2,271	290	537	8,646
Arizona	547	341	643	300	1,644	1,091	2,615	4,122	1,353	26,606
Arkansas	190	148	163	158	672	416	803	594	592	8,754
California	3,964	2,697	4,173	5,381	15,640	8,683	26,947	28,814	17,123	209,299
Colorado	512	81	975	445	1,461	1,258	3,305	2,380	1,834	26,718
Connecticut	268	372	301	440	1,358	1,429	3,769	829	1,774	27,767
Delaware	104	44	76	104	408	326	447	222	257	5,533
District of Columbia	211	43	303	88	383	236	959	1,490	13	5,436
Florida	1,714	1,852	1,837	1,179	4,886	4,176	9,317	7,190	3,632	90,276
Georgia	1,081	493	746	740	2,400	1,132	3,107	4,244	2,204	34,301
Hawaii	168	147	260	221	529	573	1,406	336	569	8,448
Idaho	154	87	109	31	419	210	561	202	295	3,985
Illinois	1,480	466	2,524	1,788	4,148	3,926	6,333	4,842	6,156	80,936
Indiana	866	230	471	589	1,906	1,176	2,907	1,782	1,093	24,071
Iowa	299	146	296	151	838	376	1,334	845	839	9,494
Kansas	190	100	196	138	943	633	1,385	834	709	12,313
Kentucky	441	203	259	178	1,011	1,490	1,512	1,188	1,447	28,994
Louisiana	349	269	410	369	1,401	1,054	1,936	1,046	2,017	20,986
Maine	117	104	56	130	424	329	978	154	412	6,346
Maryland	485	440	696	754	1,645	1,368	3,069	1,104	1,953	25,663
Massachusetts	836	393	280	1,344	2,053	3,236	5,184	3,495	2,976	65,322
Michigan	1,426	539	1,057	372	2,860	2,382	5,172	2,778	3,972	54,195
Minnesota	613	273	733	763	1,744	1,455	4,034	2,009	2,587	32,010
Mississippi	116	118	160	145	634	497	1,045	761	929	9,934
Missouri	456	143	430	467	1,303	1,038	1,916	1,518	1,848	24,244
Montana	51	55	43	82	335	210	557	122	294	3,963
Nebraska	114	67	147	113	435	256	932	2,306	312	7,906
Nevada	178	19	381	195	910	676	976	1,260	549	15,773
New Hampshire	74	79	64	155	361	406	603	354	265	7,221
New Jersey	1,112	1,048	961	941	2,801	2,377	7,569	3,024	4,080	57,590
New Mexico	119	105	205	92	626	378	759	382	745	8,603
New York	2,244	2,367	2,006	3,766	7,470	8,329	20,801	17,282	14,140	197,195
North Carolina	651	623	645	760	1,744	1,343	3,503	3,693	2,330	33,461
North Dakota	31	34	95	53	180	150	641	89	123	2,905
Ohio	1,598	456	1,038	1,449	4,651	2,695	4,283	2,909	6,628	51,344
Oklahoma	269	162	302	178	865	523	1,487	1,088	1,109	12,508
Oregon	602	132	318	483	1,590	737	2,174	1,667	1,800	18,827
Pennsylvania	1,563	620	678	1,645	3,423	4,046	6,731	4,539	5,123	83,809
Rhode Island	82	105	64	156	372	324	591	233	546	7,345
South Carolina	229	235	261	270	1,291	1,159	1,462	2,277	1,372	22,873
South Dakota	44	25	104	51	199	173	339	164	198	3,451
Tennessee	366	317	442	496	1,247	922	2,074	5,808	1,185	21,128
Texas	1,777	907	2,050	1,564	4,509	4,999	7,935	9,107	6,910	122,810
Utah	237	111	323	180	915	425	1,040	1,796	452	13,250
Vermont	42	35	31	90	255	164	315	224	97	3,028
Virginia	751	550	632	702	2,251	1,706	3,245	1,838	1,914	35,422
Washington	911	493	866	897	1,742	1,539	3,844	6,775	1,841	45,561
West Virginia	124	60	113	114	636	446	686	261	493	8,085
Wisconsin	776	396	655	314	1,551	1,457	2,725	1,239	2,980	30,327
Wyoming	44	36	78	9	243	128	391	185	172	2,388

[1] Includes items not shown separately.   [2] Based on estimated resident population as of July 1; see Table 17.   [3] Includes community development.

Source: U.S. Census Bureau; *State and Local Government Finance Estimates by State,* annual, and unpublished data. <http://www.census.gov/govs/estimate/02.html>; (accessed 8 April 2005).

Table 432. **State and Local Governments—Summary of Finances by State: 2002**

[In millions of dollars (1,807,573 represents $1,807,573,000,000), except as indicated. For fiscal year ending in year shown; see text, this section]

State	Revenue [1]						Expenditures		Debt outstanding	
	All revenue		General revenue		Taxes		Direct general expendi-tures	Per capita [2] (dol.)	Total	Per capita [2] (dol.)
	Total	Per capita [2] (dol.)	Total	Per capita [2] (dol.)	Total	Per capita [2] (dol.)				
United States ...	1,807,573	6,277	1,684,776	5,850	904,971	3,143	1,730,809	6,010	1,686,106	5,855
Alabama	24,740	5,524	23,741	5,301	9,719	2,170	24,605	5,493	19,057	4,255
Alaska	6,993	10,909	7,209	11,246	2,070	3,229	8,443	13,172	8,646	13,488
Arizona	30,083	5,529	25,524	4,691	14,420	2,650	25,252	4,641	26,606	4,890
Arkansas	13,616	5,032	13,260	4,900	6,461	2,388	13,068	4,829	8,754	3,235
California	250,725	7,163	226,644	6,475	120,424	3,440	235,627	6,732	209,299	5,980
Colorado	25,657	5,700	26,041	5,786	13,900	3,088	27,099	6,021	26,718	5,936
Connecticut	24,831	7,179	22,805	6,593	15,125	4,373	24,199	6,996	27,767	8,028
Delaware	5,972	7,410	5,600	6,948	2,687	3,334	5,357	6,646	5,533	6,864
District of Columbia	7,352	12,921	6,922	12,166	3,228	5,673	6,180	10,860	5,436	9,554
Florida	92,631	5,549	86,663	5,192	44,840	2,686	87,082	5,217	90,276	5,408
Georgia	46,166	5,403	44,360	5,192	24,058	2,816	44,951	5,261	34,301	4,015
Hawaii	7,452	6,005	7,429	5,986	4,240	3,416	8,289	6,680	8,448	6,808
Idaho	6,873	5,117	6,620	4,929	3,291	2,451	6,804	5,066	3,985	2,967
Illinois	73,588	5,847	69,098	5,490	41,570	3,303	73,819	5,865	80,936	6,431
Indiana	34,221	5,558	32,363	5,256	16,987	2,759	32,796	5,327	24,071	3,910
Iowa	17,601	5,995	16,871	5,746	8,330	2,837	17,186	5,854	9,494	3,234
Kansas	15,985	5,894	14,635	5,396	7,975	2,941	14,876	5,485	12,313	4,540
Kentucky	22,475	5,495	21,231	5,191	10,781	2,636	21,592	5,279	28,994	7,089
Louisiana	27,373	6,115	26,048	5,819	12,182	2,722	24,321	5,434	20,986	4,688
Maine	8,019	6,193	8,077	6,237	4,541	3,507	7,948	6,137	6,346	4,901
Maryland	33,468	6,140	32,319	5,929	19,874	3,646	31,796	5,833	25,663	4,708
Massachusetts	41,925	6,528	39,002	6,073	23,895	3,721	42,347	6,594	65,322	10,172
Michigan	63,099	6,283	57,942	5,769	30,644	3,051	60,723	6,046	54,195	5,396
Minnesota	35,131	6,991	33,193	6,606	18,456	3,673	34,933	6,952	32,010	6,370
Mississippi	15,905	5,548	15,293	5,334	6,524	2,275	15,384	5,366	9,934	3,465
Missouri	30,621	5,400	29,062	5,126	15,123	2,667	29,045	5,123	24,244	4,276
Montana	5,511	6,056	5,122	5,629	2,135	2,346	5,051	5,550	3,963	4,355
Nebraska	12,031	6,962	9,821	5,684	5,316	3,077	9,745	5,640	7,906	4,575
Nevada	12,809	5,911	11,417	5,269	6,433	2,968	11,766	5,430	15,773	7,279
New Hampshire	6,729	5,281	6,406	5,028	3,599	2,825	6,343	4,979	7,221	5,668
New Jersey	54,835	6,395	55,256	6,444	34,629	4,038	54,387	6,343	57,590	6,716
New Mexico	11,503	6,211	10,868	5,868	4,878	2,634	11,436	6,175	8,603	4,645
New York	170,982	8,936	155,541	8,129	88,878	4,645	161,130	8,421	197,195	10,306
North Carolina	48,597	5,851	44,165	5,317	22,576	2,718	44,540	5,362	33,461	4,028
North Dakota	4,227	6,666	3,994	6,300	1,729	2,727	3,886	6,130	2,905	4,582
Ohio	72,627	6,366	65,568	5,747	36,165	3,170	67,047	5,747	51,344	4,500
Oklahoma	19,161	5,490	18,061	5,175	8,782	2,516	18,154	5,202	12,508	3,584
Oregon	23,201	6,591	21,625	6,144	9,003	2,558	22,990	6,531	18,827	5,349
Pennsylvania	73,694	5,977	71,961	5,837	37,627	3,052	73,312	5,946	83,809	6,798
Rhode Island	6,862	6,425	6,636	6,214	3,622	3,392	6,756	6,326	7,345	6,877
South Carolina	24,985	6,088	21,239	5,175	9,752	2,376	23,820	5,804	22,873	5,573
South Dakota	3,964	5,216	3,902	5,134	1,841	2,423	3,885	5,111	3,451	4,540
Tennessee	33,483	5,783	27,484	4,747	12,974	2,241	28,952	5,000	21,128	3,649
Texas	114,018	5,245	109,128	5,020	58,981	2,713	111,604	5,134	122,810	5,650
Utah	13,789	5,946	12,499	5,390	6,026	2,599	12,861	5,546	13,250	5,714
Vermont	4,046	6,568	3,857	6,262	1,965	3,190	3,805	6,177	3,028	4,915
Virginia	38,780	5,321	39,026	5,355	22,131	3,037	39,267	5,388	35,422	4,860
Washington	42,124	6,943	36,345	5,991	19,514	3,216	38,646	6,370	45,561	7,510
West Virginia	11,345	6,285	10,111	5,602	4,641	2,571	9,848	5,456	8,085	4,479
Wisconsin	31,424	5,776	32,555	5,984	18,610	3,421	34,003	6,251	30,327	5,575
Wyoming	4,346	8,710	4,237	8,491	1,818	3,643	3,853	7,722	2,388	4,786

[1] Includes items not shown separately. [2] Based on estimated resident population as of July 1, see Table 17.

Source: U.S. Census Bureau; *State and Local Government Finance Estimates by State*, annual, and unpublished data. <http://www.census.gov/govs/estimate/02.html>; (accessed 8 April 2005).

U.S. Census Bureau, Statistical Abstract of the United States: 2006

Table 433. State and Local Governments—Indebtedness: 1980 to 2002

[In billions of dollars (335.6 represents $335,600,000,000), except per capita. For fiscal year ending in year shown; see text, this section. Local government amounts are estimates subject to sampling variation; see Appendix III and source]

Item			Debt outstanding				Long term		
	Total	Per capita [1] (dol.)	Long-term			Short-term	Net long term	Debt issued	Debt retired
			Local schools [2]	Utilities	All other				
1980: Total	335.6	1,481	32.3	55.2	235.0	13.1	262.9	42.4	17.4
State.	122.0	540	3.8	4.6	111.5	2.1	79.8	16.4	5.7
Local	213.6	943	28.5	50.6	123.5	11.0	183.1	25.9	11.7
1990: Total	858.0	3,449	60.4	134.8	643.5	19.3	474.4	108.5	64.8
State.	318.3	1,282	4.4	12.3	298.7	2.8	125.5	43.5	22.9
Local	539.8	2,169	56.0	122.4	344.8	16.5	348.9	65.0	42.0
1995: Total	1,115.4	4,244	118.2	163.9	806.2	27.0	697.3	129.3	95.1
State.	427.2	1,629	11.3	17.0	392.8	6.1	205.3	52.6	37.5
Local	688.1	2,618	107.0	146.9	413.4	20.9	491.9	76.8	57.6
1998: Total	1,283.6	4,750	159.2	182.8	924.3	17.3	842.6	204.4	144.6
State.	483.1	1,791	13.6	16.7	450.6	2.2	237.2	83.4	58.1
Local	800.4	2,962	145.5	166.1	473.8	15.1	605.4	120.9	86.5
1999: Total	1,369.3	5,021	180.7	194.9	975.7	17.8	907.3	229.4	153.1
State.	510.5	1,876	15.4	16.7	475.8	2.7	249.4	83.2	55.6
Local	858.8	3,149	165.3	178.3	500.0	15.2	657.9	146.2	97.5
2000: Total	1,451.8	5,159	197.7	200.1	1,029.8	24.3	959.6	184.8	121.9
State.	547.9	1,951	18.7	17.9	505.0	6.4	266.9	75.0	44.4
Local	903.9	3,212	179.0	182.2	524.8	17.9	692.7	109.8	77.5
2001: Total	1,554.0	5,447	225.3	210.4	1,096.2	22.1	1,038.6	199.6	130.6
State.	576.5	2,025	21.5	18.7	532.6	3.7	287.4	81.3	50.7
Local	977.5	3,426	203.8	191.7	563.5	18.5	751.2	118.3	79.9
2002: Total	1,686.1	5,855	250.2	218.5	1,174.2	43.2	1,126.6	262.3	162.5
State.	642.2	2,234	23.8	26.1	573.6	18.6	317.8	103.7	65.3
Local	1,043.9	3,625	226.4	192.4	600.5	24.6	808.8	158.6	97.2

[1] 1980, 1990, and 2000 based on enumerated resident population as of April 1; other years based on estimated resident population as of July 1.   [2] Includes debt for education activities other than higher education.
Source: U.S. Census Bureau, *1980–90, State and Local Government Finance Estimates,* annual; thereafter, <http://www.census.gov/govs/www/estimate/02.html> (accessed 8 April 2005).

Table 434. Long Term Municipal New Bond Issues for State and Local Governments: 1980 to 2002

[In billions of dollars (45.6 represents $45,600,000,000)]

Item	1980	1985	1990	1995	1997	1998	1999	2000	2001	2002
Long-Term Municipal New Issues [1] . . .	45.6	202.4	125.9	156.2	214.3	279.7	219.2	194.3	283.5	355.8
General obligation.	13.7	39.6	40.2	60.2	72.2	92.6	69.8	65.2	101.3	125.6
Revenue	31.9	162.8	85.7	96.0	142.1	187.1	149.4	129.1	182.2	230.2
Competitive	19.3	27.8	30.2	41.0	47.8	65.2	52.8	48.7	63.1	71.9
Negotiated	26.4	174.6	95.9	115.4	166.5	214.5	166.4	145.6	220.4	283.9
States with largest issuance: [2]										
New York	2.9	12.7	16.9	18.8	37.4	36.3	19.8	19.1	22.5	48.0
California	3.6	25.3	15.7	20.2	27.7	33.9	26.5	22.9	31.7	48.5
Texas	3.8	21.2	6.5	10.4	15.3	18.1	17.7	14.7	24.6	26.6
Florida	2.2	13.2	5.9	9.1	10.5	14.7	10.8	10.1	14.1	18.7
Illinois	2.3	9.2	6.3	6.6	9.6	10.1	12.4	8.9	14.1	14.7
All others . . . [3]	30.8	120.8	74.6	91.1	123.8	166.6	132.0	118.6	176.5	198.5
Type of issuer: [3]										
City, town, or village	8.5	36.5	22.7	27.9	34.8	44.3	33.0	29.3	45.6	46.9
College or university	0.2	2.9	1.5	2.5	3.3	4.6	4.1	3.8	5.6	7.1
County/parish	4.6	15.8	10.0	13.3	15.5	21.2	17.1	12.7	19.0	23.5
Direct issuer	(NA)	0.4	0.2	0.4	0.8	2.1	2.0	2.6	3.1	4.9
District	3.9	15.6	15.2	22.4	33.7	43.6	34.1	27.8	47.9	54.4
Indian Tribe	(NA)	(NA)	(NA)	(NA)	(NA)	(NA)	(NA)	(NA)	0.2	0.2
Local authority.	9.2	51.1	20.7	27.9	41.5	53.9	43.2	33.1	53.1	59.8
State authority	14.1	68.1	40.6	47.2	66.0	85.2	68.1	64.2	78.9	125.0
State	5.1	12.1	15.0	14.6	18.7	24.7	17.6	20.8	30.2	34.0
General use of proceeds:										
Airports	0.4	3.0	5.2	4.7	6.4	10.2	5.5	7.4	12.3	10.0
Combined utilities.	0.3	2.4	1.0	0.7	1.5	1.8	1.0	0.3	1.3	2.2
Economic development	0.2	2.5	2.1	2.5	2.9	3.5	3.6	2.9	3.9	4.4
Education	4.0	20.4	20.5	28.5	42.7	56.5	47.6	39.9	64.5	76.4
Health care.	3.1	30.0	12.6	11.5	22.1	33.4	22.0	14.4	20.1	22.4
Industrial development	1.0	2.9	1.9	3.2	3.5	3.6	3.5	3.4	2.9	2.3
Multifamily housing.	2.5	20.2	3.1	6.1	5.4	6.4	6.1	6.2	7.3	10.1
Nursing homes/life care retirement	0.3	1.2	1.6	1.9	3.6	4.8	4.9	1.8	3.0	3.7
Other miscellaneous.	11.1	37.3	36.2	44.2	57.0	71.5	58.4	52.8	81.2	102.4
Pollution control.	2.3	10.0	2.5	5.0	5.6	9.7	8.9	4.8	4.5	5.5
Electric & public power	4.4	23.2	5.2	4.8	6.5	15.6	4.9	5.7	11.5	23.1
Single family housing	10.6	16.4	12.5	10.0	13.6	12.9	12.6	12.0	14.0	12.4
Solid waste/resource recovery	0.4	3.8	3.0	3.3	3.6	2.4	1.2	0.5	2.1	1.9
Student loans	0.2	4.0	0.4	4.4	3.9	4.9	5.3	7.6	8.2	11.7
Transportation	1.3	11.0	7.6	11.3	16.6	20.5	16.0	15.9	18.6	33.8
Water, sewer, and gas facilities.	3.1	13.4	9.3	13.2	18.2	20.9	16.4	11.3	27.1	32.2
Waterfront/seaports	0.5	1.5	0.5	0.8	1.2	0.9	1.2	1.1	1.1	1.0

NA Not available.   [1] Excludes issues with a final maturity of less than 13 months, private placements, and not-for-profit cooperative utilities.   [2] Ranked by 2002 Long Term Municipal New Issue Volume.   [3] Includes island areas.
Source: Thomson Financial Securities Data Company, Newark, NJ, Municipal New Issues Database (copyright).

Table 435. **Bond Ratings for State Governments by State: 2004**

[As of fourth quarter. Key to investment grade ratings are in declining order of quality. The ratings from AA to CCC may be modified by the addition of a (+) or (-) sign to show relative standing within the major rating categories. *S&P:* AAA, AA, A, BBB, BB, B, CCC, CC, C; *Moody's:* Aaa, Aa, A, Baa, Ba, B, Caa, Ca, C; numerical modifiers 1, 2, and 3 are added to letter-rating. *Fitch:* AAA, AA, A, BBB, BB, B, CCC, CC, C]

State	Standard & Poor's	Moody's	Fitch	State	Standard & Poor's	Moody's	Fitch
Alabama	AA	Aa3	AA	Montana	AA-	Aa3	AAA
Alaska	AA	Aa2	AA	Nebraska	(¹)	(NA)	(NA)
Arizona	AA	(NA)	(NA)	Nevada	AA	Aa2	(NA)
Arkansas	AA	Aa2	(NA)	New Hampshire . . .	AA	Aa2	AA
California	A	A3	A-	New Jersey	AA-	Aa3	AA-
Colorado	AA-	(NA)	(NA)	New Mexico	AA+	Aa1	(NA)
Connecticut	AA	Aa3	AA	New York	AA	A1	AA-
Delaware	AAA	Aaa	AAA	North Carolina	AAA	Aa1	AAA
Florida	AA+	Aa2	AA	North Dakota	AA-	Aa2	(NA)
Georgia	AAA	Aaa	AAA	Ohio	AA+	Aa1	AA+
Hawaii	AA-	Aa3	AA-	Oklahoma	AA	Aa3	AA
Idaho	AA-	Aa2	(NA)	Oregon	AA-	Aa3	A+
Illinois	AA	Aa3	AA	Pennsylvania	AA	Aa2	(NA)
Indiana	AA	Aa1	(NA)	Rhode Island	AA-	Aa3	AA
Iowa	AA+	Aa1	AA	South Carolina	AAA	Aaa	AAA
Kansas	AA+	Aa1	(NA)	South Dakota	(¹)	(NA)	(NA)
Kentucky	AA-	Aa2	(NA)	Tennessee	AA	Aa2	AA
Louisiana	A+	A1	A+	Texas	AA	Aa1	AA+
Maine	AA	Aa2	AA+	Utah	AAA	Aaa	AAA
Maryland	AAA	Aaa	AAA	Vermont	AA+	Aa1	AA+
Massachusetts	AA-	Aa2	(NA)	Virginia	AAA	Aaa	(NA)
Michigan	AA+	Aa1	AA	Washington	AA	Aa1	AA
Minnesota	AAA	Aa1	AAA	West Virginia	AA-	Aa3	AA-
Mississippi	AA	Aa3	AA	Wisconsin	AA-	Aa3	AA-
Missouri	AAA	Aaa	AAA	Wyoming	AA	(NA)	(NA)

NA Not available   ¹ Not reviewed.

Sources: Standard & Poor's, New York, NY (copyright); <http://www2.standardandpoors.com/servlet/Satellite?pagename=sp/Page/HomePg>; Moody's Investors Service, New York, NY (copyright); <http://www.moodys.com/cust/defaultalt.asp>; Fitch Ratings, New York, NY (copyright); <http://www.fitchratings.com/>.

Table 436. **Bond Ratings for City Governments by Largest Cities: 2004**

[As of fourth quarter. See headnote in table 435]

Cities ranked by 2000 population	Standard & Poor's	Moody's	Fitch	Cities ranked by 2000 population	Standard & Poor's	Moody's	Fitch
New York, NY	A	A2	A+	Oakland, CA	A+	A1	A+
Los Angeles, CA	AA	Aa2	AA	Mesa, AZ	AA-	A1	(NA)
Chicago, IL	A+	A1	AA-	Tulsa, OK	AA	Aa2	(NA)
Houston, TX	AA-	Aa3	AA	Omaha, NE	AAA	Aaa	(NA)
Philadelphia, PA	BBB	Baa1	(NA)	Minneapolis, MN	AAA	Aa1	(NA)
Phoenix, AZ	AA+	Aa1	AAA	Honolulu, HI	AA-	Aa2	AA
San Diego, CA	(¹)	A1	AA	Miami, FL	A+	A3	(NA)
Dallas, TX	AA+	Aa1	(NA)	Colorado Springs, CO. . . .	AA	Aa3	(NA)
San Antonio, TX	AA+	Aa2	AA+	St. Louis, MO	A-	A3	A-
Detroit, MI	A-	Baa1	AAA	Wichita, KS	AA	Aa2	(NA)
San Jose, CA	AA+	Aa1	AA+	Santa Ana, CA	(¹)	(NA)	(NA)
Indianapolis, IN	AAA	(NA)	(NA)	Pittsburgh, PA.	BBB-	Ba1	BB
San Francisco, CA	AA	Aa3	AA	Arlington, TX.	AA	Aa2	(NA)
Jacksonville, FL	(¹)	Aa2	(NA)	Cincinnati, OH	AA+	Aa1	(NA)
Columbus, OH	AAA	Aaa	(NA)	Anaheim, CA	AA	Aa2	(NA)
Austin, TX	AA+	Aa2	(NA)	Toledo, OH	A	A3	(NA)
Baltimore, MD	A+	A1	A+	Tampa, FL	AA	Aa3	(NA)
Memphis, TN	AA	Aa2	AA-	Buffalo, NY	BBB-	Baa3	(NA)
Milwaukee, WI.	AA	Aa2	AA+	St. Paul, MN	AAA	Aa2	AA+
Boston, MA	AA	Aa2	AA-	Corpus Christi, TX	A+	A2	AA-
Washington, DC	A	A2	BBB+	Aurora, CO	AA	Aa2	(NA)
El Paso, TX	AA	Aa3	(NA)	Raleigh, NC	AAA	Aaa	AAA
Seattle, WA	AAA	Aaa	(NA)	Newark, NJ	AA-	Baa1	(NA)
Denver, CO	AA+	Aa1	AA+	Lexington-Fayette, KY . . .	AA+	(NA)	(NA)
Nashville-Davidson, TN. . .	AA	Aa2	AA+	Anchorage, AK	(¹)	Aa3	(NA)
Charlotte, NC	AAA	Aaa	AAA	Louisville, KY	AA	Aa2	(NA)
Fort Worth, TX	AA+	Aa1	(NA)	Riverside, CA	AA-	(NA)	(NA)
Portland, OR.	(¹)	Aaa	(NA)	St Petersburg, FL	(¹)	(NA)	(NA)
Oklahoma City, OK	AA	Aa2	(NA)	Bakersfield, CA	(¹)	Aa3	(NA)
Tucson, AZ.	AA	Aa3	(NA)	Stockton CA	A+	(NA)	(NA)
New Orleans, LA	BBB+	Baa1	(NA)	Birmingham, AL	AA	Aa3	AA-
Las Vegas, NV	AA-	Aa3	(NA)	Jersey City, NJ	BBB	Baa3	BBB
Cleveland, OH.	A	A2	A+	Norfolk, VA	AA	A1	AA
Long Beach, CA	AA-	Aa3	(NA)	Baton Rouge, LA	(¹)	(NA)	(NA)
Albuquerque, NM.	AA	Aa3	AA	Hialeah, FL.	(¹)	(NA)	(NA)
Kansas City, MO	AA	Aa3	AAA	Lincoln, NE.	AAA	Aaa	(NA)
Fresno, CA.	AA-	A1	(NA)	Greensboro, NC	AAA	Aa1	AAA
Virginia Beach, VA	AA+	Aa1	AA+	Plano, TX.	AAA	Aaa	AAA
Atlanta, GA.	AA-	Aa3	AA-	Rochester, NY	AA	A2	(NA)
Sacramento, CA	AA	Aa2	(NA)				

Not available.   ¹ Not reviewed.

Sources: Standard & Poor's, New York, NY (copyright); <http://www2.standardandpoors.com/servlet/Satellite?pagename=sp/Page/HomePg>; Moody's Investors Service, New York, NY (copyright); <http://www.moodys.com/cust/defaultalt.asp>; Fitch Ratings, New York, NY (copyright); <http://www.fitchratings.com/>.

State and Local Government Finances and Employment   289

Table 437. State Resources, Expenditures, and Balances: 2003 and 2004

[In millions of dollars (1,136,694 represents $1,136,694,000,000). For fiscal year ending in year shown; see text; this section. General funds exclude special funds earmarked for particular purposes, such as highway trust funds and federal funds; they support most on-going broad-based state services and are available for appropriation to support any governmental activity. Minus sign (-) indicates deficit]

State	Expenditures by fund source				State general fund					
	Total, 2003	2004 [1]			Resources [3,4]		Expenditures [4]		Balance [5]	
		Total [2]	General fund	Federal funds	2003	2004 [1]	2003	2004 [1]	2003	2004 [1]
United States...	1,136,694	1,187,444	516,095	358,417	524,428	544,912	508,285	523,539	10,219	18,625
Alabama.........	16,012	19,922	5,523	7,880	5,585	5,792	5,473	5,491	113	261
Alaska..........	6,496	7,578	2,331	2,792	2,496	2,301	2,496	2,301	-	-
Arizona.........	19,550	20,764	6,474	6,454	6,218	6,884	6,026	6,517	192	368
Arkansas........	12,631	14,577	3,526	5,070	3,251	3,526	3,251	3,526	-	-
California.......	161,512	165,850	78,028	57,972	79,089	80,760	77,482	77,634	[6]1,607	[6]3,127
Colorado........	13,213	13,372	5,580	3,201	6,138	6,035	5,913	5,689	225	346
Connecticut......	20,533	21,948	12,530	4,321	12,023	12,881	12,120	12,678	-97	202
Delaware........	5,825	6,145	2,545	990	2,918	3,200	2,454	2,554	[6]464	[6]646
Florida.........	48,560	53,950	21,615	15,985	21,196	23,852	20,514	21,542	682	2,310
Georgia.........	27,981	28,670	15,446	11,824	17,292	17,348	16,025	16,265	[6]1,268	[6]1,083
Hawaii..........	8,029	7,599	3,823	1,467	3,923	4,025	3,806	3,840	117	185
Idaho...........	4,359	4,901	1,994	1,860	1,941	2,087	1,926	1,987	16	100
Illinois.........	37,653	41,290	19,027	10,403	25,161	26,996	21,893	22,632	317	182
Indiana.........	19,288	20,259	11,323	6,239	10,751	11,535	10,309	11,244	442	291
Iowa...........	13,480	13,641	4,489	3,805	4,484	4,513	4,531	4,561	-46	26
Kansas.........	10,083	10,209	4,332	2,719	4,260	4,644	4,138	4,317	123	327
Kentucky........	18,376	19,534	7,236	6,683	7,444	7,620	7,179	7,294	163	250
Louisiana.......	16,989	19,465	6,536	6,371	6,662	6,826	6,457	6,743	23	45
Maine..........	6,064	6,116	2,556	2,233	2,586	2,658	2,533	2,643	29	15
Maryland........	23,037	24,106	10,275	5,852	10,469	10,493	10,347	10,262	123	230
Massachusetts....	26,058	27,322	20,287	4,876	23,376	23,949	22,439	22,470	[6]752	[6]1,479
Michigan........	39,844	39,424	8,813	11,806	8,909	8,707	8,735	8,695	174	12
Minnesota.......	23,099	23,539	13,387	5,700	14,263	14,658	13,894	13,734	[6]369	[6]924
Mississippi......	11,708	12,052	3,477	4,756	3,498	3,594	3,458	3,591	41	3
Missouri........	17,460	18,665	6,786	6,462	6,598	7,150	6,382	6,662	216	488
Montana........	3,649	3,977	1,333	1,559	1,327	1,419	1,283	1,287	43	132
Nebraska........	6,809	7,649	2,674	2,380	2,622	2,752	2,619	2,576	3	177
Nevada.........	5,756	6,271	2,260	1,663	2,146	2,461	2,037	2,320	108	141
New Hampshire....	4,065	4,095	1,313	1,240	1,260	1,321	1,260	1,305	-	16
New Jersey.......	36,217	37,451	23,855	8,702	23,941	24,761	23,568	23,939	[6]373	[6]822
New Mexico......	11,464	11,779	4,502	3,807	4,339	5,025	4,051	4,383	[6]245	[6]480
New York........	89,056	97,327	42,065	35,995	40,328	41,242	37,613	42,065	[6]815	[6]1,077
North Carolina....	28,780	29,319	14,700	8,466	14,271	15,187	13,856	14,704	251	287
North Dakota.....	2,520	2,646	884	1,018	875	971	860	894	15	77
Ohio...........	46,905	48,775	24,076	8,216	22,558	24,083	22,653	23,839	53	157
Oklahoma.......	12,922	13,986	4,287	4,711	4,687	4,936	4,653	4,833	34	102
Oregon.........	15,086	19,685	5,720	3,564	3,958	5,001	3,865	5,479	93	-478
Pennsylvania.....	47,292	48,752	21,462	16,740	20,679	22,152	20,400	21,926	209	77
Rhode Island.....	5,509	6,146	2,796	1,927	2,741	2,834	2,691	2,790	43	44
South Carolina....	16,704	15,425	4,954	5,543	5,040	5,162	4,995	4,865	[6]46	[6]55
South Dakota	2,861	2,815	904	1,222	891	892	884	889	7	3
Tennessee	20,275	21,781	8,656	8,706	8,049	8,767	7,914	8,357	64	349
Texas..........	59,057	59,269	29,434	19,814	31,105	29,787	30,656	29,434	88	981
Utah...........	7,542	7,930	3,582	2,065	3,552	3,668	3,536	3,569	16	53
Vermont........	2,674	2,896	901	991	882	973	888	915	-6	58
Virginia.........	26,925	27,989	11,299	5,756	12,204	12,660	12,118	12,387	86	274
Washington......	25,137	26,055	11,381	5,800	11,739	11,958	11,334	11,452	405	506
West Virginia.....	15,678	16,208	2,959	3,454	3,139	3,319	2,933	3,019	196	291
Wisconsin.......	31,770	23,841	10,852	6,416	10,772	10,759	11,054	10,654	[6]-282	[6]105
Wyoming	4,201	4,429	1,307	941	792	792	788	788	4	4

- Represents zero.   [1] Estimated.   [2] Includes bonds and other state funds not shown separately.   [3] Includes funds budgeted, adjustments, and balances from previous year.   [4] May or may not include budget stabilization fund transfers, depending on state accounting practices.   [5] Resources less expenditures.   [6] Ending balance includes the balance in a budget stabilization fund.

Source: National Association of State Budget Officers, Washington, DC, 2003 State Expenditure Report, and State General Fund from NASBO, Fiscal Survey of the States, semi-annual (copyright).

U.S. Census Bureau, Statistical Abstract of the United States: 2006

Table 438. State Governments—Summary of Finances: 1990 to 2002

[(673,119 represents $673,119,000,000), For fiscal year ending in year shown; see text; this section. Minsus (-) indicates net loss)]

Item	Total (million dollars)				Per capita [1] (dollars)			
	1990	2000	2001	2002	1990	2000	2001	2002
Borrowing and revenue......	673,119	1,336,798	1,257,148	1,205,999	2,712	4,760	4,415	4,196
Borrowing.................	40,948	75,968	76,843	108,170	165	270	270	376
Revenue..................	632,172	1,260,829	1,180,305	1,097,829	2,547	4,489	4,145	3,820
General revenue............	517,429	984,783	1,049,298	1,062,305	2,085	3,506	3,685	3,696
Taxes..................	300,489	539,655	559,679	535,241	1,211	1,922	1,966	1,862
Sales and gross receipts	147,069	252,147	258,018	262,361	593	898	906	913
General...............	99,702	174,461	179,319	179,665	402	621	630	625
Motor fuels............	19,379	29,968	31,026	31,968	78	107	109	111
Alcoholic beverages......	3,191	4,104	4,167	4,249	13	15	15	15
Tobacco products	5,541	8,391	8,644	8,902	22	30	30	31
Other	19,256	35,222	34,863	37,576	78	125	122	131
Licenses...............	18,842	32,598	32,866	35,391	76	116	115	123
Motor vehicles........	9,848	15,099	15,141	15,641	40	54	53	54
Corporations in general ...	3,099	6,460	6,384	5,842	12	23	22	20
Other	5,895	11,039	11,341	13,908	24	39	40	48
Individual income	96,076	194,573	208,079	185,697	387	693	731	646
Corporation net income	21,751	32,522	31,687	25,123	88	116	111	87
Property	5,848	10,996	10,430	9,702	24	39	37	34
Other	10,902	16,819	18,597	16,967	44	60	65	59
Charges and miscellaneous ..	90,612	170,747	183,998	191,641	365	608	646	667
Intergovernmental revenue	126,329	274,382	305,621	335,423	509	977	1,073	1,167
From federal government....	118,353	259,114	288,309	317,581	477	923	1,013	1,105
Public welfare..........	59,397	147,150	165,800	181,517	239	524	582	632
Education	21,271	42,086	45,760	51,103	86	150	161	178
Highways	13,931	23,790	27,894	29,641	56	85	98	103
Health and hospitals	5,475	14,223	16,426	17,875	22	51	58	62
Other	18,279	31,865	32,428	37,445	74	113	114	130
From local governments.....	7,976	15,268	17,312	17,842	32	54	61	62
Utility revenue...........	3,305	4,513	6,930	11,935	13	16	24	42
Liquor store revenue	2,907	3,895	4,092	4,288	12	14	14	15
Insurance trust revenue [2]	108,530	267,639	119,985	19,301	437	953	421	67
Employee retirement........	78,898	230,166	79,527	-25,244	318	820	279	-88
Unemployment compensation...	18,370	23,260	23,221	26,960	74	83	82	94
Expenditure and debt redemption	592,213	1,125,828	1,235,568	1,334,969	2,386	4,009	4,339	4,645
Expenditure................	572,318	1,084,097	1,186,108	1,280,290	2,306	3,860	4,166	4,455
General expenditure	508,284	964,723	1,045,296	1,109,227	2,048	3,435	3,671	3,859
Education...............	184,935	346,465	374,444	389,390	745	1,234	1,315	1,355
Public welfare	104,971	238,890	262,346	287,016	423	851	921	999
Health	20,029	42,066	43,732	50,293	81	150	154	175
Hospitals	22,637	32,578	34,538	37,393	91	116	121	130
Highways	44,249	74,415	78,786	84,198	178	265	277	293
Police protection	5,166	9,788	10,145	10,706	21	35	36	37
Corrections.............	17,266	35,129	38,165	38,918	70	125	134	135
Natural resources.........	9,909	15,967	17,309	17,821	40	57	61	62
Housing and community development	2,856	4,726	5,009	5,989	12	17	18	21
Other and unallocable........	96,267	164,698	180,823	187,504	388	586	635	652
Utility expenditure	7,131	10,723	18,632	20,279	29	38	65	71
Liquor store expenditure	2,452	3,195	3,347	3,498	10	11	12	12
Insurance trust expenditure [2]....	54,452	105,456	118,833	147,286	219	375	417	512
Employee retirement........	29,562	75,971	83,770	91,971	119	271	294	320
Unemployment compensation...	16,423	18,583	22,920	42,017	66	66	80	146
By character and object:								
Intergovernmental expenditure....	175,028	327,070	350,327	364,789	705	1,165	1,230	1,269
Direct expenditure...........	397,291	757,027	835,782	915,501	1,601	2,695	2,935	3,185
Current operation..........	258,046	523,114	580,374	620,763	1,040	1,863	2,038	2,160
Capital outlay	45,524	76,233	81,881	89,919	183	271	288	313
Construction	34,803	59,681	64,668	71,035	140	213	227	247
Land and existing structure...	3,471	4,681	4,643	5,305	14	17	16	18
Equipment.............	7,250	11,871	12,570	13,579	29	42	44	47
Assistance and subsidies	16,902	22,136	23,496	24,313	68	79	83	85
Interest on debt..........	22,367	30,089	31,198	33,220	90	107	110	116
Insurance benefits [3]	54,452	105,456	118,833	147,286	219	375	417	512
Debt redemption.	19,895	41,730	49,460	54,678	80	149	174	190
Debt outstanding, year	318,254	547,876	576,494	642,202	1,282	1,951	2,025	2,234
Long-term	315,490	541,497	572,831	623,558	1,271	1,928	2,012	2,170
Full-faith and credit	74,972	138,525	147,130	159,502	302	493	517	555
Nonguaranteed...........	240,518	402,972	425,701	464,056	969	1,435	1,495	1,615
Short-term................	2,764	6,379	3,663	18,644	11	23	13	65
Net long-term [4]...............	125,524	266,870	287,450	317,829	506	950	1,010	1,106
Full-faith and credit only	63,481	128,384	137,341	149,580	256	457	482	520

[1] 1990 and 2000 based on enumerated resident population as of April 1. Other years based on estimated resident population as of July 1. [2] Includes other items not shown separately. [3] Includes repayments. [4] Less cash and investment assets specifically held for redemption of long-term debt.

Source: U.S. Census Bureau, 1990, State Government Finances. series GF, No. 3 thereafter. <http://www.census.gov/govs/www/state02.html> (accessed 8 April 2005).

State and Local Government Finances and Employment 291

Table 439. State Governments—Revenue by State: 2002

[In millions of dollars (1,097,829 represents $1,097,829,000,000), except as noted. For fiscal year ending in year shown; See text. this section.Includes local shares of state imposed taxes. Minus sign (-) indicates net loss]

State	Total revenue [1]	General revenue Total	Per capita [2] Total (dol.)	Per capita [2] Rank	Intergovernmental revenue Total	Intergovernmental revenue From Federal government	Charges and miscellaneous Total	Charges and miscellaneous Current charges	Charges and miscellaneous Miscellaneous general revenue	Insurance trust revenue
United States. . .	1,097,829	1,062,305	3,689	(X)	335,423	317,581	191,641	99,811	91,830	19,301
Alabama	14,942	15,986	3,567	35	6,275	5,795	3,201	2,286	915	-1,204
Alaska	5,019	5,423	8,462	1	1,556	1,551	2,777	338	2,439	-421
Arizona	17,298	15,860	2,916	46	5,260	4,875	2,123	925	1,198	1,414
Arkansas	10,297	10,533	3,890	24	3,429	3,410	1,878	1,177	701	-236
California	151,245	141,481	4,044	18	43,861	40,843	19,865	11,456	8,408	5,520
Colorado	11,809	13,875	3,085	40	3,866	3,806	3,086	1,471	1,615	-2,065
Connecticut	16,993	15,382	4,447	6	3,769	3,686	2,580	1,076	1,504	1,589
Delaware	4,842	4,633	5,748	2	922	891	1,538	623	914	199
Florida	47,890	46,995	2,817	49	13,141	12,786	8,502	2,927	5,575	881
Georgia	24,847	26,114	3,058	45	8,611	8,541	3,731	1,895	1,836	-1,268
Hawaii	5,869	6,042	4,894	3	1,367	1,365	1,255	766	489	-174
Idaho	4,488	4,375	3,257	32	1,330	1,324	774	383	391	48
Illinois	41,095	40,340	3,205	39	11,435	10,449	6,430	2,669	3,761	755
Indiana	20,116	20,011	3,249	36	6,028	5,886	3,782	2,287	1,495	106
Iowa	11,130	11,026	3,757	29	3,445	3,320	2,574	1,452	1,122	-11
Kansas	9,694	9,179	3,384	43	2,992	2,964	1,379	669	710	515
Kentucky	16,073	15,810	3,866	22	5,121	5,102	2,714	1,621	1,093	263
Louisiana	18,079	17,659	3,944	23	6,049	5,994	4,253	2,218	2,035	415
Maine	5,451	5,600	4,315	13	1,830	1,817	1,143	438	706	-231
Maryland	20,788	19,909	3,659	31	5,453	5,260	3,635	1,967	1,668	784
Massachusetts	26,885	26,476	4,129	8	5,431	5,061	6,223	1,861	4,361	297
Michigan	43,950	40,886	4,071	14	11,507	11,241	7,515	4,620	2,895	2,457
Minnesota	22,439	21,910	4,360	12	5,427	5,282	3,259	1,539	1,720	529
Mississippi	11,052	11,044	3,851	27	4,535	4,374	1,780	1,193	587	-167
Missouri	19,085	18,654	3,284	41	6,819	6,693	3,106	1,444	1,662	432
Montana	4,033	3,721	4,086	20	1,427	1,419	852	387	464	266
Nebraska	6,002	5,987	3,468	33	1,823	1,780	1,172	559	613	15
Nevada	6,888	6,167	2,844	44	1,338	1,281	884	513	370	557
New Hampshire . . .	4,636	4,391	3,442	50	1,389	1,189	1,104	506	598	-81
New Jersey	32,709	33,897	3,952	16	8,677	8,235	6,891	3,682	3,209	-1,734
New Mexico	8,746	8,478	4,570	9	2,855	2,760	1,995	696	1,299	268
New York	104,534	92,897	4,851	7	37,730	32,197	11,905	5,198	6,707	6,272
North Carolina	31,524	29,972	3,606	25	10,202	9,466	4,233	2,722	1,512	1,551
North Dakota	3,017	2,868	4,526	11	1,043	1,022	708	506	202	148
Ohio	45,439	40,232	3,526	38	12,654	12,328	7,447	4,134	3,314	4,682
Oklahoma	13,134	12,761	3,658	42	4,120	4,044	2,588	1,583	1,005	55
Oregon	14,815	14,305	4,060	19	5,710	5,625	3,431	1,878	1,552	256
Pennsylvania	46,165	46,544	3,775	28	13,734	13,685	10,675	6,305	4,370	-1,339
Rhode Island	4,891	4,836	4,524	10	1,720	1,637	988	385	603	43
South Carolina	16,997	14,477	3,526	30	5,434	5,028	2,954	2,136	818	1,534
South Dakota	2,491	2,604	3,424	37	1,063	1,045	564	177	388	-113
Tennessee	17,952	17,620	3,042	47	7,316	7,078	2,506	1,713	792	332
Texas	60,588	62,181	2,862	48	21,385	20,672	12,134	6,115	6,019	-1,593
Utah	8,468	8,623	3,717	26	2,279	2,267	2,419	1,675	744	-288
Vermont	3,260	3,229	5,238	5	1,087	1,041	624	324	300	-3
Virginia	23,577	24,843	3,416	34	5,531	5,377	6,530	3,703	2,827	-1,604
Washington	23,813	22,775	3,754	21	6,348	6,216	3,798	2,353	1,445	673
West Virginia	9,130	8,053	4,461	17	2,899	2,847	1,602	772	830	1,025
Wisconsin	20,874	22,874	4,205	15	7,031	5,913	4,029	2,374	1,655	-2,000
Wyoming	2,770	2,768	5,546	4	1,169	1,113	505	112	393	-48

See footnote at end of table.

U.S. Census Bureau, Statistical Abstract of the United States: 2006

Table 439. **State Governments—Revenue by State: 2002—Con.**

[See headnote, page 292]

State	All taxes				Sales and gross receipts taxes						
		Per capita [2]		Property taxes		General sales taxes, total	Selective sales taxes [3]				
	Total [3]	Total (dol.)	Rank		Total [3]		Total [3]	Alcoholic beverages and tobacco sales	Insurance premiums	Motor fuels sales	Public utilities
United States. . .	535,241	1,862	(X)	9,702	262,361	179,665	82,695	13,151	11,158	31,968	10,288
Alabama	6,510	1,453	47	195	3,383	1,748	1,635	194	220	512	541
Alaska	1,090	1,700	32	50	142	-	142	59	37	40	3
Arizona.	8,477	1,558	40	329	5,352	4,284	1,069	214	199	625	29
Arkansas.	5,226	1,931	20	487	2,649	1,947	702	123	112	414	-
California.	77,755	2,221	8	1,952	30,702	23,816	6,886	1,395	1,596	3,296	483
Colorado.	6,923	1,538	42	-	2,835	1,902	933	96	158	569	8
Connecticut	9,033	2,611	4	-	4,516	3,044	1,472	200	207	425	167
Delaware.	2,174	2,697	2	-	323	-	323	39	76	108	30
Florida	25,352	1,519	43	428	19,456	14,409	5,048	1,014	414	1,809	1,306
Georgia	13,772	1,612	38	54	6,018	4,834	1,184	238	296	650	-
Hawaii	3,421	2,756	1	-	2,118	1,612	506	105	70	78	93
Idaho	2,271	1,691	34	-	1,116	795	321	35	66	214	2
Illinois.	22,475	1,786	24	57	11,256	6,591	4,664	605	285	1,374	1,510
Indiana	10,201	1,657	35	6	5,425	3,798	1,626	161	179	742	9
Iowa.	5,006	1,705	31	-	2,538	1,747	791	107	136	343	-
Kansas	4,808	1,773	25	55	2,432	1,799	633	134	97	376	1
Kentucky.	7,975	1,950	19	438	3,741	2,312	1,429	89	258	461	-
Louisiana	7,357	1,644	37	35	4,192	2,327	1,865	180	288	559	8
Maine.	2,627	2,028	14	48	1,237	836	401	137	60	192	7
Maryland.	10,821	1,985	16	273	4,699	2,690	2,009	236	197	703	141
Massachusetts	14,823	2,308	6	3	5,211	3,696	1,515	341	361	667	-
Michigan.	21,864	2,177	10	1,891	10,069	7,784	2,285	808	227	1,090	25
Minnesota	13,224	2,632	3	306	5,767	3,741	2,026	231	163	620	-
Mississippi.	4,729	1,649	36	1	3,183	2,340	843	95	130	410	16
Missouri	8,729	1,539	41	21	4,140	2,855	1,285	133	217	692	-
Montana.	1,443	1,585	39	182	371	-	371	32	51	191	31
Nebraska	2,993	1,732	30	6	1,505	1,069	436	62	38	308	3
Nevada.	3,945	1,821	22	113	3,338	2,070	1,268	80	156	266	11
New Hampshire . . .	1,897	1,489	44	502	605	-	605	95	69	120	64
New Jersey	18,329	2,137	12	3	8,777	5,997	2,781	488	346	524	832
New Mexico.	3,628	1,959	18	53	1,823	1,337	486	53	52	200	13
New York	43,262	2,261	7	-	13,121	8,608	4,513	1,189	585	492	1,155
North Carolina	15,537	1,871	21	-	6,565	3,741	2,824	244	348	1,209	407
North Dakota	1,117	1,762	27	1	620	336	284	27	26	111	33
Ohio.	20,130	1,764	26	18	9,328	6,391	2,936	367	366	1,372	814
Oklahoma	6,053	1,734	29	-	2,273	1,529	743	136	149	410	20
Oregon.	5,164	1,467	46	24	650	-	650	188	54	398	9
Pennsylvania	22,136	1,795	23	51	10,948	7,330	3,618	515	503	1,753	732
Rhode Island	2,128	1,992	15	1	1,161	732	429	93	32	130	80
South Carolina	6,088	1,483	45	13	3,158	2,335	823	151	113	411	43
South Dakota	977	1,285	50	-	777	523	254	30	45	123	3
Tennessee.	7,798	1,347	48	-	6,046	4,675	1,371	164	283	814	5
Texas	28,662	1,319	49	-	23,577	14,560	9,018	1,100	972	2,835	722
Utah.	3,925	1,693	33	-	2,023	1,500	523	77	88	336	2
Vermont	1,518	2,465	5	391	570	215	355	42	36	71	9
Virginia	12,781	1,754	28	21	4,782	2,800	1,983	148	293	849	87
Washington	12,629	2,082	13	1,457	9,950	7,904	2,046	505	291	743	332
West Virginia	3,552	1,968	17	4	1,921	963	958	41	89	300	187
Wisconsin	11,814	2,172	11	92	5,428	3,696	1,732	348	107	955	315
Wyoming.	1,094	2,193	9	144	544	445	98	6	15	75	2

See footnote at end of table.

Table 439. **State Governments—Revenue by State: 2002—Con.**

[See headnote, page 292]

State	License taxes					Income taxes			Other taxes	
	Total [3]	Corpo-ration license	Hunt-ing and fishing license	Motor vehicle and opera-tor's license	Occu-pancy and busi-ness license, n.e.c. [4]	Total	Indi-vidual income	Corpo-ration net income	Total [3]	Death and gift
United States ...	35,391	5,842	1,182	17,060	9,873	210,820	185,697	25,123	16,967	7,384
Alabama.........	395	72	15	196	99	2,353	2,031	323	183	83
Alaska..........	74	1	20	37	11	269	-	269	554	3
Arizona.........	271	8	20	167	62	2,437	2,091	346	88	82
Arkansas	273	10	21	129	92	1,740	1,563	177	78	39
California	5,693	48	74	1,892	3,551	38,380	33,047	5,333	1,029	1,000
Colorado........	278	7	57	168	39	3,681	3,476	205	130	72
Connecticut......	405	17	3	274	100	3,835	3,685	149	277	160
Delaware	780	534	1	32	186	968	717	252	102	41
Florida	1,557	128	13	1,062	282	1,219	-	1,219	2.692	752
Georgia	494	41	23	293	93	7,056	6,488	568	151	123
Hawaii	112	2	-	80	17	1,164	1,112	53	27	17
Idaho..........	222	1	30	117	41	919	842	77	13	10
Illinois	1,914	165	25	1,414	299	8,855	7,471	1,384	393	329
Indiana.........	377	6	23	298	36	4,250	3,541	709	143	142
Iowa , ...	520	32	20	372	70	1,858	1,769	88	90	80
Kansas.........	230	29	17	154	21	1,977	1,855	122	115	48
Kentucky	539	181	22	202	116	2,980	2,678	302	276	85
Louisiana	515	265	33	125	86	2,053	1,789	264	563	69
Maine..........	149	3	9	89	41	1,150	1,073	77	43	23
Maryland	436	15	11	220	188	5,064	4,704	359	350	183
Massachusetts....	501	19	6	328	87	8,725	7,913	812	383	201
Michigan........	1,297	12	49	934	223	8,191	6,125	2,065	416	131
Minnesota.......	864	5	51	525	248	5,977	5,443	534	310	66
Mississippi	301	62	13	135	77	1,181	985	196	62	30
Missouri	518	20	29	258	126	3,916	3,615	300	134	134
Montana	199	2	33	132	26	586	518	68	105	14
Nebraska	196	6	14	93	61	1,261	1,153	108	24	16
Nevada	439	36	7	143	157	-	-	-	56	30
New Hampshire....	185	4	8	90	57	449	71	377	157	56
New Jersey......	957	122	14	404	344	7,938	6,837	1,101	653	510
New Mexico	171	2	17	123	27	1,107	983	124	474	19
New York	1,040	66	34	767	113	27,832	25,574	2,258	1,270	768
North Carolina....	884	274	15	480	105	7,933	7,265	668	155	118
North Dakota.....	103	-	10	56	36	250	200	50	144	5
Ohio	1,562	264	28	661	576	9,097	8,336	761	125	116
Oklahoma........	823	44	16	581	171	2,460	2,286	174	497	86
Oregon.........	496	-	33	293	149	3,871	3,675	196	121	65
Pennsylvania.....	2,078	698	60	825	419	7,933	6,735	1,198	1,125	762
Rhode Island......	92	12	1	54	24	852	824	28	22	19
South Carolina....	311	59	15	112	100	2,509	2,349	160	97	64
South Dakota	133	2	22	44	56	41	-	41	26	23
Tennessee	836	421	25	277	100	649	146	503	267	100
Texas..........	3,778	1,991	64	1,101	536	-	-	-	1,307	333
Utah	148	2	22	95	25	1,716	1,605	111	38	9
Vermont	74	2	6	44	20	445	408	37	39	14
Virginia.........	543	30	20	343	137	7,019	6,711	309	416	134
Washington......	631	16	31	350	175	-	-	-	590	114
West Virginia.....	175	7	16	91	30	1,255	1,035	220	198	13
Wisconsin........	728	89	59	346	230	5,419	4,974	445	148	83
Wyoming	95	8	26	54	6	-	-	-	311	10

- Represents or rounds to zero.   X Not applicable.   [1] Duplicate intergovernmental transactions are excluded.   [2] Based on estimated population as of July 1.   [3] Includes categories not shown separately.   [4] n.e.c. Not elsewhere classified.

Source: U.S. Census Bureau, *1990, State Government Finances*, series GF, No. 3 thereafter. <http://www.census.gov/govs/www/state02.html> (accessed 8 April 2005).

Table 440. State Governments—Expenditures and Debt by State: 2002

[In millions of dollars (1,280,290 represents $1,280,290,000,000) except as indicated. For fiscal year ending in year shown; see text, this section]

State	Total expendi- ture [1]	General expenditure								
		Total		Direct expenditures						
		Amount	Per capita [2] (dol.)	Inter- govern- mental	Total	Educa- tion	Public welfare	Health and hospitals	High- ways	Police protec- tion
United States ...	1,280,290	1,109,227	3,859	364,789	744,438	162,054	239,903	66,802	71,248	9,408
Alabama	17,996	16,160	3,608	4,096	12,065	3,231	4,110	1,821	1,064	100
Alaska	7,402	6,702	10,456	1,056	5,647	882	1,029	141	667	63
Arizona	18,119	16,246	2,986	6,969	9,278	2,212	2,780	610	1,127	151
Arkansas	11,521	10,634	3,930	3,071	7,563	1,832	2,578	722	942	72
California	184,928	158,235	4,521	74,687	83,548	17,289	23,014	6,835	5,696	1,132
Colorado	16,823	14,662	3,257	4,295	10,366	3,009	2,283	894	1,134	100
Connecticut	20,117	17,536	5,070	3,735	13,802	2,218	3,362	1,749	817	164
Delaware	4,646	4,233	5,252	823	3,410	733	659	311	332	68
Florida	51,834	47,287	2,833	14,054	33,233	5,105	11,874	2,839	4,707	425
Georgia	30,053	27,166	3,180	8,645	18,521	5,011	6,013	1,094	1,990	255
Hawaii	7,446	6,684	5,386	130	6,553	2,257	1,112	620	236	6
Idaho	5,234	4,625	3,444	1,407	3,218	704	1,003	143	383	44
Illinois	49,131	42,678	3,391	13,091	29,587	6,128	9,429	3,348	2,983	359
Indiana	22,205	20,585	3,343	6,557	14,028	4,146	4,805	749	1,255	194
Iowa	12,721	11,436	3,895	3,326	8,109	2,140	2,573	865	939	86
Kansas	10,592	9,617	3,546	2,971	6,646	1,578	1,963	542	967	63
Kentucky	18,407	16,376	4,004	3,560	12,817	2,981	4,762	844	1,614	163
Louisiana	18,319	16,162	3,611	4,168	11,994	2,771	3,311	1,932	951	195
Maine	6,265	5,670	4,378	1,010	4,661	699	1,762	413	439	59
Maryland	23,317	20,704	3,798	5,236	15,469	3,414	4,625	1,249	1,196	297
Massachusetts	32,848	28,471	4,433	6,284	22,187	3,188	5,665	2,399	2,628	287
Michigan	49,184	43,827	4,364	19,067	24,760	6,590	9,069	2,318	1,250	307
Minnesota	26,693	23,478	4,672	8,271	15,206	3,496	6,071	541	1,080	178
Mississippi	12,742	11,462	3,998	3,457	8,005	1,698	3,214	894	776	67
Missouri	20,841	18,708	3,299	5,073	13,634	2,556	5,377	1,361	1,609	172
Montana	4,265	3,785	4,159	911	2,874	637	643	287	436	28
Nebraska	6,537	6,219	3,599	1,820	4,399	1,116	1,647	274	526	52
Nevada	7,348	6,242	2,881	2,433	3,809	904	1,004	310	568	64
New Hampshire	4,823	4,177	3,278	1,179	2,998	630	879	162	347	37
New Jersey	41,988	32,936	3,841	9,320	23,616	4,558	5,663	2,135	1,977	343
New Mexico	10,084	9,214	4,975	2,768	6,445	1,468	2,028	739	925	89
New York	119,199	96,529	5,045	38,982	57,547	7,619	23,328	4,756	3,222	568
North Carolina	33,124	29,537	3,556	9,451	20,087	4,602	6,522	1,921	2,574	329
North Dakota	3,020	2,813	4,436	586	2,227	563	626	80	311	14
Ohio	52,594	42,362	3,713	15,052	27,310	6,515	9,723	2,234	2,255	233
Oklahoma	14,727	12,904	3,697	3,377	9,527	2,520	3,156	527	1,010	92
Oregon	18,029	14,884	4,228	4,213	10,671	2,040	3,796	1,401	587	141
Pennsylvania	55,171	47,147	3,824	12,788	34,360	7,304	12,160	2,749	4,066	893
Rhode Island	5,767	4,843	4,534	749	4,094	672	1,659	295	260	48
South Carolina	20,009	17,048	4,154	4,241	12,807	2,763	4,360	1,542	1,276	205
South Dakota	2,772	2,554	3,361	506	2,048	377	593	125	390	22
Tennessee	20,029	18,489	3,193	4,478	14,011	3,315	6,319	1,237	1,206	125
Texas	70,274	61,771	2,842	16,681	45,090	11,558	14,607	4,385	5,111	389
Utah	10,107	9,143	3,942	2,171	6,972	2,351	1,573	685	728	104
Vermont	3,512	3,291	5,343	919	2,372	524	756	82	239	48
Virginia	28,044	25,546	3,505	8,369	17,177	4,657	3,622	2,186	2,587	232
Washington	30,378	25,160	4,147	6,806	18,354	4,825	6,151	2,088	1,254	175
West Virginia	9,409	7,560	4,189	1,454	6,107	1,181	2,136	299	986	48
Wisconsin	26,749	23,119	4,250	9,523	13,596	3,197	4,136	968	1,272	97
Wyoming	2,948	2,609	5,228	975	1,634	287	372	104	354	25

See footnote at end of table.

State and Local Government Finances and Employment **295**

Table 440. State Governments—Expenditures and Debt by State: 2002—Con.

[See headnote, page 295]

State	General expenditure-Con.									Debt outstanding	
	Direct expenditures-Con.										
	Corrections	Natural resources	Parks and recreation	Governmental administration	Interest on general debt	Utility expenditures	Liquor stores expenditures	Insurance trust expenditures	Cash and security holdings	Total	Per capita [2] (dol.)
United States ...	36,472	16,588	4,953	39,912	31,426	20,279	3,498	147,286	2,534,039	642,202	2,230
Alabama	325	228	23	415	242	-	161	1,675	26,166	6,405	1,429
Alaska	174	238	9	361	276	53	-	647	39,863	5,308	8,283
Arizona	642	199	42	459	186	27	-	1,845	33,685	4,348	799
Arkansas	284	206	75	405	138	-	-	887	16,827	3,002	1,109
California	5,334	2,977	537	6,816	3,405	5,511	-	21,181	351,945	71,263	2,037
Colorado	639	177	61	422	326	10	-	2,151	40,309	5,419	1,205
Connecticut	638	194	104	913	1,138	310	-	2,271	31,602	20,784	6,009
Delaware	245	68	50	331	255	75	-	339	10,452	4,038	5,010
Florida	2,200	1,395	178	1,914	1,052	86	-	4,460	107,567	20,266	1,215
Georgia	1,233	494	162	660	433	1	-	2,886	61,649	8,243	965
Hawaii	157	98	50	372	462	-	-	762	12,988	5,656	4,582
Idaho	170	164	37	222	142	-	51	558	10,874	2,545	1,895
Illinois	1,300	426	288	1,284	1,847	-	-	6,453	89,504	34,761	2,762
Indiana	615	281	43	763	397	-	-	1,620	32,639	9,456	1,535
Iowa	233	239	18	487	123	-	79	1,206	21,725	3,713	1,265
Kansas	268	175	5	496	127	-	-	974	11,648	2,288	844
Kentucky	413	282	123	636	450	-	-	2,031	33,446	9,039	2,210
Louisiana	480	317	185	576	506	3	-	2,154	36,321	9,233	2,062
Maine	106	146	11	253	238	-	56	538	11,215	4,321	3,330
Maryland	1,029	458	167	840	711	475	-	2,138	41,706	12,309	2,262
Massachusetts	900	243	89	1,268	2,687	333	-	4,044	58,371	45,216	7,051
Michigan	1,613	484	174	820	1,064	-	501	4,855	71,354	21,947	2,185
Minnesota	335	453	111	659	354	-	-	3,215	53,130	6,408	1,275
Mississippi	249	198	37	202	211	-	143	1,138	21,777	4,160	1,451
Missouri	606	261	49	513	568	-	-	2,133	47,734	12,693	2,235
Montana	106	181	6	207	143	-	38	442	9,877	2,752	3,022
Nebraska	176	142	29	165	110	-	-	318	8,938	2,215	1,283
Nevada	225	82	17	198	150	169	-	937	18,655	3,668	1,691
New Hampshire	80	40	5	187	322	-	279	367	8,759	5,397	4,231
New Jersey	1,139	382	506	1,346	1,199	2,262	-	6,790	85,135	32,093	3,742
New Mexico	241	138	49	349	192	-	-	870	32,745	4,493	2,422
New York	2,371	346	430	4,037	3,647	9,470	-	13,200	229,445	89,856	4,692
North Carolina	914	524	125	781	583	-	-	3,586	70,643	11,128	1,339
North Dakota	37	101	13	103	87	-	-	208	6,889	1,673	2,640
Ohio	1,297	366	91	1,911	1,135	-	327	9,904	152,620	20,009	1,754
Oklahoma	506	174	66	458	258	365	-	1,458	23,328	6,477	1,857
Oregon	494	315	46	897	251	10	127	3,008	48,973	7,668	2,176
Pennsylvania	1,456	528	149	1,300	1,073	-	885	7,138	96,330	20,983	1,702
Rhode Island	158	47	25	260	257	109	-	815	11,354	5,856	5,478
South Carolina	423	225	60	540	652	955	-	2,006	26,743	10,116	2,464
South Dakota	67	91	26	103	120	-	-	217	7,367	2,308	3,034
Tennessee	390	227	103	433	198	5	-	1,535	27,347	3,628	626
Texas	3,036	621	86	1,310	950	-	-	8,503	172,989	24,008	1,105
Utah	268	179	60	462	188	-	99	866	17,902	4,729	2,039
Vermont	80	65	15	192	134	12	33	175	4,880	2,284	3,704
Virginia	959	183	74	923	721	13	307	2,178	52,060	13,785	1,895
Washington	735	553	201	539	674	18	322	4,878	58,292	13,552	2,234
West Virginia	170	174	68	426	238	7	47	1,795	10,430	4,537	2,514
Wisconsin	873	378	54	603	737	-	-	3,630	67,155	14,870	2,733
Wyoming	83	125	22	93	72	-	43	296	10,686	1,298	2,600

- Represents or rounds to zero.   [1] Includes amounts not shown separately.   [2] Based on estimated resident population as of July 1.

Source: U.S. Census Bureau, *"State Government Finances"*; <http://www.census.gov/govs/www/state02.html> (accessed 8 April 2005).

Table 441. Local Governments—Revenue by State: 2002

[In millions of dollars (1,083,129 represents $1,083,129,000,000), except as noted. For fiscal year ending in year shown; see text, this section. Minus sign (-) indicates net loss.]

State	Total revenue [1]	General revenue Total	Per capita [2] (dol.)	Intergovernmental revenue Total	From federal government	From state governments	Taxes Total [1]	Property	Sales and gross receipts	Income [3]	Motor licenses
United States...	1,083,129	995,856	3,458	398,497	42,953	355,544	369,730	269,419	61,679	20,190	1,303
Alabama	14,528	12,486	2,788	4,719	468	4,250	3,209	1,278	1,417	96	24
Alaska	2,866	2,678	4,178	1,125	238	887	980	780	169	-	10
Arizona	19,578	16,455	3,024	7,251	844	6,407	5,943	3,925	1,729	-	1
Arkansas	6,282	5,690	2,103	3,180	235	2,944	1,235	517	691	3	-
California	174,136	159,820	4,566	79,046	7,406	71,639	42,669	28,291	10,858	-	-
Colorado	17,835	16,154	3,589	4,390	462	3,928	6,977	4,162	2,467	-	32
Connecticut	11,094	10,679	3,087	3,526	354	3,172	6,092	5,995	-	-	-
Delaware	2,052	1,889	2,343	959	68	891	513	400	3	47	-
District of Columbia	7,352	6,922	12,166	2,840	2,840	-	3,228	803	936	1,160	19
Florida	60,028	54,956	3,292	17,103	2,171	14,932	19,488	15,327	3,480	-	17
Georgia	29,982	26,908	3,149	9,409	816	8,593	10,286	6,586	3,377	-	-
Hawaii	1,739	1,543	1,243	337	183	154	819	615	126	-	54
Idaho	3,839	3,699	2,754	1,539	91	1,448	1,020	959	19	-	4
Illinois	46,218	42,484	3,375	15,007	2,268	12,739	19,095	15,816	2,620	-	116
Indiana	20,291	18,539	3,011	6,441	397	6,044	6,786	5,970	98	580	3
Iowa	9,743	9,118	3,105	3,453	306	3,147	3,324	2,878	348	45	15
Kansas	9,304	8,469	3,123	3,120	135	2,985	3,167	2,470	634	-	3
Kentucky	9,712	8,732	2,135	3,603	312	3,291	2,806	1,539	201	818	24
Louisiana	13,554	12,648	2,826	4,696	490	4,205	4,825	1,906	2,757	-	4
Maine	3,623	3,531	2,727	1,125	84	1,041	1,914	1,864	5	-	26
Maryland	17,927	17,657	3,239	5,721	668	5,054	9,053	5,139	275	2,940	-
Massachusetts	23,427	20,913	3,256	9,132	1,115	8,017	9,073	8,719	152	-	-
Michigan	36,228	34,134	3,399	18,115	1,302	16,813	8,780	7,903	169	472	-
Minnesota	21,133	19,724	3,925	9,101	806	8,296	5,232	4,909	150	-	3
Mississippi	7,998	7,394	2,579	3,236	251	2,985	1,795	1,645	72	-	-
Missouri	16,310	15,183	2,678	5,285	635	4,650	6,395	3,859	1,904	313	12
Montana	2,296	2,219	2,439	982	172	810	692	671	3	-	-
Nebraska	7,587	5,392	3,121	1,709	193	1,515	2,324	1,742	314	-	19
Nevada	8,670	7,998	3,691	3,043	352	2,691	2,487	1,590	502	-	-
New Hampshire	3,518	3,441	2,701	1,332	107	1,225	1,702	1,668	-	-	-
New Jersey	32,488	31,721	3,699	10,635	714	9,921	16,300	16,046	26	30	-
New Mexico	5,530	5,163	2,788	3,042	364	2,678	1,250	703	497	-	2
New York	108,836	105,032	5,489	40,843	3,989	36,855	45,616	26,826	9,370	7,452	147
North Carolina	27,473	24,592	2,961	10,439	775	9,664	7,039	5,422	1,287	-	27
North Dakota	1,767	1,683	2,654	670	134	536	611	531	69	-	-
Ohio	42,138	40,285	3,531	16,158	1,535	14,623	16,035	10,625	1,438	3,458	100
Oklahoma	9,182	8,455	2,423	3,448	369	3,079	2,729	1,482	1,174	-	1
Oregon	13,183	12,118	3,443	5,525	812	4,713	3,840	3,115	239	-	9
Pennsylvania	40,614	38,501	3,123	15,377	2,341	13,036	15,491	10,860	343	2,775	-
Rhode Island	2,877	2,707	2,535	953	129	824	1,495	1,461	4	-	-
South Carolina	12,136	10,911	2,659	4,046	305	3,742	3,664	3,084	267	-	19
South Dakota	1,987	1,812	2,384	601	105	496	865	668	153	-	25
Tennessee	20,001	14,333	2,476	4,757	526	4,231	5,176	3,453	1,415	-	105
Texas	71,362	64,879	2,985	19,462	2,242	17,219	30,318	24,521	5,062	-	306
Utah	7,462	6,017	2,595	2,476	347	2,129	2,101	1,420	596	-	-
Vermont	1,668	1,511	2,452	883	46	837	447	433	3	-	-
Virginia	22,755	21,735	2,982	8,255	857	7,397	9,350	6,690	1,760	-	134
Washington	26,003	21,262	3,504	8,385	826	7,559	6,885	4,333	2,026	-	29
West Virginia	3,939	3,783	2,096	1,824	152	1,672	1,090	897	59	-	-
Wisconsin	20,376	19,507	3,586	9,251	543	8,708	6,796	6,374	270	-	1
Wyoming	2,502	2,394	4,798	944	74	870	724	548	148	-	11

See footnotes at end of table.

U.S. Census Bureau, Statistical Abstract of the United States: 2006

Table 441. Local Governments—Revenue by State: 2002—Con.

[See headnote, page 297]

State	Current charges and miscellaneous general revenue	General revenue									
		Current charges				Miscellaneous general revenue			Utility revenue	Liquor store revenue	Insurance trust revenue [2]
		Total [1]	Education	Hospital	Sewerage	Total [1]	Interest earnings	Special assessment			
United States ...	227,629	153,382	17,235	41,502	27,056	74,247	35,211	4,661	90,387	777	-3,891
Alabama.........	4,558	3,706	287	2,600	257	852	438	3	1,978	-	65
Alaska..........	573	358	37	65	53	215	123	8	207	-	-20
Arizona.........	3,262	1,968	330	265	386	1,294	681	73	3,170	-	-48
Arkansas	1,275	783	138	186	171	493	287	8	595	-	-2
California	38,105	24,547	1,837	4,840	3,585	13,559	5,933	1,154	16,817	-	-2,500
Colorado........	4,787	3,133	318	811	488	1,654	744	142	1,755	-	-74
Connecticut......	1,061	688	98	16	189	373	125	25	486	-	-71
Delaware........	416	285	15	-	113	132	77	1	161	-	3
District of Columbia......	854	302	18	-	92	553	132	1	499	-	-69
Florida	18,365	12,095	1,427	3,479	1,614	6,269	3,310	1,207	5,675	-	-603
Georgia	7,213	5,068	230	2,630	650	2,145	1,017	21	3,109	-	-35
Hawaii	387	271	-	-	145	116	52	8	197	-	-
Idaho..........	1,140	916	58	497	104	223	96	28	141	-	-1
Illinois	8,382	5,217	959	610	831	3,165	1,506	145	2,781	-	953
Indiana.........	5,311	3,475	311	1,767	750	1,836	417	26	1,720	-	33
Iowa	2,340	1,836	479	708	255	504	221	17	615	-	11
Kansas.........	2,183	1,415	254	530	190	768	441	67	864	-	-29
Kentucky	2,322	1,203	91	242	282	1,120	883	34	951	-	29
Louisiana	3,127	2,223	68	1,336	235	905	584	5	895	-	10
Maine..........	492	364	40	61	116	128	53	2	92	-	-
Maryland	2,882	1,953	544	-	588	929	353	108	443	162	-335
Massachusetts.....	2,708	1,962	196	310	682	746	261	32	2,175	-	339
Michigan........	7,239	4,704	767	436	1,118	2,535	940	182	1,634	-	459
Minnesota.......	5,390	3,335	249	866	613	2,055	922	276	1,369	213	-173
Mississippi	2,364	1,873	247	1,223	139	491	234	8	604	-	-
Missouri	3,504	2,438	482	756	395	1,066	532	18	1,240	-	-112
Montana........	545	360	58	35	50	184	78	45	76	-	-
Nebraska.......	1,360	876	176	259	102	483	198	37	2,348	-	-154
Nevada	2,469	1,683	98	489	235	786	386	35	671	-	-
New Hampshire....	407	299	44	-	76	108	38	1	77	-	-
New Jersey......	4,787	3,119	599	214	1,113	1,667	541	21	767	-	-
New Mexico	871	534	81	63	114	337	176	20	367	-	-
New York	18,573	12,982	998	3,251	1,453	5,591	1,947	97	4,081	-	-277
North Carolina....	7,114	5,822	501	2,925	962	1,292	588	14	2,505	386	-10
North Dakota.....	401	200	42	-	30	201	63	46	76	-	8
Ohio	8,092	4,973	831	925	1,360	3,119	1,819	157	1,954	-	-101
Oklahoma.......	2,278	1,682	253	660	231	597	278	5	729	-	-2
Oregon.........	2,754	2,016	354	208	525	738	316	46	1,064	-	1
Pennsylvania.....	7,633	4,775	584	36	1,488	2,858	1,998	83	2,225	-	-112
Rhode Island.....	260	170	20	1	58	90	21	4	122	-	47
South Carolina....	3,201	2,443	201	1,436	262	758	409	26	1,226	-	-1
South Dakota	346	247	48	29	45	99	57	4	160	16	-
Tennessee	4,400	3,427	267	1,789	417	973	451	17	5,670	-	-2
Texas..........	15,099	10,045	1,452	2,817	1,959	5,054	3,184	93	7,220	-	-737
Utah	1,441	829	66	39	163	612	216	22	1,445	-	-
Vermont.........	181	113	18	-	36	68	17	3	167	-	-10
Virginia.........	4,130	2,817	309	294	741	1,313	581	73	1,258	-	-238
Washington......	5,992	4,246	269	1,088	907	1,746	726	104	4,798	-	-57
West Virginia.....	869	539	34	198	123	330	231	10	142	-	14
Wisconsin.......	3,460	2,483	406	102	532	977	448	91	957	-	-88
Wyoming	726	584	47	409	33	142	82	11	106	-	2

- Represents or rounds to zero.   [1] Includes items not shown separately.   [2] Based on estimated resident population as of July 1.

Source: U.S. Census Bureau, 1990, State Government Finances, series GF, No. 3 thereafter. <http://www.census.gov/govs/www/state02.html> (accessed 8 April 2005).

Table 442. Local Governments—Expenditures and Debt by State: 2002

[In millions of dollars, (1,140,082 represents $1,140,082,000,000), except as indicated. For fiscal year ending in year shown; see text, this section]

State	Total expenditure [1]	General expenditures		Direct general expenditures	Selected functions (direct expenditures)						
		Total amount	Per capita [2] (dol.)		Education	Public welfare	Health	Hospitals	Highways	Police protection	Fire protection
United States . . .	1,140,082	997,623	3,959	986,371	432,537	39,695	29,295	50,282	44,219	55,084	25,978
Alabama.	14,642	12,552	3,269	12,540	5,089	52	280	1,981	605	610	279
Alaska	3,051	2,797	4,759	2,797	1,225	6	58	63	248	201	85
Arizona.	20,404	16,221	3,750	15,975	6,584	506	204	396	786	1,108	485
Arkansas	6,123	5,507	2,263	5,505	2,951	15	22	172	365	331	148
California	181,512	153,282	5,186	152,079	59,538	12,545	7,335	6,791	5,771	9,015	4,170
Colorado.	19,363	16,736	4,302	16,732	6,002	540	212	935	1,702	972	424
Connecticut.	11,211	10,399	3,241	10,397	5,634	110	129	25	408	617	391
Delaware	2,127	1,950	2,638	1,946	1,204	-	16	-	133	122	24
District of Columbia.	7,832	6,180	13,765	6,180	1,175	1,462	378	177	69	385	136
Florida	61,756	54,078	3,700	53,849	20,690	626	526	4,126	2,013	3,968	1,856
Georgia	30,960	26,488	3,624	26,430	12,355	146	873	2,865	949	1,300	636
Hawaii	2,077	1,741	1,674	1,736	-	30	32	-	183	248	104
Idaho	3,743	3,591	2,787	3,586	1,719	32	62	400	235	197	82
Illinois	51,384	44,257	4,083	44,231	19,825	432	558	1,293	2,693	2,867	1,358
Indiana.	20,687	18,802	3,360	18,769	8,046	508	195	1,933	776	702	503
Iowa	9,928	9,149	3,382	9,077	4,328	109	293	728	823	373	161
Kansas.	9,098	8,230	3,355	8,230	3,923	40	169	520	561	414	189
Kentucky	9,995	8,778	2,444	8,775	3,896	54	343	258	337	379	266
Louisiana	13,523	12,333	3,021	12,327	5,223	51	112	1,577	580	695	359
Maine.	3,386	3,288	2,615	3,287	1,792	30	17	70	179	122	84
Maryland	17,682	16,514	3,244	16,327	8,728	112	241	-	659	1,038	523
Massachusetts. . . .	25,035	20,794	3,898	20,160	10,255	67	110	665	630	1,155	848
Michigan.	39,489	36,094	3,932	35,963	17,155	769	2,589	440	1,969	1,669	681
Minnesota.	22,200	19,832	4,418	19,727	7,770	1,402	450	974	1,600	841	265
Mississippi	8,000	7,380	2,790	7,379	3,403	22	45	1,201	460	394	173
Missouri	17,266	15,411	3,045	15,410	8,000	143	230	842	864	846	476
Montana.	2,262	2,178	2,485	2,177	1,155	28	53	38	106	142	42
Nebraska	7,769	5,354	4,496	5,346	2,681	56	36	297	397	216	126
Nevada	9,055	7,964	4,178	7,957	2,775	116	78	534	703	586	285
New Hampshire. . . .	3,493	3,416	2,741	3,345	1,809	151	22	-	157	175	119
New Jersey.	31,826	31,054	3,711	30,772	15,985	945	355	246	986	2,076	700
New Mexico	5,397	5,015	2,914	4,991	2,708	49	28	62	219	321	146
New York	123,857	109,731	6,473	103,583	40,104	9,175	2,456	5,796	3,855	6,151	2,452
North Carolina	28,577	24,865	3,441	24,453	10,660	1,135	1,367	2,799	443	1,175	573
North Dakota.	1,766	1,669	2,785	1,659	749	38	24	-	150	63	26
Ohio	42,720	40,031	3,744	39,737	17,108	2,555	2,112	1,108	1,837	2,180	1,202
Oklahoma.	9,384	8,628	2,689	8,627	4,383	36	115	663	534	477	295
Oregon.	13,916	12,320	3,953	12,318	5,503	250	559	234	609	631	376
Pennsylvania.	43,527	38,958	3,530	38,952	16,992	2,326	2,204	200	1,224	1,554	482
Rhode Island.	2,894	2,663	2,709	2,663	1,509	7	3	1	72	191	189
South Carolina.	12,374	11,049	3,015	11,013	5,616	14	142	1,459	215	518	232
South Dakota	2,011	1,837	2,646	1,837	983	12	14	31	190	83	36
Tennessee	21,128	14,982	3,649	14,941	6,152	139	239	1,825	567	851	423
Texas.	77,108	67,341	3,547	66,514	34,145	296	1,529	4,190	2,416	3,338	1,496
Utah	7,599	5,901	3,277	5,889	2,845	22	137	36	289	337	147
Vermont	1,616	1,433	2,623	1,433	937	1	6	-	123	44	35
Virginia.	24,033	22,113	3,298	22,090	10,492	1,052	667	331	515	1,077	623
Washington.	26,875	20,319	4,430	20,292	8,041	47	679	1,245	1,122	916	663
West Virginia.	3,980	3,748	2,205	3,742	2,338	3	34	183	54	139	66
Wisconsin.	22,077	20,449	4,058	20,408	9,367	1,424	919	194	1,714	1,175	490
Wyoming	2,365	2,220	4,739	2,219	991	9	35	378	123	96	42

See footnotes at end of table.

U.S. Census Bureau, Statistical Abstract of the United States: 2006

State	General expenditures–Con.									Insurance trust expenditures	Debt outstanding
	Selected functions (direct expenditures)–Con.										
	Corrections	Parks and recreation	Housing [3]	Sewerage	Solid waste	Governmental administration	Interest on general debt	Other	Utility expenditures		
United States ...	18,215	25,143	27,827	30,189	16,311	52,878	43,876	94,841	119,389	22,386	1,043,904
Alabama.........	135	317	400	612	230	539	578	834	1,999	91	12,652
Alaska..........	1	91	108	53	49	162	151	294	236	18	3,338
Arizona..........	480	602	286	547	314	1,185	905	1,588	4,095	89	22,259
Arkansas	85	88	155	177	134	266	278	318	594	22	5,752
California	3,678	3,636	5,220	3,818	1,870	8,824	5,278	14,590	23,303	4,926	138,037
Colorado........	217	914	373	512	63	1,039	933	1,896	2,369	257	21,299
Connecticut......	-	197	348	268	201	445	291	1,334	519	293	6,984
Delaware	-	26	52	104	9	78	71	108	147	29	1,494
District of Columbia......	174	303	88	211	43	383	236	959	1,490	163	5,436
Florida	1,165	1,658	1,112	1,679	1,649	2,972	3,124	6,682	7,103	575	70,010
Georgia	532	584	708	1,081	461	1,740	698	1,502	4,243	229	26,058
Hawaii	-	211	53	167	144	156	111	297	336	-	2,792
Idaho...........	59	72	27	120	87	197	68	228	150	2	1,440
Illinois	579	2,236	1,738	1,452	417	2,864	2,080	3,839	4,842	2,284	46,176
Indiana.........	226	428	418	858	213	1,143	779	2,042	1,782	103	14,615
Iowa	97	277	145	299	142	351	253	700	766	14	5,781
Kansas.........	94	190	134	190	100	447	506	753	834	33	10,025
Kentucky	186	136	160	423	165	374	1,040	756	1,188	29	19,955
Louisiana	295	226	353	349	249	825	549	883	1,043	147	11,753
Maine..........	40	45	84	117	90	171	91	357	98	-	2,025
Maryland	228	528	565	421	419	805	658	1,402	490	538	13,354
Massachusetts.....	225	190	1,036	545	341	785	549	2,760	3,162	1,079	20,106
Michigan.........	496	883	320	1,426	460	2,041	1,318	3,747	2,277	1,118	32,248
Minnesota.......	313	622	706	613	241	1,085	1,100	1,743	1,813	359	25,602
Mississippi	73	123	141	116	118	432	286	390	618	2	5,774
Missouri	209	382	332	456	117	790	470	1,253	1,518	337	11,552
Montana........	16	37	37	51	54	128	67	223	84	-	1,211
Nebraska	81	118	112	114	67	270	147	628	2,306	109	5,691
Nevada	278	364	183	178	13	712	527	622	1,091	-	12,105
New Hampshire....	35	59	85	71	71	174	84	334	76	1	1,825
New Jersey......	468	456	714	1,088	857	1,456	1,178	3,261	762	10	25,497
New Mexico	130	156	81	108	101	277	186	419	382	-	4,110
New York........	2,292	1,577	3,560	2,213	2,180	3,433	4,682	13,658	7,812	6,314	107,339
North Carolina.....	258	520	669	650	551	963	760	1,929	3,359	19	22,332
North Dakota......	23	82	48	31	34	77	64	251	89	7	1,232
Ohio	518	947	1,209	1,347	431	2,740	1,560	2,883	2,581	108	31,335
Oklahoma........	54	236	166	269	157	407	264	571	723	34	6,031
Oregon.........	333	271	360	602	107	693	486	1,304	1,530	66	11,159
Pennsylvania......	995	529	1,616	1,561	545	2,123	2,973	3,628	3,653	915	62,827
Rhode Island.....	-	38	141	53	39	112	68	240	124	106	1,489
South Carolina.....	147	201	176	229	231	751	507	575	1,322	3	12,757
South Dakota	26	77	37	44	25	96	53	128	150	9	1,143
Tennessee	299	339	480	366	299	814	723	1,424	5,803	343	17,500
Texas..........	1,365	1,965	1,245	1,777	764	3,199	4,049	4,739	9,107	659	98,801
Utah	108	264	153	237	98	453	237	527	1,698	-	8,520
Vermont	-	16	34	40	25	62	30	80	178	4	744
Virginia.........	429	558	588	694	512	1,328	984	2,241	1,518	402	21,637
Washington......	411	665	681	911	435	1,203	865	2,407	6,436	121	32,008
West Virginia.....	31	45	90	124	52	210	208	164	207	26	3,547
Wisconsin.......	303	601	294	776	305	948	720	1,177	1,239	389	15,457
Wyoming	27	56	4	44	33	150	55	174	142	3	1,090

-Represents or rounds to zero.   [1] Duplicate intergovernmental transactions are excluded.   [2] Based on estimated resident population as of July 1.   [3] Includes community development.

Source: U.S. Census Bureau, *1990, State Government Finances, series GF, No. 3* thereafter. <http://www.census.gov/govs/www/state02.html> (accessed 8 April 2005).

Table 443. Estimated State and Local Taxes Paid by a Family of Four for Selected Largest City in Each State: 2003

[Data based on average family of four (two wage earners and two school age children) owning their own home and living in a city where taxes apply. Comprises state and local sales, income, auto, and real estate taxes. For definition of median, see Guide to Tabular Presentation]

City	Total taxes paid by gross family income level (dollars)					Total taxes paid as percent of income				
	$25,000	$50,000	$75,000	$100,000	$150,000	$25,000	$50,000	$75,000	$100,000	$150,000
Albuquerque, NM	1,560	3,730	6,369	8,903	14,011	6.2	7.5	8.5	8.9	9.3
Atlanta, GA	1,970	4,933	8,261	11,203	16,771	7.9	9.9	11.0	11.2	11.2
Baltimore, MD	1,871	5,591	8,923	11,876	17,636	7.5	11.2	11.9	11.9	11.8
Boston, MA	1,990	4,880	7,878	10,254	15,123	8.0	9.8	10.5	10.3	10.1
Charlotte, NC	1,713	4,199	7,061	9,851	14,699	6.9	8.4	9.4	9.9	9.8
Chicago, IL	2,476	4,938	7,790	10,050	14,504	9.9	9.9	10.4	10.0	9.7
Columbus, OH	2,116	4,579	7,434	10,254	16,119	8.5	9.2	9.9	10.3	10.7
Denver, CO	1,320	3,296	5,535	7,247	10,648	5.3	6.6	7.4	7.2	7.1
Detroit, MI	2,463	5,246	8,257	10,904	16,139	9.9	10.5	11.0	10.9	10.8
Honolulu, HI	1,687	3,832	6,393	8,720	13,458	6.7	7.7	8.5	8.7	9.0
Houston, TX	1,564	2,974	4,612	5,843	8,187	6.3	5.9	6.1	5.8	5.5
Indianapolis, IN	2,061	4,472	6,925	9,054	13,274	8.2	8.9	9.2	9.1	8.8
Jacksonville, FL	633	1,818	3,235	4,300	6,376	2.5	3.6	4.3	4.3	4.3
Kansas City, MO	1,740	4,259	6,805	9,074	13,596	7.0	8.5	9.1	9.1	9.1
Las Vegas, NV	1,473	2,511	3,802	4,790	6,572	5.9	5.0	5.1	4.8	4.4
Los Angeles, CA	2,161	4,245	7,488	10,856	17,716	8.6	8.5	10.0	10.9	11.8
Memphis, TN	1,757	3,107	4,708	5,924	8,369	7.0	6.2	6.3	5.9	5.6
Milwaukee, WI	1,982	5,164	8,439	11,328	16,914	7.9	10.3	11.3	11.3	11.3
Minneapolis, MN	1,454	4,181	6,962	9,533	14,657	5.8	8.4	9.3	9.5	9.8
New Orleans, LA	1,084	3,538	6,798	9,435	14,517	4.3	7.1	9.1	9.4	9.7
New York City, NY . . .	1,784	5,999	10,490	14,232	22,274	7.1	12.0	14.0	14.2	14.8
Oklahoma City, OK . . .	1,223	3,991	6,593	8,571	13,351	4.9	8.0	8.8	8.6	8.9
Omaha, NE	1,901	4,214	7,138	9,864	15,234	7.6	8.4	9.5	9.9	10.2
Philadelphia, PA.	2,814	6,591	9,757	12,642	18,384	11.3	13.2	13.0	12.6	12.3
Phoenix, AZ	1,338	3,025	4,782	6,901	10,888	5.4	6.1	6.4	6.9	7.3
Portland, OR	2,580	5,907	9,273	12,573	18,997	10.3	11.8	12.4	12.6	12.7
Seattle, WA.	1,825	3,232	4,876	6,122	8,556	7.3	6.5	6.5	6.1	5.7
Virginia Beach, VA . . .	1,892	3,996	6,411	8,576	12,815	7.6	8.0	8.5	8.6	8.5
Washington, DC.	1,657	4,583	7,594	10,454	16,192	6.6	9.2	10.1	10.5	10.8
Wichita, KS	1,055	3,142	5,683	7,931	12,224	4.2	6.3	7.6	7.9	8.1
Average [1]	1,816	4,172	6,832	9,203	13,859	7.3	8.3	9.1	9.2	9.2
Median [1]	1,740	4,070	6,805	9,391	14,011	7.0	8.1	9.1	9.4	9.3

[1] Based on selected cities and District of Columbia. For complete list of cities, see Table 444.

Source: Government of the District of Columbia. Department of Finance and Revenue, *Tax Rates and Tax Burdens in the District of Columbia: A Nationwide Comparison,* annual. <http://www.cfo.dc.gov/main.asp>

Table 444. Residential Property Tax Rates for Largest City in Each State: 2003

[Effective tax rate is amount each jurisdiction considers based upon assessment level used. Assessment level is ratio of assessed value to assumed market value. Nominal rates represent the "announced" rates levied by the jurisdiction]

City	Effective tax rate per $100		Assessment level (percent)	Nominal rate per $100	City	Effective tax rate per $100		Assessment level (percent)	Nominal rate per $100
	Rank	Rate				Rank	Rate		
Providence, RI	1	3.88	100.0	3.88	Columbus, OH	28	1.45	29.6	4.91
Bridgeport, CT	2	3.86	70.0	5.52	Columbia, SC.	29	1.40	4.0	35.02
Newark, NJ	3	2.96	137.0	2.16	Little Rock, AR	30	1.38	20.0	6.90
Philadelphia, PA	4	2.64	32.0	8.26	Salt Lake City, UT	31	1.36	99.0	1.37
Houston, TX	5	2.62	100.0	2.62	Boston, MA	32	1.33	100.0	1.33
Manchester, NH	6	2.57	100.0	2.57	Minneapolis, MN.	33	1.32	86.4	1.52
Milwaukee, WI	7	2.53	100.0	2.53	Wichita, KS	34	1.31	11.5	11.36
Baltimore, MD	8	2.46	100.0	2.46	Albuquerque, NM	35	1.27	33.3	3.82
Des Moines, IA.	9	2.17	48.5	4.48	Louisville, KY	36	1.21	100.0	1.21
Indianapolis, IN	10	2.17	100.0	2.17	Phoenix, AZ.	37	1.17	10.0	11.65
Fargo, ND	11	2.12	4.4	48.66	Oklahoma City, OK . . .	38	1.16	11.0	10.59
Omaha, NE	12	2.03	94.0	2.16	Kansas City, MO.	39	1.16	19.0	6.13
Jacksonville, FL	13	1.94	100.0	1.94	Charlotte, NC.	40	1.13	98.1	1.16
Burlington, VT	14	1.86	67.6	2.75	New York City, NY	41	1.12	8.0	14.05
Detroit, MI	15	1.82	27.1	6.73	Virginia Beach, VA	42	1.11	90.6	1.22
Portland, OR	16	1.79	80.0	2.24	Las Vegas, NV.	43	1.09	35.0	3.12
Atlanta, GA	17	1.79	40.0	4.47	Los Angeles, CA.	44	1.08	100.0	1.08
Boise, ID.	18	1.75	97.8	1.79	Seattle, WA.	45	0.99	90.5	1.10
New Orleans, LA	19	1.75	10.0	17.50	Washington, DC.	46	0.96	100.0	0.96
Portland, ME	20	1.75	68.0	2.57	Charleston, WV	47	0.88	60.0	1.47
Memphis, TN	21	1.73	23.8	7.27	Birmingham, AL	48	0.70	10.0	6.95
Jackson, MS	22	1.69	10.0	16.93	Cheyenne, WY.	49	0.67	9.5	7.10
Chicago, IL	23	1.69	22.1	7.63	Denver, CO	50	0.53	8.0	6.63
Billings, MT	24	1.62	80.0	2.03	Honolulu, HI.	51	0.38	100.0	0.38
Anchorage, AK	25	1.62	100.0	1.62					
Sioux Falls, SD	26	1.50	85.0	1.77	Unweighted average . . .	(X)	1.65	60.5	$6.05
Wilmington, DE	27	1.45	53.0	2.75	Median	(X)	1.50	(X)	(X)

X Not applicable.

Source: Government of the District of Columbia, Department of Finance and Revenue, *Tax Rates and Tax Burdens in the District of Columbia: A Nationwide Comparison,* annual. <http://www.cfo.dc.gov/services/studies/index.shtm>

Table 445. Gross Revenue From Parimutuel and Amusement Taxes and Lotteries by State: 2001 to 2003

[In millions of dollars (40,004.8 represents $40,004,800,000). For fiscal years; see text, this section]

State	Gross revenue 2001	Gross revenue 2002	Total	Amusement taxes [1]	Parimutuel taxes	Total [2]	Prizes	Administration	Proceeds available from ticket sales
				2003					
						Lottery revenue		Apportionment of funds	
United States ...	40,004.8	43,653.3	46,673.7	4,485.3	302.1	41,886.3	25,342.1	2,762.4	13,781.8
Alabama........	3.6	3.7	3.5	0.1	3.4	(X)	(X)	(X)	(X)
Alaska	2.4	2.5	2.6	2.6	(X)	(X)	(X)	(X)	(X)
Arizona.........	256.6	276.2	302.0	0.6	0.6	300.8	174.0	31.0	95.9
Arkansas	6.3	4.4	4.4	(X)	4.4	(X)	(X)	(X)	(X)
California	2,742.8	2,743.4	2,634.0	(X)	42.0	2,592.0	1,451.8	164.5	975.7
Colorado........	417.9	478.2	464.6	98.1	4.6	361.9	227.5	31.8	102.6
Connecticut.....	1,177.4	1,282.8	1,302.4	424.3	10.7	867.4	523.9	87.8	255.7
Delaware	350.5	397.1	367.3	(X)	0.2	367.1	52.7	6.4	308.0
Florida	2,187.2	2,232.9	2,743.5	(X)	31.2	2,712.3	1,555.8	130.8	1,025.7
Georgia	1,945.3	2,162.8	2,284.1	(X)	(X)	2,284.1	1,389.2	143.6	751.3
Hawaii	(X)	(X)	(X)	(X)	(X)	(X)	(X)	(X)	(X)
Idaho..........	81.7	92.7	90.8	(X)	(X)	90.8	56.6	10.3	23.9
Illinois	1,882.2	2,064.4	2,152.2	681.8	11.9	1,458.5	885.2	62.2	511.1
Indiana.........	973.8	1,094.8	1,281.2	671.8	5.1	604.4	396.2	33.8	174.4
Iowa ....,...	328.9	375.4	356.8	177.6	3.2	176.1	104.2	26.3	45.6
Kansas.........	175.2	184.3	196.7	0.7	3.9	192.2	107.7	20.5	64.0
Kentucky	603.2	656.8	650.7	0.2	18.6	632.0	402.2	46.3	183.5
Louisiana	723.2	787.8	809.9	519.1	5.9	284.9	155.9	19.5	109.5
Maine..........	145.3	157.7	164.3	(X)	4.8	159.5	99.9	18.6	41.1
Maryland	1,223.9	1,314.5	1,336.9	11.4	3.3	1,322.2	743.4	138.3	440.5
Massachusetts....	3,712.7	4,214.9	4,214.1	5.5	6.5	4,202.1	3,008.4	68.0	1,125.7
Michigan........	1,577.1	1,662.9	1,666.0	90.9	11.8	1,563.2	899.7	68.6	595.0
Minnesota.......	400.3	410.0	370.5	55.7	1.4	313.4	205.0	44.8	63.6
Mississippi......	182.2	184.2	184.6	184.6	(X)	(X)	(X)	(X)	(X)
Missouri	669.0	769.2	952.6	288.5	(X)	664.1	434.6	40.2	189.3
Montana........	70.3	75.5	78.6	45.8	0.1	32.7	17.6	6.6	8.5
Nebraska	73.6	81.2	88.1	6.2	1.0	80.9	43.0	18.4	19.5
Nevada	729.4	720.7	739.3	739.3	(X)	(X)	(X)	(X)	(X)
New Hampshire....	204.0	209.5	217.1	1.7	4.2	211.2	130.0	14.9	66.4
New Jersey......	2,049.6	2,306.0	2,307.6	348.6	(X)	1,959.0	1,132.9	74.8	751.3
New Mexico	141.6	158.2	168.8	39.0	1.2	128.6	77.7	16.8	34.2
New York	3,856.1	4,506.6	5,109.8	0.6	38.1	5,071.1	3,061.7	217.7	1,791.6
North Carolina.....	11.8	11.1	11.1	11.1	(X)	(X)	(X)	(X)	(X)
North Dakota......	17.7	16.6	16.9	14.2	2.7	(X)	(X)	(X)	(X)
Ohio	1,942.4	2,000.5	2,093.8	(X)	15.5	2,078.3	1,208.2	296.7	573.4
Oklahoma.......	10.9	10.1	9.4	6.7	2.7	(X)	(X)	(X)	(X)
Oregon.........	1,308.1	1,421.8	1,526.5	0.2	2.6	1,523.6	1,107.3	257.0	159.3
Pennsylvania.....	1,693.2	1,805.7	1,987.6	0.6	28.1	1,958.9	1,124.6	47.9	786.4
Rhode Island.....	855.3	1,019.4	1,124.8	(X)	4.9	1,119.9	880.9	7.1	231.9
South Carolina.....	37.7	364.5	709.0	35.8	(X)	673.2	415.7	36.9	220.6
South Dakota.....	123.6	132.6	137.0	-	1.1	136.0	15.8	6.2	113.9
Tennessee	(X)	(X)	(X)	(X)	(X)	(X)	(X)	(X)	(X)
Texas..........	2,858.4	2,847.7	3,164.3	21.4	12.2	3,130.7	1,845.2	317.5	968.0
Utah	(X)	(X)	(X)	(X)	(X)	(X)	(X)	(X)	(X)
Vermont	81.2	82.0	74.8	(X)	(X)	74.8	51.4	7.6	15.8
Virginia.........	997.7	1,104.9	1,137.4	0.1	(X)	1,137.4	695.1	117.4	324.9
Washington.......	485.8	440.7	462.3	0.2	1.7	460.4	298.0	64.8	97.6
West Virginia......	309.2	461.5	566.8	(X)	10.5	556.3	114.7	27.6	414.1
Wisconsin.......	378.3	399.9	406.7	0.3	1.9	404.5	248.5	33.4	122.5
Wyoming	0.2	0.2	0.2	(X)	0.2	(X)	(X)	(X)	(X)

- Represents or rounds to zero. X Not applicable. [1] Represents nonlicense taxes. [2] Excludes commissions.

Source: U.S. Census Bureau, unpublished data.

Table 446. Lottery Sales—Type of Game: 1980 to 2004

[In millions of dollars (2,393 represents $2,393,000,000). For fiscal years]

Game	1980	1985	1990	1995	2000	2002	2003	2004
Total ticket sales............	2,393	9,035	20,017	31,931	37,201	41,979	43,521	47,697
Instant [1]	527	1,296	5,204	11,511	15,459	18,509	20,387	23,011
Three-digit [2]	1,554	3,376	4,572	5,737	5,341	5,356	5,394	5,389
Four-digit [2]	55	693	1,302	1,941	2,711	2,916	3,059	3,195
Lotto [3]...................	52	3,583	8,563	10,594	9,160	9,564	9,655	10,472
Other [4]...................	206	88	376	2,148	4,530	5,633	5,026	5,630
State proceeds (net income) [5]....	978	3,735	7,703	11,100	11,404	12,478	13,991	15,094

[1] Player scratches a latex section on ticket which reveals instantly whether ticket is a winner. [2] Players choose and bet on three or four digits, depending on game, with various payoffs for different straight order or mixed combination bets. [3] Players typically select six digits out of a large field of numbers. Varying prizes are offered for matching three through six numbers drawn by lottery. [4] Includes break-open tickets, spiel, keno, video lottery, etc. [5] Sales minus prizes and expenses equal net government income.

Source: TLF Publications, Inc., Boyds, MD, 2005 World Lottery Almanac annual; LaFleur's Fiscal 2004 Lottery Report; (copyright).

Table 447. City Governments—Revenue for Largest Cities: 2002

[In millions of dollars (55,349 represents $55,349,000,000). For fiscal years ending in year shown; see text, this section. Cities ranked by enumerated resident population as of April 1. Data reflect inclusion of fiscal activity of dependent school systems where applicable. Regarding intercity comparisons, see text, this section. See Appendix III]

Column groups: **General revenue** comprises *General revenue Total*, *Intergovernmental* (Total, From federal government, From State government, From local government), and *General revenue from own sources* (Total; **Taxes**: Total, Property, and *Sales and gross receipts* [Total, General sales, Public utilities]; **Current charges**: Total, Parks and recreation, Sewerage[2]; **Miscellaneous**: Total, Interest earnings). The final two columns are *Utility revenue[3]* and *Employee retirement revenue[3]*.

Cities ranked by 2000 population	Total revenue[1]	Gen. rev. Total	Intergov. Total	From federal govt	From State govt	From local govt	Own sources Total	Taxes Total	Property	Sales & gross receipts Total	General sales	Public utilities	Current charges Total	Parks & recreation	Sewerage[2]	Misc. Total	Interest earnings	Utility revenue[3]	Employee retirement revenue[3]
New York, NY	55,349	52,718	22,536	3,246	19,178	112	30,182	22,235	8,897	4,480	3,373	436	5,369	54	1,003	2,578	708	2,908	-
Los Angeles, CA[4]	7,903	6,019	1,011	407	482	122	5,007	2,421	850	983	351	531	1,727	81	467	860	438	2,811	-
Chicago, IL	4,955	4,887	1,298	410	887	-	3,589	2,042	641	1,165	196	504	925	23	144	621	275	312	-
Houston, TX	2,531	2,290	212	153	41	18	2,078	1,212	615	561	342	175	586	15	202	280	153	291	-
Philadelphia, PA[4]	5,322	4,757	2,033	451	1,434	148	2,724	2,043	374	189	108	95	544	26	166	137	84	837	-
Phoenix, AZ	2,335	2,125	749	310	412	27	1,376	751	189	512	369	110	473	47	194	152	119	233	-
San Diego, CA	2,245	1,903	433	178	139	115	1,470	745	262	390	217	51	354	29	203	372	135	210	132
Dallas, TX	1,618	1,473	114	83	31	-	1,359	798	424	211	211	-	344	29	170	217	149	194	-
San Antonio, TX	2,249	1,079	168	41	127	-	903	445	210	211	151	20	283	29	154	176	127	1,303	256
Detroit, MI	4,364	3,876	2,404	355	2,017	32	1,472	912	276	152	-	110	316	20	266	223	59	232	-
San Jose, CA[4]	1,421	1,463	257	75	104	78	1,206	667	414	256	138	101	316	20	186	223	100	18	-
Honolulu, HI	1,134	1,000	172	111	60	-	829	534	382	95	-	49	217	15	68	77	33	133	-
Indianapolis, IN[4]	2,181	1,643	518	77	429	13	1,125	629	495	41	-	-	363	24	147	134	66	534	-
San Francisco, CA[4]	4,787	4,844	1,726	378	1,344	-	3,117	1,699	747	551	341	83	1,135	35	129	283	194	319	71
Jacksonville, FL[4]	2,264	1,252	173	51	122	-	1,079	590	357	219	125	83	247	-	143	242	209	941	-
Columbus, OH	1,212	1,064	206	61	135	9	858	516	36	16	-	-	253	23	142	89	53	148	-
Austin, TX	1,806	971	82	45	33	-	889	407	195	184	123	31	309	11	72	174	117	921	-
Baltimore, MD[4]	2,373	2,419	1,381	89	1,220	72	1,037	806	495	63	-	24	129	48	60	102	40	78	98
Memphis, TN	2,967	1,602	1,031	24	506	501	571	364	303	49	-	19	140	-	31	67	31	1,268	-
Milwaukee, WI	878	884	439	78	317	44	444	208	197	37	-	-	163	-	84	74	33	55	112
Boston, MA	2,783	2,575	1,189	93	1,094	-	1,386	1,049	978	936	558	196	181	-	107	155	29	97	-
Washington, DC	6,229	6,238	2,190	2,102	-	87	4,048	3,228	803	32	-	-	302	12	93	518	100	62	-
Nashville, TN[4]	2,446	1,711	598	11	346	241	1,113	683	589	93	-	-	267	9	86	163	129	799	-
El Paso, TX	527	444	70	53	12	-	374	208	108	92	71	21	111	12	59	54	25	64	-
Seattle, WA[4]	1,971	1,297	136	35	94	-	1,162	689	253	275	132	110	318	42	242	156	46	734	19
Denver, CO[4]	2,072	1,912	233	10	223	-	1,679	733	158	462	415	14	651	38	62	296	85	151	-
Charlotte, NC	1,006	958	238	56	58	124	720	313	233	53	-	-	220	-	116	187	42	55	-
Ft Worth, TX	564	624	39	-	39	-	585	323	173	127	127	-	129	-	83	133	71	139	-
Portland, OR	810	724	118	28	38	51	607	350	199	53	-	24	197	25	163	60	29	85	-
Oklahoma City, OK	776	711	71	38	33	-	639	245	41	301	274	20	299	10	76	95	32	66	-
Tucson, AZ	694	598	241	83	145	13	357	184	44	140	100	40	135	15	10	38	16	120	-
New Orleans, LA	1,006	947	242	82	160	-	704	403	165	208	140	42	183	-	72	118	50	52	-
Las Vegas, NV	574	574	212	-	183	29	362	168	83	47	-	-	136	-	58	57	78	-	-
Cleveland, OH	1,284	954	229	74	156	-	725	425	78	29	-	-	147	-	20	153	78	329	-
Long Beach, CA	1,017	883	186	76	94	15	697	233	78	131	51	67	403	15	76	61	22	135	-

- Represents or rounds to zero.   [1] Includes revenue sources not shown separately   [2] Includes solid waste management.   [3] Includes water, electric, and transit.   [4] Represents, in effect, city-county consolidated government.

Source: U.S. Census Bureau, *Government Finances, 2001–2002*. See also <http://www.census.gov/govs/estimate.html>.

State and Local Government Finances and Employment   303

Table 448. City Governments—Expenditures and Debt for Largest Cities: 2002

[In millions of dollars (66,898 represents $66,898,000,000). For fiscal year ending in year shown; see headnote, Table 447].

Cities ranked by 2000 population	Total expen- ditures	Total direct expen- ditures	General expenditures — Total	Educa- tion	Housing and commu- nity devel- opment	Public welfare	Health and hospi- tals	Police protec- tion	Fire protec- tion	Correc- tion	High- ways	Parks and recre- ation	Sewer- age	Solid waste man- agement	Govern- mental adminis- tration[1]	Interest on general debt	Utility expen- ditures[2]	Employee retire- ment expen- ditures	Debt out- standing
New York, NY	66,898	62,966	54,502	14,414	3,175	8,789	5,731	3,764	1,378	1,388	1,212	685	1,304	1,170	1,065	2,445	6,082	6,314	63,934
Los Angeles, CA	10,669	10,622	6,503	1	174	2	40	1,128	427	2	562	335	388	183	505	461	2,973	1,193	12,121
Chicago, IL	7,071	6,946	5,529	-	206	141	189	1,109	313	15	811	73	270	180	151	589	596	945	13,145
Houston, TX	3,101	3,084	2,601	-	58	-	95	440	250	-	189	149	295	65	95	234	321	178	8,205
Philadelphia, PA[3]	6,300	6,222	4,827	22	179	437	1,002	495	156	331	99	98	182	90	352	181	1,019	455	5,158
Phoenix, AZ	2,521	2,509	1,982	17	96	-	-	301	158	-	88	190	162	139	109	176	471	68	4,387
San Diego, CA	2,254	2,245	1,774	-	168	4	25	265	111	10	56	153	284	82	85	128	324	156	2,550
Dallas, TX	2,381	2,349	2,013	-	42	-	40	233	125	8	107	161	152	41	47	251	215	153	5,108
San Antonio, TX	2,388	2,382	1,121	38	18	62	116	186	113	-	93	149	98	45	29	64	1,219	47	4,813
Detroit, MI	5,476	5,392	4,436	2,007	104	-	22	340	114	1	154	125	409	106	231	116	584	456	5,045
San Jose, CA	1,656	1,600	1,519	-	313	-	18	187	96	-	104	149	141	69	79	110	33	104	2,955
Honolulu, HI[3]	1,463	1,463	1,181	-	30	-	-	168	64	-	109	105	135	121	221	89	281	-	2,297
Indianapolis, IN[3]	2,423	2,408	1,826	93	176	-	401	144	204	50	96	237	139	36	300	185	538	59	3,024
San Francisco, CA[3]	6,042	5,893	4,793	-	63	527	963	373	145	126	49	66	268	23	71	390	825	424	8,164
Jacksonville, FL[3]	2,671	2,581	1,479	-	18	33	46	149	92	48	94	82	137	63	70	173	1,060	132	6,833
Columbus, OH	1,225	1,194	1,081	-	16	-	59	203	71	12	24	60	107	44	56	96	144	-	1,675
Austin, TX	2,097	2,097	1,028	-	13	8	82	123	101	-	117	126	71	43	116	71	981	88	4,391
Baltimore, MD	2,438	2,387	2,160	1,013	44	7	64	255	103	-	25	81	26	48	24	73	69	210	1,569
Memphis, TN	2,993	2,976	1,520	863	26	-	12	155	86	-	104	26	45	46	31	43	1,318	155	1,088
Milwaukee, WI	1,198	1,169	862	-	87	-	26	198	137	-	53	6	111	60	65	38	42	294	739
Boston, MA	2,809	2,550	2,471	823	103	120	187	257	136	-	69	26	57	43	267	64	77	261	1,697
Washington, DC	6,656	6,457	6,379	1,175	88	1,462	555	385	79	109	31	303	211	37	95	236	123	5	5,205
Nashville, TN[3]	2,573	2,572	1,642	564	24	-	148	117	49	174	18	63	33	16	20	154	825	106	3,516
El Paso, TX	590	590	438	-	46	3	16	83	96	48	104	22	158	101	159	28	99	52	807
Seattle, WA	2,309	2,195	1,900	-	36	125	17	157	71	15	83	182	48	-	38	40	935	74	3,109
Denver, CO[3]	2,087	2,033	747	-	40	-	52	150	60	64	96	155	61	33	48	262	103	84	4,995
Charlotte, NC	995	989	566	-	12	-	-	142	64	-	67	63	44	24	70	61	234	14	2,193
Ft. Worth, TX	806	806	876	-	41	-	10	121	70	-	109	69	61	3	65	31	171	69	1,120
Portland, OR	1,025	1,025	751	-	20	-	-	126	98	-	86	117	178	30	106	92	86	64	1,991
Oklahoma City, OK	859	859	543	-	46	4	-	110	42	-	50	54	80	70	64	40	97	12	937
Tucson, AZ	742	742	853	-	100	1	20	101	61	27	49	17	84	26	57	33	178	21	1,107
New Orleans, LA	1,008	1,008	556	-	12	-	2	105	70	6	62	66	28	32	106	58	106	49	1,466
Las Vegas, NV	557	466	912	-	122	-	34	88	79	-	46	61	17	5	64	20	-	-	350
Cleveland, OH	1,266	1,260	936	-	90	3	38	173	79	-	90	27	32	32	57	49	353	-	2,561
Long Beach, CA	1,118	1,114	936	-	90	-	38	149	65	-	90	27	15	58	36	81	178	3	1,881

- Represents or rounds to zero. [1] Excludes public buildings. [2] Includes water, electric, and transit. [3] Represents, in effect, city-county consolidated government.

Source: U.S. Census Bureau, Government Finances, 2001-2002. See also <http://www.census.gov/govs/estimate.html>.

Table 449. County Governments—Revenue for Largest Counties: 2002

[In millions of dollars (14,788 represents $14,788,000,000). For fiscal year ending in year shown; see text, this section. See Appendix III]

Counties ranked by 2000 population	Total revenue [1]	General revenue Total	Intergovernmental Total	From federal government Total	From federal government Housing [2]	From state government Total	From state government Public welfare	From state government Health and hospitals	From local government	General revenue from own sources Total	Taxes Total [1]	Taxes Property	Sales and gross receipts Total	Sales and gross receipts General sales	Current charges Total	Current charges Parks and recreation	Current charges Sewerage [3]	Current charges Hospitals	Miscellaneous general revenue Total	Miscellaneous general revenue Interest earnings
Los Angeles, CA	14,788	15,960	10,889	326	89	10,193	4,619	2,032	370	5,071	2,481	2,244	138	69	1,568	71	39	738	1,021	255
Cook, IL	2,758	2,425	505	56	37	443	189	123	7	1,920	1,362	785	560	337	445	47	-	228	130	63
Harris, TX	2,455	2,455	506	100	39	332	152	31	74	1,949	1,153	1,026	63	-	445	3	-	86	351	255
Maricopa, AZ	2,107	2,107	1,034	45	7	966	406	224	24	1,072	572	443	103	103	282	24	111	220	218	158
Orange, CA	2,917	2,976	1,703	151	9	1,446	518	489	106	1,273	445	388	47	45	456	3	-	-	372	141
San Diego, CA	3,149	3,023	2,194	123	75	1,961	663	1	110	829	504	423	29	21	165	24	-	-	160	49
Dade, FL	5,220	4,983	1,015	483	181	531	-	1	1	3,968	1,352	900	375	90	1,985	27	417	783	631	394
Dallas, TX	1,310	1,290	177	1	-	148	53	20	29	1,113	541	497	10	-	497	4	69	410	74	41
Wayne, MI	2,524	2,322	1,451	57	-	1,079	149	570	314	871	318	301	10	-	396	5	278	271	157	75
King, WA	1,975	1,869	494	99	16	269	-	174	126	1,375	855	381	448	370	409	7	39	-	110	66
San Bernardino, CA	2,689	2,816	1,701	515	13	1,154	434	128	31	1,115	202	164	25	20	708	4	11	391	205	71
Santa Clara, CA	2,683	2,683	1,615	31	7	1,526	814	155	57	1,069	685	502	146	144	264	5	-	151	120	59
Broward, FL	1,764	1,721	295	85	6	165	-	6	44	1,426	696	558	110	-	506	16	135	376	224	142
Riverside, CA	2,257	2,257	1,619	92	21	1,395	672	107	132	638	323	279	27	21	165	3	46	45	150	62
Tarrant, TX	507	507	148	24	15	108	17	62	17	358	214	182	12	-	41	9	-	-	102	74
Alameda, CA	2,193	2,251	1,181	16	3	1,081	621	253	85	1,070	460	427	142	132	479	9	20	383	131	49
Suffolk, NY	2,153	2,040	538	27	3	497	242	81	14	1,502	1,241	427	794	791	299	-	3	289	161	128
Cuyahoga, OH	1,819	1,819	844	19	18	816	482	186	9	976	487	278	172	158	327	-	76	271	161	83
Bexar, TX	881	881	158	4	2	138	85	40	16	723	321	280	24	-	299	15	9	376	103	83
Clark, NV	3,013	2,691	466	69	12	361	-	9	36	2,225	893	419	306	123	922	16	76	212	410	212
Nassau, NY	2,738	2,738	737	55	34	682	364	82	-	2,001	1,545	726	815	807	353	4	9	-	104	67
Allegheny, PA	1,426	1,444	919	69	31	847	256	371	3	525	298	253	43	36	186	15	-	-	41	20
Sacramento, CA	2,428	2,562	1,517	6	9	1,479	734	222	32	1,045	397	204	146	114	464	7	220	4	184	76
Oakland, MI	918	869	536	28	9	371	117	87	136	333	249	238	3	-	41	7	7	-	43	31
Palm Beach, FL	1,372	1,326	163	32	7	130	7	-	24	1,163	610	452	143	-	260	8	75	279	292	103
Hennepin, MN	1,748	1,748	751	117	6	610	326	81	29	997	450	445	3	-	432	75	51	-	115	54
Franklin, OH	1,030	1,029	414	6	3	379	181	118	3	615	391	285	100	82	71	5	3	-	153	142
St Louis, MO	580	582	64	17	17	44	-	-	2	518	416	100	304	260	54	2	3	-	49	29
Hillsborough, FL	1,494	1,359	258	47	19	209	43	74	16	1,101	575	414	148	140	306	1	65	292	220	156
Fairfax, VA	3,361	3,323	877	83	38	778	122	35	11	2,445	1,938	1,524	236	362	332	27	190	287	175	106
Erie, NY	1,493	1,428	384	8	-	366	220	121	39	1,044	552	173	367	140	378	1	4	-	114	43
Contra Costa, CA	1,827	1,676	792	101	72	652	294	135	11	883	314	257	34	-	486	39	25	292	84	36
Milwaukee, WI	1,077	1,063	538	135	12	392	85	83	14	526	252	191	59	59	234	28	24	287	40	12
Westchester, NY	2,038	2,025	488	6	-	468	269	-	14	1,537	785	463	318	309	704	1	108	521	48	38
Pinellas, FL	888	835	118	35	-	81	-	-	2	717	407	294	105	70	186	-	-	-	124	79

- Represents or rounds to zero.   [1] Includes revenue sources not shown separately.   [2] Includes urban development.   [3] Includes solid waste management.

Source: U.S. Census Bureau, Government Finances, 2001–2002. See also <http://www.census.gov/govs/estimate.html>.

Table 450. County Governments—Expenditures and Debt for Largest Counties: 2002

[In millions of dollars (16,232 represents $16,232,000,000). For fiscal year ending in year shown; see text, this section. See headnote, Table 449. See Appendix III]

Counties ranked by 2000 population	Total expenditures	Total direct expenditures	General expenditures														Utility expenditures [3]	Employee retirement expenditures [3]	Debt outstanding
			Total [1]	Education	Housing [2]	Public welfare	Health	Hospitals	Police protection	Correction	Highways	Parks and recreation	Natural resources	Sewerage and solid waste management	Governmental administration	Interest on general debt			
Los Angeles, CA	16,232	15,128	14,931	538	124	4,569	2,072	1,776	956	1,015	346	245	203	54	1,560	423	60	1,240	5,440
Cook, IL	2,906	2,886	2,694	1	19	11	45	897	91	370	124	117	-	-	605	120	-	212	2,210
Harris, TX	3,136	3,136	3,136	-	55	22	156	598	131	272	301	486	151	3	302	348	-	-	6,242
Maricopa, AZ	2,020	1,795	2,020	16	8	569	77	251	44	373	97	10	65	-	289	111	-	-	1,861
Orange, CA	3,137	2,911	2,968	252	25	718	337	-	258	253	72	64	57	95	405	193	-	169	3,081
San Diego, CA	3,370	3,174	3,175	319	80	728	479	-	201	265	92	36	11	30	459	65	16	179	725
Dade, FL	5,281	5,267	4,726	-	219	118	73	1,047	378	169	45	177	36	438	277	452	554	-	8,168
Dallas, TX	1,347	1,340	1,337	-	59	15	72	684	37	162	34	-	14	-	140	29	-	-	524
Wayne, MI	2,740	2,649	2,643	1	4	203	578	61	22	233	154	186	40	70	333	109	-	9	2,373
King, WA	2,025	1,990	1,613	-	21	6	290	24	100	117	102	64	32	321	199	153	412	97	2,671
San Bernardino, CA	2,950	2,639	2,811	298	110	751	209	302	395	139	56	10	3	37	197	27	5	133	1,650
Santa Clara, CA	2,779	2,606	2,779	203	8	573	299	377	58	238	68	29	18	36	401	147	152	-	591
Broward, FL	1,758	1,702	1,606	-	18	45	107	-	218	178	68	97	-	129	142	76	-	-	3,143
Riverside, CA	2,309	2,095	2,308	298	53	566	152	190	200	139	269	9	102	31	233	89	-	-	937
Tarrant, TX	469	468	469	-	20	4	88	-	19	85	61	-	-	-	106	58	-	-	1,445
Alameda, CA	2,474	2,368	2,314	31	26	578	261	511	69	188	17	26	83	60	260	127	168	160	1,167
Suffolk, NY	2,189	1,910	2,022	243	7	411	152	-	372	99	46	-	28	15	117	75	-	-	1,692
Cuyahoga, OH	1,806	1,788	1,806	-	20	419	304	457	25	89	22	-	8	-	229	273	-	-	2,607
Bexar, TX	879	810	879	-	1	70	43	409	25	82	55	54	92	-	80	194	-	-	1,098
Clark, NV	2,898	2,881	2,472	231	9	73	48	415	323	162	14	65	1	71	257	70	426	-	4,719
Nassau, NY	3,054	2,654	2,899	29	34	541	132	335	546	184	375	69	-	88	129	88	155	51	3,728
Allegheny, PA	1,456	1,365	1,404	143	43	295	327	29	38	64	64	58	-	-	100	13	38	117	1,375
Sacramento, CA	2,686	2,575	2,531	11	9	764	233	-	232	177	190	30	27	169	335	96	3	-	2,148
Oakland, MI	856	842	827	-	19	5	243	9	56	85	113	19	89	66	118	27	95	-	251
Palm Beach, FL	1,327	1,299	1,231	-	28	39	36	-	191	70	76	58	5	48	104	120	-	26	1,707
Hennepin, MN	1,590	1,584	1,590	-	4	367	230	372	72	96	75	31	-	66	122	14	-	-	862
Franklin, OH	1,032	1,009	1,031	-	16	275	272	-	29	61	37	33	-	120	114	105	-	-	1,806
St Louis, MO	630	436	611	-	5	15	47	-	64	33	77	51	27	48	49	133	2	18	387
Hillsborough, FL	1,292	1,270	1,060	-	76	53	26	-	107	76	45	119	46	4	100	40	1	-	2,258
Fairfax, VA	3,737	3,662	3,422	1,739	5	198	144	240	139	67	68	16	3	5	102	42	232	216	3,223
Erie, NY	1,512	1,171	1,450	81	69	539	63	360	36	88	68	-	17	54	45	31	99	-	664
Contra Costa, CA	1,845	1,795	1,707	108	16	321	157	127	70	68	21	105	-	206	141	41	62	-	803
Milwaukee, WI	1,265	1,265	1,016	-	-	264	122	532	52	122	18	54	1	13	74	-	154	138	570
Westchester, NY	2,105	1,855	2,070	79	14	407	102	-	27	74	18	32	1	146	97	-	35	95	1,237
Pinellas, FL	957	880	893	-	-	48	72	-	90	74	83	32	27	72	109	69	63	-	767

- Represents or rounds to zero.   [1] Includes expenditure categories not shown separately.   [2] Includes community development.   [3] Includes water, electric, and transit.

Source: U.S. Census Bureau, Government Finances, 2001–2002. See also <http://www.census.gov/govs/estimate.html>.

Table 451. Governmental Employment and Payrolls: 1980 to 2003

[Employees in thousands (16,213 represents 16,213,000), payroll in millions of dollars (19,935 represents $19,935,000,000). For 1980 to 1995 as of October; later years as of March. Covers both full-time and part-time employees. Local government data are estimates subject to sampling variation; see Appendix III and source]

Type of government	1980	1985	1990	1995	1998	1999	2000	2001	2002	2003
EMPLOYEES (1,000)										
Total	16,213	16,690	18,369	19,521	19,854	20,306	20,876	20,970	21,039	21,336
Federal (civilian) [1]	2,898	3,021	3,105	2,895	2,765	2,799	2,899	2,698	2,690	2,717
State and local	13,315	13,669	15,263	16,626	17,089	17,506	17,976	18,272	18,349	18,649
Percent of total	82	82	83	85	86	86	86	87	87	87
State	3,753	3,984	4,503	4,719	4,758	4,818	4,877	4,985	5,072	5,043
Local	9,562	9,685	10,760	11,906	12,271	12,689	13,099	13,288	13,277	13,606
Counties	1,853	1,891	2,167	(NA)	(NA)	(NA)	(NA)	(NA)	2,729	(NA)
Municipalities	2,561	2,467	2,642	(NA)	(NA)	(NA)	(NA)	(NA)	2,972	(NA)
School districts	4,270	4,416	4,950	(NA)	(NA)	(NA)	(NA)	(NA)	6,367	(NA)
Townships	394	392	418	(NA)	(NA)	(NA)	(NA)	(NA)	488	(NA)
Special districts	484	519	585	(NA)	(NA)	(NA)	(NA)	(NA)	721	(NA)
PAYROLLS (mil. dol.)										
Total	19,935	28,945	39,228	(NA)	51,568	54,363	58,166	60,632	63,923	67,195
Federal (civilian) [1]	5,205	7,580	8,999	(NA)	10,115	10,748	11,485	11,370	11,599	12,673
State and local	14,730	21,365	30,229	37,714	41,453	43,686	46,681	49,262	52,323	54,522
Percent of total	74	74	77	(NA)	80	81	80	81	82	81
State	4,285	6,329	9,083	10,927	11,845	12,565	13,279	14,136	14,838	15,116
Local	10,445	15,036	21,146	26,787	29,608	31,321	33,402	35,126	37,486	39,406
Counties	1,936	2,819	4,192	(NA)	(NA)	(NA)	(NA)	(NA)	7,902	(NA)
Municipalities	2,951	4,191	5,564	(NA)	(NA)	(NA)	(NA)	(NA)	9,714	(NA)
School districts	4,683	6,746	9,551	(NA)	(NA)	(NA)	(NA)	(NA)	16,720	(NA)
Townships	330	446	642	(NA)	(NA)	(NA)	(NA)	(NA)	1,124	(NA)
Special districts	546	834	1,197	(NA)	(NA)	(NA)	(NA)	(NA)	2,026	(NA)

NA Not available. [1] Includes employees outside the United States.

Source: U.S. Census Bureau, *Public Employment and Payroll Data.* See also <http://www.census.gov/govs/www/apes.html>; (accessed 12 May 2005).

Table 452. All Governments—Employment and Payroll by Function: 2003

[Employees in thousands (21,366 represents 21,366,000); payroll in millions of dollars (67,195 represents $67,195,000,000). See headnote, Table 451]

Function	Employees (1,000)					Payrolls (mil. dol.)				
	Total	Federal (civilian) [1]	State and local			Total	Federal (civilian) [1]	State and local		
			Total	State	Local			Total	State	Local
Total	21,366	2,717	18,649	5,043	13,606	67,195	12,673	54,522	15,116	39,406
National defense [2]	682	682	(X)	(X)	(X)	2,604	2,604	(X)	(X)	(X)
Postal Service	786	786	(X)	(X)	(X)	3,267	3,267	(X)	(X)	(X)
Space research and technology	19	19	(X)	(X)	(X)	136	136	(X)	(X)	(X)
Elementary and secondary education	7,480	(X)	7,480	64	7,416	20,742	-	20,742	183	20,560
Higher education	2,804	(X)	2,804	2,248	555	6,818	(X)	6,818	5,643	1,175
Other education	112	11	101	101	(X)	390	62	328	328	(X)
Health	605	134	471	183	287	2,218	758	1,460	617	843
Hospitals	1,139	155	985	428	556	3,911	810	3,101	1,333	1,768
Public welfare	541	9	532	234	298	1,652	55	1,597	719	878
Social insurance administration	161	68	93	93	(X)	640	330	309	309	(X)
Police protection	1,118	157	962	106	856	4,545	760	3,784	438	3,346
Fire protection	394	(X)	394	(X)	394	1,442	(X)	1,442	(X)	1,442
Correction	748	35	713	464	250	2,526	165	2,361	1,519	842
Streets and highways	572	3	569	249	320	1,856	20	1,836	869	967
Air transportation	95	49	46	3	43	623	447	177	13	163
Water transport/terminals . . .	18	5	12	5	8	63	14	49	18	31
Solid waste management . . .	119	(X)	119	2	117	364	(X)	364	8	356
Sewerage	134	(X)	134	2	132	466	(X)	466	9	457
Parks and recreation	408	27	381	40	340	815	112	703	97	606
Natural resources	402	194	208	164	44	1,607	981	626	508	119
Housing and community development	141	17	124	-	124	515	109	405	-	405
Water supply	174	-	174	1	173	575	-	575	3	572
Electric power	81	-	81	4	77	382	-	382	22	360
Gas supply	11	-	11	-	11	37	-	37	-	37
Transit	240	(X)	240	33	207	974	(X)	974	155	819
Libraries	188	4	183	1	183	361	25	337	2	335
State liquor stores	9	(X)	9	9	(X)	19	(X)	19	19	(X)
Financial administration	538	115	423	173	250	1,926	587	1,339	598	741
Other government administration	476	22	454	60	394	1,116	124	992	202	790
Judicial and legal	494	62	432	164	268	1,969	353	1,616	682	934
Other and unallocable	677	163	514	211	303	2,636	954	1,682	822	860

- Represents or rounds to zero.   X Not applicable.   [1] Includes employees outside the United States   [2] Includes international relations.

Source: U.S. Census Bureau, *Public Employment and Payroll Data.* See also <http://www.census.gov/govs/www/apes.html>; (accessed 12 May 2005).

U.S. Census Bureau, Statistical Abstract of the United States: 2006

Table 453. State and Local Government—Employer Costs per Hour Worked: 2004

[In dollars. As of March. Based on a sample; see source for details. For additional data, see Table 637]

Occupation and industry	Total compensation	Wages and salaries	Benefits Total	Paid leave	Supplemental pay	Insurance	Retirement and savings	Legally required benefits	Other [1]
Total workers	35.16	24.10	11.05	2.66	0.31	3.68	2.28	2.06	0.05
Occupational group:									
Management, professional, and related	42.87	30.71	12.16	2.88	0.19	4.05	2.62	2.37	0.06
Professional and related	42.67	30.90	11.77	2.56	0.19	4.03	2.57	2.35	0.07
Teachers [2]	47.58	35.34	12.24	2.42	0.11	4.14	2.97	2.53	0.07
Primary, secondary, and special education school teachers	46.25	34.05	12.21	2.41	0.11	4.40	2.81	2.38	0.09
Sales and office	24.06	15.26	8.80	2.28	0.17	3.40	1.41	1.52	0.03
Office and administrative support . . .	24.04	15.24	8.80	2.27	0.16	3.40	1.41	1.51	0.03
Service	26.61	16.58	10.04	2.40	0.60	2.98	2.31	1.69	0.06
Industry group:									
Education and health services.	36.98	26.42	10.56	2.42	0.20	3.70	2.13	2.06	0.05
Educational services	37.65	27.09	10.56	2.32	0.13	3.78	2.22	2.07	0.05
Elementary and secondary schools.	36.93	26.59	10.34	2.09	0.12	3.96	2.12	1.99	0.07
Junior colleges, colleges, and universities	40.25	28.92	11.33	3.03	0.17	3.28	2.53	2.30	-
Health care and social assistance	32.51	21.91	10.60	3.13	0.68	3.16	1.53	2.06	0.04
Hospitals	29.87	19.67	10.20	2.98	0.71	2.96	1.49	2.02	0.05
Public administration	32.49	20.60	11.88	3.06	0.46	3.66	2.65	1.98	0.06

- Represents zero   [1] Includes severance pay and supplemental unemployment benefits.

Source: U.S. Bureau of Labor Statistics, *Compensation and Working Conditions, Fall 2004.*

Table 454. State and Local Governments—Full-Time Employment and Salary by Sex and Race/Ethnic Group: 1980 to 2003

[As of June 30. (2,350 represents 2,350,000). Excludes school systems and educational institutions. Based on reports from state governments (42 in 1980; 47 in 1983; 49 in 1981 and 1984 through 1987; and 50 in 1989 through 1991) and a sample of county, municipal, township, and special district jurisdictions employing 15 or more nonelected, nonappointed full-time employees. Beginning 1993, only for State and Local Governments with 100 or more employees. For definition of median, see Guide to Tabular Presentation]

Year and occupation	Employment (1,000) Male	Female	White [1]	Minority Total [2]	Black [1]	Hispanic [3]	Median annual salary ($1,000) Male	Female	White [1]	Minority Total [2]	Black [1]	Hispanic [3]
1980	2,350	1,637	3,146	842	619	163	15.2	11.4	13.8	11.8	11.5	12.3
1981	2,740	1,925	3,591	1,074	780	205	17.7	13.1	16.1	13.5	13.3	14.7
1983	2,674	1,818	3,423	1,069	768	219	20.1	15.3	18.5	15.9	15.6	17.3
1984	2,700	1,880	3,458	1,121	799	233	21.4	16.2	19.6	17.4	16.5	18.4
1985	2,789	1,952	3,563	1,179	835	248	22.3	17.3	20.6	18.4	17.5	19.2
1986	2,797	1,982	3,549	1,230	865	259	23.4	18.1	21.5	19.6	18.7	20.2
1987	2,818	2,031	3,600	1,249	872	268	24.2	18.9	22.4	20.9	19.3	21.1
1989	3,030	2,227	3,863	1,394	961	308	26.1	20.6	24.1	22.1	20.7	22.7
1990	3,071	2,302	3,918	1,456	994	327	27.3	21.8	25.2	23.3	22.0	23.8
1991	3,110	2,349	3,965	1,494	1,011	340	28.4	22.7	26.4	23.8	22.7	24.5
1993	2,820	2,204	3,588	1,436	948	341	30.6	24.3	28.5	25.9	24.2	26.8
1995	2,960	2,355	3,781	1,534	993	379	33.5	27.0	31.4	26.3	26.8	28.6
1997	2,898	2,307	3,676	1,529	973	392	34.6	27.9	32.2	30.2	27.4	29.5
1999	2,939	2,393	3,723	1,609	1,012	417	37.0	29.9	34.8	31.1	29.6	31.2
2001	3,080	2,554	3,888	1,746	1,077	471	39.8	32.1	37.5	34.0	31.5	33.8
2003, total	3,134	2,610	3,919	1,826	1,097	508	42.2	34.7	40.0	35.9	33.6	36.6
Officials/ administrators . . .	215	126	275	65	39	17	66.4	59.2	64.0	63.0	61.5	62.8
Professionals	654	819	1,064	409	228	96	52.2	44.9	48.6	46.6	43.1	45.6
Technicians	273	204	340	138	75	40	42.2	34.6	39.6	36.3	34.5	37.8
Protective service . . .	923	209	795	337	205	107	43.0	35.5	42.2	40.1	37.3	44.0
Paraprofessionals . . .	109	301	238	172	119	39	31.0	28.0	29.8	27.2	25.7	29.8
Admin. support . . .	122	795	593	325	188	102	31.1	29.2	29.4	29.5	28.8	29.5
Skilled craft	401	23	308	116	67	37	38.6	32.9	38.4	38.0	36.2	38.2
Service/ maintenance	437	133	306	264	177	71	31.4	24.2	30.4	29.3	28.3	29.9

[1] Non-Hispanic.   [2] Includes other minority groups not shown separately.   [3] Persons of Hispanic origin may be of any race.

Source: U.S. Equal Employment Opportunity Commission. 1980–1991, *State and Local Government Information Report,* annual; beginning 1993, biennial.

Table 455. **State and Local Government Full-Time Equivalent Employment, by Selected Function and State: 2003**

[In thousands (1,656.4 represents 1,656,400). For **March**. Local government amounts are estimates subject to sampling variation; see Appendix III and source]

State	Total [1]		Education				Public welfare		Health		Hospitals	
			Elem. & secondary		Higher education							
	State	Local	State	Local	State	Local	State	Local	State	Local	State	Local
United States . . .	1,656.4	6,712.3	52.7	6,394.8	1,510.1	317.5	230.4	277.7	176.9	253.9	403.0	506.9
Alabama	39.9	97.7	-	97.7	37.3	-	3.8	1.4	5.5	4.3	12.0	21.6
Alaska	8.5	15.6	3.3	15.5	4.8	0.1	1.8	0.2	0.7	0.4	0.2	0.6
Arizona	28.8	115.7	-	103.9	25.8	11.9	5.7	1.9	2.4	2.6	0.7	4.0
Arkansas	22.0	65.4	-	65.4	19.3	-	3.8	0.1	4.7	0.3	4.4	2.4
California	143.5	756.8	-	684.5	138.9	72.3	3.8	66.0	11.9	43.4	38.5	62.0
Colorado	39.3	102.2	-	100.6	38.0	1.6	2.1	6.1	1.2	3.8	3.6	9.0
Connecticut	18.1	80.2	-	80.2	15.2	-	4.4	1.7	2.2	1.6	10.3	-
Delaware	7.8	15.0	-	15.0	7.4	-	1.6	-	2.0	0.2	1.8	-
District of Columbia	(X)	12.3	(X)	11.3	(X)	1.0	(X)	1.5	(X)	2.0	(X)	1.8
Florida	57.7	314.0	-	288.9	54.2	25.0	13.3	6.6	21.4	5.8	4.9	39.8
Georgia	49.5	219.3	-	218.9	46.4	0.4	8.9	1.2	4.6	12.7	8.1	18.6
Hawaii	36.2	-	27.5	-	8.5	-	0.8	0.2	2.4	0.2	4.0	-
Idaho	9.7	32.7	-	31.3	9.2	1.3	1.7	0.2	1.0	1.1	0.9	5.7
Illinois	57.4	291.3	-	268.8	55.0	22.5	10.8	6.9	2.8	7.8	12.3	13.0
Indiana	54.3	139.0	-	139.0	53.2	-	5.5	1.3	1.7	3.5	4.3	23.8
Iowa	25.9	79.3	-	72.7	24.8	6.6	2.6	1.3	0.4	2.3	7.1	10.1
Kansas	19.8	84.8	-	77.0	19.2	7.9	2.7	1.0	1.0	3.0	2.3	7.4
Kentucky	32.7	99.7	-	99.7	28.3	-	7.0	0.5	2.0	5.0	5.7	4.3
Louisiana	32.1	106.0	-	106.0	28.7	-	5.2	0.6	3.7	1.7	17.7	16.0
Maine	7.6	38.0	0.1	38.0	7.3	-	2.1	0.4	1.4	0.3	0.7	0.6
Maryland	28.7	124.7	-	114.6	26.6	10.1	7.2	3.4	6.9	4.5	5.4	-
Massachusetts	27.6	146.9	0.1	146.8	26.5	0.1	6.7	2.2	7.8	2.9	7.4	-
Michigan	68.7	240.0	0.9	226.8	66.4	13.2	10.3	2.5	1.5	11.5	11.7	9.1
Minnesota	37.6	123.8	-	123.8	33.4	-	2.7	11.2	2.3	3.7	4.6	10.7
Mississippi	19.9	77.3	-	70.8	18.4	6.5	2.8	0.4	3.0	0.2	12.1	17.4
Missouri	29.9	133.6	-	127.8	27.7	5.8	8.0	2.6	3.5	4.0	12.4	10.2
Montana	6.7	22.3	-	22.1	6.3	0.2	1.5	0.5	0.9	0.8	0.6	0.6
Nebraska	12.8	45.8	-	42.9	12.2	2.8	2.8	0.8	0.8	0.6	5.1	4.0
Nevada	8.9	32.7	-	32.7	8.8	-	1.1	0.7	1.1	1.0	1.0	4.8
New Hampshire	7.6	32.5	-	32.5	7.3	-	1.4	2.5	1.1	0.2	0.8	-
New Jersey	53.7	212.4	20.2	201.6	30.3	10.8	6.2	10.7	3.1	4.2	16.6	1.9
New Mexico	19.1	48.9	-	45.6	17.8	3.3	1.6	0.9	2.5	0.4	6.4	0.7
New York	53.1	491.2	-	468.5	48.4	22.7	6.7	48.7	9.4	18.3	45.5	50.1
North Carolina	51.5	194.6	-	177.6	48.8	16.9	1.9	14.6	4.0	20.2	16.5	23.8
North Dakota	8.6	14.8	-	14.8	8.3	-	0.4	0.9	1.3	0.6	1.0	-
Ohio	69.3	264.0	-	258.0	66.8	6.0	2.8	24.7	3.7	18.0	11.4	11.8
Oklahoma	27.9	83.6	-	83.1	25.9	0.5	6.2	0.2	5.9	2.6	2.6	9.7
Oregon	19.6	72.7	-	64.6	18.6	8.0	5.5	0.8	2.6	4.3	4.8	2.3
Pennsylvania	61.3	245.7	-	236.6	57.8	9.1	12.9	21.4	1.6	5.7	12.8	-
Rhode Island	6.8	23.6	0.6	23.6	5.6	-	1.5	0.2	1.3	0.0	1.2	-
South Carolina	30.2	97.4	-	97.4	27.4	-	5.0	0.3	7.0	2.2	8.1	18.0
South Dakota	5.0	20.5	-	20.0	4.6	0.6	1.0	0.3	0.6	0.2	0.9	0.5
Tennessee	37.5	119.7	-	119.7	35.6	-	5.8	1.7	3.2	3.8	9.3	20.7
Texas	94.7	642.8	-	605.4	89.8	37.4	20.0	3.5	12.7	23.4	30.8	46.0
Utah	23.3	46.1	-	46.1	22.3	-	3.2	0.5	1.9	1.5	5.6	0.4
Vermont	5.1	20.1	-	20.1	4.5	-	1.2	0.0	0.7	0.0	0.2	-
Virginia	49.3	185.4	-	184.1	46.5	1.3	2.1	7.5	5.0	6.2	13.2	3.1
Washington	49.6	99.5	-	99.5	47.6	-	8.7	1.3	5.3	3.6	8.9	12.3
West Virginia	12.1	37.4	-	37.4	10.7	-	3.2	0.0	0.8	1.3	1.7	2.3
Wisconsin	35.9	129.0	-	119.5	34.8	9.5	1.3	13.4	1.8	5.9	3.8	1.0
Wyoming	3.4	18.1	-	16.2	3.2	1.9	1.0	0.0	0.6	0.4	0.9	4.7

See footnote at end of table.

U.S. Census Bureau, Statistical Abstract of the United States: 2006

[In thousands. **For March.** Local government amounts are estimates subject to sampling variation; see Appendix III and source]

State	Highways		Police protection		Fire protection		Corrections		Parks and recreation		Government administration	
	State	Local	State	Local	State	Local	State	Local	State	Local	State	Local
United States ...	**245.1**	**300.5**	**104.1**	**790.6**	**(X)**	**311.1**	**458.9**	**241.1**	**35.3**	**226.4**	**382.7**	**687.8**
Alabama.........	4.1	7.4	1.2	12.1	(X)	5.1	4.7	3.0	0.7	3.2	6.7	8.5
Alaska..........	3.0	1.0	0.5	1.6	(X)	0.8	1.8	0.1	0.1	0.6	2.8	1.8
Arizona.........	3.0	4.4	2.0	15.5	(X)	5.5	9.1	4.8	0.4	4.5	5.6	17.0
Arkansas	3.8	3.9	1.1	6.9	(X)	2.5	4.2	1.9	0.8	1.0	3.9	6.1
California	21.8	21.7	13.5	88.3	(X)	32.1	50.2	32.4	3.3	36.5	30.4	101.3
Colorado........	3.1	6.0	1.2	12.1	(X)	5.0	6.6	3.4	0.3	6.4	6.2	11.4
Connecticut......	3.6	3.6	1.8	8.6	(X)	4.7	7.5	(X)	0.1	2.1	8.2	4.5
Delaware	1.6	0.5	0.9	1.6	(X)	0.2	2.8	(X)	0.2	0.3	2.5	1.3
District of Columbia......	(X)	0.4	(X)	4.3	(X)	1.8	(X)	1.1	(X)	0.9	(X)	3.3
Florida	8.4	15.3	4.4	55.5	(X)	24.4	26.6	15.3	1.4	19.2	27.0	43.9
Georgia	6.1	8.3	2.3	23.1	(X)	10.5	19.5	7.8	3.1	5.3	8.3	21.3
Hawaii	0.9	0.8	-	3.6	(X)	1.8	2.4	(X)	0.2	1.9	3.4	2.6
Idaho..........	1.7	1.7	0.5	3.2	(X)	1.2	1.7	1.2	0.2	0.7	2.1	3.8
Illinois	8.2	12.8	4.2	41.7	(X)	16.9	13.9	9.4	0.7	16.7	10.4	31.6
Indiana.........	4.3	6.2	2.0	15.1	(X)	6.5	8.2	5.4	0.1	3.3	4.5	16.8
Iowa...........	2.5	5.8	0.9	6.3	(X)	1.9	3.2	1.3	0.1	2.2	4.2	6.5
Kansas.........	3.6	5.0	1.1	7.5	(X)	2.8	3.5	2.5	0.6	2.3	4.8	7.1
Kentucky	5.5	3.8	2.2	7.4	(X)	3.8	3.8	3.1	1.6	1.6	9.3	6.3
Louisiana	5.4	5.6	1.7	14.8	(X)	4.8	8.0	5.8	1.2	3.1	5.8	12.2
Maine..........	2.5	1.7	0.6	2.5	(X)	1.7	1.3	0.8	0.2	0.7	2.4	3.0
Maryland	4.7	4.7	2.5	14.6	(X)	5.8	12.0	3.1	0.6	6.0	9.3	8.8
Massachusetts.....	3.8	6.4	5.6	17.8	(X)	12.9	6.9	2.6	0.8	2.0	15.3	8.7
Michigan........	2.7	10.3	3.4	22.7	(X)	8.3	18.7	5.6	0.3	5.2	8.4	26.6
Minnesota.......	5.1	7.7	0.9	10.5	(X)	2.6	3.8	4.6	0.6	4.6	6.4	13.6
Mississippi	3.3	5.1	1.2	7.8	(X)	3.4	4.2	1.8	0.3	1.3	2.4	6.8
Missouri	6.5	7.1	2.4	16.5	(X)	6.4	11.6	3.1	0.7	4.2	7.7	12.3
Montana........	2.2	1.3	0.4	1.9	(X)	0.5	1.1	0.6	0.1	0.4	2.1	2.4
Nebraska	2.2	3.2	0.7	4.0	(X)	1.3	2.5	1.3	0.3	1.2	1.5	4.6
Nevada	1.7	1.4	0.8	6.2	(X)	2.3	3.1	2.4	0.2	3.0	3.1	6.0
New Hampshire....	2.0	1.6	0.4	3.3	(X)	1.7	1.5	0.5	0.2	0.4	1.9	2.0
New Jersey......	7.1	10.5	4.1	31.3	(X)	8.0	10.1	6.7	2.2	5.9	20.8	20.3
New Mexico	2.3	2.1	0.6	5.0	(X)	2.1	4.1	1.6	0.7	2.0	4.7	4.4
New York	12.4	27.9	6.1	80.4	(X)	23.0	33.6	25.9	2.6	11.2	37.3	39.3
North Carolina....	11.8	3.9	3.3	20.4	(X)	7.3	19.1	4.2	1.0	5.1	11.0	12.2
North Dakota.....	0.9	1.0	0.2	1.2	(X)	0.3	0.6	0.3	0.1	1.0	1.5	1.3
Ohio	7.1	13.9	2.7	30.4	(X)	16.3	16.6	8.4	0.6	8.8	11.9	35.3
Oklahoma........	2.8	5.9	1.8	8.8	(X)	4.0	5.7	1.2	0.9	2.0	5.3	6.7
Oregon.........	3.5	3.8	1.2	7.1	(X)	3.5	4.6	3.7	0.4	2.3	8.1	7.4
Pennsylvania.....	13.5	10.7	5.8	26.0	(X)	6.3	16.3	12.6	1.6	3.4	14.0	32.3
Rhode Island.....	0.8	0.9	0.3	3.2	(X)	2.9	1.8	(X)	0.1	0.7	2.8	1.4
South Carolina.....	4.8	2.7	3.1	10.8	(X)	4.3	7.9	2.7	0.6	2.5	3.5	8.9
South Dakota	1.0	1.5	0.3	1.5	(X)	0.4	0.8	0.5	0.1	0.5	1.2	1.8
Tennessee	4.5	6.6	2.0	16.0	(X)	7.2	6.9	6.1	1.0	4.0	5.6	12.2
Texas	16.0	20.3	4.0	56.5	(X)	22.1	46.0	24.9	1.1	16.0	17.4	46.5
Utah	1.8	1.6	0.9	4.7	(X)	1.9	3.1	1.7	0.3	2.4	3.5	4.9
Vermont	1.1	1.0	0.4	0.8	(X)	0.4	1.0	(X)	0.1	0.2	1.8	1.0
Virginia.........	10.6	3.8	2.7	17.0	(X)	8.2	13.9	7.0	0.8	7.4	8.1	16.0
Washington.......	6.8	6.7	2.2	12.1	(X)	7.7	9.1	4.5	0.6	5.6	6.0	16.0
West Virginia.....	5.4	1.0	1.0	2.8	(X)	0.9	3.0	0.3	0.6	0.8	4.1	3.8
Wisconsin.......	1.9	9.2	0.9	15.4	(X)	4.9	9.3	3.6	0.2	3.4	6.3	12.3
Wyoming	1.8	0.8	0.2	1.9	(X)	0.4	1.0	0.5	0.1	0.7	1.2	1.7

- Represents or rounds to zero. X Not applicable. [1] Includes other categories not shown separately.

Source: U.S. Census Bureau; *Public Employment and Payroll Data*. See also<http://www.census.gov/govs/www/apes.html>; (accessed 12 May 2005).

Table 456. **State and Local Government Employment and Average Monthly Earnings by State: 1993 and 2003**

[3,891 represents 3,891,000. 1993, as of October; 2003, as of March. Full-time equivalent employment is a derived statistic that provides an estimate of a government's total full-time employment by converting part-time employees to a full-time amount.]

State	Full-time equivalent employment (1,000)				Full-time equivalent employment per 10,000 population [2]				Average monthly earnings [3] (dol.)			
	State		Local [1]		State		Local [1]		State		Local [1]	
	1993	2003	1993	2003	1993	2003	1993	2003	1993	2003	1993	2003
United States . . .	3,891	4,191	9,552	11,570	150	144	368	398	2,722	3,751	2,627	3,529
Alabama	83	86	157	184	197	190	372	409	2,307	3,393	1,908	2,649
Alaska	22	25	22	26	364	383	368	405	3,640	4,095	3,624	3,924
Arizona	57	65	149	196	139	117	366	352	2,424	3,416	2,694	3,444
Arkansas	47	54	84	99	190	198	344	364	2,261	3,041	1,754	2,404
California	344	389	1,085	1,416	110	110	347	399	3,644	4,892	3,390	4,610
Colorado	55	67	133	189	151	148	367	415	3,042	4,412	2,530	3,423
Connecticut	60	60	95	116	181	172	287	334	3,337	4,489	3,322	4,206
Delaware	20	24	18	21	289	299	249	263	2,469	3,592	2,714	3,638
District of Columbia . . .	(X)	(X)	51	44	(X)	(X)	863	793	(X)	(X)	3,315	4,679
Florida	167	187	498	620	120	110	358	365	2,266	3,298	2,355	3,312
Georgia	119	121	293	363	170	140	420	419	2,309	3,261	2,054	2,892
Hawaii	52	57	14	14	441	460	122	115	2,627	3,296	2,900	3,680
Idaho	21	23	41	55	185	171	370	404	2,280	3,277	1,999	2,813
Illinois	132	134	431	507	112	106	365	401	2,839	3,921	2,799	3,618
Indiana	88	91	203	242	153	146	355	390	2,682	3,255	2,257	2,967
Iowa	51	53	113	127	180	179	397	431	2,971	4,222	2,214	2,916
Kansas	48	44	115	134	187	161	449	492	2,289	3,412	2,227	2,763
Kentucky	72	79	122	149	188	191	320	362	2,295	3,299	1,997	2,536
Louisiana	90	90	160	189	209	201	370	420	2,242	3,171	1,844	2,515
Maine	21	22	42	53	171	167	341	407	2,455	3,473	2,175	2,777
Maryland	84	92	161	196	169	166	323	355	2,742	3,819	2,977	4,021
Massachusetts	81	91	202	229	133	142	334	357	2,914	4,187	2,817	3,919
Michigan	136	137	326	375	142	136	342	372	3,231	4,212	3,064	3,811
Minnesota	67	75	177	208	147	149	387	412	3,127	4,455	2,810	3,562
Mississippi	48	56	107	130	180	195	402	450	2,177	2,929	1,634	2,282
Missouri	79	91	177	221	150	159	335	387	2,142	2,850	2,178	2,887
Montana	17	19	35	34	205	204	413	372	2,377	3,238	2,131	2,701
Nebraska	29	34	71	80	179	193	435	462	2,214	3,004	2,292	3,086
Nevada	19	25	46	68	135	110	327	303	2,795	3,778	2,909	4,221
New Hampshire	17	20	35	48	150	158	310	371	2,510	3,402	2,558	3,208
New Jersey	110	147	304	343	139	170	382	397	3,303	4,531	3,238	4,372
New Mexico	43	46	63	76	262	247	384	403	2,223	2,964	1,980	2,682
New York	267	248	855	945	146	129	465	492	3,335	4,404	3,323	4,558
North Carolina	111	131	279	339	157	156	396	402	2,416	3,299	2,172	3,032
North Dakota	16	18	23	23	245	285	353	366	2,318	3,092	2,366	3,111
Ohio	141	137	390	483	127	120	351	422	2,777	3,764	2,504	3,397
Oklahoma	68	66	122	136	210	187	374	388	1,897	3,083	1,949	2,598
Oregon	47	57	108	125	154	160	352	350	2,780	3,639	2,653	3,542
Pennsylvania	145	159	367	410	120	129	303	331	2,804	3,865	2,713	3,598
Rhode Island	20	20	28	36	195	187	272	333	2,949	4,182	2,961	4,133
South Carolina	78	77	125	165	213	186	340	398	2,091	2,992	2,037	2,775
South Dakota	14	13	26	30	192	171	362	397	2,238	3,143	1,926	2,528
Tennessee	77	83	182	228	150	143	353	390	2,238	3,075	2,059	2,847
Texas	247	266	768	987	136	120	423	447	2,426	3,382	2,140	2,892
Utah	42	48	56	75	221	203	294	317	2,206	3,383	2,253	3,132
Vermont	13	14	22	25	219	219	381	406	2,504	3,606	2,348	2,827
Virginia	118	116	234	295	181	157	359	401	2,355	3,478	2,381	3,163
Washington	96	113	171	209	183	184	325	340	2,987	3,882	3,140	4,251
West Virginia	33	37	57	56	184	205	314	310	2,015	2,939	2,127	2,855
Wisconsin	70	71	190	217	137	130	373	396	2,913	4,072	2,689	3,567
Wyoming	11	12	25	32	230	241	527	628	2,127	3,205	2,249	2,926

X Not applicable.   [1] Estimates subject to sampling variation; see Appendix III and source.   [2] Based on estimated resident population as of July 1.   [3] For full-time employees.

Source: U.S. Census Bureau; *Public Employment and Payroll Data*. See also <http://www.census.gov/govs/www/apes> (accessed 12 May 2005).

Table 457. **City Government Employment and Payroll—Largest Cities: 1993 and 2003**

[In thousands, (421.8 represents 421,800). For 1993 as of October; 2003 as of March. See footnote 3, Table 447, for those areas representing city-county consolidated governments. See headnote, page 311 for full-time equivalent employment definition.]

Cities ranked by 2002 population [1]	Total employment (1,000)		Full-time equivalent employment				Payroll (mil. dol.)		Average monthly earnings for full-time employees (dol.)	
			Total (1,000)		Per 10,000 population [1]					
	1993	2003	1993	2002	1993	2003	1993	2003	1993	2003
New York, NY [2][3]	421.8	453.1	380.9	413.9	520	512	1,278.7	2,044.6	3,416	5,080
Los Angeles, CA	47.4	53.1	46.9	51.8	135	136	182.1	286.3	3,896	5,573
Chicago, IL	39.6	41.4	39.6	40.7	142	141	131.4	165.5	3,315	4,091
Houston, TX	22.0	22.7	22.0	22.4	135	112	53.1	73.1	2,412	3,268
Philadelphia, PA	29.8	31.1	29.0	30.1	183	202	88.6	124.8	3,071	4,157
Phoenix, AZ	11.4	13.7	10.9	13.3	111	97	34.1	59.6	3,211	4,495
San Diego, CA	10.8	12.0	10.1	11.2	91	89	30.8	53.0	3,116	4,865
Dallas, TX	13.8	15.0	13.6	14.7	135	122	35.2	59.4	2,647	4,090
San Antonio, TX	13.7	17.8	13.1	16.9	140	141	32.0	57.3	2,472	3,515
Detroit, MI	18.8	44.8	18.5	38.5	180	416	49.2	157.2	2,700	4,139
San Jose, CA	6.2	7.8	5.7	7.0	73	78	23.7	44.1	4,312	6,674
Honolulu, HI	10.3	9.8	9.7	9.1	116	101	28.3	33.5	2,966	3,737
Indianapolis, IN	12.4	16.0	11.7	15.2	161	195	26.7	45.9	2,293	3,009
San Francisco, CA	23.9	28.8	23.9	28.8	330	377	92.9	175.1	3,892	6,078
Jacksonville, FL	10.5	10.6	9.8	10.5	154	137	27.9	39.0	2,967	3,862
Columbus, OH	7.9	9.0	7.5	8.7	119	120	21.6	34.6	2,919	4,018
Austin, TX	3.7	8.4	3.5	7.9	131	113	6.7	24.7	1,936	3,160
Baltimore, MD [2]	12.4	12.5	11.8	11.9	254	178	30.6	44.4	2,650	3,752
Memphis, TN [2]	24.2	28.1	22.3	27.1	366	418	55.4	89.6	2,490	3,357
Milwaukee, WI	28.4	29.4	27.8	28.3	378	444	74.4	107.3	2,713	3,892
Boston, MA [2]	8.7	8.0	8.3	7.8	133	132	22.9	32.5	2,782	4,181
Washington DC [2][3]	21.0	21.8	20.7	20.7	360	351	61.8	89.7	3,034	4,397
Nashville-Davidson, TN	4.8	5.9	4.7	5.7	119	99	11.9	21.6	2,578	3,777
El Paso, TX	5.7	5.8	5.6	5.7	108	99	12.2	16.3	2,225	2,868
Seattle,WA	44.6	36.8	43.1	34.9	711	612	132.7	156.9	3,130	4,553
Denver, CO	11.2	13.4	10.3	11.6	199	203	36.8	56.3	3,691	5,161
Charlotte, NC	5.3	6.1	5.1	5.9	113	104	11.5	21.0	2,334	3,704
Fort Worth, TX	13.9	14.6	12.5	13.6	266	243	35.5	50.1	2,859	3,663
Portland, OR	17.7	20.9	16.6	19.9	340	365	40.4	71.1	2,430	3,649
Oklahoma City, OK	5.3	6.2	4.8	5.4	109	100	17.2	25.4	3,679	4,818
Tucson, AZ	5.0	4.9	4.6	4.5	104	87	11.7	18.5	2,567	4,218
New Orleans, LA	2.0	2.9	2.0	2.7	77	53	6.5	14.5	3,310	5,466
Las Vegas, NV	5.4	6.5	4.9	5.9	122	118	12.9	22.7	2,714	4,023
Cleveland, OH	9.8	9.7	9.6	9.4	194	199	15.5	23.3	1,623	2,474
Long Beach, CA	5.7	6.4	5.4	6.0	125	127	19.3	28.0	3,726	4,938
Albuquerque, NM	9.4	9.5	8.8	9.1	175	194	23.6	31.9	2,687	3,539
Kansas City, MO	7.4	5.8	6.0	5.6	156	120	12.6	17.8	2,148	3,304
Fresno, CA	2.7	3.7	2.7	3.6	76	80	9.1	15.6	3,396	4,565
Virginia Beach, VA [2]	6.3	6.7	6.2	6.6	143	149	15.6	25.2	2,518	3,834
Atlanta,GA	4.3	5.0	3.9	4.3	107	98	12.8	19.7	3,384	4,948
Sacramento, CA	14.7	22.7	14.0	18.4	356	423	31.5	51.4	2,273	2,964
Oakland, CA	2.5	3.9	2.5	3.8	86	88	7.6	17.0	3,091	4,605
Mesa, AZ	8.5	7.4	8.4	7.2	213	170	21.1	24.5	2,523	3,409
Tulsa, OK	6.6	7.4	5.9	6.7	154	162	13.3	19.0	2,363	3,067
Omaha, NE	5.1	5.2	4.8	5.2	128	130	18.0	35.0	4,165	6,680
Baton Rouge. LA	3.0	3.2	2.8	2.8	84	69	8.6	11.4	3,225	4,233
Minneapolis, MN	4.5	4.5	4.3	4.3	118	112	10.8	14.6	2,559	3,395
Miami, FL	6.8	6.4	6.1	5.9	165	157	19.2	24.9	3,359	4,321
Colorado Springs, CO	3.8	4.1	3.7	4.0	103	105	12.8	18.7	3,595	5,015
St Louis, MO	6.0	7.7	5.5	7.1	197	192	15.2	29.6	2,826	4,235
Wichita, KS	3.2	3.4	2.9	3.0	97	83	7.1	10.0	2,429	3,443
Santa Ana, CA	2.2	3.2	1.9	2.6	74	74	5.1	8.7	2,721	3,518
Pittsburgh, PA	2.2	2.4	1.8	2.0	63	57	8.9	10.7	5,163	5,910
Arlington, TX	7.9	7.6	7.5	7.4	190	219	17.9	27.4	2,393	3,706
Cincinnati, OH	3.6	3.4	2.4	2.7	90	81	9.4	14.3	4,251	6,381
Anaheim, CA	5.3	4.0	5.1	4.0	138	122	14.9	15.5	3,009	3,981
Toledo, OH	7.8	6.5	7.0	6.1	192	189	19.3	25.8	2,973	4,341
Tampa, FL	4.0	4.5	3.9	4.4	139	141	12.0	16.9	3,128	3,848
Buffalo, NY [2]	3.0	2.9	3.0	2.9	89	95	9.1	11.9	3,054	4,054
St Paul, MN	2.9	3.7	2.6	3.3	127	109	6.6	10.2	2,532	3,221
Corpus Christi, TX	14.4	12.6	13.3	11.3	405	393	35.4	46.1	2,862	4,266
Aurora, CO	2.0	2.6	2.0	2.6	88	90	5.5	11.1	2,796	4,279
Raleigh, NC	3.6	3.3	3.3	3.0	121	105	11.5	13.8	3,629	4,800
Newark, NJ	3.2	3.2	3.0	2.9	117	105	6.6	9.2	2,247	3,176
Lexington-Fayette, KY	6.1	7.0	5.9	6.1	214	219	16.8	28.5	2,877	4,901
Anchorage, AK	2.2	2.2	2.2	2.0	98	74	7.9	10.2	3,756	5,502
Louisville, KY	8.8	10.8	8.0	9.7	353	359	28.4	38.7	3,691	4,125
Riverside, CA	3.5	4.2	3.3	3.9	148	148	6.8	11.9	2,039	3,126
St Petersburg, FL	1.8	2.3	1.6	1.9	77	73	5.3	8.7	3,426	5,035
Bakersfield, CA	1.2	1.4	1.1	1.4	64	52	3.8	6.1	3,517	4,580
Stockton,CA	3.5	3.8	3.1	3.4	128	136	7.9	11.9	2,745	3,767
Birmingham, AL	3.5	3.9	3.3	3.6	146	148	146	16.3	3,416	4,897
Jersey City, NJ	4.2	4.8	4.1	4.6	152	193	9.3	18.5	2,320	4,063
Norfolk, VA [2]	11.6	13.9	10.3	11.8	394	495	25.5	36.5	2,523	3,146
Hialeah, FL	1.5	2.3	1.3	2.1	104	89	3.6	8.3	2,753	4,165
Lincoln, NE	3.7	2.9	3.3	2.7	170	115	8.4	10.1	2,668	3,930
Greensboro, NC	1.3	1.9	1.2	1.7	80	75	3.6	7.3	3,104	4,406

[1]2002 based on enumerated resident population as of July 1.   [2] Includes city-operated elementary and secondary schools.
[3] Includes city-operated university or college.
Source: U.S. Census Bureau; *Government Employment, March 2003.* See also <http://www.census.gov/govs/www/apes.html>; (accessed 12 May 2005).

Table 458. County Government Employment and Payroll—Largest Counties: 1993 and 2003

[In thousands, (86.5 represents 86,500). For 1993 as of October; 2003 as of March. See headnote, page 311 for full-time equivalent employment definition. See text, this section]

Counties ranked by 2002 population [1]	Total employment (1,000)		Full-time equivalent employment				Payroll (mil. dol.)		Average monthly earnings for full-time employees (dol.)	
			Total (1,000)		Per 10,000 population					
	1993	2003	1993	2003	1993	2003	1993	2003	1993	2003
Los Angeles, CA	86.5	101.1	82.9	97.1	98	103	301.0	457.9	3,582	4,773
Cook, IL	25.0	27.3	24.9	27.3	49	51	70.6	111.8	2,833	4,110
Harris, TX	19.6	22.7	18.5	22.2	70	64	45.4	79.9	2,457	3,605
Maricopa, AZ	16.3	15.6	15.6	15.2	77	47	32.8	46.8	2,108	3,074
Orange, CA	16.4	26.1	15.5	24.2	68	89	51.7	99.5	3,380	4,149
San Diego, CA	17.9	21.9	17.0	20.6	72	75	48.8	83.3	2,879	4,082
Dade, FL	36.7	42.4	34.4	41.2	190	182	101.4	172.3	2,938	4,288
Dallas, TX	11.5	14.3	10.8	13.7	62	63	25.0	52.3	2,229	3,847
Wayne, MI	5.7	6.6	5.6	6.5	27	32	16.3	28.4	2,871	4,409
King, WA	14.4	21.1	13.6	19.3	101	116	38.6	68.5	2,869	3,555
San Bernardino, CA	9.1	14.7	7.4	13.8	60	84	25.2	61.4	3,395	4,624
Santa Clara, CA	9.8	12.7	9.3	12.5	78	74	24.3	49.4	2,618	4,006
Broward, FL	12.6	20.2	11.9	19.1	108	119	38.7	82.1	3,298	4,334
Riverside, CA	17.9	19.1	16.2	18.1	119	114	55.1	97.6	3,412	5,497
Tarrant, TX	3.4	8.7	3.3	8.5	29	57	7.9	28.6	2,373	3,400
Alameda, CA	10.8	18.0	9.9	16.4	146	118	31.4	77.3	3,235	4,823
Suffolk, NY	11.0	12.6	10.0	12.0	86	85	35.7	62.6	3,495	5,255
Cuyahoga, OH	13.0	14.0	11.6	12.6	98	96	42.0	64.2	3,619	5,183
Bexar, TX	6.8	10.0	6.3	9.3	57	69	13.6	30.0	2,147	3,141
Clark, NV	18.3	15.4	15.8	14.9	130	112	37.8	52.9	2,433	3,479
Nassau, NY	18.6	19.3	16.2	17.4	145	144	60.2	84.0	3,808	4,984
Allegheny, PA	13.6	14.8	13.3	14.2	131	114	41.6	71.6	3,149	5,090
Sacramento, CA	9.0	7.3	8.6	7.1	67	57	21.9	19.9	2,664	2,855
Oakland, MI	4.4	4.6	4.1	4.4	41	38	12.1	17.7	3,009	4,151
Palm Beach, FL	8.1	9.9	7.9	9.7	94	83	20.9	37.5	2,666	3,922
Hennepin, MN	12.1	12.6	10.3	11.0	117	112	31.4	47.3	3,052	4,164
Franklin, OH	6.2	6.8	5.9	6.5	65	63	13.7	20.8	2,347	3,226
St Louis, MO	12.9	15.7	12.2	11.9	154	149	27.9	38.7	2,288	3,580
Hillsborough, FL	3.9	4.3	3.8	4.2	39	42	10.0	14.8	2,657	3,554
Fairfax, VA	33.7	43.2	29.9	37.4	411	433	85.5	150.6	3,023	4,104
Erie, NY	8.6	9.9	7.8	9.1	107	100	27.5	44.3	3,527	4,980
Contra Costa, CA	8.6	10.7	7.8	10.0	127	113	18.9	33.7	2,440	3,435
Milwaukee, WI	10.8	11.0	9.5	9.9	111	116	23.0	39.0	2,463	4,150
Westchester, NY	12.2	7.3	10.6	6.4	139	78	37.1	27.4	3,474	4,436
Pinellas, FL	10.8	8.1	10.7	7.8	113	87	26.3	29.3	2,435	3,781
Du Page, IL	5.3	6.7	5.2	6.5	63	72	12.7	23.1	2,406	3,531
Salt Lake, UT	2.8	3.7	2.6	3.4	36	40	6.4	12.8	2,500	3,831
Shelby, TN	4.3	6.3	3.5	4.6	60	68	8.5	14.8	2,662	3,487
Orange, FL	31.4	40.5	25.5	33.2	415	445	87.9	157.8	3,855	5,166
Bergen, NJ	10.8	14.5	10.1	13.7	130	160	21.2	41.9	2,122	3,065
Montgomery, MD	8.7	6.3	7.5	4.6	105	71	21.4	20.0	2,855	4,461
Hamilton, OH	6.7	7.9	6.1	7.2	101	89	14.2	23.8	2,395	3,424
Pima, AZ	3.1	4.6	2.8	4.5	54	54	6.5	14.8	2,283	3,276
Fulton, GA	8.2	9.0	8.0	8.6	123	108	21.7	31.1	2,695	3,670
Travis, TX	5.8	6.1	5.6	6.0	66	73	13.2	20.1	2,364	3,376
Prince George's, MD	24.9	31.9	22.2	28.9	341	383	67.4	104.2	3,090	3,760
Fresno, CA	5.8	7.4	5.5	7.1	89	89	13.6	26.5	2,503	3,875
Essex, NJ	2.8	3.2	2.6	2.9	39	39	6.4	10.8	2,604	3,812
Macomb, MI	8.6	5.4	8.0	5.1	110	67	20.3	22.3	2,546	4,486
Baltimore, MD	7.0	9.2	6.7	8.7	104	118	20.4	39.1	3,015	4,482
Ventura, CA	5.5	4.6	4.6	4.2	81	59	13.9	17.3	2,920	4,656
Middlesex, NJ	24.2	26.1	20.4	22.7	350	339	52.2	85.3	2,717	4,012
Montgomery, PA	3.3	3.9	3.1	3.6	49	51	6.9	11.1	2,227	3,130
Monroe, NY	7.0	6.7	6.2	5.8	98	91	17.9	22.0	2,977	3,887
San Mateo, CA	18.2	25.2	16.4	22.9	356	342	38.8	73.6	2,445	3,310
Pierce, WA	2.5	3.6	2.3	3.4	43	49	7.9	15.4	3,345	4,611
Mecklenburg, NC	5.8	7.0	5.1	6.3	89	99	18.7	32.2	3,676	5,327
Jefferson, KY	3.5	4.3	3.1	4.2	59	61	6.3	13.3	2,017	3,266
El Paso, TX	8.4	10.0	8.1	9.3	155	144	23.0	38.9	2,871	4,151
Dekalb, GA	3.1	3.7	2.9	3.6	47	53	6.2	11.5	2,120	3,219
Jefferson, AL	4.4	4.9	3.8	4.6	75	72	9.8	17.0	2,658	3,673
Kern, CA	5.4	6.8	5.3	6.6	100	101	13.2	23.6	2,488	3,605
Multnomah, OR	14.5	19.0	12.6	17.0	342	281	27.6	54.0	2,159	3,166
Oklahoma, OK	2.4	3.1	2.2	2.9	46	46	3.0	11.4	1,304	3,978
Jackson, MO	1.9	2.3	1.8	2.1	32	35	3.3	5.5	1,859	2,655
Norfolk, MA	5.0	4.9	4.8	4.8	77	74	11.6	16.6	2,377	3,440
Lake, IL	2.0	2.2	1.9	2.0	31	33	3.7	5.6	1,867	2,770
Wake, NC	0.8	0.5	0.7	0.5	12	7	1.8	1.9	2,566	4,138
Monmouth, NJ	3.6	4.7	3.3	4.3	81	72	8.1	14.6	2,493	3,543
Hudson, NJ	3.1	4.4	3.0	4.2	89	68	7.3	15.1	2,478	3,721
Cobb, GA	2.0	2.9	2.0	2.6	44	45	6.1	11.7	3,032	4,556
Snohomish, WA	5.7	6.2	4.9	5.4	104	98	12.9	21.7	2,623	4,162
Bucks, PA	1.5	2.1	1.4	2.1	38	35	2.0	5.2	1,423	2,449
Gwinnett, GA	7.2	8.4	6.6	7.5	150	136	15.4	29.3	2,364	4,091
Kent, MI	5.3	4.4	4.9	3.7	96	72	11.4	13.4	2,300	3,770
Hidalgo, TX	2.2	2.7	2.0	2.5	40	45	4.9	8.8	2,359	3,527
San Joaquin, CA	2.7	2.4	2.5	2.3	54	41	6.3	8.8	2,561	3,901

[1] 2002 based on enumerated resident population as of July 1.

Source: U.S. Census Bureau; "Government Employment, March 2003. See also <http://www.census.gov/govs/www/apes.html>; (accessed 12 May 2005).

State and Local Government Finances and Employment 313

No. 5.—AMOUNT of INTERNAL REVENUE RECEIPTS from all sources from 1863 to 1878, inclusive.

[From the Annual Report of the Commissioner of Internal Revenue.]

YEAR ENDED JUNE 30—	Spirits.	Tobacco.	Fermented liquors.	Banks and bankers.	Penalties, &c.	Adhesive stamps.a	Articles and occupations formerly taxed, but now exempt.	TOTAL.
	Dollars.	Dollars.	Dollars.	Dollars.	Dollars.	Dollars.	Dollars.	Dollars.
1863	5,176,530	3,097,020	1,658,884		27,170	4,140,175	28,032,703	41,003,193
1864	30,329,150	8,592,000	2,290,000	2,887,738	193,600	5,804,945	67,008,225	117,145,749
1865	18,731,422	11,401,373	3,734,928	4,940,871	520,303	11,162,392	100,628,180	211,129,329
1866	33,268,172	16,531,008	5,220,553	3,408,988	1,142,808	15,044,873	225,280,037	310,906,984
1867	33,542,952	19,765,148	6,087,501	2,046,562	1,459,171	16,094,718	186,954,423	265,920,473
1868	18,655,631	16,736,095	5,905,089	1,665,746	1,256,882	14,852,252	129,863,090	191,180,564
1869	45,071,231	23,430,708	6,099,879	2,196,054	877,080	10,420,710	65,943,673	100,869,344
1870	55,606,094	31,350,708	6,310,127	3,020,084	827,903	16,544,043	71,567,908	185,235,808
1871	46,281,848	32,578,907	7,389,502	3,644,342	636,980	15,342,720	37,136,958	144,013,176
1872	49,475,516	33,736,170	8,258,498	4,628,239	442,205	16,177,321	19,052,906	131,770,947
1873	52,099,372	34,386,303	9,324,938	3,711,931	461,633	7,702,377	6,329,782	114,075,450
1874	40,444,090	33,242,876	9,304,680	3,867,161	364,216	6,130,845	764,680	102,044,747
1875	52,081,991	37,303,462	9,144,004	4,007,348	281,108	6,557,230	1,080,111	110,545,154
1876	56,426,365	39,795,340	9,571,281	4,006,098	409,294	6,518,488	509,631	117,227,987
1877	57,469,430	41,106,547	9,480,789	3,829,729	419,099	6,440,429	238,301	118,905,184
1878	50,420,816	40,091,755	9,937,052	3,492,032	346,098	6,380,405	429,650	111,097,726
Total in 16 years	654,080,610	426,140,119	109,117,544	51,228,395	9,696,486	171,419,442	1,010,066,387	2,432,209,183

a These amounts represent the face value of the stamps sold, but the receipts covered into the Treasury are these amounts less the commissions allowed on such sales.

Source: Statistical Abstract of the United States: 1878 Edition.

Section 9
Federal Government Finances and Employment

This section presents statistics relating to the financial structure and the civilian employment of the federal government. The fiscal data cover taxes, other receipts, outlays, and debt. The principal sources of fiscal data are the *Budget of the United States Government* and related documents, published annually by the Office of Management and Budget (OMB), and the U.S. Department of the Treasury's *United States Government Annual Report* and its *Appendix*. Detailed data on tax returns and collections are published annually by the Internal Revenue Service. The personnel data relate to staffing and payrolls. They are published by the Office of Personnel Management and the Bureau of Labor Statistics. The primary source for data on public lands is *Public Land Statistics*, published annually by the Bureau of Land Management, Department of the Interior. Data on federally owned land and real property are collected by the General Services Administration and presented in its annual *Inventory Report on Real Property Owned by the United States Throughout the World*.

Budget concept—Under the unified budget concept, all federal monies are included in one comprehensive budget. These monies comprise both federal funds and trust funds. Federal funds are derived mainly from taxes and borrowing and are not restricted by law to any specific government purpose. Trust funds, such as the Unemployment Trust Fund, collect certain taxes and other receipts for use in carrying out specific purposes or programs in accordance with the terms of the trust agreement or statute. Fund balances include both cash balances with the Treasury and investments in U.S. securities. Part of the balance is obligated, part unobligated. Prior to 1985, the budget totals, under provisions of law, excluded some federal activities—including the Federal Financing Bank, the Postal Service, the Synthetic Fuels Corporation, and the lending activities of the Rural Electrification Administration. The Balanced Budget and Emergency Deficit Control Act of 1985 (P.L.99-177) repealed the off-budget status of these entities and placed social security (federal old-age and survivors insurance and the federal disability insurance trust funds) off-budget. Though social security is now off-budget and, by law, excluded from coverage of the congressional budget resolutions, it continues to be a federal program.

Receipts arising from the government's sovereign powers are reported as governmental receipts; all other receipts; i.e., from business-type or market-oriented activities, are offset against outlays. Outlays are reported on a checks-issued (net) basis (i.e., outlays are recorded at the time the checks to pay bills are issued).

Debt concept—For most of U.S. history, the total debt consisted of debt borrowed by the Treasury (i.e., public debt). The present debt series, includes both public debt and agency debt. The *gross federal debt* includes money borrowed by the Treasury and by various federal agencies; it is the broadest generally used measure of the federal debt. *Total public debt* is covered by a statutory debt limitation and includes only borrowing by the Treasury.

Treasury receipts and outlays—All receipts of the government, with a few exceptions, are deposited to the credit of the U.S. Treasury regardless of ultimate disposition. Under the Constitution, no money may be withdrawn from the Treasury unless appropriated by the Congress.

The day-to-day cash operations of the federal government clearing through the accounts of the U.S. Treasury are reported in the *Daily Treasury Statement*. Extensive detail on the public debt is published in the *Monthly Statement of the Public Debt of the United States*.

Budget receipts such as taxes, customs duties, and miscellaneous receipts, which are collected by government agencies, and outlays represented by checks issued and cash payments made by disbursing officers as well as government agencies are reported in the *Daily Treasury Statement of Receipts and Outlays of the United States Government* and in the Treasury's *United States Government Annual Report* and its *Appendix*. These deposits in and payments from accounts maintained by government agencies are on the same basis as the unified budget.

The quarterly *Treasury Bulletin* contains data on fiscal operations and related Treasury activities, including financial statements of government corporations and other business-type activities.

Income tax returns and tax collections—Tax data are compiled by the Internal Revenue Service of the Treasury Department. The annual *Internal Revenue Service Data Book* gives a detailed account of tax collections by kind of tax. The agency's annual *Statistics of Income* reports present detailed data from individual income tax returns and corporation income tax returns. The quarterly *Statistics of Income Bulletin* has, in general, replaced the supplemental *Statistics of Income* publications which presented data on such diverse subjects as tax-exempt organizations, unincorporated businesses, fiduciary income tax and estate tax returns, sales of capital assets by individuals, international income and taxes reported by corporations and individuals, and estate tax wealth.

Employment and payrolls—The Office of Personnel Management collects employment and payroll data from all departments and agencies of the federal government, except the Central Intelligence Agency, the National Security Agency, and the Defense Intelligence Agency. Employment figures represent the number of persons who occupied civilian positions at the end of the report month shown and who are paid for personal services rendered for the federal government, regardless of the nature of appointment or method of payment. Federal payrolls include all payments for personal services rendered during the report month and payments for accumulated annual leave of employees who separate from the service. Since most federal employees are paid on a biweekly basis, the calendar month earnings are partially estimated on the basis of the number of work days in each month where payroll periods overlap.

Federal employment and payroll figures are published by the Office of Personnel Management in its *Federal Civilian Workforce Statistics—Employment and Trends*. It also publishes biennial employment data for minority groups, data on occupations of white- and blue-collar workers, and data on employment by geographic area; reports on salary and wage distribution of federal employees are published annually. General schedule is primarily white-collar; wage system primarily blue-collar. Data on federal employment are also issued by the Bureau of Labor Statistics in its *Monthly Labor Review* and in *Employment and Earnings* and by the U.S. Census Bureau in its annual publication *Public Employment*.

Public lands—The data on applications, entries, selections, patents, and certifications refer to transactions that involve the disposal, under the public land laws (including the homestead laws), of federal public lands to nonfederal owners. In general, original entries and selections are applications to secure title to public lands that have been accepted as properly filed (i.e., allowed). Some types of applications, however, are not reported until issuance of the final certificate, which passes equitable title to the land to the applicant.

Table 459. Federal Budget—Receipts, Outlays, and Debt: 1960 to 2005

[In billions of dollars (92.5 represents $92,500,000,000), except percent. For fiscal years ending in year shown; see text, Section 8. State and Local Government Finances and Employment. The Balanced Budget and Emergency Deficit Control Act of 1985 put all the previously off-budget Federal entities into the budget and moved Social Security off-budget. Minus sign (-) indicates deficit or decrease]

Year	Receipts	Outlays	Surplus or deficit(-)	Outlays as percent of GDP [1]	Gross federal debt [2] Total	Federal gov't account	Held by the public Total	Federal Reserve System	As percent of GDP [1]
1960	92.5	92.2	0.3	17.8	290.5	53.7	236.8	26.5	56.1
1965	116.8	118.2	-1.4	17.2	322.3	61.5	260.8	39.1	46.9
1970	192.8	195.6	-2.8	19.3	380.9	97.7	283.2	57.7	37.6
1975	279.1	332.3	-53.2	21.3	541.9	147.2	394.7	85.0	34.7
1980	517.1	590.9	-73.8	21.7	909.0	197.1	711.9	120.8	33.3
1981	599.3	678.2	-79.0	22.2	994.8	205.4	789.4	124.5	32.6
1982	617.8	745.7	-128.0	23.1	1,137.3	212.7	924.6	134.5	35.2
1983	600.6	808.4	-207.8	23.5	1,371.7	234.4	1,137.3	155.5	39.9
1984	666.5	851.9	-185.4	22.2	1,564.6	257.6	1,307.0	155.1	40.7
1985	734.1	946.4	-212.3	22.9	1,817.4	310.2	1,507.3	169.8	43.9
1986	769.2	990.4	-221.2	22.4	2,120.5	379.9	1,740.6	190.9	48.1
1987	854.4	1,004.1	-149.7	21.6	2,346.0	456.2	1,889.8	212.0	50.5
1988	909.3	1,064.5	-155.2	21.3	2,601.1	549.5	2,051.6	229.2	51.9
1989	991.2	1,143.6	-152.5	21.2	2,867.8	677.1	2,190.7	220.1	53.1
1990	1,032.0	1,253.2	-221.2	21.8	3,206.3	794.7	2,411.6	234.4	55.9
1991	1,055.0	1,324.4	-269.3	22.3	3,598.2	909.2	2,689.0	258.6	60.6
1992	1,091.3	1,381.7	-290.4	22.1	4,001.8	1,002.1	2,999.7	296.4	64.1
1993	1,154.4	1,409.5	-255.1	21.4	4,351.0	1,102.6	3,248.4	325.7	66.2
1994	1,258.6	1,461.9	-203.3	21.0	4,643.3	1,210.2	3,433.1	355.2	66.7
1995	1,351.8	1,515.8	-164.0	20.7	4,920.6	1,316.2	3,604.4	374.1	67.2
1996	1,453.1	1,560.5	-107.5	20.3	5,181.5	1,447.4	3,734.1	390.9	67.3
1997	1,579.3	1,601.3	-22.0	19.6	5,369.2	1,596.9	3,772.3	424.5	65.6
1998	1,721.8	1,652.6	69.2	19.2	5,478.2	1,757.1	3,721.1	458.2	63.5
1999	1,827.5	1,701.9	125.6	18.7	5,605.5	1,973.2	3,632.4	496.6	61.4
2000	2,025.2	1,789.1	236.4	18.4	5,628.7	2,218.9	3,409.8	511.4	58.0
2001	1,991.2	1,863.9	127.4	18.5	5,769.9	2,450.3	3,319.6	534.1	57.4
2002	1,853.2	2,011.0	-157.8	19.4	6,198.4	2,658.0	3,540.4	604.2	59.7
2003	1,782.3	2,159.9	-377.6	19.9	6,760.0	2,846.6	3,913.4	656.1	62.4
2004	1,880.1	2,292.2	-412.1	19.8	7,354.7	3,059.1	4,295.5	700.3	63.7
2005, estimate. .	2,052.8	2,479.4	-426.6	20.3	8,031.4	3,310.2	4,721.2	(NA)	65.7

NA Not available.   [1] Gross domestic product as of fiscal year; for calendar year GDP, see Section 13, Income, Expenditures, and Wealth.   [2] See text, this section, for discussion of debt concept.

Source: U.S. Office of Management and Budget, *Budget of the United States Government, Historical Tables*, annual. See also <http://w3.access.gpo.gov/usbudget/fy2006/pdf/hist.pdf>.

Table 460. Federal Budget Outlays—Defense, Human and Physical Resources, and Net Interest Payments: 1990 to 2005

[In billions of dollars (1,253.2 represents $1,253,200,000,000). For fiscal year ending in year shown. Minus sign (-) indicates offsets]

Outlays	1990	1995	2000	2001	2002	2003	2004	2005, est.
Federal outlays, total	1,253.2	1,515.8	1,789.1	1,863.9	2,011.0	2,159.9	2,292.2	2,479.4
National defense.	299.3	272.1	294.5	305.5	348.6	404.9	455.9	465.9
Human resources	619.3	923.8	1,115.5	1,194.4	1,317.4	1,417.7	1,485.6	1,588.0
Education, training, employment and social services.	37.2	51.0	53.8	57.1	70.5	82.6	87.9	96.3
Health	57.7	115.4	154.5	172.3	196.5	219.6	240.1	257.5
Medicare	98.1	159.9	197.1	217.4	230.9	249.4	269.4	295.4
Income security.	148.7	223.7	253.6	269.6	312.5	334.4	332.8	350.9
Social security.	248.6	335.8	409.4	433.0	456.0	474.7	495.5	519.7
Veterans' benefits and services	29.1	37.9	47.1	45.0	51.0	57.0	59.8	68.2
Physical resources	126.0	59.1	84.7	97.9	104.4	115.6	116.3	131.7
Energy. . . . . : .	3.3	4.9	10.8	-	0.5	-0.7	-0.2	1.4
Natural resources and environment . . .	17.1	21.9	25.0	25.6	29.5	29.7	30.7	31.0
Commerce and housing credit	67.6	-17.8	3.2	5.7	-0.4	0.7	5.3	10.7
Transportation.	29.5	39.4	46.9	54.4	61.8	67.1	64.6	68.5
Community and regional development .	8.5	10.7	10.6	11.8	13.0	18.9	15.8	20.1
Net interest	184.3	232.1	222.9	206.2	170.9	153.1	160.2	177.9
International affairs.	13.8	16.4	17.2	16.5	22.4	21.2	26.9	32.0
Agriculture	12.0	9.8	36.6	26.4	22.0	22.5	15.4	30.5
Administration of justice	10.0	16.2	28.0	29.7	35.1	35.3	45.5	40.7
General government.	10.6	14.0	13.3	14.6	16.9	23.1	21.8	18.9
Undistributed offsetting receipts	-36.6	-44.5	-42.6	-47.0	-47.4	-54.4	-58.5	-65.0

-Represents zero.

Source: U.S. Office of Management and Budget, *Budget of the United States Government, Historical Tables*, annual. See also <http://w3.access.gpo.gov/usbudget/fy2006/pdf/hist.pdf>.

Table 461. Federal Budget Outlays in Constant (2000) Dollars: 1990 to 2005

[Dollar amounts in billions of dollars (1,609.9 represents $1,609,900,000,000). For fiscal year ending in year shown; see text, Section 8. Given the inherent imprecision in deflating outlays, the data shown in constant dollars present a reasonable perspective—not precision. The deflators and the categories that are deflated are as comparable over time as feasible. Minus sign (-) indicates off-set]

Type	1990	1995	2000	2001	2002	2003	2004	2005, est.
Constant (2000) dollar outlays, total	1,609.9	1,662.1	1,789.1	1,820.6	1,930.1	2,022.4	2,099.7	2,214.0
National defense [1]	333.7	305.9	294.5	297.2	330.3	366.6	404.7	406.0
Nondefense, total:	1,276.1	1,356.2	1,494.6	1,523.3	1,599.9	1,655.7	1,728.0	1,808.0
Payments for individuals	782.5	957.0	1,054.3	1,103.6	1,197.6	1,260.5	1,293.9	1,339.6
Direct payments [2]	668.9	794.4	867.5	900.1	974.2	1,023.1	1,047.4	1,085.1
Grants to state and local governments	113.5	162.6	186.8	203.5	223.4	237.3	246.5	254.6
All other grants	74.7	85.1	97.9	105.9	113.7	125.6	125.3	123.5
Net interest [2]	230.7	251.8	222.9	201.4	164.0	144.2	148.0	161.1
All other [2]	242.4	114.8	162.0	158.1	169.0	174.7	179.7	240.2
Undistributed offsetting receipts [2]	54.0	52.6	42.6	45.8	-44.4	-49.3	-52.0	-56.6
Total outlays as percent of GDP [3]	21.8	20.7	18.4	18.6	19.4	19.9	19.8	20.3
National defense [1]	5.2	3.7	3.0	3.0	3.4	3.7	3.9	3.8
Nondefense, total:	16.6	17.0	15.4	15.6	16.0	16.2	15.9	16.5
Payments for individuals	10.2	12.0	10.8	11.3	12.0	12.3	12.1	12.2
Direct payments [2]	8.8	9.9	8.9	9.2	9.7	10.0	9.8	9.9
Grants to state and local governments	1.4	2.0	1.9	2.1	2.2	2.3	2.3	2.3
All other grants	1.0	1.0	1.0	1.1	1.2	1.3	1.2	1.2
Net interest [2]	3.2	3.2	2.3	2.1	1.6	1.4	1.4	1.5
All other [2]	2.9	1.4	1.7	1.6	1.7	1.7	1.7	2.2
Percent of outlays, total	100.0	100.0	100.0	100.0	100.0	100.0	100.0	100.0
National defense [1]	23.9	17.9	16.5	16.4	17.3	18.7	19.9	18.8
Payments for individuals	46.7	57.9	58.9	60.5	61.7	61.7	61.0	60.0
Direct payments [2]	40.5	48.1	48.5	49.4	50.2	50.0	49.3	48.6
Grants to state and local governments	6.3	9.8	10.4	11.2	11.5	11.6	11.6	11.4
All other grants	4.5	5.0	5.5	5.9	6.0	6.3	6.1	5.8
Net interest [2]	14.7	15.3	12.5	11.1	8.5	7.1	7.0	7.2
All other [2]	13.1	6.8	9.0	8.7	8.8	8.7	8.6	10.9
Undistributed offsetting receipts [2]	-2.9	-2.9	-2.4	-2.5	-2.4	-2.5	-2.6	-2.6

[1] Includes a small amount of grants to state and local governments and direct payments for individuals.   [2] Includes some off-budget amounts; most of the off-budget amounts are direct payments for individuals (social security benefits).   [3] Gross domestic product in chained (2000) dollars.

Source: U.S. Office of Management and Budget, *Budget of the United States Government, Historical Tables,* annual. See also <http://w3.access.gpo.gov/usbudget/fy2006/pdf/hist.pdf>.

Table 462. Federal Outlays by Agency: 1990 to 2005

[In billions of dollars (1,253.1 represents $1,253,100,000,000). See headnote, table 459]

Department or other unit	1990	1995	2000	2002	2003	2004	2005, est.
Outlays, total [1]	1,253.1	1,515.8	1,789.1	2,011.0	2,159.9	2,292.2	2,479.4
Legislative Branch	2.2	2.6	2.9	3.2	3.4	3.9	4.1
The Judiciary Branch	1.6	2.9	4.1	4.8	5.1	5.4	5.7
Agriculture	45.9	56.6	75.5	68.7	72.4	71.8	94.9
Commerce	3.7	3.4	7.8	5.3	5.7	5.9	6.3
Defense–Military	289.7	259.5	281.2	332.0	388.9	437.1	444.1
Education	23.0	31.2	33.9	46.3	57.4	62.8	71.0
Energy	12.1	17.6	15.0	17.7	19.4	20.0	22.2
Health and Human Services	175.5	303.1	382.6	465.8	505.3	543.4	585.8
Homeland Security	7.2	9.4	13.1	17.6	32.0	26.5	33.3
Housing and Urban Development	20.2	29.0	30.8	31.9	37.5	45.0	42.6
Interior	5.8	7.5	8.0	9.7	9.2	8.9	9.4
Justice	5.9	10.1	17.3	21.1	21.5	29.0	21.2
Labor	26.1	32.8	31.9	64.7	69.6	56.7	50.0
State	4.8	6.3	6.9	9.5	9.3	10.9	11.9
Transportation	25.6	35.1	41.5	56.0	50.8	54.5	58.2
Treasury	253.9	346.9	388.6	370.6	367.0	374.8	403.0
Veterans Affairs	29.0	37.8	47.1	50.9	56.9	59.6	68.0
Corps of Engineers	3.3	3.7	4.3	4.8	4.7	4.8	4.9
Other Defense–Civil Programs	21.7	28.0	32.9	35.2	39.9	41.7	43.5
Environmental Protection Agency	5.1	6.4	7.2	7.5	8.1	8.3	7.9
Executive Office of the President	0.2	0.2	0.3	0.5	0.4	3.3	5.8
General Services Administration	-0.2	0.7	0.1	-0.7	0.6	-0.4	0.5
International Assistance Programs	10.1	11.1	12.1	13.3	13.5	13.7	14.8
National Aeronautics and Space Administration	12.4	13.4	13.4	14.4	14.6	15.2	15.7
National Science Foundation	1.8	2.8	3.5	4.2	4.7	5.1	5.6
Office of Personnel Management	31.9	41.3	48.7	52.5	54.1	56.5	61.0
Social Security Administration (on-budget)	17.3	31.0	45.1	45.8	46.3	49.0	55.8
Social Security Administration (off-budget)	245.0	330.4	396.2	442.0	461.4	481.2	503.3
Undistributed offsetting receipts	-98.9	-137.6	-173.0	-200.7	-210.5	-212.5	-228.4

[1] Includes agencies and allowances not shown separately.

Source: U.S. Office of Management and Budget, *Budget of the United States Government, Historical Tables,* annual. See also <http://w3.access.gpo.gov/usbudget/fy2006/pdf/hist.pdf>.

Table 463. **Federal Outlays by Detailed Function: 1990 to 2005**

[In billions of dollars (1,253.1 represents $1,253,100,000,000). For fiscal year ending in year shown]

Superfunction and function	1990	1995	2000	2001	2002	2003	2004	2005, est.
Outlays, total.	1,253.2	1,515.8	1,789.1	1,863.9	2,011.0	2,159.9	2,292.2	2,479.4
National defense [1]	299.3	272.1	294.5	304.9	348.6	404.9	455.9	465.9
Department of Defense–Military	289.7	259.4	281.2	290.3	332.0	387.3	436.5	443.9
Military personnel	75.6	70.8	76.0	74.0	86.8	106.7	113.6	110.0
Operation and maintenance.	88.3	91.0	105.8	112.0	130.0	151.4	174.0	174.5
Procurement.	81.0	55.0	51.7	55.0	62.5	67.9	76.2	80.2
Research, development, test, and evaluation	37.5	34.6	37.6	40.5	44.4	53.1	60.8	65.6
Military construction	5.1	6.8	5.1	5.0	5.1	5.9	6.3	6.6
Family housing	3.5	3.6	3.4	3.5	3.7	3.8	3.9	3.9
Atomic energy defense activities	9.0	11.8	12.1	12.9	14.8	16.0	16.6	18.7
International affairs	13.8	16.4	17.2	16.5	22.4	21.2	26.9	32.0
International development and humanitarian assistance	5.5	7.6	6.5	7.2	7.8	10.3	13.8	14.7
International security assistance.	8.7	5.3	6.4	6.6	7.9	8.6	8.4	8.8
Conduct of foreign affairs	3.1	4.2	4.7	5.1	7.1	6.7	7.9	8.4
Foreign information and exchange activities	1.1	1.4	0.8	0.8	0.9	1.0	1.1	1.1
International financial programs	-4.5	-2.0	-1.2	-3.1	-1.3	-5.4	-4.3	-0.9
General science, space and technology	14.4	16.7	18.6	19.8	20.8	20.9	23.1	24.0
General science and basic research	2.8	4.1	6.2	6.5	7.3	8.0	8.4	9.2
Space flight, research, and supporting activities	11.6	12.6	12.4	13.2	13.5	12.9	14.6	14.8
Energy	3.3	4.9	-0.8	-	0.5	-0.7	-0.2	1.4
Energy supply	2.0	3.6	-1.8	-1.1	-0.8	-2.1	-1.6	0.1
Energy conservation	0.4	0.7	0.7	0.8	0.9	0.9	0.9	0.9
Emergency energy preparedness.	0.4	0.2	0.2	0.2	0.2	0.2	0.2	0.2
Energy information, policy, and regulation	0.6	0.5	0.2	0.2	0.2	0.2	0.3	0.3
Natural resources and environment [1]	17.1	21.9	25.0	25.6	29.5	29.7	30.7	31.0
Water resources	4.4	4.6	5.1	5.2	5.6	5.5	5.6	6.1
Conservation and land management.	4.0	6.0	6.8	7.1	9.8	9.7	9.8	8.7
Recreational resources.	1.4	2.0	2.6	2.3	2.8	2.9	3.0	3.2
Pollution control and abatement.	5.2	6.5	7.4	7.6	7.6	8.2	8.5	8.0
Agriculture	11.8	9.7	36.5	26.3	22.0	22.5	15.4	30.5
Farm income stabilization	9.7	7.0	33.4	22.7	18.4	18.3	11.2	26.0
Agricultural research and services	2.1	2.6	3.0	3.5	3.6	4.2	4.3	4.5
Commerce and housing credit [1]	67.6	-17.8	3.2	5.7	-0.4	0.7	5.3	10.7
Mortgage credit.	3.8	-1.0	-3.3	-1.2	-7.0	-4.6	2.7	-1.0
Postal service.	2.1	-1.8	2.1	2.4	0.2	-5.2	-4.1	-0.4
Deposit insurance	57.9	-17.8	-3.1	-1.6	-1.0	-1.4	-2.0	-0.3
Transportation [1]	29.5	39.4	46.9	54.4	61.8	67.1	64.6	68.5
Ground transportation	19.0	25.3	31.7	35.8	40.2	37.5	40.7	43.7
Air transportation.	7.2	10.0	10.6	14.0	16.5	23.3	16.7	18.0
Water transportation	3.2	3.7	4.4	4.4	5.0	5.9	6.9	6.4
Community and regional development	8.5	10.7	10.6	11.8	13.0	18.9	15.8	20.1
Community development	3.5	4.7	5.5	5.3	6.0	6.3	6.2	6.4
Area and regional development	2.9	2.7	2.5	2.6	2.6	2.4	2.3	3.0
Disaster relief and insurance	2.1	3.3	2.6	3.8	4.4	10.1	7.3	10.8
Education/training/employment and social services [1]	37.2	51.0	53.8	57.1	70.5	82.6	87.9	96.3
Elementary, secondary, and vocational education . . .	9.9	14.7	20.6	22.9	25.9	31.5	34.4	38.4
Higher education.	11.1	14.2	10.1	9.6	17.0	22.7	25.3	28.8
Research and general education aids	1.6	2.1	2.5	2.8	2.9	3.0	3.0	3.3
Training and employment	5.6	7.4	6.8	7.2	8.3	8.4	7.9	7.4
Other labor services.	0.8	1.0	1.2	1.3	1.4	1.5	1.6	1.7
Social services	8.1	11.6	12.6	13.5	14.9	15.6	15.9	16.7
Health	57.7	115.4	154.5	172.3	196.5	219.6	240.1	257.5
Health care services	47.6	101.9	136.2	151.9	172.6	192.6	210.1	226.3
Health research and training	8.6	11.6	16.0	17.9	21.4	24.0	27.1	28.3
Consumer and occupational health and safety	1.5	1.9	2.3	2.4	2.6	2.9	2.9	3.0
Medicare	98.1	159.9	197.1	217.4	230.9	249.4	269.4	295.4
Income security [1]	148.7	223.7	253.6	269.6	312.5	334.4	332.8	350.9
General retirement and disability insurance (excluding social security)	5.1	5.1	5.2	5.8	5.7	7.0	6.6	6.6
Federal employee retirement and disability.	52.0	65.9	77.2	81.0	83.4	85.2	88.7	94.3
Unemployment compensation	18.9	23.6	23.0	30.2	53.3	57.1	45.0	38.1
Housing assistance	15.9	27.5	28.8	30.1	33.1	35.3	36.6	37.3
Food and nutrition assistance	24.0	37.6	32.5	34.1	38.2	42.5	46.0	53.1
Social security: Social security	248.6	335.8	409.4	433.0	456.0	474.7	495.5	519.7
Veterans benefits and services [1]	29.1	37.9	47.1	45.0	51.0	57.0	59.8	68.2
Income security for veterans	15.6	19.4	25.5	23.2	27.4	29.9	31.7	37.0
Veterans education, training and rehabilitation	0.4	1.3	1.4	1.4	1.9	2.3	2.8	3.1
Hospital and medical care for veterans	12.1	16.4	19.5	20.9	22.2	24.0	26.8	26.6
Veterans housing	0.6	0.4	0.4	-0.9	-1.0	0.5	-2.0	0.8
Administration of justice.	10.2	16.5	28.5	30.2	35.1	35.3	45.5	40.7
General government	10.5	13.8	13.0	14.3	16.9	23.1	21.8	18.9
Net interest [1]	184.3	232.1	222.9	206.2	170.9	153.1	160.2	177.9
Interest on Treasury debt securities (gross)	264.7	332.4	361.9	359.5	332.5	318.1	321.7	347.9
Interest received by on-budget trust funds	-46.3	-59.9	-69.3	-75.3	-76.5	-72.5	-67.8	-71.5
Interest received by off-budget trust funds	-16.0	-33.3	-59.8	-68.8	-76.8	-83.5	-86.2	-92.0
Undistributed offsetting receipts	-36.6	-44.5	-42.6	-47.0	-47.4	-54.4	-58.5	-65.0

-Represents zero.   [1] Includes functions not shown separately.
Source: U.S. Office of Management and Budget, *Budget of the United States Government, Historical Tables*, annual. See also
<http://w3.access.gpo.gov/usbudget/fy2006/pdf/hist.pdf>.

Table 464. **Federal Receipts by Source: 1990 to 2005**

[In billions of dollars (1,032.0 represents $1,032,000,000,000). For fiscal years ending in year shown; see text, Section 8, State and Local Government Finances and Employment. Receipts reflect collections. Covers both Federal funds and trust funds; see text, this section. Excludes government-sponsored, but privately-owned corporations, Federal Reserve System, District of Columbia government, and money held in suspense as deposit funds]

Source	1990	1995	2000	2001	2002	2003	2004	2005, est.
Total federal receipts [1]	1,032.0	1,351.8	2,025.2	1,991.2	1,853.2	1,782.3	1,880.1	2,052.8
Individual income taxes	466.9	590.2	1,004.5	994.3	858.3	793.7	809.0	893.7
Corporation income taxes	93.5	157.0	207.3	151.1	148.0	131.8	189.4	226.5
Social insurance and retirement receipts	380.0	484.5	652.9	694.0	700.8	713.0	733.4	773.7
Excise taxes	35.3	57.5	68.9	66.2	67.0	67.5	69.9	74.0
Social insurance and retirement receipts [1]	**380.0**	**484.5**	**652.9**	**694.0**	**700.8**	**713.0**	**733.4**	**773.7**
Employment and general retirement	353.9	451.0	620.5	661.4	668.5	675.0	689.4	726.6
Old-age and survivors' insurance (off-budget)	255.0	284.1	411.7	434.1	440.5	447.8	457.1	479.9
Disability insurance (off-budget)	26.6	67.0	68.9	73.5	74.8	76.0	77.6	81.5
Hospital insurance	68.6	96.0	135.5	149.7	149.0	147.2	150.6	161.4
Railroad retirement/pension fund	2.3	2.4	2.7	2.7	2.5	2.3	2.3	2.2
Unemployment insurance	21.6	28.9	27.6	27.8	27.6	33.4	39.5	42.5
Other retirement	4.5	4.6	4.8	4.7	4.6	4.6	4.6	4.6
Federal employees retirement— employee share	4.4	4.5	4.7	4.6	4.5	4.6	4.5	4.6
Excise taxes, total [1]	**35.3**	**57.5**	**68.9**	**66.2**	**67.0**	**67.5**	**69.9**	**74.0**
Federal funds	15.6	26.9	22.7	24.3	24.0	23.8	24.6	22.1
Alcohol	5.7	7.2	8.1	7.6	7.8	7.9	8.1	7.9
Tobacco	4.1	5.9	7.2	7.4	8.3	7.9	7.9	7.9
Telephone	3.0	3.8	5.7	5.8	(X)	(X)	(X)	(X)
Ozone-depleting chemicals/products	0.4	0.6	0.1	(Z)	(X)	(X)	(X)	(X)
Transportation fuels	-	8.5	0.8	1.2	0.8	0.9	1.4	-0.5
Trust funds	19.8	30.5	46.2	41.9	43.0	43.7	45.3	52.0
Highway	13.9	22.6	35.0	31.5	32.6	33.7	34.7	38.9
Airport and airway	3.7	5.5	9.7	9.2	9.0	8.7	9.2	10.5
Black-lung disability	0.7	0.6	0.5	0.5	0.6	0.5	0.6	0.6
Inland waterway	0.1	0.1	0.1	0.1	0.1	0.1	0.1	0.1
Hazardous substance superfund	0.8	0.9	(Z)	-	(X)	(X)	(X)	(X)
Oil spill liability	0.1	0.2	0.2	(X)	(X)	(X)	(X)	(X)
Aquatic resources	0.2	0.3	0.3	0.4	0.4	0.4	0.4	0.4
Vaccine injury compensation	0.2	0.1	0.1	0.1	0.1	0.1	0.1	0.2

- Represents or rounds to zero.   X Not applicable.   Z $50 million or less.   [1] Totals reflect interfund and intragovernmental transactions and/or other functions, not shown separately.

Source: U.S. Office of Management and Budget, *Budget of the United States Government, Historical Tables*, annual. See also <http://w3.access.gpo.gov/usbudget/fy2006/pdf/hist.pdf>.

Table 465. **Federal Trust Fund Receipts, Outlays, and Balances: 2000 to 2004**

[In billions of dollars (1,063 represents $1,063,000,000,000). For years ending September 30. Receipts deposited. Outlays on a checks-issued basis less refunds collected. Balances: That which have not been spent. See text, this section, for discussion of the budget concept and trust funds]

Description	Income			Outlays			Balances [1]		
	2000	2003	2004	2000	2003	2004	2000	2003	2004
Total [2]	1,063	1,185	1,243	829	1,006	1,056	2,110	2,723	2,911
Airport and airway trust fund	11	9	10	9	10	10	14	12	12
Federal employees' health benefits fund	20	26	29	20	25	27	6	9	11
Federal/civil employees' retirement funds	77	80	84	46	51	53	523	615	645
Federal old-age, survivors' and disability insurance trust funds	564	630	645	412	475	496	1,007	1,485	1,634
Foreign military sales trust fund	11	11	12	11	11	12	6	6	6
Highway trust fund	35	34	36	33	38	38	31	18	15
Health insurance trust funds (Medicare): Federal hospital insurance trust fund	160	176	179	130	154	169	168	251	261
Federal supplemental medical insurance	91	110	129	91	124	133	46	25	21
Military retirement trust fund	39	42	47	33	36	37	158	179	189
Railroad retirement trust funds	10	31	13	8	29	12	16	24	25
Unemployment trust funds	33	38	43	24	59	50	87	48	42
Veterans' life insurance trust funds	2	2	2	2	2	2	14	13	13
Other trust funds [3]	11	19	21	9	18	19	35	38	40

[1] Balances available on a cash basis (rather than an authorization basis) at the end of the year. Balances are primarily invested in Federal debt securities.   [2] Includes funds not shown separately.   [3] Effective August 9, 1989, the permanent insurance fund of the FDIC was classified under law as a Federal fund.

Source: U.S. Office of Management and Budget, *Budget of the United States Government, Analytical Perspectives*, annual. See also <http://w3.access.gpo.gov/usbudget/fy2006/pdf/spec.pdf>.

Table 466. United States Government Ledger Balance Sheet—Assets and Liabilities: 1995 to 2003

[In millions of dollars (89,349 represents $89,349,000,000). As of September 30]

Item	1995	2000	2003	2004
Assets, total	**89,349**	**181,729**	**265,170**	**237,440**
Cash and monetary assets, total	84,080	98,401	113,303	87,248
U.S. Treasury operating cash:				
Federal Reserve account	8,620	8,459	7,224	5,987
Tax and loan note accounts	29,329	44,199	27,735	30,362
Special drawing rights (SDR):				
Total holdings	11,035	10,316	12,062	12,782
SDR's certificates issued to				
Federal Reserve banks	-10,168	-3,200	-2,200	-2,200
Monetary assets with IMF[1]	14,682	13,690	24,072	19,442
Other cash and monetary assets:				
Cash and other assets held				
outside the Treasury Account	29,697	24,937	44,409	20,875
U.S. Treasury monetary assets	356	-	-	-
U.S. Treasury time deposits	528	5,977	7,200	-
Loan financing accounts:				
Guaranteed loans	-12,714	-22,013	-15,579	-25,001
Direct loans	19,732	105,459	145,801	150,663
Miscellaneous asset accounts	-1,748	-119	-55	451
Liabilities, total	**3,674,266**	**3,467,448**	**3,970,611**	**4,354,504**
Federal securities, total	4,920,944	5,629,009	6,758,722	7,352,017
Treasury debt securities, total	4,893,989	5,601,336	6,732,770	7,327,834
Agency securities outstanding	26,955	27,672	25,952	24,183
Deduct: Net Federal securities held as				
investments by government accounts	*1,317,645*	*2,218,896*	*2,859,291*	*3,075,263*
Equals: Borrowing from the public, total	3,603,299	3,410,113	3,913,291	4,292,910
Accrued interest payable	50,611	44,211	31,806	32,734
Special drawing rights allocated by IMF[1]	7,380	6,359	7,005	7,197
Deposit fund liabilities	8,186	2,625	9,941	12,851
Miscellaneous liability accounts				
(checks outstanding, etc.)	4,790	4,140	8,568	8,812

- Represents zero. [1] IMF = International Monetary Funds.

Source: U.S. Department of Treasury, 1995–2003, *United States Government Annual Report*; and beginning 2000, *Combined Statement of Receipts, Outlays, and Balances of the United States 2003.* See also <http://www.fms.treas.gov/annualreport/cs2003/sc1.pdf> (released 11 December 2003).

Table 467. U.S. Savings Bonds: 1990 to 2003

[In billions of dollars (122.5 represents $122,500,000,000), except percent. As of end of fiscal year, see text, Section 8, State and Local Government Finances and Employment]

Item	1990	1994	1995	1996	1997	1998	1999	2000	2001	2002	2003
Amounts outstanding, total[1]	122.5	176.8	181.5	184.4	182.6	180.7	166.5	177.7	179.5	185.5	192.6
Sales	7.8	9.5	7.2	5.9	5.3	4.8	6.5	5.6	8.0	12.5	13.8
Accrued discounts	8.0	9.4	9.5	9.8	9.1	9.1	8.4	6.9	8.4	7.7	7.3
Redemptions[2]	7.5	9.4	11.8	2.5	2.1	14.3	16.6	14.5	13.8	12.5	12.1
Percent of total outstanding	6.1	5.3	6.5	1.4	1.1	7.9	10.0	8.2	7.7	6.7	6.3

[1] Interest-bearing debt only for amounts end of year. [2] Matured and unmatured bonds.

Source: U.S. Department of the Treasury, *Treasury Bulletin*, quarterly.

Table 468. Internal Revenue Gross Collections by Source: 1990 to 2004

[1,078 represents $1,078,000,000,000. For fiscal year ending in year shown; see text, Section 8, State and Local Government Finances and Employment]

Source of revenue	Collections (bil. dol.)					Percent of total				
	1990	1995	2000	2003	2004	1990	1995	2000	2003	2004
All taxes	**1,078**	**1,389**	**2,097**	**1,952**	**2,018**	**100.0**	**100.0**	**100.0**	**100.0**	**100.0**
Individual income taxes	540	676	1,137	987	990	50.1	48.7	54.2	50.5	49.1
Withheld by employers	388	534	781	735	747	36.0	38.4	37.2	37.6	37.0
Employment taxes[1]	367	465	640	696	717	34.0	33.5	30.5	35.6	35.5
Old-age and disability insurance	358	455	628	685	706	33.2	32.8	29.9	35.1	35.0
Unemployment insurance	6	6	7	7	7	0.6	0.4	0.3	0.3	0.3
Corporation income taxes	110	174	236	194	231	10.2	12.5	11.2	9.9	11.4
Estate and gift taxes	12	15	30	23	26	1.1	1.1	1.4	1.2	1.3
Excise taxes	49	59	55	53	55	4.5	4.2	2.6	2.7	2.7

[1] Includes railroad retirement, not shown separately.

Source: U.S. Internal Revenue Service, *IRS Data Book*, annual. For most recent report, see <http://www.irs.gov/pub/irs-soi/04databk.pdf>.

Federal Government Finances and Employment 321

Table 469. Tax Expenditures Estimates Relating to Individual and Corporate Income Taxes by Selected Function: 2004 to 2006

[In millions of dollars (2,460 represents $2,460,000,000). For years ending Sept. 30. Tax expenditures are defined as revenue losses attributable to provisions of the Federal tax laws which allow a special exclusion, exemption, or deduction from gross income or which provide a special credit, a preferential rate of tax, or a deferral of liability]

Function and provision	2004	2005	2006	2006, rank
National defense:				
Exclusion of benefits and allowances to armed forces personnel.	2,460	2,490	2,520	36
International affairs:				
Exclusion of income earned abroad by U.S. citizens	2,680	2,750	2,810	33
Exclusion of certain allowances for Federal employees abroad.	850	900	950	59
Extraterritorial income exclusion	5,500	5,170	4,270	24
Inventory property sales source rules exception	1,500	1,620	1,770	47
Deferral of income from controlled foreign corporations (normal tax method)	7,240	7,000	7,440	18
Deferred taxes for financial firms on certain income earned overseas.	2,130	2,190	2,260	37
General science, space, and technology:				
Expensing of research and experimentation expenditures (normal tax method) . . .	2,330	4,110	7,920	17
Credit for increasing research activities.	4,680	5,130	2,140	40
Agriculture:				
Capital gains treatment of certain income	670	730	760	63
Commerce and housing:				
Financial institutions and insurance:				
Exemption of credit union income	1,270	1,330	1,390	50
Exclusion of interest on life insurance savings	20,830	22,750	24,070	12
Housing:				
Exclusion of interest on owner-occupied mortgage subsidy bonds	1,020	1,110	1,180	53
Deductibility of mortgage interest on owner-occupied homes	61,450	68,870	76,030	2
Deductibility of state and local property tax on owner-occupied homes	19,930	16,590	14,830	14
Deferral of income from post 1987 installment sales	1,100	1,120	1,140	55
Capital gains exclusion on home sales	29,730	32,840	36,270	5
Exception from passive loss rules for $25,000 of rental loss.	5,030	4,900	4,750	22
Credit for low-income housing investments	3,660	3,850	4,010	25
Accelerated depreciation on rental housing (normal tax method)	750	156	993	
Commerce:				
Capital gains (except agriculture, timber, iron ore, and coal) [1]	25,150	27,200	28,370	10
Step-up basis of capital gains at death.	24,200	26,140	28,760	9
Accelerated depreciation of buildings other than rental housing [1]	3,250	4,180	4,790	
Accelerated depreciation of machinery and equipment [1]	44,690	11,000	37,830	
Expensing of certain small investments [1]	1,520	4,820	1,650	48
Graduated corporation income tax rate [1]	2,450	3,190	3,730	29
Transportation:				
Exclusion of reimbursed employee parking expenses	2,470	2,590	2,730	35
Community and regional development:				
Empowerment zones, Enterprise communities, and renewal communities.	1,080	1,120	1,210	52
Education, training, employment, and social services:				
Education:				
Exclusion of scholarship and fellowship income [1]	1,320	1,400	1,460	49
HOPE tax credit	3,320	3,410	3,220	32
Lifetime Learning tax credit.	2,190	2,130	2,080	43
Deduction for higher education expenses	1,280	1,830	1,840	45
Parental personal exemption for students age 19 or over	3,200	2,670	2,110	41
Deductibility of charitable contributions (education)	3,690	3,420	3,680	30
Training, employment, and social services:				
Exclusion of employee meals and lodging (other than military)	810	850	890	60
Child credit	22,400	32,710	32,810	7
Credit for child and dependent care expenses	2,990	3,140	2,810	33
Deductibility of charitable contributions, other than education and health	27,370	29,670	32,550	8
Health:				
Exclusion of employer contributions for medical insurance premiums [2]	102,250	112,160	125,690	1
Self-employed medical insurance premiums	3,330	3,780	4,330	23
Deductibility of medical expenses	7,380	8,590	9,140	16
Exclusion of interest on hospital construction bonds	1,870	2,020	2,160	39
Deductibility of charitable contributions (health)	3,090	3,350	3,670	31
Income security:				
Exclusion of workers compensation benefits	5,490	5,730	5,940	20
Net exclusion of pension contributions and earnings:				
Employer plans:				
401(k) plans	46,970	50,330	51,050	3
Individual Retirement Accounts	47,730	45,870	48,140	4
Low and moderate income savers credit	7,450	7,340	7,310	19
Keogh plans	970	1,100	1,170	54
Exclusion of other employee benefits:	8,830	9,380	9,980	15
Premiums on group term life insurance	2,070	2,090	2,110	41
Special ESOP rules.	1,920	2,060	2,220	38
Additional deduction for the elderly.	1,700	1,810	1,960	44
Earned income tax credit	4,890	4,980	5,420	21
Social Security:				
Exclusion of social security benefits:				
Social Security benefits for retired workers.	19,200	19,480	19,770	13
Social Security benefits for disabled	3,580	3,740	3,870	27
Social Security benefits for dependents and survivors	4,140	4,120	3,990	26
Veterans' benefits and services:				
Exclusion of veterans' death benefits and disability compensation	3,300	3,560	3,750	28
General purpose fiscal assistance:				
Exclusion of interest on public purpose state and local bonds.	26,150	26,530	26,610	11
Deductibility of nonbusiness state & local taxes other than on owner-occupied home	45,290	39,090	34,620	6
Tax credit for corps. receiving income from doing business in U.S. possessions. . .	1,000	900	500	72

[1] Normal tax method.   [2] Includes premiums and medial care.

Source: U.S. Office of Management and Budget, *Budget of the United States Government, Analytical Perspectives, Fiscal Year 2006*. See also <http://www.whitehouse.gov/omb/budget/fy2006/pdf/spec.pdf>.

Table 470. Federal Funds—Summary Distribution by State and Outlying Area: 2003

[In millions of dollars (2,061,486 represents $2,061,486,000,000), except as indicated. For year ending Sept. 30. Data for grants, salaries and wages and direct payments to individuals are on an expenditures basis; procurement is on obligation basis]

State and outlying area	Federal funds		Defense	Non-defense	Direct payments	Procure-ment	Grants	Salaries and wages
	Total	Per capita [1] (dol.)						
United States [2]	2,061,486	6,910	319,507	1,741,979	1,082,358	327,413	441,038	210,677
Alabama	36,871	8,192	7,907	28,964	19,930	7,067	6,649	3,224
Alaska	7,944	12,244	2,307	5,636	1,625	1,680	3,022	1,617
Arizona	37,801	6,773	9,885	27,916	18,675	8,557	7,235	3,335
Arkansas	18,340	6,729	1,445	16,895	11,596	864	4,541	1,339
California	219,706	6,192	39,240	180,466	110,716	37,050	51,329	20,611
Colorado	28,874	6,345	5,184	23,690	13,389	5,142	6,014	4,329
Connecticut	28,595	8,209	8,545	20,050	13,219	8,484	5,376	1,516
Delaware	5,061	6,191	564	4,497	3,146	245	1,181	489
District of Columbia	34,750	61,681	3,321	31,429	4,304	11,376	4,310	14,760
Florida	113,341	6,660	15,969	97,372	75,233	10,899	17,463	9,746
Georgia	51,910	5,977	9,003	42,907	28,092	5,243	10,561	8,015
Hawaii	11,269	8,961	4,484	6,785	4,516	1,978	1,911	2,864
Idaho	8,654	6,334	653	8,002	4,431	1,531	1,858	834
Illinois	73,020	5,771	4,938	68,082	45,018	5,729	15,720	6,553
Indiana	35,525	5,734	3,650	31,874	22,572	3,302	7,313	2,338
Iowa	17,550	5,961	1,008	16,542	11,434	1,109	3,877	1,129
Kansas	18,208	6,686	2,520	15,688	10,665	2,020	3,415	2,108
Kentucky	31,153	7,565	5,289	25,864	16,288	5,119	6,634	3,112
Louisiana	31,646	7,038	3,605	28,042	17,984	3,195	7,820	2,648
Maine	9,966	7,632	1,813	8,152	5,156	1,312	2,610	888
Maryland	57,646	10,464	11,412	46,235	22,467	16,216	8,632	10,331
Massachusetts	51,265	7,969	7,422	43,843	26,133	8,357	13,328	3,446
Michigan	57,870	5,741	3,462	54,408	37,598	3,884	12,970	3,418
Minnesota	27,580	5,451	2,120	25,460	16,141	2,406	6,914	2,120
Mississippi	21,741	7,545	3,644	18,096	11,827	2,626	5,318	1,970
Missouri	43,874	7,691	7,991	35,883	23,395	7,992	8,655	3,832
Montana	7,092	7,729	556	6,536	3,812	497	1,938	845
Nebraska	11,000	6,324	1,099	9,901	6,688	608	2,512	1,192
Nevada	11,637	5,193	1,368	10,269	6,988	1,472	1,955	1,222
New Hampshire	7,349	5,707	827	6,522	4,174	738	1,865	571
New Jersey	53,679	6,214	5,330	48,349	32,578	5,461	11,481	4,159
New Mexico	18,736	9,995	2,158	16,578	6,669	5,819	4,322	1,926
New York	137,898	7,186	6,286	131,612	74,030	7,758	47,575	8,535
North Carolina	51,766	6,157	7,508	44,259	29,818	3,794	11,613	6,541
North Dakota	5,726	9,033	712	5,014	3,074	398	1,537	717
Ohio	69,902	6,113	6,777	63,124	42,305	6,548	15,687	5,362
Oklahoma	25,254	7,192	3,986	21,268	14,278	2,488	5,136	3,353
Oregon	21,253	5,971	1,097	20,156	13,171	1,198	5,103	1,781
Pennsylvania	90,350	7,307	8,054	82,296	57,228	8,137	18,624	6,363
Rhode Island	8,036	7,467	1,080	6,956	4,326	659	2,234	817
South Carolina	28,038	6,761	4,257	23,781	15,592	3,614	5,969	2,863
South Dakota	6,202	8,114	501	5,700	3,450	381	1,698	673
Tennessee	42,602	7,293	3,493	39,109	22,666	7,522	9,057	3,357
Texas	140,451	6,350	30,354	110,097	68,266	29,823	28,423	13,939
Utah	13,500	5,741	3,102	10,398	5,943	2,665	2,845	2,047
Vermont	4,443	7,176	610	3,833	2,186	566	1,331	360
Virginia	82,454	11,163	32,684	49,770	28,974	30,839	7,886	14,756
Washington	43,368	7,073	7,703	35,665	22,100	6,629	8,881	5,758
West Virginia	14,226	7,858	510	13,717	8,711	665	3,562	1,289
Wisconsin	30,237	5,525	1,805	28,432	18,900	2,008	7,544	1,785
Wyoming	4,226	8,432	374	3,852	1,754	346	1,616	510
Outlying areas:								
American Samoa	198	3,425	13	185	53	28	110	7
Federated States of Micronesia	145	1,343	-	145	8	1	136	(NA)
Guam	1,539	9,406	817	722	298	526	400	315
Marshall Islands	182	3,219	114	67	1	115	66	(NA)
Northern Marianas	141	1,848	9	132	37	8	90	6
Palau	53	2,697	1	53	2	1	51	(NA)
Puerto Rico	14,661	3,780	771	13,890	8,324	561	4,808	968
Virgin Islands	615	5,652	20	595	253	26	282	55
Undistributed	34,366	(X)	18,149	16,217	155	32,133	43	2,035

- Represents zero. NA Not available. X Not applicable. [1] Based on U.S. Census Bureau estimated resident population as of July 1. [2] Includes outlying areas and undistributed.

Source: U.S. Census Bureau, Consolidated Federal Funds Report, 2003. See also <http://www.census.gov/prod/2004pubs/cffr03.pdf> (issued May 2004).

Federal Government Finances and Employment **323**

Table 471. Individual Income Tax Returns Filed—Examination Coverage: 1990 to 2004

[In thousands (109,868 represents 109,868,000), except as indicated. See the annual *IRS Data Book* (Publication 55B) publications for a detailed explanation and Appendix III]

Year	Returns filed [1]	Returns examined Total [2]	Returns examined Percent coverage	Total recommended additional tax (dollars) [3]	Average recommended additional tax per return (dollars) [3]
1990	109,868	1,145	1.04	5,336,063	4,660
1991	112,305	1,313	1.17	6,892,527	5,249
1992	113,829	1,206	1.06	6,308,424	5,231
1993	114,719	1,059	0.92	5,653,094	5,338
1994	113,754	1,226	1.08	6,167,026	5,031
1995	114,683	1,919	1.67	7,756,954	4,041
1996	116,060	1,942	1.67	7,600,191	3,915
1997	118,363	1,519	1.28	8,363,918	5,505
1998	120,342	1,193	0.99	6,095,698	5,110
1999	122,547	1,100	0.90	4,458,474	4,052
2000	124,887	618	0.49	3,388,905	5,486
2001	127,097	732	0.58	3,301,860	4,512
2002	129,445	744	0.57	3,636,486	4,889
2003	130,341	849	0.65	4,559,902	5,369
2004	130,134	1,008	0.77	6,203,236	6,155

[1] Returns filed in previous calendar year. [2] Includes taxpayer examinations by correspondence and activities to protect release of funds from the U.S. Treasury in response to taxpayer efforts to recoup tax previously assessed and paid. [3] For 1990-1997, amount includes associated penalties.
Source: U.S. Internal Revenue Service, *IRS Data Book*, annual, Publication 55B.

Table 472. Tax Returns Filed—Examination Coverage: 2000 and 2004

[In thousands (124,887 represents 124,887,000), except as indicated. Return classification as Schedule C or C-EZ (nonfarm sole proprietorship) or Schedule F (farm proprietorships) for audit examination purposes was based on the largest source of income on the return and certain other characteristics. Therefore, some returns with business activity are reflected in the nonbusiness individual income tax return statistics in the table below (and vise versa), so that the statistics for the number of returns with Schedule C is not comparable to the number of nonfarm sole proprietorship returns in Table 728. For more detailed information, see the annual *IRS Data Book* (Publication 55B);

Year and type of return	Returns filed [1]	Returns examined Total [2]	Returns examined Percent coverage	Total recommended additional tax (dollars) [3]	Average recommended additional tax per return (dollars) [3]
ALL RETURNS 2000					
Individual returns, total	124,887	618	0.49	3,388,905	5,486
1040A, TPI under $25,000 [3]	42,485	257	0.60	688,256	2,682
Non-1040A, TPI under $25,000 [3]	13,763	52	0.37	161,643	3,135
Non-1040A, TPI $25,000 under $50,000 [3]	29,651	64	0.21	186,488	2,926
Non-1040A, TPI $50,000 under $100,000 [3]	22,337	52	0.23	197,035	3,792
Non-1040A, TPI $100,000 and over [3]	8,152	69	0.84	1,251,369	18,237
Sch C—TGR under $25,000 [4]	2,541	62	2.43	126,495	2,050
Sch C—TGR $25,000 under $100,000 [4]	3,351	31	0.93	159,886	5,120
Sch C—TGR $100,000 and over [4]	1,949	29	1.48	572,103	19,878
Sch F—TGR under $100,000 [4]	391	1	0.35	3,739	2,702
Sch F—TGR $100,000 and over [4]	268	2	0.80	41,891	19,484
Corporation (except S corporation)	2,509	28	1.12	10,042,559	356,334
Fiduciary	3,403	7	0.22	239,960	32,790
Estate	117	8	6.89	1,044,678	130,194
Gift	292	2	0.72	459,785	219,258
Employment	29,000	16	0.06	344,666	21,436
Excise	822	10	1.25	293,411	28,503
Miscellaneous taxable	(NA)	(Z)	(NA)	45,270	108,301
Partnerships (nontaxable)	1,975	7	0.33	(X)	(X)
S corporations (nontaxable)	2,767	15	0.55	(X)	(X)
ALL RETURNS 2004					
Individual returns, total	130,134	1,008	0.77	6,203,236	6,155
1040A, TPI under $25,000 [3]	33,695	169	0.50	475,272	2,814
Non-1040A, TPI under $25,000 [3]	19,513	245	1.26	706,715	2,879
Non-1040A, TPI $25,000 under $50,000 [3]	31,100	135	0.43	425,572	3,151
Non-1040A, TPI $50,000 under $100,000 [3]	25,616	114	0.44	350,022	3,072
Non-1040A, TPI $100,000 and over [3]	10,928	152	1.39	3,161,850	20,806
Sch C—TGR under $25,000 [4]	2,947	93	3.15	210,170	2,263
Sch C—TGR $25,000 under $100,000 [4]	3,645	53	1.47	218,650	4,089
Sch C—TGR $100,000 and over [4]	2,101	39	1.86	614,233	15,700
Sch F—TGR under $100,000 [4]	342	3	0.91	4,661	1,502
Sch F—TGR $100,000 and over [4]	248	4	1.61	36,091	9,016
Corporation (except S corporation)	2,394	17	0.71	16,840,983	985,026
Fiduciary	3,705	4	0.12	145,175	32,712
Estate	87	6	7.41	972,575	150,670
Gift	285	2	0.69	546,442	276,120
Employment	30,121	18	0.06	422,264	23,858
Excise	845	13	1.49	220,713	17,573
Miscellaneous taxable	(NA)	(Z)	(NA)	249,314	621,731
Partnerships (nontaxable)	2,405	6	0.26	(X)	(X)
S corporations (nontaxable)	3,369	6	0.19	(X)	(X)

NA Not available. X Not applicable. Z Less than 500. [1] Returns filed in previous calendar year. [2] Includes taxpayer examinations by correspondence and activities to protect release of funds from the U.S. Treasury in response to taxpayer efforts to recoup tax previously assessed and paid. [3] TPI = Total positive income, i.e., excludes losses. [4] TGR = Total gross receipts.
Source: U.S. Internal Revenue Service, *IRS Data Book*, annual, Publication 55B.

Table 473. Federal Individual Income Tax Returns With Adjusted Gross Income (AGI)—Summary: 2000 and 2002

[129,374 represents 129,374,000. Includes Puerto Rico and Virgin Islands. Includes returns of resident aliens, based on a sample of unaudited returns as filed. Data are not comparable for all years because of tax changes and other changes, as indicated. See *Statistics of Income, Individual Income Tax Returns* publications for a detailed explanation. See Appendix III]

Item	Number of returns (1,000)		Amount (mil. dol.)		Average amount (dollars)	
	2000	2002	2000	2002	2000	2002
Total returns.............................	129,374	130,076	6,365,377	6,033,586	49,202	46,385
Adjusted gross income (AGI)...................	129,374	130,076	6,365,377	6,033,586	49,202	46,385
Salaries and wages.....................	110,169	110,938	4,456,167	4,559,691	40,449	41,101
Taxable interest received.................	68,046	63,585	199,322	149,025	2,929	2,344
Tax-exempt interest.....................	4,658	4,454	53,952	54,564	11,582	12,251
Dividends in AGI.......................	34,141	31,410	146,988	103,241	4,305	3,287
Business or profession net income..........	13,313	13,751	244,598	256,879	18,373	18,681
Business or profession net loss............	4,287	4,846	30,733	36,095	7,168	7,448
Net capital gain in AGI...................	22,646	9,970	644,285	268,202	28,451	26,901
Net capital loss in AGI...................	6,875	13,280	13,742	29,834	1,999	2,247
Sales of property other than capital assets, net gain...	827	789	7,445	7,292	8,997	9,242
Sales of property other than capital assets, net loss...	873	939	8,364	9,678	9,586	10,307
Pensions and annuities in AGI.............	21,765	22,794	325,828	357,841	14,970	15,699
Unemployment compensation in AGI.........	6,478	10,335	16,913	43,129	2,611	4,173
Social security benefits in AGI.............	10,609	10,703	89,964	93,459	8,480	8,732
Rent net income......................	4,201	4,229	45,099	49,266	10,736	11,650
Rent net loss........................	4,520	4,501	30,309	34,254	6,705	7,610
Royalty net income.....................	1,104	1,118	7,998	8,014	7,245	7,168
Royalty net loss.......................	36	38	101	141	2,800	3,711
Partnerships and S Corporations net income [1]	4,180	4,329	285,425	314,665	68,291	72,688
Partnerships and S Corporations net loss [1]...	2,121	2,394	72,511	76,698	34,191	32,038
Estate or trust net income................	557	540	12,134	12,459	21,803	23,072
Estate or trust net loss..................	39	42	1,128	1,219	28,900	29,024
Farm net income......................	703	556	8,270	6,324	11,763	11,374
Farm net loss........................	1,359	1,439	17,305	20,744	12,736	14,416
Statutory adjustments, total.................	23,197	28,911	58,610	77,161	2,527	2,669
Individual retirement arrangements..........	3,505	3,278	7,477	9,462	2,133	2,887
Student loan interest deduction............	4,478	6,641	2,639	4,660	589	702
Medical savings accounts................	65	61	120	121	1,839	1,984
Self-employed retirement plans............	957	947	2,138	2,215	2,235	2,339
Deduction for self-employment tax..........	14,300	14,664	17,393	18,687	1,216	1,274
Self-employment health insurance..........	3,565	3,571	7,569	10,494	2,123	2,939
Exemptions, total [2].....................	252,332	258,716	690,109	761,440	2,735	2,943
Deductions, total.........................	128,205	128,303	1,293,181	1,390,115	10,087	10,835
Standard deductions...................	85,671	82,655	470,821	477,170	5,496	5,773
Returns with additional standard deductions for age 65 or older, or for blindness.............	11,331	10,857	14,736	14,897	1,301	1,372
Itemized deductions, total [3]..............	42,534	45,648	822,361	898,047	19,334	19,673
Medical and dental expenses...........	6,513	8,547	39,251	52,276	6,026	6,116
Taxes paid........................	41,824	44,794	294,712	302,654	7,047	6,757
Interest paid.......................	35,405	37,637	322,932	351,496	9,121	9,339
Home mortgage interest paid.........	34,914	37,216	299,963	336,571	8,591	9,044
Charitable contributions................	37,525	40,400	140,682	140,571	3,749	3,479
Taxable income.........................	105,259	102,276	4,544,242	4,096,128	43,172	40,050
Income tax before credits..................	105,278	102,294	1,018,219	836,843	9,672	8,181
Tax credits, total [2]......................	37,736	40,614	37,722	39,862	1,000	981
Child care credit......................	6,368	6,186	2,794	2,707	439	438
Elderly and disabled credit...............	156	134	33	21	209	157
Child tax credit.......................	26,405	25,940	19,689	21,520	746	830
Education credit......................	6,815	6,545	4,851	5,013	712	766
Foreign tax credit.....................	3,936	3,749	5,990	5,934	1,522	1,583
General business credit.................	275	285	764	751	2,778	2,635
Income tax after credits...................	96,816	90,964	980,497	796,980	10,127	8,761
Income tax, total [4]....................	96,818	90,964	980,645	796,986	10,129	8,762
Alternative minimum tax..................	1,304	1,911	9,601	6,854	7,361	3,587
Earned income credit.....................	19,277	21,703	32,296	38,199	1,675	1,760
Used to offset income tax before credits...........	5,416	4,169	1,969	1,115	363	267
Used to offset other taxes................	3,148	4,106	2,524	3,347	802	815
Excess earned income credit (refundable)........	16,126	18,780	27,804	33,737	1,724	1,796
Tax payments, total......................	122,244	123,463	1,084,868	998,312	8,875	8,086
Income tax withheld....................	113,733	114,862	763,901	717,492	6,717	6,247
Excess social security tax withheld............	1,641	1,145	2,185	1,564	1,332	1,366
Estimated tax payments.................	13,327	12,435	221,622	198,178	16,630	15,937
Payments with requests for extension of filing time....	1,611	1,235	63,397	36,322	39,354	29,411
Taxes due at time of filing...................	30,624	22,819	134,944	82,288	4,406	3,606
Tax overpayments, total....................	95,921	103,463	196,199	239,784	2,045	2,318
Overpayment refunds...................	93,000	100,144	167,577	205,987	1,802	2,057

[1] S Corporations are certain small corporations with up to 35 shareholders. [2] Includes items not shown separately. Total exemptions amount is after limitation. [3] Total itemized deductions are after limitation [4] Includes minimum tax or alternative minimum tax.

Source: U.S. Internal Revenue Service, *Statistics of Income Bulletin Quarterly*, and *Statistics of Income, Individual Income Tax Returns*, annual.

Federal Government Finances and Employment **325**

Table 474. Individual Income Tax Returns—Number, Income Tax, and Average Tax by Size of Adjusted Gross Income: 2000 and 2002

[In billions of dollars (6,365 represents $6,365,000,000,000), except as indicated. See Appendix III]

Size of adjusted gross income	Number of returns (1,000) 2000	2002	Adjusted gross income (AGI) 2000	2002	Income tax total [1] 2000	2002	Tax as percent of AGI [2] 2000	2002	Average tax [2] 2000	2002
Total	129,374	130,076	6,365	6,034	981	797	16	14	10,129	8,762
Less than $1,000 [3]	2,966	3,565	-58	-79	-	-	2	1	648	1,416
$1,000 to $2,999	5,385	4,833	11	10	-	-	7	5	134	94
$3,000 to $4,999	5,599	5,164	22	21	-	-	4	2	179	84
$5,000 to $6,999	5,183	5,019	31	30	1	-	5	2	297	145
$7,000 to $8,999	4,972	4,977	40	40	1	-	4	3	331	224
$9,000 to $10,999	5,089	5,062	51	51	1	1	5	3	470	259
$11,000 to $12,999	4,859	4,748	58	57	2	1	6	4	704	441
$13,000 to $14,999	4,810	4,808	67	67	3	1	6	4	883	611
$15,000 to $16,999	4,785	4,632	76	74	3	2	7	5	1,052	747
$17,000 to $18,999	4,633	4,509	83	81	4	3	7	5	1,279	948
$19,000 to $21,999	6,502	6,523	133	134	7	5	8	6	1,565	1,214
$22,000 to $24,999	5,735	5,650	135	133	8	6	8	7	1,815	1,548
$25,000 to $29,999	8,369	8,575	229	235	16	12	8	7	2,248	1,886
$30,000 to $39,999	13,548	13,980	471	486	40	33	9	8	3,094	2,622
$40,000 to $49,999	10,412	10,550	466	473	46	38	10	9	4,462	3,800
$50,000 to $74,999	17,076	17,397	1,045	1,067	116	102	11	10	6,824	5,931
$75,000 to $99,999	8,597	9,248	738	795	100	94	14	12	11,631	10,169
$100,000 to $199,999	8,083	8,423	1,066	1,110	184	175	17	16	22,783	20,831
$200,000 to $499,999	2,136	1,908	614	549	146	125	24	23	68,628	65,452
$500,000 to $999,999	396	337	269	227	76	63	28	28	192,092	188,463
$1,000,000 or more	240	169	817	476	226	136	28	29	945,172	805,212

- Represents or rounds to zero.   [1] Consists of income after credits, and alternative minimum tax.   [2] Computed using taxable returns only.   [3] In addition to low income taxpayers, this size class (and others) includes taxpayers with "tax preferences," not reflected in adjusted gross income or taxable income which are subject to the "alternative minimum tax" (included in total income tax).

Source: U.S. Internal Revenue Service, *Statistics of Income Bulletin,* quarterly and *Statistics of Income, Individual Income Tax Returns,* annual.

Table 475. Individual Income Tax Returns—Itemized Deductions and Statutory Adjustments by Size of Adjusted Gross Income: 2002

[45,648 represents 45,648,000. Based on a sample of returns, see Appendix III]

Item	Unit	Total	Under $10,000	$10,000 to $19,999	$20,000 to $29,999	$30,000 to $39,999	$40,000 to $49,999	$50,000 to $99,999	$100,000 and over
Returns with itemized deductions:									
Number of returns [1]	1,000	45,648	874	2,410	3,742	4,745	4,971	18,933	9,973
Amount	Mil. dol.	898,047	11,805	29,651	46,459	59,962	67,855	318,569	363,747
Medical and dental expenses:									
Returns	1,000	8,547	568	1,388	1,550	1,316	1,103	2,235	387
Amount	Mil. dol.	52,276	4,615	11,028	11,839	10,318	8,996	24,107	8,860
Taxes paid: Returns	1,000	44,794	782	2,230	3,574	4,616	4,910	18,751	9,930
Amount, total	Mil. dol.	302,654	1,952	4,946	8,444	13,257	17,202	96,900	159,954
State and local income taxes:									
Returns	1,000	37,596	388	1,456	2,789	3,858	4,201	16,216	8,688
Amount	Mil. dol.	181,952	350	1,051	2,779	5,637	8,158	52,249	111,729
Real estate taxes:									
Returns	1,000	39,673	644	1,825	2,802	3,783	4,267	17,029	9,323
Amount	Mil. dol.	111,013	1,526	3,602	5,088	6,917	8,180	40,642	45,059
Interest paid: Returns	1,000	37,637	536	1,478	2,686	3,676	4,124	16,457	8,680
Amount	Mil. dol.	351,496	4,217	9,564	17,863	24,904	29,011	138,482	127,455
Home mortgage interest:									
Returns	1,000	37,216	524	1,454	2,665	3,646	4,103	16,343	8,480
Amount	Mil. dol.	336,571	4,058	9,385	17,684	24,550	28,641	136,555	115,698
Charitable contributions:									
Returns	1,000	40,400	588	1,880	3,014	3,958	4,215	17,218	9,527
Amount	Mil. dol.	140,571	710	3,226	5,699	7,694	8,710	43,761	70,771
Returns with statutory adjustments: [2]									
Number of returns [2]	1,000	28,911	3,489	3,797	3,517	3,111	2,699	8,111	4,186
Amount of adjustments	Mil. dol.	77,161	3,791	4,821	5,539	5,477	5,022	20,182	32,328
Payments to IRAs: [3] Returns	1,000	3,278	104	299	462	471	376	1,007	558
Amount	Mil. dol.	9,462	215	625	1,108	1,210	1,077	3,034	2,193
Student loan interest deduction	1,000	6,641	286	644	1,029	1,038	909	2,343	393
Amount	Mil. dol.	4,470	144	345	651	678	690	1,748	214
Medical Savings Account deduction	1,000	61	1	6	6	3	8	26	12
Amount	Mil. dol.	121	2	6	7	8	7	62	30
Payments to Keogh plans	1,000	1,187	16	31	40	55	54	326	664
Amount	Mil. dol.	16,350	181	86	144	337	346	2,520	12,735
Alimony paid	1,000	587	23	43	38	58	47	207	171
Amount	Mil. dol.	7,184	320	265	346	235	248	1,862	3,907

[1] After limitations.   [2] Includes disability income exclusion, employee business expenses, moving expenses, forfeited interest penalty, alimony paid, deduction for expense of living abroad, and other data not shown separately.   [3] Individual Retirement Account.

Source: U.S. Internal Revenue Service, *Statistics of Income, Individual Income Tax Returns,* annual.

Table 476. **Federal Individual Income Tax Returns—Adjusted Gross Income (AGI) by Source of Income and Income Class for Taxable Returns: 2002**

[In millions of dollars (5,641,128 represents $5,641,128,000,000), except as indicated. Minus sign (-) indicates net loss was greater than net income. See headnote, Table 473. See Appendix III]

Item	Total [1]	Under $10,000	$10,000 to $19,999	$20,000 to $29,999	$30,000 to $39,999	$40,000 to $49,999	$50,000 to $99,999	$100,000 and over
Number of taxable returns (1,000) . . .	90,964	5,321	13,089	12,877	12,452	10,030	26,377	10,819
Source of income:								
Adjusted gross income (AGI).	5,641,128	35,362	198,171	321,667	434,002	449,963	1,844,319	2,357,643
Salaries and wages.	4,161,739	30,732	143,139	251,377	355,936	373,194	1,505,370	1,501,992
Percent of AGI for taxable returns.	73.8	86.9	72.2	78.1	82.0	82.9	81.6	63.7
Interest received.	131,825	1,592	8,505	9,520	8,776	8,026	29,991	65,414
Dividends in AGI.	94,222	811	3,133	3,934	3,819	4,176	19,287	59,063
Business; profession, net profit less loss	190,148	823	6,877	8,266	10,803	10,353	49,630	103,397
Sales of property, [2] net gain less loss	232,034	461	221	625	674	1,390	12,609	216,053
Pensions and annuities in AGI. . . .	331,764	1,695	27,094	34,786	36,411	32,422	126,825	72,532
Rents and royalties, net income less loss	30,884	55	846	897	600	84	3,148	25,253
Other sources, [3] net	468,512	-807	8,357	12,263	16,983	20,318	97,458	313,938
Percent of all returns: [4]								
Number of returns.	69.9	20.4	55.9	69.2	89.1	95.1	99.0	99.8
Adjusted gross income (AGI).	93.5	79.0	56.9	70.0	89.4	95.2	99.1	99.8
Salaries and wages.	91.3	27.1	55.3	67.5	88.8	95.0	99.2	99.9
Interest received.	88.5	14.9	69.0	87.2	91.6	95.8	97.7	98.4
Dividends in AGI.	91.3	15.6	61.4	83.3	91.9	93.3	96.4	99.1
Business; profession, net profit less loss	86.1	19.2	34.4	49.3	76.4	87.1	98.6	100.0
Sales of property, [2] net gain less loss	97.3	11.3	68.0	59.1	93.2	84.3	94.2	99.5
Pensions and annuities in AGI. . . .	92.7	16.6	70.4	90.8	96.4	98.5	99.5	99.8
Rents and royalties, net income less loss	106.6	(X)	101.1	110.5	138.5	(X)	100.2	99.6

[1] Includes a small number of taxable returns with no adjusted gross income (or a deficit). [2] Includes sales of capital assets and other property; net gain less loss. [3] Excludes rental passive losses disallowed in the computation of AGI; net income less loss. [4] Without regard to taxability.

Source: U.S. Internal Revenue Service, *Statistics of Income, Individual Income Tax Returns*, annual.

Table 477. **Federal Individual Income Tax Returns by State: 2002**

State	Number of returns [1] (1,000)	Adjusted gross income (AGI) [2] (mil. dol.)	Income Tax Total [3] (mil. dol.)	Per capita [4] (dol.)	State	Number of returns [1] (1,000)	Adjusted gross income (AGI) [2] (mil. dol.)	Income Tax Total [3] (mil. dol.)	Per capita [4] (dol.)
U.S. . . .	131,357	6,199,925	751,617	2,610					
					MT	434	15,198	1,474	1,619
AL	1,884	74,843	7,897	1,762	NE	803	33,043	3,515	2,036
AK	343	14,833	1,796	2,803	NV	1,044	52,307	6,783	3,128
AZ	2,285	102,846	11,482	2,111	NH	635	32,337	3,997	3,133
AR	1,122	41,364	4,138	1,528	NJ	4,082	247,077	34,778	4,055
CA	15,172	803,512	101,142	2,891	NM	814	29,959	3,032	1,634
CO	2,079	105,025	12,715	2,827	NY	8,590	465,512	64,517	3,369
CT	1,654	111,029	17,141	4,955	NC	3,681	157,402	16,646	2,003
DE	388	19,284	2,313	2,869	ND	302	11,285	1,140	1,799
DC	276	16,145	2,371	4,199	OH	5,444	227,754	24,760	2,170
FL	7,850	350,664	44,497	2,668	OK	1,461	56,019	5,834	1,673
GA	3,709	168,864	19,128	2,240	OR	1,572	67,956	7,097	2,014
HI.	591	25,718	2,754	2,230	PA	5,772	261,846	30,944	2,510
ID.	578	22,254	2,156	1,605	RI.	498	23,701	2,817	2,636
IL.	5,723	290,425	37,309	2,965	SC	1,805	70,931	7,045	1,716
IN.	2,817	119,765	12,963	2,105	SD	357	13,475	1,448	1,905
IA.	1,325	54,107	5,442	1,854	TN	2,565	105,526	12,129	2,094
KS.	1,219	52,503	5,730	2,112	TX	9,299	415,647	51,853	2,387
KY	1,741	68,276	6,986	1,708	UT	970	41,015	3,964	1,709
LA	1,880	70,865	7,506	1,677	VT	302	12,525	1,330	2,158
ME	615	24,727	2,503	1,928	VA	3,432	180,640	22,232	3,057
MD.	2,602	145,389	17,870	3,284	WA	2,809	141,431	17,928	2,955
MA	3,052	178,244	24,505	3,821	WV	744	26,629	2,598	1,439
MI	4,546	209,646	24,061	2,396	WI	2,590	117,029	12,865	2,365
MN	2,384	119,930	14,184	2,823	WY	241	11,092	1,389	2,782
MS.	1,170	40,610	3,827	1,335	Other [5]	1,546	43,729	5,255	(NA)
MO.	2,564	107,992	11,834	2,083					

NA Not available. [1] Includes returns constructed by Internal Revenue Service for certain self-employment tax returns. [2] Less deficit. [3] Includes additional tax for tax preferences, self-employment tax, tax from investment credit recapture and other income-related taxes. Total is before earned income credit. [4] Based on resident population as of July 1. [5] Includes returns filed from Army Post Office and Fleet Post Office addresses by members of the armed forces stationed overseas; returns by other U.S. citizens abroad; and returns filed by residents of Puerto Rico with income from sources outside of Puerto Rico or with income earned as U.S. Government employees.

Source: U.S. Internal Revenue Service, *Statistics of Income Bulletin*, quarterly.

Federal Government Finances and Employment **327**

Table 478. **Federal Individual Income Tax—Tax Liability and Effective and Marginal Tax Rates for Selected Income Groups: 1990 to 2001**

[Refers to income after exclusions. Effective rate represents tax liability divided by stated income. The marginal tax rate is the percentage of the first additional dollar of income which would be paid in income tax. Computations assume the low income allowance, standard deduction, zero bracket amount, or itemized deductions equal to 10 percent of adjusted gross income, whichever is greatest. Excludes self-employment tax]

Adjusted gross income	1990	1995	1997	1998	1999	2000	2001
TAX LIABILITY (dol.)							
Single person, no dependents:							
$5,000 [1]	-	-314	-332	-341	-347	-353	-364
$10,000 [2]	705	540	480	455	427	391	201
$20,000	2,205	2,040	1,980	1,958	1,943	1,920	1,283
$25,000	2,988	2,790	2,730	2,708	2,693	2,670	2,033
$35,000	5,718	4,973	4,692	4,559	4,479	4,372	3,595
$50,000	9,498	8,865	8,654	8,549	8,483	8,404	7,596
$75,000	16,718	15,418	15,107	14,951	14,852	14,738	13,784
Married couple, two dependents: [3, 4]							
$5,000 [5]	-700	-1,800	-2,000	-2,000	-2,000	-2,000	-2,000
$10,000 [5]	-953	-3,110	-3,556	-3,756	-3,816	-4,000	-4,000
$20,000 [5]	926	-832	-1,414	-1,811	-1,958	-2,553	-3,553
$25,000 [1]	1,703	929	389	-8	-155	-1,500	-2,120
$35,000	3,203	2,768	2,625	2,565	2,520	1,468	570
$50,000	5,960	5,018	4,875	4,815	4,770	3,718	2,820
$75,000	12,386	11,030	10,576	10,371	10,224	9,064	7,895
EFFECTIVE RATE (percent)							
Single person, no dependents:							
$5,000 [1]	-	-6.3	-6.6	-6.8	-6.9	-7.1	-7.3
$10,000 [2]	7.1	5.4	4.8	4.6	4.3	3.9	2.0
$20,000	11.0	10.2	9.9	9.8	9.7	9.6	6.4
$25,000	12.0	11.2	10.9	10.8	10.8	10.7	8.1
$35,000	16.3	14.2	13.4	13.0	12.8	12.5	10.3
$50,000	19.0	17.7	17.3	17.1	17.0	16.8	15.2
$75,000	22.3	20.6	20.1	19.9	19.8	19.7	18.4
Married couple, two dependents: [3]							
$5,000 [5]	-14.0	-36.0	-40	-40.0	-40.0	-40.0	-40.0
$10,000 [5]	-9.5	-31.1	-35.6	-37.6	38.2	-40.0	-40.0
$20,000 [5]	4.6	-4.2	-7.1	-9.1	-9.8	-12.8	-17.8
$25,000 [1]	6.8	3.7	1.6	0.0	-0.6	-6.0	-8.5
$35,000	9.2	7.9	7.5	7.3	7.2	4.2	1.6
$50,000	11.9	10.0	9.8	9.6	9.5	7.4	5.6
$75,000	16.5	14.7	14.1	13.8	13.6	12.1	10.5
MARGINAL TAX RATE (percent)							
Single person, no dependents:							
$5,000 [1]	-	-	-	-	-	-	-
$10,000 [2]	15	15	15	23	23	23	18
$20,000	15	15	15	15	15	15	15
$25,000	28	15	15	15	15	15	15
$35,000	28	28	28	28	28	28	28
$50,000	28	28	28	28	28	28	28
$75,000	33	31	31	31	31	31	28
Married couple, two dependents: [3, 4]							
$5,000 [5]	-14	-36	-40	-40	-40	-40	-40
$10,000 [5]	-	-	-	-	-	-40	-40
$20,000 [1]	25	35	36	36	36	21	11
$25,000	15	35	36	36	36	36	21
$35,000	15	15	15	15	15	15	15
$50,000	28	15	15	15	15	15	15
$75,000	28	28	28	28	28	28	28

- Represents zero. [1] Beginning 1999, includes refundable earned income credit. [2] Refundable earned income credit. [3] Only one spouse is assumed to work. [4] Beginning 1998, includes child tax credit. [5] Beginning 1994, refundable earned income credit.

Source: U.S. Dept. of the Treasury, Office of Tax Analysis, unpublished data. See also <http://www.treas.gov/ota/index.html>.

Table 479. Federal Individual Income Tax—Current Income Equivalent to 1996 Constant Income for Selected Income Groups: 1990 to 2001

[Constant 1996 dollar incomes calculated by using the NIPA Chain-Type Price Index for Personal Consumption Expenditures (1996 = 100), 1990, 85.63; 1995, 97.60; 1997, 101.98; 1998, 102.93; 1999, 104.57; 2000, 109.60; and 2001, 111.10]

Adusted gross income	1990	1995	1997	1998	1999	2000	2001 [1]
REAL INCOME EQUIVALENT (dol.)							
Single person, no dependents:							
$5,000	4,280	4,900	5,100	5,150	5,230	5,380	5,480
$10,000	8,560	9,790	10,200	10,290	10,460	10,750	10,950
$20,000	17,130	19,580	20,400	20,590	20,910	21,500	21,910
$25,000	21,410	24,480	25,500	25,730	26,140	26,880	27,380
$35,000	29,970	34,270	35,690	36,030	36,600	37,630	38,340
$50,000	42,820	48,950	50,990	51,470	52,290	53,760	54,770
$75,000	64,220	73,430	76,490	77,200	78,430	80,640	82,150
Married couple, two dependents: [2]							
$5,000	4,280	4,900	5,100	5,150	5,230	5,380	5,480
$10,000	8,560	9,790	10,200	10,290	10,460	10,750	10,950
$20,000	17,130	19,580	20,400	20,590	20,910	21,500	21,910
$25,000	21,410	24,480	25,500	25,730	26,140	26,880	27,380
$35,000	29,970	34,270	35,690	36,030	36,600	37,630	38,340
$50,000	42,820	48,950	50,990	51,470	52,290	53,760	54,770
$75,000	64,220	73,430	76,490	77,200	78,430	80,640	82,150
EFFECTIVE RATE (percent)							
Single person, no dependents:							
$5,000 [3]	-	-6.4	-6.5	-6.6	-6.6	-6.6	-6.6
$10,000	5:7	5.2	5.0	4.9	4.9	5.0	3.2
$20,000	10.4	10.1	10.0	9.9	9.9	10.0	7.2
$25,000	11.3	11.1	11.0	10.9	11.0	11.0	8.7
$35,000	14.6	13.9	13.7	13.5	13.5	13.6	11.8
$50,000	18.0	17.6	17.5	17.3	17.3	17.4	16.0
$75,000	21.0	20.4	20.3	20.2	20.2	20.2	19.1
Married couple, two dependents: [2]							
$5,000 [4]	-14.0	-36.0	-40.0	-40.0	-40.0	-40.0	-40.0
$10,000 [4]	-11.1	-31.8	-34.9	-36.5	-36.5	-37.3	-37.5
$20,000 [4]	1.2	-5.0	-6.2	-7.8	-7.8	-10.4	-14.1
$25,000	5.4	3.0	2.2	1.0	1.0	-3.2	-5.0
$35,000	8.2	7.8	7.6	7.5	7.5	4.9	2.8
$50,000	10.2	9.9	9.9	9.8	9.8	8.0	6.4
$75,000	15.1	14.5	14.3	14.2	14.1	13.0	11.8
MARGINAL TAX RATE (percent)							
Single person, no dependents:							
$5,000	-	-	-	-	-	-	-
$10,000	15.0	15.0	15.0	15.0	15.0	15.0	10.0
$20,000	15.0	15.0	15.0	15.0	15.0	15.0	15.0
$25,000	15.0	15.0	15.0	15.0	15.0	15.0	15.0
$35,000	28.0	28.0	28.0	28.0	28.0	28.0	27.5
$50,000	28.0	28.0	28.0	28.0	28.0	28.0	27.5
$75,000	33.0	31.0	31.0	31.0	31.0	31.0	30.5
Married couple, two dependents: [2]							
$5,000 [4]	-14.0	-36.0	-40.0	-40.0	-40.0	-40.0	-40.0
$10,000 [4]	-	-	-	-	-	-	-10.0
$20,000 [4]	25.0	35.2	36.1	36.1	36.1	21.1	21.1
$25,000	15.0	35.2	36.1	36.1	36.1	36.1	21.1
$35,000	15.0	15.0	15.0	15.0	15.0	15.0	15.0
$50,000	15.0	15.0	15.0	15.0	15.0	15.0	15.0
$75,000	28.0	28.0	28.0	28.0	28.0	28.0	27.5

- Represents zero. [1] Includes rate reduction tax credit. [2] Only one spouse is assumed to work. [3] Beginning 1995, refundable earned income credit. [4] Refundable earned income credit.

Source: U.S. Department of the Treasury, Office of Tax Analysis, unpublished data.

Table 480. Full-Time Federal Civilian Employment—Employees and Average Pay-by-Pay System: 1990 to 2003

[As of March 31. 2,036 represents 2,036,000. Excludes employees of Congress and Federal courts, maritime seamen of Department of Commerce, and small number for whom rates were not reported. See text, this section, for explanation of general schedule and wage system]

Pay system	Employees (1,000)				Average pay (dol.)			
	1990	2000	2002	2003	1990	2000	2002	2003
Total, excluding postal	2,036	1,671	1,681	1,755	31,174	50,429	55,715	57,480
General Schedule	1,506	1,216	1,238	1,243	31,239	49,428	54,329	56,874
Wage System	369	205	193	187	26,565	37,082	39,892	41,259
Other	161	250	250	325	41,149	66,248	74,771	69,138
Postal pay system [1]	753	788	753	729	29,264	37,627	40,434	42,119

NA Not available. [1] Source: Career employees—U.S. Postal Service, *Annual Report of the Postmaster General*. See also <http://www.usps.com/financials/cspo/welcome.htm>, Average pay—U.S. Postal Service, *Comprehensive Statement of Postal Operations*, annual.

Source: Except as noted, U.S. Office of Personnel Management, *Pay Structure of the Federal Civil Service*, annual.

Federal Government Finances and Employment 329

Table 481. Federal Civilian Employment and Annual Payroll by Branch: 1970 to 2003

[Employment in thousands (2,997 represents 2,997,000); payroll in millions of dollars (27,322 represents $27,322,000,000). For fiscal year ending in year shown; see text, Section 8, State and Local Government Finances and Employment. Includes employees in U.S. territories and foreign countries. Data represent employees in active-duty status, including intermittent employees. Annual employment figures are averages of monthly figures. Excludes Central Intelligence Agency, National Security Agency, and, as of November 1984, the Defense Intelligence Agency; and as of October 1996, the National Imagery and Mapping Agency]

Year			Employment						Payroll		
	Total	Percent of U.S. employed [1]	Executive		Legis-lative	Judicial	Total	Executive		Legis-lative	Judicial
			Total	Defense				Total	Defense		
1970 ...	[2]2,997	3.81	2,961	1,263	29	7	27,322	26,894	11,264	338	89
1971 ...	2,899	3.65	2,861	1,162	31	7	29,475	29,007	11,579	369	98
1972 ...	2,882	3.51	2,842	1,128	32	8	31,626	31,102	12,181	411	112
1973 ...	2,822	3.32	2,780	1,076	33	9	33,240	32,671	12,414	447	121
1974 ...	2,825	3.26	2,781	1,041	35	9	35,661	35,035	12,789	494	132
1975 ...	2,877	3.35	2,830	1,044	37	10	39,126	38,423	13,418	549	154
1976 ...	2,879	3.24	2,831	1,025	38	11	42,259	41,450	14,699	631	179
1977 ...	2,855	3.10	2,803	997	39	12	45,895	44,975	15,696	700	219
1978 ...	2,875	2.99	2,822	987	40	13	49,921	48,899	16,995	771	251
1979 ...	2,897	2.93	2,844	974	40	13	53,590	52,513	18,065	817	260
1980 ...	[2]2,987	3.01	2,933	971	40	14	58,012	56,841	18,795	883	288
1981 ...	2,909	2.90	2,855	986	40	15	63,793	62,510	21,227	922	360
1982 ...	2,871	2.88	2,816	1,019	39	16	65,503	64,125	22,226	980	398
1983 ...	2,878	2.85	2,823	1,033	39	16	69,878	68,420	23,406	1,013	445
1984 ...	2,935	2.80	2,879	1,052	40	17	74,616	73,084	25,253	1,081	451
1985 ...	3,001	2.80	2,944	1,080	39	18	80,599	78,992	28,330	1,098	509
1986 ...	3,047	2.77	2,991	1,089	38	19	82,598	80,941	29,272	1,112	545
1987 ...	3,075	2.73	3,018	1,084	38	19	85,543	83,797	29,786	1,153	593
1988 ...	3,113	2.71	3,054	1,073	38	21	88,841	86,960	29,609	1,226	656
1989 ...	3,133	2.67	3,074	1,067	38	22	92,847	90,870	30,301	1,266	711
1990 ...	[2]3,233	2.72	3,173	1,060	38	23	99,138	97,022	31,990	1,329	787
1991 ...	3,101	2.63	3,038	1,015	38	25	104,273	101,965	31,486	1,434	874
1992 ...	3,106	2.62	3,040	1,004	39	27	108,054	105,402	31,486	1,569	1,083
1993 ...	3,043	2.53	2,976	952	39	28	114,323	111,523	32,755	1,609	1,191
1994 ...	2,993	2.43	2,928	900	37	28	116,138	113,264	32,144	1,613	1,260
1995 ...	2,943	2.36	2,880	852	34	28	118,304	115,328	31,753	1,598	1,379
1996 ...	2,881	2.27	2,819	811	32	29	119,321	116,385	31,964	1,519	1,417
1997 ...	2,816	2.17	2,755	768	31	30	119,603	116,693	31,431	1,515	1,396
1998 ...	2,783	2.12	2,721	730	31	31	121,964	118,800	30,315	1,517	1,647
1999 ...	2,789	2.09	2,726	703	30	32	124,990	121,732	30,141	1,560	1,699
2000 ...	[2]2,879	2.10	2,816	681	31	32	130,832	127,472	29,607	1,619	1,741
2001 ...	2,704	1.97	2,641	672	30	33	131,964	128,502	28,594	1,682	1,780
2002 ...	2,699	1.98	2,635	671	31	34	136,611	132,893	28,845	1,781	1,938
2003 ...	2,743	1.99	2,677	669	31	34	143,380	139,506	29,029	1,908	1,966

[1] Civilian only. See Table 578. [2] Includes temporary census workers.
Source: U.S. Office of Personnel Management, *Federal Civilian Workforce Statistics—Employment and Trends*, bimonthly; and unpublished data.

Table 482. Paid Civilian Employment in the Federal Government by State: 2000 and 2002

[As of December 31. In thousands (2,674 represents 2,674,000). Excludes Central Intelligence Agency, Defense Intelligence Agency, seasonal and on-call employees, and National Security Agency]

State	2000 (1,000)	2002 (1,000)	Percent change, 2000-2002	State	2000 (1,000)	2002 (1,000)	Percent change, 2000-2002
United States [1]	2,674	2,653	-0.8	Missouri	54	54	-
Alabama	48	48	-	Montana	11	12	9.1
Alaska	14	14	-	Nebraska	15	15	-
Arizona	43	46	7.0	Nevada..............	13	15	15.4
Arkansas	20	20	-	New Hampshire	8	9	12.5
California.............	248	245	-1.2	New Jersey	62	63	1.6
Colorado.............	51	52	2.0	New Mexico	25	26	4.0
Connecticut	21	20	-4.8	New York	134	133	-0.7
Delaware.............	5	5	-	North Carolina	57	57	-
District of Columbia......	181	189	4.4	North Dakota	8	8	-
Florida	113	122	8.0	Ohio................	84	80	-4.8
Georgia	89	91	2.2	Oklahoma	43	44	2.3
Hawaii	23	25	8.7	Oregon	29	29	-
Idaho	11	11	0.0	Pennsylvania	107	106	-0.9
Illinois	94	92	-2.1	Rhode Island	10	11	10.0
Indiana	37	36	-2.7	South Carolina	26	27	3.8
Iowa................	18	18	-	South Dakota	9	10	11.1
Kansas	25	25	-	Tennessee...........	50	49	-2.0
Kentucky.............	30	31	3.3	Texas	162	166	2.5
Louisiana	33	33	0.0	Utah................	30	33	10.0
Maine...............	13	14	7.7	Vermont	6	6	-
Maryland.............	130	133	2.3	Virginia	145	143	-1.4
Massachusetts	53	53	-	Washington	62	65	4.8
Michigan.............	58	57	-1.7	West Virginia	18	19	5.6
Minnesota............	34	34	-	Wisconsin	30	29	-3.3
Mississippi............	24	24	-	Wyoming.............	6	6	-

- Represents zero.   [1] Includes employees outside the United States not shown separately.
Source: U.S. Office of Personnel Management, *Biennial Report of Employment by Geographic Area, 2002*.

330   Federal Government Finances and Employment

Table 483. **Federal Civilian Employment by Branch and Agency: 1990 to 2003**

[For years ending September 30; excludes Central Intelligence Agency, National Security Agency; the Defense Intelligence Agency; and, as of October 1996, the National Imagery and Mapping Agency]

Agency	1990	1995	2000	2003	Percent change 1990-2000	Percent change 2000-2003
Total, all agencies	3,128,267	2,920,277	2,708,101	2,743,063	-13.4	1.3
Legislative Branch, total.	37,495	33,367	31,157	31,297	-16.9	0.4
Judicial Branch	23,605	28,993	32,186	34,472	36.4	7.1
Executive Branch, total	3,067,167	2,857,917	2,644,758	2,677,294	-13.8	1.2
Executive Departments [1]	2,065,542	1,782,834	1,592,200	1,687,158	-22.9	6.0
State.	25,288	24,859	27,983	31,402	10.7	12.2
Treasury	158,655	155,951	143,508	134,302	-9.5	-6.4
Defense.	1,034,152	832,352	676,268	669,096	-34.6	-1.1
Justice.	83,932	103,262	125,970	115,259	50.1	-8.5
Interior.	77,679	76,439	73,818	74,818	-5.0	1.4
Agriculture	122,594	113,321	104,466	107,204	-14.8	2.6
Commerce	69,920	36,803	47,652	37,330	-31.8	-21.7
Labor	17,727	16,204	16,040	16,296	-9.5	1.6
Health & Human Services	123,959	59,788	62,605	67,240	-49.5	7.4
Housing & Urban Development	13,596	11,822	10,319	10,660	-24.1	3.3
Transportation [2]	67,364	63,552	63,598	89,262	-5.6	40.4
Energy	17,731	19,589	15,692	15,823	-11.5	0.8
Education.	4,771	4,988	4,734	4,593	-0.8	-3.0
Veterans Affairs [3]	248,174	263,904	219,547	226,171	-11.5	3.0
Homeland Security [4]	(X)	(X)	(X)	150,350	(X)	(X)
Independent agencies.	999,894	1,073,510	1,050,900	988,434	5.1	-5.9
Board of Governors Federal Reserve System. . .	1,525	1,704	2,372	1,761	55.5	-25.8
Commodity Futures Trading Commission.	542	544	574	534	5.9	-7.0
Consumer Product Safety Commission	520	486	479	482	-7.9	0.6
Environmental Protection Agency.	17,123	17,910	18,036	18,126	5.3	0.5
Equal Employment Opportunity Commission . . .	2,880	2,796	2,780	2,669	-3.5	-4.0
Federal Communications Commission	1,778	2,116	1,965	2,058	10.5	4.7
Federal Deposit Insurance Corporation	17,641	14,765	6,958	5,502	-60.6	-20.9
Federal Trade Commission.	988	996	1,019	1,076	3.1	5.6
General Services Administration	20,277	16,500	14,334	13,615	-29.3	-5.0
National Archives & Records Administration	3,120	2,833	2,702	3,027	-13.4	12.0
National Aeronautics & Space Administration . . .	24,872	21,635	18,819	18,908	-24.3	0.5
National Credit Union Administration.	900	912	1,021	930	13.4	-8.9
National Labor Relations Board	2,263	2,050	2,054	1,932	-9.2	-5.9
National Science Foundation.	1,318	1,292	1,247	1,327	-5.4	6.4
Nuclear Regulatory Commission	3,353	3,212	2,858	3,034	-14.8	6.2
Office of Personnel Management	6,636	4,354	3,780	3,410	-43.0	-9.8
Peace Corps	1,178	1,179	1,065	1,118	-9.6	5.0
Securities & Exchange Commission	2,302	2,852	2,955	3,132	28.4	6.0
Small Business Administration.	5,128	5,085	4,150	3,824	-19.1	-7.9
Smithsonian Institution.	5,092	5,444	5,065	5,133	-0.5	1.3
Social Security Administration	(X)	66,850	64,474	64,414	(X)	-0.1
Tennessee Valley Authority	28,392	16,545	13,145	13,379	-53.7	1.8
U.S. Information Agency.	8,555	7,480	2,436	2,362	-71.5	-3.0
U.S. Postal Service	816,886	845,393	860,726	801,552	5.4	-6.9

X Not applicable.   [1] Total may not add due to the use of fiscal year averages.   [2] Beginning in 2001, includes the Transportation Security Administration created within the Department of Transportation.   [3] Formerly Veterans Administration.   [4] See text, section 10.

Source: U.S. Office of Personnel Management, *Federal Civilian Workforce Statistics—Employment and Trends,* bimonthly. See also <http://www.opm.gov/feddata/index.htm>.

Table 484. **Federal Employment Trends—Individual Characteristics: 1990 to 2002**

[In percents, except as indicated. Covers only Federal civilian nonpostal employees]

Characteristics	1990	1995	1996	1997	1998	1999	2000	2001	2002
Average age (years) [1]	42.3	44.3	44.8	45.2	45.6	45.9	46.3	46.5	46.5
Average length of service (years) [1]	13.4	15.5	15.9	16.3	16.6	16.9	17.1	17.1	16.8
Retirement eligible: [1]									
Civil Service Retirement System [2]	8	10	11	12	13	15	17	19	23
Federal Employees Retirement System. . . .	3	5	6	7	8	10	11	10	11
College-conferred [3].	35	39	39	40	40	40	41	41	41
Gender:									
Men	57	56	56	56	56	55	55	55	55
Women	43	44	44	44	44	45	45	45	45
Race and national origin:									
Total minorities	27.4	28.9	29.1	29.4	29.7	30.0	30.4	30.6	30.8
Black.	16.7	16.8	16.7	16.7	16.7	17.0	17.1	17.1	17.0
Hispanic	5.4	5.9	6.1	6.2	6.4	6.5	6.6	6.7	6.9
Asian/Pacific Islander	3.5	4.2	4.3	4.4	4.5	4.5	4.5	4.6	4.7
American Indian/Alaska native	1.8	2.0	2.0	2.1	2.1	2.2	2.2	2.2	2.2
Disabled.	7.0	7.0	7.0	7.0	7.0	7.0	7.0	7.0	7.0
Veterans preference	30.0	26.0	26.0	25.0	25.0	25.0	24.0	24.0	23.0
Vietnam era veterans.	17.0	17.0	17.0	15.0	14.0	14.0	14.0	13.0	13.0
Retired military.	4.9	4.2	4.3	4.2	3.9	3.9	3.9	4.2	4.4
Retired officers.	0.5	0.5	0.5	0.5	0.5	0.5	0.5	0.6	0.7

[1] Represents full-time permanent employees.   [2] Represents full-time permanent employees under the Civil Service Retirement System (excluding hires since January 1984), and the Federal Employees Retirement System (since January 1984).   [3] Bachelor's degree or higher.

Source: U.S. Office of Personnel Management, Office of Workforce Information, *The Fact Book, Federal Civilian Workforce Statistics,* annual. See also <http://www.opm.gov/feddata/02factbk.pdf> (released June 2002).

Federal Government Finances and Employment   **331**

Table 485. Federal Executive Branch (Non-Postal) Employment by Race and National Origin: 1990 to 2003

[As of **Sept. 30**. GS pay scale effective January 2003. Covers total employment for only Executive branch agencies participating in OPM's Central Personnel Data File (CPDF). For information on the CPDF, see <http://www.opm.gov/feddata/acpdf.pdf>.]

Pay system	1990	1995	2000	2002	2003
All personnel	**2,150,359**	**1,960,577**	**1,755,689**	**1,813,047**	**1,832,626**
White, non-Hispanic	1,562,846	1,394,690	1,224,836	1,255,941	1,263,595
General schedule and related	1,218,188	1,101,108	961,261	973,957	972,094
Grades 1-4 ($15,214 - $27,234)	132,028	79,195	55,067	55,005	51,514
Grades 5-8 ($23,442 - $41,806)	337,453	288,755	239,128	237,807	234,637
Grades 9-12 ($35,519 - $66,961)	510,261	465,908	404,649	405,583	405,376
Grades 13-15 ($61,251 - $110,682)	238,446	267,250	262,417	275,562	280,567
Total executives/senior pay levels [1]	9,337	13,307	14,332	15,428	15,787
Wage pay system	244,220	186,184	146,075	138,785	133,334
Other pay systems	91,101	94,091	103,168	127,771	142,380
Black	356,867	327,302	298,701	306,128	310,622
General schedule and related	272,657	258,586	241,135	243,884	243,236
Grades 1-4 ($15,214 - $27,234)	65,077	41,381	26,895	23,841	21,857
Grades 5-8 ($23,442 - $41,806)	114,993	112,962	99,937	97,731	96,159
Grades 9-12 ($35,519 - $66,961)	74,985	79,795	82,809	86,619	87,633
Grades 13-15 ($61,251 - $110,682)	17,602	24,448	31,494	35,693	37,587
Total executives/senior pay levels [1]	479	942	1,180	1,207	1,247
Wage pay system	72,755	55,637	42,590	39,354	38,038
Other pay systems	10,976	12,137	13,796	21,683	28,101
Hispanic	115,170	115,964	115,247	124,868	130,492
General schedule and related	83,218	86,762	89,911	96,333	99,118
Grades 1-4 ($15,214 - $27,234)	15,738	11,081	8,526	8,314	8,053
Grades 5-8 ($23,442 - $41,806)	28,727	31,152	31,703	34,201	34,808
Grades 9-12 ($35,519 - $66,961)	31,615	34,056	36,813	39,310	40,998
Grades 13-15 ($61,251 - $110,682)	7,138	10,473	12,869	14,508	15,259
Total executives/senior pay levels [1]	154	382	547	594	631
Wage pay system	26,947	22,128	16,926	16,017	15,412
Other pay systems	4,851	6,692	7,863	11,924	15,331
American Indian, Alaska Natives, Asians, and Pacific Islanders	115,476	122,621	116,905	126,110	127,917
General schedule and related	81,499	86,768	86,074	92,402	92,828
Grades 1-4 ($15,214 - $27,234)	15,286	11,854	9,340	9,568	8,868
Grades 5-8 ($23,442 - $41,806)	24,960	26,580	25,691	27,479	27,060
Grades 9-12 ($35,519 - $66,961)	31,346	33,810	33,167	35,054	35,546
Grades 13-15 ($61,251 - $110,682)	9,907	14,524	17,876	20,301	21,354
Total executives/senior pay levels [1]	148	331	504	626	682
Wage pay system	24,927	21,553	17,613	17,439	16,379
Other pay systems	8,902	13,969	12,714	15,643	18,028

[1] General schedule pay rates and Senior Pay Levels effective as of January 1999.
Source: Office of Personnel Management, Central Personnel Data File.

Table 486. Federal General Schedule Employee Pay Increases: 1980 to 2005

[Percent change from prior year shown, except 1980, change from 1979. Represents legislated pay increases. For some years data based on range. For details see source]

Date	Pay increase	Date	Pay increase	Date	Pay increase
1980	9.1	1994	-	2000	3.8
1985	3.5	1995	2.0	2001	2.7
1990	3.6	1996	2.0	2002	3.6
1991	4.1	1997	2.3	2003	3.1
1992	4.2	1998	2.3	2004	2.7
1993	3.7	1999	3.1	2005	2.5

- Represents zero.
Source: U.S. Office of Personnel Management, *Pay Structure of the Federal Civil Service*, annual.

Table 487. Turnover Data for the Executive Branch—All Areas: 1990 to 2003

[Turnover data exclude Legislative and Judicial branches, U.S. Postal Service, Postal Rate Commission]

Year	Accessions [1]		Separations		Total employment		
	Total	New hires	Total	Quits	Average	Change from prior year	Percent change
1990 [2]	819,554	716,066	799,237	165,099	2,348,458	114,477	5.1
1991	495,123	351,112	515,673	134,175	2,224,389	-124,069	-5.3
1992	430,021	290,883	446,126	129,167	2,238,635	14,246	0.6
1993	382,399	253,374	423,830	127,140	2,189,416	-49,219	-2.2
1994	317,509	219,026	398,134	111,096	2,114,387	-75,029	-3.4
1995	345,166	222,025	457,246	91,909	2,037,890	-76,542	-3.6
1996	266,473	199,463	356,566	80,922	1,960,892	-76,953	-3.8
1997	283,517	208,725	333,431	81,574	1,895,295	-65,597	-3.3
1998	320,830	242,637	321,292	84,124	1,855,112	-40,183	-2.1
1999	423,500	346,988	372,778	129,196	1,846,170	-8,942	-0.5
2000 [2]	1,168,783	1,092,888	1,027,653	801,684	1,946,684	100,514	5.4
2001	308,877	233,034	301,659	82,495	1,783,239	-163,445	-8.4
2002	316,941	242,410	280,714	55,167	1,805,627	22,388	1.3
2003	508,160	254,030	461,171	53,187	1,875,695	70,068	3.9

[1] Accessions are employees who have been added to federal employment; these would include temporary and permanent new hires and those who returned to duty.   [2] Includes hiring for census enumerators.
Source: U.S. Office of Personnel Management, *Federal Civilian Workforce Statistics— Employment and Trends*, bimonthly. Also in *The Fact Book, Federal Civilian Workforce Statistics*, annual. See also <http://www.opm.gov/feddata/03factbk.pdf> (released April 2002).

Table 488. Federal Land and Buildings Owned and Leased: 1990 to 2004

[For years ending September 30. Covers federal real property throughout the world, except as noted. Cost of land figures represent total cost of property owned in year shown. For further details, see source. For data on Federal land by state, see Table 348]

Item	Unit	1990	1995	2000	2002	2003	2004
Federally-owned:							
Land, worldwide..........	1,000 acres ...	650,014	549,670	635,824	675,864	673,207	654,719
United States..........	1,000 acres ...	649,802	549,474	635,355	674,100	671,759	653,299
Buildings [1]	1,000	(NA)	(NA)	435	446	437	416
United States........	1,000	446	424	430	441	433	411
Buildings, floor area [1]	Mil. sq./ft. ...	(NA)	(NA)	3,003	3,009	3,066	2,875
United States........	Mil. sq./ft. ...	2,859	2,793	2,968	2,975	3,032	2,840
Costs................	Mil. dol.	187,865	199,387	260,069	334,708	312,415	331,451
Land	Mil. dol.	(NA)	18,972	21,008	53,930	(NA)	(NA)
Buildings.............	Mil. dol.	(NA)	113,018	139,291	174,929	(NA)	(NA)
Structures and facilities ...	Mil. dol.	(NA)	67,398	99,770	105,849	(NA)	(NA)
Federally-leased:							
Land, worldwide..........	1,000 acres ...	994	1,385	1,670	894	373	2,453
United States..........	1,000 acres ...	938	1,351	1,611	842	309	2,391
Buildings [1]	1,000	(NA)	(NA)	84	57	54	58
United States........	1,000	47	78	73	46	42	45
Buildings, floor area [1]	Mil. sq./ft. ...	(NA)	(NA)	347	374	370	381
United States........	Mil. sq./ft. ...	234	275	313	339	334	344
Annual rental	Mil. dol.	2,590	3,633	3,394	5,111	6,135	6,702
United States........	Mil. dol.	2,125	3,174	2,931	4,588	5,656	6,179

NA Not available.   [1] Excludes data for Department of Defense military functions outside of the United States.

Source: U.S. General Services Administration, *Summary Report on Real Property Owned by the United States Throughout the World,* annual; and *Summary Report of Real Property Leased by the United States Throughout the World, 2004.* See also <http://www.gsa.gov>.

Table 489. Federally-Owned Property in the United States by State: 2004

[As of September 30. For data on federal land by state, see Table 348]

State	Number of owned buildings [1]	Owned-building area (mil. sq. ft.)	Leased-building area (mil. sq. ft.)	State	Number of owned buildings [1]	Owned-building area (mil. sq. ft.)	Leased-building area (mil. sq. ft.)
U.S. ...	411,406	2,839.9	343.7				
AL.....	8,142	52.7	5.4	MO	6,689	50.6	8.4
AK.....	9,283	55.1	2.3	MT	6,944	15.7	2.4
AZ.....	13,869	53.7	4.9	NE.....	3,281	18.9	2.2
AR.....	4,803	21.6	2.8	NV.....	7,527	32.9	1.8
CA.....	54,463	344.3	27.5	NH.....	735	3.4	1.2
CO.....	9,226	60.5	7.4	NJ.....	5,461	46.7	9.6
CT.....	2,054	15.4	1.8	NM.....	14,190	61.1	3.1
DE.....	896	7.5	0.5	NY.....	10,808	100.9	15.2
DC.....	1,596	66.6	22.3	NC.....	14,499	87.0	6.7
FL.....	13,640	110.0	16.1	ND.....	3,374	20.3	1.1
GA.....	12,216	111.5	18.5	OH.....	5,135	70.1	8.5
HI.....	13,642	74.6	1.2	OK.....	8,990	57.0	7.5
ID.....	6,822	18.1	2.1	OR.....	8,690	23.1	4.1
IL.....	6,754	76.2	8.3	PA.....	7,227	77.4	11.9
IN.....	4,827	33.0	4.6	RI.....	1,321	12.7	0.8
IA.....	2,326	12.4	3.2	SC.....	8,098	61.5	3.0
KS.....	6,059	42.8	3.5	SD.....	3,159	17.4	1.5
KY.....	6,180	52.0	4.2	TN.....	7,063	68.7	4.9
LA.....	5,329	41.4	4.3	TX.....	23,548	198.5	18.7
ME.....	2,024	13.4	1.3	UT.....	7,390	31.0	3.5
MD.....	9,882	110.5	22.4	VT.....	535	2.6	1.3
MA.....	4,268	35.0	5.7	VA.....	17,532	152.1	28.0
MI.....	5,520	31.3	7.0	WA.....	14,839	86.9	6.4
MN.....	3,078	19.7	3.3	WV....	1,878	15.4	3.2
MS.....	5,470	34.1	2.9	WI	4,896	21.9	4.5
				WY	5,228	12.6	0.9

[1] Excludes data for Department of Defense military functions outside of the United States.

Source: U.S. General Services Administration, *Summary Report of Real Property Owned by the United States Throughout the World, 2004.* See also <http://www.gsa.gov/>.

No. 255.—THE MILITIA FORCE OF THE UNITED STATES ACCORDING TO THE LATEST RETURNS RECEIVED AT THE OFFICE OF THE ADJUTANT-GENERAL, U. S. ARMY, FOR THE YEAR 1893.

[From Report to Congress of the Adjutant-General.]

States and Territories	Commissioned officers.					Enlisted men.				
	Cavalry.	Light batteries.	Infantry.	Other.a	Total.	Cavalry.	Light batteries.	Infantry.	Other.a	Total.
Alabama	12	15	166	104	297	170	197	2,296	-------	2,663
Arkansas	4	3	59	13	79	40	20	842	-------	902
California	4	10	273	156	443	60	112	3,812	517	4,501
Colorado	6	3	56	41	106	83	44	562	27	721
Connecticut		9	163	18	190		104	2,381	76	2,561
Delaware	6		30	14	50	48		232	-------	280
Florida		4	80	11	95		60	856		916
Georgia	62	8	257	49	376	534	102	2,523	-------	3,159
Idaho			16	8	24			208		208
Illinois	6	8	277	56	347	99	122	4,205	4	4,430
Indiana		14	179	10	203		183	2,247		2,430
Iowa			188	42	230			2,082	3	2,085
Kansas			105	18	123			1,543	-------	1,543
Kentucky			109	17	126			1,205		1,205
Louisiana	2	35	69	14	120	52	367	710	-------	1,129
Maine			76	12	88			961	15	976
Maryland			160	10	170			1,948		1,948
Massachusetts	19	22	284	118	443	237	299	3,899	688	5,123
Michigan			158	30	188			2,613		2,613
Minnesota		11	95	28	134		88	1,579		1,667
Mississippi	7		92	49	148	93		1,197	267	1,557
Missouri		9	132	22	163		144	1,977	131	2,252
Montana		3	35	11	49		35	442		477
Nebraska	3	3	75	18	99	88	49	900		987
Nevada		3	33	18	54		58	380	1	439
New Hampshire	3	4	97	10	114	55	68	1,013	5	1,141
New Jersey	3	4	231	51	289	52	68	3,500	6	3,626
New York	6	22	626	83	737	105	367	11,517	84	12,073
North Carolina	3	------	138	43	184	37	------	1,403	158	1,598
North Dakota	10	4	33	3	50	62	50	317	-------	429
Ohio	9	45	358	18	430	81	483	5,017	114	5,695
Oregon	6	4	96	14	120	100	42	1,313		1,455
Pennsylvania	15	18	564	83	680	178	230	7,223	303	7,934
Rhode Island	13	6	68	83	170	90	90	724	402	1,306
South Carolina	169	4	331	87	591	1,375	427	3,047	-------	4,849
South Dakota		3	67	23	93		43	643		686
Tennessee		7	67	58	132		104	1,029	529	1,662
Texas	37	16	185	39	277	383	128	1,990	6	2,507
Vermont		8	48	23	79		72	585	48	705
Virginia	32	20	185	10	247	294	196	2,484	-------	2,974
Washington	17	------	81	34	132	248	------	1,322	-------	1,570
West Virginia			69	11	80			820		820
Wisconsin	4	5	169	17	195	58	56	2,412	-------	2,526
Wyoming			36	10	46			369		369
TERRITORIES.										
Alaska b										
Arizona			96	8	104			366		366
New Mexico			32	16	48			421		421
Oklahoma b										
Utah b										
District of Columbia	2	3	115	15	135	39	41	1,217	131	1,428
Total	460	333	6,859	1,626	9,278	4,616	4,449	90,332	3,515	102,912

a Includes general staff, signal corps, hospital and ambulance corps, naval brigade, cadet corps, etc.
b No organized militia.

Source: Statistical Abstract of the United States: 1893 Edition.

Section 10
National Security and Veterans Affairs

This section displays data for national security (national defense and homeland security) and benefits for veterans. Data are presented on national defense and its human and financial costs; active and reserve military personnel; and federally sponsored programs and benefits for veterans, and funding, budget and selected agencies for homeland security. The principal sources of these data are the annual *Selected Manpower Statistics* and the *Atlas/Data Abstract for the United States and Selected Areas* issued by the Office of the Secretary of Defense; *Annual Report of Secretary of Veterans Affairs*, Department of Veterans Affairs, *Budget in Brief*, Department of Homeland Security; and *The Budget of the United States Government*, Office of Management and Budget. For more data on expenditures and personnel, see Section 30.

Department of Defense (DOD)—The Department of Defense is responsible for providing the military forces of the United States. It includes the Office of the Secretary of Defense, the Joint Chiefs of Staff, the Army, the Navy, the Air Force, and the defense agencies. The President serves as Commander-in-Chief of the Armed Forces; from him, the authority flows to the Secretary of Defense and through the Joint Chiefs of Staff to the commanders of unified and specified commands (e.g., U.S. Strategic Command).

Reserve components—The Reserve Components of the Armed Forces consist of the Army National Guard of the United States, Army Reserve, Naval Reserve, Marine Corps Reserve, Air National Guard, Air Force Reserve, and Coast Guard Reserve. They provide trained personnel and units available for active duty in the Armed Forces during times of war or national emergency, and at such other times as national security may require. The National Guard has dual federal-state responsibilities and uses jointly provided equipment, facilities, and budget support. The President is empowered to mobilize the National Guard and to use such of the Armed Forces as he considers necessary to enforce federal authority in any state. There is in each Armed Force a Ready Reserve, a Standby Reserve, and a Retired Reserve. The Ready Reserve includes the Selected Reserve, which provides trained and ready units and individuals to augment the active forces during times of war or national emergency, or at other times when required; and the Individual Ready Reserves, which is a manpower pool, that can be called to active duty during times of war or national emergency and would normally be used as individual fillers for active, guard and reserve units, and as a source of combat replacements. Most of the Ready Reserve serves in an active status. The Standby Reserve cannot be called to active duty, other than for training, unless authorized by Congress under "full mobilization," and a determination is made that there are not enough qualified members in the Ready Reserve in the required categories who are readily available. The Retired Reserve represents a lower potential for involuntary mobilization.

Department of Veterans Affairs (VA)—The Department of Veterans Affairs administers laws authorizing benefits for eligible former and present members of the Armed Forces and for the beneficiaries of deceased members. Veterans benefits available under various acts of Congress include compensation for service-connected disability or death; vocational rehabilitation, education, and training; home loan insurance; life insurance; health care; special housing and automobiles or other conveyances for certain disabled veterans; burial and plot allowances; and educational assistance to families of deceased or totally disabled veterans, servicemen missing in action, or prisoners of war. Since these benefits are legislated by Congress, the dates they were enacted and the dates they apply to veterans may be different from the actual dates the conflicts occurred.

U.S. Census Bureau, Statistical Abstract of the United States: 2006

VA estimates of veterans cover all persons discharged from active U.S. military service under conditions other than dishonorable.

Homeland Security—In an effort to increase homeland security following the September 11, 2001, terrorist attacks on the United States, President George W. Bush issued the *National Strategy for Homeland Security* in July 2002 and signed legislation creating the Department of Homeland Security (DHS) in November 2002.

The *National Strategy* sets forth a plan to improve homeland security through 43 initiatives that fall within six critical mission areas. These mission areas are intelligence and warning, border and transportation security, domestic counterterrorism, protection of critical infrastructure, defense against catastrophic terrorism, and emergency preparedness and response. The first three mission areas focus primarily on preventing terrorist attacks; the next two on reducing our nation's vulnerabilities; and the final one on minimizing the damage and recovery from attacks that do occur.

The funding and activities of homeland security are not only carried out by DHS, but also by other federal agencies, state, and local entities. In addition to DHS, there are 32 other federal agencies that comprise federal homeland security funding. DHS, along with four other agencies—Department of Defense (DOD), Energy (DOE), Health and Human Services (HHS), and Justice (DOJ)—account for over 90 percent of federal spending for homeland security.

Department of Homeland Security (DHS)—The mission of DHS is to lead a unified effort to secure the United States. This effort is to prevent and deter terrorist attacks and to protect against and respond to threats and hazards to the nation. This effort is to ensure safe and secure borders, to welcome lawful immigrants and visitors, and to promote the free flow of commerce.

The creation of the Department of Homeland Security, which began operations in March 2003, represents a fusion of 22 federal agencies (legacy agencies) to coordinate and centralize the leadership of many homeland security activities under a single department. Twenty of these agencies are housed in one of the four major directorates of DHS. These four directorates are: Border and Transportation Security, Emergency Preparedness and Response, Science and Technology, and Information Analysis and Infrastruce. The Secret Service and Coast Guard remain intact and report directly to the Secretary. Immigration and Naturalization Services (INS) adjudications and benefits programs report directly to the Deputy Secretary as the U.S. Citizenship and Immigration Services (USCIS).

The Customs and Border Protection (CBP) is responsible for managing, securing, and controlling U.S. borders. This includes carrying out traditional border-related responsibilities, such as stemming the tide of illegal drugs and illegal aliens; securing and facilitating legitimate global trade and travel; and protecting the food supply and agriculture industry from pests and disease. CBP is composed of the Border Patrol and Inspections (both moved from INS) along with Customs (absorbed from the Department of Treasury) and Animal and Plant Health Inspections Services (absorbed from the Department of Agriculture).

Immigration and Customs Enforcement (ICE) is the largest investigation arm of DHS. ICE's mission is to prevent acts of terrorism by targeting the people, money, and materials that support terrorist and criminal activities. Selected responsibilities include the enforcement of immigration customs laws within the U.S., the protection of specified federal buildings, and air and marine enforcement. ICE is composed of five law enforcement divisions: Investigations, Intelligence, Federal Air Marshal Service, Federal Protective Service, and Apprehension, Detention, and Removal.

The Transportation Security Administration (TSA) was created as part of the Aviation and Transportation Security Act on November 19, 2001. TSA was originally part of the Department of Transportation, but was moved to Department of Homeland Security. TSA's mission is to provide security to our nation's transportation systems with a primary focus on aviation security.

336　National Security and Veterans Affairs

Figure 10.1
Department of Defense Manpower: 2004
(In thousands)

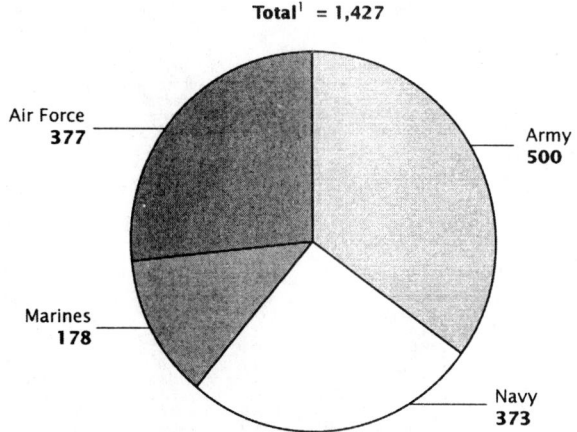

Total[1] = 1,427

Air Force
377

Army
500

Marines
178

Navy
373

[1] Includes National Guard, Reserve, and retired regular personnel on extended or continuous active duty. Excludes Coast Guard.

Source: Figure 10.1 prepared by U.S. Census Bureau. For data, see Table 501.

Figure 10.2
Living Veterans by Age: 2004
(In thousands)

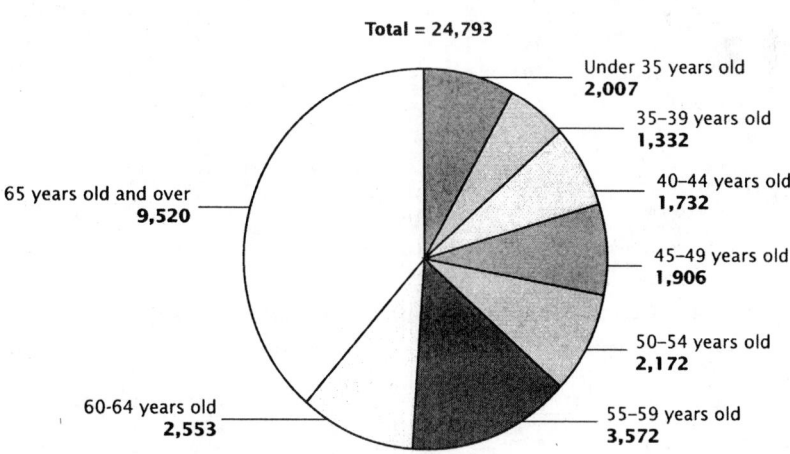

Total = 24,793

Under 35 years old
2,007

35–39 years old
1,332

40–44 years old
1,732

45–49 years old
1,906

50–54 years old
2,172

55–59 years old
3,572

65 years old and over
9,520

60-64 years old
2,553

Source: Figure 10.2 prepared by U.S. Census Bureau. For data, see Table 510.

Table 490. National Defense Outlays and Veterans Benefits: 1960 to 2006

[(53.5 represents $53,500,000,000). For fiscal year ending in year shown, see text, section 8. Includes outlays of Department of Defense, Department of Veterans Affairs, and other agencies for activities primarily related to national defense and veterans programs. For explanation of average annual percent change, see Guide to Tabular Presentation. Minus sign (-) indicates decrease]

Year	National defense and veterans outlays				Annual percent change [1]			Defense outlays percent of—	
	Total outlays (bil. dol.)	Defense outlays		Veterans' outlays (bil. dol.)	Total outlays	Defense outlays	Veterans' outlays	Federal outlays	Gross domestic product [2]
		Current dollars (bil. dol.)	Constant (FY2000) dollars (bil. dol.)						
1960	53.5	48.1	300.2	5.4	2.5	2.4	3.1	52.2	9.3
1965	56.3	50.6	291.8	5.7	-6.8	-7.6	0.7	42.8	7.4
1970	90.4	81.7	375.1	8.7	0.3	-1.0	13.6	41.8	8.1
1975	103.1	86.5	262.7	16.6	11.2	9.0	24.0	26.0	5.5
1980	155.1	134.0	267.1	21.1	13.9	15.2	6.3	22.7	4.9
1985	279.0	252.7	356.5	26.3	10.3	11.1	2.7	26.7	6.1
1990	328.4	299.3	382.7	29.1	-1.6	-1.4	-3.2	23.9	5.2
1993	326.8	291.1	340.3	35.7	-1.7	-2.4	4.7	20.7	4.4
1994	319.2	281.6	322.8	37.6	-2.3	-3.2	5.4	19.3	4.1
1995	310.0	272.1	305.9	37.9	-2.9	-3.4	0.8	17.9	3.7
1996	302.7	265.8	289.2	37.0	-2.3	-2.3	-2.4	17.0	3.5
1997	309.8	270.5	288.4	39.3	2.3	1.8	6.3	16.9	3.3
1998	310.2	268.5	282.6	41.8	0.1	-0.8	6.3	16.2	3.1
1999	320.2	274.9	283.7	43.2	3.2	2.4	3.4	16.1	3.0
2000	341.6	294.5	294.5	47.1	6.7	7.1	9.0	16.5	3.0
2001	350.5	305.5	297.5	45.0	2.6	3.7	-4.3	16.4	3.0
2002	399.5	348.6	330.8	51.0	14.0	14.1	13.2	17.3	3.4
2003	461.9	404.9	366.6	57.0	15.6	16.2	11.8	18.7	3.7
2004	515.7	455.9	404.7	59.8	11.6	12.6	4.8	19.9	3.9
2005, est. . . .	534.0	465.9	406.0	68.2	3.6	2.2	14.0	18.8	3.8
2006, est. . . .	515.8	447.4	383.4	68.4	-3.4	-4.0	0.3	17.4	3.5

[1] Change from immediate prior year; for 1960, change from 1955. [2] Represents fiscal year GDP; for definition, see text, Section 13.

Source: U.S. Office of Management and Budget, Budget of the United States Government, *Historical Tables*, annual. See also, <http://www.whitehouse.gov/omb/budget>.

Table 491. Federal Budget Outlays for Defense Functions: 1990 to 2005

[In billions of dollars (299.3 represents $299,300,000,000), except percent. For year ending September 30. Minus sign (-) indicates decrease]

Defense function	1990	1995	1997	1998	1999	2000	2001	2002	2003	2004	2005, est.
Total	299.3	272.1	270.5	268.5	274.9	294.5	305.5	348.6	404.9	455.9	465.9
Percent change [1]	-1.4	-3.4	1.8	-0.8	2.4	7.1	3.7	14.1	16.2	12.6	2.2
Defense Dept., military.	289.8	259.4	258.3	256.1	261.3	281.2	291.0	332.0	387.3	436.5	443.9
Military personnel	75.6	70.8	69.7	69.0	69.5	76.0	74.0	86.8	106.7	113.6	110.0
Operation, maintenance	88.3	91.0	92.4	93.4	96.3	105.9	112.0	130.0	151.4	174.0	174.5
Procurement.	81.0	55.0	47.7	48.2	48.8	51.7	55.0	62.5	67.9	76.2	80.2
Research and development. . .	37.5	34.6	37.0	37.4	37.4	37.6	40.5	44.4	53.1	60.8	65.6
Military construction.	5.1	6.8	6.2	6.0	5.5	5.1	5.0	5.1	5.9	6.3	6.6
Family housing	3.5	3.6	4.0	3.9	3.7	3.4	3.5	3.7	3.8	3.9	3.9
Other [2]	-1.2	-2.4	1.2	-1.9	0.1	1.6	1.1	-0.5	-1.5	1.7	3.2
Atomic energy activities [3]	9.0	11.8	11.3	11.3	12.2	12.1	12.9	14.8	16.0	16.6	18.7
Defense-related activities [4]	0.6	0.9	1.0	1.1	1.4	1.2	1.6	1.8	1.6	2.8	3.3

[1] Change from immediate prior year. [2] Revolving and management funds, trust funds, special foreign currency program, allowances, and offsetting receipts. [3] Defense activities only. [4] Includes civil defense activities.

Source: U.S. Office of Management and Budget, Budget of the United States Government, *Historical Tables*, annual. See also, <http://www.whitehouse.gov/omb/budget>.

Table 492. National Defense—Budget Authority and Outlays: 1990 to 2005

[In billions of dollars (303.3 represents $303,300,000,000). For year ending September 30.]

Item	1990	1995	1998	1999	2000	2001	2002	2003	2004	2005, est.
Defense (Budget authority) [1]	303.3	266.4	271.3	292.3	304.1	335.5	362.1	456.2	490.6	423.6
Department of Defense–Military	293.0	255.7	258.5	278.5	290.4	319.4	345.0	437.9	471.0	402.0
Atomic energy defense activities [1] . . .	9.7	10.1	11.7	12.4	12.4	14.3	15.2	16.4	16.8	18.0
Defense-related activities.	0.6	0.6	1.1	1.4	1.3	1.7	1.9	2.0	2.8	3.2
Defense (outlays) [1]	299.3	272.1	268.5	274.9	294.5	305.5	348.6	404.9	455.9	465.9
Department of Defense–Military	289.7	259.4	256.1	261.3	281.2	291.0	332.0	387.3	436.5	443.9
Atomic energy defense activities [1] . . .	9.0	11.8	11.3	12.2	12.1	12.9	14.8	16.0	16.6	18.7
Defense-related activities.	0.6	0.9	1.1	1.4	1.2	1.6	1.8	1.6	2.8	3.3

[1] Includes defense budget authority, balances, and outlays by other departments.

Source: U.S. Office of Management and Budget, Budget of the U.S. Government, *Historical Tables*, annual. See also, <http://www.whitehouse.gov/omb/budget>.

Table 493. **Military Prime Contract Awards to All Businesses by Program: 1990 to 2004**

[In billions of dollars (144.7 represents $144,700,000,000). Net values for year ending September 30. Includes all new prime contracts; debit or credit changes in contracts are also included. Actions cover official awards, amendments, or other changes in prime contracts to obtain military supplies, services, or construction. Excludes term contracts and contracts which do not obligate a firm total dollar amount or fixed quantity, but includes job orders, task orders, and delivery orders against such contracts]

DOD procurement program	1990	1995	1998	1999	2000	2001	2002	2003	2004
Total	144.7	131.4	128.8	135.2	143.0	154.1	180.6	219.5	241.0
Intragovernmental [1]	10.0	12.3	9.9	11.6	14.8	13.4	17.0	19.5	19.8
For work outside the U.S.	7.1	5.6	5.6	7.4	7.5	7.1	9.3	16.2	25.5
Educ. and nonprofit institutions	3.5	3.3	3.5	3.9	4.3	4.5	5.5	6.2	6.4
With business firms for work in the U.S. [2]	123.8	110.0	109.7	112.2	116.4	129.2	148.8	177.7	189.3
Major hard goods	79.1	56.0	56.0	57.5	59.8	67.9	76.1	90.6	99.0
Aircraft	24.0	18.8	20.8	23.3	28.8	30.5	30.6	41.1	40.4
Electronics and communication equip.	18.5	12.3	10.7	10.7	9.5	10.9	13.0	14.9	18.5
Missiles and space systems	17.1	10.6	9.9	9.5	8.2	8.2	11.2	13.3	14.6
Ships	10.3	9.1	8.6	7.8	8.3	12.0	11.4	10.2	12.3
Tanks, ammo. and weapons	9.2	5.3	6.0	6.2	5.0	6.3	9.8	11.0	13.3
Services	14.6	18.6	21.2	23.7	24.0	25.9	33.2	43.1	45.4

[1] Covers only purchases from other Federal agencies and reimbursable purchases on behalf of foreign governments.
[2] Includes Department of Defense. Includes other business not shown separately. Contracts awarded for work in U.S. possessions, and other areas subject to complete sovereignty of United States; contracts in a classified location; and any intragovernmental contracts entered into overseas.

Source: U.S. Department of Defense, Directorate for Information Operations and Reports, Prime Contract Awards, semiannual. See also <http://www.dior.whs.mil>.

Table 494. **U.S. Military Sales and Assistance to Foreign Governments: 1995 to 2003**

[In millions of dollars (8,080 represents $8,080,000,000). For year ending September 30. Department of Defense (DoD) sales deliveries cover deliveries against sales orders authorized under Arms Export Control Act, as well as earlier and applicable legislation. For details regarding individual programs, see source]

Item	1995	1996	1997	1998	1999	2000	2001	2002	2003
Military sales agreements	8,080	9,070	8,234	8,379	11,158	10,952	12,788	12,236	12,700
Military construction sales agreements	24	135	29	474	301	283	124	72	221
Military sales deliveries [1]	12,100	11,710	15,671	13,183	16,879	10,533	12,054	10,385	9,706
Military sales financing	3,712	3,836	3,530	3,420	3,370	4,333	3,535	4,040	5,956
Military assistance programs [2]	117	355	91	95	268	86	41	46	257
Military assistance program delivery [3]	14	31	113	91	13	10	15	26	175
IMET program/deliveries [4]	26	39	43	50	50	50	58	70	79

[1] Includes military construction sales deliveries. [2] Also includes Military Assistance Service Funded (MASF) program data, Section 506(a) drawdown authority, and MAP Merger Funds. [3] Includes Military Assistance Service Funded (MASF) program data and Section 506(a) drawdown authority. [4] International Military Education & Training. Includes Military Assistance Service Funded and emergency drawdowns.

Source: U.S. Department of Defense, Defense Security Cooperation Agency, DSCA Data and Statistics. See also <http://www.dsca.osd.mil/datastats.htm>.

Table 495. **U.S. Military Sales Deliveries by Selected Country: 1995 to 2003**

[In millions of dollars (12,100 represents $12,100,000,000). For year ending September 30. Represents Department of Defense military sales]

Country	1995	1996	1997	1998	1999	2000	2001	2002	2003
Total [1]	12,100	11,710	15,671	13,183	16,879	10,533	12,055	10,385	9,706
Australia	303	223	196	207	269	330	245	156	200
Bahrain	40	39	61	62	48	54	343	83	97
Belgium	8	157	107	194	250	58	170	68	72
Canada	127	154	83	111	96	84	110	85	164
China	1,332	829	2,370	1,423	2,505	785	1,166	1,418	637
Denmark	54	91	48	159	157	46	112	23	14
Egypt	1,479	1,083	897	551	448	805	862	1,950	1,032
France	65	52	57	35	248	217	142	207	169
Germany	261	404	208	191	278	136	390	222	245
Greece	220	210	691	397	463	315	448	454	1,329
Israel	327	386	456	1,195	1,214	562	741	650	829
Italy	54	77	51	43	106	41	97	103	188
Japan	693	753	488	409	442	477	494	476	411
Jordan	47	16	42	47	49	53	80	57	70
Korea, South	442	340	478	836	588	1,401	735	545	513
Kuwait	479	745	1,212	323	318	348	565	131	144
Netherlands	153	391	168	344	321	161	413	242	227
Norway	25	135	98	119	220	64	192	88	123
Portugal	88	19	70	21	12	20	42	28	116
Saudi Arabia	3,567	2,835	4,639	3,800	4,686	2,047	1,943	1,314	1,133
Singapore	59	80	133	232	549	131	244	422	169
Spain	193	411	216	133	324	141	267	178	160
Thailand	356	269	151	144	133	114	119	169	132
Turkey	368	481	1,153	532	856	217	466	280	498
United Arab Emirates	345	112	93	26	95	70	24	92	90
United Kingdom	419	401	432	430	366	347	525	386	364

[1] Includes countries not shown.
Source: U.S. Department of Defense, Defense Security Cooperation Agency, DSCA Data and Statistics. See also <http://www.dsca.osd.mil/datastats.htm>.

Table 496. Military and Civilian Personnel and Expenditures: 1990 to 2003

[Personnel in thousands (3,693 represents 3,693,000); expenditures in millions of dollars (209,904 represents 209,904,000,000). For year ending September 30. For definitions, see headnote, tables 497 and 499]

Item	1990	1995	2000	2001	2002	2003
Personnel, total [1] (1,000).............	3,693	3,391	2,791	2,781	2,811	2,806
Active duty military	1,185	1,085	984	991	1,045	1,071
Civilian	931	768	634	628	628	631
Reserve and National Guard...............	1,577	1,538	1,173	1,163	1,138	1,105
Expenditures, total [2]...............	209,904	209,695	229,072	243,778	276,281	316,648
Payroll outlays.........................	88,650	98,396	103,447	106,013	114,950	122,270
Active duty military pay.................	33,705	35,188	36,872	37,873	40,945	46,614
Civilian pay	28,230	29,932	29,935	29,879	32,805	35,041
Retired military pay	21,159	27,595	31,994	33,196	33,677	33,309
Reserve and National Guard pay	5,556	5,681	4,646	5,066	7,523	7,306
Prime contract awards [3]................	121,254	109,005	123,295	135,225	158,737	191,222
Grants	6,329	7,543	2,330	2,540	2,594	3,156

[1] Includes those based ashore and excludes those temporarily shore-based, in a transient status, or afloat.   [2] Includes expenditures not shown separately.   [3] Represents contract awards over $25,000.

Source: U.S. Department of Defense, Directorate for Information Operations and Reports, *Atlas/Data Abstract for the United States and Selected Areas*, annual. <http://www.dior.whs.mil/mmid/Pubs.htm>.

Table 497. Department of Defense Payroll and Contract Awards—States: 2003

[(In millions of dollars (122,270 represents $122,270,000,000); For year ending September 30. *Payroll outlays* include the gross earnings of civilian and active duty military personnel for services rendered to the government and for cash allowances for benefits. Excludes employer's share of employee benefits, accrued military retirement benefits and most permanent change-of-station costs. *Contracts*, refer to awards made in year specified; expenditures relating to awards may extend over several years]

State	Payroll Total	Retired military	Contract awards [1]	Grants	State	Payroll Total	Retired military	Contract awards [1]	Grants
U.S....	**122,270**	**33,309**	**191,222**	**3,156**	MO	1,804	531	6,558	50
AL	2,764	857	6,281	37	MT.......	353	118	200	25
AK	1,123	130	1,427	27	NE.......	779	221	315	38
AZ	2,314	939	7,505	69	NV.......	970	478	457	16
AR	888	390	588	39	NH.......	285	171	545	17
CA	13,272	3,467	28,681	407	NJ.......	1,657	316	3,793	66
CO	2,712	929	2,488	44	NM.......	1,245	385	973	32
CT	623	171	8,065	43	NY.......	2,017	470	4,320	155
DE	383	118	168	19	NC.......	5,632	1,275	2,091	68
DC	2,163	56	1,845	33	ND.......	435	57	280	27
FL	8,105	3,518	8,108	184	OH.......	2,523	646	4,326	76
GA	5,971	1,383	3,447	54	OK.......	2,671	517	1,515	11
HI	3,038	276	1,808	42	OR.......	660	341	491	14
ID	439	185	213	21	PA.......	2,521	708	5,491	176
IL	2,497	527	2,565	86	RI	608	102	489	18
IN	1,106	316	2,607	40	SC.......	2,807	883	1,540	51
IA	339	143	667	34	SD.......	292	91	208	38
KS	1,341	334	1,222	27	TN.......	1,297	736	2,190	33
KY	2,215	361	3,897	17	TX.......	9,799	3,244	22,868	128
LA	1,647	428	1,914	80	UT.......	1,343	217	1,899	23
ME.......	692	178	1,182	20	VT.......	136	52	464	20
MD.......	4,548	906	7,570	151	VA	14,187	3,214	19,978	64
MA.......	980	298	6,800	156	WA	4,774	1,208	3,217	56
MI	1,040	359	2,524	116	WV	316	138	207	26
MN.......	541	222	1,565	52	WI	539	235	1,271	59
MS.......	1,601	393	2,326	53	WY	279	72	76	19

[1] Military awards for supplies, services, and construction. Net value of contracts of over $25,000 for work in each state and DC. Figures reflect impact of prime contracting on state distribution of defense work. Often the State in which a prime contractor is located in is not the State where the subcontracted work is done. See also headnote, Table 493. Undistributed civilians and military personnel, their payrolls, and prime contract awards for performance in classified locations are excluded.

Source: U.S. Department of Defense, Directorate for Information Operations and Reports, *Atlas/Data Abstract for the United States and Selected Areas*, annual; <http://www.dior.whs.mil/mmid/Pubs.htm>.

Table 498. Expenditures and Personnel by Selected Major Locations: 2003

[In thousands of dollars (11,135,714 represents $11,135,714,000) except for personnel. For year ending September 30]

Major locations	Expenditures Total	Payroll outlays	Grants/ contracts	Major locations	Military and civilian personnel Total	Active duty military	Civilian
Fort Worth, TX.........	11,135,714	215,107	10,920,607	Fort Bragg, NC.......	48,206	42,634	5,572
San Diego, CA.........	7,340,029	3,180,150	4,159,879	Fort Hood, TX.......	47,163	43,522	3,641
St. Louis, MO	5,485,952	192,232	5,293,720	Camp Pendleton, CA...	37,262	35,043	2,219
Norfolk, VA	4,922,561	3,060,366	1,862,195	San Diego, CA	34,318	22,263	12,055
Long Beach, CA	4,229,385	55,972	4,173,413	Camp Lejeune, NC ...	33,628	30,845	2,783
Huntsville, AL	4,166,884	241,170	3,925,714	Fort Campbell, KY.....	28,131	25,760	2,371
Arlington, VA.........	3,953,990	1,908,465	2,045,525	Norfolk, VA..........	26,217	16,989	9,228
Sunnyvale, CA........	3,953,905	44,412	3,908,648	Arlington, VA	25,309	10,916	14,393
Washington, DC.......	3,281,861	1,403,730	1,878,131	Fort Benning, GA	22,954	19,881	3,073
Groton, CT...........	2,994,267	285,625	2,708,642	Washington, DC	22,918	8,979	13,930

Source: U.S. Department of Defense, Directorate for Information Operations and Reports, *Atlas/Data Abstract for the United States and Selected Areas*, annual. See also <http://www.dior.whs.mil/mmid/Pubs.htm>.

Table 499. Military and Civilian Personnel in Installations: 2003

[As of September 30. *Civilian employees* include United States citizens and foreign national direct- hire civilians subject to Office of Management and Budget (OMB) ceiling controls and civilian personnel involved in civil functions in the United States. Excludes indirect-hire civilians and those direct-hire civilians not subject to OMB ceiling controls. *Military personnel* include active duty personnel based ashore, excludes personnel temporarily shore-based in a transient status. or afloat]

State	Active military personnel				Reserve and National Guard, total	Civilian personnel			
	Total [1]	Army	Navy/ Marine Corps	Air Force		Total [1]	Army	Navy/ Marine Corps	Air Force
United States.	1,070,511	394,550	364,990	310,971	1,104,669	630,567	216,642	177,008	153,107
Alabama	10,815	6,018	740	4,057	28,615	20,672	16,791	41	2,408
Alaska	16,282	6,327	117	9,838	5,638	4,549	2,433	16	1,746
Arizona	24,156	5,524	6,248	12,384	17,800	8,618	3,801	441	3,350
Arkansas.	5,283	365	133	4,785	15,961	3,937	2,916	6	891
California.	130,473	8,145	101,670	20,658	90,800	57,631	7,139	32,745	10,213
Colorado	31,386	16,471	931	13,984	20,004	10,122	2,645	41	5,077
Connecticut	4,215	47	4,136	32	9,618	2,534	501	1,110	262
Delaware.	3,898	2	40	3,856	6,087	1,477	255	-	1,152
District of Columbia. . .	11,942	4,754	3,980	3,208	8,958	15,483	4,530	9,731	934
Florida	55,820	3,485	26,510	25,825	50,304	27,369	3,223	12,481	8,789
Georgia	68,016	52,424	4,945	10,647	38,088	30,588	10,701	3,993	13,653
Hawaii	34,203	15,985	13,542	4,676	11,398	16,602	4,304	9,293	1,961
Idaho	4,353	41	89	4,223	6,796	1,451	655	46	692
Illinois.	28,068	655	21,600	5,813	35,735	12,782	6,430	1,705	3,180
Indiana	1,104	526	457	121	24,244	9,032	1,812	3,285	1,070
Iowa	425	255	126	44	15,508	1,569	1,015	5	503
Kansas	16,547	13,264	163	3,120	14,962	5,925	4,456	1	1,098
Kentucky.	35,177	34,586	377	214	16,576	8,423	6,821	198	250
Louisiana	17,827	9,545	2,095	6,187	26,252	6,979	3,606	1,240	1,735
Maine.	2,764	245	2,484	35	6,812	6,267	339	5,250	273
Maryland.	30,649	7,138	15,640	7,871	24,598	31,913	12,253	15,395	2,238
Massachusetts	2,476	242	557	1,677	20,794	6,702	2,413	263	2,896
Michigan	1,372	442	791	139	24,895	7,945	5,008	24	1,169
Minnesota	763	273	402	88	22,287	2,622	1,557	18	830
Mississippi.	14,620	395	5,463	8,762	20,404	9,346	3,652	2,519	2,867
Missouri	15,685	9,358	2,227	4,100	26,935	9,131	5,837	256	1,204
Montana	3,713	25	17	3,671	5,813	1,217	481	-	684
Nebraska	7,449	121	563	6,765	8,797	3,713	1,415	16	1,908
Nevada	9,081	114	1,098	7,869	6,544	2,075	341	311	1,234
New Hampshire	347	11	276	60	5,114	1,061	567	46	285
New Jersey	6,818	1,129	824	4,865	22,003	13,776	9,301	2,092	1,546
New Mexico.	11,731	248	191	11,292	7,779	6,808	2,982	38	3,320
New York	21,450	17,715	3,297	438	45,047	11,149	6,891	156	2,556
North Carolina	96,560	42,701	43,840	10,019	31,253	16,742	6,160	7,329	1,276
North Dakota	7,740	21	28	7,691	5,470	1,747	527	2	1,126
Ohio.	7,069	463	618	5,988	38,987	21,865	1,344	70	12,322
Oklahoma	23,508	12,801	1,461	9,246	19,768	21,961	4,547	84	15,942
Oregon	808	220	511	77	14,072	3,185	2,270	21	866
Pennsylvania	3,423	1,121	2,037	265	48,013	24,777	8,269	7,711	1,544
Rhode Island	2,605	82	2,444	79	5,963	4,483	302	3,863	231
South Carolina	37,184	10,429	16,873	9,882	23,131	9,522	2,897	3,617	1,787
South Dakota	3,608	63	6	3,539	5,763	1,216	514	1	653
Tennessee.	2,648	327	2,084	237	25,343	5,338	2,619	1,000	975
Texas	114,196	63,861	7,657	42,678	76,523	38,018	18,205	1,536	14,389
Utah.	5,613	304	206	5,103	13,639	14,608	2,343	24	11,422
Vermont	53	11	28	14	4,657	590	316	1	238
Virginia	92,683	25,708	53,010	13,965	37,597	77,825	19,931	34,348	4,334
Washington	39,387	20,071	11,946	7,370	27,633	23,397	5,869	14,543	1,917
West Virginia	561	206	311	44	10,682	1,834	1,286	86	439
Wisconsin	564	280	200	84	21,623	2,957	1,960	10	892
Wyoming.	3,393	6	1	3,386	3,386	1,034	212	-	780

- Represents zero.   [1] Includes Other Defense Activities (ODA) not shown separately.

Source: U.S. Department of Defense, Directorate for Information Operations and Reports, *Selected Manpower Statistics,* annual; <http://www.dior.whs.mil/mmid/Pubs.htm>.

Table 500. Military Personnel on Active Duty by Location: 1980 to 2004

[In thousands (2,051 represents 2,051,000). As of September 30]

Location	1980	1985	1990	1995	1999	2000	2001	2002	2003	2004
Total	2,051	2,151	2,046	1,518	1,386	1,384	1,385	1,412	1,434	1,427
Shore-based [1]	1,840	1,920	1,794	1,351	1,241	1,237	1,244	1,262	1,287	1,291
Afloat [2]	211	231	252	167	145	147	141	150	147	136
United States [3]	1,562	1,636	1,437	1,280	1,133	1,127	1,130	1,181	1,182	1,139
Foreign countries	489	515	609	238	253	258	255	230	253	288

[1] Includes Navy personnel temporarily on shore.   [2] Includes Marine Corps.   [3] Includes Puerto Rico and Island areas.

Source: U.S. Department of Defense, Directorate for Information Operations and Reports, *Selected Manpower Statistics,* annual; <http://www.dior.whs.mil/mmid/Pubs.htm>.

National Security and Veterans Affairs   341

Table 501. Department of Defense Personnel: 1950 to 2004

[In thousands (1,459 represents 1,459,000.) As of end of fiscal year, see text, Section 8. Includes National Guard, Reserve, and retired regular personnel on extended or continuous active duty. Excludes Coast Guard. Other officer candidates are included under enlisted personnel]

		Army					Navy²					Marine Corps					Air Force				
Year	Total¹,²	Total¹	Male Officers	Male Enlisted	Female Officers	Female Enlisted	Total¹	Male Officers	Male Enlisted	Female Officers	Female Enlisted	Total¹	Male Officers	Male Enlisted	Female Officers	Female Enlisted	Total¹	Male Officers	Male Enlisted	Female Officers	Female Enlisted
1950	1,459	593	69	512	4.4	6.6	381	43	330	2.4	2.7	74	7	66	-	0.5	411	55	350	1.5	3.8
1955	2,935	1,109	117	978	5.2	7.7	661	72	577	2.9	5.7	205	18	185	0.1	2.1	960	134	815	3.1	8.3
1960	2,475	873	97	762	4.3	8.3	617	67	540	2.7	5.4	171	16	153	0.1	1.5	815	126	677	3.7	5.7
1965	2,654	969	108	846	3.8	8.5	670	75	583	2.6	5.3	190	17	172	0.1	1.4	825	128	685	4.1	4.7
1970	3,065	1,323	162	1,142	5.2	11.5	691	78	600	2.9	5.8	260	25	233	0.3	2.1	791	125	648	4.7	9.0
1975	2,128	784	98	640	4.6	37.7	535	62	449	3.7	17.5	196	19	174	0.3	2.8	613	100	478	5.0	25.2
1976	2,082	779	94	634	4.8	43.8	525	60	439	3.5	19.3	192	19	171	0.4	3.1	585	95	452	5.0	29.2
1977	2,075	782	92	634	5.7	46.1	530	59	443	3.8	19.5	192	19	169	0.4	3.5	571	91	435	5.4	34.6
1978	2,062	772	92	619	6.3	50.5	530	59	442	4.0	21.3	191	18	167	0.4	4.7	570	89	429	6.0	41.1
1979	2,027	759	90	602	6.9	55.2	523	58	432	4.4	25.0	185	18	161	0.5	5.5	560	89	413	7.3	46.4
1980	2,051	777	91	612	7.6	61.7	527	58	430	4.9	30.1	189	18	164	0.5	6.2	558	90	404	8.5	51.9
1981	2,083	781	94	610	8.3	65.3	540	60	435	5.3	34.6	191	17	165	0.5	7.1	570	90	413	9.1	54.4
1982	2,109	780	94	609	9.0	64.1	553	61	444	5.7	37.3	192	18	165	0.6	7.9	583	92	421	9.9	54.5
1983	2,123	780	97	602	9.5	66.5	558	62	444	6.3	40.8	194	19	166	0.6	8.3	592	94	428	10.6	55.3
1984	2,138	780	98	601	10.2	67.1	565	62	448	6.6	42.6	196	19	167	0.6	8.6	597	95	430	11.2	55.9
1985	2,151	781	99	599	10.8	68.4	571	64	449	6.9	45.7	198	19	169	0.7	9.0	602	96	431	11.9	58.1
1986	2,169	781	99	597	11.3	69.7	581	65	457	7.3	47.2	200	19	170	0.6	9.2	608	97	434	12.4	61.2
1987	2,174	781	96	596	11.6	71.6	587	65	462	7.2	47.7	200	19	170	0.6	9.1	607	94	432	12.6	63.2
1988	2,138	772	95	588	11.8	72.0	593	65	466	7.3	49.7	197	19	168	0.7	9.0	576	92	405	12.9	61.5
1989	2,130	770	95	584	12.2	74.3	593	65	464	7.5	52.1	197	19	168	0.7	9.0	571	91	399	13.4	63.7
1990	2,044	732	92	553	12.4	71.2	579	64	451	7.8	52.1	197	19	168	0.7	8.7	535	87	370	13.3	60.8
1991	1,986	711	91	535	12.5	67.8	570	63	444	8.0	51.4	194	19	166	0.7	8.3	510	84	350	13.3	59.1
1992	1,807	610	83	449	11.7	61.7	542	61	417	8.3	51.0	185	18	157	0.6	7.9	470	77	320	12.7	56.1
1993	1,705	572	77	420	11.1	60.2	510	58	390	8.3	49.3	178	17	153	0.6	7.2	444	72	302	12.3	54.5
1994	1,610	541	74	394	10.9	59.0	469	54	355	8.0	47.9	174	17	149	0.6	7.0	426	69	287	12.3	54.0
1995	1,518	509	72	365	10.8	57.3	435	51	324	7.9	47.9	175	17	150	0.7	7.4	400	66	266	12.1	52.1
1996	1,472	492	70	347	10.6	59.0	417	50	308	7.8	46.9	175	17	149	0.8	7.8	389	64	256	12.0	52.8
1997	1,439	492	69	346	10.4	62.4	396	48	290	7.8	44.8	174	17	148	0.8	8.5	377	62	246	12.0	53.8
1998	1,407	484	68	340	10.4	61.4	382	47	280	7.8	42.9	173	17	148	0.9	8.9	368	60	237	11.8	54.2
1999	1,386	479	67	337	10.5	61.5	373	46	271	7.7	43.9	173	17	145	0.9	9.3	361	58	232	11.8	54.6
2000	1,384	482	66	339	10.8	62.9	373	46	272	7.8	43.8	173	17	146	0.9	9.5	356	57	227	11.8	55.0
2001	1,385	481	65	337	11.0	62.9	378	46	273	8.0	46.6	173	17	145	1.0	9.6	354	57	224	12.0	55.6
2002	1,414	487	66	341	11.5	63.2	385	47	279	8.2	47.3	174	17	146	1.0	9.5	368	59	233	12.9	58.6
2003	1,434	499	68	352	12.0	63.5	382	47	276	8.2	47.3	178	18	149	1.1	9.6	375	61	237	13.5	60.0
2004	1,427	500	69	358	12.3	61.0	373	46	273	8.1	46.1	178	18	149	1.1	9.7	377	61	242	13.6	60.2

- Rounds to zero.   ¹ Includes cadets, midshipmen and other not shown separately.   ² Beginning 1980, excludes Navy Reserve personnel on active duty for Training and Administration of Reserves (TARS).

Source: U.S. Department of Defense. Selected Manpower Statistics. annual. See also <http://www.dior.whs.mil/mmid/pubs.htm>.

Table 502. **U.S. Military Personnel on Active Duty in Selected Foreign Countries: 1995 to 2004**

[As of September 30]

Country	1995	1998	1999	2000	2001	2002	2003	2004
In foreign countries [1]...	238,064	259,871	252,763	257,817	254,788	230,484	252,764	287,802
Ashore.............	208,836	218,957	207,131	212,858	211,947	208,479	226,570	265,594
Afloat..............	29,228	40,914	45,632	44,959	42,841	22,005	26,194	20,208
Argentina..............	26	27	24	26	22	28	28	29
Australia.............	314	322	323	175	803	171	574	196
Austria................	35	24	31	18	24	20	24	21
Bahamas, The..........	36	24	23	24	64	22	25	41
Bahrain	618	916	1,511	949	2,065	1,560	1,514	1,712
Belgium..............	1,689	1,645	1,649	1,554	1,578	1,458	1,526	1,474
Bosnia and Herzegovina.....	1	6,912	5,800	5,708	3,116	3,082	3,041	951
Brazil................	50	36	43	38	39	27	34	37
Canada	214	156	150	156	163	148	141	156
Chile	28	21	30	26	337	28	25	23
China	30	53	57	74	57	61	53	63
Colombia.............	44	30	41	224	63	39	54	55
Cuba (Guantanamo).......	5,129	1,348	1,030	688	557	549	697	682
Cyprus...............	24	52	38	41	30	28	34	20
Denmark ...[2]...........	37	38	32	26	28	22	21	22
Diego Garcia [2]	897	715	670	625	590	548	528	816
Dominican Republic	13	11	11	12	14	55	14	14
Ecuador..............	86	367	21	20	22	35	33	32
Egypt	1,123	1,041	892	499	500	433	385	348
El Salvador............	25	21	30	27	26	23	21	23
France................	67	60	73	67	71	74	93	77
Germany	73,280	69,663	65,538	69,203	70,998	68,701	74,796	76,058
Greece	489	441	652	678	506	593	583	473
Greenland	131	130	129	125	153	88	139	133
Haiti	1,616	356	59	21	13	15	13	26
Honduras.............	193	594	513	351	394	402	414	448
Hungary..............	16	1,379	87	375	29	19	15	18
Iceland	1,982	1,651	1,681	1,636	1,743	1,665	1,747	1,491
India	27	21	25	20	18	19	26	30
Indonesia.............	46	41	50	51	43	28	21	24
Israel................	46	35	35	36	35	36	36	34
Italy.................	12,007	11,519	11,530	11,190	11,704	12,466	13,152	12,606
Japan	39,134	40,364	40,338	40,159	40,217	41,848	40,519	36,365
Jordan...............	24	35	27	29	18	32	24	25
Kenya	40	86	95	21	62	43	33	33
Korea, Republic of	36,016	36,880	35,913	36,565	37,605	37,743	41,145	40,840
Kuwait...............	771	3,921	4,011	4,602	4,208	567	([3])	([3])
Macedonia, The Former Yugoslav, Republic of	591	442	1,100	347	351	146	41	40
Mexico...............	36	25	33	29	27	31	30	32
Netherlands	687	685	673	659	676	629	703	701
Norway	57	96	95	81	83	123	86	84
Oman	27	97	101	251	673	31	32	34
Pakistan..............	28	22	26	22	21	31	33	33
Philippines	126	29	84	79	35	86	107	47
Portugal..............	1,066	1,033	1,024	1,005	1,005	992	1,094	1,006
Qatar................	2	25	39	52	116	71	2,997	273
Russia...............	60	56	88	101	20	78	78	84
Saudi Arabia...........	1,077	4,873	5,552	7,053	4,805	776	953	235
Serbia and Montenegro	13	37	6,410	5,427	5,679	2,804	319	1,814
Singapore	166	152	167	411	160	167	171	237
South Africa	24	34	32	34	31	32	31	31
Spain	2,799	3,219	2,127	2,007	1,990	2,621	1,893	2,012
Switzerland............	26	21	18	19	18	19	18	18
Thailand..............	99	124	120	526	113	125	132	122
Tunisia...............	20	14	13	12	15	17	15	15
Turkey...............	3,111	2,518	2,312	2,006	2,153	1,587	2,021	1,762
Ukraine	5	15	18	16	10	13	13	14
United Arab Emirates	30	313	679	402	204	21	73	149
United Kingdom..........	12,131	10,156	11,311	11,207	11,318	10,258	11,616	11,469
Venezuela	35	28	30	28	31	27	21	28
Operation Iraqi Freedom [4]....	(X)	(X)	(X)	(X)	(X)	(X)	183,002	170,647

X Not applicable.   [1] Includes areas not shown separately.   [2] British Indian Ocean Territory.   [3] See footnote 4.   [4] Total (in/around Iraq as of September 30)-includes Reserve/National Guard.

Source: U.S. Department of Defense, *Selected Manpower Statistics*, annual. See also <http://www.dior.whs.mil/mmid/pubs.htm>.

National Security and Veterans Affairs 343

Table 503. **U.S. Active Duty Military Deaths by Manner of Death: 1980 to 2004**

[As of end of Dec. 31. Table reflects addition of calendar years 2003-2004 data and updates to death figures throughout.

Manner of death	1980-2004	1980	1990	1995	1997	1998	1999	2000	2001	2002	2003	2004
Deaths, total	**38,503**	**2,392**	**1,507**	**1,040**	**817**	**827**	**796**	**758**	**891**	**999**	**1,410**	**1,887**
Accident	21,757	1,556	880	538	433	445	436	398	437	547	560	565
Hostile action	1,331	-	-	-	-	-	-	-	3	18	344	737
Homicide	1,995	174	74	67	42	26	37	34	49	51	41	40
Illness	6,956	419	277	174	170	168	150	138	185	190	232	252
Pending	210	-	-	-	-	10	13	-	1	6	17	163
Self-inflicted	5,353	231	232	250	159	161	145	151	140	160	197	126
Terrorist attack	426	1	1	7	-	3	-	17	55	-	-	-
Undetermined	475	11	43	4	13	14	15	20	21	27	19	4

- Represents zero.

Source: U.S. Department of Defense, Directorate for Information Operations and Reports, Statistical Information Analysis Division, Personnel; <http://www.dior.whs.mil/mmid/casualty/castop.htm> (released 8 July 2005).

Table 504. **Armed Forces Personnel—Summary of Major Conflicts**

[For Revolutionary War, number of personnel serving not known, but estimates range from 184,000 to 250,000; for War of 1812, 286,730 served; for Mexican War, 78,718 served. Dates of the major conflicts may differ from those specified in various laws providing benefits for veterans]

Item	Unit	Civil War [1]	World War I	World War II	Korean conflict	Vietnam conflict	Persian Gulf War
Personnel serving [2]	1,000	2,213	4,735	[3]16,113	[4]5,720	[5]8,744	2,233
Average duration of service	Months . . .	20	12	33	19	23	(NA)
Service abroad: Personnel serving . . .	Percent . .	(NA)	53	73	[6]56	(NA)	(NA)
Average duration [7]	Months . . .	(NA)	6	16	13	(NA)	(NA)
Casualties: [8] Battle deaths [2]	1,000	140	53	292	34	[9]47	(Z)
Other deaths	1,000	224	63	114	3	11	(Z)
Wounds not mortal [2]	1,000	282	204	671	103	[9]153	(Z)
Draftees: Classified	1,000	777	24,234	36,677	9,123	[5]75,717	(X)
Examined	1,000	522	3,764	17,955	3,685	[5]8,611	(X)
Rejected	1,000	160	803	6,420	1,189	[5]3,880	(X)
Inducted	1,000	46	2,820	10,022	1,560	[5]1,759	(X)

NA Not available.   X Not applicable.   Z Fewer than 500.   [1] Union forces only. Estimates of the number serving in Confederate forces range from 600,000 to 1.5 million.   [2] Source: U.S. Department of Defense, *Selected Manpower Statistics*, annual.   [3] Covers Dec. 1, 1941, to Dec. 31, 1946.   [4] Covers June 25, 1950, to July 27, 1953.   [5] Covers Aug. 4, 1964, to Jan. 27, 1973.   [6] Excludes Navy. Covers July 1950, through Jan. 1955. Far East area only.   [7] During hostilities only.   [8] For periods covered, see footnotes 3, 4, and 5.   [9] Covers Jan.1, 1961, to Jan. 27, 1973. Includes known military service personnel who have died from combat related wounds.

Source: Except as noted, the President's Commission on Veterans' Pensions, *Veterans' Benefits in the United States*, Vol. I, 1956; and U.S. Department of Defense, unpublished data; <http://www.dior.whs.mil/mmid/casualty/castop.htm>.

Table 505. **Military Personnel on Active Duty by Rank or Grade: 1990 to 2004**

[In thousands (2,043.7 represents 2,043,700). As of Sept. 30]

Rank/grade	1990	1995	2000	2001	2002	2003	2004
Total	**2,043.7**	**1,518.2**	**1,384.3**	**1,385.1**	**1,411.6**	**1,434.4**	**1,426.8**
General-Admiral	(Z)	(Z)	(Z)	(Z)	(Z)	(Z)	(Z)
Lieutenant General-Vice Admiral	0.1	0.1	0.1	0.1	0.1	0.1	0.1
Major General-Rear Admiral (U)	0.4	0.3	0.3	0.3	0.3	0.3	0.3
Brigadier General-Rear Admiral (L) . . .	0.5	0.4	0.4	0.4	0.4	0.4	0.4
Colonel-Captain	14.0	11.7	11.3	11.2	11.4	11.6	11.5
Lieutenant Colonel-Commander	32.3	28.7	27.5	27.2	28.2	28.5	28.4
Major-Lieutenant Commander.	53.2	43.9	43.2	43.1	43.6	44.1	44.0
Captain-Lieutenant	106.6	84.3	68.1	66.0	66.5	68.1	69.5
1st Lieutenant-Lieutenant (JG)	37.9	26.1	24.7	25.7	28.1	29.9	31.1
2nd Lieutenant-Ensign	31.9	25.6	26.4	28.1	29.0	29.1	26.9
Chief Warrant Officer W-5	(Z)	(Z)	0.1	0.1	0.1	0.1	0.1
Chief Warrant Officer W-4	3.0	2.2	2.0	1.9	2.0	2.1	1.9
Chief Warrant Officer W-3	5.0	4.5	3.8	3.9	4.3	4.6	4.1
Chief Warrant Officer W-2	8.4	7.4	6.7	6.5	6.2	6.2	6.0
Warrant Officer W-1	3.2	2.0	2.1	2.2	2.3	2.4	3.1
E-9	15.3	11.1	10.2	10.4	10.6	10.8	10.7
E-8	38.0	28.8	26.0	26.7	27.0	27.7	27.1
E-7	134.1	109.3	97.7	98.4	101.9	101.4	99.6
E-6	239.1	180.5	164.9	164.9	170.0	172.4	173.1
E-5	361.5	261.4	229.5	239.7	242.5	250.7	251.1
E-4	427.8	317.2	251.0	240.1	248.1	264.5	264.1
E-3	280.1	197.1	196.3	210.4	219.6	222.1	220.1
E-2	140.3	99.7	99.0	92.4	91.8	85.1	84.3
E-1	97.6	63.4	80.0	72.5	64.7	59.2	55.8
Cadets and Midshipmen	**13.3**	**12.1**	**12.5**	**12.8**	**12.5**	**12.6**	**12.6**

Z Fewer than 50.

Source: U.S. Department of Defense, Directorate of Information Operations and Reports, *Selected Manpower Statistics*, annual. See also <http://www.dior.whs.mil/mmid/military/miltop.htm>.

Table 506. **Military Reserve Personnel: 1990 to 2004**

[As of September 30. The Ready Reserve includes the Selected Reserve which is scheduled to augment active forces during times of war or national emergency, and the Individual Ready Reserve which, during times of war or national emergency, would be used to fill out Active, Guard and Reserve units, and which would also be a source for casualty replacements; Ready Reservists serve in an active status (except for the Inactive National Guard—a very small pool within the Army National Guard). The Standby Reserve cannot be called to active duty, other than for training, unless authorized by Congress under "full mobilization," and a determination is made that there are not enough qualified members in the Ready Reserve in the required categories who are readily available. The Retired Reserve represents a lower potential for involuntary mobilization.]

Reserve status and branch·of service	1990	1995	2000	2001	2002	2003	2004
Total reserves [1]	1,688,674	1,674,164	1,276,843	1,249,043	1,222,337	1,188,851	1,166,937
Ready reserve	1,658,707	1,648,388	1,251,452	1,224,121	1,199,321	1,167,101	1,145,035
Army [2]	1,049,579	999,462	725,771	713,251	699,548	682,522	663,209
Navy	240,228	267,356	184,080	168,454	159,098	152,855	148,643
Marine Corps	81,355	103,668	99,855	99,377	97,944	98,868	101,443
Air Force [3]	270,313	263,011	229,009	230,182	229,798	219,895	219,159
Coast Guard	17,232	14,891	12,737	12,857	12,933	12,961	12,581
Standby reserve	29,967	25,776	25,391	24,922	23,016	21,750	21,902
Army	788	1,128	701	753	726	744	715
Navy	11,791	12,707	7,213	5,650	4,051	2,520	2,502
Marine Corps	1,424	216	895	507	605	685	992
Air Force	15,369	11,453	16,429	17,826	17,430	17,578	17,340
Coast Guard	595	272	153	186	204	223	353
Retired reserve	462,371	505,905	573,305	580,785	590,018	601,611	614,904
Army	223,919	259,553	296,004	299,233	304,524	308,820	315,477
Navy	111,961	97,532	109,531	111,485	112,374	113,485	115,210
Marine Corps	9,101	11,319	12,937	13,352	13,672	13,926	14,319
Air Force	117,390	137,501	154,833	156,715	159,448	165,380	169,898

[1] Less retired reserves.   [2] Includes Army National Guard.   [3] Includes Air National Guard.

Source: U.S. Department of Defense, *Official Guard and Reserve Manpower Strengths and Statistics, quarterly.* See also <http://www.dior.whs.mil/mmid/pubs.htm>.

Table 507. **Ready Reserve Personnel Profile—Race and Sex: 1990 to 2004**

[In thousands (1,658.7 represents 1,658,700). As of September 30]

Year	Race						Sex			
					American		Officer		Enlisted	
	Total [1]	White	Black	Asian	Indian	Hispanic [2]	Male	Female	Male	Female
1990	1,658.7	1,304.6	272.3	14.9	7.8	83.1	226.8	40.5	1,204.7	186.7
1992	1,876.4	1,459.5	309. ̄	20.2	9.3	95.4	232.7	44.7	1,382.4	216.6
1993	1,858.1	1,440.7	310.5	21.3	9.2	98.2	232.5	46.3	1,365.6	213.7
1994	1,795.8	1,380.9	298.3	22.4	9.0	99.1	223.9	46.2	1,315.8	210.0
1995	1,648.4	1,267.7	274.5	22.0	8.8	96.2	209.9	44.7	1,196.8	196.9
1996	1,536.6	1,179.0	249.8	21.5	8.6	93.1	196.9	43.6	1,108.8	187.4
1997	1,451.0	1,113.7	230.6	21.7	8.4	91.5	188.7	43.2	1,037.6	181.5
1998	1,353.4	1,033.9	210.4	21.7	7.8	88.2	175.9	40.3	964.1	173.1
1999	1,288.8	980.0	202.6	22.6	7.6	88.9	166.2	38.4	911.2	173.1
2000	1,251.5	942.2	199.6	26.7	8.4	91.8	159.4	36.9	879.9	175.3
2001	1,224.1	912.7	198.4	27.9	8.5	94.3	158.0	36.6	852.2	177.3
2002	1,199.3	891.3	193.2	27.9	8.8	96.0	152.1	35.6	835.2	176.4
2003	1,167.1	865.7	187.5	25.4	8.5	98.0	145.1	34.0	813.7	174.3
2004	1,145.0	845.3	181.3	26.2	9.1	100.2	141.9	33.6	799.7	169.8

[1] Race subgroups do not sum to equal the total. "Pacific Islanders, Other, and Unknowns" are not listed.   [2] Persons of Hispanic origin may be of any race.

Source: U.S. Department of Defense, *Official Guard and Reserve Manpower Strengths and Statistics,* annual. See also <http://www.dior.whs.mil/mmid/pubs.htm>.

Table 508. **National Guard—Summary: 1980 to 2004**

[In thousands (368 represents 368,000). As of September 30]

Item	Unit	1980	1985	1990	1995	2000	2001	2002	2003	2004
Army National Guard:										
Units	Number . . .	3,379	4,353	4,055	5,872	5,300	5,200	5,150	5,100	[1]5,100
Personnel [2]	1,000	368	438	444	375	353	352	352	351	343
Females	1,000	17	23	31	31	38	42	43	44	(NA)
Funds obligated [3]	Bil. dol. . . .	1.8	4.4	5.2	6.0	6.9	7.7	8.0	10.0	[4]8.3
Value of equipment	Bil. dol. . . .	7.6	18.8	29.0	33.0	35.0	35.0	35.0	36.0	[5]26.0
Air National Guard:										
Units	Number . . .	1,054	1,184	1,339	1,604	1,550	1,500	1,500	1,500	1,500
Personnel [2]	1,000	96	109	118	110	106	109	112	108	108
Females	1,000	8	12	(NA)	16	(NA)	(NA)	(NA)	(NA)	(NA)
Funds obligated [3]	Bil. dol. . . .	1.7	2.8	3.2	4.2	5.6	5.8	6.8	6.4	7.6
Value of equipment (est.) [6] . . .	Bil. dol. . . .	5.2	21.4	26.4	38.3	44.0	44.0	44.0	44.0	44.0

NA Not available.   [1] Includes units on active duty.   [2] Officers and enlisted personnel.   [3] Federal funds; includes personnel, operations, maintenance, and military construction.   [4] Decrease due to units being mobilized for Gulf war operations.   [5] Decreased due to equipment left overseas by mobilized units.   [6] Beginning 1985, increase due to repricing of aircraft to current year dollars to reflect true replacement value. Beginning 1995, includes value of aircraft and support equipment.

Source: National Guard Bureau, *Annual Review of the Chief, National Guard Bureau;* and unpublished data. See also <http://www.ang.af.mil> and <http://www.arng.army.mil>.

Table 509. Veterans by Sex, Period of Service, and State: 2004

[In thousands (24,523 represents 24,523,000). As of September 30. VetPop 2004 Ver 1.0 is the Department of Veterans Affairs (VA's) new official estimate and projection of the veteran population as of December 31, 2004. It is based on published Census 2000 data that has been supplemented by special data extracts prepared for the VA Office of the Actuary by the Census Bureau. This estimate and projection is also based on data provided by the Defense Manpower Data Center on service member separations from active duty, information from the DoD Office of the Actuary, and Department of Veterans Affairs administrative data from the Veterans Benefits Administration and the Veterans Health Administration.]

State	Total veterans [1,2] Total	Male	Female	Gulf War [3]	Vietnam era	Korean conflict	World War II	Peacetime
United States.....	24,523	22,849	1,675	4,065	8,064	3,376	3,877	6,244
Alabama............	426	396	30	81	143	62	59	108
Alaska.............	67	60	7	18	27	5	4	17
Arizona............	555	513	42	93	177	87	97	135
Arkansas...........	268	251	17	46	89	37	42	69
California..........	2,311	2,146	165	361	775	330	384	580
Colorado...........	428	393	35	89	155	50	50	108
Connecticut.........	269	254	15	28	85	41	53	69
Delaware...........	81	75	6	13	27	11	12	22
District of Columbia	37	34	3	6	12	6	7	10
Florida.............	1,788	1,659	129	277	530	294	371	434
Georgia............	760	694	66	179	258	84	78	203
Hawaii.............	107	99	9	20	39	15	16	25
Idaho..............	133	124	9	28	44	17	19	32
Illinois.............	897	844	52	133	283	123	152	228
Indiana............	551	519	32	84	178	71	80	152
Iowa..............	266	252	13	37	88	39	45	64
Kansas............	246	231	16	43	84	32	39	59
Kentucky	360	338	22	62	121	48	51	92
Louisiana	367	340	27	72	120	47	54	90
Maine..............	144	134	9	20	49	21	22	38
Maryland...........	486	443	43	95	158	59	66	132
Massachusetts.......	491	462	28	54	150	76	99	127
Michigan...........	837	790	47	116	274	109	132	224
Minnesota..........	427	404	23	55	147	58	64	114
Mississippi	240	223	18	49	76	34	34	60
Missouri	555	520	34	85	182	78	85	145
Montana...........	103	96	7	16	37	14	15	25
Nebraska	159	149	11	28	53	24	24	37
Nevada	244	225	19	41	86	35	33	64
New Hampshire.......	131	123	8	18	45	18	19	37
New Jersey.........	583	552	30	62	175	91	118	152
New Mexico	180	166	15	32	64	25	26	44
New York	1,172	1,105	67	137	350	176	225	309
North Carolina.......	767	708	59	154	253	99	102	198
North Dakota........	55	52	4	10	19	7	8	13
Ohio	1,052	990	62	155	336	137	170	281
Oklahoma..........	355	332	23	65	126	48	52	83
Oregon............	367	342	25	53	130	47	58	94
Pennsylvania........	1,146	1,083	63	134	352	170	227	296
Rhode Island........	91	86	5	11	29	14	18	23
South Carolina.......	414	382	31	86	142	54	52	106
South Dakota........	73	68	5	13	24	11	11	17
Tennessee	541	505	36	97	188	69	70	143
Texas..............	1,682	1,552	130	354	583	209	224	408
Utah	151	142	9	29	49	21	24	35
Vermont	58	54	4	7	19	8	9	16
Virginia............	751	677	74	196	263	88	86	180
Washington.........	633	583	49	122	231	76	82	160
West Virginia........	188	178	10	27	64	27	30	46
Wisconsin..........	475	448	27	65	153	65	74	129
Wyoming	55	51	4	11	20	7	7	12

[1] Veterans serving in more than one period of service are counted only once in the total. [2] Current civilians discharged from active duty, other than for training only without service-connected disability. [3] Service from August 2, 1990, to the present. Source: Department of Veterans Affairs, Office of Policy, Planning & Preparedness. Annual Report of the Secretary of Veterans Affairs <http://www.va.gov/vetdata/ProgramStatistcs/index.htm>.

Table 510. Veterans Living by Age and Period of Service: 2004

[In thousands (24,793 represents 24,793,000). As of September 30. Includes those living outside U.S. See headnote, Table 509]

Age	Total veterans	Wartime veterans Total [1]	Gulf War [2]	Vietnam era	Korean conflict	World War II	Peacetime veterans
Total...........	24,793	18,477	4,105	8,147	3,423	3,916	6,316
Under 35 years old.....	2,007	1,946	1,946	-	-	-	61
35-39 years old	1,332	768	768	-	-	-	564
40-44 years old	1,732	520	520	-	-	-	1,212
45-49 years old	1,906	738	383	393	-	-	1,168
50-54 years old	2,172	1,858	267	1,731	-	-	314
55-59 years old	3,572	3,448	151	3,409	-	-	124
60-64 years old	2,553	1,762	48	1,755	-	-	791
65 years old and over ...	9,520	7,437	22	859	3,423	3,916	2,083
Female, total.........	1,692	1,130	647	262	80	178	562

- Represents or rounds to zero. [1] Veterans who served in more than one wartime period are counted only once in the total.
[2] Service from August 2, 1990, to the present.
Source: U.S. Dept. of Veterans Affairs, VetPop 2004, Ver 1.0, VA Office of the Actuary <http://www.va.gov/vetdata/demographics>.

Table 511. **Veterans by Sex, Race, and Hispanic or Latino Origin: 2000**
[In thousands (26,403.7 represents 26,403,700). As of April 1. Data are based on a sample from the census. See Appendix III.]

Characteristics	Total number	18 to 64 years	65 years and over
Total...............................	26,403.7	16,740.2	9,663.5
Sex:			
Male	24,810.4	15,494.6	9,315.9
Female	1,593.3	1,245.6	347.7
White alone	22,573.0	13,710.5	8,862.5
Male	21,373.2	12,829.6	8,543.6
Female	1,199.9	881.0	318.9
Black or African American alone	2,572.0	2,021.9	550.1
Male	2,297.6	1,765.8	531.8
Female	274.4	256.1	18.3
American Indian/Alaska Native alone	195.9	160.3	35.6
Male	177.9	143.8	34.0
Female	18.0	16.5	1.5
Asian alone	284.3	198.4	85.9
Male	261.3	178.4	82.9
Female	23.0	20.0	3.0
Native Hawaiian, and other Pacific Islander alone...	28.6	23.9	4.6
Male	25.6	21.2	4.4
Female	3.0	2.7	0.2
Some other race alone	367.9	321.3	46.6
Male	333.3	288.5	44.8
Female	34.6	32.8	1.7
Hispanic or Latino origin [1]	1,139.2	905.5	233.7
Male	1,045.9	820.2	225.7
Female	93.3	85.3	8.0

[1] Persons of Hispanic or Latino origin may be of any race.
Source: U.S. Census Bureau, American FactFinder, 2000 Census of Population and Housing, Summary File 3, tables P39, PCT66A, PCT 66B, PCT66C, PCT66D, PCT 66E, PCT 66F, PCT66G, PCT 66H and P66 (accessed 30 March 2004) <http://www.census.gov/Press-Release/www/2002/sumfile3.html>.

Table 512. **Veterans Benefits—Expenditures by Program and Compensation for Service-Connected Disabilities: 1980 to 2004**
[In millions of dollars (23,187 represents $23,187,000,000). For year ending September 30.]

Program	1980	1990	1995	1999	2000	2001	2002	2003	2004
Total	23,187	28,998	37,775	43,166	47,086	45,037	50,882	56,892	59,555
Medical programs...............	6,042	11,582	16,255	18,223	19,637	21,330	23,049	25,188	28,158
Construction	300	661	641	521	466	421	449	411	318
General operating expenses.......	605	811	954	989	1,016	1,222	1,318	1,399	1,252
Compensation and pension	11,044	14,674	17,765	21,069	22,012	23,276	25,573	27,995	29,937
Vocational rehabilitation and education ..	2,350	452	1,317	1,584	1,610	1,786	2,170	2,565	2,684
All other [1]	2,846	818	844	780	2,345	-2,999	-1,676	-666	-2,795
**Compensation for service connected disabilities [2]	6,104	9,284	11,644	14,560	15,511	16,593	18,584	20,855	22,387

[1] Includes insurance, indemnities and miscellaneous funds and expenditures. (Excludes expenditures from personal funds of patients.)   [2] Represents Veterans receiving compensation for service-connected disabilities.
Source: U.S. Dept. of Veterans Affairs, *Expenditure and Workload*, annual. See also <http://www.va.gov/vetdata/index.htm>.

Table 513. **Veterans Compensation and Pension Benefits—Number on Rolls by Period of Service and Status: 1980 to 2004**
[In thousands (4,646 represents 4,646,000), except as indicated. As of Sept. 30. Living refers to veterans receiving compensation for disability incurred or aggravated while on active duty and war veterans receiving pension and benefits for non-service connected disabilities. Deceased refers to deceased veterans whose dependents were receiving pensions and compensation benefits]

Period of service and veteran status	1980	1990	1995	2000	2001	2002	2003	2004
Total	4,646	3,584	3,330	3,236	3,218	3,285	3,369	3,432
Living veterans	3,195	2,746	2,669	2,672	2,669	2,745	2,832	2,899
Service connected	2,273	2,184	2,236	2,308	2,321	2,398	2,485	2,556
Nonservice connected	922	562	433	364	348	347	347	343
Deceased veterans	1,451	838	662	564	549	540	538	533
Service connected	358	320	307	307	307	310	314	318
Nonservice connected	1,093	518	355	257	241	230	224	215
Prior to World War I.............	14	4	2	1	1	1	1	(Z)
Living	(Z)	(Z)	(Z)	(Z)	(Z)	(Z)	(Z)	(Z)
World War I	692	198	89	34	28	23	19	16
Living	198	18	3	(Z)	(Z)	(Z)	(Z)	(Z)
World War II....................	2,520	1,723	1,307	968	906	856	813	766
Living	1,849	1,294	961	676	624	583	546	506
Korean conflict [1]	446	390	368	323	313	308	306	302
Living	317	305	290	255	246	243	241	237
Peacetime	312	495	559	607	608	613	620	624
Living	262	444	514	567	569	575	583	587
Vietnam era [2]..................	662	774	868	969	987	1,052	1,120	1,172
Living	569	685	766	848	862	922	983	1,028
Gulf War [3]	(X)	(X)	138	334	376	431	490	552
Living	(X)	(X)	134	326	368	421	479	540

X Not applicable.   Z Fewer than 500.   [1] Service during period June 27, 1950, to Jan. 31, 1955.   [2] Service from Aug. 5, 1964, to May 7, 1975.   [3] Service from August 2, 1990 to the present.
Source: U.S. Dept. of Veterans Affairs, *Annual Report of the Secretary of Veterans Affairs to 1998; Annual Accountability Report* and unpublished data 1999 to 2004. See also <http://www.va.gov/vetdata/index.htm>.

National Security and Veterans Affairs 347

Table 514. Homeland Security Funding by Agency

[In millions of dollars. (37,118.2 represents $37,118,200,000).For year ending September 30. A total of 33 agencies comprise Federal homeland security funding. Department of Homeland Security (DHS) is the designated department to coordinate and centralize the leadership of many homeland security activites under a single department. In addition to DHS, the Departments of Defense (DoD), Energy (DoE), Health and Human Services (HHS), and Justice (DoJ), account for most of the total government-wide homeland security funding]

Agency	2003	2004	2005
Total Budget Authority, excluding Bioshield [1] [2] [3]	37,118.2	40,727.7	45,998.2
Department of Agriculture	299.9	411.1	599.9
Department of Commerce	111.6	124.6	166.7
Department of Defense [4]	8,442.0	7,024.0	8,570.1
Department of Education	5.7	8.0	23.8
Department of Energy	1,246.9	1,364.0	1,562.0
Department of Health and Human Services	4,002.4	4,062.2	4,230.3
Department of Homeland Security [5]	18,652.4	22,832.7	24,870.7
Department of Housing and Urban Development	1.6	1.7	2.0
Department of the Interior	47.4	82.9	65.0
Department of Justice	1,892.5	2,164.9	2,677.8
Department of Labor	69.4	52.4	56.1
Department of State	632.7	696.4	824.1
Department of Transportation	382.8	283.5	181.7
Department of the Treasury	80.0	90.4	101.1
Department of Veterans Affairs	154.3	271.3	280.4
Corps of Engineers	36.0	101.5	89.0
Environmental Protection Agency	132.9	131.0	106.8
Executive Office of the President	41.0	35.0	29.5
General Services Administration	67.1	78.9	65.2
National Aeronautics and Space Administration	205.0	207.0	218.0
National Science Foundation	284.6	340.0	342.2
Office of Personnel Management	3.0	3.0	3.0
Social Security Administration	132.0	143.4	159.4
District of Columbia	25.0	19.0	15.0
Federal Communications Commission	1.0	1.0	1.6
Intelligence Community Management Account	(X)	1.0	72.4
National Archives and Records Administration	10.1	16.0	17.1
Nuclear Regulatory Commission	47.0	66.8	59.2
Postal Service	(X)	(X)	503.0
Securities and Exchange Commission	5.0	5.0	5.0
Smithsonian Institution	82.8	78.3	75.0
United States Holocaust Memorial Museum	8.0	8.0	8.0
Corporation for National and Community Service	16.3	22.8	17.0

X Not applicable.   [1] Enacted Budget.   [2] The Federal spending estimates are for the Executive Branch's homeland security efforts. These estimates do not include the efforts of the Legislative or Judicial branches.   [3] The Department of Homeland Security Appropriations Act, 2004, provided $5.6 billion for Project BioShield, to remain available through 2013. Including this uneven funding stream can distort year-over-year comparisons.   [4] In all tables, classified funds for the Intelligence Comunity are combined with the Department of Defense and titled "Department of Defense".   [5] Excludes $16 million dollars in supplemental appropriations provided to the Coast Guard in 2005.

Source: U.S. Office of Management and Budget, based on *Analytical Prospectives, Budget of the United States Government*, annual; <http://www.whitehouse.gov/omb/>.

Table 515. Homeland Security Funding by National Strategy Mission Area

[In millions of dollars. (37,118.2 represents $37,118,200,000.) For homeland security funding analysis by OMB, agencies categorize their funding data based on the critical mission areas defined in the *National Strategy*.]

Mission area	2003	2004	2005
Total Budget Authority excluding Bioshield [1] [2]	37,118.2	40,727.7	45,998.2
Intelligence and Warning	125.1	242.2	349.8
Border and Transportation Security	15,170.8	15840.8	17,550.2
Domestic Counterterrorism	2,509.2	3,379.3	3,944.5
Protecting Critical Infrastructure and Key Assets	12,893.1	12,279.1	14,939.4
Defending Against Catastrophic Threats	2,428.4	2,974.2	3,399.2
Emergency Preparedness and Response	3,873.2	6,002.6	5,765.2
Other	118.3	9.6	49.8

[1] Enacted budget.   [2] See footnote 3 in Table 514.

Source: U.S. Office of Management and Budget, based on *Analytical Prospectives, Budget of the United States Government*, annual; <http://www.whitehouse.gov/omb/>.

Figure 10.3   **Department of Homeland Security Organization Chart**

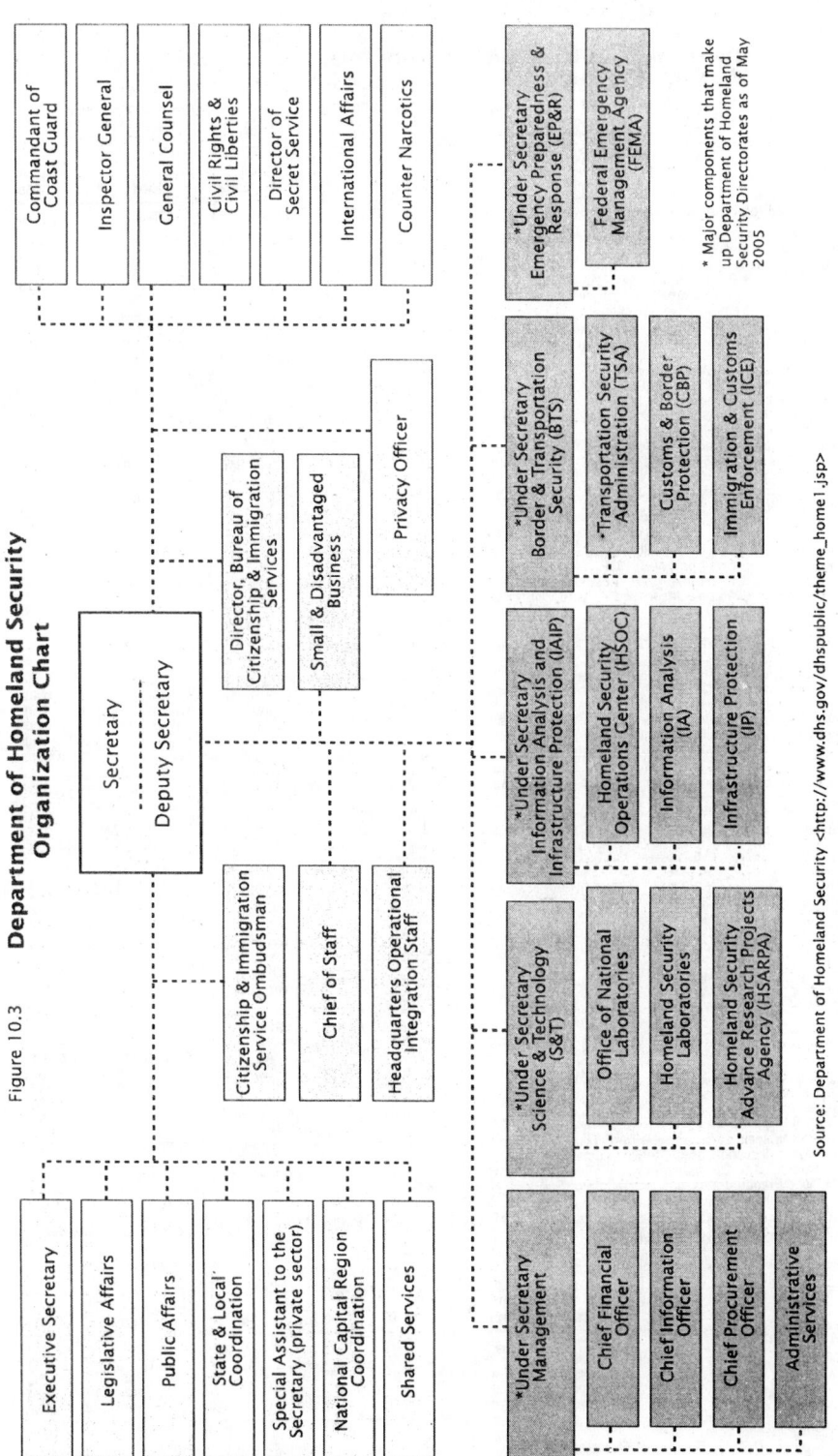

Source: Department of Homeland Security <http://www.dhs.gov/dhspublic/theme_home1.jsp>

Table 516. Department of Homeland Security Total Budget Authority and Personnel by Organization: 2004 and 2005

[Expenditures in thousands of dollars (35,604,092 represents $35,604,092,000). For the fiscal year ending September 30. Not all activities carried out by DHS constitute homeland security funding (e.g., Coast Guard search and rescue activities)]

Organization	Expenditures		Full-time employees	
	2004	2005	2004 [1]	2005
Adjusted total budget authority [2][3]	35,604,092	38,510,517	175,870	179,370
Border & Transportation Security (BTS) Under Secretary......	8,058	9,617	67	67
United States–Visitor Immigrant Status Indicator Technology (US–VISIT)............................	328,053	340,000	64	102
U.S. Customs & Border Protection.....................	5,997,287	6,416,398	40,076	40,616
U.S. Immigration & Customs Enforcement	3,669,615	3,845,178	14,751	14,486
Transportation Security Administration	4,578,043	5,405,375	51,346	52,615
Federal Law Enforcement Training Center	191,643	222,357	934	959
U.S. Coast Guard.................................	6,994,222	7,558,560	45,532	46,809
U.S. Secret Service	1,334,128	1,375,758	6,381	6,516
Federal Emergency Management Agency (FEMA), (Emergency Preparedness & Response (EP&R) Directorate) ...	4,671,782	5,038,256	4,780	4,735
U.S. Citizenship & Immigration Services.................	1,549,733	1,775,000	9,795	9,937
Information Analysis & Infrastructure Directorate (IAIP)	834,348	893,708	729	803
Science & Technology Directorate (S&T)	912,751	1,115,450	180	320
State and Local Government Coordination and Preparedness (SLGCP) [4]......................	4,192,120	3,984,846	146	220
Departmental Operations............................	394,435	524,457	632	683
Counter-Terrorism Fund............................	9,941	8,000	(X)	(X)
Inspector General................................	80,318	82,317	457	502

X Not applicable. [1] Data comes from the Budget-in-Brief, Fiscal Year 2005. [2] Reflects adjustment for recission of prior year carryover funds. [3] Excludes BioShield funding, see footnote 3, Table 514. [4] For FY 2005, the Office of Domestic Preparedness became part of SLGCP.

Source: U.S. Department of Homeland Security, "Budget-in-Brief, Fiscal Year 2006," <http://www.dhs.gov/interweb/assetlibrary/BudgetBIB-FY2006.pdf> (accessed 7 February 2005).

Table 517. Homeland Security Grants by State/Territories: 2004 and 2005

[In thousands of dollars (3,115,550 represents 3,115,550,000). For fiscal years ending September 30. Grants consist of the following programs: Citizen Corps Program (CCP), Law Enforcement Terrorism Prevention Program (LETPP), Emergency Management Performance Grant (EMPG), State Homeland Security Program (SHSP), Metropolitan Medical Response System (MMRS), and Urban Areas Security Initiative (UASI). Urban Areas Security Initiative program includes the Urban Areas Program, Transit Security Program, Port Security Grant Program and the Intercity Bus Program. 2005 grants include all the programs as in 2004 except for Port Security Grant Program and the Intercity Bus Program. These programs have not yet been awarded as of May 2005]

State/Territory	2004	2005	State/Territory	2004	2005	State/Territory	2004	2005
Total ...	3,115,550	2,518,763	LA	76,005	42,670	RI	23,485	16,074
U.S.	3,050,076	2,475,564	ME.......	23,776	16,609	SC	40,643	26,284
AL	38,723	28,153	MD.......	64,014	42,250	SD	19,996	14,809
AK	21,218	14,879	MA.......	69,288	62,436	TN	54,157	32,605
AZ	53,371	41,705	MI	76,981	64,075	TX	195,671	138,570
AR	28,815	21,561	MN.......	60,236	35,311	UT	27,033	20,308
CA	349,894	282,622	MS.......	31,795	22,081	VT	19,594	14,326
CO......	45,583	36,799	MO.......	66,618	46,952	VA	61,902	38,185
CT	46,523	24,080	MT.......	20,689	15,318	WA......	73,593	45,330
DE	20,206	14,984	NE	24,376	23,656	WV......	25,270	18,289
DC	49,231	96,144	NV	37,196	28,386	WI	51,343	37,251
FL	142,667	101,285	NH	24,110	16,776	WY......	18,809	13,934
GA	70,815	54,918	NJ	95,795	60,811			
HI.......	26,865	23,130	NM......	24,946	18,499			
ID.......	22,621	16,805	NY	178,492	298,351	PR [1]	37,864	25,169
IL.......	114,925	102,593	NC	65,392	46,609	VI	6,918	4,612
IN.......	55,534	38,996	ND	19,421	14,376	AS	5,776	4,279
IA.......	29,918	22,291	OH	103,582	77,823	GU	7,016	4,706
KS	29,064	21,784	OK.......	32,824	29,974	NM	7,960	4,333
KY	45,537	31,419	OR	41,665	34,820	RM	-	50
			PA	109,866	87,671	FM	-	50

- Represents zero. [1] PR–Puerto Rico, VI–Virgin Islands, AS–America Samoa, GU–Guam, NM–Northern Mariana Islands, RM–Marshall Islands, and FM–Micronesia.

Source: U.S. Department of Homeland Security, State and Local Government Coordination and Preparedness, Office for Domestic Preparedness, unpublished data. See also <http://www.ojp.gov/odp>.

Table 518. Coast Guard Migrant Interdictions by Nationality of Alien: 2000 to 2004

[For the year ending September 30]

Year	Total	Haiti	Dominican Republic	China	Cuba	Mexico	Ecuador	Other
2000	4,210	1,113	499	261	1,000	49	1,244	44
2001	3,948	1,391	659	53	777	17	1,020	31
2002	4,104	1,486	177	80	666	32	1,608	55
2003	6,068	2,013	1,748	15	1,555	-	703	34
2004	10,899	3,229	5,014	68	1,225	86	1,189	88

- Represents zero.

Source: U.S. Department of Homeland Security, United States Coast Guard, "Fact File, Migrants Statistics, Statistics." <http://www.uscg.mil/hq/g-cp/comrel/factfile/index.htm> (accessed 3 June 2005).

Table 519. **Customs and Border Protection (CBP)—Processed and Cleared Passengers, Planes, Vehicles, and Containers: 2000 to 2004**

[For year ending September 30]

Characteristic	2000	2001	2002	2003	2004
Air					
Passenger	80,512,207	79,674,803	69,316,987	70,854,290	78,267,680
Commercial plane [1]	829,318	839,221	768,879	789,805	823,757
Private plane	142,050	125,721	129,243	132,154	139,644
Land					
Passenger [2, 3]	397,312,173	381,477,331	333,651,738	329,998,234	326,692,741
Auto [2]	127,094,722	129,576,724	118,306,795	120,376,489	121,415,504
Rail container	2,156,537	2,257,608	2,430,107	2,473,569	2,587,565
Truck [4]	11,575,243	11,186,909	11,239,541	11,095,397	11,346,725
Sea					
Passenger [5]	10,990,098	11,281,774	12,224,397	15,127,461	18,127,781
Vessel [6]	211,242	214,610	211,922	203,635	190,701
Vessel container [7]	5,813,244	5,709,974	7,283,475	8,821,847	9,796,282

[1] A commercial aircraft is any aircraft transporting passengers and/or cargo for some payment or other consideration, including money or services rendered. [2] See Table 1256 for more details. [3] Includes pedestrians. [4] Trucks\containers entering the U.S. [5] Does not include passengers on ferries. [6] Number of vessels. The word vessel includes every description of water craft or other contrivance used or capable of being used as a means of transportation on water, does not include aircraft. [7] Number of vessel containers.

Source: U.S. Department of Homeland Security, Customs and Border Protection, *About CBP, Statistics and Accomplishments, National Workload Statistics, 2000–2004.* See also <http://www.cbp.gov/xp/cgov/toolbox/about/accomplish/> (released 1 June 2005).

Table 520. **Deportable Aliens Located by Border Patrol Program: 2000 to 2004**

[As of the end of September. Excludes Immigration and Customs Enforcement (ICE) investigations' data. Data for this table comes from the Performance Analysis System (PAS). This system captures aggregated data updated once a month by DHS offices.]

Border Patrol Sector	2000	2001	2002	2003	2004
Total	**1,676,438**	**1,266,214**	**955,310**	**931,557**	**1,160,395**
All southwest sectors	**1,643,679**	**1,235,718**	**929,809**	**905,065**	**1,139,282**
San Diego, CA	151,681	110,075	100,681	111,515	138,608
El Centro, CA.	238,126	172,852	108,273	92,099	74,467
Yuma, AZ	108,747	78,385	42,654	56,638	98,060
Tucson, AZ	616,346	449,675	333,648	347,263	491,771
El Paso, TX	115,696	112,857	94,154	88,816	104,399
Marfa, TX	13,689	12,087	11,392	10,319	10,530
Del Rio, TX	157,178	104,875	66,985	50,145	53,794
Laredo, TX	108,973	87,068	82,095	70,521	74,706
McAllen, TX	133,243	107,844	89,927	77,749	92,947
All other sectors.	**32,759**	**30,496**	**25,501**	**26,492**	**21,113**
Blaine, WA	2,581	2,089	1,732	1,380	1,354
Buffalo, NY	1,570	1,434	1,102	564	671
Detroit, MI	2,057	2,106	1,511	2,345	1,912
Grand Forks, ND	562	921	1,369	1,223	1,225
Havre, MT	1,568	1,305	1,463	1,406	986
Houlton, ME.	489	685	432	292	263
Livermore, CA	6,205	5,211	4,371	3,565	1,850
Miami, FL	6,237	5,962	5,143	5,931	4,602
New Orleans, LA	6,478	5,033	4,665	5,151	2,889
Ramey, PR	1,731	1,952	835	1,688	1,813
Spokane, WA.	1,324	1,335	1,142	992	847
Swanton, VT	1,957	2,463	1,736	1,955	2,701

Source: U.S. Department of Homeland Security, Office of Immigration Statistics, *Yearbook of Immigration Statistics, 2004.* See also <http://uscis.gov/graphics/shared/aboutus/statistics/ybpage.htm>. Data as of 10 June 2005.

Table 521. **Border Patrol Enforcement Activities: 2000 to 2004**

[As of September 30. Excludes Immigration and Customs Enforcement (ICE) investigations' data. Data for this table comes from the Performance Analysis System (PAS). This system captures aggregated data updated once a month by DHS offices.]

Activities	2000	2001	2002	2003	2004
Persons processed by the Border Patrol [1]	**1,689,195**	**1,277,577**	**967,044**	**946,684**	**1,179,296**
Deportable aliens located by the Border Patrol	**1,676,438**	**1,266,214**	**955,310**	**931,557**	**1,160,395**
Mexican aliens	1,636,883	1,224,046	917,994	882,012	1,085,006
Working in agriculture	1,330	1,248	1,821	1,908	1,647
Working in trades, crafts, industry, and service	2,167	2,678	2,897	3,856	3,634
Seeking employment	1,525,422	1,107,550	822,161	810,671	997,986
Canadian aliens	2,211	2,539	1,836	1,611	1,497
All others	37,344	39,629	35,480	47,934	73,892
Smugglers of aliens located	14,406	8,720	8,701	11,128	16,074
Aliens located who were smuggled					
into the United States	236,782	112,927	68,192	110,575	193,122
Seizures (conveyances)	17,269	5,892	7,250	9,355	18,024
Value of seizures (mil. dol.)	**1,945**	**1,581**	**1,564**	**1,680**	**1,696**
Narcotics.	1,848	1,519	1,499	1,608	1,620
Other	97	62	65	72	75

[1] Includes deportable aliens located and non-deportable (e.g., U.S. citizens).

Source: U.S. Department of Homeland Security, Office of Immigration Statistics, *Yearbook of Immigration Statistics, 2004.* See also <http://uscis.gov/graphics/shared/aboutus/statistics/ybpage.htm>. Data as of 10 June 2005.

National Security and Veterans Affairs **351**

Table 522. Immigration and Customs Enforcement (ICE) Investigations Activities: 2000 to 2003

[As of September 30. Investigative activity for 2003 carried out by Immigration and Customs Enforcement (ICE). Prior to 2003, investigation activity was carried out by Immigration and Naturalization Service (INS).]

Activities	2000	2001	2002	2003
Criminal investigations: [1]				
Cases completed.	90,519	89,222	78,841	82,236
Defendants prosecuted.	3,802	2,962	2,309	3,138
Defendants convicted.	3,022	2,219	1,496	1,858
Employer investigations: [2]				
Cases completed.	1,966	1,595	2,061	2,194
Warnings	282	169	124	479
Notice of Intent to Fine	178	100	53	162
Final orders	180	78	13	124
Arrests.	953	735	485	445
Fraud investigations: [3]				
Cases completed.	3,733	3,721	2,527	3,050
Defendants prosecuted.	483	397	253	347
Defendants convicted.	259	214	142	250
Smuggling Investigations: [4]				
Cases completed.	3,309	2,885	2,395	2,346
Smugglers arrested	4,139	3,139	3,330	2,663
Smuggled aliens arrested	46,001	32,429	19,278	14,418
Defendants prosecuted	2,618	2,124	2,106	2,185
Defendants convicted.	1,474	1,174	1,252	1,418
Entered without Inspection/status violators: [5]				
Cases completed.	38,311	25,301	23,067	27,240
Aliens arrested	14,963	11,162	10,538	9,319

[1] Criminal alien cases include large-scale organizations engaged in ongoing criminal activity and individual aliens convicted of crimes such as terrorism or drug trafficking.   [2] Employer investigations target employers of unauthorized aliens and include criminal investigations, administrative investigations, auxiliary investigations, ICE Headquarters Investigation Project, and Department of Labor ESA-91. In FY 2003, also includes statistics pertaining to Work Site Enforcement National Interest Investigations.   [3] Fraud investigations seek to penetrate fraud schemes of all sizes and degrees of complexity which are used to violate immigration and related laws or to shield the true status of illegal aliens in order to obtain entitlement benefits.   [4] Smuggling cases involve those which target persons or entities who bring, transport, harbor or smuggle illegal aliens into or within the United States. The decline in Performance Analysis System (PAS) investigation figures for smugglers arrested and smuggled aliens arrested from fiscal year 2002 to 2003, may partially be attributable to the DHS reorganization and shift of workload from some anti-smuggling units in Border Patrol Sectors to ICE Special Agent in Charge (SAC) offices.   [5] Includes Entry Without Inspection (EWI), such as stowaways, or landed crewmen who were ordered detained on board, and status violators.

Source: U.S. Department of Homeland Security, Office of Immigration Statistics, *2003 Yearbook of Immigration Statistics*. See also <http://uscis.gov/graphics/shared/aboutus/statistics/ybpage.htm>. Data as of 10 June 2005.

Table 523. Convictions for Immigration and Naturalization Violations: 2000 to 2003

[As of September 30. Data for this table comes from the Performance Analysis System (PAS). This system captures aggregated data updated once a month by DHS offices.]

Violations	2000	2001	2002	2003
All violations [1][2]	20,751	21,055	21,042	22,479
Immigration violations	20,007	20,297	20,483	21,821
Entry of aliens illegally.	12,733	13,378	13,371	14,199
Reentry of deported aliens.	4,759	4,315	4,699	4,939
Bringing in, transporting, harboring illegal aliens.	1,700	1,680	1,691	1,612
Fraud and false statements to obtain or confer immigration benefits	31	98	119	270
Fraud, forgery, misuse of visas, alien registration, and other documents.	362	327	196	253
Fraud, forgery, misuse of identification documents	363	432	367	390
Conspiring to defraud the United States	(D)	(D)	5	6
Employing unauthorized aliens, peonage, false attestations for employment	49	19	25	72
Other immigration violations	9	47	10	80
Naturalization violations	181	168	146	137
False representation as citizens of United States	93	129	98	101
Fraud, misuse of citizen naturalization papers	3	4	7	6
Fraud, forgery, misuse of U.S. passports	85	35	41	30
Other violations	563	590	413	521
Racketeering	199	185	122	173
Terrriosm, threat to national security.	-	-	-	10
Money laundering and financial fraud	29	10	17	10
Weapons trafficking, unlawful possession by aliens.	64	84	105	67
Drug trafficking.	175	226	126	158
Obstructing justice	39	57	37	35
Alien prostitution.	4	6	(D)	(D)
Other violations	53	22	5	53

D Figure withheld to avoid disclosure pertaining to a specific organization or individual.   [1] Data for fiscal years 2000-2003 have been revised due to recategorized statutes and adjusted classification for various violation codes.   [2] For FY 2000-2003, includes conviction data reported by Inspections Air. Land, Sea, Border Patrol, and Investigations offices.

Source: U.S. Department of Homeland Security, Office of Immigration Statistics, *2003 Yearbook of Immigration Statistics*. See also <http://uscis.gov/graphics/shared/aboutus/statistics/ybpage.htm> Data as of 10 June 2005.

Table 524. **Department Participation in the Control of Marijuana, Narcotics, and Dangerous Drug Traffic: 2000 to 2003**

[As of the end of September. Department participation includes Border Patrol, Inspections and Investigations. Data for this table comes from the Performance Analysis System (PAS). This system captures aggregated data updated once a month by DHS offices.]

Year and seizure	Total	Type of contraband				
		Marijuana (lbs.)	Heroin (ozs.)	Cocaine (ozs.)	Dangerous drug pills (units)	Other
2000 [1]						
Number of seizures.................	12,143	9,914	225	1,020	470	514
Amount seized.....................	(X)	1,597,395	5,487	567,341	1,426,547	(X)
Estimated value of seizures (mil. dol.)	2,314	1,289	32	946	5	41
2001 [1]						
Number of seizures.................	11,387	9,201	190	1,074	380	542
Amount seized.....................	(X)	1,449,947	6,564	446,331	736,157	(X)
Estimated value of seizures (mil. dol.)	1,959	1,144	40	744	3	28
2002						
Number of seizures.................	10,231	8,289	160	991	250	541
Amount seized.....................	(X)	1,440,488	6,887	489,491	619,004	(X)
Estimated value of seizures (mil.dol.)	1,980	1,177	32	736	2	32
2003						
Number of seizures.................	10,284	8,528	119	742	362	533
Amount seized.....................	(X)	1,562,368	6,624	336,493	395,714	(X)
Estimated value of seizures (mil. dol.)	2,107	1,434	42	598	9	24

X Not applicable   [1] Revised data.

Source: U.S. Department of Homeland Security, Office of Immigration Statistics, *2003 Yearbook of Immigration Statistics.* See also <http://uscis.gov/graphics/shared/aboutus/statistics/ybpage.htm> released 10 June 2005).

Table 525. **Prohibited Items Intercepted at U.S. Airport Screening Checkpoints: 2002 to 2004**

[Passengers boarding aircraft in thousands (612,876 represents 612,876,000). For the calendar year. Transportation Security Administration (TSA) assumed responsibility for airport security on February 17, 2002, and by November 19, 2002, TSA assumed control over all passenger screenings from private contractors. TSA data are incomplete]

Year	2002	2003	2004
Passengers boarding aircraft total (1,000) [1]	**612,876**	**646,275**	**697,701**
Domestic...	560,107	592,412	635,515
International..	52,769	53,863	62,276
Total prohibited items............................	**4,185,916**	**6,167,497**	**7,103,560**
Knife [2]	1,147,843	1,969,003	2,055,306
Other cutting items [3]............................	2,063,729	3,029,318	3,409,724
Club [4]..	13,134	25,578	28,998
Box cutter [5]...................................	37,504	21,396	22,428
Firearm [6].....................................	983	638	254
Incendiary [7]...................................	83,086	485,792	697,242
Other [8].......................................	839,637	635,772	889,608

[1] Data comes from the Air Transport Association.   [2] Knife includes any length and type except round-bladed, butter, and plastic cutlery.   [3] Other cutting instruments refers to, e.g., scissors, screwdrivers, swords, sabers, and ice picks.   [4] Club refers to baseball bats, night sticks, billy clubs, bludgeons; etc.   [5] Box cutter.   [6] Firearm refers to items like pistols, revolvers, rifles, automatic weapons, shotguns, parts of guns and firearms.   [7] Incendiaries refer to categories of ammunition and gunpowder, flammables/irritants, and explosives.   [8] Other refers to tools, self-defense items, and sporting good (excluding baseball bats).

Source: U.S. Department of Homeland Security, Transportation Security Administration, unpublished data; 13 June 2005 <http://www.tsa.gov>; Air Transport Association of America, Washington, DC, Air Transport Annual Report, <http://www.airlines.org/home/default.aspx>.

Table 526. **Federal Emergency Management Agency (FEMA) Declarations and Expenditures for Disasters: 2000 to 2004**

[Expenditures in thousands of dollars (1,747,511 represents $1,747,511,000). For calendar year. FEMA leads the federal government's role in preparing for, mitigating the effects of, responding to, and recovering from all domestic disasters, whether natural or manmade, including acts of terror]

Year	Declarations				Expenditures [1]
	Total disaster	Major disaster	Emergency	Fire Management Assistance	
2000	113	45	6	62	1,747,511
2001	100	45	10	45	11,297,969
2002	121	49	1	71	1,883,822
2003	123	56	19	48	2,377,908
2004	118	68	7	43	5,583,391

[1] Expenditures represent FEMA funding obligated as of 12/31/04. Expenditures for declared disasters within a calendar year represent obligations at the time data was collected. Figures will change as those disasters remaining open receive funding obligated for ongoing recovery and mitigation projects.

Source: U.S. Department of Homeland Security, Federal Emergency Management Agency, Library, and unpublished data. See also <http://www.fema.gov/library/drcys.shtm> (accessed 5 April 2005).

National Security and Veterans Affairs 353

No. 115.—NUMBER OF PENSION CLAIMS FILED AND ALLOWED EACH YEAR SINCE JULY, 1861, AND THE NUMBER OF PENSIONERS ON ROLL AT THE CLOSE OF EACH YEAR, TOGETHER WITH THE ANNUAL AMOUNT PAID ON ACCOUNT OF PENSIONS, SINCE JULY 1, 1860.

[From the Annual Report of the Commissioner of Pensions.]

Fiscal year ending June 30—	Army.		Navy.		Army and Navy.				War of 1812.							Total number of applications filed.	Total number of claims allowed.	Number of pensioners on the roll.			Disbursements.
	Applications filed.		Applications filed.		Applications filed.		Claims allowed.		Applications filed.				Claims allowed.					Invalids.	Widows, etc.	Total.	
	Invalids.	Widows, etc.	Invalids.	Widows, etc.	Invalids.	Widows, etc.	Invalids.	Widows, etc.	Survivors.	Widows.	Survivors.	Widows.									

Source: Statistical Abstract of the United States: 1887 Edition.

In the total number of applications filed in 1887 are included 14,735 survivors and 3,983 widows of the war with Mexico. In the total number of claims allowed in 1887 are included 7,552 survivors and 903 widows of the war with Mexico. (See act of Congress approved January 29, 1887.) In the number of pensioners on the roll under the heads of "Invalids" and "Widows, etc.," are included survivors and widows of the war of 1812, respectively, commencing with the year 1871. Survivors and widows of the war with Mexico are included in the number of pensioners on the roll June 30, 1887.

Section 11
Social Insurance and Human Services

This section presents data related to governmental expenditures for social insurance and human services; governmental programs for old-age, survivors, disability, and health insurance (OASDHI); governmental employee retirement; private pension plans; government unemployment and temporary disability insurance; federal supplemental security income payments and aid to the needy; child and other welfare services; and federal food programs. Also included here are selected data on workers' compensation and vocational rehabilitation, child support, child care, charity contributions, and philanthropic trusts and foundations.

The principal source for these data is the Social Security Administration's *Annual Statistical Supplement to the Social Security Bulletin* which presents current data on many of the programs.

Social insurance under the Social Security Act—Programs established by the Social Security Act provide protection against wage loss resulting from retirement, prolonged disability, death, or unemployment, and protection against the cost of medical care during old age and disability. The federal OASDI program provides monthly benefits to retired or disabled insured workers and their dependents and to survivors of insured workers. To be eligible, a worker must have had a specified period of employment in which OASDI taxes were paid. The age of eligibility for full retirement benefits has been 65 years old for many years. However, for persons born in 1938 or later that age will gradually increase until it reaches age 67 for those born after 1959. Reduced benefits may be obtained as early as age 62. The worker's spouse is under the same limitations. Survivor benefits are payable to dependents of deceased insured workers. Disability benefits are payable to an insured worker under full retirement age with a prolonged disability and to the disabled worker's dependents on the same basis as

dependents of retired workers. Disability benefits are provided at age 50 to the disabled widow or widower of a deceased worker who was fully insured at the time of death. Disabled children, aged 18 or older, of retired, disabled, or deceased workers are also eligible for benefits. A lump sum benefit is generally payable on the death of an insured worker to a spouse or minor children. For information on the medicare program, see Section 3, Health and Nutrition.

Retirement, survivors, disability, and hospital insurance benefits are funded by a payroll tax on annual earnings (up to a maximum of earnings set by law) of workers, employers, and the self-employed. The maximum taxable earnings are adjusted annually to reflect increasing wage levels (see Table 535). Effective January 1994, there is no dollar limit on wages and self-employment income subject to the hospital insurance tax. Tax receipts and benefit payments are administered through federal trust funds. Special benefits for uninsured persons; hospital benefits for persons aged 65 and over with specified amounts of social security coverage less than that required for cash benefit eligibility; and that part of the cost of supplementary medical insurance not financed by contributions from participants are financed from federal general revenues.

Unemployment insurance is presently administered by the U.S. Employment and Training Administration and each state's employment security agency. By agreement with the U.S. Secretary of Labor, state agencies also administer unemployment compensation for eligible ex-military personnel and federal employees. Under state unemployment insurance laws, benefits related to the individual's past earnings are paid to unemployed eligible workers. State laws vary concerning the length of time benefits are paid and their amount. In most states, benefits are payable for 26 weeks and, during periods of high unemployment, extended benefits are payable under a federal-state program to those who have exhausted their regular state benefits. Some states also supplement the basic benefit with allowances for dependents.

Unemployment insurance is funded by a federal unemployment tax levied on the taxable payrolls of most employers. Taxable payroll under the federal act and 12 state laws is the first $7,000 in wages paid each worker during a year. Forty-one states have taxable payrolls above $7,000. Employers are allowed a percentage credit of taxable payroll for contributions paid to states under state unemployment insurance laws. The remaining percent of the federal tax finances administrative costs, the federal share of extended benefits, and advances to states. About 97 percent of wage and salary workers are covered by unemployment insurance.

Retirement programs for government employees—The Civil Service Retirement System (CSRS) and the Federal Employees' Retirement System (FERS) are the two major programs providing age and service, disability, and survivor annuities for federal civilian employees. In general, employees hired after December 31, 1983, are covered under FERS and the social security program (OASDHI), and employees on staff prior to that date are members of CSRS and are covered under Medicare. CSRS employees were offered the option of transferring to FERS during 1987 and 1998. There are separate retirement systems for the uniformed services (supplementing OASDHI) and for certain special groups of federal employees. State and local government employees are covered for the most part by state and local retirement systems similar to the federal CSRS. In many jurisdictions these benefits supplement OASDHI coverage.

Workers' compensation—All states provide protection against work-connected injuries and deaths, although some states exclude certain workers (e.g., domestic workers). Federal laws cover federal employees, private employees in the District of Columbia, and longshoremen and harbor workers. In addition, the Department of Labor administers "black lung"

benefits programs for coal miners disabled by pneumoconiosis and for specified dependents and survivors. Specified occupational diseases are compensable to some extent. In most states, benefits are related to the worker's salary. The benefits may or may not be augmented by dependents' allowances or automatically adjusted to prevailing wage levels.

Income support—Income support programs are designed to provide benefits for persons with limited income and resources. The Supplemental Security Income (SSI) program and Temporary Assistance for Needy Families (TANF) program are the major programs providing monthly payments. In addition, a number of programs provide money payments or in-kind benefits for special needs or purposes. Several programs offer food and nutritional services. Also, various federal-state programs provide energy assistance, public housing, and subsidized housing to individuals and families with low incomes. General assistance may also be available at the state or local level.

The SSI program, administered by the Social Security Administration, provides income support to persons aged 65 or older and blind or disabled adults and children. Eligibility requirements and federal payment standards are nationally uniform. Most states supplement the basic SSI payment for all or selected categories of persons.

The Personal Responsibility and Work Opportunity Reconciliation Act of 1996 contained provisions that replaced the Aid to Families With Dependent Children (AFDC), Job Opportunities and Basic Skills (JOBS), and Emergency Assistance programs with the Temporary Assistance for Needy Families block grant program. This law contains strong work requirements, comprehensive child support enforcement, support for families moving from welfare to work, and other features. The TANF became effective as soon as each state submitted a complete plan implementing TANF, but no later than July 1, 1997. The AFDC program provided cash assistance based on need, income, resources, and family size.

356   Social Insurance and Human Services

Federal food stamp program—Under the food stamp program, single persons and those living in households meeting nationwide standards for income and assets may receive coupons redeemable for food at most retail food stores or provides benefits through electronic benefit transfer. The monthly amount of benefits or allotments a unit receives is determined by household size and income. Households without income receive the determined monthly cost of a nutritionally adequate diet for their household size. This amount is updated to account for food price increases. Households with income receive the difference between the amount of a nutritionally adequate diet and 30 percent of their income, after certain allowable deductions.

To qualify for the program, a household must have less than $2,000 in disposable assets ($3,000 if one member is aged 60 or older), gross income below 130 percent of the official poverty guidelines for the household size, and net income below 100 percent of the poverty guidelines. Households with a person aged 60 or older or a disabled person receiving SSI, social security, state general assistance, or veterans' disability benefits may have gross income exceeding 130 percent of the poverty guidelines. All households in which all members receive TANF or SSI are categorically eligible for food stamps without meeting these income or resource criteria. Households are certified for varying lengths of time, depending on their income sources and individual circumstances.

Health and welfare services—Programs providing health and welfare services are aided through federal grants to states for child welfare services, vocational rehabilitation, activities for the aged, maternal and child health services, maternity and infant care projects, comprehensive health services, and a variety of public health activities. For information about the Medicaid program, see Section 3, Health and Nutrition.

Noncash benefits—The U.S. Census Bureau annually collects data on the characteristics of recipients of noncash (in-kind) benefits to supplement the collection of annual money income data in the Current Population Survey (see text, Section 1, Population, and Section 14, Prices). Noncash benefits are those benefits received in a form other than money which serve to enhance or improve the economic well-being of the recipient. As for money income, the data for noncash benefits are for the calendar year prior to the date of the interview. The major categories of noncash benefits covered are public transfers (e.g., food stamps, school lunch, public housing, and Medicaid) and employer or union-provided benefits to employees.

Statistical reliability—For discussion of statistical collection, estimation, and sampling procedures and measures of statistical reliability applicable to HHS and Census Bureau data, see Appendix III.

U.S. Census Bureau, Statistical Abstract of the United States: 2006

Table 527. **Government Transfer Payments to Individuals—Summary: 1980 to 2003**

[In billions of dollars (263.4 represents $263,400,000,000)]

Year	Total	Retirement & disability insurance benefits	Medical payments	Income maintenance benefits	Unemploy- ment insurance benefits	Veterans benefits	Federal education & training assistance payments [1]	Other [2]
1980	263.4	128.8	62.6	34.3	18.7	14.7	4.1	0.2
1990	561.5	264.2	188.8	63.5	18.2	17.7	7.3	1.8
1993	759.9	321.2	283.6	90.3	34.9	19.4	9.1	1.5
1994	795.2	335.1	310.7	95.6	24.0	19.7	8.6	1.5
1995	840.0	350.3	336.5	100.4	21.8	20.5	9.0	1.4
1996	883.1	364.9	361.7	102.6	22.4	21.4	8.6	1.6
1997	912.8	379.3	377.3	100.5	20.3	22.2	11.5	1.6
1998	932.6	391.8	383.7	101.1	19.9	23.2	11.2	1.8
1999	966.5	402.5	401.1	104.8	20.8	24.1	11.4	1.9
2000	1,018.1	424.8	427.7	106.6	20.7	24.9	11.0	2.4
2001	1,117.2	450.4	482.5	109.4	32.2	26.5	13.1	3.1
2002	1,219.8	474.1	526.3	119.4	53.7	29.6	13.9	2.7
2003	1,275.1	493.1	549.0	130.5	53.5	31.9	13.7	3.4

[1] See footnote 9, Table 528.   [2] See footnote 10, Table 528.

Source: U.S. Bureau of Economic Analysis, "Regional Accounts Data, Annual State Personal Income"; <http://www.bea.doc.gov/bea/regional/spi/>; (accessed 3 May 2005).

Table 528. **Government Transfer Payments to Individuals by Type: 1990 to 2003**

[In millions of dollars (561,484 represents $561,484,000,000)]

Item	1990	1995	1999	2000	2001	2002	2003
Total.	561,484	840,034	966,502	1,018,106	1,117,218	1,219,759	1,275,144
Retirement & disability insurance benefit payments	264,230	350,310	402,507	424,810	450,415	474,144	493,132
Old age, survivors, & disability insurance. . . .	244,135	327,667	379,763	401,218	425,081	446,600	463,320
Railroad retirement and disability	7,221	8,028	8,203	8,265	8,411	8,698	8,852
Worker's compensation payments (federal & state)	8,618	10,530	10,429	10,845	11,673	12,691	13,617
Other government disability insurance & retirement [1]	4,256	4,085	4,112	4,482	5,250	6,155	7,343
Medical payments	188,808	336,506	401,097	427,689	482,527	526,299	548,986
Medicare.	107,638	179,147	209,110	219,612	243,462	261,652	270,514
Public assistance medical care [2]	78,176	155,007	189,252	205,021	234,644	258,686	274,036
Military medical insurance [3]	2,994	2,352	2,735	3,056	4,421	5,961	4,436
Income maintenance benefit payments.	63,481	100,443	104,777	106,616	109,403	119,407	130,464
Supplemental Security Income (SSI).	16,670	27,726	31,023	31,675	33,162	34,664	35,990
Family assistance [4]	19,187	22,637	17,920	18,440	18,106	17,657	18,330
Food stamps	14,741	22,447	15,473	14,896	16,000	18,659	21,860
Other income maintenance [5]	12,883	27,633	40,361	41,605	42,135	48,427	54,284
Unemployment insurance benefit payments . . .	18,208	21,838	20,756	20,680	32,155	53,737	53,512
State unemployment insurance compensation.	17,644	20,937	20,015	19,913	31,383	52,749	52,365
Unemployment compensation for federal civilian employees.	215	339	207	226	209	327	280
Unemployment compensation for railroad employees.	89	62	65	81	98	96	94
Unemployment compensation for veterans . .	144	320	201	182	183	282	365
Other unemployment compensation [6]	116	180	268	278	282	283	408
Veterans benefit payments.	17,687	20,546	24,053	24,935	26,500	29,573	31,916
Veterans pension and disability	15,550	17,565	20,904	21,895	23,287	25,926	27,912
Veterans readjustment [7]	257	1,086	1,323	1,323	1,510	1,912	2,286
Veterans life insurance benefits	1,868	1,884	1,817	1,707	1,693	1,724	1,707
Other assistance to veterans [8]	12	11	9	10	10	11	11
Federal education & training assistance payments [9]	7,300	9,007	11,367	10,985	13,129	13,948	13,708
Other payments to individuals [10]	1,770	1,384	1,945	2,391	3,089	2,651	3,426

[1] Consists largely of temporary disability payments, pension benefit guaranty payments, and black lung payments.
[2] Consists of medicaid and other medical vendor payments.   [3] Consists of payments made under the TriCare Management Program (formerly called CHAMPUS) for the medical care of dependents of active duty military personnel and of retired military personnel and their dependents at nonmilitary medical facilities.   [4] Through 1995, consists of emergency assistance and aid to families with dependent children. Beginning with 1998, consists of benefits— generally known as temporary assistance for needy families— provided under the Personal Responsibility and Work Opportunity Reconciliation Act of 1996.   [5] Consists largely of general assistance, expenditures for food under the supplemental program for women, infants, and children; refugee assistance; foster home care and adoption assistance; earned income tax credits; and energy assistance.   [6] Consists of trade readjustment allowance payments, Redwood Park benefit payments, public service employment benefit payments, and transitional benefit payments.   [7] Consists largely of veterans' readjustment benefit payments, educational assistance to spouses and children of disabled or deceased veterans, payments to paraplegics, and payments for autos and conveyances for disabled veterans.   [8] Consists largely of State and local government payments to veterans.   [9] Excludes veterans. Consists largely of federal fellowship payments (National Science Foundation fellowships and traineeships, subsistence payments to state maritime academy cadets, and other federal fellowships), interest subsidy on higher education loans, basic educational opportunity grants, and Job Corps payments.   [10] Consists largely of Bureau of Indian Affairs payments, education exchange payments, Alaska Permanent Fund dividend payments, compensation of survivors of public safety officers, compensation of victims of crime, disaster relief payments, compensation for Japanese internment, and other special payments to individuals.

Source: U.S. Bureau of Economic Analysis, "Regional Accounts Data, Annual State Personal Income"; <http://www.bea.doc.gov/bea/regional/spi/>; (accessed 3 May 2005).

Table 529. **Government Transfer Payments to Individuals by State: 2000 to 2003**

[In millions of dollars (1,018,106 represents $1,018,106,000,000)]

State	2000, total	2002, total	2003							
			Total	Retirement & disability insurance benefits	Medical payments	Income maintenance benefits	Unemployment insurance benefits	Veterans' benefits	Federal education & training assistance payments [1]	Other [2]
U.S. . . .	1,018,106	1,219,759	1,275,144	493,132	548,986	130,464	53,512	31,916	13,708	3,426
AL.	16,643	19,565	20,651	8,517	8,287	2,412	412	739	270	14
AK.	2,966	3,232	3,164	596	1,244	336	166	117	14	691
AZ.	15,959	20,490	22,242	9,157	9,222	2,090	511	743	341	177
AR.	10,006	12,098	12,596	5,149	4,986	1,354	406	522	169	11
CA.	114,559	138,572	145,642	49,747	63,463	20,621	7,281	2,694	1,648	188
CO	11,169	13,633	14,264	5,714	5,734	1,327	710	563	181	35
CT.	14,086	16,245	16,662	6,642	7,420	1,285	927	259	96	32
DE.	2,857	3,410	3,650	1,565	1,526	284	159	83	28	5
DC	2,709	3,202	3,290	666	1,821	505	116	116	47	19
FL.	64,208	76,619	80,866	34,274	34,919	6,811	1,622	2,441	742	56
GA	23,696	30,377	30,630	11,699	12,683	3,708	1,038	1,096	373	34
HI	3,844	4,468	4,642	1,972	1,685	604	167	170	40	4
ID	3,804	4,692	4,966	2,248	1,794	398	251	177	88	10
IL	41,726	49,067	51,277	20,577	21,102	5,202	3,020	748	577	51
IN	20,081	23,738	24,606	11,199	9,447	2,176	959	480	329	16
IA	10,046	12,160	12,119	5,672	4,684	852	468	257	173	13
KS.	8,908	10,532	10,746	4,818	4,133	826	525	292	140	12
KY.	15,778	18,481	19,004	7,750	7,587	2,243	644	536	235	9
LA.	16,582	20,525	20,701	6,981	9,583	2,868	400	575	282	12
ME	5,307	6,193	6,746	2,496	3,118	613	165	294	54	6
MD	16,981	20,157	21,579	8,175	10,061	1,814	752	551	190	36
MA	26,4713	31,989	32,668	11,097	15,713	2,515	2,362	693	239	49
MI	36,675	42,861	45,090	18,657	18,097	4,637	2,563	695	419	23
MN	15,748	19,365	20,402	8,146	8,907	1,596	1,030	488	215	20
MS	10,803	13,225	13,803	4,956	6,034	1,883	269	415	230	16
MO	20,904	24,993	26,145	10,655	11,411	2,389	775	631	256	28
MT	3,127	3,570	3,697	1,775	1,260	336	103	154	55	13
NE.	5,694	6,687	6,981	3,032	2,850	585	170	254	86	4
NV.	5,588	7,230	7,716	3,441	2,893	639	390	275	57	21
NH	3,918	4,711	4,803	2,223	1,914	294	154	173	40	6
NJ.	33,092	40,123	41,097	16,233	18,354	2,641	2,678	592	298	301
NM	6,014	7,450	7,955	2,816	3,435	942	180	367	117	98
NY.	95,735	112,278	117,583	35,083	62,713	12,588	3,945	1,385	1,137	732
NC	28,108	34,148	35,759	14,222	14,477	4,024	1,413	1,189	410	24
ND	2,322	2,535	2,592	1,192	1,004	191	59	79	42	24
OH	43,149	50,679	53,176	22,789	22,071	4,973	1,789	1,011	501	43
OK	11,999	14,418	15,114	6,251	5,887	1,566	397	777	211	24
OR	12,2431	14,939	15,293	6,664	5,255	1,369	1,303	507	172	24
PA.	54,928	63,454	66,136	26,446	29,259	5,060	3,608	1,205	514	45
RI	4,748	5,632	5,827	2,146	2,687	532	261	133	60	7
SC.	14,340	17,417	18,212	7,412	7,246	2,124	570	618	215	27
SD.	2,490	2,921	2,995	1,311	1,181	240	39	125	48	50
TN.	21,864	25,734	27,315	10,415	12,052	3,063	773	754	264	24
TX.	59,911	73,433	77,966	27,896	33,521	9,553	3,001	2,715	1,064	216
UT.	4,962	6,001	6,373	2,866	2,286	549	289	169	172	42
VT.	2,245	2,681	2,844	1,090	1,247	277	120	84	25	2
VA.	19,916	23,951	25,059	11,248	9,359	2,311	790	1,030	274	48
WA	20,817	25,196	26,493	11,057	9,683	2,195	2,285	975	249	47
WV	8,894	10,900	11,555	5,620	4,110	1,068	256	387	106	9
WI	17,902	21,902	22,414	9,805	8,856	1,843	1,179	515	193	22
WY	1,583	1,879	2,011	976	724	155	61	66	25	4

[1] Excludes veterans. Consists largely of federal fellowship payments (National Science Foundation, fellowships and traineeships, subsistence payments to State maritime academy cadets, and other federal fellowships), interest subsidy on higher education loans, basic educational opportunity grants, and Job Corps payments. [2] Consists largely of Bureau of Indian Affairs payments, education exchange payments, Alaska Permanent Fund dividend payments, compensation of survivors of public safety officers, compensation of victims of crime, disaster relief payments, compensation for Japanese internment, and other special payments to individuals.

Source: U.S. Bureau of Economic Analysis, "Regional Accounts Data, Annual State Personal Income"; <http://www.bea.doc.gov/bea/regional/spi/>; (accessed 3 May 2005).

Social Insurance and Human Services 359

Table 530. Number of Persons With Income by Specified Sources of Income: 2003

[In thousands (203,482 represents 203,482,000). Persons 15 years old and over as of March of the following year. Based on Current Population Survey; see text, Sections 1 and 13, and Appendix III]

Source of income	Total persons with income	Under 65 years old	65 years old and over	White [1]	Black [2]	Hispanic origin [3]
Total	203,482	169,702	33,779	168,257	22,567	22,928
Earnings	151,880	145,806	6,074	125,350	16,662	19,071
Wages and salary	142,790	137,717	5,072	117,327	16,160	18,191
Nonfarm self-employment	12,471	11,516	955	10,945	785	1,110
Farm self-employment	2,604	2,293	311	2,358	133	141
Unemployment compensation	8,219	7,999	220	6,647	1,011	1,032
Workers compensation.	2,022	1,861	162	1,659	252	273
Social security, railroad retirement	40,632	9,750	30,882	35,066	4,050	2,380
Supplemental security income (SSI) . . .	5,173	3,948	1,225	3,438	1,338	738
Public assistance	2,428	2,338	89	1,432	803	512
TANF/Welfare (AFDC) only [4]	1,644	1,600	44	888	632	367
Other assistance only	685	640	45	480	140	133
Both	99	99	-	65	31	13
Veterans' payments	2,323	1,383	940	1,938	270	96
Survivors' benefits	2,649	913	1,736	2,397	168	79
Company or union	1,204	217	987	1,090	77	33
Disability benefits	1,642	1,464	178	1,265	309	143
Company or union	469	425	45	370	77	44
Pensions	15,809	5,007	10,802	14,041	1,301	533
Company or union	11,276	3,229	8,047	10,029	909	418
Federal government	1,684	541	1,143	1,430	204	69
Military retirement	1,113	651	461	962	109	34
State or local government	3,885	1,571	2,315	3,437	330	125
Property income [5]	104,536	84,964	19,572	92,021	6,517	5,930
Interest	98,565	80,158	18,407	86,898	6,083	5,461
Dividends	35,947	29,092	6,855	32,494	1,527	1,185
Rents, royalities, estates or trusts . . .	11,255	8,479	2,776	10,118	514	673
Education	8,466	8,446	20	6,554	1,247	826
Pell grant only	1,818	1,817	1	1,228	477	242
Other government only	1,233	1,227	7	964	177	146
Scholarships only	2,409	2,401	8	1,950	243	198
Child support	5,443	5,426	17	4,202	996	556
Alimony	401	372	29	378	17	22
Financial assistance.						
Other income	1,068	815	253	884	90	74
Combinations of income types:						
Government transfer payments.	60,370	28,317	32,053	50,027	7,472	4,842
Public assistance or SSI	7,285	5,992	1,293	4,674	2,046	1,198

- Represents or rounds to zero. [1] Beginning with the 2003 CPS, respondents could choose one or more races. For example, "White" refers to people who reported White and did not report any other race category. The use of this single-race population does not imply that it is the preferred method of presenting or analyzing data. Information on people who reported more than one race, such as "Asian and Black or African American," is available from Census 2000 through American FactFinder. [2] "Black" refers to people who reported Black and did not report any other race category. [3] Persons of Hispanic origin may be of any race. [4] TANF—Temporary Assistance for Needy Families program; AFDC—Aid to Families with Dependent Children program. [5] Includes estates and trusts reported as survivor benefits.

Source: U.S. Census Bureau, "Table PINC-09. Source of Income in 2003—Number With Income and Mean Income of Specified Type in 2003 of People 15 Years Old and Over, by Race, Hispanic Origin and Sex". See also <http://pubdb3.census.gov /macro/032004/perinc/new09_000.htm>.

Table 531. Households Receiving Means-Tested Noncash Benefits: 1980 to 2002

[In thousands (82,368 represents 82,368,000), except percent. Households as of March of following year. Covers civilian noninstitutional population, including persons in the Armed Forces living off post or with their families on post. A means-tested benefit program requires that the household's income and/or assets fall below specified guidelines in order to qualify for benefits. There are general trends toward underestimation of noncash beneficiaries. Households are classified according to poverty status of family or nonfamily householder; for explanation of poverty level, see text, Section 13. Data for 1980 and 1990 based on 1980 census population controls; 1995 and 2000 based on 1990 census population controls; beginning 2002, based on Census 2000 population controls and a 28,000 household sample expansion to 78,000 households. Based on Current Population Survey; see text, Section 1 and Appendix III]

Type of benefit received	1980	1990	1995	2001	2002			
					Below poverty level			Above poverty level
					Total	Number	Percent of total	
Total households	82,368	94,312	99,627	106,418	111,278	13,505	100	97,773
Receiving at least one noncash benefit . . .	14,266	16,098	21,148	20,131	22,478	7,806	58	14,672
Not receiving cash public assistance . . .	7,860	8,819	13,335	14,465	16,890	5,003	37	11,887
Receiving cash public assistance [1]	6,407	7,279	7,813	5,667	5,588	2,803	21	2,785
Total households receiving—								
Food stamps	6,769	7,163	8,388	5,563	6,245	3,834	28	2,411
School lunch	5,532	6,252	8,607	7,185	7,930	3,092	23	4,838
Public housing	2,777	4,339	4,846	4,689	5,125	2,593	19	2,532
Medicaid	8,287	10,321	14,111	14,328	16,765	6,182	46	10,583

[1] Households receiving money from aid to families with dependent children program (beginning 2000, temporary assistance for needy families program), supplemental security income program or other public assistance programs.

Source: U.S. Census Bureau, "Table NC1. Means-Tested Noncash Benefits Received by Households, by Selected Household Characteristics, Race and Hispanic Origin, and Poverty Status: 2002"; May 2004; <http://ferret.bls.census.gov/macro/032003/noncash /toc.htm> and Current Population Reports, P-60 reports.

Table 532. **Program Participation Status of Household—Poverty Status of People: 2003**

[In thousands (287,699 represents 287,699,000), except percent. People who lived with someone (a nonrelative or a relative) who received aid. Not every person tallied here received the aid themselves. Excludes members of the Armed Forces except those living off post or with their famillies on post. Population controls for 2003 based on Census 2000 and an expanded sample of households. Based on Current Population Survey. See text section 1 and Appendix III]

Race, age, and sex	Total [1]	In household that received means-tested assistance [2]		In household that received means-tested cash assistance		In household that received food stamps		In household in which one or more persons were covered by Medicaid		Lived in public or authorized housing	
		Num-ber	Per-cent	Num-ber	Per-cent	Num-ber	Per-cent	Num-ber	Per-cent	Num-ber	Per-cent
Total	287,699	74,818	26.0	18,484	6.4	20,807	7.2	56,770	19.7	11,555	4.0
Under 18 years	72,999	28,608	39.2	5,862	8.0	9,161	12.5	21,654	29.7	4,305	5.9
18 to 24 years	27,824	7,550	27.1	1,912	6.9	2,100	7.5	5,968	21.4	1,349	4.8
25 to 34 years	39,201	10,733	27.4	2,137	5.5	2,991	7.6	8,229	21.0	1,488	3.8
35 to 44 years	43,573	10,210	23.4	2,238	5.1	2,431	5.6	7,522	17.3	1,164	2.7
45 to 54 years	41,068	7,232	17.6	2,486	6.1	1,730	4.2	5,461	13.3	984	2.4
55 to 59 years	16,158	2,420	15.0	975	6.0	613	3.8	1,901	11.8	353	2.2
60 to 64 years	12,217	2,021	16.5	783	6.4	465	3.8	1,577	12.9	318	2.6
65 years and over. . . .	34,659	6,044	17.4	2,090	6.0	1,315	3.8	4,458	12.9	1,594	4.6
65 to 74 years	18,238	3,192	17.5	1,104	6.1	720	3.9	2,474	13.6	723	4.0
75 years and over. . . .	16,421	2,852	17.4	986	6.0	595	3.6	1,985	12.1	872	5.3
Male.	140,931	34,749	24.7	8,488	6.0	9,026	6.4	26,327	18.7	4,653	3.3
Female	146,768	40,069	27.3	9,996	6.8	11,781	8.0	30,443	20.7	6,902	4.7
White alone	231,866	51,822	22.3	11,682	5.0	12,648	5.5	39,268	16.9	5,854	2.5
Black alone	35,989	17,002	47.2	5,246	14.6	6,662	18.5	12,808	35.6	4,808	13.4
Asian alone	11,856	2,838	23.9	709	6.0	416	3.5	2,199	18.6	386	3.3
Hispanic	40,300	19,881	49.3	3,571	8.9	4,928	12.2	14,444	35.8	2,325	5.8
White alone, non-Hispanic	194,595	33,490	17.2	8,469	4.4	8,229	4.2	26,072	13.4	3,858	2.0

[1] Number of persons living in households. [2] Means-tested assistance includes means-tested cash assistance, food stamps, Medicaid, and public or authorized housing.

Source: U.S. Census Bureau, *Current Population Reports*, P60-226. See also <http://pubdb3.census.gov/macro/032004/pov/new26_001.htm>.

Table 533. **Government Expenditures for Income-Tested Benefits by Type of Benefit: 1980 to 2002**

[In millions of dollars (106,036 represents $106,036,000,000). For years ending September 30. Programs covered provide cash, goods, or services to persons who make no payment and render no service in return. In case of many programs, including family cash welfare, food and housing programs, job and training programs and some educational programs, some recipients must work or study. Most of the programs base eligibility on individual, household, or family income, but some use group or area income tests; and a few offer help on the basis of presumed need. Constant dollar figures are based on the Consumer Price Index for all Urban Consumers]

Level of government and year	Total spending		Constant (2002) dollars							
	Current dollars	Constant (2002) dollars	Medical benefits	Cash aid	Food benefits	Housing benefits	Educa-tion benefits	Jobs/training	Services	Energy aid
TOTAL										
1980	106,036	237,093	72,890	64,226	30,288	24,520	11,573	19,466	10,281	3,848
1990	214,738	298,497	120,687	75,417	34,899	27,394	20,003	5,897	11,799	2,402
1995	371,115	438,553	206,362	108,243	45,654	37,477	19,016	6,425	13,388	1,988
2000	428,556	448,985	235,591	98,907	35,776	32,651	17,085	7,897	18,915	2,162
2002	522,156	522,156	282,468	102,157	39,306	35,566	30,484	7,808	22,215	2,152
FEDERAL										
1980	81,403	182,015	43,376	42,434	29,267	24,520	10,934	19,285	8,351	3,848
1990	153,673	213,614	69,817	50,661	33,182	27,394	19,129	5,525	5,677	2,230
1995	262,905	310,679	119,841	80,266	43,492	34,729	17,888	5,467	7,104	1,892
2000	305,659	320,230	136,680	78,548	33,508	32,117	15,648	6,697	14,959	2,073
2002	373,152	373,152	163,760	82,476	36,824	34,861	28,783	6,893	17,525	2,030
STATE AND LOCAL										
1980	24,633	55,079	29,515	21,792	1,022	-	639	181	1,930	-
1990	61,065	84,884	50,870	24,757	1,717	-	874	371	6,122	172
1995	108,210	127,873	86,521	27,977	2,163	2,747	1,129	958	6,283	96
2000	122,897	128,755	98,912	20,359	2,268	533	1,437	1,201	3,956	89
2002	149,004	149,004	118,708	19,681	2,482	705	1,701	915	4,690	122

- Represents or rounds to zero.

Source: Library of Congress, Congressional Research Service, "Cash and Noncash Benefits for Persons With Limited Income: Eligibility Rules, Recipient and Expenditure Data, FY2000-FY2002"; CRS Report RL 32233; November 25, 2003.

Social Insurance and Human Services 361

Table 534. Cash and Noncash Benefits for Persons With Limited Income: 2001 and 2002

[For years ending September 30, except as noted (476,863 represents $476,863,000,000). Programs covered provide cash, goods, or services to persons who make no payment and render no service in return. In case of many programs, including family cash welfare, food and housing programs, job and training programs and some educational programs, some recipients must work or study. Most of the programs base eligibility on individual, household, or family income, but some use group or area income tests; and a few offer help on the basis of presumed need]

Program	Average monthly recipients (1,000)		Expenditures (mil. dol.)					
			Total		Federal		State and local	
	2001	2002	2001	2002	2001	2002	2001	2002
Total.	(X)	(X)	476,863	522,156	342,877	373,152	133,986	149,004
Medical care [1]	(X)	(X)	249,670	282,468	145,076	163,760	104,594	118,708
Medicaid [2, 3]	44,600	50,900	228,039	258,216	129,840	146,643	98,199	111,573
Veterans [4, 5]	1,479	1,640	7,731	8,185	7,731	8,185	-	-
General assistance [5]	(NA)	(NA)	4,705	4,956	-	-	4,705	4,956
State children's health insurance program	4,601	5,315	3,826	5,407	2,672	3,776	1,154	1,631
Indian health services [2, 3]	1,600	1,600	2,629	2,758	2,629	2,758	-	-
Maternal and child health services	8,707	9,038	1,250	1,279	714	731	536	548
Consolidated health centers [2]	10,500	11,550	1,164	1,328	1,164	1,328	-	-
Cash aid [1]	(X)	(X)	101,842	102,157	82,600	82,476	19,242	19,681
Supplemental security income [3, 6]	6,751	6,887	37,080	38,522	32,584	33,871	4,496	4,651
Temporary assistance for needy families (TANF) [7]	5,420	5,147	13,596	13,035	6,731	6,481	6,865	6,554
Earned income tax credit (refunded portion) [8]	16,827	(NA)	29,428	27,830	29,428	27,830	-	-
Foster care	265	254	8,311	8,618	4,395	4,523	3,916	4,095
Child tax credit (refunded portion).	8,634	(NA)	5,015	5,060	5,015	5,060	-	-
General assistance [8]	(NA)	(NA)	2,956	3,251	-	-	2,956	3,251
Pensions for needy veterans [9, 10]	602	581	3,018	3,177	3,018	3,177	-	-
Food benefits [1]	(X)	(X)	35,490	39,306	33,177	36,824	2,313	2,482
Food stamps [3, 11]	18,400	20,150	21,046	24,054	18,813	21,657	2,233	2,397
School lunch program [12, 13]	15,500	16,000	5,659	6,064	5,659	6,064	(NA)	(NA)
Women, infants and children [3, 14]	7,300	7,500	4,123	4,350	4,123	4,350	-	-
Child and adult care food program [15]	1,900	2,000	1,533	1,638	1,533	1,638	-	-
School breakfast [12]	6,400	6,700	1,402	1,515	1,402	1,515	-	-
Housing benefits [1]	(X)	(X)	32,820	35,566	32,070	34,861	750	705
Low-income housing asst. (Sec. 8) [16] . . .	3,310	3,326	16,720	18,499	16,720	18,499	-	-
Low-rent public housing [16, 17]	1,219	1,209	7,504	8,213	7,504	8,213	(NA)	(NA)
Rural housing loans [18, 19]	46	43	3,406	3,499	3,406	3,499	-	-
Home investment partnerships [3, 19, 20]	82	84	2,541	2,500	1,796	1,796	745	704
Housing for special populations (elderly and disabled)	8	12	3,406	3,499	3,406	3,499	-	-
Education aid [21, 22]	3,696	4,812	26,018	30,484	24,401	28,783	1,617	1,701
Pell grants [21, 22]	3,696	4,812	11,314	11,364	11,314	11,364	-	-
Head Start	905	912	7,750	8,172	6,200	6,538	1,550	1,634
Stafford loans [21]	5,040	5,564	3,590	7,523	3,590	7,523	-	-
Federal Work-Study Program [21, 22]	970	1,073	1,000	1,000	1,000	1,000	-	-
Federal Trio Programs	742	865	803	827	803	827	-	-
Services [1]	(X)	(X)	20,696	22,215	16,566	17,525	4,130	4,690
Social services (Title 20).	12,826	(NA)	2,645	2,743	2,645	2,743	(NA)	(NA)
Child care for TANF recipients and ex-recipients [23]	(NA)	(NA)	2,346	2,322	1,583	1,572	763	750
Child care and development block grant [24]	1,814	(NA)	7,911	8,589	5,872	6,383	2,039	2,206
TANF services	(NA)	(NA)	5,528	6,147	4,200	4,413	1,328	1,734
Homeless assistance grants	(X)	(X)	967	1,044	967	1,044	-	-
Jobs and training [1]	(X)	(X)	8,200	7,808	6,978	6,893	1,222	915
TANF work activities	(NA)	(NA)	2,696	2,727	1,983	2,121	713	606
Training for disadvantaged adults and youth [25]	1,136	839	2,078	1,950	2,078	1,950	-	-
Job Corps	68	68	1,459	1,532	1,459	1,532	-	-
Energy assistance [1]	(X)	(X)	2,127	2,152	2,009	2,030	118	122
Low-income energy assistance [3, 26]	4,832	4,672	1,856	1,800	1,856	1,800	(NA)	(NA)

- Represents zero. NA Not available. X Not applicable. [1] Includes other programs not shown separately. [2] Recipient data represent unduplicated annual number. [3] Expenditures include administrative expenses. [4] Medical care for veterans with a nonservice-connected disability. [5] Estimated expenditures. [6] Includes state-administered SSI supplements. [7] Excludes data for child support operations. [8] Estimated families. (In previous years, individual recipients were estimated.) [9] Estimated recipients as of September. [10] Includes dependents and survivors. [11] Includes Puerto Rico's nutritional assistance program. [12] Free and reduced-price segments. [13] Includes estimate of commodity assistance. [14] Special supplemental food program for women, infants and children. [15] Recipient data are numbers of children receiving free or reduced price meals and snacks in child care centers and estimates of children in family day care homes with incomes below 185 percent of poverty. [16] Recipient data represent units eligible for payment at end of year. [17] Includes operating subsidies, capital grants, and HUD-administered Indian housing. [18] Recipient data represent total families or dwelling units during year. [19] Expenditure data represent amounts obligated. [20] Recipient data are housing units provided or rehabilitated. [21] Recipient data are total numbers for the school year ending in year shown. [22] Expenditure data are appropriations available for school year ending the fiscal year named. [23] P.L. 104-193, which created TANF, established a mandatory block grant for TANF-related child care. [24] Recipient data are estimated number of children served. [25] Recipient data are total number of participants. [26] Households served during the year with heating and winter crisis aid. Federal funds include amounts transferred to other programs serving the needy.

Source: Library of Congress, Congressional Research Service, "Cash and Noncash Benefits for Persons With Limited Income: Eligibility Rules, Recipient and Expenditure Data, FY2000-FY2002"; CRS Report RL32233; November 25, 2003.

Table 535. Social Security—Covered Employment, Earnings, and Contribution Rates: 1990 to 2004

[164.0 represents 164,000,000. Includes Puerto Rico, Virgin Islands, American Samoa, and Guam. Represents all reported employment. Data are estimated. OASDHI = Old-age, survivors, disability, and health insurance; SMI = Supplementary medical insurance]

Item	Unit	1990	1995	1997	1998	1999	2000	2001	2002	2003	2004
Workers with insured status [1]	Million	164.0	173.2	177.8	180.3	182.9	185.4	187.7	189.6	191.7	194.0
Male	Million	86.5	90.2	92.2	93.3	94.3	95.4	96.4	97.4	98.4	99.4
Female	Million	77.5	82.9	85.6	87.1	88.6	89.9	91.3	92.1	93.3	94.6
Under 25 years old	Million	21.3	18.8	19.1	19.7	20.3	20.8	21.1	21.1	21.1	21.1
25 to 34 years old	Million	41.6	39.5	38.3	37.5	37.0	36.6	36.4	36.2	36.2	36.1
35 to 44 years old	Million	36.4	40.6	41.8	42.3	42.5	42.5	42.3	41.9	41.5	41.2
45 to 54 years old	Million	22.8	29.5	31.9	33.1	34.5	35.9	36.8	37.7	38.5	39.4
55 to 59 years old	Million	8.8	9.7	10.8	11.3	11.8	12.2	13.0	13.7	14.5	15.4
60 to 64 years old	Million	8.8	8.5	8.8	9.1	9.3	9.5	10.0	10.5	10.9	11.4
65 to 69 years old	Million	8.2	8.1	8.0	8.0	8.0	8.0	8.1	8.3	8.5	8.8
70 years old and over	Million	16.3	18.4	19.1	19.4	19.6	19.8	20.0	20.2	20.4	20.6
Workers reported with—											
Taxable earnings [2]	Million	134	141	146	149	151	155	155	154	154	157
Maximum earnings [2]	Million	8	8	9	9	9	9	9	8	8	9
Earnings in covered employment [2]	Bil. dol.	2,704	3,402	3,859	4,173	4,455	4,811	4,915	4,917	5,047	5,317
Reported taxable [2]	Bil. dol.	2,358	2,919	3,285	3,528	3,749	4,007	4,169	4,241	4,350	4,515
Percent of total	Percent	87.2	85.8	85.1	84.5	84.2	83.3	84.8	86.3	86.2	84.9
Average per worker:											
Total earnings [2]	Dollars	20,238	24,126	26,403	27,980	29,317	31,090	31,682	31,826	32,670	33,970
Taxable earnings [2]	Dollars	17,650	20,703	22,478	23,653	24,671	25,898	26,876	27,451	28,160	28,849
Annual maximum taxable earnings [3]	Dollars	51,300	61,200	65,400	68,400	72,600	76,200	80,400	84,900	87,000	87,900
Contribution rates for OASDHI: [4]											
Each employer and employee	Percent	7.65	7.65	7.65	7.65	7.65	7.65	7.65	7.65	7.65	7.65
Self-employed [5]	Percent	15.30	15.30	15.30	15.30	15.30	15.30	15.30	15.30	15.30	15.30
SMI, monthly premium [6]	Dollars	28.60	46.10	43.80	43.80	45.50	45.50	50.00	54.00	58.70	66.60

[1] Estimated number fully insured for retirement and/or survivor benefits as of end of year. [2] Includes self-employment. [3] Beginning 1995 upper limit on earnings subject to HI taxes was repealed. [4] As of January 1, 2005, each employee and employer pays 7.65 percent and the self-employed pay 15.3 percent. [5] Beginning 1990, self-employed pays 15.3 percent, and half of the tax is deductible for income tax purposes and for computing self-employment income subject to social security tax. [6] As of January 1.

Source: U.S. Social Security Administration, *Annual Statistical Supplement* to the *Social Security Bulletin;* and unpublished data.

Table 536. Social Security Trust Funds: 1990 to 2004

[In billions of dollars (272.4 represents $272,400,000,000)]

Type of trust fund	1990	1995	1998	1999	2000	2001	2002	2003	2004
Old-age and survivors' insurance (OASI):									
Net contribution income [1]	272.4	310.1	380.4	407.3	433.0	453.4	468.1	468.6	487.4
Interest received [2]	16.4	32.8	44.5	49.8	57.5	64.7	71.2	75.2	79.0
Benefit payments [3]	223.0	291.6	326.8	334.4	352.7	372.3	388.1	399.8	415.0
Assets, end of year	214.2	458.5	681.6	798.8	931.0	1,071.5	1,217.5	1,355.3	1,500.6
Disability insurance (DI):									
Net contribution income [1]	28.7	54.7	59.5	63.9	71.8	75.7	78.2	78.4	81.4
Interest received [2]	0.9	2.2	4.8	5.7	6.9	8.2	9.2	9.7	10.0
Benefit payments [3]	24.8	40.9	48.2	51.4	55.0	59.6	65.7	70.9	78.2
Assets, end of year	11.1	37.6	80.8	97.3	118.5	141.0	160.5	175.4	186.2

[1] Includes deposits by states and deductions for refund of estimated employee-tax overpayment. Includes government contributions on deemed wage credits for military service in 1957–2001. Includes taxation of benefits. [2] In 1990, includes interest on advance tax transfers. Beginning 1990, includes interest on reimbursement for unnegotiated checks. [3] Includes payments for vocational rehabilitation services furnished to disabled persons receiving benefits because of their disabilities. Amounts reflect deductions for unnegotiated benefit checks.

Source: U.S. Social Security Administration, *Annual Report of Board of Trustees, OASI, DI, HI, and SMI Trust Funds.* Also published in *Social Security Bulletin,* quarterly.

Social Insurance and Human Services **363**

Table 537. **Social Security (OASDI)—Benefits by Type of Beneficiary: 1990 to 2004**

[**39,832 represents 39,832,000**. A person eligible to receive more than one type of benefit is generally classified or counted only once as a retired-worker beneficiary. OASDI = Old-age, survivors, and disability insurance. See also headnote, Table 535 and Appendix III]

Type of beneficiary	1990	1995	1997	1998	1999	2000	2001	2002	2003	2004
Number of benefits [1] (1,000)...	**39,832**	**43,387**	**43,971**	**44,246**	**44,596**	**45,415**	**45,878**	**46,444**	**47,038**	**47,688**
Retired workers [2] (1,000)	24,838	26,673	27,275	27,511	27,775	28,499	28,837	29,190	29,532	29,953
Disabled workers [3] (1,000)	3,011	4,185	4,508	4,698	4,879	5,042	5,274	5,544	5,874	6,198
Wives and husbands [2,4] (1,000)	3,367	3,290	3,129	3,054	2,987	2,963	2,899	2,833	2,773	2,722
Children (1,000)	3,187	3,734	3,772	3,769	3,795	3,803	3,839	3,910	3,961	3,986
Under age 18	2,497	2,956	2,970	2,963	2,970	2,976	2,994	3,043	3,080	3,097
Disabled children [5]	600	686	705	713	721	729	737	745	753	759
Students [6]	89	92	97	93	104	98	109	123	128	130
Of retired workers	422	442	441	439	442	459	467	477	480	483
Of deceased workers	1,776	1,884	1,893	1,884	1,885	1,878	1,890	1,908	1,910	1,905
Of disabled workers	989	1,409	1,438	1,446	1,468	1,466	1,482	1,526	1,571	1,599
Widowed mothers [7] (1,000)	304	275	230	221	212	203	197	194	190	184
Widows and widowers [2,8] (1,000)	5,111	5,226	5,053	4,990	4,944	4,901	4,828	4,771	4,707	4,643
Parents [2] (1,000)	6	4	4	3	3	3	3	2	2	2
Special benefits [9] (1,000)	7	1	(Z)	(Z)	(Z)	(Z)	(Z)	(Z)	(Z)	(Z)
AVERAGE MONTHLY BENEFIT, CURRENT DOLLARS										
Retired workers [2]	603	720	765	780	804	844	874	895	922	955
Retired worker and wife [2]	1,027	1,221	1,295	1,318	1,357	1,420	1,466	1,494	1,535	1,585
Disabled workers [3]	587	682	722	733	754	786	814	834	862	894
Wives and husbands [2,4]	298	354	379	386	398	416	430	439	450	464
Children of retired workers	259	322	349	358	373	395	413	426	444	465
Children of deceased workers	406	469	500	510	526	550	571	585	603	625
Children of disabled workers	164	183	201	208	216	228	238	245	254	265
Widowed mothers [7]	409	478	532	545	566	595	621	640	664	689
Widows and widowers, nondisabled [2]	556	680	731	749	775	810	841	861	888	920
Parents [2]	482	591	636	651	674	704	729	753	779	810
Special benefits [9]	167	192	201	204	209	217	224	227	232	238
AVERAGE MONTHLY BENEFIT, CONSTANT (2002) DOLLARS [10]										
Retired workers [2]	858	893	903	905	909	923	942	942	952	955
Retired worker and wife [2]	1,461	1,514	1,528	1,530	1,534	1,553	1,578	1,572	1,585	1,585
Disabled workers [3]	835	846	852	851	853	860	877	877	890	894
Wives and husbands [2,4]	424	439	447	449	450	455	463	462	465	464
Children of deceased workers	577	581	590	592	595	602	615	615	623	625
Widowed mothers [7]	582	593	628	633	640	651	669	673	685	689
Widows and widowers, nondisabled [2]	791	843	862	869	876	886	906	906	917	920
Number of benefits awarded (1,000)...	**3,717**	**3,882**	**3,866**	**3,800**	**3,917**	**4,290**	**4,162**	**4,336**	**4,322**	**4,459**
Retired workers [2]	1,665	1,609	1,719	1,631	1,690	1,961	1,779	1,813	1,791	1,883
Disabled workers [3]	468	646	587	608	620	622	691	750	777	796
Wives and husbands [2,4]	379	322	319	311	322	385	358	363	353	367
Children	695	809	757	763	773	777	796	846	852	859
Widowed mothers [7]	58	52	44	42	42	40	41	41	39	40
Widows and widowers [2,8]	452	445	440	444	470	505	496	523	508	514
Parents [2]	(Z)	(Z)	(Z)	(Z)	(Z)	(Z)	(Z)	(Z)	(Z)	(Z)
Special benefits [9]	(Z)	(Z)	(Z)	(Z)	(Z)	(Z)	(Z)	(Z)	(Z)	(Z)
BENEFIT PAYMENTS DURING YEAR (bil. dol.)										
Total [11]	247.8	332.6	362.0	375.0	385.8	407.6	431.9	453.8	470.8	493.3
Monthly benefits [12]	247.6	332.4	361.8	374.8	385.6	407.4	431.7	453.6	470.6	493.1
Retired workers [2]	156.8	205.3	223.6	232.3	238.5	253.5	269.0	281.6	291.5	304.3
Disabled workers [3]	22.1	36.6	41.1	43.5	46.5	49.8	54.2	59.9	64.8	71.7
Wives and husbands [2,4]	14.5	17.9	18.6	18.9	18.8	19.4	19.9	20.3	20.4	20.6
Children	12.0	16.1	17.6	18.1	18.6	19.3	20.4	21.5	22.3	23.3
Under age 18	9.0	11.9	13.0	13.3	13.6	14.1	14.8	15.7	16.2	17.0
Disabled children [5]	2.5	3.6	4.0	4.2	4.4	4.6	4.8	5.1	5.2	5.5
Students [6]	0.5	0.6	0.6	0.7	0.7	0.7	0.7	0.8	0.8	0.9
Of retired workers	1.3	1.7	1.9	1.9	2.0	2.1	2.3	2.5	2.6	2.7
Of deceased workers	8.6	10.7	11.7	11.9	12.1	12.5	13.1	13.7	14.1	14.5
Of disabled workers	2.2	3.7	4.1	4.2	4.4	4.7	4.9	5.3	5.7	6.1
Widowed mothers [7]	1.4	1.6	1.5	1.4	1.4	1.4	1.4	1.5	1.5	1.5
Widows and widowers [2,8]	40.7	54.8	59.3	60.5	61.8	63.9	66.8	68.8	70.1	71.7
Parents [2]	(Z)	(Z)	(Z)	(Z)	(Z)	(Z)	(Z)	(Z)	(Z)	(Z)
Special benefits [9]	(Z)	(Z)	(Z)	(Z)	(Z)	(Z)	(Z)	(Z)	(Z)	(Z)
Lump sum	0.2	0.2	0.2	0.2	0.2	0.2	0.2	0.2	0.2	0.2

Z Fewer than 500 or less than $50 million. [1] Number of benefit payments in current-payment status, i.e., actually being made at a specified time with no deductions or with deductions amounting to less than a month's benefit. [2] 62 years and over. [3] Disabled workers under age 65. [4] Includes wife beneficiaries with entitled children in their care and entitled divorced wives. [5] 18 years old and over. Disability began before age 18. [6] Full-time students aged 18 and 19. [7] Includes surviving divorced mothers with entitled children in their care and widowed fathers with entitled children in their care. [8] Includes widows aged 60-61, surviving divorced wives aged 60 and over, disabled widows and widowers aged 50 and over; and widowers aged 60-61. [9] Benefits for persons aged 72 and over not insured under regular or transitional provisions of Social Security Act. [10] Constant dollar figures are based on the consumer price index (CPI-U) for December as published by the U.S. Bureau of Labor Statistics. [11] Represents total disbursements of benefit checks by the U.S. Department of the Treasury during the years specified. [12] Distribution by type estimated.

Source: U.S. Social Security Administration, *Annual Statistical Supplement* to the *Social Security Bulletin;* and unpublished data.

Table 538. Social Security—Beneficiaries, Annual Payments, and Average Monthly Benefit, 1990 to 2004, and by State and Other Areas, 2004

[Number of beneficiaries in current-payment status (**39,832 represents 39,832,000**) and average monthly benefit as of **December**. Data based on 10-percent sample of administrative records. See also headnote, Table 537, and Appendix III]

Year, state, and other area	Number of beneficiaries (1,000)				Annual payments [2] (mil. dol.)				Average monthly benefit (dol.)		
	Total	Retired workers and dependents [1]	Survivors	Disabled workers and dependents	Total	Retired workers and dependents [1]	Survivors	Disabled workers and dependents	Retired workers [3]	Disabled workers	Widows and widowers [4]
1990	39,832	28,369	7,197	4,266	247,796	172,042	50,951	24,803	603	587	557
1995	43,380	30,139	7,379	5,862	332,581	224,381	67,302	40,898	720	682	680
2000	45,417	31,761	6,981	6,675	407,431	274,645	77,848	54,938	845	787	810
2002	46,453	32,362	6,870	7,220	453,601	303,983	83,973	65,645	895	834	861
2003	46,448	32,360	6,870	7,220	470,546	314,024	85,621	70,899	922	862	888
2004, total [5]	47,707	33,025	6,730	7,952	493,078	327,139	87,737	78,202	955	894	920
United States	46,531	32,278	6,510	7,743	485,123	322,792	85,828	76,505	(NA)	(NA)	(NA)
Alabama	884	536	142	207	8,697	5,062	1,686	1,949	912	866	850
Alaska	63	41	10	13	618	388	114	116	920	868	877
Arizona	888	634	108	147	9,282	6,377	1,427	1,478	973	924	954
Arkansas	546	341	81	123	5,228	3,151	935	1,142	888	846	826
California	4,412	3,162	579	671	45,788	31,216	7,760	6,812	957	910	949
Colorado	571	406	77	88	5,822	3,926	1,025	871	935	887	929
Connecticut	584	435	69	80	6,642	4,808	1,011	824	1,044	932	1,021
Delaware	149	105	19	25	1,618	1,098	259	261	1,004	936	988
District of Columbia	72	50	11	11	653	435	114	104	819	824	767
Florida	3,382	2,497	407	478	34,976	24,782	5,437	4,757	951	895	948
Georgia	1,192	771	181	239	11,958	7,464	2,167	2,326	929	878	864
Hawaii	199	154	23	23	2,039	1,516	291	232	945	915	899
Idaho	219	156	28	35	2,202	1,495	369	338	931	879	938
Illinois	1,884	1,337	276	271	20,456	13,869	3,826	2,761	993	924	984
Indiana	1,038	719	147	173	11,259	7,520	2,037	1,702	1,003	899	981
Iowa	546	396	77	73	5,689	3,926	1,061	702	952	857	940
Kansas	447	319	62	66	4,745	3,260	860	625	979	866	976
Kentucky	785	459	125	201	7,656	4,247	1,502	1,907	903	879	838
Louisiana	739	440	148	151	7,121	3,960	1,759	1,403	888	887	846
Maine	265	175	33	57	2,548	1,617	425	506	882	819	875
Maryland	761	541	113	108	8,076	5,460	1,490	1,127	962	926	939
Massachusetts	1,067	748	130	189	11,195	7,561	1,798	1,837	961	883	952
Michigan	1,716	1,172	251	293	19,067	12,497	3,522	3,048	1,029	950	992
Minnesota	775	567	101	106	8,080	5,640	1,394	1,046	955	879	938
Mississippi	546	319	88	139	5,092	2,889	964	1,239	875	835	793
Missouri	1,046	703	145	198	10,686	6,918	1,879	1,889	944	872	918
Montana	166	119	23	24	1,653	1,122	298	233	916	863	907
Nebraska	291	211	39	41	2,963	2,049	535	379	937	847	946
Nevada	341	249	38	54	3,594	2,504	512	578	962	960	964
New Hampshire	219	154	26	40	2,327	1,584	356	386	978	897	976
New Jersey	1,370	1,007	173	190	15,777	11,191	2,529	2,058	1,054	976	1,014
New Mexico	304	205	44	55	2,871	1,858	506	507	892	861	850
New York	3,045	2,162	387	497	33,354	22,849	5,364	5,141	1,011	943	973
North Carolina	1,467	977	192	299	14,779	9,565	2,302	2,912	934	877	860
North Dakota	115	82	19	14	1,125	746	251	128	891	840	879
Ohio	1,951	1,346	311	293	20,609	13,480	4,275	2,854	970	876	952
Oklahoma	623	420	96	107	6,234	3,993	1,198	1,043	916	880	894
Oregon	611	445	77	90	6,437	4,458	1,063	916	964	894	967
Pennsylvania	2,405	1,703	349	354	25,893	17,477	4,884	3,533	982	910	966
Rhode Island	192	135	22	35	2,007	1,371	294	342	955	877	962
South Carolina	751	489	104	157	7,538	4,761	1,231	1,546	931	884	854
South Dakota	140	101	21	18	1,340	913	264	163	878	835	873
Tennessee	1,070	688	161	221	10,679	6,635	1,954	2,089	929	862	874
Texas	2,865	1,939	474	452	28,664	18,429	5,923	4,312	930	884	895
Utah	262	191	36	36	2,710	1,892	476	342	959	886	982
Vermont	110	77	14	20	1,117	756	179	182	945	848	927
Virginia	1,114	757	156	201	11,381	7,408	1,987	1,986	940	898	881
Washington	913	658	114	141	9,833	6,785	1,602	1,445	993	906	983
West Virginia	407	237	71	99	4,189	2,268	905	1,016	943	936	879
Wisconsin	937	685	121	132	10,000	7,018	1,687	1,295	979	894	968
Wyoming	83	60	11	12	856	598	141	117	955	896	947
Puerto Rico	705	398	120	187	4,957	2,478	972	1,508	635	767	565
Guam	13	9	2	2	88	53	21	14	650	776	641
American Samoa	6	2	2	2	37	12	11	13	555	695	547
Virgin Islands	16	12	2	2	136	97	22	18	824	908	721
Northern Mariana Islands	2	1	1	(Z)	12	6	4	1	548	438	377
Abroad	431	322	93	16	2,685	1,679	871	135	543	766	603

NA Not available.   Z Fewer than 500.   [1] Includes special benefits for persons aged 72 and over not insured under regular or transitional provisions of Social Security Act.   [2] Unnegotiated checks not deducted. 1990 and 1995 include lump-sum payments to survivors of deceased workers.   [3] Excludes persons with special benefits.   [4] Nondisabled only.   [5] Includes those with state or area unknown.

Source: U.S. Social Security Administration, *Annual Statistical Supplement to the Social Security Bulletin.*

Social Insurance and Human Services   **365**

Table 539. Public Employee Retirement Systems—Participants and Finances: 1980 to 2002

[For fiscal year of retirement system, except data for the Thrift Savings Plan are for calendar year (4,629 represents 4,629,000)]

Retirement plan	Unit	1980	1990	1995	1997	1998	1999	2000	2001	2002, proj.
TOTAL PARTICIPANTS [1]										
Federal retirement systems:										
Defined benefit:										
Civil Service Retirement System	1,000	4,629	4,167	3,731	3,518	3,423	3,362	3,256	(NA)	(NA)
Federal Employees Retirement System [2]	1,000	(X)	1,180	1,512	1,679	1,757	1,879	1,935	(NA)	(NA)
Military Service Retirement System [3]	1,000	3,380	3,763	3,387	3,367	3,368	3,374	3,397	3,418	3,453
Thrift Savings Plan [4]	1,000	(X)	1,625	2,195	2,303	2,300	2,400	2,500	2,600	3,000
State and local retirement systems [5, 6]	1,000	(NA)	16,858	14,734	15,194	16,215	16,195	16,834	17,021	17,264
ACTIVE PARTICIPANTS										
Federal retirement systems:										
Defined benefit:										
Civil Service Retirement System	1,000	2,700	1,826	1,525	1,189	1,099	1,042	978	(NA)	(NA)
Federal Employees Retirement System [2]	1,000	(X)	1,136	1,318	1,497	1,547	1,640	1,668	(NA)	(NA)
Military Service Retirement System [3]	1,000	2,050	2,130	1,572	1,491	1,459	1,438	1,437	1,438	1,465
Thrift Savings Plan [4]	1,000	(X)	1,419	1,512	2,011	1,800	1,900	1,900	1,900	2,300
State and local retirement systems [5, 6]	1,000	(NA)	11,345	12,524	12,817	13,059	13,472	13,917	13,977	14,123
ASSETS										
Total	Bil. dol.	258	1,047	1,655	2,110	2,403	2,644	2,943	2,803	2,831
Federal retirement systems	Bil. dol.	73	326	537	631	686	738	774	645	673
Defined benefit	Bil. dol.	73	318	502	570	608	643	679	544	571
Civil Service Retirement System	Bil. dol.	73	220	311	344	361	376	390	414	414
Federal Employees Retirement System [2]	Bil. dol.	(X)	18	60	83	97	111	126	157	157
Military Service Retirement System [3]	Bil. dol.	(7)	80	131	143	150	156	163	174	174
Thrift Savings Plan [4]	Bil. dol.	(X)	8	35	61	77	95	98	102	102
State and local retirement systems [5]	Bil. dol.	185	721	1,118	1,479	1,717	1,906	2,169	2,158	2,158
CONTRIBUTIONS										
Total	Bil. dol.	83	103	127	139	137	142	143	145	151
Federal retirement systems	Bil. dol.	19	61	67	73	73	75	78	80	85
Defined benefit	Bil. dol.	19	59	61	66	65	67	69	70	73
Civil Service Retirement System	Bil. dol.	19	28	31	33	33	33	33	33	34
Federal Employees Retirement System [2]	Bil. dol.	(X)	4	6	7	6	8	8	9	10
Military Service Retirement System [3]	Bil. dol.	(7)	27	24	26	26	26	28	28	29
Thrift Savings Plan [4]	Bil. dol.	(X)	2	6	7	8	8	9	10	12
State and local retirement systems [5]	Bil. dol.	64	42	60	66	64	67	65	65	66
BENEFITS										
Total	Bil. dol.	39	89	125	142	152	160	172	185	197
Federal retirement systems	Bil. dol.	27	53	66	73	76	78	81	84	87
Defined benefit	Bil. dol.	27	53	65	72	74	76	78	81	85
Civil Service Retirement System	Bil. dol.	15	31	37	41	42	43	44	46	48
Federal Employees Retirement System [2]	Bil. dol.	(X)	(Z)	1	1	1	1	1	1	2
Military Service Retirement System [3]	Bil. dol.	12	22	28	30	31	32	33	34	35
Thrift Savings Plan [4]	Bil. dol.	(X)	(Z)	1	1	2	2	3	3	2
State and local retirement systems [5]	Bil. dol.	12	36	59	69	76	82	91	101	110

NA Not available.   X Not applicable.   Z Less than $500 million.   [1] Includes active, separated vested, retired employees, and survivors.   [2] The Federal Employees Retirement System was established June 6, 1986.   [3] Includes nondisability and disability retirees, surviving families, and all active personnel with the exception of active reserves.   [4] The Thrift Savings Plan (a defined contribution plan) was established April 1, 1987.   [5] Excludes state and local plans that are fully supported by employee contributions.   [6] Not adjusted for double counting of individuals participating in more than one plan.   [7] The Military Retirement System was unfunded until October 1, 1984.

Source: Employee Benefit Research Institute, Washington, DC, EBRI Databook on Employee Benefits, Twelfth Edition, and unpublished data (copyright). See also <http://www.ebri.org/>.

Table 540. Federal Civil Service Retirement: 1980 to 2002

[As of Sept. 30 or for year ending Sept. 30 (2,720 represents 2,720,000). Covers both Civil Service Retirement System and Federal Employees Retirement System]

Item	Unit	1980	1990	1995	1997	1998	1999	2000	2001	2002
Employees covered [1]	1,000	2,720	2,945	2,668	2,681	2,658	2,668	2,764	2,655	2,654
Annuitants, total	1,000	1,675	2,143	2,311	2,352	2,369	2,368	2,376	2,383	2,383
Age and service	1,000	905	1,288	1,441	1,474	1,488	1,491	1,501	1,509	1,513
Disability	1,000	343	297	263	257	253	246	242	239	236
Survivors	1,000	427	558	607	621	628	631	633	635	634
Receipts, total [2]	Mil. dol.	24,389	52,689	65,684	70,227	72,156	74,522	75,967	77,949	80,069
Employee contributions	Mil. dol.	3,686	4,501	4,498	4,358	4,274	4,381	4,637	4,593	4,475
Federal government contributions	Mil. dol.	15,562	27,368	33,130	35,386	36,188	36,561	37,722	38,442	39,692
Disbursements, total [3]	Mil. dol.	14,977	31,416	38,435	41,722	43,058	43,932	45,194	47,356	48,970
Age and service annuitants [4]	Mil. dol.	12,639	26,495	32,070	34,697	35,806	36,492	37,546	39,397	40,758
Survivors	Mil. dol.	1,912	4,366	5,864	6,518	6,763	6,978	7,210	7,533	7,790
Average monthly benefit:										
Age and service	Dollars	992	1,369	1,643	1,749	1,796	1,830	1,885	1,967	2,031
Disability	Dollars	723	1,008	1,164	1,204	1,216	1,221	1,240	1,269	1,286
Survivors	Dollars	392	653	819	881	905	923	952	992	1,024
Cash and security holdings	Bil. dol.	73.7	238.0	366.2	422.2	451.3	481.3	508.1	542.6	573.7

[1] Excludes employees in leave-without-pay status.   [2] Includes interest on investments.   [3] Includes refunds, death claims, and administration.   [4] Includes disability annuitants.

Source: U.S. Office of Personnel Management, Civil Service Retirement and Disability Trust Fund Annual Report.

Table 541. **State and Local Government Retirement Systems—Beneficiaries and Finances: 1990 to 2003**

[In billions of dollars, except as indicated (111.3 represents 111,300,000,000). For fiscal years closed during the 12 months ending June 30]

Year and level of government	Numbers of beneficiaries (1,000)	Receipts					Benefits and withdrawals			Cash and security holdings
		Total	Employee contributions	Government contributions		Earnings on investments	Total	Benefits	Withdrawals	
				State	Local					
1990: All systems	4,026	111.3	13.9	14.0	18.6	64.9	38.4	36.0	2.4	721
State-administered. . . .	3,232	89.2	11.6	14.0	11.5	52.0	29.6	27.6	2.0	575
Locally-administered. . .	794	22.2	2.2	(Z)	7.0	12.9	8.8	8.4	0.4	145
1995: All systems	4,979	148.8	18.6	16.6	24.4	89.2	61.5	58.8	2.7	1,118
State-administered. . . .	4,025	123.3	15.7	16.2	15.4	76.0	48.0	45.8	2.2	914
Locally-administered. . .	954	25.5	2.9	0.4	9.0	13.3	13.5	13.0	0.5	204
2000: All systems	6,292	297.0	25.0	17.5	22.6	231.9	95.7	91.3	4.4	2,169
State-administered. . . .	4,786	247.4	20.7	17.2	16.7	192.8	76.0	72.2	3.8	1,798
Locally-administered. . .	1,506	49.7	4.3	0.4	5.9	39.1	19.8	19.1	0.7	371
2002: All systems	6,198	-6.1	27.5	17.1	21.6	-72.4	121.9	110.1	4.0	2,157
State-administered. . . .	5,180	-8.4	23.0	16.7	15.2	-63.5	98.2	88.7	3.2	1,774
Locally-administered. . .	1,018	2.3	4.5	0.4	6.3	-8.9	23.7	21.4	0.8	375
2003: All systems	6,448	147.7	28.8	19.6	26.6	72.7	134.8	122.3	4.9	2,172
State-administered. . . .	5,421	130.0	24.4	19.1	18.2	68.2	109.1	98.8	4.2	1,802
Locally-administered. . .	1,027	17.8	4.4	0.4	8.4	4.5	25.8	23.5	0.7	370

Z Less than $50 million.

Source: U.S. Census Bureau, through 1995, *Finances of Employee-Retirement Systems of State and Local Governments*, Series GF, No. 2, annual; beginning 2000, "Federal, State, and Local Governments, State and Local Government Public Employee Retirement Systems"; <http://www.census.gov/govs/www/retire.html>.

Table 542. **Private Pension Plans—Summary by Type of Plan: 1990 to 2000**

[712.3 represents 712,300. "Pension plan" is defined by the Employee Retirement Income Security Act (ERISA) as "any plan, fund, or program which is heretofore or is hereafter established or maintained by an employer or an employee organization, or by both, to the extent that such plan (a) provides retirement income to employees, or (b) results in a deferral of income by employees for periods extending to the termination of covered employment or beyond, regardless of the method of calculating the contributions made to the plan, the method of calculating the benefits under the plan, or the method of distributing benefits from the plan." A defined benefit plan provides a definite benefit formula for calculating benefit amounts—such as a flat amount per year of service or a percentage of salary times years of service. A defined contribution plan is a pension plan in which the contributions are made to an individual account for each employee. The retirement benefit is dependent upon the account balance at retirement. The balance depends upon amounts contributed, investment experience, and, in the case of profit sharing plans, amounts which may be allocated to the account due to forfeitures by terminating employees. Employee Stock Ownership Plans (ESOP) and 401(k) plans are included among defined contribution plans. Data are based on Form 5500 series reports filed with the Department of Labor]

Item	Unit	Total				Defined contribution plan				Defined benefit plan			
		1990	1995	1999	2000	1990	1995	1999	2000	1990	1995	1999	2000
Number of plans [1] . . .	1,000	712.3	693.4	733.0	736.0	599.2	623.9	683.1	687.3	113.1	69.5	49.9	48.7
Total participants [2,3] . . .	Million	76.9	87.5	101.8	102.9	38.1	47.7	60.4	61.8	38.8	39.7	41.4	41.2
Active participants [2,4]	Million	61.8	66.2	73.0	72.8	35.5	42.7	50.4	50.8	26.3	23.5	22.6	22.0
Assets [5]	Million	1,674	2,724	4,408	4,193	712	1,322	2,350	2,229	962	1,402	2,058	1,964
Contributions [6]	Bil. dol. . . .	98.8	158.8	215.8	232.6	75.8	117.4	185.9	199.3	23.0	41.4	30.0	33.2
Benefits [7]	Bil. dol. . . .	129.4	183.0	314.5	341.6	63.0	97.9	195.1	215.6	66.4	85.1	119.4	126.0

[1] Excludes all plans covering only one participant. [2] Includes double counting of workers in more than one plan. [3] Total participants include active participants, vested separated workers, and retirees. [4] Any workers currently in employment covered by a plan and who are earning or retaining credited service under a plan. Includes any nonvested former employees who have not yet incurred breaks in service. [5] Asset amounts shown exclude funds held by life insurance companies under allocated group insurance contracts for payment of retirement benefits. These excluded funds make up roughly 10 to 15 percent of total private fund assets. [6] Includes both employer and employee contributions. [7] Benefits paid directly from trust and premium payments made from plan to insurance carriers. Excludes benefits paid directly by insurance carriers.

Source: U.S. Dept. of Labor, Employee Benefits Security Administration, *Private Pension Plan Bulletin* (Plan Year 2000, Preliminary), Spring 2005.

Table 543. **Percent Of Workers Participating In Retirement Benefits by Worker Characteristics: 2004**

[Based on National Compensation Survey, a sample survey of 4,703 private industry establishments of all sizes, representing over 102.3 million workers; see Appendix III. Survey covers all 50 States and the District of Columbia. See also Table 639]

Characteristic	Total [1]	Defined benefit	Defined contribution	Characteristic	Total [1]	Defined benefit	Defined contribution
Total	50	21	42	Full time	60	24	50
White-collar occupations . . .	61	24	53	Part time	20	9	14
Blue-collar occupations	50	25	38	Union	81	69	42
Service occupations	22	6	18	Nonunion	47	15	42

[1] Total is less than the sum of the individual retirement items because many employees participated in both types of plans.

Source: U.S. Bureau of Labor Statistics, *Summary*, 04-04, November, 2004. See also <http://www.bls.gov/ncs/ebs/sp/ebsm0002.pdf>.

Social Insurance and Human Services 367

Table 544. **Defined Benefit Retirement Plans—Selected Features: 2002**

[In percent. Covers full-time employees in private industry. Based on National Compensation Survey, a sample survey of 1,436 private industry establishments of all sizes, representing over 107 million workers; see Appendix III. See also Table 639]

Feature	All workers	White collar	Blue collar	Serv-ice	Goods pro-ducing	Serv-ice pro-ducing	1–99 work-ers	100 work-ers or more	Union	Non-union
Plan provisions:										
Benefits based on earnings	56	61	47	64	47	62	51	58	32	68
Early retirement benefits available	83	79	88	96	86	82	82	84	88	81
Availability of lump sum benefits at retirement	48	58	35	32	37	54	58	45	34	55
Benefit formula:										
Percent of terminal earnings	44	49	36	49	42	46	42	45	22	55
Percent of career earnings	12	13	10	16	5	16	8	13	10	13
Dollar amount formula	22	10	41	18	40	11	22	21	50	8
Percent of contribution formula	4	2	5	10	4	4	10	2	8	1
Cash balance	17	25	7	8	8	23	17	18	9	21
Pension equity	1	1	1	(Z)	1	1	1	1	(Z)	1
Requirements for normal retirement: [1]										
No age requirement	6	7	5	2	6	6	9	5	7	6
Less than 30 years of service	4	6	3	2	3	5	5	4	3	5
30 years of service	2	2	3	(S)	3	1	4	1	4	1
At age 55	4	4	5	2	3	5	3	4	6	3
At age 60	8	6	10	10	6	8	13	6	11	6
At age 62	14	8	21	25	18	11	14	14	25	8
At age 65	66	74	53	61	63	67	60	67	48	74
Sum of age plus service [2]	2	2	1	(S)	2	1	(S)	2	1	2

S Represents no employees in this category or data do not meet publication criteria.   Z Less than 0.5 percent.   [1] Normal retirement is defined as the point at which the participant could retire and immediately receive all accrued benefits by virtue of service and earnings, without reduction due to age. If a plan had alternative age and service requirements, the earliest age and associated service were tabulated; if one alternative did not specify an age, it was the requirement tabulated. Some age and service requirements are not shown separately.   [2] In some plans, participants must also satisfy a minimum age or service requirement.

Source: U.S. Bureau of Labor Statistics, National Compensation Survey: *Employee Benefits in Private Industry in the United States, 2002–2003*, Bulletin 2573. See also <http://stats.bls.gov/ncs/ebs/sp/ebbl0020.pdf>.

Table 545. **Pension Plan Coverage of Workers by Selected Characteristics: 2002**

[63,767 represents 63,767,000. Covers workers as of March 2003 who had earnings in 2002. Based on Current Population Survey; see text, Section 1, Population and Appendix III]

Sex and age	Number with coverage (1,000)				Percent of total workers			
	Total [1]	White [2]	Black [2]	His-panic [3]	Total [1]	White [2]	Black [2]	His-panic [3]
Total	63,767	53,514	6,648	4,803	41.9	42.5	40.0	25.6
Male	34,602	29,637	3,046	2,757	43.0	43.7	40.0	43.7
Under 65 years old	33,808	28,942	2,999	2,726	43.7	44.6	40.4	24.9
15 to 24 years old	1,630	1,363	190	224	13.2	13.2	15.0	10.1
25 to 44 years old	17,251	14,593	1,589	1,643	45.6	46.7	41.3	25.2
45 to 64 years old	14,926	12,986	1,220	859	55.0	55.6	52.9	38.3
65 years old and over . . .	794	694	46	32	24.9	24.4	24.2	17.6
Female.	29,165	23,878	3,602	2,046	40.8	41.2	40.0	26.9
Under 65 years old	28,509	23,312	3,548	2,019	41.3	41.8	40.3	26.9
15 to 24 years old	1,377	1,115	184	149	12.1	12.0	13.2	10.3
25 to 44 years old	14,282	11,414	1,930	1,241	43.7	44.3	41.6	29.2
45 to 64 years old	12,850	10,783	1,433	629	51.7	52.0	51.9	35.1
65 years old and over . . .	656	565	55	27	26.2	25.6	27.9	25.2

[1] Includes other races, not shown separately.   [2] Beginning with the 2003 CPS, respondents could choose one or more races. For example, White refers to people who reported White and did not report any other race category; Black refers to people who reported Black and did not report any other race category. The use of this single-race population does not imply that it is the preferred method of presenting or analyzing data. The Census Bureau uses a variety of approaches. Information on people who reported more than one race, such as "White and American Indian and Alaska Native" or "Asian and Black or African American," is available from Census 2000 through American FactFinder. About 2.6 percent of people reported more than one race in Census 2000.   [3] Hispanic persons may be of any race.

Source: U.S. Census Bureau, "Table NC8. Pension Plan Coverage of Workers by Selected Characteristics, Gender, Race and Hispanic Origin, and Poverty Status: 2002"; published May 2004; <http://ferret.bls.census.gov/macro/032003/noncash/toc.htm>.

Table 546. U.S. Households Owning IRAs: 2001 to 2004

[43.0 represents 43,000,000. Incidence of IRA ownership is based on an annual tracking survey of 3,000 randomly selected, representative U.S. households; see source for details]

Type of IRA	Number (mil.) [1]				Percent of U.S. households			
	2001	2002	2003	2004	2001	2002	2003	2004
Any type of IRA [2]	43.0	43.2	46.1	45.2	39.7	39.5	41.4	40.4
Traditional IRA	35.1	35.7	37.1	36.7	32.4	32.7	33.3	32.8
Roth IRA	12.2	13.2	16.2	14.3	11.3	12.1	14.6	12.8
SIMPLE IRA, SEP-IRA, or SAR-SEP IRA	8.3	8.5	8.3	9.6	7.7	7.8	7.5	8.6

[1] The number of U.S. households owning IRAs in 2001 through 2004 is based on the following U.S. Census Bureau's total U.S. household estimates: 108.2 million in 2001, 109.3 million in 2002, 111.3 million in 2003, and 112.0 million in 2004 (U.S. Bureau of the Census, Current Population Reports, P60-226, August 2004).   [2] Excludes ownership of Coverdell Education Savings Accounts, which were referred to as Education IRAs before July 2001.

Source: Investment Company Institute, Washington, DC, *Fundamentals, Investment Company Institute Research in Brief*, "IRA Ownership in 2004"; Vol 14, No. 1, February 2005 (copyright). See also <http://www.ici.org/statements/fundamentals /fm-v14n1.pdf>.

Table 547. 401(k) Plans—Selected Features: 2002

[In percent. Covers full-time employees in private industry. Based on National Compensation Survey, a sample survey of private industry establishments of all sizes, representing millions of workers; see Appendix III. See also Table 639]

Feature	All employees	White Collar	Blue Collar	Service
MAXIMUM PRETAX EMPLOYEE CONTRIBUTIONS [1]				
Percent of employee earnings	74	73	75	79
Specified dollar amount	2	1	1	4
Up to the Internal Revenue Code limit	23	24	21	17
Average maximum pretax contribution [2]	16.5	16.6	16.6	16.4
INVESTMENT CHOICES				
Employee permitted to choose investments	81	83	77	71
Employee not permitted to choose investments	3	2	3	9

S Indicates no employees in this category, or data do not meet publication criteria. Z Less than 0.5 percent. [1] Includes contributions that are not matched by the employer. If maximum contributions vary, such as by length of service, the highest possible contribution was tabulated.   [2] The average is presented for all covered workers; averages exclude workers without the plan provision.

Source: U.S. Bureau of Labor Statistics, National Compensation Survey: Employee Benefits in Private Industry in the United States, 2002–2003, Bulletin 2573. See also <http://stats.bls.gov/nec/home.htm>.

Table 548. State Unemployment Insurance—Summary: 1990 to 2004

[2,522 represents 2,522,000. Includes unemployment compensation for state and local government employees where covered by state law]

Item	Unit	1990	1995	1997	1998	1999	2000	2001	2002	2003	2004
Insured unemployment, avg. weekly	1,000	2,522	2,572	2,323	2,222	2,188	2,110	2,974	3,585	3,531	2,950
Percent of covered employment [1]	Percent	2.4	2.3	2.0	1.9	1.8	1.7	2.3	2.8	2.80	(NA)
Percent of civilian unemployed	Percent	35.8	34.7	34.5	35.8	38.0	38.0	45.0	44.0	39.5	36.6
Unemployment benefits, avg. weekly	Dollars	161	187	193	200	212	221	238	257	262	263
Percent of weekly wage	Percent	36.0	35.5	33.5	32.9	33.1	32.9	34.6	36.8	36.5	(NA)
Weeks compensated	Million	116.2	118.3	106.6	101.4	100.6	96.0	136.3	166.3	163.2	135.1
Beneficiaries, first payments [2]	1,000	8,629	8,035	7,325	7,332	6,951	7,033	9,877	10,088	9,935	8,369
Average duration of benefits [2]	Weeks	13.4	14.7	14.6	13.8	14.5	13.7	13.8	16.5	16.4	16.1
Claimants exhausting benefits	1,000	2,323	2,662	2,485	2,266	2,300	2,144	2,827	4,416	4,417	3,532
Percent of first payment [3]	Percent	29.4	34.3	32.8	31.8	31.4	31.8	34.1	42.5	43.4	39.0
Contributions collected [4]	Bil. dol.	15.2	22.0	21.2	19.8	19.2	19.9	19.7	19.7	25.3	31.2
Benefits paid	Bil. dol.	18.1	21.2	19.7	19.4	20.3	20.5	31.6	42.0	41.4	34.4
Funds available for benefits [5]	Bil. dol.	37.9	35.4	43.8	48.0	50.3	54.1	46.6	35.7	24.2	22.3
Average employer contribution rate [6]	Percent	1.95	2.44	2.13	1.92	1.77	1.75	1.71	1.80	2.20	(NA)

NA Not available.   [1] Insured unemployment as percent of average covered employment in preceding year.   [2] Weeks compensated divided by first payment.   [3] Based on first payments for 12-month period ending June 30.   [4] Contributions from employers; also employees in states which tax workers.   [5] End of year. Sum of balances in state clearing accounts, benefit-payment accounts, and state accounts in Federal unemployment trust funds.   [6] As percent of taxable wages.

Source: U.S. Employment and Training Administration, *Unemployment Insurance Financial Data Handbook*.

Social Insurance and Human Services   369

Table 549. **State Unemployment Insurance by State and Other Area: 2004**

[8,369 represents 8,369,000. See headnote, Table 548. For state data on insured unemployment, see Table 617]

State or other area	Beneficiaries, first payments (1,000)	Benefits paid (mil. dol.)	Avg. weekly unemploy-ment benefits (dol.)	State or other area	Beneficiaries, first payments (1,000)	Benefits paid (mil. dol.)	Avg. weekly unemploy-ment benefits (dol.)
Total	8,369	34,442	263	MT	22	69	197
AL........	119	241	177	NE	43	128	220
AK........	46	126	194	NV	66	258	245
AZ........	96	295	177	NH	21	84	251
AR	85	243	228	NJ........	332	1,943	331
CA	1,111	5,132	260	NM	32	127	220
CO	88	389	298	NY	513	2,584	271
CT........	128	590	284	NC	273	855	256
DE	28	107	247	ND	13	40	226
DC	17	91	257	OH	306	1,234	252
FL........	300	1,016	223	OK	60	204	219
GA	208	585	242	OR	148	653	252
HI	24	112	323	PA........	487	2,266	294
ID	50	145	229	RI........	41	203	324
IL	392	2,059	279	SC	123	352	211
IN	187	686	267	SD	10	30	205
IA	89	309	261	TN........	168	472	209
KS	68	279	272	TX	422	1,656	259
KY........	121	421	257	UT........	45	155	266
LA........	90	284	195	VT........	23	79	256
ME	33	116	235	VA........	126	385	240
MD	109	443	254	WA	208	1,049	310
MA	239	1,460	351	WV	44	147	219
MI	462	1,882	289	WI........	269	843	251
MN	147	678	318	WY	14	43	238
MS	60	158	172	PR	96	198	107
MO	166	534	205	VI	1	4	242

Source: U.S. Employment and Training Administration, *Unemployment Insurance Financial Data Handbook.*

Table 550. **Persons With Work Disability by Selected Characteristics: 2004**

[In thousands, except percent (19,016 represents 19,016,000). As of March. Covers civilian noninstitutional population and members of Armed Forces living off post or with their families on post. Persons are classified as having a work disability if they (1) have a health problem or disability which prevents them from working or which limits the kind or amount of work they can do; (2) have a service-connected disability or ever retired or left a job for health reasons; (3) did not work in survey reference week or previous year because of long-term illness or disability; or (4) are under age 65, and are covered by Medicare or receive supplemental security income. Based on Current Population Survey; see text, Section 1, Population, and Appendix III]

Age and participation status in assistance programs	Total [1]	Male	Female	White [2]	Black [3]	Hispanic [4]
Persons with work disability	**19,016**	**9,381**	**9,634**	**14,354**	**3,625**	**1,961**
16 to 24 years old.....................	1,504	812	692	1,045	374	178
25 to 34 years old.	2,331	1,138	1,193	1,642	527	304
35 to 44 years old.	3,741	1,892	1,849	2,801	721	434
45 to 54 years old.	5,320	2,642	2,678	4,001	1,064	550
55 to 64 years old.	6,120	2,898	3,222	4,866	938	495
Percent work disabled of total population . . .						
16 to 24 years old.....................	4.1	4.4	3.8	3.7	7.2	2.9
25 to 34 years old.....................	6.0	5.9	6.1	5.4	10.6	4.1
35 to 44 years old.....................	8.7	8.9	8.4	8.0	13.5	7.3
45 to 54 years old.....................	13.0	13.2	12.8	11.8	22.6	14.0
55 to 64 years old.....................	21.6	21.4	21.7	20.2	33.8	22.9
Percent of work disabled—						
Receiving social security income	33.7	34.4	33.0	34.4	32.8	26.0
Receiving food stamps	18.7	15.8	21.6	15.8	30.2	25.8
Covered by medicaid...................	65.3	67.6	63.1	68.6	52.3	56.5
Residing in public housing	6.6	5.8	7.5	4.8	13.7	9.1
Residing in subsidized housing	3.7	3.0	4.5	2.9	6.7	5.8

[1] Includes other races not shown separately. [2] The 2003 Current Population Survey asked respondents to choose one or more races. White alone refers to people who reported White and did not report any other race category. The use of this single-race population does not imply that it is the preferred method of presenting or analyzing data. The Census Bureau uses a variety of approaches. Information on people who reported more than one race, such as "White and American Indian and Alaska Native" or "Asian and Black or African American," is available from Census 2001 through American FactFinder. About 2.6 percent of people reported more than one race in 2000. [3] Black alone refers to people who reported Black and did not report any other race category. [4] Hispanic persons may be of any race.

Source: U.S. Census Bureau, unpublished data.

Table 551. Workers' Compensation Payments: 1990 to 2002

[In billions of dollars, except as indicated (53.1 represents $53,100,000,000). See headnote, Table 552]

Item	1990	1994	1995	1996	1997	1998	1999	2000	2001	2002
Workers covered (mil.)	106	109	113	115	118	122	124	127	127	126
Premium amounts paid [1]	**53.1**	**60.5**	**57.1**	**55.3**	**53.5**	**53.4**	**55.7**	**59.7**	**64.5**	**72.9**
Private carriers [1]	35.1	34.0	31.6	30.5	29.9	30.4	32.0	35.3	36.8	41.2
State funds	8.0	11.2	10.5	10.2	8.0	8.0	8.1	8.7	11.1	14.3
Federal programs [2].	2.2	2.5	2.6	2.6	3.4	3.5	3.5	3.6	3.8	3.9
Self-insurers	7.9	12.8	12.5	12.1	12.3	11.7	12.1	12.2	12.9	13.5
Annual benefits paid [1]	**38.2**	**43.4**	**43.5**	**41.8**	**42.4**	**43.9**	**45.9**	**48.3**	**49.8**	**53.4**
By private carriers [1]	22.2	22.7	21.4	20.4	21.6	23.0	24.6	26.5	27.3	29.0
From state funds [3]	8.8	10.6	10.9	7.6	7.3	7.2	7.3	7.5	8.0	9.4
Employers' self-insurance [4]	7.2	11.5	11.2	10.8	10.6	10.2	10.5	10.7	11.5	11.9
Type of benefit:										
Medical/hospitalization	15.1	17.1	16.6	16.5	17.2	17.9	19.2	20.6	22.1	24.2
Compensation payments	21.7	26.3	25.7	24.2	24.3	24.5	25.2	26.2	26.8	28.4
Percent of covered payroll: [1]										
Workers' compensation costs [5, 6] . . .	2.18	2.05	1.82	1.66	1.49	1.38	1.34	1.33	1.40	1.58
Benefits [6]	1.57	1.51	1.38	1.26	1.18	1.11	1.09	1.06	1.08	1.16

[1] Premium and benefit amounts include estimated payments under insurance policy deductible provisions. Deductible benefits are allocated to private carriers and state funds. [2] Years 1990–1996 include federal employer compensation program and that portion of federal black lung benefits program financed from employer contributions. Years 1997–2002 include federal employer compensation program only due to changes in reporting methods. [3] Net cash and medical benefits paid by competitive and exclusive state funds and by federal workers' compensation programs. [4] Cash and medical benefits paid by self-insurers, plus value of medical benefits paid by employers carrying workers' compensation policies that exclude standard medical coverage. [5] Premiums written by private carriers and state funds, and benefits paid by self-insurers increased by 5–10 prior to 1992 and by 11 percent for 1992–2002 for administrative costs. Also includes benefits paid and administrative costs of federal system for government employees. [6] Excludes programs financed from general revenue—black lung benefits and supplemental pensions in some states.

Source: National Academy of Social Insurance, Washington, DC, *Workers' Compensation: Benefits, Coverage, and Costs*, annual.

Table 552. Workers' Compensation Payments by State: 1998 to 2002

[In millions of dollars (43,881 represents $43,881,000,000). Calendar-year data. Payments represent compensation and medical benefits and include insurance losses paid by private insurance carriers (compiled from state workers' compensation agencies and A.M. Best Co.); disbursements of state funds (compiled from the A.M. Best Co. and state workers' compensation agencies); and self-insurance payments (compiled from state workers' compensation agencies and authors' estimates)]

State	1998	1999	2000	2001	2002	State	1998	1999	2000	2001	2002
Total	**43,881**	**45,896**	**48,284**	**49,772**	**53,443**						
						Montana	137	146	170	173	191
Alabama	602	551	529	563	565	Nebraska	164	198	211	238	293
Alaska	127	130	146	171	188	Nevada	331	384	361	385	353
Arizona	433	466	515	465	528	New Hampshire	170	190	182	216	217
Arkansas	174	185	198	207	222	New Jersey	1,164	1,240	1,299	1,363	1,471
California	7,366	7,852	8,968	9,605	11,283	New Mexico	128	136	146	163	191
Colorado	811	739	835	586	807	New York	2,601	2,796	2,909	2,978	3,142
Connecticut	715	737	667	661	748	North Carolina	810	814	853	890	1,014
Delaware	147	133	146	146	169	North Dakota	69	70	74	76	74
District of						Ohio	2,077	2,039	2,099	2,248	2,388
Columbia	90	90	89	93	102	Oklahoma	536	496	485	500	490
Florida	2,538	2,768	2,545	2,670	2,306						
Georgia	889	896	996	1,067	1,083	Oregon	431	384	412	456	448
Hawaii	233	222	231	252	268	Pennsylvania	2,418	2,467	2,403	2,440	2,532
Idaho	164	169	179	199	233	Rhode Island	110	113	114	124	131
Illinois	1,838	1,953	2,049	2,139	2,232	South Carolina	467	512	597	623	690
Indiana	481	511	546	531	577	South Dakota	67	73	67	75	79
Iowa	321	322	357	396	428	Tennessee	551	586	642	692	679
Kansas	319	326	342	340	405	Texas	1,592	1,875	2,005	2,056	2,275
Kentucky	421	478	479	482	527	Utah	189	196	188	211	240
						Vermont	91	106	112	106	148
Louisiana	442	465	494	502	499	Virginia	658	629	681	672	700
Maine	254	266	267	265	293	Washington	1,287	1,395	1,528	1,638	1,714
Maryland	691	714	730	796	784	West Virginia	644	687	690	712	829
Massachusetts	729	733	828	774	807	Wisconsin	704	724	768	924	894
Michigan	1,367	1,393	1,474	1,478	1,512	Wyoming	73	75	83	98	104
Minnesota	737	745	798	904	921						
Mississippi	235	254	269	271	287	Federal total [1]	3,471	3,496	3,620	3,069	3,154
Missouri	814	972	909	1,080	1,226	Federal employees . .	2,010	2,000	2,118	2,223	2,317

NA Not available. [1] Federal benefits include: those paid under the Federal Employees Compensation Act for civilian employees; the portion of the Black Lung benefit program that is financed by employers; and a portion of benefits under the Longshore and Harbor Workers Compensation Act that are not reflected in state data, namely, benefits paid by self-insured employers and by special funds under the LHWCA. See Appendix H of source for more information about federal programs.

Source: National Academy of Social Insurance, Washington, DC, *Workers' Compensation: Benefits, Coverage, and Costs*, annual. Also see <http://www.nasi.org/>.

Table 553. **Supplemental Security Income—Recipients and Payments: 1990 to 2003**

[As of December, except total payments, calendar year (4,817 represents 4,817,000). See also Appendix III]

Program	Unit	1990	1995	1997	1998	1999	2000	2001	2002	2003
Recipients, total [1]	1,000	4,817	6,514	6,495	6,566	6,557	6,602	6,688	6,787	6,902
Aged	1,000	1,454	1,446	1,363	1,332	1,308	1,289	1,264	1,251	1,233
Blind	1,000	84	84	81	80	79	79	78	77	77
Disabled	1,000	3,279	4,984	5,052	5,154	5,169	5,234	5,345	5,459	5,593
Payments, total [2]	Mil. dol.	16,599	27,628	29,052	30,216	30,923	31,564	33,060	34,566	35,605
Aged	Mil. dol.	3,736	4,467	4,532	4,425	4,712	4,811	4,958	5,085	5,147
Blind	Mil. dol.	334	376	375	366	391	394	407	426	419
Disabled	Mil. dol.	12,521	22,779	24,006	25,305	25,719	26,198	27,611	28,996	29,966
Average monthly payment, total [1]	Dollars	299	358	351	359	368	378	393	407	417
Aged	Dollars	213	251	268	277	289	299	314	330	342
Blind	Dollars	342	370	382	390	401	413	428	445	455
Disabled	Dollars	337	389	373	380	388	397	412	425	433

[1] Persons with a federal SSI payment and/or federally-administered state supplementation. [2] Includes payments not distributed by reason for eligibility.

Source: U.S. Social Security Administration, *Social Security Bulletin*, quarterly and *Annual Statistical Supplement to the Social Security Bulletin.*

Table 554. **Supplemental Security Income (SSI)—Recipients and Payments by State and Other Area: 2000 to 2003**

[Recipients as of December; payments for calendar year (6,602 represents 6,602,000). Data cover federal SSI payments and/or federally-administered state supplementation. For explanation of methodology, see Appendix III.]

State and other area	Recipients (1,000)		Payments for year (mil. dol.)			State and other area	Recipients (1,000)		Payments for year (mil. dol.)		
	2000	2003	2000	2002	2003		2000	2003	2000	2002	2003
Total	6,602	6,903	30,672	33,722	34,700	MO	112	115	471	515	528
U.S.	6,601	6,902	30,669	33,719	34,696	MT	14	14	57	63	64
AL	159	164	659	730	738	NE	21	22	85	93	95
AK	9	11	37	44	47	NV	25	31	108	133	144
AZ	81	92	355	406	429	NH	12	13	49	56	58
AR	85	87	333	354	361	NJ	146	150	672	721	732
CA	1,088	1,163	6,386	7,230	7,573	NM	47	50	193	217	223
CO	54	54	228	243	246	NY	617	625	3,197	3,408	3,400
CT	49	51	216	236	244	NC	191	194	732	798	825
DE	12	13	50	56	59	ND	8	8	30	32	32
DC	20	20	93	102	105	OH	240	244	1,114	1,190	1,204
FL	377	409	1,621	1,814	1,908	OK	72	75	302	328	339
GA	197	200	785	854	888	OR	52	57	228	263	271
HI	21	22	104	111	113	PA	284	311	1,367	1,551	1,599
ID	18	20	76	87	91	RI	28	29	130	146	150
IL	249	255	1,174	1,247	1,267	SC	107	106	429	454	461
IN	88	94	382	424	441	SD	13	13	48	52	52
IA	40	42	158	175	176	TN	164	161	664	705	719
KS	36	38	151	164	170	TX	409	455	1,575	1,797	1,901
KY	174	179	741	803	819	UT	20	21	87	98	99
LA	166	168	715	761	769	VT	13	13	51	55	57
ME	30	31	116	131	136	VA	132	134	535	575	587
MD	88	91	400	435	441	WA	101	109	484	540	546
MA	168	168	807	849	855	WV	71	75	318	349	357
MI	210	217	988	1,065	1,086	WI	85	89	357	386	398
MN	64	69	272	303	316	WY	6	6	23	25	25
MS	129	126	512	543	550	N. Mariana	1	1	3	3	4

Source: U.S. Social Security Administration, *Annual Statistical Supplement* to the *Social Security Bulletin.*

Table 555. **Temporary Assistance for Needy Families (TANF)—Families and Recipients: 1980 to 2004**

[In thousands (3,712 represents 3,712,000). Average monthly families and recipients for calendar year. Prior to TANF, the cash assistance program to families was called Aid to Families with Dependent Children (1980-1996). Under the new welfare law (Personal Responsibility and Work Opportunity Reconciliation Act of 1996), the program became TANF. See text, this section. Includes Puerto Rico, Guam, and Virgin Islands]

Year	Families	Recipients	Year	Families	Recipients	Year	Families	Recipients
1980	3,712	10,774	1989	3,799	10,993	1997	3,740	10,376
1982	3,542	10,258	1990	4,057	11,695	1998	3,050	8,347
1983	3,686	10,761	1991	4,467	12,930	1999	2,554	6,824
1984	3,714	10,831	1992	4,829	13,773	2000	2,215	5,778
1985	3,701	10,855	1993	5,012	14,205	2001	2,104	5,359
1986	3,763	11,038	1994	5,033	14,161	2002	2,048	5,069
1987	3,776	11,027	1995	4,791	13,418	2003	2,025	4,932
1988	3,749	10,915	1996	4,434	12,321	2004	1,987	4,783

Source: U.S. Administration for Children and Families, unpublished data.

372 Social Insurance and Human Services

Table 556. **Temporary Assistance for Needy Families (TANF)—Recipients by State and Other Areas: 2000 to 2004**

[In thousands (2,215 represents 2,215,000). Average monthly families and recipients for calendar year, except as noted. See headnote, Table 555]

State or other area	Families			Recipients			State or other area	Families			Recipients		
	2000	2003	2004	2000	2003	2004		2000	2003	2004	2000	2003	2004
Total...	2,215	2,025	1,987	5,778	4,932	4,783	MT	5	6	5	13	17	14
U.S	2,181	2,002	1,966	5,678	4,867	4,723	NE	9	11	11	24	27	27
AL	19	19	19	45	46	45	NV	6	10	9	16	24	21
AK	7	5	5	21	15	14	NH	6	6	6	14	14	14
AZ	33	49	50	84	116	115	NJ	50	43	45	125	104	108
AR	12	11	10	29	25	22	NM	23	17	18	69	45	46
CA	489	450	457	1,262	1,107	1,103	NY	250	148	147	695	336	336
CO	11	14	15	28	37	38	NC	45	40	38	98	83	77
CT	27	21	21	64	43	43	ND	3	3	3	7	9	8
DE	6	6	6	12	13	13	OH	95	84	85	235	187	186
DC	17	17	17	45	43	44	OK	14	15	14	35	37	34
FL	65	58	57	142	120	116	OR	17	19	19	38	43	42
GA	52	56	53	125	134	124	PA	88	82	88	241	214	231
HI	14	10	9	46	25	23	RI	16	13	12	44	35	32
ID	1	2	2	2	3	3	SC	18	21	17	42	51	39
IL	78	36	36	234	92	89	SD	3	3	3	7	6	6
IN	37	52	51	101	138	131	TN	57	70	72	147	185	190
IA	20	20	18	53	52	45	TX	129	129	105	347	318	250
KS	13	16	17	32	41	44	UT	8	9	9	21	22	23
KY	38	35	36	87	77	78	VT	6	5	5	16	13	12
LA	27	23	19	71	57	46	VA	31	20	9	69	47	27
ME	11	10	10	28	26	27	WA	56	55	56	148	135	137
MD	29	26	25	71	62	59	WV	13	16	15	33	41	36
MA	43	50	50	100	109	108	WI	17	21	22	38	50	54
MI	72	77	79	198	206	212	WY	1	-	-	1	1	1
MN	39	36	34	114	94	88	PR.	30	19	17	88	53	49
MS	15	20	19	34	45	42	GU	3	3	3	10	11	11
MO	47	41	41	125	101	100	VI	1	-	1	3	1	2

- Represents or rounds to zero.

Source: U.S. Administration for Children and Families, unpublished data.

Table 557. **Temporary Assistance for Needy Families (TANF)—Expenditures by State: 2000 to 2003**

[In millions of dollars (24,781 represents $24,781,000,000), except as indicated. Represents federal and state funds expended in fiscal year]

State	2000, total	2002, total	2003		State	2000, total	2002, total	2003	
			Total ¹	Expenditures on assistance				Total ¹	Expenditures on assistance
U.S. . . .	24,781	25,414	26,340	11,717	MO	321	326	299	130
AL	96	135	171	50	MT	44	61	56	35
AK	93	93	88	59	NE	79	77	79	59
AZ	261	309	342	175	NV	69	89	85	54
AR	139	70	54	22	NH	73	72	72	37
CA	6,481	5,477	5,851	3,436	NJ	321	952	842	274
CO	205	233	236	53	NM	149	123	123	79
CT	436	436	450	162	NY	3,512	3,852	4,463	2,097
DE	55	56	56	37	NC	440	471	457	136
DC	157	209	166	68	ND	33	33	42	29
FL	781	993	852	293	OH	995	901	1,007	310
GA	386	511	501	203	OK	130	148	203	174
HI	162	137	134	91	OR	169	258	226	120
ID	43	39	43	7	PA	1,327	1,063	1,109	346
IL	879	971	989	132	RI	172	174	162	91
IN	342	328	313	125	SC	245	134	148	51
IA	163	150	156	60	SD	21	23	26	19
KS	151	137	150	83	TN	293	311	274	165
KY	203	207	191	119	TX	727	741	911	405
LA	118	240	267	73	UT	100	110	131	56
ME	108	104	100	87	VT	62	69	67	42
MD	336	428	366	32	VA	418	264	273	129
MA	690	670	697	355	WA	535	628	572	269
MI	1,264	1,267	1,205	416	WV	134	214	157	88
MN	381	466	498	193	WI	382	489	489	109
MS	62	144	120	67	WY	34	22	71	17

¹ Includes other items not shown separately.

Source: U.S. Administration for Children and Families, *Temporary Assistance for Needy Families (TANF) Program, Annual Report to Congress.*

U.S. Census Bureau, Statistical Abstract of the United States: 2006

Table 558. Child Support—Award and Recipiency Status of Custodial Parent: 2001

[In thousands except as noted (13,383 represents 13,383,000). Custodial parents 15 years and older with own children under 21 years of age present from absent parents as of spring 2002. Covers civilian noninstitutional population. Based on Current Population Survey; see text, section 1 and Appendix III. For definition of mean, see Guide to Tabular Presentation]

Award and recipiency status	All custodial parents				Custodial parents below the poverty level			
	Total		Mothers	Fathers	Total		Mothers	Fathers
	Number	Percent distribution			Number	Percent distribution		
Total......................	13,383	(X)	11,291	2,092	3,131	(X)	2,823	308
With child support agreement or award ...	7,916	(X)	7,110	807	1,706	(X)	1,571	135
Supposed to receive payments in 2001...	6,924	100.0	6,212	712	1,469	100.0	1,339	130
Actually received payments in 2001 ...	5,119	73.9	4,639	480	963	65.6	885	77
Received full amount	3,099	44.8	2,821	278	453	30.8	423	30
Received partial payments........	2,020	29.2	1,818	202	510	34.7	463	47
Did not receive payments in 2001.....	1,804	26.1	1,573	232	507	34.5	454	53
Child support not awarded...........	5,466	(X)	4,181	1,285	1,425	(X)	1,253	172
MEAN INCOME AND CHILD SUPPORT								
Received child support payments in 2001:								
Mean total money income (dol.)........	29,008	(X)	28,258	36,255	7,571	(X)	7,604	7,189
Mean child support received (dol.)......	4,274	(X)	4,274	4,273	3,041	(X)	3,078	2,622
Received the full amount due:								
Mean total money income (dol.)....	32,338	(X)	31,734	38,479	7,963	(X)	7,958	8,032
Mean child support received (dol.)...	5,665	(X)	5,655	5,768	4,576	(X)	4,701	2,831
Received partial payments:								
Mean total money income (dol.)....	23,899	(X)	22,865	33,199	7,223	(X)	7,281	6,647
Mean child support received (dol.)...	2,141	(X)	2,132	2,219	1,677	(X)	1,595	2,487
Received no payments in 2001:								
Mean total money income (dol.).......	23,571	(X)	21,835	35,348	6,832	(X)	6,755	7,492
Without child support agreement or award:								
Mean total money income (dol.)........	24,055	(X)	19,339	39,396	6,113	(X)	6,089	6,287

X Not applicable.

Source: U.S. Census Bureau, unpublished data.

Table 559. Child Support Enforcement Program—Caseload and Collections: 1990 to 2004

[For years ending September 30 (12,796 represents 12,796,000). Includes Puerto Rico, Guam, and the Virgin Islands. The child support enforcement program locates absent parents, establishes paternity of children born out-of-wedlock, and establishes and enforces support orders. By law, these services are available to all families that need them. The program is operated at the state and local government level, but 68 percent of administrative costs are paid by the federal government. Child support collected for families not receiving Temporary Assistance for Needy Families (TANF) goes to the family to help it remain self-sufficient. Most of the child support collected on behalf of TANF families goes to federal and state governments to offset TANF payments. Some states pass-through a portion of the CS collections to help families become self-sufficient. Based on data reported by state agencies. Minus sign (-) indicates net outlay]

Item	Unit	1990	1995	1999	2000	2001	2002	2003	2004, prel.
Total cases [1]..............	1,000.....	12,796	19,162	17,330	17,334	17,061	16,066	15,923	15,854
Paternities established, total [2]...	1,000.....	393	659	845	867	777	697	663	692
Support orders established, total [3]...	1,000.....	1,022	1,051	1,220	1,175	1,181	1,220	1,161	1,181
FINANCES									
Collections, total	Mil. dol....	6,010	10,827	15,901	17,854	18,958	20,137	21,176	21,861
TANF/FC collections [4].......	Mil. dol....	1,750	2,689	2,482	2,593	2,592	2,893	2,972	2,239
State share	Mil. dol....	620	939	1,048	1,080	1,004	947	947	927
Incentive payments to states.....	Mil. dol....	264	400	377	353	337	338	356	361
Federal share [5]............	Mil. dol....	533	822	922	968	895	1,183	1,167	1,147
Non-TANF collections	Mil. dol....	4,260	8,138	13,419	15,261	16,366	17,244	18,204	19,598
Administrative expenditures, total....................	Mil. dol....	1,606	3,012	4,039	4,526	4,835	5,183	5,216	5,322
State share	Mil. dol....	545	918	1,359	1,519	1,613	1,752	1,765	1,803
Federal share.............	Mil. dol....	1,061	2,095	2,680	3,006	3,222	3,432	3,450	3,519
Program savings, total	Mil. dol....	-190	-852	-1,692	-2,125	-2,599	-3,053	-3,098	-3,249
State share	Mil. dol....	338	421	66	-87	-272	-466	-461	-515
Federal share.............	Mil. dol....	-528	-1,273	-1,758	-2,038	-2,327	-2,587	-2,637	-2,734

[1] Passage of the Personal Responsibility and Work Opportunity Reconciliation Act of 1996 (PRWORA) mandated new categories in 1999 and cases were no longer double counted resulting in a 2 million case reduction. [2] Does not include in-hospital paternities. [3] Through 1990, includes modifications to orders. [4] Collections for current assistance cases where the children are: (1) recipients of TANF under title IV-A of the Social Security Act, or (2) entitled to Foster Care (FC) maintenance under title IV-E of the Social Security Act plus collections distributed as assistance reimbursements. Includes medical support and payments of current assistance not shown separately. Assistance reimbursements are collections that will be divided between the state and federal governments to reimburse their respective shares of either Title IV-A assistance payments or Title IV-E Foster Care maintenance payments. [5] Prior to fiscal year 2000, incentives were paid out of the federal share of collections and the net federal share was reported.

Source: U.S. Department of Health and Human Services, Office of Child Support Enforcement, Annual Report to Congress.

Table 560. Federal Food Programs: 1990 to 2004

[20.0 represents 20,000,000. For years ending Sept. 30. Program data include Puerto Rico, Virgin Islands, Guam, American Samoa, Northern Marianas, and the former Trust Territory when a federal food program was operated in these areas. Participation data are average monthly figures except as noted. Participants are not reported for the commodity distribution programs. Cost data are direct federal benefits to recipients; they exclude Federal administrative payments and applicable state and local contributions. Federal costs for commodities and cash-in-lieu of commodities are shown separately from direct cash benefits for those programs receiving both]

Program	Unit	1990	1995	1999	2000	2001	2002	2003	2004
Food Stamp:									
Participants	Million....	20.0	26.6	18.2	17.2	17.3	19.1	21.3	23.9
Federal cost	Mil. dol....	14,186	22,764	15,769	14,983	15,547	18,256	21,404	24,628
Monthly average coupon value per recipient	Dollars...	58.96	71.27	72.27	72.62	74.82	79.67	83.90	86.02
Nutrition assistance program for Puerto Rico:									
Federal cost	Mil. dol....	937	1,131	1,236	1,268	1,296	1,351	1,395	1,413
National school lunch program (NSLP):									
Free lunches served	Million....	1,662	2,090	2,207	2,205	2,182	2,277	2,335	2,397
Reduced-price lunches served	Million....	273	308	392	409	425	441	453	462
Children participating [1]	Million....	24.1	25.7	27.0	27.3	27.5	28.0	28.4	29.0
Federal cost	Mil. dol....	3,214	4,466	5,315	5,494	5,612	6,050	6,340	6,663
School breakfast (SB):									
Children participating [1]	Million....	4.1	6.3	7.4	7.6	7.8	8.1	8.4	8.9
Federal cost	Mil. dol....	596	1,048	1,346	1,393	1,450	1,567	1,651	1,774
Special supplemental food program (WIC): [2]									
Participants	Million....	4.5	6.9	7.3	7.2	7.3	7.5	7.6	7.9
Federal cost	Mil. dol....	1,637	2,512	2,852	2,853	3,008	3,130	3,230	3,561
Child and adult care (CAC): [3]									
Participants [4]	Million....	1.5	2.3	2.7	2.7	2.7	2.9	2.9	3.0
Federal cost	Mil. dol....	719	1,296	1,438	1,500	1,548	1,658	1,727	1,813
Federal cost of commodities donated to— [5]									
Child nutrition (NSLP, CACFP, SFS, and SBP)	Mil. dol....	644	733	754	704	917	862	909	1,032
Emergency feeding [6]	Mil. dol....	282	160	234	182	333	380	396	360

[1] Average monthly participation (excluding summer months of June through August). Includes children in public and private elementary and secondary schools and in residential child care institutes. [2] WIC serves pregnant and postpartum women, infants, and children up to age five. [3] CACFP provides year-round subsidies to feed preschool children in child care centers and family day care homes. Certain care centers serving disabled or elderly adults also receive meal subsidies. [4] Average quarterly daily attendance at participating institutions. [5] Includes the Federal cost of commodity entitlements, cash-in-lieu of commodities, and bonus foods. [6] Provides free commodities to needy persons for home consumption through food banks, hunger centers, soup kitchens, and similar nonprofit agencies. Includes the Emergency Food Assistance Program, the commodity purchases for soup kitchens/food banks program (FY 1989–96), and commodity disaster relief.

Source: U.S. Dept. of Agriculture, Food and Nutrition Service, "Food and Nutrition Service, Program Data"; <http://www.fns.usda.gov/pd/>; updated monthly.

Table 561. Federal Food Stamp Program by State: 2000 to 2004

[Participation data are average monthly numbers (17,194 represents 17,194,000). For years ending Sept. 30. Food stamp costs are for benefits only and exclude administrative expenditures]

State	Persons (1,000)			Benefits (mil. dol.)			State	Persons (1,000)			Benefits (mil. dol.)		
	2000	2003	2004	2000	2003	2004		2000	2003	2004	2000	2003	2004
Total [1]	17,194	21,259	23,858	14,983	21,404	24,628	MS	276	356	377	226	335	361
U.S.	17,156	21,222	23,819	14,927	21,332	24,560	MO	423	592	700	358	568	663
							MT	59	71	77	51	69	79
AL	396	472	498	344	466	513	NE	82	99	114	61	89	109
AK	38	51	49	46	66	64	NV	61	111	120	57	113	120
AZ	259	466	530	240	498	578	NH	36	45	48	28	40	44
AR	247	310	346	206	304	347							
CA	1,830	1,709	1,859	1,639	1,806	1,990	NJ	345	339	369	304	339	378
CO	156	208	242	127	203	251	NM	169	195	223	140	184	217
CT	165	181	196	138	165	198	NY	1,439	1,436	1,598	1,361	1,677	1,876
DE	32	46	56	31	48	57	NC	488	649	747	403	645	753
DC	81	82	89	77	90	98	ND	32	40	41	25	37	40
FL	882	1,041	1,202	771	988	1,269	OH	610	855	945	520	879	1,009
							OK	253	380	412	208	362	398
GA	559	750	867	489	782	924	OR	234	398	420	198	381	415
HI	118	100	99	166	156	152	PA	777	823	961	656	785	933
ID	58	82	91	46	77	91	RI	74	74	78	59	69	74
IL	817	954	1,070	777	1,053	1,211	SC	295	451	497	249	443	501
IN	300	470	526	268	484	550	SD	43	51	53	37	51	54
IA	123	154	179	100	149	176	TN	496	728	806	415	722	812
KS	117	161	170	83	140	158	TX	1,333	1,872	2,259	1,215	1,881	2,307
KY	403	503	545	337	486	543	UT	82	106	123	68	102	123
LA	500	655	706	448	685	754	VT	41	41	43	32	38	40
ME	102	133	142	81	124	140	VA	336	393	486	263	366	476
							WA	295	404	453	241	394	455
MD	219	252	274	199	257	287	WV	227	247	256	185	216	232
MA	232	292	335	182	254	304	WI	193	297	324	129	233	269
MI	603	838	944	457	783	896	WY	22	25	26	19	24	25
MN	196	235	247	165	227	249							

[1] Includes Guam and the Virgin Islands. Several outlying areas receive nutrition assistance grants in lieu of food stamp assistance (e.g., Puerto Rico, American Samoa and the Northern Marianas).

Source: U.S. Dept. of Agriculture, Food and Nutrition Service. "Food and Nutrition Service, Program Data"; <http://www.fns.usda.gov/pd/>; updated monthly.

U.S. Census Bureau, Statistical Abstract of the United States: 2006

Table 562. **Selected Characteristics of Food Stamp Households and Participants: 1990 to 2003**

[7,803 represents 7,803,000. For years ending September 30. Data for 1990 exclude Guam and the Virgin Islands. Based on a sample of households from the Food Stamp Quality Control System]

Year	Households				Participants		
		Percent of total				Percent of total	
	Total (1,000)	With children	With elderly [1]	With disabled [2]	Total (1,000)	Children	Elderly [1]
1990	7,803	60.3	18.1	8.9	20,411	49.6	7.7
1995	10,883	59.7	16.0	18.9	26,955	51.5	7.1
1998	8,246	58.3	18.2	24.4	19,969	52.8	8.2
1999	7,670	55.7	20.1	26.5	18,149	51.5	9.4
2000	7,335	53.9	21.0	27.5	17,091	51.3	10.0
2001	7,450	53.6	20.4	27.7	17,297	51.1	9.6
2002	8,201	54.1	18.7	27.0	19,041	51.0	8.9
2003	8,971	54.7	18.0	23.3	20,934	50.8	8.5

[1] Persons 60 years old and over. [2] Beginning 1995, disabled households are defined as households with at least one member under age 65 who received SSI, or at least one member age 18 to 61 who received Social Security, veteran's benefits, or other government benefits as a result of a disability. For 1990, disabled households are defined as households with SSI but no members over age 59. The substantial increase in the percentage of households with a disabled member between 1994 and 1995 is due in part to the change in the definition of disabled households. Using the previous definition, 13.3 percent of households included a disabled person in fiscal year 1995.

Source: U.S. Dept. of Agriculture, Food and Nutrition Service, *Characteristics of Food Stamp Households: Fiscal Year 2003*, November 2004.

Table 563. **Food Stamp Households and Participants—Summary: 2003**

[8,971 represents 8,971,000. For year ending September 30. Based on a sample of 46,963 households from the Food Stamp Quality Control System]

Household type and income source	Households		Age, sex, race, and Hispanic origin	Participants	
	Number (1,000)	Percent		Number (1,000)	Percent
Total....................	8,971	100.0	Total...............	20,934	100.0
With children.................	4,909	54.7	Children..............	10,629	50.8
Single-parent households..........	3,075	34.3	Under 5 years old.........	3,541	16.9
Married-couple households.........	877	9.8	5 to 17 years old.........	7,087	33.9
Other.................	957	10.7	Adults................	10,302	49.2
With elderly.................	1,616	18.0	18 to 35 years old........	4,445	21.2
Living alone...............	1,129	14.2	36 to 59 years old........	4,069	19.4
Not living alone.............	339	3.8	60 years old and over.......	1,788	8.5
Disabled.................	2,089	23.3			
Living alone...............	1,129	12.6	Male..................	8,605	41.1
Not living alone.............	960	10.7	Female................	12,327	58.9
Earned income.................	2,533	28.2	White, non-Hispanic........	8,861	42.3
Wages and salaries...........	2,275	25.4	Black, non-Hispanic........	7,186	34.3
Unearned income.............	6,489	72.3	Hispanic..............	3,841	18.3
TANF [1]................	1,529	17.0	Asian................	559	2.7
Supplemental Security Income........	2,524	28.1	Native American..........	321	1.5
Social Security............	2,095	23.4	Other................	166	0.8
No income..................	1,049	11.7			

[1] Temporary Assistance for Needy Families (TANF) program.

Source: U.S. Dept. of Agriculture, Food and Nutrition Service, *Characteristics of Food Stamp Households: Fiscal Year 2003*, November 2004.

Table 564. **Head Start—Summary: 1980 to 2004**

[For years ending September 30 (376 represents 376,000)]

Year	Enrollment (1,000)	Appropriation (mil. dol.)	Age and race	Enrollment, 2004 (percent)	Item	Number
1980 ...	376	735	Under 3 years old.....	9	Average cost per child:	
1990 ...	541	1,552	3 years old..........	34	1995............	$4,534
1994 ...	740	3,326	4 years old..........	52	2000............	$5,951
1995 ...	751	3,534	5 years old and over ...	5	2004............	$7,222
1996 ...	752	3,569				
1997 ...	794	3,981			Paid staff (1,000):	
1998 ...	822	4,347	White.............	27	1995............	147
1999 ...	826	4,658	Black.............	31	2000............	180
2000 ...	858	5,267	Hispanic...........	31	2004............	212
2001 ...	905	6,200	American Indian.......	3	Volunteers (1,000):	
2002 ...	912	6,537	Asian.............	2	1995............	1,235
2003 ...	910	6,668	Hawaiian/..........		2000............	1,252
2004 ...	906	6,775	Pacific Islander.....	1	2004............	1,353

Source: U.S. Administration for Children and Families, "Head Start Statistical Fact Sheet"; <http://www2.acf.dhhs.gov/programs/hsb/research/2005.htm>.

Table 565. **Social Assistance—Establishments, Receipts, Payroll, and Employees by Kind of Business: 2002**

[19,172 represents $19,172,000,000. For combined social assistance taxable and tax-exempt data, see Table 737]

Kind of business	NAICS code [1]	Taxable firms				Tax-exempt firms			
		Establish-ments (number)	Receipts (mil. dol.)	Annual payroll (mil. dol.)	Paid employ-ees [2] (1,000)	Establish-ments (number)	Receipts (mil. dol.)	Annual payroll (mil. dol.)	Paid employ-ees [2] (1,000)
Social assistance	624	57,901	19,172	8,828	611.0	81,070	72,240	27,263	1,494.9
Individual & family services . . .	6241	10,811	5,204	2,316	142.4	38,405	40,342	15,240	754.4
Child & youth services	62411	1,337	761	283	13.5	8,078	8,725	3,063	136.8
Services for elderly & disabled persons	62412	4,003	2,258	1,208	93.4	11,048	13,058	4,943	276.2
Other individual & family services.	62419	5,471	2,185	824	35.5	19,279	18,559	7,234	341.4
Community/emergency & other relief services	6242	367	81	24	1.4	12,069	12,849	3,190	142.8
Community food services	62421	116	19	6	0.4	3,777	2,844	528	29.2
Community housing services	62422	147	45	14	0.7	6,579	5,584	2,038	91.4
Emergency & other relief services	62423	104	16	5	0.3	1,713	4,421	625	22.2
Vocational rehabilitation services.	6243	2,167	1,821	804	32.7	6,318	9,365	4,011	282.5
Child day care services	6244	44,556	12,066	5,684	434.3	24,278	9,684	4,822	315.3

[1] North American Industry Classification System, 2002; see text, Section 15.   [2] For pay period including March 12.

Source: U.S. Census Bureau, *2002 Economic Census, Health Care and Social Assistance*, Series EC02-621-04, issued July 2004, and *Nonemployer Statistics*.

Table 566. **Social Assistance Services—Revenue for Employer Firms: 2000 to 2003**

[In millions of dollars (74,158 represents $74,158,000,000). Based on the North American Industry Classification System, 1997, (NAICS), see text, Section 15, Business Enterprise. See Appendix III]

Kind of business	NAICS code	2000, total	2002, total	2003		
				Total	Taxable firms	Tax-exempt firms
Social assistance.	624	74,158	88,347	93,695	21,633	72,062
Individual & family services	6241	37,318	44,571	47,061	4,986	42,075
Child & youth services.	62411	9,993	11,868	12,850	977	11,873
Services for elderly & disabled persons.	62412	11,311	13,418	14,272	1,657	12,615
Other individual & family services.	62419	16,014	19,284	19,938	2,352	17,587
Community, emergency & other relief services	6242	7,736	9,055	9,598	498	9,100
Community food services	62421	2,194	2,512	2,697	(S)	2,427
Community housing services.	62422	3,855	4,651	4,815	190	4,625
Emergency & other relief services	62423	1,688	1,893	2,087	(S)	2,049
Vocational rehabilitation services.	6243	10,919	12,733	13,959	2,505	11,453
Child day care services	6244	18,184	21,988	23,078	13,644	9,434

S Figure does not meet publication standards.

Source: U.S. Census Bureau, *Service Annual Survey, 2003*. See also <http://www.census.gov/svsd/www/sas62.html>.

Social Insurance and Human Services 377

Table 567. **Social Assistance—Nonemployer Establishments and Receipts: 1997 to 2002**

[Receipts in millions of dollars (5,451 represents $5,451,000,000). Includes only firms subject to federal income tax. Nonemployers are businesses with no paid employees. Based on the North American Industry Classification System 1997 (NAICS), see text, Section 15]

Kind of business	NAICS code	Establishments			Receipts		
		1997	2000	2002	1997	2000	2002
Social assistance, total..............	624	526,512	642,946	717,105	5,451	7,539	8,670
Individual & family services.............	6241	33,227	72,433	85,304	592	1,106	1,386
Community/emergency & other relief services...	6242	1,338	3,560	4,365	24	54	67
Vocational rehabilitation services.........	6243	3,213	7,314	8,489	82	151	175
Child day care services	6244	488,734	559,639	618,947	4,754	6,228	7,041

Source: U.S. Census Bureau, *Nonemployer Statistics*; published November 2004; <http://www.census.gov/epcd/nonemployer/>.

Table 568. **Child Care Arrangements of Preschool Children by Type of Arrangement: 1991 to 2001**

[In percent, except as indicated (8,428 represents 8,428,000). Estimates are based on children 3 to 5 years old who have not entered kindergarten. Based on interviews from a sample survey of the civilian, noninstitutional population in households with telephones; see source for details. See also Appendix III]

Characteristic	Children		Type of nonparental arrangement [1]			With parental care only
	Number (1,000)	Percent distribution	In relative care	In nonrelative care	In center-based program [2]	
1991, total..............	8,428	100.0	16.9	14.8	52.8	31.0
1995, total..............	9,232	100.0	19.4	16.9	55.1	25.9
2001, total..............	8,551	100.0	22.8	14.1	56.4	26.1
Age:						
3 years old	3,795	44.4	23.6	14.7	42.8	33.8
4 years old	3,861	45.1	22.5	13.6	65.9	20.4
5 years old	896	10.5	20.9	13.1	73.0	18.0
Race-ethnicity:						
White, non-Hispanic	5,313	62.1	19.6	16.5	59.1	25.3
Black, non-Hispanic.........	1,251	14.6	36.7	8.5	63.1	15.1
Hispanic	1,506	17.6	22.8	11.3	39.9	39.0
Other	482	5.6	22.8	10.8	61.8	23.7
Household income:						
Less than $10,001	951	11.1	37.1	6.2	45.6	30.5
$10,001 to $20,000	1,156	13.5	23.5	10.8	50.6	32.3
$20,001 to $30,000	1,134	13.3	24.3	10.4	49.3	32.4
$30,001 to $40,000........	978	11.4	24.5	12.6	48.9	32.2
$40,001 to $50,000	822	9.6	21.9	15.2	42.9	36.4
$50,001 to $75,000	1,724	20.2	20.7	18.6	62.3	20.9
$75,001 or more..........	1,788	20.9	15.3	18.6	75.1	12.8

[1] Columns do not add to 100.0 because some children participated in more than one type of nonparental arrangement. [2] Center-based programs include day care centers, Head Start programs, preschools, prekindergarten, and nursery schools.

Source: U.S. Department of Education, National Center for Education Statistics, Early Childhood Program Participation Survey of the National Household Education Surveys Program (NHES), 2001.

Table 569. **Licensed Child Care Centers and Family Child Care Providers by State and Other Areas: 2004**

[Centers as of February; family child care providers as of August]

State	Licensed child care centers	Licensed family child care providers	State	Licensed child care centers	Licensed family child care providers	State	Licensed child care centers	Licensed family child care providers
US, total ...	116,351	290,425	KY.........	2,221	9,183	OH.........	3,663	15,171
AL.........	1,450	1,951	LA.........	2,156	8,032	OK.........	1,933	4,469
AK.........	213	1,579	ME.........	835	1,834	OR.........	840	5,013
AZ.........	2,101	4,218	MD.........	2,626	10,197	PA.........	3,966	5,132
AR.........	1,748	1,175	MA.........	3,216	9,484	RI.........	460	1,318
CA.........	14,637	44,800	MI.........	4,657	14,057	SC.........	1,631	1,947
CO.........	2,873	4,120	MN.........	1,600	13,645	SD.........	285	1,006
CT.........	1,588	3,296	MS.........	1,789	591	TN.........	3,574	1,811
DE.........	351	1,661	MO.........	1,826	2,045	TX.........	11,206	13,234
DC.........	360	233	MT.........	268	1,057	UT.........	336	2,485
FL.........	6,641	8,073	NE.........	851	3,106	VT.........	630	1,320
GA.........	2,572	6,660	NV.........	450	588	VA.........	2,573	3,692
HI	523	501	NH.........	1,172	352	WA.........	2,150	6,629
ID	790	1,235	NJ.........	4,132	4,072	WV.........	600	3,136
IL.........	3,125	10,774	NM.........	630	8,986	WI	2,415	8,099
IN	634	3,222	NY.........	4,653	14,438	WY.........	257	510
IA.........	1,455	5,688	NC.........	4,248	4,999	PR.........	702	41
KS.........	1,317	7,295	ND.........	122	2,306	VI	231	64

Source: Children's Foundation, Washington, DC, *Child Care Center Licensing Study and Family Child Care Licensing Study*, annual (copyright).

Table 570. Private Philanthropy Funds by Source and Allocation: 1990 to 2003

[In billions of dollars (101.4 represents $101,400,000,000). Estimates for sources of funds based on U.S. Internal Revenue Service reports of individual charitable deductions and household surveys of giving by Independent Sector and the Center on Philanthropy at Indiana University. For corporate giving, data are corporate charitable deductions from the U.S. Internal Revenue Service and the contributions made by corporate foundations as reported by the Foundation Center. Data about foundation donations are based upon surveys of foundations and data provided by the Foundation Center. Estimates of the allocation of funds were derived from surveys of nonprofits conducted by various sources]

Source and allocation	1990	1993	1994	1995	1996	1997	1998	1999	2000	2001	2002	2003
Total funds	101.4	116.5	119.2	124.0	138.6	159.4	177.4	201.0	227.7	229.0	234.1	240.7
Individuals	81.0	92.0	92.5	95.4	107.6	124.2	138.4	154.6	174.5	172.4	175.0	179.4
Foundations [1]	7.2	9.5	9.7	10.6	12.0	13.9	17.0	20.5	24.6	27.2	27.0	26.3
Corporations	5.5	6.5	7.0	7.4	7.5	8.6	8.5	10.2	10.7	11.7	12.9	13.5
Charitable bequests	7.6	8.5	10.0	10.7	11.5	12.6	13.6	15.6	17.9	17.7	19.2	21.6
Allocation:												
Religion	49.8	52.9	56.4	58.1	61.9	64.7	68.3	71.3	77.0	79.9	82.8	86.4
Health	9.9	10.8	11.5	12.6	13.9	14.0	16.9	18.0	18.8	19.3	18.9	20.9
Education	12.4	15.4	16.6	17.6	19.2	22.0	25.3	27.5	31.7	32.0	31.8	31.6
Human service	11.8	12.5	11.7	11.7	12.2	12.7	16.1	17.4	18.0	20.7	18.7	18.9
Arts, culture and humanities . .	7.9	9.6	9.7	10.0	10.9	10.6	10.5	11.1	11.5	12.1	12.2	13.1
Public/societal benefit	4.9	5.4	6.1	7.1	7.6	8.4	10.9	11.0	11.6	11.8	11.6	12.1
Environment/wildlife	2.5	3.0	3.3	3.8	3.8	4.1	5.3	5.8	6.2	6.4	6.6	7.0
International	1.3	2.2	2.4	2.9	2.8	2.6	2.9	3.6	3.7	4.1	4.6	5.3
Gifts to foundations [1, 2]	3.8	6.3	6.3	8.5	12.6	14.0	19.9	28.8	24.7	25.7	19.2	21.4
Unallocated [3]	-3.0	-1.5	-4.9	-8.2	-6.3	6.3	1.5	6.8	24.6	17.0	27.7	24.0

[1] Data are from the Foundation Center.   [2] Estimate for gifts to foundations in 2003 is from Giving USA.   [3] Money deducted as a charitable contribution by donors but not allocated to sources. May include gifts to governmental entities, in-kind giving, gifts to new charities.

Source: AAFRC Trust for Philanthropy, Indianapolis, IN, researched and written by the Center on Philanthropy at Indiana University, *Giving USA*, annual (copyright).

Table 571. Nonprofit Charitable Organizations—Information Returns: 1990 to 2001

[In billions of dollars (697.3 represents $697,300,000,000), except as indicated. Categories based on The National Taxonomy of Exempt Entities (NTEE), a classification system that uses 26 major field areas that are aggregated into 10 categories. Includes data reported by organizations described in Internal Revenue Code section 501(3), excluding private foundations and most religious organizations. Organizations with receipts under $25,000 were not required to file]

Year and category	Number of returns	Total assets	Total fund balance or net worth	Revenue Total	Revenue Program service revenue [1]	Revenue Contributions, gifts, and grants	Total expenses	Excess of revenue over expenses (net)
1990	141.8	697.3	375.3	435.6	306.9	85.3	409.4	26.1
2000	230.2	1,562.5	1,023.2	866.2	579.1	199.1	796.4	69.8
2001, total	240.6	1,631.7	1,020.3	897.0	630.8	212.4	862.7	34.3
Arts, culture, and humanities . . .	26.0	65.7	54.0	22.7	6.2	12.9	20.5	2.3
Education	41.2	518.7	377.8	157.3	90.8	52.5	148.4	8.9
Environment, animals	9.4	24.2	20.2	9.0	1.9	6.0	7.5	1.6
Health	32.2	647.0	339.4	509.0	450.0	39.6	497.1	11.9
Human services	91.1	189.4	94.5	135.8	67.2	59.1	131.2	4.7
International, foreign affairs	3.4	10.8	8.2	10.5	0.9	9.3	9.9	0.6
Mutual, membership benefit . . .	0.6	10.3	8.3	1.7	1.2	0.3	1.6	0.1
Public, societal benefit	21.5	149.6	105.1	43.7	11.4	27.4	39.8	3.8
Religion related	15.0	15.9	12.8	7.2	1.1	5.3	6.7	0.4
Unknown, unclassified [2]	0.2	0.2	0.1	0.1	(Z)	(Z)	0.1	(Z)

Z Less than $50 million.   [1] Represents fees collected by organizations in support of their tax-exempt purposes, and income such as tuition and fees at educational institutions, hospital patient charges, and admission and activity fees collected by museums and other nonprofit organizations or institutions.   [2] Estimates are based on a small sample size and should be used with caution.

Source: Internal Revenue Service, Statistics of Income, SOI Tax Stats-Charities & Other Tax-Exempt Organizations Statistics. See also <http://www.irs.gov/taxstats/charitablestats/article/0,,id=97176,00.html> (accessed 26 May 2005).

Table 572. Foundations—Number and Finances: 1990 to 2003

[142.5 represents $142,500,000,000. Covers nongovernmental nonprofit organizations with funds and programs managed by their own trustees or directors, whose goals were to maintain or aid social, educational, religious, or other activities deemed to serve the common good. Excludes organizations that make general appeals to the public for funds, act as trade associations for industrial or other special groups, or do not currently award grants. Constant dollar figures based on Consumer Price Index, all urban consumers, supplied by U.S. Bureau of Labor Statistics. Minus sign (-) indicates decrease]

Year	Number of foundations	Assets Current dollars Amt. (bil. dol.)	Assets Current dollars Percent change [1]	Assets Constant (1975) dollars Amt. (bil. dol.)	Assets Constant (1975) dollars Percent change [1]	Total giving [2] Current dollars Amt. (bil. dol.)	Total giving [2] Current dollars Percent change [1]	Total giving [2] Constant (1975) dollars Amt. (bil. dol.)	Total giving [2] Constant (1975) dollars Percent change [1]	Gifts received Current dollars Amt. (bil. dol.)	Gifts received Current dollars Percent change [1]	Gifts received Constant (1978) dollars Amt. (bil. dol.)	Gifts received Constant (1978) dollars Percent change [1]
1990 .	32,401	142.5	3.6	58.7	-1.7	8.7	9.7	3.6	4.1	5.0	-10.0	2.5	-14.6
1995 .	40,140	226.7	15.8	80.1	12.6	12.3	8.6	4.3	5.6	10.3	26.9	4.4	23.5
2000 .	56,582	486.1	8.4	154.9	4.8	27.6	18.2	8.6	14.3	27.6	-13.9	10.5	-16.7
2003 .	66,398	476.7	9.5	139.4	7.1	30.3	-0.4	8.9	-2.6	24.9	12.2	8.8	9.7

[1] Percent change from immediate preceding year.   [2] Includes grants, scholarships, and employee matching gifts.

Source: The Foundation Center, New York, NY, FC Stats; <http://fdncenter.org/fc_stats/index.html>; (copyright).

Social Insurance and Human Services   379

Table 573. Foundations—Number and Finances by Asset Size: 2003

[Figures are for latest year reported by foundations (472,810 represents $472,810,000,000). See headnote, Table 572]

| Asset size | Number | Assets (mil. dol.) | Gifts received (mil. dol.) | Expenditures (mil. dol.) | Grants (mil. dol.) | Percent distribution | | | | |
						Number	Assets	Gifts received	Expenditures	Grants
Total	66,397	472,810	24,858	37,092	30,043	100.0	100.0	100.0	100.0	100.0
Under $50,000..........	11,433	189	963	1,179	1,080	17.0	(Z)	3.7	3.0	3.5
$50,000-$99,999	4,822	355	172	230	201	7.2	(Z)	0.6	0.6	0.6
$100,000-$249,999.......	9,261	1,548	338	483	402	13.9	0.3	1.3	1.3	1.3
$250,000-$499,999........	8,549	3,116	421	597	510	12.8	0.6	1.6	1.6	1.6
$500,000-$999,999.........	9,191	6,622	649	961	812	13.8	1.4	2.6	2.5	2.7
$1,000,000-$4,999,999	15,019	33,582	3,414	4,377	3,717	22.6	7.1	13.7	11.8	12.3
$5,000,000-$9,999,999	3,391	23,761	1,648	2,147	1,783	5.1	5.0	6.6	5.7	5.9
$10,000,000-$49,999,999	3,616	77,323	5,416	6,524	5,306	5.4	16.3	21.7	17.5	17.6
$50,000,000-$99,999,999	547	38,378	2,574	3,466	2,738	0.8	8.1	10.3	9.3	9.1
$100,000,000-$249,999,999 ...	362	54,321	1,818	4,009	3,238	0.5	11.4	7.3	10.8	10.7
$250,000,000 or more.......	206	233,616	7,445	13,120	10,256	0.3	49.4	29.9	35.3	34.1

Z Less than 0.05 percent.

Source: The Foundation Center, New York, NY, Foundation Yearbook, annual (copyright).

Table 574. Domestic Private Foundations—Information Returns: 1990 to 2001

[Money amounts in billions of dollars (122.4 represents $122,400,000,000)]

Item	1990	1992	1993	1994	1995	1996	1997	1998	1999	2000	2001
Number of returns.........	40,105	42,383	43,956	45,801	47,917	50,774	55,113	56,658	62,694	66,738	70,787
Nonoperating foundations ...	36,880	38,576	40,166	41,983	43,966	46,066	50,541	52,460	58,840	61,501	63,650
Operating foundations	3,226	3,807	3,790	3,818	3,951	4,708	4,572	4,198	3,854	5,238	7,137
Total assets, book value......	122.4	144.1	155.6	169.3	195.6	232.6	280.9	325.7	384.6	409.5	413.6
Total assets, fair market value	151.0	181.4	192.3	203.6	242.9	288.6	342.7	397.1	466.9	471.6	455.4
Investments in securities....	115.0	141.3	147.6	158.9	190.7	225.1	272.4	317.9	363.4	361.4	329.4
Total revenue.............	19.0	22.5	24.5	26.5	30.8	48.2	55.5	59.7	83.3	72.8	45.3
Total expenses...........	11.3	13.6	14.6	15.7	17.2	19.9	22.4	25.9	33.9	37.4	36.7
Contributions, gifts, and grants paid	8.6	10.1	11.1	11.8	12.3	14.5	16.4	19.4	22.8	27.6	27.4
Excess of revenue over expenses (net).........	7.7	8.9	9.9	10.8	13.6	28.4	33.0	33.8	49.4	35.3	8.6
Net investment income [1]	11.9	14.1	15.1	15.0	20.4	26.2	34.8	39.3	57.1	48.8	25.7

[1] Represents income not considered related to a foundation's charitable purpose, e.g., interest, dividends, and capital gains. Foundations could be subject to an excise tax on such income.

Source: Internal Revenue Service, Statistics of Income, SOI Tax Stats-Charities & Other Tax-Exempt Organizations Statistics. See also <http://www.irs.gov/taxstats/charitablestats/article/0,,id=97176,00.html#3>(accessed 26 May 2005).

Table 575. Volunteers by Type of Main Organization: 2004

[In percent, except as noted. Data on volunteers relate to persons who performed unpaid volunteer activities for an organization at any point from September 1, 2003 through September 2004. Data represents the percent of the population involved in the activity]

Total and type of main organization [1]	Sex			Age						Race and Hispanic or Latino origin				Educational attainment [4]				Employment status			
	Total, both sexes	Men	Women	16 to 24 years	25 to 34 years	35 to 44 years	45 to 54 years	55 to 64 years	65 years and over	White [2]	Black [2]	Asian [2]	Hispanic or Latino [3]	Less than a high school diploma	High school graduate, no college [5]	Less than a bachelor's degree [6]	College graduates	Civilian labor force			Not in labor force
																		Total	Employed	Unemployed	
Total volunteers (1,000)	64,542	27,011	37,530	8,821	10,046	14,783	13,584	8,784	8,524	55,892	5,435	1,832	4,102	2,718	12,709	16,414	23,880	45,896	43,886	2,010	18,646
Percent of population [7]	28.8	25.0	32.4	24.2	25.8	34.2	32.8	30.1	24.6	30.5	20.8	19.3	14.5	9.6	21.6	34.2	45.7	30.9	31.2	25.6	24.7
Median annual hours [8]	52	52	50	36	40	51	52	60	96	52	56	40	48	40	50	52	60	48	48	46	64
Civic and political [8]	7.0	9.0	5.5	5.5	5.5	5.3	8.1	9.3	8.7	7.2	5.2	4.3	5.4	5.5	6.8	6.6	8.0	7.2	7.2	7.1	6.3
Educational or youth service	27.0	24.8	28.5	32.4	34.1	39.8	26.0	13.2	6.4	26.8	27.1	29.0	35.2	23.9	23.5	27.3	26.9	28.8	28.4	36.3	22.5
Environmental or animal care	1.7	1.7	1.6	1.5	1.4	1.4	1.5	2.0	1.4	1.8	0.2	0.7	1.1	0.6	1.3	1.7	2.0	1.8	1.7	2.2	1.4
Hospital or other health	7.5	5.4	9.1	8.6	6.4	5.5	6.9	8.9	10.9	7.9	5.0	6.8	6.3	4.4	7.6	7.6	7.5	7.2	7.3	4.9	8.5
Public safety	1.5	2.7	0.7	1.7	2.2	1.4	1.4	1.5	1.1	1.6	0.6	0.4	1.1	1.9	2.3	1.7	0.9	1.7	1.7	1.8	1.1
Religious	34.4	33.3	35.2	28.5	30.4	30.5	35.3	39.6	45.2	33.5	45.6	34.2	31.8	46.0	38.5	34.9	32.8	32.8	33.1	24.8	38.4
Social or community service	12.4	12.9	12.1	13.0	11.1	9.0	12.3	15.0	16.9	12.5	10.7	15.2	10.6	11.0	12.3	12.3	12.6	12.0	11.9	15.4	13.5
Sport and hobby [9]	3.6	4.7	2.9	3.4	2.8	3.4	4.2	4.3	3.6	3.7	1.6	5.1	2.7	1.4	3.0	3.3	4.5	3.9	4.0	3.0	2.8
Other	3.3	3.9	2.9	3.2	3.8	1.4	2.9	4.2	4.3	3.4	1.9	2.1	4.3	4.1	3.3	3.3	3.3	3.1	3.1	3.0	3.8
Not determined	1.6	1.6	1.6	2.2	1.4	1.6	1.3	1.9	1.6	1.5	2.1	2.1	1.5	1.0	1.5	1.3	1.7	1.6	1.6	1.5	1.6

[1] Main organization is defined as the organization for which the volunteer worked the most hours during the year. See headnote for more details. [2] Persons who selected this race group only; persons who selected more than one race group are not included. [3] Persons of Hispanic origin may be any race. [4] Data refer to persons 25 years and over. [5] Includes high school diploma or equivalent. [6] Includes the categories, some college, no degree; and associate's degree. [7] For those reporting annual hours. [8] Includes professional and/or international. [9] Includes cultural and/or arts.

Source: U.S. Bureau of Labor Statistics, News. USDL 04-2503. December 16, 2004. See also <http://www.bls.gov/news.release/pdf/volun.pdf>

Social Insurance and Human Services   381

No. 107.—POPULATION GAINFULLY OCCUPIED: ADULTS AND CHILDREN, BY SEX AND BY STATES AND TERRITORIES, CENSUS YEAR 1900.

[From reports of the Bureau of the Census, Department of Commerce and Labor.]

State or Territory.	Men.	Women.	Children.		Total.
			Boys.	Girls.	
Alabama	482,100	158,345	80,989	41,664	763,188
Arizona	45,226	6,162	1,358	624	53,370
Arkansas	358,195	62,532	49,747	15,321	485,795
California	549,158	85,790	7,187	2,132	644,267
Colorado	187,394	27,369	2,903	597	218,263
Connecticut	290,133	83,898	6,838	4,741	385,610
Delaware	57,243	11,894	2,781	1,078	72,996
District of Columbia	84,415	40,382	1,365	779	126,941
Florida	152,708	33,459	11,281	4,122	201,570
Georgia	568,470	182,037	77,462	36,502	864,471
Idaho	56,772	4,375	1,395	141	62,683
Illinois	1,458,400	275,105	50,994	19,541	1,804,040
Indian Territory	108,544	10,020	12,950	2,196	133,710
Indiana	755,783	111,024	26,454	5,692	898,953
Iowa	657,957	102,037	24,564	4,846	789,404
Kansas	431,865	53,386	20,304	2,185	507,740
Kentucky	593,233	98,181	53,676	7,441	752,531
Louisiana	365,562	109,484	39,620	21,427	536,093
Maine	220,868	49,917	3,979	2,013	276,777
Maryland	342,721	91,097	17,034	7,886	458,738
Massachusetts	862,981	317,558	16,393	11,475	1,208,407
Michigan	752,776	126,517	19,523	7,174	905,990
Minnesota	531,973	90,887	16,973	6,041	645,874
Mississippi	402,860	144,254	63,906	34,103	645,123
Missouri	914,245	145,498	52,621	9,028	1,121,392
Montana	104,061	9,539	929	270	114,799
Nebraska	315,072	44,121	12,282	2,495	373,970
Nevada	17,626	1,969	183	31	19,809
New Hampshire	134,414	39,807	2,547	1,951	178,719
New Jersey	584,780	142,718	18,457	11,804	757,759
New Mexico	56,723	5,766	2,987	544	66,020
New York	2,269,211	635,319	55,218	36,726	2,996,474
North Carolina	478,595	127,740	77,986	32,421	716,742
North Dakota	100,423	13,073	3,125	1,019	117,640
Ohio	1,265,716	233,177	34,165	12,894	1,545,952
Oklahoma	115,129	9,708	7,309	549	132,695
Oregon	148,869	17,916	2,331	521	169,637
Pennsylvania	1,932,857	395,656	84,195	35,881	2,448,589
Rhode Island	134,686	48,203	5,143	3,891	191,923
South Carolina	333,282	142,433	56,363	38,917	570,995
South Dakota	115,636	14,425	5,876	1,219	137,156
Tennessee	547,672	103,553	63,711	12,651	727,587
Texas	819,037	122,425	73,604	17,967	1,033,033
Utah	71,745	10,334	2,095	430	84,604
Vermont	110,011	21,852	2,170	900	134,933
Virginia	492,232	114,438	44,651	11,094	662,415
Washington	201,799	20,203	2,807	578	225,387
West Virginia	272,159	28,680	22,343	2,481	325,663
Wisconsin	595,549	106,474	20,842	9,673	732,538
Wyoming	40,469	2,893	795	111	44,268
Total	22,489,425	4,833,630	1,264,411	485,767	29,073,233
Geographical divisions.					
North Atlantic	6,539,941	1,734,928	194,940	109,382	8,579,191
South Atlantic	2,781,825	772,160	311,266	135,280	4,000,531
North Central	7,895,395	1,315,724	287,723	81,807	9,580,649
South Central	3,792,422	818,502	445,512	153,319	5,209,755
Western	1,479,842	192,316	24,970	5,979	1,703,107
Alaska	28,905	3,428	802	200	33,335
Hawaii	83,219	5,955	828	170	90,172
Military and naval	90,179	142	9	....	90,330

* For States and Territories included in each division see note *f*, page 57.

59776—s A 1908——14

Labor Force, Employment, and Earnings

This section presents statistics on the labor force; its distribution by occupation and industry affiliation; and the supply of, demand for, and conditions of labor. The chief source of these data is the Current Population Survey (CPS) conducted by the U.S. Census Bureau for the Bureau of Labor Statistics (BLS). Comprehensive historical and current data are available from the BLS Internet site <http://www.bls.gov/cps/>. These data are published on a current basis in the BLS monthly publication *Employment and Earnings*. Detailed data on the labor force are also available from the Census Bureau's decennial census of population.

Types of data—Most statistics in this section are obtained by two methods: household interviews or questionnaires and reports of establishment payroll records. Each method provides data that the other cannot suitably supply. Population characteristics, for example, are readily obtainable only from the household survey, while detailed industrial classifications can be readily derived only from establishment records.

Household data are obtained from a monthly sample survey of the population. The CPS is used to gather data for the calendar week including the 12th of the month and provides current comprehensive data on the labor force (see text, Section 1, Population). The CPS provides information on the work status of the population without duplication since each person is classified as employed, unemployed, or not in the labor force. Employed persons holding more than one job are counted only once, according to the job at which they worked the most hours during the survey week.

Monthly, quarterly, and annual data from the CPS are published by the Bureau of Labor Statistics in *Employment and Earnings*. Data presented include national totals of the number of persons in the civilian labor force by sex, race, Hispanic or Latino origin, and age; the number employed; hours of work; industry and occupational groups; and the number unemployed, reasons for, and duration of unemployment. Annual data shown in this section are averages of monthly figures for each calendar year, unless otherwise specified. Historical national CPS data are available on the Web site <http://www.bls.gov/cps/>.

The CPS also produces annual estimates of employment and unemployment for each state, 50 large metropolitan statistical areas, and selected cities. These estimates are published by BLS in its annual *Geographic Profile of Employment and Unemployment* available at <http://www.bls.gov/opub/gp/laugp.htm>. More detailed geographic data (e.g., for counties and cities) are provided by the decennial population censuses.

Data based on establishment records are compiled by BLS and cooperating state agencies as part of an ongoing Current Employment Statistics program. Survey data, gathered monthly from a sample of employers through electronic interviewing (including electronic data interchange, touchtone data entry, and computer-assisted telephone interviewing) or by mail, fax, on magnetic tape or computer diskette, are supplemented by data from other government agencies and adjusted at intervals to data from government social insurance program reports. The estimates exclude self-employed persons, private household workers, unpaid family workers, agricultural workers, and the Armed Forces. In March 2004, reporting establishments employed 4.9 million manufacturing workers (35 percent of the total manufacturing employment at the time), 21.8 million workers in private nonmanufacturing industries (23 percent of the total in private nonmanufacturing), and 15.8 million federal, state, and local government employees (72 percent of total government).

The establishment survey counts workers each time they appear on a payroll during the reference period (the payroll period that includes the 12th of the month). Thus, unlike the CPS, a person with two jobs is counted twice. The establishment survey is designed to provide detailed industry information for the nation, states, and metropolitan areas on nonfarm wage and salary employment, average weekly hours, and average hourly and weekly earnings. Establishment survey data also are published in *Employment and Earnings*. Historical national data are available on the Web site <http://www.bls.gov/ces/>. Historical data for states and metropolitan areas are available on the Web site <http://www.bls.gov/sae/>.

In June 2003, BLS completed a comprehensive sample redesign of the establishment survey begun in June 2000, changing from a quota-based sample to a probability-based sample. Also in June 2003, all establishment survey employment, hours, and earnings series were converted from being classified by the 1987 Standard Industrial Classification (SIC) system to being classified by the 2002 North American Industry Classification System (NAICS). The NAICS conversion resulted in major definitional changes to many of the previously published SIC-based series. All establishment survey historical time series were reconstructed as part of the NAICS conversion process and all published series have a NAICS-based history extending back to at least 1990. For total nonfarm industries and other high-level aggregates, NAICS history was reconstructed back to the previously existing start date for the series, 1939 in most cases. More information on the sample redesign, the conversion to NAICS, and other changes to the establishment survey implemented in June 2003 appears in "Revisions to the Current Employment Statistics National Estimates Effective May 2003" in the June 2003 issue of *Employment and Earnings*, as well as the Establishment Data portion of the Explanatory Notes and Estimates of Error section of *Employment and Earnings*.

The completion of the sample redesign and the conversion to NAICS for state and metropolitan area establishment survey

data was implemented in March 2003 with the release of January 2003 estimates. For a discussion of the changes to the state and area establishment survey data, see "Revisions to the Current Employment Statistics State and Area Estimates Effective January 2003" in the March 2003 issue of *Employment and Earnings*.

Labor force—According to the CPS definitions, the civilian labor force comprises all civilians in the noninstitutionalized population 16 years and over classified as "employed" or "unemployed" according to the following criteria: Employed civilians comprise (a) all civilians, who, during the reference week, did any work for pay or profit (minimum of an hour's work) or worked 15 hours or more as unpaid workers in a family enterprise and (b) all civilians who were not working but who had jobs or businesses from which they were temporarily absent for noneconomic reasons (illness, weather conditions, vacation, labor-management dispute, etc.) whether they were paid for the time off or were seeking other jobs. Unemployed persons comprise all civilians who had no employment during the reference week, who made specific efforts to find a job within the previous 4 weeks (such as applying directly to an employer or to a public employment service or checking with friends) and who were available for work during that week, except for temporary illness. Persons on layoff from a job and expecting recall also are classified as unemployed. All other civilian persons, 16 years old and over, are classified as "not in the labor force."

Various breaks in the CPS data series have occurred over time due to the introduction of population adjustments and other changes. For details on these breaks in series and the effect that they had on the CPS data, see the section on noncomparability of labor force levels in the Household Data portion of the Explanatory Notes and Estimates of Error section of *Employment and Earnings* available on the site <http://www.bls.gov/cps/eetech_methods.pdf>.

Beginning in January 2004, the CPS data reflect the introduction of revised population controls. The effect of the revised population controls on the monthly CPS estimates was to decrease the December 2003 employment level by 409,000 and the unemployment level by 27,000. The updated controls had little or no effect on unemployment rates and other ratios. For additional information on the effects of the revised population controls on estimates from the CPS, see "Adjustments to Household Survey Population Estimates in January 2004" in the February 2004 issue of *Employment and Earnings*, available on the Internet at <http://www.bls.gov/cps /cps04adj.pdf>.

Hours and earnings—Average hourly earnings, based on establishment data, are gross earnings (i.e., earnings before payroll deductions) and include overtime premiums; they exclude irregular bonuses and value of payments in kind. Hours are those for which pay was received. Wages and salaries from the CPS consist of total monies received for work performed by an employee during the income year. It includes wages, salaries, commissions, tips, piece-rate payments, and cash bonuses earned before deductions were made for taxes, bonds, union dues, etc. Persons who worked 35 hours or more are classified as working full-time.

Industry and occupational groups— Industry data derived from the CPS for 1983–91 utilize the 1980 census industrial classification developed from the 1972 SIC. CPS data from 1971 to 1982 were based on the 1970 census classification system, which was developed from the 1967 SIC. Most of the industry categories were not affected by the change in classification.

The occupational classification system used in the 1980 census and in the CPS for 1983–91, evolved from the 1980 Standard Occupational Classification (SOC) system, first introduced in 1977. Occupational categories used in the 1980 census classification system are so radically different from the 1970 census system used in the CPS through 1982, that their implementation represented a break in historical data series. In cases where data have not yet been converted to the 1980 classifications and still reflect the 1970 classifications (e.g., Table 634), comparisons between the two systems should not be made.

Beginning in January 1992, the occupational and industrial classification systems used in the 1990 census were introduced into the CPS. (These systems were largely based on the 1980 Standard Occupational Classification and the 1987 Standard Industrial Classification Systems, respectively.)

Beginning in 2003, the 2002 Census Bureau occupational and industrial classification systems were introduced into the CPS. These systems were derived from the 2000 Standard Occupational Classification (SOC) and the 2002 North American Industry Classification System (NAICS). The composition of detailed occupational and and industrial classifications in the new classification systems was substantially changed from the previous systems in use, as was the structure for aggregating them into broad groups. Consequently, the use of the new classification systems created breaks in existing data series at all levels of aggregation. CPS data using the new classification systems are available beginning 2000. Additional information on the 2002 Census Bureau occupational and industrial classifications systems appears in "Revisions to the Current Population Survey Effective in January 2003" in the February 2003 issue of *Employment and Earnings*, available on the BLS Web site <http://www.bls.gov /cps/rvcps03.pdf>.

For details on the changes over time in the industrial and occupational classification systems used in the CPS, see the section on changes in the occupational and industrial classification systems in the Household Data portion of the Explanatory Notes and Estimates of Error section of *Employment and Earnings* available on the site <http://www.bls.gov/cps /eetech_methods.pdf>.

Establishments responding to the establishment survey are classified according to the 2002 North American Industrial Classification System (NAICS). Previously they were classified according to the Standard Industrial Classification Manual (SIC). See text, Section 15, Business Enterprise, for information about the SIC manual and NAICS.

Labor Force, Employment, and Earnings   385

Productivity—BLS publishes data on productivity as measured by output per hour (labor productivity), output per combined unit of labor and capital input (multifactor productivity), and, for manufacturing industries, output per combined unit of capital, labor, energy, materials, and purchased service inputs. Labor productivity and related indexes are published for the business sector as a whole and its major subsectors: nonfarm business, manufacturing, and nonfinancial corporations, and for over 200 detailed industries. Labor productivity data were converted to a NAICS classification from the SIC classification in September 2003. Data for the business and nonfarm business sectors were reconstructed back to 1947; data for nonfinancial corporations back to 1958, and data for the detailed industry measures and the manufacturing sectors were reconstructed back to 1987. Multifactor productivity and related measures (currently SIC-based) are published for the private business sector and its major subsectors. Productivity indexes that take into account capital, labor, energy, materials, and service inputs are published for the 18 major industry groups that comprise most of the manufacturing sector, the utility services industry group, for 140 3-digit SIC manufacturing industries, and railroad transportation and air transportation. The major sector data are published in the BLS quarterly news release, *Productivity and Costs* and in the annual *Multifactor Productivity Trends* release. Industry productivity measures are updated and published annually in the news releases *Productivity and Costs by Industry*. The latest data are available at the BLS productivity and costs Web site <http://www.bls .gov/lpc/home.htm>. Detailed information on methods, limitations, and data sources appears in the BLS *Handbook of Methods*, BLS Bulletin 2490 (1997), Chapters 10 and 11.

Unions—As defined here, unions include traditional labor unions and employee associations similar to labor unions. Data on union membership status provided by BLS are for employed wage and salary workers and relate to their principal job. Earnings by union membership status are usual weekly earnings of full-time wage and salary workers. The information is collected through the Current Population Survey.

Work stoppages—Work stoppages include all strikes and lockouts known to BLS that last for at least 1 full day or shift and involve 1,000 or more workers. All stoppages, whether or not authorized by a union, legal or illegal, are counted. Excluded are work slowdowns and instances where employees report to work late or leave early to attend mass meetings or mass rallies.

Seasonal adjustment—Many economic statistics reflect a regularly recurring seasonal movement that can be estimated on the basis of past experience. By eliminating that part of the change which can be ascribed to usual seasonal variation (e.g., climate or school openings and closings), it is possible to observe the cyclical and other nonseasonal movements in the series. However, in evaluating deviations from the seasonal pattern—that is, changes in a seasonally adjusted series—it is important to note that seasonal adjustment is merely an approximation based on past experience. Seasonally adjusted estimates have a broader margin of possible error than the original data on which they are based, since they are subject not only to sampling and other errors, but also are affected by the uncertainties of the adjustment process itself.

Statistical reliability—For discussion of statistical collection, estimation, sampling procedures, and measures of statistical reliability applicable to Census Bureau and BLS data, see Appendix III.

Table 576. Employment Status of the Civilian Population: 1970 to 2004

[In thousands (137,085 represents 137,085,000), except as indicated. Annual averages of monthly figures. For the civilian noninstitutional population 16 years old and over. Based on Current Population Survey; see text, Section 1, and Appendix III]

Year	Civilian noninsti-tutional population	Civilian labor force Total	Civilian labor force Percent of population	Civilian labor force Employed	Employ-ment/population ratio[1]	Unemployed Number	Unemployed Percent of labor force	Not in labor force Number	Not in labor force Percent of population
1970	137,085	82,771	60.4	78,678	57.4	4,093	4.9	54,315	39.6
1980	167,745	106,940	63.8	99,303	59.2	7,637	7.1	60,806	36.2
1985	178,206	115,461	64.8	107,150	60.1	8,312	7.2	62,744	35.2
1987	182,753	119,865	65.6	112,440	61.5	7,425	6.2	62,888	34.4
1988	184,613	121,669	65.9	114,968	62.3	6,701	5.5	62,944	34.1
1989	186,393	123,869	66.5	117,342	63.0	6,528	5.3	62,523	33.5
1990 [2] . . .	189,164	125,840	66.5	118,793	62.8	7,047	5.6	63,324	33.5
1991	190,925	126,346	66.2	117,718	61.7	8,628	6.8	64,578	33.8
1992	192,805	128,105	66.4	118,492	61.5	9,613	7.5	64,700	33.6
1993	194,838	129,200	66.3	120,259	61.7	8,940	6.9	65,638	33.7
1994 [2] . . .	196,814	131,056	66.6	123,060	62.5	7,996	6.1	65,758	33.4
1995	198,584	132,304	66.6	124,900	62.9	7,404	5.6	66,280	33.4
1996	200,591	133,943	66.8	126,708	63.2	7,236	5.4	66,647	33.2
1997 [2] . . .	203,133	136,297	67.1	129,558	63.8	6,739	4.9	66,837	32.9
1998 [2] . . .	205,220	137,673	67.1	131,463	64.1	6,210	4.5	67,547	32.9
1999 [2] . . .	207,753	139,368	67.1	133,488	64.3	5,880	4.2	68,385	32.9
2000 [2] . . .	212,577	142,583	67.1	136,891	64.4	5,692	4.0	69,994	32.9
2001	215,092	143,734	66.8	136,933	63.7	6,801	4.7	71,359	33.2
2002 . . . : .	217,570	144,863	66.6	136,485	62.7	8,378	5.8	72,707	33.4
2003 [2] . . .	221,168	146,510	66.2	137,736	62.3	8,774	6.0	74,658	33.8
2004 [2] . . .	223,357	147,401	66.0	139,252	62.3	8,149	5.5	75,956	34.0

[1] Civilian employed as a percent of the civilian noninstitutional population.   [2] Data not strictly comparable with data for earlier years. See text, this section, and February 1994, March 1996, February 1997-99, and February 2003 and 2004 issues of *Employment and Earnings*.

Source: U.S. Bureau of Labor Statistics, Bulletin 2307; and *Employment and Earnings*, monthly, January 2005 issue. See Internet site <http://www.bls.gov/cps/home.htm>.

Table 577. Civilian Labor Force and Participation Rates With Projections: 1980 to 2012

[106.9 represents 106,900,000. For civilian noninstitutional population 16 years old and over. Annual averages of monthly figures. Rates are based on annual average civilian noninstitutional population of each specified group and represent proportion of each specified group in the civilian labor force. Based on Current Population Survey; see text, Section 1, and Appendix III]

Race, Hispanic origin sex, and age	Civilian labor force (millions) 1980	1990[1]	2000[1]	2003[1]	2004[1]	2012, proj.	Participation rate (percent) 1980	1990[1]	2000[1]	2003[1]	2004[1]	2012, proj.
Total [2]	106.9	125.8	142.6	146.5	147.4	162.3	63.8	66.5	67.1	66.2	66.0	67.2
White [3]	93.6	107.4	118.5	120.5	121.1	130.4	64.1	66.9	67.3	66.5	66.3	66.2
Male.	54.5	59.6	64.5	65.5	66.0	69.3	78.2	77.1	75.5	74.2	74.1	73.5
Female	39.1	47.8	54.1	55.0	55.1	61.1	51.2	57.4	59.5	59.2	58.9	59.2
Black [3]	10.9	13.7	16.4	16.5	16.6	19.8	61.0	64.0	65.8	64.3	63.8	66.3
Male.	5.6	6.8	7.7	7.7	7.8	9.3	70.3	71.0	69.2	67.3	66.7	69.1
Female	5.3	6.9	8.7	8.8	8.9	10.4	53.1	58.3	63.1	61.9	61.5	64.0
Asian [3][4]	(NA)	(NA)	6.3	6.1	6.3	9.0	(NA)	(NA)	67.2	66.4	65.9	68.7
Male.	(NA)	(NA)	3.4	3.3	3.4	4.9	(NA)	(NA)	76.1	75.6	75.0	77.3
Female	(NA)	(NA)	2.9	2.8	2.9	4.0	(NA)	(NA)	59.2	58.3	57.6	61.3
Hispanic or Latino [5] . . .	6.1	10.7	16.7	18.8	19.3	23.8	64.0	67.4	69.7	68.3	68.6	68.8
Male.	3.8	6.5	9.9	11.3	11.6	13.7	81.4	81.4	81.5	80.1	80.4	79.0
Female	2.3	4.2	6.8	7.5	7.7	10.1	47.4	53.1	57.5	55.9	56.1	58.6
Male	61.5	69.0	76.3	78.2	79.0	85.3	77.4	76.4	74.8	73.5	73.3	73.1
16 to 19 years	5.0	4.1	4.3	3.6	3.6	3.8	60.5	55.7	52.8	44.3	43.9	45.6
20 to 24 years	8.6	7.9	7.5	7.9	8.1	8.7	85.9	84.4	82.6	80.0	79.6	81.4
25 to 34 years	17.0	19.9	17.8	17.8	17.8	19.1	95.2	94.1	93.4	91.8	91.9	92.5
35 to 44 years	11.8	17.5	20.1	19.8	19.5	18.2	95.5	94.3	92.7	92.1	91.9	92.3
45 to 54 years	9.9	11.1	16.3	17.4	17.6	19.1	91.2	90.7	88.6	87.7	87.5	88.6
55 to 64 years	7.2	6.6	7.8	9.1	9.5	12.7	72.1	67.8	67.3	68.7	68.7	69.9
65 years and over. . .	1.9	2.0	2.5	2.7	2.8	3.6	19.0	16.3	17.7	18.6	19.0	20.8
Female.	45.5	56.8	66.3	68.3	68.4	77.0	51.5	57.5	59.9	59.5	59.2	61.6
16 to 19 years	4.4	3.7	4.0	3.6	3.5	3.8	52.9	51.6	51.2	44.8	43.8	47.4
20 to 24 years	7.3	6.8	6.7	7.0	7.1	8.1	68.9	71.3	73.1	70.8	70.5	75.1
25 to 34 years	12.3	16.1	14.9	14.6	14.4	16.3	65.5	73.5	76.1	74.1	73.6	78.2
35 to 44 years	8.6	14.7	17.5	16.9	16.6	16.2	65.5	76.4	77.2	76.0	75.6	79.9
45 to 54 years	7.0	9.1	14.8	15.9	16.1	17.9	59.9	71.2	76.8	76.8	76.5	79.8
55 to 64 years	4.7	4.9	6.6	8.1	8.5	11.9	41.3	45.2	51.9	56.6	56.3	60.6
65 years and over. . .	1.2	1.5	1.8	2.1	2.2	2.8	8.1	8.6	9.4	10.6	11.1	12.1

NA Not available.   [1] See footnote 2, Table 576.   [2] Includes other races, not shown separately.   [3] The 2003 Current Population Survey (CPS) allowed respondents to choose more than one race. Beginning 2003, data represent persons who selected this race group only and exclude persons reporting more than one race. The CPS in prior years only allowed respondents to report one race group. See also comments on race in the text for Section 1.   [4] Prior to 2003, includes Pacific Islanders.   [5] Persons of Hispanic or Latino origin may be of any race.

Source: U.S. Bureau of Labor Statistics. *Employment and Earnings*, monthly, January 2005 issue; *Monthly Labor Review*, February 2004; and unpublished data. See Internet site <http://www.bls.gov/cps/home.htm>.

Labor Force, Employment, and Earnings   387

Table 578. Employment Status of the Civilian Population by Sex, Race, and Ethnicity: 1970 to 2004

[In thousands (64,304 represents 64,304,000), except as indicated. Annual averages of monthly figures. See Table 576 for U.S. totals and coverage]

Year, sex, race, and Hispanic origin	Civilian noninstitutional population	Civilian labor force						Not in labor force	
		Total	Percent of population	Employed	Employ-ment/ popula-tion ratio [1]	Unemployed			
						Number	Percent of labor force	Number	Percent of population
Male: 1970	64,304	51,228	79.7	48,990	76.2	2,238	4.4	13,076	20.3
1980 [2]	79,398	61,453	77.4	57,186	72.0	4,267	6.9	17,945	22.6
1990 [2]	90,377	69,011	76.4	65,104	72.0	3,906	5.7	21,367	23.6
1995 [2]	95,178	71,360	75.0	67,377	70.8	3,983	5.6	23,818	25.0
2000 [2]	101,964	76,280	74.8	73,305	71.9	2,975	3.9	25,684	25.2
2002 [2]	104,585	77,500	74.1	72,903	69.7	4,597	5.9	27,085	25.9
2003 [2]	106,435	78,238	73.5	73,332	68.9	4,906	6.3	28,197	26.5
2004 [2]	107,710	78,980	73.3	74,524	69.2	4,456	5.6	28,730	26.7
Female:									
1970	72,782	31,543	43.3	29,688	40.8	1,855	5.9	41,239	56.7
1980 [2]	88,348	45,487	51.5	42,117	47.7	3,370	7.4	42,861	48.5
1990 [2]	98,787	56,829	57.5	53,689	54.3	3,140	5.5	41,957	42.5
1995 [2]	103,406	60,944	58.9	57,523	55.6	3,421	5.6	42,462	41.1
2000 [2]	110,613	66,303	59.9	63,586	57.5	2,717	4.1	44,310	40.1
2001	111,811	66,848	59.8	63,737	57.0	3,111	4.7	44,962	40.2
2002 [2]	112,985	67,363	59.6	63,582	56.3	3,781	5.6	45,621	40.4
2003 [2]	114,733	68,272	59.5	64,404	56.1	3,868	5.7	46,461	40.5
2004 [2]	115,647	68,421	59.2	64,728	56.0	3,694	5.4	47,225	40.8
White: [3]									
1970	122,174	73,556	60.2	70,217	57.5	3,339	4.5	48,618	39.8
1980 [2]	146,122	93,600	64.1	87,715	60.0	5,884	6.3	52,523	35.9
1990 [2]	160,625	107,447	66.9	102,261	63.7	5,186	4.8	53,178	33.1
1995 [2]	166,914	111,950	67.1	106,490	63.8	5,459	4.9	54,965	32.9
2000 [2]	176,220	118,545	67.3	114,424	64.9	4,121	3.5	57,675	32.7
2002 [2]	179,783	120,150	66.8	114,013	63.4	6,137	5.1	59,633	33.2
2003 [2]	181,292	120,546	66.5	114,235	63.0	6,311	5.2	60,746	33.5
2004 [2]	182,643	121,086	66.3	115,239	63.1	5,847	4.8	61,558	33.7
Black: [3]									
1973	14,917	8,976	60.2	8,128	54.5	846	9.4	5,941	39.8
1980 [2]	17,824	10,865	61.0	9,313	52.2	1,553	14.3	6,959	39.0
1985 [2]	19,664	12,364	62.9	10,501	53.4	1,864	15.1	7,299	37.1
1990 [2]	21,477	13,740	64.0	12,175	56.7	1,565	11.4	7,737	36.0
1995 [2]	23,246	14,817	63.7	13,279	57.1	1,538	10.4	8,429	36.3
2000 [2]	24,902	16,397	65.8	15,156	60.9	1,241	7.6	8,505	34.2
2002 [2]	25,578	16,565	64.8	14,872	58.1	1,693	10.2	9,013	35.2
2003 [2]	25,686	16,526	64.3	14,739	57.4	1,787	10.8	9,161	35.7
2004 [2]	26,065	16,638	63.8	14,909	57.2	1,729	10.4	9,428	36.2
Asian: [3][4]									
2000	9,330	6,270	67.2	6,043	64.8	227	3.6	3,060	32.8
2002 [2]	9,833	6,604	67.2	6,215	63.2	389	5.9	3,229	32.8
2003 [2]	9,220	6,122	66.4	5,756	62.4	366	6.0	3,098	33.6
2004 [2]	9,519	6,271	65.9	5,994	63.0	277	4.4	3,248	34.1
Hispanic: [5]									
1980	9,598	6,146	64.0	5,527	57.6	620	10.1	3,451	36.0
1985	11,915	7,698	64.6	6,888	57.8	811	10.5	4,217	35.4
1986	12,344	8,076	65.4	7,219	58.5	857	10.6	4,268	34.6
1990 [2]	15,904	10,720	67.4	9,845	61.9	876	8.2	5,184	32.6
1995 [2]	18,629	12,267	65.8	11,127	59.7	1,140	9.3	6,362	34.2
2000 [2]	23,938	16,689	69.7	15,735	65.7	954	5.7	7,249	30.3
2002 [2]	25,963	17,943	69.1	16,590	63.9	1,353	7.5	8,020	30.9
2003 [2]	27,551	18,813	68.3	17,372	63.1	1,441	7.7	8,738	31.7
2004 [2]	28,109	19,272	68.6	17,930	63.8	1,342	7.0	8,837	31.4
Mexican:									
1986 [2]	7,377	4,941	67.0	4,387	59.5	555	11.2	2,436	33.0
1990 [2]	9,752	6,707	68.8	6,146	63.0	561	8.4	3,045	31.2
1995 [2]	11,609	7,765	66.9	7,016	60.4	750	9.7	3,844	33.1
2000 [2]	15,333	10,783	70.3	10,144	66.2	639	5.9	4,550	29.7
2002 [2]	16,420	11,542	70.3	10,673	65.0	869	7.5	4,878	29.7
2003 [2]	17,464	12,081	69.2	11,151	63.9	930	7.7	5,383	30.8
2004 [2]	17,900	12,340	68.9	11,449	64.0	892	7.2	5,559	31.1
Puerto Rican:									
1986 [2]	1,494	804	53.8	691	46.3	113	14.0	690	46.2
1990 [2]	1,718	960	55.9	870	50.6	91	9.5	758	44.1
1995 [2]	1,896	1,098	57.9	974	51.4	123	11.2	798	42.1
2000 [2]	2,193	1,411	64.3	1,318	60.1	92	6.6	783	35.7
2002 [2]	2,484	1,546	62.2	1,401	56.4	145	9.4	938	37.8
2003 [2]	2,652	1,649	62.2	1,495	56.4	154	9.3	1,003	37.8
2004 [2]	2,547	1,610	63.2	1,481	58.1	130	8.1	936	36.7
Cuban:									
1986 [2]	842	570	67.7	533	63.3	36	6.4	272	32.3
1990 [2]	918	603	65.7	559	60.9	44	7.2	315	34.3
1995 [2]	1,019	613	60.2	568	55.7	45	7.4	406	39.8
2000 [2]	1,174	740	63.1	707	60.3	33	4.5	434	37.0
2002 [2]	1,141	635	55.6	592	51.9	43	6.7	507	44.4
2003 [2]	1,191	679	57.0	638	53.6	41	6.0	512	43.0
2004 [2]	1,264	769	60.9	735	58.1	34	4.5	495	39.2

[1] Civilian employed as a percent of the civilian noninstitutional population.   [2] See footnote 2, Table 576.   [3] Beginning 2003, for persons in this race group only. See footnote 3, Table 577.   [4] Prior to 2003, includes Pacific Islanders.   [5] Persons of Hispanic or Latino ethnicity may be of any race. Includes persons of other Hispanic or Latino ethnicity, not shown separately.
Source: U.S. Bureau of Labor Statistics, Bulletin 2307; and Employment and Earnings, monthly, January 2005 issue. See Internet site <http://www.bls.gov/cps/home.htm>.

Table 579. **Civilian Labor Force—Percent Distribution by Sex and Age: 1980 to 2004**

[106,940 represents 106,940,000. For civilian noninstitutional population 16 years old and over. Annual averages of monthly figures. Based on Current Population Survey; see text, Section 1, Population, and Appendix III]

Year and sex	Civilian labor force (1,000)	Percent distribution						
		16 to 19 years	20 to 24 years	25 to 34 years	35 to 44 years	45 to 54 years	55 to 64 years	65 yrs. and over
Total: 1980	106,940	8.8	14.9	27.3	19.1	15.8	11.2	2.9
1990 [1]	125,840	6.2	11.7	28.6	25.5	16.1	9.2	2.7
1995	132,304	5.9	10.3	25.8	27.0	19.1	9.0	2.9
2000 [1]	142,583	5.8	10.0	23.0	26.3	21.8	10.1	3.0
2004 [1]	147,401	4.8	10.3	21.8	24.5	22.9	12.2	3.4
Male: 1980	61,453	8.1	14.0	27.6	19.3	16.1	11.8	3.1
1990 [1]	69,011	5.9	11.4	28.8	25.3	16.1	9.6	2.9
1995	71,360	5.7	10.3	26.2	26.9	18.8	9.1	3.1
2000 [1]	76,280	5.6	9.9	23.4	26.3	21.3	10.2	3.3
2004 [1]	78,980	4.6	10.2	22.5	24.7	22.3	12.1	3.5
Female: 1980	45,487	9.6	16.1	26.9	19.0	15.4	10.4	2.6
1990 [1]	56,829	6.5	12.0	28.3	25.8	16.1	8.7	2.6
1995	60,944	6.1	10.4	25.5	27.2	19.4	8.8	2.7
2000 [1]	66,303	6.0	10.2	22.5	26.4	22.3	9.9	2.7
2004 [1]	68,421	5.1	10.4	21.1	24.3	23.6	12.4	3.2

[1] See footnote 2, Table 576.

Source: U.S. Bureau of Labor Statistics, Bulletin 2307, and *Employment and Earnings*, monthly, January 2005 issue. See Internet site <http://www.bls.gov/cps/home.htm>.

Table 580. Civilian Labor Force and Participation Rates by Educational Attainment, Sex, Race, and Hispanic Origin: 1992 to 2004

[106,490 represents 106,490,000 Annual averages of monthly figures. For the civilian noninstitutional population 25 years of age and older. See Table 615 for unemployment data. Based on Current Population Survey; see text, Section 1, and Appendix III]

Year, sex, and race	Civilian labor force					Participation rate [1]				
		Percent distribution								
	Total (1,000)	Less than high school diploma	High school graduate, no degree	Less than a bachelor's degree	College graduate	Total	Less than high school diploma	High school graduate, no degree	Less than a bachelor's degree	College graduate
Total: [2]										
1992	106,490	12.6	35.6	25.4	26.4	66.5	41.2	66.4	75.3	81.3
1995	110,851	10.8	33.1	27.9	28.1	66.7	39.9	65.4	74.5	81.0
2000 [3]	120,061	10.4	31.4	27.7	30.5	67.3	43.5	64.4	73.9	79.4
2003 [3]	124,412	10.2	30.5	27.4	32.0	67.2	44.9	63.8	72.8	78.2
2004 [3]	125,133	10.0	30.2	27.5	32.3	66.9	45.1	63.2	72.4	77.9
Male:										
1992	58,439	14.1	34.0	24.0	27.9	77.0	54.7	78.3	83.9	86.9
1995	59,986	12.2	32.3	26.1	29.4	76.0	52.1	76.5	82.1	85.8
2000 [3]	64,490	11.8	31.1	25.9	31.2	76.1	56.0	75.1	80.9	84.4
2003 [3]	66,717	11.9	30.5	25.4	32.2	75.5	57.7	74.0	79.5	83.2
2004 [3]	67,306	11.7	30.6	25.3	32.4	75.3	58.3	73.5	79.2	82.8
Female:										
1992	48,051	10.7	37.5	27.1	24.7	57.1	29.5	56.8	67.8	74.8
1995	50,865	9.2	34.2	30.0	26.6	58.3	29.2	56.4	68.1	75.4
2000 [3]	55,572	8.8	31.8	29.7	29.7	59.4	32.3	55.5	68.0	74.0
2003 [3]	57,695	8.2	30.4	29.6	31.8	59.6	32.7	55.0	67.2	73.1
2004 [3]	57,826	7.9	29.8	30.1	32.2	59.3	32.5	54.1	66.8	72.8
White: [4]										
1992	90,627	11.8	35.5	25.5	27.2	66.3	41.1	65.4	74.6	81.0
1995	94,139	10.1	33.0	27.8	29.1	66.7	40.0	64.8	73.8	80.6
2000 [3]	99,964	10.1	31.4	27.5	31.0	67.0	44.1	63.6	73.1	79.0
2003 [3]	102,509	10.0	30.4	27.2	32.5	66.9	45.7	62.9	72.2	77.8
2004 [3]	102,965	9.8	30.0	27.5	32.7	66.8	46.0	62.4	72.0	77.5
Black: [4]										
1992	11,583	18.2	39.5	26.4	15.9	66.7	40.6	72.9	80.9	86.2
1995	12,152	13.9	37.1	30.7	18.3	66.0	36.2	69.7	79.8	85.6
2000 [3]	13,582	12.4	36.0	31.2	20.5	68.2	39.3	69.9	79.3	84.4
2003 [3]	13,863	11.5	35.5	31.2	21.8	67.5	39.8	68.1	77.0	82.3
2004 [3]	13,951	11.2	36.2	30.3	22.3	67.0	39.6	67.6	74.9	82.9
Asian: [4][5]										
2000 [3]	5,402	9.1	20.7	20.2	50.1	70.9	46.0	65.6	76.4	79.1
2004 [3]	5,560	8.2	18.9	18.1	54.8	69.2	44.2	64.5	72.4	76.4
Hispanic: [6]										
1992	8,728	38.9	29.6	20.0	11.5	68.3	56.3	75.5	82.2	83.2
1995	9,599	37.2	29.3	21.7	11.7	67.5	55.3	74.3	79.7	83.1
2000 [3]	12,975	36.7	29.3	20.6	13.4	71.5	61.9	75.0	80.8	83.5
2003 [3]	15,181	36.4	29.2	20.4	14.0	70.7	61.6	73.9	79.2	81.8
2004 [3]	15,545	35.7	29.4	20.7	14.2	71.2	62.3	74.0	79.3	82.1

[1] See headnote, Table 577. [2] Includes other races, not shown separately. [3] See footnote 2, Table 576. [4] Beginning 2003, for persons in this race group only. See footnote 3, Table 577. [5] 2000 data include Pacific Islanders. [6] Persons of Hispanic or Latino origin may be of any race.

Source: U.S. Bureau of Labor Statistics, *Employment and Earnings*, monthly, January 2005 issue. See Internet site <http://www.bls.gov/cps/home.htm>.

Table 581. Characteristics of the Civilian Labor Force by State: 2004

[In thousands (147,401 represents 147,401,000), except ratio and rate. For civilian noninstitutional population, 16 years old and over. Annual averages of monthly figures. Because of separate processing and weighting procedures, the totals for the United States may differ from results obtained by aggregating totals for states]

State	Total		Employed		Employed popu-lation ratio [1]	Unemployed					Participation rate [3]	
						Total		Rate [2]				
	Num-ber	Female	Total	Female		Num-ber	Female	Total	Male	Female	Male	Female
United States ...	147,401	68,421	139,252	64,728	62.3	8,149	3,694	5.5	5.6	5.4	73.3	59.2
Alabama.	2,179	1,023	2,053	957	58.9	126	66	5.8	5.3	6.4	70.0	55.8
Alaska	331	152	306	141	65.8	25	11	7.5	7.9	7.2	76.6	65.6
Arizona.	2,778	1,242	2,637	1,179	61.8	141	63	5.1	5.0	5.1	73.1	57.4
Arkansas	1,308	601	1,231	562	58.5	77	38	5.9	5.5	6.4	70.1	54.9
California	17,551	7,860	16,466	7,390	61.5	1,084	470	6.2	6.3	6.0	73.9	57.6
Colorado.	2,525	1,142	2,389	1,084	68.9	137	58	5.4	5.7	5.1	80.5	65.3
Connecticut.	1,790	848	1,702	807	63.0	88	40	4.9	5.1	4.7	73.3	60.0
Delaware	426	206	409	198	63.7	17	8	3.9	3.9	4.0	72.0	61.1
District of Columbia.	299	149	275	138	62.0	25	11	8.2	9.0	7.4	73.9	62.3
Florida	8,411	3,904	8,021	3,719	59.3	390	185	4.6	4.5	4.7	69.6	55.4
Georgia	4,399	2,010	4,194	1,914	64.2	205	96	4.7	4.6	4.8	76.0	59.2
Hawaii	612	295	591	287	62.5	21	8	3.4	4.1	2.7	69.7	60.1
Idaho	706	323	669	307	64.4	37	15	5.3	5.8	4.7	74.8	61.3
Illinois	6,386	2,979	5,997	2,794	62.2	389	185	6.1	6.0	6.2	73.3	59.7
Indiana.	3,160	1,486	2,993	1,406	63.4	167	80	5.3	5.2	5.4	73.1	61.0
Iowa	1,620	774	1,545	736	67.0	75	38	4.6	4.4	4.9	75.3	65.4
Kansas.	1,480	685	1,398	644	67.6	82	40	5.5	5.2	5.9	78.9	64.5
Kentucky	1,977	920	1,874	876	58.7	103	44	5.2	5.6	4.8	68.9	55.4
Louisiana	2,058	982	1,934	926	57.3	124	56	6.0	6.3	5.7	67.7	54.9
Maine.	696	334	664	320	63.0	32	14	4.7	5.1	4.2	71.4	61.0
Maryland	2,883	1,394	2,762	1,331	65.4	121	64	4.2	3.9	4.6	75.0	62.3
Massachusetts.	3,399	1,629	3,226	1,562	64.1	172	68	5.1	5.9	4.2	73.7	61.9
Michigan.	5,114	2,394	4,758	2,241	61.4	356	153	7.0	7.5	6.4	72.8	59.7
Minnesota.	2,941	1,384	2,800	1,330	71.0	140	54	4.8	5.5	3.9	80.3	69.0
Mississippi	1,335	637	1,252	593	57.7	83	43	6.2	5.6	6.8	68.4	55.5
Missouri	3,017	1,445	2,844	1,365	64.3	173	80	5.7	5.9	5.6	74.1	62.7
Montana.	486	230	462	220	63.2	24	10	4.9	5.6	4.3	71.2	62.0
Nebraska	990	467	953	449	71.6	37	18	3.8	3.7	3.8	80.7	68.5
Nevada	1,175	518	1125	496	64.0	50	22	4.2	4.2	4.2	74.2	59.3
New Hampshire	724	337	698	326	68.5	27	11	3.7	4.0	3.3	77.9	64.7
New Jersey.	4,388	2,032	4,178	1,933	62.7	210	99	4.8	4.7	4.9	74.0	58.4
New Mexico	911	427	860	403	59.9	51	25	5.6	5.4	5.8	69.9	57.5
New York	9,370	4,406	8,823	4,151	59.2	548	254	5.8	5.9	5.8	70.3	56.2
North Carolina	4,243	1,973	4,016	1,862	62.4	227	111	5.4	5.1	5.6	73.6	58.8
North Dakota.	359	170	347	166	69.8	12	4	3.4	4.2	2.5	77.1	67.6
Ohio	5,884	2,778	5,514	2,613	62.5	370	165	6.3	6.6	5.9	73.5	60.4
Oklahoma.	1,714	798	1,630	756	61.0	84	42	4.9	4.5	5.3	71.3	57.6
Oregon.	1,850	840	1,710	780	61.1	140	60	7.6	8.0	7.1	73.5	59.0
Pennsylvania.	6,260	2,950	5,911	2,808	60.9	350	143	5.6	6.3	4.8	71.6	58.1
Rhode Island.	562	275	532	261	62.8	30	14	5.4	5.5	5.2	71.5	61.7
South Carolina.	2,077	1002	1,935	931	60.6	142	71	6.9	6.7	7.1	71.2	59.5
South Dakota.	431	207	416	200	71.0	16	8	3.7	3.5	3.8	78.1	69.4
Tennessee	2,894	1,365	2,747	1,295	60.2	147	70	5.1	5.1	5.1	69.9	57.4
Texas.	10,989	4,901	10,332	4,614	63.0	657	287	6.0	6.1	5.9	76.4	58.2
Utah	1,206	538	1,142	509	67.3	64	29	5.3	5.2	5.4	79.5	62.7
Vermont	353	169	340	163	68.1	13	6	3.7	4.0	3.4	75.9	65.8
Virginia.	3,766	1,791	3,619	1,718	64.6	147	72	3.9	3.8	4.0	74.3	60.8
Washington.	3,240	1,494	3,037	1,400	63.6	202	94	6.2	6.2	6.3	74.7	61.2
West Virginia.	795	369	753	352	51.8	42	18	5.3	5.8	4.7	60.8	49.1
Wisconsin.	3,071	1,456	2,917	1,391	68.1	155	65	5.0	5.6	4.4	77.2	66.6
Wyoming	282	130	271	125	68.6	11	5	3.8	3.4	4.2	77.3	65.3

[1] Civilian employment as a percent of civilian noninstitutional population.   [2] Percent unemployed of the civilian labor force.
[3] Percent of civilian noninstitutional population of each specified group in the civilian labor force.

Source: U.S. Bureau of Labor Statistics, Local Area Unemployment Statistics, *Geographic Profile of Employment and Unemployment, 2004 Annual Averages.* See Internet site <http://www.bls.gov/gps/>; (accessed July 2005).

Table 582. Civilian Labor Force by Selected Metropolitan Area: 2004

[147,401 represents 147,401,000. For the civilian noninstitutional population 16 years old and over. Annual averages of monthly figures. Data are derived from the Local Area Unemployment Statistics Program. For metro areas with a 2000 census population of one million or more. For definition of metropolitan areas, see Appendix II. Metropolitan areas defined as of December 2003]

Metropolitan areas ranked by population, 2000	Civilian labor force (1,000)	Unem- ploy- ment rate [1]	Metropolitan areas ranked by population, 2000	Civilian labor force (1,000)	Unem- ploy- ment rate [1]
U.S. total, 2004	147,401	5.5	Cincinnati-Middletown, OH-KY-IN	1,083	5.3
New York-Northern New Jersey-Long Island, NY-NJ-PA.	9,093	5.7	Portland-Vancouver-Beaverton, OR-WA	1,094	7.2
Los Angeles-Long Beach-Santa Ana, CA	6,396	6.0	Kansas City, MO-KS	1,035	6.0
Chicago-Naperville-Joliet, IL-IN-WI	4,733	6.1	Sacramento—Arden-Arcade—Roseville, CA	1,003	5.4
Philadelphia-Camden-Wilmington, PA-NJ-DE-MD	2,917	5.2	San Jose-Sunnyvale-Santa Clara, CA	854	6.7
Dallas-Fort Worth-Arlington, TX	2,966	5.9	San Antonio, TX	883	5.6
Miami-Fort Lauderdale-Miami Beach, FL.	2,622	5.2	Orlando, FL	961	4.5
Washington-Arlington-Alexandria, DC-VA-MD-WV.	2,801	3.7	Columbus, OH	916	5.4
Houston-Baytown-Sugar Land, TX	2,574	6.3	Virginia Beach-Norfolk-Newport News, VA-NC	778	4.1
Boston-Cambridge-Quincy, MA-NH NECTA.	2,455	4.9	Indianapolis, IN	867	4.7
Detroit-Warren-Livonia, MI	2,206	7.1	Milwaukee-Waukesha-West Allis, WI	802	5.4
Atlanta-Sandy Springs-Marietta, GA	2,454	4.6	Las Vegas-Paradise, NV	828	4.4
San Francisco-Oakland-Fremont, CA	2,179	5.6	Charlotte-Gastonia-Concord, NC-SC	778	5.6
Riverside-San Bernardino-Ontario, CA	1,648	5.7	New Orleans-Metairie-Kenner, LA	613	4.6
Phoenix-Mesa-Scottsdale, AZ	1,851	4.4	Nashville-Davidson—Murfreesboro, TN	732	4.3
Seattle-Tacoma-Bellevue, WA	1,699	5.6	Providence-Fall River-Warwick, RI-MA NECTA	698	5.4
Minneapolis-St. Paul-Bloomington, MN-WI	1,849	4.5	Austin-Round Rock, TX	778	5.1
San Diego-Carlsbad-San Marcos, CA	1,490	4.7	Memphis, TN-MS-AR	597	5.9
St. Louis, MO-IL	1,453	6.0	Buffalo-Niagara Falls, NY	587	5.8
Baltimore-Towson, MD	1,346	4.5	Louisville, KY-IN	602	5.1
Pittsburgh, PA	1,218	5.8	Jacksonville, FL	608	4.8
Tampa-St. Petersburg-Clearwater, FL	1,268	4.6	Richmond, VA	600	3.9
Denver-Aurora, CO	1,296	5.8	Oklahoma City, OK	576	4.4
Cleveland-Elyria-Mentor, OH	1,101	5.9	Hartford-West Hartford-East Hartford, CT NECTA	562	5.2
			Birmingham-Hoover, AL	533	4.8
			Rochester, NY	530	5.3

[1] Percent unemployed of the civilian labor force.

Source: U.S. Bureau of Labor Statistics, Local Area Unemployment Statistics program. See Internet site <http://www.bls.gov/lau/>.

Table 583. School Enrollment and Labor Force Status: 1990 and 2004

[In thousands (31,421 represents 31,421,000), except percent. As of October. For the civilian noninstitutional population 16 to 24 years old. Based on Current Population Survey; see text, Section 1, and Appendix III]

Characteristic	Population		Civilian labor force		Employed		Unemployed		
	1990	2004	1990	2004	1990	2004	1990, total	2004 Total	2004 Rate [1]
Total, 16 to 24 years [2]	31,421	36,504	20,679	22,484	18,317	19,847	2,363	2,637	11.7
Enrolled in school [2]	15,210	20,173	7,301	9,293	6,527	8,283	774	1,010	10.9
16 to 19 years	10,118	13,047	4,244	4,810	3,645	4,116	599	694	14.4
20 to 24 years	5,092	7,125	3,057	4,483	2,882	4,167	174	316	7.0
Sex: Male	7,704	9,847	3,635	4,296	3,215	3,761	420	535	12.5
Female	7,507	10,326	3,666	4,997	3,312	4,522	353	475	9.5
College level	8,139	10,801	4,542	6,311	4,231	5,794	311	517	8.2
Full-time	6,810	9,256	3,376	4,967	3,117	4,534	259	433	8.7
Race:									
White [3]	12,308	15,623	6,294	7,633	5,705	6,913	588	721	9.4
Below college	5,535	7,138	2,374	2,503	2,021	2,146	354	357	14.3
College level	6,772	8,486	3,919	5,130	3,685	4,767	234	364	7.1
Black [3]	2,129	2,799	718	996	576	786	142	210	21.1
Below college	1,207	1,523	306	319	212	212	94	106	33.4
College level	922	1,276	411	678	364	574	47	104	15.3
Asian [3]	(NA)	1,070	(NA)	354	(NA)	306	(NA)	48	13.5
Below college	(NA)	358	(NA)	52	(NA)	43	(NA)	9	(4)
College level	(NA)	712	(NA)	302	(NA)	263	(NA)	39	12.8
Not enrolled [2]	16,210	16,331	13,379	13,191	11,789	11,564	1,589	1,627	12.3
White [3]	13,317	12,842	11,276	10,486	10,193	9,441	1,083	1,045	10.0
Black [3]	2,441	2,465	1,752	1,924	1,298	1,484	454	440	22.9
Asian [3]	(NA)	425	(NA)	333	(NA)	296	(NA)	37	11.1

NA Not available. [1] Percent unemployed of civilian labor force in each category. [2] Includes other races, not shown separately. [3] 2004 data for persons in this race group only. See footnote 3, Table 577. [4] Data not shown where base is less than 75,000.

Source: U.S. Bureau of Labor Statistics, Bulletin 2307; College Enrollment and Work Activity of High School Graduates, News, USDL 05-487, March 25, 2005; and unpublished data. See Internet site <http://www.bls.gov/bls/newsrels.htm#OEUS>.

Table 584. **Labor Force Participation Rates by Marital Status, Sex, and Age: 1970 to 2004**

[Annual averages of monthly figures. See Table 581 for definition of participation rate. Based on Current Population Survey; see text, Section 1, and Appendix III]

Marital status and year	Male participation rate							Female participation rate						
	Total	16-19 years	20-24 years	25-34 years	35-44 years	45-64 years	65 and over	Total	16-19 years	20-24 years	25-34 years	35-44 years	45-64 years	65 and over
Single:														
1970....	65.5	54.6	73.8	87.9	86.2	75.7	25.2	56.8	44.7	73.0	81.4	78.6	73.0	19.7
1980....	72.6	59.9	81.3	89.2	82.2	66.9	16.8	64.4	53.6	75.2	83.3	76.9	65.6	13.9
1985....	73.8	56.3	81.5	89.4	84.6	65.5	15.6	66.6	52.3	76.3	82.4	80.8	67.9	9.8
1990 [1]...	74.8	55.1	81.6	89.9	84.5	67.3	15.7	66.7	51.7	74.5	80.9	80.8	66.2	12.1
1995....	73.7	54.4	80.3	88.7	81.4	67.0	17.9	66.8	52.2	72.9	80.2	79.5	67.3	11.6
1999 [1]...	73.4	52.5	79.7	89.5	83.5	70.6	17.3	68.7	51.1	76.1	84.2	80.8	69.6	9.9
2000 [1]...	73.6	52.5	80.5	89.4	82.9	69.7	17.3	68.9	51.1	76.1	83.9	80.9	69.9	10.8
2001....	72.7	50.0	79.6	89.0	83.2	69.8	15.4	68.1	49.1	75.3	83.2	81.3	69.9	12.1
2002....	71.7	47.2	78.7	88.7	83.1	69.6	16.9	67.4	47.3	74.5	83.3	79.9	69.6	14.3
2003 [1]...	70.4	44.0	77.9	87.7	82.9	67.6	19.4	66.2	44.8	72.9	82.2	79.8	69.9	15.2
2004 [1]...	70.2	43.6	77.7	87.9	82.7	67.8	20.3	65.9	43.8	73.1	81.8	80.5	70.9	14.7
Married: [2]														
1970....	86.1	92.3	94.7	98.0	98.1	91.2	29.9	40.5	37.8	47.9	38.8	46.8	44.0	7.3
1980....	80.9	91.3	96.9	97.5	97.2	84.3	20.5	49.8	49.3	61.4	58.8	61.8	46.9	7.3
1985....	78.7	91.0	95.6	97.4	96.8	81.7	16.8	53.8	49.6	65.7	65.8	68.1	49.4	6.6
1990 [1]...	78.6	92.1	95.6	96.9	96.7	82.6	17.5	58.4	49.5	66.1	69.6	74.0	56.5	8.5
1995....	77.5	89.2	94.9	96.3	95.4	82.4	18.0	61.0	51.6	64.7	72.0	75.7	62.7	9.1
1999 [1]...	77.5	83.2	93.7	96.5	95.9	83.4	18.3	61.2	49.8	64.5	70.9	74.6	65.3	9.6
2000 [1]...	77.3	79.5	94.1	96.7	95.8	83.0	19.2	61.1	53.2	63.8	70.3	74.8	65.4	10.1
2001....	77.4	77.7	94.2	95.9	95.6	83.7	19.1	61.2	45.1	63.9	69.9	74.5	66.1	10.3
2002....	77.4	81.1	93.3	95.7	95.1	83.8	19.4	61.0	49.6	63.4	69.3	73.8	66.5	10.7
2003 [1]...	77.3	76.6	93.2	95.3	95.1	83.5	19.9	61.0	46.7	62.6	68.5	73.3	67.4	11.3
2004 [1]...	77.1	77.4	92.4	95.6	95.1	83.1	20.4	60.5	41.1	60.9	67.6	72.7	67.0	11.6
Other: [3]														
1970....	60.7	(B)	90.4	93.7	91.1	78.5	19.3	40.3	48.6	60.3	64.6	68.8	61.9	10.0
1980....	67.5	(B)	92.6	94.1	91.9	73.3	13.7	43.6	50.0	68.4	76.5	77.1	60.2	8.2
1985....	68.7	(B)	95.1	93.7	91.8	72.8	11.4	45.1	51.9	66.2	76.9	81.6	61.0	7.5
1990 [1]...	68.9	(B)	93.1	93.0	90.7	74.9	12.0	47.2	53.9	65.4	77.0	82.1	65.0	8.4
1995....	66.2	(B)	92.7	90.9	88.2	72.4	12.1	47.4	55.8	67.2	77.1	80.7	67.2	8.4
1999 [1]...	65.9	(B)	90.2	92.3	88.7	73.4	12.3	49.1	45.3	73.6	82.4	83.4	69.1	8.4
2000 [1]...	66.8	60.5	88.1	93.2	89.9	73.9	12.9	49.0	46.0	74.0	83.1	82.9	69.8	8.7
2001....	66.0	57.3	85.4	92.4	89.4	73.5	13.9	49.0	47.2	75.5	81.6	82.6	69.3	8.9
2002....	65.5	57.5	87.4	91.2	89.6	74.1	13.2	49.2	46.2	74.7	80.7	82.7	69.7	8.9
2003 [1]...	65.0	45.6	88.0	91.4	89.3	72.4	14.3	49.6	44.1	71.4	79.1	81.9	70.7	9.8
2004 [1]...	64.9	53.1	87.2	90.6	88.6	72.8	14.3	49.6	48.7	70.0	79.4	81.7	69.8	10.4

B Percentage not shown where base is less than 35,000.   [1] See footnote 2, Table 576.   [2] Spouse present.   [3] Widowed, divorced, and married (spouse absent).

Source: U.S. Bureau of Labor Statistics, Bulletins 2217 and 2340; and unpublished data.

Table 585. **Marital Status of Women in the Civilian Labor Force: 1970 to 2004**

[Annual averages of monthly figures (31,543 represents 31,543,000). For civilian noninstitutional population 16 years old and over. Based on the Current Population Survey; see text, Section 1, and Appendix III]

Year	Female civilian labor force (1,000)				Female participation rate [3]			
	Total	Single	Married [1]	Other [2]	Total	Single	Married [1]	Other [2]
1970	31,543	7,265	18,475	5,804	43.3	56.8	40.5	40.3
1975	37,475	9,125	21,484	6,866	46.3	59.8	44.3	40.1
1980	45,487	11,865	24,980	8,643	51.5	64.4	49.8	43.6
1985	51,050	13,163	27,894	9,993	54.5	66.6	53.8	45.1
1987	53,658	13,885	29,381	10,393	56.0	67.4	55.9	45.7
1988	54,742	14,194	29,921	10,627	56.6	67.7	56.7	46.2
1989	56,030	14,377	30,548	11,104	57.4	68.0	57.8	47.0
1990 [4]	56,829	14,612	30,901	11,315	57.5	66.7	58.4	47.2
1991	57,178	14,681	31,112	11,385	57.4	66.2	58.5	46.8
1992	58,141	14,872	31,700	11,570	57.8	66.2	59.3	47.1
1993	58,795	15,031	31,980	11,784	57.9	66.2	59.4	47.2
1994 [4]	60,239	15,333	32,888	12,018	58.8	66.7	60.7	47.5
1995	60,944	15,467	33,359	12,118	58.9	66.8	61.0	47.4
1996	61,857	15,842	33,618	12,397	59.3	67.1	61.2	48.1
1997 [4]	63,036	16,492	33,802	12,742	59.8	67.9	61.6	48.6
1998 [4]	63,714	17,087	33,857	12,771	59.8	68.5	61.2	48.8
1999 [4]	64,855	17,575	34,372	12,909	60.0	68.7	61.2	49.1
2000 [4]	66,303	17,849	35,146	13,308	59.9	68.9	61.1	49.0
2001	66,848	18,021	35,236	13,592	59.8	68.1	61.2	49.0
2002	67,363	18,203	35,477	13,683	59.6	67.4	61.0	49.2
2003 [4]	68,272	18,397	36,046	13,828	59.5	66.2	61.0	49.6
2004 [4]	68,421	18,616	35,845	13,961	59.2	65.9	60.5	49.6

[1] Husband present.   [2] Widowed, divorced, or separated.   [3] See footnote 3, Table 581 for definition of participation rate.   [4] See footnote 2, Table 576.

Source: U.S. Bureau of Labor Statistics, Bulletin 2307; and unpublished data.

Table 586. Employment Status of Women by Marital Status and Presence and Age of Children: 1970 to 2004

[As of March (7.0 represents 7,000,000). For the civilian noninstitutional persons 16 years and over. Based on the Current Population Survey; see text, Section 1, and Appendix III]

Item	Total			With any children								
				Total			Children 6 to 17 only			Children under 6		
	Single	Mar-ried [1]	Other [2]	Single	Mar-ried [1]	Other [2]	Single	Mar-ried [1]	Other [2]	Single	Mar-ried [1]	Other [2]
IN LABOR FORCE (mil.)												
1970	7.0	18.4	5.9	(NA)	10.2	1.9	(NA)	6.3	1.3	(NA)	3.9	0.6
1980	11.2	24.9	8.8	0.6	13.7	3.6	0.2	8.4	2.6	0.3	5.2	1.0
1990	14.0	31.0	11.2	1.5	16.5	4.2	0.6	9.3	3.0	0.9	7.2	1.2
1995	15.0	33.6	12.0	2.1	18.0	4.6	0.8	10.2	3.3	1.3	7.8	1.3
2000	17.8	35.0	13.2	3.1	18.2	4.5	1.2	10.8	3.4	1.8	7.3	1.1
2002 [3]	18.1	35.6	13.7	3.2	18.3	4.6	1.4	11.1	3.4	1.8	7.2	1.2
2003 [3]	17.9	36.2	14.2	3.2	18.3	4.7	1.3	11.1	3.6	1.9	7.2	1.1
2004 [3]	18.1	35.9	14.2	3.3	18.0	4.7	1.4	10.8	3.6	1.9	7.1	1.1
PARTICIPATION RATE [4]												
1970	53.0	40.8	39.1	(NA)	39.7	60.7	(NA)	49.2	66.9	(NA)	30.3	52.2
1980	61.5	50.1	44.0	52.0	54.1	69.4	67.6	61.7	74.6	44.1	45.1	60.3
1990	66.4	58.2	46.8	55.2	66.3	74.2	69.7	73.6	79.7	48.7	58.9	63.6
1995	65.5	61.1	47.3	57.5	70.2	75.3	67.0	76.2	79.5	53.0	63.5	66.3
2000	68.6	62.0	50.2	73.9	70.6	82.7	79.7	77.2	85.0	70.5	62.8	76.6
2002 [3]	67.1	61.5	49.3	75.3	69.6	82.1	81.7	76.8	83.6	71.0	60.8	77.9
2003 [3]	65.0	61.8	50.1	73.1	69.2	82.0	77.6	77.0	84.8	70.2	59.8	74.3
2004 [3]	64.5	60.9	50.3	72.6	68.2	80.7	79.2	75.6	83.0	68.4	59.3	74.4
EMPLOYMENT (mil.)												
1970	6.5	17.5	5.6	(NA)	9.6	1.8	(NA)	6.0	1.2	(NA)	3.6	0.6
1980	10.1	23.6	8.2	0.4	12.8	3.3	0.2	8.1	2.4	0.2	4.8	0.9
1990	12.9	29.9	10.5	1.2	15.8	3.8	0.5	8.9	2.7	0.7	6.9	1.1
1995	13.7	32.3	11.3	1.8	17.2	4.2	0.7	9.8	3.1	1.1	7.3	1.2
2000	16.4	34.0	12.7	2.7	17.6	4.3	1.1	10.6	3.2	1.6	7.1	1.1
2002 [3]	16.5	34.3	12.9	2.8	17.5	4.3	1.2	10.7	3.2	1.6	6.8	1.1
2003 [3]	16.2	34.8	13.2	2.8	17.5	4.3	1.2	10.7	3.3	1.6	6.8	1.0
2004 [3]	16.5	34.6	13.3	2.8	17.2	4.4	1.2	10.4	3.3	1.6	6.8	1.0
UNEMPLOY-MENT RATE [5]												
1970	7.1	4.8	4.8	(NA)	6.0	7.2	(NA)	4.8	5.9	(NA)	7.9	9.8
1980	10.3	5.3	6.4	23.2	5.9	9.2	15.6	4.4	7.9	29.2	8.3	12.8
1990	8.2	3.5	5.7	18.4	4.2	8.5	14.5	3.8	7.7	20.8	4.8	10.2
1995	8.7	3.9	5.8	16.6	4.3	8.1	11.8	3.6	7.1	19.5	5.3	10.8
2000	7.3	2.7	4.3	11.0	2.9	5.1	8.7	2.6	4.8	12.6	3.5	5.9
2002 [3]	8.7	3.7	6.3	12.6	4.1	7.9	11.1	3.5	6.7	13.8	5.1	11.4
2003 [3]	9.4	3.8	6.5	13.4	4.1	8.9	11.6	3.6	7.7	14.7	4.9	13.0
2004 [3]	8.8	3.7	6.1	13.1	4.1	7.2	10.6	3.7	6.3	14.8	4.7	9.9

NA Not available. [1] Husband present. [2] Widowed, divorced, or separated. [3] See footnote 2, Table 576. [4] Percent of women in each specific category in the labor force. [5] Unemployed as a percent of civilian labor force in specified group.

Source: U.S. Bureau of Labor Statistics, Bulletin 2307; and unpublished data.

Table 587. Labor Force Participation Rates for Wives, Husband Present by Age of Own Youngest Child: 1975 to 2004

[As of March. For civilian noninstitutional population, 16 years old and over. For definition of participation rate, see Table 586. Based on Current Population Survey; see text, Section 1, and Appendix III]

Presence and age of child	Total			White [1]			Black [1]		
	1975	1990	2004	1975	1990	2004	1975	1990	2004
Wives, total	44.4	58.2	60.9	43.6	57.6	60.4	54.1	64.7	67.9
No children under 18	43.8	51.1	55.0	43.6	50.8	54.8	47.6	52.9	58.1
With children under 18	44.9	66.3	68.2	43.6	65.6	67.7	58.4	75.6	78.4
Under 6, total	36.7	58.9	53.3	34.7	57.8	58.4	54.9	73.1	75.1
Under 3	32.7	55.5	55.1	30.7	54.9	54.5	50.1	67.5	71.3
1 year or under	30.8	53.9	54.2	29.2	53.3	54.7	50.0	64.4	70.7
2 years	37.1	60.9	56.1	35.1	60.3	55.2	56.4	75.4	75.0
3 to 5 years	42.2	64.1	65.4	40.1	62.5	64.3	61.2	80.4	79.1
3 years	41.2	63.1	63.6	39.0	62.3	62.5	62.7	74.5	82.7
4 years	41.2	65.1	66.8	38.7	63.2	65.2	64.9	80.6	80.3
5 years	44.4	64.5	66.4	43.8	62.0	65.5	56.3	86.2	71.6
6 to 13 years	51.8	73.0	74.2	50.7	72.6	73.8	65.7	77.6	80.5
14 to 17 years	53.5	75.1	78.8	53.4	74.9	79.0	52.3	78.8	81.0

[1] 2004 for persons in this race group only. See footnote 3, Table 577.

Source: U.S. Bureau of Labor Statistics, Bulletin 2340; and unpublished data.

Table 588. Married Couples by Labor Force Status of Spouse: 1986 to 2004

[50,933 represents 50,933,000. Based on the Current Population Survey and subject to sampling error; for details see source and Appendix III]

Year	Number (1,000)					Percent distribution			
	All married couples	In labor force		Wife only	Husband and wife not in labor force	In labor force		Wife only	Husband and wife not in labor force
		Husband and wife	Husband only			Husband and wife	Husband only		
TOTAL									
1986	50,933	25,428	14,675	2,362	8,468	49.9	28.8	4.6	16.6
1990	52,317	28,056	13,013	2,453	8,794	53.6	24.9	4.7	16.8
1995	53,858	29,999	11,777	3,043	9,039	55.7	21.9	5.7	16.8
1998	54,317	30,591	11,582	3,087	9,057	56.3	21.3	5.7	16.7
1999	54,770	30,635	11,704	3,185	9,245	55.9	21.4	5.8	16.9
2000	55,311	31,095	11,815	3,301	9,098	56.2	21.4	6.0	16.4
2001	56,592	31,794	12,213	3,274	9,311	56.2	21.6	5.8	16.5
2002	56,747	31,637	12,327	3,388	9,395	55.8	21.7	6.0	16.6
2003	58,586	32,585	12,757	3,642	9,602	55.6	21.8	6.2	16.4
2004	59,064	32,199	13,328	3,771	9,766	54.5	22.6	6.4	16.5
WITH CHILDREN UNDER 18									
1986	24,630	14,606	8,916	518	590	59.3	36.2	2.1	2.4
1990	24,537	15,768	7,667	558	544	64.3	31.2	2.3	2.2
1995	25,241	17,024	6,863	756	598	67.4	27.2	3.0	2.4
1998	25,269	17,168	6,856	753	491	67.9	27.1	3.0	1.9
1999	25,066	16,887	6,998	765	418	67.4	27.9	3.1	1.7
2000	25,248	17,116	6,950	795	387	67.8	27.5	3.1	1.5
2001	25,980	17,563	7,210	784	422	67.6	27.8	3.0	1.6
2002	25,792	17,233	7,301	777	482	66.8	28.3	3.0	1.9
2003	26,445	17,383	7,660	923	480	65.7	29.0	3.5	1.8
2004	26,377	17,014	7,923	983	458	64.5	30.0	3.7	1.7
WITH CHILDREN UNDER 6									
1986	11,924	6,271	5,284	155	215	52.6	44.3	1.3	1.8
1990	12,051	6,932	4,692	192	235	57.5	38.9	1.6	2.0
1995	11,951	7,406	4,059	233	253	62.0	34.0	1.9	2.1
1998	11,773	7,310	4,079	223	161	62.1	34.6	1.9	1.4
1999	11,461	6,878	4,182	257	144	60.0	36.5	2.2	1.3
2000	11,393	6,984	4,077	211	121	61.3	35.8	1.9	1.1
2001	11,732	7,054	4,296	247	134	60.1	36.6	2.1	1.1
2002	11,531	6,796	4,311	250	175	58.9	37.4	2.2	1.5
2003	12,014	6,884	4,615	308	208	57.3	38.4	2.6	1.7
2004	12,006	6,794	4,713	326	173	56.6	39.3	2.7	1.4

Source: U.S. Census Bureau, Table MC-1, Married Couples by Labor Force Status of Spouses: 1986 to Present; released 29 June 2005; <http://www.census.gov/population/www/socdemo/hh-fam.html>.

Table 589. Employed Civilians and Weekly Hours: 1980 to 2004

[In thousands (99,303 represents 99,303,000), except as indicated. For civilian noninstitutional population 16 years old and over. Annual averages of monthly figures. Based on Current Population Survey; see text, Section 1, and Appendix III]

Item	1980	1990 [1]	1995	2000 [1]	2002	2003 [1]	2004 [1]
Total employed	99,303	118,793	124,900	136,891	136,485	137,736	139,252
Age:							
16 to 19 years old	7,710	6,581	6,419	7,189	6,332	5,919	5,907
20 to 24 years old	14,087	13,401	12,443	13,229	13,351	13,433	13,723
25 to 34 years old	27,204	33,935	32,356	31,549	30,306	30,383	30,423
35 to 44 years old	19,523	30,817	34,202	36,433	35,235	34,881	34,580
45 to 54 years old	16,234	19,525	24,378	30,310	31,281	31,914	32,469
55 to 64 years old	11,586	11,189	11,435	14,002	15,674	16,598	17,331
65 years old and over	2,960	3,346	3,666	4,179	4,306	4,608	4,819
Class of worker:							
Nonagricultural industries	95,938	115,570	121,460	134,427	134,174	135,461	137,020
Wage and salary worker	88,525	106,598	112,448	125,114	125,156	126,015	127,463
Self-employed	7,000	8,719	8,902	9,205	8,923	9,344	9,467
Unpaid family workers	413	253	110	108	95	101	90
Agriculture and related industries	3,364	3,223	3,440	2,464	2,311	2,275	2,232
Wage and salary worker	1,425	1,740	1,814	1,421	1,282	1,299	1,242
Self-employed	1,642	1,378	1,580	1,010	1,003	951	964
Unpaid family workers	297	105	45	33	26	25	27
Weekly hours:							
Nonagricultural industries:							
Wage and salary workers	38.1	39.2	39.2	39.6	39.1	39.0	39.0
Self-employed	41.2	40.8	39.4	39.7	38.7	38.4	38.4
Unpaid family workers	34.7	34.0	33.5	32.5	31.5	31.7	31.3
Agriculture and related industries:							
Wage and salary workers	41.6	41.2	41.1	43.2	42.4	42.6	42.7
Self-employed	49.3	46.8	43.5	45.3	44.9	45.1	44.4
Unpaid family workers	38.6	38.5	42.0	38.3	38.7	33.4	37.3

[1] See footnote 2, Table 576.

Source: U.S. Bureau of Labor Statistics, *Employment and Earnings*, monthly, January issues; and unpublished data. See Internet site <http://www.bls.gov/cps/home.htm>.

Table 590. Persons at Work by Hours Worked: 2004

[133,770 represents 133,770,000. For civilian noninstitutional population 16 years old and over. Annual averages of monthly figures. Based on Current Population Survey; see text, Section 1, and Appendix III. See headnote, Table 593 regarding industries]

Hours of work	Persons at work (1,000)			Percent distribution		
	Total	Agriculture and related industries	Non-agricultural industries	Total	Agriculture and related industries	Non-agricultural industries
Total	133,770	2,134	131,637	100.0	100.0	100.0
1 to 34 hours	32,378	577	31,801	24.2	27.0	24.2
1 to 4 hours	1,391	54	1,337	1.0	2.5	1.0
5 to 14 hours	5,011	143	4,868	3.7	6.7	3.7
15 to 29 hours	16,017	254	15,763	12.0	11.9	12.0
30 to 34 hours	9,959	127	9,832	7.4	5.9	7.5
35 hours and over	101,393	1,556	99,836	75.8	73.0	75.8
35 to 39 hours	9,129	103	9,026	6.8	4.8	6.9
40 hours	54,878	531	54,347	41.0	24.9	41.3
41 hours and over	37,386	922	36,464	27.9	43.2	27.7
41 to 48 hours	13,201	163	13,039	9.9	7.6	9.9
49 to 58 hours	14,085	250	13,835	10.5	11.7	10.5
60 hours and over	10,100	509	9,590	7.6	23.9	7.3
Average weekly hours: Persons at work	39.0	43.4	39.0	(X)	(X)	(X)
Persons usually working full-time	42.9	49.4	42.8	(X)	(X)	(X)

X Not applicable.

Source: U.S. Bureau of Labor Statistics, *Employment and Earnings*, monthly, January 2005 issue. See Internet site <http://www.bls.gov/cps/home.htm>.

Table 591. Persons With a Job, But Not at Work: 1980 to 2004

[In thousands (5,881 represents 5,881,000), except percent. For civilian noninstitutional population 16 years old and over. Annual averages of monthly figures. Based on Current Population Survey; see text, Section 1 and Appendix III]

Reason for not working	1980	1990[1]	1995	1997[1]	1998[1]	1999[1]	2000[1]	2001	2002	2003[1]	2004[1]
All industries, number	5,881	6,160	5,582	5,555	5,586	5,407	5,681	5,631	5,394	5,469	5,482
Percent of employed	5.9	5.2	4.5	4.3	4.2	4.1	4.2	4.1	4.0	4.0	3.9
Reason for not working:											
Vacation	3,320	3,529	2,982	2,942	3,033	2,899	3,109	3,039	2,929	2,922	2,923
Illness	1,426	1,341	1,084	1,114	1,095	1,096	1,156	1,095	1,072	1,090	1,058
Bad weather	155	90	122	146	130	104	89	100	97	123	133
Industrial dispute	105	24	21	20	10	7	14	9	7	18	10
All other	876	1,177	1,373	1,334	1,318	1,300	1,313	1,388	1,289	1,316	1,358

[1] See footnote 2, Table 576.
Source: U.S. Bureau of Labor Statistics, *Employment and Earnings*, monthly, January issues; and unpublished data. See Internet site <http://www.bls.gov/cps/home.htm>.

Table 592. Class of Worker by Sex and Selected Characteristic: 2004

[In percent, except as indicated (10,431 represents 10,431,000). For the civilian noninstitutional population 16 years old and over. Annual averages of monthly figures. Based on Current Population Survey; see text, Section 1, and Appendix III]

Characteristic	Unincorporated self-employed			Incorporated self-employed			Wage and salary workers[1]		
	Total	Male	Female	Total	Male	Female	Total	Male	Female
Total (1,000)	10,431	6,562	3,869	5,151	3,775	1,376	123,554	64,145	59,408
PERCENT DISTRIBUTION	100.0	100.0	100.0	100.0	100.0	100.0	100.0	100.0	100.0
Age: 16 to 19 years old	0.8	0.9	0.6	0.1	0.1	0.1	4.7	4.5	4.9
20 to 24 years old	3.1	3.3	2.8	1.3	1.5	0.8	10.8	10.9	10.7
25 to 34 years old	15.5	15.1	16.1	11.5	11.4	11.6	22.8	24.0	21.6
35 to 44 years old	25.1	24.2	26.7	28.5	28.4	28.9	24.7	25.0	24.3
45 to 54 years old	26.8	26.7	27.0	31.1	30.8	31.9	22.7	21.9	23.6
55 to 64 years old	19.4	19.5	19.2	20.6	20.6	20.7	11.5	11.1	12.0
65 years old and over	9.3	10.2	7.7	6.8	7.1	5.9	2.8	2.7	3.0
Race/ethnicity: White[2]	88.1	88.6	87.1	89.4	90.1	87.4	82.0	83.3	80.6
Black[2]	5.8	5.5	6.4	4.1	3.8	4.7	11.4	10.0	12.9
Asian[2]	4.0	3.7	4.4	5.3	5.0	6.2	4.3	4.4	4.2
Hispanic[3]	9.9	10.9	8.2	5.8	5.9	5.5	13.4	15.4	11.3
Country of birth: U.S. born	86.8	86.0	88.2	85.9	86.2	84.9	85.3	83.2	87.7
Foreign-born	13.4	14.2	12.0	14.1	13.8	15.0	14.7	16.8	12.3
U.S. citizen	6.0	6.0	5.9	9.6	9.2	10.7	5.8	5.8	5.7
Not a U.S. citizen	7.4	8.2	6.2	4.5	4.6	4.4	8.9	11.0	6.6

[1] Excludes the incorporated self-employed. [2] For persons in this race group only. See footnote 3, Table 577. [3] Persons of Hispanic origin may be of any race.

Source: U.S. Bureau of Labor Statistics, Current Population Survey, unpublished data.

Table 593. Self-Employed Workers by Industry and Occupation: 2000 to 2004

[In thousands (10,214 represents 10,214,000). For civilian noninstitutional population 16 years old and over. Annual averages of monthly figures. Data represent the unincorporated self-employed; the incorporated self-employed are considered wage and salary workers. Based on the occupational and industrial classification derived from those used in the 2000 census and are not comparable to those used in the 1990 Census. See text, this section. Based on the Current Population Survey; see text, Section 1, and Appendix III]

Item	2000	2001	2002	2003 [1]	2004 [1]
Total self-employed................	10,214	10,109	9,926	10,295	10,431
Industry:					
Agriculture and related industries............	1,010	988	1,003	951	964
Mining............................	12	21	13	9	13
Construction	1,728	1,675	1,598	1,717	1,848
Manufacturing	334	354	312	325	316
Wholesale and retail trade	1,221	1,195	1,163	1,247	1,153
Transportation and utilities	348	375	369	357	410
Information	139	132	145	152	146
Financial activities [2]	735	697	675	736	792
Professional and business services [2] ...	1,927	2,001	1,863	1,908	1,993
Education and health services [2]	1,107	1,090	1,119	1,138	1,105
Leisure and hospitality [2]............	660	631	627	686	660
Other services [3]	993	951	1,041	1,071	1,031
Occupation:					
Management, professional, and related occupations	4,169	4,085	4,064	4,176	4,179
Service occupations	1,775	1,775	1,786	1,690	1,757
Sales and office occupations..........	1,982	1,927	1,883	1,945	1,909
Natural resources, construction, and maintenance occupations	1,591	1,602	1,503	1,795	1,847
Production, transportation, and material moving occupations.................	698	720	690	689	739

[1] See footnote 2, Table 576.   [2] For composition of industries, see Table 613.   [3] Includes private households.

Source: U.S. Bureau of Labor Statistics, *Employment and Earnings*, monthly, January issues. See Internet site <http://www.bls.gov /cps/home.htm>.

Table 594. Persons Doing Job-Related Work at Home: 2001

[19,759 represents 19,759,000. As of May. For persons at work 16 years and over in non-agricultural industries doing job-related work at home at least once a week as part of their primary job. Based on the Current Population Survey; see text, Section 1, and Appendix III. Industry and occupational classifications not comparable to those based on the 2000 Census. See text, this section]

Characteristic			Percent distribution			Wage and salary workers paid to work at home			
			Wage and salary workers				Percent distribution		
	Total [1] (1,000)	Rate [2]	Paid [3]	Unpaid	Self-employed [4]	Total [5] (1,000)	Hours vary	Usually less than 8 hours	Usually 35 hours or more
Total [6]......................	19,759	15.0	17.4	52.0	29.7	3,436	27.4	24.5	15.7
SEX									
Male	10,291	14.8	16.0	50.5	32.6	1,642	30.9	23.3	14.8
Female	9,468	15.2	18.9	53.7	26.5	1,794	24.2	25.7	16.5
RACE AND HISPANIC ORIGIN									
White.......................	17,947	16.3	17.5	51.6	30.0	3,138	27.2	24.4	15.0
Black.......................	1,152	7.6	14.9	57.9	26.0	172	29.7	22.1	28.9
Hispanic origin [7]	937	6.7	20.4	49.2	28.4	191	32.3	15.9	27.6
OCCUPATION									
Managerial and professional	12,628	29.8	14.2	62.8	22.4	1,798	28.0	24.1	13.9
Exec., admin., and managerial	5,262	25.7	16.7	52.5	30.0	880	25.8	24.3	12.9
Professional specialty	7,366	33.5	12.5	70.1	17.0	918	30.1	23.9	14.9
Technical, sales and admin. support ..	4,669	12.2	24.7	40.2	33.9	1,155	27.3	22.1	16.7
Technicians and related support	305	6.9	36.0	48.4	14.3	110	40.2	24.6	21.2
Sales	3,133	20.0	20.3	40.3	38.9	635	27.8	18.9	13.0
Admin support, inc. clerical........	1,231	6.8	33.4	37.8	25.8	411	23.3	26.5	21.0
Service	972	5.3	24.1	18.4	55.1	234	25.6	19.6	33.1
Precision production, craft, & repair....	1,050	7.1	15.7	19.4	64.4	165	29.1	47.2	2.7
Operators, fabricators, and laborers ...	381	2.2	19.4	24.3	49.3	74	(B)	(B)	(B)
Farming, forestry, and fishing	59	8.7	(B)	(B)	(B)	10	(B)	(B)	(B)

- Represents zero.   B Base figure too small to meet statistical standards for reliability of a derived figure.   [1] Includes unpaid family workers and persons who did not report pay status.   [2] Persons working at home as a percent of the total employed.   [3] Persons with formal arrangements with their employers to be paid for the work done at home.   [4] Includes incorporated and unincorporated self-employed.   [5] Includes those not reporting usual number of hours worked.   [6] Includes other races, not shown separately.   [7] Persons of Hispanic origin may be of any race.

Source: U.S. Bureau of Labor Statistics, *Work at Home in 2001*, News, USDL 02-107, March 1, 2002. See Internet site <http://www.bls.gov/bls/newsrels.htm#OEUS>.

Table 595. Persons on Flexible Schedules: 2004

[In thousands, except percent. (99,778 represents 99,778,000) As of May. For employed full-time wage and salary workers 16 years old and over. Excludes all self-employed persons, regardless of whether or not their businesses were incorporated. Data related to the primary job. Based on the Current Population Survey; see text, Section 1, Population, and Appendix III]

Item	Total [1]	Total — Number	Total — Percent	Male — Total [1]	Male — Number	Male — Percent	Female — Total [1]	Female — Number	Female — Percent
		With flexible schedules			With flexible schedules			With flexible schedules	
Total	99,778	27,411	27.5	56,412	15,853	28.1	43,366	11,558	26.7
AGE									
16 to 19 years old	1,427	336	23.6	903	185	20.5	524	151	28.9
20 years and over	98,351	27,075	27.5	55,509	15,668	28.2	42,842	11,406	26.6
20 to 24 years old	9,004	2,058	22.9	5,147	1,065	20.7	3,856	993	25.8
25 to 34 years old	24,640	6,902	28.0	14,358	4,051	28.2	10,283	2,851	27.7
35 to 44 years old	26,766	7,807	29.2	15,424	4,605	29.9	11,342	3,202	28.2
45 to 54 years old	24,855	6,651	26.8	13,440	3,769	28.0	11,415	2,882	25.2
55 to 64 years old	11,745	3,181	27.1	6,383	1,865	29.2	5,361	1,316	24.5
65 years old and over	1,341	475	35.4	757	314	41.4	585	161	27.6
RACE AND HISPANIC ORIGIN									
White [2]	80,498	23,121	28.7	46,222	13,582	29.4	34,276	9,539	27.8
Black [2]	12,578	2,476	19.7	6,447	1,193	18.5	6,131	1,283	20.9
Asian [2]	4,136	1,132	27.4	2,300	720	31.3	1,836	412	22.4
Hispanic origin [3]	14,110	2,596	18.4	8,621	1,430	16.6	5,489	1,166	21.2
MARITAL STATUS									
Married, spouse present	57,630	16,270	28.2	34,926	10,382	29.7	22,704	5,888	25.9
Not married	42,148	11,141	26.4	21,486	5,471	25.5	20,662	5,670	27.4
Never married	25,144	6,693	26.6	14,469	3,605	24.9	10,676	3,088	28.9
Other marital status	17,004	4,448	26.2	7,018	1,866	26.6	9,986	2,582	25.9
PRESENCE AND AGE OF CHILDREN									
Without own children under 18	61,761	16,759	27.1	34,680	9,410	27.1	27,081	7,349	27.1
With own children under 18	38,018	10,652	28.0	21,733	6,443	29.6	16,285	4,209	25.8
With youngest child 6 to 17	21,739	5,960	27.4	11,477	3,341	29.1	10,262	2,619	25.5
With youngest child under 6	16,279	4,692	28.8	10,256	3,102	30.2	6,023	1,590	26.4

[1] Includes persons who did not provide information on flexible schedules. [2] For persons in the race group only. See footnote 3, Table 577. [3] Persons of Hispanic origin may be of any race.

Source: U.S. Bureau of Labor Statistics, *Workers on Flexible and Shift Schedules*, News, USDL 05-1198, July 1, 2005. See Internet site <http://www.bls.gov/bls/newsrels.htm#OEUS>.

Table 596. Persons on Shift Schedules: 2004

[In percent, except as indicated. (99,778 represents 99,778,000) As of May. See headnote, Table 595]

Item	Total workers (1,000) [1]	Regular daytime schedules [1]	Shift workers — Total	Evening shift	Night shift	Rotating shift	Split shift	Irregular shift [2]	Other shift
Total	99,778	84.6	14.8	4.7	3.2	2.5	0.5	3.1	0.7
AGE									
16 to 19 years old	1,427	64.9	34.6	14.5	4.4	6.1	1.0	8.3	0.2
20 years and over	98,351	84.9	14.6	4.6	3.2	2.5	0.5	3.0	0.7
20 to 24 years old	9,004	76.8	22.3	8.8	3.7	3.3	0.9	4.6	0.9
25 to 34 years old	24,640	84.1	15.2	5.0	3.4	2.7	0.5	2.8	0.8
35 to 44 years old	26,766	85.4	14.1	4.1	3.2	2.5	0.4	3.1	0.7
45 to 54 years old	24,855	86.8	12.8	3.6	3.2	2.3	0.5	2.5	0.7
55 to 64 years old	11,745	87.1	12.5	3.8	2.6	2.0	0.4	3.0	0.7
65 years old and over	1,341	88.8	10.3	3.5	1.8	1.4	0.5	2.9	0.2
SEX									
Male	56,412	82.7	16.7	5.2	3.6	2.8	0.5	3.6	0.9
Female	43,366	87.0	12.4	4.1	2.8	2.2	0.5	2.4	0.4
RACE AND HISPANIC ORIGIN									
White [3]	80,498	85.8	13.7	4.1	3.0	2.3	0.5	3.1	0.7
Black [3]	12,578	78.0	20.8	7.9	4.5	4.1	0.4	3.0	0.7
Asian [3]	4,136	83.6	15.7	5.4	4.1	1.6	1.2	2.6	0.8
Hispanic origin [4]	14,110	83.1	16.0	5.8	3.9	2.1	0.6	2.6	0.9
MARITAL STATUS									
Males:									
Married, spouse present	34,926	84.8	14.9	3.9	3.3	2.9	0.5	3.4	0.9
Not married	21,486	79.5	19.7	7.4	3.9	2.6	0.7	4.0	1.0
Never married	14,469	78.6	20.6	8.1	3.8	2.6	0.8	4.2	1.0
Other	7,018	81.4	17.8	5.9	4.2	2.8	0.4	3.6	1.0
Females:									
Married, spouse present	22,704	90.4	9.2	2.8	2.4	1.4	0.3	1.9	0.3
Not married	20,662	83.2	16.0	5.6	3.2	3.0	0.6	2.9	0.6
Never married	10,676	81.2	17.9	6.3	3.0	3.6	0.8	3.6	0.6
Other	9,986	85.5	13.9	4.8	3.5	2.3	0.4	2.1	0.6

[1] Includes persons who did not provide information on usual shift worked. [2] Employer arranged schedule. [3] For persons in this race group only. See footnote 3, Table 577. [4] Persons of Hispanic origin may be of any race.

Source: U.S. Bureau of Labor Statistics, *Workers on Flexible and Shift Schedules*, News, USDL 05-1198, July 1, 2005. See Internet site <http://www.bls.gov/bls/newsrels.htm#OEUS>.

Labor Force, Employment, and Earnings 397

Table 597. **Multiple Jobholders: 2004**

[Annual average of monthly figures (7,473 represents 7,473,000). For the civilian noninstitutional population 16 years old and over. Multiple jobholders are employed persons who, either 1) had jobs as wage or salary workers with two employers or more; 2) were self-employed and also held a wage and salary job; or 3) were unpaid family workers on their primary jobs but also held a wage and salary job. Based on the Current Population Survey; see text, Section 1, Population, and Appendix III]

Characteristic	Total		Male		Female	
	Number (1,000)	Percent of employed	Number (1,000)	Percent of employed	Number (1,000)	Percent of employed
Total [1]	7,473	5.4	3,835	5.1	3,638	5.6
Age:						
16 to 19 years old	274	4.6	107	3.6	167	5.7
20 to 24 years old	795	5.8	377	5.2	419	6.5
25 to 54 years old	5,361	5.5	2,800	5.3	2,561	5.7
55 to 64 years old	869	5.0	451	4.9	417	5.1
65 years old and over	173	3.6	100	3.7	74	3.4
Race and Hispanic ethnicity:						
White [2]	6,357	5.5	3,266	5.2	3,091	5.9
Black [2]	705	4.7	360	5.2	345	4.3
Asian [2]	226	3.8	118	3.6	108	3.9
Hispanic [3]	612	3.4	363	3.4	248	3.5
Marital status:						
Married, spouse present	4,125	5.2	2,408	5.3	1,718	5.0
Widowed, divorced, or separated	1,303	5.9	463	5.1	840	6.4
Single, never married	2,044	5.5	964	4.7	1,080	6.4
Full- or part-time status:						
Primary job full-time, secondary job part time . .	3,908	(X)	2,210	(X)	1,697	(X)
Both jobs part-time	1,678	(X)	540	(X)	1,138	(X)
Both jobs full-time	286	(X)	187	(X)	100	(X)
Hours vary on primary or secondary job	1,564	(X)	879	(X)	685	(X)

X Not applicable.   [1] Includes a small number of persons who work part-time on their primary job and full-time on their secondary job(s), not shown separately. Includes other races, not shown separately.   [2] For persons who selected this race group only. See footnote 3, Table 577.   [3] Persons of Hispanic or Latino ethnicity may be of any race.

Source: U.S. Bureau of Labor Statistics, *Employment and Earnings*, January 2005. See Internet site <http://www.bls.gov/cps/home.htm>.

Table 598. **Average Number of Jobs Held From Ages 18 to 38: 1978 to 2002**

[For persons 37 to 45 in 2002. A job is an uninterrupted period of work with a particular employer. Educational attainment as of 2002. Based on the National Longitudinal Survey of Youth 1979; see source for details]

Sex and educational attainment	Number of jobs held by age				
	Total [1]	Age 18 to 22 years old	Age 23 to 27 years old	Age 28 to 32 years old	Age 33 to 38 years old
Total [2]	10.2	4.4	3.3	2.6	2.5
Less than a high school diploma	10.3	3.9	3.2	2.6	2.5
High school graduates, no college	9.7	4.2	3.0	2.6	2.5
Less than a bachelor's degree	10.5	4.6	3.7	2.7	2.6
Bachelor's degree or more	10.6	5.0	3.5	2.6	2.3
Male	10.4	4.5	3.5	2.8	2.5
Less than a high school diploma	11.6	4.6	3.8	3.0	2.7
High school graduates, no college	10.2	4.5	3.4	2.8	2.4
Less than a bachelor's degree	10.6	4.6	3.4	2.9	2.7
Bachelor's degree or more	10.0	4.6	3.4	2.6	2.4
Female	9.9	4.3	3.1	2.4	2.4
Less than a high school diploma	8.5	3.0	2.4	2.1	2.2
High school graduates, no college	9.2	3.8	2.7	2.3	2.5
Less than a bachelor's degree	10.4	4.6	3.3	2.5	2.5
Bachelor's degree or more	11.1	5.4	3.7	2.7	2.2
White, non-Hispanic	10.3	4.6	3.3	2.6	2.5
Less than a high school diploma	10.8	4.3	3.3	2.7	2.6
High school graduates, no college	9.7	4.3	3.1	2.6	2.5
Less than a bachelor's degree	10.8	4.8	3.5	2.7	2.6
Bachelor's degree or more	10.6	5.1	3.5	2.6	2.3
Black, non-Hispanic	9.6	3.6	3.1	2.7	2.6
Less than a high school diploma	9.1	2.9	2.9	2.6	2.3
High school graduates, no college	9.7	3.5	3.0	2.7	2.5
Less than a bachelor's degree	9.7	3.8	3.1	2.6	2.7
Bachelor's degree or more	9.9	4.2	3.6	2.8	2.7
Hispanic or Latino	9.6	4.0	3.0	2.5	2.4
Less than a high school diploma	9.6	3.9	3.0	2.4	2.3
High school graduates, no college	9.5	3.9	2.9	2.5	2.4
Less than a bachelor's degree	9.5	4.2	3.0	2.5	2.4
Bachelor's degree or more	10.5	4.5	3.4	2.8	2.5

[1] Jobs held in more than one age category were counted in each category, but only once in the total.   [2] Includes other races, not shown separately.

Source: U.S. Bureau of Labor Statistics, Number of Jobs Held, Labor Market Activity, and *Earnings Growth Among Younger Baby Boomers: Recent results from a Longitudinal Survey*, USDL 04-1678, August 25, 2004. See Internet site <http://www.bls.gov/nls/home.htm>.

Table 599. Distribution of Workers by Tenure With Current Employer: 2004

[121,753 represents 121,753,000. As of January. For employed wage and salary workers 16 years and over. Data exclude the incorporated and unincorporated self-employed. Based on the Current Population Survey and subject to sampling error; see source and Appendix III]

Characteristic	Number employed (1,000)	Percent distribution by tenure with current employer								Median years [1]
		12 months or less	13 to 23 months	2 years	3 to 4 years	5 to 9 years	10 to 14 years	15 to 19 years	20 years or more	
Total [2]	121,753	23.0	7.0	5.7	18.5	19.8	9.9	6.4	9.7	4.0
AGE AND SEX										
16 to 19 years old	5,433	73.2	11.2	7.5	7.8	0.3	-	-	-	0.7
20 to 24 years old	13,028	49.6	12.6	10.2	20.8	6.6	0.1	-	-	1.3
25 to 34 years old	27,877	26.9	9.4	7.4	25.9	23.7	5.9	0.9	-	2.9
35 to 44 years old	30,314	17.4	5.7	4.8	19.1	25.1	13.7	9.3	5.0	4.9
45 to 54 years old	27,713	11.0	4.7	3.7	14.8	20.7	13.6	10.5	20.9	7.7
55 to 64 years old	13,983	10.4	4.0	3.4	12.8	18.8	13.9	10.6	26.0	9.6
65 years old and over	3,405	9.9	3.1	4.1	14.0	20.2	14.0	9.2	25.5	9.0
Male	63,146	22.4	6.6	5.6	18.3	19.6	10.1	6.5	10.9	4.1
16 to 19 years old	2,683	70.9	9.9	9.3	9.5	0.4	-	-	-	0.8
20 to 24 years old	6,798	50.0	11.4	9.6	21.5	7.4	0.1	-	-	1.3
25 to 34 years old	15,209	26.0	9.1	6.9	26.4	24.1	6.6	0.9	-	3.0
35 to 44 years old	15,885	16.4	5.0	4.7	18.1	25.1	14.6	10.4	5.6	5.2
45 to 54 years old	13,785	9.6	4.7	3.5	12.8	19.1	13.7	11.3	25.3	9.6
55 to 64 years old	7,026	11.4	3.9	3.5	12.0	17.5	12.9	9.1	29.7	9.8
65 years old and over	1,761	8.7	3.3	4.4	16.8	20.1	13.4	8.4	24.9	8.2
Female	58,608	23.7	7.4	5.8	18.7	20.1	9.6	6.2	8.4	3.8
16 to 19 years old	2,750	75.5	12.3	5.8	6.1	0.3	-	-	-	0.7
20 to 24 years old	6,230	49.2	13.8	10.9	20.1	5.8	0.1	-	-	1.3
25 to 34 years old	12,668	27.9	9.7	7.9	25.2	23.3	5.2	0.8	-	2.8
35 to 44 years old	14,429	18.4	6.5	4.9	20.1	25.0	12.6	8.1	4.3	4.5
45 to 54 years old	13,929	12.4	4.8	3.9	16.8	22.3	13.4	9.8	16.6	6.4
55 to 64 years old	6,957	9.4	4.1	3.3	13.6	20.2	15.0	12.1	22.2	9.2
65 years old and over	1,644	11.2	3.0	3.7	11.0	20.3	14.6	10.1	26.1	9.6
RACE AND HISPANIC ORIGIN										
White [3]	100,243	22.7	7.1	5.4	18.2	19.6	10.2	6.6	10.2	4.0
Male	52,758	22.3	6.7	5.3	17.9	19.3	10.3	6.7	11.5	4.2
Female	47,485	23.2	7.6	5.5	18.5	20.0	10.1	6.4	8.7	3.9
Black [3]	13,401	24.5	5.8	6.6	19.2	20.5	8.4	5.9	9.1	3.7
Male	6,097	23.4	5.4	7.0	18.7	20.6	9.3	5.8	9.8	3.8
Female	7,304	25.4	6.1	6.2	19.6	20.4	7.6	6.1	8.5	3.6
Asian [3]	5,131	22.3	7.2	7.5	21.5	22.8	8.6	5.3	4.9	3.6
Male	2,678	20.3	7.2	6.8	22.4	23.5	9.5	4.8	5.4	3.9
Female	2,453	24.3	7.2	8.2	20.6	21.9	7.6	5.8	4.3	3.3
Hispanic origin [4]	16,338	26.9	7.4	7.8	22.8	18.2	8.0	4.4	4.4	3.1
Male	9,778	26.4	7.5	7.4	23.2	17.9	8.2	4.5	4.7	3.1
Female	6,560	27.6	7.3	8.5	22.2	18.7	7.7	4.3	3.8	3.0

- Represents or rounds to zero. [1] For definition of median, see Guide to Tabular Presentation. [2] Includes other races, not shown separately. [3] For persons in this race group only. See footnote 3, Table 577. [4] Persons of Hispanic or Latino origin may be of any race.

Source: U. S. Bureau of Labor Statistics, News, *Employee Tenure in 2004*, USDL 04-1829, September 21, 2004; and unpublished data. See Internet site <http://www.bls.gov/bls/newsrels.htm#OEUS>.

Table 600. Part-Time Workers by Reason: 2004

[In thousands (32,378 represents 32,378,000), except hours. For persons working 1 to 34 hours per week. For civilian noninstitutional population 16 years old and over. Annual average of monthly figures. Based on the Current Population Survey and subject to sampling error; see text, Section 1, and Appendix III]

Reason	All industries			Nonagriculture industries		
		Usually work—			Usually work—	
	Total	Full-time	Part-time	Total	Full-time	Part-time
Total working fewer than 35 hours	32,378	10,053	22,325	31,801	9,865	21,936
Economic reasons	4,567	1,622	2,945	4,469	1,559	2,909
Slack work or business conditions	2,841	1,360	1,481	2,773	1,314	1,459
Could find only part-time work	1,409	-	1,409	1,399	-	1,399
Seasonal work	179	124	55	160	109	52
Job started or ended during the week	137	137	-	136	136	-
Noneconomic reasons	27,811	8,431	19,380	27,332	8,306	19,026
Child-care problems	781	72	709	777	72	705
Other family or personal obligations	5,642	704	4,938	5,556	692	4,864
Health or medical limitations	784	-	784	763	-	763
In school or training	6,284	98	6,186	6,218	97	6,121
Retired or Social Security limit on earnings	2,028	-	2,028	1,922	-	1,922
Vacation or personal day	3,510	3,510	-	3,462	3,462	-
Holiday, legal, or religious	1,045	1,045	-	1,039	1,039	-
Weather-related curtailment	562	562	-	535	535	-
Other	7,176	2,440	4,736	7,059	2,408	4,651
Average hours per week:						
Economic reasons	22.9	24.0	22.4	23.0	24.0	22.4
Noneconomic reasons	21.4	25.3	19.8	21.5	25.3	19.8

- Represents or rounds to zero.

Source: U.S. Bureau of Labor Statistics, *Employment and Earnings*, monthly, January 2005. See Internet site <http://www.bls.gov/cps/home.htm>.

Table 601. Displaced Workers by Selected Characteristics: 2004

[In percent, except total (5,329 represents 5,329,000). As of January. For persons 20 years old and over with tenure of 3 years or more who lost or left a job between January 2001 and December 2003 because of plant closings or moves, slack work, or the abolishment of their positions. Based on Current Population Survey and subject to sampling error; see source and Appendix III]

Characteristic	Total (1,000)	Employment status			Reason for job loss		
		Employed	Unemployed	Not in the labor force	Plant or company closed down or moved	Slack/ insufficient work	Position or shift abolished
Total [1]	5,329	64.8	20.2	15.0	43.1	28.3	28.6
20 to 24 years old	149	65.0	19.6	15.3	52.6	28.7	18.7
25 to 54 years old	4,087	68.9	19.5	11.6	42.2	29.3	28.5
55 to 64 years old	887	55.5	24.9	19.6	45.2	22.1	32.7
65 years old and over . . .	206	23.8	12.9	63.3	45.2	34.9	19.9
Males	3,010	67.7	20.8	11.5	40.7	31.9	27.5
20 to 24 years old	96	59.8	24.5	15.7	44.4	33.7	21.9
25 to 54 years old	2,372	71.0	20.8	8.1	39.8	33.3	27.0
55 to 64 years old	461	58.1	22.3	19.6	44.0	23.8	32.3
65 years old and over . . .	81	33.5	8.5	57.9	44.0	34.4	21.6
Females	2,319	61.1	19.3	19.6	46.3	23.7	30.1
20 to 24 years old	53	(2)	(2)	(2)	(2)	(2)	(2)
25 to 54 years old	1,715	65.9	17.7	16.4	45.6	23.8	30.7
55 to 64 years old	426	52.7	27.7	19.6	46.4	20.3	33.3
65 years old and over . . .	125	17.5	15.8	66.7	46.0	35.3	18.8
White [3]	4,273	65.6	18.9	15.5	42.7	27.4	29.9
Black [3]	695	61.6	27.1	11.2	47.1	28.9	24.1
Asian [3]	215	63.2	22.6	14.2	44.8	36.7	18.5
Hispanic origin [4]	608	64.6	20.8	14.6	41.5	36.1	22.4

[1] Includes other races, not shown separately.   [2] Data not shown where base is less than 75,000.   [3] For persons in this race group only. See footnote 3, Table 577.   [4] Persons of Hispanic or Latino origin may be of any race.
Source: U.S. Bureau of Labor Statistics, News, Worker Displacement, 1999–2001, USDL 04-1381, July 30, 2004. See Internet site <http://www.bls.gov/bls/newsrels.htm#OEUS>.

Table 602. Labor Force Status of Persons With a Work Disability by Age: 2004

[In percent, except as indicated (23,081 represents 23,081,000). As of March. For civilians 16 to 74 who have a condition which prevents them from working or limits the amount of work they can do. Data from the Current Population Survey and subject to sampling error; see text, Section 1, and Appendix III]

Labor force status	Total	Age						
		16 to 24 years old	25 to 34 years old	35 to 44 years old	45 to 54 years old	55 to 64 years old	65 to 69 years old	70 to 74 years old
Number (1,000)	23,081	1,504	2,331	3,741	5,320	6,120	2,123	1,943
In labor force.	23.3	33.5	33.1	30.9	26.2	18.7	11.9	8.3
Employed	19.9	25.3	27.2	24.9	22.8	17.3	11.2	7.1
Full-time.	11.6	11.1	16.2	15.9	14.0	10.6	4.5	2.0
Not in labor force	76.7	66.5	66.9	69.1	73.8	81.3	88.1	91.7
Unemployment rate	14.8	24.6	17.8	19.5	13.0	7.9	5.6	14.9

Source: U.S. Census Bureau, "Disability Data from the March Current Population Survey"; <http://www.census.gov/hhes/www/disability /disabcps.html>; (accessed 18 July 2005).

Table 603. Persons Not in the Labor Force: 2004

[In thousands (75,956 represents 75,956,000). Annual average of monthly figures. For the civilian noninstitutional population 16 years old and over. Based on the Current Population Survey; see text, Section 1, and Appendix III]

Status and reason	Total	Age			Sex	
		16 to 24 years old	25 to 54 years old	55 years old and over	Male	Female
Total not in the labor force	75,956	14,151	21,288	40,517	28,730	47,225
Do not want a job now [1]	71,103	12,422	19,136	39,545	26,565	44,538
Want a job now	4,852	1,729	2,152	971	2,165	2,687
In the previous year—						
Did not search for a job.	2,715	886	1,145	684	1,126	1,590
Did search for a job [2]	2,137	843	1,006	288	1,040	1,097
Not available for work now	563	279	242	42	230	333
Available for work now, not looking for work. . .	1,574	565	764	245	809	765
Reason for not currently looking for work:						
Discouraged over job prospects [3]	466	142	240	84	288	178
Family responsibilities.	157	28	104	24	38	119
In school or training	244	199	43	2	131	112
Ill health or disability	123	18	71	35	56	67
Other [4]	584	178	306	100	296	288

[1] Includes some persons who are not asked if they want a job.   [2] Persons who had a job in the prior 12 months must have searched since the end of that job.   [3] Includes such things as believes no work available, could not find work, lacks necessary schooling or training, employer thinks too young or old, and other types of discrimination.   [4] Includes such things as child care and transportation problems.

Source: U.S. Bureau of Labor Statistics, Employment and Earnings, monthly, January 2005 issue. See Internet site <http://www.bls.gov/cps/home.htm>.

Table 604. **Employed Civilians by Occupation, Sex, Race, and Hispanic Origin: 2004**

[For civilian noninstitutional population 16 years old and over (139,252 represents 139,252,000). Annual average of monthly figures. Based on Current Population Survey; see text, Section 1, and Appendix III. Occupational classifications are those used in the 2000 census and are not comparable to those used in the 1990 census]

Occupation	Total employed (1,000)	Percent of total			
		Female	Black [1]	Asian [1]	Hispanic [2]
Total	139,252	46.5	10.7	4.3	12.9
Management, professional, and related occupations	48,532	50.3	8.1	5.6	6.4
Management, business, and financial operations occupations	20,235	42.1	7.0	4.5	6.4
Management occupations [3]	14,555	36.7	5.9	4.0	6.3
Chief executives	1,680	23.3	3.2	3.4	3.7
General and operations managers.	795	26.7	5.8	3.5	7.1
Advertising and promotions managers	70	60.3	5.2	0.9	4.1
Marketing and sales managers	806	40.4	3.4	3.7	4.8
Administrative services managers	87	34.6	7.6	2.5	9.0
Computer and information systems managers	337	31.0	4.9	7.3	5.2
Financial managers	1,045	56.6	7.8	4.8	6.9
Human resources managers	262	64.4	7.3	1.3	6.6
Industrial production managers	280	18.0	4.7	1.2	6.7
Purchasing managers	170	39.1	5.6	2.9	6.3
Transportation, storage, and distribution managers.	241	14.9	7.1	2.0	8.2
Farm, ranch, and other agricultural managers	199	20.1	0.1	0.2	9.9
Farmers and ranchers.	817	25.2	0.4	0.5	1.8
Construction managers	851	6.4	2.4	1.7	8.0
Education administrators	757	62.6	12.8	2.1	5.3
Engineering managers	106	5.9	1.7	7.0	2.9
Food service managers.	916	41.2	8.2	12.1	11.1
Lodging managers	152	51.3	4.1	11.7	4.2
Medical and health services managers.	508	71.7	8.8	4.3	4.7
Property, real estate, and community association managers.	604	48.5	6.8	1.9	11.8
Social and community service managers . . . ;	280	67.0	13.6	2.2	6.1
Business and financial operations occupations [3]	5,680	55.8	9.6	5.7	6.5
Wholesale and retail buyers, except farm products	212	51.0	5.0	3.1	8.0
Purchasing agents, except wholesale, retail, and farm products . . .	285	54.2	11.6	2.5	6.2
Claims adjusters, appraisers, examiners, and investigators	281	65.9	16.2	2.4	6.1
Compliance officers, except agriculture, construction,					
health and safety, and transportation	126	51.5	14.4	1.3	8.3
Cost estimators	98	17.7	2.5	0.7	4.5
Human resources, training, and labor relations specialists	694	67.9	13.2	3.9	7.8
Management analysts.	554	41.8	6.9	4.7	4.3
Accountants and auditors	1,723	60.5	8.6	9.5	6.7
Appraisers and assessors of real estate	138	31.2	2.4	2.1	4.0
Personal financial advisors.	331	26.6	5.8	4.1	2.9
Insurance underwriters	98	71.2	8.4	4.2	4.9
Loan counselors and officers	425	56.7	10.0	4.4	8.2
Tax examiners, collectors, and revenue agents	81	63.6	19.1	4.5	5.9
Tax preparers	88	63.1	6.1	9.9	8.1
Professional and related occupations	28,297	56.1	9.0	6.4	6.4
Computer and mathematical occupations [3]	3,140	27.0	7.5	14.0	5.5
Computer scientists and systems analysts	700	29.4	9.8	10.1	6.6
Computer programmers.	564	26.7	6.9	14.1	3.9
Computer software engineers.	813	25.0	5.3	24.2	4.1
Computer support specialists	325	29.7	9.2	7.9	8.7
Database administrators	94	33.6	5.5	16.5	3.3
Network and computer systems administrators	190	20.3	8.5	6.9	6.1
Network systems and data communications analysts	312	21.9	8.0	7.7	7.0
Operations research analysts	90	43.0	9.4	10.6	5.9
Architecture and engineering occupations [3]	2,760	13.8	4.9	8.4	5.7
Architects, except naval.	207	24.0	2.6	5.8	7.1
Aerospace engineers	113	11.3	4.4	9.2	4.2
Civil engineers.	293	11.7	7.7	11.7	4.6
Computer hardware engineers	96	12.7	7.4	19.0	5.8
Electrical and electronics engineers.	343	7.9	4.8	12.3	4.0
Industrial engineers, including health and safety	177	18.8	4.9	6.1	5.4
Mechanical engineers.	311	5.8	4.2	6.5	3.9
Drafters	206	23.7	5.0	4.8	9.9
Engineering technicians, except drafters.	416	19.7	5.9	5.8	8.8
Surveying and mapping technicians.	80	12.2	1.0	0.8	7.7
Life, physical, and social science occupations [3]	1,365	43.0	5.6	9.2	5.1
Biological scientists	123	45.2	3.1	12.7	2.2
Medical scientists.	93	53.2	5.1	17.6	3.1
Chemists and materials scientists	141	32.5	7.0	14.8	4.3
Environmental scientists and geoscientists	86	27.3	5.1	1.5	2.3
Market and survey researchers.	124	48.2	6.6	7.6	4.8
Psychologists	185	66.7	3.3	1.4	4.6
Chemical technicians	84	33.3	10.6	7.8	6.3
Community and social services occupations [3]	2,170	61.1	19.1	2.8	9.4
Counselors	643	69.1	21.9	2.0	9.7
Social workers.	687	77.7	20.4	2.9	10.9
Miscellaneous community and social service specialists	283	65.6	24.7	1.7	12.3
Clergy	403	15.0	11.6	5.1	6.0
Legal occupations [3]	1,554	48.9	6.4	3.0	5.7
Lawyers	954	29.4	4.7	2.9	3.4
Paralegals and legal assistants.	322	86.4	10.4	2.8	10.7
Miscellaneous legal support workers	215	76.6	6.0	4.1	8.1

See footnotes end of table.

Table 604. Employed Civilians by Occupation, Sex, Race, and Hispanic Origin: 2004—Con.

[For civilian noninstitutional population 16 years old and over (139,252 represents 139,252,000). Annual average of monthly figures. Based on Current Population Survey; see text, Section 1, and Appendix III. Occupational classifications are those used in the 2000 census and are not comparable to those used in the 1990 census]

Occupation	Total employed (1,000)	Percent of total			
		Female	Black [1]	Asian [1]	Hispanic [2]
Professional and related occupations—con.					
Education, training, and library occupations [3]	7,900	73.4	9.4	3.4	6.9
Postsecondary teachers	1,176	46.0	5.9	11.0	3.5
Preschool and kindergarten teachers	656	98.1	15.2	2.5	8.2
Elementary and middle school teachers	2,580	81.3	9.5	1.7	6.4
Secondary school teachers	1,151	55.3	6.6	1.5	5.2
Special education teachers	384	83.3	9.7	1.3	5.0
Other teachers and instructors	667	64.7	8.6	4.8	8.6
Librarians	217	83.2	5.6	4.5	4.6
Teacher assistants	920	91.6	14.6	1.8	14.3
Arts, design, entertainment, sports, and media occupations [3]	2,687	47.0	6.1	4.8	7.5
Artists and related workers	222	50.7	2.2	3.9	6.4
Designers	792	54.0	5.0	7.1	7.4
Producers and directors	137	32.3	8.4	3.4	8.8
Athletes, coaches, umpires, and related workers	239	31.6	7.8	2.2	5.4
Musicians, singers, and related workers	179	36.4	8.6	3.4	5.4
News analysts, reporters and correspondents	81	53.7	7.4	4.7	3.4
Public relations specialists	133	61.1	7.6	3.3	4.6
Editors	164	53.9	4.1	3.3	4.1
Writers and authors	194	55.1	3.6	2.2	2.6
Broadcast and sound engineering technicians and radio operators	92	12.1	12.2	2.7	12.1
Photographers	158	37.6	8.0	6.6	7.1
Healthcare practitioner and technical occupations [3]	6,721	73.2	10.0	7.4	5.5
Chiropractors	73	22.7	0.3	2.8	1.9
Dentists	167	22.0	5.0	11.7	4.1
Dietitians and nutritionists	84	89.2	21.1	3.3	11.3
Pharmacists	233	47.0	3.1	11.0	3.7
Physicians and surgeons	830	29.4	6.1	16.5	5.3
Physician assistants	70	67.3	6.8	7.6	9.4
Registered nurses	2,464	92.2	10.1	6.8	4.4
Occupational therapists	84	92.7	5.1	8.8	3.7
Physical therapists	173	65.4	7.1	10.3	3.3
Respiratory therapists	103	54.7	11.9	3.8	6.4
Speech-language pathologists	93	95.1	6.0	0.5	2.1
Clinical laboratory technologists and technicians	333	72.0	14.6	10.2	6.9
Dental hygienists	130	98.8	2.6	1.1	4.2
Diagnostic-related technologists and technicians	284	71.8	7.3	3.4	7.4
Emergency medical technicians and paramedics	139	32.7	9.0	1.5	8.9
Health diagnosing and treating practitioner support technicians	397	84.1	10.8	4.2	7.7
Licensed practical and licensed vocational nurses	517	94.3	20.8	3.4	5.6
Medical records and health information technicians	91	88.6	16.0	4.4	18.6
Service occupations	**22,720**	**56.8**	**15.6**	**4.3**	**19.1**
Healthcare support occupations [3]	2,921	89.3	25.9	3.5	13.1
Nursing, psychiatric, and home health aides	1,806	89.3	34.6	3.7	13.4
Massage therapists	106	84.6	4.4	2.9	6.5
Dental assistants	242	96.5	5.1	2.5	15.3
Protective service occupations [3]	2,847	21.7	17.9	1.9	11.1
First-line supervisors/managers of police and detectives	133	21.2	10.2	1.4	6.5
Firefighters	268	5.1	8.4	1.3	8.6
Bailiffs, correctional officers, and jailers	373	28.4	20.2	1.4	10.3
Detectives and criminal investigators	121	20.2	17.1	1.6	7.3
Police and sheriffs patrol officers	664	13.3	15.7	1.6	12.7
Private detectives and investigators	81	33.1	7.8	2.2	8.8
Security guards and gaming surveillance officers	798	22.6	28.4	2.7	14.5
Food preparation and serving-related occupations	7,279	56.1	11.5	5.2	19.3
Chefs and head cooks	299	18.9	11.5	10.7	20.9
First-line supervisors/managers of food preparation and serving workers	644	59.0	12.7	3.9	14.6
Cooks	1,791	40.6	16.2	5.8	28.0
Food preparation workers	621	57.5	15.1	6.3	22.8
Bartenders	360	58.2	2.6	1.9	10.7
Combined food preparation and serving workers, including fast food	296	68.6	12.8	4.1	13.4
Counter attendants, cafeteria, food concession, and coffee shop	327	64.9	12.2	4.2	12.3
Waiters and waitresses	1,892	73.1	7.0	4.8	12.7
Food servers, nonrestaurant	165	64.9	19.4	8.3	16.1
Dining room and cafeteria attendants and bartender helpers	379	45.0	8.8	5.5	27.6
Dishwashers	267	23.8	14.5	3.4	34.3
Hosts and hostesses, restaurant, lounge, and coffee shop	237	90.1	4.1	4.3	9.6
Building and grounds cleaning and maintenance occupations	5,185	40.5	14.9	3.1	32.0
First-line supervisors/managers of housekeeping and janitorial workers	191	40.6	19.6	0.9	20.2
First-line supervisors/managers of landscaping, lawn service, and groundskeeping workers	227	8.1	3.3	1.1	12.7
Janitors and building cleaners	2,047	33.2	17.8	3.3	26.8
Maids and housekeeping cleaners	1,365	90.0	18.0	4.9	38.2
Pest control workers	75	7.1	11.6	1.7	13.1
Grounds maintenance workers	1,280	7.1	8.5	1.5	40.2

See footnotes end of table.

U.S. Census Bureau, Statistical Abstract of the United States: 2006

[For civilian noninstitutional population 16 years old and over (139,252 represents 139,252,000). Annual average of monthly figures. Based on Current Population Survey; see text, Section 1, and Appendix III. Occupational classifications are those used in the 2000 census and are not comparable to those used in the 1990 census]

Occupation	Total employed (1,000)	Percent of total			
		Female	Black [1]	Asian [1]	Hispanic [2]
Service occupations—con.					
Personal care and service occupations [3]	4,488	77.6	14.9	6.3	12.7
First-line supervisors/managers of gaming workers	140	42.3	8.2	1.5	8.2
First-line supervisors/managers of personal service workers	174	67.3	9.1	16.6	7.7
Nonfarm animal caretakers	128	62.0	2.8	0.2	9.8
Gaming services workers	95	52.8	7.8	19.1	7.7
Barbers	101	18.4	34.9	3.9	6.6
Hairdressers, hairstylists, and cosmetologists	722	91.5	12.1	3.3	11.5
Miscellaneous personal appearance workers	200	85.4	3.7	47.5	8.2
Baggage porters, bellhops, and concierges	70	17.5	11.1	5.6	25.1
Transportation attendants	116	71.4	15.2	4.3	11.2
Child care workers	1,332	94.5	17.8	2.1	16.5
Personal and home care aides	630	87.6	21.8	6.1	16.1
Recreation and fitness workers	314	64.9	12.6	3.2	7.0
Sales and office occupations	**35,464**	**63.9**	**11.0**	**3.9**	**10.8**
Sales and related occupations [3]	15,983	49.3	9.0	4.2	10.3
First-line supervisors/managers of retail sales workers	3,299	43.0	7.1	4.6	9.2
First-line supervisors/managers of non-retail sales workers	1,390	28.1	5.4	5.7	9.6
Cashiers	2,971	76.1	15.6	5.6	15.9
Counter and rental clerks	186	55.2	10.5	4.1	12.6
Parts salespersons	147	12.4	7.2	3.6	9.4
Retail salespersons	3,130	50.8	10.9	3.8	10.9
Advertising sales agents	211	49.2	5.3	1.3	5.7
Insurance sales agents	508	44.7	6.3	2.8	6.1
Securities, commodities, and financial services sales agents	382	28.5	7.0	3.9	6.2
Travel agents	95	82.0	7.1	7.9	10.5
Sales representatives, services, all other	476	39.4	7.1	1.9	7.4
Sales representatives, wholesale and manufacturing	1,416	25.5	3.5	2.9	7.2
Models, demonstrators, and product promoters	68	86.4	8.5	0.4	6.9
Real estate brokers and sales agents	912	54.5	5.7	3.6	6.7
Telemarketers	180	63.8	18.6	2.7	17.0
Door-to-door sales workers, news and street vendors, and related workers	312	63.6	5.6	3.1	11.8
Office and administrative support occupations [3]	19,481	75.9	12.8	3.6	11.1
First-line supervisors/managers of office and administrative support workers	1,631	71.4	11.1	3.0	8.4
Switchboard operators, including answering service	66	86.5	18.2	2.2	6.0
Bill and account collectors	229	70.2	20.1	2.9	15.4
Billing and posting clerks and machine operators	441	91.6	13.2	5.2	10.7
Bookkeeping, accounting, and auditing clerks	1,567	91.8	7.4	3.9	6.9
Payroll and timekeeping clerks	153	91.9	5.8	4.8	7.3
Tellers	424	88.1	10.9	5.0	10.0
Court, municipal, and license clerks	102	88.2	12.0	1.8	10.5
Customer service representatives	1,749	71.1	16.4	2.9	12.4
Eligibility interviewers, government programs	66	76.5	22.4	4.7	22.4
File clerks	387	79.8	14.1	7.6	11.9
Hotel, motel, and resort desk clerks	106	75.3	14.1	2.9	13.0
Interviewers, except eligibility and loan	143	84.7	19.7	2.8	13.4
Library assistants, clerical	117	83.2	6.8	5.0	9.1
Loan interviewers and clerks	186	82.9	11.5	5.2	10.6
Order clerks	114	71.9	7.9	4.6	12.2
Receptionists and information clerks	1,373	92.4	10.6	2.5	14.0
Reservation and transportation ticket agents and travel clerks	161	65.7	16.8	5.9	12.2
Couriers and messengers	293	14.8	14.4	4.2	15.0
Dispatchers	257	55.6	12.2	2.5	9.2
Postal service clerks	167	48.0	30.4	9.4	12.0
Postal service mail carriers	336	37.1	14.6	5.0	6.9
Postal service mail sorters, processors, and processing machine operators	116	43.2	29.8	15.2	12.0
Production, planning, and expediting clerks	288	53.1	7.6	3.7	6.1
Shipping, receiving, and traffic clerks	584	28.1	15.9	3.1	22.9
Stock clerks and order fillers	1,350	37.4	14.8	3.8	15.8
Secretaries and administrative assistants	3,522	96.9	9.4	2.0	8.1
Computer operators	191	55.1	14.6	5.6	9.0
Data entry keyers	504	80.3	15.7	3.7	13.1
Word processors and typists	319	93.5	19.5	4.4	8.6
Insurance claims and policy processing clerks	277	87.2	16.8	1.0	11.0
Mail clerks and mail machine operators, except postal service	154	52.2	28.4	5.1	15.4
Office clerks, general	982	83.5	12.7	6.1	14.8
Natural resources, construction, and maintenance occupations	**14,582**	**4.5**	**6.9**	**1.8**	**22.1**
Farming, fishing, and forestry occupations [3]	991	20.6	5.4	2.1	39.0
Graders and sorters, agricultural products	68	76.4	10.0	5.4	44.7
Logging workers	92	2.9	12.1	-	10.1
Construction and extraction occupations [3]	8,522	2.5	6.7	1.0	25.0
First-line supervisors/managers of construction trades and extraction workers	887	2.2	3.9	1.5	11.7
Brickmasons, blockmasons, and stonemasons	239	0.9	12.7	0.7	34.1

See footnotes end of table.

U.S. Census Bureau, Statistical Abstract of the United States: 2006

Table 604. **Employed Civilians by Occupation, Sex, Race, and Hispanic Origin: 2004—Con.**

[For civilian noninstitutional population 16 years old and over (139,252 represents 139,252,000). Annual average of monthly figures. Based on Current Population Survey; see text, Section 1, and Appendix III. Occupational classifications are those used in the 2000 census and are not comparable to those used in the 1990 census]

Occupation	Total employed (1,000)	Percent of total			
		Female	Black [1]	Asian [1]	Hispanic [2]
Construction and extraction occupations—con.					
Carpenters	1,764	1.8	5.2	0.8	21.8
Carpet, floor, and tile installers and finishers	268	1.9	3.9	1.1	35.6
Cement masons, concrete finishers, and terrazzo workers	115	0.2	9.6	0.3	44.0
Construction laborers	1,234	3.2	8.9	1.0	38.1
Operating engineers and other construction equipment operators	367	1.0	5.2	0.5	11.1
Drywall installers, ceiling tile installers, and tapers	213	1.1	6.9	0.4	49.6
Electricians	781	2.1	6.5	1.2	13.6
Painters, construction and maintenance	719	5.8	7.6	2.1	36.2
Pipelayers, plumbers, pipefitters, and steamfitters	635	0.9	8.7	1.0	17.3
Roofers	269	1.3	8.2	0.2	39.4
Sheet metal workers	152	4.0	4.0	0.9	12.8
Structural iron and steel workers	66	0.8	3.4	3.9	9.8
Helpers, construction trades	121	5.3	8.9	0.7	36.0
Construction and building inspectors	104	12.4	8.5	2.7	11.8
Highway maintenance workers	96	2.7	10.6	0.3	14.8
Installation, maintenance, and repair occupations [3]	5,069	4.6	7.6	3.0	14.1
First-line supervisors/managers of mechanics, installers, and repairers	327	7.1	7.6	0.4	9.3
Computer, automated teller, and office machine repairers	369	12.0	11.8	6.7	9.5
Radio and telecommunications equipment installers and repairers	235	13.6	14.7	4.1	10.7
Electronic home entertainment equipment installers and repairers	68	3.3	6.9	3.1	19.1
Aircraft mechanics and service technicians	135	3.4	6.2	2.6	15.5
Automotive body and related repairers	169	2.4	4.7	2.1	20.5
Automotive service technicians and mechanics	936	1.3	6.1	5.0	19.0
Bus and truck mechanics and diesel engine specialists	325	0.6	6.2	1.0	12.2
Heavy vehicle and mobile equipment service technicians and mechanics	205	0.3	6.5	2.7	12.2
Heating, air conditioning, and refrigeration mechanics and installers	351	1.5	5.3	2.1	13.1
Industrial and refractory machinery mechanics	434	3.7	7.3	2.6	10.1
Maintenance and repair workers, general	300	4.1	8.6	2.1	17.0
Electrical power-line installers and repairers	120	1.1	13.2	1.4	11.9
Telecommunications line installers and repairers	142	4.8	12.4	4.2	16.7
Production, transportation, and material occupations	**17,954**	**23.0**	**13.9**	**3.8**	**19.2**
Production occupations [3]	9,462	30.4	11.9	5.3	20.0
First-line supervisors/managers of production and operating workers	921	20.1	9.6	4.4	11.6
Electrical, electronics, and electromechanical assemblers	226	54.9	12.0	17.6	21.1
Bakers	188	45.6	13.0	6.6	28.4
Butchers and other meat, poultry, and fish processing workers	304	19.6	12.1	4.1	44.3
Food batchmakers	85	52.5	8.7	6.3	20.5
Cutting, punching, and press machine setters, operators, and tenders, metal and plastic	139	28.4	8.9	1.5	16.3
Grinding, lapping, polishing, and buffing machine tool setters, operators, and tenders, metal and plastic	74	11.0	15.5	1.1	26.2
Machinists	445	4.4	6.0	3.8	10.9
Molders and molding machine setters, operators, and tenders, metal and plastic	70	24.9	4.2	1.5	18.8
Tool and die makers	86	3.0	2.8	0.8	3.7
Welding, soldering, and brazing workers	572	5.0	7.9	1.5	23.3
Printing machine operators	195	19.3	8.7	2.5	15.2
Laundry and dry-cleaning workers	195	60.0	18.5	8.3	27.5
Pressers, textile, garment, and related materials	76	66.0	21.8	7.3	47.1
Sewing machine operators	281	77.7	13.5	15.2	32.5
Tailors, dressmakers, and sewers	101	69.9	7.8	19.7	18.3
Cabinetmakers and bench carpenters	86	4.4	1.5	0.8	18.0
Stationary engineers and boiler operators	105	1.0	11.4	2.4	9.6
Crushing, grinding, polishing, mixing, and blending workers	111	20.1	14.1	1.6	16.6
Cutting workers	83	25.6	9.9	2.9	26.4
Inspectors, testers, sorters, samplers, and weighers	690	38.0	11.0	5.7	13.3
Medical, dental, and ophthalmic laboratory technicians	92	52.0	8.4	12.7	15.4
Packaging and filling machine operators and tenders	318	54.9	20.4	3.5	42.4
Painting workers	191	13.1	6.1	2.3	24.5
Transportation and material moving occupations [3]	8,491	14.7	16.1	2.0	18.3
Supervisors, transportation and material moving workers	220	17.8	15.4	4.0	13.3
Aircraft pilots and flight engineers	118	5.3	1.7	1.5	3.2
Bus drivers	602	48.5	24.4	2.0	12.8
Driver/sales workers and truck drivers	3,276	4.5	13.4	1.4	15.8
Taxi drivers and chauffeurs	277	12.9	28.7	10.5	12.4
Parking lot attendants	77	13.3	15.5	5.5	23.0
Service station attendants	120	8.7	8.7	1.7	9.4
Dredge, excavating, and loading machine operators	80	0.1	5.4	—	11.6
Industrial truck and tractor operators	530	7.5	22.2	0.5	25.0
Cleaners of vehicles and equipment	316	11.9	16.2	2.2	29.5
Laborers and freight, stock, and material movers, hand	1,797	16.2	17.0	2.2	20.6
Packers and packagers, hand	432	60.8	14.1	3.5	44.1
Refuse and recyclable material collectors	81	8.2	29.5	0.5	14.4

- Represents or rounds to zero.   [1] For persons in this race group only. See footnote 3, Table 577.   [2] Persons of Hispanic or Latino ethnicity may be of any race.   [3] Includes other occupations, not shown separately.
Source: U.S. Bureau of Labor Statistics, *Employment and Earnings*, monthy, January 2005 issue. See Internet site <http://www.bls.gov/cps/home.htm>.

Table 605. Employed Civilians by Occupation: 2003

[In thousands (137,736 represents 137,736,000). Occupation classifications are those used in the 2000 census and are not comparable to those in other tables using 1990 census classifications. Based on the Current Population Survey and subject to sampling error; see text, Section 1, and Appendix III]

| State | Total | Management, professional, and related occupations | | Service occupations | Sales and office occupations | | Natural resources, construction, and maintenance occupations | | | Production, transportation, and material moving occupations | |
		Management, business, and financial operations	Professional and related occupations		Sales and related occupations	Office and administrative support occupations	Farming, fishing, and forestry occupations	Construction and extraction occupations	Installation, maintenance, and repair occupations	Production occupations	Transportation and material moving occupations
Total...	137,736	19,934	27,995	22,086	15,960	19,536	1,050	8,114	5,041	9,700	8,320
AL.....	2,023	267	389	292	212	288	(B)	123	82	217	135
AK.....	305	40	64	51	27	45	6	23	14	12	23
AZ.....	2,539	393	500	416	361	350	(B)	164	93	134	117
AR.....	1,186	160	198	170	135	161	(B)	61	53	128	101
CA.....	16,283	2,407	3,424	2,579	1,968	2,375	231	879	536	1,013	873
CO.....	2,328	392	478	363	283	308	(B)	161	79	116	134
CT.....	1,704	275	397	255	196	257	(B)	95	48	107	72
DE.....	399	61	81	62	41	66	(B)	25	14	24	23
DC.....	281	58	96	44	17	40	(B)	8	4	(B)	10
FL.....	7,744	1,103	1,461	1,375	1,038	1,155	45	535	300	323	410
GA.....	4,207	605	813	595	526	540	(B)	306	181	343	282
HI.....	592	86	105	126	64	93	(B)	35	23	20	34
ID.....	655	79	120	118	76	91	19	44	29	39	41
IL.....	5,908	849	1,180	904	653	869	(B)	349	220	457	406
IN.....	3,024	393	527	435	339	432	(B)	174	142	337	232
IA.....	1,540	225	296	231	164	228	(B)	66	53	157	98
KS.....	1,357	214	273	212	142	189	(B)	79	55	102	79
KY.....	1,836	245	353	301	196	255	(B)	88	74	172	134
LA.....	1,904	214	379	348	217	261	(B)	141	88	127	116
ME.....	658	81	129	115	74	88	11	41	29	51	39
MD.....	2,773	500	691	419	287	389	(B)	158	79	105	137
MA.....	3,217	527	796	498	351	440	(B)	196	86	184	128
MI.....	4,674	578	929	815	491	651	(B)	236	154	515	285
MN.....	2,778	483	607	398	309	373	(B)	168	87	188	149
MS.....	1,229	140	215	197	127	166	(B)	83	54	131	97
MO.....	2,850	395	583	435	352	416	(B)	194	107	174	183
MT.....	452	81	80	77	48	59	10	36	16	19	26
NE.....	937	163	167	139	106	135	(B)	55	39	61	57
NV.....	1,082	134	160	271	140	140	(B)	91	42	45	57
NH.....	688	106	158	94	86	87	(B)	41	27	54	32
NJ.....	4,118	702	913	583	503	640	(B)	190	117	187	271
NM.....	840	110	178	149	94	110	13	62	32	39	53
NY.....	8,726	1,217	1,986	1,616	954	1,239	32	450	263	493	476
NC.....	3,957	532	788	583	438	503	44	274	145	387	261
ND.....	333	54	61	59	38	45	7	18	13	16	22
OH.....	5,552	758	1,052	970	650	791	(B)	271	198	468	381
OK.....	1,600	241	305	245	170	229	(B)	106	77	111	98
OR.....	1,707	237	318	287	214	245	35	83	56	120	113
PA.....	5,826	824	1,267	863	630	876	(B)	283	215	460	380
RI.....	543	69	112	103	61	75	(B)	26	16	48	29
SC.....	1,866	244	318	313	235	248	(B)	106	95	174	123
SD.....	410	68	70	69	47	56	(B)	23	14	33	21
TN.....	2,740	397	492	404	325	392	(B)	161	102	239	211
TX.....	10,173	1,368	1,925	1,660	1,219	1,462	101	685	412	702	639
UT.....	1,118	161	214	159	140	177	(B)	65	43	77	74
VT.....	335	53	78	53	33	41	(B)	23	14	23	14
VA.....	3,620	609	856	520	410	475	(B)	214	140	199	182
WA.....	2,903	448	631	453	323	400	40	169	109	165	164
WV.....	739	78	140	128	86	106	(B)	54	38	46	60
WI.....	2,905	422	525	451	306	394	(B)	159	111	313	195
WY.....	266	39	44	40	29	35	(B)	26	15	12	23

B Base figure too small to meet statistical standards for reliability of a derived figure.

Source: U.S. Bureau of Labor Statistics, Local Area Unemployment Statistics, *Geographic Profile of Employment and Unemployment, 2003*, August 2005. See Internet site <http://www.bls.gov/gps/>.

Table 606. Employment Projections by Occupation: 2002 and 2012

[In thousands (365 represents 365,000), except percent and rank. Estimates based on the Current Employment Statistics Program; the Occupational Employment Statistics Survey; and the Current Population Survey. See source for methodological assumptions. Occupations based on the 2000 Standard Occupational Classification system]

Occupation	Employment (1,000)		Change 2002–2012		Quartile rank by 2002 median annual earnings [1]	Most significant source of postsecondary education or training
	2002	2012	(1,000)	Per-cent		
FASTEST GROWING						
Medical assistants	365	579	215	59	3	Moderate-term on-the-job training
Network systems and data communications analysts	186	292	106	57	1	Bachelor's degree
Physician assistants	63	94	31	49	1	Bachelor's degree
Social and human service assistants	305	454	149	49	3	Moderate-term on-the-job training
Home health aides	580	859	279	48	4	Short-term on-the-job training
Medical records and health information technicians	147	216	69	47	3	Associate's degree
Physical therapist aides	37	54	17	46	3	Short-term on-the-job training
Computer software engineers, applications	394	573	179	46	1	Bachelor's degree
Computer software engineers, systems software	281	409	128	45	1	Bachelor's degree
Physical therapist assistants	50	73	22	45	2	Associate's degree
Fitness trainers and aerobics instructors	183	264	81	44	3	Postsecondary vocational award
Database administrators	110	159	49	44	1	Bachelor's degree
Veterinary technologists and technicians	53	76	23	44	3	Associate's degree
Hazardous materials removal workers	38	54	16	43	2	Moderate-term on-the-job training
Dental hygienists	148	212	64	43	1	Associate's degree
Occupational therapist aides	8	12	4	43	3	Short-term on-the-job training
Dental assistants	266	379	113	42	3	Moderate-term on-the-job training
Personal and home care aides	608	854	246	40	4	Short-term on-the-job training
Self-enrichment education teachers	200	281	80	40	2	Work experience in a related occupation
Computer systems analysts	468	653	184	39	1	Bachelor's degree
Occupational therapist assistants	18	26	7	39	2	Associate's degree
Environmental engineers	47	65	18	38	1	Bachelor's degree
Postsecondary teachers	1,581	2,184	603	38	1	Doctoral degree
Network and computer systems administrators	251	345	94	37	1	Bachelor's degree
Environmental science and protection technicians, including health	28	38	10	37	2	Associate's degree
Preschool teachers, except special education	424	577	153	36	4	Postsecondary vocational award
Computer and information systems managers	284	387	103	36	1	Bachelor's or higher degree, plus work experience
LARGEST JOB GROWTH						
Registered nurses	2,284	2,908	623	27	1	Associate's degree
Postsecondary teachers	1,581	2,184	603	38	1	Doctoral degree
Retail salespersons	4,076	4,672	596	15	4	Short-term on-the-job training
Customer service representatives	1,894	2,354	460	24	3	Moderate-term on-the-job training
Combined food preparation and serving workers, including fast food	1,990	2,444	454	23	4	Short-term on-the-job training
Cashiers, except gaming	3,432	3,886	454	13	4	Short-term on-the-job training
Janitors and cleaners, except maids and housekeeping cleaners	2,267	2,681	414	18	4	Short-term on-the-job training
General and operations managers	2,049	2,425	376	18	1	Bachelor's or higher degree, plus work experience
Waiters and waitresses	2,097	2,464	367	18	4	Short-term on-the-job training
Nursing aides, orderlies, and attendants	1,375	1,718	343	25	3	Short-term on-the-job training
Truck drivers, heavy and tractor-trailer	1,767	2,104	337	19	2	Moderate-term on-the-job training
Receptionists and information clerks	1,100	1,425	325	29	3	Short-term on-the-job training
Security guards	995	1,313	317	32	4	Short-term on-the-job training
Office clerks, general	2,991	3,301	310	10	3	Short-term on-the-job training
Teacher assistants	1,277	1,571	294	23	4	Short-term on-the-job training
Sales representatives, wholesale and manufacturing, except technical and scientific products	1,459	1,738	279	19	1	Moderate-term on-the-job training
Home health aides	580	859	279	48	4	Short-term on-the-job training
Personal and home care aides	608	854	246	40	4	Short-term on-the-job training
Truck drivers, light or delivery services	1,022	1,259	237	23	3	Short-term on-the-job training
Landscaping and groundskeeping workers	1,074	1,311	237	22	3	Short-term on-the-job training
Elementary school teachers, except special education	1,467	1,690	223	15	2	Bachelor's degree
Medical assistants	365	579	215	59	3	Moderate-term on-the-job training
Maintenance and repair workers, general	1,266	1,472	207	16	2	Moderate-term on-the-job training
Accountants and auditors	1,055	1,261	205	19	1	Bachelor's degree
Computer systems analysts	468	653	184	39	1	Bachelor's degree
Secondary school teachers, except special and vocational education	988	1,167	180	18	1	Bachelor's degree
Computer software engineers, applications	394	573	179	46	1	Bachelor's degree

[1] Quartile ranks based on the Occupational Employment Statistics annual earnings. 1 = very high ($41,820 and over), 2 = high ($27,500 to $41,780), 3 = low ($19,710 to $27,380), and 4 = very low (up to $19,600). The rankings were based on quartiles using one-fourth of total employment to define each quartile. Earnings are for wage and salary workers.

Source: U.S. Bureau of Labor Statistics Occupational employment projections to 2012, *Monthly Labor Review*, February 2004. See Internet site <http://www.bls.gov/emp/home.htm>.

Table 607. Occupations of the Employed by Selected Characteristics: 2004

[In thousands (119,622 represents 119,622,000). Annual averages of monthly figures. For civilian noninstitutional population 25 years old and over. Based on Current Population Survey; see text, Section 1, and Appendix III. See headnote, Table 593 regarding occupations]

Sex, race, and educational attainment	Total employed	Managerial, professional, and related	Service	Sales and office	Natural resources, construction, and maintenance	Production, transportation, and material moving
Total [1]	119,622	45,661	17,016	28,875	12,472	15,598
Less than a high school diploma	11,408	734	3,293	1,491	2,661	3,229
High school graduates, no college	35,944	5,862	6,745	10,198	5,509	7,631
Less than a bachelor's degree	32,977	10,856	4,888	10,272	3,398	3,562
College graduates	39,293	28,210	2,090	6,914	903	1,175
White [2]	98,967	38,625	12,799	24,144	11,021	12,377
Less than a high school diploma	9,335	603	2,470	1,231	2,390	2,639
High school graduates, no college	29,571	5,072	4,881	8,685	4,911	6,023
Less than a bachelor's degree	27,262	9,232	3,811	8,470	2,948	2,800
College graduates	32,799	23,718	1,637	5,758	772	914
Black [2]	12,817	3,709	2,930	3,044	913	2,221
Less than a high school diploma	1,326	76	553	164	161	372
High school graduates, no college	4,606	562	1,364	1,088	407	1,185
Less than a bachelor's degree	3,911	1,084	777	1,232	275	544
College graduates	2,973	1,987	236	561	69	120
Asian [2]	5,350	2,557	814	1,129	225	625
Less than a high school diploma	429	35	162	58	36	137
High school graduates, no college	1,005	114	324	240	69	257
Less than a bachelor's degree	956	284	153	330	74	115
College graduates	2,960	2,123	175	500	46	116
Hispanic [3]	14,661	2,808	3,443	2,829	2,650	2,930
Less than a high school diploma	5,135	176	1,618	465	1,416	1,462
High school graduates, no college	4,330	501	1,063	1,032	766	968
Less than a bachelor's degree	3,068	822	551	958	361	377
College graduates	2,127	1,310	212	375	108	122

[1] Includes other races, not shown separately.   [2] For persons in this race group only. See footnote 3, Table 577.   [3] Persons of Hispanic or Latino ethnicity may be of any race.

Source: U.S. Bureau of Labor Statistics, unpublished data.

Table 608. Employment by Industry: 2000 to 2004

[In thousands (136,891 represents 136,891,000), except percent. Annual averages of monthly figures. Based on the Current Population Survey; see text, Section 1, and Appendix III. See also headnote Table 593 regarding industries]

Industry	2000	2002	2003 [1]	2004, total [1]	2004, percent [1] Female	Black [2]	Asian [2]	Hispanic [3]
Total employed	136,891	136,485	137,736	139,252	46.5	10.7	4.3	12.9
Agriculture and related industries	2,464	2,311	2,275	2,232	24.4	2.4	1.0	19.6
Mining	475	502	525	539	10.2	4.8	0.8	11.3
Construction	9,931	9,981	10,138	10,768	9.7	5.9	1.3	21.4
Manufacturing	19,644	17,233	16,902	16,484	30.3	9.4	5.1	14.3
Durable goods	12,519	10,833	10,520	10,329	26.4	8.2	5.4	11.8
Nondurable goods	7,125	6,400	6,382	6,155	36.9	11.6	4.6	18.6
Wholesale trade	4,216	4,144	4,486	4,600	29.5	7.4	4.3	13.3
Retail trade	15,763	15,665	16,220	16,269	48.8	10.0	4.2	12.0
Transportation and utilities	7,380	7,244	6,950	7,013	23.8	15.5	3.4	12.4
Transportation and warehousing	6,096	5,971	5,758	5,844	23.9	16.7	3.7	13.4
Utilities	1,284	1,273	1,193	1,168	23.6	9.5	1.8	7.0
Information	4,059	3,691	3,687	3,463	43.3	10.8	4.4	9.2
Telecommunications	1,546	1,444	1,421	1,273	40.8	15.0	5.3	9.3
Financial activities	9,374	9,565	9,748	9,969	55.9	9.9	4.3	9.2
Finance and insurance	6,641	6,749	6,834	6,940	59.8	10.6	4.9	7.8
Real estate and rental and leasing	2,734	2,816	2,914	3,029	47.0	8.2	3.0	12.3
Professional and business services	13,649	14,015	13,879	14,108	42.8	8.8	5.1	13.1
Professional and technical services	8,266	8,408	8,243	8,386	44.7	5.6	6.9	6.1
Management, administrative, and waste services	5,383	5,607	5,636	5,722	40.1	13.5	2.6	23.3
Education and health services	26,188	27,624	28,260	28,719	74.9	13.8	4.4	9.1
Educational services	11,255	11,724	11,826	12,058	68.9	10.7	3.6	8.2
Health care and social assistance	14,933	15,900	16,434	16,661	79.2	16.1	4.9	9.8
Hospitals	5,202	5,330	5,652	5,700	76.6	15.4	6.4	8.3
Health services, except hospitals	7,009	7,738	7,964	8,118	78.6	15.4	4.7	9.4
Social assistance	2,722	2,832	2,818	2,844	85.8	19.7	2.5	13.6
Leisure and hospitality	11,186	11,541	11,607	11,820	51.1	10.6	6.0	17.6
Arts, entertainment, and recreation	2,539	2,639	2,587	2,690	45.7	8.9	3.4	10.8
Accommodation and food services	8,647	8,902	9,021	9,131	52.7	11.1	6.7	19.6
Other services	6,450	6,665	6,815	6,903	51.8	10.6	5.6	15.0
Other services, except private households	5,731	5,908	6,050	6,124	46.6	10.3	5.9	12.9
Private households	718	757	764	779	92.2	13.3	2.9	31.4
Government workers	6,113	6,307	6,243	6,365	45.7	16.3	3.4	8.3

[1] See footnote 2, Table 576.   [2] Persons in this race group only. See footnote 3, Table 577.   [3] Persons of Hispanic or Latino origin may be of any race.
Source: U.S. Bureau of Labor Statistics, Employment and Earnings, monthly, January 2005 issue. See Internet site <http://www.bls.gov/cps/home.htm>.

Table 609. **Employment Projections by Industry: 2002 to 2012**

[15,047.2 represents 15,047,200. Estimates based on the Current Employment Statistics estimates. See source for methodological assumptions. Minus sign (-) indicates decline]

Industry	2002 NAICS code [1]	Employment (1,000) 2002	Employment (1,000) 2012	Change, 2002-2012 (1,000)	Average annual rate of change 2002-2012
LARGEST GROWTH					
Retail trade	44-45	15,047.2	17,129.2	2,082.0	1.3
Employment services	5613	3,248.8	5,012.3	1,763.5	4.4
State and local government education	(X)	9,876.0	11,606.0	1,730.0	1.6
Food services and drinking places	722	8,411.7	9,749.0	1,337.3	1.5
Offices of health practitioners	6211-3	3,189.9	4,418.8	1,228.9	3.3
Construction	23	6,731.7	7,745.4	1,013.7	1.4
Educational services	61	2,650.6	3,409.8	759.2	2.6
Ambulatory health care services except offices of health practitioners	6214-6,6219	1,443.6	2,113.4	669.8	3.9
State and local general government, n.e.c. [2]	(X)	6,838.4	7,508.1	669.7	0.9
Wholesale trade	42	5,641.1	6,279.3	638.2	1.1
Computer systems design and related services	5415	1,162.7	1,797.7	635.0	4.5
Hospitals	622	4,153.1	4,785.0	631.9	1.4
Individual, family, community, and vocational rehabilitation services	6241-3	1,269.3	1,866.6	597.3	3.9
Nursing care and residential mental health facilities	6231-2	2,047.8	2,607.1	559.3	2.4
Truck transportation and couriers and messengers	484,492	1,897.1	2,404.3	507.2	2.4
Business support and investigation and security services and support services, n.e.c. [2]	5614,5616,5619	1,772.3	2,260.8	488.5	2.5
Religious, grantmaking and giving services, and social advocacy organizations	8131-3	1,944.2	2,372.0	427.8	2.0
Amusement, gambling, and recreation industries	713	1,307.6	1,717.3	409.7	2.8
MOST RAPID GROWTH					
Software publishers	5112	256.0	429.7	173.7	5.3
Management, scientific, and technical consulting services	5416	731.8	1,137.4	405.6	4.5
Community care facilities for the elderly and residential care facilities, n.e.c. [2]	6233,6239	695.3	1,077.6	382.3	4.5
Computer systems design and related services	5415	1,162.7	1,797.7	635.0	4.5
Employment services	5613	3,248.8	5,012.3	1,763.5	4.4
Individual, family, community, and vocational rehabilitation services	6241-3	1,269.3	1,866.6	597.3	3.9
Ambulatory health care services except offices of health practitioners	6214-6,6219	1,443.6	2,113.4	669.8	3.9
Water, sewage, and other systems	2213	48.5	71.0	22.5	3.9
Internet services, data processing, and other information services	516,518,519	528.8	773.1	244.3	3.9
Child day care services	6244	734.2	1,050.3	316.1	3.6
Commercial and industrial machinery and equipment rental and leasing	5324	102.2	142.8	40.6	3.4
Offices of health practitioners	6211-3	3,189.9	4,418.8	1,228.9	3.3
Consumer goods rental and general rental centers	5322,5323	352.9	484.2	131.3	3.2
Cable and other subscription programming and program distribution	5152,5175	220.9	299.8	78.9	3.1
Amusement, gambling, and recreation industries	713	1,307.6	1,717.3	409.7	2.8
Transit and ground passenger transportation	485	371.5	487.7	116.2	2.8
Specialized design services	5414	122.9	160.8	37.9	2.7
Office administrative and facilities support services	5611,2	390.3	507.6	117.3	2.7
MOST RAPID DECLINE					
Cut and sew apparel manufacturing	3152	281.8	77.1	-204.7	-12.2
Apparel knitting mills	3151	49.6	20.0	-29.6	-8.7
Textile and fabric finishing and fabric coating mills	3133	82.4	40.1	-42.3	-6.9
Leather and hide tanning and finishing	3161	8.6	4.5	-4.1	-6.3
Textile mills	313	293.2	156.9	-136.3	-6.1
Other leather and allied product manufacturing	3169	19.9	10.8	-9.1	-5.9
Fabric mills	3132	146.6	79.6	-67.0	-5.9
Apparel accessories and other apparel manufacturing	3159	26.2	15.1	-11.1	-5.4
Fiber, yarn, and thread mills	3131	64.2	37.2	-27.0	-5.3
Tobacco manufacturing	3122	33.2	20.2	-13.0	-4.8
Metal ore mining	2122	29.4	18.0	-11.4	-4.8
Federal Government enterprises, n.e.c. [2]	(X)	51.9	32.4	-19.5	-4.6
Coal mining	2121	74.9	52.3	-22.6	-3.5
Other chemical product and preparation manufacturing	3259	112.4	79.4	-33.0	-3.4
Iron and steel mills and ferroalloy manufacturing	3311	107.1	76.0	-31.1	-3.4
Oil and gas extraction	211	122.5	88.4	-34.1	-3.2
Computer and peripheral equipment manufacturing	3341	249.8	182.1	-67.7	-3.1
Forestry, fishing, hunting, and trapping	1131-2,114	67.6	50.4	-17.2	-2.9

X Not applicable. [1] Based on the North American Industry Classification System, 2002; see text, this section. [2] N.e.c. means not elsewhere classified.

Source: U.S. Bureau of Labor Statistics, "Industry output and employment projections to 2012" *Monthly Labor Review*, February 2004. See Internet site <http://www.bls.gov/emp/home.htm>.

Table 610. Unemployed Workers—Summary: 1980 to 2004

[In thousands (7,637 represents 7,637,000), except as indicated. For civilian noninstitutional population 16 years old and over. Annual averages of monthly figures. For data on unemployment insurance, see Table 548]

Age, sex, race, Hispanic origin	1980	1985	1990 [1]	1995	2000 [1]	2002	2003 [1]	2004 [1]
UNEMPLOYED								
Total [2]	7,637	8,312	7,047	7,404	5,692	8,378	8,774	8,149
16 to 19 years old	1,669	1,468	1,212	1,346	1,081	1,253	1,251	1,208
20 to 24 years old	1,835	1,738	1,299	1,244	1,022	1,430	1,495	1,431
25 to 44 years old	2,964	3,681	3,323	3,390	2,340	3,581	3,775	3,362
45 to 64 years old	1,075	1,331	1,109	1,269	1,117	1,950	2,069	1,970
65 years and over	94	93	105	153	132	163	183	179
Male	4,267	4,521	3,906	3,983	2,975	4,597	4,906	4,456
16 to 19 years old	913	806	667	744	599	700	697	664
20 to 24 years old	1,076	944	715	673	547	792	841	811
25 to 44 years old	1,619	1,950	1,803	1,776	1,159	1,920	2,085	1,819
45 to 64 years old	600	766	662	697	587	1,098	1,176	1,057
65 years and over	58	55	59	94	83	87	107	104
Female	3,370	3,791	3,140	3,421	2,717	3,781	3,868	3,694
16 to 19 years old	755	661	544	602	483	553	554	543
20 to 24 years old	760	794	584	571	475	638	654	619
25 to 44 years old	1,345	1,732	1,519	1,615	1,181	1,661	1,690	1,543
45 to 64 years old	473	566	447	574	529	854	894	914
65 years and over	36	39	46	60	50	76	76	75
White [3]	5,884	6,191	5,186	5,459	4,121	6,137	6,311	5,847
16 to 19 years old	1,291	1,074	903	952	795	925	909	890
20 to 24 years old	1,364	1,235	899	866	682	977	1,012	959
Black [3]	1,553	1,864	1,565	1,538	1,241	1,693	1,787	1,729
16 to 19 years old	343	357	268	325	230	260	255	241
20 to 24 years old	426	455	349	311	281	365	375	353
Asian [3, 4]	(NA)	(NA)	(NA)	(NA)	227	389	366	277
16 to 19 years old	(NA)	(NA)	(NA)	(NA)	40	41	31	20
20 to 24 years old	(NA)	(NA)	(NA)	(NA)	41	63	47	46
Hispanic [3, 5]	620	811	876	1,140	954	1,353	1,441	1,342
16 to 19 years old	145	141	161	205	194	221	192	203
20 to 24 years old	138	171	167	209	190	265	273	255
Full-time workers	6,269	6,793	5,677	5,909	4,538	7,063	7,361	6,762
Part-time workers	1,369	1,519	1,369	1,495	1,154	1,314	1,413	1,388
UNEMPLOYMENT RATE (percent) [6]								
Total [2]	7.1	7.2	5.6	5.6	4.0	5.8	6.0	5.5
16 to 19 years old	17.8	18.6	15.5	17.3	13.1	16.5	17.5	17.0
20 to 24 years old	11.5	11.1	8.8	9.1	7.2	9.7	10.0	9.4
25 to 44 years old	6.0	6.2	4.9	4.8	3.3	5.2	5.5	4.9
45 to 64 years old	3.7	4.5	3.5	3.4	2.5	4.0	4.1	3.8
65 years and over	3.1	3.2	3.0	4.0	3.1	3.7	3.8	3.6
Male	6.9	7.0	5.7	5.6	3.9	5.9	6.3	5.6
16 to 19 years old	18.3	19.5	16.3	18.4	14.0	18.1	19.3	18.4
20 to 24 years old	12.5	11.4	9.1	9.2	7.3	10.2	10.6	10.1
25 to 44 years old	5.6	5.9	4.8	4.7	3.1	5.1	5.6	4.9
45 to 64 years old	3.5	4.5	3.7	3.5	2.4	4.2	4.4	3.9
65 years and over	3.1	3.1	3.0	4.3	3.3	3.4	4.0	3.7
Female	7.4	7.4	5.5	5.6	4.1	5.6	5.7	5.4
16 to 19 years old	17.2	17.6	14.7	16.1	12.1	14.9	15.6	15.5
20 to 24 years old	10.4	10.7	8.5	9.0	7.1	9.1	9.3	8.7
25 to 44 years old	6.4	6.6	4.9	5.0	3.6	5.2	5.4	5.0
45 to 64 years old	4.0	4.6	3.2	3.3	2.5	3.7	3.7	3.7
65 years and over	3.1	3.3	3.1	3.7	2.7	3.9	3.6	3.4
White [3]	6.3	6.2	4.8	4.9	3.5	5.1	5.2	4.8
16 to 19 years old	15.5	15.7	13.5	14.5	11.4	14.5	15.2	15.0
20 to 24 years old	9.9	9.2	7.3	7.7	5.9	8.1	8.4	7.9
Black [3]	14.3	15.1	11.4	10.4	7.6	10.2	10.8	10.4
16 to 19 years old	38.5	40.2	30.9	35.7	24.5	29.8	33.0	31.7
20 to 24 years old	23.6	24.5	19.9	17.7	15.0	19.1	19.8	18.4
Asian [3, 4]	(NA)	(NA)	(NA)	(NA)	3.6	5.9	6.0	4.4
16 to 19 years old	(NA)	(NA)	(NA)	(NA)	14.2	16.2	17.5	11.5
20 to 24 years old	(NA)	(NA)	(NA)	(NA)	6.9	10.2	9.0	8.6
Hispanic [3, 5]	10.1	10.5	8.2	9.3	5.7	7.5	7.7	7.0
16 to 19 years old	22.5	24.3	19.5	24.1	16.6	20.1	20.0	20.4
20 to 24 years old	12.1	12.6	9.1	11.5	7.5	9.9	10.2	9.3
Experienced workers [7]	6.9	6.8	5.3	5.4	3.8	5.7	5.8	5.3
Women maintaining families	9.2	10.4	8.3	8.0	5.9	8.0	8.5	8.0
Married men, wife present	4.2	4.3	3.4	3.3	2.0	3.6	3.8	3.1
Percent without work for—								
Fewer than 5 weeks	43.2	42.1	46.3	36.5	44.9	34.5	31.7	33.1
5 to 10 weeks	23.4	22.2	23.5	22.0	23.0	20.7	19.8	19.6
11 to 14 weeks	9.0	8.0	8.5	9.6	8.9	10.1	10.0	9.7
15 to 26 weeks	13.8	12.3	11.7	14.6	11.8	16.3	16.4	15.9
27 weeks and over	10.7	15.4	10.0	17.3	11.4	18.3	22.1	21.8
Unemployment duration, average (weeks)	11.9	15.6	12.0	16.6	12.6	16.6	19.2	19.6

NA Not available.   [1] See footnote 2, Table 576.   [2] Includes other races, not shown separately.   [3] Includes other ages, not shown separately. Also beginning 2003, for this race group only. See footnote 3, Table 577.   [4] Prior to 2003, includes Pacific Islanders.   [5] Persons of Hispanic or Latino origin may be of any race.   [6] Unemployed as percent of civilian labor force in specified group.   [7] Wage and salary workers.

Source: U.S. Bureau of Labor Statistics, *Employment and Earnings*, monthly, January 2005 issue; and unpublished data. See Internet site <http://www.bls.gov/cps/>.

Labor Force, Employment, and Earnings   409

Table 611. Unemployed Jobseekers Job Search Activities: 2004

[8,149 represents 8,149,000. For the civilian non-institutional population 16 years old and over. Annual average of monthly data. Based on the Current Population Survey and subject to sampling error; see text, Section 1 and Appendix III]

Characteristic	Population (1,000)		Jobseekers jobsearch methods (percent)						
	Total unemployed	Total jobseekers [1]	Employer directly	Sent out a resume or filled out applications	Placed or answered ads	Friends or relatives	Public employment agency	Private employment agency	Average number of methods used
Total, 16 years and over [2] ...	8,149	7,151	62.7	54.5	16.4	18.0	19.9	7.7	**1.92**
16 to 19 years old	1,208	1,149	60.4	60.4	10.7	12.6	8.1	2.5	1.61
20 to 24 years old	1,431	1,313	64.1	55.2	14.8	15.9	18.0	6.0	1.85
25 to 34 years old	1,784	1,542	63.1	53.8	16.8	17.8	22.5	8.8	1.95
35 to 44 years old	1,578	1,348	64.1	54.1	19.2	20.5	24.0	9.0	2.04
45 to 54 years old	1,288	1,097	62.9	53.7	19.9	21.7	25.4	10.7	2.10
55 to 64 years old	682	562	61.2	49.6	18.2	21.2	23.3	10.7	2.00
65 years old and over	179	139	55.4	39.1	14.5	20.0	11.7	5.6	1.58
Male	4,456	3,807	63.9	52.4	15.9	19.5	20.0	8.2	1.93
16 to 19 years old......	664	628	59.6	60.0	9.3	14.1	8.5	2.8	1.61
20 to 24 years old......	811	726	64.4	53.4	13.4	17.8	17.2	6.6	1.84
25 to 34 years old......	980	810	65.1	50.7	16.8	19.3	22.1	9.0	1.97
35 to 44 years old......	839	693	67.0	50.1	19.4	22.3	24.8	9.8	2.09
45 to 54 years old......	684	567	64.4	52.1	19.7	22.7	26.2	11.9	2.14
55 to 64 years old......	373	301	61.9	48.5	19.1	22.5	25.0	11.4	2.07
65 years old and over ...	104	81	56.4	37.6	11.3	19.1	11.7	5.4	1.56
Female..............	3,694	3,344	61.4	57.0	17.1	16.4	19.8	7.1	1.90
16 to 19 years old......	543	520	61.4	60.9	12.4	10.9	7.6	2.2	1.61
20 to 24 years old......	619	587	63.6	57.5	16.4	13.6	18.9	5.4	1.87
25 to 34 years old......	804	732	60.8	57.2	16.8	16.0	23.0	8.5	1.94
35 to 44 years old......	739	655	61.0	58.4	18.9	18.7	23.2	8.1	2.00
45 to 54 years old......	605	529	61.3	55.4	20.2	20.6	24.5	9.4	2.05
55 to 64 years old......	309	261	60.4	50.9	17.2	19.7	21.3	9.9	1.93
65 years old and over ...	75	59	54.0	41.3	18.9	21.4	11.7	5.8	1.62
White [3].............	5,847	5,029	62.6	55.0	17.4	18.1	18.4	7.5	1.92
Male	3,282	2,742	64.0	52.4	17.0	19.5	19.1	8.2	1.94
Female	2,565	2,287	60.9	58.0	17.8	16.3	17.6	6.6	1.89
Black [3].............	1,729	1,599	63.4	52.9	14.5	17.0	25.5	7.6	1.91
Male	860	784	64.1	51.0	13.2	17.6	23.8	7.2	1.87
Female	868	815	62.8	54.7	15.8	16.4	27.0	8.0	1.94
Asian [3].............	277	258	62.2	51.6	14.5	26.1	16.4	11.9	1.98
Male............	153	142	63.6	53.6	14.6	29.1	17.3	14.6	2.08
Female	124	115	60.4	49.1	14.4	22.4	15.3	8.7	1.85
Hispanic [4].............	1,342	1,142	63.2	46.3	12.5	21.9	19.7	6.9	1.80
Male	755	619	66.1	42.7	12.6	23.3	19.9	7.4	1.82
Female	587	524	59.7	50.6	12.4	20.1	19.5	6.3	1.76

[1] Excludes persons on temporary layoff.   [2] Includes other races, not shown separately.   [3] Data for this race group only. See footnote 3, Table 577.   [4] Persons of Hispanic or Latino origin may be of any race.

Source: U.S. Bureau of Labor Statistics, *Employment and Earnings*, monthly, January 2005 issue. See Internet site <http://www.bls.gov/cps/home.htm>.

Table 612. Unemployed Persons by Sex and Reason: 1980 to 2004

[In thousands (4,267 represents 4,267,000). For civilian noninstitutional population 16 years old and over. Annual averages of monthly figures. Based on Current Population Survey; see text, Section 1, Population, and Appendix III]

Sex and reason	1980	1985	1990 [1]	1995	1997 [1]	1998 [1]	1999 [1]	2000 [1]	2001	2002	2003 [1]	2004 [1]
Male, total	4,267	4,521	3,906	3,983	3,577	3,266	3,066	2,975	3,690	4,597	4,906	4,456
Job losers [2]......	2,649	2,749	2,257	2,190	1,902	1,703	1,563	1,516	2,119	2,820	3,024	2,603
Job leavers	438	409	528	407	414	368	389	387	422	434	422	437
Reentrants	776	876	806	1,113	1,004	931	895	854	925	1,068	1,141	1,070
New entrants......	405	487	315	273	257	264	219	217	223	274	320	346
Female, total	3,370	3,791	3,140	3,421	3,162	2,944	2,814	2,717	3,111	3,781	3,868	3,694
Job losers [2]......	1,297	1,390	1,130	1,286	1,135	1,119	1,059	1,001	1,356	1,787	1,814	1,595
Job leavers	453	468	513	417	381	366	394	393	413	432	397	421
Reentrants	1,152	1,380	1,124	1,412	1,334	1,201	1,111	1,107	1,105	1,300	1,336	1,338
New entrants......	468	552	373	306	312	257	250	217	237	262	321	340

[1] See footnote 2, Table 576.   [2] Beginning 1995, persons who completed temporary jobs are identified separately and are included as job losers.

Source: U.S. Bureau of Labor Statistics, *Employment and Earnings*, monthly, January issues; Bulletin 2307; and unpublished data. See Internet site <http://www.bls.gov/cps/home.htm>.

Table 613. **Unemployment Rates by Industry, 2000 to 2004, and by Sex, 2000 and 2004**

[In percent. For civilian noninstitutional population 16 years old and over. Annual averages of monthly figures. Rate represents unemployment as a percent of labor force in each specified group. Based on Current Population Survey; see text, Section 1, and Appendix III. See headnote, Table 593 regarding industries]

Industry	2000	2002	2003 [1]	2004 [1]	Male 2000	Male 2004 [1]	Female 2000	Female 2004 [1]
All unemployed [2]	4.0	5.8	6.0	5.5	3.9	5.6	4.1	5.4
Industry: [3]								
Agriculture and related industries	9.0	10.1	10.2	9.9	8.3	9.5	11.5	11.2
Mining	4.4	6.3	6.7	3.9	4.6	3.9	2.8	4.4
Construction	6.2	9.2	9.3	8.4	6.4	8.5	5.1	7.1
Manufacturing	3.5	6.7	6.6	5.7	3.0	5.2	4.5	6.8
Wholesale trade	3.3	5.0	5.1	4.6	2.8	4.0	4.4	5.9
Retail trade	4.6	6.4	6.3	6.1	4.0	5.6	5.1	6.6
Transportation and utilities	3.4	4.9	5.3	4.4	3.2	4.3	4.2	5.0
Transportation and warehousing	3.8	5.4	5.7	4.9	1.9	4.8	4.6	5.4
Utilities	1.9	2.5	3.1	1.9	2.8	1.6	2.1	3.0
Information	3.2	6.9	6.8	5.7	2.7	5.4	3.7	6.0
Telecommunications	2.3	7.9	7.5	6.0	1.5	5.5	3.3	6.8
Financial activities	2.4	3.5	3.5	3.6	2.1	3.6	2.6	3.5
Finance and insurance	2.2	3.3	3.3	3.4	1.7	3.3	2.5	3.5
Real estate and rental and leasing	3.1	4.3	4.1	4.1	2.9	4.4	3.2	3.7
Professional and business services	4.8	7.9	8.2	6.8	4.4	6.6	5.2	7.1
Professional and technical services	2.5	5.5	5.4	4.1	2.2	3.8	2.9	4.4
Management, administrative, and waste services	8.1	11.2	12.1	10.6	7.6	10.1	8.8	11.3
Education and health services	2.5	3.4	3.6	3.4	2.2	3.1	2.5	3.5
Educational services	2.4	3.9	4.5	3.7	2.1	3.4	2.5	3.9
Health care and social assistance	2.5	3.2	3.4	3.4	2.3	3.0	2.5	3.4
Leisure and hospitality	6.6	8.4	8.7	8.3	6.2	8.0	7.0	8.6
Arts, entertainment, and recreation	5.9	8.2	7.8	7.2	6.1	7.5	5.7	6.9
Accommodation and food services	6.8	8.4	8.9	8.6	6.2	8.2	7.3	8.9
Other services [4]	3.9	5.1	5.7	5.3	3.7	5.3	4.0	5.3
Government workers	2.1	2.5	2.8	2.7	2.1	2.9	2.2	2.5

[1] See footnote 2, Table 576. [2] Includes the self-employed, unpaid family workers, and persons with no previous work experience, not shown separately. [3] Covers unemployed wage and salary workers. [4] Includes private household workers.

Source: U.S. Bureau of Labor Statistics, Employment and Earnings, monthly, January 2005 issue; and unpublished data. See Internet site <http://www.bls.gov/cps/home.htm>.

Table 614. **Unemployment by Occupation, 2000 to 2004, and by Sex, 2004**

[5,692 represents 5,692,000. For civilian noninstitutional population 16 years old and over. Annual averages of monthly data. Rate represents unemployment as a percent of the labor force for each specified group. Based on Current Population Survey; see text, Section 1, and Appendix III. See also headnote, Table 593 regarding occupations]

Occupation	Number (1,000) 2000	Number (1,000) 2003 [1]	Number (1,000) 2004 [1]	Unemployment rate 2000	Unemployment rate 2003 [1]	2004 [1] Total	2004 [1] Male	2004 [1] Female
Total [2]	5,692	8,774	8,149	4.0	6.0	5.5	5.6	5.4
Management, professional, and related occupations	827	1,556	1,346	1.8	3.1	2.7	2.7	2.7
Management, business, and financial operations	320	627	544	1.6	3.1	2.6	2.5	2.8
Management	214	430	369	1.5	2.9	2.5	2.4	2.5
Business and financial operations	106	198	175	2.0	3.5	3.0	2.7	3.2
Professional and related occupations	507	929	801	1.9	3.2	2.8	3.0	2.6
Computer and mathematical	74	181	136	2.2	5.5	4.2	4.0	4.5
Architecture and engineering	51	124	80	1.7	4.4	2.8	2.7	3.4
Life, physical, and social science	18	48	35	1.4	3.3	2.5	2.6	2.4
Community and social services	40	57	65	2.0	2.5	2.9	2.7	3.1
Legal	18	35	31	1.2	2.3	1.9	1.5	2.4
Education, training, and library	136	225	207	1.8	2.8	2.5	2.6	2.5
Arts, design, entertainment, sports, and media	97	171	157	3.5	6.0	5.5	5.6	5.5
Healthcare practitioner and technical	73	88	90	1.2	1.3	1.3	1.1	1.4
Service occupations	1,132	1,681	1,617	5.2	7.1	6.6	6.7	6.6
Healthcare support	101	171	169	4.0	5.5	5.5	5.4	5.5
Protective service	70	129	113	2.7	4.5	3.8	3.6	4.6
Food preparation and serving related	469	683	656	6.6	8.6	8.3	8.5	8.1
Building and grounds cleaning and maintenance	301	447	421	5.8	8.3	7.5	7.6	7.3
Personal care and service	190	250	257	4.4	5.6	5.4	5.3	5.5
Sales and office occupations	1,446	2,070	1,937	3.8	5.5	5.2	5.0	5.3
Sales and related	673	995	912	4.1	5.9	5.4	4.2	6.6
Office and administrative support	773	1,076	1,025	3.6	5.2	5.0	6.4	4.6
Natural resources, construction, and maintenance	758	1,244	1,140	5.3	8.1	7.3	7.0	11.6
Farming, fishing, and forestry	133	136	132	10.2	11.4	11.8	10.1	17.6
Construction and extraction	507	814	786	6.2	9.1	8.4	8.3	12.2
Installation, maintenance, and repair	119	295	222	2.4	5.5	4.2	4.2	4.9
Production, transportation, and material moving	1,081	1,555	1,393	5.1	7.9	7.2	6.5	9.4
Production	575	807	714	4.8	7.7	7.0	5.9	9.4
Transportation and material moving	505	748	679	5.6	8.2	7.4	7.0	9.5

[1] See footnote 2, Table 576. [2] Includes persons with no previous work experience and those whose last job was in the Armed Forces.

Source: U.S. Bureau of Labor Statistics, Employment and Earnings, monthly, January 2005 issue; and unpublished data. See Internet site<http://www.bls.gov/cps/home.htm>.

Labor Force, Employment, and Earnings 411

[6,543 represents 6,543,000. Annual averages of monthly figures. For the civilian noninstitutional population 25 years old and over. See Table 580 for civilian labor force and participation rate data. Based on Current Population Survey; see text, Section 1, and Appendix III]

Year, sex, and race	Unemployed (1,000)					Unemployment rate [1]				
	Total	Less than high school diploma	High school graduates, no degree	Less than a bachelor's degree	College graduate	Total	Less than high school diploma	High school graduate, no degree	Less than a bachelor's degree	College graduate
Total: [2]										
1992	6,543	1,533	2,590	1,527	893	6.1	11.5	6.8	5.6	3.2
2000 [3]	3,589	791	1,298	890	610	3.0	6.3	3.4	2.7	1.7
2004 [3]	5,511	1,062	1,890	1,462	1,098	4.4	8.5	5.0	4.2	2.7
Male:										
1992	3,767	942	1,462	829	533	6.4	11.4	7.4	5.9	3.3
2000 [3]	1,829	411	682	427	309	2.8	5.4	3.4	2.6	1.5
2004 [3]	2,980	602	1,049	732	597	4.4	7.6	5.1	4.3	2.7
Female:										
1992	2,776	591	1,128	697	361	5.8	11.5	6.3	5.4	3.0
2000 [3]	1,760	380	616	463	301	3.2	7.8	3.5	2.8	1.8
2004 [3]	2,531	460	841	730	500	4.4	10.0	4.9	4.2	2.7
White: [4]										
1992	4,978	1,145	1,928	1,162	743	5.5	10.7	6.0	5.0	3.0
2000 [3]	2,644	564	924	667	489	2.6	5.6	2.9	2.4	1.6
2004 [3]	3,998	752	1,354	1,038	854	3.9	7.5	4.4	3.7	2.5
Black: [4]										
1992	1,269	322	565	301	81	11.0	15.3	12.3	9.8	4.4
2000 [3]	731	179	315	169	68	5.4	10.7	6.4	4.0	2.5
2004 [3]	1,134	243	438	321	133	8.1	15.5	8.7	7.6	4.3
Asian: [4][5]										
2000 [3]	146	28	34	35	49	2.7	5.7	3.0	3.2	1.8
2004 [3]	211	27	47	48	89	3.8	5.9	4.5	4.8	2.9
Hispanic: [6]										
1992	853	434	235	134	50	9.8	12.8	9.1	7.7	5.0
2000 [3]	569	297	150	85	38	4.4	6.2	3.9	3.2	2.2
2004 [3]	884	417	236	154	77	5.7	7.5	5.2	4.8	3.5

[1] Percent unemployed of the civilian labor force. [2] Includes other races, not shown separately. [3] See footnote 2, Table 576. [4] 2004 data are for persons in this race group only. See footnote 3, Table 577. [5] 2000 data include Pacific Islanders. [6] Persons of Hispanic or Latino origin may be of any race.

Source: U.S. Bureau of Labor Statistics, *Employment and Earnings*, monthly, January 2005 issue. See Internet site <http://www.bls.gov/cps/home.htm>.

Table 616. **Unemployed Persons by Reason of Unemployment: 2004**

[8,149 represents 8,149,000. Annual averages of monthly data. Based on Current Population Survey; see text, Section 1, and Appendix III]

Age, sex, and reason	Total unemployed (1,000)	Percent distribution by duration				
		Less than 5 weeks	5 to 14 weeks	15 weeks and over		
				Total	15 to 26 weeks	27 weeks or longer
Total 16 years old and over	8,149	33.1	29.2	37.7	15.9	21.8
16 to 19 years old	1,208	44.6	32.1	23.4	11.6	11.8
Total 20 years old and over	6,941	31.1	28.7	40.2	16.6	23.6
Males	3,791	31.1	28.0	40.9	16.2	24.7
Job losers and persons who completed temporary jobs	2,503	31.9	28.1	39.9	16.6	23.3
On temporary layoff	613	49.5	31.7	18.8	12.1	6.7
Not on temporary layoff	1,890	26.3	27.0	46.7	18.1	28.6
Permanent job losers	1,366	23.2	25.7	51.1	18.5	32.6
Persons who completed temporary jobs	524	34.3	30.4	35.4	17.0	18.4
Job leavers	398	35.6	29.6	34.8	14.8	20.0
Reentrants	791	27.4	26.5	46.1	15.7	30.4
New entrants	99	21.3	30.5	48.2	13.3	34.9
Females	3,150	31.1	29.6	39.3	17.1	22.2
Job losers and persons who completed temporary jobs	1,529	31.0	29.2	39.8	17.7	22.0
On temporary layoff	326	55.4	32.0	12.6	7.7	4.8
Not on temporary layoff	1,202	24.4	28.4	47.1	20.4	26.7
Permanent job losers	949	22.1	27.8	50.0	21.2	28.8
Persons who completed temporary jobs	253	33.0	30.7	36.3	17.5	18.7
Job leavers	384	38.0	30.8	31.3	17.5	14.4
Reentrants	1,107	29.5	29.3	41.2	16.6	24.6
New entrants	131	24.4	33.1	42.5	16.0	26.5

Source: U.S. Bureau of Labor Statistics, *Employment and Earnings*, January 2005 issue. See Internet site <http://www.bls.gov/cps/home.htm>.

Table 617. **Total Unemployed and Insured Unemployed by State: 1980 to 2004**

[7,637 represents 7,637,000. For civilian noninstitutional population 16 years old and over. Annual averages of monthly figures. Total unemployment estimates based on the Current Population Survey; see text, Section 1, and Appendix III. U.S. totals derived by independent population controls; therefore state data may not add to U.S. totals]

State	Total unemployed								Insured unemployed [3]			
	Number (1,000)				Percent [1]				Number (1,000)		Percent [4]	
	1980	1990 [2]	2000 [2]	2004 [2]	1980	1990 [2]	2000 [2]	2004 [2]	2000	2003	2000	2003
United States ...	7,637	7,047	5,692	8,149	7.1	5.6	4.0	5.5	[5]2,110	[5]3,531	[5]1.7	[5]2.8
Alabama.........	147	130	97	126	8.8	6.9	4.5	5.8	29.0	39.1	1.6	2.2
Alaska..........	18	19	21	25	9.7	7.0	6.7	7.5	12.3	14.3	4.9	5.3
Arizona.........	83	99	98	141	6.7	5.5	4.0	5.1	20.5	47.6	1.0	2.2
Arkansas	76	78	55	77	7.6	7.0	4.4	5.9	23.9	34.9	2.2	3.2
California	790	874	835	1,084	6.8	5.8	4.9	6.2	338.5	531.9	2.4	3.6
Colorado........	88	89	65	137	5.9	5.0	2.8	5.4	15.0	41.3	0.7	2.0
Connecticut......	94	95	40	88	5.9	5.2	2.2	4.9	28.3	53.3	1.7	3.3
Delaware	22	19	16	17	7.7	5.2	3.9	3.9	5.9	9.8	1.5	2.5
District of Columbia......	24	22	18	25	7.3	6.6	5.7	8.2	5.7	7.3	1.3	1.6
Florida	251	390	281	390	5.9	6.0	3.6	4.6	70.8	120.0	1.1	1.7
Georgia	163	182	156	205	6.4	5.5	3.7	4.7	34.5	70.0	0.9	1.9
Hawaii	21	16	25	21	4.9	2.9	4.3	3.4	8.4	10.4	1.7	2.0
Idaho..........	34	29	32	37	7.9	5.9	4.9	5.3	12.1	19.4	2.3	3.5
Illinois	459	369	281	389	8.3	6.2	4.3	6.1	103.8	182.8	1.8	3.2
Indiana.........	252	149	100	167	9.6	5.3	3.2	5.3	31.8	65.1	1.1	2.3
Iowa	82	62	41	75	5.8	4.3	2.6	4.6	19.4	31.6	1.4	2.3
Kansas.........	53	57	52	82	4.5	4.5	3.7	5.5	15.6	30.9	1.2	2.4
Kentucky	133	104	81	103	8.0	5.9	4.1	5.2	25.4	39.6	1.5	2.4
Louisiana	121	117	111	124	6.7	6.3	5.4	6.0	24.0	36.6	1.3	2.0
Maine..........	39	33	24	32	7.8	5.2	3.5	4.7	8.9	13.1	1.6	2.3
Maryland	140	122	107	121	6.5	4.7	3.8	4.2	28.9	48.3	0.3	2.1
Massachusetts.....	162	195	88	172	5.6	6.0	2.6	5.1	60.1	107.8	1.9	3.4
Michigan........	534	350	183	356	12.4	7.6	3.5	7.0	81.6	155.0	1.8	3.6
Minnesota.......	125	117	91	140	5.9	4.9	3.3	4.8	31.4	60.7	1.2	2.4
Mississippi	79	90	74	83	7.5	7.6	5.6	6.2	19.7	26.4	1.8	2.4
Missouri	167	151	102	173	7.2	5.8	3.4	5.7	41.8	68.5	1.6	2.7
Montana........	23	24	24	24	6.1	6.0	5.0	4.9	7.8	9.9	2.2	2.6
Nebraska.......	31	18	28	37	4.1	2.2	3.0	3.8	7.3	14.4	0.9	1.7
Nevada	27	33	42	50	6.2	4.9	4.0	4.2	19.5	27.8	2.0	2.7
New Hampshire....	22	36	19	27	4.7	5.7	2.8	3.7	3.1	9.5	0.5	1.6
New Jersey.......	260	206	160	210	7.2	5.1	3.7	4.8	84.8	132.5	2.3	3.5
New Mexico......	42	46	42	51	7.5	6.5	5.0	5.6	9.5	14.8	1.4	2.1
New York	597	467	419	548	7.5	5.3	4.6	5.8	146.2	240.1	1.8	3.0
North Carolina.....	187	144	150	227	6.6	4.2	3.6	5.4	54.3	105.2	1.5	2.9
North Dakota......	15	13	11	12	5.0	4.0	3.0	3.4	3.9	4.5	1.3	1.5
Ohio	426	310	233	370	8.4	5.7	4.0	6.3	71.6	128.9	1.3	2.5
Oklahoma.......	66	86	51	84	4.8	5.7	3.1	4.9	12.2	28.4	0.9	2.0
Oregon.........	107	83	88	140	8.3	5.6	4.9	7.6	41.2	68.5	2.7	4.4
Pennsylvania.....	425	315	251	350	7.8	5.4	4.1	5.6	132.4	215.5	2.5	4.0
Rhode Island.....	34	35	22	30	7.2	6.8	4.1	5.4	12.2	14.4	2.7	3.2
South Carolina.....	96	83	75	142	6.9	4.8	3.8	6.9	27.1	48.6	1.5	2.8
South Dakota	16	13	9	16	4.9	3.9	2.3	3.7	2.0	3.5	0.6	1.0
Tennessee	152	126	110	147	7.3	5.3	3.9	5.1	42.2	58.0	1.6	2.3
Texas..........	352	544	441	657	5.2	6.3	4.2	6.0	107.9	198.7	1.2	2.2
Utah	40	35	37	64	6.3	4.3	3.3	5.3	10.5	18.3	1.1	1.8
Vermont	16	15	10	13	6.4	5.0	2.9	3.7	4.8	8.4	1.7	2.9
Virginia.........	128	141	79	147	5.0	4.3	2.2	3.9	22.2	50.2	0.7	1.5
Washington......	156	125	159	202	7.9	4.9	5.2	6.2	70.6	102.5	2.7	4.0
West Virginia.....	74	64	45	42	9.4	8.4	5.5	5.3	14.1	19.1	2.1	2.9
Wisconsin.......	167	114	105	155	7.2	4.4	3.6	5.0	53.1	91.5	2.0	3.4
Wyoming	9	13	10	11	4.0	5.5	3.9	3.8	2.9	4.1	1.3	1.8

[1] Total unemployment as percent of civilian labor force. [2] See footnote 2, Table 576. [3] Source: U.S. Employment and Training Administration, *Unemployment Insurance, Financial Handbook*, annual updates. [4] Insured unemployment as percent of average covered employment in the previous year. [5] Includes 49,800 in Puerto Rico and the Virgin Islands in 2000; and 47,500 in 2003.

Source: Except as noted, U.S. Bureau of Labor Statistics, *Geographic Profile of Employment and Unemployment*, annual. See Internet site <http://www.bls.gov/gps/>.

Table 618. Nonfarm Establishments—Employees, Hours, and Earnings by Industry: 1990 to 2004

[Annual averages of monthly data. (109,487 represents 109,487,000). Based on data from establishment reports. Includes all full- and part-time employees who worked during, or received pay for, any part of the pay period reported. Excludes proprietors, the self-employed, farm workers, private household workers, and Armed Forces. Establishment data shown here conform to industry definitions in the 2002 North American Industry Classification System (NAICS) and are adjusted to March 2004 employment benchmarks. Based on the Current Employment Statistics Program; see source and Appendix III]

Item and year	Total nonfarm	Total [1]	Construction	Manufacturing	Wholesale trade	Retail trade	Transportation and warehousing	Utilities	Information	Finance and insurance	Real estate and rental and leasing	Professional and technical services	Administrative and waste services	Educational services	Health care and social insurance	Arts, entertainment, and recreation	Accommodations and food services	Government
EMPLOYEES (1,000)																		
1990	109,487	91,072	5,263	17,695	5,268	13,182	3,476	740	2,688	4,979	1,635	4,557	4,624	1,688	9,296	1,132	8,156	18,415
1995	117,298	97,866	5,274	17,241	5,433	13,897	3,838	666	2,843	5,072	1,755	5,101	6,057	2,010	11,278	1,459	9,042	19,432
2000	131,785	110,996	6,787	17,263	5,933	15,280	4,410	601	3,631	5,680	2,007	6,734	8,136	2,390	12,718	1,788	10,074	20,790
2001	131,826	110,707	6,826	16,441	5,773	15,239	4,372	599	3,629	5,773	2,035	6,902	7,795	2,511	13,134	1,824	10,211	21,118
2002	130,341	108,828	6,716	15,259	5,652	15,025	4,224	596	3,395	5,817	2,030	6,676	7,595	2,643	13,556	1,783	10,203	21,513
2003	129,999	108,416	6,735	14,510	5,608	14,917	4,185	577	3,188	5,923	2,054	6,630	7,670	2,695	13,893	1,813	10,360	21,583
2004	131,480	109,862	6,964	14,329	5,655	15,035	4,250	570	3,138	5,966	2,086	6,762	7,934	2,766	14,187	1,833	10,646	21,618
WEEKLY EARNINGS [2] (dol.)																		
1990	(NA)	349.29	513.43	436.16	444.48	235.62	471.72	670.40	479.50	378.21	286.81	504.87	272.70	(NA)	319.80	219.02	143.52	(NA)
1995	(NA)	399.53	571.57	509.26	515.14	272.56	513.37	811.52	564.98	477.39	321.69	583.41	306.54	(NA)	379.66	240.57	160.46	(NA)
2000	(NA)	480.41	685.78	590.65	631.40	333.38	562.31	955.66	700.89	589.64	385.85	745.83	386.33	(NA)	449.27	273.79	201.09	(NA)
2001	(NA)	493.20	695.89	595.19	643.45	346.16	562.70	977.18	731.11	612.36	409.75	769.63	400.95	(NA)	473.04	283.17	203.35	(NA)
2002	(NA)	506.07	711.82	618.75	644.38	360.81	579.75	979.09	738.17	632.34	419.76	784.51	417.44	(NA)	495.17	301.84	207.67	(NA)
2003	(NA)	517.30	726.83	635.99	657.29	367.15	598.41	1,017.27	760.81	670.86	437.20	801.82	427.02	(NA)	516.03	305.85	210.35	(NA)
2004	(NA)	528.56	735.70	658.53	666.93	371.15	614.90	1,048.82	777.42	683.96	455.03	828.39	424.54	(NA)	538.00	312.90	214.47	(NA)
WEEKLY HOURS [2]																		
1990	(NA)	34.3	38.3	40.5	38.4	30.6	37.7	41.5	35.8	36.4	33.1	36.1	32.3	(NA)	31.8	26.1	25.9	(NA)
1995	(NA)	34.3	38.8	41.3	38.6	30.8	38.9	42.3	36.8	36.5	32.7	35.8	32.5	(NA)	31.9	26.3	25.8	(NA)
2000	(NA)	34.3	39.2	41.3	38.8	30.7	37.4	42.0	36.8	37.1	32.6	36.2	33.1	(NA)	32.1	25.6	26.2	(NA)
2001	(NA)	34.0	38.7	40.3	38.0	30.7	36.7	41.4	36.9	36.9	32.7	35.9	32.8	(NA)	32.3	25.5	25.8	(NA)
2002	(NA)	33.9	38.4	40.5	38.0	30.9	36.8	40.9	36.5	36.6	32.8	35.6	33.0	(NA)	32.3	25.5	25.8	(NA)
2003	(NA)	33.7	38.4	40.4	37.9	30.9	36.8	41.1	36.2	36.5	32.8	35.6	32.9	(NA)	32.5	25.7	25.6	(NA)
2004	(NA)	33.7	38.3	40.8	37.8	30.7	37.2	40.9	36.3	36.5	32.8	35.7	32.9	(NA)	32.7	—	25.6	(NA)
HOURLY EARNINGS [2] (dol.)																		
1990	(NA)	10.19	13.42	10.78	11.58	7.71	12.50	16.14	13.40	10.40	8.66	13.99	8.45	(NA)	10.05	8.41	5.53	(NA)
1995	(NA)	11.64	14.73	12.34	13.34	8.85	13.18	19.19	15.68	13.07	9.85	16.32	9.43	(NA)	11.89	9.14	6.22	(NA)
2000	(NA)	14.00	17.48	14.32	16.28	10.86	15.05	22.75	19.07	15.90	12.14	20.61	11.66	(NA)	13.90	10.68	7.68	(NA)
2001	(NA)	14.53	18.00	14.76	16.77	11.29	15.33	23.58	19.80	16.59	12.53	21.42	12.21	(NA)	14.67	11.10	7.88	(NA)
2002	(NA)	14.95	18.52	15.29	16.98	11.67	15.76	23.96	20.20	17.28	12.79	22.02	12.66	(NA)	15.32	11.75	8.04	(NA)
2003	(NA)	15.35	18.95	15.74	17.36	11.90	16.25	24.77	21.01	18.37	13.32	22.54	13.00	(NA)	15.88	11.99	8.22	(NA)
2004	(NA)	15.67	19.23	16.14	17.66	12.08	16.53	25.62	21.42	18.71	13.88	23.23	12.90	(NA)	16.46	12.17	8.36	(NA)

NA Not available. [1] Includes other industries, not shown separately. [2] Average hours and earnings of production workers for natural resources and mining, manufacturing, and construction; average hours and earnings of nonsupervisory workers for the service-providing industries.

Source: U.S. Bureau of Labor Statistics, the Current Employment Statistics program Internet site <http://www.bls.gov/ces/home.htm>.

Table 619. Employees in Nonfarm Establishments—States: 2004

[In thousands (131,480 represents 131,480,000). For coverage, see headnote, Table 618. National totals differ from the sum of the state figures because of differing benchmarks among states and differing industrial and geographic stratification. Based on North American Industry Classification System, 2002; see text, this section]

State	Total [1]	Construction	Manufacturing	Trade, transportation, and utilities	Information	Financial activities [2]	Professional and business services [3]	Education and health services [4]	Leisure and hospitality [5]	Other services [6]	Government
U.S.. .	131,480	6,964	14,329	25,510	3,138	8,052	16,414	16,954	12,479	5,431	21,618
AL. . . .	1,902	104	291	376	31	97	197	192	160	82	360
AK. . . .	304	18	12	62	7	15	23	35	30	12	81
AZ. . . .	2,374	190	176	462	48	164	334	260	241	89	401
AR. . . .	1,159	52	204	242	20	51	108	143	91	41	201
CA. . . .	14,539	847	1,533	2,753	483	903	2,099	1,562	1,442	505	2,390
CO. . . .	2,179	151	155	407	81	155	299	219	252	87	359
CT. . . .	1,651	66	198	308	39	141	198	268	128	63	242
DE. . . .	424	[7]26	35	81	7	45	62	52	40	19	58
DC. . . .	672	[7]12	3	28	24	31	143	92	51	59	231
FL. . . .	7,504	491	388	1,498	168	501	1,290	919	854	320	1,069
GA . . .	3,890	198	445	828	119	218	511	407	358	156	638
HI	582	[7]29	15	112	11	29	71	67	104	24	120
ID	587	40	62	118	10	28	73	65	56	18	114
IL	5,807	267	697	1,179	121	400	796	728	507	259	844
IN	2,930	148	572	576	41	140	266	369	275	109	426
IA	1,456	68	223	306	34	97	107	191	128	56	244
KS. . . .	1,323	63	176	261	42	70	127	160	110	53	252
KY. . . .	1,796	84	264	372	29	87	162	231	161	78	309
LA. . . .	1,920	117	152	380	29	103	184	252	204	72	383
ME . . .	614	31	63	126	12	35	50	111	59	20	105
MD . . .	2,520	[7]178	143	468	51	156	373	348	225	114	466
MA . . .	3,180	138	314	573	87	220	449	582	292	116	408
MI. . . .	4,391	190	696	810	68	218	584	553	403	179	682
MN . . .	2,678	127	343	523	60	176	302	377	235	118	411
MS . . .	1,125	49	179	220	15	46	83	119	125	38	243
MO . . .	2,693	138	312	533	64	163	303	359	267	119	429
MT . . .	412	25	19	86	8	21	33	54	55	17	87
NE. . . .	923	[7]48	101	196	22	63	94	127	78	35	160
NV. . . .	1,152	118	46	205	15	62	133	80	313	35	139
NH . . .	627	30	80	140	13	38	57	95	64	21	90
NJ. . . .	4,002	166	339	876	99	278	582	547	327	154	634
NM . . .	791	50	36	138	15	35	90	103	83	29	198
NY. . . .	8,447	318	596	1,483	271	702	1,054	1,521	662	352	1,483
NC . . .	3,830	217	580	724	72	192	429	446	345	168	651
ND . . .	337	17	25	73	8	19	24	49	31	15	75
OH . . .	5,407	235	825	1,038	93	312	624	744	495	227	802
OK . . .	1,470	62	142	276	31	84	161	179	129	74	302
OR . . .	1,594	82	200	320	33	97	177	193	156	57	270
PA. . . .	5,640	248	691	1,121	112	336	633	996	476	263	745
RI	488	21	57	80	11	34	54	93	50	23	66
SC. . . .	1,823	113	269	353	26	93	192	176	201	68	328
SD. . . .	383	20	39	77	7	28	24	57	41	16	74
TN. . . .	2,701	118	412	587	50	142	301	320	253	102	414
TX. . . .	9,478	543	890	1,943	226	595	1,088	1,145	883	359	1,656
UT. . . .	1,103	73	115	219	30	65	138	123	102	33	199
VT. . . .	303	17	37	59	6	13	21	53	33	10	52
VA. . . .	3,584	231	299	647	100	189	577	380	320	180	652
WA . . .	2,698	164	264	519	92	152	302	319	255	100	523
WV . . .	736	35	63	137	12	31	58	111	68	55	143
WI	2,803	126	502	540	50	158	251	376	250	135	412
WY . . .	255	19	10	49	4	11	15	22	31	10	65

[1] Includes natural resources and mining, not shown separately.   [2] Finance and insurance; real estate and rental and leasing.   [3] Professional, scientific and technical services; management of companies and enterprises; administrative and support and waste management and remediation services.   [4] Education services; health care and social assistance.   [5] Arts, entertainment and recreation; accommodations and food services.   [6] Includes repair and maintenance; personal and laundry services; and membership associations and organizations.   [7] Natural resources and mining included with construction.

Source: U.S. Bureau of Labor Statistics, the Current Employment Statistics program Internet site <http://www.bls.gov/ces/home.htm>. Compiled from data supplied by cooperating state agencies.

Labor Force, Employment and Earnings   415

Table 620. Nonfarm Industries—Employees and Earnings: 1990 to 2004

[Annual averages of monthly figures (109,487 represents 109,487,000). Covers all full- and part-time employees who worked during, or received pay for, any part of the pay period including the 12th of the month. See also headnote, Table 618]

Industry	2002 NAICS [1] code	All employees (1,000)					Average hourly earnings [2] (dollars)		
		1990	2000	2002	2003	2004	2000	2003	2004
Total nonfarm	(X)	109,487	131,785	130,341	129,999	131,480	(NA)	(NA)	(NA)
Goods-producing [3]	(X)	23,723	24,649	22,557	21,816	21,884	15.27	16.80	17.19
Service-providing [4]	(X)	85,764	107,136	107,784	108,182	109,596	(NA)	(NA)	(NA)
Total private	(X)	91,072	110,996	108,828	108,416	109,862	14.00	15.35	15.67
Natural resources and mining	(X)	765	599	583	572	591	16.55	17.56	18.08
Mining	21	680	520	512	503	523	16.94	17.90	18.45
Oil and gas extraction	211	190	125	122	120	123	19.43	18.95	18.58
Mining, except oil and gas	212	302	225	211	203	207	18.07	19.14	19.85
Support activities for mining	213	188	171	180	180	193	14.55	16.07	16.92
Construction	23	5,263	6,787	6,716	6,735	6,964	17.48	18.95	19.23
Construction of buildings	236	1,413	1,633	1,575	1,576	1,632	16.74	18.35	18.73
Residential building	2361	673	823	804	838	894	15.18	16.86	17.38
Nonresidential building	2362	741	809	771	738	738	18.18	19.85	20.18
Heavy and civil engineering construction . .	237	813	937	931	903	903	16.80	18.70	19.18
Highway, street, and bridge construction .	2373	289	340	346	340	348	18.17	19.50	19.82
Specialty trade contractors [5]	238	3,037	4,217	4,210	4,256	4,430	17.91	19.20	19.40
Building foundation and exterior contractors	2381	703	919	920	951	1,006	16.93	18.03	18.30
Building equipment contractors	2382	1,282	1,897	1,835	1,822	1,863	19.52	20.66	20.90
Building finishing contractors	2383	665	857	876	884	926	16.44	18.44	18.66
Manufacturing	31-33	17,695	17,263	15,259	14,510	14,329	14.32	15.74	16.14
Durable goods	(X)	10,736	10,876	9,483	8,963	8,923	14.93	16.45	16.82
Wood products	321	541	613	555	538	548	11.63	12.71	13.03
Nonmetallic mineral products	327	528	554	516	494	505	14.53	15.76	16.25
Cement and concrete products	3273	195	234	230	224	235	14.64	16.06	16.37
Primary metals	331	689	622	509	477	466	16.64	18.13	18.57
Foundries	3315	214	217	178	166	165	14.72	16.51	16.91
Fabricated metal products [5]	332	1,610	1,753	1,549	1,479	1,498	13.77	15.01	15.31
Architectural and structural metals	3323	357	428	399	380	390	13.43	14.54	14.71
Machine shops and threaded products . .	3327	309	365	318	311	326	14.53	15.78	15.91
Machinery [5]	333	1,408	1,455	1,230	1,149	1,142	15.22	16.30	16.68
Agricultural, construction, and mining machinery	3331	229	222	200	188	195	14.21	14.66	15.16
HVAC and commercial refrigeration equipment	3334	165	194	167	157	152	13.10	14.23	14.82
Metalworking machinery	3335	267	274	217	205	202	16.66	17.81	17.80
Computer and electronic products [5]	334	1,903	1,820	1,507	1,355	1,326	14.73	16.69	17.28
Computer and peripheral equipment . . .	3341	367	302	250	224	212	18.39	20.18	20.56
Communications equipment	3342	232	248	186	155	151	14.39	16.84	16.86
Semiconductors and electronic components	3344	574	676	525	461	453	13.46	15.37	16.24
Electronic instruments	3345	626	479	450	430	432	15.83	17.09	17.37
Electrical equipment and appliances	335	633	591	497	460	447	13.23	14.36	14.90
Electrical equipment	3353	244	210	175	160	153	13.28	14.40	14.86
Transportation equipment [5]	336	2,133	2,056	1,829	1,774	1,764	18.89	21.23	21.49
Motor vehicles	3361	271	291	265	265	256	24.45	28.04	28.35
Motor vehicle parts	3363	653	840	734	708	689	17.95	20.39	20.40
Aerospace products and parts	3364	841	517	470	442	444	20.52	22.93	23.93
Furniture and related products	337	601	680	604	573	573	11.72	12.98	13.16
Household and institutional furniture . . .	3371	398	440	400	382	384	11.39	12.69	12.82
Miscellaneous manufacturing	339	690	733	688	663	656	11.93	13.30	13.85
Medical equipment and supplies	3391	288	310	308	304	304	12.70	13.82	14.32
Nondurable goods	(X)	6,959	6,388	5,775	5,547	5,406	13.31	14.63	15.05
Food manufacturing [5]	311	1,507	1,553	1,526	1,518	1,497	11.77	12.80	12.98
Fruit and vegetable preserving and specialty	3114	218	197	183	185	182	11.90	12.79	12.86
Animal slaughtering and processing . . .	3116	427	507	517	516	505	10.27	11.30	11.53
Bakeries and tortilla manufacturing	3118	292	306	297	292	288	11.45	12.63	12.64
Beverages and tobacco products	312	218	207	207	200	194	17.40	17.96	19.12
Beverages	3121	173	175	174	169	165	17.19	17.43	18.70
Textile mills	313	492	378	291	261	239	11.23	11.99	12.13
Textile product mills	314	209	216	195	179	178	10.43	11.23	11.39
Apparel	315	929	497	360	312	285	8.60	9.56	9.75
Cut-and-sew apparel	3152	776	394	283	243	220	8.40	9.39	9.61
Leather and allied products	316	133	69	50	45	43	10.35	11.66	11.63
Paper and paper products	322	647	605	547	516	499	15.91	17.33	17.90
Pulp, paper, and paperboard mills	3221	238	191	165	151	147	20.62	22.62	23.00
Converted paper products	3222	409	413	382	365	352	13.58	14.94	15.56
Printing and related support activities	323	809	807	707	681	665	14.09	15.37	15.72
Petroleum and coal products	324	153	123	118	114	113	22.80	23.63	24.38
Chemicals [5]	325	1,036	980	928	906	887	17.09	18.50	19.16
Basic chemicals	3251	249	188	170	162	156	21.06	22.12	23.13
Pharmaceuticals and medicines	3254	207	274	291	292	291	17.27	19.77	20.90
Plastics and rubber products	326	826	952	848	815	807	12.69	14.18	14.58
Plastics products	3261	619	738	664	639	634	12.04	13.42	13.83
Rubber products	3262	207	214	184	177	173	14.82	16.80	17.13

See footnotes at end of table.

416   Labor Force, Employment, and Earnings

Table 620. **Nonfarm Industries—Employees and Earnings: 1990 to 2004—Con.**

[Annual averages of monthly figures (109,487 represents 109,487,000). Covers all full- and part-time employees who worked during, or received pay for, any part of the pay period including the 12th of the month. See also headnote, Table 618]

Industry	2002 NAICS [1] code	All employees (1,000)					Average hourly earnings [2] (dollars)		
		1990	2000	2002	2003	2004	2000	2003	2004
Trade, transportation, and utilities	(X)	22,666	26,225	25,497	25,287	25,510	13.31	14.34	14.59
Wholesale trade	42	5,268	5,933	5,652	5,608	5,655	16.28	17.36	17.66
Durable goods [5]	423	2,834	3,251	3,008	2,941	2,949	16.71	17.90	18.31
Motor vehicles and parts	4231	309	356	346	342	340	14.27	15.74	16.08
Lumber and construction supplies	4233	181	227	225	229	240	13.61	15.58	16.03
Commercial equipment	4234	597	722	665	653	643	20.29	22.14	22.88
Electric goods	4236	357	425	366	346	340	19.43	20.03	20.60
Hardware and plumbing	4237	216	247	233	231	234	15.07	16.37	16.22
Machinery and supplies	4238	690	725	673	644	653	16.47	17.46	17.77
Nondurable goods [5]	424	1,900	2,065	2,015	2,005	2,007	14.33	15.66	15.88
Paper and paper products	4241	162	177	159	152	150	15.65	16.20	17.33
Druggists' goods	4242	136	192	211	211	219	18.98	19.08	18.89
Grocery and related products	4244	623	689	680	685	688	13.57	15.08	15.29
Electronic markets and agents and brokers	425	535	618	629	662	699	20.79	20.42	20.15
Retail trade	44,45	13,182	15,280	15,025	14,917	15,035	10.86	11.90	12.08
Motor vehicle and parts dealers [5]	441	1,494	1,847	1,879	1,883	1,901	14.94	16.07	16.09
Automobile dealers	4411	983	1,217	1,253	1,254	1,254	16.95	17.85	17.68
Auto parts, accessories, and tire stores	4413	418	499	485	480	490	11.04	11.97	12.28
Furniture and home furnishings stores	442	432	544	539	547	560	12.33	13.28	13.46
Furniture stores	4421	244	289	281	284	289	13.37	14.41	14.44
Home furnishings stores	4422	188	254	258	263	271	11.06	11.99	12.35
Electronics and appliance stores	443	382	564	525	512	514	13.67	16.14	16.96
Building material and garden supply stores	444	891	1,142	1,177	1,185	1,226	11.25	12.67	12.80
Building material and supplies dealers	4441	753	982	1,025	1,038	1,081	11.30	12.86	12.92
Food and beverage stores	445	2,779	2,993	2,882	2,838	2,826	9.76	10.82	10.86
Grocery stores	4451	2,406	2,582	2,487	2,453	2,447	9.71	10.76	10.79
Specialty food stores	4452	232	270	256	247	244	9.97	11.00	11.13
Beer, wine, and liquor stores	4453	141	141	139	138	136	10.40	11.60	11.87
Health and personal care stores	446	792	928	939	938	942	11.68	13.12	13.73
Gasoline stations	447	910	936	896	882	877	8.05	8.72	8.84
Clothing & clothing accessories stores	448	1,313	1,322	1,313	1,305	1,362	9.96	10.48	10.55
Clothing stores	4481	930	954	960	956	1,008	9.88	10.30	10.26
Shoe stores	4482	216	193	183	179	185	8.96	9.22	9.46
Jewelry, luggage, and leather goods stores	4483	167	175	170	169	168	11.48	12.30	12.94
Sporting goods, hobby, book, and music stores	451	532	686	661	647	639	9.33	10.23	10.42
Sporting goods and musical instrument stores	4511	352	437	435	428	430	9.55	10.57	10.83
Book, periodical, and music stores	4512	180	249	227	219	209	8.91	9.49	9.53
General merchandise stores	452	2,500	2,820	2,812	2,822	2,844	9.22	10.10	10.32
Department stores	4521	1,494	1,755	1,684	1,621	1,613	9.59	10.42	10.67
Miscellaneous store retailers [5]	453	738	1,007	960	931	919	10.20	10.93	10.98
Florists	4531	121	130	122	113	107	8.95	9.53	9.71
Office supplies, stationery, and gift stores	4532	358	471	435	416	407	10.46	11.61	11.39
Nonstore retailers	454	419	492	444	427	425	13.22	13.77	13.87
Electronic shopping and mail-order houses	4541	157	257	224	218	223	13.38	13.53	13.35
Transportation and warehousing	48,49	3,476	4,410	4,224	4,185	4,250	15.05	16.25	16.53
Air transportation	481	529	614	564	528	515	(NA)	(NA)	(NA)
Scheduled air transportation	4811	503	570	520	485	470	(NA)	(NA)	(NA)
Rail transportation	482	272	232	218	218	224	(NA)	(NA)	(NA)
Water transportation	483	57	56	53	55	57	(NA)	(NA)	(NA)
Truck transportation	484	1,122	1,406	1,339	1,326	1,351	15.86	16.30	16.61
General freight trucking	4841	807	1,013	952	935	950	16.37	16.70	17.14
Specialized freight trucking	4842	315	393	388	390	401	14.51	15.25	15.28
Transit and ground passenger transportation	485	274	372	381	382	386	11.88	12.79	12.84
Pipeline transportation	486	60	46	42	40	39	19.86	23.03	23.94
Scenic and sightseeing transportation	487	16	28	26	27	27	12.49	14.02	13.67
Support activities for transportation	488	364	537	525	520	536	14.57	17.63	17.69
Freight transportation arrangement	4885	111	178	168	167	170	13.46	16.50	16.87
Couriers and messengers	492	375	605	561	562	561	13.51	15.68	15.45
Couriers	4921	340	546	507	510	510	13.92	16.58	16.09
Warehousing and storage	493	407	514	517	528	556	14.46	14.80	14.90
Utilities	22	740	601	596	577	570	22.75	24.77	25.62
Power generation and supply	2211	550	434	434	418	412	23.13	25.65	26.49
Natural gas distribution	2212	155	121	115	113	112	23.41	23.84	25.32
Water, sewage and other systems	2213	35	46	48	47	46	16.93	18.62	18.30

See footnotes at end of table.

U.S. Census Bureau, Statistical Abstract of the United States: 2006

Table 620. Nonfarm Industries—Employees and Earnings: 1990 to 2004—Con.

[Annual averages of monthly figures (109,487 represents 109,487,000). Covers all full- and part-time employees who worked during, or received pay for, any part of the pay period including the 12th of the month. See also headnote, Table 618]

Industry	2002 NAICS [1] code	All employees (1,000)					Average hourly earnings [2] (dollars)		
		1990	2000	2002	2003	2004	2000	2003	2004
Information.	51	2,688	3,631	3,395	3,188	3,138	19.07	21.01	21.42
Publishing industries, except Internet	511	871	1,035	964	925	910	20.18	21.93	23.43
Newspaper, book, and directory publishers.	5111	773	774	711	686	671	15.06	16.46	17.78
Software publishers	5112	98	261	253	239	239	28.48	33.78	36.90
Motion picture and sound recording industries.	512	255	383	388	376	389	21.25	21.32	19.90
Motion picture and video industries	5121	232	352	361	352	368	21.33	21.35	20.02
Broadcasting, except Internet	515	284	344	334	324	327	16.74	19.39	19.75
Radio and television broadcasting.	5151	232	253	241	238	241	17.13	20.24	20.49
Cable and other subscription programming.	5152	52	91	93	86	86	(NA)	(NA)	(NA)
Internet publishing and broadcasting.	516	17	51	34	29	31	(NA)	(NA)	(NA)
Telecommunications [5]	517	980	1,263	1,187	1,082	1,043	17.81	20.66	21.27
Wired telecommunications carriers.	5171	673	719	651	579	548	18.52	22.21	23.09
Wireless telecommunications carriers.	5172	36	186	197	190	189	14.41	17.91	18.36
Telecommunications resellers.	5173	180	214	180	155	150	19.99	21.66	21.94
Cable and other program distribution	5175	70	123	130	133	130	14.67	16.61	16.81
ISPs, search portals, and data processing	518	252	510	441	402	388	20.57	21.26	20.43
ISPs and Web search portals	5181	41	194	137	122	118	25.60	24.22	21.58
Data processing and related services	5182	211	316	304	280	271	16.97	19.91	19.93
Other information services.	519	30	46	47	49	51	10.68	14.67	16.00
Financial activities	(X)	6,614	7,687	7,847	7,977	8,052	14.98	17.14	17.53
Finance and insurance [5]	52	4,979	5,680	5,817	5,923	5,966	15.90	18.37	18.71
Credit intermediation and related activities	522	2,425	2,548	2,686	2,792	2,832	13.14	15.64	15.62
Depository credit intermediation.	5221	1,909	1,681	1,733	1,749	1,761	11.97	13.54	13.80
Commercial banking	52211	1,362	1,251	1,278	1,280	1,285	11.83	13.30	13.48
Nondepository credit intermediation	5222	398	644	695	750	768	15.30	19.82	19.32
Activities related to credit intermediation.	5223	119	222	258	294	303	15.39	17.08	16.28
Securities, commodity contracts, investments.	523	458	805	789	758	767	20.20	23.69	25.15
Securities and commodity contracts brokerage and exchanges	5232	338	566	528	493	494	20.07	23.42	25.74
Other financial investment activities	5239	120	239	261	264	273	20.48	24.21	24.11
Insurance carriers and related activities	524	2,016	2,221	2,233	2,266	2,260	17.37	19.88	20.39
Insurance carriers.	5241	1,338	1,433	1,413	1,429	1,403	17.92	20.50	21.19
Insurance agencies, brokerages, and related services	5242	678	788	820	837	857	16.28	18.75	18.96
Funds, trusts, and other financial vehicles	525	56	85	85	84	85	17.66	21.73	21.95
Real estate and rental and leasing [5]	53	1,635	2,007	2,030	2,054	2,086	12.14	13.32	13.88
Real estate.	531	1,107	1,312	1,353	1,384	1,417	12.24	13.54	14.21
Lessors of real estate	5311	564	607	606	604	601	11.16	12.68	13.09
Offices of real estate agents and brokers	5312	217	281	298	310	332	12.57	13.39	14.35
Activities related to real estate	5313	327	424	449	470	485	13.60	14.87	15.56
Rental and leasing services [5]	532	514	667	649	643	644	11.69	12.59	13.00
Automotive equipment rental and leasing	5321	163	208	195	193	198	10.70	11.96	12.57
Consumer goods rental	5322	220	292	288	288	281	9.53	10.12	10.72
Professional and business services	(X)	10,848	16,666	15,976	15,987	16,414	15.52	17.21	17.46
Professional and technical services	54	4,557	6,734	6,676	6,630	6,762	20.61	22.54	23.23
Legal services	5411	944	1,066	1,115	1,142	1,162	21.38	22.25	22.91
Accounting and bookkeeping services	5412	664	866	837	815	816	14.42	16.49	16.87
Architectural and engineering services	5413	942	1,238	1,246	1,227	1,261	20.49	22.50	23.24
Computer systems design and related services	5415	410	1,254	1,153	1,117	1,147	27.13	29.49	30.15
Management and technical consulting services	5416	324	705	734	745	779	20.86	23.58	23.60
Scientific research and development services	5417	494	515	538	539	548	21.39	25.24	26.88
Advertising and related services	5418	382	497	441	430	425	16.99	17.84	18.71
Other professional and technical services. . . .	5419	317	462	487	494	503	13.55	15.23	15.48
Management of companies & enterprises. . .	55	1,667	1,796	1,705	1,687	1,718	15.28	16.76	17.18
Administrative and waste services	56	4,624	8,136	7,595	7,670	7,934	11.66	13.00	12.90
Administrative and support services [5]	561	4,395	7,823	7,277	7,348	7,609	11.49	12.77	12.68
Office administrative services	5611	211	264	289	308	319	14.68	16.59	16.93
Employment services	5613	1,494	3,817	3,247	3,300	3,470	11.83	13.36	12.94
Temporary help services.	56132	1,156	2,636	2,194	2,224	2,393	11.79	12.63	12.07
Business support services	5614	505	787	757	750	755	11.08	12.21	12.53
Travel arrangement and reservation services	5615	250	299	252	235	226	12.72	14.47	14.05
Investigation and security services.	5616	507	689	724	712	730	9.78	10.88	11.29
Services to buildings and dwellings	5617	1,175	1,571	1,606	1,636	1,694	10.02	11.00	11.16
Waste management and remediation services	562	229	313	318	322	325	15.29	17.33	17.26

See footnotes at end of table.

Table 620. Nonfarm Industries—Employees and Earnings: 1990 to 2004—Con.

[Annual averages of monthly figures (109,487 represents 109,487,000). Covers all full- and part-time employees who worked during, or received pay for, any part of the pay period including the 12th of the month. See also headnote, Table 618]

Industry	2002 NAICS [1] code	All employees (1,000)					Average hourly earnings [2] (dollars)		
		1990	2000	2002	2003	2004	2000	2003	2004
Education and health services	(X)	10,984	15,109	16,199	16,588	16,954	13.95	15.64	16.16
Educational services	61	1,688	2,390	2,643	2,695	2,766	(NA)	(NA)	(NA)
Elementary and secondary schools.	6111	461	716	786	801	829	(NA)	(NA)	(NA)
Junior colleges	6112	44	79	84	79	84	(NA)	(NA)	(NA)
Colleges and universities	6113	939	1,196	1,339	1,361	1,378	(NA)	(NA)	(NA)
Business, computer, and management training	6114	60	86	82	81	80	(NA)	(NA)	(NA)
Technical and trade schools	6115	72	91	95	96	99	(NA)	(NA)	(NA)
Other schools and instruction.	6116	96	184	207	221	230	(NA)	(NA)	(NA)
Educational support services	6117	17	39	50	56	67	(NA)	(NA)	(NA)
Health care and social assistance	62	9,296	12,718	13,556	13,893	14,187	13.98	15.88	16.46
Ambulatory health care services [5]	621	2,842	4,320	4,633	4,786	4,946	14.99	16.87	17.44
Offices of physicians.	6211	1,278	1,840	1,968	2,003	2,054	15.65	17.91	18.41
Offices of dentists.	6212	513	688	725	744	760	15.96	18.38	18.96
Offices of other health practitioners	6213	276	438	486	503	523	14.24	15.54	16.00
Outpatient care centers	6214	261	386	413	427	446	15.29	17.68	18.57
Medical and diagnostic laboratories	6215	129	162	175	182	189	15.74	17.56	18.15
Home health care services.	6216	288	633	680	733	773	12.86	13.69	14.41
Hospitals [5]	622	3,513	3,954	4,160	4,245	4,294	16.71	19.37	20.31
General medical and surgical hospitals. .	6221	3,305	3,745	3,930	4,005	4,051	16.75	19.48	20.41
Psychiatric and substance abuse hospitals	6222	113	86	90	92	92	14.97	16.55	17.04
Nursing and residential care facilities [5] . . .	623	1,856	2,583	2,743	2,786	2,815	10.67	11.86	12.05
Nursing care facilities	6231	1,170	1,514	1,573	1,580	1,575	11.08	12.52	12.75
Residential mental health facilities.	6232	269	437	473	484	491	9.96	10.83	11.10
Community care facilities for the elderly	6233	330	478	532	558	583	9.83	10.84	10.89
Social assistance	624	1,085	1,860	2,020	2,075	2,133	9.78	10.82	11.06
Individual and family services	6241	389	678	773	813	853	10.57	11.84	12.14
Emergency and other relief services . . .	6242	67	117	127	128	131	10.95	12.01	12.79
Vocational rehabilitation services.	6243	242	370	376	379	381	9.57	10.79	10.78
Child day care services	6244	388	696	744	755	767	8.88	9.54	9.76
Leisure and hospitality	(X)	9,288	11,862	11,986	12,173	12,479	8.11	8.76	8.91
Arts, entertainment, and recreation	71	1,132	1,788	1,783	1,813	1,833	10.68	11.99	12.17
Performing arts and spectator sports.	711	273	382	364	372	365	13.11	16.71	17.35
Museums, historical sites, zoos, and parks.	712	68	110	114	115	117	12.21	12.62	12.92
Amusements, gambling, and recreation . . .	713	791	1,296	1,305	1,327	1,351	9.86	10.60	10.72
Accommodations and food services	72	8,156	10,074	10,203	10,360	10,646	7.68	8.22	8.36
Accommodations.	721	1,616	1,884	1,779	1,775	1,796	9.48	10.27	10.58
Traveler and other longer-term accommodations	7211	1,582	1,837	1,738	1,724	1,745	9.49	10.29	10.62
RV parks and recreational camps	7212	34	47	41	52	51	9.03	9.42	9.18
Food services and drinking places	722	6,540	8,189	8,425	8,584	8,850	7.18	7.73	7.84
Full-service restaurants	7221	3,070	3,845	3,992	4,089	4,226	7.15	7.77	7.95
Limited-service eating places	7222	2,765	3,462	3,537	3,602	3,727	6.85	7.31	7.36
Special food services	7223	392	491	513	516	524	9.45	10.29	10.42
Drinking places, alcoholic beverages . . .	7224	312	391	382	378	373	7.24	7.61	7.77
Other services	81	4,261	5,168	5,372	5,401	5,431	12.73	13.84	13.98
Repair and maintenance	811	1,009	1,242	1,247	1,234	1,228	13.28	14.31	14.38
Automotive repair and maintenance	8111	659	888	900	894	891	12.45	13.51	13.68
Personal and laundry services.	812	1,120	1,243	1,257	1,264	1,274	10.18	11.44	11.69
Personal care services	8121	430	490	529	542	561	10.18	11.64	12.07
Death care services	8122	123	136	140	140	138	13.04	14.32	15.04
Dry-cleaning and laundry services	8123	371	388	368	358	352	9.17	9.86	10.04
Dry-cleaning and laundry services, except coin-operated.	81232	215	211	197	190	184	8.14	8.75	8.99
Other personal services	8129	196	229	221	223	223	10.52	12.07	11.77
Pet care services, except veterinary . .	81291	23	31	36	38	40	(NA)	(NA)	(NA)
Membership associations & organizations [5] . .	813	2,132	2,683	2,868	2,904	2,929	13.66	14.67	14.78
Social advocacy organizations	8133	126	143	171	175	178	12.08	13.97	13.74
Civic and social organizations	8134	377	404	412	413	410	9.85	10.67	10.86
Professional and similar organizations. . . .	8139	379	473	501	503	517	15.98	18.20	17.78
Government	92	18,415	20,790	21,513	21,583	21,618	(NA)	(NA)	(NA)
Federal.	(X)	3,196	2,865	2,766	2,761	2,728	(NA)	(NA)	(NA)
State government.	(X)	4,305	4,786	5,029	5,002	4,985	(NA)	(NA)	(NA)
Local government.	(X)	10,914	13,139	13,718	13,820	13,905	(NA)	(NA)	(NA)

NA Not available.　　X Not applicable.　　[1] Based on the North American Industry Classification System, 2002 (NAICS). See text, this section.　　[2] Production workers in the goods-producing industries and non-supervisory workers in service-producing industries. See footnotes 3 and 4.　　[3] Natural resources and mining, construction, and manufacturing.　　[4] Trade, transportation and utilities, information, financial activities, professional and business services, education and health services, leisure and hospitality, other services, and government.　　[5] Includes other industries not shown separately.

Source: U.S. Bureau of Labor Statistics, the Current Employment Statistics program Internet site <http://www.bls.gov/ces/home.htm>

Table 621. **Private Sector Job Gains and Losses: 1992 to 2004**

[In thousands (455 represents 455,000). **For the three months ending in month shown.** Based on the Quarterly Census of Employment and Wages; for details see source. Minus sign (-) indicates loss]

Year and month ending	Net change [1]	Gross job gains			Gross job losses		
		Total	Expanding establish-ments	Opening establish-ments	Total	Contracting establish-ments	Closing establish-ments
1992:							
September...........	455	7,377	5,632	1,745	6,922	5,351	1,571
December...........	216	7,101	5,465	1,636	6,885	5,487	1,398
1993:							
March.............	313	7,309	5,410	1,899	6,996	5,354	1,642
June..............	786	7,330	5,794	1,536	6,544	5,136	1,408
September..........	874	7,523	5,881	1,642	6,649	5,316	1,333
December..........	641	7,436	5,840	1,596	6,795	5,420	1,375
1994:							
March.............	517	7,400	5,807	1,593	6,883	5,435	1,448
June..............	1,021	7,807	6,060	1,747	6,786	5,295	1,491
September..........	1,175	7,972	6,227	1,745	6,797	5,493	1,304
December..........	507	7,630	5,998	1,632	7,123	5,647	1,476
1995:							
March.............	746	7,782	6,129	1,653	7,036	5,660	1,376
June..............	402	7,714	6,017	1,697	7,312	5,839	1,473
September..........	771	7,970	6,291	1,679	7,199	5,680	1,519
December..........	407	7,877	6,153	1,724	7,470	5,934	1,536
1996:							
March.............	460	7,943	6,190	1,753	7,483	5,957	1,526
June..............	642	8,080	6,302	1,778	7,438	5,894	1,544
September..........	632	8,189	6,326	1,863	7,557	5,998	1,559
December..........	861	8,278	6,409	1,869	7,417	5,889	1,528
1997:							
March.............	799	8,292	6,448	1,844	7,493	5,900	1,593
June..............	594	8,098	6,342	1,756	7,504	5,925	1,579
September..........	854	8,593	6,680	1,913	7,739	5,981	1,758
December..........	702	8,731	6,727	2,004	8,029	6,068	1,961
1998:							
March.............	747	8,788	6,633	2,155	8,041	6,107	1,934
June..............	666	8,722	6,569	2,153	8,056	6,218	1,838
September..........	659	8,539	6,574	1,965	7,880	6,161	1,719
December..........	759	8,576	6,778	1,798	7,817	6,060	1,757
1999:							
March.............	380	8,744	6,733	2,011	8,364	6,466	1,898
June..............	569	8,800	6,788	2,012	8,231	6,419	1,812
September..........	548	8,817	6,871	1,946	8,269	6,397	1,872
December..........	1,105	9,144	7,112	2,032	8,039	6,264	1,775
2000:							
March.............	818	8,906	6,988	1,918	8,088	6,361	1,727
June..............	541	8,764	6,975	1,789	8,223	6,509	1,714
September..........	146	8,724	6,834	1,890	8,578	6,719	1,859
December..........	336	8,690	6,862	1,828	8,354	6,582	1,772
2001:							
March.............	-101	8,555	6,768	1,787	8,656	6,756	1,900
June..............	-771	8,254	6,439	1,815	9,025	7,149	1,876
September..........	-1,380	7,749	5,990	1,759	9,129	7,174	1,955
December..........	-871	7,893	6,055	1,838	8,764	6,995	1,769
2002:							
March.............	-1	8,128	6,324	1,804	8,129	6,400	1,729
June..............	-80	8,050	6,246	1,804	8,130	6,411	1,719
September..........	-211	7,763	6,083	1,680	7,974	6,345	1,629
December..........	-175	7,702	6,059	1,643	7,877	6,267	1,610
2003							
March.............	-404	7,472	5,932	1,540	7,876	6,321	1,555
June..............	-142	7,560	6,033	1,527	7,702	6,138	1,564
September..........	72	7,396	5,897	1,499	7,324	5,893	1,431
December..........	344	7,646	6,063	1,583	7,302	5,816	1,486
2004							
March.............	435	7,745	6,231	1,514	7,310	5,871	1,439
June..............	594	7,857	6,292	1,565	7,263	5,726	1,537
September..........	191	7,789	6,123	1,666	7,598	5,953	1,645
December..........	869	8,081	6,365	1,716	7,212	5,727	1,485

[1] Difference between the total gross job gains and total gross job losses.

Source: U.S. Bureau of Labor Statistics, *Business Employment Dynamics: Fourth Quarter 2004*, USDL 05-1562, August 18, 2005. See Internet site: <http://www.bls.gov/bdm/home.htm>

Table 622. Annual Indexes of Output Per Hour for Selected NAICS Industries: 1987 to 2003

[For a discussion of productivity measures, see text, this section. Minus sign (-) indicates decrease]

Industry	2002 NAICS code [1]	Indexes (1997 = 100)						Average annual percent change [2]
		1987	1990	1995	2000	2002	2003	
Mining:.	21	85.5	85.1	101.7	111.2	113.9	116.2	1.9
Oil and gas extraction	211	80.1	75.7	95.3	119.4	124.0	130.5	3.1
Mining, except oil and gas	212	69.8	79.3	94.0	106.8	111.4	113.6	3.1
Utilities:								
Power generation and supply	2211	65.6	71.1	88.5	107.0	102.9	105.1	3.0
Natural gas distribution	2212	67.8	71.4	89.0	113.2	115.4	114.3	3.3
Manufacturing:								
Sugar and confectionery products	3113	87.6	89.5	93.2	109.8	108.2	112.2	1.6
Fruit and vegetable preserving and specialty	3114	92.4	87.6	98.3	111.8	126.7	121.8	1.7
Dairy products	3115	82.7	91.1	97.6	95.9	105.0	110.1	1.8
Animal slaughtering and processing	3116	97.4	94.3	99.0	102.6	107.8	107.0	0.6
Bakeries and tortilla manufacturing	3118	100.9	94.5	100.7	108.3	110.7	110.9	0.6
Other food products	3119	97.5	92.4	104.0	112.7	113.6	118.9	1.2
Beverages	3121	77.1	87.6	103.2	90.8	99.8	105.0	2.0
Fabric mills	3132	68.0	75.3	95.5	110.1	125.7	136.1	4.4
Textile furnishings mills	3141	91.2	88.0	92.3	104.5	103.5	111.9	1.3
Cut-and-sew apparel	3152	69.8	70.1	85.2	119.8	110.9	123.5	3.6
Sawmills and wood preservation	3211	77.6	79.4	90.4	105.4	114.4	120.6	2.8
Plywood and engineered wood products	3212	99.8	102.9	101.5	98.9	110.3	106.5	0.4
Other wood products	3219	103.2	105.5	99.8	103.1	114.2	112.9	0.6
Pulp, paper, and paperboard mills	3221	81.7	84.0	98.4	116.3	133.1	138.0	3.3
Converted paper products	3222	89.0	90.1	97.2	101.1	105.5	109.3	1.3
Printing and related support activities	3231	97.7	97.6	98.8	104.6	110.0	110.7	0.8
Petroleum and coal products	3241	72.1	76.1	89.9	113.5	117.9	118.9	3.2
Basic chemicals	3251	94.6	93.4	91.3	117.5	124.0	132.0	2.1
Resin, rubber, and artificial fibers	3252	77.4	76.4	95.4	109.8	123.0	120.9	2.8
Pharmaceuticals and medicines	3254	87.3	91.3	95.9	95.6	96.0	98.6	0.8
Soap, cleaning compounds, and toiletries	3256	84.4	84.8	96.1	102.8	124.5	114.6	1.9
Other chemical products and preparations	3259	75.4	77.8	93.5	119.7	118.9	122.7	3.1
Plastics products	3261	83.1	85.2	94.5	112.3	122.7	127.6	2.7
Rubber products	3262	75.5	83.5	92.9	101.7	107.9	111.7	2.5
Glass and glass products	3272	82.3	79.1	87.5	108.2	107.4	115.2	2.1
Cement and concrete products	3273	93.6	96.6	99.7	101.6	102.4	106.9	0.8
Iron and steel mills and ferroalloy production	3311	64.8	70.2	90.0	106.0	123.8	125.5	4.2
Foundries	3315	81.4	86.5	93.1	103.6	117.0	117.5	2.3
Forging and stamping	3321	85.4	89.0	93.9	121.1	125.3	132.9	2.8
Architectural and structural metals	3323	88.7	87.9	93.3	100.7	106.3	109.1	1.3
Boilers, tanks, and shipping containers	3324	86.0	90.1	97.3	94.7	99.7	102.0	1.1
Machine shops and threaded products	3327	76.9	79.2	98.3	108.2	115.6	115.8	2.6
Coating, engraving, and heat treating metals	3328	75.5	81.3	102.2	105.5	115.2	116.9	2.8
Other fabricated metal products	3329	91.0	86.5	96.3	99.9	106.5	111.2	1.3
Agriculture, construction, and mining machinery	3331	74.6	83.3	95.4	100.3	103.7	116.6	2.8
Industrial machinery	3332	75.1	81.6	97.1	130.0	106.0	109.0	2.4
Commercial and service industry machinery	3333	86.9	95.6	103.6	100.9	102.0	109.7	1.5
HVAC and commercial refrigeration equipment	3334	84.0	90.6	96.4	107.9	117.6	127.5	2.6
Metalworking machinery	3335	85.1	86.5	99.2	106.1	115.6	117.4	2.0
Turbine and power transmission equipment	3336	80.2	85.9	91.3	114.9	132.7	141.8	3.6
Other general purpose machinery	3339	83.5	86.8	94.0	113.7	117.6	124.5	2.5
Computer and peripheral equipment	3341	11.0	14.7	49.9	234.9	297.3	379.6	24.8
Communications equipment	3342	39.8	48.4	74.4	164.1	128.1	142.2	8.3
Semiconductors and electronic components	3344	17.0	21.9	63.8	232.4	264.1	322.1	20.2
Electronic instruments	3345	70.2	78.5	97.9	116.7	119.3	128.5	3.9
Household appliances	3352	73.3	76.5	91.8	117.2	136.0	151.6	4.6
Electrical equipment	3353	68.7	73.6	98.0	99.4	103.2	104.9	2.7
Other electrical equipment and components	3359	78.7	76.0	92.0	119.6	115.6	116.9	2.5
Motor vehicles	3361	75.4	85.6	88.5	109.7	126.3	138.7	3.9
Motor vehicle bodies and trailers	3362	85.0	75.9	97.4	98.8	105.5	109.3	1.6
Motor vehicle parts	3363	78.7	76.0	92.3	112.3	130.7	135.9	3.5
Aerospace products and parts	3364	86.5	89.1	94.9	103.2	117.8	121.7	2.2
Ship and boat building	3366	95.5	99.6	93.1	121.9	131.0	133.8	2.1
Household and institutional furniture	3371	85.2	88.2	97.2	101.9	115.7	118.2	2.1
Office furniture and fixtures	3372	85.8	82.2	84.9	100.2	115.2	125.3	2.4
Medical equipment and supplies	3391	76.3	82.9	96.6	114.6	128.6	137.1	3.7
Other miscellaneous manufacturing	3399	85.4	90.5	95.9	113.6	129.5	135.3	2.9
Wholesale trade	42	73.5	78.5	93.4	115.7	124.3	128.6	3.6
Durable goods	423	62.1	66.7	88.8	120.2	127.5	133.7	4.9
Nondurable goods	424	93.3	97.9	99.6	106.3	112.0	117.1	1.4
Electronic markets and agents and brokers	425	65.7	73.2	92.6	126.5	139.7	131.0	4.4
Retail trade	44-45	80.8	83.1	94.6	114.8	123.2	129.8	3.0
Motor vehicle and parts dealers	441	85.6	90.7	97.6	107.6	111.1	112.9	1.7
Automobile dealers	4411	87.1	92.4	97.7	106.0	107.2	106.4	1.3
Other motor vehicle dealers	4412	73.3	73.3	91.0	110.3	117.5	131.6	3.7
Auto parts, accessories, and tire stores	4413	78.4	86.3	98.7	114.2	120.0	130.0	3.2
Furniture and home furnishings stores	442	76.7	80.1	94.7	116.3	124.8	135.3	3.6
Furniture stores	4421	76.3	83.3	93.5	113.8	124.3	131.4	3.5
Home furnishings stores	4422	77.0	75.8	96.1	119.5	125.6	140.4	3.8
Electronics and appliance stores	443	36.9	45.9	89.4	179.7	242.6	311.0	14.3
Building material and garden supply stores	444	77.4	81.5	93.1	114.4	120.8	129.3	3.3
Building material and supplies dealers	4441	78.2	83.0	94.2	115.7	121.6	130.4	3.2
Lawn and garden equipment & supplies stores	4442	73.1	73.8	86.8	105.9	115.1	121.6	3.2

See footnotes at end of table.

Table 622. **Annual Indexes of Output Per Hour for Selected NAICS Industries: 1987 to 2003—Con.**

[For a discussion of productivity measures, see text, this section. Minus sign (-) indicates decrease]

Industry	2002 NAICS code [1]	Indexes (1997 = 100)						Average annual percent change [2]
		1987	1990	1995	2000	2002	2003	
Food and beverage stores	445	109.6	106.6	101.9	104.5	109.8	114.3	0.3
Grocery stores	4451	110.6	106.5	102.8	104.5	110.5	113.7	0.2
Specialty food stores	4452	127.0	119.3	97.6	102.0	108.0	123.2	-0.2
Beer, wine and liquor stores	4453	95.6	98.7	95.1	112.1	112.8	127.2	1.8
Health and personal care stores	446	85.8	92.9	91.6	110.6	119.9	129.5	2.6
Gasoline stations	447	83.0	83.7	99.7	107.0	121.8	117.6	2.2
Clothing and clothing accessories stores	448	65.8	69.2	92.8	123.2	130.2	138.9	4.8
Clothing stores	4481	66.6	69.1	91.5	124.6	134.8	141.2	4.8
Shoe stores	4482	65.3	71.4	96.7	111.2	123.5	132.1	4.5
Jewelry, luggage, and leather goods stores	4483	63.6	67.8	95.7	128.6	117.8	135.3	4.8
Sporting goods, hobby, book, & music stores	451	73.7	81.1	94.3	122.8	131.7	131.7	3.7
Sporting goods & musical instrument stores	4511	69.4	78.3	94.0	129.7	136.7	137.8	4.4
Book, periodical, and music stores	4512	84.4	87.3	95.0	110.1	122.7	121.1	2.3
General merchandise stores	452	73.7	75.3	92.0	120.1	129.2	135.6	3.9
Department stores	4521	87.7	84.2	94.7	106.7	103.2	106.6	1.2
Other general merchandise stores	4529	54.8	61.4	87.2	145.9	176.5	184.6	7.9
Miscellaneous store retailers	453	65.7	69.5	88.8	110.7	114.5	120.8	3.9
Florists	4531	77.9	73.3	82.5	114.8	117.9	130.0	3.2
Office supplies, stationery and gift stores	4532	56.6	61.1	91.7	125.3	135.8	145.4	6.1
Used merchandise stores	4533	78.5	82.2	86.2	118.0	129.2	131.1	3.3
Other miscellaneous store retailers	4539	74.9	81.7	88.9	96.4	93.2	99.2	1.8
Nonstore retailers	454	52.7	56.4	80.0	150.1	175.1	203.0	8.8
Electronic shopping and mail-order houses	4541	40.0	43.9	71.3	158.1	204.8	242.2	11.9
Vending machine operators	4542	98.7	97.2	88.5	127.1	117.8	128.4	1.7
Direct selling establishments	4543	74.9	77.8	94.3	114.6	117.2	127.8	3.4
Transportation and warehousing:								
Air transportation	481	81.1	77.5	95.3	98.2	102.0	112.1	2.0
Line-haul railroads	482111	58.9	69.8	92.0	114.3	131.9	142.0	5.7
General freight trucking, long-distance	48412	86.8	87.5	95.2	101.0	106.6	108.8	1.4
Used household and office goods moving	48421	102.3	115.5	102.3	100.2	81.8	88.7	-0.9
Postal service	491	92.4	96.1	98.3	104.9	107.0	108.7	1.0
Couriers and messengers	492	147.8	138.8	101.5	122.1	131.4	134.4	-0.6
Information:								
Newspaper, book, and directory publishers	5111	104.8	96.6	93.4	106.1	102.6	105.8	0.1
Software publishers	5112	10.2	28.5	73.2	112.2	122.5	138.4	17.7
Motion picture and video exhibition	51213	90.4	109.2	99.8	107.2	100.7	104.8	0.9
Broadcasting, except Internet	515	99.0	97.9	103.4	105.9	106.5	108.4	0.6
Radio and television broadcasting	5151	97.2	97.2	105.9	95.7	97.1	99.0	0.1
Cable and other subscription programming	5152	105.9	100.6	93.2	140.2	135.4	138.0	1.7
Wired telecommunications carriers	5171	56.1	65.3	87.2	119.2	129.0	134.7	5.6
Wireless telecommunications carriers	5172	79.4	72.1	90.2	142.8	218.9	247.7	7.4
Cable and other program distribution	5175	105.4	100.3	93.5	89.3	92.2	97.2	-0.5
Finance and insurance:								
Commercial banking	52211	72.8	80.7	95.6	100.8	98.6	101.5	2.1
Real estate and rental leasing:								
Passenger car rental	532111	90.9	88.7	100.2	112.1	114.2	120.4	1.8
Truck, trailer and RV rental and leasing	53212	60.7	69.0	88.6	105.1	105.1	105.7	3.5
Video tape and disc rental	53223	71.5	92.9	115.7	140.6	135.8	154.0	4.9
Professional and technical services:								
Tax preparation services	541213	89.9	91.9	96.9	101.3	115.9	114.9	1.5
Advertising agencies	54181	94.3	105.2	100.7	119.5	128.1	138.3	2.4
Photography studios, portrait	541921	104.8	107.7	118.7	101.6	103.3	113.2	0.5
Administrative and waste management:								
Travel agencies	56151	91.4	95.6	93.6	120.0	130.8	151.9	3.2
Janitorial services	56172	70.2	85.4	90.0	111.1	104.4	115.9	3.2
Health care and social assistance:								
Medical and diagnostic laboratories	62151	(NA)	(NA)	91.2	134.5	142.7	136.8	5.2
Medical laboratories	621511	(NA)	(NA)	91.4	125.1	126.3	117.0	3.1
Diagnostic imaging centers	621512	(NA)	(NA)	90.8	153.2	173.2	172.0	8.3
Accommodation and food services:								
Traveler accommodations	7211	83.8	80.8	97.9	113.0	113.2	115.6	2.0
Food services and drinking places	722	96.5	102.7	100.4	103.8	105.0	108.4	0.7
Full-service restaurants	7221	91.9	99.1	96.3	101.1	102.2	105.3	0.9
Limited-service eating places	7222	96.0	103.1	104.4	105.4	108.2	111.5	0.9
Special food services	7223	100.0	108.1	98.8	111.3	104.3	107.4	0.4
Drinking places, alcoholic beverages	7224	136.2	123.0	104.8	103.0	105.7	118.0	-0.9
Other services:								
Automotive repair and maintenance	8111	85.9	90.6	102.4	108.5	103.5	104.3	1.2
Hair, nail and skin care services	81211	83.3	81.5	92.8	106.6	110.0	124.8	2.6
Funeral homes and funeral services	81221	100.2	93.1	100.7	94.9	93.1	95.5	-0.3
Dry cleaning and laundry services	8123	96.4	94.2	99.1	110.9	114.0	110.1	0.8
Photofinishing	81292	100.0	110.8	106.5	84.0	96.0	91.6	-0.5

NA Not available. [1] North American Industry Classification System (NAICS), 2002; see text, this section. [2] Average annual percent change, 1987 to 2003, based on compound rate formula. For NAICS industries 62151, 621511, and 621512, annual percent changes are for 1995-2003.

Source: U.S. Bureau of Labor Statistics. Latest data available at: <http://www.bls.gov/lpc/home.htm> (accessed 26 August 2005).

Table 623. Productivity and Related Measures: 1980 to 2004

[See text, this section. Minus sign (-) indicates decrease]

Item	1980	1985	1990	1995	2000	2001	2002	2003	2004
INDEXES (1992 = 100)									
Output per hour, business sector	79.1	87.1	94.5	101.6	116.1	119.0	124.2	129.6	134.7
Nonfarm business	80.6	87.4	94.5	102.1	115.6	118.5	123.6	129.0	134.2
Manufacturing	(NA)	(NA)	92.9	109.9	134.1	136.9	147.3	154.8	163.0
Output, [1] business sector	68.8	82.2	96.9	111.4	140.5	141.0	143.5	149.0	156.7
Nonfarm business	69.2	82.2	97.1	111.8	140.8	141.3	143.9	149.4	157.3
Manufacturing	(NA)	(NA)	97.6	115.0	138.6	132.3	132.2	132.2	138.6
Hours, [2] business sector	87.0	94.3	102.6	109.6	121.0	118.4	115.6	115.0	116.3
Nonfarm business	85.9	94.0	102.7	109.4	121.8	119.3	116.3	115.8	117.2
Manufacturing	(NA)	(NA)	105.0	104.6	103.4	96.6	89.8	85.4	85.0
Compensation per hour, [3] business sector	54.1	72.5	90.6	105.9	134.5	140.2	144.6	150.4	157.8
Nonfarm business	54.4	72.6	90.4	106.0	134.0	139.3	143.8	149.6	156.8
Manufacturing	(NA)	(NA)	90.5	107.3	134.7	137.8	147.0	159.7	167.3
Real hourly compensation, [3] business sector	89.1	92.0	96.3	98.8	111.9	113.4	115.1	117.1	119.6
Nonfarm business	89.5	92.2	96.0	98.9	111.4	112.6	114.5	116.4	118.9
Manufacturing	(NA)	(NA)	96.1	100.1	112.0	111.5	117.0	124.3	126.8
Unit labor costs, [4] business sector	68.4	83.2	96.0	104.2	115.9	117.8	116.4	116.1	117.2
Nonfarm business	67.5	83.1	95.7	103.7	115.9	117.5	116.3	116.0	116.9
Manufacturing	(NA)	(NA)	97.3	97.6	100.5	100.7	99.8	103.2	102.6
ANNUAL PERCENT CHANGE [5]									
Output per hour, business sector	-0.2	2.3	2.0	0.2	2.8	2.5	4.3	4.4	3.9
Nonfarm business	-0.2	1.5	1.9	0.5	2.7	2.5	4.3	4.3	4.0
Manufacturing	(NA)	(NA)	2.9	3.6	4.7	2.1	7.5	5.2	5.3
Output, [1] business sector	-1.1	4.6	1.5	2.9	3.9	0.3	1.8	-3.8	5.1
Nonfarm business	-1.0	4.2	1.5	3.2	3.8	0.4	1.8	3.8	5.3
Manufacturing	(NA)	(NA)	0.3	4.5	3.0	-4.6	-0.1	0.0	4.8
Hours, [2] business sector	-0.9	2.3	-0.4	2.7	1.1	-2.2	-2.4	-0.5	1.2
Nonfarm business	-0.8	2.6	-0.4	2.7	1.1	-2.0	-2.5	-0.5	1.2
Manufacturing	(NA)	(NA)	-2.5	0.8	-1.6	-6.5	-7.1	-4.9	-0.4
Compensation per hour, [3] business sector	10.8	4.8	6.3	2.1	7.0	4.2	3.1	4.0	4.9
Nonfarm business	10.8	4.6	6.1	2.1	7.0	4.0	3.2	4.0	4.8
Manufacturing	(NA)	(NA)	4.4	1.9	9.2	2.3	6.6	8.7	4.7
Real hourly compensation, [3] business sector	-0.2	1.4	1.2	-0.3	3.5	1.4	1.5	1.7	2.2
Nonfarm business	-0.2	1.2	1.1	-0.3	3.6	1.1	1.6	1.7	2.1
Manufacturing	(NA)	(NA)	-0.5	-0.5	5.6	-0.5	5.0	6.2	2.0
Unit labor costs, [4] business sector	11.0	2.5	4.1	1.9	4.0	1.6	-1.1	-0.3	1.0
Nonfarm business	11.0	3.0	4.1	1.6	4.2	1.4	-1.1	-0.3	0.8
Manufacturing	(NA)	(NA)	1.5	-1.7	4.2	0.2	-0.8	3.3	-0.5

NA Not available. [1] Refers to gross sectoral product, annual weighted. [2] Hours at work of all persons engaged in the business and nonfarm-business sectors (employees, proprietors, and unpaid family workers); employees' and proprietors' hours in manufacturing. [3] Wages and salaries of employees plus employers' and contributions for social insurance and private benefit plans. Also includes an estimate of same for self-employed. Real compensation deflated by the consumer price index for all urban consumers, see text, Section 14. [4] Hourly compensation divided by output per hour. [5] All changes are from the immediate prior year.

Source: U.S. Bureau of Labor Statistics, *Productivity and Costs, News* USDL 05-964, June 2, 2005; and Internet site <http://www.bls.gov/lpc/home.htm>.

Table 624. Employed Persons Using Computers at Work by Sex and Occupation: 2001

[In percent, except as indicated (135,089 represents 135,089,000). As of September. For persons 16 years old and over, except as indicated. Based on the Current Population Survey and subject to sampling error; see Appendix III and source]

Characteristic	Total employed (1,000)	Total using a computer at work (1,000)	Percent of employed	Word processing [1]	Internet or e-mail	Calendar or scheduling	Spreadsheets or databases	Graphics or design	Programming
Total, 16 years and over	135,089	72,277	53.5	67.0	71.8	52.9	62.3	28.8	15.2
Sex: Male	72,306	34.663	47.9	64.3	75.1	55.2	64.9	32.0	20.4
Women	62,784	37,614	59.9	69.4	68.8	50.9	59.9	25.8	10.5
Occupation:									
Managerial and professional	41,936	33,374	79.6	78.3	82.7	60.8	70.3	37.2	18.6
Executive, administrative, and managerial	20,279	16,297	80.4	79.0	83.5	65.3	76.9	34.4	16.6
Professional specialty	21,657	17,077	78.9	77.6	81.9	56.5	63.9	39.9	20.5
Technical, sales, and administrative support	38,761	26.056	67.2	62.6	67.3	48.4	59.7	22.5	12.4
Technicians and related support	4,617	3,462	75.0	58.5	70.4	52.3	59.3	29.5	27.0
Sales occupations	15,905	9,173	57.7	59.9	69.3	48.6	60.1	25.6	11.1
Administrative support, including clerical	18,238	13,421	73.6	65.6	65.1	47.2	59.6	18.5	9.6
Service occupations	18,279	4,259	23.3	52.6	51.1	45.7	43.8	17.2	8.9
Precision production, craft, and repair	14,850	4,447	29.9	46.5	59.9	45.4	51.7	23.7	17.4
Operators, fabricators, and laborers	17,737	3,465	19.5	35.7	43.1	32.4	41.2	17.1	9.5
Farming, forestry, and fishing	3,527	675	19.1	60.9	67.1	43.7	61.3	21.7	10.6

[1] Or desktop publishing.

Source: U.S. Bureau of Labor Statistics, *Computer and Internet Use at Work, 2001, News*, USDL 02-601, October 23, 2002. See Internet site <http://www.bls.gov/bls/newsrels.htm#OEUS>.

Table 625. **Average Hours per Day Worked by Employed Persons: 2003**

[145,466 represents 145,466,000]. For the civilian noninstitutional population 15 years old and over. Based on the American Time Use Survey, a survey conducted continuously throughout the year, and subject to sampling error; see source for details]

Characteristic	Total employed (1,000)	Employed persons who worked on their diary day						
		Number (1,000)	Percent of employed	Hours of work	Worked at workplace		Worked at home [1]	
					Percent of employed [2]	Hours of work	Percent of employed [2]	Hours of work
Total...............	145,466	98,069	67.4	7.59	87.0	7.83	18.9	2.54
Work status:								
Full-time workers [3]......	112,347	80,033	71.2	8.09	88.8	8.22	18.3	2.60
Part-time workers [3]......	33,120	18,035	54.5	5.40	79.3	5.86	21.6	2.29
Male...........	78,092	55,288	70.8	8.01	88.2	8.21	18.6	2.50
Full-time workers [3]......	66,243	48,534	73.3	8.33	89.5	8.45	18.4	2.52
Part-time workers [3]......	11,848	6,754	57.0	5.74	79.1	6.29	20.0	2.35
Female...........	67,374	42,781	63.5	7.06	85.6	7.31	19.4	2.58
Full-time workers [3]......	46,103	31,500	68.3	7.72	87.7	7.87	18.2	2.73
Part-time workers [3]......	21,271	11,281	53.0	5.19	79.5	5.60	22.5	2.25
Jobholding status:								
Single jobholders.......	131,462	86,928	66.1	7.57	87.8	7.83	17.0	2.46
Multiple jobholders......	14,005	11,141	79.6	7.79	81.4	7.78	33.6	2.84
Educational attainment: [4]								
Less than high school....	10,830	7,116	65.7	7.71	91.8	7.80	9.3	(B)
High school diploma [5]....	38,089	25,623	67.3	7.89	90.5	7.90	12.8	3.28
Some college..........	32,748	22,338	68.2	7.69	87.4	7.92	18.9	2.49
BA degree or higher.....	41,004	29,725	72.5	7.50	80.1	7.98	32.5	2.33

B Percent not shown where base is less than 800,000. [1] Represents doing activities that were "part of one's job." [2] Percent of employed who worked on their diary day. [3] Full-time workers usually worked 35 or more hours per week at all jobs combined; part-time workers fewer than 35 hours per week. [4] For those 25 years old and over. [5] Or equivalent.

Source: U.S. Bureau of Labor Statistics, *Time Use Survey—First Results Announced by BLS, News*, USDL 04-1797, September 14, 2004. See Internet site <http://www.bls.gov/tus/home.htm>.

Table 626. **Adults in Selected Work-Related Informal Learning Activities: 2000–01**

[(198,803 represents 198,803,000). For the civilian noninstitutional population 16 years old and over not enrolled in elementary or secondary school. Based on the Adult Education and Lifelong Learning Survey of the National Household Education Survey Program and subject to sampling error; see source and Appendix III for details]

Characteristic	Total adults (1,000)	Adults participating in work-related informal learning activities (percent)						
		Any activities	Self-paced study with books [1]	Self-paced study with software	Informal presentations [2]	Attended conferences [3]	Read journals [4]	Received supervised training [5]
Total...............	198,803	63	30	21	20	25	43	46
Age:								
16 to 30 years old..........	46,905	72	36	24	21	26	38	58
31 to 40 years old..........	41,778	71	35	25	24	30	50	46
41 to 50 years old..........	41,255	73	37	28	25	31	54	43
51 to 65 years old..........	39,523	58	26	20	18	24	44	35
65 years old and over.......	29,342	28	9	5	4	6	22	22
Sex:								
Male.................	94,955	67	34	23	21	29	48	44
Female................	103,848	59	27	20	18	21	38	49
Educational attainment:								
Less than high school.......	31,343	34	16	5	4	8	16	35
High school diploma or equivalent..............	64,606	52	22	14	12	16	28	40
Some college............	52,559	72	36	27	21	25	48	52
BA degree or higher.........	50,295	84	42	36	38	46	73	50
Employment/occupation:								
Employed in the past 12 months:								
Professional or managerial...	42,230	91	47	39	41	52	77	49
Sales, service, or support...	65,298	73	36	25	21	27	43	48
Trades...............	37,722	62	29	15	14	17	33	38
Not employed in the past 12 months..............	53,553	28	11	8	4	6	22	(X)

X Not applicable. [1] Includes procedure manuals and video tapes. [2] Such as "brown bag" events. [3] Includes conventions. [4] Professional journals or magazines. [5] Asked to those who were employed in the prior 12 months. Includes mentoring.

Source: U.S. National Center for Education Statistics, NCES 2004-050, September 2004.

Table 627. Annual Total Compensation and Wages and Salary Accruals Per Full-Time Equivalent Employee by Industry: 2000 to 2003

[In dollars. Wage and salary accruals include executives' compensation, bonuses, tips, and payments-in-kind; total compensation includes in-addition-to wages and salaries, employer contributions for social insurance, employer contributions to private and welfare funds, director's fees, jury and witness fees, etc. Based on the 1997 North American Industry Classification System (NAICS); see text, this section]

Industry	Annual total compensation				Annual wages and salary			
	2000	2001	2002	2003	2000	2001	2002	2003
Domestic industries	46,407	47,523	49,045	51,024	38,762	39,538	40,219	41,414
Private industries	45,240	46,204	47,520	49,426	38,446	39,104	39,601	40,745
Agriculture, forestry, fishing, and hunting	29,332	26,418	26,421	27,572	25,847	23,246	23,228	24,229
Mining	70,413	73,275	74,917	78,789	58,291	60,595	61,051	63,394
Utilities	78,147	81,365	86,579	92,144	64,271	66,470	68,313	69,758
Construction	44,764	47,802	48,754	49,537	37,196	39,647	40,399	40,965
Manufacturing	54,219	54,158	57,765	62,691	44,216	43,778	44,866	46,743
Wholesale trade	56,264	59,902	61,248	63,382	48,017	50,974	51,510	52,945
Retail trade	30,225	30,038	31,235	32,301	26,307	26,027	26,691	27,412
Transportation and warehousing	48,336	48,588	49,771	51,151	39,463	39,426	40,129	40,800
Information	74,196	71,915	71,438	75,031	63,217	60,917	59,696	61,930
Finance and insurance	74,821	77,992	79,348	81,823	64,049	66,562	65,722	67,804
Real estate and rental and leasing	41,906	42,171	43,675	45,177	36,178	36,227	37,399	38,670
Professional, scientific, and technical services	68,436	72,062	73,605	75,340	58,886	61,756	62,025	63,557
Management of companies and enterprises [1]	89,496	85,400	86,720	88,922	75,984	72,270	72,787	74,052
Administrative and waste management services	28,540	30,508	31,636	32,874	25,181	26,784	27,659	28,543
Educational services	32,736	34,181	35,461	37,164	28,974	30,086	31,094	32,368
Health care and social assistance	40,897	42,087	43,923	45,633	35,127	36,011	37,411	38,651
Arts, entertainment, and recreation	35,898	35,884	37,166	39,601	31,259	31,115	32,162	34,053
Accommodation and food services	19,092	20,493	21,196	21,834	16,830	17,973	18,421	18,843
Other services, except government	28,630	29,413	30,534	31,820	25,495	26,091	27,050	28,027
Government	52,845	54,679	57,032	59,279	40,501	41,895	43,454	44,872
Federal	70,004	73,764	79,166	83,907	46,646	48,815	52,081	55,055
State and local	48,020	49,579	51,209	52,768	38,773	40,046	41,185	42,179

[1] Consists of offices of bank and other holding companies and of corporate, subsidiary, and regional managing offices.

Source: U.S. Bureau of Economic Analysis, Survey of Current Business, May 2005; and Internet site <http://www.bea.gov/bea/dn/nipaweb/SelectTable.asp?Selected=N>.

Table 628. Average Hourly Earnings by Private Industry Group: 1990 to 2004

[In dollars. Average earnings include overtime. Data are for production workers in natural resources and mining, manufacturing, and construction, and nonsupervisory employees in other industries. See headnote, Table 618]

Private industry group	Current dollars					Constant (1982) dollars [1]				
	1990	2000	2002	2003	2004	1990	2000	2002	2003	2004
AVERAGE HOURLY EARNINGS										
Total private	10.19	14.00	14.95	15.35	15.67	7.66	8.03	8.24	8.27	8.23
Natural resources and mining	13.40	16.55	17.19	17.56	18.08	10.07	9.50	9.47	9.46	9.50
Construction	13.42	17.48	18.52	18.95	19.23	10.08	10.03	10.20	10.21	10.10
Manufacturing	10.78	14.32	15.29	15.74	16.14	8.10	8.22	8.42	8.48	8.48
Trade, transportation and utilities	9.83	13.31	14.02	14.34	14.59	7.39	7.64	7.72	7.73	7.66
Information	13.40	19.07	20.20	21.01	21.42	10.07	10.94	11.13	11.32	11.25
Financial activities [2]	9.99	14.98	16.17	17.14	17.53	7.51	8.59	8.91	9.23	9.21
Professional and business services [2]	11.14	15.52	16.81	17.21	17.46	8.37	8.90	9.26	9.27	9.17
Education and health services [2]	10.00	13.95	15.21	15.64	16.16	7.51	8.00	8.38	8.43	8.49
Leisure and hospitality [2]	5.88	8.11	8.58	8.76	8.91	4.42	4.65	4.73	4.72	4.68
Other services	9.08	12.73	13.72	13.84	13.98	6.82	7.30	7.56	7.46	7.34
AVERAGE WEEKLY EARNINGS										
Total private	349.29	480.41	506.07	517.30	528.56	262.43	275.62	278.83	278.72	277.61
Natural resources and mining	602.54	734.92	741.97	765.94	804.03	452.70	421.64	408.80	412.68	422.28
Construction	513.43	685.78	711.82	726.83	735.70	385.75	393.45	392.19	391.61	386.40
Manufacturing	436.16	590.65	618.75	635.99	658.53	327.69	338.87	340.91	342.67	345.87
Trade, transportation and utilities	331.55	449.88	471.27	481.14	488.58	249.10	258.11	259.65	259.23	256.61
Information	479.50	700.89	738.17	760.81	777.42	360.26	402.12	406.71	409.92	408.31
Financial activities [2]	354.65	537.37	575.51	609.08	622.99	266.45	308.30	317.09	328.17	327.20
Professional and business services [2]	380.61	535.07	574.66	587.02	596.96	285.96	306.98	316.62	316.28	313.53
Education and health services [2]	319.27	449.29	492.74	505.69	523.83	239.87	257.77	271.48	272.46	275.12
Leisure and hospitality [2]	152.47	211.79	221.26	224.30	228.63	114.55	121.51	121.91	120.85	120.08
Other services	297.91	413.41	439.76	434.41	433.04	223.82	237.18	242.29	234.06	227.44

[1] Earnings in current dollars divided by the Consumer Price Index (CPI-W) on a 1982 base; see text, Section 14. Prices.
[2] For composition of industries, see Table 619.

Source: U.S. Bureau of Labor Statistics, the Current Employment Statistics program Internet site <http://www.bls.gov/ces/home.htm>.

Labor Force, Employment, and Earnings **425**

Table 629. Mean Hourly Earnings and Weekly Hours by Selected Characteristics: 2003

[Covers civilian workers in private industry establishments and state and local governments in the 50 states and DC. Excludes private households, federal government and agriculture. Based on establishment survey; see source and Appendix III for details]

Item	Mean hourly earnings (dol.) [1]			Mean weekly hours		
	Total	Private industry	State and local government	Total	Private industry	State and local government
Total	17.75	16.98	22.22	35.7	35.5	36.8
WORKER CHARACTERISTIC						
White-collar occupations	21.85	21.12	25.09	36.1	36.0	36.6
Professional specialty and technical	28.37	27.73	29.80	36.2	36.3	36.1
Professional	30.60	30.32	31.08	36.3	36.5	35.9
Technical	20.85	21.27	18.11	36.1	35.9	37.6
Executive, administrative, and managerial	32.20	32.60	30.06	40.0	40.2	38.5
Sales	15.05	15.05	13.58	32.4	32.4	33.9
Administrative support	13.77	13.69	14.17	36.3	36.3	36.7
Blue-collar occupations	15.03	14.91	17.11	38.0	38.0	37.6
Precision production, craft, and repair	18.89	18.84	19.52	39.6	39.5	39.8
Machine operators, assemblers, and inspectors	13.30	13.29	16.52	39.1	39.1	38.5
Transportation and material moving	14.78	14.66	15.96	37.5	37.9	34.1
Handlers, equipment cleaners, helpers and laborers	11.27	11.09	14.22	35.0	34.9	38.7
Service occupations	10.40	8.90	16.70	31.5	30.4	37.1
Protective service	17.17	10.50	20.78	31.5	33.0	39.8
Food service	7.46	7.31	10.53	28.4	28.3	30.1
Health service	10.68	10.42	12.59	33.6	33.2	37.1
Cleaning and building service	10.52	9.92	12.65	34.6	33.6	38.5
Personal service	10.13	9.93	11.62	29.3	29.4	28.4
Full-time [2]	18.79	18.07	22.62	39.6	39.7	38.8
Part-time [2]	9.93	9.56	15.12	20.5	20.5	19.2
Union [3]	21.45	19.52	24.22	36.9	36.9	36.8
Nonunion	16.96	16.63	20.29	35.4	35.3	36.8
Time [4]	17.45	16.57	22.22	35.6	35.4	36.8
Incentive [4]	22.82	22.82	(NA)	36.9	36.9	(NA)
ESTABLISHMENT CHARACTERISTIC						
Goods producing [5]	(X)	18.46	(X)	(X)	39.50	(X)
Service producing [5]	(X)	16.44	(X)	(X)	34.20	(X)
1 to 99 workers [6]	15.06	15.03	17.32	34.5	34.5	36.5
100 to 499 workers	17.20	16.78	20.67	36.4	36.4	35.7
500 to 999 workers	19.48	18.57	22.56	36.9	37.1	36.1
1,000 to 2,499 workers	20.99	20.71	21.73	36.6	36.6	36.6
2,500 workers or more	24.09	24.99	23.23	36.9	36.4	37.5
GEOGRAPHIC REGION [7]						
New England	19.55	18.70	25.45	34.3	34.1	35.6
Middle Atlantic	20.03	19.08	25.53	34.9	34.8	35.6
East North Central	17.97	17.16	23.33	35.5	35.4	36.0
West North Central	17.03	16.30	21.09	35.1	34.7	37.4
South Atlantic	16.46	15.88	19.34	36.2	35.8	38.2
East South Central	14.45	13.97	18.34	36.2	36.1	36.9
West South Central	15.75	15.22	18.52	36.6	36.3	38.4
Mountain	16.63	15.65	22.34	35.8	35.6	37.2
Pacific	20.12	19.11	25.76	35.8	35.8	35.6

NA Not available.   X Not applicable.   [1] Earnings are straight time hourly wages or salary, including incentive pay, cost-of-living adjustments, and hazard pay. Excludes premium pay for overtime, vacations and holidays, nonproduction bonuses and tips.   [2] Based on definition used by each establishment.   [3] Workers whose wages are determined through collective bargaining.   [4] Time worker wages are based solely on an hourly rate or salary. Incentive workers wages are based at least in part on productivity payments such as piece rates or commissions.   [5] For private industry only.   [6] Private establishments employing 1 to 99 workers and state and local government establishments employing 50 to 99 workers.   [7] Composition of regions: NEW ENGLAND: Maine, New Hampshire, Vermont, Massachusetts, Rhode Island, Connecticut. MIDDLE ATLANTIC: New York, New Jersey, and Pennsylvania. EAST NORTH CENTRAL: Ohio, Indiana, Illinois, Michigan, Wisconsin. WEST NORTH CENTRAL: Minnesota, Iowa, Missouri, North Dakota, South Dakota, Nebraska, and Kansas. SOUTH ATLANTIC: Delaware, Maryland, District of Columbia, Virginia, West Virginia. North Carolina, South Carolina, Georgia, Florida. EAST SOUTH CENTRAL: Kentucky, Tennessee, Alabama, Mississippi. WEST SOUTH CENTRAL: Arkansas, Louisiana, Oklahoma, and Texas. MOUNTAIN: Montana, Idaho, Wyoming, Colorado, New Mexico, Arizona, Utah, Nevada. PACIFIC: Washington, Oregon, California, Alaska, and Hawaii.

Source: U.S. Bureau of Labor Statistics, National Compensation Survey: Occupational Wages in the United States, July 2003, Bulletin 2568, September 2004. See Internet site <http://www.bls.gov/ncs/home.htm>.

Table 630. **Average Annual Wage by State: 2002 and 2003**

[In dollars, except percent change. For workers covered by state unemployment insurance laws and for federal civilian workers covered by unemployment compensation for federal employees, approximately 99 percent of wage and salary civilian employment in 2002. Excludes most agricultural workers on small farms, all Armed Forces, elected officials in most states, railroad employees, most domestic workers, most student workers at school, employees of certain nonprofit organizations, and most self-employed individuals. Pay includes bonuses, stock options, cash value of meals and lodging, and tips and other gratuities]

State	Average annual pay 2002	Average annual pay 2003	Percent change, 2002-03	State	Average annual pay 2002	Average annual pay 2003	Percent change, 2002-03
United States.	36,764	37,765	2.7	Missouri	33,118	33,788	2.0
Alabama	31,163	32,236	3.4	Montana	26,001	26,907	3.5
Alaska	37,134	37,804	1.8	Nebraska	29,448	30,382	3.2
Arizona.	34,036	35,056	3.0	Nevada.	33,993	35,329	3.9
Arkansas.	28,074	28,893	2.9	New Hampshire	36,176	37,321	3.2
California.	41,419	42,592	2.8	New Jersey	45,182	46,351	2.6
Colorado.	38,005	38,942	2.5	New Mexico.	29,431	30,202	2.6
Connecticut	46,852	48,328	3.2	New York	46,328	47,247	2.0
Delaware.	39,684	40,954	3.2	North Carolina	32,689	33,532	2.6
District of Columbia. . . .	57,914	60,417	4.3	North Dakota	26,550	27,628	4.1
Florida	32,426	33,544	3.4	Ohio.	34,214	35,153	2.7
Georgia	35,734	36,626	2.5	Oklahoma	28,654	29,699	3.6
Hawaii	32,671	33,742	3.3	Oregon.	33,684	34,450	2.3
Idaho	28,163	28,677	1.8	Pennsylvania	35,808	36,995	3.3
Illinois.	39,688	40,540	2.1	Rhode Island	34,810	36,415	4.6
Indiana	32,603	33,379	2.4	South Carolina	30,003	30,750	2.5
Iowa.	29,668	30,708	3.5	South Dakota	26,360	27,210	3.2
Kansas.	30,825	31,489	2.2	Tennessee	32,531	33,581	3.2
Kentucky.	30,904	31,855	3.1	Texas.	36,248	36,968	2.0
Louisiana	30,115	30,782	2.2	Utah.	30,585	31,106	1.7
Maine	29,736	30,750	3.4	Vermont	31,041	32,086	3.4
Maryland.	39,382	40,686	3.3	Virginia	37,222	38,585	3.7
Massachusetts	44,954	46,323	3.0	Washington	38,242	39,021	2.0
Michigan	38,135	39,433	3.4	West Virginia	28,612	29,284	2.3
Minnesota	37,458	38,610	3.1	Wisconsin	32,464	33,425	3.0
Mississippi	26,665	27,591	3.5	Wyoming.	28,975	29,924	3.3

Source: U.S. Bureau of Labor Statistics. "Employment and Wages, Annual Averages," 2002 and 2003. See Internet site <http://www.bls.gov/cew/home.htm>.

Table 631. **Employment and Wages: 1995 to 2003**

[(115,488 represents 115,488,000). See headnote, Table 630]

Employment and wages	Unit	1995	1998	1999	2000	2001	2002	2003
Average annual employment:								
Total	1,000	115,488	124,184	127,042	129,877	129,636	128,234	127,796
Excluding federal	1,000	112,540	121,401	124,256	127,006	126,883	125,475	125,032
Private	1,000	96,895	105,082	107,619	110,015	109,305	107,577	107,066
State government	1,000	4,202	4,241	4,297	4,370	4,452	4,485	4,482
Local governments	1,000	11,442	12,078	12,340	12,620	13,126	13,413	13,484
Federal government.	1,000	2,948	2,783	2,787	2,871	2,753	2,759	2,764
Annual wages:								
Total	Bil. dol. . . .	3,216	3,967	4,236	4,588	4,695	4,714	4,826
Excluding federal	Bil. dol. . . .	3,102	3,845	4,112	4,455	4,561	4,571	4,676
Private	Bil. dol. . . .	2,659	3,338	3,578	3,888	3,952	3,931	4,016
State government	Bil. dol. . . .	128	143	149	159	168	176	180
Local governments	Bil. dol. . . .	315	365	385	409	440	464	481
Federal government.	Bil. dol. . . .	114	122	123	133	135	144	150
Annual wage per employee:								
Total	Dol.	27,846	31,945	33,340	35,323	36,219	36,764	37,765
Excluding federal	Dol.	27,567	31,676	33,094	35,077	35,943	36,428	37,401
Private	Dol.	27,441	31,762	33,244	35,337	36,157	36,539	37,508
State government	Dol.	30,497	33,605	34,681	36,296	37,814	39,212	40,057
Local governments	Dol.	27,552	30,251	31,234	32,387	33,521	34,605	35,669
Federal government.	Dol.	38,523	43,688	44,287	46,228	48,940	52,050	54,239
Average weekly wage per employee:								
Total	Dol.	536	614	641	679	697	707	726
Excluding federal	Dol.	530	609	636	675	691	701	719
Private	Dol.	528	611	639	680	695	703	721
State government	Dol.	586	646	667	698	727	754	770
Local governments	Dol.	530	582	601	623	645	665	686
Federal government.	Dol.	741	840	852	889	941	1,001	1,043

Source: U.S. Bureau of Labor Statistics. "Employment and Wages, Annual Averages, 2003". See Internet site <http://www.bls.gov/cew/home.htm>.

Labor Force, Employment, and Earnings 427

Table 632. Full-Time Wage and Salary Workers—Number and Earnings: 2000 to 2004

[In current dollars of usual weekly earnings. Data represent annual averages (101,210 represents 101,210,000). Occupational classifications are those used in the 2000 census; see text, this section. Based on the Current Population Survey; see text, Section 1, and Appendix III. For definition of median, see Guide to Tabular Presentation]

Characteristic	Number of workers (1,000)			Median weekly earnings (dol.)		
	2000	2003 [1]	2004 [1]	2000	2003 [1]	2004 [1]
All workers [2]	101,210	100,302	101,224	576	620	638
SEX						
Male	57,107	56,227	57,001	641	695	713
16 to 24 years old	6,770	6,158	6,243	375	398	400
25 years old and over	50,337	50,069	50,758	693	744	762
Female	44,103	44,076	44,223	493	552	573
16 to 24 years old	5,094	4,632	4,633	344	371	375
25 years old and over	39,009	39,444	39,590	516	584	599
RACE/ETHNICITY						
White [3]	83,228	81,916	82,468	590	636	657
Male	48,085	47,001	47,495	662	715	732
Female	35,143	34,916	34,972	502	567	584
Black [3]	12,410	11,887	12,032	474	514	525
Male	5,911	5,585	5,706	510	555	569
Female	6,500	6,301	6,326	429	491	505
Asian [3][4]	4,598	4,314	4,457	615	693	708
Male	2,538	2,442	2,504	685	772	802
Female	2,060	1,872	1,953	547	598	613
Hispanic origin [5]	12,761	13,634	14,061	399	440	456
Male	8,077	8,677	8,996	417	464	480
Female	4,684	4,957	5,065	366	410	419
OCCUPATION						
Management, professional, and related occupations	34,831	35,680	36,149	810	887	918
Management, business, and financial operations	14,240	14,493	14,778	877	961	965
Management occupations	9,952	10,115	10,221	937	1,023	1,052
Business and financial operations occupations	4,288	4,378	4,558	760	842	847
Professional and related occupations	20,590	21,186	21,371	770	845	883
Computer and mathematical occupations	3,051	2,790	2,793	938	1,049	1,114
Architecture and engineering occupations	2,781	2,487	2,500	949	1,053	1,098
Life, physical, and social science occupations	989	1,085	1,073	811	891	957
Community and social services occupations	1,641	1,814	1,846	629	686	707
Legal occupations	1,039	1,024	1,111	919	1,051	1,070
Education, training, and library occupations	5,467	5,884	5,941	704	754	781
Arts, design, entertainment, sports, and media	1,488	1,473	1,426	724	745	768
Healthcare practitioner and technical occupations	4,134	4,630	4,680	727	816	852
Service occupations	12,595	13,333	13,763	365	403	411
Healthcare support occupations	1,731	2,023	1,985	358	400	407
Protective service occupations	2,281	2,405	2,509	591	630	700
Food preparation and serving-related occupations	3,483	3,819	3,863	317	349	360
Building and grounds cleaning and maintenance	3,354	3,280	3,436	351	390	385
Personal care and service occupations	1,746	1,806	1,969	351	391	402
Sales and office occupations	25,606	25,108	24,950	492	545	558
Sales and related occupations	9,650	9,924	9,984	525	598	604
Office and administrative support occupations	15,956	15,184	14,966	480	523	535
Natural resources, construction, and maintenance occupations	10,958	11,082	11,280	582	608	621
Farming, fishing, and forestry occupations	842	778	718	310	369	356
Construction and extraction occupations	5,852	5,973	6,232	580	599	604
Installation, maintenance, and repair occupations	4,263	4,331	4,330	628	673	704
Production, transportation, and material moving occupations	17,221	15,100	15,082	475	519	523
Production occupations	10,378	8,599	8,478	471	519	526
Transportation and material moving occupations	6,843	6,501	6,604	481	520	520

[1] See footnote 2, Table 576. [2] Includes other races, not shown separately. [3] Beginning 2003, for persons in this race group only. See footnote 3, table 577. [4] Prior to 2003, includes Pacific Islanders. [5] Persons of Hispanic or Latino origin may be of any race.

Source: U.S. Bureau of Labor Statistics, Bulletin 2307, and *Employment and Earnings*, monthly, January 2005 issue and unpublished data. See Internet site <http://www.bls.gov/cps/home.htm>.

Table 633. Workers With Earnings by Occupation of Longest Held Job and Sex: 2003

[Covers persons 15 years old and over as of March 2004. (71,372 represents 71,372,000). Based on Current Population Survey; see text, Section 1, and Appendix III. For definition of median, see Guide to Tabular Presentation. Occupational classifications are those used in the 2000 Census and are not comparable to those used in the 1990 Census]

Major occupation of longest job held in 2003	All workers				Full-time, year-round			
	Women		Men		Women		Men	
	Number (1,000)	Median earnings (dol.)	Number (1,000)	Median earnings (dol.)	Number (1,000)	Median earnings (dol.)	Number (1,000)	Median earnings (dol.)
Total	71,372	22,004	80,508	32,048	41,908	30,724	58,772	40,668
Management, business, and financial occupations	9,033	35,201	11,903	55,454	6,971	42,064	10,253	60,447
Professional and related occupations . . .	17,071	32,309	12,763	51,679	10,370	40,298	10,023	58,867
Service occupations	14,510	11,546	11,065	16,991	6,386	19,970	6,490	26,447
Sales and office occupations.	25,044	21,122	14,151	30,402	14,773	27,803	10,022	39,491
Natural resources, construction, and maintenance	817	15,597	14,845	28,472	383	27,658	10,417	33,807
Production, transportation, and material moving occupations	4,806	17,337	15,063	27,271	2,944	22,430	10,931	31,942
Armed Forces	92	31,446	718	35,183	81	32,198	636	36,326

Source: U.S. Census Bureau Internet site <http://pubdb3.census.gov/macro/032004/perinc/toc.htm>, Table PINC-06, "Occupation of Longest Job in 2003—People 15 years Old and Over, by Total Money Earnings in 2003, Work Experience in 2003, Race, Hispanic Origin, and Sex" (accessed 2 March 2005).

Table 634. Employment Cost Index (ECI), Total Compensation by Occupation and Industry: 1985 to 2004

[As of December. The ECI is a measure of the rate of change in employee compensation (wages, salaries, and employer costs for employee benefits). Data are not seasonally adjusted: 1985 based on fixed employment counts from 1970 Census of Population; 1990 based on fixed employment counts from the 1980 Census of Population; beginning 1995 based primarily on 1990 Occupational Employment Survey]

Item	Indexes (June 1989 = 100)						Percent change for 12 months ending Dec.—				
	1985	1990	1995	2000	2003	2004	1985	1990	1995	2000	2004
Civilian workers [1]	86.8	107.6	127.2	150.6	168.4	174.7	4.3	4.9	2.7	4.1	3.7
Workers, by occupational group:											
White-collar occupations	85.8	108.3	128.0	152.5	170.7	176.6	4.9	5.2	2.9	4.2	3.5
Blue-collar occupations	88.4	106.5	125.8	146.5	163.7	170.9	3.3	4.4	2.5	4.2	4.4
Service occupations	87.2	108.0	127.4	150.0	167.9	173.6	3.9	5.1	2.5	3.6	3.4
Workers, by industry division:											
Manufacturing	87.8	107.2	128.3	149.3	167.1	175.4	3.3	5.1	2.6	4.0	5.0
Nonmanufacturing [2]	86.4	107.8	126.8	150.7	168.6	174.4	4.7	4.9	2.8	4.1	3.4
Service industries . . . [3]	84.1	110.2	129.4	152.4	169.5	175.5	4.7	6.3	2.4	4.0	3.5
Public administration [3]	85.4	108.7	128.3	148.3	168.1	175.4	4.9	5.3	3.3	2.7	4.3
State and local government. . .	84.6	110.4	129.3	148.9	166.8	172.6	5.6	5.8	2.9	3.0	3.5
Workers, by occupational group:											
White-collar occupations	84.2	110.9	129.1	148.3	165.7	171.2	5.8	6.0	2.9	3.0	3.3
Blue-collar workers	86.7	108.7	128.0	147.2	165.2	171.0	5.3	4.8	2.6	3.3	3.5
Workers, by industry division:											
Service industries.	84.0	111.3	129.6	148.9	165.7	170.8	5.9	6.3	2.8	3.0	3.1
Schools.	83.6	111.6	129.8	149.0	165.3	170.3	6.2	6.0	2.8	3.0	3.0
Elementary and secondary	83.6	112.1	130.1	148.1	163.7	169.2	6.4	6.3	2.8	2.8	3.4
Colleges and universities [4]	(NA)	110.2	128.7	151.7	170.0	173.2	(NA)	5.3	2.5	3.5	1.9
Services, excluding schools [4]	85.2	110.2	129.4	148.8	168.2	173.8	4.7	6.8	3.0	3.5	3.3
Public administration [3] . . . . [5]	85.4	108.7	128.3	148.3	168.1	175.4	4.9	5.3	3.3	2.7	4.3
Private industry workers [5]	87.3	107.0	126.7	150.9	168.8	175.2	3.9	4.6	2.6	4.4	3.8
Workers, by occupational group:											
White-collar occupations	86.4	107.4	127.6	153.6	172.0	178.1	4.9	4.9	2.8	4.6	3.5
Blue-collar occupations	88.5	106.4	125.6	146.4	163.6	170.8	3.1	4.4	2.4	4.2	4.4
Service occupations	88.4	107.3	125.2	148.1	164.9	169.7	3.0	4.7	1.9	3.9	2.9
Workers, by industry division:											
Manufacturing	87.8	107.2	128.3	149.3	167.1	175.4	3.3	5.1	2.6	4.0	5.0
Nonmanufacturing [2]	87.0	106.9	125.9	151.1	169.0	174.7	4.3	4.5	2.7	4.6	3.4
Service industries [2]	84.1	109.3	129.4	154.1	171.4	177.9	(NA)	6.2	2.2	4.4	3.8
Business services	(NA)	107.4	125.3	158.4	172.6	179.1	(NA)	6.0	2.7	4.3	3.8
Health services	83.7	110.8	132.2	150.6	170.8	178.0	(NA)	6.8	2.7	4.4	4.2
Hospitals	(NA)	110.7	131.3	151.1	175.9	183.2	(NA)	7.0	2.1	4.5	4.2
Workers by bargaining status:											
Union.	90.1	106.2	127.7	146.9	166.8	176.2	2.6	4.3	2.8	4.0	5.6
Nonunion	86.3	107.3	126.5	151.6	169.1	174.9	4.6	4.8	2.7	4.4	3.4

NA Not available. [1] Includes private industry and state and local government workers and excludes farm, household, and federal government workers. [2] Includes other industries, not shown separately. [3] Consists of executive, legislative, judicial, administrative, and regulatory activities. [4] Includes library, social, and health services. Formerly called hospitals and other services. [5] Excludes farm and household workers.

Source: U.S. Bureau of Labor Statistics, News, Employment Cost Index, quarterly; and Internet site <http://www.bls.gov/ncs/ect/home.htm>.

Table 635. **Federal Minimum Wage Rates: 1950 to 2000**

Year	Current dollars	Year	Current dollars
1950	0.75	1976	2.30
1951	0.75	1977	2.30
1952	0.75	1978	2.65
1953	0.75	1979	2.90
1954	0.75		
1955	0.75	1980	3.10
1956	1.00	1981	3.35
1957	1.00	1982	3.35
1958	1.00	1983	3.35
1959	1.00	1984	3.35
		1985	3.35
1960	1.00	1986	3.35
1961	1.15	1987	3.35
1962	1.15	1988	3.35
1963	1.25	1989	3.35
1964	1.25		
1965	1.25	1990	3.80
1966	1.25	1991	4.25
1967	1.40	1992	4.25
1968	1.60	1993	4.25
1969	1.60	1994	4.25
		1995	4.25
1970	1.60	1996	4.75
1971	1.60	1997	5.15
1972	1.60	1998	5.15
1973	1.60	1999	5.15
1974	2.00		
1975	2.10	2000	5.15

Source: U.S. Employment Standards Administration, Internet site: <http://www.dol.gov/esa/whd/flsa/>.

Table 636. **Workers Paid Hourly Rates by Selected Characteristics: 2004**

[Data are annual averages (73,939 represents 73,939,000). For employed wage and salary workers. Based on Current Population Survey; see text, Section 1, and Appendix III]

Characteristic	Number of workers [1] (1,000)				Percent of all workers paid hourly rates				Median hourly earnings of workers paid hourly rates [2]
	Total paid hourly rates	At or below $5.15				At or below $5.15			
		Total	At $5.15	Below $5.15		Total	At $5.15	Below $5.15	
Total, 16 years and over [3]	73,939	2,003	520	1,483		2.7	0.7	2.0	11.00
16 to 24 years	16,174	1,022	272	750		6.3	1.7	4.6	7.98
16 to 19 years........	5,433	497	168	329		9.1	3.1	6.1	7.00
25 years and over	57,765	982	249	733		1.7	0.4	1.3	12.23
Male, 16 years and over	36,806	680	210	470		1.8	0.6	1.3	12.02
16 to 24 years	8,305	366	127	239		4.4	1.5	2.9	8.21
16 to 19 years.......	2,672	179	78	101		6.7	2.9	3.8	7.15
25 years and over	28,500	314	83	231		1.1	0.3	0.8	13.74
Women, 16 years and over...	37,133	1,323	310	1,013		3.6	0.8	2.7	10.17
16 to 24 years	7,869	655	145	510		8.3	1.8	6.5	7.71
16 to 19 years.......	2,761	319	90	229		11.6	3.3	8.3	6.86
25 years and over	29,265	668	166	502		2.3	0.6	1.7	11.23
White [4]	59,877	1,681	395	1,286		2.8	0.7	2.1	11.13
Black [4]	9,417	227	99	128		2.4	1.1	1.4	10.19
Asian [4]	2,672	38	8	30		1.4	0.3	1.1	11.10
Hispanic origin [5]	12,073	250	82	168		2.1	0.7	1.4	9.81
Full-time workers [6]	55,739	760	177	583		1.4	0.3	1.0	12.12
Part-time workers [6]	18,046	1,240	343	897		6.9	1.9	5.0	8.09
Private sector industries.....	64,708	1,890	467	1,423		2.9	0.7	2.2	10.72
Public sector	9,231	113	53	60		1.2	0.6	0.6	13.34

[1] Excludes the incorporated self-employed. [2] For definition of median, see Guide to Tabular Presentation. [3] Includes races not shown separately. Also includes a small number of multiple jobholders whose full- or part-time status can not be determined for their principal job. [4] For persons in this race group only. See footnote 3, Table 577. [5] Persons of Hispanic or Latino origin may be of any race. [6] Working fewer than 35 hours per week.

Source: U.S. Bureau of Labor Statistics, *Employment and Earnings*, January 2005, and unpublished data. See Internet site <http://www.bls.gov/cps.home.htm>.

U.S. Census Bureau, Statistical Abstract of the United States: 2006

Table 637. Employer Costs for Employee Compensation Per Hour Worked: 2004

[In dollars. As of March, for private industry workers. Based on a sample of establishments from the National Compensation Survey; see source for details. See also Appendix III]

Compensation component	Total	Goods producing[1]	Service producing[2]	Employment size 1 to 99 workers	Employment size 100 or more workers	Union workers	Non-union workers	Full-time workers	Part-time workers
Total compensation	**24.17**	**28.48**	**23.11**	**20.22**	**28.94**	**33.17**	**23.09**	**27.58**	**13.17**
Wages and salaries	17.15	18.66	16.78	14.94	19.82	20.76	16.72	19.23	10.41
Total benefits	7.02	9.82	6.34	5.28	9.12	12.41	6.38	8.34	2.75
Paid leave	1.54	1.72	1.50	1.07	2.12	2.25	1.46	1.91	0.38
Vacation	0.76	0.89	0.73	0.52	1.05	1.14	0.72	(NA)	(NA)
Holiday	0.53	0.63	0.51	0.38	0.72	0.72	0.51	(NA)	(NA)
Sick	0.19	0.13	0.20	0.13	0.25	0.28	0.18	(NA)	(NA)
Other	0.06	0.07	0.06	0.04	0.10	0.11	0.06	(NA)	(NA)
Supplemental pay	0.68	1.24	0.54	0.52	0.87	1.09	0.63	0.83	0.18
Insurance	1.76	2.45	1.59	1.27	2.36	3.63	1.54	2.14	0.53
Health insurance	1.64	2.28	1.48	1.19	2.17	3.41	1.42	(NA)	(NA)
Retirement and savings	0.90	1.59	0.73	0.49	1.39	2.39	0.72	1.11	0.19
Defined benefit	0.45	1.08	0.30	0.17	0.78	1.86	0.28	(NA)	(NA)
Defined contributions	0.45	0.51	0.43	0.32	0.60	0.53	0.44	(NA)	(NA)
Legally required	2.10	2.73	1.95	1.92	2.32	2.95	2.00	2.30	1.46
Social Security and Medicare	1.43	1.61	1.39	1.24	1.67	1.80	1.39	(NA)	(NA)
Social Security	1.15	1.29	1.12	0.99	1.34	1.45	1.12	(NA)	(NA)
Medicare	0.28	0.31	0.28	0.24	0.33	0.35	0.28	(NA)	(NA)
Federal unemployment	0.03	0.03	0.03	0.04	0.03	0.03	0.03	(NA)	(NA)
State unemployment	0.16	0.20	0.15	0.15	0.17	0.22	0.15	(NA)	(NA)
Workers compensation	0.48	0.89	0.37	0.50	0.45	0.90	0.43	(NA)	(NA)
Other benefits[3]	0.04	0.08	0.03	-	0.07	0.11	0.03	0.05	-

- Represents or rounds to zero.   NA Not available.   [1] Based on the North American Industry Classification System, 2002 (NAICS). See text, this section. Includes mining, construction, and manufacturing. The agriculture, forestry, farming and hunting sector is excluded.   [2] Based on the 2002 NAICS. Includes utilities; wholesale and retail trade; transportation and warehousing; information; finance and insurance; real estate and rental and leasing; professional and technical services; management of companies and enterprises, administrative and waste services; education services; health care and social assistance; arts, entertainment, and recreation; accommodations and food services; and other services, except public administration.   [3] Includes severance pay, and supplemental unemployment benefits.

Source: U.S. Bureau of Labor Statistics, *Employer Costs for Employee Compensation, News*, USDL 05-1056, June 16, 2005. See Intenet site <http://www.bls.gov/ncs/ect/home.htm>.

Table 638. Employees With Employer- or Union-Provided Pension Plans or Group Health Plans: 2001

[Total in thousands (151,608 represents 151,608,000). For wage and salary workers 15 years old and over as of March 2002. Based on the Current Population Survey, Annual Demographic Survey, March Supplement; see text, Section 1, Population, and Appendix III. Data based on 1990 population controls]

Occupation	Total (1,000)	Percent— Included in pension plan	Percent— With group health plan	Characteristic	Total (1,000)	Percent— Included in pension plan	Percent— With group health plan
Total	**151,608**	**43.2**	**53.7**	AGE			
Executive, admin., managerial	21,951	58.5	68.9	Total	151,608	43.2	53.7
Professional specialty	23,078	60.8	67.3	15 to 24 years	24,593	12.7	21.9
				25 to 44 years old	71,281	47.0	58.5
Technical/related support	4,884	55.3	65.4	45 to 64 years	50,230	54.7	63.7
Sales workers	18,236	32.7	43.8	65 years and over	5,504	23.6	42.6
Admin. support, inc. clerical	20,449	47.3	56.2	WORK EXPERIENCE			
				Worked	151,608	43.2	53.7
Precision prod., craft/repair	16,040	41.9	56.1	Full-time	122,001	50.1	62.4
				50 weeks or more	100,379	54.5	67.1
Mach. operators, assemblers[1]	7,601	44.3	60.5	27 to 49 weeks	13,177	36.7	49.8
Transportation/material moving	6,397	40.3	55.8	26 weeks or fewer	8,445	19.0	26.2
Handlers, equipment cleaners[2]	6,516	25.5	38.8	Part-time	29,607	14.4	17.9
				50 weeks or more	14,094	19.1	22.9
Service workers	21,941	22.8	33.4	27 to 49 weeks	6,187	15.8	19.2
Private households	860	3.5	9.6	26 weeks or fewer	9,326	6.4	9.6
Other	21,080	23.5	34.4	EMPLOYER SIZE			
				Under 25 persons	44,717	17.2	29.6
Farming, forestry and fishing	3,853	11.9	22.2	25 to 99 persons	19,311	37.4	54.1
				100 to 499 persons	19,777	50.2	62.9
Armed Forces	653	70.2	36.2	500 to 999 persons	8,467	56.4	65.9
				Over 1,000 persons	59,336	60.4	67.0

[1] Includes inspectors.   [2] Includes helpers and laborers.

Source: U.S. Census Bureau, "Pension Plan Coverage of Workers by Selected Characteristic, Sex, Race, and Hispanic Origin and Poverty Status: 2001," and "All Workers and Poor Workers With Their Own Employment-Based Health Insurance Policy, by Employer Contribution and Selected Characteristics: 2001." See Internet site <http://pubdb3.census.gov/macro/032002/noncash /toc.htm>.

Labor Force, Employment, and Earnings   431

Table 639. Percent of Workers With Access to Selected Employee Benefits in Private Industry: 2004

[As of March. Based on National Compensation Survey, a sample survey of 4,703 private industry establishments of all sizes, representing over 102 million workers; see Appendix III. See also Tables 145 and 147]

Characteristic	Paid holidays	Paid vacation	Paid jury duty	Paid military leave	Employer assistance for child care				Adoption assistance	Long-term care insurance	Flexible work plans[1]	Employer-provided home personal computer	Sub-sidized com-muting[2]
					Total	Employer-provided funds	On-site and off-site child care	Child care resource and referral services					
Total	77	77	70	49	14	3	5	10	9	11	4	3	5
WORKER CHARACTERISTICS													
White-collar occupations	85	83	80	58	19	4	7	14	13	17	7	4	7
Blue-collar occupations	81	80	66	43	8	2	2	6	6	6	1	1	3
Service occupations	48	58	47	33	9	2	4	4	2	4	1	1	2
Full-time[3]	89	90	77	54	16	4	6	11	11	13	5	3	6
Part-time[3]	37	35	44	31	8	1	3	5	4	5	2	1	2
Union[4]	84	85	83	56	16	3	6	15	12	13	2	2	6
Nonunion[4]	76	77	68	48	13	3	5	9	9	11	5	3	5
Average wage less than $15 per hour	68	70	60	41	8	2	3	5	5	6	2	1	2
Average wage $15 per hour or more	88	88	83	61	22	5	8	16	15	18	8	5	8
ESTABLISHMENT CHARACTERISTICS													
Goods producing	85	85	73	53	12	3	3	10	9	10	3	3	4
Service producing	74	75	69	48	14	3	6	10	9	12	5	2	5
1 to 99 workers	69	71	57	37	4	1	2	3	3	4	4	1	2
100 or more workers	86	86	84	63	25	5	9	18	16	20	5	4	8
GEOGRAPHIC AREAS[5]													
New England division	79	75	78	59	17	2	9	14	14	14	4	3	11
Middle Atlantic division	80	82	77	54	16	4	5	11	12	13	6	4	7
East North Central division	78	78	71	51	15	3	6	11	10	12	5	3	2
West North Central division	73	72	65	46	16	2	9	7	7	6	2	2	4
South Atlantic division	77	79	71	50	11	4	4	8	9	11	3	2	4
East South Central division	76	77	69	43	9	3	4	5	4	7	4	2	3
West South Central division	77	77	67	48	14	2	4	10	9	13	5	3	6
Mountain division	71	74	66	47	16	3	3	13	8	10	5	3	6
Pacific division	74	76	61	41	11	3	3	9	7	13	4	2	8

[1] Arrangements permitting employees to work at home several days of the workweek. [2] Employers subsidize employees' cost of commuting to and from work via public transportation, company-sponsored van pool, discounted subway fares, etc. [3] Employees are classified as working either a full-time or part-time schedule based on the definition used by each establishment. [4] Union workers are those whose wages are determined through collective bargaining. [5] For composition of divisions, see map, inside front cover.

Source: U.S. Bureau of Labor Statistics, Employee Benefits in Private Industry in the United States, March 2004, Summary 04-04, November 2004. See Internet site <http://www.bls.gov/ncs/ebs/home.htm>.

Table 640. **Workers Killed or Disabled on the Job: 1970 to 2003**

[Data for 2003 are preliminary estimates (13.8 represents 13,800). Excludes homicides and suicides. Estimates based on data from the U.S. National Center for Health Statistics, state vital statistics departments, state industrial commissions and beginning 1995, Bureau of Labor Statistics, Census of Occupational Fatalities. Numbers of workers based on data from the U.S. Bureau of Labor Statistics]

	Deaths						Deaths, 2003		
					Non-	Dis-			Dis-
Year	Total		Manufacturing		manufacturing	abling	Year and industry group			abling injur-
	Num-ber (1,000)	Rate [1]	Num-ber (1,000)	Rate [1]	Num-ber (1,000)	Rate [1]	injur-ies [2] (mil.)	Num-ber	Rate [1]	ies 2003 [2] (1,000)
1970 . . .	13.8	18	1.7	9	12.1	21	2.2	Total [3]	4,500	3.2	3,400
1975 . . .	13.0	15	1.6	9	11.4	17	2.2	Agriculture [4]	710	20.9	110
1980 . . .	13.2	13	1.7	8	11.5	15	2.2	Mining and quarrying [5] . . .	120	22.3	20
1985 . . .	11.5	11	1.2	6	10.3	12	2.0	Construction	1,060	11.4	390
1990 . . .	10.1	9	1.0	5	9.1	9	3.9	Manufacturing	490	2.8	460
1995 . . .	5.0	4	0.6	3	4.4	4	3.6	Transportation and			
2000 . . .	5.0	4	0.6	3	4.4	4	3.9	utilities	770	10.0	320
2001 . . .	5.0	4	0.5	3	4.5	4	3.9	Trade [6]	380	1.3	710
2002 . . .	4.7	3	0.5	3	4.2	3	3.7	Services [7]	550	1.1	890
2003 . . .	4.5	3	0.5	3	4.0	3	3.4	Government.	420	2.0	500

[1] Per 100,000 workers. [2] Disabling injury defined as one which results in death, some degree of physical impairment, or renders the person unable to perform regular activities for a full day beyond the day of the injury. Due to change in methodology, data beginning 1990 not comparable with prior years. [3] Includes deaths where industry is not known. [4] Includes forestry and fishing. [5] Includes oil and gas extraction. [6] Includes wholesale and retail trade. [7] Includes finance, insurance, and real estate. Source: National Safety Council, Itasca, IL, *Accident Facts*, annual through 1998 edition; thereafter, *Injury Facts*, annual (copyright).

Table 641. **Worker Deaths, Injuries, and Production Time Lost: 1995 to 2003**

[45.7 represents 45,700. Data may not agree with Table 640 because data here are not revised]

| Item | Deaths (1,000) | | | Disabling injuries [1] (mil.) | | | Production time lost (mil. days) | | | | | |
| | | | | | | | In the current year | | | In future years [2] | | |
	1995	2000	2003	1995	2000	2003	1995	2000	2003	1995	2000	2003
All accidents.	45.7	47.0	46.8	9.9	10.5	9.9	225	240	230	455	460	460
On the job	5.3	5.2	4.5	3.6	3.9	3.4	75	80	70	65	60	55
Off the job.	40.4	41.8	42.3	6.3	6.6	6.5	150	160	160	390	400	405
Motor vehicle.	22.9	22.8	23.1	1.2	1.2	1.2	(NA)	(NA)	(NA)	(NA)	(NA)	(NA)
Public nonmotor vehicle. . . .	7.5	8.3	7.2	2.3	2.8	2.4	(NA)	(NA)	(NA)	(NA)	(NA)	(NA)
Home.	10.0	10.7	12.0	2.8	2.6	2.9	(NA)	(NA)	(NA)	(NA)	(NA)	(NA)

NA Not available. [1] See footnote 2, Table 640 for a definition of disabling injuries. [2] Based on an average of 5,850 days lost in future years per fatality and 565 days lost in future years per permanent injury. Source: National Safety Council, Itasca, IL, *Accident Facts*, annual through 1998 edition; thereafter, *Injury Facts*, annual (copyright).

Table 642. **Industries With the Highest Total Case Incidence Rates for Nonfatal Injuries and Illnesses: 2003**

[Rates per 100 full-time employees. Rates refer to any OSHA-recordable occupational injury or illness, whether or not it resulted in days away from work, job transfer, or restriction. Incidence rates were calculated as: Number of injuries and illnesses divided by total hours worked by all employees during the year multiplied by 200,000 as base for 100 full-time equivalent workers (working 40 hours per week, 50 weeks per year)]

Industry	2002 NAICS [1] code	Rate	Industry	2002 NAICS [1] code	Rate
Private industry [2]	(X)	5.0	Sugarcane mills	311311	12.7
			Fabricated structural metal mfg.	332312	12.3
Light truck and utility vehicle mfg..	336112	18.0	Motor vehicle metal stamping	33637	12.2
Bottled water manufacturing	312112	16.7	Amusement parks and arcades	7131	12.2
Iron foundries	331511	16.0	Framing contractors	23813	12.0
Steel foundries, except investment	331513	15.2	Aluminum die-casting foundries	331521	11.7
Manufactured home, mobile home, mfg. . . .	321991	14.9	Scheduled air transportation	4811	11.7
Truss manufacturing	321214	14.7	Ship building and repairing	336611	11.5
Iron and steel forging.	332111	14.7	Rendering & meat by-product processing. . .	311613	11.4
Cutlery & flatware, except precious, mfg. . . .	332211	14.6	Other metal valve & pipe fitting mfg.	332919	11.4
Motorhome manufacturing.	336213	14.0	Wood window and door manufacturing	321911	11.3
Vitreous china table and kitchenware	327111	13.9	Other fabricated wire product mfg.	332618	11.3
Soft drink manufacturing.	312111	13.8	Industrial & commercial fan & blower mfg. . .	333412	11.3
Truck trailer manufacturing.	336212	13.6	Meat processed from carcasses.	311612	11.2
Automobile manufacturing.	336111	13.3	Enameled iron & metal sanitary ware		
Refrigerated warehousing and storage	49312	13.1	manufacturing.	332998	11.2
Animal, except poultry, slaughtering	311611	12.9	Overhead traveling crane, hoist, and		
Couriers	4921	12.8	monorail system manufacturing	333923	11.2

X Not applicable. [1] Based on the North American Industry Classification System, 2002 (NAICS). See text, this section. [2] Excludes farms with fewer than 11 employees.
Source: U.S. Bureau of Labor Statistics, *Workplace Injuries and Illnesses in 2003*. See Internet site <http://www.bls.gov/iif/>.

Labor Force, Employment, and Earnings   **433**

Table 643. Nonfatal Occupational Injury and Illness Incidence Rates: 2003

[Rates per 100 full-time employees. Except as noted, rates refer to any Occupational Safety and Health Administration (OSHA) recordable occupational injury or illness, whether or not it resulted in days away from work, job transfer, or restriction. Incidence rates were calculated as: Number of injuries and illnesses divided by total hours worked by all employees during the year multiplied by 200,000 as base for 100 full-time equivalent workers (working 40 hours, per week, 50 weeks per year)]

Industry	2002 NAICS code [1]	Rate	Industry	2002 NAICS code [1]	Rate
Private industry [2]	(X)	5.0	Building material and garden equipment		
Goods producing [2]	(X)	6.7	and supplies dealers	444	6.4
Natural resources and mining [2, 3]	(X)	5.1	Food and beverage stores	445	6.8
Agriculture, forestry, fishing & hunting [2, 4]	11	6.2	General merchandise stores	452	7.2
Crop production [2]	111	6.1	Nonstore retailers	454	5.6
Animal production [2]	112	8.2	Transportation and warehousing [4, 5]	48-49	7.8
Forestry and logging	113	6.2	Air transportation	481	11.0
Support activities for agriculture & forestry	115	5.5	Truck transportation	484	6.8
Mining [3]	21	3.3	Transit and ground passenger		
Construction	(X)	6.8	transportation	485	6.4
Construction of buildings	236	5.7	Support activities for transportation	488	5.6
Heavy and civil engineering construction	237	6.5	Couriers and messengers	492	12.1
Specialty trade contractors	238	7.3	Warehousing and storage	493	10.1
Manufacturing [4]	(X)	6.8	Utilities	22	4.4
Food manufacturing	311	8.6	**Information**	(X)	2.2
Beverage and tobacco product mfg	312	10.7	**Financial activities**	(X)	1.7
Textile mills	313	5.0	Finance and insurance	52	1.1
Textile product mills	314	5.5	Real estate & rental & leasing	53	3.9
Apparel manufacturing	315	3.6	**Professional and business services**	(X)	2.5
Leather and allied product mfg	316	7.8	Professional, scientific, and technical		
Wood product manufacturing	321	10.0	services	54	1.3
Printing and related support activities	323	4.5	Management of companies & enterprises	55	3.0
Plastics and rubber products mfg	326	7.4	Administrative & support & waste		
Nonmetallic mineral product mfg	327	7.9	management & remediation services	56	4.0
Primary metal manufacturing	331	9.6	Waste mgmt and remediation services	562	8.3
Fabricated metal product mfg	332	8.5	**Education and health services**	(X)	6.0
Machinery manufacturing	333	6.9	Educational services	61	2.7
Electrical equipment, appliance, and			Health care & social assistance [4]	62	6.5
component manufacturing	335	6.1	Hospitals	622	8.7
Transportation equipment manufacturing	336	9.3	Nursing & residential care facilities	623	10.1
Furniture and related product mfg	337	8.7	**Leisure and hospitality**	(X)	5.1
Miscellaneous manufacturing	339	5.0	Arts, entertainment, and recreation [4]	71	5.9
Service providing	(X)	4.4	Performing arts, spectator sports, and		
Trade, transportation, and utilities [5]	(X)	5.5	related industries	711	6.7
Wholesale trade [4]	42	4.7	Amusement, gambling, & recreation		
Merchant wholesalers, nondurable goods	424	5.7	industries	713	5.8
Retail trade [4]	44-45	5.3	Accommodation and food services	72	5.0
Motor vehicle and parts dealers	441	5.1	Accommodation	721	6.7
Furniture and home furnishings stores	442	5.2	Other services	(X)	3.4

[1] North American Industry Classification System, 2002; see text, this section. [2] Excludes farms with fewer than 11 employees. [3] Data for mining operators in coal, metal, and nonmetal mining are provided to BLS by the Mine Safety and Health Administration (MHSA), U.S. Department of Labor. Independent mining contractors are excluded. Data provided by MSHA do not reflect 2002 OSHA recordkeeping requirements; therefore, estimates for these industries are not comparable with estimates for other industries. [4] Includes other industries, not shown separately. [5] Data for employers in railroad transportation are provided to BLS by the Federal Railroad Administration, U.S. Department of Transportation. Data do not reflect the 2002 OSHA recordkeeping requirements; therefore, estimates for these industries are not comparable with estimates for other industries.

Source: U.S. Bureau of Labor Statistics, *Workplace Injuries and Illnesses in 2003*. See Internet site <http://www.bls.gov/iif/>.

Table 644. Fatal Work Injuries by Event or Exposure: 2003

[See headnote, Table 645]

Cause	Number of fatalities	Percent distribution	Cause	Number of fatalities	Percent distribution
Total	**5,575**	**100**	Contacts with objects and equipment [1]	913	16
			Struck by object [1]	531	10
Transportation accidents [1]	2,364	42	Struck by falling objects	324	6
Highway accidents [1]	1,353	24	Struck by flying object	57	1
Collision between vehicles,			Caught in or compressed by—		
mobile equipment	648	12	Equipment or objects	238	4
Noncollision accidents	321	6	Collapsing materials	126	2
Nonhighway accident (farm,					
industrial premises)	347	6	Falls	696	12
Aircraft accidents	211	4	Exposure to harmful substances or		
Workers struck by a vehicle	337	6	environments [1]	486	9
Water vehicle accidents	69	1	Contact with electric current	246	4
Railway accidents	43	1	Exposure to caustic, noxious		
			or allergenic substances	122	2
Assaults and violent acts [1]	902	16	Oxygen deficiency	73	1
Homicides [1]	632	11	Drowning, submersion	52	1
Shooting	487	9	Fires and explosions	198	4
Stabbing	58	1	Other events and exposures	16	(Z)
Self-inflicted injury	218	4			

Z Less than 0.5 percent. [1] Includes other causes, not shown separately.

Source: U.S. Bureau of Labor Statistics, Census of Fatal Occupational Injuries (CFOI)—Current and Revised Data. See Internet site <http://www.bls.gov/iif/oshcfoi1.htm>.

Table 645. **Fatal Occupational Injuries by Industry and Event or Exposure: 2003**

[For the 50 states and DC. Based on the Census of Fatal Occupational Injuries. For details, see source. Due to methodological differences, data differ from National Safety Council data]

Industry	2002 NAICS [1] code	Fatali-ties [2]	Event or exposure—Percent distribution					Rate [5]
			Trans-portation incidents	Assaults/ violent acts	Contact with objects [3]	Falls	Expo-sure [4]	
Total, 2003	(X)	5,575	42	16	16	13	9	4
Private industry	(X)	5,043	41	16	18	13	9	4
Goods producing	(X)	2,401	34	6	26	19	12	8
Natural resources and mining.	11,21	850	47	7	30	5	7	31
Construction	23	1,131	26	3	20	32	16	12
Manufacturing	31-33	420	28	10	31	9	11	2
Service providing	(X)	2,642	47	25	10	8	6	3
Trade, transportation, and utilities . . .	42, 44-45, 48-49, 22	1,375	59	22	9	5	4	5
Wholesale trade	42	191	48	12	21	8	6	4
Retail trade	44-45	344	24	57	7	7	4	2
Transportation & warehousing. . . .	48-49	808	77	9	7	3	2	18
Utilities	22	32	34	9	13	-	28	4
Information	51	64	61	13	-	11	11	2
Financial activities	52, 53	129	36	37	8	11	6	1
Finance and insurance.	52	45	49	36	-	7	-	1
Real estate and renting and leasing	53	84	29	38	10	13	8	3
Professional & business services . . .	54, 55, 56	453	38	13	18	15	12	3
Professional and technical services.	54	97	54	25	3	8	6	1
Administration and waste management services	56	356	34	10	23	17	13	7
Education and health services	61, 62	143	55	19	4	13	8	1
Education services	61	41	78	-	-	10	-	1
Health and social assistance.	62	102	46	25	4	15	11	1
Leisure and hospitality.	71, 72	275	22	54	4	9	7	2
Arts, entertainment, and recreation	71	88	34	30	10	11	9	4
Accommodation and food services.	72	187	16	66	-	8	6	2
Other.	81	194	21	37	17	9	8	3
Government	92	532	60	19	5	6	8	3

- No data reported or data do not meet publication standards.   X Not applicable.   [1] North American Industry Classification System, 2002. See text, this section. [2] Includes 9 fatalities in service-producing private industries in 2003 for which there was insufficient information to determine industry classification. Includes fatalities caused by other events and exposures, not shown separately. [3] Includes equipment. [4] Exposure to harmful substances or environments. [5] Rate per 100,000 employed civilians 16 years old and over.

Source: U.S. Bureau of Labor Statistics, "Census of Fatal Occupational Injuries (CFOI)—Current and Revised Data." See Internet site <http://www.bls.gov/iif/oshcfoil.htm>.

Table 646. **Work Stoppages: 1960 to 2004**

[896 represents 896,000. Excludes work stoppages involving fewer than 1,000 workers and lasting less than 1 day. Information is based on reports of labor disputes appearing in daily newspapers, trade journals, and other public sources. The parties to the disputes are contacted by telephone, when necessary, to clarify details of the stoppages]

Year	Number of stop-pages [1]	Workers involved [2] (1,000)	Days idle		Year	Number of stop-pages [1]	Workers involved [2] (1,000)	Days idle	
			Number [3] (1,000)	Percent estimated working time [4]				Number [3] (1,000)	Percent estimated working time [4]
1960	222	896	13,260	0.09	1987	46	174	[5]4,481	0.02
1965	268	999	15,140	0.10	1988	40	118	[5]4,381	0.02
1970	381	2,468	52,761	0.29	1989	51	452	16,996	0.07
1972	250	975	16,764	0.09	1990	44	185	5,926	0.02
1973	317	1,400	16,260	0.08	1991	40	392	4,584	0.02
1974	424	1,796	31,809	0.16	1992	35	364	3,989	0.01
1975	235	965	17,563	0.09	1993	35	182	3,981	0.01
1976	231	1,519	23,962	0.12	1994	45	322	5,020	0.02
1977	298	1,212	21,258	0.10	1995	31	192	5,771	0.02
1978	219	1,006	23,774	0.11	1996	37	273	4,889	0.02
1979	235	1,021	20,409	0.09	1997	29	339	4,497	0.01
1980	187	795	20,844	0.09	1998	34	387	5,116	0.02
1981	145	729	16,908	0.07	1999	17	73	1,996	0.01
1982	96	656	9,061	0.04	2000	39	394	20,419	0.06
1983	81	909	17,461	0.08	2001	29	99	1,151	(Z)
1984	62	376	8,499	0.04	2002	19	46	660	(Z)
1985	54	324	7,079	0.03	2003	14	129	4,091	0.01
1986	69	533	11,861	0.05	2004	17	171	3,344	0.01

Z Less than 0.005 percent.   [1] Beginning in year indicated.   [2] Workers counted more than once if involved in more than one stoppage during the year.   [3] Resulting from all stoppages in effect in a year, including those that began in an earlier year. [4] Agricultural and government employees are included in the total working time; private household and forestry and fishery employees are excluded. [5] Revised since originally published.

Source: U.S. Bureau of Labor Statistics. Major Work Stoppages in 2004, News, USDL 05-598, April 8, 2005. See Internet site <http://www.bls.gov/cba/>.

Labor Force, Employment and Earnings 435

Table 647. **Labor Union Membership by Sector: 1983 to 2004**

[See headnote, Table 640. **(17,717.4 represents 17,717,400)**]

Sector	1983	1985	1990	1995	2000	2001	2002	2003	2004
TOTAL (1,000)									
Wage and salary workers:									
Union members	17,717.4	16,996.1	16,739.8	16,359.6	16,258.2	16,288.8	15,978.7	15,776.0	15,471.6
Covered by unions	20,532.1	19,358.1	19,057.8	18,346.3	17,944.1	17,878.1	17,501.6	17,448.4	17,087.3
Public sector workers:									
Union members	5,737.2	5,743.1	6,485.0	6,927.4	7,110.5	7,147.5	7,327.2	7,324.1	7,267.1
Covered by unions. . . .	7,112.2	6,920.6	7,691.4	7,986.6	7,975.6	7,975.4	8,131.9	8,184.7	8,131.1
Private sector workers:									
Union members.	11,980.2	11,253.0	10,254.8	9,432.1	9,147.7	9,141.3	8,651.5	8,451.8	8,204.5
Covered by unions. . . .	13,419.9	12,437.5	11,366.4	10,359.8	9,968.5	9,902.7	9,369.7	9,263.7	8,956.2
PERCENT									
Wage and salary workers:									
Union members	20.1	18.0	16.1	14.9	13.5	13.5	13.3	12.9	12.5
Covered by unions	23.3	20.5	18.3	16.7	14.9	14.8	14.6	14.3	13.8
Public sector workers:									
Union members.	36.7	35.7	36.5	37.7	37.5	37.4	37.8	37.2	36.4
Covered by unions. . . .	45.5	43.1	43.3	43.5	42.0	41.7	41.9	41.5	40.7
Private sector workers:									
Union members.	16.5	14.3	11.9	10.3	9.0	9.0	8.6	8.2	7.9
Covered by unions. . . .	18.5	15.9	13.2	11.3	9.8	9.7	9.3	9.0	8.6

Source: The Bureau of National Affairs, Inc., Washington, DC, *Union Membership and Earnings Data Book: Compilations from the Current Population Survey (2005 edition)*, (copyright by BNA PLUS); authored by Barry Hirsch of Trinity University, San Antonio, TX and David Macpherson of Florida State University. Internet sites <http://www.bna.com/bnaplus/labor/laborrpts.html> and <http://www.unionstats.com>.

Table 648. **Union Members by Selected Characteristics: 2004**

[**Annual averages of monthly data (123,554 represents 123,554,000).** Covers employed wage and salary workers 16 years old and over. Excludes self-employed workers whose businesses are incorporated although they technically qualify as wage and salary workers. Based on Current Population Survey, see text, Section 1, and Appendix III]

Characteristic	Employed wage and salary workers			Median usual weekly earnings [3] (dol.)			
		Percent					
	Total (1,000)	Union members [1]	Repre-sented by unions [2]	Total	Union members [1]	Repre-sented by unions [2]	Not repre-sented by unions
Total [4]	**123,554**	**12.5**	**13.8**	**638**	**781**	**776**	**612**
16 to 24 years old	19,109	4.7	5.3	390	498	494	385
25 to 34 years old	28,202	10.6	11.8	604	724	717	590
35 to 44 years old	30,470	13.7	15.1	713	813	808	690
45 to 54 years old	28,039	17.0	18.7	743	834	831	718
55 to 64 years old	14,239	16.8	18.4	725	835	835	693
65 years and over	3,495	7.5	9.0	560	728	744	520
Men	64,145	13.8	15.0	713	829	828	685
Women	59,408	11.1	12.5	573	723	719	541
White [5]	**101,340**	**12.2**	**13.5**	**657**	**808**	**802**	**626**
Men	53,432	13.6	14.7	732	855	854	704
Women	47,908	10.7	12.1	584	738	734	557
Black [5]	**14,090**	**15.1**	**16.7**	**525**	**656**	**651**	**507**
Men	6,409	16.9	18.5	569	679	679	534
Women	7,681	13.6	15.2	505	629	621	490
Asian [5]	**5,280**	**11.4**	**12.7**	**708**	**765**	**774**	**691**
Men	2,815	11.7	13.2	802	775	786	809
Women	2,465	11.1	12.1	613	756	762	594
Hispanic [6]	**16,533**	**10.1**	**11.4**	**456**	**679**	**670**	**428**
Men	9,857	10.3	11.5	480	697	690	455
Women	6,676	9.9	11.4	419	623	616	401
Private sector industry	103,584	7.9	8.6	615	739	734	604
Agriculture and related industries.	1,023	2.2	2.9	403	(B)	(B)	402
Mining.	496	11.4	11.7	874	905	911	865
Construction	7,550	14.7	15.4	618	893	884	588
Manufacturing	15,754	12.9	13.9	662	694	692	654
Wholesale and retail trade	18,754	5.5	5.9	550	596	590	547
Transportation and utilities	4,893	24.9	26.3	711	854	850	662
Information	3,058	14.2	15.4	828	893	887	808
Financial activities [7]	8,490	2.0	2.5	706	657	649	708
Professional and business services [7] . .	10,815	2.3	2.8	709	679	694	710
Education and health services [7]	16,870	8.3	9.4	613	717	728	603
Leisure and hospitality [7]	10,326	3.1	3.6	407	518	508	402
Other services	5,556	2.8	3.3	528	749	750	521
Public sector	19,970	36.4	40.7	751	832	827	683

B Data not shown where base is less than 50,000.   [1] Members of a labor union or an employee association similar to a labor union.   [2] Members of a labor union or an employee association similar to a union as well as workers who report no union affiliation but whose jobs are covered by a union or an employee association contract.   [3] For full-time employed wage and salary workers.   [4] Includes races not shown separately. Also includes a small number of multiple jobholders whose full- and part-time status can not be determined for their principal job.   [5] For persons in this race group only. See footnote 3, Table 577.   [6] Persons of Hispanic or Latino ethnicity may be of any race.   [7] For composition of industries, see Table 613.

Source: U.S. Bureau of Labor Statistics, *Employment and Earnings*, January 2005. See Internet site <http://www.bls.gov /cps/home.htm>.

Table 649. **Labor Union Membership by State: 1983 and 2004**

[Annual averages of monthly figures (17,717.4 represents 17,717,400). For wage and salary workers in agriculture and non-agriculture. Data represent union members by place of residence. Based on the Current Population Survey and subject to sampling error. For methodological details, see source]

State	Union members (1,000)		Workers covered by unions (1,000)		Percent of workers					
					Union members		Covered by unions		Private sector union members	
	1983	2004	1983	2004	1983	2004	1983	2004	1983	2004
United States.....	17,717.4	15,471.60	20,532.1	17,087.30	20.1	12.5	23.3	13.8	16.5	7.9
Alabama [1].........	228.2	181.3	268.2	213.1	16.9	9.7	19.8	11.5	15.3	5.7
Alaska	41.7	53.9	49.2	60.0	24.9	20.1	29.3	22.4	17.3	10.9
Arizona [1].........	125.0	145.3	156.4	183.2	11.4	6.3	14.3	7.9	8.6	3.9
Arkansas [1]........	82.2	50.9	103.2	65.3	11.0	4.8	13.8	6.2	10.2	3.2
California	2,118.9	2,384.7	2,505.2	2,587.6	21.9	16.5	25.9	18.0	17.7	9.4
Colorado...........	177.9	172.0	209.6	191.3	13.6	8.4	16.0	9.3	11.2	5.2
Connecticut.........	314.0	234.7	345.1	255.8	22.7	15.3	25.0	16.6	16.7	7.3
Delaware	49.2	46.1	54.1	49.2	20.1	12.4	22.1	13.2	15.9	7.7
District of Columbia	52.4	32.7	69.4	37.5	19.5	12.7	25.9	14.5	15.2	8.8
Florida [1]..........	393.7	414.2	532.9	532.9	10.2	6.0	13.8	7.7	7.1	2.8
Georgia [1].........	267.0	242.2	345.1	282.3	11.9	6.4	15.3	7.5	11.1	4.3
Hawaii.............	112.6	126.4	124.9	132.2	29.2	23.7	32.4	24.8	21.9	16.2
Idaho [1]...........	41.3	32.8	53.7	44.4	12.5	5.8	16.2	7.9	10.3	3.7
Illinois	1,063.8	908.3	1,205.1	970.6	24.2	16.8	27.4	17.9	21.5	12.1
Indiana............	503.3	310.7	544.5	337.5	24.9	11.4	27.0	12.4	25.0	9.0
Iowa [1]	185.9	141.0	231.3	170.7	17.2	10.5	21.5	12.7	14.6	7.2
Kansas [1]	125.2	103.0	170.4	131.7	13.7	8.4	18.7	10.8	12.2	6.1
Kentucky	223.7	163.7	259.8	197.2	17.9	9.6	20.8	11.6	18.2	7.5
Louisiana [1]........	204.2	129.3	267.8	157.2	13.8	7.6	18.1	9.3	11.0	4.8
Maine.............	88.0	63.7	100.4	74.4	21.0	11.3	24.0	13.2	14.2	5.9
Maryland	346.5	272.0	423.1	312.9	18.5	10.9	22.6	12.5	14.4	6.0
Massachusetts.......	603.2	393.3	661.4	429.9	23.7	13.5	26.0	14.7	17.6	7.7
Michigan...........	1,005.4	929.8	1,084.6	965.6	30.4	21.6	32.8	22.4	25.3	15.9
Minnesota..........	393.9	424.2	439.4	443.4	23.2	17.5	25.9	18.3	17.1	11.1
Mississippi [1]	79.4	52.9	99.7	70.1	9.9	4.8	12.5	6.3	9.0	4.0
Missouri	374.4	314.8	416.7	356.5	20.8	12.4	23.2	14.0	21.5	10.9
Montana	49.5	42.7	55.5	46.1	18.3	11.7	20.5	12.6	14.8	5.5
Nebraska [1]	80.6	69.2	94.8	83.3	13.6	8.3	16.0	10.0	9.7	5.0
Nevada [1]	90.0	126.0	106.7	143.9	22.4	12.5	26.6	14.3	19.6	10.0
New Hampshire.......	48.5	60.9	60.8	68.3	11.5	9.9	14.4	11.0	7.5	4.8
New Jersey.........	822.1	744.8	918.2	813.5	26.9	19.8	30.0	21.6	21.1	11.6
New Mexico	52.6	49.0	70.6	65.3	11.8	6.7	15.8	8.9	10.1	3.4
New York	2,155.6	1,995.8	2,385.9	2,084.6	32.5	25.3	36.0	26.4	24.0	15.1
North Carolina [1]......	178.7	97.0	238.1	126.5	7.6	2.7	10.2	3.6	5.4	1.6
North Dakota [1].......	28.4	22.4	35.1	26.2	13.2	7.7	16.3	9.0	9.5	4.1
Ohio	1,011.0	758.6	1,125.0	820.3	25.1	15.2	27.9	16.4	22.5	10.5
Oklahoma [2]........	131.5	86.2	168.2	100.2	11.5	6.1	14.7	7.1	9.1	3.5
Oregon............	222.9	223.5	261.9	243.2	22.3	15.2	26.2	16.5	16.4	8.1
Pennsylvania........	1,195.7	792.7	1,350.0	841.7	27.5	15.0	31.1	15.9	23.2	9.7
Rhode Island........	85.8	79.4	93.7	82.6	21.5	16.3	23.5	17.0	13.7	8.8
South Carolina [1]	69.6	53.5	100.6	74.3	5.9	3.0	8.6	4.2	3.9	2.6
South Dakota [1]	26.8	20.8	34.8	26.8	11.5	6.0	14.9	7.7	8.0	2.9
Tennessee [1]	252.4	164.2	300.9	191.0	15.1	6.7	18.0	7.7	12.4	4.9
Texas [1]...........	583.7	457.3	712.8	572.8	9.7	5.0	11.9	6.3	8.1	2.7
Utah [1]	81.6	57.5	100.9	66.6	15.2	5.8	18.9	6.7	11.3	2.9
Vermont............	25.9	28.7	31.5	33.3	12.6	9.8	15.3	11.4	6.7	4.2
Virginia [1]	268.3	176.1	346.1	217.8	11.7	5.3	15.1	6.6	10.2	3.4
Washington.........	419.9	509.8	499.7	535.7	27.1	19.3	32.3	20.3	22.0	13.2
West Virginia........	142.7	99.4	160.6	109.6	25.3	14.2	28.5	15.7	26.1	10.5
Wisconsin..........	465.5	414.3	526.7	439.1	23.8	16.0	26.9	16.9	19.8	10.4
Wyoming [1]	27.1	17.8	31.8	21.9	13.9	8.0	16.2	9.8	10.4	5.3

[1] Right to work state.   [2] Passed right to work law in 2001.

Source: The Bureau of National Affairs, Inc., Washington, DC, *Union Membership and Earnings Data Book: Compilations from the Current Population Survey (2004 edition)*, (copyright by BNA PLUS); authored by Barry Hirsch of Trinity University, San Antonio, TX, and David Macpherson of Florida State University. Internet site <http://www.bna.com/bnaplus/labor/laborrpts.html>. and <http://www.unionstats.com>

No. 346.—CONSUMER INCOMES: Distribution of Families and Single Individuals and of Aggregate Income Received by Income Level,[1] 1935–36

Note.—These figures are estimates based primarily on sample data collected in the Study of Consumer Purchases, a Works Progress Administration project conducted by the Bureau of Home Economics and the Bureau of Labor Statistics in cooperation with the National Resources Committee and the Central Statistical Board. Findings of that study were supplemented by income tax statistics and by other sample data on family and individual incomes

Income level	Families and single individuals, total			Families			Single individuals		
	Number or amount	Per cent at each level	Cumulative per cent	Number or amount	Per cent at each level	Cumulative per cent	Number or amount	Per cent at each level	Cumulative per cent
	Number of units								
All levels	39,458,300	100.00		29,400,300	100.00		10,058,000	100.00	
Under $250	2,123,534	5.38	5.38	1,162,890	3.95	3.95	960,644	9.55	9.55
$250–$500	4,587,377	11.63	17.01	3,015,394	10.26	14.21	1,571,983	15.63	25.18
$500–$750	5,771,960	14.63	31.64	3,799,215	12.92	27.13	1,972,745	19.62	44.80
$750–$1,000	5,876,078	14.90	46.54	4,277,048	14.55	41.68	1,599,030	15.91	60.71
$1,000–$1,250	4,990,995	12.65	59.19	3,882,444	13.20	54.88	1,108,551	11.02	71.73
$1,250–$1,500	3,743,428	9.49	68.68	2,865,472	9.75	64.63	877,956	8.73	80.46
$1,500–$1,750	2,889,904	7.32	76.00	2,343,358	7.97	72.60	546,546	5.43	85.89
$1,750–$2,000	2,296,022	5.82	81.82	1,897,037	6.45	79.05	398,985	3.97	89.86
$2,000–$2,250	1,704,535	4.32	86.14	1,420,883	4.83	83.88	283,652	2.82	92.68
$2,250–$2,500	1,254,076	3.18	89.32	1,043,977	3.55	87.43	210,099	2.09	94.77
$2,500–$3,000	1,475,474	3.74	93.06	1,314,199	4.47	91.90	161,275	1.60	96.37
$3,000–$3,500	851,919	2.16	95.22	743,559	2.53	94.43	108,360	1.08	97.45
$3,500–$4,000	502,159	1.27	96.49	438,428	1.49	95.92	63,731	.63	98.08
$4,000–$4,500	286,053	.72	97.21	249,948	.85	96.77	36,105	.36	98.44
$4,500–$5,000	178,138	.45	97.66	152,647	.52	97.29	25,491	.25	98.69
$5,000–$7,500	380,266	.96	98.62	322,950	1.10	98.39	57,316	.57	99.26
$7,500–$10,000	215,642	.55	99.17	187,060	.64	99.03	28,582	.28	99.54
$10,000–$15,000	152,682	.39	99.56	131,821	.45	99.48	20,861	.21	99.75
$15,000–$20,000	67,923	.17	99.73	58,487	.20	99.68	9,436	.09	99.84
$20,000–$25,000	39,825	.10	99.83	34,208	.12	99.80	5,617	.06	99.90
$25,000–$30,000	28,583	.06	99.89	22,233	.08	99.88	3,350	.03	99.93
$30,000–$40,000	17,959	.05	99.94	15,561	.05	99.93	2,398	.02	99.95
$40,000–$50,000	8,340	.02	99.96	6,603	.02	99.95	1,737	.02	99.97
$50,000–$100,000	13,041	.03	99.99	10,571	.04	99.99	2,470	.02	99.99
$100,000–$250,000	4,144	.01	100.00	3,336	.01	100.00	808	.01	100.00
$250,000–$500,000	916	(2)		699	(2)		217	(2)	
$500,000–$1,000,000	240	(2)		197	(2)		43	(2)	
$1,000,000 and over	87	(2)		75	(2)		12	(2)	
	Amount of aggregate income (in thousands of dollars)								
All levels	59,258,628	100.00		47,679,238	100.00		11,579,390	100.00	
Under $250	294,138	0.50	0.50	135,836	0.28	0.28	158,302	1.37	1.37
$250–$500	1,767,363	2.98	3.48	1,166,509	2.45	2.73	600,854	5.19	6.56
$500–$750	3,615,653	6.10	9.58	2,384,017	5.00	7.73	1,231,636	10.63	17.19
$750–$1,000	5,129,506	8.65	18.23	3,738,014	7.84	15.57	1,391,492	12.01	29.20
$1,000–$1,250	5,589,111	9.42	27.65	4,348,429	9.12	24.69	1,240,682	10.71	39.91
$1,250–$1,500	5,109,112	8.62	36.27	3,907,765	8.20	32.89	1,201,347	10.37	50.28
$1,500–$1,750	4,660,793	7.87	44.14	3,777,570	7.92	40.81	883,223	7.63	57.91
$1,750–$2,000	4,214,263	7.11	51.25	3,468,803	7.27	48.08	745,400	6.44	64.35
$2,000–$2,250	3,602,861	6.08	57.33	3,002,082	6.30	54.38	600,779	5.19	69.54
$2,250–$2,500	2,968,932	5.01	62.34	2,471,672	5.18	59.56	497,260	4.29	73.83
$2,500–$3,000	4,004,774	6.76	69.10	3,568,624	7.48	67.04	436,150	3.77	77.60
$3,000–$3,500	2,735,457	4.62	73.72	2,385,963	5.00	72.04	349,494	3.02	80.62
$3,500–$4,000	1,863,384	3.14	76.86	1,625,887	3.41	75.45	237,497	2.05	82.67
$4,000–$4,500	1,202,826	2.03	78.89	1,048,368	2.20	77.65	154,458	1.33	84.00
$4,500–$5,000	841,766	1.42	80.31	719,447	1.51	79.16	122,319	1.06	85.06
$5,000–$7,500	2,244,406	3.79	84.10	1,900,091	3.99	83.15	344,315	2.97	88.03
$7,500–$10,000	1,847,820	3.12	87.22	1,605,632	3.37	86.52	242,188	2.09	90.12
$10,000–$15,000	1,746,925	2.95	90.17	1,496,600	3.14	89.66	250,325	2.16	92.28
$15,000–$20,000	1,174,574	1.98	92.15	1,013,664	2.13	91.79	160,910	1.39	93.67
$20,000–$25,000	889,114	1.50	93.65	762,240	1.60	93.39	126,874	1.10	94.77
$25,000–$30,000	720,268	1.22	94.87	627,567	1.32	94.71	92,701	.80	95.57
$30,000–$40,000	641,272	1.08	95.95	560,390	1.18	95.89	80,882	.70	96.27
$40,000–$50,000	390,311	.66	96.61	314,689	.66	96.55	75,622	.65	96.92
$50,000–$100,000	908,485	1.53	98.14	755,017	1.58	98.13	153,468	1.33	98.25
$100,000–$250,000	539,006	.91	99.05	440,554	.92	99.05	98,452	.85	99.10
$250,000–$500,000	264,498	.45	99.50	200,174	.42	99.47	64,324	.56	99.66
$500,000–$1,000,000	134,803	.23	99.73	110,954	.23	99.70	23,849	.21	99.87
$1,000,000 and over	157,237	.27	100.00	142,650	.30	100.00	14,587	.13	100.00

[1] The estimates cover all consumers with the exception of 2,000,000 persons living in institutions or quasi-institutional groups. A family is defined as 2 or more persons sharing a common income and living under a common roof. Single individuals include persons lodging in rooming houses and hotels, living as lodgers or servants in private homes, or maintaining independent living quarters as 1-person families. Income includes the total net money income received during the year by all members of the economic family plus the value of certain items of nonmoney income, such as the occupancy of an owned home and food produced by rural families for their own use. The estimates apply to the 12-month period from July 1935 through June 1936. [2] Less than 0.005 percent.

Source: National Resources Committee—Report on "Consumer Incomes in the United States—their distribution in 1935–36."

Source: Statistical Abstract of the United States: 1938 Edition.

Section 13
Income, Expenditures, and Wealth

This section presents data on gross domestic product (GDP), gross national product (GNP), national and personal income, saving and investment, money income, poverty, and national and personal wealth. The data on income and expenditures measure two aspects of the U.S. economy. One aspect relates to the National Income and Product Accounts (NIPA), a summation reflecting the entire complex of the nation's economic income and output and the interaction of its major components; the other relates to the distribution of money income to families and individuals or consumer income. New information from the American Community Survey may be found in Tables 689–692.

The primary source for data on GDP, GNP, national and personal income, gross saving and investment, and fixed reproducible tangible wealth is the *Survey of Current Business*, published monthly by the Bureau of Economic Analysis (BEA). A comprehensive revision to the NIPA was released beginning in October 1999. Discussions of the revision appeared in the January, June, August, September and the December 2003 issues of the *Survey of Current Business*. Summary historical estimates appeared in the February 2004 issue of the *Survey of Current Business*. Detailed historical data on the NIPA are available on an interactive Web site at <http://www.bea.doc.gov/bea/dn/nipaweb/index.asp>.

Sources of income distribution data are the decennial censuses of population and the Current Population Survey (CPS), both products of the U.S. Census Bureau (see text, Section 1 and Section 4). Annual data on income of families, individuals, and households are presented in *Current Population Reports, Consumer Income*, P60 Series, in print, and many data series found on the Census Web site at <http://www.census.gov/hhes/www/income.html>. Data on the household sector's saving and assets are published

by the Board of Governors of the Federal Reserve System in the quarterly *Flow of Funds Accounts*. The Board also periodically conducts the *Survey of Consumer Finances*, which presents financial information on family assets and net worth. Detailed information on personal wealth is published periodically by the Internal Revenue Service (IRS) in *SOI Bulletin*.

National income and product—Gross domestic product is the total output of goods and services produced by labor and property located in the United States, valued at market prices. GDP can be viewed in terms of the expenditure categories that comprise its major components purchases of goods and services by consumers and government, gross private domestic investment, and net exports of goods and services. The goods and services included are largely those bought for final use (excluding illegal transactions) in the market economy. A number of inclusions, however, represent imputed values, the most important of which is rental value of owner-occupied housing. GDP, in this broad context, measures the output attributable to the factors of production located in the United States. Gross state product (GSP) is the gross market value of the goods and services attributable to labor and property located in a state. It is the state counterpart of the nation's gross domestic product.

In January 1996, BEA replaced its fixed weighted index as the featured measure of real GDP with an index based on chain type annual weights. Changes in this measure of real output and prices are calculated as the average of changes based on weights for the current and preceding years. (Components of real output are weighted by price, and components of prices are weighted by output.) These annual changes are "chained" (multiplied) together to form a time series that allows for the effects of changes in relative prices and changes in the composition of output over time. Quarterly and monthly changes are also based on annual weights. The new output indexes are expressed as 2000=100, and for recent years, in 2000 dollars; the new price indexes are based to 2000=100. For more information on chain-dollar indexes, see the article on this subject in the November 2003 issue of the *Survey of Current Business.*

Chained (2000) dollar estimates of most components of GDP are not published for periods prior to 1990, because during periods far from the base period, the levels of the components may provide misleading information about their contributions to an aggregate. Values are published in index form (2000=100) for 1929 to the present to allow users to calculate the percent changes for all components, changes that are accurate for all periods.

Gross national product measures the output attributable to all labor and property supplied by United States residents. GNP differs from "national income" mainly in that GNP includes allowances for depreciation consumption of fixed capital.

National Income includes all net incomes (net of CFC) earned in production. National income is the sum of compensation of employees, proprietors' income with inventory valuation adjustment (IVA) and capital consumption adjustment (CCAdj), rental income of persons with CCAdj, corporate profits with IVA and CCAdj, net interest and miscellaneous payments, taxes on production and imports, business current transfer payments, current surplus of government enterprises, less subsidies.

Capital consumption adjustment for corporations and for nonfarm sole proprietorships and partnerships is the difference between capital consumption based on income tax returns and capital consumption measured using empirical evidence on prices of used equipment and structures in resale markets, which have shown that depreciation for most types of assets approximates a geometric pattern. The tax return data are valued at historical costs and reflect changes over time in service lives and depreciation patterns as permitted by tax regulations. *Inventory*

valuation adjustment represents the difference between the book value of inventories used up in production and the cost of replacing them.

Personal income is the current income received by persons from all sources minus their personal contributions for government social insurance. Classified as "persons" are individuals (including owners of unincorporated firms), nonprofit institutions that primarily serve individuals, private trust funds, and private noninsured welfare funds. Personal income includes personal current transfer receipts (payments not resulting from current production) from government and business such as social security benefits, public assistance, etc., but excludes transfers among persons. Also included are certain nonmonetary types of income chiefly, estimated net rental value to owner-occupants of their homes and the value of services furnished without payment by financial intermediaries. Capital gains (net losses) are excluded.

Disposable personal income is personal income less personal current taxes. It is the income available to persons for spending or saving. Personal current taxes are tax payments (net of refunds) by persons (except personal contributions for government social insurance) that are not chargeable to business expense and certain personal payments to general government that are treated like taxes. Personal taxes include income, estate and gift, and personal property taxes andmotor vehicle licenses. Nontax payments include passport fees, fines and forfeitures, and donations.

Gross domestic product by industry—The BEA also prepares estimates of value added by industry. *Value added* is a measure of the contribution of each private industry and of government to the Nation's GDP. It is defined as an industry's gross output (which consists of sales or receipts and other operating income, commodity taxes, and inventory change) minus its intermediate inputs (which consists of energy, raw materials, semi-finished goods, and services that are purchased from domestic industries or from foreign sources). These estimates of value added are produced for 61 private industries and for 4 government classifications—federal general government and government enterprises and state and local general government and government enterprises.

The estimates by industry are available in current dollars and are derived from the estimates of gross domestic income, which consists of three components the compensation of employees, gross operating surplus, and taxes on production and imports, less subsidies. Real, or inflation-adjusted, estimates are also prepared.

Regional Economic Accounts—These accounts consist of estimates of state and local area personal income and of gross state product and are consistent with estimates of personal income and gross domestic product in the Bureau's national economic accounts. BEA's estimates of state and local area personal income provide a framework for analyzing individual state and local economies, and they show how the economies compare with each other. The *personal income* of a state and/or local area is the income received by, or on behalf of, the residents of that state or area. Estimates of labor and proprietors' earnings by place of work indicate the economic activity of business and government within that area, and estimates of personal income by place of residence indicate the income within the area that is available for spending. BEA prepares estimates for states, counties, metropolitan areas, and BEA economic areas.

Gross state product estimates measure the value added to the Nation's production by the labor and property in each state. GSP is often considered the state counterpart of the Nation's GDP. The GSP estimates provide the basis for analyzing the regional impacts of national economic trends. GSP is measured as the sum of the distributions by industry and state of the components of gross domestic income that is, the sum of the costs incurred and incomes earned in the production of GDP. The GSP estimates are presented in current dollars and in real (chained dollars) for 63 industries.

Consumer Expenditure Survey—The Consumer Expenditure Survey program was begun in late 1979. The principal objective of the survey is to collect current consumer expenditure data, which provide a continuous flow of data on the buying habits of American consumers. The data are necessary for future revisions of the Consumer Price Index.

The survey conducted by the Census Bureau for the Bureau of Labor Statistics consists of two components: (1) an interview panel survey in which the expenditures of consumer units are obtained in five interviews conducted every 3 months, and (2) a diary or recordkeeping survey completed by participating households for two consecutive 1-week period.

Each component of the survey queries an independent sample of consumer units representative of the U.S. total population. Over 52 weeks of the year, 5,000 consumer units are sampled for the diary survey. Each consumer unit keeps a diary for two 1-week periods yielding approximately 10,000 diaries a year. The interview sample is selected on a rotating panel basis, targeted at 5,000 consumer units per quarter. Data are collected in 88 urban and 16 rural areas of the country that are representative of the U.S. total population. The survey includes students in student housing. Data from the two surveys are combined; integration is necessary to permit analysis of total family expenditures because neither the diary nor quarterly interview survey was designed to collect a complete account of consumer spending.

Distribution of money income to families and individuals—Money income statistics are based on data collected in various field surveys of income conducted since 1936. Since 1947, the Census Bureau has collected the data on an annual basis and published them in *Current Population Reports*, P60 Series. In each of the surveys, field representatives interview samples of the population with respect to income received during the previous year. *Money income* as defined by the Census Bureau differs from the BEA concept of "personal income." Data on consumer income collected in the CPS by the Census Bureau cover money income

Income, Expenditures, and Wealth   441

received (exclusive of certain money receipts such as capital gains) before payments for personal income taxes, social security, union dues, medicare deductions, etc. Therefore, money income does not reflect the fact that some families receive part of their income in the form of noncash benefits (see Section 11) such as food stamps, health benefits, and subsidized housing; that some farm families receive noncash benefits in the form of rent-free housing and goods produced and consumed on the farm; or that noncash benefits are also received by some nonfarm residents which often take the form of the use of business transportation and facilities, full or partial payments by business for retirement programs, medical and educational expenses, etc. These elements should be considered when comparing income levels. None of the aggregate income concepts (GDP, national income, or personal income) is exactly comparable with money income, although personal income is the closest.

In October 1983, the Census Bureau began to collect data under the new Survey of Income and Program Participation-(SIPP). The data collected in SIPP will be used to study federal and state aid programs (such as food stamps, welfare, medicaid, and subsidized housing), to estimate program costs and coverage, and to assess the effects of proposed changes in program eligibility rules or benefit levels. The core questions are repeated at each interview and cover labor force activity, the types and amounts of income received, and participation status in various programs. The core also contains questions covering attendance in postsecondary schools and private health insurance coverage. Various supplements or topical modules covering areas such as educational attainment, assets and liabilities, and pension plan coverage are periodically included.

Poverty—Families and unrelated individuals are classified as being above or below the poverty level using the poverty index originated at the Social Security Administration in 1964 and revised by Federal Interagency Committees in 1969 and 1980.

The poverty index is based solely on money income and does not reflect the fact that many low-income persons receive noncash benefits such as food stamps, medicaid, and public housing. The index is based on the Department of Agriculture's 1961 Economy Food Plan and reflects the different consumption requirements of families based on their size and composition. The poverty thresholds are updated every year to reflect changes in the Consumer Price Index. The following technical changes to the thresholds were made in 1981: (1) distinctions based on sex of householder have been eliminated, (2) separate thresholds for farm families have been dropped, and (3) the matrix has been expanded to families of nine or more persons from the old cutoff of seven or more persons. These changes have been incorporated in the calculation of poverty data beginning with 1981. Besides the Census Bureau Web site at <http://www.census.gov/hhes/www/poverty.html>, information on poverty guidelines and research may be found at the U.S. Department of Human Services Web site at <http://aspe.hhs.gov/poverty/poverty.shtml>.

In the recent past, the Census Bureau has published a number of technical papers that presented experimental poverty estimates based on income definitions that counted the value of selected government noncash benefits. The Census Bureau has also published annual reports on aftertax income. In addition, in July 1999, the Census Bureau released a report (P60-205) that showed the effect of using experimental poverty following the recommendations of a National Academy of Sciences panel on redefining our nation's poverty measure and recently published a report entitled *Alternative Poverty Estimates in the United States: 2003.*

Statistical reliability—For a discussion of statistical collection and estimation, sampling procedures, and measures of statistical reliability pertaining to Census Bureau data, see Appendix III.

442   Income, Expenditures, and Wealth

U.S. Census Bureau. Statistical Abstract of the United States: 2006

Table 650. Gross Domestic Product in Current and Real (2000) Dollars: 1960 to 2004

[In billions of dollars (526,400,000,000). For explanation of gross domestic product and chained dollars, see text, this section]

Item	1960	1970	1980	1990	1992	1993	1994	1995	1996	1997	1998	1999	2000	2001	2002	2003	2004
CURRENT DOLLARS																	
Gross domestic product	526.4	1,038.5	2,789.5	5,803.1	6,337.7	6,657.4	7,072.2	7,397.7	7,816.9	8,304.3	8,747.0	9,268.4	9,817.0	10,128.0	10,487.0	11,004.0	11,735.0
Personal consumption expenditures	331.7	648.5	1,757.1	3,839.9	4,235.3	4,477.9	4,743.3	4,975.8	5,256.8	5,547.4	5,879.5	6,282.5	6,739.4	7,055.0	7,376.1	7,760.9	8,229.9
Durable goods	43.3	85.0	214.2	474.2	483.6	526.7	582.2	611.6	652.5	692.7	750.2	817.6	863.3	883.7	916.2	950.7	993.9
Nondurable goods	152.8	272.0	696.1	1,249.9	1,330.5	1,379.4	1,437.2	1,485.1	1,555.5	1,619.0	1,683.6	1,804.8	1,947.2	2,017.1	2,080.1	2,200.1	2,377.0
Services	135.6	291.5	846.9	2,115.9	2,421.2	2,571.8	2,723.9	2,879.1	3,048.7	3,235.8	3,445.7	3,660.0	3,928.8	4,154.3	4,379.8	4,610.1	4,859.0
Gross private domestic investment	78.9	152.4	479.3	861.0	864.8	953.4	1,097.1	1,144.0	1,240.3	1,389.8	1,509.1	1,625.7	1,735.5	1,614.3	1,579.2	1,665.8	1,927.3
Fixed investment	75.7	150.4	485.6	846.4	848.5	932.5	1,033.3	1,112.9	1,209.5	1,317.8	1,438.4	1,558.8	1,679.0	1,646.1	1,568.0	1,667.0	1,884.0
Change in business inventories	3.2	2.0	-6.3	14.5	16.3	20.8	63.8	31.1	30.8	72.0	70.8	66.9	56.5	-31.7	11.2	-1.2	43.4
Net exports of goods and services	4.2	4.0	-13.1	-78.0	-33.2	-65.0	-93.6	-91.4	-96.2	-101.6	-159.9	-260.5	-379.5	-367.0	-424.9	-498.1	-606.2
Exports	27.0	59.7	280.8	552.4	635.3	655.8	720.9	812.2	868.6	955.3	955.9	991.2	1,096.3	1,032.8	1,005.0	1,046.2	1,175.5
Imports	22.8	55.8	293.8	630.3	668.6	720.9	814.5	903.6	964.8	1,056.9	1,115.9	1,251.7	1,475.8	1,399.8	1,429.9	1,544.3	1,781.6
Government consumption expenditures and gross investment	111.6	233.8	566.2	1,180.2	1,271.0	1,291.2	1,325.5	1,369.2	1,416.0	1,468.7	1,518.3	1,620.8	1,721.6	1,825.6	1,956.6	2,075.5	2,183.9
Federal	64.1	113.5	243.8	508.3	533.9	525.2	519.1	519.2	524.4	530.9	530.4	555.8	578.8	612.9	680.8	752.2	809.9
National defense	53.4	87.6	168.0	374.0	376.9	362.9	353.7	348.7	354.6	349.6	345.7	360.6	370.3	392.6	437.4	496.4	547.9
Nondefense	10.7	25.8	75.8	134.3	157.0	162.4	165.5	170.5	172.8	181.3	184.7	195.2	208.5	220.3	243.4	255.7	262.0
State and local	47.5	120.3	322.4	671.9	737.0	766.0	806.3	850.0	888.6	937.8	987.9	1,065.0	1,142.8	1,212.8	1,275.8	1,323.3	1,373.9
CHAINED (2000) DOLLARS																	
Gross domestic product	2,501.8	3,771.9	5,161.7	7,112.5	7,336.6	7,532.7	7,835.5	8,031.7	8,328.9	8,703.5	9,066.9	9,470.3	9,817.0	9,890.7	10,074.8	10,381.3	10,841.9
Personal consumption expenditures	1,597.4	2,451.9	3,374.1	4,770.3	4,934.8	5,099.8	5,290.7	5,433.5	5,619.4	5,831.8	6,125.8	6,438.6	6,739.4	6,910.4	7,123.4	7,355.6	7,632.5
Durable goods	(NA)	(NA)	(NA)	453.5	453.0	484.8	529.4	552.6	595.9	646.9	720.3	804.6	863.3	900.7	959.6	1,030.6	1,099.3
Nondurable goods	(NA)	(NA)	(NA)	1,484.0	1,510.1	1,550.4	1,603.9	1,638.6	1,680.4	1,725.3	1,794.4	1,876.6	1,947.2	1,986.7	2,037.4	2,112.4	2,208.5
Services	(NA)	(NA)	(NA)	2,851.7	3,000.0	3,085.7	3,176.6	3,259.9	3,356.0	3,468.0	3,615.0	3,758.0	3,928.8	4,023.2	4,128.6	4,220.3	4,338.3
Gross private domestic investment	266.6	427.1	645.3	895.1	889.0	968.3	1,099.6	1,134.0	1,234.3	1,387.7	1,524.1	1,642.6	1,735.5	1,598.4	1,560.7	1,628.8	1,843.5
Fixed investment	(NA)	(NA)	(NA)	886.6	878.3	953.5	1,042.3	1,109.6	1,200.2	1,320.6	1,455.0	1,576.3	1,679.0	1,629.9	1,548.9	1,627.3	1,794.4
Change in business inventories	(NA)	(NA)	(NA)	15.4	16.5	20.6	63.6	29.9	28.7	71.2	72.6	68.9	56.5	-31.7	11.7	-0.8	45.7
Net exports of goods and services	(NA)	(NA)	(NA)	-54.7	-15.9	-52.1	-79.4	-71.0	-79.6	-104.6	-203.7	-296.2	-379.5	-399.1	-472.1	-518.5	-583.7
Exports	90.6	161.4	323.5	552.5	629.7	650.0	706.5	778.2	843.4	943.7	966.5	1,008.2	1,096.3	1,036.7	1,012.3	1,031.8	1,120.3
Imports	103.3	213.4	310.9	607.1	645.6	702.1	785.9	849.1	923.0	1,048.3	1,170.3	1,304.4	1,475.8	1,435.8	1,484.4	1,550.3	1,704.0
Government consumption expenditures and gross investment	715.4	1,012.9	1,115.4	1,530.0	1,555.3	1,541.1	1,541.3	1,549.7	1,564.9	1,594.0	1,624.4	1,686.9	1,721.6	1,780.3	1,857.9	1,909.4	1,946.5
Federal	(NA)	(NA)	(NA)	659.1	646.6	619.6	596.4	580.3	573.5	567.6	561.2	573.7	578.8	601.4	646.6	689.6	721.7
National defense	(NA)	(NA)	(NA)	479.4	450.7	425.3	404.6	389.2	383.8	373.0	365.3	372.2	370.3	384.9	414.6	451.8	484.4
Nondefense	(NA)	(NA)	(NA)	178.6	195.4	194.1	191.7	191.0	189.6	194.5	195.9	201.5	208.5	216.5	232.0	237.6	236.4
State and local	(NA)	(NA)	(NA)	868.4	906.5	919.5	943.3	968.3	990.5	1,025.9	1,063.0	1,113.2	1,142.8	1,179.0	1,211.4	1,219.8	1,224.8
Residual	-64.9	-68.0	14.3	-91.1	-89.1	-78.6	-63.7	-51.1	-38.5	-23.8	-14.6	-5.8	0.2	1.6	3.7	0.8	-10.6

NA Not available.

Source: U.S. Bureau of Economic Analysis. *Survey of Current Business*, May 2005. See also <http://www.bea.doc.gov/bea/dn/nipaweb/SelectTable.asp?Selected=N> (released 28 April 2005).

Income, Expenditures, and Wealth 443

Table 651. Gross Domestic Product in Current and Real (2000) Dollars by Industry: 2000 to 2004

[In billions of dollars (9,817.0 represents $9,817,000,000,000). Data are based on the 1997 NAICS. Data include nonfactor charges (capital consumption allowances, indirect business taxes, etc.) as well as factor charges against gross product; corporate profits and capital consumption allowances have been shifted from a company to an establishment basis]

Industry	Current dollars				Chained (2000) dollars			
	2000	2002	2003	2004	2000	2002	2003	2004
Gross domestic product [1]	9,817.0	10,487.0	11,004.0	11,735.0	9,817.0	10,074.8	10,381.4	10,841.9
Private industries	8,614.3	9,154.1	9,604.2	10,276.0	8,614.3	8,851.6	9,123.0	9,543.5
Agriculture, forestry, and fishing	98.0	96.9	113.9	116.6	98.0	98.1	103.5	96.9
Farms	71.5	70.8	84.8	(NA)	71.5	69.9	72.7	(NA)
Agricultural services	26.5	26.1	29.1	(NA)	26.5	28.3	31.1	(NA)
Mining	121.3	104.9	130.3	147.5	121.3	112.4	104.6	106.9
Metal mining	81.0	60.4	83.2	(NA)	81.0	77.6	65.3	(NA)
Coal mining	27.0	27.4	27.7	(NA)	27.0	24.7	25.1	(NA)
Oil and gas extraction	13.4	17.1	19.4	(NA)	13.4	10.9	12.7	(NA)
Utilities	189.3	210.7	222.2	241.2	189.3	190.7	202.0	213.0
Construction	435.9	479.1	501.3	541.4	435.9	425.1	424.1	433.4
Manufacturing	1,426.2	1,347.2	1,402.3	1,494.0	1,426.2	1,378.2	1,440.0	1,501.3
Durable goods	865.3	771.9	798.0	862.6	865.3	824.2	874.5	925.7
Wood products	31.4	30.0	32.0	(NA)	31.4	29.9	29.9	(NA)
Nonmetallic mineral products	45.7	43.3	43.3	(NA)	45.7	42.8	43.4	(NA)
Primary metals	48.2	41.6	38.9	(NA)	48.2	43.6	41.9	(NA)
Fabricated metal products	121.7	109.4	112.2	(NA)	121.7	106.3	109.9	(NA)
Machinery	109.3	97.6	96.4	(NA)	109.3	94.5	93.7	(NA)
Computer and electronic products	185.6	130.5	147.6	(NA)	185.6	195.3	250.9	(NA)
Electronic equipment, appliances, and components	50.6	46.1	47.3	(NA)	50.6	46.4	48.9	(NA)
Motor vehicles, bodies and trailers, and parts	118.1	114.1	121.9	(NA)	118.1	120.3	131.0	(NA)
Other transportation equipment	64.4	70.0	67.6	(NA)	64.4	64.5	60.1	(NA)
Furniture and related products	32.7	30.0	28.9	(NA)	32.7	28.2	27.2	(NA)
Miscellaneous manufacturing	57.5	59.4	62.0	(NA)	57.5	55.9	57.8	(NA)
Nondurable goods	561.0	575.3	604.4	631.4	561.0	553.0	566.2	578.4
Food & beverage & tobacco	154.8	172.5	173.3	(NA)	154.8	153.0	154.6	(NA)
Textile mills & textile product mills	26.5	22.3	21.7	(NA)	26.5	21.7	21.9	(NA)
Apparel and leather and allied products	25.1	24.7	25.0	(NA)	25.1	25.0	25.5	(NA)
Paper products	55.6	50.8	51.5	(NA)	55.6	51.3	53.6	(NA)
Printing & related support activities	49.0	46.0	45.2	(NA)	49.0	44.2	43.2	(NA)
Petroleum and coal products	26.2	25.7	38.2	(NA)	26.2	31.5	28.1	(NA)
Chemical products	157.1	167.0	181.5	(NA)	157.1	163.3	174.0	(NA)
Plastics and rubber products	66.7	66.2	68.0	(NA)	66.7	63.6	66.1	(NA)
Wholesale trade	591.7	624.9	645.4	688.1	591.7	643.0	631.0	651.6
Retail trade	662.4	744.3	770.5	797.6	662.4	746.4	788.4	829.7
Transportation and warehousing	301.6	304.4	319.3	338.6	301.6	299.1	314.2	324.7
Air transportation	57.7	50.0	56.5	(NA)	57.7	61.1	73.8	(NA)
Rail transportation	25.5	25.8	26.6	(NA)	25.5	24.2	24.3	(NA)
Water transportation	7.2	7.0	7.7	(NA)	7.2	6.3	6.4	(NA)
Truck transportation	92.8	95.4	97.2	(NA)	92.8	87.9	88.0	(NA)
Transit & ground passenger transport	14.5	15.8	16.3	(NA)	14.5	14.7	14.5	(NA)
Pipeline transportation	8.7	9.7	7.6	(NA)	8.7	8.0	7.7	(NA)
Other transportation & support	70.2	72.5	75.5	(NA)	70.2	69.6	71.2	(NA)
Warehousing and storage	25.0	28.3	31.9	(NA)	25.0	27.1	30.3	(NA)
Information	458.3	470.0	493.8	547.2	458.3	475.5	502.4	551.7
Publishing industries (incl. software)	116.7	116.1	120.9	(NA)	116.7	113.6	121.3	(NA)
Motion picture and sound recording	32.5	36.4	41.2	(NA)	32.5	33.5	35.5	(NA)
Broadcasting & telecommunications	271.3	272.8	283.0	(NA)	271.3	285.7	299.2	(NA)
Information and data processing services	37.7	44.7	48.6	(NA)	37.7	42.5	46.1	(NA)
Finance and insurance [2]	740.5	818.2	882.9	972.4	740.5	793.8	856.3	923.1
Real estate and rental and leasing	1,190.5	1,330.0	1,367.4	1,451.3	1,190.5	1,239.7	1,244.1	1,295.7
Professional, scientific, and technical services	675.1	712.9	743.3	792.1	675.1	681.2	701.8	730.5
Legal services	136.1	149.2	160.6	(NA)	136.1	135.8	140.8	(NA)
Computer systems design, related services	125.7	123.1	126.6	(NA)	125.7	123.5	129.8	(NA)
Miscellaneous	413.3	440.6	456.1	(NA)	413.3	421.9	431.2	(NA)
Management of companies & enterprises	183.4	178.0	191.3	213.6	183.4	179.8	186.5	197.2
Administrative and waste management	282.4	299.1	309.7	335.6	282.4	286.7	299.6	317.7
Educational services	79.2	91.5	94.5	99.5	79.2	79.2	77.8	77.3
Health care and social assistance	599.2	707.6	756.7	804.4	599.2	647.6	669.3	690.0
Ambulatory health care services	307.6	367.8	391.1	(NA)	307.6	348.7	363.6	(NA)
Hospitals, nursing, residential care	238.6	276.8	298.2	(NA)	238.6	241.7	246.8	(NA)
Social assistance	53.0	63.0	67.3	(NA)	53.0	57.9	59.9	(NA)
Arts, entertainment, and recreation	88.7	102.5	106.6	111.8	88.7	94.7	95.6	97.5
Performing arts, spectator sports, museums, and related activities	40.0	46.8	49.0	(NA)	40.0	43.0	43.3	(NA)
Amusements, gambling, & recreation	48.7	55.7	57.6	(NA)	48.7	51.6	52.3	(NA)
Accommodation and food services	261.4	279.8	289.9	308.1	261.4	259.4	265.2	279.8
Accommodation	90.7	90.4	93.2	(NA)	90.7	87.9	89.2	(NA)
Food services and drinking places	170.8	189.4	196.6	(NA)	170.8	171.5	176.0	(NA)
Government	1,202.7	1,332.9	1,399.9	1,458.4	1,202.7	1,230.4	1,247.3	1,262.4
Federal	378.7	415.8	447.1	465.4	378.7	380.6	390.3	395.6
State and local	823.9	917.1	952.8	993.0	823.9	849.7	856.9	866.6

NA Not available. [1] Includes industries, not shown separately.

Source: U.S. Bureau of Economic Analysis, Survey of Current Business, May 2005. See also <http://www.bea.doc.gov/bea/newsrelarchive/2005/gdpind04.pdf> (released 20 April 2005).

Table 652. **Gross Domestic Product in Current and Real (2000) Dollars by Type of Product and Sector: 1990 to 2004**

[In billions of dollars (5,803.1 represents $5,803,100,000,000). For explanation of chained dollars, see text, this section]

Type of product and sector	1990	1995	1998	1999	2000	2001	2002	2003	2004
CURRENT DOLLARS									
Gross domestic product	5,803.1	7,397.7	8,747.0	9,268.4	9,817.0	10,128.0	10,487.0	11,004.0	11,735.0
PRODUCT									
Goods	2,155.8	2,661.1	3,143.4	3,311.3	3,449.3	3,412.6	3,439.5	3,564.5	3,837.2
Durable goods	957.9	1,235.7	1,530.5	1,616.5	1,689.4	1,588.6	1,570.9	1,618.8	1,752.0
Nondurable goods	1,198.0	1,425.4	1,612.8	1,694.8	1,760.0	1,824.0	1,868.6	1,945.7	2,085.2
Services	3,113.7	4,098.4	4,789.8	5,081.8	5,425.6	5,725.6	6,056.8	6,384.7	6,727.5
Structures	533.5	638.1	813.8	875.3	942.1	989.8	990.7	1,054.8	1,170.3
SECTOR									
Business	4,462.6	5,700.6	6,827.1	7,243.4	7,666.7	7,841.2	8,057.1	8,472.3	9,061.3
Nonfarm	4,386.0	5,632.0	6,748.2	7,174.7	7,595.1	7,768.0	7,986.3	8,387.5	8,974.6
Farm	76.6	68.5	78.9	68.8	71.5	73.1	70.8	84.8	86.7
Households and institutions	618.9	815.5	949.7	1,012.3	1,080.7	1,160.4	1,235.2	1,276.5	1,367.6
General government	721.6	881.6	970.3	1,012.7	1,069.6	1,126.4	1,194.8	1,255.3	1,306.1
Federal	258.9	284.7	293.1	300.9	315.4	325.7	350.4	378.4	393.5
State and local	462.6	596.9	677.2	711.8	754.2	800.8	844.3	876.9	912.6
CHAINED (2000) DOLLARS									
Gross domestic product	7,112.5	8,031.7	9,066.9	9,470.3	9,817.0	9,890.7	10,074.8	10,381.3	10,841.9
PRODUCT									
Goods	2,252.7	2,639.0	3,132.7	3,312.6	3,449.3	3,390.9	3,432.8	3,581.8	3,846.3
Durable goods	877.2	1,124.5	1,473.1	1,594.1	1,689.4	1,613.0	1,625.8	1,719.7	1,896.2
Nondurable goods	1,407.1	1,531.6	1,661.8	1,718.9	1,760.0	1,776.9	1,805.6	1,862.5	1,956.1
Services	4,170.0	4,654.7	5,057.5	5,245.1	5,425.6	5,553.2	5,718.0	5,850.9	6,006.0
Structures	718.3	753.5	879.1	913.0	942.1	945.6	922.8	950.4	1,001.3
SECTOR									
Business	5,287.0	6,076.8	7,017.1	7,376.8	7,666.7	7,691.0	7,831.0	8,132.1	8,549.7
Nonfarm	5,237.9	6,030.2	6,955.3	7,314.2	7,595.1	7,625.7	7,761.3	8,059.6	8,488.2
Farm	49.3	49.6	61.6	62.9	71.5	65.6	69.9	72.7	65.5
Households and institutions	841.2	945.1	1,010.4	1,042.3	1,080.7	1,110.0	1,135.8	1,132.5	1,170.3
General government	1,003.9	1,020.6	1,041.0	1,051.4	1,069.6	1,089.3	1,107.4	1,120.1	1,129.6
Federal	371.6	334.1	315.2	312.7	315.4	317.0	323.2	331.7	334.3
State and local	633.6	686.5	725.8	738.7	754.2	772.3	784.3	788.3	795.2

Source: U.S. Bureau of Economic Analysis, *Survey of Current Business*, May 2005. See also <http://www.bea.doc.gov/bea /dn/nipaweb/SelectTable.asp?Selected=N> (released as 28 April 2005).

Table 653. **GDP Components in Real (2000) Dollars—Annual Percent Change: 1990 to 2004**

[Change from previous year; for 1990, change from 1989 and for 1996, change from 1995. Minus sign (-) indicates decrease]

Component	1990	1996	1997	1998	1999	2000	2001	2002	2003	2004
Gross domestic product (GDP). . .	1.9	3.7	4.5	4.2	4.5	3.7	0.8	1.9	3.0	4.4
Personal consumption expenditures	2.0	3.4	3.8	5.0	5.1	4.7	2.5	3.1	3.3	3.8
Durable goods.	(NA)	7.8	8.6	11.3	11.7	7.3	4.3	6.5	7.4	6.7
Nondurable goods	(NA)	2.6	2.7	4.0	4.6	3.8	2.0	2.6	3.7	4.6
Services.	(NA)	2.9	3.3	4.2	4.0	4.5	2.4	2.6	2.2	2.8
Gross private domestic investment	-3.4	8.8	12.4	9.8	7.8	5.7	-7.9	-2.4	4.4	13.2
Fixed investment	(NA)	9.0	9.2	10.2	8.3	6.5	-3.0	-4.9	5.1	10.3
Nonresidential	(NA)	9.3	12.1	11.1	9.2	8.7	-4.2	-8.9	3.3	10.6
Structures	(NA)	5.7	7.3	5.1	-0.4	6.8	-2.3	-17.8	-5.6	1.4
Equipment and software	(NA)	10.6	13.8	13.3	12.7	9.4	-4.9	-5.5	6.4	13.6
Residential	(NA)	8.0	1.9	7.6	6.0	0.7	0.4	4.8	8.8	9.7
Exports	9.0	8.4	11.9	2.4	4.3	8.7	-5.4	-2.3	1.9	8.6
Goods	(NA)	8.8	14.4	2.2	3.8	11.2	-6.1	-4.1	2.2	8.8
Services.	(NA)	7.2	6.0	2.9	5.6	2.9	-3.7	1.8	1.4	8.0
Imports	3.6	8.7	13.6	11.6	11.5	13.1	-2.7	3.4	4.4	9.9
Goods	(NA)	9.3	14.4	11.7	12.4	13.5	-3.2	3.7	4.7	10.8
Services.	(NA)	5.5	9.4	11.4	6.9	11.1	-0.3	1.9	3.1	5.8
Government consumption expenditures and gross investment	3.2	1.0	1.9	1.9	3.9	2.1	3.4	4.4	2.8	1.9
Federal	(NA)	-1.2	-1.0	-1.1	2.2	0.9	3.9	7.5	6.6	4.7
National defense	(NA)	-1.4	-2.8	-2.1	1.9	-0.5	3.9	7.7	9.0	7.3
Nondefense.	(NA)	-0.7	2.6	0.7	2.8	3.5	3.9	7.1	2.4	-0.5
State and local	(NA)	2.3	3.6	3.6	4.7	2.7	3.2	2.8	0.7	0.4

NA Not available.

Source: U.S. Bureau of Economic Analysis, *Survey of Current Business*, May 2005. See also <http://www.bea.doc.gov/bea /dn/nipaweb/SelectTable.asp?Selected=N> (released as 28 April 2005).

Table 654. Gross State Product in Current and Real (2000) Dollars by State: 1990 to 2004

[In billions of dollars (5,674.0 represents $5,674,000,000,000). For definition of gross state product or chained dollars, see text, this section]

State	Current dollars					Chained (2000) dollars [1]				
	1990	2000	2002	2003	2004, prel	1990	2000	2002	2003	2004, prel.
United States	5,674.0	9,749.1	10,412.2	10,923.8	11,649.8	6,939.7	9,749.1	10,009.4	10,289.2	10,720.3
Alabama.	71.1	114.2	123.8	130.8	138.5	86.6	114.2	118.2	122.7	126.9
Alaska	25.0	27.6	29.7	31.7	33.9	31.9	27.6	28.7	28.1	29.0
Arizona.	69.3	157.6	173.1	183.3	199.7	81.1	157.6	168.0	175.5	187.3
Arkansas	38.1	66.2	71.2	74.5	80.1	45.1	66.2	68.1	69.7	72.8
California	788.3	1,291.1	1,363.6	1,438.1	1,543.8	955.9	1,291.1	1,324.3	1,369.2	1,438.7
Colorado.	74.2	171.4	181.2	188.4	200.0	91.3	171.4	174.7	178.3	185.2
Connecticut.	99.0	160.7	167.2	174.1	187.1	124.6	160.7	160.1	164.1	172.4
Delaware	20.1	42.4	47.0	50.5	54.5	28.1	42.4	44.5	47.0	49.4
District of Columbia	40.1	58.4	67.2	70.7	75.3	55.1	58.4	62.6	64.1	66.9
Florida	257.2	470.1	522.3	553.7	594.5	320.5	470.1	497.7	517.9	543.8
Georgia	139.5	291.0	307.4	321.2	340.7	172.1	291.0	294.8	303.0	314.3
Hawaii	31.9	40.2	43.8	46.7	50.1	41.0	40.2	41.4	43.0	45.4
Idaho	17.8	35.2	38.3	40.4	43.4	19.6	35.2	37.4	38.8	40.8
Illinois	277.2	464.3	486.2	499.7	528.9	336.3	464.3	465.8	470.1	485.2
Indiana.	110.1	194.7	203.3	213.3	227.3	131.0	194.7	195.0	201.3	208.4
Iowa	55.9	90.8	97.8	102.4	114.3	64.5	90.8	93.2	95.6	103.3
Kansas.	51.3	83.4	89.9	93.3	99.1	62.4	83.4	85.8	86.8	89.9
Kentucky	67.5	112.7	121.6	128.3	135.4	81.3	112.7	116.3	120.5	124.1
Louisiana	93.6	134.8	134.4	144.3	152.0	121.7	134.8	130.6	130.7	133.3
Maine.	23.3	35.7	39.0	40.8	43.3	29.3	35.7	37.1	38.1	39.5
Maryland	113.7	180.0	202.8	213.1	226.5	145.2	180.0	192.5	198.3	206.4
Massachusetts.	158.9	276.8	287.2	297.1	317.7	195.7	276.8	278.2	284.3	298.0
Michigan.	189.7	337.2	347.0	359.4	372.8	234.2	337.2	333.7	341.0	346.0
Minnesota.	100.3	185.4	199.3	210.2	225.6	121.5	185.4	191.7	198.5	207.8
Mississippi	38.8	64.1	68.6	71.9	76.2	46.7	64.1	65.2	66.6	68.9
Missouri	104.1	176.4	187.1	193.8	203.2	128.0	176.4	178.6	181.6	185.8
Montana	13.4	21.4	23.9	25.6	27.7	16.2	21.4	22.6	23.5	24.7
Nebraska	33.8	55.7	60.6	65.4	67.9	40.3	55.7	57.6	60.7	61.2
Nevada	31.8	74.8	82.4	89.7	99.4	40.5	74.8	78.2	83.6	90.4
New Hampshire	23.8	43.6	46.1	48.2	52.1	27.7	43.6	44.5	45.9	48.6
New Jersey	214.8	344.0	377.8	394.0	415.9	266.6	344.0	363.0	371.8	383.7
New Mexico	26.9	50.4	53.4	57.1	60.9	28.7	50.4	52.5	54.2	56.4
New York	503.6	769.4	802.9	838.0	899.7	624.3	769.4	777.1	801.0	843.1
North Carolina	140.3	274.3	301.3	315.5	335.4	173.6	274.3	286.9	295.9	307.6
North Dakota	11.5	18.1	20.0	21.6	23.6	13.5	18.1	19.0	19.9	21.1
Ohio	228.3	371.2	385.7	398.9	418.3	274.9	371.2	369.4	375.7	384.0
Oklahoma.	57.7	89.9	95.3	101.2	107.2	70.0	89.9	91.8	93.8	96.7
Oregon.	57.3	113.0	115.1	120.0	128.1	63.2	113.0	112.9	116.1	121.4
Pennsylvania	248.3	391.5	424.8	443.7	468.8	305.2	391.5	404.6	415.3	427.8
Rhode Island	21.5	33.8	37.0	39.4	41.9	27.2	33.8	35.0	36.5	38.0
South Carolina.	65.7	112.8	122.3	128.0	135.3	79.0	112.8	116.4	120.0	124.1
South Dakota	12.8	23.2	25.8	27.3	29.4	14.9	23.2	24.7	25.6	26.8
Tennessee	94.6	174.3	191.4	203.1	216.9	115.5	174.3	183.2	191.2	199.5
Texas	384.1	722.8	775.5	821.9	880.9	462.0	722.8	755.4	769.4	803.7
Utah	31.4	67.9	73.6	76.7	82.4	38.8	67.9	70.1	71.6	75.1
Vermont	11.7	17.7	19.4	20.5	22.1	13.8	17.7	18.7	19.6	20.6
Virginia	147.0	260.3	288.8	304.1	326.6	187.9	260.3	274.5	283.9	299.4
Washington	115.7	221.3	234.0	245.1	259.8	145.6	221.3	223.5	229.7	238.3
West Virginia.	28.3	41.7	45.3	46.7	49.8	33.2	41.7	42.7	43.2	44.3
Wisconsin	100.3	176.2	189.5	198.1	211.7	119.1	176.2	181.2	186.4	194.1
Wyoming	13.2	17.4	20.3	22.3	24.3	15.2	17.4	19.5	19.9	20.7

[1] For chained (2000) dollar estimates, states will not add to U.S. total.

Source: U.S. Bureau of Economic Analysis, *Survey of Current Business*, July 2005; and Internet site at <http://www.bea.doc.gov/bea /regional/gsp/> and <http://www.bea.doc.gov/bea/newsrelarchive/2005/gsp0605.pdf> (released 23 June 2005).

446 Income, Expenditures, and Wealth

Table 655. Gross State Product in Chained (2000) Dollars by Selected Industries and State: 2003

[In billions of dollars (10,289.2 represents $10,289,200,000,000). For definition of gross state product or chained dollars, see text, this section. Industries based on 1997 North American Industry Classification System; see text, Section 12, Labor]

State	Total [1]	Construction	Manufacturing	Wholesale trade	Retail trade	Finance, and insurance	Information	Professional services	Health care and social assistance	Government [2]
United States [3] . . .	10,289.2	424.1	1,440.0	631.0	788.4	856.3	502.4	701.8	669.3	1,175.3
Alabama.	122.7	4.9	21.6	7.2	11.3	6.6	4.0	7.2	8.1	19.0
Alaska	28.1	1.4	0.6	0.7	1.8	1.0	0.9	1.0	1.6	5.5
Arizona.	175.5	9.2	26.0	10.0	16.0	14.5	5.9	9.6	10.9	20.3
Arkansas	69.7	2.9	13.4	4.7	5.9	3.2	3.1	2.4	5.1	8.6
California	1,369.2	53.8	181.5	80.1	106.9	96.3	85.4	109.0	75.3	142.9
Colorado.	178.3	9.7	14.8	9.9	13.2	12.4	17.2	15.1	9.8	20.4
Connecticut.	164.1	4.9	21.1	9.2	11.4	27.1	6.8	12.7	11.6	13.8
Delaware	47.0	1.4	4.8	1.8	2.4	15.2	0.9	2.8	2.2	3.8
District of Columbia	64.1	0.7	0.2	0.7	1.0	3.6	4.7	12.7	2.9	22.1
Florida	517.9	26.7	31.0	35.3	47.4	37.3	24.6	31.4	37.0	59.0
Georgia	303.0	13.4	43.0	23.7	22.8	18.8	21.3	18.8	16.2	37.2
Hawaii	43.0	2.0	0.8	1.6	3.6	2.0	1.3	2.0	2.9	9.2
Idaho	38.8	2.2	7.1	2.1	3.5	1.6	0.8	2.5	2.4	5.0
Illinois	470.1	20.3	66.2	34.0	31.4	46.8	20.5	38.1	28.6	43.9
Indiana.	201.3	· 8.5	58.4	11.0	15.0	12.0	4.9	7.4	13.4	18.6
Iowa	95.6	3.5	20.5	5.8	7.3	9.9	3.3	3.0	6.2	10.7
Kansas.	86.8	3.4	12.9	5.7	7.3	5.5	7.4	3.9	5.8	11.5
Kentucky	120.5	4.8	26.5	7.2	9.5	5.9	3.3	5.3	8.8	16.8
Louisiana	130.7	5.4	14.1	7.3	10.8	5.2	3.8	6.1	8.8	16.6
Maine.	38.1	1.6	4.9	2.1	4.0	2.6	1.2	1.7	3.7	5.2
Maryland	198.3	10.3	13.5	11.0	15.0	14.1	7.9	20.1	14.0	32.3
Massachusetts.	284.3	12.7	38.0	17.5	17.5	33.2	13.6	27.7	21.9	23.3
Michigan.	341.0	13.5	76.4	20.3	26.0	19.8	10.0	27.1	22.2	33.5
Minnesota.	198.5	9.1	28.8	14.3	14.7	20.9	7.4	11.7	14.7	19.3
Mississippi	66.6	2.6	10.9	3.6	6.6	2.9	1.9	2.3	4.6	11.1
Missouri	181.6	7.9	28.8	11.8	14.7	11.6	9.2	10.4	12.7	20.1
Montana	23.5	1.3	1.2	1.4	2.1	1.2	0.8	1.2	2.0	3.8
Nebraska	60.7	2.4	7.8	4.1	4.5	5.0	2.3	2.6	4.1	8.5
Nevada	83.6	7.3	3.1	3.5	7.5	6.9	2.3	4.3	4.0	8.1
New Hampshire	45.9	2.2	6.6	3.0	4.6	3.9	1.5	2.8	3.5	4.0
New Jersey.	371.8	14.0	43.3	32.0	27.5	32.5	18.0	30.3	23.7	35.4
New Mexico	54.2	2.1	7.1	2.0	4.3	2.0	1.7	3.6	3.4	10.1
New York	801.0	23.5	60.6	43.8	48.6	138.3	57.0	66.0	58.5	78.5
North Carolina	295.9	11.4	68.7	16.8	21.8	29.1	9.9	13.9	16.5	35.4
North Dakota.	19.9	0.8	2.1	1.6	1.7	1.3	0.7	0.8	1.7	3.0
Ohio	375.7	13.6	80.8	23.4	30.3	28.0	11.6	20.1	27.6	39.4
Oklahoma.	93.8	3.6	11.2	5.1	8.4	4.9	4.2	4.4	6.3	15.3
Oregon.	116.1	4.8	21.4	8.1	7.9	6.5	4.0	5.7	8.1	13.8
Pennsylvania.	415.3	16.3	72.2	24.2	31.7	31.0	17.2	27.9	34.7	38.4
Rhode Island.	36.5	2.0	3.9	1.9	2.8	4.9	1.5	1.9	3.1	4.2
South Carolina.	120.0	6.1	24.8	6.8	10.7	5.8	3.4	5.1	6.5	17.6
South Dakota	25.6	1.0	3.2	1.4	2.3	4.4	0.7	0.6	2.1	3.1
Tennessee	191.2	6.7	35.1	13.2	18.1	11.8	6.3	9.0	14.8	22.1
Texas.	769.4	32.1	101.3	54.3	61.3	50.6	38.5	49.4	44.7	86.1
Utah	71.6	3.6	8.0	3.9	6.3	6.6	2.9	4.4	3.8	9.9
Vermont	19.6	0.8	3.2	1.1	1.8	1.2	0.8	1.0	1.7	2.4
Virginia.	283.9	12.0	36.4	12.8	19.8	18.9	16.6	29.3	14.1	45.9
Washington.	229.7	9.7	21.0	14.1	18.5	13.8	21.4	15.4	14.3	31.2
West Virginia.	43.2	1.6	5.1	2.1	4.0	1.7	1.4	1.7	4.0	7.1
Wisconsin	186.4	7.5	43.6	10.6	13.9	13.6	6.0	7.7	14.1	19.5
Wyoming	19.9	1.0	1.3	0.8	1.4	0.6	0.4	0.6	0.9	2.8

- Represents zero.   [1] Includes industries not shown separately.   [2] Includes Federal civilian and military and state and local government.   [3] States will not add to U.S. total as chained-dollar estimates are usually not additive.

Source: U.S. Bureau of Economic Analysis, *Survey of Current Business,* July 2005; and Internet site at <http://www.bea.doc.gov /bea/regional/gsp/> and <http://www.bea.doc.gov/bea/newsrelarchive/2005/gsp0605.pdf> (released 23 June 2005).

Income, Expenditures, and Wealth 447

Table 656. Relation of GDP, GNP, Net National Product, National Income, Personal Income, Disposable Personal Income, and Personal Saving: 1990 to 2004

[In billions of dollars (5,803.1 represents $5,803,100,000,000). For definitions, see text, this section]

Item	1990	1995	1999	2000	2001	2002	2003	2004
Gross domestic product	5,803.1	7,397.7	9,268.4	9,817.0	10,128.0	10,487.0	11,004.0	11,735.0
Plus: Income receipts from the rest of the world	189.1	233.9	320.8	382.7	322.4	301.8	329.0	405.8
Less: Income payments to the rest of the world	154.3	198.1	287.0	343.7	278.8	274.7	273.9	361.9
Equals: Gross national product	5,837.9	7,433.4	9,302.2	9,855.9	10,171.6	10,514.1	11,059.2	11,778.9
Less: Consumption of fixed capital	682.5	878.4	1,101.3	1,187.8	1,281.5	1,303.9	1,353.9	1,407.3
Equals: Net national product	5,155.4	6,555.1	8,200.9	8,668.1	8,890.2	9,210.1	9,705.2	10,371.6
Less: Statistical discrepancy	66.2	101.2	-35.7	-127.2	-89.6	-15.3	25.6	50.9
Equals: National income	5,089.1	6,453.9	8,236.7	8,795.2	8,979.8	9,225.4	9,679.6	10,320.6
Less: Corporate profits [1]	437.8	696.7	851.3	817.9	767.3	874.6	1,021.1	1,181.6
Taxes on production and imports less subsidies	398.7	524.2	629.8	664.6	673.3	724.4	751.3	800.6
Contributions for government social insurance	410.1	532.8	661.4	702.7	731.1	748.3	773.2	820.2
Net interest and miscellaneous payments on assets	442.2	367.1	495.4	559.0	566.3	532.9	543.0	549.5
Business current transfer payments (net)	39.4	46.9	67.4	87.1	92.8	80.9	77.7	82.1
Current surplus of government enterprises	1.6	11.4	10.1	5.3	-1.4	2.8	9.5	6.9
Wage accruals less disbursements . . .	0.1	16.4	5.2	-	-	-	-	-
Plus: Personal income receipts on assets	924.0	1,016.4	1,264.2	1,387.0	1,380.0	1,334.6	1,322.7	1,387.3
Personal current transfer receipts	595.2	877.4	1,022.1	1,084.0	1,193.9	1,282.7	1,335.4	1,405.9
Equals: Personal income	4,878.6	6,152.3	7,802.4	8,429.7	8,724.1	8,878.9	9,161.8	9,673.0
Less: Personal current taxes	592.8	744.1	1,107.5	1,235.7	1,237.3	1,051.2	1,001.9	1,038.9
Equals: Disposable personal income	4,285.8	5,408.2	6,695.0	7,194.0	7,486.8	7,827.7	8,159.9	8,634.0
Less: Personal outlays	3,986.4	5,157.3	6,536.4	7,025.6	7,354.5	7,668.5	8,049.3	8,531.9
Equals: Personal saving	299.4	250.9	158.6	168.5	132.3	159.2	110.6	102.1

- Represents zero or rounds to zero.   [1] Corporate profits with inventory valuation and capital consumption adjustments.

Source: U.S. Bureau of Economic Analysis, *Survey of Current Business,* May 2005. See also <http://www.bea.doc.gov/bea /dn/nipaweb/SelectTable.asp?Selected=N> (released as 28 April 2005).

Table 657. Selected Per Capita Income and Product Measures in Current and Real (2000) Dollars: 1960 to 2004

[In dollars. Based on U.S. Census Bureau estimated population including Armed Forces abroad; based on quarterly averages. For explanation of chained dollars, see text, this section]

Year	Current dollars					Chained (2000) dollars			
	Gross domestic product	Gross national product	Personal income	Disposable personal income	Personal consumption expenditures	Gross domestic product	Gross national product	Disposable personal income	Personal consumption expenditures
1960	2,912	2,929	2,277	2,022	1,835	13,840	13,938	9,735	8,837
1965	3,700	3,727	2,860	2,563	2,283	16,420	16,554	11,594	10,331
1970	5,064	5,095	4,090	3,587	3,162	18,391	18,520	13,563	11,955
1975	7,586	7,646	6,181	5,498	4,789	19,961	20,133	15,291	13,320
1980	12,249	12,400	10,134	8,822	7,716	22,666	22,956	16,940	14,816
1981	13,601	13,745	11,266	9,765	8,439	23,007	23,259	17,217	14,879
1982	14,017	14,174	11,951	10,426	8,945	22,346	22,607	17,418	14,944
1983	15,092	15,251	12,635	11,131	9,775	23,146	23,396	17,828	15,656
1984	16,638	16,792	13,915	12,319	10,589	24,593	24,828	19,011	16,343
1985	17,695	17,806	14,787	13,037	11,406	25,382	25,548	19,476	17,040
1986	18,542	18,616	15,466	13,649	12,048	26,024	26,137	19,906	17,570
1987	19,517	19,590	16,255	14,241	12,766	26,664	26,770	20,072	17,994
1988	20,827	20,923	17,358	15,297	13,685	27,514	27,647	20,740	18,554
1989	22,169	22,275	18,545	16,257	14,546	28,221	28,358	21,120	18,898
1990	23,195	23,335	19,500	17,131	15,349	28,429	28,600	21,281	19,067
1991	23,650	23,770	19,923	17,609	15,722	28,007	28,150	21,109	18,848
1992	24,668	24,783	20,870	18,494	16,485	28,556	28,693	21,548	19,208
1993	25,578	25,700	21,356	18,872	17,204	28,940	29,079	21,493	19,593
1994	26,844	26,944	22,176	19,555	18,004	29,741	29,850	21,812	20,082
1995	27,749	27,884	23,078	20,287	18,665	30,128	30,271	22,153	20,382
1996	28,982	29,112	24,176	21,091	19,490	30,881	31,015	22,546	20,835
1997	30,424	30,544	25,334	21,940	20,323	31,886	32,010	23,065	21,365
1998	31,674	31,752	26,880	23,161	21,291	32,833	32,912	24,131	22,183
1999	33,181	33,302	27,933	23,968	22,491	33,904	34,027	24,564	23,050
2000	34,759	34,897	29,847	25,472	23,862	34,759	34,897	25,472	23,862
2001	35,491	35,644	30,572	26,236	24,723	34,660	34,810	25,698	24,216
2002	36,386	36,480	30,806	27,159	25,592	34,955	35,049	26,229	24,715
2003	37,805	37,995	31,476	28,034	26,663	35,666	35,846	26,570	25,270
2004	39,921	40,071	32,907	29,372	27,998	36,883	37,023	27,240	25,965

Source: U.S. Bureau of Economic Analysis, *Survey of Current Business,* May 2005. See also <http://www.bea.doc.gov/bea /dn/nipaweb/SelectTable.asp?Selected=N> (released as 28 April 2005).

Table 658. **Personal Consumption Expenditures in Current and Real (2000) Dollars by Type: 1990 to 2003**

[In billions of dollars (3,839.9 represents $3,839,900,000,000). For definition of "chained" dollars, see text, this section]

Expenditure	Current dollars				Chained (2000) dollars			
	1990	2000	2002	2003	1990	2000	2002	2003
Total expenditures [1]	3,839.9	6,739.4	7,376.1	7,760.9	4,770.3	6,739.4	7,123.4	7,355.6
Food and tobacco [1]	677.8	1,003.7	1,095.0	1,152.6	867.1	1,003.7	1,034.4	1,068.4
Food purchased for off-premise consumption	401.6	566.7	615.6	647.1	485.7	566.7	589.8	609.2
Purchased meals and beverages [2]	227.7	348.8	380.0	406.5	289.6	348.8	358.7	375.6
Tobacco products	41.0	78.5	89.1	88.1	87.7	78.5	76.3	74.2
Clothing, accessories, and jewelry [1]	261.5	397.0	404.4	412.3	247.7	397.0	416.8	433.6
Shoes	31.5	47.0	49.3	50.7	30.4	47.0	50.3	52.5
Clothing	172.4	250.4	252.5	256.0	157.7	250.4	266.1	277.2
Jewelry and watches	30.3	50.6	51.0	53.6	26.5	50.6	52.5	57.1
Personal care	56.9	93.4	95.8	96.9	68.5	93.4	93.1	93.7
Housing [1]	597.9	1,006.5	1,144.8	1,188.4	802.2	1,006.5	1,062.0	1,076.1
Owner-occupied nonfarm dwellings- space rent	412.8	712.2	820.7	859.6	551.6	712.2	759.4	776.4
Tenant-occupied nonfarm dwellings-space rent	150.7	227.5	258.7	262.3	199.9	227.5	238.8	235.6
Household operation [1]	433.3	719.3	746.0	779.6	485.0	719.3	738.8	763.8
Furniture [3]	38.4	67.6	68.3	69.5	41.8	67.6	70.9	73.1
Semidurable house furnishings [4]	22.5	36.5	37.4	37.9	20.1	36.5	39.4	43.2
Cleaning and polishing preparations	38.9	61.6	66.6	69.1	46.2	61.6	63.8	67.2
Household utilities	141.1	209.9	221.9	242.4	174.5	209.9	212.1	215.5
Electricity	74.2	102.3	111.7	116.1	81.1	102.3	104.5	106.2
Gas	26.8	41.0	40.8	51.2	36.6	41.0	40.2	41.0
Water and other sanitary services	27.1	50.8	55.2	58.2	41.1	50.8	52.0	52.8
Fuel oil and coal	12.9	15.8	14.1	16.9	16.7	15.8	15.4	15.4
Telephone and telegraph	60.5	125.1	128.3	129.8	58.3	125.1	130.7	133.4
Medical care [1]	635.1	1,218.3	1,444.9	1,557.2	905.9	1,218.3	1,355.6	1,414.6
Drug preparations and sundries [5]	65.4	169.4	213.0	233.7	90.1	169.4	195.4	208.6
Physicians	138.6	236.8	278.3	298.2	194.7	236.8	270.6	285.6
Dentists	32.4	61.8	72.2	75.0	53.5	61.8	66.4	66.2
Hospitals and nursing homes [6]	270.9	482.6	574.0	616.8	386.4	482.6	531.0	546.5
Health insurance [7]	43.4	84.0	96.1	106.0	70.1	84.0	92.1	96.4
Medical care [7]	31.8	68.4	79.7	88.1	52.8	68.4	73.9	76.9
Personal business [1]	250.9	539.1	552.1	577.7	330.0	539.1	531.3	547.3
Expense of handling life insurance [8]	53.2	96.1	84.8	91.5	86.2	96.1	79.4	82.6
Legal services	40.9	63.9	71.3	77.3	62.2	63.9	63.9	66.0
Funeral and burial expenses	9.5	14.0	14.6	15.7	15.0	14.0	13.5	13.9
Transportation	471.7	853.4	877.5	925.5	590.1	853.4	889.0	911.0
User-operated transportation [1]	434.7	793.8	827.2	872.9	546.6	793.8	833.4	854.4
New autos	89.7	103.6	101.6	97.5	102.5	103.6	103.3	101.0
Net purchases of used autos	29.3	60.7	58.4	53.9	42.4	60.7	57.6	56.9
Tires, tubes, accessories, etc.	29.9	49.0	50.7	53.2	29.3	49.0	48.7	50.6
Repair, greasing, washing, parking, storage, rental, and leasing	84.9	183.5	186.0	186.2	109.4	183.5	175.4	172.5
Gasoline and oil	111.2	175.7	163.4	191.3	141.8	175.7	180.7	182.0
Purchased local transportation	8.4	12.2	12.4	12.6	10.9	12.2	11.8	11.1
Mass transit systems	5.8	9.1	9.0	8.8	7.5	9.1	8.5	7.8
Taxicab	2.6	3.1	3.4	3.7	3.4	3.1	3.2	3.3
Purchased intercity transportation [1]	28.6	47.4	37.9	40.0	32.5	47.4	43.6	45.3
Railway (commutation)	0.6	0.5	0.6	0.6	0.8	0.5	0.5	0.5
Bus	1.3	2.4	2.3	2.3	1.5	2.4	2.2	2.0
Airline	22.7	36.7	28.1	30.3	24.8	36.7	34.0	36.1
Recreation [1, 9]	290.2	585.7	628.3	660.7	276.5	585.7	646.0	689.6
Magazines, newspapers, and sheet music	21.6	35.0	35.3	36.6	29.3	35.0	34.0	34.6
Nondurable toys and sport supplies	32.8	56.6	59.0	60.2	28.3	56.6	65.0	70.2
Video and audio products, including musical instruments and computer goods	53.0	116.6	119.1	121.3	18.6	116.6	154.4	176.7
Computers, peripherals, and software	8.9	43.8	44.2	46.1	(NA)	(NA)	(NA)	(NA)
Education and research	83.7	163.8	190.7	201.7	125.6	163.8	173.7	174.7
Higher education	43.8	86.4	103.9	112.2	69.6	86.4	93.5	95.7
Religious and welfare activities	88.7	172.3	202.9	211.2	121.2	172.3	191.5	193.7
Foreign travel and other, net [1]	-7.7	-13.0	-6.4	-2.7	-13.1	-13.0	-9.1	-8.5
Foreign travel by U.S. residents	42.7	84.4	77.4	79.2	53.3	84.4	73.7	71.0
Expenditures abroad by U.S. residents	3.6	4.6	5.6	6.6	3.6	4.6	5.2	5.2
Less: Expenditures in the United States by nonresidents	53.0	100.7	87.9	86.7	68.8	100.7	86.6	83.0

NA - Not available. [1] Includes other expenditures not shown separately. [2] Consists of purchases (including tips) of meals and beverages from retail, service, and amusement establishments; hotels; dining and buffet cars; schools; school fraternities; institutions; clubs; and industrial lunch rooms. Includes meals and beverages consumed both on- and off-premise. [3] Includes mattresses and bedsprings. [4] Consists largely of textile house furnishings including piece goods allocated to house furnishing use. Also includes lamp shades, brooms, and brushes. [5] Excludes drug preparations and related products dispensed by physicians, hospitals, and other medical services. [6] Consists of (1) current expenditures (including consumption of fixed capital) of nonprofit hospitals and nursing homes and (2) payments by patients to proprietary and government hospitals and nursing homes. [7] Consists of (1) premiums, less benefits and dividends, for health hospitalization and accidental death and dismemberment insurance provided by commercial insurance carriers and (2) administrative expenses (including consumption of fixed capital) of Blue Cross and Blue Shield plans and of other independent prepaid and self-insured health plans. [8] Consists of (1) operating expenses of life insurance carriers and private noninsured pension plans and (2) premiums less benefits and dividends of fraternal benefit societies. Excludes expenses allocated by commercial carriers to accident and health insurance. [9] For additional details, see Table 1222.

Source: U.S. Bureau of Economic Analysis, *Survey of Current Business*, August 2004. See also <http://www.bea.doc.gov/bea/dn/nipaweb/SelectTable.asp?Selected=N> (released as 05 August 2004).

Income, Expenditures, and Wealth 449

Table 659. Personal Income and Its Disposition: 1990 to 2004

[In billions of dollars (4,878.6 represents $4,878,600,000,000), except as indicated. For definition of personal income and chained dollars, see text, this section]

Item	1990	1995	1999	2000	2001	2002	2003	2004
Personal income	4,878.6	6,152.3	7,802.4	8,429.7	8,724.1	8,878.9	9,161.8	9,673.0
Compensation of employees, received . .	3,338.2	4,177.0	5,352.0	5,782.7	5,942.1	6,069.5	6,289.0	6,632.0
Wage and salary disbursements	2,754.0	3,419.3	4,466.3	4,829.2	4,942.8	4,976.3	5,103.6	5,355.7
Supplements to wages and salaries . .	584.2	757.7	885.7	953.4	999.3	1,093.2	1,185.5	1,276.3
Proprietors' income [1]	380.6	492.1	678.3	728.4	771.9	769.6	834.1	902.8
Farm	31.9	22.7	28.6	22.7	19.7	9.7	21.8	18.2
Nonfarm	348.7	469.5	649.7	705.7	752.2	759.9	812.3	884.6
Rental income of persons [1]	50.7	122.1	147.3	150.3	167.4	170.9	153.8	165.1
Personal income receipts on assets . . .	924.0	1,016.4	1,264.2	1,387.0	1,380.0	1,334.6	1,322.7	1,387.3
Personal interest income	755.2	763.2	928.6	1,011.0	1,011.0	946.7	929.9	946.2
Personal dividend income	168.8	253.2	335.6	376.1	369.0	387.9	392.8	441.1
Personal current transfer receipts	595.2	877.4	1,022.1	1,084.0	1,193.9	1,282.7	1,335.4	1,405.9
Government social benefits to persons	573.1	858.4	988.0	1,041.6	1,143.9	1,248.9	1,306.4	1,373.2
Old-age, survivors, disability, and health insurance benefits	351.8	506.8	588.9	620.8	668.5	708.3	733.8	779.2
Other current transfer receipts, from business(net)	22.2	19.0	34.1	42.4	50.0	33.7	28.9	32.7
Less: Contributions for government social insurance	410.1	532.8	661.4	702.7	731.1	748.3	773.2	820.2
Less: Personal current taxes	592.8	744.1	1,107.5	1,235.7	1,237.3	1,051.2	1,001.9	1,038.9
Equals: Disposable personal income . .	**4,285.8**	**5,408.2**	**6,695.0**	**7,194.0**	**7,486.8**	**7,827.7**	**8,159.9**	**8,634.0**
Less: Personal outlays	3,986.4	5,157.3	6,536.4	7,025.6	7,354.5	7,668.5	8,049.3	8,531.9
Personal consumption expenditures . . .	3,839.9	4,975.8	6,282.5	6,739.4	7,055.0	7,376.1	7,760.9	8,229.9
Personal interest payments	116.1	132.7	181.0	204.7	212.2	197.2	185.3	188.5
Personal current transfer payments	30.4	48.9	73.0	81.5	87.2	95.3	103.1	113.5
Equals: Personal saving	**299.4**	**250.9**	**158.6**	**168.5**	**132.3**	**159.2**	**110.6**	**102.1**
Personal saving as a percentage of disposable personal income	7.0	4.6	2.4	2.3	1.8	2.0	1.4	1.2
Addenda:								
Disposable personal income:								
Total, billions of chained (2000) dollars .	5,324.2	5,905.7	6,861.3	7,194.0	7,333.3	7,559.5	7,733.8	8,007.3
Per capita:								
Current dollars	17,131	20,287	23,968	25,472	26,236	27,159	28,034	29,372
Chained (2000) dollars	21,281	22,153	24,564	25,472	25,698	26,229	26,570	27,240

[1] With inventory valuation adjustments and capital consumption adjustment.
Source: U.S. Bureau of Economic Analysis, *Survey of Current Business,* May 2005. See also <http://www.bea.doc.gov/bea/dn /nipaweb/SelectTable.asp?Selected=N> (released as 28 April 2005).

Table 660. Gross Saving and Investment: 1990 to 2004

[In billions of dollars (940.4 represents $940,400,000,000)]

Item	1990	1995	1999	2000	2001	2002	2003	2004
Gross saving	**940.4**	**1,184.5**	**1,674.3**	**1,770.5**	**1,657.6**	**1,484.3**	**1,487.7**	**1,620.0**
Net saving	258.0	306.2	573.0	582.7	376.1	180.3	133.8	212.7
Net private saving	422.7	491.1	419.0	343.3	324.6	459.8	501.5	570.7
Personal saving	299.4	250.9	158.6	168.5	132.3	159.2	110.6	102.1
Undistributed corporate profits with IVA and CCA [1]	123.3	223.8	255.3	174.8	192.3	300.7	390.9	468.5
Wage accruals less disbursements	-	16.4	5.2	-	-	-	-	-
Net government saving	-164.8	-184.9	154.0	239.4	51.5	-279.5	-367.8	-358.0
Federal	-172.0	-197.0	103.6	189.5	46.7	-254.5	-364.5	-375.6
State and local	7.2	12.0	50.4	50.0	4.8	-25.0	-3.2	17.6
Consumption of fixed capital	682.5	878.4	1,101.3	1,187.8	1,281.5	1,303.9	1,353.9	1,407.3
Private	551.6	713.4	914.3	990.8	1,075.5	1,092.8	1,135.9	1,178.3
Domestic business	466.4	600.2	769.8	836.1	903.7	912.6	942.6	967.3
Households and institutions	85.1	113.2	144.5	154.8	171.7	180.2	193.3	211.0
Government	130.9	165.0	187.0	197.0	206.0	211.2	218.1	229.0
Federal	67.9	81.9	84.8	87.2	88.2	89.0	90.2	93.0
State and local	63.0	83.1	102.1	109.8	117.8	122.1	127.9	136.0
Gross domestic investment, capital account transactions, and net lending	**1,006.7**	**1,285.7**	**1,638.5**	**1,643.3**	**1,567.9**	**1,468.9**	**1,513.3**	**1,671.0**
Gross domestic investment	1,076.7	1,376.7	1,912.4	2,040.0	1,938.3	1,926.6	2,024.2	2,307.0
Gross private domestic investment.	861.0	1,144.0	1,625.7	1,735.5	1,614.3	1,579.2	1,665.8	1,927.3
Gross government investment.	215.7	232.7	286.8	304.5	324.0	347.4	358.5	379.7
Capital account transactions (net)	6.6	0.9	4.8	0.8	1.1	3.3	3.1	1.3
Net lending or net borrowing	-76.6	-91.9	-278.7	-397.4	-371.5	-458.9	-514.0	-637.3
Statistical discrepancy	66.2	101.2	-35.7	-127.2	-89.6	-15.3	25.6	50.9
Addenda:								
Gross private saving	974.3	1,204.5	1,333.3	1,334.1	1,400.1	1,552.6	1,637.4	1,749.0
Gross government saving	-33.8	-19.9	341.0	436.4	257.5	-68.4	-149.7	-129.0
Federal	-104.1	-115.1	188.5	276.6	134.9	-165.5	-274.3	-282.5
State and local	70.3	95.2	152.5	159.8	122.6	97.1	124.7	153.6
Net domestic investment	394.2	498.4	811.2	852.1	656.9	622.7	670.3	899.7
Gross saving as a percentage of gross national income	16.3	16.2	17.9	17.7	16.2	14.1	13.5	13.8
Net saving as a percentage of gross national income	4.5	4.2	6.1	5.8	3.7	1.7	1.2	1.8

- Represents or rounds to zero.   [1] IVA and CCA = Inventory valuation adjustment and capital consumption adjustment.
Source: U.S. Bureau of Economic Analysis, *Survey of Current Business,* May 2005. See also <http://www.bea.doc.gov/bea/dn /nipaweb/SelectTable.asp?Selected=N> (released as 28 April 2005).

450   Income, Expenditures, and Wealth

U.S. Census Bureau. Statistical Abstract of the United States: 2006

Table 661. **Personal Income in Current and Constant (2000) Dollars by State: 1990 to 2004**

[In billions of dollars (4,861.9 represents $4,861,900,000,000). Represents a measure of income received from all sources during the calendar year by residents of each state. Data exclude federal employees overseas and U.S. residents employed by private U.S. firms on temporary foreign assignment. Totals may differ from those in Tables 656, 657, and 659

State	Current dollars					Constant (2000) dollars [1]				
	1990	2000	2002	2003	2004, prel.	1990	2000	2002	2003	2004, prel.
United States ..	4,861.9	8,422.1	8,869.8	9,151.7	9,672.2	6,039.9	8,422.1	8,565.9	8,673.7	8,970.4
Alabama..........	63.7	105.8	114.7	119.4	125.9	79.1	105.8	110.8	113.1	116.8
Alaska	12.6	18.7	20.9	21.5	22.6	15.7	18.7	20.2	20.4	20.9
Arizona..........	62.6	132.6	145.1	151.9	163.4	77.8	132.6	140.1	144.0	151.5
Arkansas	34.1	58.7	63.5	66.5	70.8	42.3	58.7	61.4	63.0	65.7
California	648.3	1,103.8	1,149.2	1,185.0	1,257.0	805.3	1,103.8	1,109.8	1,123.1	1,165.8
Colorado.........	64.7	144.4	154.0	157.2	165.9	80.4	144.4	148.7	149.0	153.9
Connecticut.......	87.3	141.6	147.1	149.8	159.1	108.4	141.6	142.0	142.0	147.5
Delaware	14.3	24.3	26.7	28.0	29.8	17.8	24.3	25.8	26.5	27.6
District of Columbia ...	16.0	23.1	26.2	27.0	28.7	19.9	23.1	25.3	25.6	26.6
Florida	255.0	457.5	492.9	511.6	547.2	316.8	457.5	476.0	484.9	507.5
Georgia	114.6	230.4	245.0	251.6	265.3	142.4	230.4	236.6	238.5	246.1
Hawaii	24.7	34.5	36.5	38.0	40.6	30.7	34.5	35.2	36.0	37.7
Idaho...........	15.9	31.3	34.4	35.4	37.8	19.8	31.3	33.2	33.6	35.0
Illinois	238.5	400.4	409.1	417.0	436.7	296.3	400.4	395.1	395.2	405.0
Indiana..........	97.2	165.3	172.2	178.8	187.7	120.8	165.3	166.3	169.4	174.1
Iowa	48.4	77.8	81.7	83.4	90.3	60.1	77.8	78.9	79.0	83.7
Kansas..........	44.9	74.6	78.3	80.2	84.3	55.7	74.6	75.6	76.0	78.2
Kentucky	57.0	98.8	105.4	109.4	114.9	70.8	98.8	101.8	103.7	106.5
Louisiana	64.1	103.2	114.5	118.2	124.6	79.6	103.2	110.5	112.1	115.5
Maine...........	21.4	33.2	36.6	38.2	40.3	26.6	33.2	35.3	36.2	37.3
Maryland	109.7	182.0	198.9	206.4	218.1	136.3	182.0	192.1	195.6	202.3
Massachusetts.......	138.8	240.2	249.9	253.6	268.2	172.4	240.2	241.4	240.4	248.8
Michigan..........	176.2	294.2	301.8	314.3	323.1	218.9	294.2	291.4	297.9	299.7
Minnesota.........	87.3	158.0	166.7	172.3	182.9	108.5	158.0	161.0	163.3	169.7
Mississippi	33.8	59.8	64.6	67.6	71.6	41.9	59.8	62.3	64.1	66.4
Missouri	90.4	152.7	163.1	168.5	176.1	112.3	152.7	157.5	159.7	163.4
Montana..........	12.4	20.7	22.4	23.3	24.9	15.4	20.7	21.6	22.1	23.1
Nebraska	28.4	47.3	49.5	52.4	54.8	35.3	47.3	47.8	49.7	50.8
Nevada	24.8	61.4	66.9	71.5	78.0	30.9	61.4	64.6	67.8	72.3
New Hampshire......	22.8	41.4	44.1	45.3	48.1	28.3	41.4	42.6	42.9	44.6
New Jersey........	190.8	323.6	334.3	342.0	359.5	237.0	323.6	322.9	324.2	333.5
New Mexico	22.7	40.3	44.9	47.0	49.8	28.2	40.3	43.4	44.5	46.2
New York	423.9	663.0	676.6	693.8	735.0	526.6	663.0	653.4	657.6	681.7
North Carolina......	114.9	218.7	229.7	236.4	249.8	142.8	218.7	221.9	224.0	231.7
North Dakota.......	10.2	16.1	16.9	18.3	19.9	12.6	16.1	16.4	17.4	18.5
Ohio	203.6	320.5	333.5	344.6	358.9	253.0	320.5	322.1	326.6	332.9
Oklahoma.........	51.0	84.3	90.5	93.7	99.0	63.3	84.3	87.4	88.8	91.8
Oregon..........	51.5	96.4	100.3	102.4	107.7	64.0	96.4	96.8	97.1	99.9
Pennsylvania.......	234.3	364.8	382.6	394.8	413.7	291.1	364.8	369.5	374.1	383.7
Rhode Island.......	20.1	30.7	33.2	34.5	36.5	25.0	30.7	32.0	32.7	33.8
South Carolina......	55.6	98.3	104.6	108.5	114.1	69.1	98.3	101.1	102.8	105.8
South Dakota	11.3	19.4	20.4	22.1	23.8	14.0	19.4	19.7	20.9	22.1
Tennessee	81.7	148.8	160.3	167.4	177.1	101.5	148.8	154.8	158.7	164.2
Texas............	297.1	593.1	623.9	642.6	679.7	369.1	593.1	602.5	609.1	630.4
Utah	25.8	53.6	58.1	59.8	63.6	32.1	53.6	56.1	56.6	59.0
Vermont	10.1	16.9	18.4	19.1	20.4	12.5	16.9	17.8	18.1	18.9
Virginia..........	127.1	220.8	239.8	248.4	264.7	157.9	220.8	231.6	235.5	245.4
Washington........	97.4	187.9	198.4	203.9	219.0	121.0	187.9	191.6	193.2	203.1
West Virginia......	26.0	39.6	43.0	44.5	47.0	32.3	39.6	41.6	42.1	43.6
Wisconsin.........	88.6	153.5	162.9	168.0	177.2	110.1	153.5	157.3	159.2	164.3
Wyoming	8.2	14.1	15.5	16.3	17.4	10.1	14.1	15.0	15.4	16.1

[1] Constant dollar estimates are computed by the U.S. Census Bureau using the national implicit price deflator for personal consumption expenditures from the Bureau of Economic Analysis. Any regional differences in the rate of inflation are not reflected in these constant dollar estimates.

Source: Except as noted, U.S. Bureau of Economic Analysis, *Survey of Current Business*, April 2005. See also <http://www.bea.doc.gov/bea/regional/spi/> (released 28 March 2005).

Income, Expenditures, and Wealth 451

Table 662. **Personal Income Per Capita in Current and Constant (2000) Dollars by State: 1990 to 2004**

[In dollars, except as indicated. 2004 preliminary. See headnote, Table 661]

State	Current dollars				Constant (2000) dollars [1]				Income rank	
	1900	2000	2003	2004	1990	2000	2003	2004	2000	2004
United States . . .	19,477	29,845	31,472	32,937	24,196	29,845	29,828	30,547	(X)	(X)
Alabama	15,723	23,764	26,505	27,795	19,532	23,764	25,121	25,778	44	40
Alaska	22,804	29,867	33,213	34,454	28,329	29,867	31,478	31,954	15	13
Arizona	17,005	25,660	27,232	28,442	21,125	25,660	25,810	26,378	37	38
Arkansas	14,460	21,925	24,384	25,725	17,963	21,925	23,110	23,858	48	49
California	21,638	32,464	33,415	35,019	26,881	32,464	31,670	32,478	8	12
Colorado	19,575	33,370	34,561	36,063	24,318	33,370	32,756	33,446	7	7
Connecticut	26,504	41,489	42,972	45,398	32,925	41,489	40,728	42,104	1	1
Delaware	21,422	30,869	34,199	35,861	26,612	30,869	32,413	33,259	13	8
District of Columbia . . .	26,473	40,456	48,446	51,803	32,887	40,456	45,916	48,044	(X)	(X)
Florida	19,564	28,509	30,098	31,455	24,304	28,509	28,526	29,173	20	23
Georgia	17,603	27,989	29,000	30,051	21,868	27,989	27,485	27,870	26	34
Hawaii	22,186	28,422	30,441	32,160	27,561	28,422	28,851	29,826	22	20
Idaho	15,724	24,075	25,902	27,098	19,534	24,075	24,549	25,132	42	44
Illinois	20,824	32,185	32,965	34,351	25,869	32,185	31,243	31,858	9	14
Indiana	17,491	27,132	28,838	30,094	21,729	27,132	27,332	27,910	31	33
Iowa	17,389	26,554	28,340	30,560	21,602	26,554	26,860	28,342	33	31
Kansas	18,085	27,694	29,438	30,811	22,467	27,694	27,900	28,575	27	28
Kentucky	15,437	24,412	26,575	27,709	19,177	24,412	25,187	25,698	40	41
Louisiana	15,173	23,078	26,312	27,581	18,849	23,078	24,938	25,580	45	42
Maine	17,376	25,969	29,164	30,566	21,586	25,969	27,641	28,348	35	30
Maryland	22,852	34,257	37,446	39,247	28,389	34,257	35,490	36,399	5	4
Massachusetts	23,043	37,756	39,504	41,801	28,626	37,756	37,441	38,768	3	2
Michigan	18,922	29,552	31,178	31,954	23,506	29,552	29,550	29,635	17	22
Minnesota	19,891	32,017	34,031	35,861	24,710	32,017	32,254	33,259	10	8
Mississippi	13,089	21,005	23,466	24,650	16,260	21,005	22,240	22,861	50	50
Missouri	17,627	27,241	29,464	30,608	21,898	27,241	27,925	28,387	30	29
Montana	15,448	22,929	25,406	26,857	19,191	22,929	24,079	24,908	46	45
Nebraska	17,983	27,625	30,179	31,339	22,340	27,625	28,603	29,065	29	25
Nevada	20,346	30,437	31,910	33,405	25,275	30,437	30,243	30,981	14	17
New Hampshire	20,512	33,396	35,140	37,040	25,482	33,396	33,305	34,352	6	6
New Jersey	24,572	38,365	39,577	41,332	30,525	38,365	37,510	38,333	2	3
New Mexico	14,924	22,135	24,995	26,191	18,540	22,135	23,689	24,291	47	47
New York	23,523	34,897	36,112	38,228	29,222	34,897	34,226	35,454	4	5
North Carolina	17,246	27,068	28,071	29,246	21,424	27,068	26,605	27,124	32	37
North Dakota	15,943	25,106	28,922	31,398	19,806	25,106	27,411	29,120	38	24
Ohio	18,743	28,207	30,129	31,322	23,284	28,207	28,555	29,049	24	26
Oklahoma	16,187	24,407	26,719	28,089	20,109	24,407	25,323	26,051	41	39
Oregon	18,010	28,097	28,734	29,971	22,374	28,097	27,233	27,796	25	36
Pennsylvania	19,687	29,695	31,911	33,348	24,457	29,695	30,244	30,928	16	18
Rhode Island	20,006	29,214	32,038	33,733	24,853	29,214	30,365	31,285	18	16
South Carolina	15,894	24,424	26,144	27,172	19,745	24,424	24,778	25,200	39	43
South Dakota	16,172	25,720	28,856	30,856	20,090	25,720	27,349	28,617	36	27
Tennessee	16,692	26,097	28,641	30,005	20,736	26,097	27,145	27,828	34	35
Texas	17,421	28,313	29,074	30,222	21,642	28,313	27,555	28,029	23	32
Utah	14,913	23,878	25,407	26,606	18,526	23,878	24,080	24,675	43	46
Vermont	17,876	27,680	30,888	32,770	22,207	27,680	29,275	30,392	28	19
Virginia	20,449	31,087	33,730	35,477	25,403	31,087	31,968	32,903	12	10
Washington	19,865	31,779	33,254	35,299	24,678	31,779	31,517	32,738	11	11
West Virginia	14,493	21,900	24,542	25,872	18,004	21,900	23,260	23,995	49	48
Wisconsin	18,072	28,570	30,685	32,157	22,451	28,570	29,082	29,824	19	21
Wyoming	18,002	28,460	32,433	34,306	22,364	28,460	30,739	31,817	21	15

X Not applicable. [1] Constant dollar estimates are computed by the U.S. Census Bureau using the national implicit price deflator for personal consumption expenditures from the Bureau of Economic Analysis. Any regional differences in the rate of inflation are not reflected in these constant dollar estimates.

Source: Except as noted, U.S. Bureau of Economic Analysis, *Survey of Current Business*, April 2005. See also <http://www.bea.doc.gov/bea/regional/spi/> (released 28 March 2005).

Table 663. Disposable Personal Income Per Capita in Current and Constant (2000) Dollars by State: 1990 to 2004

[In dollars, except percent. 2004 preliminary. Disposable personal income is the income available to persons for spending or saving; it is calculated as personal income less personal tax and nontax payments]

State	Current dollars				Constant (2000) dollars [1]				Percent of U.S. average	
	1990	2000	2003	2004	1990	2000	2003	2004	1990	2004
United States . . .	17,108	25,471	28,031	29,404	21,253	25,471	26,567	27,270	100.0	100.0
Alabama.	14,047	21,046	24,169	25,416	17,450	21,046	22,907	23,572	82.6	86.4
Alaska	20,147	26,425	30,228	31,454	25,028	26,425	28,649	29,172	103.7	107.0
Arizona.	15,131	22,326	24,625	25,770	18,797	22,326	23,339	23,900	87.7	87.6
Arkansas	12,987	19,375	22,193	23,453	16,134	19,375	21,034	21,751	76.1	79.8
California	18,871	26,716	29,467	30,964	23,443	26,716	27,928	28,717	104.9	105.3
Colorado.	17,201	28,235	30,743	32,207	21,368	28,235	29,137	29,870	110.9	109.5
Connecticut.	23,121	33,383	36,461	38,559	28,723	33,383	34,557	35,761	131.1	131.1
Delaware	18,474	26,278	30,301	31,900	22,950	26,278	28,718	29,585	103.2	108.5
District of Columbia	22,858	33,408	42,220	45,213	28,396	33,408	40,015	41,932	131.2	153.8
Florida	17,525	24,810	27,212	28,515	21,771	24,810	25,791	26,446	97.4	97.0
Georgia	15,464	24,054	25,885	26,891	19,211	24,054	24,533	24,940	94.4	91.5
Hawaii	19,269	24,842	27,296	28,808	23,938	24,842	25,870	26,718	97.5	98.0
Idaho.	13,988	20,959	23,559	24,692	17,377	20,959	22,328	22,900	82.3	84.0
Illinois	18,168	27,412	29,292	30,616	22,570	27,412	27,762	28,394	107.6	104.1
Indiana	15,368	23,647	25,926	27,125	19,091	23,647	24,572	25,157	92.8	92.2
Iowa	15,369	23,390	25,666	27,794	19,093	23,390	24,325	25,777	91.8	94.5
Kansas.	15,971	24,047	26,497	27,799	19,840	24,047	25,113	25,782	94.4	94.5
Kentucky	13,621	21,344	23,826	24,929	16,921	21,344	22,582	23,120	83.8	84.8
Louisiana	13,689	20,574	24,068	25,256	17,006	20,574	22,811	23,423	80.8	85.9
Maine.	15,387	22,489	26,200	27,512	19,115	22,489	24,832	25,516	88.3	93.6
Maryland	19,591	28,800	32,683	34,282	24,338	28,800	30,976	31,794	113.1	116.6
Massachusetts.	19,795	30,310	34,174	36,169	24,591	30,310	32,389	33,544	119.0	123.0
Michigan.	16,571	25,435	27,967	28,719	20,586	25,435	26,506	26,635	99.9	97.7
Minnesota.	17,304	27,187	29,960	31,702	21,496	27,187	28,395	29,402	106.7	107.8
Mississippi	11,910	18,935	21,669	22,823	14,796	18,935	20,537	21,167	74.3	77.6
Missouri	15,536	23,676	26,499	27,614	19,300	23,676	25,115	25,610	93.0	93.9
Montana.	13,795	20,233	22,989	24,334	17,137	20,233	21,788	22,568	79.4	82.8
Nebraska	16,031	24,090	27,249	28,316	19,915	24,090	25,826	26,261	94.6	96.3
Nevada	17,866	26,322	28,767	30,177	22,195	26,322	27,264	27,987	103.3	102.6
New Hampshire	18,292	28,566	31,637	33,453	22,724	28,566	29,985	31,026	112.2	113.8
New Jersey.	21,381	32,010	34,544	36,223	26,561	32,010	32,740	33,595	125.7	123.2
New Mexico	13,413	19,578	22,732	23,929	16,663	19,578	21,545	22,193	76.9	81.4
New York	20,183	28,881	31,010	32,743	25,073	28,881	29,390	30,367	113.4	111.4
North Carolina	15,196	23,396	25,081	26,232	18,878	23,396	23,771	24,329	91.9	89.2
North Dakota.	14,457	22,596	26,647	29,041	17,960	22,596	25,255	26,934	88.7	98.8
Ohio	16,446	24,263	26,825	27,981	20,431	24,263	25,424	25,951	95.3	95.2
Oklahoma.	14,280	21,517	24,191	25,496	17,740	21,517	22,927	23,646	84.5	86.7
Oregon.	15,823	23,905	25,442	26,580	19,657	23,905	24,113	24,651	93.9	90.4
Pennsylvania.	17,344	25,573	28,472	29,789	21,546	25,573	26,985	27,627	100.4	101.3
Rhode Island.	17,639	25,059	28,427	29,996	21,913	25,059	26,942	27,819	98.4	102.0
South Carolina.	14,095	21,501	23,727	24,712	17,510	21,501	22,488	22,919	84.4	84.0
South Dakota	14,822	23,163	26,747	28,711	18,413	23,163	25,350	26,628	90.9	97.6
Tennessee	15,122	23,409	26,467	27,794	18,786	23,409	25,085	25,777	91.9	94.5
Texas.	15,623	24,965	26,577	27,722	19,408	24,965	25,189	25,710	98.0	94.3
Utah	13,197	20,801	22,980	24,122	16,394	20,801	21,780	22,372	81.7	82.0
Vermont	15,759	24,010	27,842	29,640	19,577	24,010	26,388	27,489	94.3	100.8
Virginia.	17,872	26,215	29,672	31,277	22,202	26,215	28,122	29,007	102.9	106.4
Washington.	17,676	27,309	30,178	32,219	21,959	27,309	28,602	29,881	107.2	109.6
West Virginia.	12,965	19,535	22,393	23,676	16,106	19,535	21,223	21,958	76.7	80.5
Wisconsin.	15,801	24,498	27,258	28,645	19,629	24,498	25,834	26,566	96.2	97.4
Wyoming	16,149	24,497	29,194	30,972	20,062	24,497	27,669	28,725	96.2	105.3

[1] Constant dollar estimates are computed by the Census Bureau using the national implicit price deflator for personal consumption expenditures from the Bureau of Economic Analysis. Any regional differences in the rate of inflation are not reflected in these constant dollar estimates.

Source: Except as noted, U.S. Bureau of Economic Analysis, *Survey of Current Business*, April 2005. See also <http://www.bea.doc.gov/bea/regional/spi/> (released 28 March 2005).

Income, Expenditures, and Wealth   453

Table 664. **Personal Income by Selected Large Metropolitan Area: 2000 to 2003**

[8,422,074 represents $8,422,074,000,000. Metropolitan areas as defined December 2003. See Appendix II]

Metropolitan area ranked by 2003 population	Personal income				Per capita personal income			
	2000 (mil. dol.)	2002 (mil. dol.)	2003 (mil. dol.)	Annual percent change, 2002-2003	2000 (dol.)	2002 (dol.)	2003 (dol.)	Percent of national average, 2003
United States	8,422,074	8,869,809	9,151,694	3.2	29,845	30,804	31,472	100.0
New York-Northern New Jersey-Long Island, NY-NJ-PA MSA . .	732,799	747,054	763,575	2.2	39,915	40,186	40,899	130.0
Los Angeles-Long Beach-Santa Ana, CA MSA	385,053	413,328	427,523	3.4	31,046	32,567	33,347	106.0
Chicago-Naperville-Joliet, IL-IN-WI MSA	318,439	325,145	330,867	1.8	34,918	35,085	35,464	112.7
Philadelphia-Camden-Wilmington, PA-NJ-DE-MD MSA.	193,919	206,186	213,917	3.7	34,059	35,909	37,059	117.8
Detroit-Warren-Livonia, MI MSA	151,793	154,629	161,421	4.4	34,046	34,526	35,972	114.3
Boston-Cambridge-Quincy, MA-NH MSA	182,380	188,595	191,107	1.3	41,436	42,546	43,135	137.1
Washington-Arlington-Alexandria, DC-VA-MD-WV MSA . . .	196,093	214,919	223,394	3.9	40,672	42,987	44,056	140.0
San Francisco-Oakland-Fremont, CA MSA . . .	199,989	192,993	195,174	1.1	48,343	46,359	46,958	149.2
Miami-Ft. Lauderdale-Miami Beach, FL MSA	157,015	169,151	174,652	3.3	31,224	32,493	33,094	105.2
Houston-Sugar Land-Baytown, TX MSA	161,398	170,887	175,431	2.7	34,041	34,401	34,578	109.9
Dallas-Fort Worth-Arlington, TX MSA	176,530	184,821	188,747	2.1	33,972	33,770	33,790	107.4
Pittsburgh, PA MSA.	74,361	77,723	79,552	2.4	30,610	32,190	33,015	104.9
St. Louis, MO-IL MSA	84,222	89,751	92,348	2.9	31,172	32,807	33,535	106.6
Atlanta-Sandy Springs-Marietta, GA MSA . . .	141,817	149,854	153,379	2.4	33,122	33,270	33,308	105.8
Minneapolis-St. Paul-Bloomington, MN-WI MSA.	109,818	115,401	119,080	3.2	36,838	37,773	38,601	122.7
Baltimore-Towson, MD MSA	85,144	93,311	96,501	3.4	33,293	35,940	36,733	116.7
Cleveland-Elyria-Mentor, OH MSA	67,935	69,022	71,051	2.9	31,625	32,219	33,196	105.5
Seattle-Tacoma-Bellevue, WA MSA . . .	115,203	119,799	122,568	2.3	37,746	38,374	39,008	123.9
San Diego-Carlsbad-San Marcos, CA MSA . . .	92,654	101,118	104,614	3.5	32,803	34,915	35,841	113.9
Cincinnati-Middletown, OH-KY-IN MSA	61,393	65,470	67,508	3.1	30,476	32,159	32,979	104.8
Tampa-St. Petersburg-Clearwater, FL MSA . .	68,891	73,620	75,634	2.7	28,653	29,596	29,881	94.9
Phoenix-Mesa-Scottsdale, AZ MSA	92,975	101,447	106,327	4.8	28,364	29,080	29,590	94.0
Riverside-San Bernardino-Ontario, CA MSA	74,787	84,500	89,399	5.8	22,807	24,119	24,526	77.9
Kansas City, MO-KS MSA	58,247	62,020	63,540	2.5	31,607	32,863	33,015	105.9
Denver-Aurora, CO MSA	82,196	88,602	90,239	1.8	37,847	38,923	39,203	124.6
Providence-New Bedford-Fall River, RI-MA MSA.	45,976	49,888	51,522	3.3	28,973	30,933	31,743	100.9
Milwaukee-Waukesha-West Allis, WI MSA. . . .	49,151	51,910	53,182	2.5	32,718	34,384	35,133	111.6
Portland-Vancouver-Beaverton, OR-WA MSA.	62,190	64,395	65,629	1.9	32,123	31,988	32,152	102.2
San Jose-Sunnyvale-Santa Clara, CA MSA . .	92,947	79,599	79,801	0.3	53,415	46,003	46,072	146.4
New Orleans-Metairie-Kenner, LA MSA.	34,606	38,211	39,595	3.6	26,302	29,091	30,092	95.6
Columbus, OH MSA	49,770	53,554	55,227	3.1	30,743	32,312	32,930	104.6
Buffalo-Niagara Falls, NY MSA	31,806	32,725	33,751	3.1	27,209	28,212	29,145	92.6
Virginia Beach-Norfolk-Newport News, VA-NC MSA	41,659	45,999	47,675	3.6	26,364	28,659	29,337	93.2
Indianapolis, IN MSA	48,862	52,040	53,816	3.4	31,916	32,983	33,618	106.8
San Antonio, TX MSA	45,997	47,797	49,733	4.1	26,752	26,832	27,381	87.0
Sacramento-Arden-Arcade-Roseville, CA MSA	54,236	59,439	62,079	4.4	29,988	30,864	31,425	99.9
Louisville, KY-IN MSA	34,250	37,276	38,664	3.7	29,395	31,579	32,485	103.2
Hartford-West Hartford-East Hartford, CT MSA	42,568	44,169	44,992	1.9	36,981	37,782	38,131	121.2
Memphis, TN-MS-AR MSA	34,459	37,767	39,244	3.9	28,518	30,787	31,677	100.7
Rochester, NY MSA	30,455	31,374	32,329	3.0	29,327	30,184	31,057	98.7
Birmingham-Hoover, AL MSA	29,898	32,746	33,873	3.4	28,383	30,723	31,540	100.2
Nashville-Davidson-Murfreesboro, TN MSA . . .	40,309	43,734	45,785	4.7	30,601	32,326	33,368	106.0
Oklahoma City, OK MSA	29,092	31,573	32,817	3.9	26,502	28,195	28,958	92.0
Charlotte-Gastonia-Concord, NC-SC MSA	43,120	46,485	47,850	2.9	32,182	33,045	33,251	105.7
Richmond, VA MSA.	33,603	36,421	37,432	2.8	30,546	32,384	32,879	104.5
Dayton, OH MSA	24,210	25,168	26,000	3.3	28,549	29,780	30,748	97.7
Orlando-Kissimmee, FL MSA	44,751	48,096	50,670	5.4	27,018	27,407	28,114	89.3
Bridgeport-Stamford-Norwalk, CT MSA	52,190	53,777	54,703	1.7	58,986	60,098	60,803	193.2
Albany-Schenectady-Troy, NY MSA	25,168	26,224	27,075	3.2	30,444	31,439	32,208	102.3
Honolulu, HI MSA	26,605	27,936	29,002	3.8	30,393	31,522	32,463	103.1
New Haven-Milford, CT MSA	28,379	29,757	30,399	2.2	34,396	35,643	36,127	114.8
Jacksonville, FL MSA	33,151	34,974	36,548	4.5	29,436	29,793	30,525	97.0
Tulsa, OK MSA	24,984	26,800	27,196	1.5	29,004	30,587	30,908	98.2
Salt Lake City, UT MSA	27,081	29,316	29,935	2.1	27,851	29,456	29,768	94.6
Akron, OH MSA	20,593	20,945	21,645	3.3	29,590	29,942	30,878	98.1
Youngstown-Warren-Boardman, OH-PA MSA.	14,806	15,114	15,635	3.4	28,584	25,371	26,361	83.8
Toledo, OH MSA.	18,305	18,904	19,759	4.5	27,769	28,673	29,963	95.2
Omaha-Council Bluffs, NE-IA MSA.	24,230	25,678	26,578	3.5	31,506	32,793	33,537	106.6
Worcester, MA MSA	24,539	25,401	25,972	2.2	32,600	33,008	33,479	106.4
Springfield, MA MSA	18,766	19,842	20,229	1.9	27,576	29,000	29,432	93.5

Source: U.S. Bureau of Economic Analysis, *Survey of Current Business*, May 2005. See also <http://www.bea.doc.gov/bea/regional/reis/> and <http://www.bea.doc.gov/bea/newsrelarchive/2005/mpi0405.pdf> (released 27 April 2005).

Table 665. **Flow of Funds Accounts—Composition of Individuals' Savings: 1990 to 2003**

[In billions of dollars (540.6 represents $540,600,000,000).** Combined statement for households, farm business, and nonfarm noncorporate business. Minus sign (-) indicates decrease]

Composition of savings	1990	1995	1997	1998	1999	2000	2001	2002	2003
Increase in financial assets	540.6	536.0	601.3	929.5	709.6	677.9	880.4	719.6	909.9
Foreign deposits	1.4	4.6	6.5	0.1	5.2	15.0	-5.0	10.7	3.5
Checkable deposits and currency	-9.8	-27.1	-11.3	18.7	-35.8	-63.8	90.8	-23.0	-53.4
Time and savings deposits	33.6	131.4	142.6	175.6	101.3	308.7	257.8	295.8	342.6
Money market fund shares	27.8	99.6	83.5	139.4	118.3	154.2	158.2	-37.9	-98.4
Securities	191.8	21.1	2.7	133.4	107.0	-347.1	-57.1	91.4	188.9
Open market paper	6.2	1.3	1.5	7.5	4.1	4.8	-30.8	5.8	-1.6
U.S. government securities	109.3	5.6	-112.4	-7.7	164.5	-129.5	-161.6	-232.5	134.6
Municipal securities	27.6	-52.4	37.3	5.8	23.5	10.2	52.3	106.6	62.5
Corporate and foreign bonds	74.8	93.9	67.7	127.1	51.9	65.8	117.8	165.3	-116.6
Corporate equities [1]	-48.6	-102.8	-257.4	-247.1	-308.1	-470.0	-231.7	-72.5	-183.1
Mutual fund shares	22.5	75.5	266.0	247.8	171.2	171.6	196.8	118.8	293.1
Life insurance reserves	26.5	45.8	59.3	48.0	50.8	50.2	77.2	60.1	56.7
Pension fund reserves	207.7	158.9	201.3	217.4	181.8	209.1	210.9	215.2	232.7
Investment in bank personal trusts	32.9	6.4	-53.0	-46.1	-8.1	56.6	-59.9	-2.4	-26.3
Miscellaneous assets	28.7	95.4	169.5	242.9	189.1	295.1	207.4	109.6	263.5
Gross investment in tangible assets	829.5	1,033.3	1,148.7	1,253.5	1,380.5	1,489.2	1,554.6	1,558.2	1,655.7
Minus: Consumption of fixed capital	*567.4*	*696.5*	*753.9*	*791.1*	*837.0*	*890.7*	*936.8*	*974.3*	*991.0*
Equals: Net investment in tangible assets . . .	262.1	336.8	394.8	462.4	543.5	598.6	617.8	584.0	664.7
Net increase in liabilities	234.5	419.0	561.0	801.1	887.1	927.0	828.7	942.9	1,151.2
Mortgage debt on nonfarm homes	207.1	176.9	258.1	383.2	422.2	416.2	531.1	723.3	818.2
Other mortgage debt [2]	-0.3	5.7	31.8	105.6	101.2	114.9	107.4	102.0	109.2
Consumer credit	15.1	147.0	62.1	96.8	112.1	165.2	137.7	81.4	100.2
Policy loans	4.1	10.5	3.2	0.1	-5.1	2.8	2.2	1.1	-0.2
Security credit	-3.7	3.5	36.8	21.6	75.2	7.2	-38.8	-48.2	32.6
Other liabilities [2]	12.2	75.4	169.0	193.8	181.4	220.6	89.1	83.3	91.4
Personal savings with consumer durables [3] . .	583.4	474.5	462.8	623.8	403.4	385.9	706.3	394.9	453.8
Personal savings, without consumer durable [3] . .	495.2	337.6	298.3	417.2	182.3	143.6	436.1	146.7	181.7
Personal savings (NIPA, excludes consumer durables) [4]	299.4	250.9	218.3	276.8	158.6	168.4	127.2	183.2	165.6

[1] Only directly held and those in closed-end funds. Other equities are included in mutual funds, life insurance and pension reserves, and bank personal trusts. [2] Includes corporate farms. [3] Flow of Funds measure. [4] National Income and Product Accounts measure.

Source: Board of Governors of the Federal Reserve System, *Flow of Funds Accounts,* quarterly. See also <http://www.federalreserve.gov/releases/Z1/20030306/z1.pdf> (released 04 March 2004).

Table 666. **Annual Expenditure Per Child by Husband-Wife Families by Family Income and Expenditure Type: 2004**

[In dollars. Expenditures based on data from the 1990–92 Consumer Expenditure Survey updated to 2004 dollars using the Consumer Price Index. Excludes expenses for college. For more on the methodology, see report cited below]

Family income and age of child				Expenditure type				
	Total	Housing	Food	Trans-por-tation	Clothing	Health care	Child care and educa-tion	Miscel-lan-eous [1]
INCOME: LESS THAN $41,700								
Less than 2 yrs. old	7,040	2,680	980	820	350	530	1,020	660
3 to 5 yrs. old	7,210	2,650	1,090	800	340	500	1,150	680
6 to 8 yrs. old	7,250	2,560	1,400	930	380	580	680	720
9 to 11 yrs. old	7,220	2,310	1,680	1,010	420	630	410	760
12 to 14 yrs. old	8,070	2,580	1,770	1,130	710	640	290	950
15 to 17 yrs. old	8,000	2,080	1,910	1,530	630	680	480	690
INCOME: $41,700–$70,200								
Less than 2 yrs. old	9,840	3,630	1,170	1,230	410	690	1,680	1,030
3 to 5 yrs. old	10,120	3,600	1,350	1,200	400	660	1,860	1,050
6 to 8 yrs. old	10,030	3,510	1,720	1,330	440	750	1,190	1,090
9 to 11 yrs. old	9,910	3,260	2,030	1,410	490	820	780	1,120
12 to 14 yrs. old	10,640	3,520	2,050	1,540	830	820	570	1,310
15 to 17 yrs. old	10,900	3,030	2,270	1,950	740	870	980	1,060
INCOME: MORE THAN $70,200								
Less than 2 yrs. old	14,620	5,770	1,550	1,720	540	790	2,530	1,720
3 to 5 yrs. old	14,960	5,730	1,760	1,690	530	760	2,750	1,740
6 to 8 yrs. old	14,710	5,640	2,120	1,820	580	870	1,900	1,780
9 to 11 yrs. old	14,470	5,400	2,460	1,900	630	940	1,320	1,820
12 to 14 yrs. old	15,270	5,660	2,580	2,030	1,040	940	1,010	2,010
15 to 17 yrs. old	15,810	5,160	2,720	2,460	950	990	1,780	1,750

[1] Expenses include personal care items, entertainment, and reading materials.

Source: Department of Agriculture, Center for Nutrition Policy and Promotion, *Expenditures on Children by Families, 2004 Annual Report.* See also <http://www.cnpp.usda.gov/Crc/crc2004.pdf> (released April 2005).

Income, Expenditures, and Wealth   **455**

Table 667. **Average Annual Expenditures of All Consumer Units by Selected Major Types of Expenditure: 1990 to 2003**

[In dollars, except as indicated (96,968 represents 96,968,000). Based on Consumer Expenditure Survey. Data are averages for the noninstitutional population. Expenditures reported here are out-of-pocket]

Type	1990	1995	1998	1999	2000	2001	2002	2003
Number of consumer units (1,000)......	96,968	103,123	107,182	108,465	109,367	110,339	112,108	115,356
Expenditures, total............	**28,381**	**32,264**	**35,535**	**36,995**	**38,045**	**39,518**	**40,677**	**40,817**
Food	4,296	4,505	4,810	5,031	5,158	5,321	5,375	5,340
Food at home [1]	2,485	2,803	2,780	2,915	3,021	3,086	3,099	3,129
Meats, poultry, fish, and eggs	668	752	723	749	795	828	798	825
Dairy products	295	297	301	322	325	332	328	328
Fruits and vegetables	408	457	472	500	521	522	552	535
Other food at home.............	746	856	858	896	927	952	970	999
Food away from home............	1,811	1,702	2,030	2,116	2,137	2,235	2,276	2,211
Alcoholic beverages	293	277	309	318	372	349	376	391
Housing [1]	8,703	10,458	11,713	12,057	12,319	13,011	13,283	13,432
Shelter	4,836	5,928	6,680	7,016	7,114	7,602	7,829	7,887
Fuels, utilities, public services	1,890	2,191	2,405	2,377	2,489	2,767	2,684	2,811
Apparel and services	1,618	1,704	1,674	1,743	1,856	1,743	1,749	1,640
Transportation [1]	5,120	6,014	6,616	7,011	7,417	7,633	7,759	7,781
Vehicle purchases	2,129	2,638	2,964	3,305	3,418	3,579	3,665	3,732
Gasoline and motor oil...........	1,047	1,006	1,017	1,055	1,291	1,279	1,235	1,333
Other vehicles expenses	1,642	2,015	2,206	2,254	2,281	2,375	2,471	2,331
Health care..................	1,480	1,732	1,903	1,959	2,066	2,182	2,350	2,416
Entertainment	1,422	1,612	1,746	1,891	1,863	1,953	2,079	2,060
Reading	153	162	161	159	146	141	139	127
Tobacco products, smoking supplies	274	269	273	300	319	308	320	290
Personal insurance and pensions	2,592	2,964	3,381	3,436	3,365	3,737	3,899	4,055
· Life and other personal insurance	345	373	398	394	399	410	406	397
Pensions and Social Security	2,248	2,591	2,982	3,042	2,966	3,326	3,493	3,658

[1] Includes expenditures not shown separately.

Source: U.S. Bureau of Labor Statistics, *Consumer Expenditures in 2003;* and earlier reports. See also <http://www.bls.gov /news.release/pdf/cesan.pdf> (released 30 November 2004).

Table 668. **Average Annual Expenditures of All Consumer Units by Metropolitan Area: 2002-2003**

[In dollars. Metropolitan areas defined June 30, 1983. CMSA = Consolidated Metropolitan Statistical Area; MSA = Metropolitan Statistical Area; PMSA = Primary Metropolitan Statistical Area. See text, Section 1, Population, and Appendix II. See headnote, Table 667]

Metropolitan area	Total expendi- tures [1]	Food	Housing			Transportation			Health care
			Total [1]	Shel- ter	Utility, fuels [2]	Total [1]	Vehicle pur- chases	Gaso- line and motor oil	
Anchorage, AK MSA	54,229	6,898	17,178	10,591	2,703	10,765	5,487	1,450	2,595
Atlanta, GA MSA	39,549	5,085	14,548	8,783	3,421	7,400	3,610	1,222	1,903
Baltimore, MD MSA..............	39,909	5,411	13,801	8,648	2,767	5,605	1,852	1,139	2,108
Boston-Lawrence-Salem, MA-NH CMSA....................	41,814	5,627	15,211	10,145	2,676	7,175	3,518	1,159	2,007
Chicago-Gary-Lake County, IL-IN-WI CMSA....................	47,016	6,001	17,059	10,290	3,190	7,961	3,570	1,325	2,462
Cincinnati-Hamilton, OH-KY- IN CMSA..................	39,030	5,303	13,072	7,715	2,520	7,803	3,917	1,152	2,126
Cleveland-Akron-Lorain, OH CMSA ...	37,487	4,574	12,335	7,262	3,079	7,702	3,716	1,107	2,035
Dallas-Fort Worth, TX CMSA	49,899	6,537	15,726	9,209	3,538	9,815	4,939	1,510	2,833
Denver-Boulder-Greeley, CO CMSA...	50,208	6,489	16,584	10,272	2,660	9,652	4,301	1,327	2,652
Detroit-Ann Arbor, MI CMSA	44,039	5,511	14,429	8,814	2,911	9,024	3,955	1,354	1,999
Honolulu, HI MSA..............	44,505	5,819	15,156	10,067	2,492	8,023	3,724	1,142	2,617
Houston-Galveston-Brazoria, TX CMSA....................	47,434	5,822	15,121	8,515	3,284	9,891	5,243	1,467	2,494
Kansas City, MO-Kansas City, KS CMSA....................	43,450	5,672	14,022	7,848	3,329	8,794	4,255	1,559	2,533
Los Angeles-Long Beach, CA PMSA	49,765	6,402	17,986	11,852	2,568	9,162	4,019	1,580	2,196
Miami-Fort Lauderdale, FL CMSA	42,656	5,704	16,178	10,161	3,068	8,348	3,709	1,324	2,059
Milwaukee, WI PMSA	40,890	5,234	14,364	8,786	2,558	6,797	3,002	1,284	2,429
Minneapolis-St. Paul, MN-WI MSA....	54,088	6,235	17,451	10,575	2,766	9,280	4,209	1,400	2,576
New York-Northern New Jersey- Long Island, NY-NJ-CT CMSA......	50,319	7,005	18,919	12,402	3,055	7,729	2,928	1,101	2,235
Philadelphia-Wilmington-Trenton, PA-NJ-DE-MD CMSA............	40,986	4,862	14,780	8,843	3,105	6,510	2,399	1,142	2,138
Phoenix-Mesa, AZ MSA..........	44,078	5,615	14,515	8,411	2,773	8,659	3,947	1,266	2,551
Pittsburgh-Beaver Valley, PA CMSA ...	42,102	5,295	12,310	6,528	2,902	6,972	2,769	1,164	2,459
Portland-Vancouver, OR-WA CMSA ...	45,172	5,423	15,590	9,457	2,778	6,807	2,417	1,253	2,751
San Diego, CA MSA	47,137	5,929	17,797	11,553	2,608	8,652	3,600	1,513	2,275
San Francisco-Oakland-San Jose, CA CMSA	53,135	6,551	20,349	14,552	2,566	8,802	3,776	1,455	2,580
Seattle-Tacoma, WA CMSA	49,114	6,465	16,619	10,850	2,687	9,347	4,592	1,342	2,730
St. Louis-East St. Louis-Alton, MO-IL CMSA	44,654	5,662	13,961	7,980	3,083	8,359	4,231	1,261	2,588
Tampa-St. Petersburg-Clearwater, FL MSA...................	35,776	4,074	13,355	7,800	3,021	7,291	3,546	1,142	2,167
Washington, DC-MD-VA MSA	50,985	6,288	18,863	12,189	3,067	7,853	3,374	1,318	2,289

[1] Includes expenditures not shown separately. [2] Includes public services.

Source: U.S. Bureau of Labor Statistics, *Consumer Expenditures in 2003;* and earlier reports. See also <http://www.bls.gov/news.release /pdf/cesan.pdf> (released 30 November 2004).

456 Income, Expenditures, and Wealth

Table 669. **Average Annual Expenditures of All Consumer Units by Race, Hispanic Origin, and Age of Householder: 2003**

[In dollars. Based on Consumer Expenditure Survey. Data are averages for the noninstitutional population. Expenditures reported here are out-of-pocket]

Type	All con-sumer units	Black or African Ameri-can	His-panic or Latino	Age of householder					
				Under 25 yrs.	25 to 34 yrs.	35 to 44 yrs.	45 to 54 yrs.	55 to 64 yrs.	65 yrs. and over
Expenditures, total	**40,817**	**28,708**	**34,575**	**22,396**	**40,525**	**47,175**	**50,101**	**44,191**	**29,376**
Food	5,340	4,007	5,717	3,401	5,318	6,272	6,381	5,530	3,896
Food at home	3,129	2,664	3,597	1,766	2,976	3,600	3,693	3,315	2,575
Cereals and bakery products	442	370	486	256	421	523	509	427	387
Cereals and cereal products	150	139	183	96	156	183	168	140	120
Bakery products	292	231	303	160	265	340	341	287	267
Meats, poultry, fish, and eggs	825	882	1,059	438	769	933	1,002	914	661
Beef	246	232	327	131	227	265	320	287	178
Pork	171	206	212	88	142	188	208	192	157
Other meats	102	90	113	53	90	123	123	108	83
Poultry	145	177	190	85	151	174	171	142	105
Fish and seafood	124	140	158	57	124	139	140	148	103
Eggs	37	36	59	23	35	44	40	36	36
Dairy products	328	227	374	193	317	388	378	326	277
Fresh milk and cream	127	94	160	76	127	157	138	118	108
Other dairy products	201	133	214	116	191	230	240	209	169
Fruits and vegetables	535	438	686	272	495	593	621	593	484
Fresh fruits	171	128	231	75	157	190	204	189	153
Fresh vegetables	172	133	240	87	157	187	199	192	160
Processed fruits	108	100	131	66	104	123	122	115	95
Processed vegetables	84	77	83	44	77	93	96	97	76
Other food at home	999	747	992	607	974	1,164	1,184	1,054	767
Nonalcoholic beverages	268	202	289	159	256	317	329	291	191
Food away from home	2,211	1,343	2,120	1,636	2,342	2,672	2,688	2,215	1,321
Alcoholic beverages	391	169	315	509	446	424	477	372	184
Housing	13,432	10,622	12,300	7,095	14,392	16,098	15,624	13,714	9,729
Shelter	7,887	6,117	7,672	4,574	8,915	9,678	9,237	7,571	5,201
Owned dwellings	5,263	3,042	3,889	765	4,837	6,940	6,893	5,769	3,515
Mortgage interest and charges	2,954	1,848	2,471	449	3,373	4,541	4,088	2,739	851
Property taxes	1,344	748	779	230	910	1,479	1,625	1,770	1,399
Rented dwellings	2,179	2,946	3,560	3,593	3,835	2,315	1,656	1,179	1,331
Other lodging	445	129	224	216	243	423	688	623	355
Utilities, fuels, and public services	2,811	2,910	2,490	1,329	2,580	3,142	3,335	3,089	2,484
Natural gas	392	465	301	118	341	427	468	432	396
Electricity	1,028	1,094	860	470	915	1,145	1,199	1,153	946
Fuel oil and other fuels	110	46	57	23	62	109	129	146	138
Telephone	956	1,027	968	616	1,001	1,097	1,156	981	673
Water and other public services	326	278	305	102	261	365	383	376	332
Household operations	707	453	454	230	872	949	633	604	635
Personal services	294	247	238	135	571	521	121	71	206
Other household expenses	414	206	216	95	301	428	512	533	429
Housekeeping supplies	529	357	476	225	455	597	618	618	485
Household furnishings & equipment	1,497	785	1,208	737	1,571	1,731	1,801	1,831	923
Household textiles	113	61	89	42	109	108	155	140	90
Furniture	401	234	403	203	499	518	450	447	184
Floor coverings	52	11	19	8	32	61	62	76	48
Major appliances	196	118	201	67	216	209	217	231	165
Misc. household equipment	648	318	415	369	647	743	807	810	373
Apparel and services	1,640	1,601	1,756	1,117	1,849	2,091	1,953	1,562	908
Men and boys	372	292	435	259	391	530	467	314	170
Women and girls	634	565	564	352	625	764	809	654	419
Children under 2 years old	81	104	121	115	175	95	52	60	17
Footwear	294	440	368	206	331	413	334	237	167
Other apparel products and services	258	201	268	184	327	289	291	297	135
Transportation	7,781	5,074	6,780	4,674	8,106	8,892	9,766	8,680	4,824
Vehicle purchases (net outlay)	3,732	2,097	3,063	2,241	3,932	4,255	4,632	4,289	2,247
Cars and trucks, new	2,052	929	1,441	991	1,757	2,221	2,569	2,624	1,591
Cars and trucks, used	1,611	1,164	1,562	1,231	2,080	1,937	1,951	1,645	637
Gasoline and motor oil	1,333	1,016	1,328	947	1,388	1,582	1,644	1,411	792
Other vehicle expenses	2,331	1,728	2,057	1,299	2,446	2,643	3,013	2,484	1,487
Vehicle finance charges	371	308	331	224	483	476	485	336	125
Maintenance and repair	619	413	520	352	558	677	782	728	467
Vehicle insurance	905	730	812	504	910	997	1,197	932	640
Public transportation	385	233	331	187	340	411	476	495	298
Health care [1]	2,416	1,309	1,439	546	1,468	2,105	2,479	3,059	3,741
Entertainment [2]	2,060	1,007	1,245	950	1,958	2,519	2,407	2,414	1,469
Personal care products and services	527	461	490	326	498	602	616	549	440
Reading	127	52	48	53	99	114	150	168	141
Education	783	442	477	1,490	684	694	1,377	743	129
Tobacco products & smoking supplies	290	180	171	230	285	312	385	337	162
Miscellaneous	606	447	419	251	532	601	830	675	533
Cash contributions	1,370	832	594	371	754	1,256	1,651	1,568	1,969
Personal insurance and pensions	4,055	2,504	2,824	1,382	4,137	5,196	6,003	4,819	1,251
Life and other personal insurance	397	295	160	40	200	382	600	570	388
Pensions and Social Security	3,658	2,209	2,664	1,342	3,937	4,814	5,403	4,249	864
Personal taxes	**2,532**	**966**	**680**	**421**	**1,979**	**2,817**	**3,949**	**2,827**	**1,878**

[1] For additional health care expenditures, see Table 129. [2] For additional recreation expenditures, see Section 26.

Source: U.S. Bureau of Labor Statistics, *Consumer Expenditures in 2003*. See also <http://www.bls.gov/cex/2003/Standard /race.pdf> and <http://www.bls.gov/cex/2003/Standard/hispanic.pdf> and <http://www.bls.gov/cex/2003/Standard/age.pdf> (released 30 November 2004).

Table 670. **Average Annual Expenditures of All Consumer Units by Region and Size of Unit: 2003**

[In dollars. For composition of regions, see map, inside front cover. See headnote, Table 667]

Type	Region				Size of consumer unit				
	North-east	Mid-west	South	West	One person	Two per-sons	Three per-sons	Four per-sons	Five or more
Expenditures, total	42,162	40,280	37,625	45,381	23,657	43,693	47,406	55,201	52,565
Food	5,730	5,088	4,960	5,876	2,831	5,432	6,173	7,472	8,178
Food at home.	3,306	2,904	2,996	3,428	1,525	3,128	3,664	4,472	5,157
Cereals and bakery products	485	411	413	482	217	425	508	644	772
Cereals and cereal products	158	135	142	173	71	139	174	227	274
Bakery products	327	276	271	310	146	286	334	418	498
Meats, poultry, fish, and eggs	889	734	835	849	359	824	976	1,213	1,422
Beef	239	225	262	247	94	253	292	368	425
Pork	168	161	181	167	73	173	203	252	286
Other meats	132	98	94	92	47	100	116	153	179
Poultry.	165	123	141	157	66	135	167	222	266
Fish and seafood.	146	97	121	141	59	126	156	168	205
Eggs.	38	31	36	45	20	38	43	50	62
Dairy products	353	323	298	359	161	324	383	467	555
Fresh milk and cream.	130	126	117	139	62	116	145	185	241
Other dairy products.	222	197	181	220	99	208	238	282	314
Fruits and vegetables.	586	472	489	633	280	552	609	740	832
Fresh fruits.	185	152	149	213	88	177	191	235	276
Fresh vegetables.	190	142	154	217	89	184	192	237	257
Processed fruits	123	96	98	125	60	105	124	153	177
Processed vegetables	88	81	88	78	44	86	103	115	122
Other food at home	994	962	961	1,104	507	1,003	1,188	1,407	1,577
Nonalcoholic beverages	272	254	258	297	131	265	327	382	436
Food away from home.	2,424	2,184	1,964	2,449	1,306	2,304	2,509	3,000	3,020
Alcoholic beverages	427	403	345	421	280	468	419	436	358
Housing	14,811	12,634	12,006	15,371	8,768	13,536	15,596	18,322	16,930
Shelter	9,134	7,086	6,660	9,630	5,614	7,730	8,949	10,622	9,801
Owned dwellings.	5,932	4,908	4,528	6,244	2,692	5,263	6,220	8,299	7,304
Mortgage interest and charges.	2,901	2,578	2,567	4,020	1,230	2,626	3,732	5,299	4,752
Property taxes.	2,004	1,427	1,018	1,211	802	1,487	1,507	1,790	1,635
Maintenance, repair, insurance, other	1,026	903	942	1,013	659	1,150	982	1,211	917
Rented dwellings.	2,664	1,720	1,802	2,848	2,679	1,869	2,229	1,818	2,109
Other lodging	537	458	330	538	242	597	501	505	388
Utilities, fuels, and public services	2,889	2,855	2,891	2,569	1,758	2,905	3,320	3,615	3,762
Natural gas.	512	593	243	320	254	396	449	506	548
Electricity.	926	931	1,251	854	621	1,082	1,216	1,306	1,393
Fuel oil and other fuels.	287	99	61	44	70	120	126	144	119
Telephone	932	917	1,002	941	623	965	1,161	1,227	1,229
Water and other public services	232	315	333	409	190	342	369	432	472
Household operations	813	614	666	778	343	565	1,026	1,337	899
Personal services	373	274	265	291	93	104	512	801	476
Other household expenses	440	340	402	487	251	461	513	536	423
Housekeeping supplies	523	575	496	537	284	582	636	685	690
Household furnishings and equipment. . .	1,452	1,504	1,294	1,858	769	1,754	1,666	2,064	1,778
Household textiles.	126	105	91	147	52	150	107	147	139
Furniture	391	411	357	471	194	457	475	608	438
Floor coverings	66	44	38	71	26	65	54	70	58
Major appliances	176	195	179	240	91	219	250	243	282
Small appliances, misc. housewares . . .	75	87	87	101	48	112	96	87	114
Miscellaneous household equipment. .	617	663	542	828	358	751	685	909	746
Apparel and services.	1,859	1,563	1,451	1,834	837	1,547	1,916	2,503	2,698
Men and boys	426	369	303	437	177	325	441	622	647
Women and girls.	709	612	548	732	331	619	746	978	932
Children under 2 years old	76	92	74	87	17	42	153	158	186
Footwear.	357	249	283	305	156	258	285	470	585
Other apparel products and services . . .	291	242	242	273	156	303	289	275	348
Transportation	7,043	7,817	7,621	8,645	3,839	8,683	9,562	10,459	10,185
Vehicle purchases (net outlay).	3,040	3,775	3,893	4,028	1,692	4,363	4,644	4,929	4,720
Cars and trucks, new.	1,688	2,039	2,208	2,131	1,027	2,703	2,189	2,663	1,963
Cars and trucks, used	1,294	1,654	1,627	1,820	620	1,593	2,369	2,193	2,653
Gasoline and motor oil	1,157	1,357	1,321	1,479	674	1,388	1,619	1,859	1,956
Other vehicle expenses	2,307	2,314	2,154	2,659	1,217	2,458	2,910	3,220	3,122
Vehicle finance charges	268	391	408	379	144	373	520	535	583
Maintenance and repair	565	580	555	811	362	685	728	803	748
Vehicle insurance	924	860	905	936	493	928	1,129	1,258	1,233
Public transportation	539	371	253	479	256	473	389	452	387
Health care [1]	2,127	2,586	2,396	2,525	1,558	3,093	2,532	2,581	2,379
Entertainment [2]	2,117	1,978	1,812	2,494	1,041	2,421	2,263	2,821	2,554
Personal care products and services	532	499	494	606	316	563	603	693	689
Reading	153	141	93	146	93	159	130	135	110
Education	1,040	796	581	875	498	597	938	1,426	1,119
Tobacco products and smoking supplies	306	363	275	224	193	310	351	329	364
Miscellaneous	548	647	556	695	423	650	658	801	661
Cash contributions	1,161	1,469	1,344	1,491	1,032	1,810	1,179	1,270	1,385
Personal insurance and pensions	4,308	4,295	3,690	4,179	1,948	4,424	5,087	5,952	4,956
Life and other personal insurance	454	423	381	347	159	496	488	498	511
Pensions and Social Security	3,855	3,872	3,309	3,832	1,790	3,928	4,599	5,454	4,446
Personal taxes.	2,294	2,853	2,268	2,840	1,592	3,701	2,332	2,838	1,444

[1] For additional health care expenditures, see Table 129. [2] For additional recreation expenditures, see Section 26.
Source: U.S. Bureau of Labor Statistics, *Consumer Expenditures in 2003*. See also <http://www.bls.gov/cex/2003/Standard/region.pdf> and <http://www.bls.gov/cex/2003/Standard/cusize.pdf> (released 30 November 2005).

Table 671. Average Annual Expenditures of All Consumer Units by Income Level: 2003

[In dollars. Based on Consumer Expenditure Survey. Data are averages for the noninstitutional population. Expenditures reported here are out-of-pocket]

Income level	Total expendi- tures [1]	Food	Housing			Transportation			Health care
			Total [1]	Shelter	Utility fuels [2]	Total [1]	Vehicle pur- chases	Gaso- line and motor oil	
All consumer units	**40,817**	**5,340**	**13,432**	**7,887**	**2,811**	**7,781**	**3,732**	**1,333**	**2,416**
Consumer units with complete reporting	42,742	5,593	13,653	7,921	2,820	8,041	3,871	1,353	2,495
Less than $70,000	31,737	4,619	10,464	6,046	2,450	6,138	2,884	1,134	2,199
$70,000 to $79,999	57,128	7,548	17,081	9,912	3,433	11,540	5,698	1,861	2,700
$80,000 to $99,999	65,957	7,840	19,841	10,899	3,779	13,295	6,834	2,038	3,335
$100,000 and over	93,515	9,926	28,941	17,253	4,336	15,526	7,604	2,123	3,809
$100,000 to $119,999	75,601	8,714	23,204	13,623	3,895	14,178	7,295	2,063	3,465
$120,000 to $149,999	86,451	9,689	26,719	16,128	4,146	15,785	7,932	2,195	3,478
$150,000 and over	118,674	11,435	36,971	22,117	4,969	16,799	7,683	2,133	4,447

[1] Includes expenditures not shown separately. [2] Includes public service.

Source: U.S. Bureau of Labor Statistics, *Consumer Expenditures in 2003*. See also <http://www.bls.gov/cex/2003/share/higherincome.pdf> (released 30 November 2004).

Table 672. Money Income of Households—Distribution of Income and Median Income by Race and Hispanic Origin: 1999

[In thousands, except as indicated. (105,539 represents 105,539,000). Households as of April 2000. Based on sample data from the 2000 Census of Population and Housing; see text, Section 1, Population, and Appendix III]

Income Interval	All house- holds	Race of householder							Hispanic or Latino [1]
		White alone	Black or African American alone	American Indian and Alaska Native alone	Asian alone	Native Hawaiian and other Pacific Islander alone	Some other race alone	Two or more races	
All households	**105,539**	**83,698**	**12,024**	**770**	**3,129**	**100**	**3,834**	**1,984**	**9,273**
Under $10,000	10,067	6,584	2,294	128	314	9	469	268	1,150
$10,000 to $14,999	6,657	4,955	1,038	68	143	5	300	148	723
$15,000 to $19,999	6,601	4,974	960	63	143	6	315	141	739
$20,000 to $24,999	6,936	5,303	935	63	153	7	331	145	768
$25,000 to $29,999	6,801	5,259	874	56	146	7	319	140	727
$30,000 to $34,999	6,718	5,281	787	54	157	6	299	134	682
$35,000 to $39,999	6,236	4,953	697	47	149	6	261	122	605
$40,000 to $44,999	5,966	4,794	624	42	154	6	235	111	546
$45,000 to $49,999	5,244	4,249	522	35	136	5	202	95	466
$50,000 to $59,999	9,537	7,834	879	60	267	9	323	165	773
$60,000 to $74,999	11,003	9,161	918	62	349	12	323	180	796
$75,000 to $99,999	10,799	9,121	797	51	396	11	258	164	683
$100,000 to $124,999	5,492	4,695	343	21	247	5	102	78	296
$125,000 to $149,999	2,656	2,285	148	9	136	2	40	36	127
$150,000 to $199,999	2,322	2,023	106	6	128	2	28	29	97
$200,000 and over	2,503	2,227	102	6	111	1	27	28	96
Median income (dollars)	41,994	44,687	29,423	30,599	51,908	42,717	32,694	35,587	33,676
Aggregate household income (mil. dol)	5,978,107	4,996,446	479,476	30,917	211,949	5,318	159,556	94,444	410,310

[1] Persons of Hispanic origin or Latino may be of any race.

Source: U.S. Census Bureau, *2000 Census of Population and Housing, Summary File 3*, using American FactFinder, tables P52, P53, P54, P151A-H, P152A-H, and P153A-H (accessed 05 September 2003).

Income, Expenditures, and Wealth   459

Table 673. **Money Income of Households—Percent Distribution by Income Level, Race, and Hispanic Origin, in Constant (2003) Dollars: 1980 to 2003**

[Constant dollars based on CPI-U-RS deflator. Households as of March of following year. (82,368 represents 82,368,000). Based on Current Population Survey; see text, Sections 1 and 13. and Appendix III. For data collection changes over time, see <http://www.census.gov/hhes/income/histinc/hstchg.html>. For definition of median, see Guide to Tabular Presentation]

Year	Number of households (1,000)	Percent distribution							Median income (dollars)
		Under $15,000	$15,000-$24,999	$25,000-$34,999	$35,000-$49,999	$50,000-$74,999	$75,000-$99,999	$100,000 and over	
ALL HOUSEHOLDS [1]									
1980	82,368	18.8	14.3	14.0	17.9	20.0	8.6	6.3	37,447
1990	94,312	17.0	13.6	12.9	17.0	19.2	10.0	10.3	40,865
2000 [2]	108,209	15.0	12.5	12.3	15.2	18.6	11.3	15.2	44,853
2002	111,278	15.7	12.9	12.2	14.9	18.2	11.2	14.7	43,381
2003	112,000	15.9	13.1	11.9	15.0	18.0	11.0	15.1	43,318
WHITE									
1980	71,872	16.8	13.9	14.0	18.4	21.0	9.1	6.9	39,506
1990	80,968	14.8	13.4	12.9	17.4	19.9	10.6	11.0	42,622
2000 [2]	90,030	13.5	12.1	12.2	15.2	19.1	11.8	16.1	46,910
2002 [3 4]	91,645	14.1	12.6	12.0	15.0	18.9	11.8	15.6	46,119
2003	91,962	14.2	12.8	11.8	15.0	18.5	11.5	16.1	45,631
BLACK									
1980	8,847	35.8	18.0	14.0	14.6	11.9	4.1	1.7	22,760
1990	10,671	33.7	15.8	13.4	14.4	13.5	5.1	4.1	25,488
2000 [2]	13,174	24.7	16.1	13.7	15.8	15.4	7.2	7.0	31,690
2002 [3 5]	13,465	27.4	16.0	13.3	15.0	14.6	7.0	6.7	29,691
2003	13,629	27.4	16.0	13.3	15.0	14.6	7.0	6.7	29,645
ASIAN AND PACIFIC ISLANDER									
1990 [2]	1,958	13.1	10.6	8.7	14.8	22.1	13.1	17.7	52,475
2000 [2]	3,963	11.0	8.5	10.0	13.6	18.4	14.2	24.3	59,559
2002 [3 6]	3,917	11.9	10.4	10.5	13.4	18.3	12.8	22.7	53,832
2003	4,040	15.2	9.5	7.1	13.8	18.4	12.5	23.4	55,699
HISPANIC [7]									
1980	3,906	24.1	19.4	16.3	17.0	15.7	4.8	2.8	28,864
1990 [2]	6,220	24.3	18.0	14.7	17.3	15.1	5.9	4.7	30,475
2000 [2]	10,034	17.9	16.7	14.9	17.6	17.4	8.3	7.2	35,429
2002	11,339	18.9	16.9	15.8	16.3	16.9	7.8	7.6	33,861
2003	11,693	18.9	17.6	15.8	16.7	15.9	7.7	7.5	32,997

[1] Includes other races not shown separately. [2] Data reflect implementation of Census 2000-based population controls and a 28,000 household sample expansion to 78,000 households. [3] Beginning with the 2003 Current Population Survey (CPS), the questionnaire allowed respondents to choose more than one race. For 2002 and later, data represent persons who selected this race group only and excludes persons reporting more than one race. The CPS in prior years allowed respondents to report only one race group. See also comments on race in the text for Section 1, Population. [4] Data represents White alone, which refers to people who reported White and did not report any other race category. [5] Data represents Black alone, which refers to people who reported Black and did not report any other race category. [6] Data represents Asian alone, which refers to people who reported Asian and did not report any other race category. [7] People of Hispanic origin may be of any race.

Table 674. **Money Income of Households—Median Income by Race and Hispanic Origin, in Current and Constant (2003) Dollars: 1980 to 2003**

[In dollars. See headnote, Table 673]

Year	Median income in current dollars					Median income in constant (2003) dollars				
	All households [1]	White [2]	Black [3]	Asian, Pacific Islander [4]	Hispanic [5]	All households [1]	White [2]	Black [3]	Asian, Pacific Islander [4]	Hispanic [5]
1980	17,710	18,684	10,764	(NA)	13,651	37,447	39,506	22,760	(NA)	28,864
1985	23,618	24,908	14,819	(NA)	17,465	38,510	40,614	24,163	(NA)	28,478
1990	29,943	31,231	18,676	38,450	22,330	40,865	42,622	25,488	52,475	30,475
1991	30,126	31,569	18,807	36,449	22,691	39,679	41,580	24,771	48,007	29,887
1992	30,636	32,209	18,755	37,801	22,597	39,364	41,385	24,098	48,570	29,035
1993	31,241	32,960	19,533	38,347	22,886	39,165	41,320	24,487	48,073	28,690
1994	32,264	34,028	21,027	40,482	23,421	39,613	41,779	25,816	49,703	28,756
1995	34,076	35,766	22,393	40,614	22,860	40,845	42,871	26,842	48,680	27,401
1996	35,492	37,161	23,482	43,276	24,906	41,431	43,379	27,411	50,517	29,073
1997	37,005	38,972	25,050	45,249	26,628	42,294	44,542	28,630	51,716	30,434
1998	38,885	40,912	25,351	46,637	28,330	43,825	46,110	28,572	52,562	31,929
1999	40,696	42,325	27,910	50,960	30,746	44,922	46,720	30,808	56,251	33,938
2000 [6]	41,990	43,916	29,667	55,757	33,168	44,853	46,910	31,690	59,559	35,429
2001	42,228	44,517	29,470	53,635	33,565	43,882	46,261	30,625	55,736	34,880
2002 [7]	42,409	45,086	29,026	52,626	33,103	43,381	46,119	29,691	53,832	33,861
2003	43,318	45,631	29,645	55,699	32,997	43,318	45,631	29,645	55,699	32,997

NA Not available. [1] Includes other races not shown separately. [2] Beginning with 2002, data represents White alone, which refers to people who reported White and did not report any other race category. [3] Beginning with 2002, data represents Black alone, which refers to people who reported Black and did not report any other race category. [4] Beginning with 2002, data represents Asian alone, which refers to people who reported Asian and did not report any other race category. [5] People of Hispanic origin may be any race. [6] Implementation of Census 2000-based population controls and sample expanded by 28,000 households. [7] See footnote 2, Table 673. See also comments on race in the text for Section 1, Population.

Source of Tables 673 and 674: U.S. Census Bureau, *Current Population Reports*, P60-226; and Internet sites <http://www.census.gov/prod/2004pubs/p60-226.pdf> (released 26 August 2004) and <http://www.census.gov/hhes/www/income/histinc/inchtoc.html>.

Table 675. **Money Income of Households—Distribution by Income Level and Selected Characteristics: 2003**

[111,278 represents 111,278,000. Households as of **March of the following year.** Based on Current Population Survey; see text, Sections 1 and 13, and Appendix III]

Characteristic	Number of households (1,000)	Number (1,000)							Median income (dollars)
		Under $15,000	$15,000-$24,999	$25,000-$34,999	$35,000-$49,999	$50,000-$74,999	$75,000-$99,999	$100,000 and over	
Total [1]	112,000	17,851	14,649	13,277	16,773	20,191	12,313	16,945	43,318
Age of householder:									
15 to 24 years	6,610	1,766	1,319	1,079	1,047	865	316	219	27,053
25 to 34 years	19,159	2,385	2,277	2,517	3,479	4,082	2,263	2,157	44,779
35 to 44 years	23,222	2,199	2,130	2,442	3,579	5,092	3,325	4,454	55,044
45 to 54 years	23,137	2,243	1,848	2,157	3,311	4,686	3,404	5,490	60,242
55 to 64 years	16,824	2,446	1,823	1,833	2,415	3,095	1,957	3,254	49,215
65 years and over.......	23,048	6,812	5,255	3,249	2,941	2,370	1,051	1,371	23,787
Region: [2]									
Northeast	21,017	3,461	2,536	2,164	2,859	3,732	2,452	3,812	46,742
Midwest	25,643	3,720	3,292	3,104	3,925	4,945	3,027	3,629	44,732
South	40,742	7,146	5,799	5,219	6,373	6,936	4,054	5,214	39,823
West...................	24,598	3,523	3,023	2,789	3,614	4,577	2,781	4,290	46,820
Size of household:									
One person	29,586	10,532	5,733	4,017	4,085	3,093	1,117	1,012	21,930
Two people	37,366	3,804	5,013	4,923	6,085	7,243	4,426	5,874	46,924
Three people	17,968	1,647	1,766	1,785	2,744	3,982	2,554	3,489	55,726
Four people	16,065	1,037	1,217	1,436	2,167	3,559	2,587	4,060	64,374
Five people	7,150	551	581	688	1,090	1,511	1,109	1,621	60,128
Six people	2,476	167	217	281	392	524	312	583	58,109
Seven or more people	1,388	113	122	149	210	280	208	306	60,521
Type of household:									
Family households	76,217	6,760	8,247	8,533	11,590	15,691	10,376	15,019	53,991
Married-couple	57,719	2,861	5,078	5,622	8,490	12,727	9,073	13,866	62,405
Male householder, wife absent..........	4,717	510	668	709	853	959	500	518	41,959
Female householder, husband absent.......	13,781	3,390	2,500	2,202	2,247	2,003	805	634	29,307
Nonfamily households	35,783	11,089	6,402	4,744	5,180	4,502	1,938	1,926	25,741
Male householder	16,136	3,807	2,624	2,219	2,649	2,538	1,123	1,178	31,928
Female householder	19,647	7,283	3,779	2,525	2,532	1,963	816	748	21,313
Educational attainment of householder: [3]									
Total	105,390	16,084	13,331	12,199	15,726	19,327	11,998	16,726	45,016
Less than 9th grade	6,385	2,553	1,438	863	715	499	199	119	18,787
9th to 12th grade (no diploma)	9,043	2,979	1,890	1,365	1,187	986	373	266	22,718
High school graduate	31,860	5,505	5,005	4,559	5,480	5,688	3,064	2,559	36,835
Some college, no degree	18,837	2,436	2,380	2,280	3,113	3,948	2,312	2,367	45,854
Associate's degree	9,117	902	866	995	1,538	2,111	1,254	1,449	51,970
Bachelor's degree or more	30,149	1,712	1,752	2,137	3,691	6,097	4,795	9,967	73,446
Bachelor's degree	19,307	1,191	1,246	1,520	2,548	4,099	3,160	5,544	68,728
Master's degree	7,449	346	357	442	893	1,480	1,217	2,711	78,541
Professional degree	1,834	85	96	107	121	250	229	950	100,000
Doctorate degree	1,558	88	54	68	130	266	191	761	96,830
Number of earners:									
No earners	23,932	11,507	5,511	2,909	2,013	1,186	370	434	15,661
One earner	40,769	5,547	7,233	6,904	7,863	6,903	2,838	3,482	35,977
Two earners and more......	47,299	796	1,904	3,466	6,896	12,105	9,105	13,029	71,496
2 earners	37,917	767	1,801	3,135	6,014	9,910	6,953	9,337	67,348
3 earners.............	6,998	28	89	285	745	1,846	1,595	2,411	82,464
4 earners or more	2,384	-	15	44	138	351	555	1,281	100,000
Work experience of householder:									
Total	112,000	17,851	14,649	13,277	16,773	20,191	12,313	16,945	43,318
Worked................	77,597	5,482	7,704	8,871	12,667	16,907	10,925	15,039	54,989
Worked at full-time jobs ...	66,138	3,215	6,018	7,443	11,052	15,038	9,845	13,525	57,475
50 weeks or more	55,952	1,666	4,474	6,110	9,346	13,192	8,824	12,344	60,852
27 to 49 weeks	6,393	660	381	836	1,165	1,251	747	854	45,532
26 weeks or less........	3,792	889	663	496	543	596	277	327	31,224
Worked at part-time jobs. ..	11,459	2,267	1,685	1,429	1,615	1,869	1,079	1,515	37,833
50 weeks or more	6,211	946	952	763	912	1,078	668	891	41,789
27 to 49 weeks........	2,435	476	341	267	359	422	222	351	40,750
26 weeks or less	2,813	846	393	398	344	371	188	272	28,704
Did not work	34,403	12,367	6,946	4,406	4,105	3,284	1,389	1,905	21,476
Tenure:									
Owner-occupied	77,092	8,196	8,253	8,030	11,312	15,568	10,478	15,257	53,584
Renter-occupied	33,414	9,151	6,118	5,059	5,250	4,426	1,783	1,629	27,561
Occupier paid no cash rent	1,494	504	280	188	210	197	56	59	23,662

[1] Includes other races not shown separately.　[2] For composition of regions, see map inside front cover.　[3] People 25 years old and over.

Source: U.S. Census Bureau, *Current Population Reports*, P60-226; and Internet site <http://pubdb3.census.gov/macro/032004/hhinc/new01001.htm> (accessed 08 June 2005).

Income, Expenditures, and Wealth　461

Table 676. **Money Income of Households—Number and Distribution by Race and Hispanic Origin: 2003**

[Households as of **March of the following year. (112,000 represents 112,000,000).** Based on Current Population Survey (CPS); see text, Sections 1 and 13, and Appendix III. The 2004 CPS allowed respondents to choose more than one race. Data represent persons who selected this race group only and excludes persons reporting more than one race. See also comments on race in the text for Section 1, Population]

Income interval	Number (1,000)					Percent distribution				
	All races	White	Black	Asian	His-panic [1]	All races	White	Black	Asian	His-panic [1]
All households [1] . . .	**112,000**	**91,962**	**13,629**	**4,040**	**11,693**	**100.0**	**100.0**	**100.0**	**100.0**	**100.0**
Under $10,000	10,111	7,012	2,409	432	1,264	9.0	7.6	17.7	10.7	10.8
$10,000 to $14,999	7,740	6,035	1,329	181	942	6.9	6.6	9.8	4.5	8.1
$15,000 to $19,999	7,434	5,926	1,107	231	1,042	6.6	6.4	8.1	5.7	8.9
$20,000 to $24,999	7,215	5,827	1,071	153	1,014	6.4	6.3	7.9	3.8	8.7
$25,000 to $29,999	6,718	5,479	959	124	940	6.0	6.0	7.0	3.1	8.0
$30,000 to $34,999	6,559	5,412	857	162	907	5.9	5.9	6.3	4.0	7.8
$35,000 to $39,999	6,024	4,954	768	187	752	5.4	5.4	5.6	4.6	6.4
$40,000 to $44,999	5,801	4,765	712	199	700	5.2	5.2	5.2	4.9	6.0
$45,000 to $49,999	4,948	4,096	562	172	500	4.4	4.5	4.1	4.3	4.3
$50,000 to $59,999	9,151	7,676	972	299	879	8.2	8.3	7.1	7.4	7.5
$60,000 to $74,999	11,040	9,346	1,018	445	977	9.9	10.2	7.5	11.0	8.4
$75,000 to $84,999	5,815	4,993	455	246	458	5.2	5.4	3.3	6.1	3.9
$85,000 to $99,999	6,498	5,619	495	260	446	5.8	6.1	3.6	6.4	3.8
$100,000 to $149,999. . . .	10,719	9,309	659	575	572	9.6	10.1	4.8	14.2	4.9
$150,000 to $199,999. . . .	3,372	2,933	153	234	171	3.0	3.2	1.1	5.8	1.5
$200,000 to $249,999. . . .	1,307	1,157	61	67	58	1.2	1.3	0.4	1.7	0.5
$250,000 and above	1,547	1,421	42	71	70	1.4	1.5	0.3	1.8	0.6

[1] Persons of Hispanic origin may be of any race.

Source: U.S. Census Bureau, Current Population Reports, *Income, Poverty, and Health Insurance 2003*, P60-226; and Internet site at <http://ferret.bls.census.gov/macro/032004/hhinc/new06000.htm> (accessed 10 June 2005).

Table 677. **Money Income of Families—Number and Distribution by Race and Hispanic Origin: 2003**

[Households as of **March of the following year. (76,232 represents 76,232,000).** Based on Current Population Survey (CPS); see text, Sections 1 and 13, and Appendix III. The 2004 CPS allowed respondents to choose more than one race. For 2003, data represent persons who selected this race group only and excludes persons reporting more than one race. The CPS in prior years only allowed respondents to report one race group. See also comments on race in the text for Section 1, Population]

Income interval	Number (1,000)					Percent distribution				
	All races	White	Black	Asian	His-panic [1]	All races	White	Black	Asian	His-panic [1]
All families [1]	**76,232**	**62,620**	**8,914**	**3,064**	**9,274**	**100.0**	**100.0**	**100.0**	**100.0**	**100.0**
Under $10,000	4,246	2,684	1,221	196	813	5.6	4.3	13.7	6.4	8.8
$10,000 to $14,999	3,120	2,234	692	104	715	4.1	3.6	7.8	3.4	7.7
$15,000 to $19,999	4,148	3,177	724	144	852	5.4	5.1	8.1	4.7	9.2
$20,000 to $24,999	4,341	3,433	684	114	841	5.7	5.5	7.7	3.7	9.1
$25,000 to $29,999	4,435	3,606	626	92	786	5.8	5.8	7.0	3.0	8.5
$30,000 to $34,999	4,222	3,443	561	117	708	5.5	5.5	6.3	3.8	7.6
$35,000 to $39,999	4,038	3,284	525	135	602	5.3	5.2	5.9	4.4	6.5
$40,000 to $44,999	3,885	3,172	483	153	526	5.1	5.1	5.4	5.0	5.7
$45,000 to $49,999	3,520	2,910	394	133	424	4.6	4.6	4.4	4.3	4.6
$50,000 to $59,999	6,650	5,571	687	251	710	8.7	8.9	7.7	8.2	7.7
$60,000 to $74,999	8,702	7,365	771	378	827	11.4	11.8	8.6	12.3	8.9
$75,000 to $84,999	4,723	4,067	368	199	361	6.2	6.5	4.1	6.5	3.9
$85,000 to $99,999	5,434	4,717	404	214	373	7.1	7.5	4.5	7.0	4.0
$100,000 to $149,999. . . .	9,312	8,106	561	504	489	12.2	12.9	6.3	16.4	5.3
$150,000 to $199,999. . . .	2,948	2,570	132	211	128	3.9	4.1	1.5	6.9	1.4
$200,000 to $249,999. . . .	1,142	1,014	52	57	55	1.5	1.6	0.6	1.9	0.6
$250,000 and above	1,366	1,264	29	64	63	1.8	2.0	0.3	2.1	0.7

[1] Persons of Hispanic origin may be of any race.

Source: U.S. Census Bureau, Current Population Reports, *Income, Poverty, and Health Insurance 2003*, P60-226; and Internet site at <http://ferret.bls.census.gov/macro/032004/faminc/new07000.htm> (accessed 10 June 2005).

Table 678. Money Income of Families—Percent Distribution by Income Level in Constant (2003) Dollars: 1980 to 2003

[Constant dollars based on CPI-U-RS deflator. Families as of March of the following year (60,309 represents 60,309,000). Based on Current Population Survey; see text, Sections 1 and 13, and Appendix III. For data collection changes over time, see <http://www.census.gov/hhes/income/histinc/hstchg.html>. For definition of median, see Guide to Tabular Presentation]

Year	Number of families (1,000)	Percent distribution							Median income (dollars)
		Under $15,000	$15,000-$24,999	$25,000-$34,999	$35,000-$49,999	$50,000-$74,999	$75,000-$99,999	$100,000 and over	
ALL FAMILIES [1]									
1980	60,309	11.4	12.6	13.7	19.6	24.0	10.7	7.9	44,452
1990 [2]	66,322	10.9	11.5	12.1	17.6	22.4	13.0	7.9	48,248
2000 [2]	73,778	8.8	10.4	11.5	15.5	20.9	12.4	13.0	54,191
2002	75,616	9.5	11.0	11.7	15.1	20.5	13.7	19.1	52,864
2003	76,232	9.6	11.1	11.4	15.0	20.1	13.7	18.6	52,680
WHITE								13.3	19.4
1980	52,710	9.4	11.9	13.7	20.0	25.2	11.3	8.6	46,315
1990 [2]	56,803	8.6	11.0	12.0	18.0	23.3	13.2	13.9	50,380
2000 [2] [3] [4]	61,330	7.4	9.7	11.3	15.5	21.6	14.3	20.3	56,645
2002	62,313	7.9	10.3	11.2	15.0	21.2	14.5	19.8	55,885
2003	62,620	7.9	10.6	11.3	15.0	20.7	14.0	20.7	55,768
BLACK									
1980	6,317	28.4	18.6	14.6	16.2	14.7	5.2	2.2	26,798
1990 [2]	7,471	28.6	15.6	13.5	15.3	15.6	6.4	5.1	29,237
2000 [2] [3] [5]	8,731	19.1	15.9	14.2	16.2	17.3	8.8	8.7	35,972
2002	8,932	21.5	15.8	13.3	15.7	16.3	8.7	8.7	34,293
2003	8,914	21.5	15.8	13.3	15.7	16.3	8.7	8.7	34,369
ASIAN AND PACIFIC ISLANDER									
1990 [2]	1,536	9.5	9.8	8.5	14.3	22.2	15.5	20.3	57,655
2000 [2]	2,982	7.4	7.5	9.1	13.2	19.0	15.8	28.1	66,886
2002 [3] [6]	2,845	6.9	8.5	10.0	13.6	20.1	14.2	26.7	62,381
2003	3,064	9.8	8.4	6.8	13.7	20.5	13.5	27.3	63,251
HISPANIC ORIGIN [7]									
1980	3,235	20.0	19.5	16.9	18.4	17.1	5.2	3.0	31,116
1990 [2]	4,981	21.7	18.4	14.6	17.7	16.1	6.5	5.1	31,977
2000 [2]	8,017	15.7	17.0	15.1	17.9	17.9	8.7	7.7	36,790
2002	9,094	16.4	17.8	16.1	16.7	17.2	8.0	7.8	34,968
2003	9,274	16.5	18.3	16.1	16.7	16.6	7.9	7.9	34,272

[1] Includes other races not shown separately. [2] Data reflect implementation of Census 2000-based population controls and a 28,000 household sample expansion to 78,000 households. [3] Beginning with the 2003 Current Population Survey (CPS), the questionnaire allowed respondents to choose more than one race. For 2002 and later, data represent persons who selected this race group only and excludes persons reporting more than one race. The CPS in prior years allowed respondents to report only one race group. See also comments on race in the text for Section 1, Population. [4] Data represents White alone, which refers to people who reported White and did not report any other race category. [5] Data represents Black alone, which refers to people who reported Black and did not report any other race category. [6] Data represents Asian alone, which refers to people who reported Asian and did not report any other race category. [7] People of Hispanic origin may be of any race.

Table 679. Money Income of Families—Median Income by Race and Hispanic Origin in Current and Constant (2003) Dollars: 1980 to 2003

[See headnote, Table 678]

Year	Median income in current dollars					Median income in constant (2003) dollars				
	All families [1]	White [2]	Black [3]	Asian, Pacific Islander [4]	His-panic [5]	All families [1]	White [2]	Black [3]	Asian, Pacific Islander [4]	His-panic [5]
1980	21,023	21,904	12,674	(NA)	14,716	44,452	46,315	26,798	(NA)	31,116
1985	27,735	29,152	16,786	(NA)	19,027	45,223	47,534	27,370	(NA)	31,025
1990	35,353	36,915	21,423	42,246	23,431	48,248	50,380	29,237	57,655	31,977
1991	35,939	37,783	21,548	40,974	23,895	47,336	49,764	28,381	53,967	31,472
1992	36,573	38,670	21,103	42,255	23,555	46,992	49,687	27,115	54,293	30,266
1993	36,959	39,300	21,542	44,456	23,654	46,333	49,268	27,006	55,731	29,653
1994	38,782	40,884	24,698	46,122	24,318	47,615	50,196	30,324	56,627	29,857
1995	40,611	42,646	25,970	46,356	24,570	48,679	51,118	31,129	55,565	29,451
1996	42,300	44,756	26,522	49,105	26,179	49,378	52,245	30,960	57,321	30,559
1997	44,568	46,754	28,602	51,850	28,142	50,938	53,436	32,690	59,260	32,164
1998	46,737	49,023	29,404	52,826	29,608	52,675	55,251	33,140	59,538	33,370
1999	48,831	51,079	31,850	56,127	31,523	53,901	56,383	35,157	61,955	34,796
2000 [6] . . .	50,732	53,029	33,676	62,617	34,442	54,191	56,645	35,972	66,886	36,790
2001	51,407	54,067	33,598	60,158	34,490	53,421	56,185	34,914	62,515	35,841
2002 [7] . . .	51,680	54,633	33,525	60,984	34,185	52,864	55,885	34,293	62,381	34,968
2003	52,680	55,768	34,369	63,251	34,272	52,680	55,768	34,369	63,251	34,272

NA Not available. [1] Includes other races not shown separately. [2] Beginning with 2002, data represents White alone, which refers to people who reported White and did not report any other race category. [3] Beginning with 2002, data represents Black alone, which refers to people who reported Black and did not report any other race category. [4] Beginning with 2002, data represents Asian alone, which refers to people who reported Asian and did not report any other race category. [5] People of Hispanic origin may be of any race. [6] Implementation of Census 2000-based population controls and sample expanded by 28,000 households. [7] See footnote 3, Table 678.

Source of Tables 678 and 679: U.S. Census Bureau, Current Population Reports, P60-226; and Internet site <http://www.census.gov/hhes/www/income/histinc/incfamdet.html> (revised 13 May 2005).

[Families as of March of the following year (60,309 represents 60,309,000). Income in constant 2003 CPI-U-RS adjusted dollars. Based on the Current Population Survey; see text, Sections 1 and 13, and Appendix III. For data collection changes over time, see <http://www.census.gov/hhes/income/histinc/hstchg.html>

Year	Number of families (1,000)	Income at selected positions (dollars)					Percent distribution of aggregate income					
		Upper limit of each fifth				Top 5 percent	Lowest 5th	Second 5th	Third 5th	Fourth 5th	Highest 5th	Top 5 percent
		Lowest	Second	Third	Fourth							
1980	60,309	21,990	37,024	52,438	73,583	116,294	5.3	11.6	17.6	24.4	41.1	14.6
1985	63,558	21,662	37,317	54,056	78,640	128,757	4.8	11.0	16.9	24.3	43.1	16.1
1986	64,491	22,418	38,592	56,238	80,978	133,550	4.7	10.9	16.9	24.1	43.4	16.5
1987	65,204	22,606	38,996	56,988	82,584	134,645	4.6	10.7	16.8	24.0	43.8	17.2
1988	65,837	22,565	39,120	57,525	83,532	137,463	4.6	10.7	16.7	24.0	44.0	17.2
1989	66,090	22,926	40,113	58,451	85,313	141,776	4.6	10.6	16.5	23.7	44.6	17.9
1990	66,322	22,991	39,638	57,374	83,918	139,693	4.6	10.8	16.6	23.8	44.3	17.4
1991	67,173	22,391	38,342	56,636	82,966	135,430	4.5	10.7	16.6	24.1	44.2	17.1
1992	68,216	21,474	38,128	56,535	82,297	136,214	4.3	10.5	16.5	24.0	44.7	17.6
1993	68,506	21,274	37,609	56,451	83,735	141,888	4.1	9.9	15.7	23.3	47.0	20.3
1994	69,313	22,026	38,429	57,705	85,942	147,386	4.2	10.0	15.7	23.3	46.9	20.1
1995	69,597	22,858	39,538	58,716	86,615	148,221	4.4	10.1	15.8	23.2	46.5	20.0
1996	70,241	22,973	40,057	59,634	87,918	149,417	4.2	10.0	15.8	23.1	46.8	20.3
1997	70,884	23,528	41,145	61,279	91,433	156,671	4.2	9.9	15.7	23.0	47.2	20.7
1998	71,551	24,344	42,481	63,137	94,326	163,647	4.2	9.9	15.7	23.0	47.3	20.7
1999	73,206	25,163	43,593	65,424	97,174	171,116	4.3	9.9	15.6	23.0	47.2	20.3
2000 [1] . . .	72,388	25,636	43,795	65,563	97,952	171,176	4.3	9.8	15.5	22.8	47.4	20.8
2001	74,340	24,940	42,738	64,949	97,839	170,533	4.2	9.7	15.4	22.9	47.7	21.0
2002	75,616	24,550	42,389	64,443	96,633	168,088	4.2	9.7	15.5	23.0	47.6	20.8
2003	76,232	24,117	42,057	65,000	98,200	170,082	4.1	9.6	15.5	23.2	47.6	20.5

[1] Data reflect implementation of Census 2000-based population controls and a 28,000 household sample expansion to 78,000 households.

Source: U.S. Census Bureau, Current Population Reports, P60-226, Income, Poverty, and Health Insurance Coverage in the United States: 2003; and Internet sites at <http://www.census.gov/prod/2004pubs/p60-226.pdf> (released 26 August 2004), and <http://www.census.gov/hhes/income/histinc/f01.html> and <http://www.census.gov/hhes/income/histinc/f02.html> (revised 13 May 2005).

Table 681. **Money Income of Families—Distribution by Family Characteristics and Income Level: 2003**

[(76,232 represents 76,232,000). See headnote, Table 678. For composition of regions, see map inside front cover]

Characteristic	Number of families (1,000)	Income level (1,000)							Median income (dollars)
		Under $15,000	$15,000 to $24,999	$25,000 to $34,999	$35,000 to $49,999	$50,000 to $74,999	$75,000 to $99,999	$100,000 and over	
All families	76,232	7,366	8,489	8,657	11,443	15,352	10,157	14,768	52,680
Age of householder:									
15 to 24 years old.	3,592	1,027	696	571	545	450	163	139	26,198
25 to 34 years old.	13,561	1,808	1,560	1,668	2,186	2,942	1,698	1,701	46,554
35 to 44 years old.	18,329	1,493	1,585	1,784	2,655	4,081	2,799	3,927	59,122
45 to 54 years old.	17,137	956	1,097	1,336	2,242	3,619	2,942	4,946	70,149
55 to 64 years old.	11,621	891	988	1,106	1,661	2,391	1,667	2,916	60,976
65 years old and over	11,991	1,191	2,563	2,192	2,153	1,871	883	1,139	35,310
Region:									
Northeast	13,994	1,222	1,368	1,378	1,926	2,774	1,977	3,350	59,874
Midwest	17,378	1,342	1,710	2,003	2,650	3,804	2,658	3,214	55,613
South	28,000	3,217	3,537	3,475	4,476	5,378	3,326	4,591	47,322
West.	16,860	1,584	1,875	1,801	2,392	3,397	2,198	3,613	55,095
Type of family:									
Married-couple families	57,725	2,873	5,107	5,661	8,505	12,721	9,058	13,802	62,281
Male householder, wife absent	4,717	632	755	768	813	875	416	458	38,032
Female householder, husband absent	13,791	3,861	2,628	2,227	2,125	1,759	684	508	26,550
Unrelated subfamilies	509	199	92	115	53	29	3	20	20,160
Education attainment of householder: [1]									
Total	72,640	6,337	7,793	8,087	10,896	14,901	9,993	14,629	54,739
Less than 9th grade	4,056	922	1,072	729	619	448	160	106	25,313
9th to 12th grade (no diploma) . . .	5,996	1,250	1,281	1,108	966	841	322	230	28,848
High school graduate (includes equivalency)	21,966	2,171	2,843	3,138	4,110	4,723	2,682	2,297	44,620
Some college, no degree.	13,145	996	1,366	1,489	2,111	3,133	2,007	2,045	54,255
Associate's degree	6,537	375	461	597	1,033	1,685	1,100	1,289	61,208
Bachelor's degree or more.	20,940	624	771	1,029	2,056	4,075	3,724	8,662	86,921
Bachelor's degree.	13,497	418	569	731	1,455	2,871	2,524	4,927	81,094
Master's degree	5,080	130	136	193	458	915	927	2,319	93,867
Professional degree	1,274	31	39	77	67	141	131	787	100,000
Doctorate degree	1,089	46	28	28	75	146	136	629	100,000

[1] Persons 25 years old and over.

Source: U.S. Census Bureau, Current Population Reports, Income, Poverty, and Health Insurance Coverage in the United States, 2003, and Internet sites <http://www.census.gov/prod/2004pubs/p60-226.pdf> (released 26 August 2004) and <http://pubdb3.census.gov/macro/032004/faminc/new01000.htm> (accessed 13 June 2005).

Table 682. Median Income of Families by Type of Family in Current and Constant (2003) Dollars: 1980 to 2003

[In dollars. See headnote, Table 678. For definition of median, see Guide to Tabular Presentation]

	Current dollars						Constant (2003) dollars					
	Married-couple families				Female		Married-couple families				Female
Year			Wife in paid labor force	Wife not in paid labor force	Male house- holder, no wife present	house- holder, no hus- band present	Total	Total	Wife in paid labor force	Wife not in paid labor force	Male house- holder, no wife present	house- holder, no husband present
	Total	Total										
1980 . . .	21,023	23,141	26,879	18,972	17,519	10,408	44,452	48,930	56,834	40,115	37,043	22,007
1990 . . .	35,353	39,895	46,777	30,265	29,046	16,932	48,248	54,447	63,839	41,304	39,640	23,108
1995 . . .	40,611	47,062	55,823	32,375	30,358	19,691	48,679	56,411	66,913	38,807	36,389	23,603
1996 . . .	42,300	49,707	58,381	33,748	31,600	19,911	49,378	58,024	68,149	39,395	36,887	23,243
1997 . . .	44,568	51,591	60,669	36,027	32,960	21,023	50,938	58,964	69,340	41,176	37,671	24,028
1998 . . .	46,737	54,180	63,751	37,161	35,681	22,163	52,675	61,064	71,851	41,882	40,214	24,979
1999 . . .	48,831	56,501	66,478	38,480	37,339	23,762	53,901	62,368	73,381	42,475	41,216	26,229
2000 . . .	50,732	59,099	69,235	39,982	37,727	25,716	54,191	63,128	73,956	42,708	40,299	27,469
2001 . . .	51,407	60,335	70,834	40,782	36,590	25,745	53,421	62,699	73,609	42,380	38,024	26,754
2002 . . .	51,680	61,130	72,806	40,102	37,739	26,423	52,864	62,530	74,474	41,021	38,604	27,028
2003 . . .	52,680	62,281	75,170	41,122	38,032	26,550	52,680	62,281	75,170	41,122	38,032	26,550

Table 683. Married-Couple Families—Number and Median Income by Work Experience of Husbands and Wives and Presence of Children: 2003

[(57,725 represents 57,725,000). See headnote, Table 678. For definition of median, see Guide to Tabular Presentation]

| | Number (1,000) | | | | | Median income (dollars) | | | | |
| Work experience of husband or wife | All married- couple families | No related chil- dren | One or more related children under 18 years old | | | All married- couple families | No related chil- dren | One or more related children under 18 years old | | |
			Total	One child	Two or more			Total	One child	Two or more
All married-couple families .	**57,725**	**30,766**	**26,959**	**10,261**	**16,698**	**62,281**	**58,514**	**66,419**	**68,427**	**65,091**
Husband worked	45,446	20,170	25,277	9,470	15,807	71,685	75,766	68,712	71,119	66,991
Wife worked	33,256	15,292	17,963	7,213	10,750	77,899	81,422	75,396	77,319	74,119
Wife did not work	12,191	4,877	7,314	2,257	5,057	51,303	53,533	50,422	50,333	50,450
Husband year-round, full-time worker	37,582	15,749	21,833	8,129	13,704	75,644	80,987	71,702	74,212	70,526
Wife worked	27,801	12,342	15,459	6,194	9,265	81,255	85,293	77,808	80,259	76,488
Wife did not work	9,781	3,407	6,374	1,935	4,439	55,616	60,189	52,841	53,406	52,509
Husband did not work	12,279	10,596	1,682	792	891	31,042	31,205	29,935	30,917	29,020
Wife worked	3,568	2,502	1,066	469	597	43,931	46,680	37,693	40,027	36,392
Wife did not work	8,711	8,094	616	322	294	27,130	27,589	17,943	20,518	14,826

Source of Tables 682 and 683: U.S. Census Bureau, Current Population Reports, P60-226; and <http://www.census.gov/prod/2004pubs/p60-226.pdf> (released 26 August 2004) and <http://pubdb3.census.gov/macro/032004/faminc/toc.htm> (accessed June 13 2005).

Table 684. Median Income of People With Income in Constant (2003) Dollars by Sex, Race, and Hispanic Origin: 1980 to 2003

[People 15 years old and over. Constant dollars based on CPI-U-RS deflator. Based on the Current Population Survey; see text, Sections 1 and 13, and Appendix III. For data collection changes over time, see <http://www.census.gov/hhes/income/histinc/hstchg.html>].

| Race and Hispanic origin | Male | | | | | Female | | | | |
	1980	1990	2000 [1]	2002 [2]	2003	1980	1990	2000 [1]	2002 [2]	2003
All races [3]	26,494	27,695	30,275	29,908	29,931	10,403	13,743	17,158	17,197	17,259
White [4]	28,181	28,892	31,829	31,079	30,732	10,460	14,080	17,175	17,224	17,422
Black [5]	16,935	17,562	22,798	22,055	21,986	9,684	11,366	16,964	17,112	16,581
Asian alone [6]	(NA)	(NA)	(NA)	31,797	32,291	(NA)	(NA)	(NA)	18,087	17,679
Hispanic [7]	20,423	18,383	20,827	21,176	21,053	9,314	10,279	13,083	13,670	13,642
White non-Hispanic	(NA)	29,967	33,656	32,768	32,331	(NA)	14,440	17,801	17,787	18,301

NA Not available. [1] Implementation of Census 2000-based population controls and sample expanded by 28,000 households. [2] Beginning with the 2003 Current Population Survey (CPS), the questionnaire allowed respondents to choose more than one race. For 2002 and later, data represent persons who selected this race group only and excludes persons reporting more than one race. The CPS in prior years allowed respondents to report only one race group. See also comments on race in the text for Section 1, Population. [3] Includes other races not shown separately. [4] Beginning with 2002, data represents White alone, which refers to people who reported White and did not report any other race category. [5] Beginning with 2002, data represents Black alone, which refers to people who reported Black and did not report any other race category. [6] Beginning with 2002, data represents Asian alone, which refers to people who reported Asian and did not report any other race category. [7] People of Hispanic origin may be of any race.

Source: U.S. Census Bureau, Current Population Reports. P60-226; and Internet site <http://www.census.gov/hhes/www/income/histinc/incpertoc.html> (revised 13 May 2005).

Table 685. Money Income of People—Selected Characteristics by Income Level: 2002

[People as of March 2003 (108,814 represents 108,814,000). Covers people 15 years old and over. For definition of median, see Guide to Tabular Presentation. For composition of regions, see map, inside front cover. Based on the Current Population Survey (CPS), see Appendix III]

Characteristic	All persons (1,000)	Persons with income								
			Number (1,000)								Median income (dollars)
		Total (1,000)	Under $5,000 [1]	$5,000 to $9,999	$10,000 to $14,999	$15,000 to $24,999	$25,000 to $34,999	$35,000 to $49,999	$50,000 to $74,999	$75,000 and over	
MALE											
Total	110,257	100,769	8,169	7,848	9,654	17,566	14,458	15,746	14,394	12,934	29,931
15 to 24 years old	20,699	14,237	4,742	2,394	1,990	2,832	1,315	656	222	86	9,961
25 to 34 years old	19,598	18,684	860	1,110	1,608	3,772	3,524	3,749	2,543	1,518	30,562
35 to 44 years old	21,530	20,781	843	941	1,081	2,989	3,268	4,055	3,994	3,610	39,195
45 to 54 years old	20,082	19,417	725	959	1,068	2,389	2,561	3,628	4,069	4,018	42,079
55 to 64 years old	13,551	13,097	505	760	1,001	1,906	1,744	2,186	2,357	2,638	38,915
65 yrs. old and over. . . .	14,797	14,554	496	1,682	2,907	3,679	2,045	1,474	1,208	1,063	20,363
Region:											
Northeast	20,589	18,834	1,589	1,415	1,792	2,860	2,516	2,972	2,807	2,883	31,412
Midwest	24,977	23,231	2,011	1,748	2,017	3,925	3,426	3,846	3,541	2,717	30,289
South	39,272	35,654	2,733	2,967	3,589	6,761	5,437	5,426	4,665	4,076	27,613
West	25,418	23,050	1,835	1,718	2,255	4,022	3,081	3,502	3,380	3,257	30,426
Education attainment of householder: [2]											
Total	89,558	86,532	3,432	5,454	7,663	14,733	13,144	15,091	14,169	12,846	33,517
Less than 9th grade. . .	5,804	5,405	349	1,042	1,209	1,628	634	345	151	47	15,461
9th to 12th grade [3]	7,766	7,245	497	944	1,311	1,938	1,226	772	410	147	18,990
High school graduate [4]. . .	27,889	26,800	1,174	1,849	2,575	5,699	5,154	5,209	3,578	1,562	28,763
Some college, no degree.	15,012	14,586	548	721	1,205	2,288	2,510	3,060	2,729	1,525	35,073
Associate's degree	6,751	6,618	181	264	383	909	1,152	1,532	1,403	794	39,015
Bachelor's degree or more	26,336	25,879	687	634	980	2,273	2,468	4,170	5,898	8,769	55,751
Bachelor's degree	16,632	16,295	450	464	680	1,584	1,803	2,909	3,877	4,528	50,916
Master's degree.	6,157	6,076	141	129	184	451	480	904	1,434	2,353	61,698
Professional degree . . .	1,925	1,901	36	29	68	121	112	161	271	1,103	88,530
Doctorate degree	1,621	1,606	57	12	49	117	74	195	315	787	73,853
Tenure:											
Owner-occupied	80,538	74,163	5,894	4,822	6,047	11,193	10,233	12,314	12,171	11,489	33,218
Renter-occupied	28,429	25,437	2,172	2,910	3,442	6,070	4,024	3,283	2,139	1,397	21,403
Occupier paid no cash rent	1,290	1,169	100	118	164	303	204	150	83	47	21,580
FEMALE											
Total	117,327	102,713	16,335	16,155	13,409	19,291	13,859	12,037	7,462	4,165	17,259
15 to 24 years old	20,009	13,594	5,189	2,687	1,841	2,436	965	384	72	20	7,435
25 to 34 years old	19,603	17,156	2,511	1,695	1,886	3,446	3,124	2,628	1,255	611	21,992
35 to 44 years old	22,043	20,010	2,877	1,884	1,969	3,739	3,160	3,151	2,051	1,179	23,472
45 to 54 years old	20,987	19,303	2,121	1,772	1,738	3,627	3,244	3,207	2,297	1,297	25,866
55 to 64 years old	14,824	13,424	1,950	2,065	1,439	2,336	1,907	1,689	1,263	775	20,368
65 yrs. old and over.	19,862	19,225	1,681	6,051	4,536	3,708	1,461	982	525	281	11,845
Region:											
Northeast	22,599	20,104	3,206	3,122	2,510	3,554	2,675	2,482	1,527	1,028	17,951
Midwest	26,353	23,897	3,765	3,681	3,070	4,696	3,429	2,744	1,675	837	17,498
South	42,226	36,262	5,753	6,019	4,914	6,894	4,897	4,108	2,432	1,245	16,663
West	26,149	22,449	3,617	3,332	2,915	4,147	2,858	2,701	1,831	1,048	17,499
Education attainment of householder: [2]											
Total	97,319	89,118	11,142	13,468	11,567	16,857	12,895	11,654	7,391	4,144	19,679
Less than 9th grade. . .	5,943	4,734	833	1,795	1,053	759	177	69	33	15	9,296
9th to 12th grade [3]	8,233	6,965	1,087	2,096	1,566	1,470	449	184	65	48	10,786
High school graduate [4]. . .	31,921	28,976	3,899	5,158	4,622	6,703	4,400	2,757	1,036	401	15,962
Some college, no degree.	16,796	15,691	1,828	2,044	1,978	3,294	2,798	2,207	1,157	385	21,007
Associate's degree	9,013	8,523	904	804	923	1,661	1,571	1,458	890	312	24,808
Bachelor's degree or more	25,413	24,229	2,596	1,570	1,426	2,968	3,496	4,980	4,208	2,985	35,125
Bachelor's degree	17,134	16,198	1,942	1,142	1,023	2,289	2,614	3,272	2,424	1,492	31,309
Master's degree.	6,451	6,268	527	334	345	525	693	1,473	1,428	943	41,334
Professional degree . . .	1,027	990	81	52	37	109	98	122	183	308	48,536
Doctorate degree	801	773	44	43	23	46	93	108	174	242	53,003
Tenure:											
Owner-occupied	84,718	75,289	12,241	10,874	8,982	13,345	10,331	9,574	6,305	3,637	18,777
Renter-occupied	31,221	26,255	3,818	5,023	4,238	5,735	3,416	2,395	1,119	511	15,068
Occupier paid no cash rent	1,389	1,169	279	258	188	212	112	67	38	15	11,089

[1] Includes persons with income deficit. [2] Persons 25 years and over. [3] No diploma attained. [4] Includes high school equivalency.

Source: U.S. Census Bureau, Current Population Reports, *Income, Poverty, and Health Insurance Coverage in the United States, 2003*, series P60-226. See also <http://www.census.gov/prod/2004pubs/p60-226.pdf> (released 26 August 2004) and <http://pubdb3.census.gov/macro/032004/perinc/toc.htm> (accessed 10 June 2005).

Table 686. **Average Earnings of Year-Round, Full-Time Workers by Educational Attainment: 2003**

[In dollars. For people 18 years old and over as of March 2004. See headnote. Table 684]

| Sex and Age | All workers | Less than 9th grade | High school | | College | | Bachelor's degree or more |
			9th to 12th grade (no diploma)	High school graduate[1]	Some college, no degree	Associate's degree	
Male, total	**53,039**	**23,972**	**29,100**	**38,331**	**46,332**	**48,683**	**81,007**
18 to 24 years old	23,785	16,805	20,156	23,119	23,872	26,554	33,952
25 to 34 years old	41,993	20,977	26,797	33,509	40,417	42,200	58,500
35 to 44 years old	56,515	25,733	30,968	40,885	49,498	50,832	85,368
45 to 54 years old	61,291	26,139	33,781	43,638	52,314	53,701	89,499
55 to 64 years old	65,765	29,067	34,341	44,619	54,630	55,888	95,568
65 years old and over	58,398	23,499	32,695	38,108	59,160	(B)	86,713
Female, total	**37,197**	**20,979**	**21,426**	**27,956**	**31,655**	**36,528**	**53,215**
18 to 24 years old	20,812	(B)	16,698	18,915	19,727	23,070	27,650
25 to 34 years old	35,845	23,142	19,646	26,132	27,927	32,145	49,339
35 to 44 years old	39,234	17,401	23,908	28,975	33,814	38,078	57,208
45 to 54 years old	40,335	21,853	22,076	29,729	36,008	40,785	56,596
55 to 64 years old	39,448	20,496	22,625	30,590	36,032	37,467	55,511
65 years old and over	30,927	28,687	(B)	27,955	31,018	(B)	44,576

B Base figure too small to meet statistical standards for reliability of derived figure.   [1] Includes equivalency.

Table 687. **Per Capita Money Income in Current and Constant (2003) Dollars by Race and Hispanic Origin: 1980 to 2003**

[In dollars. Constant dollars based on CPI-U-RS deflator. People as of March of following year. Based on the Current Population Survey; see text, Sections 1 and 13, and Appendix III. For data collection changes over time, see <http://www.census.gov/hhes/income/histinc/hstchg.html>]

| Year | Current dollars | | | | | Constant (2003) dollars | | | | |
	All races[1]	White[2]	Black[3]	Asian, Pacific Islander[4]	His-panic[5]	All races[1]	White[2]	Black[3]	Asian, Pacific Islander[4]	His-panic[5]
1980	7,787	8,233	4,804	(NA)	4,865	16,465	17,408	10,158	(NA)	10,287
1990	14,387	15,265	9,017	(NA)	8,424	19,635	20,833	12,306	(NA)	11,497
1995 [6]	17,227	18,304	10,982	16,567	9,300	20,649	21,940	13,164	19,858	11,148
2000 [6]	22,346	23,582	14,796	23,350	12,651	23,870	25,190	15,805	24,942	13,514
2001 [7]	22,851	24,127	14,953	24,277	13,003	23,746	25,072	15,539	25,228	13,512
2002 [7]	22,794	24,142	15,441	24,131	13,487	23,316	24,695	15,795	24,684	13,796
2003	23,276	24,626	15,775	24,604	13,492	23,276	24,626	15,775	24,604	13,492

NA Not available.   [1] Includes other races not shown separately.   [2] Beginning with 2002, data represents White alone, which refers to people who reported White and did not report any other race category.   [3] Beginning with 2002, data represents Black alone, which refers to people who reported Black and did not report any other race category.   [4] Beginning with 2002, data represents Asian alone, which refers to people who reported Asian and did not report any other race category.   [5] People of Hispanic origin may be of any race.   [6] Implementation of Census 2000-based population controls and sample expanded by 28,000 households.   [7] Beginning with the 2003 Current Population Survey (CPS), the questionnaire allowed respondents to choose more than one race. For 2002 and later, data represent persons who selected this race group only and excludes persons reporting more than one race. The CPS in prior years allowed respondents to report only one race group. See also comments on race in the text for Section 1, Population.

Table 688. **Money Income of People—Number by Income Level and by Sex, Race, and Hispanic Origin: 2003**

[In thousands. People as of March of the following year. (110,257 represents 110,257,000). Based on Current Population Survey (CPS); see text, Sections 1 and 13, and Appendix III]

| Income interval | Male | | | | | Female | | | | |
	All races[1]	White[2]	Black[3]	Asian[4]	His-panic[5]	All races[1]	White[2]	Black[3]	Asian[4]	His-panic[5]
All households[1]	**110,257**	**90,980**	**12,008**	**4,617**	**14,664**	**117,327**	**94,958**	**14,671**	**4,982**	**13,902**
Under $10,000	25,505	18,906	4,456	1,300	4,196	47,104	37,362	6,132	2,296	7,562
$10,000 to $19,999	18,662	15,492	2,070	643	3,660	23,652	19,238	3,108	783	2,879
$20,000 to $29,999	15,777	13,099	1,761	513	2,694	16,526	13,394	2,270	563	1,567
$30,000 to $39,999	13,043	11,077	1,251	451	1,644	11,444	9,437	1,370	410	844
$40,000 to $49,999	9,942	8,411	920	391	932	6,974	5,791	770	267	460
$50,000 to $59,999	7,280	6,318	565	254	542	3,984	3,312	405	191	209
$60,000 to $74,999	7,114	6,205	429	346	442	3,478	2,894	325	190	193
$75,000 to $84,999	3,139	2,755	169	175	136	1,241	1,014	111	103	48
$85,000 to $99,999	2,751	2,401	168	127	136	960	821	59	61	51
$100,000 to $149,999	4,260	3,772	144	291	181	1,317	1,147	78	73	56
$150,000 to $199,999	1,362	1,231	40	68	49	337	297	21	17	15
$200,000 to $249,999	526	482	17	20	15	136	110	7	12	8
$250,000 and above	897	832	16	36	37	174	140	16	15	12

[1] Includes races not shown separately.   [2] White alone refers to people who reported Black and did not report any other race category.   [3] Black alone refers to people who reported Black and did not report any other race category.   [4] Asian alone refers to people who reported Asian and did not report any other race category.   [5] Persons of Hispanic origin may be of any race.

Source of tables 687 and 688: U.S. Census Bureau, Current Population Reports, P60-226; and Internet site at <http://www.census.gov/hhes/www/income/histinc/histinctb.html> and <http://pubdb3.census.gov/macro/032004/perinc/toc.htm> (released 13 May 2005).

Table 689. Household Income—Distribution by Income Level and State: 2003

[In thousands (108,420 represents 108,420,000), except as indicated. The American Community Survey universe is limited to the household population and excludes the population living in institutions, college dormitories, and other group quarters. Based on a sample and subject to sampling variability; see Appendix III. For definition of median, see Guide to Tabular Presentation]

State	Number of house- holds (1,000)	Number of households by income level (1,000)							Median income (dol.)
		Under $25,000	$25,000- $49,999	$50,000- $74,999	$75,000- $99,999	$100,000- $149,999	$150,000- $199,999	$200,000 and over	
United States ...	108,420	30,465	30,288	20,705	11,785	9,700	2,906	2,571	43,564
Alabama	1,743	638	522	281	153	104	24	22	35,158
Alaska	229	46	62	49	32	28	7	5	52,499
Arizona	2,049	597	626	377	203	155	49	41	40,762
Arkansas	1,076	378	352	183	82	58	13	11	34,246
California	11,857	2,880	3,020	2,243	1,399	1,400	485	430	50,220
Colorado	1,821	424	474	396	222	195	56	54	50,538
Connecticut	1,323	272	307	260	187	166	62	70	56,803
Delaware	304	68	82	62	40	36	10	6	50,583
District of Columbia	247	78	60	41	22	24	11	12	42,118
Florida	6,638	2,044	1,992	1,189	656	478	145	133	39,871
Georgia	3,153	893	907	607	334	268	75	70	42,742
Hawaii	419	94	112	85	55	48	15	11	50,787
Idaho	503	151	158	99	52	31	6	6	39,492
Illinois	4,625	1,162	1,231	929	554	463	152	133	47,977
Indiana	2,351	657	711	495	254	157	41	36	42,067
Iowa	1,158	333	365	237	113	77	18	15	40,526
Kansas	1,059	313	315	212	103	78	22	16	41,075
Kentucky	1,607	588	482	283	131	87	18	18	34,368
Louisiana	1,673	661	437	277	151	100	25	21	34,141
Maine	535	159	175	106	50	33	5	7	39,838
Maryland	2,048	401	489	399	287	297	98	77	57,218
Massachusetts	2,436	585	545	454	335	318	107	92	53,610
Michigan	3,884	1,034	1,115	769	445	358	93	70	44,407
Minnesota	2,012	451	553	449	254	201	59	45	50,100
Mississippi	1,056	416	319	168	78	51	10	14	32,466
Missouri	2,285	669	703	460	225	161	34	32	40,725
Montana	366	127	120	65	29	17	4	4	35,399
Nebraska	675	197	211	135	71	43	9	9	41,406
Nevada	834	209	249	164	99	79	18	15	45,395
New Hampshire	493	107	119	109	71	60	16	11	53,910
New Jersey	3,123	626	697	597	419	457	174	152	58,588
New Mexico	698	250	218	113	54	44	11	8	34,805
New York	7,119	2,006	1,769	1,311	804	722	250	256	46,195
North Carolina	3,271	1,035	1,017	585	310	217	54	53	38,234
North Dakota	254	84	79	51	21	12	3	4	37,554
Ohio	4,480	1,325	1,311	896	463	342	81	62	41,350
Oklahoma	1,341	482	420	229	107	73	17	14	35,129
Oregon	1,409	436	408	279	130	102	29	25	40,319
Pennsylvania	4,801	1,396	1,421	920	495	383	99	88	41,478
Rhode Island	412	110	99	86	53	42	13	8	48,854
South Carolina	1,568	513	460	282	158	106	29	20	38,467
South Dakota	299	90	105	59	23	15	4	3	38,415
Tennessee	2,296	732	702	419	217	152	40	34	38,247
Texas	7,635	2,340	2,157	1,389	764	627	189	169	40,674
Utah	752	168	231	161	96	67	15	12	46,873
Vermont	242	66	73	50	28	18	4	4	43,697
Virginia	2,790	650	721	562	346	325	103	84	50,805
Washington	2,382	593	674	493	283	230	57	53	46,868
West Virginia	732	306	212	110	62	31	7	4	31,008
Wisconsin	2,159	571	642	486	241	153	36	30	44,084
Wyoming	199	55	60	43	23	13	3	2	43,332

Source: U.S. Census Bureau, <http://www.census.gov/acs/www/Products/Profiles/Single/2003/ACS/index.htm> (revised 28 June 2005).

Table 690. Family Income—Distribution by Income Level and State: 2003

[In thousands (73,058 represents 73,058,000), except as indicated. The American Community Survey universe is limited to the household population and excludes the population living in institutions, college dormitories, and other group quarters. Based on a sample and subject to sampling variability; see Appendix III. For definition of median, see Giide to Tabular Presentation]

State	Number of families (1,000)	Number of families by income level (1,000)							Median income (dol.)
		Under $25,000	$25,000-$49,999	$50,000-$74,999	$75,000-$99,999	$100,000-$149,999	$150,000-$199,999	$200,000 and over	
United States...	73,058	14,633	19,996	15,717	9,731	8,279	2,489	2,213	52,273
Alabama.........	1,194	314	365	238	138	96	20	21	43,307
Alaska	156	23	38	37	25	23	6	4	61,117
Arizona..........	1,390	319	413	282	167	135	37	36	47,219
Arkansas.........	738	190	255	149	74	50	11	9	41,072
California.........	8,106	1,572	2,022	1,574	1,084	1,123	385	346	56,530
Colorado.........	1,210	194	297	283	176	165	49	47	59,252
Connecticut.......	904	115	189	186	152	143	55	63	69,917
Delaware.........	200	26	51	45	33	32	8	5	61,270
District of Columbia......	113	32	24	17	11	12	8	8	50,243
Florida	4,339	966	1,312	903	529	393	123	113	47,442
Georgia	2,165	466	601	465	278	231	64	60	50,647
Hawaii	289	42	72	65	46	43	12	9	60,647
Idaho	360	78	115	84	46	27	6	4	46,783
Illinois..........	3,097	531	790	682	443	400	132	120	57,385
Indiana	1,587	281	481	393	222	141	36	32	51,338
Iowa............	758	129	235	193	101	70	16	14	51,336
Kansas..........	709	129	215	170	90	71	20	15	51,157
Kentucky.........	1,123	310	353	235	116	77	16	16	41,898
Louisiana	1,152	352	312	226	129	90	23	19	41,831
Maine...........	348	68	112	86	43	29	5	6	48,541
Maryland.........	1,401	179	303	278	233	250	88	70	69,087
Massachusetts.....	1,585	237	321	317	268	269	89	83	67,527
Michigan.........	2,600	455	715	585	381	316	84	63	55,018
Minnesota	1,334	175	325	348	215	181	52	39	61,417
Mississippi........	739	227	230	142	71	46	10	13	39,182
Missouri	1,539	304	476	364	190	146	33	27	49,441
Montana	238	55	84	53	25	14	4	3	44,503
Nebraska	440	77	138	111	61	36	8	9	50,756
Nevada..........	538	95	159	116	77	64	15	13	52,502
New Hampshire	338	44	78	82	58	52	14	9	63,439
New Jersey.......	2,206	291	448	438	336	400	154	138	70,263
New Mexico.......	473	133	150	87	48	38	10	7	41,661
New York	4,650	959	1,127	948	623	580	202	211	55,309
North Carolina	2,235	523	703	461	262	190	50	47	45,540
North Dakota	161	32	51	42	19	11	3	3	48,386
Ohio............	2,982	590	843	711	403	309	74	53	51,522
Oklahoma........	909	235	292	193	98	64	15	12	43,259
Oregon..........	911	200	257	215	108	84	24	22	49,800
Pennsylvania......	3,166	586	943	721	420	331	89	76	51,339
Rhode Island......	265	46	59	61	44	37	12	7	60,165
South Carolina.....	1,079	264	306	227	140	97	27	18	47,081
South Dakota......	199	36	71	51	22	13	4	3	46,824
Tennessee........	1,549	348	480	340	181	134	35	30	46,654
Texas...........	5,414	1,322	1,510	1,077	645	550	163	147	47,479
Utah............	570	90	172	136	87	62	13	11	52,481
Vermont	156	29	44	38	23	16	4	3	52,895
Virginia	1,891	301	464	408	281	273	91	73	60,174
Washington	1,529	258	407	357	223	190	51	44	56,461
West Virginia	490	151	153	93	56	27	7	4	38,568
Wisconsin	1,400	232	394	369	212	137	30	26	54,500
Wyoming.........	133	24	40	34	19	11	3	2	51,627

Source: U.S. Census Bureau, <http://www.census.gov/acs/www/Products/Profiles/Single/2003/ACS/index.htm> (revised 28 June 2005).

Income, Expenditures, and Wealth   469

Table 691. **Household Income, Family Income, and Per Capita Income and Individuals and Families Below Poverty Level by City: 2003**

[For number and percent below poverty, see headnote, Table 692. The American Community Survey universe is limited to the household population and excludes the population living in institutions, college dormitories, and other group quarters. Based on a sample and subject to sampling variability; see Appendix III. For definition of median, see Guide to Tabular Presentation]

City	Median household income (dol.)	Median family income (dol.)	Per capita income (dol.)	Number below poverty level		Percent below poverty level	
				Individuals	Families	Individuals	Families
Albuquerque, NM	40,061	49,677	21,772	58,671	11,003	12.5	8.9
Anaheim, CA	45,707	52,639	20,758	37,461	6,421	12.6	9.5
Arlington, TX	48,775	57,156	21,895	41,166	8,448	11.3	9.4
Atlanta, GA	32,635	40,614	27,409	86,796	13,682	23.5	19.2
Aurora, CO	44,401	51,554	22,107	32,405	6,073	11.5	8.4
Austin, TX	40,921	51,519	24,764	104,916	18,840	16.0	12.6
Baltimore, MD	32,452	38,510	19,924	124,314	24,189	20.6	17.3
Boston, MA	42,567	53,635	29,449	102,857	15,971	19.1	14.9
Buffalo, NY	28,499	35,620	18,704	60,496	13,613	22.0	20.5
Charlotte, NC	44,375	54,294	26,072	64,783	16,017	11.5	10.8
Chicago, IL	40,879	43,848	21,773	523,772	98,358	19.3	16.6
Cincinnati, OH	30,850	38,151	21,192	61,531	12,251	21.1	18.5
Cleveland, OH	22,978	28,108	14,188	132,896	30,039	31.3	27.9
Colorado Springs, CO	50,667	59,035	25,773	31,714	7,450	8.3	7.8
Columbus, OH	40,042	49,046	21,550	114,764	21,922	16.5	13.2
Dallas, TX	36,678	41,049	22,454	252,858	45,949	21.0	17.3
Denver, CO	43,978	51,686	27,341	68,072	11,989	12.6	9.7
Detroit, MI	26,157	30,520	14,418	263,800	53,189	30.1	25.9
El Paso, TX	32,495	36,338	14,599	138,889	31,429	24.5	22.3
Fort Worth, TX	39,729	45,492	21,214	81,908	15,413	14.9	11.2
Fresno, CA	36,537	37,200	16,026	128,804	23,350	28.4	22.5
Honolulu, HI [1]	46,839	60,348	25,444	48,904	7,509	12.7	8.3
Houston, TX	35,597	40,043	21,290	392,184	82,645	20.3	18.0
Indianapolis, IN [2]	41,349	50,587	22,647	103,662	22,285	13.6	11.6
Jacksonville, FL	41,167	50,551	21,342	105,590	20,972	14.2	10.7
Kansas City, MO	38,639	48,532	20,026	73,889	13,177	16.4	12.2
Las Vegas, NV	44,078	51,968	21,341	64,418	12,154	12.5	9.8
Long Beach, CA	36,652	42,049	20,334	114,247	20,431	24.1	20.7
Los Angeles, CA	40,733	44,479	22,251	743,732	131,608	20.1	16.7
Memphis, TN	32,315	35,309	18,045	139,981	31,858	23.5	21.8
Mesa, AZ	41,230	48,339	21,751	52,091	8,938	11.7	8.1
Miami, FL	23,774	28,623	16,384	105,622	22,575	27.9	25.1
Milwaukee, WI	32,291	39,443	16,876	122,561	22,796	22.1	17.3
Minneapolis, MN	42,010	52,661	27,117	57,724	10,279	17.6	15.2
Nashville-Davidson, TN [2]	39,794	51,055	23,175	75,996	14,273	14.6	11.3
New Orleans, LA	28,645	35,677	17,757	93,156	16,320	20.8	15.9
New York, NY	39,937	44,131	24,596	1,499,718	301,887	19.0	16.6
Oakland, CA	44,129	51,898	27,119	56,234	10,653	14.7	13.4
Oklahoma City, OK	35,694	44,565	20,740	83,188	16,297	17.0	12.9
Omaha, NE	40,436	51,519	22,956	50,368	9,764	13.5	10.5
Philadelphia, PA	33,062	41,577	18,399	315,042	58,564	22.3	17.2
Phoenix, AZ	40,919	43,872	19,984	230,723	42,978	17.6	13.9
Pittsburgh, PA	30,976	46,157	22,748	44,388	5,697	16.1	9.4
Portland, OR	40,855	51,543	24,204	81,921	12,635	15.6	10.9
Raleigh, NC	44,452	58,728	27,543	32,028	4,119	11.2	6.5
Sacramento, CA	42,142	47,286	22,328	53,021	8,721	13.1	9.0
San Antonio, TX	36,994	44,329	18,969	220,163	42,811	18.5	14.9
San Diego, CA	47,631	56,905	25,719	176,198	29,221	14.5	10.8
San Francisco, CA	57,833	67,809	37,590	69,410	10,679	9.5	7.4
San Jose, CA	70,240	73,978	28,684	69,729	12,433	8.2	6.3
Santa Ana, CA	36,968	36,962	12,887	54,097	10,111	16.4	15.5
Seattle, WA	49,469	66,752	32,492	52,598	5,278	10.0	4.9
St. Louis, MO	30,032	35,912	17,778	69,648	12,273	21.8	16.1
Tampa, FL	33,424	41,307	23,748	63,281	12,727	21.3	18.1
Toledo, OH	31,982	43,379	17,235	60,461	12,846	20.3	17.4
Tucson, AZ	32,414	40,108	17,997	90,029	15,571	18.8	13.7
Tulsa, OK	36,581	44,458	21,788	55,710	10,401	15.2	11.8
Virginia Beach, VA	52,175	60,611	24,493	27,333	6,030	6.3	5.3
Washington, DC	42,118	50,243	32,840	105,050	20,840	19.9	18.5
Wichita, KS	38,846	49,789	21,390	46,571	8,529	13.3	9.3

[1] Data shown for census designated place (CDP).   [2] Represents the portion of a consolidated city that is not within one or more separately incorporated places.

Source: U.S. Census Bureau, <http://www.census.gov/acs/www/Products/Profiles/Single/2003/ACS/index.htm> (revised 28 June 2005).

Table 692. **Individuals and Families Below Poverty Level—Number and Rate by State: 2000 and 2003**

[In thousands (33,311 represents 33,311,000), except as indicated. Represents number and percent below poverty in the past 12 months. The American Community Survey universe is limited to the household population and excludes the population living in institutions, college dormitories, and other group quarters. Based on a sample and subject to sampling variability; see Appendix III. For definition of median, see Guide to Tabular Presentation]

| State | Number below poverty level (1,000) | | | | Percent below poverty level | | | |
| | Individuals | | Families | | Individuals | | Families | |
	2000	2003	2000	2003	2000	2003	2000	2003
United States	33,311	35,846	6,615	7,143	12.2	12.7	9.3	9.8
Alabama	672	748	146	164	15.6	17.1	12.4	13.7
Alaska	55	61	11	13	9.1	9.7	6.8	8.0
Arizona	780	839	150	166	15.6	15.4	11.6	11.9
Arkansas	439	421	96	89	17.0	16.0	13.0	12.1
California	4,520	4,610	832	849	13.7	13.4	10.7	10.5
Colorado	363	433	64	88	8.7	9.8	5.7	7.3
Connecticut	254	273	51	58	7.7	8.1	5.8	6.4
Delaware	70	69	14	12	9.3	8.7	6.7	5.8
District of Columbia	94	105	17	21	17.5	19.9	15.4	18.5
Florida	1,987	2,174	387	422	12.8	13.1	9.3	9.7
Georgia	999	1,125	206	234	12.6	13.4	10.0	10.8
Hawaii	103	132	19	21	8.8	10.9	6.8	7.4
Idaho	144	183	26	35	11.4	13.8	7.7	9.8
Illinois	1,335	1,389	262	265	11.1	11.3	8.6	8.5
Indiana	592	633	113	119	10.1	10.6	7.1	7.5
Iowa	281	286	53	53	10.0	10.1	7.0	6.9
Kansas	247	284	43	51	9.5	10.8	6.2	7.1
Kentucky	640	696	148	159	16.4	17.4	13.5	14.2
Louisiana	862	882	182	191	20.0	20.3	16.0	16.6
Maine	124	133	22	26	10.1	10.5	6.6	7.6
Maryland	477	439	89	86	9.3	8.2	6.6	6.1
Massachusetts	586	582	110	118	9.6	9.4	7.1	7.5
Michigan	975	1,118	196	224	10.1	11.4	7.7	8.6
Minnesota	328	383	66	75	6.9	7.8	5.1	5.6
Mississippi	498	553	104	121	18.2	19.9	14.2	16.4
Missouri	606	646	118	133	11.2	11.7	7.7	8.6
Montana	117	126	23	24	13.4	14.2	9.5	9.9
Nebraska	158	182	28	36	9.6	10.8	6.5	8.2
Nevada	194	252	34	47	9.9	11.5	6.9	8.7
New Hampshire	63	96	11	17	5.3	7.7	3.5	5.1
New Jersey	651	704	126	145	7.9	8.4	6.0	6.6
New Mexico	320	340	64	70	18.0	18.6	14.2	14.8
New York	2,391	2,501	491	499	13.1	13.5	10.7	10.7
North Carolina	1,018	1,136	203	239	13.1	14.0	9.6	10.7
North Dakota	71	71	14	13	11.6	11.7	8.1	8.4
Ohio	1,216	1,343	246	280	11.1	12.1	8.4	9.4
Oklahoma	459	546	100	112	13.8	16.1	11.0	12.4
Oregon	439	481	84	88	13.2	13.9	9.5	9.7
Pennsylvania	1,240	1,296	247	260	10.5	10.9	7.8	8.2
Rhode Island	108	117	23	22	10.7	11.3	8.5	8.2
South Carolina	557	563	123	121	14.4	14.1	11.7	11.3
South Dakota	83	81	16	14	11.5	11.1	8.4	7.2
Tennessee	745	780	158	164	13.5	13.8	10.5	10.6
Texas	3,056	3,508	639	712	15.1	16.3	12.3	13.1
Utah	192	244	40	43	8.8	10.6	7.2	7.6
Vermont	63	57	12	10	10.7	9.7	7.5	6.4
Virginia	630	642	124	126	9.2	9.0	6.8	6.6
Washington	667	654	127	121	11.6	11.0	8.6	7.9
West Virginia	327	326	72	76	18.6	18.5	14.7	15.5
Wisconsin	461	554	75	101	8.9	10.5	5.6	7.2
Wyoming	55	47	10	10	11.4	9.7	7.9	7.3

Source: U.S. Census Bureau, American Community Survey, "Multi-Year Profiles 2003 - Economic Characteristics"; <http://www.census.gov/acs/www/Products/Profiles/Chg/2003/ACS/index.htm> (revised 28 June 2005).

Table 693. People Below Poverty Level and Below 125 Percent of Poverty Level by Race and Hispanic Origin: 1980 to 2003

[People as of March of the following year (29,272 represents 29,272,000). Based on Current Population Survey; see text, Section 1, and Appendix III. For data collection changes over time, see <http://www.census.gov/hhes/income/histinc/hstchg.html>]

Year	Number below poverty level (1,000)					Percent below poverty level					Below 125 percent of poverty level	
	All races [1]	White [2]	Black [3]	Asian and Pacific Islander [4]	His-panic [5]	All races [1]	White [2]	Black [3]	Asian and Pacific Islander [4]	His-panic [5]	Number (1,000)	Percent of total population
1980....	29,272	19,699	8,579	(NA)	3,491	13.0	10.2	32.5	(NA)	25.7	40,658	18.1
1985....	33,064	22,860	8,926	(NA)	5,236	14.0	11.4	31.3	(NA)	29.0	44,166	18.7
1986....	32,370	22,183	8,983	(NA)	5,117	13.6	11.0	31.1	(NA)	27.3	43,486	18.2
1987....	32,221	21,195	9,520	1,021	5,422	13.4	10.4	32.4	16.1	28.0	43,032	17.9
1988....	31,745	20,715	9,356	1,117	5,357	13.0	10.1	31.3	17.3	26.7	42,551	17.5
1989....	31,528	20,785	9,302	939	5,430	12.8	10.0	30.7	14.1	26.2	42,653	17.3
1990....	33,585	22,326	9,837	858	6,006	13.5	10.7	31.9	12.2	28.1	44,837	18.0
1991....	35,708	23,747	10,242	996	6,339	14.2	11.3	32.7	13.8	28.7	47,527	18.9
1992....	38,014	25,259	10,827	985	7,592	14.8	11.9	33.4	12.7	29.6	50,592	19.7
1993....	39,265	26,226	10,877	1,134	8,126	15.1	12.2	33.1	15.3	30.6	51,801	20.0
1994....	38,059	25,379	10,196	974	8,416	14.5	11.7	30.6	14.6	30.7	50,401	19.3
1995....	36,425	24,423	9,872	1,411	8,574	13.8	11.2	29.3	14.6	30.3	48,761	18.5
1996....	36,529	24,650	9,694	1,454	8,697	13.7	11.2	28.4	14.5	29.4	49,310	18.5
1997....	35,574	24,396	9,116	1,468	8,308	13.3	11.0	26.5	14.0	27.1	47,853	17.8
1998....	34,476	23,454	9,091	1,360	8,070	12.7	10.5	26.1	12.5	25.6	46,036	17.0
1999....	32,791	22,169	8,441	1,285	7,876	11.9	9.8	23.6	10.7	22.7	44,286	16.2
2000 [6]..	31,581	21,645	7,982	1,258	7,747	11.3	9.5	22.5	9.9	21.5	43,612	15.6
2001 [7]..	32,907	22,739	8,136	1,275	7,997	11.7	9.9	22.7	10.2	21.4	45,320	16.1
2002 [7]..	34,570	23,466	8,602	1,161	8,555	12.1	10.2	24.1	10.1	21.8	47,084	16.5
2003....	35,861	24,272	8,781	1,401	9,051	12.5	10.5	24.4	11.8	22.5	48,687	16.9

NA Not available. [1] Includes other races not shown separately. [2] Beginning 2002, data represents White alone, which refers to people who reported White and did not report any other race category. [3] Beginning 2002, data represents Black alone, which refers to people who reported Black and did not report any other race category. [4] Beginning 2002, data represents Asian alone, which refers to people who reported Asian and did not report any other race category. [5] People of Hispanic origin may be of any race. [6] Implementation of Census 2000-based population controls and sample expanded by 28,000 households. [7] Beginning with the 2003 Current Population Survey (CPS), the questionnaire allowed respondents to choose more than one race. For 2002 and later, data represent persons who selected this race group only and excludes persons reporting more than one race. The CPS in prior years allowed respondents to report only one race group. See also comments on race in the text for Section 1, Population.

Source: U.S. Census Bureau, Current Population Reports, P60-226; and Internet sites <http://www.census.gov/prod/2004pubs/p60-226.pdf> (released 26 August 2004) and <http://www.census.gov/hhes/poverty/histpov/hstpov3.html> (revised 13 May 2005).

Table 694. Children Below Poverty Level by Race and Hispanic Origin: 1980 to 2003

[Persons as of March of the following year. (11,114 represents 11,114,000). Covers only related children in families under 18 years old. Based on Current Population Survey; see text, this section and Section 1, and Appendix III. For data collection changes over time, see <http://www.census.gov/hhes/income/histinc/hstchg.html>]

Year	Number below poverty level (1,000)					Percent below poverty level				
	All races [1]	White [2]	Black [3]	Asian and Pacific Islander [4]	His-panic [5]	All races [1]	White [2]	Black [3]	Asian and Pacific Islander [4]	His-panic [5]
1980......	11,114	6,817	3,906	(NA)	1,718	17.9	13.4	42.1	(NA)	33.0
1985......	12,483	7,838	4,057	(NA)	2,512	20.1	15.6	43.1	(NA)	39.6
1986......	12,257	7,714	4,037	(NA)	2,413	19.8	15.3	42.7	(NA)	37.1
1987......	12,275	7,398	4,234	432	2,606	19.7	14.7	44.4	22.7	38.9
1988......	11,935	7,095	4,148	458	2,576	19.0	14.0	42.8	23.5	37.3
1989......	12,001	7,164	4,257	368	2,496	19.0	14.1	43.2	18.9	35.5
1990......	12,715	7,696	4,412	356	2,750	19.9	15.1	44.2	17.0	37.7
1991......	13,658	8,316	4,637	348	2,977	21.1	16.1	45.6	17.1	39.8
1992......	14,521	8,752	5,015	352	3,440	21.6	16.5	46.3	16.0	39.0
1993......	14,961	9,123	5,030	358	3,666	22.0	17.0	45.9	17.6	39.9
1994......	14,610	8,826	4,787	308	3,956	21.2	16.3	44.9	17.9	41.1
1995......	13,999	8,474	4,644	532	3,938	20.2	15.5	41.5	18.6	39.3
1996......	13,764	8,488	4,411	553	4,090	19.8	15.5	39.5	19.1	39.9
1997......	13,422	8,441	4,116	608	3,865	19.2	15.4	36.8	19.9	36.4
1998......	12,845	7,935	4,073	542	3,670	18.3	14.4	36.4	17.5	33.6
1999......	11,678	7,194	3,698	367	3,561	16.6	13.1	32.8	11.5	29.9
2000 [6]..	11,005	6,834	3,495	407	3,342	15.6	12.4	30.9	12.5	27.6
2001 [7]..	11,175	7,086	3,423	353	3,433	15.8	12.8	30.0	11.1	27.4
2002 [7]..	11,646	7,203	3,570	302	3,653	16.3	13.1	32.1	11.4	28.2
2003......	12,340	7,624	3,750	331	3,982	17.2	13.9	33.6	12.1	29.5

NA Not available. [1] Includes other races not shown separately. [2] Beginning 2002, data represents White alone, which refers to people who reported White and did not report any other race category. [3] Beginning 2002, data represents Black alone, which refers to people who reported Black and did not report any other race category. [4] Beginning 2002, data represents Asian alone, which refers to people who reported Asian and did not report any other race category. [5] People of Hispanic origin may be of any race. [6] Implementation of Census 2000-based population controls and sample expanded by 28,000 households. [7] Beginning with the 2003 Current Population Survey (CPS), the questionnaire allowed respondents to choose more than one race. For 2002 and later, data represent persons who selected this race group only and excludes persons reporting more than one race. The CPS in prior years allowed respondents to report only one race group. See also comments on race in the text for Section 1, Population.

Source: U.S. Census Bureau, Current Population Reports, P60-226; and Internet site <http://www.census.gov/prod/2004pubs/p60-226.pdf> (released 26 August 2004) and <http://www.census.gov/hhes/poverty/histpov/hstpov3.html> (revised 13 May 2005).

Table 695. Weighted Average Poverty Thresholds by Size of Unit: 1980 to 2003

[**In dollars.** For information on the official poverty thresholds; see text, this section]

Size of family unit	1980[1]	1990	1995	1998	1999	2000	2001	2002	2003
One person (unrelated individual) . . .	4,190	6,652	7,763	8,316	8,499	8,791	9,039	9,183	9,393
Under 65 years.	4,290	6,800	7,929	8,480	8,667	8,959	9,214	9,359	9,573
65 years and over	3,949	6,268	7,309	7,818	7,990	8,259	8,494	8,628	8,825
Two persons	5,363	8,509	9,933	10,634	10,864	11,235	11,569	11,756	12,015
Householder under 65 years	5,537	8,794	10,259	10,972	11,213	11,589	11,920	12,110	12,384
Householder 65 years and over . . .	4,983	7,905	9,219	9,862	10,075	10,418	10,715	10,885	11,133
Three persons	6,565	10,419	12,158	13,003	13,289	13,740	14,128	14,348	14,680
Four persons	8,414	13,359	15,569	16,660	17,030	17,604	18,104	18,392	18,810
Five persons	9,966	15,792	18,408	19,680	20,128	20,815	21,405	21,744	22,245
Six persons	11,269	17,839	20,804	22,228	22,730	23,533	24,195	24,576	25,122
Seven persons.	13,955	20,241	23,552	25,257	25,918	26,750	27,517	28,001	28,544
Eight persons.	14,199	22,582	26,237	28,166	28,970	29,701	30,627	30,907	31,589
Nine or more persons	16,896	26,848	31,280	33,339	34,436	35,150	36,286	37,062	37,656

[1] Poverty levels for nonfarm families.

Source: U.S. Census Bureau, Current Population Reports, *Poverty in the United States, 2002*, P60-222. See also <http://www.census.gov/prod/2003pubs/p60-222.pdf> (released September 2003).

Table 696. Persons Below Poverty Level by Selected Characteristics: 2003

[**People as of March 2003 (35,861 represents 35,861,000).** Based on Current Population Survey (CPS); see text, this section, Section 1, and Appendix III. The 2004 CPS allowed respondents to choose more than one race. For 2003, data represent persons who selected this race group only and excludes persons reporting more than one race. The CPS in prior years allowed respondents to report only one race group. See also comments on race in the text for Section 1, Population. For composition of regions, see map, inside front cover]

Characteristic	Number below poverty level (1,000)					Percent below poverty level				
	All races[1]	White	Black	Asian	His-panic[2]	All races[1]	White	Black	Asian	His-panic[2]
Total	35,861	24,272	8,781	1,401	9,051	12.5	10.5	24.4	11.8	22.5
Male.	15,783	10,830	3,671	668	4,262	11.2	9.5	22.0	11.6	20.6
Female	20,078	13,443	5,110	733	4,790	13.7	11.5	26.5	12.0	24.4
Under 18 years old	12,866	7,985	3,877	344	4,077	17.6	14.3	34.1	12.5	29.7
18 to 24 years old	4,596	3,202	1,026	192	1,043	16.5	14.6	26.9	17.0	21.0
25 to 34 years old	5,037	3,430	1,108	287	1,589	12.8	11.1	22.0	13.0	21.4
35 to 44 years old	4,164	2,957	898	164	1,058	9.6	8.4	16.6	8.1	17.6
45 to 54 years old	3,136	2,167	715	164	541	7.6	6.4	15.2	9.9	13.8
55 to 59 years old	1,322	985	245	48	168	8.2	7.2	15.9	7.8	13.1
60 to 64 years old	1,188	880	232	52	169	9.7	8.5	18.8	12.3	19.3
65 years old and over	3,552	2,666	680	151	406	10.2	8.8	23.7	14.3	19.5
65 to 74 years old	1,647	1,197	330	81	239	9.0	7.6	20.5	12.7	18.8
75 years old and over. . .	1,905	1,469	351	69	167	11.6	10.1	27.6	16.9	20.7
Northeast.	6,052	4,095	1,538	308	1,373	11.3	9.3	23.3	13.6	25.1
Midwest.	6,932	4,710	1,798	199	680	10.7	8.5	27.4	12.9	19.4
South	14,548	9,096	4,770	277	3,449	14.1	11.5	24.4	11.7	24.0
West	8,329	6,372	675	617	3,549	12.6	11.9	20.7	10.8	21.0
Native.	29,965	19,957	8,331	450	5,298	11.8	9.6	25.1	10.7	22.0
Foreign born.	5,897	4,315	450	951	3,754	17.2	18.8	16.0	12.5	23.1
Naturalized citizen	1,309	822	147	307	555	10.0	10.7	11.9	7.9	13.8
Not a citizen	4,588	3,493	303	644	3,199	21.7	23.0	19.3	17.2	26.1

[1] Includes other races not shown separately.   [2] Persons of Hispanic origin may be any race.

Source: U.S. Census Bureau, Current Population Reports, *Income, Poverty, and Health Insurance Coverage in the United States, 2003*, P60-226. See also <http://www.census.gov/prod/2004pubs/p60-226.pdf> (released 26 August 2004) and <http://pubdb3.census.gov/macro/032004/pov/toc.htm> (revised 22 November 2004).

Income, Expenditures, and Wealth   **473**

Table 697.
Table 697. Work Experience During 2003 by Poverty Status, Sex, and Age: 2003

[Number in thousands (100,700 represents 100,700,000). Covers only persons 16 years old and over. Based on Current Population Survey; see text, this section and Section 1, and Appendix III]

Sex and age	Worked full-time year-round			Did not work full-time year-round			Did not work		
	Number (1,000)	Below poverty level		Number (1,000)	Below poverty level		Number (1,000)	Below poverty level	
		Number (1,000)	Percent		Number (1,000)	Percent		Number (1,000)	Percent
BOTH SEXES									
Total............	100,700	2,636	2.6	50,854	6,183	12.2	71,868	15,446	21.5
16 to 17 years old.....	74	4	(B)	2,716	180	6.6	5,931	1,086	18.3
18 to 64 years old.....	98,174	2,600	2.6	44,506	5,892	13.2	37,360	10,951	29.3
18 to 24 years old....	7,692	361	4.7	12,676	1,945	15.3	7,455	2,290	30.7
25 to 34 years old....	23,428	876	3.7	9,379	1,657	17.7	6,394	2,504	39.2
35 to 54 years old....	53,717	1,152	2.1	16,945	1,938	11.4	13,980	4,210	30.1
55 to 64 years old....	13,336	211	1.6	5,506	351	6.4	9,532	1,948	20.4
65 years old and over...	2,451	32	1.3	3,631	112	3.1	28,577	3,408	11.9
MALE									
Total............	58,778	1,469	2.5	21,539	2,467	11.5	27,737	5,888	21.2
16 to 17 years old.....	43	2	(B)	1,370	86	6.3	2,895	519	17.9
18 to 64 years old.....	57,237	1,444	2.5	18,350	2,341	12.8	13,363	4,353	32.6
18 to 24 years old....	4,482	180	4.0	6,177	764	12.4	3,530	964	27.3
25 to 34 years old....	13,935	536	3.8	3,855	613	15.9	1,808	843	46.6
35 to 54 years old....	31,170	619	2.0	6,020	816	13.6	4,422	1,796	40.6
55 to 64 years old....	7,650	108	1.4	2,299	149	6.5	3,602	751	20.8
65 years old and over...	1,498	23	1.5	1,819	40	2.2	11,480	1,016	8.9
FEMALE									
Total............	41,921	1,167	2.8	29,315	3,716	12.7	44,131	9,557	21.7
16 to 17 years old.....	31	2	(B)	1,346	94	7.0	3,037	567	18.7
18 to 64 years old....	40,937	1,156	2.8	26,156	3,551	13.6	23,998	6,599	27.5
18 to 24 years old....	3,210	181	5.6	6,500	1,181	18.2	3,925	1,326	33.8
25 to 34 years old....	9,493	340	3.6	5,523	1,044	18.9	4,586	1,661	36.2
35 to 54 years old....	22,548	532	2.4	10,925	1,123	10.3	9,557	2,414	25.3
55 to 64 years old....	5,686	103	1.8	3,208	203	6.3	5,930	1,197	20.2
65 years old and over...	953	9	1.0	1,812	72	4.0	17,097	2,392	14.0

B Base figure too small to meet statistical standards for reliability of a derived figure.
Source: U.S. Census Bureau, <http://ferret.bls.census.gov/macro/032004/pov/new22100.htm> (revised 22 November 2004).

Table 698. Families Below Poverty Level and Below 125 Percent of Poverty by Race and Hispanic Origin: 1980 to 2003

[Families as of March of the following year (6,217 represents 6,217,000). Based on Current Population Survey; see text, this section 1, and Appendix III. For data collection changes over time, see <http://www.census.gov/hhes/income/histinc/hstchg.html>]

Year	Number below poverty level (1,000)					Percent below poverty level					Below 125 percent of poverty level	
	All races [1]	White [2]	Black [3]	Asian and Pacific Islander [4]	His-panic [5]	All races [1]	White [2]	Black [3]	Asian and Pacific Islander [4]	His-panic [5]	Num-ber (1,000)	Percent
1980....	6,217	4,195	1,826	(NA)	751	10.3	8.0	28.9	(NA)	23.2	8,764	14.5
1981....	6,851	4,670	1,972	(NA)	792	11.2	8.8	30.8	(NA)	24.0	9,568	15.7
1982 [3]...	7,512	5,118	2,158	(NA)	916	12.2	9.6	33.0	(NA)	27.2	10,279	16.7
1983 [3]...	7,277	4,925	2,094	(NA)	991	11.6	9.1	30.9	(NA)	25.2	10,358	16.7
1984....	7,223	4,983	1,983	(NA)	1,074	11.4	9.1	28.7	(NA)	25.5	9,901	15.8
1985....	7,647	5,220	2,161	(NA)	981	12.3	9.7	32.3	(NA)	25.9	9,753	15.3
1986 [4]...	7,023	4,811	1,987	(NA)	1,085	10.9	8.6	28.0	(NA)	24.7	9,476	14.7
1987....	7,005	4,567	2,117	199	1,168	10.7	8.1	29.4	13.5	25.5	9,338	14.3
1988....	6,874	4,471	2,089	201	1,141	10.4	7.9	28.2	13.6	23.7	9,284	14.1
1989....	6,784	4,409	2,077	182	1,133	10.3	7.8	27.8	11.9	23.4	9,267	14.0
1990....	7,098	4,622	2,193	169	1,244	10.7	8.1	29.3	11.0	25.0	9,564	14.4
1991....	7,712	5,022	2,343	210	1,372	11.5	8.8	30.4	13.0	26.5	10,244	15.3
1992....	8,144	5,255	2,484	215	1,529	11.9	9.1	31.1	12.2	26.7	10,959	16.1
1993....	8,393	5,452	2,499	235	1,625	12.3	9.4	31.3	13.5	27.3	11,203	16.4
1994....	8,053	5,312	2,212	208	1,724	11.6	9.1	27.3	13.1	27.8	10,771	15.5
1995....	7,532	4,994	2,127	264	1,695	10.8	8.5	26.4	12.4	27.0	10,223	14.7
1996....	7,708	5,059	2,206	284	1,748	11.0	8.6	26.1	12.7	26.4	10,476	14.9
1997....	7,324	4,990	1,985	244	1,721	10.3	8.4	23.6	10.2	24.7	10,032	14.2
1998....	7,186	4,829	1,981	270	1,648	10.0	8.0	23.4	11.0	22.7	9,714	13.6
1999....	6,792	4,447	1,887	258	1,593	9.3	7.3	21.8	10.3	20.5	9,320	12.9
2000 [6]...	6,400	4,333	1,686	233	1,540	8.7	7.1	19.3	7.8	19.2	9,032	12.2
2001 [7]...	6,813	4,579	1,829	234	1,649	9.2	7.4	20.7	7.8	19.4	9,525	12.8
2002 [7]...	7,229	4,862	1,923	210	1,792	9.6	7.8	21.5	7.4	19.7	9,998	13.2
2003....	7,607	5,058	1,986	311	1,925	10.0	8.1	22.3	10.2	20.8	10,360	13.6

NA Not available. [1] Includes other races not shown separately. [2] Beginning 2002, data represents White alone, which refers to people who reported White and did not report any other race category. [3] Beginning 2002, data represents Black alone, which refers to people who reported Black and did not report any other race category. [4] Beginning 2002, data represents Asian alone, which refers to people who reported Asian and did not report any other race category. [5] People of Hispanic origin may be of any race. [6] Data reflect implementation of Census 2000-based population controls and a 28,000 household sample expansion to 78,000 households. [7] Beginning with the 2003 Current Population Survey (CPS), the questionnaire allowed reponsdents to choose more than one race. For 2002 and later, data represent persons who selected this race group only and excludes persons reporting more than one race. The CPS in prior years allowed respondents to report only one race group. See also comments on race in the text for Section 1, Population.
Source: U.S. Census Bureau, Current Population Reports, P60-226; and Internet site <http://www.census.gov/prod/2004pubs/p60-226.pdf> (released 26 August 2004) and <http://www.census.gov/hhes/www/poverty/histpov/hstpov4.html> (revised 13 May 2005).

Table 699. **Families Below Poverty Level by Selected Characteristics: 2003**

[Families as of March 2004. (7,607 represents 7,607,000). Based on Current Population Survey (CPS); see text, this section and Section 1, and Appendix III. The 2004 CPS allowed respondents to choose more than one race. For 2003, data represent persons who selected this race group only and exclude persons reporting more than one race. The CPS in prior years allowed respondents to report only one race group. See also comments on race in the text for Section 1, Population]

Characteristic	Number below poverty level (1,000)					Percent below poverty level				
	All races [1]	White	Black	Asian	His-panic [2]	All races [1]	White	Black	Asian	His-panic [2]
Total	7,607	5,058	1,986	311	1,925	10.0	8.1	22.3	10.2	20.8
Age of householder:										
15 to 24 years old	1,048	614	361	25	255	30.9	25.1	52.3	19.5	31.9
25 to 34 years old	2,150	1,377	613	79	695	15.9	13.0	31.3	12.0	26.6
35 to 44 years old	1,835	1,257	451	59	500	10.0	8.5	19.7	7.2	19.4
45 to 54 years old	1,025	691	232	76	241	6.0	4.9	12.2	10.7	14.6
55 to 64 years old	763	561	151	32	111	6.6	5.6	14.2	7.8	12.1
65 years old and over	745	530	166	37	113	6.2	5.0	17.1	11.6	17.2
Region:										
Northeast	1,218	799	327	70	313	8.7	6.8	21.2	11.7	24.0
Midwest	1,403	915	409	39	131	8.1	6.1	24.9	9.8	17.6
South	3,263	2,029	1,097	73	749	11.7	9.2	22.3	12.2	21.7
West	1,723	1,315	152	130	732	10.2	9.5	18.8	8.8	19.4
Type of family:										
Married couple	3,115	2,504	321	200	976	5.4	5.0	7.8	8.0	15.7
Female householder, no husband present	3,856	2,171	1,473	83	792	28.0	24.0	36.9	23.8	37.0
Male household, no wife present	636	383	192	28	157	13.5	10.8	24.5	12.8	17.3
Education of householder: [3]										
No high school diploma	2,296	1,625	529	73	1,011	22.8	20.5	35.3	21.4	28.9
High school diploma, no college.	2,229	1,454	638	71	411	10.1	8.0	22.4	16.3	18.0
Some college, less than bachelor's degree.	1,415	917	395	45	197	7.2	5.7	16.4	8.3	11.7
Bachelor's degree or more	577	420	52	95	42	2.8	2.4	3.6	5.9	4.4

[1] Includes other races not shown separately. [2] Hispanic persons may be of any race. [3] Householder 25 years old and over.
Source: U.S. Census Bureau, Current Population Reports, *Income, Poverty, and Health Insurance Coverage in the United States, 2003*, P60-226. See also <http://www.census.gov/prod/2004pubs/p60-226.pdf> (released 26 August 2004) and <http://pubdb3.census.gov/macro/032004/pov/toc.htm> (revised 22 November 2004).

Table 700. **Asset Ownership Rates for Households by Type of Asset and Household Characteristic: 2000**

[In percent. Excludes group quarters. Based on the Survey of Income and Program Participation and subject to sampling variability. Data are similar, but not comparable to those found in Tables 701 and 702, which are based on the Survey of Consumer Finances]

Characteristic	Interest-earning assets at financial institutions	Stocks and mutual fund shares	Own business or profession	Motor vehicles	Own home	Rental property	IRA or Keogh accounts	401K or thrift savings plans
Total	65.0	27.1	10.8	85.8	67.2	4.9	23.1	29.9
White	68.6	29.7	11.6	88.3	70.7	5.2	25.7	31.4
White, not of Hispanic origin	71.1	31.9	12.0	89.2	73.0	5.4	27.5	32.9
Black	41.6	10.2	4.7	70.2	46.8	2.2	6.5	19.6
Hispanic origin	44.6	9.2	8.1	77.5	47.8	3.0	8.1	17.4
Not of Hispanic origin	67.0	28.9	11.0	86.6	69.1	5.0	24.6	31.1
Age of householder:								
Less than 35 years	55.7	18.4	7.7	85.5	42.2	1.6	12.0	30.4
35 to 44 years	64.6	26.9	14.0	88.8	67.0	4.1	20.7	41.1
45 to 54 years	67.6	31.3	14.7	89.5	74.5	5.8	28.0	40.5
55 to 64 years	67.7	32.3	13.5	87.8	78.8	7.9	33.9	30.5
65 years and over	70.5	29.0	4.8	78.0	78.4	6.1	25.4	6.3
65 to 69 years	69.1	29.8	7.5	84.9	81.3	6.7	33.7	12.1
70 to 74 years	70.4	29.9	6.0	83.3	80.7	7.2	33.4	7.2
75 and over	71.4	28.1	2.8	71.6	75.6	5.3	16.7	2.8
Educational attainment:								
No high school diploma	42.8	6.9	5.5	71.1	56.1	2.3	6.7	8.4
High school graduate only.	59.6	19.5	9.5	85.7	67.3	3.9	16.4	23.8
Some college, no degree	66.7	27.3	11.2	88.7	65.0	4.8	22.9	32.1
Associate's degree	72.0	29.9	11.1	91.8	70.7	5.1	24.6	38.8
Bachelor's degree or higher. . . .	82.6	49.3	15.7	91.4	74.9	7.7	42.3	46.8
Region:								
Northeast	71.8	30.1	10.4	77.5	64.1	4.2	26.2	32.2
Midwest	70.3	30.0	11.0	87.4	72.5	4.6	26.4	33.8
South	57.0	23.1	10.3	86.9	69.3	4.5	17.9	26.2
West	65.7	28.0	11.7	89.3	60.7	6.4	25.1	29.5
Tenure:								
Owner	74.4	34.4	13.3	92.0	100.0	6.7	29.8	35.2
Renter	45.5	12.3	5.6	73.2	-	1.2	9.4	19.1

- Represents zero.
Source: U.S. Census Bureau, *Asset Ownership of Households: 1998 and 2000*, P70-88, May 2003. See also <http://www.census.gov/hhes/www/wealth/19982000/wealth9800.html>.

Income, Expenditures, and Wealth 475

Table 701. Nonfinancial Assets Held by Families by Type of Asset: 2001

[Median value in thousands of dollars. Constant dollar figures are based on consumer price index for all urban consumers published by U.S. Bureau of Labor Statistics. Families include one-person units and, as used in this table, are comparable to the U.S. Census Bureau household concept. For definition of family, see text, Section 1, Population. Based on Survey of Consumer Finance; see Appendix III. For data on financial assets, see Section 25, Banking. For definition of median, see Guide to Tabular Presentation]

Age of family head, and family income	Total	Vehicles	Primary residence	Other residential property	Equity in nonresidential property	Business equity	Other	Any nonfinancial asset
PERCENT OF FAMILIES HOLDING ASSET								
All families, total	96.7	84.8	67.7	11.3	8.3	11.8	7.6	90.7
Age of family head:								
Under 35 years old	93.1	78.8	39.9	3.4	2.8	7.0	6.9	83.0
35 to 44 years old	97.4	88.9	67.8	9.2	7.6	14.2	8.0	93.2
45 to 54 years old	98.1	90.5	76.2	14.7	10.0	17.1	7.2	95.2
55 to 64 years old	98.2	90.7	83.2	18.3	12.3	15.6	7.9	95.4
65 to 74 years old	97.1	81.3	82.5	13.7	12.9	11.6	9.7	91.6
75 years old and over	97.8	73.9	76.2	15.2	8.3	2.4	6.2	86.4
Race or ethnicity of respondent:								
White non-Hispanic	99.0	89.1	74.1	12.9	9.6	13.9	9.0	94.7
Non-White or Hispanic	89.4	70.9	47.0	6.4	4.1	5.1	2.9	77.9
Tenure:								
Owner-occupied	100.0	92.2	100.0	14.9	11.0	15.5	8.7	100.0
Renter-occupied or other	89.7	69.3	(X)	3.9	2.6	4.2	5.1	71.3
MEDIAN VALUE [1] ($1,000)								
All families, total	147.4	13.5	122.0	80.0	49.0	100.0	12.0	113.2
Age of family head:								
Under 35 years old	39.4	11.3	95.0	75.0	33.3	50.0	10.0	30.5
35 to 44 years old	157.6	14.8	125.0	75.0	39.5	100.0	9.0	117.8
45 to 54 years old	211.6	15.7	135.0	65.0	56.4	102.0	11.0	140.3
55 to 64 years old	226.3	15.1	130.0	80.0	78.5	100.0	11.0	147.9
65 to 74 years old	214.6	13.6	129.0	145.0	50.0	100.0	30.0	149.2
75 years old and over	169.6	8.8	111.0	80.0	28.0	510.9	20.0	122.6
Race or ethnicity of respondent:								
White non-Hispanic	183.9	14.6	130.0	80.0	50.0	100.0	15.0	131.4
Non-White or Hispanic	56.8	10.0	92.0	60.0	22.5	50.0	5.0	58.2
Tenure:								
Owner-occupied	240.1	16.2	122.0	80.0	50.0	105.0	15.0	156.9
Renter-occupied or other	13.4	7.6	(X)	60.0	32.5	35.0	6.0	8.9

X Not applicable. [1] Median value of financial asset for families holding such assets.

Source: Board of Governors of the Federal Reserve System, *Federal Reserve Bulletin*, January 2003, and unpublished data found at <http://www.federalreserve.gov/pubs/oss/oss2/2001/scf2001home.html>.

Table 702. Family Net Worth—Mean and Median Net Worth in Constant (2001) Dollars by Selected Family Characteristics: 1992 to 2001

[Net worth in thousands of constant (2001) dollars (230.5 represents $230,500). Constant dollar figures are based on consumer price index for all urban consumers published by U.S. Bureau of Labor Statistics. Families include one-person units and, as used in this table, are comparable to the Census Bureau household concept. Based on Survey of Consumer Finance; see Appendix III. For definition of median, see Guide to Tabular Presentation]

Family characteristic	1992		1995		1998		2001	
	Mean	Median	Mean	Median	Mean	Median	Mean	Median
All families	230.5	61.3	244.8	66.4	307.4	78.0	395.5	86.1
Age of family head:								
Under 35 years old	56.2	11.4	49.9	13.9	69.5	9.9	90.7	11.6
35 to 44 years old	164.8	55.1	165.9	60.3	213.6	69.0	259.5	77.6
45 to 54 years old	331.7	96.8	342.4	107.5	394.1	114.8	485.8	133.0
55 to 64 years old	418.0	141.1	442.3	133.2	579.3	139.2	727.0	181.5
65 to 74 years old	354.6	121.7	402.9	128.0	507.9	159.5	673.8	176.3
75 years old and over	264.0	107.5	298.5	107.5	338.3	136.7	465.9	151.4
Race or ethnicity of respondent:								
White non-Hispanic	274.8	86.2	289.8	88.5	363.9	103.4	482.9	120.9
Non-White or Hispanic	95.8	14.8	89.1	18.3	109.9	17.9	115.3	17.1
Tenure:								
Owner-occupied	333.7	122.3	350.8	120.2	439.9	143.8	558.2	171.7
Renter-occupied or other	47.8	4.0	50.5	5.6	47.3	4.6	55.0	4.8

Source: Board of Governors of the Federal Reserve System, *Federal Reserve Bulletin*, January 2003, and unpublished data found at <http://www.federalreserve.gov/pubs/oss/oss2/2001/scf2001home.html>.

Table 703. **Household and Nonprofit Organization Sector Balance Sheet: 1980 to 2004**

[In billions of dollars (10,872 represents $10,872,000,000,000). As of December 31. For details of financial assets and liabilities, see Table 1158]

Item	1980	1990	1995	1998	1999	2000	2001	2002	2003	2004
Assets.......................	10,872	24,082	32,781	43,775	49,271	49,481	49,245	48,295	54,165	59,232
Tangible assets [1]...............	4,272	9,351	11,252	13,414	14,503	15,803	17,035	18,428	20,073	22,473
Real estate................	3,338	7,378	8,777	10,606	11,534	12,643	13,736	14,996	16,522	18,645
Consumer durable goods	910	1,899	2,371	2,683	2,835	3,015	3,144	3,269	3,376	3,639
Financial assets [1]..............	6,600	14,731	21,529	30,362	34,768	33,679	32,211	29,867	34,092	36,759
Deposits..................	1,521	3,259	3,298	3,854	4,032	4,340	4,801	5,072	5,252	5,694
Checkable deposits and currency	219	412	544	422	364	229	332	361	324	408
Time and savings deposits......	1,239	2,465	2,281	2,681	2,799	3,076	3,281	3,552	3,877	4,291
Money market fund shares......	62	369	450	713	825	971	1,129	1,085	985	894
Credit market instruments [1]......	425	1,555	1,955	2,264	2,398	2,336	2,176	2,075	2,242	2,265
Treasury..................	160	471	806	747	833	619	487	345	465	468
Savings bonds	73	126	185	187	186	185	190	195	204	204
Corporate equities	875	1,770	4,123	7,122	9,170	7,806	6,604	5,048	6,376	6,522
Mutual fund shares...........	46	457	1,153	2,397	2,987	2,833	2,666	2,326	3,009	3,570
Pension fund reserves	970	3,376	5,676	8,120	9,113	8,831	8,330	7,612	8,835	9,638
Equity in noncorporate business	2,182	3,065	3,512	4,258	4,465	4,834	4,949	5,140	5,496	5,930
Liabilities.....................	1,453	3,719	5,071	6,252	6,827	7,407	7,987	8,677	9,583	10,707
Credit market instruments..........	1,402	3,597	4,874	5,955	6,448	7,018	7,639	8,369	9,232	10,264
Home mortgages	932	2,504	3,342	4,079	4,453	4,821	5,286	5,909	6,643	7,543
Consumer credit	358	824	1,168	1,448	1,561	1,739	1,879	1,962	2,050	2,151
Net worth....................	9,419	20,363	27,710	37,524	42,445	42,074	41,258	39,618	44,583	48,525
Replacement cost value of structures:.										
Residential..................	2,553	4,624	6,105	7,304	7,887	8,468	9,142	9,768	10,566	11,625
Households..................	2,449	4,367	5,817	6,978	7,542	8,106	8,761	9,372	10,150	11,183
Farm households..............	35	149	171	197	211	223	235	245	258	274
Nonprofit organizations	70	108	117	129	134	140	146	151	158	168
Nonresidential (nonprofits).........	263	472	591	710	760	813	867	909	955	1,066
Disposable personal income	2,116	4,351	5,479	6,522	6,846	7,309	7,525	7,879	8,321	8,878
Owners'equity in household real estate..................	1,935	4,072	4,648	5,464	5,944	6,589	7,217	7,792	8,490	9,622

[1] Includes types of assets and/or liabilities not shown separately.
Source: Board of Governors of the Federal Reserve System, "Federal Reserve Statistical Release, Z.1, Flow of Funds Accounts of the United States"; published: 10 March 2005; <http://www.federalreserve.gov/releases/Z1/20050310/data.htm>.

Table 704. **Net Stock of Fixed Reproducible Tangible Wealth in Current and Real (2000) Dollars: 1980 to 2003**

[In billions of dollars (10,108 represents $10,108,000,000,000). As of December 31]

Item	1980	1990	1995	1998	1999	2000	2001	2002	2003
CURRENT DOLLARS									
Net stock, total.............	10,108	18,111	22,670	26,405	28,081	29,917	31,609	33,046	34,693
Fixed assets.................	9,198	16,212	20,299	23,722	25,246	26,902	28,465	29,778	31,317
Private	7,049	12,611	15,794	18,621	19,847	21,190	22,485	23,530	24,824
Nonresidential.............	3,545	6,500	7,954	9,320	9,860	10,514	11,020	11,334	11,698
Equipment and software	1,396	2,469	3,067	3,584	3,822	4,077	4,203	4,279	4,425
Information processing equipment and software	(NA)	622	811	999	1,109	1,238	1,294	1,322	1,383
Structures.................	2,149	4,031	4,887	5,737	6,038	6,437	6,817	7,055	7,273
Residential................	3,505	6,111	7,840	9,300	9,987	10,676	11,465	12,196	13,125
Housing units	(NA)	4955	6354	7546	8106	8663	9320	9925	10679
Government.................	2,149	3,601	4,505	5,101	5,399	5,713	5,980	6,248	6,493
Nonresidential..............	2,071	3,452	4,317	4,894	5,179	5,481	5,733	5,989	6,220
Equipment and software	252	551	675	677	698	703	711	725	742
Structures.................	1,820	2,900	3,642	4,217	4,481	4,778	5,022	5,264	5,477
Residential.................	78	149	188	207	220	232	247	259	274
Federal	(NA)	1,079	1,291	1,356	1,399	1,425	1,447	1,469	1,498
Defense.................	(NA)	735	865	872	891	896	904	913	927
State and local	(NA)	2,522	3,213	3,745	4,000	4,288	4,533	4,779	4,995
Consumer durable goods	910	1,899	2,371	2,683	2,835	3,015	3,144	3,269	3,376
Motor vehicles and parts	(NA)	670	842	950	1,021	1,092	1,156	1,214	1,257
Furniture and household equipment	(NA)	814	1,011	1,147	1,196	1,260	1,292	1,332	1,360
Other	(NA)	415	518	586	618	662	696	723	760
CHAINED (2000) DOLLARS									
Net stock, total	(NA)	22,580	25,156	27,553	28,524	29,528	30,393	31,178	31,952
Fixed assets.................	(NA)	20,726	22,939	24,928	25,700	26,498	27,170	27,757	28,389
Private.....................	(NA)	16,029	17,804	19,523	20,190	20,880	21,438	21,897	22,399
Nonresidential..............	(NA)	7,809	8,638	9,605	9,986	10,392	10,669	10,826	10,986
Equipment and software	(NA)	2,532	2,972	3,567	3,823	4,091	4,249	4,337	4,446
Structures................	(NA)	5,347	5,702	6,042	6,163	6,302	6,422	6,493	6,548
Residential	(NA)	8,223	9,174	9,919	10,203	10,488	10,769	11,069	11,404
Government.................	(NA)	4,700	5,137	5,406	5,510	5,618	5,731	5,860	5,991
Nonresidential..............	(NA)	4,507	4,926	5,185	5,285	5,390	5,501	5,626	5,754
Equipment and software	(NA)	631	686	690	699	706	714	727	742
Structures.................	(NA)	3,872	4,237	4,494	4,587	4,684	4,786	4,899	5,011
Residential	(NA)	201	220	221	225	227	231	234	237
Consumer durable goods	(NA)	1,903	2,242	2,629	2,824	3,030	3,228	3,437	3,658

NA Not available.
Source: U.S. Bureau of Economic Analysis, *Survey of Current Business*, periodic articles, and <http://www.bea.doc.gov/bea/dn/FA2004/SelectTable.asp> (released 08 March 2005).

No. 204.—ANNUAL AVERAGE CURRENCY PRICES IN THE NEW YORK MARKET OF MIDDLING COTTON AND THE STAPLE MANUFACTURES OF COTTON FOR EACH YEAR FROM 1847 TO 1888, INCLUSIVE.

[Prepared by Mr. Joshua Reece, jr., of the Dry Goods Economist, New York.]

Year.	Middling cotton per pound.	Standard sheetings per yard.	Standard drillings per yard.	New York Mills bleached sheetings per yard.	Standard prints per yard.	64 by 64 printing-cloths per yard.
	Cents.	Cents.	Cents.	Cents.	Cents.	Cents.
1847	11.21	8.28	8.34	14.96	11.83	6.01
1848	8.03	6.78	6.83	14.21	10.17	4.35
1849	7.55	6.91	6.90	14.21	9.33	4.58
1850	12.34	7.87	7.97	14.96	10.62	5.19
1851	12.14	7.09	7.75	14.75	10.50	4.59
1852	9.50	6.96	7.70	14.50	10.50	4.70
1853	11.02	7.92	7.93	14.50	10.50	6.15
1854	10.97	7.96	7.84	15.00	10.50	5.81
1855	10.39	7.64	7.77	15.00	9.80	5.11
1856	10.30	7.50	8.10	15.00	9.50	5.26
1857	13.51	8.90	9.04	15.00	10.19	5.98
1858	12.23	8.25	8.70	15.00	9.50	5.60
1859	12.08	8.50	8.82	15.42	9.50	5.67
1860	11.00	8.73	8.92	15.50	9.50	5.44
1861	13.01	10.00	9.58	15.33	9.71	5.23
1862	31.29	18.55	18.94	21.00	14.40	9.81
1863	67.21	36.64	33.41	35.33	21.24	15.20
1864	101.50	52.07	53.02	48.35	33.25	23.42
1865	83.38	32.04	37.33	49.58	29.00	20.24
1866	43.20	24.21	25.14	45.90	21.15	14.13
1867	31.59	18.28	18.79	35.21	16.58	9.12
1868	24.85	16.79	16.49	26.65	13.83	8.18
1869	29.01	16.19	16.49	24.79	14.00	8.30
1870	23.98	14.58	14.98	22.50	12.41	7.14
1871	16.95	12.00	13.64	20.83	11.62	7.41
1872	23.19	14.27	15.14	20.66	12.00	7.88
1873	20.14	12.31	14.13	19.41	11.37	6.69
1874	17.95	11.42	11.75	18.04	9.75	5.57
1875	15.46	10.41	11.12	15.12	8.71	5.33
1876	12.98	8.85	8.71	13.58	7.06	4.10
1877	11.82	8.46	8.46	12.46	6.77	4.38
1878	11.22	7.80	7.65	11.00	6.09	3.44
1879	10.84	7.97	7.57	11.62	6.25	3.93
1880	11.51	8.51	8.51	12.74	7.41	4.51
1881	12.03	8.51	a8.06	12.74	7.00	3.95
1882	11.56	8.45	a8.25	12.95	6.50	3.76
1883	11.88	8.32	a7.11	12.93	6.00	3.60
1884	10.88	7.28	a6.86	10.46	6.00	3.36
1885	10.45	6.75	a6.36	10.37	6.00	3.12
1886	9.28	6.75	a6.25	10.65	6.00	3.31
1887	10.21	7.15	6.58	10.88	6.00	3.33
1888	10.03	7.45	6.89	10.94	6.50	3.81

a Including 1881 and since, the prices of standard drillings are net; raw cotton prices are also net for the entire period.

Source: Statistical Abstract of the United States: 1889 Edition.

Section 14
Prices

This section presents indexes of producer and consumer prices, actual prices for selected commodities, and energy prices. The primary sources of these data are monthly publications of the Department of Labor, Bureau of Labor Statistics (BLS), which include *Monthly Labor Review, Consumer Price Index, Detailed Report, Producer Price Indexes,* and *U.S. Import and Export Price Indexes.* The Department of Commerce, Bureau of Economic Analysis is the source for gross domestic product measures.

Producer price index (PPI)—This index, dating from 1890, is the oldest continuous statistical series published by BLS. It is designed to measure average changes in prices received by producers of all commodities, at all stages of processing, produced in the United States.

The index has undergone several revisions (see *Monthly Labor Review,* February 1962, April 1978, and August 1988). It is now based on approximately 10,000 individual products and groups of products along with about 100,000 quotations per month. Indexes for the net output of manufacturing and mining industries have been added in recent years. Prices used in constructing the index are collected from sellers and generally apply to the first significant large-volume commercial transaction for each commodity—i.e., the manufacturer's or other producer's selling price or the selling price on an organized exchange or at a central market.

The weights used in the index represent the total net selling value of commodities produced or processed in this country. Values are f.o.b. (free on board) production point and are exclusive of excise taxes. Effective with the release of data for January 1988, many important producer price indexes were changed to a new reference base year, 1982 = 100, from 1967 = 100. The reference year of the PPI shipment weights has been taken primarily from the 1987 Census of Manufactures. For further detail regarding the PPI, see the BLS *Handbook of Methods,* Bulletin 2490 (April 1997), Chapter 16. The PPI Web page is <http://stats.bls.gov/ppihome.htm>.

Consumer price indexes (CPI)—The CPI is a measure of the average change in prices over time in a "market basket" of goods and services purchased either by urban wage earners and clerical workers or by all urban consumers. In 1919, BLS began to publish complete indexes at semiannual intervals, using a weighting structure based on data collected in the expenditure survey of wage-earner and clerical-worker families in 1917–19 (BLS Bulletin 357, 1924). The first major revision of the CPI occurred in 1940, with subsequent revisions in 1953, 1964, 1978, 1987, and 1998.

Beginning with the release of data for January 1988 in February 1988, most consumer price indexes shifted to a new reference base year. All indexes previously expressed on a base of 1967 = 100, or any other base through December 1981, have been rebased to 1982–84 = 100. The expenditure weights are based upon data tabulated from the Consumer Expenditure Surveys for 1993, 1994, and 1995.

BLS publishes CPIs for two population groups: (1) a CPI for all urban consumers (CPI-U), which covers approximately 80 percent of the total population; and (2) a CPI for urban wage earners and clerical workers (CPI-W), which covers 32 percent of the total population. The CPI-U includes, in addition to wage earners and clerical workers, groups which historically have been excluded from CPI coverage, such as professional, managerial, and technical workers; the self-employed; short-term workers; the unemployed; and retirees and others not in the labor force.

The current CPI is based on prices of food, clothing, shelter, fuels, transportation fares, charges for doctors' and dentists' services, drugs, etc. purchased for day-to-day living. Prices are collected in 87 areas across the country from over 50,000 housing units and 23,000 establishments. Area selection was based on the 1990 census. All taxes directly associated with the purchase and use of items are included in the index. Prices of food, fuels, and a few other items are obtained every month in all 87 locations. Prices of most other commodities and services are collected monthly in the three largest geographic areas and every other month in other areas.

In calculating the index, each item is assigned a weight to account for its relative importance in consumers' budgets. Price changes for the various items in each location are then averaged. Local data are then combined to obtain a U.S. city average. Separate indexes are also published for regions, area size-classes, cross-classifications of regions and size-classes, and for 26 local areas, usually consisting of the Metropolitan Statistical Area (MSA); see Appendix II. Area definitions are those established by the Office of Management and Budget in 1983. Definitions do not include revisions made since 1992. Area indexes do not measure differences in the level of prices among cities; they only measure the average change in prices for each area since the base period. For further detail regarding the CPI, see the BLS *Handbook of Methods*, Bulletin 2490, Chapter 17; the *Consumer Price Index*, and the CPI home page: <http://stats.bls.gov/cpihome.htm>. In January 1983, the method of measuring homeownership costs in the CPI-U was changed to a rental equivalence approach. This treatment calculates homeowner costs of shelter based on the implicit rent owners would pay to rent the homes they own. The rental equivalence approach was introduced into the CPI-W in 1985. The CPI-U was used to prepare the consumer price tables in this section.

Other price indexes—Chain-weighted price indexes, produced by the Bureau of Economic Analysis (BEA), are weighted averages of the detailed price indexes used in the deflation of the goods and services that make up the gross domestic product (GDP) and its major components. Growth rates are constructed for years and quarters using quantity weights for the current and preceding year or quarter; these growth rates are used to move the index for the preceding period forward a year or quarter at a time. The gross domestic purchases chained price index measures the average price of goods and services purchased in the United States. It differs from the GDP chained price index, which measures the average price of goods produced in the United States, by excluding net exports. All chain-weighted price indexes are expressed in terms of the reference year value 1996 = 100.

Personal consumption expenditures (PCE) price and quantity indexes are based on market transactions for which there are corresponding price measures. The price index provides a measure of the prices paid by persons for domestic purchases of goods and services, which may be a useful measure of consumer prices for some analytical purposes. PCEs are defined as market value of spending by individuals and not-for-profit institutions on all goods and services. Personal consumption expenditures also include the value of certain imputed goods and services—such as the rental value of owner-occupied homes and compensation paid in kind—such as employer-paid health and life insurance premiums.

The index is composed of PCE components that are deflated by either a detailed CPI or a PPI. It excludes most imputed expenditures. It excludes expenses of nonprofit institutions serving households, most insurance purchases, gambling, margins on used light motor vehicles, and expenditures by U.S. residents working and traveling abroad. Household insurance premiums, which are deflated by the CPI for tenants' and household insurance, are included in market-based PCE; medical and hospitalization and income loss insurance, expense of handling life insurance, motor vehicle insurance, and workers' compensation are excluded.

Measures of inflation—Inflation is defined as a time of generally rising prices for goods and factors of production. The Bureau of Labor Statistics samples prices of items in a representative market basket and publishes the result as the CPI. The media invariably announce the inflation rate as the percent change in the CPI from month to month. A much more meaningful indicator of inflation is the percent change from the same month of the prior year. The producer price index measures prices at the producer level only. The PPI shows the same general pattern of inflation as does the CPI but is more volatile. The PPI can be roughly viewed as a leading indicator. It often tends to foreshadow trends that later occur in the CPI.

Other measures of inflation include the gross domestic purchases chain-weighted price index, the index of industrial materials prices; the Dow Jones Commodity Spot Price Index; Futures Price Index; the Employment Cost Index, the Hourly Compensation Index, or the Unit Labor Cost Index as a measure of the change in cost of the labor factor of production; and changes in long-term interest rates that are often used to measure changes in the cost of the capital factor of production.

International price indexes—The BLS International Price Program produces export and import price indexes for non-military goods traded between the United States and the rest of the world.

The export price index provides a measure of price change for all products sold by U.S. residents to foreign buyers. The import price index provides a measure of price change for goods purchased from other countries by U.S. residents. The reference period for the indexes is 2000 = 100, unless otherwise indicated.

The product universe for both the import and export indexes includes raw materials, agricultural products, semifinished manufactures, and finished manufactures, including both capital and consumer goods. Price data for these items are collected primarily by mail questionnaire. In nearly all cases, the data are collected directly from the exporter or importer, although in a few cases, prices are obtained from other sources.

To the extent possible, the data gathered refer to prices at the U.S. border for exports and at either the foreign border or the U.S. border for imports. For nearly all products, the prices refer to transactions completed during the first week of the month. Survey respondents are asked to indicate all discounts, allowances, and rebates applicable to the reported prices, so that the price used in the calculation of the indexes is the actual price for which the product was bought or sold.

In addition to general indexes for U.S. exports and imports, indexes are also published for detailed product categories of exports and imports. These categories are defined according to the five-digit level of detail for the Bureau of Economic Analysis End-Use Classification, the 3-digit level of detail for the Standard International Trade Classification (SITC), and the 4-digit level of detail for the Harmonized System. Aggregate import indexes by country or region of origin are also available.

Table 705. **Purchasing Power of the Dollar: 1980 to 2004**

[Indexes: PPI, 1982 = $1.00; CPI, 1982–84 = $1.00. Producer prices prior to 1961, and consumer prices prior to 1964, exclude Alaska and Hawaii. Producer prices based on finished goods index. Obtained by dividing the average price index for the 1982 = 100, PPI: 1982–84 = 100, CPI base periods (100.0) by the price index for a given period and expressing the result in dollars and cents. Annual figures are based on average of monthly data]

Year	Annual average as measured by—		Year	Annual average as measured by—	
	Producer prices	Consumer prices		Producer prices	Consumer prices
1980	1.136	1.215	1993	0.802	0.692
1981	1.041	1.098	1994	0.797	0.675
1982	1.000	1.035			
1983	0.984	1.003	1995	0.782	0.656
1984	0.964	0.961	1996	0.762	0.638
			1997	0.759	0.623
1985	0.955	0.928	1998	0.765	0.614
1986	0.969	0.913	1999	0.752	0.600
1987	0.949	0.880			
1988	0.926	0.846	2000	0.725	0.581
1989	0.880	0.807	2001	0.711	0.565
			2002	0.720	0.556
1990	0.839	0.766	2003	0.698	0.544
1991	0.822	0.734	2004	0.673	0.530
1992	0.812	0.713			

Source: U.S. Bureau of Labor Statistics. Monthly data in U.S. Bureau of Economic Analysis, *Survey of Current Business.*

Table 706. Consumer Price Indexes (CPI-U) by Major Groups: 1980 to 2004

[1982-84 = 100. except as indicated. Represents annual averages of monthly figures. Reflects buying patterns of all urban consumers. Minus sign (-) indicates decrease. See text, this section]

Year	All items	Com-modities	Ser-vices	Food	Energy	All items less food and energy	Food and bever-ages	Shelter	Transpor-tation	Medi-cal care	Apparel	Education and communi-cation [1]
1980	82.4	86.0	77.9	86.8	86.0	80.8	86.7	81.0	83.1	74.9	90.9	(NA)
1990	130.7	122.8	139.2	132.4	102.1	135.5	132.1	140.0	120.5	162.8	124.1	(NA)
1991	136.2	126.6	146.3	136.3	102.5	142.1	136.8	146.3	123.8	177.0	128.7	(NA)
1992	140.3	129.1	152.0	137.9	103.0	147.3	138.7	151.2	126.5	190.1	131.9	(NA)
1993	144.5	131.5	157.9	140.9	104.2	152.2	141.6	155.7	130.4	201.4	133.7	85.5
1994	148.2	133.8	163.1	144.3	104.6	156.5	144.9	160.5	134.3	211.0	133.4	88.8
1995	152.4	136.4	168.7	148.4	105.2	161.2	148.9	165.7	139.1	220.5	132.0	92.2
1996	156.9	139.9	174.1	153.3	110.1	165.6	153.7	171.0	143.0	228.2	131.7	95.3
1997	160.5	141.8	179.4	157.3	111.5	169.5	157.7	176.3	144.3	234.6	132.9	98.4
1998	163.0	141.9	184.2	160.7	102.9	173.4	161.1	182.1	141.6	242.1	133.0	100.3
1999	166.6	144.4	188.8	164.1	106.6	177.0	164.6	187.3	144.4	250.6	131.3	101.2
2000	172.2	149.2	195.3	167.8	124.6	181.3	168.4	193.4	153.3	260.8	129.6	102.5
2001	177.1	150.7	203.4	173.1	129.3	186.1	173.6	200.6	154.3	272.8	127.3	105.2
2002	179.9	149.7	209.8	176.2	121.7	190.5	176.8	208.1	152.9	285.6	124.0	107.9
2003	184.0	151.2	216.5	180.0	136.5	193.2	180.5	213.1	157.6	297.1	120.9	109.8
2004	188.9	154.7	222.8	186.2	151.4	196.6	186.6	218.8	163.1	310.1	120.4	111.6
PERCENT CHANGE [2]												
1980	13.5	12.3	15.4	8.6	30.9	12.4	8.5	17.6	17.9	11.0	7.1	(NA)
1990	5.4	5.2	5.5	5.8	8.3	5.0	5.8	5.4	5.6	9.0	4.6	(NA)
1991	4.2	3.1	5.1	2.9	0.4	4.9	3.6	4.5	2.7	8.7	3.7	(NA)
1992	3.0	2.0	3.9	1.2	0.5	3.7	1.4	3.3	2.2	7.4	2.5	(NA)
1993	3.0	1.9	3.9	2.2	1.2	3.3	2.1	3.0	3.1	5.9	1.4	(NA)
1994	2.6	1.7	3.3	2.4	0.4	2.8	2.3	3.1	3.0	4.8	-0.2	3.9
1995	2.8	1.9	3.4	2.8	0.6	3.0	2.8	3.2	3.6	4.5	-1.0	3.8
1996	3.0	2.6	3.2	3.3	4.7	2.7	3.2	3.2	2.8	3.5	-0.2	3.4
1997	2.3	1.4	3.0	2.6	1.3	2.4	2.6	3.1	0.9	2.8	0.9	3.3
1998	1.6	0.1	2.7	2.2	-7.7	2.3	2.2	3.3	-1.9	3.2	0.1	1.9
1999	2.2	1.8	2.5	2.1	3.6	2.1	2.2	2.9	2.0	3.5	-1.3	0.9
2000	3.4	3.3	3.4	2.3	16.9	2.4	2.3	3.3	6.2	4.1	-1.3	1.3
2001	2.8	1.0	4.1	3.2	3.8	2.6	3.1	3.7	0.7	4.6	-1.8	2.6
2002	1.6	-0.7	3.1	1.8	-5.9	2.4	1.8	3.7	-0.9	4.7	-2.6	2.6
2003	2.3	1.0	3.2	2.2	12.2	1.4	2.1	2.4	3.1	4.0	-2.5	1.8
2004	2.7	2.3	2.9	3.4	10.9	1.8	3.4	2.7	3.5	4.4	-0.4	1.6

NA Not available. [1] Dec. 1997 = 100. [2] Change from immediate prior year. 1980 change from 1979; 1990 change from 1989.

Source: U.S. Bureau of Labor Statistics, Monthly Labor Review.

Table 707. Annual Percent Changes From Prior Year in Consumer Price Indexes (CPI-U)—Selected Areas: 2004

[Represents percent changes of annual averages of monthly figures. Local area CPI indexes are by-products of the national CPI program. Each local index has a smaller sample size than the national index and is therefore subject to substantially more sampling and other measurement error. As a result, local area indexes show greater volatility than the national index, although their long-term trends are similar. Area definitions are those established by the Office of Management and Budget in 1983. For further detail, see the U.S. Bureau of Labor Statistics Handbook of Methods, Bulletin 2285, Chapter 19, the Consumer Price Index, and Report 736, the CPI: 1987 Revision. See also text, this section and Appendix III]

Area	All items	Food and bever-ages	Food	Hous-ing	Apparel	Trans-porta-tion	Medical care	Fuel and other utilities
U.S. city average	2.7	3.4	3.4	2.5	-0.4	3.5	4.4	4.8
Anchorage, AK MSA	2.6	4.4	4.8	1.6	0.6	2.8	(NA)	9.2
Atlanta, GA MSA	1.3	4.0	4.1	-0.2	-8.7	6.2	2.4	5.5
Boston, MA MSA	2.7	3.3	3.3	3.3	-5.6	3.4	4.7	7.1
Chicago-Gary, IL-IN CMSA	2.2	2.9	2.8	1.6	1.9	3.5	4.3	4.1
Cincinnati-Hamilton, OH-KY-IN CMSA	1.8	1.9	2.0	0.8	1.1	3.7	4.6	5.4
Cleveland-Akron-Lorain, OH CMSA	3.1	2.3	2.3	2.8	3.7	5.1	3.4	5.6
Dallas-Fort Worth, TX CMSA	1.4	3.6	3.5	-0.1	-2.1	3.1	2.5	5.9
Denver-Boulder-Greely, CO CMSA	0.1	2.5	2.3	-0.8	2.0	-3.1	1.9	8.5
Detroit-Ann Arbor-Flint, MI CMSA	1.6	1.3	1.3	1.3	-1.2	2.4	3.9	8.3
Honolulu, HI MSA	3.3	3.0	3.1	4.4	2.7	3.4	(NA)	4.5
Houston-Galveston-Brazoria, TX CMSA	3.5	3.1	3.2	4.2	2.1	3.9	4.3	7.1
Kansas City, MO-KS CMSA	2.1	2.8	2.9	2.4	-1.0	3.5	-0.7	5.2
Los Angeles-Anaheim-Riverside, CA CMSA	3.3	2.8	2.9	3.9	-1.3	3.9	3.4	-1.2
Miami-Fort Lauderdale, FL CMSA	2.8	3.3	3.3	3.6	-6.2	3.2	4.9	4.6
Milwaukee, WI PMSA	1.4	4.1	4.1	0.4	-4.0	3.7	1.5	3.8
Minneapolis-St. Paul, MN-WI MSA	2.8	3.8	4.1	2.9	-2.1	3.4	4.9	6.0
New York-Northern New Jersey-Long Island, NY-NJ-CT CMSA	3.5	4.1	4.2	4.2	1.9	3.4	3.2	5.3
Philadelphia-Wilmington-Trenton, PA-NJ-DE-MD CMSA	4.1	3.2	3.1	4.4	6.4	4.2	4.1	6.0
Pittsburgh, PA MSA	3.1	4.6	4.7	3.5	-3.2	2.5	5.4	5.0
Portland, OR MSA	2.6	4.1	4.2	1.9	0.6	3.8	3.4	4.2
San Diego, CA MSA	3.7	2.3	2.2	4.3	2.4	4.5	2.7	1.2
San Francisco-Oakland-San Jose, CA CMSA	1.2	4.7	4.8	-1.0	-1.3	3.2	6.8	-0.7
Seattle-Tacoma, WA CMSA	1.2	2.6	2.6	0.1	2.1	4.1	3.9	3.6
St. Louis-East St. Louis, MO-IL CMSA	4.0	3.7	3.8	5.0	4.8	3.3	(NA)	4.7
Tampa-St. Petersburg-Clearwater, FL MSA	2.5	3.1	3.1	3.4	-8.2	1.8	5.1	11.8
Washington-Baltimore, DC-MD-VA-WV CMSA	2.8	4.8	5.1	3.5	-4.4	3.3	2.8	4.6

NA Not available.
Source: U.S. Bureau of Labor Statistics, Monthly Labor Review and CPI Detailed Report, January issues.

Table 708. Consumer Price Indexes for All Urban Consumers (CPI-U) for Selected Items and Groups: 1990 to 2004

[1982-84 = 100 except as noted. Annual averages of monthly figures. See headnote, Table 706]

Item	1990	1995	2000	2001	2002	2003	2004	Annual percentage change. 2003-2004
All items	**130.7**	**152.4**	**172.2**	**177.1**	**179.9**	**184.0**	**188.9**	**2.7**
Food and beverages	132.1	148.9	168.4	173.6	176.8	180.5	186.6	3.4
Food	132.4	148.4	167.8	173.1	176.2	180.0	186.2	3.4
Food at home	132.3	148.8	167.9	173.4	175.6	179.4	186.2	3.8
Cereals and bakery products	140.0	167.5	188.3	193.8	198.0	202.8	206.0	1.6
Cereals and cereal products	141.1	167.1	175.9	178.7	181.8	185.2	186.2	0.5
Breakfast Cereal	158.6	192.5	198.0	199.7	203.0	204.3	203.5	-0.4
Rice, pasta, and cornmeal	122.0	140.2	150.7	154.6	155.8	160.3	164.5	2.6
Rice [1, 2]	(NA)	(NA)	(NA)	(NA)	(NA)	100.8	108.0	7.1
Bakery products	139.2	167.4	194.1	201.3	206.1	211.7	216.2	2.1
Bread [1]	(NA)	(NA)	(NA)	(NA)	(NA)	118.5	121.1	2.2
White bread	136.4	165.5	199.1	208.3	213.4	218.6	223.3	2.2
Bread other than white [1]	(NA)	(NA)	(NA)	(NA)	(NA)	224.2	227.8	1.6
Cookies [1]	(NA)	(NA)	(NA)	(NA)	(NA)	202.6	205.2	1.3
Other bakery products	(NA)	(NA)	(NA)	(NA)	(NA)	207.3	211.8	2.2
Meats, poultry, fish and eggs	130.0	138.8	154.5	161.3	162.1	169.3	181.7	7.3
Meats	128.5	135.5	150.7	159.3	160.3	169.0	183.2	8.4
Beef and veal	128.8	134.9	148.1	160.5	160.6	175.1	195.3	11.5
Uncooked ground beef	(NA)	(NA)	(NA)	(NA)	(NA)	149.2	166.3	11.5
Uncooked beef roasts [2]	(NA)	(NA)	(NA)	(NA)	(NA)	129.3	142.3	10.1
Uncooked beef steaks [2]	(NA)	(NA)	(NA)	(NA)	(NA)	127.6	144.7	13.4
Pork	129.8	134.8	156.5	162.4	161.8	164.9	174.2	5.6
Bacon, breakfast sausage, and related product	(NA)	(NA)	(NA)	(NA)	(NA)	116.1	123.1	6.0
Ham	132.4	139.6	152.7	157.3	160.0	161.9	166.0	2.5
Pork chops	140.2	144.2	152.2	159.0	156.0	160.9	170.4	5.9
Poultry	132.5	143.5	159.8	164.9	167.0	169.1	181.7	7.5
Chicken [2]	(NA)	(NA)	(NA)	(NA)	(NA)	108.9	118.2	8.5
Fresh whole chicken	134.9	142.2	162.9	168.0	169.1	165.8	182.4	10.0
Fish and seafood	146.7	171.6	190.4	191.1	188.1	190.0	194.3	2.3
Eggs	124.1	120.5	131.9	136.4	138.2	157.3	167.0	6.2
Dairy products	126.5	132.8	160.7	167.1	168.1	167.9	180.2	7.3
Milk [2]	(NA)	(NA)	(NA)	(NA)	(NA)	111.5	125.0	12.1
Fresh whole milk	126.7	131.1	156.9	165.9	162.1	162.5	183.4	12.9
Other dairy and related products [2]	(NA)	(NA)	(NA)	(NA)	(NA)	115.0	120.2	4.5
Fruits and vegetables	149.0	177.7	204.6	212.2	220.9	225.9	232.7	3.0
Fresh fruits and vegetables	(NA)	206.0	238.8	247.9	258.4	265.3	274.7	3.5
Fresh fruits	170.9	219.0	258.3	265.1	270.2	279.1	286.8	2.8
Apples	147.5	183.5	212.6	213.9	230.7	244.4	251.7	3.0
Bananas	138.2	153.8	162.5	166.6	166.5	164.8	163.0	-1.1
Citrus fruits [2]	(NA)	(NA)	(NA)	(NA)	(NA)	152.5	162.1	6.3
Oranges, tangerines	160.6	224.5	257.0	271.7	294.6	302.0	330.8	9.5
Fresh vegetables	151.1	193.1	219.4	230.6	245.4	250.5	261.2	4.3
Potatoes	162.6	174.7	196.3	202.3	238.5	228.1	231.1	1.3
Lettuce	150.3	221.2	228.1	233.8	252.1	246.2	239.8	-2.6
Tomatoes	160.8	188.3	234.7	250.0	251.0	271.0	296.8	9.5
Processed fruits and vegetables [2]	(NA)	(NA)	105.6	109.0	113.1	114.1	115.5	1.2
Nonalcoholic beverages	113.5	131.7	137.8	139.2	139.2	139.8	140.4	0.4
Juices and nonalcoholic drinks [2]	(NA)	(NA)	(NA)	(NA)	(NA)	108.0	108.5	0.5
Carbonated drinks	112.1	119.5	123.4	125.4	125.6	125.6	127.9	1.8
Coffee	117.5	163.1	154.0	146.7	142.6	144.9	145.3	0.3
Food away from home	(NA)	149.0	169.0	173.9	178.3	182.1	187.5	3.0
Alcoholic beverages	129.3	153.9	174.7	179.3	183.6	187.2	192.1	2.6
Alcoholic beverages at home	123.0	143.1	158.1	161.1	164.0	166.5	170.2	2.2
Alcoholic beverages away from home	144.4	176.5	207.1	215.2	222.5	228.6	236.6	3.5
Housing	128.5	148.5	169.6	176.4	180.3	184.8	189.5	2.5
Shelter	140.0	165.7	193.4	200.6	208.1	213.1	218.8	2.7
Owners' equivalent rent of primary residence [2]	144.8	171.3	198.7	206.3	214.7	219.9	224.9	2.3
Fuels and utilities	111.6	123.7	137.9	150.2	143.6	154.5	161.9	4.8
Fuels	104.5	111.5	122.8	135.4	127.2	138.2	144.4	4.5
Fuel oil and other	99.3	88.1	129.7	129.3	115.5	139.5	160.5	15.1
Gas (piped) and electricity	109.3	119.2	128.0	142.4	134.4	145.0	150.6	3.9
Electricity	117.4	129.6	128.5	137.8	136.2	139.5	142.1	1.9
Utility (piped) gas	97.3	102.9	132.0	158.3	135.3	166.3	180.1	8.3
Water and sewer and trash collection services [2]	(NA)	(NA)	(NA)	(NA)	(NA)	117.2	124.0	5.8
Water and sewerage maintenance	150.2	196.5	227.5	234.6	242.5	251.7	268.1	6.5
Garbage and trash collection [3]	171.2	241.2	269.8	275.5	283.0	291.9	303.3	3.9

See footnotes at end of table.

U.S. Census Bureau, Statistical Abstract of the United States: 2006

[1982-84 = 100 except as noted. Annual averages of monthly figures. See headnote, Table 706]

Item	1990	1995	2000	2001	2002	2003	2004	Annual percentage change, 2003-2004
Household furnishings and operations	113.3	123.0	128.2	129.1	128.3	126.1	125.5	-0.5
Furniture and bedding	115.7	130.9	134.4	132.2	129.4	127.7	127.3	-0.3
Bedroom furniture	118.5	136.4	138.4	136.6	135.3	133.9	137.3	2.5
Housekeeping supplies	125.2	137.1	153.4	158.4	159.8	157.5	157.4	-0.1
Apparel	124.1	132.0	129.6	127.3	124.0	120.9	120.4	-0.4
Men's and boy's apparel	120.4	126.2	129.7	125.7	121.7	118.0	117.5	-0.4
Women's and girl's apparel.	122.6	126.9	121.5	119.3	115.8	113.1	113.0	-0.1
Footwear	117.4	125.4	123.8	123.0	121.4	119.6	119.3	-0.3
Transportation	120.5	139.1	153.3	154.3	152.9	157.6	163.1	3.5
Private transportation.	118.8	136.3	149.1	150.0	148.8	153.6	159.4	3.8
New and used motor vehicles [2]	(NA)	(NA)	(NA)	(NA)	(NA)	96.5	94.2	-2.4
New vehicles.	121.4	141.0	142.8	142.1	140.0	137.9	137.1	-0.6
New cars and trucks	(NA)	(NA)	(NA)	(NA)	(NA)	95.6	95.1	-0.5
New cars	121.0	139.0	139.6	138.9	137.3	134.7	133.9	-0.6
Used cars and trucks	117.6	156.5	155.8	158.7	152.0	142.9	133.3	-6.7
Motor fuel	101.2	100.0	129.3	124.7	116.1	135.8	160.4	18.1
Public transportation	142.6	175.9	209.6	210.6	207.4	209.3	209.1	-0.1
Airline fares	148.4	189.7	239.4	239.4	231.6	231.3	227.2	-1.8
Medical care	162.8	220.5	260.8	272.8	285.6	297.1	310.1	4.4
Medical care commodities	163.4	204.5	238.1	247.6	256.4	262.8	289.3	2.5
Prescription drugs and medical supplies . .	181.7	235.0	285.4	300.9	316.5	326.3	337.1	3.3
Nonprescription drugs, and medical supplies [4]	120.6	140.5	149.5	150.6	150.4	152.0	153.3	0.2
Medical care services	162.7	224.2	266.0	278.8	292.9	306.0	321.3	5.0
Professional medical services	156.1	201.0	237.7	246.5	253.9	261.2	271.5	3.9
Recreation [2]	(NA)	(NA)	103.3	104.9	106.2	107.5	108.6	1.0
Video and audio	80.8	73.9	101.0	101.5	102.8	103.6	104.2	0.6
Televisions	74.6	68.1	49.9	44.8	40.1	34.9	30.0	-14.0
Sporting goods.	114.9	123.5	119.0	118.5	116.4	115.3	115.0	-0.3
Photography	(NA)	(NA)	99.2	99.0	97.9	96.0	92.9	-3.2
Other recreational goods	(NA)	(NA)	87.8	84.6	80.5	76.1	73.3	-3.7
Recreation services.	(NA)	(NA)	111.7	116.1	119.6	124.5	127.5	2.4
Recreational reading materials	(NA)	(NA)	188.3	191.4	195.8	197.5	201.2	1.9
Education and communication [1]	(NA)	92.2	102.5	105.2	107.9	109.8	111.6	1.6
Education [1]	(NA)	(NA)	112.5	118.5	126.0	134.4	143.7	6.9
Educational books and supplies	171.3	214.4	279.9	295.9	317.6	335.4	351.0	4.7
Tuition/and child care fees and other school fees	175.7	253.8	324.0	341.1	362.1	386.7	414.3	7.1
College tuition	175.0	264.8	331.9	348.8	372.6	403.9	442.1	9.5
Communication.	(NA)	99.0	93.0	93.3	92.3	89.7	86.7	-3.3
Postage and delivery services [2]	(NA)	(NA)	(NA)	(NA)	(NA)	119.4	119.8	0.3
Postage	125.1	160.3	165.1	171.5	181.8	190.9	190.9	0.0
Delivery services [1]	(NA)	(NA)	114.5	123.0	127.9	134.9	150.1	11.3
Information and information processing [1] . .	(NA)	98.9	92.8	92.3	90.8	87.8	84.6	-3.6
Telephone services [1]	(NA)	(NA)	98.5	99.3	99.7	98.3	95.8	-2.5
Commodities	122.8	136.4	149.2	150.7	149.7	151.2	154.7	2.3
Commodities less food and beverages	(NA)	(NA)	(NA)	(NA)	(NA)	134.5	136.7	1.6
Energy.	102.1	105.2	124.6	129.3	121.7	136.5	151.4	10.9

NA Not available. [1] December 1997 = 100. [2] December 1982 = 100. [3] December 1988 = 100. [4] December 1986 = 100.

Source: U.S. Bureau of Labor Statistics, *Monthly Labor Review* and *CPI Detailed Report*, January issues.

Table 709. **Cost of Living Index—Selected Metropolitan Areas: Fourth Quarter 2004**

[Measures relative price levels for consumer goods and services in participating areas for a mid-management standard of living. The nationwide average equals 100, and each index is read as a percent of the national average. The index does not measure inflation, but compares prices at a single point in time. Excludes taxes. Metropolitan areas as defined by the Office of Management and Budget. For definitions and components of metropolitan areas, see source for details]

Metropolitan areas (MA)	Com- posite index (100%)	Grocery items (14%)	Housing (29%)	Utilities (10%)	Transpor- tation (10%)	Health care (4%)	Misc. goods and services (33%)
Birmingham, AL	92.9	104.1	76.8	113.2	91.1	82.5	99.1
Decatur-Hartselle, AL.	88.9	94.9	72.0	91.4	101.9	89.1	97.1
Florence, AL	88.3	89.2	76.6	90.7	90.5	82.2	97.6
Huntsville, AL.	92.7	93.3	79.8	90.1	102.7	85.4	102.6
Mobile, AL.	89.6	92.8	80.0	93.4	89.6	83.1	96.4
Montgomery, AL	95.5	96.3	90.9	97.6	100.1	79.8	99.1
Tuscaloosa, AL.	98.7	105.6	92.0	99.0	97.7	85.9	103.6
Fairbanks, AK	127.8	130.6	133.8	148.1	112.2	166.5	116.1
Flagstaff, AZ	109.7	110.2	122.6	97.6	106.7	113.8	101.8
Phoenix, AZ.	98.7	98.2	94.7	94.4	108.2	106.6	100.2
Tucson, AZ	94.4	102.4	85.4	97.0	98.8	98.4	97.0
Fayetteville, AR	90.7	86.2	86.1	105.0	94.1	93.4	91.5
Fort Smith, AR.	85.5	83.1	74.6	91.3	92.1	83.9	92.8
Jonesboro, AR	85.1	92.6	72.2	88.6	90.8	82.9	91.2
Fresno, CA	119.4	118.4	145.0	99.5	121.2	112.4	103.3
Los Angeles-Long Beach, CA	156.4	125.7	251.9	115.9	114.8	105.8	112.8
Riverside City, CA.	121.0	109.4	157.3	87.8	119.2	108.7	104.7
San Diego, CA.	147.7	125.5	222.1	90.6	127.3	124.3	114.7
San Francisco, CA	183.6	149.4	311.8	103.2	121.7	128.2	129.4
Colorado Springs, CO	98.3	99.6	99.2	92.2	106.6	106.4	95.6
Denver, CO	103.3	106.2	108.7	82.2	96.4	120.6	102.7
Fort Collins, CO	99.2	109.5	98.8	88.0	97.4	87.1	100.4
Pueblo, CO	90.5	102.6	81.0	85.4	96.0	88.8	94.3
Dover, DE	99.0	100.7	96.3	110.5	94.2	93.9	99.6
Wilmington, DE	106.7	124.6	100.7	109.2	108.2	91.8	105.9
Washington-Arlington-Alexandria, DC-VA. . .	144.5	125.7	208.2	98.4	120.8	137.6	115.5
Fort Walton, FL	101.5	105.5	99.4	91.5	106.7	100.3	103.2
Jacksonville, FL	94.3	105.3	92.2	82.2	100.3	104.3	92.3
Orlando, FL.	95.8	98.1	92.1	97.2	100.0	86.0	97.7
Panama City, FL.	97.6	102.3	88.7	96.3	106.7	98.1	101.4
Pensacola, FL	100.2	104.3	100.8	94.0	97.6	85.2	102.3
Sarasota, FL	103.4	100.5	110.4	91.9	113.1	102.1	99.1
St. Petersburg-Clearwater, FL	93.9	94.5	93.0	97.6	103.8	83.8	92.1
Tampa, FL.	98.6	94.9	101.8	92.8	100.8	103.8	97.5
Albany, GA	88.7	102.5	69.3	88.7	91.9	90.3	99.0
Atlanta, GA	96.5	95.4	90.7	86.9	102.3	110.7	101.2
Augusta-Aiken, GA-SC	90.6	103.6	73.8	94.2	102.1	88.2	96.5
Boise, ID.	95.8	84.3	93.7	93.8	100.5	104.5	100.2
Peoria, IL	97.3	98.4	99.1	106.2	97.9	91.2	93.5
Springfield, IL.	91.7	89.8	83.8	96.8	103.3	93.1	94.7
Evansville, IN	98.1	100.2	87.0	97.8	104.6	98.6	105.1
Lafayette, IN	94.4	91.9	83.1	115.3	99.9	104.6	97.2

See source at end of table.

Prices **485**

Table 709. Cost of Living Index—Selected Metropolitan Areas: Fourth Quarter 2004—Con.

[See headnote, page 485]

Metropolitan areas (MA)	Composite index (100%)	Grocery items (14%)	Housing (29%)	Utilities (10%)	Transportation (10%)	Health care (4%)	Misc. goods and services (33%)
South Bend, IN	95.3	87.8	91.5	108.5	96.8	102.3	96.8
Terre Haute, IN	90.4	94.8	80.4	95.3	94.3	103.8	93.6
Cedar Rapids, IA	91.5	90.6	78.0	101.0	98.6	98.3	98.5
Waterloo-Cedar Falls, IA	93.7	86.4	94.9	90.6	101.5	90.5	94.5
Lawrence, KS	95.3	85.7	91.8	97.2	98.6	91.0	100.9
Covington, KY	93.0	90.5	81.5	96.5	98.7	93.5	101.3
Hopkinsville, KY	86.6	89.5	73.2	101.3	86.3	85.2	93.6
Lexington, KY	95.5	92.1	87.7	118.7	93.4	99.3	97.5
Louisville, KY	93.3	96.4	80.9	97.9	111.4	87.2	97.7
Baton Rouge, LA	105.6	111.2	93.2	116.6	110.2	110.8	109.6
Monroe, LA	94.0	95.6	84.0	91.7	101.2	90.4	101.1
Shreveport-Bossier City, LA	89.1	85.8	84.2	87.3	94.1	73.1	95.4
Baltimore, MD	112.3	104.8	126.0	119.7	107.5	107.8	103.3
Bethesda-Frederick-Gaithersburg, MD	139.4	123.8	184.2	111.5	122.4	114.3	121.1
Boston, MA	138.6	119.9	178.6	135.8	107.6	150.4	118.6
Grand Rapids, MI	101.0	105.7	91.2	111.9	105.9	96.6	104.0
Rochester, MN	99.0	90.2	96.7	106.2	102.7	110.7	100.0
St. Cloud, MN	101.9	95.4	100.5	103.7	100.5	105.5	104.9
Hattiesburg, MS	94.3	96.3	80.7	99.5	91.0	96.0	104.4
Jackson, MS	88.3	86.7	76.0	114.5	91.3	84.7	92.3
Columbia, MO	91.8	88.7	87.2	93.7	95.6	90.9	95.6
St. Louis, MO-IL	98.1	101.8	93.1	99.3	99.2	114.8	98.6
Springfield, MO	87.7	96.9	74.4	73.5	95.4	94.9	96.5
Billings, MT	95.3	101.2	84.3	101.2	94.8	106.6	99.9
Missoula, MT	99.7	112.8	86.1	89.6	99.3	125.0	106.4
Lincoln, NE	96.4	85.4	99.6	98.4	100.6	104.4	95.3
Omaha, NE	90.9	88.0	82.6	102.0	101.0	98.3	92.6
Las Vegas, NV	112.7	112.2	122.5	103.8	109.5	133.9	105.3
Reno-Sparks, NV	109.2	96.6	114.7	112.6	124.2	103.8	105.1
Buffalo, NY	98.9	97.8	90.1	130.7	103.3	96.5	97.7
Glens Falls, NY	103.0	99.0	92.9	122.5	110.4	94.7	107.2
New York (Manhattan), NY	211.6	132.8	387.4	147.7	116.9	142.5	138.9
New York (Queens), NY	137.1	121.8	173.6	138.1	120.3	103.9	119.4
Asheville, NC	104.1	94.8	117.6	89.0	104.8	105.0	99.6
Fayetteville, NC	93.9	108.2	81.5	89.3	92.5	104.2	99.5
Wilmington, NC	95.6	99.6	90.1	99.3	96.7	102.4	96.9
Bismarck-Mandan, ND	91.7	95.3	78.1	104.4	97.8	88.6	97.4
Akron, OH	92.8	110.7	83.3	103.2	99.8	84.7	90.8
Cincinnati, OH	94.1	86.6	88.8	108.7	101.5	92.6	95.8
Cleveland, OH	101.3	112.0	98.1	119.6	101.1	96.3	95.8
Dayton, OH	93.0	99.8	81.1	92.3	96.8	95.3	99.7
Lima, OH	95.4	107.8	85.8	104.9	103.7	88.0	95.4
Mansfield, OH	92.7	100.9	78.1	110.5	101.3	84.2	96.4
Toledo, OH	94.6	102.2	81.5	108.0	101.7	93.0	97.8
Youngstown-Warren, OH	91.1	98.1	82.8	112.7	91.6	85.4	90.5

See source at end of table.

U.S. Census Bureau, Statistical Abstract of the United States: 2006

Table 709. Cost of Living Index—Selected Metropolitan Areas: Fourth Quarter 2004—Con.

[See headnote, page 485]

Metropolitan areas (MA)	Composite index (100%)	Grocery items (14%)	Housing (29%)	Utilities (10%)	Transportation (10%)	Health care (4%)	Misc. goods and services (33%)
Muskogee, OK.	91.0	102.0	85.4	106.9	78.2	91.3	90.7
Oklahoma City, OK.	92.3	86.4	85.9	94.0	99.3	102.1	96.6
Corvallis, OR.	112.7	118.1	116.5	113.9	104.4	137.8	106.3
Philadelphia, PA.	118.7	118.2	124.1	127.6	107.6	105.3	116.4
Pittsburgh, PA.	94.6	97.5	85.0	97.5	113.5	81.5	97.8
York County, PA.	98.3	93.3	98.8	105.2	93.8	83.2	100.8
Camden, SC.	94.1	99.4	89.9	89.0	88.3	93.0	98.6
Columbia, SC	95.4	93.5	94.1	104.5	92.6	103.1	94.7
Myrtle Beach, SC.	92.7	99.4	81.3	94.5	100.5	103.9	96.3
Sumter, SC Metro.	90.6	98.0	80.2	91.0	96.9	92.3	94.9
Chattanooga, TN-GA	93.8	93.1	85.5	86.3	100.8	104.8	100.0
Jackson-Madison County, TN	89.1	91.1	78.9	81.5	97.6	92.1	96.4
Johnson City, TN	89.2	88.1	79.0	92.6	84.9	92.5	98.3
Knoxville, TN.	86.3	91.3	74.3	89.7	85.8	88.7	93.7
Memphis, TN.	88.4	91.8	77.0	87.4	96.4	99.0	94.1
Abilene, TX.	88.9	86.6	81.2	87.5	96.0	95.0	94.3
Amarillo, TX	86.7	87.6	82.4	87.3	88.4	91.2	88.9
Arlington, TX	92.1	94.7	82.3	100.3	96.9	92.8	96.2
Beaumont, TX.	90.4	94.3	73.1	106.6	102.6	93.3	96.2
El Paso, TX.	91.8	103.9	81.2	97.3	98.0	96.4	92.8
Fort Worth, TX.	91.7	96.8	78.1	99.0	100.2	109.5	95.5
Houston, TX	88.0	83.7	72.0	99.2	103.1	102.4	94.8
Longview, TX.	87.3	84.2	80.7	73.4	90.0	92.6	96.3
Lubbock, TX	87.3	86.9	76.5	77.5	93.4	104.5	95.5
Odessa, TX.	87.6	87.6	76.3	94.3	94.9	96.0	92.8
San Antonio, TX.	92.0	84.1	92.5	75.1	87.2	97.9	99.6
Sherman-Denison, TX.	91.2	91.1	75.1	109.9	91.5	100.4	99.1
Tyler, TX.	90.6	85.6	79.9	96.3	101.1	104.9	95.9
Salt Lake City, UT	94.4	106.1	89.6	87.3	97.4	92.0	95.4
Burlington-Chittenden County, VT	114.2	108.2	125.9	116.3	101.0	108.2	109.9
Roanoke, VA.	92.0	89.5	88.5	91.8	90.4	96.6	95.9
Hampton Roads-SE Virginia, VA	101.2	99.2	105.8	114.7	101.7	96.0	95.1
Bellingham, WA	105.6	113.7	112.0	83.6	100.9	121.0	102.2
Olympia, WA.	103.1	107.8	98.8	87.3	103.7	130.3	105.8
Spokane, WA	103.8	106.5	100.3	87.1	96.6	130.2	108.8
Yakima, WA	96.4	110.7	88.5	76.5	99.3	134.9	98.0
Huntington, WV	93.5	101.7	83.9	104.5	95.2	101.8	94.5
Appleton, WI.	91.5	89.3	81.2	100.6	96.6	106.0	95.9
Eau Claire, WI.	99.9	96.7	95.9	95.8	96.6	113.7	104.7
Green Bay, WI.	93.3	84.6	89.6	95.5	99.0	100.2	96.9
Wausau, WI.	93.1	82.9	89.0	110.4	97.6	101.7	93.7
Marshfield, WI.	93.9	89.5	90.4	112.7	95.9	104.9	91.9
Cheyenne, WY	108.7	113.8	117.7	112.3	98.3	96.7	102.2

Source: ACCRA, 4232 King St., Alexandria, VA 22302-1507, *ACCRA Cost of Living Index*, Fourth Quarter 2004 (copyright)

Table 710. Annual Percent Changes From Prior Year in Consumer Prices— United States and OECD Countries: 1990 to 2004

[Covers member countries of Organization for Economic Cooperation (OECD). For consumer price indexes for OECD countries, see Section 30. 1990 change from1989; 1995 change from 1994; 1999 change from 1998]

Country	1990	1995	1999	2000	2001	2002	2003	2004
United States	5.4	2.8	2.2	3.4	2.8	1.5	2.3	2.7
OECD	7.0	5.7	3.4	4.0	3.0	(NA)	(NA)	(NA)
Australia	7.3	4.6	1.5	4.5	3.0	3.0	2.8	2.4
Canada	4.8	2.2	1.7	2.7	4.6	2.2	2.8	1.9
Japan	3.1	-0.1	-0.3	-0.7	-0.2	-2.0	0.8	0.0
New Zealand	6.1	3.8	-0.1	2.6	2.7	2.7	1.8	2.3
Austria	3.3	2.2	0.6	2.4	1.7	1.8	1.3	2.1
Belgium	3.4	1.5	1.1	2.5	1.8	1.8	1.6	2.1
Denmark	2.6	2.1	2.5	2.9	2.9	2.4	2.1	1.2
Finland	6.1	0.8	1.2	3.4	1.9	1.5	0.9	0.2
France	3.6	1.8	0.5	1.7	2.6	1.9	2.1	2.1
Germany	2.7	1.7	0.6	1.9	1.3	1.4	1.0	1.6
Greece	20.4	8.9	2.6	3.2	4.4	3.6	3.6	2.9
Ireland	3.3	2.5	1.6	5.6	5.1	4.7	3.5	2.1
Italy [1]	6.5	5.2	1.7	2.5	2.7	2.5	2.7	2.2
Luxembourg	3.3	1.9	1.0	3.2	2.5	2.1	2.0	2.2
Netherlands	2.5	1.9	2.2	2.5	2.7	3.3	2.2	1.2
Norway [2]	4.1	2.4	2.3	3.1	4.8	1.3	2.5	0.5
Portugal [2]	13.4	4.2	2.3	2.9	4.1	3.5	3.3	2.3
Spain	6.7	4.7	2.3	3.4	3.8	3.1	3.0	3.1
Sweden	10.4	2.9	0.3	1.3	3.3	2.3	2.1	0.5
Switzerland	5.4	1.8	0.8	1.6	1.3	0.7	0.6	0.8
Turkey [2]	60.3	89.1	64.9	54.9	27.0	45.0	25.3	10.7
United Kingdom	9.5	3.4	1.6	2.9	3.2	1.6	2.9	3.0

[1] Households of wage and salary earners. [2] Excludes rent.

Source: Organization for Economic Cooperation and Development, Paris, France, *Main Economic Indicators*, monthly (copyright).

Table 711. Producer Price Indexes by Stage of Processing: 1980 to 2004

[1982 = 100, except as indicated. See Appendix III]

Year	Crude materials				Intermediate materials, supplies, and components	Finished goods		Finished consumer foods		Finished consumer goods excl. food
	Total	Foodstuffs and feedstuffs	Fuel	Crude nonfood materials except fuel		Consumer goods	Capital equipment	Crude	Processed	
1980	95.3	104.6	69.4	91.8	90.3	88.6	85.8	93.9	92.3	87.1
1985	95.8	94.8	102.7	94.3	102.7	103.8	107.5	102.9	104.8	103.3
1990	108.9	113.1	84.8	107.3	114.5	118.2	122.9	123.0	124.4	115.3
1991	101.2	105.5	82.9	97.5	114.4	120.5	126.7	119.3	124.4	118.7
1992	100.4	105.1	84.0	94.2	114.7	121.7	129.1	107.6	124.4	120.8
1993	102.4	108.4	87.1	94.1	116.2	123.0	131.4	114.4	126.5	121.7
1994	101.8	106.5	82.4	97.0	118.5	123.3	134.1	111.3	127.9	121.6
1995	102.7	105.8	72.1	105.8	124.9	125.6	136.7	118.8	129.8	124.0
1996	113.8	121.5	92.6	105.7	125.7	129.5	138.3	129.2	133.8	127.6
1997	111.1	112.2	101.3	103.5	125.6	130.2	138.2	126.6	135.1	128.2
1998	96.8	103.9	86.7	84.5	123.0	128.9	137.6	127.2	134.8	126.4
1999	98.2	98.7	91.2	91.1	123.2	132.0	137.6	125.5	135.9	130.5
2000	120.6	100.2	136.9	118.0	129.2	138.2	138.8	123.5	138.3	138.4
2001	121.0	106.1	151.4	101.5	129.7	141.5	139.7	127.7	142.4	141.4
2002	108.1	99.5	117.3	101.0	127.8	139.4	139.1	128.5	141.0	138.8
2003	135.3	113.5	185.7	116.9	133.7	145.3	139.5	130.0	147.2	144.7
2004, prel.	159.0	126.9	211.8	149.0	142.5	151.6	141.5	137.9	153.7	150.9
PERCENT CHANGE [1]										
1980	10.9	4.6	21.1	21.6	15.2	14.3	10.7	1.7	6.3	18.5
1985	-7.4	-9.5	-2.3	-6.6	-0.4	0.5	2.2	-7.6	-0.1	1.1
1990	5.6	1.7	-0.6	12.0	2.2	5.4	3.5	2.8	4.9	5.9
1991	-7.1	-6.7	-2.2	-9.1	-0.1	1.9	3.1	-3.0	-	2.9
1992	-0.8	-0.4	1.3	-3.4	0.3	1.0	1.9	-9.8	-	1.8
1993	2.0	3.1	3.7	-0.1	1.3	1.1	1.8	6.3	1.7	0.7
1994	-0.6	-1.8	-5.4	3.1	2.0	0.2	2.1	-2.7	1.1	-0.1
1995	0.9	-0.7	-12.5	9.1	5.4	1.9	1.9	6.7	1.5	2.0
1996	10.8	14.8	28.4	-0.1	0.6	3.1	1.2	8.8	3.1	2.9
1997	-2.4	-7.7	9.4	-2.1	-0.1	0.5	-0.1	-2.0	1.0	0.5
1998	-12.9	-7.4	-14.4	-18.4	-2.1	-1.0	-0.4	0.5	-0.2	-1.4
1999	1.4	-5.0	5.2	7.8	0.2	2.4	-	-1.3	0.8	3.2
2000	22.8	1.5	50.1	29.5	4.9	4.7	0.9	-1.6	1.8	6.1
2001	0.3	5.9	10.6	-14.0	0.4	2.4	0.6	3.4	3.0	2.2
2002	-10.7	-6.2	-22.5	-0.5	-1.5	-1.5	-0.4	0.6	-1.0	-1.8
2003	25.2	14.1	58.3	15.7	4.6	4.2	0.3	1.2	4.4	4.3
2004, prel.	17.5	11.8	14.1	27.5	6.6	4.3	1.4	6.1	4.4	4.3

- Represents or rounds to zero. [1] Change from immediate prior year.

Source: U.S. Bureau of Labor Statistics, *Producer Price Indexes*, monthly and annual.

Table 712. **Producer Price Indexes by Stage of Processing: 1990 to 2004**

[1982 = 100, except as indicated. See Appendix III]

Stage of processing	1990	1995	1999	2000	2001	2002	2003	2004[1]
Finished goods	**119.2**	**127.9**	**133.0**	**138.0**	**140.7**	**138.9**	**143.3**	**148.5**
Finished consumer goods	**118.2**	**125.6**	**132.0**	**138.2**	**141.5**	**139.4**	**145.3**	**151.6**
Finished consumer foods	**124.4**	**129.0**	**135.1**	**137.2**	**141.3**	**140.1**	**145.9**	**152.6**
Fresh fruits and melons	118.1	85.8	103.6	91.4	97.7	91.5	84.1	104.3
Fresh and dry vegetables	118.1	144.4	118.0	126.7	124.7	136.5	135.7	129.4
Eggs for fresh use (Dec. 1991 = 100)	(NA)	86.3	77.9	84.9	81.8	82.9	106.6	100.0
Bakery products	141.0	164.3	178.0	182.3	187.7	189.9	195.0	195.9
Milled rice	102.5	113.1	121.3	101.2	87.3	80.3	102.5	135.4
Pasta products (June 1985 = 100)	114.1	125.0	122.1	121.6	122.1	121.7	126.4	127.1
Beef and veal	116.0	100.9	106.3	113.7	120.6	114.7	137.9	141.2
Pork	119.8	101.5	96.0	113.4	120.3	109.0	115.7	132.6
Processed young chickens	111.0	113.5	113.4	110.4	117.2	109.7	119.7	138.9
Processed turkeys	107.6	104.9	94.8	98.7	98.9	95.3	92.5	107.4
Finfish and shellfish	147.2	170.8	190.9	198.1	190.8	191.2	195.3	206.0
Dairy products	117.2	119.7	139.2	133.7	145.2	136.2	139.4	156.0
Processed fruits and vegetables	124.7	122.4	128.1	128.6	129.6	132.6	133.8	135.1
Confectionery end products	140.0	160.7	170.4	170.6	171.4	175.6	183.7	188.8
Soft drinks	122.3	133.1	137.9	144.1	148.2	151.3	153.0	156.8
Roasted coffee	113.0	146.5	134.7	133.5	124.2	121.5	127.3	129.2
Shortening and cooking oils	123.2	142.5	140.4	132.4	132.9	140.8	160.8	193.8
Finished consumer goods excluding foods . . .	**115.3**	**124.0**	**130.5**	**138.4**	**141.4**	**138.8**	**144.7**	**150.9**
Alcoholic beverages	117.2	128.5	136.7	140.6	145.4	147.0	148.9	153.1
Women's apparel	116.1	119.6	123.9	124.6	123.7	122.7	124.4	(NA)
Men's and boy's apparel	120.2	130.3	133.1	133.2	132.4	129.0	127.2	(NA)
Girls', children's, and infants' apparel	115.3	121.6	118.2	117.4	116.6	118.4	119.5	(NA)
Textile house furnishings	109.5	119.5	122.7	122.0	122.5	122.3	122.4	123.4
Footwear	125.6	139.2	144.5	144.9	145.8	146.0	147.1	146.3
Residential electric power (Dec. 1990 = 100)	(NA)	111.8	109.5	110.8	116.6	115.4	118.8	121.5
Residential gas (Dec. 1990 = 100)	(NA)	104.4	114.3	135.5	158.7	131.9	167.6	183.1
Gasoline	78.7	63.7	64.7	94.6	90.5	83.3	102.7	128.1
Fuel oil No. 2	73.3	56.6	56.1	93.5	84.3	75.0	95.3	120.6
Soaps and synthetic detergents	117.7	122.9	126.3	128.2	130.6	130.0	130.9	133.0
Cosmetics and other toilet preparations	121.6	129.0	135.4	137.4	138.5	139.4	140.4	140.5
Tires, tubes, and tread	96.8	100.2	92.9	93.0	94.1	95.2	97.9	102.4
Sanitary papers and health products	135.3	144.4	144.3	146.7	147.3	149.3	150.5	148.5
Newspaper circulation	144.1	185.6	207.1	210.0	219.5	225.6	230.5	233.6
Periodical circulation	150.3	176.6	196.9	198.9	200.7	210.0	219.9	223.2
Book publishing	153.4	185.0	213.0	218.2	225.5	234.8	243.1	252.7
Household furniture	125.1	141.8	150.5	152.7	154.9	157.1	158.2	160.5
Floor coverings	119.0	123.7	127.2	129.6	130.2	130.5	133.6	136.7
Household appliances	110.8	112.4	108.5	107.3	105.3	104.6	102.4	101.5
Home electronic equipment	82.7	78.9	73.7	71.8	70.4	69.0	67.7	65.0
Household glassware	132.5	153.2	163.9	166.0	169.6	169.9	168.9	171.4
Household flatware	122.1	138.3	139.7	142.6	142.8	144.7	145.2	145.4
Lawn and garden equipment, except tractors	123.0	130.4	132.0	132.0	132.8	133.9	133.5	134.6
Passenger cars	118.3	134.1	131.3	132.8	132.0	129.5	129.5	131.8
Toys, games, and children's vehicles	118.1	124.3	123.1	121.9	123.4	124.8	124.9	125.1
Sporting and athletic goods	112.6	122.0	126.2	126.1	126.3	125.5	124.0	123.7
Tobacco products	221.4	231.3	374.0	397.2	441.9	459.4	431.6	433.7
Mobile homes	117.5	145.6	158.4	161.3	164.1	166.6	169.6	186.7
Jewelry, platinum, and karat gold	122.8	127.8	127.1	127.2	128.5	130.0	132.4	135.3
Costume jewelry and novelties	125.3	135.1	140.1	141.6	144.0	144.2	144.9	147.3
Capital equipment	**122.9**	**136.7**	**137.6**	**138.8**	**139.7**	**139.1**	**139.5**	**141.5**
Agricultural machinery and equipment	121.7	142.9	152.1	153.7	156.1	158.5	160.9	165.9
Construction machinery and equipment	121.6	136.7	147.2	148.6	149.1	151.1	153.2	158.6
Metal cutting machine tools	129.8	148.0	160.7	161.9	158.8	152.4	150.6	151.5
Metal forming machine tools	128.7	145.7	159.7	161.8	164.8	166.8	167.6	171.6
Tools, dies, jigs, fixtures, and industrial molds	117.2	133.8	139.8	141.1	141.3	140.6	139.5	139.4
Pumps, compressors, and equipment	119.2	139.4	151.7	154.1	157.6	161.0	162.9	167.4
Industrial material handling equipment	115.0	125.3	132.9	134.7	136.8	136.9	137.9	143.4

See footnote at end of table.

U.S. Census Bureau, Statistical Abstract of the United States: 2006

Table 712. **Producer Price Indexes by Stage of Processing: 1990 to 2004—Con.**

[1982 = 100, except as indicated]

Stage of processing	1990	1995	1999	2000	2001	2002	2003	2004[1]
Capital Equipment—Continued								
Electronic computers (Dec. 1990 = 100)	(NA)	237.2	87.2	73.0	56.7	42.8	34.1	29.9
Textile machinery	128.8	146.7	154.2	156.2	158.0	157.0	157.6	158.3
Paper industries machinery (June 1982 = 100)	134.8	151.0	162.6	164.7	166.8	168.9	170.3	173.7
Printing trades machinery	124.9	133.6	141.0	142.1	143.3	143.7	143.1	143.4
Transformers and power regulators	120.9	128.9	132.6	135.8	134.4	131.7	131.9	135.9
Communication/related equip.(Dec. 1985 = 100)	106.1	112.1	112.7	110.6	109.5	107.6	105.5	103.5
X-ray and electromedical equipment	109.8	111.8	104.3	101.5	100.2	100.9	100.5	97.6
Oil field and gas field machinery	102.4	114.1	126.5	128.2	134:3	135.8	139.6	143.5
Mining machinery and equipment	121.0	135.6	144.2	146.1	148.5	151.8	155.2	163.3
Office and store machines and equipment	109.5	111.5	112.3	112.7	112.7	112.5	113.2	113.6
Commercial furniture.	133.4	148.2	156.6	158.4	160.3	160.9	162.3	165.5
Light motor trucks.	130.0	159.0	157.5	157.6	155.0	150.5	150.2	151.4
Heavy motor trucks.	120.3	144.1	146.5	148.0	147.7	152.2	154.2	155.3
Truck trailers	110.8	131.7	136.3	139.4	138.8	138.1	139.4	148.1
Civilian aircraft (Dec. 1985 = 100)	115.3	141.8	151.7	159.6	168.5	171.3	179.9	190.4
Ships (Dec. 1985 = 100)	110.1	132.8	145.8	146.9	148.9	150.6	159.4	171.9
Railroad equipment.	118.6	134.8	135.2	135.7	135.2	134.9	136.3	143.6
Intermediate materials, supplies,								
and components.	**114.5**	**124.9**	**123.2**	**129.2**	**129.7**	**127.8**	**133.7**	**142.5**
Intermediate foods and feeds	**113.3**	**114.8**	**111.1**	**111.7**	**115.9**	**115.5**	**125.9**	**137.0**
Flour	103.6	123.0	104.3	103.8	109.9	116.2	123.6	129.0
Refined sugar	122.7	119.3	121.0	110.6	109.9	117.7	121.8	120.9
Confectionery materials.	101.2	109.1	94.0	94.2	105.8	117.4	125.1	125.3
Crude vegetable oils	115.8	130.0	90.2	73.6	70.1	87.6	128.3	(NA)
Prepared animal feeds	107.4	109.1	98.3	102.9	105.1	105.7	112.8	124.6
Intermediate materials less foods and feed. . . .	**114.5**	**125.5**	**123.9**	**130.1**	**130.5**	**128.5**	**134.2**	**142.9**
Synthetic fibers	106.7	109.4	103.8	107.2	108.6	106.2	106.4	106.5
Processed yarns and threads.	112.6	112.8	108.6	107.9	105.6	102.6	103.6	108.6
Gray fabrics	117.2	121.2	114.4	113.2	114.0	112.6	111.1	112.8
Leather	177.5	191.4	176.3	182.2	200.9	202.5	214.0	220.8
Liquefied petroleum gas	77.4	65.1	73.7	127.1	119.0	104.5	150.9	192.6
Commercial electric power.	115.3	131.7	129.1	131.5	139.6	137.5	140.9	142.7
Industrial electric power.	119.6	130.8	128.9	131.5	141.1	139.9	145.8	147.5
Commercial natural gas (Dec. 1990 = 100).	(NA)	96.5	108.1	134.7	168.3	135.0	173.6	194.8
Industrial natural gas (Dec. 1990 = 100).	(NA)	90.9	103.3	139.0	177.3	136.5	180.5	201.2
Natural gas to electric utilities (Dec. 1990 = 100) . . .	(NA)	87.7	81.6	120.7	146.5	103.9	158.2	171.2
Jet fuels	76.0	55.0	52.5	88.5	77.4	71.6	86.3	111.4
No. 2 Diesel fuel	74.1	57.0	57.3	93.3	83.4	77.9	100.5	128.2
Residual fuel	57.7	52.6	51.5	84.7	74.6	75.4	101.2	100.2
Industrial chemicals	113.2	128.4	118.9	129.1	128.4	127.3	141.7	162.5
Prepared paint.	124.8	142.1	157.4	160.8	164.4	166.9	170.8	175.7
Paint materials.	136.3	139.4	144.1	148.5	149.8	165.9	172.9	180.1
Medicinal and botanical chemicals.	102.2	128.3	142.2	146.2	141.2	132.6	135.3	135.0
Fats and oils, inedible	88.1	126.9	88.4	70.1	77.6	90.3	123.4	152.8
Mixed fertilizers	103.3	111.1	113.7	112.4	116.6	113.9	119.1	127.8
Nitrogenates	92.3	129.4	94.6	118.2	143.0	106.0	146.5	168.7
Phosphates.	96.5	109.1	112.0	96.9	95.2	99.8	109.6	120.9
Other agricultural chemicals	119.9	144.3	144.5	146.1	148.3	148.5	148.8	149.3
Plastic resins and materials	124.1	143.5	125.8	141.6	134.2	130.7	146.1	162.4
Synthetic rubber.	111.9	126.3	113.9	119.1	122.9	119.3	125.7	132.4
Plastic construction products	117.2	133.8	128.0	135.8	132.9	136.1	138.6	144.8
Unsupported plastic film, sheet, and shapes	119.0	135.6	127.5	133.2	138.0	136.5	142.8	148.6
Plastic parts and components for manufacturing	112.9	115.9	117.4	117.3	116.9	116.2	116.3	116.6
Softwood lumber	123.8	178.5	196.0	178.6	170.1	170.8	170.8	210.0
Hardwood lumber.	131.0	167.0	177.3	185.9	181.3	178.3	188.8	199.3
Millwork	130.4	163.8	174.7	176.4	179.2	179.8	181.8	191.9
Plywood.	114.2	165.3	176.4	157.6	154.3	151.7	167.0	198.5
Woodpile	151.3	183.2	119.7	145.3	125.8	116.2	121.4	132.4
Paper.	128.8	159.0	141.8	149.8	150.6	144.7	146.1	149.4
Paperboard.	135.7	183.1	153.2	176.7	172.1	164.3	162.7	170.3
Paper boxes and containers.	129.9	163.8	158.0	172.6	175.2	172.8	172.9	177.5
Building paper and board.	112.2	144.9	141.6	138.8	129.3	129.3	159.9	192.1

See footnotes at end of table.

490 Prices

Table 712. **Producer Price Indexes by Stage of Processing: 1990 to 2004—Con.**

[1982 = 100, except as indicated]

Stage of processing	1990	1995	1999	2000	2001	2002	2003	2004 [1]
Intermediate materials less foods and feeds—Continued								
Commercial printing (June 1982 = 100)	128.0	144.5	152.2	155.2	157.6	157.0	158.3	159.5
Foundry and forge shop products	117.2	129.3	135.1	136.5	136.9	136.8	137.4	143.9
Steel·mill products	112.1	120.1	105.3	108.4	101.3	104.8	109.5	147.0
Primary nonferrous metals	133.4	146.8	101.5	113.6	105.2	100.8	104.8	133.6
Aluminum mill shapes	127.9	160.4	138.1	149.0	148.7	143.3	143.3	150.9
Copper and brass mill shapes	174.6	195.2	151.2	162.3	155.0	149.6	152.3	199.9
Nonferrous wire and cable	142.6	151.5	135.6	143.7	140.4	134.3	134.5	152.0
Metal containers.	114.0	117.2	106.4	106.8	106.3	107.8	109.2	115.8
Hardware	125.9	141.1	148.7	151.2	154.4	156.0	156.5	161.5
Plumbing fixtures and brass fittings	144.3	166.0	176.7	180.4	180.8	181.9	183.4	188.1
Heating equipment	131.6	147.5	154.0	155.6	157.1	157.9	163.2	169.5
Fabricated structural metal products	121.8	135.1	143.3	144.9	144.6	145.0	145.5	163.4
Fabricated ferrous wire products (June 1982 = 100)	114.6	125.7	130.6	130.0	129.8	129.7	131.3	149.4
Other miscellaneous metal products	120.7	124.9	125.5	126.0	127.0	126.8	127.4	132.0
Mechanical power transmission equipment	125.3	146.9	161.1	163.9	167.0	169.5	171.7	179.2
Air conditioning and refrigeration equipment	122.1	130.2	135.5	135.3	136.0	136.9	137.2	139.5
Metal valves, excluding fluid power (Dec. 1982 = 100)	125.3	145.3	160.2	162.1	164.7	167.2	169.4	176.3
Ball and roller bearings	130.6	152.0	166.8	168.8	169.5	170.0	171.3	177.2
Wiring devices	132.2	147.2	152.5	152.9	153.5	153.8	152.9	169.1
Motors, generators, motor generator sets	132.9	143.9	145.9	146.2	146.8	146.8	147.4	149.8
Switchgear and switchboard equipment	124.4	140.3	151.0	153.0	156.9	158.4	159.9	163.7
Electronic components and accessories	118.4	113.6	98.2	97.1	93.9	92.4	90.8	88.9
Internal combustion engines.	120.2	135.6	143.0	143.8	143.9	144.4	144.6	145.9
Machine shop products	124.3	131.3	136.8	138.0	140.1	140.0	140.7	144.5
Flat glass	107.5	113.2	106.4	109.7	112.0	111.2	111.0	108.7
Cement	103.7	128.1	150.6	150.1	150.2	152.6	152.0	156.5
Concrete products	113.5	129.4	143.7	147.8	151.7	152.7	153.6	161.2
Asphalt felts and coatings	97.1	100.0	99.2	104.1	107.5	110.9	116.4	117.9
Gypsum products	105.2	154.5	208.0	201.4	156.4	168.9	171.5	199.0
Glass containers	120.4	130.5	125.9	127.4	132.9	135.6	140.2	144.4
Motor vehicle parts.	111.2	116.0	114.0	113.6	113.3	112.9	111.8	112.0
Aircraft engines and engine parts (Dec. 1985 = 100)	113.5	132.8	138.5	141.0	145.1	145.7	153.8	163.0
Aircraft parts and auxiliary equipment, n.e.c. [2] (June 1985 = 100)	117.7	135.7	143.7	145.7	149.2	151.1	150.6	151.9
Photographic supplies.	127.6	126.8	128.3	125.2	128.5	121.6	117.5	115.2
Medical/surgical/personal aid devices.	127.3	141.3	144.6	146.0	148.3	150.9	154.7	158.0
Crude materials for further processing . . .	**108.9**	**102.7**	**98.2**	**120.6**	**121.0**	**108.1**	**135.3**	**159.0**
Crude foodstuffs and feedstuffs	113.1	105.8	98.7	100.2	106.1	99.5	113.5	126.9
Wheat	87.6	118.6	79.5	80.3	85.5	97.9	98.5	106.0
Corn	100.9	109.0	78.2	76.4	78.8	89.4	93.8	97.5
Slaughter cattle	122.5	99.5	97.6	104.1	108.4	100.8	124.3	126.2
Slaughter hogs	94.1	70.2	53.8	72.7	73.4	55.4	66.1	87.8
Slaughter broilers/fryers.	119.5	129.1	134.5	127.6	138.4	125.9	149.3	188.5
Slaughter turkeys	116.9	120.3	120.0	120.7	110.3	104.3	102.8	122.0
Fluid milk	100.8	93.6	106.3	92.0	111.8	90.8	93.8	119.9
Soybeans	100.8	102.2	80.1	83.4	78.6	87.7	108.8	130.0
Cane sugar, raw.	119.2	119.7	113.7	101.8	111.4	110.9	114.0	(NA)
Crude nonfood materials.	101.5	96.8	94.3	130.4.	126.8	111.4	148.2	179.2
Raw cotton	118.2	156.2	87.4	95.2	67.2	61.5	92.9	85.6
Leaf tobacco	95.8	102.5	101.6	(NA)	105.2	(NA)	102.0	92.7
Cattle hides.	217.8	209.9	141.9	169.4	(NA)	(NA)	(NA)	(NA)
Coal.	97.5	95.0	90.7	87.9	96.2	99.8	99.9	109.3
Natural gas.	80.4	66.6	92.5	155.5	171.8	122.5	214.5	246.4
Crude petroleum	71.0	51.1	50.3	85.2	69.2	67.9	83.0	107.9
Logs and timber.	142.8	220.4	202.0	196.4	182.8	180.1	181.8	193.4
Wastepaper.	138.9	371.1	183.6	282.5	148.6	173.1	197.3	231.5
Iron ore	83.3	91.8	94.9	94.8	96.2	95.2	95.9	98.6
Iron and steel scrap	166.0	202.7	139.2	142.1	120.0	141.4	182.6	322.9
Nonferrous metal ores (Dec. 1983 = 100)	98.3	101.6	63.1	68.0	63.7	68.1	78.5	113.1
Copper base scrap.	181.3	193.5	108.2	123.7	114.8	111.4	128.4	187.0
Aluminum base scrap	172.6	209.4	161.7	177.0	156.5	158.0	168.7	193.6
Construction sand, gravel, and crushed stone	125.4	142.3	157.2	163.1	168.8	173.0	177.1	183.3

NA Not available. [1] Preliminary data. [2] n.e.c. Not elsewhere classified.

Source: U.S. Bureau of Labor Statistics, *Producer Price Indexes*, monthly and annual.

Table 713. Producer Price Indexes for the Net Output of Selected Industries: 2000 to 2004

[Indexes are based on selling prices reported by establishments of all sizes by probability sampling. Manufacturing industries selected by shipment value. n.e.c.= not elsewhere classified. See text, Section 22, Domestic Trade. See Appendix III]

Industry	NAICS code [1]	Index base [2]	2000	2001	2002	2003	2004 [3]
Logging.	113310	12/81	177.6	167.6	165.1	168.8	175.4
Total mining industries	21	12/84	113.5	114.3	96.6	131.3	153.4
Crude petroleum & natural gas extraction	211111	06/02	(NA)	(NA)	(NA)	152.3	183.6
Natural gas liquid extraction	211112	06/02	(NA)	(NA)	(NA)	181.2	216.0
Bituminous coal & lignite surface mining	212111	12/01	(NA)	(NA)	101.9	101.5	107.5
Anthracite mining	212113	12/79	157.3	161.0	163.0	168.4	180.9
Iron ore mining	212210	12/84	93.9	95.2	94.2	95.0	97.6
Gold ore mining	212221	06/85	84.2	81.5	92.4	107.6	121.3
Silver ore mining	212222	12/83	(NA)	(NA)	(NA)	(NA)	(NA)
Copper ore & nickel ore mining	212234	06/88	88.7	81.7	80.1	90.1	150.4
Metal ores, n.e.c.	212299	12/85	85.8	77.9	91.6	113.2	(NA)
Dimension stone mining and quarrying	212311	06/85	153.4	156.9	164.0	169.9	173.2
Crushed and broken limestone mining and quarrying. . .	212312	12/83	145.6	150.9	154.7	159.2	165.3
Crushed and broken granite mining and quarrying.	212313	12/83	182.3	188.3	193.2	197.5	203.5
Other crushed and broken stone mining and quarrying. . .	212319	12/83	153.1	156.8	160.8	164.0	170.3
Construction sand and gravel mining	212321	06/82	175.5	181.6	185.8	188.9	195.1
Industrial sand mining	212322	06/82	148.0	154.3	157.1	162.1	167.2
Kaolin and ball clay mining	212324	06/84	113.3	119.6	118.8	121.0	122.7
Clay and ceramic and refractory minerals mining	212325	06/84	135.7	140.3	140.9	142.5	144.4
Potash, soda, and borate mineral mining.	212391	12/84	111.6	110.0	107.7	106.1	110.7
Drilling oil and gas wells.	213111	12/85	138.2	173.9	153.5	153.5	167.9
Oil & gas operations support activities.	213112	12/85	123.3	142.4	137.4	135.6	142.2
Nonmetallic minerals support activity (except fuels)	213115	06/85	107.2	109.3	110.5	114.6	119.7
Total manufacturing industries	31-33	12/84	133.5	134.6	133.7	137.1	142.9
Dog & cat food mfg.	311111	12/85	131.3	134.7	135.7	136.2	144.0
Flour milling	311211	06/83	97.2	101.9	107.6	113.7	117.3
Rice milling	311212	06/84	89.3	81.9	72.2	87.6	113.0
Soybean processing	311222	12/79	69.1	67.3	72.1	87.1	101.7
Fats and oils refining and blending	311225	12/81	131.8	131.5	138.1	158.1	186.8
Chocolate & confectionery mfg. from cacao beans	311320	06/83	132.1	138.6	148.1	156.2	155.0
Confectionery mfg. (purchased chocolate)	311330	12/03	(NA)	(NA)	(NA)	(NA)	100.1
Frozen fruit, juice, & vegetable mfg.	311411	06/81	141.0	140.2	144.1	147.8	149.1
Frozen specialty food mfg.	311412	12/82	136.1	138.8	139.0	139.2	142.1
Fruit and vegetable canning	311421	06/81	139.1	142.2	143.7	144.8	146.3
Specialty canning	311422	12/82	171.5	173.8	174.6	176.1	177.6
Fluid milk.	311511	12/82	141.8	153.6	146.4	147.7	162.3
Ice cream and frozen dessert mfg.	311520	06/83	150.4	157.1	158.8	160.6	165.8
Animal (except poultry) slaughtering	311611	12/80	113.4	120.3	113.1	130.1	137.7
Meat processed from carcasses	311612	12/82	121.3	125.8	121.1	129.7	132.4
Poultry processing.	311615	12/81	118.3	121.5	115.9	121.9	137.4
Seafood canning	311711	12/82	103.8	108.9	110.3	110.2	115.3
Fresh & frozen seafood processing	311712	12/82	171.5	161.7	157.2	161.5	164.1
Frozen cakes, pies, & other pastries mfg.	311813	06/91	116.8	119.5	120.9	124.8	127.6
Cookie and cracker manufacturing	311821	06/83	172.0	173.3	175.0	181.6	183.4
Flour mixes & dough mfg. from purch flour.	311822	06/85	122.0	124.6	126.4	131.9	133.9
Dry pasta manufacturing	311823	06/85	121.9	122.4	122.0	126.3	127.0
Coffee and tea manufacturing	311920	06/81	144.3	136.4	133.8	139.4	141.4
Mayonnaise, dressing, & other sauces mfg.	311941	12/03	(NA)	(NA)	(NA)	(NA)	101.6
Spice and extracts manufacturing	311942	12/03	(NA)	(NA)	(NA)	(NA)	100.4
Soft drinks manufacturing	312111	06/81	152.0	156.5	159.5	161.5	165.7
Bottled water manufacturing	312112	12/03	(NA)	(NA)	(NA)	(NA)	100.7
Breweries	312120	06/82	136.1	140.5	142.7	145.8	152.4
Wineries	312130	12/83	139.9	141.3	141.7	140.8	139.7
Distilleries	312140	06/83	153.5	165.1	164.9	165.1	164.7
Tobacco stemming & redrying	312210	06/84	109.0	112.3	114.7	117.5	119.4
Cigarettes	312221	12/82	379.2	425.8	442.8	411.7	412.4
Other tobacco product mfg.	312229	12/03	(NA)	(NA)	(NA)	(NA)	99.6
Broadwoven fabric finishing mills	313311	12/03	(NA)	(NA)	(NA)	(NA)	100.1
Textile/fabric finishing (exc broadwoven) mills	313312	12/03	(NA)	(NA)	(NA)	(NA)	99.5
Underwear & nightwear knitting mills.	315192	06/82	134.5	131.5	130.1	129.1	128.6
Men's/boys' cut & sew trouser/slack/jean mfg.	315224	12/81	134.8	135.1	132.2	128.4	126.4
Women's/girls' cut & sew dress mfg.	315233	12/80	125.8	123.6	122.1	122.8	124.9
Women's/girls' cut & sew other outerwear mfg.	315239	06/83	113.3	112.1	111.5	112.9	112.2
Sawmills	321113	12/80	140.8	141.2	139.1	141.1	163.5
Wood preservation	321114	06/85	156.2	152.7	151.6	154.0	167.7
Hardwood veneer & plywood manufacturing.	321211	06/85	142.7	142.5	142.3	138.6	143.7
Softwood veneer or plywood, mfg.	321212	12/80	140.4	135.8	131.8	154.4	189.1
Engineered wood member (exc truss) mfg.	321213	12/03	(NA)	(NA)	(NA)	(NA)	110.0
Truss mfg.	321214	12/03	(NA)	(NA)	(NA)	(NA)	112.5
Reconstituted wood product mfg.	321219	06/91	121.1	112.5	112.3	139.1	167.8
Wood window & door mfg.	321911	12/03	(NA)	(NA)	(NA)	(NA)	101.9
Manufactured homes (mobile homes) mfg.	321991	06/81	167.1	170.0	172.6	175.8	190.1
Pulp mills.	322110	12/82	143.4	122.9	116.5	120.9	131.5
Paper (except newsprint) mills	322121	12/03	(NA)	(NA)	(NA)	(NA)	102.4
Newsprint mills	322122	12/03	(NA)	(NA)	(NA)	(NA)	104.0
Paperboard mills	322130	12/82	192.4	187.4	179.7	180.4	190.3
Digital printing.	323115	12/03	(NA)	(NA)	(NA)	(NA)	99.4
Book printing	323117	12/83	153.1	154.1	150.7	150.2	151.5
Petroleum refineries.	324110	06/85	111.6	103.1	96.3	121.2	151.3
Petroleum lubricating oils and greases	324191	12/80	172.3	183.3	185.5	191.5	199.3
Industrial gas manufacturing	325120	12/03	(NA)	(NA)	(NA)	(NA)	108.2

See footnotes at end of table.

[See headnote, page 492]

Industry	NAICS code [1]	Index base [2]	2000	2001	2002	2003	2004 [3]
Plastics material and resins manufacturing	325211	12/80	164.3	159.9	148.9	167.8	191.5
Synthetic rubber manufacturing.	325212	06/81	119.2	122.5	119.1	125.2	131.6
Nitrogenous fertilizer manufacturing.	325311	12/79	144.7	171.7	131.6	177.0	203.9
Phosphatic fertilizer manufacturing	325312	12/79	119.0	129.4	132.8	145.4	161.3
Fertilizer (mixing only) manufacturing.	325314	12/79	142.3	147.0	143.3	149.2	157.1
Pesticide and other agricultural chemical mfg.	325320	06/82	136.6	138.0	138.2	138.1	138.5
Pharmaceutical preparation mfg.	325412	06/81	306.6	314.5	326.7	343.3	360.3
Photo film, paper, plate & chemical mfg.	325992	12/03	(NA)	(NA)	(NA)	(NA)	99.2
Plastics pipe and pipe fitting manufacturing.	326122	06/93	128.5	107.8	114.6	124.7	141.1
Cement manufacturing	327310	06/82	148.7	148.7	151.1	150.5	155.1
Lime	327410	12/85	120.0	122.7	126.1	128.1	133.0
Cut stone and stone products.	327991	12/84	144.8	147.9	149.3	149.7	149.5
Steel investment foundries	331512	06/81	203.8	205.0	205.6	199.8	197.5
Steel foundries (except investment)	331513	06/81	137.3	136.7	135.3	137.5	144.6
Aluminum die-casting foundries.	331521	06/91	109.9	110.0	109.6	111.5	113.9
Iron & steel forging.	332111	12/83	115.8	114.7	112.9	112.8	117.4
Hand and edge tools, except machine tools and handsaws	332212	06/83	158.4	162.5	164.7	165.1	168.7
Saw blade & handsaw mfg.	332213	06/83	139.4	139.9	142.0	142.9	142.9
Metal window and door manufacturing	332321	06/83	156.1	158.1	159.2	161.0	166.5
Sheet metal work mfg.	332322	12/82	141.8	141.5	142.9	144.4	159.3
Heating equipment (except warm air furnaces) mfg.	333414	06/80	192.8	195.0	196.3	199.8	206.2
Electronic computer mfg.	334111	12/98	80.8	71.3	61.1	49.1	43.1
Computer storage device mfg.	334112	12/98	85.2	78.2	64.2	55.4	49.5
Computer terminal mfg.	334113	12/93	91.0	90.7	88.5	86.4	85.3
Telephone apparatus mfg.	334210	12/85	113.1	108.8	104.6	100.9	96.0
Radio/TV broadcast & wireless comm equip mfg.	334220	12/91	101.5	101.7	98.2	95.1	93.5
Audio & video equipment mfg.	334310	03/80	76.1	74.6	74.0	72.8	70.9
Laboratory apparatus and furniture	339111	12/91	127.1	129.4	132.7	137.3	140.9
Surgical and medical instrument mfg.	339112	06/82	127.2	128.7	130.8	133.1	134.7
Services industries							
Recyclable materials wholesalers	421930	12/86	152.8	123.9	129.3	151.6	220.7
New car dealers.	441110	12/99	99.7	103.1	108.7	111.5	113.6
Recreational vehicle dealers.	441210	06/01	(NA)	(NA)	112.2	109.7	121.6
Boat dealers	441222	06/01	(NA)	(NA)	107.9	113.8	116.2
Automotive parts and accessories stores	441310	12/03	(NA)	(NA)	(NA)	(NA)	106.0
Household appliance stores	443111	06/03	(NA)	(NA)	(NA)	(NA)	93.9
Radio, TV, and other electronics stores	443112	06/03	(NA)	(NA)	(NA)	(NA)	100.1
Computer and software stores	443120	06/03	(NA)	(NA)	(NA)	(NA)	93.8
Hardware stores.	444130	06/03	(NA)	(NA)	(NA)	(NA)	103.3
Nursery, garden, and farm supply stores.	444220	12/02	(NA)	(NA)	(NA)	102.1	112.5
Grocery (except convenience) stores.	445110	12/99	104.2	109.9	113.6	117.9	123.5
Specialty food stores	445200	12/03	(NA)	(NA)	(NA)	(NA)	107.0
Beer, wine, and liquor stores	445310	06/00	(NA)	102.9	103.5	106.9	110.7
Food (health) supplement stores	446191	12/99	102.3	123.5	130.6	139.1	145.3
Gasoline stations with convenience stores	447110	12/03	(NA)	(NA)	(NA)	(NA)	102.1
Men's clothing stores	448110	06/02	(NA)	(NA)	(NA)	102.2	103.0
Women's clothing stores	448120	06/03	(NA)	(NA)	(NA)	(NA)	105.0
Family clothing stores	448140	06/03	(NA)	(NA)	(NA)	(NA)	103.9
Luggage and leather goods stores	448320	06/00	(NA)	103.6	93.6	94.7	98.5
Sporting goods stores	451110	06/00	(NA)	103.6	107.2	104.4	99.3
Book stores.	451211	06/00	(NA)	108.0	106.9	113.7	118.7
Discount department stores	452112	12/03	(NA)	(NA)	(NA)	(NA)	105.9
Office supplies and stationery stores	453210	06/00	(NA)	107.3	114.8	124.3	125.7
Manufactured (mobile) home dealers	453930	12/02	(NA)	(NA)	(NA)	103.6	114.3
Mail-order houses.	454113	06/00	(NA)	90.9	93.5	92.8	94.5
Scheduled passenger air transportation	481111	12/89	186.5	200.6	200.4	205.7	205.9
Scheduled freight air transportation	481112	12/03	(NA)	(NA)	(NA)	(NA)	100.4
General freight trucking, local	484110	12/03	(NA)	(NA)	(NA)	(NA)	104.9
General freight trucking, long-distance	484121	12/03	(NA)	(NA)	(NA)	(NA)	102.6
Used household and office goods moving.	484210	12/03	(NA)	(NA)	(NA)	(NA)	102.4
Marine cargo handling.	488320	12/91	109.1	111.4	110.9	111.5	113.1
Navigational services to shipping.	488330	12/92	124.2	125.4	127.4	129.3	132.9
Freight transportation arrangement	488510	12/94	100.3	100.3	99.5	99.9	101.0
United States Postal Service	491110	06/89	135.2	143.4	150.2	155.0	155.0
Couriers	492110	12/03	(NA)	(NA)	(NA)	(NA)	106.3
Newspaper publishers.	511110	12/79	351.2	367.9	381.8	395.6	409.5
Periodical publishers.	511120	12/79	292.6	305.9	320.4	332.3	338.7
Software publishers	511210	12/97	100.8	101.4	98.0	96.9	94.2
Commercial banking.	522110	12/03	(NA)	(NA)	(NA)	(NA)	102.6
Savings institutions.	522120	12/03	(NA)	(NA)	(NA)	(NA)	100.8
Direct life insurance carriers.	524113	12/98	99.2	100.1	101.6	103.4	105.2
Direct health and medical insurance carriers	524114	12/02	(NA)	(NA)	(NA)	106.2	111.7
Direct property and casualty insurance carriers	524126	06/98	102.0	104.4	108.8	115.1	118.8
Insurance agencies and brokerages	524210	12/02	(NA)	(NA)	(NA)	102.3	104.4
Nursing care facilities	623110	12/94	131.0	139.3	144.6	149.4	155.4
Hotels (exc. casino hotels) and motels	721110	12/03	(NA)	(NA)	(NA)	(NA)	103.1
Casino hotels	721120	12/03	(NA)	(NA)	(NA)	(NA)	105.0

NA Not available.   n.e.c. Not elsewhere classified.   [1] North American Industry Classification System.   [2] Index base year equals 100.   [3] Preliminary data.

Source: U.S. Bureau of Labor Statistics, *Producer Price Indexes*, monthly.

Prices   493

Table 714. Commodity Research Bureau Futures Price Index: 1980 to 2004

[1967 = 100. Index computed daily. Represents unweighted geometric average of commodity futures prices (through 6 months forward) of 17 major commodity futures markets. Represents end-of-year index]

Item	1980	1985	1990	1995	1997	1998	1999	2000	2001	2002	2003	2004
All commodities	308.5	229.2	222.6	243.2	229.1	191.2	205.1	227.8	190.6	234.5	255.3	283.9
Softs [1]	426.0	398.2	276.0	354.4	408.7	344.8	280.9	254.4	252.8	303.7	250.5	343.5
Industrials	324.6	211.7	245.5	272.5	210.9	185.3	192.9	211.0	141.8	176.6	256.6	232.1
Grains and oilseeds [2]	312.1	198.5	171.2	218.6	210.7	172.8	156.6	174.9	159.0	188.2	225.8	177.0
Energy	(NA)	96.5	246.0	180.0	180.4	135.0	221.0	355.8	204.9	320.7	358.7	457.3
Oilseeds [3]	314.6	245.4	223.6	277.5	(³)	(³)	(³)	(³)	(³)	(³)	(³)	(³)
Livestock and meats	217.4	206.9	226.2	192.4	238.1	186.7	239.6	253.6	247.4	251.0	237.8	303.6
Metals (precious)	531.4	256.6	257.8	276.0	249.3	234.3	253.4	265.7	246.8	289.1	364.1	396.6

NA Not available. [1] Prior to 1997, reported as Imported. Softs include commodities that are grown and not mined such as coffee, cocoa, lumber, cotton and sugar. [2] Prior to 1997, reported as Grains. [3] Incorporated into Grains and Oilseeds beginning 1997.

Source: Commodity Research Bureau (CRB), Chicago, IL, *CRB Commodity Index Report*, weekly (copyright).

Table 715. Indexes of Spot Primary Market Prices: 1980 to 2004

[1967 = 100. Computed weekly for 1980; daily thereafter. Represents unweighted geometric average of price quotations of 23 commodities; much more sensitive to changes in market conditions than is a monthly producer price index]

Items and number of commodities	1980	1985	1990	1995	1998	1999	2000	2001	2002	2003	2004
All commodities (23)	283.5	236.7	258.1	289.1	235.2	227.3	224.0	212.1	244.3	283.6	293.0
Foodstuffs (10)	269.5	235.2	206.4	236.4	197.5	178.1	184.7	201.6	238.1	250.2	256.0
Raw industrials (13)	293.5	237.6	301.2	332.2	265.3	268.9	255.8	217.3	248.6	309.1	321.5
Livestock and products (5)	281.0	271.1	292.7	307.4	232.3	265.7	265.5	257.2	317.8	365.9	365.0
Metals (5)	288.3	207.7	283.2	300.6	218.5	261.6	214.0	172.5	184.5	276.7	357.7
Textiles and fibers (4)	240.4	206.7	257.6	274.3	237.5	223.8	245.7	217.4	230.2	255.2	237.9
Fats and oils (4)	255.9	220.2	188.7	226.7	236.0	174.8	163.6	175.8	234.0	297.2	262.6

Source: Commodity Research Bureau, Chicago, IL, *CRB Commodity Index Report*, weekly (copyright).

Table 716. Chain-Type Price Indexes for Gross Domestic Product: 1980 to 2004

[2000 = 100. For explanation of "chain-type," see text, Section 13, Income]

Item	1980	1985	1990	1995	2000	2003	2004
Gross domestic product	54.1	69.7	81.6	92.1	100.0	106.0	108.3
Personal consumption expenditures. . . .	52.1	69.7	80.5	91.6	100.0	105.5	107.8
Durable goods	83.3	96.6	104.6	110.7	100.0	92.2	90.4
Nondurable goods.	60.4	71.5	84.2	90.6	100.0	104.2	107.6
Services	42.3	59.3	74.2	88.3	100.0	109.2	112.0
Gross private domestic investment	74.4	86.7	96.4	100.9	100.0	102.3	104.9
Fixed investment	72.9	85.5	95.5	100.3	100.0	102.4	105.0
Nonresidential.	83.2	95.9	104.7	106.2	100.0	98.5	99.3
Structures	51.7	63.9	74.0	83.9	100.0	110.2	115.6
Equipment and software	100.9	111.4	118.2	115.2	100.0	94.8	94.4
Residential.	51.4	63.2	74.9	85.8	100.0	112.0	118.3
Net exports of goods and services:							
Exports	86.8	92.0	100.0	104.4	100.0	101.4	104.9
Goods	101.3	102.0	108.0	109.2	100.0	100.6	104.4
Services	57.0	70.9	82.5	93.1	100.0	103.2	106.1
Imports	94.5	88.8	103.8	106.4	100.0	99.6	104.5
Goods	101.7	94.2	108.2	108.6	100.0	98.1	102.9
Services	67.1	67.6	85.7	96.1	100.0	107.8	113.0
Government consumption expenditures and gross investment	50.8	67.0	77.1	88.4	100.0	108.7	112.2
Federal	53.3	70.0	77.1	89.5	100.0	109.1	112.2
National defense	53.9	71.6	78.0	89.6	100.0	109.9	113.0
Nondefense	51.7	65.7	75.3	89.4	100.0	107.6	110.8
State and local	48.9	64.7	77.4	87.8	100.0	108.5	112.2

Source: U.S. Bureau of Economic Analysis, *The National Income and Product Accounts of the United States, 1929–2004*, and *Survey of Current Business*, April 2005. See also <http://www.bea.gov/bea/dn/nipaweb/SelectTable.asp?Selected=N#S2>.

Table 717. Chain-Type Price Indexes for Personal Consumption Expenditures (PCE): 1980 to 2003

[2000 = 100. For explanation of "chain-type," see text, Section 13, Income]

Item	1980	1985	1990	1995	2000	2002	2003
Personal consumption expenditures . . .	**52.1**	**66.9**	**80.5**	**91.6**	**100.0**	**103.5**	**105.5**
Durable goods	**83.3**	**96.6**	**104.6**	**110.7**	**100.0**	**95.5**	**92.2**
Motor vehicles and parts	60.4	73.8	83.1	98.0	100.0	99.4	97.3
Furniture and household equipment	133.8	146.3	143.2	131.9	100.0	88.7	83.3
Other	70.3	81.1	96.9	104.6	100.0	99.5	97.9
Nondurable goods	**60.4**	**71.5**	**84.2**	**90.6**	**100.0**	**102.1**	**104.2**
Food	56.0	67.2	81.2	89.6	100.0	104.9	107.0
Food purchased for off-premise consumption	59.6	69.0	82.7	90.4	100.0	104.4	106.2
Purchased meals and beverages	49.4	63.9	78.6	88.2	100.0	106.0	108.2
Food furnished to employees (including military) and food produced and consumed on farms	54.8	67.6	83.1	90.4	100.0	103.0	107.4
Clothing and shoes	90.7	97.8	108.5	106.3	100.0	95.4	93.0
Shoes	85.8	93.0	103.7	106.2	100.0	98.1	96.6
Women's and children's clothing and accessories, except shoes.	99.0	103.5	114.2	109.1	100.0	95.5	93.2
Men's and boys' clothing and accessories, except shoes.	79.8	90.8	101.4	101.8	100.0	93.9	91.0
Gasoline, fuel oil, and other energy goods. . .	74.5	76.7	78.3	77.1	100.0	90.5	105.5
Gasoline and oil	75.5	76.6	78.4	77.8	100.0	90.4	105.2
Fuel oil and coal	68.2	76.1	76.9	69.9	100.0	91.8	109.6
Other [1]	46.9	63.2	78.9	89.2	100.0	105.0	105.2
Tobacco products	18.9	30.3	46.7	57.6	100.0	116.8	118.8
Drug preparations and sundries	35.7	53.9	72.7	87.2	100.0	109.0	112.0
Magazines, newspapers, and sheet music	44.2	61.4	73.9	89.4	100.0	103.8	105.9
Services	**42.3**	**59.3**	**74.2**	**88.3**	**100.0**	**106.1**	**109.2**
Housing	41.8	59.0	74.5	86.1	100.0	107.8	110.4
Owner-occupied nonfarm dwellings—space rent.	41.9	59.1	74.8	86.2	100.0	108.1	110.7
Tenant-occupied nonfarm dwellings—rent	42.0	60.1	75.4	86.2	100.0	108.3	111.3
Household operation	54.9	79.8	85.3	95.5	100.0	103.8	107.8
Electricity	59.1	84.9	91.5	100.9	100.0	106.9	109.4
Gas	49.5	78.9	73.2	77.3	100.0	101.6	124.7
Water and other sanitary services.	31.7	48.8	66.1	87.1	100.0	106.2	110.1
Telephone and telegraph.	74.0	104.8	103.8	107.0	100.0	98.2	97.2
Domestic service.	51.7	64.0	72.7	85.8	100.0	107.6	110.3
Other	43.8	60.8	71.0	86.7	100.0	109.4	114.7
Transportation	46.8	61.4	75.5	89.6	100.0	102.9	105.9
Medical care	34.0	51.5	69.7	88.0	100.0	106.2	109.9
Physicians	33.8	50.1	71.2	92.3	100.0	102.8	104.4
Dentists	30.8	44.6	60.6	80.1	100.0	108.7	113.2
Other professional services	42.3	58.6	74.6	89.0	100.0	105.7	107.9
Hospitals and nursing homes.	34.6	51.8	70.1	87.7	100.0	108.1	112.9
Health insurance	24.6	49.1	62.0	82.4	100.0	104.4	109.9
Recreation.	47.7	60.2	73.8	85.7	100.0	106.4	109.2
Other	45.7	59.6	74.1	88.4	100.0	105.9	108.8
Personal care	47.7	63.7	78.0	88.3	100.0	106.5	109.0
Cleaning, storage, and repair of clothing and shoes	46.4	64.1	79.4	90.5	100.0	106.9	109.4
Barbershops, beauty parlors, and health clubs.	49.1	63.3	76.3	85.7	100.0	105.7	108.4
Other.	46.5	64.0	79.2	90.3	100.0	107.1	109.6
Personal business	44.6	61.1	76.0	90.3	100.0	103.9	105.6
Brokerage charges and investment counseling.	171.8	184.0	189.0	154.6	100.0	87.0	90.1
Bank service charges, trust services, and safe deposit box rentals	24.8	44.0	55.6	76.3	100.0	104.9	106.9
Services furnished without payment by financial intermediaries, except life insurance carriers	51.0	60.1	70.8	87.3	100.0	107.1	104.8
Expense of handling life insurance and pension plans	32.1	45.3	61.7	75.2	100.0	106.7	110.8
Legal services	28.5	48.5	65.7	80.5	100.0	111.5	117.1
Funeral and burial expenses	28.7	48.6	63.7	82.1	100.0	108.7	113.0
Other.	39.1	54.1	68.3	82.9	100.0	108.0	111.4
Education and research	37.2	51.9	66.6	82.6	100.0	109.8	115.5
Higher education	31.2	46.8	62.9	82.8	100.0	111.1	117.2
Nursery, elementary, and secondary schools.	45.2	59.1	73.1	84.5	100.0	107.8	111.1
Other.	46.6	58.2	69.8	80.5	100.0	108.7	115.4
Religious and welfare activities.	48.4	60.3	73.1	84.5	100.0	105.9	109.0

[1] Includes other items not shown separately.

Source: U.S. Bureau of Economic Analysis, *The National Income and Product Accounts of the United States*, 1929-2004, Vol. 2; and *Survey of Current Business,* April 2005. See also <http://www.bea.gov/bea/dn/nipaweb/SelectTable.asp?Selected=N#S2>.

Table 718. Weekly Food Cost by Type of Family: 2000 and 2004

[**In dollars**. Assumes that food for all meals and snacks is purchased at the store and prepared at home. See source for details on estimation procedures]

Family type	December 2000				December 2004			
	Thrifty plan	Low-cost plan	Moderate-cost plan	Liberal-plan	Thrifty-plan	Low-cost plan	Moderate-cost plan	Liberal-plan
FAMILIES								
Family of two:								
20-50 years.................	60.60	78.20	96.40	120.00	69.60	88.40	109.40	137.10
51 years and over	57.60	75.20	93.10	111.50	66.40	85.30	105.70	127.20
Family of four:								
Couple, 20-50 years and children—								
1-2 and 3-5 years	88.40	112.60	137.60	169.40	100.80	126.70	156.00	192.70
6-8 and 9-11 years	101.90	132.60	165.30	199.20	116.70	149.70	186.90	226.40
INDIVIDUALS [1]								
Child:								
1 year	16.10	19.80	23.20	28.20	17.90	22.30	26.30	31.80
2 years.....................	16.00	19.80	23.20	28.20	17.80	22.10	26.50	31.80
3-5 years...................	17.30	21.70	26.80	32.10	19.70	24.30	30.10	36.20
6-8 years	21.50	28.80	35.90	41.70	24.60	32.70	40.30	47.00
9-11 years	25.30	32.70	41.80	48.40	28.80	36.70	47.20	54.80
Male:								
12-14 years.................	26.20	36.90	45.70	53.80	30.10	41.50	51.40	60.80
15-19 years. :...............	27.00	38.00	47.40	54.70	31.10	42.70	53.60	62.40
20-50 years.................	28.90	37.90	47.20	57.20	33.20	42.90	53.60	65.50
51 years and over	26.40	36.10	44.50	53.40	30.50	41.10	50.60	60.90
Female:								
12-19 years.................	26.30	31.80	38.60	46.70	30.00	36.00	43.80	52.80
20-50 years.................	26.20	33.20	40.40	51.90	30.10	37.50	45.80	59.10
51 years and over	26.00	32.30	40.10	48.00	29.80	36.50	45.50	54.70

[1] The costs given are for individuals in 4-person families. For individuals in other size families, the following adjustments are suggested: 1-person, add 20 percent; 2-person, add 10 percent; 3-person, add 5 percent; 5- or 6-person, subtract 5 percent; 7- (or more) person, subtract 10 percent.

Source: U.S. Department of Agriculture, *Official USDA Food Plans: Cost of Food at Home at Four Levels*, monthly. See also <http://www.usda.gov/cnpp/FoodPlans/Updates/fooddec04.pdf>.

Table 719. Food—Retail Prices of Selected Items: 2000 to 2004

[**In dollars per pound, except as indicated. As of December.** See Appendix III]

Food	2000	2003	2004	Food	2000	2003	2004
Cereals and bakery products:				Fresh fruits and vegetables:			
Flour, white, all purpose	0.28	0.29	0.29	Apples, red Delicious	0.82	0.96	0.95
Rice, white, lg. grain, raw	(NA)	0.48	0.57	Bananas	0.49	0.50	0.47
Spaghetti and macaroni	0.88	0.93	0.95	Oranges, navel.................	0.62	0.86	0.87
Bread, white, pan	0.99	0.95	0.97	Grapefruit	0.58	0.68	0.95
Bread, whole wheat	1.36	(NA)	1.30	Grapes, Thompson seedless	2.36	2.25	3.09
Meats, poultry, fish and eggs:				Lemons.......................	1.11	1.26	1.16
Ground beef, 100% beef..........	1.63	2.23	2.14	Pears, Anjou....................	(NA)	(NA)	1.17
Ground chuck, 100% beef.	1.98	2.62	2.47	Potatoes, white.................	0.35	0.44	0.51
Ground beef, lean and extra lean	2.33	2.93	2.99	Lettuce, iceberg	0.85	1.26	0.99
Round steak, USDA Choice........	3.28	4.27	4.26	Tomatoes, field grown	1.57	1.53	2.86
Sirloin steak, boneless	4.81	6.93	6.09	Processed fruits and vegetables:			
Pork:				Orange juice, frozen concentrate,			
Bacon, sliced	3.03	3.18	3.37	12 oz. can, per 16 oz.	1.88	1.83	1.96
Chops, center cut, bone-in	3.46	2.91	2.89	Potatoes, frozen, french-fried.......	1.09	1.00	0.93
Ham, boneless, excluding canned	2.75	2.89	3.25	Other foods at home:			
Poultry:				Sugar and sweets:			
Chicken, fresh, whole............	1.08	1.05	1.03	Sugar, white, all sizes.	0.41	0.42	0.43
Chicken legs, bone-in............	1.26	1.27	1.37	Sugar, white, 33-80 oz. pkg.	0.40	0.42	0.42
Turkey, frozen, whole	0.99	1.05	1.00	Fats and oils:.................			
Tuna, light, chunk, canned	1.92	1.83	1.78	Margarine, stick................	(NA)	1.03	0.91
Eggs, Grade A, large, (dozen)	0.96	1.56	0.98	Margarine, tubs, soft	0.84	0.98	1.13
Dairy products:				Shortening, vegetable oil blends......	1.07	1.12	1.29
Milk, fresh, whole, fortified (per gal.) ...	2.79	2.95	3.23	Peanut butter, creamy, all sizes	1.96	1.89	1.76
Butter, salted, grade AA, stick	2.80	2.80	3.46	Nonalcoholic beverages:			
American processed cheese	3.69	3.84	3.94	Coffee, 100% ground roast, all sizes...	3.21	2.88	2.78
Cheddar cheese, natural..........	3.76	4.07	4.16	Other prepared foods:			
Ice cream, prepack., bulk,				Potato chips, per 16 oz.	3.44	3.58	3.35
reg. (1/2 gal.)	3.66	3.90	3.85				

NA Not available.

Source: U.S. Bureau of Labor Statistics, *Monthly Labor Review* and *CPI Detailed Report*, January issues.

Table 720. Export Price Indexes—Selected Commodities: 1990 to 2004

[2000 = 100. Indexes are weighted by 2000 export values according to the Schedule B classification system of the U.S. Census Bureau. Prices used in these indexes were collected from a sample of U.S. manufacturers of exports and are factory transaction prices, except as noted. n.e.s. = Not elsewhere specified]

Commodities	1990	1995	1999	2000 [1]	2001	2002	2003	2004
All commodities	95.1	104.5	98.2	100.1	99.4	98.0	99.5	103.4
Food and live animals	102.4	112.1	102.6	100.6	101.1	99.8	107.5	123.9
Meat	81.4	95.7	87.6	104.8	106.1	90.0	102.9	127.3
Fish	86.8	107.1	123.0	100.6	90.8	97.9	108.2	108.6
Cereals and cereal preparations	126.5	133.2	106.0	100.0	102.6	106.5	118.5	141.2
Wheat	116.9	132.5	101.4	99.4	111.3	113.5	121.4	136.2
Maize	144.0	144.6	108.3	101.0	95.9	104.8	121.3	146.5
Fruits and vegetables	93.2	107.2	109.9	97.9	98.6	99.0	99.6	111.1
Feeding stuff for animals	99.5	104.9	92.5	100.4	101.1	101.2	108.8	131.9
Miscellaneous food products	94.0	94.8	100.1	100.0	100.1	100.7	101.5	101.6
Beverages and tobacco	84.9	98.2	99.4	100.0	98.4	98.2	98.2	101.6
Tobacco and tobacco manufactures	85.0	98.1	99.2	99.9	98.2	97.6	96.6	100.0
Crude materials	96.7	125.4	90.2	101.6	92.6	95.3	103.9	125.7
Oil seeds and oleaginous fruits	116.1	115.6	94.8	103.3	95.6	102.9	122.7	168.5
Cork and wood	76.5	117.5	94.4	99.8	92.8	87.1	90.4	98.3
Pulp and waste paper	70.9	122.2	72.3	106.9	80.6	89.3	90.1	100.8
Textile fibers	118.2	154.3	99.1	100.5	90.9	88.6	103.2	108.7
Metalliferous ores and metal scrap	105.9	132.2	89.7	99.2	91.0	99.8	109.0	167.5
Mineral fuels and related materials	67.2	68.5	68.5	97.4	103.2	93.9	107.6	131.8
Coal, coke and briquettes	109.5	106.4	104.3	99.5	106.9	110.9	(NA)	(NA)
Crude petroleum and petroleum products	57.5	59.6	61.9	96.8	101.8	87.9	102.7	129.7
Chemicals and related products	90.4	108.4	96.4	100.9	96.2	95.8	100.8	105.8
Organic chemicals	93.9	122.8	86.4	102.1	90.6	90.8	103.1	114.6
Chemical materials and products, n.e.s.	86.4	100.7	100.3	99.7	99.1	97.5	101.6	104.9
Intermediate manufactured products	86.8	100.6	96.7	100.2	99.5	98.1	100.0	107.0
Rubber manufactures	81.4	95.7	101.2	100.1	99.8	102.7	110.1	111.2
Paper and paperboard products	90.8	115.6	93.3	100.5	97.4	94.8	98.3	99.2
Textiles	91.2	102.8	100.8	100.2	98.5	100.0	102.7	105.4
Nonmetallic mineral manufactures	85.8	94.3	100.2	100.4	100.8	102.2	100.4	99.9
Nonferrous metals	87.1	98.2	83.7	98.5	98.0	85.3	80.3	95.4
Manufactures of metals, n.e.s.	81.2	92.3	100.2	100.9	101.5	102.5	104.8	108.4
Machinery and transport equipment [2]	97.9	102.8	100.3	100.0	100.3	98.9	97.8	98.2
Power generating machinery [3]	77.0	88.5	97.6	99.7	102.3	104.5	107.2	108.7
Rotating electric plant and parts thereof, n.e.s.	87.0	97.9	100.1	100.1	99.8	107.8	106.9	105.5
Machinery specialized for particular industries	82.7	94.0	98.9	100.3	100.3	101.8	102.6	105.4
Agricultural machinery and parts [4]	86.0	95.6	98.9	99.9	98.9	99.8	98.9	100.5
Civil engineering and contractors, plant and equipment	81.8	93.6	100.4	100.3	100.4	101.6	104.9	107.6
Metalworking machinery	82.1	92.3	100.4	99.3	101.0	99.9	101.0	100.0
General industrial machines, parts, n.e.s.	82.5	92.0	99.2	100.1	101.3	102.3	102.4	104.9
Computer equipment and office machines	193.2	147.5	104.8	99.9	95.6	90.4	88.1	87.2
Computer equipment	234.5	160.7	106.1	99.7	96.0	92.1	88.1	83.9
Telecommunications [5]	97.3	103.8	100.2	100.3	99.8	97.7	93.8	91.8
Electrical machinery and equipment	112.7	117.2	103.1	99.8	98.3	93.9	89.7	88.2
Electronic valves, diodes, transistors and integrated circuits	135.0	135.1	105.0	99.5	95.4	87.5	80.7	78.1
Road vehicles	88.7	96.1	98.6	100.0	100.2	100.3	101.1	102.4
Miscellaneous manufactured articles	90.5	98.6	99.6	99.7	100.1	100.4	101.2	100.9

NA Not available. [1] June 2000 may not equal 100 because indexes were reweighted to an "average" trade value in 2000. [2] Excludes military and commercial aircraft. [3] Includes equipment. [4] Excludes tractors. [5] Includes sound recording and reproducing equipment.

Source: U.S. Bureau of Labor Statistics, *U.S. Import and Export Price Indexes*, monthly.

Prices 497

Table 721. Import Price Indexes—Selected Commodities: 1990 to 2004

[2000 = 100. As of June. Indexes are weighted by the 2000 Tariff Schedule of the United States Annotated, a scheme for describing and reporting product composition and value of U.S. imports. Import prices are based on U.S. dollar prices paid by importer]

Commodity	1990	1995 [1]	1999	2000 [1]	2001	2002	2003	2004
All commodities	90.8	101.4	92.9	100.2	97.6	94.1	96.2	101.7
Food and live animals	92.1	108.6	101.2	99.0	96.0	94.5	99.4	106.9
Meat	118.4	100.8	96.1	100.8	106.2	104.0	102.9	128.9
Fish	70.9	92.5	94.9	99.3	90.0	79.8	81.3	84.1
Crustaceans; fresh, chilled, frozen, salted or dried	65.2	91.9	88.0	100.9	83.6	70.0	69.9	71.8
Beverages and tobacco	76.5	88.6	98.1	100.4	101.7	103.0	103.9	105.3
Crude materials	90.4	109.5	99.1	99.4	102.8	96.4	99.5	125.8
Mineral fuels and related products	54.7	61.9	54.6	101.3	90.4	86.1	101.7	131.5
Crude petroleum and petroleum products	54.8	63.0	54.6	102.2	89.3	85.9	97.6	130.0
Natural gas	54.9	49.3	51.8	95.2	97.4	83.6	130.1	140.0
Chemicals and related products	93.7	106.8	96.2	99.8	100.5	97.0	100.1	103.8
Intermediate manufactured products	91.3	102.7	94.6	100.4	98.0	92.8	94.4	106.1
Machinery and transport equipment	100.8	112.4	110.9	100.1	98.5	97.1	95.8	95.1
Computer equipment and office machines	198.5	167.2	105.1	99.9	93.6	87.8	81.8	75.5
Computer equipment	284.6	198.4	108.9	100.4	89.3	80.3	71.9	64.9
Telecommunications [2]	120.9	119.1	103.8	100.2	97.2	94.4	89.3	84.7
Electrical machinery and equipment	111.5	122.9	100.1	100.7	98.8	97.1	95.4	94.7
Road vehicles	82.0	97.3	99.6	100.1	99.8	100.2	100.7	102.4
Miscellaneous manufactured articles	94.7	103.2	100.5	99.7	99.8	98.6	99.7	99.9
Plumbing, heating and lighting fixtures	102.0	107.4	99.5	99.2	99.2	98.5	94.8	93.5
Furniture and parts	96.0	103.1	101.1	99.6	98.5	98.8	100.2	102.3
Articles of apparel and clothing	96.5	99.0	100.6	99.6	100.6	99.7	100.6	100.7
Footwear	96.5	99.3	100.0	99.6	100.1	99.2	100.0	100.4

[1] June 1995 and 2000 may not equal 100 because indexes were reweighted to an "average" trade value in 1995 and 2000.
[2] Includes sound recording and reproducing equipment.

Source: U.S. Bureau of Labor Statistics, *U.S. Import and Export Price Indexes*, monthly.

Table 722. Average Prices of Selected Fuels and Electricity: 1990 to 2004

[In dollars per unit, except electricity, in cents per kWh. Represents price to end-users, except as noted]

Type	Unit [1]	1990	1995	1997	1998	1999	2000	2001	2002	2003	2004
Crude oil, composite [2]	Barrel	22.22	17.23	19.04	12.52	17.51	28.26	22.95	24.10	28.53	36.97
Motor gasoline: [3]											
Unleaded regular	Gallon	1.16	1.15	1.23	1.06	1.17	1.51	1.46	1.36	1.59	1.88
Unleaded premium	Gallon	1.35	1.34	1.42	1.25	1.36	1.69	1.66	1.56	1.78	2.07
No. 2 heating oil	Gallon	1.06	0.87	0.98	0.85	0.88	1.31	1.25	1.13	(NA)	(NA)
No. 2 diesel fuel	Gallon	0.73	0.56	0.64	0.49	0.58	0.94	0.84	0.76	0.94	1.24
Residual fuel oil	Gallon	0.44	0.39	0.42	0.31	0.37	0.60	0.53	0.57	0.70	0.74
Natural gas, residential	1,000 cu./ft.	5.80	6.06	6.94	6.82	6.69	7.76	9.63	7.91	9.52	10.74
Electricity, residential	kWh	7.83	8.40	8.43	8.26	8.16	8.24	8.62	8.46	8.70	8.94

NA Not available. [1] See headnote. [2] Refiner acquisition cost. [3] Average, all service.

Source: U.S. Energy Information Administration, *Monthly Energy Review*.

Table 723. Refiner/Reseller Sales Price of Gasoline by State: 2003 to 2005

[In cents per gallon. As of March. Represents all refinery and gas plant operators' sales through company-operated retail outlets. Gasoline prices exclude taxes]

State	Gaso-line excise taxes 2004	Average, all grades 2003	2004	2005	Midgrade 2003	2004	2005	Premium 2003	2004	2005
United States	(NA)	126.7	131.6	164.4	132.9	138.1	170.4	142.5	148.0	180.6
Alabama	18.0	119.4	125.8	162.1	125.7	132.2	168.2	133.3	140.2	174.7
Alaska	8.0	(NA)	147.5	187.2	(NA)	154.1	181.6	178.5	164.9	190.8
Arizona	18.0	151.8	158.5	172.4	160.8	166.8	181.1	169.9	177.5	188.6
Arkansas	21.5	120.3	124.2	159.0	128.0	131.3	166.2	133.2	135.5	170.3
California	18.0	159.8	164.1	181.8	168.6	173.1	188.9	174.7	179.4	198.4
Colorado	22.0	129.6	132.8	167.0	135.8	139.2	173.5	145.6	148.7	182.4
Connecticut	25.0	125.6	133.3	161.5	131.5	139.0	169.1	140.2	148.8	176.8
Delaware	23.0	121.2	127.2	154.2	128.0	134.0	159.9	137.3	142.5	168.5
District of Columbia . .	20.0	(D)	(D)	(D)	(D)	(D)	(D)	(D)	(D)	(D)
Florida	14.5	125.2	130.1	162.1	131.3	136.5	168.7	139.9	144.1	176.9
Georgia	7.5	120.7	127.9	164.9	128.1	135.5	171.4	135.3	142.9	180.3
Hawaii	16.0	156.0	161.6	198.0	151.7	166.0	202.0	169.1	174.1	209.9
Idaho	25.0	127.9	136.8	157.2	135.8	144.7	161.8	141.4	151.1	171.9
Illinois	19.0	126.5	131.3	164.7	134.0	138.6	170.4	142.8	148.0	182.7
Indiana	18.0	123.8	127.3	163.3	131.8	135.0	171.0	139.6	143.8	180.3
Iowa	20.5	120.1	124.3	159.8	123.0	129.0	161.9	132.7	133.1	171.1
Kansas	24.0	119.3	124.1	164.5	126.5	130.0	170.2	135.8	140.9	180.6
Kentucky	17.4	125.2	129.7	168.9	132.3	136.3	175.7	142.3	146.0	185.5
Louisiana	20.0	119.5	122.3	157.9	126.6	129.3	165.3	135.8	137.7	175.3
Maine	25.2	126.8	134.4	165.6	134.9	142.2	174.6	140.2	149.5	181.9
Maryland	23.5	121.8	128.0	160.3	128.1	134.2	166.1	134.9	140.8	173.5
Massachusetts	21.0	128.2	130.9	158.2	134.8	137.6	165.1	143.7	146.3	176.4
Michigan	19.0	124.1	128.7	166.6	129.1	135.1	174.0	136.0	141.7	180.7
Minnesota	20.0	124.4	133.2	166.9	126.2	135.8	169.3	137.0	146.3	180.4
Mississippi	18.4	124.4	129.3	164.6	130.1	135.7	171.8	140.6	144.4	181.4
Missouri	17.0	120.6	126.6	163.3	129.9	136.6	173.5	137.3	143.7	182.4
Montana	27.0	123.4	123.2	160.8	129.6	129.6	167.4	138.4	137.9	178.1
Nebraska	25.4	118.7	125.0	164.6	120.8	127.6	165.2	129.6	134.4	177.0
Nevada	23.0	151.8	161.7	180.6	163.6	174.7	188.3	163.9	176.7	197.4
New Hampshire.	19.5	126.7	131.7	161.7	135.3	140.5	169.9	141.7	147.6	175.9
New Jersey	10.5	127.0	133.5	158.6	132.7	139.5	165.1	141.0	147.8	173.8
New Mexico	18.9	126.1	131.7	170.3	135.9	137.8	179.2	140.3	146.6	183.2
New York	23.2	124.0	133.3	158.3	130.6	141.1	165.2	137.2	149.1	173.2
North Carolina.	26.6	120.7	124.4	157.5	127.8	131.8	164.7	136.2	139.9	171.9
North Dakota	21.0	128.3	135.2	170.7	129.0	136.0	173.6	135.3	143.4	177.7
Ohio	26.0	124.1	129.4	164.2	132.4	137.3	172.1	140.9	146.8	182.3
Oklahoma	17.0	115.6	121.7	161.7	121.6	127.9	166.5	128.8	135.4	174.4
Oregon	24.0	144.2	138.5	171.7	154.2	147.7	181.1	162.3	155.7	192.0
Pennsylvania	30.0	118.9	125.8	156.5	125.0	131.5	162.9	133.4	140.1	172.5
Rhode Island	30.0	123.4	127.9	155.8	130.5	135.3	164.6	138.2	143.4	173.8
South Carolina	16.0	120.8	126.9	160.3	127.8	134.2	167.8	137.3	143.7	178.1
South Dakota	22.0	123.0	131.1	166.8	125.8	134.3	168.2	135.1	144.9	181.3
Tennessee	21.0	119.2	124.4	161.2	126.2	131.2	167.9	134.6	139.1	177.1
Texas	20.0	118.4	120.0	157.2	124.9	126.4	163.7	132.3	134.3	170.8
Utah	24.5	124.7	136.2	158.0	129.6	141.4	164.9	138.0	151.1	172.1
Vermont	20.0	128.4	136.5	167.5	134.6	143.9	174.5	141.4	149.5	183.8
Virginia	17.5	122.5	127.9	159.6	128.2	134.2	165.5	137.2	142.4	173.7
Washington	28.0	142.1	135.1	169.7	152.2	144.5	179.8	161.1	154.0	188.4
West Virginia	27.0	125.6	129.8	164.7	132.0	135.8	171.5	139.2	144.2	180.2
Wisconsin	29.1	124.1	129.1	165.4	125.0	131.0	165.0	137.3	141.7	180.7
Wyoming	14.0	131.1	130.6	164.9	138.6	136.8	170.3	144.3	142.3	176.8

D Withheld to avoid disclosure of individual company data.   NA Not available.

Source: U.S. Energy Information Administration, *Petroleum Marketing Monthly*.

Table 724. Retail Gasoline Prices—Selected Areas: 2003 and 2004

[Prices are annual averages.]

Area	Regular 2003	2004	Midgrade 2003	2004	Premium 2003	2004
Boston, MA	158.9	185.8	168.9	195.8	178.5	205.6
Chicago, IL	161.9	190.0	171.9	200.1	181.8	209.9
Cleveland, OH	151.8	180.2	161.7	190.2	172.1	200.4
Denver, CO	151.9	180.4	163.4	191.9	173.7	201.8
Houston, TX	143.3	171.2	153.3	181.0	163.3	190.7
Los Angeles, CA	181.9	214.7	192.6	224.8	202.3	234.6
Miami, FL	219.3	191.3	234.7	202.0	246.1	210.5
New York, NY	163.1	190.4	173.1	201.0	181.2	209.2
San Francisco, CA	189.8	214.8	200.7	225.9	210.5	235.7
Seattle, WA	162.5	194.9	173.1	205.9	183.1	216.0

Source: U.S. Energy Information Administration, *Weekly U.S. Retail Gasoline Prices*, Gasoline Historical Data. See also <http://www.eia.doe.gov/oil_gas/petroleum/data_publications/wrgp/mogas_history.html>.

No. 200.—COMPARATIVE STATEMENT OF THE BUSINESS OF THE UNITED STATES PATENT OFFICE FOR EACH CALENDAR YEAR FROM 1839 TO 1889, INCLUSIVE.

[From the Report of the Commissioner of Patents.]

Year.	Applications.	Caveats filed.	Patents and reissues.	Cash received.	Cash expended.	Surplus.
				Dollars.	Dollars.	Dollars.
1839			325	37,260.00	34,543.51	2,716.49
1840	765	228	473	38,056.51	39,020.67	
1841	847	312	495	40,413.01	52,666.87	
1842	761	291	517	36,505.68	31,241.48	5,264.20
1843	819	315	510	35,315.81	30,776.96	4,538.85
1844	1,045	380	495	42,509.26	36,244.73	6,264.53
1845	1,246	452	504	51,076.14	39,395.65	11,680.49
1846	1,272	448	638	50,264.16	46,158.71	4,105.45
1847	1,531	553	569	63,111.19	41,878.35	21,232.84
1848	1,628	607	652	67,576.69	58,905.84	8,670.85
1849	1,955	595	1,068	80,752.98	77,716.44	3,036.54
1850	2,193	602	983	86,927.05	80,100.95	6,816.10
1851	2,258	760	872	95,738.61	86,916.93	8,821.68
1852	2,639	996	1,019	112,656.34	95,916.91	16,739.43
1853	2,673	901	961	121,527.45	132,869.83	
1854	3,328	868	1,844	163,789.84	167,146.32	
1855	4,435	906	2,012	216,459.35	179,540.33	36,919.02
1856	4,960	1,024	2,506	192,588.03	199,931.02	
1857	4,771	1,010	2,896	196,132.01	211,582.09	
1858	5,364	934	3,695	203,716.16	193,193.74	10,522.42
1859	6,225	1,097	4,504	245,942.15	210,278.41	35,663.74
1860	7,653	1,084	4,778	256,352.59	252,820.80	3,531.79
1861	4,643	700	3,320	137,351.44	221,491.91	
1862	5,038	824	3,532	215,754.99	182,810.39	32,944.60
1863	6,014	787	4,184	195,593.29	189,414.14	6,179.15
1864	6,932	1,063	5,025	240,919.78	229,868.00	11,051.98
1865	10,664	1,937	6,616	348,791.84	274,199.34	74,592.50
1866	15,269	2,723	9,458	495,665.38	361,724.28	133,941.10
1867	21,276	3,597	13,026	646,581.92	639,263.32	7,318.60
1868	20,420	3,705	13,410	681,363.86	628,679.77	52,886.09
1869	19,271	3,624	13,997	693,145.81	486,430.73	206,715.03
1870	19,171	3,273	13,333	669,456.76	557,149.19	112,307.57
1871	19,472	3,365	13,056	678,716.46	560,595.08	118,121.38
1872	18,246	3,090	13,613	699,726.39	665,591.36	34,135.03
1873	20,414	3,248	12,864	703,191.77	691,178.98	12,012.79
1874	21,602	3,181	13,599	738,278.17	679,288.41	58,989.76
1875	21,638	3,094	14,837	743,453.36	721,657.71	21,795.65
1876	21,425	2,697	15,595	757,987.65	652,542.60	105,445.05
1877	20,308	2,809	14,187	732,342.85	613,152.62	119,190.23
1878	20,260	2,755	13,414	725,375.55	593,082.89	132,292.66
1879	20,059	2,620	13,213	703,931.47	529,938.97	174,292.50
1880	23,012	2,490	13,947	749,685.32	538,865.17	210,820.15
1881	26,059	2,406	16,584	853,665.89	605,173.28	248,492.61
1882	31,522	2,553	19,267	1,009,219.45	683,867.67	325,351.78
1883	35,577	2,741	22,353	1,146,240.00	675,234.86	471,005.14
1884	35,600	2,582	20,413	1,075,798.80	970,579.76	105,219.04
1885	35,717	2,552	24,233	1,186,098.15	1,024,378.85	163,710.30
1886	35,968	2,513	22,508	1,154,551.40	992,503.40	162,047.95
1887	35,613	2,622	21,477	1,144,509.60	994,472.22	150,037.38
1888	35,797	2,251	20,506	1,118,516.10	973,108.78	145,407.32
1889	40,575	2,481	24,158	1,281,728.05	1,052,955.96	228,772.09

Source: Statistical Abstract of the United States: 1889 Edition.

Section 15
Business Enterprise

This section relates to the place and behavior of the business firm and to business initiative in the American economy. It includes data on the number, type, and size of businesses; financial data of domestic and multinational U.S. corporations; business investments, expenditures, and profits; and sales and inventories.

The principal sources of these data are the *Survey of Current Business*, published by the Bureau of Economic Analysis (BEA), the *Statistical Supplement to the Federal Reserve Bulletin*, issued by the Board of Governors of the Federal Reserve System, the annual *Statistics of Income (SOI)* reports of the Internal Revenue Service (IRS), and the Census Bureau's Economic Census, *County Business Patterns, Quarterly Financial Report for Manufacturing, Mining, and Trade Corporations (QFR)*, *Surveys of Minority- and Women-Owned Business Enterprises*, and *Annual Capital Expenditures Survey*.

Business firms—A firm is generally defined as a business organization under a single management and may include one or more establishments. The terms firm, business, company, and enterprise are used interchangeably throughout this section. A firm doing business in more than one industry is classified by industry according to the major activity of the firm as a whole.

The IRS concept of a business firm relates primarily to the legal entity used for tax reporting purposes. A sole proprietorship is an unincorporated business owned by one person and may include large enterprises with many employees and hired managers and part-time operators. A partnership is an unincorporated business owned by two or more persons, each of whom has a financial interest in the business. A corporation is a business that is legally incorporated under state laws. While many corporations file consolidated tax returns, most corporate tax returns represent individual corporations, some of which are affiliated through common ownership or control with other corporations filing separate returns.

Economic census—The economic census is the major source of facts about the structure and functioning of the nation's economy. It provides essential information for government, business, industry, and the general public. It furnishes an important part of the framework for such composite measures as the gross domestic product estimates, input/output measures, production and price indexes, and other statistical series that measure short-term changes in economic conditions. The Census Bureau takes the economic census every 5 years, covering years ending in "2" and "7." The economic census forms an integrated program at 5-year intervals since 1967, and before that for 1963, 1958, and 1954. Prior to that time, the individual censuses were taken separately at varying intervals.

The economic census is collected on an establishment basis. A company operating at more than one location is required to file a separate report for each store, factory, shop, or other location. Each establishment is assigned a separate industry classification based on its primary activity and not that of its parent company. Establishments responding to the establishment survey are classified into industries on the basis of their principal product or activity (determined by annual sales volume). The statistics issued by industry in the 2002 Economic Census are classified primarily on the 2002 North American Industry Classification System (NAICS), and, to a lesser extent, on the 1997 NAICS used in the previous census (see below).

More detailed information about the scope, coverage, methodology, classification system, data items, and publications for each of the economic censuses and related surveys is published in the *Guide to the 2002 Economic Census* at <http://www.census.gov/econ/census02/guide/index.html>.

Data from the 2002 Economic Census were released through the Census Bureau's American FactFinder service, on CD-ROM, in Adobe Acrobat PDF reports and in hypertext "drill-down" tables available on the Census Bureau Web site. For more information on these various media of release, see the following page on the Census Bureau Web site <http://www.census.gov/econ/census02/>.

North American Industry Classification System (NAICS)—NAICS has replaced the previous Standard Industrial Classification (SIC) system. This new system of industrial classification was developed by experts on classification in the United States, Canada, and Mexico.

NAICS 2002 is the same as NAICS 1997 for 14 of the 20 sectors. Construction and wholesale trade are substantially changed, but the revisions also modify a number of retail classifications and the organization of the information sector. Very minor boundary adjustments affect administrative and support services and mining. NAICS also reflects, in a much more explicit way, the enormous changes in technology and in the growth and diversification of services that have marked recent decades. A key feature of NAICS is the revision for the Information sector. A few of the new and important industries created in this section include:

Internet service providers and Web search portals, and Internet publishing and broadcasting. Also included in the Information sector is electronic shopping and electronic auctions.

Most of the 1997 and 2002 Economic Census data are issued on a NAICS basis as seen in the industry and geographic series from the census. Current survey data from the Census Bureau as well as other statistical agencies are converting over time to NAICS after benchmarking to the 1997 Economic Census where appropriate or implementation of data collection on a NAICS basis.

Quarterly Financial Report—The Quarterly Financial Report (QFR) program publishes quarterly aggregate statistics on the financial conditions of U.S. corporations. The QFR requests companies to report estimates from their statements of income and retained earnings, balance sheets, and related financial and operating ratios for domestic operations. The statistical data are classified and aggregated by type of industry and asset size. The QFR sample includes large manufacturing companies, mostly with $250 million or more in assets. It also includes a small sample of manufacturing companies, mostly with assets between $250 thousand and $250 million, and a sample of mining, wholesale, and retail companies, mostly with assets of $50 million or more. The data are published quarterly in the *Quarterly Financial Report for Manufacturing, Mining, and Trade Corporations* and on the Internet at <http://www.census.gov/csd/qfr/>.

502   Business Enterprise

Table 725. Number of Returns, Receipts, and Net Income by Type of Business: 1980 to 2002

[8,932 represents 8,932,000. Covers active enterprises only. Figures are estimates based on sample of unaudited tax returns; see Appendix III. Minus sign (-) indicates net loss]

Item	Number of returns (1,000)			Business receipts [2] (bil. dol.)			Net income (less loss) [3] (bil. dol.)		
	Nonfarm proprietorships [1]	Partnerships	Corporations	Nonfarm proprietorships [1]	Partnerships	Corporations	Nonfarm proprietorships [1]	Partnerships	Corporations
1980	8,932	1,380	2,711	411	286	6,172	55	8	239
1985	11,929	1,714	3,277	540	349	8,050	79	-9	240
1990	14,783	1,554	3,717	731	541	10,914	141	17	371
1991	15,181	1,515	3,803	713	539	10,963	142	21	345
1992	15,495	1,485	3,869	737	571	11,272	154	43	402
1993	15,848	1,468	3,965	757	627	11,814	156	67	498
1994	16,154	1,494	4,342	791	732	12,858	167	82	577
1995	16,424	1,581	4,474	807	854	13,969	169	107	714
1996	16,955	1,654	4,631	843	1,042	14,890	177	145	806
1997	17,176	1,759	4,710	870	1,297	15,890	187	168	915
1998	17,409	1,855	4,849	918	1,534	16,543	202	187	838
1999	17,576	1,937	4,936	969	1,829	18,009	208	228	929
2000	17,905	2,058	5,045	1,021	2,316	19,593	215	269	928
2001	18,338	2,132	5,136	1,017	2,569	19,308	217	276	604
2002	18,926	2,242	5,267	1,030	2,669	18,849	221	271	564

[1] In 1980, represents individually-owned businesses, including farms; thereafter, represents only nonfarm proprietors, i.e., business owners. [2] Excludes investment income except for partnerships and corporations in finance, insurance, and real estate before 1998. Beginning 1998 finance and insurance, real estate, and management of companies included investment income for partnerships and corporations. Starting 1985, investment income no longer included for S corporations. [3] Net income (less loss) is defined differently by form of organization, basically as follows: (a) Proprietorships: Total taxable receipts less total business deductions, including cost of sales and operations, depletion, and certain capital expensing, excluding charitable contributions and owners' salaries; (b) Partnerships: Total taxable receipts (including investment income except capital gains) less deductions, including cost of sales and operations and certain payments to partners, excluding charitable contributions, oil and gas depletion, and certain capital expensing; (c) Corporations: Total taxable receipts (including investment income, capital gains, and income from foreign subsidiaries deemed received for tax purposes, except for S corporations beginning 1985) less business deductions, including cost of sales and operations, depletion, certain capital expensing, and officers' compensation excluding S corporation charitable contributions and investment expenses starting 1985; net income is before income tax.

Source: U.S. Internal Revenue Service, *Statistics of Income,* various publications.

Table 726. Number of Returns and Business Receipts by Size of Receipts: 1990 to 2002

[3,717 represents 3,717,000. Covers active enterprises only. Figures are estimates based on sample of unaudited tax returns; see Appendix III]

Size-class of receipts	Returns (1,000)					Business receipts [1] (bil. dol.)				
	1990	1995	2000	2001	2002	1990	1995	2000	2001	2002
Corporations	3,717	4,474	5,045	5,136	5,267	10,914	13,969	19,593	19,308	18,849
Under $25,000 [2]	879	1,030	1,220	1,248	1,283	5	4	4	3	4
$25,000 to $49,999	252	288	302	296	314	9	11	10	11	12
$50,000 to $99,999	359	447	477	485	514	26	33	35	36	38
$100,000 to $499,999	1,162	1,393	1,515	1,550	1,583	291	350	397	388	395
$500,000 to $999,999	416	513	582	601	611	294	361	407	428	434
$1,000,000 or more	649	803	946	956	962	10,289	13,210	18,738	18,442	17,967
Partnerships	1,554	1,581	2,058	2,132	2,242	541	854	2,316	2,569	2,669
Under $25,000 [2]	963	931	1,105	1,130	1,204	4	4	5	5	5
$25,000 to $49,999	126	133	183	183	185	5	5	7	7	7
$50,000 to $99,999	133	142	187	192	195	10	10	13	14	14
$100,000 to $499,999	222	245	353	373	394	51	56	82	88	92
$500,000 to $999,999	52	59	92	103	105	36	42	66	73	74
$1,000,000 or more	57	69	137	151	159	435	738	2,143	2,383	2,478
Nonfarm proprietorships	14,783	16,424	17,905	18,338	18,926	731	807	1,021	1,017	1,030
Under $25,000 [2]	10,196	11,317	11,997	12,345	12,716	69	76	82	86	87
$25,000 to $49,999	1,660	1,983	2,247	2,239	2,358	58	71	80	79	83
$50,000 to $99,999	1,282	1,393	1,645	1,704	1,752	91	99	117	121	124
$100,000 to $499,999	1,444	1,514	1,733	1,759	1,803	296	310	355	353	362
$500,000 to $999,999	143	147	190	197	203	97	100	126	133	138
$1,000,000 or more	57	70	92	93	93	119	151	261	245	234

[1] Excludes investment income except for partnerships and corporations in finance, insurance, and real estate before 1998. Beginning 1998, finance and insurance, real estate, and management of companies included investment income for partnerships and corporations. [2] Includes firms with no receipts.

Source: U.S. Internal Revenue Service, *Statistics of Income Bulletin;* and unpublished data.

U.S. Census Bureau, Statistical Abstract of the United States: 2006

Table 727. Number of Returns, Receipts, and Net Income by Type of Business and Industry: 2002

[18,926 represents 18,926,000. Covers active enterprises only. Figures are estimates based on sample of unaudited tax returns; see Appendix III. Based on the North American Industry Classification System (NAICS), 2002; see text, this section. Minus sign (-) indicates net loss]

Industry	NAICS code	Number of returns (1,000)			Business receipts [1] (bil. dol.)			Net income (less loss) (bil. dol.)		
		Nonfarm proprietorships	Partnerships	Corporations	Nonfarm proprietorships	Partnerships	Corporations	Nonfarm proprietorships	Partnerships	Corporations
Total [2]	(X)	18,926	2,242	5,267	1,030	2,669	18,849	221	271	564
Agriculture, forestry, fishing, and hunting [3]	11	305	118	140	15	18	108	1	-1	(Z)
Mining	21	110	30	30	6	55	142	1	12	1
Utilities	22	7	3	8	(Z)	147	537	(Z)	1	-1
Construction	23	2,278	134	649	168	170	1,080	28	11	28
Special trade contractors	235	1,708	46	383	108	28	434	21	2	10
Manufacturing	31-33	310	38	280	23	485	4,823	3	23	119
Wholesale and retail trade [4]	(X)	2,629	160	965	215	538	5,279	12	9	87
Wholesale trade	42	308	38	360	35	257	2,440	5	7	37
Retail trade [5]	44-45	2,321	122	601	179	281	2,837	8	2	50
Motor vehicle and parts dealers	441	154	16	89	35	79	738	1	1	8
Food and beverage stores	445	108	16	86	30	46	457	1	(Z)	7
Gasoline stations	447	22	6	37	20	25	141	(Z)	(Z)	(Z)
Transportation and warehousing	48-49	949	26	178	55	52	511	8	3	-9
Information	51	223	29	120	6	167	799	1	-7	-34
Finance and insurance	52	647	263	224	76	316	2,606	16	89	247
Real estate and rental and leasing	53	1,015	1,000	571	53	168	205	23	55	3
Professional, scientific, and technical services [5]	54	2,672	146	736	125	218	652	49	54	2
Legal services	5411	357	29	91	34	94	71	14	33	6
Accounting, tax preparation, bookkeeping, and payroll services	5412	366	16	60	11	37	24	4	7	2
Management, scientific, and technical consulting services	5416	662	32	205	27	23	131	13	4	4
Management of companies and enterprises	55	(NA)	19	48	(NA)	25	690	(NA)	7	85
Administrative and support and waste management and remediation services	56	1,754	44	231	45	51	338	12	4	5
Educational services	61	396	6	41	5	2	25	2	(-Z)	1
Health care and social assistance	62	1,722	47	334	97	102	448	41	13	17
Arts, entertainment and recreation	71	1,106	43	111	23	47	73	6	-2	1
Accommodation and food services	72	362	78	272	37	93	372	2	-1	8
Accommodation	721	64	25	34	5	44	108	(Z)	-2	1
Food services and drinking places	722	298	52	238	32	49	264	1	(Z)	7
Other services [5]	81	2,226	57	321	75	15	159	17	1	3
Auto repair and maintenance	8111	316	21	103	23	6	59	3	(Z)	1
Personal and laundry services	812	1,225	26	127	33	5	62	10	(Z)	1
Religious, grantmaking, civic, professional, and similar organizations	813	257	1	38	3	(Z)	10	2	(Z)	(Z)
Unclassified	(X)	212	3	8	4	(Z)	(Z)	1	(Z)	(Z)

NA Not available.   Z Less than $500 million.   [1] Includes investment income for partnerships and corporations in finance and insurance, real estate, and management of companies' industries.   Excludes investment income for S corporations.   [2] For corporations, includes businesses not allocable to individual industries.   [3] For corporations, represents agricultural services only.   [4] For corporations, includes trade business not identified as wholesale or retail.   [5] Includes other industries not shown separately.

Source: U.S. Internal Revenue Service, *Statistics of Income*, various publications.

504 Business Enterprise

Table 728. Nonfarm Sole Proprietorships—Selected Income and Deduction Items: 1990 to 2002

[In billions of dollars (731 represents $731,000,000,000) except as indicated. All figures are estimates based on samples. Tax law changes have affected the comparability of the data over time; see *Statistics of Income* reports for a description. See Appendix III]

Item	1990	1995	1996	1997	1998	1999	2000	2001	2002
Number of returns (1,000)	14,783	16,424	16,955	17,176	17,409	17,576	17,905	18,338	18,926
Returns with net income (1,000).	11,222	12,213	12,524	12,703	13,080	13,159	13,308	13,604	13,751
Business receipts	731	807	843	870	918	969	1,021	1,017	1,030
Income from sales and operations . . .	719	797	832	858	905	955	1,008	1,002	1,015
Business deductions [1]	589	638	666	684	716	761	806	800	809
Cost of goods sold/operations [1]	291	307	316	320	341	370	387	363	352
Purchases	210	219	220	224	231	256	269	247	227
Labor costs.	23	24	26	25	27	29	29	28	30
Materials and supplies	30	34	40	38	42	42	43	44	46
Advertising	(NA)	(NA)	(NA)	9	9	9	10	11	11
Car and truck expenses	22	33	37	39	40	41	46	47	50
Commissions	9	10	11	11	11	11	12	12	14
Depreciation.	24	27	28	29	29	31	32	33	37
Insurance.	13	13	13	13	13	13	14	14	16
Interest paid.	13	10	11	11	11	11	12	13	11
Office expenses	(NA)	(NA)	(NA)	9	10	10	10	11	11
Rent paid.	23	28	29	29	30	31	33	34	35
Repairs.	9	10	11	11	11	12	12	12	13
Salaries and wages (net)	47	54	56	58	59	61	63	64	66
Supplies	(NA)	(NA)	(NA)	20	20	22	22	23	25
Taxes paid	10	13	14	14	14	14	14	14	15
Utilities	14	17	18	19	18	18	19	20	21
Net income (less loss) [2].	141	169	177	187	202	208	215	217	221
Net income [2]	162	192	200	210	226	233	245	250	257
Constant (2000) Dollars [3]									
Business receipts	896	877	899	912	952	991	1,021	993	991
Business deductions	722	693	710	717	742	778	806	781	778
Net income (less loss)	173	184	188	196	210	213	215	212	213
Net income.	198	208	213	221	235	239	245	244	248

NA Not available. [1] Includes other amounts not shown separately. [2] After adjustment for the passive loss carryover from prior years. Therefore, "business receipts" minus "total deductions" do not equal "net income." [3] Based on the overall implicit price deflator for gross domestic product.

Source: U.S. Internal Revenue Service, *Statistics of Income Bulletin.*

Table 729. Partnerships—Selected Income and Balance Sheet Items: 1990 to 2002

[In billions of dollars (1,735 represents $1,735,000,000,000), except as indicated. Covers active partnerships only. All figures are estimates based on samples. See Appendix III]

Item	1990	1995	1996	1997	1998	1999	2000	2001	2002
Number of returns (1,000)	1,554	1,581	1,654	1,759	1,855	1,937	2,058	2,132	2,242
Returns with net income (1,000).	854	955	1,010	1,092	1,171	1,226	1,261	1,301	1,325
Number of partners (1,000).	17,095	15,606	15,662	16,184	15,663	15,924	13,660	14,232	14,328
Assets [1][2]	1,735	2,719	3,368	4,171	5,127	5,999	6,694	8,428	8,867
Depreciable assets (net)	681	767	848	980	1,153	1,314	1,487	1,646	1,792
Inventories, end of year	57	88	137	147	176	174	150	208	203
Land	215	221	232	257	291	326	359	392	423
Liabilities [1][2]	1,415	1,886	2,235	2,658	3,151	3,453	3,696	4,835	4,972
Accounts payable	67	91	121	159	191	244	230	362	346
Short-term debt [3].	88	124	126	127	230	232	252	289	283
Long-term debt [4]	498	544	607	706	884	989	1,132	1,286	1,375
Nonrecourse loans	470	466	474	492	523	582	639	700	770
Partners' capital accounts [2]	320	832	1,133	1,513	1,976	2,546	2,999	3,593	3,895
Receipts [1]	566	890	1,089	1,354	1,603	1,907	2,405	2,665	2,773
Business receipts [5]	483	854	1,042	1,297	1,534	1,829	2,316	2,569	2,669
Interest received	21	31	33	41	51	62	82	85	70
Deductions [1]	550	784	943	1,186	1,416	1,679	2,136	2,389	2,502
Cost of goods sold/operations	243	395	486	625	737	902	1,226	1,338	1,430
Salaries and wages	56	80	94	115	143	170	201	231	238
Taxes paid	9	13	15	18	24	27	31	35	36
Interest paid.	30	43	49	60	73	74	93	97	68
Depreciation.	60	23	29	38	43	52	59	72	83
Net income (less loss)	17	107	145	168	187	228	269	276	271
Net income.	116	179	228	262	298	348	410	446	440

[1] Includes items not shown separately. [2] Assets, liabilities, and partners' capital accounts are understated because not all partnerships file complete balance sheets. [3] Mortgages, notes, and bonds payable in less than 1 year. [4] Mortgages, notes, and bonds payable in 1 year or more. [5] Excludes investment income except for partnerships in finance, insurance, and real estate from 1995 to 1997. Beginning 1998 finance and insurance, real estate, and management of companies included investment income for partnerships.

Source: U.S. Internal Revenue Service, *Statistics of Income,* various issues.

Business Enterprise 505

Table 730. Partnerships—Selected Items by Industry: 2002

[In billions of dollars (8,867 represents $8,867,000,000,000), except as indicated. Covers active partnerships only. Figures are estimates based on samples. Based on the North American Industry Classification System (NAICS), 2002; see text, this section. See Appendix III]

INDUSTRY	NAICS code	Number of partnerships (1,000)			Total assets [1]	Business receipts [2]	Total deductions	Net income less loss	Net income	Net loss
		Total	With net income	With net loss						
Total [3]	(X)	2,242	1,325	917	8,867	2,669	2,502	270.7	439.8	169.1
Agriculture, forestry, fishing and hunting	11	118	61	57	80	18	25	-1.1	4.5	5.7
Mining	21	30	20	10	141	55	49	12.0	17.6	5.6
Utilities	22	3	1	1	165	147	148	1.1	5.6	4.5
Construction	23	134	79	56	145	170	164	10.7	15.8	5.0
Manufacturing	31-33	38	18	20	366	485	478	23.4	37.3	14.0
Wholesale trade	42	38	17	21	71	257	256	6.6	9.3	2.7
Retail trade	44-45	122	58	64	86	281	284	2.1	6.9	4.8
Transportation and warehousing	48-49	26	13	13	108	52	53	2.9	6.2	3.3
Information	51	29	11	18	383	167	186	-6.5	19.1	25.6
Finance and insurance	52	263	201	62	4,377	316	227	89.3	108.8	19.5
Real estate and rental and leasing	53	1,000	596	404	2,235	168	122	55.0	102.1	47.1
Professional, scientific, and technical services	54	146	94	52	109	218	177	54.4	61.0	6.6
Management of companies and enterprises	55	19	11	8	296	25	19	6.7	12.1	5.3
Admin/support waste mgt/remediation services	56	44	26	19	30	51	50	3.7	5.0	1.3
Educational services	61	6	4	3	6	2	3	-0.4	0.4	0.8
Health care and social assistance	62	47	31	17	61	102	94	13.4	16.6	3.2
Arts, entertainment and recreation	71	43	15	27	59	47	55	-1.8	4.2	6.0
Accommodation and food services	72	78	38	40	136	93	98	-1.4	5.5	6.9
Other services	81	57	31	26	12	15	15	0.5	1.6	1.1

X Not applicable.   [1] Total assets are understated because not all partnerships file complete balance sheets.   [2] Finance and insurance, real estate, and management of companies includes investment income for partnerships.   [3] Includes businesses not allocable to individual industries.

Source: U.S. Internal Revenue Service, *Statistics of Income*, various issues.

Table 731. Nonfarm Noncorporate Business-Sector Balance Sheet: 1990 to 2004

[In billions of dollars (3,733 represents $3,733,000,000,000), except as noted. Represents year-end outstandings]

Item	1990	1995	1998	1999	2000	2001	2002	2003	2004
Assets	3,733	4,116	5,378	5,850	6,511	6,812	7,143	7,685	8,325
Tangible assets	3,376	3,568	4,387	4,675	5,091	5,236	5,488	5,896	6,364
Real estate [1]	3,066	3,218	3,997	4,261	4,654	4,792	5,035	5,429	5,869
Residential	2,131	2,370	2,956	3,166	3,462	3,623	3,847	4,193	4,586
Nonresidential	935	848	1,041	1,095	1,191	1,169	1,188	1,237	1,283
Equipment and software [2]	263	294	329	348	367	377	384	397	419
Residential [3]	32	36	37	37	39	40	40	40	42
Nonresidential	232	259	292	311	329	338	344	357	377
Inventories [2]	47	56	61	66	70	67	69	70	77
Financial assets	356	548	991	1,175	1,420	1,575	1,655	1,789	1,960
Checkable deposits and currency	71	105	179	218	274	275	280	288	291
Time and savings deposits	51	71	98	118	138	145	156	164	173
Money market fund shares	7	17	33	41	49	59	61	53	50
Treasury securities	13	24	38	37	40	43	43	44	46
Municipal securities	-	2	3	3	2	4	3	4	4
Mortgages	31	22	25	23	21	23	23	25	25
Trade receivables	98	140	233	273	342	344	363	418	482
Miscellaneous assets	86	167	382	464	554	684	725	794	889
Insurance receivables	39	44	46	46	46	48	52	57	61
Equity investment in GSEs [4]	1	1	2	2	2	2	2	2	2
Other	47	122	335	416	506	634	671	735	826
Liabilities	1,349	1,396	2,021	2,332	2,674	2,890	3,085	3,331	3,595
Credit market instruments	1,093	1,062	1,405	1,600	1,797	1,959	2,108	2,264	2,432
Bank loans n.e.c. [5]	136	165	262	313	361	405	430	420	436
Other loans and advances	94	92	108	117	128	125	128	133	139
Mortgages	863	805	1,035	1,170	1,308	1,429	1,550	1,711	1,857
Trade payables	60	86	179	213	260	255	281	325	383
Taxes payable	32	33	44	53	65	69	70	80	84
Miscellaneous liabilities	164	215	393	467	553	607	626	663	695
Net worth	2,384	2,720	3,357	3,518	3,838	3,921	4,058	4,354	4,730
Debt/net worth (percent)	45.9	39.0	41.9	45.5	46.8	50.0	51.9	52.0	51.4

- Represents or rounds to zero.   [1] At market value.   [2] At replacement (current) cost.   [3] Durable goods in rental properties.   [4] GSEs = government-sponsored enterprises. Equity in the Farm Credit System.   [5] Not elsewhere classified.

Source: Board of Governors of the Federal Reserve System, "Federal Reserve Statistical Release, Z.1, Flow of Funds Accounts of the United States"; published: 10 March 2005; <http://www.federalreserve.gov/releases/Z1/20050310/data.htm>.

Table 732. Nonfinancial Corporate Business-Sector Balance Sheet: 1990 to 2004

[In billions of dollars (9,680 represents $9,680,000,000,000). Represents year-end outstandings]

Item	1990	1995	1998	1999	2000	2001	2002	2003	2004
Assets	9,680	11,459	14,838	16,627	18,928	19,019	19,353	20,322	21,423
Tangible assets	6,104	6.501	8,022	8,534	9,155	9,120	9,391	9,788	10,327
Real estate [1]	3,384	3,144	4,170	4,417	4,755	4,687	4,868	5,139	5,396
Equipment and software [2]	1,819	2,287	2,687	2,864	3,067	3,167	3,220	3,319	3,477
Inventories [2]	901	1,070	1,165	1,252	1,334	1,266	1,303	1,330	1,454
Financial assets [3]	3,575	4,959	6,816	8,094	9,772	9,899	9,962	10,534	11,097
Checkable deposits and currency	166	205	275	331	381	332	313	401	405
Time and savings deposits	75	100	113	137	137	131	128	172	204
Money market fund shares	20	60	126	155	191	302	329	291	280
Commercial paper	14	20	39	48	58	60	65	80	81
Treasury securities	38	57	24	19	18	16	31	52	68
Consumer credit	67	85	88	86	90	89	86	70	74
Trade receivables	967	1,185	1,440	1,648	1,931	1,802	1,722	1,841	2,022
Mutual fund shares [1]	10	46	98	127	124	111	97	121	129
Liabilities [3]	4,729	6,010	7,458	8,407	9,611	9,809	9,949	10,151	10,377
Credit market instruments	2,533	2,910	3,778	4,186	4,536	4,758	4,786	4,954	5,194
Commercial paper	117	157	193	230	278	190	126	86	102
Municipal securities [4]	115	135	148	153	154	158	161	164	170
Corporate bonds [5]	1,008	1,344	1,846	2,068	2,230	2,579	2,711	2,869	2,947
Bank loans n.e.c. [6]	545	602	769	809	853	744	636	571	580
Other loans and advances	473	454	562	585	651	659	675	681	707
Mortgages	274	218	261	341	369	429	477	582	688
Trade payables	626	878	1,050	1,228	1,541	1,438	1,462	1,571	1,732
Taxes payable	38	40	64	71	78	81	93	85	90
Net worth (market value)	4,950	5,450	7,380	8,220	9,316	9,209	9,404	10,171	11,047
Debt/net worth (percent)	51.2	53.4	51.2	50.9	48.7	51.7	50.9	48.7	47.0

[1] At market value. [2] At replacement (current) cost. [3] Includes items not shown separately. [4] Industrial revenue bonds. Issued by state and local governments to finance private investment and secured in interest and principal by the industrial user of the funds. [5] Through 1992, corporate bonds include net issues by Netherlands Antillean financial subsidiaries. [6] Not elsewhere classified.

Source: Board of Governors of the Federal Reserve System, Federal Reserve Statistical Release, Z.1, Flow of Funds Accounts of the United States; published: 10 March 2005; <http://www.federalreserve.gov/releases/Z1/20050310/data.htm>.

Table 733. Corporate Funds—Sources and Uses: 1990 to 2004

[In billions of dollars (238 represents $238,000,000,000). Covers nonfarm nonfinancial corporate business]

Item	1990	1995	1998	1999	2000	2001	2002	2003	2004
Profits before tax (book)	238	419	449	457	422	310	323	397	488
- Taxes on corporate income	98	141	158	171	170	111	89	130	157
- Net dividends	117	177	240	223	250	243	253	273	305
+ Capital consumption allowance [1]	365	463	558	598	629	678	746	804	884
= U.S. internal funds, book	388	564	609	661	632	632	728	798	911
+ Foreign earnings retained abroad	51	60	60	80	116	129	115	156	151
+ Inventory valuation adjustment (IVA)	-13	-18	20	1	-14	11	-1	-14	-38
= Internal funds + IVA	426	606	690	742	734	773	842	940	1,024
Gross investment	369	653	733	846	900	885	802	984	1,073
Capital expenditures [2]	429	618	779	864	929	802	763	770	900
Fixed investment [3]	422	577	715	806	882	841	761	781	867
Inventory change + IVA	12	40	66	66	55	-30	12	-1	43
Net financial investment	-59	36	-46	-18	-28	82	39	214	172
Net acquisition of financial assets [2]	124	426	570	970	1,209	178	151	488	524
Time and savings deposits	-6	3	-7	24	(Z)	-6	-4	44	31
Money market fund shares	9	23	39	28	37	111	27	-38	-11
Treasury securities	-14	6	-3	-4	-1	-2	15	20	16
Agency- and GSE-backed securities [4]	-6	4	3	2	3	2	(Z)	8	9
Trade receivables	29	78	79	208	283	-129	-80	119	182
Miscellaneous assets [2]	114	320	431	666	811	256	188	221	283
U.S. direct investment abroad [5]	35	90	129	194	128	119	119	142	164
Insurance receivables	13	8	2	1	(Z)	10	17	18	22
Investment in finance company subsidiaries	10	5	-6	27	7	-2	-5	6	9
Net increase in liabilities [2]	184	391	616	988	1,237	95	111	273	352
Net funds raised in markets	71	169	180	260	232	174	-14	87	30
Net new equity issues	-63	-58	-216	-110	-118	-47	-42	-58	-210
Credit market instruments [2]	134	227	396	370	350	221	28	145	240
Commercial paper	10	18	24	37	48	-88	-64	-40	16
Corporate bonds [5]	47	91	235	222	163	348	132	158	78
Bank loans n.e.c. [6]	3	75	76	40	44	-110	-108	-64	9
Other loans and advances [2]	56	32	54	23	66	8	16	6	26
Finance companies	16	24	33	49	57	-10	7	2	15
Mortgages	19	8	(Z)	43	29	59	49	82	106
Trade payables	28	81	58	178	313	-104	24	109	161
Miscellaneous liabilities [2]	84	141	373	542	685	22	89	86	155
Foreign direct investment in U.S.	59	54	144	247	181	88	22	9	37

Z Less than $500 million. [1] Consumption of fixed capital plus capital consumption adjustment. [2] Includes other items not shown separately. [3] Nonresidential fixed investment plus residential fixed investment. [4] GSE = government-sponsored enterprises. [5] 1990, corporate bonds include net issues by Netherlands Antillean financial subsidiaries, and U.S. direct investment abroad excludes net inflows from those bond issues. [6] Not elsewhere classified.

Source: Board of Governors of the Federal Reserve System, Federal Reserve Statistical Release, Z.1, Flow of Funds Accounts of the United States; published: 10 March 2005; <http://www.federalreserve.gov/releases/Z1/20050310/data.htm>.

U.S. Census Bureau, Statistical Abstract of the United States: 2006

Table 734. **Corporations—Selected Financial Items: 1990 to 2002**

[In billions of dollars (18,190 represents $18,190,000,000,000), except as noted. Covers active corporations only. All corporations are required to file returns except those specifically exempt. See source for changes in law affecting comparability of historical data. Based on samples; see Appendix III]

Item	1990	1995	1996	1997	1998	1999	2000	2001	2002
Number of returns (1,000)	3,717	4,474	4,631	4,710	4,849	4,936	5,045	5,136	5,267
Number with net income (1,000) . . .	1,911	2,455	2,588	2,647	2,761	2,812	2,819	2,822	2,800
S Corporation returns [1] (1,000)	1,575	2,153	2,304	2,452	2,588	2,726	2,860	2,986	3,154
Assets [2]	18,190	26,014	28,642	33,030	37,347	41,464	47,027	49,154	50,414
Cash	771	962	1,097	1,299	1,336	1,597	1,820	1,926	1,923
Notes and accounts receivable	4,198	5,307	5,783	6,632	7,062	7,745	8,754	8,756	8,886
Inventories.	894	1,045	1,079	1,114	1,139	1,198	1,272	1,208	1,221
Investments in government									
obligations	921	1,363	1,339	1,343	1,366	1,340	1,236	1,392	1,527
Mortgage and real estate	1,538	1,713	1,825	2,029	2,414	2,555	2,822	3,229	3,687
Other investments.	4,137	7,429	8,657	10,756	13,201	15,799	17,874	18,344	18,728
Depreciable assets	4,318	5,571	5,923	6,208	6,541	6,936	7,292	7,614	7,678
Depletable assets	129	154	169	177	193	184	191	199	226
Land.	210	242	254	262	271	286	303	320	326
Liabilities [2]	18,190	26,014	28,642	33,030	37,347	41,464	47,027	49,154	50,414
Accounts payable	1,094	1,750	1,905	2,111	2,501	2,792	3,758	3,927	4,074
Short-term debt [3]	1,803	2,034	2,328	2,582	3,216	3,658	4,020	4,132	3,814
Long-term debt [4]	2,665	3,335	3,651	4,072	4,813	5,448	6,184	6,782	7,185
Net worth	4,739	8,132	9,495	11,353	13,108	15,363	17,349	17,615	17,545
Capital stock.	1,585	2,194	2,278	2,951	3,244	3,522	3,966	4,253	4,000
Paid-in or capital surplus.	2,814	5,446	6,427	7,253	8,610	10,186	12,265·	13,920	15,287
Retained earnings [5]	1,410	2,191	2,519	3,113	3,373	3,970	3,627	2,131	1,177
Receipts [2, 6]	11,410	14,539	15,526	16,610	17,324	18,892	20,606	20,273	19,749
Business receipts [6, 7]	9,860	12,786	13,659	14,461	15,010	16,314	17,637	17,504	17,297
Interest [8]	977	1,039	1,082	1,140	1,277	1,354	1,628	1,549	1,281
Rents and royalties	133	145	156	176	200	223	254	251	252
Deductions [2, 6]	11,033	13,821	14,728	15,704	16,489	17,967	19,692	19,683	19,199
Cost of sales and operations [7]	6,611	8,206	8,707	9,114	9,362	10,284	11,135	11,042	10,607
Compensation of officers	205	304	319	336	357	374	401	383	381
Rent paid on business property	185	232	248	265	308	347	380	398	411
Taxes paid.	251	326	341	350	355	371	390	392	397
Interest paid.	825	744	771	866	967	1,019	1,272	1,203	913
Depreciation	333	437	474	513	542	584	614	650	711
Advertising	126	463	177	188	198	216	234	220	218
Net income (less loss) [6, 9]	371	714	806	915	838	929	928	604	564
Net income	553	881	987	1,118	1,091	1,229	1,337	1,112	1,053
Deficit.	182	166	180	202	253	300	409	508	490
Income subject to tax	366	565	640	684	663	694	760	635	601
Income tax before credits [10]	119	194	220	235	231	242	266	221	210
Tax credits	32	42	53	55	50	49	62	54	56
Foreign tax credit	25	30	40	42	37	38	49	41	42
Income tax after credits [11]	96	156	171	184	182	193	204	167	154

[1] Represents certain small corporations with up to 75 shareholders (35 for 1990–1996), mostly individuals, electing to be taxed at the shareholder level. [2] Includes items not shown separately. [3] Payable in less than 1 year. [4] Payable in 1 year or more. [5] Appropriated and unappropriated and "adjustments to shareholders' equity." [6] Receipts, deductions and net income of S corporations are limited to those from trade or business. Those from investments are excluded. [7] Includes gross sales and cost of sales of securities, commodities, and real estate by exchanges, brokers, or dealers selling on their own accounts. Excludes investment income. [8] Includes tax-exempt interest in state and local government obligations. [9] Excludes regulated investment companies. [10] Consists of regular (and alternative) tax only. [11] Includes minimum tax, alternative minimum tax, adjustments for prior year credits, and other income-related taxes.

Source: U.S. Internal Revenue Service, *Statistics of Income, Corporation Income Tax Returns*, annual.

Table 735. **Corporations by Receipt-Size Class and Industry: 2002**

[Number of returns in thousands (5,267 represents 5,267,000); receipts and net income in billions of dollars (18,849 represents $18,849,000,000,000). Covers active enterprises only. Figures are estimates based on a sample of unaudited tax returns; see Appendix III. Numbers in parentheses represent North American Industry Classification System 2002 codes, see text, this section]

Industry	Total	Under $1 mil. [1]	$1 mil.-$4.9 mil.	$5 mil.-$9.9 mil.	$10 mil.-$49.9 mil.	$50 mil. or more
Total: [2]						
Number of returns . . .	5,267	4,304	720	115	102	25
Business receipts [3] . . .	18,849	882	1,528	793	2,070	13,575
Net income (less loss) . . .	564	-14	23	16	59	479
Agriculture, forestry, fishing, and hunting (11):						
Number . . .	140	125	13	2	1	(Z)
Business receipts [3] . . .	108	19	26	12	21	30
Mining (21):						
Number . . .	30	25	4	(Z)	(Z)	(Z)
Business receipts [3] . . .	142	4	9	3	12	115
Utilities (22):						
Number . . .	8	5	(Z)	(Z)	(Z)	(Z)
Business receipts [3] . . .	537	1	1	(Z)	3	533
Construction (23):						
Number . . .	649	502	113	18	13	2
Business receipts [3] . . .	1,080	124	242	125	256	333
Manufacturing (31-33):						
Number . . .	280	173	69	16	17	6
Business receipts [3] . . .	4,823	47	161	110	348	4,157
Wholesale and retail trade (42,44-45):						
Number . . .	965	657	217	40	41	10
Business receipts [3] . . .	5,279	176	475	274	858	3,496
Transportation and warehousing (48-49):						
Number . . .	178	143	27	5	3	1
Business receipts [3] . . .	511	28	55	31	60	336
Information (51):						
Number . . .	120	103	12	2	2	1
Business receipts [3] . . .	799	15	24	13	45	701
Finance and insurance (52):						
Number . . .	224	188	23	5	6	3
Business receipts [3] . . .	2,606	33	51	37	123	2,361
Real estate and rental and leasing (53):						
Number . . .	571	547	21	2	1	(Z)
Business receipts [3] . . .	205	48	43	13	25	75
Professional, scientific, and technical services (54):						
Number . . .	736	654	65	10	6	1
Business receipts [3] . . .	652	112	128	67	120	225
Management of companies & enterprises (55):						
Number . . .	48	42	2	1	2	(Z)
Business receipts [3] . . .	690	1	7	10	36	637
Administrative and support and waste management and remediation services (56):						
Number . . .	231	195	31	3	2	1
Business receipts [3] . . .	338	41	63	22	41	171
Educational services (61):						
Number . . .	41	38	3	(Z)	(Z)	(Z)
Business receipts [3] . . .	25	5	6	1	4	9
Health care and social services (62):						
Number . . .	334	273	51	5	4	1
Business receipts [3] . . .	448	83	104	36	69	156
Arts, entertainment, and recreation (71):						
Number . . .	111	101	9	1	(Z)	(Z)
Business receipts [3] . . .	73	16	17	4	9	26
Accommodation and food services (72):						
Number . . .	272	231	37	3	1	(Z)
Business receipts [3] . . .	372	65	71	19	27	190
Other services (81):						
Number . . .	321	295	24	2	1	(Z)
Business receipts [3] . . .	159	63	44	15	13	25

Z Less than 500 returns or $500 million.   [1] Includes businesses without receipts.   [2] Includes businesses not allocable to individual industries.   [3] Includes investment income for corporations in finance and insurance and management of companies' industries. Excludes investment income for S corporations (certain small corporations with up to 75 shareholders, mostly individuals, electing to be taxed at the shareholder level).

Source: U.S. Internal Revenue Service, unpublished data.

Table 736. **Corporations by Asset-Size Class and Industry: 2002**

[In millions of dollars (119,151 represents $119,151,000,000), except number of returns. Covers active corporations only. Excludes corporations not allocable by industry. Numbers in parentheses represent North American Industry Classification System 2002 codes, see text, this section]

Industry	Total	Asset-size class					
		Under $10 mil. [1]	$10-$24.9 mil.	$25-$49.9 mil.	$50-$99.9 mil.	$100-$249.9 mil.	$250 mil. and over
Agriculture, forestry, fishing, and hunting (11):							
Returns.	140,223	139,364	537	172	82	49	18
Total receipts	119,151	79,413	8,895	6,712	6,031	7,970	10,129
Mining (21):							
Returns.	30,287	29,242	470	211	107	101	155
Total receipts	157,299	21,003	5,442	5,086	3,878	7,969	113,921
Utilities (22):							
Returns.	7,863	7,491	100	51	28	45	149
Total receipts	578,343	5,955	1,386	1,142	3,912	4,165	561,783
Construction (23):							
Returns.	648,535	642,992	3,877	941	420	171	134
Total receipts	1,098,819	674,750	111,621	57,354	49,700	36,825	168,569
Manufacturing (31-33):							
Returns.	280,185	265,959	7,098	2,754	1,638	1,245	1,492
Total receipts	5,257,106	497,855	184,681	140,290	156,330	233,178	4,044,773
Wholesale and retail trade (42, 44-45):							
Returns.	964,523	948,963	10,165	2,763	1,221	697	715
Total receipts	5,403,354	1,747,075	494,596	275,465	217,122	249,334	2,419,761
Transportation and warehousing (48-49):							
Returns.	177,745	176,165	906	270	154	116	133
Total receipts	533,613	160,844	25,744	14,569	14,467	20,743	297,246
Information (51):							
Returns.	120,271	117,516	1,262	516	323	253	401
Total receipts	909,195	77,821	19,850	15,647	17,485	28,018	750,374
Finance and insurance (52):							
Returns.	224,352	205,743	3,662	2,722	2,848	3,519	5,859
Total receipts	2,605,572	178,984	24,103	23,234	28,496	64,354	2,286,400
Real estate and rental and leasing (53):							
Returns.	570,639	565,531	3,389	960	409	217	134
Total receipts	230,647	119,176	14,631	9,533	7,755	15,635	63,918
Professional, scientific, and technical services (54):							
Returns.	736,005	732,836	1,773	650	309	254	183
Total receipts	683,880	417,620	41,895	30,225	22,138	40,987	131,014
Management of companies and enterprises (55):							
Returns.	48,053	41,573	1,120	1,065	1,348	1,585	1,363
Total receipts	689,799	5,762	1,434	2,277	6,820	17,045	656,462
Administrative and support and waste management and remediation services (56):							
Returns.	231,412	230,438	488	200	114	72	99
Total receipts	350,217	172,795	19,611	14,352	14,838	14,541	114,080
Educational services (61):							
Returns.	41,317	41,169	76	28	22	11	11
Total receipts	25,972	14,243	1,800	1,223	2,018	1,574	5,115
Health care and social assistance (62):							
Returns.	334,305	333,314	533	190	112	79	76
Total receipts	463,254	301,150	16,230	11,957	10,758	18,392	104,766
Arts, entertainment, and recreation (71):							
Returns.	110,609	109,958	379	137	51	55	28
Total receipts	78,918	45,005	4,520	3,107	3,326	7,498	15,462
Accommodation and food services (72):							
Returns.	271,527	270,295	695	203	115	95	121
Total receipts	399,787	172,084	13,098	8,584	8,731	17,715	179,574
Other services (81):							
Returns.	321,134	320,686	284	70	40	31	22
Total receipts	164,353	130,982	5,917	2,874	4,350	6,411	13,819

[1] Includes returns with zero assets.

Source: U.S. Internal Revenue Service, *Statistics of Income, Corporation Income Tax Returns*, annual.

Table 737. Economic Census Summary (NAICS 1997 Basis): 1997 and 2002

[25 represents 25,000. Data for 2002 are preliminary. Data are based on the 1997 and 2002 economic censuses which are subject to nonsampling error. Data for the construction sector are also subject to sampling errors. For details on survey methodology and nonsampling and sampling errors, see Appendix III]

Kind of business	NAICS code [1]	Establishments (1,000)		Sales, receipts or shipments (bil. dol.)		Annual payroll (bil. dol.)		Paid employees [2] (1,000)	
		1997	2002	1997	2002	1997	2002	1997	2002
Mining	21	25	(S)	174	(S)	20.8	(S)	509	(S)
Oil & gas extraction	211	8	8	103	107	5.5	5.4	111	100
Mining (except oil & gas)	212	7	7	51	54	9.4	8.9	229	200
Mining support activities	213	9	(S)	20	(S)	5.9	(S)	169	(S)
Utilities	22	16	19	412	478	36.6	45.1	703	739
Construction [3]	23	656	698	859	1,140	174.2	235.5	5,665	6,944
Manufacturing	31-33	363	344	3,835	3,833	569.8	568.4	16,805	14,543
Wholesale trade	42	453	442	4,060	4,379	214.9	255.6	5,797	6,035
Wholesale trade, durable goods	421	291	288	2,180	2,354	133.2	159.0	3,398	3,565
Wholesale trade, nondurable goods	422	163	154	1,880	2,025	81.7	96.6	2,398	2,470
Retail trade	44-45	1,118	1,112	2,461	3,171	237.2	306.0	13,991	15,029
Motor vehicle & parts dealers	441	123	123	645	812	50.2	64.3	1,719	1,884
Furniture & home furnishings stores	442	65	65	72	94	10.0	13.0	483	554
Electronics & appliance stores	443	43	47	69	88	7.1	10.0	345	418
Building material & garden equipment & supply dealers	444	93	(S)	228	(S)	25.6	(S)	1,118	(S)
Food & beverage stores	445	149	150	402	488	40.6	49.1	2,893	2,896
Health & personal care stores	446	83	79	118	183	15.2	20.6	904	1,043
Gasoline stations	447	127	(S)	198	(S)	11.5	(S)	922	(S)
Clothing & clothing accessories stores	448	157	149	136	170	16.6	21.2	1,280	1,425
Sporting goods, hobby, book, & music stores	451	69	63	62	78	7.1	9.0	561	633
General merchandise stores	452	36	40	330	451	30.9	42.6	2,508	2,549
Miscellaneous store retailers	453	130	129	78	95	10.2	13.7	753	849
Nonstore retailers	454	44	56	123	171	12.3	17.6	506	587
Transportation & warehousing [4][5]	48-49	178	201	318	(S)	82.3	116.8	2,921	3,751
Information [4]	51	114	137	623	905	129.5	189.7	3,066	3,846
Publishing industries	511	34	32	179	235	43.4	64.1	1,006	1,132
Motion picture & sound recording industries	512	22	23	56	77	9.4	11.7	276	334
Broadcasting & telecommunications	513	43	57	346	499	63.5	83.7	1,434	1,740
Information & data processing services [4]	514	15	25	42	94	13.3	30.2	350	638
Finance & insurance [6]	52	395	449	2,198	2,616	264.6	343.5	5,835	6,664
Real estate & rental & leasing [6]	53	288	326	241	348	41.6	61.8	1,702	2,136
Professional, scientific, & technical services [4]	54	621	747	595	896	231.4	374.5	5,361	7,509
Management of companies & enterprises	55	47	(S)	92	(S)	154.2	(S)	2,618	(S)
Admin/support waste management/ remediation services [4]	56	276	276	296	414	137.3	193.5	7,347	8,345
Administrative & support services [4]	561	260	258	257	362	128.4	181.4	7,067	8,003
Waste management & remediation services [4]	562	16	18	39	51	8.9	12.1	281	342
Educational services [4]	61	41	50	20	32	6.4	10.2	321	452
Health care and social assistance	62	646	712	885	1,234	378.2	497.8	13,562	15,347
Ambulatory health care services	621	455	492	355	500	155.9	204.3	4,414	5,071
Hospitals	622	7	7	379	511	155.8	196.2	4,933	5,165
Nursing & residential care facilities	623	57	70	93	130	42.2	59.8	2,471	2,878
Social assistance	624	126	144	57	93	24.4	37.6	1,744	2,233
Arts, entertainment, & recreation	71	99	111	105	138	32.8	43.1	1,588	1,896
Performance arts, spectator sports, & related industries	711	31	39	38	55	14.5	19.6	327	438
Museums, historical sites, & like institutions	712	6	7	7	9	1.8	2.9	92	124
Amusement, gambling, & recreation industries	713	63	66	60	74	16.5	20.6	1,169	1,334
Accommodation & food services	72	545	565	350	452	97.0	127.5	9,451	10,836
Accommodation	721	58	(S)	98	(S)	26.7	(S)	1,697	(S)
Food services & drinking places	722	487	(S)	252	(S)	70.3	(S)	7,755	(S)
Other services (except public administration) [4]	81	520	528	266	315	65.5	82.7	3,256	3,528
Repair & maintenance [4]	811	235	233	105	120	29.9	35.5	1,276	1,367
Personal and laundry services [4]	812	185	192	58	73	18.6	22.6	1,217	1,311
Religious/grantmaking/prof/like organizations	813	99	102	103	122	17.1	24.6	763	849

S Estimates did not meet publication standards. [1] Based on North American Industry Classification System, 1997; see text this section. [2] For pay period including March 12. [3] For detailed industries, see Table 922. [4] Enterprise support establishments are included in the 2002 data, but not in the 1997 data affecting comparability for this industry. [5] For detailed industries, see Table 1048. [6] For detailed industries, see Table 1152.

Source: U.S. Census Bureau, 2002 Economic Census Advance Report, published 29 March 2004; <http://www.census.gov/econ/census02/>.

Business Enterprise **511**

Table 738. **Nonemployer Establishments and Receipts by Industry: 1997 to 2002**

[**Establishments: 15,440 represents 15,440,000.** Includes only firms subject to federal income tax. Nonemployers are businesses with no paid employees. Data originate chiefly from administrative records of the Internal Revenue Service; see Appendix III. Based on the North American Industry Classification System (NAICS), 1997; see text, this section]

Kind of business	NAICS code	Establishments (1,000)			Receipts (mil. dol)		
		1997	2000	2002	1997	2000	2002
All industries	(X)	**15,440**	**16,530**	**17,646**	**586,316**	**709,379**	**770,032**
Forestry, fishing & ag support services	113-115	240	223	220	8,533	9,196	8,994
Mining	21	92	86	83	4,964	5,227	4,924
Utilities.	22	16	14	13	515	504	549
Construction	23	1,890	2,014	2,071	87,101	107,538	115,269
Manufacturing	31-33	303	285	290	12,319	13,022	13,402
Wholesale trade	42	406	388	364	30,759	31,684	30,022
Retail trade	44-45	1,831	1,743	1,839	69,418	73,810	77,896
Transportation & warehousing	48-49	646	747	809	29,428	37,824	40,698
Information	51	174	238	233	5,767	7,620	7,550
Finance & insurance	52	679	692	660	36,966	49,058	44,139
Real estate & rental & leasing	53	1,397	1,696	1,880	101,704	133,398	161,790
Professional, scientific, & technical services	54	2,650	2,420	2,553	81,165	90,272	96,395
Admin/support waste mgt/ remediation services	56	892	1,032	1,263	16,975	23,754	26,910
Educational services	61	235	283	345	2,798	3,736	4,581
Health care & social assistance	62	1,168	1,317	1,457	31,203	36,550	42,268
Arts, entertainment, & recreation	71	693	782	866	14,366	17,713	20,000
Accommodation & food services	72	191	218	242	9,035	13,418	14,178
Other services (except public administration)	81	1,936	2,350	2,459	43,299	55,056	60,468

X Not applicable.

Source: U.S. Census Bureau, "Nonemployer Statistics"; <http://www.census.gov/epcd/nonemployer/> and *2002 Economic Census: Advance Nonemployer Statistics*; published 21 May 2004; <http://www.census.gov/epcd/nonemployer/2002/us/US000.HTM>.

Table 739. **Establishments, Employees, and Payroll by Employment-Size Class: 1990 to 2002**

[**6,176 represents 6,176,000.** Excludes most government employees, railroad employees, self-employed persons. Employees are for the week including March 12. Covers establishments with payroll. An *establishment* is a single physical location where business is conducted or where services or industrial operations are performed. For statement on methodology, see Appendix III]

Employment-size class	Unit	1990	1995	1997	1998	1999	2000	2001	2002
Establishments, total. . . .	**1,000**	**6,176**	**6,613**	**6,895**	**6,942**	**7,008**	**7,070**	**7,095**	**7,201**
Under 20 employees.	1,000	5,354	5,733	5,968	5,991	6,036	6,069	6,083	6,199
20 to 99 employees	1,000	684	730	767	786	802	826	836	835
100 to 499 employees.	1,000	122	135	143	147	152	157	157	149
500 to 999 employees.	1,000	10	10	11	11	12	12	12	11
1,000 or more employees . . .	1,000	6	6	6	6	7	7	7	7
Employees, total	**1,000**	**93,476**	**100,335**	**105,299**	**108,118**	**110,706**	**114,065**	**115,061**	**112,401**
Under 20 employees.	1,000	24,373	25,785	26,883	27,131	27,289	27,569	27,681	28,116
20 to 99 employees	1,000	27,414	29,202	30,631	31,464	32,193	33,147	33,555	33,335
100 to 499 employees.	1,000	22,926	25,364	26,993	27,842	28,707	29,736	29,692	28,101
500 to 999 employees.	1,000	6,551	7,021	7,422	7,689	7,923	8,291	8,357	7,743
1,000 or more employees . . .	1,000	12,212	12,962	13,370	13,991	14,594	15,322	15,776	15,105
Annual payroll, total	**Bil. dol. . . .**	**2,104**	**2,666**	**3,048**	**3,309**	**3,555**	**3,879**	**3,989**	**3,943**
Under 20 employees.	Bil. dol. . . .	485	608	688	734	773	818	839	866
20 to 99 employees	Bil. dol. . . .	547	696	796	866	925	1,006	1,037	1,041
100 to 499 employees.	Bil. dol. . . .	518	675	786	858	931	1,031	1,052	1,021
500 to 999 employees.	Bil. dol. . . .	174	219	254	277	298	336	342	329
1,000 or more employees . . .	Bil. dol. . . .	381	467	524	575	628	690	719	685

Source: U.S. Census Bureau, "County Business Patterns"; published November 2004; <http://www.census.gov/epcd/cbp/view/cbpview.html>.

Table 740. Establishments, Employees, and Payroll by Employment-Size Class and Industry: 2000 to 2002

[Establishments and employees in thousands (7,070.0 represents 7,070,000); payroll in billions of dollars. See headnote, Table 739. Based on the North American Industry Classification System (NAICS), 1997; see text, this section]

Industry	NAICS code	2000, total	2001, total	2002 Total	2002 Under 20 employees	2002 20 to 99 employees	2002 100 to 499 employees	2002 500 to 999 employees	2002 1,000 or more employees
Establishments, total	(X)	7,070.0	7,095.3	7,200.8	6,198.5	835.2	148.9	11.4	6.7
Agriculture, forestry, fishing & hunting	11	26.1	26.4	26.6	24.9	1.5	0.2	(Z)	(Z)
Mining	21	23.7	24.3	23.9	19.6	3.6	0.7	0.1	(Z)
Utilities	22	17.3	17.7	18.4	13.2	3.9	1.2	0.1	0.1
Construction	23	709.6	698.9	710.3	647.4	55.6	6.8	0.3	0.1
Manufacturing	31-33	354.5	352.6	344.3	236.5	77.6	26.4	2.6	1.2
Wholesale trade	42	446.2	438.9	436.9	374.7	54.2	7.4	0.4	0.1
Retail trade	44-45	1,113.6	1,120.0	1,125.7	977.5	123.6	24.0	0.5	0.1
Transportation and warehousing	48-49	190.0	190.7	195.1	165.1	25.1	4.5	0.3	0.3
Information	51	133.6	137.3	138.6	109.9	22.0	5.7	0.7	0.3
Finance and insurance	52	423.7	425.0	450.4	403.6	38.5	6.9	0.9	0.5
Real estate and rental and leasing	53	300.2	307.0	323.0	307.8	13.4	1.7	0.1	(Z)
Professional, scientific, and technical services	54	722.7	736.5	772.4	712.2	51.6	7.7	0.6	0.3
Management of companies and enterprises	55	47.4	47.6	49.4	33.1	10.9	4.3	0.7	0.4
Admin/support waste mgt/remediation services	56	351.5	362.7	343.5	284.7	43.4	13.7	1.1	0.7
Educational services	61	68.0	70.9	73.7	55.7	14.3	2.9	0.4	0.4
Health care and social assistance	62	658.6	671.4	703.5	600.1	80.9	19.1	1.7	1.8
Arts, entertainment, and recreation	71	103.8	106.0	110.4	92.2	15.3	2.5	0.2	0.1
Accommodation and food services	72	542.4	548.6	565.1	405.4	151.3	8.0	0.3	0.2
Other services [1]	81	723.3	719.4	740.1	691.1	45.0	3.9	0.1	(Z)
Auxiliaries [2]	95	14.8	14.9	13.6	8.3	3.5	1.4	0.3	0.1
Unclassified establishments	99	99.0	78.6	35.7	35.7	0.1	(Z)	-	-
Employees, total	(X)	114,065	115,061	112,401	28,116	33,335	28,101	7,743	15,105
Agriculture, forestry, fishing & hunting	11	184	183	181	91	(D)	(D)	(D)	(D)
Mining	21	456	486	466	93	(D)	137	(D)	56
Utilities	22	655	654	648	69	172	227	87	93
Construction	23	6,573	6,492	6,307	2,457	2,137	1,229	228	258
Manufacturing	31-33	16,474	15,950	14,394	1,365	3,401	5,332	1,780	2,515
Wholesale trade	42	6,112	6,142	5,860	1,815	2,104	1,358	291	293
Retail trade	44-45	14,841	14,890	14,820	5,181	4,960	4,254	321	104
Transportation and warehousing	48-49	3,790	3,751	3,581	679	1,024	826	187	865
Information	51	3,546	3,755	3,536	507	935	1,126	445	523
Finance and insurance	52	5,963	6,248	6,415	1,784	1,487	1,388	628	1,127
Real estate and rental and leasing	53	1,942	2,014	2,017	1,080	503	313	(D)	(D)
Professional, scientific, and technical services	54	6,816	7,157	7,046	2,464	1,984	1,473	403	722
Management of companies and enterprises	55	2,874	2,879	2,914	175	490	919	501	829
Admin/support waste mgt/remediation services	56	9,138	9,062	8,299	1,120	1,906	2,659	735	1,878
Educational services	61	2,532	2,612	2,702	267	599	566	266	1,003
Health care and social assistance	62	14,109	14,535	14,900	3,152	3,231	3,549	1,176	3,793
Arts, entertainment, and recreation	71	1,741	1,780	1,801	346	643	460	111	241
Accommodation and food services	72	9,881	9,972	10,049	2,467	5,763	1,273	198	348
Other services [1]	81	5,293	5,370	5,420	2,921	1,641	668	84	105
Auxiliaries [2]	95	1,001	1,022	1,011	52	155	316	190	299
Unclassified establishments	99	144	105	33	30	(D)	(D)	-	-
Annual payroll, total	(X)	3,879	3,989	3,943	866	1,041	1,021	329	685
Agriculture, forestry, fishing & hunting	11	5	5	5	2	(D)	(D)	(D)	(D)
Mining	21	22	25	24	4	(D)	8	(D)	4
Utilities	22	41	42	42	4	10	15	7	7
Construction	23	240	247	247	82	89	56	10	11
Manufacturing	31-33	644	618	580	44	121	205	75	135
Wholesale trade	42	270	276	263	75	92	64	15	17
Retail trade	44-45	303	315	321	104	113	93	8	4
Transportation and warehousing	48-49	126	130	127	21	34	28	7	37
Information	51	209	207	188	24	44	61	25	33
Finance and insurance	52	347	374	373	83	86	89	38	76
Real estate and rental and leasing	53	59	64	65	32	18	11	(D)	(D)
Professional, scientific, and technical services	54	362	374	369	111	110	91	24	32
Management of companies and enterprises	55	211	213	205	13	32	61	35	64
Admin/support waste mgt/remediation services	56	210	221	212	35	52	62	17	46
Educational services	61	62	67	72	6	14	15	6	32
Health care and social assistance	62	431	466	499	118	98	95	40	150
Arts, entertainment, and recreation	71	43	46	48	12	12	15	3	5
Accommodation and food services	72	126	129	131	32	66	20	4	9
Other services [1]	81	110	115	119	59	36	18	3	3
Auxiliaries [2]	95	55	53	53	3	7	15	9	19
Unclassified establishments	99	4	2	1	1	(D)	(D)	-	-

- Represents zero.   D Data withheld to avoid disclosure.   X Not applicable.   Z Less than 50 establishments.   [1] Except public administration.   [2] Excludes corporate, subsidiary and regional management.

Source: U.S. Census Bureau, "County Business Patterns"; published November 2004; <http://www.census.gov/epcd/cbp/view/cbpview.html>.

Business Enterprise   513

[5,698 represents 5,698,000. A firm is an aggregation of all establishments owned by a parent company (within a geographic location and/or industry) with some annual payroll. A firm may be a single location or it can include multiple locations. Employment is measured in March and payroll is annual leading to some firms with zero employment. Numbers in parentheses represent North American Industry Classification System codes, 1997; see text, this section]

Industry and data type	Unit		All industries—employment size of enterprise							
		Total	0	1 to 4	5 to 9	10 to 19	20 to 99	100 to 499	Less than 500	500 or more
Total [1]:										
Firms	1,000 . . .	5,698	770	2,696	1,011	614	508	82	5,681	17
Employment	1,000 . . .	112,401	-	5,698	6,640	8,246	19,874	15,909	56,366	56,034
Annual payroll	Bil. dol. . .	3,943	38	156	182	241	624	536	1,777	2,166
Construction (23):										
Firms	1,000 . . .	701	117	338	118	69	52	6	700	1
Employment	1,000 . . .	6,307	-	715	774	930	1,946	997	5,361	946
Annual payroll	Bil. dol. . .	247	5	20	23	32	79	44	203	45
Manufacturing (31-33):										
Firms	1,000 . . .	298	22	97	56	47	58	14	294	4
Employment	1,000 . . .	14,394	-	220	372	639	2,376	2,488	6,095	8,299
Annual payroll	Bil. dol. . .	580	2	6	11	20	82	91	212	368
Wholesale trade (42):										
Firms	1,000 . . .	345	36	156	61	42	39	8	342	3
Employment	1,000 . . .	5,860	-	328	405	565	1,421	960	3,679	2,181
Annual payroll	Bil. dol. . .	263	2	12	15	22	58	41	150	112
Retail trade (44-45):										
Firms	1,000 . . .	736	85	344	150	86	60	9	734	2
Employment	1,000 . . .	14,820	-	771	988	1,131	2,204	1,268	6,361	8,459
Annual payroll	Bil. dol. . .	321	3	14	19	24	61	37	157	164
Transportation & warehousing (48-49):										
Firms	1,000 . . .	159	24	78	23	16	15	3	158	1
Employment	1,000 . . .	3,581	-	152	151	212	555	421	1,491	2,090
Annual payroll	Bil. dol. . .	127	1	4	4	6	16	14	45	83
Information (51):										
Firms	1,000 . . .	78	12	34	12	8	8	2	77	1
Employment	1,000 . . .	3,536	-	68	78	114	319	324	904	2,632
Annual payroll	Bil. dol. . .	188	1	3	3	4	15	16	42	146
Finance & insurance (52):										
Firms	1,000 . . .	238	29	138	34	16	15	4	236	2
Employment	1,000 . . .	6,415	-	282	215	214	600	652	1,963	4,451
Annual payroll	Bil. dol. . .	373	2	10	10	12	33	37	102	270
Professional, scientific & technical services (54):										
Firms	1,000 . . .	708	113	394	100	55	38	6	706	2
Employment	1,000 . . .	7,046	-	761	652	726	1,392	992	4,523	2,523
Annual payroll	Bil. dol. . .	369	6	28	26	33	76	58	228	141
Management of companies & enterprises (55):										
Firms	1,000 . . .	28	1	4	1	1	6	8	22	7
Employment	1,000 . . .	2,914	-	6	5	9	77	280	377	2,536
Annual payroll	Bil. dol. . .	205	(Z)	(Z)	(Z)	1	4	15	20	185
Admin/support waste mgt/ remediation services (56):										
Firms	1,000 . . .	289	54	128	44	27	26	8	286	3
Employment	1,000 . . .	8,299	-	269	285	361	1,026	1,345	3,286	5,014
Annual payroll	Bil. dol. . .	212	3	7	7	10	27	31	85	127
Educational services (61):										
Firms	1,000 . . .	66	9	23	10	8	12	3	65	1
Employment	1,000 . . .	2,702	-	48	63	112	516	535	1,275	1,427
Annual payroll	Bil. dol. . .	72	(Z)	1	1	2	11	14	30	42
Health care and social assistance (62):										
Firms	1,000 . . .	560	51	236	130	73	52	14	556	4
Employment	1,000 . . .	14,900	-	533	857	961	2,064	2,730	7,145	7,755
Annual payroll	Bil. dol. . .	499	4	21	31	36	69	73	232	267
Accommodation & food services (72):										
Firms	1,000 . . .	427	61	128	83	71	75	8	426	2
Employment	1,000 . . .	10,049	-	304	550	970	2,844	1,417	6,087	3,962
Annual payroll	Bil. dol. . .	131	3	4	6	10	34	17	73	58
Other services (except public administration) (81):										
Firms	1,000 . . .	675	60	367	135	67	41	4	674	1
Employment	1,000 . . .	5,420	-	791	876	881	1,482	640	4,670	750
Annual payroll	Bil. dol. . .	119	1	14	17	18	32	16	99	20

- Represents zero.   Z Less than $500 million.   [1] Includes other industries not shown separately.

Source: U.S. Small Business Administration, Office of Advocacy, "Statistics of U.S. Businesses and Nonemployer Statistics: Firm Size Data provided by U.S. Census Bureau"; <http://www.sba.gov/advo/research/data.html>; accessed 4 May 2005.

Table 742. Employer Firms, Establishments, Employment, and Annual Payroll by Enterprise Size: 1990 to 2002

[In thousands except as noted (5,074 represents 5,074,000). Firms are an aggregation of all establishments owned by a parent company with some annual payroll. Establishments are locations with active payroll in any quarter. Employment is measured in March and payroll is annual leading to some enterprises with zero employment. This table illustrates the changing importance of enterprise sizes over time, not job growth, as enterprises can grow or decline and change enterprise size cells over time]

Item		All industries—employment size of enterprise						
	Total	0-4 [1]	5-9	10-19	20-99	100-499	Less than 500	500 or more
Firms:								
1990	5,074	3,021	952	563	454	70	5,060	14
1995	5,369	3,250	981	577	470	76	5,354	15
1997	5,542	3,358	1,007	594	487	80	5,526	16
1998	5,579	3,376	1,012	600	494	80	5,563	16
1999	5,608	3,389	1,013	606	502	81	5,591	17
2000	5,653	3,397	1,021	617	516	84	5,635	17
2001	5,658	3,402	1,019	616	518	85	5,640	17
2002	5,698	3,466	1,011	614	508	82	5,681	17
Establishments:								
1990	6,176	3,032	971	600	590	255	5,448	728
1995	6,613	3,260	998	618	639	284	5,799	814
1997	6,895	3,364	1,023	639	683	309	6,018	877
1998	6,942	3,383	1,026	640	675	307	6,030	911
1999	7,008	3,398	1,027	643	671	307	6,048	911
2000	7,070	3,406	1,035	652	674	309	6,080	960
2001	7,095	3,410	1,034	650	670	316	6,080	1,015
2002	7,201	3,471	1,024	653	693	333	6,173	1,028
Employment:								
1990	93,469	5,117	6,252	7,543	17,710	13,545	50,167	43,302
1995	100,315	5,395	6,440	7,734	18,422	14,660	52,653	47,662
1997	105,299	5,546	6,610	7,962	19,110	15,317	54,545	50,754
1998	108,118	5,584	6,643	8,048	19,378	15,411	55,064	53,053
1999	110,706	5,606	6,652	8,130	19,703	15,638	55,729	54,977
2000	114,065	5,593	6,709	8,286	20,277	16,260	57,124	56,941
2001	115,061	5,630	6,698	8,275	20,370	16,410	57,383	57,678
2002	112,401	5,698	6,640	8,246	19,874	15,909	56,366	56,034
Annual payroll (bil. dol.):								
1990	2,104	117	114	144	352	279	1,007	1,097
1995	2,666	142	137	175	437	361	1,252	1,414
1997	3,048	158	151	194	495	418	1,416	1,632
1998	3,309	168	160	207	531	446	1,513	1,797
1999	3,555	177	167	218	565	475	1,601	1,954
2000	3,879	186	174	231	608	528	1,727	2,152
2001	3,989	188	179	237	624	539	1,768	2,222
2002	3,943	194	182	241	624	536	1,777	2,166

[1] Employment is measured in March, thus some firms (start-ups after March, closures before March, and seasonal firms) will have zero employment and some annual payroll.

Source: U.S. Small Business Administration, Office of Advocacy, "Statistics of U.S. Businesses and Nonemployer Statistics: Firm Size Data provided by U.S. Census Bureau"; <http://www.sba.gov/advo/research/data.html>; accessed 4 May 2005.

Table 743. Firm Births and Deaths by Employment Size of Enterprise: 1990 to 2002

[In thousands (541.1 represents 541,100). Data represent activity from March of the beginning year to March of the ending year. Establishments with no employment in the first quarter of the beginning year were excluded. This table provides the number of births and deaths of initial establishments (based on plant number) as an approximation of firm births and deaths]

Item	Births (initial locations)				Deaths (initial locations)			
	Total	Less than 20	Less than 500	500 or more	Total	Less than 20	Less than 500	500 or more
Firms:								
1990 to 1991	541.1	515.9	540.9	0.3	546.5	517.0	546.1	0.4
1995 to 1996	597.8	572.4	597.5	0.3	512.4	485.5	512.0	0.4
1996 to 1997	590.6	564.2	590.3	0.3	530.0	500.0	529.5	0.5
1997 to 1998	590.0	564.8	589.7	0.3	540.6	511.6	540.1	0.5
1998 to 1999	579.6	554.3	579.3	0.3	544.5	514.3	544.0	0.4
1999 to 2000	574.3	548.0	574.0	0.3	542.8	514.2	542.4	0.5
2000 to 2001	585.1	558.0	584.8	0.3	553.3	524.0	552.8	0.5
2001 to 2002 [1]	569.8	541.5	568.3	1.5	586.9	557.1	586.5	0.4
Employment:								
1990 to 1991	3,105	1,713	2,907	198	3,208	1,723	3,044	164
1995 to 1996	3,256	1,845	3,056	200	3,100	1,560	2,808	291
1996 to 1997	3,228	1,814	3,030	198	3,275	1,621	2,961	314
1997 to 1998	3,205	1,812	3,002	203	3,233	1,662	2,992	242
1998 to 1999	3,225	1,670	2,991	235	3,180	1,645	2,969	210
1999 to 2000	3,229	1,793	3,031	198	3,177	1,654	2,946	230
2000 to 2001	3,418	1,821	3,109	310	3,262	1,701	2,946	212
2001 to 2002	3,370	1,748	3,034	336	3,660	1,755	3,257	403

[1] A change in methodology has affected the allocation of firms by employment size.

Source: U.S. Small Business Administration, Office of Advocacy, "Statistics of U.S. Businesses and Nonemployer Statistics: Firm Size Data provided by U.S. Census Bureau"; <http://www.sba.gov/advo/research/data.html>; accessed 4 May 2005.

Table 744. Employer Firms, Employment, and Payroll by Employment Size of Enterprise and State: 2000 and 2002

[5,652.5 represents 5,652,500. A firm is an aggregation of all establishments owned by a parent company (within a state) with some annual payroll. A firm may be a single location or it can include multiple locations. Employment is measured in March and payroll is annual leading to some firms with zero employment]

| State | Employer firms (1,000) | | | | | Employment, 2002 (mil.) | | | Annual payroll, 2002 (bil. dol.) | | |
| | 2000 | | 2002 | | | | | | | | |
	Total	Less than 20 employ-ees	Total	Less than 20 employ-ees	Less than 500 employ-ees	Total	Less than 20 employ-ees	Less than 500 employ-ees	Total	Less than 20 employ-ees	Less than 500 employ-ees
U.S	5,652.5	5,035.0	5,697.8	5,090.3	5,680.9	112.4	20.6	56.4	3,943.2	617.6	1,777.0
AL.......	79.9	68.2	78.7	67.2	76.6	1.6	0.3	0.8	45.5	7.1	20.6
AK.......	15.9	14.0	16.0	14.1	15.5	0.2	0.1	0.1	8.4	1.9	4.5
AZ.......	93.0	79.3	95.9	81.8	93.2	1.9	0.3	0.9	61.1	9.5	26.9
AR.......	52.4	45.4	52.1	45.1	50.6	1.0	0.2	0.5	25.9	4.3	11.2
CA.......	664.6	581.1	674.6	591.1	669.1	12.9	2.4	6.8	510.8	82.9	243.4
CO	116.2	101.5	119.6	104.8	116.8	1.9	0.4	1.0	67.8	12.0	31.7
CT.......	78.5	67.2	77.3	66.0	75.2	1.6	0.3	0.8	68.5	10.3	29.5
DE.	20.2	16.6	20.2	16.3	18.8	0.4	0.1	0.2	14.7	1.9	5.4
DC	16.3	12.4	16.4	12.3	15.3	0.4	0.1	0.2	21.4	2.7	9.9
FL.......	354.0	319.3	370.8	335.8	366.7	6.4	1.2	2.9	192.9	35.0	85.6
GA	160.4	138.3	164.3	141.9	160.4	3.4	0.6	1.5	113.8	16.6	45.8
HI	24.3	20.8	24.9	21.2	24.1	0.4	0.1	0.3	13.4	2.5	7.1
ID	32.2	28.0	33.2	29.0	32.2	0.5	0.1	0.3	12.6	2.7	6.4
IL	254.1	218.1	253.7	218.5	249.4	5.2	0.9	2.6	197.8	29.3	88.7
IN	116.3	98.1	116.0	98.3	113.2	2.5	0.4	1.3	79.4	11.1	35.0
IA	65.6	56.2	65.1	56.0	63.5	1.2	0.2	0.6	34.8	5.4	16.4
KS.......	61.6	52.4	60.9	51.9	59.1	1.1	0.2	0.6	33.2	5.3	15.7
KY.......	72.3	61.0	71.9	60.8	69.8	1.5	0.3	0.7	42.5	6.4	18.8
LA.......	81.7	69.5	81.7	69.5	79.7	1.6	0.3	0.9	45.6	7.6	21.9
ME	34.1	30.1	34.4	30.3	33.6	0.5	0.1	0.3	14.4	3.0	8.0
MD	106.0	90.4	108.0	92.2	105.4	2.1	0.4	1.1	75.0	12.2	36.5
MA	148.2	127.8	146.1	125.8	143.2	3.0	0.5	1.5	127.9	18.6	57.7
MI	193.9	167.2	192.3	166.7	189.3	3.9	0.7	2.0	142.4	21.5	63.0
MN	116.2	99.4	118.7	102.0	116.2	2.4	0.4	1.2	84.5	12.0	37.6
MS	48.3	41.5	48.0	41.1	46.5	0.9	0.2	0.5	22.8	3.9	10.4
MO	118.1	101.1	119.6	102.6	116.9	2.4	0.4	1.2	74.1	11.0	33.1
MT	28.0	25.0	28.8	25.7	28.2	0.3	0.1	0.2	7.4	2.1	4.8
NE.......	41.4	35.5	41.5	35.7	40.2	0.7	0.1	0.4	21.7	3.4	9.9
NV.......	40.3	33.4	42.5	35.3	40.7	0.9	0.1	0.4	29.3	4.5	12.7
NH	32.1	27.3	32.3	27.4	31.2	0.6	0.1	0.3	18.7	3.6	10.0
NJ.......	202.2	178.4	203.5	179.5	200.3	3.6	0.7	1.8	152.4	24.8	67.8
NM	35.5	30.1	35.6	30.2	34.2	0.6	0.1	0.3	15.1	3.0	7.9
NY.......	424.8	379.2	428.4	383.6	424.3	7.2	1.4	3.8	329.8	50.0	143.3
NC	163.6	142.0	165.0	143.3	161.8	3.3	0.6	1.6	101.8	15.7	43.3
ND	17.2	14.7	17.2	14.6	16.6	0.3	0.1	0.2	6.6	1.3	3.8
OH	212.5	180.5	211.0	180.1	207.3	4.7	0.8	2.3	154.8	22.2	68.4
OK	70.2	61.0	70.3	61.0	68.5	1.2	0.2	0.6	33.6	5.9	16.1
OR	85.1	74.2	85.1	74.4	83.2	1.3	0.3	0.7	43.5	7.7	21.2
PA.......	237.5	204.6	237.4	204.8	233.6	5.0	0.9	2.5	169.2	24.4	75.5
RI	25.2	21.5	25.5	21.7	24.6	0.4	0.1	0.2	13.5	2.6	7.3
SC.......	78.4	67.2	78.6	67.5	76.5	1.5	0.3	0.7	44.0	7.1	19.0
SD.......	20.6	17.7	20.9	18.0	20.2	0.3	0.1	0.2	7.7	1.6	4.4
TN.......	102.4	86.7	100.7	85.3	97.9	2.3	0.4	1.0	71.3	9.8	29.8
TX.......	369.0	321.3	373.1	324.8	368.1	8.0	1.4	3.8	277.8	40.8	114.7
UT.......	46.2	39.3	49.3	42.3	47.6	0.9	0.2	0.4	26.2	4.4	12.0
VT.......	19.1	16.7	19.0	16.5	18.4	0.3	0.1	0.2	7.4	1.7	4.4
VA.......	139.7	120.3	142.6	122.8	139.5	2.9	0.5	1.4	101.7	15.2	45.3
WA	138.2	120.9	138.3	121.6	135.7	2.2	0.5	1.2	83.1	14.0	38.6
WV	33.5	28.8	32.7	28.0	31.6	0.6	0.1	0.3	14.8	2.5	7.0
WI	115.6	98.2	116.0	98.8	113.6	2.4	0.4	1.3	75.3	11.5	35.8
WY	15.9	13.9	16.5	14.3	15.9	0.2	0.1	0.1	5.1	1.3	3.2

Source: U.S. Small Business Administration, Office of Advocacy, "Statistics of U.S. Businesses and Nonemployer Statistics: Firm Size Data provided by U.S. Census Bureau"; <http://www.sba.gov/advo/research/data.html>; accessed 4 May 2005.

Table 745. **Employer Firm Births and Deaths and Business Bankruptcies by State: 2000 to 2004**

[2003 and 2004 births and deaths data are estimated. At the state level, births represent requests for new employer codes, deaths represent the elimination of all employees, and a third category, successor firms or the rebirth of terminated firms, is not listed; so state deaths greater than state births does not necessarily indicate a loss of state employer firms]

State	Births			Deaths			Business bankruptcies		
	2000	2003	2004	2000	2003	2004	2000	2003	2004
United States [1]	574,300	553,500	580,900	542,831	572,300	576,200	35,219	34,765	34,019
Alabama	10,067	9,014	9,413	9,302	10,927	10,104	445	287	325
Alaska	2,333	2,441	1,848	2,671	2,507	2,650	118	121	64
Arizona	15,175	13,322	12,421	11,984	15,488	17,553	765	701	480
Arkansas	4,680	7,253	7,852	5,581	6,918	6,481	261	429	376
California	167,047	113,500	117,016	134,541	140,435	143,115	4,595	4,501	3,748
Colorado	25,462	22,400	23,694	7,561	13,243	9,734	373	552	786
Connecticut	9,910	8,501	9,064	11,528	11,044	11,018	139	187	132
Delaware	3,682	3,439	3,270	3,052	3,148	3,362	2,320	505	276
District of Columbia	4,472	4,052	4,393	4,996	3,874	3,440	58	55	41
Florida	59,912	69,711	77,754	55,186	56,665	54,498	1,447	1,534	1,183
Georgia	28,925	24,217	29,547	26,754	25,898	27,835	1,012	1,585	2,090
Hawaii	3,745	3,658	3,698	3,521	4,010	3,754	63	72	47
Idaho	5,829	5,998	7,814	6,249	6,742	5,716	269	225	160
Illinois	28,875	28,933	28,453	31,361	41,112	33,472	1,270	991	912
Indiana	14,112	13,452	13,906	15,738	15,137	15,282	398	640	524
Iowa	5,668	5,534	5,954	7,485	7,378	7,391	214	323	360
Kansas	6,483	7,625	6,742	6,981	8,392	7,250	169	303	268
Kentucky	8,637	8,155	8,807	7,508	10,801	8,597	355	327	319
Louisiana	10,468	9,298	9,875	13,708	12,171	9,668	619	499	622
Maine	5,135	4,033	4,300	· 4,906	4,715	4,987	162	105	138
Maryland	20,539	20,687	21,751	19,563	21,697	20,636	677	523	417
Massachusetts	18,640	18,984	18,822	18,164	21,870	20,270	393	396	315
Michigan	23,760	22,022	24,625	30,240	24,748	24,584	577	684	681
Minnesota	13,906	14,652	15,167	4,829	17,928	15,209	1,492	1,379	1,374
Mississippi	6,439	6,020	6,141	7,555	7,267	7,380	203	282	170
Missouri	13,996	15,947	16,155	17,580	20,190	17,924	369	378	354
Montana	4,418	4,548	4,588	2,435	4,679	4,896	141	98	109
Nebraska	4,441	4,311	4,849	5,234	5,050	5,051	115	238	207
Nevada	8,587	9,749	10,483	7,761	8,939	9,012	332	321	257
New Hampshire	4,677	4,653	4,865	7,341	4,598	5,401	302	178	158
New Jersey	27,885	29,236	35,895	23,950	36,827	50,034	660	734	684
New Mexico	5,836	5,508	5,683	6,451	5,770	5,592	513	774	727
New York	61,507	60,569	62,854	57,423	61,199	64,013	1,960	1,987	4,070
North Carolina	23,310	22,465	23,387	23,467	23,234	22,055	445	528	486
North Dakota	1,493	1,456	1,747	2,191	2,049	2,621	92	105	85
Ohio	22,290	22,227	22,725	24,276	23,544	21,328	1,471	1,426	1,432
Oklahoma	8,979	8,802	9,263	8,848	8,434	8,018	876	612	659
Oregon	14,729	13,842	13,481	16,102	14,194	14,407	1,453	1,591	852
Pennsylvania	35,104	31,214	33,188	34,893	32,917	34,507	1,455	1,193	1,138
Rhode Island	3,675	3,465	3,932	4,170	4,103	4,250	74	48	74
South Carolina	11,114	10,759	11,745	11,721	10,711	10,975	138	142	175
South Dakota	2,138	1,338	1,691	1,809	1,899	2,251	133	110	108
Tennessee	15,793	17,700	17,415	17,563	16,315	16,520	641	597	548
Texas	54,330	52,677	54,098	57,300	55,461	55,792	2,592	3,153	3,094
Utah	9,875	10,656	11,357	10,135	10,368	11,597	451	519	440
Vermont	2,511	2,122	2,322	2,653	2,584	2,578	71	78	85
Virginia	22,219	22,069	24,134	20,569	20,539	19,919	815	956	750
Washington	40,357	36,136	31,955	41,793	35,345	47,141	717	737	665
West Virginia	4,177	4,126	3,937	5,542	5,550	5,136	277	290	247
Wisconsin	12,436	12,400	13,093	15,151	12,629	12,711	685	722	742
Wyoming	2,314	2,419	2,519	2,908	2,921	2,737	47	44	65

[1] State births and deaths do not necessarily add to the U.S. as firms enter and exit multiple states and the U.S. data is based upon a different data source.

Source: U.S. Small Business Administration, Office of Advocacy, "Small Business Economy," forthcoming; based on data provided by U.S. Employment and Training Administration, U.S. Census Bureau, and Administrative Office of the U.S. Courts.

Table 746. **Small Business Administration Loans to Minority Small Businesses: 1990 to 2004**

[576 represents $576,000,000. For year ending September 30. A small business must be independently owned and operated, must not be dominant in its particular industry, and must meet standards set by the Small Business Administration as to its annual receipts or number of employees]

Minority group	Number of loans					Amount (mil. dol.)				
	1990	2000	2002	2003	2004	1990	2000	2002	2003	2004
Total minority loans	2,367	11,999	14,305	20,182	25,406	576	3,634	4,228	4,215	5,143
Percent of all loans	12.0	24.8	25.0	27.2	28.4	(NA)	(NA)	(NA)	(NA)	(NA)
African American	513	2,120	2,148	3,769	4,826	96	388	419	399	481
Asian American	1,075	5,838	7,249	9,507	12,100	317	2,383	2,799	2,756	3,399
Hispanic American	694	3,500	4,272	6,112	7,684	149	761	885	942	1,151
Native American	85	541	636	794	796	14	101	126	118	112

NA Not available.

Source: U.S. Small Business Administration, Management Information Summary, unpublished data.

Business Enterprise 517

Table 747. **Selected Characteristics of Employer Business Owners: 2002**

[The preliminary estimates in this report are based on responses from owners of businesses with paid employees operating in the United States. Data were collected on the 2002 Survey of Business Owners (SBO). Businesses were asked to report information about the characteristics of up to 3 individuals with the largest share of ownership. If a business had more than 3 owners, no characteristics information was requested from the additional owners. The data represent the characteristics of approximately 7.7 million owners. The estimates in this report are subject to sampling variability as well as nonsampling errors. Sources of nonsampling error include errors of response, nonreporting and coverage. For information on sampling error and nonsampling error, see <http://www.census.gov/econ/census02/sbo/intro.htm#reliability>]

Characteristic	Percent of employer business owners	Characteristic	Percent of employer business owners
Owner's age:		Ethnicity:	
Under 25 years old.	1	Hispanic [2].	4
25 to 34 years old	8	Non-Hispanic	93
35 to 44 years old	24	Not reported	3
45 to 64 years old	53	Owner's educational level:	
65 years old and over.	10	High school or less.	24
Not reported	4	Some college	28
Sex:		Undergraduate	24
Male	71	Post graduate	19
Female	27	Not reported	4
Not reported	3	Average number of hours owner spent managing or working in the business:	
Race: [1]		None	7
White.	88	Less than 20.	13
Black or African American	2	20 to 39	12
American Indian and Alaska Native	1	40.	14
Asian.	6	41 to 59	30
Native Hawaiian and Other Pacific Islander.	(Z)	60 or more	19
Not reported	4	Not reported	4

Z Less than 0.5 percent.   [1] Owners reporting more than one race are counted in each race group reported.   [2] Persons of Hispanic origin may be of any race.

Source: U.S. Census Bureau, "2002 Survey of Business Owners, Advance Report on Characteristics of Employer Business Owners: 2002"; published 2 February 2005; <http://www.census.gov/econ/census02/sbo/sboadvance.htm>.

Table 748. **U.S. Firms—Ownership by Women, Race and Hispanic Origin Groups: 1997**

[**20,822 represents 20,822,000.** A Hispanic firm may be of any race and, therefore may be included in more than one race group. See Appendix III]

Group	All firms		Firms with paid employees			
	Firms (1,000)	Sales and receipts (mil. dol.)	Firms (1,000)	Sales and receipts (mil. dol.)	Employees (1,000)	Annual payroll (mil. dol.)
All firms	**20,822**	**18,553,243**	**5,295**	**17,907,940**	**103,360**	**2,936,493**
Women	5,417	818,669	847	717,764	7,076	149,116
Black	823	71,215	93	56,378	718	14,322
Hispanic	1,200	186,275	212	158,675	1,389	29,830
Cuban	125	26,492	30	23,873	176	4,163
Mexican, Mexican American, Chicano.	472	73,707	91	62,271	695	13,015
Puerto Rican	70	7,461	11	5,814	62	1,497
Spaniard	57	16,923	13	15,264	76	2,046
Hispanic Latin American.	287	40,998	43	34,798	239	5,863
Other Spanish/Hispanic/Latino.	188	20,694	24	16,654	140	3,247
American Indian and Alaska Native	197	34,344	33	29,226	299	6,624
Asian and Pacific Islander	913	306,933	290	278,294	2,203	46,180
Asian Indian.	167	67,503	67	61,760	491	12,586
Chinese	253	106,197	91	98,233	692	12,945
Filipino	85	11,078	15	8,966	110	2,667
Japanese	86	43,741	23	41,295	262	7,107
Korean	136	45,936	50	40,746	334	5,789
Vietnamese	98	9,323	19	6,768	79	1,166
Other Asian	71	19,016	22	16,801	202	3,136
Native Hawaiian	16	2,250	2	1,957	21	498
Other Pacific Islander	4	1,888	1	1,768	13	286
White non-Hispanic.	17,317	7,763,011	4,373	7,252,270	54,084	1,395,150
Fifty-percent minority/fifty-percent nonminority	85	37,732	39	34,632	302	8,619
Other [1]	382	10,161,242	(S)	10,104,058	44,458	1,437,195

S Does not meet publication standards.   [1] Includes publicly-held corporations, foreign-owned companies, and not-for-profit companies.

Source: U.S. Census Bureau, 1997 Economic Census, Company Statistics Series, *Company Summary 1997*, EC97CS-1; and *Survey of Minority-Owned Business Enterprises—Asians and Pacific Islanders 1997*, EC97CS-5; and *Hispanic 1997*, EC97CS-4.

Table 749. Bankruptcy Petitions Filed and Pending by Type and Chapter: 1990 to 2004

[For years ending June 30. Covers only bankruptcy cases filed under the Bankruptcy Reform Act of 1978. *Bankruptcy:* legal recognition that a company or individual is insolvent and must restructure or liquidate. Petitions "filed" means the commencement of a proceeding through the presentation of a petition to the clerk of the court; "pending" is a proceeding in which the administration has not been completed]

Item	1990	1995	1998	1999	2000	2001	2002	2003	2004
Total filed	725,484	858,104	1,429,451	1,391,964	1,276,922	1,386,606	1,505,306	1,650,279	1,635,725
Business [1]	64,688	51,288	50,202	39,934	36,910	37,135	39,201	37,182	35,739
Nonbusiness [2]	660,796	806,816	1,379,249	1,352,030	1,240,012	1,349,471	1,466,105	1,613,097	1,599,986
Chapter 7 [3]	468,171	552,244	984,745	968,807	864,183	950,724	1,030,372	1,144,658	1,146,761
Chapter 11 [4]	2,116	1,755	981	731	722	745	894	966	935
Chapter 13 [5]	190,509	252,817	393,523	382,492	375,107	397,996	434,835	467,466	452,286
Voluntary	723,886	856,991	1,428,550	1,391,130	1,276,146	1,385,840	1,504,500	1,649,543	1,635,099
Involuntary	1,598	1,113	901	834	776	766	806	736	626
Chapter 7 [3]	505,337	581,390	1,015,453	993,414	885,447	972,659	1,053,230	1,165,993	1,167,101
Chapter 9 [6]	7	12	5	3	8	10	8	7	7
Chapter 11 [4]	19,591	13,221	9,613	8,684	9,947	10,272	11,401	10,602	11,048
Chapter 12 [7]	1,351	904	845	829	732	206	367	775	302
Chapter 13 [5]	199,186	262,551	403,501	389,004	380,770	403,418	440,231	472,811	457,171
Section 304 [8]	12	26	34	30	18	41	69	91	96
Total pending	961,919	1,090,446	1,389,917	1,394,794	1,400,416	1,535,903	1,613,742	1,729,139	1,697,751

[1] Business bankruptcies include those filed under chapters 7, 9, 11, or 12. [2] Includes Section 304 petitions not shown separately. [3] Chapter 7, liquidation of nonexempt assets of businesses or individuals. [4] Chapter 11, individual or business reorganization. [5] Chapter 13, adjustment of debts of an individual with regular income. [6] Chapter 9, adjustment of debts of a municipality. [7] Chapter 12, adjustment of debts of a family farmer with regular income, effective November 26, 1986. [8] Chapter 11, U.S.C., Section 304, cases ancillary to foreign proceedings.

Source: Administrative Office of the U.S. Courts, *Statistical Tables for the Federal Judiciary* and "Bankruptcy Statistics"; <http://www.uscourts.gov/bnkrpctystats/statistics.htm>.

Table 750. Bankruptcy Cases Filed by State: 2000 to 2004

[In thousands (1,276.9 represents 1,276,900). For years ending June 30. Covers only bankruptcy cases filed under the Bankruptcy Reform Act of 1978. *Bankruptcy:* legal recognition that a company or individual is insolvent and must restructure or liquidate. Petitions "filed" means the commencement of a proceeding through the presentation of a petition to the clerk of the court]

State	2000	2002	2003	2004	State	2000	2002	2003	2004
Total [1]	1,276.9	1,505.3	1,650.3	1,635.7	Missouri	26.3	31.5	37.3	38.0
					Montana	3.3	4.1	4.3	4.4
Alabama	31.4	39.6	42.0	42.4	Nebraska	5.6	7.3	8.3	8.8
Alaska	1.4	1.4	1.6	1.5	Nevada	14.3	18.6	20.7	19.4
Arizona	21.7	27.3	31.7	31.8	New Hampshire	3.9	3.7	4.3	4.5
Arkansas	16.3	21.8	24.5	24.2					
California	160.6	148.4	148.6	132.5	New Jersey	38.7	40.5	42.0	42.5
					New Mexico	7.1	8.7	10.0	9.4
Colorado	15.6	19.2	24.2	27.4	New York	61.7	67.9	75.0	80.2
Connecticut	11.4	11.2	12.2	11.8	North Carolina	25.8	34.9	38.6	37.7
Delaware	4.9	4.0	3.9	3.8	North Dakota	2.0	2.0	2.3	2.3
District of Columbia . . .	2.6	2.5	2.5	2.1					
Florida	74.0	88.0	94.9	92.2	Ohio	53.6	73.2	85.4	90.9
Georgia	57.9	72.6	80.2	79.8	Oklahoma	19.3	23.3	26.1	27.2
Hawaii	5.0	4.7	4.1	3.5	Oregon	18.1	23.5	25.5	24.9
Idaho	7.3	8.5	9.3	9.7	Pennsylvania	43.8	52.0	57.9	59.1
Illinois	62.3	77.3	86.9	81.3	Rhode Island	4.8	4.7	4.8	4.3
Indiana	37.5	50.6	55.3	55.7					
Iowa	8.2	11.2	12.4	13.0	South Carolina	11.7	15.1	15.9	15.9
Kansas	11.4	14.0	16.0	16.3	South Dakota	2.1	2.7	2.8	2.9
Kentucky	20.8	26.3	28.7	29.3	Tennessee	47.1	61.5	65.9	62.9
Louisiana	23.1	26.5	28.4	30.2	Texas	62.9	77.0	88.4	92.2
Maine	4.1	4.4	4.6	4.6	Utah	14.4	20.7	22.8	21.3
Maryland	31.1	34.5	35.8	32.0	Vermont	1.6	1.7	1.9	1.8
Massachusetts	16.7	16.9	18.0	18.2	Virginia	37.1	41.9	44.1	42.1
Michigan	36.4	50.2	60.8	63.0	Washington	31.2	37.3	40.7	40.1
Minnesota	15.4	19.1	20.6	19.1	West Virginia	8.2	9.7	11.0	11.4
Mississippi	17.9	22.0	23.0	21.2	Wisconsin	18.0	23.2	27.7	27.7
					Wyoming	2.0	2.2	2.5	2.4

[1] Includes outlying areas not shown separately.

Source: Administrative Office of the U.S. Courts, *Statistical Tables for the Federal Judiciary* and "Bankruptcy Statistics"; <http://www.uscourts.gov/bnkrpctystats/statistics.htm>.

U.S. Census Bureau, Statistical Abstract of the United States: 2006

Table 751. Mergers and Acquisitions—Summary: 1990 to 2003

[206 represents $206,000,000,000. Covers transactions valued at $5 million or more. Values based on transactions for which price data revealed. *All activity* includes mergers, acquisitions, acquisitions of partial interest that involve a 40-percent stake in the target or an investment of at least $100 million, divestitures, and leveraged transactions that result in a change in ownership. *Divestiture:* sale of a business, division, or subsidiary by corporate owner to another party. *Leveraged buyout:* acquisition of a business in which buyers use mostly borrowed money to finance purchase price and incorporate debt into capital structure of business after change in ownership]

Item	Unit	1990	1995	1997	1998	1999	2000	2001	2002	2003
All activity: Number	Number	4,239	4,981	8,770	9,634	9,599	11,169	7,713	7,032	7,743
Value	Bil. dol.	206	896	1,610	2,480	3,402	3,440	1,688	1,185	1,318
Divestitures: Number	Number	1,907	2,227	3,189	3,304	3,184	3,497	2,816	2,631	3,090
Value	Bil. dol.	91	365	616	555	678	892	644	473	501
Leveraged buyouts: Number	Number	177	206	198	238	344	476	329	303	366
Value	Bil. dol.	18	24	24	27	58	86	60	83	86
Foreign acquisitions of U.S. companies:										
Number	Number	773	80	441	483	560	741	448	336	321
Value	Bil. dol.	56	4	65	233	297	335	125	68	58
U.S. acquisitions overseas:										
Number	Number	392	317	539	746	608	746	470	378	398
Value	Bil. dol.	21	63	88	128	158	136	108	56	106
U.S. companies acquiring U.S. companies:										
Number	Number	(NA)	2,250	3,753	3,882	3,353	3,119	2,079	1,994	2,070
Value	Bil. dol.	(NA)	462	834	1,379	1,259	1,400	638	370	463

NA Not available.

Source: Thomson Financial, Newark, NJ, Mergers & Corporate Transactions Database (copyright).

Table 752. Mergers and Acquisitions by Industry: 2003

[462,808 represents $462,808,000,000. See headnote, Table 751]

Industry	U.S. company acquiring U.S. company		Foreign company acquiring U.S. company		U.S. company acquiring foreign company	
	Number	Value (mil. dol.)	Number	Value (mil. dol.)	Number	Value (mil. dol.)
Total activity [1]	2,070	462,808	321	58,371	398	106,423
Business services	209	33,417	33	1,562	56	5,391
Chemicals and allied products	31	9,192	15	1,739	13	4,409
Commercial banks, bank holding companies	130	65,995	3	227	13	7,154
Credit institutions	23	11,423	7	961	6	720
Drugs	70	15,914	14	7,502	19	11,548
Electric, gas, water distribution	75	26,240	16	1,386	4	246
Electronic and electrical equipment	72	9,577	16	1,827	17	932
Food and kindred products	36	7,033	10	1,339	8	5,999
Health services	54	10,935	2	217	1	10
Insurance	56	54,893	4	13,366	5	3,095
Investment & commodity firms, dealers, exchanges	59	18,522	10	910	28	3,563
Measuring, medical, photo equip; clocks	69	12,239	11	997	21	5,394
Metal and metal products	46	6,542	8	669	8	856
Motion picture production and distribution	15	14,584	3	335	-	-
Oil and gas; petroleum refining	111	20,742	19	1,585	12	3,827
Other financial	7	7,615	1	11	2	292
Prepackaged software	134	11,884	19	1,261	38	982
Printing, publishing, and allied services	17	2,612	7	1,650	3	4,099
Radio & television broadcasting stations	71	13,132	-	-	11	5,420
Real estate, mortgage bankers and brokers	123	26,559	21	3,005	13	16,378
Soaps, cosmetics, & personal-care products	7	425	2	3,089	3	6,951
Telecommunications	49	5,973	5	8,237	11	2,789

- Represents zero. [1] Includes other industries not shown separately.

Source: Thomson Financial, Newark, NJ, Merger & Corporate Transactions Database (copyright).

Table 753. Private Equity Commitments: 1990 to 2004

Type of capital	Number of funds						Amount (mil. dol.)					
	1990	1995	2000	2002	2003	2004	1990	1995	2000	2002	2003	2004
Private equity capital, total	151	280	794	276	235	274	11,166	36,655	182,789	35,533	41,357	62,244
Venture capital	88	176	634	192	147	175	3,390	10,212	106,060	9,037	11,521	18,227
Buyouts and mezzanine capital [1]	63	104	160	84	88	99	7,777	26,443	76,729	26,496	29,835	44,016

[1] Mezzanine capital is a fund investment strategy involving subordinated debt (the level of financing senior to equity and below senior debt).

Source: Thomson Venture Economics, New York, NY, unpublished data.

Table 754. Patents and Trademarks: 1990 to 2004

[In thousands (99.2 represents 99,200). Calendar year data. Covers U.S. patents issued to citizens of the United States and residents of foreign countries. For data on foreign countries, see Table 1339]

Type	1990	1995	1998	1999	2000	2001	2002	2003	2004
Patents issued	99.2	113.8	163.1	169.1	176.0	184.0	184.4	187.0	181.3
Inventions	90.4	101.4	147.5	153.5	157.5	166.0	167.3	169.0	164.3
Individuals	17.3	17.4	22.5	22.8	22.4	21.7	20.5	19.6	17.6
Corporations:									
United States	36.1	44.0	66.1	69.4	70.9	74.3	74.2	75.3	73.0
Foreign[1]	36.0	39.1	57.9	60.3	63.3	69.0	71.8	73.2	72.9
U.S. Government	1.0	1.0	1.0	1.0	0.9	1.0	0.9	0.9	0.8
Designs	8.0	11.7	14.8	14.7	17.4	16.9	15.5	16.6	15.7
Botanical plants	0.3	0.4	0.6	0.4	0.5	0.6	1.1	1.0	1.0
Reissues	0.4	0.3	0.3	0.4	0.5	0.5	0.5	0.4	0.3
U.S. residents	52.8	64.4	90.6	94.0	96.9	98.6	97.1	98.6	94.1
Foreign country residents	46.2	49.4	72.5	75.1	79.1	85.4	87.3	88.5	87.2
Percent of total	46.7	43.4	44.4	44.4	44.9	46.4	47.3	47.3	48.1
Trademarks:									
Applications filed	127.3	181.0	238.0	328.6	361.8	277.3	264.1	271.7	304.5
Issued	60.8	92.5	136.1	191.9	115.2	142.9	176.0	166.6	146.0
Trademarks	53.6	85.6	129.9	184.9	106.4	109.6	146.9	130.9	113.7
Trademark renewals	7.2	6.9	6.2	7.0	8.8	33.3	29.2	35.6	32.3

[1] Includes patents to foreign governments.

Source: U.S. Patent and Trademark Office, "Statistical Reports Available For Viewing, Calendar Year Patent Statistics"; <http://www.uspto.gov/web/offices/ac/ido/oeip/taf/reports.htm> and unpublished data.

Table 755. Patents by State: 2004

[Includes only U.S. patents granted to residents of the United States and territories]

State	Total	Inventions	Designs	Botanical plants	Reissues	State	Total	Inventions	Designs	Botanical plants	Reissues
U.S.[1]	94,110	84,271	9,252	428	159	Missouri	895	768	117	10	-
Alabama	412	375	33	4	-	Montana	131	119	11	-	1
Alaska	49	39	10	-	-	Nebraska	229	191	37	1	-
Arizona	1,730	1,621	103	2	4	Nevada	476	410	65	-	1
Arkansas	160	132	27	1	-	New Hampshire	681	626	52	2	1
California	21,601	19,488	1,861	210	42	New Jersey	3,352	2,957	380	5	10
Colorado	2,289	2,099	189	1	-	New Mexico	383	370	12	-	1
Connecticut	1,722	1,577	141	:	4	New York	6,618	5,846	760	1	11
Delaware	406	342	62	1	1	North Carolina	2,075	1,794	268	10	3
District of Columbia	80	75	5	-	-	North Dakota	66	53	12	1	-
Florida	2,989	2,456	464	64	5	Ohio	3,417	2,889	525	-	3
Georgia	1,492	1,326	155	6	5	Oklahoma	490	447	40	2	1
Hawaii	86	76	9	-	1	Oregon	1,967	1,725	218	20	4
Idaho	1,822	1,785	36	1	-	Pennsylvania	3,223	2,883	322	10	8
Illinois	3,754	3,162	570	17	5	Rhode Island	368	309	55	1	3
Indiana	1,485	1,280	194	10	1	South Carolina	581	524	54	3	-
Iowa	736	658	77	1	-	South Dakota	88	82	6	-	-
Kansas	540	448	92	-	-	Tennessee	874	681	193	-	-
Kentucky	463	407	56	-	-	Texas	6,239	5,930	290	7	12
Louisiana	387	343	38	6	-	Utah	784	683	100	-	1
Maine	138	134	4	-	-	Vermont	428	400	28	-	-
Maryland	1,436	1,313	116	2	5	Virginia	1,181	1,077	103	1	-
Massachusetts	3,904	3,672	225	2	5	Washington	2,442	2,221	214	3	4
Michigan	4,122	3,757	351	8	6	West Virginia	111	100	6	5	-
Minnesota	2,996	2,754	230	7	5	Wisconsin	1,975	1,658	310	2	5
Mississippi	159	135	22	1	1	Wyoming	55	52	3	-	-

- Represents zero. [1] Includes U.S. territories not shown separately.

Source: U.S. Patent and Trademark Office, unpublished data.

Table 756. Copyright Registration by Subject Matter: 1990 to 2004

[In thousands (590.7 represents 590,700). For years ending September 30. Comprises claims to copyrights registered for both U.S. and foreign works. Semiconductor chips and renewals are not considered copyright registration claims]

Subject matter	1990	2000	2003	2004	Subject matter	1990	2000	2003	2004
Total copyright claims	590.7	497.6	514.1	642.0	Works of the visual arts[3]	76.7	85.8	93.4	107.8
Monographs[1]	179.7	169.7	188.0	227.5					
Serials	111.5	69.0	56.3	68.2	Semiconductor chip				
Sound recordings	37.5	34.2	47.0	68.0	products	1.0	0.7	0.4	0.3
Musical works[2]	185.3	138.9	129.4	170.5	Renewals	51.8	16.8	19.5	18.9

[1] Includes computer software and machine readable works. [2] Includes dramatic works, accompanying music, choreography, pantomimes, motion pictures, and filmstrips. [3] Two-dimensional works of fine and graphic art, including prints and art reproductions; sculptural works; technical drawings and models; photographs; commercial prints and labels; works of applied arts, cartographic works, and multimedia works.

Source: The Library of Congress, Copyright Office, *Annual Report*.

Table 757. Net Stock of Private Fixed Assets by Industry: 2000 to 2003

[In billions of dollars (21,190 represents $21,190,000,000,000). Estimates as of Dec. 31. Net stock estimates are presented in terms of current cost and cover equipment, software, and structures]

Industry	NAICS code [1]	2000	2001	2002	2003
Private fixed assets	(X)	21,190	22,485	23,530	24,824
Agriculture, forestry, fishing, and hunting.	11	406	421	433	449
Farms [2]	111, 112	379	394	405	421
Forestry, fishing, and related activities.	113-115	27	27	28	28
Mining	21	580	642	636	632
Oil and gas extraction	211	442	500	495	489
Mining, except oil and gas	212	92	93	93	94
Support activites for mining.	213	46	49	49	49
Utilities.	22	1,039	1,090	1,139	1,180
Construction	23	173	179	184	191
Manufacturing	31-33	1,759	1,800	1,812	1,833
Durable goods	(X)	996	1,028	1,040	1,057
Wood products	321	31	32	32	32
Nonmetallic mineral products	327	55	57	58	59
Primary metals	331	124	124	123	121
Fabricated metal products	332	112	114	115	115
Machinery	333	140	147	151	155
Computer and electronic products	334	245	261	268	278
Electrical equipment, appliances, and components	335	45	46	47	47
Motor vehicles, bodies and trailers, and parts	3361-3363	105	107	107	107
Other transportation equipment	3364, 3365, 3369	79	80	81	81
Furniture and related products	337	16	16	17	17
Miscellaneous manufacturing	339	43	44	45	45
Nondurable goods.	(X)	763	773	772	776
Food and beverage and tobacco products	311, 312	182	185	185	185
Textile mills and textile product mills	313, 314	44	43	43	42
Apparel and leather and allied products	315, 316	17	17	17	17
Paper products	322	100	100	98	98
Printing and related support activities	323	41	42	42	43
Petroleum and coal products	324	92	94	94	95
Chemical products	325	220	225	226	228
Plastics and rubber products	326	67	68	68	69
Wholesale trade	42	348	358	366	380
Retail trade	44-45	641	677	706	733
Transportation and warehousing	48-49	805	835	855	880
Air transportation	481	196	216	227	239
Railroad transportation.	482	267	272	274	280
Water transportation	483	39	40	41	42
Truck transportation.	484	68	66	66	66
Transit and ground passenger transportation	485	34	35	36	37
Pipeline transportation.	486	74	77	81	84
Other transportation and support activites [3]	487, 488, 492	105	106	107	109
Warehousing and storage.	493	22	23	23	24
Information	51	817	865	894	927
Publishing industries (includes software)	511	50	51	51	52
Motion picture and sound recording industries	512	32	32	32	32
Broadcasting and telecommunications	513	716	761	788	819
Information and data processing services	514	19	21	23	24
Finance and insurance	52	822	855	878	910
Federal Reserve banks	521	11	12	12	13
Credit intermediation and related activities.	522	465	480	489	506
Securities, commodity contracts, and investments.	523	86	89	94	99
Insurance carriers and related activities.	524	165	171	174	178
Funds, trusts, and other financial vehicles	525	95	104	110	115
Real estate and rental and leasing	53	11,476	12,300	13,062	14,030
Real estate	531	11,233	12,038	12,784	13,726
Rental and leasing services and lessors of intangible assets [4]	532, 533	243	263	278	305
Professional, scientific, and technical services	54	205	221	229	240
Legal services	5411	20	20	21	21
Computer systems design and related services	5415	50	55	58	61
Miscellaneous professional, scientific, and technical services [5]	(5)	135	145	150	157
Management of companies and enterprises [6]	551111, 551112	269	279	285	291
Administrative and waste management services.	56	153	161	167	172
Administrative and support services	561	84	91	96	101
Waste management and remediation services	562	68	70	71	71
Educational services	61	213	232	249	265
Health care and social assistance	62	693	734	770	813
Ambulatory health care services	621	190	199	206	214
Hospitals.	622	449	479	505	536
Nursing and residential care facilities	623	29	31	33	34
Social assistance	624	24	26	27	28
Arts, entertainment, and recreation	71	128	140	149	158
Performing arts, spectator sports, museums, and related activities	711, 712	48	52	55	58
Amusements, gambling, and recreation industries.	713	80	88	93	99
Accommodation and food services	72	336	350	359	368
Accommodation	721	177	183	186	189
Food services and drinking places	722	160	167	173	178
Other services, except government	81	329	346	359	373

X Not applicable.   [1] Based on North American Industry Classification System, 1997; see text this section.   [2] NAICS crop and animal production.   [3] Consists of scenic and sightseeing transportation; transportation support activities; and couriers and messengers.   [4] Intangible assets include patents, trademarks, and franchise agreements, but not copyrights.   [5] Consists of accounting, tax preparation, bookkeeping, and payroll services (NAICS code 5412); architectural, engineering, and related services (5413); specialized design services (5414); management, scientific, and technical consulting services (5416); scientific research and development services (5417); advertising and related services (5418); and other professional, scientific, and technical services (5419).   [6] Consists of bank and other holding companies.

Source: U.S. Bureau of Economic Analysis, "Table 3.1ES. Current-Cost Net Stock of Private Fixed Assets by Industry, 1987-2003"; <http://www.bea.doc.gov/bea/dn/FA2004/Table View.asp>; accessed 14 April 2005.

Table 758. Gross Private Domestic Investment in Current and Real (2000) Dollars: 1990 to 2003

[In billions of dollars (861 represents $861,000,000,000). Covers equipment, software, and structures]

Item	1990	1995	1998	1999	2000	2001	2002	2003
CURRENT DOLLARS								
Gross private domestic investment . . .	861	1,144	1,509	1,626	1,736	1,614	1,579	1,666
Less: Consumption of fixed capital	552	713	851	914	991	1,076	1,093	1,136
Equals: Net private domestic investment	309	431	658	711	745	539	486	530
Fixed investment	846	1,113	1,438	1,559	1,679	1,646	1,568	1,667
Less: Consumption of fixed capital . . .	552	713	851	914	991	1,076	1,093	1,136
Equals: Net fixed investment	295	400	587	644	688	571	475	531
Nonresidential	622	810	1,053	1,134	1,232	1,177	1,064	1,095
Residential	224	303	386	425	447	469	504	572
Change in private inventories	15	31	71	67	57	-32	11	-1
CHAINED (2000) DOLLARS								
Gross private domestic investment . . .	895	1,134	1,524	1,643	1,736	1,598	1,561	1,629
Less: Consumption of fixed capital	572	707	856	922	991	1,072	1,091	1,124
Equals: Net private domestic investment	323	427	669	721	745	527	470	505
Fixed investment	887	1,110	1,455	1,576	1,679	1,629	1,549	1,627
Nonresidential	595	763	1,038	1,133	1,232	1,181	1,076	1,111
Residential	299	353	418	444	447	449	470	511
Change in private inventories	15	30	73	69	57	-32	12	-1

Source: U.S. Bureau of Economic Analysis, *National Income and Product Accounts, Volume 1, 1929–2000*, and *Survey of Current Business*, May 2005. See also <http://www.bea.gov/bea/dn/nipaweb/selecttable.asp>.

Table 759. Capital Expenditures: 2000 to 2003

[In billions of dollars (1,161 represents $1,161,000,000,000). Based on a sample survey and subject to sampling error; see source for details]

Item	All companies				Companies with employees				Companies without employees			
	2000	2001	2002	2003	2000	2001	2002	2003	2000	2001	2002	2003
Capital expenditures, total	1,161	1,109	997	984	1,090	1,052	917	896	71	57	80	88
Structures	364	364	358	344	338	346	325	313	26	18	33	31
New	329	336	321	304	309	324	300	281	20	12	21	23
Used	35	28	37	40	29	22	25	32	6	6	12	7
Equipment and software	797	745	639	640	752	706	592	583	45	39	47	57
New	751	706	598	590	718	679	564	551	32	27	34	39
Used	46	39	41	50	34	27	28	32	12	12	13	18
Capital leases	20	16	15	16	19	16	15	15	(Z)	(Z)	(Z)	(Z)

Z Less than $500 million.

Source: U.S. Census Bureau, *Annual Capital Expenditures, 2003*, Series ACE.

Table 760. Capital Expenditures by Industry: 2000 and 2003

[In billions of dollars (1,090 represents $1,090,000,000,000). Covers only companies with employees. Based on the North American Industry Classification System (NAICS), 1997; see text, this section. Based on a sample survey and subject to sampling error; see source for details]

Industry	NAICS code	2000	2003	Industry	NAICS code	2000	2003
Total expenditures	(X)	1,090	896	Professional, scientific, and technical services	54	34	25
Forestry, fishing, and agricultural services	113-115	1	2	Management of companies and enterprises	55	5	3
Mining	21	43	51	Admin/support waste mgt. /remediation services	56	18	16
Utilities	22	61	55	Educational services	61	18	17
Construction	23	25	23	Health care and social assistance	62	52	61
Manufacturing	31-33	215	149	Arts, entertainment, and recreation	71	19	11
Durable goods	321, 327, 33	134	81	Accommodation and food services	72	26	21
Nondurable goods	31, 322-326	81	68	Other services (except public administration)	81	21	26
Wholesale trade	42	34	28	Structure and equipment expenditures serving multi- ple industry categories	(X)	2	1
Retail trade	44-45	70	66				
Transportation and warehousing	48-49	60	45				
Information	51	160	82				
Finance and insurance	52	134	125				
Real estate and rental and leasing	53	92	89				

X Not applicable.

Source: U.S. Census Bureau, *Annual Capital Expenditures, 2003* Series ACE.

Table 761. **Composite Indexes of Leading, Coincident, and Lagging Economic Indicators: 1990 to 2004**
[385.4 represents 385,400]

Item	Unit	1990	2000	2001	2002	2003	2004
Leading index, composite	1996 = 100	95.0	109.4	108.5	110.8	112.3	115.6
Average weekly hours, manufacturing	Hours	40.5	41.2	40.4	40.4	40.4	40.8
Average weekly initial claims for unemployment insurance	1,000	385.4	299.1	406.1	403.9	401.4	343.1
Manufacturers' new orders, consumer goods and materials (1982 dol.)	Mil. dol.	112,431	152,073	142,731	142,629	141,912	146,678
Vendor performance, slower deliveries diffusion index [1]	Percent	47.9	53.3	48.0	53.3	53.1	62.7
Manufacturers' new orders, nondefense capital goods (1982 dol.)	Mil. dol.	31,882	49,869	41,859	39,008	41,062	45,983
Building permits, new private housing units	1,000	1,155	1,598	1,637	1,749	1,889	2,035
Stock prices, 500 common stocks [1]	1941-43 = 10	334.6	1,426.8	1,192.1	995.6	963.7	1,130.6
Money supply, M2 (chain 2000 dol.)	Bil. dol.	4,010	4,802	5,115	5,423	5,684	5,813
Interest rate spread, 10-year Treasury bonds less federal funds	Percent	0.45	-0.21	1.13	2.94	2.89	2.93
Index of consumer expectations [1]	1966:1 = 100	70.2	102.7	82.3	84.6	81.4	88.5
Coincident index, composite	1996=100	88.5	115.4	114.8	114.1	114.5	117.4
Employees on nonagricultural payrolls	1,000	109,489	131,792	131,833	130,345	129,999	131,473
Personal income less transfer payments (chain 2000 dol.)	Bil. dol.	5,321	7,345	7,376	7,336	7,417	7,654
Industrial production	1997 = 100	77.4	115.4	111.3	111.0	110.9	115.5
Manufacturing and trade sales (chain 2000 dol.)	Mil. dol.	592,717	844,794	834,827	846,205	866,894	919,736
Lagging index, composite	1996 = 100	101.4	106.7	105.2	102.8	100.9	98.8
Average duration of unemployment	Weeks	12.0	12.7	13.1	16.7	19.2	19.6
Inventories to sales ratio, manufacturing and trade (chain 2000 dol.)	Ratio	1.43	1.38	1.41	1.36	1.35	1.29
Change in labor cost per unit of output, manufacturing	Percent	1.2	2.4	-11.4	0.5	3.6	-1.2
Average prime rate	Percent	10.0	9.2	6.9	4.7	4.1	4.3
Commercial and industrial loans outstanding (chain 2000 dol.)	Mil. dol.	670,015	941,727	835,394	677,212	579,641	518,965
Consumer installment credit to personal income ratio	Percent	16.5	19.2	20.4	21.3	21.6	21.4
Change in consumer price index for services	Percent	5.8	3.8	3.9	3.2	3.1	3.0

[1] Data are from private sources and provided through the courtesy of the compilers and are subject to their copyrights: stock prices, Standard & Poors Corporation; index of consumer expectations, University of Michigan's Survey Research Center; vendor perfomance, Institute for Supply Management.

Source: The Conference Board, New York, NY 10022-6601, *Business Cycle Indicators*, monthly, <http://www.conference-board.org/economics/bci/> (copyright).

Table 762. **Business Cycle Expansions and Contractions—Months of Duration: 1918 to 2001**
[A trough is the low point of a business cycle; a peak is the high point. Contraction, or recession, is the period from peak to subsequent trough; expansion is the period from trough to subsequent peak. Business cycle reference dates are determined by the National Bureau of Economic Research, Inc.]

Business cycle reference date				Contraction (peak to trough)	Expansion (previous trough to this peak)	Length of cycle	
Peak		Trough				Trough from previous trough	Peak from previous peak
Month	Year	Month	Year				
August	1918	March	1919	7	[1]44	[1]51	[2]67
January	1920	July	1921	18	10	28	17
May	1923	July	1924	14	22	36	40
October	1926	November	1927	13	27	40	41
August	1929	March	1933	43	21	64	34
May	1937	June	1938	13	50	63	93
February	1945	October	1945	8	80	88	93
November	1948	October	1949	11	37	48	45
July	1953	May	1954	10	45	55	56
August	1957	April	1958	8	39	47	49
April	1960	February	1961	10	24	34	32
December	1969	November	1970	11	106	117	116
November	1973	March	1975	16	36	52	47
January	1980	July	1980	6	58	64	74
July	1981	November	1982	16	12	28	18
July	1990	March	1991	8	92	100	108
March	2001	November	2001	8	120	128	128
Average, all cycles:							
1854 to 2001 (32 cycles)				17	38	55	[3]56
1854 to 1919 (16 cycles)				22	27	48	[4]49
1919 to 1945 (6 cycles)				18	35	53	53
1945 to 2001 (10 cycles)				10	57	67	67
Average, peacetime cycles:							
1854 to 2001 (27 cycles)				18	33	51	[5]52
1854 to 1919 (14 cycles)				22	24	46	[6]47
1919 to 1945 (5 cycles)				20	26	46	45
1945 to 2001 (8 cycles)				10	52	63	63

[1] Previous trough: December 1914.   [2] Previous peak: January 1913.   [3] 31 cycles.   [4] 15 cycles.   [5] 26 cycles.   [6] 13 cycles.

Source: National Bureau of Economic Research, Inc., Cambridge, MA, "Business Cycle Expansions and Contractions"; <http://www.nber.org/cycles.html>; (accessed: 5 May 2005).

Table 763. Industrial Production Indexes by Industry: 1980 to 2004

[Except as noted, based on the North American Industry Classification System (NAICS): 1997; see text, this section. Minus sign (-) indicates decrease]

Industry	NAICS code	Index (1997 = 100)															Percent change		
		1980	1985	1990	1993	1994	1995	1996	1997	1998	1999	2000	2001	2002	2003	2004	2001-2002	2002-2003	2003-2004
Total index	(X)	62.6	68.2	77.4	80.9	85.3	89.4	93.2	100.0	105.8	110.6	115.4	111.3	111.0	110.9	115.5	-0.3	-	4.1
Manufacturing (SIC) [1]	(X)	58.2	65.1	75.0	78.9	83.7	88.1	92.2	100.0	106.6	112.2	117.3	112.3	111.9	111.9	117.2	-0.4	-	4.8
Manufacturing (NAICS)	31-33	57.2	63.9	73.9	78.3	83.3	87.9	92.2	100.0	106.6	112.3	117.6	112.7	112.7	112.7	118.1	-0.1	-	4.8
Durable goods	(X)	48.9	55.4	64.6	69.6	75.7	82.1	89.1	100.0	110.5	120.1	129.4	123.1	122.8	124.4	133.0	-0.3	1.3	7.0
Wood products	321	68.3	75.3	86.8	86.7	91.8	94.0	97.1	100.0	104.5	108.8	107.3	100.4	102.6	100.9	104.8	2.1	-1.6	3.8
Nonmetallic mineral products	327	77.6	77.7	85.1	83.6	88.3	90.9	96.7	100.0	105.6	105.8	105.8	101.8	101.6	100.9	105.7	-0.3	-0.6	4.7
Primary metals	331	102.4	75.3	85.6	86.2	92.7	93.8	96.0	100.0	101.6	101.4	98.1	88.7	90.3	87.4	92.3	1.8	-3.3	5.6
Fabricated metal products	332	75.9	75.2	78.3	80.0	87.1	92.3	95.8	100.0	103.1	104.0	108.1	100.0	97.6	93.5	96.5	-2.4	-4.2	3.2
Machinery	333	79.2	69.4	77.6	78.1	85.5	91.5	94.8	100.0	102.5	100.3	105.4	93.1	88.3	86.4	96.4	-5.2	-2.1	11.6
Computers and electronic products	334	10.2	20.3	29.2	37.7	44.8	58.1	74.3	100.0	128.5	169.7	224.9	227.3	222.2	251.5	288.2	-2.2	13.2	14.6
Electrical equip, appliances, and components	335	75.3	76.8	79.7	85.2	91.4	93.5	96.4	100.0	103.7	105.5	110.8	99.6	91.5	88.9	94.4	-8.1	-2.9	6.2
Motor vehicles and parts	3361-3	45.0	62.9	64.7	77.8	89.4	92.0	92.7	100.0	105.2	116.7	115.9	105.7	115.7	119.9	124.5	9.5	3.6	3.8
Aerospace and other misc transportation equipment	3364-9	103.3	99.6	121.4	101.1	90.7	86.2	89.6	100.0	115.9	111.8	98.2	104.4	98.2	96.0	99.9	-5.9	-2.3	4.0
Furniture and related products	337	65.8	76.2	82.0	85.2	88.0	89.6	90.3	100.0	107.1	110.6	112.4	105.2	109.7	103.7	108.9	4.3	-5.5	5.0
Miscellaneous products	339	53.4	61.4	79.0	88.8	89.6	92.8	97.5	100.0	105.9	108.2	114.1	112.6	119.1	117.2	121.3	5.8	-1.6	3.5
Nondurable goods	(X)	70.3	76.9	88.1	91.3	94.5	96.2	96.4	100.0	101.5	102.2	102.8	99.4	99.6	98.1	100.1	0.2	-1.5	2.1
Food, beverage and tobacco products	311	77.1	84.0	91.2	92.8	96.0	98.7	97.9	100.0	103.0	101.2	102.6	102.4	100.9	101.0	104.2	-1.4	0.1	3.2
Textile and product mills	313,4	76.1	77.2	85.9	92.8	97.9	96.9	94.7	100.0	99.2	99.0	97.1	87.1	85.8	78.5	75.9	-1.4	-8.5	-3.4
Apparel and leather	315,6	109.7	106.8	98.4	102.4	103.6	102.8	100.4	100.0	94.3	90.2	86.1	73.2	61.2	52.6	49.5	-16.3	-14.1	-5.9
Paper	322	74.4	81.4	92.0	95.5	99.7	101.1	98.0	100.0	100.8	101.6	102.7	93.8	94.1	93.4	94.8	0.4	-0.7	-1.5
Printing and related support	323	56.9	76.3	92.6	94.9	95.9	97.3	98.0	100.0	101.2	102.0	102.7	96.4	91.1	87.3	87.8	-5.5	-4.1	0.6
Petroleum and coal products	324	92.2	86.0	91.5	90.4	92.9	94.5	96.8	100.0	98.1	102.2	102.1	101.4	105.9	106.0	109.7	4.4	0.2	3.5
Chemical	325	65.4	69.8	86.7	88.8	91.1	92.5	94.4	100.0	101.7	103.7	105.3	103.4	107.9	107.2	110.3	4.4	-0.6	2.8
Plastics and rubber products	326	41.4	56.3	72.0	82.1	88.9	91.2	94.2	100.0	103.6	109.0	110.2	103.8	105.5	102.6	104.0	1.7	-2.8	1.4
Other manufacturing (non-NAICS) [2]	1133, 5111	82.0	94.8	99.1	93.8	93.1	93.0	92.3	100.0	106.5	109.9	112.2	105.7	100.5	99.5	103.4	-5.0	-0.9	3.9
Mining	21	106.7	102.9	99.0	94.6	96.8	96.7	98.3	100.0	98.5	93.6	95.8	96.7	92.6	92.2	91.4	-4.2	-0.4	-0.9
Utilities	2211,2	69.1	74.0	86.8	92.0	93.9	97.2	100.0	100.0	102.6	105.5	108.6	108.1	111.4	111.9	115.0	3.1	0.4	2.8
Electric power generation, transmission and distribution	2211	64.3	72.6	86.9	91.7	93.7	97.1	99.6	100.0	104.1	107.1	110.2	109.9	113.4	113.7	117.6	3.2	0.3	3.4
Natural gas distribution	2212	93.0	81.4	86.0	94.2	94.9	97.3	102.0	100.0	93.5	102.0	99.0	97.6	100.3	100.9	98.1	2.7	0.6	-2.7

- Represents or rounds to zero.   X Not applicable.   [1] Standard Industrial Classification (SIC); see text, this section.   [2] Those industries—logging and newspaper, periodical, book, and directory publishing—that have traditionally been considered to be manufacturing.

Source: Board of Governors of the Federal Reserve System, *Statistical Supplement to the Federal Reserve Bulletin*, monthly; and *Industrial Production and Capacity Utilization, Statistical Release G.17*, monthly.

Table 764. Index of Industrial Capacity: 1980 to 2004

[**1997 output = 100.** Annual figures are averages of monthly data. Capacity represents estimated quantity of output relative to output in 1997 which the current stock of plant and equipment was capable of producing]

Year	Index of capacity		Relation of output to capacity (percent)				
				Stage of process			
	Total industry	Manufacturing	Total industry	Crude [1]	Primary and semifinished [2]	Finished [3]	Manufacturing
1980	77.4	74.0	80.9	89.2	78.9	79.6	78.8
1985	85.7	83.0	79.5	83.3	80.2	77.2	78.5
1990	93.9	92.0	82.4	89.1	82.3	80.5	81.6
1991	95.7	93.9	79.6	86.1	79.4	78.1	78.3
1992	97.6	96.0	80.3	85.7	80.9	78.3	79.4
1993	99.6	98.3	81.3	85.4	83.1	78.2	80.3
1994	102.2	101.3	83.5	87.3	86.3	79.2	82.6
1995	106.8	106.5	83.7	88.3	86.4	79.2	82.8
1996	112.7	113.2	82.7	88.0	85.2	78.3	81.4
1997	119.4	120.8	83.7	89.3	85.7	80.1	82.8
1998	127.7	130.4	82.9	86.6	84.3	80.4	81.8
1999	134.6	138.4	82.2	86.4	84.6	78.4	81.1
2000	140.7	145.6	82.0	87.8	84.7	77.5	80.6
2001	145.3	150.9	76.6	85.3	78.0	73.0	74.5
2002	147.4	152.2	75.3	83.4	77.6	71.1	73.5
2003	146.9	151.8	75.5	84.7	77.3	71.5	73.7
2004	148.0	152.9	78.1	85.6	79.8	74.6	76.7

[1] Crude processing, covers a relatively small portion of total industrial capacity and consists of logging (NAICS 1133), much of mining (excluding stone, sand, and gravel mining, and oil and gas drilling, which are NAICS 21231, 21221-2, and 213111) and some basic manufacturing industries, including basic chemicals (NAICS 3251); fertilizers, pesticides, and other agricultural chemicals (NAICS 32531,2); pulp, paper, and paperboard mills (NAICS 3221); and alumina, aluminum, and other nonferrous production and processing mills (NAICS 3313,4). [2] Primary and semifinished processing loosely corresponds to the previously published aggregate, primary processing. Includes utilities and portions of several 2-digit SIC industries included in the former advanced processing group. These include printing and related support activities (NAICS 3231); paints and adhesives (NAICS 3255); and newspaper, periodical, book, and directory publishers (NAICS 5111). [3] Finished processing generally corresponds to the previously published aggregate, advanced processing. Includes oil and gas well drilling and carpet and rug mills.

Source: Board of Governors of the Federal Reserve System, *Industrial Production and Capacity Utilization*, Statistical Release G.17, monthly. (Based on data from Federal Reserve Board, U.S. Dept. of Commerce, U.S. Bureau of Labor Statistics, and McGraw-Hill Information Systems Company, New York, NY; and other sources.)

Table 765. Manufacturing and Trade—Sales and Inventories: 1992 to 2004

[**In billions of dollars (541 represents $541,000,000,000),** except ratios. Based on North American Industry Classification System (NAICS) 1997; see text, this section]

Year	Sales, average monthly [1]				Inventories [2]				Inventory-sales ratios [3]			
	Total	Manu-factur-ing	Retail trade	Mer-chant whole-salers	Total	Manu-factur-ing	Retail trade	Mer-chant whole-salers	Total	Manu-factur-ing	Retail trade	Mer-chant whole-salers
1992	541	242	150	149	837	379	259	199	1.52	1.57	1.67	1.31
1993	568	252	161	155	864	380	277	207	1.50	1.51	1.67	1.30
1994	611	270	175	166	927	400	303	224	1.46	1.44	1.66	1.29
1995	655	290	184	181	986	425	320	240	1.48	1.44	1.71	1.30
1996	688	300	196	192	1,005	431	331	243	1.46	1.43	1.66	1.27
1997	724	320	205	200	1,046	444	341	261	1.42	1.37	1.64	1.26
1998	743	325	214	203	1,078	449	355	274	1.43	1.39	1.62	1.32
1999	787	336	233	217	1,139	464	384	291	1.40	1.35	1.59	1.30
2000	834	351	249	235	1,198	481	406	310	1.41	1.35	1.59	1.29
2001	819	331	256	232	1,145	452	395	297	1.44	1.42	1.58	1.32
2002	821	324	262	235	1,163	444	419	301	1.40	1.37	1.55	1.26
2003	852	333	273	246	1,180	439	435	307	1.38	1.33	1.57	1.23
2004	941	369	293	278	1,271	471	460	340	1.31	1.24	1.54	1.17

[1] Averages of monthly not-seasonally-adjusted figures. [2] Seasonally-adjusted end-of-year data. [3] Averages of seasonally-adjusted monthly ratios.

Source: U.S. Council of Economic Advisors, *Economic Indicators*, March 2005.

Table 766. Corporate Profits, Taxes, and Dividends: 1990 to 2004

[In billions of dollars (438 represents $438,000,000,000). Covers corporations organized for profit and other entities treated as corporations. Represents profits to U.S. residents, without deduction of depletion charges and exclusive of capital gains and losses; intercorporate dividends from profits of domestic corporations are eliminated; net receipts of dividends, reinvested earnings of incorporated foreign affiliates, and earnings of unincorporated foreign affiliates are added. CCA = capital consumption adjustment]

Item	1990	1995	2000	2001	2002	2003	2004
Corporate profits with IVA and CCA	438	697	818	767	875	1,021	1,182
Taxes on corporate income	145	219	265	204	184	235	269
Profits after tax with IVA and CCA	292	478	553	563	691	786	912
Net dividends	169	254	378	371	390	395	444
Undistributed profits with IVA and CCA. . .	123	224	175	192	301	391	469
Cash flow:							
Net cash flow with IVA and CCA	491	711	865	945	1,059	1,173	1,265
Undistributed profits with IVA and CCA. . .	123	224	175	192	301	391	469
Consumption of fixed capital	368	487	690	753	758	783	796
Less: Inventory valuation adjustment							
(IVA)	-13	-18	-14	11	-1	-14	-43
Equals: Net cash flow	504	729	879	934	1,060	1,188	1,308

Source: U.S. Bureau of Economic Analysis, *National Income and Product Accounts, Volume 1, 1929–2000*, and *Survey of Current Business*, monthly. See also <http://www.bea.gov/bea/dn/nipaweb/selecttable.asp>.

Table 767. Corporate Profits Before Taxes by Industry: 1999 to 2003

[In millions of dollars (775,876 represents $775,876,000,000). Profits are without inventory valuation and capital consumption adjustments. Minus sign (-) indicates loss. See headnote, Table 766]

Industry	NAICS code [1]	1999	2000	2001	2002	2003
Corporate profits before tax	(X)	775,876	773,398	707,909	758,026	874,465
Domestic industries	(X)	654,363	627,695	538,212	600,246	697,553
Agriculture, forestry, fishing, and hunting	11	1,934	1,621	1,322	440	325
Mining.	21	3,509	14,733	15,504	4,427	16,320
Utilities	221	33,237	24,896	24,121	11,695	18,962
Construction	23	41,051	41,867	43,949	40,643	40,867
Manufacturing	31-33	148,151	153,317	47,645	49,279	75,478
Wholesale trade	42	55,080	61,693	48,160	53,763	52,740
Retail trade	44-45	66,267	61,297	69,939	77,510	77,949
Transportation and warehousing	48-49	16,482	15,164	804	-1,014	10,633
Information	51	10,214	-17,748	-26,071	-11,893	-1,376
Finance and insurance.	52	126,704	113,371	125,861	157,288	179,616
Real estate and rental and leasing.	53	9,807	9,407	9,898	9,490	11,023
Professional, scientific, and technical services . . .	54	20,686	8,991	8,991	16,445	19,369
Management of companies and enterprises [2]. . . .	551111,551112	67,550	86,801	101,707	118,893	120,230
Admin/support waste mgt/remediation services. . .	56	9,438	8,534	9,972	9,820	9,837
Educational services	61	1,588	1,885	1,911	2,360	2,398
Health care and social assistance	62	20,550	24,913	31,616	38,009	41,468
Arts, entertainment, and recreation.	71	2,738	2,170	2,912	3,366	2,925
Accommodation and food services.	72	11,737	13,934	11,248	12,634	11,651
Other services, except public administration. . . .	81	7,640	8,424	8,723	7,091	7,138
Rest of the world [3]	(X)	121,513	145,703	169,697	157,780	176,912

X Not applicable.   [1] Based on North American Industry Classification System, 1997; see text, this section.   [2] Consists of bank and other holding companies.   [3] Consists of receipts by all U.S. residents, including both corporations and persons, of dividends from foreign corporations, and, for U.S. corporations, their share of reinvested earnings of their incorporated foreign affiliates, and earnings of unincorporated foreign affiliates, net of corresponding payments.

Source: U.S. Bureau of Economic Analysis, *National Income and Product Accounts, Volume 1, 1929–2000*, and *Survey of Current Business*, August 2004. See also <http://www.bea.gov/bea/dn/nipaweb/selecttable.asp>.

Table 768. Corporate Profits With Inventory Valuation and Capital Consumption Adjustments—Financial and Nonfinancial Industries: 1999 to 2004

[In billions of dollars (851 represents $851,000,000,000). Based on the North American Industry Classification System 1997; see text, this section. Minus sign (-) indicates loss. See headnote, Table 766]

Item	1999	2000	2001	2002	2003	2004
Corporate profits with IVA/CCA [1] . . .	851	818	767	875	1,021	1,182
Domestic industries	730	672	598	717	844	990
Rest of the world	122	146	170	158	177	192
Corporate profits with IVA [1]	777	759	719	757	860	942
Domestic industries	655	614	550	599	683	750
Financial [2]	194	200	228	276	300	294
Nonfinancial.	461	413	322	323	384	456
Utilities	33	24	25	11	19	23
Manufacturing.	151	144	53	51	67	106
Wholesale trade	56	60	52	51	48	55
Retail trade	65	60	71	78	78	72
Transportation and warehousing.	16	15	1	-1	11	10
Information.	11	-18	-26	-11	-1	10
Other nonfinancial [3]	130	128	146	144	162	181
Rest of the world	122	146	170	158	177	192

[1] Inventory valuation adjustment and capital consumption adjustment.   [2] Consists of finance and insurance and bank and other holding companies.   [3] Consists of agriculture, forestry, fishing, and hunting; mining; construction; real estate and rental and leasing; professional, scientific, and technical services; administrative and waste management services; educational services; health care and social assistance; arts, entertainment, and recreation; accommodation and food services; and other services, except government.

Source: U.S. Bureau of Economic Analysis, *National Income and Product Accounts, Volume 1, 1929–2000*, and *Survey of Current Business*, monthly. See also <http://www.bea.gov/bea/dn/nipaweb/selecttable.asp>.

Table 769. **Manufacturing, Mining, and Trade Corporations—Profits and Stockholders' Equity by Industry: 2003 and 2004**

[Averages of quarterly figures at annual rates. Manufacturing data exclude estimates for corporations with less than $250,000 in assets at time of sample selection. Based on sample; see source for discussion of methodology. Based on North American Industry Classification System (NAICS), 1997; see text, this section. Minus sign (-) indicates loss]

Industry	NAICS code	Ratio of profits after taxes to stockholders' equity (percent)		Profits after taxes per dollar of sales (cents)		Ratio of stockholders' equity to debt	
		2003	2004	2003	2004	2003	2004
Manufacturing	31-33	12.1	15.7	5.4	7.0	1.5	1.7
Nondurable manufacturing	(X)	16.4	19.4	7.1	8.0	1.3	1.4
Food	311	16.5	18.4	4.4	5.0	1.0	1.0
Beverage and tobacco products	312	24.7	28.0	12.3	16.1	0.8	1.0
Textile mills and textile product mills	313, 314	7.2	5.4	2.1	1.5	1.1	1.3
Apparel and leather products	315, 316	24.2	20.9	7.7	6.7	1.6	2.0
Paper	322	4.2	8.2	1.7	3.1	0.7	0.8
Printing and related support activities	323	15.1	22.2	2.9	3.8	0.8	0.7
Petroleum and coal products	324	17.1	26.2	7.3	9.3	2.6	2.5
Chemicals	325	16.9	15.5	10.7	10.3	1.4	1.5
Plastics and rubber products	326	7.2	14.0	1.9	3.0	0.8	0.7
Durable manufacturing	(X)	8.4	12.7	3.9	6.1	1.8	2.1
Wood products	321	12.7	23.1	3.2	5.8	1.1	1.4
Nonmetallic mineral products	327	5.0	-3.8	1.8	-1.3	1.0	1.1
Primary metals	331	-2.1	22.0	-0.7	6.9	1.0	1.3
Fabricated metal products	332	8.7	17.6	3.0	5.8	1.3	1.4
Machinery	333	5.5	12.1	2.6	5.2	1.5	1.7
Computer and electronic products	334	4.9	10.3	4.3	9.2	3.2	4.0
Electrical equipment, appliances, & components	335	18.0	16.8	11.1	11.8	2.7	3.5
Transportation equipment	336	12.2	13.4	2.7	3.4	1.1	1.3
Furniture and related products	337	10.8	11.7	3.1	3.3	1.6	1.8
Miscellaneous manufacturing	339	15.2	15.1	8.5	9.4	1.6	1.9
All mining	21	9.8	14.3	12.0	17.2	1.7	1.9
All wholesale trade	42	9.3	14.7	1.4	2.2	1.5	1.6
Durable goods	421	7.7	13.1	1.5	2.5	1.5	1.8
Nondurable goods	422	11.7	17.3	1.4	1.9	1.3	1.4
All retail trade	44-45	15.8	16.6	3.0	3.2	1.4	1.4
Food and beverage stores	445	9.8	11.4	1.2	1.4	0.8	0.9
Clothing and general merchandise stores	448, 452	17.6	17.1	3.9	3.9	1.4	1.4
All other retail trade	(X)	15.6	17.9	3.0	3.4	1.8	2.0

X Not applicable.

Source: U.S. Census Bureau, *Quarterly Financial Report for Manufacturing, Mining, and Trade Corporations.*

Table 770. **Value Added, Employment, and Capital Expenditures of Nonbank U.S. Multinational Companies: 1990 to 2002**

[Value added and capital expenditures in billions of dollars (1,717 represents $1,717,000,000,000); employees in thousands. See headnote, table 771. MNC = Multinational company. MOFA = Majority-owned foreign affiliate. Minus sign (-) indicates decrease]

Item	1990	1994	1995	1999 [1]	2000 [1]	2001 [1]	2002 [1]	Percent change at annual rates	
								1994-2001	2001-2002
VALUE ADDED									
MNCs worldwide:									
Parents and all affiliates	(NA)	(NA)	(NA)	(NA)	(NA)	(NA)	(NA)	(NA)	(NA)
Parents and MOFAs	(NA)	1,717	1,831	2,481	2,748	2,478	2,469	5.3	-0.4
Parents	(NA)	1,314	1,365	1,914	2,141	1,892	1,857	5.2	-1.9
Affiliates, total	(NA)	(NA)	(NA)	(NA)	(NA)	(NA)	(NA)	(NA)	(NA)
MOFAs	356	404	466	566	607	586	611	5.3	4.4
Other	(NA)	(NA)	(NA)	(NA)	(NA)	(NA)	(NA)	(NA)	(NA)
EMPLOYEES									
MNCs worldwide:									
Parents and all affiliates	25,264	25,670	25,921	32,227	33,598	32,539	32,109	3.4	-1.3
Parents and MOFAs	23,786	24,273	24,500	30,773	32,057	30,929	30,597	3.5	-1.1
Parents	18,430	18,565	18,576	23,007	23,885	22,735	22,413	2.9	-1.4
Affiliates, total	6,834	7,105	7,345	9,220	9,713	9,804	9,696	4.6	-1.1
MOFAs	5,356	5,707	5,924	7,766	8,171	8,194	8,184	5.2	-0.1
Other	1,478	1,398	1,421	1,454	1,542	1,610	1,512	2.0	-6.1
CAPITAL EXPENDITURES									
MNCs worldwide:									
Parents and all affiliates	(NA)	328	(NA)	514	(NA)	(NA)	(NA)	(NA)	(NA)
Parents and MOFAs	275	303	324	483	507	524	454	8.0	-13.3
Parents	213	232	248	370	396	413	341	8.4	-17.5
Affiliates, total	(NA)	96	(NA)	144	(NA)	(NA)	(NA)	(NA)	(NA)
MOFAs	62	71	76	113	111	111	113	6.3	2.2
Other	(NA)	25	(NA)	31	(NA)	(NA)	(NA)	(NA)	(NA)

NA Not available. [1] Data for 1999 through 2002 are not strictly comparable with data prior to 1999; see source.

Source: U.S. Bureau of Economic Analysis, *Survey of Current Business*, July 2004.

528 Business Enterprise

Table 771. U.S. Multinational Companies—Selected Characteristics: 2002

[Preliminary. In billions of dollars (14,647 represents $14,647,000,000,000), except as indicated. Consists of nonbank U.S. parent companies and their nonbank foreign affiliates. U.S. parent comprises the domestic operations of a multinational and is a U.S. person that owns or controls directly or indirectly, 10 percent or more of the voting securities of an incorporated foreign business enterprise, or an equivalent interest in an unincorporated foreign business enterprise. A U.S. person can be an incorporated business enterprise. A majority-owned foreign affiliate (MOFA) is a foreign business enterprise in which a U.S. parent company owns or controls more than 50 percent of the voting securities]

Industry [1]	NAICS code	U.S. parents				MOFAs		
		Total assets	Capital expenditures	Value added	Employment (1,000)	Capital expenditures	Value added	Employment (1,000)
All Industries	(X)	14,647	341.2	1,857	22,413	113.2	611	8,184
Mining	21	166	12.7	24	127	29.2	58	149
Utilities	22	692	34.8	80	373	3.8	8	71
Manufacturing [2]	31-33	4,294	137.0	829	8,374	45.4	317	4,318
Chemicals	325	698	19.7	147	986	10.1	68	600
Transportation equipment	336	1,107	30.1	147	1,738	10.9	45	889
Wholesale trade	42	398	18.3	88	911	6.0	94	776
Information [2]	51	1,274	56.0	227	1,877	5.8	23	345
Broadcasting & telecommunications	513	865	46.3	148	1,154	4.1	5	99
Finance (except depository institutions) and insurance	52 exc. 521, 522	6,524	20.4	140	1,388	7.7	24	311
Professional, scientific, and technical services	54	242	8.6	99	976	2.4	31	414
Other industries [2]	(X)	1,057	53.3	370	8,388	12.9	57	1,801
Retail trade	44-45	396	27.1	162	3,971	3.0	22	556
Transportation and warehousing	48-49	193	9.2	73	985	1.3	7	137
Admin/support waste management /remediation services	56	60	2.3	33	990	0.4	10	455

X Not applicable. [1] Represents North American Industry Classification System 1997 based industry of U.S. parent or industry of foreign affiliate. [2] Includes other industries not shown separately.
Source: U.S. Bureau of Economic Analysis, *Survey of Current Business*, July 2004.

Table 772. U.S. Multinational Companies—Value Added: 2000 and 2002

[In billions of dollars (2,748.1 represents $2,748,100,000,000). See headnote, Table 771. Data are by industry of U.S. parent. Based on the North American Industry Classification System, 1997 (NAICS); see text this section]

Industry	NAICS code	U.S. multinationals		U.S. parents		Majority-owned foreign affiliates	
		2000	2002	2000	2002	2000	2002
All Industries	(X)	2,748.1	2,468.8	2,141.5	1,857.4	606.6	611.5
Mining	21	39.0	37.4	27.7	24.1	11.3	13.3
Utilities	22	85.7	86.9	80.5	80.0	5.1	6.9
Manufacturing [1]	31-33	1,410.5	1,247.0	995.1	829.1	415.3	417.9
Chemicals	325	212.0	227.9	141.3	146.9	70.7	81.0
Transportation equipment	336	270.8	199.9	208.6	147.3	62.2	52.6
Wholesale trade	42	132.7	113.8	99.0	88.1	33.8	25.7
Information [1]	51	324.7	250.1	302.3	227.2	22.4	22.9
Broadcasting & telecommunications	513	226.3	152.8	218.3	147.6	8.0	5.2
Finance (except depository institutions) and insurance	52 exc. 521, 522	181.1	167.8	156.7	139.8	24.4	28.0
Professional, scientific, and technical services	54	141.4	137.8	100.7	98.7	40.8	39.2
Other industries [1]	(X)	433.0	428.0	379.5	370.3	53.5	57.7
Retail trade	44-45	166.2	184.7	148.7	162.3	17.5	22.4
Transportation and warehousing	48-49	90.8	79.3	85.3	73.5	5.5	5.8
Admin/support waste mgt/remediation services	56	56.3	42.8	44.6	33.4	11.7	9.4

X Not applicable. [1] Includes other industries not shown separately.
Source: U.S. Bureau of Economic Analysis, *Survey of Current Business*, November 2003 and July 2004.

Table 773. U.S. Multinational Companies—Value Added by Industry of Affiliate and Country: 2002

[In millions of dollars (611,456 represents $611,456,000,000. See headnote, Table 771. Numbers in parentheses represent North American Industry Classification System 1997 codes, see text, this section]

Country	All industries [1]	Mining (21)	Manufacturing (31-33)			Wholesale trade (42)	Professional, scientific, and technical services (54)
			Total [1]	Chemicals (325)	Transportation equipment (336)		
All countries [2]	611,456	58,175	316,621	67,808	45,316	94,447	30,962
United Kingdom	105,056	8,039	43,450	6,408	4,232	14,461	9,224
Canada	71,139	8,135	40,723	5,032	10,693	5,524	1,202
Germany	60,738	814	35,196	4,758	9,667	15,613	2,772
France	35,864	24	19,693	5,275	2,154	5,757	1,411
Japan	34,606	7	16,763	3,746	463	5,921	4,666
Ireland	23,511	2	19,713	12,738	94	1,824	340
Mexico	22,233	99	16,734	3,499	5,478	955	368
Italy	21,665	13	15,919	3,217	918	3,358	736
Netherlands	21,406	1,211	11,857	3,334	1,067	4,353	839
Australia	19,511	2,669	7,538	1,217	1,360	3,308	1,839

[1] Includes other industries not shown separately. [2] Includes other countries not shown separately.
Source: U.S. Bureau of Economic Analysis, *Survey of Current Business*, July 2004.

Business Enterprise 529

No. 559.—RESEARCH AND DEVELOPMENT EXPENDITURES: 1941 TO 1952

[Government data derived from actual Federal budget expenditures for research and development plus estimates of procurement expenditures used for research and development. Industry data based on nationwide survey conducted in mid-1952 (see table 560). University data based on sample survey completed early in 1953]

YEAR	Total	SOURCE OF FUNDS			USE OF FUNDS BY—		
		Government	Industry	University	Government	Industry	University
EXPENDITURES (million dollars)							
1941	900	370	510	20	200	660	40
1942	1,070	490	560	20	240	780	50
1943	1,210	780	410	20	300	850	60
1944	1,380	940	420	20	390	910	80
1945	1,520	1,070	430	20	430	990	100
1946	1,780	910	840	30	470	1,190	120
1947	2,260	1,160	1,050	50	520	1,570	170
1948	2,610	1,390	1,150	70	570	1,820	220
1949	2,610	1,550	990	70	550	1,790	270
1950	2,870	1,610	1,180	80	570	1,980	320
1951	3,360	1,980	1,300	80	700	2,300	360
1952	3,750	2,240	1,430	80	800	2,530	420
PERCENT OF TOTAL							
1941	100.0	41.0	57.0	2.0	22.0	73.0	5.0
1942	100.0	46.0	52.0	2.0	22.0	73.0	5.0
1943	100.0	64.0	34.0	2.0	25.0	70.0	5.0
1944	100.0	68.0	30.0	2.0	28.0	66.0	6.0
1945	100.0	70.0	28.0	2.0	28.0	65.0	7.0
1946	100.0	51.0	47.0	2.0	26.0	67.0	7.0
1947	100.0	51.0	47.0	2.0	23.0	69.0	8.0
1948	100.0	53.0	44.0	3.0	22.0	70.0	8.0
1949	100.0	59.0	38.0	3.0	21.0	69.0	10.0
1950	100.0	56.0	41.0	3.0	20.0	69.0	11.0
1951	100.0	59.0	39.0	2.0	21.0	68.0	11.0
1952	100.0	60.0	38.0	2.0	21.0	68.0	11.0

Source: Department of Defense, Research and Development Board.

No. 560.—INDUSTRIAL RESEARCH AND DEVELOPMENT—RESEARCH COST AND PERSONNEL, BY INDUSTRY: 1951

[Figures cover approximately 85 percent of all industrial research and development. Based on nationwide survey of companies engaged in scientific and engineering research and development conducted in mid-1952]

INDUSTRY	Number of companies reporting	COST OF RESEARCH			RESEARCH PERSONNEL		COST RATIOS [1]	
		Total cost ($1,000)	Percent of total sales	Percent financed by Federal government	Total research employees	Number of engineers and scientists [2]	Average cost per research employee	Average cost per engineer or scientist [2]
All Industries	1,934	[4] 1,783,662	2.0	47.0	[4] 220,157	[4] 89,851	$8,900	$22,100
Manufacturing	1,527	1,613,493	2.0	46.5	196,517	79,303	9,000	22,700
Food and kindred products	72	23,764	.3	3.7	2,941	1,357	8,700	16,900
Textile mill products and apparel	49	15,817	.9	14.4	1,989	734	8,500	19,300
Chemicals and allied products	275	204,170	2.5	7.1	25,211	13,181	7,900	16,500
Petroleum refining	49	92,942	.6	3.1	12,393	4,953	8,100	20,900
Stone, clay, and glass products	38	20,752	1.3	2.7	3,115	1,210	6,600	18,600
Primary metal industries	49	34,415	.4	9.5	3,705	1,703	10,100	21,600
Fabricated metal products	150	38,404	.9	31.1	5,311	2,491	8,000	16,500
Machinery (except electrical)	182	99,334	1.5	23.9	12,668	5,333	8,100	18,500
Electrical machinery	233	431,948	6.4	57.0	51,172	17,243	9,400	28,100
Transportation equipment	104	510,608	4.5	70.7	59,243	21,857	10,000	27,700
Motor vehicles and equipment	26	94,303	1.2	9.4	8,895	1,445	10,900	68,600
Aircraft and parts	62	410,085	12.7	85.0	49,915	20,168	9,700	21,300
Other transportation equipment	16	6,217	.9	52.8	433	246	15,500	30,800
Professional, scientific, and controlling instruments	152	91,447	5.7	57.6	13,442	5,694	7,500	17,900
Photographic equipment and supplies	24	30,794	4.8	29.1	4,330	1,954	7,500	17,300
Other professional, scientific, and controlling instruments	128	60,653	6.4	72.8	9,112	3,740	7,500	18,200
Other manufacturing	174	49,895	.8	31.4	7,327	3,547	8,400	16,300
Nonmanufacturing	407	170,169	1.7	50.8	23,640	10,548	8,300	18,000
Commercial consulting services	281	43,620	47.2	65.5	7,181	3,391	7,400	15,500
Nonprofit research agencies	37	28,517	86.3	56.0	4,588	2,518	6,900	11,700
Other nonmanufacturing	89	98,032	1.0	42.9	11,871	4,639	9,300	23,300

[1] Based on reports from 1,650 companies reporting both research cost and employment.
[2] Professional research staff.
[3] Operating cost of all research and development divided by average employment of research engineers and scientists.
[4] Based on reports from 1,754 companies; total including estimates for 180 companies not reporting is $1,959,100,000.
[5] Based on reports from 1,801 companies; total including estimates for 133 companies not reporting is 234,000.
[6] Based on reports from 1,795 companies; total including estimates for 139 companies not reporting is 94,000.

Source: Department of Labor, Bureau of Labor Statistics, and Department of Defense, Research and Development Board; *Industrial Research and Development,* January 1953 (a preliminary report).

Source: Statistical Abstract of the United States: 1953 Edition.

Section 16
Science and Technology

This section presents statistics on scientific, engineering, and technological resources, with emphasis on patterns of research and development (R&D) funding and on scientific, engineering, and technical personnel; education; and employment. Also included are statistics on space program outlays and accomplishments. Principal sources of these data are the National Science Foundation (NSF) and the National Aeronautics and Space Administration (NASA).

NSF gathers data chiefly through recurring surveys. Current NSF publications containing data on funds for research and development and on scientific and engineering personnel include detailed statistical tables; issue briefs; and annual, biennial, triennial, and special reports. Titles or the areas of coverage of these reports include the following: *Science and Engineering Indicators; National Patterns of R&D Resources; Women, Minorities, and Persons with Disabilities in Science and Engineering*—science and technology data presented in chart and tabular form in a pocket-sized publication—*Federal Funds for Research and Development; Federal R&D Funding by Budget Function; Federal Support to Universities, Colleges, and Selected Nonprofit Institutions; Research and Development in Industry*; R&D expenditures and graduate enrollment and support in academic science and engineering; and characteristics of doctoral scientists and engineers and of recent graduates in the United States. Statistical surveys in these areas pose problems of concept and definition and the data should therefore be regarded as broad estimates rather than precise, quantitative statements. See sources for methodological and technical details.

The National Science Board's biennial *Science and Engineering Indicators* contains data and analysis of international and domestic science and technology, including measures of inputs and outputs.

The *Budget of the United States Government,* published by the U.S. Office of Management and Budget, contains summary financial data on federal R&D programs.

Research and development outlays— NSF defines research as "systematic study directed toward fuller scientific knowledge of the subject studied" and development as "the systematic use of scientific knowledge directed toward the production of useful materials, devices, systems, or methods, including design and development of prototypes and processes."

National coverage of R&D expenditures is developed primarily from periodic surveys in four principal economic sectors: (1) *Government,* made up primarily of federal executive agencies; (2) *industry,* consisting of manufacturing and nonmanufacturing firms and the federally funded research and development centers (FFRDCs) they administer; (3) *universities and colleges,* composed of universities, colleges, and their affiliated institutions, agricultural experiment stations, and associated schools of agriculture and of medicine, and FFRDCs administered by educational institutions; and (4) *other nonprofit institutions,* consisting of such organizations as private philanthropic foundations, nonprofit research institutes, voluntary health agencies, and FFRDCs administered by nonprofit organizations.

The R&D funds reported consist of current operating costs, including planning and administration costs, except as otherwise noted. They exclude funds for routine testing, mapping and surveying, collection of general-purpose data, dissemination of scientific information, and training of scientific personnel.

Scientists, engineers, and technicians—Scientists and engineers are defined as persons engaged in scientific and engineering work at a level requiring a knowledge of sciences equivalent at least to that acquired through completion

U.S. Census Bureau, Statistical Abstract of the United States: 2006

of a 4-year college course. Technicians are defined as persons engaged in technical work at a level requiring knowledge acquired through a technical institute, junior college, or other type of training less extensive than 4-year college training. Craftsmen and skilled workers are excluded.

Table 774. **Research and Development (R&D) Expenditures by Source and Objective: 1970 to 2003**

[In millions of dollars (26,271 represents $26,271,000,000) except as indicated. For calendar years]

Year		Sources of funds					Objective (percent of total)			Character of work		
	Total	Federal govern-ment	Indus-try	Univer sities/ colleges	Non-profit	Non-federal govern-ment [1]	Defense related [2]	Space related [3]	Other	Basic research	Applied research	Devel-opment
1970....	26,271	14,984	10,449	259	343	237	33	10	56	3,594	5,752	16,925
1971....	26,952	15,210	10,824	290	366	262	33	10	58	3,720	5,833	17,399
1972....	28,740	16,039	11,715	312	393	282	33	8	59	3,850	6,147	18,743
1973....	30,952	16,587	13,299	343	422	302	32	7	61	4,099	6,655	20,197
1974....	33,359	17,287	14,885	393	474	320	29	7	64	4,511	7,344	21,504
1975....	35,671	18,533	15,824	432	534	348	28	8	65	4,875	8,091	22,706
1976....	39,435	20,292	17,702	480	592	369	27	8	65	5,373	8,976	25,085
1977....	43,338	22,071	19,642	569	662	394	27	7	66	6,008	9,662	27,667
1978....	48,719	24,414	22,457	679	727	443	26	6	68	6,959	10,704	31,056
1979....	55,379	27,225	26,097	785	791	482	25	6	70	7,836	12,097	35,445
1980....	63,213	29,975	30,929	920	871	519	24	5	70	8,790	13,745	40,678
1981....	72,269	33,715	35,948	1,058	967	581	24	5	70	9,830	16,391	46,047
1982....	80,783	37,168	40,692	1,207	1,095	621	26	5	69	10,824	18,280	51,679
1983....	89,971	41,472	45,264	1,357	1,220	658	28	4	68	12,059	20,373	57,540
1984....	102,251	46,477	52,187	1,514	1,351	721	29	3	68	13,484	22,505	66,261
1985....	114,685	52,655	57,962	1,743	1,491	834	30	3	67	14,857	25,410	74,417
1986....	120,259	54,633	60,991	2,019	1,647	969	31	3	66	17,247	27,259	75,754
1987....	126,217	58,466	62,576	2,262	1,849	1,065	32	3	65	18,498	27,915	79,804
1988....	133,880	60,130	67,977	2,527	2,081	1,165	30	4	66	19,786	29,528	84,566
1989....	141,889	60,463	74,966	2,852	2,333	1,274	28	4	69	21,889	32,277	87,723
1990....	151,990	61,607	83,208	3,187	2,589	1,399	25	4	71	23,028	34,896	94,067
1991....	160,872	60,780	92,300	3,457	2,852	1,483	22	4	73	27,139	38,629	95,104
1992....	165,347	60,912	96,229	3,568	3,113	1,525	22	4	74	27,604	37,933	99,810
1993....	165,723	60,522	96,549	3,708	3,387	1,557	21	4	74	28,739	37,280	99,704
1994....	169,195	60,769	99,203	3,937	3,664	1,622	20	5	76	29,644	36,615	102,936
1995....	183,611	62,959	110,870	4,109	3,924	1,750	19	4	77	29,602	40,932	113,077
1996....	197,330	63,383	123,416	4,434	4,238	1,860	18	4	78	32,790	43,165	121,375
1997....	212,134	64,561	136,227	4,836	4,589	1,921	17	4	79	36,918	46,542	128,674
1998....	226,321	66,356	147,843	5,168	4,984	1,970	16	4	80	35,256	46,353	144,712
1999....	243,517	67,015	163,229	5,630	5,549	2,095	15	3	82	38,710	51,865	152,941
2000....	264,634	66,327	183,688	6,211	6,170	2,238	13	2	84	42,321	56,481	165,827
2001....	274,211	73,341	184,892	6,778	6,818	2,382	14	2	84	47,112	64,401	162,698
2002 [4]..	276,434	80,490	178,514	7,332	7,550	2,548	15	3	82	50,807	65,559	160,068
2003 [4]..	283,795	85,279	179,615	7,944	8,247	2,710	16	3	81	54,103	67,780	161,911

[1] Nonfederal R&D expenditures to university and college performers. [2] R&D spending by the Department of Defense, including space activities, and a portion of the Department of Energy funds. [3] For the National Aeronautics and Space Administration only. [4] Preliminary.

Source: U.S. National Science Foundation, *National Patterns of R&D Resources*, annual. See also <http://www.nsf.gov/sbe/srs/>.

Table 775. Performance Sector of R&D Expenditures: 1995 to 2003

[In millions of dollars (183,611 represents $183,611,000,000). For calendar year. FFRDCs are federally-funded research and development centers. For most academic institutions and the Federal Government before 1997, began on July 1 instead of October 1]

Year	Total	Federal government	Industry — Total	Industry — Funded by Federal government	Industry — Funded by Industry[1]	Industry FFRDCs	Universities and colleges — Total	Univ — Funded by Federal government	Univ — Funded by Nonfederal government[2]	Univ — Funded by Industry	Univ — Funded by Universities & colleges	Univ — Funded by Nonprofits	Universities & colleges FFRDCs[3]	Other nonprofit institutions — Total	Other — Funded by Federal government	Other — Funded by Industry	Other — Funded by Nonprofits
RESEARCH AND DEVELOPMENT TOTAL																	
1995	183,611	16,904	129,830	21,178	108,652	2,273	22,603	13,582	1,750	1,547	4,109	1,616	5,367	5,827	2,847	671	2,308
1999	243,517	17,851	180,672	20,496	160,176	2,039	28,135	16,223	2,095	2,077	5,630	2,110	5,652	8,175	3,761	975	3,440
2000	264,634	17,917	197,539	17,118	180,421	2,000	30,566	17,637	2,238	2,165	6,211	2,316	5,742	9,404	4,447	1,103	3,854
2001	274,211	21,048	198,505	16,899	181,606	2,020	33,518	19,654	2,382	2,117	6,778	2,528	6,225	10,702	5,302	1,110	4,290
2002, prel.	276,434	23,788	192,379	17,085	175,294	2,235	36,846	22,052	2,548	2,150	7,332	2,764	7,132	11,766	5,910	1,070	4,786
2003, prel.	283,795	24,959	193,729	17,314	176,415	2,383	40,262	24,499	2,710	2,123	7,944	2,986	7,421	12,661	6,323	1,077	5,261
BASIC RESEARCH																	
1995	29,602	2,689	5,569	190	5,379	530	15,139	9,629	1,069	945	2,509	987	2,702	2,899	1,170	390	1,338
1999	38,710	3,347	6,560	1,198	5,362	557	20,900	12,773	1,429	1,417	3,841	1,439	2,765	4,185	1,734	541	1,910
2000	42,321	3,765	6,942	925	6,017	547	22,726	13,836	1,539	1,488	4,271	1,592	2,873	4,852	2,099	612	2,140
2001	47,112	4,317	7,911	754	7,157	552	24,862	15,299	1,643	1,501	4,675	1,744	3,041	5,518	2,520	616	2,382
2002, prel.	50,807	4,617	7,671	762	6,908	611	27,369	17,122	1,765	1,489	5,079	1,915	3,484	6,105	2,854	594	2,657
2003, prel.	54,103	4,463	7,725	773	6,952	651	29,940	19,022	1,877	1,470	5,503	2,069	3,625	6,709	3,190	598	2,921
APPLIED RESEARCH																	
1995	40,932	4,952	26,919	3,164	23,755	535	5,655	2,775	559	494	1,311	516	1,050	1,692	934	170	589
1999	51,865	5,530	36,418	3,109	33,309	274	5,843	2,740	546	542	1,467	550	1,251	2,419	1,300	247	872
2000	56,481	6,105	38,812	2,682	36,130	269	6,661	3,349	573	554	1,591	593	1,330	3,087	1,831	279	977
2001	64,491	7,164	43,486	3,603	39,883	916	7,366	3,839	606	554	1,724	643	1,548	3,570	2,202	281	1,087
2002, prel.	65,559	8,083	42,140	3,643	38,497	955	8,146	4,418	642	542	1,848	697	1,938	3,933	2,448	271	1,213
2003, prel.	67,780	8,837	42,434	3,691	38,743	1,040	8,927	4,954	683	535	2,002	753	1,968	4,215	2,609	273	1,333
DEVELOPMENT																	
1995	113,077	9,262	97,342	17,824	79,518	1,208	1,810	1,178	123	108	288	113	1,616	1,236	744	111	381
1999	152,941	8,974	137,694	16,189	121,505	1,208	1,392	711	120	119	322	121	1,636	1,570	726	187	658
2000	165,827	8,047	151,784	13,510	138,274	1,185	1,179	452	126	122	349	130	1,540	1,461	513	211	737
2001	162,698	9,567	147,108	12,542	134,566	552	1,290	516	133	122	378	141	1,636	1,614	581	212	821
2002, prel.	160,068	11,088	142,569	12,680	129,889	669	1,331	512	141	119	406	153	1,710	1,728	608	205	916
2003, prel.	161,911	11,658	143,569	12,850	130,719	692	1,395	523	150	117	439	165	1,828	1,736	524	206	1,006

[1] Includes all non-federal sources of industry R&D expenditures. [2] Includes all non-federal sources. [3] Includes all R&D expenditures of FFRDCs administered by academic institutions and funded by the federal government.

Source: National Science Foundation. Data derived from: *Research and Development in Industry*, annual; *Academic Research and Development Expenditures*, annual; and *Federal Funds for Research and Development*, annual. Also see <http://www.nsf.gov/sbe/srs/nprdf/start.htm>.

Science and Technology **533**

Table 776. National R&D Expenditures as a Percent of Gross Domestic Product by Country: 1985 to 2001

Year	Total R&D						Nondefense R&D [1]					
	United States	Japan	Unified Germany	France	United Kingdom	Italy	United States	Japan	Unified Germany	France	United Kingdom	Italy
1985	2.76	2.54	2.68	2.22	2.24	1.12	1.9	2.5	2.6	1.8	1.8	1.1
1990	2.65	2.78	2.67	2.37	2.15	1.29	2.0	2.8	2.5	1.9	1.7	1.3
1995	2.51	2.69	2.26	2.31	1.95	1.00	2.0	2.8	2.2	2.0	1.7	1.0
1996	2.55	2.77	2.26	2.30	1.88	1.01	2.1	2.7	2.2	2.0	1.6	1.0
1997	2.58	2.83	2.29	2.22	1.81	1.05	2.1	2.8	2.2	2.0	1.5	1.1
1998	2.60	2.94	2.31	2.17	1.80	1.07	2.2	2.9	2.3	2.0	1.5	1.1
1999	2.65	2.94	2.44	2.18	1.88	1.04	2.3	2.9	2.4	2.0	1.6	1.0
2000	2.72	2.98	2.49	2.18	1.85	1.10	2.4	3.0	2.4	2.0	1.6	1.1
2001	2.82	(NA)	2.53	2.20	(NA)	(NA)	2.4	(NA)	2.5	2.0	(NA)	(NA)

NA Not available.   [1] Estimated.

Source: National Science Foundation, *National Patterns of R&D Resources,* annual; and Organization .for Economic Cooperation and Development.

Table 777. Federal Obligations for Research in Current and Constant (1996) Dollars by Field of Science: 1980 to 2003

[In millions of dollars (11,597 represents $11,597,000,000). For fiscal years ending in year shown; see text, Section 8. Excludes R&D plant]

Field of science	1980	1985	1990	1995	1999	2000	2001	2002, prel.	2003, prel.
CURRENT DOLLARS									
Research, total	11,597	16,133	21,622	28,434	33,528	38,471	44,714	49,809	53,377
Basic	4,674	7,819	11,286	13,877	17,444	19,570	21,958	24,174	25,977
Applied	6,923	8,315	10,337	14,557	16,084	18,901	22,756	25,635	27,400
Life sciences	4,192	6,363	8,830	11,811	15,422	17,965	23,057	25,868	28,673
Psychology	199	327	449	623	633	1,627	742	839	955
Physical sciences	2,001	3,046	3,809	4,278	4,066	4,788	4,601	5,145	5,200
Environmental sciences	1,261	1,404	2,174	2,854	3,095	3,329	3,252	3,668	3,879
Mathematics and computer sciences . . .	241	575	841	1,579	1,981	2,206	2,611	2,751	2,866
Engineering	2,830	3,618	4,227	5,708	6,263	6,346	8,197	8,951	9,161
Social sciences	524	460	630	679	855	1,050	1,009	1,027	1,050
Other sciences, n.e.c. [1]	350	342	664	902	1,212	1,160	1,246	1,559	1,593
CONSTANT (1996) DOLLARS [2]									
Research, total	20,713	21,953	25,127	29,002	32,011	35,988	40,872	44,954	47,569
Basic	8,348	10,640	13,116	14,154	16,655	18,307	20,071	21,817	23,150
Applied	12,365	11,314	12,013	14,848	15,356	17,681	20,800	23,136	24,419
Life sciences	7,487	8,658	10,261	12,047	14,724	16,805	21,076	23,347	25,553
Psychology	355	445	522	635	604	1,522	678	757	851
Physical sciences	3,574	4,145	4,426	4,364	3,882	4,479	4,205	4,644	4,635
Environmental sciences	2,252	1,910	2,526	2,911	2,955	3,114	2,972	3,310	3,457
Mathematics and computer sciences . . .	430	782	977	1,611	1,891	2,064	2,386	2,483	2,554
Engineering	5,054	4,923	4,912	5,822	5,980	5,936	7,493	8,079	8,164
Social sciences	936	626	732	693	816	982	922	927	936
Other sciences, n.e.c. [1]	625	465	772	920	1,157	1,085	1,139	1,407	1,419

[1] Not elsewhere classified.   [2] Based on gross domestic product implicit price deflator.

Source: U.S. National Science Foundation, *Federal Funds for Research and Development,* annual. See also <http://www.nsf.gov/statistics/publication.cfm>.

Table 778. Federal Budget Authority for R&D in Current and Constant (1996) Dollars by Selected Budget Functions: 2001 to 2004

[In millions of dollars (86,756 represents $86,756,000,000). For year ending September 30. Excludes R&D plant. Represents budget authority. Functions shown are those for which $1 billion or more was authorized since 1995]

Function	Current dollars				Constant (2000) dollars [1]			
	2001	2002	2003	2004, prel.	2001	2002	2003	2004, prel.
Total [2]	86,756	97,624	112,544	122,045	84,772	93,734	106,324	113,805
National defense	45,713	53,016	63,048	69,852	44,668	50,904	59,564	65,136
Health	20,758	23,560	26,517	28,188	20,283	22,621	25,052	26,285
Space research and technology	6,126	6,270	7,355	7,597	5,986	6,021	6,948	7,084
Energy	1,314	1,327	1,403	1,441	1,284	1,274	1,325	1,343
General science	5,468	5,753	6,129	6,388	5,343	5,524	5,790	5,957
Natural resources and environment	2,096	2,160	2,151	2,220	2,048	2,074	2,032	2,070
Transportation	1,640	1,838	1,869	1,908	1,602	1,765	1,766	1,779
Agriculture	1,657	1,606	1,708	1,747	1,619	1,542	1,614	1,629

[1] Based on gross domestic product implicit price deflator.   [2] Includes other functions, not shown separately.

Source: U.S. National Science Foundation, *Federal R&D Funding by Budget Function,* annual. See also <http://www.nsf.gov/statistics/nsf04329/htmstart.htm> (released December 2004).

Table 779. R&D Expenditures in Science and Engineering at Universities and Colleges in Current and Constant (1996) Dollars: 1990 to 2002

[In millions of dollars (16,286 represents $16,286,000,000). Totals may not add due to rounding]

Characteristic	Current dollars				Constant (1996) dollars [1]			
	1990	1995	2000	2002	1990	1995	2000	2002
Total	16,286	22,170	30,063	36,333	18,926	22,613	28,134	32,943
Basic research [2]	10,643	14,808	22,243	26,959	12,368	15,104	20,815	24,443
Applied R&D [2]	5,643	7,362	7,820	9,374	6,558	7,509	7,318	8,499
Source of funds:								
All governments	9,638	13,331	17,518	21,834	11,200	13,598	16,394	19,797
Institutions' own funds	1,324	1,689	2,198	2,501	1,539	1,723	2,057	2,268
Industry.	3,006	4,047	5,940	7,109	3,493	4,128	5,559	6,446
Other	1,127	1,489	2,153	2,188	1,310	1,519	2,015	1,984
Fields:								
Physical sciences	1,807	2,256	2,711	3,008	2,100	2,301	2,537	2,727
Environmental sciences . . .	1,069	1,434	1,764	2,022	1,242	1,463	1,651	1,833
Mathematical sciences. . . .	222	279	341	387	258	285	319	351
Computer sciences	515	682	876	1,126	598	696	820	1,021
Life sciences	8,726	12,188	17,468	21,404	10,141	12,432	16,347	19,407
Psychology	253	371	516	671	294	378	483	608
Social sciences.	703	1,019	1,298	1,583	817	1,039	1,215	1,435
Other sciences.	336	427	535	627	390	436	501	568
Engineering	2,656	3,515	4,554	5,504	3,087	3,585	4,262	4,990

[1] Based on gross domestic product implicit price deflator. [2] Basic research and applied R&D statistics were re-estimated for FY 2001 and forward. These data are not directly comparable to those from earlier years.
Source: U.S. National Science Foundation, *Survey of Research and Development Expenditures at Universities and Colleges,* annual.

Table 780. Federal R&D Obligations to Selected Universities and Colleges: 2001 and 2002

[In millions of dollars (19,390.2 represents $19,390,200,000), except rank. For years ending September 30. For the top 40 institutions receiving Federal R&D funds in 2002. Awards to the administrative offices of university systems are excluded from totals for individual institutions because that allocation of funds is unknown, but those awards are included in "total all institutions"]

Major institution ranked by total 2002 Federal R&D obligations	2001	2002	Major institution ranked by total 2002 Federal R&D obligations	2001	2002
Total, all institutions [1]	19,390.2	21,117.9	Massachusetts Institute of		
Johns Hopkins University	838.0	974.7	Technology	252.5	268.8
University of Washington	474.5	525.6	Baylor College of Medicine	231.7	266.8
University of Pennsylvania	412.0	447.2	University Southern California	232.5	254.3
University of Michigan	403.4	419.7	University of Alabama—Birmingham. .	201.6	224.2
University of California—Los Angeles .	363.9	415.7	Vanderbilt University	166.1	215.5
Stanford University	351.1	381.0	Case Western Reserve University . . .	200.0	213.4
University of California—San Diego . .	333.9	373.6	University of Illinois—Urbana in		
University of California—San			Champaign	186.9	194.0
Francisco.	344.9	361.0	The Scripps Research Institute	157.4	193.6
Washington University	314.7	348.0	University of Rochester	171.2	189.2
University of Pittsburgh	300.8	335.8	University of California—Berkeley . . .	210.6	187.3
Columbia University—Main Division . .	305.8	330.2	University of California—Davis	166.2	185.3
University of Wisconsin—Madison . . .	290.2	327.9	Boston University	154.4	182.9
Duke University	274.1	327.5	Emory University	161.9	180.6
Harvard University	321.7	313.4	Ohio State University.	156.6	174.7
University of Colorado	290.7	308.3	Northwestern University	164.0	174.0
Yale University	276.2	306.9	University of Iowa	163.9	172.7
University of North Carolina at			University of Arizona	166.9	168.5
Chapel Hill.	275.9	297.9	University of Florida	157.4	167.1
University of Minnesota	273.1	291.9	University of Texas SW Medical		
Pennsylvania State University	253.6	287.1	Center Dallas.	146.9	162.3
Cornell University	271.9	283.1	University of Chicago.	160.1	161.5

[1] Includes other institutions, not shown separately.
Source: U.S. National Science Foundation, *Federal S&E Support to Universities and Colleges and Nonprofit Institutions,* annual.

Table 781. Graduate Science/Engineering Students in Doctorate-Granting Colleges by Characteristic and Field: 1990 to 2003

[In thousands (397.8 represents 397,800). As of fall. Includes outlying areas]

Field of science or engineering	Characteristic										
	Total			Female			Foreign		Part-time		
	1990	2000	2003	1990	2000	2003	2000	2003	1990	2000	2003
Total, all surveyed fields. . .	397.8	433.3	507.2	149.7	195.3	233.4	122.3	148.0	123.2	118.2	135.5
Science/engineering	350.6	366.7	428.0	113.4	145.6	174.2	116.9	141.0	100.7	94.7	107.8
Engineering, total	99.9	98.4	119.3	13.6	19.6	25.5	46.1	58.2	35.9	27.8	31.6
Sciences, total	250.7	268.3	308.7	99.8	126.0	148.7	70.8	82.7	64.8	66.9	76.2
Physical sciences	32.5	29.3	33.3	7.6	8.7	10.4	11.5	13.9	3.6	3.2	3.3
Environmental.	12.9	12.7	13.5	3.8	5.2	6.0	2.6	2.7	3.0	2.6	2.5
Mathematical sciences	17.3	13.8	17.4	5.3	4.9	6.3	5.7	7.1	4.0	2.7	3.5
Computer sciences	27.7	39.5	46.7	6.4	11.4	12.5	19.3	21.6	12.9	16.3	18.4
Agricultural sciences	10.9	11.2	12.4	3.2	4.7	5.6	2.4	2.5	2.0	2.3	2.9
Biological sciences.	46.0	52.3	60.6	21.0	27.4	33.4	11.5	14.5	6.8	7.2	8.2
Psychology.	35.8	37.7	41.8	23.6	27.0	30.8	2.1	2.8	10.3	9.5	11.6
Social sciences	67.7	71.8	82.8	29.0	36.8	43.8	15.7	17.6	22.1	23.0	25.9
Health fields, total.	47.2	66.6	79.3	36.3	49.6	59.2	5.4	7.0	22.5	23.5	27.6

Source: U.S. National Science Foundation, *Survey of Graduate Science Engineering Students and Postdoctorates,* annual.

U.S. Census Bureau, Statistical Abstract of the United States: 2006

Table 782. **Science and Engineering Degree Recipients, 1999 and 2000, and Post-Graduate Employment Status, 2001**

[In thousands (758.3 represents 758,300). FT represents full-time. Based on a survey and subject to sampling error; see source for details]

Degree and field	Graduates 1999 and 2000 (1,000)	2001 [1]				
		In school [2]	Employed		Not employed or not FT students	Median salary [4] ($1,000)
			In S&E [3][4] ($1,000)	In other		
Bachelor's recipients	758.3	168.4	171.5	373.8	44.6	34
All science fields	649.0	154.5	94.7	358.4	41.4	31
Computer and information sciences	61.5	(B)	35.6	19.5	4.4	51
Mathematical sciences	24.4	4.3	3.8	14.6	(B)	33
Life and related sciences	159.4	52.9	17.8	81.6	7.1	29
Physical and related sciences	32.2	10.1	10.6	9.9	1.6	34
Psychology	152.9	41.0	11.1	91.2	9.6	28
Social and related sciences	218.7	44.2	15.9	141.7	17.0	30
All engineering fields	109.2	13.8	76.8	15.3	3.3	49
Aerospace and related engineering	2.2	0.4	1.3	0.4	(B)	44
Chemical engineering	10.8	2.2	6.4	1.7	(B)	50
Civil and architectural engineering	16.8	1.5	12.5	2.2	(B)	42
Electrical, electronics, computer and communications engineering	34.2	4.3	25.8	3.3	(B)	54
Industrial engineering	6.9	(B)	4.6	1.7	(B)	49
Mechanical engineering	25.8	2.7	18.8	3.6	(B)	48
Other engineering	12.6	2.3	7.5	2.2	(B)	45
Master's recipients	160.1	29.5	77.3	45.9	7.4	51
All science fields	115.3	23.9	44.1	41.4	5.8	45
Computer and mathematical sciences . . .	24.3	1.6	17.1	4.4	(B)	65
Mathematical sciences	6.2	1.6	2.5	2.0	(B)	45
Life and related sciences	16.2	4.7	5.9	5.0	(B)	37
Physical and related sciences	8.6	3.2	3.9	1.1	(B)	45
Psychology	33.0	5.8	9.1	16.1	2.0	35
Social and related sciences	27.1	7.1	5.6	12.8	1.5	43
All engineering fields	44.8	5.6	33.2	4.5	1.5	60
Aerospace and related engineering	1.2	0.2	0.8	(B)	(B)	62
Chemical engineering	2.0	0.6	1.2	(B)	(B)	58
Civil and architectural engineering	6.3	(B)	5.1	(B)	(B)	50
Electrical, electronics, computer and communications engineering	16.4	1.7	13.0	1.0	(B)	66
Industrial engineering	3.2	(B)	2.4	(B)	(B)	62
Mechanical engineering	6.1	1.0	4.5	(B)	(B)	60
Other engineering	9.5	1.6	6.3	1.2	(B)	61

B Base figure too small to meet statistical standards of reliability of a derived figure.   [1] As of April.   [2] Full-time students.   [3] In science and engineering.   [4] For the principal job. Excludes full-time students, the self-employed, and persons whose principal job is less than 35 hours per week. For definition of median, see Guide to Tabular Presentation.
Source: National Science Foundation, *National Survey of Recent College Graduates: 2001*.

Table 783. **Doctorates Conferred by Characteristics of Recipients: 2000 and 2003**

[In percent, except as indicated. Based on the Survey of Earned Doctorate Awards; for description of methodology, see <http://www.nsf.gov/sbe/srs/ssed/sedmeth.htm>]

Characteristic	2000, total	2003									
		All fields [1]	Engineering	Physical sciences [2]	Earth sciences	Mathematics	Computer sciences	Biological sciences [3]	Agricultural	Social sciences [4]	Psychology
Total conferred (number).	41,368	40,710	5,265	3,284	783	994	866	5,694	922	4,139	3,275
Male	56.0	54.5	83.0	73.2	66.9	73.5	79.8	54.3	66.1	55.4	31.9
Female.	43.8	45.2	17.0	26.8	33.1	26.5	20.2	45.6	33.9	44.6	67.1
Median age [5].	33.6	33.3	31.4	31.8	32.7	30.3	32.5	30.4	33.4	33.8	32.2
CITIZENSHIP [6]											
Total conferred (number).	39,485	38,629	4,807	3,011	702	910	763	8,183	835	3,748	2,973
U.S. citizen	75.6	72.6	39.5	59.6	67.5	51.6	50.3	46.2	53.1	67.5	93.4
Foreign citizen	24.4	27.4	60.5	40.4	32.5	48.4	49.7	17.1	46.9	32.5	6.6
RACE/ETHNICITY [7]											
Total conferred (number).	29,837	28,044	2,166	1,949	514	516	443	4,065	481	2,690	2,853
White [8].	79.3	76.6	71.8	78.7	83.5	78.9	68.6	75.1	82.3	75.8	79.0
Black [8].	5.9	6.4	3.5	2.8	3.3	3.1	3.8	2.7	3.3	7.0	5.9
Asian/Pacific [8]. . . .	7.8	7.2	15.8	9.5	5.1	9.9	18.5	13.3	4.8	6.6	4.4
Indian/Alaskan [8]. . . .	0.6	0.5	0.5	0.1	0.4	0.4	0.5	0.3	0.8	0.6	0.8
Hispanic	4.3	5.1	4.8	3.7	3.5	3.1	2.3	4.3	4.6	5.7	5.9
Other/unknown [9] . . .	2.2	4.2	3.6	5.2	4.3	4.7	6.3	4.3	4.2	4.4	4.0

[1] Includes other fields, not shown separately.   [2] Astronomy, physics, and chemistry.   [3] Biochemistry, botany, microbiology, physiology, zoology, and related fields.   [4] Anthropology, sociology, political science, economics, international relations and related fields.   [5] For definition of median, see Guide to Tabular Presentation.   [6] For those with known citizenship. Includes those with temporary visas.   [7] Excludes those with temporary visas.   [8] Non-Hispanic.   [9] For the year 2003, includes Native Hawaiians and Other Pacific Islanders, respondents choosing multiple races (excluding those selecting an Hispanic ethnicity), and respondents with unknown race/ethnicity.
Source: U.S. National Science Foundation, *Science and Engineering Doctorate Awards*, annual. See also <http://www.nsf.gov/statistics/pubseri.cfm?TopID=2&SubID=5&SeriID=11> (released December 2004).

Table 784. Doctorates Awarded, by Field of Study and Year of Doctorate: 1995 to 2003

	1995	1998	1999	2000	2001	2002	2003
Grand total, all fields	41,748	42,645	41,090	41,357	40,808	39,964	40,710
Science and engineering, total	26,535	27,278	25,932	25,966	25,540	24,571	25,258
Engineering, total	6,008	5,924	5,330	5,321	5,502	5,071	5,265
Aeronautical/astronautical	252	241	206	214	203	208	199
Chemical	708	776	674	725	728	705	643
Civil	656	650	584	556	594	625	672
Electrical	1,731	1,596	1,478	1,544	1,576	1,392	1,463
Industrial/manufacturing	284	229	211	176	205	230	211
Materials/metallurgical	588	565	469	451	497	396	473
Mechanical	1,025	1,022	855	864	953	827	814
Other	764	845	853	791	746	688	790
Science, total	20,527	21,354	20,602	20,645	20,038	19,500	19,993
Biological/agricultural sciences	6,412	6,882	6,548	6,797	6,543	6,580	6,616
Agricultural sciences	1,036	1,037	966	943	853	893	922
Biological sciences	5,376	5,845	5,582	5,854	5,690	5,687	5,694
Earth, atmospheric, and ocean sciences, total	780	814	805	758	749	785	783
Atmospheric	130	125	124	143	116	117	139
Earth	454	504	452	386	393	428	373
Oceanography	115	112	130	134	121	128	133
Other environmental sciences	81	73	99	95	119	112	138
Mathematical/computer sciences, total	2,187	2,104	1,938	1,909	1,833	1,725	1,860
Computer sciences	997	927	855	859	826	807	866
Mathematics	1,190	1,177	1,083	1,050	1,007	918	994
Physical sciences, total	3,841	3,824	3,579	3,407	3,393	3,209	3,320
Astronomy	173	206	159	185	186	144	167
Chemistry	2,162	2,216	2,132	1,989	1,980	1,923	2,037
Physics	1,479	1,378	1,271	1,204	1,197	1,124	1,080
Other	27	24	17	29	30	18	36
Psychology	3,429	3,675	3,668	3,618	3,442	3,198	3,275
Social sciences, total	3,878	4,055	4,064	4,156	4,078	4,003	4,139
Economics	1,152	1,156	1,075	1,086	1,081	1,023	1,051
Political science	894	959	1,016	987	984	938	1,026
Sociology	555	579	572	637	577	565	612
Other social sciences	1,277	1,361	1,401	1,446	1,436	1,477	1,450
Non-science and engineering, total	15,213	15,367	15,158	15,391	15,268	15,393	15,452
Education	6,650	6,571	6,546	6,429	6,337	6,487	6,627
Health	1,329	1,500	1,407	1,591	1,620	1,655	1,633
Humanities	4,691	5,116	5,034	5,213	5,160	5,009	5,015
Professional/other/unknown	2,543	2,180	2,171	2,158	2,151	2,242	2,177

Source: U.S. National Science Foundation, *Science and Engineering Doctorate Awards*, annual. See also <http://www.nsf.gov/sbe/srs/nsf05300/start.htm> (released December 2004).

Table 785. R&D Funds in R&D-Performing Manufacturing and Nonmanufacturing Companies by Industry: 2000 to 2002

Industry	NAICS [1] code	Total R&D funds as a percent of net sales			Company R&D funds as a percent of net sales		
		2000	2001	2002	2000	2001	2002
All industries, total	(X)	3.8	4.1	3.9	3.4	3.8	3.6
All manufacturing industries, total	(X)	3.6	4.0	3.6	3.3	3.6	3.2
Food	311	(D)	0.5	(D)	0.4	0.5	0.6
Paper, printing, and support activities	322, 326	(D)	(D)	(D)	1.6	2.1	1.3
Petroleum and coal products	324	(D)	(D)	(D)	0.3	0.3	0.4
Chemicals	325	5.9	4.9	6.0	5.9	4.8	5.9
Plastic and rubber products	326	(D)	(D)	(D)	1.8	2.9	1.8
Nonmetallic mineral products	327	1.8	2.4	(D)	1.8	2.3	1.2
Primary metals	331	0.5	0.7	0.7	0.5	0.7	0.7
Fabricated metal products	332	1.4	1.7	1.5	1.4	1.6	1.4
Machinery	333	3.9	4.3	4.4	3.8	4.2	4.3
Navigational, measuring, electromedical, and control instruments	3345	12.0	12.6	8.7	8.0	7.3	5.4
Electrical equipment, appliances, and components	335	(D)	3.1	2.8	2.1	2.9	2.7
Motor vehicles, trailers, and parts	3361-3363	(D)	(D)	(D)	3.2	3.5	3.1
Aerospace products and parts	3364	7.3	5.7	4.1	2.8	3.0	2.3
All nonmanufacturing industries, total	(X)	4.1	4.3	4.4	3.3	4.0	4.1
Transportation and warehousing services	48, 49	(D)	2.5	(D)	0.4	2.4	0.5
Software publishing	5112	20.5	19.4	21.5	1.6	19.3	21.4
Architectural, engineering, and relelated services	5413	10.8	7.5	7.8	0.3	5.2	5.3
Computer systems design and related services	5415	12.3	17.4	16.5	5.9	16.5	14.3
Scientific R&D services	5417	42.9	47.7	21.3	1.8	36.5	17.6
Management of companies and enterprises	55	4.4	7.8	7.6	1.8	7.8	7.6

D Figure withheld to avoid disclosure of information pertaining to a specific organization or individual.   X Not applicable.
[1] North American Industry Classification System 1997 (NAICS); see text, Section 15.

Source: U.S. National Science Foundation, *Research and Development in Industry,* annual. See also <http://www.nsf.gov/statistics /pubseri.cfm?TopID=2&SubID=5&SerilD=26>.

Table 786. Civilian Employment of Scientists, Engineers, and Technicians by Occupation and Industry: 2002

[In thousands (6,703.1 represents 6,703,100). Based on sample and subject to sampling error. For details, see source]

Occupation	Total [1]	Wage and salary workers							Self-employed [3]
		Mining [2]	Construction	Manufacturing	Information	Professional, scientific and technical services	Government	Other service-providing industries	
Scientists, engineers, and technicians, total	6,703.1	42.2	86.8	1,301.9	529.8	1,799.2	1,075.1	1,544.3	304.7
Scientists	998.6	7.0	1.4	99.3	29.4	210.0	323.6	224.3	93.5
Physical scientists	251.1	6.8	(NA)	47.7	1.3	77.4	84.3	22.4	10.2
Life scientists	214.0	(NA)	(NA)	23.5	0.1	43.4	90.1	38.9	9.6
Mathematical science occupations	107.0	(NA)	0.2	9.7	7.4	24.0	20.7	39.8	5.1
Social scientists and related occupations	426.4	0.2	1.2	18.3	20.6	65.2	128.4	123.3	68.6
Computer specialists	2,911.2	5.0	11.9	269.6	407.9	853.4	313.8	916.9	131.5
Engineers [4]	1,478.3	16.0	42.5	565.6	59.8	354.5	191.6	192.9	54.8
Civil engineers	228.1	0.7	19.8	4.1	0.8	106.2	72.0	9.1	15.3
Electrical/electronics engineers	291.9	0.5	5.5	106.7	34.1	62.3	31.6	41.9	9.3
Mechanical engineers	215.1	0.7	5.2	116.2	2.4	44.8	12.8	26.4	6.6
Drafters, engineering, and mapping technicians [5]	904.8	5.0	27.6	297.7	31.3	268.9	119.5	133.9	20.2
Electrical/electronics engineering technicians	203.6	0.9	3.5	82.9	22.0	26.3	17.0	49.9	0.9
Other engineering technicians	274.7	1.3	5.4	105.6	3.5	70.7	51.4	35.6	1.1
Drafters	216.1	0.6	14.3	60.5	1.9	105.4	6.7	18.6	8.1
Surveying and mapping technicians	60.1	0.7	1.0	(NA)	0.4	38.7	11.0	3.9	3.3
Life, physical, and social science technicians	345.9	8.3	0.3	69.6	0.9	66.3	118.0	73.3	2.4
Surveyors, cartographers, and photogrammetrists	64.3	0.8	3.1	0.1	0.4	46.1	8.6	2.9	2.2

NA Not available.   [1] Includes agriculture, forestry, and fishing not shown separately.   [2] Includes oil and gas extraction.   [3] Includes secondary jobs.   [4] Includes kinds of engineers and technicians not shown separately.   [5] Includes other drafters, technicians, and mapping technnicians not shown separately.

Source: U.S. Bureau of Labor Statistics, *National Industry-Occupation Employment Matrix,* February 2004. (Data collected biennially.)

Table 787. Funds for Performance of Industrial R&D by Selected Industries: 2000 to 2002

[In millions of dollars (199,539 represents $199,539,000,000). For calendar years. Covers basic research, applied research, and development. Based on the Survey of Industry Research and Development]

Industry	NAICS [1] code	2000	2001	2002 Total	2002 Percent from company funds
CURRENT DOLLARS					
Total funds [2]............................	(X)	199,539	198,505	190,809	91.4
Chemicals and allied products...................	325	20,918	17,892	20,641	98.8
Machinery..................................	333	6,580	6,404	6,429	99.0
Navigational, measuring, electromedical, and control instruments...	3345	15,116	12,947	13,729	62.3
Electrical equipment, appliances, and components............	335	(D)	4,980	2,039	97.0
Aerospace products and parts....................	3364	10,319	7,868	9,654	55.4
CONSTANT (1996) DOLLARS [3]					
Total funds [2]............................	(X)	186,677	181,416	172,491	91.4
Chemicals.................................	325	19,570	16,352	18,659	98.8
Machinery..................................	333	6,156	5,853	5,812	99.0
Navigational, measuring, electromedical, and control instruments...	3345	14,142	11,832	12,411	62.3
Electrical equipment, appliances, and components............	335	(D)	4,551	1,843	97.0
Aerospace products and parts....................	3364	9,654	7,191	8,727	55.4

D Figure withheld to avoid disclosure of information pertaining to a specific organization or individual.   X Not applicable.
[1] North American Industry Classification System, 1997; see text, Section 15.   [2] Includes other industries not shown separately.
[3] Based on gross domestic product implicit price deflator.

Source: U.S. National Science Foundation, *Research and Development in Industry*, annual.

Table 788. R&D Scientists and Engineers—Employment and Cost, by Industry: 2000 to 2002

[1,037.5 represents 1,037,500]

Industry	NAICS [1] code	Employed scientists and engineers [2] (1,000)			Cost per scientist or engineer, Constant (1996) dollars [3, 4] ($1,000)		
		2000	2001	2002	2000	2001	2002
All industries [5]......................	(X)	1,037.5	1,050.8	1,063.2	179.9	172.7	170.9
Chemicals............................	325	82.0	81.4	84.2	238.6	200.9	225.3
Machinery............................	333	51.9	53.8	56.2	118.7	108.8	108.7
Electrical equipment, appliances, and components...	335	23.3	11.4	7.0	(D)	(D)	(D)
Motor vehicles, trailers, and parts...............	3361-3363	75.4	74.4	78.4	(D)	(D)	(D)
Aerospace products and parts..............	3364	40.2	22.1	25.8	(D)	325.9	(D)
Transportation and warehousing services.........	48, 49	1.5	1.3	0.4	(D)	(D)	(D)
Software publishing......................	5112	79.7	82.2	81.0	148.3	145.8	153.6
Architectural, engineering, and related services.....	5413	33.0	28.9	28.0	95.9	107.3	143.8
Computer systems design and related services.....	5415	41.6	54.6	76.8	116.2	153.2	125.5
Scientific R&D services....................	5417	52.4	58.4	55.0	230.3	223.1	245.1
Management of companies and enterprises........	55	0.4	0.9	1.5	124.4	386.1	157.9

D Withheld to avoid disclosure.   X Not applicable.   [1] North American Industry Classification System 1997 (NAICS); see text, Section 15.   [2] The mean number of full-time equivalent R&D scientists and engineers employed in January of the year shown and the following January.   [3] Based on gross domestic product implicit price deflator.   [4] Represents the arithmetic mean of the numbers of R&D scientists and engineers reported in each industry for January in 2 consecutive years divided into total R&D expenditures in each industry.   [5] Includes other industries not shown separately.

Source: U.S. National Science Foundation, *Research and Development in Industry*, annual.

Table 789. Space Vehicle Systems—Net Sales and Backlog Orders: 1970 to 2003

[In millions of dollars (1,956 represents $1,956,000,000). Backlog orders as of Dec. 31. Based on data from major companies engaged in manufacture of aerospace products. Includes parts but excludes engines and propulsion units, except where noted]

Year	Net sales Total	Military	Non-military	Backlog orders Total	Military	Non-mili-tary	Year	Net sales Total	Military	Non-military	Backlog orders Total	Military	Non-mili-tary
1970...	1,956	1,025	931	1,184	786	398	1998...	9,490	4,227	5,264	20,371	7,970	12,402
1975...	2,119	1,096	1,023	1,304	1,019	285	1999...	9,022	5,107	3,915	22,356	10,666	11,690
1980...	3,483	1,461	2,022	1,814	951	863	2000...	8,164	3,723	4,441	21,395	8,942	12,453
1985...	6,300	4,241	2,059	6,707	4,941	1,766	2001...	5,112	3,605	1,507	18,893	8,039	10,854
1990...	9,691	6,556	3,135	12,462	8,130	4,332	2002 [1]..	7,946	(D)	(D)	21,968	(D)	(D)
1995...	11,314	4,782	6,532	15,650	5,872	9,778	2003 [1]..	7,392	(D)	(D)	14,365	(D)	(D)

D Withheld to avoid disclosing data for individual companies.   [1] Includes engines and/or propulsion units for space vehicles, including parts.

Source: U.S. Census Bureau, *Current Industrial Reports*, M336G, *Civil Aircraft and Aircraft Engines*, annual. See also <http://www.census.gov/industry/1/m336g0313.pdf>.

Table 790. Federal Outlays for General Science, Space, and Other Technology, 1970 to 2004, and Projections, 2005 and 2006

[In billions of dollars (4.5 represents $4,500,000,000). For fiscal years ending in year shown; see text, Section 8]

Year	Current dollars			Constant (2000) dollars		
	Total	General science/ basic research	Space and other technologies	Total	General science/ basic research	Space and other technologies
1970	4.5	0.9	3.6	19.3	4.0	15.2
1980	5.8	1.4	4.5	12.0	2.8	9.1
1985	8.6	2.0	6.6	13.7	3.2	10.5
1990	14.4	2.8	11.6	20.0	3.9	16.1
1995	16.7	4.1	12.6	18.7	4.6	14.1
2000	18.6	6.2	12.4	18.6	6.2	12.4
2001	19.7	6.5	13.2	19.3	6.4	12.9
2002	20.7	7.2	13.5	19.7	6.9	12.8
2003	20.8	7.9	12.9	19.3	7.4	12.0
2004	23.0	8.3	14.6	20.9	7.6	13.3
2005, proj...	23.9	9.0	14.8	21.2	8.0	13.2
2006, proj...	23.8	8.9	14.9	20.8	7.8	13.0

Source: U.S. Office of Management and Budget, *Budget of the United States, Historical Tables, Fiscal Year 2006*, annual. See also <http://www.gpoaccess.gov/usbudget/fy06/hist.html>.

Table 791. U.S. and Worldwide Commercial Space Industry Revenue by Type: 2000 to 2003

[In billions of dollars (35.4 represents $35,400,000,000). For calendar years]

Industry	U.S.				World			
	2000	2001	2002	2003	2000	2001	2002	2003
Revenue, total	35.4	20.8	22.7	24.9	73.7	78.6	86.1	91.0
Satellite manufacturing [1]	6.0	3.8	4.4	4.6	11.5	9.5	12.1	9.8
Launch industry [2]	2.7	1.1	1.0	2.1	5.3	3.0	3.7	3.2
Satellite services [2]	11.8	15.9	16.6	18.2	39.2	46.5	49.1	55.9
Ground equipment manufacturing [3]	10.7	(NA)	(NA)	(NA)	17.7	19.6	21.2	22.1

NA Not available. [1] Includes revenues from the construction and sale of satellites to both commercial and government. [2] Includes revenues derived from transponder leasing and subscription/retail services such as direct-to-home television and satellite mobile and data communications. [3] Includes revenues from the manufacture of gateways and satellite control stations, satellite news-gathering trucks, very small aperture terminals, direct-to-home television equipment and mobile satellite phones.

Source: Satellite Industry Association/Futron Corporation, Bethesda, MD, *2002-2003 Satellite Industry Indicators Survey* (copyright). See also <http://www.sia.org/>.

Table 792. World-Wide Successful Space Launches: 1957 to 2004

[Criterion of success is attainment of Earth orbit or Earth escape]

Country	Total, 1957-04	1957-64	1965-69	1970-74	1975-79	1980-84	1985-89	1990-94	1995-2002	2003	2004
Total	4,358	289	586	555	607	605	550	466	586	61	53
Soviet Union/Russia [1] ...	2,723	82	302	405	461	483	447	283	217	21	22
United States	1,293	207	279	139	126	93	61	122	227	23	16
Japan	60	-	-	5	10	12	11	9	11	2	-
ESA [2]	155	-	-	-	1	8	21	33	85	4	3
China	83	-	-	2	6	6	9	15	31	6	8
France	10	-	4	3	3	-	-	-	-	-	-
India	15	-	-	-	-	3	-	3	6	2	1
Israel	4	-	-	-	-	-	1	1	2	-	-
Ukraine [1]	13	-	-	-	-	-	-	-	7	3	3
Australia	1	-	1	-	-	-	-	-	-	-	-
United Kingdom	1	-	-	1	-	-	-	-	-	-	-

- Represents zero. [1] Launches conducted by the former Soviet Union are listed separately as Russia or Ukraine. [2] European Space Agency. Includes launches by Arianespace.

Source: Library of Congress, Congressional Research Service, Science Policy Research Division, *Space Activities of the United States, CIS, and Other Launching Countries/Organizations 1957-1999;* thereafter, Resources, Science, and Industry Division, 2004.

Table 793. **National Aeronautics and Space Administration—Budget Appropriations, 2005 and Projections, 2006 to 2010**

[In millions of dollars (16,070.4 represents $16,070,400,000). Figures may not add due to rounding]

Item	2005	2006	2007	2008	2009	2010
Appropriation, total.	16,070.4	16,456.3	16,962.0	17,305.9	17,611.9	18,027.1
Science, exploration, & aeronautics	9,334.7	9,661.0	10,549.8	11,214.6	12,209.6	12,796.1
Science	5,527.2	5,476.3	5,960.3	6,503.4	6,853.0	6,797.6
Solar system exploration.	1,858.1	1,900.5	2,347.7	2,831.8	2,998.9	3,066.1
The universe	1,513.2	1,512.2	1,531.5	1,539.4	1,495.0	1,406.7
Earth-sun system	2,155.8	2,063.6	2,081.2	2,132.2	2,359.0	2,324.8
Exploration systems	2,684.5	3,165.4	3,707.0	3,825.9	4,473.7	5,125.5
Constellation systems	526.0	1,120.1	1,579.5	1,523.7	1,990.9	2,452.2
Exploration systems research & technology	722.8	919.2	907.3	989.2	1,050.3	1,078.5
Prometheus nuclear systems & technology	431.7	319.6	423.5	500.6	614.0	779.0
Human systems research & technology	1,003.9	806.5	796.7	812.4	818.5	815.8
Aeronautics research & technology	906.2	852.3	727.6	730.7	727.5	717.6
Education programs	216.7	166.9	154.9	154.7	155.4	155.4
Exploration capabilities	6,704.4	6,763.0	6,378.6	6,056.7	5,367.1	5,193.8
Space operations	6,704.4	6,763.0	6,378.6	6,056.7	5,367.1	5,193.8
International space station	1,676.3	1,856.7	1,835.3	1,790.9	2,152.3	2,375.5
Space shuttle	4,543.0	4,530.6	4,172.4	3,865.7	2,815.1	2,419.2
Space & flight support	485.1	375.6	370.9	400.0	399.7	399.1
Inspector General	31.1	32.4	33.5	34.6	35.2	37.3

Source: U.S. National Aeronautics and Space Administration, *Fiscal Year 2006 Budget* <http://www.nasa.gov/pdf/107486mainFY06high.pdf> (accessed June 2005).

Table 794. **Nobel Prize Laureates in Selected Sciences: 1901 to 2003**

[Presented by location of award-winning research and by date of award]

Country	Total	Physics	Chemistry	Physiology/Medicine	1901–1930	1931–1945	1946–1960	1961–1975	1976–1990	1991–2002	2003
Total	494	171	143	180	93	49	74	92	98	82	7
United States	219	74	51	90	6	14	38	41	63	54	5
United Kingdom	76	21	27	28	15	11	14	20	9	5	1
Germany [1]	63	19	29	15	27	11	4	8	7	4	-
France	25	11	7	7	13	2	-	5	2	3	-
Soviet Union	12	9	1	2	2	-	4	3	1	1	1
Japan	8	4	4	-	-	-	1	2	1	4	-
Other countries	91	30	22	39	30	11	13	13	15	4	-

- Represents zero. [1] Between 1946 and 1991, data are for the former West Germany only.

Source: U.S. National Science Foundation, unpublished data.

No. 147.—ESTIMATED. ANNUAL PRODUCT, ACREAGE, and VALUE of the POTATO CROP of the UNITED STATES, from 1868 to 1877, inclusive.

[From the Annual Reports of the Department of Agriculture.]

YEAR.	Bushels.	Acres.	Value.	Value per bushel.	Yield per acre.	Value per acre.
			Dollars.	Cents.	Bushels.	Dollars.
1868....................	106,090,000	1,131,552	84,150,040	79.3	93.7	74 36
1869....................	133,886,000	1,222,250	71,651,730	53.5	109.5	58 62
1870....................	114,775,000	1,325,119	82,668,590	72.0	86.6	62 38
1871....................	120,461,700	1,220,912	71,836,671	59.6	98.6	58 83
1872....................	113,516,000	1,331,331	68,081,120	59.9	85.2	51 14
1873....................	106,089,000	1,295,139	74,774,890	70.5	81.9	57 73
1874....................	105,981,000	1,310,041	71,823,330	67.7	80.9	54 82
1875....................	106,877,000	1,510,041	65,019,420	38.9	110.5	43 05
1876....................	124,827,000	1,741,983	83,861,390	65.5	71.6	48 14
1877....................	170,092,000	1,792,287	76,249,500	44.8	94.9	42 54
Total	1,262,594,700	13,880,655	750,116,681	....	....	....
Average..........	126,259,470	1,388,065	75,011,668	59.4	90.9	54 04

No. 148.—ESTIMATED ANNUAL PRODUCT, ACREAGE, and VALUE of the HAY CROP of the UNITED STATES, from 1868 to 1877, inclusive.

[From the Annual Reports of the Department of Agriculture.]

YEAR.	Tons.	Acres.	Value.	Value per ton.	Yield per acre.	Value per acre.
			Dollars.	Dollars.	Tons.	Dollars.
1868....................	26,141,900	21,541,573	351,941,930	16 33	1.21	16 33
1869....................	26,420,000	18,591,281	337,662,600	12 78	1.42	18 16
1870....................	24,525,000	19,861,805	338,969,680	13 82	1.23	17 06
1871....................	22,239,400	19,009,052	351,717,035	15 81	1.17	18 50
1872....................	23,812,800	20,318,936	345,969,079	14 52	1.17	17 02
1873....................	25,085,100	21,894,084	339,895,486	13 55	1.14	15 52
1874....................	24,133,900	21,769,772	331,420,738	13 73	1.11	15 22
1875....................	27,873,600	23,507,964	342,203,445	12 27	1.18	14 55
1876....................	30,867,100	25,282,797	300,901,252	9 74	1.22	11 90
1877....................	31,629,300	25,367,708	271,934,950	8 59	1.24	10 72
Total	262,728,100	217,144,972	3,312,616,595	....	....	....
Average..........	26,272,810	21,714,497	331,261,659	12 60	1.21	15 25

Source: Statistical Abstract of the United States: 1878 Edition.

Section 17

Agriculture

This section presents statistics on farms and farm operators; land use; farm income, expenditures, and debt; farm output, productivity, and marketings; foreign trade in agricultural products; specific crops; and livestock, poultry, and their products.

The principal sources are the reports issued by the National Agricultural Statistics Service (NASS) and the Economic Research Service (ERS) of the U.S. Department of Agriculture. The information from the 2002 Census of Agriculture is available in printed form in the Volume 1, Geographic Area Series; in electronic format on CD-ROM; and on the Internet site <http://www.nass.usda.gov/census/>. The Department of Agriculture publishes annually *Agricultural Statistics*, a general reference book on agricultural production, supplies, consumption, facilities, costs, and returns. The ERS publishes data on farm assets, debt, and income on the Internet site <http://www.ers.usda .gov/briefing/farmincome/>. Sources of current data on agricultural exports and imports include *Outlook for U.S. Agricultural Trade*, published by the ERS; the ERS Internet site <http://www.ers.usda.gov /briefing/AgTrade>; and the reports of the U.S. Census Bureau, particularly *U.S. Imports of Merchandise on CD-ROM*, and *U.S. Exports of Merchandise on CD-ROM*.

The 45 field offices of the NASS collect data on crops, livestock and products, agricultural prices, farm employment, and other related subjects mainly through sample surveys. Information is obtained on some 75 crops and 50 livestock items as well as scores of items pertaining to agricultural production and marketing. State estimates and supporting information are sent to the Agricultural Statistics Board of NASS, which reviews the estimates and issues reports containing state and national data. Among these reports are annual summaries such as *Crop Production, Crop Values, Agricultural Prices*, and *Livestock Production, Disposition and*

Income. For more information about concepts and methods underlying USDA's statistical series, see *Major Statistical Series of the U.S. Department of Agriculture* (Agricultural Handbook No. 671), a 12-volume set of publications.

Farms and farmland—The definitions of a farm have varied through time. Since 1850, when minimum criteria defining a farm for census purposes first were established, the farm definition has changed nine times. The current definition, first used for the 1974 census, is any place from which $1,000 or more of agricultural products were produced and sold, or normally would have been sold, during the census year.

Acreage designated as "land in farms" consists primarily of agricultural land used for crops, pasture, or grazing. It also includes woodland and wasteland not actually under cultivation or used for pasture or grazing, provided it was part of the farm operator's total operation. Land in farms includes acres set aside under annual commodity acreage programs as well as acres in the Conservation Reserve and Wetlands Reserve Programs for places meeting the farm definition. Land in farms is an operating unit concept and includes land owned and operated as well as land rented from others. All grazing land, except land used under government permits on a per-head basis, was included as "land in farms" provided it was part of a farm or ranch.

An evaluation of coverage has been conducted for each census of agriculture since 1945 to provide estimates of the completeness of census farm counts. The 2002 coverage evaluation shows the census covered 96 percent of the farms with $50,000 or more in sales, but only 78 percent of farms with less than $50,000 in sales. The overall coverage of all farms was 82 percent. The census covered nearly 98 percent of all land in farms and

97 percent of the market value of agricultural products sold. In 2002, census farm counts and totals were statistically adjusted for coverage and reported at the county level. The size of the adjustments varies considerably by state. In general, farms not on the census mail list tended to be small in acreage, production, and sales of farm products. For more explanation about census mail list compilation, collection methods, coverage measurement, and adjustments, see Appendixes A and C, 2002 Census of Agriculture, Volume 1 reports.

Farm income—The final agricultural sector output comprises cash receipts from farm marketings of crops and livestock, federal government payments made directly to farmers for farm-related activities, rental value of farm homes, value of farm products consumed in farm homes, and other farm-related income such as machine hire and custom work. Farm marketings represent quantities of agricultural products sold by farmers multiplied by prices received per unit of production at the local market. Information on prices received for farm products is generally obtained by the NASS Agricultural Statistics Board from surveys of firms (such as grain elevators, packers, and processors) purchasing agricultural commodities directly from producers. In some cases, the price information is obtained directly from the producers.

Crops—Estimates of crop acreage and production by the NASS are based on current sample survey data obtained from individual producers and objective yield counts, reports of carlot shipments, market records, personal field observations by field statisticians, and reports from other sources. Prices received by farmers are marketing year averages. These averages are based on U.S. monthly prices weighted by monthly marketings during specific periods. U.S. monthly prices are state average prices weighted by marketings during the month. Marketing year average prices do not include allowances for outstanding loans, government purchases, deficiency payments or disaster payments.

All state prices are based on individual state marketing years, while U.S. marketing year averages are based on standard marketing years for each crop. For a listing of the crop marketing years and the participating states in the monthly program, see *Crop Values*. Value of production is computed by multiplying state prices by each state's production. The U.S. value of production is the sum of state values for all states. Value of production figures shown in Tables 825–828, 832, and 833 should not be confused with cash receipts from farm marketings which relate to sales during a calendar year, irrespective of the year of production.

Livestock—Annual inventory numbers of livestock and estimates of livestock, dairy, and poultry production prepared by the Department of Agriculture are based on information from farmers and ranchers obtained by probability survey sampling methods.

Statistical reliability—For a discussion of statistical collection and estimation, sampling procedures, and measures of statistical reliability pertaining to Department of Agriculture data, see Appendix III.

Table 795. Farms by Size and Type of Organization: 1974 to 2002

[2,314 represents 2,314,000. For comments on adjustment, see text, this section. See also Appendix III]

Size and type of organization	Unit	Not adjusted for coverage						1997 [1]	2002 [1]
		1974	1978	1982	1987	1992	1997		
Farms.	1,000	2,314	2,258	2,241	2,088	1,925	1,912	2,216	2,129
Land in farms.	Mil. acres. . .	1,017	1,015	987	964	946	932	955	938
Average size of farm	Acres	440	449	440	462	491	487	431	441
Farms by size:									
Under 10 acres.	1,000	128	151	188	183	166	154	205	179
10 to 49 acres	1,000	380	392	449	412	388	411	531	564
50 to 179 acres.	1,000	828	759	712	645	584	593	694	659
180 to 499 acres.	1,000	616	582	527	478	428	403	428	389
500 to 999 acres.	1,000	207	213	204	200	186	176	179	162
1,000 to 1,999 acres	1,000	93	98	97	102	102	101	103	99
2,000 acres or more	1,000	62	63	65	67	71	75	74	78
Farms by type of organization:									
Family or individual	1,000	(NA)	1,966	1,946	1,809	1,653	1,643	1,923	1,910
Partnership	1,000	(NA)	233	223	200	187	169	186	130
Corporation	1,000	(NA)	50	60	67	73	84	90	74
Other [2]	1,000	(NA)	9	12	12	12	15	17	16

NA Not available. [1] Data have been adjusted for coverage; see text, this section. [2] Cooperative, estate or trust, institutional, etc.

Source: U.S. Dept. of Agriculture, National Agricultural Statistics Service, *2002 Census of Agriculture*, Vol. 1.

Table 796. Farm Operators—Tenure and Characteristics: 1997 and 2002

[In thousands, except as indicated (2,216 represents 2,216,000). An "operator" is a person who operates a farm, either doing the work or making day-to-day decisions. A family operation may have more than one operator. A principal operator is the person primarily responsible for the on-site, day-to-day operation of the farm or ranch business. Data on operator characteristics were collected up to a maximum of three operators per farm, though operations were asked to report the total number of operators. Data have been adjusted for coverage; see text, this section and Appendix III]

Characteristic	Principal operators, 1997	2002			Characteristic	Principal operators, 1997	2002		
		Total operators	Principal operators	Other operators			Total operators	Principal operators	Other operators
Total	**2,216**	**3,054**	**2,129**	**925**					
					Average age (years)	54.0	53.2	55.3	(NA)
White	2,154	2,966	2,067	899	Full owner	1,385	(NA)	1,428	(NA)
Black or					Part owner	616	(NA)	551	(NA)
African American	27	36	29	7	Tenant.	215	(NA)	150	(NA)
American Indian or					**Principal occupation:**				
Alaska Native	13	24	15	9	Farming	1,044	1,658	1,224	434
Native Hawaiian or					Other.	1,171	1,396	905	491
Other Pacific Islander [1]	(NA)	2	1	1	**Place of residence:** [3]				
Asian [1]	10	13	8	5	On farm operated.	1,577	2,391	1,680	711
More than one race					Not on farm operated . . .	475	662	449	214
reported	(NA)	12	8	4	**Years on present farm:** [3]				
Other	12	(NA)	(NA)	(NA)	2 years or less.	115	143	75	68
					3 to 4 years	157	251	144	108
Operators of Hispanic [2]					5 to 9 years	318	587	375	212
origin.	33	72	51	22	10 years or more	1,253	2,073	1,536	537
					Average years on				
Female	210	822	238	585	present farm	19.4	(NA)	20.7	(NA)
					Days worked off farm: [3]				
Under 25 years old	24	60	17	43	None	833	1,354	962	392
25 to 34 years old	155	201	106	95	1 to 49 days	121	183	122	61
35 to 44 years old	444	590	366	224	50 to 99 days	65	102	66	36
45 to 54 years old	552	838	573	265	100 to 199 days.	(NA)	224	146	78
55 to 64 years old	481	690	509	181	200 days or more.	871	1,190	832	358
65 to 74 years old	(NA)	439	354	85					
75 years old and over	(NA)	236	203	32					

NA Not available. [1] In 1997, Asians and Native Hawaiians or Other Pacific Islanders were tabulated in one group. [2] Operators of Hispanic origin may be of any race. [3] Data for 1997 exclude "not reported."

Source: U.S. Dept. of Agriculture, National Agricultural Statistics Service, *2002 Census of Agriculture*, Vol. 1.

Agriculture 545

Table 797. Farms—Number and Acreage by Size of Farm: 1997 and 2002

[2,216 represents 2,216,000. Data have been adjusted for coverage; see text, this section and Appendix III]

Size of farm	Number of farms (1,000) 1997	2002	Land in farms (mil. acres) 1997	2002	Cropland harvested (mil. acres) 1997	2002	Percent distribution, 2002 Number of farms	All land in farms	Cropland harvested
Total	2,216	2,129	954.8	938.3	318.9	302.7	100.0	100.0	100.0
Under 10 acres	205	179	0.9	0.8	0.3	0.2	8.4	0.1	0.1
10 to 49 acres.......	531	564	14.0	14.7	4.3	4.1	26.5	1.6	1.4
50 to 69 acres	154	152	9.0	8.8	2.7	2.5	7.1	0.9	0.8
70 to 99 acres......	200	191	16.5	15.7	5.2	4.7	9.0	1.7	1.5
100 to 139 acres	187	175	21.7	20.2	7.0	6.1	8.2	2.2	2.0
140 to 179 acres	153	142	24.1	22.3	8.4	7.3	6.7	2.4	2.4
180 to 219 acres	100	91	19.8	18.0	7.2	6.2	4.3	1.9	2.1
220 to 259 acres	79	72	18.8	17.1	7.5	6.5	3.4	1.8	2.1
260 to 499 acres	249	226	89.2	80.6	40.1	34.1	10.6	8.6	11.3
500 to 999 acres	179	162	124.6	112.4	66.5	56.7	7.6	12.0	18.7
1,000 to 1,999 acres...	103	99	140.7	135.7	75.9	72.8	4.7	14.5	24.0
2,000 acres or more ...	74	78	475.6	491.9	94.1	101.6	3.7	52.4	33.6

Source: U.S. Dept. of Agriculture, National Agricultural Statistics Service, *2002 Census of Agriculture*, Vol. 1.

Table 798. Farms—Number, Acreage, and Value by Tenure of Principal Operator and Type of Organization: 1997 and 2002

[2,216 represents 2,216,000. Full owners own all the land they operate. Part owners own a part and rent from others the rest of the land they operate. A principal operator is the person primarily responsible for the on-site, day-to-day operation of the farm or ranch business. Data have been adjusted for coverage; see text, this section and Appendix III]

Item and year	Unit	Total [1]	Tenure of operator Full owner	Part owner	Tenant	Type of organization Family or indi-vidual	Partner-ship	Corpora-tion
NUMBER OF FARMS								
1997.......................	1,000	2,216	1,385	616	215	1,923	186	90
2002, total	1,000	2,129	1,428	551	150	1,910	130	74
Under 50 acres...............	1,000	743	639	64	41	697	24	18
50 to 179 acres..............	1,000	659	487	131	41	611	31	12
180 to 499 acres.............	1,000	389	203	153	33	344	29	12
500 to 999 acres	1,000	162	54	91	17	133	17	10
1,000 acres or more...........	1,000	177	46	112	18	125	29	21
LAND IN FARMS								
1997.......................	Mil. acres...	955	332	512	111	605	151	133
2002.......................	Mil. acres...	938	357	495	87	622	146	108
Value of land and buildings, 2002 [2] ...	Bil. dol.	1,145	495	551	99	836	158	129
Value of farm products sold, 2002	Bil. dol.	201	88	91	22	104	37	57

[1] Includes other types, not shown separately.   [2] Based on a sample of farms.

Source: U.S. Dept. of Agriculture, National Agricultural Statistics Service, *2002 Census of Agriculture*, Vol. 1.

Table 799. Farms—Number, Acreage, and Value of Sales by Size of Sales: 2002

[2,129 represents 2,129,000. Data have been adjusted for coverage; see text, this section and Appendix III]

Market value of agricultural products sold	Farms (1,000)	Acreage Total (mil.)	Average per farm	Value of sales Total (mil. dol.)	Average per farm (dol.)	Percent distribution Farms	Acreage	Value of sales
Total	2,129	938.3	441	200,646	94,244	100.0	100.0	100.0
Less than $2,500	827	107.0	129	485	586	38.8	11.4	0.2
$2,500 to $4,999	213	23.1	108	763	3,582	10.0	2.5	0.4
$5,000 to $9,999	223	34.8	156	1,577	7,072	10.5	3.7	0.8
$10,000 to $24,999	256	69.5	271	4,068	15,891	12.0	7.4	2.0
$25,000 to $49,999	158	77.9	494	5,594	35,405	7.4	8.3	2.8
$50,000 to $99,999	140	110.1	784	10,024	71,600	6.6	11.7	5.0
$100,000 to $249,999	159	189.4	1,191	25,401	159,755	7.5	20.2	12.7
$250,000 to $499,999	82	140.8	1,723	28,530	347,927	3.9	15.0	14.2
$500,000 to $999,999	42	94.0	2,241	28,944	689,143	2.0	10.0	14.4
$1,000,000 or more	29	91.7	3,198	95,259	3,284,793	1.4	9.8	47.5

Source: U.S. Dept. of Agriculture, National Agricultural Statistics Service, *2002 Census of Agriculture*, Vol. 1.

Table 800. Farms—Number, Acreage, and Value by State: 1997 and 2002

[2,216 represents 2,216,000. Data have been adjusted for coverage; see text, this section and Appendix III]

State	Number of farms (1,000)		Land in farms (mil. acres)		Average size of farm (acres)		Total value of land and buildings [1] (bil. dol.)		Market value of agricultural products sold and government payments, 2002 (mil. dol.)	Total number of operators, 2002 (1,000)
	1997	2002	1997	2002	1997	2002	1997	2002		
U.S....	2,216	2,129	954.8	938.3	431	441	921.6	1,144.9	207,192	3,115
AL.......	50	45	9.5	8.9	191	197	14.1	15.1	3,343	63
AK.......	1	1	0.9	0.9	1,608	1,479	0.3	0.3	48	1
AZ.......	9	7	27.2	26.6	3,194	3,645	11.0	10.6	2,427	12
AR.......	49	47	14.8	14.5	300	305	17.5	21.2	5,189	70
CA.......	88	80	28.8	27.6	327	346	73.8	96.1	25,906	125
CO.......	30	31	32.4	31.1	1,071	991	20.3	23.8	4,651	50
CT.......	5	4	0.4	0.4	83	85	2.5	3.5	474	7
DE.......	3	2	0.6	0.5	221	226	1.5	2.3	627	4
FL.......	46	44	10.7	10.4	233	236	24.8	29.3	6,264	64
GA.......	49	49	11.3	10.7	228	218	17.9	22.6	5,030	67
HI.......	5	5	1.4	1.3	263	241	3.5	4.6	534	8
ID.......	26	25	12.1	11.8	470	470	12.5	15.3	4,002	39
IL.......	79	73	27.7	27.3	350	374	58.2	66.7	8,089	102
IN.......	67	60	15.5	15.1	233	250	32.4	38.4	5,008	86
IA.......	97	91	32.3	31.7	334	350	54.1	64.2	12,813	127
KS.......	65	64	46.7	47.2	712	733	27.3	32.6	9,074	90
KY.......	91	87	13.9	13.8	153	160	20.3	25.5	3,174	123
LA.......	30	27	8.4	7.8	275	286	10.3	12.2	1,939	39
ME.......	7	7	1.3	1.4	177	190	1.7	2.3	472	11
MD.......	13	12	2.2	2.1	165	170	7.1	8.5	1,326	19
MA.......	7	6	0.6	0.5	79	85	3.1	4.6	389	10
MI.......	54	53	10.4	10.1	195	190	18.0	27.1	3,917	80
MN.......	79	81	27.6	27.5	350	340	31.4	41.8	8,926	114
MS.......	42	42	11.4	11.1	271	263	12.6	15.6	3,262	58
MO.......	111	107	30.2	29.9	272	280	32.7	45.3	5,248	158
MT.......	28	28	58.4	59.6	2,115	2,139	18.0	23.3	2,093	43
NE.......	55	49	45.9	45.9	841	930	30.0	35.7	10,051	71
NV.......	3	3	6.4	6.3	2,000	2,118	2.5	2.8	451	5
NH.......	4	3	0.5	0.4	118	132	1.2	1.4	149	6
NJ.......	10	10	0.9	0.8	85	81	5.7	7.4	754	15
NM.......	18	15	46.2	44.8	2,583	2,954	9.7	10.6	1,750	23
NY.......	38	37	7.8	7.7	204	206	10.4	12.9	3,228	58
NC.......	59	54	9.4	9.1	160	168	20.7	28.0	7,059	76
ND.......	32	31	39.7	39.3	1,227	1,283	16.0	15.8	3,526	42
OH.......	79	78	14.7	14.6	187	187	30.3	39.6	4,461	114
OK.......	84	83	34.1	33.7	405	404	21.6	23.8	4,606	121
OR.......	40	40	17.7	17.1	442	427	17.7	20.4	3,248	66
PA.......	60	58	7.8	7.7	130	133	19.9	26.3	4,343	87
RI.......	1	1	0.1	0.1	65	71	0.4	0.6	56	1
SC.......	26	25	5.0	4.8	193	197	7.6	10.1	1,528	34
SD.......	33	32	44.1	43.8	1,330	1,380	15.7	19.6	4,050	46
TN.......	92	88	12.0	11.7	131	133	22.4	28.5	2,259	123
TX.......	228	229	134.0	129.9	587	567	82.5	100.5	14,664	335
UT.......	16	15	12.0	11.7	760	768	7.2	9.0	1,143	24
VT.......	7	7	1.3	1.2	186	189	2.1	2.5	497	11
VA.......	49	48	8.8	8.6	177	181	17.6	23.3	2,416	70
WA.......	40	36	15.8	15.3	393	426	20.9	22.4	5,465	56
WV.......	22	21	3.7	3.6	172	172	4.2	4.8	488	30
WI.......	80	77	16.2	15.7	204	204	20.6	35.8	5,871	118
WY.......	9	9	34.3	34.4	3,633	3,651	7.6	10.2	902	16

[1] Based on reports for a sample of farms.

Source: U.S. Dept. of Agriculture, National Agricultural Statistics Service, 2002 Census of Agriculture, Vol. 1.

Table 801. Farms—Number and Acreage: 1980 to 2004

[As of June 1 (2,440 represents 2,440,000). Based on 1974 census definition; for definition of farms and farmland, see text of this section. Activities included as agriculture have undergone changes in recent years. Data for period 1995 to 2004 are not directly comparable with data for 1980 to 1990. Data for 2002 have been adjusted for underenumeration. Minus sign (-) indicates decrease]

Year	Unit	1980	1985	1990	1995	2000	2001	2002	2003	2004
Number of farms	1,000	2,440	2,293	2,146	2,196	2,167	2,149	2,135	2,127	2,113
Annual change [1]	1,000	3	-41	-29	-1	-21	-18	-13	-9	-13
Land in farms	Mil. acres	1,039	1,012	987	963	945	942	940	939	937
Average per farm	Acres	426	441	460	438	436	438	440	441	443

[1] Annual change from immediate preceding year.

Source: U.S. Dept. of Agriculture, National Agricultural Statistics Service, *Farms and Land in Farms, Final Estimates by States, 1979–1987; Farms and Land in Farms, Final Estimates, 1988–1992; Farms and Land in Farms, Final Estimates, 1993–1997; Farm Numbers and Land in Farms, Final Estimates, 1998–2002;* and *Farms, Land In Farms, and Livestock Operations,* annual.

Table 802. Farms—Number and Acreage by State: 2000 and 2004

[2,167 represents 2,167,000. See headnote, Table 801]

State	Farms (1,000) 2000	Farms (1,000) 2004	Acreage (mil.) 2000	Acreage (mil.) 2004	Acreage per farm 2000	Acreage per farm 2004	State	Farms (1,000) 2000	Farms (1,000) 2004	Acreage (mil.) 2000	Acreage (mil.) 2004	Acreage per farm 2000	Acreage per farm 2004
U.S	2,167	2,113	945	937	436	443	Montana	28	28	59	60	2,133	2,146
Alabama	47	44	9	9	191	198	Nebraska	52	48	46	46	887	950
Alaska	1	1	1	1	1,569	1,452	Nevada	3	3	6	6	2,065	2,100
Arizona	11	10	27	26	2,514	2,588	New						
Arkansas	48	48	15	14	304	303	Hampshire	3	3	(Z)	(Z)	133	132
California	83	77	28	27	337	347	New Jersey	10	10	1	1	86	83
Colorado	30	31	32	31	1,053	1,000	New Mexico	18	18	45	45	2,494	2,554
Connecticut	4	4	(Z)	(Z)	86	86	New York	38	36	8	8	205	211
Delaware	3	2	1	1	215	230	North Carolina	56	52	9	9	166	173
Florida	44	43	10	10	236	235	North Dakota	31	30	39	39	1,279	1,300
Georgia	49	49	11	11	222	218	Ohio	79	77	15	15	187	189
Hawaii	6	6	1	1	251	236	Oklahoma	85	84	34	34	400	404
Idaho	25	25	12	12	486	472	Oregon	40	40	17	17	433	430
Illinois	77	73	28	28	357	377	Pennsylvania	59	58	8	8	130	132
Indiana	63	59	15	15	240	253	Rhode Island	1	1	(Z)	(Z)	75	71
Iowa	94	90	33	32	346	353	South Carolina	24	24	5	5	203	199
Kansas	65	65	48	47	736	732	South Dakota	32	32	44	44	1,358	1,386
Kentucky	90	85	14	14	152	162	Tennessee	88	85	12	12	134	136
Louisiana	29	27	8	8	277	289	Texas	228	229	131	130	573	568
Maine	7	7	1	1	190	190	Utah	16	15	12	12	748	758
Maryland	12	12	2	2	172	169	Vermont	7	6	1	1	192	195
Massachusetts	6	6	1	1	89	85	Virginia	49	48	9	9	180	181
Michigan	53	53	10	10	192	190	Washington	37	35	16	15	420	434
Minnesota	81	80	28	28	344	346	West Virginia	21	21	4	4	173	173
Mississippi	42	42	11	11	266	262	Wisconsin	78	77	16	16	206	203
Missouri	109	106	30	30	277	284	Wyoming	9	9	35	34	3,750	3,743

Z Less than 500,000 acres.

Source: U.S. Department of Agriculture, National Agricultural Statistics Service, *Farm Numbers* and *Land in Farms, Final Estimates, 1998–2002* and *Farms, Land In Farms, and Livestock Operations,* annual.

Table 803. Certified Organic Farmland Acreage and Livestock: 1997 to 2001

Item	Unit	1997	2000	2001	Crop	Certified organic acreage (1,000) 1997	Certified organic acreage (1,000) 2001
Certified growers	Number	5,021	6,592	6,949	Corn	43	94
					Wheat	126	195
Certified organic acreage,					Oats	30	33
total	1,000	1,347	2,029	2,344	Barley	30	31
Pastureland and							
rangeland	1,000	496	810	1,040	Rice	11	32
Cropland	1,000	850	1,219	1,305	Millet	12	23
					Buckwheat	8	14
Certified animals:					Soybeans	82	174
Beef cows	Number	4,429	13,829	15,197	Dry beans	5	15
Milk cows	Number	12,897	38,196	48,677	Hay and silage	127	254
Hogs and pigs	Number	482	1,724	3,135	Sunflowers	11	15
Sheep and lambs	Number	705	2,279	4,207	Lettuce	6	16
Layer hens	1,000	538	1,114	1,612	Apples	9	12
Broilers	1,000	38	1,925	3,286	Grapes	19	15
Turkeys	Number	(NA)	9,138	98,653	Cotton	10	11
Unclassified/other	Number	226,105	111,359	17,244	Trees for maple syrup	14	12

NA Not available.

Source: U.S. Dept. of Agriculture, Economic Research Service, *U.S. Organic Farming Emerges in the 1990s: Adoption of Certified Systems,* AIB No. 770, June 2001; *U.S. Organic Farming in 2000–2001: Adoption of Certified Systems,* AIB No. 780, February 2003; and "U.S. Organic Agriculture Data Tables"; <http://www.ers.usda.gov/data/organic/>.

Table 804. Farm Sector Output and Value Added: 1990 to 2003

[In billions of dollars (180.1 represents $180,100,000,000). For definition of value added, see text, Section 13. Minus sign (-) indicates decrease]

Item	1990	1994	1995	1996	1997	1998	1999	2000	2001	2002	2003
CURRENT DOLLARS											
Farm output, total.	180.1	197.6	192.0	215.9	222.0	208.9	198.5	203.6	210.8	201.9	223.8
Cash receipts from farm marketings	172.1	181.1	194.3	201.6	211.2	199.0	190.2	196.6	200.1	194.9	211.4
Farm products consumed on farms	0.7	0.6	0.5	0.5	0.5	0.5	0.5	0.6	0.5	0.5	0.5
Other farm income	4.9	5.1	6.3	6.1	7.4	8.5	9.4	8.4	9.5	9.3	11.3
Change in farm finished goods inventories	2.4	10.8	-9.2	7.8	2.8	0.8	-1.6	-2.0	0.6	-2.8	0.6
Less: Intermediate goods and services consumed [1]	103.5	115.9	123.5	125.2	133.9	130.0	129.8	132.1	137.7	131.1	139.0
Equals: **Gross farm value added**	76.6	81.6	68.5	90.7	88.1	78.9	68.8	71.5	73.1	70.8	84.8
Less: Consumption of fixed capital	18.6	19.2	19.6	19.9	20.3	20.9	21.2	21.3	27.4	28.0	29.0
Equals: Net farm value added.	58.0	62.4	48.9	70.8	67.8	58.0	47.6	50.2	45.7	42.8	55.8
Compensation of employees.	13.4	14.4	15.4	16.0	17.1	18.2	18.9	19.7	20.9	20.5	20.4
Taxes on production and imports	3.8	4.0	4.2	4.2	4.4	4.3	4.9	4.7	4.8	5.0	5.3
Less: Subsidies to operators	7.6	6.6	6.1	6.2	6.4	10.5	18.6	19.6	18.3	9.4	13.6
Net operating surplus	48.5	50.6	35.4	56.7	52.6	46.0	42.4	45.4	38.3	26.6	43.7
CHAINED (2000) DOLLARS [2]											
Farm output, total.	164.5	187.4	179.6	183.3	198.4	198.4	200.5	203.6	200.7	200.3	203.5
Cash receipts from farm marketings	159.0	173.3	183.5	172.1	189.2	189.2	192.0	196.6	190.1	193.5	191.8
Farm products consumed on farms	0.7	0.6	0.5	0.5	0.5	0.6	0.6	0.6	0.5	0.5	0.5
Other farm income	4.8	4.9	5.8	5.2	6.5	7.9	9.5	8.4	9.4	8.7	10.1
Change in farm finished goods inventories	2.1	10.0	-8.8	6.0	2.5	0.9	-1.8	-2.0	0.6	-2.8	0.6
Less: Intermediate goods and services consumed [1]	117.5	126.7	134.4	128.5	133.7	137.5	138.1	132.1	135.3	130.4	130.7
Equals: **Gross farm value added**	49.3	60.9	49.6	56.1	64.4	61.6	62.9	71.5	65.6	69.9	72.7
Less: Consumption of fixed capital	23.0	21.4	21.3	21.1	21.3	21.6	21.6	21.3	27.0	27.3	27.7
Equals: Net farm value added.	29.4	40.1	30.4	36.0	42.9	40.2	41.5	50.2	39.0	42.9	45.3

[1] Includes rent paid to nonoperator landlords.   [2] See text, Section 13.

Source: U.S. Bureau of Economic Analysis, *National Income and Product Accounts, Volume 1, 1929-2000*, and *Survey of Current Business*, May 2005. See also <http://www.bea.gov/bea/dn/nipaweb/selecttable.asp>.

Table 805. Value Added to Economy by Agricultural Sector: 1990 to 2003

[In billions of dollars (188.5 represents $188,500,000,000). Data are consistent with the net farm income accounts and include income and expenses related to the farm operator dwellings. The concept presented is consistent with that employed by the Organization for Economic Co-operation and Development]

Item	1990	1994	1995	1996	1997	1998	1999	2000	2001	2002	2003
Value of agricultural sector production	188.5	208.2	203.6	228.5	230.7	220.0	212.9	218.4	227.6	219.7	240.9
Value of crop production [1]	83.2	100.5	95.9	115.7	112.6	102.1	92.7	94.9	95.1	98.7	108.0
Value of livestock production [1]	90.0	89.7	87.8	92.1	96.3	94.1	95.1	99.1	106.3	93.3	104.7
Services and forestry	15.3	18.0	19.9	20.7	21.7	23.8	25.1	24.4	26.1	27.7	28.2
Machine hire and customwork	1.8	2.1	1.9	2.2	2.4	2.2	2.0	2.2	2.1	2.2	2.6
Forest products sold	1.8	2.6	2.8	2.6	2.8	3.0	2.7	2.8	2.6	2.6	2.4
Other farm income	4.5	4.3	5.8	6.2	6.9	8.7	10.1	8.7	10.1	11.2	11.3
Gross imputed rental value of farm dwellings	7.2	9.0	9.4	9.8	9.7	9.9	10.2	10.7	11.4	11.8	11.9
Less: Purchased inputs	92.2	103.9	108.8	112.1	119.9	117.7	118.7	121.8	126.1	123.8	127.4
Farm origin	39.5	41.3	41.8	42.7	46.9	44.8	45.5	47.9	48.6	48.7	52.6
Feed purchased	20.4	22.6	23.8	25.2	26.3	25.0	24.5	24.5	24.8	24.9	26.6
Livestock and poultry purchased	14.6	13.3	12.5	11.3	13.8	12.6	13.8	15.9	15.7	14.9	16.7
Seed purchased	4.5	5.4	5.5	6.2	6.7	7.2	7.2	7.5	8.2	8.9	9.3
Manufactured inputs [2]	22.0	24.4	26.1	28.6	29.2	28.1	27.1	28.7	29.4	28.0	28.3
Fertilizers and lime.	8.2	9.2	10.0	10.9	10.9	10.6	9.9	10.0	10.3	9.6	10.0
Other purchased inputs [2]	30.7	38.2	40.8	40.8	43.8	44.7	46.1	45.2	48.0	47.0	46.5
Repair and maintenance of capital items	8.6	9.2	9.6	10.4	10.5	10.5	10.6	10.9	11.2	11.7	10.9
Plus: Net government transactions [3]	3.1	1.2	0.4	0.4	0.4	5.2	14.3	15.5	13.3	3.7	8.7
Direct Government payments	9.3	7.9	7.3	7.3	7.5	12.4	21.5	22.9	20.7	11.0	15.9
Property taxes	5.8	6.3	6.4	6.6	6.7	6.7	6.8	6.9	6.9	6.8	6.8
Equals: Gross value added	99.3	105.5	95.2	116.7	111.1	107.5	108.5	112.1	114.8	99.7	122.2
Less: Capital consumption	18.1	18.5	18.9	19.1	19.3	19.6	19.9	20.2	20.7	20.9	20.8
Equals: Net value added	81.2	87.1	76.2	97.6	91.8	87.8	88.7	91.9	94.1	78.8	101.4
Less: Employee compensation	12.4	13.4	14.3	15.1	15.9	16.8	17.4	17.9	18.8	18.7	18.3
Less: Net rent received by nonoperator landlords	9.0	10.6	9.6	11.4	11.3	10.8	10.4	11.2	11.1	9.8	10.7
Less: Real estate and nonreal estate interest	13.5	11.7	12.7	13.2	13.4	13.7	13.8	14.9	13.6	13.0	12.3
Equals: Net farm income	46.3	51.3	39.6	57.9	51.3	46.5	47.1	47.9	50.6	37.3	59.2

[1] Includes home consumption and value of inventory adjustment.   [2] Includes other outlays not shown separately.   [3] Direct government payments minus motor vehicle registration and licensing fees and property taxes.

Source: U.S. Dept. of Agriculture, Economic Research Service, "United States and State Farm Income Data"; <http://www.ers.usda.gov/Data/farmincome/finfidmu.htm>; accessed 12 October 2004.

Agriculture 549

Table 806. Farm Income—Cash Receipts From Farm Marketings: 2000 to 2003

[In millions of dollars (192,078 represents $192,078,000,000). Represents gross receipts from commercial market sales as well as net Commodity Credit Corporation loans. The source estimates and publishes individual cash receipt values only for major commodities and major producing states. The U.S. receipts for individual commodities, computed as the sum of the reported states, may understate the value of sales for some commodities. The degree of underestimation in some of the minor commodities can be substantial]

Commodity	2000	2001	2002	2003
Total	192,078	200,075	195,072	211,647
Livestock and products [1]	99,585	106,659	93,816	105,471
Cattle and calves	40,783	40,541	38,095	45,095
Hogs	11,758	12,395	9,602	10,629
Sheep and lambs	470	397	421	496
Dairy products	20,587	24,686	20,582	21,228
Broilers	13,989	16,695	15,438	15,214
Chicken eggs	4,346	4,446	4,281	5,315
Turkeys	2,771	2,736	2,643	2,652
Horses/mules	1,239	1,014	982	1,018
Aquaculture [1][2]	876	824	777	783
Catfish	469	444	410	425
Crops [1]	92,494	93,416	101,257	106,176
Rice	837	1,029	882	1,214
Wheat	5,654	5,344	5,927	6,713
Barley	556	550	513	652
Corn	15,162	15,317	17,884	18,336
Hay	3,844	4,575	4,643	4,394
Sorghum grain	864	901	934	849
Cotton	2,950	3,639	3,418	5,025
Tobacco	2,316	1,894	1,742	1,551
Peanuts	897	1,001	600	779
Soybeans	12,047	11,779	13,826	15,942
Sunflower [1]	305	304	323	315
Vegetables [1]	15,554	15,450	17,160	16,808
Beans, dry	436	413	464	460
Potatoes	2,376	2,593	2,916	2,571
Beans, snap	393	390	404	386
Broccoli	622	484	568	644

Commodity	2000	2001	2002	2003
Corn, sweet	709	749	718	789
Cucumbers	382	375	377	368
Lettuce [1]	1,863	1,840	2,358	2,103
Head	1,202	1,229	1,429	1,185
Romaine	299	291	469	526
Leaf	312	314	454	389
Onions	713	684	758	997
Peppers, green	531	474	464	505
Tomatoes	1,845	1,680	1,934	1,866
Fresh	1,195	1,132	1,254	1,290
Processing	650	547	680	576
Cantaloups	372	429	399	372
Fruits/nuts [1]	12,497	11,950	12,958	13,098
Oranges	1,775	1,546	1,733	1,423
Apples	1,523	1,303	1,472	1,524
Avocados	353	354	346	383
Cherries	327	328	302	426
Grapes [1]	3,100	2,952	2,839	2,577
Wine	1,909	1,820	1,683	1,543
Table	437	437	456	408
Peaches	470	483	488	455
Strawberries	1,045	1,069	1,162	1,321
Almonds	666	740	1,201	1,600
Walnuts	296	342	330	355
Sugarbeets	1,113	1,025	1,089	1,093
Cane for sugar	881	905	931	1,003
Greenhouse/nursery [1]	13,611	14,476	15,071	15,193
Floriculture	4,576	4,803	5,090	5,073
Christmas trees	470	513	521	521
Mushrooms	867	863	873	859

[1] Includes other commodities not shown separately.   [2] See also Table 860.

Source: U.S. Department of Agriculture, Economic Research Service, "United States and State Farm Income Data"; <http://www.ers.usda.gov/Data/farmincome/finfidmu.htm>; accessed 12 October 2004.

Table 807. Balance Sheet of the Farming Sector: 1990 to 2003

[In billions of dollars, except as indicated (841 represents $841,000,000,000). As of December 31]

Item	1990	1994	1995	1996	1997	1998	1999	2000	2001	2002	2003
Assets	841	935	966	1,003	1,051	1,083	1,139	1,203	1,256	1,304	1,379
Real estate	619	704	740	770	808	840	887	946	996	1,046	1,112
Livestock and poultry [1]	71	68	58	60	67	63	73	77	79	76	79
Machinery, motor vehicles [2]	86	87	88	88	89	90	90	90	93	94	96
Crops [3]	23	23	27	32	33	30	28	28	25	23	24
Purchased inputs	3	5	3	4	5	5	4	5	4	6	6
Financial assets	38	48	49	49	50	55	57	57	59	60	62
Claims	841	935	966	1,003	1,051	1,083	1,139	1,203	1,256	1,304	1,379
Debt [4]	131	139	143	149	157	165	168	178	186	193	198
Real estate debt	68	70	72	74	79	83	87	91	96	103	108
Non-real estate debt	63	69	71	74	78	82	80	87	90	90	90
Equity	709	796	823	854	894	919	971	1,026	1,070	1,111	1,181
FINANCIAL RATIOS (percent)											
Farm debt/equity ratio	18.5	17.5	17.4	17.4	17.5	17.9	17.3	17.3	17.4	17.4	16.8
Farm debt/asset ratio	15.6	14.9	14.8	14.8	14.9	15.2	14.7	14.8	14.8	14.8	14.4
Rate of return on assets from:											
Total	3.5	5.2	4.3	5.8	5.7	5.1	5.3	5.1	4.6	3.2	6.6
Current income [5]	4.1	3.8	2.2	4.1	3.0	2.4	1.8	2.0	2.0	0.7	2.2
Real capital gains [6]	-0.7	1.5	2.1	1.7	2.7	2.7	3.4	3.1	2.6	2.5	4.4
Rate of return on equity from:											
Total	3.0	5.0	3.9	5.6	5.5	4.8	5.1	5.0	4.4	2.8	6.8
Current income [7]	3.0	3.0	1.1	3.3	2.0	1.4	0.7	0.9	1.1	-0.4	1.5
Real capital gains [8]	0.1	2.0	2.8	2.3	3.5	3.4	4.3	4.1	3.4	3.2	5.2

[1] Excludes horses, mules, and broilers.   [2] Includes only farm share value for trucks and autos.   [3] All non-CCC crops held on farms plus the value above loan rate for crops held under Commodity Credit Corporation.   [4] Excludes debt for nonfarm purposes.   [5] Returns to farm assets from current income/farm business assets. Measures how efficiently the farm business uses its assets; the per dollar return on farm assets from current income only.   [6] Real capital gains on farm business assets/farm business assets. The per dollar return on farm assets from real capital gains.   [7] Returns to farm assets from current income minus interest/farm business equity. Measures the returns to equity capital employed in farm business from current income less interest.   [8] Real capital gains on farm business assets/farm business equity. The per dollar return on farm equity from real capital gains.

Source: U.S. Dept. of Agriculture, Economic Research Service, "Farm Business Balance Sheet and Financial Ratios"; published 3 December 2004; <http://www.ers.usda.gov/Data/FarmBalanceSheet/fbsdmu.htm>.

Table 808. Farm Assets, Debt, and Income by State: 2000 and 2003

[Assets and debt, as of December 31 (1,203,215 represents $1,203,215,000,000). Farm income data are after inventory adjustment and include income and expenses related to the farm operator's dwelling]

State	Assets (mil. dol.)		Debt (mil. dol.)		Debt/asset ratio (percent)		Final agricultural sector output (mil. dol.)		Net farm income (mil. dol.)	
	2000	2003	2000	2003	2000	2003	2000	2003	2000	2003
United States [1]	1,203,215	1,378,757	177,637	197,998	14.8	14.4	218,381	240,915	47,897	59,229
Alabama	16,521	18,917	2,054	2,361	12.4	12.5	3,927	4,128	1,195	1,604
Alaska	624	685	24	26	3.8	3.7	58	57	16	10
Arizona	35,823	44,348	1,448	1,575	4.0	3.6	2,624	3,029	720	1,078
Arkansas	22,372	25,973	4,315	4,884	19.3	18.8	5,251	5,952	1,591	1,914
California	88,124	96,678	17,837	19,955	20.2	20.6	27,086	29,377	5,402	8,475
Colorado	25,108	27,150	3,686	4,143	14.7	15.3	5,045	5,562	711	1,172
Connecticut	2,318	2,824	284	338	12.3	12.0	589	561	183	93
Delaware	1,795	1,906	378	433	21.0	22.7	829	859	144	156
Florida	28,959	34,550	4,771	5,372	16.5	15.6	7,082	6,833	2,627	1,831
Georgia	24,535	30,027	3,600	4,115	14.7	13.7	5,775	6,195	2,010	2,971
Hawaii	3,808	4,463	254	283	6.7	6.3	556	600	112	122
Idaho	16,874	18,883	3,012	3,289	17.9	17.4	3,832	4,440	957	1,218
Illinois	76,078	87,558	9,383	10,480	12.3	12.0	7,894	9,289	1,502	1,657
Indiana	40,218	46,035	5,655	6,391	14.1	13.9	5,230	5,957	852	1,328
Iowa	73,326	83,330	13,117	14,434	17.9	17.3	11,710	13,122	2,341	2,023
Kansas	36,983	38,248	7,141	7,820	19.3	20.4	8,655	10,365	1,016	1,387
Kentucky	25,704	29,843	3,433	3,907	13.4	13.1	4,604	4,299	1,677	864
Louisiana	11,798	12,925	1,777	1,976	15.1	15.3	1,953	2,272	504	711
Maine	1,923	2,212	395	423	20.5	19.1	573	563	137	84
Maryland	7,887	9,184	1,087	1,283	13.8	14.0	1,725	1,757	390	327
Massachusetts	3,490	4,257	387	445	11.1	10.5	471	469	69	40
Michigan	24,548	30,403	3,074	3,513	12.5	11.6	3,795	4,403	259	444
Minnesota	46,958	56,585	8,969	9,982	19.1	17.6	8,352	9,249	1,301	1,568
Mississippi	15,197	17,194	2,887	3,202	19.0	18.6	3,309	3,934	750	1,148
Missouri	45,005	53,787	6,015	6,725	13.4	12.5	5,442	5,728	955	1,539
Montana	24,516	27,160	2,685	2,900	11.0	10.7	1,980	2,382	260	576
Nebraska	44,121	47,932	9,325	10,085	21.1	21.0	9,492	11,960	1,374	3,228
Nevada	3,311	3,550	259	303	7.8	8.5	454	460	100	111
New Hampshire	988	1,148	104	123	10.5	10.7	174	181	20	17
New Jersey	5,972	7,239	465	539	7.8	7.4	954	963	248	127
New Mexico	11,441	12,143	1,419	1,612	12.4	13.3	2,193	2,275	501	716
New York	13,967	15,725	2,509	2,808	18.0	17.9	3,386	3,581	569	597
North Carolina	26,880	30,726	3,688	4,235	13.7	13.8	9,473	8,840	3,296	1,629
North Dakota	22,485	25,995	3,981	4,357	17.7	16.8	3,411	4,377	1,027	1,315
Ohio	38,537	44,514	4,239	4,898	11.0	11.0	5,392	6,012	1,241	1,470
Oklahoma	26,587	30,310	4,413	4,717	16.6	15.6	4,618	5,041	996	2,037
Oregon	18,659	21,026	2,519	2,763	13.5	13.1	3,691	3,990	409	493
Pennsylvania	23,442	26,636	2,828	3,230	12.1	12.1	4,829	5,034	1,100	1,107
Rhode Island	377	457	39	46	10.2	10.1	62	66	12	10
South Carolina	8,338	9,703	1,143	1,330	13.7	13.7	1,757	1,959	547	681
South Dakota	24,696	28,661	4,198	4,479	17.0	15.6	4,331	4,787	1,358	1,321
Tennessee	26,990	30,649	2,605	3,013	9.7	9.8	2,665	2,953	541	480
Texas	98,539	112,521	11,970	13,286	12.2	11.8	14,895	17,966	3,868	5,939
Utah	11,424	13,249	857	951	7.5	7.2	1,195	1,385	232	368
Vermont	2,699	3,178	378	435	14.0	13.7	589	562	144	102
Virginia	21,619	24,800	2,069	2,441	9.6	9.8	2,884	2,761	690	529
Washington	20,786	22,483	3,504	3,788	16.9	16.9	5,962	5,921	1,005	680
West Virginia	4,567	5,458	408	456	8.9	8.4	508	503	45	15
Wisconsin	36,065	43,642	5,983	6,699	16.6	15.4	6,069	6,756	756	1,626
Wyoming	10,217	11,884	1,067	1,150	10.5	9.7	1,052	1,204	137	291

[1] The U.S. total will exceed the sum of the states because data for some states are not included in the state's statistics due to disclosure issues.

Source: U.S. Dept. of Agriculture, Economic Research Service, "Farm Income Summary Totals for 50 States"; <http://www.ers.usda.gov/Data/FarmIncome/50State/50stmenu.htm>; accessed 12 October 2004; and "Farm Business Balance Sheet and Financial Ratios"; published 3 December 2004; <http://www.ers.usda.gov/Data/FarmBalanceSheet/fbsdmu.htm>.

Table 809. Cash Receipts for Selected Commodities—Leading States: 2003

[In millions of dollars (45,095 represents $45,095,000,000). See headnote, Table 806]

State	Value	State	Value	State	Value	State	Value
Cattle and calves	45,095	Dairy products	21,228	Corn	18,336	Vegetables	16,808
Texas	7,872	California	4,029	Iowa	3,709	California	7,199
Nebraska	5,904	Wisconsin	2,838	Illinois	3,259	Florida	1,409
Kansas	5,618	New York	1,560	Nebraska	2,041	Washington	928
Colorado	2,944	Pennsylvania	1,446	Minnesota	1,666	Arizona	743
Oklahoma	2,375	Minnesota	1,044	Indiana	1,449	Idaho	697

Source: U.S. Department of Agriculture, Economic Research Service, "Farm Income"; published 2 September 2004; <http://www.ers.usda.gov/Data/farmincome/finfidmu.htm>.

Agriculture 551

Table 810. **Farm Income—Farm Marketings, 2002 and 2003, and Principal Commodities, 2003 by State**

[In millions of dollars (195,072 represents $195,072,000,000). Livestock includes products; cattle include calves; and greenhouse includes nursery]

State	2002 Total	2002 Crops	2002 Live-stock	2003 Total	2003 Crops	2003 Live-stock	State rank for total farm marketings and four principal commodities in order of marketing receipts
U.S.: . . .	195,072	101,257	93,816	211,647	106,176	105,471	Cattle, dairy products, corn, soybeans
AL	2,920	534	2,386	3,415	676	2,739	25-Broilers, cattle, chicken eggs, greenhouse
AK	50	22	28	51	23	28	50-Greenhouse, hay, dairy products, potatoes
AZ	3,065	1,972	1,093	2,586	1,327	1,259	29-Cattle, dairy products, lettuce, cotton
AR	4,505	1,547	2,959	5,298	2,083	3,215	12-Broilers, soybeans, rice, cotton
CA	26,606	20,345	6,261	27,805	20,812	6,993	1-Dairy products, greenhouse, grapes, lettuce
CO	4,958	1,458	3,500	4,964	1,289	3,676	16-Cattle, dairy products, greenhouse, corn
CT	472	310	162	485	320	165	43-Greenhouse, dairy products, chicken eggs, aquaculture
DE	718	171	547	760	168	593	40-Broilers, soybeans, corn, greenhouse
FL	6,663	5,448	1,214	6,450	5,244	1,206	9-Greenhouse, oranges, sugar cane, tomatoes
GA	4,475	1,585	2,889	5,246	2,024	3,222	13-Broilers, cotton, chicken eggs, peanuts
HI	540	454	86	549	464	86	41-Pineapples, greenhouse, sugar cane, macadamia nuts
ID	3,985	1,986	1,999	3,953	1,776	2,177	21-Cattle, dairy products, potatoes, wheat
IL	7,732	6,183	1,549	8,290	6,490	1,800	7-Corn, soybeans, hogs, cattle
IN	4,719	3,183	1,536	5,162	3,363	1,799	14-Corn, soybeans, hogs, dairy products
IA	11,394	6,248	5,146	12,633	6,560	6,073	3-Corn, hogs, soybeans, cattle
KS	8,070	2,747	5,323	9,046	2,867	6,179	5-Cattle, wheat, corn, soybeans
KY	3,166	1,193	1,973	3,469	1,243	2,226	24-Horses/mules, cattle, broilers, tobacco
LA	1,723	1,073	649	1,993	1,296	697	33-Sugar cane, cotton, cattle, rice
ME	465	214	251	499	227	272	42-Potatoes, dairy products, chicken eggs, aquaculture
MD	1,396	612	784	1,467	620	847	36-Broilers, greenhouse, dairy products, corn
MA	388	298	89	385	298	87	47-Greenhouse, cranberries, dairy products, sweet corn
MI	3,465	2,175	1,290	3,821	2,422	1,399	22-Dairy products, greenhouse, corn, soybeans
MN	7,866	4,245	3,622	8,588	4,516	4,072	6-Corn, soybeans, hogs, dairy products
MS	2,841	890	1,952	3,411	1,246	2,165	26-Broilers, cotton, soybeans, aquaculture
MO	4,263	1,979	2,284	4,973	2,344	2,628	15-Cattle, soybeans, corn, hogs
MT	1,768	767	1,001	1,892	787	1,105	34-Cattle, wheat, barley, hay
NE	9,422	3,582	5,840	10,621	3,754	6,867	4-Cattle, corn, soybeans, hogs
NV	362	149	213	396	141	254	45-Cattle, hay, dairy products, onions
NH	147	85	63	150	88	62	48-Greenhouse, dairy products, apples, cattle
NJ	869	680	189	846	658	188	39-Greenhouse, horses/mules, blueberries, chicken eggs
NM	1,970	573	1,398	2,140	543	1,597	32-Dairy products, cattle, hay, pecans
NY	3,115	1,241	1,875	3,139	1,225	1,915	28-Dairy products, greenhouse, hay, cattle
NC	6,600	2,660	3,940	6,916	2,759	4,158	8-Hogs, broilers, greenhouse, tobacco
ND	3,344	2,546	798	3,778	2,907	870	23-Wheat, cattle, soybeans, barley
OH	4,372	2,742	1,629	4,662	2,853	1,809	17-Soybeans, corn, dairy products, greenhouse
OK	3,835	912	2,923	4,526	1,022	3,504	18-Cattle, wheat, hogs, broilers
OR	3,098	2,288	809	3,284	2,479	805	27-Greenhouse, cattle, dairy products, hay
PA	4,065	1,389	2,676	4,266	1,407	2,859	19-Dairy products, cattle, greenhouse, chicken eggs
RI	56	47	8	57	49	9	49-Greenhouse, dairy products, sweet corn, cattle
SC	1,449	688	761	1,644	754	890	35-Broilers, greenhouse, turkeys, tobacco
SD	3,775	1,730	2,046	4,018	1,899	2,119	20-Cattle, soybeans, corn, wheat
TN	2,054	1,120	934	2,339	1,268	1,071	30-Cattle, broilers, greenhouse, soybeans
TX	12,594	4,505	8,089	15,342	5,031	10,311	2-Cattle, cotton, greenhouse, broilers
UT	1,067	254	813	1,138	258	880	37-Cattle, dairy products, hogs, hay
VT	475	76	399	482	79	403	44-Dairy products, cattle, greenhouse, hay
VA	2,155	703	1,451	2,227	695	1,532	31-Broilers, cattle, dairy products, greenhouse
WA	5,267	3,715	1,553	5,345	3,818	1,527	11-Apples, dairy products, cattle, wheat
WV	363	70	294	390	73	317	46-Broilers, cattle, chicken eggs, turkeys
WI	5,521	1,729	3,792	5,876	1,782	4,094	10-Dairy products, cattle, corn, greenhouse
WY	887	136	751	874	150	724	38-Cattle, hay, sugar beets, sheep/lambs

Source: U.S. Dept. of Agriculture, Economic Research Service, "Farm Income"; published 2 September 2004; <http://www.ers.usda.gov/Data/farmincome/finfidmu.htm>.

Table 811. **Indexes of Prices Received and Paid by Farmers: 2000 to 2004**

[1990-92 = 100, except as noted]

Item	2000	2002	2003	2004	Item	2000	2002	2003	2004
Prices received, all products	96	98	107	119	**Prices paid, total [2] . . . .**	118	121	126	132
					Production	116	119	124	131
					Feed	102	112	114	118
Crops	96	105	111	117	Livestock & poultry	110	102	109	128
Food grains	85	104	108	120	Seed	124	142	154	158
Feed grains and hay	86	100	104	109	Fertilizer	110	108	124	138
Cotton	82	56	85	91	Agricultural chemicals	120	119	121	120
Tobacco	107	108	107	98	Fuels	134	112	140	163
Oil-bearing crops	85	88	107	134	Supplies & repairs	124	131	134	137
Fruits and nuts . . . . , . .	98	105	106	120	Autos and trucks	119	116	115	114
Commercial vegetables [1]	121	137	138	137	Farm machinery	139	148	151	162
Potatoes & dry beans	93	129	104	102	Building materials	121	122	124	134
All other crops	110	114	114	115	Farm services	119	120	123	124
					Rent	110	119	120	120
Livestock and products	97	90	103	122	Interest	113	104	102	103
Meat animals	94	87	103	116	Taxes	123	126	128	130
Dairy products	94	93	96	123	Wage rates	140	153	157	161
Poultry and eggs	106	94	110	133	Parity ratio (1910-14 = 100) [3] . . .	38	38	40	43

[1] Excludes potatoes and dry beans. [2] Includes production items, interest, taxes, wage rates, and a family living component. The family living component is the Consumer Price Index for all urban consumers from the Bureau of Labor Statistics. See text, Section 14, and Table 706. [3] Ratio of prices received by farmers to prices paid.

Source: U.S. Dept. of Agriculture, National Agricultural Statistics Service. *Agricultural Prices: Annual Summary.*

552 Agriculture

Table 812. Civilian Consumer Expenditures for Farm Foods: 1990 to 2003

[In billions of dollars, except percent (449.8 represents $449,800,000,000). Excludes imported and nonfarm foods, such as coffee and seafood, as well as food consumed by the military, or exported]

Item	1990	1994	1995	1996	1997	1998	1999	2000	2001	2002	2003
Consumer expenditures, total. . .	449.8	512.2	529.5	546.7	566.5	585.0	625.3	661.1	687.5	709.4	744.2
Farm value, total	106.2	109.6	113.8	122.2	121.9	119.6	122.2	123.3	130.0	132.5	140.2
Marketing bill, total [1]	343.6	402.6	415.7	424.5	444.6	465.4	503.1	537.8	557.5	576.9	604.0
Percent of total consumer expenditures	76.4	78.6	78.5	77.6	78.5	79.6	80.5	81.3	81.1	81.3	81.2
At-home expenditures [2]	276.2	308.7	316.9	328.0	339.2	346.8	370.7	390.2	403.9	416.8	437.2
Farm value	80.2	75.3	76.1	81.6	79.0	77.0	78.7	79.6	83.9	85.7	91.4
Marketing bill [1]	196.0	233.4	240.8	246.4	260.2	269.8	292.0	310.6	320.0	331.1	345.8
Away-from-home expenditures	173.6	203.5	212.6	218.7	227.3	238.2	254.6	270.9	283.6	292.6	307.0
Farm value	26.0	34.3	37.7	40.6	42.9	42.6	43.5	43.7	46.1	46.8	48.8
Marketing bill [1]	147.6	169.2	174.9	178.1	184.4	195.6	211.1	227.2	237.5	245.8	258.2
Marketing bill cost components:											
Labor cost	154.0	186.1	196.6	204.6	216.9	229.9	241.5	252.9	263.8	273.1	285.9
Packaging materials	36.5	43.3	48.2	47.7	48.7	50.4	50.9	53.5	55.0	56.8	59.5
Rail and truck transport	19.8	21.8	22.3	22.9	23.6	24.4	25.2	26.4	27.5	28.4	29.7
Corporate profits before taxes	13.2	20.9	19.5	20.7	22.3	25.5	29.2	31.1	32.0	33.0	34.6
Fuels and electricity.	15.2	17.9	18.6	19.6	20.2	20.7	22.0	23.1	24.1	24.9	26.1
Advertising	17.1	19.3	19.8	20.9	22.1	23.4	24.8	26.1	27.5	28.1	29.4
Depreciation	16.3	18.1	18.9	20.1	21.0	21.6	23.0	24.2	24.5	25.3	26.5
Net interest	13.5	11.0	11.6	11.4	12.5	12.9	14.4	16.9	18.6	19.2	20.1
Net rent	13.9	18.9	19.8	21.0	21.8	23.7	25.3	26.7	29.4	30.3	31.7
Repairs	6.2	7.8	7.9	8.5	8.8	9.0	9.6	10.1	10.6	10.9	11.4
Taxes	15.7	18.7	19.1	19.4	19.8	20.9	22.2	23.5	24.1	24.9	26.1
Other	22.2	18.8	13.4	7.7	6.9	3.0	15.0	23.3	23.3	20.4	22.0	23.0

[1] The difference between expenditures for domestic farm-originated food products and the farm value or payment farmers received for the equivalent farm products.   [2] Food primarily purchased from retail food stores for use at home.

Source: U.S. Dept. of Agriculture, Economic Research Service, *Food Cost Review, 1950-97*, ERS Agricultural Economic Report No. AER780, June 1999; and "ERS/USDA Briefing Room - Food marketing and price spreads: USDA marketing bill"; <http://www.ers.usda.gov/Briefing/FoodPriceSpreads/bill/>.

Table 813. Agricultural Exports and Imports—Volume by Principal Commodities: 1990 to 2004

[In thousands of metric tons, except fruit juices, wine and malt beverages in thousands of hectoliters (7,703 represents 7,703,000). Includes Puerto Rico, U.S. territories, and shipments under foreign aid programs]

Commodity	1990	1995	2000	2001	2002	2003	2004
EXPORTS							
Fruit juices and wine	7,703	10,688	14,356	13,503	15,118	13,714	15,351
Beef, pork, and poultry meats	1,451	3,723	4,935	5,369	5,074	5,127	4,026
Wheat, unmilled	27,384	32,317	27,568	25,585	24,159	25,100	31,040
Wheat products	863	1,142	844	631	707	420	378
Rice, paddy, milled	2,534	3,275	3,241	2,889	3,808	4,469	3,525
Feed grains	61,066	66,795	54,946	54,702	53,218	48,400	52,260
Feed grain products	1,430	2,018	2,062	2,234	3,153	4,353	4,517
Feeds and fodders [1]	10,974	13,338	13,065	12,587	12,677	11,839	11,475
Fresh fruits and nuts	2,648	3,323	3,450	3,432	3,493	3,490	3,430
Fruit products	390	462	471	474	475	502	528
Vegetables, fresh	1,297	1,708	2,029	2,002	2,059	1,997	1,954
Vegetables, frozen and canned	529	892	1,112	1,087	1,065	1,010	1,045
Oilcake and meal	5,079	6,404	6,462	7,426	6,672	5,653	4,826
Oilseeds	15,820	23,596	28,017	29,974	29,139	32,253	26,727
Vegetable oils	1,226	2,532	2,043	2,193	2,682	2,251	1,942
Tobacco, unmanufactured	223	209	180	186	153	156	164
Cotton, excluding linters	1,696	2,039	1,485	1,868	2,108	2,674	2,882
IMPORTS							
Fruit juices	33,116	21,922	31,154	29,615	29,047	35,488	33,744
Wine	2,510	2,781	4,584	4,888	5,655	6,214	6,551
Malt beverages	10,382	13,251	23,464	25,533	27,087	27,618	27,946
Coffee, including products	1,214	989	1,370	1,229	1,238	1,302	1,323
Rubber and allied gums, crude	840	1,044	1,232	1,002	1,213	1,120	1,158
Beef, pork, lamb, and poultry meats	1,169	1,050	1,579	1,635	1,704	1,665	1,876
Grains	2,071	4,553	4,622	5,234	4,472	3,484	3,730
Biscuits, pasta, and noodles	300	489	711	761	834	904	934
Feeds and fodders [1]	959	1,247	1,224	1,219	1,266	1,160	1,075
Fruits, nuts, and preparations [2]	5,401	6,530	8,354	8,139	8,711	9,052	9,191
Vegetables, fresh or frozen	1,898	2,777	3,763	4,064	4,457	4,765	5,003
Tobacco, unmanufactured	173	190	216	233	260	288	254
Oilseeds and oilnuts	509	713	1,056	964	825	622	897
Vegetable oils and waxes	1,204	1,509	1,846	1,898	1,931	1,841	2,290
Oilcake and meal	316	805	1,254	1,070	1,008	1,314	1,780

[1] Excluding oil meal.   [2] Includes bananas and plantains.

Source: U.S. Dept. of Agriculture, Economic Research Service, "foreign agricultural trade of the united states (fatus)"; <http://www.ers.usda.gov/data/fatus/> and "U.S. Trade Internet System"; <http://www.fas.usda.gov/ustrade>.

Agriculture 553

Table 814. Agricultural Exports and Imports—Value: 1990 to 2004

[In billions of dollars, except percent (16.6 represents $16,600,000,000). Includes Puerto Rico, U.S. territories, and shipments under foreign aid programs. Excludes fish, forest products, distilled liquors, manufactured tobacco, and products made from cotton; but includes raw tobacco, raw cotton, rubber, beer and wine, and processed agricultural products]

Year	Trade balance	Exports, domestic products	Percent of all exports	Imports for consumption	Percent of all imports	Year	Trade balance	Exports, domestic products	Percent of all exports	Imports for consumption	Percent of all imports
1990...	16.6	39.5	11	22.9	5	1998...	14.9	51.8	8	36.9	4
1992...	18.3	43.1	10	24.8	5	1999...	10.7	48.4	8	37.7	4
1993...	17.7	42.9	10	25.1	4	2000...	12.3	51.2	7	39.0	3
1994...	19.2	46.2	10	27.0	4	2001...	14.3	53.7	8	39.4	3
1995...	26.0	56.3	10	30.3	4	2002...	11.1	53.1	8	41.9	4
1996...	26.8	60.3	10	33.5	4	2003...	12.2	59.6	8	47.3	4
1997...	21.0	57.2	9	36.1	4	2004...	7.3	61.3	7	54.0	4

Source: U.S. Dept. of Agriculture, Economic Research Service, *U.S. Agricultural Trade Update*, February 11, 2005; and "foreign agricultural trade of the united states (fatus)"; <http://www.ers.usda.gov/data/fatus/> and U.S. Dept. of Agriculture, Foreign Agricultural Service, "U.S. Trade Internet System"; <http://www.fas.usda.gov/ustrade>.

Table 815. Agricultural Imports—Value by Selected Commodity: 1990 to 2004

[In millions of dollars (22,918 represents $22,918,000,000). See headnote, Table 814]

Commodity	1990	1995	1998	1999	2000	2001	2002	2003	2004
Total [1]..............	22,918	30,255	36,896	37,673	38,974	39,366	41,909	47,342	54,019
Cattle, live........	978	1,413	1,144	1,001	1,152	1,461	1,446	867	544
Beef and veal	1,872	1,447	1,842	2,136	2,399	2,712	2,741	2,623	3,625
Pork.................	938	686	682	753	997	1,048	1,001	1,189	1,367
Dairy products	891	1,118	1,465	1,557	1,671	1,789	1,783	1,978	2,424
Grains and feeds	1,188	2,312	2,878	2,989	3,076	3,320	3,666	3,921	4,299
Fruits and preparations ...	2,167	2,759	3,387	3,966	3,846	3,977	4,351	4,715	5,082
Vegetables and preparations.........	2,317	3,189	4,374	4,583	4,740	5,252	5,614	6,393	7,163
Sugar and related products	1,213	1,335	1,682	1,589	1,555	1,600	1,854	2,129	2,107
Wine	917	1,153	1,876	2,187	2,207	2,250	2,671	3,264	3,418
Malt beverages	923	1,166	1,712	1,893	2,179	2,348	2,581	2,680	2,768
Oilseeds and products....	952	1,746	2,067	1,818	1,847	1,630	1,789	2,064	3,035
Coffee and products	1,915	3,263	3,431	2,893	2,700	1,677	1,693	1,958	2,263
Cocoa and products	1,072	1,106	1,666	1,522	1,404	1,536	1,761	2,432	2,491
Rubber, crude natural ...	707	1,629	977	704	842	613	751	1,047	1,466

[1] Includes other commodities not shown separately.

Source: U.S. Dept. of Agriculture, Economic Research Service, "foreign agricultural trade of the united states (fatus)"; <http://www.ers.usda.gov/data/fatus/> and U.S. Dept. of Agriculture, Foreign Agricultural Service, "U.S. Trade Internet System"; <http://www.fas.usda.gov/ustrade>.

Table 816. Imports' Share of Food Consumption by Selected Commodity: 1990 to 2003

[In percent. Import share is the total quantity imported divided by the quantity available for domestic human food consumption. Calculated from supply and utilization balance sheets. A portion of the imports of some commodities is exported plus, some is diverted to such nonfood uses as feed, seed, alcohol and fuel production, and industrial uses. These can overstate the importance of imports]

Commodity	1990	2000	2003	Commodity	1990	2000	2003
Total food consumption [1] ..	9.7	11.3	12.1	Wine.................	13.9	21.3	26.1
Red meat................	7.6	8.2	9.4	Vegetables...........	5.7	8.5	10.5
Beef	9.8	11.1	11.1	Vegetables—fresh	9.9	13.9	16.4
Pork	5.6	5.2	6.1	Cucumbers	33.7	42.4	43.6
Fish and shellfish	56.3	68.3	82.1	Onions..............	10.1	9.3	14.1
Dairy products	1.9	2.7	2.9	Peppers, bell	19.7	22.2	27.1
Cheese	4.8	4.8	5.3	Potatoes............	5.8	6.0	4.3
Fruits—fresh.............	29.4	39.8	39.5	Tomatoes...........	20.5	32.4	38.7
Citrus................	3.3	13.8	15.0	Vegetables—processed.......	2.2	2.9	3.6
Non-citrus.............	35.7	44.7	45.5	Beans, dry...........	5.0	6.1	6.8
Apples	4.3	7.3	8.9	Mushrooms	24.2	36.2	31.3
Grapes.............	40.5	45.0	49.4	Olives..............	36.4	38.0	50.6
Melons.............	14.2	22.9	21.6	Tomatoes	5.7	3.0	5.2
Strawberries	13.0	11.4	13.9	Vegetable oils	41.8	40.9	37.4
Fruits—processed.........	2.9	3.2	3.9	Spices..............	88.1	106.9	102.6
Fruit juices..............	50.1	33.0	38.8	Wheat..............	4.7	9.5	7.0
Apple juice	55.0	60.6	76.5	Rice	11.2	19.2	25.4
Grape juice..........	33.7	39.3	44.2	Beet and cane sugar	34.3	17.7	17.6
Orange juice	38.0	21.3	20.0	Confectionery products........	6.0	10.9	17.3
Tree nuts................	32.5	41.1	44.9	Malt beverages	4.5	9.9	11.4

[1] Computed from units of weight, weight equivalents, or content weight.

Source: U.S. Dept. of Agriculture, Economic Research Service, "The Import Share of U.S.-Consumed Food Continues to Rise," *Electronic Outlook Report*, FAU-66-01, July 2002, and online at <http://www.ers.usda.gov/data/foodconsumption>.

Table 817. **Selected Farm Products—United States and World Production and Exports: 2000 to 2004**

[In metric tons, except as indicated (61 represents 61,000,000). Metric ton = 1.102 short tons or .984 long tons]

Commodity	Unit	Amount						United States as percent of world		
		United States			World					
		2000	2003	2004	2000	2003	2004	2000	2003	2004
PRODUCTION [1]										
Wheat	Million	61	64	59	581	553	624	10.4	11.5	9.4
Corn for grain	Million	252	256	300	590	623	706	42.7	41.1	42.5
Soybeans	Million	75	67	85	176	189	219	42.7	35.4	39.0
Rice, milled	Million	5.9	6.4	7.3	398	390	402	1.5	1.6	1.8
Cotton [2]	Million bales [3] . . .	17.0	17.2	18.3	87.7	88.3	95.1	19.3	19.5	19.2
EXPORTS [4]										
Wheat [5]	Million	28.0	32.3	28.0	104.0	105.0	107.6	26.9	30.7	26.0
Corn	Million	48.3	48.6	45.5	76.4	78.9	74.1	63.3	61.7	61.4
Soybeans	Million	27.1	24.1	29.4	53.8	55.6	62.4	50.4	43.3	47.1
Rice, milled basis	Million	2.5	3.1	3.5	24.4	26.7	25.4	10.4	11.6	13.6
Cotton [2]	Million bales [3] . . .	6.8	11.9	13.8	27.1	30.4	33.1	24.9	39.1	41.6

[1] Production years vary by commodity. In most cases, includes harvests from July 1 of the year shown through June 30 of the following year. [2] For production and trade years ending in year shown. [3] Bales of 480 lb. net weight. [4] Trade years may vary by commodity. Wheat, corn, soybean, and rice data are for trade year beginning in year shown. [5] Includes wheat flour on a grain equivalent.

Source: U.S. Dept. of Agriculture, Foreign Agricultural Service, *Foreign Agricultural Commodity Circular Series*, periodic.

Table 818. **Percent of U.S. Agricultural Commodity Output Exported: 1980 to 2003**

[All export shares are estimated from export and production weights]

Commodity group	1980-84, average	1985-89, average	1990-94, average	1995-99, average	2000	2001	2002	2003
Total agriculture	**22.9**	**19.1**	**18.2**	**18.2**	**17.6**	**17.7**	**16.5**	**17.9**
Livestock [1]	2.3	2.3	4.1	4.5	4.5	4.7	4.4	4.6
Red meat	1.2	2.1	4.1	7.1	8.1	8.4	8.6	9.0
Poultry meat	4.0	3.8	7.4	15.5	15.5	16.8	14.2	14.2
Dairy products [2]	2.4	2.1	1.4	1.4	1.0	1.0	1.0	1.2
Crops	31.2	26.5	24.4	24.2	23.3	23.4	22.1	23.8
Wheat and rice	60.9	56.2	51.3	49.3	44.7	47.1	45.7	51.8
Coarse grains [3]	27.4	23.4	21.2	21.5	21.0	20.5	17.7	19.4
Oilseeds/meal/oil	34.6	28.7	25.0	26.8	27.2	27.3	27.7	27.9
Fruits and nuts [4]	9.5	9.5	13.4	14.2	13.7	15.2	15.4	15.2
Vegetables [5]	5.1	4.0	5.7	6.4	6.6	6.8	6.7	6.4
Cotton and tobacco	49.0	41.7	40.7	38.1	43.7	57.1	60.3	66.7

[1] Excludes hides, animal fats, and live animals. [2] Includes butter, cheese, and nonfat dried milk. [3] Includes corn, barley, sorghum, oats, and rye. [4] Includes fruit juices and wine, whose volumes are converted to weight units using 8 pounds per gallon. [5] Total vegetable production is estimated from U.S. per capita use of major fresh and processing vegetables.

Source: U.S. Dept. of Agriculture, Economic Research Service, USDA's commodity yearbooks, "Foreign Agricultural Trade of the U.S."; <http://www.ers.usda.gov/data/fatus/>, and "Production, Supply, and Distribution database"; <http://www.fas.usda.gov/psd/>.

Table 819. **Top 10 U.S. Export Markets for Selected Commodities: 2004**

[In thousands of metric tons (47,556 represents 47,556,000)]

Corn		Wheat [1]		Soybeans		Cotton [2]	
Country	Amount	Country	Amount	Country	Amount	Country	Amount
World, total . . .	**47,556**	**World, total. . .**	**31,040**	**World, total . . .**	**24,976**	**World, total. . .**	**2,882**
Japan	15,304	Japan	3,093	China [3]	9,403	China [3]	905
Mexico [3]	5,473	China [3]	2,940	Japan	3,108	Mexico	353
Taiwan [3]	4,516	Mexico	2,811	Mexico	2,688	Turkey	328
Korea, South	4,333	Egypt	2,731	Germany	1,630	Indonesia	196
Egypt	3,106	Nigeria	2,360	Taiwan [3]	1,059	Thailand	133
Canada	1,997	Korea, South	1,430	Indonesia	884	Pakistan	127
Colombia	1,755	Philippines	1,348	Korea, South	864	Korea, South	108
Algeria	1,169	Taiwan [3]	1,082	Spain	813	Taiwan [3]	106
Israel	878	Peru	937	Canada	498	Canada	71
Syria	794	Israel	720	Thailand	358	Japan	57
Rest of world	8,231	Rest of world. . . .	11,589	Rest of world. . . .	3,671	Rest of world. . . .	498

[1] Unmilled. [2] Excluding linters. [3] See footnote 2, Table 1314.

Source: U.S. Dept. of Agriculture, Foreign Agricultural Service, "FAS Online, U.S.Trade Exports - FATUS Commodity Aggregations"; <http://www.fas.usda.gov/ustrade/USTExFatus.asp>; accessed 16 May 2005.

Agriculture **555**

Table 820. **Agricultural Exports—Value by Principal Commodities: 1990 to 2004**

[(39,492 represents $39,492,000,000). Includes Puerto Rico, U.S. territories, and shipments under foreign aid programs. Excludes fish, forest products, distilled liquors, manufactured tobacco, and products made from cotton; but includes raw tobacco, raw cotton, rubber, beer and wine, and processed agricultural products]

Commodity	Value (mil. dol.)							Percent		
	1990	1995	2000	2001	2002	2003	2004	1990	2000	2004
Total agricultural exports	39,492	56,251	51,246	53,659	53,115	59,561	61,309	100.0	100.0	100.0
Animals and animal products [1]	6,648	10,889	11,600	12,431	11,087	12,357	10,365	16.8	22.6	16.9
Meat and meat products	2,558	4,522	5,276	5,284	5,042	5,741	3,239	6.5	10.3	5.3
Beef and veal	1,580	2,647	2,986	2,632	2,585	3,145	552	4.0	5.8	0.9
Poultry and poultry products	910	2,348	2,235	2,636	2,064	2,287	2,569	2.3	4.4	4.2
Dairy products	353	795	1,018	1,130	993	1,048	1,503	0.9	2.0	2.5
Fats, oils, and greases.	424	827	383	334	461	538	575	1.1	0.7	0.9
Hides and skins, including furskins. . .	1,751	1,748	1,562	1,963	1,745	1,782	1,749	4.4	3.0	2.9
Bovine hides, whole	1,337	1,388	1,193	1,471	1,042	1,062	1,076	3.4	2.3	1.8
Grains and feeds [1]	14,409	18,644	13,687	13,923	14,459	15,122	17,642	36.5	26.7	28.8
Wheat and products	4,035	5,734	3,578	3,560	3,845	4,097	5,273	10.2	7.0	8.6
Rice	801	996	855	692	769	1,024	1,166	2.0	1.7	1.9
Feed grains and products.	7,150	8,341	5,372	5,503	5,875	5,810	6,787	18.1	10.5	11.1
Corn	6,026	7,304	4,469	4,502	4,845	4,719	5,741	15.3	8.7	9.4
Fruits and preparations	2,009	2,660	2,742	2,768	2,775	2,968	3,140	5.1	5.4	5.1
Fresh fruits	1,486	1,973	2,080	2,125	2,134	2,273	2,379	3.8	4.1	3.9
Nuts and preparations.	976	1,410	1,319	1,292	1,525	1,762	2,220	2.5	2.6	3.6
Vegetables and preparations	2,225	3,637	4,457	4,483	4,554	4,813	5,282	5.6	8.7	8.6
Fresh vegetables	696	1,017	1,207	1,180	1,232	1,293	1,345	1.8	2.4	2.2
Oilseeds and products [1]	5,728	8,953	8,586	9,219	9,632	11,658	10,422	14.5	16.8	17.0
Soybeans	3,548	5,400	5,258	5,403	5,677	7,960	6,672	9.0	10.3	10.9
Soybean meal	979	986	1,169	1,386	1,216	1,180	1,034	2.5	2.3	1.7
Vegetable oils and waxes.	832	1,852	1,259	1,250	1,634	1,691	1,678	2.1	2.5	2.7
Tobacco, unmanufactured	1,441	1,400	1,204	1,269	1,050	1,038	1,044	3.6	2.3	1.7
Cotton, excluding linters	2,783	3,681	1,873	2,162	2,015	3,361	4,223	7.0	3.7	6.9
Other	3,273	4,977	5,777	6,112	6,017	6,482	6,970	8.3	11.3	11.4

[1] Includes commodities not shown separately.

Source: U.S. Dept. of Agriculture, Economic Research Service, *U.S. Agricultural Trade Update*, February 11, 2005; and "foreign agricultural trade of the united states (fatus)"; <http://www.ers.usda.gov/data/fatus/> and U.S. Dept. of Agriculture, Foreign Agricultural Service, "U.S. Trade Internet System"; <http://www.fas.usda.gov/ustrade>.

Table 821. **Agricultural Exports—Value by Selected Countries of Destination: 1990 to 2004**

[(39,492 represents $39,492,000,000). See headnote, Table 820.]

Country	Value (mil. dol.)							Percent		
	1990	1995	2000	2001	2002	2003	2004	1990	2000	2004
Total agricultural exports [1] . . .	39,492	56,251	51,246	53,659	53,115	59,561	61,309	100.0	100.0	100.0
Canada	4,217	5,791	7,640	8,121	8,660	9,314	9,669	10.7	14.9	15.8
Mexico	2,561	3,538	6,410	7,404	7,226	7,879	8,494	6.5	12.5	13.9
Caribbean.	1,016	1,282	1,408	1,399	1,518	1,589	1,840	2.6	2.7	3.0
Central America.	482	873	1,120	1,233	1,250	1,337	1,428	1.2	2.2	2.3
South America [2]	1,063	2,348	1,701	1,703	1,788	1,909	1,948	2.7	3.3	3.2
Brazil	177	522	263	221	329	383	278	0.4	0.5	0.5
Colombia	119	465	415	452	520	512	593	0.3	0.8	1.0
Asia, excluding Middle East [2]	15,862	25,704	19,872	20,312	19,724	23,681	23,002	40.2	38.8	37.5
Japan	8,146	11,161	9,290	8,883	8,382	8,903	8,148	20.6	18.1	13.3
Korea, South	2,650	3,754	2,546	2,588	2,672	2,884	2,489	6.7	5.0	4.1
Taiwan [3]	1,663	2,597	1,996	2,009	1,966	2,025	2,063	4.2	3.9	3.4
China [3, 4]	818	2,633	1,716	1,939	2,067	5,016	5,542	2.1	3.3	9.0
Hong Kong	704	1,502	1,262	1,227	1,091	1,113	912	1.8	2.5	1.5
India.	108	194	210	353	274	317	256	0.3	0.4	0.4
Indonesia	274	816	668	907	810	996	925	0.7	1.3	1.5
Philippines.	381	765	901	794	776	625	694	1.0	1.8	1.1
Thailand	275	591	493	570	611	684	685	0.7	1.0	1.1
Australia	226	339	317	290	338	611	405	0.6	0.6	0.7
Europe/Eurasia [2]	7,751	10,699	7,669	8,425	7,692	7,811	8,341	19.6	15.0	13.6
European Union [5]	7,244	8,967	6,483	6,626	6,335	6,656	6,808	18.3	12.7	11.1
Former Soviet Union [6]	(X)	1,251	670	1,060	695	739	1,112	(X)	1.3	1.8
Russia	(X)	1,046	580	917	551	578	802	(X)	1.1	1.3
Middle East [2]	1,816	2,437	2,322	2,223	2,259	2,547	2,816	4.6	4.5	4.6
Saudi Arabia	564	527	477	429	342	331	362	1.4	0.9	0.6
Turkey	226	536	658	571	675	921	945	0.6	1.3	1.5
Africa [2]	1,935	3,073	2,308	2,105	2,297	2,489	2,951	4.9	4.5	4.8
Egypt	692	1,448	1,050	1,022	862	966	938	1.8	2.0	1.5
South Africa	81	293	134	99	148	148	168	0.2	0.3	0.3
Oceania	343	507	489	471	511	820	596	0.9	1.0	1.0

X Not applicable. [1] Totals include transshipments through Canada, but transshipments are not distributed by country after 1998. [2] Includes areas not shown separately. [3] See footnote 2, Table 1314. [4] China includes Macao. However, Hong Kong remains separate economically until 2050 and is not included. [5] For consistency, data for all years are shown on the basis of 25 countries in the European Union; see footnote 1, Table 1351. [6] Includes the 12 member states of the Former Soviet Union.

Source: U.S. Dept. of Agriculture, Economic Research Service, *U.S. Agricultural Trade Update*, February 11, 2005; and "foreign agricultural trade of the united states (fatus)"; <http://www.ers.usda.gov/data/fatus/> and U.S. Dept. of Agriculture, Foreign Agricultural Service, "U.S. Trade Internet System"; <http://www.fas.usda.gov/ustrade>.

Table 822. **Cropland Used for Crops and Acreages of Crops Harvested: 1990 to 2004**

[In millions of acres, except as indicated (341 represents 341,000,000)]

Item	1990	1995	1997	1998	1999	2000	2001	2002	2003	2004
Cropland used for crops.....	341	332	349	345	344	345	340	340	342	337
Index (1977 = 100).........	90	88	92	91	91	91	90	90	90	89
Cropland harvested [1]........	310	302	321	315	316	314	311	307	315	312
Crop failure	6	8	7	10	8	11	10	17	10	9
Cultivated summer fallow	25	22	21	20	20	20	19	16	16	16
Cropland idled by all federal programs	62	55	33	30	30	31	32	34	34	34
Acres of crops harvested [2] ...	322	314	332	326	327	325	321	316	324	321

[1] Land supporting one or more harvested crops. [2] Area in principal crops harvested as reported by Crop Reporting Board plus acreages in fruits, vegetables for sale, tree nuts, and other minor crops.

Source: U.S. Dept. of Agriculture, Economic Research Service, *Major Uses of Land in the United States, 1997*, SB-973, 2001. Also in *Agricultural Statistics*, annual. Beginning 1995 *Agricultural Resources and Environmental Indicators*, periodic, and *AREI Updates: Cropland Use*. See also ERS Briefing Room at <http://www.ers.usda.gov/Briefing/LandUse/majorlandusechapter.htm#trends>.

Table 823. **Percent of Corn, Soybean, and Cotton Acreage Planted With Genetically Modified Seed: 2000 and 2003**

[In percent. Based on the June Agricultural Survey. Randomly selected farmers across the United States were asked if they planted corn, soybeans, or upland cotton seed that, through biotechnology, is resistant to herbicides, insects, or both. The states published individually below represent 81 percent of all corn planted acres, 89 percent of all soybean planted acres, and 82 percent of all upland cotton planted acres. Conventionally bred herbicide resistant varieties were excluded. Insect resistant varieties include only those containing bacillus thuringiensis (Bt). The acreage estimates are subject to sampling variability because all operations planting biotech varieties are not included in the sample]

State	Corn		State	Soybeans		State	Cotton	
	2000	2003		2000	2003		2000	2003
US, total	25	40	US, total	54	75	US, total	61	73
IL.....................	17	28	AR............	43	84	AR............	70	95
IN.....................	11	16	IL.............	44	77	CA............	24	39
IA.....................	30	45	IN.............	63	88	GA............	82	93
KS....................	33	47	IA.............	59	84	LA............	80	91
MI....................	12	35	KS............	66	87	MS............	78	92
MN....................	37	53	MI............	50	73	NC............	76	93
MO....................	28	42	MN............	46	79	TX............	46	53
NE....................	34	52	MS............	48	89	Other states [1]	74	88
OH....................	9	9	MO............	62	83			
SD....................	48	75	NE............	72	86			
WI.....................	18	32	ND............	22	74			
Other states [1]	17	36	OH............	48	74			
			SD............	68	91			
			WI............	51	84			
			Other states [1].....	54	76			

[1] Includes all other states in the specified commodity estimating program.

Source: U.S. Dept. of Agriculture, National Agricultural Statistics Service, *Acreage*, annual.

Table 824. **Quantity of Pesticides Applied to Selected Crops: 1990 to 2003**

[In million pounds of active ingredients, except as indicated (497.7 represents 497,700,000)]

Type of pesticide and commodity	1990	1995	1998	1999	2000	2001	2002	2003
Total	497.7	543.3	544.4	553.7	539.4	511.1	486.0	499.0
Herbicides	344.6	324.9	340.3	316.8	308.6	307.6	285.5	300.5
Insecticides	57.4	69.9	52.0	75.4	77.4	62.0	55.6	40.8
Fungicides	27.8	47.5	45.7	42.3	36.6	33.3	33.6	35.7
Other	67.9	101.0	106.4	119.1	116.8	108.3	111.3	122.1
Corn	240.7	201.3	212.4	186.0	176.1	187.3	153.5	169.6
Cotton.....................	50.9	83.7	55.4	90.6	94.5	72.8	64.5	55.9
Wheat.....................	17.8	21.5	23.9	21.4	19.2	18.3	13.9	14.8
Soybeans	74.4	68.7	78.8	77.3	79.1	72.2	90.7	90.6
Potatoes	43.8	53.1	63.6	64.6	61.8	60.5	55.3	66.3
Other vegetables.............	39.8	78.0	67.8	70.5	70.1	66.5	75.4	75.3
Citrus fruit	11.0	14.0	14.1	13.3	13.0	12.8	12.4	7.5
Apples	8.3	9.0	9.3	7.9	7.6	7.6	7.2	8.6
Other deciduous fruit	10.9	14.1	19.2	22.2	18.1	13.1	13.1	10.4
POUNDS OF ACTIVE INGREDIENT PER PLANTED ACRE								
Total......................	2.2	2.4	2.3	2.3	2.2	2.2	2.1	2.1
Herbicides	1.5	1.4	1.4	1.3	1.3	1.3	1.2	1.3
Insecticides	0.3	0.3	0.2	0.3	0.3	0.3	0.2	0.2
Fungicides	0.1	0.2	0.2	0.2	0.2	0.1	0.1	0.2
Other	0.3	0.4	0.4	0.5	0.5	0.5	0.5	0.5

Source: U.S. Dept. of Agriculture, Economic Research Service, *Production Practices for Major Crops in U.S. Agriculture, 1990–97*, Statistical Bulletin No. 969, August 2000 and unpublished data.

Agriculture 557

Table 825. Principal Crops—Production, Supply, and Disappearance: 1990 to 2004

[67.0 represents 67,000,000. Marketing year beginning January 1 for potatoes, May 1 for hay, June 1 for wheat, August 1 for cotton, September 1 for soybeans and corn. Acreage, production, and yield of all crops periodically revised on basis of census data]

Item	Unit	1990	1995	2000	2001	2002	2003	2004
CORN FOR GRAIN								
Acreage harvested	Million	67.0	65.2	72.4	68.8	69.3	70.9	73.6
Yield per acre	Bushel	119	114	137	138	129	142	160
Production	Mil. bu.	7,934	7,400	9,915	9,503	8,967	10,089	11,807
Farm price [1]	Dol./bu.	2.28	3.24	1.85	1.97	2.32	2.42	1.95
Farm value	Mil. dol.	18,192	24,118	18,499	18,888	20,882	24,477	23,033
Total supply [2]	Mil. bu.	9,282	8,974	11,639	11,412	10,578	11,190	12,775
Total disappearance [3]	Mil. bu.	7,761	8,548	9,740	9,815	9,491	10,232	10,720
Ethanol	Mil. bu.	(NA)	(NA)	(NA)	(NA)	996	1,168	1,425
Exports	Mil. bu.	1,725	2,228	1,941	1,905	1,588	1,897	1,850
Ending stocks	Mil. bu.	1,521	426	1,899	1,596	1,087	958	2,055
SOYBEANS								
Acreage harvested	Million	56.5	61.5	72.4	73.0	72.5	72.5	74.0
Yield per acre	Bushel	34.1	35.3	38.1	39.6	38.0	33.9	42.5
Production	Mil. bu.	1,926	2,174	2,758	2,891	2,756	2,454	3,141
Farm price [1]	Dol./bu.	5.74	6.72	4.54	4.38	5.53	7.34	5.10
Farm value	Mil. dol.	11,042	14,617	12,467	12,606	15,253	18,014	16,098
Total supply [2]	Mil. bu.	2,169	2,514	3,052	3,141	2,969	2,638	3,258
Total disappearance [3]	Mil. bu.	1,840	2,330	2,804	2,933	2,791	2,525	2,848
Exports	Mil. bu.	557	849	996	1,064	1,044	885	1,045
Ending stocks	Mil. bu.	329	183	248	208	178	112	410
HAY								
Acreage harvested	Million	61.0	59.8	59.9	63.5	63.9	63.4	61.9
Yield per acre	Sh. tons	2.40	2.58	2.54	2.46	2.34	2.49	2.55
Production	Mil. sh. tons	146	154	152	156	149	158	158
Farm price [4, 5]	Dol./ton	80.60	82.20	84.60	96.50	92.40	85.50	89.70
Farm value	Mil. dol.	10,462	11,042	11,417	12,597	12,338	12,007	12,197
WHEAT								
Acreage harvested	Million	69.1	61.0	53.1	48.5	45.8	53.1	50.0
Yield per acre	Bushel	39.5	35.8	42.0	40.2	35.0	44.2	43.2
Production	Mil. bu.	2,730	2,183	2,228	1,947	1,606	2,345	2,158
Farm price [1]	Dol./bu.	2.61	4.55	2.62	2.78	3.56	3.40	3.38
Farm value	Mil. dol.	7,184	9,787	5,782	5,440	5,637	7,929	7,192
Total supply [2]	Mil. bu.	3,303	2,757	3,268	2,931	2,460	2,899	2,770
Total disappearance [3]	Mil. bu.	2,435	2,381	2,392	2,154	1,969	2,353	2,217
Exports	Mil. bu.	1,069	1,241	1,062	962	850	1,159	1,050
Ending stocks	Mil. bu.	868	376	876	777	491	546	553
COTTON								
Acreage harvested	Million	11.7	16.0	13.1	13.8	12.4	12.0	13.1
Yield per acre	Pounds	634	537	632	705	665	730	846
Production [6]	Mil. bales [7]	15.5	17.9	17.2	20.3	17.2	18.3	23.0
Farm price [1]	Cents/lb.	68.2	76.5	51.6	32.0	45.7	63.0	48.0
Farm value	Mil. dol.	5,076	6,575	4,260	3,122	3,777	5,517	5,300
Total supply [2]	Mil. bales [7]	18.5	21.0	21.1	26.3	24.7	23.7	26.6
Total disappearance [3]	Mil. bales [7]	16.5	18.3	15.6	18.7	19.2	20.3	19.5
Exports	Mil. bales [7]	7.8	7.7	6.7	11.0	11.9	13.8	13.2
Ending stocks [8]	Mil. bales [7]	2.3	2.6	6.0	7.4	5.4	3.5	7.1
POTATOES								
Acreage harvested	Million	1.4	1.4	1.3	1.2	1.3	1.2	1.2
Yield per acre	Cwt.	293	323	381	358	362	367	391
Production	Mil. cwt.	402	445	514	438	458	458	456
Farm price [1]	Dol./cwt.	6.08	6.77	5.08	6.99	6.67	5.89	5.62
Farm value	Mil. dol.	2,431	2,992	2,591	3,058	3,045	2,686	2,564

NA Not available. [1] Marketing year average price. U.S. prices are computed by weighting U.S. monthly prices by estimated monthly marketings and do not include an allowance for outstanding loans and government purchases and payments. [2] Comprises production, imports, and beginning stocks. [3] Includes feed, residual, and other domestic uses not shown separately. [4] Prices are for hay sold baled. [5] Season average prices received by farmers. U.S. prices are computed by weighting state prices by estimated sales. [6] State production figures, which conform with annual ginning enumeration with allowance for cross-state ginnings, rounded to thousands and added for U.S. totals. [7] Bales of 480 pounds, net weight. [8] Stock estimates based on Census Bureau data which results in an unaccounted difference between supply and use estimates and changes in ending stocks.

Source: Production—U.S. Dept. of Agriculture, National Agricultural Statistics Service. In Crop Production, annual; and Crop Values, annual. Supply and disappearance—U.S. Dept. of Agriculture, Economic Research Service, Feed Situation, quarterly; Fats and Oils Situation, quarterly; Wheat Situation, quarterly; Cotton and Wool Outlook Statistics, periodic; and Agricultural Supply and Demand Estimates, periodic. Data are also in Agricultural Statistics, annual; and "Agricultural Outlook: Statistical Indicators"; <http://www.ers.usda.gov/publications/agoutlook/aotables/>.

Table 826. Corn—Acreage, Production, and Value by Leading States: 2002 to 2004

[69,330 represents 69,330,000. One bushel of corn = 56 pounds]

State	Acreage harvested (1,000 acres)			Yield per acre (bu.)			Production (mil. bu.)			Price ($/bu.)			Farm value (mil. dol.)		
	2002	2003	2004	2002	2003	2004	2002	2003	2004	2002	2003	2004	2002	2003	2004
U.S. [1] . . .	69,330	70,944	73,632	129	142	160	8,967	10,089	11,807	2.32	2.42	1.95	20,882	24,477	23,033
IA	11,850	11,900	12,400	163	157	181	1,932	1,868	2,244	2.22	2.37	1.90	4,288	4,428	4,264
IL	10,900	11,050	11,600	135	164	180	1,472	1,812	2,088	2.35	2.42	2.00	3,458	4,386	4,176
NE.	7,350	7,700	7,950	128	146	166	941	1,124	1,320	2.32	2.39	1.95	2,183	2,687	2,573
MN	6,700	6,650	7,050	157	146	159	1,052	971	1,121	2.15	2.35	1.85	2,262	2,282	2,074
IN	5,220	5,390	5,530	121	146	168	632	787	929	2.41	2.53	1.75	1,522	1,991	1,626
SD.	3,250	3,850	4,150	95	111	130	309	427	540	2.17	2.28	1.65	670	974	890
OH	2,970	3,070	3,110	89	156	158	264	479	491	2.48	2.45	1.85	656	1,173	909
MO	2,700	2,800	2,880	105	108	162	284	302	467	2.45	2.46	1.90	695	744	886
KS.	2,600	2,500	2,880	116	120	150	302	300	432	2.48	2.51	2.15	748	753	929
WI	2,900	2,850	2,600	135	129	136	392	368	354	2.22	2.35	2.00	869	864	707
MI	2,000	2,030	1,920	117	128	134	234	260	257	2.34	2.37	1.80	548	616	463
TX.	1,790	1,650	1,680	113	118	139	202	195	234	2.57	2.59	2.55	520	504	595
KY.	1,070	1,080	1,140	104	137	152	111	148	173	2.58	2.53	2.05	287	374	355
CO	720	890	1,040	150	135	135	108	120	140	2.53	2.49	2.15	273	299	302
PA	840	890	980	68	115	140	57	102	137	2.97	2.96	2.00	170	303	274
ND	995	1,170	1,150	114	112	105	113	131	121	2.16	2.37	1.80	245	311	217
NC	680	680	740	83	106	117	56	72	87	2.89	2.68	2.35	163	193	203
TN.	610	620	615	107	131	140	65	81	86	2.58	2.37	2.10	168	192	181
MD	425	410	425	74	123	153	31	50	65	2.85	2.83	2.15	90	143	140
NY.	460	440	500	97	121	122	45	53	61	2.87	2.82	2.40	128	150	146
MS	530	530	440	120·	135	136	64	72	60	2.33	2.28	2.40	148	163	144

[1] Includes other states, not shown separately.

Source: U.S. Dept. of Agriculture, National Agricultural Statistics Service, *Crop Production*, annual; and *Crop Values*, annual.

Table 827. Soybeans—Acreage, Production, and Value by Leading States: 2002 to 2004

[72,497 represents 72,497,000. One bushel of soybeans = 60 pounds]

State	Acreage harvested (1,000 acres)			Yield per acre (bu.)			Production (mil. bu.)			Price ($/bu.)			Farm value (mil. dol.)		
	2002	2003	2004	2002	2003	2004	2002	2003	2004	2002	2003	2004	2002	2003	2004
U.S. [1] . . .	72,497	72,476	73,958	38	34	43	2,756	2,454	3,141	5.53	7.34	5.10	15,253	18,014	16,098
IL	10,550	10,260	9,900	43	37	51	454	380	500	5.66	7.51	5.05	2,568	2,851	2,525
IA	10,400	10,550	10,150	48	33	49	499	343	497	5.54	7.70	5.05	2,766	2,640	2,512
IN	5,770	5,370	5,520	42	38	52	239	204	287	5.55	7.67	5.00	1,329	1,565	1,435
MN	7,100	7,450	7,050	44	32	34	309	238	236	5.42	7.26	5.35	1,674	1,731	1,264
MO	5,000	4,950	4,960	34	30	45	170	146	223	5.54	7.52	4.95	942	1,098	1,105
NE.	4,580	4,500	4,750	39	41	47	176	182	221	5.43	7.02	5.05	957	1,279	1,115
OH	4,720	4,280	4,420	32	39	47	151	165	208	5.59	7.20	5.15	844	1,186	1,070
SD.	4,090	4,200	4,120	31	28	34	127	116	140	5.33	6.96	4.95	676	804	693
AR.	2,880	2,890	3,150	34	39	40	96	111	124	5.65	7.11	5.55	545	791	691
KS.	2,540	2,480	2,710	23	23	41	58	57	111	5.49	7.68	4.75	321	438	528
ND	2,630	3,050	3,570	33	29	23	87	88	82	5.32	6.62	5.35	462	586	439
MI	2,040	1,990	1,980	39	28	38	79	55	75	5.62	7.30	5.05	441	399	380
MS	1,370	1,430	1,640	32	39	38	44	56	62	5.52	6.61	5.90	242	369	368
KY	1,290	1,240	1,300	33	44	44	43	54	57	5.74	7.40	5.20	244	399	297

[1] Includes other states, not shown separately.

Source: U.S. Dept. of Agriculture, National Agricultural Statistics Service, *Crop Production*, annual; and *Crop Values*, annual.

Table 828. Wheat—Acreage, Production, and Value by Leading States: 2002 to 2004

[45,824 represents 45,824,000. One bushel of wheat = 60 pounds]

State	Acreage harvested (1,000 acres)			Yield per acre (bu.)			Production (mil. bu.)			Price ($/bu.)			Farm value (mil. dol.)		
	2002	2003	2004	2002	2003	2004	2002	2003	2004	2002	2003	2004	2002	2003	2004
U.S. [1] . . .	45,824	53,063	49,999	35.0	44.2	43.2	1,606	2,345	2,158	3.56	3.40	3.38	5,637	7,929	7,192
KS.	8,200	10,000	8,500	33.0	48.0	37.0	271	480	315	3.41	3.15	3.25	923	1,512	1,022
ND	7,915	8,500	7,775	27.3	37.3	39.4	216	317	307	3.80	3.63	3.30	821	1,150	1,015
MT	4,795	5,200	5,025	23.1	27.4	34.5	111	142	173	4.04	3.73	3.55	449	527	612
OK	3,700	4,600	4,700	28.0	39.0	35.0	104	179	165	3.37	3.31	3.30	349	594	543
WA	2,390	2,345	2,275	54.3	59.4	63.1	130	139	144	3.83	3.75	3.65	497	521	519
SD.	1,677	2,797	2,798	26.4	42.3	46.0	44	118	129	3.81	3.46	3.25	168	408	417
TX.	2,700	3,450	3,500	29.0	28.0	31.0	78	97	109	3.02	3.06	3.35	236	296	363
ID	1,090	1,130	1,190	71.9	74.9	85.5	78	85	102	3.67	3.49	3.50	288	294	357

[1] Includes other states, not shown separately.

Source: U.S. Dept. of Agriculture, National Agricultural Statistics Service, *Crop Production*, annual; and *Crop Values*, annual.

Agriculture **559**

Table 829. Floriculture and Nursery Crops—Value of Production, Trade, and Consumption: 1990 to 2003

[In millions of dollars, except as noted (8,764 represents $8.764,000,000). Includes all floriculture and nursery crops except cut Christmas trees, seeds, and food crops grown under cover. Domestic production based on grower wholesale receipts. Domestic consumption equals supply minus exports. Supply equals domestic production plus imports]

Year	Production and trade				Consumption			
	Domestic production	Imports	Supply	Exports	Domestic consumption	Per household (dol.)	Per capita (dol.)	Import share (percent)
1990	8,764	538	9,302	204	9,098	99	36	5.9
1992	9,654	604	10,258	222	10,036	106	39	6.0
1993	9,840	654	10,494	242	10,253	108	39	6.4
1994	10,294	712	11,007	252	10,754	112	41	6.6
1995	10,800	859	11,659	241	11,418	117	43	7.5
1996	11,300	952	12,252	242	12,010	122	45	7.9
1997	12,355	1,004	13,358	283	13,076	131	48	7.7
1998	12,559	1,080	13,640	306	13,334	132	48	8.1
1999	13,096	1,101	14,197	299	13,897	135	50	7.9
2000	13,612	1,160	14,771	279	14,493	137	51	8.0
2001	13,566	1,151	14,717	264	14,453	135	51	8.0
2002	14,455	1,133	15,588	250	15,338	142	53	7.4
2003	14,321	1,250	15,570	272	15,299	140	53	8.2

Source: U.S. Dept. of Agriculture, Economic Research Service, *Floriculture and Nursery Crops Yearbook.*

Table 830. Fresh Fruits and Vegetables—Supply and Use: 2000 to 2004

[In millions of pounds, except per capita in pounds (8,355 represents 8,355,000,000)]

Year	Utilized production [1]	Imports [2]	Supply, [1] total	Consumption		Exports [2]
				Total	Per capita	
FRUITS						
Citrus:						
2000	8,355	720	9,075	6,630	23.5	2,445
2001	8,331	871	9,202	6,810	23.9	2,392
2002	8,256	707	8,962	6,718	23.4	2,245
2003	8,440	969	9,409	6,953	23.9	2,456
2004	8,164	860	9,024	6,585	18.2	2,438
Noncitrus: [3]						
2000	13,850	11,225	25,074	21,685	76.6	3,389
2001	12,781	10,911	23,692	20,588	72.0	3,104
2002	12,833	11,552	24,385	21,483	74.4	2,902
2003	13,078	11,766	24,844	22,078	75.6	2,767
2004	13,148	11,444	24,593	21,757	72.8	2,835
VEGETABLES and MELONS						
2000	46,649	6,719	54,713	48,293	171.0	4,197
2001	46,086	7,304	54,656	48,311	169.3	4,115
2002	46,405	7,691	55,437	49,064	170.3	4,265
2003	46,655	8,037	55,942	49,704	170.8	4,207
2004	48,589	8,199	58,040	51,231	174.3	4,327
POTATOES						
2000	13,185	806	13,990	13,314	47.1	677
2001	13,252	671	13,923	13,287	46.6	636
2002	12,567	883	13,450	12,757	44.3	693
2003	13,468	872	14,341	13,751	47.3	590
2004	13,398	755	14,155	13,676	46.5	479

[1] Crop-year basis for fruits.   [2] Fiscal year for fruits; calendar year for vegetables and potatoes.   [3] Includes bananas.

Source: U.S. Department of Agriculture, Economic Research Service, *Fruit and Tree Nuts Situation and Outlook Yearbook,* and *Vegetables and Melons Situation and Outlook Yearbook.*

Table 831. Nuts—Supply and Use: 2000 to 2003

[In millions of pounds (shelled) (365.6 represents 365,600,000)]

Year	Beginning stocks	Marketable production [1]	Imports	Supply, total	Consumption	Exports	Ending stocks
2000	365.6	1,110.1	297.0	1,772.7	647.0	851.1	274.5
2001	274.3	1,334.5	322.5	1,931.3	805.5	845.2	280.7
2002	280.7	1,561.9	346.1	2,188.6	898.3	927.8	362.5
2003	362.5	1,506.3	384.3	2,253.1	931.4	971.7	350.0

[1] Utilized production minus inedibles and noncommercial usage.

Source: U.S. Dept. of Agriculture, Economic Research Service, *Fruit and Tree Nuts Situation and Outlook Yearbook.*

Table 832. **Commercial Vegetable and Other Specified Crops—Area, Production, and Value, 2002 to 2004, and Leading Producing States, 2004**

[300 represents 300,000. Except as noted, relates to commercial production for fresh market and processing combined. Includes market garden areas but excludes minor producing acreage in minor producing states. Excludes production for home use in farm and nonfarm gardens. Value is for season or crop year and should not be confused with calendar-year income]

Crop	Area [1] (1,000 acres)			Production [2] (1,000 short tons)			Value [3] (mil. dol.)			Leading states in order of production, 2004
	2002	2003	2004	2002	2003	2004	2002	2003	2004	
Beans, snap	300	283	291	1,092	1,012	1,116	404	395	399	WI, OR, NY [4]
Beans, dry edible	1,739	1,347	1,219	1,516	1,125	890	519	423	445	OR, MI, NE
Broccoli	130	132	138	919	973	1,037	568	616	677	CA, AZ
Cabbage [5]	76	75	76	1,211	1,132	1,252	308	295	347	CA, NY, TX
Cantaloupes [5]	90	86	90	1,122	1,105	1,014	398	372	301	CA, AZ, TX
Carrots	102	102	100	1,695	1,805	1,766	521	552	577	CA, MI, CO [5]
Cauliflower	41	39	42	311	327	353	198	226	231	CA, AZ
Celery	27	28	27	937	963	940	240	259	284	CA, MI
Corn, sweet	663	673	652	4,392	4,691	4,424	718	780	833	(NA)
Fresh market	246	247	246	1,324	1,425	1,456	509	551	619	FL, CA, GA
Processed	417	427	406	3,068	3,266	2,968	209	230	214	MN, WA, WI
Cucumbers	173	174	170	1,166	1,120	1,070	377	366	370	FL, GA, MI [5]
Lettuce, head [5]	185	183	189	3,407	3,412	3,498	1,435	1,235	1,176	CA, AZ
Lettuce, leaf [5]	54	57	54	671	702	646	452	440	376	CA, AZ
Lettuce, Romaine [5]	58	77	81	928	1,127	1,342	467	622	514	CA, AZ
Mushrooms [6]	31	30	32	416	418	422	871	856	880	PA, CA
Onions	163	166	167	3,492	3,668	4,045	765	982	863	CA, WA, OR
Peppers, bell	54	54	55	783	806	840	464	495	576	CA, FL, NJ
Potatoes	1,266	1,249	1,168	22,909	22,891	22,818	3,045	2,686	2,564	ID, WA, WI
Spinach	43	51	53	337	399	452	171	220	260	CA, AZ [5]
Squash	52	51	53	440	384	388	203	197	223	CA, FL, GA
Sweet potatoes	82	93	93	640	795	820	215	305	287	NC, CA, MS
Tomatoes	441	416	427	13,650	11,599	14,072	1,933	1,909	2,062	(NA)
Fresh market	129	122	126	1,979	1,779	1,806	1,253	1,332	1,342	FL, CA, VA
Processed	312	294	301	11,671	9,820	12,266	680	576	719	CA, IN, OH
Watermelons	153	150	141	1,979	1,911	1,841	328	343	313	FL, CA, TX

NA Not available. [1] Area of crops for harvest for fresh market, including any partially harvested or not harvested because of low prices or other factors, plus area harvested for processing. [2] Excludes some quantities not marketed. [3] Fresh market vegetables valued at f.o.b. shipping point. Processing vegetables are equivalent returns at packinghouse door. [4] Processed only. [5] Fresh market only. [6] Area is shown in million square feet. All data are for marketing year ending June 30.

Source: U.S. Dept. of Agriculture, National Agricultural Statistics Service, *Vegetables, 2004 Summary*, January 2005. Also in *Agricultural Statistics*, annual.

Table 833. **Fruits and Nuts—Utilized Production and Value, 2002 to 2004, and Leading Producing States, 2004**

[4,187 represents 4,187,000]

Fruit or nut	Unit	Utilized production [1]			Farm value (mil. dol.)			Leading states in order of production, 2004
		2002	2003	2004	2002	2003	2004	
Apples [2]	1,000 tons	4,187	4,312	4,964	1,581	1,811	1,758	WA, NY, MI
Apricots	1,000 tons	80	98	92	29	35	35	CA, WA
Avocados	1,000 tons	199	234	(NA)	382	396	(NA)	(NA)
Blueberries	1,000 tons	126	134	137	212	248	295	MI, ME, NJ
Cherries, sweet	1,000 tons	177	244	278	274	342	436	WA, CA, OR
Cherries, tart	1,000 tons	31	113	107	28	81	71	MI, UT, WA
Cranberries	1,000 tons	284	310	318	183	209	222	WI, MA, OR
Grapefruit	1,000 tons	2,424	2,063	2,152	292	263	297	FL, TX, CA
Grapes (13 states)	1,000 tons	7,337	6,399	5,961	2,842	2,606	2,879	CA, WA, NY
Lemons	1,000 tons	801	1,026	798	328	291	270	CA, AZ
Nectarines (CA)	1,000 tons	300	273	252	115	119	86	CA
Olives (CA)	1,000 tons	103	118	104	59	48	61	CA
Oranges	1,000 tons	12,374	11,545	12,930	1,846	1,565	1,646	FL, CA
Peaches	1,000 tons	1,218	1,205	1,227	488	454	461	CA, SC, GA
Pears	1,000 tons	889	923	888	264	270	296	WA, CA, OR
Pineapples	1,000 tons	320	300	215	101	101	80	HI
Plums (CA)	1,000 tons	201	209	144	76	87	64	CA
Prunes (dried basis) (CA)	1,000 tons	163	168	48	132	130	72	CA
Raspberries	1,000 tons	57	68	68	85	172	196	CA, WA
Strawberries	1,000 tons	942	1,078	1,107	1,162	1,375	1,471	CA, FL
Tangerines	1,000 tons	420	382	435	125	117	125	FL, CA, AZ
Almonds (shelled basis) (CA)	Mil. lb	1,090	1,040	1,020	1,201	1,600	2,052	CA
Hazelnuts (in the shell)	1,000 tons	20	38	37	20	39	51	OR
Macadamia nuts	1,000 tons	27	27	26	30	32	33	HI
Pecans (in the shell) (11 states)	1,000 tons	87	141	91	165	278	301	GA, TX, NM
Pistachios	1,000 tons	152	60	174	333	145	438	CA
Walnuts, English (in the shell)	1,000 tons	282	326	325	330	375	(NA)	CA

NA Not available. [1] Excludes quantities not harvested or not marketed. [2] Production in commercial orchards with 100 or more bearing age trees.

Source: U.S. Dept. of Agriculture, National Agricultural Statistics Service, *Noncitrus Fruits and Nuts, 2004 Preliminary Summary*, January 2005; and *Citrus Fruits, 2004 Summary*, September 2004.

Agriculture 561

Table 834. **Meat Supply and Use: 1990 to 2004**

[**In millions of pounds** (carcass weight equivalent) (**62,255 represents 62,255,000,000**). Carcass weight equivalent is the weight of the animal minus entrails, head, hide, and internal organs; includes fat and bone. Covers federal and state inspected, and farm slaughter]

Year and type of meat	Production	Imports	Supply [1]	Consumption [2]	Exports	Ending stocks
RED MEAT AND POULTRY						
1990	62,255	3,295	66,673	62,937	2,472	1,263
1995	74,068	2,838	78,636	69,911	6,956	1,768
2000	82,372	4,137	88,481	77,069	9,344	2,069
2002	85,384	4,464	91,969	80,185	9,445	2,339
2003	85,187	4,375	91,902	80,134	9,743	2,025
2004	85,140	4,995	92,159	81,896	8,072	2,191
ALL RED MEATS						
1990	38,787	3,295	42,742	40,784	1,250	707
1995	43,675	2,832	47,511	43,967	2,614	929
2000	46,299	4,128	51,341	46,560	3,760	1,021
2002	47,305	4,448	52,913	47,610	4,065	1,238
2003	46,710	4,359	52,307	47,005	4,243	1,059
2004	45,555	4,961	51,575	47,739	2,649	1,187
Beef:						
1990	22,743	2,356	25,434	24,031	1,006	397
1995	25,222	2,104	27,874	25,534	1,821	519
2000	26,888	3,032	30,332	27,338	2,468	525
2002	27,192	3,218	31,016	27,878	2,447	691
2003	26,339	3,006	30,036	26,999	2,519	518
2004	24,650	3,680	28,848	27,750	461	637
Pork:						
1990	15,354	898	16,565	16,031	238	296
1995	17,849	664	18,952	17,768	787	396
2000	18,952	967	20,407	18,643	1,287	478
2002	19,685	1,070	21,291	19,147	1,611	533
2003	19,966	1,185	21,684	19,435	1,717	532
2004	20,529	1,100	22,161	19,439	2,179	543
Veal:						
1990	327	(NA)	331	325	(NA)	6
1995	319	(NA)	326	319	(NA)	7
2000	225	(NA)	230	225	(NA)	5
2002	205	(NA)	211	204	(NA)	7
2003	202	(NA)	209	204	(NA)	5
2004	176	(NA)	181	177	(NA)	4
Lamb and mutton:						
1990	363	41	412	397	6	8
1995	285	64	359	346	6	8
2000	234	130	372	354	5	13
2002	223	160	395	381	7	7
2003	203	168	378	367	7	4
2004	200	181	385	373	9	3
POULTRY, TOTAL						
1990	23,468	-	23,931	22,153	1,222	556
1995	30,393	6	31,125	25,944	4,342	839
2000	36,073	9	37,140	30,508	5,584	1,048
2002	38,079	16	39,056	32,575	5,380	1,101
2003	38,477	16	39,595	33,129	5,500	966
2004	39,585	34	40,584	34,157	5,423	1,004
Broilers:						
1990	18,430	-	18,651	17,266	1,143	242
1995	24,827	1	25,286	20,832	3,894	560
2000	30,209	6	31,011	25,295	4,918	798
2002	31,895	12	32,619	27,049	4,807	763
2003	32,399	12	33,173	27,645	4,920	608
2004	33,699	27	34,334	28,853	4,768	713
Mature chicken:						
1990	523	-	530	496	25	9
1995	496	3	513	406	99	7
2000	531	2	540	311	220	9
2002	547	3	557	418	134	5
2003	502	3	510	411	96	3
2004	504	2	509	293	213	3
Turkeys:						
1990	4,514	-	4,750	4,390	54	306
1995	5,069	2	5,326	4,706	348	271
2000	5,333	1	5,589	4,902	445	241
2002	5,638	1	5,879	5,108	439	333
2003	5,576	2	5,911	5,074	484	354
2004	5,383	5	5,742	5,011	443	288

- Represents zero.   NA Not available.   [1] Total supply equals production plus imports plus ending stocks of previous year.
[2] Includes shipments to territories.

Source: U.S. Department of Agriculture, Economic Research Service, *Food Consumption, Prices, and Expenditures, 1970–1997*; and "Agricultural Outlook: Statistical Indicators"; <http://www.ers.usda.gov/publications/agoutlook/aotables/>.

562 Agriculture

Table 835. Livestock Inventory and Production: 1990 to 2005

[95.8 represents 95,800,000. **Production in live weight**; includes animals-for-slaughter market, younger animals shipped to other states for feeding or breeding purposes, farm slaughter and custom slaughter consumed on farms where produced, minus livestock shipped into states for feeding or breeding with an adjustment for changes in inventory]

Type of livestock	Unit	1990	1995	1998	1999	2000	2001	2002	2003	2004	2005
ALL CATTLE [1]											
Inventory: [2] Number on farms	Mil.	95.8	102.8	99.7	99.1	98.2	97.3	96.7	96.1	94.9	95.8
Total value.	Bil. dol. . . .	59.0	63.2	60.2	58.8	67.1	70.5	72.3	69.9	77.6	87.8
Value per head.	Dol	616	615	603	594	683	725	747	728	818	916
Production: Quantity	Bil. lb	39.2	42.5	41.7	42.6	43.0	42.6	42.4	42.2	41.5	(NA)
Beef, price per 100 lb.	Dol. . . .	74.60	61.80	59.60	63.40	68.60	71.30	66.50	79.70	85.90	(NA)
Calves, price per 100 lb.	Dol.	95.60	73.10	78.80	87.70	104.00	106.00	96.40	102.00	119.00	(NA)
Value of production	Bil. dol. . . .	29.3	24.7	24.2	26.1	28.5	29.4	27.1	32.1	34.9	(NA)
HOGS AND PIGS											
Inventory: [3] Number on farms	Mil.	53.8	59.7	61.2	62.2	59.3	59.1	59.7	59.6	60.4	60.6
Total value.	Bil. dol. . . .	4.3	3.2	5.0	2.8	4.3	4.5	4.6	4.2	4.0	6.2
Value per head.	Dol.	79	53	82	44	72	77	77	71	67	102
Production: Quantity	Bil. lb. . . .	21.3	24.4	25.8	25.9	25.7	25.9	26.3	26.3	26.7	(NA)
Price per 100 lb.	Dol.	53.70	40.50	34.40	30.30	42.30	44.40	33.40	37.20	49.30	(NA)
Value of production	Bil. dol. . . .	11.3	9.8	8.7	7.8	10.8	11.4	8.7	9.7	13.1	(NA)
SHEEP AND LAMBS											
Inventory: [2] Number on farms	Mil.	11.4	9.0	7.8	7.2	7.0	6.9	6.6	6.3	6.1	6.1
Total value.	Mil. dol. . . .	901	663	798	641	670	690	614	657	724	799
Value per head.	Dol.	79	75	102	88	95	100	92	104	119	130
Production: Quantity	Mil. lb. . . .	781	602	554	537	512	501	485	470	465	(NA)
Sheep, price per 100 lb. . . .	Dol.	23.20	28.00	30.60	31.10	34.30	34.60	28.20	34.90	38.80	(NA)
Lambs, price per 100 lb.	Dol.	55.50	78.20	72.30	74.50	79.80	66.90	74.10	94.40	101.00	(NA)
Value of production	Mil. dol. . . .	374	414	355	352	365	303	314	392	412	(NA)

NA Not available.   [1] Includes milk cows.   [2] As of January 1.   [3] As of December 1 of preceding year.

Source: U.S. Dept. of Agriculture, National Agricultural Statistics Service, *Meat Animals—Production, Disposition, and Income Final Estimates 1998-2002*, May 2004; *Meat Animals Production, Disposition, and Income*, annual; and annual livestock summaries. Also in *Agricultural Statistics*, annual.

Table 836. Livestock Operations by Size of Herd: 2000 to 2004

[In thousands (1,076 represents 1,076,000). An operation is any place having one or more head on hand at any time during the year]

Size of herd	2000	2003	2004	Size of herd	2000	2003	2004
CATTLE [1]				**MILK COWS** [2]			
Total operations	1,076	1,014	989	Total operations	105	86	81
1 to 49 head.	671	633	619	1 to 49 head.	53	42	39
50 to 99 head.	186	170	164	50 to 99 head.	31	26	24
100 to 499 head	192	182	179	100 head or more	21	19	18
500 to 999 head	19	18	18				
1,000 head or more	10	10	10	**HOGS AND PIGS**			
				Total operations	87	65	61
BEEF COWS [2]				1 to 99 head.	50	44	42
Total operations	831	792	775	100 to 499 head	17	11	10
1 to 49 head.	655	620	602	500 to 999 head	8	3	4
50 to 99 head.	100	96	96	1,000 to 1,999 head.	6	3	3
100 to 499 head	71	70	72	2,000 to 4,999 head.	5	2	2
500 head or more	6	5	5	5,000 head or more	2	1	1

[1] Includes calves.   [2] Included in operations with cattle.

Source: U.S. Dept. of Agriculture, National Agricultural Statistics Service, *Livestock Operations Final Estimates 1998-2002*, April 2004; *Farms, Land in Farms, and Livestock Operations 2004 Summary*, January 2005; *Agricultural Statistics*, annual and unpublished data.

Table 837. Hogs and Pigs—Number, Production, and Value by State: 2002 to 2004

[59,554 represents 59,554,000. See headnote, Table 835]

State	Number on farms [1] (1,000)			Quantity produced (mil. lb.)			Value of production (mil. dol.)			Commercial slaughter [2] (mil. lb.)	
	2002	2003	2004	2002	2003	2004	2002	2003	2004	2003	2004
U.S. [3]	59,554	60,444	60,645	26,274	26,334	26,678	8,691	9,729	13,072	26,876	27,588
IA.	15,500	15,900	16,200	6,701	6,831	7,196	2,030	2,247	3,264	7,788	8,012
NC.	9,700	10,000	9,800	3,875	3,768	3,849	1,393	1,531	2,065	2,765	2,728
MN.	6,100	6,500	6,500	2,786	3,016	3,098	937	1,127	1,505	2,357	2,398
IL.	4,150	4,000	4,050	1,811	1,828	1,733	651	752	938	2,278	2,544
IN.	3,250	3,100	3,150	1,466	1,568	1,437	462	560	685	1,847	1,870
NE	3,000	2,900	2,850	1,508	1,427	1,374	560	583	717	1,824	1,846
OK	2,240	2,380	2,390	1,102	1,169	1,230	342	415	578	1,295	1,362

[1] As of December 1.   [2] Includes slaughter in federally-inspected and other slaughter plants; excludes animals slaughtered on farms.   [3] Includes other states not shown separately.

Source: U.S. Dept. of Agriculture, National Agricultural Statistics Service, *Meat Animals-Production, Disposition and Income*, annual; and *Livestock Slaughter*, annual.

Agriculture 563

Table 838. **Cattle and Calves—Number, Production, and Value by State: 2002 to 2005**

[96,100 represents 96,100,000. Includes milk cows. See headnote, Table 835]

State	Number on farms [1] (1,000)			Quantity produced (mil. lb.)			Value of production (mil. dol.)			Commercial slaughter [2] (mil. lb.)	
	2003	2004	2005	2002	2003	2004	2002	2003	2004	2003	2004
U.S. [3]	96,100	94,888	95,848	42,385	42,243	41,501	27,083	32,113	34,888	43,705	40,589
TX........	14,000	13,900	13,800	7,183	7,767	7,334	4,658	6,029	6,135	7,671	7,343
NE........	6,200	6,250	6,350	4,493	4,401	4,392	2,630	3,380	3,605	9,648	8,822
KS........	6,350	6,650	6,650	4,067	4,025	3,900	2,364	3,033	2,827	8,926	8,752
CA........	5,250	5,200	5,400	1,833	1,987	1,983	848	1,148	1,267	1,759	1,731
OK........	5,400	5,100	5,400	2,006	2,044	1,978	1,499	1,671	1,951	34	32
CO........	2,650	2,400	2,500	2,015	1,865	1,915	1,454	1,522	1,849	3,063	3,001
IA.........	3,550	3,450	3,600	1,815	1,797	1,611	1,138	1,420	1,329	1,002	(⁴)
SD........	3,700	3,650	3,750	1,557	1,482	1,546	1,142	1,220	1,451	(⁴)	(⁴)
MO........	4,500	4,350	4,450	1,186	1,155	1,195	909	991	1,212	120	(⁴)
MN........	2,450	2,400	2,400	1,150	1,096	1,067	683	789	810	1,082	973
ID.........	2,000	2,000	2,070	1,143	1,096	1,054	705	810	845	949	729

[1] As of January 1. [2] Data cover cattle only. Includes slaughter in federally-inspected and other slaughter plants; excludes animals slaughtered on farms. [3] Includes other states not shown separately. [4] Included in U.S. total. Not printed to avoid disclosing individual operation.

Source: U.S. Dept. of Agriculture, National Agricultural Statistics Service, *Meat Animals-Production, Disposition and Income,* annual; and *Livestock Slaughter,* annual.

Table 839. **Milk Cows—Number, Production, and Value by State: 2002 to 2004**

[9,139 represents 9,139,000]

State	Number on farms [1] (1,000)			Milk produced on farms (mil. lb.)			Value of production [2] (mil. dol.)		
	2002	2003	2004	2002	2003	2004	2002	2003	2004
United States [3] ...	9,139	9,083	9,010	170,063	170,394	170,805	20,720	21,381	27,549
California........	1,648	1,688	1,725	35,065	35,437	36,465	3,836	4,033	5,371
Wisconsin........	1,271	1,256	1,241	22,074	22,266	22,085	2,693	2,872	3,732
New York........	675	671	655	12,218	11,952	11,650	1,564	1,566	1,957
Pennsylvania	585	575	562	10,775	10,338	10,062	1,487	1,447	1,771
Idaho...........	388	404	424	8,155	8,774	9,093	922	1,009	1,364
Minnesota	487	473	463	8,458	8,258	8,102	1,023	1,057	1,353
New Mexico.......	301	317	326	6,316	6,666	6,710	752	800	1,013
Michigan........	301	302	303	6,120	6,375	6,315	741	803	1,029
Texas...........	317	319	319	5,300	5,630	6,009	684	732	979

[1] Average number during year. Represents cows and heifers that have calved, kept for milk; excluding heifers not yet fresh. [2] Valued at average returns per.100 pounds of milk in combined marketings of milk and cream. Includes value of milk fed to calves. [3] Includes other states not shown separately.

Source: U.S. Dept. of Agriculture, National Agricultural Statistics Service, *Dairy Products,* annual; and *Milk: Production, Disposition, and Income,* annual.

Table 840. **Milk Production and Manufactured Dairy Products: 1990 to 2004**

[193 represents 193,000]

Item	Unit	1990	1995	1998	1999	2000	2001	2002	2003	2004
Number of farms with milk cows	1,000	193	140	117	111	105	97	91	86	81
Cows and heifers that have calved, kept for milk.	Mil. head...	10.0	9.5	9.2	9.2	9.2	9.1	9.1	9.1	9.0
Milk produced on farms...............	Bil. lb.....	148	155	157	163	167	165	170	170	171
Production per cow...............	1,000 lb....	14.8	16.4	17.2	17.8	18.2	18.2	18.6	18.8	19.0
Milk marketed by producers [1]	Bil. lb.....	146	154	156	161	166	164	169	169	170
Value of milk produced	Bil. dol.....	20.4	20.1	24.3	23.4	20.8	24.9	20.7	21.4	27.5
Cash receipts from marketing of milk and cream [1]	Bil. dol.....	20.1	19.9	24.1	23.2	20.6	24.7	20.6	21.2	27.4
Number of dairy manufacturing plants	Number....	1,723	1,495	1,323	1,192	1,164	1,179	1,149	1,119	1,096
Manufactured dairy products:										
Butter (incl. whey butter)............	Mil. lb....	1,302	1,264	1,168	1,277	1,256	1,232	1,355	1,242	1,250
Cheese, total [2]	Mil. lb....	6,059	6,917	7,492	7,941	8,258	8,261	8,547	8,557	8,876
American (excl. full-skim American)...	Mil. lb....	2,894	3,131	3,315	3,568	3,642	3,544	3,591	3,622	3,739
Cream and Neufchatel	Mil. lb....	431	544	621	639	687	645	686	677	699
All Italian varieties	Mil. lb....	2,207	2,674	3,005	3,152	3,289	3,426	3,470	3,622	3,660
Cottage cheese: Creamed [3]	Mil. lb....	832	711	728	720	735	742	748	769	768
Curd, pot, and bakers............	Mil. lb....	493	469	466	465	461	453	437	448	458
Condensed bulk milk	Mil. lb....	1,426	1,372	1,263	1,365	1,202	1,110	1,191	1,047	1,021
Nonfat dry milk [4]	Mil. lb....	902	1,243	1,140	1,364	1,457	1,419	1,596	1,589	1,406
Dry whey [5]	Mil. lb....	1,143	1,147	1,178	1,147	1,188	1,046	1,115	1,085	1,035
Yogurt, plain and fruit-flavored	Mil. lb....	(NA)	1,646	1,639	1,717	1,837	2,003	2,311	2,506	2,709
Ice cream, regular	Mil. gal...	824	862	935	972	980	970	1,005	999	944
Ice cream, lowfat [6]	Mil. gal...	352	357	407	381	373	380	339	398	415

NA Not available. [1] Comprises sales to plants and dealers, and retail sales by farmers direct to consumers. [2] Includes varieties not shown separately. [3] Includes partially creamed (low fat). [4] Includes dry skim milk for animal feed. [5] Includes animal, but excludes modified whey production. [6] Includes freezer-made milkshake in most states.

Source: U.S. Dept. of Agriculture, National Agricultural Statistics Service, *Dairy Products,* annual; and *Milk: Production, Disposition, and Income,* annual.

Table 841. **Milk Production and Commercial Use: 1990 to 2004**

[In billions of pounds milkfat basis (147.7 represents 147,700,000,000) except as noted.]

Year	Pro- duction	Farm use	Commercial Farm marketings	Beginning stock	Imports	Commer- cial supply, total	CCC net removals [1]	Commercial Ending stock	Disappear- ance	Milk price per 100 lb. [2] (dol.)
1990	147.7	2.0	145.7	4.1	2.7	152.5	8.5	5.1	138.8	13.68
1995	155.3	1.6	153.7	4.3	2.9	160.9	2.1	4.1	154.7	12.78
1999	162.6	1.3	161.3	5.3	4.8	171.3	0.3	6.1	164.8	14.38
2000	167.4	1.3	166.1	6.1	4.4	176.7	0.8	6.8	169.0	12.40
2001	165.3	1.2	164.1	6.8	5.7	176.7	0.1	7.0	169.5	15.04
2002	170.1	1.1	168.9	7.0	5.1	181.1	0.3	9.9	170.9	12.19
2003	170.4	1.1	169.3	9.9	5.0	184.2	1.2	8.3	174.7	12.55
2004	170.8	1.1	169.8	8.3	5.2	183.3	-0.1	7.2	176.2	16.03

[1] Removals from commercial supply by Commodity Credit Corporation (CCC). [2] Wholesale price received by farmers for all milk delivered to plants and dealers.

Source: U.S. Dept. of Agriculture, Economic Research Service, "Agricultural Outlook: Statistical Indicators"; <http://www.ers.usda.gov/publications/agoutlook/aotables/>.

Table 842. **Broiler, Turkey, and Egg Production: 1990 to 2004**

[For year ending November 30 (353 represents 353,000,000)]

Item	Unit	1990	1995	1997	1998	1999	2000	2001	2002	2003	2004
Chickens: [1]											
Number [2]	Million	353	388	410	425	437	437	444	444	450	454
Value per head [2]	Dollars	2.29	2.41	2.72	2.69	2.64	2.44	2.41	2.38	2.48	2.47
Value, total [2]	Mil. dol. . . .	808	935	1,113	1,143	1,156	1,064	1,069	1,055	1,116	1,121
Number sold	Million	208	180	191	200	214	218	202	200	190	192
Price per lb.	Cents	9.6	6.5	7.7	8.1	7.1	5.7	4.5	4.8	4.9	5.8
Value of sales	Mil. dol. . . .	94	60	71	80	75	64	47	50	48	58
PRODUCTION											
Broilers: [3]											
Number.	Million	5,864	7,326	7,764	7,934	8,146	8,284	8,390	8,591	8,493	8,741
Weight	Bil. lb.	25.6	34.2	37.5	38.6	40.8	41.6	42.5	44.1	44.0	45.8
Price per lb	Cents	32.6	34.4	37.7	39.3	37.1	33.6	39.3	30.5	34.6	44.6
Production value. . . .	Mil. dol. . . .	8,366	11,762	14,159	15,147	15,129	13,989	16,696	13,437	15,215	20,446
Turkeys:											
Number.	Million	282	292	301	286	270	270	273	275	274	264
Weight	Bil. lb.	6.0	6.8	7.2	7.1	6.9	7.0	7.2	7.5	7.5	7.3
Price per lb	Cents	39.6	41.0	39.9	38.0	40.8	40.6	39.0	36.5	36.1	42.0
Production value. . . .	Mil. dol. . . .	2,393	2,769	2,884	2,683	2,807	2,828	2,797	2,732	2,700	3,065
Eggs:											
Number.	Billion	68.1	74.8	77.5	79.8	82.9	84.7	86.1	87.3	87.5	89.1
Price per dozen	Cents	70.8	62.5	70.3	66.8	62.0	61.6	62.0	58.9	73.2	71.4
Production value. . . .	Mil. dol. . . .	4,021	3,893	4,540	4,439	4,287	4,346	4,446	4,281	5,333	5,303

[1] Excludes commercial broilers. [2] As of December 1. [3] Young chickens of the heavy breeds and other meat-type birds, to be marketed at 2-5 lbs. live weight and from which no pullets are kept for egg production.

Source: U.S. Dept. of Agriculture, National Agricultural Statistics Service, *Poultry Production and Value Final Estimates 1998–2002*, April 2004; *Turkeys Final Estimates 1998–2002*, April 2004; *Chickens and Eggs Final Estimates 1998–2002*, April 2004; *Poultry—Production and Value*, annual; *Turkeys*, annual; and *Chickens and Eggs*, annual.

Table 843. **Broiler and Turkey Production by State: 2002 to 2004**

[In millions of pounds, liveweight production (44,059 represents 44,059,000,000)]

State	Broilers 2002	2003	2004	Turkeys 2002	2003	2004	State	Broilers 2002	2003	2004	Turkeys 2002	2003	2004
U.S. [1] . . .	44,059	43,958	45,796	7,495	7,487	7,305	MS	4,078	4,189	4,387	(NA)	(NA)	(NA)
AL	5,362	5,405	5,470	(NA)	(NA)	(NA)	MO	(NA)	(NA)	(NA)	783	724	667
AR	5,813	5,843	6,208	522	540	527	NC	4,411	4,320	4,537	1,160	1,105	1,069
CA	(NA)	(NA)	(NA)	439	419	414	ND	(NA)	(NA)	(NA)	50	35	26
DE	1,544	1,507	1,492	(Z)	(NA)	(NA)	OH	215	226	225	219	212	220
FL.	631	511	463	(NA)	(NA)	(NA)	OK	1,141	1,115	1,243	(NA)	(NA)	(NA)
GA.	6,453	6,303	6,495	(NA)	(NA)	(NA)	PA	706	687	708	234	216	234
IL	(NA)	(NA)	(NA)	90	90	89	SC	1,080	1,145	1,186	369	456	463
IN	(NA)	(NA)	(NA)	403	397	410	SD	(NA)	(NA)	(NA)	159	153	151
IA	(NA)	(NA)	(NA)	261	268	324	TN	895	948	999	(NA)	(NA)	(NA)
KY	1,404	1,490	1,570	(NA)	(NA)	(NA)	TX	2,882	2,947	3,166	(NA)	(NA)	(NA)
MD	1,377	1,374	1,366	16	15	13	VA	1,301	1,299	1,341	446	492	435
MI.	(NA)	(NA)	(NA)	180	191	188	WV	359	358	354	89	92	71
MN	230	229	232	1,148	1,215	1,228	WI	145	155	152	(NA)	(NA)	(NA)

NA Not available. Z Less than 500,000 pounds. [1] Includes other states not shown separately.

Source: U.S. Dept. of Agriculture, National Agricultural Statistics Service, *Poultry—Production and Value*, annual.

No. 161.—QUANTITY of COAL PRODUCED in each STATE and TERRITORY of the UNITED STATES, during the Calendar Years 1869, 1876, 1877, 1878, 1879, and 1880.

[Weight expressed in tons of 2,240 pounds.]

STATE OR TER- RITORY.	1869. a	1876.	1877.	1878.	1879.	1880.
ANTHRACITE.	Tons.	Tons.	Tons.	Tons.	Tons.	Tons.
Pennsylvania	13,866,180	b21,436,667	b23,619,911	b20,605,262	b26,142,689	b26,437,242
BITUMINOUS.						
Pennsylvania	7,798,517	11,500,000	12,500,000	13,500,000	14,500,000	19,000,000
Illinois	2,629,563	3,500,000	3,500,000	3,500,000	3,500,000	4,000,000
Ohio	2,527,285	3,500,000	5,250,000	5,000,000	5,000,000	7,000,000
Maryland	1,819,824	1,835,081	1,574,339	1,679,322	1,730,709	2,136,160
Missouri	621,930	900,000	900,000	900,000	900,000	1,500,000
West Virginia	608,878	800,000	1,000,000	1,000,000	1,250,000	1,400,000
Indiana	437,870	950,000	1,000,000	1,000,000	1,000,000	1,196,490
Iowa	263,487	1,500,000	1,500,000	1,500,000	1,600,000	1,600,000
Kentucky	150,582	650,000	850,000	900,000	1,000,000	1,000,000
Tennessee	133,418	550,000	750,000	375,000	450,000	641,042
Virginia	61,803	90,000	90,000	75,000	90,000	100,000
Kansas	32,938	125,000	200,000	300,000	400,000	550,000
Oregon		200,000	200,000	200,000	200,000	200,000
Michigan	21,150	30,000	30,000	30,000	35,000	35,000
California		600,000	600,000	600,000	600,000	600,000
Rhode Island	14,000	14,000	14,000	14,000	15,000	15,000
Alabama	11,000	100,000	175,000	200,000	250,000	340,000
Nebraska	1,425	30,000	50,000	75,000	75,000	100,000
Wyoming	50,000	500,000	100,000	100,000	175,000	225,000
Washington	17,844	100,000	150,000	150,000	170,000	175,000
Utah	5,800	45,000	45,000	60,000	225,000	275,000
Colorado	4,500	250,000	300,000	367,000	400,000	575,000
Georgia					100,000	100,000
Totals	31,077,994	49,005,748	54,308,250	52,130,584	62,808,398	69,200,934

a The statistics for 1869 are derived from the United States Census. The statistics for 1876, 1877, 1878, 1879, and 1880 are compiled from data collected and estimates made by Mr. Frederick E. Saward, editor of the Coal Trade Journal of New York.

b Includes 3,000,000 tons estimated as the local consumption.

Source: Statistical Abstract of the United States: 1880 Edition.

Section 18

Natural Resources

This section presents data on the area, ownership, production, trade, reserves, and disposition of natural resources. Natural resources is defined here as including forestry, fisheries, and mining and mineral products.

Forestry—Presents data on the area, ownership, and timber resource of commercial timberland; forestry statistics covering the National Forests and Forest Service cooperative programs; product data for lumber, pulpwood, woodpulp, paper and paperboard, and similar data.

The principal sources of data relating to forests and forest products are *Forest Resources of the United States, 1991; Timber Demand and Technology Assessment, 2003; U.S. Timber Production, Trade, Consumption, and Price Statistics; Land Areas of the National Forest System,* issued annually by the Forest Service of the Department of Agriculture; *Agricultural Statistics* issued by the Department of Agriculture; and reports of the annual survey of manufactures, and the annual *Current Industrial Reports,* issued by the Census Bureau on the Internet and in print in the annual *Manufacturing Profiles.* Additional information is published in the monthly *Survey of Current Business* of the Bureau of Economic Analysis, and the annual *Wood Pulp* and *Fiber Statistics* and *The Statistics of Paper, Paperboard, and Wood Pulp* of the American Forest and Paper Association, Washington, DC.

The completeness and reliability of statistics on forests and forest products vary considerably. The data for forest land area and stand volumes are much more reliable for areas that have been recently surveyed than for those for which only estimates are available. In general, more data are available for lumber and other manufactured products such as particle board and softwood panels, etc., than for the primary forest products such as poles and piling and fuelwood.

Fisheries—The principal source of data relating to fisheries is *Fisheries of the United States,* issued annually by the National Marine Fisheries Service (NMFS), National Oceanic and Atmospheric Administration (NOAA). The NMFS collects and disseminates data on commercial landings of fish and shellfish. Annual reports include quantity and value of commercial landings of fish and shellfish disposition of landings and number and kinds of fishing vessels and fishing gear. Reports for the fish-processing industry include annual output for the wholesaling and fish processing establishments, annual and seasonal employment. The principal source for these data is the annual *Fisheries of the United States.*

Mining and mineral products—Presents data relating to mineral industries and their products, general summary measures of production and employment, and more detailed data on production, prices, imports and exports, consumption, and distribution for specific industries and products. Data on mining and mineral products may also be found in Sections 19, 21, and 28 of this *Abstract;* data on mining employment may be found in Section 12.

Mining comprises the extraction of minerals occurring naturally (coal, ores, crude petroleum, natural gas) and quarrying, well operation, milling, refining and processing, and other preparation customarily done at the mine or well site or as a part of extraction activity. (Mineral preparation plants are usually operated together with mines or quarries.) Exploration for minerals is included as is the development of mineral properties.

The principal governmental sources of these data are the *Minerals Yearbook* and *Mineral Commodity Summaries,* published by the U.S. Geological Survey, Department of the Interior, and various monthly and annual publications of the Energy Information Administration, Department of

U.S. Census Bureau, Statistical Abstract of the United States: 2006

Energy. See text, Section 19, for a list of Department of Energy publications. In addition, the Census Bureau conducts a census of mineral industries every 5 years.

Nongovernment sources include the *Annual Statistical Report* of the American Iron and Steel Institute, Washington, DC; *Metals Week* and the monthly *Engineering and Mining Journal,* issued by the McGraw-Hill Publishing Co., New York, NY; *The Iron Age,* issued weekly by the Chilton Co., Philadelphia, PA; and the *Joint Association Survey of the U.S. Oil and Gas Industry,* conducted jointly by the American Petroleum Institute, Independent Petroleum Association of America, and Mid-Continent Oil and Gas Association.

Mineral statistics, with principal emphasis on commodity detail, have been collected by the U.S. Geological Survey and the former Bureau of Mines since 1880. Current data in U.S. Geological Survey publications include quantity and value of nonfuel minerals produced, sold or used by producers, or shipped; quantity of minerals stocked; crude materials treated and prepared minerals recovered; and consumption of mineral raw materials.

Censuses of mineral industries have been conducted by the Census Bureau at various intervals since 1840. Beginning with the 1967 census, legislation provides for a census to be conducted every 5 years for years ending in "2" and "7." The most recent results, published for 2002, are based on the North American Industry Classification System (NAICS). The censuses provide, for the various types of mineral establishments, information on operating costs, capital expenditures, labor, equipment, and energy requirements in relation to their value of shipments and other receipts. Commodity statistics on many manufactured mineral products are also collected by the Census Bureau at monthly, quarterly, or annual intervals and issued in its *Current Industrial Reports* series.

In general, figures shown in the individual commodity tables include data for outlying areas and may therefore not agree with summary tables. Except for crude petroleum and refined products, the export and import figures include foreign trade passing through the customs districts of United States and Puerto Rico but exclude shipments between U.S. territories and the customs districts.

Table 844. **Gross Domestic Product of Natural Resource-Related Industries in Current and Real (2000) Dollars by Industry: 2000 to 2003**

[In billions of dollars (9,817.0 represents $9,817,000,000,000). Data are based on the 1997 NAICS Codes. Data include nonfactor charges (capital consumption allowances, indirect business taxes, etc.) as well as factor charges against gross product; corporate profits and capital consumption allowances have been shifted from a company to an establishment basis]

Industry	Current dollars				Chained (2000) dollars			
	2000	2002	2003	2004	2000	2002	2003	2004
All industries, total [1]	9,817.0	10,487.0	11,004.0	11,735.0	9,817.0	10,074.8	10,381.4	10,841.9
Industries covered	306.3	282.6	327.7	(NA)	306.3	291.7	291.6	(NA)
Percent of all industries	3.1	2.7	3.0	(NA)	3.1	2.9	2.8	(NA)
Agriculture, forestry, and fishing	98.0	96.9	113.9	116.6	98.0	98.1	103.5	96.9
Farms	71.5	70.8	84.8	(NA)	71.5	69.9	72.7	(NA)
Agricultural services	26.5	26.1	29.1	(NA)	26.5	28.3	31.1	(NA)
Mining	121.3	104.9	130.3	147.5	121.3	112.4	104.6	106.9
Metal mining	81.0	60.4	83.2	(NA)	81.0	77.6	65.3	(NA)
Coal mining	27.0	27.4	27.7	(NA)	27.0	24.7	25.1	(NA)
Oil and gas extraction	13.4	17.1	19.4	(NA)	13.4	10.9	12.7	(NA)
Nonmetallic minerals	45.7	43.3	43.3	(NA)	45.7	42.8	43.4	(NA)
Timber-related manufacturing	87.0	80.8	83.5	(NA)	87.0	81.2	83.5	(NA)
Wood products	31.4	30.0	32.0	(NA)	31.4	29.9	29.9	(NA)
Paper products	55.6	50.8	51.5	(NA)	55.6	51.3	53.6	(NA)

Source: U.S. Bureau of Economic Analysis, *Survey of Current Business,* May 2005. See also <http://www.bea.doc.gov/bea/newsrelarchive/2005/gdpind04.pdf> (released 20 April 2005).

Table 845. Natural Resource-Related Industries—Establishments, Employees, and Annual Payroll, by Industry: 2000 and 2002

[1,791.3 represents 1,791,300. Excludes government employees, railroad employees, self-employed persons, etc. See "General Explanation" in source for definitions and statement on reliability of data. An establishment is a single physical location where business is conducted or where services or industrial operations are performed]

Industry	NAICS code [1]	2000			2002		
		Estab- lish- ments	Number of employ- ees [2] (1,000)	Annual payroll (bil. dol.)	Estab- lish- ments	Number of employ- ees [2] (1,000)	Annual payroll (bil. dol.)
Natural resource-related industries, total	(X)	72,932	1,791.3	66.58	73,021	1,676.9	66.68
Forestry, fishing, hunting and agriculture support	11	26,076	183.6	4.68	26,552	181.2	4.98
Forestry and logging	113	13,347	83.1	2.26	12,509	75.8	2.21
Timber tract operations	1131	469	3.3	0.13	680	4.2	0.16
Forest nurseries & gathering forest products	1132	258	1.7	0.07	352	2.7	0.08
Logging	1133	12,620	78.1	2.06	11,477	69.0	1.97
Fishing, hunting & trapping	114	2,671	10.0	0.34	2,385	9.2	0.34
Fishing	1141	2,308	7.5	0.27	1,916	6.5	0.25
Hunting & trapping	1142	363	2.5	0.08	469	2.7	0.08
Agriculture & forestry support activities . .	115	10,058	90.4	2.08	11,658	96.1	2.44
Crop production support activities	1151	5,061	57.6	1.35	5,324	58.5	1.51
Animal production support activities . .	1152	3,450	18.2	0.38	4,537	22.9	0.50
Forestry support activities	1153	1,547	14.7	0.35	1,797	14.7	0.42
Mining	21	23,738	456.1	22.09	23,871	465.8	23.96
Oil & gas extraction	211	7,740	83.0	5.39	7,629	88.3	6.41
Mining (except oil & gas)	212	7,231	204.3	9.34	7,205	194.2	9.12
Coal mining	2121	1,253	70.7	3.54	1,194	74.9	3.81
Metal ore mining	2122	522	34.8	1.72	351	25.7	1.37
Nonmetallic mineral mining & quarrying	2123	5,456	98.8	4.08	5,660	93.6	3.94
Mining support activities	213	8,767	168.8	7.35	9,037	183.3	8.43
Timber-related manufacturing	(X)	23,118	1,151.6	39.80	22,598	1,030.0	37.74
Wood product manufacturing	321	17,328	597.7	16.51	17,052	534.0	15.92
Sawmills & wood preservation	3211	4,695	131.4	3.78	4,368	116.0	3.55
Veneer, plywood & engineered wood product mfg.	3212	1,904	120.6	3.75	1,844	111.0	3.67
Other wood product mfg	3219	10,729	345.8	8.95	10,840	307.0	8.70
Paper manufacturing	322	5,790	553.9	23.29	5,546	496.0	21.81
Pulp, paper & paperboard mills	3221	597	177.1	9.48	628	163.0	9.11
Converted paper product manufacturing	3222	5,193	376.8	13.82	4,918	333.0	12.71

X Not applicable.   [1] North American Industry Classification System, 1997.   [2] Covers full- and part-time employees who are on the payroll in the pay period including March 12.

Source: U.S. Census Bureau, "County Business Patterns"; published November 2004; <http://www.census.gov/epcd/cbp/view/cbpview.html>.

Table 846. Oil and Gas Extraction Industry—Establishments, Employees and Payroll by State: 2002

[5,036,621 represents $5,036,621,000. Covers establishments with payroll. Employees are for the week including March 12. Data based on the 2002 Economic Census. Offshore areas refer to those areas not associated with a state. For statement on methodology, see Appendix III]

State	Crude petroleum and natural gas extraction (211111)[1]			State	Natural gas liquid extraction (211112) [1]		
	Establish- ments	Paid employees	Annual payroll ($1,000)		Establish- ments	Paid employees	Annual payroll ($1,000)
United States . . .	7,178	94,886	5,036,621	United States . . .	511	9,693	528,190
Alabama	37	1,042	64,411	Alabama	10	204	11,004
California	215	3,666	224,144	California	18	708	38,567
Colorado	344	4,057	254,900	Colorado	21	401	22,276
Illinois	175	899	32,210	Illinois	9	281	15,946
Kansas	375	2,325	104,281	Kansas	10	126	6,526
Louisiana	425	11,270	634,319	Louisiana	76	1,341	72,969
Michigan	88	926	41,363	Michigan	11	156	7,920
New Mexico	167	2,097	118,118	New Mexico	39	840	47,263
Oklahoma	1,039	9,382	438,850	Oklahoma	35	581	30,090
Pennsylvania	145	1,629	81,514	Texas	180	3,631	200,008
Texas	2,794	40,408	2,172,312	Wyoming	35	583	35,671
Utah	55	1,860	56,946				
West Virginia	210	1,720	71,397				
Wyoming	180	2,553	127,296				
Offshore Areas	5	501	36,626				
Alabama	10	204	11,004				
California	18	708	38,567				

[1] Based on North American Industry Classification System, 2002;

Source: U.S. Census Bureau, 2002 Economic Census, issued October 2004. See also <http://www.census.gov/econ/census02>.

Natural Resources 569

Table 847. Natural Resource-Related Industries—Establishments, Sales, Payroll and Employees by Industry: 1997 and 2002

[174 represents $174,000,000,000. Includes only establishments of firms with payroll. See Appendix III]

Industry	NAICS code [1]	1997				2002			
		Estab-lish-ments	Sales, receipts, revenue, or ship-ments (bil. dol.)	Annual payroll (bil. dol.)	Paid employ-ees (1,000)	Estab-lish-ments	Sales, receipts, revenue, or ship-ments (bil. dol.)	Annual payroll (bil. dol.)	Paid employ-ees (1,000)
Mining	21	25,000	174	21	509	23,932	184	21	485
Oil & gas extraction	211	8,312	103	6	111	7,689	115	6	105
Mining (except oil & gas)	212	7,348	51	9	229	7,220	48	9	197
Mining support activities	213	9,340	20	6	169	9,023	21	7	183
Manufacturing [2]	31-33	362,829	3,835	570	16,805	350,054	3,906	574	14,693
Wood product mfg	321	17,367	88	14	570	17,178	88	16	540
Paper mfg	322	5,868	150	22	574	5,501	153	21	488
Petroleum & coal products manufacturing	324	2,146	177	6	108	2,240	216	6	103

[1] North American Industry Classification System, 1997.　[2] Includes other industries not shown separately.
Source: U.S. Census Bureau, 2002 Economic Census, Comparative Statistics for the United States 1997 NAICS Basis. See also <http://www.census.gov/econ/census02>.

Table 848. Timber-Based Manufacturing Industries—Establishments, Shipments, Payroll and Employees: 2002

[3,906,024,316 represents $3,906,024,316,000. Data based on the 2002 Economic Census. See Appendix III]

Industry	NAICS code [1]	Estab-lish-ments	Value of shipments ($1,000)	Annual payroll ($1,000)	Paid employees (1,000)
Manufacturing	31-33	350,054	3,906,024,316	573,802,788	14,692,765
Wood product manufacturing	321	17,178	88,294,243	15,909,908	539,784
Sawmills and wood preservation	3211	4,322	25,761,530	3,490,857	107,728
Saw mills	321113	3,807	21,339,251	3,118,252	95,452
Wood preservation	321114	515	4,422,279	372,605	12,276
Veneer, plywood, & engineered wood product mfg.	3212	1,916	20,093,795	3,659,563	113,589
Other wood product manufacturing	3219	10,940	42,438,918	8,759,488	318,467
Millwork	32191	4,717	22,353,587	4,386,903	150,073
Wood container and pallet manufacturing	32192	2,946	5,075,309	1,152,608	50,896
All other wood product manufacturing	32199	3,277	15,010,022	3,219,977	117,498
Paper manufacturing	322	5,501	152,651,488	21,336,257	487,906
Pulp, paper, and paperboard mills	3221	560	70,483,801	8,879,983	158,857
Pulp mills	32211	32	3,531,242	469,688	7,730
Paper mills	32212	329	46,098,951	5,849,652	104,938
Paperboard mills	32213	199	20,853,608	2,560,643	46,189
Converted paper product manufacturing	3222	4,941	82,167,687	12,456,274	329,049
Paperboard container manufacturing	32221	2,664	43,271,298	7,033,538	184,008
Paper bag and coated and treated paper mfg.	32222	924	17,658,326	2,551,871	64,520
Stationery product manufacturing	32223	636	7,903,016	1,302,387	38,647
Other converted paper product manufacturing	32229	717	13,335,047	1,568,478	41,874
Printing and related support activities	323	37,532	95,653,027	25,738,613	718,542
Petroleum and coal products manufacturing	324	2,240	216,019,846	6,202,508	102,976

[1] North American Industry Classification System, 1997.
Source: U.S. Census Bureau, 2002 Economic Census, Comparative Statistics for the United States 1997 NAICS Basis. See also <http://www.census.gov/econ/census02>.

Table 849. National Forest System Land—State and Other Areas: 2004

[In thousands of acres (232,489 represents 232,489,000). As of September 30]

State and other area	Gross area within unit boundaries [1]	National Forest System Land [2]	State and other area	Gross area within unit boundaries [1]	National Forest System Land [2]	State and other area	Gross area within unit boundaries [1]	National Forest System Land [2]
Total	232,489	192,858	KS	116	108	OH	834	237
U.S.	232,433	192,830	KY	2,208	811	OK	579	400
			LA	1,025	604	OR	17,502	15,667
AL	1,288	667	ME	93	53	PA	743	513
AK	24,359	21,974	MD	-	-	RI	-	-
AZ	11,891	11,263	MA	-	-	SC	1,379	624
AR	3,522	2,593	MI	4,894	2,868	SD	2,369	2,014
CA	24,430	20,770	MN	5,467	2,840	TN	1,276	701
CO	16,019	14,499	MS	2,317	1,171	TX	1,994	755
CT	-	-	MO	3,060	1,489	UT	9,209	8,194
DE	-	-	MT	19,117	16,924	VT	817	394
DC	-	-	NE	442	352	VA	3,223	1,664
FL	1,434	1,157	NV	6,275	5,836	WA	10,112	9,276
GA	1,857	865	NH	828	732	WV	1,877	1,041
HI	-	-	NJ	-	-	WI	2,023	1,527
ID	21,904	20,716	NM	10,455	9,419	WY	9,703	9,238
IL	857	293	NY	16	16			
IN	644	201	NC	3,165	1,255	PR	56	28
IA	-	-	ND	1,106	1,106	VI	-	-

- Represents zero or rounds to zero.　[1] Comprises all publicly- and privately-owned land within authorized boundaries of national forests, purchase units, national grasslands, land utilization projects, research and experimental areas, and other areas. [2] Federally-owned land within the "gross area within unit boundaries."
Source: U.S. Forest Service, Land Areas of the National Forest System, annual.

570　Natural Resources

Table 850. Timber-Based Manufacturing Industries—Employees, Payroll, and Shipments: 2003

[13,876 represents 13,876,000. Based on the Annual Survey of Manufactures; for description, see Appendix III]

Selected industries	1997 NAICS code [1]	All employees			Production workers, total (1,000)	Value added by manufactures		Value of shipments (mil. dol.)
		Number (1,000)	Payroll			Total (mil. dol.)	Per production worker (dol.)	
			Total (mil. dol.)	Per employee (dol.)				
Manufacturing, all industries [2] ..	31-33	13,876	565,026	40,721	9,795	1,912,124	195,224	3,979,917
Wood product manufacturing	321	511	15,631	30,564	420	36,571	87,148	91,240
Sawmills & wood preservation.	3211	104	3,453	33,295	89	8,404	94,516	26,680
Veneer, plywood, & engineered wood product	3212	110	3,639	33,004	89	8,872	99,177	21,571
Other wood product.	3219	297	8,539	28,707	241	19,295	79,973	42,990
Millwork.	32191	148	4,371	29,599	121	10,117	83,720	23,677
Wood container & pallet	32192	47	1,116	23,996	39	2,352	60,562	4,933
All other wood product	32199	103	3,051	29,554	82	6,826	83,664	14,379
Paper.	322	464	20,773	44,737	361	72,084	199,920	149,270
Pulp, paper, & paperboard mills. . . .	3221	145	8,261	57,048	115	35,000	303,438	66,651
Pulp mills.	32211	8	491	60,916	6	1,723	273,276	3,891
Paper mills.	32212	92	5,230	56,829	74	23,048	313,286	42,169
Paperboard mills	32213	45	2,540	56,801	35	10,229	288,372	20,591
Converted paper product	3222	320	12,512	39,158	245	37,084	151,227	82,620
Paperboard container.	32221	176	6,948	39,379	135	17,407	128,894	43,108
Paper bag & coated & treated paper.	32222	64	2,627	40,942	48	8,608	180,218	18,197
Stationery product	32223	39	1,345	34,448	31	3,398	109,958	7,706
Other converted paper product. . .	32229	40	1,592	39,920	32	7,670	243,500	13,609

[1] North American Industry Classification System, 1997; see text, Section 15.　[2] Includes other industries not shown separately.

Source: U.S. Census Bureau, *Annual Survey of Manufactures, 2003*, Series M03(AS)-1 (RV). See also <http://www.census.gov/prod/ec02/am0331gs1.pdf> (issued April 2005).

Table 851. Timber Products—Production, Foreign Trade, and Consumption by Type of Product: 1990 to 2004

[In millions of cubic feet, roundwood equivalent (15,577 represents 15,577,000,000)]

Type of product	1990	1995	1996	1997	1998	1999	2000	2001	2002	2003	2004
Industrial roundwood:											
Domestic production.	15,577	15,537	15,413	15,703	15,620	15,632	15,436	14,634	14,902	14,819	15,301
Softwoods.	10,968	10,191	10,153	10,180	10,097	10,381	10,201	9,859	10,124	10,001	10,251
Hardwoods	4,609	5,347	5,260	5,523	5,523	5,251	5,235	4,775	4,778	4,817	5,050
Imports	3,091	3,907	3,885	4,008	4,157	4,370	4,529	4,605	4,505	4,954	5,575
Exports	2,307	2,282	2,264	2,290	1,951	1,964	1,996	1,759	1,769	1,698	2,139
Consumption.	16,361	17,161	17.034	17,421	17,827	18,038	17,969	17,481	17,637	18,075	18,737
Softwoods.	11,779	11,961	11,996	12,072	12,339	12,754	12,659	12,552	12,790	12,944	13,303
Hardwoods	4,582	5,200	5,038	5,349	5,488	5,284	5,310	4,929	4,847	5,131	5,434
Lumber:											
Domestic production	7,317	6,815	6,886	7,103	7,093	7,379	7,199	6,820	7,060	7,240	7,347
Imports.	1,909	2,522	2,616	2,619	2,721	2,807	2,845	2,903	3,036	3,193	3,697
Exports.	589	460	449	452	350	404	428	354	353	360	644
Consumption	8,637	8,877	9,053	9,270	9,463	9,782	9,616	9,369	9,744	10,073	10,400
Plywood and veneer:											
Domestic production	1,423	1,303	1,281	1,213	1,201	1,208	1,187	1,067	1,074	1,044	930
Imports.	97	107	97	114	131	160	155	173	205	240	244
Exports.	109	89	87	103	55	45	42	32	31	35	20
Consumption	1,410	1,321	1,291	1,224	1,277	1,323	1,300	1,208	1,249	1,249	1,154
Pulp products:											
Domestic production	5,313	6,079	5,908	6,097	6,114	5,813	5,881	5,691	5,708	5,706	5,750
Imports.	1,038	1,248	1,144	1,249	1,269	1,355	1,459	1,458	1,180	1,437	1,488
Exports.	646	905	891	929	818	768	842	801	810	793	801
Consumption	5,704	6,422	6,161	6,417	6,565	6,400	6,498	6,348	6,078	6,351	6,437
Logs:											
Imports	4	13	18	20	30	47	68	70	81	80	146
Exports	674	451	422	384	316	326	331	307	309	356	474
Pulpwood chips, exports.	288	377	416	422	412	422	353	265	265	155	200
Fuelwood consumption.	3,019	2,937	2,739	2,542	2,523	2,542	2,561	2,571	2,581	2,591	1,500

Source: U.S. Forest Service, *U.S. Timber Production, Trade, Consumption, and Price Statistics, 1965–1999*, Research Paper FPL-RP-595; and unpublished data. See also <http://www.fpl.fs.fed.us/documents/fplrp/fplrp595.pdf>.

Natural Resources **571**

Table 852. **Selected Timber Products—Imports and Exports: 1990 to 2004**

[In million board feet (13,063 represents 13,063,000,000), exceptions indicated]

Product	Unit	1990	1995	1998	1999	2000	2001	2002	2003	2004
IMPORTS [1]										
Lumber, total [2]	Mil. bd. ft.	13,063	17,524	19,012	19,576	19,906	20,443	21,434	21,981	25,493
From Canada	Percent.	91.3	97.1	96.0	93.0	92.0	93.0	90.4	90.0	83.3
Logs, total	Mil. bd. ft.[3]	23	80	185	294	435	452	525	497	454
From Canada	Percent.	84	70	91	95	96	97	97	98	97
Paper and board [4]	1,000 tons	12,195	14,292	14,538	16,917	17,555	18,513	19,433	20,034	21,146
Woodpulp	1,000 tons	4,893	5,969	5,984	6,660	7,227	7,348	7,247	6,691	6,726
Plywood	Mil. sq. ft.[5]	1,687	1,951	2,429	2,987	2,917	3,246	3,868	4,489	5,896
EXPORTS										
Lumber, total [2]	Mil. bd. ft.	4,614	2,958	2,189	2,549	2,700	2,190	2,186	2,193	3,842
To: Canada	Percent.	14	22	26	26	26	26	27	29	12
Japan	Percent.	28	33	16	14	12	10	7	7	11
Europe	Percent.	15	17	26	21	19	18	16	16	9
Logs, total	Mil. bd. ft.[3]	4,213	2,820	1,978	2,038	2,068	1,918	1,934	2,224	2,287
To: Canada	Percent.	9	25	39	39	41	46	50	54	49
Japan	Percent.	62	61	51	49	45	39	34	29	28
China	Percent.	9	1	1	-	-	1	2	2	3
Paper and board [4]	1,000 tons	5,163	7,621	9,103	9,477	10,003	11,504	11,564	11,868	12,566
Woodpulp	1,000 tons	5,905	8,261	6,025	5,936	6,409	6,167	6,254	5,847	6,225
Plywood	Mil. sq. ft.[5]	1,766	1,517	970	797	754	580	563	640	783

- Represents zero. [1] Customs value of imports; see text, Section 28. [2] Includes railroad ties. [3] Log scale. [4] Includes paper and board products. Excludes hardboard. [5] 3/8 inch basis.

Source: U.S. Forest Service, *U.S. Timber Production, Trade, Consumption, and Price Statistics, 1965–1999*, Research Paper FPL-RP-595; and unpublished data. See also <http://www.fpl.fs.fed.us/documnts/fplrp/fplrp595.pdf>.

Table 853. **Lumber Consumption by Species Group and End Use: 1995 to 2004**

[In million board feet (59.3 represents 59,300,000), except per capita in board feet. Per capita consumption based on estimated resident population as of July 1]

Item	1995	2000	2002	2003	2004	End-use	1995	2000	2002	2003	2004
Total	59.3	66.1	67.5	67.5	73.0	New housing	15.9	20.6	20.0	20.0	21.0
						Residential upkeep and improvements	14.3	16.4	17.3	17.5	17.9
Per capita	225	240	235	232	248	New nonresidential					
Species group:						construction [1]	5.8	7.7	5.5	5.5	5.5
Softwoods	47.6	54.0	56.4	56.2	62.5	Manufacturing	5.5	(NA)	(NA)	8.1	7.9
Hardwoods	11.7	12.2	11.1	11.3	10.5	Shipping	8.5	7.7	8.0	7.5	7.8
						Other [2]	10.2	6.7	7.5	6.9	7.0

NA Not available. [1] In addition to new construction, includes railroad ties laid as replacements in existing track and lumber used by railroads for railcar repair. [2] Includes upkeep and improvement of nonresidential buildings and structures; made-at-home projects, such as furniture, boats, and picnic tables; made-on-the-job items such as advertising and display structures; and miscellaneous products and uses.

Source. U.S. Forest Service, *U.S. Timber Production, Trade, Consumpiton, and Price Statistics, 1965-1999*, Resesearch Paper FPL-RP-595. See also <http://www.fpl.fs.fed.us/documnts/fplrp/fplrp595.pdf>.

Table 854. **Selected Timber Products—Producer Price Indexes: 1990 to 2004**

[1982 = 100. For information about producer prices, see text, Section 14, Prices]

Product	1990	1995	1998	1999	2000	2001	2002	2003	2004
Lumber and wood products	129.7	178.1	179.1	183.6	178.2	174.4	173.3	177.4	195.6
Lumber	124.6	173.4	179.5	188.2	178.8	171.6	170.6	174.3	203.7
Softwood lumber	123.8	178.5	182.7	196.0	178.6	170.1	170.8	170.8	210.0
Hardwood lumber	131.0	167.0	178.7	177.3	185.9	181.3	178.3	188.8	199.3
Millwork	130.4	163.8	171.1	174.7	176.4	179.2	179.8	181.8	191.9
General millwork	132.0	165.4	172.4	176.6	178.0	181.8	183.3	185.4	193.1
Prefabricated structural members	122.3	163.5	170.1	178.1	175.1	173.5	168.5	171.0	193.6
Plywood	114.2	165.3	157.3	176.4	157.6	154.3	151.7	167.0	198.5
Softwood plywood	119.6	188.1	174.9	207.0	173.3	167.8	164.1	195.9	250.9
Hardwood plywood and related products	102.7	122.2	126.9	128.6	130.2	130.4	131.5	129.0	134.4
Other wood products	114.7	143.7	135.2	131.1	130.5	130.5	127.2	129.9	134.3
Boxes	119.1	145.0	150.7	152.3	155.2	154.5	154.3	157.6	162.7
Pulp, paper, and allied products	141.2	172.2	171.7	174.1	183.7	184.8	185.9	190.0	195.6
Pulp, paper, and prod, ex bldg paper	132.9	163.4	147.0	147.9	161.4	157.7	155.3	157.1	162.1
Woodpulp	151.3	183.2	122.6	119.7	145.3	125.8	116.2	121.4	132.4
Wastepaper	138.9	371.1	145.4	183.6	282.5	148.6	173.1	197.3	231.5
Paper	128.8	159.0	145.4	141.8	149.8	150.6	144.7	146.1	149.4
Writing and printing papers	129.1	158.4	139.9	137.8	146.6	146.4	143.8	144.7	146.1
Newsprint	119.6	161.8	143.4	(NA)	127.5	138.6	105.7	112.1	124.3
Paperboard	135.7	183.1	151.6	153.2	176.7	172.1	164.3	162.7	170.3
Converted paper and paperboard products	135.2	157.0	152.2	153.5	162.7	164.5	163.8	165.3	168.2
Office supplies and accessories	121.4	134.9	131.2	129.5	133.8	136.9	135.7	137.4	137.7
Building paper & building board mill prods	112.2	144.9	132.9	141.6	138.8	129.3	129.3	159.9	192.1

NA Not available.

Source: U.S. Bureau of Labor Statistics, *Producer Price Indexes*, monthly.

Table 855. **Selected Species—Stumpage Prices In Current and Constant (1996) Dollars: 1990 to 2004**

[In dollars per 1,000 board feet. Stumpage prices are based on sales of sawtimber from National Forests]

Species	1990	1995	1996	1997	1998	1999	2000	2001	2002	2003	2004
CURRENT DOLLARS											
Softwoods:											
Douglas fir [1]	466	454	436	331	254	315	433	258	185	193	93
Southern pine [2]	127	248	241	307	288	269	258	168	166	164	183
Sugar pine [3]	285	397	318	234	200	229	187	192	209	95	94
Ponderosa pine [3, 4]	218	150	274	270	205	181	155	143	118	111	65
Western hemlock [5]	203	297	248	211	161	96	46	34	73	86	63
Hardwoods:											
All eastern hardwoods [6]	146	309	259	287	241	195	341	264	384	279	427
Oak, white, red, and black [6]	188	297	237	265	270	317	258	153	207	304	291
Maple, sugar [7]	135	286	238	357	395	448	314	271	485	560	618
CONSTANT (1996) DOLLARS [8]											
Softwoods:											
Douglas fir [1]	428	417	436	304	233	289	397	237	170	152	69
Southern pine [2]	117	228	241	282	264	247	237	154	153	129	136
Sugar pine [3]	262	364	318	215	183	210	172	176	191	49	70
Ponderosa pine [3, 4]	200	138	274	248	188	166	142	131	108	88	49
Western hemlock [5]	186	272	248	194	148	88	42	31	67	68	47
Hardwoods:											
All eastern hardwoods [6]	134	283	259	263	221	179	313	242	353	224	317
Oak, white, red, and black [6]	172	272	237	243	248	291	237	140	190	239	216
Maple, sugar [7]	124	262	238	328	362	411	288	249	445	441	459

[1] Western Washington and western Oregon. [2] Southern region. [3] Pacific Southwest region (formerly California region). [4] Includes Jeffrey pine. [5] Pacific Northwest region. [6] Eastern and Southern regions. [7] Eastern region. [8] Deflated by the producer price index, all commodities.

Source: U.S. Forest Service, *Timber Demand and Technology Assessment*, RWU-4851. Also in *Agricultural Statistics*, annual.

Table 856. **Paper and Paperboard—Production and New Supply: 1990 to 2003**

[In millions of short tons (80.45 represents 80,450,000]

Item	1990	1995	1997	1998	1999	2000	2001	2002	2003, prel.
Production, total	80.45	91.33	96.92	96.40	98.65	96.05	90.38	91.11	89.81
Paper, total	39.36	42.87	44.70	44.76	45.98	45.52	42.10	41.56	40.37
Paperboard, total	39.32	46.64	50.40	49.83	51.04	48.97	46.81	48.13	48.02
Unbleached kraft	20.36	22.70	23.22	23.20	23.11	21.80	20.44	21.09	21.73
Semichemical	5.64	5.66	6.05	5.89	6.01	5.95	5.58	5.84	6.10
Bleached kraft	4.40	5.30	5.55	5.49	5.71	5.44	5.30	5.30	5.36
Recycled	8.92	12.98	15.58	15.25	16.21	15.79	15.50	15.91	14.83
Wet machine board E	0.15	0.15	0.10	0.10	0.06	0.06	0.05	0.05	0.05
Building paper E	0.81	0.81	0.79	0.79	0.66	0.64	0.58	0.55	0.55
Insulating board E	0.86	0.86	0.93	0.93	0.91	0.86	0.85	0.83	0.83
New supply, all grades, excluding products	87.68	98.16	101.27	103.01	106.90	105.02	99.12	100.41	99.73
Paper, total	49.49	52.77	54.15	55.13	57.30	57.13	53.23	53.50	53.19
Newsprint	13.41	12.76	12.61	12.80	13.09	12.92	11.47	11.18	11.05
Printing/writing papers	25.46	29.55	30.75	31.38	32.53	32.99	30.38	30.93	31.00
Packaging and ind. conv. papers	4.72	4.24	4.27	4.29	4.71	4.27	4.31	4.20	3.96
Tissue	5.90	6.22	6.52	6.66	6.98	6.95	7.07	7.20	7.18
Paperboard, total	36.30	43.45	45.13	45.67	47.59	46.02	44.09	45.29	44.95
Construction and other	1.90	1.95	1.99	2.20	2.00	1.88	1.80	1.62	1.59

Source: American Forest and Paper Association, Washington, DC, *Monthly Statistical Summary of Paper, Paperboard and Woodpulp*.

U.S. Census Bureau, Statistical Abstract of the United States: 2006

Table 857. Fishery Products—Domestic Catch, Imports, and Disposition: 1990 to 2003

[Live weight, in millions of pounds (16,349 represents 16,349,000,000). For data on commercial catch for selected countries, see Table 1347, Section 30]

Item	1990	1995	1997	1998	1999	2000	2001	2002	2003
Total	16,349	16,484	17,131	16,897	17,378	17,338	18,118	19,028	19,848
For human food	12,662	13,584	13,739	14,175	14,462	14,738	15,306	16,007	17,185
For industrial use	3,687	2,900	3,392	2,722	2,916	2,599	2,812	3,021	2,663
Domestic catch	9,404	9,788	9,846	9,194	9,339	9,069	9,492	9,397	9,505
For human food	7,041	7,667	7,248	7,174	6,832	6,912	7,314	7,205	7,519
For industrial use	2,363	2,121	2,597	2,020	2,507	2,157	2,178	2,192	1,986
Imports [1]	6,945	6,696	7,286	7,703	8,039	8,269	8,626	9,631	10,343
For human food [2]	5,621	5,917	6,491	7,001	7,630	7,827	7,992	8,802	9,666
For industrial use [2]	1,324	779	795	702	409	442	634	829	677
Exports [1]	4,627	5,166	5,537	4,889	5,208	5,757	7,107	6,979	6,756
For human food [2]	3,832	4,175	4,326	3,709	4,130	4,586	5,774	5,587	5,392
For industrial use [2]	795	991	1,211	1,180	1,078	1,171	1,333	1,392	1,364
Disposition of domestic catch	9,404	9,788	9,846	9,194	9,339	9,069	9,492	9,397	9,505
Fresh and frozen	6,501	7,099	6,877	6,870	6,416	6,657	7,085	6,826	7,264
Canned	751	769	648	516	712	530	536	652	498
Cured	126	90	108	129	133	119	123	117	119
Reduced to meal, oil, etc.	2,026	1,830	2,213	1,679	2,078	1,763	1,748	1,802	1,624

[1] Excludes imports of edible fishery products consumed in Puerto Rico; includes landings of tuna caught by foreign vessels in American Samoa. [2] Fish meal and sea herring.

Source: U.S. National Oceanic and Atmospheric Administration, National Marine Fisheries Service, *Fisheries of the United States*, annual. See also <http://www.st.nmfs.gov/st1/fus/fus01/2003-fus.pdf> (released September 2004).

Table 858. Fisheries—Quantity and Value of Domestic Catch: 1980 to 2003

Year	Quantity (mil. lb. [1])			Value (mil. dol.)	Average price per lb. (cents)	Year	Quantity (mil. lb. [1])			Value (mil. dol.)	Average price per lb. (cents)
	Total	For human food	For industrial products [2]				Total	For human food	For industrial products [2]		
1980	6,482	3,654	2,828	2,237	34.5	1997	9,846	7,248	2,597	3,447	35.0
1985	6,258	3,294	2,964	2,326	37.2	1998	9,194	7,174	2,020	3,128	34.0
1990	9,404	7,041	2,363	3,522	37.5	1999	9,339	6,832	2,507	3,464	37.1
1992	9,637	7,618	2,019	3,678	38.2						
1993	[3]10,467	8,214	2,253	3,471	33.2	2000	9,069	6,912	2,157	3,549	39.1
1994	10,461	7,936	2,525	3,807	36.8	2001	9,492	7,314	2,178	3,228	34.0
1995	9,788	7,667	2,121	3,770	38.5	2002	9,397	7,205	2,192	3,092	32.9
1996	9,565	7,474	2,091	3,487	36.5	2003	9,505	7,519	1,986	3,342	35.2

[1] Live weight. [2] Meal, oil, fish solubles, homogenized condensed fish, shell products, bait, and animal food. [3] Represents record year.

Source: U.S. National Oceanic and Atmospheric Administration, National Marine Fisheries Service, *Fisheries of the United States*, annual. See also <http://www.st.nmfs.gov/st1/fus/fus01/2003-fus.pdf> (released September 2004).

Table 859. Domestic Fish and Shellfish Catch and Value by Major Species Caught: 1990 to 2003

Species	Quantity (1,000 lb.)				Value ($1,000)			
	1990	2000	2002	2003	1990	2000	2002	2003
Total	9,403,571	9,068,985	9,397,164	9,505,448	3,521,995	3,549,481	3,092,318	3,342,184
Fish, total [1]	8,091,068	7,689,661	8,089,987	8,248,374	1,900,097	1,594,815	1,359,392	1,519,522
Cod: Atlantic	95,881	25,060	29,841	23,586	61,329	26,384	30,715	27,494
Pacific	526,396	530,505	512,827	567,544	91,384	142,330	96,206	159,619
Flounder	254,519	412,723	372,697	364,560	112,921	109,910	102,370	94,427
Halibut	70,454	75,190	82,044	79,515	96,700	143,826	135,603	172,191
Herring, sea: Atlantic	113,095	160,269	135,871	211,713	5,746	9,972	9,106	15,496
Herring, sea: Pacific	108,120	74,835	78,408	74,337	32,178	12,043	11,534	10,424
Menhaden	1,962,160	1,760,498	1,750,609	1,599,344	93,896	112,403	105,102	96,080
Pollock, Alaska	3,108,031	2,606,802	3,341,105	3,361,802	268,344	160,525	203,696	203,183
Salmon	733,146	628,638	567,179	674,096	612,367	270,213	155,010	200,838
Tuna	62,393	50,779	49,358	61,912	105,040	95,176	84,116	86,934
Whiting (Atlantic, silver)	44,500	26,855	17,622	19,019	11,281	11,370	7,454	9,316
Whiting (Pacific, hake)	21,232	452,718	285,714	309,363	1,229	18,809	13,584	17,153
Shellfish, total [1]	1,312,503	1,379,324	1,307,177	1,257,074	1,621,898	1,954,666	1,732,926	1,822,662
Clams	139,198	118,482	130,076	127,794	130,194	153,973	167,215	162,294
Crabs	499,416	299,006	307,601	338,854	483,837	405,006	397,695	483,586
Lobsters: American	61,017	83,180	82,252	71,735	154,677	301,300	293,329	284,814
Oysters	29,193	41,146	34,397	37,046	93,718	90,667	89,071	103,045
Scallops, sea	39,917	32,747	53,056	56,018	153,696	164,609	203,707	229,140
Shrimp	346,494	332,486	316,727	313,628	491,433	690,453	460,878	424,027
Squid, Pacific	36,082	259,508	160,677	88,229	2,636	27,077	18,262	23,137

[1] Includes other types of fish and shellfish, not shown separately.

Source: U.S. National Oceanic and Atmospheric Administration, National Marine Fisheries Service, *Fisheries of the United States*, annual. See also <http://www.st.nmfs.gov/st1/fus/fus01/2003-fus.pdf> (released September 2004).

Table 860. U.S. Private Aquaculture—Trout and Catfish Production and Value: 1990 to 2004

[67.8 represents 67,800,000. Periods are from September 1 of the previous year to August 31 of stated year. Data are for foodsize fish, those over 12 inches long]

Item	Unit	1990	1995	1999	2000	2001	2002	2003	2004
TROUT FOODSIZE									
Number sold	Millions	67.8	60.2	61.0	58.5	54.5	50.2	46.1	47.5
Total weight	Mil. lb	56.8	55.6	60.2	59.2	56.9	54.5	50.8	55.0
Total value of sales	Mil. dol	64.6	60.8	64.7	63.7	64.4	58.3	52.9	57.1
Average price received	Dol./lb	1.14	1.09	1.07	1.08	1.13	1.07	1.04	1.04
Percent sold to processors	Percent	58	68	68	70	68	69	68	72
CATFISH FOODSIZE									
Number sold	Millions	272.9	321.8	424.5	420.1	406.9	405.8	381.7	389.3
Total weight	Mil. lb	392.4	481.5	635.2	633.8	647.5	673.7	699.3	682.2
Total value of sales	Mil. dol	305.1	378.1	464.7	468.8	410.7	378.5	397.1	450.9
Average price received	Dol./lb	0.78	0.79	0.73	0.74	0.63	0.56	0.57	0.66
Fish sold to processors	Mil. lb	360.4	446.9	596.6	593.6	597.1	630.6	661.5	630.0
Avg. price paid by processors	Cents/lb	75.8	78.6	73.7	75.1	64.7	56.8	58.1	69.7
Processor sales	Mil. lb	183.1	227.0	292.7	297.2	296.4	317.6	319.3	306.8
Avg. price received by processors	Cents/lb	224.1	240.3	234.0	236.0	226.0	207.0	205.0	223.0
Inventory (January 1)	Mil. lb	9.4	10.9	12.6	13.6	15.0	12.3	13.6	15.2

Source: U.S. Department of Agriculture, National Agricultural Statistics Service, *Trout Production*, released February; *Catfish Production*, released February; and *Catfish Processing*, released February. Also in *Agricultural Statistics*, annual.

Table 861. Supply of Selected Fishery Items: 1990 to 2003

[In millions of pounds (734 represents 734,000,000). Totals available for U.S. consumption are supply minus exports plus imports. Round weight is the complete or full weight as caught]

Species	Unit	1990	1995	1997	1998	1999	2000	2001	2002	2003
Shrimp	Heads-off weight	734	832	923	1,002	1,084	1,172	1,312	1,430	1,607
Tuna, canned	Canned weight	856	875	829	912	1,020	980	796	922	982
Snow crab	Round weight	37	42	110	254	216	122	171	172	198
Clams	Meat weight	152	144	124	119	125	133	139	144	143
Salmon, canned	Canned weight	148	147	82	83	123	95	81	135	111
American lobster	Round weight	95	94	112	110	122	124	125	135	126
Spiny lobster	Round weight	89	89	76	100	91	99	79	87	93
Scallops	Meat weight	74	62	66	58	64	78	76	91	94
Sardines, canned	Canned weight	61	44	49	50	57	(NA)	(NA)	(NA)	(NA)
Oysters	Meat weight	56	63	58	61	55	71	58	62	69
King crab	Round weight	19	21	45	62	52	41	38	47	47
Crab meat, canned	Canned weight	9	12	15	22	26	29	35	44	47

NA Not available.

Source: U.S. National Oceanic and Atmospheric Administration, National Marine Fisheries Service, *Fisheries of the United States*, annual. See also <http://www.st.nmfs.gov/st1/fus/fus03/2003-fus.pdf (released September 2004).

Table 862. Canned, Fresh, and Frozen Fishery Products—Production and Value: 1990 to 2003

[In millions of pounds (1,178 represents 1,178,000,000). Fresh fishery products exclude Alaska and Hawaii. Canned fishery products data are for natural pack only]

Product	Production (mil. lb.)					Value (mil. dol.)				
	1990	1995	2000	2002	2003	1990	1995	2000	2002	2003
Canned, total [1]	1,178	1,927	1,747	1,317	1,301	1,562	1,887	1,626	1,290	1,224
Tuna	581	667	671	547	529	902	939	856	675	669
Salmon	196	244	171	224	188	366	419	288	296	242
Clam products	110	129	127	140	126	76	110	120	118	113
Sardines, Maine	13	14	(Z)	(Z)	(Z)	17	24	(Z)	(Z)	(Z)
Shrimp	1	1	2	2	1	3	7	11	9	5
Crabs	1	(Z)	(Z)	(Z)	(Z)	4	(Z)	(Z)	(Z)	(Z)
Oysters [2]	1	(Z)	(Z)	(Z)	(Z)	1	(Z)	1	(Z)	(Z)
Fish fillets and steaks [3]	441	385	368	517	611	843	841	823	981	1,126
Cod	65	65	56	50	56	132	152	167	155	172
Flounder	54	35	27	25	21	154	86	71	73	62
Haddock	7	3	6	8	8	24	11	24	32	35
Ocean perch, Atlantic	1	(Z)	(Z)	(Z)	1	1	1	1	1	2
Rockfish	33	25	11	8	5	53	38	25	15	12
Pollock, Atlantic	12	4	2	4	7	21	10	4	11	10
Pollock, Alaska	164	135	160	308	367	174	184	178	330	395
Other	105	118	106	114	146	284	359	353	364	438

Z Less than 500,000 pounds or $500,000. [1] Includes other products, not shown separately. [2] Includes oyster specialties. [3] Fresh and frozen.

Source: U.S. National Oceanic and Atmospheric Administration, National Marine Fisheries Service, *Fisheries of the United States*, annual. See also <http://www.st.nmfs.gov/st1> (released September 2004).

U.S. Census Bureau, Statistical Abstract of the United States: 2006

Table 863. Mining and Primary Metal Production Indexes: 1990 to 2004

[Index 1997 = 100]

Industry group	1990	1995	1997	1998	1999	2000	2001	2002	2003	2004
Mining	99.0	96.7	100.0	98.5	93.6	95.8	96.7	92.6	92.2	91.4
Coal	96.1	94.6	100.0	101.6	98.9	97.0	101.6	97.7	95.3	99.1
Oil and gas extraction	103.2	100.0	100.0	99.2	96.6	97.1	98.1	96.3	95.3	92.3
Crude oil and natural gas	104.7	100.4	100.0	99.6	96.4	96.6	97.8	95.9	95.6	91.8
Oil and gas drilling	92.9	81.3	100.0	93.5	73.4	104.0	125.9	90.8	105.5	115.3
Metal mining	84.9	92.8	100.0	99.6	91.4	91.0	82.7	75.7	70.4	72.3
Iron ore	89.2	98.9	100.0	99.2	91.3	99.2	73.2	81.1	73.2	83.1
Nonferrous ores	91.9	100.4	100.0	107.5	99.4	94.5	89.3	(NA)	(NA)	(NA)
Copper ore	89.4	104.7	100.0	105.4	90.7	81.4	76.9	(NA)	(NA)	(NA)
Primary metals, manufacturing	85.6	93.8	100.0	101.6	101.4	98.1	88.7	90.3	87.4	92.3
Nonferrous metals	89.6	99.1	100.0	105.7	97.5	89.5	81.3	81.4	69.2	73.8
Copper	60.6	111.9	100.0	102.9	89.1	56.9	47.7	42.5	38.8	38.9
Aluminum	97.6	93.4	100.0	105.2	106.3	98.5	87.9	96.4	94.2	97.7
Iron and steel	85.3	94.8	100.0	99.8	100.5	99.5	90.0	92.0	93.3	100.6

NA Not available.
Source: Board of Governors of the Federal Reserve System, *Federal Reserve Bulletin*, monthly; and *Industrial Production and Capacity Utilization*, Statistical Release G.17, monthly.

Table 864. Mineral Industries—Employment, Hours, and Earnings: 1990 to 2004

[In thousands (680 represents 680,000). Based on the Current Employment Statistics Program, see Appendix III]

Industry and item	Unit	1990	1995	1999	2000	2001	2002	2003	2004
All mining:									
All employees	1,000	680	558	517	520	533	512	503	523
Production workers	1,000	469	391	374	383	398	378	364	385
Avg. weekly hours	Number...	46.1	46.8	45.4	45.5	45.5	43.9	44.4	45.4
Avg. weekly earnings	Dollars ...	630	711	760	771	789	769	796	838
Coal mining:									
All employees	1,000	136	97	79	72	74	74	70	72
Production workers	1,000	110	78	65	59	63	63	59	60
Avg. weekly hours	Number...	44.7	45.7	45.6	45.6	47.0	45.4	46.2	47.7
Avg. weekly earnings	Dollars ...	822	929	953	945	957	934	964	1,030
Oil and gas extraction:									
All employees	1,000	190	152	131	125	124	121.9	122.9	123
Production workers	1,000	84	73	71	67	68	68	68	70
Avg. weekly hours	Number...	44.4	43.6	41.9	41.3	41.3	39.5	41.1	43.5
Avg. weekly earnings	Dollars ...	591	677	802	802	825	761	778	807
Metal mining:									
All employees	1,000	53	48	42	38	33	29	27	27
Production workers	1,000	43	39	32	29	25	22	20	20
Avg. weekly hours	Number...	42.5	43.4	44.1	43.4	43.4	42.8	43.7	45.1
Avg. weekly earnings	Dollars ...	646	788	874	871	866	878	957	1,034
Nonmetallic minerals, except fuels:									
All employees	1,000	113	108	114	115	111	107	105	108
Production workers	1,000	85	81	87	87	83	50	78	82
Avg. weekly hours	Number...	45.0	46.3	45.9	46.1	46.3	45.2	45.1	44.6
Avg. weekly earnings	Dollars ...	532	632	702	722	745	749	773	791

Source: U.S. Bureau of Labor Statistics, *Bulletin 2370* and *Employment and Earnings*, March and June issues.

Table 865. Selected Mineral Products—Average Prices: 1990 to 2004

[Excludes Alaska and Hawaii, except as noted]

	Nonfuels								Fuels		
Year	Copper, electrolytic (cents per lb.)	Platinum [1] (dol./ troy oz.)	Gold (dol./ fine oz.)	Silver (dol./ fine oz.)	Lead (cents per lb.)	Tin (New York) (cents per lb.)	Zinc (cents per lb.)	Sulfur, crude [2] (dol./ metric ton)	Bituminous coal [3][4] (dol./ short ton)	Crude petroleum [3] (dol./ bbl.)	Natural gas [3] (dol./ 1,000 cu. ft.)
1990	123	467	385	4.82	46	386	75	80.14	27.43	20.03	1.71
1991	109	371	363	4.04	34	363	53	71.45	27.49	16.54	1.64
1992	107	356	345	3.94	35	402	58	48.14	26.78	15.99	1.74
1993	92	370	361	4.30	32	350	46	31.86	26.15	14.25	2.04
1994	111	411	385	5.29	37	369	49	30.08	25.68	13.19	1.85
1995	138	425	386	5.15	42	416	56	44.46	25.56	14.62	1.55
1996	109	398	389	5.19	49	412	51	34.11	25.17	18.46	2.17
1997	107	397	332	4.89	47	381	65	36.06	24.64	17.23	2.32
1998	79	375	295	5.54	45	373	51	29.14	24.87	10.87	1.96
1999	76	379	280	5.25	44	366	53	37.81	23.88	15.56	2.19
2000	88	549	280	5.00	44	370	56	24.73	24.15	26.72	3.69
2001	77	533	272	4.39	44	315	44	10.01	25.36	21.84	4.12
2002	76	543	311	4.62	44	292	39	11.84	26.57	22.51	2.95
2003	85	694	365	4.91	44	340	41	28.71	26.57	27.56	4.98
2004	134	852	410	6.46	53	643	52	28.00	(NA)	(NA)	(NA)

NA Not available. [1] Average annual dealer prices. [2] F.o.b. works. [3] Average value at the point of production or domestic first purchase price. [4] Includes lignite.
Source: Nonfuels, through 1994, U.S. Bureau of Mines, thereafter, U.S. Geological Survey, *Minerals Yearbook* and *Mineral Commodities Summaries*, annual; fuels, U.S. Energy Information Administration, *Annual Energy Review* and most recent year from the *Monthly Energy Review*.

Table 866. Mineral Production: 1990 to 2004

[In millions of short tons (1,029.1 represents 1,029,100,000). Data represent production as measured by mine shipments, mine sales or marketable production]

Minerals and Metals	Unit	1990	1995	2000	2003	2004, est.
FUEL MINERALS						
Coal, total	Mil. sh. tons	1,029.1	1,033.0	1,073.6	1,069.5	(NA)
Bituminous	Mil. sh. tons	693.2	613.8	574.3	559.2	(NA)
Sub-bituminous	Mil. sh. tons	244.3	328.0	409.2	428.4	(NA)
Lignite	Mil. sh. tons	88.1	86.5	85.6	80.6	(NA)
Anthracite	Mil. sh. tons	3.5	4.7	4.6	1.3	(NA)
Natural gas (marketed production)	Tril. cu. ft.	18.59	19.51	20.00	20.07	(NA)
Petroleum (crude)	Mil. bbl. [1]	2,686	2,394	2,125	2,074	1,982
Uranium (recoverable content)	Mil. lb.	8.9	6.0	4.0	2.0	(NA)
NONFUEL MINERALS						
Asbestos (sales)	1,000 metric tons	(D)	9	5	-	-
Barite, primary, sold/used by producers	1,000 metric tons	430	543	392	468	550
Boron minerals, sold or used by producers	1,000 metric tons	1,090	1,190	1,070	1,150	1,160
Bromine, sold or used by producers	1,000 metric tons	177	218	228	216	222
Cement:						
Portland	Mil. metric tons	67	73	84	88	93
Masonry	Mil. metric tons	3	4	4	5	5
Clays	1,000 metric tons	42,200	43,100	40,800	40,000	48,900
Diatomite	1,000 metric tons	631	722	677	620	635
Feldspar [2]	1,000 metric tons	630	880	790	800	790
Fluorspar, finished shipments	1,000 metric tons	64	51	-	-	-
Garnet (industrial)	1,000 metric tons	47	46	60	29	30
Gypsum, crude	Mil. metric tons	15	17	20	17	18
Helium [3]	Mil. cu. meters	85	101	98	87	85
Lime, sold or used by producers	Mil. metric tons	16	19	20	18	20
Mica, scrap & flake, sold/used by producers	1,000 metric tons	109	108	101	79	76
Peat, sales by producers	1,000 metric tons	721	660	847	632	624
Perlite, processed, sold or used	1,000 metric tons	576	700	672	493	510
Phosphate rock (marketable)	Mil. metric tons	46	44	39	35	37
Potash (K₂O equivalent) sales	1,000 metric tons	1,710	1,480	1,300	1,100	1,200
Pumice & pumicite, producer sales	1,000 metric tons	443	529	1,050	870	1,070
Salt, common, sold/used by producers	Mil. metric tons	37	41	46	44	45
Sand & gravel, sold/used by producer	Mil. metric tons	855	935	1,148	1,158	1,219
Construction	Mil. metric tons	829	907	1,120	1,160	1,190
Industrial	Mil. metric tons	26	28	28	28	29
Sodium carbonate (natural) (soda ash)	1,000 metric tons	9,100	10,100	10,200	10,600	10,800
Sodium sulfate (natural)	1,000 metric tons	349	327	(NA)	472	425
Stone [4]	Mil. metric tons	1,110	2,420	2,810	2,840	2,900
Crushed and broken	Mil. metric tons	1,110	1,260	1,560	1,530	1,600
Dimension [5]	1,000 metric tons	1,120	1,160	1,250	1,340	1,300
Sulfur: Total shipments	1,000 metric tons	11,500	12,100	10,700	9,600	10,000
Sulfur: Frasch mines (shipments)	1,000 metric tons	3,680	3,150	900	-	-
Talc, and pyrophyllite, crude	1,000 metric tons	1,270	1,060	851	869	911
Vermiculite concentrate	1,000 metric tons	209	171	150	(NA)	(NA)
METALS						
Antimony ore and concentrate	Metric tons	(D)	262	(D)	-	-
Aluminum	1,000 metric tons	4,048	3,375	3,668	2,703	2,500
Bauxite (dried)	1,000 metric tons	(D)	(D)	(NA)	(NA)	(NA)
Copper (recoverable content)	1,000 metric tons	1,590	1,850	1,450	1,120	1,160
Gold (recoverable content)	Metric tons	294	317	353	277	247
Iron ore (gross weight) [6]	Mil. metric tons	56	63	63	49	55
Lead (recoverable content)	1,000 metric tons	484	386	449	449	(NA)
Magnesium metal	1,000 metric tons	139	142	(D)	(D)	(D)
Manganiferous ore (gross weight) [7]	1,000 metric ton	(D)	(D)	-	(NA)	(NA)
Mercury [8]	Metric tons	(NA)	(D)	(NA)	(NA)	(NA)
Molybdenum (concentrate)	1,000 metric tons	62	61	41	34	40
Nickel	1,000 metric tons	(Z)	2	-	-	-
Palladium metal	Kilograms	5,930	5,260	10,300	14,000	14,200
Platinum metal	Kilograms	1,810	1,590	4,390	4,170	4,200
Silicon (silicon content)	1,000 metric tons	418	396	367	248	240
Silver (recoverable content)	Metric tons	2,120	1,560	1,860	1,240	1,200
Titanium concentrate: Ilmenite (gross weight)	1,000 metric tons	(D)	(D)	(D)	(D)	(D)
Tungsten ore and concentrate [9]	Metric tons	(D)	-	-	(NA)	-
Zinc (recoverable content)	1,000 metric tons	515	603	805	738	712

- Represents zero. D Withheld to avoid disclosing individual company data. NA Not available. Z Less than half of the unit of measure. [1] 42 gal. bbl. [2] Beginning 1995, includes aplite. [3] Refined. [4] Excludes abrasive stone, bituminous limestone and sandstone, and ground soapstone, all included elsewhere in table. Includes calcareous marl and slate. [5] Includes Puerto Rico. [6] Represents shipments; includes by-product ores. [7] 5- to 35-percent manganiferous ore. [8] Covers mercury recovered as a by-product of gold ores only. [9] Content of ore and concentrate.

Source: Nonfuels, through 1995, U.S. Bureau of Mines, thereafter, U.S. Geological Survey, *Minerals Yearbook* and *Mineral Commodities Summaries*, annual; fuels, U.S. Energy Information Administration, *Annual Energy Review* and *Uranium Industry Annual*.

Natural Resources 577

Table 867. Nonfuel Mineral Commodities—Summary: 2004

[In thousands of metric tons (2,500 represents except as indicated. Preliminary estimates. Average price in dollars per metric tons except as noted]

Mineral	Unit	Mineral disposition		Net import reliance [1] (percent)	Consumption, apparent	Average price per unit (dollars)	Employment (number)
		Production	Exports				
Aluminum	1,000 metric tons	2,500	1,700	41	6,300	[2]0.82	58,200
Antimony (contained)	Metric tons	[3]4,100	3,680	85	27,040	[2]1.27	30
Asbestos	1,000 metric tons	-	2	100	3	[4]255.00	-
Barite	1,000 metric tons	550	78	79	2,600	[4]30.00	340
Bauxite and alumina	1,000 metric tons	(NA)	744	100	2,600	[4]22.00	(NA)
Beryllium (contained)	Metric tons	100	80	55	220	(NA)	(NA)
Bismuth (contained)	Metric tons	-	120	90	(NA)	[2]3.10	(NA)
Boron (B$_2$O$_3$ content)	1,000 metric tons	562	192	(5)	509	[4 6]400-425	1,300
Bromine (contained)	1,000 metric tons	222	8	(5)	220	[7 8]0.70	1,500
Cadmium (contained)	Metric tons	[3]600	400	(5)	500	[2 9]0.60	(NA)
Cement	1,000 metric tons	95,000	840	23	121,200	[4]85.00	18,100
Chromium	1,000 metric tons	[10]130	70	72	450	[4 11](NA)	(NA)
Clays	1,000 metric tons	48,900	5,580	(5)	43,500	(NA)	6,230
Cobalt (contained)	Metric tons	[10]2,500	2,700	76	10,200	[2]24.50	(NA)
Copper (mine, contained)	1,000 metric tons	1,160	750	43	2,640	[12]134.00	7.0
Diamond (industrial)	Million carats	254	83	40	421	[13]0.24	(NA)
Diatomite	1,000 metric tons	635	136	(5)	500	[4]258	1,000
Feldspar	1,000 metric tons	790	8	2	810	[4]54.00	400
Fluorspar	1,000 metric tons	-	22	100	622	(NA)	-
Garnet (industrial)	Metric tons	29,700	10,500	34	50,400	[4]50-2,000	180
Germanium (contained)	Kilograms	15,000	(NA)	(NA)	(NA)	[7 14]640.00	65
Gold (contained)	Metric tons	247	500	(5)	(NA)	[15]410.00	7,000
Gypsum (crude)	1,000 metric tons	18,000	130	26	39,300	[4]6.90	5,900
Iodine	Metric tons	1,340	1,330	74	5,210	[7 16]12.91	30
Iron ore (usable)	Million metric tons	54.60	8.8	8	58.8	[4 17]31.00	4,800
Iron and steel slag (metal)	1,000 metric tons	20,000	100	5	19,900	[4]15.75	2,700
Lead (contained)	1,000 metric tons	1,610	275	(5)	1,520	[2]53.00	2,720
Lime	1,000 metric tons	20,400	86	(Z)	20,500	90.00	5,350
Magnesium compounds	1,000 metric tons	280	50	48	540	(NA)	370
Magnesium metal	1,000 metric tons	(NA)	15	68	110	(NA)	400
Mercury	Metric tons	[10](NA)	300	(NA)	(NA)	[18]350.00	(NA)
Mica, scrap and flake	1,000 metric tons	166	10	35	117	[4]245.00	(NA)
Molybdenum (contained)	Metric tons	39,900	54,100	(5)	1,700	[7]29.67	568
Nickel (contained)	Metric tons	-	55,900	[19]49	126,000	[20]13,823.00	-
Nitrogen (fixed)-ammonia	1,000 metric tons	8,900	430	38	14,200	[4 21]275.00	1,300
Peat	1,000 metric tons	607	30	56	1,370	[4]29.28	700
Perlite	1,000 metric tons	510	40	23	660	[4]35.22	135
Phosphate rock	1,000 metric tons	37,000	40	6	(NA)	[4]27.12	3,300
Platinum-group metals	Kilograms	18,400	49,600	90	(NA)	[16 22](NA)	1,500
Potash (K$_2$O equivalent)	1,000 metric tons	1,200	200	70	5,800	[4 23]170.00	1,130
Pumice and pumicite	1,000 metric tons	1,070	25	26	1,450	[4]24.12	100
Salt	1,000 metric tons	45,100	800	20	53,900	[4 24]122.00	4,100
Silicon (contained)	1,000 metric tons	240	23	56	560	[25]59.00	(NA)
Silver (contained)	Metric tons	1,200	340	54	6,200	[16]6.46	900
Sodium carbonate (soda ash)	1,000 metric tons	10,800	4,700	(5)	6,300	[26]105.00	2,500
Sodium sulfate	1,000 metric tons	425	140	(5)	330	[27]114.00	225
Stone (crushed)	Million metric tons	1,600	2	(Z)	1,610	[4]6.08	78,700
Sulfur (all forms)	1,000 metric tons	10,000	675	20	12,400	[4 28]28.00	2,700
Talc	1,000 metric tons	911	210	1	921	[4]112.00	450
Thallium (contained)	Kilograms	-	1500	100	(NA)	[7]1,300.00	(NA)
Tin (contained)	Metric tons	[10]9,000	4,600	88	50,400	[4]4.12	(NA)
Titanium dioxide	1,000 metric tons	1,430	590	(5)	1,120	[2 29]0.93	4,400
Tungsten (contained)	Metric tons	[10]3,600	4,340	73	11,800	[30]47.00	(NA)
Vermiculite	1,000 metric tons	NA	10	(NA)	(NA)	143.00	100
Zinc (contained)	1,000 metric tons	1,130	712	56	1,470	[2 31]0.53	1,800
Zirconium (Z,02) content	Metric tons	(D)	41,000	(5)	(D)	[4 32]400.00	(NA)

- Represents or rounds to zero. D Withheld to avoid disclosure. NA Not available. Z Less than half the unit of measure. [1] Calculated as a percent of apparent consumption. [2] Dollars per pound. [3] Refinery production. [4] Dollars per metric ton. [5] Net exporter. [6] Metal, vacuum-cast ingot. [7] Granulated pentahydrate borax in bulk, f.o.b mine. [8] Dollars per kilogram. [9] Bulk, purified bromine. [10] 1- to 5-short ton lots. [11] Secondary production. [12] Columbite price. [13] Value of imports, dollars per carat. [14] Reported consumption. [15] Zone refined. [16] Price of flake imports. [17] Includes employment at calcining plants. [18] Price of eastern Canadian ore. [19] Delivered, No. 1 Heavy, Melting composite price. [20] Year-end price. [21] 46%-48% metallurgical ore, per unit contained Mn, c.i.f. U.S. ports. [22] Dollars per 76-pound flask. [23] London Metal Exchange cash price. [24] F.o.b. Gulf Coast. [25] Dealer price of platinum. [26] Price of K20, muriate. [27] Vacuum and open pan, bulk, pellets and packaged, f.o.b. mine and plant. [28] Ferrosilicon, 50% Si. [29] Quoted year-end price, dense, bulk, f.o.b. Green River, WY, dollars per short ton. [30] Quoted price, bulk, f.o.b. works, East, dollars per short ton. [31] Elemental sulfur, f.o.b. mine and/or plant. [32] Rutile, list, year-end.

Source: U.S. Geological Survey, *Mineral Commodity Summaries*, annual.

Table 868. Value of Domestic Nonfuel Mineral Production by State: 1990 to 2004

[In millions of dollars (33,445 represents $33,445,000,000), except as indicated. For similar data on fuels, see Table 875]

State	1990	1995	2000	2002	2003	2004 Total	2004 Rank	2004 Percent of U.S.
United States [1] ..	33,445	38,506	40,100	38,000	37,600	44,000	(X)	100.00
Alabama	559	706	1,070	968	863	982	17	2.23
Alaska...........	577	538	1,140	1,030	1,060	1,320	12	3.01
Arizona	3,085	4,190	2,550	1,920	2,100	3,000	3	6.83
Arkansas........	381	492	506	543	445	514	29	1.17
California........	2,771	2,760	3,350	3,440	3,170	3,620	1	8.23
Colorado	377	570	566	619	672	762	22	1.73
Connecticut	122	93	[2]100	142	142	132	42	0.30
Delaware [2]......	10	9	[2]12	18	16	21	50	0.05
Florida..........	1,574	1,540	1,920	2,020	2,000	2,220	5	5.05
Georgia..........	1,504	1,690	1,660	1,450	1,670	1,830	6	4.15
Hawaii..........	106	114	91	75	74	75	45	0.17
Idaho	375	510	398	307	294	322	37	0.73
Illinois	667	828	907	950	911	1,030	16	2.35
Indiana	428	589	729	740	734	774	21	1.76
Iowa	310	456	510	487	477	533	28	1.21
Kansas	349	498	624	661	688	741	23	1.69
Kentucky	359	432	497	372	559	674	24	1.53
Louisiana........	368	434	404	294	331	364	34	0.83
Maine	55	68	[2]102	106	100	122	43	0.28
Maryland	368	324	357	375	382	478	32	1.09
Massachusetts	128	190	210	235	186	221	38	0.50
Michigan	1,440	1,520	1,670	1,580	1,350	1,530	10	3.49
Minnesota	1,482	1,530	1,570	1,090	1,230	1,590	8	3.62
Mississippi	111	131	157	176	174	189	40	0.43
Missouri.........	1,105	1,140	1,320	1,290	1,290	1,540	9	3.50
Montana	573	574	582	442	492	582	27	1.32
Nebraska........	90	146	170	89	94	95	44	0.22
Nevada	2,621	3,060	[2]2,800	2,900	2,940	3,250	2	7.40
New Hampshire	36	50	[2]59	68	64	65	47	0.15
New Jersey	229	243	286	285	272	330	36	0.75
New Mexico.......	1,103	1,130	812	571	533	811	20	1.85
New York.........	773	886	970	1,010	978	1,060	15	2.41
North Carolina	586	735	779	708	676	822	19	1.87
North Dakota	25	31	42	39	38	52	48	0.12
Ohio	733	891	1,060	1,060	968	1,090	13	2.48
Oklahoma	259	357	453	462	479	498	30	1.13
Oregon	205 ●	239	[2]439	320	311	356	35	0.81
Pennsylvania	1,031	1,080	[2]1,250	1,270	1,260	1,400	11	3.18
Rhode Island	18	31	24	17	26	37	49	0.08
South Carolina	450	447	560	460	484	586	26	1.33
South Dakota	319	332	260	186	206	210	39	0.48
Tennessee........	663	665	770	629	606	660	25	1.50
Texas	1,459	1,680	2,050	2,180	2,030	2,400	4	5.47
Utah	1,335	1,850	[2]1,420	1,240	1,260	1,740	7	3.95
Vermont	87	60	43	71	73	69	46	0.16
Virginia	507	515	692	697	727	868	18	1.97
Washington	483 ●	582	691	450	430	447	33	1.02
West Virginia	133	181	[2]182	173	168	179	41	0.41
Wisconsin	215	416	349	340	404	487	31	1.11
Wyoming.........	911	973	922	1,010	1,010	1,090	14	2.48

X Not applicable. [1] Includes undistributed not shown separately. [2] Partial data only; excludes values withheld to avoid disclosing individual company data.

Source: U.S. Geological Survey, *Minerals Yearbook*, annual, and *Mineral Commodities Summaries*, annual. See also <http://minerals.er.usgs.gov/minerals/pubs/mcs/2004/mcs2004.pdf> (released 31 January 2004).

U.S. Census Bureau, Statistical Abstract of the United States: 2006

Table 869. **Principal Fuels, Nonmetals, and Metals—World Production and the U.S. Share: 1990 to 2004**

[In millions of short tons (5,386 represents 5,386,000,000), except as indicated]

Mineral	Unit	World production				Percent U.S. of world			
		1990	1995	2000	2004 [1]	1990	1995	2000	2004 [1]
Fuels: [2]									
Coal	Mil. sh. ton	5,386	5,218	5,059	(NA)	19	20	22	(NA)
Petroleum (crude)	Bil. bbl	22.1	22.8	24.9	26.5	12	11	9	7
Natural gas (dry, marketable)	Tril. cu. ft.	73.6	78.0	88.0	(NA)	24	24	19	(NA)
Natural gas plant liquids	Bil. bbl	1.7	2.0	2.3	(NA)	34	32	31	(NA)
Nonmetals:									
Asbestos	1,000 metric tons	4,010	2,180	2,110	2,280	(D)	(Z)	(Z)	-
Barite	1,000 metric tons	5,770	4,870	6,470	6,900	7	11	6	8
Feldspar	1,000 metric tons	5,990	7,910	9,580	11,000	11	11	8	7
Fluorspar	1,000 metric tons	5,120	4,170	4,470	4,930	1	1	(NA)	-
Gypsum	Mil. metric tons	104	98	106	106	15	17	19	17
Mica (incl. scrap)	1,000 metric tons	217	328	328	300	51	43	31	25
Nitrogen, (fixed) - ammonia	Mil. metric tons	98	100	108	109	13	13	11	8
Phosphate rock, gross wt.	Mil. metric tons	162	130	132	138	29	33	30	27
Potash (K₂O equivalent)	Mil. metric tons	28	25	27	30	6	6	4	4
Sulfur, elemental	Mil. metric tons	58	54	58	63	20	22	19	16
Metals, mine basis:									
Bauxite	Mil. metric tons	113	112	136	156	(D)	(D)	(NA)	(NA)
Columbian concentrates (Nb content)	1,000 metric tons	12	18	33	33	-	-	-	-
Copper	1,000 metric tons	8,950	10,100	13,200	14,500	18	18	11	8
Gold	Metric tons	2,180	2,230	2,590	2,470	14	14	14	10
Iron ore	Mil. metric tons	983	1,030	1,070	1,250	6	6	6	4
Lead [3]	1,000 metric tons	3,370	2,830	3,184	3,150	15	14	15	14
Mercury	Metric tons	4,523	3,160	1,350	1,750	12	(D)	(NA)	(D)
Molybdenum	1,000 metric tons	111	126	133	139	55	48	31	29
Nickel [3]	1,000 metric tons	974	1,040	1,270	1,400	(Z)	(Z)	(Z)	-
Silver	1,000 metric tons	16	15	18	20	13	10	11	6
Tantalum concentrates	Metric tons	344	356	1,040	1,270	-	-	-	-
Titanium concentrates:									
Ilmenite	1,000 metric tons	4,070	4,010	5,010	4,800	(D)	(D)	7	6
Rutile	1,000 metric tons	481	416	387	400	(D)	(D)	(D)	(D)
Tungsten [3]	1,000 metric tons	52	39	44	60	(D)	-	(NA)	-
Vanadium [3]	1,000 metric tons	33	34	56	44	6	6	-	-
Zinc [3]	1,000 metric tons	7,150	7,280	8,788	9,100	7	8	10	8
Metals, smelter basis:									
Aluminum	1,000 metric tons	19,300	19,700	24,400	28,900	21	17	15	9
Cadmium	1,000 metric tons	20	19	20	17	8	7	10	3
Copper	1,000 metric tons	9,472	10,400	11,000	12,700	15	15	9	4
Iron, pig	Mil. metric tons	551	536	573	703	9	10	8	6
Lead [4]	1,000 metric tons	5,950	5,590	6,580	NA	22	25	22	(D)
Magnesium [5]	1,000 metric tons	354	395	428	570	39	36	(D)	(D)
Raw Steel	Mil. metric tons	771	752	845	1,030	12	13	12	9
Tin [6]	1,000 metric tons	220	189	271	250	-	-	2	-
Zinc	1,000 metric tons	7,180	7,370	9,137	10,100	5	5	4	3

- Represents or rounds to zero. D Withheld to avoid disclosing company data. NA Not available. Z Less than half the unit of measure. [1] Preliminary data. [2] Source: Energy Information Administration, *International Energy Annual.* [3] Content of ore and concentrate. [4] Refinery production. [5] Primary production; no smelter processing necessary. [6] Production from primary sources only.

Source: Nonfuels, through 1990, U.S. Bureau of Mines, thereafter, U.S. Geological Survey, *Minerals Yearbook,* annual, and *Mineral Commodities Summaries,* annual; fuels, U.S. Energy Information Administration, *International Energy Annual. See also* <http://minerals.er.usgs.gov/minerals/pubs/mcs/2005/mcs2005.pdf>.

Table 870. **Net U.S. Imports of Selected Minerals and Metals as Percent of Apparent Consumption: 1980 to 2004**

[In percent. Based on net imports which equal the difference between imports and exports plus or minus Government stockpile and industry stock changes]

Minerals in rank of net imports	1980	1990	1995	1999	2000	2001	2002	2003	2004
Bauxite [1]	94	98	99	100	100	100	100	100	100
Columbium	100	100	100	100	100	100	100	100	100
Manganese	98	100	100	100	100	100	100	100	100
Mica (sheet)	100	100	100	100	100	100	100	100	100
Strontium	100	100	100	100	100	100	100	100	100
Vanadium	35	(D)	84	76	100	100	100	100	100
Tin	79	71	84	85	88	86	88	89	88
Tantalum	90	86	80	80	80	80	80	80	80
Barite	44	71	65	67	84	86	78	77	79
Cobalt	93	84	79	75	78	76	72	79	76
Tungsten	53	81	90	65	66	64	69	63	73
Chromium	67	80	75	79	77	63	69	73	72
Potash	65	68	75	80	80	80	80	80	70
Zinc [2]	60	64	71	72	72	73	75	72	70
Silver	7	(NA)	(NA)	39	43	44	68	56	54
Nickel	76	64	60	63	56	46	46	48	49
Copper	16	15	27	27	37	22	37	40	43
Aluminum	([3])	([3])	23	31	33	38	39	38	41
Gypsum	35	46	29	25	27	26	23	23	26
Iron and steel	25	13	21	17	18	16	15	10	18
Iron ore	25	21	18	18	10	26	10	13	8

D Withheld to avoid disclosure. NA Not available. [1] Includes alumina. [2] Beginning 1990, effect of sharp rise in exports of concentrates. If calculated on a refined zinc-only basis, reliance would be about the same as pre-1990 level; 1990, 64%; 1995, 71%; and 1999, 71%. [3] Net exports.

Source: Through 1994, U.S. Bureau of Mines; thereafter, U.S. Geological Survey, *Mineral Commodity Summaries;* import and export data from U.S. Census Bureau.

Table 871. Federal Offshore Leasing, Exploration, Production, and Revenue: 1990 to 2004

[In millions (56.79 represents 56,790,000), except as indicated. See source for explanation of terms and for reliability statement]

Item	Unit	1990	1995	1999	2000	2001	2002	2003	2004
Tracts offered.	Number. . . .	10,459	10,995	7,453	7,992	8,790	8,548	10,349	8,676
Tracts leased.	Number. . . .	825	835	333	553	942	804	923	888
Acres offered.	Millions. . . .	56.79	59.70	40.22	42.89	49.15	45.69	55.31	46.14
Acres leased	Millions. . . .	4.30	4.34	1.77	2.92	5.00	4.20	4.85	4.69
Bonus paid for leased tracts	Bil. dol	0.6	0.4	0.3	0.3	1.0	0.1	0.4	0.6
New wells being drilled:									
Active	Number. . . .	120	124	219	224	213	119	135	156
Suspended.	Number. . . .	266	247	110	146	97	72	48	56
Wells completed.	Number. . . .	13,167	13,475	13,676	13,718	13,921	13,282	13,619	13,556
Cumulative wells (since 1953):									
Wells plugged and abandoned. . .	Number. . . .	14,677	18,008	22,115	22,814	24,218	25,232	26,867	28,076
Revenue, total [1]	Bil. dol	3.4	2.7	3.2	5.2	[2]5.8	5.0	5.9	5.3
Bonuses	Bil. dol	0.8	0.4	0.2	0.4	[2]0.5	0.1	1.1	0.52
Oil and gas royalties [1]	Bil. dol	2.6	2.1	2.6	4.1	[2]4.8	4.7	4.4	4.5
Rentals	Bil. dol	0.09	0.09	0.21	0.21	[2]0.13	0.44	0.25	0.21
Sales value [3]	Bil. dol	17.0	13.8	17.4	27.4	[2]31.4	31.0	29	30.6
Oil	Bil. dol	7.0	6.3	6.5	11.5	[2]11.3	12.1	8.3	8.4
Natural gas	Bil. dol	9.5	7.5	10.9	15.9	[2]20.1	18.9	20.7	22.2
Sales volume: [4]									
Oil	Mil. bbls. . . .	324	409	513	566	[2]463	612	310	248
Natural gas	Bil. cu. ft. . . .	5,093	4,692	4,992	4,723	[2]3,470	4,971	3,501	3,941

[1] Includes condensate royalties. [2] Covers January through September 2001 only. [3] Production value is value at time of production, not current value. [4] Excludes sales volumes for gas lost, gas plant products or sulfur.

Source: U.S. Department of the Interior, Minerals Management Service, *Federal Offshore Statistics*, annual.

Table 872. Uranium Concentrate (U₃O₈) Industry—Summary: 1990 to 2004

[In million feet (1.7 represents 1,700,000), except as indicated. See also Table 911 in Section 19, Energy and Utilities]

Item	Unit	1990	1995	1998	1999	2000	2001	2002	2003	2004
Exploration and development, surface drilling.	Mil. ft.	1.7	1.3	4.6	2.5	1.0	0.7	(D)	(D)	1.2
Expenditures	Mil. dol.	(NA)	2.6	18.1	7.9	5.6	2.7	(D)	(D)	10.6
Number of mines operated.	Number.	39	12	15	14	10	7	6	4	6
Underground	Number.	27	-	4	3	1	-	-	1	2
Openpit.	Number.	2	-	-	-	-	-	-	-	-
In situ leaching	Number.	7	5	6	6	4	3	3	2	3
Other sources	Number.	3	7	5	5	5	4	3	1	1
Mine production	1,000 pounds .	5,876	3,528	4,782	4,548	3,123	2,647	2,405	2,200	2,452
Underground	1,000 pounds .	(D)	-	(D)	(D)	(D)	(D)	(D)	(D)	(D)
Openpit.	1,000 pounds .	1,881	-	-	-	-	-	-	-	-
In situ leaching.	1,000 pounds .	(D)	3,372	3,721	3,830	2,995	(D)	(D)	(D)	(D)
Other sources	1,000 pounds .	3,995	156	1,062	718	128	(D)	(D)	(D)	(D)
Uranium concentrate production . .	1,000 pounds .	8,886	6,043	4,705	4,611	3,958	2,639	2,344	2,000	2,282
Concentrate shipments from mills and plants	1,000 pounds .	12,957	5,500	4,863	5,527	3,187	2,203	3,810	1,600	2,280
Employment	Person-years . .	1,335	1,107	1,120	848	627	423	426	321	420

- Represents zero. D Data withheld to avoid disclosing figures for individual companies. NA Not available.

Source: U.S. Department of Energy, *Uranium Industry*, annual. See also <http://www.eia.doe.gov/fuelnuclear.html>.

Natural Resources 581

Table 873. Petroleum Industry—Summary: 1980 to 2003

[548 represents 548,000. Includes all costs incurred for drilling and equipping wells to point of completion as productive wells or abandonment after drilling becomes unproductive. Based on sample of operators of different size drilling establishments]

Item	Unit	1980	1990	1995	1998	1999	2000	2001	2002	2003
Crude oil producing wells										
Dec. 31).....	1,000	548	602	574	562	546	534	530	529	520
Daily output per well......	Bbl......	15.9	12.2	11.4	11.1	10.8	10.9	10.9	10.9	11.0
Completed wells drilled, total.....	1,000	57.73	26.50	17.75	20.77	16.53	25.68	31.46	23.46	27.56
Crude oil	1,000	30.88	11.54	7.09	6.77	4.02	7.09	7.74	5.83	5.48
Gas................	1,000	15.25	10.36	7.78	10.80	10.34	15.85	21.10	15.28	19.15
Dry	1,000	11.60	4.60	2.88	3.19	2.17	2.74	2.63	2.35	2.93
Average depth per well [1]	Feet	4,172	4,649	5,500	6,059	5,254	4,890	5,361	5,305	5,842
Average cost per well [1]	$1,000 ...	368	384	513	769	856	755	943	1,054	(NA)
Average cost per foot [1]	Dollars ...	77.02	76.07	87.22	128.97	152.02	142.16	181.94	195.31	(NA)
Crude oil production, total.......	Mil. bbl....	3,138	2,685	2,394	2,282	2,147	2,125	2,117	2,097	2,094
Value at wells.............	Bil. dol....	67.9	53.8	35.0	24.8	33.4	56.9	46.3	47.21	57.71
Average price per barrel	Dollars ...	21.59	20.03	14.62	10.87	15.56	26.72	21.84	22.51	27.56
Lower 48 states...........	Mil. bbl...	2,548	2,037	1,853	1,853	1,764	1,771	1,766	1,738	1,738
Alaska.................	Mil. bbl...	590	647	542	429	383	354	351	359	356
Onshore................	Mil. bbl...	2,760	2,290	1,838	1,664	1,508	1,478	1,416	1,366	1,335
Offshore...............	Mil. bbl...	377	395	557	618	639	647	702	731	759
Imports: Crude oil	Mil. bbl....	1,921	2,151	2,639	3,178	3,187	3,311	3,405	3,336	3,521
Refined petroleum products....	Mil. bbl....	601	775	586	731	775	872	928	872	952
Exports: Crude oil	Mil. bbl....	104.8	39.8	34.7	40.2	43.1	18.3	7.3	3.3	4.4
Proved reserves	Bil. bbl. ...	29.8	26.3	22.4	21.0	21.8	22.0	22.4	22.7	21.9
Operable refineries	Number...	319	205	175	163	159	158	155	153*	149
Capacity (Jan. 1).......	Mil. bbl...	6,566	5,683	5,632	5,734	5,935	6,026	6,057	6,127	6,116
Refinery input, total	Mil. bbl...	5,119	5,325	5,555	5,893	5,878	5,948	5,979	5,955	6,032
Crude oil	Mil. bbl...	4,921	4,894	5,100	5,434	5,403	5,499	5,522	5,456	5,586
Natural gas plant liquids.....	Mil. bbl...	169	170	172	147	136	139	157	157	153
Other liquids	Mil. bbl...	30	260	775	311	338	310	301	343	293
Refinery output, total	Mil. bbl...	5,337	5,574	5,838	6,216	6,201	6,294	6,309	6,305	6,383
Motor gasoline...........	Mil. bbl...	2,370	2,540	2,723	2,881	2,896	2,902	2,928	2,987	2,992
Jet fuel...............	Mil. bbl...	365	543	517	557	571	586	558	553	543
Distillate fuel oil	Mil. bbl...	971	1,068	1,152	1,250	1,241	1,307	1,349	1,311	1,356
Residual fuel oil	Mil. bbl...	577	347	288	278	255	254	263	219	242
Liquefied petroleum gases ...	Mil. bbl...	120	182	239	246	250	257	243	245	240
Utilization rate.............	Percent ...	75.4	87.1	92.0	95.6	92.6	92.6	92.6	90.7	92.5

NA Not available. [1] Source: American Petroleum Institute, *Joint Association Survey on Drilling Costs,* annual.

Source: Except as noted, U.S. Energy Information Administration, *Annual Energy Review, Petroleum Supply Annual; U.S. Crude Oil, Natural Gas,* and *Natural Gas Liquids Reserves;* and *Monthly Energy Review.*

Table 874. U.S. Petroleum Balance: 1980 to 2003

[In millions of barrels (6,242 represents 6,242,000,000). Minus sign (-) indicates decreased]

Item	1980	1990	1995	1998	1999	2000	2001	2002	2003
Petroleum products supplied for domestic use	6,242	6,201	7,087	6,905	7,125	7,211	7,172	7,213	7,312
Production of products	5,765	5,934	6,940	6,733	6,774	6,903	6,942	6,925	6,979
Crude input to refineries	4,934	4,894	5,718	5,434	5,403	5,514	5,522	5,456	5,586
Oil, field production.............	3,138	2,685	2,406	2,282	2,147	2,125	2,118	2,097	2,073
Alaska..................	592	647	542	429	383	354	351	359	356
Lower 48 States	2,555	2,037	1,853	1,853	1,764	1,771	1,766	1,738	1,718
Net imports	1,821	2,112	2,604	3,137	3,144	3,301	3,398	3,333	3,523
Imports (gross excluding SPR) [1] ...	1,910	2,142	2,639	3,178	3,184	3,317	3,401	3,330	3,528
SPR [1] imports	16	10	-	-	3	3	4	6	-
Exports..................	-105	40	35	40	43	18	7	3	5
Other sources	33	98	102	15	113	82	7	26	-1▸
Natural gas liquids (NGL), supply	577	574	708	717	757	799	801	798	756
Other liquids	253	465	514	582	614	589	619	671	637
Net imports of refined products	484	326	101	225	252	305	303	249	312
Imports	578	598	407	508	537	648	636	581	660
Exports	94	272	307	283	284	343	333	332	348
Stock withdrawal, refined products	-7	-59	46	-53	98	2	-73	39	21
TYPE OF PRODUCT SUPPLIED									
Total products supplied	6,242	6,201	6,469	6,905	7,125	7,211	7,172	7,213	7,312
Finished motor gasoline	2,407	2,641	2,843	3,012	3,077	3,101	3,143	3,229	3,261
Distillate fuel oil..................	1,049	1,103	1,170	1,263	1,304	1,362	1,404	1,378	1,433
Residual fuel oil	918	449	311	324	303	333	296	255	282
Liquified petroleum gases [2]..........	414	568	693	713	801	816	746	789	757
Other	1,454	1,440	1,452	1,593	1,639	1,598	1,583	1,561	1,579
ENDING STOCKS									
Ending stocks, all oils...........	1,392	1,621	1,563	1,647	1,493	1,468	1,586	1,548	1,568
Crude oil and lease condensate..........	358	323	303	324	284	286	312	278	269
Strategic Petroleum Reserve (SPR) [1]	108	586	592	571	567	541	550	599	638
Other	926	712	668	752	641	641	724	671	661

- Represents zero. [1] SPR = Strategic petroleum reserve. For more information, see Table 914. [2] Includes ethane.

Source: U.S. Energy Information Administration, *Petroleum Supply Annual,* volume 1. See also <http://www.eia.doe.gov/pub/oilgas /petroleum/datapublications/petroleumsupplyannual/psavolume1/current/pdf/volume1all.pdf> (released June 2004).

Table 875. **Crude Petroleum and Natural Gas—Production and Value by Major Producing States: 1990 to 2003**

[2,685 mil. bbl. represents 2,685,000,000 bbl. or 18,594 bil. cu. ft. represents 18,594,000,000,000 cu. ft.]

| State | Crude petroleum | | | | | | Natural gas marketed production [1] | | | | | |
| | Quantity (mil. bbl.) | | | Value (mil. dol.) | | | Quantity (bil. cu. ft.) | | | Value (mil. dol.) | | |
	1990	2000	2003	1990	2000	2003	1990	2000	2003	1990	2000	2003
Total [2]	2,685	2,131	2,073	53,772	56,932	57,144	18,594	20,198	19,912	31,658	74,339	97,250
AL	18	10	8	387	289	228	135	523	346	373	2,087	2,051
AK	658	355	356	10,086	8,439	8,503	403	459	490	554	807	1,179
AR	10	7	7	222	193	192	175	172	170	360	898	877
CA	322	271	250	5,732	6,729	6,608	363	377	337	857	1,812	1,698
CO	31	18	21	722	533	648	243	753	1,011	377	2,765	4,591
FL	6	5	3	(NA)	(NA)	(NA)	6	6	3	15	(NA)	(NA)
IL	20	12	12	467	343	340	1	(Z)	(Z)	1	(NA)	(NA)
IN	3	2	2	73	59	53	(Z)	1	1	1	3	8
KS	59	34	34	1,359	970	974	574	526	419	893	1,690	1,815
KY	5	3	3	124	92	69	75	82	88	169	258	398
LA	148	105	90	3,409	3,060	2,750	5,242	5,069	1,350	9,587	18,642	7,614
MI	20	8	7	458	222	190	140	297	237	420	724	950
MS	30	20	17	630	520	456	95	89	134	167	293	688
MT	20	15	19	429	429	554	50	70	86	90	198	321
NE	5	3	3	119	83	79	1	1	1	2	3	5
NM	66	67	66	1,472	1,935	1,952	965	1,687	1,604	1,629	5,790	7,307
NY	(Z)	(Z)	(Z)	9	(NA)	(NA)	25	18	36	55	67	209
ND	39	33	29	849	922	861	52	52	56	93	206	197
OH	8	7	6	196	181	159	155	105	94	393	426	552
OK	117	70	65	2,690	2,035	1,942	2,258	1,613	1,558	3,548	5,857	7,737
PA	2	2	2	54	43	72	178	201	160	417	(NA)	(NA)
TX	674	443	406	15,060	12,681	11,821	6,343	6,205	5,244	9,939	24,384	27,171
UT	23	16	13	524	446	378	146	269	268	249	883	1,103
WV	2	1	1	43	38	37	178	264	188	568	(NA)	(NA)
WY	103	61	52	2,169	1,633	1,396	736	1,088	1,539	856	3,640	6,362
Federal offshore	296	558	599	6,468	15,252	17,073	(NA)	(NA)	(NA)	(NA)	(NA)	(NA)
Lower 48 states	2,027	1,776	1,718	(NA)	(NA)	(NA)	18,191	19,739	19,422	(NA)	(NA)	(NA)

NA Not available.   Z Less than 500,000 barrels or 500 million cubic feet.   [1] Excludes nonhydrocarbon gases.   [2] Includes other states not shown separately. State production does not include state offshore production. U.S. level totals shown in Tables 879 and 880 may contain revisions not carried to state level.

Source: U.S. Energy Information Administration, *Petroleum Supply Annual*, Vol. 2, and *Petroleum Marketing Annual;* and *Natural Gas Annual*, and *Natural Gas Monthly.*

Table 876. **Crude Oil, Natural Gas, and Natural Gas Liquids—Reserves by State: 1990 to 2003**

[26,254 mil. bbl. represents 26,254,000,000 bbl. As of December 31. Proved reserves are estimated quantities of the mineral, which geological and engineering data demonstrate with reasonable certainty, to be recoverable in future years from known reservoirs under existing economic and operating conditions. Based on a sample of operators of oil and gas wells]

| Area | 1990 | | | 2000 | | | 2003 | | |
	Crude oil proved reserves (mil. bbl.)	Natural gas (bil. cu. ft.)	Natural gas liquids (mil. bbl.)	Crude oil proved reserves (mil. bbl.)	Natural gas (bil. cu. ft.)	Natural gas liquids (mil. bbl.)	Crude oil proved reserves (mil. bbl.)	Natural gas (bil. cu. ft.)	Natural gas liquids (mil. bbl.)
United States [1]	26,254	169,346	7,586	22,045	177,427	8,345	21,891	189,044	7,459
Alabama	44	[4]4,125	170	34	4149	150	52	4,301	60
Alaska	6,524	9,300	340	4,861	9,237	277	4,446	8,285	387
Arkansas	60	1,731	9	48	1,581	5	50	1,663	3
California	[2]4,658	[2]3,185	[2]105	3,813	2,849	101	3,452	2,450	101
Colorado	305	4,555	169	217	10,428	316	217	15,436	395
Florida	(NA)	(NA)	(NA)	76	82	11	68	79	17
Illinois	(NA)	(NA)	(NA)	111	(NA)	(NA)	125	(NA)	(NA)
Indiana	131	(NA)	(NA)	15	(NA)	(NA)	19	(NA)	(NA)
Kansas	(NA)	(NA)	(NA)	237	5,299	306	243	4,819	248
Kentucky	321	9,614	313	24	1,760	56	25	1,889	66
Louisiana	33	1,016	25	529	9,239	436	452	9,325	295
Michigan	(NA)	(NA)	(NA)	56	2,729	35	75	3,428	48
Mississippi	(NA)	(NA)	(NA)	182	618	8	169	746	7
Montana	(NA)	(NA)	(NA)	235	885	4	315	1,059	8
Nebraska	221	899	15	18	(NA)	(NA)	16	(NA)	(NA)
New Mexico	(NA)	(NA)	(NA)	719	17,322	896	677	17,020	875
New York	687	17,260	990	(NA)	322	(NA)	(NA)	365	(NA)
North Dakota	285	586	60	270	433	54	353	448	45
Ohio	65	1,214	(NA)	59	1,185	(NA)	66	1,126	(NA)
Oklahoma	734	16,151	657	610	13,699	734	588	15,401	686
Pennsylvania	22	1,720	(NA)	15	1,741	(NA)	13	2,487	(NA)
Texas	[2]7,106	[2]38,192	[2]2,575	5,273	42,082	2,819	4,583	45,730	2,517
Utah	249	1,510	[3]	283	4,235	[3]	221	3,516	[3]
Virginia	(NA)	138	(NA)	(NA)	1,704	(NA)	·	1,717	(NA)
West Virginia	31	2,207	86	12	2,900	105	13	3,306	68
Wyoming	794	9,944	[4]812	561	16,158	947	517	21,744	[4]898
Federal offshore	2,805	31,433	619	3,770	26,748	1,078	5,120	22,570	725
Lower 48 States	19,730	160,046	7,246	17,184	168,190	8,068	17,445	180,759	7,072

NA Not available.   [1] Includes miscellaneous not shown separately.   [2] Excludes Federal offshore.   [3] Included with Wyoming.   [4] Includes Utah.

Source: Energy Information Administration, *U.S. Crude Oil, Natural Gas, and Natural Gas Liquids Reserves, 2003 Annual Report*, December 2004.

Natural Resources 583

Table 877. **World Daily Crude Oil Production by Major Producing Country: 1980 to 2002**

[In thousands of barrels per day (59,600 barrels represents 59,600,000 barrels)]

Country	1980	1990	1995	1997	1998	1999	2000	2001	2002
World, total [1]	59,600	60,566	62,335	65,690	66,921	65,848	68,342	67,942	66,842
Algeria	1,106	1,175	1,202	1,277	1,246	1,202	1,254	1,310	1,306
Angola	150	475	646	714	735	745	746	742	896
Argentina	491	483	715	834	847	802	761	802	757
Australia	380	575	562	588	544	539	722	657	626
Brazil	182	631	695	841	969	1,132	1,269	1,295	1,455
Canada	1,435	1,553	1,805	1,922	1,981	1,977	1,977	2,029	2,171
China	2,114	2,774	2,990	3,200	3,198	3,195	3,249	3,300	3,390
Colombia	126	440	585	652	733	816	691	625	577
Egypt	595	873	920	856	834	852	748	698	631
India	182	660	703	675	661	653	646	642	665
Indonesia	1,577	1,462	1,503	1,520	1,518	1,472	1,423	1,340	1,267
Iran	1,662	3,088	3,643	3,664	3,634	3,557	3,696	3,724	3,444
Iraq	2,514	2,040	560	1,155	2,150	2,508	2,571	2,390	2,023
Kazakhstan	(X)	(X)	362	466	476	530	610	721	818
Kuwait	1,656	1,175	2,057	2,007	2,085	1,898	2,079	1,998	1,894
Libya	1,787	1,375	1,390	1,446	1,390	1,319	1,410	1,367	1,319
Malaysia	283	619	682	700	720	693	690	659	698
Mexico	1,936	2,553	2,618	3,023	3,070	2,906	3,012	3,157	3,177
Nigeria	2,055	1,810	1,993	2,132	2,153	2,130	2,165	2,256	2,118
Norway	528	1,704	2,768	3,143	3,017	3,018	3,197	3,117	2,990
Oman	282	685	851	904	900	910	970	913	897
Qatar	472	406	442	550	696	665	737	714	679
Russia	(X)	(X)	5,995	5,920	5,854	6,079	6,479	6,917	7,408
Saudi Arabia	9,900	6,410	8,231	8,362	8,389	7,833	8,404	8,031	7,634
Syria	164	388	575	561	553	538	523	518	511
United Arab Emirates	1,709	2,117	2,233	2,316	2,345	2,169	2,368	2,205	2,082
United Kingdom	1,622	1,820	2,489	2,518	2,616	2,684	2,275	2,282	2,292
United States	8,597	7,355	6,560	6,452	6,252	5,881	5,822	5,801	5,746
Venezuela	2,168	2,137	2,750	3,280	3,167	2,826	3,155	3,010	2,604
Yemen	(X)	193	345	362	388	409	440	438	443

X Not applicable. [1] Includes countries not shown separately.

Source: U.S. Energy Information Administration, *International Energy Annual, 2002.* See also <http://tonto.eia.doe.gov/FTPROOT/international/021901.pdf> (issued March 2004).

Table 878. **Liquefied Petroleum Gases—Summary: 1980 to 2004**

[In millions of 42-gallon barrels (561 barrels represents 561,000,000 barrels). Includes ethane]

Item	1980	1990	1995	1999	2000	2001	2002	2003	2004
Production	561	638	760	814	843	813	822	767	795
At natural gas plants	441	456	521	564	587	570	577	527	560
At refineries	121	182	234	250	258	243	245	240	235
Imports	79	68	53	66	79	75	67	82	95
Refinery input	85	107	105	87	87	88	90	83	84
Exports	9	14	21	18	27	16	24	20	16
Stocks, Dec. 31	116	98	93	89	83	121	106	94	104

Source: U.S. Energy Information Administration, *Petroleum Supply Annual,* volume 1.

Table 879. **Natural Gas Plant Liquids—Production and Value: 1980 to 2004**

[Barrels of 42 gallons (567 represents 567,000,000)]

Item	Unit	1980	1990	1995	1999	2000	2001	2002	2003	2004
Field production [1]	Mil. bbl.	567	566	643	675	699	682	686	686	628
Pentanes plus	Mil. bbl.	126	112	122	111	112	112	109	109	100
Liquefied petroleum gases	Mil. bbl.	441	454	521	564	587	570	577	577	527
Natural gas processed	Tril. cu. ft.	15	15	17	17	17	17	16	15	(NA)

NA Not available [1] Includes other finished petroleum products, not shown separately.

Source: U.S. Energy Information Administration, *Petroleum Supply Annual* and *Natural Gas Annual.*

Table 880. **Natural Gas—Supply, Consumption, Reserves, and Marketed Production: 1980 to 2003**

[182 represents 182,000]

Item	Unit	1980	1990	1995	1998	1999	2000	2001	2002	2003
Producing wells (year-end)	1,000	182	269	299	317	302	342	373	384	366
Production value at wells	Bil. dol.	32.1	31.8	30.2	38.2	43.4	74.3	82.3	58.8	97.9
Avg. per 1,000 cu. ft.	Dollars	1.59	1.71	1.55	1.96	2.19	3.68	4.00	2.95	4.88
Proved reserves [1]	Tril. cu. ft.	199	169	165	164	167	177	183	187	189
Marketed production [2]	Bil. cu. ft.	20,180	18,594	19,506	19,961	19,805	20,198	20,570	19,921	20,070
Minus: Extraction losses [3]	Bil. cu. ft.	777	784	908	938	973	1,016	954	957	964
Equals: Dry production	Bil. cu. ft.	19,403	17,810	18,599	19,024	18,832	19,182	19,616	18,964	19,106
Plus: Supplemental gas supplies	Bil. cu. ft.	155	123	110	102	98	90	86	68	65
Equals: Dry production with supplemental gas	Bil. cu. ft.	19,558	17,932	18,709	19,126	18,931	19,272	19,702	19,032	19,171
Plus: Withdrawals from storage	Bil. cu. ft.	1,972	1,986	3,025	2,432	2,808	3,550	2,344	3,180	3,095
Plus: Imports [4]	Bil. cu. ft.	985	1,532	2,841	3,152	3,586	3,782	3,977	4,015	3,928
Plus: Balancing item	Bil. cu. ft.	-640	307	396	657	-119	-306	99	18	-320
Equals: Total supply	Bil. cu. ft.	21,875	21,758	24,971	25,367	25,206	26,298	26,122	26,245	25,874
Minus: Exports	Bil. cu. ft.	49	86	154	159	163	244	373	516	692
Minus: Additions to storage [5]	Bil. cu. ft.	1,949	2,499	2,610	2,961	2,636	2,721	3,510	2,712	3,288
Equals: Consumption, total	Bil. cu. ft.	19,877	19,174	22,207	22,246	22,405	23,333	22,239	23,018	21,894
Lease and plant fuel	Bil. cu. ft.	1,026	1,236	1,220	1,173	1,079	1,151	1,119	1,114	1,123
Pipeline fuel	Bil. cu. ft.	635	660	700	635	645	642	625	667	635
Residential	Bil. cu. ft.	4,752	4,391	4,850	4,520	4,726	4,996	4,771	4,890	5,101
Commercial [6]	Bil. cu. ft.	2,611	2,623	3,031	2,999	3,045	3,182	3,023	3,103	3,129
Industrial	Bil. cu. ft.	7,172	7,018	8,164	8,320	8,079	8,142	7,344	7,557	6,967
Vehicle fuel	Bil. cu. ft.	(NA)	-	5	9	12	13	15	15	15
Electric utilities	Bil. cu. ft.	3,682	3,245	4,237	4,588	4,820	5,206	5,342	5,672	4,924
World production (dry)	Tril. cu. ft.	53.5	73.6	78.0	83.0	84.9	88.3	90.5	92.2	95.2
U.S. production (dry)	Tril. cu. ft.	19.4	17.8	18.6	19.0	18.8	19.2	19.6	18.9	19.0
Percent U.S. of world	Percent	36.3	24.2	23.9	22.9	22.2	21.7	21.7	20.5	20.0

- Represents zero. NA Not available. [1] Estimated, end of year. Source: U.S. Energy Information Administration, *U.S. Crude Oil, Natural Gas,* and *Natural Gas Liquids Reserves,* annual. [2] Marketed production includes gross withdrawals from reservoirs less quantities used for reservoir repressuring and quantities vented or flared. Excludes nonhydrocarbon gases subsequently removed. [3] Volumetric reduction in natural gas resulting from the extraction of natural gas constituents at natural gas processing plants. [4] Includes imports of liquefied natural gas. [5] Includes liquefied natural gas (LNG) storage in above ground tanks. [6] Includes deliveries to municipalities and public authorities for institutional heating and other purposes.
Source: Except as noted, U.S. Energy Information Administration, *Annual Energy Review, International Energy Annual, Natural Gas Annual,* Volume I and II, and *Monthly Energy Review.*

Table 881. **World Natural Gas Production by Major Producing Country: 1980 to 2003**

[In trillion cubic feet (53.35 represents 53,350,000,000,000]

Country	1980	1990	1995	1998	1999	2000	2001	2002	2003
World Total [1]	**53.35**	**73.57**	**77.96**	**83.03**	**84.93**	**88.29**	**90.45**	**92.15**	**95.18**
Russia	(NA)	(NA)	21.01	20.87	20.83	20.63	20.51	21.03	21.77
United States	19.40	17.81	18.60	19.02	18.83	19.18	19.62	18.93	19.04
Canada	2.76	3.85	5.60	5.98	6.27	6.47	6.60	6.63	6.45
Algeria	0.41	1.79	2.05	2.60	2.88	2.94	2.79	2.80	2.91
Iran	0.25	0.84	1.25	1.77	2.04	2.13	2.33	2.65	2.79
Indonesia	0.63	1.53	2.24	2.27	2.51	2.36	2.34	2.48	2.62
Norway	0.92	0.98	1.08	1.63	1.76	1.87	1.95	2.41	2.59
Netherlands	3.40	2.69	2.98	2.84	2.65	2.56	2.75	2.66	2.58
Saudi Arabia	0.33	1.08	1.34	1.65	1.63	1.76	1.90	2.00	2.12
Turkmenistan	(NA)	(NA)	1.14	0.47	0.79	1.64	1.70	1.89	2.08
Uzbekistan	(NA)	(NA)	1.70	1.94	1.96	1.99	2.23	2.04	2.03
Malaysia	0.06	0.65	1.02	1.37	1.42	1.50	1.66	1.71	1.89
United Arab Emirates	0.20	0.78	1.11	1.31	1.34	1.36	1.39	1.53	1.58
Mexico	0.90	0.90	0.96	1.27	1.29	1.31	1.30	1.33	1.49
Argentina	0.28	0.63	0.88	1.04	1.22	1.32	1.31	1.28	1.45
Australia	0.31	0.72	1.03	1.10	1.12	1.16	1.19	1.23	1.26
China	0.51	0.51	0.60	0.78	0.85	0.96	1.07	1.15	1.21
Qatar	0.18	0.28	0.48	0.69	0.78	1.03	0.95	1.04	1.09
Venezuela	0.52	0.76	0.89	1.11	0.95	0.96	1.12	1.05	1.05
India	0.05	0.40	0.63	0.76	0.75	0.79	0.85	0.88	0.96
Egypt	0.03	0.29	0.44	0.49	0.52	0.65	0.87	0.94	0.95
Trinidad and Tobago	0.08	0.18	0.27	0.33	0.41	0.49	0.54	0.61	0.87
Pakistan	0.29	0.48	0.65	0.71	0.78	0.86	0.77	0.81	0.84
Thailand	0.00	0.21	0.37	0.57	0.63	0.66	0.66	0.69	0.79
Germany	(NA)	(NA)	0.74	0.77	0.82	0.78	0.79	0.79	0.78
Ukraine	(NA)	(NA)	0.62	0.64	0.63	0.64	0.64	0.65	0.69
Nigeria	0.04	0.13	0.18	0.21	0.25	0.44	0.53	0.50	0.68
Oman	0.03	0.10	0.15	0.25	0.20	0.32	0.49	0.53	0.58
Kazakhstan	(NA)	(NA)	0.17	0.19	0.16	0.31	0.36	0.46	0.49
Italy	0.44	0.61	0.72	0.67	0.62	0.59	0.54	0.51	0.48
Romania	1.20	1.00	0.68	0.52	0.50	0.48	0.51	0.47	0.43
Bangladesh	0.05	0.16	0.26	0.29	0.32	0.34	0.36	0.38	0.42
Brunei	0.32	0.32	0.33	0.32	0.33	0.35	0.37	0.38	0.40
Bahrain	0.10	0.21	0.23	0.29	0.30	0.30	0.31	0.33	0.34
Kuwait	0.24	0.19	0.21	0.32	0.31	0.34	0.30	0.29	0.29

NA Not available. [1] Includes countries not shown separately.
Source: U. S. Energy Information Administration, *International Energy Annual.* See also <http://www.eia.doe.gov>.

Natural Resources 585

Table 882. Coal Supply, Disposition, and Prices: 1998 to 2003

[In millions of short tons (1,089.9 represents 1,089,900,000)]

Item	1998	1999	2000	2001	2002	2003	2004
United States, total	**1,117.5**	**1,100.4**	**1,073.6**	**1,127.7**	**1,094.3**	**1,071.8**	**1,111.5**
Consumption by sector:							
Total.	1,038.3	1,045.3	1,084.1	1,060.1	1,066.4	1,094.9	1,104.3
Electric power	937.8	946.8	985.8	964.4	977.5	1,005.1	1,015.1
Electric utilities.	910.9	894.1	(NA)	(NA)	(NA)	(NA)	(NA)
Other power producers [1]	26.9	52.7	(NA)	(NA)	(NA)	(NA)	(NA)
Coke plants.	28.2	28.1	28.9	26.1	23.7	24.2	23.7
Other industrial plants	67.4	65.5	65.2	65.3	60.7	61.3	61.2
Residential/commercial users	4.9	4.9	4.1	4.4	4.4	4.2	4.2
Year-end coal stocks:							
Total.	164.6	183.0	140.0	181.9	192.1	165.5	147.2
Electric power	120.5	136.0	102.0	138.5	141.7	121.6	106.7
Coke plants.	2.0	1.9	1.5	1.5	1.4	0.9	1.3
Other industrial plants	5.5	5.6	4.6	6.0	5.8	4.7	4.8
Producers/distributors	36.5	39.5	31.9	35.9	43.3	38.3	34.4
U.S. coal trade:							
Net exports	69.3	49.4	46.0	28.9	22.7	18.0	20.7
Exports	78.0	58.5	58.5	48.7	39.6	43.0	48.0
Steam coal.	31.0	26.3	25.7	23.3	18.1	20.9	21.2
Metallurgical coal.	47.1	32.1	32.8	25.4	21.5	22.1	26.8
Imports	8.7	9.1	12.5	19.8	16.9	25.0	27.3
Average delivered price (dollars per short ton):							
Electric utilities	25.64	24.72	24.28	24.68	24.74	25.72	27.28
Coke plants	46.06	45.85	44.38	46.42	50.67	50.63	61.50
Other industrial plants	32.26	31.59	31.46	32.26	35.49	34.70	39.30
Average free alongside ship (f.a.s.)							
Exports.	38.89	36.50	34.90	36.97	40.44	35.98	54.11
Steam coal	30.24	29.91	29.67	31.88	34.51	26.94	42.03
Metallurgical coal	44.58	41.91	38.99	41.63	45.41	44.55	63.63
Imports.	32.18	30.77	30.10	34.00	35.51	31.45	37.52

NA Not available. [1] Includes utility coal-fired power plants sold to nonutilities during 1998, 1999, and 2000. Coal consumption by cogenerators are included in the end-use sector.

Source: U.S. Energy Information Administration, *U.S. Coal Supply and Demand: 2003 Review*, annual. See also <http://tonto.eia.doe.gov/FTPROOT/coal/coalpubs.htm>.

Table 883. Coal and Coke—Summary: 1980 to 2004

[(830 represents 830,000,000). Includes coal consumed at mines. Recoverability varies between 40 and 90 percent for individual deposits; 50 percent or more of overall U.S. coal reserve base is believed to be recoverable]

Item	Unit	1980	1990	1995	2000	2001	2002	2003	2004
COAL									
Coal production, total [1]	Mil. sh. tons . . .	830	1,029	1,033	1,074	1,128	1,094	1,072	1,111
Value	Bil. dol.	20.45	22.39	19.45	18.02	19.60	19.68	19.27	(NA)
Anthracite production.	Mil. sh. tons . . .	6.1	3.5	4.7	4.6	1.9	1.4	1.3	(NA)
Bituminous coal and lignite.	Mil. sh. tons . . .	824	1,026	1,028	1,069	1,126	1,093	1,068	(NA)
Underground	Mil. sh. tons . . .	337	425	396	374	381	357	353	(NA)
Surface.	Mil. sh. tons . . .	487	605	637	700	747	737	718	(NA)
Exports	Mil. sh. tons . . .	92	106	89	58	49	40	43	48
Imports	Mil. sh. tons . . .	1	3	9	13	20	17	25	27
Consumption [2]	Mil. sh. tons . . .	703	896	941	1,081	1,060	1,066	1,095	(NA)
Electric power utilities	Mil. sh. tons . . .	569	774	829	859	964	978	1,004	(NA)
Industrial	Mil. sh. tons . . .	126	115	106	94	91	84	86	(NA,
Number of mines	Number	5,598	3,243	2,104	1,453	1,512	1,426	1,316	(NA)
Daily employment	1,000	225	131	90	72	77	75	71	(NA)
Production, by state:									
Alabama	Mil. sh. tons . . .	26	29	25	19	19	19	20	22
Illinois	Mil. sh. tons . . .	63	60	48	33	34	33	32	32
Indiana	Mil. sh. tons . . .	31	36	26	28	37	35	35	35
Kentucky	Mil. sh. tons . . .	150	173	154	131	134	124	113	114
Montana	Mil. sh. tons . . .	30	38	39	38	39	37	37	40
Ohio	Mil. sh. tons . . .	39	35	26	22	25	21	22	23
Pennsylvania	Mil. sh. tons . . .	93	71	62	75	74	68	64	66
Virginia	Mil. sh. tons . . .	41	47	34	33	33	30	32	31
West Virginia	Mil. sh. tons . . .	122	169	163	158	162	150	140	148
Wyoming	Mil. sh. tons . . .	95	184	264	339	369	373	376	396
Other States.	Mil. sh. tons . . .	140	187	192	197	201	202	202	204
World production	Mil. sh. tons . . .	4,200	5,386	5,079	4,929	5,227	5,252	(NA)	(NA)
Percent U.S. of world	Percent	19.8	19.1	20.3	21.8	21.6	20.8	(NA)	(NA)
COKE									
Coke production [3]	Mil. sh. tons . . .	46.1	27.6	23.7	20.8	18.9	16.8	17.2	16.9
Imports.	Mil. sh. tons . . .	0.7	0.8	3.8	3.8	2.5	3.2	2.8	6.9
Exports.	Mil. sh. tons . . .	2.1	0.6	1.4	1.1	1.3	0.8	0.7	1.3
Consumption	Mil. sh. tons . . .	41.3	27.8	25.8	23.2	20.2	19.6	19.4	22.5

NA Not available. [1] Includes bituminous coal, subbituminous coal, lignite, and anthracite. [2] Includes some categories not shown separately. [3] Includes beehive coke.

Source: U.S. Energy Information Administration, *Coal Industry*, annual; *Annual Energy Review, International Energy Annual*, and *Annual Coal Report*.

586 Natural Resources

Table 884. **World Coal Production by Major Producing Country: 1980 to 2002**

[In millions of short tons (4,181.6 represents 4,181,600,000)]

Country	1980	1990	1995	1997	1998	1999	2000	2001	2002
World, total	4,181.6	5,347.5	5,078.6	5,135.9	5,048.2	4,943.0	4,929.2	5,227.1	5,252.5
China.	683.6	1,190.4	1,537.0	1,507.1	1,429.0	1,364.9	1,314.4	1,458.7	1,521.2
United States	829.7	1,029.1	1,033.0	1,089.9	1,117.5	1,100.4	1,073.6	1,127.7	1,093.8
India	125.8	247.6	320.6	338.1	343.1	356.3	368.9	385.2	392.6
Australia	116.1	225.8	266.5	291.5	316.8	320.8	338.2	362.9	377.7
South Africa	131.9	193.2	227.3	244.3	246.9	243.0	248.4	250.3	245.3
Russia	(X)	(X)	270.9	252.8	241.0	259.2	264.9	273.4	259.3
Germany [1]	(X)	(X)	274.2	251.7	233.0	226.0	225.3	225.7	231.0
Poland	253.5	237.1	220.2	221.5	196.2	187.6	178.3	178.9	177.8
Korea, North	48.6	51.0	34.5	30.0	27.1	30.6	32.8	33.7	36.6
Ukraine	(X)	(X)	94.6	84.8	85.1	88.0	89.3	92.5	92.6
Kazakhstan.	(X)	(X)	91.9	80.1	76.9	64.3	79.7	82.5	80.7
Canada	40.4	75.3	82.7	86.7	82.8	79.9	76.2	77.6	73.2
Turkey	20.2	52.3	60.6	66.0	74.3	73.9	69.6	72.5	58.7
Indonesia	0.6	11.6	45.4	60.5	68.4	81.3	84.4	102.0	111.6
Czech Republic	(X)	(X)	82.6	81.6	74.4	65.2	71.8	72.9	70.4
Greece.	25.6	57.2	63.6	64.9	67.1	68.4	70.4	73.1	75.0
Colombia	4.5	22.6	28.4	35.9	37.2	36.1	42.0	47.9	48.3
United Kingdom	143.8	104.1	52.5	51.8	44.1	39.9	33.7	34.7	32.6
Romania.	38.8	42.1	45.3	37.3	28.9	25.2	32.3	36.7	33.6
Bulgaria	33.3	34.9	30.5	32.7	33.2	27.9	29.1	29.4	28.4
Spain	31.2	39.6	31.4	29.1	28.6	26.8	25.9	25.0	24.3
Thailand	1.6	13.7	20.3	25.8	22.0	20.1	19.6	21.6	21.8
Hungary	28.3	19.7	16.1	17.2	16.1	16.0	15.5	15.3	14.2
Mexico	4.0	8.6	10.3	11.5	12.4	11.4	12.5	12.8	12.1

X Not applicable.   [1] For 1980 and 1990, represents East and West Germany combined.

Source: U.S. Energy Information Administration, *International Energy Annual, 2002*. See also <http://tonto.eia.doe .gov/FTPROOT/international/021901.pdf> (issued March 2004).

Table 885. **Demonstrated Coal Reserves by Major Producing State: 2002 and 2003**

[In millions of short tons (497,708 represents 497,708,000,000). As of January 1. The demonstrated reserve base represents the sum of coal in both measured and indicated resource categories of reliability. Measured resources of coal are estimates that have a high degree of geologic assurance from sample analyses and measurements from closely spaced and geological well known sample sites. Indicated resources are estimates based partly from sample and analyses and measurements and partly from reasonable geologic projections]

State	2002			2003		
		Method of mining			Method of mining	
	Total reserves	Under ground	Surface	Total reserves	Under ground	Surface
United States [1] . . .	497,708	336,928	160,780	496,092	336,199	159,893
Alabama.	4,318	1,097	3,221	4,282	1,066	3,215
Alaska	6,115	5,423	692	6,114	5,423	691
Colorado.	16,430	11,661	4,769	16,365	11,599	4,766
Illinois	104,648	88,077	16,570	104,589	88,025	16,563
Indiana.	9,637	8,801	835	9,586	8,784	802
Iowa	2,189	1,732	457	2,189	1,732	457
Kentucky	30,614	17,484	13,130	30,422	17,346	13,076
Kentucky, Eastern	10,977	1,491	9,486	10,824	1,387	9,437
Kentucky, Western . . .	19,637	15,993	3,644	19,597	15,959	3,639
Missouri	5,991	1,479	4,512	5,991	1,479	4,512
Montana	119,377	70,958	48,418	119,330	70,958	48,372
New Mexico	12,249	6,199	6,051	12,212	6,187	6,025
North Dakota.	9,166		9,166	9,128	(NA)	9,128
Ohio	23,419	17,631	5,788	23,382	17,606	5,777
Oklahoma	1,562	1,233	328	1,559	1,233	327
Pennsylvania.	27,838	23,541	4,297	27,719	23,437	4,283
Anthracite	7,204	3,845	3,359	7,203	3,845	3,358
Bituminous	20,634	19,696	938	20,517	19,592	925
Texas	12,559	-	12,559	12,500	(NA)	12,500
Utah	5,534	5,267	268	5,488	5,221	268
Virginia	1,850	1,247	603	1,794	1,204	590
Washington.	1,356	1,332	23	1,348	1,332	16
West Virginia	33,713	29,722	3,991	33,473	29,548	3,925
Wyoming	65,291	42,501	22,790	64,821	42,501	22,320

- Represents or rounds to zero.   NA Not available.   [1] Includes other states not shown separately.

Source: U.S. Energy Information Administration, unpublished data from the Coal Reserves Database.

Natural Resources   587

No. 331.—CENTRAL ELECTRIC STATIONS: EQUIPMENT, EMPLOYEES, OUTPUT, AND SALES

[NOTE.—A central electric station is one selling current to public or private consumers, or a municipal plant supplying current for streets, public buildings, etc. Isolated or private plants operated solely for the benefit of the owner in connection with factories, mines, stores, hotels, institutions, etc., which in the aggregate produce great quantities of current, are not included. The business of electric street railways is shown only so far as that portion of their business relating to the sale of current can be segregated. Electric plants operated by the Federal or State Governments are excluded even when they sell current to private consumers. One central electric station often sells current to another, so that there is considerable duplication in total sales. Net sales are considerably less than current generated because of wire losses, self consumption, etc. Part of the sales reported as made to other public-service corporations, however, go to street railways, and the exact amount of duplication in the central station sales is not known. The separate data given for hydroelectric stations relate only to those with a capacity of 1,000 horsepower or more]

	All central electric stations				Commercial stations, 1922	Municipal stations, 1922	Larger hydro-electric stations, 1922[1]
	1907	1912	1917	1922			
Number of stations[2]	4,714	5,221	6,542	6,355	3,774	2,581	267
Prime movers, horsepower,							
total	4,098,188	7,530,044	12,936,755	20,296,235	19,016,107	1,280,128	8,444,288
Steam engines	1,875,863	1,895,382	1,701,677	1,816,665	1,495,055	321,610	163,439
Steam turbines	817,410	3,054,396	6,747,399	12,354,557	11,815,231	539,326	2,646,294
Water wheels and turbines	1,349,087	2,469,231	4,277,273	5,822,018	5,515,298	306,810	5,628,065
Internal-combustion engines	55,828	111,035	210,406	302,995	189,613	113,382	6,490
Dynamos:							
Number	12,173	12,610	13,428	12,701	9,082	3,619	2,645
Kilowatt capacity	2,709,225	5,165,439	8,994,407	14,313,438	13,407,041	906,397	5,915,485
Output, 1,000 kilowatt hours		14,182,613	31,044,049	50,274,212	47,833,036	2,441,176	22,070,101
Generated	5,862,277	11,569,110	25,438,303	40,291,536	38,413,240	1,878,296	18,700,047
Purchased	(3)	2,613,503	5,605,746	9,982,676	9,419,796	562,880	3,370,054
Sold, total	(3)	(3)	25,751,985	41,964,785	39,912,345	2,052,440	18,758,285
For light	(3)	(3)	5,112,517	9,777,114	8,483,425	1,293,689	2,573,194
Per capita[4]			50.0	92.9	81.1	11.8	27.8
For power	(3)	(3)	13,174,827	18,613,367	17,918,135	695,252	9,565,718
Per capita[4]			128.9	170.4	164.0	6.4	87.6
To other public service corporations	(3)	(3)	7,464,621	13,574,284	13,510,785	63,499	6,619,377
Stationary motors served:							
Number	167,184	435,473	555,924	(3)	(3)	(3)	(4)
Horsepower capacity	1,649,026	4,130,619	9,216,330	(3)	(3)	(4)	(4)
Number of customers	1,946,979	3,837,518	7,178,703	12,709,868	11,065,124	1,644,744	3,305,684
Salaried employees..number	12,990	26,093	35,406	55,112	50,667	4,445	[6] 38,602
Salaries..dollars	11,735,787	24,307,304	36,787,701	86,951,301	81,338,448	5,612,853	(3)
Wage earners..number	[6] 34,642	[7] 53,242	[8] 70,135	[9] 95,650	85,438	10,212	(3)
Wages..dollars	23,686,537	36,854,637	58,454,157	125,481,354	112,809,673	12,671,681	(6)

Source: Bureau of the Census, Department of Commerce.

[1] Data related to stations of 1,000 or more horsepower capacity.
[2] The term "station" as here used may represent a single electric station or a number of stations operated under the same ownership.
[3] Figures not available.
[4] Based on estimated total population of the United States.
[5] Wage earners included.
[6] Average number for the year.
[7] Number Sept. 16, 1912, or nearest representative day.
[8] Number Sept. 29, 1917, or nearest representative day.
[9] Number June 30, 1922, or nearest representative day.

337

Source: Statistical Abstract of the United States: 1924 Edition.

Section 19
Energy and Utilities

This section presents statistics on fuel resources, energy production and consumption, electric energy, hydroelectric power, nuclear power, solar energy, wood energy, and the electric and gas utility industries. The principal sources are the U.S. Department of Energy's Energy Information Administration (EIA), the Edison Electric Institute, Washington, DC, and the American Gas Association, Arlington, VA. The Department of Energy was created in October 1977 and assumed and centralized the responsibilities of all or part of several agencies including the Federal Power Commission (FPC), the U.S. Bureau of Mines, the Federal Energy Administration, and the U.S. Energy Research and Development Administration. For additional data on transportation, see Section 23; on fuels, see Section 18; and on energy-related housing characteristics, see Section 20.

The EIA, in its *Annual Energy Review*, provides statistics and trend data on energy supply, demand, and prices. Information is included on petroleum and natural gas, coal, electricity, hydroelectric power, nuclear power, solar, wood, and geothermal energy. Among its annual reports are *Annual Energy Review, Electric Power Annual, Natural Gas Annual, Petroleum Supply Annual, State Energy Data Report, State Energy Price and Expenditure Report, Performance Profiles of Major Energy Producers, Annual Energy Outlook*, and *International Energy Annual*. These various publications contain state, national, and international data on production of electricity, net summer capability of generating plants, fuels used in energy production, energy sales and consumption, and hydroelectric power. The EIA also issues the *Monthly Energy Review*, which presents current supply, disposition, and price data and monthly publications on petroleum, coal, natural

gas, and electric power. Data on residential energy consumption, expenditures, and conservation activities are available from EIA's Residential Energy Consumption Survey and are published every 4 years.

The Edison Electric Institute's monthly bulletin and annual *Statistical Year Book of the Electric Utility Industry for the Year* contain data on the distribution of electric energy by public utilities; information on the electric power supply, expansion of electric generating facilities, and the manufacture of heavy electric power equipment is presented in the annual *Year-End Summary of the Electric Power Situation in the United States*. The American Gas Association, in its monthly and quarterly bulletins and its yearbook, *Gas Facts*, presents data on gas utilities and financial and operating statistics.

Btu conversion factors—Various energy sources are converted from original units to the thermal equivalent using British thermal units (Btu). A Btu is the amount of energy required to raise the temperature of 1 pound of water 1 degree Fahrenheit (F) at or near 39.2 degrees F. Factors are calculated annually from the latest final annual data available; some are revised as a result. The following list provides conversion factors used in 2002 for production and consumption, in that order, for various fuels: Petroleum, 5.800 and 5.324 mil. Btu per barrel; total coal, 20.620 and 20.814 mil. Btu per short ton; and natural gas (dry), 1,027 Btu per cubic foot for both. The factors for the production of nuclear power and geothermal power were 10,442 and 21,017 Btu per kilowatt-hour, respectively. The fossil fuel steam-electric power plant generation factor of 10,119 Btu per kilowatt-hour was used for hydroelectric power generation and for wood and waste, wind, photovoltaic, and solar thermal energy consumed at electric utilities.

U.S. Census Bureau, Statistical Abstract of the United States: 2006

In the past few years, EIA has restructured the industry categories it once used to gather and report electricity statistics. The electric power industry, previously divided into electric utilities and non-utilities, now consists of the Electric Power Sector, the Commercial Sector, and the Industrial Sector (see Table 904).

The Electric Power Sector is composed of electricity-only and combined-heat-and-power (CHP) plants whose primary business is to sell electricity, or electricity and heat to the public.

Electricity-only plants are composed of traditional electric utilities, and nontraditional participants, including energy service providers, power marketers, independent power producers (IPPs), and the portion of combined-heat-and-power plants (CHPs) that produce only electricity.

A utility is defined as a corporation, person, agency, authority, or other legal entity or instrumentality aligned with distribution facilities for delivery of electric energy for use primarily by the public. Electric utilities include investor-owned electric utilities, municipal and state utilities, federal electric utilities, and rural electric cooperatives. In total, there are more than 3,100 electric utilities in the United States.

An independent power producer is an entity defined as a corporation, person, agency, authority, or other legal entity or instrumentality that owns or operates facilities whose primary business is to produce electricity for use by the public. They are not generally aligned with distribution facilities and are not considered electric utilities.

Combined-heat-and-power producers are plants designed to produce both heat and electricity from a single heat source. These types of electricity producers can be independent power producers or industrial or commercial establishments. As some independent power producers are combined-heat-and-power producers, their information is included in the data for the combined-heat-and-power sector. There are approximately 2,800 unregulated independent power producers and combined-heat-and-power plants in the United States.

The Commercial Sector consists of commercial CHP and commercial electricity-only plants. Industrial CHP and industrial electricity-only plants make up the Industrial Sector. For more information, please refer to the *Electric Power Annual 2003* Web site located at <http://www.eia.doe.gov/cneaf/electricity/epa/epa_sum.html>.

U.S. Census Bureau, Statistical Abstract of the United States: 2006

Table 886. Utilities—Establishments, Revenue, Payroll, and Employees by Kind of Business (NAICS Basis): 2002

[478,268 represents $478,268,000,000. See headnote, Table 737 and Appendix III]

Kind of business	NAICS code [1]	Estab- lish- ments (number)	Revenue		Annual payroll		Paid employee for pay period including March 12 (number)
			Total (mil. dol.)	Per paid employee (dol.)	Total (mil. dol.)	Per paid employee (dol.)	
Utilities	22	18,594	478,268	647,524	45,111	61,076	738,611
Electric power generation, transmission, & distribution	2211	9,676	337,033	625,827	35,921	66,701	538,540
Electric power generation	22111	2,138	78.163	641,913	9,195	75,513	121,766
Hydroelectric power generation.	221111	416	3,260	425,084	483	62,952	7,668
Fossil fuel electric power generation . . .	221112	1,233	53,329	792,480	4,945	73,484	67,294
Nuclear electric power generation	221113	78	11,909	375,696	2,507	79,094	31,698
Other electric power generation	221119	411	9,666	639,857	1,260	83.415	15,106
Electric power transmission, control & distribution	22112	7,538	258,870	621,128	26,726	64,126	416,774
Electric bulk power transmission & control	221121	158	12,738	847,369	1,173	78,021	15,032
Electric power distribution	221122	7,380	246,132	612,662	25,553	63,606	401,742
Natural gas distribution	2212	2,431	71,827	771,772	5,973	64,179	93,068
Water, sewage, & other systems	2213	5,780	7,594	166,333	1,600	35,040	45,654
Water supply & irrigation systems.	22131	4,830	5,860	162,575	1,252	34,731	36,046
Sewage treatment facilities	22132	866	1,051	137,443	241	31,472	7,647
Steam & air-conditioning supply	22133	84	683	348,056	107	54,628	1,961

[1] North American Industry Classification System, 2002; see text, Section 15.

Source: U.S. Census Bureau, *2002 Economic Census*, Series EC02-221-US, issued December 2004. See also <http://www.census.gov /econ/census02/>.

Table 887. Private Utilities—Employees, Annual Payroll, and Establishments by Industry: 2002

[41,845 represents 41,845,000,000. Excludes government employees, railroad employees, self-employed persons, etc. See "General Explanation" in source for definitions and statement on reliability of data. An establishment is a single physical location where business is conducted or where services or industrial operations are performed. See Appendix III]

Year and industry	NAICS code [1]	Number of employ- ees [2]	Annual payroll (mil. dol.)	Aver- age payroll per em- ployee (dol.)	Establishment by employment size-class				
					Total	Under 20 em- ployees	20 to 99 em- ployees	100 to 499 em- ployees	500 and over employ- ees
Utilities, total	22	648,254	41,845	64,550	18,432	13,216	3,869	1,166	181
Electric power generation, transmission and distribution	2211	515,769	34,828	67,527	9,493	5,449	2,941	938	165
Electric power generation	22111	135,521	9,766	72,060	2,349	1,394	654	251	50
Hydroelectric power generation. . . .	221111	7,597	522	68,776	428	339	71	18	-
Fossil fuel electric power generation.	221112	78,790	5,558	70,547	1,427	744	466	207	10
Nuclear electric power generation.	221113	34,904	2,769	79,339	80	21	12	14	33
Other electric power generation. . .	221119	14,230	916	64,340	414	290	105	12	7
Electric power transmission, control and distribution	22112	380,248	25,063	65,912	7,144	4,055	2,287	687	115
Electric bulk power transmission and control	221121	18,590	1,365	73,441	217	131	54	21	11
Electric power distribution.	221122	361,658	23,697	65,525	6,927	3,924	2,233	666	104
Natural gas distribution.	2212	86,890	5,342	61,482	2,897	2,100	600	182	15
Water, sewage & other systems	2213	45,595	1,674	36,718	6,042	5,667	328	46	1
Water supply & irrigation systems . . .	22131	37,041	1,357	36,625	5,114	4,829	246	38	1
Sewage treatment facilities	22132	7,022	233	33,240	831	769	55	7	-
Steam & air-conditioning supply . . .	22133	1,532	84	54,906	97	69	27	1	-

- Represents zero. [1] North American Industry Classification System, 2002. [2] Covers full- and part-time employees who are on the payroll in the pay period including March 12.

Source: U.S. Census Bureau, *County Business Patterns 2002*. See also <http://censtats.census.gov/cgi-bin/cbpnaic /cbpdetl.pl> (accessed March 2005).

Table 888. Energy Supply and Disposition by Type of Fuel: 1960 to 2003

[In quadrillion British thermal units (Btu) (42.80 represents 42,800,000,000,000,000 Btu). For Btu conversion factors, see source and text, this section]

Year	Production										Consumption					
	Total [1]	Crude oil [2]	Natural gas	Coal	Nuclear power [3]	Renewable energy [4] Total [1]	Hydro-electric power	Biofuel [5]	Solar energy	Net imports [6] total	Total [1]	Petro-leum [7]	Natural gas [8]	Coal	Nuclear power	Renewable energy [4] total
1960	42.80	14.93	12.66	10.82	(Z)	2.93	1.61	1.32	(NA)	2.71	45.09	19.92	12.39	9.84	(Z)	2.93
1970	63.50	20.40	21.67	14.61	0.24	4.08	2.63	1.43	(NA)	5.71	67.84	29.52	21.79	12.26	0.24	4.08
1973	63.58	19.49	22.19	13.99	0.91	4.43	2.86	1.53	(NA)	12.58	75.71	34.84	22.51	12.97	0.91	4.43
1974	62.37	18.57	21.21	14.07	1.27	4.77	3.18	1.54	(NA)	12.10	73.99	33.45	21.73	12.66	1.27	4.77
1975	61.36	17.73	19.64	14.99	1.90	4.72	3.15	1.50	(NA)	11.71	72.00	32.73	19.95	12.66	1.90	4.72
1976	61.60	17.26	19.48	15.65	2.11	4.77	2.98	1.71	(NA)	14.59	76.01	35.17	20.35	13.58	2.11	4.77
1977	62.05	17.45	19.57	15.75	2.70	4.25	2.33	1.84	(NA)	17.90	78.00	37.12	19.93	13.92	2.70	4.25
1978	63.14	18.43	19.49	14.91	3.02	5.04	2.94	2.04	(NA)	17.19	79.99	37.97	20.00	13.77	3.02	5.04
1979	65.95	18.10	20.08	17.54	2.78	5.17	2.93	2.15	(NA)	16.60	80.90	37.12	20.67	15.04	2.78	5.17
1980	67.24	18.25	19.91	18.60	2.74	5.49	2.90	2.48	(NA)	12.10	78.29	34.20	20.39	15.42	2.74	5.49
1981	67.01	18.15	19.70	18.38	3.01	5.47	2.76	2.59	(NA)	9.41	76.34	31.93	19.93	15.91	3.01	5.47
1982	66.57	18.31	18.32	18.64	3.13	5.99	3.27	2.62	(NA)	7.25	73.25	30.23	18.51	15.32	3.13	5.99
1983	64.11	18.39	16.59	17.25	3.20	6.49	3.53	2.83	(NA)	8.06	73.10	30.05	17.36	15.89	3.20	6.49
1984	68.83	18.85	18.01	19.72	3.55	6.43	3.39	2.88	(Z)	8.68	76.74	31.05	18.51	17.07	3.55	6.43
1985	67.65	18.99	16.98	19.33	4.08	6.03	2.97	2.86	(Z)	7.58	76.47	30.92	17.83	17.48	4.08	6.03
1986	67.09	18.38	16.54	19.51	4.38	6.13	3.07	2.84	(Z)	10.13	76.78	32.20	16.71	17.26	4.38	6.13
1987	67.61	17.67	17.14	20.14	4.75	5.69	3.07	2.82	(Z)	11.59	79.23	32.87	17.74	18.01	4.75	5.69
1988	68.95	17.28	17.60	20.74	5.59	5.49	2.33	2.94	(Z)	12.93	82.84	34.22	18.55	18.85	5.59	5.49
1989 [9]	69.36	16.12	17.85	21.35	5.60	6.29	2.84	3.06	0.06	14.11	84.96	34.21	19.71	19.07	5.60	6.29
1990	70.73	15.57	18.33	22.46	6.10	6.13	3.05	2.66	0.06	14.06	84.67	33.55	19.73	19.17	6.10	6.13
1991	70.36	15.70	18.23	21.59	6.42	6.16	3.02	2.70	0.06	13.19	84.60	32.85	20.15	18.99	6.42	6.16
1992	69.93	15.22	18.38	21.63	6.48	5.91	2.62	2.85	0.06	14.44	85.95	33.53	20.84	19.12	6.48	5.91
1993	68.26	14.49	18.58	20.25	6.41	6.16	2.89	2.80	0.07	17.01	87.58	33.84	21.35	19.84	6.41	6.16
1994	70.68	14.10	19.35	22.11	6.69	6.06	2.68	2.94	0.07	18.33	89.25	34.67	21.84	19.91	6.69	6.06
1995	71.16	13.89	19.08	22.03	7.08	6.67	3.21	3.07	0.07	17.75	91.22	34.55	22.78	20.09	7.08	6.67
1996	72.47	13.72	19.34	22.68	7.09	7.14	3.59	3.13	0.07	19.07	94.22	35.76	23.20	21.00	7.09	7.14
1997	72.39	13.66	19.39	23.21	6.60	7.08	3.64	3.01	0.07	20.70	94.73	36.27	23.33	21.45	6.60	7.08
1998	72.79	13.24	19.61	23.94	7.07	6.56	3.30	2.83	0.07	22.28	95.15	36.93	22.94	21.66	7.07	6.56
1999	71.65	12.45	19.34	23.19	7.61	6.60	3.27	2.89	0.07	23.54	96.77	37.96	23.01	21.62	7.61	6.60
2000	71.22	12.36	19.66	22.62	7.86	6.16	2.81	2.91	0.07	24.97	98.90	38.40	23.92	22.58	7.86	6.16
2001	71.79	12.28	20.20	23.53	8.03	5.29	2.20	2.64	0.07	26.39	96.38	38.33	22.91	21.95	8.03	5.29
2002	70.93	12.16	19.49	22.70	8.14	5.96	2.67	2.79	0.06	25.74	98.03	38.40	23.66	21.98	8.14	5.96
2003 [10]	70.47	12.15	19.64	22.31	7.97	6.15	2.78	2.88	0.06	26.97	98.16	39.07	22.51	22.71	7.97	6.15

NA Not available. Z Less than 5 trillion. [1] Includes types of fuel not shown separately. [2] Includes lease condensate. [3] Data on the generation of electricity in the United States represent net generation, which is gross output of electricity (measured at the generator terminals) minus power plant use. Nuclear electricity generation data are gross outputs of electricity. [4] Nuclear electricity net generation. End-use consumption and electricity net generation. [5] Wood, waste, and alcohol (ethanol blended into motor gasoline). [6] Imports minus exports. [7] Petroleum products supplied, including natural gas plant liquids and crude oil burned as fuel. [8] Includes supplemental gaseous fuels. [9] There is a discontinuity in this time series between 1989 and 1990 due to the expanded coverage of nonelectric utility use of renewable energy beginning in 1990. [10] Preliminary.

Source: U.S. Energy Information Administration, *Annual Energy Review 2003*. See also <http://www.eia.doe.gov/emeu/aer/overview.html> (released September 2004).

Figure 19.1
Energy Production, Trade, and Consumption: 1980 to 2003

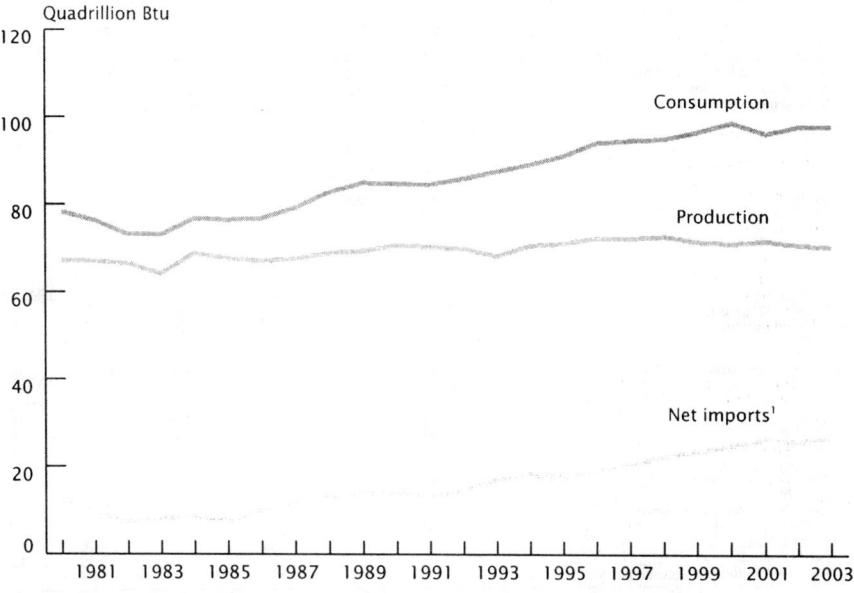

¹Imports minus exports.
Source: Figure 19.1 prepared by U.S. Census Bureau. For data, see Table 888.

Figure 19.2
Top Suppliers of U.S. Crude Oil Imports: 2004
(In millions of barrels)

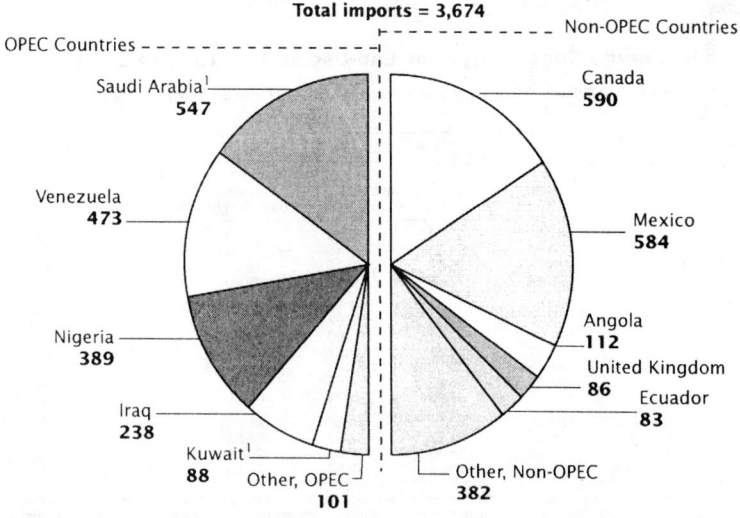

¹Imports from the neutral zone between Kuwait and Saudi Arabia are included in Saudi Arabia.
Source: Figure 19.2 prepared by U.S. Census Bureau. For data, see Table 900.

Energy and Utilities 593

Table 889. Energy Supply and Disposition by Type of Fuel—Estimates, 2002 and 2003, and Projections, 2005 to 2020

[Quadrillion Btu (71.94 represents 71,940,000,000,000,000) per year. Btu = British thermal unit. Projections are "reference" or mid-level forecasts. See report for methodology and assumptions used in generating projections]

Type of fuel	2002	2003	Projections			
			2005	2010	2015	2020
Production, total	**71.94**	**71.42**	**74.44**	**77.79**	**77.73**	**80.35**
Crude oil and lease condensate	12.15	12.03	12.19	12.75	11.63	11.03
Natural gas plant liquids	2.56	2.34	2.48	2.66	2.67	2.80
Natural gas, dry	19.48	19.58	19.80	20.97	21.33	22.48
Coal	22.70	22.66	24.15	25.10	25.56	27.04
Nuclear power	8.14	7.97	8.31	8.49	8.62	8.67
Renewable energy [1]	5.79	5.89	6.49	6.85	7.13	7.57
Other [2]	1.12	0.93	1.02	0.97	0.78	0.77
Imports, total	**29.35**	**30.95**	**32.74**	**37.38**	**44.37**	**49.22**
Crude oil [3]	19.93	21.08	21.92	24.69	28.98	32.29
Petroleum products [4]	4.75	5.16	5.86	6.06	6.32	6.83
Natural gas	4.11	4.02	4.22	5.71	8.00	8.95
Other imports [5]	0.56	0.69	0.75	0.92	1.07	1.15
Exports, total	**3.60**	**3.95**	**4.17**	**3.86**	**3.90**	**4.01**
Petroleum [6]	2.05	2.13	2.20	2.14	2.21	2.26
Natural gas	0.52	0.70	0.76	0.65	0.81	0.86
Coal	1.03	1.12	1.21	1.06	0.88	0.89
Consumption, total	**97.99**	**98.22**	**101.85**	**111.27**	**118.29**	**125.60**
Petroleum products [7]	38.41	39.09	40.81	44.84	48.07	51.30
Natural gas	23.59	22.54	22.92	26.11	28.69	30.73
Coal	21.98	22.71	23.30	24.95	25.71	27.27
Nuclear power	8.14	7.97	8.31	8.49	8.62	8.67
Renewable energy [1], other [8]	5.86	5.91	6.51	6.88	7.20	7.62
Net imports of petroleum	**22.64**	**24.10**	**25.57**	**28.61**	**33.10**	**36.87**
Prices (1999 dollars per unit):						
World oil price (dol. per bbl.) [9]	24.10	27.73	33.99	25.00	26.75	28.50
Gas wellhead price (dol. per mcf.) [10]	3.06	4.98	5.30	3.64	4.16	4.53
Coal minemouth price (dol. per ton)	18.23	17.93	18.61	17.30	16.89	17.25
Average electric price (cents per kWh)	7.4	7.4	7.4	6.6	6.9	7.2

[1] Includes grid-connected electricity from conventional hydroelectric; wood and wood waste; landfill gas; municipal solid waste; other biomass; wind; photovoltaic and solar thermal sources; non-electric energy from renewable sources, such as active and passive solar systems, and wood; and both the ethanol and gasoline components of E85, but not the ethanol components of blends less than 85 percent. Excludes electricity imports using renewable sources and nonmarketed renewable energy. See Table A18 of source for selected nonmarketed residential and commercial renewable energy. [2] Includes liquid hydrogen, methanol, supplemental natural gas, and some domestic inputs to refineries. [3] Includes imports of crude oil for the Strategic Petroleum Reserve. [4] Includes imports of finished petroleum products, imports of unfinished oils, alcohols, ethers, and blending components. [5] Includes coal, coal coke (net), and electricity (net). [6] Includes crude oil and petroleum products. [7] Includes natural gas plant liquids, crude oil consumed as a fuel, and nonpetroleum-based liquids for blending, such as ethanol. [8] Includes net electricity imports, methanol, and liquid hydrogen. [9] Average refiner acquisition cost for imported crude oil. [10] Represents lower 48 onshore and offshore supplies.

Source: U.S. Energy Information Administration, *Annual Energy Outlook 2005*, DOE/EIA-0383(2005). See also <http://eia.doe.gov/oiaf/aeo/pdf/aeotab_1.pdf>.

Table 890. Energy Consumption by End-Use Sector: 1970 to 2003

[67.84 represents 67,840,000,000,000,000 Btu. Btu = British thermal units. For Btu conversion factors, see source and text, this section. See Appendix III]

Year	Total (quad. Btu)	Residential and commercial [1] (quad. Btu)	Industrial [2] (quad. Btu)	Transportation (quad. Btu)	Percent of total		
					Residential and commercial [1]	Industrial [2]	Transportation
1970	67.84	22.11	29.64	16.10	32.6	43.7	23.7
1975	72.00	24.31	29.45	18.24	33.8	40.9	25.3
1980	78.29	26.44	32.15	19.70	33.8	41.1	25.2
1985	76.47	27.49	28.89	20.09	36.0	37.8	26.3
1990	84.67	30.36	31.89	22.42	35.9	37.7	26.5
1994	89.25	32.32	33.57	23.37	36.2	37.6	26.2
1995	91.22	33.37	34.00	23.85	36.6	37.3	26.1
1996	94.22	34.81	34.97	24.44	36.9	37.1	25.9
1997	94.73	34.73	35.24	24.75	36.7	37.2	26.1
1998	95.15	35.02	34.88	25.26	36.8	36.7	26.5
1999	96.77	36.03	34.79	25.95	37.2	36.0	26.8
2000	98.90	37.67	34.68	26.55	38.1	35.1	26.8
2001	96.38	37.57	32.53	26.28	39.0	33.7	27.3
2002	98.03	38.50	32.86	26.65	39.3	33.5	27.2
2003 [3]	98.16	38.78	32.52	26.86	39.5	33.1	27.4

[1] Commercial sector fuel use, including that at commercial combined-heat-and-power (CHP) and industrial electricity-only plants. [2] Industrial sector fuel use, including that at industrial combined-heat-and-power (CHP) and industrial electricity-only plants. [3] Preliminary.

Source: U.S. Energy Information Administration, *Annual Energy Review 2003*. See also <http://www.eia.doe.gov/emeu/aer/pdf/pages/sec2_4.pdf> (released September 2004).

Table 891. Energy Consumption—End-Use Sector and Selected Source by State: 2001

[In trillions of Btu (96,275 represents 96,275,000,000,000,000), except as indicated]

State	Total [1]	Per capita [2] (mil. Btu)	End-use sector [3] Resi-dential	Com-mercial	Indus-trial [1]	Trans-portation	Source Petro-leum	Natural gas (dry) [4]	Coal	Hydro electric power [5]	Nuclear electric power
United States	**96,275**	**338**	**20,241**	**17,332**	**32,431**	**26,272**	**38,333**	**22,845**	**21,905**	**2,118**	**8,033**
Alabama	1,943	435	380	254	863	446	540	342	846	85	317
Alaska.........	737	1,164	53	65	413	206	292	413	16	14	-
Arizona	1,353	255	344	312	221	476	524	245	424	80	300
Arkansas	1,106	411	219	148	462	278	379	232	274	26	154
California	7,853	227	1,446	1,509	1,928	2,971	3,604	2,514	68	256	347
Colorado	1,270	287	303	287	294	386	462	385	400	13	-
Connecticut	853	249	267	215	134	238	439	149	40	3	161
Delaware.......	293	368	62	52	113	66	147	52	38	-	-
District of Columbia	168	294	34	104	4	26	34	31	1	-	-
Florida.........	4,135	253	1,193	958	598	1,386	1,990	570	726	2	330
Georgia	2,881	343	642	503	876	860	1,034	363	772	21	352
Hawaii.........	282	230	35	39	77	132	240	3	18	1	-
Idaho..........	501	379	105	95	180	122	155	82	11	74	-
Illinois	3,870	309	928	829	1,173	939	1,304	971	994	2	965
Indiana	2,802	457	504	397	1,296	604	837	514	1,567	6	-
Iowa	1,151	392	229	179	472	270	401	225	445	9	40
Kansas	1,044	387	215	192	385	252	391	274	355	(Z)	108
Kentucky	1,880	462	339	246	846	449	704	217	1,011	39	-
Louisiana	3,500	784	348	264	2,135	753	1,491	1,340	240	7	181
Maine	491	382	111	74	199	107	233	101	8	27	-
Maryland	1,420	264	391	372	252	405	568	191	317	12	143
Massachusetts ...	1,549	242	461	379	261	447	762	364	109	(-Z)	54
Michigan	3,120	312	790	598	928	804	1,042	929	797	4	279
Minnesota	1,745	350	381	336	526	502	674	345	353	9	123
Mississippi	1,173	410	234	163	427	349	486	341	198	-	104
Missouri........	1,815	322	496	389	374	556	719	289	716	9	88
Montana	366	404	70	60	128	108	168	67	184	67	-
Nebraska.......	627	365	152	130	182	163	218	124	228	11	91
Nevada	629	301	147	108	169	205	250	181	189	26	-
New Hampshire...	322	256	87	65	68	102	178	25	40	10	91
New Jersey	2,500	294	573	554	491	882	1,246	586	112	-1	318
New Mexico	679	371	107	122	220	230	251	262	297	2	-
New York.......	4,135	217	1,194	1,303	667	970	1,713	1,206	315	225	422
North Carolina....	2,591	316	641	513	743	694	950	216	757	26	395
North Dakota	407	640	61	56	203	88	138	63	420	14	-
Ohio	3,982	350	892	682	1,429	979	1,305	836	1,343	5	162
Oklahoma	1,540	444	298	233	544	466	588	548	377	23	-
Oregon	1,064	307	252	208	298	307	368	236	43	291	-
Pennsylvania	3,923	319	931	709	1,286	997	1,454	669	1,379	11	770
Rhode Island	227	215	73	63	26	66	100	99	(Z)	(Z)	-
South Carolina ...	1,549	382	322	235	609	383	470	147	414	2	521
South Dakota ...	248	327	60	50	54	83	112	37	44	35	-
Tennessee	2,195	382	500	369	746	581	708	265	688	63	299
Texas	12,029	564	1,570	1,356	6,426	2,677	5,521	4,435	1,493	12	399
Utah	725	318	140	140	233	213	261	168	390	5	-
Vermont........	164	267	48	33	31	52	89	8	(Z)	9	44
Virginia	2,315	322	549	534	547	685	911	247	482	-13	269
Washington	2,034	339	471	377	586	600	843	323	100	557	86
West Virginia	762	423	157	111	311	183	215	152	872	10	-
Wisconsin.......	1,863	345	401	313	729	422	668	363	495	21	120
Wyoming	439	890	39	51	238	111	157	104	500	9	-

- Represents zero.   Z Less than .5 trillion Btus.   [1] U.S. total energy and U.S. industrial sector include 29.3 trillion Btus of net imports of coal coke that is not allocated to the states. State and U.S. totals include 81.8 trillion Btus of net imports of electricity generated from nonrenewable energy sources.   [2] Based on estimated resident population as of July 1.   [3] End-use sector data include electricity sales and associated electrical system energy losses.   [4] Includes supplemental gaseous fuels.   [5] Includes net imports of hydroelectricity. A negative number in this column results from pumped storage for which, overall, more electricity is expended than created to provide electricity during peak demand periods.

Source: U.S. Energy Information Administration, *State Energy Data Report, 2001.* See also<http://www.eia.doe.gov /emeu/states/sep_use/total/pdf/use_all.pdf> (released December 2004).

Energy and Utilities   595

Table 892. Renewable Energy Consumption Estimates by Source: 1995 to 2003

[In quadrillion Btu (6.66 represents 6,660,000,000,000,000. Renewable energy is obtained from sources that are essentially inexhaustible unlike fossil fuels of which there is a finite supply]

Source and sector	1995	1998	1999	2000	2001	2002	2003 [1]
Consumption, total	**6.66**	**6.55**	**6.59**	**6.15**	**5.27**	**5.95**	**6.13**
Conventional hydroelectric power [2]	3.21	3.30	3.27	2.81	2.20	2.68	2.78
Geothermal energy [3]	0.29	0.33	0.33	0.32	0.31	0.33	0.31
Biomass [4]	3.06	2.82	2.87	2.89	2.63	2.77	2.87
Solar energy [5]	0.07	0.07	0.07	0.07	0.07	0.06	0.06
Wind energy [6]	0.03	0.03	0.05	0.06	0.07	0.11	0.11
Residential [7]	0.67	0.46	0.49	0.50	0.44	0.38	0.44
Biomass [4]	0.60	0.39	0.41	0.43	0.37	0.31	0.36
Geothermal [3]	0.01	0.01	0.01	0.01	0.01	0.01	0.02
Solar [5, 8]	0.07	0.07	0.06	0.06	0.06	0.06	0.06
Commercial [9]	0.09	0.11	0.11	0.11	0.09	0.09	0.11
Biomass [4]	0.09	0.10	0.11	0.10	0.08	0.08	0.09
Geothermal [3]	0.01	0.01	0.01	0.01	0.01	0.01	0.02
Hydroelectric [2]	(Z)	(Z)	(Z)	(Z)	(Z)	(Z)	(Z)
Industrial [10]	1.91	1.84	1.84	1.83	1.63	1.75	1.75
Biomass [4]	1.85	1.78	1.79	1.78	1.59	1.71	1.69
Geothermal [3]	(Z)	(Z)	(Z)	(Z)	0.01	0.01	0.01
Hydroelectric [2]	0.06	0.06	0.05	0.04	0.03	0.04	0.06
Transportation:							
Alcohol fuels [11]	0.11	0.11	0.11	0.13	0.13	0.16	0.22
Electric power [12]	3.89	4.03	4.03	3.58	2.98	3.57	3.62
Electric utilities [13]	3.17	3.28	3.12	2.61	2.03	2.53	2.55
Biomass [4]	0.02	0.02	0.02	0.02	0.02	0.05	0.04
Geothermal [3]	0.10	0.11	0.04	(Z)	(Z)	(Z)	0.01
Hydroelectric [2]	3.06	3.15	3.07	2.58	2.01	2.45	2.50
Solar [5]	(Z)	(Z)	(Z)	(Z)	(Z)	(Z)	(Z)
Wind [6]	(Z)	(Z)	(Z)	(Z)	(Z)	(Z)	(Z)

Z Less than 5 trillion Btu. [1] Preliminary. [2] Power produced from natural streamflow as regulated by available storage. [3] As used at electric power plants, hot water or steam extracted from geothermal reservoirs in the Earth's crust that is supplied to steam turbines at electric power plants that drive generators to produce electricity. [4] Organic nonfossil material of biological origin constituting a renewable energy source. [5] Includes small amounts of distributed solar thermal and photovoltaic energy. [6] Energy present in wind motion that can be converted to mechanical energy for driving pumps, mills, and electric power generators. Wind pushes against sails, vanes, or blades radiating from a central rotating shaft. [7] Consists of living quarters for private households, but excludes institutional living quarters. [8] The radiant energy of the sun, which can be converted into other forms of energy, such as heat or electricity. [9] Consists of service-providing facilities and equipment of businesses, governments, and other private and public organizations. Includes institutional living quarters and sewage treatment facilities. [10] Consists of all facilities and equipment used for producing, processing, or assembling goods. [11] Ethanol primarily derived from corn. [12] Consists of electricity only and combined heat and power plants who sell electricity and heat to the public. [13] A corporation or other legal entity aligned with distribution facilities for delivery of electric energy, primarily for public use.

Source: U.S. Energy Information Administration, *Renewable Energy Annual 2003*. See also <http://www.eia.doe.gov/cneaf/solar.renewables/page/rea_data/trends.pdf> (issued December 2004).

Table 893. Energy Expenditures and Average Fuel Prices by Source and Sector: 1970 to 2001

[In millions of dollars (82,911 represents $82,911,000,000). For definition of Btu, see text, this section. End-use sector and electric utilities exclude expenditures and prices on energy sources such as hydropower, solar, wind, and geothermal. Also excludes expenditures for reported amounts of energy consumed by the energy industry for production, transportation, and processing operations]

Source and sector	1970	1980	1985	1990	1995	1997	1998	1999	2000	2001
EXPENDITURES (mil. dol.)										
Total	82,911	374,367	437,586	471,951	514,126	566,515	524,439	555,018	689,384	693,599
Natural gas	10,891	51,061	72,938	65,281	75,020	93,392	83,634	84,971	119,091	139,526
Petroleum products	47,955	237,676	223,906	235,347	236,863	267,233	231,864	262,795	360,735	336,362
Motor gasoline	31,596	124,408	118,048	126,558	136,647	149,668	132,730	149,260	193,947	185,892
Coal	4,630	22,607	29,678	28,602	27,431	28,278	27,888	27,310	28,080	28,195
Electricity sales	23,345	98,095	149,233	176,737	205,932	213,645	216,928	216,737	231,653	244,814
Residential sector [2]	20,213	69,438	99,669	111,099	128,482	138,664	134,914	137,421	156,095	168,618
Commercial sector [2]	10,628	46,932	70,396	79,237	91,746	100,355	98,327	98,186	112,843	125,772
Industrial sector [3]	16,691	94,316	106,518 [4]	102,402	107,060	119,097	107,386	111,529	141,692	137,820
Transportation sector	35,379	163,680	161,003	179,212	186,838	208,398	183,811	207,883	278,754	261,390
Motor gasoline	30,525	121,809	115,205	123,845	134,641	147,164	130,709	147,592	191,620	182,122
Electric utilities [1]	4,329	37,788	43,421	40,155	38,727	42,466	42,649	43,932	57,596	62,115
AVERAGE FUEL PRICES (dol. per mil. Btu)										
All sectors	1.65	6.89	8.37	8.25	8.28	8.80	8.18	8.50	10.33	10.72
Residential sector [2]	2.10	7.46	10.93	11.88	12.59	13.29	13.46	13.17	14.27	15.72
Commercial sector [2]	1.98	7.85	11.65	11.90	12.65	13.06	13.04	12.74	13.94	15.56
Industrial sector [3]	0.84	4.71	6.03	5.23 [4]	4.97	5.33	4.89	5.09	6.48	6.78
Transportation sector	2.31	8.61	8.26	8.28	8.09	8.70	7.48	8.23	10.78	10.21
Electric utilities [1]	0.32	1.76	1.88	1.47	1.28	1.36	1.30	1.31	1.64	1.78

[1] There are no direct fuel costs for geothermal, photovoltaic, or solar thermal energy. [2] There are no direct fuel costs for hydroelectric, geothermal, photovoltaic, or solar thermal energy. [3] There are no direct fuel costs for hydroelectric, geothermal, wind, photovoltaic, or solar thermal energy. [4] There is a discontinuity in the total time series and the industrial time series between 1988 and 1989 due to the expanded coverage of nonelectric utility use of wood and waste beginning in 1989.

Source: U.S. Energy Information Administration, *State Energy Price and Expenditure Report 2001*. See also <http://www.eia.doe.gov/emeu/states/main_us.html> (published January 2005).

596 Energy and Utilities

Table 894. Energy Expenditures—End-Use Sector and Selected Source by State: 2001

[In millions of dollars (693,599 represents $693,599,000,000). End-use sector and electric utilities exclude expenditures on energy sources such as hydroelectric, photovoltaic, solar thermal, wind, and geothermal. Also excludes expenditures for reported amounts of energy consumed by the energy industry for production, transportation, and processing operations]

State	Total [1]	End-use sector				Source			
		Residen-tial	Commer-cial	Industrial	Transpor-tation	Petroleum products	Natural gas	Coal	Electricity sales
U.S....	693,599	168,618	125,772	137,820	261,390	336,362	139,526	28,195	244,814
AL	11,580	2,798	1,628	2,827	4,327	5,142	2,077	1,219	4,345
AK	2,780	428	453	310	1,589	2,071	250	31	567
AZ	10,672	2,664	2,046	1,136	4,826	5,351	1,381	540	4,526
AR	7,340	1,702	915	1,968	2,755	3,510	1,419	250	2,464
CA	72,924	15,504	15,832	10,676	30,913	33,751	20,824	99	27,483
CO	9,279	2,268	1,653	1,155	4,203	4,864	2,092	374	2,638
CT	8,062	2,672	1,743	886	2,762	4,273	1,125	67	2,937
DE	1,985	522	352	425	686	1,020	338	80	744
DC	1,479	310	826	25	318	381	363	1	740
FL	31,605	9,257	6,341	2,891	13,116	16,036	3,195	1,250	15,376
GA	19,361	4,935	3,198	3,441	7,788	9,072	2,616	1,294	7,484
HI.	2,812	519	515	474	1,304	1,849	48	22	1,349
ID.	3,142	660	483	712	1,287	1,583	517	19	1,037
IL.	29,387	7,737	5,578	5,687	10,384	12,676	7,469	1,220	9,311
IN.	17,066	3,710	2,211	5,117	6,028	7,311	4,122	1,966	5,130
IA.	8,161	1,847	1,108	2,387	2,820	4,085	1,593	403	2,408
KS	7,082	1,667	1,208	1,792	2,416	3,457	1,500	373	2,223
KY	11,018	2,005	1,292	3,232	4,489	6,082	1,475	1,158	3,361
LA	18,026	2,696	1,891	7,487	5,952	8,991	4,960	314	5,070
ME	3,625	1,112	651	660	1,201	2,131	409	15	1,270
MD.	11,446	3,179	2,433	1,170	4,663	5,777	1,891	496	3,983
MA.	15,957	4,966	3,790	2,130	5,071	7,394	3,176	183	6,062
MI	21,913	5,551	3,881	3,996	8,484	10,711	4,440	1,057	7,068
MN	12,447	2,932	2,050	2,135	5,330	6,495	2,305	376	3,618
MS	7,459	1,788	1,088	1,611	2,972	3,886	1,493	324	2,719
MO.	13,822	3,786	2,404	1,914	5,717	7,005	2,531	700	4,414
MT	2,484	469	361	489	1,164	1,408	343	177	720
NE	4,412	1,040	740	904	1,729	2,216	869	134	1,333
NV	5,127	1,218	808	962	2,139	2,459	1,447	239	2,172
NH	3,128	927	600	446	1,155	1,768	239	67	1,129
NJ	20,178	4,951	4,433	2,732	8,063	10,236	3,659	255	6,785
NM.	4,313	921	825	629	1,938	2,418	769	437	1,316
NY	39,903	13,371	12,961	3,297	10,274	15,374	9,889	463	16,449
NC	18,865	5,170	3,170	3,414	7,111	9,167	1,786	1,210	7,804
ND	2,243	417	307	707	812	1,296	241	412	535
OH.	29,071	7,375	5,198	6,212	10,286	12,376	6,404	1,790	10,200
OK.	10,181	2,193	1,441	2,349	4,197	4,920	3,011	348	3,016
OR.	7,411	1,605	1,129	1,306	3,372	3,855	1,335	48	2,494
PA	29,888	8,713	5,393	5,632	10,150	13,222	5,736	1,796	10,757
RI.	2,313	771	578	209	755	1,067	601	(Z)	847
SC	9,867	2,397	1,447	2,228	3,795	4,412	1,012	665	4,317
SD	1,881	449	301	282	849	1,127	220	46	548
TN	13,808	3,217	2,304	2,799	5,489	6,319	1,971	864	5,325
TX	72,653	12,999	9,310	26,995	23,349	38,721	17,441	1,993	22,979
UT	4,533	959	749	659	2,166	2,442	889	454	1,198
VT	1,660	536	310	200	615	991	61	(Z)	607
VA	16,290	4,325	2,963	2,025	6,977	8,523	1,917	784	5,928
WA	12,906	2,920	2,048	1,927	6,012	7,014	2,316	115	4,141
WV	4,297	999	603	986	1,710	2,148	656	1,116	1,392
WI	13,358	3,190	1,951	3,361	4,855	6,645	2,727	552	3,931
WY	2,322	275	275	746	1,026	1,339	384	402	564

Z Less than $500,000. [1] Includes sources not shown separately. Total expenditures are the sum of purchases for each source (including electricity sales) less electric utility purchases of fuel.

Source: U.S. Energy Information Administration, *State Energy Price and Expenditure Report 2001.* See also <http://tonto.eia.doe.gov/FTPROOT/state/pr_all.pdf> (released January 2005).

Energy and Utilities **597**

Table 895. **Residential Energy Consumption, Expenditures, and Average Price: 1980 to 2001**

[9.32 represents 9,320,000,000,000,000 Btu. For period April to March for 1980; January to December for 1987 to 2001. Excludes Alaska and Hawaii in 1980. Covers occupied units only. Excludes household usage of gasoline for transportation and the use of wood or coal. Based on Residential Energy Consumption Survey; see source. Btu = British thermal unit; see text, this section]

Type of fuel	Unit	1980	1987	1990	1993	1997	2001
CONSUMPTION							
Total.	Quad. Btu . .	9.32	9.13	9.22	10.01	10.25	9.86
Average per household . . .	Mil. Btu . .	114	101	98	104	101	92
Natural gas	Quad. Btu . .	4.97	4.83	4.86	5.27	5.28	4.84
Electricity, site	Quad. Btu . .	2.48	2.76	3.03	3.28	3.54	3.89
Fuel oil, kerosene	Quad. Btu . .	1.52	1.22	1.04	1.07	1.07	0.76
Liquid petroleum gas	Quad. Btu . .	0.35	0.32	0.28	0.38	0.36	0.38
EXPENDITURES							
Total.	Bil. dol.	75.6	97.8	110.2	123.9	135.8	159.7
Average per household . . .	Dollars	926	1,080	1,172	1,282	1,338	1,493
Natural gas	Bil. dol.	19.8	26.2	27.3	32.0	35.8	47.0
Electricity	Bil. dol.	40.8	61.6	71.5	81.1	88.3	100.3
Fuel oil, kerosene	Bil. dol.	12.2	7.2	8.3	7.0	7.6	6.8
Liquid petroleum gas	Bil. dol.	2.8	2.8	3.1	3.8	4.0	5.6
AVERAGE PRICE							
Total.	Dol./mil. Btu.	8.12	10.71	11.95	12.38	13.25	16.19
Natural gas	Dol./mil. Btu .	3.98	5.41	5.61	6.07	6.78	9.70
Electricity	Dol./mil. Btu .	16.46	22.34	23.60	24.69	24.97	25.80
Fuel oil, kerosene	Dol./mil. Btu .	8.03	5.89	7.92	6.53	7.13	9.05
Liquid petroleum gas	Dol./mil. Btu .	8.00	8.91	11.18	10.04	11.23	14.87

Source: U.S. Energy Information Administration, *Residential Energy Consumption Survey: Household Energy Consumption and Expenditures*, 1980, 1987, 1990, 1993, 1997, and 2001. See also <http://www.eia.doe.gov/emeu/recs/contents.html>.

Table 896. **Residential Energy Consumption and Expenditures, by Type of Fuel and Selected Household Characteristic: 2001**

[Quad. = quadrillion. (9.86 represents 9,860,000,000,000,000 Btu). See headnote, Table 895]

Characteristic	Consumption (Btus)					Expenditures				
	Total [1] (quad.)	Avg. per house-hold [1, 2] (mil.)	Natural gas (quad.)	Electric-ity (quad.)	Fuel oil [3] (quad.)	Total [1] (bil. dol.)	Avg. per house-hold [1, 2] (dol.)	Natural gas (bil. dol.)	Electric-ity (bil. dol.)	Fuel oil [3] (bil. dol.)
Total households . . .	9.86	92.2	4.84	3.89	0.71	159.74	1,493	46.98	100.34	6.83
Single family.	7.91	107.3	3.98	3.01	0.59	125.02	1,697	38.04	76.69	5.32
Two-to-four unit building . . .	0.74	78.1	0.45	0.23	0.06	11.97	1,261	4.70	6.68	0.54
Five-or-more unit building . .	0.70	41.0	0.28	0.36	0.05	13.66	803	2.98	10.29	0.37
Mobile home	0.52	75.9	0.14	0.29	0.01	9.09	1,336	1.26	6.68	0.08
Year house built:										
1949 or earlier.	2.92	109.8	1.68	0.76	0.34	42.18	1,586	16.47	20.65	3.04
1950 to 1959	1.39	97.9	0.75	0.46	0.14	21.25	1,500	7.15	12.34	1.29
1960 to 1969	1.19	86.5	0.61	0.45	0.09	19.48	1,414	6.00	12.09	0.77
1970 to 1979	1.48	79.0	0.57	0.77	0.07	26.03	1,388	5.28	18.99	0.61
1980 to 1989	1.45	79.7	0.57	0.78	0.04	26.22	1,438	5.53	19.37	0.40
1990 to 2001 [4]	1.43	92.5	0.66	0.68	0.02	24.59	1,591	6.54	16.90	0.21

[1] Includes liquid petroleum gas, not shown separately. [2] The averages are over the set of all households; otherwise the averages are over the set of households using a given fuel or end use. [3] Includes kerosene. [4] New construction for 2001 includes only those housing units built and occupied between January and the April-August period when the household interviews were conducted.

Source: U.S. Energy Information Administration, *Residential Energy Consumption Survey: Household Energy Consumption and Expenditures*, 2001. See also <http://www.eia.doe.gov/emeu/recs/contents.html>.

Table 897. **Fossil Fuel Prices by Type of Fuel: 1990 to 2003**

[In cents per million British thermal units (Btu), except as indicated. All fuel prices taken as close to the point of production as possible. See text, this section, for explanation of Btu conversions from mineral fuels]

Fuel	Current dollars					Constant (2000) dollars				
	1990	1995	2000	2002	2003 [1]	1990	1995	2000	2002	2003 [1]
Composite [2] . .	1.84	1.47	2.60	2.21	3.12	2.26	1.60	2.60	2.12	2.95
Crude oil [3]	3.45	2.52	4.61	3.88	4.75	4.23	2.74	4.61	3.73	4.50
Natural gas [4] . . .	1.55	1.40	3.32	2.67	4.50	1.90	1.52	3.32	2.56	4.26
Bituminous coal [5] .	1.00	0.88	0.80	0.87	0.86	1.22	0.96	0.80	0.83	0.82

[1] Preliminary. [2] Derived by multiplying the price per Btu of each fossil fuel by the total Btu content of the production of each fossil fuel and dividing this accumulated value of total fossil fuel production by the accumulated Btu content of total fossil fuel production. [3] Domestic first purchase prices. [4] Wellhead prices. [5] Includes bituminous coal, subbituminous coal, and lignite.

Source: U.S. Energy Information Administration. *Annual Energy Review 2003.* See also <http://www.eia.doe.gov/emeu/aer/finan.html> (released September 2004).

598   Energy and Utilities

U.S. Census Bureau. Statistical Abstract of the United States: 2006

Table 898. **Energy Imports and Exports by Type of Fuel: 1980 to 2003**

[In quadrillion of Btu. (12.10 represents 12,100,000,000,000,000 Btu). For definition of Btu, see text, this section]

Type of fuel	1980	1985	1990	1995	1997	1998	1999	2000	2001	2002	2003 [1]
Net imports, total [2]	12.10	7.58	14.06	17.75	20.70	22.28	23.54	24.97	26.39	25.74	26.97
Coal	-2.39	-2.39	-2.70	-2.08	-2.01	-1.87	-1.30	-1.21	-0.77	-0.61	-0.49
Natural gas (dry).	0.96	0.90	1.46	2.74	2.90	3.06	3.50	3.62	3.69	3.58	3.32
Petroleum [3]	13.50	8.95	15.29	16.89	19.64	20.94	21.18	22.38	23.36	22.63	24.07
Other [4]	0.04	0.13	0.01	0.19	0.16	0.16	0.16	0.18	0.10	0.14	0.07
Imports, total	15.80	11.78	18.82	22.26	25.22	26.58	27.25	28.97	30.16	29.41	31.02
Coal	0.03	0.05	0.07	0.24	0.19	0.22	0.23	0.31	0.49	0.42	0.63
Natural gas (dry).	1.01	0.95	1.55	2.90	3.06	3.22	3.66	3.87	4.07	4.10	4.02
Petroleum [3]	14.66	10.61	17.12	18.88	21.74	22.91	23.13	24.53	25.40	24.68	26.21
Other [4]	0.10	0.17	0.08	0.24	0.22	0.23	0.23	0.26	0.19	0.20	0.17
Exports, total	3.69	4.20	4.75	4.51	4.51	4.30	3.71	4.01	3.77	3.66	4.05
Coal	2.42	2.44	2.77	2.32	2.19	2.09	1.53	1.53	1.27	1.03	1.12
Natural gas (dry).	0.05	0.06	0.09	0.16	0.16	0.16	0.16	0.25	0.38	0.52	0.70
Petroleum	1.16	1.66	1.82	1.99	2.10	1.97	1.95	2.15	2.04	2.04	2.13
Other [4]	0.07	0.04	0.07	0.05	0.06	0.07	0.07	0.08	0.09	0.07	0.10

[1] Preliminary. [2] Net imports equals imports minus exports. Minus sign (-) denotes an excess of exports over imports.
[3] Includes imports into the Strategic Petroleum Reserve, which began in 1977. [4] Coal coke and small amounts of electricity transmitted across U.S. borders with Canada and Mexico.

Source: U.S. Energy Information Administration, *Annual Energy Review 2003.* See also <http://www.eia.doe.gov/emeu/aer /pdf/pages/sec1_11.pdf> (released September 2004).

Table 899. **U.S. Foreign Trade in Selected Mineral Fuels: 1980 to 2003**

[985 represents 985,000,000,000 cu. ft. Minus sign (-) indicates an excess of imports over exports]

Mineral fuel	Unit	1980	1985	1990	1995	1999	2000	2001	2002	2003 [1]
Natural gas:										
Imports	Bil. cu. ft.	985	950	1,532	2,841	3,586	3,782	3,977	4,015	3,928
Exports	Bil. cu. ft.	49	55	86	154	164	244	373	516	692
Net trade	Bil. cu. ft.	-936	-894	-1,447	-2,687	-3,422	-3,538	-3,604	-3,499	-3,236
Crude oil:										
Imports [2]	Mil. bbl.	1,926	1,168	2,151	2,639	3,187	3,320	3,405	3,336	3,521
Exports	Mil. bbl.	105	75	40	35	43	18	7	3	5
Net trade	Mil. bbl.	-1,821	-1,094	-2,112	-2,604	-3,144	-3,301	-3,398	-3,333	-3,516
Petroleum products:										
Imports	Mil. bbl.	603	681	775	586	774	874	928	872	952
Exports	Mil. bbl.	94	211	273	312	300	362	347	356	367
Net trade	Mil. bbl.	-508	-471	-502	-274	-474	-512	-581	-517	-585
Coal:										
Imports	Mil. sh. tons . . .	1.2	2.0	2.7	9.5	9.1	12.5	19.8	16.9	25.0
Exports	Mil. sh. tons . . .	91.7	92.7	105.8	88.5	58.5	58.5	48.7	39.6	43.0
Net trade	Mil. sh. tons . . .	90.5	90.7	103.1	79.1	49.4	46.0	28.9	22.7	18.0

[1] Preliminary. [2] Includes strategic petroleum reserve imports.

Source: U.S. Energy Information Administration, *Annual Energy Review 2003.* See also <http://www.eia.doe.gov/emeu/aer/contents.html> (issued September 2004).

Table 900. **Crude Oil Imports Into the U.S. by Country of Origin: 1980 to 2004**

[In millions of barrels (1,921 represents 1,921,000,000). Barrels contain 42 gallons. Total OPEC excludes, and Non-OPEC includes, petroleum imported into the United States indirectly from members of OPEC, primarily from Carribean and West European areas, as petroleum products that were refined from crude oil produced by OPEC]

Country of origin	1980	1985	1990	1995	1998	1999	2000	2001	2002	2003	2004
Total imports . . .	1,921	1,168	2,151	2,639	3,178	3,187	3,311	3,405	3,336	3,521	3,674
OPEC, [1, 2, 3] total	1,410	479	1,283	1,219	1,522	1,543	1,659	1,770	1,490	1,671	1,836
Algeria	166	31	23	10	4	9	(Z)	4	11	41	79
Iraq	10	17	188	-	123	265	226	290	168	171	238
Kuwait [4]	10	1	29	78	110	90	96	87	79	75	88
Libya	200	-	-	-	-	-	-	-	-	-	7
Saudi Arabia [4]	456	48	436	460	512	506	556	588	554	629	547
Indonesia	115	107	36	23	18	26	13	15	18	10	12
Nigeria	307	102	286	227	251	227	319	307	215	306	389
Venezuela	57	112	243	420	503	420	446	471	438	436	473
Non-OPEC, total [5]	511	689	869	1,419	1,656	1,643	1,652	1,635	1,846	1,850	1,838
Angola	(NA)	(NA)	86	131	170	130	108	117	117	132	112
Canada	73	171	235	380	462	430	492	495	527	565	590
Colombia	(NA)	(NA)	51	76	127	165	116	95	86	59	51
Ecuador [2]	6	20	(NA)	35	36	42	46	41	37	50	83
Gabon [3]	9	19	(NA)	84	76	61	52	51	52	48	52
Mexico	185	261	251	375	482	458	479	509	548	580	584
Norway	53	11	35	94	81	96	110	103	127	60	54
Russia	(NA)	(NA)	(Z)	5	3	8	3	-	31	54	55
United Kingdom	63	101	57	124	59	104	106	89	148	127	86

- Represents zero. NA Not available. Z Represents less than 500,000 barrels. [1] OPEC (Organization of Petroleum Exporting Countries) includes the Persian Gulf nations shown below, except Bahrain, which is not a member of OPEC, and also includes nations not shown. [2] Ecuador withdrew from OPEC on December 31, 1992; therefore, it is included under OPEC for the period 1973 to 1992. [3] Gabon withdrew from OPEC on December 31, 1994; therefore, it is included under OPEC for the period 1973 to 1994. [4] Imports from the Neutral Zone between Kuwait and Saudi Arabia are included in Saudi Arabia. [5] Non-OPEC total includes nations not shown.

Source: U.S. Energy Information Administration, *Petroleum Supply Monthly,* February 2005. See also <http://www.eia.doe.gov/pub/oil_gas/petroleum/data_publications/petroleum_supply_monthly/historical/2005/2005_02/pdf/table40.pdf>.

Table 901. Crude Oil and Refined Products—Summary: 1980 to 2004

[13,481 represents 13,481,000 bbl. Barrels (bbl.) of 42 gallons. Data are averages]

Year	Crude oil (1,000 bbl. per day)					Refined oil products (1,000 bbl. per day)			Total oil imports [3] (1,000 bbl. per day)	Crude oil stocks [4] (mil. bbl.)	
	Input to refiner-ies	Domestic produc-tion	Imports			Domestic demand	Imports	Exports		Total	Strategic reserve [5]
			Total [1]	Strategic reserve [2]	Exports						
1980 ...	13,481	8,597	5,263	44	287	17,056	1,646	258	6,909	[6]466	108
1985 ...	12,002	8,971	3,201	118	204	15,726	1,866	577	5,067	814	493
1990 ...	13,409	7,355	5,894	27	109	16,988	2,123	748	8,018	908	586
1994 ...	13,866	6,662	7,063	12	99	17,718	1,933	843	8,996	929	592
1995 ...	13,973	6,560	7,230	-	95	17,725	1,605	855	8,835	895	592
1996 ...	14,195	6,465	7,508	-	110	18,309	1,971	871	9,478	850	566
1997 ...	14,662	6,452	8,225	-	108	18,620	1,936	896	10,162	868	563
1998 ...	14,889	6,252	8,706	-	110	18,917	2,002	835	10,708	895	571
1999 ...	14,804	5,881	8,731	8	118	19,519	2,122	822	10,852	852	567
2000 ...	15,067	5,822	9,071	8	50	19,701	2,389	990	11,459	826	541
2001 ...	15,128	5,801	9,328	11	20	19,649	2,543	951	11,871	862	550
2002 ...	14,947	5,746	9,140	16	9	19,761	2,390	975	11,530	877	599
2003 ...	15,304	5,681	9,665	-	12	20,034	2,599	1,014	12,264	907	638
2004 ...	15,479	5,430	10,038	75	27	20,517	2,861	1,021	12,899	962	676

- Represents zero. [1] Includes Strategic Petroleum Reserve. [2] SPR is the Strategic Petroleum Reserve. Through 2003, includes imports by SPR only; beginning in 2004, includes imports by SPR, and imports into SPR by others. [3] Crude oil (including Strategic Petroleum Reserve imports) plus refined products. [4] Crude oil at end of period. Includes commercial and Strategic Petroleum Reserve stocks. [5] Crude oil stocks in the Strategic Petroleum Reserve include non-U.S. stocks held under foreign or commercial storage agreements. [6] Stocks of Alaskan crude oil in transit are included from January 1985 forward.

Source: U.S. Energy Information Administration, *Monthly Energy Review*, March 2005 issue.

Table 902. Petroleum and Coal Products Corporations—Sales, Net Profit, and Profit Per Dollar of Sales: 1990 to 2004

[318.5 represents $318,500,000,000. Represents SIC group 29 (NAICS group 324). Through 2000 based on Standard Industrial Classification code; beginning 2001 based on North American Industry Classification System, 1997 (NAICS). Profit rates are averages of quarterly figures at annual rates. Beginning 1990, excludes estimates for corporations with less than $250,000 in assets]

Item	Unit	1990	1995	1996	1997	1998	1999	2000	2001	2002	2003	2004
Sales.	Bil. dol. . . .	318.5	283.1	323.5	320.0	250.4	277.0	455.2	472.5	474.9	597.8	762.7
Net profit:												
Before income taxes	Bil. dol. . . .	23.1	16.5	32.6	36.8	9.7	20.3	55.5	47.2	22.4	52.8	88.0
After income taxes	Bil. dol. . . .	17.8	13.9	26.6	29.4	8.3	17.2	42.6	35.8	19.5	43.6	71.4
Depreciation[1]	Bil. dol. . . .	18.7	16.7	15.9	15.6	14.7	13.5	15.5	17.2	17.8	19.4	18.4
Profits per dollar of sales:												
Before income taxes	Cents	7.3	5.8	10.1	11.5	3.5	7.1	12.2	9.7	4.6	10.4	15.1
After income taxes	Cents	5.6	4.9	8.2	9.2	3.1	6.0	9.4	7.4	4.2	8.6	12.3
Profits on stockholders' equity:												
Before income taxes	Percent . . .	16.4	12.6	23.2	23.5	6.0	13.0	29.4	21.8	9.7	20.9	32.3
After income taxes	Percent . . .	12.7	10.6	18.9	18.9	5.2	11.0	22.6	16.5	8.4	17.2	26.2

[1] Includes depletion and accelerated amortization of emergency facilities.

Source: U.S. Census Bureau, *Quarterly Financial Report for Manufacturing, Mining and Trade Corporations.*

Table 903. Major Petroleum Companies—Financial Summary: 1980 to 2004

[32.9 represents $32,900,000,000. Data represent a composite of approximately 42 major worldwide petroleum companies aggregated on a consolidated total company basis]

Item	1980	1990	1995	1998	1999	2000	2001	2002	2003	2004
FINANCIAL DATA (bil. dol.)										
Net income	32.9	26.8	24.3	14.5	35.3	76.4	62.0	44.3	85.5	120.5
Depreciation, depletion, etc.	32.5	38.7	43.1	61.0	45.0	53.3	63.4	61.2	68.0	76.9
Cash flow [1]	65.4	65.5	67.4	75.5	75.3	129.7	140.0	118.0	157.7	205.1
Dividends paid	9.3	15.9	17.6	20.9	21.7	23.0	29.7	27.3	27.5	33.5
Net internal funds available for investment or debt repayment [2]	56.1	49.6	49.8	54.6	54.1	106.7	110.4	90.7	130.3	171.5
Capital and exploratory expenditures	62.1	59.6	59.8	83.9	67.7	72.8	99.9	88.7	90.7	112.4
Long-term capitalization	211.4	300.0	304.3	382.0	456.2	516.9	543.8	548.1	606.1	685.0
Long-term debt.	49.8	90.4	85.4	103.9	105.4	112.8	143.2	153.5	142.1	145.6
Preferred stock.	2.0	5.2	5.7	3.9	4.8	5.4	6.7	2.5	2.2	1.3
Common stock and retained earnings [3] . . .	159.6	204.4	213.2	274.2	346.0	398.7	393.9	392.1	461.8	538.1
Excess of expenditures over cash income [4]	6.0	10.0	10.0	29.3	13.6	-33.9	-10.5	-2.0	-39.5	-59.2
RATIOS [5] (percent)										
Long-term debt to long-term capitalization. . .	23.6	30.1	28.1	27.2	23.1	21.8	26.7	28.3	26.5	24.1
Net income to total average capital	17.0	9.1	8.1	3.8	8.9	15.7	12.3	8.7	15.2	18.9
Net income to average common equity	22.5	13.5	11.6	5.2	12.4	20.5	16.3	11.5	20.1	24.2

[1] Generally represents internally-generated funds from operations. Sum of net income and noncash charges such as depreciation, depletion, and amortization. [2] Cash flow minus dividends paid. [3] Includes common stock, capital surplus, and earned surplus accounts after adjustments. [4] Capital and exploratory expenditures plus dividends paid minus cash flow. [5] Represents approximate year-to-year comparisons because of changes in the makeup of the group due to mergers and other corporate changes.

Source: Carl H. Pforzheimer & Co., New York, NY, *Comparative Oil Company Statements*, annual.

600   Energy and Utilities

Table 904. Electric Power Industry—Sales, Prices, Net Generation, Net Summer Capacity, and Consumption of Fuels: 1990 to 2004

[2,837.1 represents 2,837,100,000,000 kWh. Net generation for calendar years; capacity as of December 31]

Item	Unit	1990	2000	2001	2002	2003	2004 [1]
ELECTRIC POWER INDUSTRY, ALL SECTORS							
Consumption, total	Bil. kWh	2,837.1	3,592.4	3,532.4	3,628.7	3,656.5	3,716.5
Net generation, total	Bil. kWh	3,038.0	3,802.1	3,736.6	3,858.5	3,883.2	3,953.4
Electric power sector	Bil. kWh	2,901.3	3,637.5	3,580.1	3,698.5	3,721.2	3,793.6
Commercial sector	Bil. kWh	5.8	7.9	7.4	7.4	7.5	7.4
Industrial sector	Bil. kWh	130.8	156.7	149.2	152.6	154.5	152.4
Electricity imports	Bil. kWh	18.4	48.6	38.5	36.4	30.4	34.2
Electricity exports	Bil. kWh	16.1	14.8	16.5	13.6	24.0	22.9
Electricity losses and unaccounted for	Bil. kWh	203.2	243.5	226.2	252.6	233.1	248.2
Retail sales of electricity	Bil. kWh	2,712.6	3,421.4	3,369.8	3,462.5	3,488.2	3,550.5
Direct use of electricity	Bil. kWh	124.5	170.9	162.6	166.2	168.3	166.0
Electricity retail prices per kWh:							
All sectors, current dollars	Cents	6.57	6.81	7.32	7.21	7.42	7.57
All sectors, real (1996) dollars	Cents	8.05	6.81	7.15	6.93	7.00	6.99
Residential, current dollars	Cents	7.83	8.24	8.62	8.46	8.70	8.94
Residential, real (1996) dollars	Cents	9.60	8.24	8.42	8.13	8.21	8.26
Commercial, current dollars	Cents	7.34	7.43	7.93	7.86	7.98	8.17
Commercial, real (1996) dollars	Cents	9.00	7.43	7.74	7.55	7.53	7.55
Industrial, current dollars	Cents	4.74	4.64	5.04	4.88	5.13	5.11
Industrial, real (1996) dollars	Cents	5.81	4.64	4.92	4.69	4.84	4.72
Transportation, current dollars	Cents	(NA)	(NA)	(NA)	(NA)	7.58	6.48
Transportation, real (1996) dollars	Cents	(NA)	(NA)	(NA)	(NA)	7.15	5.99
Other users, current dollars	Cents	6.40	6.56	7.03	6.73	(NA)	(NA)
Other users, real (1996) dollars	Cents	7.84	6.56	6.87	6.47	(NA)	(NA)
Net generation, total [2]	Bil. kWh	3,038.0	3,802.1	3,736.6	3,858.5	3,883.2	3,953.4
Coal	Bil. kWh	1,594.0	1,966.3	1,904.0	1,933.1	1,973.7	1,976.3
Petroleum	Bil. kWh	126.6	111.2	124.9	94.6	119.4	117.6
Natural gas	Bil. kWh	372.8	601.0	639.1	691.0	649.9	699.6
Nuclear	Bil. kWh	576.9	753.9	768.8	780.1	763.7	788.6
Hydroelectric pumped storage plants	Bil. kWh	-3.5	-5.5	-8.8	-8.7	-8.5	-8.1
Conventional hydroelectric power plants	Bil. kWh	292.9	275.6	217.0	264.3	275.8	269.6
Geothermal	Bil. kWh	15.4	14.1	13.7	14.5	14.4	14.4
Net summer capacity, total [2]	Mil. kW	734.1	811.7	848.3	905.3	948.4	968.1
Coal-fired plants	Mil. kW	307.4	315.1	314.2	315.4	313.0	313.3
Petroleum-fired plants	Mil. kW	49.0	35.9	39.7	38.2	36.4	36.6
Natural-gas-fired plants	Mil. kW	56.2	95.7	125.8	171.7	208.4	222.9
Dual-fired plants	Mil. kW	113.6	149.8	153.5	162.3	171.3	175.4
Nuclear electric power plants	Mil. kW	99.6	97.9	98.2	98.7	99.2	99.6
Hydroelectric-pumped storage plants	Mil. kW	19.5	19.5	19.1	20.4	20.5	20.5
Conventional hydroelectric power plants	Mil. kW	73.9	79.4	79.5	79.4	78.7	78.7
Geothermal energy plants	Mil. kW	2.7	2.8	2.2	2.3	2.1	2.1
Fuel consumption:							
Coal	Mil. sh. tons	792.5	994.9	972.7	987.6	1,014.1	1,029.6
Distillate fuel and kerosene	Mil. bbl	18.1	31.7	31.1	23.3	29.7	19.7
Residual fuel	Mil. bbl	190.8	143.4	165.3	109.2	142.5	147.9
Petroleum coke	Mil. sh. tons	1.9	3.7	3.9	6.8	6.3	7.5
Natural gas	Bil. cu. ft	3,691.6	5,691.5	5,832.3	6,126.1	5,616.1	6,020.3
ELECTRIC POWER SECTOR							
Net generation, total [2]	Bil. kWh	2,901.3	3,637.5	3,580.1	3,698.5	3,721.2	3,793.6
Coal	Bil. kWh	1,572.1	1,943.1	1,882.8	1,910.6	1,952.7	1,954.0
Petroleum	Bil. kWh	118.9	105.2	119.1	89.7	113.7	112.5
Natural gas	Bil. kWh	309.5	518.0	554.9	607.7	567.3	618.6
Nuclear	Bil. kWh	576.9	753.9	768.8	780.1	763.7	788.6
Net summer capacity, total [2]	Mil. kW	709.9	782.1	818.8	875.8	918.6	938.3
Coal-fired plants	Mil. kW	302.3	310.2	309.8	311.0	308.5	308.9
Petroleum-fired plants	Mil. kW	48.0	34.9	38.4	37.3	35.5	35.6
Natural-gas-fired plants	Mil. kW	47.9	82.6	111.1	157.4	193.9	208.3
Dual-fired plants	Mil. kW	110.8	147.9	152.0	160.4	169.4	173.6
Nuclear electric power plants	Mil. kW	99.6	97.9	98.2	98.7	99.2	99.6
COMBINED HEAT-AND-POWER PLANTS							
Commercial:							
Net generation, total [2]	Bil. kWh	5.8	7.9	7.4	7.4	7.5	7.4
Coal	Bil. kWh	0.8	1.1	1.0	1.0	1.2	1.1
Petroleum	Bil. kWh	0.6	0.4	0.4	0.4	0.4	0.4
Natural gas	Bil. kWh	3.3	4.3	4.4	4.3	3.9	4.0
Net summer capacity, total [2]	Mil. kW	1.4	2.2	2.9	2.2	2.1	2.1
Coal-fired plants	Mil. kW	0.3	0.3	0.3	0.3	0.3	0.3
Petroleum-fired plants	Mil. kW	0.2	0.3	0.3	0.3	0.3	0.3
Natural-gas-fired plants	Mil. kW	0.2	0.6	1.4	0.5	0.5	0.5
Dual-fired plants	Mil. kW	0.6	0.6	0.6	0.7	0.6	0.6
Industrial:							
Net generation, total [2]	Bil. kWh	130.8	156.7	149.2	152.6	154.5	152.4
Coal	Bil. kWh	21.1	22.1	20.1	21.5	19.8	21.2
Petroleum	Bil. kWh	7.2	5.6	5.3	4.4	5.3	4.7
Natural gas	Bil. kWh	60.0	78.8	79.8	79.0	78.7	77.0
Net summer capacity, total [2]	Mil. kW	22.9	27.3	26.6	27.3	27.7	27.6
Coal-fired plants	Mil. kW	4.8	4.6	4.2	4.0	4.1	4.1
Petroleum-fired plants	Mil. kW	0.9	0.8	1.0	0.6	0.7	0.7
Natural-gas-fired plants	Mil. kW	8.1	12.5	13.3	13.7	14.1	14.0
Dual-fired plants	Mil. kW	2.2	1.3	0.9	1.1	1.3	1.3

- Represents zero.   (NA) Not available.   [1] Preliminary.   [2] Includes types not shown separately.

Source: U.S. Energy Information Administration, *Annual Energy Review 2004*. See also <http://www.eia.doe.gov/emeu/aer/elect.html>

Table 905. **Electric Power Industry—Net Generation and Net Summer Capacity by State: 2000 to 2003**

[Capacity as of December 31. (3,802.1 represents 3,802,100,000,000) Covers utilities for public use]

State	Net generation (bil. kWh)			2003		Net summer capacity (mil. kW)			
	2000	2001	2002	Total	Percent from coal	2000	2001	2002	2003
United States.	3,802.1	3,736.6	3,858.5	3,883.2	50.8	809.4	846.6	905.3	948.4
Alabama.	124.4	125.3	132.9	137.5	55.8	23.5	23.8	26.6	30.2
Alaska	6.2	6.7	6.8	6.3	8.7	2.1	2.1	2.0	1.9
Arizona.	88.9	89.9	94.1	94.4	100.0	15.3	16.7	19.4	23.5
Arkansas	43.9	47.2	47.6	50.4	46.6	9.7	10.1	11.3	13.5
California	208.1	198.6	184.2	192.8	1.2	51.9	54.2	56.7	57.9
Colorado.	44.2	46.9	45.6	46.6	77.5	8.4	8.9	9.4	10.4
Connecticut.	33.0	30.5	31.3	29.5	14.2	6.4	7.9	7.4	7.6
Delaware	6.0	6.8	6.0	7.4	54.5	2.1	2.7	3.4	3.4
District of Columbia	0.1	0.1	0.3	0.1	-	0.8	0.8	0.8	0.8
Florida	191.8	190.9	203.4	212.6	31.8	41.5	42.8	47.1	49.4
Georgia	123.9	118.3	126.5	124.1	63.4	27.8	29.5	34.6	34.8
Hawaii	10.6	10.6	11.7	11.0	15.0	2.4	2.3	2.3	2.3
Idaho	11.9	9.3	9.8	10.4	0.9	3.0	3.2	3.3	3.0
Illinois	178.5	179.2	188.1	189.1	46.5	36.3	40.0	44.7	45.5
Indiana	127.8	122.6	125.6	124.9	94.3	23.3	23.6	25.3	25.6
Iowa	41.5	40.7	42.5	42.1	85.1	9.1	9.2	9.3	10.1
Kansas.	44.8	44.7	47.2	46.6	75.4	10.1	10.4	10.4	10.9
Kentucky	93.0	95.4	92.1	91.7	91.7	16.8	17.6	19.1	19.1
Louisiana	92.9	87.9	95.0	94.9	24.1	21.0	21.7	25.6	25.7
Maine.	14.0	19.6	22.5	19.0	2.0	4.2	4.2	4.3	4.3
Maryland	51.1	49.1	48.3	52.2	57.3	10.4	11.8	11.9	12.5
Massachusetts.	38.7	38.5	42.0	48.4	22.5	12.4	11.8	12.2	13.9
Michigan.	104.2	111.8	117.9	111.3	60.9	25.8	26.9	29.3	30.4
Minnesota.	51.4	48.5	52.8	55.1	64.8	10.3	11.1	11.3	11.5
Mississippi	37.6	53.4	42.9	40.1	42.5	9.0	11.1	13.7	17.3
Missouri	76.6	79.5	81.2	87.2	85.1	17.3	18.9	19.8	20.0
Montana	26.5	24.2	25.5	26.3	64.9	5.2	5.1	5.2	5.2
Nebraska	29.1	30.5	31.6	30.5	68.8	6.0	6.0	6.1	6.7
Nevada	35.5	33.9	32.1	33.2	51.5	6.7	6.9	6.9	7.5
New Hampshire	15.0	15.1	16.0	21.6	18.2	2.9	2.8	3.4	4.2
New Jersey.	58.1	59.4	61.6	57.4	17.1	16.5	16.1	18.4	18.6
New Mexico	34.0	33.6	30.7	32.7	88.0	5.6	5.7	5.9	6.3
New York	138.1	143.9	139.6	137.6	17.1	35.6	35.7	36.0	36.7
North Carolina	122.3	117.5	124.5	127.6	58.6	24.5	26.1	26.7	27.3
North Dakota	31.3	30.3	31.3	31.3	94.0	4.7	4.7	4.7	4.7
Ohio	149.1	142.3	147.1	146.6	90.7	28.4	29.5	31.5	34.1
Oklahoma	55.6	55.2	59.2	60.6	60.5	14.1	14.9	16.2	18.2
Oregon.	51.8	45.1	47.1	49.0	8.8	11.3	11.8	12.5	12.9
Pennsylvania.	201.7	196.6	204.3	206.3	56.2	36.7	37.6	39.8	42.4
Rhode Island.	6.0	7.5	7.1	5.6	-	1.2	1.2	1.7	1.7
South Carolina.	93.3	89.2	96.6	93.8	39.9	18.7	19.4	20.4	20.7
South Dakota	9.7	7.4	7.7	7.9	43.2	2.8	2.8	2.9	2.7
Tennessee	95.8	96.2	96.1	92.2	59.6	19.5	20.2	20.7	20.9
Texas.	377.7	372.6	385.6	379.2	38.8	81.7	87.8	94.5	99.6
Utah	36.6	35.9	36.6	38.0	94.6	5.2	5.3	5.8	5.8
Vermont	6.3	5.5	5.5	6.0	-	1.0	1.0	1.0	1.0
Virginia.	77.2	74.1	75.0	75.3	49.3	19.4	20.1	20.2	21.3
Washington.	108.2	83.0	102.8	100.1	11.1	26.1	26.6	27.1	27.7
West Virginia.	92.9	81.8	94.8	94.7	97.6	15.0	15.7	16.2	16.1
Wisconsin	59.6	58.8	58.4	60.1	69.4	13.6	14.1	14.2	14.3
Wyoming	45.5	44.8	43.8	43.6	97.1	6.2	6.3	6.3	6.6

- Represents zero.

Source: U.S. Energy Information Administration, *Electric Power Annual 2003*. See also <http://www.eia.doe.gov/cneaf/electricity/epa /epa_sprdshts.html> (accessed June 1, 2005).

Table 906. Electric Utility Industry—Capability, Peak Load, and Capacity Margin:1980 to 2003

[558,237 represents 558,237,000 kW. Excludes Alaska and Hawaii. Capability represents the maximum kilowatt output with all power sources available and with hydraulic equipment under actual water conditions, allowing for maintenance, emergency outages, and system operating requirements. Capacity margin is the difference between capability and peak load]

Year	Capability at the time of— Summer peak load (1,000 kW)		Winter peak load (1,000 kW)		Noncoincident peak load		Capacity margin Summer		Winter	
	Amount	Change from prior year	Amount	Change from prior year	Summer (1,000 kW)	Winter (1,000 kW)	Amount (1,000 kW)	Percent of capability	Amount (1,000 kW)	Percent of capability
1980	558,237	13,731	572,195	17,670	427,058	384,567	131,179	23.5	187,628	32.8
1983	596,449	10,307	612,453	14,387	447,526	410,779	148,923	25.0	201,674	32.9
1984	604,240	7,791	622,125	9,672	451,150	436,374	153,090	25.3	185,751	29.9
1985	621,597	17,357	636,475	14,350	460,503	423,660	161,094	25.9	212,815	33.4
1986	633,291	11,694	646,721	10,246	476,320	422,857	156,971	24.8	223,864	34.6
1987	648,118	14,827	662,977	16,256	496,185	448,277	151,933	23.4	214,700	32.4
1988	661,580	13,462	676,940	13,963	529,460	466,533	132,120	20.0	210,407	31.1
1989	673,316	11,736	685,249	8,309	524,110	496,378	149,206	22.2	188,871	27.6
1990	685,091	11,775	696,757	11,508	546,331	484,231	138,760	20.3	212,526	30.5
1991	690,915	5,824	703,212	6,455	551,418	485,761	139,497	20.2	217,451	30.92
1992	695,436	4,521	707,752	4,540	548,707	492,983	146,729	21.1	214,769	30.35
1993	694,250	-1,186	711,957	4,205	575,356	521,733	118,894	17.1	190,224	26.72
1994	702,985	8,735	715,090	3,133	585,320	518,253	117,665	16.7	196,837	27.53
1995	714,222	11,237	727,679	12,589	620,249	544,684	93,973	13.2	182,995	25.15
1996	724,728	10,506	737,637	9,958	616,790	554,081	107,938	14.9	183,556	24.88
1997	725,829	1,101	736,666	-971	637,677	529,874	88,152	12.1	206,792	28.07
1998	724,193	-1,636	735,090	-1,576	660,293	567,558	63,900	8.8	167,532	22.79
1999	733,481	9,288	748,271	13,181	682,122	570,915	51,359	7.0	177,356	23.70
2000	750,771	17,290	767,505	19,234	678,413	588,426	72,358	9.6	179,079	23.33
2001	783,737	32,966	806,598	39,093	687,812	576,312	95,925	12.2	230,286	28.55
2002	825,145	41,408	850,984	44,386	714,565	604,986	110,580	13.4	245,998	28.91
2003 [1]	853,649	28,504	882,120	31,136	709,375	593,874	144,274	16.9	288,246	32.68

[1] Preliminary.

Source: Edison Electric Institute, Washington, DC, *Statistical Yearbook of the Electric Utility Industry,* annual.

Table 907. Electric Energy Retail Sales by Class of Service and State: 2003

[In billions of kilowatt-hours (3,488.2 represents 3,488,200,000,000)]

State	Total [1]	Residential	Commercial	Industrial	State	Total [1]	Residential	Commercial	Industrial
United States	3,488.2	1,273.5	1,199.7	1,008.0	Missouri	74.2	31.4	28.0	14.8
Alabama	83.8	29.4	20.4	34.0	Montana	12.7	4.1	4.1	4.5
Alaska	5.6	2.0	2.5	1.1	Nebraska	25.9	8.9	8.6	8.4
Arizona	64.1	27.7	25.4	10.9	Nevada	30.1	10.3	8.2	11.6
Arkansas	43.1	15.6	10.6	16.9	New Hampshire	11.0	4.3	4.3	2.5
California	238.7	80.7	108.0	49.2					
Colorado	46.5	15.7	19.7	11.1	New Jersey	76.6	27.3	36.1	13.1
Connecticut	31.8	13.2	12.9	5.5	New Mexico	19.3	5.4	8.1	5.8
Delaware	12.6	4.2	3.9	4.5	New York	144.2	47.1	72.5	21.7
District of Columbia	10.9	1.9	8.4	0.3	North Carolina	121.3	49.3	41.7	30.3
Florida	217.4	112.6	85.3	19.4	North Dakota	10.5	3.7	3.8	3.0
Georgia	123.7	48.2	40.6	34.8	Ohio	151.4	49.5	44.1	57.8
Hawaii	10.4	3.0	3.5	3.8	Oklahoma	50.4	20.2	17.0	13.3
Idaho	21.2	7.1	5.5	8.7	Oregon	45.2	17.7	15.5	12.0
Illinois	136.0	43.2	51.1	41.2	Pennsylvania	141.0	49.8	46.2	44.2
Indiana	100.5	30.7	22.4	47.3	Rhode Island	7.8	3.0	3.5	1.3
Iowa	41.2	12.8	11.6	16.8	South Carolina	77.1	26.4	19.3	31.3
Kansas	36.7	12.6	13.8	10.4	South Dakota	9.1	3.7	3.7	1.6
Kentucky	85.2	24.7	17.9	42.6	Tennessee	97.5	37.7	27.5	32.3
Louisiana	77.8	28.6	21.9	27.3	Texas	322.7	121.4	96.7	104.5
Maine	12.0	4.2	4.0	3.8	Utah	23.9	7.2	9.0	7.6
Maryland	71.3	26.7	17.0	27.2	Vermont	5.4	2.0	1.9	1.5
Massachusetts	54.7	19.3	25.6	9.6	Virginia	101.5	40.9	41.2	19.3
Michigan	108.9	33.7	35.4	39.8	Washington	78.1	31.9	28.0	18.2
Minnesota	63.1	20.6	20.5	21.9	West Virginia	28.3	10.5	7.1	10.7
Mississippi	45.5	17.7	12.6	15.3	Wisconsin	67.2	21.4	20.1	25.8
					Wyoming	13.3	2.3	3.3	7.7

[1] Includes transportation, not shown separately.

Source: U.S. Energy Information Administration, *Electric Sales and Revenue 2003.* See also <http://www.eia.doe.gov/cneaf/electricity/esr/esr_sum.html> (issued January 2005).

Table 908. Electric Energy Price by Class of Service and State: 2003

[Revenue (in cents) per kilowatt-hour (kWh). Data include both bundled and unbundled consumers]

State	Total [1]	Residential	Commercial	Industrial	State	Total [1]	Residential	Commercial	Industrial
United States . . .	**7.42**	**8.70**	**7.98**	**5.13**	Missouri	6.02	6.96	5.78	4.49
Alabama	5.88	7.39	6.85	3.98	Montana	6.16	7.56	7.10	4.01
Alaska	10.50	11.98	10.49	7.86	Nebraska	5.64	6.87	5.81	4.18
Arizona	7.34	8.35	7.09	5.37	Nevada	8.29	9.02	8.79	7.30
Arkansas	5.57	7.24	5.54	4.04	New Hampshire	10.80	11.98	10.44	9.39
California	11.62	12.00	12.19	9.85	New Jersey	9.46	10.69	9.25	7.47
Colorado	6.77	8.14	6.60	5.10	New Mexico	7.00	8.69	7.36	4.95
Connecticut	10.17	11.31	9.99	7.92	New York	12.44	14.31	12.93	7.14
Delaware	6.96	8.59	7.31	5.15	North Carolina	6.86	8.32	6.65	4.79
District of Columbia . . .	7.43	7.66	7.43	5.61	North Dakota	5.47	6.49	5.64	3.96
Florida	7.72	8.55	7.13	5.41	Ohio	6.75	8.27	7.60	4.79
Georgia	6.32	7.70	6.66	4.02	Oklahoma	6.35	7.47	6.38	4.59
Hawaii	14.47	16.73	15.02	12.20	Oregon	6.18	7.06	6.38	4.63
Idaho	5.22	6.24	5.56	4.16	Pennsylvania	7.98	9.55	8.07	6.14
Illinois	6.88	8.38	7.22	4.91	Rhode Island	10.47	11.62	10.00	9.06
Indiana	5.37	7.04	6.12	3.92	South Carolina	6.08	8.01	6.81	4.00
Iowa	6.11	8.57	6.24	4.16	South Dakota	6.35	7.47	6.04	4.51
Kansas	6.35	7.71	6.42	4.61	Tennessee	5.84	6.55	6.68	4.29
Kentucky	4.42	5.81	5.37	3.21	Texas	7.50	9.16	7.84	5.27
Louisiana	6.93	7.84	7.42	5.57	Utah	5.41	6.90	5.59	3.79
Maine	9.79	12.37	10.34	6.35	Vermont	10.98	12.82	11.29	8.05
Maryland	6.45	7.73	6.95	4.89	Virginia	6.27	7.76	5.74	4.23
Massachusetts	10.63	11.68	10.49	9.11	Washington	5.86	6.31	6.07	4.76
Michigan	6.85	8.35	7.55	4.96	West Virginia	5.13	6.24	5.45	3.81
Minnesota	6.01	7.65	6.12	4.36	Wisconsin	6.64	8.67	6.97	4.71
Mississippi	6.46	7.60	7.25	4.48	Wyoming	4.76	7.04	5.74	3.65

[1] Includes transportation, not shown separately.

Source: U.S. Energy Information Administration, *Electric Sales and Revenue 2003*. Also see <http://www.eia.doe.gov/cneaf/electricity/esr/esr_tabs.html>

Table 909. Electric Utilities—Generation, Sales, Revenue, and Customers: 1990 to 2004

[2,808 represents 2,808,000,000,000 kWh. Sales and revenue are to and from ultimate customers. Commercial and Industrial are not wholly comparable on a year-to-year basis due to changes from one classification to another. For the 2003 period forward, the Energy Information Administration replaced the "Other" sector with the Transportation sector. The Transportation sector consists entirely of electrified rail and urban transit systems. Data previously reported in "Other" have been relocated to the Commercial sector, except for Agriculture (i.e., irrigation load), which have been relocated to the Industrial sector]

Class	Unit	1990	1995	1998	1999	2000	2001	2002	2003	2004
Generation [1]	Bil. kWh. . .	2,808	2,995	3,212	3,174	3,015	2,630	2,549	2,462	2,494
Sales [2]	**Bil. kWh** . .	**2,713**	**3,013**	**3,264**	**3,312**	**3,421**	**3,370**	**3,463**	**3,488**	**3,551**
Residential or domestic	Bil. kWh. . .	924	1,043	1,130	1,145	1,192	1,203	1,267	1,273	1,293
Percent of total	Percent . . .	34.1	34.6	34.6	34.6	34.9	35.7	36.6	36.5	36.4
Commercial [3]	Bil. kWh. . .	751	863	979	1,002	1,055	1,089	1,116	1,200	1,229
Industrial [4]	Bil. kWh. . .	946	1,013	1,051	1,058	1,064	964	972	1,008	1,021
Revenue [2]	**Bil. dol** . .	**178.2**	**207.7**	**219.8**	**219.8**	**233.2**	**246.6**	**249.6**	**258.8**	**268.6**
Residential or domestic	Bil. dol. . . .	72.4	87.6	93.4	93.5	98.2	103.7	107.2	110.8	115.6
Percent of total	Percent . . .	40.6	42.2	42.5	42.5	42.1	42.0	43.0	42.8	43.0
Commercial [3]	Bil. dol. . . .	55.1	66.4	72.6	72.8	78.4	86.4	87.7	95.8	100.3
Industrial [4]	Bil. dol. . . .	44.9	47.2	47.0	46.4	48.4	48.6	47.5	51.7	52.2
Ultimate customers, Dec. 31 [2] .	Million	110.1	118.3	124.4	125.9	127.6	130.8	132.9	135.1	136.7
Residential or domestic	Million	97.0	103.9	109.0	110.4	111.7	114.3	116.0	117.6	119.1
Commercial [3]	Million	12.1	12.9	13.9	14.1	14.3	14.9	15.2	16.8	16.9
Industrial [4]	Million	0.5	0.6	0.5	0.6	0.5	0.6	0.6	0.7	0.7
Avg. kWh used per customer	1,000	24.6	25.5	26.2	26.3	26.8	25.8	26.1	25.8	26.0
Residential	1,000	9.5	10.0	10.4	10.4	10.7	10.5	10.9	10.8	10.9
Commercial [3]	1,000	62.0	66.6	70.5	71.2	73.5	72.9	73.3	71.4	72.6
Avg. annual bill per customer	Dollar	1,619	1,756	1,767	1,746	1,828	1,885	1,879	1,915	1,965
Residential	Dollar	746	843	856	847	879	907	925	942	971
Commercial [3]	Dollar	4,553	5,124	5,226	5,171	5,464	5,780	5,757	5,697	5,929
Avg. revenue per kWh sold . .	Cents	6.57	6.89	6.74	6.64	6.81	7.32	7.21	7.42	7.57
Residential	Cents	7.83	8.40	8.26	8.17	8.24	8.62	8.46	8.70	8.94
Commercial [3]	Cents	7.34	7.69	7.41	7.26	7.43	7.93	7.86	7.98	8.17
Industrial [4]	Cents	4.74	4.66	4.48	4.43	4.64	5.04	4.88	5.13	5.11

NA Not available. [1] "Generation" includes batteries, chemicals, hydrogen, pitch, sulfur, and purchased steam. [2] Includes other types not shown separately. [3] Small light and power. [4] Large light and power.

Source: Edison Electric Institute, Washington, DC, *Statistical Yearbook of the Electric Utility Industry*, annual.

Table 910. Revenue and Expense Statistics for Major U.S. Investor-Owned Electric Utilities: 1995 to 2003

[In millions of nominal dollars (199,967 represents $199,967,000,000). Covers approximately 180 investor-owned electric utilities that during each of the last 3 years met any one or more of the following conditions—1 mil. megawatt-hours of total sales; 100 megawatt-hours of sales for resale, 500 megawatt-hours of gross interchange out, and 500 megawatt-hours of wheeling for other]

Item	1995	1998	1999	2000	2001	2002	2003
Utility operating revenues	199,967	218,175	214,160	235,336	267,525	219,389	226,227
Electric utility	183,655	201,970	197,578	214,707	244,219	200,135	202,369
Other utility	16,312	16,205	16,583	20,630	23,306	19,254	23,858
Utility operating expenses	165,321	186,498	182,258	210,324	235,198	188,745	197,459
Electric utility	150,599	171,689	167,266	191,329	213,733	171,291	175,473
Operation	91,881	110,759	108,461	132,662	159,929	116,374	122,723
Production	68,983	85,956	83,555	107,352	136,089	90,649	96,181
Cost of fuel	29,122	31,252	29,826	32,555	29,490	24,132	26,476
Purchased power	29,981	42,612	43,258	61,969	98,231	58,828	62,173
Other	9,880	12,092	10,470	12,828	8,368	7,688	7,532
Transmission	1,425	2,197	2,423	2,699	2,365	3,494	3,585
Distribution	2,561	2,804	2,956	3,115	3,217	3,113	3,185
Customer accounts	3,613	4,021	4,195	4,246	4,434	4,165	4,180
Customer service	1,922	1,955	1,889	1,839	1,856	1,821	1,893
Sales	348	514	492	403	282	261	234
Administrative and general	13,028	13,311	12,951	13,009	11,686	12,872	13,466
Maintenance	11,767	12,486	12,276	12,185	11,167	10,843	11,141
Depreciation	19,885	24,122	23,968	22,761	20,845	17,319	16,962
Taxes and other	27,065	24,322	22,561	23,721	21,792	26,755	24,648
Other utility	14,722	14,809	14,992	18,995	21,465	17,454	21,986
Net utility operating income	34,646	31,677	31,902	25,012	32,327	30,644	28,768

Source: U.S. Energy Information Administration, *Electric Power Annual 2003*. See also <http://www.eia.doe.gov/cneaf/electricity/epa/epat8p1.html> (released December 2004).

Table 911. Uranium Concentrate—Supply, Inventories, and Average Prices: 1980 to 2003

[43.70 represents 43,700,000 pounds (lbs.) Years ending Dec. 31. For additional data on uranium, see Section 18]

Item	Unit	1980	1990	1995	1998	1999	2000	2001	2002	2003
Production [1]	Mil. lb.	43.70	8.89	6.04	4.71	4.61	3.96	2.64	2.34	2.00
Exports [2]	Mil. lb.	5.8	2.0	9.8	15.1	8.5	13.6	11.7	15.4	13.2
Imports [2]	Mil. lb.	3.6	23.7	41.3	43.7	47.6	44.9	46.7	52.7	53.0
Electric plant purchases from domestic suppliers	Mil. lb.	(NA)	20.5	22.3	21.6	21.4	24.3	27.5	22.7	21.7
Loaded into U.S. nuclear reactors [3]	Mil. lb.	(NA)	(NA)	51.1	38.2	58.8	51.5	52.7	57.2	62.3
Inventories, total	Mil. lb.	(NA)	129.1	72.5	136.5	127.1	111.3	103.8	102.1	85.2
At domestic suppliers	Mil. lb.	(NA)	26.4	13.7	70.7	68.8	56.5	48.1	48.7	39.5
At electric utilities	Mil. lb.	(NA)	102.7	58.7	65.8	58.3	54.8	55.6	53.5	45.7
Average price per pound:										
Purchased imports	Dollars	(NA)	12.55	10.20	11.19	10.55	9.84	9.51	10.05	10.59
Domestic purchases	Dollars	(NA)	15.70	11.11	12.31	11.88	11.45	10.45	10.35	10.84

NA Not available. [1] Data are for uranium concentrate, a yellow or brown powder obtained by the milling of uranium ore, processing of in situ leach mining solutions, or as a byproduct of phosphoric acid production. [2] Trade data prior to 1982 were for transactions conducted by uranium suppliers only. For 1982 forward, transactions by uranium buyers (consumers) have been included. Buyer imports and exports prior to 1982 are believed to be small. [3] Does not include any fuel rods removed from reactors and later reloaded into the reactor.

Source: U.S. Energy Information Administration, *Annual Energy Review 2003*. See also <http://www.eia.doe.gov/emeu/aer/nuclear.html> (released September 2004).

Table 912. Nuclear Power Plants—Number, Capacity, and Generation: 1980 to 2004

[51.8 represents 51,800,000 kW]

Item	1980	1985	1990	1995	1997	1998	1999	2000	2001	2002	2003	2004
Operable generating units [1, 2] . . .	71	96	112	109	107	104	104	104	104	104	104	104
Net summer capacity [2, 3] (mil. kW)	51.8	79.4	99.6	99.5	99.7	97.1	97.4	97.9	98.2	98.7	99.2	99.2
Net generation (bil. kWh)	251.1	383.7	576.9	673.4	628.6	673.7	728.3	753.9	768.8	780.1	763.7	788.6
Percent of total electricity net generation	11.0	15.5	19.0	20.1	18.0	18.6	19.7	19.8	20.6	20.2	19.7	19.9
Capacity factor [4] (percent)	56.3	58.0	66.0	77.4	71.1	78.2	85.3	88.1	89.4	90.3	87.9	90.5

[1] Total of nuclear generating units holding full-power licenses, or equivalent permission to operate, at the end of the year. Although Browns Ferry 1 was shut down in 1985, the unit has remained fully licensed and thus has continued to be counted as operable during the shutdown. [2] As of year-end. [3] Net summer capacity is the peak steady hourly output that generating equipment is expected to supply to system load, exclusive of auxiliary and other power plant, as demonstrated by test at the time of summer peak demand. [4] Weighted average of monthly capacity factors. Monthly factors are derived by dividing actual monthly generation by the maximum possible generation for the month (number of hours in the month multiplied by the net summer capacity at the end of the month).

Source: U.S. Energy Information Administration, *Monthly Energy Review, 2005*. See also <http://www.eia.doe.gov/emeu /mer/nuclear.html> (accessed June 2, 2005).

Table 913. Nuclear Power Plants—Number of Units, Net Generation, and Net Summer Capacity by State: 2003

[763,733 represents 763,733,000,000 kWh]

State	Number of units	Net generation		Net summer capacity		State	Number of units	Net generation		Net summer capacity	
		Total (mil. kWh)	Percent of total[1]	Total (mil. kW)	Percent of total[1]			Total (mil. kWh)	Percent of total[1]	Total (mil. kW)	Percent of total[1]
U.S.	104	763,733	19.7	99.21	10.5	MS	1	10,902	27.2	1.26	7.3
AL	5	31,677	23.0	4.97	16.5	MO	1	9,700	11.1	1.14	5.7
AZ	3	28,581	30.3	3.83	16.3	NE	2	7,997	26.3	1.23	18.4
AR	2	14,689	29.1	1.84	13.6	NH	1	9,276	43.0	1.16	27.3
CA	4	35,594	18.5	4.32	7.5	NJ	4	29,709	51.8	3.91	21.0
CT	2	16,078	54.4	2.00	26.4	NY	6	40,679	29.6	5.03	13.7
FL	5	30,979	14.6	3.90	7.9	NC	5	40,907	32.1	4.78	17.5
GA	4	33,257	26.8	4.04	11.6	OH	2	8,475	5.8	2.11	6.2
IL	11	189	0.1	11.47	25.2	PA	9	74,361	36.0	9.18	21.7
IA	1	3,988	9.5	0.56	5.6	SC	7	50,418	53.8	6.47	31.3
KS	1	8,890	19.1	1.17	10.7	TN	3	24,153	26.2	3.40	16.3
LA	2	16,126	17.0	2.07	8.0	TX	4	33,437	8.8	4.77	4.8
MD	2	13,691	26.2	1.70	13.7	VT	1	4,444	73.7	0.51	50.7
MA	1	4,978	10.3	0.68	4.9	VA	4	24,816	33.0	3.47	16.3
MI	4	27,954	25.1	3.97	13.0	WA	1	7,615	7.6	1.11	4.0
MN	3	13,414	24.4	1.61	14.0	WI	3	12,215	20.3	1.57	10.9

[1] For total generation and capacity, see Table 905.

Source: U.S. Energy Information Administration, *Electric Power Annual 2003*. See also <http://www.eia.doe.gov/cneaf /electricity/epa/epa_sprdshts.html>.

Table 914. Solar Collector Shipments by Type, End Use, and Market Sector: 1980 to 2003

[Shipments in thousands of square feet (19,398 represents 19,398,000). Solar collector is a device for intercepting sunlight, converting the light to heat, and carrying the heat to where it will be either used or stored. 1985 data are not available. Based on the Annual Solar Thermal Collector Manufacturers Survey]

Year	Number of manufacturers	Total shipments [1, 2, 3]	Collector type		End use			Market sector		
			Low temperature [1, 2]	Medium temperature, special, other [2]	Pool heating	Hot water	Space heating	Residential	Commercial	Industrial
1980	233	19,398	12,233	7,165	12,029	4,790	1,688	16,077	2,417	488
1986 [4]	98	9,360	3,751	1,111	3,494	1,181	127	4,131	703	13
1990 [4]	51	11,409	3,645	2,527	5,016	1,091	2	5,835	294	22
1995	36	7,666	6,813	840	6,763	755	132	6,966	604	82
1999	29	8,583	8,152	427	8,141	373	42	7,774	785	18
2000	26	8,354	7,948	400	7,863	367	99	7,473	810	57
2001	26	11,189	10,919	268	10,797	274	70	10,125	1,012	17
2002	27	11,663	11,046	615	11,073	423	146	11,000	595	62
2003	26	11,444	10,877	559	10,778	-	65	9,993	813	71

- Represents zero. [1] Includes shipments of high temperature collectors to the government, including some military, but excluding space applications. Also includes end uses such as process heating, utility, and other market sectors not shown separately. [2] Includes imputation of shipment data to account for nonrespondents. [3] Total shipments include all domestic and export shipments and may include imported collectors that subsequently were shipped to domestic or foreign customers. [4] Declines between 1986 and 1990 are primarily due to the expiration of the Federal energy tax credit and industry consolidation.

Source: U.S. Energy Information Administration, 1980–1990, *Solar Collector Manufacturing Activity*, annual reports; thereafter, *Renewable Energy Annual 2003*. See also <http://www.eia.doe.gov/cneaf/solar.renewables/page/rea_data/rea_sum.html> (released December 2004).

Table 915. Total Renewable Net Generation by Source and State: 2001

[In millions of kilowatt hours (294,946 represents 294,946,000,000) MSW = municipal solid waste]

State	Total [1]	Hydro-electric	MSW/landfill gas	Other Bio-mass [2]	Wood/Wood Waste	State	Total [1]	Hydro-electric	MSW/landfill gas	Other Bio-mass [2]	Wood/Wood Waste
U.S.	294,946	216,961	19,931	1,834	35,200	MO	1,167	1,104	(X)	62	(X)
AL	12,553	8,356	3	21	4,172	MT	6,679	6,613	(X)	(X)	65
AK	1,347	1,346	(X)	(X)	(X)	NE	1,143	1,124	(X)	17	(X)
AZ	7,663	7,624	34	5	(X)	NV	3,714	2,514	(X)	(X)	(X)
AR	4,060	2,548	(X)	7	1,505	NH	2,075	991	226	(X)	859
CA	47,359	25,542	1,861	410	3,324	NJ	1,321	18	1,290	13	(X)
CO	1,608	1,495	(X)	64	(X)	NM	256	237	(X)	19	(X)
CT	2,064	286	1,567	211	(X)	NY	25,694	23,084	2,087	(X)	503
DE	(X)	(X)	(X)	(X)	(X)	NC	4,376	2,596	129	9	1,642
DC	(X)	(X)	(X)	(X)	(X)	ND	1,340	1,332	(X)	8	(X)
FL	5,191	148	2,990	225	1,828	OH	942	511	28	(X)	403
GA	5,606	2,596	29	6	2,974	OK	2,575	2,345	(X)	(X)	231
HI	767	101	402	56	(X)	OR	29,522	28,645	87	(X)	701
ID	7,756	7,223	(X)	(X)	533	PA	4,312	1,650	2,020	34	597
IL	872	144	641	87	(X)	RI	107	3	104	(X)	(X)
IN	701	571	126	4	(X)	SC	2,141	1,225	49	1	866
IA	1,445	845	97	15	(X)	SD	3,433	3,432	(X)	(X)	(X)
KS	65	26	(X)	(X)	(X)	TN	7,775	6,947	49	(X)	779
KY	3,865	3,856	(X)	(X)	(X)	TX	3,395	1,200	51	59	898
LA	3,480	732	(X)	107	2,641	UT	671	508	10	(X)	(X)
ME	6,734	2,645	400	158	3,530	VT	1,267	884	(X)	(X)	370
MD	1,804	1,184	609	-	12	VA	3,158	1,014	991	5	1,148
MA	2,786	703	1,929	24	130	WA	56,021	54,734	175	47	1,065
MI	4,069	1,562	743	64	1,700	WV	978	952	25	(X)	1
MN	3,090	832	780	7	575	WI	3,321	2,056	401	86	705
MS	1,432	(X)	(X)	-	1,432	WY	1,244	879	(X)	(X)	(X)

X Not applicable. - Represents zero. [1] Includes types not shown separately. [2] Agriculture byproducts/crops, sludge waste, tires and other biomass solids, liquids and gases.

Source: Energy Information Administration, *Renewable Energy Annual 2003*. See also <http://www.eia.doe.gov/cneaf/solar.renewables/page/rea_data/trends.pdf> (released December 2004).

Table 916. Privately-Owned Gas Utility Industry—Balance Sheet and Income Account: 1990 to 2003

[In millions of dollars (121,686 represents $121,686,000,000). The gas utility industry consists of pipeline and distribution companies. Excludes operations of companies distributing gas in bottles or tanks]

Item	1990	1995	1997	1998	1999	2000	2001	2002	2003
COMPOSITE BALANCE SHEET									
Assets, total	121,686	141,965	134,715	119,715	155,413	165,709	171,681	185,064	174,756
Total utility plant	112,863	143,636	140,268	135,092	166,134	162,206	175,530	197,717	188,807
Depreciation and amortization	49,483	62,723	62,554	61,226	73,823	69,366	73,753	85,038	76,642
Utility plant (net)	63,380	80,912	77,714	73,866	92,311	92,839	101,777	112,679	112,165
Investment and fund accounts	23,872	26,489	22,812	12,337	17,344	10,846	10,237	13,000	13,430
Current and accrued assets	23,268	18,564	19,084	17,348	22,443	35,691	29,345	25,786	22,905
Deferred debits [1]	9,576	13,923	12,844	13,721	20,922	24,279	28,553	31,928	24,663
Liabilities, total	121,686	141,965	134,775	119,715	155,413	165,709	171,681	185,064	174,756
Capitalization, total	74,958	90,581	78,887	71,718	95,244	96,079	107,310	117,362	112,089
Capital stock	43,810	54,402	42,530	37,977	[2]859	760	701	333	305
Long-term debts	31,148	35,548	35,971	33,386	46,906	48,267	49,739	58,962	54,179
Current and accrued liabilities	29,550	28,272	33,507	26,953	32,683	42,312	34,962	30,856	28,599
Deferred income taxes [3]	11,360	14,393	13,636	13,239	17,120	17,157	20,445	24,612	23,888
Other liabilities and credits	5,818	8,715	8,745	7,806	10,365	10,161	8,964	12,235	10,179
COMPOSITE INCOME ACCOUNT									
Operating revenues, total	66,027	58,390	62,617	57,117	59,142	72,042	79,276	68,352	75,527
Minus: Operating expenses [4]	60,137	50,760	59,375	50,896	38,752	64,988	71,209	60,041	66,677
Operation and maintenance	51,627	37,966	46,070	41,026	41,415	54,602	58,873	48,521	55,036
Federal, state, and local taxes	4,957	6,182	7,182	5,429	5,605	6,163	7,394	6,249	6,581
Equals: Operating income	5,890	7,630	3,242	6,220	20,390	7,053	8,068	8,310	8,852
Utility operating income	6,077	7,848	3,337	6,361	16,614	7,166	8,192	8,564	9,198
Income before interest charges	8,081	9,484	4,193	7,779	17,531	7,589	8,266	9,305	10,053
Net income	4,410	5,139	48	4,379	10,420	4,245	4,038	4,792	6,198
Dividends	3,191	4,037	6,258	2,263	5,595	3,239	3,560	3,887	3,765

[1] Includes capital stock discount and expense and reacquired securities. [2] Data not comparable to earlier years. [3] Includes reserves for deferred income taxes. [4] Includes expenses not shown separately.

Source: American Gas Association, Arlington, VA; *Gas Facts*, annual (copyright).

Table 917. **Gas Utility Industry—Summary: 1990 to 2003**

[54,261 represents 54,261,000. Covers natural, manufactured, mixed, and liquid petroleum gas. Based on a questionnaire mailed to all privately- and municipally-owned gas utilities in United States, except those with annual revenues less than $25,000]

Item	Unit	1990	1995	1998	1999	2000	2001	2002	2003
End users [1]	1,000	**54,261**	**58,728**	**61,528**	**60,778**	**61,262**	**61,385**	**62,034**	**62,610**
Residential	1,000	49,802	53,955	56,517	56,017	56,494	56,680	57,293	57,802
Commercial	1,000	4,246	4,530	4,825	4,599	4,610	4,546	4,590	4,661
Industrial and other	1,000	166	181	183	159	157	156	149	145
Sales [2]	Tril. Btu [3]	**9,842**	**9,221**	**8,781**	**8,975**	**9,232**	**8,667**	**8,864**	**8,927**
Residential	Tril. Btu	4,468	4,803	4,534	4,622	4,741	4,525	4,589	4,722
Percent of total	Percent	45	52	52	51	51	52	52	53
Commercial	Tril. Btu	2,192	2,281	2,063	2,067	2,077	2,053	2,055	2,125
Industrial	Tril. Btu	3,010	1,919	1,370	1,553	1,698	1,461	1,748	1,672
Other	Tril. Btu	171	218	814	734	715	627	472	408
Revenues [2]	Mil. dol.	**45,153**	**46,436**	**47,084**	**47,202**	**59,243**	**69,150**	**57,112**	**72,606**
Residential	Mil. dol.	25,000	28,742	30,130	30,095	35,828	42,454	35,062	43,664
Percent of total	Percent	55	62	64	64	60	61	61	60
Commercial	Mil. dol.	10,604	11,573	11,020	10,731	13,339	16,848	13,512	17,349
Industrial	Mil. dol.	8,996	5,571	4,189	4,715	7,432	7,513	6,841	11,525
Other	Mil. dol.	553	549	1,745	1,662	2,645	2,335	1,698	2,115
Prices per mil. Btu [3]	Dollars	**4.59**	**5.05**	**5.36**	**5.26**	**6.42**	**7.98**	**6.44**	**8.13**
Residential	Dollars	5.60	6.00	6.64	6.51	7.56	9.38	7.64	9.25
Commercial	Dollars	4.84	5.07	5.34	5.19	6.42	8.20	6.57	8.17
Industrial	Dollars	2.99	2.98	3.06	3.04	4.38	5.14	3.84	5.67
Gas mains mileage	1,000	**1,189**	**1,278**	**1,351**	**1,340**	**1,369**	**1,374**	**1,411**	**1,424**
Field and gathering	1,000	32	31	29	32	27	20	22	22
Transmission	1,000	292	297	300	301	297	287	310	304
Distribution	1,000	865	950	1,022	1,008	1,046	1,066	1,080	1,098
Construction expenditures [4]	Mil. dol.	**7,899**	**10,760**	**10,978**	**8,320**	**8,624**	**9,516**	**11,552**	**13,034**
Transmission	Mil. dol.	2,886	3,380	3,656	1,785	1,590	3,212	5,184	7,317
Distribution	Mil. dol.	3,714	5,394	5,035	4,180	5,437	4,546	4,890	3,870
Production and storage	Mil. dol.	309	367	598	161	138	113	73	258
General	Mil. dol.	770	1,441	1,389	1,974	1,273	1,457	1,156	1,350
Underground storage	Mil. dol.	219	177	299	220	185	187	249	239

[1] Annual average. [2] Excludes sales for resale. [3] For definition of Btu, see text, this section. [4] Includes general.

Source: American Gas Association, Arlington, VA, *Gas Facts,* annual (copyright).

Table 918. **Gas Utility Industry—Customers, Sales, and Revenues by State: 2003**

[62,610 represents 62,610,000. See headnote, Table 917. For definition of Btu, see text, this section]

State	Customers [1] (1,000) Total	Resi-dential	Sales [2] (tril. Btu) Total	Resi-dential	Revenues [2] (mil. dol.) Total	Resi-dential
U.S.	62,610	57,802	8,927	4,722	72,606	43,664
AL	877	809	105	48	988	550
AK	114	100	113	17	267	74
AZ	1,014	957	83	36	727	400
AR	625	553	72	39	633	393
CA	10,224	9,765	708	494	6,137	4,467
CO	1,593	1,454	198	125	1,224	821
CT	515	467	85	46	935	575
DE	142	130	21	11	192	113
DC	121	113	16	11	209	142
FL	649	607	45	16	520	252
GA	353	319	56	19	480	205
HI	33	30	3	1	54	15
ID	307	274	31	20	218	144
IL	3,787	3,548	555	430	4,627	3,668
IN	1,737	1,588	264	164	2,209	1,434
IA	929	832	120	74	1,021	677
KS	935	850	102	71	861	630
KY	800	720	111	60	919	533
LA	1,023	959	185	50	1,290	487
ME	26	18	5	1	57	15
MD	886	831	98	73	1,054	803
MA	1,438	1,315	230	130	2,415	1,571
MI	3,251	3,011	522	374	3,617	2,655
MN	1,433	1,308	280	138	2,170	1,184
MS	491	439	85	28	642	259
MO	1,486	1,344	176	116	1,588	1,087
MT	264	233	32	21	220	145
NE	457	418	63	36	457	282
NV	645	611	80	34	595	266
NH	103	88	17	8	178	91
NJ	2,646	2,437	397	241	3,154	1,971
NM	544	499	53	33	398	266
NY	4,269	3,930	550	360	5,953	4,209
NC	1,064	954	145	68	1,357	751
ND	126	110	24	12	168	86
OH	2,225	2,056	299	215	2,723	2,009
OK	953	872	109	67	882	581
OR	701	625	75	38	640	367
PA	2,558	2,349	357	248	3,657	2,615
RI	244	221	30	21	331	239
SC	574	516	122	30	981	321
SD	171	151	25	13	189	112
TN	1,158	1,024	173	73	1,425	683
TX	4,186	3,860	1,417	213	8,547	1,907
UT	731	679	90	58	575	401
VT	35	31	8	3	63	31
VA	1,007	924	134	78	1,360	890
WA	986	896	132	73	1,002	600
WV	395	360	59	35	463	293
WI	1,699	1,541	255	143	2,153	1,317
WY	83	73	13	7	82	48

[1] Averages for the year. [2] Excludes sales for resale.

Source: American Gas Association, Arlington, VA, *Gas Facts,* annual (copyright).

Table 919. Public Drinking Water Systems by Size of Community Served and Source of Water: 2004

[As of **September.** Covers systems that provide water for human consumption through pipes and other constructed conveyances to a least 15 service connections or serve an average of at least 25 persons for at least 60 days a year. Based on reported data in the Safe Drinking Water Information System maintained by the Environmental Protection Agency]

Type of system	Total	Size of community served					Water source	
		500 or fewer persons	501 to 3,300 persons	3,301 to 10,000 persons	10,001 to 100,000	100,000 persons or more	Ground water	Surface water
Total systems	**159,796**	**131,291**	**19,632**	**4,913**	**3,584**	**376**	**145,498**	**14,298**
COMMUNITY WATER SYSTEMS [1]								
Number of systems	52,838	30,006	14,212	4,707	3,541	372	41,264	11,574
Percent of systems	100	57	27	9	7	1	78	22
Population served (1,000)	272,496	4,957	20,138	27,346	99,809	120,246	90,500	181,996
Percent of population	100	2	7	10	37	44	33	67
NON-TRANSIENT NON-COMMUNITY WATER SYSTEM [2]								
Number of systems	19,375	16,545	2,720	96	14	(NA)	18,647	728
Percent of systems	100	85	14	-	-	(NA)	96	4
Population served (1,000)	5,933	2,302	2,713	517	402	(NA)	5,357	577
Percent of population	100	39	46	9	7	(NA)	90	10
TRANSIENT NON-COMMUNITY WATER SYSTEM [3]								
Number of systems	87,583	84,740	2,700	110	29	4	85,587	1,996
Percent of systems	100	97	3	-	-	-	98	2
Population served (1,000)	18,485	7,318	2,668	612	618	7,269	15,691	2,793
Percent of population	100	40	14	3	3	39	85	15

- Represents zero.   [1] A public water system that supplies water to the same population year-round.   [2] A public water system that regularly supplies water to at least 25 of the same people at least 6 months per year, but not year-round. Some examples are schools, factories, and office buildings which have their own water systems.   [3] A public water system that provides water in a place such as a gas station or campground where people do not remain for long periods of time.

Source: U.S. Environmental Protection Agency, *Factoids: Drinking Water and Ground Water Statistics for 2004*, annual reports. See also <http://www.epa.gov/safewater/data/getdata.html> (accessed June 2005).

Table 920. Sewage Treatment Facilities: 2002

[Based on the North American Industry Classification System (NAICS), 2002; see text, Section 15]

State	Sewage Treatment Facilities (NAICS 22132)		State	Sewage Treatment Facilities (NAICS 22132)	
	Number of establishments	Paid employees		Number of establishments	Paid employees
U.S.	831	7022	MO	21	(2)
AL	13	(1)	MT	9	(1)
AK	5	25	NE	5	(3)
AZ	14	(1)	NV	4	(3)
AR	7	(1)	NH	2	(1)
CA	32	199	NJ	15	(4)
CO	14	(1)	NM	3	32
CT	8	(2)	NY	22	(2)
DE	1	(3)	NC	19	108
DC	(NA)	(NA)	ND	(NA)	(NA)
FL	71	805	OH	16	(1)
GA	6	(4)	OK	9	(1)
HI	12	87	OR	6	(3)
ID	8	71	PA	116	582
IL	42	(4)	RI	5	(1)
IN	31	(2)	SC	11	82
IA	5	(1)	SD	4	(2)
KS	5	(1)	TN	7	(1)
KY	10	(2)	TX	71	(5)
LA	24	(2)	UT	1	(3)
ME	7	(3)	VT	3	(3)
MD	6	(1)	VA	17	116
MA	20	(2)	WA	17	(1)
MI	16	(1)	WV	19	93
MN	22	(1)	WI	25	(1)
MS	19	113	WY	6	(1)

NA Not available.   [1] 20-99 employees.   [2] 100-249 employees.   [3] 0-19 employees.   [4] 250-499 employees.   [5] 1,000-2,499 employees.

Source: U.S. Census Bureau, *County Business Patterns 2002*. See also <http://censtats.census.gov/cgi-bin/cbpnaic/cbpcomp.pl> (accessed June 2005).

No. 106.—AVERAGE VALUE, AVERAGE ENCUMBRANCE, TOTAL ANNUAL AND AVERAGE ANNUAL INTEREST CHARGE, AND AVERAGE ANNUAL RATE OF INTEREST FOR ENCUMBERED HOMES OCCUPIED BY OWNERS, BY STATES AND TERRITORIES, IN 1890

[From Abstract of the Eleventh Census.]

States and Territories.	Average value of encumbered homes.	Average encumbrance.	Annual interest charge.	Average annual interest charge.	Average annual rate of interest.
	Dollars.	Dollars.	Dollars.	Dollars.	Per cent.
Alabama	3,132	1,190	81,080	98	8.25
Arizona	3,305	1,172	35,022	158	13.46
Arkansas	1,999	845	103,790	81	9.60
California	5,205	1,805	2,637,770	154	8.51
Colorado	4,552	1,583	814,318	137	8.64
Connecticut	3,926	1,694	2,008,090	92	5.45
Delaware	3,616	1,633	299,512	92	5.65
District of Columbia	7,054	2,439	385,426	146	5.99
Florida	2,647	1,017	78,949	105	10.32
Georgia	2,396	1,020	82,945	80	7.89
Idaho	2,946	915	33,474	102	11.15
Illinois	3,114	1,164	5,252,861	78	6.69
Indiana	1,861	628	1,376,556	43	6.89
Iowa	1,987	659	1,374,741	51	7.74
Kansas	2,202	820	1,712,326	09	8.42
Kentucky	2,651	842	204,648	57	6.74
Louisiana	3,731	1,457	123,996	116	7.94
Maine	1,830	681	373,525	41	6.06
Maryland	2,346	937	720,311	55	5.85
Massachusetts	3,990	1,797	5,840,785	98	5.48
Michigan	1,842	636	2,068,534	46	7.18
Minnesota	3,692	1,268	2,074,436	94	7.43
Mississippi	1,556	762	55,117	72	9.45
Missouri	2,616	1,011	2,134,146	76	7.30
Montana	3,612	1,303	162,428	143	10.97
Nebraska	3,268	1,052	1,236,702	85	8.13
Nevada	4,513	1,555	30,255	158	10.19
New Hampshire	2,336	873	298,518	52	5.92
New Jersey	3,829	1,660	3,709,176	93	5.62
New Mexico	2,891	1,637	52,670	112	10.80
New York	4,657	1,979	13,220,703	107	5.38
North Carolina	1,795	864	105,706	67	7.80
North Dakota	2,049	771	93,359	73	9.42
Ohio	2,366	879	4,051,017	58	6.63
Oklahoma					
Oregon	4,914	1,398	577,405	122	8.72
Pennsylvania	3,416	1,473	7,610,464	81	5.52
Rhode Island	4,207	1,864	732,256	108	5.78
South Carolina	2,356	1,104	109,711	90	8.17
South Dakota	1,894	681	270,558	65	9.49
Tennessee	1,847	824	122,043	51	6.20
Texas	2,589	1,090	278,672	103	9.42
Utah	3,711	1,028	138,734	100	9.71
Vermont	2,026	754	325,865	45	5.94
Virginia	2,067	1,056	129,934	67	6.32
Washington	4,788	1,382	486,545	129	9.31
West Virginia	1,809	631	176,747	40	6.34
Wisconsin	2,314	756	1,526,974	51	6.70
Wyoming	3,171	1,324	63,229	142	10.73
The United States	3,250	1,293	65,182,029	80	6.23

Source: Statistical Abstract of the United States: 1896 Edition.

Section 20
Construction and Housing

This section presents data on the construction industry and on various indicators of its activity and costs; on housing units and their characteristics and occupants; and on the characteristics and vacancy rates for commercial buildings. This edition contains data from the 2003 American Housing Survey.

The principal source of these data is the U.S. Census Bureau, which issues a variety of current publications, as well as data from the decennial census. Current construction statistics compiled by the Census Bureau appear in its *New Residential Construction* and *New Residential Sales* press releases and Web site <http://www.census.gov/const/www/>. Statistics on expenditures by owners of residential properties are issued quarterly and annually in *Expenditures for Residential Improvements and Repairs. Value of New Construction Put in Place* presents data on all types of construction. Reports of the censuses of construction industries (see below) are also issued on various topics.

Other Census Bureau publications include the *Current Housing Reports* series, which comprise the quarterly *Housing Vacancies,* the quarterly *Market Absorption of Apartments,* the biennial *American Housing Survey* (formerly *Annual Housing Survey),* and reports of the censuses of housing and of construction industries.

Other sources include the monthly *Dodge Construction Potentials* of McGraw-Hill Construction, New York, NY, which present national and state data on construction contracts; the National Association of Home Builders with state-level data on housing starts; the NATIONAL ASSOCIATION OF REALTORS®, which presents data on existing home sales; the Society of Industrial and Office Realtors and Oncor

International on commercial office and industrial space; the Bureau of Economic Analysis, which presents data on residential capital and gross housing product; and the U.S. Energy Information Administration, which provides data on commercial buildings through its periodic sample surveys.

Censuses and surveys—Censuses of the construction industry were first conducted by the Census Bureau for 1929, 1935, and 1939; beginning in 1967, a census has been taken every 5 years (through 2002, for years ending in "2" and "7"). The latest reports are part of the 2002 Economic Census. See text, Section 15, Business Enterprise.

The construction sector of the economic census, covers all employer establishments primarily engaged in (1) building construction by general contractors or operative builders; (2) heavy (nonbuilding) construction by general contractors; and (3) construction by special trade contractors. This sector includes construction management and land subdividers and developers. The 2002 census was conducted in accordance with the 2002 North American Industrial Classification System (NAICS). See text, Section 15, Business Enterprise, for general information on the SIC and NAICS.

From 1850 through 1930, the Census Bureau collected some housing data as part of its censuses of population and agriculture. Beginning in 1940, separate censuses of housing have been taken at 10-year intervals. For the 1970 and 1980 censuses, data on year-round housing units were collected and issued on occupancy and structural characteristics, plumbing facilities, value, and rent; for 1990 such characteristics were presented for all housing units.

U.S. Census Bureau, Statistical Abstract of the United States: 2006

The American Housing Survey (*Current Housing Reports* Series H-150 and H-170), which began in 1973, provided an annual and ongoing series of data on selected housing and demographic characteristics until 1983. In 1984, the name of the survey was changed from the Annual Housing Survey. Currently, national data are collected every other year, and data for selected metropolitan areas are collected on a rotating basis. All samples represent a cross section of the housing stock in their respective areas. Estimates are subject to both sampling and nonsampling errors; caution should therefore be used in making comparisons between years.

Data on residential mortgages were collected continuously from 1890 to 1970, except 1930, as part of the decennial census by the Census Bureau. Since 1973, mortgage status data, limited to single family homes on less than 10 acres with no business on the property, have been presented in the American Housing Survey. Data on mortgage activity are covered in Section 25, Banking and Finance.

Housing units—In general, a housing unit is a house, an apartment, a group of rooms or a single room occupied or intended for occupancy as separate living quarters; that is, the occupants live separately from any other individual in the building, and there is direct access from the outside or through a common hall. Transient accommodations, barracks for workers, and institutional-type quarters are not counted as housing units.

Statistical reliability—For a discussion of statistical collection and estimation, sampling procedures, and measures of statistical reliability applicable to Census Bureau data, see Appendix III.

U.S. Census Bureau, Statistical Abstract of the United States: 2006

Table 921. **Construction—Establishments, Employees, and Payroll by Kind of Business (NAICS Basis): 2000 and 2002**

[For establishments with payroll. (6,572.8 represents 6,572,800). See Appendix III]

Industry	1997 NAICS code [1]	Establishments		Paid employees [2] (1,000)		Annual payroll (mil. dol.)	
		2000	2002	2000	2002	2000	2002
Construction	23	709,590	710,325	6,572.8	6,307.4	239,910.1	247,302.5
Building, developing, & general contracting . . .	233	216,354	226,394	1,604.9	1,585.7	60,798.1	65,730.5
Land subdivision & land development.	2331	13,111	14,044	77.9	90.7	3,269.2	4,100.1
Residential building construction	2332	159,550	170,720	781.0	770.9	25,519.7	28,410.1
Single-family housing construction	23321	151,296	161,677	713.3	696.9	23,058.3	25,396.8
Multifamily housing construction	23322	8,254	9,043	67.7	74.0	2,461.3	3,013.3
Nonresidential building construction	2333	43,693	41,630	746.0	724.2	32,009.3	33,220.3
Mfg. & industrial building construction . . .	23331	7,039	2,402	164.9	86.9	6,797.3	3,828.8
Commercial & institutional building construction	23332	36,654	39,224	581.2	637.3	25,212.0	29,391.5
Heavy construction.	234	39,516	39,949	901.0	856.3	38,628.0	39,321.5
Highway, street, bridge, & tunnel construction	2341	11,795	11,818	304.9	310.8	14,316.1	15,755.1
Highway & street construction	23411	10,889	10,985	265.7	274.1	12,328.6	13,767.5
Bridge & tunnel construction	23412	906	833	39.3	36.7	1,987.5	1,987.6
Other heavy construction	2349	27,721	28,131	596.1	545.5	24,311.9	23,566.4
Water, sewer, & pipeline construction . . .	23491	7,483	10,652	165.8	198.8	7,033.0	8,785.6
Power & communication transmission line construction	23492	3,644	4,325	97.5	98.5	3,815.8	3,909.7
Industrial nonbuilding structure construction	23493	689	527	101.7	91.9	4,137.8	4,087.5
All other heavy construction.	23499	15,905	12,627	231.0	156.3	9,325.3	6,783.7
Special trade contractors	235	453,720	443,982	4,066.9	3,865.3	140,484.1	142,250.4
Plumbing, heating, & air-conditioning contractors.	2351	90,487	90,341	897.9	879.9	33,406.0	34,806.1
Painting & wall covering contractors	2352	40,973	40,935	221.8	216.8	6,121.4	6,459.8
Electrical contractors	2353	66,802	65,858	815.1	770.6	32,698.0	31,707.1
Masonry, drywall, insulation, & tile contractors.	2354	53,625	50,021	565.0	515.4	17,389.8	17,208.7
Masonry & stone contractors	23541	25,030	21,720	197.9	170.0	5,667.8	5,460.5
Drywall, plastering, acoustical, & insulation contractors	23542	21,774	19,944	319.3	293.8	10,224.4	10,055.0
Tile, marble, terrazzo, & mosaic contractors	23543	6,821	8,357	47.8	51.5	1,497.7	1,693.2
Carpentry & floor contractors.	2355	58,525	60,754	347.3	338.8	9,963.6	10,438.9
Carpentry contractors	23551	45,028	46,918	269.8	262.6	7,533.3	7,809.9
Floor laying & other floor contractors. . . .	23552	13,497	13,836	77.5	76.2	2,430.3	2,629.0
Roofing, siding, & sheet metal contractors.	2356	30,966	31,538	260.8	244.4	7,928.8	7,882.3
Concrete contractors	2357	30,238	34,820	292.6	306.6	9,501.2	10,993.2
Water well drilling contractors	2358	3,797	4,028	21.6	23.7	688.5	841.1
Other special trade contractors	2359	78,307	65,687	644.9	567.1	22,786.6	21,913.4
Structural steel erection contractors	23591	5,382	3,799	93.6	76.2	3,585.8	3,130.3
Glass & glazing contractors	23592	5,772	5,205	45.8	46.2	1,570.1	1,773.3
Excavation contractors . . . . .'.	23593	27,005	22,812	152.5	145.8	5,253.6	5,666.4
Wrecking & demolition contractors	23594	1,752	1,874	21.9	26.9	808.7	950.1
Building equip. & other machinery installation contractors	23595	4,820	3,912	80.9	66.5	3,859.6	3,448.3
All other special trade contractors	23599	33,576	28,085	250.1	205.4	7,708.7	6,945.1

[1] North American Industry Classification System code, 1997; see text, Section 15. [2] Employees on the payroll for the pay period including March 12.

Source: U.S. Census Bureau, "County Business Patterns"; 2002 data issued November 2004; <http://www.census.gov/epcd/cbp /view/cbpview.html>

Construction and Housing **613**

Table 922. **Construction—Establishments, Employees, Payroll, Value of Construction, Costs, and Capital Expenditures by Kind of Business (NAICS Basis): 2002**

[Preliminary. For establishments with payroll. (11,771 represents $11,771,000,000). Based on the 2002 Economic Censuses; See Appendix III]

Kind of business	2002 NAICS code [1]	Number of establishments	Number of employees	Total payroll (mil. dol.)	Average number of construction workers	Total payroll construction workers (mil. dol.)	Value of construction work (mil. dol.)	Net value of construction work (mil. dol.)	Value added (mil. dol.)	Cost of materials, components, supplies, and fuels (mil. dol.)	Capital expenditures, excluding land (mil. dol.)
New single-family general contractors	236115	104,930	423,323	11,771	272,973	6,394	96,902	60,685	27,437	33,964	1,244
New multifamily general contractors	236116	4,397	44,384	1,731	27,856	935	16,673	7,638	4,411	3,550	191
New housing operative builders	236117	15,191	186,814	8,570	87,820	3,167	118,968	74,872	44,778	31,026	720
Residential remodelers	236118	46,627	220,026	6,598	140,579	3,742	29,974	21,085	12,805	8,482	380
Industrial building construction	236210	2,777	93,931	3,827	70,567	2,535	17,029	9,581	6,252	3,486	164
Commercial building construction	236220	37,208	715,896	29,210	478,923	16,517	241,065	108,229	71,882	38,142	1,441
Water and sewer system construction	237110	12,357	204,085	7,381	162,096	5,312	32,501	26,838	16,022	11,004	1,201
Oil and gas pipeline construction	237120	1,403	93,176	3,985	78,317	3,172	11,459	10,224	7,663	2,696	303
Power and communication system construction	237130	6,034	253,506	10,601	192,704	7,743	34,810	30,475	23,045	8,209	786
Land subdivision	237210	8,403	66,105	2,396	25,630	699	20,481	16,044	14,374	2,169	395
Highway, street, and bridge construction	237310	11,239	434,714	15,791	339,437	11,487	81,660	62,319	36,211	28,071	2,903
Other heavy construction	237990	10,502	154,071	4,997	119,355	3,531	21,801	18,108	12,042	6,419	1,134
Poured concrete structure contractors	238110	27,151	309,955	9,203	261,917	7,187	33,982	30,665	18,211	12,574	819
Steel and precast concrete contractors	238120	4,321	78,266	2,900	63,625	2,214	8,722	7,985	5,823	2,208	199
Framing contractors	238130	14,455	158,003	4,410	134,663	3,515	14,432	12,651	8,587	4,216	195
Masonry contractors	238140	25,720	260,703	7,173	221,790	5,801	20,274	19,212	13,174	6,088	426
Glass and glazing contractors	238150	5,294	50,800	1,764	34,086	1,092	6,285	6,017	3,513	2,633	75
Roofing contractors	238160	23,192	226,203	6,019	176,512	4,100	22,991	21,100	12,801	8,393	450
Siding contractors	238170	6,632	43,042	1,185	30,284	797	4,253	3,810	2,262	1,610	67
Other building exterior contractors	238190	2,786	31,972	1,153	23,444	773	3,494	3,246	2,046	1,233	52
Electrical contractors	238210	62,586	771,184	29,324	606,403	22,228	82,141	77,672	51,677	26,647	1,188
Plumbing and HVAC contractors	238220	87,501	974,368	35,942	712,452	25,620	117,786	105,323	66,878	39,400	1,838
Other building equipment contractors	238290	6,087	126,559	4,941	90,504	3,587	14,503	13,680	10,093	3,823	286
Drywall and insulation contractors	238310	19,598	311,077	9,767	261,239	7,593	30,822	27,046	18,042	9,091	349
Painting and wall covering contractors	238320	38,943	234,562	6,005	184,328	4,448	16,853	15,317	11,516	3,891	326
Flooring contractors	238330	12,865	79,813	2,421	51,933	1,446	9,775	8,623	4,869	3,887	138
Tile and terrazzo contractors	238340	8,950	60,001	1,835	44,729	1,260	5,858	5,640	3,754	1,943	96
Finish carpentry contractors	238350	35,087	179,476	4,712	129,888	3,240	18,154	15,641	9,762	6,184	322
Other building finishing contractors	238390	3,729	50,617	1,719	37,353	1,167	4,862	4,560	3,404	1,201	75
Site preparation contractors	238910	30,496	285,430	9,702	223,045	7,112	37,442	32,286	23,115	9,706	2,325
All other specialty trade contractors	238990	33,452	248,065	6,965	178,700	4,669	27,072	23,833	15,339	9,307	949

[1] North American Industry Classification System, 2002; see text, this section Section 15.

Source: U.S. Census Bureau, "2002 Economic Census Industry Series Reports, Construction." See Internet site: <http://www.census.gov/econ/census02/guide/INDRPT23.HTM> (accessed 28 April 2005).

Table 923. Construction Materials—Producer Price Indexes: 1990 to 2004

[1982 = 100, except as noted. Data for 2004 are preliminary. For discussion of producer price indexes, see text, Section 14. This index, more formally known as the special commodity grouping index for construction materials, covers materials incorporated as integral part of a building or normally installed during construction and not readily removable. Excludes consumer durables such as kitchen ranges, refrigerators, etc. This index is not the same as the stage-of-processing index of intermediate materials and components for construction]

Commodity	1990	1995	1998	1999	2000	2001	2002	2003	2004
Construction materials	**119.6**	**138.8**	**141.4**	**142.8**	**144.1**	**142.8**	**144.0**	**147.1**	**161.4**
Interior solvent-based paint	133.0	164.5	185.7	188.0	191.1	190.2	190.5	199.1	(NA)
Construction products from plastics	117.2	133.8	126.2	128.0	135.8	132.9	136.1	138.6	144.8
Douglas fir, dressed	138.4	198.8	186.1	212.1	185.2	178.1	178.5	176.9	(NA)
Southern pine, dressed	111.2	166.9	177.3	185.7	161.0	152.5	145.2	145.8	(NA)
Millwork	130.4	163.8	171.1	174.7	176.4	179.2	179.8	181.8	191.9
Softwood plywood	119.6	188.1	174.9	207.0	173.3	167.8	164.1	195.6	250.9
Hardwood plywood and related products	102.7	122.2	126.9	128.6	130.2	130.4	131.5	129.0	134.4
Softwood plywood veneer, ex. reinforced/backed . . .	142.3	203.5	180.1	197.4	182.2	175.5	172.8	183.9	209.5
Building paper and building board mill products	112.2	144.9	132.9	141.6	138.8	129.3	129.3	159.7	192.1
Steel pipe and tubes [1]	102.6	104.4	109.4	102.5	106.6	104.0	106.7	113.5	165.9
Builders hardware	133.0	153.2	160.8	161.9	163.8	166.4	169.3	170.2	172.7
Plumbing fixtures and brass fittings	144.3	166.0	175.1	176.7	180.4	180.8	181.9	183.4	188.1
Heating equipment	131.6	147.5	153.3	154.0	155.6	157.1	157.9	163.3	169.5
Metal doors, sash, and trim	131.4	156.5	161.3	162.2	165.1	167.1	168.0	169.9	175.7
Siding, aluminum [2]	(NA)	132.4	134.5	135.4	142.2	141.5	141.0	(NA)	(NA)
Outdoor lighting equipment, including parts [3]	113.0	120.8	122.8	122.3	124.7	125.7	126.2	126.9	129.8
Commercial fluorescent fixtures [4]	113.0	121.0	119.0	118.7	117.7	113.6	114.0	115.5	119.3
Architectural and ornamental metalwork [5]	118.7	128.0	135.4	136.2	139.8	141.7	144.2	147.2	172.5
Fabricated ferrous wire products [1]	114.6	125.7	130.1	130.6	130.0	129.8	129.7	131.4	149.4
Elevators, escalators, and other lifts.	110.1	113.0	116.0	117.5	118.7	119.4	120.0	118.6	120.7
Stamped metal switch and receptacle box	158.0	183.5	191.5	192.8	183.0	195.4	195.4	196.1	205.2
Concrete ingredients and related products	115.3	134.7	147.6	152.1	155.6	159.1	162.6	164.9	170.3
Concrete products	113.5	129.4	140.0	143.7	147.8	151.7	152.7	153.5	161.2
Clay construction products, exc. refractories	129.9	141.3	144.9	148.3	152.8	155.7	152.8	154.5	158.0
Prep. asphalt and tar roofing and siding products. . .	95.8	97.8	95.7	95.2	100.0	103.3	106.6	110.6	111.6
Gypsum products.	105.2	154.5	177.6	208.0	201.4	156.4	168.9	171.4	199.0
Insulation materials.	108.4	118.8	119.7	131.7	126.8	127.3	128.3	128.7	137.2
Paving mixtures and blocks	101.2	105.8	112.5	112.9	130.4	134.6	136.2	142.7	144.9

NA Not available. [1] June 1982 = 100. [2] December 1982 = 100. [3] June 1985 = 100. [4] Recessed nonair. [5] December 1983 = 100.

Source: U.S. Bureau of Labor Statistics, *Producer Price Indexes*, monthly and annual. See Internet site <http://www.bls.gov/ppi/home.htm>.

Table 924. Value of New Construction Put in Place: 1980 to 2004

[In millions of dollars (273,936 represents $273,936,000,000). Represents value of construction put in place during year; differs from building permit and construction contract data in timing and coverage. Includes installed cost of normal building service equipment and selected types of industrial production equipment (largely site fabricated). Excludes cost of shipbuilding, land, and most types of machinery and equipment. For methodology, see Appendix III]

Year	Total	Private			Public		
		Total	Residential buildings	Non-residential	Total	Federal	State and local
1980	273,936	210,290	100,381	109,909	63,646	9,642	54,004
1981	289,070	224,378	99,241	125,137	64,691	10,413	54,278
1982	279,332	216,268	84,676	131,592	63,064	10,008	53,056
1983	311,887	248,437	125,833	122,604	63,450	10,557	52,893
1984	370,190	299,952	155,015	144,937	70,238	11,240	58,998
1985	403,416	325,601	160,520	165,081	77,815	12,004	65,811
1986	433,454	348,872	190,677	158,195	84,582	12,412	72,170
1987	446,643	355,994	199,652	156,342	90,648	14,052	76,596
1988	462,012	367,277	204,496	162,781	94,735	12,264	82,471
1989	477,502	379,328	204,255	175,073	98,174	12,155	86,018
1990	476,778	369,300	191,103	178,197	107,478	12,099	95,379
1991	432,592	322,483	166,251	156,232	110,109	12,845	97,264
1992	463,661	347,814	199,393	148,421	115,847	14,376	101,471
1993	491,033	375,073	225,067	150,006	115,960	14,424	101,535
1994	539,193	418,999	258,561	160,438	120,193	14,440	105,753
1995	557,818	427,885	247,351	180,534	129,933	15,751	114,181
1996	615,900	476,638	281,115	195,523	139,263	15,325	123,938
1997	653,429	502,734	289,014	213,720	150,695	14,087	136,608
1998	706,303	552,001	314,607	237,394	154,302	14,318	139,984
1999	769,461	599,729	350,562	249,167	169,732	14,025	155,706
2000	835,279	649,750	374,457	275,293	185,529	14,166	171,362
2001	868,310	662,247	388,324	273,922	206,063	15,081	190,981
2002	876,802	659,651	421,912	237,739	217,150	16,578	200,572
2003	925,069	701,601	475,941	225,660	223,468	17,913	205,556
2004	1,027,736	798,487	563,376	235,110	229,250	17,955	211,294

Source: U.S. Census Bureau, "Construction Spending," Internet site <http://www.census.gov/const/www/c30index.html>.

U.S. Census Bureau, Statistical Abstract of the United States: 2006

Table 925. **Value of Private Construction Put in Place: 1995 to 2004**

[In millions of dollars (427,885 represents $427,885,000,000). Represents value of construction put in place during year; differs from building permit and construction contract data in timing and coverage. See Appendix III]

Type of construction	1995	1997	1998	1999	2000	2001	2002	2003	2004
Total construction [1]	**427,885**	**502,734**	**552,001**	**599,729**	**649,750**	**662,247**	**659,651**	**701,601**	**798,487**
Residential	247,351	289,014	314,607	350,562	374,457	388,324	421,912	475,941	563,376
New single family	153,515	175,179	199,409	223,837	236,788	249,086	265,889	310,575	377,557
New multifamily	17,889	22,883	24,574	27,434	28,259	30,305	32,952	35,116	38,495
Improvements	75,947	90,951	90,624	99,290	109,410	108,933	123,071	130,250	147,324
Nonresidential	180,534	213,720	237,394	249,167	275,293	273,922	237,739	225,660	235,110
Lodging	7,131	12,898	14,818	15,955	16,304	14,519	10,467	9,930	11,542
Office [1]	22,996	32,813	40,394	45,052	52,407	49,745	35,296	30,579	33,112
General	20,569	29,301	37,615	41,745	49,637	47,136	32,356	27,380	28,966
Financial	2,339	3,157	2,636	3,125	2,689	2,586	2,857	3,174	4,116
Commercial [1]	44,096	53,088	55,681	59,376	64,055	63,606	59,008	57,235	61,582
Automotive [1]	4,191	5,736	5,270	5,904	5,967	5,650	5,807	5,039	5,282
Sales	883	1,743	1,542	1,573	1,629	2,014	2,235	2,099	2,508
Service/parts	2,448	3,213	2,527	3,270	3,009	2,394	2,308	1,866	1,981
Parking	860	781	1,200	1,062	1,330	1,242	1,265	1,074	793
Food/beverage [1]	7,169	8,566	9,118	8,277	8,786	8,765	7,914	8,369	8,167
Food	3,062	4,658	4,665	4,610	4,792	4,300	4,207	4,234	3,740
Dining/drinking	3,408	3,058	3,817	2,874	2,935	3,441	2,916	3,321	3,698
Fast food	699	850	636	793	1,058	1,024	792	813	729
Multiretail [1]	11,976	12,157	13,254	15,234	14,911	16,373	15,581	15,400	18,281
General merchandise	5,339	4,083	3,778	4,668	5,100	5,066	6,009	5,341	6,476
Shopping center	4,086	5,694	6,045	7,187	6,803	7,769	6,605	6,867	8,649
Shopping mall	2,175	1,949	2,917	2,873	2,523	2,701	2,108	2,231	2,104
Other commercial [1]	8,432	10,203	11,050	11,179	13,537	11,945	12,083	11,249	12,735
Drug store	536	1,007	1,409	1,645	1,682	1,185	1,644	1,790	1,404
Building supply store	1,372	1,323	1,742	1,588	2,592	3,016	2,471	2,268	2,584
Other stores	5,653	7,090	7,025	6,849	8,136	6,995	7,145	6,214	7,548
Warehouse	9,299	12,563	12,698	13,702	14,822	15,691	11,908	12,345	11,994
General commercial	8,944	11,501	11,732	12,756	13,511	14,440	10,934	11,004	10,703
Farm	3,014	3,815	4,284	5,059	5,498	5,135	5,611	4,833	5,123
Health care	15,259	17,390	17,737	18,388	19,455	19,506	22,438	24,217	26,706
Hospital	8,807	9,968	9,469	9,491	10,183	11,313	13,925	15,234	16,492
Medical building	4,064	4,001	4,070	4,910	5,066	4,638	4,924	6,068	7,706
Special care	2,388	3,421	4,197	3,987	4,206	3,555	3,538	2,915	2,509
Educational [1]	5,699	8,802	9,829	9,756	11,683	12,846	13,109	13,424	12,722
Preschool	326	531	619	663	770	874	593	711	682
Primary/secondary	1,245	2,032	2,174	2,420	2,948	3,536	3,605	3,204	3,229
Higher education [1]	3,055	4,327	4,945	5,204	6,333	6,597	6,875	7,259	6,472
Instructional	1,712	1,991	2,469	2,258	3,058	3,210	3,619	3,701	3,200
Dormitory	483	789	955	1,274	1,356	1,555	1,528	1,761	1,663
Sports/recreation	192	475	403	515	645	755	772	677	756
Other educational	817	1,714	1,798	1,232	1,318	1,421	1,651	1,785	1,993
Gallery/museum	571	1,107	1,127	778	920	990	1,312	1,371	1,311
Religious [1]	4,348	5,782	6,604	7,371	8,030	8,393	8,335	8,559	8,080
House of worship	2,951	3,844	4,549	5,057	5,656	6,040	6,021	6,238	5,962
Other religious	1,389	1,935	2,054	2,314	2,347	2,330	2,312	2,322	2,118
Auxiliary building	619	874	992	1,252	1,280	1,247	1,358	1,296	1,221
Public safety	185	569	586	465	423	274	217	185	289
Amusement and recreation [1]	5,886	8,537	8,589	9,550	8,768	7,828	7,478	7,781	8,553
Theme/amusement park	563	723	866	919	747	462	230	270	182
Sports	910	1,333	1,136	1,495	1,068	1,067	1,427	1,306	1,044
Fitness	637	801	889	1,137	1,152	1,294	1,286	1,262	1,116
Performance/meeting center	365	628	603	546	732	977	900	844	1,060
Social center	1,558	1,979	2,093	2,006	2,368	2,337	2,285	1,996	2,577
Movie theater/studio	848	2,199	2,441	2,376	1,461	792	568	855	1,245
Transportation [1]	4,759	6,208	7,290	6,525	6,879	7,058	6,773	6,250	6,642
Air	666	901	1,093	1,106	1,804	1,993	1,281	1,012	880
Land	4,008	5,183	6,112	5,164	4,907	4,883	5,325	5,144	5,612
Railroad	3,509	4,922	5,736	4,670	4,263	4,456	4,584	4,533	5,211
Communication	11,112	12,452	12,473	18,405	18,799	19,596	18,384	12,708	13,382
Power	22,006	16,362	21,690	22,040	29,344	31,499	32,608	32,280	27,735
Electricity	14,274	11,325	12,993	15,489	23,374	25,270	24,998	24,236	19,462
Gas	6,279	4,006	7,372	4,918	4,891	5,078	6,080	6,327	6,840
Oil	929	969	1,265	1,489	1,003	943	1,193	1,117	1,136
Sewage and waste disposal	576	468	339	516	508	402	246	278	342
Water supply	670	448	543	413	714	563	397	393	406
Manufacturing [1]	35,364	37,624	40,485	35,126	37,583	37,815	22,744	21,434	23,517
Food/beverage/tobacco	4,525	3,957	3,536	3,654	3,985	4,088	2,817	2,695	3,135
Textile/apparel/leather & allied	824	584	713	490	413	307	284	218	200
Wood	616	522	492	460	483	343	477	376	486
Paper	1,448	1,548	1,232	896	479	1,265	584	818	566
Print/publishing	1,197	930	1,103	924	848	1,232	666	630	665
Petroleum/coal	4,741	1,186	1,064	1,004	1,255	1,171	887	717	1,263
Chemical	5,531	6,034	8,266	6,632	3,798	4,896	5,625	5,368	5,318
Plastic/rubber	1,475	1,959	2,139	2,388	1,645	1,379	776	659	932
Nonmetallic mineral	856	1,004	1,481	1,282	1,898	2,216	536	865	906
Primary metal	2,533	2,802	2,606	2,137	1,976	773	241	436	198
Fabricated metal	808	2,162	2,037	2,046	2,148	1,447	833	662	535
Machinery	1,275	1,106	1,256	1,040	864	863	797	707	640
Computer/electronic/electrical	6,332	7,537	7,552	4,748	6,392	6,029	1,918	1,444	2,911
Transportation equipment	2,382	3,453	3,498	3,683	6,318	6,901	3,832	3,314	2,617
Furniture	213	167	413	232	148	232	148	278	223

[1] Includes other types of construction, not shown separately.

Source: U.S. Census Bureau, "Construction Spending", Internet site <http://www.census.gov/const/www/c30index.html>.

Table 926.

Table 926. Value of State and Local Government Construction Put in Place: 1995 to 2004

[In millions of dollars (114,181 represents $114,181,000,000). See headnote, Table 925]

Type of construction	1995	1997	1998	1999	2000	2001	2002	2003	2004
Total construction [1]	114,181	136,608	139,984	155,706	171,362	190,981	200,572	205,556	211,294
Residential	4,043	4,336	4,340	4,603	4,200	5,005	5,320	4,965	5,191
Multifamily	3,976	4,238	4,242	4,584	4,175	4,929	5,204	4,791	4,990
Nonresidential	110,138	132,272	135 644	151,103	167,163	185,976	195,252	200,591	206,104
Office :	3,914	4,619	4,605	4,521	6,256	7,196	8,156	8,456	8,616
Commercial [1]	1,329	2,227	1,993	2,519	2,543	3,189	3,149	3,052	2,888
Automotive	965	1,553	1,603	1,915	1,719	2,486	2,224	2,210	2,122
Parking	794	1,425	1,549	1,703	1,596	2,467	2,198	2,158	1,898
Warehouse	231	295	258	342	464	394	384	442	399
Health care	3,156	3,501	2,884	3,166	3,944	3,805	4,541	5,542	6,531
Hospital	1,960	2,498	1,980	2,220	2,716	2,749	3,303	3,718	4,253
Medical building	801	657	515	494	684	630	664	1,211	1,563
Special care	395	345	389	452	545	427	575	614	716
Educational [1]	25,743	33,758	35,015	41,117	45,616	51,289	54,571	54,998	57,923
Primary/secondary [1]	17,545	23,853	26,064	30,494	32,888	35,621	38,498	37,374	39,490
Elementary	5,242	8,015	9,492	10,314	11,939	13,697	13,893	12,434	13,692
Middle/junior high	3,745	3,988	3,930	5,992	5,676	6,727	7,735	7,354	7,807
High	4,833	6,687	7,627	11,053	12,988	13,673	15,711	17,211	17,425
Higher education [1]	6,883	8,198	7,721	8,914	10,483	12,974	13,120	14,313	15,563
Instructional	4,277	4,459	4,307	5,272	6,163	7,646	7,332	8,371	8,379
Parking	158	262	331	369	498	545	398	472	702
Administration	128	189	179	270	287	192	418	219	295
Dormitory	324	388	548	802	1,051	1,386	1,489	1,923	2,572
Library	300	695	368	327	300	363	402	503	506
Student union/cafeteria	238	405	318	298	314	601	947	650	612
Sports/recreation	625	873	795	767	942	1,250	1,425	1,232	1,305
Infrastructure	788	654	780	701	814	808	501	570	808
Other educational	1,110	1,250	1,128	1,372	1,602	2,100	2,420	2,491	2,288
Library/archive	704	779	566	945	948	1,625	1,947	1,680	1,468
Public safety [1]	5,928	6,668	7,575	7,858	8,146	7,845	7,747	8,086	7,746
Correctional	4,854	5,701	6,588	6,575	6,611	6,342	5,909	5,815	5,403
Detention	4,049	4,786	5,618	5,338	5,431	4,977	4,440	4,353	4,004
Police/sheriff	804	916	970	1,237	1,180	1,366	1,469	1,462	1,399
Other public safety	1,025	967	988	1,284	1,534	1,503	1,838	2,272	2,343
Fire/rescue	652	773	795	1,095	1,387	1,284	1,606	1,882	1,969
Amusement and recreation [1]	6,142	6,857	7,666	9,159	10,563	11,834	11,978	11,556	10,878
Sports	1,637	2,311	3,173	3,402	3,181	3,516	3,339	2,855	2,241
Performance/meeting center	1,751	1,629	1,343	1,572	2,905	3,779	3,784	3,122	2,952
Convention center	1,224	938	835	1,099	1,957	2,933	2,760	2,134	1,932
Social center	772	961	947	1,399	1,605	1,846	1,881	2,224	2,103
Neighborhood center	581	673	622	1,059	1,234	1,375	1,216	1,691	1,864
Park/camp	1,696	1,874	2,020	2,584	2,681	2,386	2,512	2,768	3,284
Transportation	8,967	9,708	10,197	11,296	14,231	16,076	17,678	17,886	18,467
Air [1]	3,855	4,852	5,594	5,960	7,347	7,940	8,308	8,839	9,915
Passenger terminal	1,209	2,086	2,196	2,217	3,198	2,815	3,113	4,099	4,558
Runway	2,176	2,260	2,563	3,100	3,520	4,391	4,403	4,117	4,563
Land [1]	4,009	3,642	3,823	4,275	5,649	6,340	7,447	7,820	7,049
Passenger terminal	1,147	1,237	1,222	1,249	1,366	1,580	1,905	2,276	1,569
Mass transit	1,734	1,607	1,548	1,347	1,624	2,519	3,442	3,428	3,301
Railroad	462	401	564	1,033	1,607	1,121	684	488	389
Water [1]	1,103	1,214	780	1,061	1,236	1,796	1,923	1,227	1,502
Dock/marina	690	729	421	657	940	1,286	1,222	971	1,180
Dry dock/marine terminal	204	477	352	404	257	484	702	256	323
Power	2,879	3,101	2,495	3,228	3,891	3,995	4,365	6,244	5,920
Electrical	2,231	2,893	2,052	2,538	3,714	3,751	3,738	5,571	4,979
Distribution	733	1,650	1,511	1,494	1,479	1,038	1,349	1,981	1,584
Highway and street [1]	37,616	43,017	44,782	49,174	53,081	59,125	58,286	58,417	59,205
Pavement	29,164	32,416	33,180	36,464	39,048	43,095	42,130	40,808	41,520
Lighting	659	812	1,180	910	878	1,286	913	1,202	1,190
Retaining wall	187	493	711	816	1,133	653	764	587	568
Tunnel	346	539	862	926	919	1,120	676	644	543
Bridge	6,615	7,299	7,229	8,479	9,568	11,429	12,084	13,476	13,603
Toll/weigh	152	219	247	277	331	109	222	187	239
Maintenance building	53	307	362	354	302	426	306	253	175
Rest facility/streetscape	167	722	838	940	901	1,008	1,189	1,260	1,368
Sewage and waste disposal [1]	8,419	10,515	9,943	10,524	10,249	11,084	12,919	13,687	14,822
Sewage/dry waste [1]	4,825	6,830	6,589	7,082	6,836	7,079	8,386	8,595	9,385
Plant	1,641	1,969	1,925	2,178	2,025	1,879	2,259	2,396	2,706
Line/pump station	2,960	4,639	4,422	4,612	4,629	4,996	5,963	6,073	6,529
Waste water	3,522	3,664	3,317	3,436	3,413	4,005	4,533	5,092	5,437
Plant	2,467	2,680	2,276	2,613	2,363	2,987	3,561	3,856	4,057
Line/drain	1,055	984	1,041	823	1,050	1,018	972	1,236	1,380
Water supply [1]	4,713	6,493	6,678	6,967	6,972	8,972	9,835	10,250	10,309
Plant	1,204	1,664	1,912	2,154	2,246	3,185	3,221	3,770	3,784
Well	212	179	247	254	277	308	467	320	277
Line	2,516	3,353	3,106	3,089	3,395	4,156	4,378	4,328	4,567
Pump station	286	349	418	571	458	536	717	670	615
Reservoir	208	514	429	409	195	325	390	395	437
Tank/tower	246	433	565	491	402	462	662	767	630
Conservation and development [1]	1,265	1,503	1,444	1,346	1,304	1,396	1,316	1,414	2,372
Dam/levee	329	631	597	525	425	316	363	321	481
Breakwater/jetty	358	360	456	382	377	635	510	712	1,047

[1] Includes other types of construction, not shown separately.

Source: U.S. Census Bureau, "Construction Spending", Internet site <http://www.census.gov/const/www/c30index.html>.

Construction and Housing 617

Table 927. **Construction Contracts—Value of Construction and Floor Space of Buildings by Class of Construction: 1980 to 2004**

[151.8 reresents $151,800,000,000. Building construction includes new structures and additions; nonbuilding construction includes major alterations to existing structures which affect only valuation, since no additional floor area is created by "alteration"]

Year	Total	Residential buildings	Nonresidential buildings Total	Commercial [1]	Manufacturing	Educational [2]	Health	Public buildings	Religious	Social and recreational	Miscellaneous	Nonbuilding construction
VALUE (bil. dol.)												
1980	151.8	60.4	56.9	27.7	9.2	7.4	5.4	1.6	1.2	2.7	1.7	34.5
1985	235.6	102.1	92.1	54.6	8.1	10.0	7.8	3.1	2.0	4.0	2.5	41.4
1990	246.0	100.9	95.4	44.8	8.4	16.6	9.2	5.7	2.2	5.3	3.1	49.7
1995	306.5	127.9	114.2	46.6	13.8	22.9	10.8	6.3	2.8	7.1	3.8	64.4
1996	332.0	146.5	120.5	51.9	13.1	23.0	11.1	6.3	2.9	8.1	4.1	65.1
1997	362.4	153.6	138.9	59.8	14.0	28.4	11.9	7.0	3.8	10.0	4.0	69.8
1998	405.6	179.8	154.5	74.0	12.1	30.1	12.9	6.6	4.3	10.8	3.6	71.3
1999	447.2	195.0	168.7	77.2	11.3	37.1	13.6	8.2	4.5	11.6	5.1	83.5
2000	472.9	208.3	173.3	80.9	8.9	40.9	12.4	7.5	4.6	13.8	4.4	91.3
2001	496.6	219.7	169.2	70.3	8.1	47.0	14.4	7.8	4.8	12.0	4.8	107.7
2002	504.1	248.7	155.2	59.7	5.5	45.4	16.1	7.3	5.1	11.5	4.7	100.2
2003	530.7	283.1	155.6	58.9	6.7	47.8	15.6	7.0	4.5	10.8	4.3	92.0
2004	587.0	331.8	161.4	65.6	7.4	43.6	17.2	7.2	4.4	11.7	4.3	93.8
FLOOR SPACE (mil. sq. ft.)												
1980	3,102	1,839	1,263	738	220	103	55	18	28	49	52	(X)
1985	3,853	2,324	1,529	1,039	165	111	73	28	32	44	38	(X)
1990	3,020	1,817	1,203	694	128	152	69	47	29	51	32	(X)
1995	3,454	2,172	1,281	700	163	186	70	40	33	56	33	(X)
1996	3,776	2,479	1,297	723	155	177	77	41	32	60	33	(X)
1997	4,126	2,586	1,540	855	191	204	89	48	42	77	35	(X)
1998	4,812	3,015	1,797	1,107	166	219	96	42	47	85	34	(X)
1999	5,091	3,253	1,838	1,115	141	261	98	49	48	87	39	(X)
2000	4,982	3,113	1,869	1,180	111	273	88	44	49	94	29	(X)
2001	4,830	3,159	1,671	989	93	295	92	44	50	81	27	(X)
2002	4,793	3,355	1,438	811	68	277	97	37	52	71	28	(X)
2003	5,084	3,685	1,399	794	72	270	92	35	45	66	26	(X)
2004	5,469	4,044	1,424	853	79	229	93	34	42	68	26	(X)

X Not applicable.   [1] Includes nonindustrial warehouses.   [2] Includes science.

Source: McGraw-Hill Construction Dodge, a Division of the McGraw-Hill Companies, New York, NY (copyright).

Table 928. **Construction Contracts—Value by State: 2000 to 2004**

[In millions of dollars (472,930 represents $472,930,000,000). Represents value of construction in states in which work was actually done. See headnote, Table 927]

State	2000	2003	2004 Total [1]	2004 Residential	2004 Nonresidential	State	2000	2003	2004 Total [1]	2004 Residential	2004 Nonresidential
U.S.	472,930	530,712	586,986	331,751	161,397	MO	7,498	9,406	10,061	5,754	2,731
AL	7,225	7,510	8,329	4,137	2,211	MT	1,004	974	1,206	631	242
AK	1,327	1,836	1,919	528	636	NE	2,646	3,475	3,400	1,651	1,033
AZ	13,966	17,793	21,188	15,030	3,831	NV	6,978	9,512	11,206	6,619	3,334
AR	3,739	3,999	4,421	2,409	1,230	NH	2,514	2,171	2,576	1,435	773
CA	52,858	60,321	65,984	38,513	17,370	NJ	10,940	11,813	11,233	5,063	4,263
CO	12,491	11,543	13,950	8,946	3,267	NM	3,140	3,108	3,949	1,884	1,329
CT	5,181	4,820	5,080	2,610	1,950	NY	20,756	21,202	23,064	9,819	8,694
DE	1,350	1,555	1,455	964	228	NC	17,258	18,934	21,488	14,120	4,729
DC	1,763	1,806	1,663	336	1,151	ND	854	1,115	1,194	463	297
FL	35,079	49,501	58,162	40,955	11,064	OH	16,270	16,777	18,394	8,582	6,613
GA	20,419	20,202	23,628	14,605	5,970	OK	5,330	5,129	5,449	2,991	1,514
HI	1,409	2,308	2,363	1,613	292	OR	6,020	7,334	7,719	4,983	1,651
ID	2,521	3,060	3,867	2,768	702	PA	14,861	14,820	15,881	7,098	5,795
IL	17,167	19,071	21,251	10,930	7,310	RI	1,063	1,163	1,314	534	499
IN	11,011	12,680	13,155	6,683	4,182	SC	7,759	9,737	11,731	6,506	2,810
IA	3,776	6,514	5,832	2,370	1,970	SD	1,221	1,209	1,541	699	372
KS	4,463	4,568	4,943	2,481	1,399	TN	10,108	10,138	12,037	7,329	3,044
KY	6,625	7,147	7,559	3,863	2,333	TX	41,124	44,789	48,535	26,921	13,035
LA	5,528	6,602	6,193	3,121	1,951	UT	4,420	4,962	6,528	3,798	1,619
ME	1,710	2,096	2,246	1,337	552	VT	602	891	1,177	573	364
MD	7,836	9,170	9,416	4,442	3,205	VA	13,634	14,966	15,840	9,236	4,338
MA	11,983	8,800	9,856	4,928	3,782	WA	10,332	13,285	14,193	7,604	3,977
MI	14,735	13,975	14,319	7,757	4,384	WV	1,856	1,699	2,053	829	527
MN	8,838	10,455	10,974	6,537	2,559	WI	8,044	10,070	12,352	6,237	2,900
MS	2,917	3,665	3,995	1,959	1,186	WY	778	1,028	1,121	574	196

[1] Includes nonbuilding construction, not shown separately.

Source: McGraw-Hill Construction Dodge, a Division of the McGraw-Hill Companies, New York, NY, (copyright).

618 Construction and Housing

Table 929. **New Privately-Owned Housing Units Authorized by State: 2000 and 2004**

[1,592.3 represents 1,592,300. Based on about 19,000 places in United States having building permit systems in 2000 and 20,000 in 2004]

State	Housing units (1,000)			Valuation (mil. dol.)			State	Housing units (1,000)			Valuation (mil. dol.)		
		2004			2004				2004			2004	
	2000	Total	1 unit	2000	Total	1 unit		2000	Total	1 unit	2000	Total	1 unit
U.S.	**1,592.3**	**2,070.1**	**1,613.4**	**185,744**	**292,414**	**255,511**	MO	24.3	32.8	26.3	2,569	4,286	3,809
AL	17.4	27.4	22.4	1,718	3,293	2,850	MT	2.6	5.0	3.4	235	645	522
AK	2.1	3.1	1.8	333	540	365	NE	9.1	10.9	9.1	830	1,373	1,255
AZ	61.5	90.6	80.8	7,158	13,531	12,819	NV	32.3	44.6	38.9	3,312	5,461	5,061
AR	9.2	15.9	10.6	859	1,764	1,509	NH	6.7	8.7	7.0	937	1,385	1,238
CA	145.6	207.4	151.6	23,344	36,059	30,865	NJ	34.6	35.9	22.4	3,376	4,294	3,302
CO	54.6	46.5	40.8	6,822	8,050	7,522	NM	8.9	12.6	11.7	1,073	1,747	1,701
CT	9.4	11.8	9.3	1,425	2,032	1,850	NY	44.1	53.5	24.1	4,992	6,945	4,532
DE	4.6	7.9	7.5	414	893	880	NC	78.4	93.1	77.1	8,643	12,845	11,830
DC	0.8	1.9	0.2	54	225	22	ND	2.1	4.0	2.5	190	434	343
FL	155.3	255.9	187.5	17,462	36,959	29,601	OH	49.7	51.7	42.5	6,154	7,974	7,366
GA	91.8	108.4	87.7	8,722	12,884	11,486	OK	11.1	17.1	14.1	1,204	2,184	2,023
HI	4.9	9.0	5.6	823	1,742	1,184	OR	19.9	27.3	20.7	2,533	4,458	3,950
ID	10.9	18.1	15.3	1,359	2,624	2,443	PA	41.1	49.7	41.5	4,616	6,767	6,181
IL	51.9	59.8	46.2	6,528	9,551	8,388	RI	2.6	2.5	1.9	296	362	325
IN	37.9	39.2	32.2	4,414	5,610	5,160	SC	32.8	43.2	36.1	3,533	5,641	5,061
IA	12.5	16.3	12.4	1,333	2,231	1,933	SD	4.2	5.8	4.7	369	656	577
KS	12.5	13.3	11.5	1,397	1,926	1,804	TN	32.2	44.8	37.8	3,378	5,863	5,423
KY	18.5	22.6	18.5	1,767	2,679	2,453	TX	141.2	188.8	149.1	15,418	22,487	20,380
LA	14.7	23.0	20.7	1,553	2,626	2,489	UT	17.6	24.3	20.2	2,138	3,633	3,304
ME	6.2	8.8	8.1	723	1,249	1,190	VT	2.5	3.6	2.7	319	494	412
MD	30.4	27.4	21.6	3,232	3,823	3,385	VA	48.4	63.2	49.0	5,052	8,094	7,218
MA	18.0	22.5	14.8	2,741	3,790	3,021	WA	39.0	50.1	36.5	4,426	7,535	6,376
MI	52.5	54.7	45.9	6,256	7,625	6,955	WV	3.8	5.7	5.1	360	735	700
MN	32.8	41.8	32.6	4,204	6,583	5,629	WI	34.2	40.0	29.7	3,917	5,783	4,986
MS	11.3	14.5	11.2	918	1,517	1,345	WY	1.6	3.3	2.8	314	525	490

Source: U.S. Census Bureau, Construction Reports, Series C40, *Building Permits*, monthly; publication discontinued in 2001. See Internet site <http://www.census.gov/const/www/newresconstindex.html> and *New Residential Construction*, monthly.

Table 930. **New Privately-Owned Housing Units Started—Selected Characteristics: 1970 to 2004**

[In thousands (1,434 represents 1,434,000). For composition of regions, see map inside front cover]

Year	Total units	Structures with—			Region				Units for sale		
		One unit	2 to 4 units	5 or more units	North-east	Mid-west	South	West	Total	Single-family	Multi-family
1970	1,434	813	85	536	218	294	612	311	(NA)	(NA)	(NA)
1975	1,160	892	64	204	149	294	442	275	576	531	45
1978	2,020	1,433	125	462	200	451	824	545	1,032	901	131
1979	1,745	1,194	122	429	178	349	748	470	915	742	173
1980	1,292	852	110	331	125	218	643	306	689	526	163
1981	1,084	705	91	288	117	165	562	240	584	426	158
1982	1,062	663	80	320	117	149	591	205	549	409	140
1983	1,703	1,068	113	522	168	218	935	382	923	713	210
1984	1,750	1,084	121	544	204	243	866	436	934	728	206
1985	1,742	1,072	93	576	252	240	782	468	867	713	154
1986	1,805	1,179	84	542	294	296	733	483	925	782	143
1987	1,621	1,146	65	409	269	298	634	420	862	732	130
1988	1,488	1,081	59	348	235	274	575	404	808	709	99
1989	1,376	1,003	55	318	179	266	536	396	735	648	87
1990	1,193	895	38	260	131	253	479	329	585	529	56
1991	1,014	840	36	138	113	233	414	254	531	490	41
1992	1,200	1,030	31	139	127	288	497	288	659	618	41
1993	1,288	1,126	29	133	127	298	562	302	760	716	44
1994	1,457	1,198	35	224	138	329	639	351	815	763	52
1995	1,354	1,076	34	244	118	290	615	331	763	712	51
1996	1,477	1,161	45	271	132	322	662	361	833	774	59
1997	1,474	1,134	45	296	137	304	670	363	843	784	59
1998	1,617	1,271	43	303	149	331	743	395	941	882	59
1999	1,641	1,302	32	307	156	347	746	392	981	912	69
2000	1,569	1,231	39	299	155	318	714	383	946	871	75
2001	1,603	1,273	37	293	149	330	732	391	990	919	71
2002	1,705	1,359	39	308	158	350	782	416	1,070	999	71
2003	1,848	1,499	34	315	163	374	839	472	1,207	1,120	87
2004	1,956	1,611	42	303	175	356	909	516	1,360	1,240	120

NA Not available.

Source: U.S. Census Bureau, Current Construction Reports, Series C20, *Housing Starts*, monthly; publication discontinued in 2001. See Internet site <http://www.census.gov/const/www/newresconstindex.html> and *New Residential Construction*, monthly.

Table 931. New Privately-Owned Housing Units Started by State: 2000 to 2006

[In thousands of units (1,573 represents 1,573,000)]

State	2000	2004, est.	2005, est.	2006, est. Total units	2006, est. Single-family units	State	2000	2004, est.	2005, est.	2006, est. Total units	2006, est. Single-family units
U.S.	1,573	1,724	1,658	1,614	1,319	MO	27.4	27.7	27.5	27.5	24.3
AL	21.2	20.8	20.9	21.1	18.2	MT	2.4	2.9	2.9	2.8	2.0
AK	2.0	2.3	2.3	2.3	1.6	NE	9.2	10.5	10.0	9.7	8.5
AZ	59.4	64.4	61.9	60.1	53.2	NV	31.0	37.8	36.1	35.0	27.9
AR	12.5	13.8	13.6	13.6	10.4	NH	6.4	7.4	7.0	6.6	5.6
CA	137.1	177.7	165.0	154.2	120.3	NJ	31.4	27.2	26.5	26.1	20.7
CO	52.5	35.9	36.8	37.7	31.7	NM	7.3	10.6	10.3	10.1	8.9
CT	8.9	8.6	8.5	8.5	7.7	NY	41.1	41.0	38.8	37.5	22.0
DE	4.4	6.2	5.9	5.7	5.4	NC	76.1	72.8	71.1	70.2	59.3
DC	0.4	0.4	0.4	0.4	0.1	ND	2.4	3.6	3.4	3.3	2.3
FL	147.9	185.7	173.6	165.4	123.7	OH	47.8	51.2	49.7	48.8	41.7
GA	90.4	89.3	86.1	84.1	71.0	OK	14.1	14.6	14.3	14.2	12.6
HI	4.7	6.8	6.5	6.2	5.1	OR	18.8	19.2	19.6	20.0	15.6
ID	11.3	13.5	13.1	12.8	11.1	PA	39.2	40.4	39.4	39.0	34.6
IL	51.3	61.5	58.5	56.6	45.2	RI	2.6	2.4	2.4	2.4	2.0
IN	38.2	40.4	39.4	38.8	33.5	SC	31.6	35.1	33.4	32.3	27.2
IA	12.8	15.3	14.6	14.1	11.5	SD	4.4	5.2	4.9	4.8	4.0
KS	13.4	14.0	13.8	13.8	11.7	TN	34.6	34.3	34.2	34.3	30.4
KY	21.8	20.4	20.4	20.5	17.9	TX	145.0	163.3	154.9	149.1	117.8
LA	15.5	18.7	18.0	17.7	15.2	UT	18.1	20.2	19.9	19.8	16.7
ME	6.3	7.3	6.8	6.5	6.0	VT	2.6	2.8	2.7	2.6	2.4
MD	28.7	27.4	27.1	27.0	22.5	VA	47.5	53.4	51.8	50.6	43.2
MA	17.1	16.2	16.0	16.0	12.8	WA	36.9	38.8	38.3	38.2	29.9
MI	50.4	53.4	51.7	50.7	45.2	WV	5.3	5.4	5.4	5.4	5.1
MN	32.9	41.7	39.0	37.1	31.9	WI	32.6	38.1	36.7	35.8	27.9
MS	14.1	12.8	12.8	12.9	11.1	WY	1.9	2.2	2.2	2.3	2.1

Source: National Association of Home Builders, Economics Division, Washington, DC. Data provided by the Econometric Forecasting Service.

Table 932. Characteristics of New Privately-Owned One-Family Houses Completed: 1990 to 2004

[Percent distribution, except total houses. (966 represents 966,000). Data are percent distribution of characteristics for all houses completed (includes new houses completed, houses built-for-sale completed, contractor-built and owner-built houses completed, and houses completed for rent). Percents exclude houses for which characteristics specified were not reported]

Characteristic	1990	1995	2000	2004	Characteristic	1990	1995	2000	2004
Total houses (1,000)	966	1,066	1,242	1,532	Bedrooms	100	100	100	100
					2 or less	15	13	11	11
Construction type	100	100	100	100	3	57	57	54	51
Site built	(NA)	94	94	95	4 or more	29	30	35	37
Modular	(NA)	3	3	3					
Other	(NA)	3	3	2	Bathrooms	100	100	100	100
					1-1/2 or less	13	11	7	5
Exterior wall material	100	100	100	100	2	42	41	39	39
Brick	18	20	20	19	2-1/2 or more	45	48	54	57
Wood	39	25	14	7					
Stucco	18	16	17	22	Heating fuel	100	100	100	100
Vinyl siding [1]	(NA)	30	39	38	Gas	59	67	70	69
Aluminum siding	5	3	1	1	Electricity	33	28	27	29
Other [1]	20	6	7	14	Oil	5	3	3	2
					Other	3	1	1	1
Floor area	100	100	100	100					
Under 1,200 sq. ft	11	10	6	4	Heating system	100	100	100	100
1,200 to 1,599 sq. ft	22	22	18	17	Warm air furnace	65	67	71	70
1,600 to 1,999 sq. ft	22	23	23	21	Electric heat pump	23	25	23	26
2,000 to 2,399 sq. ft	17	17	18	18	Other	12	9	6	4
2,400 sq. ft. and over	29	28	35	39					
Average (sq. ft.)	2,080	2,095	2,266	2,349	Central air-conditioning	100	100	100	100
Median (sq. ft.)	1,905	1,920	2,057	2,140	With	76	80	85	90
					Without	24	20	15	10
Number of stories	100	100	100	100					
1	46	49	47	47	Fireplaces	100	100	100	100
2 or more	49	48	52	52	No fireplace	34	37	40	45
Split level	4	3	1	1	1 or more	66	63	60	55
Foundation	100	100	100	100	Parking facilities	100	100	100	100
Full or partial basement	38	39	37	31	Garage	82	84	89	90
Slab	40	42	46	54	Carport	2	2	1	1
Crawl space	21	19	17	15	No garage or carport	16	14	11	9

NA Not available. [1] Prior to 1995 "other" includes vinyl siding.

Source: U.S. Census Bureau and U.S. Department of Housing and Urban Development, Current Construction Reports, Series C25, New One-Family Houses Sold, monthly, and Characteristics of New Housing, annual; publication discontinued in 2001, see Internet site <http://www.census.gov/const/www/charindex.html>.

Table 933. Average Length of Time from Start to Completion of New Privately-Owned 1 Unit Residential Buildings: 1971 to 2004

[In months. For buildings started in permit issuing places]

Year	Total [1]	Purpose of construction			Region [2]			
		Built-for-sale	Contractor-built	Owner-built	Northeast	Midwest	South	West
1971	4.8	4.4	4.0	7.2	5.9	5.2	4.4	4.4
1972	5.2	4.8	4.4	7.8	6.0	5.6	4.9	5.0
1973	6.0	5.7	4.9	7.9	6.5	6.0	5.8	5.9
1974	6.2	6.1	4.9	8.0	6.6	6.5	6.0	6.2
1975	6.1	5.7	4.6	8.5	6.3	6.6	5.8	6.1
1976	5.5	5.2	4.6	7.4	6.1	6.0	5.0	5.5
1977	5.7	5.4	4.7	7.6	5.8	5.8	5.4	6.0
1978	6.2	5.9	5.3	8.5	6.5	6.6	5.7	6.7
1979	6.7	6.2	5.8	9.0	7.0	7.1	6.1	7.0
1980	6.9	6.2	5.5	10.1	7.7	8.0	6.1	7.4
1981	6.6	5.8	5.2	9.6	7.7	7.4	5.7	7.4
1982	6.6	5.6	5.5	10.4	8.0	7.5	5.9	7.2
1983	5.8	4.8	4.8	10.0	7.2	6.5	5.1	6.2
1984	6.1	5.2	4.8	10.7	7.0	6.7	5.4	6.7
1985	6.2	5.4	4.9	10.6	7.2	6.0	5.7	6.7
1986	6.2	5.4	4.9	11.1	7.3	6.5	5.6	6.4
1987	6.2	5.6	5.1	10.3	7.6	5.9	5.7	6.4
1988	6.5	5.8	5.3	10.4	8.8	5.8	5.7	6.6
1989	6.4	5.9	5.3	10.2	9.3	5.8	5.6	6.5
1990	6.4	5.9	5.3	10.3	9.3	5.6	5.7	6.9
1991	6.3	5.6	5.1	10.2	8.9	5.6	5.5	6.9
1992	5.8	5.0	5.0	9.5	7.6	5.6	5.1	6.1
1993	5.6	4.9	5.4	9.0	7.2	5.5	5.2	6.0
1994	5.6	4.9	5.3	9.1	7.1	5.7	5.3	5.6
1995	5.9	5.2	5.8	9.5	7.4	6.0	5.4	6.0
1996	6.0	5.2	5.8	9.9	8.2	6.1	5.6	5.6
1997	6.0	5.2	5.9	9.8	7.3	6.2	5.6	5.8
1998	6.0	5.4	6.0	9.5	7.1	6.2	5.5	6.1
1999	6.1	5.5	6.4	9.2	7.0	6.4	5.7	6.3
2000	6.2	5.6	6.5	9.2	7.5	6.4	5.9	6.0
2001	6.2	5.6	7.0	9.2	7.6	6.5	5.8	6.3
2002	6.1	5.5	6.6	9.6	7.3	6.4	5.6	6.2
2003	6.2	5.5	6.8	9.9	7.5	6.7	5.7	6.2
2004	6.2	5.7	7.0	9.1	7.3	6.7	5.8	6.3

[1] Includes units built for rent, not shown separately.   [2] For composition of regions, see map inside front cover.

Source: U.S. Census Bureau, *New Residential Construction.* See Internet site <http://www.census.gov/const/www/newresconstindex.html>.

Table 934. Price Indexes of New One-Family Houses Sold, by Region: 1979 to 2004

[1996 = 100. Based on kinds of homes sold in 1996. Includes value of the lot. For composition of regions, see map, inside front cover]

Year	Total	Northeast	Midwest	South	West
1979	54.0	43.7	54.3	56.6	52.1
1980	59.5	48.0	56.8	63.2	58.4
1981	64.2	52.1	62.1	68.7	62.0
1982	65.7	54.0	63.9	70.9	62.8
1983	67.1	57.3	63.7	72.8	64.0
1984	69.8	62.2	67.5	75.2	66.3
1985	70.7	68.5	66.4	76.7	66.7
1986	73.4	78.6	70.2	79.0	68.4
1987	77.4	89.2	74.9	81.9	72.0
1988	80.3	91.5	78.2	83.7	75.9
1989	83.5	94.1	80.0	86.1	80.7
1990	85.1	92.2	80.7	86.3	84.6
1991	86.2	89.2	82.8	87.9	85.1
1992	87.3	96.1	84.3	88.8	85.6
1993	91.1	93.3	90.0	93.0	88.7
1994	95.5	94.5	94.4	96.4	94.9
1995	98.2	96.7	98.1	99.4	96.5
1996	100.0	100.0	100.0	100.0	100.0
1997	102.9	102.8	103.3	102.8	102.9
1998	105.5	104.5	105.3	106.0	105.1
1999	110.7	108.8	110.3	110.5	111.7
2000	115.4	114.6	114.4	114.7	117.3
2001	119.5	122.6	115.8	117.8	123.9
2002	124.8	127.5	120.7	121.2	132.5
2003	131.9	137.5	124.7	126.5	144.3
2004	141.9	149.1	132.6	133.0	161.5

Source: U.S. Census Bureau, *New Residential Sales.* See Internet site <http://www.census.gov/const/www/newressalesindex.html>.

Table 935. New Privately-Owned One-Family Houses Sold by Region and Type of Financing, 1980 to 2004, and by Sales-Price Group, 2004

[In thousands (545 represents 545,000). Based on a national probability sample of monthly interviews with builders or owners of one-family houses for which building permits have been issued or, for nonpermit areas, on which construction has started. For details, see source and Appendix III. For composition of regions, see map inside front cover]

Year and sales-price group	Total sales	Region				Financing type			
		North-east	Midwest	South	West	Conven-tional [1]	FHA and VA	Rural Housing Service [2]	Cash
1980	545	50	81	267	145	302	196	14	32
1985	688	112	82	323	170	403	208	11	64
1990	534	71	89	225	149	337	138	10	50
1995	667	55	125	300	187	490	129	9	39
1997	804	78	140	363	223	616	137	6	46
1998	886	81	164	398	243	693	136	9	48
1999	880	76	168	395	242	689	143	6	41
2000	877	71	155	406	244	695	138	4	40
2001	908	66	164	439	239	726	141	2	39
2002	973	65	185	450	273	788	140	4	42
2003	1,086	79	189	511	307	911	130	4	41
2004.	**1,203**	**83**	**210**	**562**	**348**	**1,047**	**105**	**6**	**46**
Under $100,000	48	1	6	39	2	(NA)	(NA)	(NA)	(NA)
$100,000 to $149,999	222	5	40	142	34	(NA)	(NA)	(NA)	(NA)
$150,000 to $199,999	254	7	54	136	56	(NA)	(NA)	(NA)	(NA)
$200,000 to $299,999	312	26	61	129	96	(NA)	(NA)	(NA)	(NA)
$300,000 and over	368	45	49	115	159	(NA)	(NA)	(NA)	(NA)

NA Not available.   [1] Includes all other types of financing.   [2] Prior to 1997, the Farmers Home Administration.

Source: U.S. Census Bureau and U.S. Department of Housing and Urban Development, Current Construction Reports, Series C25, *Characteristics of New Housing*, annual; and *New One-Family Houses Sold*, monthly; publications discontinued in 2001. See Internet site <http://www.census.gov/const/www/newressalesindex.html> and *New Residential Sales*, monthly.

Table 936. Median Sales Price of New Privately-Owned One-Family Houses Sold by Region: 1980 to 2004

[In dollars. For definition of median, see Guide to Tabular Presentation. For composition of regions, see map inside front cover. See Appendix III. See also headnote, table 935]

Year	U.S.	North-east	Mid-west	South	West	Year	U.S.	North-east	Mid-west	South	West
1980 ...	64,600	69,500	63,400	59,600	72,300	1999 ...	161,000	210,500	164,000	145,900	173,700
1985 ...	84,300	103,300	80,300	75,000	92,600	2000 ...	169,000	227,400	169,700	148,000	196,400
1990 ...	122,900	159,000	107,900	99,000	147,500	2001 ...	175,200	246,400	172,600	155,400	213,600
1995 ...	133,900	180,000	134,000	124,500	141,400	2002 ...	187,600	264,300	178,000	163,400	238,500
1997 ...	146,000	190,000	149,900	129,600	160,000	2003 ...	195,000	264,500	184,300	168,150	260,900
1998 ...	152,500	200,000	157,500	135,800	163,500	2004 ...	221,000	315,800	205,000	181,100	283,100

Source: U.S. Census Bureau and U.S. Department of Housing and Urban Development, Current Construction Reports, Series C25, *Characteristics of New Housing*, annual; and *New One-Family Houses Sold*, monthly; publications discontinued in 2001. See Internet site <http://www.census.gov/const/www/newressalesindex.html> and *New Residential Sales*, monthly.

Table 937. New Manufactured (Mobile) Homes Placed for Residential Use and Average Sales Price by Region: 1980 to 2004

[233.7 represents 233,700. A mobile home is a moveable dwelling, 8 feet or more wide and 40 feet or more long, designed to be towed on its own chassis, with transportation gear integral to the unit when it leaves the factory, and without need of permanent foundation. Excluded are travel trailers, motor homes, and modular housing. Data are based on a probability sample and subject to sampling variability; see source. For composition of regions, see map inside front cover]

Year	Units placed (1,000)					Average sales price (dol.)				
	Total	North-east	Mid-west	South	West	U.S.	North-east	Mid-west	South	West
1980	233.7	12.3	32.3	140.3	48.7	19,800	18,500	18,600	18,200	25,400
1985	283.4	20.2	38.6	187.6	36.9	21,800	22,700	21,500	20,400	28,700
1990	195.4	18.8	37.7	108.4	30.6	27,800	30,000	27,000	24,500	39,300
1994	290.9	16.3	53.3	177.7	43.6	32,800	32,900	34,000	30,200	41,900
1995	319.4	15.0	57.5	203.2	43.7	35,300	35,800	35,700	33,300	44,100
1996	337.7	16.2	58.8	218.2	44.4	37,200	37,300	38,000	35,500	45,000
1997	336.3	14.3	55.3	219.4	47.3	39,800	41,300	40,300	38,000	47,300
1998	373.7	14.7	58.3	250.3	50.4	41,600	42,200	42,400	40,100	48,400
1999	338.3	14.1	53.6	227.2	43.5	43,300	44,000	44,400	41,900	49,600
2000	280.9	14.9	48.7	178.7	38.6	46,400	47,000	47,900	44,300	54,100
2001	196.2	12.2	37.6	116.4	30.0	48,900	50,000	49,100	46,500	58,000
2002	174.3	11.8	34.2	101.0	27.2	51,300	53,200	51,700	48,000	62,600
2003	139.8	11.8	25.2	77.2	26.1	54,900	57,300	55,100	50,500	67,700
2004	124.2	10.9	20.3	67.7	25.3	58,100	60,100	58,900	52,100	73,300

Source: U.S. Census Bureau, *Manufactured Housing Statistics*. See Internet site <http://www.census.gov/const/www/mhsindex .html>.

Table 938. Profile of Homebuyers by Characteristic: 2004

[In percent, except as indicated. 67.1 represents $67,100. Includes condos. For the 12-month period ending July 2004, except income for 2003. Based on survey consumers who bought a home between August 2003 and July 2004. See source for details. Data by region represent region where home was purchased. For composition of regions, see map inside front cover]

Characteristic	Total	Northeast	Midwest	South	West	1st time buyers	Repeat buyers
Age	100	100	100	100	100	100	100
Under 25 years old	5	3	7	5	5	12	1
25 to 34 years old	34	35	37	33	30	54	20
35 to 44 years old	26	29	25	25	24	21	28
45 to 54 years old	18	18	16	18	19	9	24
55 to 64 years old	12	10	9	12	14	3	17
65 to 74 years old	5	3	4	5	6	1	7
75 years old and over	2	2	1	2	2	-	3
Median age (years)	39	39	37	39	41	32	45
Household income	100	100	100	100	100	100	100
Under $25,000	4	3	4	4	5	7	3
$25,000 to 34,999	9	6	10	10	10	14	6
$35,000 to 44,999	11	8	12	10	13	16	6
$45,000 to 54,999	12	10	12	12	12	15	10
$55,000 to 64,999	13	15	15	13	12	15	11
$65,000 to 74,999	10	10	9	10	10	9	10
$75,000 to 84,999	9	9	8	9	9	8	10
$85,000 to 94,999	7	8	7	8	7	5	9
$95,000 to 104,999	7	7	8	7	6	4	9
$105,000 to 114,999	4	4	4	4	4	2	5
$115,000 to 124,999	3	3	2	3	3	2	4
$125,000 to 134,999	2	3	3	2	2	1	3
$135,000 to 149,999	2	3	1	2	2	1	3
$150,000 to 174,999	3	3	2	3	3	1	4
$175,000 to 199,999	1	2	1	2	1	1	2
$200,000 or more	4	6	3	4	4	1	6
Median income [1] ($1,000)	67.1	72.4	63.4	67.3	65.0	54.5	79.1
Race	100	100	100	100	100	100	100
White	84	87	82	81	77	77	88
Black/African American	6	5	8	9	3	10	4
Asian/Pacific Islander	3	2	3	3	9	4	3
Hispanic/Latino	5	4	4	6	11	7	4
Other	2	1	2	2	3	3	2

- Represents or rounds to zero.   [1] For definition of median, see Guide to Tabular Presentation.

Source: NATIONAL ASSOCIATION OF REALTORS®, Washington, DC, *Profile of Home Buyers and Sellers, 2004 (copyright)*. See Internet site <http://www.realtor.org/research>.

Table 939. Profile of Second-Home Buyers by Characteristic: 2004

[In percent, except as indicated. (2,805 represents 2,805,000). See headnote, table 938]

Characteristic	Total	Vacation homes	Investment properties	Characteristic	Total	Vacation homes	Investment properties
Total (1,000)	2,805	1,014	1,791	Age	100	100	100
Household income	100	100	100	Under 25 years old	1	1	1
Under $25,000	3	5	2	25 to 34 years old	16	21	15
$25,000 to 34,999	11	23	7	35 to 44 years old	23	11	28
$35,000 to 44,999	6	5	7	45 to 54 years old	24	16	26
$45,000 to 54,999	9	9	9	55 to 64 years old	22	25	20
$55,000 to 64,999	10	6	12	65 to 74 years old	10	14	7
$65,000 to 74,999	6	5	7	75 years old and over	5	12	3
$75,000 to 84,999	6	4	5	Median age (years) [1]	50	55	47
$85,000 to 94,999	7	2	9				
$95,000 to 104,999	6	3	6	Home attributes [2]	100	100	100
$105,000 to 124,999	7	5	8	Close to primary residence	31	24	34
$125,000 to 149,999	8	11	8	Close to family members	12	18	11
$150,000 to 199,999	8	8	8	Close to job/school	19	33	13
$200,000 or more	13	15	11	Close to preferred recreation activities	16	22	13
Median income [1] ($1,000)	83.7	71.0	85.7	Close to ocean/river/lake	16	18	16
Reason for buying [2]	100	100	100	Close to mountains	9	7	9
Diversifies investments	30	13	36	Close to preferred vacation area	9	16	6
Provides rental income	28	7	37	In safer area than primary residence	9	22	5
Residence after retirement	18	27	14	Child can occupy while attending school	6	4	6
Personal or family retreat	14	29	8	Other	9	2	12
Vacation use	6	16	2				
Had extra money to spend	5	4	5				
Other	22	47	12				

[1] For definition of median, see Guide to Tabular Presentation.   [2] Multiple reasons and attributes allowed but counted once in total.

Source: NATIONAL ASSOCIATION OF REALTORS®, Washington, DC, *Profile of Second-Home Buyers, 2005 (copyright)*. See Internet site <http://www.realtor.org/research>.

Construction and Housing   623

Table 940. Existing One-Family Homes Sold and Price by Region: 1980 to 2004

[2,973 represents 2,973,000. Includes existing detached single-family homes and townhomes; excludes condos and co-ops. Data shown here reflect revisions to previous estimates. Based on data (adjusted and aggregated to regional and national totals) reported by participating real estate multiple listing services. For definition of median, see Guide to Tabular Presentation. See Table 943 for data on condos and co-ops. For composition of regions, see map inside front cover]

Year	Homes sold (1,000)					Median sales price (dol.)				
	Total	North-east	Mid-west	South	West	Total	North-east	Mid-west	South	West
1980	2,973	403	806	1,092	672	62,200	60,800	51,900	58,300	89,300
1985	3,134	561	806	1,063	704	75,500	88,900	58,900	75,200	95,400
1987	3,436	618	892	1,163	763	85,600	133,300	66,000	80,400	113,200
1988	3,513	606	865	1,224	817	89,300	143,000	68,400	82,200	124,900
1989 [1]	3,010	545	829	1,003	633	89,500	127,700	71,800	84,400	127,100
1990	2,914	510	806	1,010	587	92,000	126,400	75,300	85,100	129,600
1991	2,885	515	808	992	569	97,100	129,100	79,500	88,500	135,300
1992	3,150	578	906	1,049	618	99,700	128,900	83,000	91,500	131,500
1993	3,427	611	961	1,173	681	103,100	129,100	86,000	94,300	132,500
1994	3,544	615	963	1,220	746	107,200	129,100	89,300	95,700	139,400
1995	3,519	609	944	1,219	747	110,500	126,700	94,800	97,700	141,000
1996	3,797	652	988	1,289	868	115,800	127,800	101,000	103,400	147,100
1997	3,964	678	1,009	1,363	914	121,800	131,800	107,000	109,600	155,200
1998	4,495	741	1,136	1,598	1,020	128,400	135,900	114,300	116,200	164,800
1999	4,651	729	1,144	1,705	1,072	133,300	139,000	119,600	120,300	173,900
2000	4,604	715	1,115	1,706	1,066	139,000	139,400	123,600	128,300	183,000
2001	4,733	710	1,155	1,793	1,075	147,800	146,500	130,200	137,400	194,500
2002	4,974	730	1,217	1,871	1,155	158,100	164,300	136,000	147,300	215,400
2003	5,452	771	1,323	2,072	1,280	170,000	190,500	141,300	157,100	234,200
2004	5,964	822	1,388	2,312	1,440	184,100	220,000	149,000	169,000	265,800

[1] Beginning 1989 data not comparable to earlier years due to rebenchmarking.

Source: NATIONAL ASSOCIATION OF REALTORS®, Washington, DC, prior to 1990, Home Sales, monthly, and Home Sales Yearbook: 1990; (copyright); thereafter, Real Estate Outlook; Market Trends & Insights, monthly, (copyright). See Internet site <http://www.realtor.org/research>.

Table 941. Median Sales Price of Existing One-Family Homes by Selected Metropolitan Area: 2002 to 2004

[In thousands of dollars (158.1 represents $158,100). Includes existing detached single-family homes and townhouses. Areas are metropolitan statistical areas defined by Office of Management and Budget as of 1992, except as noted]

Metropolitan area	2002	2003	2004	Metropolitan area	2002	2003	2004
United States, total	158.1	170.0	184.1	NY: Middlesex-Somerset-Hunterdon, NJ	284.1	314.0	352.4
Albany-Schenectady-Troy, NY . . .	126.0	141.9	162.1	NY: Monmouth-Ocean, NJ	251.7	288.3	319.1
Anaheim-Santa Ana, (Orange County), CA [1]	412.7	487.0	627.3	NY: Nassau-Suffolk, NY	312.9	364.5	413.5
Atlanta, GA	146.5	152.4	156.9	NY: New York-North NJ-Long Island, NY	309.8	353.0	395.8
Atlantic City, NJ [2]	143.6	174.4	197.9	NY: Newark, NJ	300.5	331.2	370.5
Aurora-Elgin, IL [2]	193.3	208.1	224.3	Norfolk-Virginia Beach-Newport News, VA	(NA)	138.8	163.0
Austin/San Marcos, TX	156.5	156.7	154.7	Orlando, FL	136.6	145.1	169.6
Baltimore, MD	179.6	208.9	239.6	Philadelphia, PA-NJ	146.1	168.0	184.6
Boston, MA	(NA)	354.8	389.7	Phoenix, AZ	143.8	152.5	169.4
Bradenton, FL [2]	150.0	172.7	220.1	Portland, ME	180.0	199.1	232.2
Charleston, SC.	159.4	168.9	183.5	Portland, OR	180.4	192.0	210.0
Chicago, IL	220.9	238.9	246.3	Providence, RI	193.2	233.4	268.0
Colordo Springs, CO	176.9	184.5	188.2	Raleigh-Durham, NC	172.2	174.7	182.9
Denver, CO	228.1	238.2	239.1	Reno, NV	183.2	204.9	284.3
Eugene-Springfield, OR	143.7	151.7	164.9	Richmond-Petersburg, VA	142.3	155.1	170.7
Ft. Lauderdale-Hollywood-Pompano Beach, FL	197.0	227.6	278.0	Riverside-San Bernadino, CA [1] . .	176.5	221.0	296.4
Ft. Myers-Cape Coral-Punta Gorda,FL	133.6	147.6	181.5	Sacramento, CA [1]	210.2	247.6	317.6
Gainesville, FL	130.0	145.0	159.0	Salt Lake City-Ogden, UT.	148.8	148.0	158.0
Hartford, CT.	175.9	202.3	226.6	San Diego, CA [1]	364.2	424.9	551.6
Honolulu, HI.	335.0	380.0	460.0	San Francisco, CA Area [1]	517.1	558.1	641.7
Lake County, IL	240.0	257.9	265.1	Sarasota, FL [2]	176.2	207.9	264.1
Las Vegas, NV	159.8	179.2	266.4	Seattle, WA	254.0	268.8	294.9
Los Angeles-Long Beach, CA [1] . .	290.0	354.7	446.4	Springfield, MA	139.8	153.4	161.4
Madison, WI	177.0	188.7	207.0	Tacoma, WA	170.4	178.1	208.9
Melbourne-Titusville-Palm Bay, FL	112.7	131.3	158.6	Tampa-St.Petersburg-Clearwater, FL	133.5	138.1	159.7
Miami-Hialeah, FL.	189.8	226.8	277.2	Trenton, NJ	179.5	212.4	234.1
Milwaukee, WI	173.8	182.1	197.1	Tucson, AZ	146.4	156.3	177.3
Minneapolis-St. Paul, MN-WI . . .	185.0	199.6	217.4	Washington, DC-MD-VA.	250.2	286.2	351.1
New Haven-Meriden, CT	192.3	225.3	252.6	West Palm Beach-Boca Raton-Delray Beach, FL	(NA)	241.3	300.9
NY: Bergen-Passaic, NJ.	337.9	370.7	410.5	Wilmington, DE-NJ-MD	150.1	166.2	186.0
				Worcester, MA	225.6	252.6	275.9

NA Not available. [1] California data supplied by the California Association of REALTORS. [2] In 1992, Bradenton and Sarasota were merged and Aurora-Elgin was incorporated into Chicago. The source still collects price data on the previous jurisdictions.

Source: NATIONAL ASSOCIATION OF REALTORS®, Washington, DC, Real Estate Outlook: Market Trends & Insights, monthly, (copyright). See Internet site <http://www.realtor.org/research>.

Table 942. Existing Home Sales by State: 2000 to 2004

[In thousands (5,171 represents 5,171,000). Includes condos and co-ops as well as single-family homes. Data shown here reflect revisions from prior estimates]

State	2000	2002	2003	2004	State	2000	2002	2003	2004
United States . . .	5,171	5,631	6,183	6,784	Missouri	110.2	115.2	131.1	141.8
Alabama	67.0	82.2	93.7	112.0	Montana	17.4	22.6	23.2	24.2
Alaska	14.3	17.2	18.4	23.0	Nebraska	32.3	34.3	38.0	39.8
Arizona	104.8	128.2	149.6	186.8	Nevada	44.6	63.5	80.9	99.8
Arkansas	45.0	52.2	53.8	60.9	New Hampshire	26.7	23.8	25.4	27.2
California	573.5	565.1	577.6	610.1	New Jersey	160.8	166.8	174.3	188.7
Colorado	111.5	109.4	112.4	126.0	New Mexico	29.9	38.9	43.3	50.6
Connecticut	61.5	64.2	63.5	72.5	New York	273.3	290.4	282.6	307.5
Delaware	12.9	14.5	15.8	18.9	North Carolina	134.2	142.1	156.3	192.6
District of Columbia . . .	10.6	11.2	12.1	13.4	North Dakota	10.8	12.3	12.9	14.5
Florida	393.6	429.3	476.1	526.5	Ohio	216.4	237.0	253.1	275.7
Georgia	143.6	173.9	174.0	215.8	Oklahoma	67.3	79.5	85.1	93.6
Hawaii	22.1	28.1	34.4	35.5	Oregon	62.6	72.1	78.3	90.7
Idaho	24.1	25.7	27.6	32.0	Pennsylvania	194.0	204.7	219.6	244.6
Illinois	246.8	269.0	275.1	307.5	Rhode Island	17.0	17.1	16.9	19.2
Indiana	111.0	125.2	120.4	130.5	South Carolina	64.3	72.7	83.0	99.3
Iowa	53.3	58.4	62.4	71.1	South Dakota	12.6	14.9	15.6	17.3
Kansas	52.6	60.0	65.3	73.4	Tennessee	100.4	112.0	128.8	156.1
Kentucky	66.0	73.5	81.1	89.3	Texas	381.8	412.4	425.4	485.5
Louisiana	66.8	71.7	76.2	79.6	Utah	35.5	40.9	43.9	43.6
Maine	27.6	28.8	30.7	33.6	Vermont	12.1	13.0	14.5	14.2
Maryland	100.5	117.6	120.8	140.6	Virginia	130.0	150.1	158.3	186.0
Massachusetts	112.3	115.9	118.3	141.7	Washington	112.4	116.3	132.3	147.6
Michigan	185.0	203.5	207.4	213.4	West Virginia	22.9	28.1	28.9	36.0
Minnesota	96.3	122.6	126.7	137.4	Wisconsin	91.6	105.5	105.9	116.8
Mississippi	38.7	48.0	51.5	58.1	Wyoming	9.6	10.6	11.4	13.2

Source: NATIONAL ASSOCIATION OF REALTORS®, Washington, DC, *Real Estate Outlook: Market Trends & Insights*, monthly (copyright). See Internet site <http://www.realtor.org/research>.

Table 943. Existing Apartment Condos and Co-ops—Units Sold and Median Sales Price by Region: 1990 to 2004

[272 represents 272,000. Data shown here reflect revisions from prior estimates. For definition of median, see Guide to Tabular Presentation. For composition of regions, see map inside front cover]

Year	Units sold (1,000)					Median sales price (dol.)				
	Total	North-east	Mid-west	South	West	U.S.	North-east	Mid-west	South	West
1990	272	73	55	80	64	85,200	110,200	70,200	66,800	105,200
1995	333	108	66	96	63	87,400	94,800	90,700	70,600	105,300
1996	370	120	72	105	73	90,900	97,500	95,200	73,500	109,900
1997	407	134	79	111	83	95,500	101,100	99,100	76,300	118,300
1998	471	157	92	126	95	100,600	103,400	106,400	80,000	126,400
1999	539	183	103	147	106	108,000	112,500	114,600	84,100	132,100
2000	567	197	98	161	110	111,800	111,200	121,700	87,700	136,800
2001	599	203	114	174	108	123,200	124,200	134,900	91,700	147,200
2002	657	220	129	194	114	142,200	147,000	148,600	114,500	171,600
2003	731	251	145	210	124	165,400	182,400	162,600	132,300	204,000
2004	820	292	161	230	137	193,600	219,300	181,000	163,200	236,700

Source: NATIONAL ASSOCIATION OF REALTORS®, Washington, DC, *Real Estate Outlook: Market Trends & Insights*, monthly (copyright). See Internet site <http://www.realtor.org/research>.

Table 944. New Apartments Completed and Rented in 3 Months by Region: 2000 to 2004

[226.2 represents 226,200. Structures with five or more units, privately-financed, nonsubsidized, unfurnished rental apartments. Based on sample and subject to sampling variability; see source for details. For composition of regions, see map, inside front cover]

Year and rent	Number (1,000)					Percent rented in 3 months				
	U.S.	North-east	Mid-west	South	West	U.S.	North-east	Mid-west	South	West
2000	226.2	14.8	39.5	125.9	45.9	72	85	76	67	77
2002	204.1	19.4	34.5	96.2	54.0	59	51	69	57	58
2003	166.5	19.8	35.5	72.0	39.2	61	72	62	56	63
2004, prel.	155.0	13.1	31.7	73.0	37.1	62	75	59	60	65
Less than $650	18.7	0.1	8.1	8.1	2.4	70	89	71	67	77
$650 to $749	19.3	0.2	5.5	12.0	1.6	60	93	47	64	69
$750 to $849	18.0	0.2	5.3	9.1	3.5	66	100	67	64	67
$850 to $949	17.9	0.5	4.3	9.7	3.4	53	21	42	54	68
$950 to $1,049	14.5	0.4	1.9	8.5	3.6	61	89	67	55	66
$1,050 or more	66.6	11.7	6.6	25.6	22.6	63	77	57	58	62
Median monthly asking rent (dol.) . . .	$947	(¹)	$791	$925	(¹)	(X)	(X)	(X)	(X)	(X)

X Not applicable.   ¹ Over $1,050.

Source: U.S. Census Bureau, *Current Housing Reports*, Series H130, *Market Absorption of Apartments*, and unpublished data. See Internet site: <http://www.census.gov/prod/www/abs/apart.html>.

Construction and Housing   625

Table 945. **Total Housing Inventory for the United States: 1980 to 2004**

[In thousands (87,739 represents 87,739,000), except percent. Based on the Current Population Survey and the Housing Vacancy Survey and subject to sampling error; see source and Appendix III for details]

Item	1980	1985	1990	1995	1999	2000	2001	2002 [1]	2003	2004
All housing units	87,739	97,333	106,283	112,655	119,044	119,628	121,480	119,297	120,834	122,187
Vacant	8,101	9,446	12,059	12,669	14,116	13,908	14,470	14,332	15,274	15,599
Year-round vacant	5,996	7,400	9,128	9,570	10,848	10,439	10,916	10,771	11,631	11,884
For rent.	1,575	2,221	2,662	2,946	3,119	3,024	3,203	3,347	3,676	3,802
For sale only	734	1,006	1,064	1,022	1,184	1,148	1,301	1,220	1,308	1,307
Rented or sold	623	664	660	810	956	856	882	842	976	991
Held off market.	3,064	3,510	4,742	4,793	5,589	5,411	5,530	5,362	5,671	5,784
Occasional use.	814	977	1,485	1,667	1,948	1,892	1,887	1,819	1,989	1,967
Usual residence elsewhere . . .	568	659	1,068	801	965	1,037	1,064	995	994	1,068
Other	1,683	1,875	2,189	2,325	2,676	2,482	2,579	2,548	2,688	2,749
Seasonal [2]	2,106	2,046	2,931	3,099	3,268	3,469	3,554	3,561	3,643	3,715
Total occupied	79,638	87,887	94,224	99,985	104,928	105,720	107,010	104,965	105,560	106,588
Owner	52,223	56,152	60,248	64,739	70,097	71,250	72,593	71,278	72,054	73,575
Renter	27,415	31,736	33,976	35,246	34,831	34,470	34,417	33,687	33,506	33,013
PERCENT DISTRIBUTION										
All housing units	100.0	100.0	100.0	100.0	100.0	100.0	100.0	100.0	100.0	100.0
Vacant	9.2	9.7	11.3	11.2	11.9	11.6	11.9	12.0	12.6	12.8
Total occupied	90.8	90.3	88.7	88.8	88.1	88.4	88.1	88.0	87.4	87.2
Owner	59.5	57.7	56.7	57.5	58.9	59.6	59.8	59.7	59.6	60.2
Renter	31.2	32.6	32.0	31.3	29.3	28.8	28.3	28.3	27.7	27.0

[1] Revised. Based on 2000 census controls. [2] Beginning 1990, includes vacant seasonal mobile homes. For years shown, seasonal vacant housing units were underreported prior to 1990.

Source: U.S. Census Bureau, "Housing Vacancies and Home Ownership"; <http://www.census.gov/hhes/www/hvs.html>.

Table 946. **Occupied Housing Inventory by Age of Householder: 1985 to 2004**

[In thousands (87,887 represents 87,887,000). Based on the Current Population Survey/Housing Vacancy Survey; See source for details]

Age of householder	1985	1990	1995	1998	1999	2000	2001	2002 [1]	2003	2004
Total [2]	87,887	94,224	99,986	103,534	104,929	105,719	107,009	104,965	105,560	106,588
Less than 25 years old . . .	5,483	5,143	5,502	5,750	6,000	6,221	6,460	6,372	6,441	6,538
25 to 29 years old.	9,543	9,508	8,662	8,666	8,661	8,482	8,358	8,231	8,213	8,491
30 to 34 years old.	10,288	11,213	11,206	10,494	10,400	10,219	10,301	10,176	10,084	9,865
35 to 39 years old.	9,615	10,914	11,993	12,026	11,950	11,834	11,587	10,924	10,777	10,438
40 to 44 years old.	7,919	9,893	11,151	12,141	12,206	12,377	12,504	11,839	11,748	11,768
45 to 49 years old.	6,517	8,038	10,080	10,744	10,973	11,164	11,529	11,204	11,341	11,583
50 to 54 years old.	6,157	6,532	7,882	9,040	9,412	9,834	10,288	10,123	10,194	10,316
55 to 59 years old.	6,558	6,182	6,355	7,051	7,389	7,602	7,827	8,261	8,550	8,928
60 to 64 years old.	6,567	6,446	5,860	6,055	6,183	6,215	6,345	6,422	6,776	7,112
65 to 69 years old.	5,976	6,407	6,088	5,852	5,845	5,816	5,749	5,644	5,570	5,656
70 to 74 years old.	5,003	5,397	5,693	5,583	5,621	5,567	5,496	5,137	5,163	5,065
75 years old and over	7,517	8,546	9,514	10,131	10,289	10,388	10,565	10,632	10,703	10,827

[1] Revised. Based on 2000 census controls. [2] 1985 total includes ages not reported. Thereafter cases allocated by age.

Source: U.S. Census Bureau, "Housing Vacancies and Home Ownership"; <http://www.census.gov/hhes/www/hvs.html>.

Table 947. **Vacancy Rates for Housing Units—Characteristics: 2000 to 2004**

[In percent. Rate is relationship between vacant housing for rent or for sale and the total rental and homeowner supply, which comprises occupied units, units rented or sold and awaiting occupancy, and vacant units available for rent or sale. Based on the Current Population/Housing Vacancy Survey; see source for details. For composition of regions, see map, inside front cover]

Characteristic	Rental units				Homeowner units			
	2000	2002 [1]	2003	2004	2000	2002 [1]	2003	2004
Total units	8.0	8.9	9.8	10.2	1.6	1.7	1.8	1.7
Northeast.	5.6	5.8	6.6	7.3	1.2	1.2	1.2	1.1
Midwest.	8.8	10.1	10.8	12.2	1.3	1.8	1.7	2.0
South	10.5	11.6	12.5	12.6	1.9	1.9	2.1	2.0
West	5.8	6.9	7.7	7.5	1.5	1.6	1.6	1.4
Units in structure:								
1 unit.	7.0	8.0	8.4	9.0	1.5	1.5	1.6	1.6
2 units or more	8.7	9.7	10.7	11.1	4.7	4.8	5.5	5.4
5 units or more	9.2	10.4	11.4	11.7	5.8	4.7	5.3	4.7
Units with—								
3 rooms or less	10.3	11.3	12.2	12.3	10.4	8.9	8.1	9.0
4 rooms	8.2	9.0	10.0	10.3	2.9	2.8	3.4	3.2
5 rooms	6.9	8.3	8.9	9.4	2.0	2.0	2.1	2.0
6 rooms or more	5.2	6.2	7.0	8.3	1.1	1.2	1.3	1.2

[1] Revised. Based on 2000 census controls.

Source: U.S. Census Bureau, "Housing Vacancies and Home Ownership"; <http://www.census.gov/hhes/www/hvs.html>.

626 Construction and Housing

Table 948. Housing Units and Tenure—States: 2003

[120,879 represents 120,879,000. The American Community Survey universe is limited to the household population and excludes the population living in institutions, college dormitories, and other group quarters. Based on a sample and subject to sampling variability; see Appendix III]

State	Housing units						Housing tenure			
	Total (1,000)	Occu-pied (1,000)	Vacant (1,000) Total	For sea-sonal use [1]	Vacancy rate Home-owner [2]	Renter [3]	Owner-occupied units Total (1,000)	Average house-hold size	Renter-occupied units Total (1,000)	Average house-hold size
United States . . .	120,879	108,420	12,460	3,757	1.7	8.0	72,419	2.72	36,001	2.39
Alabama	2,032	1,743	288	55	2.2	12.3	1,250	2.59	494	2.32
Alaska.	268	229	39	21	1.6	6.2	143	2.85	86	2.56
Arizona	2,393	2,049	344	162	2.1	10.4	1,399	2.74	650	2.52
Arkansas	1,214	1,076	138	23	1.9	10.0	730	2.50	346	2.38
California.	12,657	11,857	800	242	0.9	4.8	6,883	3.00	4,974	2.81
Colorado	1,974	1,821	152	24	1.5	11.7	1,283	2.54	539	2.21
Connecticut	1,410	1,323	87	22	1.1	5.2	896	2.70	427	2.22
Delaware.	357	304	54	28	1.3	11.0	221	2.71	83	2.33
District of Columbia . . .	272	247	26	2	1.4	4.7	104	2.28	143	2.04
Florida.	7,789	6,638	1,151	582	2.0	11.2	4,662	2.54	1,975	2.41
Georgia	3,576	3,153	424	98	2.3	10.9	2,152	2.79	1,001	2.44
Hawaii.	476	419	57	27	0.6	5.1	237	3.07	182	2.71
Idaho	564	503	61	27	2.4	7.1	374	2.71	129	2.49
Illinois	5,031	4,625	406	30	1.8	7.9	3,172	2.77	1,453	2.43
Indiana	2,651	2,351	301	69	1.8	9.8	1,688	2.68	662	2.25
Iowa	1,270	1,158	112	20	1.5	8.3	853	2.58	305	2.11
Kansas	1,171	1,059	112	13	1.9	8.8	726	2.63	332	2.21
Kentucky	1,815	1,607	207	39	2.2	7.6	1,129	2.56	478	2.32
Louisiana	1,897	1,673	224	25	1.3	9.5	1,123	2.68	550	2.46
Maine	671	535	136	102	1.1	4.9	378	2.51	157	2.05
Maryland	2,219	2,048	171	38	1.0	6.6	1,421	2.77	627	2.30
Massachusetts	2,661	2,436	225	101	0.7	5.3	1,572	2.78	864	2.15
Michigan	4,383	3,884	499	211	1.8	7.5	2,893	2.67	991	2.13
Minnesota	2,167	2,012	155	54	0.9	7.0	1,542	2.59	470	1.98
Mississippi	1,207	1,056	151	24	2.4	9.7	739	2.69	316	2.53
Missouri.	2,533	2,285	248	23	1.6	8.3	1,608	2.55	677	2.13
Montana	420	366	54	21	1.5	5.9	252	2.50	114	2.32
Nebraska	746	675	71	15	1.8	8.7	458	2.64	218	2.20
Nevada	936	834	102	23	2.2	11.4	516	2.76	318	2.46
New Hampshire	569	493	76	53	0.8	5.3	359	2.68	134	2.15
New Jersey	3,398	3,123	276	97	1.2	6.1	2,081	2.86	1,041	2.40
New Mexico	816	698	118	35	2.7	9.6	485	2.75	213	2.36
New York	7,802	7,119	684	216	1.4	4.8	3,860	2.80	3,258	2.39
North Carolina	3,779	3,271	508	166	1.8	10.9	2,234	2.55	1,036	2.36
North Dakota	297	254	42	16	1.2	8.2	171	2.60	84	1.97
Ohio	4,919	4,480	438	47	1.9	9.4	3,144	2.61	1,337	2.20
Oklahoma	1,553	1,341	211	39	3.4	11.0	912	2.63	429	2.33
Oregon	1,515	1,409	106	18	1.6	7.2	890	2.57	519	2.31
Pennsylvania	5,365	4,801	564	179	1.6	6.5	3,447	2.63	1,354	2.12
Rhode Island	446	412	34	12	0.7	4.9	259	2.70	152	2.21
South Carolina	1,855	1,568	287	96	2.0	13.6	1,095	2.66	473	2.32
South Dakota	337	299	38	12	1.7	6.3	207	2.61	92	2.12
Tennessee	2,553	2,296	257	48	2.1	10.2	1,591	2.56	705	2.28
Texas	8,658	7,635	1,024	202	2.0	11.6	4,918	2.96	2,717	2.57
Utah	827	752	75	23	2.1	10.7	551	3.22	201	2.65
Vermont	302	242	60	46	1.5	5.4	172	2.63	70	2.08
Virginia	3,059	2,790	269	66	1.4	8.2	1,929	2.67	861	2.32
Washington	2,567	2,382	185	54	1.4	6.2	1,532	2.66	850	2.25
West Virginia	855	732	123	39	2.1	7.2	540	2.53	191	2.09
Wisconsin	2,417	2,159	258	155	1.1	6.1	1,492	2.61	667	2.13
Wyoming	230	199	31	15	1.8	5.8	144	2.52	55	2.28

[1] For seasonal, recreational or occasional use. [2] Proportion of the homeowner housing inventory which is vacant for sale.
[3] Proportion of the rental inventory which is vacant for rent.

Source: U.S. Census Bureau, American FactFinder, 2003 American Community Survey Summary Tables, H002. Occupancy Status, H003. Tenure, H004. Vacancy Status, Internet site <http://factfinder.census.gov/>; and American Community Survey, Multi-Year Profiles 2003—Demographic Characteristics, Internet site <http://www.census.gov/acs/www/Products/Profiles/Chg/2003/ACS/index.htm>; (accessed 13 July 2005)

Construction and Housing **627**

Table 949. **Housing Units—Characteristics by Tenure and Region: 2003**

[In thousands of units (120,777 represents 120,777,000), except as indicated. As of fall. Based on the American Housing Survey; see Appendix III. For composition of regions, see map, inside front cover]

| Characteristic | Total housing units | Seasonal | Year-round units | | | | | | | Vacant |
| | | | Occupied | | | | | | | |
			Total	Owner	Renter	Northeast	Midwest	South	West	
Total units	120,777	3,566	105,842	72,238	33,604	20,133	24,488	38,145	23,077	11,369
Percent distribution	100.0	3.0	87.6	59.8	27.8	16.7	20.3	31.6	19.1	9.4
Units in structure:										
Single family detached	74,916	2,034	67,753	59,642	8,111	10,990	17,334	25,003	14,426	5,129
Single family attached	7,227	205	6,272	3,679	2,593	1,828	1,020	2,111	1,313	750
2 to 4 units	9,965	102	8,474	1,426	7,048	2,599	1,923	2,120	1,832	1,390
5 to 9 units	6,012	73	5,135	501	4,634	992	1,046	1,763	1,334	803
10 to 19 units	5,433	77	4,468	485	3,983	751	859	1,731	1,127	887
20 to 49 units	3,964	116	3,294	389	2,905	919	550	834	990	554
50 or more units	4,289	129	3,592	601	2,991	1,485	617	722	769	568
Manufactured/ mobile home or trailer	8,971	829	6,854	5,514	1,340	568	1,140	3,861	1,286	1,288
Year structure built:										
Median year	1971	1972	1971	1972	1968	1955	1965	1976	1974	1970
1980 or later	38,692	1,110	34,071	25,343	8,727	3,629	6,450	15,734	8,253	3,512
1970 to 1979	23,502	836	20,474	13,359	7,115	2,767	4,332	8,298	5,075	2,192
1960 to 1969	15,482	480	13,781	9,187	4,594	2,480	3,188	4,916	3,197	1,221
1950 to 1959	13,433	400	11,933	8,696	3,237	2,610	3,060	3,675	2,587	1,101
1940 to 1949	8,152	237	7,098	4,643	2,456	1,652	1,644	2,270	1,531	816
1939 and earlier	21,513	501	18,486	11,009	7,475	6,993	5,813	3,248	2,431	2,527
Stories in structure: [1]										
1 story	39,248	1,378	34,244	25,777	8,468	1,214	3,999	18,778	10,254	3,626
2 stories	39,318	865	34,915	22,715	12,199	6,173	9,849	10,426	8,467	3,538
3 stories	25,118	285	22,842	15,560	7,282	8,178	8,206	4,056	2,402	1,991
4 to 6 stories	5,802	101	5,126	2,246	2,880	2,963	983	684	496	576
7 or more stories	2,320	108	1,862	426	1,436	1,037	312	341	173	351
Foundation: [2]										
Full basement	26,201	315	24,449	21,908	2,542	8,484	10,503	3,646	1,817	1,436
Partial building	9,250	160	8,618	7,701	917	2,382	3,543	1,571	1,122	472
Crawlspace	21,917	870	18,869	15,506	3,363	773	2,601	9,907	5,587	2,178
Concrete slab	24,069	686	21,674	17,909	3,765	1,133	1,619	11,797	7,125	1,709
Other	706	207	416	299	117	46	88	194	88	83
Equipment:										
Lacking complete facilities	5,704	560	1,553	303	1,250	317	352	450	434	3,591
With complete facilities	115,073	3,005	104,289	71,935	32,354	19,816	24,136	37,695	22,643	7,778
Kitchen sink	119,763	3,381	105,635	72,199	33,435	20,098	24,442	38,100	22,995	10,747
Refrigerator	117,605	3,219	105,667	72,166	33,501	20,111	24,444	38,085	23,028	8,719
Cooking stove or range	116,761	3,029	105,054	71,918	33,135	19,985	24,331	37,844	22,893	8,678
Burners only, no stove or range	159	-	143	63	81	40	22	52	29	16
Microwave oven only	477	49	340	146	194	45	86	140	69	88
Dishwasher	69,658	1,222	63,776	50,303	13,473	10,537	13,455	24,244	15,540	4,660
Washing machine	91,336	1,508	86,029	69,207	16,822	14,923	20,389	32,591	18,126	3,800
Clothes dryer	89,071	1,794	82,538	67,262	15,276	13,802	20,149	31,111	17,476	4,740
Disposal in kitchen sink	54,372	915	49,624	35,559	14,064	4,808	11,661	16,907	16,248	3,832
Trash compactor	4,270	105	3,913	3,247	667	571	605	1,550	1,186	252
Main heating equipment:										
Warm-air furnace	73,404	1,571	65,380	48,111	17,270	8,142	19,792	22,550	14,897	6,453
Steam or hot water system	14,437	104	13,257	7,801	5,456	9,650	2,152	647	808	1,076
Electric heat pump	13,188	515	11,347	8,278	3,069	283	586	9,196	1,282	1,325
Built-in electric units	5,758	356	4,760	2,190	2,570	1,172	1,061	887	1,640	642
Floor, wall, or pipeless furnace	6,074	175	5,322	2,293	3,030	430	420	1,426	3,046	577
Room heaters with flue	1,747	101	1,432	812	620	176	208	730	318	214
Room heaters without flue	1,901	58	1,509	996	513	29	33	1,393	55	334
Portable electric heaters	899	77	731	346	386	13	18	507	194	90
Stoves	1,346	214	1,040	864	176	153	163	376	348	92
Fireplaces with inserts	152	13	139	124	14	9	25	43	62	-
Fireplaces without inserts	97	39	52	42	10	1	5	24	22	5
Other	475	57	285	124	161	29	19	171	66	133
Cooking stoves	175	13	149	58	91	46	-	64	39	13
None	1,126	273	439	200	240	2	6	132	299	414
Air conditioning: Central	67,991	1,165	61,880	47,098	14,783	5,582	15,527	30,665	10,106	4,945
Percent of total units	56.3	32.7	58.5	65.2	44.0	27.7	63.4	80.4	43.8	43.5
One or more room units	29,743	770	26,364	15,201	11,165	10,364	6,298	6,360	3,344	2,608
Source of water:										
Public system or private company	104,567	2,237	92,324	60,327	31,997	16,972	20,551	33,162	21,638	10,007
Percent of total units	86.6	62.7	87.2	83.5	95.2	84.3	83.9	86.9	93.8	88.0
Well serving 1 to 5 units	15,426	1,112	13,097	11,566	1,531	3,072	3,864	4,774	1,387	1,217
Other	784	217	422	346	77	89	73	208	52	145
Means of sewage disposal:										
Public sewer	94,618	1,721	84,064	53,069	30,996	15,989	19,737	27,953	20,386	8,833
Percent of total units	78.3	48.3	79.4	73.5	92.2	79.4	80.6	73.3	88.3	77.7
Septic tank, cesspool, chemical toilet	25,741	1,652	21,697	19,129	2,568	4,138	4,735	10,149	2,675	2,392
Other	417	192	81	40	41	6	16	43	16	144

- Represents or rounds to zero. [1] Excludes mobile homes; includes basements and finished attics. [2] Limited to single-family units.

Source: U.S. Census Bureau, Current Housing Reports, Series H150/03, *American Housing Survey for the United States.* See Internet site <http://www.census.gov/hhes/www/housing/ahs/nationaldata.html>.

Table 950. Housing Units by Units in Structure and State: 2003

[In percent, except as indicated (120,879 represents 120,879,000). The American Community Survey universe is limited to the household population and excludes the population living in institutions, college dormitories, and other group quarters. Based on a sample and subject to sampling variability; see Appendix III]

State	Total housing units (1,000)	Percent of units by units in structure—								
		1-unit detached	1-unit attached	2 units	3 or 4 units	5 to 9 units	10 to 19 units	20 or more units	Mobile homes	Boat, RV, van, etc.
U.S....	120,879	60.8	5.5	4.2	4.8	5.0	4.6	7.8	7.2	0.1
AL........	2,032	67.4	1.7	2.5	3.6	4.8	2.9	2.8	14.3	(Z)
AK........	268	59.1	7.6	4.7	7.8	6.3	2.6	4.4	7.6	(Z)
AZ........	2,393	59.2	5.4	1.3	3.0	4.3	5.5	7.8	13.1	0.5
AR........	1,214	71.3	2.1	3.7	3.4	2.4	2.5	1.9	12.6	0.1
CA........	12,657	57.1	7.1	2.4	5.8	6.4	5.5	11.0	4.4	0.1
CO........	1,974	63.8	6.3	1.7	3.6	4.4	6.2	8.6	5.4	(Z)
CT........	1,410	57.7	6.1	8.7	9.4	5.2	3.5	8.4	1.0	0.5
DE........	357	56.2	13.0	2.1	2.4	4.4	5.3	5.3	11.1	(Z)
DC........	272	12.5	26.7	2.7	7.7	8.0	12.3	30.0	0.1	(Z)
FL........	7,789	52.9	5.8	2.7	4.3	5.4	5.7	12.4	10.8	0.1
GA........	3,576	65.7	2.4	2.4	3.4	5.3	5.6	3.4	11.7	0.1
HI........	476	52.4	5.6	3.0	4.7	6.9	4.2	23.0	0.2	(Z)
ID........	564	71.4	2.3	2.6	4.1	2.4	1.8	3.6	11.6	0.2
IL........	5,031	58.5	5.3	6.0	7.0	6.6	4.3	9.4	2.9	(Z)
IN........	2,651	71.2	3.3	2.8	3.8	4.8	3.6	3.7	6.6	(Z)
IA........	1,270	74.6	2.6	3.6	3.2	3.0	3.8	4.3	4.8	(Z)
KS........	1,171	72.1	3.1	3.0	3.8	4.5	4.0	4.5	5.0	(Z)
KY........	1,815	66.5	2.3	2.8	3.5	4.5	2.8	2.9	14.7	0.1
LA........	1,897	64.0	4.1	3.9	5.0	3.4	3.4	3.6	12.6	(Z)
ME........	671	67.1	2.2	5.8	5.5	4.3	2.1	3.0	10.2	(Z)
MD........	2,219	52.5	20.4	2.0	2.8	5.5	8.5	6.4	1.9	(Z)
MA........	2,661	53.5	4.6	10.7	11.5	5.8	4.1	8.8	1.0	(Z)
MI........	4,383	70.9	4.6	2.8	3.1	4.3	3.6	4.5	6.2	(Z)
MN........	2,167	69.7	6.3	2.8	2.1	2.3	2.8	10.6	3.5	(Z)
MS........	1,207	69.8	1.2	3.3	3.8	3.7	2.0	1.7	14.5	(Z)
MO........	2,533	69.9	3.4	3.6	5.0	4.6	2.7	3.7	7.1	(Z)
MT........	420	69.0	2.8	3.1	4.8	2.4	1.6	2.7	13.5	(Z)
NE........	746	72.4	3.4	2.0	3.0	3.8	4.4	6.0	4.9	(Z)
NV........	936	55.6	4.2	2.0	9.2	9.3	4.6	6.9	7.9	0.4
NH........	569	63.6	5.1	6.0	5.8	4.4	3.3	5.5	6.3	(Z)
NJ........	3,398	54.1	9.3	9.6	6.6	5.1	5.6	8.9	0.9	(Z)
NM........	816	61.8	4.1	2.0	4.1	3.0	2.5	3.7	18.7	0.1
NY........	7,802	41.0	4.8	11.5	7.7	5.5	4.1	22.6	2.6	0.1
NC........	3,779	63.6	2.7	2.3	3.1	4.2	3.8	2.5	17.6	0.1
ND........	297	63.1	4.2	2.6	4.3	4.3	5.3	8.9	7.3	(Z)
OH........	4,919	68.5	4.3	4.7	4.6	4.9	3.7	5.1	4.1	(Z)
OK........	1,553	72.2	1.9	2.2	3.2	4.1	3.4	3.4	9.4	0.1
OR........	1,515	62.6	4.0	3.7	4.2	5.0	4.1	7.2	9.1	0.2
PA........	5,365	56.7	18.4	5.1	4.6	3.2	2.6	4.8	4.7	(Z)
RI........	446	53.9	3.0	13.1	13.4	5.7	3.3	6.3	1.4	(Z)
SC........	1,855	60.8	2.3	2.7	3.8	6.0	3.2	3.2	17.9	0.1
SD........	337	66.5	2.6	3.1	3.6	3.0	4.4	5.6	11.2	(Z)
TN........	2,553	68.5	2.5	3.4	3.6	4.9	3.9	4.0	9.1	0.1
TX........	8,658	64.2	2.6	2.3	3.5	5.7	7.4	6.2	8.0	0.1
UT........	827	68.3	5.4	3.7	5.4	2.7	3.2	6.6	4.5	(Z)
VT........	302	64.9	3.0	7.5	6.8	6.1	1.6	3.1	7.0	(Z)
VA........	3,059	61.3	10.2	2.2	3.0	5.4	6.1	5.3	6.4	(Z)
WA........	2,567	61.8	2.9	3.1	4.1	4.9	6.4	9.0	7.7	0.2
WV........	855	67.8	1.8	2.8	3.4	2.9	1.5	2.4	17.5	(Z)
WI........	2,417	65.5	3.3	7.5	4.1	4.8	3.1	5.6	6.1	(Z)
WY........	230	65.6	3.2	2.7	5.2	3.3	2.1	2.5	15.2	0.1

Z Less than .05 percent.

Source: U.S. Census Bureau, American FactFinder, 2003 American Community Survey Summary Tables, H027. Units in Structure, Internet site <http://factfinder.census.gov/>; and American Community Survey, Multi-Year Profiles 2003—Housing Characteristics, Internet site <http://www.census.gov/acs/www/Products/Profiles/Chg/2003/ACS/index.htm>; (accessed 25 July 2005)

Construction and Housing 629

Table 951. Housing Units—Size of Units and Lot: 2003

[In thousands (120,777 represents 120,777,000), except as indicated. As of fall. Based on the American Housing Survey; see Appendix III. For composition of regions, see map inside front cover]

Item	Total hous- ing units	Sea- sonal	Year-round units Occupied Total	Owner	Renter	North- east	Mid- west	South	West	Vacant
Total units	120,777	3,566	105,842	72,238	33,604	20,133	24,488	38,145	23,077	11,369
Rooms:										
1 room.	520	54	344	13	331	131	54	32	127	122
2 rooms	1,432	130	984	58	320	157	210	297	318	
3 rooms	10,939	621	8,617	982	7,635	2,220	1,695	2,473	2,228	1,701
4 rooms	23,360	1,291	18,558	6,974	11,584	3,377	4,071	6,611	4,499	3,511
5 rooms	27,961	793	24,415	16,805	7,610	3,934	5,758	9,689	5,034	2,753
6 rooms	24,657	418	22,554	19,055	3,499	4,314	5,375	8,412	4,453	1,685
7 rooms	14,662	152	13,835	12,639	1,195	2,552	3,354	5,022	2,908	675
8 rooms or more	17,246	107	16,536	15,712	823	3,285	4,023	5,696	3,531	604
Complete bathrooms:										
No bathrooms	2,263	500	642	270	371	169	131	214	128	1,121
1 bathroom	48,264	1,690	40,814	17,620	23,193	9,982	10,289	12,427	8,116	5,760
1 and one-half bathrooms	17,626	314	16,240	12,716	3,523	3,939	5,206	4,369	2,726	1,072
2 or more bathrooms	52,625	1,062	48,147	41,631	6,516	6,044	8,862	21,135	12,107	3,415
Square footage of unit:										
Single detached and mobile homes [1]	83,887	2,863	74,607	65,157	9,450	11,557	18,474	28,864	15,711	6,417
Less than 500	1,235	345	686	426	261	99	99	315	173	203
500 to 749	3,049	485	2,046	1,267	779	269	455	935	386	518
750 to 999	6,697	520	5,248	3,804	1,444	636	1,394	2,195	1,023	928
1,000 to 1,499	20,354	539	18,057	15,118	2,940	2,048	4,211	7,576	4,223	1,758
1,500 to 1,999	18,807	302	17,491	15,748	1,743	2,405	4,019	6,830	4,236	1,014
2,000 to 2,499	12,605	200	11,827	11,128	699	1,979	3,102	4,363	2,382	578
2,500 to 2,999	6,439	91	6,047	5,798	248	1,148	1,517	2,247	1,135	302
3,000 to 3,999	5,784	78	5,434	5,235	198	1,107	1,431	1,841	1,054	272
4,000 or more	3,379	30	3,145	2,968	178	743	823	1,071	508	204
Other [2]	5,537	272	4,626	3,665	961	1,122	1,422	1,491	591	639
Median square footage	1,708	974	1,756	1,822	1,299	1,950	1,794	1,695	1,707	1,352
Lot size:										
Single detached and attached units and mobile homes	88,780	2,869	79,003	67,288	11,715	12,999	19,119	30,432	16,452	6,908
Less than one-eighth acre	12,590	607	10,581	8,035	2,545	2,187	2,552	2,824	3,019	1,402
One-eighth to one-quarter acre	24,985	724	22,169	18,190	3,978	2,726	5,611	7,239	6,593	2,092
One-quarter to one-half acre.	16,817	495	15,297	13,503	1,795	2,418	3,759	5,953	3,168	1,025
One-half up to one acre.	11,393	285	10,464	9,351	1,113	2,028	2,225	4,929	1,282	644
1 up to 5 acres	16,005	456	14,428	12,723	1,705	2,748	3,065	7,033	1,582	1,120
5 up to 10 acres.	2,582	101	2,331	2,185	147	318	656	1,014	343	150
10 acres or more	4,408	202	3,733	3,301	431	574	1,252	1,442	465	474
Median acreage	0.35	0.30	0.36	0.39	0.23	0.41	0.34	0.47	0.22	0.25

[1] Does not include selected vacant units.   [2] Represents units not reported or size unknown.

Source: U.S. Census Bureau, Current Housing Reports, Series H150/03, *American Housing Survey for the United States.* See Internet site <http://www.census.gov/hhes/www/housing/ahs/nationaldata.html>.

Table 952. Occupied Housing Units—Tenure by Race of Householder: 1991 to 2003

[In thousands (93,147 represents 93,147,000), except percent. As of fall. Based on the American Housing Survey; see Appendix III]

Race of householder and tenure	1991	1993	1995	1997	1999	2001	2003 [1]
ALL RACES [2]							
Occupied units, total	93,147	94,724	97,693	99,487	102,803	106,261	105,842
Owner-occupied.	59,796	61,252	63,544	65,487	68,796	72,265	72,238
Percent of occupied.	64.2	64.7	65.0	65.8	66.9	68.0	68.3
Renter-occupied.	33,351	33,472	34,150	34,000	34,007	33,996	33,604
WHITE [3]							
Occupied units, total	79,140	80,029	81,611	82,154	83,624	85,292	87,483
Owner-occupied.	53,749	54,878	56,507	57,781	60,041	62,465	63,126
Percent of occupied.	67.9	68.6	69.2	70.3	71.8	73.2	72.2
Renter-occupied.	25,391	25,151	25,104	24,372	23,583	22,826	24,357
BLACK [3]							
Occupied units, total	10,832	11,128	11,773	12,085	12,936	13,292	13,004
Owner-occupied.	4,635	4,788	5,137	5,457	6,013	6,318	6,193
Percent of occupied.	42.8	43.0	43.6	45.2	46.5	47.5	47.6
Renter-occupied.	6,197	6,340	6,637	6,628	6,923	6,974	6,811
HISPANIC ORIGIN [4]							
Occupied units, total	6,239	6,614	7,757	8,513	9,041	9,814	11,038
Owner-occupied.	2,423	2,788	3,245	3,646	4,087	4,731	5,106
Percent of occupied.	38.8	42.2	41.8	42.8	45.2	48.2	46.3
Renter-occupied.	3,816	3,826	4,512	4,867	4,955	5,083	5,931

[1] Based on 2000 census controls.   [2] Includes other races, not shown separately.   [3] The 2003 American Housing Survey (AHS) allowed respondents to choose more than one race. Beginning in 2003, data represent householders who selected this race group only and exclude householders reporting more than one race. The AHS in prior years only allowed respondents to report one race group. See also comments on race in the text for Section 1 and the below cited source.   [4] Persons of Hispanic origin may be of any race.

Source: U.S. Census Bureau, Current Housing Reports, Series H150/91, H150/93, H150/95RV, H150/97, H150/99, H150/01, and H150/03, *American Housing Survey for the United States.* See Internet site <http://www.census.gov/hhes/www/housing /ahs/nationaldata.html>.

Table 953. Homeownership Rates by Age of Householder and Household Type: 1985 to 2004

[In percent. Represents the proportion of owner households to the total number of occupied households. Based on the Current Population Survey/Housing Vacancy Survey; see source and Appendix III for details]

Age of householder and household type	1985	1990	1995	1998	1999	2000	2001	2002	2003	2004
United States	**63.9**	**63.9**	**64.7**	**66.3**	**66.8**	**67.4**	**67.8**	**67.9**	**68.3**	**69.0**
AGE OF HOUSEHOLDER										
Less than 25 years old.	17.2	15.7	15.9	18.2	19.9	21.7	22.5	22.9	22.8	25.2
25 to 29 years old.	37.7	35.2	34.4	36.2	36.5	38.1	38.9	38.8	39.8	40.2
30 to 34 years old.	54.0	51.8	53.1	53.6	53.8	54.6	54.8	54.9	56.5	57.4
35 to 39 years old.	65.4	63.0	62.1	63.7	64.4	65.0	65.5	65.2	65.1	66.2
40 to 44 years old.	71.4	69.8	68.6	70.0	69.9	70.6	70.8	71.7	71.3	71.9
45 to 49 years old.	74.3	73.9	73.7	73.9	74.5	74.7	75.4	74.8	75.4	76.3
50 to 54 years old.	77.5	76.8	77.0	77.8	77.8	78.5	78.2	77.9	77.9	78.2
55 to 59 years old.	79.2	78.8	78.8	79.8	80.7	80.4	81.0	80.8	80.9	81.2
60 to 64 years old.	79.9	79.8	80.3	82.1	81.3	80.3	81.8	81.6	81.9	82.4
65 to 69 years old.	79.5	80.0	81.0	81.9	82.9	83.0	82.4	82.9	82.5	83.2
70 to 74 years old.	76.8	78.4	80.9	82.2	82.8	82.6	82.5	82.5	82.0	84.4
75 years old and over	69.8	72.3	74.6	76.2	77.1	77.7	78.1	78.4	78.7	78.8
Less than 35 years old.	39.9	38.5	38.6	39.3	39.7	40.8	41.2	41.3	42.2	43.1
35 to 44 years old.	68.1	66.3	65.2	66.9	67.2	67.9	68.2	68.6	68.3	69.2
45 to 54 years old.	75.9	75.2	75.2	75.7	76.0	76.5	76.7	76.3	76.6	77.2
55 to 64 years old.	79.5	79.3	79.5	80.9	81.0	80.3	81.3	81.1	81.4	81.9
65 years and over.	74.8	76.3	78.1	79.3	80.1	80.4	80.3.	80.6	80.5	81.1
TYPE OF HOUSEHOLD										
Family households:										
Married-couple families	78.2	78.1	79.6	81.5	81.8	82.4	82.9	82.9	83.3	84.0
Male householder, no spouse present.	57.8	55.2	55.3	55.7	56.1	57.5	57.9	57.3	57.9	59.6
Female householder, no spouse present.	45.8	44.0	45.1	47.0	48.2	49.1	49.9	49.2	49.6	50.9
Nonfamily households:										
One-person	45.8	49.0	50.5	52.1	52.7	53.6	54.4	54.9	55.2	55.8
Male householder.	38.8	42.4	43.8	45.7	46.3	47.4	48.2	48.6	50.0	50.5
Female householder	51.3	53.6	55.4	56.9	57.6	58.1	59.0	59.6	59.1	59.9
Other:										
Male householder.	30.1	31.7	34.2	36.7	37.2	38.0	38.6	38.7	40.0	41.7
Female householder	30.6	32.5	33.0	40.3	41.5	40.6	41.0	41.9	43.1	43.5

Source: U.S. Census Bureau, "Housing Vacancies and Home Ownership". See Internet site <http://www.census.gov/hhes/www/hvs.html>.

Table 954. Homeownership Rates by State: 1985 to 2004

[In percent. See headnote, Table 953]

State	1985	1990	1995	2000	2003	2004	State	1985	1990	1995	2000	2003	2004
United States. . .	63.9	63.9	64.7	67.4	68.3	69.0	Missouri	69.2	64.0	69.4	74.2	74.0	72.4
Alabama	70.4	68.4	70.1	73.2	76.2	78.0	Montana	66.5	69.1	68.7	70.2	71.5	72.4
Alaska	61.2	58.4	60.9	66.4	70.0	67.2	Nebraska	68.5	67.3	67.1	70.2	69.5	71.2
Arizona	64.7	64.5	62.9	68.0	67.0	68.7	Nevada	57.0	55.8	58.6	64.0	64.8	65.7
Arkansas.	66.6	67.8	67.2	68.9	69.6	69.1	New Hampshire . . .	65.5	65.0	66.0	69.2	74.4	73.3
California.	54.2	53.8	55.4	57.1	58.9	59.7	New Jersey	62.3	65.0	64.9	66.2	66.9	68.8
Colorado.	63.6	59.0	64.6	68.3	71.3	71.1	New Mexico	68.2	68.6	67.0	73.7	70.3	71.5
Connecticut	69.0	67.9	68.2	70.0	73.0	71.7	New York	50.3	53.3	52.7	53.4	54.3	54.8
Delaware.	70.3	67.7	71.7	72.0	77.2	77.3	North Carolina	68.0	69.0	70.1	71.1	70.0	69.8
Dist. of Columbia . .	37.4	36.4	39.2	41.9	43.0	45.6	North Dakota	69.9	67.2	67.3	70.7	68.7	70.0
Florida	67.2	65.1	66.6	68.4	69.5	72.2	Ohio.	67.9	68.7	67.9	71.3	72.8	73.1
Georgia	62.7	64.3	66.6	69.8	71.4	70.9	Oklahoma	70.5	70.3	69.8	72.7	69.1	71.1
Hawaii	51.0	55.5	50.2	55.2	58.3	60.9	Oregon.	61.5	64.4	63.2	65.3	68.0	69.0
Idaho	71.0	69.4	72.0	70.5	74.4	73.7	Pennsylvania	71.6	73.8	71.5	74.7	73.7	74.9
Illinois.	60.6	63.0	66.4	67.9	70.7	72.7	Rhode Island	61.4	58.5	57.9	61.5	59.9	61.5
Indiana	67.6	67.0	71.0	74.9	74.4	75.8	South Carolina	72.0	71.4	71.3	76.5	75.0	76.2
Iowa	69.9	70.7	71.4	75.2	73.4	73.2	South Dakota	67.6	66.2	67.5	71.2	70.9	68.5
Kansas	68.3	69.0	67.5	69.3	70.3	69.9	Tennessee.	67.6	68.3	67.0	70.9	70.8	71.6
Kentucky.	68.5	65.8	71.2	73.4	74.4	74.3	Texas	60.5	59.7	61.4	63.8	64.5	65.6
Louisiana	70.2	67.8	65.3	68.1	67.5	70.6	Utah.	71.5	70.1	71.5	72.7	73.4	74.9
Maine	73.7	74.2	76.7	76.5	73.7	74.7	Vermont	69.5	72.6	70.4	68.7	71.4	72.0
Maryland	65.6	64.9	65.8	69.9	71.6	72.1	Virginia	68.5	69.8	68.1	73.9	75.0	73.4
Massachusetts	60.5	58.6	60.2	59.9	64.3	63.8	Washington	66.8	61.8	61.6	63.6	65.9	66.0
Michigan	70.7	72.3	72.2	77.2	75.6	77.1	West Virginia	75.9	72.0	73.1	75.9	78.1	80.3
Minnesota	70.0	68.0	73.3	76.1	77.2	76.4	Wisconsin	63.8	68.3	67.5	71.8	72.8	73.3
Mississippi.	69.6	69.4	71.1	75.2	73.4	74.0	Wyoming.	73.2	68.9	69.0	71.0	72.9	72.8

Source: U.S. Census Bureau, "Housing Vacancies and Home Ownership". See Internet site <http://www.census.gov/hhes/www/hvs.html>.

Construction and Housing 631

Table 955. Occupied Housing Units—Costs by Region: 2003

[72,238 represents 72,238,000. As of fall. Specified owner-occupied units are limited to one-unit structures on less than 10 acres and no business on property. Specified renter-occupied units exclude one-unit structures on 10 acres or more. See headnote, Table 956, for an explanation of housing costs. Based on the American Housing Survey; see Appendix III. For composition of regions, see map inside front cover]

Category	Number (1,000)					Percent distribution				
	Total units	North-east	Mid-west	South	West	Total units	North-east	Mid-west	South	West
OWNER-OCCUPIED UNITS										
Total	72,238	12,964	17,889	26,699	14,686	100.0	100.0	100.0	100.0	100.0
Monthly housing costs:										
Less than $300	15,067	1,367	3,462	7,898	2,339	20.9	10.5	19.4	29.6	15.9
$300 to $399	6,493	1,129	1,980	2,303	1,081	9.0	8.7	11.1	8.6	7.4
$400 to $499	5,191	1,131	1,453	1,754	853	7.2	8.7	8.1	6.6	5.8
$500 to $599	4,414	932	1,230	1,578	674	6.1	7.2	6.9	5.9	4.6
$600 to $699	4,219	809	1,242	1,608	560	5.8	6.2	6.9	6.0	3.8
$700 to $799	4,121	788	1,099	1,629	605	5.7	6.1	6.1	6.1	4.1
$800 to $999	7,399	1,367	2,048	2,642	1,342	10.2	10.5	11.4	9.9	9.1
$1,000 to $1,249	7,381	1,299	1,895	2,510	1,676	10.2	10.0	10.6	9.4	11.4
$1,250 to $1,499	5,462	1,077	1,383	1,596	1,406	7.6	8.3	7.7	6.0	9.6
$1,500 or more	12,492	3,065	2,096	3,180	4,150	17.3	23.6	11.7	11.9	28.3
Median (dol.) [1]	718	848	666	588	984	(X)	(X)	(X)	(X)	(X)
RENTER-OCCUPIED UNITS										
Total	33,604	7,169	6,599	11,446	8,390	100.0	100.0	100.0	100.0	100.0
Monthly housing costs:										
Less than $300	3,182	821	647	1,142	573	9.5	11.5	9.8	10.0	6.8
$300 to $399	2,244	971	603	937	334	6.7	5.2	9.1	8.2	4.0
$400 to $499	3,724	693	930	1,473	630	11.1	9.7	14.1	12.9	7.5
$500 to $599	4,366	793	1,096	1,605	872	13.0	11.1	16.6	14.0	10.4
$600 to $699	4,252	824	890	1,522	1,016	12.7	11.5	13.5	13.3	12.1
$700 to $799	3,762	828	714	1,274	945	11.2	11.5	10.8	11.1	11.3
$800 to $999	4,612	1,058	711	1,354	1,488	13.7	14.8	10.8	11.8	17.7
$1,000 to $1,249	2,787	697	332	669	1,089	8.3	9.7	5.0	5.8	13.0
$1,250 to $1,499	1,167	303	117	245	502	3.5	4.2	1.8	2.1	6.0
$1,500 or more	1,291	393	85	249	564	3.8	5.5	1.3	2.2	6.7
No cash rent	2,218	389	476	976	378	6.6	5.4	7.2	8.5	4.5
Median (dol.) [1]	651	686	581	605	762	(X)	(X)	(X)	(X)	(X)

X Not applicable.   [1] For explanation of median, see Guide to Tabular Presentation.

Source: U.S. Census Bureau, Current Housing Reports, Series H150/03, *American Housing Survey for the United States.* See Internet site <http://www.census.gov/hhes/www/housing/ahs/nationaldata.html>.

Table 956. Occupied Housing Units—Financial Summary by Selected Characteristics of the Householder: 2003

[In thousands of units (105,842 represents 105,842,000), except as indicated. As of fall. Housing costs include real estate taxes, property insurance, utilities, fuel, water, garbage collection, and mortgage. Based on the American Housing Survey; see Appendix III]

Characteristic	Total occupied units	Tenure		Black [1]		Hispanic origin [2]		Elderly [3]		Households below poverty level	
		Owner	Renter	Owner	Renter	Owner	Renter	Owner	Renter	Owner	Renter
Total units [4]	105,842	72,238	33,604	6,193	6,811	5,106	5,931	17,350	4,277	6,058	7,902
Monthly housing costs:											
Less than $300	18,249	15,067	3,182	1,604	993	938	453	7,060	886	2,733	1,841
$300 to $399	8,736	6,493	2,244	490	462	393	326	2,876	396	709	750
$400 to $499	8,916	5,191	3,724	437	861	270	634	1,877	454	506	1,064
$500 to $599	8,780	4,414	4,366	381	915	290	820	1,247	455	370	941
$600 to $699	8,471	4,219	4,252	442	877	297	827	847	448	352	788
$700 to $799	7,882	4,121	3,762	371	767	312	750	677	298	232	607
$800 to $999	12,010	7,399	4,612	771	882	601	899	887	375	370	596
$1,000 or more [5]	30,580	25,335	5,245	1,698	631	2,004	989	1,879	471	785	573
Median amount (dol.) [5]	684	718	651	642	596	817	674	350	534	340	494
Monthly housing costs as percent of income: [6]											
Less than 5 percent	5,287	5,016	271	378	49	249	36	1,131	32	31	34
5 to 9 percent	12,309	11,223	1,085	739	184	612	139	2,902	84	117	26
10 to 14 percent	14,459	11,917	2,542	973	465	696	321	2,895	192	245	90
15 to 19 percent	14,686	11,165	3,521	888	658	692	447	2,400	274	321	115
20 to 24 percent	12,506	8,476	4,030	701	713	641	656	1,699	281	313	232
25 to 29 percent	9,693	6,148	3,545	529	781	516	649	1,256	429	309	429
30 to 34 percent	7,081	4,234	2,847	413	626	417	559	941	358	283	369
35 to 39 percent	4,860	2,782	2,078	287	424	280	463	622	210	232	312
40 percent or more	20,176	9,969	10,206	1,133	2,137	934	2,216	3,027	1,779	2,987	4,430
Median amount (percent) [5]	22	18	30	20	31	22	34	18	39	57	68

[1] For persons who selected this race group only. See footnote 3, Table 952.   [2] Persons of Hispanic origin may be of any race.   [3] Householders 65 years old and over.   [4] Includes units with "mortgage payment not reported" and "no cash rent" not shown separately.   [5] For explanation of median, see Guide to Tabular Presentation.   [6] Money income before taxes.

Source: U.S. Census Bureau, Current Housing Reports, Series H150/03, *American Housing Survey for the United States.* See Internet site <http://www.census.gov/hhes/www/housing/ahs/nationaldata.html>.

Table 957. Specified Owner-Occupied Housing Units—Value and Costs by State: 2003

[In percent, except as indicated (58,809 represents 58,809,000). Specified owner-occupied units include only 1-family houses on less than 10 acres without a business or medical office on the property. The American Community Survey universe is limited to the household population and excludes the population living in institutions, college dormitories, and other group quarters. Based on a sample and subject to sampling variability; see Appendix III. For definition of median, see Guide to Tabular Presentation]

State	Total (1,000)	Percent of units with value of—			Median value (dol.)	Median selected monthly owner costs [1] (dol.)	Selected monthly owner costs as a percent of household income in the past 12 months [1]			
		$99,999 or less	$100,000 to $199,999	$200,000 or more			Less than 20 percent	20.0 to 24.9 percent	25.0 to 34.9 percent	35 percent or more
U.S. . . .	58,809	29.6	36.9	33.5	147,275	1,204	39.5	17.2	20.7	22.1
AL.	947	52.8	35.0	12.2	96,106	871	48.2	16.7	15.9	18.5
AK.	112	13.2	50.9	35.9	174,146	1,374	41.8	19.0	22.7	16.3
AZ.	1,165	20.5	52.2	27.4	146,124	1,146	39.0	18.1	19.8	22.7
AR.	556	63.0	28.5	8.5	83,699	806	53.3	15.4	17.1	13.8
CA.	5,921	5.1	17.8	77.1	334,426	1,660	28.3	16.0	23.8	31.4
CO	1,062	4.3	41.1	54.5	210,398	1,358	36.6	16.8	22.1	24.2
CT.	765	4.7	37.4	58.0	226,202	1,598	37.9	19.6	20.8	21.5
DE.	185	14.5	49.6	35.8	165,739	1,184	46.9	19.3	18.6	15.2
DC.	76	9.1	31.5	59.5	248,171	1,482	39.5	15.7	19.6	24.2
FL.	3,508	26.4	44.4	29.1	144,507	1,151	35.8	16.9	20.7	26.1
GA	1,745	28.0	45.9	26.1	140,734	1,155	41.4	16.7	19.5	21.9
HI	185	6.2	16.0	77.8	324,661	1,666	31.3	17.2	24.5	27.0
ID	284	35.4	49.0	15.6	118,174	917	43.7	18.8	18.9	18.1
IL	2,563	27.8	35.5	36.8	160,551	1,340	39.8	17.2	21.3	21.4
IN	1,419	45.5	43.1	11.4	106,840	952	47.6	16.4	19.6	16.2
IA	688	56.6	34.5	8.9	91,427	913	49.8	19.2	16.8	14.0
KS.	611	49.9	37.0	13.1	100,257	993	49.1	18.2	18.3	14.3
KY.	812	47.5	39.5	13.0	104,103	906	47.0	15.0	18.9	18.7
LA.	892	50.6	37.0	12.5	99,215	911	48.5	14.8	16.1	20.1
ME	267	31.6	43.0	25.4	134,846	1,025	42.6	17.6	18.9	20.5
MD	1,255	16.6	38.1	45.3	186,139	1,395	41.9	19.7	20.0	18.3
MA	1,259	3.5	19.9	76.7	309,736	1,571	38.0	16.8	22.2	22.8
MI	2,417	28.6	45.5	25.9	141,413	1,122	41.1	18.1	20.3	20.2
MN	1,259	20.0	44.3	35.7	169,778	1,212	43.0	19.0	20.3	17.4
MS	560	61.3	30.3	8.4	85,142	849	41.8	17.2	19.1	21.5
MO	1,256	45.2	39.8	15.0	108,625	945	47.7	16.4	18.0	17.4
MT.	173	38.8	45.7	15.5	118,887	951	39.8	18.9	19.9	20.9
NE.	389	49.6	39.8	10.6	100,539	1,002	46.0	19.5	19.4	14.7
NV.	433	9.3	54.3	36.4	170,333	1,279	34.4	15.6	22.3	26.6
NH	280	9.3	37.4	53.3	208,403	1,420	36.8	20.4	22.2	20.4
NJ.	1,795	8.1	28.4	63.5	245,573	1,723	34.7	17.9	22.7	24.2
NM	363	38.1	45.6	16.4	118,764	963	44.4	14.1	19.5	21.3
NY.	2,804	26.9	23.3	49.8	198,883	1,474	38.8	16.2	19.7	25.0
NC	1,678	34.9	44.9	20.2	125,428	1,079	41.9	17.6	20.3	19.8
ND	129	64.3	30.6	5.1	81,796	904	51.7	20.0	16.4	11.1
OH	2,727	37.8	45.4	16.8	118,956	1,068	41.6	17.7	20.2	20.1
OK	749	63.3	30.2	6.5	85,502	861	47.8	15.3	18.1	18.5
OR	709	9.2	54.7	36.1	171,039	1,216	35.1	17.5	22.8	24.0
PA.	3,002	45.0	37.0	18.1	110,020	1,094	41.7	17.1	20.4	20.4
RI	212	4.6	43.4	52.1	205,244	1,381	39.0	18.4	23.2	19.1
SC.	818	37.4	40.9	21.6	121,290	1,037	42.3	18.2	18.3	21.0
SD.	146	52.7	38.3	8.9	96,977	918	47.2	18.8	19.9	14.0
TN.	1,281	43.8	40.4	15.8	110,000	963	42.9	16.1	20.1	20.6
TX.	4,179	50.6	34.8	14.6	99,139	1,166	40.1	18.2	19.8	21.4
UT.	488	11.2	60.8	28.0	156,657	1,173	37.4	18.2	22.4	21.5
VT.	111	27.3	49.3	23.4	138,457	1,142	37.2	21.2	21.4	20.0
VA.	1,632	25.2	35.2	39.6	162,080	1,278	42.3	17.0	22.2	18.0
WA	1,254	9.1	40.8	50.1	200,235	1,380	32.0	17.0	24.9	25.7
WV	387	62.0	30.4	7.6	85,709	783	51.5	16.5	14.6	16.2
WI	1,193	29.9	49.7	20.4	131,908	1,138	39.2	19.0	22.4	19.1
WY	105	38.5	44.7	16.8	116,360	920	49.3	17.3	16.7	16.5

[1] For homes with a mortgage. Includes all forms of debt where the property is pledged as security for repayment of the debt, including deeds of trust, land contracts, home equity loans, etc.

Source: U.S. Census Bureau, American Community Survey, Multi-Year Profiles 2003 - Housing Characteristics, Internet site <http://www.census.gov/acs/www/Products/Profiles/Chg/2003/ACS/index.htm>; (accessed 1 August 2005).

Construction and Housing 633

Table 958. Specified Renter-Occupied Housing Units—Gross Rent by State: 2003

[In percent, except as indicated (35,545 represents 35,545,000. Specified renter-occupied units include all renter-occupied units except one-family houses on 10 or more acres. The American Community Survey universe is limited to the household population and excludes the population living in institutions, college dormitories, and other group quarters. Based on a sample and subject to sampling variability; see Appendix III]

State	Total [1] (1,000)	Percent of units with gross rent of—					Median gross rent (dol.)	Gross rent as a percent of household income in the past 12 months			
		$299 or less	$300 to $499	$500 to $749	$750 to $999	$1,000 or more		Less than 15 percent	15 to 24 percent	25 to 34 percent	35 percent or more
U.S. . . .	35,545	7.9	16.6	31.2	20.9	17.8	679	13.4	25.1	19.0	35.2
AL	484	14.0	30.6	30.7	9.5	3.5	498	14.1	22.3	15.8	32.4
AK	85	3.1	9.7	26.0	25.5	20.8	780	14.3	23.3	18.2	29.3
AZ	646	5.3	15.7	39.0	20.0	13.7	662	9.8	24.7	21.1	35.4
AR	337	10.7	31.5	36.9	7.5	3.5	513	15.5	25.6	15.3	32.7
CA	4,941	3.9	8.2	22.0	24.5	38.1	890	10.7	24.0	20.6	39.7
CO	532	5.6	9.2	32.7	27.3	21.3	754	10.3	26.1	21.6	36.9
CT	427	8.0	9.0	28.8	27.8	22.0	766	13.6	25.6	21.0	33.7
DE	82	8.2	11.6	31.3	26.9	14.9	718	15.4	26.0	22.4	28.6
DC	143	11.0	9.9	30.6	18.5	26.7	721	12.2	27.9	17.5	35.6
FL	1,971	6.6	11.7	32.9	27.0	16.8	724	10.5	23.7	19.0	40.1
GA	989	7.4	16.9	29.0	25.2	13.4	687	12.1	24.1	19.0	35.4
HI	181	4.8	5.9	21.3	24.8	30.9	863	12.4	23.0	18.3	32.2
ID	125	9.5	27.4	37.4	12.1	6.4	565	12.3	24.7	23.2	31.9
IL	1,438	7.0	14.9	32.4	23.8	17.2	699	14.0	26.3	18.6	34.4
IN	646	7.3	23.2	42.0	15.0	5.9	581	15.7	25.9	17.6	32.6
IA	293	13.0	27.5	37.4	12.3	3.8	531	16.4	28.7	16.9	31.4
KS	322	11.5	29.3	32.0	14.7	5.9	535	15.5	28.7	17.1	30.4
KY	459	14.3	31.2	30.2	8.8	3.1	491	17.2	22.7	16.3	29.0
LA	546	11.8	27.8	32.2	10.4	4.9	525	14.9	19.2	14.5	35.7
ME	154	14.5	22.7	31.8	15.4	6.5	562	16.2	27.5	20.0	26.2
MD	623	6.9	8.3	24.7	28.5	27.9	817	13.2	27.7	20.6	33.2
MA	862	11.7	9.2	20.2	21.7	33.1	820	13.0	26.6	20.3	34.6
MI	977	10.3	19.6	39.1	17.6	8.8	608	15.3	26.4	18.8	33.5
MN	455	12.2	15.5	31.7	22.6	13.6	657	12.4	27.6	22.5	32.2
MS	309	13.9	25.8	33.7	11.5	3.0	525	13.1	21.5	16.5	35.2
MO	656	9.1	27.0	37.2	15.3	5.2	556	16.1	28.8	15.4	32.2
MT	107	14.4	30.3	34.4	8.4	4.1	506	16.0	26.0	17.2	31.5
NE	209	11.5	27.5	34.9	11.9	6.5	540	16.7	28.1	19.0	27.1
NV	317	2.8	9.4	32.8	32.1	19.7	771	12.4	27.1	20.0	35.8
NH	132	7.1	9.6	27.6	31.0	20.8	780	11.1	27.2	21.1	33.9
NJ	1,039	6.8	5.3	21.6	31.9	30.4	856	13.9	27.1	20.0	33.6
NM	211	11.1	30.1	33.8	9.5	7.3	523	15.7	21.0	18.3	34.9
NY	3,243	8.2	12.0	25.9	24.4	26.2	770	15.2	23.1	18.2	38.1
NC	1,020	8.5	21.1	37.8	16.4	6.5	601	13.0	23.8	18.8	32.7
ND	80	17.3	37.7	28.3	5.0	2.2	456	22.0	27.8	14.4	24.4
OH	1,314	9.0	24.8	38.8	15.9	6.4	575	14.7	26.3	18.5	33.6
OK	421	9.7	32.4	33.9	11.4	4.0	519	16.9	23.6	17.9	30.0
OR	509	6.6	13.6	42.9	21.1	12.5	657	9.4	24.1	21.3	40.3
PA	1,334	9.9	23.4	33.7	18.0	9.9	602	15.8	26.2	19.1	32.4
RI	151	11.0	12.1	34.6	24.5	13.6	686	13.8	27.2	19.9	33.0
SC	466	9.9	21.9	36.7	14.3	6.4	586	13.6	23.1	17.8	32.6
SD	87	15.4	31.0	31.5	7.5	3.6	490	16.6	27.3	17.2	26.5
TN	688	11.8	26.4	35.5	14.7	4.5	548	16.4	25.1	17.3	32.2
TX	2,695	6.4	18.8	37.2	20.2	11.4	639	13.7	25.5	19.2	33.8
UT	201	5.1	15.7	44.3	19.4	11.7	632	11.6	25.3	22.0	35.7
VT	67	11.5	15.0	38.2	18.5	10.7	624	12.8	25.7	21.3	33.5
VA	841	6.5	14.5	25.9	22.8	24.2	751	13.9	28.1	17.7	32.8
WA	845	5.8	11.8	32.1	25.2	20.0	734	11.0	25.1	20.2	37.7
WV	186	18.5	34.2	24.5	6.1	1.9	432	12.8	18.3	19.3	33.1
WI	646	8.2	22.5	40.6	17.1	7.1	595	14.7	28.4	18.5	32.6
WY	53	11.2	36.5	29.2	8.3	7.7	494	23.9	27.7	14.8	25.7

[1] Includes units with no cash rent.

Source: U.S. Census Bureau, American FactFinder, 2003 American Community Survey Summary Tables. H060. Gross Rent - Specified Renter-Occupied Housing Units and H067. Gross Rent as a Percentage of Household Income In the Past 12 Months - Specified Renter-Occupied Housing Units, Internet site <http://factfinder.census.gov/>; and (accessed 13 July 2005)

Table 959. **Mortgage Characteristics—Owner Occupied Units: 2003**

[In thousands (72,238 represents 72,238,000). As of fall. Based on the American Housing Survey; see Appendix III]

Mortgage characteristic	Total owner-occupied units	New construction [1]	Mobile homes	Black [2]	His-panic [3]	Elderly [4]	Moved in past year	Below poverty level
ALL OWNERS								
Total	72,238	4,673	5,514	6,193	5,106	17,350	5,609	6,058
Mortgages currently on property:								
None, owned free and clear.	25,020	798	3,100	2,036	1,452	12,476	1,083	3,618
Regular and home equity mortgages	45,471	3,770	2,319	3,968	3,537	4,446	4,397	2,211
Regular mortgage.	42,261	3,678	2,225	3,790	3,445	3,598	4,301	2,066
Home equity lump-sum mortage	3,791	186	88	261	171	457	173	127
Home equity line of credit.	7,217	414	86	303	296	984	340	194
Not reported	1,700	105	95	187	112	385	129	213
Number of regular and home equity mortgages: [5]								
1 mortgage.	33,429	2,934	2,080	3,076	2,865	3,307	3,502	1,602
2 mortgages	8,127	599	118	468	457	543	585	200
3 mortgages or more	855	50	4	57	40	85	53	43
Type of mortgage:								
Regular and home equity lump sum [5] . . .	2,374	136	23	145	120	157	123	67
With home equity line of credit	451	22	-	25	16	50	23	15
No home equity line of credit . . ˌ . . .	1,902	114	23	120	100	104	98	52
Regular no home equity lump sum [5]	39,887	3,542	2,202	3,645	3,325	3,441	4,178	1,999
With home equity line of credit ˙.	4,703	346	54	197	233	327	265	94
No home equity line of credit . . ˌ . . .	32,205	3,017	2,032	3,082	2,921	2,616	3,664	1,553
Home equity lump sum no regular [5] . . .	1,418	51	65	116	51	300	49	60
With home equity line of credit	271	5	3	18	6	58	6	-
No home equity line of credit . . . ˌ . .	1,123	42	62	96	45	242	40	55
No regular or home equity lump sum [5] . .	28,560	944	3,224	2,287	1,610	13,453	1,259	3,933
With home equity line of credit	1,792	41	29	62	41	549	47	85
No home equity line of credit	25,068	798	3,100	2,037	1,457	12,519	1,083	3,634
OWNERS WITH ONE OR MORE REGULAR OR LUMP-SUM HOME EQUITY MORTGAGES, 2003								
Total [5]	43,678	3,729	2,290	3,906	3,496	3,898	4,350	2,125
Type of primary mortgage:								
FHA	5,341	486	118	930	750	282	614	299
VA.	1,981	225	54	269	142	155	230	76
RHS/RD [6].	398	29	7	47	48	50	58	42
Other types.	32,527	2,789	1,949	2,235	2,346	2,796	3,161	1,311
Mortgage origination:								
Placed new mortgage(s)	43,315	3,722	2,266	3,840	3,443	3,866	4,316	2,085
Primary obtained when property acquired	26,276	2,882	1,930	2,896	2,439	2,108	4,156	1,526
Obtained later	17,040	840	335	944	1,004	1,758	159	559
Assumed	278	6	21	49	41	28	27	32
Wrap-around	8	-	-	2	6	-	3	-
Combination of the above	76	-	3	14	6	4	5	9
Payment plan of primary mortgage:								
Fixed payment, self amortizing	36,221	3,188	1,959	3,133	2,980	2,931	3,542	1,507
Adjustable rate mortgage	1,695	127	49	144	137	137	179	57
Adjustable term mortgage	113	3	3	15	2	30	11	12
Graduated payment mortgage	286	36	10	21	16	2	76	24
Balloon	410	34	60	23	20	37	62	16
Combination of the above	291	35	2	13	22	25	45	7
Payment plan of secondary mortgage:								
Units with two or more mortgages [5]	4,234	317	67	320	271	254	385	153
Fixed payment, self amortizing	3,373	232	55	265	214	197	292	118
Adjustable rate mortgage	183	26	2	2	17	1	26	5
Adjustable term mortgage	129	13	-	10	6	21	11	7
Graduated payment mortgage.	18	-	-	-	-	-	3	3
Balloon	105	5	-	1	15	4	19	3
Other	5	-	-	-	-	-	-	-
Combination of the above	79	5	-	2	5	5	9	-
Reason primary refinanced:								
Units with a refinanced primary mortgage [7]	16,595	937	292	850	1,050	1,225	194	415
To get a lower interest rate.	14,918	903	214	722	914	959	184	343
To increase payment period	378	23	8	15	22	40	5	12
To reduce payment period	1,931	97	20	73	124	100	7	56
To renew or extend a loan that has fallen due	144	6	7	29	10	19	-	7
To receive cash	1,925	35	33	99	161	229	13	71
Other reason	1,372	44	61	90	122	146	17	37
Cash received in primary mortgage refinance:								
Units receiving refinance cash	1,925	35	33	99	161	229	13	71
Median amount received (dol.)	25,080	-	-	16,519	22,917	21,206	-	18,562

- Represents or rounds to zero. [1] Constructed in the past 4 years. [2] For persons who selected this race group only. See footnote 3, Table 952. [3] Persons of Hispanic origin may be of any race. [4] 65 years old and over. [5] Includes "don't know" and "not reported." [6] Rural Housing Service/Rural Development Mortgage, formerly Farmers Home Administration [7] Persons reporting "more than one reason" are counted once in the total.

Source: U.S. Census Bureau, *Current Housing Reports*, Series H150/03, *American Housing Survey for the United States.* See Internet site <http://www.census.gov/hhes/www/housing/ahs/nationaldata.html>.

Construction and Housing 635

Table 960. Occupied Housing Units—Neighborhood Indicators by Selected Characteristics of the Householder: 2003

[In thousands (105,842 represents 105,842,000). As of fall. Based on the American Housing Survey; see Appendix III]

Characteristic	Total occupied units	Tenure		Black [1]		Hispanic origin [2]		Elderly [3]		Households below poverty level	
		Owner	Renter	Owner	Renter	Owner	Renter	Owner	Renter	Owner	Renter
Total units	105,842	72,238	33,604	6,193	6,811	5,106	5,931	17,350	4,277	6,058	7,902
Street noise or traffic present [4]	27,888	16,469	11,419	1,745	2,611	1,198	1,889	4,078	1,360	1,585	2,929
Condition not bothersome	16,556	9,728	6,828	1,030	1,601	634	1,063	2,771	967	951	1,744
Condition bothersome	11,235	6,712	4,523	713	990	563	815	1,301	383	628	1,159
So bothersome they want to move	4,140	2,153	1,988	275	538	205	396	290	121	222	556
Neighborhood crime present [4]	15,489	8,400	7,088	1,222	2,061	713	1,379	1,634	620	876	1,906
Condition not bothersome	6,393	3,615	2,778	458	791	276	446	877	312	384	721
Condition bothersome	9,021	4,765	4,256	762	1,250	437	921	754	297	491	1,166
So bothersome they want to move	3,716	1,500	2,216	305	747	181	512	192	95	210	723
Odors present [4]	5,625	3,197	2,428	392	662	319	545	637	206	386	743
Condition not bothersome	2,048	1,225	823	133	190	127	163	272	88	145	245
Condition bothersome	3,554	1,960	1,594	254	471	186	379	364	111	240	497
So bothersome they want to move	1,409	561	848	99	265	62	242	65	28	93	290
Other problems:											
Noise	2,487	1,391	1,096	149	229	146	201	295	93	86	282
Litter or housing deterioration	1,902	1,182	719	210	193	100	148	265	51	91	214
Poor city or county services	779	494	285	120	102	51	66	102	23	52	82
People	4,005	2,358	1,647	293	390	200	325	476	132	235	464
With public transportation	57,910	34,211	23,699	3,805	5,451	3,272	4,739	8,086	3,085	2,568	5,674
Household uses it at least weekly	11,356	4,005	7,351	886	2,231	625	2,034	749	953	424	2,331
Household uses it less than weekly	8,754	5,170	3,585	671	893	460	660	1,070	539	372	868
Household does not use	36,634	24,449	12,186	2,186	2,176	2,155	1,985	6,111	1,531	1,705	2,340
Not reported	1,165	587	578	63	151	33	60	155	62	66	135
No public transportation	44,197	35,539	8,658	2,205	1,139	1,667	1,070	8,698	1,079	3,234	1,985
Not reported	3,736	2,488	1,247	183	221	167	122	566	113	256	242
Police protection:											
Satisfactory	93,968	64,487	29,481	5,266	5,720	4,475	5,103	15,643	3,924	4,988	6,669
Unsatisfacory	7,712	5,223	2,488	657	707	473	593	1,097	177	741	764
Not reported	4,163	2,527	1,635	270	385	158	236	610	177	329	470
Secured communities [5]:											
Community access secured with walls or fences	6,958	3,014	3,944	228	885	321	1,008	914	504	212	806
Community access not secured	97,871	68,570	29,301	5,896	5,826	4,746	4,882	16,250	3,716	5,760	6,994
Secured multiunits [5]:											
Multiunit access secured	5,271	907	4,364	88	983	83	744	359	1,003	72	1,059
Multiunit access not secured	19,243	2,429	16,814	230	3,590	279	3,196	674	1,944	224	4,012
Not reported	448	66	382	10	111	7	55	15	50	6	91
Senior citizen communities:											
Households with persons 55 years old and over	40,356	32,523	7,833	2,668	1,407	1,804	1,060	17,350	4,277	3,888	2,213
Community age restricted [6]	2,048	1,025	1,023	27	151	37	90	787	882	159	366
Community quality:											
Some or all activities present	38,190	24,839	13,351	2,058	2,740	1,621	2,142	6,360	2,168	1,826	2,956
Community center or clubhouse	23,287	14,179	9,108	1,129	1,957	883	1,333	4,148	1,649	1,052	1,881
Golf in the community	10,976	8,440	2,535	375	288	381	298	2,306	330	562	471
Trails in the community	18,318	13,001	5,317	866	797	795	767	2,931	706	842	900
Shuttle bus	9,996	6,192	3,803	480	566	400	653	2,084	985	519	963
Daycare	15,548	10,413	5,135	1,198	1,320	711	992	2,314	630	832	1,316
Private or restricted beach, park or shoreline	6,580	4,741	1,838	307	352	220	298	1,061	236	327	397
Trash, litter or junk on street: [7]											
None	93,829	65,765	28,064	5,236	5,240	4,400	4,772	15,997	3,767	5,233	6,161
Minor accumulation	6,683	3,181	3,502	521	916	381	729	645	293	446	1,071
Major accumulation	2,630	1,369	1,261	215	400	177	306	295	85	157	454
Not reported	2,700	1,923	777	221	254	148	125	412	132	221	216

[1] For persons who selected this race group only. See footnote 3, Table 952. [2] Persons of Hispanic origin may be of any race. [3] Householders 65 years old and over. [4] Includes those not reporting if condition is bothersome. [5] Public access is restricted (walls, gates, private security). Includes high rise apartments, retirement communities, resorts, etc. [6] At least one family member must be aged 55 years old or older. [7] Or on any properties within 300 feet.

Source: U.S. Census Bureau, Current Housing Reports, Series H150/03, American Housing Survey for the United States. See Internet site <http://www.census.gov/hhes/www/housing/ahs/nationaldata.html>.

Table 961. **Heating Equipment and Fuels for Occupied Units: 1995 to 2003**

[97,693 represents 97,693,000. As of fall. Based on American Housing Survey. See Appendix III]

Type of equipment or fuel	Number (1,000)					Percent distribution	
	1995	1997	1999	2001	2003	1995	2003 [1]
Occupied units, total	**97,693**	**99,487**	**102,803**	**106,261**	**105,842**	**100.0**	**100.0**
Heating equipment:							
Warm air furnace	53,165	58,603	62,018	65,262	65,380	54.4	61.8
Steam or hot water	13,669	12,929	13,153	13,441	13,257	14.0	12.5
Heat pumps	9,406	11,101	10,992	11,080	11,347	9.6	10.7
Built-in electric units	7,035	4,531	4,939	5,063	4,760	7.2	4.5
Floor, wall, or pipeless furnace	4,963	5,588	5,310	5,343	5,322	5.1	5.0
Room heaters with flue	1,620	1,584	1,624	1,542	1,432	1.7	1.4
Room heaters without flue	1,642	1,754	1,790	1,558	1,509	1.7	1.4
Fireplaces, stoves, portable heaters or other	5,150	2,780	2,434	2,571	2,396	5.3	2.3
None	1,044	617	544	401	439	1.1	0.4
House main heating fuel:							
Electricity.	26,771	29,202	31,142	32,590	32,341	27.4	30.6
Utility gas	49,203	51,052	52,366	54,689	54,928	50.4	51.9
Bottled, tank, or LP gas	4,251	5,398	5,905	6,079	6,134	4.4	5.8
Fuel oil, kerosene, etc..	12,029	10,855	10,750	10,473	10,136	12.3	9.6
Coal or coke	210	183	168	128	126	0.2	0.1
Wood and other fuel	4,186	2,177	1,927	1,902	1,735	4.3	1.6
None	1,042	620	545	400	441	1.1	0.4
Cooking fuel:							
Electricity.	57,621	58,818	61,315	63,685	62,859	59.0	59.4
Gas [2]	39,218	40,083	41,051	42,161	42,612	40.1	40.3
Other fuel	566	113	69	66	62	0.6	0.1
None	287	473	368	349	309	0.3	0.3

[1] Based on 2000 census controls.   [2] Includes utility, bottled, tank, and LP gas.
Source: U.S. Census Bureau, Current Housing Reports, Series H150/95RV, H150/97, H150/99, H150/01, and H150/03, *American Housing Survey for the United States.* See Internet site <http://www.census.gov/hhes/www/housing/ahs /nationaldata.html>.

Table 962. **Occupied Housing Units—Housing Indicators by Selected Characteristics of the Householder: 2003**

[In thousands of units (105,842 represents 105,842,000). As of fall. Based on the American Housing Survey; see Appendix III]

Characteristic	Total occu- pied units	Tenure		Black [1]		Hispanic origin [2]		Elderly [3]		Households below poverty level	
		Owner	Renter	Owner	Renter	Owner	Renter	Owner	Renter	Owner	Renter
Total units	**105,842**	**72,238**	**33,604**	**6,193**	**6,811**	**5,106**	**5,931**	**17,350**	**4,277**	**6,058**	**7,902**
Amenities:											
Porch, deck, balcony or patio	89,562	66,021	23,541	5,318	4,540	4,580	3,865	15,626	2,645	5,284	5,116
Telephone available	102,873	70,601	32,272	6,010	6,486	4,953	5,684	16,992	4,153	5,883	7,486
Usable fireplace.	35,458	31,593	3,865	1,859	541	1,647	546	6,444	293	1,579	522
Separate dining room	50,690	41,317	9,373	3,758	2,030	2,569	1,530	9,274	899	2,960	1,865
With 2 or more living rooms or recreation rooms	30,254	28,149	2,106	1,990	344	1,353	195	5,871	209	1,327	328
Garage or carport with home.	65,251	54,664	10,587	3,500	1,293	3,799	1,875	13,341	1,261	3,721	1,724
Cars and trucks available:											
No cars, trucks, or vans	9,089	2,416	6,673	495	2,083	178	1,304	1,536	1,882	712	2,996
Other households without cars.	12,794	9,031	3,763	532	445	784	860	1,456	231	830	758
1 car with or without trucks or vans.	50,875	33,952	16,923	2,940	3,443	2,293	2,688	10,241	1,893	3,273	3,434
2 cars	25,189	19,894	5,294	1,707	705	1,288	905	3,456	229	994	608
3 or more cars	7,896	6,946	950	519	136	564	174	662	42	250	106
Selected deficiencies:											
Signs of rats in last 3 months.	829	409	420	60	125	73	154	85	38	75	147
Signs of mice in last 3 months.	6,304	3,864	2,440	452	727	259	587	755	193	463	793
Holes in floors.	978	420	558	66	163	46	138	81	36	68	216
Open cracks or holes	5,232	2,665	2,566	371	739	217	465	444	168	363	764
Broken plaster or peeling paint (interior of unit).	2,340	1,098	1,242	210	355	90	269	216	81	173	430
No electrical wiring.	74	45	29	2	-	-	11	8	10	16	12
Exposed wiring	643	390	253	28	39	49	42	88	17	53	83
Rooms without electric outlet	1,486	837	649	117	147	61	123	172	46	89	215
Water leakage from inside structure [4]	8,468	4,816	3,652	494	894	350	612	714	255	392	921
Water leakage from outside structure [4]	10,968	7,888	3,081	746	691	449	492	1,483	197	649	748

- Represents or rounds to zero.   [1] For persons who selected this race group only. See footnote 3, Table 952.   [2] Persons of Hispanic origin may be of any race.   [3] Householders 65 years old and over.   [4] During the 12 months prior to the survey.
Source: U.S. Census Bureau, Current Housing Reports, Series H150/03, *American Housing Survey for the United States.* See Internet site <http://www.census.gov/hhes/www/housing/ahs/nationaldata.html>.

U.S. Census Bureau, Statistical Abstract of the United States: 2006

Table 963. Appliances and Office Equipment Used by Households by Region and Household Income: 2001

[In millions (107.0 represents 107,000,000). Represents appliances possessed and generally used by the household. Based on Residential Energy Consumption Survey; see source. For composition of regions, see map, inside front cover]

Type of appliance	House-holds using appli-ance	Region				Household income in 2001			
		North-east	Midwest	South	West	Under $15,000	$15,000 -$29,999	$30,000 -$49,999	$50,000 and over
Total households.	107.0	20.3	24.5	38.9	23.3	18.7	22.9	27.1	38.3
Oven [1]	101.7	19.6	23.8	36.2	22.1	18.0	22.0	26.1	35.6
Electric	63.0	9.9	14.0	26.0	13.1	10.1	12.9	16.2	23.8
Natural gas	34.3	8.6	8.7	8.8	8.2	7.1	7.8	8.6	10.9
Self-cleaning oven	48.2	10.2	12.3	16.1	9.6	4.1	8.5	12.4	23.2
Range [1]	105.7	20.1	24.1	38.6	22.9	18.5	22.5	26.9	37.7
Electric	64.2	10.0	13.9	27.2	13.2	10.4	13.2	16.5	24.2
Natural gas	36.7	8.9	9.1	9.8	8.9	7.3	8.0	9.1	12.4
Refrigerator.	106.8	20.2	24.5	38.9	23.2	18.6	22.8	27.1	38.3
Frost-free	96.9	18.3	21.7	36.3	20.7	15.5	19.9	25.0	36.5
Freezer	34.2	4.9	9.6	13.6	6.2	4.4	6.9	9.2	13.7
1	30.8	4.5	8.6	12.2	5.6	3.9	6.1	8.4	12.4
2 or more	3.4	0.4	1.0	1.4	0.6	0.4	0.9	0.8	1.3
Most used defrost method:									
Frost-free	12.2	1.8	2.8	5.7	1.8	1.3	2.0	3.2	5.7
Manual	22.0	3.1	6.7	7.9	4.4	3.0	4.9	6.0	8.1
Dishwasher.	56.7	9.2	12.1	22.1	13.2	3.3	9.1	14.9	29.3
Electric coffee maker	65.5	12.4	16.1	23.0	14.0	8.7	12.8	16.7	27.3
Electric toaster oven	36.1	8.5	5.5	14.7	7.4	5.1	7.7	8.9	14.3
Microwave oven. . . . :	92.1	15.2	22.3	34.7	19.9	14.0	19.4	23.8	35.0
Air conditioning	80.8	14.2	20.2	36.9	9.6	11.9	16.7	21.0	31.2
Central system	57.5	5.7	14.3	30.4	7.1	6.2	10.7	15.2	25.3
Room	23.3	8.5	5.8	6.4	2.5	5.7	6.0	5.8	5.9
Color TV.	105.8	20.0	24.4	38.4	22.9	18.1	22.7	26.9	38.0
1	29.3	5.8	6.4	9.8	7.3	8.5	8.6	6.5	5.7
2	38.4	8.1	8.2	13.7	8.4	6.4	8.5	10.7	12.8
3	23.3	3.8	5.9	9.2	4.3	2.5	3.8	6.1	10.9
4	10.2	1.6	2.7	3.9	2.0	0.6	1.4	2.6	5.7
5 or more	4.5	0.7	1.1	1.8	0.9	(S)	0.4	1.1	2.9
Large screen TV [2]	36.6	7.1	8.1	13.3	8.0	4.7	6.7	9.8	15.3
1	27.3	5.3	5.9	9.7	6.5	3.7	5.1	7.0	11.4
2	7.9	1.4	1.8	3.3	1.4	0.9	1.5	2.2	3.2
3 or more	1.4	(S)	(S)	0.4	(S)	(S)	(S)	0.5	0.7
Cable/Satellite dish antenna.	82.2	16.3	19.1	30.2	16.6	12.1	16.2	20.9	33.0
VCR and DVD players	96.1	18.0	22.5	34.6	21.0	13.9	19.8	25.3	37.0
Stereo equipment.	80.3	15.1	18.2	28.5	18.5	10.2	15.4	20.9	33.8
Clothes washer	84.1	14.7	19.8	32.7	16.9	10.7	16.4	22.1	34.9
Clothes dryer [1]	78.8	13.3	19.2	30.3	16.0	8.4	15.0	21.3	34.1
Electric	61.1	9.2	13.4	26.6	11.9	6.9	12.2	16.8	25.1
Natural gas	16.9	4.0	5.4	3.4	4.1	1.4	2.6	4.2	8.7
Water heater [1]	107.0	20.3	24.5	38.9	23.3	18.7	22.9	27.1	38.3
Electric	40.8	4.7	6.3	22.4	7.3	8.3	9.5	10.6	12.4
Natural gas	58.0	10.8	16.9	15.4	14.9	9.3	11.7	14.1	23.0
Personal computers	60.0	10.9	14.1	20.7	14.3	3.7	8.7	16.0	31.6
Access to Internet.	50.7	9.7	11.8	16.9	12.2	2.8	6.6	13.1	28.3
Cell/mobile telephone	56.8	10.3	12.8	21.4	12.3	4.4	8.6	14.7	29.1

S Figure does not meet publication standards.   [1] Includes other types, not shown separately.   [2] Determined by respondent.

Source: U.S. Energy Information Administration, "Residential Energy Consumption Survey—Detailed Tables"; <http://www.eia.doe.gov/emeu/recs/recs2001/detail_tables.html> (accessed 04 May 2004).

Table 964. Net Stock of Residential Fixed Assets: 1990 to 2003

[In billions of dollars (6,260.2 represents $6,260,200,000,000). End of year estimates]

Item	1990	1995	1997	1998	1999	2000	2001	2002	2003
Total residential fixed assets. . .	6,260.2	8,028.0	8,927.5	9,507.0	10,206.7	10,907.4	11,711.5	12,454.9	13,399.1
By type of owner and legal form of organization:									
Private	6,111.0	7,839.8	8,730.6	9,300.1	9,986.7	10,675.7	11,464.8	12,195.9	13,125.4
Corporate.	65.7	76.6	84.6	90.0	94.5	99.5	105.0	110.1	116.2
Noncorporate.	6,045.3	7,763.3	8,646.0	9,210.1	9,892.2	10,576.1	11,359.8	12,085.8	13,009.2
Government.	149.2	188.2	196.8	206.9	219.9	231.7	246.7	259.0	273.7
Federal	51.8	61.6	65.9	68.7	72.2	75.4	79.2	82.0	85.8
State and local	97.3	126.6	130.9	138.2	147.7	156.4	167.5	177.0	187.8
By tenure group: [1]									
Owner-occupied	4,515.6	5,987.9	6,712.4	7,174.7	7,752.3	8,328.7	8,996.0	9,616.9	10,407.9
Farm.	48.7	51.3	57.9	62.0	67.0	72.2	77.2	80.6	85.6
Nonfarm	4,467.0	5,936.7	6,654.5	7,112.7	7,685.3	8,256.4	8,918.8	9,536.3	10,322.2
Tenant-occupied	1,718.8	2,011.3	2,184.6	2,300.6	2,420.6	2,543.0	2,677.2	2,797.7	2,948.2

[1] Excludes stocks of other nonfarm residential assets, which consists primarily of dormitories, and of fraternity and sorority houses.

Source: U.S. Bureau of Economic Analysis, Internet site <http://www.bea.gov/bea/dn/FA2004/SelectTable.asp> (accessed 10 May 2005).

Table 965. **Expenditures by Residential Property Owners for Improvements and Maintenance and Repairs by Type of Payment and Year Structure Built: 1995 to 2004**

[In millions of dollars (124,971 represents $124,971,000,000). Based on personal interviews and mail surveys; see source for details]

Type of expenditure	All residential properties	Owner-occupied one-unit properties							
				Materials pruchased by owners			Year structure built		
		Total [1]	Payments to contractors	Total	For jobs done by owners	For jobs done under contract	Before 1960	1960 to 1979	1980 to 2003
Total:									
1995	124,971	79,003	63,017	15,987	12,305	3,682	30,080	28,157	14,718
2000	152,975	100,161	84,778	15,382	11,682	3,700	30,451	27,872	32,717
2001	157,765	105,997	88,220	17,777	13,428	4,349	35,133	25,714	39,872
2002	173,324	116,193	99,190	17,002	13,017	3,985	42,798	25,597	47,051
2003	176,899	115,876	101,207	14,669	11,750	2,920	40,497	29,498	45,881
2004	198,557	136,080	114,197	21,883	17,213	4,671	39,452	36,036	60,594
Maintenance and repairs:									
1995	47,032	25,460	19,487	5,973	5,498	476	9,979	8,388	5,511
2000	42,236	22,411	18,260	4,151	3,384	767	8,074	5,226	6,788
2001	47,491	23,642	19,220	4,422	3,481	942	9,233	5,992	7,427
2002	47,377	21,885	18,279	3,607	3,048	559	7,734	5,232	8,867
2003	44,094	18,381	15,714	2,667	2,387	279	5,583	4,545	8,253
2004	50,612	26,575	20,655	5,920	5,356	564	8,198	6,399	11,976
Improvements:									
1995	77,940	53,543	43,530	10,013	6,807	3,206	20,101	·19,768	9,208
2000	110,739	77,750	66,517	11,232	8,298	2,934	22,377	22,646	25,929
2001	110,274	82,355	69,000	13,355	9,947	3,408	25,900	19,722	32,444
2002	125,946	94,308	80,911	13,395	9,969	3,426	35,064	20,363	38,184
2003	132,804	97,495	85,494	12,003	9,362	2,640	34,914	24,953	37,628
2004	147,945	109,506	93,542	15,962	11,857	4,106	31,255	29,633	48,618

[1] Includes year built not reported, not shown separately.

Source: U.S. Census Bureau, "Residential Improvement and Repair Statistics". See Internet site <http://www.census.gov/const/www/c50index.html>

Table 966. **Home Remodeling—Work Done and Amount Spent: 2004**

[In thousands, except percent (4,055 representrs 4,055,000). As of fall 2004. For work done in the prior 12 months. Based on household survey and subject to sampling error; see source]

Remodeling project	Households with work done [1]			Amount spent (dol.)		
	Number	Percent of households	Done by outside contractor	Under $1,000	$1,000 to $2,999	Over $3,000
Conversion of garage/attic/basement into living space	4,055	1.9	857	1,040	973	1,274
Remodel bathroom	15,503	7.3	3,901	6,385	3,243	2,492
Remodel kitchen	10,652	5.0	2,828	2,914	1,951	3,054
Remodel bedroom	8,142	3.8	852	4,659	1,090	400
Remodel/convert room to home office	2,375	1.1	350	1,063	133	362
Remodel other rooms	8,360	3.9	1,289	3,780	1,347	962
Add bathroom	1,736	0.8	572	164	405	444
Add/extend garage	1,255	0.6	340	100	198	513
Add other rooms—exterior addition	2,181	1.0	815	114	444	1,036
Add deck/porch/patio	5,692	2.7	1,717	1,721	1,744	1,182
Roofing	11,636	5.5	6,622	2,187	2,838	4,452
Siding—vinyl/metal	3,562	1.7	1,604	634	688	1,247
Aluminum windows	1,349	0.6	421	356	188	336
Clad-wood/Wood windows	1,134	0.5	339	326	259	261
Vinyl windows	4,781	2.2	2,382	1,175	1,109	1,579
Ceramic tile floors	7,839	3.7	2,756	3,455	1,544	900
Hardwood floors	5,116	2.4	1,993	1,392	1,369	1,105
Laminate flooring	4,268	2.0	1,372	2,000	944	428
Vinyl flooring	4,387	2.1	1,317	2,787	405	101
Carpeting	10,815	5.1	6,074	3,950	3,161	1,265
Kitchen cabinets	5,830	2.7	2,001	1,356	952	1,685
Kitchen counter tops	5,579	2.6	2,494	1,735	1,105	1,219
Skylights	1,212	0.6	572	552	227	125
Exterior doors	6,528	3.1	2,317	3,445	989	499
Interior doors	4,307	2.0	1,162	2,129	694	321
Garage doors	4,093	1.9	2,110	2,059	978	158
Concrete or masonry work	5,678	2.7	2,597	1,974	1,168	1,327
Swimming pool—in ground	735	0.3	506	45	121	430
Wall paneling	1,493	0.7	143	807	91	38
Ceramic wall tile	2,268	1.1	670	1,175	267	119

[1] Includes no response and amount unknown.

Source: Mediamark Research Inc., New York, NY, *Top-Line Reports*, (copyright); Intemet site <http://www.mediamark.com/>.

Table 967. Commercial Office Space—Overview for Selected Market Areas: 2004

[As of mid-October (4,088,087 represents 4,088,087,000). For the 76 market areas with the highest vacancy rates in 2004. Data based on responses from individuals knowledgeable in the local markets]

Market area	Inventory (1,000 sq. ft.)	Vacant space (1,000 sq. ft.)	Vacancy rate (percent)	Construction (1,000 sq. ft.)	Net absorption [1] (1,000 sq. ft.)
United States, all market areas [2] . . .	4,088,087	629,585	15.4	59,468	73,542
Albuquerque	13,058	1,946	14.9	222	29
Allentown	5,928	1,531	25.8	-	226
Atlanta	115,245	20,664	17.9	1,225	1,108
Austin	34,130	6,838	20.0	-	211
Baltimore	53,523	8,559	16.0	1,101	2,452
Binghamton.	4,788	677	14.1	6	1
Boston	56,798	7,300	12.9	-	783
Bridgeport/Stratford	6,403	1,202	18.8	-	-45
Cedar Rapids	2,702	434	16.1	68	112
Charlotte.	34,338	5,188	15.1	914	321
Chicago	250,083	46,260	18.5	4,641	673
Cincinnati	28,154	6,046	21.5	465	972
Cleveland	37,296	7,115	19.1	189	-328
Columbia	6,058	1,255	20.7	170	87
Columbus	39,889	5,685	14.3	469	760
Dallas	211,812	39,670	18.7	2,343	9,293
Dayton	14,224	2,303	16.2	35	163
Denver.	107,779	20,446	19.0	-	964
Des Moines.	9,608	1,236	12.9	900	561
Detroit.	92,878	14,752	15.9	-	-1,369
El Paso	8,205	2,071	25.2	-	43
Grand Rapids	12,137	1,658	13.7	146	381
Greensboro, High-Point, Winston-Salem. . .	16,716	3,488	20.9	106	34
Greenville	7,370	1,718	23.3	212	431
Hartford	21,917	4,101	18.7	-	195
Houston	168,454	25,288	15.0	185	-872
Indianapolis.	26,627	4,835	18.2	-	145
Jacksonville.	20,819	3,394	16.3	444	1,247
Kansas City.	44,009	8,730	19.8	580	-347
Knoxville.	8,276	1,070	12.9	196	220
Lake Charles.	646	143	22.2	-	26
Lansing	8,914	1,413	15.8	199	-243
Las Vegas	18,869	2,848	15.1	1,092	957
Los Angeles-Central	179,405	26,968	15.0	2,449	1,015
Los Angeles-South Bay	29,018	5,392	18.6	36	1,265
Los Angeles-West	42,347	6,648	15.7	971	1,919
Louisville	17,426	3,546	20.4	450	-31
Marin County.	6,303	820	13.0	-	73
Memphis.	21,392	3,997	18.7	64	-116
Minneapolis/St. Paul	68,117	15,052	22.1	-	4,498
Mobile	3,255	749	23.0	600	50
Nashua	2,296	463	20.2	-	166
New Haven.	14,570	2,828	19.4	-	-268
New Jersey Central	83,969	15,884	18.9	650	1,039
New Jersey Northern	93,728	16,448	17.5	550	42
New Orleans.	14,830	2,390	16.1	-	20
Oakland	50,317	7,576	15.1	-	-
Oklahoma City.	15,363	3,807	24.8	125	11
Omaha.	12,202	1,870	15.3	600	678
Orlando	23,187	2,983	12.9	774	509
Peoria	2,053	509	24.8	-	-50
Philadelphia	91,494	20,096	22.0	402	-721
Phoenix	31,424	6,233	19.8	82	954
Pittsburgh	73,251	11,428	15.6	2,005	2,745
Raleigh.	33,599	5,709	17.0	1,120	1,876
Reno	5,081	672	13.2	64	-28
Richmond.	24,983	3,650	14.6	652	1,333
Roanoke.	3,104	437	14.1	-	30
Sacramento	41,537	7,077	17.0	1,495	211
Salt Lake City	18,459	3,287	17.8	975	-
San Antonio	19,067	3,223	16.9	268	519
San Francisco	80,405	13,905	17.3	850	1,081
San Jose	18,434	2,547	13.8	-	345
Santa Rosa/Sonoma Valley	11,874	1,831	15.4	107	540
Savannah.	1,462	237	16.2	-	-74
Seattle	112,142	15,523	13.8	339	941
South Bend.	3,020	437	14.5	-	36
Spokane.	2,519	421	16.7	-	-78
St. Louis.	40,735	9,044	22.2	120	1,225
Stamford/Norwalk.	29,968	5,233	17.5	700	-461
Tampa	40,698	7,072	17.4	339	386
Toledo	9,765	1,462	15.0	15	89
Tulsa	15,656	2,928	18.7	-	-230
Washington DC/Suburban MD	59,908	7,843	13.1	1,346	753
Wichita.	7,991	1,536	19.2	-	252
Wilmington.	12,412	1,660	13.4	157	199

- Represents zero.   [1] Net change in occupied stock.   [2] Includes other market areas, not shown separately.

Source: Society of Industrial and Office REALTORS, Washington DC, *2005 Comparative Statistics of Industrial and Office Real Estate Markets* (copyright).

U.S. Census Bureau, Statistical Abstract of the United States: 2006

Table 968. Commercial Buildings—Summary: 2003

[4,645 represents 4,645,000. Excludes mall buildings. Building type based on predominant activity in which the occupants were engaged. Based on a sample survey of building representatives conducted in 2003, therefore subject to sampling variability]

Characteristic	All buildings (1,000)	Floor-space (mil. sq.ft.)	Mean sq. ft. per building (1,000)	Characteristic	All buildings (1,000)	Floor-space (mil. sq.ft.)	Mean sq. ft. per building (1,000)
All buildings	4,645	64,783	13.9	1990 to 1999.	876	12,360	14.1
				2000 to 2003.	334	5,533	16.6
Building floorspace (sq. ft.):				Workers (main shift):			
1,001 to 5,000	2,552	6,789	2.7	Fewer than 5.	2,653	15,492	5.8
5,001 to 10,000	889	6,585	7.4	5 to 9	778	6,166	7.9
10,001 to 25,000	738	11,535	15.6	10 to 19	563	7,803	13.9
25,001 to 50,000	241	8,668	35.9	20 to 49	398	10,989	27.6
50,001 to 100,000	129	9,057	70.4	50 to 99	147	7,934	53.8
100,001 to 200,000.	65	9,064	138.8	100 to 249	77	6,871	89.7
200,001 to 500,000.	25	7,176	289.0	250 or more	30	9,528	320.4
Over 500,000	7	5,908	896.1	Energy sources: [1]			
Principal activity within building:				Electricity	4,404	63,307	14.4
Education	386	9,874	25.6	Natural gas	2,392	43,500	18.2
Food sales	226	1,255	5.6	Fuel oil	452	15,185	33.6
Food service	297	1,654	5.6	District heat.	67	5,454	81.6
Health care	129	3,163	24.6	District chilled water	32	2,831	88.7
Inpatient	8	1,905	241.4	Propane	502	7,076	14.1
Outpatient	121	1,258	10.4	Wood.	62	289	4.6
Lodging	142	5,096	35.8	Heating equipment: [1]			
Retail (other than mall).	443	4,317	9.7	Heat pumps	474	8,771	18.5
Office.	824	12,208	14.8	Furnaces	1,868	19,672	10.5
Public assembly.	277	3,939	14.2	Individual space heaters	818	12,581	15.4
Public order and safety	71	1,090	15.5	District heat.	65	5,177	79.9
Religious worship	370	3,754	10.1	Boilers	580	20,383	35.2
Service.	622	4,050	6.5	Packaged heating units	949	18,054	19.0
Warehouse and storage	597	10,078	16.9	Other.	197	3,249	16.5
Other.	79	1,738	21.9	Cooling equipment: [1]			
Vacant	182	2,567	14.1	Residential-type central A/C . . .	1,005	11,069	11.0
Year constructed:				Heat pumps	493	9,041	18.3
1919 or before.	330	3,769	11.4	Individual A/C	752	12,578	16.7
1920 to 1945.	527	6,871	13.0	District chilled water	32	2,831	88.7
1946 to 1959.	562	7,045	12.5	Central chillers.	112	11,700	104.2
1960 to 1969.	579	8,101	14.0	Packaged A/C units	1,608	29,822	18.5
1970 to 1979.	731	10,772	14.7	Swamp coolers	118	1,554	13.2
1980 to 1989.	707	10,332	14.6	Other.	38	1,227	32.3

[1] More than one type may apply.

Source: U.S. Energy Information Administration, "2003 Commercial Buildings Energy Consumption Buildings (CBECS) Detailed Tables"; Table B1. See Internet site <http://www.eia.doe.gov/emeu/cbecs/cbecs2003/detailed_tables_2003/2003set1 /2003set1.htm> (accessed 19 July 2005).

Table 969. Office Building Markets—Summary: 2003

[As of end-of-year. In thousands of square feet, except as indicated. (159,907 represents 159,907,000). For the top 25 areas in market size. Excludes government-owned, and occupied, owner-occupied, and medical office buildings. CBD means central business district]

Market area	Total market size	Total market vacancy rate (percent)	CBD market size	Suburban market size	CBD market construction	Suburban market construction	CBD rental rate [1] (dol.)
Atlanta.	159,907	21.74	50,558	109,349	1,424	309	21.50
Boston.	142,295	20.27	55,366	86,929	1,582	605	34.01
Charlotte	38,735	15.20	14,293	24,443	(NA)	645	19.19
Chicago	206,328	21.79	127,789	78,539	3,544	(NA)	28.22
Dallas	203,970	25.80	42,880	161,090	(NA)	863	16.89
Denver.	84,366	22.65	23,349	61,017	(NA)	658	17.50
Detroit	76,390	20.66	15,991	60,399	(NA)	783	(NA)
Houston.	260,337	17.14	43,410	216,927	(NA)	380	19.73
Kansas City	64,068	20.64	12,009	52,059	(NA)	654	15.61
Los Angeles	391,596	13.65	63,404	328,192	(NA)	1,292	22.93
Miami	59,177	13.27	14,334	44,843	423	639	24.05
Minneapolis	54,333	20.95	26,111	28,221	(NA)	77	21.03
New Jersey Central	77,323	26.44	(X)	77,323	(NA)	646	(NA)
New Jersey North	113,301	20.90	14,820	98,481	30	139	25.32
New York City (Manhattan) . . .	480,955	12.72	480,955	(X)	(NA)	(NA)	40.91
Orlando	53,633	14.29	8,861	44,771	(NA)	403	21.75
Philadelphia	43,661	15.46	43,661	(X)	(NA)	(NA)	22.60
Raleigh/Durham.	36,094	20.32	4,774	31,320	783	927	16.23
Sacramento	56,660	16.11	5,366	51,294	(NA)	1,213	30.60
San Diego	56,951	11.71	9,128	47,823	410	987	25.80
San Francisco.	89,503	17.56	53,261	36,242	(NA)	(NA)	(NA)
Seattle.	35,479	15.78	19,208	16,271	(NA)	133	25.99
St. Louis	40,647	21.02	10,144	30,503	(NA)	(NA)	(NA)
Tampa	63,141	14.42	11,876	51,265	(NA)	(NA)	(NA)
Washington, D.C	114,031	7.39	114,031	(X)	6,321	(NA)	39.00

NA Not available.   X Not applicable.   [1] Per square foot. Direct asking rental rate (not including sublease).

Source: ONCOR International, Houston, TX, Year-End 2003 Market Data Book (copyright).

Construction and Housing **641**

No. 84.—MANUFACTURES: Gross and Net Values of Products,[a] Census Years 1900 and 1905, by Industry Groups.

[From reports of the Bureau of the Census, Department of Commerce and Labor.]

Group.	1900[b] Gross Value.	1900 Gross Rank.	1900 Net Value.	1900 Net Rank.	1905 Gross Value.	1905 Gross Rank.	1905 Net Value.	1905 Net Rank.
	Dollars.		Dollars.		Dollars.		Dollars.	
Food and kindred products	2,273,880,874	1	1,780,811,817	1	2,845,234,900	1	2,176,489,026	1
Textiles	1,637,484,484	3	1,081,961,248	3	2,147,441,418	3	1,367,009,940	2
Iron and steel and their products	1,793,490,908	2	983,821,918	2	2,176,739,720	2	1,239,490,273	3
Lumber and its remanufactures	1,030,606,350	5	547,227,860	6	1,223,730,330	4	805,315,333	4
Leather and its finished products	588,731,046	9	829,614,905	11	706,747,470	9	401,011,414	10
Paper and printing	600,317,768	8	419,798,101	7	857,112,258	8	596,872,380	7
Liquors and beverages	425,504,167	12	349,157,618	10	501,266,605	11	431,735,398	9
Chemicals and allied products	552,797,877	10	372,538,857	8	1,031,965,203	5	714,489,549	5
Clay, glass, and stone products	293,504,235	13	246,447,118	13	391,230,422	14	334,971,057	11
Metals and metal products, other than iron and steel	748,705,464	7	371,154,446	7	922,262,456	7	442,912,699	8
Tobacco	283,076,546	14	294,062,573	14	331,117,681	13	307,100,175	13
Vehicles for land transportation	508,524,510	11	250,622,377	11	643,924,442	10	324,109,901	12
Shipbuilding	74,578,158	15	42,492,618	15	82,769,239	15	46,707,258	14
Miscellaneous industries	1,004,092,294	6	628,191,538	6	941,604,873	6	602,990,604	6
Hand trades	1,183,615,473	4	721,104,869	4	(c)	(c)	(c)	(c)
Total	13,000,149,159		8,367,967,844		14,802,147,067		9,921,205,387	

[a] The gross value of manufactures as reported by the Census contains many duplications because the finished products of some factories frequently become the material for other factories. In this way not only one but several duplications of the cost of materials often occur. The net value of productions eliminates these duplications by deducting from the gross value the cost of all materials which have undergone any process of manufacture covered by the census reports on manufactures.
[b] The figures of production for 1900 differ from those shown in other portions of this volume by reason of the fact that they exclude 10 lumber establishments reported for Alaska with products valued at $4,250,984.
[c] "Hand trades" not included in the census of 1905.

Source: Statistical Abstract of the United States: 1908 Edition.

Section 21

Manufactures

This section presents summary data for manufacturing as a whole and more detailed information for major industry groups and selected products. The types of measures shown at the different levels include data for establishments, employment and payroll, plant and equipment expenditures, value and quantity of production and shipments, value added by manufacture, inventories, and various indicators of financial status.

The principal sources of these data are U.S. Census Bureau reports of the censuses of manufactures conducted every 5 years, the *Annual Survey of Manufactures,* and *Current Industrial Reports.* Reports on current activities of industries or current movements of individual commodities are compiled by such government agencies as the Bureau of Labor Statistics; the Economic Research Service of the Department of Agriculture; the International Trade Administration; and by private research or trade associations.

Data on financial aspects of manufacturing industries are collected by the U.S. Census Bureau (see especially Tables 986–988 as part of the Quarterly Financial Report. Industry aggregates in the form of balance sheets, profit and loss statements, analyses of sales and expenses, lists of subsidiaries, and types and amounts of security issues are published for leading manufacturing corporations registered with the Securities and Exchange Commission. The BEA issues data on capital in manufacturing industries and capacity utilization rates in manufacturing. See also Section 15, Business Enterprise.

Several private trade associations provide industry coverage for certain sections of the economy. They include the Aluminum Association (Table 995), American Iron and Steel Institute (Tables 996 and 997), Consumer Electronics Association (Table 1003), and the Aerospace Industries Association (Tables 1008 and 1010). Machine tool consumption data (Table 999) is produced jointly by the Association for Manufacturing Technology and American Machine Tool Distributors Association.

Censuses and annual surveys—The first census of manufactures covered the year 1809. Between 1809 and 1963, a census was conducted at periodic intervals. Since 1967, it has been taken every 5 years (for years ending in "2" and "7"). Results from the 2002 census are presented in this section utilizing the new NAICS (North American Industry Classification System). For additional information see text, Section 15, Business Enterprise, and the Census Bureau Web site at <http://www.census.gov/ econ /census02/>. Census data, either directly reported or estimated from administrative records, are obtained for every manufacturing plant with one or more paid employees.

The *Annual Survey of Manufactures* (ASM), conducted for the first time in 1949, collects data for the years between censuses for the more general measure of manufacturing activity covered in detail by the censuses. The annual survey data are estimates derived from a scientifically selected sample of establishments. The 2003 annual survey is based on a sample of about 57,000 from a universe of 366,000 establishments. These establishments represent all manufacturing establishments of multiunit companies and all single-establishment manufacturing companies mailed schedules in the 2002 Census of Manufactures. For the current panel of the ASM sample, all establishments of companies with 2002 shipments in manufacturing in excess of $500 million were included in the survey with certainty. For the remaining portion of the mail survey, the establishment was defined as the sampling unit. For this portion, all establishments with 500 employees or more and establishments with a very large value of shipments also were included. Therefore, of the 57,000 establishments included in the ASM panel, approximately

Manufactures   643

17,000 are selected with certainty. These establishments account for approximately 62 percent of total value of shipments in the 2002 census. Smaller establishments in the remaining portion of the mail survey were selected by sample.

Establishments and classification—
Each of the establishments covered in the 2002 Economic Census—Manufacturing was classified in 1 of 480 industries (473 manufacturing industries and 7 former manufacturing industries) in accordance with the industry definitions in the 2002 NAICS Manual. In the NAICS system, an industry is generally defined as a group of establishments that have similar production processes. To the extent practical, the system uses supply-based or production-oriented concepts in defining industries. The resulting group of establishments must be significant in terms of number, value added by manufacture, value of shipments, and number of employees.

Establishments frequently make products classified both in their industry (primary products) and other industries (secondary products). Industry statistics (employment, payroll, value added by manufacture, value of shipments, etc.) reflect the activities of the establishments, which may make both primary and secondary products. Product statistics, however, represent the output of all establishments without regard for the classification of the producing establishment. For this reason, when relating the industry statistics, especially the value of shipments, to the product statistics, the composition of the industry's output should be considered.

The censuses of manufactures for 1947 through 1992 cover operating manufacturing establishments as defined in the Standard Industrial Classification Manual (SIC), issued by the U.S. Office of Management and Budget (see text, Section 12). The Manual is also used for classifying establishments in the annual surveys. The comparability of manufactures data over time is affected by changes in the official definitions of industries as presented in the Manual. It is important to note, therefore, that the 1987 edition of the Manual was used for the 1987 and 1992 censuses; and the 1972 edition of the Manual and the 1977 Supplement were used for the 1972 through 1982 censuses.

Establishment—Establishment signifies a single physical plant site or factory. It is not necessarily identical to the business unit or company, which may consist of one or more establishments. A company operating establishments at more than one location is required to submit a separate report for each location and include establishments with payroll at any time during the year. An establishment engaged in distinctly different lines of activity and maintaining separate payroll and inventory records is also required to submit separate reports.

Durable goods—Items with a normal life expectancy of 3 years or more. Automobiles, furniture, household appliances, and mobile homes are common examples.

Nondurable goods—Items which generally last for only a short time (3 years or less). Food, beverages, clothing, shoes, and gasoline are common examples.

Statistical reliability—For a discussion of statistical collection and estimation, sampling procedures, and measures of statistical reliability applicable to Census Bureau data, see Appendix III.

Table 970. **Gross Domestic Product in Manufacturing in Current and Real (2000) Dollars by Industry: 1998 to 2004**

[In billions of dollars (8,747.0 represents $8,747,000,000,000), except as indicated. Data are based on the 1997 NAICS. Data include nonfactor charges (capital consumption allowances, indirect business taxes, etc.) as well as factor charges against gross product; corporate profits and capital consumption allowances have been shifted from a company to an establishment basis]

Industry	1998	1999	2000	2001	2002	2003	2004
CURRENT DOLLARS							
Gross domestic product, total [1]	8,747.0	9,268.4	9,817.0	10,128.0	10,487.0	11,004.0	11,735.0
Manufacturing, total.	1,343.9	1,373.1	1,426.2	1,341.3	1,347.2	1,402.3	1,494.0
Percent of total.	15.36	14.81	14.53	13.24	12.85	12.74	12.73
Durable goods	806.9	820.4	865.3	778.9	771.9	798.0	862.6
Wood products	29.4	31.9	31.4	31.3	30.0	32.0	(NA)
Nonmetallic mineral products	42.3	45.1	45.7	44.9	43.3	43.3	(NA)
Primary metals	49.4	47.3	48.2	41.1	41.6	38.9	(NA)
Fabricated metal products	112.7	116.4	121.7	112.0	109.4	112.2	(NA)
Machinery.	111.5	105.6	109.3	103.2	97.6	96.4	(NA)
Computer and electronic products	165.7	162.8	185.6	136.9	130.5	147.6	(NA)
Electrical equipment, appliances, and components	44.7	48.2	50.6	49.2	46.1	47.3	(NA)
Motor vehicles, bodies and trailers, and parts . . .	108.8	115.4	118.1	103.7	114.1	121.9	(NA)
Other transportation equipment.	63.3	64.3	64.4	69.2	70.0	67.6	(NA)
Furniture and related products	29.1	31.0	32.7	30.2	30.0	28.9	(NA)
Miscellaneous manufacturing	49.9	52.5	57.5	57.2	59.4	62.0	(NA)
Nondurable goods	537.0	552.7	561.0	562.5	575.3	604.4	631.4
Food and beverage and tobacco products	137.5	153.6	154.8	167.1	172.5	173.3	(NA)
Textile mills and textile product mills	27.1	26.4	26.5	22.7	22.3	21.7	(NA)
Apparel and leather and allied products	26.0	24.7	25.1	22.8	24.7	25.0	(NA)
Paper products	52.2	54.2	55.6	48.9	50.8	51.5	(NA)
Printing and related support activities.	46.5	48.2	49.0	46.9	46.0	45.2	(NA)
Petroleum and coal products	30.6	22.4	26.2	33.4	25.7	38.2	(NA)
Chemical products	153.4	157.1	157.1	157.2	167.0	181.5	(NA)
Plastics and rubber products	63.6	66.1	66.7	63.4	66.2	68.0	(NA)
CHAINED (2000) DOLLARS							
Gross domestic product, total [1]	9,066.9	9,470.3	9,817.0	9,890.6	10,074.8	10,381.4	10,841.9
Manufacturing, total.	1,286.2	1,342.1	1,426.2	1,346.9	1,378.2	1,440.0	1,501.3
Percent of total.	14.19	14.17	14.53	13.62	13.68	13.87	13.85
Durable goods	729.9	775.5	865.3	813.6	824.2	874.5	925.7
Wood products	29.9	30.4	31.4	30.9	29.9	29.9	(NA)
Nonmetallic mineral products	44.1	45.1	45.7	45.2	42.8	43.4	(NA)
Primary metals	45.9	48.1	48.2	43.2	43.6	41.9	(NA)
Fabricated metal products	114.4	114.9	121.7	109.4	106.3	109.9	(NA)
Machinery.	113.8	105.0	109.3	100.4	94.5	93.7	(NA)
Computer and electronic products	96.3	125.4	185.6	181.9	195.3	250.9	(NA)
Electrical equipment, appliances, and components	44.6	48.0	50.6	48.5	46.4	48.9	(NA)
Motor vehicles, bodies and trailers, and parts . . .	111.8	114.6	118.1	104.6	120.3	131.0	(NA)
Other transportation equipment.	68.3	67.4	64.4	65.2	64.5	60.1	(NA)
Furniture and related products	30.2	31.5	32.7	29.1	28.2	27.2	(NA)
Miscellaneous manufacturing	50.4	52.1	57.5	55.3	55.9	57.8	(NA)
Nondurable goods	559.6	568.2	561.0	533.1	553.0	566.2	578.4
Food and beverage and tobacco products	153.1	155.1	154.8	156.0	153.0	154.6	(NA)
Textile mills and textile product mills	26.3	25.6	26.5	21.5	21.7	21.9	(NA)
Apparel and leather and allied products	26.4	24.4	25.1	22.7	25.0	25.5	(NA)
Paper products	60.0	61.0	55.6	48.8	51.3	53.6	(NA)
Printing and related support activities.	47.7	48.5	49.0	45.3	44.2	43.2	(NA)
Petroleum and coal products	36.5	33.5	26.2	23.9	31.5	28.1	(NA)
Chemical products	149.8	157.1	157.1	153.1	163.3	174.0	(NA)
Plastics and rubber products	62.4	64.7	66.7	61.4	63.6	66.1	(NA)

NA Not available.   [1] For additional industry detail, see Table 651.

Source: U.S. Bureau of Economic Analysis, *Survey of Current Business*, May 2005. See also <http://www.bea.doc.gov/bea /newsrelarchive/2005/gdpind04.pdf> (released 20 April 2005).

Manufactures **645**

Table 971. Manufacturing—Establishments, Employees, and Annual Payroll by Industry: 2001 and 2002

[(115,061 represents 115,061,000). Excludes government employees, railroad employees, self-employed persons, etc. See "General Explanation" in source for definitions and statement on reliability of data. An *establishment* is a single physical location where business is conducted or where services or industrial operations are performed. See Appendix III]

Industry	NAICS code [1]	2001			2002		
		Establish- ments, number	Employ- ees [2] (1,000)	Annual payroll (mil. dol.)	Establish- ments, number	Employ- ees [2] (1,000)	Annual payroll (mil. dol.)
All industries, total	(X)	7,095,302	115,061	3,989,086	7,200,770	112,401	3,943,180
Manufacturing, total	31-33	352,619	15,950	617,699	344,341	14,394	580,356
Percent of all industries	(X)	5.07	13.86	15.48	4.78	12.81	14.72
Food manufacturing.	311	26,785	1,470	44,085	25,698	1,444	44,480
Beverage & tobacco product	312	3,212	171	7,258	3,232	163	7,154
Textile mills	313	4,452	308	8,403	4,045	262	7,608
Textile product mills	314	6,966	202	5,059	7,332	190	5,113
Apparel manufacturing	315	16,152	442	9,262	13,359	350	8,152
Leather & allied product	316	1,763	61	1,496	1,549	48	1,269
Wood product.	321	17,289	558	15,829	17,052	534	15,922
Paper	322	5,739	533	22,501	5,546	496	21,813
Printing & related support activities.	323	37,895	785	27,051	36,902	706	25,062
Petroleum & coal products	324	2,253	104	6,336	2,296	100	6,456
Chemical	325	13,361	870	46,395	13,096	827	46,431
Plastics & rubber products	326	15,981	1,003	32,641	15,462	926	32,036
Nonmetallic mineral product	327	16,732	524	19,350	16,674	475	18,120
Primary metal	331	6,684	573	23,642	6,229	501	21,623
Fabricated metal product	332	60,791	1,761	61,803	61,652	1,582	57,682
Machinery	333	28,922	1,333	54,714	27,941	1,166	50,101
Computer & electronic product.	334	16,764	1,593	84,522	15,883	1,300	71,698
Electrical equip, appliance & component	335	6,940	575	20,873	6,601	502	18,849
Transportation equipment	336	12,627	1,753	83,440	12,202	1,579	78,771
Furniture & related product	337	20,593	619	17,434	22,083	575	16,806
Miscellaneous.	339	30,718	713	25,605	29,507	665	25,208

X Not applicable.   [1] North American Industry Classification System, 1997; see text, Section 15.   [2] Covers full- and part-time employees who are on the payroll in the pay period including March 12.

Source: U.S. Census Bureau, *County Business Patterns*, annual. See also <http://www.census.gov/prod/2004pubs/02cbp /cbp02-1.pdf> (released November 2004).

Table 972. Manufacturing Establishments, Employees, and Annual Payroll by State: 2002

[14,394 represents 14,394,000) Excludes government employees, railroad employees, self-employed persons, etc. See "General Explanation" in source for definitions and statement on reliability of data. An *establishment* is a single physical location where business is conducted or where services or industrial operations are performed]

State	Establish- ments	Em- ployees [1] (1,000)	Annual payroll (mil.dol.)	State	Establish- ments	Em- ployees [1] (1,000)	Annual payroll (mil.dol.)
United States . . .	344,341	14,394	580,356	Missouri	7,112	308	11,090
Alabama	5,053	283	9,712	Montana	1,201	19	631
Alaska	495	11	364	Nebraska	1,930	102	3,367
Arizona	4,796	168	6,993	Nevada	1,728	39	1,462
Arkansas	3,146	214	6,293	New Hampshire	2,184	87	3,523
California	47,558	1,560	71,082	New Jersey	10,454	347	16,705
Colorado	5,250	149	6,235	New Mexico	1,545	34	1,265
Connecticut	5,280	211	10,338	New York	20,778	625	25,892
Delaware	688	39	1,607	North Carolina	10,548	613	20,398
District of Columbia . . .	144	2	80	North Dakota	689	22	721
Florida	14,880	372	13,880	Ohio	17,189	829	34,319
Georgia	8,636	450	15,650	Oklahoma	3,960	148	5,180
Hawaii	915	13	440	Oregon	5,521	178	7,336
Idaho	1,763	60	2,056	Pennsylvania	16,399	711	27,870
Illinois.	16,556	727	30,024	Rhode Island	2,086	60	2,255
Indiana	9,053	552	22,748	South Carolina	4,360	290	10,750
Iowa	3,718	223	8,049	South Dakota	897	37	1,120
Kansas	3,181	179	6,803	Tennessee.	6,833	408	14,927
Kentucky	4,166	260	9,951	Texas	21,051	851	34,760
Louisiana	3,427	149	6,433	Utah.	3,018	110	3,995
Maine	1,827	65	2,484	Vermont	1,140	44	1,759
Maryland	3,929	145	6,465	Virginia	5,773	313	12,049
Massachusetts	8,686	330	15,856	Washington	7,365	269	11,872
Michigan	14,947	691	31,978	West Virginia	1,454	69	2,574
Minnesota	7,953	336	13,932	Wisconsin	9,771	500	19,342
Mississippi.	2,766	183	5,355	Wyoming.	542	10	386

[1] Covers full- and part-time employees who are on the payroll in the pay period including March 12.

Source: U.S. Census Bureau, *County Business Patterns*, annual. See also <http://www.census.gov/prod/2004pubs/02cbp/cbp02-1pdf> issued November 2004).

Table 973. Manufactures—Summary by Selected Industry: 2003

[13,875.5 represents 13,875,500. Based on the Annual Survey of Manufactures; see Appendix III]

Industry based on shipments	NAICS code [1]	All employees [2]			Produc- tion workers [2] (1,000)	Value added by manufac- tures [3] (mil.dol.)	Value of ship- ments [4] (mil. dol.)
		Number (1,000)	Payroll				
			Total (mil. dol.)	Per employee (dol.)			
Manufacturing, total	31-33	13,875.5	565,026	40,721	9,794.5	1,912,124	3,979,917
Food [5]	311	1,467.4	45,685	31,134	1,121.2	211,697	482,815
Beverage and tobacco product	312	151.3	6,866	45,391	85.8	69,125	106,873
Textile mills	313	247.5	7,167	28,959	210.8	18,531	42,557
Textile product mills	314	169.9	4,596	27,058	135.4	13,480	30,827
Apparel [5]	315	296.1	6,704	22,644	233.9	20,396	40,624
Wood product [5]	321	511.4	15,631	30,564	419.6	36,571	91,240
Paper	322	464.3	20,773	44,737	360.6	72,084	149,270
Pulp, paper, and paperboard mills	3221	144.8	8,261	57,048	115.3	35,000	66,651
Printing and related support activities. . . .	323	675.4	25,127	37,205	488.1	56,590	92,192
Petroleum and coal products	324	101.4	6,411	63,234	65.8	45,415	237,011
Chemical [5]	325	829.5	45,082	54,348	480.5	260,288	477,360
Pharmaceutical and medicine	3254	244.8	14,388	58,773	119.9	110,502	148,099
Plastics and rubber products	326	933.9	32,165	34,442	731.6	91,591	176,344
Plastics product	3261	762.7	25,360	33,250	598.0	74,063	142,769
Nonmetallic mineral product [5]	327	462.5	17,733	38,340	360.5	54,768	96,349
Primary metal [5]	331	455.5	20,196	44,337	357.4	54,194	136,839
Iron and steel mills and ferroalloy.	3311	108.8	5,919	54,383	86.6	17,637	47,230
Fabricated metal product [5]	332	1,484.1	55,882	37,655	1,107.6	137,232	244,662
Machinery [5]	333	1,101.1	48,123	43,703	694.9	126,232	253,673
Industrial machinery	3332	144.3	7,270	50,381	73.5	15,156	28,965
Metalworking machinery.	3335	174.3	7,950	45,624	120.8	15,437	24,466
Computer and electronic product [5]	334	1,163.0	63,097	54,255	539.6	203,514	353,665
Computer and peripheral equipment. . .	3341	142.2	8,529	59,959	42.4	30,489	68,768
Communications equipment	3342	163.5	9,249	56,560	62.2	30,557	60,506
Semiconductor and other electronic components	3344	388.7	18,614	47,882	231.2	72,776	113,206
Navigational, measuring, medical, control instruments	3345	406.8	24,306	59,757	161.9	62,283	95,560
Electrical equipment, appliance, and component [5]	335	453.3	17,266	38,089	320.9	52,298	101,771
Electrical equipment	3353	149.5	5,904	39,502	98.7	16,476	30,611
Transportation equipment [5]	336	1,580.9	80,994	51,233	1,142.1	258,540	653,489
Motor vehicle	3361	209.5	14,192	67,730	184.1	78,236	259,578
Motor vehicle parts	3363	670.5	31,401	46,834	524.9	84,234	200,491
Aerospace product and parts	3364	374.6	23,101	61,676	188.0	65,389	124,071
Furniture and related product [5]	337	556.0	16,808	30,229	433.5	43,531	76,621

[1] North American Industry Classification System, 1997; see text, Section 15. [2] Includes employment and payroll at administrative offices and auxiliary units. All employees represents the average of production workers plus all other employees for the payroll period ended nearest the 12th of March. Production workers represents the average of the employment for the payroll periods ended nearest the 12th of March, May, August, and November. [3] Adjusted value added; takes into account (a) value added by merchandising operations (that is, difference between the sales value and cost of merchandise sold without further manufacture, processing, or assembly), plus (b) net change in finished goods and work-in-process inventories between beginning and end of year. [4] Includes extensive and unmeasurable duplication from shipments between establishments in the same industry classification. [5] Includes industries not shown separately.

Source: U.S. Census Bureau, Annual Survey of Manufactures, Statistics for Industry Groups and Industries, Series M03(AS)-1. See also <http://www.census.gov/prod/2005pubs/am0331gs1.pdf> (issued March 2005).

Table 974. Manufactures—Summary by State: 2003

[13,865.8 represents 13,865,800. Sum of state totals may not add to U.S. total because U.S. and state figures were independently derived. See Appendix III]

State	All employees [1]			Production workers [1]		Value added by manufactures [2]		Value of shipments [3] (mil. dol.)
		Payroll					Per production worker (dol.)	
	Number (1,000)	Total (mil. dol.)	Per employee (dol.)	Total (1,000)	Wages (mil. dol.)	Total (mil. dol.)		
United States	13,865.8	564,771	40,731	9,795	329,730	1,909,616	137,721	3,977,165
Alabama..........	260.3	9,406	36,130	205	6,434	29,768	114,342	70,048
Alaska...........	11.4	371	32,647	10	276	1,413	124,424	4,371
Arizona..........	161.2	7,120	44,159	101	3,367	29,017	179.964	44,900
Arkansas	193.0	6,120	31,717	154	4,379	22,730	117,800	47,560
California	1,523.3	64,840	42,565	978	30,195	197.547	129,682	378,468
Colorado.........	141.9	6,338	44,650	90	3,161	17,243	121,478	33,775
Connecticut.......	194.5	9,248	47,547	117	4,478	25,771	132,499	41,587
Delaware	36.5	1,630	44,667	26	965	4,607	126,240	14,445
District of Columbia ...	1.9	84	43,383	1	18	196	100,722	293
Florida	358.3	13,972	38,994	233	6,919	42,391	118,310	78,900
Georgia	430.8	15,422	35,801	330	10,082	58,683	136,229	125,099
Hawaii	13.6	434	32,022	9	269	1,224	90,275	3,880
Idaho...........	58.2	2,159	37,087	44	1,434	7,701	132,311	15,788
Illinois	704.7	29,021	41,180	493	16,611	93,534	132,722	190,421
Indiana..........	536.4	22,484	41,916	408	15,219	80,988	150,981	167,437
Iowa	217.8	8,183	37,567	158	5,148	32,739	150,290	70,323
Kansas..........	167.7	6,702	39,959	117	3,988	20,429	121,794	50,368
Kentucky	251.7	10,108	40,168	192	6,825	35,562	141,317	89,652
Louisiana	144.8	6,392	44,152	105	4,158	30,605	211,407	94,387
Maine...........	64.5	2,535	39,312	48	1,682	7,377	114,393	13,925
Maryland	143.8	6,515	45,312	92	3,118	18,490	128,611	35,456
Massachusetts......	325.8	14,962	45,929	201	6,864	46,266	142,025	78,023
Michigan.........	685.4	32,549	47,489	506	21,951	97,552	142,330	223,853
Minnesota........	333.4	14,045	42,127	224	7,615	41,451	124,335	82,691
Mississippi	167.6	5,257	31,363	134	3,628	17,169	102,437	39,995
Missouri.........	306.1	12,405	40,532	226	8,111	43,120	140,887	95,941
Montana.........	16.6	587	35,412	12	379	1,794	108,273	5,334
Nebraska	100.9	3,388	33,592	78	2,296	11,844	117,426	32,962
Nevada	44.3	1,821	41,116	28	947	5,040	113,829	9,103
New Hampshire......	83.7	3,563	42,549	54	1,730	8,909	106,398	16,205
New Jersey........	345.2	15,386	44,569	226	7,902	51,979	150,570	96,325
New Mexico	29.9	1,169	39,087	22	723	6,150	205,683	10,670
New York	592.1	24,434	41,269	398	13,169	80,199	135,453	142,252
North Carolina......	569.4	19,792	34,761	434	12,590	89,017	156,340	157,359
North Dakota.......	21.2	721	34,006	16	469	2,520	118,813	6,419
Ohio	811.2	34,337	42,330	596	22,446	109,282	134,723	240,066
Oklahoma.........	138.6	5,158	37,223	102	3,314	17,686	127,619	41,345
Oregon..........	176.1	6,984	39,653	125	4,205	25,109	142,575	44,512
Pennsylvania.......	675.6	26,880	39,787	479	16,125	93,777	138,805	183,721
Rhode Island.......	60.4	2,296	38,020	41	1,211	6,039	100,007	10,653
South Carolina......	279.3	10,412	37,275	212	6,756	39,228	140,438	84,526
South Dakota	36.0	1,138	31,639	27	769	3,776	105,013	10,356
Tennessee	384.7	14,345	37,286	291	9,259	51,130	132,902	113,789
Texas...........	806.8	33,636	41,690	558	18,647	123,846	153,503	326,718
Utah	105.8	3,980	37,608	71	2,162	12,720	120,177	25,624
Vermont..........	41.5	1,716	41,309	28	936	4,972	119,669	9,469
Virginia..........	295.9	11,530	38,973	218	7,221	46,849	158,349	82,760
Washington........	258.6	10,930	42,266	165	5,535	38,896	150,404	79,891
West Virginia.......	64.6	2,613	40,435	49	1,720	8,205	126,972	19,463
Wisconsin.........	481.9	19,239	39,925	352	12,021	65,355	135,630	131,134
Wyoming	11.1	416	37,552	9	301	1,722	155,466	4,924

[1] Includes employment and payroll at administrative offices and auxiliary units. All employees represents the average of production workers plus all other employees for the payroll period ended nearest the 12th of March. Production workers represents the average of the employment for the payroll periods ended nearest the 12th of March, May, August, and November. [2] Adjusted value added; takes into account (a) value added by merchandising operations (that is, difference between the sales value and cost of merchandise sold without further manufacture, processing, or assembly), plus (b) net change in finished goods and work-in-process inventories between beginning and end of year. [3] Includes extensive and unmeasurable duplication from shipments between establishments in the same industry classification.

Source: U.S. Census Bureau, *Annual Survey of Manufactures, Geographic Area Statistics*, Series M03(AS)-3. See also <http://www.census.gov/prod/2005pubs/m03as-3.pdf> (issued May 2005).

Table 975. **Manufacturing Industries—Export-Related Shipments and Employment by Industry: 2001**

[(3,970,499.8 represents $3,970,499,800,000) Exports include both "direct" exports (exports manufactured in the U.S. and consumed in foreign markets and "indirect" exports (intermediate goods and services required to manufacture export goods). For methodology, see report]

Industry	NAICS code [1]	Value of manufacturers' shipments (mil. dol.)	Export-related shipments (mil. dol.)	All manufacturing employment (1,000)	Export-related manufacturing employment (1,000)	Export-related as percent of all manufacturers	
						Shipments	Employment
Manufacturing, total	31-33	3,970,499.8	806,189.2	15,879.5	3,251.7	20.3	20.5
Food manufacturing	311	451,385.9	31,806.1	1,504.7	90.5	7.0	6.0
Beverage and tobacco products	312	118,785.6	4,354.7	177.5	4.9	3.7	2.8
Textile mills	313	45,680.7	12,667.7	293.9	85.6	27.7	29.1
Textile products	314	31,970.6	2,547.7	209.7	18.9	8.0	9.0
Apparel	315	54,598.3	6,570.3	456.5	57.7	12.0	12.6
Leather and allied products	316	8,834.4	2,519.9	61.7	14.7	28.5	23.8
Wood products	321	87,250.0	6,727.9	555.9	41.1	7.7	7.4
Paper	322	155,846.0	27,284.1	530.2	90.2	17.5	17.0
Printing and related support activities	323	100,792.2	10,677.3	799.2	86.1	10.6	10.8
Petroleum and coal products	324	219,074.8	17,502.0	101.5	8.5	8.0	8.4
Chemicals	325	438,410.2	109,148.4	875.0	225.1	24.9	25.7
Plastics and rubber products	326	170,716.8	29,377.3	1,028.1	178.6	17.2	17.4
Nonmetallic mineral products	327	94,860.6	11,449.2	507.3	63.8	12.1	12.6
Primary metals	331	138,245.4	56,706.4	532.8	209.8	41.0	39.4
Fabricated metal products	332	253,113.4	53,257.4	1,724.7	383.8	21.0	22.3
Machinery	333	266,552.9	75,829.6	1,314.7	372.5	28.4	28.3
Computers and electronic products	334	429,470.8	155,184.4	1,598.8	610.4	36.1	38.2
Electrical equipment, appliances, and components	335	114,067.0	28,855.7	556.6	146.8	25.3	26.4
Transportation equipment	336	602,495.9	141,758.6	1,717.6	418.6	23.5	24.4
Furniture and related products	337	72,147.1	2,869.1	608.0	24.6	4.0	4.0
Miscellaneous	339	116,201.1	19,095.4	725.1	119.7	16.4	16.5

[1] North American Industry Classification System, 1997; see text, Section 15, Business Enterprise.
Source: U.S. Census Bureau, *Exports from Manufacturing Establishments: 2001*, series AR(01)-1. See also <http://www.census.gov/mcd/exports/ar01.pdf> (released July 2004).

Table 976. **Manufacturing Industries—Export-Related Shipments and Employment by State: 2001**

[806,189 represents $806,189,000,000. Exports include both "direct" exports (exports manufactured in the U.S. and consumed in foreign markets and "indirect" exports (intermediate goods and services required to manufacture export goods). For methodology, see report]

State	Export-related shipments (mil. dol.)	Export-related manufacturing employment (1,000)	Export-related as percent of all manufacturers		State	Export-related shipments (mil. dol.)	Export-related manufacturing employment (1,000)	Export-related as percent of all manufacturers	
			Shipments	Employment				Shipments	Employment
U.S.	806,189	3,252	20.3	20.5	Mississippi	4,750	20	12.3	9.9
					Missouri	13,486	56	15.0	16.2
Alabama	12,452	46	18.5	14.7	Montana	442	1	8.2	6.4
Alaska	599	2	15.0	11.9	Nebraska	4,581	15	14.7	14.7
Arizona	11,218	48	26.6	25.5	Nevada	1,120	6	14.8	15.8
Arkansas	7,421	30	15.9	13.1	New Hampshire	3,656	20	21.5	20.8
California	110,597	471	26.7	26.3	New Jersey	15,933	64	16.2	16.9
Colorado	7,113	34	20.0	20.9	New Mexico	3,368	8	29.4	23.2
Connecticut	11,561	55	24.5	24.0	New York	29,325	140	20.0	19.7
Delaware	1,131	4	6.8	9.7	North Carolina	28,668	140	17.2	20.1
District					North Dakota	666	2	10.2	8.1
of Columbia	1	(D)	0.3	(D)	Ohio	53,214	215	22.0	23.3
Florida	11,561	59	15.1	14.7	Oklahoma	6,100	27	15.2	16.7
Georgia	20,387	73	16.0	15.0	Oregon	12,016	50	27.8	24.9
Hawaii	197	1	6.2	9.0	Pennsylvania	29,667	133	16.6	17.3
Idaho	4,040	16	26.8	24.4	Rhode Island	1,925	12	17.6	17.6
Illinois	37,336	151	19.0	18.6	South Carolina	20,046	80	25.5	25.6
Indiana	31,067	120	20.1	20.1	South Dakota	2,192	7	19.8	17.2
Iowa	10,623	41	16.2	17.4	Tennessee	17,404	77	16.7	17.5
Kansas	6,987	26	13.2	13.5	Texas	69,444	216	21.6	22.7
Kentucky	14,967	50	17.8	17.9	Utah	4,800	23	18.5	18.8
Louisiana	11,691	22	13.7	14.1	Vermont	4,048	18	45.4	38.4
Maine	2,500	12	16.6	14.9	Virginia	14,071	57	15.2	17.4
Maryland	4,948	24	13.7	15.0	Washington	44,121	127	49.4	41.0
Massachusetts	20,721	98	25.9	26.0	West Virginia	3,026	12	18.7	17.0
Michigan	47,700	190	22.8	25.4	Wisconsin	18,356	87	14.5	15.9
Minnesota	12,794	68	15.5	18.2	Wyoming	204	-	5.3	4.4

- Represents or rounds to zero. D Data withheld to avoid disclosure of individual companies.
Source: U.S. Census Bureau, *Exports from Manufacturing Establishments: 2001*, series AR(01)-1. See also <http://www.census.gov/mcd/exports/ar01.pdf> (released July 2004).

Manufactures 649

Table 977. Manufacturers' E-Commerce Shipments by Industry: 2002 and 2003

[(3,920,632 represents $3,920,632,000,000). Based on the Annual Survey of Manufactures; subject to sampling variability. E-commerce is the value of goods and services sold over computer-mediated networks (open or proprietary)]

Industry	NAICS code [1]	2002				2003			
		Ship-ments, total (mil. dol)	E-commerce			Ship-ments, total (mil.dol)	E-commerce		
			Ship-ments, total (mil.dol)	Percent of total ship-ments	Percent distri-bution		Ship-ments, total (mil.dol)	Percent of total ship-ments	Percent distri-bution
Manufacturing, total	31-33	3,920,632	751,985	19.2	100.0	3,979,917	842,666	21.2	100.0
Food products	311	460,020	51,094	11.1	6.8	482,815	59.576	12.3	7.1
Beverage and tobacco	312	105,691	45,419	43.0	6.0	106,873	46,998	44.0	5.6
Textile mills	313	45,549	3,977	8.7	0.5	42,557	3,639	8.6	0.4
Textile product mills	314	31,807	7,491	23.6	1.0	30,827	7,244	23.5	0.9
Apparel	315	44,515	9,726	21.8	1.3	40,624	9,137	22.5	1.1
Leather and allied products	316	6,299	783	12.4	0.1	6,003	653	10.9	0.1
Wood products	321	88,985	4,567	5.1	0.6	91,240	5,753	6.3	0.7
Paper.	322	153,655	18,385	12.0	2.4	149,270	18,683	12.5	2.2
Printing and related support activities	323	95,388	4,725	5.0	0.6	92,192	4,452	4.8	0.5
Petroleum and coal products	324	215,190	25,523	11.9	3.4	237,011	51,586	21.8	6.1
Chemicals.	325	460,451	68,674	14.9	9.1	477,360	85,186	17.8	10.1
Plastics and rubber products	326	173,901	23,953	13.8	3.2	176,344	26,954	15.3	3.2
Nonmetallic mineral products	327	95,265	7,144	7.5	1.0	96,349	8,631	9.0	1.0
Primary metals.	331	139,449	12,828	9.2	1.7	136,839	12,578	9.2	1.5
Fabricated metal products	332	246,734	21,427	8.7	2.8	244,662	23,735	9.7	2.8
Machinery.	333	253,135	30,390	12.0	4.0	253,673	34,797	13.7	4.1
Computer and electronic products	334	358,258	73,406	20.5	9.8	353,666	67,476	19.1	8.0
Electrical equipment, appliances, and components.	335	104,472	23,043	22.1	3.1	101,771	23,722	23.3	2.8
Transportation equipment	336	637,675	297,280	46.6	39.5	653,489	327,401	50.1	38.9
Furniture and related products . . .	337	77,242	8,082	10.5	1.1	76,621	9,983	13.0	1.2
Miscellaneous	339	126,951	14,068	11.1	1.9	129,731	14,482	11.2	1.7

[1] North American Industry Classification System, 1997; see text, Section 15.

Source: U.S. Census Bureau, Internet site <http://www.census.gov/eos/www/papers/2003/2003finaltables.pdf> (released 11 May 2005).

Table 978. Manufacturing Employer Costs for Employee Compensation Per Hour Worked: 1990 to 2004

[As of March, for private industry workers. Based on a sample of establishments in the National Compensation Survey; see Appendix III and source for details. See also Table 637, Section 12]

Compensation component	Cost (dol.)					Percent distribution				
	1990	2000	2002	2003	2004	1990	2000	2002	2003	2004
Total compensation	17.33	23.41	25.20	26.02	28.10	100.0	100.0	100.0	100.0	100.0
Wages and salaries.	11.86	16.01	17.19	17.43	18.14	68.4	68.4	68.2	67.0	64.6
Total benefits	5.47	7.40	8.01	8.59	9.96	31.6	31.6	31.8	33.0	35.4
Paid leave	1.31	1.74	1.91	1.97	2.05	7.6	7.4	7.6	7.6	7.3
Vacation.	0.67	0.86	0.97	1.00	1.03	3.9	3.7	3.8	3.8	3.7
Holiday	0.48	0.65	0.70	0.73	0.76	2.8	2.8	2.8	2.8	2.7
Sick.	0.12	0.13	0.14	0.16	0.16	0.7	0.6	0.6	0.6	0.6
Other.	0.05	0.10	0.10	0.10	0.10	0.3	0.4	0.4	0.4	0.4
Supplemental pay	0.65	1.04	1.13	1.23	1.20	3.8	4.4	4.5	4.7	4.3
Premium pay.	0.34	0.58	0.56	0.60	0.60	2.0	2.5	2.2	2.3	2.1
Nonproduction bonuses. . .	0.22	0.36	0.46	0.51	0.48	1.3	1.5	1.8	2.0	1.7
Shift pay.	0.09	0.10	0.11	0.11	0.12	0.5	0.4	0.4	0.4	0.4
Insurance.	1.37	1.85	2.11	2.27	2.59	7.9	7.9	8.4	8.7	9.2
Health insurance	(NA)	1.69	1.92	2.08	2.40	(NA)	7.2	7.6	8.0	8.5
Retirement and savings	0.56	0.75	0.74	0.86	1.56	3.2	3.2	2.9	3.3	5.6
Defined benefit	(NA)	0.34	0.30	0.41	1.06	(NA)	1.5	1.2	1.6	3.8
Defined contributions	(NA)	0.41	0.44	0.45	0.50	(NA)	1.8	1.7	1.7	1.8
Legally required	1.54	1.92	2.05	2.18	2.43	8.9	8.2	8.1	8.4	8.6
Social Security.	1.02	1.38	1.48	1.51	1.57	5.9	5.9	5.9	5.8	5.6
Federal unemployment . . .	0.03	0.03	0.03	0.03	0.03	0.2	0.1	0.1	0.1	0.1
State unemployment.	0.12	0.11	0.11	0.13	0.18	0.7	0.5	0.4	0.5	0.6
Workers compensation . . .	0.36	0.40	0.43	0.51	0.64	2.1	1.7	1.7	2.0	2.3
Other benefits [1]	0.04	0.09	0.07	0.08	0.13	0.2	0.4	0.3	0.3	0.5

NA Not available. [1] Includes severance pay and supplemental unemployment benefits.

Source: U.S. Bureau of Labor Statistics, *Employer Costs for Employee Compensation Historical Listing, annual, 1986-2001*, and *Employer Costs for Employee Compensation, March 2005*. See also <ftp://ftp.bls.gov/pub/special.requests/ocwc/ect/ecechist.pdf> (issued 19 June 2002) and <http://www.bls.gov/news.release/pdf/ecec.pdf> (issued 16 March 2005).

Table 979. **Manufacturing Industries—Employment by Industry: 1990 to 2004**

[Annual averages of monthly figures (109,487 represents 109,487,000). Covers all full- and part-time employees who worked during, or received pay for, any part of the pay period including the 12th of the month. Minus sign (-) indicates decrease. See also headnote, Table 618]

Industry	2002 NAICS code [1]	All employees (1,000)						Percent change	
		1990	2000	2001	2002	2003	2004	1990-2000	2000-2004
All industries	(X)	109,487	131,785	131,826	130,341	129,999	131,480	20.4	-0.2
Manufacturing	31-33	17,695	17,263	16,441	15,259	14,510	14,329	-2.4	-17.0
Percent of all industries	(X)	16.16	13.10	12.47	11.71	11.16	10.90	(X)	(X)
Durable goods	(X)	10,736	10,876	10,335	9,483	8,963	8,923	1.3	-18.0
Wood products	321	541	613	574	555	538	548	13.4	-10.5
Sawmills and wood preservation	3211	148	134	127	121	117	118	-9.6	-12.2
Plywood and engineered wood products	3212	96	122	116	116	114	117	28.2	-4.2
Other wood products	3219	297	357	331	318	306	314	20.1	-12.1
Nonmetallic mineral products	327	528	554	545	516	494	505	4.9	-8.9
Clay products and refractories	3271	84	82	77	72	66	66	-1.9	-20.1
Glass and glass products	3272	152	141	136	124	115	112	-7.6	-20.2
Cement and concrete products	3273	195	234	236	230	224	235	20.1	0.4
Lime, gypsum, and other nonmetallic mineral products	3279	98	97	95	91	89	92	-0.3	-5.5
Primary metals	331	689	622	571	509	477	466	-9.7	-25.1
Iron and steel mills and ferroalloy production	3311	187	135	122	107	102	95	-27.7	-29.3
Steel products from purchased steel . .	3312	70	73	68	63	61	61	4.0	-16.9
Alumina and aluminum production . .	3313	108	101	92	80	75	73	-7.3	-27.4
Other nonferrous metal production . . .	3314	109	96	90	81	74	71	-11.7	-26.0
Foundries	3315	214	217	200	178	166	165	1.4	-23.7
Fabricated metal products	332	1,610	1,753	1,676	1,549	1,479	1,498	8.9	-14.6
Forging and stamping	3321	128	138	125	113	109	110	7.9	-20.5
Cutlery and hand tools	3322	79	79	72	64	61	59	0.3	-25.6
Architectural and structural metals . . .	3323	357	428	422	399	380	390	20.0	-9.0
Boilers, tanks, and shipping containers	3324	117	107	103	96	91	92	-9.1	-13.3
Hardware	3325	57	50	46	42	40	38	-12.8	-23.2
Spring and wire products	3326	78	81	76	70	64	62	4.3	-23.4
Machine shops and threaded products	3327	309	365	348	318	311	326	18.4	-10.7
Coating, engraving, and heat treating metals	3328	143	175	163	149	143	142	22.7	-18.5
Other fabricated metal products	3329	344	330	321	296	281	278	-4.0	-15.6
Machinery	333	1,408	1,455	1,368	1,230	1,149	1,142	3.3	-21.5
Agricultural, construction, and mining machinery	3331	229	222	217	200	188	195	-2.8	-12.3
Industrial machinery	3332	152	163	149	131	123	119	7.5	-27.1
Commercial and service industry machinery	3333	147	147	143	130	118	115	0.3	-21.9
HVAC and commercial refrigeration equipment	3334	165	194	184	167	157	152	17.8	-21.5
Metalworking machinery	3335	267	274	249	217	205	202	2.5	-26.3
Turbine and power transmission equipment	3336	114	111	106	101	94	93	-2.4	-16.7
Other general purpose machinery	3339	335	343	321	285	265	266	2.4	-22.5
Computer and electronic products	334	1,903	1,820	1,749	1,507	1,355	1,326	-4.3	-27.1
Computer and peripheral equipment . .	3341	367	302	286	250	224	212	-17.8	-29.7
Communications equipment	3342	232	248	234	186	155	151	7.0	-39.2
Audio and video equipment	3343	60	52	47	42	37	32	-13.3	-38.8
Semiconductors and electronic components	3344	574	676	645	525	461	453	17.8	-33.0
Electronic instruments	3345	626	479	475	450	430	432	-23.6	-9.8
Magnetic media manufacturing and reproduction	3346	43	63	61	55	48	47	46.4	-25.7
Electrical equipment and appliances	335	633	591	557	497	460	447	-6.7	-24.4
Electric lighting equipment	3351	81	85	79	72	67	65	5.0	-23.1
Household appliances	3352	114	106	102	98	93	90	-7.0	-14.8
Electrical equipment	3353	244	210	197	175	160	153	-13.9	-27.0
Other electrical equipment and components	3359	195	191	180	152	140	139	-2.3	-27.3
Transportation equipment [2]	336	2,133	2,056	1,938	1,829	1,774	1,764	-3.6	-14.2
Motor vehicles	3361	271	291	279	265	265	256	7.4	-12.1
Motor vehicle bodies and trailers	3362	130	183	159	152	153	165	40.8	-10.0
Motor vehicle parts	3363	653	840	775	734	708	689	28.6	-18.0
Aerospace products and parts	3364	841	517	511	470	442	444	-38.5	-14.1
Ship and boat building	3366	173	153	147	146	146	148	-11.4	-3.1
Other transportation equipment	3369	35	40	39	39	38	38	14.0	-4.8

See footnotes at end of table.

Manufactures   651

Table 979. Manufacturing Industries—Employment by Industry: 1990 to 2004—Con.

[Annual averages of monthly figures (109,487 represents 109,487,000). Covers all full- and part-time employees who worked during, or received pay for, any part of the pay period including the 12th of the month. See also headnote, Table 618]

Industry	2002 NAICS code [1]	All employees (1,000)						Percent change	
		1990	2000	2001	2002	2003	2004	1990-2000	2000-2004
Furniture and related products.	337	601	680	642	604	573	573	13.0	-15.7
Household and institutional furniture	3371	398	440	416	400	382	384	10.6	-12.7
Office furniture and fixtures	3372	156	181	171	151	139	136	16.0	-24.9
Other furniture-related products	3379	47	58	56	54	52	52	23.1	-10.2
Miscellaneous manufacturing	339	690	733	715	688	663	656	6.2	-10.6
Medical equipment and supplies.	3391	288	310	311	308	304	304	7.7	-1.9
Other miscellaneous manufacturing	3399	403	423	403	380	359	351	5.1	-16.9
Nondurable goods	(X)	6,959	6,388	6,107	5,775	5547	5406	-8.2	-15.4
Food manufacturing	311	1,507	1,553	1,551	1,526	1518	1497	3.0	-3.6
Animal food	3111	57	55	53	51	50	51	-4.2	-7.1
Grain and oilseed milling.	3112	71	65	63	62	62	61	-9.1	-6.5
Sugar and confectionery products.	3113	99	92	89	84	85	84	-7.3	-9.1
Fruit and vegetable preserving and specialty.	3114	218	197	193	183	185	182	-9.5	-7.9
Dairy products	3115	145	136	137	137	135	132	-5.9	-2.9
Animal slaughtering and processing	3116	427	507	516	517	516	505	18.6	-0.3
Seafood product preparation and packaging.	3117	54	45	47	44	42	42	-17.2	-7.3
Bakeries and tortilla manufacturing	3118	292	306	303	297	292	288	4.9	-6.1
Other food products	3119	143	150	152	151	152	154	5.0	2.5
Beverages and tobacco products.	312	218	207	209	207	200	194	-4.9	-6.1
Beverages	3121	173	175	177	174	169	165	1.2	-5.7
Textile mills	313	492	378	333	291	261	239	-23.1	-36.9
Fiber, yarn, and thread mills	3131	102	81	71	63	57	54	-20.5	-32.8
Fabric mills.	3132	270	192	168	145	130	116	-29.0	-39.7
Textile and fabric finishing mills	3133	120	105	95	83	74	69	-12.1	-35.0
Textile product mills.	314	209	216	206	195	179	178	3.3	-17.8
Textile furnishings mills.	3141	127	129	121	116	105	103	1.3	-20.2
Other textile product mills	3149	82	88	84	78	74	75	6.4	-14.4
Apparel.	315	929	497	427	360	312	285	-46.5	-42.7
Apparel knitting mills	3151	112	69	61	50	45	42	-38.4	-39.0
Cut and sew apparel	3152	776	394	335	283	243	220	-49.3	-44.1
Accessories and other apparel.	3159	41	34	31	27	24	23	-16.9	-33.1
Leather and allied products.	316	133	69	58	50	45	43	-48.3	-37.6
Footwear	3162	83	31	26	22	20	19	-62.8	-36.8
Leather and hide tanning and finishing and other leather products	3169	51	38	32	28	25	24	-25.0	-38.2
Paper and paper products	322	647	605	578	547	516	499	-6.6	-17.5
Pulp, paper, and paperboard mills	3221	238	191	179	165	151	147	-19.7	-23.2
Converted paper products.	3222	409	413	398	382	365	352	1.1	-14.8
Printing and related support activities	323	809	807	768	707	681	665	-0.2	-17.6
Petroleum and coal products.	324	153	123	121	118	114	113	-19.4	-8.4
Chemicals	325	1,036	980	959	928	906	887	-5.3	-9.5
Basic chemicals	3251	249	188	181	170	162	156	-24.4	-17.1
Resin, rubber, and artificial fibers	3252	158	136	126	115	112	109	-14.2	-19.8
Agricultural chemicals.	3253	52	48	46	45	42	41	-8.8	-14.0
Pharmaceuticals and medicines	3254	207	274	283	291	292	291	32.4	6.0
Paints, coatings, and adhesives	3255	85	79	75	72	69	68	-6.6	-13.6
Soaps, cleaning compounds, and toiletries	3256	132	129	127	121	119	114	-2.4	-11.0
Other chemical products and preparations	3259	153	127	120	114	111	108	-17.1	-15.2
Plastics and rubber products.	326	826	952	897	848	815	807	15.3	-15.3
Plastics products	3261	619	738	699	664	639	634	19.3	-14.1
Rubber products	3262	207	214	199	184	177	173	3.5	-19.3

X Not applicable.   [1] Based on the North American Industry Classification System, 2002 (NAICS). See text, this section.   [2] Includes railroad rolling stock manufacturing not shown separately.

Source: U.S. Bureau of Labor Statistics, *Employment and Earnings*, monthly, March 2005 issue; and the Current Employment Statistics program Internet site <http://www.bls.gov/ces/home.htm>.

Table 980. Average Hourly Earnings of Production Workers in Manufacturing Industries by State: 2001 to 2003

[In dollars. These data are now on a NAICS (North American Industry Classification System) basis and not comparable to previous data, which were based on the Standard Industrial Classification system]

State	2001	2002	2003	State	2001	2002	2003
United States	14.76	15.29	15.74	Mississippi	11.93	12.32	12.88
				Missouri	16.11	16.79	18.21
Alabama	12.76	13.10	13.56	Montana	14.03	14.43	14.02
Alaska	11.70	13.24	12.16	Nebraska	13.64	14.05	14.86
Arizona	13.80	14.16	14.38	Nevada	13.79	14.62	14.63
Arkansas	12.90	13.30	13.55	New Hampshire	13.98	14.20	14.85
California	14.69	14.89	15.05	New Jersey	14.74	15.20	15.46
Colorado	14.72	15.85	16.89	New Mexico	13.27	13.43	13.19
Connecticut	16.42	17.25	17.74	New York	16.24	16.74	16.78
Delaware . . . . ¹ .	16.56	16.62	16.90	North Carolina	12.81	13.18	13.66
District of Columbia ¹	15.14	15.39	15.80	North Dakota	12.77	13.17	14.04
Florida	12.68	13.30	14.09	Ohio	16.79	17.49	18.00
Georgia	12.50	13.39	14.08	Oklahoma	13.66	14.12	14.13
Hawaii	13.18	13.07	12.90	Oregon	14.74	15.06	15.20
				Pennsylvania	14.37	14.75	14.98
Idaho	13.85	13.80	13.72	Rhode Island	12.68	12.75	12.88
Illinois	14.66	14.99	15.20	South Carolina	13.79	14.00	14.19
Indiana	16.42	17.16	17.84	South Dakota	12.11	12.60	13.13
Iowa	14.67	15.31	15.70	Tennessee	12.88	13.15	13.56
Kansas	15.48	15.98	15.83	Texas	14.04	13.93	13.94
Kentucky	15.44	15.73	16.02	Utah	13.76	14.12	14.90
Louisiana	16.18	17.03	16.86	Vermont	14.18	14.33	14.54
Maine	14.71	15.55	16.28	Virginia	14.49	15.25	15.88
Maryland	14.56	15.21	15.75	Washington	17.96	18.15	18.03
Massachusetts	15.75	16.25	16.53	West Virginia	14.80	15.40	16.05
Michigan	19.45	20.48	21.28	Wisconsin	15.44	15.86	16.12
Minnesota	14.76	15.06	15.43	Wyoming	17.26	17.73	16.74

¹ Washington PMSA (primary metropolitan statistical area).

Source: U.S. Bureau of Labor Statistics, *Employment and Earnings*, May 2004 issue and earlier issues.

Table 981. Manufacturing Full-Time Equivalent Employees and Wages by Industry: 2000 to 2003

[124,707 represents 124,707,000. Full-time equivalent employees equals the number of employees on full-time schedules converted to full-time basis]

Industry	NAICS code ¹	Full-time equivalent (FTE) employees (1,000)				Wage and salary accruals per FTE worker (dol.)			
		2000	2001	2002	2003	2000	2001	2002	2003
All industries, total	(X)	124,707	125,144	123,865	123,364	38,762	39,538	40,219	41,415
Manufacturing	31-33	16,947	16,190	15,049	14,308	44,216	43,778	44,867	46,742
Percent of all industries	(X)	13.6	12.9	12.1	11.6	114.1	110.7	111.6	112.9
Durable goods	(X)	10,713	10,193	9,363	8,860	47,007	46,063	47,041	49,032
Wood products	321	606	576	566	544	30,360	30,642	31,081	32,127
Nonmetallic mineral products . . .	327	545	535	510	491	38,879	39,204	40,494	41,664
Primary metals	331	611	560	499	466	45,745	45,791	46,585	48,442
Fabricated metal products	332	1,738	1,645	1,524	1,457	37,688	38,178	39,159	40,336
Machinery	333	1,420	1,348	1,211	1,136	46,882	46,024	47,135	49,057
Computer and electronic products	334	1,813	1,728	1,480	1,337	71,372	65,518	66,344	70,874
Electrical equipment, appliances, and components	335	568	548	490	456	42,732	40,854	41,976	43,950
Motor vehicles, bodies and trailers, and parts	3361-3363 3364-	1,283	1,198	1,141	1,113	49,727	48,743	51,415	53,760
Other transportation equipment . .	3365	736	714	666	638	52,612	55,148	57,823	59,970
Furniture and related products . . .	337	664	630	592	558	29,660	29,917	30,807	32,086
Miscellaneous manufacturing . . .	339	728	711	684	663	38,504	39,646	40,975	43,161
Nondurable goods	(X)	6,235	5,997	5,687	5,447	39,420	39,893	41,281	43,025
Food and beverage and tobacco products	311-312	1,719	1,718	1,698	1,668	34,110	34,698	35,491	36,787
Textile mills and textile product mills	313-314	584	521	476	436	29,018	29,532	30,693	31,220
Apparel and leather and allied products	315	538	486	408	360	24,769	24,574	26,350	28,003
Paper products	322	596	564	531	501	45,578	46,888	48,586	50,124
Printing and related support activities	323	767	764	707	671	38,966	37,492	38,358	39,362
Petroleum and coal products . . .	324	120	118	117	113	62,310	64,898	65,821	69,159
Chemical products	325	968	946	912	892	60,928	61,364	62,786	66,175
Plastics and rubber products . . .	326	942	880	839	805	35,375	35,799	37,257	38,431

¹ North American Industry Classification System, 1997; see text, this section.

Source: U.S. Bureau of Economic Analysis, *Survey of Current Business*, May 2005, and earlier issues. See also <http://www.bea.doc.gov/bea/dn/nipaweb/SelectTable.asp?Selected=N> (released 31 March 2005).

Manufactures **653**

Table 982. **Manufactures' Shipments, Inventories, and New Orders: 1992 to 2004**

[In billions of dollars (2,904 represents $2,904,000,000,000), except ratio. Based on a sample survey; for methodology, see publication cited below. These data are now on a NAICS (North American Industry Classification System) basis and not comparable to previous data, which were based on the Standard Industrial Classification system]

Year	Shipments	Inventories (Dec. 31)[1]	Ratio of inventories to shipments [2]	New orders (Dec. 31)	Unfilled orders (Dec. 31)
1992	2,904	370	1.57	(NA)	448
1993	3,020	371	1.51	2,960	422
1994	3,238	391	1.48	3,200	431
1995	3,480	415	1.47	3,427	443
1996	3,597	421	1.44	3,567	485
1997	3,835	433	1.39	3,780	508
1998	3,900	439	1.38	3,808	492
1999	4,032	453	1.38	3,957	501
2000	4,209	470	1.37	4,161	545
2001	3,970	442	1.37	3,875	513
2002	3,892	434	1.37	3,801	481
2003	3,999	428	1.32	3,950	502
2004	4,430	460	1.28	4,389	547

NA Not available. [1] Inventories are stated at current cost. [2] Ratio based on December seasonally-adjusted data.

Source: U.S. Census Bureau, *Current Industrial Reports, Manufacturers' Shipments, Inventories, and Orders: 1992–2002,* Series M3-1(02). See also <http://www.census.gov/prod/2003pubs/m3-02.pdf> (released August 2003) and <http://www.census.gov /indicator/www/m3/>.

Table 983. **Ratios of Manufacturers' Inventories to Shipments and Unfilled Orders to Shipments by Industry Group: 1998 to 2004**

[Based on a sample survey; for methodology, see publication cited below.]

Industry	1998	1999	2000	2001	2002	2003	2004
INVENTORIES-TO-SHIPMENTS RATIO							
All manufacturing industries	1.38	1.38	1.37	1.37	1.37	1.32	1.28
Durable goods	1.56	1.53	1.55	1.57	1.53	1.47	1.43
Wood products	1.26	1.26	1.32	1.34	1.33	1.24	1.10
Nonmetallic mineral products.	1.17	1.17	1.23	1.21	1.29	1.27	1.26
Primary metals	1.59	1.69	1.68	1.67	1.67	1.58	1.57
Fabricated metals	1.55	1.56	1.55	1.55	1.51	1.52	1.57
Machinery	2.01	2.05	2.08	2.06	2.04	1.97	1.88
Computers and electronic products.	1.41	1.42	1.55	1.59	1.57	1.37	1.26
Electrical equipment, appliances, and components	1.45	1.42	1.44	1.47	1.47	1.47	1.47
Transportation equipment	1.57	1.42	1.34	1.39	1.31	1.31	1.28
Furniture and related products.	1.34	1.35	1.35	1.32	1.34	1.30	1.36
Miscellaneous products	1.85	1.89	1.90	1.87	1.83	1.74	1.74
Nondurable goods	1.14	1.18	1.14	1.13	1.18	1.14	1.10
Food products	0.82	0.86	0.88	0.85	0.87	0.86	0.83
Beverages and tobacco products	1.63	1.55	1.51	1.47	1.58	1.65	1.62
Textile mills	1.45	1.52	1.49	1.48	1.38	1.51	1.38
Textile product mills.	1.63	1.62	1.76	1.83	1.72	1.76	1.68
Apparel.	1.75	1.89	1.89	1.68	1.58	1.62	1.54
Leather and allied products.	2.05	2.18	2.13	2.10	1.91	1.92	1.98
Paper products.	1.15	1.16	1.11	1.16	1.17	1.09	1.04
Printing	0.80	0.81	0.79	0.77	0.78	0.78	0.86
Petroleum and coal products.	0.84	0.90	0.71	0.74	0.90	0.75	0.62
Basic chemicals	1.31	1.38	1.40	1.39	1.44	1.38	1.36
Plastics and rubber products	1.19	1.20	1.21	1.18	1.30	1.33	1.41
UNFILLED ORDERS-TO- SHIPMENTS RATIO							
All manufacturing industries	1.53	1.51	1.57	1.56	1.50	1.52	1.50
Durable goods.	2.67	2.61	2.78	2.86	2.74	2.83	2.79
Primary metals	1.56	1.69	1.45	1.47	1.33	1.51	1.42
Fabricated metals	2.00	2.02	2.02	1.93	1.80	1.90	2.03
Machinery	2.40	2.50	2.51	2.46	2.04	2.08	2.10
Computers and electronic products.	2.57	2.93	3.07	3.56	3.66	3.71	3.63
Electrical equipment, appliances, and components	1.56	1.78	1.75	1.54	1.62	1.61	1.71
Transportation equipment	5.00	4.24	4.93	5.03	4.72	4.89	4.88
Furniture and related products.	1.19	1.27	1.14	1.09	0.94	0.96	0.99
Miscellaneous products	0.46	0.49	0.62	0.44	0.45	0.58	0.64

Source: U.S. Census Bureau, *Current Industrial Reports, Manufacturers' Shipments, Inventories, and Orders: 1992–2002,* Series M3-1(02). See also <http://www.census.gov/prod/2003pubs/m3-02.pdf> (released August 2003) and <http://www.census.gov /indicator/www/m3/>.

Table 984. Value of Manufacturers' Shipments, Inventories, and New Orders by Industry: 1998 to 2004

[In millions of dollars (3,899,813 represents $3,899,813,000,000). Based on a sample survey; for methodology, see publication cited below. These data are on a NAICS (North American Industry Classification System) basis and not comparable to previous data, which were based on the Standard Industrial Classification system]

Industry	1998	1999	2000	2001	2002	2003	2004
SHIPMENTS							
All manufacturing industries	3,899,813	4,031,887	4,208,584	3,970,499	3,891,753	3,999,124	4,429,700
Durable goods	2,231,588	2,326,736	2,373,688	2,174,406	2,131,404	2,150,638	2,373,410
Wood products	91,175	97,311	93,669	87,250	87,652	93,238	110,314
Nonmetallic mineral products.	92,501	96,153	97,329	94,861	88,222	87,500	91,299
Primary metals	166,109	156,648	156,598	138,246	135,930	131,307	165,790
Fabricated metals	253,720	257,071	268,213	253,113	252,232	245,469	272,504
Machinery	280,651	276,904	291,548	266,554	255,651	253,516	294,446
Computers and electronic products.	443,768	467,059	510,639	429,471	392,026	418,651	469,794
Electrical equipment, appliances, and components	116,024	118,313	125,443	114,068	103,673	101,415	106,479
Transportation equipment	612,882	676,328	639,861	602,495	624,129	618,670	648,681
Furniture and related products.	69,616	72,659	75,107	72,147	69,999	69,870	75,369
Miscellaneous products	105,142	108,290	115,281	116,201	121,890	131,002	138,734
Nondurable goods . . . . : .	1,668,225	1,705,151	1,834,896	1,796,093	1,760,349	1,848,486	2,056,290
Food products	428,479	426,001	435,229	451,385	450,183	461,064	487,358
Beverages and tobacco products	102,359	106,920	111,692	118,786	109,832	105,310	108,824
Textile mills	57,416	54,306	52,112	45,681	43,170	39,775	41,415
Textile product mills	31,137	32,689	33,654	31,971	34,232	35,247	37,979
Apparel . . . . : . . .	64,932	62,305	60,339	54,598	53,621	52,970	56,282
Leather and allied products.	10,186	9,653	9,647	8,834	10,408	10,903	10,467
Paper products	154,984	156,915	165,298	155,845	151,530	159,611	172,508
Printing	100,297	101,536	104,396	100,792	97,968	95,036	95,043
Petroleum and coal products.	137,957	162,620	235,134	219,074	206,879	244,097	337,643
Basic chemicals	416,742	420,321	449,159	438,410	424,143	459,110	505,957
Plastics and rubber products	163,736	171,885	178,236	170,717	178,383	185,363	202,814
INVENTORIES (Dec. 31)							
All manufacturing industries	438,845	452,803	470,084	441,527	433,756	428,176	459,690
Durable goods	282,698	288,362	298,232	275,855	264,446	255,969	275,766
Wood products	9,684	10,289	10,329	9,664	9,566	9,598	9,843
Nonmetallic mineral products.	8,877	9,279	9,799	9,440	9,306	9,051	9,393
Primary metals	22,305	22,309	22,199	19,502	19,144	17,420	22,005
Fabricated metals	32,215	32,800	34,085	32,145	31,227	30,504	34,992
Machinery	45,728	46,050	49,151	44,532	42,296	40,512	44,857
Computers and electronic products.	50,066	52,838	63,024	54,598	49,287	45,945	47,524
Electrical equipment, appliances, and components	13,503	13,510	14,505	13,488	12,234	11,949	12,463
Transportation equipment	77,014	76,781	69,199	67,188	65,769	65,146	66,744
Furniture and related products.	7,599	7,983	8,261	7,765	7,632	7,375	8,359
Miscellaneous products	15,707	16,523	17,680	17,533	17,985	18,469	19,586
Nondurable goods	156,147	164,441	171,852	165,672	169,310	172,207	183,924
Food products	29,419	30,650	31,882	31,865	32,534	33,082	33,865
Beverages and tobacco products	14,294	14,167	14,331	14,855	14,717	14,725	14,776
Textile mills	6,684	6,648	6,243	5,411	4,759	4,817	4,602
Textile product mills	4,024	4,219	4,698	4,648	4,691	4,951	5,063
Apparel	9,114	9,454	9,170	7,363	6,784	6,901	7,009
Leather and allied products.	1,667	1,675	1,634	1,479	1,580	1,673	1,655
Paper products	14,688	15,034	15,205	14,950	14,621	14,352	14,806
Printing	6,212	6,394	6,445	6,046	5,985	5,754	6,438
Petroleum and coal products.	9,102	11,375	12,840	12,479	14,302	13,973	16,259
Basic chemicals	44,943	47,806	51,623	50,052	50,363	51,917	56,263
Plastics and rubber products	16,000	17,019	17,781	16,524	18,974	20,062	23,188
NEW ORDERS							
All manufacturing industries	3,808,143	3,957,242	4,161,472	3,875,329	3,800,930	3,949,998	4,389,035
Durable goods	2,139,918	2,252,091	2,326,576	2,079,236	2,040,581	2,101,512	2,332,745
Wood products	91,175	97,311	93,669	87,250	87,652	93,238	110,314
Nonmetallic mineral products.	92,501	96,153	97,329	94,861	88,222	87,500	91,299
Primary metals . . . . : . .	160,743	156,968	153,625	136,291	134,089	132,850	168,653
Fabricated metals	253,847	258,116	270,021	248,872	249,408	246,590	279,101
Machinery	278,100	278,277	294,608	260,392	244,559	253,978	301,965
Computers and electronic products.	372,433	402,216	436,415	363,049	325,378	358,127	396,431
Electrical equipment, appliances, and components	115,711	120,774	126,196	110,628	103,013	101,038	107,916
Transportation equipment	600,205	660,215	663,326	591,756	617,098	625,535	661,199
Furniture and related products.	69,098	73,393	74,532	71,614	68,959	69,972	76,009
Miscellaneous products	106,105	108,668	116,855	114,523	122,203	132,684	139,858
Nondurable goods	1,668,225	1,705,151	1,834,896	1,796,093	1,760,349	1,848,486	2,056,290

Source: U.S. Census Bureau, *Current Industrial Reports, Manufacturers' Shipments, Inventories, and Orders: 1992-2002,* Series M3-1(02). See also <http://www.census.gov/prod/2003pubs/m3-02.pdf> (released August 2003) and <http://www.census.gov /indicator/www/m3/>.

U.S. Census Bureau, Statistical Abstract of the United States: 2006

Table 985. **Value of Manufactures' Shipments, Inventories, and New Orders by Market Grouping: 1998 to 2004**

[In millions of dollars (3,899,813 represents $3,899,813,000,000). Based on a sample survey; for methodology, see publication cited below.

Market grouping	1998	1999	2000	2001	2002	2003	2004
SHIPMENTS							
All manufacturing industries	3,899,813	4,031,887	4,208,584	3,970,499	3,891,753	3,999,124	4,429,700
Consumer goods	1,364,326	1,438,519	1,514,377	1,493,707	1,472,647	1,529,699	1,686,162
Consumer durable goods	385,918	426,337	405,308	380,734	396,590	400,023	422,014
Consumer nondurable goods.	978,408	1,012,182	1,109,069	1,112,973	1,076,057	1,129,676	1,264,148
Aircraft and parts	116,812	120,242	111,658	118,226	111,726	107,161	114,768
Defense aircraft and parts.	26,938	27,719	24,560	27,928	35,127	39,856	43,676
Nondefense aircraft and parts	89,874	92,523	87,098	90,298	76,599	67,305	71,092
Construction materials and supplies.	418,756	434,138	444,812	424,517	419,040	421,903	471,590
Motor vehicles and parts	439,590	498,716	471,180	427,715	450,136	442,840	461,920
Computers and related products	114,482	113,162	110,242	89,529	81,449	93,449	105,677
Information technology industries.	362,564	374,384	399,751	353,237	319,391	337,316	371,050
Nondefense capital goods	747,046	768,799	808,345	727,980	673,223	683,195	760,579
Excluding aircraft	695,717	713,042	757,617	677,991	634,549	652,339	730,796
Defense capital goods.	74,690	70,955	67,051	74,019	79,825	91,883	99,688
Durables excluding capital goods	1,409,852	1,486,982	1,498,292	1,372,407	1,378,356	1,375,560	1,513,143
INVENTORIES (Dec. 31)							
All manufacturing industries	438,845	452,803	470,084	441,527	433,756	428,176	459,690
Consumer goods	116,715	123,218	129,478	126,855	129,445	131,660	138,358
Consumer durable goods	25,137	26,307	27,438	25,704	26,289	25,932	28,481
Consumer nondurable goods.	91,578	96,911	102,040	101,151	103,156	105,728	109,877
Aircraft and parts	46,921	42,599	36,091	36,393	34,978	34,293	34,240
Defense aircraft and parts.	11,376	11,052	9,423	9,384	9,610	11,296	12,035
Nondefense aircraft and parts	35,545	31,547	26,668	27,009	25,368	22,997	22,205
Construction materials and supplies.	45,617	47,510	49,389	46,344	46,196	45,350	50,223
Motor vehicles and parts	20,764	22,102	22,283	19,653	20,256	19,604	20,779
Computers and related products	8,017	7,963	8,350	6,341	5,975	5,639	6,048
Information technology industries.	43,592	44,375	50,795	46,650	41,802	38,432	39,004
Nondefense capital goods	122,415	121,653	127,162	119,258	109,106	102,129	107,531
Excluding aircraft	94,045	96,254	106,669	98,483	90,539	85,879	91,701
Defense capital goods.	17,775	19,754	17,153	17,677	17,705	19,270	19,719
Durables excluding capital goods	142,508	146,955	153,917	138,920	137,635	134,570	148,516
NEW ORDERS							
All manufacturing industries	3,808,143	3,957,242	4,161,472	3,875,329	3,800,930	3,949,998	4,389,035
Consumer goods	1,364,268	1,440,903	1,515,799	1,491,143	1,471,270	1,530,443	1,687,479
Consumer durable goods	385,860	428,721	406,730	378,170	395,213	400,767	423,331
Consumer nondurable goods.	978,408	1,012,182	1,109,069	1,112,973	1,076,057	1,129,676	1,264,148
Aircraft and parts	108,004	107,336	130,575	111,432	105,382	105,544	118,738
Defense aircraft and parts.	23,854	25,717	31,326	37,311	40,087	44,662	35,579
Nondefense aircraft and parts	84,150	81,619	99,249	74,121	65,295	60,882	83,159
Construction materials and supplies.	419,330	435,034	446,792	420,300	418,315	422,639	476,295
Motor vehicles and parts	440,934	499,527	468,470	425,580	450,183	444,327	462,965
Computers and related products	115,806	114,481	107,656	89,320	82,398	94,130	106,147
Information technology industries.	365,723	389,160	409,500	350,726	314,473	349,234	382,624
Nondefense capital goods	745,600	772,703	831,335	700,027	647,894	689,340	784,070
Excluding aircraft	698,279	728,089	767,754	665,899	617,878	663,352	741,821
Defense capital goods.	64,127	67,900	79,598	83,033	79,264	104,824	109,315
Durables excluding capital goods	1,330,191	1,411,488	1,415,643	1,296,176	1,313,423	1,307,348	1,439,360

Source: U.S. Census Bureau, *Current Industrial Reports, Manufacturers' Shipments, Inventories, and Orders: 1992-2002*, Series M3-1(02). See also <http://www.census.gov/prod/2003pubs/m3-02.pdf> (released August 2003) and <http://www.census.gov/indicator/www/m3/>.

Table 986. **Finances and Profits of Manufacturing Corporations: 1990 to 2004**

[In billions of dollars (2,811 represents $2,811,000,000,000). Data exclude estimates for corporations with less than $250,000 in assets at time of sample selection. For 1990-2001, based on Standard Industrial Classification system; thereafter, based on North American Industry Classification System. See Table 769 for individual industry data]

Item	1990	1995	1998	1999	2000	2001 [1]	2001 [2]	2002 [2]	2003 [2]	2004 [2]
Net sales.	2,811	3,528	3,949	4,149	4,548	4,308	4,295	4,217	4,397	4,929
Net operating profit	173	268	298	317	348	185	186	225	237	326
Net profit:										
Before taxes	160	274	315	355	381	82	83	196	306	445
After taxes	112	198	234	258	275	36	36	135	237	346
Cash dividends.	62	81	121	104	132	102	103	106	115	142
Net income retained in business . .	49	117	114	154	143	-67	-66	28	122	204

[1] Based on Standard Industrial Classification system. [2] Based on the North American Industry Classification System; see Text, Section 15.

Source: U.S. Census Bureau, *Quarterly Financial Report for Manufacturing, Mining, and Trade Corporations*. See also <http://www.census.gov/prod/2005pubs/qfr04-q4.pdf> (released April 2005).

Table 987. Manufacturing Corporations—Assets and Profits by Asset Size: 1990 to 2004

[In millions of dollars. Corporations and assets as of end of 4th quarter; profits for entire year (2,629,458 represents $2,629,458,000,000). Through 2000 based on Standard Industrial Classification code; beginning 2001 based on North American Industry Classification System (see footnote 3). For corporations above a certain asset value based on complete canvass. The asset value for complete canvass was raised in 1988 to $50 million and in 1995 to $250 million. Asset sizes less than these values are sampled, except as noted. For details regarding methodology, see source for first quarter, 1988. Minus sign (-) indicates loss]

Year	Unit	Total [1]	Under $10 mil. [1]	$10– $25 mil.	$25– $50 mil.	$50– $100 mil.	$100– $250 mil.	$250– $1 bil.	$1 bil. and over
Assets:									
1990.	Mil. dol	2,629,458	142,498	74,477	55,914	72,554	123,967	287,512	1,872,536
1991.	Mil. dol	2,688,422	140,056	70,567	58,549	72,694	127,748	295,743	1,923,066
1992.	Mil. dol	2,798,625	143,766	70,446	65,718	75,967	132,742	302,287	2,007,698
1993.	Mil. dol	2,904,869	149,763	72,854	61,243	81,389	134,388	317,774	2,087,457
1994.	Mil. dol	3,080,231	148,751	81,505	66,405	82,116	138,950	358,100	2,204,404
1995.	Mil. dol	3,345,229	155,618	87,011	68,538	87,262	159,133	370,263	2,417,403
1996.	Mil. dol	3,574,407	163,928	87,096	69,722	93,205	156,702	398,651	2,605,102
1997.	Mil. dol	3,746,797	167,921	87,398	76,034	85,186	157,130	397,559	2,775,570
1998.	Mil. dol	3,967,309	170,068	87,937	69,627	86,816	148,060	419,153	2,985,647
1999.	Mil. dol	4,382,814	170,058	85,200	67,352	97,810	138,143	398,881	3,425,370
2000.	Mil. dol	4,852,106	171,666	85,482	72,122	90,866	149,714	389,537	3,892,720
2001 [2]. . . .	Mil. dol	4,747,789	169,701	84,664	67,493	88,088	131,617	393,752	3,812,474
2002.	Mil. dol	4,823,219	166,191	82,369	62,654	81,667	134,821	407,423	3,888,095
2003.	Mil. dol	5,162,852	161,462	80,681	62,592	77,205	126,826	392,192	4,261,894
2004.	Mil. dol	5,525,256	163,919	79,902	71,714	82,918	128,015	431,699	4,567,089
Net profit: [3]									
1990.	Mil. dol	110,128	8,527	5,160	2,769	2,661	3,525	7,110	80,377
1991.	Mil. dol	66,407	6,820	4,271	2,564	1,704	1,707	5,027	44,316
1992.	Mil. dol	22,085	9,567	4,748	3,245	3,034	4,553	5,919	-8,979
1993.	Mil. dol	83,156	11,195	5,415	3,439	3,218	3,584	4,555	51,750
1994.	Mil. dol	174,874	14,131	7,057	4,072	4,996	6,745	14,626	123,250
1995.	Mil. dol	198,151	13,224	5,668	3,767	5,771	7,000	16,549	146,172
1996.	Mil. dol	224,869	15,802	6,872	4,266	5,664	7,935	16,059	168,271
1997.	Mil. dol	244,505	17,948	8,383	4,153	4,675	7,074	18,433	183,836
1998.	Mil. dol	234,386	18,350	6,421	3,790	4,681	5,610	14,364	181,170
1999.	Mil. dol	257,805	17,398	7,618	3,504	4,798	4,795	12,756	206,934
2000.	Mil. dol	275,313	16,578	6,820	3,403	2,742	3,510	15,121	227,136
2001 [2]. . . .	Mil. dol	36,168	8,387	3,366	-408	403	-543	-6,782	31,746
2002.	Mil. dol	134,686	10,003	2,784	807	1,699	3,356	-1,227	117,262
2003.	Mil. dol	237,041	9,821	3,374	2,005	2,256	2,973	4,115	212,497
2004.	Mil. dol	345,608	15,007	5,794	3,905	3,065	5,428	13,783	298,625

[1] Excludes estimates for corporations with less than $250,000 in assets at time of sample selection.   [2] Beginning 2001, data reported on a NAICS basis.   [3] After taxes.

Source: U.S. Census Bureau, *Quarterly Financial Report for Manufacturing, Mining and Trade Corporations.* See also <http://www.census.gov/prod/2005pubs/qfr04-q4.pdf> (released April 2005).

Table 988. Manufacturing Corporations—Selected Finances: 1990 to 2004

[In billions of dollars (2,811 represents $2,811,000,000,000). Data are not necessarily comparable from year to year due to changes in accounting procedures, industry classifications, sampling procedures, etc.; for detail, see source. Through 2000 based on Standard Industrial Classification code; beginning 2001, based on North American Industry Classification System (NAICS)]

Year	All manufacturing corporations			Durable goods industries			Nondurable goods industries		
		Profits [1]			Profits [1]			Profits [1]	
	Sales	Before taxes	After taxes	Sales	Before taxes	After taxes	Sales	Before taxes	After taxes
1990. . . .	2,811	158	110	1,357	57	41	1,454	101	69
1991. . . .	2,761	99	66	1,304	14	7	1,457	85	59
1992 [2]. . .	2,890	31	22	1,390	-34	-24	1,500	65	46
1993. . . .	3,015	118	83	1,490	39	27	1,525	79	56
1994. . . .	3,256	244	175	1,658	121	87	1,598	123	88
1995. . . .	3,528	275	198	1,808	131	94	1,721	144	104
1996. . . .	3,758	307	225	1,942	147	106	1,816	160	119
1997. . . .	3,922	331	244	2,076	167	121	1,847	164	123
1998. . . .	3,949	315	234	2,169	175	128	1,781	140	107
1999. . . .	4,149	355	258	2,314	199	140	1,835	157	117
2000. . . .	4,548	381	275	2,457	191	132	2,091	190	144
2001. . . .	4,295	83	36	2,321	-69	-76	1,974	152	112
2002. . . .	4,217	196	135	2,261	45	21	1,955	149	113
2003. . . .	4,397	306	237	2,283	118	85	2,114	188	149
2004. . . .	4,929	445	346	2,538	197	154	2,391	248	192

[1] Beginning 1998, profits before and after income taxes reflect inclusion of minority stockholders' interest in net income before and after income taxes.   [2] Data for 1992 (most significantly 1992:I qtr.) reflect the early adoption of Financial Accounting Standards Board Statement 106 (Employer's Accounting for Post-Retirement Benefits Other Than Pensions) by a large number of companies during the fourth quarter of 1992. Data for 1993:I qtr. also reflect adoption of Statement 106. Corporations must show the cumulative effect of a change in accounting principle in the first quarter of the year in which the change is adopted.

Source: U.S. Census Bureau, *Quarterly Financial Report for Manufacturing, Mining and Trade Corporations.* See also <http://www.census.gov/prod/2005pubs/qfr04-q4.pdf> (released April 2005).

Manufactures 657

Table 989. Tobacco Products—Summary: 1990 to 2004

[Production data are for calendar years. Excludes cigars produced in customs bonded manufacturing warehouses]

Item	Unit	1990	1995	1998	1999	2000	2001	2002	2003	2004
PRODUCTION										
Cigarettes, total	Billions	710	747	680	607	565	562	532	499	493
Nonfilter tip	Billions	23	15	12	8	7	6	5	6	5
Filter tip	Billions	687	732	669	599	558	556	527	494	487
Cigars	Billions	1.9	2.1	2.8	2.9	2.8	3.7	3.8	4.0	4.4
Tobacco [1]	Mil. lb.	142	131	131	133	133	130	133	137	135
Smoking	Mil. lb.	16	12	13	15	14	13	16	18	16
Chewing tobacco	Mil. lb.	73	63	53	51	49	47	45	43	39
Snuff	Mil. lb.	53	60	66	67	70	70	73	76	79
EXPORTS										
Cigarettes	Bil. Pieces	164.3	231.1	201.3	151.4	147.9	133.9	127.4	121.5	118.7
Cigars	Bil. Cigars	72.0	94.0	93.0	84.0	113.0	124.0	122.7	130.0	171.0
Smoking tobacco	Bil. lb.	0.8	0.3	1.1	1.6	0.5	11.0	7.9	0.7	1.1
IMPORTS										
Cigarettes	Bil. Pieces	1.4	3.0	4.3	8.7	11.3	14.7	20.8	23.1	22.7
Cigars	Bil. Cigars	111.0	195.0	502.3	463.4	497.0	543.4	413.5	508.0	616.0
Smoking tobacco	Bil. lb.	2.9	4.2	4.3	4.3	4.2	1.9	2.1	2.1	1.7
CONSUMPTION										
Consumption per person [2]	Lb. [3]	5.6	4.7	4.5	4.2	4.1	4.1	4.2	3.9	3.8
Cigarettes	1,000	2.8	2.5	2.3	2.1	2.1	2.0	2.0	1.8	1.8
EXPENDITURES										
Consumer expenditures, total	Bil. dol.	43.8	48.7	57.3	72.1	77.5	82.9	88.2	86.7	86.1
Cigarettes	Bil. dol.	41.6	45.8	53.2	68.3	72.9	77.8	82.8	81.1	80.0
Cigars	Bil. dol.	0.7	1.0	1.6	1.8	1.8	2.1	2.2	2.5	2.7
Other	Bil. dol.	1.5	2.5	2.4	2.7	2.7	3.0	3.1	3.2	3.4

[1] Smoking and chewing tobaccos and snuff output. [2] Based on estimated population, 18 years old and over, as of July 1, including Armed Forces abroad. [3] Unstemmed processing weight equivalent.

Source: U.S. Dept. of Agriculture, Economic Research Service, *Tobacco Situation and Outlook*, quarterly. See also <http://usda.mannlib.cornell.edu/reports/erssor/specialty/tbs-bb/2005/tbs258.pdf> (released 15 April 2005).

Table 990. Cotton, Wool, and Manmade Fibers—Consumption by End-Use: 1990 to 2003

[14,011 represents 14,011,000,000. Represents products manufactured by U.S. mills. Excludes glass fiber]

Year	Total (mil. lb.)	Cotton Total (mil. lb.)	Cotton Percent of end-use	Wool Total (mil. lb.)	Wool Percent of end-use	Manufactured fibers Total (mil. lb.)	Manufactured fibers Percent of end-use	Artificial [1] Total (mil. lb.)	Artificial [1] Percent of end-use	Synthetic [2] Total (mil. lb.)	Synthetic [2] Percent of end-use
Total:											
1990	14,011	4,699	33.5	185	1.3	9,127	65.1	599.0	4.3	8,528.0	60.9
1995	16,815	5,508	32.8	184	1.1	11,123	66.1	540.2	3.2	10,582.5	62.9
2000	17,904	5,128	28.6	132	0.7	12,645	70.6	304.9	1.7	12,340.2	68.9
2001	16,231	4,619	28.5	116	0.7	11,496	70.8	282.1	1.7	11,214.2	69.1
2002	15,715	4,102	26.1	96	0.6	11,518	73.3	250.3	1.6	11,267.4	71.7
2003	14,816	3,512	23.7	99	0.7	11,205	75.6	225.0	1.5	10,980.3	74.1
Apparel:											
1990	5,204	2,897	55.7	118	2.3	2,189	42.1	287.0	5.5	1,902.0	36.5
1995	6,877	3,640	52.9	132	1.9	3,106	45.2	305.6	4.4	2,799.9	40.7
2000	6,039	3,089	51.2	79	1.3	2,871	47.5	153.9	2.5	2,717.2	45.0
2001	5,335	2,648	49.6	73	1.4	2,613	49.0	134.7	2.5	2,478.6	46.5
2002	4,733	2,232	47.2	64	1.4	2,437	51.5	112.8	2.4	2,324.5	49.1
2003	4,133	1,912	46.3	65	1.6	2,157	52.2	93.2	2.3	2,063.6	49.9
Home textiles:											
1990	2,235	1,325	59.3	14	0.6	896	40.1	104.0	4.7	792.0	35.4
1995	2,530	1,487	58.8	12	0.5	1,030	40.7	93.2	3.7	936.7	37.0
2000	2,862	1,644	57.4	15	0.5	1,203	42.0	61.2	2.1	1,142.1	39.9
2001	2,678	1,587	59.3	13	0.5	1,079	40.3	56.3	2.1	1,022.3	38.2
2002	2,504	1,492	59.6	10	0.4	1,002	40.0	49.2	2.0	952.6	38.0
2003	2,173	1,278	58.8	12	0.6	883	40.6	43.0	2.0	839.9	38.7
Floor coverings:											
1990	3,075	18	0.6	21	0.7	3,036	98.7	-	-	3,036.0	98.7
1995	3,731	25	0.7	25	0.7	3,681	98.7	0.1	-	3,680.6	98.7
2000	4,519	31	0.7	25	0.6	4,464	98.8	-	-	4,463.5	98.8
2001	4,059	30	0.7	20	0.5	4,009	98.8	-	-	4,008.7	98.8
2002	4,261	30	0.7	14	0.3	4,218	99.0	-	-	4,217.8	99.0
2003	4,377	29	0.7	14	0.3	4,334	99.0	-	-	4,333.8	99.0
Industrial: [3]											
1990	2,965	313	10.6	10	0.3	2,642	89.1	179.0	6.0	2,463.0	83.1
1995	3,677	355	9.7	15	0.4	3,307	89.9	141.3	3.8	3,165.3	86.1
2000	4,484	364	8.1	13	0.3	4,107	91.6	89.8	2.0	4,017.4	89.6
2001	4,160	354	8.5	10	0.2	3,796	91.3	91.1	2.2	3,704.6	89.1
2002	4,216	347	8.2	8	0.2	3,861	91.6	88.3	2.1	3,772.8	89.5
2003	4,133	293	7.1	8	0.2	3,832	92.7	88.8	2.1	3,743.0	90.6

- Represents or rounds to zero. [1] Rayon and acetate. [2] Nylon, polyester, acrylic, and olefin. [3] Includes consumer-type products.

Source: Fiber Economics Bureau, Inc., Arlington. VA, *Fiber Organon*, monthly (copyright).

Table 991. Broadwoven and Knit Fabrics—Shipments and Foreign Trade: 2003

[2,422,538 represents 2,422,538,000. Fabric blends as shown in the report are reported based on the chief weight of the fiber; whereas, fabrics blends as shown for imports are based on the chief value of the fiber]

Product description	Manufac-turers' ship-ments (quantity)	Imports for consumption		Percent imports to manufac-turers' ship-ments	Exports of domestic merchandise		Percent exports to manufac-turers' ship-ments
		Quantity	Value [1] ($1,000)		Quantity	Value ($1,000)	
BROADWOVEN FABRICS (quantity 1,000 sq. meters)							
Cotton fabrics [2]	2,422,538	1,589,724	1,647,063	65.6	541,690	1,053,648	22.4
Manmade fiber fabrics	7,001,405	1,088,511	1,228,537	15.5	543,766	1,133,688	7.8
Silk fabrics	(D)	42,595	253,384	(D)	3,707	22,748	(D)
Wool fabrics	19,205	25,093	181,045	130.7	9,994	49,577	52.0
KNIT FABRICS (quantity in 1,000 kilograms)							
Total	497,035	238,753	1,391,524	48.0	188,824	1,175,425	38.0
Pile fabrics	34,125	19,619	162,858	57.5	37,259	218,826	109.2
Elastic fabric	24,073	40,936	390,658	(S)	38,943	389,752	161.8
Other warp knit fabrics	51,467	12,049	72,275	23.4	21,860	134,479	42.5
Other narrow knit fabrics	9,802	3,382	20,943	34.5	1,147	12,393	11.7
Other knit fabrics	377,568	162,767	744,790	43.1	89,615	419,975	23.7

D Data withheld to avoid disclosing figures for individual companies.   [1] Dollar value represents the c.i.f. (cost, insurance, and freight) at the first port of entry in the United States plus calculated import duty.   [2] Includes all cotton and chiefly. cotton mixed with manmade fiber.

Source: U.S. Census Bureau, *Current Industrial Reports*, Series MQ313 and MA313K, annual. See also <http://www.census.gov/industry/1/mq313t035.pdf> (issued May 2004) and <http://www.census.gov/industry/1/ma313k03.pdf> (issued September 2004).

Table 992. Footwear—Production, Foreign Trade, and Apparent Consumption: 2002

[Quantity in thousands of pairs (38,248 represents 38,248,000 pairs), value in thousands of dollars (298,025 represents 298,025,000)]

Product description	Manufac-turers' ship-ments (quantity)	Exports of domestic merchandise		Percent exports to domestic produc-tion	Imports for consumption		Apparent consump-tion (quantity)	Percent imports to apparent consump-tion
		Quantity	Value		Quantity	Value		
Total	38,248	25,251	298,025	66.0	1,214,261	13,409,050	1,227,258	98.9
Rubber or plastic uppers and rubber or plastic	3,484	8,426	100,546	241.8	517,768	2,814,299	512,826	101.0
Waterproof	(D)	905	8,664	(D)	12,972	75,854	(D)	(D)
Not waterproof	(D)	7,521	91,882	(D)	504,796	2,738,445	(D)	(D)
Leather uppers	18,401	7,187	146,901	39.1	696,493	9,296,097	707,707	98.4
Athletic	1,217	4,000	70,942	328.7	533,513	6,077,663	530,730	100.5
Leather soles	5,204	1,717	46,455	33.0	44,518	1,217,348	48,005	92.7
Other soles	11,980	1,464	29,504	12.2	118,462	2,001,086	128,978	91.8
Fabric uppers	16,363	9,638	50,578	58.9	339,272	1,298,654	345,997	98.1

D Data withheld to avoid disclosing figures for individual companies

Source: U.S. Census Bureau, *Current Industrial Reports*, Series MA316A, annual. See also <http://www.census.gov/industry/1/ma316a03.pdf> (released October 2004).

Table 993. Pharmaceutical Preparations—Value of Shipments: 1990 to 2003

[In millions of dollars (33,954 represents 33,954,000,000]

Product description	NAICS product code [1]	1990	1995	2000	2001	2002	2003
Pharmaceutical preparations, except biologicals	(X)	33,954	48,864	79,262	90,182	100,741	103,758
Affecting neoplasms, endocrine systems, and metabolic disease.	3254121100	2,743	4,076	9,784	14,819	17,499	20,077
Acting on the central nervous system and sense organs.	3254124100	7,219	9,228	18,508	18,975	24,345	24,705
Acting on the cardiovascular system	3254127100	4,815	5,988	8,993	9,798	10,339	9,644
Acting on the respiratory system	325412A100	3,724	5,196	10,179	11,692	12,504	11,202
Acting on the digestive system	325412D100	4,840	8,593	10,046	12,616	13,373	14,112
Acting on the skin.	325412G100	1,558	2,171	2,941	2,708	2,844	2,943
Vitamin, nutrient, and hematinic preps. . . .	325412L100	2,588	4,812	5,676	5,884	6,029	6,878
Affecting parasitic and infective disease . . .	325412P100	5,411	7,196	11,037	11,193	11,337	11,544
Pharmaceutical preps. for veterinary use . .	325412T100	1,057	1,605	2,096	2,497	2,471	2,653

X Not applicable.   [1] North American Industry Classification System, 1997, see text, Section 15.

Source: U.S. Census Bureau, 1990, *Current Industrial Reports*, Series MA28G; thereafter, MA325G(01)-1. See also <http://www.census.gov/industry/1/ma325g03.pdf> (released November 2004).

Manufactures   659

Table 994. **Inorganic Chemicals and Fertilizers—Production: 1995 to 2003**

[17,402 represents 17,402,000]

Product description	Unit	1995	1999	2000	2001	2002	2003
INORGANIC FERTILIZERS							
Ammonia, synthetic anhydrous	1,000 sh. tons	17,402	17,337	15,809	12,227	13,863	11,539
Ammonium nitrate, original solution	1,000 sh. tons	8,489	7,630	7,979	6,431	7,096	6,321
Ammonium sulfate	1,000 sh. tons	2,647	2,875	2,808	2,588	2,945	2,871
Urea (100%)	1,000 sh. tons	8,117	8,907	7,682	6,702	7,758	6,375
Nitric acid (100%)	1,000 sh. tons	8,839	8,945	8,708	7,074	7,651	7,493
Phosphoric acid (100% P2O5)	1,000 sh. tons	13,134	13,708	12,492	11,546	12,289	12,485
Sulfuric acid, gross (100%)	1,000 sh. tons	47,519	44,756	43,643	40,064	39,760	41,205
Superphosphates and other fertilizer materials (100% P2O5)	1,000 sh. tons	10,364	9,133	8,899	8,109	8,756	8,895
INORGANIC CHEMICALS							
Chlorine gas	1,000 metric tons	12,395	12,114	14,000	11,489	11,438	10,361
Sodium hydroxide, total liquid	1,000 metric tons	11,408	11,974	11,523	9,813	9,461	8,796
Potassium hydroxide liquid	1,000 metric tons	(D)	430	539	465	470	471
Finished sodium bicarbonate	1,000 metric tons	520	505	536	513	535	540
Titanium dioxide, composite and pure	1,000 metric tons	1,382	1,355	1,547	1,327	1,409	1,422
Hydrochloric acid	1,000 metric tons	3,904	4,191	4,717	3,970	4,028	4,181
Aluminum oxide	1,000 metric tons	4,764	4,016	(D)	2,863	(D)	(D)
Aluminum sulfate (commercial)	1,000 metric tons	1,144	1,052	1,076	1,020	1,054	961
Sodium chlorate	1,000 metric tons	617	742	940	792	721	669
Sodium phosphate tripoly	1,000 metric tons	(D)	(D)	(D)	(D)	(D)	(D)
Sodium silicates [1]	1,000 metric tons	1,203	992	1,136	1,070	1,054	1,074
Sodium metasilicates	1,000 metric tons	93	63	72	63	58	61
Sodium sulfate	1,000 metric tons	(D)	599	509	76	74	88
Carbon activated [2]	1,000 metric tons	156	151	166	(S)	(D)	143
Hydrogen peroxide	1,000 metric tons	355	342	1,083	(S)	(S)	(S)
Phosphorous, oxychloride and trichlorde.	1,000 metric tons	226	163	(D)	(D)	(D)	(D)

D Withheld to avoid disclosing data for individual companies. S Does not meet publication standards. [1] Other than metasilicates. [2] Granular and pulverized.

Source: U.S. Census Bureau, Current Industrial Reports, Series MAQ325A, and MA325B, annual. See also <http://www.census.gov/industry/1/mq325a035.pdf> (released December 2004) and <http://www.census.gov/industry/1/mq325b035.pdf> (released December 2004).

Table 995. **Aluminum—Supply, Shipments, and Foreign Trade: 1990 to 2004**

[In millions of pounds (17,334 represents 17,334,000,000)]

Item	1990	1995	1999	2000	2001	2002	2003	2004
SUPPLY								
Aluminum supply, total	17,334	20,425	24,590	23,586	20,071	21,118	21,147	22,278
Primary production	8,925	7,441	8,330	8,087	5,812	5,964	5,962	5,549
Recovery from scrap	5,276	7,028	8,146	7,606	6,572	6,452	6,216	6,665
Imports of ingot and mill products	3,133	5,956	8,113	7,893	7,687	8,702	8,969	10,064
Aluminum net shipments, total [1]	17,188	21,019	24,673	24,496	22,519	23,601	23,393	24,820
PRODUCT								
Mill products, total	13,013	15,716	17,989	17,676	15,467	15,715	15,675	17,109
Sheet, plate, and foil	9,297	11,168	12,437	12,116	10,376	10,573	10,561	11,481
Rod, bar, and wire	370	534	670	690	571	172	139	141
Electrical conductor	542	566	676	681	676	705	694	771
Extruded shapes and tube	2,546	3,102	3,817	3,792	3,482	3,903	3,944	4,355
Powder and paste	106	108	130	142	142	142	146	146
Forgings and impacts	152	238	259	255	220	220	191	215
Ingot for castings and other [2]	4,175	5,303	6,684	6,820	7,052	7,886	7,718	7,711
MARKET								
Domestic, total	14,637	18,152	21,707	21,680	20,531	21,245	21,385	22,900
Building and construction	2,663	2,679	3,237	3,204	3,297	3,447	3,442	3,702
Transportation	3,205	5,749	7,938	7,947	7,035	7,516	7,757	8,465
Consumer durables	1,122	1,369	1,675	1,692	1,502	1,592	1,518	1,609
Electrical	1,309	1,395	1,646	1,704	1,513	1,493	1,439	1,593
Machinery and equipment	992	1,257	1,458	1,496	1,414	1,359	1,439	1,611
Containers and packaging	4,772	5,088	5,106	4,992	4,961	4,979	4,941	5,088
Other	574	615	647	645	809	859	849	832
Exports	2,551	2,867	2,967	2,816	1,988	2,356	2,008	1,920
FOREIGN TRADE [3]								
Exports	3,753	3,846	3,865	4,097	3,712	3,729	3,662	4,410
Imports	3,718	6,910	9,506	9,357	8,853	9,680	9,885	11,222

[1] Data presented on this report have been adjusted to represent total U.S. producer's shipments and inventories plus imports by consumers. [2] Net ingot for foundry castings, export and destructive uses. [3] U.S. imports and exports of aluminum ingot, mill products and scrap.

Source: The Aluminum Association, Inc., Washington, DC, Aluminum Statistical Review, annual.

Table 996. Iron and Steel Industry—Summary: 1990 to 2002

[95.5 represents 95,500,000 tons. For financial data, the universe in 1992 consists of the companies that produced 68 percent of the total reported raw steel production. The financial data represent the operations of the steel segment of the companies. Minus sign (-) indicates net loss]

Item	Unit	1990	1995	1999	2000	2001	2002, final	2003, final	2004
Steel mill products, apparent supply...	Mil. tons [1]	95.5	109.6	127.9	131.9	116.4	117.8	116.1	131.8
Net shipments	Mil. tons [1]	85.0	97.5	106.2	109.1	98.9	100.0	106.0	111.4
Exports	Mil. tons [1]	4.3	7.1	5.4	6.5	6.1	6.0	8.2	7.9
Imports	Mil. tons [1]	17.2	24.4	31.2	29.4	30.1	32.6	23.1	35.8
Scrap consumed	Mil. tons [1]	50.1	62.0	62.0	65.0	63.0	62.0	61.8	57.3
Scrap inventory	Mil. tons [1]	3.6	4.1	5.3	5.3	4.9	4.2	4.5	4.8
Iron and steel products: Exports	Mil. tons [1]	5.3	8.2	6.7	7.7	7.2	7.0	9.3	9.6
Imports	Mil. tons [1]	21.9	27.3	40.2	42.6	34.4	37.3	27.9	41.2
Capacity by steelmaking process.....	Mil. net tons ...	116.7	112.4	128.2	130.3	125.5	113.7	121.6	116.1
Revenue	Bil. dol.	30.9	35.1	36.3	38.8	31.0	31.6	34.3	51.1
Net income	Bil. dol.	0.1	1.5	-0.5	-1.1	-3.9	-1.3	-6.9	4.4
Stockholders' equity	Bil. dol.	4.3	8.6	11.8	9.9	5.5	1.4	-5.0	11.2
Total assets...............	Bil. dol.	28.3	35.1	43.7	43.9	38.1	34.1	29.8	37.3
Capital expenditures	Bil. dol.	2.6	2.5	2.8	2.1	1.1	1.1	2.1	1.6
Working capital ratio [2]	Ratio.	1.6	1.5	1.7	1.7	1.6	1.3	0.9	2.1
Inventories	Bil. dol.	4.7	5.1	6.5	6.8	5.7	5.5	4.9	6.5
Average employment.........	1,000	169.0	122.6	102.2	99.5	88.0	74.4	42.5	39.7
Hours worked.............	Million	350.0	269.2	222.7	219.7	186.4	157.1	90.6	87.8
Index of output, all employees [3]	1997 = 100 ..	106.5	89.7	106.5	108.5	106.7	(NA)	(NA)	(NA)

NA Not available. [1] In millions of short tons. [2] Current assets to current liabilities. [3] NAICS code 3311. Output per hour.
Source: U.S. Bureau of Labor Statistics, Internet site <http://stats.bls.gov/iprhome.htm>.
Source: Except as noted, American Iron and Steel Institute, Washington, DC, *Annual Statistical Report* (copyright).

Table 997. Steel Products—Net Shipments by Market Classes: 1990 to 2002

[In thousands of short tons (84,981 represents 84,981,000). Comprises carbon, alloy, and stainless steel]

Market class	1990	1995	1999	2000	2001	2002	2003	2004
Net shipments, total [1]	84,981	97,494	106,201	109,050	99,448	100,000	105,974	111,385
Automotive.................	11,100	14,622	16,771	16,063	14,059	13,998	15,883	13,858
Steel service centers, distributors	21,111	23,751	28,089	30,108	27,072	27,473	28,551	34,667
Construction, incl. maintenance [2]	9,245	14,892	18,428	20,290	21,543	20,536	23,787	23,810
Containers, packaging, shipping.....	4,474	4,139	3,842	3,708	3,232	3,237	3,082	2,592
Machinery, industrial equipment, tools...	2,388	2,310	1,722	1,784	1,456	1,402	1,178	1,853
Steel for converting and processing	9,441	10,440	11,309	12,708	10,311	9,710	9,448	8,151
Rail transportation.............	1,080	1,373	1,031	1,307	981	1,042	938	1,185
Contractors' products.............	2,870	(2)	(2)	(2)	(2)	(2)	(2)	(2)
Oil and gas industries	1,892	2,643	2,151	2,885	2,953	2,098	2,112	2,487
Electrical equipment.............	2,453	2,397	2,267	2,055	1,684	1,341	1,099	2,026
Appliances, utensils, and cutlery	1,540	1,589	1,789	1,907	1,820	1,714	2,018	919

[1] Includes nonclassified shipments and other classes not shown separately. [2] Beginning 1994, contractors' products included with construction.
Source: American Iron and Steel Institute, Washington, DC, *Annual Statistical Report* (copyright).

Table 998. Metalworking Machinery—Value of Shipments: 1990 to 2003

[In millions of dollars (3,426.1 represents $3,426,100,000)]

Product	NAICS product code	1990	1995	1999	2000	2001	2002	2003
Metalworking machinery........	(X)	3,426.1	4,547.1	3,783.3	3,632.4	2,987.6	2,002.1	1,965.7
Metal cutting type [1]	(X)	2,371.3	3,036.6	2,512.6	2,552.4	2,163.7	1,418.7	1,399.2
Boring machines..	333512A1	(2)	172.4	53.8	87.2	124.8	128.3	76.6
Drilling machines [2]	333512A1	184.1	78.9	50.6	23.7	22.6	17.1	52.7
Gear cutting machines...........	33351211	102.7	137.1	132.0	180.6	137.2	111.0	287.1
Grinding and polishing machines	33351221	433.6	549.6	477.1	454.3	367.7	210.7	168.6
Lathes [3]	33351231	355.6	478.0	297.4	287.0	262.0	132.4	119.5
Milling machines [4]	33351241	214.3	194.8	200.5	150.5	137.8	56.1	39.3
Machining centers [5]	33351271	437.0	698.8	597.9	629.7	435.5	273.6	318.3
Station type machines	33351281	502.1	477.0	407.1	401.8	347.9	169.9	(D)
Other metal cutting machine tools [6] ...	33351291	141.9	246.2	291.7	333.2	276.4	238.3	250.1
Remanufactured tools	3335126111	(NA)	(NA)	(NA)	(NA)	49.2	50.4	42.4
Metal forming type	(X)	1,080.2	1,510.5	1,270.7	1,080.0	823.9	583.4	566.5
Punching and shearing machines	33351311 pt.	200.1	326.3	220.0	203.8	155.3	105.9	103.1
Bending and forming machines	33351311 pt.	222.9	256.9	265.8	262.4	202.6	141.3	132.5
Presses, except forging	33351331	308.3	379.2	433.7	303.1	180.3	140.1	120.9
Forging machines [7]	33351351 pt.	73.9	(D)	(D)	(D)	(D)	(D)	(D)
Other metal forming [7]	33351351 pt.	275.0	548.1	351.2	310.7	275.8	187.4	169.1

D Data withheld to avoid disclosure. X Not applicable. [1] Beginning 1995, data for "All lathes (turning machines)" and "All milling machines," valued at under $3,025 each are included in total "Metal cutting type" for 1995 through 2000. [2] For 1990, data for "Boring machines" were combined with "Drilling machines" to avoid disclosing individual company data. [3] Beginning 1995, product code 33351230, "Lathes," excludes the value for product code 3335123031, All lathes valued under $3,025 each. [4] Beginning 1995, product code 33351240, "Milling machines," excludes the value for product code 3335124001, "All milling machines valued under $3,025 each." [5] Multi-function numerically controlled machines. [6] Excludes those designed primarily for home workshops, labs, etc. [7] For 1995 through 2003, data for "Forging machines" have been combined with "Other metal forming machines" to avoid disclosing individual company data.
Source: U.S. Census Bureau, 1990, *Current Industrial Reports*, Series MQ35W; and thereafter, MQ333W. See also <http://www.census.gov/industry/1/mq333w025.pdf> (released July 2004).

Manufactures 661

Table 999. **U.S. Machine Tool Consumption—Gross New Orders and Exports: 2003 and 2004**

[Value in millions of dollars (2,388 represents $2,388,000,000)]

Item	2003				2004			
	Total	Metal cutting machines	Metal forming machines	Other manufac-turing technol-ogy	Total	Metal cutting machines	Metal forming machines	Other manufac-turing technol-ogy
New order units, total . . .	**16,671**	**14,082**	**1,323**	**1,266**	**22,254**	**19,674**	**1,184**	**1,396**
Northeast [1]	2,761	2,308	222	231	3,756	3,368	157	231
South [2]	3,035	2,524	258	253	3,626	3,064	270	292
Midwest [3]	5,448	4,479	440	529	6,792	5,883	369	540
Central [4]	3,294	2,834	299	161	4,611	4,142	249	220
West [5]	2,134	1,938	104	92	3,469	3,217	139	113
New order value, total . . .	**2,388**	**1,900**	**190**	**298**	**3,395**	**2,809**	**185**	**401**
Northeast [1]	305	262	17	25	509	432	18	59
South [2]	445	350	41	54	515	396	57	62
Midwest [3]	996	744	89	163	1,325	1,098	59	169
Central [4]	410	340	30	41	632	516	34	81
West [5]	231	204	12	15	413	366	18	29
Export order units [6]	1,178	859	112	207	1,761	1,423	159	179
Export order value [6]	332	220	31	81	447	345	35	67

[1] Covers Maine, New Hampshire, Vermont, New York, Massachusetts, Connecticut, Rhode Island, New Jersey, and Pennsylvania. [2] Covers Delaware, Maryland, Virginia, West Virginia, Kentucky, North Carolina, South Carolina, Tennessee, Mississippi, Alabama, Georgia, and Florida. [3] Covers Wisconsin, Michigan, Ohio, Illinois, and Indiana. [4] Covers Minnesota, North Dakota, South Dakota, Montana, Wyoming, Idaho, Iowa, Nebraska, Kansas, Missouri, Oklahoma, Arkansas, Louisiana, Texas, New Mexico, Colorado, and Utah. [5] Covers Washington, Oregon, California, Nevada, and Arizona. [6] Represents orders placed with U.S. builders.

Source: The Association for Manufacturing Technology, McLean, VA, (copyright); and American Machine Tool Distributors Association, Rockville, MD, *U.S. Machine Tool Consumption Report*, monthly.

Table 1000. **Semiconductors, Printed Circuit Boards, and Other Electronic Components—Value of Shipments by Class of Product: 1990 to 2003**

[In millions of dollars (56,301 represents $56,301,000,000). n.e.c. = not elsewhere classified]

Class of product	NAICS product code [1]	1990	1995	2000	2001	2002	2003
Total . . .	(X)	**56,301**	**118,906**	**164,854**	**118,868**	**104,897**	**103,001**
Transmittal, industrial, and special-purpose electron tubes (except x-ray)	3344111	1,097	855	703	700	584	631
Electron tubes, receiving type	(X)	24	(2)	(2)	(2)	(2)	(2)
Receiving type electron tubes and cathode ray picture tubes	3344114	1,344	2,907	3,458	2,847	2,486	1,459
Electron tube parts	3344117	143	120	144	125	91	75
Printed circuit boards	3344120	7,175	8,367	11,892	8,911	5,764	5,005
Integrated microcircuits (semiconductor networks)	3344131	16,623	48,438	73,664	46,337	49,726	54,588
Transistors	3344134	682	943	1,569	913	818	649
Diodes and rectifiers	3344137	668	1,067	621	403	370	392
Other semiconductor devices	334413A	5,741	12,639	9,757	7,632	6,632	6,534
Capacitors for electronic applications	3344140	1,392	1,785	2,786	1,734	1,338	1,199
Resistors	3344150	800	953	982	776	653	648
Coils, transformers, reactors, and chokes for electronic applications	3344160	976	1,412	1,719	1,362	1,153	964
Coaxial connectors	3344171	420	732	805	506	464	430
Cylindrical connectors	3344174	514	553	725	688	528	563
Rack and panel connectors	3344177	500	541	532	359	264	274
Printed circuit connectors	334417A	805	1,026	1,811	1,147	776	818
Other connectors including parts	334417D	1,085	1,402	2,059	2,052	1,436	1,415
Filters (except microwave) and piezoelectric devices	3344191	457	729	1,168	984	726	585
Transducers, electrical/electronic input or output	3344194	741	1,111	1,519	1,331	1,203	1,247
Switches, mechanical types for electronic circuitry	3344197	579	666	903	828	836	769
Printed circuit assemblies	334418B	8,269	24,448	37,273	31,214	23,171	19,231
Microwave components and devices	334419A	1,369	1,233	2,435	1,848	1,511	1,396
All other electronic components n.e.c.	334419D	4,898	6,978	8,332	6,173	4,366	4,131

X Not applicable. [1] North American Industry Classification System, 1997; see text, Section 15. [2] Product codes combined to avoid disclosing figures for individual companies.

Source: U.S Census Bureau, 1990, Current Industrial Reports, Series MA36Q; thereafter, MA334Q. See also <http://www.census.gov/industry/1/ma334q03.pdf> (released December 2004).

662 Manufactures

Table 1001. **Computers and Office and Accounting Machines—Value of Shipments: 1990 to 2003**

[In millions of dollars (25,630 represents $25,630,000,000)]

Selected products	1990	1995	1999	2000	2001	2002	2003
Electronic computers [1]	25,630	49,038	64,696	62,857	48,541	40,448	38,461
Host computers (multi-users).	(NA)	(NA)	21,089	22,877	16,469	13,053	12,106
Single user computers.	(NA)	(NA)	42,765	38,981	31,492	26,586	25,470
Other computers.	(NA)	(NA)	(D)	998	581	809	886
Loaded computer processor boards and board subassemblies [2]	2,247	24,448	30,091	37,273	31,214	23,171	19,231
Computer storage devices & equipment . . .	7,488	7,903	9,827	8,995	7,319	5,027	5,121
Parts for computer storage devices & subassemblies.	955	2,236	2,254	1,692	1,699	1,578	1,129
Computer terminals	2,067	1,086	541	415	361	266	257
Computer peripheral equipment, n.e.c.	7,697	12,331	12,889	12,434	10,637	10,460	9,387
Parts for input/output equipment	3,706	2,391	2,388	2,766	2,360	1,905	1,833
Calculating and accounting machines	(D)	1,279	1,196	1,210	1,191	845	920
Magnetic and optical recording media	3,695	5,106	3,907	3,206	2,228	2,207	2,135

NA Not available. D Withheld to avoid disclosing data for individual companies. [1] Beginning 1998, computer industry data are not entirely comparable to previous years. [2] These data are collected on two Current Industrial Report forms, MA35R, Computers and Office and Accounting Machines (Shipments) and MA36Q, Semiconductors, Printed Circuit Boards, And Other Electronic Components.

Source: U.S. Census Bureau, *Current Industrial Reports*, Series MA334R. See also <http://www.census.gov/industry/1/ma334r03.pdf>. (released December 2004).

Table 1002. **Computers and Office and Accounting Machines—Shipments: 2002 and 2003**

[Quantity in thousands of units (21,252 represents 21,252,000, value in millions of dollars (40,448.3 represents $40,448,300,000)]

Product	Number of companies, 2003	Quantity (1,000)		Value (mil. dol.)	
		2002	2003	2002	2003
Electronic computers (automatic data processors)	111	21,252	23,183	40,448.3	38,461.0
Host computers (multi-users):					
Large scale systems and unix servers	12	127	175	3,196.7	3,010.8
Medium-scale systems and unix servers	17	285	(D)	6,703.8	(D)
PC servers	21	(D)	1,111	(D)	8,946.2
Other host computers	8	(D)	(D)	(D)	(D)
Single user computers:					
Personal computers	29	14,138	14,950	16,030.2	14,708.4
Workstations	35	1,186	1,309	2,407.4	2,288.0
Laptops (AC/DC)	8	8	9	23.4	24.9
Notebooks, subnotebooks (battery operated)	13	4,491	5,107	7,850.2	8,161.2
Personal digital assistants	5	(D)	(D)	(D)	(D)
Other portable computers.	4	(D)	(D)	(D)	(D)
Other single user computers	5	317	316	274.8	287.1
Other computers	28	112	175	809.1	885.7
Computer storage devices and equipment	51	(X)	(X)	5,026.9	5,121.5
Parts for computer storage devices and subassemblies.	16	(X)	(X)	1,578.0	1,129.5
Computer terminals	24	(X)	(X)	266.1	256.9
Computer peripheral equipment, n.e.c. [1].	185	(X)	(X)	10,460.4	9,386.6
Keyboards.	21	(D)	1,100	(D)	46.4
Computer printers:					
Laser	22	2,327	2,040	1,853.7	1,998.4
Inkjet.	8	(D)	(D)	(D)	(D)
Calculating and accounting machines	34	(X)	(X)	844.6	920.2
Printed circuit assemblies	618	(X)	(X)	23,170.8	19,231.0
Magnetic and optical recording media	34	(X)	(X)	2,207.3	2,135.2

X Not applicable. D Withheld to avoid disclosure of individual companies. [1] n.e.c. = not elsewhere classssified.

Source: U.S. Census Bureau. *Current Industrial Reports*, Series MA334R. See also <http://www.census.gov/industry/1/ma334r03.pdf>. (released December 2004).

Table 1003. **Consumer Electronics and Electronic Components—Factory Sales by Product Category: 1990 to 2004**

[In millions of dollars (43,033 represents $43,033,000,000). Factory sales include imports]

Product category	1990	1995	2000	2001	2002	2003	2004
Total [1]	43,033	67,905	96,943	94,211	95,793	102,611	113,545
Video products, total	12,440	15,376	17,927	16,607	18,506	19,267	21,654
Analog direct-view color TV	6,197	6,798	6,503	5,130	5,782	4,756	3,505
Analog projection TV	626	1,417	1,481	1,060	733	293	85
Monochrome TV	99	34	15	15	12	9	5
Digital direct-view and projection TV	(NA)	(NA)	1,355	2,485	3,574	4,351	6,099
LCD TV	83	75	64	62	246	664	2,022
Plasma TV	(NA)	(NA)	(NA)	116	515	1,590	2,518
TV Combinations	178	723	1,292	790	733	778	665
Videocassette players	65	59	14	5	4	2	2
VCR decks	2,439	2,767	1,869	1,058	826	407	134
Camcorders	2,260	2,130	2,838	2,236	2,361	2,002	1,701
Direct-to-home satellite	421	1,265	790	1,175	1,116	1,476	1,886
Personal video recorders	(NA)	(NA)	77	144	57	178	541
Digital versatile disc players (DVD)	(NA)	(NA)	1,717	2,097	2,427	3,050	(NA)
Home and portable products, total	5,210	6,378	6,323	5,726	5,111	4,779	5,531
Compact audio systems	1,270	1,162	1,776	1,357	965	731	900
Separate audio components	1,935	1,911	1,545	1,261	1,202	981	1,140
Home radios	360	284	351	326	300	318	334
Portable audio equipment	1,645	2,506	2,156	1,846	1,526	1,355	980
Portable MP3 players	(NA)	(NA)	80	100	205	424	1,204
Mobile electronics, total	5,733	11,422	17,071	16,799	16,189	17,184	19,006
Aftermarket autosound equipment	1,192	1,931	2,169	2,098	2,211	2,090	2,210
Mobile video and navigation	(NA)	(NA)	386	436	586	580	782
Factory installed autosound	3,100	3,100	2,700	2,850	2,950	3,245	3,569
Wireless (cellular) telephones	1,133	2,574	8,995	8,651	8,106	9,163	10,538
Pagers	118	300	750	790	810	729	675
Family Radio Services (FRS)	(NA)	(NA)	418	461	251	235	201
Vehicle security	190	142	218	266	265	260	255
PDAs	(NA)	(NA)	1,265	1,077	875	759	657
Home office products, total	11,021	24,140	36,854	34,924	33,505	38,282	41,433
Cordless telephones	842	1,141	1,562	1,960	1,261	1,268	1,157
Corded telephones	638	557	386	294	266	256	264
Telephone answering devices	827	1,077	984	1,062	1,060	1,210	1,302
Caller ID devices	(NA)	(NA)	54	35	20	12	14
Home computers	4,187	12,600	16,400	12,960	12,609	15,584	17,201
Computer printers	(NA)	2,430	5,116	5,245	4,829	4,734	5,019
Modems/fax modems	(NA)	770	1,564	1,564	1,445	1,419	1,386
Computer peripherals	1,980	816	1,950	2,150	2,256	2,707	3,032
Computer software (incl. CDROM)	971	2,500	4,480	5,062	4,961	5,060	5,162
Home fax machines	920	919	386	349	297	242	160
Digital cameras	(NA)	(NA)	1,825	1,972	2,794	3,921	4,516
Electronic gaming, total	3,375	4,500	8,550	9,689	10,848	10,253	10,970
Electronic gaming hardware	975	1,500	2,700	3,250	3,750	3,188	3,162
Electronic gaming software	2,400	3,000	5,850	6,439	7,098	7,065	7,808
Blank media, total	1,638	1,415	2,169	2,679	3,210	3,750	5,255
Blank audio cassettes	376	334	162	129	98	77	66
Blank videocassettes	948	708	351	357	602	527	433
Blank computer media	314	373	1,200	1,550	1,600	1,800	1,692
Flash media	(NA)	(NA)	456	643	910	1,346	3,064
Accessories and batteries, total	2,176	3,544	6,299	5,968	6,460	7,041	7,545
Electronic accessories	793	944	1,356	1,378	1,500	1,635	1,815
Batteries	1,383	2,600	4,943	4,590	4,960	5,406	5,730
Home security systems	1,440	1,130	1,750	1,820	1,965	2,055	2,150

NA Not available.   [1] Includes categories, not shown separately.
Source: Consumer Electronics Association, Washington, DC, *Electronic Market Data Book*, annual (copyright).

Table 1004. **Communication Equipment—Value of Shipments: 1990 to 2003**

[In millions of dollars (36,990 represents $36,990,000,000]

Product description	NAICS product code [1]	1990	1995	2000	2001	2002	2003
Total	(X)	36,990	56,362	104,389	93,803	62,212	56,755
Telephone switching and switchboard equipment	3342101	7,537	8,178	15,174	12,188	7,437	4,921
Carrier line equipment and modems	3342104	5,014	5,869	13,112	10,943	4,488	3,048
Other telephone and telegraph equipment and components	3342107	3,181	10,510	28,971	22,841	13,886	12,407
Communication systems and equipment (except broadcast)	3342201	14,768	23,032	36,357	36,501	25,104	25,778
Broadcast, studio, and related electronic equip.	3342203	1,856	2,845	4,029	3,491	3,304	2,880
Intercommunications systems, including inductive paging systems (selective calling)	3342903	346	296	447	451	385	427
Alarm systems	3342901	1,027	1,662	2,755	2,374	2,440	2,254
Vehicular and pedestrian traffic control equipment and electrical railway signals and attachments	3342902	471	711	838	806	928	945
Electronic teaching machines, teaching aids, trainers and simulators	3333197	1,209	913	782	1,172	1,168	1,205
Laser sources [2]	3359997	(NA)	788	(S)	1,051	929	832
Ultrasonic equipment	335999A	109	172	272	233	174	195
Other electronic systems and equipment, n.e.c.	335999C	1,473	1,387	1,652	1,752	1,971	1,861

NA Not available.   S Does not meet publication standards.   [1] North American Industry Classification System, 1997; see text, Section 15.   [2] Beginning in 1995, data for laser equipment, instrumentation, and components were eliminated from this survey. Only laser sources are being collected.
Source: U.S. Census Bureau, *Current Industrial Reports*, Series MA334P. See also <http://www.census.gov/industry/1/ma334p03.pdf>. (released December 2004).

664   Manufactures

Table 1005. **Motor Vehicle Manufactures—Summary by Selected Industry: 2003**

[Payroll of 49,925 represents $49,925,000,000. Based on the Annual Survey of Manufactures; see Appendix III]

Industry	NAICS code [1]	All employees [2] Number	Payroll Total (mil. dol.)	Payroll Per employee (dol.)	Production workers [2]	Value of shipments [3] (mil. dol.)
Motor vehicle manufacturing, total	3361-3363	1,007,422	49,925	49,558	811,017	485,921
Motor vehicle, total	3361	209,537	14,192	67,730	184,149	259,578
Automobile & light duty motor vehicle	33611	183,033	13,060	71,352	163,554	243,656
Automobile	336111	74,366	5,068	68,146	64,243	85,118
Light truck & utility vehicle	336112	108,667	7,992	73,546	99,311	158,538
Heavy duty truck	33612	26,504	1,132	42,718	20,594	15,922
Motor vehicle body & trailer	3362	127,420	4,333	34,003	101,985	25,852
Motor vehicle body & trailer	33621	127,420	4,333	34,003	101,985	25,852
Motor vehicle body	336211	40,391	1,451	35,920	30,785	8,565
Truck trailer	336212	23,716	774	32,628	19,623	4,396
Motor home	336213	21,775	758	34,809	18,019	6,163
Travel trailer & camper	336214	41,538	1,350	32,502	33,559	6,728
Motor vehicle parts	3363	670,465	31,401	46,834	524,883	200,491
Motor vehicle gasoline engine & engine parts	33631	87,365	4,620	52,887	68,302	34,546
Motor vehicle electrical & electronic equipment	33632	92,339	3,903	42,269	67,735	24,923
Motor vehicle steering & suspension equipment	33633	39,696	1,918	48,313	31,609	10,641
Motor vehicle brake system	33634	41,217	1,604	38,918	32,232	12,975
Motor vehicle transmission & power train parts	33635	89,281	5,365	60,094	72,770	32,731
Motor vehicle seating & interior trim	33636	54,852	2,165	39,462	41,741	16,850
Motor vehicle metal stamping	33637	106,292	5,753	54,120	86,813	25,155
Other motor vehicle parts	33639	159,422	6,073	38,093	123,682	42,670

[1] North American Industry Classification System, 1997; see text, Section 15.   [2] Includes employment and payroll at administrative offices and auxiliary units. All employees represents the average of production workers plus all other employees for the payroll period ended nearest the 12th of March. Production workers represents the average of the employment for the payroll periods ended nearest the 12th of March and May.   [3] Includes extensive and unmeasurable duplication from shipments between establishments in the same industry classification.

Source: U.S. Census Bureau, *Annual Survey of Manufactures, Statistics for Industry Groups and Industries*, Series M03(AS)-1. See also <http://www.census.gov/prod/2005pubs/am0331gs1.pdf> (issued March 2005).

Table 1006. **Motor Vehicle Manufactures—Employees, Payroll, and Shipments by Major State: 2001**

[12,647 represents $12,647,000,000. Industry based on the North American Industry Classification System (NAICS), 1997; see text, Section 15]

Major State based on employment	Motor vehicle manufacturing (NAICS 3361) Employees, total	Payroll (mil. dol.)	Shipments (mil. dol.)	Motor vehicle body and trailer manufacturing (NAICS 3362) Employees, total	Payroll (mil. dol.)	Shipments (mil. dol.)	Motor vehicle parts manufacturing (NAICS 3363) Employees, total	Payroll (mil. dol.)	Shipments (mil. dol.)
United States ...	213,981	12,647	216,128	123,120	3,807	24,209	736,003	31,501	186,839
Alabama	(D)	(D)	(D)	3,158	94	754	11,531	565	3,315
Arkansas	(NA)	(NA)	(NA)	1,549	35	281	7,522	173	873
California	7,429	416	2,965	11,287	341	4,693	25,824	771	3,849
Florida	(NA)	(NA)	(NA)	3,793	134	806	4,409	124	625
Georgia	7,620	386	8,130	2,977	80	(S)	9,394	273	2,114
Illinois	8,083	481	7,863	3,719	127	649	28,464	930	5,271
Indiana	11,867	618	10,811	24,414	867	4,845	93,497	4,226	22,712
Iowa	(NA)	(NA)	(NA)	8,000	247	1,403	9,169	307	1,693
Kentucky	18,810	1,287	22,470	(NA)	(NA)	(NA)	27,764	934	7,240
Michigan	42,260	2,722	51,873	3,925	113	599	178,681	9,230	52,242
Mississippi	(NA)	(NA)	(NA)	780	22	109	9,718	296	1,673
Missouri	(D)	(D)	(D)	2,049	52	227	19,520	569	4,030
Nebraska	(NA)	(NA)	(NA)	1,109	29	190	3,609	123	668
New York	(NA)	(NA)	(NA)	1,088	32	768	30,232	1,737	8,703
North Carolina	(D)	(D)	(D)	3,714	141	961	18,661	619	4,512
Ohio	29,972	1,784	32,648	4,387	142	809	96,775	4,881	29,924
Oklahoma	(D)	(D)	(D)	4,086	105	691	5,531	165	1,031
Oregon	1,749	60	781	4,635	113	552	2,525	98	500
Pennsylvania	(D)	(D)	(D)	7,243	191	1,118	15,328	581	3,328
South Carolina	6,210	298	4,501	(S)	(S)	(S)	16,109	557	4,570
Tennessee	14,241	840	7,552	1,818	52	381	32,130	1,065	8,098
Texas	(D)	(D)	(D)	5,963	169	800	16,186	468	3,389
Utah	(NA)	(NA)	(NA)	1,085	27	177	5,341	223	2,387
Virginia	(D)	(D)	(D)	(D)	(D)	(D)	6,747	253	1,718
Wisconsin	(D)	(D)	(D)	5,258	188	909	23,387	970	5,412

NA Not available.   D Withheld to avoid disclosing data on individual companies.   S Does not meet publication standards.

Source: U.S. Census Bureau, Annual Survey of Manufactures, *Geographic Area Statistics*, Series M01(AS)-3. See also <http://www.census.gov/prod/2003pubs/m01as-3.pdf> (issued January 2003).

Manufactures   665

Table 1007. Aerospace—Sales, New Orders, and Backlog: 1990 to 2003

[In billions of dollars (136.6 represents $136,600,000,000), except as indicated. Reported by establishments in which the principal business is the development and/or production of aerospace products]

Item	1990	1995	1999	2000	2001	2002	2003
Net sales	136.6	102.8	124.2	109.3	117.1	115.2	116.2
Percent U.S. Government	53.8	50.5	36.3	37.5	38.6	46.1	52.9
Complete aircraft and parts [1]	49.9	42.5	68.0	57.2	58.7	53.9	49.0
Aircraft engines and parts	16.4	12.5	14.4	12.5	15.9	14.8	13.9
Missiles and space vehicles, parts	22.0	18.4	15.7	15.6	15.5	15.6	16.0
Other products, services	48.3	29.4	26.1	24.0	26.9	30.9	37.3
Net, new orders	146.0	109.1	115.3	140.1	122.3	114.8	116.7
Backlog, December 31	250.1	202.6	188.4	215.0	220.1	222.5	222.9

[1] Except engines sold separately.

Source: U.S. Census Bureau, 1990–1997. *Current Industrial Reports*, Series M37G; thereafter M336G. See also <http://www.census.gov/industry/1/m336g0313.pdf> (released June 2005).

Table 1008. Net Orders for U.S. Civil Jet Transport Aircraft: 1990 to 2004

[1990 data are net new firm orders; beginning 1995, net announced orders. Minus sign (-) indicates net cancellations. In 1997, Boeing acquired McDonnell Douglas]

Type of aircraft and customer	1990	1995	1999	2000	2001	2002	2003	2004
Total number [1]	670	421	346	585	271	174	237	267
U.S. customers	259	138	192	412	49	89	84	23
Foreign customers	411	283	70	193	130	172	185	204
Boeing 737, total	189	189	258	378	184	117	204	142
U.S. customers	38	85	155	302	51	64	74	16
Foreign customers	151	104	45	86	73	127	145	92
Boeing 747, total	153	35	22	24	16	17	4	10
U.S. customers	24	2	1	1	7	-	-	1
Foreign customers	129	33	19	18	13	13	9	10
Boeing 757, total	66	-7	18	43	23	-	-1	-
U.S. customers	33	-6	7	38	15	2	-7	-
Foreign customers	33	-1	2	14	6	-	6	-
Boeing 767, total	60	26	32	6	32	-2	10	9
U.S. customers	23	4	21	-2	-1	1	-	-
Foreign customers	37	22	1	14	9	12	15	1
Boeing 777, total	34	83	21	113	30	26	12	42
U.S. customers	34	-	8	60	-	-1	11	-
Foreign customers	-	83	8	53	20	27	8	43
Boeing 787, total	-	-	-	-	-	-	-	56
U.S. customers	-	-	-	-	-	-	-	-
Foreign customers	-	-	-	-	-	-	-	56
Unidentified	-	-	-	-	-	-	-	-
McDonnell Douglas MD-11, total	52	-6	-	-	-	-	-	-
U.S. customers	16	3	-	-	-	-	-	-
Foreign customers	36	-9	-	-	-	-	-	-
McDonnell Douglas MD-80/90, total	116	51	-20	-	-	-	-	-
U.S. customers	91	-	-	-	-	-	-	-
Foreign customers	25	51	-20	-	-	-	-	-
McDonnell Douglas MD-95, total	-	50	15	21	-14	16	8	8
U.S. customers	-	50	-	13	-23	23	6	6
Foreign customers	-	-	15	8	9	-7	2	2

- Represents zero. [1] Includes types of aircraft not shown separately. Beginning 1999, includes unidentified customers.

Source: Aerospace Industries Association of America, Washington, DC, Research Center, Statistical Series 23, Internet site at <http://www.aia-aerospace.org/stats/aerostats/aerostats.cfm>.

Table 1009. U.S. Aircraft Shipments, 1980 to 2003, and Projections, 2004

[Value in millions of dollars (18,929 represents $18,929,000,000)]

Year	Total		Civil						Military	
			Large transports		General aviation [1]		Helicopters			
	Units	Value	Units	Value	Units	Value	Units	Value	Units	Value
1980	14,677	18,929	387	9,895	11,877	2,486	1,366	656	1,047	5,892
1985	3,610	27,269	278	8,448	2,029	1,431	384	506	919	16,884
1990	3,321	38,585	521	22,215	1,144	2,007	603	254	1,053	14,109
1991	3,092	44,657	589	26,856	1,021	1,968	571	211	911	15,622
1992	2,585	47,397	567	28,750	941	1,840	324	142	753	16,665
1993	2,585	41,166	408	24,133	964	2,144	258	113	955	14,776
1994	2,309	36,568	309	18,124	928	2,357	308	185	764	15,902
1995	2,436	33,658	256	15,263	1,077	2,842	292	194	811	15,359
1996	2,220	55,583	269	18,915	1,115	3,048	278	193	558	33,427
1997	2,757	65,129	374	26,929	1,549	4,593	346	231	488	33,376
1998	3,533	75,724	559	35,663	2,193	5,534	363	252	418	34,275
1999	3,799	80,974	620	38,171	2,475	6,803	345	200	359	35,800
2000	4,113	72,669	485	30,327	2,802	8,040	493	270	333	34,032
2001	3,902	77,586	526	34,155	2,616	7,991	415	247	345	35,193
2002	3,248	72,850	379	27,547	2,196	7,261	318	157	355	37,885
2003	3,238	66,571	281	20,500	2,080	6,205	517	366	360	39,500
2004, proj.	(NA)	(NA)	285	20,000	2,050	6,180	545	400	(NA)	(NA)

NA Not available. [1] Excludes off-the-shelf military aircraft.

Source: U.S. Department of Commerce, International Trade Administration, Internet site <http://www.ita.doc.gov/td/aerospace/inform/information.htm>

Table 1010. Aerospace Industry Sales by Product Group and Customer: 1990 to 2005

[In billions of dollars (134.4 represents $134,400,000,000). Due to reporting practices and tabulating methods, figures may differ from those in Table 1007]

Product group and customer	1990	1995	1998	1999	2000	2001	2002	2003	2004 [1]	2005 [2]
Current dollars										
Total sales.	134.4	107.8	148.0	153.7	144.7	154.2	153.4	147.1	160.7	172.8
Product group:										
Aircraft, total	71.4	55.0	84.0	88.7	81.6	86.4	80.2	73.2	80.8	87.0
Civil [4]	31.3	24.0	49.7	52.9	47.6	51.3	42.3	33.7	34.6	38.7
Military.	40.1	31.1	34.3	35.8	34.0	35.2	37.9	39.5	46.2	48.3
Missiles.	14.2	7.4	7.7	8.8	9.3	10.4	12.7	12.9	14.8	16.0
Space.	26.4	27.4	31.6	30.5	29.7	31.7	35.0	35.1	38.3	40.9
Related products and services [5] . . .	22.4	18.0	24.7	25.6	24.1	25.7	25.6	25.9	26.8	28.8
Customer group:										
Aerospace, total	112.0	89.8	123.3	128.1	120.6	128.5	127.8	121.2	133.9	144.0
DOD [6]	60.5	42.4	42.9	45.7	47.5	50.1	57.0	59.1	71.4	76.3
NASA [7] and other agencies.	11.1	11.4	13.3	13.4	13.4	14.5	16.4	16.5	16.1	17.6
Other customers [8]	40.4	36.0	67.0	69.0	59.7	63.9	54.5	45.6	46.4	50.1
Related products and services [5] . . .	22.4	18.0	24.7	25.6	24.1	25.7	25.6	25.9	26.8	28.8
Constant (1987)dollars [3]										
Total sales.	123.7	86.6	115.2	118.8	108.6	112.6	110.7	104.2	108.9	113.7
Product group:										
Aircraft, total	65.7	44.2	65.3	68.6	61.2	63.1	57.8	51.8	54.7	57.3
Civil [4]	28.8	19.2	38.7	40.9	35.7	37.4	30.5	23.9	23.4	25.5
Military.	36.9	25.0	26.7	27.7	25.5	25.7	27.3	28.0	31.3	31.8
Missiles.	13.1	5.9	6.0	6.8	7.0	7.6	9.1	9.1	10.0	10.5
Space.	24.4	22.0	24.6	23.6	22.3	23.1	25.2	24.9	25.9	26.9
Related products and services [5] . . .	20.6	14.4	19.2	19.8	18.1	18.8	18.4	18.3	18.1	18.9
Customer group:										
Aerospace, total	103.1	72.1	96.0	99.0	90.5	93.9	92.2	85.8	90.7	94.7
DOD [6]	55.7	34.1	33.4	35.3	35.6	36.6	41.1	41.9	48.4	50.2
NASA [7] and other agencies.	10.0	9.2	10.4	10.4	10.0	10.6	11.8	11.7	10.9	11.6
Other customers [8]	36.5	28.9	52.2	53.3	44.8	46.7	39.3	32.3	31.4	32.9
Related products and services [5] . . .	20.6	14.4	19.2	19.8	18.1	18.8	18.4	18.3	18.1	18.9

[1] Preliminary. [2] Estimate. [3] Based on AIA's aerospace composite price deflator. [4] All civil sales of aircraft (domestic and export sales of jet transports, commuters, business, and personal aircraft and helicopters). [5] Electronics, software, and ground support equipment, plus sales of non-aerospace products which are produced by aerospace-manufacturing use technology, processes, and materials derived from aerospace products. [6] Department of Defense. [7] National Aeronautics and Space Administration. [8] Includes civil aircraft sales (see footnote 4), commercial space sales, all exports of military aircraft and missiles and related propulsion and parts.

Source: Aerospace Industries Association of America, Inc., Washington, DC, 2005 Year-end Review and Forecast; and Internet site <http://www.aia-aerospace.org>

Table 1011. Major Household Appliances—Value of Shipments: 1990 to 2003

[In millions of dollars (11,670.0 represents $11,670,000,000)]

Product	NAICS product code	1990	1995	1999	2000	2001	2002	2003
Total.	33522	11,670.0	13,966.2	16,622.3	17,041.0	16,710.6	17,672.8	18,010.4
Electric household ranges, ovens, and surface cooking units, equipment and parts. . .	3352211	1,659.8	1,791.8	2,197.1	2,170.3	2,004.5	1,823.5	2,122.8
Gas household ranges, ovens, and surface cooking units, equipment and parts. . .	3352213	739.4	654.1	786.3	779.1	902.0	929.4	1,089.9
Other household ranges, cooking equipment, outdoor cooking equipment incl. parts and accessories.	3352215	581.1	911.6	1,218.6	1,251.1	1,027.0	1,050.8	909.4
Household refrigerators [1] [2].	3352221	3,208.1	4,739.4	4,968.8	5,395.8	5,227.1	5,080.3	5,499.1
Food freezers, complete units, for freezing and/or storing frozen food (household type) [2]	3352222	226.6	(D)	(D)	(D)	(D)	(D)	(D)
Parts and attachments for household refrigerators and freezers.	3352223	134.0	111.8	92.4	99.4	63.7	78.4	85.0
Household laundry machines and parts.	3352240	2,924.5	3,095.4	4,029.7	4,046.6	4,162.0	4,446.5	4,699.2
Water heaters, electric	3352281	433.8	513.0	580.0	572.7	555.7	576.0	580.7
Water heaters, except electric.	3352283	577.2	681.8	842.8	843.6	799.3	842.0	985.2
Household appliances, n.e.c. and parts	3352285	1,185.5	1,579.2	1,998.8	2,066.1	2,033.1	2,008.9	2,039.1

D Withheld to avoid disclosing data for individual companies. [1] Includes combination refrigerator-freezers. [2] Product code 33522210000 and 3352222000 are combined to avoid disclosing data for individual companies.

Source: U.S. Census Bureau, 1990, Current Industrial Reports, Series MA36F; thereafter Series MA335F. See also <http://www.census.gov/industry/1/ma335f03.pdf> (released December 2004).

No. 288.—INDEXES OF VALUE OF WHOLESALE SALES

[NOTE.—Monthly average 1919=100. Sales in this and the two following tables are much affected by changes in price levels. For certain branches they are also highly seasonal]

Period	Total, 6 branches	Groceries	Meats	Dry goods	Shoes	Hardware	Drugs	General wholesale price index
1920	112	113		115	88	116	112	226
1921	78	77	55	83	68	82	97	147
1922	74	76	56	83	65	86	90	149
1923	83	83	65	95	68	104	111	154
1924	82	85	65	91	58	99	113	150
1924								
January	80	80	66	97	49	91	116	151
February	78	77	63	98	49	90	110	152
March	80	80	62	90	65	104	118	150
April	78	79	61	81	69	108	114	148
May	77	81	64	72	56	104	110	147
June	76	83	64	70	52	96	105	145
July	78	83	67	79	44	93	110	147
August	83	83	68	102	56	93	108	150
September	92	93	71	116	69	106	117	149
October	95	100	78	104	67	111	128	152
November	84	89	69	88	57	98	109	153
December	79	83	66	77	57	99	109	157

No. 289.—INDEXES OF VALUE OF SALES OF 359 DEPARTMENT STORES: For the UNITED STATES AND BY FEDERAL RESERVE DISTRICTS

[NOTE.—Monthly average 1919=100. See headnote Table 288]

Month	Unadjusted					Adjusted for seasonal variations				
	1920	1921	1922	1923	1924	1920	1921	1922	1923	1924
Year	120	110	111	124	125					
January	106	103	90	101	109	121	117	102	116	125
February	90	91	81	90	102	116	117	104	117	127
March	122	117	102	124	115	122	117	102	124	115
April	121	115	113	119	133	117	110	109	117	130
May	127	113	116	128	127	123	110	112	124	123
June	122	111	110	126	120	122	111	111	126	120
July	94	80	80	89	91	126	107	107	119	122
August	94	85	89	100	93	121	108	113	128	119
September	109	95	107	113	119	120	104	117	124	131
October	132	124	131	148	141	118	110	116	130	124
November	137	120	132	142	141	122	107	117	126	126
December	184	173	188	202	210	114	108	117	126	132

Period	Total (359 stores)	Boston	New York	Philadelphia	Cleveland	Richmond	Atlanta	Chicago	Minneapolis [1]	Dallas [1]	San Francisco
1920	120	118	119	118	128	113	119	123	112	120	121
1921	110	114	114	112	114	106	101	110	103	99	116
1922	111	119	116	114	114	104	94	114	99	92	121
1923	124	127	127	127	130	111	104	132	105	98	139
1924	125	126	132	126	128	117	101	133	104	102	143

No. 290.—INDEXES OF VALUE OF SALES OF CHAIN STORES

[NOTE.—Monthly average 1919=100. See headnote Table 288]

Period	Grocery (27 chains)	5-and-10 (5 chains)	Drug (9 chains)	Cigar (3 chains)	Shoe (6 chains)	Music (4 chains)	Candy (4 chains)
1920	146	120	121	133	120	109	138
1921	130	124	123	132	113	86	142
1922	151	140	127	128	114	101	147
1923	188	165	144	135	123	113	176
1924	215	185	150	138	133	101	190

Source of Tables 288, 289, and 290: Federal Reserve Board

Source: Statistical Abstract of the United States: 1924 Edition.

Section 22
Domestic Trade

This section presents statistics relating to the distributive trades, specifically wholesale trade and retail trade. Data shown for the trades are classified by kind of business and cover sales, establishments, employees, payrolls, and other items. The principal sources of these data are from the Census Bureau and include the *2002 Economic Census*, annual surveys, and the *County Business Patterns* program. These data are supplemented by several tables from trade associations, such as the National Automobile Dealers Association (Table 1023). Several notable research groups are also represented, such as Claritas (Table 1021), National Research Bureau (Tables 1037 and 1038), Jupiter Research, Inc. (Table 1035), and Forrester Research, Inc. (Table 1034).

Data on retail and wholesale trade also appear in several other sections. For instance, labor force employment and earnings data appear in Section 12, Labor Force, Employment, and Earnings; gross domestic product of the industry (Table 651) appear in Section 13, Income, Expenditures, and Wealth; financial data (several tables) from the quarterly *Statistics of Income Bulletin,* published by the Internal Revenue Service, appear in Section 15, Business Enterprise.

Censuses—Censuses of retail trade and wholesale trade have been taken at various intervals since 1929. Beginning with the 1967 census, legislation provides for a census of each area to be conducted every 5 years (for years ending in "2" and "7"). For more information on these censuses, see the *History of the 1997 Economic Census* found at <http://www.census.gov/prod/ec97/pol00-hec.pdf>. The industries covered in the censuses and surveys of business are those classified in 13 sectors defined in the *North American Industry Classification System,* called NAICS (see below). *Retail trade* refers to places of business primarily engaged in retailing merchandise to the general public; and *wholesale trade,* to

establishments primarily engaged in selling goods to other businesses and normally operating from a warehouse or office that have little or no display of merchandise. All Census Bureau tables in this section are utilizing the 2002 NAICS codes, which replaced the Standard Industrial Classification (SIC) system. NAICS makes substantial structural improvements and identifies over 350 new industries. At the same time, it causes breaks in time series far more profound than any prior revision of the previously used SIC system. For information on this system and how it affects the comparability of retail and wholesale statistics historically, see text, Section 15, Business Enterprise, and especially the Census Bureau Web site at <http://www.census .gov/epcd/www /naics.html>. In general, the 2002 Economic Census has two series of publications for these two sectors: 1) subject series with reports such as product lines and establishment and firm sizes, and 2) geographic reports with individual reports for each state. For information on these series, see the Census Bureau Web site at <http://www.census.gov/econ/census02/>.

Current surveys—Current sample surveys conducted by the Census Bureau cover various aspects of retail and wholesale trade. Its *Monthly Retail Trade and Food Services* report contains monthly estimates of sales, inventories, and inventory/sales ratios for the United States, by kind of business. Annual figures on sales, year-end inventories, and inventory/sales ratios, purchases, accounts receivable, and gross margins by kind of business, appear in the *Annual Benchmark Report for Retail Trade and Food Services.* Statistics from the Bureau's monthly wholesale trade survey include national estimates of sales, inventories, and inventory/sales ratios for merchant wholesales excluding manufacturers' sales branches and offices. Data are presented by major summary groups "durable and nondurable," and 4-digit

U.S. Census Bureau, Statistical Abstract of the United States: 2006

NAICS industry groups. Merchant wholesalers excluding manufacturers' sales branches and offices are those wholesalers who take title to the goods they sell (e.g., jobbers, exporters, importers, industrial distributors). These data, based on reports submitted by a sample of firms, appear in the *Monthly Wholesale Trade Report.* Annual figures on sales, inventory/sales ratios, year-end inventories, purchases, and gross margins appear in the *Annual Benchmark Report for Wholesale Trade.* Data on manufacturers' sales branches and offices were collected for the first time in the 2004 *Annual Trade Survey* and appear in the *Annual Report for Wholesale Trade.* Data are presented by major summary groups "durable and nondurable" and 4-digit NAICS industry groups for sales, end-of-year inventories, and operating expenses. The reports just mentioned may appear in print in some cases, but principally are available as documents on the Census Bureau Web site at <http://www.census .gov/econ/www/retmenu.html>.

E-commerce—Electronic commerce (or e-commerce) are sales of goods and services over the Internet and extranet, electronic data interchange (EDI), or other online systems. Payment may or may not be made online. This edition has several tables on e-commerce sales, such as Tables 1020 and 1034 to 1036 in this section, 977 in Section 21, Manufactures, and 1261 in Section 27, Accommodation, Food Services, and Other Services. Also, there are several private sources for similar data such as Forrester Research Inc., Cambridge MA; BizRate.com, Los Angeles, CA; and Jupiter Research, Inc., New York, NY. These sources show estimated and projected online retail sales by key categories from business to consumers or to other businesses. Their methods of collecting the data vary widely between the sources and consequently these estimates of this activity vary also. Users of these estimates may want to contact the sources for descriptions of their methodology. Methodology for Census Bureau estimates can be found at <www.census- .gov /estats>.

Statistical reliability—For a discussion of statistical collection and estimation, sampling procedures, and measures of statistical reliability applicable to Census Bureau data, see Appendix III.

Table 1012. **Wholesale and Retail Trade—Establishments, Sales, Payroll and Employees: 2002**

[**4,376 represents $4,376,000,000,000.** Covers establishments with payroll. These data are preliminary and are subject to change. For statement on methodology, see Appendix III]

Kind of business	NAICS code [1] 2002	Establishments	Sales, receipts, revenue, or shipments (bil. dol.)	Annual payroll (bil. dol.)	Paid employees (1,000)
Wholesale trade.	42	**438,301**	**4,376**	**255**	**6,011**
Durable goods wholesalers (except agents, brokers, and electronic markets)	423	262,751	2,086	153	3,404
Nondurable goods wholesalers (except agents, brokers, and electronic markets) . . .	424	143,274	1,838	93	2,382
Wholesale trade, agents, brokers, and electronic markets.	425	32,276	452	9	225
Retail trade	44-45	**1,115,092**	**3,173**	**307**	**15,053**
Motor vehicle and parts dealers.	441	126,201	814	65	1,907
Furniture and home furnishings stores	442	65,088	94	13	554
Electronics and appliance stores	443	46,724	88	10	418
Building material and garden equipment and supplies dealers	444	(S)	(S)	(S)	(S)
Food and beverage stores	445	149,802	488	49	2,896
Health and personal care stores	446	79,360	183	21	1,043
Gasoline stations	447	(S)	(S)	(S)	(S)
Clothing and clothing accessories stores. . . .	448	149,318	170	21	1,425
Sporting goods, hobby, book, and music stores.	451	63,033	78	9	633
General merchandise stores	452	39,846	451	43	2,549
Miscellaneous store retailers.	453	129,070	95	14	849
Nonstore retailers	454	55,764	171	18	587

S Figures does not meet publication standards. [1] North American Industry Classification System, 2002; see text, Section 15.

Source: U.S. Census Bureau, 2002 Economic Census, Advance Summary Statistics for the United States, issued March 2004. See also <http://www.census.gov/econ/census02/advance/TABLE1.HTM>.

Table 1013. **Retail Trade—Establishments, Employees, and Payroll: 1997 and 2002**

[**4,060 represents $4,060,000,000,000.** Covers establishments with payroll. These data are preliminary and are subject to change. For statement on methodology, see Appendix III]

Kind of business	NAICS code [1] 1997	1997				2002			
		Establishments	Sales, receipts, revenue, or shipments (bil. dol.)	Annual payroll (bil. dol.)	Paid employees (1,000)	Establishments	Sales, receipts, revenue, or shipments (bil. dol.)	Annual payroll (bil. dol.)	Paid employees (1,000)
Wholesale trade	42	**453,470**	**4,060**	**215**	**5,797**	**441,810**	**4,379**	**256**	**6,035**
Wholesale trade, durable goods	421	290,629	2,180	133	3,398	288,286	2,354	159	3,565
Wholesale trade, nondurable goods. . .	422	162,841	1,880	82	2,398	153,524	2,025	97	2,470
Retail trade.	44-45	**1,118,447**	**2,461**	**237**	**13,991**	**1,111,583**	**3,171**	**306**	**15,029**
Motor vehicle and parts dealers	441	122,633	645	50	1,719	122,692	812	64	1,884
Furniture and home furnishings stores.	442	64,725	72	10	483	65,088	94	13	554
Electronics and appliance stores	443	43,373	69	7	345	46,724	88	10	418
Building material and garden equipment and supplies dealers	444	93,117	228	26	1,118	(S)	(S)	(S)	(S)
Food and beverage stores	445	148,528	402	41	2,893	149,802	488	49	2,896
Health and personal care stores	446	82,941	118	15	904	79,360	183	21	1,043
Gasoline stations	447	126,889	198	11	922	(S)	(S)	(S)	(S)
Clothing and clothing accessories stores.	448	156,601	136	17	1,280	149,318	170	21	1,425
Sporting goods, hobby, book, and music stores	451	69,149	62	7	561	63,033	78	9	633
General merchandise stores.	452	36,171	330	31	2,508	39,846	451	43	2,549
Miscellaneous store retailers	453	129,838	78	10	753	129,070	95	14	849
Nonstore retailers.	454	44,482	123	12	506	55,764	171	18	587

S Figure does not meet publication standards. [1] North American Industry Classification System; see text, Section 15, Business Enterprise.

Source: U.S. Census Bureau, 2002 Economic Census, Advance Comparative Statistics for the United States, issued March 2004. See also <http://www.census.gov/econ/census02/advance/TABLE2.HTM>.

Domestic Trade 671

Table 1014. **Wholesale and Retail Trade—Establishments, Employees, and Payroll by State: 2000 and 2002**

[6,112 represents 6,112,000. Covers establishments with payroll. Employees are for the week including March 12. Excludes most government employees, railroad employees, and self-employed persons. Kind-of-business classification based on North American Industry Classification System (NAICS); see text, Section 15, Business Enterprise. For statement on methodology, see Appendix III]

State	Wholesale establishments (NAICS 42)						Retail establishments (NAICS 44,45)					
	Number of establishments		Number of employees (1,000)		Annual payroll (mil. dol.)		Number of establishments		Number of employees (1,000)		Annual payroll (mil. dol.)	
	2000	2002	2000	2002	2000	2002	2000	2002	2000	2002	2000	2002
U.S. . . .	446,237	436,900	6,112	5,860	270,122	262,528	1,113,573	1,125,693	14,841	14,820	302,553	320,707
AL	6,132	5,792	82	76	2,892	2,691	19,723	19,601	230	225	4,074	4,245
AK	752	748	7	7	281	295	2,733	2,683	33	34	790	846
AZ	6,731	6,636	86	85	3,627	3,562	16,911	17,431	255	280	5,694	6,664
AR	3,505	3,535	45	42	1,402	1,403	12,211	12,151	135	136	2,268	2,457
CA	58,326	58,700	808	811	40,011	39,506	107,987	110,510	1,491	1,535	36,073	39,534
CO	7,452	7,458	97	100	4,906	4,900	18,748	19,200	252	252	5,883	5,990
CT	5,076	4,796	77	75	4,481	4,096	14,111	14,060	191	196	4,540	4,982
DE	1,009	953	19	23	1,117	1,404	3,742	3,800	52	54	1,048	1,149
DC	372	338	5	5	282	260	1,945	1,930	19	19	431	438
FL.	30,671	30,760	315	300	12,536	11,895	67,396	70,622	903	909	18,044	19,419
GA	13,892	13,618	199	196	9,064	8,882	33,788	34,531	464	460	9,365	9,531
HI	1,809	1,828	19	19	627	663	4,924	4,997	63	64	1,313	1,359
ID	2,012	1,978	24	26	845	971	5,871	5,920	70	70	1,347	1,447
IL	21,509	20,597	344	323	16,683	15,537	43,800	43,623	637	599	12,992	13,363
IN	8,642	8,440	120	113	4,607	4,394	24,261	24,358	354	345	6,332	6,630
IA	5,155	5,003	65	62	2,173	2,120	14,382	13,937	184	177	3,169	3,331
KS	4,876	4,719	62	55	2,333	2,108	12,261	11,980	153	149	2,747	2,854
KY	4,939	4,713	74	70	2,536	2,545	16,988	16,985	221	215	3,804	3,981
LA	6,192	5,965	79	75	2,723	2,702	17,755	17,746	232	228	4,032	4,211
ME	1,740	1,707	22	21	744	768	7,015	7,096	77	80	1,436	1,607
MD	6,098	6,022	95	93	4,526	4,501	19,539	19,734	285	289	6,062	6,504
MA	9,735	9,439	156	149	9,114	8,328	25,813	25,932	353	361	7,729	8,455
MI	13,576	13,055	191	175	8,887	8,292	38,862	38,829	545	524	10,667	11,069
MN	9,294	9,166	137	131	6,399	6,537	20,862	21,095	304	310	5,980	6,730
MS	3,116	2,968	40	35	1,222	1,142	12,794	12,644	141	139	2,384	2,515
MO	9,072	8,701	146	133	5,458	4,875	23,911	23,803	318	313	6,258	6,576
MT	1,537	1,566	15	14	433	451	5,101	5,193	52	54	920	1,042
NE	3,061	2,972	41	40	1,346	1,384	8,248	8,222	110	107	1,895	2,024
NV	2,556	2,586	31	33	1,238	1,345	6,940	7,310	108	114	2,533	2,804
NH	2,105	2,045	25	23	1,184	1,152	6,545	6,678	93	94	1,930	2,111
NJ.	17,157	16,548	279	265	14,724	14,657	34,841	35,410	439	447	9,897	10,651
NM	2,162	2,089	22	21	753	713	7,249	7,261	91	91	1,745	1,941
NY	36,606	35,628	422	393	20,941	20,170	75,500	77,532	844	848	18,116	19,166
NC	12,364	12,071	173	164	7,153	6,773	35,785	36,082	450	440	8,739	8,822
ND	1,543	1,517	18	16	532	524	3,435	3,435	42	41	719	757
OH	16,646	16,203	261	245	10,437	10,153	42,708	42,608	644	623	11,903	12,452
OK	5,005	4,835	62	56	2,126	1,935	14,147	13,942	168	168	2,913	3,104
OR	5,836	5,815	79	76	3,266	3,294	14,256	14,328	193	188	4,126	4,170
PA	16,796	16,272	243	240	10,287	10,399	48,518	48,444	668	669	12,556	13,229
RI	1,530	1,481	21	18	768	738	4,342	4,203	53	56	1,149	1,335
SC	5,091	4,940	65	64	2,353	2,522	18,619	18,487	224	213	4,083	4,022
SD	1,390	1,342	16	15	472	471	4,181	4,272	50	51	879	965
TN	8,006	7,614	127	123	4,848	5,017	24,624	24,288	311	307	5,908	6,154
TX	32,631	31,876	458	433	20,176	19,145	74,758	76,973	1,021	1,049	21,846	22,769
UT	3,294	3,346	44	43	1,583	1,662	7,952	8,275	124	124	2,455	2,486
VT	889	869	11	11	401	448	3,974	3,926	38	41	750	836
VA	7,893	7,636	110	105	4,651	4,468	28,794	29,194	399	406	7,949	8,499
WA	9,869	9,672	125	118	5,412	5,164	22,700	22,706	313	300	7,181	7,219
WV	1,869	1,708	22	21	698	684	7,788	7,510	92	89	1,493	1,513
WI	7,928	7,801	119	117	4,636	4,625	21,354	21,366	322	309	5,891	6,179
WY	790	833	7	7	229	252	2,881	2,850	28	29	515	571

Source: U.S. Census Bureau, "County Business Patterns"; published November 2004. See also <http://www.census.gov/prod/2004pubs/02cbp/cbp02-1.pdf>.

Table 1015. **Retail Trade—Establishments, Employees, and Payroll: 2000 and 2002**

[1,113.6 represents 1,113,600. Covers establishments with payroll. Employees are for the week including March 12. Most government employees are excluded. For statement on methodology, see Appendix III]

Kind of business	NAICS code [1] 1997	Establishments (1,000)		Employees (1,000)		Payroll (bil. dol.)	
		2000	2002	2000	2002	2000	2002
Retail trade, total....................	44-45	1,113.6	1,125.7	14,841	14,820	302.6	320.7
Motor vehicle & parts dealers [2]...............	441	124.5	126.6	1,866	1,891	63.9	68.0
Automobile dealers......................	4411	50.9	52.0	1,225	1,259	47.8	51.3
New car dealers.....................	44111	26.2	25.6	1,112	1,139	44.8	47.9
Used car dealers....................	44112	24.7	26.4	110	120	3.1	3.5
Automotive parts, accessories & tire stores......	4413	59.1	58.4	517	491	12.2	12.1
Furniture & home furnishing stores..............	442	64.8	66.4	549	552	13.4	13.8
Electronics & appliance stores..................	443	45.6	49.6	407	419	11.2	11.6
Appliance, TV & all other electronics stores......	44311	29.6	34.2	279	305	6.6	7.9
Computer & software stores.................	44312	12.9	12.5	106	94	4.2	3.3
Camera & photographic supplies stores........	44313	3.1	2.9	22	20	0.4	0.4
Bldg material & garden equip & supp dealers......	444	91.9	94.1	1,235	1,271	32.5	35.1
Building material & supplies dealers...........	4441	70.9	71.7	1,055	1,092	28.4	30.8
Lawn & garden equip & supplies stores........	4442	21.0	22.4	180	179	4.0	4.3
Food & beverage stores....................	445	154.5	155.7	3,004	2,884	48.4	50.1
Grocery stores.........................	4451	98.3	97.2	2,717	2,569	44.0	44.9
Grocery (except convenience) stores........	44511	68.8	62.9	2,544	2,388	41.8	42.5
Convenience stores..................	44512	29.5	34.2	*173	182	2.2	2.4
Specialty food stores.....................	4452	27.8	29.3	154	177	2.4	3.0
Meat markets.......................	44521	6.5	6.5	41	42	0.6	0.7
Fish & seafood markets...............	44522	1.9	2.2	8	10	0.1	0.2
Fruit & vegetable markets.............	44523	3.2	3.6	18	22	0.3	0.4
Other specialty food stores............	44529	16.2	17.1	86	104	1.3	1.7
Beer, wine & liquor stores [3]...............	4453	28.5	29.2	134	138	2.1	2.2
Health & personal care stores...............	446	81.2	82.6	914	988	19.3	22.2
Pharmacies & drug stores.................	44611	40.6	40.2	680	731	14.5	16.8
Cosmetics, beauty supplies & perfume stores.....	44612	9.6	11.3	61	83	0.8	1.2
Optical goods stores....................	44613	14.3	13.0	74	73	1.7	1.7
Other health & personal care stores...........	44619	16.7	18.2	98	102	2.2	2.5
Food (health) supplement stores...........	446191	8.7	9.7	49	51	0.7	0.8
All other health & personal care stores.......	446199	8.0	8.5	49	51	1.5	1.7
Gasoline stations.........................	447	119.6	117.1	937	896	13.3	13.5
Gasoline stations with convenience stores.......	44711	80.5	84.7	653	653	8.9	9.4
Other gasoline stations.................	44719	39.1	32.4	284	243	4.4	4.1
Clothing & clothing accessories stores...........	448	150.9	151.9	1,369	1,409	20.2	21.9
Clothing stores.........................	4481	90.0	93.1	1,015	1,046	13.7	15.4
Men's clothing stores..................	44811	10.7	10.4	85	83	1.6	1.6
Women's clothing stores...............	44812	35.6	34.6	302	300	3.9	4.1
Children's & infants' clothing stores.......	44813	5.6	6.1	59	62	0.7	0.7
Family clothing stores................	44814	20.6	22.9	453	474	5.9	7.0
Clothing accessories stores............	44815	5.7	6.4	28	31	0.4	0.5
Other clothing stores.................	44819	11.8	12.7	88	95	1.2	1.4
Shoe stores............................	4482	29.7	28.0	185	201	2.6	2.7
Jewelry, luggage & leather goods stores.........	4483	31.3	30.9	168	162	3.9	3.8
Jewelry stores.......................	44831	29.3	28.9	156	151	3.6	3.6
Luggage & leather goods stores...........	44832	2.0	1.9	12	11	0.2	0.2
Sporting goods, hobby, book & music stores........	451	65.0	65.9	616	618	8.8	9.3
Sporting goods, hobby, musical instrument stores...	4511	43.6	44.3	389	405	6.0	6.5
Book, periodical & music stores...............	4512	21.4	21.7	228	213	2.8	2.8
Prerecorded tape, CD & record stores........	45122	7.7	7.5	76	66	0.9	0.8
General merchandise stores..................	452	39.6	41.1	2,526	2,546	39.8	43.7
Department stores......................	4521	10.4	10.4	1,766	1,742	27.2	29.2
Other general merchandise stores............	4529	29.2	30.7	760	804	12.6	14.5
Warehouse clubs & superstores.............	45291	2.0	2.2	478	498	8.7	10.1
All other general merchandise stores........	45299	27.2	28.4	283	306	3.8	4.4
Miscellaneous store retailers [2]................	453	131.0	130.0	850	823	13.8	14.1
Used merchandise stores.................	4533	17.5	18.0	114	118	1.6	1.8
Other miscellaneous store retailers...........	4539	46.4	43.6	264	252	5.4	5.3
Nonstore retailers.......................	454	44.8	44.7	567	524	18.1	17.3
Electronic shopping & mail-order houses........	4541	11.8	11.9	277	250	10.4	9.5
Vending machine operators................	4542	6.2	5.9	67	58	1.5	1.4
Direct selling establishments...............	4543	26.8	27.0	223	216	6.1	6.5
Fuel dealers........................	45431	11.8	11.3	106	102	3.1	3.3
Other direct selling establishments........	45439	15.0	15.6	117	114	3.0	3.2

[1] Based on North American Industry Classification System; see text, Section 15. [2] Includes other kinds of business not shown separately. [3] Includes government employees.

Source: U.S. Census Bureau, "County Business Patterns"; published November 2004. See also <http://www.census.gov/prod/2004pubs/02cbp/cbp02-1.pdf>.

Domestic Trade   673

Table 1016. Retail Trade and Food Services—Sales by Kind of Business: 1992 to 2004

[In billions of dollars (2,007.9 represents $2,007,900,000,000)]

Kind of business	NAICS code [1]	1992	1995	1999	2000	2001	2002	2003	2004
Retail and food services sales,									
total	44–45, 72	2,007.9	2,441.1	3,083.0	3,288.7	3,388.0	3,473.7	3,624.8	3,901.7
Retail sales, total	44–45	1,804.5	2,207.5	2,797.9	2,983.0	3,069.8	3,141.5	3,275.4	3,521.7
GAFO, total [2]		529.0	644.7	813.3	862.1	884.1	915.6	949.6	1,010.2
Motor vehicle and parts dealers	441	414.6	576.9	764.4	797.3	818.7	821.7	845.8	882.0
Automobile and other motor vehicle dealers	4411, 4412	377.2	528.7	703.4	734.9	757.9	758.7	781.2	814.7
Automobile dealers	4411	359.1	502.5	663.5	689.7	710.9	708.9	725.4	754.0
New car dealers	44111	333.8	464.6	606.7	631.0	651.5	647.0	661.8	686.5
Used car dealers	44112	25.3	37.8	56.8	58.7	59.4	61.8	63.5	67.5
Auto parts, access., and tire stores	4413	37.3	48.2	61.0	62.4	60.8	63.0	64.6	67.3
Furniture, home furnishings, electronics and appliance stores	442, 443	90.1	122.6	160.4	172.1	172.3	180.1	185.8	198.3
Furniture and home furnishings stores	442	49.8	61.3	83.3	90.5	91.4	94.9	97.7	103.8
Furniture stores	4421	29.5	35.3	46.2	50.1	50.4	51.5	52.2	56.7
Home furnishings stores	4422	20.4	26.0	37.0	40.4	41.0	43.4	45.5	47.0
Electronics and appliance stores [3]	443	40.3	61.2	77.2	81.6	80.9	85.2	88.1	94.5
Appl. T.V., and other elect. stores	44311	29.0	42.1	52.4	58.6	60.8	64.2	66.9	72.3
Computer and software stores	44312	9.0	16.8	21.7	19.6	16.8	17.7	17.9	18.6
Building mat. garden equip. & supply stores	444	129.7	162.7	216.9	228.1	238.8	248.7	264.9	303.1
Building mat. & supply dealers	4441	109.6	140.6	187.9	197.7	206.9	217.2	231.7	267.9
Food and beverage stores [3]	445	371.5	391.3	434.6	445.9	463.7	466.2	477.3	498.2
Grocery stores	4451	337.9	356.9	394.6	403.1	418.8	420.5	432.0	447.7
Beer, wine and liquor stores	4453	21.8	22.1	26.6	28.6	29.8	30.2	30.6	32.0
Health and personal care stores	446	89.9	101.8	143.4	156.3	168.1	182.1	194.0	205.4
Pharmacies and drug stores	44611	77.8	85.9	121.8	131.7	143.0	155.8	166.5	175.6
Gasoline stations	447	156.6	181.3	212.8	250.2	251.8	251.0	274.1	320.6
Clothing and clothing access. stores [3]	448	120.3	131.6	160.1	168.0	167.7	172.7	178.6	190.0
Clothing stores [3]	4481	85.5	90.8	111.8	118.2	119.4	123.0	127.4	136.8
Men's clothing stores	44811	10.2	9.3	9.7	9.5	8.6	8.1	8.5	9.5
Women's clothing stores	44812	31.8	28.7	29.7	31.6	31.7	31.5	32.9	35.2
Family clothing stores	44814	33.2	40.0	55.2	58.8	60.0	64.1	65.9	70.6
Shoe stores	4482	18.6	20.4	22.7	23.0	23.0	23.3	23.3	23.7
Jewelry stores	44831	15.2	19.2	23.8	24.9	23.7	24.7	26.2	27.4
Sporting goods, hobby, book & music stores [3]	451	49.3	60.9	72.7	76.1	77.1	76.9	77.3	80.1
Sporting goods stores	45111	15.7	20.0	23.9	25.5	26.3	26.4	27.4	29.7
Book stores	451211	8.3	11.2	14.1	14.8	15.0	15.3	16.1	16.2
General merchandise stores	452	248.0	300.6	380.2	404.4	427.6	444.8	468.9	502.8
Department stores (excl. L.D.) [4]	4521	177.1	205.9	230.5	232.8	228.8	221.3	215.0	216.0
Department stores (incl. L.D.) [4]	4521	181.3	210.9	236.1	238.7	234.0	224.5	219.3	218.7
Other general merchandise stores	4529	70.9	94.7	149.7	171.6	198.7	225.4	253.8	286.8
Warehouse clubs and superstores	45291	40.0	65.1	118.9	139.9	165.1	191.8	217.0	247.3
Miscellaneous stores retail	453	55.5	76.7	105.4	108.0	104.6	104.6	103.6	107.9
Nonstore retailers [3]	454	79.1	101.0	146.9	176.6	179.5	190.8	205.2	233.3
Electronic shopping and mail order	4541	35.2	49.7	88.9	109.2	112.8	122.6	131.2	148.3
Fuel dealers	45431	17.2	20.2	20.1	27.0	26.4	24.4	29.3	33.7
Food services and drinking places [3]	722	203.4	233.6	285.1	305.7	318.1	332.2	349.4	380.0
Full service restaurants	7221	86.5	99.4	125.6	134.2	140.6	148.1	154.2	166.2
Limited service eating places	7222	87.4	103.1	120.1	128.1	133.3	138.8	147.7	163.0
Drinking places	7224	12.4	12.5	14.6	15.5	15.8	16.5	17.6	19.6

[1] North American Industry Classification System, 2002; see text, Section 15, Business Enterprise. [2] GAFO (General Merchandise, Apparel, Furniture, and Office Supplies) represents store classified in the following NAICS codes: 442, 443, 448, 451, 452, and 4532. [3] Includes other kinds of business not shown separately. [4] L.D. represents leased departments.

Source: U.S. Census Bureau, *Current Business Reports, Annual Benchmark Report for Retail Trade and Food Services, January 1992 Through February 2005*, Series BR/04-A.

Table 1017. Retail Trade Corporations—Sales, Net Profit, and Profit Per Dollar of Sales: 2004

[Represents North American Industry Classification System, 1997 (NAICS) groups 44 and 45. Profit rates are averages of quarterly figures at annual rates. Covers corporations with assets of $50,000,000 or more]

Item	Unit	Total retail trade	Food and beverage stores (NAICS 445)	Clothing and general merchandise stores (NAICS 448 and 452)	All other retail stores
Sales	Bil. dol.	1,657.0	358.6	634.2	664.2
Net profit:					
Before income taxes	Bil. dol.	79.2	7.3	38.4	33.4
After income taxes	Bil. dol.	52.7	5.0	25.1	22.7
Profits per dollar of sales:					
Before income taxes	Cents	4.8	2.0	6.0	5.0
After income taxes	Cents	3.2	1.4	3.9	3.4
Profits on stockholders' equity:					
Before income taxes	Percent	25.0	16.8	26.1	26.5
After income taxes	Percent	16.6	11.4	17.1	17.9

Source: U.S. Census Bureau, *Quarterly Financial Report for Manufacturing, Mining and Trade Corporations.*

Table 1018. **Retail Trade and Food Services—Estimated Per Capita Sales by Selected Kinds of Business: 1992 to 2004**

[In dollars. **As of December 31.** Based on estimated resident population estimates as of July. For statement on methodology, see Appendix III]

Kind of business	NAICS code [1]	1992	1995	1997	1998	1999	2000	2001	2002	2003	2004
Retail and food service sales	44-45, 72	6,051	6,860	7,435	7,699	8,197	8,508	8,692	8,882	9,221	9,929
Retail sales, total.	44-45	7,076	8,400	9,172	9,518	10,260	10,571	10,767	10,910	11,264	11,993
Total (Excluding motor vehicle and parts dealers)	44-45 ex 441	5,450	6,204	6,737	6,974	7,457	7,745	7,896	8,057	8,355	8,989
Motor vehicle and parts dealers	441	1,625	2,195	2,435	2,544	2,803	2,825	2,872	2,854	2,909	3,004
Furniture & home furnishings. . .	442	195	233	265	281	305	321	321	330	336	353
Electronics and appliance stores	443	158	233	248	265	283	289	284	296	303	322
Building material and garden equipment and supply stores	444	508	619	704	741	795	808	838	864	911	1,032
Food and beverage stores	445	1,456	1,489	1,532	1,545	1,594	1,580	1,627	1,619	1,641	1,696
Health and personal care stores	446	352	387	444	481	526	554	589	633	667	699
Gasoline stations	447	614	690	746	710	780	887	883	872	943	1,092
Clothing & clothing accessories stores .	448	472	501	525	553	587	595	588	600	614	647
Sporting goods, hobby, book, and music stores	451	193	232	245	255	267	270	270	267	266	273
General merchandise stores.	452	972	1,144	1,238	1,299	1,394	1,433	1,500	1,551	1,612	1,712
Miscellaneous store retailers	453	218	292	341	368	387	383	367	363	356	368
Nonstore retailers.	454	310	384	448	475	539	626	630	663	706	794
Food services and drinking places.	722	798	889	964	1,007	1,045	1,083	1,116	1,154	1,202	1,294

[1] North American Industry Classification System, 1997; see text, Section 15.

Source: U.S. Census Bureau, *Current Business Reports, Annual Benchmark Report for Retail Trade and Food Services, January 1992 Through February 2005,* Series BR/04-A.

Table 1019. **Retail Trade—Merchandise Inventories and Inventory/Sales Ratio by Kind of Business: 2000 to 2004**

[Inventories in billions of dollars (406.3 represents $406,300,000,000. As of December 31. Estimates exclude food services. Includes warehouses. Adjusted for seasonal variations. Sales data also adjusted for holiday and trading-day differences]

Kind of business	NAICS code [1]	Inventories				Inventory/Sales Ratio			
		2000	2002	2003	2004	2000	2002	2003	2004
Total.	44-45	406.3	418.6	435.0	459.7	1.62	1.57	1.56	1.51
Excluding motor vehicle and parts dealers	44-45 ex 441	277.8	281.8	287.5	304.4	1.49	1.44	1.38	1.34
Motor vehicle and parts dealers	441	128.5	136.8	147.6	155.3	2.01	1.96	2.08	2.01
Furniture, home furnishings, electronics, and appliance stores. . .	442, 443	25.2	25.4	26.5	28.3	1.83	1.69	1.65	1.69
Building material and garden equipment & supplies dealers	444	34.5	36.9	38.5	45.0	1.77	1.81	1.68	1.71
Food and beverage stores	445	32.0	32.7	32.4	33.5	0.84	0.84	0.81	0.79
Clothing and clothing accessories stores.	448	36.5	36.7	37.4	37.8	2.58	2.49	2.42	2.36
General merchandise stores.	452	64.9	65.9	66.7	70.7	1.87	1.75	1.66	1.64
Department stores	4521	42.8	39.0	38.1	38.2	2.17	2.17	2.13	2.11

[1] North American Industry Classification System, 1997; see text, Section 15, Business Enterprise.

Source: U.S. Census Bureau, *Current Business Reports, Annual Benchmark Report for Retail Trade and Food Services, January 1992 Through February 2005,* Series BR/04-A.

Table 1020. **Retail Trade Sales—Total and E-Commerce by Kind of Business: 2003**

[3,275,407 represents $3,275,407,000,000. Covers retailers with and without payroll. Based on Annual Retail Trade Survey, See Appendix III]

Kind of business	NAICS code [1]	Value of sales (mil. dol.)		E-commerce as percent of total sales	Percent distribution of e-commerce sales
		Total	E-commerce		
Retail trade, total.	44-45	3,275,407	55,731	1.7	100.0
Motor vehicle and parts dealers	441	845,772	9,540	1.1	17.1
Electronics and appliance stores.	443	88,084	755	0.9	1.4
Building material and garden equipment and supplies stores	444	264,911	456	0.2	0.8
Clothing and clothing accessories stores	448	178,642	747	0.4	1.3
Sporting goods, hobby, book, and music stores. . . .	451	77,280	828	1.1	1.5
Miscellaneous store retailers	453	103,558	933	0.9	1.7
Nonstore retailers	454	205,243	41,562	20.3	74.6
Electronic shopping and mail-order houses	454110	131,173	40,379	30.8	72.5

[1] North American Industry Classification System, 1997; see text, Section 15.

Source: U.S. Census Bureau, *2004 Annual Retail Trade Survey,* "2003 E-Commerce Multi-Sector Report"; published May 2005. See also <http://www.census.gov/eos/www/ebusiness614.htm>.

Domestic Trade 675

Table 1021. Retail Trade and Food Services—Sales by Type of Store and State: 2004

[In millions of dollars, (3,522,754 represents $3,522,754,000,000) except as indicated. Kind-of-business classification based on North American Industry Classification System (NAICS), 1997; see text, Section 15. Data are estimates]

State	All retail stores [1] (NAICS 44-45)	Total Retail sales + food and drink (NAICS 44-45, 722)	Motor vehicle and parts dealers (NAICS 441)	Furniture and home furnishings (NAICS 442)	Electronics and appliances (NAICS 443)	Building material & garden equip. & supp. dealers (NAICS 444)	Food and beverage stores (NAICS 445)	Health and personal care (NAICS 446)
U.S....	3,522,754	3,906,482	906,076	104,986	98,252	355,220	526,194	215,424
AL	45,859	50,618	12,200	1,185	744	4,581	6,090	2,745
AK	8,028	9,076	1,697	132	172	1,100	1,353	133
AZ	67,909	74,855	18,436	2,203	1,867	5,930	9,388	3,887
AR	28,926	31,464	8,170	663	482	3,041	3,234	1,305
CA	428,851	481,895	111,604	13,186	19,075	41,457	70,435	27,118
CO	61,285	68,426	15,999	2,429	1,942	7,262	9,272	2,021
CT	48,829	53,814	11,560	1,508	1,414	5,180	8,685	3,299
DE	11,909	13,236	3,122	585	376	1,425	1,472	812
DC	2,783	4,681	122	119	100	277	668	417
FL.	209,355	229,956	63,010	6,348	5,704	17,747	32,838	14,234
GA	103,516	115,211	28,583	3,446	2,334	12,945	15,870	4,688
HI	14,260	16,685	2,306	253	215	954	2,854	1,245
ID.	18,211	19,564	4,881	505	442	2,463	2,456	557
IL	144,755	162,211	35,026	4,167	4,054	13,950	23,488	11,044
IN	72,222	79,750	18,839	1,726	1,584	8,049	8,808	4,489
IA.	37,089	40,101	9,436	943	920	5,254	5,229	1,956
KS	34,263	37,215	8,615	982	994	3,512	4,878	1,534
KY	41,326	46,500	10,182	860	661	4,835	5,589	2,765
LA	47,385	52,810	12,409	1,074	744	4,835	6,663	3,106
ME	19,001	20,547	4,138	368	229	1,967	3,742	756
MD	69,072	76,380	17,301	2,165	2,253	6,545	13,341	4,287
MA	83,465	94,893	20,257	2,274	1,812	7,592	14,953	5,702
MI.	123,244	135,626	33,550	3,501	2,783	11,169	15,785	10,038
MN	74,127	80,931	17,209	2,607	2,197	9,594	9,642	3,494
MS	28,192	30,884	7,499	822	426	3,260	3,875	1,534
MO	68,687	76,046	17,963	1,704	1,494	6,778	8,553	3,592
MT	9,577	10,723	2,280	235	187	1,358	1,691	312
NE	21,486	23,563	4,802	1,090	437	2,819	2,997	1,040
NV	29,721	33,846	6,762	1,064	787	2,871	4,367	1,456
NH	25,328	27,265	7,184	707	876	2,142	3,651	1,014
NJ.	116,147	126,940	29,067	4,232	3,696	9,324	19,018	9,965
NM	20,859	23,040	4,883	635	393	1,802	2,614	1,129
NY	205,165	229,401	44,139	6,255	5,602	18,477	33,300	18,133
NC	94,049	104,764	25,471	3,516	2,062	11,885	13,074	5,228
ND	8,374	9,097	1,855	219	187	1,719	841	498
OH	139,302	154,089	35,807	4,081	3,912	13,955	18,683	10,483
OK	38,292	42,369	11,229	922	1,019	3,196	4,470	2,170
OR	44,357	49,091	11,312	1,161	1,057	5,150	6,722	1,407
PA	140,302	155,423	35,614	3,544	2,780	12,925	22,867	10,891
RI.	10,990	12,911	2,547	311	239	824	1,941	1,161
SC	45,705	51,079	11,995	1,202	710	6,204	6,785	2,332
SD	15,516	16,433	2,379	218	174	1,476	1,356	409
TN	73,920	81,572	19,586	2,033	1,283	7,066	12,338	4,127
TX	288,967	319,203	82,487	8,650	9,148	25,172	35,674	12,671
UT	27,310	29,708	7,122	1,015	876	3,464	4,428	460
VT	8,175	8,905	2,104	190	186	1,045	1,459	404
VA	92,453	101,475	22,821	3,436	3,548	9,889	12,960	4,384
WA	74,935	84,161	16,493	2,106	1,906	8,671	11,178	3,720
WV	18,126	19,875	4,561	343	204	1,828	2,573	1,685
WI	74,044	80,444	17,837	1,931	1,864	9,522	10,892	3,446
WY	7,109	7,727	1,626	135	100	736	1,151	143

See footnotes at end of table.

Table 1021. **Retail Trade and Food Services—Sales by Type of Store and State: 2004—Con.**

[See headnote, page 676]

State	Gasoline stations (NAICS 447)	Clothing and clothing accessories (NAICS 448)	Sporting goods, hobby, book & music stores (NAICS 451)	General merchandise (NAICS 452)	Miscellaneous stores (NAICS 453)	Nonstore retailers (NAICS 454)	Food services & drinking places (NAICS 722)
U.S....	249,258	184,752	81,733	504,356	99,566	196,938	383,728
AL	4,232	2,086	771	8,820	1,323	1,082	4,759
AK	503	353	192	1,826	192	374	1,048
AZ	5,438	2,493	1,561	10,189	2,715	3,802	6,946
AR	2,794	1,107	495	6,099	829	708	2,538
CA	27,174	25,282	11,937	56,316	12,122	13,146	53,044
CO	4,097	2,562	2,183	8,703	2,082	2,733	7,141
CT	2,481	2,846	1,204	3,986	1,240	5,426	4,985
DE	591	681	361	1,590	378	514	1,327
DC	234	390	167	87	136	66	1,897
FL......	12,323	11,736	4,037	25,911	5,734	9,733	20,601
GA	9,024	5,095	1,815	14,283	2,761	2,672	11,695
HI.....	1,029	1,584	357	2,769	561	134	2,425
ID.....	1,289	532	514	2,884	560	1,127	1,354
IL.....	8,719	8,824	3,019	17,734	3,574	11,155	17,456
IN.....	5,970	2,468	1,231	12,109	1,708	5,242	7,527
IA.....	4,007	1,238	661	5,341	769	1,334	3,013
KS	2,900	1,563	775	6,777	915	819	2,952
KY	4,286	1,456	689	7,683	1,340	978	5,174
LA	4,646	2,150	745	8,906	1,180	927	5,425
ME	1,540	809	370	2,119	465	2,497	1,547
MD	4,049	4,398	2,033	8,518	1,860	2,321	7,308
MA	4,683	5,663	2,351	9,090	2,341	6,747	11,428
MI....	7,465	5,245	3,697	21,820	4,299	3,891	12,382
MN	5,847	2,792	2,170	9,493	2,003	7,080	6,805
MS	2,992	1,012	338	5,150	720	564	2,692
MO	6,875	2,457	1,406	11,597	1,930	4,337	7,359
MT	749	273	292	1,704	262	234	1,147
NE	1,792	863	391	2,939	421	1,895	2,077
NV	1,759	2,260	639	3,667	1,366	2,724	4,125
NH	1,420	1,091	676	3,345	588	2,635	1,937
NJ.....	5,462	7,484	3,512	12,708	3,143	8,535	10,793
NM	1,944	855	514	3,660	1,101	1,329	2,182
NY	10,471	20,293	5,868	23,525	7,154	11,948	24,236
NC	7,220	4,310	1,609	13,057	3,251	3,366	10,715
ND	660	242	248	1,279	203	424	723
OH	9,720	6,089	2,719	22,837	3,299	7,719	14,786
OK	3,833	1,060	763	7,553	1,089	987	4,077
OR	2,465	1,703	1,241	8,074	1,514	2,550	4,734
PA	8,919	7,648	2,817	15,694	3,118	13,484	15,121
RI......	702	683	271	1,105	283	921	1,921
SC	4,332	2,280	628	6,893	1,562	782	5,375
SD	916	302	210	1,396	235	6,446	917
TN	6,251	3,664	1,324	12,532	2,034	1,680	7,653
TX	21,918	14,367	5,830	45,371	7,862	19,816	30,236
UT	1,952	1,151	775	4,341	504	1,222	2,398
VT	711	309	203	537	190	837	730
VA	7,894	4,890	2,072	13,634	2,051	4,873	9,022
WA	4,094	3,043	2,317	13,368	2,538	5,500	9,226
WV....	1,888	712	268	3,217	456	391	1,750
WI.....	5,913	2,176	1,326	10,870	1,386	6,881	6,400
WY.....	1,084	179	137	1,250	217	351	618

[1] Includes other types of stores, not shown separately.

Source: Market Statistics, a division of Claritas Inc., Arlington, VA, *The Survey of Buying Power Data Service*, annual (copyright).

Table 1022. Retail Trade—Nonemployer Establishments and Receipts by Kind of Business: 2000 to 2002

[1,743 represents 1,743,000. Includes only firms subject to federal income tax. Nonemployers are businesses with no paid employees. Based on the North American Industry Classification System (NAICS), 1997. see text, Section 15]

Kind of business	NAICS code	Establishments (1,000)			Receipts (mil. dol.)		
		2000	2001	2002	2000	2001	2002
Retail trade, total	44-45	1,743	1,739	1,839	73,810	73,675	77,896
Motor vehicle & parts dealers [1]	441	122	127	138	17,355	17,404	18,529
Used car dealers	44112	74	76	83	13,255	13,197	13,835
Motorcycle & boat & other MV dealers	44122	21	23	24	1,969	2,062	2,217
Automotive parts, accessories, & tire stores . . .	4413	25	25	28	1,872	1,885	2,150
Furniture & home furnishings stores	442	37	37	41	2,574	2,592	2,794
Furniture stores	4421	14	14	14	1,034	1,054	1,120
Home furnishings stores	4422	23	23	26	1,540	1,538	1,674
Electronics & appliance stores	443	29	28	29	1,688	1,658	1,669
Bldg material & garden equip & supp dealers [1] . . .	444	28	28	30	2,182	2,196	2,326
Building material & supplies dealers	4441	20	20	22	1,677	1,691	1,803
Food & beverage stores	445	82	82	88	8,493	8,505	8,851
Grocery stores	4451	39	39	41	4,609	4,591	4,673
Specialty food stores	4452	33	33	36	2,135	2,149	2,362
Beer, wine, & liquor stores.	4453	10	10	10	1,749	1,765	1,815
Health & personal care stores	446	92	97	104	1,915	2,012	2,196
Gasoline stations	447	10	10	9	1,721	1,665	1,628
Clothing & clothing accessories stores [1]	448	89	91	96	4,464	4,472	4,683
Clothing stores	4481	60	61	62	2,718	2,724	2,823
Jewelry stores.	44831	23	24	29	1,416	1,419	1,512
Sporting goods, hobby, book, & music stores [1] . . .	451	96	94	94	3,761	3,733	3,776
Sporting goods stores	45111	23	23	23	1,340	1,337	1,340
Book, periodical, & music stores.	4512	32	31	31	1,007	982	973
General merchandise stores	452	28	28	30	1,291	1,318	1,423
Miscellaneous store retailers [1]	453	339	329	338	12,963	12,617	13,350
Gift, novelty, & souvenir stores	45322	73	72	76	2,104	2,097	2,161
Used merchandise stores	4533	76	72	73	2,115	1,927	1,953
Nonstore retailers [1]	454	792	787	843	15,401	15,504	16,670
Electronic shopping & mail-order houses	4541	49	50	48	1,391	1,531	1,584
Direct selling establishments	4543	708	704	761	13,047	13,019	14,138

[1] Includes other kinds of business not shown separately.

Source: U.S. Census Bureau, "Nonemployer Statistics"; published March 2004;<http://www.census.gov/epcd/nonemployer/>.

Table 1023. Franchised New Car Dealerships—Summary: 1980 to 2004

[130.5 represents $130,500,000,000]

Item	Unit	1980	1985	1990	1995	1999	2000	2001	2002	2003	2004
Dealerships [1]	Number .	27,900	24,725	24,825	22,800	22,400	22,250	21,800	21,725	21,650	21,640
Sales	Bil. dol. .	130.5	251.6	316.0	456.2	606.5	650.3	690.4	679.5	699.2	714.3
New cars sold [2]	Millions .	9.0	11.0	9.3	8.6	8.7	8.8	8.4	8.1	7.6	7.5
Used vehicles sold	Millions .	9.7	13.3	14.2	18.5	20.1	20.5	21.4	19.4	19.5	19.7
Employment	1,000. . .	745	856	924	996	1,081	1,114	1,130	1,130	1,130	1,130
Annual payroll	Bil. dol .	11.0	20.1	24.0	33.1	42.5	46.1	48.0	48.8	50.0	50.5
Advertising expenses	Bil. dol .	1.2	2.8	3.7	4.6	5.6	6.4	6.6	7.5	8.5	8.3
Dealer pretax profits as a percentage of sales	Percent .	0.6	2.2	1.0	1.4	1.8	1.6	2.0	1.9	1.7	1.7
Inventory: [3] Domestic: [4]											
Total	1,000. . .	2,112	2,339	2,537	2,974	2,901	3,183	2,824	2,727	3,085	3,267
Days' supply.	Days . . .	57	60	73	71	62	68	63	63	63	75
Imported: [4]											
Total	1,000. . .	269	345	707	445	378	468	508	521	618	646
Days' supply.	Days . . .	31	30	72	72	47	50	51	49	49	59

[1] At beginning of year. [2] Data provided by "Ward's Automotive Reports." [3] Annual average. Includes light trucks. [4] Classification based on where automobiles are produced (i.e., automobiles manufactured by foreign companies but produced in the U.S. are classified as domestic).

Source: National Automobile Dealers Association, McLean, VA, NADA Data, annual.

Table 1024. Retail Sales—New Passenger Cars: 1990 to 2003

[In thousands 9,300 represents 9,300,000, except as indicated. Retail new car sales include both sales to individuals and to corporate fleets. It also includes leased cars]

Item	1990	1995	1997	1998	1999	2000	2001	2002	2003
Total retail new passenger car sales	9,300	8,635	8,272	8,142	8,698	8,847	8,423	8,103	7,610
Domestic [1]	6,897	7,129	6,917	6,762	6,979	6,831	6,325	5,878	5,527
Imports	2,403	1,506	1,355	1,380	1,719	2,016	2,098	2,226	2,083
Japan	1,719	982	726	691	758	863	837	923	817
Germany	265	207	297	367	467	517	523	547	544
Other	419	317	332	322	494	637	738	756	722

[1] Includes cars produced in Canada and Mexico.

Source: U.S. Bureau of Transportation Statistics, National Transportation Statistics 2004. Data supplied by following sources: Motor Vehicle Facts & Figures, 1997, Southfield, MI; Ward's Motor Vehicle Facts & Figures, 2002, Southfield, MI: 2002. See also: <http://www.bts.gov>.

Table 1025. Retail Sales of New Cars by Sector: 1990 to 2003

[In thousands, 9,300 represents 9,300,000 except as indicated. Includes imported cars, but not vans, trucks, or sport utility vehicles]

Item	1990	1995	1997	1998	1999	2000	2001	2002	2003
Total, Sales of new cars	9,300	8,636	8,273	8,142	8,697	8,852	8,422	8,102	7,615
Consumer	5,677	4,326	3,908	3,981	4,389	4,680	4,634	4,521	4,336
Business	3,477	4,070	4,166	3,943	4,076	3,949	3,566	3,376	3,082
Government	147	241	199	218	232	224	222	205	197
Percentage of total sales									
Consumer	61.0	50.1	47.2	48.9	50.5	52.9	55.0	55.8	56.9
Business	37.4	47.1	50.4	48.4	46.9	44.6	42.3	41.7	40.5
Government	1.6	2.8	2.4	2.7	2.7	2.5	2.6	2.5	2.6

Source: U.S. Bureau of Transportation Statistics, *National Transportation Statistics 2004*. Data supplied by following source: U.S. Bureau of Economic Analysis, unpublished data. See also <http://www.bts.gov>.

Table 1026. New and Used Car Sales and Leases: 1990 to 2004

[In thousands (51,390 represents 51,390,000) except as indicated]

Item	1990	1995	1998	1999	2000	2001	2002	2003	2004
Total, vehicle sales and leases [1] . . .	51,390	56,476	56,375	57,618	58,964	59,742	59,835	60,215	59,410
New vehicle sales and leases.	13,860	14,718	15,534	16,879	17,344	17,118	16,810	16,643	16,865
Used vehicle sales [2]	37,530	41,758	40,841	40,739	41,620	42,624	43,025	43,572	42,545
Total value, new and used vehicle sales (bil. dol.) [3]	446	611	651	698	737	737	721	738	759
New vehicle sales (bil. dol.)	227	292	316	348	380	369	371	382	392
Used vehicle sales (bil. dol.).	219	319	335	350	357	367	350	356	367
Average price (current dol.) [3]	8,672	10,818	11,545	12,098	12,491	12,321	12,034	12,253	12,774

[1] Vehicle sales, value of sales, and average prices are from different sources and cannot be calculated from the data presented in this table. [2] Used car or vehicle sales include sales from franchised dealers, independent dealers, and casual sales. [3] Includes leased vehicles.

Source: U.S. Bureau of Transportation Statistics, *National Transportation Statistics 2004*. Data supplied by following sources: New vehicle leases: CNW Marketing/Research, personal communication, Mar. 2, 2005; Used vehicle sales, value, and average price: Manheim, *Used Car Market Report* (Atlanta, GA: Annual issues), See also <http://www.bts.gov>.

Table 1027. New Motor Vehicle Sales and Expenditures by Model Year: 1990 to 2004

[In thousands of units (14,169 represents 14,169,000), except as indicated. A model year begins on October 1 and ends on September 30. It covers the fourth quarter of one calendar year and the first three quarters of the next calendar year]

Sales and expenditures	1990	1995	1999	2000	2001	2002	2003	2004
New motor vehicle sales	14,169	15,204	17,401	17,806	17,468	17,132	16,968	17,297
New-car sales.	9,436	8,687	8,697	8,852	8,422	8,102	7,615	7,505
Domestic	6,790	7,178	6,982	6,833	6,323	5,871	5,527	5,350
Import	2,645	1,510	1,715	2,019	2,099	2,231	2,087	2,155
New-truck sales	4,733	6,517	8,704	8,954	9,046	9,030	9,353	9,792
Light	4,428	6,089	8,183	8,492	8,696	8,708	9,025	9,360
Domestic	3,996	5,694	7,420	7,651	7,718	7,647	7,801	8,115
Import	432	395	763	841	978	1,061	1,224	1,245
Other.	306	429	521	462	350	322	328	432
Domestic-car production	6,231	6,351	5,638	5,542	4,878	5,019	4,510	4,230
Avg. expenditure per new car [1] (dollar) . .	14,371	17,959	20,381	20,600	20,945	21,248	21,338	21,969
Domestic (dollar)	13,936	16,864	18,339	18,577	18,755	18,897	18,857	19,607
Import (dollar)	15,510	23,202	28,695	27,447	27,539	27,436	27,906	27,835

[1] BEA estimate based on the manufacturer's suggested retail price.

Source: U.S. Bureau of Economic Analysis, *Survey of Current Business*, February 2005 and unpublished data. Data on unit sales and production are mainly from "Ward's Automotive Reports" published by Ward's Communications, Southfield, MI.

Table 1028. Annual U.S. Motor Vehicle Production and Factory (Wholesale) Sales: 1990 to 2003

[In thousands (9,783 represents 9,783,000) except as indicated]

Item	1990	1995	1997	1998	1999	2000	2001	2002	2003
Production, total [1]	9,783	11,985	12,119	12,006	13,025	12,771	11,425	12,280	12,087
Passenger cars	6,077	6,351	5,927	5,554	5,638	5,542	4,879	5,019	4,510
Commercial vehicles [2]	3,706	5,635	6,192	6,452	7,387	7,228	6,546	7,261	7,577
Factory (wholesale) sales, total [1]. . .	9,775	12,023	12,223	12,112	12,127	12,527	11,108	(NA)	(NA)
Passenger cars	6,050	6,310	6,070	5,677	5,428	5,504	4,884	(NA)	(NA)
Commercial vehicles [2]	3,725	5,713	6,153	6,435	6,699	7,022	6,224	6,964	7,143

NA Not available. [1] Factory sales can be greater than production total because of sales from previous year's inventory. [2] Includes trucks under 10,000 pounds gross vehicle weight rating (GVWR), such as compact and conventional pickups, sport utility vehicles, minivans and vans, and trucks and buses.

Source: U.S. Bureau of Transportation Statistics, *National Transportation Statistics 2004*. Data supplied by following source: Ward's *Motor Vehicle Facts & Figures, 2004*, Southfield, MI: 2004; See also: <http://www.bts.gov>.

Domestic Trade 679

Table 1029. **Retail Foodstores—Number and Sales by Type: 1990 to 2003**

[133.6 represents 133,600. Beginning with 2002 data based on North American Industry Classification System (NAICS), 2002. All other years based on StandardIndustrial Classification (SIC) codes]

Type of foodstore	Number [1] (1,000)					Sales [2] (bil. dol.)					Percent distribution			
											Number		Sales	
	1990	1995	2000	2002	2003	1990	1995	2000	2002	2003	2000	2003	2000	2003
Total.	133.6	118.5	119.6	120.0	120.2	335.8	369.2	430.0	458.4	473.8	100.0	100.0	100.0	100.0
Grocery stores	109.1	97.0	95.9	95.5	95.3	324.6	356.9	415.3	441.7	455.5	80.2	79.3	96.6	96.1
Supermarkets [3]	24.5	25.3	24.6	24.1	25.9	261.7	300.4	337.3	359.1	357.9	20.6	21.5	78.4	75.5
Conventional	13.2	12.3	9.9	8.3	8.9	92.3	76.4	63.4	74.0	42.6	8.3	7.4	14.7	9.0
Superstore [4]	5.8	6.8	7.9	7.9	8.1	87.6	116.7	142.4	147.1	164.3	6.6	6.7	33.1	34.7
Warehouse [5]	3.4	2.7	2.4	2.7	3.2	33.1	20.7	22.0	24.0	16.1	2.0	2.7	5.1	3.4
Combination food and drug [6]	1.6	2.7	3.7	4.5	5.0	29.3	59.3	81.8	85.7	114.4	3.1	4.2	19.0	24.1
Superwarehouse [7] . . .	0.3	0.6	0.5	0.5	0.5	12.6	17.8	17.4	17.1	14.3	0.4	0.4	4.0	3.0
Hypermarket [8]	0.1	0.2	0.2	0.3	0.2	6.8	9.5	10.3	11.2	6.2	0.2	0.2	2.4	1.3
Convenience stores [9] . .	28.0	27.2	28.2	29.4	29.4	20.3	17.0	19.2	20.9	21.0	23.6	24.5	4.5	4.4
Superette [10]	56.6	44.4	43.1	42.0	40.1	42.5	39.5	58.8	61.7	76.6	36.0	33.4	13.7	16.2
Specialized food stores [11] .	24.5	21.5	23.7	24.5	24.9	11.2	12.2	14.7	16.7	18.3	19.8	20.7	3.4	3.9

[1] Estimated.   [2] Includes nonfood items.   [3] A grocery store, primarily self-service in operation, providing a full range of departments, and having at least $2.5 million in annual sales in 1985 dollars.   [4] Contains greater variety of products than conventional supermarkets, including specialty and service departments, and considerable nonfood (general merchandise) products.   [5] Contains limited product variety and fewer services provided, incorporating case lot stocking and shelving practices.   [6] Contains a pharmacy, a nonprescription drug department, and a greater variety of health and beauty aids than that carried by conventional supermarkets.   [7] A larger warehouse store that offers expanded product variety and often service meat, deli, or seafood departments.   [8] A very large store offering a greater variety of general merchandise—like clothes, hardware, and seasonal goods—and personal care products than other grocery stores.   [9] A small grocery store selling a limited variety of food and nonfood products, typically open extended hours.   [10] A grocery store, primarily self-service in operation, selling a wide variety of food and nonfood products with annual sales below $2.5 million (1985 dollars).   [11] Primarily engaged in the retail sale of a single food category such as meat and seafood stores and retail bakeries.

Source: U.S. Department of Agriculture, Economic Research Service, *Food Marketing Review*, annual.

Table 1030. **Percent of Supermarkets Offering Selected Services and Product Lines: 1990 to 2003**

[In percent. Based on a sample survey of chain and independent supermarkets and subject to sampling variability; for details, see source]

Service or product line offered	1990	1996	1997	1998	1999	2000	2001	2002	2003
Service delicatessen	73	80	81	81	81	81	80	80	79
Service bakery	60	69	69	69	69	71	72	72	71
Service meat	42	74	60	59	60	62	66	66	64
Service seafood	33	46	43	43	45	45	51	43	41
Specialty cheese department	33	31	30	31	32	33	42	36	35
Salad bar	18	27	24	24	24	25	22	22	21
Automated teller machines (ATMs) . . .	20	60	62	62	63	64	65	68	67
Banking in store	(NA)	14	22	21	22	21	20	22	21
Pharmacy	15	26	26	32	30	32	36	34	35
Warehouse aisle	(NA)	10	16	17	17	16	14	14	13

NA Not available.

Source: Progressive Grocer, New York, NY, *Progressive Grocer 71st Annual Report* (copyright). Used by permission of Progressive Grocer magazine(A VNU company).

Table 1031. **Food and Alcoholic Beverage Sales by Sales Outlet: 1990 to 2003**

[In billions of dollars (556.6 represents $556,600,000,000)]

Sales outlet	1990	1995	1996	1997	1998	1999	2000	2001	2002	2003
Food sales, total [1]	**556.6**	**655.1**	**680.6**	**704.4**	**737.4**	**780.4**	**825.6**	**870.0**	**903.7**	**948.6**
Food at home	308.1	352.7	368.0	375.7	391.1	417.9	439.8	469.1	485.7	503.5
Food stores [2]	256.4	276.2	285.8	290.0	296.4	310.1	326.2	348.4	356.3	370.6
Other stores [3]	32.3	53.1	57.3	61.8	70.4	81.8	85.6	93.2	102.0	104.5
Home-delivered, mail order	5.3	8.6	10.0	10.6	10.6	11.4	12.1	11.8	12.2	12.5
Farmers, manufacturers, wholesalers.	6.3	7.8	8.1	7.7	7.6	8.1	9.4	9.6	8.8	9.3
Home production and donations .	7.7	7.0	6.8	5.7	6.0	6.5	6.4	6.0	6.3	6.6
Food away from home [4]	248.5	302.4	312.6	328.7	346.4	362.4	385.8	400.9	418.0	445.1
Alcoholic beverage sales, total.	**72.6**	**80.4**	**83.7**	**86.7**	**92.1**	**97.6**	**102.4**	**106.6**	**111.1**	**115.9**
Packaged alcoholic beverages. . . .	38.0	41.5	43.6	44.9	48.5	51.9	53.8	56.3	58.9	60.6
Liquor stores.	18.6	19.0	20.0	20.9	22.2	23.3	25.2	26.2	26.7	27.7
Food stores	10.8	12.3	13.0	12.8	13.8	14.4	14.7	15.3	16.1	17.0
All other.	8.6	10.3	10.6	11.2	12.4	14.1	13.9	14.8	16.1	15.9
Alcoholic drinks.	34.5	38.9	40.1	41.8	43.6	45.7	48.6	50.3	52.2	55.3
Eating and drinking places [5] . . .	26.6	30.3	31.5	33.5	35.0	36.6	39.1	40.5	42.3	45.1
Hotels and motels [5]	3.8	3.9	3.9	4.0	4.1	4.3	4.6	4.7	4.7	4.9
All other.	4.1	4.7	4.7	4.3	4.5	4.8	5.0	5.1	5.2	5.3

[1] Includes taxes and tips.   [2] Excludes sales to restaurants and institutions.   [3] Includes eating and drinking establishments, trailer parks, commissary stores, and military exchanges.   [4] Includes food furnished and donations.   [5] Includes tips.

Source: U.S. Department of Agriculture, Economic Research Service, "food cpi, prices, and expenditures: food expenditure tables"; published 18 June 2004; See also <http://www.ers.usda.gov/briefing/CPIFoodAndExpenditures/Data/>.

Table 1032. General Merchandise Stores—Number and Sales by Product Lines: 2002

[396,097 represents $396,097,000,000. Represents North American Industry Classification System (NAICS), 2002, code 452. Covers establishments with payroll. For statement on methodology, see Appendix III]

Product line	2002 Product line code	Establishments with the product line		Product line sales (mil. dol.)
		Number	Total sales (mil. dol.)	
General merchandise stores	(X)	40,907	(X)	444,664
Groceries and other food items for human consumption off the premises, including bottled, canned, or packaged soft drinks; candy; gum; packaged snacks; etc.	20100	35,520	396,097	82,677
Drugs, health aids, beauty aids, including cosmetics	20160	38,249	440,384	46,820
Soaps, detergents, and household cleaners.	20180	32,936	338,914	12,023
Men's wear	20200	36,219	438,996	24,224
Women's, juniors', and misses' wear	20220	37,041	439,187	46,557
Children's wear, including boys' (sizes 2 to 7 and 8 to 20), girls' (sizes 4 to 6x and 7 to 14), and infants' and toddlers' clothing and accessories	20240	35,574	406,992	19,400
Footwear, including accessories	20260	31,553	369,315	10,483
Curtains, draperies, blinds, slipcovers, bed and table coverings.	20280	35,981	432,009	12,082
Small electric appliances, including mixers; blenders; can openers; toasters; coffee makers; fry pans; and personal care appliances, such as hair dryers, curling irons, shavers, etc.	20310	33,335	398,088	5,903
Audio equipment, musical instruments, radios, stereos, compact discs, records, tapes, audio tape books, sheet music, accessories. . .	20330	27,222	375,195	9,992
Furniture, sleep equipment and outdoor/patio furniture.	20340	27,222	406,328	8,047
Kitchenware and home furniture, including cookware, cooking accessories, dinnerware, glassware, giftware, decorative accessories and lighting, clocks, mirrors, closet and bathroom accessories, outdoor charcoal grills, planters, etc.	20380	38,507	440,381	14,298
Toys, hobby goods, and games, including stuffed animals, video and electronic games, electronic game devices, and wheel goods, except bicycles.	20460	37,052	409,960	14,519

X Not applicable.

Source: U.S. Census Bureau, 2002 Economic Census, General Merchandise Stores, issued October 2004. See also <http://www.census.gov/econ/census02>.

Table 1033. Food and Beverage Stores—Number and Sales by Product Lines: 2002

[443,370 represents $443,370,000,000. Represents North American Industry Classification System (NAICS), 2002, code 445. Covers establishments with payroll. For statement on methodology, see Appendix III]

Product line	2002 Product line code	Establishments with the product line		Product line sales (mil.dol.)
		Number	Total sales (mil. dol.)	
Food and beverage stores	(X)	148,901	(X)	456,136
Groceries and other food items for human consumption off the premises, including bottled, canned, or packaged soft drinks; candy; gum; packaged snacks; etc.	20100	135,419	443,370	311,813
Meals, unpacked snacks, sandwiches, ice cream and yogurt, bakery items and nonalcoholic beverages generally served for immediate consumption	20120	44,345	229,604	9,008
Alcoholic drinks served at the establishment	20130	2,730	2,297	250
Cigars, cigarettes, tobacco, and smokers' accessories, excluding sales from vending machines operated by others	20150	90,681	414,041	13,972
Drugs, health aids, beauty aids, including cosmetics	20160	75,070	404,909	36,742
Soaps, detergents, and household cleaners.	20180	71,139	395,995	10,087
Paper and related products, including paper towels, toilet tissue, wraps, bags, foils, etc.	20190	72,551	396,934	10,344
Kitchenware and home furniture, including cookware, cooking accessories, dinnerware, glassware, giftware, decorative accessories and lighting, clocks, mirrors, closet and bathroom accessories, outdoor charcoal grills, planters, etc.	20380	17,231	171,361	1,394
Lawn, garden, and farm equipment and supplies; cut flowers; plants and shrubs; fertilizers; animal feed, other than for pets; etc.	20620	22,465	257,992	3,090

X Not applicable.

Source: U.S. Census Bureau, 2002 Economic Census, Food and Beverage Stores, issued October 2004. See also <http://www.census.gov/econ/census02>.

Domestic Trade 681

Table 1034. U.S. Projected Online Retail Sales: 2003 to 2005

[In billions of dollars (95.7 represents $95,700,000,000,000), except as indicated]

Online product or service	Projected online sales			Percent change	
	2003	2004	2005	2003–2004	2004–2005
Retail trade, total [1]	95.7	144.6	175.3	51.1	21.2
Event tickets	3.3	4.3	5.4	30.3	25.6
Flowers	0.8	1.2	1.7	50.0	41.7
Apparel	8.6	11.7	13.8	36.0	17.9
Leisure travel	27.3	52.4	62.8	91.9	19.8
Automobiles	7.2	8.1	9.3	12.5	14.8
Home products	10.6	15.4	20.7	45.3	34.4
Pet supplies	0.3	0.4	0.6	33.3	50.0
Health and beauty	1.5	2.4	3.2	60.0	33.3
Food and beverage	3.7	5.1	6.3	37.8	23.5

[1] Includes items sold to consumers in product categories not shown separately.
Source: Forrester Research, Inc., Cambridge, MA, *Online Retail Ripple Effect* (copyright).

Table 1035. Online Consumer Spending Forecast by Kind of Business: 2003 to 2005

[Forecast data: October 2004. (53.1 represents $53,100,000,000). Figures below reflect a partial revision of the Jupiter Internet Shopping Model]

Category	Online retail spending (bil.dol.)			Percentage of spending online			Total retail sales by category (bil. dol.)		
	2003	2004	2005	2003	2004	2005	2003	2004	2005
Total	53.1	66.0	79.2	(X)	(X)	(X)	(X)	(X)	(X)
Personal computers	8.9	9.9	10.9	36.0	37.3	39.6	24.8	26.4	27.5
Peripherals	2.6	2.9	3.1	24.9	26.0	26.8	10.4	11.1	11.5
Software	3.0	3.3	3.6	36.1	37.8	39.2	8.4	8.8	9.1
Consumer electronics	2.6	3.4	4.1	5.5	6.6	7.5	47.8	51.6	55.0
Books	3.2	3.6	3.9	13.1	14.4	15.4	24.4	25.0	25.6
Music	0.8	1.1	1.5	7.0	9.1	11.9	12.0	12.2	12.6
Videos	1.2	1.5	1.7	7.5	8.7	9.5	15.9	17.1	18.1
Movie tickets	0.4	0.6	0.7	4.4	5.2	6.2	9.8	10.6	11.1
Event tickets	2.7	3.3	3.8	14.5	16.6	18.5	18.9	19.8	20.7
Over-the-counter drugs	0.2	0.3	0.5	1.0	1.4	2.0	21.8	22.8	23.8
Medical supplies & contact lenses	0.3	0.4	0.6	2.0	2.7	3.8	14.3	14.9	15.7
Apparel	6.2	7.7	9.1	2.9	3.4	3.8	211.8	224.5	235.8
Footwear	1.1	1.4	1.6	1.9	2.4	2.7	57.9	59.3	60.7
Jewelry	1.4	1.7	1.9	4.2	4.7	5.3	33.3	35.1	36.4
Grocery	1.7	2.5	3.3	0.3	0.4	0.6	551.9	569.6	587.8
Pets	0.4	0.5	0.7	1.6	2.4	3.2	21.9	22.2	23.0
Toys	0.8	0.8	0.9	3.7	4.0	4.2	20.7	21.3	21.9
Sporting goods	1.3	1.6	2.0	5.4	6.7	7.9	23.4	24.2	25.1
Flowers	1.0	1.3	1.5	6.2	7.2	8.1	16.8	17.4	18.0
Specialty gifts	1.1	1.4	1.7	2.8	3.6	4.3	37.7	38.8	40.0
Furniture	0.5	0.7	0.9	0.7	0.9	1.3	68.9	70.0	71.8
Large appliances	0.7	0.9	1.1	3.0	3.9	4.7	22.3	23.0	23.6
Housewares/small appliances	2.0	3.0	4.1	2.7	3.9	5.3	73.0	75.2	77.4
Art and collectibles	0.6	0.8	1.1	2.2	2.9	3.6	28.7	29.4	30.1
Home improvement	1.0	1.6	2.2	0.6	0.9	1.2	168.4	176.8	185.2
Garden supplies	0.4	0.5	0.7	0.8	1.2	1.5	43.6	45.8	48.0
Office products	1.8	2.6	3.3	5.2	7.3	9.1	34.0	35.0	36.0

X Not applicable.
Source: Jupiter Research, Inc., New York, NY unpublished data.

Table 1036. Electronic Shopping and Mail-Order Houses—Total and E-Commerce Sales by Merchandise Line: 2003

[131,173 represents $131,173,000,000 in sales. Represents NAICS code 454110. Covers establishments with payroll. Based on 2003 Annual Retail Trade Survey; see Appendix III]

Merchandise line	Value of sales		E-Commerce as percent of total sales	Percent distribution	
	Total (mil.dol.)	E-Commerce (mil.dol.)		Total sales	E-Commerce sales
Electronic shopping and mail-order houses, total [1]	131,173	40,379	30.8	100.0	100.0
Books and magazines	4,160	2,143	51.5	3.2	5.3
Clothing & clothing accessories (includes footwear)	15,125	5,525	36.5	11.5	13.7
Computer hardware	23,714	6,745	28.4	18.1	16.7
Computer software	3,887	1,173	30.2	3.0	2.9
Drugs, health aids, beauty aids	27,205	1,966	7.2	20.7	4.9
Electronics and appliances	5,967	2,902	48.6	4.5	7.2
Furniture and home furnishings	8,302	3,436	41.4	6.3	8.5
Music and videos	3,823	1,733	45.3	2.9	4.3
Office equipment and supplies	6,962	3,473	49.9	5.3	8.6
Toys, hobby goods, and games	3,942	1,638	41.6	3.0	4.1
Other merchandise [2]	17,456	4,962	28.4	13.3	12.3
Nonmerchandise receipts [3]	5,788	2,629	45.4	4.4	6.5

[1] This industry comprises businesses primarily engaged in retailing all types of merchandise through catalogs, television, and the Internet. Data are preliminary and, therefore, subject to revision.   [2] Includes other merchandise such as jewelry, collectibles, souvenirs, auto parts and accessories, hardware, and lawn and garden equipment and supplies.   [3] Includes nonmerchandise receipts such as auction commissions, shipping and handling, customer training, customer support, and online advertising.
Source: U.S. Census Bureau, *2003 Annual Retail Trade Survey*, "2003 E-Commerce Multi-Sector Report"; published May 2005 <http://www.census.gov/eos/www/ebusiness614.htm>.

682 Domestic Trade

Table 1037. Shopping Centers—Number, Gross Leasable Area, and Retail Sales: 1990 to 2004

[4,390 represents 4,390,000,000. As of December 31. A shopping center is a group of architecturally unified commercial establishments built on a site that is planned, developed, owned, and managed as an operating unit related in its location, size, and type of shops to the trade area that the unit serves. The unit provides on-site parking in definite relationship to the types and total size of the stores. The data base attempts to include all centers with three or more stores. Estimates are based on a sample of data available on shopping center properties; for details, contact source]

Year	Total	Gross leasable area (sq. ft.)					
		Less than 100,001	100,001-200,000	200,001-400,000	400,001-800,000	800,001-1,000,000	More than 1 million
NUMBER							
1990	36,515	23,231	8,756	2,781	1,102	288	357
1995	41,235	26,001	9,974	3,345	1,234	301	380
2000	45,115	28,062	10,958	3,935	1,424	326	410
2002	46,438	28,819	11,220	4,137	1,507	332	424
2003	47,104	29,234	11,336	4,233	1,540	334	427
2004	47,835	29,710	11,471	4,315	1,573	335	430
Percent distribution	100.0	62.1	24.0	9.0	3.3	0.7	0.9
Percent change, 2003-2004	1.6	1.6	1.2	1.9	2.1	0.3	0.7
GROSS LEASABLE AREA							
1990 (mil. sq. ft.)	4,390	1,125	1,197	734	618	259	457
1995 (mil. sq. ft.)	4,967	1,267	1,368	886	689	271	486
2000 (mil. sq. ft.)	5,566	1,383	1,514	1,059	790	294	526
2002 (mil. sq. ft.)	5,774	1,424	1,552	1,119	836	299	544
2003 (mil. sq. ft.)	5,865	1,446	1,569	1,147	854	301	548
2004 (mil. sq. ft.)	5,953	1,469	1,588	1,171	872	302	552
Percent distribution	100.0	24.7	26.7	19.7	14.6	5.1	9.3
Percent change, 2003-2004	1.5	1.6	1.2	2.0	2.1	0.3	0.8
RETAIL SALES							
1990 (bil. dol.)	706.4	205.1	179.5	108.0	91.7	45.1	77.0
1995 (bil. dol.)	893.8	259.6	227.1	136.4	115.8	57.0	97.8
2000 (bil. dol.)	1,181.1	342.8	300.0	180.5	152.8	75.2	129.8
2002 (bil. dol.)	1,277.2	370.6	324.4	195.3	165.1	81.3	140.6
2003 (bil. dol.)	1,339.2	388.5	340.1	204.8	173.1	85.2	147.5
2004 (bil. dol.)	1,432.6	415.5	363.8	219.2	185.1	91.1	158.0
Percent distribution	100.0	29.0	25.4	15.3	12.9	6.4	11.0
Percent change, 2003-2004	7.0	7.0	7.0	7.0	6.9	6.9	7.1

Source: National Research Bureau, Chicago, IL (copyright, 2005).

Table 1038. Shopping Centers—Gross Leasable Area and Retail Sales, by State: 2004

[5,953 represents 5,953,000,000. See headnote, Table 1037]

State	Gross leasable area, (mil. sq. ft.)	Retail sales, (bil. dol.)	Retail sales per sq. ft. (dol.)	Percent change, 2003-2004		State	Gross leasable area, (mil. sq. ft.)	Retail sales, (bil. dol.)	Retail sales per sq. ft. (dol.)	Percent change, 2003-2004	
				Gross leasable area	Retail sales					Gross leasable area	Retail sales
U.S.	5,953	1,432.6	241	1.5	7.0						
AL	83	20.5	246	2.1	5.9	MO	127	31.0	244	1.6	6.6
AK	8	3.0	395	-	8.7	MT	10	2.8	274	-	6.9
AZ	145	34.4	236	1.3	7.2	NE	39	7.8	198	4.5	6.4
AR	38	9.7	253	2.4	5.5	NV	62	9.5	152	2.9	7.6
CA	743	171.4	231	1.0	6.8	NH	27	6.9	258	0.5	10.1
CO	119	32.8	275	2.7	7.7	NJ	187	40.8	218	1.4	7.9
CT	101	27.6	272	2.1	8.5	NM	32	8.6	265	1.0	6.2
DE	24	6.4	269	4.1	8.4	NY	265	61.1	231	1.6	6.7
DC	11	2.4	222	6.1	6.9	NC	200	39.5	198	2.9	6.6
FL	477	134.3	282	1.7	7.8	ND	10	2.9	294	-	6.8
GA	201	42.8	213	0.9	6.5	OH	267	56.4	211	1.5	6.4
HI	21	6.7	321	2.0	10.3	OK	62	16.9	274	0.7	5.2
ID	20	4.4	216	-	5.8	OR	62	13.3	214	1.7	7.5
IL	279	59.1	212	1.5	7.4	PA	267	56.0	210	1.7	7.0
IN	131	28.9	221	1.5	6.3	RI	23	5.3	228	6.4	7.1
IA	51	10.2	201	7.4	6.5	SC	93	21.0	227	1.5	6.3
KS	62	15.7	255	2.1	6.5	SD	7	1.7	250	-	6.5
KY	70	18.6	266	0.2	6.3	TN	140	31.5	225	0.6	6.7
LA	90	25.3	281	1.7	6.5	TX	399	119.3	299	0.9	6.6
ME	19	6.2	323	3.6	8.8	UT	41	8.6	211	3.0	5.8
MD	134	34.5	256	1.0	6.9	VT	9	2.6	294	-	8.4
MA	120	33.2	276	1.3	7.6	VA	184	44.7	242	0.5	7.4
MI	154	34.7	226	1.2	6.7	WA	106	24.9	235	1.3	7.3
MN	75	19.3	258	0.5	7.0	WV	23	4.8	205	-	5.3
MS	46	10.5	230	1.1	5.0	WI	82	20.3	249	2.5	7.1
						WY	6	1.8	291	-	6.0

- Represents zero.

Source: National Research Bureau, Chicago, IL (copyright, 2005).

U.S. Census Bureau, Statistical Abstract of the United States: 2006

Table 1039. **Merchant Wholesalers—Summary: 1995 to 2004**

[In billions of dollars (2,176.4 represents $2,176,400,000,000) except ratios. Inventories and stock/sales ratios, as of December. Data reflect latest revision. Based on Annual Trade Survey; see Appendix III]

Kind of business	NAICS code [1]	1995	1999	2000	2001	2002	2003	2004
SALES								
Merchant wholesalers	42	2,176.4	2,609.4	2,820.6	2,783.3	2,824.4	2,946.5	3,338.4
Durable goods	423	1,155.8	1,415.7	1,488.9	1,418.7	1,412.1	1,441.6	1,683.8
Motor vehicles, parts, and supplies	4231	173.6	213.9	222.7	234.1	249.9	255.2	274.1
Furniture and home furnishings	4232	38.9	48.2	53.6	52.7	53.2	55.3	61.2
Lumber and construction materials	4233	67.8	87.9	86.5	89.1	94.4	105.1	140.6
Professional and commercial equipment	4234	205.1	288.5	285.6	267.6	269.2	270.7	292.4
Computer, peripheral equip. & software	42343	(NA)	182.9	178.6	153.5	147.5	141.1	161.5
Metals and minerals, except petroleum	4235	87.0	86.6	93.9	84.9	81.8	81.5	120.8
Electrical goods	4236	184.4	222.8	256.0	227.6	217.5	221.6	256.4
Hardware, plumbing & heating equipment	4237	56.7	68.8	72.2	69.0	70.2	70.8	77.5
Machinery, equipment and supplies	4238	192.5	249.0	257.2	248.4	229.3	232.6	279.3
Miscellaneous durable goods	4239	149.9	150.1	161.1	145.4	146.7	148.8	181.7
Nondurable goods	424	1,020.6	1,193.7	1,331.8	1,364.6	1,412.3	1,504.9	1,654.5
Paper and paper products	4241	66.5	73.5	78.0	76.3	72.6	73.9	79.3
Drugs, proprietaries, and sundries	4242	83.7	148.7	176.1	209.0	241.0	268.2	299.8
Apparel, piece goods, and notions	4243	67.6	90.2	96.3	98.7	105.5	103.9	109.1
Groceries and related products	4244	309.0	356.4	375.3	377.9	386.8	401.8	413.1
Farm-product raw materials	4245	125.5	101.8	104.6	103.4	106.6	118.7	129.0
Chemicals and allied products	4246	50.3	57.5	61.9	63.7	67.0	69.0	74.1
Petroleum and petroleum products	4247	127.7	139.1	194.4	189.2	189.4	223.5	282.9
Beer, wine, and distilled beverages	4248	52.5	67.1	71.0	74.4	78.5	81.4	85.2
Miscellaneous nondurable goods	4249	137.8	159.3	174.2	172.0	164.7	164.5	182.1
INVENTORIES								
Merchant wholesalers	42	241.3	291.7	310.5	298.5	302.2	308.6	341.3
Durable goods	423	153.5	188.8	199.1	182.3	181.6	184.3	211.4
Motor vehicles, parts, and supplies	4231	22.7	26.9	28.6	27.1	29.3	30.6	31.8
Furniture and home furnishings	4232	5.1	5.9	6.6	6.2	6.5	7.0	7.4
Lumber and construction materials	4233	6.7	8.1	8.3	8.3	8.7	9.8	13.0
Professional and commercial equipment	4234	24.5	28.9	28.6	24.9	25.4	25.7	28.3
Computer, peripheral equip. & software	42343	(NA)	14.2	12.5	9.5	9.1	9.4	10.9
Metals and minerals, except petroleum	4235	11.2	13.0	13.6	12.2	12.4	12.6	20.3
Electrical goods	4236	23.1	27.1	30.6	25.6	24.3	23.6	26.0
Hardware, plumbing & heating equipment	4237	8.6	10.5	11.4	10.8	10.8	10.8	12.3
Machinery, equipment and supplies	4238	35.8	49.9	51.2	49.1	46.6	44.9	50.6
Miscellaneous durable goods	4239	15.8	18.6	20.1	17.9	17.5	19.2	21.8
Nondurable goods	424	87.8	102.9	111.5	116.2	120.6	124.3	129.8
Paper and paper products	4241	5.4	6.1	6.9	6.2	5.9	6.0	6.9
Drugs, proprietaries, and sundries	4242	10.7	18.9	23.3	29.7	30.8	31.2	30.8
Apparel, piece goods, and notions	4243	11.7	13.6	14.0	14.3	14.6	14.0	14.8
Groceries and related products	4244	18.5	20.7	21.2	20.3	21.9	22.4	23.3
Farm-product raw materials	4245	13.1	10.7	11.6	11.5	11.9	14.5	11.0
Chemicals and allied products	4246	4.9	6.1	6.1	6.3	6.8	6.8	7.1
Petroleum and petroleum products	4247	4.5	4.2	4.9	4.7	5.2	5.4	7.6
Beer, wine, and distilled beverages	4248	4.7	6.2	6.5	6.4	7.0	7.2	7.8
Miscellaneous nondurable goods	4249	14.3	16.4	17.0	16.8	16.5	16.7	20.5
STOCK/SALES RATIO								
Merchant wholesalers	42	1.33	1.25	1.34	1.37	1.28	1.18	1.15
Durable goods	423	1.59	1.50	1.71	1.67	1.59	1.44	1.41
Motor vehicles, parts, and supplies	4231	1.57	1.39	1.54	1.41	1.36	1.30	1.31
Furniture and home furnishings	4232	1.65	1.42	1.60	1.56	1.62	1.50	1.44
Lumber and construction materials	4233	1.40	1.21	1.42	1.34	1.39	1.21	1.25
Professional and commercial equipment	4234	1.31	1.06	1.24	1.11	1.06	1.00	1.00
Computer, peripheral equip. & software	42343	(NA)	0.80	0.89	0.74	0.69	0.66	0.65
Metals and minerals, except petroleum	4235	1.73	1.77	2.00	2.23	2.20	1.90	2.02
Electrical goods	4236	1.53	1.33	1.50	1.51	1.42	1.24	1.19
Hardware, plumbing & heating equipment	4237	1.93	1.96	2.20	2.13	2.15	1.96	2.01
Machinery, equipment and supplies	4238	2.14	2.33	2.53	2.61	2.47	2.12	1.88
Miscellaneous durable goods	4239	1.27	1.37	1.61	1.62	1.51	1.44	1.29
Nondurable goods	424	1.03	0.96	0.98	1.06	0.98	0.93	0.89
Paper and paper products	4241	1.05	0.99	1.10	1.07	0.98	0.94	1.00
Drugs, proprietaries, and sundries	4242	1.46	1.30	1.47	1.57	1.42	1.23	1.11
Apparel, piece goods, and notions	4243	2.63	2.18	2.17	2.18	2.12	1.79	1.78
Groceries and related products	4244	0.70	0.65	0.67	0.65	0.67	0.66	0.65
Farm-product raw materials	4245	1.19	1.18	1.19	1.37	1.03	1.11	0.96
Chemicals and allied products	4246	1.25	1.29	1.26	1.33	1.35	1.23	1.12
Petroleum and petroleum products	4247	0.41	0.30	0.27	0.36	0.29	0.28	0.31
Beer, wine, and distilled beverages	4248	0.98	0.91	0.98	0.90	0.88	0.87	0.86
Miscellaneous nondurable goods	4249	1.26	1.15	1.19	1.24	1.23	1.16	1.31

NA Not available.   [1] North American Industry Classification System, 2002; see text, Section 15, Business Enterprise.

Source: U.S. Census Bureau, *Current Business Reports, Annual Benchmark Report for Wholesale Trade,* January 1992 through January 2005, Series BW/04-A. See also <http://www.census.gov/prod/www/abs/bw_month.html>.

Table 1040. Merchant Wholesale Trade Sales—Total and E-Commerce: 2003

[2,946,473 represents $2,946,473,000,000. Covers only businesses with paid employees. Based on the Annual Trade Survey, see Appendix III]

Kind of business	NAICS code [1]	Value of sales (mil. dol.)		E-commerce as percent of total sales	Percent distribution of E-commerce sales
		Total	E-commerce		
Merchant wholesale trade, total	42	2,946,473	386,922	13.1	100.0
Durable goods [2]	423	1,441,566	173,834	12.1	44.9
Motor vehicles, parts and supplies.	4231	255,198	64,142	25.1	16.6
Furniture and home furnishings.	4232	55,315	6,679	12.1	1.7
Professional & commercial equipment & supplies. . .	4234	270,702	38,515	14.2	10.0
Computer, peripheral equipment and software . . .	42343	141,056	20,470	14.5	5.3
Electrical goods	4236	221,568	21,983	9.9	5.7
Hardware, and plumbing and heating equipment and supplies	4237	70,765	9,059	12.8	2.3
Machinery, equipment and supplies	4238	232,603	11,122	4.8	2.9
Miscellaneous durable goods	4239	148,802	16,368	11.0	4.2
Nondurable goods [2]	424	1,504,907	213,088	14.2	55.1
Drugs and druggists' sundries.	4242	268,158	131,540	49.1	34.0
Apparel, piece goods and notions	4243	103,949	20,814	20.0	5.4
Groceries and related products	4244	401,810	27,931	7.0	7.2
Farm product raw materials	4245	118,663	3,681	3.1	1.0

[1] North American Industry Classification System, 2002; see text, Section 15, Business Enterprise. [2] Includes kinds of business not shown separately.

Source: U.S. Census Bureau, "2003 E-Commerce Multi-Sector Report"; published 11 May 2005; <http://www.census.gov/eos/www/ebusiness614.htm>.

Table 1041. Wholesale Trade—Establishments, Employees, and Payroll: 2000 and 2002

[446.2 represents 446,200. Covers establishments with payroll. Employees are for the week including March 12. Excludes most government employees, railroad employees, and self-employed persons. Kind-of-business classification based on North American Industry Classification System (NAICS), 1997; see text, Section 15, Business Enterprise. For statement on methodology, see Appendix III]

Kind of business	NAICS code	Establishments (1,000)		Employees (1,000)		Payroll	
		2000	2002	2000	2002	2000	2002
Wholesale trade	42	446.2	436.9	6,112	5,860	270.1	262.5
Wholesale trade, durable goods	421	288.6	283.0	3,625	3,444	171.8	162.4
Motor vehicle/motor vehicle parts & supply whsle . . .	4211	28.4	27.4	402	390	14.1	14.0
Furniture & home furnishing whsle	4212	14.9	14.5	167	155	6.6	6.4
Lumber & other construction materials whsle	4213	15.1	16.1	184	183	7.2	7.5
Professional & commercial equip. & supply whsle. . .	4214	44.4	41.6	763	723	44.9	41.8
Metal & mineral (except petroleum) whsle	4215	12.1	11.6	173	154	7.6	6.9
Electrical goods wholesale	4216	38.3	36.6	535	512	33.9	30.2
Hardware, & plumbing & heating equipment & supply wholesale	4217	21.4	21.6	249	237	10.4	10.1
Machinery, equipment, & supplies wholesale	4218	73.7	71.3	796	748	34.2	32.4
Miscellaneous durable goods wholesale	4219	40.2	42.2	355	341	12.9	13.0
Wholesale trade, nondurable goods	422	157.7	153.9	2,487	2,417	98.4	100.1
Paper & paper product wholesale	4221	14.9	13.7	232	209	8.9	8.2
Drugs & druggists' sundries wholesale	4222	7.4	7.2	210	218	12.0	12.8
Apparel, piece goods & notions wholesale.	4223	20.0	19.0	214	201	8.9	9.3
Grocery & related product wholesale	4224	39.7	38.6	875	861	31.6	32.7
Farm product raw material wholesale	4225	9.5	8.8	92	84	2.5	2.4
Chemical & allied products wholesale	4226	15.3	15.6	166	157	8.3	8.0
Petroleum & petroleum products wholesale	4227	10.7	9.8	132	122	5.2	5.2
Beer/wine/distilled alcoholic beverage wholesale. . .	4228	4.6	4.4	157	163	6.8	7.3
Miscellaneous nondurable goods wholesale.	4229	35.4	36.9	409	401	14.3	14.2

Source: U.S. Census Bureau, "County Business Patterns"; published November 2004; <http://www.census.gov/prod/2004pubs/02cbp/cbp02-1.pdf>

Domestic Trade 685

No. 97.—NUMBER OF MILES OF RAILROAD IN OPERATION IN EACH STATE AND TERRITORY OF THE UNITED STATES DURING THE YEARS ENDING DECEMBER 31, 1850, 1860, 1870, AND FROM 1880 TO 1887, INCLUSIVE.

[From Poor's Railroad Manual.]

State or Territory.	1850.	1860.	1870.	1880.	1881.	1882.	1883.	1884.	1885.	1886.	1887.
Maine	245	472	786	1,005	1,027	1,056	1,099	1,142	1,135	1,149	1,179
New Hampshire	467	661	736	1,015	1,021	1,038	1,042	1,044	1,044	1,050	1,073
Vermont	290	554	614	914	916	925	937	944	947	947	947
Massachusetts	1,035	1,264	1,480	1,915	1,959	1,967	1,979	1,990	1,998	2,018	2,069
Rhode Island	68	108	136	210	211	211	211	211	210	210	210
Connecticut	402	601	742	923	960	963	963	976	976	976	976
New England	2,507	3,660	4,494	5,982	6,094	6,158	6,231	6,307	6,310	6,350	6,454
New York	1,361	2,682	3,928	5,991	6,260	6,991	7,349	7,335	7,385	7,481	7,576
New Jersey	206	560	1,125	1,684	1,773	1,862	1,874	1,889	1,921	1,957	1,972
Pennsylvania	1,240	2,598	4,656	6,191	6,356	6,884	7,236	7,546	7,667	7,872	7,993
Delaware	39	127	197	275	275	282	282	307	316	335	335
Maryland	} 259	386	671	1,040	1,065	{ 1,079	1,099	1,082	1,189	1,225	1,243
District of Columbia						18	18	18	22	22	22
West Virginia	97	352	387	691	706	813	948	1,626	1,039	1,147	1,198
Middle States	3,202	6,795	10,964	15,872	16,435	17,929	18,806	19,203	19,539	20,039	20,339
Virginia	384	1,379	1,449	1,893	2,220	2,450	2,553	2,688	2,693	2,730	2,794
North Carolina	283	937	1,178	1,486	1,645	1,781	1,812	1,938	2,028	2,292	2,377
South Carolina	289	973	1,139	1,427	1,479	1,508	1,549	1,564	1,687	1,814	1,918
Georgia	643	1,420	1,845	2,459	2,561	2,878	2,933	2,978	3,116	3,391	3,618
Florida	21	402	446	518	693	964	1,157	1,324	1,603	1,918	2,111
Alabama	183	743	1,167	1,843	1,859	1,901	2,059	2,191	2,226	2,280	2,801
Mississippi	75	862	990	1,127	1,182	1,303	1,616	1,844	1,929	2,111	2,210
Louisiana	80	335	450	652	914	1,010	1,204	1,316	1,370	1,381	1,446
Tennessee		1,253	1,492	1,843	1,909	2,065	2,112	2,166	2,158	2,199	2,267
Kentucky	78	534	1,017	1,530	1,672	1,745	1,852	1,887	2,010	2,117	2,278
Southern States	2,036	8,838	11,173	14,778	16,125	17,605	18,847	19,896	20,811	22,143	23,820
Ohio	575	2,946	3,538	5,792	6,289	6,901	7,217	7,276	7,338	7,456	7,606
Michigan	342	779	1,638	3,938	4,283	4,614	5,072	5,233	5,269	5,636	6,322
Indiana	228	2,163	3,177	4,373	4,759	5,372	5,543	5,534	5,690	5,711	5,813
Illinois	111	2,790	4,823	7,851	8,260	8,676	8,865	8,909	8,965	9,276	9,597
Wisconsin	20	905	1,525	3,155	3,457	3,811	4,039	4,289	4,418	4,869	5,226
Minnesota			1,092	3,151	3,338	3,735	3,906	4,193	4,331	4,823	5,019
Dakota Territory			65	1,225	1,668	2,084	2,495	2,759	2,877	3,898	4,440
Iowa		655	2,683	5,400	6,164	6,967	7,216	7,510	7,504	7,935	8,291
Nebraska			705	1,953	2,277	2,498	2,696	2,794	2,988	3,616	4,676
Kansas			1,501	3,400	3,609	3,820	3,964	4,205	4,441	6,119	8,119
Missouri		817	2,000	3,965	4,207	4,501	4,619	4,710	4,969	5,068	5,628
Indian Territory				289	295	350	353	353	353	432	910
Arkansas		38	256	859	1,002	1,488	1,732	1,764	2,146	2,196	2,349
Texas		307	711	3,244	4,913	6,009	6,075	6,198	6,687	7,295	8,350
Colorado			157	1,570	2,187	2,766	2,832	2,842	2,884	2,944	3,768
New Mexico Territory				758	1,047	1,089	1,140	1,191	1,195	1,233	1,237
Wyoming Territory			429	512	576	625	625	616	617	778	911
Idaho Territory				206	276	494	777	811	798	811	805
Utah Territory			257	842	877	1,062	1,124	1,134	1,139	1,139	1,145
Montana Territory				106	271	633	1,035	1,047	1,047	1,062	1,663
Western States, etc	1,276	11,400	24,557	52,589	59,755	67,495	71,328	73,368	75,506	82,097	91,935
Nevada			593	739	895	948	948	948	954	954	954
California		23	925	2,195	2,369	2,636	2,861	2,911	3,044	3,297	3,677
Arizona Territory				349	497	713	866	906	906	989	1,059
Oregon			159	508	573	756	950	1,165	1,181	1,219	1,267
Washington Territory				289	472	472	598	675	736	898	997
Pacific States, etc		23	1,677	4,080	4,746	5,525	6,243	6,605	6,821	7,357	7,954

RECAPITULATION.

	1850.	1860.	1870.	1880.	1881.	1882.	1883.	1884.	1885.	1886.	1887.
New England States	2,507	3,660	4,494	5,982	6,094	6,158	6,231	6,307	6,310	6,351	6,454
Middle States	3,202	6,705	10,964	15,872	16,435	17,929	18,806	19,203	19,539	20,039	20,339
Southern States	2,036	8,838	11,173	14,778	16,125	17,605	18,847	19,896	20,811	22,143	23,820
Western States and Ter	1,276	11,400	24,557	52,589	59,755	67,495	71,328	73,368	75,506	82,097	91,935
Pacific States and Ter		23	1,677	4,080	4,746	5,525	6,243	6,605	6,821	7,357	7,954
Grand total	9,021	30,626	52,865	93,301	103,155	114,712	121,455	125,379	128,987	137,986	150,502

Section 23

Transportation

This section presents data on civil air transportation, both passenger and cargo, and on water transportation, including inland waterways, oceanborne commerce, the merchant marine, cargo, and vessel tonnages.

This section also presents statistics on revenues, passenger and freight traffic volume, and employment in various revenue-producing modes of the transportation industry, including motor vehicles, trains, and pipelines. Data are also presented on highway mileage and finances, motor vehicle travel, accidents, and registrations; and characteristics of public transit, railroads, and pipelines. Data from the 2001 National Household Travel Survey are now included in Section 26.

Principal sources of air and water transportation data are the annual *National Transportation Statistics*, issued by the U.S. Bureau of Transportation Statistics; the *Annual Report* issued by the Air Transport Association of America, Washington, DC; and the annual *Waterborne Commerce of the United States* issued by the Corps of Engineers of the Department of the Army. In addition, the U.S. Census Bureau in its commodity flow survey (part of the census of transportation, taken every 5 years through 2002, for years ending in "2" and "7") provides data on the type, weight, and value of commodities shipped by manufacturing establishments in the United States, by means of transportation, origin, and destination. The latest reports for 2002 are part of the 2002 Economic Census. This census was conducted in accordance with the 2002 North American Industry Classification System (NAICS). See text, Section 15, Business Enterprise, for a discussion of the 2002 Economic Census and NAICS.

The principal compiler of data on public roads and on operation of motor vehicles is the U.S. Department of Transportation's (DOT) Federal Highway Administration (FHWA). These data appear in FHWA's annual *Highway Statistics* and other publications.

The U.S. National Highway Traffic Safety Administration issues data on traffic accident deaths and death rates in two annual reports: the *Fact Book* and the *Fatal Accident Reporting System Annual Report*. DOT's Federal Railroad Administration presents data on accidents involving railroads in its annual *Accident/Incident Bulletin*, and the *Rail-Highway Crossing Accident/Incident and Inventory Bulletin*.

Data are also presented in many nongovernment publications. Among them are the weekly and annual *Cars of Revenue Freight Loaded* and the annual *Yearbook of Railroad Facts*, both published by the Association of American Railroads, Washington, DC; *Transit Fact Book*, containing electric railway and motorbus statistics, published annually by the American Public Transit Association, Washington, DC; *Injury Facts*, issued by the National Safety Council, Chicago, IL; and *Transportation in America*, issued by the Eno Foundation for Transportation, Washington, DC.

Civil aviation—Federal promotion and regulation of civil aviation have been carried out by the FAA and the Civil Aeronautics Board (CAB). The CAB promoted and regulated the civil air transportation industry within the United States and between the United States and foreign countries. The Board granted licenses to provide air transportation service, approved or disapproved proposed rates and fares, and approved or disapproved proposed agreements and corporate relationships involving air carriers. In December 1984, the CAB ceased to exist as an agency. Some of its functions were transferred to the Department of Transportation (DOT), as outlined below. The responsibility for investigation of aviation accidents resides with the National Transportation Safety Board.

U.S. Census Bureau, Statistical Abstract of the United States: 2006

The Office of the Secretary, DOT aviation activities include: negotiation of international air transportation rights, selection of U.S. air carriers to serve capacity-controlled international markets, oversight of international rates and fares, maintenance of essential air service to small communities, and consumer affairs. DOT's Bureau of Transportation Statistics (BTS) handles aviation information functions formerly assigned to CAB. Prior to BTS, the Research and Special Programs Administration handled these functions.

The principal activities of the FAA include: the promotion of air safety; controlling the use of navigable airspace; prescribing regulations dealing with the competency of airmen, airworthiness of aircraft and air traffic control; operation of air route traffic control centers, airport traffic control towers, and flight service stations; the design, construction, maintenance, and inspection of navigation, traffic control, and communications equipment; and the development of general aviation.

The CAB published monthly and quarterly financial and traffic statistical data for the certificated route air carriers. BTS continues these publications, including both certificated and noncertificated (commuter) air carriers. The FAA annually publishes data on the use of airway facilities; data related to the location of airmen, aircraft, and airports; the volume of activity in the field of nonair carrier (general aviation) flying; and aircraft production and registration.

General aviation comprises all civil flying (including such commercial operations as small demand air taxis, agriculture application, powerline patrol, etc.) but excludes certificated route air carriers, supplemental operators, large-aircraft commercial operators, and commuter airlines.

Air carriers and service—The CAB previously issued "certificates of public convenience and necessity" under Section 401 of the Federal Aviation Act of 1958 for scheduled and nonscheduled (charter) passenger services and cargo services. It also issued certificates under Section 418 of the Act to cargo air carriers for domestic all-cargo service only. The DOT Office

of the Secretary now issues the certificates under a "fit, willing, and able" test of air carrier operations. Carriers operating only a 60-seat-or-less aircraft are given exemption authority to carry passengers, cargo, and mail in scheduled and nonscheduled service under Part 298 of the DOT (formerly CAB) regulations. Exemption authority carriers who offer scheduled passenger service to an essential air service point must meet the "fit, willing, and able" test.

Vessel shipments, entrances, and clearances—Shipments by dry cargo vessels comprise shipments on all types of watercraft, except tanker vessels; shipments by tanker vessels comprise all types of cargo, liquid and dry, carried by tanker vessels.

A vessel is reported as entered only at the first port which it enters in the United States, whether or not cargo is unloaded at that port. A vessel is reported as cleared only at the last port at which clearance is made to a foreign port, whether or not it takes on cargo. Army and Navy vessels entering or clearing without commercial cargo are not included in the figures.

Units of measurement—Cargo (or freight) tonnage and shipping weight both represent the gross weight of the cargo including the weight of containers, wrappings, crates, etc. However, shipping weight excludes lift and cargo vans and similar substantial outer containers. Other tonnage figures generally refer to stowing capacity of vessels, 100 cubic feet being called 1 ton. Gross tonnage comprises the space within the frames and the ceiling of the hull, together with those closed-in spaces above deck available for cargo, stores, passengers, or crew, with certain minor exceptions. Net or registered tonnage is the gross tonnage less the spaces occupied by the propelling machinery, fuel, crew quarters, master's cabin, and navigation spaces. Substantially, it represents space available for cargo and passengers. The net tonnage capacity of a ship may bear little relation to weight of cargo. Deadweight tonnage is the weight in long tons required to depress a vessel from light water line (that is, with only the machinery and equipment on board)

688   Transportation

to load line. It is, therefore, the weight of the cargo, fuel, etc., which a vessel is designed to carry with safety.

Federal-aid highway systems—The Intermodal Surface Transportation Efficiency Act (ISTEA) of 1991 eliminated the historical Federal-Aid Highway Systems and created the National Highway System (NHS) and other federal-aid highway categories. The final NHS was approved by Congress in December of 1995 under the National Highway System Designation Act.

Functional systems—Roads and streets are assigned to groups according to the character of service intended. The functional systems are (1) arterial highways that generally handle the long trips, (2) collector facilities that collect and disperse traffic between the arterials and the lower systems, and (3) local roads and streets that primarily serve direct access to residential areas, farms, and other local areas.

Regulatory bodies—The ICC, created by the U.S. Congress to regulate transportation in interstate commerce, has jurisdiction over railroads, trucking companies, bus lines, freight forwarders, water carriers, coal slurry pipelines, and transportation brokers. The Federal Energy Regulatory Commission is responsible for setting rates and charges for transportation and sale of natural gas and for establishing rates or charges for transportation.

Motor carriers—For 1960–73, Class I for-hire motor carriers of freight were classified by the ICC as those with $1 million or more of gross annual operating revenue; 1974–79, the class minimum was $3 million. Effective January 1, 1980, Class I carriers are those with $5 million or more in revenue. For 1960–68, Class I motor carriers of passengers were classified by the ICC as those with $200,000 or more of gross annual operating revenue; for 1969–76, as those with revenues of $1 million or more; and since 1977, as those with $3 million or more. Effective January 1, 1988, Class I motor carriers of passengers are those with $5 million or more in operating revenues; Class II less than $5 million in operating revenues.

Railroads—Railroad companies reporting to the ICC are divided into specific groups as follows: (1) regular line-haul (interstate) railroads (and their nonoperating subsidiaries), (2) switching and terminal railroads, (3) private railroads prior to 1964 (identified by ICC as "circular" because they reported on brief circulars), and (4) unofficial railroads, so designated when their reports are received too late for tabulation. For the most part, the last three groups are not included in the statistics shown here.

For years prior to 1978, Class I railroads were those with annual revenues of $1 million or more for 1950–55; $3 million or more for 1956–64; $5 million or more for 1965–75; and $10 million or more for 1976–77. In 1978, the classification became Class I, those having more than $50 million gross annual operating revenue; Class II, from $10 million to $50 million; and Class III, less than $10 million. Effective January 1, 1982, the ICC adopted a procedure to adjust the threshold for inflation by restating current revenues in constant 1978 dollars. In 1988, the criteria for Class I and Class II railroads were $92.0 million and $18.4 million, respectively. Also effective January 1, 1982, the ICC adopted a Carrier Classification Index Survey Form for carriers not filing annual report Form R-1 with the commission. Class II and Class III railroads are currently exempted from filing any financial report with the Commission. The form is used for reclassifying carriers.

The Surface Transportation Board (STB) was established pursuant to the ICC Termination Act of 1995, Pub. L. No. 104-88, 109 Stat. 803 (1995) (ICCTA), to assume certain of the regulatory functions that had been administered by the Interstate Commerce Commission. The Board has broad economic regulatory oversight of railroads, addressing such matters as rate reasonableness, car service and interchange, mergers and line acquisitions, line construction, and line abandonments (49 U.S.C. 10101-11908). Other ICC regulatory functions were either eliminated or transferred to the Federal Highway Administration or the Bureau of Transportation Statistics within DOT.

Class I Railroads are regulated by the STB and subject to the Uniform System of Accounts and required to file annual and periodic reports. Railroads are classified based on their annual operating revenues. The class to which a carrier belongs is determined by comparing its adjusted operating revenues for 3 consecutive years to the following scale: Class I, $250 million or more; Class II, $20 million to $250 million; and Class III, $0 to $20 million.

Postal Service—The Postal Service provides mail processing and delivery services within the United States. The Postal Reorganization Act of 1970 created the Postal Service, effective July 1971, as an independent establishment of the Federal Executive Branch.

Revenue and cost analysis describes the Postal Service's system of attributing revenues and costs to classes of mail and service. This system draws primarily upon probability sampling techniques to develop estimates of revenues, volumes, and weights, as well as costs by class of mail and special service. The costs attributed to classes of mail and special services are primarily incremental costs which vary in response to changes in volume; they account for roughly 60 percent of the total costs of the Postal Service. The balance represents "institutional costs." Statistics on revenues, volume of mail, and distribution of expenditures are presented in the Postal Service's annual report, *Cost and Revenue Analysis*, and its *Annual Report of the Postmaster General* and its annual *Comprehensive Statement on Postal Operations*.

Statistical reliability—For a discussion of statistical collection and estimation, sampling procedures, and measures of statistical reliability applicable to Census Bureau data, see Appendix III.

Table 1042. **Transportation-Related Components of U.S. Gross Domestic Product: 1995 to 2004**

[In billions dollars (7,397.7 represents $7,397,700,000,000), except percent]

Item	1995	2000	2001	2002	2003	2004
CURRENT DOLLARS						
Total transportation-related final demand [1]	(NA)	1,089.5	1,103.9	1,100.6	1,150.0	(NA)
Total gross domestic product (GDP)	7,397.7	9,817.0	10,128.0	10,487.0	11,004.0	11,733.5
Transportation as a percent of GDP	(NA)	11.1	10.9	10.5	10.5	(NA)
Personal consumption of transportation	594.6	853.5	872.3	877.5	925.4	975.5
Motor vehicles and parts	266.7	386.5	407.9	426.1	440.1	449.3
Gasoline and oil	120.2	175.7	171.6	163.4	191.3	224.5
Transportation services	207.7	291.3	292.8	288.0	294	301.7
Gross private domestic investment	(NA)	167.4	148.6	132.6	132.9	(NA)
Transportation structures	(NA)	6.6	6.9	6.6	6.3	(NA)
Transportation equipment	116.1	160.8	141.7	126.0	126.6	(NA)
Net exports of transportation-related goods and service [2]	-43.6	-109.0	-108.2	-112.1	-125.2	-132.5
Exports (+)	132.4	179.0	174.3	175.5	174.9	194.3
Civilian aircraft, engines, and parts	26.1	48.1	52.6	50.4	46.7	50.1
Automotive vehicles, engines, and parts	61.3	80.4	75.4	78.9	80.7	87.9
Passenger fares	18.9	20.7	17.9	17.0	15.7	18.5
Other transportation	26.1	29.8	28.4	29.2	31.8	37.8
Imports (-)	176.0	288.0	282.5	287.6	300.1	326.8
Civilian aircraft, engines,and parts	10.7	26.4	31.4	25.5	24.1	24.3
Automotive vehicles, engines, and parts	123.6	195.9	189.8	203.7	210.2	228.0
Passenger fares	14.7	24.3	22.6	20.0	21.0	22.5
Other transportation	27.0	41.4	38.7	38.4	44.8	52.0
Government transportation-related purchases	133.8	177.6	191.2	202.6	216.9	(NA)
Federal purchases [3]	16.1	19.2	21.1	26.2	29.9	(NA)
State and local purchases [3]	109.3	149.4	160.3	165.8	170.6	(NA)
Defense-related purchases [4]	8.4	9.0	9.8	10.6	16.4	16.5
CHAINED (2000) DOLLARS						
Total transportation-related final demand [1]	(NA)	1,089.5	1,098.7	1,098.2	1,112.8	(NA)
Total gross domestic product (GDP)	8,031.7	9,817.0	9,890.7	10,074.8	10,381.3	10,837.2
Transportation as a percent of GDP	(NA)	11.1	11.1	10.9	10.7	(NA)
Personal consumption of transportation	658.6	853.5	872.1	889.3	911.8	929.5
Motor vehicles and parts	272.3	386.5	405.8	428.7	452.1	467.4
Gasoline and oil	154.5	175.7	178.3	180.7	182.0	181.4
Transportation services	231.8	291.3	288.0	279.9	277.7	280.7
Gross private domestic investment	(NA)	167.4	149.4	131.8	127.3	(NA)
Transportation structures	(NA)	6.6	6.6	6.2	5.7	(NA)
Transportation equipment	120.6	160.8	142.8	125.6	121.6	(NA)
Net exports of transportation-related goods and service [2]	-46.9	-109.0	-108.5	-114.4	-126.1	-130.4
Exports (+)	142.1	179.0	171.6	170.8	164.8	177.9
Civilian aircraft, engines, and parts	30.3	48.1	49.9	46.5	41.5	42.8
Automotive vehicles, engines, and parts	63.4	80.4	75.2	78.3	79.4	85.9
Passenger fares	19.6	20.7	17.8	16.5	13.5	14.5
Other transportation	28.8	29.8	28.7	29.5	30.4	34.7
Imports (-)	189.0	288.0	280.1	285.2	290.9	308.3
Civilian aircraft, engines, and parts	12.4	26.4	30.2	24.2	22.8	22.2
Automotive vehicles, engines, and parts	126.6	195.9	189.9	203.3	208.6	222.3
Passenger fares	17.3	24.3	20.7	17.4	17.9	19.5
Other transportation	32.7	41.4	39.3	40.3	41.6	44.3
Government transportation-related purchases	156.5	177.6	185.7	191.5	199.8	(NA)
Federal purchases [3]	18.0	19.2	20.6	25.0	27.8	(NA)
State and local purchases [3]	128.8	149.4	155.8	156.8	157.9	(NA)
Defense-related purchases [4]	9.7	9.0	9.3	9.7	14.1	13.8

NA Not available. [1] Sum of total personal consumption of transportation, total gross private domestic investment, net exports of transportation-related goods and services, and total government transportation related purchases. [2] Sum of exports and imports. [3] Federal purchases and state and local purchases are the sum of consumption expenditures and gross investment. [4] Defense-related purchases are the sum of transportation of material and travel.

Source: U.S. Bureau of Transportation Statistics, *National Transportation Statistics, 2004*. See Internet site <http://www.bts.gov/publications/nationaltransportationstatistics/2004/>

Transportation 691

Table 1043. **Transportation System Mileage Within the U.S.: 1980 to 2003**

[3,860 represents 3,860,000]

System	1980	1995	1990	1995	1999	2000	2001	2002	2003
Highway (1,000)............	3,860	3,864	3,867	3,912	3,917	3,936	3,948	3,966	3,974
Class 1 rail..............	164,822	145,764	119,758	108.264	99,430	99,250	97,817	100,125	99,126
Amtrak...............	24,000	24,000	24,000	24,000	23,000	23,000	23,000	23,000	22,675
Transit:									
Commuter rail [1].........	(X)	3,574	4,132	4,160	5,191	5,209	5,209	4,440	(NA)
Heavy rail [2]...........	(X)	1,293	1,351	1,458	1,540	1,558	1,572	1,572	(NA)
Light rail [3]............	(X)	384	483	568	802	834	897	943	(NA)
Navigable channels.........	26,000	26,000	26,000	26,000	26,000	26,000	26,000	26,000	26,000
Oil pipeline [4]..........	218,393	213,605	208,752	181,912	177,463	176,996	158,489	161,189	160,868
Gas pipeline [5] (1,000)......	1,052	1,119	1,189	1,278	1,340	1,369	1,374	1,411	(NA)

NA Not available.   X Not applicable.   [1] Also called metropolitan rail or regional rail.   [2] Also called metro, subway, rapid transit, or rapid rail.   [3] Also called streetcar, tramway, or trolley.   [4] Includes trunk and gathering lines for crude-oil pupeline.   [5] Excludes service pipelines.

Source: U.S. Bureau of Transportation Statistics, *National Transportation Statistics, 2004.* See Internet site <http://www.bts.gov/publications /nationaltransportationstatistics/2004/>.

Table 1044. **U.S. Aircraft, Vehicles, and Other Conveyances: 1980 to 2003**

[121,601 represents 121,601,000]

System	1980	1990	1995	1998	1999	2000	2001	2002	2003
Air:									
Air carrier [1].............	3,808	6,083	7,411	8,111	8,228	8,055	8,497	8,194	(NA)
General aviation [2] (active fleet) ...	211,045	198,000	188,089	204,710	219,464	217,533	211,446	211,244	(NA)
Highway, registered vehicles (1,000):									
Passenger car	121,601	133,700	128,387	131,839	132,432	133,621	137,633	135,921	135,670
Motorcycle	5,694	4,259	3,897	3,879	4,152	4,346	4,903	5,004	5,370
Vans, pick-ups, SUVs.........	27,876	48,275	65,738	71,330	75,356	79,085	84,188	85,011	87,032
Trucks..................	5,791	6,196	6,719	7,732	7,791	8,023	7,858	7,927	7,912
Bus..................	529	627	686	716	729	746	750	760	777
Transit: [3]									
Motor bus	59,411	58,714	67,107	72,142	74,228	75,013	76,075	76,190	(NA)
Light rail cars [4]...........	1,013	913	999	1,220	1,297	1,577	1,366	1,445	(NA)
Heavy rail cars [5]..........	9,641	10,419	10,157	10,301	10,306	10,591	10,718	10,718	(NA)
Trolley bus.............	823	832	885	880	859	951	600	600	(NA)
Commuter rail cars and									
locomotives	4,500	4,415	4,565	4,963	4,883	5,073	5,124	5,300	(NA)
Demand response	(X)	16,471	29,352	29,646	31,884	33,080	34,661	34,699	(NA)
Other [6]	(X)	1,197	2,809	4,703	5,059	5,208	5,727	6,330	(NA)
Rail:									
Class I, Freight cars 1,000)......	1,168	659	583	576	579	560	500	478	467
Class I, Locomotive	28,094	18,835	18,812	20,261	20,256	20,028	19,745	20,506	20,774
Nonclass I freight cars	102,161	103,527	84,724	121,659	126,762	132,448	125,470	130,590	124,580
Car companies and shippers									
freight cars	440,552	449,832	550,717	618,404	662,934	688,194	688,806	691,329	687,337
Amtrak, Passenger train car	2,128	1,863	1,722	1,962	1,992	1,894	2,084	2,896	1,623
Amtrak, Locomotive	419	318	313	345	329	378	401	372	442
Water:									
Nonself-propelled vessels [7].....	31,662	31,209	31,360	33,509	33,387	33,152	33,042	32,381	31,335
Self-propelled vessels [8]	7,126	8,236	8,281	8,523	8,379	8,202	8.546	8,621	8,648
Oceangoing steam and motor ships									
(1,000 gross tons and over).....	864	636	509	470	463	454	443	426	412
Recreational boats (1,000)	8,578	10,996	11,735	12,566	12,738	12,782	12,876	12,854	12,795

NA Not available.   X Not applicable.   [1] Air carrier aircraft are those carrying passengers or cargo for hire under 14 CFR 121 and 14 CFR 135. [2] Includes air taxi aircraft.   [3] 2002 data are preliminary.   [4] Fixed rail streetcar or trolley, for example. [5] Metro, subway, or rapid transit, for example.   [6] Includes aerial tramway, automated guideway transit, cablecar, ferry boat, inclined plane, monorail, and vanpool.   [7] Includes dry-cargo barges, tank barges, and railroad-car floats.   [8] Includes dry-cargo and/or passenger, offshore supply vessels, railroad-car ferries, tankers, and towboats.

Source: U.S. Bureau of Transportation Statistics, *National Transportation Statistics, 2004.* See Internet site <http://www.bts.gov/publications /nationaltransportationstatistics/2004/>.

Table 1045. **U.S. Freight Gateways: 2003**

[In billions of dollars, **except as indicated (1,983 represents $1,983,000,000,000)** For the top 50 gateways ranked by value of shipments. Excludes imports of less than $1,250, exports less than $2,500, and intransit shipments]

Port	Mode	Rank	Total trade	Exports	Imports	Exports as a percent of total
Total U.S. merchandise trade	(X)	(X)	1,983	724	1,259	36.5
Top 50 gateways	(X)	(X)	1,587	576	1,011	36.3
As a percent of total	(X)	(X)	80.0	79.6	80.2	(X)
Port of Los Angeles, CA.	Water	1	122	17	105	13.8
JFK International Airport, NY.	Air	2	112	47	65	41.7
Port of Detroit, MI	Land	3	102	55	47	53.5
Port of New York and New Jersey	Water	4	101	24	77	24.0
Port of Long Beach, CA.	Water	5	96	17	79	17.9
Port of Laredo, TX	Land	6	79	32	46	41.1
Los Angeles International Airport, CA	Air	7	64	33	31	51.1
Port Huron, MI.	Land	8	62	23	40	36.4
Port of Buffalo-Niagara Falls, NY	Land	9	59	27	32	46.1
Chicago, IL	Air	10	54	21	34	37.9
Port of Houston, TX	Water	11	50	21	28	43.0
San Francisco International Airport, CA.	Air	12	47	21	26	44.1
Port of Charleston, SC.	Water	13	39	13	26	34.0
Port of El Paso, TX	Land	14	39	17	22	42.6
Port of Norfolk Harbor, VA	Water	15	29	11	18	37.4
New Orleans, LA . . . . • . .	Air	16	27	14	14	50.0
Port of Tacoma, WA	Water	17	26	5	21	19.8
Port of Baltimore, MD	Water	18	26	6	20	21.9
Port of Oakland, CA	Water	19	25	8	17	30.9
Dallas-Fort Worth, TX	Air	20	24	11	12	48.3
Port of Seattle, WA	Water	21	23	6	17	24.6
Miami International Airport, FL.	Air	22	23	14	9	61.5
Anchorage, AK.	Air	23	22	6	16	25.5
Port of Savannah, GA	Water	24	21	7	14	34.7
Port of Otay Mesa Station, CA	Land	25	20	8	11	42.0
Port of New Orleans, LA	Water	26	19	11	8	57.9
Cleveland, OH	Air	27	19	10	9	51.3
Atlanta, GA	Air	28	18	8	10	45.6
Port of Miami, FL	Water	29	17	7	10	41.1
Port of Champlain-Rouses Point, NY	Land	30	14	5	9	36.2
Port of Hidalgo, TX	Land	31	14	6	8	43.6
Newark, NJ	Air	32	13	3	10	20.1
San Juan International Airport, PR	Air	33	12	5	7	42.4
Port of Blaine, WA	Land	34	12	5	7	43.6
Port of Portland, OR	Water	35	12	3	9	25.1
Port of Jacksonville, FL	Water	36	11	2	9	20.8
Port Everglades, FL	Water	37	10	4	6	41.4
Port of Nogales, AZ.	Land	38	10	· 4	7	34.2
Port of Philadelphia, PA.	Water	39	10	1	10	6.1
Port of Morgan City, LA	Water	40	10	-	10	1.8
Port of Brownsville, TX	Land	41	10	5	5	51.5
Port of Alexandria Bay, NY	Land	42	10	4	6	38.2
Port of Corpus Christi, TX	Water	43	10	2	8	19.8
Port of Beaumont, TX	Water	44	10	1	9	9.9
Port of Pembina, ND.	Land	45	9	5	4	53.1
Boston Logan Airport, MA	Air	46	9	6	3	62.0
Port of Calexico-East, CA.	Land	47	9	4	5	42.4
Philadelphia International Airport, PA	Air	48	9	5	4	53.8
Port of Sweetgrass, MT.	Land	49	7	3	4	48.1
Seattle-Tacoma International Airport, WA.	Air	50	7	4	3	56.8

- Represents or rounds to zero. X Not applicable.

Source: U.S. Bureau of Transportation Statistics, *America's Freight Transportation Gateways*, 2004. See Internet site <http://www.bts.gov/publications/americasfreighttransportationgateways/>.

Transportation 693

Table 1046. **Transportation Outlays by Type of Transport: 1970 to 2001**

[In billions of dollars (97.0 represents $97,000,000,000)]

Type of transport	1970	1980	1985	1990	1995	2000	2001
Private transportation	**97.0**	**305.2**	**434.7**	**517.2**	**629.8**	**831.3**	**862.1**
Automobiles	95.0	297.1	426.8	507.3	619.4	809.4	835.6
New and used cars	32.0	71.5	137.1	148.1	169.6	205.4	200.6
Other motor vehicles [1]	2.7	11.8	40.8	57.5	80.2	125.9	149.0
Tires, tubes, accessories	7.0	20.6	27.9	32.9	40.6	45.9	45.8
Gasoline and oil	27.4	99.7	111.8	118.0	124.6	164.4	162.1
Tolls	0.8	1.3	1.7	2.5	3.7	4.6	4.9
Insurance less claims	4.4	10.8	11.5	19.9	32.7	30.7	32.1
Interest on debt	4.7	39.1	21.0	28.2	38.0	48.7	51.0
Auto registration fees	1.7	2.9	4.8	6.1	7.0	7.6	7.7
Operators' permit fees	0.2	0.4	0.5	0.6	0.8	0.7	0.8
Repair, greasing, washing, parking, leasing, rentals	14.1	39.1	69.6	93.4	122.2	175.5	181.6
Air	2.0	8.1	7.9	9.9	10.4	21.9	26.5
Aircraft	0.3	2.9	2.3	3.4	4.3	14.3	18.5
Operating costs	1.7	5.2	5.6	6.5	6.1	7.6	8.0
For-hire transportation	**14.9**	**51.0**	**71.9**	**99.6**	**117.6**	**159.9**	**148.1**
Local	5.0	17.3	25.3	31.6	41.0	52.5	53.4
Bus and transit [2]	1.8	9.3	13.5	16.7	21.6	30.6	30.6
Taxi	1.7	2.8	3.8	4.0	5.0	5.6	5.7
Railroad commutation [2]	0.2	1.5	2.2	2.8	4.5	4.2	4.5
School bus	1.2	3.8	5.7	8.0	9.9	12.1	12.6
Intercity	7.7	28.4	39.5	53.1	57.8	79.9	70.2
Air [3]	6.6	25.1	35.9	49.5	54.0	75.1	64.9
Bus	0.8	1.7	2.0	1.8	1.5	2.0	2.2
Rail [4]	0.3	1.5	1.6	1.7	2.2	2.7	2.9
Water	(Z)	(Z)	0.1	0.1	0.1	0.2	0.1
International	2.2	5.3	7.1	14.9	18.8	27.5	24.5
Air [3]	1.9	5.0	6.6	13.6	16.8	23.0	20.4
Water	0.3	0.3	0.5	1.3	2.0	4.5	4.0
Freight, total	**84.0**	**213.7**	**273.6**	**351.0**	**442.6**	**575.8**	**579.6**
Highway	62.5	155.3	205.6	270.8	348.1	460.8	467.3
Truck, intercity [5]	33.6	94.6	123.2	162.3	219.6	305.2	309.4
Truck, local [6]	28.8	60.5	82.2	108.4	128.4	155.5	157.7
Bus, intercity	0.1	0.2	0.2	0.1	0.1	0.1	0.1
Rail	11.9	27.9	29.2	30.1	34.6	36.5	36.7
Water	5.3	15.5	18.4	20.1	22.7	28.7	27.6
Oil pipeline	1.4	7.5	8.9	8.5	9.1	9.0	9.1
Air carrier	1.2	4.0	6.8	13.7	18.8	27.6	25.8
Other carriers	0.4	1.1	1.7	4.0	5.0	7.8	7.7
Other shipper costs	1.4	2.4	3.0	3.7	4.4	5.4	5.4

Z Less than $50,000,000.   [1] Includes small pickup trucks, vans, recreational vehicles, and mobile homes.   [2] Includes federal, state, and local government operating subsidies and capital grants, except 1970 data for railroad commutations.   [3] Includes domestic and international air passenger federal excise taxes.   [4] Includes federal operating subsidies and capital grants for Amtrak and the Northeast Corridor.   [5] Includes freight, mail, express, and where applicable, subsidies and user fees.   [6] Excludes use of small trucks/vans used almost exclusively for personal travel.

Source: Eno Transportation Foundation, Inc., Washington, DC, *Transportation in America*, annual (copyright).

Table 1047. **Volume of Domestic Intercity Freight and Passenger Traffic by Type of Transport: 1980 to 2001**

[Freight traffic in billions ton-miles (2,487 represents 2,487,000,000,000); passenger traffic in billions passenger-miles. A ton-mile is the movement of 1 ton (2,000 pounds) of freight for the distance of 1 mile. A passenger-mile is the movement of 1 passenger for the distance of 1 mile. Comprises public and private traffic, both revenue and nonrevenue. ICC = Interstate Commerce Commission]

Type of transport	1980	1985	1990	1994	1995	1996	1997	1998	1999	2000	2001, est.
Freight traffic, total [1]	2,487	2,458	2,896	3,261	3,407	3,516	3,534	3,591	3,686	3,746	3,733
Railroads	932	895	1,091	1,275	1,375	1,426	1,421	1,442	1,499	1,534	1,558
Truck:											
ICC truck	242	250	311	391	401	428	436	459	474	483	471
Non-ICC truck	313	360	424	517	520	544	560	568	585	591	580
Water:											
Rivers/canals	311	306	390	388	406	392	392	392	403	409	400
Great Lakes	96	76	85	87	91	93	95	96	92	97	94
Oil pipelines	588	564	584	591	601	619	617	620	618	617	616
Domestic airways [2]	5	7	10	12	13	14	14	14	15	16	15
Passenger traffic, total	**1,468**	**1,636**	**1,847**	**2,065**	**2,098**	**2,182**	**2,247**	**2,328**	**2,424**	**2,494**	**2,498**
Private automobiles [3]	1,210	1,310	1,452	1,625	1,641	1,693	1,740	1,806	1,873	1,911	1,938
Air, private carrier [4]	15	12	13	10	11	12	13	13	14	15	16
Air, public carrier	204	278	346	388	404	435	451	463	488	515	488
Bus	27	24	23	28	28	29	31	32	35	38	42
Railroads [5]	11	11	13	14	14	13	13	14	14	15	15

[1] Includes both for-hire and private carrier freight, mail and express.   [2] Includes both scheduled and nonscheduled carriers.   [3] Includes small trucks used for travel purposes.   [4] General aviation including air taxi and small air commuter.   [5] Traffic by other than Amtrak and classified as noncommutation.

Source: Eno Transportation Foundation, Inc., Washington, DC, *Transportation in America*, annual (copyright).

694   Transportation

Table 1048. **Transportation and Warehousing—Establishments, Revenue, Payroll, and Employees by Industry: 2002**

[17,973 represents $17,973,000,000. Data are preliminary. For establishments with payroll. Based on the 2002 Economic Censuses; See Appendix III]

Kind of business	2002 NAICS code [1]	Number of establishments	Revenue (mil. dol.)	Annual payroll (mil. dol.)	Paid employees (1,000)
Air transportation [2]	481	3,847	17,973	3,549	85.9
Scheduled air transportation [2]	4811	1,674	10,532	2,028	54.6
Nonscheduled air transportation	4812	2,173	7,441	1,522	31.3
Water transportation	483	1,924	23,124	3,032	65.3
Deep sea, coastal, and Great Lakes water transportation	4831	1,334	20,631	2,438	52.0
Truck transportation	484	112,698	165,561	47,834	1,437.3
General freight trucking	4841	59,120	111,550	34,230	992.9
Specialized freight trucking	4842	53,578	54,011	13,603	444.3
Transit and ground passenger transportation [3]	485	17,333	18,770	7,575	404.8
Urban transit systems	4851	1,234	3,603	2,047	65.6
Interurban and rural bus transportation	4852	360	769	231	9.2
Taxi and limousine service	4853	6,998	4,160	1,146	67.5
School and employee bus transportation	4854	4,407	5,901	2,570	175.7
Charter bus industry	4855	1,222	1,700	532	28.8
Pipeline transportation [3]	486	2,512	27,641	3,083	46.6
Pipeline transportation of crude oil	4861	271	3,334	506	6.9
Pipeline transportation of natural gas	4862	1,701	19,968	2,120	32.5
Scenic and sightseeing transportation	487	2,493	1,773	500	22.1
Scenic and sightseeing transportation, water	4872	1,726	964	267	11.6
Support activities for transportation [3]	488	34,223	62,316	16,558	478.2
Support activities for air transportation	4881	4,972	13,151	3,961	132.7
Support activities for rail transportation	4882	840	2,068	745	21.6
Support activities for water transportation	4883	2,502	9,801	2,764	69.6
Support activities for road transportation	4884	8,000	4,153	1,360	56.3
Freight transportation arrangement	4885	16,570	31,040	7,086	175.9
Couriers and messengers	492	12,754	59,373	17,432	578.3
Couriers	4921	7,485	56,028	16,296	523.0
Local messengers and local delivery	4922	5,269	3,345	1,136	55.2
Warehousing and storage	493	12,637	17,925	18,689	639.2

[1] North American Industry Classification System, 2002; see text, Section 15. [2] Excludes large certificated passenger carriers that do not report to the Office of Airline Information, U.S. Department of Transportation. [3] Includes other industries, not shown separately.

Source: U.S. Bureau of the Census, "2002 Economic Census Industry Series Reports, Transporation and Warehousing." See Internet site <http://www.census.gov/econ/census02/guide/INDRPT48.HTM> (accessed 2 May 2005).

Table 1049. **Employment and Earnings in Transportation and Warehousing by Industry: 1990 to 2004**

[3,476 represents 3,476,000. Annual average of monthly figures. Earnings data for air, rail and water transportation are not available. Based on Current Employment Statistics program; see Appendix III]

Industry	2002 NAICS code [1]	1990	1995	2000	2001	2002	2003	2004
EMPLOYEES (1,000)								
Transportation & warehousing	48,49	3,476	3,838	4,410	4,372	4,224	4,185	4,250
Air transportation	481	529	511	614	615	564	528	515
Rail transportation	482	272	233	232	227	218	218	224
Water transportation	483	57	51	56	54	53	55	57
Truck transportation	484	1,122	1,249	1,406	1,387	1,339	1,326	1,351
Transit and ground	485	274	328	372	375	381	382	386
Pipeline transportation	486	60	54	46	45	42	40	39
Scenic and sightseeing	487	16	22	28	29	26	27	27
Support activities	488	364	430	537	539	525	520	536
Couriers and messengers	492	375	517	605	587	561	562	561
Warehousing and storage	493	407	444	514	514	517	528	556
AVG. WEEKLY EARNINGS [2] (dol.)								
Transportation & warehousing	48,49	471.72	513.37	562.31	562.70	579.75	598.41	614.90
Truck transportation	484	489.65	554.10	635.18	603.79	626.32	652.07	686.43
Transit and ground	485	315.91	355.78	399.59	400.17	421.93	426.46	415.61
Pipeline transportation	486	610.40	750.77	826.00	860.35	936.68	1,077.76	1,100.50
Scenic and sightseeing	487	288.86	303.32	360.05	360.05	361.05	368.64	352.10
Support activities	488	437.09	490.92	549.04	577.97	616.04	658.20	657.26
Couriers and messengers	492	235.75	342.66	384.31	390.42	398.07	403.86	414.96
Warehousing and storage	493	404.59	462.91	558.49	564.78	571.73	567.40	557.79

[1] North American Industry Classification System 2002, see text, sections 12 and 15. [2] For nonsupervisory workers.

Source: U.S. Bureau of Labor Statistics, *Employment and Earnings*, monthly, March 2005 issue. See also Internet site: <http://www.bls.gov/ces/home.htm>.

Table 1050. **Transportation and Warehousing—Establishments, Employees, and Payroll by Kind of Business (NAICS Basis): 2000 and 2002**

[3,790.0 **represents 3,790,000.** For establishments with payroll. See Appendix III. County Business Patterns excludes rail transportation (NAICS 482) and the National Postal Service (NAICS 491)]

Industry	1997 NAICS code [1]	Establishments		Paid employees [2] (1,000)		Annual payroll (mil. dol.)	
		2000	2002	2000	2002	2000	2002
Transportation & warehousing	48-49	190,044	195,143	3,790.0	3,581.0	125,592.4	127,251.9
Air transportation	481	5,429	5,512	615.6	548.3	26,569.3	27,470.9
Scheduled air transportation	4811	3,324	3,297	570.9	513.6	24,484.5	25,739.1
Scheduled passenger air transportation	481111	2,740	2,739	536.2	486.7	23,470.7	24,889.8
Scheduled freight air transportation	481112	584	558	34.7	26.9	1,013.8	849.3
Nonscheduled air transportation	4812	2,105	2,215	44.7	34.6	2,084.8	1,731.8
Water transportation	483	1,900	1,902	67.6	64.3	3,003.2	3,164.7
Deep sea, coastal, & Great Lakes water transportation	4831	1,254	1,222	47.8	45.5	2,214.2	2,360.3
Inland water transportation	4832	646	680	19.7	18.7	789.0	804.4
Inland water freight transportation	483211	402	419	16.3	15.1	673.9	681.2
Inland water passenger transportation	483212	244	261	3.5	3.6	115.1	123.2
Truck transportation	484	110,416	111,308	1,415.8	1,333.3	46,451.5	45,067.4
General freight trucking	4841	55,874	56,746	922.7	882.0	31,614.0	30,866.7
General freight trucking, local	48411	20,329	21,172	153.3	156.1	4,529.8	4,903.5
General freight trucking, long distance	48412	35,545	35,574	769.5	725.9	27,084.2	25,963.3
Specialized freight trucking	4842	54,542	54,562	493.1	451.3	14,837.5	14,200.7
Used household & office goods moving	48421	9,147	8,781	128.9	114.6	3,661.4	3,314.1
Specialized freight (except used goods) trucking, local	48422	32,493	33,326	200.4	189.6	5,692.4	5,650.5
Specialized freight (except used goods) trucking, long-distance	48423	12,902	12,455	163.7	147.1	5,483.7	5,236.1
Transit & ground passenger transportation	485	16,383	17,073	386.9	387.3	7,214.7	7,780.1
Urban transit systems	4851	705	751	43.1	46.2	1,295.8	1,482.7
Mixed mode systems	485111	152	151	6.2	5.2	146.9	129.3
Commuter rail	485112	15	16	(D)	(D)	(D)	(D)
Bus and other motor vehicle mode systems	485113	505	542	31.4	35.6	925.1	1,074.4
Other	485119	33	42	(D)	(D)	(D)	(D)
Interurban & rural bus transportation	4852	444	579	26.8	20.7	709.7	730.8
Taxi & limousine service	4853	6,806	7,146	67.8	65.6	1,244.3	1,269.2
Taxi service	48531	3,116	3,164	30.4	29.1	485.2	492.8
Limousine service	48532	3,690	3,982	37.5	36.5	759.1	776.5
School & employee bus transportation	4854	4,217	4,352	162.9	171.6	2,322.6	2,612.2
Charter bus industry	4855	1,451	1,473	34.1	32.2	668.7	667.0
Other transit & ground passenger transportation	4859	2,760	2,772	52.2	51.1	973.6	1,018.2
Special needs transportation	485991	1,914	1,886	34.8	35.0	648.9	704.0
Pipeline transportation	486	2,802	2,701	53.0	50.4	3,828.6	3,915.5
Pipeline transportation of crude oil	4861	307	261	6.7	6.0	425.6	472.3
Pipeline transportation of natural gas	4862	1,938	1,936	39.2	37.5	2,961.1	2,994.1
Other pipeline transportation	4869	557	504	7.0	6.9	441.9	449.0
Scenic & sightseeing transportation	487	2,254	2,503	23.6	19.3	583.5	497.5
Scenic & sightseeing transportation, land	4871	454	538	8.7	7.2	192.8	164.4
Scenic & sightseeing transportation, water	4872	1,642	1,784	13.0	10.5	331.2	281.6
Scenic & sightseeing transportation, other	4879	158	181	2.0	1.7	59.5	51.5
Support activities for transportation	488	31,440	33,342	472.4	475.5	16,507.0	17,553.4
Support activities for air transportation	4881	4,368	4,926	126.7	126.3	3,634.0	3,899.4
Airport operations	48811	1,834	1,942	67.9	67.6	1,569.5	1,762.7
Air traffic control	488111	137	156	0.8	1.0	29.9	45.9
Other support activities for air transportation	48819	2,534	2,984	58.8	58.8	2,064.6	2,136.7
Support activities for rail transportation	4882	821	924	21.4	20.7	714.4	733.9
Support activities for water transportation	4883	2,543	2,453	81.6	77.2	3,250.7	3,577.0
Port and harbor operations	48831	196	212	7.4	6.3	265.8	246.0
Marine cargo handling	48832	607	595	53.5	50.4	2,194.7	2,425.2
Navigational services to shipping	48833	863	828	11.8	11.2	478.7	510.0
Other	48839	877	818	8.9	9.2	311.5	395.9
Support activities for road transportation	4884	7,010	8,238	56.2	62.0	1,308.8	1,575.9
Motor vehicle towing	48841	6,078	6,813	41.8	43.3	961.7	1,064.8
Freight transportation arrangement	4885	15,177	15,476	161.7	164.4	6,620.3	6,809.9
Other support activities for transportation	4889	1,521	1,325	24.7	24.9	978.6	957.2
Couriers & messengers	492	12,297	13,173	619.3	553.3	17,399.4	17,189.3
Couriers	4921	6,667	7,447	548.9	497.4	15,890.5	15,936.1
Local messengers & local delivery	4922	5,630	5,726	70.5	55.9	1,508.9	1,253.2
Warehousing & storage	493	7,123	7,629	135.9	149.4	4,035.3	4,613.2

D Figure withheld to avoid disclosure pertaining to individual companies.   [1] North American Industry Classification System, 1997; see text, Section 15.   [2] For employees on the payroll for the pay period including March 12.

Source: U.S. Census Bureau, "County Business Patterns; 2002" issued November 2004; <http://www.census.gov/epcd/cbp/view/cbpview.html>.

Table 1051. **Transportation Accidents, Deaths, and Injuries: 1980 to 2003**

[6,216 represents 6,216,000]

Year and casualty	High way [1] (1,000)	Rail-road [2]	Air U.S. Air carrier [3]	Air Commuter air car-riers [4]	Air On demand air car-riers [5]	Air Gen-eral aviation	Recre-ational boat-ing [6]	Pipeline [7] Gas	Pipeline [7] Hazard-ous liquid	Water-borne (vessel related) [8]	Rail Rapid Trans-it [9]	Hazard-ous materi-als [10]
Accidents:												
1980...	6,216	8,205	19	38	171	3,590	5,513	1,524	246	4,624	6,789	15,719
1990...	6,471	2.879	24	15	107	2,241	6,411	198	180	3,613	12.178	8,879
2000...	6,394	2,983	56	12	80	1,837	7,740	234	146	3,887	12,782	17,566
2003...	6,328	2,958	54	2	75	1,741	3,888	241	128	3,090	(NA)	15,191
Deaths:												
1980...	51.1	584	1	37	105	1,239	1,360	15	4	206	83	19
1990...	44.6	599	39	6	51	767	865	6	3	85	117	8
2000...	41.9	512	92	5	71	596	701	37	1	49	80	16
2003...	42.6	531	22	2	45	63¹	703	12	-	46	(NA)	8
Injuries:												
1980...	2,848	58,696	19	14	43	681	2,650	177	15	180	6,801	626
1990...	3,231	22,736	29	11	36	409	3,822	69	7	175	10,036	423
2000...	3,189	10,424	29	7	12	309	4,355	77	4	130	10,848	251
2003...	2,889	7,956	30	1	15	326	3,888	66	5	205	(NA)	117

- Represents zero. NA Not available. [1] Data on deaths are from U.S. National Highway Traffic Safety Administration and are based on 30-day definition. Includes only police reported crashes. For more detail, see Table 1094. [2] Accidents,which result in damages to railroad property. Grade crossing accidents are also included when classified as a train accident. Deaths exclude fatalities in railroad-highway grade crossing accidents. [3] Includes scheduled and nonscheduled (charter) air carriers. Represents serious injuries. [4] All scheduled service. Represents serious injuries. [5] All nonscheduled service. Represents serious injuries. [6] Accidents resulting in death, injury or requiring medical treatment beyond first aid; damages exceeding $500; or a person's disappearance. [7] Beginning 1990, pipeline accidents/incidents are credited to year of occurrence; 1980 data are credited to the year filed. [8] Covers accidents involving commercial vessels which must be reported to U.S. Coast Guard if there is property damage exceeding $25,000; material damage affecting the seaworthiness or efficiency of a vessel; stranding or grounding; loss of life; or injury causing a person's incapacity for more than 3 days. [9] Reporting criteria and source of data changed between 1989 and 1990; these data from 1990 to present are not comparable to earlier years. [10] Incidents, deaths, and injuries involving hazardous materials cover all types of transport.

Source: U.S. Bureau of Transportation Statistics, *National Transportation Statistics*, annual. See Internet site <http://www.bts.gov/publications/nts/index.html>.

Table 1052. **U. S. Scheduled Airline Industry—Summary: 1995 to 2004**

[For calendar years or Dec. 31 (547.8 represents 547,800,000). For domestic and international operations. Covers carriers certificated under Section 401 of the Federal Aviation Act. Minus sign (-) indicates loss]

Item	Unit	1995	1998	1999	2000	2001 [1]	2002 [1]	2003 [2]	2004
SCHEDULED SERVICE									
Revenue passengers enplaned...	Mil....	547.8	612.9	636.0	666.2	622.1	612.9	646.3	697.8
Revenue passenger miles......	Bil....	540.7	618.1	652.0	692.8	651.7	641.1	656.9	731.9
Available seat miles..........	Bil....	807.1	874.1	918.4	957.0	930.5	892.6	893.8	969.0
Revenue passenger load factor..	Percent...	67.0	70.7	71.0	72.4	70.0	71.8	73.5	75.5
Mean passenger trip length [3]...	Miles.....	987	1,008	1,025	1,040	1,048	1,046	1,016	1,049
Cargo ton miles.............	Mil....	16,921	20,496	21,613	23,888	22,003	24,591	26,735	28,003
Aircraft departures..........	1,000	8,062	8,292	8,627	9,035	8,788	9,187	10,839	11,182
FINANCES									
Total operating revenue [4]....	Mil. dol. ..	95,117	113,810	119,455	130,839	115,526	106,985	117,920	131,510
Passenger revenue	Mil. dol....	69,835	81,052	84,383	93,622	80,947	73,577	77,379	85,657
Freight and express revenue	Mil. dol....	8,616	10,697	11,415	12,486	12,066	12,865	14,101	14,911
Mail revenue...............	Mil. dol....	1,266	1,708	1,739	1,970	1,063	660	902	701
Charter revenue.............	Mil. dol....	3,742	4,059	4,284	4,913	4,449	4,225	5,589	5,550
Total operating expense	Mil. dol....	89,266	104,528	111,119	123,840	125,852	115,552	120,028	132,874
Operating profit (or loss)	Mil. dol...	5,852	9,283	8,337	6,999	-10,326	-8,566	-2,108	-1,364
Interest income (or expense)	Mil. dol....	-2,426	-1,753	-1,833	-2,193	-2,506	-3,263	-3,442	-3,633
Net profit (or loss)	Mil. dol....	2,283	4,847	5,277	2,486	-8,275	-11,312	-3,658	-9,071
Revenue per passenger mile	Cents	12.9	13.1	12.9	13.5	12.4	11.5	11.8	11.7
Operating profit margin	Percent...	6.2	8.2	7.0	5.3	-8.9	-8.0	-1.8	-1.0
Net profit margin	Percent...	2.4	4.3	4.4	1.9	-7.2	-10.6	-3.1	-6.9
EMPLOYEES [5]									
Total	1,000	547.0	621.1	646.4	680.0	672.0	601.4	569.8	569.1
Pilots and copilots	1,000	55.4	64.1	67.2	72.4	73.8	68.8	67.8	65.6
Other flight personnel	1,000	8.6	11.1	12.4	10.8	9.6	7.5	8.2	5.1
Flight attendants	1,000	86.7	97.6	105.6	112.6	111.0	97.7	89.7	89.0
Mechanics	1,000	50.5	69.9	70.3	72.1	70.8	61.7	57.3	57.2
Aircraft and traffic servicing personnel..........	1,000	251.1	290.1	295.6	311.7	303.9	280.9	267.3	270.6
All other.................	1,000	94.8	88.3	95.3	100.3	102.9	84.9	79.4	81.6

[1] Includes cash compensation remitted to carriers under the Air Transportation Safety and System Stabilization Act (P.L. 107-42). [2] Includes security costs reimbursements remitted to carriers under the Emergency Wartime Supplemental Appropriations Act (P.L. 108-11). [3] For definition of mean, see Guide to Tabular Presentation. [4] Includes other types of revenues, not shown separately. [5] Average number of full-time equivalents.

Source: Air Transport Association of America, Washington, DC, *Air Transport Annual Report*.

U.S. Census Bureau, Statistical Abstract of the United States: 2006

Table 1053. Airline Cost Indexes: 1980 to 2003

[1982 = 100. Covers U.S. major and national passenger carriers. Major carriers have operating revenues of $1 billion or more; nationals have operating revenues from $100 million to $1 billion]

Index	1980	1985	1990	1995	1997	1998	1999	2000	2001	2002	2003
Composite index [1]	87.2	108.8	142.2	161.1	168.4	171.4	173.8	176.5	182.0	187.6	188.0
Labor costs.	84.7	109.6	121.1	152.2	159.1	160.0	162.0	169.9	182.0	193.6	204.2
Fuel.	92.0	91.0	77.4	54.9	63.4	50.4	52.2	77.2	76.7	71.5	85.2
Aircraft ownership [2]	91.7	138.6	207.3	247.2	254.1	259.6	277.5	296.8	298.6	309.3	307.9
Non-aircraft ownership	79.9	111.7	184.0	212.3	191.0	195.5	202.4	206.4	230.2	226.3	229.4
Professional services	83.2	134.9	196.8	248.0	258.8	281.1	282.6	285.6	290.9	279.7	284.9
Food and beverage	93.4	99.5	128.8	109.7	101.7	103.7	104.8	102.4	102.5	89.1	77.4
Landing fees	90.1	98.7	141.2	171.1	176.6	170.2	178.3	174.3	180.6	201.9	216.0
Maintenance material	108.3	127.3	191.5	147.2	179.4	176.2	163.3	168.8	148.2	127.1	106.5
Aircraft insurance	93.4	150.7	56.8	119.5	99.4	53.6	36.0	36.0	50.9	94.7	63.0
Non-aircraft insurance	91.6	160.4	84.0	266.0	242.5	179.9	124.7	120.7	218.0	686.1	532.2
Passenger commissions	77.1	112.5	163.9	134.8	122.9	109.1	95.2	77.2	61.5	38.5	28.7
Communication	70.3	98.4	114.2	115.0	110.0	116.2	134.8	131.4	144.5	133.2	112.6
Advertising and promotion . . .	69.8	95.1	96.8	64.0	56.3	60.6	61.0	59.7	55.1	44.6	41.6
Utilities and office supplies. . .	88.8	113.2	128.4	115.4	128.7	127.8	128.1	137.8	143.2	120.2	107.4
Other operating expenses . . .	86.1	111.2	130.6	148.1	153.9	155.8	158.0	161.3	163.2	165.9	169.0
Interest [3]	87.9	98.5	97.9	94.7	71.2	60.2	53.8	54.4	50.6	53.6	50.7

[1] Weighted average of all components, including interest. [2] Includes lease, aircraft and engine rentals, depreciation and amortization. [3] Interest on long-term debt and capital and other interest expense.

Source: Air Transport Association of America, Washington, DC, *Airline Cost Index, Major and National Carriers, Third Quarter 2004*. See Internet site <http://www.airlines.org/econ/econ.aspx> (accessed 07 June 2005).

Table 1054. Top 40 Airports in 2004—Passengers Enplaned: 1994 and 2004

[In thousands (501,197 represents 501,197,000), except rank. For calendar year. Airports ranked by total passengers enplaned by large certificated air carriers on scheduled and nonscheduled operations]

Airport	1994		2004		Airport	1994		2004	
	Total	Rank	Total	Rank		Total	Rank	Total	Rank
All airports.	501,197	(X)	652,712	(X)	Baltimore, MD (BWI)	5,481	27	9,735	22
Total, top 40	382,759	(X)	502,609	(X)	Washington, DC (Dulles				
Atlanta, GA (Hartsfield Intl) . .	25,630	2	40,399	1	Intl).	4,218	35	9,389	23
Chicago, IL (O'Hare Intl) . . .	29,700	1	33,653	2	Chicago, IL (Midway).	4,049	36	9,236	24
Dallas/Ft.Worth, Intl, TX	25,117	3	27,563	3	Fort Lauderdale-Hollywood				
Los Angeles Intl, CA	19,721	4	22,892	4	Intl, FL	4,500	32	9,173	25
Denver Intl, CO	14,640	5	19,856	5	Salt Lake City Intl, UT	7,825	23	8,868	26
Las Vegas, NV (McCarran					San Diego, CA (Lindbergh				
Intl).	10,435	14	19,413	6	Field)	6,160	26	8,089	27
Phoenix Sky Harbor Intl,					Tampa Intl, FL	5,416	29	8,065	28
AZ	12,427	7	19,123	7	Honolulu Intl, HI	8,494	22	7,830	29
Minneapolis/St. Paul Intl,					Wash, DC (Ronald Reagan				
MN.	10,456	13	17,282	8	Washington National). . . .	6,975	25	7,184	30
Detroit, MI (Wayne County) .	11,822	8	16,784	9	Metropolitan Oakland Intl,				
Houston Intercontinental,					CA	3,992	38	6,825	31
TX	9,626	17	16,707	10	Portland Intl, OR.	4,826	30	6,267	32
Newark Intl, NJ.	11,782	9	14,026	11	St. Louis, MO (Lambert-St.				
Orlando Intl, FL	8,863	21	13,752	12	Louis Intl)	11,453	10	5,880	33
Seattle-Tacoma Intl, WA. . . .	9,936	15	13,744	13	Pittsburgh Intl, PA.	8,928	19	5,704	34
San Francisco Intl, CA.	14,309	6	13,504	14	Memphis Intl, TN	3,454	43	5,285	35
New York, NY (JFK Intl)	8,894	20	13,222	15	San Jose Intl, CA	4,016	37	5,190	36
Philadelphia Intl, PA	7,537	24	12,480	16	Cleveland, OH (Cleveland-				
Miami Intl, FL.	10,810	11	11,521	17	Hopkins Intl).	4,665	31	5,151	37
Charlotte-Douglas Intl, NC . .	9,370	18	11,306	18	San Juan, PR (Luis Munoz				
Boston, MA (Logan Intl)	10,609	12	11,094	19	Marin Intl)	4,377	33	5,074	38
New York, NY (La Guardia) .	9,780	16	10,980	20	Kansas City Intl, MO	4,236	34	5,003	39
Greater Cincinnati, OH.	5,441	28	10,594	21	Sacramento Intl, CA	2,791	50	4,768	40

X Not applicable.

Source: U.S. Bureau of Transportation Statisics, Office of Airline Information, BTS Form 41, Schedule T-3, unpublished data.

Table 1055. Domestic Airline Markets: 2004

[In thousands (3,885 represents 3,885,000). For calendar year. Data are for the 25 top markets and include all commercial airports in each metro area. Data represent origin and final destination of travel]

Market	Passengers	Market	Passengers
New York to—from Fort Lauderdale	3,885	New York to—from Boston	1,625
New York to—from Orlando	3,277	New York to—from Tampa	1,614
New York to—from Chicago	2,861	Dallas/Fort Worth to—from Houston	1,543
New York to—from Los Angeles	2,747	Chicago to—from Orlando	1,374
New York to—from Atlanta	2,509	Chicago to—from Phoenix	1,367
New York to—from Washington.	1,922	New York to—from Miami.	1,365
New York to—from West Palm Beach.	1,873	New York to—from Dallas/Fort Worth	1,354
New York to—from San Francisco	1,821	Los Angeles to—from Las Vegas	1,332
New York to—from Las Vegas.	1,817	Atlanta to—from Washington.	1,285
New York to—from San Juan	1,809	Los Angeles to—from Oakland	1,259
Chicago to—from Las Vegas	1,712	Chicago to—from Washington.	1,253
Chicago to—from Los Angeles	1,692	Chicago to—from Atlanta	1,184
Honolulu to—from Kahului, Maui	1,632		

Source: Air Transport Association of America, Washington, DC, *Annual Report.*

Table 1056. **Worldwide Airline Fatalities: 1986 to 2004**

[For scheduled air transport operations]

Year	Fatal accidents	Passenger deaths	Death rate [1]	Death rate [2]	Year	Fatal accidents	Passenger deaths	Death rate [1]	Death rate [2]
1986	24	641	0.07	0.04	1996	24	1,146	0.07	0.05
1987	25	900	0.09	0.06	1997	25	921	0.06	0.04
1988	29	742	0.07	0.04	1998	20	904	0.05	0.03
1989	29	879	0.08	0.05	1999	21	499	0.03	0.02
1990	27	544	0.05	0.03	2000	18	757	0.04	0.03
1991	29	638	0.06	0.03	2001	13	577	0.03	0.02
1992	28	1,070	0.09	0.06	2002	14	791	0.04	0.03
1993	33	864	0.07	0.04	2003	7	466	0.02	0.02
1994	27	1,170	0.09	0.05	2004	9	203	0.01	0.01
1995	25	711	0.05	0.03					

[1] Rate per 100 million passenger miles flown.   [2] Rate per 100 million passenger kilometers flown.

Source: International Civil Aviation Organization, Montreal, Canada, *Civil Aviation Statistics of the World*, annual.

Table 1057. **Aircraft Accidents: 1990 to 2004**

[For years ending December 31]

Item	Unit	1990	1995	2000	2001	2002	2003	2004, prel.
Air carrier accidents, all services [1]	Number...	24	36	56	46	41	54	28
Fatal accidents	Number...	6	3	3	6	-	2	2
Fatalities [2]	Number...	39	168	92	531	-	22	14
Aboard	Number...	12	162	92	525	-	21	14
Rates per 100,000 flight hours:								
Accidents	Rate	0.198	0.267	0.306	0.236	0.237	0.310	0.159
Fatal accidents	Rate	0.049	0.022	0.016	0.011	-	0.011	0.011
Commuter air carrier accidents [3]	Number...	15	12	12	7	7	2	5
Fatal accidents	Number...	3	2	1	2	-	1	-
Fatalities	Number...	6	9	5	13	-	2	-
Aboard	Number...	4	9	5	13	-	2	-
Rates per 100,000 flight hours:								
Accidents	Rate	0.641	0.457	3.247	2.33	2.559	0.627	1.515
Fatal accidents	Rate	0.128	0.076	0.271	0.666	-	0.313	-
On-demand air taxi accidents [4]	Number...	107	75	80	72	60	75	68
Fatal accidents	Number...	29	24	22	18	18	18	24
Fatalities	Number...	51	52	71	60	35	42	65
Aboard	Number...	49	52	68	59	35	40	64
Rates per 100,000 flight hours:								
Accidents	Rate	4.76	3.02	2.04	2.40	2.06	2.56	2.21
Fatal accidents	Rate	1.29	0.97	0.56	0.60	0.62	0.61	0.78
General aviation accidents [5]	Number...	2,242	2,056	1,837	1,727	1,715	1,741	1,614
Fatal accidents	Number...	444	413	345	325	345	352	312
Fatalities	Number...	770	735	596	562	581	632	556
Aboard	Number...	765	728	585	558	575	629	556
Rates per 100,000 flight hours:								
Accidents	Rate	7.85	8.21	6.57	6.78	6.69	6.77	6.22
Fatal accidents	Rate	1.55	1.63	1.21	1.27	1.33	1.37	1.20

- Represents zero.   [1] U.S. air carriers operating under 14 CFR 121. Beginning 2000, includes aircraft with 10 or more seats, previously operating under 14 CFR 135.   [2] Other than persons aboard aircraft who were killed, fatalities resulting from the September 11, 2001, terrorist acts are excluded.   [3] All scheduled service of U.S. air carriers operating under 14 CFR 135. Beginning 2000, only aircraft with fewer than 10 seats.   [4] All nonscheduled service of U.S. air carriers operating under 14 CFR 135.   [5] U.S. civil registered aircraft not operated under 14 CFR 121 or 135.

Source: U.S. National Transportation Safety Board, "Aviation Accident Statistics," Internet site <http://www.ntsb.gov/aviation/stats.htm> (accessed 14 June 2005).

Table 1058. **U.S. Carrier Delays, Cancellations, and Diversions: 1995 to 2004**

[In thousands (5,327.4 represents 5,327,400). For calendar year. See headnote, table 1059]

Item	1995	1996	1997	1998	1999	2000	2001	2002	2003	2004
Total operations	5,327.4	5,352.0	5,411.8	5,384.7	5,527.9	5,683.0	5,967.8	5,271.4	6,488.5	7,129.3
Delays:										
Late departures [1]	827.9	973.9	846.9	870.4	937.3	1,131.7	953.8	717.4	834.4	1,187.6
Late arrivals [2]	1,039.3	1,220.0	1,083.8	1,070.1	1,152.7	1,356.0	1,104.4	868.2	1,057.8	1,421.4
Cancellations [3]	91.9	128.5	97.8	144.5	154.3	187.5	231.2	65.1	101.5	127.8
Diversions [4]	10.5	14.1	12.1	13.2	13.6	14.3	12.9	8.4	11.4	13.8

[1] Late departures comprise flights departing 15 minutes or more after the scheduled departure time.   [2] Late arrivals comprise flights arriving 15 minutes or more after the scheduled arrival time.   [3] A cancelled flight is one that was not operated, but was listed in a carrier's computer reservation system within seven days of the scheduled departure.   [4] A diverted flight is one that left from the scheduled departure airport but flew to a destination point other than the scheduled destination point.

Source: U.S. Bureau of Transportation Statistics, *National Transportation Statistics*, annual. See Internet site <http://www.bts.gov/publications/nts/index.html>.

Transportation   699

Table 1059. On-Time Flight Arrivals and Departures at Major U.S. Airports: 2004

[In percent. Quarterly, based on gate arrival and departure times for domestic scheduled operations of U.S. major airlines. All U.S. airlines with 1 percent or more of total U.S. domestic scheduled airline passenger revenues are required to report on-time data. A flight is considered on time if it operated less than 15 minutes after the scheduled time shown in the carrier's computerized reservation system. See source for data on individual airlines]

Airport	On-time arrivals				On-time departures			
	1st qtr.	2d qtr.	3d qtr.	4th qtr.	1st qtr.	2d qtr.	3d qtr.	4th qtr.
Total, all airports	77.9	77.9	79.3	77.2	82.2	81.7	82.0	80.3
Total major airports.	77.6	77.8	78.9	77.2	81.4	81.2	80.9	79.9
Atlanta, Hartsfield International	73.6	73.1	73.9	70.9	78.4	76.7	76.0	73.3
Baltimore/Washington International	82.1	78.7	79.9	82.7	81.6	78.1	80.0	82.4
Boston, Logan International	79.7	78.0	76.4	77.8	82.9	83.0	80.6	81.9
Charlotte Douglas.	84.2	83.4	83.3	81.7	84.5	83.1	82.4	82.5
Chicago Midway.	78.8	77.5	79.8	81.2	78.7	76.4	77.3	78.6
Chicago, O'Hare	60.2	67.6	78.6	74.5	65.5	71.1	78.9	76.3
Cincinnati International	80.6	81.5	81.4	76.1	82.6	81.9	80.6	77.1
Dallas/Ft. Worth Regional	81.2	80.8	83.4	79.2	81.7	80.7	81.7	79.0
Denver International	83.3	82.1	83.9	83.0	85.7	85.3	85.2	84.2
Detroit, Metro Wayne	80.0	80.4	83.7	81.5	83.5	81.3	83.0	83.0
Fort Lauderdale	75.9	77.1	71.2	77.9	81.5	83.7	77.7	82.3
Houston George Bush.	81.6	75.4	86.3	80.6	89.7	83.0	89.7	86.4
Las Vegas, McCarran International	78.8	78.5	78.5	74.9	80.0	79.1	77.7	74.8
Los Angeles International.	83.4	82.4	82.0	78.9	86.1	86.1	84.9	82.8
Miami International.	78.7	79.8	72.2	80.4	83.6	81.5	71.1	84.2
Minneapolis/St. Paul International	76.2	81.0	83.2	81.4	83.1	84.6	85.6	85.5
Newark International.	77.8	77.3	72.5	77.3	81.3	83.3	76.7	80.6
New York, Kennedy International.	73.6	74.0	71.8	74.0	81.8	83.3	79.5	82.6
New York, LaGuardia	73.4	70.5	69.7	71.3	81.7	80.4	78.3	80.3
Orlando International	80.3	78.4	71.7	81.4	84.7	82.9	75.2	84.9
Philadelphia International.	77.3	74.0	72.5	70.8	78.0	75.8	72.8	71.0
Phoenix, Sky Harbor International	81.5	82.1	81.2	75.2	81.5	79.8	79.9	76.0
Pittsburgh, Greater International	82.2	80.2	80.7	79.3	86.2	82.9	82.8	82.1
Portland International	77.8	81.9	81.4	76.2	83.2	87.8	86.3	81.5
Washington, Ronald Reagan National	78.1	83.4	86.4	80.9	82.8	88.4	89.1	83.9
St. Louis, Lambert	82.4	81.4	80.5	76.0	85.7	85.5	84.5	79.9
Salt Lake City International	74.9	79.6	79.2	73.8	84.3	88.1	87.0	81.7
San Diego International, Lindbergh	77.4	79.2	78.8	75.5	81.7	82.0	79.7	77.3
San Francisco International	80.2	80.1	81.3	80.6	83.9	83.0	84.9	82.3
Seattle-Tacoma International	81.0	79.7	75.4	80.7	86.0	84.6	79.8	84.9
Tampa International	82.6	80.3	78.7	81.3	88.1	86.8	84.3	86.0
Washington/Dulles	84.1	79.3	74.9	77.5	85.6	81.9	78.6	76.9

Source: U.S. Department of Transportation, Aviation Consumer Protection Division, *Air Travel Consumer Report*, monthly. See Internet site <http://airconsumer.ost.dot.gov>.

Table 1060. Consumer Complaints Against U.S. Airlines: 1990 to 2004

[Calendar year data. Represents complaints filed by consumers to the U.S. Department of Transportation, Aviation Consumer Protection Division, regarding service problems with air carrier personnel. See source for data on individual airlines]

Complaint category	1990	1995	1998	1999	2000	2001	2002	2003	2004
Total	7,703	4,629	7,980	17,345	20,564	14,076	7,697	4,601	5,863
Flight problems [1]	3,034	1,133	2,270	6,449	8,698	5,048	1,808	1,049	1,479
Customer service [2]	758	667	1,716	3,657	4,074	2,531	1,478	584	749
Baggage.	1,329	628	1,105	2,351	2,753	1,965	1,082	802	1,088
Ticketing/boarding [3]	624	666	805	1,329	1,405	1,310	898	643	639
Refunds	701	576	601	935	803	942	737	428	377
Fares [4]	312	185	276	584	708	568	436	243	180
Disability [5]	(NA)	(NA)	331	520	612	457	420	325	463
Oversales [6]	399	263	387	673	759	539	364	223	265
Discrimination [7]	(NA)	(NA)	(NA)	(NA)	(NA)	164	176	71	92
Advertising	96	66	39	57	42	42	43	13	41
Tours	29	18	23	28	25	11	([8])	([8])	([8])
Animals	(NA)	(NA)	(NA)	(NA)	1	6	-	2	3
Smoking.	74	15	([9])	([9])	([9])	([9])	([9])	([9])	([9])
Credit.	5	4	([9])	([9])	([9])	([9])	([9])	([9])	([9])
Other	342	408	427	762	684	493	255	218	487

- Represents zero. NA Not available. [1] Cancellations, delays, etc. from schedule. [2] Unhelpful employees, inadequate meals or cabin service, treatment of delayed passengers. [3] Errors in reservations and ticketing; problems in making reservations and obtaining tickets. [4] Incorrect or incomplete information about fares, discount fare conditions, and availability, etc. [5] Prior to 1998, included in ticketing/boarding. [6] All bumping problems, whether or not airline complied with DOT regulations. [7] Allegations of discrimination by airlines due to factors other than disability, such as race, religion, national origin or sex. [8] Included in "Other" beginning 2002. [9] Included in "Other" beginning 1998.

Source: U.S. Department of Transportation, Aviation Consumer Protection Division, *Air Travel Consumer Report*, monthly. See Internet site <http://airconsumer.ost.dot.gov>.

Table 1061. Commuter/Regional Airline Operations—Summary: 1990 to 2004

[Calendar year data (42.1 represents 42,100,000). Commuter/regional airlines operate primarily aircraft of predominately 75 passengers or less and 18,000 pounds of payload capacity serving short haul and small community markets. Represents operations within all North America by U.S. Regional Carriers. Averages are means. For definition of mean, see Guide to Tabular Presentation]

Item	Unit	1990	1995	2000	2001	2002	2003	2004
Passenger carriers operating	Number...	150	124	94	91	91	82	74
Passengers enplaned	Millions...	42.1	57.2	84.6	82.8	98.4	113.0	134.7
Average passengers enplaned per carrier...	1,000	277.5	461.4	830.4	910.2	1,080.9	1,379.3	1,820.0
Revenue passenger miles (RPM)	Billions...	7.61	12.75	25.27	25.74	32.77	43.34	56.21
Average RPMs per carrier	Millions...	50.75	102.80	268.83	282.83	360.11	528.51	759.54
Airports served	Number...	811	780	729	726	707	709	735
Average trip length	Miles.....	183	223	299	311	333	384	417
Passenger aircraft operated	Number...	1,917	2,138	2,271	2,323	2,385	2,569	2,757
Average seating capacity (seats)	Number...	22.1	24.6	31.7	33.5	35.1	37.7	39.9
Fleet flying hours [1]	1,000	3,447	4,659	5,362	5,161	5,248	6,088	6,587
Average annual utilization per aircraft	Hours....	1,798	2,179	2,368	2,222	2,201	2,370	2,389

[1] Prior to 1995, utilization results reflected airborne rather than block hours.

Source: Regional Airline Association and AvStat Associates, Washington, DC, *Annual Report of the Regional Airline Industry* (copyright).

Table 1062. Airports, Aircraft, and Airmen: 1980 to 2003

[As of December 31 or for years ending December 31]

Item	1980	1985	1990	1995	2000	2001	2002	2003
Airports, total [1]	15,161	16,319	17,490	18,224	19,281	19,356	19,572	19,581
Public	4,814	5,858	5,589	5,415	5,317	5,294	5,286	5,286
Percent—with lighted runways	66.2	68.1	71.4	74.3	75.9	76.2	76	76.2
With paved runways	72.3	66.7	70.7	73.3	74.3	74.6	75	74.5
Private	10,347	10,461	11,901	12,809	13,964	14,062	14,286	14,295
Percent—with lighted runways	15.2	9.1	7.0	6.4	7.2	8.0	8.3	9.8
With paved runways	13.3	17.4	31.5	33.0	32.0	32.4	32.4	37.4
Certificated [2]	730	700	680	667	651	635	633	628
Civil	(X)	(X)	(X)	572	563	560	558	555
Civil military	(X)	(X)	(X)	95	88	75	75	73
General aviation	14,431	15,619	16,810	17,557	18,630	18,721	18,939	18,953
Active air carrier fleet [3]	3,808	4,678	6,083	7,411	8,055	8,497	8,194	8,176
Fixed wing	3,803	4,673	6,072	7,293	8,016	8,370	8,161	8,144
Helicopter	2	5	11	118	39	127	33	32
General aviation fleet [4]	211,043	196,500	198,000	188,089	217,533	211,446	211,244	(NA)
Fixed-wing	200,097	184,700	184,500	162,342	183,276	177,697	176,283	(NA)
Turbojet	2,992	4,100	4,100	4,559	7,001	7,787	8,355	(NA)
Turboprop	4,090	5,000	5,300	4,995	5,762	6,596	6,841	(NA)
Piston	193,014	175,600	175,200	152,788	170,513	163,314	161,087	(NA)
Rotocraft	6,001	6,000	6,900	5,830	7,150	6,783	6,648	(NA)
Other	4,945	5,800	6,600	4,741	6,700	6,545	6,377	(NA)
Gliders	(NA)	(NA)	(NA)	2,182	2,041	1,904	1,951	(NA)
Lighter than air	(NA)	(NA)	(NA)	2,559	4,660	4,641	4,426	(NA)
Experimental	(NA)	(NA)	(NA)	15,176	20,407	20,421	21,936	(NA)
Airman certificates held: [5]								
Pilot, total	827,071	709,540	702,659	639,184	625,581	612,274	631,762	625,011
Women	52,902	43,082	40,515	38,032	36,757	34,257	38,257	37,694
Student	199,833	146,652	128,663	101,279	93,064	86,731	85,991	87,296
Recreational	(NA)	(NA)	87	232	340	316	317	310
Airplane:								
Private	357,479	311,086	299,111	261,399	251,561	243,823	245,230	241,045
Commercial	183,442	151,632	149,666	133,980	121,858	120,502	125,920	123,990
Air transport	69,569	82,740	107,732	123,877	141,596	144,702	144,708	143,504
Rotocraft only [6]	6,030	8,123	9,567	7,183	7,775	7,727	7,770	7,916
Glider only	7,039	8,168	7,833	11,234	9,387	8,473	21,826	20,950
Flight instructor certificates	60,440	58,940	63,775	77,613	80,931	82,875	86,089	87,816
Instrument ratings	260,462	258,559	297,073	298,798	311,944	315,276	317,389	315,413
Nonpilot [7]	368,356	395,139	492,237	651,341	547,453	513,100	515,570	509,835
Mechanic	250,157	274,100	344,282	405,294	344,434	310,850	315,928	313,032
Repairmen	(NA)	(NA)	(NA)	61,233	38,208	40,085	37,114	37,248
Parachute rigger	9,547	9,395	10,094	11,824	10,477	7,927	8,063	7,883
Ground instructor	61,550	58,214	66,882	96,165	72,326	72,261	73,658	72,692
Dispatcher	6,799	8,511	11,002	15,642	16,340	16,070	16,695	16,955
Flight navigator	1,936	1,542	1,290	916	570	509	431	382
Flight engineer	38,367	43,377	58,687	60,267	65,098	65,398	63,681	61,643

NA Not available. X Not applicable. [1] Existing airports, heliports, seaplane bases, etc. recorded with FAA. Includes military airports with joint civil and military use. Includes U.S. outlying areas. Airport-type definitions: Public—publicly owned and under control of a public agency; private—owned by a private individual or corporation. May or may not be open for public use. [2] Certificated airports serve air-carriers with aircraft seating more that 30 passengers. [3] Air-carrier aircraft are aircraft carrying passengers or cargo for hire under 14 CFR 121 (large aircraft—more than 30 seats) and 14 CFR 135 (small aircraft— 30 seats or fewer). [4] Beginning 1995 excludes commuters. [5] Source: U.S. Federal Aviation Administration. See Internet site <http://apo.faa.gov/pubs.asp>. Prior years in the *Statistical Handbook of Aviation*, annual. [6] Data for 1980 and 1985 are for helicopters only. [7] All certificates on record. No medical examination required

Source: Except as noted, U.S. Bureau of Transportation Statistics, *National Transportation Statistics*, annual. See Internet site <http://www.bts.gov/publications/nts/index.html>.

Table 1063. **Freight Carried on Major U.S. Waterways: 1980 to 2003**

[In millions of tons (4.0 represents 4,000,000)]

Item	1980	1985	1990	1995	1999	2000	2001	2002	2003
Atlantic intracoastal waterway	4.0	3.1	4.2	3.5	3.4	3.1	2.5	1.9	1.9
Great Lakes.	183.5	148.1	167.1	177.8	182.9	187.5	171.4	167.2	156.5
Gulf intracoastal waterway	94.5	102.5	115.4	118.0	109.6	113.8	112.2	107.7	117.8
Mississippi River system [1]	584.2	527.8	659.1	707.2	716.9	715.5	714.8	712.8	676.8
Mississippi River mainstem	441.5	384.0	475.3	520.3	512.3	515.6	504.2	501.7	478.0
Ohio River system [2]	179.3	203.9	260.0	267.6	277.9	274.4	281.8	280.9	261.3
Columbia River.	49.2	42.4	51.4	57.1	50.7	55.2	50.3	45.0	47.2
Snake River.	5.1	3.5	4.8	6.8	5.8	6.7	5.6	4.3	5.3

[1] Main channels and all tributaries of the Mississippi, Illinois, Missouri and Ohio Rivers. [2] Main channels and all navigable tributaries and embayments of the Ohio, Tennessee, and Cumberland Rivers.

Source: U.S. Army Corps of Engineers, *Waterborne Commerce of the United States*, annual. See Internet site <http://www.iwr.usace.army.mil/ndc/wcsc/wcsc.htm>

Table 1064. **Waterborne Commerce by Type of Commodity: 1995 to 2003**

[In millions of short tons (2,240.4 represents 2,240,400,000). Domestic trade includes all commercial movements between United States ports and on inland rivers, Great Lakes, canals, and connecting channels of the United States, Puerto Rico, and Virgin Islands]

Commodity	1995	2000	2002	2003			
				Total	Domestic	Foreign imports	Foreign exports
Total	2,240.4	2,424.6	2,340.3	2,394.3	1,016.1	1,004.8	373.3
Coal.	324.5	297.0	286.9	281.2	213.5	25.0	42.6
Petroleum and petroleum products	907.1	1,044.0	1,017.9	1,080.5	360.8	661.5	58.2
Crude petroleum	504.6	571.4	566.0	604.5	87.5	515.7	1.2
Petroleum products [1]	402.5	472.4	451.9	476.1	273.3	145.8	57.0
Gasoline	114.4	125.2	122.6	126.4	87.5	32.3	6.6
Distillate fuel oil.	76.7	91.7	88.4	101.7	65.6	29.1	7.0
Residual fuel oil.	111.9	131.6	117.0	116.7	76.0	31.3	9.4
Chemicals and related products	153.7	172.4	167.6	171.3	75.7	42.0	53.6
Fertilizers.	35.7	35.1	32.4	35.2	13.7	8.6	12.9
Other chemicals and related products. . . .	118.0	137.3	135.2	136.1	62.0	33.4	40.7
Crude material, inedible.	381.7	380.3	352.0	358.0	211.6	102.2	44.2
Forest products, wood and chips	47.2	33.1	25.1	23.6	8.1	7.4	8.1
Pulp and waste paper	14.9	13.6	14.0	16.1	0.2	1.6	14.3
Soil, sand, gravel, rock, and stone [1]	152.5	165.0	166.1	170.8	130.8	37.5	2.5
Limestone	54.0	67.4	68.8	64.7	50.3	12.5	1.8
Phosphate rock	10.7	3.4	6.2	5.7	3.1	2.5	0.0
Sand & gravel.	77.0	79.0	76.0	85.3	73.7	11.1	0.5
Iron ore and scrap. . . . . :	104.9	97.9	85.8	80.9	52.9	16.9	11.1
Marine shells	0.5	0.3	0.3	0.1	0.1	0.0	0.0
Non-ferrous ores and scrap.	27.9	29.2	24.3	26.2	6.9	16.9	2.4
Sulphur, clay and salt.	23.4	11.3	9.8	8.4	0.9	2.8	4.7
Slag	1.9	4.0	3.1	3.6	1.7	1.8	0.0
Other nonmetal minerals	8.4	25.9	23.3	28.3	9.9	17.4	1.0
Primary manufactured goods	106.3	153.0	140.8	134.7	41.7	76.4	16.5
Papers products	13.1	12.1	11.0	11.8	0.3	5.6	6.0
Lime, cement and glass	33.9	55.9	51.2	49.1	18.1	29.8	1.2
Primary iron and steel products	44.1	57.1	46.3	41.7	14.3	24.5	2.9
Primary nonferrous metal products.	12.3	25.5	29.3	28.6	8.9	13.6	6.2
Primary wood products.	2.9	2.5	3.1	3.3	0.1	2.9	0.3
Food and farm products.	303.2	283.3	280.0	265.7	90.9	32.8	142.0
Fish	3.6	2.4	2.7	2.6	0.1	1.6	0.9
Grain [1]	167.9	145.2	139.3	130.1	52.4	1.6	76.2
Wheat	48.5	43.4	36.0	37.3	10.8	0.2	26.4
Corn	105.0	88.2	89.8	78.2	36.7	0.1	41.4
Oilseeds	46.1	57.6	60.5	56.9	23.3	0.3	33.4
Soybeans.	42.0	47.3	49.8	49.7	20.4	0.0	29.3
Vegetables products	9.0	8.9	8.5	8.3	0.9	3.5	3.9
Processed grain and animal feed.	33.0	23.1	21.9	20.3	7.2	0.9	12.2
Other agricultural products	43.5	46.1	47.2	47.5	7.1	25.0	15.5
All manufactured equipment, machinery and products.	57.0	83.6	81.9	90.0	18.7	58.5	12.8
Waste and scrap, n.e.c.[2]	5.4	4.3	2.7	3.1	3.1	-	-
Unknown or not elsewhere classified	1.6	6.8	10.4	9.7	0.1	6.3	3.3

- Represents or rounds to zero. [1] Includes commodities not shown separately. [2] n.e.c. Not elsewhere classified.

Source: U.S. Army Corps of Engineers, *Waterborne Commerce of the United States*, annual. See Internet site <http://www.iwr.usace.army.mil/ndc/wcsc/wcsc.htm>.

Table 1065. Cargo-Carrying U.S.-Flag Fleet by Area of Operation: 2002

[Tons in thousands of metric tons (30,495 represents 30,495,000). As of July 1. One ton equals 100 cubic feet of space. Represents active vessels]

Area of operation	Total fleet Number	Total fleet Tons	Liquid carriers Number	Liquid carriers Tons	Dry bulk carriers Number	Dry bulk carriers Tons	Containerships Number	Containerships Tons	Other freighters[1] Number	Other freighters[1] Tons
VESSELS OF 1,000 GROSS TONS AND OVER										
Grand total[2]	3,869	30,495	2,196	15,714	759	5,889	123	3,108	791	5,784
Foreign waterborne trade[2]	268	5,319	53	946	116	1,115	61	2,510	38	748
Domestic trade	3,430	21,921	2,116	13,887	643	4,774	57	512	614	2,748
Coastal	1,344	13,299	567	8,770	355	2,146	57	512	365	1,871
Inland waterway	2,000	6,454	1,542	5,075	227	576	-	-	231	803
Great Lakes	86	2,168	7	42	61	2,052	-	-	18	74
Government	171	3,255	27	881	-	-	5	86	139	2,288
Total self-propelled	462	14,914	114	6,230	69	2,600	90	2,898	189	3,186
Foreign waterborne trade[2]	127	4,588	17	771	12	579	61	2,510	37	728
Domestic trade	164	7,071	70	4,578	57	2,021	24	302	13	170
Coastal	105	5,063	68	4,559	2	71	24	302	11	131
Inland waterway	-	-	-	-	-	-	-	-	-	-
Great Lakes	59	2,008	2	19	55	1,950	-	-	2	39
Government	171	3,255	27	881	-	-	5	86	139	2,288
Total non-self-propelled[3]	3,407	15,581	2,082	9,484	690	3,289	33	210	602	2,598
Foreign waterborne trade[2]	141	731	36	175	104	536	-	-	1	20
Domestic trade	3,266	14,850	2,046	9,309	586	2,753	33	210	601	2,578
Coastal	1,239	8,236	499	4,211	353	2,075	33	210	354	1,740
Inland waterway	2,000	6,454	1,542	5,075	227	576	-	-	231	803
Great Lakes	27	160	5	23	6	102	-	-	16	35
VESSELS LESS THAN 1,000 GROSS TONS										
Grand total[2]	32,229	46,381	2,214	3,965	23,010	36,438	4	2	7,001	5,976
Foreign waterborne trade[2]	109	50	3	1	106	49	-	-	-	-
Domestic trade	32,120	46,331	2,211	3,964	22,904	36,389	4	2	7,001	5,976
Coastal	3,930	3,562	241	982	573	741	1	1	3,115	1,838
Inland waterway	27,890	42,394	1,961	2,975	22,211	35,478	3	1	3,715	3,940
Great Lakes	300	375	9	7	120	170	-	-	171	198
Total self-propelled	384	948	77	797	4	2	-	-	303	149
Domestic trade	384	948	77	797	4	2	-	-	303	149
Coastal	256	902	71	795	-	-	-	-	185	107
Inland waterway	109	27	2	-	-	-	-	-	107	27
Great Lakes	19	19	4	2	4	2	-	-	11	15
Total non-self-propelled[3]	31,845	45,433	2,137	3,168	23,006	36,436	4	2	6,698	5,827
Foreign waterborne trade[2]	109	50	3	1	106	49	-	-	-	-
Domestic trade	31,736	45,383	2,134	3,167	22,900	36,387	4	2	6,698	5,827
Coastal	3,674	2,660	170	187	573	741	1	1	2,930	1,731
Inland waterway	27,781	42,367	1,959	2,975	22,211	35,478	3	1	3,608	3,913
Great Lakes	281	356	5	5	116	168	-	-	160	183

- Represents zero. [1] Includes general cargo, ro-ro (roll-on roll-off), multi-purpose, LASH (lighter aboard ship) vessels and deck barges. Excludes offshore supply vessels. [2] Includes U.S./Canada TransLakes. [3] Includes Integrated Tug Barge (ITB) Units.

Source: U.S. Maritime Administration, Office of Statistical & Economic Analysis; adapted from Corps of Engineers, Lloyds Maritime Information Service, U.S. Coast Guard and Customs Service data.

Table 1066. **Selected U.S. Ports by Tons of Traffic: 2003**

[In thousands of short tons, except rank (7,656 represents 7,656,000). For calendar year for the top 70 ports. Represents tons of cargo shipped from or received by the specified port. Excludes cargo carried on general ferries; coal and petroleum products loaded from shore facilities directly onto bunkers of vessels for fuel; and amounts of less than 100 tons of government owned-equipment in support of Corps projects]

Port name	Rank	Total	Foreign Total	Foreign Inbound	Foreign Outbound	Domestic
Albany, NY	62	7,656	1,644	1,326	318	6,012
Anacortes, WA.	41	15,820	2,598	1,492	1,106	13,222
Ashtabula, OH	50	10,427	5,838	960	4,878	4,589
Baltimore, MD	18	40,183	24,096	18,985	5,111	16,087
Baton Rouge, LA	10	61,264	23,152	18,702	4,450	38,112
Beaumont, TX	4	87,541	68,787	63,337	5,451	18,754
Boston, MA	31	24,832	16,442	15,634	807	8,391
Burns Waterway Harbor, IN	60	8,069	1,655	1,270	385	6,414
Calcite, MI	64	6,880	579	70	509	6,302
Camden-Gloucester, NJ.	65	6,819	4,334	3,764	570	2,484
Charleston, SC	30	25,199	18,779	13,042	5,737	6,420
Chicago, IL	36	22,610	1,734	1,057	677	20,876
Cincinnati, OH	48	11,828	-	-	-	11,828
Cleveland, OH	47	12,621	3,112	2,708	404	9,509
Conneaut, OH	67	6,705	3,117	178	2,939	3,588
Corpus Christi, TX	7	77,225	53,394	44,759	8,635	23,831
Detroit, MI	43	14,308	3,883	3,494	389	10,425
Duluth-Superior, MN and WI.	19	38,343	13,083	529	12,554	25,261
Freeport, TX	24	30,537	25,101	22,666	2,435	5,436
Galveston, TX	63	7,545	3,788	1,065	2,723	3,757
Gary, IN	56	9,010	573	394	179	8,437
Honolulu, HI	40	17,836	5,408	4,919	489	12,428
Houston, TX	2	190,923	126,893	90,336	36,558	64,030
Huntington - Tristate	6	77,641	-	-	-	77,641
Indiana Harbor, IN	44	14,133	360	314	46	13,773
Jacksonville, FL	37	21,731	10,831	9,879	952	10,900
Kalama, WA	61	7,659	6,658	220	6,438	1,001
Lake Charles, LA	12	53,364	31,805	27,825	3,980	21,558
Long Beach, CA	8	69,195	52,371	37,970	14,402	16,824
Los Angeles, CA	13	51,327	42,791	29,962	12,829	8,536
Louisville, KY.	59	8,477	-	-	-	8,477
Marcus Hook, PA	29	26,164	16,087	16,077	10	10,076
Matagorda Ship Channel, TX	49	11,673	8,024	6,451	1,573	3,649
Memphis, TN.	39	18,191	-	-	-	18,191
Miami, FL	55	9,165	7,796	4,916	2,881	1,369
Mobile, AL.	14	50,214	25,028	17,553	7,475	25,186
New Castle, DE	58	8,538	1,329	1,329	-	7,209
New Haven, CT.	51	10,385	3,070	2,954	116	7,315
New Orleans, LA	5	83,847	48,876	20,890	27,987	34,970
New York, NY and NJ	3	145,889	79,685	70,251	9,434	66,204
Newport News, VA	52	10,257	4,791	936	3,855	5,466
Nikishka, AK	70	6,420	3,311	227	3,084	3,109
Norfolk Harbor, VA	23	31,195	24,304	9,219	15,085	6,891
Oakland, CA	46	12,627	10,063	4,203	5,860	2,564
Pascagoula, MS.	22	31,292	20,783	17,514	3,269	10,509
Paulsboro, NJ	26	27,283	18,219	17,908	310	9,065
Philadelphia, PA.	20	33,249	18,793	18,616	177	14,456
Pittsburgh, PA	17	41,675	-	-	-	41,675
Plaquemines, LA, Port of	11	55,917	19,002	8,520	10,482	36,915
Port Arthur, TX.	27	27,170	18,467	14,259	4,207	8,703
Port Everglades, FL	33	23,040	10,408	8,427	1,981	12,633
Portland, ME.	25	29,161	27,307	27,134	173	1,854
Portland, OR.	28	26,796	15,753	4,398	11,354	11,043
Presque Isle, MI.	57	8,776	1,144	-	1,144	7,632
Providence, RI.	54	9,214	4,674	4,402	271	4,540
Richmond, CA.	34	23,001	10,875	10,017	858	12,125
San Juan, PR	42	14,556	5,444	5,009	436	9,111
Savannah, GA.	32	23,369	21,502	13,175	8,328	1,866
Seattle, WA.	38	19,448	13,573	6,749	6,825	5,875
South Louisiana, LA, Port of.	1	198,825	80,433	30,857	49,576	118,392
St. Louis, MO and IL.	21	32,431	-	-	-	32,431
Stoneport, MI	69	6,445	55	-	55	6,390
Tacoma, WA.	35	22,966	15,409	5,703	9,707	7,556
Tampa, FL	16	48,252	17,369	9,231	8,138	30,883
Texas City, TX.	9	61,338	43,392	40,185	3,207	17,946
Toledo, OH	53	9,864	7,695	4,243	3,452	2,169
Two Harbors, MN.	45	13,033	-	-	-	13,033
Valdez, AK	15	49,857	6	-	6	49,851
Vancouver, WA	68	6,631	4,557	681	3,876	2,074
Wilmington, NC	66	6,811	3,501	2,740	762	3,310

- Represents zero.

Source: U.S. Army Corps of Engineers, *Waterborne Commerce of the United States, 2003.* See Internet site <http://www.iwr.usace.army.mil/ndc/>

Table 1067. **Highway Mileage—Urban and Rural by Ownership: 1980 to 2003**

[In thousands (3,955 represents 3,955,000). As of Dec. 31. Includes Puerto Rico beginning 1999]

Type and control	1980	1985	1990	1995	1999	2000	2001	2002	2003
Total mileage [1]	[2]3,955	3,862	3,880	3,912	3,932	3,951	3,963	3,982	3,990
Urban mileage [3]	624	691	757	819	853	859	884	902	954
Under state control	79	111	96	112	111	112	110	112	124
Under local control	543	578	661	706	740	746	771	787	831
Rural mileage	3,331	3,171	3,123	3,093	3,079	3,092	3,079	3,080	3,036
Under state control	702	773	703	691	663	664	665	665	653
Under local control	2,270	2,173	2,242	2,231	2,299	2,311	2,295	2,297	2,263
Under federal control	262	225	178	170	117	117	119	118	120

[1] Beginning 1985, includes only public road mileage as defined 23 USC 402. [2] Includes 98,000 miles of nonpublic road mileage previously contained in other rural categories. [3] Includes a small amount of road owned by the federal government, such as roads in federal parks that are not part of a state or local highway system.
Source: U.S. Federal Highway Administration, *Highway Statistics*, annual. See Internet site <http://www.fhwa.dot.gov/policy/ohpi/hss/hsspubs.htm>.

Table 1068. **Highway Mileage—Functional Systems and Urban/Rural: 2003**

[As of Dec. 31. Excludes Puerto Rico. For definition of fuctional systems see text, this section]

State	Total	Functional systems					Urban	Rural
		Interstate	Other freeways and expressways	Arterial	Collector	Local		
U.S.	3,974,107	46,508	9,870	383,392	788,926	2,745,411	940,969	3,033,138
AL	94,434	905	21	8,795	20,530	64,183	20,958	73,476
AK	14,230	1,082	-	1,513	2,753	8,882	2,070	12,160
AZ	57,529	1,167	150	4,664	8,549	42,999	21,900	35,629
AR	98,541	656	90	6,839	20,077	70,879	10,808	87,733
CA	169,549	2,458	1,434	27,133	32,074	106,450	85,622	83,927
CO	86,821	956	279	8,191	16,586	60,809	18,128	68,693
CT	21,089	346	236	2,785	3,037	14,685	14,969	6,120
DE	5,894	41	14	630	939	4,270	2,029	3,865
DC	1,536	13	22	264	152	1,085	1,536	-
FL	120,375	1,471	470	12,162	14,194	92,078	68,479	51,896
GA	116,534	1,245	123	13,126	23,342	78,698	28,557	87,977
HI	4,309	55	34	752	831	2,637	2,128	2,181
ID	46,927	611	-	3,841	10,075	32,400	4,410	42,517
IL	138,526	2,170	88	14,030	21,701	100,537	37,007	101,519
IN	94,597	1,169	136	7,963	22,663	62,666	20,600	73,997
IA	113,516	782	-	9,680	31,485	71,569	10,705	102,811
KS	135,012	874	133	9,197	33,364	91,444	10,593	124,419
KY	77,011	763	65	5,850	16,040	54,293	11,982	65,029
LA	60,937	904	34	5,246	10,132	44,621	13,950	46,987
ME	22,693	367	18	2,288	5,975	14,045	2,633	20,060
MD	30,688	481	287	3,732	4,825	21,363	16,780	13,908
MA	35,590	569	288	6,188	4,836	23,709	27,681	7,909
MI	122,222	1,243	306	12,101	25,814	82,758	35,088	87,134
MN	131,893	912	153	12,702	29,602	88,524	16,209	115,684
MS	74,105	685	46	7,372	15,286	50,716	10,661	63,444
MO	124,685	1,181	326	9,414	24,976	88,788	17,576	107,109
MT	69,450	1,192	-	6,038	16,368	45,852	2,753	66,697
NE	93,198	482	21	8,007	20,778	63,910	5,767	87,431
NV	33,977	560	52	2,875	5,210	25,280	5,727	28,250
NH	15,630	235	37	1,609	2,789	10,960	3,036	12,594
NJ	38,952	431	402	5,538	3,839	28,742	31,541	7,411
NM	63,953	1,000	5	5,028	7,234	50,686	6,814	57,139
NY	113,124	1,674	798	13,502	20,557	76,593	41,145	71,979
NC	102,160	1,019	299	8,937	17,621	74,284	24,410	77,750
ND	86,782	572	-	5,879	11,736	68,595	1,834	84,948
OH	123,522	1,574	484	10,868	22,518	88,078	43,262	80,260
OK	112,578	930	186	8,163	25,305	77,994	14,991	97,587
OR	65,951	728	53	6,818	17,503	40,849	11,067	54,884
PA	120,423	1,758	516	13,194	19,802	85,153	37,689	82,734
RI	6,415	71	85	832	879	4,548	5,193	1,222
SC	66,230	842	71	6,876	13,378	45,063	10,685	55,545
SD	83,688	679	-	6,352	19,234	57,423	2,264	81,424
TN	88,518	1,073	146	8,935	17,905	60,459	20,418	68,100
TX	301,987	3,233	1,170	28,537	63,508	205,539	83,287	218,700
UT	42,716	940	7	3,360	7,838	30,571	8,189	34,527
VT	14,359	320	19	1,299	3,129	9,592	1,382	12,977
VA	71,242	1,118	224	8,250	14,081	47,569	21,011	50,231
WA	82,264	764	290	7,324	16,807	57,079	19,458	62,806
WV	36,993	549	9	3,170	8,777	24,488	3,190	33,803
WI	113,270	745	238	11,870	21,408	79,009	20,293	92,977
WY	27,482	913	5	3,673	10,884	12,007	2,504	24,978

- Represents zero.
Source: U.S. Federal Highway Administration, *Highway Statistics*, annual. See Internet site <http://www.fhwa.dot.gov/policy/ohpi/hss/hsspubs.htm>.

Table 1069. Commodity Shipments—Value, Tons, and Ton-Miles: 1997 and 2002

[6,859,805 represents $6,859,805,000,000. For business establishments in mining, manufacturing, wholesale trade and selected retail industries. 2002 industries classified by the 1997 North American Classification System (NAICS); 1997 classified by the Standard Industry Classification (SIC) Manual. Selected auxiliary establishments are also included. See source for details. Based on the Economic Census; see Appendix III]

Mode of transportation	Value (mil. dol.)		Tons (1,000)		Ton-miles (mil.)	
	1997	2002	1997	2002	1997	2002
All modes	6,859,805	8,397,210	10,566,330	11,667,919	2,592,590	3,137,898
Single modes	5,673,920	7,049,383	9,928,296	11,086,660	2,317,973	2,867,938
Truck [1]	4,936,491	6,235,001	7,292,256	7,842,836	998,035	1,255,908
Rail	318,915	310,884	1,543,727	1,873,884	1,021,250	1,261,612
Water	75,765	89,344	535,558	681,227	240,572	282,659
Air (includes truck and air)	229,272	264,959	4,378	3,760	6,124	5,835
Pipeline [2]	113,476	149,195	552,377	684,953	(S)	(S)
Multiple modes	913,164	1,079,185	212,981	216,686	202,602	225,715
Parcel, U.S. Postal Service or courier	823,311	987,746	22,100	25,513	16,729	19,004
Truck and rail	75,566	69,929	53,730	42,984	55,371	45,525
Other multiple modes	14,287	21,510	137,151	148,189	130,503	161,187
Other and unknown modes	272,722	268,642	425,053	364,573	72,015	44,245

S Data do not meet publication standards due to high sampling variability or other reasons. [1] Truck as a single mode includes shipments that went by private truck only, for hire truck only, or a combination of private truck and for-hire truck. [2] Commodity Flow Survey data exclude shipments of crude oil.

Source: U.S. Bureau of Transportation Statistics and U.S. Census Bureau, "2002 Economic Census, Transportation, 2002 Commodity Flow Survey," Series EC02TCF-US, issued December 2004. See Internet site <http://www.census.gov/cfs>.

Table 1070. Hazardous Shipments—Value, Tons, and Ton-Miles: 2002

[660,181 represents $660,181,000,000. Based on the Economic Census; see Appendix III. See also headnote, table 1069]

Mode of transportation	Value (mil. dol.)		Tons (1,000)		Ton-miles (mil.)		Average miles per shipment
	Total	Percent	Total	Percent	Total	Percent	
All modes	660,181	100.0	2,191,519	100.0	326,727	100.0	136
Single modes	644,489	97.6	2,158,533	98.5	311,897	95.5	105
Truck [1]	419,630	63.6	1,159,514	52.9	110,163	33.7	86
For-hire truck	189,803	28.8	449,503	20.5	65,112	19.9	285
Private truck	226,660	34.3	702,186	32.0	44,087	13.5	38
Rail	31,339	4.7	109,369	5.0	72,087	22.1	695
Water	46,856	7.1	228,197	10.4	70,649	21.6	(S)
Air (includes truck and air)	1,643	0.2	64	-	85	-	2,080
Pipeline [2]	145,021	22.0	661,390	30.2	(S)	(S)	(S)
Multiple modes	9,631	1.5	18,745	0.9	12,488	3.8	849
Parcel, U.S. Postal Service or courier	4,268	0.6	245	-	119	-	837
Other multiple modes	5,363	0.8	18,500	0.8	12,369	3.8	1,371
Other and unknown modes	6,061	0.9	14,241	0.6	2,342	0.7	57
Class of material	660,181	100.0	2,191,519	100.0	326,727	100.0	136
Class 1, explosives	7,901	1.2	5,000	0.2	1,568	0.5	651
Class 2, gasses	73,932	11.2	213,358	9.7	37,262	11.4	95
Class 3, flammable liquids	490,238	74.3	1,788,986	81.6	218,574	66.9	106
Class 4, flammable solids	6,566	1.0	11,300	0.5	4,391	1.3	158
Class 5, oxidizers and organic peroxides . . .	5,471	0.8	12,670	0.6	4,221	1.3	407
Class 6, toxic (poison)	8,275	1.3	8,459	0.4	4,254	1.3	626
Class 7, radioactive materials	5,850	0.9	57	-	44	-	(S)
Class 8, corrosive materials	38,324	5.8	90,671	4.1	36,260	11.1	301
Class 9, miscellaneous dangerous goods . . .	23,625	3.6	61,018	2.8	20,153	6.2	368

- Rounds to zero. S Data do not meet publication standards due to high sampling variability or other reasons. [1] Truck as a single mode includes shipments that went by private truck only, for-hire truck only, or a combination of private truck and for-hire truck. [2] Commodity Flow Survey data exclude shipments of crude oil.

Source: U.S. Bureau of Transportation Statistics and U.S. Census Bureau, "2002 Economic Census, Transportation, 2002 Commodity Flow Survey, Hazardous Shipments Series EC02TCF-US(HM)," issued December 2004. See Internet site <http://www.census.gov/cfs>.

Table 1071. Shipments by Commodity: 2002

[8,397,210 represents $8,397,210,000,000. Based on the Economic Census; see Appendix III. See also headnote, table 1069]

Mode of transportation	Value (mil. dol.) Total	Percent	Tons (1,000) Total	Percent	Ton-miles (mil.) Total	Percent	Average miles per shipment
Total	8,397,210	100.0	11,667,919	100.0	3,137,898	100.0	546
Live animals and live fish	7,410	-	6,118	-	1,586	-	530
Cereal grains	53,835	0.6	561,089	4.8	264,239	8.4	138
Other agricultural products	129,471	1.5	259,178	2.2	109,362	3.5	481
Animal feed and products of animal origin, n.e.c. [1]	52,142	0.6	227,991	2.0	51,158	1.6	167
Meat, fish, seafood, and their preparations	201,304	2.4	84,506	0.7	41,352	1.3	162
Milled grain products and preparations, and bakery products	113,379	1.4	109,311	0.9	49,001	1.6	189
Other prepared foodstuffs and fats and oils	355,561	4.2	448,924	3.8	161,565	5.1	179
Alcoholic beverages	108,991	1.3	89,434	0.8	25,735	0.8	55
Tobacco products	69,868	0.8	4,370	-	983	-	334
Monumental or building stone	3,039	-	22,451	0.2	1,571	-	170
Natural sands	3,644	-	472,975	4.1	29,990	1.0	45
Gravel and crushed stone	12,850	0.2	1,866,487	16.0	105,826	3.4	30
Nonmetallic minerals, n.e.c.	10,066	0.1	184,632	1.6	56,630	1.8	185
Metallic ores and concentrates	14,027	0.2	98,267	0.8	63,028	2.0	474
Coal	22,875	0.3	1,239,862	10.6	686,279	21.9	120
Gasoline and aviation turbine fuel	279,407	3.3	1,063,569	9.1	117,219	3.7	52
Fuel oils	116,119	1.4	549,007	4.7	55,464	1.8	32
Coal and petroleum products, n.e.c. [1]	82,130	1.0	447,975	3.8	93,001	3.0	102
Basic chemicals	153,656	1.8	347,670	3.0	115,961	3.7	417
Pharmaceutical products	479,117	5.7	24,270	0.2	11,337	0.4	693
Fertilizers	34,049	0.4	264,319	2.3	87,605	2.8	157
Chemical products and preparations, n.e.c. [1]	226,598	2.7	105,962	0.9	53,657	1.7	385
Plastics and rubber	325,673	3.9	139,973	1.2	80,827	2.6	424
Logs and other wood in the rough	5,756	-	(S)	(S)	7,790	0.2	(S)
Wood products	158,586	1.9	345,940	3.0	120,151	3.8	242
Pulp, newsprint, paper, and paperboard	102,495	1.2	137,053	1.2	78,160	2.5	206
Paper or paperboard articles	103,713	1.2	69,211	0.6	23,360	0.7	282
Printed products	134,452	1.6	34,015	0.3	17,037	0.5	816
Textiles, leather, and articles of textiles or leather	466,429	5.6	51,232	0.4	31,787	1.0	940
Nonmetallic mineral products	149,951	1.8	967,978	8.3	135,937	4.3	357
Base metal in primary or semifinished forms and in finished basic shapes	259,834	3.1	328,053	2.8	121,330	3.9	270
Articles of base metal	234,571	2.8	116,447	1.0	42,680	1.4	392
Machinery	484,152	5.8	63,390	0.5	34,535	1.1	377
Electronic and other electrical equipment and components and office equipment	890,803	10.6	49,592	0.4	30,269	1.0	713
Motorized and other vehicles (including parts)	748,550	8.9	133,088	1.1	59,029	1.9	395
Transportation equipment, n.e.c. [1]	155,013	1.8	18,352	0.2	10,649	0.3	1,074
Precision instruments and apparatus	225,070	2.7	18,352	0.2	3,912	0.1	922
Furniture, mattresses and mattress supports, lamps, lighting fittings and illuminated signs	139,727	1.7	32,546	0.3	13,705	0.4	515
Miscellaneous manufactured products	387,426	4.6	79,208	0.7	34,467	1.1	995
Waste and scrap	37,896	0.5	217,234	1.9	48,009	1.5	166
Mixed freight	840,346	10.0	299,926	2.6	52,823	1.7	329
Commodity unknown	17,229	0.2	24,266	0.2	8,889	0.3	485

- Rounds to zero. S Data do not meet publication standards due to high sampling variability or other reasons. [1] n.e.c. Means not elsewhere classified.

Source: U.S. Bureau of Transportation Statistics and U.S. Census Bureau, 2002 Economic Census, Transportation, 2002 Commodity Flow Survey, Series EC02TCF-US, issued December 2004. See Internet site <http://www.census.gov/cfs>.

Table 1072. **Bridge Inventory—Total and Deficient, 1996 to 2004, and by State, 2004**

[Based on the National Bridge Inventory program]

State and year	Number of bridges	Deficient and obsolete					
		Total number	Percent	Structurally deficient [1]		Functionally obsolete [2]	
				Number	Percent	Number	Percent
1996, total............	581,862	182,726	31.4	101,518	17.4	81,208	14.0
1997, total............	582,751	175,885	30.2	98,475	16.9	77,410	13.3
1998, total............	582,984	172,582	29.6	93,076	16.0	79,506	13.6
1999, total............	585,542	170,050	29.0	88,150	15.1	81,900	14.0
2000, total............	587,755	167,993	28.6	87,106	14.8	80,887	13.8
2001, total............	590,066	165,099	28.0	83,630	14.2	81,469	13.8
2002, total............	591,220	163,010	27.6	81,437	13.8	81,573	13.8
2003, total............	592,246	160,819	27.2	79,811	13.5	81,008	13.7
U.S. total, 2004.....	**593,865**	**158,318**	**26.7**	**77,758**	**13.1**	**80,560**	**13.6**
Alabama	15,648	4,679	29.9	2,393	15.3	2,286	14.6
Alaska	1,187	353	29.7	151	12.7	202	17.0
Arizona..............	7,119	717	10.1	163	2.3	554	7.8
Arkansas.............	12,456	3,132	25.1	1,238	9.9	1,894	15.2
California.............	23,823	6,668	28.0	2,894	12.1	3,774	15.8
Colorado.............	8,182	1,387	17.0	604	7.4	783	9.6
Connecticut	4,167	1,363	32.7	345	8.3	1,018	24.4
Delaware.............	850	122	14.4	42	4.9	80	9.4
District of Columbia.....	251	157	62.5	23	9.2	134	53.4
Florida	11,469	2,118	18.5	317	2.8	1,801	15.7
Georgia	14,461	2,948	20.4	1,187	8.2	1,761	12.2
Hawaii	1,099	513	46.7	156	14.2	357	32.5
Idaho	4,047	730	18.0	316	7.8	414	10.2
Illinois...............	25,727	4,361	17.0	2,436	9.5	1,925	7.5
Indiana	18,171	4,016	22.1	1,993	11.0	2,023	11.1
Iowa................	24,902	6,958	27.9	5,259	21.1	1,699	6.8
Kansas	25,525	5,900	23.1	3,330	13.0	2,570	10.1
Kentucky.............	13,500	4,104	30.4	1,283	9.5	2,821	20.9
Louisiana	13,362	4,324	32.4	2,070	15.5	2,254	16.9
Maine...............	2,371	843	35.6	355	15.0	488	20.6
Maryland.............	5,064	1,479	29.2	428	8.5	1,051	20.8
Massachusetts.........	4,954	2,546	51.4	614	12.4	1,932	39.0
Michigan.............	10,818	3,121	28.9	1,764	16.3	1,357	12.5
Minnesota............	13,026	1,633	12.5	1,163	8.9	470	3.6
Mississippi............	16,838	4,697	27.9	3,379	20.1	1,318	7.8
Missouri	23,791	8,244	34.7	5,028	21.1	3,216	13.5
Montana	5,043	1,074	21.3	576	11.4	498	9.9
Nebraska	15,455	3,975	25.7	2,550	16.5	1,425	9.2
Nevada..............	1,611	198	12.3	54	3.4	144	8.9
New Hampshire	2,357	788	33.4	355	15.1	433	18.4
New Jersey...........	6,484	2,370	36.6	890	13.7	1,480	22.8
New Mexico...........	3,839	724	18.9	404	10.5	320	8.3
New York	17,301	6,552	37.9	2,172	12.6	4,380	25.3
North Carolina	17,340	5,196	30.0	2,322	13.4	2,874	16.6
North Dakota	4,507	1,062	23.6	803	17.8	259	5.7
Ohio................	27,907	7,102	25.4	3,052	10.9	4,050	14.5
Oklahoma	23,312	8,757	37.6	7,307	31.3	1,450	6.2
Oregon	7,261	1,848	25.5	659	9.1	1,189	16.4
Pennsylvania..........	22,253	9,404	42.3	5,464	24.6	3,940	17.7
Rhode Island	749	405	54.1	193	25.8	212	28.3
South Carolina	9,201	2,130	23.1	1,286	14.0	844	9.2
South Dakota	5,961	1,490	25.0	1,072	18.0	418	7.0
Tennessee............	19,688	4,499	22.9	1,499	7.6	3,000	15.2
Texas	48,950	10,195	20.8	2,580	5.3	7,615	15.6
Utah................	2,805	506	18.0	256	9.1	250	8.9
Vermont	2,690	954	35.5	484	18.0	470	17.5
Virginia..............	13,160	3,348	25.4	1,186	9.0	2,162	16.4
Washington	7,543	2,056	27.3	420	5.6	1,636	21.7
West Virginia	6,881	2,555	37.1	1,078	15.7	1,477	21.5
Wisconsin	13,611	2,339	17.2	1,495	11.0	844	6.2
Wyoming.............	3,033	629	20.7	409	13.5	220	7.3
Puerto Rico	2,135	1,049	49.1	261	12.2	788	36.9

[1] Bridges are structurally deficient if they have been restricted to light vehicles, require immediate rehabilitation to remain open, or are closed. [2] Bridges are functionally obsolete if they have deck geometry, load caring capacity, clearance or approach roadway alignment that no longer meet the criteria for the system of which the bridge is carrying a part.

Source: U.S. Federal Highway Administration, Office of Bridge Technology, Internet site <http://www.fhwa.dot.gov/bridge/britab.htm>.

Table 1073. Funding for Highways and Disposition of Highway-User Revenue: 1990 to 2003

[In millions of dollars (75,444 represents $75,444,000,0000. Data compiled from reports of state and local authorities]

Type	1990	1995	1998	1999	2000	2001	2002	2003
Total receipts	75,444	96,269	111,581	121,650	131,115	132,324	134,765	138,195
Current income	69,880	87,620	102,533	110,376	119,815	119,659	122,018	123,770
Highway user revenues	44,346	59,331	68,951	74,222	81,335	77,719	79,587	79,860
Other taxes and fees	19,827	21,732	25,395	29,380	31,137	34,190	34,353	35,967
Investment income, other receipts . . .	5,707	6,557	8,187	6,774	7,342	7,749	8,078	7,943
Bond issue proceeds [1]	5,564	8,649	9,048	11,274	11,301	12,665	12,747	14,425
Funds from (+) or to (-) reserves	-36	-2,791	-3,606	-5,639	-8,418	-2,423	1,154	5,612
Total funds available	75,408	93,478	107,975	116,011	122,697	129,900	135,919	143,807
Total disbursements	75,408	93,478	107,975	116,011	122,697	129,900	135,919	143,807
Current disbursements	72,457	88,994	102,828	111,097	117,592	124,815	129,137	136,979
Capital outlay	35,151	44,228	52,308	57,227	61,323	65,968	68,175	69,876
Maintenance and traffic services	20,365	24,319	28,173	29,997	30,636	31,677	33,180	35,467
Administration and research	6.501	8,419	8,523	9,130	10,020	10,423	10,695	12,142
Law enforcement and safety	7,235	8,218	9,445	10,393	11,031	11,977	11,672	13,649
Interest on debt	3,205	3,810	4,379	4,350	4,583	4,770	5,416	5,846
Bond retirement [1]	2,951	4,484	5,147	5,644	4,914	5,105	5,086	6,828

[1] Excludes issue and redemption of short-term notes or refunding bonds.

Source: U.S. Federal Highway Administration, *Highway Statistics*, annual. See Internet site <http://www.fhwa.dot.gov/policy/ohpi/hss/hsspubs.htm>.

Table 1074. Federal Aid to State and Local Governments for Highway Trust Fund and Federal Transit Administration (FTA) by State: 2003

[Year ending Sept. 30. (28,614 represents $28,614,000,0000)]

State	Highway trust fund Total (mil. dol.)	Highway trust fund Per capita (dol.)[1]	FTA Total (mil. dol.)	FTA Per capita (dol.)[1]	State	Highway trust fund Total (mil. dol.)	Highway trust fund Per capita (dol.)[1]	FTA Total (mil. dol.)	FTA Per capita (dol.)[1]	State	Highway trust fund Total (mil. dol.)	Highway trust fund Per capita (dol.)[1]	FTA Total (mil. dol.)	FTA Per capita (dol.)[1]
U.S. [2] . . .	28,614	97.0	5,841	19.8	KS	358	131.3	13	4.9	ND	182	287.8	6	9.7
U.S. [3] . . .	28,272	97.2	5,720	19.7	KY	509	123.6	39	9.4	OH	918	80.3	171	15.0
AL	530	117.7	39	8.6	LA	514	114.3	71	15.9	OK	398	113.5	20	5.6
AK	381	587.7	35	53.9	ME	181	138.3	13	9.8	OR	378	106.3	55	15.6
AZ	469	84.0	41	7.4	MD	425	77.2	147	26.6	PA	1,347	108.9	329	26.6
AR	392	143.7	22	8.0	MA	497	77.3	164	25.5	RI	142	131.5	13	11.7
CA	2,727	76.9	1,276	36.0	MI	776	77.0	65	6.4	SC	438	105.7	29	7.0
CO	401	88.1	38	8.4	MN	367	72.5	105	20.8	SD	204	266.5	4	5.7
CT	387	111.0	80	23.0	MS	364	126.4	22	7.6	TN	532	91.1	53	9.1
DE	97	118.7	16	19.7	MO	725	127.1	75	13.2	TX	2,595	117.3	264	12.0
DC	152	269.2	189	335.2	MT	1	1.3	7	7.2					
FL	1,650	97.0	199	11.7	NE	222	127.8	8	4.6	UT	215	91.5	39	16.6
GA	778	89.6	113	13.0	NV	180	80.4	26	11.4	VT	108	173.9	11	17.4
HI	115	91.2	6	4.8	NH	140	109.0	6	4.8	VA	697	94.3	83	11.2
ID	209	152.8	7	4.8	NJ	720	83.3	212	24.5	WA	554	90.4	179	29.2
IL	869	68.7	406	32.0	NM	261	139.4	16	8.7	WV	328	181.3	23	12.8
IN	615	99.2	53	8.6	NY	1,250	65.2	787	41.0	WI	579	105.8	42	7.7
IA	345	117.3	21	7.0	NC	815	97.0	79	9.4	WY	233	464.8	3	6.6

[1] Based on estimated population as of July 1. [2] Includes outlying areas and undistributed funds, not shown separately.
[3] For the 50 states and D.C.

Source: U.S. Census Bureau, *Federal Aid to States for Fiscal Year, 2003*. See Inernet site <http://www.census.gov/prod/2004pubs/03fas.pdf> (issued September 2004).

Table 1075. State Motor Fuel Tax Receipts, 2002 and 2003, and Gasoline Tax Rates, 2003

[571 represents $571,000,000]

State	Net receipts (mil.dol) 2002	Net receipts (mil.dol) 2003	Tax rate,[1] 2003	State	Net receipts (mil.dol) 2002	Net receipts (mil.dol) 2003	Tax rate,[1] 2003	State	Net receipts (mil dol) 2002	Net receipts (mil dol) 2003	Tax rate,[1] 2003
AL	571	566	18.00	KY	498	499	16.40	ND	100	104	21.00
AK	23	28	8.00	LA	554	573	20.00	OH	1,410	1,432	24.00
AZ	608	656	18.00	ME	171	217	22.00	OK	410	407	17.00
AR	427	436	21.70	MD	707	709	23.50	OR	395	404	24.00
CA	3,237	3,248	18.00	MA	667	676	21.00	PA	1,677	1,754	25.90
CO	539	544	22.00	MI	1,083	1,093	19.00	RI	131	135	30.00
CT	420	447	25.00	MN	619	639	20.00	SC	447	463	16.00
DE	111	107	23.00	MS	386	391	18.40	SD	128	127	22.00
DC	27	30	20.00	MO	669	680	17.00	TN	723	752	21.40
FL	1,750	1,841	13.90	MT	183	184	27.00	TX	2,836	2,863	20.00
GA	423	465	7.50	NE	299	305	24.60	UT	334	330	24.50
HI	72	75	16.00	NV	387	401	25.70	VT	86	86	20.00
ID	212	209	25.00	NH	143	157	19.50	VA	818	849	17.50
IL	1,294	1,310	19.00	NJ	489	554	10.50	WA	736	750	28.00
IN	759	1,047	18.00	NM	229	253	18.50	WV	301	290	25.35
IA	408	413	20.30	NY	1,519	1,499	22.65	WI	865	902	28.50
KS	393	407	24.00	NC	1,212	1,160	24.20	WY	99	89	14.00

[1] State gasoline tax rates in cents per gallon. In effect December 31.

Source: U.S. Federal Highway Administration, *Highway Statistics*, annual. See Internet site <http://www.fhwa.dot.gov/policy/ohpi/hss/hsspubs.htm>

U.S. Census Bureau, Statistical Abstract of the United States: 2006

Table 1076. **Public Highway Debt—State and Local Governments: 1980 to 2003**

[In millions of dollars (2,381 represents $2,381,000,000). Long-term obligations. Data are for varying calendar and fiscal years. Excludes duplicated and interunit obligations]

Item	1980	1985	1990	1995	1999	2000	2001	2002	2003
Total debt issued	2,381	8,194	5,708	11,305	12,822	14,513	15,697	19,089	(NA)
State...................	1,160	5,397	3,147	4,718	9,554	9,067	11,012	13.250	16,571
Local [1]	1,221	2,797	2,561	6,587	3,268	5,446	4,685	5,839	(NA)
Total debt redeemed......	1,987	5,294	3,120	5,634	5,808	8,623	7,230	13,537	(NA)
State..................	1,114	3,835	1,648	2,939	3,609	3,897	4,660	9,988	11,541
Local [1]	873	1,459	1,472	2,695	2,199	4,726	2,570	3,549	(NA)
Total debt outstanding [2] ...	27,616	32,690	46,586	68,733	89,778	96,383	103,342	111,226	(NA)
State..................	20,210	21,277	28,362	39,228	55,646	61,434	66,256	70,826	77,205
Local [1]	7,406	11,413	18,224	29,505	34,132	34,949	37,086	40,400	(NA)

NA Not available. [1] Local data estimated. [2] End-of-year.

Source: U.S. Federal Highway Administration, *Highway Statistics*, annual. See Internet site <http://www.fhwa.dot.gov/policy/ohpi/hss/hsspubs.htm>.

Table 1077. **State Disbursements for Highways by State: 1995 to 2003**

[In millions of dollars (67,615 represents $67,615,000,000). Comprises disbursements from current revenues or loans for construction, maintenance, interest and principal payments on highway bonds, transfers to local units, and miscellaneous. Includes transactions by state toll authorities. Excludes amounts allocated for collection expenses and nonhighway purposes, and bonds redeemed by refunding]

State	1995	1997	1998	1999	2000	2001	2002	2003
United States............	67,615	73,994	80,518	83,675	89,832	94,513	104,977	109,203
Alabama.................	1,002	1,019	1,053	1,085	1,246	1,433	1,575	1,572
Alaska..................	438	435	404	416	501	482	541	618
Arizona.................	1,199	1,359	1,430	1,860	2,040	2,149	2,445	2,453
Arkansas	666	832	815	736	817	976	1,161	1,176
California	5,966	6,219	6,574	6,876	6,750	6,795	8,570	9,349
Colorado................	922	887	1,166	1,260	1,392	1,616	2,195	1,788
Connecticut..............	1,153	1,173	1,427	1,094	1,304	1,236	1,848	1,743
Delaware	441	449	647	507	595	647	738	929
District of Columbia	140	151	259	242	244	406	336	368
Florida..................	3,421	3,734	4,024	3,992	4,208	4,348	4,985	6,664
Georgia	1,437	1,372	1,613	1,763	1,567	1,748	1,945	1,756
Hawaii	360	387	326	355	272	263	275	375
Idaho...................	350	403	414	445	492	480	508	547
Illinois..................	3,006	2,992	3,306	2,957	3,147	3,788	4,286	4,595
Indiana.................	1,433	1,636	1,652	1,522	1,932	3,202	1,975	2,445
Iowa	1,078	1,173	1,177	1,253	1,494	1,388	1,405	1,419
Kansas.................	1,019	1,087	1,306	1,155	1,206	1,271	1,951	1,891
Kentucky	1,397	1,331	1,481	1,578	1,651	1,612	1,776	2,152
Louisiana	1,198	1,189	1,400	1,237	1,301	1,154	1,287	1,498
Maine..................	379	474	485	458	488	505	744	579
Maryland	1,289	1,489	1,492	1,554	1,599	1,673	1,803	1,885
Massachusetts...........	2,501	3,287	3,351	4,407	3,524	3,965	3,783	3,547
Michigan................	1,974	2,100	2,745	2,629	2,748	2,920	2,859	2,799
Minnesota...............	1,210	1,450	1,377	1,534	1,692	1,683	1,866	1,969
Mississippi	662	809	843	968	1,039	911	1,040	1,014
Missouri................	1,313	1,492	1,438	1,600	1,818	2,044	2,110	2,120
Montana................	388	379	378	434	474	469	535	578
Nebraska...............	578	611	589	681	745	661	867	839
Nevada	484	431	446	557	651	668	631	807
New Hampshire...........	328	360	371	416	387	445	522	453
New Jersey..............	2,102	2,247	2,513	2,905	4,503	4,276	4,863	6,364
New Mexico	535	546	570	753	1,162	1,119	983	862
New York	4,584	4,778	6,051	5,347	5,307	5,301	7,161	6,592
North Carolina...........	1,871	2,099	2,352	2,441	2,621	2,868	3,001	3,013
North Dakota............	270	326	306	413	385	358	385	379
Ohio...................	2,637	2,940	3,327	3,158	3,351	3,493	3,580	3,660
Oklahoma...............	828	867	944	1,322	1,417	1,443	1,839	1,379
Oregon.................	888	992	1,051	1,009	1,010	984	1,029	983
Pennsylvania............	3,153	3,764	3,902	4,143	4,517	4,875	5,365	5,258
Rhode Island............	290	225	339	316	256	380	380	299
South Carolina...........	668	741	766	885	970	1,104	1,201	1,191
South Dakota............	286	349	305	371	466	463	437	441
Tennessee	1,230	1,351	1,420	1,398	1,440	1,563	1,622	1,661
Texas..................	3,593	4,253	4,295	4,840	5,665	5,716	6,019	6,758
Utah	431	802	1,129	1,072	1,072	941	956	879
Vermont	194	213	222	252	287	297	265	312
Virginia.................	2,107	2,358	2,619	2,771	2,678	2,909	3,185	3,419
Washington..............	1,909	1,851	1,805	1,780	1,871	2,042	2,276	2,288
West Virginia............	781	940	893	930	1,170	1,289	1,210	1,169
Wisconsin...............	1,252	1,354	1,398	1,614	1,663	1,793	2,204	1,904
Wyoming................	272	284	321	386	396	360	460	468

Source: U.S. Federal Highway Administration, *Highway Statistics*, annual. See Internet site <http://www.fhwa.dot.gov/policy/ohpi/hss/hsspubs.htm>.

Table 1078. **State Motor Vehicle Registrations: 1980 to 2003**

[In thousands (155,796 represents 155,796,000). Compiled principally from information obtained from state authorities, but it was necessary to draw on other sources and to make numerous estimates in order to complete series. See also Table 1081]

Item	1980	1990	1995	2000	2001	2002	2003
All motor vehicles	155,796	188,798	201,530	221,475	230,428	229,620	231,390
Private and commercial	153,265	185,541	197,941	217,567	226,646	225,772	227,476
Publicly-owned	2,531	3,257	3,589	3,908	3,782	3,848	3,914
Automobiles [1]	121,601	133,700	128,387	133,621	137,633	135,921	135,670
Private and commercial	120,743	132,164	126,900	132,247	136,341	134,605	134,337
Publicly-owned	857	1,536	1,487	1,374	1,293	1,316	1,333
Buses	529	627	686	746	750	761	777
Private and commercial	254	275	288	314	318	320	325
Publicly-owned	275	351	398	432	432	441	452
Trucks [1]	33,667	54,470	72,458	87,108	92,045	92,939	94,943
Private and commercial	32,268	53,101	70,754	85,005	89,988	90,847	92,814
Publicly-owned	1,399	1,369	1,704	2,103	2,058	2,091	2,129

[1] Trucks include pickups, panels and delivery vans. Beginning 1990, personal passenger vans, passenger minivans and utility-type vehicles are no longer included in automobiles, but are included in trucks.

Source: U.S. Federal Highway Administration, *Highway Statistics*, annual. See Internet site <http://www.fhwa.dot.gov/policy/ohpi/hss /hsspubs.htm>.

Table 1079. **Alternative Fueled Vehicles in Use by Fuel Type: 2002 to 2004**

[2004 data are projections. 378,589 represents 378,589,000]

Fuel type	Alternative fueled vehicles			Fuel consumption (1,000 gasoline-equivalent gallons)		
	2002	2003	2004	2002	2003	2004
Total....................	471,098	510,805	547,904	378,589	412,725	447,198
Liquified petroleum gases (LPG)	187,680	190,438	194,389	223,143	230,486	242,368
Compressed natural gas (CNG)	120,839	132,988	143,742	120,670	141,726	159,464
Liquified natural gas (LNG)	2,708	3,030	3,134	9,382	10,514	10,868
Methanol, 85 percent (M85) [1]	5,873	4,917	4,592	337	274	257
Ethanol, 85 percent (E85) [1]	120,951	133,776	146,195	17,783	20,092	22,405
Electricity [2]	33,047	45,656	55,852	7,274	9,633	11,836

[1] The remaining portion is gasoline. [2] Excludes gasoline-electric hybrids.

Source: Energy Information Administration, *Alternatives to Traditional Transportation Fuels*. See Internet site <http://www.eia.doe.gov /fuelalternate.html> (released February 2004).

Table 1080. **Number of Households Leasing Vehicles and Number of Vehicles Leased Per Household: 1992 to 2001**

[Based on the Survey of Consumer Finances; see Appendix III]

Item	Share of households leasing a vehicle for personal use (percent)				Average number of leased vehicles, among households having such vehicles			
	1992	1995	1998	2001	1992	1995	1998	2001
All households	2.9	4.5	6.4	5.8	1.1	1.1	1.2	1.2
Household income:								
Less than $10,000.............	(Z)	(Z)	(Z)	(Z)	(Z)	(Z)	1.1	(Z)
$10,000 to $24,999	(Z)	1.3	4.1	1.8	(Z)	1.0	1.1	1.1
$25,000 to $49,999	3.1	3.2	4.6	5.3	1.1	1.0	1.1	1.0
$50,000 to $99,999	3.7	9.2	9.2	7.6	1.1	1.1	1.2	1.2
$100,000 and over.............	9.5	12.6	13.8	12.9	1.1	1.3	1.3	1.3
Age of household head:								
Less than 35 years	3.2	4.8	8.2	7.3	1.0	1.0	1.1	1.1
35 to 44 years...............	4.3	5.4	8.3	5.9	1.1	1.1	1.2	1.2
45 to 54 years...............	3.2	7.9	7.6	6.1	1.2	1.2	1.3	1.2
55 to 64 years...............	3.2	4.1	4.4	5.5	1.2	1.2	1.1	1.2
65 to 74 years...............	1.0	1.3	2.9	6.3	1.0	1.1	1.2	1.1
75 years and over	(Z)	0.5	1.9	1.6	(Z)	1.0	1.0	1.0
Race/ethnicity of respondent:								
White non-Hispanic	3.1	4.4	6.3	6.3	1.1	1.1	1.1	1.2
Non-White and Hispanic	2.3	4.9	6.5	4.2	1.1	1.1	1.3	1.1
Work status of household head:								
Work for someone else...........	3.4	6.0	8.1	6.2	1.1	1.1	1.2	1.2
Self-employed.................	7.2	5.2	9.0	9.4	1.1	1.3	1.1	1.3
Retired......................	0.7	1.4	1.5	3.1	1.3	1.0	1.2	1.1
Other not working	(Z)	2.6	(Z)	(Z)	(Z)	1.0	(Z)	(Z)
Homeownership status:								
Owner......................	3.5	5.8	7.2	6.2	1.1	1.2	1.2	1.2
Renter or other	1.8	2.3	4.8	5.0	1.1	1.1	1.1	1.1
Net worth percentile:								
Bottom 25 percent	2.1	2.7	4.9	3.9	1.1	1.1	1.1	1.2
25 to 49.9 percent	1.6	4.2	5.4	4.4	1.0	1.0	1.1	1.1
50 to 74.9 percent	2.9	4.3	7.1	6.3	1.1	1.1	1.2	1.3
75 to 89.9 percent	3.7	6.2	7.0	7.6	1.0	1.2	1.2	1.2
Top 10 percent	6.5	8.2	9.9	10.2	1.2	1.3	1.2	1.2

Z Ten or fewer observations.

Source: Board of Governors of the Federal Reserve System, unpublished data. See Internet site <http://www.federalreserve.gov /pubs/oss/oss2/2001/scf2001home.html>.

Table 1081. **State Motor Vehicle Registrations, 1980 to 2003, and Licensed Drivers and Motorcycle Registrations by State, 2003**

[In thousands (155,796 represents 155,796,000). Motor vehicle registrations cover publicly, privately, and commercially owned vehicles. For uniformity, data have been adjusted to a calendar-year basis as registration years in states differ; figures represent net numbers where possible, excluding re-registrations and nonresident registrations. See also Table 1078]

| State | Motor vehicle registrations [1] | | | | | | 2003 | | 2003 | |
| | | | | | | | | | Auto-mobiles (incl. taxis) | Motor-cycle registra-tion [2] | Licensed drivers |
	1980	1985	1990	1995	2000	2002	Total			
U.S.	155,796	171,689	188,798	201,530	221,475	229,620	231,390	135,670	5,328	196,166
AL......	2,938	3,383	3,744	3,553	3,960	4,428	4,329	1,771	70	3,598
AK......	262	353	477	542	594	620	637	261	20	481
AZ......	1,917	2,235	2,825	2,873	3,795	3,940	3,574	1,992	208	3,819
AR......	1,574	1,384	1,448	1,613	1,840	1,873	1,889	955	38	1,998
CA.	16,873	18,899	21,926	22,432	27,698	29,619	30,248	18,699	547	22,657
CO	2,342	2,759	3,155	2,812	3,626	2,151	2,027	888	8	2,975
CT.	2,147	2,465	2,623	2,622	2,853	2,915	2,964	2,041	63	2,660
DE......	397	465	526	592	630	674	687	419	15	585
DC	268	306	262	243	242	238	228	184	1	313
FL......	7,614	9,865	10,950	10,369	11,781	13,964	14,526	8,564	386	12,906
GA	3,818	4,580	5,489	6,120	7,155	7,648	7,730	4,192	118	5,758
HI......	570	651	771	802	738	893	903	525	22	834
ID......	834	854	1,054	1,043	1,178	1,386	1,301	554	44	921
IL......	7,477	7,527	7,873	8,973	8,973	9,577	9,250	5,769	261	8,054
IN......	3,826	3,824	4,366	5,072	5,571	5,665	5,739	3,252	144	4,536
IA......	2,329	2,696	2,632	2,814	3,106	3,310	3,369	1,883	140	1,978
KS......	2,007	2,148	2,012	2,085	2,296	2,337	2,314	834	56	1,987
KY......	2,593	2,615	2,909	2,631	2,826	3,601	3,389	1,959	51	3,120
LA......	2,779	3,012	2,995	3,286	3,557	3,660	3,714	1,997	57	3,120
ME	724	840	977	967	1,024	968	1,052	619	35	932
MD	2,803	3,276	3,607	3,654	3,848	3,884	3,877	2,479	64	3,552
MA	3,749	3,738	3,726	4,502	5,265	5,407	5,479	3,615	130	4,646
MI......	6,488	6,727	7,209	7,674	8,436	8,534	8,540	4,805	214	7,065
MN	3,091	3,385	3,508	3,882	4,630	4,520	4,525	2,502	174	3,036
MS	1,577	1,746	1,875	2,144	2,289	1,955	1,951	1,139	27	1,886
MO	3,271	3,558	3,905	4,255	4,580	4,235	4,460	2,600	74	3,966
MT	680	652	783	968	1,026	1,056	1,010	437	66	705
NE.	1,254	1,258	1,384	1,467	1,619	1,656	1,677	855	27	1,311
NV......	655	709	853	1,047	1,220	1,253	1,222	624	37	1,488
NH	704	974	946	1,122	1,052	1,143	1,145	656	60	968
NJ......	4,761	5,164	5,652	5,906	6,390	6,688	6,712	4,449	140	5,729
NM	1,068	1,226	1,301	1,484	1,529	1,538	1,509	694	32	1,236
NY......	8,002	9,042	10,196	10,274	10,235	10,456	10,802	8,313	150	11,357
NC	4,532	4,501	5,162	5,682	6,223	6,149	6,119	3,654	95	6,015
ND	627	655	630	695	694	698	694	346	19	460
OH	7,771	8,102	8,410	9,810	10,467	10,470	10,536	6,519	285	7,656
OK	2,583	2,911	2,649	2,856	3,014	3,071	3,074	1,623	72	2,348
OR	2,081	2,204	2,445	2,785	3,022	3,069	3,061	1,545	75	2,590
PA......	6,926	7,209	7,971	8,481	9,260	9,525	9,724	6,121	268	8,370
RI......	623	610	672	699	760	776	806	549	25	731
SC......	1,996	2,222	2,521	2,833	3,095	3,202	3,162	1,915	57	2,919
SD......	601	657	704	709	793	814	827	388	38	555
TN......	3,271	3,754	4,444	5,400	4,820	4,777	4,796	2,782	94	4,204
TX......	10,475	12,444	12,800	13,682	14,070	14,664	14,889	7,842	258	13,498
UT......	992	1,099	1,206	1,447	1,628	1,847	2,006	1,014	38	1,548
VT......	347	398	462	492	515	537	516	272	26	543
VA......	3,626	4,253	4,938	5,613	6,046	6,273	6,346	4,044	73	5,046
WA	3,225	3,526	4,257	4,503	5,116	5,336	5,379	2,969	141	4,407
WV	1,320	1,143	1,225	1,425	1,442	1,463	1,409	756	19	1,272
WI......	2,941	3,187	3,815	3,993	4,366	4,557	4,647	2,578	240	3,766
WY......	467	500	528	601	586	603	620	232	28	378

[1] Automobiles, trucks, and buses. Excludes vehicles owned by military services. [2] Private and commercial.

Source: U.S. Federal Highway Administration, *Highway Statistics,* annual. See Internet site <http://www.fhwa.dot.gov/policy/ohpi/hss/hsspubs.htm>.

U.S. Census Bureau, Statistical Abstract of the United States: 2006

Table 1082. **Roadway Congestion: 2003**

[**15,919 represents 15,919,000.** Various federal, state, and local information sources were used to develop the data base with the primary source being the Federal Highway Administration's Highway Performance Monitoring System. Areas shown are rated the top 73 in annual per-person hours of delay]

Urbanized areas	Freeway daily vehicle miles of travel		Annual person hours of delay		Annual congestion cost		
	Total miles (1,000)	Per lane-mile of freeway	Total hours (1,000)	Per person	Per person (dol.)	Delay and fuel cost (mil. dol.)	Fuel wasted (gal. per person)
Total, average	**15,919**	**16,206**	**43,802**	**25**	**422**	**742**	**15**
Akron, OH.	5,435	12,494	3,672	6	105	62	4
Albany-Schenectady, NY	5,820	10,582	3,784	7	122	64	4
Albuquerque, NM	4,285	12,985	9,258	16	269	156	9
Allentown-Bethlehem, PA-NJ.	4,600	11,646	5,618	9	151	95	6
Atlanta, GA	43,590	19,077	103,618	34	584	1,754	24
Austin, TX	9,200	15,726	23,201	27	457	391	16
Baltimore, MD	26,050	17,026	62,436	27	458	1,057	17
Beaumont, TX	1,685	12,481	1,101	8	127	18	4
Birmingham, AL	9,020	13,363	9,705	14	242	165	10
Boston, MA-NH-RI	37,300	15,738	100,237	25	424	1,692	15
Bridgeport-Stamford, CT-NY	10,000	16,667	14,550	17	291	250	13
Buffalo, NY	6,720	10,500	6,981	6	104	118	3
Cape Coral, FL.	435	9,667	2,712	8	141	46	5
Charleston-North Charleston, SC. . .	3,130	12,275	6,364	14	228	107	8
Charlotte, NC-SC	7,755	15,990	16,692	23	389	282	15
Chicago, IL-IN	52,010	19,516	252,822	31	526	4,274	19
Cincinnati, OH-KY-IN.	17,635	15,203	27,288	17	287	461	10
Cleveland, OH	17,390	12,647	10,709	6	97	182	4
Colorado Springs, CO	3,435	11,845	6,953	14	243	117	8
Columbus, OH	14,665	15,356	18,550	16	264	314	10
Dallas-Fort Worth-Arlington, TX	51,870	16,705	151,840	35	592	2,545	19
Dayton, OH	6,870	12,491	4,438	6	102	75	4
Denver-Aurora, CO	17,960	15,754	64,506	31	530	1,087	18
Detroit, MI	33,465	17,521	119,581	30	499	2,019	18
El Paso, TX-NM	4,030	14,393	6,491	10	164	110	6
Fresno, CA	3,280	12,377	4,180	7	120	72	5
Grand Rapids, MI	4,515	12,203	5,852	10	169	99	6
Hartford, CT.	10,425	13,196	7,434	8	144	127	6
Honolulu, HI.	5,930	14,289	7,476	11	184	129	6
Houston, TX	46,665	18,970	135,652	36	609	2,283	22
Indianapolis, IN	11,290	15,466	21,358	21	350	362	14
Jacksonville, FL	10,275	13,980	16,850	18	308	285	11
Kansas City, MO-KS	20,185	11,404	13,874	9	156	235	6
Las Vegas, NV	8,275	17,062	22,245	16	279	380	11
Los Angeles-Long Beach-Santa Ana, CA	136,000	23,248	623,796	50	855	10,686	33
Louisville, KY-IN	11,500	15,972	19,916	22	377	336	14
Memphis, TN-MS-AR.	7,815	14,081	17,465	18	295	294	10
Miami, FL	36,685	19,057	147,294	29	487	2,486	17
Milwaukee, WI	10,465	14,950	18,249	13	214	310	8
Minneapolis-St. Paul, MN	27,580	17,346	57,537	23	394	975	15
Nashville-Davidson, TN	13,085	13,702	18,890	20	331	318	11
New Haven, CT	7,450	14,327	5,848	11	181	100	7
New Orleans, LA	5,960	14,024	10,853	10	167	183	6
New York-Newark, NY-NJ-CT	112,555	15,698	404,480	23	383	6,780	11
Oklahoma City, OK	9,500	12,102	7,218	7	112	122	4
Omaha, NE-IA	3,600	12,000	7,984	13	211	134	7
Orlando, FL.	10,570	13,551	38,157	30	510	643	18
Oxnard-Ventura, CA	6,700	18,873	10,249	18	307	176	12
Pensacola, FL-AL.	1,200	10,909	2,977	10	162	50	5
Philadelphia, PA-NJ-DE-MD	33,875	14,728	112,309	21	357	1,884	11
Phoenix, AZ.	23,610	17,819	76,662	26	431	1,294	15
Pittsburgh, PA	12,210	9,768	14,530	8	135	243	4
Portland, OR-WA	12,945	18,105	33,387	20	341	569	13
Providence, RI-MA	11,095	12,328	21,668	18	295	363	9
Raleigh-Durham, NC	8,145	13,352	11,481	15	248	194	10
Richmond, VA	10,830	10,995	8,305	9	153	140	5
Riverside-San Bernardino, CA.	19,500	21,429	50,155	30	517	863	21
Sacramento, CA	13,705	19,303	35,929	22	374	619	15
Salem, OR	1,245	12,450	1,714	8	135	29	5
Salt Lake City, UT.	8,300	15,660	15,094	16	279	257	11
San Antonio, TX	16,100	14,977	23,788	18	301	401	11
San Diego, CA	36,195	19,460	81,756	28	492	1,411	21
San Francisco-Oakland, CA	48,985	20,242	152,352	37	631	2,605	23
San Jose, CA.	16,565	18,508	48,134	29	492	823	18
Sarasota-Bradenton, FL	825	12,692	5,772	10	170	97	6
Seattle, WA	30,700	17,593	72,461	25	427	1,237	17
St. Louis, MO-IL	26,145	14,647	39,936	19	326	675	13
Tampa-St. Petersburg, FL	9,855	14,600	51,360	25	422	865	14
Toledo, OH-MI	4,115	12,470	3,391	7	110	57	4
Tucson, AZ	3,285	13,408	13,767	19	324	233	12
Tulsa, OK	7,025	10,036	5,419	7	113	91	4
Virginia Beach, VA	12,875	13,697	21,746	14	239	367	9
Washington, DC-VA-MD.	37,815	18,537	145,484	34	577	2,465	21

Source: Texas Transportation Institute, College Station, Texas; *2005 Urban Mobility Study* (issued May 2005). (Copyright). See <http://mobility.tamu.edu/ums/>.

Transportation 713

Table 1083. **Commuting to Work by State: 2003**

[In percent, except as indicated (129,412 represents 129,412,000). For workers 16 years old and over. The American Community Survey universe is limited to the household population and excludes the population living in institutions, college dormitories, and other group quarters. Based on a sample and subject to sampling variability; see Appendix III]

State	Total workers (1,000)	Commuted by car, truck, or van		Used public transportation [1]	Walked	Used other means	Worked at home	Mean travel time to work (min.)
		Drove alone	Car-pooled					
U.S.	**129,142**	**77.8**	**10.4**	**4.8**	**2.3**	**1.2**	**3.5**	**24.3**
AL	1,885	85.0	10.6	0.6	1.0	0.8	2.1	22.7
AK	288	69.9	14.4	1.8	6.2	3.0	4.7	18.9
AZ	2,336	77.6	12.9	2.1	2.1	2.1	3.3	23.4
AR	1,171	82.1	12.3	0.5	1.6	0.9	2.5	19.9
CA	15,189	74.2	12.6	5.0	2.3	1.5	4.3	26.5
CO	2,221	77.8	10.3	2.7	2.0	1.5	5.8	22.9
CT	1,637	80.8	8.9	3.9	2.1	1.0	3.4	23.6
DE	378	80.8	10.6	2.4	1.8	0.5	3.8	22.5
DC	254	38.9	7.8	38.8	8.9	2.4	3.2	28.4
FL	7,259	81.3	10.7	1.9	1.3	1.4	3.4	24.8
GA	3,915	80.6	12.0	2.0	1.3	1.2	3.0	26.1
HI	575	68.5	16.1	6.0	3.3	2.0	4.1	24.5
ID	614	77.2	12.1	0.7	3.3	1.4	5.3	19.5
IL	5,670	75.4	9.5	8.4	2.5	1.1	3.1	27.0
IN	2,768	83.0	9.7	1.0	1.5	1.5	3.3	21.2
IA	1,425	81.2	10.0	0.9	2.4	1.1	4.4	18.1
KS	1,298	83.3	8.4	0.3	2.6	1.2	4.2	17.5
KY	1,730	83.3	10.3	1.0	1.7	1.1	2.5	22.1
LA	1,834	82.3	10.8	1.9	1.4	1.3	2.2	23.3
ME	631	80.3	10.5	0.8	2.8	0.9	4.7	22.6
MD	2,636	75.2	10.5	8.1	2.0	1.1	3.1	30.2
MA	2,993	74.9	8.0	9.2	3.3	1.0	3.5	26.0
MI	4,409	84.4	8.6	1.1	1.8	0.8	3.2	22.7
MN	2,530	79.4	9.0	3.3	2.5	1.0	4.8	21.7
MS	1,188	83.9	10.7	0.6	1.1	1.2	2.5	21.6
MO	2,626	82.7	9.9	1.3	1.5	0.9	3.7	23.3
MT	440	75.6	10.9	0.5	5.3	1.5	6.3	16.9
NE	852	82.0	8.9	0.6	2.7	1.0	4.8	16.5
NV	1,023	78.5	11.3	2.9	2.4	2.2	2.7	21.8
NH	644	82.7	9.4	0.5	2.6	1.0	3.8	24.6
NJ	3,919	72.5	10.6	10.3	2.9	0.7	3.0	28.5
NM	786	78.8	11.6	0.9	2.1	1.9	4.7	19.4
NY	8,307	57.0	7.9	25.7	5.1	0.9	3.4	30.4
NC	3,710	82.0	11.7	1.0	1.4	0.9	3.1	23.2
ND	315	80.0	8.2	0.6	4.4	1.0	5.7	15.4
OH	5,077	84.4	8.1	1.9	1.8	0.8	3.1	22.1
OK	1,485	84.4	9.4	0.5	1.3	1.2	3.1	19.1
OR	1,588	74.2	11.3	4.0	2.8	2.2	5.4	21.0
PA	5,470	78.2	9.2	5.3	3.3	0.9	3.1	23.8
RI	503	85.1	8.3	1.7	1.6	1.0	2.3	21.8
SC	1,782	83.8	10.9	1.1	1.0	1.0	2.3	23.0
SD	373	79.2	8.9	0.5	2.9	1.0	7.5	15.2
TN	2,650	85.9	9.2	0.6	0.8	0.8	2.7	23.4
TX	9,525	80.4	12.0	1.9	1.4	1.2	3.0	23.7
UT	1,046	77.4	13.8	2.0	1.7	1.4	3.7	19.7
VT	312	77.3	10.2	0.8	4.3	1.1	6.2	20.3
VA	3,497	78.9	11.1	3.8	1.7	1.3	3.3	25.8
WA	2,794	73.8	11.3	5.0	3.2	2.2	4.6	24.8
WV	702	83.1	10.4	1.1	2.2	1.1	2.1	24.7
WI	2,636	81.0	9.0	2.0	3.1	1.2	3.6	20.4
WY	247	77.7	11.0	1.5	3.4	1.7	4.7	17.5

[1] Including taxicabs.

Source: U.S. Census Bureau, American FactFinder, 2003 American Community Survey Summary Table, P047, Means of Transportation to Work for Workers 16 Years Old and Over, Internet site <http://factfinder.census.gov/>; and American Community Survey, Multi-Year Profiles 2003 - Economic Characteristics, Internet site <http://www.census.gov/acs/www/Products/Profiles/Chg/2003/ACS/index.htm>; (accessed 13 July 2005).

Table 1084. Motor Vehicle Distance Traveled by Type of Vehicle: 1970 to 2003

[1,110 represents 1,110,000,000,000. Travel estimates based on automatic traffic recorder data]

Year	Vehicle-miles of travel (bil.)					Average miles per vehicle (1,000)				
		Passenger vehicles		Vans, pickups,			Passenger vehicles		Vans, pickups,	
	Total[1]	Cars[1]	Buses[2]	SUVs	Trucks[3]	Total	Cars[1]	Buses[2]	SUVs	Trucks[3]
1970	1,110	920	4.5	123	62	10.0	10.0	12.0	8.7	13.6
1980	1,527	1,122	6.1	291	108	9.5	8.8	11.5	10.4	18.7
1981	1,555	1,144	6.2	296	109	9.5	8.9	11.5	10.2	19.0
1982	1,595	1,172	5.8	306	111	9.6	9.1	10.4	10.3	19.9
1983	1,653	1,204	5.2	328	116	9.8	9.1	8.9	10.5	21.1
1984	1,720	1,236	4.6	358	122	10.0	9.2	8.0	11.2	22.6
1985	1,775	1,256	4.5	391	124	10.0	9.4	7.5	10.5	20.6
1986	1,835	1,280	4.7	424	127	10.1	9.5	7.9	10.8	22.1
1987	1,921	1,325	5.3	457	134	10.5	9.7	8.9	11.1	23.3
1988	2,026	1,380	5.5	502	138	10.7	10.0	8.9	11.5	22.5
1989	2,096	1,412	5.7	536	143	10.9	10.2	9.1	11.7	22.9
1990	2,144	1,418	5.7	575	146	11.1	10.3	9.1	11.9	23.6
1991	2,172	1,367	5.8	649	150	11.3	10.3	9.1	12.2	24.2
1992	2,247	1,381	5.8	707	153	11.6	10.6	9.0	12.4	25.4
1993	2,296	1,385	6.1	746	160	11.6	10.5	9.4	12.4	26.3
1994	2,358	1,416	6.4	765	170	11.7	10.8	9.6	12.2	25.8
1995	2,423	1,438	6.4	790	178	11.8	11.2	9.4	12.0	26.5
1996	2,486	1,470	6.6	817	183	11.8	11.3	9.4	11.8	26.1
1997	2,562	1,503	6.8	851	191	12.1	11.6	9.8	12.1	27.0
1998	2,632	1,550	7.0	868	196	12.2	11.8	9.8	12.2	25.4
1999	2,691	1,569	7.7	901	203	12.2	11.9	10.5	12.0	26.0
2000	2,747	1,600	7.6	923	206	12.2	11.9	10.2	11.7	25.7
2001	2,797	1,628	7.1	943	209	11.9	11.8	9.4	11.2	26.6
2002	2,856	1,658	6.8	966	215	12.2	12.2	9.0	11.4	27.1
2003	2,891	1,661	6.6	998	216	12.2	12.2	8.5	11.5	27.3

[1] Motorcycles included with cars through 1994; thereafter in total, not shown separately. [2] Includes school buses. [3] Includes combinations.

Source: U.S. Federal Highway Administration, *Highway Statistics*, annual. See Internet site <http://www.fhwa.dot.gov/policy/ohpi/hss/hsspubs.htm>.

Table 1085. Domestic Motor Fuel Consumption by Type of Vehicle: 1970 to 2003

[92.3 represents 92,300,000,000. Comprises all fuel types used for propulsion of vehicles under state motor fuels laws. Excludes federal purchases for military use. Minus sign (-) indicates decrease]

Year	Annual fuel consumption (bil. gal.)						Average miles per gallon				
	All vehicles[1]	Avg. annual percent change[2]	Cars[1]	Buses[3]	Vans, pickups, SUVs	Trucks[4]	All vehicles[1]	Cars[1]	Buses[3]	Vans, pickups, SUVs	Trucks[4]
1970 . . .	92.3	4.8	67.8	0.8	12.3	11.3	12.0	13.5	5.5	10.0	5.5
1980 . . .	115.0	-5.9	70.2	1.0	23.8	20.0	13.3	16.0	6.0	12.2	5.4
1981 . . .	114.5	-0.4	69.3	1.1	23.7	20.4	13.6	16.5	5.9	12.5	5.3
1982 . . .	113.4	-1.0	69.3	1.0	22.7	20.4	14.1	16.9	5.9	13.5	5.5
1983 . . .	116.1	2.4	70.5	0.9	23.9	20.8	14.2	17.1	5.9	13.7	5.6
1984 . . .	118.7	2.2	70.8	0.8	25.6	21.4	14.5	17.4	5.7	14.0	5.7
1985 . . .	121.3	2.2	71.7	0.8	27.4	21.4	14.6	17.5	5.4	14.3	5.8
1986 . . .	125.2	3.2	73.4	0.9	29.1	21.9	14.7	17.4	5.3	14.6	5.8
1987 . . .	127.5	1.8	73.5	0.9	30.6	22.5	15.1	18.0	5.8	14.9	5.9
1988 . . .	130.1	2.0	73.5	0.9	32.7	22.9	15.6	18.8	5.8	15.4	6.0
1989 . . .	131.9	1.4	74.1	0.9	33.3	23.5	15.9	18.0	6.0	16.1	6.1
1990 . . .	130.8	-0.8	69.8	0.9	35.6	24.5	16.4	20.3	6.4	16.1	6.0
1991 . . .	128.6	-1.7	64.5	0.9	38.2	25.0	16.9	21.2	6.7	17.0	6.0
1992 . . .	132.9	3.3	65.6	0.9	40.9	25.5	16.9	21.0	6.6	17.3	6.0
1993 . . .	137.3	3.3	67.2	0.9	42.9	26.2	16.7	20.6	6.6	17.4	6.1
1994 . . .	140.8	2.5	68.1	1.0	44.1	27.7	16.7	20.8	6.6	17.3	6.1
1995 . . .	143.8	2.1	68.1	1.0	45.6	29.0	16.8	21.1	6.6	17.3	6.1
1996 . . .	147.4	2.5	69.2	1.0	47.4	29.6	16.9	21.2	6.6	17.2	6.2
1997 . . .	150.4	2.0	69.9	1.0	49.4	29.9	17.0	21.5	6.7	17.2	6.4
1998 . . .	155.4	3.3	71.7	1.1	50.5	32.0	16.9	21.6	6.7	17.2	6.1
1999 . . .	161.4	3.9	73.2	1.1	52.8	33.9	16.7	21.4	6.7	17.0	6.0
2000 . . .	162.5	0.7	73.1	1.1	52.9	35.2	16.9	21.9	6.8	17.4	5.8
2001 . . .	163.5	0.6	73.6	1.0	53.5	35.2	17.1	22.1	6.9	17.6	5.9
2002 . . .	168.7	3.2	75.5	1.0	55.2	36.8	16.9	22.0	6.8	17.5	5.8
2003 . . .	169.6	0.5	74.6	1.0	56.3	37.6	17.0	22.3	6.9	17.7	5.7

[1] Motorcycles included with through 1994; thereafter in total, not shown separately. [2] Change from immediate prior year. [3] Includes school buses. [4] Includes combinations.

Source: U.S. Federal Highway Administration, *Highway Statistics*, annual. See Internet site <http://www.fhwa.dot.gov/policy/ohpi/hss/hsspubs.htm>.

Table 1086. Motor Vehicle Accidents—Number and Deaths: 1980 to 2003

[17.9 represents 17,900,000]

Item	Unit	1980	1985	1990	1995	1999	2000	2001	2002	2003
ACCIDENTS										
Motor vehicle accidents [1]	Million . . .	17.9	19.3	11.5	10.7	11.4	13.4	12.5	18.3	11.8
Vehicles involved:										
Cars	Million . . .	22.8	25.6	14.3	12.3	11.6	15.9	13.6	18.1	11.5
Trucks	Million . . .	5.5	6.1	4.4	4.5	6.2	8.8	7.4	12.2	8.2
Motorcycles	1,000 . . .	560	480	180	152	70	130	119	190	150
DEATHS										
Motor vehicle deaths within 1 yr. [2]	1,000 . . .	53.2	45.9	46.8	43.4	43.0	43.0	43.7	44.0	44.8
Noncollision accidents	1,000 . . .	(NA)	(NA)	4.9	4.4	4.3	4.6	5.2	5.5	5.2
Collision accidents:										
With other motor vehicles	1,000 . . .	23.0	19.9	19.9	19.0	18.8	20.6	18.4	18.2	19.9
With pedestrians	1,000 . . .	9.7	8.5	7.3	6.4	5.8	5.3	6.1	5.7	5.6
With fixed objects.	1,000 . . .	(NA)	(NA)	13.1	12.1	11.1	11.2	12.8	13.5	13.0
Deaths within 30 days [3]	1,000 . . .	51.1	43.8	44.6	41.8	41.7	41.9	42.2	43.0	42.6
Occupants	1,000 . . .	36.8	31.5	33.9	33.1	33.4	33.5	33.2	34.1	33.5
Passenger cars	1,000 . . .	27.4	23.2	24.1	22.4	20.9	20.7	20.3	20.6	19.5
Light trucks.	1,000 . . .	7.5	6.7	8.6	9.6	11.3	11.5	11.7	12.3	12.4
Large trucks	1,000 . . .	1.3	1.0	0.7	0.6	0.8	0.8	0.7	0.7	0.7
Buses	1,000 . . .	(Z)	0.1	(Z)	(Z)	0.1	(Z)	(Z)	(Z)	(Z)
Other/unknown	1,000 . . .	0.5	0.5	0.5	0.4	0.4	0.5	0.5	0.5	0.8
Motorcycle riders [4].	1,000 . . .	5.1	4.6	3.2	2.2	2.5	2.9	3.2	3.3	3.7
Nonoccupants.	1,000 . . .	9.2	7.8	7.5	6.5	5.8	5.6	5.8	5.6	5.5
Pedestrians.	1,000 . . .	8.1	6.8	6.5	5.6	4.9	4.8	4.9	4.9	4.7
Pedalcyclist.	1,000 . . .	1.0	0.9	0.9	0.8	0.8	0.7	0.7	0.7	0.6
Other/unknown	1,000 . . .	0.1	0.1	0.1	0.1	0.1	0.1	0.1	0.1	0.1
Traffic death rates: [3] [5]										
Per 100 million vehicle miles	Rate	3.3	2.5	2.1	1.7	1.6	1.5	1.5	1.5	1.5
Per 100,000 licensed drivers	Rate	35.2	27.9	26.7	23.7	22.3	22.0	22.1	22.1	21.7
Per 100,000 registered vehicles . . .	Rate	34.8	26.4	24.2	21.2	19.6	19.3	19.1	19.1	18.5
Per 100,000 resident population. . .	Rate	22.5	18.4	17.9	15.9	15.3	14.9	14.8	14.9	14.7

NA Not available.   Z Fewer than 50.   [1] Covers only accidents occurring on the road. Data are estimated. Year-to-year comparisons should be made with caution.   [2] Deaths that occur within 1 year of accident. Includes collision categories not shown separately.   [3] Within 30 days of accident. Source: U.S. National Highway Traffic Safety Administration, *Traffic Safety Facts,* annual; and unpublished data. See Internet site <http://www.nhtsa.dot.gov/people/Crash/Index.html>.   [4] Includes motorized cycles.   [5] Based on 30-day definition of traffic deaths.

Source: Except as noted, National Safety Council, Itasca, IL, *Injury Facts,* annual (copyright). See Internet site <http://www.nsc.org/>.

Table 1087. Traffic Fatalities by State: 1980 to 2003

[For deaths within 30 days of the accident]

State	1980	1990	2000	2003	Fatality rate [1] 1980	Fatality rate [1] 2003	State	1980	1990	2000	2003	Fatality rate [1] 1980	Fatality rate [1] 2003
U.S.	51,091	44,599	41,945	42,643	3.3	1.5	MO	1,175	1,097	1,157	1,232	3.4	1.8
							MT.	325	212	237	262	4.9	2.4
AL	940	1,121	996	1,001	3.2	1.7	NE	396	262	276	293	3.5	1.5
AK	88	98	106	95	3.3	1.9	NV	346	343	323	368	5.7	1.9
AZ	947	869	1,036	1,120	5.3	2.1	NH	194	158	126	127	3.0	1.0
AR	588	604	652	627	3.6	2.1	NJ	1,120	886	731	747	2.2	1.1
CA	5,496	5,192	3,753	4,215	3.5	1.3	NM	606	499	432	439	5.4	1.9
CO	709	544	681	632	3.2	1.5	NY	2,610	2,217	1,460	1,491	3.4	1.1
CT	575	385	341	294	3.0	0.9	NC	1,503	1,385	1,557	1,531	3.6	1.6
DE	153	138	123	142	3.6	1.6	ND	151	112	86	105	2.9	1.4
DC	41	48	48	67	1.2	1.6	OH	2,033	1,638	1,366	1,277	2.8	1.2
FL	2,825	2,891	2,999	3,169	3.6	1.7	OK	959	641	650	668	3.5	1.5
GA	1,508	1,562	1,541	1,603	3.5	1.5	OR	646	579	451	512	3.4	1.5
HI	186	177	132	135	3.3	1.5	PA	2,089	1,646	1,520	1,577	2.9	1.5
ID	331	244	276	293	4.8	2.1	RI	129	84	80	104	2.4	1.2
IL	1,975	1,589	1,418	1,453	3.0	1.4	SC	852	979	1,065	968	3.8	2.0
IN	1,166	1,049	886	834	3.0	1.2	SD	228	153	173	203	3.7	2.4
IA	626	465	445	441	3.3	1.4	TN	1,153	1,177	1,307	1,193	3.4	1.7
KS	595	444	461	471	3.4	1.6	TX	4,366	3,250	3,779	3,675	3.8	1.6
KY	820	849	820	928	3.2	2.0	UT	334	272	373	309	3.1	1.3
LA	1,219	959	938	894	5.0	2.0	VT	137	90	76	69	3.7	0.8
ME	265	213	169	207	3.5	1.4	VA	1,045	1,079	929	943	2.7	1.2
MD	756	707	588	649	2.6	1.2	WA	971	825	631	600	3.4	1.1
MA	881	605	433	462	2.5	0.9	WV	523	481	411	394	4.9	2.0
MI	1,750	1,571	1,382	1,283	2.8	1.3	WI	972	769	799	848	3.1	1.4
MN	848	566	625	657	3.0	1.2	WY	245	125	152	165	4.9	1.8
MS	695	750	949	871	4.2	2.3							

[1] Deaths per 100 million vehicle miles traveled.

Source: U.S. National Highway Safety Traffic Administration, *Traffic Safety Facts,* annual. See Internet site <http://www.nhtsa.dot.gov/people/Crash/Index.html>.

716 Transportation

Table 1088. Fatal Motor Vehicle Accidents—National Summary: 1990 to 2003

[Based on data from the Fatality Analysis Reporting System (FARS). FARS gathers data on accidents that result in loss of human life. FARS is operated and maintained by National Highway Traffic Safety Administration's (NHTSA) National Center for Statistics and Analysis (NCSA). FARS data are gathered on motor vehicle accidents that occurred on a roadway customarily open to the public, resulting in the death of a person within 30 days of the accident. Collection of these data depend on the use of police, hospital, medical examiner/coroner, and Emergency Medical Services reports; State vehicle registration, driver licensing, and highway department files; and vital statistics documents and death certificates. See source for further detail]

Item	1990	1995	1998	1999	2000	2001	2002	2003
Fatal crashes, total	39,836	37,241	37,107	37,140	37,526	37,862	38,491	38,252
One vehicle involved	23,445	21,250	20,900	20,911	21,117	21,510	22,164	21,668
Two or more vehicles involved	16,391	15,991	16,207	16,229	16,409	16,352	16,327	16,584
Persons killed in fatal crashes	44,599	41,817	41,501	41,717	41,945	42,196	43,005	42,643
Occupants	37,134	35,291	35,382	35,875	36,348	36,440	37,375	37,132
Drivers	25,750	24,390	24,743	25,257	25,567	25,869	26,659	26,640
Passengers	11,276	10,782	10,530	10,521	10,695	10,469	10,604	10,387
Other	108	119	109	97	86	102	112	105
Nonmotorists	7,465	6,526	6,119	5,842	5,597	5,756	5,630	5,511
Pedestrians	6,482	5,584	5,228	4,939	4,763	4,901	4,851	4,749
Pedalcyclists	859	833	760	754	693	732	665	622
Other	124	109	131	149	141	123	114	140
Occupants killed by vehicle type:								
Passenger cars	24,092	22,423	21,194	20,862	20,699	20,320	20,569	19,460
Mini-compact (95 inches)	3,556	2,207	1,480	1,224	1,113	887	813	633
Subcompact (95 to 99 inches)	4,753	4,584	4,034	3,663	3,660	3,571	3,435	3,048
Compact (100 to 104 inches)	5,310	6,899	6,804	6,942	7,022	6,731	7,061	6,663
Intermediate (105 to 109) inches	4,849	4,666	4,617	4,721	5,204	5,402	5,514	5,502
Full-size (110 to 114) inches	2,386	2,116	2,014	2,179	2,287	2,344	2,434	2,424
Largest (115 inches and over)	2,249	1,297	1,092	708	897	864	828	767
Unknown	989	654	1,153	1,425	516	521	484	423
Motorcycles	3,129	2,114	2,186	2,374	2,783	3,077	3,150	3,534
Other motorized cycles	115	113	108	109	114	120	120	127
Light Trucks	8,601	9,568	10,705	11,265	11,526	11,723	12,274	12,444
Pickup	5,979	5,938	5,921	6,127	6,003	6,139	6,100	5,904
Utility	1,214	1,935	2,713	3,026	3,358	3,530	4,031	4,446
Van	1,154	1,639	2,042	2,088	2,129	2,019	2,109	2,066
Other	254	56	29	24	36	35	34	28
Medium trucks	134	96	99	90	106	82	87	81
Heavy trucks	571	552	643	669	648	620	602	642
Buses	32	33	38	59	22	34	45	40
Other vehicles	296	307	336	355	401	401	424	470
Unknown	164	85	73	92	49	63	104	334
Persons involved in fatal crashes	107,777	102,102	101,100	100,666	100,716	101,175	101,784	101,157
Occupants	99,297	94,621	94,241	93,959	94,325	94,706	95,403	94,807
Drivers	58,893	56,164	56,604	56,502	57,280	57,586	58,113	58,156
Passengers	40,229	38,252	37,448	37,280	36,889	36,892	37,080	36,439
Other	175	205	189	177	156	228	210	212
Nonoccupants	8,480	7,481	6,859	6,707	6,391	6,469	6,381	6,350
Vehicle miles traveled (VMT) (100 mil.)	21,444	24,227	26,315	26,911	27,469	27,973	28,556	28,909
Licensed drivers (1,000)	167,015	176,628	184,861	187,170	190,625	191,276	194,602	196,166
Registered vehicles (1,000)	184,275	197,065	208,076	212,685	217,028	221,230	225,685	230,788
Percent distribution of fatal accidents by the highest blood alcohol concentration (BAC) in accident:								
0.00 percent	49.5	57.7	59.8	60.2	58.7	58.9	59.2	60.1
0.01 to 0.07 percent	6.5	5.7	5.8	5.5	5.9	5.9	5.6	5.5
0.08 percent and over	44.0	36.7	34.4	34.3	35.4	35.2	35.3	34.3
Fatalities per 100,000 population:								
Under 5 years old	4.9	4.3	4.0	3.9	3.7	3.4	3.1	3.1
5 years to 15 years old	6.4	6.0	5.2	5.1	4.7	4.3	4.3	4.4
16 years to 24 years old	35.2	30.7	28.5	28.9	28.5	28.6	29.3	27.9
25 years to 44 years old	19.7	17.2	16.4	16.4	16.1	16.2	16.2	15.9
45 years to 64 years old	14.9	13.6	14.0	13.8	13.8	13.5	13.8	13.9
65 years to 79 years old	18.8	18.5	18.7	18.3	17.1	17.1	17.0	16.2
80 years old and over	26.8	28.0	28.4	27.3	25.0	24.5	23.3	24.1
Fatalities per 100 million VMT [1]	2.1	1.7	1.6	1.6	1.5	1.5	1.5	1.5
Fatalities per 100,000 licensed drivers	26.7	23.7	22.4	22.3	22.0	22.1	22.1	21.7
Licensed driver per person	0.7	0.7	0.7	0.7	0.7	0.7	0.7	0.7
VMT [1] per registered vehicle	11,637	12,294	12,647	12,653	12,657	12,644	12,652	12,526
Fatalities per 100,000 registered vehicles	24.2	21.2	19.9	19.6	19.3	19.1	19.1	18.5
Fatal crashes per 100 million VMT [1]	1.9	1.5	1.4	1.4	1.4	1.4	1.3	1.3
Involved vehicles per fatal crash	1.5	1.5	1.5	1.5	1.5	1.5	1.5	1.5
Fatalities per fatal crash	1.1	1.1	1.1	1.1	1.1	1.1	1.1	1.1
Average occupants per fatal crash	2.5	2.5	2.5	2.5	2.5	2.5	2.5	2.5
Fatalities per 100,000 population	17.9	15.9	15.4	15.3	14.9	14.8	14.9	14.7

[1] VMT = vehicle miles of travel.

Source: U.S. National Highway Traffic Safety Administration, *Fatality Analysis Reporting System,* annual. See Internet site <http://www.nhtsa.dot.gov/people/Crash/Index.html>.

U.S. Census Bureau, Statistical Abstract of the United States: 2006

Table 1089. Motor Vehicle Occupants and Nonoccupants Killed and Injured: 1980 to 2003

[For deaths within 30 days of the accident. (3,416 represents 3,416,000)]

Year	Total	Occupants Total	Passenger cars	Light trucks[1]	Large trucks[1]	Buses	Other/unknown[3]	Motorcycle riders[2]	Nonoccupants Total	Pedestrian	Pedalcyclist	Other/unknown[3]
KILLED												
1980	51,091	36,783	27,449	7,486	1,262	46	540	5,144	9,164	8,070	965	129
1985	43,825	31,479	23,212	6,689	977	57	544	4,564	7,782	6,808	890	84
1990	44,599	33,890	24,092	8,601	705	32	460	3,244	7,465	6,482	859	124
1991	41,508	31,934	22,385	8,391	661	31	466	2,806	6,768	5,801	843	124
1992	39,250	30,485	21,387	8,098	585	28	387	2,395	6,370	5,549	723	98
1993	40,150	31,125	21,566	8,511	605	18	425	2,449	6,576	5,649	816	111
1994	40,716	31,998	21,997	8,904	670	18	409	2,320	6,398	5,489	802	107
1995[4]	41,817	33,064	22,423	9,568	648	33	392	2,227	6,526	5,584	833	109
1996	42,065	33,534	22,505	9,932	621	21	455	2,161	6,368	5,449	765	154
1997	42,013	33,609	22,199	10,249	723	18	420	2,116	6,288	5,321	814	153
1998	41,501	33,088	21,194	10,705	742	38	409	2,294	6,119	5,228	760	131
1999	41,717	33,392	20,862	11,265	759	59	447	2,483	5,842	4,939	754	149
2000	41,945	33,451	20,699	11,526	754	22	450	2,897	5,597	4,763	693	141
2001	42,196	33,243	20,320	11,723	708	34	458	3,197	5,756	4,901	732	123
2002	43,005	34,105	20,569	12,274	689	45	528	3,270	5,630	4,851	665	114
2003	42,643	33,471	19,460	12,444	723	40	804	3,661	5,511	4,749	622	140
INJURED (1,000)												
1988	3,416	3,119	2,585	478	37	15	4	105	192	110	75	8
1990	3,231	2,960	2,376	505	42	33	4	84	187	105	75	7
1991	3,097	2,851	2,235	563	28	21	4	80	166	88	67	11
1992	3,070	2,843	2,232	545	34	20	12	65	162	89	63	10
1993	3,149	2,919	2,265	601	32	17	4	59	171	94	68	9
1994	3,266	3,045	2,364	631	30	16	4	57	164	92	62	9
1995	3,465	3,246	2,469	722	30	19	4	57	162	86	67	10
1996	3,483	3,277	2,458	761	33	20	4	55	151	82	58	11
1997	3,348	3,149	2,341	755	31	17	6	53	146	77	58	11
1998	3,192	3,012	2,201	763	29	16	4	49	131	69	53	8
1999	3,236	3,047	2,138	847	33	22	7	50	140	85	51	3
2000	3,189	2,997	2,052	887	31	18	10	58	134	78	51	5
2001	3,033	2,841	1,927	861	29	15	9	60	131	78	45	8
2002	2,926	2,735	1,805	879	26	19	6	65	126	71	48	7
2003	2,889	2,697	1,756	889	27	18	7	67	124	70	46	8

[1] See footnotes 2 and 3 in Table 1090. [2] Includes motorized cycles. [3] Includes combination trucks. [4] Includes two fatalities of unknown person type.

Source: U.S. National Highway Traffic Safety Administration, *Traffic Safety Facts*, annual; and unpublished data. See Internet site <http://www.nhtsa.dot.gov/people/Crash/Index.html>.

Table 1090. Vehicles Involved in Crashes by Vehicle Type, Rollover Occurrence, and Crash Severity: 2003

[Numbers in thousands (11,107.6 represents 11,107,600]

Vehicle type	Total Number	Total Percent	Rollover occurrence Yes Number	Yes Percent	No Number	No Percent
All crashes [1]	11,107.6	100.0	280.8	2.5	10,826.8	97.5
Passenger cars	6,511.1	100.0	112.5	1.7	6,398.7	98.3
Light trucks: [2]						
Pickup	1,697.8	100.0	58.8	3.5	1,639.0	96.5
Utility	1,431.1	100.0	75.4	5.3	1,355.7	94.7
Van	835.0	100.0	15.7	1.9	819.2	98.1
Other	95.0	100.0	2.4	2.5	92.7	97.5
Large truck [3]	456.6	100.0	14.4	3.1	442.2	96.9
Bus	58.0	100.0	(Z)	0.1	58.0	99.9
Other/unknown	23.0	100.0	1.6	7.1	21.3	92.9
Fatal crashes	54.8	100.0	11.0	20.0	43.8	80.0
Passenger cars	26.2	100.0	4.1	15.8	22.0	84.2
Light trucks: [2]						
Pickup	11.0	100.0	2.7	24.5	8.3	75.5
Utility	7.2	100.0	2.6	35.7	4.6	64.3
Van	3.7	100.0	0.7	18.7	3.0	81.3
Other	0.1	100.0	(Z)	9.8	0.1	90.2
Large truck [3]	4.7	100.0	0.6	13.0	4.1	87.0
Bus	0.3	100.0	(Z)	4.5	0.3	95.5
Other/unknown	1.6	100.0	0.2	13.7	1.4	86.3

Z Less than 500. [1] Includes injury and property-only crashes, not shown separately. [2] Trucks of 10,000 pounds gross vehicle weight rating or less including pickups, vans, truck-based station wagons and utility vehicles. [3] Trucks over 10,000 pounds gross vehicle weight rating.

Source: U.S. National Highway Safety Traffic Administration, *Traffic Safety Facts*, annual; and unpublished data. See Internet site <http://www.nhtsa.dot.gov/people/Crash/Index.html>.

Table 1091. Speeding-Related Traffic Fatalities by State and Road Type and Speed Limit: 2003

[Speeding consists of exceeding the posted speed limit or driving too fast for the road conditions or any speed-related violation charged (Racing, driving above speed limit, speed greater than reasonable, exceeding special speed limit)]

State	Traffic fatali- ties, total	Interstate			Noninterstate					
		Total [1]	Over 55 mph	At or under 55 mph	55 mph	50 mph	45 mph	40 mph	35 mph	Under 35 mph
United States	42,643	13,380	1,403	396	3,743	482	1,652	821	1,447	1,488
Alabama............	1,001	469	46	6	124	16	148	31	45	24
Alaska	95	39	9	3	6	-	6	5	-	4
Arizona............	1,120	432	76	16	52	18	71	38	39	31
Arkansas	627	118	7	-	69	-	10	3	14	31
California	4,215	1,507	242	26	397	58	142	107	173	156
Colorado...........	632	239	23	17	38	5	29	22	23	37
Connecticut.........	294	111	9	15	6	1	16	8	8	43
Delaware	142	37	-	4	4	13	2	5	4	4
District of Columbia ...	67	22	-	-	-	-	-	2	4	4
Florida	3,169	539	35	11	80	13	150	49	2	16
Georgia	1,603	328	25	14	101	8	61	11	80	75
									68	20
Hawaii	135	66	-	7	6	1	11	-	22	10
Idaho	293	82	17	-	8	13	4	-	11	5
Illinois	1,453	566	46	50	226	3	22	47	69	88
Indiana............	834	217	16	14	68	12	20	19	22	34
Iowa	441	68	3	2	24	4	6	1	8	14
Kansas	471	144	17	-	51	2	6	8	7	25
Kentucky	928	122	11	2	75	-	11	-	19	1
Louisiana	894	223	16	3	103	8	26	9	24	20
Maine.............	207	79	3	2	12	16	18	2	14	10
Maryland	649	198	11	6	24	40	10	35	28	43
Massachusetts.......	462	156	17	5	3	5	14	13	26	52
Michigan...........	1,283	293	27	7	132	6	19	5	26	47
Minnesota..........	657	194	13	7	94	10	9	4	3	28
Mississippi.........	871	170	18	-	59	15	35	12	12	11
Missouri	1,232	519	66	12	187	4	32	24	49	58
Montana...........	262	113	18	-	3	2	6	1	14	7
Nebraska	293	38	2	-	3	13	5	1	-	2
Nevada	368	125	14	1	5	3	28	1	26	11
New Hampshire.......	127	31	2	-	1	2	3	8	5	6
New Jersey.........	747	48	4	-	6	6	4	6	4	11
New Mexico	439	172	29	2	28	4	6	13	19	16
New York	1,491	481	9	24	177	10	23	30	23	80
North Carolina.......	1,531	566	31	10	298	8	119	2	71	9
North Dakota........	105	32	-	-	13	-	-	2	1	3
Ohio	1,277	264	25	6	123	2	23	7	38	25
Oklahoma..........	668	273	43	1	34	14	55	15	15	13
Oregon............	512	167	9	11	82	1	13	12	14	9
Pennsylvania........	1,577	652	42	30	177	12	124	66	115	47
Rhode Island........	104	54	1	5	1	1	7	7	7	25
South Carolina.......	968	410	35	1	146	11	91	13	28	28
South Dakota........	203	87	18	1	31	1	1	2	2	6
Tennessee	1,193	272	16	13	72	14	42	26	16	45
Texas.............	3,675	1,509	207	43	225	43	113	94	119	143
Utah	309	93	34	1	10	3	1	9	7	5
Vermont	69	33	4	-	1	13	3	5	3	3
Virginia	943	286	25	11	127	6	43	7	38	23
Washington.........	600	234	20	2	16	38	15	18	53	43
West Virginia........	394	112	14	1	50	2	12	14	5	9
Wisconsin..........	848	306	22	3	161	-	29	-	25	48
Wyoming	165	84	26	1	4	2	8	2	-	4

- Represents zero. [1] Includes fatalities that occurred on roads for which the speed limit was unknown.

Source: U.S. National Highway Traffic Safety Administration, Traffic Safety Facts, Speeding, annual; and unpublished data. See Internet site <http://www.nhtsa.dot.gov/people/Crash/Index.html>.

U.S. Census Bureau, Statistical Abstract of the United States: 2006

Table 1092. Traffic Fatalities by State and Highest Blood Alcohol Concentration (BAC) in the Crash: 2003

[BAC means blood alcohol concentration; g/dl means grams per deciliter]

State	Traffic fatalities, total	No alcohol (BAC = 0.00 g/dl)		Any alcohol (BAC = 0.01 g/dl or more)		Low alcohol (BAC = 0.01–0.07 g/dl)		High alcohol (BAC = 0.08 g/dl or more)	
		Number	Percent	Number	Percent	Number	Percent	Number	Percent
United States ...	42,643	25,630	60	17,013	40	2,383	6	14,630	34
Alabama	1,001	586	59	415	41	40	4	376	38
Alaska	95	60	63	35	37	3	4	31	33
Arizona	1,120	650	58	470	42	63	6	408	36
Arkansas	627	373	59	254	41	51	8	203	32
California	4,215	2,589	61	1,626	39	249	6	1,378	33
Colorado	632	386	61	246	39	26	4	221	35
Connecticut	294	163	55	131	45	17	6	114	39
Delaware	142	82	58	60	42	9	6	51	36
District of Columbia ...	67	33	50	34	50	4	6	29	44
Florida	3,169	1,895	60	1,274	40	185	6	1,089	34
Georgia	1,603	1,115	70	488	30	68	4	420	26
Hawaii	135	63	47	72	53	18	14	54	40
Idaho	293	186	63	107	37	18	6	90	31
Illinois	1,453	814	56	639	44	99	7	539	37
Indiana	834	572	69	262	31	40	5	223	27
Iowa	441	296	67	145	33	26	6	119	27
Kansas	471	265	56	206	44	24	5	182	39
Kentucky	928	652	70	276	30	36	4	240	26
Louisiana	894	488	55	406	45	44	5	363	41
Maine	207	132	64	75	36	6	3	69	33
Maryland	649	368	57	281	43	73	11	208	32
Massachusetts	462	255	55	207	45	37	8	170	37
Michigan	1,283	802	63	481	37	86	7	395	31
Minnesota	657	390	59	267	41	36	5	231	35
Mississippi	871	551	63	320	37	32	4	288	33
Missouri	1,232	728	59	504	41	80	6	425	34
Montana	262	134	51	128	49	20	8	108	41
Nebraska	293	172	59	121	41	22	8	99	34
Nevada	368	186	50	182	50	24	6	159	43
New Hampshire	127	75	59	52	41	8	7	43	34
New Jersey	747	472	63	275	37	35	5	240	32
New Mexico	439	241	55	198	45	28	6	170	39
New York	1,491	962	65	529	35	71	5	458	31
North Carolina	1,531	977	64	554	36	80	5	474	31
North Dakota	105	53	50	52	50	6	5	47	44
Ohio	1,277	810	63	467	37	66	5	402	31
Oklahoma	668	413	62	255	38	35	5	220	33
Oregon	512	305	60	207	40	32	6	175	34
Pennsylvania	1,577	959	61	618	39	77	5	542	34
Rhode Island	104	47	45	57	55	5	5	52	50
South Carolina	968	480	50	488	50	64	7	423	44
South Dakota	203	105	52	98	48	8	4	90	44
Tennessee	1,193	746	63	447	37	43	4	404	34
Texas	3,675	1,966	53	1,709	47	209	6	1,500	41
Utah	309	263	85	46	15	8	2	39	12
Vermont	69	41	59	29	41	8	11	21	30
Virginia	943	580	61	364	39	55	6	309	33
Washington	600	341	57	259	43	31	5	228	38
West Virginia	394	246	63	148	37	22	6	126	32
Wisconsin	848	461	54	387	46	47	6	340	40
Wyoming	165	103	62	62	38	12	7	50	30

Source: U.S. National Highway Traffic Safety Administration, *Traffic Safety Facts*, annual; and unpublished data. See Internet site <http://www.nhtsa.dot.gov/people/Crash/Index.html>.

Table 1093. Fatalities by Highest Blood Alcohol Concentration in the Crash: 1985 to 2003

[BAC means blood alcohol concentration; g/dl means grams per deciliter]

Item	1985	1990	1995	1999	2000	2001	2002	2003
Total fatalities	43,825	44,599	41,817	41,717	41,945	42,196	43,005	42,643
Fatalities in alcohol-related crashes	23,167	22,587	17,732	16,572	17,380	17,400	17,524	17,013
Percent	52.9	50.6	42.4	39.7	41.4	41.2	40.7	39.9
BAC = 0.01–0.07 g/dl:								
Number	3,081	2,980	2,490	2,321	2,511	2,542	2,432	2,383
Percent	7.0	6.7	6.0	5.6	6.0	6.0	5.7	5.6
BAC = 0.08 g/dl or more:								
Number	20,086	19,607	15,242	14,250	14,870	14,858	15,093	14,630
Percent	45.8	44.0	36.5	34.2	35.5	35.2	35.1	34.3
Fatalities with BAC = 0.00 g/dl:								
Number	20,659	22,012	24,085	25,145	24,565	24,796	25,481	25,630
Percent	47.1	49.4	57.6	60.3	58.6	58.8	59.3	60.1

Source: U.S. National Highway Traffic Safety Administration, *Traffic Safety Facts*, annual; and unpublished data. See Internet site <http://www.nhtsa.dot.gov/people/Crash/Index.html>.

Table 1094. **Crashes by Crash Severity: 1990 to 2003**

[6,471 represents 6,471,000. A crash is a police-reported event that produces injury and/or property damage, involves a vehicle in transport and occurs on a trafficway or while the vehicle is in motion after running off the trafficway]

Item	1990	1995	1997	1998	1999	2000	2001	2002	2003
Crashes (1,000).............	6,471	6,699	6,624	6,335	6,279	6,394	6,323	6,316	6,328
Fatal......................	39.8	37.2	37.3	37.1	37.1	37.5	37.9	38.5	38.3
Nonfatal injury.............	2,122	2,217	2,149	2,029	2,054	2,070	2,003	1,929	1,925
Property damage only	4,309	4,446	4,438	4,269	4,188	4,286	4,282	4,348	4,365
Percent of total crashes:									
Fatal.....................	0.6	0.6	0.6	0.6	0.6	0.6	0.6	0.6	0.6
Nonfatal injury.............	32.8	33.1	32.4	32.0	32.7	32.4	31.7	30.5	30.4
Property damage only	66.6	66.4	67.0	67.4	66.7	67.0	67.7	68.8	69.0

Source: U.S. National Highway Safety Traffic Administration, *Traffic Safety Facts,* annual. See Internet site <http://www.nhtsa.dot.gov/people/Crash/Index.html>.

Table 1095. **Alcohol Involvement for Drivers in Fatal Crashes: 1993 and 2003**

[BAC = blood alcohol concentration]

Age, sex, and vehicle type	1993		2003	
	Number of drivers	Percentage with BAC of .08% or greater	Number of drivers	Percentage with BAC of .08% or greater
Total drivers involved in fatal crashes [1]...............	53,401	24	58,156	21
Drivers by age group:				
16 to 20 years old............	7,256	18	7,693	19
21 to 24 years old............	6,406	34	6,234	32
25 to 34 years old............	13,038	32	11,218	27
35 to 44 years old............	9,738	27	10,967	24
45 to 54 years old............	5,970	18	8,972	19
55 to 64 years old............	3,824	14	5,407	12
65 to 74 years old............	3,031	8	3,094	8
75 years old and over	2,817	4	3,294	5
Drivers by sex:				
Male.....................	39,556	27	42,314	24
Female...................	13,082	14	15,091	12
Drivers by vehicle type:				
Passenger cars	30,060	24	26,030	22
Light trucks................	15,207	27	21,944	22
Large trucks...............	4,271	2	4,608	1
Motorcycles...............	2,471	38	3,749	29

[1] Includes age, sex, and types of vehicles unknown.

Source: U.S. National Highway Safety Traffic Administration, *Traffic Safety Facts,* annual. See Internet site <http://www.nhtsa.dot.gov/people/Crash/Index.html>.

Table 1096. **Licensed Drivers and Number in Accidents by Age: 2003**

[196,700 represents 196,700,000]

Age group	Licensed drivers		Drivers in accidents				Accidents per number of drivers	
			Fatal		All			
	Number (1,000)	Percent	Number	Percent	Number (1,000)	Percent	Fatal [1]	All [2]
Total.............	196,700	100.0	54,000	100.0	20,000	100.0	27	10
19 years old and under	9,503	4.8	9,200	17.0	4,410	22.1	97	46
Under 16 years old	58	(Z)	600	1.1	170	0.9	(3)	(3)
16 years old..........	1,311	0.7	1,500	2.8	830	4.2	114	63
17 years old..........	2,239	1.1	2,100	3.9	1,100	5.5	94	49
18 years old..........	2,748	1.4	2,400	4.4	1,190	6.0	87	43
19 years old..........	3,147	1.6	2,600	4.8	1,120	5.6	83	36
20 to 24 years old	16,496	8.4	9,900	18.3	3,660	18.3	60	22
20 years old..........	3,322	1.7	2,400	4.4	1,050	5.3	72	32
21 years old..........	3,294	1.7	2,000	3.7	720	3.6	61	22
22 years old..........	3,221	1.6	2,000	3.7	680	3.4	62	21
23 years old..........	3,342	1.7	1,700	3.1	630	3.2	51	19
24 years old..........	3,317	1.7	1,800	3.3	580	2.9	54	17
25 to 34 years old	34,021	17.3	7,600	14.1	3,580	17.9	22	11
35 to 44 years old	40,876	20.8	9,100	16.9	3,150	15.8	22	8
45 to 54 years old	40,740	20.7	8,200	15.2	2,490	12.5	20	6
55 to 64 years old	26,168	13.3	4,300	8.0	1,400	7.0	16	5
65 to 74 years old	16,165	8.2	2,800	5.2	730	3.6	17	5
75 years old and over	12,731	6.5	2,900	5.4	580	2.9	23	5

Z Less than 0.05. [1] Per 100,000 licensed drivers. [2] Per 100 licensed drivers. [3] Rates for drivers under age 16 are substantially overstated due to the high proportion of unlicensed drivers involved.

Source: National Safety Council, Itasca, IL, *Injury Facts, 2004,* (copyright). See Internet site <http://www.nsc.org/>.

Table 1097. **Passenger Transit Industry—Summary: 1980 to 2003**

[6,510 represents $6,510,000,000. Includes Puerto Rico. Includes aggregate information for all transit systems in the United States. Excludes nontransit services such as taxicab, school bus, unregulated jitney, sightseeing bus, intercity bus, and special application mass transportation systems (e.g., amusement parks, airports, island, and urban park ferries). Includes active vehicles only]

Item	Unit	1980	1985	1990	1995	2000	2002	2003
Operating systems	Number . . .	1,044	4,972	5,078	5,973	6,000	6,000	5,804
Motor bus systems	Number . . .	1,040	2,631	2,688	2,250	2,262	2,264	1,982
Revenue vehicles. active	Number . . .	75,388	94,368	93,553	116,473	131,918	135,706	139,139
Motor bus	Number . . .	59,411	64,258	58,714	67,107	75,013	76,190	77,328
Commuter rail	Number . . .	4,500	4,035	5,007	5,164	5,498	5,724	5,959
Demand response	Number . . .	(NA)	14,490	16,471	29,352	33,080	34,699	35,954
Heavy rail	Number . . .	9,641	9,326	10,419	10,157	10,591	10,718	10,754
Light rail	Number . . .	1,013	717	913	999	1,577	1,445	1,482
Trolley bus	Number . . .	823	676	832	885	951	600	672
Other	Number . . .	(NA)	867	1,197	2,809	5,208	6,330	6,990
Operating funding, total	Mil. dol. . . .	6,510	12,195	16,053	18,241	24,243	26,632	28,086
Passenger funding	Mil. dol. . . .	2,557	4,575	5,891	6,801	8,746	8,649	9,153
Other operating funding [1]	Mil. dol. . . .	248	702	895	2,812	4,217	4,602	5,083
Operating assistance.	Mil. dol. . . .	3,705	6,918	9,267	8,628	11,280	13,382	13,850
Federal	Mil. dol. . . .	1,094	940	970	817	994	1,319	1,617
Local [2]	Mil. dol. . . .	2,611	5,979	5,327	3,981	5,319	5,344	5,577
State [2]	Mil. dol. . . .	(NA)	(NA)	2,970	3,830	4,967	6,719	6,656
Total expense	Mil. dol. . . .	6,711	14,077	17,979	21,540	28,194	30,918	33,439
Operating expense	Mil. dol. . . .	6,247	12,381	15,742	17,849	22,646	24,834	26,859
Vehicle operations	Mil. dol. . . .	3,248	5,655	6,654	8,282	10,111	11,057	11,937
Maintenance	Mil. dol. . . .	1,774	3,672	4,631	.5,047	6,445	6,999	7,369
General administration	Mil. dol. . . .	1,224	2,505	3,450	2,590	3,329	3,808	3,965
Purchased transportation	Mil. dol. . . .	(NA)	549	1,008	1,930	2,761	2,970	3,588
Reconciling expense	Mil. dol. . . .	464	1,696	2,237	3,691	5,548	6,084	6,580
Capital and planning grants, federal [3] . . .	Mil. dol. . . .	2,787	2,559	2,428	5,534	7,366	7,323	7,390
Capital expenditures	Mil. dol. . . .	(NA)	(NA)	(NA)	7,230	9,587	12,848	13,243
Vehicle-miles operated	Million	2,287	2,791	3,242	3,550	4,081	4,277	4,375
Motor bus	Million	1,677	1,863	2,130	2,184	2,315	2,411	2,421
Trolley bus	Million	13	16	14	14	14	14	14
Heavy rail	Million	385	451	537	537	595	621	630
Light rail	Million	18	17	24	35	53	61	64
Commuter rail	Million	179	183	213	238	271	284	286
Demand response.	Million	(NA)	247	306	507	759	803	864
Other	Million	15	14	18	37	74	84	96
Passengers carried.	Million	8,567	8,636	8,799	7,763	9,363	9,623	9,436
Motor bus	Million	5,837	5,675	5,677	4,848	5,678	5,868	5,692
Trolley bus	Million	142	154	126	119	122	116	109
Heavy rail	Million	2,108	2,290	2,346	2,033	2,632	2,688	2,667
Light rail	Million	133	132	175	251	320	337	338
Commuter rail	Million	280	275	328	344	413	414	410
Demand response	Million	(NA)	59	68	88	105	103	111
Other	Million	67	63	79	80	93	97	111
Avg. funding per passenger	Cents	29.8	53.0	66.9	87.6	93.4	89.0	97.0
Employees, number (avg.) [4]	1,000	187	270	273	311	360	374	351
Payroll, employee	Mil. dol. . . .	3,281	5,843	7,226	8,213	10,400	11,197	11,635
Fringe benefits, employee	Mil. dol. . . .	1,353	2,868	3,986	4,484	5,413	6,247	6,914

NA Not available. [1] Beginning 1995, includes taxes levied directly by transit agency and other dedicated funds, formerly included in Local. [2] Includes other operating revenue, nonoperating revenue, and auxiliary income. Data for 1985 are state and local combined. [3] 1980, capital grants only. [4] Through 1990, represents employee equivalents of 2,080 hours = one employee; beginning 1995, equals actual employees.

Source: American Public Transportation Association, Washington, DC, *Public Transportation Fact Book*, annual. See Internet site <http://www.apta.com/>.

Table 1098. **Transit Buses Equipped for Disabilities: 1995 to 2002**

[Represents ADA (Americans with Disabilities Act of 1992) lift- or ramp-equipped buses. Includes buses of transit agencies receiving federal funding for bus purchases and buses of agencies not receiving federal funds that voluntarily report data to the Federal Transit Administration]

Item	1995	1996	1997	1998	1999	2000	2001	2002
Transit buses, total	57,322	57,369	58,975	60,830	63,618	65,324	67,379	68,418
Percent ADA equipped	61.7	66.8	69.4	76.1	80.5	83.6	87.2	91.4
Small buses, total [1]	5,372	5,998	6,853	7,147	8,265	8,850	9,622	9,822
Percent ADA equipped	84.5	87.8	90.4	91.6	93.4	94.5	95.4	99.2
Medium buses, total [1]	3,879	4,233	5,136	5,929	6,613	7,455	7,830	8,693
Percent ADA equipped	66.0	72.8	80.7	86.9	90.1	92.9	93.7	98.4
Large buses, total [1]	46,355	45,587	45,502	46,188	46,891	47,017	47,925	47,764
Percent ADA equipped	59.2	63.8	65.2	72.6	76.8	79.9	84.5	92.2
Articulated buses, total [1]	1,716	1,551	1,484	1,566	1,849	2,002	2,002	2,139
Percent ADA equipped	50.2	57.6	61.4	68.4	81.3	85.5	88.5	97.2

[1] Small buses have fewer than 25 seats; medium buses have 25 to 35 seats; large ones have more than 35 seats; articulated buses are extra-long and measure between 54 and 60 feet.

Source: U.S. Bureau of Transportation Statistics, *National Transportation Statistics*, annual. See Internet site <http://www.bts.gov /publications/nts/index.html>.

722 Transportation

U.S. Census Bureau. Statistical Abstract of the United States: 2006

Table 1099. Characteristics of Rail Transit by Transit Authority: 2002

Mode and transit agency	Primary city served	States served	Directional route-miles [1]	Number of highway-rail crossings	Number of stations	Number of ADA-accessible stations [2]
Total [3]	33	28	9,397.3	5,940	2,768	1,444
Heavy rail.	11	12	1,572.0	27	994	366
Chicago Transit Authority.	Chicago	IL	206.3	25	144	64
Greater Cleveland Regional Transit Authority.	Cleveland	OH	38.1	-	18	9
L.A. County Metropolitan Transportation Authority.	Los Angeles	CA	31.9	-	16	16
Maryland Transit Administration.	Baltimore	MD	29.4	-	14	14
Massachusetts Bay Transportation Authority.	Boston	MA	76.3	-	53	40
Metropolitan Atlanta Rapid Transit Authority.	Atlanta	GA	96.1	-	38	38
Miami-Dade Transit Agency	Miami	FL	42.2	-	21	21
MTA New York City Transit.	New York	NY	493.8	-	468	44
MTA Staten Island Railway.	New York	NY	28.6	-	23	4
Port Authority Trans-Hudson Corp.	New York	NY, NJ	25.0	2	11	5
Port Authority Transit Corporation	Philadelphia	PA, NJ	31.5	-	13	5
San Francisco Bay Area Rapid Transit District.	San Francisco	CA	190.1	-	39	39
Southeastern Pennsylvania Transportation Authority.	Philadelphia	PA	76.1	-	53	13
Washington Metropolitan Area Transit Authority.	Washington	DC, MD, VA	206.6	-	83	54
Commuter rail [4].	17	19	6,835.2	2,505	1,139	628
Alaska Railroad Corporation.	Anchorage	AK	92.4	27	7	7
Altamont Commuter Express Authority . . .	San Jose	CA	172.0	127	10	10
Central Puget Sound Regional Transit Authority.	Seattle	WA	78.6	39	7	7
Connecticut Department of Transportation.	New Haven	CT	101.2	3	8	8
Maryland Transit Administration.	Baltimore	MD, DC, WV	400.4	40	40	19
Massachusetts Bay Transportation Authority.	Boston	MA, RI	711.3	-	124	78
MTA Long Island Rail Road	New York	NY	638.2	402	124	99
MTA Metro-North Railroad	New York	NY, NJ, CT	545.7	162	109	29
New Jersey Transit Corporation	New York	NY, NJ, PA	975.2	329	162	46
North San Diego County Transit Development Board	San Diego	CA	82.2	8	8	8
NE Illinois Regional Commuter Rail Corporation.	Chicago	IL, WI	940.4	512	227	131
Northern Indiana Commuter Trans District	Chicago	IL, IN	179.8	117	20	11
ON TRACK.	Syracuse	NY	3.5	(NA)	3	3
Peninsula Corridor Joint Powers Board.	San Francisco	CA	153.7	49	34	22
Pennsylvania Department of Transportation	Philadelphia	PA	144.4	7	4	3
South Florida Regional Transportation Authority.	Miami	FL	142.2	72	18	18
Southeastern Pennsylvania Transportation Authority.	Philadelphia	PA	449.2	116	153	48
Southern California Regional Rail Authority.	Los Angeles	CA	768.8	438	51	51
Trinity Railway Express	Dallas	TX	69.5	34	9	9
Vermont Transportation Authority.	Burlington	VT	25.0	(NA)	3	3
Virginia Railway Express	Washington	DC, VA	161.5	23	18	18

- Represents zero. NA Not available. [1] The mileage in each direction over which public transportation vehicles travel while in revenue service. The mileage is computed without regard to the number of traffic lanes or rail tracks existing in the right-of-way. [2] Number of stations that comply with the American with Disabilities Act of 1992 (ADA). Additional stations may be wheelchair-accessible, but not comply with other provisions of the ADA. [3] Includes light rail, not shown separately. [4] Excludes commuter-type services operated independently by AMTRAK.

Source: U.S. Bureau of Transportation Statistics, State Transportation Statistics, 2004. See internet site <http://www.bts.gov/publications>. /statetransportationprofiles/>

Table 1100. **Transit Ridership in 50 Largest Urbanized Areas: 2002**

[Areas ranked by 2000 population size]

Urbanized area	2000 Population [1]		Annual unlinked passenger trips [2] (mil.)	Percent distribution				
	Total (1,000)	Rank		Motor bus	Heavy rail [3]	Light rail [4]	Commuter rail [5]	Other [6]
U.S. urbanized area total [7] . . .	**195,984**	**(X)**	**9,017.8**	**58.4**	**29.8**	**3.7**	**4.6**	**3.4**
Top 50, total	127,900	(X)	8,315.4	55.8	32.3	4.0	5.0	2.9
Atlanta, GA	3,500	11	162.3	49.1	50.7	-	-	0.2
Austin, TX	902	40	35.6	98.2	-	-	-	1.8
Baltimore, MD	2,076	18	114.1	76.6	12.5	7.7	2.6	0.6
Boston, MA-NH-RI	4,032	7	395.0	29.1	40.8	18.7	9.7	1.6
Bridgeport-Stamford, CT-NY	889	41	38.1	60.7	-	-	38.4	1.0
Buffalo, NY	977	38	24.5	76.1	-	23.6	-	0.2
Charlotte, NC-SC	759	47	16.6	96.6	-	-	-	3.4
Chicago, IL-IN	8,308	3	595.5	56.7	30.3	-	12.3	0.7
Cincinnati, OH-KY-IN	1,503	26	29.0	98.6	-	-	-	1.4
Cleveland, OH	1,787	21	64.4	82.5	11.2	4.8	-	1.6
Columbus, OH	1,133	36	16.5	97.9	-	-	-	2.1
Dallas-Fort Worth-Arlington, TX . . .	4,146	6	80.8	77.7	-	17.0	2.7	2.7
Denver-Aurora, CO	1,985	20	80.9	86.1	-	12.9	-	1.0
Detroit, MI	3,903	9	53.8	94.1	-	0.1	-	5.8
Hartford, CT.	852	45	19.2	95.6	-	-	1.5	2.8
Houston, TX.	3,823	10	96.9	97.8	-	-	-	2.2
Indianapolis, IN	1,219	33	10.2	96.9	-	-	-	3.1
Jacksonville, FL	882	43	9.3	86.7	-	-	-	13.3
Kansas City, MO-KS	1,362	29	15.2	96.3	-	-	-	3.7
Las Vegas, NV	1,314	31	52.1	98.6	-	-	-	1.4
Los Angeles-Long Beach-Santa Ana, CA	11,789	2	646.9	87.8	5.3	5.0	0.9	0.9
Louisville, KY-IN	864	44	15.0	97.5	-	-	-	2.5
Memphis, TN-MS-AR.	972	39	13.0	81.9	-	16.5	-	1.6
Miami, FL	4,919	5	126.2	81.3	10.9	-	2.0	5.8
Milwaukee, WI	1,309	32	65.6	98.1	-	-	-	1.9
Minneapolis-St. Paul, MN	2,389	16	75.1	97.5	-	-	-	2.5
Nashville-Davidson, TN	750	48	7.1	98.4	-	-	-	1.6
New Orleans, LA	1,009	37	61.1	85.5	-	8.8	-	5.7
New York-Newark, NY-NJ-CT	17,800	1	3,373.3	40.1	52.2	0.2	6.6	0.9
Oklahoma City, OK	747	49	6.0	97.5	-	-	-	2.5
Orlando, FL	1,157	35	24.8	94.8	-	-	-	5.2
Philadelphia, PA-NJ-DE-MD	5,149	4	332.5	52.5	28.3	6.8	9.7	2.8
Phoenix-Mesa, AZ.	2,907	13	44.5	96.5	-	-	-	3.5
Pittsburgh, PA	1,753	22	77.5	85.5	-	9.7	-	4.8
Portland, OR-WA	1,583	23	106.7	72.5	-	26.5	-	1.0
Providence, RI-MA	1,175	34	16.6	89.7	-	-	4.7	5.6
Richmond, VA	819	46	14.5	97.8	-	-	-	2.2
Riverside-San Bernardino, CA. . . .	1,507	25	26.1	90.3	-	-	6.1	3.6
Sacramento, CA	1,393	28	28.6	68.9	-	29.9	-	1.2
Salt Lake City, UT.	888	42	28.3	61.9	-	34.4	-	3.6
San Antonio, TX	1,328	30	45.2	97.7	-	-	-	2.3
San Diego, CA	2,674	15	97.4	70.3	-	26.1	1.6	2.0
San Francisco-Oakland, CA	3,229	12	438.3	45.1	22.2	10.9	1.0	20.8
San Jose, CA.	1,538	24	59.0	77.3	-	13.2	7.7	1.7
Seattle, WA	2,712	14	140.2	66.8	-	0.3	0.6	32.4
St. Louis, MO-IL	2,078	17	49.6	68.7	-	29.6	-	1.7
Tampa-St. Petersburg, FL.	2,062	19	20.3	98.0	-	-	-	2.0
Tucson, AZ	720	50	15.5	98.2	-	-	-	1.8
Virginia Beach, VA	1,394	27	17.6	95.5	-	-	-	4.5
Washington, DC-VA-MD.	3,934	8	432.8	42.3	56.1	-	1.3	0.3
Top 50 as percent of total	65	(X)	92.2	88.0	100.0	100.0	100.0	77.5

- Represents zero. X Not applicable. [1] As of April 1. Based on the 2000 decennial census. [2] The number of times passengers board public transportation vehicles. [3] Also called metro, subway, rapid transit, or rapid rail. [4] Also called streetcar, tramway, or trolley. [5] Also called metropolitan rail or regional rail. [6] Includes such modes as trolley bus, ferry, cable car, vanpool, and demand response. [7] Includes Puerto Rico.

Source: U.S. Bureau of Transportation Statistics, *State Transportation Statistics, 2004.* See Internet site <http://www.bts.gov/publications/statetransportationprofiles/>.

Table 1101. Truck Transportation, Couriers and Messengers, and Warehousing and Storage—Estimated Revenue: 2000 to 2003

[In millions of dollars (234,749 represents $234,749,000,000). For taxable employer firms. Estimates have been adjusted to the results of the 1997 Economic Census. Based on the North American Industry Classification System, 1997; see text, Section 15]

Kind of business	1997 NAICS code [1]	2000	2002	2003
Selected transportation and warehousing industries				
Truck transportation	48, 49	234,749	235,478	242,067
General freight trucking	484	168,621	167,308	171,539
General freight trucking, local	4841	106,277	108,474	111,445
General freight trucking, long-distance	48411	15,152	15,240	16,356
General freight trucking, long-distance, truckload	48412	91,125	93,234	95,089
General freight trucking, long-distance, less than truckload	484121	61,909	65,397	68,767
Specialized freight trucking	484122	29,216	27,837	26,322
Used household and office goods moving	4842	62,344	58,834	60,093
Specialized freight (except used goods) trucking, local	48421	15,875	13,851	14,071
Specialized freight (except used goods) trucking, long-distance	48422	25,332	25,877	26,433
Couriers and messengers	48423	21,138	19,106	19,589
Couriers	492	52,686	52,932	54,409
Local messengers and local delivery	4921	48,258	48,888	50,378
Warehousing and storage	4922	4,428	4,044	4,031
General warehousing and storage	493	13,442	15,238	16,119
Refrigerated warehousing and storage	49311	7,004	8,205	8,728
Farm product warehousing and storage	49312	2,653	2,698	2,732
Other warehousing and storage	49313	647	636	624
	49319	3,139	3,699	4,035

[1] Based on the 1997 North American Industry Classification System; see text Section 15.

Source: U.S. Census Bureau, "2003 Service Annual Survey, Truck Transportation, Messenger Services and Warehousing." Internet site: <http://www.census.gov/econ/www/servmenu.html> (issued December 04).

Table 1102. Truck Transportation—Summary: 2000 to 2003

[In millions of dollars (168,621 represents $168,621,000,000). For taxable employer firms. Covers NAICS 484. Estimates have been adjusted to the results of the 1997 Economic Census. Based on the North American Industry Classification System, 1997; see text, Section 15]

Item	2000	2001	2002	2003
Total operating revenue	168,621	165,994	167,308	171,539
Total motor carrier revenue	157,223	155,418	156,650	161,066
Local trucking [1]	51,854	52,071	53,224	56,235
Long-distance trucking [1]	105,369	103,347	103,427	104,831
Size of shipments:				
Less-than-truckload	44,692	44,496	45,405	45,871
Truckload	112,531	110,923	111,245	115,195
Commodities handled:				
Agricultural and fish products	12,026	11,739	11,103	12,794
Grains, alcohol, and tobacco products	5,608	6,278	7,229	7,018
Stone, nonmetallic minerals, and metallic ores	10,292	10,629	11,238	11,778
Coal and petroleum products	5,877	6,045	5,961	6,297
Pharmaceutical and chemical products	9,074	8,245	7,692	8,135
Wood products, textiles, and leathers	15,792	16,132	15,015	15,598
Base metal and machinery	12,265	12,161	13,100	12,827
Electronic, motorized vehicles, and precision instruments	9,682	9,723	11,239	10,805
Used household and office goods	10,261	9,639	8,671	8,958
New furniture and miscellaneous manufactured products	14,979	15,276	15,755	15,752
Other goods	51,368	49,554	49,649	51,105
Hazardous materials	9,854	9,611	9,570	9,471
Origin and destination of shipments:				
U.S. to U.S.	151,350	150,196	151,698	155,918
U.S. to Canada	1,713	1,580	1,605	1,662
U.S. to Mexico	1,246	1,129	1,079	1,106
Canada to U.S.	1,187	1,034	978	1,031
Mexico to U.S.	1,079	950	754	823
All other destinations	647	531	537	526
Inventory of revenue generating equipment (1,000):				
Trucks	210	211	217	218
Owned	178	179	193	192
Leased	33	32	23	26
Truck-tractors	935	955	908	891
Owned	790	813	762	748
Leased	145	142	147	143
Trailers	1,923	1,991	1,903	1,888
Owned	1,599	1,668	1,614	1,607
Leased	324	323	301	282
Highway miles traveled (mil.):				
Total	86,252	86,350	86,938	86,484
By loaded or partially loaded vehicles	68,404	68,625	68,850	69,252

[1] Local trucking is the carrying of goods within a single metro area and its adjacent nonurban areas; long-distance trucking is the carrying of goods between metro areas.

Source: U.S. Census Bureau, "2003 Service Annual Survey, Truck Transportation, Messenger Services and Warehousing." Internet site: <http://www.census.gov/econ/www/servmenu.html> (issued December 04).

Table 1103. **Railroads, Class I—Summary: 1990 to 2003**

[As of December 31, or calendar year data, except as noted (216 represents 216,000). Compiled from annual reports of Class-I railroads only, except where noted. Minus sign (-) indicates deficit]

Item	Unit	1990	1995	1998	1999	2000	2001	2002	2003
Class-I line-hauling companies [1]	Number . . .	14	11	9	9	8	8	7	7
Employees [2]	1,000	216	188	178	178	168	162	157	155
Compensation	Mil. dol. . .	8,654	9,070	9,938	9,603	9,623	9,430	9,387	9,576
Average per hour.	Dollars . . .	15.83	19	21.3	21	21.5	22.1	22.7	23.4
Average per year.	Dollars . . .	39,987	48,188	55,764	54,082	57,157	58,153	59,650	61,920
Mileage:									
Railroad line-owned [3]	1,000	146	137	132	122	121	119	118	117
Railroad track-owned [4]	1,000	244	228	224	207	205	204	200	200
Equipment:									
Locomotives in service.	Number . . .	18,835	18,812	20,261	20,256	20,028	19,745	20,506	20,774
Average horsepower	1,000 lb. . .	2,665	2,927	3,126	3,200	3,261	3,275	3,378	3,415
Cars in service:									
Freight train [5]	1,000	1,212	1,219	1316	1,369	1,381	1,314	1,300	1,279
Freight cars [6]	1,000	659	583	576	579	560	500	478	467
Income and expenses:									
Operating revenues.	Mil. dol. . . .	28,370	32,279	33,151	33,521	34,102	34,576	35,327	36,639
Operating expenses	Mil. dol. . . .	24,652	27,897	27,916	28,011	29,040	29,164	29,592	31,440
Net revenue from operations.	*Mil. dol. . .*	*3,718*	*4,383*	*5,235*	*5,510*	*5,062*	*5,412*	*5,735*	*5,199*
Income before fixed charges.	Mil. dol. . . .	4,627	5,016	5,803	6,001	5,361	5,517	6,179	5,220
Provision for taxes [7]	Mil. dol. . . .	1,088	1,556	1,573	1,664	1,430	1,614	1,823	1,494
Ordinary income.	Mil. dol. . . .	1,961	2,439	2,807	2,976	2,501	2,740	3,201	2,683
Net income	Mil. dol. . . .	1,977	2,324	2,807	2,971	2,500	2,740	3,201	2,687
Net railway operating income	Mil. dol. . . .	2,648	2,858	3,698	4,047	3,924	4,111	4,248	4,078
Total taxes [8]	Mil. dol. . . .	3,780	4,075	4,411	4,459	4,379	4,673	4,724	4,316
Indus. return on net investment . . .	Percent . . .	8.1	7	7	6.9	6.5	6.9	7	6.3
Gross capital expenditures	Mil. dol. . . .	3,591	5,720	7,357	6,193	5,290	5,113	5,605	5,989
Equipment	Mil. dol. . . .	996	2,343	2,321	2,183	1,508	1,013	1,021	1,300
Roadway and structures	Mil. dol. . . .	2,644	3,651	4,875	4,446	4,549	4,421	4,645	4,561
Other	Mil. dol. . . .	-49	-275	161	-436	-767	-321	-61	128
Balance sheet:									
Total property investment	Mil. dol. . . .	70,348	86,186	102,171	103,424	106,136	108,588	117,770	122,902
Accrued depreciation and									
amortization	Mil. dol. . . .	22,222	23,439	23,338	23,177	23,989	24,635	26,649	29,215
Net investment	Mil. dol. . . .	48,126	62,746	78,832	80,247	82,147	83,953	91,121	93,686
Shareholder's equity	Mil. dol. . . .	23,662	31,419	32,976	30,478	32,401	34,822	39,675	41,151
Net working capital	Mil. dol. . . .	-3,505	-2,634	-4,443	-4,834	-5,783	-6,282	-6,037	-6,750
Cash dividends.	Mil. dol. . . .	2,074	1,518	1,521	2,084	819	2,120	870	1,406
AMTRAK passenger traffic:									
Passenger revenue	Mil. dol. . . .	941.9	734.1	821.5	1,067.8	1,201.6	1,299.9	1,304.3	1,421.1
Revenue-passengers carried.	1,000	22,382	20,349	21,248	21,544	22,985	23,444	23,269	24,595
Revenue-passenger miles	Million . . .	6,125	5,401	5,325	5,289	5,574	5,571	5,314	5,680
Averages:									
Revenue per passenger	Dollars . . .	42.1	36.1	38.7	49.6	52.3	55.4	56.1	57.8
Revenue per passenger mile . . .	Cents . . .	15.4	13.6	15.4	20.2	21.6	23.3	24.5	25.0
Freight service:									
Freight revenue	Mil. dol. . . .	24,471	31,356	32,247	32,680	33,083	33,533	34,110	35,413
Per ton-mile	Cents . . .	2.7	2.4	2.3	2.3	2.3	2.2	2.3	2.3
Per ton originated	Dollar . . .	19.3	20.2	19.6	19.0	19.0	19.3	19.3	19.7
Revenue-tons originated	Million . . .	1,425	1,550	1,649	1,717	1,738	1,742	1,767	1,799
Revenue-tons carried	Million . . .	2,024	2,322	2,158	2,155	2,179	2,187	2,207	2,240
Tons carried one mile	Billion . . .	1,034	1,306	1,377	1,433	1,466	1,495	1,507	1,551
Average miles of road operated . . .	1,000 . . .	133	125	120	121	121	121	123	122
Revenue ton-miles per mile of									
road	1,000 . . .	7,763	10,439	11,491	11,848	12,156	12,358	12,245	12,686
Revenue per ton-mile	Cents . . .	3	2	2	2	2	2	2	2
Train miles.	Million . . .	380	458	475	490	504	500	500	516
Net ton-miles per train-mile [9]	Number . . .	2,755	2,870	2,923	2,947	2,923	3,005	3,030	3,024
Net ton-miles per loaded									
car-mile [9]	Number . . .	69.1	73.6	73.2	73.8	73.1	72.4	71.5	71.4
Train-miles per train-hour	Miles. . . .	23.7	21.8	19	20	21	21	21	20
Haul per ton, U.S. as a system . . .	Miles. . . .	726	843	835	835	843	858	853	862
Accidents/incidents: [10]									
Casualties—all railroads:									
Persons killed.	Number . . .	1,297	1,146	1,008	932	937	971	951	865
Persons injured.	Number . . .	25,143	14,440	11,459	11,700	11,643	10,985	11,103	9,151
Class-I railroads:									
Persons killed.	Number . . .	1,166	994	900	808	778	805	796	738
Persons injured.	Number . . .	19,284	9,571	7,532	7,805	7,655	7,232	7,722	5,878

[1] See text, this section, for definition of Class I.   [2] Average midmonth count.   [3] Represents the aggregate length of roadway of all line-haul railroads. Excludes yard tracks, sidings, and parallel lines. (Includes estimate for Class-II and -III railroads). [4] Includes multiple main tracks, yard tracks, and sidings owned by both line-haul and switching and terminal. (Includes estimate for Class-II and -III railroads).   [5] Includes cars owned by all railroads, private car companies, and shippers.   [6] Class-I railroads only.   [7] Includes State income taxes.   [8] Includes payroll, income, and other taxes.   [9] Revenue and nonrevenue freight. [10] Source: Federal Railroad Admin., *Accident Bulletin*, annual. Includes highway grade crossing casualties. See Internet site <http://www.fra.dot.gov/>.

Source: Except as noted, Association of American Railroads, Washington, DC, *Railroad Facts, Statistics of Railroads of Class-I*, annual, and *Analysis of Class-I Railroads*, annual. See Internet site <http://www.aar.org/AboutTheIndustry/AboutTheIndustry.asp>.

Table 1104. Railroads, Class-I Cars of Revenue Freight Loaded, 1970 to 2004, and by Commodity Group, 2003 and 2004

[In thousands (27,160 represents 27,160,000). Figures are 52-week totals]

Year	Carloads [1]	Commodity group	Carloads 2003 [3]	Carloads 2004 [3]	Commodity group	Carloads 2003 [3]	Carloads 2004 [3]
1970....	27,160	Coal	6,633	6,821	Metals and products	599	644
1980....	22,598	Metallic ores	252	257	Stone, clay, and glass products	513	527
1990....	16,177	Chemicals, allied products	1,464	1,522	Crushed stone, gravel, sand	891	938
1995....	16,706	Grain	1,095	1,126	Nonmetallic minerals	381	391
1997 [2]..	16,568	Motor vehicles and equipment	1,217	1,181	Waste and scrap materials	472	515
1998 [2]..	16,914	Pulp, paper, allied products	442	446	Lumber, wood products	277	297
1999 [3]..	16,407	Primary forest products	186	173	Coke	248	278
2000 [3]..	16,354	Food and kindred products	433	420	Petroleum products	282	298
2001 [3]..	16,286	Grain mill products	471	462	All other carloads	304	301
2002 [3]..	16,101						
2003 [3]..	16,159						
2004 [3]..	16,598						

[1] Beginning 1990 excludes intermodal. [2] Excludes 2 Class-I railroads. [3] Excludes 3 Class-I railroads. 2004 data preliminary.

Source: Association of American Railroads, Washington, DC, *Weekly Railroad Traffic*, annual. See Internet site <http://www.aar.org/AboutTheIndustry/AboutTheIndustry.asp>.

Table 1105. Railroads, Class-I Line-Haul-Revenue Freight Originated by Commodity Group: 1990 to 2004

[21,401 represents 21,401,000]

Commodity group	1990	1995	1998	1999	2000	2001	2002	2003	2004
Carloads (1,000) [1]	21,401	23,726	25,705	27,096	27,763	27,205	27,901	28,870	30,095
Farm products	1,689	1,692	1,404	1,477	1,437	1,461	1,471	1,519	1,519
Metallic ores	508	463	311	295	322	251	328	331	339
Coal	5,912	6,095	7,027	6,965	6,954	7,295	7,088	7,037	7,102
Nonmetallic minerals	1,202	1,159	1,256	1,306	1,309	1,280	1,310	1,370	1,430
Food and kindred products	1,307	1,377	1,282	1,354	1,377	1,446	1,472	1,478	1,461
Lumber and wood products	780	719	645	673	648	603	619	612	616
Pulp, paper, allied products	611	628	547	612	633	601	646	667	669
Chemicals, allied products	1,531	1,642	1,653	1,814	1,820	1,777	1,866	1,913	1,981
Petroleum and coal products	573	596	510	543	565	547	533	606	651
Stone, clay, and glass products	539	516	475	538	541	528	559	581	594
Primary metal products	477	575	644	682	723	642	656	648	701
Fabricated metal products	31	32	27	27	30	51	38	36	39
Machinery, exc. electrical	39	41	37	34	35	46	38	38	45
Transportation equipment	1,091	1,473	1,671	1,896	1,984	1,777	1,831	1,811	1,849
Waste and scrap materials	439	623	581	624	619	591	617	651	725
Tons (mil.) [1]	1,425	1,550	1,649	1,717	1,738	1,742	1,767	1,799	1,844
Farm products	147	154	129	139	136	137	138	141	142
Metallic ores	47	44	31	29	32	25	31	33	33
Coal	579	627	749	751	758	801	785	784	792
Nonmetallic minerals	109	110	120	125	126	123	126	133	140
Food and kindred products	81	91	87	92	94	98	102	102	100
Lumber and wood products	53	51	47	50	49	46	48	47	47
Pulp, paper, allied products	33	36	31	35	36	34	37	39	38
Chemicals, allied products	126	138	139	154	155	150	157	162	167
Petroleum and coal products	40	43	38	40	42	42	42	49	54
Stone, clay, and glass products	44	43	41	47	48	46	49	51	53
Primary metal products	38	47	53	56	60	53	55	54	59
Fabricated metal products	1	1	1	1	1	1	1	1	1
Machinery, exc. electrical	1	1	1	1	1	1	1	1	1
Transportation equipment	23	30	36	40	42	37	38	36	37
Waste and scrap materials	28	38	36	40	40	37	39	41	46
Gross revenue (mil. dol.) [1]	29,775	33,782	34,898	35,441	36,063		36,742	38,434	41,622
Farm products	2,422	3,020	2,529	2,720	2,673	2,741	2,711	2,870	3,176
Metallic ores	408	394	373	336	338	288	285	289	317
Coal	6,954	7,356	7,997	7,739	7,794	8,181	7,797	7,890	8,418
Nonmetallic minerals	885	875	920	955	969	945	967	1,041	1,131
Food and kindred products	2,188	2,464	2,378	2,400	2,424	2,579	2,657	2,760	2,892
Lumber and wood products	1,390	1,385	1,487	1,528	1,524	1,519	1,628	1,745	1,924
Pulp, paper, allied products	1,486	1,543	1,472	1,457	1,526	1,457	1,567	1,646	1,730
Chemicals, allied products	3,933	4,553	4,610	4,616	4,636	4,504	4,658	4,779	5,100
Petroleum and coal products	918	997	991	980	1,010	1,014	1,026	1,123	1,268
Stone, clay, and glass products	931	1,044	1,056	1,089	1,113	1,090	1,149	1,211	1,323
Primary metal products	979	1,199	1,304	1,289	1,371	1,292	1,288	1,349	1,518
Fabricated metal products	42	44	37	38	48	65	61	47	50
Machinery, exc. electrical	67	69	64	55	61	73	61	60	72
Transportation equipment	3,100	3,269	3,339	3,582	3,843	3,590	3,731	3,707	3,746
Waste and scrap materials	504	685	693	689	706	685	717	799	956

[1] Includes commodity groups and small packaged freight shipments, not shown separately.

Source: Association of American Railroads, Washington, DC, *Freight Commodity Statistics*, annual. See Internet site <http://www.aar.org/AboutTheIndustry/AboutTheIndustry.asp>.

Transportation 727

Table 1106. Railroad Freight—Producer Price Indexes: 1990 to 2004

[Dec. 1984 = 100. Reflects prices for shipping a fixed set of commodities under specified and unchanging conditions]

Commodity	1990	1995	1999	2000	2001	2002	2003	2004
Railroad line-haul operating ...	107.5	111.7	113.0	114.5	116.6	118.9	121.4	126.1
Coal	104.2	107.3	107.3	108.7	110.6	110.1	111.4	113.3
Farm products	110.4	115.6	121.7	123.1	124.5	125.5	132.1	146.1
Food products	105.4	111.2	99.7	100.4	102.8	102.7	101.7	107.4
Metallic ores	106.5	101.9	103.8	105.9	107.0	107.0	105.9	109.9
Chemicals and allied products	111.7	120.0	119.1	121.3	122.3	126.2	131.7	139.7
Nonmetallic minerals	111.7	119.5	121.7	122.1	123.0	124.3	125.7	131.4
Lumber and wood products	107.5	110.0	109.8	109.0	112.2	120.5	123.3	131.5
Transportation equipment	107.5	112.8	113.3	112.6	118.7	130.5	136.6	141.7
Pulp, paper, and allied products	108.0	108.7	115.5	119.0	122.4	122.4	124.4	130.6
Primary metal products	113.1	115.6	118.4	124.1	128.8	132.5	136.1	141.2
Stone, clay, glass, and concrete products	114.1	121.4	122.6	128.7	129.0	124.3	127.1	132.8
Petroleum and coal products	109.2	114.3	123.0	124.6	126.8	127.5	129.6	132.1

Source: U.S. Bureau of Labor Statistics, *Producer Price Indexes*, monthly and annual. See Internet site <http://www.bls.gov/ppi/>.

Table 1107. Petroleum Pipeline Companies—Characteristics: 1980 to 2003

[173 represents 173,000. Covers pipeline companies operating in interstate commerce and subject to jurisdiction of the Federal Energy Regulatory Commission]

Item	Unit	1980	1985	1990	1995	1999	2000	2001	2002	2003
Miles of pipeline, total ...	1,000	173	171*	168	177	154	152	155	150	140
Gathering lines	1,000	36	35	32	35	20	18	17	16	14
Trunk lines	1,000	136	136	136	142	134	134	138	133	126
Total deliveries	Mil. bbl.	10,600	10,745	11,378	12,862	13,317	14,450	13,352	13,343	13,236
Crude oil	Mil. bbl.	6,405	6,239	6,563	6,952	7,551	6,923	7,082	7,019	6,941
Products	Mil. bbl.	4,195	4,506	4,816	5,910	5,766	7,527	6,270	6,324	6,295
Total trunk line traffic	Bil. bbl-miles.	3,405	3,342	3,500	3,619	3,738	3,508	3,505	3,563	3,591
Crude oil	Bil. bbl-miles.	1,948	1,842	1,891	1,899	1,815	1,602	1,566	1,620	1,609
Products	Bil. bbl-miles.	1,458	1,500	1,609	1,720	1,923	1,906	1,939	1,943	1,982
Carrier property value ...	Mil. dol.	19,752	21,605	25,828	27,460	33,780	29,648	32,148	32,605	32,018
Operating revenues	Mil. dol.	6,356	7,461	7,149	7,220	7,711	7,483	7,730	7,812	7,704
Net income	Mil. dol.	1,912	2,431	2,340	2,670	2,928	2,705	3,007	3,409	3,470

Source: PennWell Publishing Co., Houston, Texas, *Oil & Gas Journal*, annual (copyright).

Table 1108. U.S. Postal Service Rates for Letters and Postcards: 1958 to 2002

[Domestic airmail letters discontinued in 1973 at 13 cents per ounce; superseded by express mail. Prior to February 3, 1991, international airmail rates were based on international zones which have been discontinued. Rates exclude Canada and Mexico]

Domestic mail date rate of change	Surface mail — Letters Each ounce	Surface mail — Letters First ounce	Surface mail — Letters Each added ounce	Postcards	Express mail[1]	International air mail date of rate change	Letters First 1/2 ounce	Letters Second 1/2 ounce	Letters Each added 1/2 ounce	Postcards	Aerogrammes
1958 (Aug. 1) ...	0.04	(X)	(X)	0.03	(X)	1961 (July 1)	(X)	(X)	(X)	0.11	0.11
1963 (Jan. 7) ...	0.05	(X)	(X)	0.04	(X)	1967 (May 1) ...	(X)	(X)	(X)	0.13	0.13
1968 (Jan. 7) ...	0.06	(X)	(X)	0.05	(X)	1971 (July 1) ...	(X)	(X)	(X)	0.13	0.13
1971 (May 16) ...	0.08	(X)	(X)	0.06	(X)	1974 (Mar. 2) ...	(X)	(X)	(X)	0.18	0.18
1974 (Mar. 2) ...	0.10	(X)	(X)	0.08	(X)	1976 (Jan. 3) ...	(X)	(X)	(X)	0.21	0.22
1975 (Sept. 14) ..	(X)	0.10	0.09	0.07	(X)	1981 (Jan. 1) ...	(X)	(X)	(X)	0.28	0.30
1975 (Dec. 31) ..	[2](X)	[2]0.13	[2]0.11	[2]0.09	(X)	1985 (Feb. 17) ...	(X)	(X)	(X)	0.33	0.36
1978 (May 29) ..	(X)	0.15	0.13	0.10	(X)	1988 (Apr. 17)...	(X)	(X)	[3] (X)	0.36	0.39
1981 (Mar. 22) ..	(X)	0.18	0.17	0.12	(X)	1991 (Feb. 3) ...	0.50	0.45	[3]0.39	0.40	0.45
1981 (Nov. 1) ...	(X)	0.20	0.17	0.13	9.35	1995 (July 9)...	0.60	[3]0.40	(X)	0.40	0.45
1985 (Feb.17) ...	(X)	0.22	0.17	0.14	10.75	1999 (Jan. 10) ..	0.60	[3]0.40	(X)	0.50	0.50
1988 (Apr. 3) ...	(X)	0.25	0.20	0.15	[4]12.00	2001 (Jan. 7) ...	[3,5]0.80	[3,5] 1.70	(X)	0.70	0.70
1991 (Feb. 3) ...	(X)	0.29	0.23	0.19	[4]13.95	2002 (June 30) ..	[3]0.80	[3]1.70	(X)	0.70	0.70
1995 (Jan. 1) ...	(X)	0.32	0.23	0.20	[4]15.00						
1999 (Jan. 10) ..	(X)	0.33	0.22	0.20	[4]15.75						
2001 (Jan. 7) ...	(X)	0.34	0.21	0.20	[4]16.00						
2002 (June 30) ..	(X)	0.37	0.23	0.23	[4]17.85						

X Not applicable. [1] Post Office to addressee rates. Rates shown are for weights up to 2 pounds, all zones. Beginning Feb. 17, 1985, for weights between 2 and 5 lbs, $12.85 is charged. Prior to Nov. 1, 1981, rate varied by weight and distances. Over 5 pounds still varies by distance. [2] As of October 11, 1975, surface mail service upgraded to level of airmail. [3] Up to the limit of 64 ounces. [4] Over 8 ounces and up to 2 pounds. [5] The rate increments changed to 1 ounce.

Source: U.S. Postal Service, United States Domestic Postage Rate: Recent History, and unpublished data. See Internet site <http://www.usps.com/common/category/postage.htm>.

Table 1109. **U.S. Postal Service—Summary: 1980 to 2004**

[106,311 represents 106,311,000,000. For years ending September 30. Includes Puerto Rico and all outlying areas. See text, this section]

Item	1980	1990	1995	2000	2002	2003	2004
Offices, stations, and branches	39,486	40,067	39,149	38,060	37,683	37,579	37,159
Number of post offices	30,326	28,959	28,392	27,876	27,791	27,556	27,505
Number of stations and branches	9,160	11,108	10,757	10,184	9,892	10,023	9,654
Delivery Points (mil.)	(NA)	(NA)	(NA)	135.9	139.5	141.4	142.3
Residential	(NA)	(NA)	(NA)	123.9	127.0	128.7	129.6
City	(NA)	(NA)	(NA)	76.1	77.0	77.5	78.0
P.O. Box	(NA)	(NA)	(NA)	15.9	15.8	15.7	15.6
Rural/highway contract	(NA)	(NA)	(NA)	31.9	34.2	35.5	36.0
Business	(NA)	(NA)	(NA)	12.1	12.5	12.7	12.7
Pieces of mail handled (mil.)	106,311	166,301	180,734	207,882	202,822	202,185	206,106
Domestic [1]	105,348	165,503	179,933	206,782	201,918	201,380	205,262
First class mail [2]	60,276	89,270	96,296	103,526	102,379	99,059	97,926
Express Mail	17	59	57	71	61	56	54
Priority Mail	248	518	869	1,223	998	860	849
Periodicals (formerly 2d class)	10,220	10,680	10,194	10,365	9,690	9,320	9,135
Standard Mail (formerly Standard A)	30,381	63,725	71,112	90,057	87,231	90,492	95,564
Package Services (formerly Standard B)	633	663	936	1,128	1,075	1,129	1,132
Mailgram	39	14	5	4	3	3	2
U.S. Postal Service	(NA)	538	412	363	425	392	529
Free for the blind	28	35	52	47	57	70	71
International economy mail (surface)	450	166	106	79	39	30	26
International airmail	513	632	696	1,021	865	775	818
Employees, total (1,000)	667	843	875	901	854	827	808
Career	643	761	753	788	753	729	708
Headquarters	3	2	2	2	2	2	3
Headquarters support	(NA)	6	4	6	4	4	3
Inspection Service	5	4	4	4	4	4	4
Inspector General	(X)	(X)	(X)	1	1	1	1
Field Career	635	747	745	775	743	719	697
Postmasters	29	27	27	26	26	26	26
Supervisors/managers	36	43	35	39	38	35	34
Professional, administrative, and technical	5	10	11	10	10	9	9
Clerks	263	290	274	282	257	242	226
Mail handlers	37	51	57	61	59	57	55
City carriers	187	236	240	241	234	229	228
Motor vehicle operators	6	7	8	9	9	9	9
Rural carriers	33	42	46	57	61	62	63
Special delivery messengers	3	2	2	(X)	(X)	(X)	(X)
Building and equipment maintenance	27	33	38	42	42	41	40
Vehicle maintenance	5	5	5	6	6	6	6
Other [3]	4	1	2	2	2	2	2
Noncareer	25	83	122	114	101	98	100
Casuals	5	27	26	30	19	17	21
Transitional	(X)	(X)	32	13	13	11	10
Rural substitutes	20	43	50	58	56	56	56
Relief/Leave replacements	(X)	12	13	12	12	12	12
Nonbargaining temporary	(X)	(Z)	1	1	1	1	1
Compensation and employee benefits (mil. dol.)	16,541	34,214	41,931	49,532	51,557	50,428	52,134
Average salary per employee (dol.) [4]	24,799	37,570	45,001	50,103	54,225	57,051	60,261
Pieces of mail per employee, (1,000)	159	197	207	231	237	244	255
Total revenue (mil. dol.) [5]	19,253	40,074	54,509	64,540	66,463	68,529	68,996
Operating postal revenue	17,143	39,201	54,176	64,476	66,415	68,498	68,960
Mail revenue [6]	16,377	37,892	52,490	62,284	63,761	65,701	65,869
First class mail	10,146	24,023	31,955	35,516	36,483	37,048	36,377
Priority mail [7]	612	1,555	3,075	4,837	4,723	4,494	4,421
Express mail [8]	184	630	711	996	911	888	852
Mailgram	15	8	2	2	1	1	1
Periodicals (formerly 2d class)	863	1,509	1,972	2,171	2,165	2,235	2,192
Standard Mail (formerly Standard A)	2,412	8,082	11,792	15,193	15,819	17,231	18,123
Package Services (formerly Standard B)	805	919	1,525	1,912	2,080	2,216	2,207
International economy mail (surface)	154	222	205	180	150	146	145
International airmail	442	941	1,254	1,477	1,429	1,441	1,551
Service revenue	765	1,310	1,687	2,191	2,655	2,798	3,091
Registry [9]	157	174	118	98	87	82	75
Certified [9]	120	310	560	385	606	624	630
Insurance [9]	55	47	52	109	135	138	128
Collect-on-delivery	21	26	21	22	14	11	11
Special delivery [10]	73	6	3	(X)	(X)	(X)	(X)
Money orders	95	155	196	235	239	231	231
Other [9]	244	592	737	1,342	1,574	1,711	2,017
Operating expenses (mil. dol.) [11]	19,413	40,490	50,730	62,992	65,234	63,902	65,851

NA Not available.   X Not applicable.   Z Fewer than 500.   [1] Data for 1980 includes penalty and franked mail, not shown separately.   [2] Items mailed at 1st class rates and weighing 11 ounces or less.   [3] Includes discontinued operations, area offices, and nurses.   [4] For career bargaining unit employees. Includes fringe benefits.   [5] Net revenues after refunds of postage. Includes operating reimbursements, stamped envelope purchases, indemnity claims, and miscellaneous revenue and expenditure offsets. Shown in year which gave rise to the earnings.   [6] For 1980, includes penalty and franked mail, not shown separately. Later years have that mail distributed into the appropriate class.   [7] Provides 2 to 3 day delivery service.   [8] Overnight delivery of packages weighing up to 70 pounds.   [9] Beginning 1998, return receipt revenue broken out from registry, certified, and insurance and included in "other."   [10] Special delivery discontinued June 8, 1997.   [11] Shown in year in which obligation was incurred.

Source: U.S. Postal Service, *Annual Report of the Postmaster General* and *Comprehensive Statement on Postal Operations,* annual; and unpublished data.

Transportation 729

No. 234.—MILEAGE OF LINES AND WIRES, NUMBER OF OFFICES, AND TRAFFIC OF THE WESTERN UNION TELEGRAPH COMPANY FOR EACH YEAR ENDING JUNE 30, FROM 1866 TO 1891, INCLUSIVE.

[From A. R. Spofford's American Almanac.]

Year.	Miles of line.	Miles of wire.	Number of offices.	Number of messages sent.	Receipts.	Expenses.	Profits.	Average tolls per message.	Average cost per message.	Average profit per message.
					Dollars.	Dollars.	Dollars.	Cents.	Cents.	Cents.
1866....	37,380	75,686	2,250	....						
1867....	46,270	85,291	2,565	5,879,282	6,568,925	3,944,006	2,624,920	.....	.....	.....
1868....	50,183	97,594	3,219	6,404,595	7,004,560	4,362,849	2,641,711	104.7	63.4	41.3
1869....	52,099	104,584	3,607	7,934,933	7,316,918	4,568,117	2,748,801	89.3	54.7	34.6
1870....	54,109	112,191	3,972	9,157,646	7,138,738	4,910,772	2,227,966	75.5	51.2	24.3
1871....	56,032	121,151	4,606	10,646,077	7,637,449	5,104,787	2,532,662	69.5	45.7	23.8
1872....	62,033	137,190	5,237	12,444,499	8,457,096	5,666,863	2,790,223	66.2	43.8	22.4
1873....	65,757	154,472	5,740	14,456,832	9,333,019	6,575,056	2,757,963	62.5	43.4	19.1
1874....	71,585	175,735	6,188	16,329,256	9,262,654	6,755,734	2,506,920	54.9	39.5	15.4
1875....	72,833	179,496	6,565	17,153,710	9,564,575	6,335,415	3,229,158	54.9	35.2	18.8
1876....	73,532	183,832	7,072	18,729,567	10,034,984	6,635,474	3,399,510	50.9	33.5	17.4
1877....	76,955	194,323	7,500	21,158,941	9,812,353	6,672,225	3,140,128	45.6	29.8	13.8
1878....	81,002	206,202	8,014	23,918,894	9,861,356	6,309,813	3,551,543	38.9	26.0	13.0
1879....	83,987	211,566	8,534	25,070,106	10,960,640	6,160,200	4,800,440	38.6	25.2	19.1
1880....	85,645	233,534	9,077	29,215,509	12,782,895	6,948,957	5,833,938	38.5	25.4	19.1
1881....	110,340	327,171	10,737	32,500,000	14,393,544	8,485,264	5,908,280	38.4	25.6	18.1
1882....	131,069	374,368	12,068	38,842,247	17,114,166	9,996,096	7,118,070	38.2	25.8	18.3
1883....	144,294	432,726	12,917	41,181,177	19,454,909	11,794,553	7,660,356	38.0	26.0	13.9
1884....	145,037	450,571	13,761	42,076,226	19,632,940	13,022,504	6,610,436	36.5	25.2	11.3
1885....	147,500	462,283	14,184	42,096,583	17,706,834	12,005,910	5,700,924	32.1	24.9	7.2
1886....	151,832	489,607	15,142	43,289,807	16,298,639	12,378,783	3,919,855	31.3	23.4	9.1
1887....	156,814	524,641	15,658	47,304,530	17,191,910	13,154,629	4,037,281	30.4	23.9	8.5
1888....	171,375	616,248	17,241	51,463,955	19,711,164	14,640,592	5,070,572	31.2	23.2	8.0
1889....	178,754	647,697	18,470	54,108,326	20,783,194	14,565,153	6,218,041	31.2	23.4	8.8
1890....	183,917	678,997	19,382	55,878,762	22,387,029	15,074,304	7,312,725	32.4	22.7	8.7
1891....	187,981	715,591	20,098	59,148,343	23,034,327	16,428,742	6,605,585	32.5	23.2	9.3

The greatly increased mileage since 1880 is principally due to the fact that in 1881 the Western Union Telegraph Company absorbed by purchase all the lines of the American Union and the Atlantic and Pacific Telegraph Companies, the former having previously in operation over 12,000 miles of line and the latter 8,706 miles. Capital stock of the Western Union, $86,200,000.

The Western Union has exclusive contracts with several international cable companies, operating eight Atlantic cables, and guarantees 5 per cent annual dividends on the stock of the American Cable Company; amount, $14,000,000.

Besides the above, there are many new lines of telegraph which have complied with the United States telegraph act of 1866, and are operating wires with or without connection with railway companies.

The New York Mutual Telegraph Company, established in 1881, has about 8,000 miles of line, 60,000 miles of wire, 1,200 offices, and has extended its lines north and south, operating from Boston to Chicago, St. Louis, Washington, etc. Capital stock, $2,500,000. This line is now leased and operated by the Western Union Telegraph Company, at a rental of 6 per cent per annum on the stock.

The Baltimore and Ohio Railroad Telegraph, having lines coextensive with its railway system and branches, besides many newly extended wires south and west, constituting 6,711 miles of line and 54,087 miles of wire, was purchased in 1887 for

Information and Communications

This section presents statistics on the various information and communications media: publishing, including newspapers, periodicals, books, and software; motion pictures, sound recordings, broadcasting, and telecommunications; and information services, such as libraries. Statistics on computer use and Internet access are also included. Data on the usage, finances, and operations of the Postal Service previously shown in this section are now presented in Section 23, Transportation.

Information industry—The U.S. Census Bureau's *Service Annual Survey, Information Services Sector,* provides estimates of operating revenue of taxable firms and revenues and expenses of firms exempt from federal taxes for industries in the information sector of the economy. Similar estimates were previously issued in the *Annual Survey of Communications Services.* Data beginning 1998 are based on the North American Industry Classification System (NAICS), 1997 and the information sector is a newly created economic sector. It comprises establishments engaged in the following processes: (a) producing and distributing information and cultural products, (b) providing the means to transmit or distribute these products as well as data or communications, and (c) processing data. It includes establishments previously classified in the Standard Industrial Classification (SIC) in manufacturing (publishing); transportation, communications, and utilities (telecommunications and broadcasting); and services (software publishing, motion picture production, data processing, online information services, and libraries).

This new sector is comprised of industries which existed previously, were revised from previous industry definitions, or are completely new industries. Among those which existed previously are newspaper publishers, motion picture and video production, and online information services.

Revised industries include book publishers and libraries and archives. Newly created industries include database and directory publishers, record production, music publishers, sound recording studios, cable networks, wired telecommunications carriers, paging, and satellite telecommunications. The following URL contains detailed information about NAICS and provides a comparison of the SIC and NAICS <http://www.census.gov /epcd/www/naics.html>. See also the text in Section 15, Business Enterprise.

Beginning 2001, the Service Annual Survey estimates reflect the introduction of the provisional North American Product Classification System (NAPCS) for the information sector. Data for prior years are not comparable. See <http://www.census.gov/eos/www /napcs/napcs.htm>.

The 1997 Economic Census was the first economic census to cover the new information sector of the economy. The census, conducted every 5 years, for the years ending "2" and "7," provides information on the number of establishments, receipts, payroll, and paid employees for the United States and various geographic levels. The most recent reports are from the 2002 Economic Census. This census was conducted in accordance with the 2002 NAICS.

The Federal Communications Commission (FCC), established in 1934, regulates wire and radio communications. Only the largest carriers and holding companies file annual financial reports which are publically available. The FCC has jurisdiction over interstate and foreign communication services but not over intrastate or local services. The gross operating revenues of the telephone carriers reporting publically available data annually to the FCC, however, are estimated to cover about 90 percent of the revenues of all U.S. telephone companies. Data are not comparable with Census Bureau *Annual*

U.S. Census Bureau, Statistical Abstract of the United States: 2006

Survey because of coverage and different accounting practices for those telephone companies which report to the FCC.

Reports filed by the broadcasting industry cover all radio and television stations operating in the United States. The private radio services represent the largest and most diverse group of licensees regulated by the FCC. These services provide voice, data communications, point-to-point, and point-to-multipoint radio communications for fixed and mobile communicators. Major users of these services are small businesses, the aviation industry, the maritime trades, the land transportation industry, the manufacturing industry, state and local public safety and governmental authorities, emergency medical service providers, amateur radio operators, and personal radio operations (CB and the General Mobile Radio Service). The FCC also licenses entities as private and common carriers. Private and common carriers provide fixed and land mobile communications service on a for-profit basis. Principal sources of wire, radio, and television data are the FCC's *Annual Report* and its annual *Statistics of Communications Common Carriers*.

Statistics on publishing are available from the Census Bureau, as well as from various private agencies. Editor & Publisher Co., New York, NY, presents annual data on the number and circulation of daily and Sunday newspapers in its *International Year Book*. Data on book production and prices are available from Information Today, Medford, NJ. The Book Industry Study Group, New York, NY, collects data on books sold and domestic consumer expenditures. Book purchasing data are from Ipsos, NPD, Inc., Rosemont, IL. Data on academic and public libraries are collected by the U.S. National Center for Education Statistics. Public library data are also gathered by Information Today, Medford, NJ, and the National Commission on Libraries and Information Science, Washington, DC.

Advertising—Data on advertising previously shown in this section are now presented in Section 27, Accommodation, Food Services, and Other Services.

Statistical reliability—For a discussion of statistical collection and estimation, sampling procedures, and measures of statistical reliability applicable to Census Bureau data, see Appendix III.

Table 1110. Information—Establishments, Receipts, Payroll, and Employees by Kind of Business (NAICS Basis): 2002

[Preliminary. For establishments with payroll. (45,660 represents $45,660,000,000). Based on the 2002 Economic Censuses; see Appendix III]

Kind of business	2002 NAICS code [1]	Number of establishments	Receipts (mil. dol.)	Annual payroll (mil. dol.)	Paid employees (1,000)
Newspaper publishers	51111	8,574	45,660	13,570	398.8
Periodical publishers	51112	7,146	39,279	8,131	148.8
Book publishers	51113	3,570	27,163	4,880	95.2
Directory & mailing list publishers	51114	1,839	16,564	2,465	53.7
Other publishers	51119	994	7,487	1,074	26.5
Software publishers	51121	9,899	103,737	34,593	353.3
Motion picture & video industries [2]	5121	19,101	62,013	10,236	275.4
Motion picture & video production	51211	11,106	45,019	7,137	110.2
Motion picture & video exhibition	51213	5,268	11,211	1,307	133.1
Postproduction & other motion picture & video industries	51219	2,207	4,395	1,531	27.3
Sound recording industries	5122	3,468	15,530	2,280	32.9
Sound recording studios	51224	1,498	695	241	6.2
Broadcasting (except Internet)	515	9,570	75,326	14,838	295.1
Radio & television broadcasting	5151	8,856	49,298	11,903	254.5
Radio broadcasting	51511	6,897	15,793	4,825	128.9
Cable & other subscription programming	5152	714	26,028	2,935	40.6
Internet publishing & broadcasting	516	2,060	6,427	2,301	39.5
Telecommunications [2]	517	49,055	411,808	71,486	1,428.0
Wired telecommunications carriers	5171	27,891	238,263	46,949	835.4
Wireless telecommunications carriers (except satellite)	5172	11,175	100,106	13,348	286.1
Cable & other program distribution	5175	6,118	56,710	8,328	247.1
Internet service providers, Web search portals, & data processing	518	18,642	79,212	26,048	521.0
Internet service providers & Web search portals	5181	4,863	23,327	4,540	83.3
Data processing, hosting, & related services	5182	13,779	55,885	21,508	437.7
Other information services	519	3,476	4,826	1,639	54.3
Libraries & archives	51912	2,714	1,674	730	34.5

[1] North American Industry Classification System, 2002; see text, this section and Section 15.　[2] Includes other industries, not shown separately.

Source: U.S. Census Bureau, "2002 Economic Census Industry Series Reports, Information." See Internet site: <http://www.census.gov/econ/census02/guide/INDRPT51.HTM> (accessed 16 May 2005).

Table 1111. Information Sector Services—Estimated Revenue: 2000 to 2003

[In millions of dollars (845,687 represents $845,687,000,000). For taxable and tax-exempt employer firms. Except as indicated, estimates adjusted to the results of the 1997 Economic Census. Based on the Service Annual Survey; see Appendix III]

Industry	1997 NAICS code [1]	2000	2001	2002	2003
Information industries	51	845,687	868,917	875,323	889,276
Publishing industries	511	232,069	231,714	230,916	232,427
Newspaper, periodical, book, database, and other publishers [2,3]	5111	144,483	141,123	142,070	142,538
Newspaper publishers	51111	51,507	47,153	47,524	48,591
Periodical publishers	51112	39,834	39,266	38,844	38,651
Book publishers	51113	25,236	26,096	27,203	26,326
Database and directory publishers	51114	15,855	16,512	16,564	16,728
Software publishers	5112	87,585	90,591	88,846	89,889
Motion picture and sound recording industries	512	67,745	69,152	74,020	77,901
Motion picture and video [3]	5121	54,040	55,937	60,486	64,096
Motion picture and video production and distribution	51211,12	39,076	40,503	44,728	47,824
Motion picture and video exhibition	51213	9,900	10,371	11,074	11,698
Sound recording	5122	13,705	13,215	13,535	13,804
Integrated record production/distribution	51222	10,839	10,199	10,393	10,400
Broadcasting and telecommunications	513	469,349	485,410	482,496	490,390
Radio and television broadcasting	5131	52,668	47,840	51,822	51,904
Radio broadcasting	51311	14,811	13,740	14,774	14,967
Radio stations	513112	13,188	12,201	12,977	13,037
Television broadcasting	51312	37,858	34,100	37,048	36,937
Cable networks and program distribution [2]	5132	67,930	74,420	80,536	90,456
Cable networks	51321	20,878	21,871	24,041	26,969
Cable and other program distribution	51322	47,052	52,549	56,495	63,488
Telecommunications [3]	5133	348,751	363,151	350,137	348,030
Wired telecommunications carriers	51331	265,704	260,122	237,376	222,563
Wireless telecommunications carriers (except satellite) [2]	51332	64,309	83,249	95,018	107,059
Cellular and other wireless telecommunications	513322	57,547	78,239	91,521	104,228
Telecommunications resellers	51333	8,833	8,634	8,587	9,120
Satellite telecommunications	51334	8,278	9,512	7,922	8,213
Information services and data processing services	514	76,524	82,641	87,891	88,558
Information services	5141	34,575	35,422	34,971	35,457
Online information services	514191	26,577	28,623	27,832	27,160
Data processing services	5142	41,950	47,219	52,920	53,101

[1] North American Industry Classification System, 1997; see text this section and Section 15.　[2] Estimates not adjusted to the 1997 Economic Census.　[3] Includes other industries, not shown separately.

Source: U.S. Census Bureau, "Service Annual Survey: 2003", SAS/03. See <http://www.census.gov/econ/www/servmenu.html> (released December 2004).

Table 1112. **Information Industries—Establishments, Employees and Payroll: 2000 and 2002**

[For establishments with payroll (3,545.7 represents 3,545,700). Excludes most government employees, railroad employees, and self-employed persons. See Appendix III]

Industry	1997 NAICS code [1]	Establishments (number) 2000	Establishments (number) 2002	Paid employees [2] (1,000) 2000	Paid employees [2] (1,000) 2002	Annual payroll (mil. dol.) 2000	Annual payroll (mil. dol.) 2002
Information industries	51	133,590	138,590	3,545.7	3,536.1	209,394	188,077
Publishing industries	511	32,545	32,577	1,080.7	1,020.0	75,348	60,592
Newspaper, periodical, book, & database publishers	5111	21,946	22,488	749.2	707.9	31,258	30,661
Newspaper publishers.	51111	8,586	8,728	412.6	388.0	14,216	14,040
Periodical publishers.	51112	6,252	6,912	135.6	127.2	7,676	7,191
Book publishers.	51113	2,661	2,713	87.2	90.0	4,310	4,863
Database & directory publishers	51114	1,370	1,566	46.2	46.9	2,418	2,276
Other publishers	51119	3,077	2,569	67.5	55.8	2,637	2,291
Greeting card publishers	511191	112	106	17.8	16.1	631	642
All other publishers	511199	2,965	2,463	49.7	39.7	2,006	1,649
Software publishers	5112	10,599	10,089	331.5	312.1	44,090	29,930
Motion picture & sound recording industries.	512	22,899	23,021	304.2	278.4	11,736	11,700
Motion picture & video industries	5121	19,730	19,652	276.6	253.4	9,806	9,986
Motion picture & video production	51211	10,018	10,943	84.5	85.7	5,723	6,663
Motion picture & video distribution	51212	678	541	13.9	5.3	1,119	312
Motion picture & video exhibition.	51213	5,884	5,198	144.0	134.1	1,130	1,341
Motion picture theaters (except drive-ins)	512131	5,593	4,895	142.3	132.4	1,107	1,315
Drive-in motion picture theaters	512132	291	303	1.7	1.7	23	26
Post production & other motion picture & video industries.	51219	3,150	2,970	34.2	28.4	1,834	1,671
Teleproduction & other postproduction services	512191	2,816	2,594	29.7	23.8	1,591	1,414
Other motion picture & video industries.	512199	334	376	4.5	4.6	243	257
Sound recording industries	5122	3,169	3,369	27.6	25.0	1,930	1,714
Record production	51221	276	370	1.1	1.9	55	115
Integrated record production/ distribution	51222	310	303	9.0	8.7	1,100	955
Music publishers	51223	670	706	5.1	4.5	283	289
Sound recording studios	51224	1,516	1,517	8.1	6.4	327	234
Other sound recording industries.	51229	397	473	4.3	3.5	166	122
Broadcasting & telecommunications	513	54,971	58,712	1,631.8	1,698.4	88,766	87,613
Radio & television broadcasting	5131	8,492	9,038	253.6	254.3	12,292	12,215
Radio broadcasting.	51311	6,442	7,029	121.5	130.8	4,841	5,062
Radio networks	513111	334	475	9.3	9.0	516	514
Radio stations	513112	6,108	6,554	112.1	121.9	4,325	4,548
Television broadcasting	51312	2,050	2,009	132.2	123.4	7,451	7,154
Cable networks & program distribution . . .	5132	5,270	6,891	212.7	300.1	10,084	12,450
Cable networks	51321	689	1,292	39.1	61.8	2,654	3,446
Cable & other program distribution	51322	4,581	5,599	173.6	238.3	7,430	9,005
Telecommunications.	5133	41,209	42,783	1,165.5	1,144.0	66,389	62,947
Wired telecommunications carriers	51331	26,223	26,883	870.2	848.0	49,010	47,962
Wireless telecommunications carriers (except satellite).	51332	10,424	11,079	202.5	216.8	11,027	10,418
Paging	513321	4,098	2,832	72.4	42.6	3,396	1,709
Cellular & other wireless telecommunications	513322	6,326	8,247	130.1	174.2	7,631	8,709
Telecommunications resellers	51333	2,458	3,060	54.6	49.8	3,342	2,666
Satellite telecommunications	51334	728	746	21.3	16.0	1,680	1,053
Other telecommunications	51339	1,379	1,015	16.9	13.4	1,330	848
Information services & data processing services.	514	23,175	24,280	529.0	539.3	33,544	28,173
Information services.	5141	14,139	13,203	232.5	208.2	19,023	11,672
News syndicates	51411	567	543	11.3	10.2	648	584
Libraries & archives	51412	2,754	2,875	33.8	33.6	679	724
Other information services	51419	10,818	9,785	187.4	164.4	17,696	10,364
Online information services.	514191	10,257	8,594	177.3	149.1	15,690	9,256
All other information services	514199	561	1,191	10.1	15.3	2,006	1,108
Data processing services	5142	9,036	11,077	296.6	331.2	14,521	16,501

[1] North American Industry Classification System, 1997; see text, this section and Section 15. [2] For employees on the payroll for the pay period including March 12.

Source: U.S. Census Bureau, "County Business Patterns"; 2002 data, issued November 2004; <http://www.census.gov/epcd/cbp/view/cbpview.html>.

[In millions of dollars (911,784 represents $911,784,000,000), except as noted]

Industry	2002 NAICS [1] code	2000	2001	2002	2003 est.	2004 est.
Total IT-producing industries	(X)	911,784	860,536	821,928	831,108	906,632
Share of the economy	(X)	9.2	8.4	7.8	7.6	7.8
Hardware [3]	(X)	271,259	211,828	210,709	217,814	245,307
Computer and office equipment	([2])	59,863	44,885	45,448	47,167	53,300
Computers and equipment wholesale sales	421430pt.	79,513	72,126	78,826	81,808	92,445
Computer and equipment retail sales	443120pt.	7,243	6,307	4,557	4,729	5,344
Printed circuit boards	334412	6,627	4,730	3,374	3,478	3,949
Semiconductors	334413	67,897	46,499	47,264	48,731	55,330
Semiconductor machinery	333295	11,636	5,662	4,445	4,659	4,953
Passive electronic components	334414,5,6 9	14,779	11,040	9,613	9,911	11,253
Industrial instruments for measurement	334513	4,802	4,558	4,419	4,447	4,781
Instruments for measuring electricity	334515	10,347	7,758	6,054	6,092	6,551
Laboratory analytical instruments	334516	4,730	4,723	5,127	5,159	5,547
Software and computer services [3]	(X)	323,444	332,891	325,617	320,738	353,360
Computer programming services	541,511	63,262	61,145	54,829	53,019	58,411
Prepackaged software	5112, 334611	75,961	77,709	76,353	77,249	85,106
Prepackaged software wholesale sales	421430pt.	12,064	16,893	15,550	15,101	16,637
Computer integrated-system design	541512	75,137	73,733	71,396	70,172	77,309
Data processing services	5142	33,603	37,850	44,914	42,755	47,104
Information retrieval services	51419	25,313	26,156	26,443	26,818	29,546
Computer services management	541513	12,780	14,891	13,054	13,194	14,536
Office machinery rental and leasing	532420	7,404	6,234	4,551	3,456	3,808
Computer maintenance and repair	811212	7,758	7,817	7,508	7,065	7,783
Computer related services, n.e.c. [4]	541519	9,330	9,548	10,023	10,869	11,975
Communications equipment	(X)	67,262	53,527	37,512	34,858	36,982
Household audio and video equipment	334310	3,221	3,230	3,422	3,180	3,374
Telephone equipment, exc. ext. modems	334210	35,843	26,448	14,909	13,854	14,698
Radio & TV broadcasting and wireless equip.	334220	23,962	19,302	14,679	13,641	14,472
Other communications equipment	334290	2,795	3,421	3,262	3,031	3,216
Magnetic and optical and recording media	334613	1,441	1,127	1,240	1,153	1,223
Communications services	(X)	249,820	262,291	248,090	257,698	270,983
Telephone and telegraph communications	517 less 5175	208,000	220,007	208,095	216,155	227,298
Cable and other pay TV services	5175	41,820	42,284	39,995	41,544	43,685

X Not applicable. [1] North American Industry Classification System, 2002; see text, this section and Section 15. [2] NAICS 334111, 2, 3, 9, 334418, 333311, 3. [3] Includes other industries, not shown separately. [4] N.e.c. Not elsewhere classified.

Source: U.S. Department of Commerce, Economics and Statistics Administration, *The Digital Economy 2005*, forthcoming report. See Internet site <https://www.esa.doc.gov/reports.cfm>.

[110,996 represents 110,996,000]

Industry	2002 NAICS [1] code	Employment (1,000)			Annual wages per worker (dol.)	
		2000	2003	2004	2000	2003
Total private	(X)	110,996	108,416	109,862	35,350	37,510
IT producing industries	(X)	5,381.7	4,356.0	4,283.0	72,330	70,100
Computer hardware [2]	(X)	1,679.8	1,232.2	1,195.4	77,800	73,350
Electronic computers	334111	168.6	123.6	115.5	130,720	101,250
Computer and software wholesalers	423430	299.4	241.1	233.7	92,910	88,160
Computer and software retailers	443120	190.5	140.3	132.4	53,650	52,960
Bare printed circuit boards	334412	139.5	65.6	62.0	38,810	43,300
Semiconductors and related devices	334413	289.2	225.5	223.1	95,300	82,480
Miscellaneous electronic components	334415,6,7,9	146.0	98.5	97.9	42,320	45,640
Industrial process variable instruments	334513	70.1	58.4	59.9	54,760	55,280
Electricity and signal testing instruments	334515	65.8	46.8	45.2	82,790	79,000
Software and computer services [2]	(X)	2,127.4	1,845.6	1,860.0	77,310	74,520
Software publishers	511210	260.6	238.9	238.7	114,410	102,310
Data processing and related services	518210	315.7	280.0	270.5	53,610	58,440
Custom computer programming services	541511	540.0	489.8	505.0	78,070	77,350
Computer systems design services	541512	502.9	456.6	475.1	77,040	74,890
Computer facilities management services	541513	64.9	58.1	59.4	62,340	62,550
Communications equipment [2]	(X)	322.0	201.7	189.8	66,990	69,110
Telephone apparatus	334210	106.5	50.7	47.2	80,960	80,790
Broadcast and wireless communications equipment	334220	107.3	77.9	75.7	63,160	68,230
Audio and video equipment	334310	52.1	37.1	31.9	43,920	51,550
Communications services [2]	(X)	1,252.5	1,076.4	1,037.8	58,810	59,180
Wired telecommunications carriers	517110	719.2	579.2	548.4	62,560	63,870
Telecommunications resellers	517310	213.6	154.9	149.8	54,850	58,290
Cable and other program distribution	517510	123.0	132.5	129.7	42,170	46,480

X Not applicable. [1] North American Industry Classification System, 2002; see text, this section and Section 15. [2] Includes other industries, not shown separately.

Source: U.S. Department of Commerce, Economics and Statistics Administration, *The Digital Economy 2005*, forthcoming report. See Internet site <https://www.esa.doc.gov/reports.cfm>.

Table 1115. **Communications Industry—Finances: 2000 to 2003**

[In millions of dollars (293,954 represents $293,954,000,000). Covers 299 publicly-reporting media and communications companies with revenues of over $1 million in 12 media and communication industry segments. Minus sign (-) indicates loss]

Industry	Revenue				Operating income			
	2000	2001	2002	2003	2000	2001	2002	2003
Total	293,954	303,693	329,367	361,164	26,474	15,285	29,463	53,982
Advertising, specialty media and marketing services [1]	45,292	46,297	47,076	50,786	7,715	7,826	8,622	9,259
Marketing services holding companies	24,980	25,964	26,913	30,369	3,296	2,355	2,732	3,112
Telephone directory publishing	10,883	11,100	11,128	10,663	4,242	5,450	5,390	5,301
Broadcast television	34,778	34,563	37,731	39,753	6,888	5,521	6,532	7,666
Television network companies	25,812	26,230	28,365	29,928	4,346	3,891	4,057	4,999
Cable and satellite television	52,451	60,818	67,551	77,342	-2,275	-7,518	-8,501	8,564
Cable and satellite providers	39,467	46,578	52,100	58,068	-2,241	-7,718	-11,830	6,344
Radio station owners and networks	8,275	8,840	9,498	9,625	1,321	355	3,344	3,406
Entertainment [1]	52,484	49,584	58,324	66,030	2,345	2,010	3,604	5,752
Filmed entertainment	32,572	33,380	39,327	45,313	1,278	1,694	3,406	4,798
Recorded music	11,404	9,315	9,995	10,694	34	-378	-1,146	-558
Consumer Internet	10,661	11,504	12,714	13,989	920	-582	359	1,212
Internet service providers	8,701	9,974	10,663	10,359	1,454	1,749	545	603
Newspaper publishing	24,953	23,851	23,707	24,824	5,307	4,005	5,049	5,315
Consumer book publishing	2,535	2,984	3,161	3,596	339	383	412	443
Consumer magazine publishing	9,281	9,780	10,105	10,353	-23	-976	824	1,030
Business-to-business communications	5,043	4,534	4,126	4,184	769	395	283	551
Professional, educational and training media	13,178	13,028	14,980	16,561	1,164	1,220	1,968	2,421
Professional and educational media	9,087	8,090	9,264	9,592	1,287	1,024	1,578	1,549
Business information services	35,023	37,911	40,393	44,121	2,003	2,647	6,968	8,362
Financial information	16,667	17,637	18,724	19,878	2,692	3,052	3,178	3,676

[1] Includes other industries, not shown separately.

Source: Veronis Suhler Stevenson, New York, NY, *Communications Industry Forecast & Report*, annual (copyright).

Table 1116. **Media Usage and Consumer Spending: 2000 to 2008**

[Estimates of time spent were derived using rating data for television, cable and satellite television and radio, survey research and consumer purchase data (units, admissions, access) for books, home video, Internet, interactive TV, magazines, movies in theaters, newspapers, recorded music, and video games. Adults 18 and older were the basis for estimates for television, cable and satellite television, daily newspapers, consumer books, consumer magazines, home video and interactive TV. Persons 12 and older were the basis for estimates for radio, recorded music, movies in theaters, video games and consumer Internet]

Item	2000	2001	2002	2003	2004, proj.	2005, proj.	2006, proj.	2007, proj.	2008, proj.
HOURS PER PERSON PER YEAR									
Total	3,492	3,540	3,606	3,663	3,757	3,809	3,890	3,949	4,059
Television	1,635	1,676	1,705	1,745	1,792	1,826	1,858	1,887	1,931
Broadcast TV	866	833	787	769	782	785	790	794	800
Network stations [1]	799	767	721	704	717	721	726	731	738
Cable & satellite TV	769	843	918	975	1,010	1,042	1,068	1,093	1,131
Basic cable and satellite TV [1]	633	692	760	809	834	861	882	903	934
Premium cable and satellite TV [1]	136	151	158	167	176	181	186	190	197
Broadcast and satellite radio [2]	943	955	990	1,002	1,035	1,040	1,070	1,080	1,120
Box office	12	13	14	13	13	13	13	13	14
Home video [2,3]	51	56	65	70	78	85	94	103	110
Interactive TV [4]	2	2	2	2	3	3	4	4	5
Recorded music [2]	258	229	200	184	180	176	174	170	167
Video games [2]	59	60	64	69	71	75	81	86	98
Consumer Internet [2]	107	139	158	176	189	200	213	225	236
Daily newspapers [2]	180	177	175	171	169	168	165	165	164
Consumer books [2]	109	106	109	108	107	106	106	105	104
Consumer magazines [2]	135	127	125	121	118	116	113	111	110
CONSUMER SPENDING PER PERSON PER YEAR (dol.)									
Total	632.03	678.79	738.15	777.73	825.29	871.73	921.54	974.01	1,030.22
Cable and satellite TV [1]	187.93	202.73	221.52	234.65	248.02	261.47	275.06	289.09	303.49
Basic cable & satellite networks [1]	144.24	155.16	169.73	181.09	192.56	204.11	215.63	227.74	240.58
Premium cable and satellite services [1]	43.70	47.57	51.79	53.56	55.47	57.36	59.44	61.36	62.91
Broadcast and satellite radio [2]	-	-	0.07	0.37	1.32	2.59	4.20	5.97	7.69
Box office	32.75	35.45	39.54	39.00	41.16	42.31	44.46	46.13	48.72
Home video [2,3]	100.01	114.26	135.02	151.94	172.04	188.86	206.17	225.51	241.08
Interactive TV [4]	2.25	2.47	2.89	3.82	4.96	6.39	8.04	9.61	10.81
Recorded music [2]	61.24	57.92	52.39	48.72	47.63	46.26	45.55	44.64	44.38
Video games [2]	25.89	26.89	29.59	29.78	31.00	33.29	36.72	39.25	44.89
Consumer Internet [2]	49.64	68.94	84.76	96.35	107.02	117.72	127.76	140.15	154.29
Daily newspapers [2]	52.48	52.84	53.30	53.68	53.29	53.88	54.19	54.69	55.33
Consumer books [2]	86.13	84.45	87.51	89.68	90.30	91.49	92.72	93.02	93.7
Consumer magazines [2]	47.70	46.96	46.79	41.24	45.77	45.51	45.35	45.17	44.93

- Represents zero. [1] UPN, WB, and PAX affiliates included in network-affiliated stations, superstations included in basic cable, and pay-per-view included in premium service. [2] Does not include Internet-related use of traditional media. Some examples include: listening to downloaded music directly on the computer or from a burned disc on a MP3 player, reading a downloaded e-book, listening to a radio station transmitted by a Windows media player, and reading a Web-based newspaper article. Such activities are included in the time spent data under consumer Internet, although the media content was orginally provided on a traditional medium. [3] Playback of prerecorded VHS cassettes and DVDs only. [4] Video-on-demand (VOD) only. Personal video recorders (PVRs) included in total TV.

Source: Veronis Suhler Stevenson, New York, NY, *Communications Industry Forecast & Report*, annual (copyright).

Table 1117. Utilization of Selected Media: 1980 to 2003

[78.6 represents 78,600,000]

Item	Unit	1980	1990	1995	1997	1998	1999	2000	2001	2002	2003
Households with—											
Telephone service [1]	Percent . . .	93.0	93.3	93.9	93.9	94.1	94.0	94.6	94.6	95.5	95.5
Radio [2]	Millions . . .	78.6	94.4	98.0	98.0	(NA)	(NA)	(NA)	(NA)	(NA)	99.0
Percent of total households. . .	Percent . .	99.0	99.0	99.0	99.0	99.0	99.0	99.0	99.0	99.0	99.0
Average number of sets	Number . .	5.5	5.6	5.6	5.6	5.6	5.6	5.6	(NA)	(NA)	8.0
Television [3]	Millions . .	76	92	95	97	98	99	101	102	106	107
Percent of total households. . .	Percent . .	97.9	98.2	98.3	98.4	98.3	98.2	98.2	98.2	98.2	98.2
Television sets in homes.	Millions . .	128	193	217	229	235	240	245	248	254	260
Average number of sets per home	Number. . .	1.7	2.0	2.3	2.4	2.4	2.4	2.4	2.4	2.4	2.4
Color set households.	Millions . .	63	90	94	97	98	99	101	102	105	107
Cable television [4]	Millions . .	15	52	60	64	66	67	69	69	73	74
Percent of TV households. . . .	Percent . .	19.9	56.4	63.4	66.5	67.2	67.5	68.0	68.0	69.4	69.8
VCRs [4]	Millions . .	1	63	77	82	83	84	86	88	96	98
Percent of TV households. . . .	Percent . .	1.1	68.6	81.0	84.2	84.6	84.6	85.1	86.2	91.2	91.5
Computers [5]	Percent . .	(NA)	(NA)	(NA)	36.6	42.1	(NA)	51.0	56.2	(NA)	61.8
Internet connections [5]	Percent . .	(NA)	(NA)	(NA)	18.6	26.2	(NA)	41.5	50.3	(NA)	54.6
Broadband Internet [5]	Percent . .	(NA)	(NA)	(NA)	(NA)	(NA)	(NA)	4.4	9.1	(NA)	19.9
Commercial radio stations: [2]											
AM	Number. . .	4,589	4,987	4,909	4,762	4,793	4,783	4,685	4,727	4,804	4,802
FM.	Number. . .	3,282	4,392	5,296	5,542	5,662	5,766	5,892	6,051	6,161	6,207
Television stations: [6] Total	Number. . .	1,011	1,442	1,532	1,564	1,589	1,615	1,663	1,686	1,714	1,730
Commercial	Number. . .	734	1,092	1,161	1,195	1,221	1,243	1,288	1,309	1,333	1,349
VHF	Number. . .	516	547	562	555	561	561	567	572	581	587
UHF	Number. . .	218	545	599	640	660	682	721	737	752	762
Cable television:											
Systems [7]	Number. . .	4,225	9,575	11,218	10,950	10,845	10,700	10,243	9,924	9,339	9,038
Households served [8]	Millions . . .	17.7	54.9	63.0	65.9	67.0	74.9	76.5	79.5	85.5	85.9
Daily newspaper circulation [9]	Millions . . .	62.2	62.3	58.2	56.7	56.2	56.0	55.8	55.6	55.2	55.2

NA Not available. [1] For occupied housing units. 1980 as of April 1; all other years as of March. Source: U.S. Census Bureau, *1980 Census of Housing*, vol. 1; thereafter Federal Communications Commission, *Trends in Telephone Service*, annual. [2] 1980-1995 as of December 31. Source: M Street Corp. as reported by Radio Advertising Bureau New York, NY, through 1990, Radio Facts, annual (copyright); beginning 1995, Radio Marketing Guide and Fact Book for Advertisers, annual (copyright). Number of stations on the air compiled from Federal Communications Commission reports. 1985 d:ta as of February 1986. Beginning 1997, Federal Communications Commission, unpublished data as of Sept. 30. See Internet site <http://www.fcc.gov/mb/audio/totals>. [3] As of January of year shown. Excludes Alaska and Hawaii. Source: Television Bureau of Advertising, Inc., *Trends in Television*, annual (copyright). [4] As of February. Excludes Alaska and Hawaii. Source: See footnote 3. [5] As of October 1997, December 1998, August 2000, September 2001 and October 2003. Source: U.S. Department of Commerce, National Telecommunications and Information Administration, *A Nation Online: Entering the Broadband Age*, September 2004. See Internet site <http://www.ntia.doc.gov/reports/anol/index.html>. [6] Source: Beginning 1997, Federal Communications Commission, unpublished data. See Internet site <http://www.fcc.gov/mb/audio/totals>. 1997 and 1998 as of December; beginning 1999, as of September. For prior years data, see footnote 3. [7] As of January 1. Source: Warren Communications News, Washington DC, *Television and Cable Factbook* (copyright). [8] Source: Nielsen Media Research, New York, NY, (copyright). [9] As of September 30. Source: Editor & Publisher, Co., New York, NY, *Editor & Publisher International Year Book*, annual (copyright).

Source: Compiled from sources mentioned in footnotes.

Table 1118. Multimedia Audiences—Summary: 2004

[In percent, except total (213,454 represents 213,454,000). As of fall. For persons 18 years old and over. Represents the percent of persons participating during the prior week, except as indicated. Based on sample and subject to sampling error; see source for details]

Item	Total population (1,000)	Television viewing	Television prime time viewing	Cable viewing [1]	Radio listening	Newspaper reading	Accessed Internet [2]
Total.	213,454	94.1	83.2	78.1	84.2	78.8	61.4
18 to 24 years old	27,556	92.5	74.6	72.8	90.7	72.7	72.7
25 to 34 years old	39,380	92.5	82.1	76.3	91.1	74.1	72.1
35 to 44 years old	44,230	92.9	82.0	79.1	89.9	79.0	70.7
45 to 54 years old	40,387	94.4	83.8	80.0	88.2	81.6	68.0
55 to 64 years old	27,520	95.8	86.5	81.9	80.4	83.2	57.0
65 years old and over	34,381	97.2	89.2	77.6	62.3	81.6	23.6
Male.	102,533	94.3	82.9	78.5	85.4	78.1	61.6
Female.	110,921	94.0	83.4	77.6	83.1	79.4	61.2
Not high school graduate. . . .	35,023	93.6	82.5	65.0	73.6	61.2	20.1
High school graduate	67,779	95.4	85.1	78.6	83.6	77.9	47.9
Attended college	57,820	94.4	82.4	81.3	88.1	82.8	76.1
College graduate	52,832	92.5	81.9	82.6	87.8	87.0	89.8
Employed:							
Full-time	113,475	93.4	82.1	80.1	90.7	80.7	73.2
Part-time	23,165	92.5	79.6	76.6	87.6	80.1	70.0
Not employed.	76,815	95.7	85.8	75.6	73.6	75.4	41.3
Household income:							
Less than $10,000	13,236	93.5	80.0	59.8	73.7	62.2	25.5
$10,000 to $19,999	22,029	93.9	84.7	62.6	71.6	69.2	27.7
$20,000 to $29,999	24,350	94.9	83.9	69.5	77.9	72.1	36.7
$30,000 to $34,999	12,224	94.6	84.9	74.0	82.8	78.9	47.5
$35,000 to $39,999	11,290	95.1	84.3	75.3	84.6	76.9	52.2
$40,000 to $49,999	21,118	95.2	83.2	78.7	85.2	77.2	58.8
$50,000 or more.	109,207	93.7	82.7	85.9	89.4	84.6	81.0

[1] In the past 7 days. [2] In the last 30 days.

Source: Mediamark Research Inc., New York, NY, *Multimedia Audiences*, fall 2004 (copyright).

Information and Communications 737

[In millions of dollars (47,153 represents $47,153,000,000). For taxable and tax-exempt employer firms. Estimates have been adjusted to the results of the 1997 Economic Census. Based on the North American Industry ClassificationSystem, 1997; see text, this section and Section 15. See also Appendix III]

Item	Newspaper publishers (NAICS 51111)			Periodical publishers (NAICS 51112)			Database and directory publishers (NAICS 51114)		
	2001	2002	2003	2001	2002	2003	2001	2002	2003
Revenue	47,153	47,524	48,591	39,266	38,844	38,651	16,512	16,564	16,728
Source of revenue:									
Print	42,134	42,099	42,766	31,033	30,404	29,243	11,856	11,748	11,777
Subscription and sales	9,314	9,436	9,610	13,073	12,971	11,848	693	622	650
Advertising	32,820	32,664	33,156	17,960	17,434	17,396	11,162	11,126	11,127
Internet	410	597	735	1,282	1,298	1,412	433	520	663
Subscription and sales	(S)	(S)	(S)	868	894	1,047	(S)	(S)	(S)
Advertising	303	466	568	(S)	(S)	366	241	275	418
Other media	154	165	153	2,158	2,350	2,586	1,566	1,578	1,270
Subscription and sales	53	61	(S)	2,070	2,276	2,514	1,513	1,541	1,234
Advertising	101	103	96	(S)	74	72	(S)	36	37
Contract printing	1,770	1,749	1,667	922	690	628	201	(S)	(S)
Distribution of flyers, inserts, etc..	930	1,020	1,191	105	118	(S)	(NA)	(NA)	(NA)
Graphic design services	(S)	(S)	(S)	(S)	(S)	(S)	(NA)	(NA)	(NA)
Market research	2	2	(S)	(NA)	(NA)	(NA)	(NA)	(NA)	(NA)
Archival services	24	23	26	(NA)	(NA)	(NA)	(NA)	(NA)	(NA)
Sales or licensing of rights of content	69	45	74	241	274	293	98	72	(S)
Rental or sales of mailing lists	13	(S)	7	160	168	164	1,051·	1,162	1,172
Non-newspaper publishing	258	306	369	(NA)	(NA)	(NA)	(NA)	(NA)	(NA)
Publishing services for others	11	12	19	339	(S)	314	31	29	57
Other revenue	1,368	1,485	1,574	2,966	3,141	3,816	1,278	1,256	1,498
Breakdown of revenue:									
General interest publications	41,534	41,246	41,916	16,613	16,309	16,019	(X)	(X)	(X)
Special interest publications	1,164	1,169	1,075	17,860	16,312	15,683	(X)	(X)	(X)
Other publications	(NA)	(S)	662	(NA)	1,431	(S)	(X)	(X)	(X)
Inventories at end of year	748	717	780	1,634	1,671	1,542	374	(S)	(S)
Finished goods and work-in-process	63	80	108	1,223	1,252	1,156	355	(S)	(S)
Materials, supplies, fuel, etc.	685	636	672	411	419	(S)	19	(S)	(S)

NA Not available.   S Data do not meet publication standards.   X Not applicable.

Source: U.S. Census Bureau, *Service Annual Survey: 2003*, SAS/03. See <http://www.census.gov/econ/www/servmenu.html> (released December 2004).

Table 1120. **Daily and Sunday Newspapers—Number and Circulation: 1970 to 2004**

[Number of newspapers as of February 1 the following year. Circulation figures as of September 30 of year shown (62.1 represents 62,100,000). For English language newspapers only]

Type	1970	1975	1980	1985	1990	1995	1999	2000	2001	2002	2003	2004
NUMBER												
Daily: Total [1]	1,748	1,756	1,745	1,676	1,611	1,533	1,483	1,480	1,468	1,457	1,456	1,456
Morning	334	339	387	482	559	656	736	766	776	777	787	813
Evening	1,429	1,436	1,388	1,220	1,084	891	760	727	704	692	680	653
Sunday	586	639	736	798	863	888	905	917	913	913	917	914
NET PAID CIRCULATION (mil.)												
Daily: Total [1]	62.1	60.7	62.2	62.8	62.3	58.2	56.0	55.8	55.6	55.2	55.2	54.6
Morning	25.9	25.5	29.4	36.4	41.3	44.3	46.0	46.8	46.8	46.6	46.9	46.9
Evening	36.2	35.2	32.8	26.4	21.0	13.9	10.0	9.0	8.8	8.6	8.3	7.7
Sunday	49.2	51.1	54.7	58.8	62.6	61.5	59.9	59.4	59.1	58.8	58.5	57.8
PER CAPITA CIRCULATION [2]												
Daily: Total [1]	0.30	0.28	0.27	0.26	0.25	0.22	0.20	0.20	0.20	0.19	0.19	0.19
Morning	0.13	0.12	0.13	0.15	0.17	0.17	0.16	0.17	0.16	0.16	0.16	0.16
Evening	0.18	0.16	0.14	0.11	0.08	0.05	0.04	0.03	0.03	0.03	0.03	0.03
Sunday	0.24	0.24	0.24	0.25	0.25	0.23	0.21	0.21	0.21	0.20	0.20	0.20

[1] All-day newspapers are counted in both morning and evening columns, but only once in total. Circulation is divided equally between morning and evening.   [2] Based on U.S. Census Bureau estimated resident population as of July 1.

Source: Editor & Publisher Co., New York, NY. *Editor & Publisher International Year Book*, annual (copyright).

Table 1121. Daily Newspapers—Number and Circulation by Size of City: 1980 to 2004

[Number of newspapers as of February 1 the following year. Circulation as of September 30 (29,413 represents 29,413,000). For English language newspapers only. See Table 28 for number of cities by population size. All-day newspapers are counted in both morning and evening columns; circulation is divided equally between morning and evening]

Type of daily and population-size class	Number					Net paid circulation (1,000)				
	1980	1990	1995	2000	2004	1980	1990	1995	2000	2004
Morning dailies, total. . .	387	559	656	766	813	29,413	41,311	44,310	46,772	46,887
In cities of—										
1,000,001 or more	20	18	25	26	29	8,795	6,508	10,173	10,820	10,735
500,001 to 1,000,000	27	22	22	25	33	5,705	4,804	5,587	5,412	6,514
100,001 to 500,000	99	138	153	163	164	8,996	20,051	17,214	17,469	16,838
50,001 to 100,000	75	100	138	162	164	2,973	4,373	5,602	5,887	5,579
25,001 to 50,000	64	102	115	141	154	1,701	3,209	3,150	3,899	3,799
Less than 25,000	102	179	203	249	269	1,243	2,365	2,584	3,285	3,423
Evening dailies, total. . .	1,388	1,084	891	727	653	32,788	21,017	13,883	9,000	7,739
In cities of—										
1,000,001 or more	11	7	3	1	1	2,984	1,423	390	1	1
500,001 to 1,000,000	23	12	7	3	6	4,101	1,350	1,017	519	812
100,001 to 500,000	123	71	45	32	24	8,178	4,687	2,529	1,603	1,186
50,001 to 100,000	156	94	72	54	38	4,896	2,941	2,029	1,332	981
25,001 to 50,000	246	204	158	124	113	5,106	4,278	2,819	1,898	1,617
Less than 25,000	829	696	606	513	471	7,523	6,338	5,099	3,648	3,141

Source: Editor & Publisher Co., New York, NY, *Editor & Publisher International Year Book*, annual (copyright).

Table 1122. Daily and Sunday Newspapers—Number and Circulation, 1991 to 2003 and by State, 2004

[Number of newspapers as of February 1 the following year. Circulation as of September 30 (60,687 represents 60,687,000). For English language newspapers only. California, New York, Massachusetts, and Virginia Sunday newspapers include national circulation]

State	Daily			Sunday		State	Daily			Sunday	
		Circulation [1]			Net paid circula-tion			Circulation [1]			Net paid circula-tion
	Num-ber	Net paid (1,000)	Per capita [2]	Num-ber	(1,000)		Num-ber	Net paid (1,000)	Per capita [2]	Num-ber	(1,000)
Total, 1991 . . .	1,586	60,687	0.24	875	62,068						
Total, 1992 . . .	1,570	60,164	0.23	891	62,160	ME	7	227	0.17	4	194
Total, 1993 . . .	1,556	59,812	0.23	884	62,566	MD	13	558	0.10	9	901
Total, 1994 . . .	1,548	59,305	0.23	886	62,294	MA	32	1,535	0.24	16	1,508
Total, 1995 . . .	1,533	58,193	0.22	888	61,529	MI	48	1,637	0.16	27	1,873
Total, 1996 . . .	1,520	56,983	0.21	890	60,798	MN	25	864	0.17	15	1,154
Total, 1997 . . .	1,509	56,728	0.21	903	60,484	MS	23	363	0.13	18	365
Total, 1998 . . .	1,489	56,182	0.20	898	60,066	MO	42	926	0.16	23	1,156
Total, 1999 . . .	1,483	55,979	0.20	905	59,894	MT	11	187	0.20	7	186
Total, 2000 . . .	1,480	55,421	0.20	917	59,421	NE	17	407	0.23	6	390
Total, 2001 . . .	1,468	55,578	0.19	913	59,090	NV	8	304	0.13	4	329
Total, 2002 . . .	1,457	55,186	0.19	913	58,780	NH	11	217	0.17	8	224
Total, 2003 . . .	1,456	55,185	0.19	917	58,495	NJ	17	1,273	0.15	14	1,567
						NM	18	274	0.14	13	281
Total, 2004 . . .	1,456	54,626	0.19	914	57,753	NY	59	6,843	0.36	38	5,330
AL	24	619	0.14	20	699	NC	47	1,308	0.15	39	1,436
AK	7	105	0.16	5	121	ND	10	159	0.25	7	164
AZ	16	750	0.13	11	863	OH	84	2,286	0.20	41	2,556
AR	28	467	0.17	16	538	OK	42	605	0.17	34	753
CA	90	5,764	0.16	61	6,575	OR	19	662	0.18	12	693
CO	30	990	0.22	15	1,138	PA	81	2,596	0.21	41	3,015
CT	17	679	0.19	13	762	RI	6	217	0.20	3	264
DE	2	132	0.16	2	164	SC	16	611	0.15	14	699
DC	2	808	1.46	2	1,051	SD	11	153	0.20	4	134
FL	40	3,044	0.17	37	3,849	TN	26	836	0.14	18	1,007
GA	34	1,007	0.11	29	1,313	TX	85	2,923	0.13	78	3,688
HA	6	267	0.21	6	299	UT	6	331	0.14	6	363
ID	12	210	0.15	8	224	VT	8	116	0.19	3	89
IL	67	2,284	0.18	32	2,434	VA	25	3,209	0.43	17	1,146
IN	68	1,257	0.20	25	1,234	WA	23	1,059	0.17	17	1,198
IA	37	594	0.20	12	618	WV	20	327	0.18	12	338
KS	43	403	0.15	14	363	WI	35	871	0.16	18	1,065
KY	23	583	0.14	14	612	WY	9	87	0.17	5	70
LA	26	692	0.15	21	763						

[1] Circulation figures based on the principal community served by a newspaper which is not necessarily the same location as the publisher's office.   [2] Per capita based on estimated resident population as of July 1, except 2000, enumerated resident population as of April 1.

Source: Editor & Publisher Co., New York, NY, *Editor & Publisher International Year Book*, annual (copyright).

U.S. Census Bureau, Statistical Abstract of the United States: 2006

Table 1123. **Periodicals—Average Retail Prices: 2001 to 2005**

[In dollars. Reflects prices for an annual subscription]

Subject	2001	2002	2003	2004	2005
Agriculture	585	626	677	749	799
Anthropology	246	266	287	312	328
Art and architecture	107	109	117	126	135
Astronomy	918	1,088	1,160	1,253	1,235
Biology	1,094	1,171	1,276	1,392	1,494
Botany	814	864	931	1,017	1,109
Business and economics	491	539	594	646	702
Chemistry	2,140	2,321	2,505	2,699	2,868
Education	261	285	308	335	367
Engineering	1,217	1,323	1,430	1,550	1,683
Food science	818	860	926	1,014	1,107
General science	755	828	914	988	1,059
General works	76	78	87	98	110
Geography	685	769	835	912	945
Geology	884	951	1,025	1,115	1,197
Health sciences	781	839	915	999	1,081
History	115	121	134	149	163
Language and literature	108	115	127	141	154
Law	158	173	190	207	221
Library and information science	267	285	314	345	386
Math and computer science	968	1,031	1,103	1,197	1,267
Military and naval science	345	329	355	385	447
Music	77	86	93	97	114
Philosophy and religion	140	150	166	183	197
Physics	2,012	2,192	2,365	2,550	2,719
Political science	212	243	271	303	333
Psychology	340	371	397	435	472
Recreation	120	138	145	156	179
Sociology	311	340	371	419	455
Technology	1,057	1,152	1,252	1,359	1,460
Zoology	820	888	954	988	1,053

Source: Library Journal, New York, NY, *Library Journal,* April 15, 2005. (Copyright 2005, used with permission of Library Journal, a publication of Reed Business Information, a division of Reed Elsevier.)

Table 1124. **Periodicals—Percent Change in Average Retail Prices: 2002 to 2005**

[Reflects change in prices for an annual subscription. Minus sign (-) indicates decrease]

Subject	2001–2002	2002–2003	2003–2004	2004–2005
Agriculture	7.0	8.1	10.6	6.7
Anthropology	8.1	7.9	8.7	5.1
Art and architecture	1.9	7.3	7.7	7.1
Astronomy	18.5	6.6	8.0	-1.4
Biology	7.0	9.0	9.1	7.3
Botany	6.1	7.8	9.2	9.0
Business and economics	9.8	10.2	8.8	8.7
Chemistry	8.5	7.9	7.7	6.3
Education	9.2	8.1	8.8	9.6
Engineering	8.7	8.1	8.4	8.6
Food science	5.1	7.7	9.5	9.2
General science	9.7	10.4	8.1	7.2
General works	2.6	11.5	12.6	12.2
Geography	12.3	8.6	9.2	3.6
Geology	7.6	7.8	8.8	7.4
Health sciences	7.4	9.1	9.2	8.2
History	5.2	10.7	11.2	9.4
Language and literature	6.5	10.4	11.0	9.2
Law	9.5	9.8	8.9	6.8
Library and information science	6.7	10.2	9.9	11.9
Math and computer science	6.5	7.0	8.5	5.8
Military and naval science	-4.6	7.9	8.5	16.1
Music	11.7	8.1	4.3	17.5
Philosophy and religion	7.1	10.7	10.2	7.7
Physics	8.9	7.9	7.8	6.6
Political science	14.6	11.5	11.8	9.9
Psychology	9.1	7.0	9.6	8.5
Recreation	15.0	5.1	7.6	14.7
Sociology	9.3	9.1	12.9	8.6
Technology	9.0	8.7	8.5	7.4
Zoology	8.3	7.4	3.6	6.6

Source: Library Journal, New York, NY, *Library Journal,* April 15, 2005. (Copyright 2005, used with permission of Library Journal, a publication of Reed Business Information, a division of Reed Elsevier.)

740 Information and Communications

Table 1125. Quantity of Books Sold: 2000 to 2005

[In millions (2,461.9 represents 2,461,900,000). **Represents net publishers' shipments after returns.** Includes all titles released by publishers in the United States and imports which appear under the imprints of American publishers. Multivolume sets, such as encyclopedias, are counted as one unit]

Type of publication	2000	2001	2002	2003	2004	2005, proj.
Total	**2,461.9**	**2,357.7**	**2,365.2**	**2,338.7**	**2,295.0**	**2,342.2**
Trade	1,051.8	979.0	986.8	964.7	944.4	958.0
Adult	473.9	458.3	462.2	449.9	463.7	473.9
Hardback	235.4	223.5	225.5	224.3	234.2	237.4
Paperback	238.5	234.8	236.7	225.6	229.5	236.5
Juvenile	577.9	520.7	524.6	514.8	480.7	484.1
Hardback	234.1	175.3	177.0	177.9	147.2	156.1
Paperback	343.8	345.4	347.6	336.9	333.5	328.0
Mass market paperbacks—rack sized	584.2	564.0	570.2	562.6	535.6	540.1
Bookclubs	124.0	123.9	122.2	121.6	112.4	109.7
Hardback	40.3	40.1	38.6	39.0	35.8	34.8
Paperback	83.7	83.8	83.6	82.6	76.6	74.9
Mail order publications	65.4	54.3	54.6	56.0	53.9	51.4
Religious	197.7	201.1	204.4	203.9	221.2	236.4
Hardback	69.4	70.8	71.8	71.9	78.2	84.2
Paperback	128.3	130.3	132.6	131.9	142.9	152.2
Professional	187.3	168.6	170.3	172.1	175.9	176.4
Hardback	71.6	64.5	65.1	69.7	70.0	69.9
Paperback	115.7	104.2	105.2	102.3	105.9	106.5
University press	25.7	24.5	24.9	24.5	23.5	23.7
Hardback	7.8	7.4	7.5	7.5	7.2	7.3
Paperback	17.9	17.1	17.4	17.1	16.3	16.5
Elhi text	160.4	174.3	162.2	162.8	158.9	178.2
Hardback	56.9	61.8	57.4	57.3	55.9	62.7
Paperback	103.5	112.5	104.8	105.5	103.0	115.6
College text	64.3	66.8	68.4	69.2	68.0	67.1
Hardback	28.6	29.9	30.6	30.9	30.2	29.8
Paperback	35.7	36.9	37.8	38.3	37.8	37.3
Subscription reference	1.2	1.2	1.2	1.2	1.2	1.2

Source: Book Industry Study Group, Inc., New York, NY, *Book Industry Trends, 2005,* annual (copyright).

Table 1126. Books Sold—Value of U.S. Domestic Consumer Expenditures: 2000 to 2005

[In millions of dollars (36,136.2 represents $36,136,200,000). Includes all titles released by publishers in the United States and imports which appear under the imprints of American publishers]

Type of publication	2000	2001	2002	2003	2004	2005, proj.
Total	**36,136.2**	**36,060.0**	**36,796.0**	**37,908.2**	**39,202.1**	**41,070.7**
Trade	11,583.2	11,276.7	11,496.0	11,786.1	11,943.9	12,303.6
Adult	8,124.2	8,061.5	8,288.0	8,400.6	8,823.8	9,035.5
Hardback	4,753.8	4,650.1	4,914.1	4,989.2	5,333.5	5,461.5
Paperback	3,370.4	3,411.4	3,373.9	3,411.4	3,490.3	3,574.0
Juvenile	3,459.0	3,215.2	3,208.0	3,385.5	3,120.1	3,268.1
Hardback	2,126.1	1,644.1	1,601.1	1,761.7	1,446.4	1,567.2
Paperback	1,332.9	1,571.1	1,606.9	1,623.8	1,673.7	1,700.9
Mass market paperbacks—rack sized	2,934.7	2,911.2	2,966.8	2,997.9	2,946.1	2,899.3
Bookclubs	1,753.0	1,794.5	1,799.5	1,842.5	1,753.1	1,704.0
Hardback	1,387.1	1,417.6	1,419.8	1,453.7	1,383.2	1,334.9
Paperback	365.9	376.9	379.7	388.8	369.9	369.1
Mail order publications	576.5	490.5	510.1	530.7	518.6	517.6
Religious	2,782.7	2,912.6	2,969.6	3,207.5	3,763.8	4,143.9
Hardback	1,665.0	1,744.6	1,765.1	1,904.9	2,235.3	2,568.8
Paperback	1,117.7	1,168.0	1,204.5	1,302.6	1,528.5	1,575.1
Professional	6,340.1	5,857.7	6,104.3	6,294.9	6,600.5	6,864.6
Hardback	4,621.9	4,264.3	4,334.1	4,469.8	4,601.7	4,777.2
Paperback	1,718.2	1,593.4	1,770.2	1,825.1	1,998.8	2,087.4
University press	541.4	533.3	533.8	539.3	547.1	567.7
Hardback	262.8	258.2	262.3	263.6	267.4	275.9
Paperback	278.6	275.1	271.5	275.7	279.7	291.8
Elhi text	4,373.3	4,714.1	4,496.9	4,568.0	4,585.5	5,272.9
Hardback	2,382.6	2,564.5	2,445.2	2,280.6	2,289.6	2,610.5
Paperback	1,990.7	2,149.6	2,051.7	2,287.4	2,295.9	2,662.4
College text	4,265.2	4,570.7	4,899.1	5,085.9	5,478.6	5,703.2
Hardback	2,851.0	3,085.1	3,287.3	3,408.2	3,671.2	3,821.7
Paperback	1,414.2	1,485.6	1,611.8	1,677.7	1,807.4	1,881.5
Subscription reference	986.1	998.7	1,019.9	1,045.4	1,064.9	1,093.9

Source: Book Industry Study Group, Inc., New York, NY, *Book Industry Trends, 2005,* annual (copyright).

U.S. Census Bureau, Statistical Abstract of the United States: 2006

Table 1127. **Book Publishers—Estimated Revenue and Inventories: 2001 to 2003**

[In millions of dollars (26,096 represents $26,096,000,000), except percent. For taxable and tax-exempt employer firms. For NAICS 51113. Estimates have been adjusted to the results of the 1997 Economic Census. Based on the North American Industry Classification. System, 1997; see text, this section and Section 15. See also Appendix III. Minus sign (-) indicates decrease]

Item	2001	2002	2003	Percent change, 2001-02	Percent change, 2002-03
Revenue, total	26,096	27,203	26,326	4.2	-3.2
Books, print, total	21,211	22,436	21,822	5.8	-2.7
Books, internet, total.	1,499	1,404	1,454	-6.3	3.5
Books, other media, total.	819	992	816	21.2	-17.8
Sale or licensing of rights to content	298	274	230	-7.9	-16.2
Contract printing services.	186	235	(S)	26.4	(S)
Fulfillment services.	141	144	150	2.3	4.0
Rental or sale of mailing lists	(S)	7	(S)	(S)	(S)
Publishing services for others.	37	52	58	39.3	11.4
Other services revenue	1,896	1,657	1,561	-12.6	-5.8
Inventories at end of year	4,092	4,325	4,220	5.7	-2.4
Finished goods and work-in-process. . . .	3,936	4,154	4,076	5.5	-1.9
Materials, supplies, fuel, etc.	156	171	145	9.8	-15.2

S Data do not meet publication standards.

Source: U.S. Census Bureau, "Service Annual Survey: 2003", SAS/03. See <http://www.census.gov/econ/www/servmenu.html> (released December 2004)

Table 1128. **Book Purchasing for Adults: 2000 and 2004**

[In percent. Excludes all books purchased for children under age 14. Based on an ongoing survey of 16,000 households conducted over 12 months ending in December of year shown. For details, see source]

Characteristic	Total		Mass market [1]		Trade [2]		Hardcover		Audio, 2004 [3]
	2000	2004	2000	2004	2000	2004	2000	2004	
Total	100.0	100.0	100.0	100.0	100.0	100.0	100.0	100.0	100.0
Age of purchaser:									
Under 25 years old	5.0	5.1	4.4	3.2	6.3	8.4	4.6	5.2	6.4
25 to 34 years old	13.7	11.0	10.9	7.7	17.9	16.0	14.6	11.2	10.6
35 to 44 years old	19.4	17.4	15.4	15.7	24.5	20.4	22.0	17.4	17.9
45 to 54 years old	24.2	22.8	23.4	20.4	24.8	23.7	26.3	24.7	24.1
55 to 64 years old	17.2	21.0	20.2	23.6	14.1	18.1	15.0	20.5	17.0
65 years old and over	20.5	22.8	25.8	29.4	12.6	13.5	17.6	21.1	24.0
Education of household head:									
Not a high school graduate	12.0	12.5	11.6	15.2	7.8	8.1	12.5	11.2	5.9
High school graduate	54.3	54.5	61.4	59.8	46.9	48.0	49.0	52.8	46.9
College graduate.	17.2	17.0	15.6	14.8	21.4	20.8	18.3	17.2	28.9
Post college	16.5	16.0	11.4	10.2	23.9	23.1	20.2	18.8	18.3
Household income:									
Under $30,000	34.7	32.6	37.9	36.4	27.3	29.7	29.4	27.2	32.3
$30,000 to 49,999	20.3	20.0	21.0	19.3	21.2	19.6	20.1	21.6	13.1
$50,000 to 74,999	16.8	17.8	16.5	16.9	18.1	18.6	18.2	18.4	28.1
$75,000 and over	28.2	29.6	24.6	27.4	33.4	32.1	32.3	32.8	26.5
Household size:									
One member	28.8	30.5	29.6	29.6	27.2	30.8	27.9	30.4	43.0
Two members.	41.1	42.1	39.7	44.7	41.7	38.7	42.8	42.6	32.7
Three or more members.	30.2	27.5	30.7	25.6	31.2	30.6	29.3	27.0	24.4
Age of intended reader:									
Under 25 years old	7.5	7.4	5.3	4.2	11.5	13.0	6.9	7.5	7.1
25 to 34 years old	14.0	11.3	11.1	7.9	18.1	16.9	15.5	11.4	11.0
35 to 44 years old	18.9	16.8	15.1	15.0	22.7	19.5	22.0	17.1	18.4
45 to 54 years old	23.4	21.9	23.2	20.6	23.4	21.1	24.9	23.7	24.2
55 to 64 years old	16.4	20.4	19.5	23.2	12.6	16.8	14.2	20.1	15.0
65 years old and over	19.9	22.3	25.8	29.2	11.6	12.6	16.5	20.3	24.2
Category of book:									
Popular fiction.	51.3	53.7	94.8	89.0	21.6	23.5	33.6	39.9	42.2
General nonfiction	5.3	6.9	1.8	2.3	9.6	11.0	9.2	11.2	11.8
Cooking/crafts.	6.4	5.2	0.1	0.1	15.6	12.7	11.4	7.6	1.8
Other	37.0	34.2	3.3	8.6	53.2	52.8	45.7	41.3	44.2
Where purchased (channel):									
Book stores [4]	30.8	35.2	29.6	31.1	43.9	45.7	26.1	33.6	28.8
Mass merchandisers	9.4	7.9	17.3	14.5	4.5	3.9	3.3	2.8	8.0
Book clubs.	19.9	18.8	19.9	22.1	8.2	8.1	29.1	23.4	8.0
Online retailer/Internet	6.8	10.5	3.9	4.2	10.5	15.5	9.4	15.1	9.0
Other [5]	33.1	27.6	29.3	28.1	33.0	26.9	32.1	25.1	46.2

NA Not available. [1] "Pocket size" books sold primarily through magazine and news outlets, supermarkets, variety stores, etc. [2] All paperbound books, except mass market. [3] Audio and digital books were added to questionnaire in January 2001. Sample size for digital book purchasing (i.e. e-Books) was too small to show detailed breaks. [4] Includes independent, chain and used bookstores. [5] Includes mail order, price clubs, discount stores, food/drug stores, multimedia, and other outlets.

Source: Ipsos-NPD, Inc., Chicago IL., *Ipsos BookTrends*, a service mark of Ipsos-NPD, Inc. (copyright).

742   Information and Communications

Table 1129. **Software Publishers—Estimated Revenue and Inventories: 2001 to 2003**

[In millions of dollars (90,591 represents $90,591,000,000). For taxable and tax-exempt employer firms. Covers NAICS 5112. Estimates have been adjusted to the results of the 1997 Economic Census. Based on the North American Industry Classification System, 1997; see text this section, and Section 15]

Item	2001	2002	2003	Percent change, 2001-02	Percent change, 2002-03
Revenue [1]	90,591	88,846	89,889	-1.9	1.2
Source of revenue:					
System software publishing, total	31,842	31,459	31,497	-1.2	0.1
Operating system software	9,217	10,010	10,390	8.6	3.8
Network software	7,543	7,963	8,493	5.6	6.6
Database management software	9,929	8,602	8,077	-13.4	-6.1
Development tools and programming languages software	3,717	3,535	3,233	-4.9	-8.5
Other systems software	1,437	1,348	1,305	-6.1	-3.2
Application software publishing, total	37,297	37,473	38,492	0.5	2.7
General business productivity and home use applications	16,980	17,940	19,113	5.7	6.5
Cross-industry application software	11,580	10,643	10,561	-8.1	-0.8
Vertical market application software	7,414	7,717	7,699	4.1	-0.2
Utilities software	943	850	845	-9.9	-0.6
Other application software	380	323	274	-15.0	-15.1
Customization and integration of packaged software	4,045	4,029	3,357	-0.4	-16.7
Information technology consulting services	5,847	5,004	4,743	-14.4	-5.2
Information technology-related training services	1,245	1,173	885	-5.8	-24.5
Other services revenue	7,667	7,459	8,768	-2.7	17.5
Breakdown of revenue:					
System software [1]	31,842	31,459	31,497	-1.2	0.1
Personal computer software	5,759	6,767	7,357	17.5	8.7
Enterprise software	17,931	16,504	16,456	-8.0	-0.3
Mainframe computer software	8,153	7,798	7,300	-4.4	-6.4
Application software [1]	37,297	37,473	38,492	0.5	2.7
Personal computer software	12,218	13,116	14,270	7.4	8.8
Enterprise software	23,362	22,457	21,403	-3.9	-4.7
Mainframe computer software	1,717	(S)	(S)	(S)	(S)
Inventories at end of year	1,671	2,072	1,811	24.0	-12.6
Finished goods and work-in-process	1,310	1,691	1,417	29.1	-16.2
Materials, supplies, fuel, etc.	361	381	394	5.5	3.4

S Data do not meet publication standards.   [1] Includes other sources and types of revenue, not shown separately.

Source: U.S. Census Bureau, "Service Annual Survey: 2003", SAS/03. See <http://www.census.gov/econ/www/servmenu.html>. (released December 2004)

Table 1130. **Motion Picture and Sound Recording Industries—Estimated Revenue and Inventories: 1998 to 2003**

[In millions of dollars (59,404 represents $59,404,000,000), except percent. For taxable and tax-exempt employer firms. Except where indicated, estimates have been adjusted to results of the 1997 Economic Census. Based on the North American Industry Classification System, 1997; see text, this section, and Section 15]

Item	1998	1999	2000	2001	2002	2003
Motion picture and recording industries (NAICS 512):						
Operating revenue	59,404	64,023	67,745	69,152	74,020	77,901
Total inventories	13,853	14,837	15,270	15,266	16,145	18,627
Finished goods and work-in-process	13,686	14,656	15,062	15,041	15,943	18,437
Materials, supplies, fuel, etc.	168	181	208	225	202	190
Motion picture and video (NAICS 5121):						
Operating revenue	48,002	51,448	54,040	55,937	60,486	64,096
Total inventories	13,536	14,531	14,912	14,874	15,731	18,225
Finished goods and work-in-process	13,420	14,408	14,777	14,729	15,603	18,117
Materials, supplies, fuel, etc.	117	123	135	(S)	(S)	107
Sound recording (NAICS 5122): [1]						
Operating revenue	11,403	12,575	13,705	13,215	13,535	13,804
Total inventories	317	306	359	393	414	402
Finished goods and work-in-process	266	248	286	313	340	320
Materials, supplies, fuel, etc.	51	58	73	80	74	82

S Data do not meet publication standards.   [1] Estimates not adjusted to the results of the 1997 Economic Census.

Source: U.S. Census Bureau, "Service Annual Survey: 2003", SAS/03. See <http://www.census.gov/econ/www/servmenu.html>. (released December 2004)

Information and Communications **743**

Table 1131. Recording Media—Manufacturers' Shipments and Value: 1990 to 2004

[865.7 represents 865,700,000. Based on reports of RIAA member companies who distributed about 84 percent of the prerecorded music in 2004. These data are supplemented by other sources. Minus sign (-) indicates returns greater than shipments]

Medium	1990	1995	1999	2000	2001	2002	2003	2004
UNIT SHIPMENTS [1] (mil.)								
Total [2]	865.7	1,112.7	1,160.6	1,079.2	968.5	859.7	798.4	814.1
CDs	286.5	722.9	938.9	942.5	881.9	803.3	745.9	766.9
CD singles	1.1	21.5	55.9	34.2	17.3	4.5	8.3	3.1
Cassettes	442.2	272.6	123.6	76.0	45.0	31.1	17.2	5.2
Cassette singles	87.4	70.7	14.2	1.3	-1.5	-0.5	(NA)	(NA)
Albums—LPs and EPs	11.7	2.2	2.9	2.2	2.3	1.7	1.5	1.3
Vinyl singles	27.6	10.2	5.3	4.8	5.5	4.4	3.8	3.5
Music video	9.2	12.6	19.8	18.2	17.7	14.7	19.9	32.7
DVD video	(X)	(X)	2.5	3.3	7.9	10.7	17.5	29.0
DVD audio	(X)	(X)	(X)	(X)	0.3	0.4	0.4	0.35
VALUE (mil. dol.)								
Total [2]	7,541.1	12,320.3	14,584.7	14,323.7	13,740.9	12,614.2	11,854.4	12,154.7
CDs	3,451.6	9,377.4	12,816.3	13,214.5	12,909.4	12,044.1	11,232.9	11,446.5
CD singles	6.0	110.9	222.4	142.7	79.4	19.6	35.9	14.9
Cassettes	3,472.4	2,303.6	1,061.6	626.0	363.4	209.8	108.1	23.6
Cassette singles	257.9	236.3	48.0	4.6	-5.3	-1.6	(NA)	(NA)
Albums—LPs and EPs	86.5	25.1	31.8	27.7	27.4	20.5	21.7	19.2
Vinyl singles	94.4	46.7	27.9	26.3	31.4	24.9	21.5	19.8
Music video	172.3	220.3	376.7	281.9	329.2	288.4	399.9	607.2
DVD video	(X)	(X)	66.3	80.3	190.7	236.3	369.6	561.1
DVD audio	(X)	(X)	(X)	(X)	6.0	8.5	8.0	6.4

X Not applicable. [1] Net units, after returns. [2] Includes discontinued media. Beginning 2003 includes super audio compact disks (SACD), not shown separately.

Source: Recording Industry Association of America, Washington, DC, 2004 Year End Statistics and earlier issues (copyright). See Internet site <http://www.riaa.com> (accessed 20 May 2005).

Table 1132. Profile of Consumer Expenditures for Sound Recordings—Percent Distribution: 1990 to 2003

[In percent. Based on monthly telephone surveys of the population 10 years old and over]

Item	1990	1995	1998	1999	2000	2001	2002	2003
Total [1]	100.0	100.0	100.0	100.0	100.0	100.0	100.0	100.0
Age: 10 to 14 years	7.6	8.0	9.1	8.5	8.9	8.5	8.9	8.6
15 to 19 years	18.3	17.1	15.8	12.6	12.9	13.0	13.3	11.4
20 to 24 years	16.5	15.3	12.2	12.6	12.5	12.2	11.5	10.0
25 to 29 years	14.6	12.3	11.4	11.4	10.5	10.3	10.8	10.9
30 to 34 years	13.2	12.1	11.4	10.1	9.8	10.2	9.8	11.2
35 to 39 years	10.2	10.8	12.6	10.4	10.6	10.3	9.9	10.0
40 to 44 years	7.8	7.5	8.3	9.3	9.6	10.3	9.9	10.0
45 years and over	11.1	16.1	18.1	24.7	23.8	23.7	25.5	26.6
Sex: Male	54.4	53.0	48.7	50.3	50.6	48.8	49.4	49.1
Female	45.6	47.0	51.3	49.7	49.4	51.2	50.6	50.9
Sales outlet:								
Record store	69.8	52.0	50.8	44.5	42.4	42.5	36.8	33.2
Other store	18.5	28.2	34.4	38.3	40.8	42.4	50.7	52.8
Tape/record club	8.9	14.3	9.0	7.9	7.6	6.1	4.0	4.1
Ad or 800 number	2.5	4.0	2.9	2.5	2.4	3.0	2.0	1.5
Internet [2]	(NA)	(NA)	1.1	2.4	3.2	2.9	3.4	5.0
Music type: [3]								
Rock	36.1	33.5	25.7	25.2	24.8	24.4	24.7	25.2
Rap/Hip Hop	8.5	6.7	9.7	10.8	12.9	11.4	13.8	13.3
R&B/Urban	11.6	11.3	12.8	10.5	9.7	10.6	11.2	10.6
Country	9.6	16.7	14.1	10.8	10.7	10.5	10.7	10.4
Pop	13.7	10.1	10.0	10.3	11.0	12.1	9.0	8.9
Religious	2.5	3.1	6.3	5.1	4.8	6.7	6.7	5.8
Classical	3.1	2.9	3.3	3.5	2.7	3.2	3.1	3.0
Jazz	4.8	3.0	1.9	3.0	2.9	3.4	3.2	2.9
Soundtracks	0.8	0.9	1.7	0.8	0.7	1.4	1.1	1.4
Oldies	0.8	1.0	0.7	0.7	0.9	0.8	0.9	1.3
New age	1.1	0.7	0.6	0.5	0.5	1.0	0.5	0.5
Children's	0.5	0.5	0.4	0.4	0.6	0.6	0.4	0.6
Other	5.6	7.0	7.9	9.1	8.3	7.9	8.1	7.6
Media type: CDs	31.1	65.0	74.8	83.2	89.3	89.2	90.5	87.8
Cassettes	54.7	25.1	14.8	8.0	4.9	3.4	2.4	2.2
Singles (all types)	8.7	7.5	6.8	5.4	2.5	2.4	1.9	2.4
Music video [4]	(NA)	0.9	1.0	0.9	0.8	1.1	0.7	0.6
DVD audio	(NA)	(NA)	(NA)	(NA)	(NA)	1.1	1.3	2.7
Digital download	(NA)	(NA)	(NA)	(NA)	(NA)	0.2	0.5	1.3
SACD [5]	(NA)	(NA)	(NA)	(NA)	(NA)	(NA)	(NA)	0.5
Vinyl LPs	4.7	0.5	0.7	0.5	0.5	0.6	0.7	0.5

NA Not available. [1] Percent distributions exclude nonresponses and responses of "Don't know." [2] Excludes record club purchases over the Internet. [3] As classified by respondent. [4] Beginning 2001 includes video DVDs. [5] Super audio compact disks.

Source: Recording Industry Association of America, Washington, DC, 2004 Year End Statistics and earlier issues (copyright). See Internet site <http://www.riaa.com> (accessed 20 May 2005).

Table 1133. Radio and Television Broadcasting—Estimated Revenue and Expenses: 2001 to 2003

[In millions of dollars (47,840 represents $47,840,000,000). For taxable and tax-exempt employer firms. Estimates have been adjusted to the results of the 1997 Economic Census. Based on the North American Industry Classification System, 1997; see text, this section, and Section 15]

Item	Total (NAICS 5131)			Radio broadcasting (NAICS 51311)			TV broadcasting (NAICS 51312)		
	2001	2002	2003	2001	2002	2003	2001	2002	2003
Operating revenue	47,840	51,822	51,904	13,740	14,774	14,967	34,100	37,048	36,937
Station time sales	28,820	31,197	31,273	11,489	12,120	12,041	17,331	19,077	19,232
Network compensation	514	486	468	91	97	90	424	390	378
National/regional advertising	9,502	10,729	10,415	2,538	2,807	2,722	6,964	7,922	7,692
Local advertising revenue	18,803	19,982	20,391	8,861	9,217	9,229	9,943	10,766	11,163
Network time sales	14,322	15,655	15,653	935	1,122	1,156	13,387	14,534	14,497
Program rights	177	272	251	171	259	241	(S)	(S)	(S)
Production and post-production services	(S)	66	90	(S)	(S)	(S)	(S)	(S)	(S)
Public and non-commercial programming rights	2,126	2,035	2,145	(S)	(S)	(S)	1,604	1,479	1,534
Other operating services revenue	2,339	2,597	2,492	619	695	911	1,720	1,901	1,581
Operating Expenses [1]	39,714	40,724	40,667	11,242	11,256	11,437	28,472	29,468	29,229
Annual payroll	11,242	11,824	12,178	4,476	4,564	4,531	6,766	7,261	7,647
Employer contributions to employee benefit plans	1,541	1,475	1,594	566	582	558	975	893	1,037
Contract labor	(NA)	313	293	(NA)	208	194	(NA)	105	99
Total materials and supplies	(NA)	(NA)	423	(NA)	(NA)	152	(NA)	(NA)	271
Total purchased services [1]	(NA)	(NA)	5,954	(NA)	(NA)	2,696	(NA)	(NA)	3,258
Data processing and other computer services	(NA)	(NA)	120	(NA)	(NA)	11	(NA)	(NA)	109
Communication services	(NA)	350	397	(NA)	156	174	(NA)	194	223
Advertising and promotional services	1,445	1,559	1,824	523	624	767	923	934	1,058
Electricity	(NA)	300	335	(NA)	127	134	(NA)	173	202
Professional services [2]	(NA)	(NA)	592	(NA)	(NA)	251	(NA)	(NA)	342
Lease and rental payments	787	871	787	386	354	357	401	517	430
Broadcast rights and music license fees	11,898	12,750	12,141	728	657	704	11,170	12,092	11,436
Depreciation	4,048	2,855	2,761	1,572	904	1,020	2,475	1,951	1,741
Taxes and license fees	(NA)	694	766	(NA)	461	489	(NA)	233	277
Other	7,852	6,531	4,557	2,623	2,136	1,093	5,229	4,395	3,464

NA Not available. S Does not meet publication standards. [1] Includes other expenses, not shown separately. [2] Management consulting, administrative, and other.

Source: U.S. Census Bureau, "Service Annual Survey: 2003", SAS/03. See <http://www.census.gov/econ/www/servmenu.html> (released December 2004).

Table 1134. Cable and Pay TV—Summary: 1975 to 2004

[9,800 represents 9,800,000. Cable TV for calendar year. Pay TV as of December 31 of year shown]

Year	Cable TV				Pay TV					
	Avg. basic subscribers (1,000)	Avg. monthly basic rate (dol.)	Revenue [1] (mil. dol.) Total	Basic	Units [2] (1,000) Total pay [3]	Pay cable	Noncable delivered premium	Monthly rate (dol.) All-pay weighted average [3]	Pay cable	Noncable delivered premium
1975	9,800	6.50	804	764	194	194	(NA)	(NA)	7.85	(NA)
1980	17,500	7.69	2,609	1,615	8,581	7,336	(NA)	8.91	8.62	(NA)
1985	35,440	9.73	8,831	4,138	29,885	29,418	(NA)	10.29	10.25	(NA)
1990	50,520	16.78	17,582	10,174	39,902	39,751	(NA)	10.35	10.30	(NA)
1991	52,570	18.10	19,426	11,418	39,983	36,569	(NA)	10.35	10.27	(NA)
1992	54,300	19.08	21,079	12,433	40,893	36,879	(NA)	10.29	10.17	(NA)
1993	56,200	[4] 19.39	22,809	13,528	42,010	37,113	(NA)	9.27	9.11	(NA)
1994	58,373	21.62	21,531	15,144	47,478	42,528	4,950	8.19	8.33	6.99
1995	60,550	23.07	24,137	16,763	55,723	46,798	8,925	8.29	8.54	6.99
1996	62,300	24.41	26,195	18,249	63,705	49,728	13,977	7.98	8.12	7.50
1997	63,600	26.48	28,931	20,213	72,785	51,933	20,852	8.31	8.43	8.00
1998	64,650	27.81	31,191	21,574	80,605	55,280	25,325	8.58	8.74	8.22
1999	65,500	28.92	34,095	22,732	88,455	59,005	29,450	8.73	8.85	8.50
2000	66,250	30.37	37,070	24,142	102,590	65,918	36,672	8.69	8.81	8.48
2001	66,732	32.87	42,577	26,324	115,325	75,433	39,892	8.95	9.10	8.66
2002	66,472	34.71	48,733	27,690	118,575	77,292	41,283	9.19	9.29	9.00
2003	66,050	36.59	54,285	29,000	119,927	78,939	40,988	9.37	9.45	9.23
2004 est.	65,853	38.23	59,846	30,214	122,248	80,753	41,495	10.03	10.11	9.88

NA Not available. [1] Includes installation revenue, subscriber revenue, and nonsubscriber revenue; excludes telephony and high-speed access. [2] Individual program services sold to subscribers. [3] Includes multipoint distribution service (MDS), satellite TV (STV), multipoint multichannel distribution service (MMDS), satellite master antenna TV (SMATV), C-band satellite, and DBS satellite. Includes average pay unit price based on data for major premium pay movie services. [4] Weighted average representing 8 months of unregulated basic rate and 4 months of FCC rolled-back rate.

Source: Kagan Research LLC. From the Broadband Cable Financial Databook 2003, 2004 (copyright); The Pay TV Newsletter, June 28, 2002, July 31, 2002; and Cable Program Investor, Dec. 23, 2003, December 16, 2004, and various other publications.

Information and Communications 745

Table 1135. Cable Networks and Program Distribution Services—Estimated Revenue and Expenses: 2001 to 2003

[In millions of dollars (74,420 represents $74,420,000,000). For taxable and tax-exempt employer firms. Covers NAICS 5132. Estimates have been adjusted to the results of the 1997 Economic Census. Based on the North American Industry Classification System; see text, this section, and Section 15. Minus sign (-) indicates decrease]

Item	2001	2002	2003	Percent change, 2001-02	Percent change. 2002-03
Operating revenue [1]	74,420	80,536	90,456	8.2	12.3
Air time (advertising)	12,225	12,835	14,269	5.0	11.2
Specialty programming service	12,466	14,087	15,635	13.0	11.0
Basic programming service	32,148	34,340	37,626	6.8	9.6
Premium cable programming packages	5,215	5,353	5,022	2.6	-6.2
Pay-per-view service	1,927	2,133	2,352	10.7	10.3
Program distribution equipment sales and rentals	1,779	1,775	1,907	-0.2	7.4
Other program distribution related services	2,350	2,303	2,338	-2.0	1.5
Internet access services	2,314	3,664	6,561	58.4	79.0
Basic fixed local telephony	844	873	1,418	3.4	62.5
Operating expenses [1]	70,821	69,677	74,586	-1.6	7.0
Annual payroll	10,640	10,705	11,354	0.6	6.1
Employer contributions to employee benefit plans	2,019	1,897	2,243	-6.1	18.3
Contract labor	(NA)	958	1,406	(NA)	46.8
Total materials and supplies	(NA)	(NA)	702	(NA)	(NA)
Total purchased services [1]	(NA)	(NA)	7,311	(NA)	(NA)
Communication services	(NA)	607	867	(NA)	42.9
Advertising and promotional services	2,319	2,703	2,886	16.6	6.8
Electricity	(NA)	340	340	(NA)	0.1
Professional services [2]	(NA)	(NA)	649	(NA)	(NA)
Lease and rental payments	1,058	974	1,119	-7.9	14.9
Program and production costs	22,177	24,430	27,957	10.2	14.4
Depreciation	16,869	12,726	14,149	-24.6	11.2
Taxes and license fees	(NA)	878	1,076	(NA)	22.5
Other	14,062	11,380	8,389	-19.1	-26.3

NA Not available. [1] Includes other revenues and expenses, not shown separately. [2] Management consulting, administration, and other.

Source: U.S. Census Bureau, "Service Annual Survey: 2003", SAS/03. See <http://www.census.gov/econ/www/servmenu.html> (released December 2004).

Table 1136. Telecommunications—Estimated Revenue and Expenses: 2001 to 2003

[In millions of dollars (363,151 represents $363,151,000,000), except percent. For taxable and tax-exempt employer firms. Except for NAICS 51332, wireless telecommunications carriers (except satellite), estimates have been adjusted to the results of the 1997 Economic Census. Based on the North American Industry Classification System, 1997; see text, this section, and Section 15. See Table 1137 for cellular and other wireless telecommunications carriers, NAICS 513322]

Item	Telecommunucations (NAICS 5133)			Wired telecommunications carriers (NAICS 51331)		
	2001	2002	2003	2001	2002	2003
Operating revenue	363,151	350,137	348,030	260,122	237,376	222,563
Fixed total [1]	185,214	168,854	153,980	175,627	159,711	145,465
Fixed local	85,692	81,501	75,611	84,370	80,011	74,134
Basic service	70,258	67,680	62,774	69,052	66,360	61,460
Fixed long-distance	75,078	64,204	56,392	71,025	60,753	53,102
Outbound service	64,475	55,035	48,983	61,219	52.224	46,102
Dedicated network services	11,342	10,956	10,001	8,107	7,883	7,245
Data transmission services	7,970	7,911	7,677	7,196	7,155	6,932
Mobile total	74,824	85,659	94,981	(S)	(S)	(S)
Mobile telephony services	69,446	81,426	91,235	(X)	(X)	(X)
Local access and use	49,963	59,887	69,633	(X)	(X)	(X)
Carrier services	61,190	58,423	57,380	54,755	53,547	52,166
Network access	52,835	52,153	51,176	50,171	49,334	47,723
Other telecommunications services	10,494	10,649	11,752	5,918	4,752	4,418
Other services revenue	31,429	26,552	29,939	(S)	(S)	19,142
Operating expenses	331,185	303,046	302,264	235,258	202,764	196,783
Annual payroll	66,373	56,317	57,876	50,931	42,640	42,804
Employer contributions to Social Security and other supplemental benefits	15,459	15,649	17,170	12,473	12,909	13,802
Contract labor	(NA)	4,011	4,466	(NA)	2,118	2,382
Total materials and supplies	(NA)	(NA)	6,462	(NA)	(NA)	4,828
Total purchased services [1]	(NA)	(NA)	43,500	(NA)	(NA)	25,966
Communication services	(NA)	7,523	6,345	(NA)	5,593	4,236
Advertising and promotional services	8,827	8,194	8,510	4,357	3,401	3,270
Professional services [2]	(NA)	(NA)	6,110	(NA)	(NA)	4,409
Lease and rental payments	8,986	9,193	8,887	4,893	4,674	3,875
Access charges	40,641	37,568	38,235	31,410	28.872	29,715
Depreciation	73,846	62,084	64,397	52,661	43,396	42,520
Universal service contributions and other similar charges	4,017	3,510	3,434	3,274	2,825	2,543
Taxes and license fees	(NA)	6,229	6,966	(NA)	5,395	6,019
Other	91,435	70,910	59,757	58,363	(S)	26,205

NA Not available. S Does not meet publication standards. X Not applicable. [1] Includes other revenue sources and expenses, not shown separately. [2] Includes management consulting, administration, and other professional services.

Source: U.S. Census Bureau, "Service Annual Survey: 2003", SAS/03. See <http://www.census.gov/econ/www/servmenu.html> (released December 2004)

Table 1137. Cellular and Other Wireless Telecommunications Carriers— Estimated Revenue and Expenses: 2001 to 2003

[In millions of dollars (78,239 represents $78,239,000,000). For taxable and tax-exempt employer firms. For NAICS 513322. Estimates have been adjusted to the results of the 1997 Economic Census. Based on the North American Industry Classification System, 1997; see text, this section and Section 15. See Table 1136 for telecommunications total and wired carriers (NAICS 5133 and 51331). Minus sign (-) indicates decrease]

Item	2001	2002	2003	Percent change, 2001-02	Percent change, 2002-03
Operating revenue	**78,239**	**91,521**	**104,228**	**17.0**	**13.9**
Mobile total	67,819	79,526	89,898	17.3	13.0
Mobile telephony services [1]	67,224	78,995	89,368	17.5	13.1
Local access and use	49,632	59,246	69,050	19.4	16.5
Mobile long distance	4,861	5,758	5,122	18.5	-11.0
Mobile all distance	8,219	9,631	10,238	17.2	6.3
Messaging services	418	333	366	-20.3	9.8
Mobile dispatch services	178	198	(S)	11.8	(S)
Carrier services	2,719	2,596	2,289	-4.5	-11.8
Network access	1,090	1,135	1,265	4.1	11.5
Other telecommunications services	2,385	3,015	3,688	26.4	22.3
Other services revenue	5,316	6,384	8,353	20.1	30.8
Operating expenses	**71,665**	**82,140**	**87,243**	**14.6**	**6.2**
Annual payroll	10,585	9,898	11,377	-6.5	14.9
Employer contributions to social security and other supplemental benefits	2,043	2,226	2,786	9.0	25.2
Contract labor	(NA)	1,640	1,728	(NA)	5.4
Total materials and supplies	(NA)	(NA)	1,372	(NA)	(NA)
Total purchased services [1]	(NA)	(NA)	13,832	(NA)	(NA)
Data processing and other computer services	(NA)	(NA)	404	(NA)	(NA)
Communication services	(NA)	1,265	1,408	(NA)	11.3
Advertising and promotional services	4,078	4,482	4,934	9.9	10.1
Electricity	(NA)	233	262	(NA)	12.5
Professional services [2]	(NA)	(NA)	1,135	(NA)	(NA)
Lease and rental payments	2,974	3,387	4,011	13.9	18.4
Access charges	6,544	6,223	6,455	-4.9	3.7
Depreciation	15,871	15,397	18,357	-3.0	19.2
Universal service contributions and other similar charges	617	584	797	-5.4	36.4
Taxes and license fees	(NA)	646	729	(NA)	12.9
Other	26,300	30,218	29,809	14.9	-1.4

NA Not available. S Data do not meet publication standards. [1] Includes other revenue source and expenses, not shown separately. [2] Includes management consulting, administration, and other professional services.

Source: U.S. Census Bureau, "Service Annual Survey: 2003", SAS/03. See <http://www.census.gov/econ/www/servmenu.html> (released December 2004).

Table 1138. Telecommunications Industry—Carriers and Revenue: 1995 to 2003

[Revenue in millions of dollars (190,076 represents $190,076,000,000). Data based on carrier filings to the FCC. Because of reporting changes, data beginning 2000 are not strictly comparable with previous years; see source for details]

Category	Carriers					Telecommunications revenue				
	1995	2000	2001	2002 [1]	2003	1995	2000	2001	2002	2003
Total [2]	**3,058**	**4,879**	**5,001**	**4,390**	**4,636**	**190,076**	**292,762**	**301,799**	**292,341**	**291,123**
Local service providers	1,675	2,641	2,755	2,531	2,681	103,792	128,075	133,502	130,941	126,860
Incumbent local exchange carriers (ILECs)	1,347	1,335	1,335	1,310	1,303	102,820	116,158	117,885	114,990	109,480
Pay telephone providers	271	699	751	606	605	349	972	836	641	523
Competitors of ILECs [3]	57	607	669	615	773	623	10,945	14,781	15,310	16,857
CAPs and CLECs [3]	57	479	511	451	601	623	9,814	12,998	13,043	15,509
Local resellers	(⁴)	105	132	100	100	(⁴)	879	1,393	1,538	721
Other local exchange carriers	(⁴)	23	26	64	72	(⁴)	11	329	406	338
Private carriers	(⁴)	(⁴)	(⁴)	(⁴)	(⁴)	(⁴)	39	15	281	267
Shared tenant service providers	(⁴)	(⁴)	(⁴)	(⁴)	(⁴)	(⁴)	202	46	42	22
Wireless service providers [5]	930	1,430	1,306	927	939	18,627	63,280	74,596	80,467	89,342
Telephony [6]	792	783	670	422	413	17,208	59,823	71,887	78,568	88,168
Paging service providers	138	425	425	346	347	(⁴)	3,102	2,197	1,473	1,007
Toll service providers	453	808	940	932	1,026	76,447	101,407	93,702	80,934	74,920
Interexchange carriers	130	212	233	229	232	70,938	87,311	81,272	68,146	61,246
Operator service providers	25	20	19	18	17	500	635	611	554	567
Prepaid service providers	8	23	27	27	50	16	727	133	460	812
Satellite service carriers	(⁴)	25	34	33	40	(⁴)	336	373	406	663
Toll resellers	260	493	558	574	642	4,220	10,641	8,797	9,279	9,294
Other toll carriers	30	35	69	51	45	773	1,758	2,516	2,089	2,339

[1] Counts dropped in 2002 because many affiliated filers were allowed to file consolidated reports. [2] Revenue data include adjustments, not shown separately. For 1995, revenue data include some nontelecommunications revenue, formerly reported as local exchange wireless revenue. [3] Competitive access providers (CAPs) and competitive local exchange carriers (CLECs). [4] Data not available separately. [5] Beginning 2000, includes specialized mobile radio services and other services, not shown separately. [6] Cellular service, personal communications service, and specialized mobile radio.

Source: U.S. Federal Communications Commission, Trends in Telephone Service, annual.

Information and Communications **747**

Table 1139. **Telephone Systems—Summary: 1985 to 2003**

[112 represents 112,000,000. Covers principal carriers filing annual reports with Federal Communications Commission]

Item	Unit	1985	1990	1995	1998	1999	2000	2001 [1]	2002 [1]	2003 [1]
LOCAL EXCHANGE CARRIERS [2]										
Carriers [3]	Number .	55	51	53	52	52	52	30	29	28
Access lines	Millions .	112	130	166	205	228	245	253	262	268
Business access lines	Millions .	31	36	46	57	57	58	54	54	49
Residential access lines	Millions .	79	89	101	110	115	115	112	103	99
Other access lines (public, mobile, special)	Millions .	2	6	19	38	55	72	87	105	120
Number of local calls (originating)	Billions. .	365	402	484	544	554	537	515	459	425
Number of toll calls (originating)	Billions. .	(NA)	63	94	97	102	106	98	90	81
Gross book cost of plant	Bil. dol. .	191	240	284	325	342	362	360	367	368
Depreciation and amortization reserves. . .	Bil. dol. .	49	89	127	163	176	190	194	210	222
Net plant	Bil. dol. .	142	151	157	161	166	172	166	157	146
Total assets	Bil. dol. .	162	180	197	200	204	214	208	195	182
Total stockholders' equity	Bil. dol. .	63	74	72	70	67	72	66	58	47
Operating revenues	Bil. dol. .	73	84	96	108	113	117	109	103	108
Local revenues .	Bil. dol. .	32	37	46	55	58	60	55	51	51
Operating expenses [4]	Bil. dol. .	48	62	72	78	79	81	77	79	83
Net operating income [5]	Bil. dol. .	13	14	14	18	20	20	19	23	9
Net income	Bil. dol. .	9	11	11	12	13	15	11	8	4
Employees	(1,000). .	(NA)	569	447	436	436	434	386	333	303
Compensation of employees	Bil. dol. .	(NA)	23	21	23	24	24	23	23	23
Average monthly residential local telephone rate [6]	Dollars. .	(NA)	19.24	20.01	19.76	19.93	20.78	22.62	23.38	24.31
Average monthly single-line business telephone rate [7]	Dollars. .	(NA)	41.21	41.80	41.29	41.21	41.80	42.43	43.59	43.75
LONG DISTANCE CARRIERS										
Number of carriers with presubscribed lines	Number .	(NA)	325	583	(NA)	(NA)	(NA)	(NA)	(NA)	(NA)
Number of presubscribed lines	Millions .	(NA)	132	153	(NA)	(NA)	(NA)	(NA)	(NA)	(NA)
Total toll service revenues [7]	Bil. dol. .	55	67	90	105	108	110	99	84	77
Interstate switched-access minutes	Bil. min. .	167	307	432	519	553	567	538	486	444
INTERNATIONAL TELEPHONE SERVICE [8]										
Number of U.S. billed calls	Millions .	425	984	2,830	4,477	5,305	5,742	6,265	5,926	7,350
Number of U.S. billed minutes	Millions .	3,446	8,030	15,889	24,250	28,515	30,135	33,287	35,063	42,664
U.S. billed revenues	Mil. dol. .	3,487	8,059	14,335	14,726	14,980	14,909	11,380	9,773	8,944
U.S. carrier revenue net of settlements with foreign carriers	Mil. dol. .	2,332	5,188	9,397	10,242	10,379	10,982	8,034	6,931	5,964
Revenue from private-line service	Mil. dol. .	172	201	514	921	1,216	1,480	1,467	988	620
Revenue from resale service	Mil. dol. .	(NA)	167	1,756	4,798	4,528	7,600	5,341	4,871	5,420

NA Not available. [1] Beginning 2001, detailed financial data only filed by regional Bell-operating companies. Access lines and calls reported by 50 reporting companies. [2] Gross operating revenues, gross plant, and total assets of reporting carriers estimated at more than 90 percent of total industry. New accounting rules became effective in 1990; prior years may not be directly comparable on a one-to-one basis. Includes Virgin Islands, and prior to 1995, Puerto Rico. [3] The reporting threshold for carriers is $100 million in annual operating revenue. [4] Excludes taxes. [5] After tax deductions. [6] Based on surveys conducted by FCC. [7] Series revised to include all toll revenues: toll, wireless, ILECs, carriers (ILECs) and competitive local exchange carriers (CLECs). [8] Beginning 1995, data are for all U.S. points, and include calls to and from Alaska, Hawaii, Puerto Rico, Guam, the U.S. Virgin Islands, and offshore U.S. points. Beginning 1995, carriers first started reporting traffic to and from Canada and Mexico. Data for Canada and Mexico in prior years are staff estimates.

Source: U.S. Federal Communications Commission, *Statistics of Communications Common Carriers*, annual; *Trends in Telephone Service*, annual; and *Trends in the International Telecommunications Industry*, annual.

Table 1140. **Cellular Telecommunications Industry: 1990 to 2004**

[Calendar year data, except as noted (5,283 represents 5,283,000). Based on a survey mailed to all cellular, personal communications services, and enhanced special mobile radio (ESMR) systems. For 2003 data, the universe was 3,123 systems and the response rate was 87 percent; the 2004 system count is not yet available. The number of operational systems beginning 2000 differs from that reported for previous periods as a result of the consolidated operation of ESMR systems in a broader service area instead of by a city-to-city basis]

Item	Unit	1990	1995	1999	2000	2001	2002	2003	2004
Systems	Number. . .	751	1,627	3,518	2,440	2,587	2,846	3,123	(NA)
Subscribers	1,000	5,283	33,786	86,047	109,478	128,375	140,766	158,722	182,140
Cell sites [1]	Number. . .	5,616	22,663	81,698	104,288	127,540	139,338	162,986	175,725
Employees	Number. . .	21,382	68,165	155,817	184,449	203,580	192,410	205,629	226,016
Service revenue	Mil. dol. . . .	4,548	19,081	40,018	52,466	65,016	76,508	87,624	102,121
Roamer revenue [2]	Mil. dol. . . .	456	2,542	4,085	3,883	3,936	3,896	3,766	4,210
Capital investment	Mil. dol. . . .	6,282	24,080	71,265	89,624	105,030	126,922	145,867	173,794
Average monthly bill [3]	Dollars . . .	80.90	51.00	41.24	45.27	47.37	48.40	49.91	50.64
Average length of call [3]	Minutes . . .	2.20	2.15	2.38	2.56	2.74	2.73	2.87	3.05

NA Not available. [1] The basic geographic unit of a wireless PCS or cellular system. A city or county is divided into smaller "cells," each of which is equipped with a low-powered radio transmitter/receiver. The cells can vary in size depending upon terrain, capacity demands, etc. By controlling the transmission power, the radio frequencies assigned to one cell can be limited to the boundaries of that cell. When a wireless PCS or cellular phone moves from one cell toward another, a computer at the Switching Office monitors the movement and at the proper time, transfers or hands off the phone call to the new cell and another radio frequency. [2] Service revenue generated by subscribers' calls outside of their system areas. [3] As of December 31.

Source: Cellular Telecommunications & Internet Association, Washington, DC, *Semi-annual Wireless Survey* (copyright).

Table 1141. **Information Services and Data Processing Services—Estimated Revenue: 2001 to 2003**

[In millions of dollars (82,641 represents $82,641,000,000), except percent. For taxable and tax-exempt employer firms. Estimates have been adjusted to results of the 1997 Economic Census. Based on the 1997 North American Industry Classification System; see text, this section, and Section 15]

Item	2001	2002	2003	Percent change, 2001-02	Percent change, 2002-03
Total (NAICS 514)	82,641	87,891	88,558	6.4	0.8
News syndicates (NAICS 51411):					
Revenue	1,960	1,917	1,947	-2.2	1.6
Fees from supplying information	1,838	1,838	1,826	(Z)	-0.7
Other services revenue	122	79	121	-35.4	54.3
Libraries and archives (NAICS 51412):					
Revenue [1]	1,116	1,212	1,243	8.6	2.6
Subsidies, contributions, gifts, and grants	812	904	885	11.4	-2.1
Fees and dues from providing access to collections	49	47	53	-3.9	12.0
On-line information services (NAICS 514191):					
Revenue	28,623	27,832	27,160	-2.8	-2.4
Internet access services	14,222	14,632	14,318	2.9	-2.1
Advertising	3,516	2,866	2,640	-18.5	-7.9
Web site hosting	839	731	724	-12.9	-0.9
Internet backbone services	(S)	(S)	(S)	(S)	(S)
Internet telecommunications services	(S)	(S)	(S)	(S)	(S)
Information technology consulting services	(S)	(S)	(S)	(S)	(S)
Information technology design and development	(S)	(S)	(S)	(S)	(S)
Application service provisioning	(S)	(S)	(S)	(S)	(S)
Business process management	(S)	(S)	(S)	(S)	(S)
Video and audio streaming services	(S)	(S)	(S)	(S)	(S)
Other services revenue	4,429	4,315	4,809	-2.6	11.4
All other information services (NAICS 514199):					
Revenue [1]	3,724	4,011	5,107	7.7	27.3
Advertising	1,670	1,408	1,339	-15.6	-4.9
Web hosting and design	(S)	48	49	(S)	2.1
Information search services	713	849	1,364	19.0	60.6
Stock photo services	719	750	788	4.3	5.2
Video and audio streaming services	(S)	33	24	(S)	-27.6
Data processing services (NAICS 5142):					
Revenue	47,219	52,920	53,101	12.1	0.3
Business process management	15,953	20,124	20,817	26.1	3.4
Information and document transformation	1,183	(S)	(S)	(S)	(S)
Information technology design and development	13,660	13,441	12,733	-1.6	-5.3
Data storage services	224	214	(S)	-4.1	(S)
Data management services	3,238	4,321	3,876	33.4	-10.3
Collocation services	(S)	(S)	(S)	(S)	(S)
Information technology consulting services	1,161	(S)	(S)	(S)	(S)
Web site hosting	(S)	(S)	(S)	(S)	(S)
Software publishing	771	743	768	-3.6	3.3
Rental and leasing of computer hardware	(S)	(S)	(S)	(S)	(S)
Application service provisioning	973	1,066	1,175	9.5	10.3
Video and audio streaming services	43	39	(S)	-8.4	(S)
Other services revenue	8,476	8,713	9,355	2.8	7.4

S Data do not meet publication standards. Z Represents or rounds to zero. [1] Includes other sources of revenue, not shown separately.

Source: U.S. Census Bureau, "Service Annual Survey: 2003", SAS/03. See <http://www.census.gov/econ/www/servmenu.html>. (released December 2004)

Table 1142. **Academic Libraries—Summary: 2000**

[For fiscal year 193,963 represents 193,963,000. For 2- and 4-year degree granting institutions. Based on the Academic Libraries Survey; see source for details]

Item	Number of libraries	Circulation [1] (1,000)	Gate count [2] (1,000)	Volumes held [3] (1,000)	Staff [4] Total	Staff [4] Librarians (percent)	Expenditures Total (mil. dol.)	Expenditures Salary [5] (percent)	Percent with access from within library to— Electronic catalog	Percent with access from within library to— Internet
Total	3,527	193,963	16,457	913,547	95,665	26.3	5,026	50.1	93.7	98.6
Control: Public	1,566	127,848	10,890	544,917	58,277	25.6	3,080	51.5	98.9	99.6
Private	1,961	66,115	5,567	368,630	37,388	27.4	1,946	47.9	88.9	97.8
Level: [6]										
4-year degree and above [7]	2,148	166,442	12,563	856,414	81,800	25.9	4,473	48.0	95.6	98.7
Doctorate	568	117,186	7,449	605,978	55,090	24.9	3,284	46.6	98.0	98.6
Master's	884	34,228	3,667	179,758	19,193	27.3	859	52.4	96.1	99.1
Bachelor's	660	12,814	1,278	66,740	6,887	28.8	286	51.7	92.4	98.2
Less than 4-year	1,379	27,521	3,894	57,133	13,864	28.9	553	66.6	90.6	98.5
Enrollment: [4]										
Less than 1,500	1,910	25,131	2,982	117,713	14,385	30.2	596	53.4	87.9	97.6
1,500 to 4,999	1,051	39,563	4,395	176,512	22,355	27.5	1,041	53.0	99.4	99.8
5,000 or more	566	129,268	9,079	619,323	58,925	24.9	3,389	48.6	99.8	99.6

[1] Includes reserves. [2] In a typical week. [3] At end-of-year. [4] Full-time equivalent. [5] Salary and wages. [6] Level of highest degree offered. [7] Includes 36 institutions granting other degrees, not shown separately.

Source: U.S. National Center for Education Statistics, *Academic Libraries: 2000*, NCES 2004-317, November, 2003.

Information and Communications 749

Table 1143. **Public Library Outlets Offering Programs for Adults: 2000**

[In percent of outlets. For activities offered during a typical week during the prior year. Represents programs for which the outlet provided funding, materials, or staff to support the program or the library system ran the program within or on behalf of the outlet. Based on the Fast Response Survey System and subject to sampling error; see source for details]

Program	All outlets	Number of visits per week			Metropolitan status [1]		
		Less than 300	300 to 1,400	1,500 or more	Urban	Suburban	Rural
Computer/Internet instruction	56	36	59	77	68	59	49
Book/film discussions or presentations	43	22	45	69	56	50	34
Cultural performances	41	11	48	71	60	51	28
Recreational activities [2]	39	24	40	59	52	50	29
Parenting skills.	20	6	22	38	28	24	15
Financial planning/investment information . . .	18	4	19	38	30	26	11
Employment/career guidance	17	8	20	24	31	18	12
College/continuing education guidance	15	9	18	18	21	14	13
Citizenship preparation	5	5	4	5	7	6	3

[1] Urban = inside central city; Suburban = In metro area, outside of a central city; Rural = outside a metro area.   [2] Such as crafts and hobbies.

Source: U.S. National Center for Education Statistics, Fast Response Survey System. *Programs for Adults in Public Library Outlets,* NCES 2003-010, November 2002.

Table 1144. **Public Libraries by Selected Characteristics: 2002**

[8,586 represents $8,586,000,000. Based on survey of public libraries. Data are for public libraries in the 50 states and the District of Columbia. The response rates for these items are between 98 and 100 percent]

Population of service area	Number of—		Operating income—			Paid staff [3]		Libraries with Internet access
	Public libraries	Stationary outlets [1]	Total (mil. dol.) [2]	Source (percent)		Total	Librarians with ALA-MLS [4]	
				State govern-ment	Local govern-ment			
Total	9,137	16,486	8,586	11.7	79.1	136,219	30,428	8,876
1,000,000 or more . . .	23	960	1,217	9.3	77.9	15,933	4,483	23
500,000 to 999,000	54	1,152	1,375	14.0	78.0	19,634	4,876	54
250,000 to 499,999	94	1,086	983	11.8	80.8	15,212	3,733	94
100,000 to 249,999	329	2,023	1,418	10.8	81.7	22,833	4,940	329
50,000 to 99,999	530	1,616	1,110	13.3	78.8	17,929	3,977	529
25,000 to 49,999	922	1,738	1,039	12.0	79.8	17,359	4,002	918
10,000 to 24,999	1,758	2,260	889	11.5	78.6	15,662	3,157	1,754
5,000 to 9,999	1,446	1,612	324	11.3	76.2	6,252	900	1,436
2,500 to 4,999	1,315	1,358	131	7.1	75.1	2,893	242	1,288
1,000 to 2,499	1,631	1,644	77	6.3	69.9	1,931	99	1,571
Fewer than 1,000	1,035	1,037	22	7.4	66.8	581	18	880

[1] The sum of central and branches libraries. The total number of central libraries was 8,986; the total of branch libraries was 7,500.   [2] Includes income from the federal government (0.6%) and other sources (8.7%), not shown separately.   [3] Full-time equivalents.   [4] Librarians with master's degrees from a graduate library education program accredited by the American Library Association (ALA). Total librarians, including those without ALA-MLS, were 44,920.

Source: U.S. National Center for Education Statistics, *Public Libraries in the United States: 2002,* NCES 2005-356, March 2005.

Table 1145. **Public Library Use of the Internet: 2004**

[In percent, except number of outlets. As of spring. Based on sample survey; see source for details]

Item	Metropolitan status [1]				Poverty status [2]		
	Total	Urban	Sub-urban	Rural	Less than 20 percent	20 to 40 percent	More than 40 percent
All libraries outlets [3]	16,192	2,868	5,270	8,054	13,579	2,432	181
Connected to the Internet.	99.6	99.7	99.7	99.5	99.7	99.2	100.0
Connected with public access	98.9	98.5	99.4	98.7	99.0	96.3	98.1
Average number of workstations	10.4	17.3	13.0	6.7	9.7	12.5	27.2
Speed of access: [4]							
128kbps or less	12.8	5.6	6.5	18.6	12.1	16.6	18.0
129kbps-1.5mbps	45.2	51.7	46.1	42.7	45.1	45.6	49.0
Greater than 1.5mbps	20.3	33.0	25.9	13.2	19.3	25.4	23.5
Public access Internet content or service filtering/blocking:							
The library does not filter	58.2	68.3	58.1	56.6	58.7	53.8	62.3
Each public access workstation	16.7	10.4	14.1	19.2	16.5	19.5	7.9
Entire network in the library	13.4	16.3	13.1	13.0	12.7	19.3	21.8
All computers due to local community network with a public school	2.6	0.9	1.6	3.5	2.7	2.6	(NA)
All computers due to library consortium. . .	6.2	5.4	12.3	3.2	6.7	2.2	7.9

NA Not available.   [1] Urban = inside central city; Suburban = in metro area, outside of a central city; Rural = outside a metro area.   [2] Determined by the 2000 poverty status of the service area of the outlet.   [3] Central libraries and branches; excludes bookmobiles.

Source: Information Use Management and Policy Institute, College of Information, Florida State University, Tallahassee, FL, *Public Libraries and the Internet 2004: Survey Results and Findings,* by John Carlo Bertot, Charles R. McClure, and Paul T. Jaeger, Florida State University, Tallahassee, FL.

Table 1146. **Internet Access and Usage and Online Service Usage: 1997 to 2004, and by Characteristic, 2004**

[For persons 18 years old and over (193,462 represents 193,462,000). As of spring for 1997 and 2000; as of fall 2003 and 2004. Based on sample and subject to sampling error; see source for details]

Item	Total adults	Any online/ Internet usage in the past 30 days	Have Internet access			Used the Internet in the last 30 days		
			Home or work or other	Home only	Work only	Home or work or other	Home only	Work only
Total adults, 1997 (1,000)	193,462	31,686	46,305	25,500	22,931	29,127	16,640	13,806
Total adults, 2000 (1,000)	199,438	90,458	112,949	77,621	50,476	86,289	65,471	40,449
Total adults, 2003 (1,000)	209,657	131,839	165,898	128,549	73,315	128,417	107,604	62,159
Total adults, 2004 [1] (1,000).	**213,454**	**134,440**	**168,582**	**132,395**	**73,570**	**130,964**	**111,052**	**61,469**
PERCENT DISTRIBUTION	100.0	100.0	100.0	100.0	100.0	100.0	100.0	100.0
Age:								
18 to 34 years old	31.4	36.8	33.7	31.7	33.4	37.0	34.3	33.3
35 to 54 years old	39.6	44.7	42.7	45.9	52.9	44.8	46.5	53.5
55 years old and over	29.0	18.5	23.5	22.4	13.7	18.2	19.2	13.2
Sex:								
Male	48.0	48.2	48.2	49.2	51.2	48.2	48.7	50.8
Female	52.0	51.8	51.8	50.8	48.8	51.8	51.3	49.2
Census region: [2]								
Northeast	19.1	20.1	19.8	20.5	20.9	20.2	20.7	21.1
Midwest	22.6	23.4	23.9	22.9	23.0	23.3	22.7	22.1
South	36.2	33.2	34.1	33.4	33.1	33.0	33.1	32.8
West	22.1	23.3	22.2	23.2	23.0	23.4	23.5	24.0
Household size:								
1 to 2 persons	47.4	41.7	43.5	40.3	42.1	41.7	40.6	42.3
3 to 4 persons	37.1	42.9	40.9	43.4	44.0	43.0	43.9	44.0
5 or more persons	15.5	15.4	15.5	16.3	13.9	15.3	15.4	13.7
Any child in household	41.3	45.6	44.1	45.9	46.9	45.6	46.0	46.9
Marital status:								
Single	24.5	26.7	25.2	22.8	23.6	26.8	24.4	23.5
Married	56.6	59.7	59.3	64.2	62.7	59.7	63.0	63.3
Other	19.0	13.6	15.5	13.0	13.7	13.5	12.5	13.2
Educational attainment:								
Graduated college plus	24.8	35.7	30.1	34.8	46.1	36.2	38.6	50.0
Attended college	27.1	33.4	30.8	31.5	31.3	33.6	33.0	31.0
Did not attend college	48.2	30.9	39.1	33.7	22.5	30.2	28.4	18.9
Employed full-time	53.2	63.2	58.9	60.7	87.9	63.4	62.3	89.3
Employed part-time	10.9	12.3	11.8	12.2	11.4	12.4	12.8	10.3
Occupation of the employed:								
Professional	12.7	18.6	15.7	17.8	29.2	18.9	19.7	30.2
Management/business/financial. . .	9.9	14.0	12.0	13.5	22.4	14.2	14.5	24.9
Sales/office	16.0	20.9	18.7	18.9	29.3	21.2	20.1	30.0
Natural resources/construction/ maintenance	6.6	5.7	6.2	6.0	5.1	5.6	5.5	4.2
Other	18.9	16.3	18.1	16.8	13.4	16.0	15.4	10.4
Type of firm of employed:								
Business	35.0	39.8	37.5	38.2	51.2	40.0	39.5	51.7
Government	10.1	13.8	12.1	12.9	21.1	13.9	13.6	21.2
Other	18.8	21.9	21.0	21.8	27.0	21.9	22.0	26.8
Household income:								
Less than $50,000	48.8	32.9	39.5	31.5	21.9	32.5	29.0	19.5
$50,000 to $74,999.	20.3	24.3	23.0	24.5	24.6	24.3	24.6	23.4
$75,000 to $149,999.	24.1	33.1	29.0	33.7	40.7	33.3	35.5	43.0
$150,000 or more.	6.8	9.7	8.4	10.3	12.9	9.9	10.9	14.1

[1] Includes other labor force status, not shown separately.   [2] For composition of regions, see map inside front cover.

Source: Mediamark Research Inc., New York, NY, *CyberStats*, fall 2003 and 2004; and spring 1997 and 2000 (copyright). See Internet site <http://www.mriplus.com/pocketpiece.html>.

Information and Communications **751**

Table 1147. Online Activities, 2001 and 2003, and by Type of Home Internet Connection, 2003

[In percent. As of September 2001 and October 2003. Represents percent of Internet users 15 years old and over. Based on the Current Population Survey and subject to sampling error; see source and Appendix III]

Activity	Online activities from any location		Online activities by type of home Internet connection, 2003		
	2001	2003	None	Dial-up	Broadband
E-mail or instant messaging....................	86.9	87.8	71.2	88.9	93.0
Playing games	36.5	38.1	29.6	37.1	43.1
Listening to radio or viewing TV or movies	18.9	21.7	16.1	17.3	30.9
Purchase products or services....................	44.1	52.1	33.5	49.2	64.3
Take a course online	4.0	6.4	5.2	5.7	8.0
Trade stocks, bonds or mutual funds..............	8.6	6.8	3.0	5.8	9.9
Bank online	17.4	27.8	16.3	23.8	38.7
Search for product or service information	73.2	76.5	63.1	75.7	83.3
Get news, weather or sports information	66.0	66.5	50.4	64.4	76.2
Search for information on health services or practices ...	34.1	41.6	32.2	40.0	47.9
Search for information about government services or agencies...............................	30.1	35.7	29.5	33.4	41.9
Search for a job............................	16.0	18.7	19.9	16.9	21.1

Source: U.S. Department of Commerce, National Telecommunications and Information Administration, *A Nation Online: Entering the Broadband Age,* September 2004. See Internet site <http://www.ntia.doc.gov/reports/anol/index.html>.

Table 1148. Household Internet Connections by Type: 2003

[As of October. Based on the Current Population Survey and subject to sampling error; see source and Appendix III]

Characteristic	Internet households [1]		Type of Internet connection—percent distribution					
	Total	Percent of all house- holds	Dial-up telephone		Cable modem		Digital subscriber line	
			Number	Percent	Number	Percent	Number	Percent
All households [2]	**61,481**	**54.6**	**38,593**	**62.8**	**12,638**	**20.6**	**9,335**	**15.2**
Age of householder:								
Under 25 years old	3,295	46.9	1,833	55.6	803	24.4	614	18.6
25 to 34 years old..........	11,750	60.2	6,920	58.9	2,640	22.5	2,020	17.2
35 to 44 years old..........	15,447	65.2	9,434	61.1	3,344	21.7	2,497	16.2
45 to 54 years old..........	14,885	65.1	9,060	60.9	3,208	21.6	2,402.	16.1
55 years old and over	16,103	40.8	11,346	70.5	2,643	16.4	1,802	11.2
Sex of householder:								
Male..................	34,921	58.6	21,430	61.4	7,460	21.4	5,518	15.8
Female	26,559	50.1	17,163	64.6	5,179	19.5	3,817	14.4
Educational attainment:								
Elementary school	926	14.0	734	79.3	98	10.6	84	9.1
Some high school	2,507	24.3	1,829	73.0	359	14.3	275	11.0
High school diploma/GED.....	14,750	43.0	10,478	71.0	2,380	16.1	1,691	11.5
Some college............	18,793	62.4	12,037	64.1	3,794	20.2	2,661	14.2
Bachelor's degree or more	24,504	78.3	13,514	55.2	6,007	24.5	4,624	18.9
Employment status of householder:								
Employed	46,008	63.9	28,074	61.0	9,930	21.6	7,346	16.0
Unemployed	1,873	50.0	1,207	64.5	379	20.3	274	14.7
Not in the labor force........	13,600	36.9	9,311	68.5	2,329	17.1	1,714	12.6
Family income:								
Less than $15,000	3,681	22.9	2,555	69.4	584	15.9	477	13.0
15,000 to 24,999	3,839	33.5	2,786	72.6	600	15.6	418	10.9
25,000 to 34,999	5,855	45.6	4,137	70.7	921	15.7	694	11.9
35,000 to 49,999	8,867	62.8	6,213	70.1	1,391	15.7	1,138	12.8
50,000 to 74,999	12,429	76.0	7,918	63.7	2,531	20.4	1,814	14.6
75,000 to 99,999	7,774	84.1	4,440	57.1	1,919	24.7	1,321	17.0
100,000 to 149,999.........	5,811	90.4	2,726	46.9	1,771	30.5	1,207	20.8
150,000 and over	3,753	92.4	1,482	39.5	1,242	33.1	961	25.6

[1] Includes households with other types of connections, not shown separately. [2] Includes households with family income not reported.

Source: U.S. Department of Commerce, National Telecommunications and Information Administration, *A Nation Online: Entering the Broadband Age,* September 2004; and unpublished data. See Internet site <http://www.ntia.doc.gov/reports/anol/index.html>.

Table 1149. **Households With Computers and Internet Access by Selected Characteristic: 2003**

[Percent of households in specified group. As of October. Based on the Current Population Survey and subject to sampling error; for details, see source. See also text, Section 1, and Appendix III]

Characteristic	Households with computers				Households with Internet access			
	Total	Rural [1]	Urban [1]	Central city [1]	Total	Rural [1]	Urban [1]	Central city [1]
All households	61.8	61.9	61.7	56.9	54.6	54.1	54.8	49.3
Age of householder:								
Under 25 years old	56.5	52.5	57.2	56.6	46.9	43.3	47.5	46.0
25 to 34 years old	68.6	71.6	67.8	64.3	60.2	62.1	59.7	56.1
35 to 44 years old	73.2	75.3	72.6	65.8	65.2	66.2	64.9	57.0
45 to 54 years old	71.9	71.5	72.1	65.3	65.1	63.9	65.6	58.4
55 years old or over	46.6	46.7	46.6	41.5	40.8	40.3	40.9	35.4
Sex:								
Male	65.6	64.2	66.2	61.3	58.6	56.3	59.5	54.2
Female	57.4	58.6	57.1	52.5	50.1	51.1	49.8	44.4
Education of householder:								
Elementary	20.6	18.1	21.6	20.7	14.0	12.7	14.5	13.2
Some high school	32.7	34.7	32.0	28.0	24.3	26.3	23.6	20.1
High school graduate or GED	51.1	56.5	48.7	43.0	43.0	47.5	41.1	34.6
Some college	70.6	73.3	69.7	65.4	62.4	64.8	61.6	56.7
BA degree or more	83.3	84.4	83.0	80.1	78.3	79.3	78.1	74.3
Household income:								
Under $5,000	35.6	29.8	37.0	33.6	26.8	20.0	28.4	24.3
$5,000 to $9,000	26.9	24.4	27.5	27.0	20.0	17.7	20.6	20.4
$10,000 to $14,999	31.7	31.7	31.7	32.2	23.7	23.6	23.7	23.2
$15,000 to $19,999	38.2	36.7	38.8	37.8	29.4	26.9	30.3	28.8
$20,000 to $24,999	46.1	47.7	45.5	45.6	36.7	36.6	36.7	37.8
$25,000 to $34,999	55.4	55.7	55.4	54.7	45.6	46.3	45.4	44.5
$35,000 to $49,999	71.1	72.6	70.6	70.0	62.8	62.3	63.0	62.0
$50,000 to $74,999	81.9	82.4	81.7	81.7	76.0	75.8	76.1	75.1
$75,000 to $99,999	88.1	87.9	88.2	85.6	84.1	84.1	84.1	81.7
$100,000 to $149,999	92.9	92.2	93.2	89.8	90.4	89.7	90.6	86.0
$150,000 or more	94.7	95.0	94.7	92.3	92.4	91.6	92.5	91.8

[1] See text, Section 1, and Appendix II.

Source: U.S. Department of Commerce, National Telecommunications and Information Administration, *A Nation Online: Entering the Broadband Age*, September 2004; and unpublished data. See Internet site <http://www.ntia.doc.gov/reports/anol/index.html>.

Table 1150. **Households With Computers and Internet Access: 1998 and 2003**

[Percent of all households. As of October. Based on survey and subject to sampling error; for details, see source]

State	1998		2003		State	1998		2003	
	Computers	Internet access	Computers	Internet access		Computers	Internet access	Computers	Internet access
U.S.	**42.1**	**26.2**	**61.8**	**54.6**	MO	41.8	24.3	60.7	53.0
AL	34.3	21.6	53.9	45.7	MT	40.9	21.5	59.5	50.4
AK	62.4	44.1	72.7	67.6	NE	42.9	22.9	66.1	55.4
AZ	44.3	29.3	64.3	55.2	NV	41.6	26.5	61.3	55.2
AR	29.8	14.7	50.0	42.4	NH	54.2	37.1	71.5	65.2
CA	47.5	30.7	66.3	59.6	NJ	48.1	31.3	65.5	60.5
CO	55.3	34.5	70.0	63.0	NM	42.2	25.8	53.9	44.5
CT	43.8	31.8	69.2	62.9	NY	37.3	23.7	60.0	53.3
DE	40.5	25.1	64.3	56.8	NC	35.0	19.9	57.7	51.1
DC	41.4	24.2	59.5	53.2	ND	40.2	20.6	61.2	53.2
FL	39.5	27.8	61.0	55.6	OH	40.7	24.6	58.8	52.5
GA	35.8	23.9	60.6	53.5	OK	37.8	20.4	55.4	48.4
HI	42.3	27.9	63.3	55.0	OR	51.3	32.7	67.0	61.0
ID	50.0	27.4	69.2	56.4	PA	39.3	24.9	60.2	54.7
IL	42.7	26.5	60.0	51.1	RI	41.0	27.1	62.3	55.7
IN	43.5	26.1	59.6	51.0	SC	35.7	21.4	54.9	45.6
IA	41.4	21.8	64.7	57.1	SD	41.6	23.9	62.1	53.6
KS	43.7	25.7	63.8	54.3	TN	37.5	21.3	56.7	48.9
KY	35.9	21.1	58.1	49.6	TX	40.9	24.5	59.0	51.8
LA	31.1	17.8	52.3	44.1	UT	60.1	35.8	74.1	62.6
ME	43.4	26.0	67.8	57.9	VT	48.7	31.8	65.5	58.1
MD	46.3	31.0	66.0	59.2	VA	46.4	27.9	66.8	60.3
MA	43.4	28.1	64.1	58.1	WA	56.3	36.6	71.4	62.3
MI	44.0	25.4	59.9	52.0	WV	28.3	17.6	55.0	47.6
MN	47.6	29.0	67.9	61.6	WI	43.0	25.1	63.8	57.4
MS	25.7	13.6	48.3	38.9	WY	46.1	22.7	65.4	57.7

Source: U.S. Department of Commerce, National Telecommunications and Information Administration, *Falling through the Net: Defining the Digital Divide*, July 1999; and *A Nation Online: Entering the Broadband Age*, September 2004; and unpublished data. See Internet site <http://www.ntia.doc.gov/reports/anol/index.html>.

Information and Communications 753

No. 10.—AMOUNT of RESOURCES and LIABILITIES of the NATIONAL BANKS in operation for the last nine years at the dates named.

[Compiled by the Comptroller of the Currency.]

RESOURCES AND LIABILITIES.	Oct. 2, 1871.	Oct. 3, 1872.	Sept. 12, 1873.	Oct. 2, 1874.	Oct. 1, 1875.	Oct. 2, 1876.	Oct. 1, 1877.	Oct. 1, 1878.	Jan. 1, 1879.
	1,767 banks.	1,919 banks.	1,976 banks.	2,004 banks.	2,087 banks.	2,089 banks.	2,080 banks.	2,053 banks.	2,051 banks.
RESOURCES.	Millions	Millions	Millions	Millions	Millions	Millions	Millions	Millions	Millions
Loans	831.6	877.2	944.2	954.4	984.7	931.3	891.9	834.0	823.9
Bonds for circulation	364.5	382.0	388.3	383.3	370.3	337.2	336.8	347.6	347.1
Other United States bonds	45.8	27.6	23.6	28.0	28.1	47.8	45.0	94.7	110.8
Other stocks, bonds, &c	24.5	23.5	23.7	27.8	33.5	34.4	34.5	36.9	35.6
Due from other banks	143.2	128.2	149.5	134.8	144.7	146.9	129.9	138.9	134.0
Real estate	30.1	32.3	34.7	38.1	42.4	43.1	45.2	46.7	47.1
Specie	13.2	10.2	18.9	21.2	8.1	21.4	22.7	30.7	41.5
Legal-tender notes	107.0	102.1	92.4	80.0	76.5	84.2	66.9	64.4	70.5
National-bank notes	14.3	15.8	16.1	18.5	18.5	15.9	15.6	16.9	19.5
Clearing-house exchanges	115.2	125.0	100.3	109.7	87.9	100.0	74.5	82.4	100.0
United States certificates of deposit	......	6.7	20.6	42.8	48.8	29.2	33.4	32.7	28.9
Due from United States Treasurer	......	......	......	20.3	19.6	16.7	16.0	16.5	17.2
Other resources	41.2	25.2	17.3	18.3	19.1	19.1	28.7	24.9	24.5
Totals	1,730.6	1,755.8	1,830.6	1,877.2	1,882.2	1,827.2	1,741.1	1,767.7	1,800.6
LIABILITIES.									
Capital stock	458.3	479.6	491.0	493.8	504.8	499.8	479.5	466.2	462.0
Surplus fund	101.1	110.3	120.3	129.0	134.4	132.2	122.8	116.9	116.2
Undivided profits	42.0	46.6	54.5	51.5	53.0	46.4	44.5	40.9	36.8
Circulation	317.4	335.1	340.3	334.2	319.1	292.2	291.9	301.9	303.9
Due to depositors	631.4	628.9	640.0	683.8	679.4	666.2	630.4	668.4	712.4
Due to other banks	171.9	143.8	173.0	175.8	179.7	179.8	161.6	165.1	162.4
Other liabilities	8.5	11.5	11.5	9.1	11.8	10.6	10.4	7.9	6.9
Totals	1,730.6	1,755.8	1,830.6	1,877.2	1,882.2	1,827.2	1,741.1	1,767.3	1,800.6

Source: Statistical Abstract of the United States: 1878 Edition.

Section 25
Banking, Finance, and Insurance

This section presents data on the nation's finances, various types of financial institutions, money and credit, securities, insurance, and real estate. The primary sources of these data are publications of several departments of the federal government, especially the Treasury Department, and independent agencies such as the Federal Deposit Insurance Corporation, the Federal Reserve Board, and the Securities and Exchange Commission. National data on insurance are available primarily from private organizations, such as the American Council of Life Insurers and the Insurance Information Institute.

Flow of funds—The flow of funds accounts of the Federal Reserve Board bring together statistics on all of the major forms of financial instruments to present an economy-wide view of asset and liability relationships. In flow form, the accounts relate borrowing and lending to one another and to the nonfinancial activities that generate income and production. Each claim outstanding is included simultaneously as an asset of the lender and as a liability of the debtor. The accounts also indicate the balance between asset totals and liability totals over the economy as a whole. Several publications of the Board of Governors of the Federal Reserve System contain information on the flow of funds accounts: Summary data on flows and outstandings, in the *Statistical Supplement to the Federal Reserve Bulletin*, and *Flow of Funds Accounts of the United States* (quarterly); and concepts and organization of the accounts in *Guide to the Flow of Funds Accounts* (2000). Data are also available at the Board's Web site <http://www.federalreserve.gov/releases/>.

Survey of Consumer Finances (SCF)—The Federal Reserve Board in cooperation with the Department of the Treasury sponsors this survey, which is conducted every 3 years to provide detailed information on the finances of U.S. families. Among the topics covered are the balance sheet, pension, income, and other demographic characteristics of U.S. families. The survey also gathers information on the use of financial institutions. Since 1992, data for the SCF have been collected by the National Organization for Social Science and Survey Research at the University of Chicago. Data from the survey are published periodically in the *Federal Reserve Bulletin*. The latest survey is available in the January 2003 issue of the Bulletin. More data and information on the survey are available at the following Web site of the Federal Reserve Board: <http://www.federalreserve.gov/pubs/oss/oss2/scfindex.html>.

Banking system—Banks in this country are organized under the laws of both the states and the federal government and are regulated by several bank supervisory agencies. National banks are supervised by the Comptroller of the Currency. *Reports of Condition* have been collected from national banks since 1863. Summaries of these reports are published in the Comptroller's *Annual Report,* which also presents data on the structure of the national banking system.

The Federal Reserve System was established in 1913 to exercise central banking functions, some of which are shared with the U.S. Treasury. It includes national banks and such state banks that voluntarily join the system. Statements of state bank members are consolidated by the Board of Governors of the Federal Reserve System with data for national banks collected by the Comptroller of the Currency into totals for all member banks of the system. Balance sheet data for member banks and other commercial banks are published quarterly in the *Statistical Supplement to the Federal Reserve Bulletin.* The Federal Deposit Insurance Corporation (FDIC), established in 1933, insures each depositor up to $100,000. Major item balance sheet and income data for all insured financial institutions are published in the *FDIC Quarterly Banking Profile.* This publication is also available on the Internet at the following address: <http://www.fdic.gov>. Quarterly financial information for individual institutions is available through the FDIC and Federal Financial Institutions Examination Council Web sites at <http://www.fdic.gov> and <http://www.ffiec.gov>.

Credit unions—Federally chartered credit unions are under the supervision of the National Credit Union Administration. State-chartered credit unions are supervised by the respective state supervisory authorities. The administration publishes comprehensive program and statistical information on all federal and federally insured state credit unions in the *Annual Report of the National Credit Union Administration.* Deposit insurance (up to $100,000 per account) is provided to members of all federal and those state credit unions that are federally insured by the National Credit Union Share Insurance Fund which was established in 1970. Deposit insurance for state chartered credit unions is also available in some states under private or state-administered insurance programs.

Other credit agencies—Insurance companies, finance companies dealing primarily in installment sales financing, and personal loan companies represent important sources of funds for the credit market. Statistics on loans, investments, cash, etc., of life insurance companies are published principally by the American Council of Life Insurers in its *Life Insurers Fact Book.* Consumer credit data are published currently in the *Statistical Supplement to the Federal Reserve Bulletin.*

Government corporations and credit agencies make available credit of specified types or to specified groups of private borrowers, either by lending directly or by insuring or guaranteeing loans made by private lending institutions. Data on operations of government credit agencies, along with other government corporations, are available in reports of individual agencies; data on their debt outstanding are published in the *Statistical Supplement to the Federal Reserve Bulletin.*

Securities—The Securities and Exchange Commission (SEC) was established in 1934 to protect the interests of the public and investors against malpractices in the securities and financial markets and to provide the fullest possible disclosure of information regarding securities to the investing public. Statistical data are published in the *SEC Annual Report.*

Data on the securities industry and securities transactions are also available from a number of private sources. The Securities Industry Association, New York, NY, <http://www.sia.com/>, publishes the *SIA Annual Report, Securities Industry Yearbook,* and the periodic *Securities Industry Trends.* The Investment Company Institute, Washington, DC, <http://www.ici.org/>, publishes a reference book, research newsletters, and a variety of research reports that examine the industry, its shareholders, or industry issues. The annual *Mutual Fund Fact Book* is a guide to trends and statistics observed in the investment company industry. *Fundamentals* is a newsletter summarizing the findings of major Institute research projects. Institute research reports provide a detailed examination of shareholder demographics and other aspects of fund ownership.

Among the many sources of data on stock and bond prices and sales are the New York Stock Exchange, New York, NY, <http://www.nyse.com/>; NASDAQ, Washington, DC, <http://www.nasdaq.com/>; Global Financial Data, Los Angeles, CA, <http://www.globalfindata.com/>; Dow-Jones & Company, Inc., New York, NY, <http://www.dj.com/>; and the Bond Market Association, New York, NY, <http://www.bondmarkets.com/>.

Insurance—Insuring companies, which are regulated by the various states or the District of Columbia, are classified as either life or property. Both life and property insurance companies may underwrite health insurance. Insuring companies, other than those classified as life, are permitted to underwrite one or more property lines provided they are so licensed and have the necessary capital or surplus.

There are a number of published sources for statistics on the various classes of insurance—life, health, fire, marine, and casualty. Organizations representing certain classes of insurers publish reports for these classes. The American Council of Life Insurers publishes statistics on life insurance purchases, ownership, benefit payments, and assets in its *Life Insurers Fact Book.*

Table 1151. Gross Domestic Product in Finance, Insurance, Real Estate, Rental and Leasing in Current and Real (2000) Dollars: 2000 to 2004

[In billions of dollars, except percent (740 represents $740,000,000,000). Represents value added by industry. For definition of gross domestic product and explanation of chained dollars, see text, Section 13]

Industry	NAICS code [1]	Current dollars				Chained (2000) dollars			
		2000	2002	2003	2004	2000	2002	2003	2004
Finance & insurance, total	52	740	818	883	972	741	794	856	923
Percent of gross domestic product . . .		7.5	7.8	8.0	8.3	7.5	7.9	8.2	8.5
Monetary authorities—central bank, credit intermediation & related activities.	521,522	319	414	440	(NA)	319	376	399	(NA)
Security, commodity contracts & like activity	523	168	151	168	(NA)	168	184	218	(NA)
Insurance carriers & related activities	524	238	235	256	(NA)	238	222	229	(NA)
Funds, trusts, & other financial vehicles (part).	525	16	18	18	(NA)	16	12	14	(NA)
Real estate & rental & leasing, total. . .	53	1,191	1,330	1,367	1,451	1,191	1,240	1,244	1,296
Percent of gross domestic product . . .		12.1	12.7	12.4	12.4	12.1	12.3	12.0	12.0
Real estate	531	1,082	1,228	1,261	(NA)	1,082	1,136	1,141	(NA)
Rental & leasing services [2]	532,533	108	102	107	(NA)	108	103	103	(NA)

NA Not available. [1] See footnote 1, Table 1152. [2] Includes lessors of other nonfinancial intangible assets.

Source: U.S. Bureau of Economic Analysis, *Survey of Current Business*, May 2005. See also <http://www.bea.doc.gov/bea/newsrelarchive/2005/gdpind04.pdf> (released 20 April 2005).

Table 1152. Finance and Insurance, and Real Estate and Rental and Leasing—Establishments, Revenue, Payroll, and Employees by Kind of Business (1997 NAICS Basis): 1997 and 2002

[2,198 represents $2,198,000,000,000. For establishments with payroll. Data for 2002 are preliminary. Based on the 1997 and 2002 Economic Censuses; see Appendix III]

Kind of business	NAICS code [1]	Number of establishments		Revenue (bil. dol.)		Annual payroll (bil. dol.)		Paid employees (1,000)	
		1997	2002	1997	2002	1997	2002	1997	2002
Finance & insurance	52	395,203	449,134	2,198	2,616	264.6	343.5	5,835	6,664
Monetary authorities-central bank	521	42	47	25	29	0.9	1.2	22	22
Credit intermediation & related activities	522	166,882	194,822	809	923	98.7	127.0	2,745	3,055
Security, commodity contracts & like activity	523	54,491	80,493	275	316	71.3	95.6	706	976
Insurance carriers & related activities. . .	524	172,239	170,795	1,073	1,320	92.2	118.0	2,327	2,579
Funds, trusts, and other financial vehicles (part)	525	1,489	2,977	17	27	1.4	1.6	35	30
Real estate & rental & leasing.	53	288,273	325,590	241	348	41.6	61.8	1,702	2,136
Real estate.	531	221,650	258,639	153	238	27.9	42.8	1,117	1,450
Rental & leasing services.	532	64,472	64,624	76	95	12.6	17.5	559	658
Lessors of other nonfinancial intangible assets	533	2,151	2,327	11	14	1.1	1.5	26	28

[1] North American Industry Classification System, 1997; see text, Section 15.

Source: U.S. Census Bureau, 2002 Economic Census, *Advance Report*, issued March 2004. See Internet site: <http://www.census.gov/econ/census02/>

Table 1153. Finance and Insurance—Nonemployer Establishments and Receipts by Kind of Business: 1997 to 2002

[679.2 represents 679,200. Includes only firms subject to federal income tax. Nonemployers are businesses with no paid employees. Data originate chiefly from administrative records of the Internal Revenue Service; see Appendix III]

Kind of business	NAICS code [1]	Establishments (1,000)			Receipts (mil. dol.)		
		1997	2000	2002	1997	2000	2002
Finance and insurance	52	679.2	691.8	660.3	36,966	49,058	44,139
Credit intermediation & related activities	522	163.7	165.3	66.0	8,693	4,848	3,796
Depository credit intermediation.	5221	6.5	6.5	6.4	215	197	224
Nondepository credit intermediation	5222	142.7	134.1	22.9	7,920	3,624	1,845
Activities related to credit intermediation	5223	14.5	24.7	36.7	557	1,028	1,727
Security, commodity contracts & like activity	523	188.4	181.5	240.5	16,438	29,379	24,172
Scrty & comdty contracts interm & brokerage. . . .	5231	29.3	29.6	32.0	6,159	6,395	5,433
Securities & commodity exchanges	5232	1.2	1.6	1.8	315	1,495	867
Other financial investment activities	5239	158.0	150.2	206.7	9,965	21,488	17,872
Insurance carriers & related activities.	524	327.1	345.0	353.8	11,834	14,831	16,171
Insurance carriers	5241	0.9	1.0	0.5	76	98	55
Agencies & other insurance related activities	5242	326.2	344.0	353.2	11,758	14,733	16,117
Insurance agencies & brokerages	52421	258.0	245.5	246.5	9,718	11,570	12,357
Other insurance related activities	52429	68.1	98.5	106.7	2,040	3,163	3,760

[1] North American Industry Classification System, 1997; see text, section 15.

Source: U.S. Census Bureau, "Nonemployer Statistics"; <http://www.census.gov/epcd/nonemployer/> and "2002 Economic Census, Nonemployer Statistics, Finance and Insurance, United States"; published 24 November 2004; <http://www.census.gov/epcd/nonemployer/2002/us/US00052.HTM>.

Table 1154. **Finance and Insurance—Establishments, Employees, and Payroll: 2000 and 2002**

[423.7 represents 423,700. Covers establishments with payroll. Employees are for the week including March 12. Most government employees are excluded. For statement on methodology, see Appendix III]

Kind of business	NAICS code [1]	Establishments (1,000)		Employees (1,000)		Payroll (bil. dol.)	
		2000	2002	2000	2002	2000	2002
Finance & insurance, total	52	423.7	450.4	5,963	6,415	346.8	372.7
Monetary authorities—central bank	521	0.1	0.1	22	23	1.1	1.3
Credit intermediation & related activities	522	176.3	196.2	2,753	3,006	116.1	136.3
Depository credit intermediation [2]	5221	105.6	114.3	1,935	2,110	78.5	87.7
Commercial banking	52211	73.9	80.4	1,493	1,630	63.6	69.8
Savings institutions	52212	15.9	17.3	244	263	9.2	10.7
Credit unions	52213	15.6	16.3	192	211	5.4	6.8
Nondepository credit intermediation [2]	5222	49.3	53.0	621	662	29.6	37.1
Real estate credit	522292	19.8	21.9	238	267	10.8	17.7
Activities related to credit intermediation	5223	21.4	28.8	198	234	7.9	11.5
Security, commodity contracts & like activity	523	72.9	81.7	866	1,009	119.5	115.1
Security & commodity contracts intermediation & brokerage [2]	5231	38.1	42.3	539	628	80.2	76.7
Investment banking & securities dealing	52311	6.3	7.1	138	165	31.2	27.7
Securities brokerage	52312	29.5	32.8	378	443	47.0	47.2
Securities & commodity exchanges [2]	5232	(Z)	0.2	7	7	0.5	0.7
Other financial investment activities [2]	5239	34.8	39.2	320	374	38.8	37.7
Portfolio management	52392	11.6	11.3	156	178	24.9	21.0
Insurance carriers & related activities	524	172.2	169.0	2,290	2,342	108.1	117.6
Insurance carriers [2]	5241	37.4	31.3	1,489	1,501	74.7	78.5
Direct life/health/med. insurance carriers	52411	13.9	12.7	813	798	40.0	40.9
Direct life insurance carriers	5241f3	10.7	9.8	491	478	25.7	24.9
Direct health & med. insurance carriers	524114	3.1	2.9	322	320	14.3	16.0
Other direct insurance carriers [2]	52412	23.0	18.1	660	688	33.5	36.3
Direct property & casualty insurance carriers	524126	19.8	13.0	609	602	31.1	31.4
Agencies & other insurance-related activities	5242	134.8	137.7	801	841	33.3	39.1
Insurance agencies & brokerages	52421	121.5	125.2	596	641	24.7	30.0
Other insurance-related activities	52429	13.3	12.5	205	200	8.6	9.2
Funds, trusts, & other financial vehicles (part)	525	2.3	3.5	32	34	2.1	2.4

Z Less than 50. [1] North American Industry Classification System, 1997; see text, Section 15. [2] Includes industries not shown separately.
Source: U.S. Census Bureau, "County Business Patterns"; published November 2004; <http://www.census.gov/epcd/cbp/view/cbpview.html>.

Table 1155. **Flow of Funds Accounts—Financial Assets of Financial and Nonfinancial Institutions by Holder Sector: 1990 to 2004**

[In billions of dollars (36,639 represents $36,639,000,000,000). As of December 31]

Sector	1990	1995	1997	1998	1999	2000	2001	2002	2003	2004
All sectors	36,639	54,347	68,275	76,914	87,876	91,060	91,770	90,242	100,763	109,183
Households [1]	14,731	21,529	27,424	30,362	34,768	33,679	32,211	29,867	34,092	36,759
Nonfinancial business	3,979	5,568	6,644	7,871	9,334	11,257	11,542	11,689	12,400	13,139
Farm business	47	61	62	64	65	65	67	72	77	82
Nonfarm noncorporate	356	548	774	991	1,175	1,420	1,575	1,655	1,789	1,960
Nonfinancial corporations	3,575	4,959	5,809	6,816	8,094	9,772	9,899	9,962	10,534	11,097
State and local government	1,020	1,122	1,287	1,463	1,587	1,683	1,756	1,795	1,905	2,033
U.S. Government	442	442	442	445	561	514	615	611	653	615
Monetary authorities	342	472	534	567	697	636	683	754	797	841
Commercial banking	3,337	4,494	5,175	5,629	5,982	6,469	6,829	7,329	7,809	8,487
U.S.-chartered commercial banks	2,644	3,322	3,742	4,081	4,431	4,774	5,015	5,427	5,840	6,398
Foreign banking offices in U.S.	367	666	811	806	751	789	792	801	733	570
Bank-holding companies	298	467	575	686	741	842	942	1,026	1,152	1,422
Banks in U.S.-affiliated areas	28	39	46	56	59	63	80	75	84	98
Savings institutions	1,323	1,013	1,029	1,089	1,150	1,218	1,299	1,357	1,475	1,691
Credit unions	217	311	354	391	415	441	506	561	617	655
Bank personal trusts, estates	522	775	918	976	1,104	1,068	929	808	899	925
Life insurance	1,351	2,064	2,515	2,770	3,068	3,136	3,225	3,335	3,773	4,160
Other insurance	533	740	843	876	873	862	860	930	1,060	1,183
Private pension funds	1,627	2,889	3,689	4,105	4,571	4,355	3,916	3,309	4,025	4,444
State and local government employee retirement funds	801	1,308	1,749	1,965	2,247	2,124	1,965	1,727	1,967	2,072
Federal government retirement funds	340	541	659	716	774	797	860	894	959	1,024
Money market mutual funds	493	741	1,043	1,330	1,579	1,812	2,241	2,224	2,016	1,880
Mutual funds	608	1,853	2,989	3,613	4,538	4,435	4,135	3,638	4,653	5,435
Closed-end funds	53	136	146	149	152	142	140	151	206	246
Exchange-traded funds	-	1	7	16	34	66	83	102	151	226
Government-sponsored enterprises (GSE)	478	897	1,101	1,406	1,723	1,965	2,309	2,549	2,786	2,895
Agency- and GSE-backed mortgage pools	1,020	1,571	1,826	2,019	2,294	2,493	2,832	3,159	3,489	3,543
Asset-backed securities issuers	284	763	1,056	1,353	1,548	1,738	1,994	2,219	2,486	2,817
Finance companies	547	672	764	853	1,004	1,140	1,159	1,193	1,385	1,458
Mortgage companies	49	33	32	32	32	32	32	32	32	32
Real estate investment trusts	28	33	64	71	67	75	84	109	143	223
Security brokers and dealers	262	568	779	921	1,001	1,221	1,466	1,335	1,613	1,836
Funding corporations	251	383	603	765	998	1,118	1,135	1,123	1,178	1,276
Rest of the world	1,998	3,428	4,602	5,162	5,776	6,585	6,966	7,441	8,194	9,288

- Represents zero. [1] Includes nonprofit organizations.
Source: Board of Governors of the Federal Reserve System, "Federal Reserve Statistical Release, Z.1, Flow of Funds Accounts of the United States"; published: 10 March 2005; <http://www.federalreserve.gov/releases/z1/20050310/>.

Table 1156. **Flow of Funds Accounts—Credit Market Debt Outstanding: 1990 to 2004**

[In billions of dollars (13,769 represents $13,769,000,000,000). As of December 31]

Item	1990	1995	1997	1998	1999	2000	2001	2002	2003	2004
Credit market debt..........	13,769	18,462	21,213	23,347	25,482	27,193	29,162	31,350	34,099	36,911
U.S. Government...............	2,498	3,637	3,805	3,752	3,681	3,385	3,379	3,637	4,033	4,396
Nonfederal domestic nonfinancial	8,351	10,036	11,351	12,442	13,581	14,725	15,846	16,904	18,216	19,785
Households [1]...............	3,597	4,874	5,518	5,955	6,448	7,018	7,639	8,369	9,232	10,264
Corporations.................	2,533	2,910	3,382	3,778	4,186	4,536	4,758	4,786	4,954	5,194
Nonfarm noncorporate business	1,093	1,062	1,225	1,405	1,600	1,797	1,959	2,108	2,264	2,432
Farm business................	135	145	155	165	171	181	192	200	208	220
State and local government	992	1,045	1,071	1,138	1,177	1,192	1,298	1,442	1,560	1,675
Rest of the world...............	289	456	608	639	653	710	660	665	650	715
Financial sectors...............	2,630	4,334	5,450	6,513	7,567	8,374	9,277	10,143	11,199	12,016
Commercial banking...........	198	251	309	382	449	509	562	612	661	739
Savings institutions...........	140	115	160	212	260	288	286	262	268	333
Credit unions................	-	-	1	1	3	3	5	7	9	11
Life insurance companies	-	1	2	2	3	2	3	5	8	11
Government-sponsored enterprises (GSE)...................	399	807	997	1,275	1,594	1,826	2,131	2,350	2,594	2,694
Agency- and GSE-backed mortgage pools	1,020	1,571	1,826	2,019	2,294	2,493	2,832	3,159	3,489	3,543
Asset-backed securities issuers.....	286	766	1,066	1,365	1,558	1,744	2,001	2,225	2,492	2,822
Finance companies.............	374	484	568	625	696	778	779	821	940	1,058
Mortgage companies.........	25	17	16	16	16	16	16	16	16	16
Real estate investment trusts	28	45	96	159	163	168	171	196	228	299
Security brokers and dealers	15	29	35	43	25	41	42	41	47	62
Funding corporations	147	249	373	413	504	504	449	449	447	429

- Represents or rounds to zero.   [1] Includes nonprofit organizations.

Source: Board of Governors of the Federal Reserve System, "Federal Reserve Statistical Release, Z.1, Flow of Funds Accounts of the United States"; published: 10 March 2005; <http://www.federalreserve.gov/releases/z1/20050310/>.

Table 1157. **Flow of Funds Accounts—Financial Assets and Liabilities of Foreign Sector: 1990 to 2004**

[In billions of dollars (1,998 represents $1,998,000,000,000). As of December 31]

Type of instrument	1990	1995	1997	1998	1999	2000	2001	2002	2003	2004
Total financial assets [1]	1,998	3,428	4,602	5,162	5,776	6,585	6,966	7,441	8,194	9,288
Net interbank assets	53	229	173	146	140	161	116	120	120	47
U.S. checkable deposits and currency. . .	108	194	244	257	279	287	306	327	351	402
U.S. time deposits..............	49	50	74	129	126	109	121	152	125	153
Security RPs [2]	20	68	91	72	80	91	151	190	460	647
Credit market instruments..........	889	1,490	2,085	2,231	2,316	2,591	2,917	3,395	3,898	4,705
Open market paper	11	43	78	87	86	90	87	98	108	128
Treasury securities.............	438	817	1,153	1,166	1,058	1,021	1,063	1,254	1,499	1,870
Official....................	286	490	615	623	618	640	705	796	957	1,196
Private....................	152	327	538	543	441	382	358	458	543	674
Agency- and GSE-backed securities [3]										
Official....................	50	146	209	228	300	441	535	650	667	799
Private....................	5	18	33	47	76	116	127	158	188	239
U.S. corporate business	45	129	176	181	224	325	408	492	478	561
U.S. corporate bonds [4]	217	361	502	608	752	921	1,116	1,267	1,500	1,775
Loans to U.S. corporate business	172	122	143	142	120	117	116	126	125	131
U.S. corporate equities............	244	550	953	1,250	1,612	1,643	1,573	1,261	1,669	1,906
Trade receivables..............	45	53	59	53	47	47	44	47	49	46
Miscellaneous assets.............	591	795	924	1,024	1,175	1,656	1,740	1,950	1,521	1,383
Foreign direct investment in U.S [5].	505	680	824	920	1,102	1,421	1,514	1,505	1,554	1,717
Other......................	85	115	100	104	74	235	226	445	-33	-334
Total liabilities [1]	1,389	2,014	2,562	2,776	3,148	3,490	3,650	3,982	4,064	4,116
U.S. official foreign exchange and net IMF position	61	64	49	60	50	46	47	56	62	62
U.S. private deposits	298	419	618	628	676	803	810	831	831	909
Credit market instruments [1].........	289	456	608	639	653	710	660	665	650	715
Commercial paper	75	56	65	73	89	121	107	143	165	229
Bonds	115	302	428	451	453	468	443	410	382	384
Bank loans n.e.c. [6]............	19	35	52	59	59	71	63	69	61	63
Miscellaneous liabilities [1]	713	1,030	1,238	1,404	1,720	1,881	2,086	2,392	2,474	2,390
U.S. direct investment abroad [4][5]	629	886	1,068	1,196	1,414	1,532	1,687	1,840	2,069	2,264

[1] Includes other items not shown separately.   [2] Repurchase agreements.   [3] GSE = Government-sponsored enterprises. [4] Through 1992, corporate bonds include net issues by Netherlands Antillean financial subsidiaries; U.S. direct investment abroad excludes net inflows from those bond issues.   [5] Direct investment is valued on a current-cost basis.   [6] Not elsewhere classified.

Source: Board of Governors of the Federal Reserve System, "Federal Reserve Statistical Release, Z.1, Flow of Funds Accounts of the United States"; published: 10 March 2005; <http://www.federalreserve.gov/releases/z1/20050310/>.

Banking, Finance, and Insurance 759

Table 1158. **Flow of Funds Accounts—Assets and Liabilities of Households: 1990 to 2004**

[As of December 31 (14,731 represents $14,731,000,000,000). Includes nonprofit organizations. n.e.c. = Not elsewhere classified]

Type of instrument	Total (bil. dol.)							Percent distribution		
	1990	1995	2000	2001	2002	2003	2004	1990	2000	2004
Total financial assets	14,731	21,529	33,679	32,211	29,867	34,092	36,759	100.0	100.0	100.0
Deposits	3,259	3,298	4,340	4,801	5,072	5.252	5,694	22.1	12.9	15.5
Foreign deposits	13	23	64	59	74	65	101	0.1	0.2	0.3
Checkable deposits and currency....	412	543	229	332	361	324	408	2.8	0.7	1.1
Time and savings deposits	2,465	2,281	3,076	3,281	3,552	3,877	4,291	16.7	9.1	11.7
Money market fund shares	369	450	971	1,129	1,085	985	894	2.5	2.9	2.4
Credit market instruments.........	1,555	1,955	2,336	2,176	2,075	2,242	2,265	10.6	6.9	6.2
Open-market paper	63	48	83	86	99	95	127	0.4	0.2	0.3
Treasury securities	471	806	619	487	345	465	468	3.2	1.8	1.3
Agency and GSE-backed securities [1]..................	69	72	432	350	201	390	349	0.5	1.3	1.0
Municipal securities	575	429	438	489	586	617	662	3.9	1.3	1.8
Corporate and foreign bonds......	234	483	645	638	707	527	498	1.6	1.9	1.4
Mortgages	143	116	119	127	138	149	161	1.0	0.4	0.4
Corporate equities [2]	1,770	4,123	7,806	6,604	5,048	6,376	6,522	12.0	23.2	17.7
Mutual fund shares	457	1,153	2,833	2,666	2,326	3,009	3,570	3.1	8.4	9.7
Security credit	62	128	412	454	413	475	572	0.4	1.2	1.6
Life insurance reserves	392	566	819	880	921	1,013	1,109	2.7	2.4	3.0
Pension fund reserves..........	3,376	5,676	8,831	8,330	7,612	8,835	9,638	22.9	26.2	26.2
Investment in bank personal trusts....	552	803	1,096	961	841	932	959	3.7	3.3	2.6
Equity in noncorporate business	3,065	3,512	4,834	4,949	5,140	5,496	5,930	20.8	14.4	16.1
Miscellaneous assets...........	243	316	371		420	462	501	1.6	1.1	1.4
Total liabilities	3,719	5,071	7,407	7,987	8,677	9,583	10,707	100.0	100.0	100.0
Credit market instruments.........	3,597	4,874	7,018	7,639	8,369	9,232	10,264	96.7	94.7	95.9
Home mortgages [3]	2,504	3,342	4,821	5,286	5,909	6,643	7,543	67.3	65.1	70.5
Consumer credit	824	1,168	1,739	1,879	1,962	2,050	2,151	22.2	23.5	20.1
Municipal securities	87	98	143	157	170	184	194	2.3	1.9	1.8
Bank loans, n.e.c.	18	57	74	58	54	94	97	0.5	1.0	0.9
Other loans	82	116	120	120	121	119	120	2.2	1.6	1.1
Commercial mortgages..........	83	92	121	139	153	141	159	2.2	1.6	1.5
Security credit	39	79	235	196	148	183	263	1.0	3.2	2.5
Trade payables	67	101	135	133	140	148	157	1.8	1.8	1.5
Unpaid life insurance premiums [4]	16	18	20	19	20	21	22	0.4	0.3	0.2

[1] GSE = government-sponsored enterprises. [2] Only those directly held and those in closed-end and exchange-traded funds. Other equities are included in mutual funds, life insurance and pension reserves, and bank personal trusts. [3] Includes loans made under home equity lines of credit and home equity loans secured by junior liens. [4] Includes deferred premiums.

Source: Board of Governors of the Federal Reserve System, "Federal Reserve Statistical Release, Z.1, Flow of Funds Accounts of the United States"; published: 10 March 2005; <http://www.federalreserve.gov/releases/z1/20050310/>.

Table 1159. **Percent of Families Owing Financial Assets by Type of Asset: 1995 to 2001**

[All dollar figures are adjusted to 2001 dollars using the "current methods" version of the consumer price index for all urban consumers published by U.S. Bureau of Labor Statistics. Families include one-person units; for definition of family, see text, Section 1. Based on Survey of Consumer Finances; see Appendix III]

Age of family head and family income	Any financial asset [1]	Transaction accounts [2]	Certificates of deposit	Savings bonds	Stocks [3]	Mutual funds [4]	Retirement accounts [5]	Life insurance [6]	Other managed [7]
1995, total	91.0	87.0	14.3	22.8	15.2	12.3	45.2	32.0	3.9
1998, total	92.9	90.5	15.3	19.3	19.2	16.5	48.8	29.6	5.9
2001, total	93.1	90.9	15.7	16.7	21.3	17.7	52.2	28.0	6.6
Under 35 years old........	89.2	86.0	6.3	12.7	17.4	11.5	45.1	15.0	2.1
35 to 44 years old	93.3	90.7	9.8	22.6	21.6	17.5	61.4	27.0	3.1
45 to 54 years old	94.4	92.2	15.2	21.0	22.0	20.2	63.4	31.1	6.4
55 to 64 years old	94.8	93.6	14.4	14.3	26.7	21.3	59.1	35.7	13.0
65 to 74 years old	94.6	93.8	29.7	11.3	20.5	19.9	44.0	36.7	11.8
75 years old and over......	95.1	93.7	36.5	12.5	21.8	19.5	25.7	33.3	11.2
Percentiles of income: [8]									
Less than 20 ($10,300) ...	74.8	70.9	10.0	3.8	3.8	3.6	13.2	13.8	2.2
20-39.9 ($24,400).......	93.0	89.4	14.7	11.0	11.2	9.5	33.3	24.7	3.3
40-59.9 ($39,900).......	98.3	96.1	17.4	14.1	16.4	15.7	52.8	25.6	5.4
60-79.9 ($64,800).......	99.6	98.8	16.0	24.4	26.2	20.6	75.7	35.7	8.5
80-89.9 ($98,700).......	99.8	99.7	18.3	30.3	37.0	29.0	83.7	38.6	10.7
90-100 ($302,700)	99.7	99.2	22.0	29.7	60.6	48.8	88.3	41.8	16.7

[1] Includes other types of financial assets, not shown separately. [2] Checking, savings, and money market deposit accounts, money market mutual funds, and call accounts at brokerages. [3] Covers only those stocks that are directly held by families outside mutual funds, retirement accounts and other managed assets. [4] Excludes money market mutual funds and funds held through retirement accounts or other managed assets. [5] The tax-deferred retirement accounts consist of IRAs, Keogh accounts, and certain employer-sponsored accounts. Employer-sponsored accounts include 401(k), 403(b), and thrift saving accounts from current or past jobs; other current job plans from which loans or withdrawals can be made; and accounts from past jobs from which the family expects to receive the account balance in the future. [6] Cash value. [7] Includes personal annuities and trusts with an equity interest and managed investment accounts. [8] Value in parentheses represents median income for that percentile group. Percentile: A value on a scale of zero to 100 that indicates the percent of a distribution that is equal to or below it. For example, a family with income in the 80th percentile has income equal to or better than 80 percent of all other families.

Source: Board of Governors of the Federal Reserve System, *Federal Reserve Bulletin*, January 2003, and unpublished revisions.

Table 1160. **Percent of Families Holding Debt by Type of Debt: 1995 to 2001**

[See headnote, Table 1159]

Age of family head and family income	Any debt	Home-secured debt [1]	Other residential property	Installment	Credit card balances [2]	Other lines of credit	Other debt [3]
1995, total	74.5	41.0	4.9	45.9	47.3	1.9	8.5
1998, total	74.1	43.1	5.1	43.7	44.1	2.3	8.8
2001, total	75.1	44.6	4.7	45.2	44.4	1.5	7.2
Under 35 years old	82.7	35.7	2.7	63.8	49.6	1.7	8.8
35 to 44 years old	88.6	59.6	4.9	57.1	54.1	1.7	8.0
45 to 54 years old	84.6	59.8	6.5	45.9	50.4	1.5	7.4
55 to 64 years old	75.4	49.0	8.0	39.3	41.6	3.1	7.4
65 to 74 years old	56.8	32.0	3.4	21.1	30.0	(B)	5.0
75 years old and over	29.2	9.5	2.0	9.5	18.4	(B)	3.6
Percentiles of income: [4]							
Less than 20 ($10,300)	49.3	13.8	(B)	25.5	30.3	1.3	5.9
20-39.9 ($24,400)	70.2	27.0	1.8	43.2	44.5	1.5	5.6
40-59.9 ($39,900)	82.1	44.4	3.2	51.9	52.8	1.5	7.7
60-79.9 ($64,800)	85.6	61.8	5.4	56.7	52.6	1.5	7.7
80-89.9 ($98,700)	91.4	76.9	10.3	55.7	50.3	2.6	9.3
90-100 ($302,700)	85.3	75.4	14.9	41.2	33.1	1.4	8.8

B Base figure too small. [1] First and second mortgages and home equity loans and lines of credit secured by the primary residence. [2] Families that had an outstanding balance on any of their credit cards after paying their most recent bills. [3] Includes loans on insurance policies, loans against pension accounts, borrowing on margin accounts and unclassified loans. [4] Value in parentheses represents median income for that percentile group. See footnote 8, Table 1159.

Source: Board of Governors of the Federal Reserve System, *Federal Reserve Bulletin*, January 2003, and unpublished revisions.

Table 1161. **Household Debt-Service Payments and Financial Obligations as a Percentage of Disposable Personal Income: 1980 to 2004**

[Household debt service ratio is an estimate of the ratio of debt payments to disposable personal income. Debt payments consist of the estimated required payments on outstanding mortgage and consumer debt. The financial obligations ratio adds automobile lease payments, rental payments on tenant-occupied property, homeowners' insurance, and property tax payments to the debt service ratio]

Year	Household debt service ratio	Financial obligations ratio Total	Home-owner	Renter	Year	Household debt service ratio	Financial obligations ratio Total	Home-owner	Renter
1980 . . .	10.60	15.39	13.34	23.70	2000 . . .	12.84	18.20	15.72	30.55
1990 . . .	11.99	17.38	15.52	24.69	2001 . . .	13.30	18.79	16.17	31.79
1995 . . .	11.87	17.48	15.18	27.00	2002 . . .	13.36	18.84	16.21	32.15
1998 . . .	12.10	17.53	15.21	28.25	2003 . . .	13.15	18.36	15.78	32.22
1999 . . .	12.42	17.90	15.49	29.41	2004 . . .	13.26	18.32	15.96	31.12

Source: Board of Governors of the Federal Reserve System, "Household Debt Service and Financial Obligations Ratios"; <http://www.federalreserve.gov/releases/housedebt/default.htm>.

Table 1162. **Selected Financial Institutions—Number and Assets by Asset Size: 2004**

[As of December. 8,412.8 represents $8,412,800,000,000. FDIC = Federal Deposit Insurance Corporation]

Asset size	Number of institutions F.D.I.C.-insured Commercial banks	Savings institutions	Credit unions [1]	Assets (bil. dol.) F.D.I.C.-insured Commercial banks [2]	Savings institutions	Credit unions [1]
Total	7,630	1,345	9,014	8,412.8	1,691.8	647.0
Less than $25.0 million	626	85	5,975	10.6	1.3	43.9
$25.0 million to $49.9 million	1,164	131	1,112	43.2	4.9	39.4
$50.0 million to $99.9 million	1,865	222	772	135.3	16.4	54.3
$100.0 million to $499.9 million . . .	3,125	609	910	676.0	142.7	196.2
$500.0 million to $999.9 million. . .	405	146	147	277.4	103.0	100.5
$1.0 billion to $2.9 billion	265	79	88	433.8	124.9	138.4
$3.0 billion or more.	180	73	10	6,836.6	1,298.5	74.4
			Percent distribution			
Total	100.0	100.0	100.0	100.0	100.0	100.0
Less than $25.0 million	8.2	6.3	66.3	0.1	0.1	6.8
$25.0 million to $49.9 million	15.3	9.7	12.3	0.5	0.3	6.1
$50.0 million to $99.9 million	24.4	16.5	8.6	1.6	1.0	8.4
$100.0 million to $499.9 million. . .	41.0	45.3	10.1	8.0	8.4	30.3
$500.0 million to $999.9 million. . .	5.3	10.9	1.6	3.3	6.1	15.5
$1.0 billion to $2.9 billion	3.5	5.9	1.0	5.2	7.4	21.4
$3.0 billion or more.	2.4	5.4	0.1	81.3	76.8	11.5

[1] Source: National Credit Union Administration, *National Credit Union Administration Year-end Statistics 2004*. Excludes nonfederally-insured state chartered credit unions and federally-insured corporate credit unions. [2] Includes foreign branches of U.S. banks.

Source: Except as noted, U.S. Federal Deposit Insurance Corporation, *Statistics on Banking, 2004*.

Banking, Finance, and Insurance 761

Table 1163. **FDIC-Insured Financial Institutions—Number, Assets, and Liabilities: 1990 to 2004**

[In billions of dollars, except as indicated (4,649 represents $4,649,000,000,000). As of Dec. 31. 2004 data preliminary. Includes island areas. Except as noted, includes foreign branches of U.S. banks]

Item	1990	1995	1998	1999	2000	2001	2002	2003	2004
All banking offices	84,353	81,350	84,587	86,040	85,952	86,506	87,429	88,447	90,267
Commercial bank offices, total [1]	62,723	65,888	70,052	71,534	71,911	72,458	73,527	74,638	76,579
Number of main offices	12,376	9,971	8,793	8,597	8,331	8,095	7,903	7,783	7,630
Number of branches	50,347	55,917	61,259	62,937	63,580	64,363	65,624	66,855	68,949
Savings institutions offices, total	21,630	15,462	14,535	14,506	14,041	14,048	13,902	13,809	13,688
Number of main offices	2,815	2,030	1,690	1,642	1,589	1,534	1,466	1,411	1,345
Number of branches	18,815	13,432	12,845	12,864	12,452	12,514	12,436	12,398	12,343
Assets, total [2]	4,649	5,338	6,531	6,884	7,462	7,868	8,436	9,075	10,105
Net loans and leases	2,867	3,198	3,896	4,187	4,576	4,687	4,968	5,349	6,037
Real estate loans	1,586	1,690	1,990	2,181	2,396	2,561	2,850	3,144	3,683
1-4 family residential mortgages . . .	859	1,006	1,170	1,251	1,340	1,380	1,513	1,611	1,837
Commercial real estate	328	349	418	471	525	570	628	682	752
Construction and development	171	90	130	165	197	232	245	272	337
Home equity loans [3]	86	98	113	121	151	184	256	346	491
Commercial and industrial loans	646	674	920	996	1,086	1,020	953	922	968
Loans to individuals	451	576	624	618	672	701	772	848	930
Credit cards and related plans	142	224	242	227	266	250	292	339	399
Farm loans	33	40	47	46	49	48	47	47	49
Other loans and leases	245	294	385	416	448	440	435	478	492
Less: Reserve for losses	65	60	64	66	71	80	85	86	82
Less: Unearned income	29	15	4	4	3	3	4	3	3
Securities	890	1,099	1,249	1,338	1,361	1,465	1,633	1,771	1,862
Domestic office assets	4,259	4,753	5,807	6,144	6,702	7,119	7,684	8,251	9,159
Foreign office assets	390	585	724	740	760	749	752	824	945
Liabilities and capital, total	4,649	5,338	6,531	6,884	7,462	7,868	8,436	9,075	10,105
Noninterest-bearing deposits	511	641	761	745	802	927	1,002	1,028	1,121
Interest-bearing deposits	3,127	3,129	3,625	3,793	4,113	4,262	4,566	4,926	5,463
Other borrowed funds	569	849	1,171	1,376	1,467	1,496	1,571	1,735	1,905
Subordinated debt	28	46	76	79	90	99	99	107	119
Other liabilities	128	238	341	315	356	377	422	450	459
Equity capital	286	436	557	575	634	707	776	831	1,039
Domestic office deposits	3,344	3,315	3,814	3,882	4,208	4,560	4,911	5,213	5,718
Foreign office deposits	293	454	572	656	707	630	658	741	867
Estimated insured deposits [4]	2,629	2,662	2,849	2,868	3,054	3,210	3,382	3,452	3,623

[1] Includes insured branches of foreign banks that file a Call Report. [2] Includes other items not shown separately. [3] For one- to four-family residential properties. [4] Excludes foreign office deposits which are uninsured.

Source: U.S. Federal Deposit Insurance Corporation, *The FDIC Quarterly Banking Profile*, Annual Report, *Statistics on Banking*, annual; and *FDIC Quarterly Banking Profile Graph Book*.

Table 1164. **FDIC-Insured Financial Institutions—Income and Selected Measures of Financial Condition: 1990 to 2004**

[In billions of dollars, except as indicated (437.7 represents $437,700,000,000). 2004 data preliminary. Includes island areas. Includes foreign branches of U.S. banks]

Item	1990	1995	1998	1999	2000	2001	2002	2003	2004
Interest income	437.7	373.4	433.1	441.5	512.2	486.8	429.5	404.6	418.8
Interest expense	295.9	190.7	221.2	218.0	276.5	235.0	152.9	122.6	124.0
Net interest income	141.8	182.7	211.9	223.5	235.7	251.8	276.6	281.9	294.8
Provisions for loan losses	41.4	14.7	24.0	23.4	32.0	46.3	51.5	37.3	29.0
Noninterest income	62.2	89.5	132.9	154.2	164.8	168.8	183.5	202.7	203.0
Percent of net operating revenue [1]	30.5	32.9	38.5	40.8	41.1	40.1	39.9	41.8	40.8
Noninterest expense	144.2	171.6	217.7	228.2	241.6	251.1	263.7	279.7	295.6
Income taxes	9.1	30.3	37.2	45.5	43.7	44.0	51.9	58.9	58.2
Net income	11.3	56.4	72.0	82.4	81.7	87.2	105.0	120.5	123.0
PERFORMANCE RATIOS									
Return on assets [2] (percent)	0.24	1.10	1.16	1.25	1.14	1.14	1.30	1.38	1.29
Return on equity [3] (percent)	3.95	13.63	13.49	14.71	13.55	12.99	14.12	15.03	13.28
Net interest margin [4] (percent)	3.47	4.05	3.91	3.90	3.78	3.78	3.96	3.73	3.53
Net charge-offs [5]	34.8	14.4	22.2	21.6	26.3	38.9	47.0	40.8	32.1
Net charge-offs to loans and leases, total (percent)	1.19	0.46	0.59	0.53	0.59	0.83	0.97	0.78	0.56
Net charge-off rate, credit card loans (percent) . . .	3.39	3.39	5.17	4.40	4.37	5.15	5.47	5.78	4.94
CONDITION RATIOS									
Equity capital to assets (percent)	6.16	8.16	8.52	8.35	8.49	8.99	9.20	9.15	10.28
Noncurrent assets plus other real estate owned to assets [6] (percent)	3.16	0.92	0.66	0.63	0.71	0.88	0.90	0.75	0.53
Percentage of banks losing money	16.5	3.1	6.0	7.6	7.5	8.2	6.7	6.0	5.8
Number of problem institutions	1,492	193	84	79	94	114	136	116	80
Assets of problem institutions	640	31	11	10	24	40	39	30	28
Number of failed/assisted institutions	169	6	3	8	7	4	11	3	4

[1] Net operating revenue equals net interest income plus noninterest income. [2] Net income (including securities transactions and nonrecurring items) as a percentage of average total assets. [3] Net income as a percentage of average total equity capital. [4] Interest income less interest expense as a percentage of average earning assets (i.e. the profit margin a bank earns on its loans and investments). [5] Total loans and leases charged off (removed from balance sheet because of uncollectibility), less amounts recovered on loans and leases previously charged off. [6] Noncurrent assets: the sum of loans, leases, debt securities and other assets that are 90 days or more past due, or in nonaccrual status. Other real estate owned: Primarily foreclosed property.

Source: U.S. Federal Deposit Insurance Corporation, *Annual Report*; *Statistics on Banking*, annual; and *FDIC Quarterly Banking Profile*.

Table 1165. FDIC-Insured Financial Institutions by Asset Size: 2004

[In percent, except as indicated (8,413 represents $8,413,000,000,000). Preliminary. See headnote, Table 1164]

Item	Total	Less than $100 million	$100 million to $1 billion	$1 billion to $10 billion	Greater than $10 billion
COMMERCIAL BANKS					
Number of institutions reporting	7,630	3,655	3,530	360	85
Assets, total (bil. dol.)	8,413	189	954	973	6,297
Deposits (bil. dol.)	5,593	158	771	667	3,997
Net income (bil. dol.)	105	2	12	13	78
Return on assets	1.31	0.99	1.28	1.46	1.30
Return on equity	13.82	8.46	12.88	13.48	14.24
Equity capital to assets	10.10	11.52	10.00	10.90	9.95
Noncurrent assets plus other real estate owned to assets	0.55	0.73	0.59	0.51	0.54
Net charge-offs to loans and leases	0.63	0.27	0.31	0.43	0.73
Percentage of banks losing money	5.7	9.9	2.1	1.9	1.2
SAVINGS INSTITUTIONS					
Number of institutions reporting	1,345	438	755	120	32
Assets, total (bil. dol.)	1,692	23	246	343	1,080
Deposits (bil. dol.)	991	17	185	223	566
Net income (bil. dol.)	18.0	0.3	2.0	4.5	11.5
Return on assets	1.17	1.14	0.83	1.39	1.18
Return on equity	10.87	8.36	7.73	13.21	10.95
Equity capital to assets	11.18	14.33	10.84	10.73	11.33
Noncurrent assets plus other real estate owned to assets	0.46	0.79	0.46	0.52	0.43
Net charge-offs to loans and leases	0.27	0.31	0.11	0.31	0.29
Percentage of banks losing money	6.2	11.6	3.3	5.8	-

- Represents zero.

Source: U.S. Federal Deposit Insurance Corporation, *Annual Report; Statistics on Banking*, annual; and *FDIC Quarterly Banking Profile*. See also <http://www.fdic.gov/bank/index.html>.

Table 1166. FDIC-Insured Financial Institutions—Number and Assets by State: 2004

[In billions of dollars, except as indicated (10,104.6 represents $10,104,600,000,000). As of Dec. 31. Information is obtained primarily from the Federal Financial Institutions Examination Council (FFIEC) Call Reports and the Office of Thrift Supervision's Thrift Financial Reports. Data are based on the location of each reporting institution's main office. Reported data may include assets located outside of the reporting institution's home state]

State	Number of insti- tutions	Assets by asset size of bank Total	Less than $1 bil.	$1 bil. to $10 bil.	Greater than $10 bil.	State	Number of insti- tutions	Assets by asset size of bank Total	Less than $1 bil.	$1 bil. to $10 bil.	Greater than $10 bil.
Total	8,975	10,104.6	1,410.8	1,316.4	7,377.4						
AL	164	237.3	25.5	6.0	205.7	NV	38	56.1	5.4	32.3	18.3
AK	7	3.9	1.7	2.1	-	NH	30	31.2	7.8	10.1	13.4
AZ	49	59.3	7.3	7.6	44.4	NJ	139	167.7	32.2	58.3	77.2
AR	168	40.7	28.3	12.4	-	NM	58	15.8	9.2	6.6	-
CA	295	838.5	56.1	145.6	636.8	NY	200	1,166.2	44.5	101.1	1,020.5
CO	177	39.4	27.9	11.5	-	NC	108	1,302.3	26.7	9.5	1,266.1
CT	57	60.7	15.1	18.1	27.5	ND	103	15.4	9.8	5.6	-
DE	34	436.0	5.2	35.6	395.2	OH	290	1,579.5	44.5	39.4	1,495.8
DC	6	0.9	0.9	-	-	OK	274	56.4	28.2	16.6	11.6
FL	295	127.3	58.5	68.8	-	OR	40	23.6	7.1	16.5	-
GA	344	224.7	59.2	34.7	130.8	PA	262	331.0	60.7	73.5	196.9
HI	8	33.8	1.1	22.2	10.6	RI	15	246.1	2.6	13.2	230.2
ID	17	5.5	5.5	-	-	SC	96	44.5	16.2	28.2	-
IL	746	340.6	116.3	69.0	155.3	SD	91	442.5	12.8	8.7	421.0
IN	197	102.8	38.9	35.4	28.5	TN	208	133.5	36.0	6.4	91.1
IA	414	51.1	44.8	6.3	-	TX	681	215.4	88.9	80.6	45.9
KS	372	57.8	34.9	22.9	-	UT	67	193.3	10.2	13.6	169.5
KY	237	51.5	33.0	18.5	-	VT	19	7.9	3.7	4.2	-
LA	166	59.8	25.0	12.6	22.3	VA	140	221.2	31.4	17.9	172.0
ME	39	43.0	11.5	2.8	28.7	WA	98	78.5	21.6	30.1	26.8
MD	116	46.2	24.0	22.2	-	WV	72	19.8	9.9	10.0	-
MA	200	224.2	52.5	39.0	132.7	WI	308	118.4	45.9	24.3	48.2
MI	173	194.6	30.7	21.8	142.2	WY	44	5.7	5.7	-	-
MN	478	63.5	47.0	4.0	12.4	AS	1	0.1	0.1	-	-
MS	102	42.1	15.7	15.5	10.8	GU	3	1.0	1.0	-	-
MO	373	91.8	50.2	28.8	12.8	FM	1	0.1	0.1	-	-
MT	80	14.6	10.5	4.2	-	PR	10	93.5	-	28.8	64.7
NE	263	46.1	21.3	13.4	11.5	VI	2	0.2	0.2	-	-

- Represents zero.

Source: U.S. Federal Deposit Insurance Corporation, *Statistics on Banking*, annual.

Banking, Finance, and Insurance 763

Table 1167. **FDIC-Insured Financial Institutions—Number of Offices and Deposits by State: 2004**

[As of June 30 (5,464.8 represents $5,464,800,000,000). Includes insured U.S. branches of foreign banks. The term "offices" includes both main offices and branches. "Banking office" is defined to include all offices and facilities that actually hold deposits, and does not include loan production offices, computer centers, and other nondeposit installations, such as automated teller machines (ATMs). Several institutions have designated home offices that do not accept deposits; these have been included to provide a more complete listing of all offices. The figures for each geographical area only include deposits of offices located within that area. Based on the Summary of Deposits survey]

State or other area	Number of offices	Total deposits (bil. dol.)	State or other area	Number of offices	Total deposits (bil. dol.)	State or other area	Number of offices	Total deposits (bil. dol.)
Total [1] .	89,786	5,464.8	KS	1,485	46.5	ND	421	11.4
U.S.	89,153	5,416.4	KY	1,724	56.9	OH	3,950	200.2
			LA	1,525	55.2	OK	1,242	46.3
AL	1,446	62.6	ME	505	16.7	OR	1,030	39.2
AK	129	6.0	MD	1,676	82.1	PA	4,608	210.7
AZ	1,071	61.8	MA	2,115	172.7	RI	233	19.9
AR	1,341	38.7	MI	3,001	136.1	SC	1,269	48.1
CA	6,423	671.1	MN	1,715	94.4	SD	448	53.3
CO	1,418	64.5	MS	1,124	33.5	TN	2,094	90.2
CT	1,188	73.8	MO	2,189	87.1	TX	5,480	310.3
DE	255	105.8	MT	365	11.9	UT	583	102.0
DC	199	18.6	NE	997	32.9	VT	273	9.0
FL	4,897	301.0	NV	474	40.5	VA	2,377	147.8
GA	2,596	132.0	NH	415	29.4	WA	1,799	87.4
HI	294	23.1	NJ	3,157	211.3	WV	638	22.7
ID	478	13.8	NM	490	18.2	WI	2,254	96.1
IL	4,394	281.9	NY	4,837	637.6	WY	205	7.9
IN	2,275	81.1	NC	2,510	163.9			
IA	1,541	51.2						

[1] Includes Puerto Rico and other areas, not shown separately.

Source: U.S. Federal Deposit Insurance Corporation, *Bank and Thrift Branch Office Data Book*, annual.

Table 1168. **U.S. Banking Offices of Foreign Banks—Summary: 1990 to 2004**

[In billions of dollars, except as indicated (791 represents $791,000,000,000). As of December. Data cover foreign-bank branches and agencies in the 50 states and the District of Columbia, New York investment companies (through September 1996), U.S. commercial banks of which more than 25 percent is owned by foreign banks, and International Banking Facilities. Foreign banks are those owned by institutions located outside of the United States and its affiliated insular areas]

Item	1990	1995	1999	2000	2001	2002	2003	2004	Share [1]			
									1990	1995	2000	2004
Assets	791	984	1,228	1,299	1,385	1,338	1,369	1,551	21.4	21.7	19.9	18.1
Loans, total	398	461	499	531	523	471	445	503	18.0	17.3	13.7	10.5
Business	193	249	279	296	271	238	192	199	30.8	35.1	27.1	21.5
Deposits	384	523	697	709	743	665	686	808	14.5	17.6	17.6	15.3

[1] Percent of "domestically-owned" commercial banks plus U.S. offices of foreign banks.
Source: Board of Governors of the Federal Reserve System, "Share Data for U.S. Offices of Foreign Banks"; published 16 March 2005; <http://www.federalreserve.gov/releases/Iba/Share/SHRTBL1.html>.

Table 1169. **Selected Financial Institutions—Revenue by Product Line: 2002**

[In millions of dollars (598,871 represents $598,871,000,000. Preliminary. Covers only establishments of firms with payroll. Based on the 2002 Economic Census; see Appendix III. Numbers in parentheses represent North American Industry Classification System 1997 codes, see text, this section]

Product line	Total [1] (5221)	Commercial banking (52211)	Savings institutions (52212)	Credit unions (52213)
Total product line revenue [2]	598,871	481,231	78,840	37,397
Loan income:				
Loans to financial businesses	33,919	22,232	11,242	389
Loans to nonfinancial businesses—secured	90,849	80,902	9,338	530
Loans to nonfinancial businesses—unsecured	21,987	21,197	765	23
Loans to consumers—secured [2]	157,560	101,205	32,577	23,381
Interest income:				
Residential mortgage loans	95,559	64,937	23,355	7,255
Home equity loans	12,430	7,085	2,444	2,899
Vehicle loans	20,079	7,785	2,096	10,021
Other loans to consumers . . [2]	19,484	15,947	1,518	1,986
Loans to consumers—unsecured [2]	18,096	14,731	329	3,027
Interest income: Personal lines of credit	14,697	13,096	122	1,476
Credit card cardholder and merchant fees [2]	21,290	17,830	802	2,468
Interest income	17,600	14,951	648	1,812
Trading debt instruments on own account—net gains	12,675	11,835	840	(NA)
Fees for individual deposit account services	36,650	30,096	3,869	2,679
Trust products for business and governments—fiduciary fees .	14,098	13,738	290	(NA)
Other products supporting financial services—fees	91,239	81,518	6,505	3,164

NA Not available. [1] Represents depository credit intermediation business. Includes Other depository credit intermediation (52219) not shown separately. [2] Includes other product lines not shown separately.

Source: U.S. Census Bureau, 2002 Economic Census, Finance and Insurance, Industry Series, *Depository Credit Intermediation* (EC02-521-07), December 2004.

Table 1170. **Federal and State-Chartered Credit Unions—Summary: 1990 to 2004**

[Except as noted, as of December 31 (36,241 represents 36,241,000). Federal data include District of Columbia, Puerto Rico, Guam, and Virgin Islands. Excludes state-insured, privately-insured, and noninsured state-chartered credit unions and corporate central credit unions which have mainly other credit unions as members]

Year	Operating credit unions		Number of failed institutions [1]	Members (1,000)		Assets (mil. dol.)		Loans outstanding (mil. dol.)		Savings (mil. dol.)	
	Federal	State		Federal	State	Federal	State	Federal	State	Federal	State
1990 ...	8,511	4,349	164	36,241	19,454	130,073	68,133	83,029	44,102	117,892	62,082
1995 ...	7,329	4,358	26	42,163	24,927	193,781	112,860	120,514	71,606	170,300	99,838
1997 ...	6,981	4,257	16	43,491	27,921	215,104	136,074	140,104	92,117	187,822	119,359
1998 ...	6,814	4,181	17	43,865	29,674	231,890	156,811	144,849	100,890	202,651	137,348
1999 ...	6,566	4,062	23	44,076	31,308	239,316	172,086	155,578	116,366	207,614	149,305
2000 ...	6,336	3,980	29	43,883	33,705	242,881	196,931	163,851	137,485	210,188	169,053
2001 ...	6,118	3,866	22	43,817	35,560	270,123	231,432	170,326	152,112	235,201	201,923
2002 ...	5,953	3,735	15	44,600	36,300	301,238	255,837	181,768	160,881	261,819	222,372
2003 ...	5,776	3,593	13	46,153	36,287	336,611	273,572	202,898	173,236	291,484	236,856
2004 ...	5,572	3,442	21	46,858	36,710	358,701	288,294	223,878	190,376	308,317	247,804

[1] 1990 for year ending September 30; 1995 reflects 15-month period from October 1994 through December 1995; beginning 1997 reflects calendar year. A failed institution is defined as a credit union which has ceased operation because it was involuntarily liquidated or merged with assistance from the National Credit Union Share Insurance Fund.

Source: National Credit Union Administration, *Annual Report of the National Credit Union Administration*, and unpublished data.

Table 1171. **Percentage of Households Using Selected Electronic Banking Technologies: 1995 to 2003**

[Covers only those households that have an account at a bank, thrift institution, or credit union. Based on sample surveys. For details of Survey of Consumer Finances, see Appendix III. For Surveys of Consumers, based on data from approximately 1,000 respondents; for details, see source]

Technology	Survey of Consumer Finances			Surveys of Consumers	
	1995	1998	2001	1999	2003
ELECTRONIC					
Direct deposit of any type	53	67	73	65	70
ATM card	35	55	58	59	65
Debit card [1]	20	37	50	(NA)	54
Preauthorized debts	25	40	44	31	46
Automated phone system	(NA)	26	23	40	44
Computer banking	4	7	21	10	32
Smart card [2]	1	2	3	(NA)	6
Prepaid card [2]	(NA)	(NA)	(NA)	(NA)	73
NON-ELECTRONIC					
In person	87	81	78	(NA)	(NA)
Mail	59	55	52	(NA)	(NA)
Phone (talk in person)	(NA)	43	43	(NA)	(NA)

NA Not available. [1] A debit card is a card that automatically deducts the amount of a purchase from the money in an account. [2] A smart card is a type of payment card containing a computer chip which is set to hold a sum of money. As the card is used, purchases are subtracted from that sum. Prepaid cards are cards that contain a stored value, or a value that has been paid up-front, allowing you to use the card much like cash. As you use the card, the prepaid value is drawn down. Examples are phone cards and gift cards. Smart cards are different from prepaid cards in that you can add money to the card at special machines designed for smart cards or sometimes at ATMs.

Source: Board of Governors of the Federal Reserve System, *Federal Reserve Bulletin*, winter 2004.

Table 1172. **Percent of U.S. Households That Use Selected Payment Instruments: 1995 and 2001**

[In percent. Based on Survey of Consumer Finances, conducted by the Board of Governors of the Federal Reserve System; see Appendix III]

Age and education of head of household	Any of these instruments		ATM [1]		Debit card		Direct deposit		Automatic bill paying		Smart card [1]	
	1995	2001	1995	2001	1995	2001	1995	2001	1995	2001	1995	2001
All households	76.5	88.4	61.2	69.8	17.6	47.0	46.8	67.3	21.8	40.3	1.2	2.9
Under 30 years old	75.2	83.0	71.1	78.1	24.5	60.6	31.1	48.8	17.9	32.1	1.8	2.6
30 to 60 years old	77.4	89.3	67.2	76.8	19.7	53.4	42.9	64.8	24.5	44.1	1.5	3.3
61 years old and over	75.2	89.2	43.1	48.9	9.6	24.6	63.2	83.2	18.2	35.9	0.3	2.1
No college degree	69.8	84.7	52.8	63.7	14.3	42.3	40.4	61.8	18.2	33.7	0.8	2.4
College degree	91.5	95.6	80.1	81.6	25.2	56.2	61.0	78.0	30.1	53.2	2.1	3.8

[1] The questions on ATMs and smart cards asked whether any member of the household had an ATM card or a smart card, not whether the member used it. The other questions asked about usage.

Source: Mester, Loretta J., "Changes in the Use of Electronic Means of Payment: 1995-2001," *Business Review*, Third Quarter 2003, published by Federal Reserve Bank of Philadelphia. See also <http://www.phil.frb.org/files/br/brq303lm2.pdf>.

Table 1173. **Consumer Payment Systems by Method of Payment, 2000 and 2003, and Projections, 2008**

[112.3 represents 112,300,000,000. Excludes mortgage payments]

Method of payment	Transactions					Volume				
	Number (bil.)			Percent distribution		Amount (bil. dol.)			Percent distribution	
	2000	2003	2008, proj.	2000	2008, proj.	2000	2003	2008, proj.	2000	2008, proj.
Total	112.3	123.7	146.9	100.0	100.0	5,291	6,030	7,357	100.0	100.0
Paper	80.4	79.0	73.1	71.6	49.8	3,482	3,475	2,718	65.8	36.9
Direct check payments [1]	28.8	26.8	23.5	25.6	16.0	2,271	2,093	1,459	42.9	19.8
Cash [2]	50.3	51.1	48.7	44.8	33.1	1,092	1,263	1,152	20.6	15.7
Money orders	0.9	0.8	0.7	0.8	0.5	82	82	74	1.5	1.0
Travelers cheques	0.2	0.2	0.1	0.2	(Z)	13	11	6	0.2	0.1
Food stamps	0.2	0.1	-	0.1	-	4	2	-	0.1	-
Official checks [3]	0.1	0.1	0.1	0.1	0.1	22	24	27	0.4	0.4
Cards	29.8	40.7	64.5	26.6	43.9	1,589	2,110	3,594	30.0	48.9
Credit cards	19.9	21.4	27.3	17.7	18.6	1,238	1,438	2,178	23.4	29.6
Debit cards	8.2	16.1	30.5	7.3	20.8	309	583	1,213	5.8	16.5
Prepaid cards [4]	1.3	2.5	5.6	1.1	3.8	31	69	171	0.6	2.3
Electronic benefits transfer cards	0.5	0.8	1.2	0.4	0.8	11	20	32	0.2	0.4
Electronic	2.1	4.0	9.3	1.8	6.3	219	445	1,045	4.1	14.2
Preauthorized payments [5]	1.5	2.4	4.7	1.4	3.2	166	276	567	3.1	7.7
Remote payments [6]	0.5	1.5	4.5	0.5	3.1	53	169	478	1.0	6.5

- Represents zero.   Z Less than 0.05 percent.   [1] Checks access funds on deposit at financial institutions. Only direct payments are included here. Repayments and prepayments involving other payment systems are excluded.   [2] Cash includes cash advances/withdrawals on credit and debit cards and personal checks written solely for cash.   [3] Official checks include cashier's checks, teller checks, and certified checks.   [4] Prepaid cards are used primarily as gift certificates and for telephone calls.   [5] Preauthorized payments are handled electronically "end-to-end" through an automated clearing house.   [6] Remote payments are made using a telephone or a computer and include check conversions at the point-of-sale and utility-bill payments made at ATMs, self-service kiosks, and clerk-assisted machines at supermarkets.

Source: HSN Consultants Inc., Carpinteria, CA, *The Nilson Report*, twice-monthly. (Copyright used by permission.)

Table 1174. **Debit Cards—Holders, Number, Transactions, and Volume, 2000 and 2003, and Projections, 2008**

[170 represents 170,000,000]

Type of debit card	Cardholders (mil.)		Number of cards (mil.)			Number of transactions (mil.)			Volume (bil. dol.)		
	2003	2008, proj.	2000	2003	2008, proj.	2000	2003	2008, proj.	2000	2003	2008, proj.
Total [1]	170	188	235	268	293	9,797	18,442	33,936	448	820	1,630
Bank [2]	166	146	137	199	234	6,797	12,010	20,619	327	577	1,044
EFT systems [3]	169	178	223	256	283	2,979	6,414	13,298	119	242	586
Other [4]	11	10	11	11	10	22	19	19	1	1	1

[1] Cardholders may hold more than one type of card. Bank cards and EFT cards are the same pieces of plastic that carry multiple brands. The total card figure shown does not include any duplication.   [2] Visa and MasterCard debit cards.   [3] Cards issued by financial institution members of regional and national switches. EFT = Electronic funds transfer.   [4] Retail cards such as those issued by supermarkets.

Source: HSN Consultants Inc., Carpinteria, CA, *The Nilson Report*, twice-monthly. (Copyright used by permission.)

Table 1175. **Credit Cards—Holders, Number, Spending, and Debt, 2000 and 2003, and Projections, 2008**

[159 represents 159,000,000]

Type of credit card	Cardholders (mil.)			Number of cards (mil.)			Credit card spending (bil. dol.)			Credit card debt outstanding (bil. dol.)		
	2000	2003	2008, proj.	2000	2003	2008, proj.	2000	2003	2008, proj.	2000	2003	2008, proj.
Total [1]	159	164	176	1,425	1,460	1,513	1,458	1,735	2,604	680	786	965
Bank [2]	107	117	129	455	556	653	938	1,164	1,744	480	581	711
Phone	125	122	112	181	175	151	21	19	16	3	2	2
Store	114	115	114	597	542	510	120	133	146	92	89	98
Oil company	76	73	69	98	86	80	50	48	64	5	6	7
Other [3]	7	7	6	94	101	119	329	371	634	100	108	148

[1] Cardholders may hold more than one type of card.   [2] Visa and MasterCard credit cards. Excludes debit cards.   [3] Includes Universal Air Travel Plan (UATP), automobile rental, and miscellaneous cards. Except for data on cardholders, also includes Discover, American Express, and Diners Club.

Source: HSN Consultants Inc., Carpinteria, CA, *The Nilson Report*, twice-monthly. (Copyright used by permission.)

Table 1176. Usage of General Purpose Credit Cards by Families: 1992 to 2001

[General purpose credit cards include Mastercard, Visa, Optima, and Discover cards. Excludes cards used only for business purposes. All dollar figures are given in constant 2001 dollars based on consumer price index data as published by U.S. Bureau of Labor Statistics. Families include one-person units; for definition of family, see text, Section 1, Population. Based on Survey of Consumer Finances; see Appendix III. For definition of median, see Guide to Tabular Presentation]

Age of family head and family income	Percent having a general purpose credit card	Median number of cards	Median new charges on last month's bills (dol.)	Percent having a balance after last month's bills	Median balance (dol.) [1]	Percent of cardholding families who—		
						Almost always pay off the balance	Some-times pay off the balance	Hardly ever pay off the balance
1992, total	62.4	2	100	52.6	1,200	53.0	19.6	27.4
1995, total	66.5	2	200	56.0	1,700	52.4	20.1	27.5
1998, total	67.5	2	200	54.7	2,000	53.8	19.3	26.9
2001, total	72.7	2	200	53.7	1,800	55.3	19.1	25.6
Under 35 years old	64.2	2	100	68.2	1,800	40.6	24.1	35.4
35 to 44 years old	76.9	2	200	62.9	2,000	47.0	22.8	30.2
45 to 54 years old	80.0	2	200	57.3	2,000	54.3	19.3	26.4
55 to 64 years old	76.0	2	300	48.2	2,000	59.8	17.8	22.3
65 to 74 years old	76.5	2	200	30.0	1,100	75.8	11.0	13.2
75 years old and over	59.7	2	200	24.2	700	81.2	9.3	9.4
Less than $10,000	28.5	1	-	67.4	1,000	45.3	23.0	31.7
$10,000 to $24,999	56.1	2	100	57.0	1,000	49.5	19.9	30.6
$25,000 to $49,999	76.1	2	100	61.3	1,700	46.7	19.7	33.6
$50,000 to $99,999	87.9	2	200	53.9	2,000	55.2	20.8	24.0
$100,000 and more	95.8	2	1,000	36.1	3,000	75.2	13.9	10.9

- Represents zero.   [1] Among families having a balance.

Source: Board of Governors of the Federal Reserve System, unpublished data.

Table 1177. Consumer Credit Outstanding and Finance Rates: 1990 to 2004

[In billions of dollars, except percent (808 represents $808,000,000,000). Covers most short- and intermediate-term credit extended to individuals, excluding loans secured by real estate. Estimated amounts of seasonally-adjusted credit outstanding as of end of year; finance rates, annual averages]

Type of credit	1990	1995	1997	1998	1999	2000	2001	2002	2003	2004
Total	808	1,141	1,313	1,417	1,530	1,705	1,842	1,924	2,011	2,105
Revolving	239	443	530	579	608	678	722	738	759	794
Nonrevolving [1]	570	698	783	838	923	1,027	1,120	1,186	1,253	1,312
FINANCE RATES (percent)										
Commercial banks:										
New automobiles (48 months)	11.78	9.57	9.02	8.73	8.44	9.34	8.50	7.62	6.93	6.60
Other consumer goods (24 months)	15.46	13.94	13.90	13.76	13.39	13.90	13.22	12.54	11.95	11.89
Credit-card plans	18.17	15.90	15.77	15.71	15.21	15.71	14.89	13.42	12.73	13.22
Finance companies:										
New automobiles	12.54	11.19	7.12	6.30	6.66	6.61	5.65	4.29	3.40	4.36
Used automobiles	15.99	14.48	13.27	12.64	12.60	13.55	12.18	10.74	9.72	8.96

[1] Comprises automobile loans and all other loans not included in revolving credit, such as loans for mobile homes, education, boats, trailers, or vacations. These loans may be secured or unsecured.

Source: Board of Governors of the Federal Reserve System, *Statistical Supplement to the Federal Reserve Bulletin*, monthly.

Table 1178. Insured Commercial Banks—Delinquency Rates on Loans: 1990 to 2004

[In percent. Annual averages of quarterly figures, not seasonally adjusted. Delinquent loans are those past due 30 days or more and still accruing interest as well as those in nonaccrual status. They are measured as a percentage of end-of-period loans]

Type of loan	1990	1995	1998	1999	2000	2001	2002	2003	2004
Total loans	5.33	2.48	2.19	2.13	2.18	2.61	2.69	2.33	1.80
Real estate	6.10	2.94	2.16	1.93	1.89	2.13	1.99	1.76	1.44
Residential [1]	(NA)	2.20	2.16	2.08	2.11	2.29	2.11	1.83	1.55
Commercial [2]	(NA)	3.94	2.04	1.69	1.49	1.79	1.71	1.54	1.20
Consumer	3.83	3.09	3.74	3.61	3.55	3.67	3.51	3.28	3.08
Credit cards	(NA)	3.74	4.73	4.54	4.50	4.86	4.87	4.47	4.11
Other	(NA)	2.67	3.13	3.09	2.98	3.03	2.79	2.67	2.46
Leases	1.97	0.79	1.04	1.28	1.59	2.11	2.24	1.91	1.33
Commercial and industrial	5.34	1.95	1.68	1.91	2.22	3.08	3.84	3.34	2.19
Agricultural	3.84	2.50	2.73	3.00	2.54	2.63	2.51	2.50	1.68

NA Not available.   [1] Residential real estate loans include loans secured by one- to four-family properties, including home equity lines of credit.   [2] Commercial real estate loans include construction and land development loans, loans secured by multifamily residences, and loans secured by nonfarm, nonresidential real estate.

Source: Federal Financial Institutions Examination Council (FFIEC), *Consolidated Reports of Condition and Income* (1990-2000: FFIEC 031 through 034; beginning 2001: FFIEC 031 & 041).

Banking, Finance, and Insurance   767

Table 1179. Characteristics of Conventional First Mortgage Loans for Purchase of Single-Family Homes: 1990 to 2004

[In percent, except as indicated (154.1 represents $154,100). Annual averages. Covers fully amortized conventional mortgage loans used to purchase single-family nonfarm homes. Excludes refinancing loans, nonamortized and balloon loans, loans insured by the Federal Housing Administration, and loans guaranteed by the Veterans Administration. Based on a sample of mortgage lenders, including savings and loans associations, savings banks, commercial banks, and mortgage companies]

Loan characteristics	New homes						Previously-occupied homes					
	1990	1995	2000	2002	2003	2004	1990	1995	2000	2002	2003	2004
Contract interest rate, [1]												
all loans	9.7	7.7	7.4	6.3	5.7	5.7	9.8	7.7	7.9	6.5	5.7	5.7
Fixed-rate loans . . . . ., . . .	10.1	8.0	8.0	6.6	5.9	6.0	10.1	8.0	8.2	6.6	5.8	6.0
Adjustable-rate loans [2]	8.9	7.2	6.5	5.6	5.1	5.4	8.9	7.0	7.2	5.6	5.0	5.1
Initial fees, charges [3]	1.98	1.20	0.69	0.61	0.63	0.50	1.74	0.93	0.66	0.44	0.32	0.37
Effective interest rate, [4]												
all loans	10.1	7.9	7.5	6.4	5.8	5.8	10.1	7.8	8.1	6.5	5.7	5.7
Fixed-rate loans . . . ., ...	10.4	8.2	8.2	6.7	6.0	6.0	10.4	8.2	8.3	6.7	5.9	6.0
Adjustable-rate loans [2]	9.2	7.4	6.5	5.6	5.2	5.4	9.2	7.1	7.2	5.7	5.0	5.2
Term-to-maturity (years)	27.3	27.7	29.2	28.9	28.7	28.8	27.0	27.4	28.6	27.1	26.5	27.7
Purchase price ($1,000)	154.1	175.4	234.9	261.7	275.3	293.6	140.3	137.3	191.8	227.5	237.0	253.2
Loan-to-price ratio	74.9	78.6	77.4	77.7	77.9	76.0	74.9	80.1	77.9	74.8	72.6	74.6
Percent of number of loans with adjustable rates	31	37	40	27	21	42	27	31	21	16	17	33

[1] Initial interest rate paid by the borrower as specified in the loan contract.   [2] Loans with a contractual provision for periodic adjustments in the contract interest rate.   [3] Includes all fees, commissions, discounts and "points" paid by the borrower, or seller, in order to obtain the loan. Excludes those charges for mortgage, credit, life or property insurance; for property transfer; and for title search and insurance.   [4] Contract interest rate plus fees and charges amortized over a 10-year period.

Source: U.S. Federal Housing Finance Board, *Rates & Terms on Conventional Home Mortgages, Annual Summary.*

Table 1180. Mortgage Debt Outstanding by Type of Property and Holder: 1990 to 2004

[In billions of dollars (3,807 represents $3,807,000,000,000). As of December 31]

Type of property and holder	1990	1995	1997	1998	1999	2000	2001	2002	2003	2004
Total mortgages [1]	3,807	4,566	5,160	5,648	6,254	6,812	7,486	8,309	9,313	10,507
Home [2]	2,619	3,467	3,936	4,295	4,717	5,126	5,636	6,310	7,105	8,071
Multifamily residential	288	276	300	334	375	406	448	486	557	601
Commercial	821	739	833	922	1,059	1,170	1,285	1,387	1,517	1,693
Farm	79	85	91	97	104	110	118	125	134	142
Household sector	143	116	101	98	106	119	127	138	149	161
State and local government	110	114	121	126	131	132	130	124	133	141
Commercial banking	849	1,090	1,245	1,337	1,495	1,660	1,790	2,058	2,256	2,594
Savings institutions	802	597	632	644	668	723	758	781	871	1,058
Credit unions	50	66	86	97	111	125	141	159	183	211
Life insurance companies	268	213	207	214	231	236	243	250	261	270
Government-sponsored enterprises (GSE)	156	250	239	247	242	264	297	357	463	475
Agency- and GSE-backed mortgage pools	1,020	1,571	1,826	2,019	2,294	2,493	2,832	3,159	3,489	3,543
Asset-backed securities issuers	68	261	373	513	593	660	775	862	1,045	1,495
Finance companies	65	72	97	121	146	172	161	175	199	243
HOME MORTGAGES [2]										
Total [1]	2,619	3,467	3,936	4,295	4,717	5,126	5,636	6,310	7,105	8,071
Household sector	129	96	78	73	80	87	95	104	113	123
Commercial banking	430	647	746	797	880	966	1,024	1,222	1,347	1,568
Savings institutions	600	482	521	534	548	594	621	631	703	876
Credit unions	50	66	86	97	111	125	141	159	183	211
Government-sponsored enterprises (GSE)	115	205	194	200	189	205	226	271	363	368
Agency- and GSE-backed mortgage pools	991	1,543	1,788	1,970	2,235	2,426	2,749	3,064	3,367	3,417
Asset-backed securities issuers	55	206	277	355	395	426	496	552	683	1,072
Finance companies	38	43	68	90	108	131	120	135	152	190

[1] Includes other holders not shown separately.   [2] Mortgages on one- to four-family properties.

Source: Board of Governors of the Federal Reserve System, "Federal Reserve Statistical Release, Z.1, Flow of Funds Accounts of the United States"; published: 10 March 2005; <http://www.federalreserve.gov/releases/z1/20050310/>.

Table 1181. Mortgage Delinquency and Foreclosure Rates: 1990 to 2004

[In percent. Covers one- to four-family residential nonfarm mortgage loans]

Item	1990	1995	1998	1999	2000	2001	2002	2003	2004
Delinquency rates: [1]									
Total	4.7	4.2	4.4	4.3	4.4	5.1	5.1	4.7	4.4
Prime conventional loans.	(NA)	(NA)	2.6	2.3	2.3	2.7	2.6	2.5	2.3
Subprime conventional loans . . .	(NA)	(NA)	10.9	11.4	11.9	14.0	14.3	12.2	10.4
FHA loans	6.7	7.6	8.5	8.6	9.1	10.8	11.5	12.2	12.2
VA loans. . . . . , ...	6.3	6.4	7.1	6.8	6.8	7.7	7.9	8.0	7.3
Foreclosure rates: [2]									
Total	0.9	0.9	1.2	1.2	1.2	1.5	1.5	1.3	1.1
Prime conventional loans.	(NA)	(NA)	0.6	0.5	0.4	0.5	0.5	0.6	0.5
Subprime conventional loans . . .	(NA)	(NA)	4.4	6.3	9.4	9.4	8.0	5.6	4.0
FHA loans	1.3	1.3	2.4	2.0	1.7	2.2	2.8	2.9	2.7
VA loans.	1.2	1.3	1.9	1.7	1.2	1.3	1.6	1.6	1.5

NA Not available.   [1] Number of loans delinquent 30 days or more as percentage of mortgage loans serviced in survey. Annual average of quarterly figures.   [2] Percentage of loans in the foreclosure process at year-end, not seasonally adjusted.

Source: Mortgage Bankers Association of America, Washington, DC, *National Delinquency Survey, quarterly.*

Table 1182. Money Stock: 1980 to 2004

[In billions of dollars (408 represents $408,000,000,000). As of December. Seasonally-adjusted averages of daily figures]

Item	1980	1985	1988	1989	1990	1991	1992	1993	1994	1995	1996	1997	1998	1999	2000	2001	2002	2003	2004
M1, total [1]	**408**	**620**	**787**	**793**	**825**	**897**	**1,025**	**1,130**	**1,151**	**1,127**	**1,080**	**1,072**	**1,095**	**1,122**	**1,087**	**1,179**	**1,217**	**1,299**	**1,367**
Currency [1]	115	168	212	222	246	267	292	322	354	372	394	424	460	517	531	581	626	662	697
Travelers checks [2]	3	6	7	7	8	8	8	8	9	9	9	8	9	9	8	8	8	8	8
Demand deposits [3]	261	267	287	278	277	290	340	386	384	389	402	394	377	353	309	332	302	318	333
Other checkable deposits [4]	28	180	281	285	294	332	385	415	404	356	275	245	250	243	238	258	280	311	329
M2, total	**1,600**	**2,496**	**2,994**	**3,158**	**3,279**	**3,379**	**3,433**	**3,485**	**3,498**	**3,641**	**3,817**	**4,032**	**4,384**	**4,650**	**4,934**	**5,451**	**5,804**	**6,083**	**6,428**
M1	408	620	787	793	825	897	1,025	1,130	1,151	1,127	1,080	1,072	1,095	1,122	1,087	1,179	1,217	1,299	1,367
Non-M1 components of M2	1,192	1,876	2,208	2,366	2,454	2,482	2,408	2,355	2,347	2,514	2,737	2,960	3,290	3,527	3,847	4,272	4,587	4,784	5,061
Retail money funds	64	175	244	321	358	372	353	353	381	449	517	592	732	832	924	985	914	801	716
Savings deposits (including MMDAs) [5]	400	815	926	894	923	1,044	1,187	1,219	1,150	1,134	1,273	1,400	1,605	1,741	1,879	2,314	2,781	3,174	3,530
Commercial banks	186	457	542	541	581	665	754	785	753	774	906	1,022	1,188	1,289	1,424	1,740	2,062	2,341	2,638
Thrift institutions	215	359	384	353	342	380	433	434	397	359	367	377	417	452	455	574	719	834	892
Small time deposits [6]	729	886	1,037	1,151	1,173	1,066	868	782	816	931	947	968	952	954	1,045	973	892	809	815
Commercial banks	286	386	451	534	611	602	508	468	503	575	593	625	626	635	700	634	590	536	545
Thrift institutions	442	499	586	618	563	463	360	314	314	357	354	343	326	320	345	339	302	273	271
M3, total	**1,996**	**3,208**	**3,929**	**4,077**	**4,155**	**4,210**	**4,223**	**4,286**	**4,370**	**4,636**	**4,985**	**5,461**	**6,052**	**6,552**	**7,120**	**8,035**	**8,573**	**8,886**	**9,445**
M2	1,600	2,496	2,994	3,158	3,279	3,379	3,433	3,485	3,498	3,641	3,817	4,032	4,384	4,650	4,934	5,451	5,804	6,083	6,428
Non-M2 components of M3	396	713	935	919	876	831	790	801	872	995	1,168	1,429	1,668	1,902	2,186	2,584	2,769	2,802	3,016
Large time deposits [7]	260	422	512	528	482	419	356	339	379	439	521	631	684	759	836	801	812	882	1,066
Commercial banks [8]	215	270	338	367	361	335	288	278	314	365	443	546	596	667	734	686	696	762	906
Thrift institutions	45	152	175	161	121	83	67	62	65	74	78	85	88	92	102	114	117	120	160
Repurchase agreements [9]	58	121	197	169	151	131	142	173	196	199	211	254	294	336	364	376	477	509	509
Eurodollars [10]	61	104	132	109	103	92	80	73	86	94	115	147	150	171	195	212	231	293	373
Institutional money funds	16	65	94	112	140	188	213	216	210	264	322	396	540	637	788	1,196	1,249	1,119	1,069

[1] Currency outside U.S. Treasury, Federal Reserve Banks, and the vaults of depository institutions. [2] Outstanding amount of U.S. dollar-denominated travelers checks of nonbank issuers. Travelers checks issued by depository institutions are included in demand deposits. [3] Demand deposits at domestically-chartered commercial banks, U.S. branches and agencies of foreign banks, and Edge Act corporations (excluding those amounts held by depository institutions, the U.S. government, and foreign banks and official institutions) less cash items in the process of collection and Federal Reserve float. [4] Negotiable order of withdrawal (NOW) and automatic transfer service (ATS) balances at depository institutions, credit union share draft balances, and demand deposits at thrift institutions. [5] Money market deposit accounts (MMDA). [6] Small-denomination time deposits are those issued in amounts of less than $100,000. All Individual Retirement Account (IRA) and Keogh account balances at commercial banks and thrift institutions are subtracted from small time deposits. [7] Large-denomination time deposits are those issued in amounts of $100,000 or more, excluding those booked at international banking facilities. [8] Large-denomination time deposits at domestically-chartered commercial banks, U.S. branches and agencies of foreign banks, and Edge Act corporations, excluding those amounts held by depository institutions, the U.S. Government, foreign banks and official institutions, and money market mutual funds. [9] Repurchase liabilities of depository institutions, in denominations of $100,000 or more, on U.S. government and federal agency securities, excluding those amounts held by depository institutions, the U.S. government, foreign banks and official institutions, and money market mutual funds. [10] Eurodollars held by U.S. addressees at foreign branches of U.S. banks worldwide and at all banking offices in the United Kingdom and Canada, excluding those amounts held by depository institutions, the U.S. government, foreign banks and official institutions, and money market mutual funds.

Source: Board of Governors of the Federal Reserve System, Statistical Supplement to the Federal Reserve Bulletin, monthly, and Money Stock Measures, Federal Reserve Statistical Release H.6, weekly.

Table 1183. **Money Market Interest Rates and Mortgage Rates: 1980 to 2004**

[Percent per year. Annual averages of monthly data, except as indicated]

Type	1980	1985	1990	1992	1993	1994	1995	1996	1997	1998	1999	2000	2001	2002	2003	2004
Federal funds, effective rate	13.35	8.10	8.10	3.52	3.02	4.21	5.83	5.30	5.46	5.35	4.97	6.24	3.88	1.67	1.13	1.35
Prime rate charged by banks	15.26	9.93	10.01	6.25	6.00	7.15	8.83	8.27	8.44	8.35	8.00	9.23	6.91	4.67	4.12	4.34
Discount rate	11.77	7.69	6.98	3.25	3.00	3.60	5.21	5.02	5.00	4.92	4.62	5.73	3.40	1.17	2.12	2.34
Eurodollar deposits, 3-month	14.00	8.27	8.16	3.70	3.18	4.63	5.93	5.38	5.61	5.45	5.31	6.45	3.70	1.73	1.14	1.55
Large negotiable CDs:																
3-month, secondary market	13.02	8.04	8.15	3.68	3.17	4.63	5.92	5.39	5.62	5.47	5.33	6.46	3.71	1.73	1.15	1.57
6-month, secondary market	12.94	8.24	8.17	3.76	3.28	4.96	5.98	5.47	5.73	5.44	5.46	6.59	3.66	1.81	1.17	1.74
Taxable money market funds [2]	12.68	7.71	7.82	3.36	2.70	3.75	5.48	4.95	5.10	5.04	4.64	5.89	3.67	1.29	0.64	0.82
Tax-exempt money market funds [2]	(NA)	4.90	5.45	2.58	1.97	2.38	3.39	2.99	3.14	2.94	2.72	3.54	2.24	0.94	0.53	0.66
Certificates of deposit (CDs): [3]																
6-month	(NA)	8.05	7.79	3.51	2.88	3.42	4.92	4.68	4.86	4.58	4.27	5.09	3.43	1.67	1.02	1.14
1-year	(NA)	8.53	7.92	3.78	3.16	4.01	5.39	4.95	5.15	4.81	4.56	5.46	3.60	1.98	1.20	1.45
2½-year	(NA)	9.32	7.96	4.56	3.80	4.58	5.69	5.14	5.40	4.93	4.74	5.64	3.97	2.74	1.77	2.21
5-year	(NA)	9.99	8.06	5.76	4.98	5.42	6.00	6.46	5.66	5.08	4.93	5.97	4.58	3.96	2.93	3.34
U.S. Government securities: Secondary market: [4]																
3-month Treasury bill	11.39	7.47	7.50	3.43	3.00	4.25	5.49	5.01	5.06	4.78	4.64	5.82	3.40	1.61	1.01	1.37
6-month Treasury bill	11.32	7.65	7.46	3.54	3.12	4.64	5.56	5.08	5.18	4.83	4.75	5.90	3.34	1.68	1.05	1.58
Auction average: [5]																
3-month Treasury bill	11.51	7.48	7.51	3.45	3.02	4.29	5.51	5.02	5.07	4.81	4.66	5.85	3.45	1.62	1.02	1.38
Home mortgages:																
New-home mortgage yields [6]	12.66	11.55	10.05	8.24	7.20	7.49	7.87	7.80	7.71	7.07	7.04	7.52	7.00	6.43	5.80	5.77
Conventional, 15-yr. fixed [3]	(NA)	11.48	9.73	7.80	6.65	7.77	7.39	7.28	7.16	6.58	7.09	7.76	6.53	6.02	5.25	5.23
Conventional, 30-yr. fixed [3]	(NA)	11.85	9.97	8.27	7.17	8.28	7.86	7.76	7.57	6.92	7.46	8.08	7.01	6.56	5.89	5.86

NA Not available. [1] Rate for the Federal Reserve Bank of New York. Beginning 2003, the rate charged for discounts made and advances extended under the Federal Reserve's primary credit discount window program, which became effective January 9, 2003. The rate replaced that for adjustment credit, which was discontinued after January 8, 2003. [2] 12-month return for period ending December 31. Source: iMoneyNet, Inc., Westborough, MA, Money Market Insight, monthly, <http://www.imoneynet.com> (copyright). [3] Annual averages. Source: Bankrate, Inc., North Palm Beach, FL, Bank Rate Monitor, weekly (copyright). [4] Averages based on daily closing bid yields in secondary market, bank discount basis. [5] Averages computed on an issue-date basis; bank discount basis. Source: U.S. Council of Economic Advisors, Economic Indicators, monthly. [6] Effective rate (in the primary market) on conventional mortgages, reflecting fees and charges as well as contract rate and assumed, on the average, repayment at end of ten years. Source: U.S. Federal Housing Finance Board, Rates & Terms on Conventional Home Mortgages, Annual Summary.

Source: Except as noted, Board of Governors of the Federal Reserve System, Statistical Supplement to the Federal Reserve Bulletin, monthly.

Table 1184. Bond Yields: 1980 to 2004

[**Percent per year.** Annual averages of daily figures, except as indicated]

Type	1980	1985	1990	1995	1998	1999	2000	2001	2002	2003	2004
U.S. Treasury, constant maturities: [1,2]											
1-year	12.00	8.42	7.89	5.94	5.05	5.08	6.11	3.49	2.00	1.24	1.89
2-year	11.73	9.27	8.16	6.15	5.13	5.43	6.26	3.83	2.64	1.65	2.38
3-year	11.51	9.64	8.26	6.25	5.14	5.49	6.22	4.09	3.10	2.10	2.78
5-year	11.45	10.12	8.37	6.38	5.15	5.55	6.16	4.56	3.82	2.97	3.43
7-year	11.40	10.50	8.52	6.50	5.28	5.79	6.20	4.88	4.30	3.52	3.87
10-year	11.43	10.62	8.55	6.57	5.26	5.65	6.03	5.02	4.61	4.01	4.27
20-year	(NA)	(NA)	(NA)	6.95	5.72	6.20	6.23	5.63	5.43	4.96	5.04
State and local govt. bonds, Aaa	7.84	8.60	6.96	5.79	4.93	5.29	5.58	5.01	4.87	4.52	4.51
State and local govt. bonds, Baa	8.99	9.59	7.30	6.05	5.14	5.70	6.19	5.75	5.63	5.20	5.09
Municipal (Bond Buyer, 20 bonds)	8.55	9.11	7.27	5.95	5.09	5.43	5.71	5.15	5.04	4.75	4.68
High-grade municipal bonds (Standard & Poor's) [3]	8.51	9.18	7.25	5.95	5.12	5.43	5.77	5.19	5.05	4.73	4.73
Corporate Aaa seasoned [4]	11.94	11.37	9.32	7.59	6.53	7.05	7.62	7.08	6.49	5.66	5.63
Corporate Baa seasoned [4]	13.67	12.72	10.36	8.20	7.22	7.88	8.37	7.95	7.80	6.76	6.39
Corporate seasoned, all industries [4]	12.75	12.05	9.77	7.83	6.87	7.45	7.98	7.49	7.10	6.24	6.00

NA Not available. [1] Yields on actively traded non-inflation-indexed issues adjusted to constant maturities. Data from U.S. Treasury. [2] Through 1995, yields are based on closing bid prices quoted by at least five dealers. Beginning 1998, yields are based on closing indicative prices quoted by secondary market participants. [3] Source: U.S. Council of Economic Advisors, *Economic Indicators*, monthly. [4] Source: Moody's Investors Service, New York, NY.

Source: Except as noted, Board of Governors of the Federal Reserve System, *Statistical Supplement to the Federal Reserve Bulletin*, monthly.

Table 1185. Volume of Debt Markets by Type of Security: 1990 to 2004

[**In billions of dollars (2,764 represents $2,764,000,000,000).** Covers debt markets as represented by the source]

Type of security	1990	1995	2000	2001	2002	2003	2004
NEW ISSUE VOLUME							
Total	2,764	6,789	12,637	15,969	16,915	19,599	19,044
U.S. Treasury securities [1]	1,531	2,331	2,038	2,743	3,812	4,249	4,689
Federal agency debt	637	3,531	8,746	10,496	9,236	10,496	10,422
Municipal	163	198	241	343	430	452	419
Mortgage-backed securities [2]	235	269	483	1,089	2,296	3,072	1,764
Asset-backed securities [3]	50	143	387	420	489	585	897
Corporate debt [4]	149	317	742	879	652	745	853
DAILY TRADING VOLUME							
Total	111.2	246.3	357.7	508.8	613.4	733.8	798.5
U.S. Treasury securities [1,5]	111.2	193.2	206.6	297.9	366.4	433.5	497.9
Federal agency debt [5]	(NA)	23.7	72.8	90.2	81.8	81.7	78.8
Municipal [6]	(NA)	(NA)	8.8	8.8	10.7	12.6	14.8
Mortgage-backed securities [2,5]	(NA)	29.4	69.5	112.0	154.5	206.0	207.0
VOLUME OF SECURITIES OUTSTANDING							
Total	7,745	11,229	16,969	18,500	20,224	22,096	23,585
U.S. Treasury securities [1]	2,196	3,307	2,967	2,968	3,205	3,575	3,944
Federal agency debt [7]	435	845	1,852	2,143	2,359	2,637	2,745
Municipal	1,184	1,294	1,481	1,604	1,765	1,892	2,019
Mortgage-backed securities [2]	1,333	2,352	3,565	4,126	4,705	5,309	5,473
Asset-backed securities [3,7]	90	316	1,072	1,281	1,543	1,694	1,828
Money market instruments [8]	1,157	1,177	2,661	2,542	2,551	2,526	2,872
Corporate debt [4,7]	1,350	1,938	3,372	3,836	4,096	4,462	4,705

NA Not available. [1] Marketable public debt. [2] Includes only Government National Mortgage Association (GNMA), Federal National Mortgage Association (FNMA), Federal Home Loan Mortgage Corporation (FHLMC) mortgage-backed securities (MBS) and collateralized mortgage obligations (CMOs) and private-label MBS/CMOs. [3] Excludes mortgage-backed assets. [4] Includes non-convertible corporate debt, Yankee bonds, and MTNs (Medium-Term Notes), but excludes all issues with maturities of one year or less, agency debt, and all certificates of deposit. [5] Primary dealer transactions. [6] Beginning 2000 includes customer-to-dealer and dealer-to-dealer transactions. [7] The Bond Market Association estimates. [8] Commercial paper, bankers' acceptances, and large time deposits.

Source: The Bond Market Association, New York, NY. Copyright. Based on data supplied by Board of Governors of the Federal Reserve System, U.S. Department of Treasury, Thompson Financial Securities Data Company, Inside MBS & ABS, FHLMC, FNMA, GNMA, Federal Home Loan Banks, Student Loan Marketing Association, Federal Farm Credit Banks, Tennessee Valley Authority, and Municipal Securities Rulemaking Board.

Banking, Finance, and Insurance 771

Table 1186. **Table 1186. Total Returns of Stocks, Bonds, and Treasury Bills: 1970 to 2004**

[In percent. Average annual percent change. Stock return data are based on the Standard & Poor's 500 index. Minus sign (-) indicates loss]

Period	Stocks				Treasury bills, total return	Bonds (10-year), total return
	Total return	Capital gains	Dividends and reinvestment	Total return after inflation		
1970 to 1979...............	5.88	1.60	4.20	-1.38	6.48	5.94
1980 to 1989...............	17.55	12.59	4.40	11.85	9.13	13.01
1990 to 1999...............	18.21	15.31	2.51	14.85	4.95	8.02
2000 to 2004...............	-2.30	-3.38	1.54	-4.67	2.66	8.41
2002	-22.10	-23.37	1.65	-23.91	1.61	15.15
2003	28.68	26.38	1.82	26.31	1.03	0.54
2004	10.88	8.99	1.73	7.38	1.43	4.59

Source: Global Financial Data, Los Angeles, CA, "GFD Guide to Total Returns"; <http://www.globalfindata.com/articles/totalreturnworksheet.xls>; and unpublished data. (copyright).

Table 1187. Equities, Corporate Bonds, and Municipal Securities—Holdings and Net Purchases by Type of Investor: 1990 to 2004

[In billions of dollars (3,531 represents $3,531,000,000,000). Holdings as of Dec. 31. Minus sign (-) indicates net sales]

Type of investor	Holdings					Net purchases				
	1990	2000	2002	2003	2004	1990	2000	2002	2003	2004
EQUITIES [1]										
Total [2].................	3,531	17,627	11,871	15,497	17,204	-45.7	5.3	47.0	105.6	16.4
Household sector [3]	1,770	7,806	5,048	6,376	6,522	-48.9	-446.6	-20.8	-60.7	-274.7
Rest of the world [4]	244	1,643	1,261	1,669	1,906	-16.0	193.6	54.2	36.9	33.2
Bank personal trusts and estates ...	190	357	181	213	223	0.5	-2.5	-39.4	-18.7	-12.0
Life insurance companies	82	892	709	919	1,092	-5.7	111.3	52.7	45.5	69.6
Other insurance companies.......	80	194	152	183	209	-7.0	0.7	-1.1	-2.7	-
Private pension funds	606	1,915	1,097	1,492	1,690	0.6	-82.7	-121.4	-44.8	-45.1
State and local retirement funds....	285	1,223	870	1,084	1,205	22.5	-18.4	20.0	-26.9	0.5
Mutual funds	233	3,227	2,188	3,052	3,697	14.4	193.1	31.4	136.8	157.8
Exchange-traded funds	-	66	98	146	218	-	42.4	41.6	15.1	51.2
CORPORATE & FOREIGN BONDS										
Total [2].................	1,720	4,925	5,979	6,620	7,227	139.6	365.5	465.0	641.4	591.9
Household sector [3]	234	645	707	527	498	69.3	56.3	68.9	-102.3	-43.6
Rest of the world [4]	217	921	1,267	1,500	1,775	5.3	168.4	151.0	232.6	275.9
Commercial banking	89	266	360	482	560	4.6	56.0	-3.2	44.6	77.4
Life insurance companies	567	1,222	1,449	1,620	1,754	56.5	49.0	106.8	171.0	133.5
Other insurance companies.......	89	188	199	219	246	10.4	6.4	2.4	20.0	26.7
Private pension funds	158	290	307	315	331	19.8	-57.6	12.7	8.2	15.5
State and local retirement funds....	142	340	335	339	333	-10.5	29.7	-4.6	4.6	-5.9
Mutual funds	59	362	471	548	623	4.7	-6.2	50.9	77.4	74.5
Government-sponsored enterprises.................	-	131	189	226	250	-	19.1	33.5	36.6	23.8
Brokers and dealers...........	29	113	192	228	252	-4.0	19.3	30.7	36.4	23.9
MUNICIPAL SECURITIES [5]										
Total [2].................	1,184	1,481	1,763	1,898	2,029	49.3	23.6	159.4	135.1	130.4
Household sector [3]	575	438	586	617	662	27.6	6.0	96.3	31.2	44.9
Other insurance companies.......	137	184	183	224	252	1.8	-14.9	9.2	41.2	27.4
Money market mutual funds	84	245	283	297	319	13.9	34.3	1.8	14.6	21.5
Mutual funds	113	230	277	290	294	13.9	-8.9	23.8	12.9	4.3

- Represents or rounds to zero. [1] Excludes mutual fund shares. [2] Includes other types not shown separately. [3] Includes nonprofit organizations. [4] Holdings and net purchases of U.S. issues by foreign residents. [5] Includes loans.

Source: Board of Governors of the Federal Reserve System, "Federal Reserve Statistical Release, Z.1, Flow of Funds Accounts of the United States"; published: 10 March 2005; <http://www.federalreserve.gov/releases/z1/20050310/>.

Table 1188. New Security Issues of Corporations by Type of Offering: 2000 to 2004

[In billions of dollars (1,082.2 represents $1,082,200,000,000). Represents gross proceed of issues maturing in more than one year. Figures are the principal amount or the number of units multiplied by the offering price. Excludes secondary offerings, employee stock plans, investment companies other than closed-end, intracorporate transactions, and Yankee bonds. Stock data include ownership securities issued by limited partnerships]

Type of offering	2000	2003	2004	Type of offering	2000	2003	2004
Total [1]	1,082.2	1,815.6	2,070.7	Stocks, total	311.9	182.4	(NA)
Bonds, total	947.3	1,692.3	1,923.1	Public..................	134.9	123.3	147.6
Sold in the United States.....	824.5	1,579.3	1,737.3	Nonfinancial...........	118.4	44.4	64.3
Sold abroad	122.8	112.9	185.8	Financial	16.5	78.9	83.2
Nonfinancial	259.2	362.3	260.0	Private placement	177.0	59.1	(NA)
Financial..............	688.1	1,329.9	1,663.1				

NA Not available. [1] Excludes private placements of stocks.

Source: Board of Governors of the Federal Reserve System, Statistical Supplement to the Federal Reserve Bulletin, monthly.

Table 1189. Purchases and Sales by U.S. Investors of Foreign Bonds and Stocks, 1990 to 2004, and by Selected Country, 2004

[In billions of dollars (31.2 represents $31,200,000,000). Covers transactions in all types of long-term foreign securities as reported by banks, brokers, and other entities in the United States. Data cover new issues of securities, transactions in outstanding issues, and redemptions of securities. Includes transactions executed in the United States for the account of foreigners, and transactions executed abroad for the account of reporting institutions and their domestic customers. Data by country show the country of location of the foreign buyers and sellers who deal directly with reporting institutions in the United States. The data do not necessarily indicate the country of beneficial owner or issuer. The term "foreigner" covers all institutions and individuals domiciled outside the United States, including U.S. citizens domiciled abroad, and the foreign branches, subsidiaries and other affiliates abroad of U.S. banks and businesses; the central governments, central banks, and other official institutions of foreign countries; and international and regional organizations. "Foreigner" also includes persons in the United States to the extent that they are known by reporting institutions to be acting on behalf of foreigners. Minus sign (-) indicates net sales by U.S. investors or a net inflow of capital into the United States]

Year and country	Net purchases			Total transactions [1]			Bonds		Stocks	
	Total	Bonds	Stocks	Total	Bonds	Stocks	Purchases	Sales	Purchases	Sales
1990	31.2	21.9	9.2	907	652	255	337	315	132	123
1992	47.9	15.6	32.3	1,375	1,043	332	529	514	182	150
1993	143.1	80.4	62.7	2,126	1,572	554	826	746	308	245
1994	57.3	9.2	48.1	2,526	1,706	820	858	848	434	386
1995	98.7	48.4	50.3	2,569	1,827	741	938	890	396	346
1996	110.6	51.4	59.3	3,239	2,279	960	1,165	1,114	510	450
1997	89.1	48.1	40.9	4,505	2,952	1,553	1,500	1,452	797	756
1998	11.1	17.3	-6.2	4,527	2,674	1,853	1,346	1,328	923	930
1999	-10.0	5.7	-15.6	3,941	1,602	2,339	804	798	1,162	1,177
2000	17.1	4.1	13.1	5,539	1,922	3,617	963	959	1,815	1,802
2001	19.6	-30.5	50.1	5,135	2,290	2,845	1,130	1,160	1,448	1,398
2002	-27.0	-28.5	1.5	5,253	2,716	2,537	1,344	1,372	1,269	1,268
2003	65.9	-18.9	84.8	5,854	3,101	2,752	1,541	1,560	1,419	1,334
2004, total [2]	108.9	25.5	83.4	6,348	2,937	3,411	1,481	1,456	1,747	1,664
United Kingdom	105.1	69.8	35.3	2,976	1,605	1,371	837	768	703	668
Japan	20.6	-12.5	33.2	581	187	394	87	100	214	181
Cayman Islands	-7.2	-1.6	-5.6	577	262	315	130	132	155	160
Canada	1.1	0.4	0.8	384	227	157	114	113	79	78
Hong Kong	-4.9	-2.9	-2.0	179	31	148	14	17	73	75
Bermuda	-1.1	-0.3	-0.8	164	52	112	26	26	56	57
France	5.4	1.6	3.7	137	39	98	20	19	51	47
Germany	1.8	-0.7	2.4	126	86	40	43	43	21	19
Australia	3.3	1.2	2.0	110	21	88	11	10	45	43
Bahamas, The	0.1	-1.1	1.1	93	52	41	25	26	21	20
Singapore	-8.9	-8.9	(Z)	70	22	47	7	16	24	24
Switzerland	-2.6	-1.9	-0.7	67	17	50	8	10	25	25
Mexico	-3.1	-0.9	-2.1	55	35	20	17	18	9	11
Ireland	-4.7	-2.7	-2.0	53	22	31	10	12	14	16
Netherlands	-0.1	0.1	-0.3	47	11	36	6	6	18	18
Brazil	0.6	-0.5	1.1	45	29	17	14	15	9	8

Z Less than $50 million. [1] Total purchases plus total sales. [2] Includes other countries, not shown separately.

Source: U.S. Department of Treasury, Treasury Bulletin, quarterly.

Table 1190. U.S. Holdings of Foreign Stocks and Bonds by Country: 2002 to 2004

[In billions of dollars (1,374.7 represents $1,374,700,000,000)]

Country	Stocks			Country	Bonds		
	2002	2003	2004		2002	2003	2004
Total holdings	1,374.7	2,079.4	2,520.1	Total holdings	705.2	874.4	916.7
Europe [1]	789.4	1,135.3	1,382.7	Western Europe [1]	343.2	442.4	506.9
United Kingdom	289.5	426.2	540.3	United Kingdom	110.9	148.3	213.3
France	94.3	130.8	156.1	France	60.6	71.4	72.6
Switzerland	75.6	117.9	136.3	Netherlands	42.5	58.0	59.7
Netherlands	88.1	115.8	134.2	France	34.4	43.0	45.8
Germany	66.5	103.2	122.6	Italy	17.0	25.0	24.5
Spain	29.9	43.8	53.0	Belgium & Luxembourg	16.1	20.2	17.2
Italy	28.2	39.0	47.4	Sweden	11.1	12.8	13.3
Finland	34.3	35.2	40.8	Canada	131.9	139.4	143.6
Sweden	19.2	27.5	39.9	Latin America & Caribbean [1]	119.7	165.0	167.8
Canada	88.2	149.3	188.5	Cayman Islands	47.2	75.7	80.1
Latin America & Caribbean [1]	191.6	260.4	302.8	Mexico	23.8	27.6	27.4
Bermuda	88.6	107.5	124.1	Asia [1]	66.0	69.3	38.2
Cayman Islands	32.9	45.3	53.8	Japan	38.3	37.2	25.1
Brazil	19.7	31.8	39.4	Africa [1]	5.3	6.6	5.1
Mexico	22.0	28.5	31.7	South Africa	2.5	2.7	2.9
Asia [1]	258.7	454.4	575.3	Other countries [1]	39.1	51.7	55.1
Japan	148.1	255.5	333.3	Australia	21.6	29.2	31.3
Korea, South	27.8	49.1	60.9				
Hong Kong	22.0	36.2	39.5				
Taiwan [2]	8.5	27.0	35.5				
Africa [1]	9.6	18.7	22.5				
South Africa	7.9	15.1	18.3				
Other countries [1]	37.2	61.3	48.3				
Australia	34.6	56.5	42.5				

[1] Includes other countries not shown separately. [2] See footnote 3, Table 1192.

Source: U.S. Bureau of Economic Analysis, Survey of Current Business, July 2005.

Table 1191. **Foreign Purchases and Sales of U.S. Securities by Type of Security, 1990 to 2004, and by Selected Country, 2004**

[In billions of dollars (18.7 represents $18,700,000,000). Covers transactions in all types of long-term domestic securities by foreigners as reported by banks, brokers, and other entities in the United States (except nonmarketable U.S. Treasury notes, foreign series; and nonmarketable U.S. Treasury bonds and notes, foreign currency series). See headnote, Table 1189. Minus sign (-) indicates net sales by foreigners or a net outflow of capital from the United States]

Year and country	Net purchases					Total transactions [4]				
	Total	Treasury bonds and notes [1]	U.S. Govt. corporations [2] bonds	Corporate bonds [3]	Corporate stocks	Total	Treasury bonds and notes [1]	U.S. Govt. corporations [2] bonds	Corporate bonds [3]	Corporate stocks
1990	18.7	17.9	6.3	9.7	-15.1	4,204	3,620	104	117	362
1992	73.2	39.3	18.3	20.8	-5.1	5,282	4,444	204	187	448
1993	111.1	23.6	35.4	30.6	21.6	6,314	5,195	263	239	618
1994	140.4	78.8	21.7	38.0	1.9	6,562	5,343	297	222	699
1995	231.9	134.1	28.7	57.9	11.2	7,243	5,828	222	278	915
1996	370.2	232.2	41.7	83.7	12.5	8,965	7,134	241	422	1,169
1997	388.0	184.2	49.9	84.4	69.6	12,759	9,546	469	617	2,126
1998	277.8	49.0	56.8	121.9	50.0	14,989	10,259	992	641	3,097
1999	350.2	-10.0	92.2	160.4	107.5	14,617	8,586	880	577	4,574
2000	457.8	-54.0	152.8	184.1	174.9	16,910	7,795	1,305	775	7,036
2001	520.8	18.5	164.0	222.0	116.4	20,003	10,517	2,239	1,260	5,986
2002	547.6	119.9	195.1	182.3	50.2	25,498	14,409	3,261	1,459	6,369
2003	738.8	276.7	159.4	267.1	35.6	28,029	16,376	3,758	1,716	6,179
2004, total [5]	904.0	352.0	226.4	297.9	27.8	29,636	17,519	2,192	2,021	7,904
United Kingdom	245.5	78.7	53.2	98.3	15.3	9,812	6,675	324	822	1,991
Cayman Islands	68.8	18.9	21.6	33.7	-5.5	4,645	1,662	788	474	1,720
Bermuda	-6.7	-20.2	1.7	10.7	1.1	2,333	1,153	198	92	891
France	-3.8	-10.2	-0.2	7.5	-0.9	1,983	1,158	10	36	779
Japan	244.2	166.4	44.4	30.5	2.8	1,580	1,236	181	71	93
Canada	29.6	16.1	6.0	6.1	1.4	1,082	827	28	43	184
Ireland	17.5	1.0	4.2	10.2	2.1	915	754	37	43	81
Bahamas, The	9.2	4.7	2.5	-0.4	2.4	596	367	21	38	170
Norway	16.7	10.0	1.6	3.5	1.6	588	541	19	6	22
China [6]	47.3	18.9	16.4	12.3	-0.3	487	361	106	16	4
Germany	17.9	8.8	-0.1	11.6	-2.4	461	268	11	36	146
Hong Kong	17.3	1.1	11.3	5.7	-0.8	286	204	42	14	26
Switzerland	11.1	5.3	3.0	4.0	-1.2	274	111	14	21	128
Netherlands	1.0	-3.2	-0.2	2.1	2.2	248	139	13	15	81
Netherlands Antilles	13.2	11.6	0.2	0.5	1.0	247	127	2	5	114

[1] Marketable bonds and notes. [2] Includes federally-sponsored agencies. [3] Includes transactions in directly placed issues abroad by U.S. corporations and issues of states and municipalities. [4] Total purchases plus total sales. [5] Includes other countries, not shown separately. [6] See footnote 3, Table 1192.

Source: U.S. Department of Treasury, *Treasury Bulletin*, quarterly.

Table 1192. Foreign Holdings of U.S. Securities by Country: 2002 to 2004

[In billions of dollars (1,285.5 represents $1,285,500,000,000). Covers only private holdings of U.S. securities, except as noted]

Type of security and country	2002	2003	2004	Type of security and country	2002	2003	2004
U.S. Treasury securities [1, 2]	1,285.5	1,533.6	1,900.2	Asia [2]	240.3	234.3	309.4
Japan	392.7	549.5	694.2	Japan	167.2	159.8	215.6
China [3]	124.4	175.9	236.2	Africa	1.4	1.6	1.8
United Kingdom	63.6	44.1	76.5	Other countries	13.6	13.6	17.8
Taiwan [3]	15.4	16.8	72.8				
Cayman Islands	40.8	56.4	68.1	**Corporate stocks**	1,248.1	1,700.9	1,928.5
Korea, South	48.2	55.6	55.1	Europe [2]	711.4	939.8	1,081.2
Germany	38.4	44.7	54.0	United Kingdom	199.5	246.1	308.1
Hong Kong	45.0	46.9	45.2	Belgium and Luxembourg	103.1	140.0	159.7
OPEC Asia [4]	26.5	26.4	42.5	Netherlands	96.4	124.2	136.9
Switzerland	39.1	42.7	42.4	Switzerland	96.6	121.5	129.0
				Germany	60.9	76.1	80.2
Corporate and agency bonds	1,531.0	1,707.2	2,059.3	France	36.4	57.0	64.5
Europe [2]	1,034.3	1,130.8	1,302.9	Ireland	29.5	48.7	56.6
United Kingdom	566.4	489.8	517.1	Sweden	30.6	43.0	50.0
Belgium and Luxembourg	301.0	414.3	487.0	Italy	26.3	33.6	35.4
Germany	31.4	44.6	66.6	Canada	148.9	204.3	221.2
Ireland	33.5	47.6	59.9	Latin America & Caribbean [2]	178.9	270.1	288.1
Netherlands	29.4	40.5	48.6	Cayman Islands	64.8	114.0	121.2
Switzerland	27.3	31.4	36.6	Bermuda	38.6	51.7	55.3
France	17.9	24.9	33.0	Netherlands Antilles	15.0	21.8	24.2
Canada	39.4	47.1	52.6	Asia [2]	166.7	230.8	264.7
Latin America & Caribbean [2]	202.0	279.8	374.8	Japan	116.5	155.7	178.3
Cayman Islands	97.7	144.4	201.6	Africa	2.6	4.2	5.3
Bermuda	59.1	78.6	94.5	Other countries [2]	39.6	51.7	68.0
				Australia	34.8	45.0	60.2

[1] Includes foreign official holdings. [2] Includes other countries not shown separately. [3] With the establishment of diplomatic relations with China on January 1, 1979, the U.S. government recognized the People's Republic of China as the sole legal government of China and acknowledged the Chinese position that there is only one China and that Taiwan is part of China. [4] Comprises Indonesia, Iran, Iraq, Kuwait, Qatar, Saudi Arabia, and the United Arab Emirates.

Source: U.S. Bureau of Economic Analysis, *Survey of Current Business*, July 2005.

774　Banking, Finance, and Insurance

Table 1193. **Stock Prices and Yields: 1990 to 2004**

[Closing values as of end of December, except as noted]

Index	1990	1995	2000	2001	2002	2003	2004
STOCK PRICES							
Standard & Poor's indices: [1]							
S&P 500 composite (1941-43 = 10)	330.2	615.9	1,320.3	1,148.1	879.8	1,111.9	1,211.9
S&P 400 MidCap Index (1982 = 100)	100.0	217.8	516.7	508.3	429.8	576.0	663.3
S&P 600 Small Cap Index (Dec. 31, 1993 = 100)	(NA)	121.1	219.6	232.2	196.6	270.4	328.8
S&P 500/Barra Value Index (Dec. 31, 1974 = 35)	177.7	325.1	636.2	552.0	428.0	551.9	625.5
S&P 500/Barra Growth Index (Dec. 31, 1974 = 35) . . .	159.9	302.0	687.6	594.6	448.8	555.9	582.0
Russell indices: [2]							
Russell 1000 (Dec. 31, 1986 = 130)	171.2	328.9	700.1	604.9	466.2	594.6	651.0
Russell 2000 (Dec. 31, 1986 = 135)	132.2	316.0	483.5	488.5	383.1	556.9	651.6
Russell 3000 (Dec. 31, 1986 = 140)	180.9	351.9	725.8	634.2	489.5	630.1	693.6
N.Y. Stock Exchange common stock index:							
Composite (Dec. 31, 2002 = 5000)	1,908.5	3,484.2	6,945.6	6,236.4	5,000.0	6,440.3	7,250.1
Yearly high	2,126.7	3,501.7	7,164.6	7,048.1	6,445.0	6,469.5	7,373.2
Yearly low	1,715.1	2,651.2	6,094.9	5,331.4	4,452.5	4,418.6	6,211.3
American Stock Exchange Composite Index							
(Dec. 29, 1995 = 550)	(NA)	550.0	897.8	847.6	824.4	1,173.6	1,434.3
NASDAQ composite index (Feb. 5, 1971 = 100)	373.8	1,052.1	2,470.5	1,950.4	1,335.5	2,003.4	2,175.4
Nasdaq-100 (Jan. 31, 1985 = 125)	200.5	576.2	2,341.7	1,577.1	984.4	1,467.9	1,621.1
Industrial (Feb. 5, 1971 = 100)	406.1	964.7	1,483.0	1,389.2	1,029.7	1,603.7	1,857.7
Banks (Feb. 5, 1971 = 100)	254.9	1,009.4	1,939.5	2,134.9	2,231.3	2,899.2	3,217.9
Computers (Oct. 29, 1993 = 200).	(NA)	366.1	1,295.0	980.5	622.6	934.9	965.3
Transportation (Feb. 5, 1971 = 100)	417.1	816.4	1,160.4	1,285.0	1,297.6	1,754.4	2,229.5
Telecommunications (October 29, 1993 = 200).	84.0	208.4	463.4	236.6	108.8	183.6	198.3
Biotech (Oct. 29, 1993 = 200)	(NA)	304.3	1,084.5	908.8	496.9	724.1	768.5
Dow-Jones and Co., Inc.:							
Composite (65 stocks)	920.6	1,693.2	3,317.4	2,892.2	2,375.0	3,000.8	3,395.8
Industrial (30 stocks)	2,633.7	5,117.1	10,786.9	10,021.5	8,341.6	10,453.9	10,783.1
Transportation (20 stocks)	910.2	1,981.0	2,946.6	2,640.0	2,310.0	3,007.1	3,797.5
Utility (15 stocks)	209.7	225.4	412.2	293.9	215.2	266.9	335.0
Wilshire 5000 Total Market Index [3]							
(Dec. 31, 1980 = 1404.596)	3,101.4	6,057.2	12,175.9	10,707.7	8,343.2	10,799.4	11,971.1
COMMON STOCK YIELDS (percent)							
Standard & Poor's composite index (500 stocks): [4]							
Dividend-price ratio [5]	3.61	2.56	1.15	1.32	1.61	1.77	1.72
Earnings-price ratio [6]	6.47	6.09	3.63	2.95	2.92	3.84	4.89

NA Not available. [1] Standard & Poor's Indices are market-value weighted and are chosen for market size, liquidity, and industry group representation. The S&P 500 index represents 500 large publicly-traded companies. The S&P MidCap Index tracks mid-cap companies. The S&P SmallCap Index consists of 600 domestic small-cap stocks. [2] The Russell 1000 and 3000 indices show respectively the 1000 and 3000 largest capitalization stocks in the United States. The Russell 2000 index shows the 2000 largest capitalization stocks in the United States after the first 1000. [3] The Wilshire 5000 Total Market Index measures the performance of all U.S. headquartered equity securities with readily available prices. Source: Dow Jones & Company, Inc., New York, NY, Dow Jones Indexes, (copyright). [4] Source: U.S. Council of Economic Advisors, Economic Indicators, monthly. [5] Aggregate cash dividends (based on latest known annual rate) divided by aggregate market value based on Wednesday closing prices. Averages of monthly figures. [6] Averages of quarterly ratios which are ratio of earnings (after taxes) for 4 quarters ending with particular quarter to price index for last day of that quarter.

Source: Except as noted, Global Financial Data, Los Angeles, CA, <http://www.globalfindata.com/trial/index2.html>; (copyright).

Table 1194. **Dow Jones U.S. Total Market Index by Industry: 1995 to 2004**

[As of end of year]

Industry	1995	1999	2000	2001	2002	2003	2004
U.S. Total Market Index, total	147.49	341.57	306.88	266.71	204.51	262.68	289.38
Basic materials	139.19	187.16	154.49	153.22	136.97	181.10	200.33
Consumer goods	146.35	215.21	219.82	212.88	198.48	240.91	266.44
Consumer services	128.48	381.26	279.11	284.94	212.34	280.07	306.85
Oil and gas	134.54	219.71	272.96	236.74	200.29	246.08	319.76
Financial	176.60	354.55	440.91	404.50	346.36	445.96	492.54
Healthcare	127.77	263.62	360.18	310.76	242.87	286.04	295.22
Industrial	156.39	308.19	276.11	245.14	179.78	235.69	272.24
Technology	229.18	1,188.60	749.01	535.89	327.84	493.02	499.78
Telecommunications	154.84	356.97	210.38	180.62	115.04	119.12	136.84
Utilities	109.07	118.12	177.80	127.04	95.75	114.54	136.79

Source: Dow Jones & Company, Inc., New York, NY, Dow Jones Indexes, (copyright).

U.S. Census Bureau, Statistical Abstract of the United States: 2006

Table 1195. **Transaction Activity in Equities, Options, and Security Futures, 1990 to 2004, and by Exchange, 2004**

[In billions of dollars. Market value of all sales of equities and options listed on an exchange or subject to last-sale reporting. Also reported are the value of such options that were exercised and the value of single-stock futures that were delivered. Excludes options and futures on indexes]

Year and exchange	Total	Equity trading	Option trading	Option exercises and futures deliveries
1990	2,229	2,154	27	48
1995	6,321	6,208	51	63
1996	8,266	8,124	68	75
1997	11,693	11,488	105	100
1998	15,164	14,903	140	121
1999	23,219	22,813	260	145
2000	36,275	35,557	485	233
2001	26,138	25,636	278	224
2002	23,028	22,658	161	209
2003	22,737	22,291	164	282
2004, total [1]	**27,808**	**27,091**	**223**	**495**
American Stock Exchange	682	558	37	86
Boston Stock Exchange	682	667	5	9
Chicago Board Options Exchange	185	7	54	123
Chicago Stock Exchange	434	434	-	-
International Securities Exchange	221	-	66	155
National Association of Securities Dealers	7,961	7,961	-	-
National Stock Exchange	2,907	2,907	-	-
New York Stock Exchange	11,656	11,656	-	-
The Pacific Exchange	2,892	2,811	29	52
Philadelphia Stock Exchange	187	89	32	66

- Represents zero. [1] Includes other exchanges not shown separately.

Source: U.S. Securities and Exchange Commission, *Annual Report.*

Table 1196. **Volume of Trading on New York Stock Exchange: 1990 to 2004**

[39,946 represents 39,946,000,000. *Round lot:* A unit of trading or a multiple thereof. On the NYSE the unit of trading is generally 100 shares in stocks. For some inactive stocks, the unit of trading is 10 shares. *Odd lot:* An amount of stock less than the established 100-share unit or 10-share unit of trading]

Item	Unit	1990	1995	1998	1999	2000	2001	2002	2003	2004
Shares traded	**Million**	**39,946**	**87,873**	**171,188**	**206,299**	**265,499**	**311,290**	**369,069**	**356,767**	**372,718**
Round lots	Million	39,665	87,218	169,745	203,914	262,478	307,509	363,136	352,398	367,099
Average daily shares	Million	157	346	674	809	1,042	1,240	1,441	1,398	1,457
High day	Million	292	653	1,216	1,350	1,561	2,368	2,813	1,886	2,690
Low day	Million	57	118	247	312	403	414	462	360	509
Odd lots	Million	282	656	1,443	2,384	3,021	3,781	5,933	4,370	5,619
Value of shares traded	**Bil. dol.**	**1,336**	**3,110**	**7,395**	**9,073**	**11,205**	**10,645**	**10,491**	**9,847**	**11,841**
Round lots	Bil. dol.	-1,325	3,083	7,318	8,945	11,060	10,489	10,278	9,692	11,618
Odd lots	Bil. dol.	11	27	77	128	145	155	213	154	223
Bond volume [1]	**Mil. dol.**	**10,893**	**6,979**	**3,838**	**3,221**	**2,328**	**2,668**	**3,646**	**2,502**	**1,291**
Daily average	Mil. dol.	43.1	27.7	15.2	12.8	9.2	10.8	14.5	10.0	5.1

[1] Par value.

Source: New York Stock Exchange, Inc., New York, NY, *Fact Book*, annual (copyright).

Table 1197. **Securities Listed on New York Stock Exchange: 1990 to 2004**

[As of December 31, except cash dividends are for calendar year (1,689 represents $1,689,000,000,000)]

Item	Unit	1990	1995	1996	1997	1998	1999	2000	2001	2002	2003	2004
BONDS												
Number of issuers	Number	743	564	563	533	474	416	392	369	343	312	228
Number of issues	Number	2,912	2,097	2,064	1,965	1,858	1,736	1,627	1,447	1,323	1,273	1,059
Face value	Bil. dol.	1,689	2,773	2,845	2,625	2,554	2,402	2,125	1,654	1,378	1,355	1,080
STOCKS												
Companies	Number	1,774	2,675	2,907	3,047	3,114	3,025	2,862	2,798	2,783	2,750	2,768
Number of issues	Number	2,284	3,126	3,285	3,358	3,382	3,286	3,072	2,984	2,959	2,938	3,010
Shares listed	Billions	90.7	154.7	176.9	207.1	239.3	280.9	313.9	341.5	349.9	359.7	380.8
Market value	Bil. dol.	2,820	6,013	7,300	9,413	10,864	12,296	12,372	11,714	9,603	12,158	13,728
Average price [1]	Dollars	31.08	38.86	41.26	45.45	45.40	43.77	42.14	34.11	28.39	33.80	36.05

[1] This average cannot be used as an index of price trend due to changes in shares listed caused by new listings, suspensions, stock splits and stock dividends.

Source: New York Stock Exchange, Inc., New York, NY, *Fact Book*, annual (copyright).

Table 1198. **Household Ownership of Equities: 2002**

[**52.7 represents 52,700,000**. Based on a national probability sample of 4,009 household financial decision-makers. Further questions about equity ownership were asked of those 1,986 decision-makers who indicated they owned equities]

Type of holding	Households owning equities		Number of individual investors (mil.)
	Number (mil.)	Percent of all households	
Any type of equity (net) [1]	52.7	49.5	84.3
Any equity inside employer-sponsored retirement plans	36.2	34.0	57.9
Any equity outside employer-sponsored retirement plans	35.9	33.7	57.4
Individual stock (net) [1]	25.4	23.9	38.1
Individual stock inside employer-sponsored retirement plans.	8.8	8.3	12.3
Individual stock outside employer-sponsored retirement plans.	21.0	19.7	31.5
Stock mutual funds (net) [1]	47.0	44.2	70.5
Stock mutual funds inside employer-sponsored retirement plans	33.2	31.2	46.5
Stock mutual funds outside employer-sponsored retirement plans . . .	28.7	27.0	43.1

[1] Multiple responses included.

Source: Investment Company Institute, Washington, DC, and Securities Industry Association, New York, NY, *Equity Ownership in America*, Fall 2002 (copyright).

Table 1199. **Characteristics of Equity Owners: 2002**

[**In percent, except as indicated**. See headnote, Table 1198. For definition of median, see Guide to Tabular Presentation]

Item	Total	Age					Household income		
		18 to 34 years old	35 to 44 years old	45 to 54 years old	55 to 64 years old	65 years old and over	Less than $50,000	$50,000 to $99,999	$100,000 and over
Median age of owner (years)	47	29	40	50	59	73	46	44	47
Median household income (dol.)	62,500	60,000	70,000	68,000	62,500	45,000	34,000	70,000	125,000
Median household financial assets [1] (dol.)	100,000	32,500	99,100	136,800	274,300	415,100	37,500	100,000	421,500
Equity investments owned:									
Individual stock (net) [2]	49	41	49	50	50	56	39	48	64
Inside retirement plans [3]	17	18	21	18	16	6	11	18	22
Outside retirement plans [3]	41	33	40	42	44	50	31	40	57
Stock mutual funds (net) [2]	89	85	90	93	93	83	88	90	91
Inside retirement plans [3]	66	67	76	77	61	28	57	73	73
Outside retirement plans [3]	56	47	54	52	67	67	50	50	67
Non-equity investments owned: [2]									
Savings accounts, MMDAs, or CDs [4]	86	88	87	84	82	86	78	89	87
Bond investments (net) [2]	36	28	31	35	44	48	26	35	43
Individual bonds	17	13	15	16	21	28	13	15	21
Bond mutual funds	26	19	23	25	31	34	17	25	31
Fixed or variable annuities	23	13	19	25	31	33	21	23	24
Hybrid mutual funds	52	43	51	55	60	52	43	51	61
Money market mutual funds	35	27	35	35	43	36	25	33	44
Investment real estate	24	15	20	29	32	30	17	22	40
Have retirement plan coverage [3] . . .	79	81	87	84	78	58	75	87	83
Have Individual Retirement Account (IRA)	57	46	56	62	66	55	43	58	72

[1] Includes assets in employer-sponsored retirement plans, but excludes value of primary residence. [2] Multiple responses included. [3] Employer-sponsored. [4] MMDA = money market deposit account; CD = certificate of deposit.

Source: Investment Company Institute, Washington, DC, and Securities Industry Association, New York, NY, *Equity Ownership in America*, Fall 2002 (copyright).

Table 1200. **Households Owning Mutual Funds by Age and Income: 2000 and 2004**

[**In percent**. Includes money market, stock, bond and hybrid, variable annuity, IRA, Keogh, and employer-sponsored retirement plan fund owners. In 2004 an estimated 53,900,000 households own mutual funds. Based on a sample survey of 3,000 households; for details, see source]

Age of household head and household income	Percent distribution, 2004	As percent of all households		Age of household head and household income	Percent distribution, 2004	As percent of all households	
		2000	2004			2000	2004
Total	100	49	48				
Less than 25 years old. . .	3	23	25	Less than $25,000.	8	17	15
25 to 34 years old	16	49	43	$25,000 to $34,999	9	37	32
35 to 44 years old	26	58	57	$35,000 to $49,999	13	49	40
45 to 54 years old	24	59	55	$50,000 to $74,999	26	66	61
55 to 64 years old	17	54	55	$75,000 to $99,999	19	77	77
65 years old and over . . .	14	32	37	$100,000 and over	25	79	83

Source: Investment Company Institute, Washington, DC, *Fundamentals, Investment Company Institute Research in Brief*, Vol. 9, No. 4, August 2000, and Vol. 13, No. 3, October 2004 (copyright).

Table 1201. Characteristics of Mutual Fund Owners: 2004

[In percent, except as indicated. Mutual fund ownership includes holdings of money market, stock, bond, and hybrid mutual funds; and funds owned through variable annuities, Individual Retirement Accounts (IRAs), Keoghs, and employer-sponsored retirement plans. Based on a national probability sample of 3,613 primary financial decision-makers in households with mutual fund investments. For definition of median, see Guide to Tabular Presentation]

Characteristic	Total	Age			Household income		
		Under 40 years old	40 to 64 years old	65 years old and over	Less than $50,000	$50,000 to $99,999	$100,000 or more
Median age (years).............	48	33	51	71	48	46	46
Median household income (dol.)	68,700	65,000	75,000	45,000	32,500	70,000	130,000
Median household financial assets [1] (dol.)	125,000	50,000	200,000	207,100	50,000	110,000	350,000
Own an IRA	69	63	72	64	58	65	77
Household has a defined contribution retirement plan(s), net [2]	84	86	87	67	74	89	88
401(k) plan	67	78	71	28	56	72	76
403(b) plan	14	12	15	6	9	13	19
State, local, or federal government plan	35	27	37	46	32	38	31
Median mutual fund assets (dol.)...........	48,000	20,000	70,000	60,000	17,600	43,800	95,000
Median number of mutual funds owned	4	4	5	3	3	4	6
Own: [2]							
Equity funds.....................	80	79	83	74	70	80	91
Bond funds	44	41	46	39	35	41	50
Hybrid funds	34	34	36	28	30	31	39
Money market mutual funds	49	45	51	47	38	47	54
Own mutual funds bought: [2]							
Outside employer-sponsored retirement plan(s)..........................	68	59	69	84	63	60	74
Inside employer-sponsored retirememt plan(s)..........................	63	69	67	30	55	68	68

[1] Includes assets in employer-sponsored retirement plans, but excludes value of primary residence.   [2] Multiple responses included.

Source: Investment Company Institute, Washington, DC, *Profile of Mutual Fund Shareholders, 2004* (copyright).

Table 1202. Mutual Funds—Summary: 1990 to 2004

[Number of funds and assets as of December 31 (1,065 represents $1,065,000,000,000). A mutual fund is an open-end investment company that continuously issues and redeems shares that represent an interest in a pool of financial assets. Excludes data for funds that invest in other mutual funds. Minus sign (-) indicates net redemptions]

Type of fund	Unit	1990	1995	1998	1999	2000	2001	2002	2003	2004
Number of funds, total	Number...	3,079	5,725	7,314	7,791	8,155	8,305	8,244	8,126	8,044
Equity funds	Number ...	1,099	2,139	3,512	3,952	4,385	4,716	4,747	4,599	4,550
Hybrid funds	Number ...	193	412	526	532	523	483	473	508	510
Bond funds	Number ...	1,046	2,177	2,250	2,262	2,208	2,091	2,035	2,045	2,041
Money market funds, taxable [1]	Number ...	506	674	685	702	703	689	679	662	639
Money market funds, tax-exempt [2] ...	Number ...	235	323	341	343	336	326	310	312	304
Assets, total	Bil. dol.	1,065	2,811	5,525	6,846	6,965	6,975	6,390	7,414	8,107
Equity funds	Bil. dol.	239	1,249	2,978	4,042	3,962	3,418	2,662	3,684	4,384
Hybrid funds	Bil. dol.	36	210	365	379	346	346	325	430	519
Bond funds	Bil. dol.	291	599	831	812	811	925	1,130	1,248	1,290
Money market funds, taxable [1]	Bil. dol.	415	630	1,163	1,409	1,607	2,013	1,997	1,763	1,603
Money market funds, tax-exempt [2] ...	Bil. dol.	84	123	189	204	238	272	275	288	310
Equity, hybrid and bond funds:										
Sales	Bil. dol.	149	475	1,058	1,274	1,630	1,383	1,434	1,430	1,494
Redemptions	Bil. dol.	98	313	748	1,021	1,330	1,177	1,228	1,148	1,201
Net sales...............	Bil. dol.	51	163	310	252	300	206	206	282	293
Money market funds, taxable: [1]										
Sales	Bil. dol.	1,219	2,729	5,534	7,083	8,691	10,701	11,011	10,150	9,717
Redemptions	Bil. dol.	1,183	2,617	5,289	6,866	8,499	10,314	11,075	10,402	9,874
Net sales...............	Bil. dol.	36	112	244	217	192	387	-64	-252	-157
Money market funds, tax-exempt: [2]										
Sales	Bil. dol.	197	396	639	687	788	783	750	873	1,082
Redemptions	Bil. dol.	190	385	612	675	757	751	736	866	1,066
Net sales...............	Bil. dol.	7	11	27	12	31	31	14	7	16

[1] Funds invest in short-term, high-grade securities sold in the money market.   [2] Funds invest in municipal securities with relatively short maturities.

Source: Investment Company Institute, Washington, DC, *Mutual Fund Fact Book*, annual (copyright).

Table 1203. Mutual Fund Shares—Holdings and Net Purchases by Type of Investor: 1990 to 2004

[In billions of dollars (608 represents $608,000,000,000). Holdings as of December 31. Minus sign (-) indicates net sales]

Type of investor	Holdings					Net purchases				
	1990	2000	2002	2003	2004	1990	2000	2002	2003	2004
Total	608	4,435	3,638	4,653	5,435	53.7	239.4	182.4	288.0	294.1
Households, nonprofit organizations	457	2,833	2,326	3,009	3,570	22.3	83.4	71.2	267.3	280.2
Nonfinancial corporate business. . .	10	124	97	121	129	-1.0	12.0	10.5	-4.6	-4.6
State and local governments.....	5	21	24	26	28	3.5	3.7	8.9	-6.2	-0.4
Commercial banking	2	15	20	17	18	-0.3	2.5	1.7	-6.2	-0.9
Credit unions	1	2	4	4	3	0.2	-0.3	-0.2	0.5	-0.9
Bank personal trusts and estates. .	63	397	339	391	413	9.7	48.5	37.3	-15.0	-5.4
Life insurance companies	31	97	77	92	100	12.6	5.6	2.6	0.5	0.4
Private pension funds	40	946	752	994	1,174	6.6	84.0	50.4	51.7	25.8

Source: Board of Governors of the Federal Reserve System, "Federal Reserve Statistical Release, Z.1, Flow of Funds Accounts of the United States"; published: 10 March 2005; <http://www.federalreserve.gov/releases/z1/20050310/>.

Table 1204. **Mutual Fund Retirement Assets: 1990 to 2003**

[In billions of dollars, except percent (206 represents $206,000,000,000). Based on data from the Institute's Annual Questionnaire for Retirement Statistics. The 2003 survey gathered data from 14,059 mutual fund share classes representing approximately 83 percent of mutual fund industry assets. Assets were estimated for all non-reporting funds. Estimates of retirement assets in street name and omnibus accounts were derived from data reported on the Annual Questionnaire for Retirement Statistics and the Annual Institutional Survey]

Type of account	1990	1995	1998	1999	2000	2001	2002	2003
Mutual fund retirement assets	206	913	1,948	2,535	2,478	2,342	2,078	2,662
Percent of total retirement assets . . .	5	13	19	22	21	21	20	22
Individual retirement accounts (IRAs)	139	470	968	1,259	1,230	1,160	1,032	1,306
Employer-sponsored defined contribution retirement plans	67	443	980	1,276	1,248	1,182	1,046	1,356
401(k) plans [1]	35	266	619	814	820	799	711	922
Percent of total 401(k) assets.	9	31	40	45	46	47	47	49
403(b) plans [2]	15	119	233	289	264	238	200	263
457 plans [3]	2	8	24	40	38	37	31	38
Other defined contribution plans [4]	15	50	104	133	127	109	105	133
Percent of all mutual funds:								
Mutual fund retirement assets	19	32	35	37	36	34	33	36
Individual retirement accounts (IRAs)	13	17	18	18	18	17	16	18
Employer-sponsored retirement plans.	6	16	18	19	18	17	16	18

[1] A 401(k) plan is a qualified retirement plan that allows participants to have a portion of their compensation (otherwise payable in cash) contributed pretax to a retirement account on their behalf. 401(k) assets, but may also include some profit-sharing plan assets that do not have a 401(k) feature. [2] Section 403(b) of the Internal Revenue Code permits employees of certain charitable organizations, nonprofit hospitals, universities, and public schools to establish tax-sheltered retirement programs. These plans may invest in either annuity contracts or mutual fund shares. [3] These plans are deferred compensation arrangements for government employees and employees of certain tax-exempt organizations. [4] Includes Keoghs; target benefit plans; thrift savings plans, stock bonus plans, and money purchase plans without a 401(k) feature; and all other defined contribution plans not specified elsewhere.

Source: Investment Company Institute, Washington, DC, *Fundamentals, Investment Company Institute Research in Brief, "Mutual Funds and the Retirement Market in 2003"*; Vol. 13, No. 2, June 2004; <http://www.ici.org> (copyright).

Table 1205. **Individual Retirement Accounts (IRA) Plans—Value by Institution: 1990 to 2003**

[As of December 31 (637 represents $637,000,000,000). Estimated]

Institution	Amount (bil. dol.)								Percent distribution		
	1990	1995	1998	1999	2000	2001	2002	2003	1990	2000	2003
Total IRA assets	637	1,288	2,150	2,651	2,629	2,619	2,445	3,007	100	100	100
Bank and thrift deposits [1]	266	261	249	244	252	255	263	268	42	10	9
Life insurance companies [2]	40	81	156	202	202	210	267	315	6	8	10
Mutual funds.	139	470	968	1,259	1,230	1,160	1,032	1,306	22	47	43
Securities held in brokerage accounts [3]	191	477	776	947	945	994	883	1,117	30	36	37

[1] Includes Keogh deposits. [2] Annuities held by IRAs, excluding variable annuity mutual fund IRA assets. [3] Excludes mutual fund assets held through brokerage accounts, which are included in mutual funds.

Source: Investment Company Institute, Washington, DC, *Fundamentals, Investment Company Institute Research in Brief, "Mutual Funds and the Retirement Market in 2003"*; Vol. 13, No. 2, June 2004; <http://www.ici.org> (copyright).

Table 1206. **Assets of Private and Public Pension Funds by Type of Fund: 1990 to 2004**

[In billions of dollars (3,337 represents $3,337,000,000,000). As of end of year. Except for corporate equities, represents book value. Excludes social security trust funds, see Table 536]

Type of pension fund	1990	1995	1998	1999	2000	2001	2002	2003	2004
Total, all types	3,337	5,619	8,034	9,020	8,742	8,236	7,514	8,738	9,544
Private funds	2,197	3,769	5,353	5,999	5,821	5,411	4,893	5,812	6,447
Insured [1]	570	881	1,248	1,428	1,466	1,495	1,584	1,786	2,003
Noninsured [2, 3]	1,627	2,889	4,105	4,571	4,355	3,916	3,309	4,025	4,444
Credit market instruments [3]	464	608	621	720	624	637	663	677	712
Agency- and GSE-backed securities [4]	133	214	195	233	207	215	220	227	240
Corporate and foreign bonds	158	240	298	348	290	295	307	315	331
Corporate equities	606	1,278	1,948	2,081	1,915	1,562	1,097	1,492	1,690
Mutual fund shares.	40	327	668	898	946	862	752	994	1,174
Unallocated insurance contracts [5] . .	215	332	385	396	369	340	271	334	342
State and local pension funds [3]	801	1,308	1,965	2,247	2,124	1,965	1,727	1,967	2,072
Credit market instruments [3]	402	510	661	707	753	712	698	707	708
Agency- and GSE-backed securities [4]	63	63	106	129	167	152	152	158	159
Corporate and foreign bonds	142	189	280	310	340	339	335	339	333
Corporate equities	285	704	1,188	1,408	1,223	1,084	870	1,084	1,205
Federal government retirement funds [6] . .	340	541	716	774	797	860	894	959	1,024

[1] Annuity reserves held by life insurance companies, excluding unallocated contracts held by private pension funds. [2] Private defined benefit plans and defined contribution plans (including 401(k) type plans). [3] Includes other types of assets not shown separately. [4] GSE = Government-sponsored enterprises. [5] Assets held at life insurance companies (e.g., guaranteed investment contracts (GICs), variable annuities). [6] Includes the Federal Employees Thrift Savings Plan, the National Railroad Retirement Investment Trust, and nonmarketable government securities held by federal government retirement funds.

Source: Board of Governors of the Federal Reserve System, "Federal Reserve Statistical Release, Z.1, Flow of Funds Accounts of the United States"; published: 10 March 2005; <http://www.federalreserve.gov/releases/z1/20050310/>.

Banking, Finance, and Insurance **779**

Table 1207. Annual Revenues of Selected Securities Industries: 2000 to 2003

[In millions of dollars (331,497 represents $331,497 000,000). Covers taxable and tax-exempt employer firms only. Based on the North American Industry Classification System (NAICS), 1997; see text, Section 15. Based on Service Annual Survey; see Appendix III]

Kind of business	NAICS code	2000	2001	2002	2003
Total	523x	331,497	288,417	256,879	273,847
Securities and commodity contracts intermediation and brokerage	5231	227,841	191,007	163,080	173,111
Investment banking & securities dealing	52311	116,244	97,479	79,083	86,428
Securities brokerage	52312	106,933	88,757	79,257	81,838
Commodity contracts dealing	52313	1,920	1,980	1,985	2,171
Commodity contracts brokerage	52314	2,744	2,791	2,754	2,675
Other financial investment activities [1]	5239x	103,656	97,410	93,799	100,736
Portfolio management	52392	86,395	81,855	77,247	82,022
Investment advice	52393	17,261	15,555	16,553	18,714

[1] Excludes NAICS 52391 (miscellaneous intermediation) and NAICS 52399 (all other financial investment activities).

Source: U.S. Census Bureau, *Service Annual Survey: 2003.*

Table 1208. Securities Industry—Financial Summary: 1990 to 2003

[In billions of dollars, except as indicated. (71.4 represents $71,400,000,000)]

Type	1990	1995	1997	1998	1999	2000	2001	2002	2003
Number of firms	8,437	7,722	7,796	7,685	7,461	7,258	7,002	6,768	6,565
Revenues, total	71.4	143.4	207.2	235.0	266.8	349.5	280.1	221.8	219.0
Commissions	12.0	23.2	32.7	36.7	45.9	54.1	44.8	45.0	45.5
Trading/investment gains	15.7	29.0	36.0	32.8	55.5	70.8	39.0	24.2	38.8
Underwriting profits	3.7	8.9	14.6	16.2	17.8	18.7	16.9	14.7	17.2
Margin interest	3.2	6.5	10.6	12.7	15.2	24.5	13.9	6.4	5.3
Mutual fund sales	3.2	7.4	12.4	14.8	16.7	19.4	16.4	15.7	16.2
Other	33.4	68.5	101.0	121.7	115.7	161.9	149.1	115.8	96.0
Expenses, total	70.6	132.1	187.3	217.8	237.7	310.4	260.7	206.5	193.3
Interest expense	28.1	56.9	80.7	98.1	87.5	131.9	98.9	56.4	44.4
Compensation	22.9	41.5	58.6	65.0	81.7	95.2	83.5	74.9	77.4
Commissions/clearance paid	3.0	5.7	8.9	10.3	13.5	15.5	14.0	15.0	16.3
Other	16.6	28.0	39.2	44.3	55.0	67.8	64.2	60.3	55.1
Net income, pretax	0.8	11.3	20.0	17.2	29.1	39.1	19.4	15.3	25.7
Pre-tax profit margin (percent)	1.1	7.9	9.6	7.3	10.9	11.2	6.9	6.9	11.7
Pre-tax return on equity (percent) . .	2.2	20.1	27.1	19.4	27.8	31.1	13.8	10.7	17.6
Assets	657	1,494	2,079	2,187	2,537	2,866	3,371	3,261	3,980
Liabilities	623	1,435	1,997	2,092	2,423	2,728	3,227	3,119	3,831
Ownership equity	34	59	82	95	114	138	144	142	149

Source: U.S. Securities and Exchange Commission, *Annual Report.*

Table 1209. Insurance Carriers—Revenue by Product Line: 2002

[In billions of dollars (1,189.2 represents $1,189,200,000,000). Preliminary. Unless otherwise noted, represents net premiums earned. Covers only establishments of firms with payroll. Based on the 2002 Economic Census; see Appendix III. Numbers in parentheses represent North American Industry Classification System (NAICS), 1997 codes, see text, this section]

Product line	Total (5241)	Direct life/ health/ medical insurance carriers (52411)	Other direct insurance carriers (52412)	Reinsurance carriers (52413)
Total product line revenue	1,189.2	755.0	398.5	35.7
Life insurance	116.9	115.7	0.1	1.1
Accident, health and medical insurance	349.7	345.8	3.7	0.1
Property and casualty direct	321.0	0.7	319.3	1.0
Title insurance premiums earned—net	10.5	(NA)	10.5	(NA)
Other insurance premiums earned—net	12.5	5.5	7.0	(NA)
Reinsurance premiums—assumed.	59.9	14.1	17.0	28.8
Annuity revenue [1]	149.7	149.4	0.2	0.2
Realized capital gains (losses) on investment accounts	-7.2	-6.7	-0.6	0.1
Other investment income—net	133.7	102.5	27.1	4.1
Administrative services fees	24.0	24.0	(NA)	(Z)
Title fees [2]	2.5	(NA)	2.5	(Z)
Gross rents from real properties	2.2	1.9	0.3	(Z)
Other revenue	13.9	2.2	11.4	0.3

NA Not available.   Z Less than $50 million.   [1] Includes considerations and annuity fund deposit.   [2] Covers title search, title reconveyance, and title abstract service fees.

Source: U.S. Census Bureau, 2002 Economic Census, Finance and Insurance, Industry Series, *Insurance Carriers* (EC02-521-06), December 2004.

Table 1210. Life Insurance in Force and Purchases in the United States—Summary: 1990 to 2003

[As of December 31 or calendar year, as applicable (389 represents 389,000,000). Covers life insurance with life insurance companies only. Represents all life insurance in force on lives of U.S. residents whether issued by U.S. or foreign companies]

Year	Number of policies, total (mil.)	Life insurance in force			Life insurance purchases [2]					
		Value (bil. dol.)			Number (1,000)			Amount (bil. dol.)		
		Total [1]	Individual	Group	Total	Individual	Group	Total	Individual	Group
1990....	389	9,393	5,391	3,754	28,791	14,199	14,592	1,529	1,070	459
1995....	370	11,696	6,890	4,605	31,999	12,595	19,404	1,577	1,039	538
1996....	355	12,704	7,426	5,068	30,783	12,022	18,761	1,704	1,089	615
1997....	351	13,364	7,873	5,279	31,707	11,734	19,973	1,892	1,204	689
1998....	358	14,471	8,523	5,735	31,891	11,559	20,332	2,064	1,325	740
1999....	367	15,496	9,172	6,110	38,584	11,673	26,912	2,367	1,400	967
2000....	369	15,953	9,376	6,376	34,882	13,345	21,537	2,515	1,594	921
2001....	377	16,290	9,346	6,765	40,095	14,059	26,036	2,773	1,600	1,172
2002....	375	16,346	9,312	6,876	38,713	14,692	24,020	2,767	1,753	1,014
2003....	370	16,764	9,375	7,236	35,456	13,510	21,946	2,799	1,749	1,050

[1] Includes other types of policy not shown separately. [2] Excludes revivals, increases, dividend additions, and reinsurance acquired. Includes long-term credit insurance (life insurance on loans of more than 10 years' duration).

Source: American Council of Life Insurers, Washington, DC, *Life Insurers Fact Book*, annual (copyright).

Table 1211. U.S. Life Insurance Companies—Summary: 1990 to 2003

[As of December 31 or calendar year, as applicable (402.2 represents $402,200,000,000). Covers domestic and foreign business of U.S. companies. Beginning 1995 includes annual statement data for companies that primarily are health insurance companies]

Item	Unit	1990	1995	1996	1997	1998	1999	2000	2001	2002	2003
U.S. companies [1]	Number. . .	2,195	2,079	1,679	1,620	1,563	1,470	1,269	1,225	1,171	1,123
Income	**Bil. dol.** ...	**402.2**	**528.1**	**561.1**	**610.6**	**663.4**	**726.9**	**811.5**	**724.4**	**734.0**	**723.6**
Life insurance premiums......	Bil. dol. ...	76.7	102.8	107.6	115.0	119.9	120.3	130.6	125.3	134.5	124.2
Annuity considerations [2]	Bil. dol. ...	129.1	158.4	178.4	197.5	229.5	270.2	306.7	251.3	269.3	264.3
Health insurance premiums....	Bil. dol. ...	58.3	90.0	92.2	92.7	94.9	100.0	105.6	103.4	108.7	115.4
Investment and other........	Bil. dol. ...	138.2	176.9	182.9	205.3	219.1	236.4	268.5	244.5	221.5	219.6
Payments under life insurance and annuity contracts........	Bil. dol. ...	88.4	227.6	246.9	276.6	301.8	355.3	375.2	304.9	301.3	301.9
Payments to life insurance beneficiaries	Bil. dol. ...	24.6	34.5	36.3	37.5	40.1	41.4	44.1	46.5	48.2	50.6
Surrender values under life insurance [3]	Bil. dol. ...	18.0	19.5	24.5	24.0	26.8	32.8	27.2	30.7	32.9	35.2
Surrender values under annuity contracts [3, 4]	Bil. dol. ...	(NA)	105.4	115.7	140.8	154.5	198.3	214.0	151.3	142.9	139.0
Policyholder dividends	Bil. dol. ...	12.0	17.8	18.1	18.0	18.9	19.1	20.0	20.0	21.0	20.0
Annuity payments	Bil. dol. ...	32.6	48.5	51.1	55.1	60.4	62.5	68.7	55.2	55.9	55.9
Matured endowments........	Bil. dol. ...	0.7	1.0	0.7	0.6	0.6	0.5	0.6	0.5	0.6	0.6
Other payments	Bil. dol. ...	0.6	0.9	0.6	0.6	0.6	0.6	0.6	0.6	0.6	0.6
Health insurance benefit payments	Bil. dol. ...	40.0	64.7	66.7	67.4	70.0	74.5	78.8	76.3	78.7	81.7
BALANCE SHEET											
Assets	**Bil. dol.** ...	**1,408**	**2,144**	**2,328**	**2,579**	**2,827**	**3,071**	**3,182**	**3,269**	**3,380**	**3,806**
Government bonds	Bil. dol. ...	211	409	411	391	379	362	364	377	481	521
Corporate securities........	Bil. dol. ...	711	1,241	1,416	1,658	1,898	2,180	2,238	2,263	2,266	2,616
Percent of total assets....	Percent . .	50	58	61	64	67	71	70	69	67	69
Bonds	Bil. dol. ...	583	869	962	1,060	1,140	1,190	1,241	1,354	1,475	1,602
Stocks	Bil. dol. ...	128	372	454	598	758	990	997	909	791	1,014
Mortgages	Bil. dol. ...	270	212	212	210	216	230	237	244	251	261
Real estate	Bil. dol. ...	43	52	50	46	41	38	36	32	33	30
Policy loans	Bil. dol. ...	63	96	102	105	105	99	102	104	105	105
Other	Bil. dol. ...	110	133	137	169	187	163	204	248	244	273
Interest earned on assets [5]....	Percent . .	8.89	7.41	7.25	7.35	6.95	6.71	7.05	6.31	5.38	5.01
Obligations and surplus funds [6] ...	Bil. dol. ...	1,408	2,144	2,328	2,579	2,826	3,071	3,182	3,269	3,380	3,806
Policy reserves	**Bil. dol.** ...	**1,197**	**1,812**	**1,966**	**2,165**	**2,377**	**2,610**	**2,712**	**2,446**	**2,507**	**2,832**
Annuities [7]	Bil. dol. ...	798	1,213	1,312	1,455	1,608	1,781	1,841	1,516	1,550	1,807
Group...............	Bil. dol. ...	516	619	690	762	845	907	960	571	570	662
Individual	Bil. dol. ...	282	594	622	693	763	874	881	945	980	1,144
Supplementary contracts [8]..	Bil. dol. ...	17	25	28	28	31	32	34	13	14	14
Life insurance	Bil. dol. ...	349	511	556	606	656	705	742	816	833	889
Health insurance	Bil. dol. ...	33	63	70	75	82	92	96	101	111	122
Liabilities for deposit-type contracts [9]	Bil. dol. ...	18	20	20	20	21	21	21	338	364	405
Capital and surplus	Bil. dol. ...	91	151	147	160	173	181	188	191	202	224

NA Not available. [1] Beginning 1995 includes life insurance companies that sell accident and health insurance. [2] Beginning 2001 excludes certain deposit-type funds from income due to codification. [3] Beginning with 1995, "surrender values" include annuity withdrawals of funds, which were not included in prior years. [4] Beginning 2001, excludes payments under deposit-type contracts. [5] Net rate. [6] Includes other obligations not shown separately. [7] Beginning 2001, excludes reserves for guaranteed interest contracts (GICs). [8] Through 2000, includes reserves for contracts with and without life contingencies; beginning 2001 includes only reserves for contracts with life contingencies. [9] Policyholder dividend accumulations for all years. Beginning 2001, also includes liabilities for guaranteed interest contracts, supplementary contracts without life contingencies, and premium and other deposits.

Source: American Council of Life Insurers, Washington, DC, *Life Insurers Fact Book*, annual (copyright).

Table 1212. **Property and Casualty Insurance—Summary: 1998 to 2003**
[In billions of dollars (286.3 represents $286,300,000,000). Minus sign (-) indicates loss]

Item	1998	1999	2000	2001	2002	2003
Premiums, net written [1]	286.3	296.6	304.3	327.8	372.7	407.6
Automobile, private [2]	117.9	122.7	120.0	128.0	139.6	151.3
Automobile, commercial [2]	18.4	18.4	19.8	21.7	24.6	25.5
Liability other than auto [3]	34.0	33.0	34.2	38.9	48.8	58.7
Fire and allied lines	7.7	7.6	7.7	8.8	12.2	14.5
Homeowners' multiple peril	29.2	30.8	32.7	35.4	40.3	46.0
Commercial multiple peril [4]	10.4	10.3	11.7	13.0	15.3	16.3
Workers' compensation	24.2	23.1	26.2	27.1	30.0	32.9
Marine, inland and ocean	7.8	7.8	8.3	8.7	9.4	10.4
Accident and health	11.0	13.8	14.5	15.6	15.6	11.9
Other lines	25.7	29.1	29.2	30.6	36.9	40.1
Losses and expenses	(NA)	302.6	321.3	361.8	377.4	390.9
Underwriting gain/loss	(NA)	-19.9	-27.3	-50.2	-28.3	-3.2
Net investment income	(NA)	40.3	42.0	38.7	39.8	39.8
Operating earnings after taxes	(NA)	8.8	4.4	-13.6	4.3	22.9
Assets	938.0	947.3	946.8	984.1	1,055.1	1,239.8
Policyholders' surplus	339.5	342.0	324.5	295.4	291.9	359.7

NA Not available. [1] Excludes state funds. [2] Includes premiums for automobile liability and physical damage. [3] Includes the liability portion of commercial multiple peril, medical malpractice, product liability and other liability. [4] Nonliability portion only.
Source: Insurance Information Institute, New York, NY, *The III Insurance Fact Book*, annual (copyright).

Table 1213. **Automobile Insurance—Average Expenditures Per Insured Vehicle by State: 1995 to 2002**

[In dollars. Average expenditure equals total premiums written divided by liability car-years. A car-year is equal to 365 days of insured coverage for a single vehicle. The average expenditures for automobile insurance in a state are affected by a number of factors, including the underlying rate structure, the coverages purchased, the deductibles and limits selected, the types of vehicles insured, and the distribution of driver characteristics]

State	1995	2000	2002	State	1995	2000	2002	State	1995	2000	2002
U.S.	667	687	774	KS	474	540	586	ND	381	477	533
				KY	555	616	685	OH	531	579	639
AL	549	594	626	LA	788	806	926	OK	526	603	650
AK	730	770	884	ME	472	528	585	OR	565	625	682
AZ	727	792	877	MD	732	757	837	PA	667	699	783
AR	500	606	670	MA	898	946	984	RI	870	825	937
CA	794	667	778	MI	645	702	839	SC	582	620	702
CO	722	755	914	MN	628	696	800	SD	428	482	540
CT	881	871	965	MS	579	654	679	TN	519	592	632
DE	784	849	907	MO	573	612	666	TX	711	678	791
DC	959	996	1,040	MT	468	530	628	UT	547	620	700
FL	739	746	870	NE	452	533	589	VT	512	568	644
GA	597	674	739	NV	759	829	887	VA	553	576	625
HI	963	702	736	NH	609	665	731	WA	650	722	788
ID	447	505	560	NJ	1,013	977	1,113	WV	646	680	776
IL	612	652	726	NM	639	674	699	WI	506	545	609
IN	542	570	646	NY	906	939	1,087	WY	433	496	580
IA	429	479	547	NC	501	564	588				

Source: National Association of Insurance Commissioners (NAIC), Kansas City, MO, *Auto Insurance Database Report*, annual (copyright). Reprinted with permission of the NAIC. Further reprint or distribution strictly prohibited without prior written permission of the NAIC.

Table 1214. **Average Premiums for Renters and Homeowners Insurance by State: 2002**

[In dollars. Average premium equals premiums divided by exposure per house-years. A house-year is equal to 365 days of insured coverage for a single dwelling and is the standard measurement for homeowners insurance]

State	Renters [1]	Homeowners [2]	State	Renters [1]	Homeowners [2]	State	Renters [1]	Homeowners [2]
U.S.	186	593	KS	172	684	ND	121	528
			KY	155	480	OH	155	410
AL	182	533	LA	244	840	OK	269	800
AK	167	668	ME	128	416	OR	158	398
AZ	215	543	MD	145	477	PA	141	477
AR	213	616	MA	198	611	RI	176	606
CA	260	660	MI	184	577	SC	176	604
CO	183	660	MN	151	590	SD	119	469
CT	193	652	MS	240	668	TN [3]	193	536
DE	150	390	MO	177	550	TX [3]	269	1,238
DC	165	697	MT	152	547	UT	150	416
FL	217	786	NE	145	596	VT	138	493
GA	210	517	NV	220	531	VA	142	476
HI	201	565	NH	150	482	WA	168	501
ID	150	382	NJ	173	538	WV	154	447
IL	182	516	NM	200	490	WI	107	340
IN	174	508	NY	207	661	WY	152	551
IA	139	450	NC	164	527			

[1] Based on the HO-4 renters insurance policy for tenants. Includes broad named-peril coverage for the personal property of tenants. [2] Based on the HO-3 homeowner package policy for owner-occupied dwellings, 1-4 family units. Provides "all risks" coverage (except those specifically excluded in the policy) on buildings, broad named-peril coverage on personal property, and is the most common package written. [3] The Texas Insurance Commissioner promulgates residential policy forms which are similar but not identical to the standard forms. Insurers can use State-promulgated or standard forms.
Source: National Association of Insurance Commissioners (NAIC), Kansas City, MO, *Dwelling Fire, Homeowners Owner-Occupied, and Homeowners Tenant and Condominium/Cooperative Unit Owners Insurance* (copyright). Reprinted with permission of the NAIC. Further reprint or distribution strictly prohibited without prior written permission of the NAIC.

Table 1215. **Real Estate, Rental, and Leasing—Nonemployer Establishments and Receipts by Kind of Business: 1997 to 2002**

[1,397 represents 1,397,000. Includes only firms subject to federal income tax. Nonemployers are businesses with no paid employees. Data originate chiefly from administrative records of the Internal Revenue Service; see Appendix III. Based on the North American Industry Classification System 1997 (NAICS), see text, Section 15]

Kind of business	NAICS code	Establishments (1,000)			Receipts (mil. dol.)		
		1997	2000	2002	1997	2000	2002
Real estate & rental & leasing, total	53	1,397	1,696	1,880	101,704	133,398	161,790
Real estate	531	1,336	1,616	1,799	98,845	127,862	156,150
Lessors of real estate	5311	572	714	753	68,718	86,934	100,504
Offices of real estate agents & brokers	5312	530	522	570	17,556	22,623	26,007
Activities related to real estate	5313	235	380	476	12,571	18,305	29,640
Rental & leasing services	532	60	79	80	2,806	5,440	5,519
Automotive equipment rental & leasing	5321	15	19	20	591	995	904
Consumer goods rental	5322	14	17	17	521	766	705
General rental centers	5323	1	3	3	53	252	301
Commercial/industrial equipment rental & leasing	5324	31	41	40	1,641	3,426	3,610
Lessors of other nonfinancial intangible assets	533	(Z)	1	1	53	96	121

Z Less than 500.

Source: U.S. Census Bureau, "Nonemployer Statistics"; <http://www.census.gov/epcd/nonemployer/> and "2002 Economic Census, Nonemployer Statistics, Real estate and rental and leasing, United States"; published 24 November 2004; <http://www.census.gov/epcd/nonemployer/2002/us/US00053.HTM>.

Table 1216. **Real Estate, Rental and Leasing—Establishments, Employees, and Payroll: 2000 and 2002**

[300.2 represents 300,200. Covers establishments with payroll. Employees are for the week including March 12. Most government employees are excluded. For statement on methodology, see Appendix III]

Kind of business	NAICS code [1]	Establishments (1,000)		Employees (1,000)		Payroll (bil. dol.)	
		2000	2002	2000	2002	2000	2002
Real estate & rental & leasing, total	53	300.2	323.0	1,942	2,017	59.2	65.2
Real estate	531	234.9	257.2	1,280	1,352	40.4	45.8
Lessors of real estate	5311	108.2	109.1	501	515	12.5	14.2
Offices of real estate agents & brokers	5312	65.1	76.0	271	278	10.6	11.3
Activities related to real estate	5313	61.6	72.1	507	559	17.3	20.3
Rental & leasing services	532	63.2	63.6	636	641	17.2	18.0
Automotive equipment rental & leasing	5321	11.1	11.9	182	182	5.1	5.4
Passenger car rental & leasing	53211	5.2	5.6	129	131	3.4	3.6
Truck, utility trailer & RV rental & leasing	53212	5.8	6.3	53	51	1.7	1.8
Consumer goods rental [2]	5322	33.1	32.0	255	253	4.2	4.5
Video tape & disk rental	53223	19.6	18.4	152	151	1.6	1.7
General rental centers	5323	6.4	6.7	42	41	1.2	1.3
Commercial/industrial equipment rental & leasing	5324	12.6	13.0	157	166	6.7	6.8
Lessors of other nonfinancial intangible assets	533	2.1	2.2	26	24	1.6	1.4

[1] North American Industry Classification System, 1997; see text, Section 15. [2] Includes other kinds of business not shown separately.

Source: U.S. Census Bureau, "County Business Patterns"; published November 2004; <http://www.census.gov/epcd/cbp/view/cbpview.html>.

Table 1217. **Rental and Leasing Services—Revenue by Kind of Business: 1998 to 2003**

[In millions of dollars (85,002 represents $85,002,000,000). Based on the North American Industry Classification System (NAICS) 1997; see text, Section 15. Covers taxable and tax-exempt employer firms. Estimates have been adjusted using the results of the 1997 Economic Census. Based on Service Annual Survey; see Appendix III]

Kind of business	NAICS code	1998	1999	2000	2001	2002	2003
Rental & leasing services	532	85,002	93,605	101,188	99,126	96,910	97,806
Automotive equipment rental & leasing	5321	30,918	34,132	36,501	35,367	35,174	36,328
Passenger car rental & leasing	53211	20,072	22,137	23,769	23,288	23,500	23,848
Truck, utility trailer, & RV rental & leasing	53212	10,846	11,994	12,732	12,079	11,674	12,480
Consumer goods rental [1]	5322	15,776	17,392	18,029	18,445	18,271	19,360
Video tape & disk rental	53223	7,646	8,905	9,159	9,174	8,962	9,622
General rental centers	5323	4,317	4,904	5,252	4,819	4,892	5,215
Commercial/industrial equipment rental & leasing	5324	33,992	37,177	41,407	40,495	38,573	36,902

[1] Includes other kinds of business not shown separately.

Source: U.S. Census Bureau, *Service Annual Survey: 2003*.

No. 925.—PLACES OF AMUSEMENT—SUMMARY, BY KIND OF BUSINESS: 1939

NOTE.— The census covers places of amusement, except those operated by educational institutions; religious, charitable, or fraternal agencies; governmental or civic bodies; and nonprofit organizations.

KIND OF BUSINESS	Number of establishments	Receipts (thousands of dollars)	Active proprietors of unincorporated businesses	Employees, full-time and part-time (average for year)[1]	PAY ROLL (THOUSANDS OF DOLLARS)[1]		
					Total	Full-time	Part-time
Total	44, 917	998, 079	33, 971	223, 229	225, 481	205, 211	20, 270
Amusement devices	1, 093	7, 314	705	1, 600	1, 504	1, 363	141
Amusement parks	245	10, 123	148	3, 798	2, 997	2, 535	462
Bands and orchestras	550	4, 946	831	3, 467	3, 654	2, 978	676
Bathing beaches (not including municipal)	344	1, 994	264	682	534	465	69
Bicycle rentals	247	433	247	76	46	41	5
Billiard and pool parlors	12, 998	38, 631	12, 773	9, 261	5, 892	5, 348	544
Boat and canoe rental service	1, 382	1, 944	1, 341	413	276	211	65
Bowling alleys	4, 646	48, 819	4, 037	31, 557	17, 347	12, 862	4, 485
Clubs, baseball (professional)	276	24, 940	36	6, 430	10, 942	9, 910	1, 032
Dance halls, studios, and academies	2, 191	14, 156	2, 029	8, 128	4, 498	2, 872	1, 626
Race tracks, automobile	36	978	24	337	132	51	81
Race tracks, dog	11	2, 775	3	314	720	633	87
Race tracks, horse	45	40, 732	3	3, 795	7, 312	6, 028	1, 284
Riding academies	840	2, 875	765	1, 108	777	722	55
Shooting galleries	324	850	255	207	160	148	12
Skating rinks, ice	59	1, 693	24	493	503	441	62
Skating rinks, roller	1, 134	6, 550	1, 088	2, 624	1, 641	1, 243	398
Sports and athletic fields	78	5, 845	35	1, 354	1, 355	1, 145	210
Sports promoters	110	3, 409	78	1, 623	575	236	339
Swimming pools (not including municipal)	668	2, 815	516	1, 009	712	572	140
Theaters, motion-picture (including motion-picture theaters with vaudeville)	15, 115	673, 045	6, 717	125, 184	131, 583	124, 165	7, 418
Theaters, legitimate stage and opera; and theatrical productions	231	32, 461	83	4, 579	11, 459	11, 267	192
Other places of amusement [2]	2, 294	70, 751	1, 969	15, 190	20, 862	19, 975	887

[1] Employees and pay roll include paid executives of corporations but not the number and compensation of proprietors of unincorporated businesses.
[2] Includes statistics for the New York World's Fair and the Golden Gate International Exposition.

Source: Department of Commerce, Bureau of the Census; Census of Business, 1939; special report, Places of Amusement, and Vol. III, Service Businesses.

Source: Statistical Abstract of the United States: 1941 Edition.

Arts, Entertainment, and Recreation

This section presents data on the arts, entertainment, and recreation economic sector of the economy, and personal recreational activities, the arts and humanities, and domestic and foreign travel.

Arts, Entertainment, and Recreation Industry—The U.S. Census Bureau's *Service Annual Survey, Arts, Entertainment, and Recreation Sector*, provides estimates of operation revenue of taxable firms and revenues and expenses of firms exempt from federal taxes for industries in this sector of the economy. Data beginning 1998 are based on the North American Industry Classification System (NAICS). Most establishments were previously classified in the Standard Industrial Classification (SIC) in services, some in retail trade.

This new sector is comprised of industries which existed previously, were revised from previous industry definitions, or are completely new industries. Among those which existed previously are amusement and theme parks. Revised industries include museums. New industries include theater companies and dinner theaters. The following URL contains detailed information about NAICS and provides a comparison of the SIC and NAICS <http://www.census.gov/epcd/www /naics.html>. See also the text in Section 15, Business Enterprise.

The 1997 Economic Census was the first economic census to cover the new Information Sector of the economy. The Census, conducted every 5 years, for the years ending "2" and "7," provides information on the number of establishments, receipts, payroll and paid employees for the U.S. and various geographic levels.

Recreation and leisure activities— Data on the participation in various recreation and leisure time activities are based on several sample surveys. Data on participation in fishing, hunting, and other forms of wildlife-associated recreation are

published periodically by the U.S. Department of Interior, Fish and Wildlife Service. The most recent data are from the 2001 survey. Data on participation in various sports recreation activities are published by the National Sporting Goods Association. Mediamark, Inc. also conducts periodic surveys on sports and leisure activities, as well as other topics.

Parks and recreation—The Department of the Interior has responsibility for administering the national parks. The National Park Service publishes information on visits to national park areas in its annual report, *National Park Statistical Abstract. The National Parks: Index (year)* is an annual report which contains brief descriptions, with acreages, of each area administered by the service, plus certain "related" areas. The annual *Federal Recreation Fee Report* summarizes the prior year's recreation fee receipts and recreation visitation statistics for seven federal land managing agencies. Statistics for state parks are compiled by the National Association of State Park Directors.

Travel— Statistics on arrivals and departures to the United States are reported by the International Trade Administration (ITA), Office of Travel & Tourism Industries (OTTI). Data on domestic travel, business receipts and employment of the travel industry, and travel expenditures are published by the research department of the Travel Industry Association (TIA) and the national nonprofit center for travel and tourism research located in Washington, DC. Other data on household transportation characteristics are in Section 23, Transportation.

Statistical reliability—For a discussion of statistical collection and estimation, sampling procedures, and measures of statistical reliability applicable to Census Bureau data, see Appendix III.

U.S. Census Bureau, Statistical Abstract of the United States: 2006

Table 1218. **Arts, Entertainment and Recreation Services—Estimated Revenue: 2002 and 2003**

[(In millions of dollars (137,436 represents $137,436,000,000), except percent. For taxable and tax-exempt employer firms. Except where indicated, estimates adjusted using the results of the 1997 Economic Census. Minus sign (-) indicates decrease. Based on the Service Annual Survey, see Appendix III]

Industry	NAICS code [1]	Total			Taxable		
		2002	2003	Percent change, 2002-2003	2002	2003	Percent change, 2002-2003
Arts, entertainment, and recreation............	**71**	**137,436**	**145,771**	**6.1**	**114,329**	**121,935**	**6.7**
Performing arts, spectator sports..............	711	50,286	52,252	3.9	44,417	46,375	4.4
Performing arts companies [2]..............	7111	9,321	9,508	2.0	5,568	5,724	2.8
Spectator sports.......................	7112	20,224	20,386	0.8	20,224	20,386	0.8
Sports teams and clubs.................	711211	12,619	12,844	1.8	12,619	12,844	1.8
Racetracks...........................	711212	5,526	5,427	-1.8	5,526	5,427	-1.8
Other spectator sports	711219	2,078	2,116	1.8	2,078	2,116	1.8
Promoters of performing arts, sports and similar events................................	7113	9,385	10,137	8.0	7,268	8,044	10.7
Agents and managers for artists, athletes, entertainers and other public figures	7114	3,604	3,606	0.1	3,604	3,606	0.1
Independent artists, writers, and performers......	7115	7,753	8,615	11.1	7,753	8,615	11.1
Museums, historical sites, and similar institutions	712	7,735	8,205	6.1	913	1,001	9.6
Amusement, gambling, and recreation industries	713	79,415	85,314	7.4	68,999	74,559	8.1
Amusement parks and arcades	7131	9,295	9,778	5.2	9,295	9,778	5.2
Amusement and theme parks..............	71311	8,084	8,641	6.9	8,084	8,641	6.9
Amusement arcades....................	71312	1,211	1,138	-6.0	1,211	1,138	-6.0
Gambling industries......................	7132	24,300	28,756	18.3	24,300	28,756	18.3
Casinos (except casino hotels)..............	71321	16,923	19,947	17.9	16,923	19,947	17.9
Other gambling industries	71329	7,378	8,809	19.4	7,378	8,809	19.4
Other amusement and recreation industries	7139	45,820	46,780	2.1	35,404	36,024	1.8
Golf courses and country clubs.............	71391	16,738	16,195	-3.2	10,258	9,603	-6.4
Skiing facilities........................	71392	1,729	1,765	2.1	1,729	1,765	2.1
Marinas [3]...........................	71393	3,228	3,257	0.9	3,228	3,257	0.9
Fitness and recreational sports centers	71394	15,079	16,237	7.7	12,016	13,034	8.5
Bowling centers.......................	71395	3,315	3,550	7.1	3,315	3,550	7.1
All other amusement and recreation	71399	5,731	5,775	0.8	4,858	4,815	-0.9

[1] Based on the North American Industry Classification System 1997; see text, this section and Section 15, Business Enterprise. [2] Estimates for NAICS 71113 and 71119, not shown separately, have not been adjusted to the 1997 Economic Census. [3] Estimates not adjusted to the 1997 Economic Census.

Source: U.S. Census Bureau, "2003 Service Annual Survey, Arts, Entertainment, and Recreation Services". See <http://www.census.gov /econ/www/servmenu.html> issued February 2005.

Table 1219. **Arts, Entertainment and Recreation—Establishments, Revenue, Payroll, and Employees by Kind of Business (1997 NAICS Basis): 1997 and 2002**

[(104,715 represents $104,715,000,000) For establishments with payroll. Numbers in parentheses represent North American Industry Classification System (NAICS) 1997 codes, see text, Section 15. Based on the 1997 and 2002 Economic Census; see Appendix III]

Kind of business	NAICS code	Number of establishments		Revenue (mil. dol.)		Annual payroll (mil. dol.)		Paid employees (1,000)	
		1997	2002	1997	2002	1997	2002	1997	2002
Arts, entertainment and recreation, total	**71**	**99,099**	**111,128**	**104,715**	**137,782**	**32,787**	**43,075**	**1,588**	**1,896**
Performing arts, spectator sports, and related industries............	711	30,566	38,181	37,619	57,708	14,456	21,145	327	422
Performing arts	7111	9,199	9,353	8,570	10,697	2,725	3,206	122	138
Spectator sports	7112	3,881	4,314	13,656	21,933	6,151	10,175	92	107
Promoters of performing arts, sports and similar events........	7113	3,941	4,603	6,622	11,612	1,401	2,071	72	100
Agents and managers for artists, athletes, entertainers and others...	7114	2,532	4,043	2,410	4,189	911	1,457	13	22
Museums, historical sites, and similar institutions	712	5,580	6,651	6,764	8,577	1,837	2,912	92	122
Amusement, gambling, and recreation industries.............	713	62,859	65,462	57,832	76,293	15,776	21,070	1,134	1,303
Amusement parks and arcades	7131	3,344	3,196	8,418	9,622	1,962	2,111	139	123
Gambling industries	7132	2,005	2,201	13,042	20,181	2,504	3,726	133	162
Other amusement and recreation services	7139	57,510	60,065	36,372	46,490	11,310	15,233	862	1,018

Source: U.S. Census Bureau, "2002 Economic Census, Industry Series Reports, Arts, Entertainment and Recreation"; published summer 2004; <http://www.census.gov/econ/census02/guide/INDRPT71.HTM>.

786 Arts, Entertainment, and Recreation

Table 1220. **Arts, Entertainment, and Recreation—Nonemployer Establishments and Receipts by Kind of Business (NAICS Basis): 1997 to 2002**

[693.3 represents 693,300. Includes only firms subject to federal income tax. Nonemployers are businesses with no paid employees]

Kind of business	NAICS code [1]	Establishments (1,000)			Receipts (mil. dol.)		
		1997	2000	2002	1997	2000	2002
Arts, entertainment, and recreation	71	693.3	781.7	866.0	14,366	17,713	20,000
Performing arts, spectator sports, and related industries	711	536.0	645.4	732.9	10,252	13,008	14,808
Performing arts companies	7111	10.8	19.3	26.0	320	576	677
Spectator sports	7112	65.8	67.3	95.7	1,433	1,481	1,774
Promoters of performing arts, sports, and similar events	7113	12.8	23.1	29.3	513	851	1,100
Agents/managers for artists, athletes, and other public figures	7114	15.5	27.1	28.1	529	857	969
Independent artists, writers and performers	7115	431.1	508.6	553.8	7,456	9,244	10,289
Museums, historical sites, and similar institutions	712	1.8	3.6	4.4	37	52	66
Amusement, gambling, and recreation industries	713	155.6	132.7	128.7	4,077	4,653	5,125
Amusement parks and arcades	7131	7.2	5.4	5.2	463	291	322
Gambling industries	7132	2.7	5.9	7.3	197	532	875
Other amusement and recreation services. . .	7139	145.7	121.3	116.2	3,417	3,830	3,929

[1] Based on the North American Industry Classification System 1997, see text, Section 15.

Source: U.S. Census Bureau, Nonemployer Statistics; <http://www.census.gov/epcd/nonemployer/> and 2002 Economic Census: Nonemployer Statistics; published 30 November 2004; <http://www.census.gov/epcd/nonemployer/2002/us/US000.HTM>.

Table 1221. **Arts, Entertainment, and Recreation—Establishments, Payroll, and Employees by Kind of Business (NAICS Basis): 2000 and 2002**

[(1,741.5 represents 1,741,500). For establishments with payroll. See Appendix III]

Kind of business	NAICS code [1]	Establishments		Paid employees [2] (1,000)		Annual payroll (mil. dol.)	
		2000	2002	2000	2002	2000	2002
Arts, entertainment, & recreation	71	103,816	110,375	1,741.5	1,801.0	43,204	47,724
Performing arts, spectator sports	711	33,859	38,191	351.9	370.3	19,090	21,655
Performing arts companies	7111	9,253	9,366	126.4	132.5	3,251	3,331
Theater companies & dinner theaters	71111	3,367	3,449	63.4	66.9	1,469	1,603
Dance companies	71112	584	648	10.7	10.0	216	210
Musical groups & artists	71113	4,497	4,552	44.0	49.0	1,341	1,316
Other performing arts companies	71119	805	717	8.3	6.7	226	202
Spectator sports	7112	4,461	4,418	100.2	101.5	9,215	10,516
Sports teams & clubs	711211	684	767	36.3	38.4	7,587	8,783
Racetracks	711212	899	879	45.8	44.9	994	1,028
Other spectator sports	711219	2,878	2,772	18.1	18.3	633	705
Promoters of performing arts, sports, and similar events	7113	4,394	5,008	71.8	80.0	1,917	2,209
Promoters of performing arts, sports, & similar events with facilities	71131	1,107	1,451	44.3	51.1	787	1,069
Promoters of performing arts, sports, & similar events without facilities	71132	3,287	3,557	27.6	28.9	1,130	1,139
Agents/managers for artists, athletes, and other public figures	7114	3,048	3,551	16.0	17.1	1,117	1,281
Independent artists, writers, & performers.	7115	12,703	15,848	37.5	39.2	3,589	4,318
Museums, historical sites, & similar institutions . . .	712	5,777	6,633	110.4	116.1	2,549	2,900
Museums	71211	3,988	4,464	75.4	78.0	1,765	1,973
Historical sites	71212	892	1,002	8.3	8.9	143	164
Zoos & botanical gardens	71213	414	525	20.5	22.3	509	582
Nature parks & other similar institutions	71219	483	642	6.2	7.0	133	182
Amusement, gambling, & recreation industries . . .	713	64,180	65,551	1,279.2	1,314.5	21,564	23,169
Amusement parks & arcades	7131	2,879	2,992	124.0	116.5	2,277	2,150
Amusement & theme parks	71311	716	772	102.8	94.1	2,011	1,858
Amusement arcades	71312	2,163	2,220	21.3	22.4	266	291
Gambling industries	7132	2,191	2,224	202.6	221.9	4,757	5,504
Casinos (except casino hotels)	71321	537	562	150.2	164.0	3,592	4,121
Other gambling industries	71329	1,654	1,662	52.4	57.9	1,165	1,383
Other amusement & recreation services.	7139	59,110	60,335	952.6	976.1	14,531	15,515
Golf courses & country clubs	71391	11,885	11,842	297.9	290.0	6,243	6,591
Skiing facilities	71392	389	379	56.9	63.9	452	521
Marinas	71393	4,126	4,021	24.8	23.0	640	676
Fitness & recreational sports centers	71394	23,003	25,477	382.8	422.3	4,499	5,024
Bowling centers	71395	5,234	4,898	87.9	81.6	888	919
All other amusement & recreation industries	71399	14,473	13,718	102.4	95.2	1,808	1,784

[1] North American Industry Classification System 1997 code; see text, this section and Section 15, Business Enterprise. [2] For employees on the payroll for the period including March 12.

Source: U.S. Census Bureau, "County Business Patterns"; 2002 data published November 2004; <http://www.census.gov/prod/www/abs/cbptotal.html>.

Arts, Entertainment, and Recreation **787**

Table 1222. Expenditures Per Consumer Unit for Entertainment and Reading: 1985 to 2003

[Data are annual averages. In dollars, except as indicated. Based on Consumer Expenditure Survey; see text, Section 13, Income, Expenditures, and Wealth for description of survey. See also headnote, Table 669. For composition of regions, see map, inside front cover]

Year and characteristic	Entertainment and reading Total	Percent of total expenditures	Entertainment Total	Fees and admissions	Television, radios, and sound equipment	Other equipment and services [1]	Reading
1985	1,311	5.6	1,170	320	371	479	141
1987	1,335	5.5	1,193	323	379	491	142
1988	1,479	5.7	1,329	353	416	560	150
1989	1,581	5.7	1,424	377	429	618	157
1990	1,575	5.6	1,422	371	454	597	153
1991	1,635	5.5	1,472	378	468	627	163
1992	1,662	5.6	1,500	379	492	629	162
1993	1,792	5.8	1,626	414	590	621	166
1994	1,732	5.5	1,567	439	533	595	165
1995	1,775	5.5	1,612	433	542	637	163
1996	1,993	5.9	1,834	459	561	814	159
1997	1,977	5.7	1,813	471	577	766	164
1998	1,907	5.4	1,746	449	535	762	161
1999	2,050	5.5	1,891	459	608	824	159
2000	2,009	5.3	1,863	515	622	727	146
2001	2,094	5.3	1,953	526	660	767	141
2002	2,218	5.5	2,079	542	692	845	139
2003, total	**2,187**	**5.4**	**2,060**	**494**	**730**	**835**	**127**
Age of reference person:							
Under 25 years old	1,003	4.5	950	233	463	254	53
25 to 34 years old	2,057	5.1	1,958	402	780	776	99
35 to 44 years old	2,633	5.6	2,519	638	874	1,007	114
45 to 54 years old	2,557	5.1	2,407	624	865	918	150
55 to 64 years old	2,582	5.8	2,414	597	744	1,073	168
65 to 74 years old	2,165	6.4	2,016	383	560	1,072	149
75 years old and over	1,043	4.2	909	244	415	249	134
Origin of reference person:							
Hispanic	1,293	3.7	1,245	250	621	373	48
Non-Hispanic	2,289	5.5	2,153	522	742	889	136
Race of reference person:							
White and other	2,339	5.5	2,202	539	745	916	137
Black	1,059	3.7	1,007	163	616	228	52
Region of residence:							
Northeast	2,270	5.4	2,117	614	776	726	153
Midwest	2,119	5.3	1,978	489	738	751	141
South	1,905	5.1	1,812	365	696	751	93
West	2,640	5.8	2,494	606	736	1,152	146
Size of consumer unit:							
One person	1,134	4.8	1,041	253	475	314	93
Two or more persons	2,624	5.5	2,482	595	836	1,050	142
Two persons	2,580	5.9	2,421	507	740	1,173	159
Three persons	2,393	5.0	2,263	595	858	810	130
Four persons	2,956	5.4	2,821	773	957	1,091	135
Five persons or more	2,664	5.1	2,554	639	947	967	110
Income before taxes:							
Total complete reporting [2]	2,288	5.4	2,155	511	745	899	133
Quintiles of income:							
Lowest 20 percent	761	4.1	703	131	370	202	58
Second 20 percent	1,395	5.2	1,307	187	530	589	88
Third 20	1,890	5.2	1,776	323	690	764	114
Fourth 20	2,622	5.2	2,471	573	874	1,004	151
Highest 20	4,770	5.8	4,516	1,340	1,260	1,915	254
Incomplete reporting of income	1,729	5.4	1,634	404	647	582	95

[1] Other equipment and services include pets, toys, and playground equipment; sports, exercise, and photographic equipment; and recreational vehicles. [2] Income values derived from "complete income reporters" only. Represents the combined income of all consumer unit members 14 years or over during the 12 months preceding the interview. A complete reporter is a consumer unit providing values for at least one of the major sources of income.

Source: U.S. Bureau of Labor Statistics, Consumer Expenditure Survey, annual. See also <http://www.bls.gov/cex/>.

Table 1223. **Personal Consumption Expenditures for Recreation: 1990 to 2003**

[In billions of dollars (290.2 represents $290,200,000,000), except percent. Represents market value of purchases of goods and services by individuals and nonprofit institutions. See also headnote from Table 418]

Type of product or service	1990	1995	1999	2000	2001	2002	2003
Total recreation expenditures	290.2	418.1	546.1	585.7	604.0	628.3	660.7
Percent of total personal consumption [1]	7.6	8.4	8.7	8.7	8.6	8.5	8.5
Books and maps	16.2	23.2	31.5	33.7	34.6	36.9	38.5
Magazines, newspapers, and sheet music	21.6	27.5	33.5	35.0	35.0	35.3	36.6
Nondurable toys and sport supplies	32.8	44.4	54.7	56.6	57.6	59.0	60.2
Wheel goods, sports and photographic equipment [2]	29.7	39.7	52.6	57.6	59.2	60.6	68.0
Video and audio products, computer equipment, and							
musical instruments	53.0	81.5	108.1	116.6	115.5	119.1	121.3
Video and audio goods, including musical instruments	44.1	57.2	67.8	72.8	73.6	74.9	75.2
Computers, peripherals, and software	8.9	24.3	40.4	43.8	42.0	44.2	46.1
Radio and television repair	3.2	3.6	4.1	4.2	4.0	4.0	4.0
Flowers, seeds, and potted plants	10.9	14.0	17.1	18.0	18.0	18.0	18.8
Admissions to specified spectator amusements	15.1	21.1	28.4	30.4	32.2	34.6	35.6
Motion picture theaters	5.1	5.6	7.9	8.6	9.0	9.6	9.9
Legitimate theaters and opera, and entertainments							
of nonprofit institutions [3]	5.2	8.1	9.9	10.3	10.9	11.5	11.6
Spectator sports [4]	4.8	7.4	10.6	11.5	12.4	13.5	14.1
Clubs and fraternal organizations except insurance [5]	13.5	17.4	18.0	19.0	20.0	21.1	22.1
Commercial participant amusements [6]	25.2	48.8	68.8	75.8	79.6	83.5	89.2
Pari-mutuel net receipts	3.5	3.7	4.9	5.0	5.1	5.3	5.3
Other [7]	65.4	93.4	124.3	133.9	143.2	151.1	160.9

[1] See Table 658. [2] Includes boats and pleasure aircraft. [3] Except athletic. [4] Consists of admissions to professional and amateur athletic events and to racetracks, including horse, dog, and auto. [5] Consists of current expenditures (including consumption of fixed capital) of nonprofit clubs and fraternal organizations and dues and fees paid to proprietary clubs. [6] Consists of billiard parlors; bowling alleys; dancing, riding, shooting, skating, and swimming places; amusement devices and parks; golf courses; sightseeing buses and guides; private flying operations; casino gambling; and other commercial participant amusements. [7] Consists of net receipts of lotteries and expenditures for purchases of pets and pet care services, cable TV, film processing, photographic studios, sporting and recreation camps, video cassette rentals, and recreational services, not elsewhere classified.

Source: U.S. Department of Commerce, Bureau of Economic Analysis, National Income and Product Accounts, 1929–2003; and Survey of Current Business. See also <http://www.bea.doc.gov/bea/dn/nipaweb/selecttable.asp?selected=N> (revised as 5 August 2004).

Table 1224. **Performing Arts—Selected Data: 1985 to 2003**

[Sales, receipts and expenditures in millions of dollars (209 represents $209,000,000). For season ending in year shown, except as indicated]

Item	1985	1990	1995	1997	1998	1999	2000	2001	2002	2003
Legitimate theater: [1]										
Broadway shows:										
New productions	33	40	33	37	33	39	37	28	37	36
Attendance (mil.)	7.3	8.0	9.0	10.6	11.5	11.7	11.4	11.9	11.0	11.4
Playing weeks [2, 3]	1,078	1,070	1,120	1,349	1,442	1,441	1,464	1,484	1,434	1,544
Gross ticket sales	209	282	406	499	558	588	603	666	643	721
Broadway road tours:										
Attendance (mil.)	8.2	11.1	15.6	17.6	15.2	14.6	11.7	11.0	11.7	12.4
Playing weeks	993	944	1,242	1,334	1,127	1,082	888	823	863	877
Gross ticket sales	226	367	701	782	721	707	572	541	593	642
Nonprofit professional theatres: [4]										
Companies reporting [5]	217	185	215	197	189	313	262	363	1,146	1,274
Gross income	234.7	307.6	444.4	565.0	570.0	740.0	791.0	961.1	1,436.0	1,481.0
Earned income	146.1	188.4	281.2	349.9	342.0	442.0	466.0	554.5	761.0	787.0
Contributed income	88.6	119.2	163.1	215.1	228.0	298.0	325.0	406.6	675.0	694.0
Gross expenses	239.3	306.3	444.9	526.6	518.5	701.0	708.0	923.6	1,405.0	1,476.0
Productions	2,710	2,265	2,646	2,295	2,135	3,921	3,241	4,787	10,000	13,000
Performances	52,341	46,131	56,608	51,453	46,628	64,556	66,123	81,828	157,000	170,000
Total attendance (mil.)	14.2	15.2	18.6	17.2	14.6	18.0	22.0	21.1	32.2	34.3
OPERA America professional										
member companies: [6]										
Number of companies reporting [7] . . .	97	98	88	91	89	95	98	96	86	89
Expenses [7]	216.4	321.2	435.0	534.1	556.3	591.1	636.7	685.1	684.4	691.6
Performances [8]	1,909	2,336	2,251	2,137	2,222	2,200	2,153	2,031	1,868.0	1,730
Total attendance (mil.) [8, 9]	6.7	7.5	6.5	6.9	6.6	6.6	6.7	6.5	4.9	5.9
Main season attendance (mil.) [8, 10] . .	3.3	4.1	3.9	4.0	3.7	4.0	4.3	4.2	3.2	3.1
Symphony orchestras: [11]										
Concerts	19,573	18,931	29,328	26,906	31,766	31,549	33,154	36,437	37,118	38,182
Attendance (mil.)	24.0	24.7	30.9	31.9	32.2	30.8	31.7	31.5	30.3	27.8
Gross revenue	252.4	377.5	536.2	575.5	627.6	671.8	734.0	774.7	763.6	781.2
Operating expenses	426.1	621.7	858.8	937.1	1,012.0	1,088.0	1,126.3	1,285.9	1,311.9	1,314.8
Support	188.1	257.8	351.0	401.1	459.7	486.0	521.0	559.6	580.0	575.7

[1] Source: The League of American Theaters and Producers, Inc, New York, NY. For season ending in year shown. [2] All shows (new productions and holdovers from previous seasons). [3] Eight performances constitute one playing week. [4] Source: Theatre Communications Group, New York, NY. For years ending on or prior to August 31. [5] Beginning in 2002, nonprofit theatre data is based on survey responses and extrapolated data from IRS Form 990. [6] Source: OPERA America, Washington, DC. For years ending on or prior to August 31. [7] U.S. companies. [8] Prior to 1993, and for 1999, U.S. and Canadian companies; 1993 to 1998, U.S. companies only, "2000 - 2004 U.S. companies only". [9] Includes educational performances, outreach, etc. [10] For paid performances. [11] Source: American Symphony Orchestra League, Inc., New York, NY. For years ending August 31. Prior to 1995, represents 254 U.S. orchestras; beginning 1995, represents all U.S. orchestras, excluding college/university and youth orchestras. Also, beginning 1995, data based on 1,200 orchestras.

Source: Compiled from sources listed in footnotes; <http://www.broadway.org>; <http://www.tcg.org>; <http://www.operaam.org>; <http://www.symphony.org>.

Arts, Entertainment, and Recreation 789

Table 1225. **Arts and Humanities—Selected Federal Aid Programs: 1990 to 2003**

[In millions of dollars (170.8 represents $170,800,000), except as indicated. For fiscal year ending September 30]

Type of fund and program	1990	1995	1997	1998	1999	2000	2001	2002	2003
National Endowment for the Arts:									
Funds available [1]	170.8	152.1	98.4	85.3	85.0	85.2	94.0	98.6	101.0
Program appropriation	124.3	109.0	65.8	64.3	66.0	66.0	86.7	95.8	95.1
Grants awarded (number).	4,475	3,685	1,098	1,459	1,675	1,882	2,093	2,138	1,925
Funds obligated [2, 3]	157.6	147.9	94.4	82.3	82.6	83.5	92.5	96.2	99.3
National Endowment for the Humanities:									
Funds available [1]	140.6	152.3	94.8	94.0	95.5	102.6	106.8	110.1	111.6
Program appropriation	114.2	125.7	80.0	80.0	80.0	82.7	86.4	89.9	89.3
Matching funds [4]	26.3	25.7	13.9	13.9	13.9	15.1	15.6	16.1	16.0
Grants awarded (number).	2,195	1,871	900	852	874	1,230	1,290	1,252	963
Funds obligated [2]	141.0	151.8	94.8	92.7	92.1	100.0	105.7	106.1	100.1
Education programs	16.3	19.2	10.5	10.8	10.3	13.0	12.1	12.1	11.3
State programs	29.6	32.0	29.5	29.1	29.3	30.6	32.1	32.8	33.0
Research grants	22.5	22.2	8.5	7.7	6.6	6.9	7.0	7.0	7.9
Fellowship program	15.3	16.5	5.6	5.7	5.6	6.1	7.0	7.7	6.9
Challenge [5]	14.6	13.8	9.9	9.9	9.9	10.8	11.9	13.4	8.3
Public programs	25.4	25.8	12.6	11.1	12.2	11.8	16.3	13.2	12.7
Preservation and access	17.5	22.2	18.2	18.4	18.2	20.7	19.2	19.8	20.7

[1] Includes other funds, shown separately. Excludes administrative funds. [2] Includes obligations for new grants, supplemental awards on previous years' grants, and program contracts. [3] Beginning with 1997 data, the grantmaking structure changed from discipline-based categories to thematic ones. [4] Represents federal funds obligated only upon receipt or certification by Endowment of matching nonfederal gifts. [5] Program designed to stimulate new sources and higher levels of giving to institutions for the purpose of guaranteeing long-term stability and financial independence. Program usually requires a match of at least 3 private dollars to each federal dollar. Funds for challenge grants are not allocated by program area because they are awarded on a grant-by-grant basis.

Source: U.S. National Endowment for the Arts, *Annual Report;* and U.S. National Endowment for the Humanities, *Annual Report.* <http://arts.endow.gov/>and <http://www.neh.gov/>.

Table 1226. **Attendance Rates for Various Arts Activities: 2002**

[In percent. For persons 18 years old and over. Represents attendance at least once in the prior 12 months. Excludes elementary and high school performances. Based on the 2002 household survey Public Participation in the Arts. Data are subject to sampling error; see source. See also Tables 1227 and 1228]

Item	Jazz perfor- mance	Classical music perfor- mance	Musical plays	Non- musical play	Ballet	Art museum	Arts/ craft fairs	Historic parks	Reading liter- ature [1]
Total	10.8	11.6	17.1	12.3	3.9	26.5	33.4	31.6	46.7
Sex:									
Male	10.7	10.3	14.0	10.3	2.5	24.6	27.0	30.5	37.6
Female	10.8	12.7	20.0	14.2	5.1	28.2	39.2	32.5	55.1
Race and ethnicity:									
Hispanic	6.2	5.5	6.9	6.2	1.6	16.1	20.3	17.2	26.5
White alone	11.4	13.7	20.1	14.2	4.7	29.5	38.0	36.0	51.4
African American alone. . .	12.7	4.5	10.3	7.1	1.5	14.8	9.7	17.8	37.1
Other alone	7.3	10.3	11.9	10.0	2.3	32.7	25.8	30.4	43.7
Age:									
18 to 24 years old	10.5	7.8	14.8	11.4	2.6	23.7	29.2	28.3	42.8
25 to 34 years old	10.8	9.0	15.4	10.7	3.5	26.7	33.5	33.3	47.7
35 to 44 years old	13.0	10.7	19.1	13.0	4.9	27.4	37.2	35.8	46.6
45 to 54 years old	13.9	15.2	19.3	15.2	5.1	32.9	38.8	38.0	51.6
55 to 64 years old	8.8	15.6	19.7	13.8	3.3	27.8	35.1	31.6	48.9
65 to 74 years old	7.6	12.5	16.6	13.0	3.3	23.4	31.1	24.2	45.3
75 years old and older . . .	3.9	9.5	10.1	5.4	2.2	13.4	15.7	12.8	36.7
Education:									
Grade school	0.9	1.5	1.6	1.1	-	4.5	8.4	6.3	14.0
Some high school	2.7	1.9	4.1	3.7	0.8	7.7	14.0	11.4	23.4
High school graduate	5.3	4.5	9.1	5.7	1.2	14.2	25.7	20.2	37.7
Some college	12.2	11.5	19.4	12.7	3.9	29.0	38.2	36.5	52.9
College graduate	19.4	21.9	30.2	22.5	7.2	46.6	49.3	51.2	63.1
Graduate school	24.0	34.1	37.6	31.8	12.9	58.6	51.9	56.8	74.3
Income:									
Less than $10,000	5.1	6.7	7.6	5.3	1.5	12.4	19.7	14.1	32.1
$10,000 to $19,999	5.4	5.2	8.2	5.4	1.9	14.0	21.4	14.9	37.5
$20,000 to $29,999	6.3	6.3	8.6	6.0	2.4	16.2	24.5	20.8	37.5
$30,000 to $39,999	10.9	10.3	13.6	10.0	2.8	23.3	33.2	28.6	44.1
$40,000 to $49,999	10.3	12.9	16.1	12.2	3.6	25.3	34.6	32.7	47.9
$50,000 to $74,999	11.2	12.4	21.5	14.0	4.3	30.4	40.3	39.1	52.3
$75,000 or More	18.2	19.9	29.3	21.8	7.2	44.6	46.5	50.9	60.8

- Represents or rounds to zero. [1] Includes novels, short stories, poetry, and/or plays.

Source: U.S. National Endowment for the Arts. Research Division Report # 45, *2002 Survey of Public Participation in the Arts.* See also <http://www.nea.gov/pub/ResearchReportschrono.html>.

790 Arts, Entertainment, and Recreation

Table 1227. Participation in Various Leisure Activities: 2002

[In percent, except as indicated (205.9 represents 205,900,000). **For persons 18 years old and over.** Covers activities engaged in at least once in the prior 12 months. See headnote, Table 1226.]

Item	Adult popu-lation (mil.)	Attendance at—			Participation in—				
		Movies	Sports events	Amuse-ment park	Exercise program	Playing sports	Charity work	Home improve-ment/ repair	Garden-ing
Total	205.9	60.0	35.0	41.7	55.1	30.4	29.0	42.4	47.3
Sex:									
Male	98.7	59.5	41.4	40.4	55.0	38.8	25.6	46.3	37.1
Female	107.2	60.5	29.2	42.9	55.1	22.7	32.1	38.9	56.7
Race and Ethnicity:									
Hispanic	22.7	52.5	26.4	38.9	40.1	22.3	15.3	28.0	34.8
White alone	150.1	63.0	38.4	42.8	59.1	33.0	32.5	47.7	52.3
African American alone. . .	23.7	49.2	27.0	36.6	46.1	23.1	22.7	26.3	30.3
Other alone	9.5	58.1	22.3	43.9	50.4	26.9	22.5	33.8	41.3
Age:									
18 to 24 years old	26.8	82.8	46.0	57.6	61.3	49.4	25.3	21.1	20.7
25 to 34 years old	36.9	73.3	41.8	56.2	60.2	39.6	26.0	41.1	41.4
35 to 44 years old	44.2	68.0	42.2	53.3	59.5	36.6	33.2	53.0	51.8
45 to 54 years old	39.0	60.4	35.8	37.1	58.6	28.6	33.4	54.9	55.4
55 to 74 years old	25.9	46.6	25.5	27.1	48.4	16.0	28.1	44.8	56.6
65 to 74 years old	17.6	32.2	19.7	18.4	47.0	13.7	28.8	38.4	57.2
75 years old and over . . .	15.5	19.5	11.1	9.6	31.3	6.0	21.3	22.1	47.9
Education:									
Grade school	11.6	19.5	9.4	17.2	21.0	6.9	8.2	19.5	32.5
Some high school	20.1	39.4	17.4	30.6	32.7	17.2	12.5	24.9	31.2
High school graduate	63.8	51.7	28.3	37.9	45.6	22.6	20.2	35.6	43.8
Some college	56.9	68.7	39.9	48.9	62.3	35.2	33.1	46.5	49.6
College graduate	36.1	77.1	51.0	50.1	73.2	45.2	42.6	56.0	56.1
Graduate school	17.4	77.5	48.3	44.0	77.3	43.6	53.1	61.6	63.3
Income:									
Less than $10,000.	14.4	38.7	16.5	30.4	36.5	15.0	16.2	19.7	32.2
$10,000 to $19,999	22.7	41.8	20.1	30.7	42.0	18.5	18.8	23.5	38.8
$20,000 to $29,999	25.0	48.3	23.0	34.7	45.2	21.4	20.7	28.4	40.9
$30,000 to $39,999	24.2	57.5	30.0	39.3	53.3	26.6	27.4	42.0	46.6
$40,000 to $49,999	17.6	63.1	34.8	42.6	55.0	29.3	29.1	46.0	49.1
$50,000 to $74,999	34.7	69.3	44.8	50.2	63.0	36.0	35.3	53.6	54.4
$75,000 or more	45.8	79.4	53.3	54.0	72.5	48.0	41.5	61.2	56.3
Not reported	21.5	51.0	28.4	31.4	45.1	22.6	23.2	33.6	42.9

Source: U.S. National Endowment for the Arts. *Research Division Report #45. 2002 Survey of Public Participation in the Arts.* See also <http://www.nea.gov/pub/ResearchReportschrono.html>.

Table 1228. Participation in Various Arts Activities: 2002

[In percent. **For persons 18 years old and over.** Covers activities engaged in at least once in the prior 12 months. See headnote in Table 1226]

Item	Playing classical music	Other dancing [1]	Drawing	Pottery work [2]	Weaving	Photog-raphy [3]	Creative writing	Buying art work	Singing in groups
Total	1.8	4.2	8.6	6.9	16.0	11.5	7.0	29.5	4.8
Sex:									
Male	1.5	3.3	6.4	4.9	2.4	10.8	5.8	29.7	3.8
Female	2.1	4.9	10.6	8.7	28.5	12.1	8.2	29.3	5.7
Race and Ethnicity:									
Hispanic	0.7	4.2	6.8	5.1	12.5	6.7	4.0	37.5	2.9
White alone	2.1	4.1	9.4	7.6	17.6	12.8	7.6	28.9	4.5
African American alone. . .	0.4	3.5	5.6	4.1	9.4	7.6	7.4	35.9	9.1
Other alone	2.3	5.8	7.4	6.5	14.9	11.9	5.3	26.3	3.5
Age:									
18 to 24 years old	2.5	6.0	15.4	9.3	10.4	12.9	12.7	41.0	4.9
25 to 34 years old	1.4	4.5	10.2	7.8	13.0	12.3	7.9	39.1	3.9
35 to 44 years old	1.8	3.9	8.1	7.4	15.3	14.1	6.7	31.2	4.8
45 to 54 years old	2.5	4.2	8.2	7.5	18.6	12.1	6.8	27.9	5.1
55 to 64 years old	1.5	3.4	6.7	5.6	19.1	10.5	5.0	26.1	5.6
65 to 74 years old	1.4	3.7	4.8	4.6	20.5	8.1	4.1	23.7	5.3
75 years old and older . . .	0.7	2.5	3.1	2.4	18.0	3.8	3.7	11.4	3.7
Education:									
Grade school	0.4	0.7	1.7	1.6	12.0	1.7	1.7	22.8	1.1
Some high school	0.4	3.5	5.2	3.9	11.1	4.7	2.8	24.1	2.6
High school graduate	0.6	2.8	6.3	6.1	15.0	8.1	4.1	23.2	3.4
Some college	1.8	5.7	11.6	9.0	18.3	13.4	9.1	28.3	6.0
College graduate	3.6	4.9	11.0	8.0	17.4	17.3	10.6	31.4	6.4
Graduate school	5.4	5.7	11.0	7.3	17.6	20.1	12.7	34.4	7.3
Income:									
Less than $10,000.	1.5	3.1	7.3	6.6	15.7	6.7	7.8	23.4	3.3
$10,000 to $19,999	0.8	3.2	7.1	5.5	17.5	7.1	5.5	21.6	4.8
$20,000 to $29,999	0.5	4.5	7.4	5.7	15.9	6.8	5.6	26.5	4.0
$30,000 to $39,999	1.9	4.6	9.7	6.9	16.8	10.5	7.6	26.9	5.5
$40,000 to $49,999	2.9	4.2	9.4	6.8	17.8	13.8	7.4	24.1	5.3
$50,000 to $74,999	2.5	4.6	8.4	8.1	16.9	13.3	7.0	31.0	5.6
$75,000 or more	2.4	4.0	10.6	8.1	15.2	17.2	8.5	33.6	4.6
Not reported	1.2	4.6	6.7	5.4	12.3	9.1	5.9	25.5	4.3

[1] Dancing other than ballet (e.g. folk and tap).   [2] Includes ceramics, jewelry, leatherwork, and metalwork.   [3] Includes making movies or video as an artistic activity.

Source: U.S. National Endowment for the Arts. *Research Division Report #45. 2002 Survey of Public Participation in the Arts.* <http://www.nea.gov/pub/ResearchReportschrono.html>.

Arts, Entertainment, and Recreation 791

Table 1229. Adult Attendance at Sports Events by Frequency: 2004

[In thousands (2,251 represents 2,251,000), except percent. For fall 2004. Based on survey and subject to sampling error; see source]

Event	Attend one or more times a month Number	Attend one or more times a month Percent	Attend less than once a month Number	Attend less than once a month Percent	Event	Attend one or more times a month Number	Attend one or more times a month Percent	Attend less than once a month Number	Attend less than once a month Percent
Auto racing - NASCAR	2,251	1.05	6,653	3.12	Weekend professional games	3,785	1.77	7,829	3.67
Auto racing - Other	2,446	1.15	4,618	2.16	Golf	1,737	0.81	3,629	1.70
Baseball	8,524	3.99	16,217	7.60	High school sports	11,578	5.42	6,658	3.12
Basketball:					Horse racing:				
College games	3,492	1.64	5,756	2.70	Flats, runners	1,236	0.58	2,986	1.40
Professional games	2,853	1.34	7,379	3.46	Trotters/harness	446	0.21	1,930	0.90
Bowling	1,426	0.67	2,063	0.97	Ice hockey	2,576	1.21	5,731	2.68
Boxing	742	0.35	1,993	0.93	Motorcycle racing	809	0.38	2,319	1.09
Equestrian events	599	0.28	1,862	0.87	Pro beach volleyball	196	0.09	1,569	0.73
Figure skating	551	0.26	2,029	0.95	Rodeo/Bull Riding	1,029	0.48	3,190	1.49
Fishing tournaments	708	0.33	1,994	0.93	Soccer	2,848	1.33	2,929	1.37
Football:					Tennis	841	0.39	2,291	1.07
College games	5,487	2.57	8,406	3.94	Truck/tractor pull/mud racing	680	0.32	2,986	1.40
Monday night professional games	1,945	0.91	3,501	1.64	Wrestling—professional	1,158	0.54	2,387	1.12

Source: Mediamark Research, Inc., New York, NY Top-line Reports (copyright). Internet site <http://www.mediamark.com/mri/docs/TopLineReports.html>.

Table 1230. Adult Participation in Selected Leisure Activities by Frequency: 2004

[In thousands (13,478 represents 13,478,000), except percent. For fall 2004. Based on sample and subject to sampling error; see source]

Activity	Participated in the last 12 months[1] Number	Participated in the last 12 months[1] Percent	Two or more times a week Number	Two or more times a week Percent	Once a week Number	Once a week Percent	Two to three times a month Number	Two to three times a month Percent	Once a month Number	Once a month Percent
Adult education courses	13,478	6.3	2,605	1.2	2,418	1.1	634	0.3	574	0.3
Album Scrapbooking	8,901	4.2	537	0.3	539	0.3	1,094	0.5	1,648	0.8
Attend auto shows	16,631	7.8	151	0.1	321	0.2	577	0.3	683	0.3
Attend country music performances	11,227	5.3	115	0.1	114	0.1	151	0.1	391	0.2
Attend dance performances	7,921	3.7	198	0.1	111	0.1	240	0.1	300	0.1
Attend horse races	5,430	2.5	194	0.1	165	0.1	308	0.1	255	0.1
Attend music performances[2]	30,115	14.1	250	0.1	471	0.2	1,167	0.6	3,480	1.6
Attend rock music performances	19,550	9.2	183	0.1	220	0.1	427	0.2	947	0.4
Backgammon	4,301	2.0	529	0.3	408	0.2	503	0.2	608	0.3
Baking	37,705	17.7	7,805	3.7	5,762	2.7	8,875	4.2	5,174	2.4
Barbecuing	68,462	32.1	10,637	5.0	10,476	4.9	16,390	7.7	9,191	4.3
Billiards/pool	18,302	8.6	1,689	0.8	1,470	0.7	2,139	1.0	2,121	1.0
Birdwatching	10,082	4.7	5,021	2.4	709	0.3	896	0.4	553	0.3
Board games	35,645	16.7	2,471	1.2	3,248	1.5	6,463	3.0	6,332	3.0
Book clubs	6,750	3.2	455	0.2	449	0.2	740	0.4	2,114	1.0
Ceramics/pottery	2,439	1.1	268	0.1	278	0.1	72	(Z)	163	0.1
Chess	7,581	3.6	623	0.3	823	0.4	839	0.4	1,130	0.5
Concerts on radio	7,324	3.4	1,371	0.6	762	0.4	847	0.4	807	0.4
Cooking for fun	34,756	16.3	12,328	5.8	5,508	2.6	5,437	2.6	2,996	1.4
Crossword puzzles	33,481	15.7	14,734	6.9	4,002	1.9	3,295	1.5	2,261	1.1
Dance/go dancing	19,646	9.2	1,570	0.7	1,673	0.8	2,755	1.3	2,321	1.1
Dining out	102,610	48.1	20,137	9.4	25,106	11.8	23,083	10.8	10,820	5.1
Electronic games (not TV)	18,318	8.6	5,939	2.8	1,872	0.9	2,759	1.3	1,657	0.8
Entertain friends/relatives at home	81,524	38.2	7,238	3.4	10,162	4.8	17,933	8.4	16,922	7.9
Fly kites	7,079	3.3	109	0.1	44	(Z)	203	0.1	453	0.2
Furniture refinishing	7,642	3.6	267	0.1	172	0.1	197	0.1	420	0.2
Go to bars/night clubs	40,640	19.0	3,930	1.8	4,439	2.1	6,703	3.1	6,151	2.9
Go to beach	47,175	22.1	2,398	1.1	1,643	0.8	4,133	1.9	4,249	2.0
Go to live theater	28,824	13.5	168	0.1	507	0.2	1,296	0.6	3,320	1.6
Go to museums	29,441	13.8	131	0.1	390	0.2	841	0.4	2,795	1.3
Model making	3,370	1.6	274	0.1	140	0.1	299	0.1	364	0.2
Painting, drawing	14,020	6.6	2,406	1.1	1,582	0.7	2,051	1.0	1,718	0.8
Photography	24,645	11.6	3,074	1.4	2,840	1.3	5,169	2.4	4,259	2.0
Picnic	24,544	11.5	279	0.1	555	0.3	1,938	0.9	3,181	1.5
Play bingo	9,117	4.3	957	0.5	1,017	0.5	714	0.3	848	0.4
Play cards	50,318	23.6	6,277	2.9	5,486	2.6	8,027	3.8	7,709	3.6
Play musical instrument	16,680	7.8	6,536	3.1	1,650	0.8	1,495	0.7	1,213	0.6
Reading books	77,472	36.3	42,861	20.1	7,727	3.6	6,896	3.2	4,420	2.1
Surf the Net	57,095	26.8	37,380	17.5	6,354	3.0	3,718	1.7	1,961	0.9
Trivia games	13,387	6.3	1,857	0.9	939	0.4	1,756	0.8	1,736	0.8
Video games	27,580	12.9	10,613	5.0	3,034	1.4	2,839	1.3	2,145	1.0
Woodworking	11,054	5.2	2,268	1.1	1,113	0.5	1,768	0.8	1,192	0.6
Word games	17,349	8.1	6,443	3.0	1,969	0.9	1,990	0.9	1,372	0.6
Zoo attendance	25,124	11.8	126	0.1	74	(Z)	546	0.3	1,264	0.6

Z represents less than 0.05 percent. [1] Includes those participating less than once a month not shown separately. [2] Excluding country and rock.

Source: Mediamark Research, Inc., New York, NY, Top-line Reports (copyright). Internet site <http://www.mediamark.com/mri/docs/TopLineReports.html>

792 Arts, Entertainment, and Recreation

Table 1231. Retail Sales and Household Participation in Lawn and Garden Activities: 2000 to 2004

[(33,404 represents $33,404,000,000). For calendar year. Based on national household sample survey conducted by the Gallup Organization. Subject to sampling variability; see source]

Activity	Retail sales (mil. dol.)					Percent households engaged in activity				
	2000	2001	2002	2003	2004	2000	2001	2002	2003	2004
Total.............	33,404	37,734	39,635	38,371	36,778	72	80	79	78	75
Lawn care............	9,794	12.672	11,963	10,413	8,887	50	56	55	54	48
Indoor houseplants........	1,332	1,784	2,128	1,571	1,495	39	46	44	41	39
Flower gardening..........	4,167	3,926	3,131	3,025	2,735	45	43	41	38	36
Insect control..........	1,232	2,058	2,281	2,053	1,823	27	33	32	30	28
Shrub care............	1,429	1,298	1,072	1,042	1,027	31	30	27	27	26
Vegetable gardening.......	2,169	1,535	1,270	1,408	1,058	27	25	25	24	22
Tree care..............	1,872	2,121	2,790	2,359	3,067	23	25	26	25	24
Landscaping..........	6,809	6,310	8,854	10,507	11,346	30	37	34	33	33
Flower bulbs..........	912	1,188	1,191	1,036	892	28	31	29	26	26
Fruit trees..............	284	748	695	635	589	13	15	12	12	11
Container gardening.......	1,257	1,202	1,362	1,219	1,196	18	22	23	24	21
Raising transplants [1]......	334	291	262	230	258	11	12	12	10	9
Herb gardening..........	204	413	444	345	367	12	14	15	14	14
Growing berries..........	147	227	171	345	141	8	8	7	6	6
Ornamental gardening.....	519	756	580	831	769	8	9	8	9	9
Water gardening	943	1,205	1,441	1,565	1,128	10	13	14	15	13

[1] Starting plants in advance of planting in ground.

Source: The National Gardening Association, Burlington, VT, *National Gardening Survey,* annual (copyright). <http://www.garden.org/home>

Table 1232. Household Pet Ownership: 2001

[Based on a sample survey of 80,000 households in 2001; for details, see source]

Item	Unit	Dogs	Cats	Birds	Horses
Percent of households owning companion pets [1].........	Percent ...	36.1	31.6	4.6	1.7
Average number owned......................	Number...	1.6	2.1	2.1	2.9
Households obtaining veterinary care [2].............	Percent ...	85.0	66.8	12.9	56.7
Average visits per household per year	Number...	2.7	1.8	0.3	2.1
PERCENT OF HOUSEHOLDS OWNING PETS					
Annual household income:					
Under $20,000.............................	Percent ...	29.7	28.1	5.1	1.0
$20,000 to $34,999........................	Percent ...	33.9	30.9	4.5	1.3
$35,000 to $54,999........................	Percent ...	37.9	32.2	4.8	2.0
$55,000 to $84,999........................	Percent ...	40.5	34.3	4.4	2.1
$85,000 and over.........................	Percent ...	39.7	33.7	4.2	2.1
Household size: [1]					
One person..............................	Percent ...	20.8	23.5	2.8	0.7
Two persons.............................	Percent ...	34.3	31.3	4.0	1.6
Three persons...........................	Percent ...	46.2	37.4	5.9	2.2
Four persons............................	Percent ...	50.6	38.2	6.3	2.3
Five or more persons......................	Percent ...	53.0	39.7	8.3	3.2
Veterinary Expenditures:					
Per household per year (mean).................	Dollars ...	261	160	18	263
Per animal (mean)	Dollars ...	179	85	9	112

[1] As of December 31, 2001. [2] During 2001.

Source: American Veterinary Medical Association, Schaumburg, IL, *U.S. Pet Ownership and Demographics Sourcebook, 2002* (copyright) <http://www.avma.org/>.

Table 1233. College and Professional Football Summary: 1985 to 2004

[34,952 represents 34,952,000. For definition of median, see Guide to Tabular Presentation]

Sport	Unit	1985	1990	1995	2000	2001	2002	2003	2004
Football:									
NCAA college: [1]									
Teams	Number...	509	533	565	606	608	617	617	612
Attendance	1,000 ...	34,952	35,330	35,638	39,059	40,481	44,556	46,145	43,106
National Football League: [2]									
Teams	Number...	28	28	30	31	31	32	32	32
Attendance, total [3] ...	1,000 ...	14,058	17,666	19,203	20,954	20,590	21,505	21,639	21,709
Regular season	1,000 ...	13,345	13,960	15,044	16,387	16,166	16,833	16,914	17,001
Average per game...	Number...	59,567	62,321	62,682	66,078	65,187	65,755	66,328	66,409
Postseason games [4] ...	1,000 ...	711	848	(NA)	809	767	782	806	789
Players' salaries: [5]									
Average	$1,000 ...	217	354	584	787	986	1,180	1,259	1,331
Median base salary	$1,000 ...	160	275	301	441	501	525	534	537

[1] Source: National Collegiate Athletic Assn., Indianapolis, IN; <www.ncca.com> (copyright). [2] Source: National Football League, New York, NY; <http://www.nfl.com/>. [3] Beginning 1987 includes preseason attendance, not shown separately. [4] Includes Pro Bowl, a nonchampionship game and Super Bowl. [5] Source: National Football League Players Association, Washington, DC;<http://www.nflpa.org/>.

Source: Compiled from sources listed in footnotes.

Table 1234. Selected Recreational Activities: 1985 to 2004

[8,042 represents 8,042,000]

Activity	Unit	1985	1990	1995	2000	2001	2002	2003	2004
Adult golfers (eight rounds or more) [1][2]	1,000 ...	8,042	11,835	11,581	14,072	12,028	12,853	13,381	12,750
Golf facilities	Number.	12,346	12,846	14,074	15,489	15,689	15,827	15,899	16,057
Tennis players [3][4]	1,000 ...	13,000	21,000	17,820	22,900	22,000	23,200	24,100	24,000
Tenpin bowling:									
Establishments [4]	Number.	8,275	7,611	7,049	6,247	6,022	5,973	5,811	5,761.0
Membership, total [5]	1,000 ...	8,064	6,588	4,925	3,756	3,553	3,382	3,246	3,112.0
Skiing [6]									
Skier visits [7]	Million...	51.4	50.0	52.7	52.2	57.3	54.4	57.6	57.1
Operating resorts [6]	Number..	727	591	520	503	490	493	490	494
Motion picture screens [8]	1,000 ...	21	24	28	38	37	36	37	37
Receipts, box office	Mil. dol..	3,749	5,022	5,494	7,661	8,413	9,520	9,489	9,539
Attendance	Million...	1,056	1,189	1,263	1,421	1,487	1,639	1,574	1,536
Boating: [9]									
Recreational boats owned [10]	1,000 ...	13,778	15,987	15,375	16,820	17,030	17,340	17,360	17,610
Retail expenditures on boating [11]	Mil. dol..	13,284	13,731	17,226	27,066	29,710	31,563	30,283	32,953
Retail units purchased:									
Total all boats [12]	1,000 ...	675	525	664	577	880	844	838	870
Outboard boats	1,000 ...	305	227	231	241	218	212	207	217
Inboard boats	1,000 ...	17	15	12	24	22	22	19	20

[1] Source: National Golf Foundation, Jupiter, FL. [2] Definition for golfer has changed to persons 18 years of age and over. Data for all the years shown have been revised. [3] Source: Tennis Industry Association, Hilton Head, SC. Players for persons 12 years old and over who played at least once. [4] Source: Bowling Headquarters, Greendale, WI. [5] Membership totals are for U.S., Canada, and for U.S. military personnel worldwide. [6] Source: National Ski Areas Association, Kottke National End of Season Survey 2003/04, final report (copyright). [7] Represents one person visiting a ski area for all or any part of a day or night for the purpose of skiing, snowboarding or other downhill sliding. Data are estimated and are for the season ending in the year shown. [8] Source: Motion Picture Association of America, Inc., Encino, CA. [9] Source: National Marine Manufacturers Association, Chicago, IL. (copyright). [10] 2004 data are estimated. [11] Represents estimated expenditures for new and used boats, motors and engines, accessories, safety equipment, fuel, insurance, docking, maintenance, launching, storage, repairs, and other expenses. [12] Includes other boats not shown separately.

Source: Compiled from sources listed in footnotes.

Table 1235. Selected Spectator Sports: 1985 to 2004

[47,742 represents 47,742,000]

Sport	Unit	1985	1990	1995	2000	2001	2002	2003	2004
Baseball, major leagues: [1]									
Attendance	1,000 ...	47,742	55,512	51,288	74,339	73,881	69,428	69,501	74,822
Regular season	1,000 ...	46,824	54,824	50,469	72,748	72,267	67,859	67,568	73,023
National League	1,000 ...	22,292	24,492	25,110	39,851	39,558	36,949	36,661	40,221
American League	1,000 ...	24,532	30,332	25,359	32,898	32,709	30,910	30,908	32,802
Playoffs [2]	1,000 ...	591	479	533	1,314	1,247	1,262	1,568	1,625
World Series	1,000 ...	327	209	286	277	366	306	365	174
Players' salaries: [3]									
Average	$1,000 ..	371	598	1,111	1,896	2,139	2,296	2,372	2,313
Basketball: [4][5]									
NCAA—Men's college:									
Teams	Number.	753	767	868	932	937	936	967	981
Attendance	1,000 ...	26,584	28,741	28,548	29,025	28,949	29,395	30,124	30,761
NCAA—Women's college:									
Teams	Number.	746	782	864	956	958	975	1,009	1,008
Attendance	1,000 ...	2,072	2,777	4,962	8,698	8,825	9,533	10,164	10,016
Pro: [6]									
Teams	Number..	23	27	27	29	29	29	29	30
Attendance, total	1,000 ...	11,534	18,586	19,883	21,503	21,436	21,571	21,760	22,953
Regular season	1,000 ...	10,506	17,369	18,516	20,059	19,956	20,182	20,074	21,296
Average per game...	Number..	11,141	15,690	16,727	16,870	16,784	16,974	16,883	17,314
Playoffs	1,000 ...	985	1,203	1,347	1,427	1,460	1,370	1,685	1,639
Average per game...	Number..	14,479	16,704	18,457	19,202	20,565	19,296	19,152	19,507
All-Star game	Number..	43,146	14,810	18,755	18,325	20,374	19,581	19,445	18,227
National Hockey League: [7]									
Regular season attendance..	1,000 ...	11,634	12,580	9,234	18,800	20,373	20,615	20,409	22,065
Playoffs attendance	1,000 ...	1,108	1,356	1,329	1,525	1,584	1,691	1,636	1,709
Professional rodeo: [8]									
Rodeos	Number..	617	754	739	688	668	666	657	671
Performances	Number..	1,887	2,159	2,217	2,081	2,015	2,207	1,949	1,982
Members	Number..	5,239	5,693	6,894	6,255	5,913	6,209	6,158	6,247
Permit-holders (rookies)	Number..	2,534	3,290	3,835	3,249	2,544	2,543	3,121	2,990
Total prize money	Mil dol..	15.1	18.2	24.5	32.3	33.1	33.3	34.3	35.5

[1] Source: Major League Baseball (previously, The National League of Professional Baseball Clubs), New York, NY, *National League Green Book*; and The American League of Professional Baseball Clubs, New York, NY, *American League Red Book*. [2] Beginning 1997, two rounds of playoffs were played. Prior years had one round. [3] Source: Major League Baseball Players Association, New York, NY. [4] Season ending in year shown. [5] Source: National Collegiate Athletic Assn., Indianapolis, IN (copyright). For women's attendance total, excludes double-headers with men's teams. [6] Source: National Basketball Assn., New York, NY. For season ending in year shown. [7] For season ending in year shown. Source: National Hockey League, Montreal, Quebec. [8] Source: Professional Rodeo Cowboys Association, Colorado Springs, CO., *Official Professional Rodeo Media Guide*, annual (copyright).

Source: Compiled from sources listed in footnotes.

Table 1236. **High School Students Engaged in Organized Physical Activity by Sex, Race and Hispanic Origin: 2003**

[In percent. For students in grades 9 to 12. Based on the Youth Risk Behavior Survey, a school-based survey and subject to sampling error; for details see source]

Characteristic	Enrolled in physical education class			Played on a sports team
	Total	Attended daily	Exercised 20 minutes or more per class [1]	
All students	**55.7**	**28.4**	**80.3**	**57.6**
Male	58.5	30.4	84.5	64.0
Grade 9	70.8	37.7	84.8	65.0
Grade 10	63.0	33.5	83.2	62.0
Grade 11	50.5	26.0	83.7	66.3
Grade 12	44.5	21.4	87.2	62.3
Female	52.8	26.4	75.3	51.0
Grade 9	71.2	38.0	75.7	55.2
Grade 10	58.0	29.1	77.0	53.9
Grade 11	40.8	19.2	71.6	47.8
Grade 12	34.6	15.2	74.9	45.9
White, non-Hispanic	53.7	24.9	81.5	60.8
Male	55.9	26.8	85.8	65.4
Female	51.5	23.1	76.6	55.9
Black, non-Hispanic	56.0	33.0	74.0	53.2
Male	63.1	37.1	80.0	67.5
Female	49.3	29.0	66.7	39.6
Hispanic	58.8	36.7	78.2	49.5
Male	61.4	39.5	82.5	56.2
Female	56.1	34.0	73.5	42.8

[1] For students enrolled in physical education classes.

Source: U.S. Centers for Disease Control and Prevention, Atlanta, GA, *Youth Risk Behavior Surveillance—United States, 2003, Morbidity and Mortality Weekly Report*, Vol. 53, No. SS-2, May 21, 2004. See also <http://www.cdc.gov/mmwr/preview/mmwrhtml/ss5302a1.htm>.

Table 1237. **Participation in High School Athletic Programs by Sex: 1972 to 2004**

[Data based on number of state associations reporting and may underrepresent the number of schools with and participants in athletic programs]

Year	Participants [1]		Sex and sport	Most popular sports, 2003-2004 [2]	
	Males	Females		Schools	Participants
1972-73	3,770,621	817,073	MALE		
1973-74	4,070,125	1,300,169			
1975-76	4,109,021	1,645,039	Football (11-player)	13,680	1,032,682
1977-78	4,367,442	2,083,040	Basketball	17,389	544,811
1978-79	3,709,512	1,854,400	Track & field (outdoor)	15,221	504,801
1979-80	3,517,829	1,750,264	Baseball	14,984	457,146
1980-81	3,503,124	1,853,789	Soccer	10,219	349,785
1981-82	3,409,081	1,810,671	Wrestling	9,526	238,700
1982-83	3,355,558	1,779,972	Cross country	12,649	196,428
1983-84	3,303,599	1,747,346	Golf	12,921	163,341
1984-85	3,354,284	1,757,884	Tennis	9,427	152,938
			Swimming & diving	5,758	96,562
1985-86	3,344,275	1,807,121			
1986-87	3,364,082	1,836,356	FEMALE		
1987-88	3,425,777	1,849,684			
1988-89	3,416,844	1,839,352	Basketball	17,061	457,986
1989-90	3,398,192	1,858,659	Track & field (outdoor)	15,089	418,322
1990-91	3,406,355	1,892,316	Volleyball	14,181	396,322
1991-92	3,429,853	1,940,801	Softball (fast pitch)	14,181	362,468
1992-93	3,416,389	1,997,489	Soccer	9,490	309,032
1993-94	3,472,967	2,130,315	Cross country	9,559	167,758
1994-95	3,536,359	2,240,461	Tennis	12,235	166,287
			Swimming & diving	6,176	144,565
1995-96	3,634,052	2,367,936	Competitive spirit squads	3,693	89,443
1996-97	3,706,225	2,474,043	Golf	8,171	63,173
1997-98	3,763,120	2,570,333			
1998-99	3,832,352	2,652,726			
1999-00	3,861,749	2,675,874			
2000-01	3,921,069	2,784,154			
2001-02	3,960,517	2,806,998			
2002-03	3,988,738	2,856,358			
2003-04	4,038,253	2,865,299			

[1] A participant is counted in the number of sports participated in. [2] Ten most popular sports for each sex in terms of number of participants.

Source: National Federation of State High School Associations, Indianapolis, IN, *The 2003–2004 High School Athletics Participation Survey* (copyright). <http://www.nfhs.org/scriptcontent/Index.cfm>.

Arts, Entertainment, and Recreation 795

Table 1238. Participation in Selected Sports Activities: 2003

[In thousands (256,152 represents 256,152,000), except rank. For persons 7 years of age or older. Except as indicated, a participant plays a sport more than once in the year]

Activity	All persons		Sex		Age								Household income (dol.)					
	Number	Rank	Male	Female	7-11 years	12-17 years	18-24 years	25-34 years	35-44 years	45-54 years	55-64 years	65 years and over	Under 15,000	15,000-24,999	25,000-34,999	35,000-49,000	50,000-74,999	75,000 and over
SERIES I SPORTS [1]																		
Total	256,152	(X)	124,656	131,496	19,859	24,654	27,981	36,882	43,667	40,150	27,328	35,631	28,468	29,900	30,971	41,056	53,759	71,998
Number participated in—																		
Aerobic exercising [2]	28,038	10	7,005	21,034	856	2,115	4,718	6,933	5,801	4,149	1,690	1,778	2,066	2,522	2,838	4,160	5,957	10,495
Backpacking [3]	13,722	18	8,400	5,322	1,274	2,163	2,162	3,056	2,779	1,536	513	237	1,105	1,057	1,834	2,644	3,265	3,818
Baseball	14,632	17	11,368	3,264	4,514	4,079	1,371	1,322	1,659	971	408	308	912	972	1,251	1,949	3,884	5,663
Basketball	27,879	11	19,240	8,639	6,299	7,871	3,890	4,227	3,100	1,607	681	203	1,996	2,222	2,449	3,617	6,789	10,806
Bicycle riding [2]	36,257	7	20,355	15,902	8,591	6,537	2,644	5,151	6,064	3,874	1,767	1,627	2,649	2,951	3,665	5,157	8,559	13,276
Billiards	30,452	9	19,140	11,312	1,458	2,900	6,800	7,866	6,109	3,427	1,143	750	2,474	3,274	3,703	5,480	7,027	8,493
Bowling [2]	39,406	5	20,691	18,714	4,502	5,762	7,212	7,628	6,956	4,017	1,678	1,649	2,763	3,674	4,141	6,121	9,417	13,290
Camping [2]	51,421	2	27,112	24,308	5,949	6,491	6,947	9,345	9,866	6,566	3,551	2,706	3,594	4,742	6,190	9,452	12,972	14,470
Exercising with equipment [2]	48,631	3	22,312	26,319	678	4,217	6,516	10,594	10,700	7,548	4,299	4,081	2,420	3,925	4,536	6,711	11,370	19,668
Exercise walking [2]	79,496	1	29,215	50,281	3,210	4,183	7,815	13,952	16,071	13,657	9,302	11,305	8,208	8,474	9,495	11,551	16,475	25,293
Fishing (net) [2]	38,153	6	26,889	11,264	4,060	4,511	3,816	5,951	8,224	5,426	3,434	2,731	3,267	4,325	4,908	5,827	9,058	10,768
Fishing—fresh water	33,205	8	23,656	9,549	3,684	4,062	3,642	5,195	7,031	4,553	2,897	2,143	2,923	4,000	4,311	5,058	8,089	8,824
Fishing—salt water	10,628	21	7,652	2,975	809	1,008	915	1,607	2,699	1,657	1,040	893	693	1,085	1,173	1,602	2,164	3,911
Football—tackle	8,650	25	7,863	786	1,370	3,162	1,793	1,146	516	281	149	232	823	972	1,051	1,245	2,199	2,360
Football—touch	9,331	24	7,512	1,819	1,818	2,753	1,830	1,561	951	245	174	-	1,061	678	795	1,350	2,054	3,393
Golf	25,650	13	19,665	5,986	1,293	2,304	2,143	4,976	5,373	4,228	2,734	2,604	691	939	1,990	3,859	5,703	12,467
Hiking	25,032	14	13,281	11,751	2,208	2,800	2,846	5,177	5,325	3,285	1,842	1,544	1,170	1,732	3,027	3,766	5,504	9,588
Hunting with firearms	17,901	16	15,763	2,138	689	2,364	2,400	2,964	3,860	2,839	1,717	1,069	1,332	1,848	3,027	2,603	4,268	4,823
Martial arts	4,821	27	3,337	1,484	1,059	1,271	580	782	673	260	147	50	652	133	491	782	1,121	1,641
Running/jogging [2]	22,937	15	12,353	10,584	1,448	4,043	4,229	6,111	4,011	1,931	729	435	2,068	1,462	2,294	3,105	5,030	8,977
Soccer	11,085	20	6,939	4,146	4,711	3,552	862	984	570	159	110	133	492	706	695	1,615	2,520	5,056
Softball [2]	11,840	19	6,352	5,488	1,919	2,890	1,617	2,321	1,840	901	278	74	792	699	1,185	1,728	2,941	4,495
Swimming [2]	47,027	4	22,022	25,005	7,957	8,308	5,223	6,843	8,203	5,205	2,780	2,509	2,381	4,018	4,545	6,180	11,298	18,606
Tai Chi/Yoga	5,573	26	933	4,640	275	200	879	1,613	1,169	859	242	337	574	677	692	796	1,106	1,728
Tennis	9,572	23	5,150	4,421	997	2,054	1,161	2,312	1,609	683	429	327	213	670	442	1,308	2,325	4,614
Volleyball	10,444	22	4,567	5,877	1,274	3,359	1,405	2,082	1,370	694	175	84	704	968	1,014	991	2,703	4,063
Weightlifting	25,875	12	16,864	9,011	182	4,011	5,210	6,583	5,220	2,688	1,054	926	1,700	2,128	2,274	3,882	5,831	10,060

See footnote at end of table.

U.S. Census Bureau, Statistical Abstract of the United States: 2006

Household income (dol.)

Activity	All persons		Sex		Age								Household income (dol.)					
	Number	Rank	Male	Female	7-11 years	12-17 years	18-24 years	25-34 years	35-44 years	45-54 years	55-64 years	65 years and over	Under 15,000	15,000-24,999	25,000-34,999	35,000-49,999	50,000-74,999	75,000 and over
Total	256,156	(X)	124,657	131,498	19,858	24,654	27,982	36,881	43,667	40,152	27,328	35,633	28,126	30,511	30,016	42,723	53,888	70,892

SERIES II SPORTS [5]

Number participating in—

Activity	Number	Rank	Male	Female	7-11 years	12-17 years	18-24 years	25-34 years	35-44 years	45-54 years	55-64 years	65 years and over	Under 15,000	15,000-24,999	25,000-34,999	35,000-49,999	50,000-74,999	75,000 and over
Archery (target)	3,855	15	3,030	826	461	899	306	730	801	515	89	55	171	534	375	598	787	1,390
Boating—motor/power . . .	24,192	2	13,960	10,232	2,139	2,484	2,724	4,547	5,209	3,658	2,004	1,428	1,009	2,046	1,840	3,958	6,353	8,986
Hockey (ice)	1,829	21	1,586	244	388	410	265	272	310	137	15	33	104	96	71	207	424	926
Hunting with bow and arrow .	4,953	13	4,522	431	203	553	490	1,076	1,177	779	450	226	236	623	593	898	1,167	1,436
Ice/figure skating	5,100	12	1,837	3,263	1,795	1,185	514	460	668	316	104	59	292	280	385	897	1,552	1,693
In-line roller skating . . .	15,968	4	7,477	8,491	5,949	3,693	1,934	2,100	1,392	600	156	142	878	1,724	1,694	2,944	3,743	4,986
Kayaking/rafting	4,721	14	2,818	1,903	428	523	861	843	877	746	335	107	148	345	591	618	1,459	1,561
Kick boxing	3,030	18	581	2,449	258	206	639	994	664	179	49	40	259	363	170	526	535	1,177
Mountain biking—off road .	8,207	7	5,610	2,597	976	1,043	1,213	2,403	1,598	622	288	64	451	1,007	686	1,237	2,550	2,274
Muzzleloading	3,057	17	2,761	296	24	149	178	767	869	591	328	151	151	322	332	660	833	759
Paintball games	7,379	8	5,779	1,599	653	2,400	1,913	1,239	728	310	72	63	476	676	809	1,313	1,721	2,383
Sailing	2,649	19	1,505	1,143	275	191	290	384	553	291	365	301	119	184	184	573	690	1,037
Scooter riding	11,649	5	6,145	5,503	5,918	3,144	553	541	480	447	206	360	940	1,023	993	2,494	2,399	3,800
Skateboarding	8,981	6	6,989	1,992	3,484	3,568	804	586	292	54	84	109	555	1,133	969	1,478	1,954	2,893
Skiing—alpine	6,772	9	3,888	2,884	778	868	836	1,074	1,899	780	403	133	121	227	291	804	1,329	4,000
Skiing—cross country . . .	1,935	20	1,013	921	166	212	201	173	493	448	159	83	27	95	114	334	410	954
Snowboarding	6,309	10	4,144	2,165	1,146	2,029	1,892	811	215	193	-	23	179	632	515	935	1,255	2,793
Target shoot	17,006	3	13,154	3,851	731	1,867	2,476	4,225	3,263	2,317	1,270	857	1,427	1,945	1,594	3,340	3,940	4,760
Target shoot—airgun . . .	3,776	16	3,181	596	951	827	501	464	410	294	207	122	208	371	391	941	1,158	707
Water skiing	5,451	11	3,265	2,186	441	562	994	1,614	954	562	213	111	149	585	508	659	1,686	1,863
Work-out at club	29,455	1	13,130	16,325	292	1,790	4,804	7,031	6,798	4,153	2,206	2,382	1,311	2,104	2,339	4,260	7,654	11,786

- Represents or rounds to zero. X Not applicable. [1] Based on a sampling of 15,000 households. [2] Participant engaged in activity at least six times in the year. [3] Includes wilderness camping. [4] Vacation/overnight. [5] Based on a sampling of 20,000 households

Source: National Sporting Goods Association, Mt. Prospect, IL. Sports Participation in 2003: Series 1 and Series II (copyright) <http://www.nsga.org/public/pages/index.cfm?pageid=864>.

Table 1239. Participation in NCAA Sports: 2003-2004

Sport	Males Teams	Males Athletes	Males Average squad	Females Teams	Females Athletes	Females Average squad
Total [1]	8,121	217,309	(X)	9,032	162,752	(X)
Baseball	864	27,262	31.6	(X)	(X)	(X)
Basketball	994	16,028	16.1	1,022	14,596	14.3
Bowling [2]	1	25	(NA)	42	358	8.5
Cross country	871	11,273	12.9	942	12,678	13.5
Equestrian [2]	4	49	12.3	41	1,120	27.3
Fencing [3]	37	610	16.5	44	653	14.8
Field hockey	(X)	(X)	(X)	255	5,430	21.3
Football	617	59,980	97.2	(X)	(X)	(X)
Golf	758	7,738	10.2	477	3,628	7.6
Gymnastics	20	326	16.3	86	1,380	16.0
Ice hockey [4]	133	3,782	28.4	72	1,600	22.2
Lacrosse	211	7,103	33.7	258	5,545	21.5
Rifle [3]	35	192	5.5	39	205	5.3
Rowing [5]	55	1,758	32.0	143	6,805	47.6
Sailing [2]	26	259	10.0	(X)	(X)	(X)
Skiing [3]	39	467	12.0	42	457	10.9
Soccer	729	18,512	25.4	895	20,437	22.8
Softball	(X)	(X)	(X)	908	16,079	17.7
Squash [2]	23	325	14.1	27	389	14.4
Swimming/diving	387	7,333	18.9	488	10,539	21.6
Synchronized swimming [4]	(X)	(X)	(X)	8	104	13.0
Tennis	744	7,219	9.7	880	8,448	9.6
Track, indoor	563	18,157	32.3	617	18,065	29.3
Track, outdoor	657	20,869	31.8	701	19,658	28.0
Volleyball	81	1,195	14.8	978	13,310	13.6
Water polo	46	865	18.8	59	1,126	19.1
Wrestling	223	5,943	26.7	(X)	(X)	(X)

X Not applicable. [1] Includes other sports, not shown separately. [2] Sport recognized by the NCAA, but does not have an NCAA championship. [3] Co-ed championship sport. [4] Sport recognized by the NCAA, but does not have an NCAA championship for women. [5] Sport recognized by the NCAA, but does not have an NCAA championship for men.

Source: The National Collegiate Athletic Association (NCAA), Indianapolis, IN, 2003-04 Participation Study (copyright). <http://www2.ncaa.org/mediaandevents/ncaapublications/research/>

Table 1240. Sporting Goods Sales by Product Category: 1990 to 2004

[In millions of dollars (50,725 represents $50,725,000,000), except percent. Based on a sample survey of consumer purchases of 80,000 households, (100,000 beginning 1995), except recreational transport, which was provided by industry associations. Excludes Alaska and Hawaii. Minus sign (-) indicates decrease]

Selected product category	1990	1995	1998	1999	2000	2001	2002	2003	2004, proj.
Sales, all products	50,725	59,794	69,848	71,161	74,442	74,337	77,725	78,910	80,982
Annual percent change [1]	(NA)	6.5	3.7	1.9	4.6	-0.1	4.6	1.5	2.6
Percent of retail sales	(NA)	2.6	2.6	2.5	2.4	2.4	2.4	2.3	2.3
Athletic and sport clothing	10,130	10,311	12,844	10,307	11,030	10,217	9,801	9,573	9,728
Athletic and sport footwear [2]	11,654	11,415	13,068	12,546	13,026	13,814	14,144	14,446	14,732
Aerobic shoes	611	372	334	275	292	281	239	222	227
Basketball shoes	918	999	1,000	821	786	761	789	890	934
Cross training shoes	679	1,191	1,402	1,364	1,528	1,476	1,421	1,407	1,400
Golf shoes	226	225	220	208	226	223	243	222	220
Gym shoes, sneakers	2,536	1,741	2,010	1,936	1,871	2,004	2,042	2,059	2,120
Jogging and running shoes	1,110	1,043	1,469	1,502	1,638	1,670	1,733	1,802	1,838
Tennis shoes	740	480	515	505	533	505	503	544	555
Walking shoes	2,950	2,841	3,192	3,099	3,317	3,280	3,415	3,468	3,538
Athletic and sport equipment [2]	14,439	18,809	19,192	20,343	21,608	21,594	21,699	21,779	22,169
Archery	265	287	255	262	259	276	279	281	282
Baseball and softball	217	251	304	329	319	316	334	341	348
Billiards and pool	192	304	347	354	516	528	574	625	637
Camping	1,072	1,205	1,204	1,265	1,354	1,371	1,442	1,484	1,500
Exercise equipment	1,824	2,960	3,233	3,396	3,610	3,889	4,378	4,727	4,869
Fishing tackle	1,910	2,010	1,903	1,917	2,030	2,058	2,024	1,981	2,021
Golf	2,514	3,194	3,658	3,567	3,805	3,871	3,258	3,017	3,077
Hunting and firearms	2,202	3,003	2,200	2,437	2,274	2,206	2,449	2,509	2,559
In-line skating and wheel sports	150	646	509	473	1,074	726	826	840	857
Optics	438	655	710	718	729	783	826	840	857
Skin diving and scuba	294	328	345	363	355	348	348	338	334
Skiing, alpine	475	562	718	648	495	515	527	464	468
Tennis	333	297	318	338	383	371	358	343	347
Recreational transport	14,502	19,259	24,743	27,965	28,779	28,712	32,083	33,113	34,353
Bicycles and supplies	2,423	3,390	4,957	4,770	5,131	4,725	4,961	4,961	4,961
Pleasure boats	7,644	9,064	10,539	11,962	13,224	14,558	15,382	15,382	15,382
Recreational vehicles	4,113	5,895	8,364	10,413	9,529	8,598	10,960	12,058	13,270
Snowmobiles	322	910	883	820	894	831	779	712	740

NA Not available. [1] Represents change from immediate prior year. [2] Includes other products not shown separately.

Source: National Sporting Goods Association, Mt. Prospect, IL, The Sporting Goods Market in 2004; and prior issues (copyright), <http://www.nsga.org/public/pages/index.cfm?pageid=869>.

Table 1241. **Participants in Wildlife-Related Recreation Activities: 2001**

[Preliminary. In thousands (37,805 represents 37,805,000). For persons 16 years old and over engaging in activity at least once in 2001. Based on survey and subject to sampling error; see source for details]

Participant	Number	Days of partici- pation	Trips	Participant	Number	Days of partici- pation
Total sportsmen [1] ...	37,805	785,762	636,787	Wildlife watchers [1]	66,105	(X)
Total anglers	34,071	557,394	436,662	Nonresidential [2]	21,823	372,006
Freshwater	28,439	466,984	365,076	Observe wildlife	20,080	295,345
Excluding Great Lakes. . .	27,913	443,247	349,188	Photograph wildlife	9,427	76,324
Great Lakes.	1,847	23,138	15,888	Feed wildlife	7,077	103,307
Saltwater.	9,051	90,838	71,586	Residential [3]	62,928	(X)
Total hunters	13,034	228,368	200,125	Observe wildlife	42,111	(X)
Big game	10,911	153,191	114,445	Photograph wildlife	13,937	(X)
Small game	5,434	60,142	46,450	Feed wildlife	53,988	(X)
Migratory birds	2,956	29,310	24,155	Visit public parks	10,981	(X)
Other animals	1,047	19,207	15,074	Maintain plantings or natural areas	13,072	(X)

X Not applicable.   [1] Detail does not add to total due to multiple responses and nonresponse.   [2] Persons taking a trip of at least 1 mile for activity.   [3] Activity within 1 mile of home.

Source: U.S. Fish and Wildlife Service, *2001 National Survey of Fishing, Hunting, and Wildlife Associated Recreation*, May 2002. Internet links: <http://www.census.gov/prod/www/abs/fishing.html> <http://federalaid.fws.gov/surveys/surveys.html>.

Table 1242. **Consumer Purchases of Sporting Goods by Consumer Characteristics: 2003**

[In percent. Based on sample survey of consumer purchases of 100,000 households. Excludes Alaska and Hawaii]

Characteristic	Total house- holds	Footwear					Equipment				
		Aero- bic shoes	Gym shoes/ sneak- ers	Jog- ging/ run- ning shoes	Skate- board- ing shoes	Walk- ing shoes	Multi pur- pose home gyms	Rod/ reel combi- nation	Golf club set	Rifles	Soccer balls
Total	100	100	100	100	100	100	100	100	100	100	100
Age of user:											
Under 14 years old	20	10	50	12	36	6	1	6	3	-	56
14 to 17 years old	6	4	9	9	41	3	5	1	4	1	14
18 to 24 years old	10	8	6	10	15	5	2	6	5	5	8
25 to 34 years old	13	23	12	25	4	12	35	23	22	24	4
35 to 44 years old	16	24	10	20	4	15	25	27	14	27	3
45 to 64 years old	23	26	10	22	1	40	29	29	46	38	1
65 years old and over . . .	13	6	3	2	-	19	2	5	8	5	-
Multiple ages	-	-	-	-	-	-	2	5	-	-	14
Sex of user:											
Male	49	17	56	56	82	39	68	80	77	90	66
Female.	51	83	44	44	18	61	22	13	23	10	28
Both sexes	-	-	-	-	-	-	10	7	-	-	6
Annual household income:											
Under $15,000	14	3	8	5	4	9	-	6	1	6	5
$15,000 to $24,999.	13	8	9	8	8	11	10	7	7	5	11
$25,000 to $34,999.	12	8	11	8	11	11	19	10	5	8	11
$35,000 to $49,999.	15	18	16	14	12	14	17	15	14	14	16
$50,000 to $74,999.	19	23	26	22	30	23	23	31	10	31	23
$75,000 to $99,999.	13	21	15	17	20	14	14	13	29	20	17
$100,000 and over	13	19	16	27	15	19	17	18	34	16	18

- Represents or rounds to zero.
Source: National Sporting Goods Association, Mt. Prospect, IL, *The Sporting Goods Market in 2003* (copyright), <http://www.nsga.org/public/pages/index.cfm?pageid=869>.

Table 1243. **Direct Tourism Sales and Employment by Commodity Group: 2001 to 2004**

[Sales in billions of dollars, (492.1 represents $492,100,000,000). Employment in thousands (5,424 represents 5,424,000) Direct tourism-related sales comprise all output consumed directly by visitors.(e.g., traveler accommodations, passenger air transportation, souvenirs). Direct tourism-related employment comprises all jobs where the workers are engaged in the production of direct tourism-related output (e.g., hotel staff, airline pilots, and souvenir sellers)]

Tourism commodity group	Direct tourism sales				Tourism industry group	Direct tourism employment			
	2001	2002	2003	2004		2001	2002	2003	2004
All tourism commodities [1] ..	492.1	494.1	512.2	546.4	All tourism industries . . .	5,624	5,500	5,402	5,424
Traveler accommodations	81.2	81.1	81.8	86.8	Traveler accommodations. .	1,370	1,323	1,313	1,321
Passenger air transportation . . .	87.3	82.6	86.4	92.3	Air transportation services .	595	545	524	523
All other transportation- related commodities	101.5	100.1	103.9	108.7	All other transportation- related industries.	700	660	621	603
Food services and drinking places	83.7	87.9	91.8	100.7	Food and beverage services.	1,595	1,635	1,631	1,655
Recreation and entertainment . .	60.6	64.3	67.2	71.5	Recreation and entertainment	597	596	590	600
Shopping (Retailers).	77.8	77.9	81.1	86.4	Shopping (Retailers)	567	546	529	526
					All other industries	201	196	195	196

[1] Commodities that are typically purchased by visitors from the producer: such as airline passenger fares, meals, or hotel services.
Source: U.S. Bureau of Economic Analysis, Industry Economic Accounts, Satellite Industry Accounts, Travel and Tourism. <http://www.bea.doc.gov/bea/dn2/home/tourism.htm>.

Arts, Entertainment and Recreation 799

Table 1244. National Park System—Summary: 1990 to 2004

[For year ending September 30, except as noted. (986 represents $986,000,000) Includes data for five areas in Puerto Rico and Virgin Islands, one area in American Samoa, and one area in Guam]

Item	1990	1995	1999	2000	2001	2002	2003	2004
Finances (mil. dol.): [1]								
Expenditures reported	986	1,445	1,530	1,833	1,985	2,161	2,315	2,371
Salaries and wages	459	633	733	799	840	876	934	956
Improvements, maintenance	160	234	289	299	305	311	344	332
Construction	109	192	62	215	199	296	293	354
Other	259	386	446	520	641	678	744	729
Funds available	1,506	2,225	2,972	3,316	3,642	3,940	4,099	4,087
Appropriations.	1,053	1,325	1,867	1,881	2,241	2,257	2,298	2,388
Other [2]	453	900	1,105	1,435	1,401	1,683	1,801	1,699
Revenue from operations	79	106	215	234	246	245	274	264
Recreation visits (millions): [3]								
All areas	258.7	269.6	287.1	285.9	279.9	277.3	266.1	276.9
National parks [4]	57.7	64.8	64.3	66.1	64.1	64.5	63.4	63.8
National monuments	23.9	23.5	24.3	23.8	21.8	20.3	20.0	19.8
National historical, commemorative, archaeological [5]	57.5	56.9	72.6	72.2	66.7	70.2	66.6	77.0
National parkways	29.1	31.3	34.6	34.0	34.4	35.7	31.1	31.7
National recreation areas [4]	47.2	53.7	52.8	50.0	48.3	48.2	47.7	46.6
National seashores and lakeshores. . .	23.3	22.5	22.7	22.5	22.2	23.3	22.6	21.3
National Capital Parks	7.5	5.5	3.9	5.4	4.6	3.8	3.5	4.7
Recreation overnight stays (millions). . . .	17.6	16.8	15.9	15.4	15.3	14.7	14.2	13.7
In commercial lodgings	3.9	3.8	3.7	3.7	3.6	3.5	3.5	3.5
In Park Service campgrounds	7.9	7.1	6.2	5.9	5.7	5.8	5.7	5.4
In backcountry	1.7	2.2	2.0	1.9	2.0	1.9	1.8	1.7
Other	4.2	3.7	4.1	3.8	3.9	3.5	3.2	3.1
Land (1,000 acres): [6]								
Total	76,362	77,355	78,166	78,153	78,943	78,811	79,006	79,023
Parks	46,089	49,307	49,859	49,785	49,862	49,639	49,823	49,892
Recreation areas	3,344	3,353	3,404	3,388	3,388	3,390	3,391	3,391
Other	26,929	24,695	24,903	24,980	25,693	25,782	25,792	25,740
Acquisition, net.	21	27	44	187	20	115	135	13

[1] Financial data are those associated with the National Park System. Certain other functions of the National Park Service (principally the activities absorbed from the former Heritage Conservation and Recreation Service in 1981) are excluded. [2] Includes funds carried over from prior years. [3] For calendar year. Includes other areas, not shown separately. [4] For 1990, combined data for North Cascades National Park and two adjacent National Recreation Areas are included in National Parks total. [5] Includes military areas. [6] Federal land only, as of December 31. Federal land acreages, in addition to National Park Service administered lands, also include lands within national park system area boundaries but under the administration of other agencies. Year-to-year changes in the Federal lands figures include changes in the acreages of these other lands and hence often differ from "net acquisition."

Source: U.S. National Park Service, Visits, *National Park Statistical Abstract,* annual; and unpublished data. <http://www2.nature.nps.gov /stats/>.

Table 1245. State Parks and Recreation Areas by State: 2003

[For year ending June 30 (13,571 represents 13,571,000). Data are shown as reported by state park directors. In some states, park agency has under its control forests, fish and wildlife areas, and/or other areas. In other states, agency is responsible for state parks only]

State	Acreage (1,000)	Visitors (1,000) [1]	Revenue Total ($1,000)	Percent of operating expenditures	State	Acreage (1,000)	Visitors (1,000) [1]	Revenue Total ($1,000)	Percent of operating expenditures
United States. . .	13,571	734,990	666,231	36.4	Missouri	140	17,016	3,949	14.1
					Montana	71	1,575	1,228	20.1
Alabama	50	4,871	23,897	74.7	Nebraska	135	9,726	12,697	63.1
Alaska	3,353	4,301	1,478	25.4	Nevada	133	3,288	2,357	26.9
Arizona	61	2,201	5,302	31.7	New Hampshire . . .	86	5,472	8,500	100.0
Arkansas	52	9,970	14,003	43.4	New Jersey	380	14,943	2,324	6.4
California.	1,481	85,779	58,065	20.0	New Mexico.	91	3,983	3,838	22.8
Colorado	360	11,378	17,861	67.3	New York	1,532	57,001	54,103	33.1
Connecticut	202	7,033	-	-	North Carolina	171	13,213	3,187	11.0
Delaware.	24	5,549	7,758	42.6	North Dakota	17	1,134	776	29.0
Florida	602	18,241	32,075	45.6	Ohio	164	57,238	29,501	45.2
Georgia	84	12,405	27,114	47.4	Oklahoma	72	14,247	22,989	55.0
Hawaii	28	4,499	1,759	25.2	Oregon	95	39,244	15,414	37.2
Idaho	45	2,438	4,055	20.5	Pennsylvania	290	36,031	16,925	21.4
Illinois	327	37,137	16,851	29.8	Rhode Island	9	6,572	-	-
Indiana	179	14,798	35,683	81.6	South Carolina	80	7,544	13,769	58.0
Iowa	63	14,534	3,431	29.4	South Dakota	105	9,081	7,541	60.4
Kansas	32	8,250	5,736	68.9	Tennessee	154	27,020	32,516	50.7
Kentucky	45	7,668	47,559	62.2	Texas	668	17,620	13,385	26.4
Louisiana	41	2,064	200	1.1	Utah	122	5,806	7,991	46.6
Maine	99	2,542	-	-	Vermont	69	674	5,827	93.1
Maryland	266	10,219	14,361	33.8	Virginia	62	5,623	6,578	38.2
Massachusetts	295	10,512	2,199	7.1	Washington	259	44,991	15,720	32.7
Michigan	286	22,430	24,098	46.7	West Virginia	196	8,343	18,862	61.0
Minnesota	220	7,782	7,588	26.5	Wisconsin	132	15,739	8,648	43.8
Mississippi.	24	3,051	6,542	48.0	Wyoming.	119	2,214	-	-

-Represents or rounds to zero. [1] Includes overnight visitors.
Source: The National Association of State Park Directors, Raleigh, NC, *2004 Annual Information Exchange;* <http://www.indiana.edu /naspd/>.

Table 1246. Domestic Travel by U.S. Resident Households—Summary: 1998 to 2004

[In millions (656.3 represents 656,300,000). See headnote, Table 1247]

Type of trip	1998	1999	2000	2001	2002	2003	2004
All travel: [1]							
Household trips	656.3	640.8	637.7	645.6	637.0	643.5	663.5
Person-trips	1.108.0	1,089.5	1,100.8	1,123.1	1,127.0	1,140.0	1,163.9
All overnight travel:							
Household trips	479.4	475.5	477.5	483.7	482.7	491.2	508.4
Person-trips	800.0	804.9	822.4	839.2	855.4	871.6	893.1
Business travel:							
Household trips	195.8	192.9	184.9	179.0	166.6	163.5	168.2
Person-trips	245.4	240.9	235.1	227.6	214.7	210.5	219.0
Leisure travel: [2]							
Household trips	460.5	447.9	452.8	466.6	470.4	480.0	490.1
Person-trips	862.6	848.6	865.7	895.5	912.3	929.5	944.3

[1] Includes personal and other trips (e.g. medical, funerals, weddings), not shown separately. All domestic travel included. 95% of U.S. resident person-trips are domestic. [2] Includes visiting friends/relatives, outdoor recreation, entertainment and travel for other pleasure/personal reasons, etc.

Source: Travel Industry Association of America, Washington, DC, *TravelScope*, annual (copyright). <http://www.tia.org/home.asp>.

Table 1247. Characteristics of Domestic Overnight Leisure Trips by U.S. Resident Households: 1999 to 2004

[In millions except as indicated (331.1 represents 331,100,000). Represents household trips to destinations 50 miles or more, one-way, away from home and including one or more overnights. "Leisure" includes visiting friends/relatives, outdoor recreation, entertainment, and travel for other pleasure/personal reasons, etc. Other pleasure/personal trips are trips such as for medical reasons, funerals, weddings, etc. Based on a monthly mail panel survey of 25,000 U.S. households. For details, see source]

Overnight leisure trip characteristics	Unit	1999	2000	2001	2002	2003	2004
Total overnight leisure trips	Millions	331.1	337.1	349.1	354.0	360.3	375.4
Average nights per trip	Number	4.2	4.2	4.2	4.2	4.1	4.1
Traveled primarily by auto, truck, RV, or rental car	Percent	74	74	74	75	74	73
Traveled primarily by air	Percent	18	18	18	17	17	19
Stayed in a hotel/motel/B&B while on trip	Percent	42	43	42	43	44	44
Household income:							
Less than $50,000	Percent	(NA)	48	44	45	43	42
$50,000 or more	Percent	(NA)	52	56	55	57	58

NA Not available.

Source: Travel Industry Association of America, Washington, DC, *TravelScope*, annual (copyright); <http://www.tia.org/home.asp>

Table 1248. Domestic Travel Expenditures by State: 2003

[490,870 represents $490,870,000,000. Represents U.S. spending on domestic overnight trips and day trips of 50 miles or more, one way, away from home. Excludes spending by foreign visitors and by U.S. residents in U.S. territories and abroad]

State	Total (mil. dol.)	Percent distri- bution	Rank	State	Total (mil. dol.)	Percent distri- bution	Rank	State	Total (mil. dol.)	Percent distri- bution	Rank
U.S., total	490,870	100.0	(X)	IA	4,629	0.9	32	NC	12,632	2.6	11
				KS	3,846	0.8	37	ND	1,237	0.3	50
				KY	5,433	1.1	30	OH	12,419	2.5	12
AL	5,549	1.1	29	LA	9,055	1.8	19	OK	4,208	0.9	34
AK	1,380	0.3	48	ME	1,988	0.4	43	OR	5,557	1.1	28
AZ	9,153	1.9	20	MD	9,012	1.8	20	PA	15,237	3.1	7
AR	3,973	0.8	36	MA	9,952	2.0	15	RI	1,427	0.3	47
CA	61,075	12.4	1	MI	11,990	2.4	13	SC	7,215	1.5	24
CO	9,193	1.9	16	MN	7,952	1.6	22	SD	1,521	0.3	46
CT	6,709	1.4	26	MS	5,432	1.1	31	TN	10,580	2.2	14
DE	1,135	0.2	51	MO	9,177	1.9	17	TX	31,471	6.4	3
DC	4,280	0.9	33	MT	2,059	0.4	42	UT	3,725	0.8	38
FL	42,893	8.7	2	NE	2,773	0.6	39	VT	1,372	0.3	49
GA	14,524	3.0	9	NV	19,319	3.9	6	VA	13,890	2.8	10
HI	7,487	1.5	23	NH	2,688	0.5	40	WA	8,040	1.6	21
ID	2,206	0.4	41	NJ	14,728	3.0	8	WV	1,798	0.4	44
IL	21,595	4.4	5	NM	4,076	0.8	35	WI	7,157	1.5	25
IN	6,689	1.4	27	NY	27,726	5.6	4	WY	1,708	0.3	45

X Not applicable.

Source: Travel Industry Association of America, Washington, DC, *Impact of Travel on State Economies, 2003* (copyright); <http://www.tia.org/home.asp>.

Table 1249. International Travelers and Expenditures: 1990 to 2004

[(47,880 represents $47,880,000,000). For coverage, see Table 1250. Some traveler data revised since originally issued]

Year	Travel and passenger fare (mil. dol.)				U.S. net travel and passenger receipts (mil. dol.)	U.S. travelers to foreign countries (1,000)	International travelers to the U.S. (1,000)
	Payments by U.S. travelers		Receipts from international visitors				
	Total [1]	Expenditures abroad	Total [1]	Travel receipts			
1990	47,880	37,349	58,305	43,007	10,425	44,623	39,363
1995	59,579	44,916	82,304	63,395	22,725	51,285	43,491
1997	70,189	52,051	94,294	73,426	24,105	53,228	47,875
1998	76,454	56,483	91,423	71,325	14,969	55,697	46,377
1999	80,278	58,963	94,586	74,801	14,308	57,222	48,510
2000	88,979	64,705	103,087	82,400	14,108	61,327	51,237
2001	82,833	60,200	89,819	71,893	6,986	59,442	46,927
2002	78,013	58,044	83,593	66,547	5,761	58,066	43,582
2003 [2]	77,570	56,613	80,652	65,054	2,632	56,250	41,218
2004 [2]	87,900	64,590	93,707	74,768	5,807	61,509	46,077

[1] Includes passenger fares not shown separately. [2] Preliminary estimates for the receipt and payment figures.
Source: U.S. Department of Commerce; International Trade Administration; Office of Travel and Tourism Industries and Bureau of Economic Analysis (BEA); released: March 2005 <http://www.tinet.ita.doc.gov>.

Table 1250. International Travel: 1990 to 2004

[In thousands (44,623 represents 44,623,000). U.S. travelers cover residents of the United States, its territories and possessions. International travelers to the U.S. include travelers for business and pleasure, excludes travel by international personnel and international businessmen employed in the United States. Some traveler data revised since originally issued]

Item and area	1990	1995	1999	2000	2001	2002	2003	2004
U.S. travelers to international countries [1][2]	44,623	51,285	57,318	61,327	59,442	58,066	56,250	61,509
Canada	12,252	13,005	15,276	15,188	15,570	16,168	14,232	15,038
Mexico.	16,381	19,221	17,463	10,285	18,623	18,501	17,566	19,369
Total overseas [3].	15,990	19,059	24,579	26,853	25,249	23,397	24,452	27,102
Europe [3]	8,043	8,596	11,577	13,373	11,438	10,131	10,319	(N/A)
International travelers to the U.S. . . .	39,363	43,491	48,510	51,237	46,927	43,582	41,218	46,077
Canada	17,263	14,663	14,116	14,666	13,527	13,025	12,666	13,849
Mexico.	7,041	8,189	9,928	10,596	11,567	11,440	10,526	11,906
Total overseas [3].	15,059	20,639	24,466	25,975	21,833	19,117	18,026	20,322
Europe	6,659	8,793	11,243	11,597	9,496	8,603	8,639	9,686
South America	4,360	6,616	6,935	7,554	6,316	5,689	5,003	5,802
Central America	1,328	2,449	2,733	2,941	2,531	1,815	1,522	1,645
Caribbean	1,137	1,044	1,258	1,331	1,202	1,053	998	1,095
Far East	412	509	731	822	771	704	656	692
Middle East	662	588	667	731	586	529	525	660
Oceania	365	454	625	702	644	483	447	502
Africa	137	186	274	295	287	241	236	241

NA Not available [1] A person is counted in each area visited, but only once in the total. [2] 2004 U.S. Outbound totals are preliminary estimates. [3] Overseas excludes Canada and Mexico.
Source: U.S. Dept. of Commerce, International Trade Administration, Tourism Industries, Internet site <http://www.tinet.ita.doc.gov>

Table 1251. Top States and Cities Visited by Overseas Travelers: 2000 and 2004

[25,975 represents 25,975,000. Includes travelers for business and pleasure, and excludes travel by international personnel and international businessmen employed in the United States]

State	Overseas visitors [1] (1,000)		Market share (percent)		City	Overseas visitors [1] (1,000)		Market share (percent)	
	2000	2004	2000	2004		2000	2004	2000	2004
Total overseas travelers [2] . .	25,975	20,322	100.0	100	New York City, NY	5,714	5,162	22.0	25.4
New York	5,922	5,426	22.8	26.7	Los Angeles, CA	3,533	2,276	13.6	11.2
Florida	6,026	4,430	23.2	21.8	Miami, FL	2,935	2,195	11.3	10.8
California	6,364	4,207	24.5	20.7	Orlando, FL	3,013	1,951	11.6	9.6
Hawaiian Islands	2,727	2,215	10.5	10.9	Oahu/Honolulu, HI	2,234	1,870	8.6	9.2
Nevada	2,364	1,626	9.1	8.0	San Francisco, CA	2,831	1,870	10.9	9.2
Guam	1,325	1,036	5.1	5.1	Las Vegas, NV	2,260	1,565	8.7	7.7
Illinois	1,377	975	5.3	4.8	Washington, DC	1,481	1,057	5.7	5.2
Massachusetts	1,429	935	5.5	4.6	Chicago, IL	1,351	935	5.2	4.6
Texas	1,169	874	4.5	4.3	Boston, MA	1,325	833	5.1	4.1
New Jersey	909	833	3.5	4.1	San Diego, CA	701	508	2.7	2.5
Pennsylvania	649	691	2.5	3.4	Philadelphia, PA	390	427	1.5	2.1
Arizona	883	630	3.4	3.1	Houston, TX	442	386	1.7	1.9
Georgia	805	427	3.1	2.1	Tampa/St. Petersburg, FL. .	519	386	2.0	1.9
Michigan	494	366	1.9	1.8	Atlanta, GA	701	366	2.7	1.8
Washington	468	366	1.8	1.8	Ft. Lauderdale, FL.	468	345	1.8	1.7
Colorado	519	345	2.0	1.7	San Jose, CA	494	345	1.9	1.7
Ohio	390	325	1.5	1.6	Anaheim, CA	494	325	1.9	1.6
Utah	416	325	1.6	1.6	Dallas/Ft. Worth, TX	494	325	1.9	1.6
North Carolina	416	305	1.6	1.5	Seattle, WA	416	325	1.6	1.6
Virginia	364	305	1.4	1.5	Florida Keys	286	285	1.1	1.4
Louisiana	390	285	1.5	1.4	New Orleans, LA	364	244	1.4	1.2
Connecticut	260	264	1.0	1.3	Denver, CO	286	224	1.1	1.0

[1] Excludes Canada and Mexico. [2] Includes other states and cities, not shown separately.
Source: U.S. Dept. of Commerce, International Trade Administration, Office of Travel and Tourism Industries, Internet site <http://www.tinet.ita.doc.gov>.

Table 1252. Impact of International Travel on States' Economies: 2003

[Preliminary. (64,509.0 represents $64,509,000,000)]

State	Travel expenditures (mil. dol.)	Travel generated payroll (mil. dol.)	Travel generated employment (1,000)	Travel generated tax receipts (mil. dol.)	State	Travel expenditures (mil. dol.)	Travel generated payroll (mil. dol.)	Travel generated employment (1,000)	Travel generated tax receipts (mil. dol.)
U.S., total...	64,509.0	18,425.2	814.5	10,291.6	MO	121.4	40.0	2.0	23.3
AL	(NA)	(NA)	(NA)	(NA)	MT	(NA)	(NA)	(NA)	(NA)
AK	(NA)	(NA)	(NA)	(NA)	NE	(NA)	(NA)	(NA)	(NA)
AZ	1,384.0	462.7	20.9	221.1	NV	2,021.1	758.2	34.8	291.4
AR	(NA)	(NA)	(NA)	(NA)	NH	120.7	21.4	1.2	11.6
CA	10,485.1	3,122.5	130.2	1,770.0	NJ	688.5	224.4	9.2	127.0
CO	616.4	213.5	9.8	135.1	NM	(NA)	(NA)	(NA)	(NA)
CT	202.4	42.2	1.8	32.5	NY	7,708.0	2,422.8	89.4	1,582.5
DE	(NA)	(NA)	(NA)	(NA)	NC	417.8	134.4	6.8	73.3
DC	1,400.9	345.4	12.7	207.2	ND	(NA)	(NA)	(NA)	(NA)
FL	13,372.4	3,942.3	187.8	2,076.5	OH	556.0	133.6	7.2	96.9
GA	1,124.5	457.7	16.3	257.3	OK	(NA)	(NA)	(NA)	(NA)
HI	5,416.0	1,504.0	62.3	783.8	OR	303.0	79.8	4.3	45.9
ID	(NA)	(NA)	(NA)	(NA)	PA	1,181.6	378.8	16.5	204.6
IL	1,368.4	416.1	18.2	282.5	RI	(NA)	(NA)	(NA)	(NA)
IN	209.1	57.9	3.2	33.1	SC	514.2	117.7	7.8	76.4
IA	(NA)	(NA)	(NA)	(NA)	SD	(NA)	(NA)	(NA)	(NA)
KS	(NA)	(NA)	(NA)	(NA)	TN	270.0	77.2	3.9	58.8
KY	(NA)	(NA)	(NA)	(NA)	TX	3,118.7	1,058.7	47.8	573.5
LA	363.6	82.3	4.6	49.5	UT	318.3	123.9	7.2	66.0
ME	(NA)	(NA)	(NA)	(NA)	VT	(NA)	(NA)	(NA)	(NA)
MD	319.0	101.3	4.4	64.9	VA	413.7	120.8	6.2	66.4
MA	1,246.6	372.1	14.3	222.3	WA	779.0	219.0	10.2	138.6
MI	582.0	171.8	7.5	106.9	WV	(NA)	(NA)	(NA)	(NA)
MN	329.7	128.7	5.7	101.1	WI	229.2	64.5	4.0	39.6
MS	(NA)	(NA)	(NA)	(NA)	WY	(NA)	(NA)	(NA)	(NA)

[1] NA not available due to small sample size for international visitors.

Source: Travel Industry Association of America, Washington, DC, Impact of Travel on State Economies, 2003 Edition (copyright); <http://www.tia.org/default.asp>.

Table 1253. Foreign Visitors for Pleasure Admitted by Country of Citizenship: 1990 to 2003

[In thousands (13,418 represents 13,418,000). For years ending September 30. Represents non-U.S. citizens admitted to the country for a temporary period of time (also known as nonimmigrants)]

Country	1990	1995	2000	2003	Country	1990	1995	2000	2003
All countries [1]	13,418	17,612	30,511	20,143	United Arab Emirates	7	14	36	2
Europe [1]	5,383	7,012	11,806	8,331	Africa [1]	105	137	327	192
Austria	87	146	182	95	Egypt	16	16	44	17
Belgium	95	153	254	119	Nigeria	11	10	27	36
Czech Republic	(X)	12	44	24	South Africa	26	59	114	51
Denmark	75	78	150	111	Oceania [1]	562	478	748	570
Finland	83	47	95	54	Australia	380	327	535	398
France	566	738	1,113	758	New Zealand [4]	153	115	170	160
Germany [2]	969	1,550	1,925	1,033	North America [1]	2,463	2,240	6,501	4,979
Greece	43	44	60	33	Canada	119	127	277	16
Hungary	15	29	58	25	Mexico	1,061	893	3,972	3,568
Iceland	10	14	27	18	Caribbean [1]	963	831	1,404	841
Ireland	81	126	325	298	Aruba	10	19	24	7
Italy	308	427	626	483	Bahamas, The	332	234	377	268
Netherlands	214	308	559	405	Barbados	34	36	57	33
Norway	80	71	144	96	British Virgin Islands	8	9	31	4
Poland	55	36	116	93	Cayman Islands	31	31	53	19
Portugal	30	40	86	64	Dominican Republic	137	138	195	136
Russia	(X)	33	74	38	Haiti	57	43	72	58
Spain	183	248	370	334	Jamaica	132	130	240	144
Sweden	230	142	321	173	Netherlands Antilles	31	32	43	8
Switzerland	236	321	400	196	Trinidad and Tobago	81	64	133	96
United Kingdom	1,899	2,342	4,671	3,744	Central America [1]	320	387	792	554
Asia [1]	3,830	5,666	7,853	4,612	Costa Rica	62	91	172	96
China [3]	187	378	656	277	El Salvador	46	63	175	156
Hong Kong	111	162	195	40	Guatemala	91	99	177	128
India	75	75	253	198	Honduras	52	37	87	66
Indonesia	28	44	62	31	Nicaragua	13	28	47	31
Israel	128	160	319	191	Panama	43	54	106	59
Japan	2,846	3,986	4,946	3,000	South America [1]	1,016	1,978	2,867	1,294
Korea	120	427	606	478	Argentina	136	320	515	119
Malaysia	27	40	64	21	Bolivia	14	16	48	19
Pakistan	27	27	47	32	Brazil	300	710	706	273
Philippines	76	85	163	135	Chile	54	117	194	81
Saudi Arabia	33	45	67	6	Colombia	122	174	411	254
Singapore	32	61	131	43	Ecuador	57	77	122	102
Thailand	25	59	76	30	Peru	97	98	190	144
Turkey	20	27	93	51	Uruguay	16	37	66	39
					Venezuela	199	400	570	234

X Not applicable.   [1] Includes other countries and countries unknown, not shown separately.   [2] Data for 1990 are for former West Germany.   [3] Includes People's Republic of China and Taiwan.   [4] Prior to fiscal year 1995, data for Niue are included in New Zealand.

Source: U.S. Department of Homeland Security, Office of Immigration Statistics, 2003 Yearbook of Immigration Statistics,. See also <http://www.uscis.gov/graphics/shared/aboutus/statistics/ybpage.htm>.

Arts, Entertainment, and Recreation 803

Table 1254. Summary of Travel Trends: 1977 to 2001

[108,826 represents 108,826,000,000. Data obtained by collecting information on all trips taken by the respondent on a specific day (known as travel day), combined with longer trips taken over a 4-week period (known as travel period). For comparability with previous survey data, all data are based only on trips taken during travel day. Be aware that terminology changes from survey to survey. See source for details]

Characteristics	Unit	1977	1983	1990	1995	2001
Vehicle trips	Millions	108,826	126,874	158,927	229,745	233,040
Vehicle miles of travel (VMT)	Millions	907,603	1,002,139	1,409,600	2,068,368	2,274,797
Person trips	Millions	211,778	224,385	249,562	378,930	407,262
Person miles of travel	Millions	1,879,215	1,946,662	2,315,300	3,411,122	3,972,749
Average annual VMT per household [1]	Miles	12,036	11,739	15,100	20,895	21,188
To or from work	Miles	3,815	3,538	4,853	6,492	5,724
Shopping	Miles	1,336	1,567	1,743	2,807	3,062
Other family or personal business	Miles	1,444	1,816	3,014	4,307	3,956
Social and recreational	Miles	3,286	3,534	4,060	4,764	5,186
Average annual vehicle trips per household [1]	Number	1,442	1,486	1,702	2,321	2,171
To or from work	Number	423	414	448	553	479
Shopping	Number	268	297	345	501	458
Other family or personal business	Number	215	272	411	626	537
Social and recreational	Number	320	335	349	427	441
Average vehicle trip length [1]	Miles	8.35	7.90	8.98	9.06	9.87
To or from work	Miles	9.02	8.55	10.97	11.80	12.08
Shopping	Miles	4.99	5.28	5.10	5.64	6.74
Other family or personal business	Miles	6.72	6.68	7.43	6.93	7.45
Social and recreational	Miles	10.27	10.55	11.80	11.24	11.94
Average vehicle occupancy [1]	Persons	1.9	1.8	1.6	1.6	1.6
To or from work	Persons	1.3	1.3	1.1	1.1	1.1
Shopping	Persons	2.1	1.8	1.7	1.7	1.8
Other family or personal business	Persons	2.0	1.8	1.8	1.8	1.8
Social and recreational	Persons	2.4	2.1	2.1	2.0	2.0
Workers by usual mode to work	Percent	100.0	100.0	100.0	100.0	100.0
Auto	Percent	93.0	92.4	87.8	91.0	91.0
Public transit	Percent	4.7	5.8	5.3	5.1	5.0
Other	Percent	2.3	1.8	6.9	3.9	4.0

[1] Includes other purposes not shown separately.

Source: 1995 and prior years—U.S. Federal Highway Administration, Summary of Travel Trends, 1995 National Personal Transportation Survey, December 1999; 2001—U.S. Federal Highway Administration and the U.S. Bureau of Transportation Statistics, 2001 National Household Travel Survey, January 2004 Release. See Internet site <http://www.bts.gov/programs/nationalhouseholdtravelsurvey/>.

Table 1255. Travel in the United States by Selected Trip Characteristics: 2001

[In thousands (2,554,068 represents 2,554,068,000). Trips of 50 miles or more, one way. U.S. destinations only. Data based on a sample and subject to sampling variability]

Trip characteristics	Person trips		Person miles		Personal use vehicle trips		Personal use vehicle miles	
	Number (1,000)	Per-cent	Number (1,000)	Per-cent	Number (1,000)	Per-cent	Number (1,000)	Per-cent
Total	2,554,068	100.0	1,138,322,697	100.0	1,470,475	100.0	434,764,422	100.0
Principal means of transportation:								
Personal use vehicles	2,310,376	90.5	735,882,255	64.7	1,470,475	100.0	434,764,422	100.0
Airplane	165,039	6.5	367,888,741	32.3	(X)	(X)	(X)	(X)
Commercial airplane	158,880	6.2	361,717,015	31.8	(X)	(X)	(X)	(X)
Bus [1]	52,962	2.1	23,747,433	2.1	(X)	(X)	(X)	(X)
Intercity bus	3,456	0.1	1,765,696	0.2	(X)	(X)	(X)	(X)
Charter, tour, or school bus	45,952	1.8	21,019,942	1.9	(X)	(X)	(X)	(X)
Train	20,672	0.8	9,266,373	0.8	(X)	(X)	(X)	(X)
Ship, boat, or ferry	(B)	(B)	(B)	(B)	(X)	(X)	(X)	(X)
Other	(B)	(B)	(B)	(B)	(X)	(X)	(X)	(X)
Round trip distance:								
100 to 299 miles	1,688,358	66.1	284,586,370	25.0	1,086,375	73.9	179,729,832	41.3
300 to 499 miles	373,550	14.6	143,571,597	12.6	207,377	14.1	79,094,901	18.2
500 to 999 miles	261,802	10.3	180,669,482	15.9	126,324	8.6	85,265,168	19.6
1,000 to 1,999 miles	125,665	4.9	178,629,838	15.7	36,180	2.5	48,308,222	11.1
2,000 miles or more	104,694	4.1	350,865,409	30.8	14,219	1.0	42,366,300	9.7
Mean (miles)	446	(X)	(X)	(X)	296	(X)	(X)	(X)
Median [2] (miles)	206	(X)	(X)	(X)	180	(X)	(X)	(X)
Main purpose of trip:								
Commuting	329,395	12.9	65,877,968	5.8	273,779	18.6	49,068,646	11.3
Other business	405,866	15.9	242,353,212	21.3	268,688	18.3	82,157,090	18.9
Personal/leisure	1,406,411	55.1	667,471,358	58.7	708,145	48.2	235,475,184	54.2
Personal business	322,645	12.6	130,020,982	11.4	162,832	11.1	48,761,452	11.2
Other	88,230	3.5	32,031,679	2.8	56,085	3.8	19,062,128	4.4
Mean travel party size:								
Household members	2.1	(X)	(X)	(X)	1.8	(X)	(X)	(X)
Non-Household members	1.0	(X)	(X)	(X)	(X)	(X)	(X)	(X)
Nights away from home:								
1 to 3 nights	808,281	31.7	414,219,147	36.4	406,995	27.7	153,687,767	35.4
4 to 7 nights	214,464	8.4	269,265,597	23.7	82,548	5.6	59,427,600	13.7
8 or more nights	76,475	3.0	150,368,429	13.2	25,793	1.8	36,215,748	8.3
Mean excluding none (nights)	3.3	(X)	(X)	(X)	2.9	(X)	(X)	(X)

- Represents or rounds to zero. B Base figure too small to meet statistical standards for reliability of a derived figure. X Not applicable. [1] Includes other types of buses. [2] For definition of median, see Guide to Tabular Presentation.

Source: U.S. Department of Transportation, Bureau of Transportation Statistics and the Federal Highway Administration, National Household Travel Survey. <http://www.bts.gov/programs/nationalhouseholdtravelsurvey/>.

[(30,433 represents 30,433,000)]

Item and gateway	Entering the U.S. (1,000)	Item and gateway	Entering the U.S. (1,000)
All U.S.-Canadian land gateways [1]		**All U.S.-Mexican land gateways**	
Personal vehicles	30,433	Personal vehicles	91,342
Personal vehicle passengers.	64,848	Personal vehicle passengers.	190,937
Buses.	164	Buses.	269
Bus passengers	3,890	Bus passengers	3,389
Train passengers	223	Train passengers	13
Pedestrians	826	Pedestrians	48,084
Personal vehicles—top 5 gateways:		Personal vehicles—top 5 gateways:	
Buffalo-Niagara Falls, NY	6,149	San Ysidro, CA	17,621
Detroit, MI	6,131	El Paso, TX	14,817
Blaine, WA	2,524	Brownsville, TX	7,211
Port Huron, MI	1,996	Hidalgo, TX	7,184
Calais, ME	1,200	Laredo, TX	6,725
Personal vehicle passengers—top 5 gateways:		Personal vehicle passengers—top 5 gateways:	
Buffalo-Niagara Falls, NY	13,195	San Ysidro, CA	33,383
Detroit, MI	10,574	El Paso, TX	28,108
Blaine, WA	4,936	Hidalgo, TX	15,515
Port Huron, MI	3,909	Brownsville, TX	15,374
Massena, NY	3,598	Laredo, TX	15,033
Buses—top 5 gateways:		Buses—top 5 gateways:	
Buffalo-Niagara Falls, NY	40	San Ysidro, CA	110
Detroit, MI	37	Otay Mesa, CA	41
Sault Ste. Marie, MI	17	Laredo, TX	38
Champlain-Rouses Point, NY.	16	Hidalgo, TX	33
Blaine, WA	14	El Paso, TX	18
Bus passengers—top 5 gateways:		Bus passengers—top 5 gateways:	
Buffalo-Niagara Falls, NY	1,223	San Ysidro, CA	1,032
Detroit, MI	931	Laredo, TX	803
Blaine, WA	329	Hidalgo, TX	650
Champlain-Rouses Point, NY.	277	El Paso, TX	265
Sault Ste. Marie, MI	224	Otay Mesa, CA	251
Train passengers—top 5 gateways:		Train passengers—top 5 gateways:	
Skagway, AK.	52	Eagle Pass, TX	7
Blaine, WA	42	El Paso, TX	7
Buffalo-Niagara Falls, NY	31	Nogales, AZ	2
Champlain-Rouses Point, NY.	30	Calexico East, CA	2
Port Huron, MI	18	Otay Mesa/San Ysidro, CA	1
Pedestrians—top 5 gateways:		Pedestrians—top 5 gateways:	
Buffalo-Niagara Falls, NY	547	San Ysidro, CA	9,458
Sumas, WA	55	El Paso, TX	8,442
Calais, ME	45	Nogales, AZ	6,131
International Falls, MN	28	Calexico, CA.	4,847
Portland, ME (ferry crossing)	22	Laredo, TX	4,507

[1] Data reflect all personal vehicles, buses, passengers, and pedestrians entering the U.S.-Canadian border, regardless of nationality.

Source: U.S. Department of Transportation, Research and Innovative Technology Administration, Bureau of Transportation Statistics, special tabulations, May 2005. Based on the following primary data source: U.S. Department of Treasury, Customs and Border Protection, Office of Field Operations, Operations Management Database (Washington, DC, 2004) <http://www.bts.gov /programs/international/bordercrossingentrydata/>.

No. 834.—POWER LAUNDRIES, CLEANING AND DYEING ESTABLISHMENTS, AND RUG-CLEANING ESTABLISHMENTS: SUMMARY OF CENSUS STATISTICS

NOTE.—All money figures in thousands of dollars. Statistics cover establishments reporting receipts of $5,000 or more. Data for power laundries relate to commercial laundries. Data for cleaning and dyeing establishments are restricted to establishments using mechanical power; they include cleaning and dyeing departments of laundries where separate data could be obtained. Rug-cleaning, which was given a separate classification beginning with 1933, was treated in general as an activity of the power laundry industry at prior censuses; statistics include rug-cleaning departments of laundries and of cleaning and dyeing plants so far as they were reported separately. Data for 1933 are incomplete, as about 15 percent of the laundries and 24 percent of the cleaning and dyeing establishments that had reported for 1931 failed to supply any information as to their status or activities in 1933. The laundries that failed to report accounted for around 8 percent of the 1931 totals for number of wage earners and receipts for work done for all laundries, while the cleaning and dyeing establishments that did not report accounted for about 15 percent of the 1931 totals for these two items for cleaning and dyeing establishments.

	Number of laundries	Proprietors and firm members	Salaried employees [1]	Wage earners (average for the year)	Salaries [1]	Wages	Cost of supplies, fuel, and purchased electric energy	Cost of contract work	Receipts for work done
Power laundries:									
1919	4,881	[2]	[2]	130,489	[2]	91,926	52,842	1,555	233,816
1925	4,859	3,851	15,412	169,200	31,613	162,466	55,407	1,107	362,295
1927	6,013	5,224	17,828	203,216	35,781	201,132	68,283	[2]	454,034
1929	6,776	5,220	21,964	233,187	49,833	228,861	80,265	[2]	541,158
1931	6,400	[2]	[2]	217,138	[2]	202,197	67,267	2,372	465,969
1933	5,122	3,416	13,767	175,545	17,858	126,838	47,706	1,971	295,641
1935	6,316	4,244	19,920	208,354	34,586	154,791	62,796	2,356	[4]309,452
Cleaning and dyeing establishments:									
1919	1,748	[2]	[2]	18,408	[2]	17,866	11,511	461	53,183
1925	2,406	2,263	5,769	29,386	10,550	37,590	15,188	814	102,394
1927	3,175	3,106	7,332	40,251	14,474	52,542	18,829	1,340	142,814
1929	5,296	4,912	9,244	59,148	20,390	75,931	26,837	[2]	201,255
1931	4,508	[2]	[2]	50,643	[2]	57,829	20,250	1,234	147,514
1933	3,594	3,090	4,981	43,619	5,048	36,894	15,470	695	93,314
1935	5,510	4,980	9,334	57,286	12,483	49,792	21,656	1,129	[4]130,657
Rug-cleaning establishments:									
1933	270	250	146	1,596	186	1,404	772	28	4,400
1935	506	395	670	2,344	1,136	2,260	1,211	90	[4]8,001

[1] Figures for 1933 exclude data for salaried officers of corporations included in figures for other years.
[2] Not available.
[3] Included in figures for supplies, fuel, and purchased electric energy.
[4] Figures for power laundries include $876,000 receipts for rug cleaning and $25,574,000 receipts for cleaning and dyeing; figures for cleaning and dyeing establishments include $1,683,000 receipts for rug cleaning and $1,365,000 receipts for laundry work; figures for rug-cleaning establishments include $173,000 receipts for cleaning and dyeing.

Source: Bureau of the Census, Department of Commerce. The 1933 figures were collected in cooperation with the Laundry Owners National Association and the National Association of Dyers and Cleaners.

No. 835.—HOTELS: COMPARATIVE STATISTICS FOR YEAR-ROUND HOTELS OF 25 OR MORE GUEST ROOMS, 1929, 1933, AND 1935, AND SUMMARY FOR ALL HOTELS, BY SIZE, 1935

NOTE.—Receipts and pay roll in thousands of dollars. The census includes principally establishments designating themselves as hotels and providing accommodations as their main business activity. Establishments reporting a total of less than six guest rooms or receipts from room rentals amounting to less than $500 for a full year's operations, are excluded from the 1935 figures. Owing to differences in coverage for 1929, 1933, and 1935, comparable data for these years are available only for year-round hotels of 25 or more guest rooms

Item	1929	1933	1935	Size (based on number of guest rooms)	Number	Receipts	Proprietors, etc. [4]	Employees [5]
				All hotels, 1935	28,822	720,145	24,573	291,165
YEAR-ROUND HOTELS WITH 25 OR MORE GUEST ROOMS [1]				Hotels having				
Number of hotels	11,873	10,680	11,373	Less than 25 rooms	13,092	54,671	12,912	22,365
Number of guest rooms	1,005,684	890,866	934,661	25 to 49 rooms	8,352	69,810	7,741	30,534
Receipts	873,508	398,674	565,317	50 to 99 rooms	4,436	96,619	3,084	40,389
Employees (full-time and part-time) [3]	207,903	190,183	234,491	100 to 299 rooms	2,423	212,836	813	88,682
Total pay roll [3]	232,137	118,489	158,400	300 rooms and over	519	286,209	23	109,195

[1] Data for California are not included as comparable figures for all years are not available.
[2] Average number based on number of employees for April, July, October, and December.
[3] Includes no compensation for proprietors and firm members of unincorporated businesses.
[4] Active proprietors and firm members.
[5] Full-time and part-time, average for year.

Source: Bureau of the Census, Department of Commerce.

Section 27
Accommodation, Food Services, and Other Services

This section presents statistics relating to services other than those covered in the previous few sections (22 to 26) on domestic trade, transportation, communications, financial services, and recreation services. Data shown for services are classified by kind of business and cover sales or receipts, establishments, employees, payrolls, and other items. The principal sources of these data are from the Census Bureau and include the *2002 Economic Census* , annual surveys, and the *County Business Patterns* program. These data are supplemented by data from several sources such as the National Restaurant Association on food and drink sales (Table 1269), the American Hotel & Lodging Association on lodging (Table 1268), and Universal McCann on advertising (Table 1265).

Data on these services also appear in several other sections. For instance, labor force employment and earnings data appear in Section 12, Labor Force, Employment, and Earnings; gross domestic product of the industry (Table 651) appear in Section 13, Income, Expenditures, and Wealth; and financial data (several tables) from the quarterly *Statistics of Income Bulletin*, published by the Internal Revenue Service, appear in Section 15, Business Enterprise.

Censuses—Limited coverage of the service industries started in 1933. Beginning with the 1967 census, legislation provides for a census of each area to be conducted every 5 years (for years ending in "2" and "7"). For more information on the most current census, see the *History of the 1997 Economic Census* found at <http://www.census.gov/prod/ec97/pol00-hec.pdf>. The industries covered in the censuses and surveys of business are those classified in 13 sectors defined in the *North American Industry Classification System,* called NAICS (see below). All Census Bureau tables in this section are utilizing the new NAICS codes, which

replaced the Standard Industrial Classification (SIC) system. NAICS makes substantial structural improvements and identifies over 350 new industries. At the same time, it causes breaks in time series far more profound than any prior revision of the previously used SIC system. For information on this system and how it affects the comparability of statistics historically, see text, Section 15, Business Enterprise, and especially the Census Web site at <http://www.census.gov/epcd/www/naics.html>.

The *Accommodation and Food Services sector* (NAICS sector 72) comprises establishments providing customers with lodging and/or preparing meals, snacks, and beverages for immediate consumption. The *Other Services (Except Public Administration) sector* (NAICS sector 81) comprises establishments with payroll engaged in providing services not specifically provided for elsewhere in the NAICS. Establishments in this sector are primarily engaged in activities such as repair and maintenance of equipment and machinery, personal and laundry services, and religious, grantmaking, civic, professional, and similar organizations. Establishments providing death care services, pet care services, photofinishing services, temporary parking services, and dating services are also included. Private households that employ workers on or about the premises in activities primarily concerned with the operation of the household are included in this sector but are not included in the scope of the census. In general, the 2002 Economic Census has two series of publications for these two sectors: 1) subject series with reports such as product lines, and establishment and firm sizes, and 2) geographic reports with individual reports for each state. For information on these series, see the Census Bureau Web site at <http://www.census.gov/econ/census02>.

Current surveys—The Service Annual Survey provides annual estimates of nationwide receipts for selected personal,

U.S. Census Bureau, Statistical Abstract of the United States: 2006

business, leasing and repair, amusement and entertainment, social and health, and other professional service industries in the United States. For selected social, health, and other professional service industries, separate estimates are developed for receipts of taxable firms and revenue and expenses for firms and organizations exempt from federal income taxes. Several service sectors from this survey are covered in other sections of this publication. The estimates for tax exempt firms in these industries are derived from a sample of employer firms only. Estimates obtained from annual and monthly surveys are based on sample data and are not expected to agree exactly with results that would be obtained from a complete census of all establishments. Data include estimates for sampling units not reporting.

Statistical reliability—For a discussion of statistical collection and estimation, sampling procedures, and measures of statistical reliability applicable to Census Bureau data, see Appendix III.

Table 1257. **Service Related Industries—Establishments, Employees, and Payroll: 2002**

[In thousands; 917,006,982 represents $917,006,982,000 except as indicated. Covers establishments with payroll. These data are preliminary and are subject to change. For statement on methodology, see Appendix III]

Kind of business	NAICS code [1]	Establishments, (Number)	Sales, receipts, revenue, or shipments ($1,000)	Annual payroll ($1,000)	Paid employees, number
Professional, scientific, and technical services	54	771,311	890,775,381	373,735,771	7,301,980
Management of companies and enterprises.	55	50,102	119,477,966	190,807,531	2,853,788
Administrative and support and waste management and remediation services.	56	351,415	435,579,740	207,603,519	8,905,178
Administrative and support services	561	333,010	384,366,388	195,425,035	8,574,136
Waste management and remediation services.	562	18,405	51,213,352	12,178,484	331,042
Accommodation and food services.	72	565,300	452,340,621	127,507,055	10,141,955
Accommodation.	721	60,870	130,320,114	34,874,261	1,827,097
Food services and drinking places	722	504,430	322,020,507	92,632,794	8,314,858
Other services (except public administration)	81	538,404	310,912,392	83,838,731	3,512,350
Repair and maintenance	811	230,817	119,700,261	35,266,671	1,286,510
Personal and laundry services	812	192,659	70,019,133	22,269,074	1,256,337
Religious, grantmaking, civic, professional, and similar organizations	813	102,129	116,001,791	24,264,673	840,769

S Estimates did not meet publication standards.   [1] North American Industry Classification System, 2002; see text, Section 15.

Source: U.S. Census Bureau, *2002 Economic Census, Industry Series;* published 2 August 2005. See also <http://www.census.gov/econ/census02/data/us/US000.HTM>.

U.S. Census Bureau, Statistical Abstract of the United States: 2006

Table 1258. Services Related Industries—Establishments, Sales, Employees, and Payroll: 1997 and 2002

[In millions of dollars 595,251 represents $595,251,000,000 except as indicated. Covers establishments with payroll. These data are preliminary and are subject to change. For statement on methodology, see Appendix III]

Kind of business	NAICS code [1]	1997				2002			
		Establishments (number)	Sales, receipts, revenue, or shipments (mil. dol.)	Annual payroll (mil. dol.)	Paid employees	Establishments (number)	Sales, receipts, revenue, or shipments (mil. dol.)	Annual payroll (mil. dol.)	Paid employees
Professional, scientific, & technical services	54	621,129	595,251	231,399	5,361,210	746,964	896,343	374,515	7,508,866
Professional, scientific, & technical services	541	621,129	595,251	231,399	5,361,210	746,964	896,343	374,515	7,508,866
Administrative & support & waste management & remediation services	56	276,393	295,936	137,337	7,347,366	276,040	413,623	193,517	8,344,783
Administrative & support services	561	260,025	256,591	128,438	7,066,658	257,569	362,310	181,411	8,002,725
Waste management & remediation services	562	16,368	39,346	8,899	280,708	18,471	51,313	12,106	342,058
Accommodation & food services	72	545,068	350,399	97,007	9,451,226	562,059	463,375	128,683	10,836,365
Accommodation.	721	58,162	98,457	26,674	1,696,659	(S)	(S)	(S)	(S)
Food services and drinking places	722	486,906	251,942	70,334	7,754,567	(S)	(S)	(S)	(S)
Other services (except public administration)	81	519,715	265,898	65,520	3,256,178	527,508	315,049	82,670	3,527,621
Repair & maintenance	811	235,466	105,154	29,875	1,276,389	232,949	120,365	35,459	1,366,997
Personal & laundry services	812	185,484	57,879	18,577	1,217,185	192,333	72,893	22,591	1,311,387
Religious, grantmaking, civic, professional, & similar organizations.	813	98,765	102,864	17,068	762,604	102,226	121,790	24,619	849,237

S Estimates did not meet publication standards. [1] North American Industry Classification System; 2002; see text, Section 15.

Source: U.S. Census Bureau, 2002 Economic Census, Industry Series, issued December 2004.

Table 1259. Service-Related Industries—Nonemployer Establishments and Receipts by Kind of Business: 2000 to 2002

[2,420 represents 2,420,000. Includes only firms subject to federal income tax. Nonemployers are businesses with no paid employees. Based on the North American Industry Classification System, 1997 (NAICS), see text, Section 15]

Kind of business	NAICS code	Establishments (1,000)			Receipts (mil. dol.)		
		2000	2001	2002	2000	2001	2002
Professional, scientific & technical services	54	2,420	2,446	2,553	90,272	91,292	96,395
Management, sci & tech consulting services	5416	383	380	465	17,123	16,947	18,637
Admin/support waste mgt/remediation services.	56	1,032	1,076	1,263	23,754	24,851	26,910
Administrative & support services.	561	1,017	1,061	1,244	22,858	23,940	25,826
Accommodation & food services	72	218	226	242	13,418	13,472	14,178
Accommodation	721	51	52	52	3,528	3,554	3,766
Food services & drinking places	722	167	174	190	9,890	9,917	10,412
Other services (except public administration) [1]	81	2,350	2,433	2,459	55,056	57,653	60,468
Repair & maintenance [1]	811	624	632	643	21,139	21,844	22,817
Automotive R&M	8111	263	265	271	11,492	11,915	12,182
Personal & household goods R&M	8114	264	271	274	6,109	6,344	6,831
Personal & laundry services	812	1,562	1,632	1,642	31,459	33,234	35,127
Personal care services	8121	598	631	666	11,631	12,643	13,582

[1] Includes other kinds of business not shown separately.

Source: U.S. Census Bureau, "Nonemployer Statistics"; published May 2004; <http://www.census.gov/epcd/nonemployer/>.

U.S. Census Bureau, Statistical Abstract of the United States: 2006

Table 1260. Service-Related Industries—Establishments, Employees, and Payroll by Industry: 2000 and 2002

[7,070 represents 7,070,000. Covers establishments with payroll. Employees are for the week including March 12. Excludes most government employees, railroad employees, and self-employed persons. Kind-of-business classification based on North American Industry Classification System, 1997 (NAICS); see text, Section 15. For statement on methodology, see Appendix III]

Kind of business	NAICS code	Establishments (1,000)		Employees (1,000)[1]		Payroll (bil. dol.)	
		2000	2002	2000	2002	2000	2002
All industries, total	(X)	7,070	7,201	114,065	112,401	3,879	3,943
Professional, scientific, & technical services	54	723	772	6,816	7,046	362	369
Professional, scientific, & technical services	541	723	772	6,816	7,046	362	369
Legal services	5411	177	179	1,089	1,138	62	70
Accounting/tax prep/bookkeep/payroll services. . .	5412	100	111	1,164	1,241	38	39
Architectural, engineering & related services	5413	102	108	1,213	1,237	65	67
Specialized design services	5414	28	31	140	132	6	6
Computer systems design & related services. . . .	5415	100	103	1,171	1,089	85	74
Management, sci & tech consulting services	5416	97	117	712	820	44	50
Scientific R&D services	5417	13	14	359	399	25	26
Advertising & related services.	5418	40	38	472	412	23	20
Other professional/scientific/technical services . . .	5419	65	72	496	577	14	17
Management of companies & enterprises.	55	47	49	2,874	2,914	211	205
Admin/support waste mgt/remediation services . . .	56	352	344	9,138	8,299	210	212
Administrative & support services [2]	561	336	326	8,847	7,999	200	201
Employment services	5613	42	41	4,573	3,881	98	93
Temporary help services.	56132	28	26	3,013	2,391	59	53
Business support services	5614	35	34	702	693	17	18
Travel arrangement & reservation services	5615	33	28	308	258	10	8
Waste management & remediation services	562	16	18	291	301	11	12
Accommodation & food services.	72	542	565	9,881	10,049	126	131
Accommodation [2]	721	60	62	1,768	1,697	35	34
Traveler accommodation	7211	50	52	1,714	1,642	34	33
RV parks & recreational camps.	7212	7	7	38	39	1	1
Food services & drinking places	722	483	503	8,113	8,352	91	97
Full-service restaurants	7221	192	199	3,897	4,000	47	50
Limited-service eating places	7222	211	223	3,385	3,463	33	36
Special food services	7223	29	31	502	541	7	8
Drinking places (alcoholic beverages).	7224	51	51	329	348	3	4
Other services (except public administration).	81	723	740	5,293	5,420	110	119
Repair & maintenance [2]	811	233	233	1,334	1,335	37	38
Automotive R&M	8111	164	165	856	869	21	22
Electronic & precision equipment R&M.	8112	15	14	144	138	6	6
Personal and laundry services	812	199	207	1,293	1,314	23	24
Religious/grantmaking/prof/like organizations.	813	291	300	2,666	2,771	50	56

X Not applicable. [1] Includes employees on the payroll for the pay period including March 12. [2] Includes other kinds of business not shown separately.

Source: U.S. Census Bureau, "County Business Patterns"; published November 2004. See also <http://www.census.gov/prod/2004pubs/02cbp/cbp02-1.pdf>.

Table 1261. Selected Service Industries—E-Commerce Revenue: 2002 and 2003

[41,185 represents $41,185,000,000. Includes data only for businesses with paid employees, except for accommodation and food services, which also includes businesses with and without paid employees. Except as noted, based on the Service Annual Survey]

Kind of business	NAICS code[1]	E-commerce revenue (mil. dol.)		E-commerce as percent of total revenue, 2003	E-commerce revenue, percent distribution, 2003
		2002	2003		
Selected service industries, total [2]	(X)	41,185	49,945	1.0	100.0
Selected transportation and warehousing [2]	48-49	3,317	4,296	1.8	8.6
Information [3]	51	11,058	12,367	1.4	25.3
Publishing industries	511	5,362	5,989	2.6	12.0
Online information services.	51419	1,823	2,304	7.1	4.6
Selected finance [4]	52	4,191	4,464	1.6	8.9
Securities and commodity contracts intermediation and brokerage	5231	4,071	4,371	2.5	8.8
Rental and leasing services	532	(S)	(S)	(S)	(S)
Selected professional, scientific, and technical services [5]	54	6,487	8,171	0.9	16.3
Computer systems design and related services	5415	4,264	5,466	3.2	10.9
Selected administrative and support and waste management and remediation services [6]	56	10,544	11,611	2.7	23.2
Health care and social assistance services	62	(S)	(S)	(S)	(S)
Arts, entertainment, and recreation services	71	(S)	(S)	(S)	(S)
Accommodation and food services [7]	72	(S)	(S)	(S)	(S)
Selected other services [8]	81	1,097	1,905	0.6	3.8

S Data do not meet publication standards because of high sampling variability or poor response quality. X Not applicable. [1] North American Industry Classification System, 1997; see text, Section 15. [2] Excludes NAICS 481 (air transportation), 482 (rail transportation), 483 (water transportation), 485 (transit and ground passenger transportation), 487 (scenic and sightseeing transportation), 488 (support activities for transportation) and 491 (postal service). [3] Includes other industries not listed separately. [4] Excludes NAICS 521 (monetary authorities-central bank), 522 (credit intermediation and related activities), 5232 (securities and commodity exchanges), 52391 (miscellaneous intermediation), 52399 (all other financial investment activities), 524 (insurance carriers and related activities) and 525 (funds and trusts). [5] Excludes NAICS 54112 (offices of notaries) and 54132 (landscape architectural services). [6] Excludes NAICS 56173 (landscaping services). [7] Based on Annual Retail Trade Survey. [8] Excludes NAICS 81311 (religious organizations), 81393 (labor and similar organizations), 81394 (political organizations) and 814 (private households).

Source: U.S. Census Bureau, "E-Stats"; published 15 April 2005; <http://www.census.gov/eos/www/ebusiness614.htm>.

Table 1262. **Service-Related Industries—Establishments, Employees, and Annual Payroll by State: 2002**

[368,778,080 represents $368,778,000,000. Covers establishments with payroll. Employees are for the week including March 12. Excludes most government employees, railroad employees, and self-employed persons. Kind-of-business classification based on North American Industry Classification System, 1997 (NAICS); see text, Section 15. For statement on methodology, see Appendix III]

State	Professional, scientific, & technical services (NAICS 54)			Admin/support waste mgt/remediation services (NAICS 56)			Accommodation and food services (NAICS 72)		
	Establish-ments	Employ-ees [1]	Annual payroll (mil. dol.)	Establish-ments	Employ-ees [1]	Annual payroll (mil. dol.)	Establish-ments	Employ-ees [1]	Annual payroll (mil. dol.)
United States . . .	772,365	7,046,205	368,778	343,544	8,299,217	212,189	565,149	10,048,875	131,111
Alabama	8,756	80,586	3,582	3,823	118,977	2,336	7,070	128,964	1,356
Alaska	1,719	13,231	666	892	10,147	361	1,882	21,917	408
Arizona	13,697	113,699	5,026	6,823	192,657	4,405	9,913	206,185	2,577
Arkansas.	5,017	32,992	1,115	2,224	42,375	741	4,676	78,020	777
California.	100,549	1,130,867	61,402	39,856	980,573	27,749	66,543	1,150,913	16,552
Colorado.	19,391	142,815	7,759	7,110	174,014	4,888	10,810	206,139	2,689
Connecticut	10,368	100,002	5,723	5,312	100,261	2,911	7,032	98,980	1,472
Delaware.	2,342	19,482	1,086	1,128	25,599	590	1,568	27,171	382
District of Columbia. . .	4,372	84,447	6,752	990	26,733	828	1,780	41,406	900
Florida	56,941	403,902	18,703	27,007	954,424	22,599	30,203	621,996	8,213
Georgia	23,722	204,197	11,268	9,931	282,607	7,015	15,512	298,695	3,644
Hawaii	2,993	19,947	870	1,699	34,419	958	3,079	84,529	1,653
Idaho	3,303	34,455	1,263	1,714	27,860	632	3,081	44,893	452
Illinois.	36,580	334,517	19,346	15,035	422,207	10,022	24,118	409,906	5,269
Indiana	12,134	93,517	3,470	6,488	136,589	3,361	11,791	222,565	2,395
Iowa.	5,818	39,933	1,464	3,148	57,901	1,256	6,573	103,784	998
Kansas	6,719	53,603	2,150	3,232	61,682	1,379	5,610	93,969	931
Kentucky	7,546	56,633	2,028	3,491	71,155	1,417	6,689	135,844	1,506
Louisiana	10,792	79,488	3,067	4,119	103,732	2,271	7,566	165,326	2,013
Maine.	3,318	22,031	896	1,703	24,643	617	3,700	43,358	630
Maryland.	17,856	198,181	11,113	7,113	142,970	4,003	9,442	174,466	2,307
Massachusetts	21,895	238,817	16,237	8,998	187,815	5,904	14,999	237,586	3,653
Michigan.	22,244	220,283	11,144	11,668	289,529	8,068	18,925	331,587	3,679
Minnesota	15,559	119,240	6,191	6,557	132,438	3,430	10,265	198,460	2,323
Mississippi.	4,461	30,367	1,103	2,107	41,772	738	4,327	100,700	1,290
Missouri	12,876	123,952	5,877	6,635	137,093	3,515	11,303	214,111	2,478
Montana	2,931	15,491	492	1,260	11,872	211	3,230	40,568	420
Nebraska	3,889	34,735	1,506	2,314	54,441	1,493	3,982	62,124	603
Nevada.	6,350	45,410	2,141	3,298	78,603	2,249	4,262	269,300	6,294
New Hampshire	4,008	26,016	1,269	1,867	37,500	1,143	3,142	48,345	672
New Jersey	31,473	260,901	15,048	12,568	299,418	8,288	17,484	264,215	4,471
New Mexico.	4,432	31,662	1,280	1,740	35,891	878	3,756	69,220	789
New York	55,780	531,735	33,092	22,104	452,508	13,540	39,324	513,746	8,482
North Carolina	19,179	154,959	7,058	9,926	209,802	4,677	15,731	284,263	3,291
North Dakota	1,331	9,492	293	762	11,106	222	1,758	25,546	229
Ohio.	24,976	225,274	10,287	13,072	296,388	7,029	22,763	418,058	4,398
Oklahoma	8,366	55,437	2,171	3,705	87,769	1,787	6,518	113,087	1,143
Oregon	10,101	69,727	3,020	4,626	70,237	1,611	8,785	128,477	1,588
Pennsylvania	28,466	284,647	14,781	13,304	273,566	6,666	24,729	380,450	4,404
Rhode Island	2,961	19,760	839	1,570	25,150	669	2,707	38,538	525
South Carolina	8,431	63,665	2,756	4,663	126,125	2,587	8,202	156,452	1,818
South Dakota.	1,598	8,996	270	874	9,952	206	2,200	31,373	332
Tennessee.	10,579	99,722	4,161	5,802	163,975	3,874	10,053	204,191	2,384
Texas	52,357	485,623	26,062	22,340	716,557	19,280	36,710	721,493	8,766
Utah.	6,235	51,726	2,169	2,906	80,560	1,686	4,100	81,838	869
Vermont	2,019	13,899	506	873	5,898	151	1,956	29,243	374
Virginia	23,164	309,536	18,043	9,122	210,002	5,401	13,310	254,362	3,187
Washington	16,930	137,769	7,483	7,680	112,995	3,423	13,743	197,616	2,685
West Virginia	2,963	21,096	658	1,387	31,574	569	3,285	52,992	569
Wisconsin	11,278	90,826	3,864	6,229	111,379	2,443	13,229	198,215	1,988
Wyoming.	1,591	6,917	227	749	5,777	113	1,733	23,693	282

[1] Includes employees on the payroll for the pay period including March 12.

Source: U.S. Census Bureau, "County Business Patterns"; published November 2004. See also <http://www.census.gov/prod/2004pubs /02cbp/cbp02-1.pdf>.

Table 1263. **Professional, Scientific, and Technical Services—Estimated Revenue for Employer and Nonemployer Firms: 2000 to 2003**

[In millions of dollars (902,157 represents $902,157,000,000). Estimates are based on data from the 2003 Service Annual Survey and administrative data. Estimates for 2002 and prior years are revised to reflect the latest administrative data for nonemployers. Except where indicated, estimates have been adjusted using the results of the 1997 Economic Census. Based on North American Industry Classification System, 1997 (NAICS)]

Kind of business	NAICS code	Employer and nonemployer firms				Taxable employer firms			
		2000	2001	2002	2003	2000	2001	2002	2003
Professional, scientific, and technical services (except notaries and landscape architectural services)	54	902,157	936,863	949,748	988,337	793,828	827,164	833,575	864,537
Legal services (except notaries)	5411	164,572	175,620	184,121	203,743	151,082	161,340	169,257	187,507
Offices of lawyers	54111	158,602	168,964	176,987	194,428	145,617	155,263	162,742	178,950
Other legal services [1]	54119	5,970	6,656	7,133	9,314	5,465	6,077	6,515	8,557
Accounting, tax preparation, bookkeeping, and payroll services	5412	79,397	84,157	84,847	87,371	73,561	77,960	78,424	80,640
Architectural, engineering, & related services (except landscape architectural services)	5413	165,008	173,008	173,804	176,931	157,404	165,179	166,114	168,828
Specialized design services	5414	23,120	23,017	22,384	23,664	18,276	18,133	17,311	18,274
Computer systems design & services	5415	194,128	190,668	181,601	179,677	184,415	180,873	171,111	168,792
Management, scientific, and technical consulting services	5416	105,663	115,026	122,659	128,378	88,540	98,079	104,022	108,223
Scientific research and development services	5417	51,427	57,434	62,992	65,462	33,221	38,796	42,917	44,937
Advertising and related services	5418	73,592	71,883	70,029	72,262	68,267	66,753	64,535	66,689
Advertising agencies	54181	26,349	25,936	25,827	27,467	25,149	24,780	24,589	26,094
Public relations agencies	54182	8,693	8,247	8,373	8,493	7,699	7,290	7,348	7,466
Display advertising	54185	6,701	6,362	6,528	6,985	6,409	6,081	6,226	6,642
Direct mail advertising	54186	10,359	10,708	10,559	10,696	9,830	10,198	10,013	10,112
All other advertising	5418x	21,489	20,628	18,740	18,619	19,181	18,405	16,360	16,375
Other professional, scientific, and technical services (except veterinary services)[2]	5419	45,246	46,046	47,308	50,844	19,026	20,052	19,884	20,647
Marketing research and public opinion polling	54191	10,176	9,947	9,654	9,838	9,478	9,257	8,834	9,019
Photographic services	54192	8,237	8,286	7,932	8,199	6,000	6,125	5,883	6,091

[1] Estimates for NAICS 541191 (title abstract and settlement offices), not shown separately, have not been adjusted using the results of the 1997 Economic Census.　[2] Includes other kinds of business not shown separately.

Source: U.S. Census Bureau, "Service Annual Survey 2003"; published February 2005; <http://www.census.gov/prod/2005pubs/sas-03.pdf>.

Table 1264. **Computer Systems Design and Related Services—Estimated Revenue for Employer Firms: 2003**

[In millions of dollars (168,792 represents 168,792,000,000). Estimates are based on data from the 2003 Service Annual Survey and administrative data. Except where indicated, estimates have been adjusted using the results of the 1997 Economic Census. Based on North American Industry Classification System, 1997 (NAICS)]

Kind of business	Amount	Kind of business	Amount
Computer systems design and related services (NAICS 5415) total revenue	168,792	Information technology infrastructure (computer) and network management services	2,497
		Information technology technical support services	4,901
Information technology design and development total [1]	71,298	Software publishing	2,742
Custom application design and development	27,096	Information technology related training services	612
Computer systems design, development, and integration services	36,031	Other services revenue	3,235
Network design and development services	8,171	**Computer systems design services (NAICS 541512) total revenue**	85,019
Information technology infrastructure (computer) and network management services	20,984	Information technology design and development, total	41,325
Information technology technical support services	21,068	Custom application design and development	6,312
Information technology consulting services	15,408	Computer systems design, development, and integration services	28,201
Software publishing	7,376	Network design and development services	6,812
Data management services	3,000	Information technology infrastructure (computer) and network management services	5,618
Information technology related training services	2,130	Information technology technical support services	12,052
Internet access services	641	Information technology consulting services	5,346
Web site hosting services	(S)	Software publishing	3,311
Application service provisioning	3,452	Data storage services	398
Re-sale of computer hardware and software	8,204	Data management services	1,965
Other services revenue	8,832	Information technology related training services	998
		Internet access services	413
Custom computer programming services (NAICS 541511) total revenue	55,731	Web site hosting services	661
Information technology design and development, total	27,187	Application service provisioning	2,263
Custom application design and development	19,496	Business process management services	1,463
Computer systems design, development, and integration services	6,741	Re-sale of computer hareware and software	4,649
Network design and development services	950	Other services revenue	4,531

Source: U.S. Census Bureau, "Service Annual Survey 2003; published February 2005"; <http://www.census.gov/prod/2005pubs/sas-03.pdf>.

Table 1265. **Advertising—Estimated Expenditures by Medium: 1990 to 2004**

[In millions of dollars (129,968 represents $129,968,000,000). See source for definitions of types of advertising]

Medium	1990	1995	1998	1999	2000	2001	2002	2003	2004 [1]
Total	129,968	165,147	206,697	222,308	247,472	231,287	236,875	245,477	263,699
National	73,638	96,933	122,271	132,170	151,664	141,797	145,429	152,482	165,994
Local	56,330	68,214	84,426	90,138	95,808	89,490	91,446	92,995	97,705
Newspapers	32,281	36,317	44,292	46,648	49,050	44,255	44,031	44,843	46,935
National	3,867	3,996	5,402	6,358	7,229	6,615	6,806	7,357	7,762
Local	28,414	32,321	38,890	40,290	41,821	37,640	37,225	37,486	39,173
Magazines	6,803	8,580	10,518	11,433	12,370	11,095	10,995	11,435	12,121
Broadcast TV	26,616	32,720	39,173	40,011	44,802	38,881	42,068	41,932	46,020
Four TV networks	9,863	11,600	13,736	13,961	15,888	14,300	15,000	15,030	16,458
Syndication	1,109	2,016	2,609	2,870	3,108	3,102	3,034	3,434	3,949
Spot (National)	7,788	9,119	10,659	10,500	12,264	9,223	10,920	9,948	10,943
Spot (Local)	7,856	9,985	12,169	12,680	13,542	12,256	13,114	13,520	14,670
Cable TV	2,631	6,166	10,340	12,570	15,455	15,736	16,297	18,814	21,069
Cable TV networks	2,000	4,500	7,640	9,405	11,765	11,777	12,071	13,954	15,628
Spot (Local)	631	1,666	2,700	3,165	3,690	3,959	4,226	4,860	5,441
Radio	8,726	11,338	15,073	17,215	19,295	17,861	18,877	19,100	19,779
Network	482	480	622	684	780	711	775	798	852
Spot (National)	1,635	1,959	2,823	3,275	3,668	2,956	3,340	3,540	3,575
Spot (Local)	6,609	8,899	11,628	13,256	14,847	14,194	14,762	14,762	15,352
Yellow Pages	8,926	10,236	11,990	12,652	13,228	13,592	13,776	13,896	14,035
National	1,132	1,410	1,870	1,986	2,093	2,087	2,087	2,114	2,135
Local	7,794	8,826	10,120	10,666	11,135	11,505	11,689	11,782	11,900
Direct mail	23,370	32,866	39,620	41,403	44,591	44,725	46,067	48,370	52,240
Business papers	2,875	3,559	4,232	4,274	4,915	4,468	3,976	4,004	4,094
Out-of-home [2]	1,084	1,263	1,576	1,725	5,176	5,134	5,175	5,443	5,790
National	640	701	845	925	2,068	2,051	2,061	2,298	2,440
Local	444	562	731	800	3,108	3,083	3,114	3,145	3,350
Internet [3]	(NA)	(NA)	1,383	2,832	6,507	5,645	4,883	5,650	7,062
Miscellaneous [3]	16,656	22,102	28,500	31,545	32,083	29,895	30,730	31,990	34,554
National	12,074	16,147	20,312	22,264	24,418	23,042	23,414	24,550	26,735
Local	4,582	5,955	8,188	9,281	7,665	6,853	7,316	7,440	7,819

NA Not available. [1] Preliminary data. [2] Prior to 2000, represents only "outdoor" billboards. Beginning 2000 includes other forms of outdoor advertising (i.e. transportation vehicles, bus shelters, telephone kiosks, etc.) previously covered under "Miscellaneous." [3] Beginning 2000, part of miscellaneous now included under "Out-of-home" advertising. See footnote 2.

Source: Universal McCann, New York, N.Y. (copyright). See also <http://www.universalmccann.com>.

Table 1266. **Administrative and Support and Waste Management and Remediation Services—Estimated Revenue: 2000 to 2003**

[In millions of dollars (407,806 represents $407,806,000,000), except percent. For taxable and tax-exempt employer firms. Except as indicated, estimates adjusted to the results of the 1997 Economic Census. Based on the Service Annual Survey; see Appendix III. Minus sign (-) indicates decrease]

Kind of business	NAICS code [1]	2000	2002	2003	Percent change, 2002-2003
Admin/support waste mgt/remediation services	56	407,806	418,091	436,833	4.5
Administrative & support services	561	361,738	372,327	388,004	4.2
Office administrative services	56111	48,732	59,471	64,060	7.7
Facilities support services	56121	9,271	9,093	8,532	-6.2
Employment services [2]	5613	124,774	112,094	116,087	3.6
Temporary help services	56132	74,054	63,421	65,021	2.5
Employee leasing services	56133	42,448	38,816	41,319	6.4
Business support services [2]	5614	47,412	50,972	53,206	4.4
Telephone call centers	56142	16,115	14,818	14,426	-2.6
Business service centers	56143	10,173	10,099	10,186	0.9
Travel arrangement & reservation services [2]	5615	26,509	26,461	27,589	4.3
Travel agencies	56151	10,940	8,824	9,173	4.0
Other travel arrangement & reservation services	56159	12,616	14,994	15,754	5.1
Investigation and security services	5616	25,869	29,654	30,313	2.2
Investigation, guard, & armored car services	56161	14,895	16,517	17,782	7.7
Security systems services	56162	10,975	13,137	12,531	-4.6
Services to buildings & dwellings	5617	41,065	45,809	49,765	8.6
Janitorial services	56172	30,097	33,054	35,863	8.5
Other support services	5619	38,107	38,774	38,452	-0.8
Waste management & remediation services	562	46,068	45,765	48,829	6.7
Waste collection	5621	25,498	24,863	26,636	7.1
Waste treatment & disposal [3]	5622	10,261	9,830	10,299	4.8
Remediation & other waste management services	5629	10,310	11,072	11,894	7.4

[1] North American Industry Classification System, 1997; see text, Section 15. [2] Includes other kinds of business not shown separately. [3] Estimates have not been adjusted to the results of the 1997 Economic Census.

Source: U.S. Census Bureau, Service Annual Survey 2003; published February 2005; <http://www.census.gov/prod/2005pubs/sas-03.pdf>.

Table 1267. Accomodation Service Businesses—Number and Sales by Product Lines: 2002

[130,320 represents $130,320,000,000. Represents North American Industry Classification System, 2002 (NAICS) code 721; see text Section 15. Covers establishments with payroll. Employees are for the week including March 12. Most government employees are excluded. For statement on methodology, see Appendix III]

Product line code	2002 Product line code	Establishments with the product line		Amount (mil. dol.)
		Number	Total sales (mil. dol.)	
Accommodation	(X)	60,870	(X)	130,320
Guestroom or unit rentals, including campground & RV rental fees excluding occupancy taxes	20010	57,715	128,811	73,102
Telephone service charges.	20030	23,902	89,136	1,194
Rental of public rooms & areas, including conference/ convention meeting rooms.	20050	15,187	71,840	1,763
Groceries & other food items, consumption off the premises	20100	9,399	27,399	209
Meals & nonalcoholic beverages for immediate consumption off the premises.	20120	15,124	101,531	17,177
Food/nonalcoholic beverages prepared for consumption on the premises.	20122	14,054	98,903	16,547
Alcoholic drinks served at the establishment	20130	9,517	88,820	4,331
Cigars, cigarettes, tobacco, & smokers' accessories	20150	2,069	27,689	93
All other nonmerchandise receipts, excl. sales and other taxes. . .	29980	14,782	71,868	4,645

Source: U.S. Census Bureau, 2002 Economic Census, General Merchandise Stores, issued October 2004. See also <http://www.census.gov/econ/census02>.

Table 1268. Lodging Industry Summary: 1990 to 2003

Year	Average occupancy rate (percent)	Average room rate (dol.)	Room size of property	2003		Item	2003	
				Establishments	Rooms (mil.)		Business traveler	Leisure traveler
1990	63.3	57.96	Total	47,584	4.4	Typical night:		
1995	65.5	66.65				Made reservations		
1998	64.0	78.62	Percent:			(percent).	90	84
1999	63.2	81.33	Under 75 rooms . . .	57.5	25.9	Amount paid	$91.00	$87.00
2000	63.7	85.89	75-149 rooms	30.0	34.5	Length of stay (percent):		
2001	60.3	88.27	150-299 rooms	9.1	19.5	One night	40	47
2002	59.1	83.54	300-500 rooms	2.3	9.2	Two nights	24	26
2003	61.6	82.52	Over 500 rooms . . .	1.1	10.8	Three or more	36	27

Source: American Hotel & Motel Association, Washington, DC, Lodging Industry Profile (copyright).

Table 1269. Commercial and Noncommercial Groups—Food and Drink Establishments and Sales: 1990 to 2005

[(238,149 represents $238,149,000,000). Excludes military. Data refer to sales to consumers of food and alcoholic beverages. Sales are estimated. For details, see source]

Type of group	Establishments, 2002	Sales (mil. dol.)						
		1990	1995	2000	2002	2003	2004	2005 [1]
Total	876,044	238,149	294,631	377,652	410,141	428,246	451,815	474,001
Commercial restaurant services [2, 3]	692,060	211,606	265,910	345,345	376,475	393,335	415,583	436,873
Eating places [2]	432,664	155,552	198,293	259,743	281,201	293,933	310,771	326,485
Full-service restaurants	195,492	77,811	96,396	133,834	142,663	148,940	156,983	164,832
Limited-service restaurants [4]	187,019	[5]69,798	[5]92,901	107,147	115,717	121,040	128,182	134,206
Snack & nonalcoholic beverage bars	35,954	(5)	(5)	12,867	13,259	14,271	15,498	16,862
Bars and taverns [6]	48,855	9,533	9,948	12,412	13,631	14,114	14,692	15,265
Managed services [2]	20,575	14,149	18,186	24,841	26,757	27,584	29,633	31,591
Manufacturing & industrial plants . .	(NA)	3,856	4,814	6,223	6,118	6,142	6,257	6,560
Colleges and universities.	(NA)	2,788	3,989	5,879	7,046	7,324	8,302	9,008
Lodging places	14,427	13,568	15,561	19,438	21,443	18,771	23,903	25,190
Retail hosts [2, 7]	132,203	9,513	12,589	14,869	18,627	16,971	20,869	21,992
Department store restaurants	4,127	876	1,038	903	547	(NA)	(NA)	(NA)
Grocery store restaurants [7]	61,318	5,432	6,624	7,116	10,220	(NA)	(NA)	(NA)
Gasoline service stations.	53,571	1,718	2,520	4,693	5,193	(NA)	(NA)	(NA)
Recreation and sports	36,221	2,871	3,866	4,772	5,142	5,349	5,427	5,648
Noncommercial restaurant services [2] . . .	183,984	26,543	28,722	32,307	33,666	34,911	36,232	37,128
Employee restaurant services	3,733	1,864	1,364	986	742	708	658	615
Industrial, commercial organizations.	1,379	1,603	1,129	717	475	(NA)	(NA)	(NA)
Educational restaurant services	103,392	7,671	9,059	9,977	10,332	(NA)	(NA)	(NA)
Elementary & secondary schools . .	99,287	3,700	4,533	5,039	5,111	5,075	5,097	5,082
Hospitals	5,772	8,968	9,219	9,982	10,596	11,181	12,041	12,450
Miscellaneous [3]	34,305	2,892	3,673	4,898	5,163	(NA)	(NA)	(NA)
Clubs.	10,551	1,993	2,278	3,164	3,314	(NA)	(NA)	(NA)

NA Not available. [1] Projection. [2] Includes other types of groups, not shown separately. [3] Data for establishments with payroll. [4] Fast-food restaurants. [5] Snack and nonalcoholic beverage bars included in limited service restaurants. [6] For establishments serving food. [7] Includes a portion of delicatessen sales in grocery stores.

Source: National Restaurant Association, Washington, DC, Restaurant Numbers: 25 Year History, 1970-1995, 1998; Restaurant Industry in Review, annual; and National Restaurant Association Restaurant Industry Forecast, December 2004 (copyright).

Table 1270. **Other Services—Estimated Revenue for Employer Firms: 2000 to 2003**

[In millions of dollars (322,475 represents $322,475,000,000), except percent. Except where indicated, results have been adjusted to the results of the 1997 Economic Census. Based on the Service Annual Survey. See text, this section and Appendix III]

Kind of business	NAICS code [1]	2000	2002	2003	Percent change, 2002–2003
Other services (except public administration, religious, labor, and political organizations, and private households)	81	322,475	325,504	337,577	3.7
Repair & maintenance	811	125,210	131,537	136,533	3.8
Automotive R&M	8111	74,292	76,407	79,827	4.5
Electronic and precision equipment R&M [2]	8112	17,383	18,001	17,836	-0.9
Commercial equipment (exc. auto. elec.) R&M	8113	20,753	24,232	25,787	6.4
Personal and household goods R&M	8114	12,594	12,898	13,083	1.4
Personal & laundry services	812	68,798	72,586	73,758	1.6
Personal care services	8121	17,150	19,124	19,996	4.6
Hair, nail, & skin care services	81211	14,225	15,133	15,670	3.5
Death care services	8122	13,268	13,887	14,940	7.6
Drycleaning & laundry services	8123	20,972	21,490	20,548	-4.4
Coin-operated laundries & drycleaners.	81231	3,615	3,722	3,485	-6.4
Drycleaning and laundry services, (exc. coin-op)	81232	8,150	8,063	7,564	-6.2
Linen & uniform supply	81233	9,207	9,705	9,499	-2.1
Other personal services	8129	17,408	18,085	18,274	1.0
Religious/grantmaking/prof./like organizations (except religious, labor, and political organizations)	813	128,467	121,381	127,286	4.9
Grantmaking and giving services [3]	8132	63,057	51,006	51,980	1.9
Social advocacy organizations	8133	10,438	11,668	13,166	12.8
Civic & social organizations.	8134	12,175	13,043	14,173	8.7
Business, professional, and other organizations (except labor and political organizations)	8139	42,798	45,664	47,967	5.0

[1] North American Industry Classification System, 1997; see text, Section 15. [2] Estimates for NAICS 811219 (other electronics and precision equipment repair and maintenance) have not been adjusted to the results of the 1997 Economic Census. [3] Estimates for NAICS 813211 (grantmaking foundations) have not been adjusted to the results of the 1997 Economic Census.

Source : U.S. Census Bureau, *Service Annual Survey*, annual. See also <http://www.census.gov/prod/2005pubs/sas-03.pdf>

Table 1271. **Religious, Grantmaking, Civic, Professional, and Similar Organizations—Number and Sales by Product Lines: 2002**

[119,727 represents $119,727,000,000. Represents North American Industry Classification System, 2002 (NAICS) code 813; see text Section 15. Covers establishments with payroll. For statement on methodology, see Appendix III]

Kind of business	2002 Product line code	Establishments with the product line		Product line sales (mil. dol.)
		Number	Total sales (mil. dol.)	
Religious, grantmaking, civic, professional, and similar organizations	(X)	106,781	(X)	119,727
Membership dues.	30400	57,475	48,469	21,229
Condominium and homeowners' association fees and assessments . .	30930	16,873	9,234	8,405
Sales of advertising	30950	11,129	16,252	1,620
Merchandise sales	39000	14,844	14,498	1,240
Sales of food and beverages	39200	18,201	7,930	2,669

X Not applicable.

Source: U.S. Census Bureau, 2002 Economic Census, issued October 2004. See also <http://www.census.gov/econ/census02>.

Table 1272. **National Nonprofit Associations—Number by Type: 1980 to 2004**

[Data compiled during last few months of year previous to year shown and the beginning months of year shown]

Type	1980	1985	1990	1995	1998	1999	2000	2001	2002	2003	2004
Total	14,726	19,121	22,289	22,663	22,049	22,474	21,840	22,449	22,141	22,464	22,659
Trade, business, commercial .	3,118	3,719	3,918	3,757	3,714	3,815	3,880	3,922	3,883	3,818	3,812
Agriculture and environment. .	677	882	940	1,122	1,107	1,113	1,103	1,120	1,125	1,137	1,140
Legal, governmental, public admin., military	529	658	792	776	755	778	790	807	814	832	839
Scientific, engineering, tech . .	1,039	1,270	1,417	1,355	1,306	1,332	1,302	1,317	1,309	1,326	1,354
Educational	[1]2,376	[1]2,822	1,291	1,290	1,274	1,321	1,297	1,346	1,307	1,301	1,313
Cultural	([1])	([1])	1,886	1,918	1,841	1,876	1,786	1,812	1,766	1,749	1,735
Social welfare	994	1,450	1,705	1,885	1,896	1,913	1,829	1,925	1,917	1,941	1,972
Health, medical	1,413	1,886	2,227	2,348	2,383	2,481	2,495	2,574	2,601	2,808	2,921
Public affairs	1,068	1,935	2,249	2,148	1,855	1,877	1,776	1,857	1,808	1,836	1,881
Fraternal, nationality, ethnic . .	435	492	573	552	552	525	537	529	557	547	
Religious	797	953	1,172	1,230	1,156	1,151	1,123	1,160	1,154	1,155	1,157
Veteran, hereditary, patriotic . .	208	281	462	686	861	877	835	834	785	802	803
Hobby, avocational	910	1,311	1,475	1,549	1,468	1,463	1,330	1,408	1,380	1,435	1,449
Athletic sports	504	737	840	838	765	782	717	762	730	760	755
Labor unions	235	252	253	245	235	235	232	233	218	211	213
Chambers of Commerce [2] . . .	105	142	168	168	129	146	143	142	141	139	136
Greek and non-Greek letter societies	318	331	340	336	313	313	296	312	301	309	305
Fan clubs	(NA)	(NA)	581	460	449	449	381	381	373	348	327

NA Not available. [1] Data for cultural associations included with educational associations. [2] National and binational. Includes trade and tourism organizations.

Source: Gale Group, Farmington Hills, MI. Compiled from *Encyclopedia of Associations*, annual (copyright).

Accommodation, Food Services, and Other Services 815

No. 126.—VALUES of IMPORTED COMMODITIES ENTERED for CONSUMPTION in the UNITED STATES, with the Amounts of Duty Received on the same, during the TWELVE FISCAL YEARS, from 1867 to 1878, inclusive.

FISCAL YEAR ENDED JUNE 30—	Value of Free Commodities a	Discriminating Duty collected on Commodities otherwise Free	Value of Dutiable Commodities	DUTY COLLECTED Ordinary	DUTY COLLECTED Additional and Discriminating	Total value of Free and Dutiable Commodities	DUTY COLLECTED Ordinary	DUTY COLLECTED Additional and Discriminating	Total Duty Collected	AVERAGE AD VALOREM RATE OF DUTY ON— Value of Dutiable	AVERAGE AD VALOREM RATE OF DUTY ON— Value of Free and Dutiable
	Dollars.	Dollars.	Dollars.	Dollars.	Dollars.	Dollars.	Dollars.	Dollars.	Dollars.	Per cent.	Per cent.
1867	39,103,605 00	....	361,195,559 50	168,503,749 58	....	400,299,157 50	168,299,157 50	....	168,503,749 58	46.667	42.101
1868	28,071,796 00	21,099 40	329,661,302 30	160,309,941 90	201,738 09	358,733,098 80	160,309,941 29	222,837 49	160,532,778 78	48.658	44.687
1869	41,499,601 78	21,124 60	372,756,641 51	176,114,904 19	421,554 93	414,256,243 29	176,114,904 19	442,679 53	176,557,583 72	47.919	42.561
1870	46,743,760 69	13,560 80	406,131,904 99	191,221,768 94	278,644 71	452,875,665 68	191,221,768 94	292,205 51	191,513,974 45	47.083	42.223
1871	59,163,460 46	43,084 14	458,597,057 86	201,985,574 93	418,014 95	518,759,518 32	201,985,574 93	461,099 39	202,446,673 32	43.946	38.936
1872	61,177,600 98	28,158 00	512,735,287 38	212,030,727 17	560,220 28	573,912,888 36	212,030,727 17	588,378 38	212,619,105 45	41.352	36.944
1873	109,886,874 80	134,978 25	464,746,861 97	184,556,045 02	228,018 47	684,633,736 07	184,556,045 02	372,996 72	184,929,041 74	38.072	26.556
1874	160,117,061 45	133,379 92	415,748,692 65	160,185,382 72	303,522 09	595,865,754 10	160,185,382 91	336,901 91	160,522,284 63	38.530	26.883
1875	167,253,004 42	109,729 92	378,795,113 48	154,271,805 33	173,447 30	547,050,147 90	154,271,805 33	283,177 22	154,554,982 55	40.617	28.901
1876	156,268,347 06	73,173 52	324,034,925 96	144,982,441 91	124,987 32	480,303,273 02	144,982,441 91	196,160 84	145,178,602 75	44.744	30.186
1877	161,528,251 47	81,662 17	294,988,239 93	128,222,207 41	121,473 86	480,517,491 40	128,222,207 41	205,136 03	128,428,343 44	42.885	26.684
1878	171,144,273 38	67,383 60	297,083,409 48	127,015,185 30	113,500 09	468,227,682 86	127,015,185 30	179,973 69	127,195,158 99	42.754	27.127

a Commodities subject to a Discriminating Duty only, are classed in the statements of imported commodities, under the head of "Free of Duty."

Source: Statistical Abstract of the United States: 1878 Edition.

Section 28
Foreign Commerce and Aid

This section presents data on the flow of goods, services, and capital between the United States and other countries; changes in official reserve assets of the United States; international investments; and foreign assistance programs.

The Bureau of Economic Analysis publishes current figures on U.S. international transactions and the U.S. international investment position in its monthly *Survey of Current Business*. Statistics for the foreign aid programs are presented by the Agency for International Development (AID) in its annual *U.S. Overseas Loans and Grants and Assistance from International Organizations* and by the Department of Agriculture in its *Foreign Agricultural Trade of the United States*.

The principal source of merchandise import and export data is the U.S. Census Bureau. Current data are presented monthly in *U.S. International Trade in Goods and Services* report Series FT 900. The *Guide to Foreign Trade Statistics*, found on the Census Bureau Web site at <http://www.census.gov/foreign-trade /guide/index.html>, lists the Bureau's monthly and annual products and services in this field. In addition, the International Trade Administration and the Bureau of Economic Analysis present summary as well as selected commodity and country data for U.S. foreign trade in the *U.S. Foreign Trade Highlights* and the *Survey of Current Business*, respectively. The Web site for these data are found at <http://ita.doc.gov/td/industry/otea/> and <http://www.bea.doc.gov/bea/di /home/trade.htm>. The merchandise trade data in the latter source include balance of payments adjustments to the Census Bureau data. The Treasury Department's *Monthly Treasury Statement of Receipts and Outlays of the United States Government* contains information on import duties. The International Trade Commission, U.S. Department of Agriculture (agricultural products), U.S. Department of Energy (mineral fuels, like petroleum and coal), and the U.S. Geological Survey (minerals) release various reports and specialized products on U.S. trade.

International accounts—The international transactions tables (Tables 1273 to 1275) show, for given time periods, the transfer of goods, services, grants, and financial assets and liabilities between the United States and the rest of the world. The international investment position table (Table 1276) presents, for specific dates, the value of U.S. investments abroad and of foreign investments in the United States. The movement of foreign and U.S. capital as presented in the balance of payments is not the only factor affecting the total value of foreign investments. Among the other factors are changes in the valuation of assets or liabilities, including changes in prices of securities, defaults, expropriations, and write-offs.

Direct investment abroad means the ownership or control, directly or indirectly, by one person of 10 percent or more of the voting securities of an incorporated business enterprise or an equivalent interest in an unincorporated business enterprise. Direct investment position is the value of U.S. parents' claims on the equity of and receivables due from foreign affiliates, less foreign affiliates receivables due from their U.S. parents. Income consists of parents' shares in the earnings of their affiliates plus net interest received by parents on intercompany accounts, less withholding taxes on dividends and interest.

Foreign aid—Foreign assistance is divided into three major categories—grants (military supplies and services and other grants), credits, and other assistance (through net accumulation of foreign currency claims from the sale of agricultural commodities). *Grants* are transfers for which no payment is expected (other than a limited percentage of the foreign currency "counterpart" funds generated by the grant), or which at most involve an obligation on the part of the receiver to extend aid to the United States or other countries to achieve a common objective. *Credits* are loan disbursements or transfers under other agreements which give rise to specific obligations to repay, over a period of years, usually with interest. All known returns to the U.S. government stemming from grants and credits (reverse grants, returns of grants, and payments of principal) are taken into account in net grants and net credits, but no allowance is made for interest or commissions. *Other assistance* represents the transfer of U.S. farm products in exchange for foreign currencies (plus, since enactment of Public Law 87-128, currency claims from principal and interest collected on credits extended under the farm products program), less the government's disbursements of the currencies as grants, credits, or for purchases. The net acquisition of currencies represents net transfers of resources to foreign countries under the agricultural programs, in addition to those classified as grants or credits.

The basic instrument for extending military aid to friendly nations has been the Mutual Defense Assistance Program authorized by the Congress in 1949. Prior to 1952, economic and technical aid was authorized in the Foreign Assistance Act of 1948, the 1950 Act for International Development, and other legislation which set up programs for specific countries. In 1952, these economic, technical, and military aid programs were combined under the Mutual Security Act, which in turn was followed by the Foreign Assistance Act passed in 1961. Appropriations to provide military assistance were also made in the Department of Defense Appropriation Act (rather than the Foreign Assistance Appropriation Act) beginning in 1966 for certain countries in Southeast Asia and in other legislation concerning programs for specific countries (such as Israel). Figures on activity under the Foreign Assistance Act as reported in the *Foreign Grants and Credits* series differ from data published by AID or its immediate predecessors, due largely to differences in reporting, timing, and treatment of particular items.

Exports—The Census Bureau compiles export data primarily from Shipper's Export Declarations required to be filed

with customs officials for shipments leaving the United States. They include U.S. exports under mutual security programs and exclude shipments to U.S. Armed Forces for their own use.

The value reported in the export statistics is generally equivalent to a free alongside ship (f.a.s.) value at the U.S. port of export, based on the transaction price, including inland freight, insurance, and other charges incurred in placing the merchandise alongside the carrier at the U.S. port of exportation. This value, as defined, excludes the cost of loading merchandise aboard the exporting carrier and also excludes freight, insurance, and any other charges or transportation and other costs beyond the U.S. port of exportation. The country of destination is defined as the country of ultimate destination or country where the merchandise is to be consumed, further processed, or manufactured, as known to the shipper at the time of exportation. When ultimate destination is not known, the shipment is statistically credited to the last country to which the shipper knows the merchandise will be shipped in the same form as exported.

Effective January 1990, the United States began substituting Canadian import statistics for U.S. exports to Canada. As a result of the data exchange between the United States and Canada, the United States has adopted the Canadian import exemption level for its export statistics based on shipments to Canada.

Data are estimated for shipments valued under $2,501 to all countries, except Canada, using factors based on the ratios of low-valued shipments to individual country totals.

Prior to 1989, exports were based on Schedule B, Statistical Classification of Domestic and Foreign Commodities Exported from the United States. These statistics were retabulated and published using Schedule E, Standard International Trade Classification, Revision 2. Beginning in 1989, Schedule B classifications were based on the Harmonized System and made to coincide with the Standard International Trade Classification, Revision 3.

This revision will affect the comparability of most export series beginning with the 1989 data for commodities.

Imports—The Census Bureau compiles import data from various customs forms required to be filed with customs officials. Data on import values are presented on two valuations bases in this section: The c.i.f. (cost, insurance, and freight) and the customs import value (as appraised by the U.S. Customs Service in accordance with legal requirements of the Tariff Act of 1930, as amended). This latter valuation, primarily used for collection of import duties, frequently does not reflect the actual transaction value. Country of origin is defined as country where the merchandise was grown, mined, or manufactured. If country of origin is unknown, country of shipment is reported.

Imports are classified either as "General imports" or "Imports for consumption." *General imports* are a combination of entries for immediate consumption, entries into customs bonded warehouses, and entries into U.S. Foreign Trade Zones, thus generally reflecting total arrivals of merchandise. *Imports for consumption* are a combination of entries for immediate consumption, withdrawals from warehouses for consumption, and entries of merchandise into U.S. customs territory from U.S. Foreign Trade Zones, thus generally reflecting the total of the commodities entered into U.S. consumption channels.

Prior to 1989, imports were based on the Tariff Schedule of the United States Annotated. The statistics were retabulated and published using Schedule A, Standard International Trade Classification, Revision 2. Beginning in 1989, the statistics are based on the Harmonized Tariff Schedule of the United States, which coincides with the Standard International Trade Classification, Revision 3. This revision will affect the comparability of most import series beginning with the 1989 data.

Area coverage—Except as noted, the geographic area covered by the export and import trade statistics is the United States Customs area (includes the 50 states, the District of Columbia, and Puerto Rico), the U.S. Virgin Islands (effective January 1981), and U.S. Foreign Trade Zones (effective July 1982). Data for selected tables and total values for 1980 have been revised to reflect the U.S. Virgin Islands' trade with foreign countries, where possible.

Statistical reliability—For a discussion of statistical collection and estimation, sampling procedures, and measures of statistical reliability applicable to Census Bureau data, see Appendix III.

U.S. Census Bureau, Statistical Abstract of the United States: 2006

Table 1273. U.S. International Transactions by Type of Transaction: 1990 to 2004

[In millions of dollars (706,975 represents $706,975,000,000). Minus sign (-) indicates debits. n.i.e. = Not included elsewhere]

Type of transaction	1990	1995	1996	1997	1998	1999	2000	2001	2002	2003	2004
Exports of goods and services and income receipts	706,975	1,004,631	1,077,731	1,191,441	1,195,314	1,260,368	1,422,402	1,295,441	1,248,068	1,332,397	1,530,975
Exports of goods and services	535,233	794,387	851,602	934,637	933,495	966,443	1,071,484	1,007,138	977,276	1,022,567	1,151,448
Goods, balance of payments basis [1]	387,401	575,204	612,113	678,366	670,416	683,965	771,994	718,712	682,422	713,421	807,536
Services [2]	147,832	219,183	239,489	256,271	263,079	282,478	299,490	288,426	294,854	309,146	343,912
Transfers under U.S. military agency sales contracts [3]	9,932	14,643	16,446	16,675	17,405	15,928	13,790	12,539	11,943	12,769	14,814
Travel	43,007	63,395	69,809	73,426	71,325	74,801	82,400	71,893	66,605	64,348	74,481
Passenger fares	15,298	18,909	20,422	20,868	20,098	19,785	20,687	17,926	17,046	15,693	18,858
Other transportation	22,042	26,081	26,074	27,006	25,604	26,916	29,803	28,442	29,195	31,329	36,862
Royalties and license fees [4]	16,634	30,289	32,470	33,228	35,626	39,670	43,233	40,696	44,489	48,137	52,643
Other private services	40,251	65,048	73,340	84,113	92,095	104,493	108,791	116,099	124,781	136,060	145,433
U.S. government miscellaneous services	668	818	928	955	926	885	786	831	795	810	821
Income receipts	171,742	210,244	226,129	256,804	261,819	293,925	350,918	288,303	270,792	309,830	379,527
Income receipts on U.S.-owned assets abroad	170,570	208,065	223,948	254,534	259,382	291,177	348,083	285,372	267,849	306,854	376,489
Direct investment receipts	65,973	95,260	102,505	115,323	103,963	131,626	151,839	128,665	145,590	193,289	233,067
Other private receipts	94,072	108,092	116,852	135,652	151,818	156,354	192,398	153,146	118,956	108,868	140,424
U.S. government receipts	10,525	4,713	4,591	3,559	3,601	3,197	3,846	3,561	3,303	4,597	2,998
Compensation of employees	1,172	2,179	2,181	2,270	2,437	2,748	2,835	2,931	2,943	2,976	3,038
Imports of goods and services and income payments	-759,290	-1,080,124	-1,159,478	-1,287,142	-1,356,058	-1,509,874	-1,779,620	-1,632,987	-1,659,233	-1,780,907	-2,118,119
Imports of goods and services	-616,097	-890,771	-955,667	-1,042,947	-1,098,504	-1,229,837	-1,449,756	-1,369,867	-1,398,457	-1,517,381	-1,769,031
Goods, balance of payments basis [1]	-498,438	-749,374	-803,113	-876,470	-917,103	-1,029,980	-1,224,408	-1,145,900	-1,164,720	-1,260,717	-1,472,926
Services [2]	-117,659	-141,397	-152,554	-166,477	-181,401	-199,857	-225,348	-223,967	-233,737	-256,664	-296,105
Direct defense expenditures	-17,531	-10,043	-11,061	-11,707	-12,185	-13,335	-13,473	-14,835	-19,101	-25,296	-29,299
Travel	-37,349	-44,916	-48,078	-52,051	-56,483	-58,963	-64,705	-60,200	-58,715	-57,444	-65,635
Passenger fares	-10,531	-14,663	-15,809	-18,138	-19,971	-21,315	-24,274	-22,633	-19,969	-20,957	-23,701
Other transportation	-24,966	-27,034	-27,403	-28,959	-30,363	-34,139	-41,425	-38,682	-38,407	-44,705	-54,169
Royalties and license fees [4]	-3,135	-6,919	-7,837	-9,161	-11,235	-13,107	-16,468	-16,538	-19,335	-19,380	-23,901
Other private services	-22,229	-35,199	-39,679	-43,699	-48,315	-56,177	-62,120	-68,197	-75,290	-85,741	-95,666
U.S. government miscellaneous services	-1,919	-2,623	-2,687	-2,762	-2,849	-2,821	-2,883	-2,882	-2,920	-3,131	-3,734
Income payments	-143,192	-189,353	-203,811	-244,195	-257,554	-280,037	-329,864	-263,120	-260,776	-263,526	-349,088
Income payments on foreign-owned assets in the U.S.	-139,728	-183,090	-197,511	-237,529	-250,560	-272,082	-322,345	-255,034	-252,396	-255,020	-340,255
Direct investment payments	-3,450	-30,318	-33,093	-42,950	-38,418	-53,437	-56,910	-12,783	-45,820	-71,447	-105,146
Other private payments	-95,508	-97,149	-97,800	-112,878	-127,988	-138,120	-180,918	-159,825	-129,934	-110,105	-145,370
U.S. government payments	-40,770	-55,623	-66,618	-81,701	-84,154	-80,525	-84,517	-82,426	-76,642	-73,468	-89,739
Compensation of employees	-3,464	-6,263	-6,300	-6,666	-6,994	-7,955	-7,519	-8,086	-8,380	-8,506	-8,833
Unilateral current transfers, net [3]	-26,654	-38,177	-43,147	-45,205	-53,320	-50,554	-58,781	-51,910	-64,046	-71,169	-80,930
U.S. government grants [3]	-10,359	-11,190	-15,401	-12,472	-13,270	-13,774	-16,714	-11,517	-17,097	-21,834	-23,317
U.S. government pensions and other transfers [5]	-3,224	-3,451	-4,466	-4,191	-4,305	-4,406	-4,705	-5,798	-5,125	-5,341	-6,264
Private remittances and other transfers	-13,070	-23,536	-23,280	-28,542	-35,745	-32,374	-37,362	-34,595	-41,824	-43,994	-51,349

See footnotes at end of table.

Table 1273. U.S. International Transactions by Type of Transaction: 1990 to 2004—Con.

[See headnote, Page 820]

Type of transaction	1990	1995	1996	1997	1998	1999	2000	2001	2002	2003	2004
Capital account transactions, net	-6,579	-927	-631	-1,014	-702	-4,888	-929	-1,223	-1,363	-3,214	-1,648
U.S. assets abroad, net (increase/financial outflow (-))	**-81,234**	**-352,264**	**-413,409**	**-485,475**	**-353,829**	**-504,062**	**-560,523**	**-382,616**	**-294,027**	**-328,397**	**-855,509**
U.S. official reserve assets, net	-2,158	-9,742	6,668	-1,010	-6,783	8,747	-290	-4,911	-3,681	1,523	2,805
Gold [6]											
Special drawing rights	-192	-808	370	-350	-147	10	-722	-630	475	601	-398
Reserve position in the International Monetary Fund . .	731	-2,466	-1,280	-3,575	-5,119	5,484	2,308	-3,600	-2,632	1,494	3,826
Foreign currencies	-2,697	-6,468	7,578	2,915	-1,517	3,253	-1,876	-681	-574	-572	-623
U.S. government assets, other than official reserve assets, net	2,317	-984	-989	68	-422	2,750	-941	-486	345	537	1,215
U.S. credits and other long-term assets . .	-8,410	-4,859	-5,025	-5,417	-4,678	-6,175	-5,182	-4,431	-5,251	-7,279	-3,044
Repayments on U.S. credits and other long-term assets [7]	10,856	4,125	3,930	5,438	4,111	9,559	4,265	3,873	5,701	7,981	4,221
U.S. foreign currency holdings and U.S. short-term assets, net	-130	-250	106	47	145	-634	-24	72	-105	-165	38
U.S. private assets, net	-81,393	-341,538	-419,088	-484,533	-346,624	-515,559	-559,292	-377,219	-290,691	-330,457	-859,529
Direct investment	-37,183	-98,750	-91,885	-104,803	-142,644	-224,934	-159,212	-142,349	-154,460	-140,579	-252,012
Foreign securities	-28,765	-122,394	-149,315	-116,852	-130,204	-122,236	-127,908	-90,644	-48,568	-156,064	-102,383
U.S. claims on unaffiliated foreigners reported by U.S. nonbanking concerns.	-27,824	-45,286	-86,333	-121,760	-38,204	-97,704	-138,790	-8,520	-49,403	-24,240	-149,001
U.S. claims reported by U.S. banks, n.i.e. . .	12,379	-75,108	-91,555	-141,118	-35,572	-70,685	-133,382	-135,706	-38,260	-9,574	-356,133
Foreign-owned assets in the United States, net (increase/financial inflow (+))	**141,571**	**438,562**	**551,096**	**706,809**	**423,569**	**740,210**	**1,046,896**	**782,859**	**794,343**	**889,043**	**1,440,105**
Foreign official assets in the U.S., net . .	33,910	109,880	126,724	19,036	-19,903	43,543	42,758	28,059	115,945	278,275	394,710
U.S. government securities	30,243	72,712	120,679	-2,161	-3,589	32,527	35,710	54,620	90,971	224,874	311,133
Other U.S. government liabilities . .	1,868	-105	-982	-881	-3,326	-2,863	-1,825	-2,309	137	-517	488
U.S. liabilities reported by U.S. banks, n.i.e. .	3,385	34,008	5,704	22,286	-9,501	12,964	5,746	-29,978	21,221	48,643	70,329
Other foreign official assets . . .	-1,586	3,265	1,323	-208	-3,487	915	3,127	5,726	3,616	5,275	12,760
Other foreign assets in U.S., net . . .	107,661	328,682	424,372	687,773	443,472	696,667	1,004,138	754,800	678,398	610,768	1,045,396
Direct investments in U.S.	48,494	57,776	86,502	105,603	179,045	289,444	321,274	167,021	80,841	67,091	106,832
U.S. Treasury securities	-2,534	91,544	147,022	130,435	28,581	-44,497	-69,983	-14,378	100,403	104,380	106,958
U.S. securities other than U.S. Treasury securities	1,592	77,249	103,272	161,409	156,315	298,834	459,889	393,885	283,299	226,306	369,793
U.S. currency flows	18,800	12,300	17,362	24,782	16,622	22,407	5,315	23,783	21,513	16,640	14,827
U.S. nonbanking concerns	45,133	59,637	53,736	116,518	23,140	76,247	170,672	66,110	95,932	99,676	124,358
U.S. liabilities reported by U.S. banks, n.i.e.	-3,824	30,176	16,478	149,026	39,769	54,232	116,971	118,379	96,410	96,675	322,627
Statistical discrepancy	25,211	28,299	-12,162	-79,414	145,026	68,800	-69,445	-9,564	-23,742	-37,753	85,126
Balance on goods	-111,037	-174,170	-191,000	-198,104	-246,687	-346,015	-452,414	-427,188	-482,298	-547,296	-665,390
Balance on services	30,173	77,786	86,935	89,794	81,678	82,621	74,142	64,459	61,117	52,482	47,807
Balance on income	28,550	20,891	22,318	12,609	4,265	13,888	21,054	25,183	10,016	46,304	30,439
Balance on current account [8] . . .	-78,968	-113,670	-124,894	-140,906	-214,064	-300,060	-415,999	-389,456	-475,211	-519,679	-668,074

- Represents or rounds to zero. [1] Excludes exports of goods under U.S. military agency sales contracts identified in census export documents, excludes imports of goods under direct defense expenditures identified in census import documents, and reflects various other adjustments (for valuation, coverage, and timing) of census statistics to balance of payments basis. [2] Includes some goods: Mainly military equipment; major equipment, other materials, supplies, and petroleum products purchased abroad by U.S. military agencies; and fuels purchased by airline and steamship operators. [3] Includes transfers of goods and services under U.S. military grant programs. [4] These lines are presented on a gross basis. The definition of exports is revised to exclude U.S. parents' payments to foreign affiliates and to include U.S. affiliates' receipts from foreign parents. The definition of imports is revised to include U.S. parents' receipts from foreign affiliates and to exclude U.S. affiliates' receipts from foreign parents. [5] The "other transfers" component includes taxes paid by U.S. private residents to foreign governments and taxes paid by private nonresidents to the United States. Includes sales of foreign obligations to foreigners. [6] At the present time, all U.S. Treasury-owned gold is held in the United States. [7] Conceptually, "Balance on current account" is equal to "net foreign investment" in the national income and product accounts (NIPAs). However, the foreign transactions account in the NIPAs (a) includes adjustments to the international transactions accounts for the treatment of gold, (b) includes adjustments for the different geographical treatment of transactions with U.S. territories and Puerto Rico, and (c) includes services furnished without payment by financial pension plans except life insurance carriers and private noninsured pension plans.

Source: U.S. Bureau of Economic Analysis, *Survey of Current Business*, July 2005, and <http://www.bea.gov/bea/international/bpweb/list.cfm?anon=71&registered=0> (released 17 June 2005).

Table 1274. U.S. Balances on International Transactions by Area and Selected Country: 2003 and 2004

[In millions of dollars (-547,296 represents -$547,296,000,000). Minus sign (-) indicates debits]

Area or country	2003, balance on—				2004, balance on—			
	Goods [1]	Services	Income	Current account	Goods [1]	Services	Income	Current account
All areas	-547,296	52,482	46,304	-519,679	-665,390	47,807	30,439	-668,074
Europe	-116,367	9,047	8,941	-102,282	-131,497	10,364	-1,694	-127,671
European Union [2]	-97,553	8,776	4,669	-85,336	-110,484	9,107	-5,705	-108,809
Belgium-Luxembourg	4,929	1,319	-5,660	373	4,687	1,247	-14,809	-9,044
France	-12,358	889	1,155	-10,423	-10,504	1,032	622	-8,656
Germany	-39,716	-5,298	4,146	-41,564	-46,286	-5,690	-679	-52,152
Italy	-15,105	-57	1,881	-13,721	-17,666	-714	1,963	-16,839
Netherlands	9,015	1,266	9,502	18,403	11,715	1,173	4,672	17,427
United Kingdom	-9,703	2,904	-18,375	-23,978	-10,912	6,490	-11,744	-14,406
Canada	-54,320	7,610	16,546	-30,354	-69,052	9,214	18,342	-42,181
Latin America, other Western Hemisphere	-68,913	5,025	9,860	-80,834	-83,875	-42	12,227	-104,692
Mexico	-41,771	4,732	-1,235	-45,582	-46,407	4,315	720	-51,346
Venezuela	-14,353	1,747	-72	-12,824	-20,179	1,854	-65	-18,489
Japan [3]	-67,781	11,390	-18,847	-75,166	-77,519	14,212	-29,314	-92,095
Australia	6,303	2,855	3,765	12,575	6,246	2,881	2,960	11,705
Other Asia and Africa	-246,218	14,756	6,806	-255,701	-309,693	10,951	6,990	-324,114
South Africa	-1,809	137	735	-1,211	-2,777	182	957	-2,107
International and unallocated	(X)	1,799	19,233	12,083	(X)	227	20,928	10,974

X Not applicable. [1] Adjusted to balance of payments basis; excludes exports under U.S. military sales contracts and imports under direct defense expenditures. [2] Includes Denmark, Greece, Ireland, Spain, Portugal, European Atomic Energy Community, European Coal and Steel Community, and European Investment Bank, not shown separately. [3] Includes Ryukyu Islands.

Source: U.S. Bureau of Economic Analysis, *Survey of Current Business*, July 2005, and <http://www.bea.gov/bea/international /bpweb/list.cfm?anon=71&registered=0> (released 17 June 2005).

Table 1275. Private International Service Transactions by Selected Type of Service and Selected Country: 2000 to 2004

[In millions of dollars (284,914 represents $284,914,000,000). For all transactions, see Table 1273]

Type of service and country	Exports				Imports			
	2000	2002	2003	2004	2000	2002	2003	2004
Private Services, total	284,914	282,116	295,567	328,277	208,992	211,716	228,237	263,072
TYPE OF SERVICE								
Travel	82,400	66,605	64,348	74,481	64,705	58,715	57,444	65,635
Passenger fares	20,687	17,046	15,693	18,858	24,274	19,969	20,957	23,701
Other transportation	29,803	29,195	31,329	36,862	41,425	38,407	44,705	54,169
Freight	12,547	12,289	14,037	15,814	27,388	25,973	31,772	39,225
Port services	17,256	16,906	17,292	21,048	14,037	12,434	12,933	14,944
Royalties and license fees	43,233	44,489	48,137	52,643	16,468	19,335	19,390	23,901
Affiliated	30,479	32,751	35,885	39,024	12,536	15,116	15,683	18,750
Unaffiliated	12,754	11,738	12,252	13,619	3,932	4,219	3,707	5,151
Industrial processes	4,662	4,039	4,627	5,560	1,692	2,049	2,034	2,554
Other	8,092	7,699	7,625	8,059	2,241	2,169	1,673	2,598
Other private services	108,791	124,781	136,060	145,433	62,120	75,290	85,741	95,666
Affiliated	35,857	42,869	47,304	50,639	28,776	31,688	35,312	39,446
Unaffiliated	72,935	81,912	88,755	94,794	33,344	43,602	50,429	56,220
Education	10,348	12,626	13,261	13,523	2,031	2,701	3,184	3,525
Financial services	16,026	17,746	19,081	21,897	4,840	4,160	4,232	4,968
Insurance services	3,631	4,467	5,880	6,125	11,284	22,150	26,561	29,882
Telecommunications	3,883	3,890	4,514	4,374	5,428	4,233	4,259	4,365
Business, professional, and tech. services	25,318	29,230	31,473	33,773	9,129	9,688	11,393	12,519
Other unaffiliated services	13,729	13,954	14,548	15,101	632	671	801	962
AREA AND COUNTRY								
Canada	24,563	24,921	27,376	29,696	17,929	18,184	19,743	20,258
Europe	108,238	110,832	119,002	132,701	90,537	92,874	102,300	112,462
Belgium-Luxembourg	3,306	4,257	3,994	4,241	2,396	2,123	2,340	2,518
France	10,574	11,071	11,190	12,966	10,683	10,188	10,249	11,714
Germany	16,169	16,127	17,759	19,432	12,617	15,650	16,709	18,283
Italy	5,457	5,198	5,642	5,815	5,063	4,506	4,799	5,539
Netherlands	7,060	7,378	7,456	7,735	5,701	6,014	6,204	6,530
United Kingdom	31,996	32,426	35,290	40,130	28,338	27,276	31,880	32,979
Latin America & Other Western Hemisphere	54,714	53,419	53,171	57,928	38,759	43,090	47,918	57,550
Mexico	14,333	16,258	16,606	17,975	10,773	11,018	11,681	13,467
Venezuela	3,310	2,837	2,132	2,389	610	457	378	528
Australia	5,575	5,282	6,051	6,852	3,494	3,065	3,232	3,877
Japan	33,411	30,178	29,779	35,197	17,405	17,039	17,209	19,638
Other Asia and Africa	52,207	51,622	54,768	60,144	36,922	34,023	34,224	43,766
International organizations and unallocated	6,206	5,862	5,420	5,759	3,946	3,441	3,611	5,521
Addenda:								
European Union	94,519	96,357	102,590	115,588	78,180	79,292	87,070	97,186

Source: U.S. Bureau of Economic Analysis, *Survey of Current Business*, July 2005.

Table 1276. **International Investment Position by Type of Investment: 1990 to 2004**

[In millions of dollars (-245,347 represents -$245,347,000,000). Estimates for end of year; subject to considerable error due to nature of basic data. Unless otherwise specified, types below refer to current-cost method. For information on current-cost method and market value, see article cited in source]

Type of investment	1990	1995	2000	2001	2002	2003	2004
U.S. net international investment position:							
Current cost	-245,347	-458,462	-1,381,196	-1,919,430	-2,107,267	-2,156,703	-2,484,219
Market value	-164,495	-305,836	-1,581,007	-2,339,448	-2,455,114	-2,372,370	-2,542,245
U.S.-owned assets abroad:							
Current cost	2,178,978	3,486,272	6,238,785	6,308,681	6,645,679	7,640,986	9,052,796
Market value	2,294,085	3,964,558	7,401,192	6,930,484	6,807,849	8,296,638	9,972,783
U.S. official reserve assets	174,664	176,061	128,400	129,961	158,602	183,577	189,591
Gold	102,406	101,279	71,799	72,328	90,806	108,866	113,947
Special drawing rights	10,989	11,037	10,539	10,783	12,166	12,638	13,628
Reserve position in IMF	9,076	14,649	14,824	17,869	21,979	22,535	19,544
Foreign currencies	52,193	49,096	31,238	28,981	33,651	39,538	42,472
U.S. government assets, other	84,344	85,064	85,168	85,654	85,309	84,772	83,556
U.S. loans and other long-term assets	83,716	82,802	82,574	83,132	82,682	81,980	80,803
Repayable in dollars	82,602	82,358	82,293	82,854	82,406	81,706	80,530
Other	1,114	444	281	278	276	274	273
U.S. foreign currency holdings and short-term assets	628	2,262	2,594	2,522	2,627	2,792	2,753
U.S. private assets:							
Current cost	1,919,970	3,225,147	6,025,217	6,093,066	6,401,768	7,372,637	8,779,649
Market value	2,035,077	3,703,433	7,187,624	6,714,869	6,563,938	8,028,289	9,699,636
Direct investments abroad:							
Current cost	616,655	885,506	1,531,607	1,693,131	1,860,418	2,062,551	2,367,386
Market value	731,762	1,363,792	2,694,014	2,314,934	2,022,588	2,718,203	3,287,373
Foreign securities	342,313	1,203,925	2,425,534	2,169,735	2,079,891	2,953,778	3,436,718
Bonds	144,717	413,310	572,692	557,062	705,226	874,356	916,655
Corporate stocks	197,596	790,615	1,852,842	1,612,673	1,374,665	2,079,422	2,520,063
U.S. claims on unaffiliated foreigners [1]	265,315	367,567	836,559	839,303	902,002	596,961	801,536
U.S. claims reported by U.S. banks [2]	695,687	768,149	1,231,517	1,390,897	1,559,457	1,759,347	2,174,009
Foreign-owned assets in the U.S.:							
Current cost	2,424,325	3,944,734	7,619,981	8,228,111	8,752,946	9,797,689	11,537,015
Market value	2,458,580	4,270,394	8,982,199	9,269,932	9,262,963	10,669,008	12,515,028
Foreign official assets in the U.S	373,293	682,873	1,030,708	1,109,072	1,250,977	1,567,124	1,981,992
U.S. government securities	291,228	507,460	756,155	847,005	970,359	1,192,242	1,499,577
U.S. Treasury securities	285,911	489,952	639,796	720,149	811,995	990,411	1,260,502
Other	5,317	17,508	116,359	126,856	158,364	201,831	239,075
Other U.S. government liabilities. . .	17,243	23,573	19,316	17,007	17,144	16,627	17,115
U.S. liabilities reported by U.S. banks	39,880	107,394	153,403	134,655	155,876	201,054	271,471
Other foreign official assets	24,942	44,446	101,834	110,405	107,598	157,201	193,829
Other foreign assets in the U.S:							
Current cost	2,051,032	3,261,861	6,589,273	7,119,039	7,501,969	8,230,565	9,555,023
Market value	2,085,287	3,587,521	7,951,491	8,160,860	8,011,986	9,101,884	10,533,036
Direct investments:							
Current cost	505,346	680,066	1,421,017	1,518,473	1,517,403	1,585,898	1,708,877
Market value	539,601	1,005,726	2,783,235	2,560,294	2,027,420	2,457,217	2,686,890
U.S. Treasury securities	152,452	326,995	381,630	375,059	473,503	543,209	639,716
U.S. securities other than U.S. Treasury securities	460,644	969,849	2,623,014	2,821,372	2,779,067	3,408,113	3,987,797
Corporate and other bonds	238,903	459,080	1,068,566	1,343,071	1,530,982	1,707,206	2,059,250
Corporate stocks	221,741	510,769	1,554,448	1,478,301	1,248,085	1,700,907	1,928,547
U.S. currency	85,933	169,484	255,972	279,755	301,268	317,908	332,735
U.S. liabilities to unaffiliated foreigners [1]	213,406	300,424	738,904	798,314	892,574	454,317	581,258
U.S. liabilities reported by U.S. banks [2]	633,251	815,043	1,168,736	1,326,066	1,538,154	1,921,120	2,304,640

[1] Reported by U.S. nonbanking concerns. [2] Not included elsewhere.

Source: U.S. Bureau of Economic Analysis, *Survey of Current Business*, July 2005.

Table 1277. **U.S. Reserve Assets: 1990 to 2004**

[In billions of dollars ($83.3 represents $83,300,000,000). As of end of year, except as indicated]

Type	1990	1995	1998	1999	2000	2001	2002	2003	2004
Total	83.3	85.8	81.8	71.5	67.6	68.7	79.0	85.9	86.8
Gold stock	11.1	11.1	11.0	11.0	11.0	11.0	11.0	11.0	11.0
Special drawing rights	11.0	11.0	10.6	10.3	10.5	10.8	12.2	12.6	13.6
Foreign currencies	52.2	49.1	36.0	32.2	31.2	29.0	33.8	39.7	42.7
Reserve position in IMF [1]	9.1	14.6	24.1	18.0	14.8	17.9	22.0	22.5	19.5

[1] International Monetary Fund.

Source: Board of Governors of the Federal Reserve System, *Federal Reserve Bulletin*, monthly; and Department of the Treasury, *Treasury Bulletin*, quarterly. For latest issue, see <http://fms.treas.gov/bulletin/index.html>.

Table 1278. Foreign Direct Investment Position in the United States on a Historical-Cost Basis by Industry and Selected Country: 1990 to 2004

[In millions of dollars (394,911 represents $394,911,000,000)]

Country	1990	2000	2002	2003	2004 Total[1]	2004 Manufacturing	2004 Wholesale	2004 Information
All countries	394,911	1,256,867	1,344,697	1,410,672	1,526,306	519,410	201,101	117,190
Canada	29,544	114,309	95,344	101,568	133,761	29,148	3,159	5,368
Europe	247,320	887,014	980,036	1,021,349	1,078,287	402,349	114,590	93,509
Austria	625	3,007	3,727	3,775	3,720	2,122	472	1
Belgium.	3,900	14,787	10,278	10,871	11,285	3,966	1,767	(D)
Denmark.	819	4,025	4,430	4,561	5,450	3,116	601	2
Finland	1,504	8,875	6,328	5,446	5,509	(D)	1,392	(D)
France	18,650	125,740	141,588	139,265	148,242	48,318	13,512	26,670
Germany.	28,232	122,412	139,247	156,290	163,372	59,749	14,612	21,405
Ireland	1,340	25,523	27,781	24,228	21,153	4,074	(D)	410
Italy	1,524	6,576	6,833	6,820	7,421	761	1,174	(D)
Luxembourg.	2,195	58,930	95,037	108,124	107,842	25,137	1,688	6,486
Netherlands	64,671	138,894	150,263	152,708	167,280	81,420	7,265	5,097
Norway.	773	2,665	3,759	4,036	3,136	1,996	674	(D)
Spain	792	5,068	4,560	5,603	5,669	1,726	(D)	-57
Sweden	5,484	21,991	20,515	20,388	23,853	9,998	6,917	61
Switzerland.	17,674	64,719	123,867	129,032	122,944	77,280	4,918	(D)
United Kingdom	98,676	277,613	215,531	219,735	251,562	66,959	57,497	11,726
Latin America and other								
Western Hemisphere	20,168	53,691	74,561	81,768	85,864	21,473	7,213	4,556
South and Central America.	6,140	13,384	19,058	22,172	26,295	938	5,571	121
Mexico	575	7,462	7,623	7,707	7,880	1,251	218	104
Panama.	4,188	3,819	6,111	9,203	10,707	-380	-4	-5
Other Western Hemisphere.	14,028	40,307	55,502	59,596	59,569	20,534	1,642	4,435
Bahamas	1,535	1,254	1,177	1,112	1,179	(D)	555	1
Netherlands Antilles	12,974	3,807	4,098	4,144	4,749	643	(D)	(D)
United Kingdom Is., Caribbean. . .	-2,979	15,191	23,871	25,575	24,243	2,030	1,601	338
Africa	505	2,700	2,242	2,179	1,611	661	-147	(D)
Middle East	4,425	6,506	7,319	7,641	8,200	1,705	2,918	(D)
Israel	640	3,012	3,627	3,777	4,107	1,677	205	227
Kuwait	1,805	908	1,017	1,069	1,238	(D)	(Z)	-
Saudi Arabia	1,811	(D)	(D)	(D)	(D)	-2	(D)	13
Asia and Pacific	92,948	192,647	185,196	196,169	218,583	64,075	73,369	13,482
Australia	6,542	18,775	23,776	24,934	28,083	3,788	431	(D)
Hong Kong	1,511	1,493	1,888	1,831	1,709	560	247	(D)
Japan.	83,091	159,690	151,333	160,452	176,906	59,980	68,192	1,748
Singapore	1,289	5,087	804	1,484	1,801	-2,048	491	38
Taiwan	836	3,174	2,723	2,956	3,227	1,158	802	35

- Represents or rounds to zero.   D Suppressed to avoid disclosure of data of individual companies.   Z Less than $500,000.   [1] Includes other industries not shown separately.

Source: U.S. Bureau of Economic Analysis, Survey of Current Business, July 2005. For most recent copy and historical issues, see <http://www.bea.doc.gov/bea/pubs.htm>.

Table 1279. U.S. Majority-Owned Affiliates of Foreign Companies—Assets, Sales, Employment, Land, Exports, and Imports by Industry: 2002

[(4,556,582 represents $4,556,582,000,000). A U.S. affiliate is a U.S. business enterprise in which one foreign owner (individual, branch, partnership, association, trust, corporation, or government) has a direct or indirect voting interest of 10 percent or more. Estimates cover the universe of nonbank affiliates. These data are now on a NAICS (North American Industry Classification System) basis and not comparable to previous data, which were based on the Standard Industrial Classification system]

Industry	Total assets (mil. dol.)	Sales (mil. dol.)[1]	Employment (1,000)[2]	Employee compensation (mil. dol.)	Gross book value (mil. dol.) P & E[3]	Gross book value (mil. dol.) Land	Merchandise exports[4] (mil. dol.)	Merchandise imports[4] (mil. dol.)
All industries.	4,556,582	2,043,500	5,420	307,133	1,016,004	49,184	137,037	324,578
Manufacturing [5]	1,009,551	855,354	2,228	145,242	482,408	17,713	86,839	132,928
Petroleum and coal products.	(D)	(D)	(D)	(D)	6,104	(D)	1,104	(D)
Chemicals	238,898	153,073	329	27,824	109,155	2,759	15,470	18,315
Computers & electronic products . . .	94,273	90,738	246	18,960	33,522	776	12,265	24,426
Transportation equipment	209,892	192,516	367	22,744	101,670	1,168	27,957	50,326
Wholesale trade [5].	409,360	583,646	516	36,542	187,058	5,172	45,412	183,395
Motor vehicles and motor vehicle parts and supplies	86,686	129,931	54	4,710	37,198	671	2,591	64,305
Petroleum & petroleum products . . .	126,928	157,577	54	4,911	(D)	(D)	9,221	24,434
Retail trade	60,095	111,580	583	15,348	35,594	2,485	711	4,037
Information	248,147	75,109	246	16,728	44,269	650	1,046	853
Finance (except depository institutions) and insurance	2,293,786	185,248	233	30,735	29,788	756	(Z)	4
Real estate and rental and leasing . . .	88,670	17,709	34	2,122	68,306	11,068	215	467
Professional, scientific, and technical services	54,932	41,620	163	12,281	8,671	173	384	234
Other industries	392,039	173,234	1,418	48,134	159,910	11,166	2,430	2,658

D Withheld to avoid disclosure of data of individual companies.   Z Less than $500,000.   [1] Excludes returns, discounts, allowances, and sales and excise taxes.   [2] Average number of full-time and part-time employees.   [3] Plant and equipment (P & E). Includes mineral rights and minor amounts of property other than land.   [4] F.a.s. value at port of exportation.   [5] Includes industries not shown separately.

Source: U.S. Bureau of Economic Analysis, Survey of Current Business, June 2005, and previous issues. For most recent copy and historical issues, see <http://www.bea.doc.gov/bea/pubs.htm>. Foreign Direct Investment in the United States: Operations of U.S. Affiliates of Foreign Companies, Preliminary 2002 Estimates.

Table 1280. Foreign Direct Investment in the United States—Gross Book Value and Employment of U.S. Affiliates of Foreign Companies by State: 1990 to 2002

[(578,355 represents $578,355,000,000. A U.S. affiliate is a U.S. business enterprise in which one one foreign owner (individual, branch, partnership, association, trust corporation, or government) has a direct or indirect voting interest of 10 percent or more. Estimates cover the universe of nonbank U.S. affiliates]

State and other area	Gross book value of property, plant, and equipment (mil. dol.)				Total employment (1,000)				
	1990	2000	2001	2002, prel.	1990	2000	2001	2002, prel. Total	2002, prel. Percent of all businesses
Total	578,355	1,175,628	1,181,091	1,016,004	4,734.5	6,524.6	6,268.3	5,420.3	(X)
United States	552,902	1,070,422	1,054,827	912,452	4,704.4	6,498.3	6,237.5	5,394.2	4.8
Alabama	7,300	16,646	17,037	15,210	55.7	77.9	92.0	72.7	4.6
Alaska	19,435	28,964	(D)	30,064	13.2	12.0	12.2	11.2	5.1
Arizona	7,234	10,716	9,390	8,442	57.1	73.2	65.6	55.4	2.9
Arkansas	2,344	4,613	6,103	4,724	29.2	40.9	40.7	32.9	3.3
California	75,768	121,040	118,426	91,936	555.9	749.4	707.0	616.4	4.9
Colorado	6,544	15,319	12,654	12,580	56.3	102.6	91.2	76.7	4.1
Connecticut	5,357	13,604	14,468	12,789	75.9	118.0	126.0	113.0	7.7
Delaware	5,818	6,114	6,603	6,433	43.1	31.8	28.0	23.3	6.4
District of Columbia	3,869	4,247	5,187	4,433	11.4	17.1	18.6	17.0	3.7
Florida	18,659	38,755	35,481	28,446	205.7	312.1	305.3	244.9	3.8
Georgia	16,729	29,510	29,362	24,973	161.0	227.9	220.7	190.1	5.7
Hawaii	11,830	10,369	9,787	8,198	53.0	44.8	41.0	38.3	8.4
Idaho	776	2,749	2,598	2,131	11.7	14.2	14.1	12.5	2.6
Illinois	23,420	48,425	48,910	41,723	245.8	325.8	315.8	268.4	5.2
Indiana	13,426	30,179	29,744	28,139	126.9	168.2	164.3	137.4	5.4
Iowa	2,712	7,186	7,169	6,017	32.8	40.9	45.6	37.4	3.0
Kansas	5,134	9,036	5,098	4,837	29.6	61.0	39.7	33.8	3.0
Kentucky	9,229	22,091	23,116	23,731	65.7	106.0	100.8	87.7	5.8
Louisiana	17,432	31,160	32,551	27,182	61.4	61.3	58.9	48.9	3.1
Maine	2,080	5,087	5,266	5,873	26.6	33.9	34.1	33.0	6.4
Maryland	5,713	13,157	12,866	10,191	79.6	112.9	114.8	106.3	5.1
Massachusetts	8,890	23,875	25,563	23,265	131.2	226.8	221.7	191.0	6.5
Michigan	12,012	39,238	52,465	40,201	139.6	249.9	220.1	204.1	5.3
Minnesota	11,972	13,472	12,089	9,763	89.8	106.2	102.9	93.9	4.0
Mississippi	2,989	4,121	4,800	4,924	23.6	24.2	27.9	22.2	2.4
Missouri	5,757	15,773	14,918	15,044	73.7	107.4	113.1	96.7	4.1
Montana	2,181	3,099	(D)	1,716	5.1	6.8	7.3	5.8	1.8
Nebraska	776	2,737	2,106	1,748	14.9	21.7	23.5	19.3	2.5
Nevada	5,450	10,128	8,164	6,532	22.7	36.3	31.7	26.5	2.8
New Hampshire	1,446	5,124	5,321	4,300	25.9	46.5	42.5	38.4	7.0
New Jersey	18,608	35,115	36,918	31,829	227.0	272.2	268.5	228.6	6.7
New Mexico	4,312	5,801	5,482	4,454	17.4	16.7	15.9	12.7	2.2
New York	36,424	68,522	68,860	63,047	347.5	479.1	469.3	394.7	5.5
North Carolina	15,234	29,931	22,875	20,571	181.0	264.8	238.6	212.7	6.5
North Dakota	1,251	1,824	1,753	830	3.1	7.7	9.7	7.6	2.9
Ohio	20,549	37,530	35,158	32,000	219.1	260.3	244.1	212.8	4.5
Oklahoma	6,049	7,635	7,743	7,301	43.6	41.9	42.2	36.5	3.0
Oregon	3,427	13,178	12,265	9,286	39.1	62.1	56.3	48.8	3.6
Pennsylvania	16,587	34,106	33,528	30,666	221.6	283.4	260.4	233.4	4.6
Rhode Island	1,120	3,394	3,310	3,055	13.3	24.2	24.1	21.8	5.2
South Carolina	10,067	23,563	22,762	20,272	104.7	138.4	137.7	123.4	8.1
South Dakota	553	1,011	1,157	684	4.5	6.9	7.7	7.1	2.3
Tennessee	10,280	20,842	20,961	18,650	116.9	153.2	150.8	131.0	5.6
Texas	57,079	110,032	103,573	85,802	299.5	445.2	417.5	351.4	4.4
Utah	3,918	14,340	13,552	10,463	21.0	38.1	34.6	31.1	3.4
Vermont	631	2,146	2,614	1,537	7.7	11.5	11.7	12.0	4.7
Virginia	10,702	23,570	20,668	15,332	113.3	181.9	171.3	146.4	5.0
Washington	7,985	22,257	18,946	16,098	77.5	106.8	99.4	84.1	3.7
West Virginia	7,975	7,061	7,115	7,299	34.9	28.1	28.2	22.4	3.9
Wisconsin	5,088	13,961	15,842	17,192	81.4	110.3	111.9	112.5	4.7
Wyoming	2,782	8,072	10,215	10,539	5.8	7.8	10.4	8.1	4.2
Puerto Rico	1,499	2,169	2,337	2,271	16.1	17.9	18.3	15.6	(NA)
Other territories and offshore . .	18,484	34,105	35,404	40,157	9.0	7.9	12.0	10.1	(NA)
Foreign	5,470	2,406	3,582	2,476	5.0	0.5	0.5	0.4	(NA)
Unspecified [1]	(NA)	66,526	84,941	58,648	(NA)	(NA)	(NA)	(NA)	(NA)

NA Not available.   X Not applicable.   [1] Covers property, plant, and equipment not located in a particular state, including aircraft, railroad rolling stock, satellites, undersea cable, and trucks engaged in interstate transportation.

Source: U.S. Bureau of Economic Analysis, *Survey of Current Business*, August 2004 issue, and *Foreign Direct Investment in the United States, Operations of U.S. Affiliates of Foreign Companies*, annual.

Foreign Commerce and Aid   825

Table 1281. U.S. Businesses Acquired or Established by Foreign Direct Investors—Investment Outlays by Industry of U.S. Business Enterprise and Country of Ultimate Beneficial Owner: 1990 to 2004

[In millions of dollars (65,932,000,000). Foreign direct investment is the ownership or control directly or indirectly, by one foreign individual branch, partnership, association, trust, corporation, or government of 10 percent or more of the voting securities of a U.S. business enterprise or an equivalent interest in an unincorporated one. Data represent number and full cost of acquisitions of existing U.S. business enterprises, including business segments or operating units of existing U.S. business enterprises and establishments of new enterprises. Investments may be made by the foreign direct investor itself, or indirectly by an existing U.S. affiliate of the foreign direct investor. Covers investments in U.S. business enterprises with assets of over $1 million, or ownership of 200 acres of U.S. land]

Industry and country	1990	1995	1999	2000	2001	2002	2003	2004, prel.
Total	65,932	57,195	274,956	335,629	147,109	54,519	63,591	79,820
U.S. businesses acquired	(NA)	47,179	265,127	322,703	138,091	43,442	50,212	72,546
U.S. businesses established	(NA)	10,016	9,829	12,926	9,017	11,077	13,379	7,274
By type of investor:								
Foreign direct investors...........	(NA)	11,927	120,878	105,151	23,134	13,650	27,866	33,529
U.S. affiliates.................	(NA)	45,268	154,078	230,478	123,975	40,869	35,725	46,291
INDUSTRY								
Manufacturing.................	(NA)	(NA)	73,122	143,285	37,592	16,446	10,750	17,178
Wholesale trade	(NA)	(NA)	(D)	8,561	3,982	871	1,086	951
Retail trade	(NA)	(NA)	3,458	1,672	1,913	551	941	3,055
Information...................	(NA)	(NA)	90,855	67,932	27,599	14,181	9,236	3,102
Depository institutions	(NA)	(NA)	(D)	2,636	5,709	613	4,864	14,095
Finance, (except depository institutions) and insurance......	(NA)	(NA)	46,380	44,420	40,780	4,344	23,511	24,904
Real estate and rental and leasing	(NA)	(NA)	5,206	4,526	3,572	5,266	2,817	4,823
Professional, scientific, and technical services	(NA)	(NA)	9,366	32,332	7,044	4,012	1,955	4,048
Other industries	(NA)	(NA)	32,680	30,264	18,917	8,234	8,429	7,664
COUNTRY [1]								
Canada.....................	3,430	8,029	9,271	28,346	16,646	4,333	9,157	32,378
Europe	36,011	38,195	196,288	249,167	78,328	39,644	39,024	39,424
France.....................	10,217	1,129	23,750	26,114	5,772	15,196	2,955	4,661
Germany	2,363	13,117	21,514	18,452	12,733	3,067	8,830	5,020
Netherlands	2,247	1,061	22,265	47,686	14,879	3,476	1,077	253
Switzerland	3,905	7,533	7,512	22,789	16,468	2,656	649	3,523
United Kingdom..............	13,096	9,094	109,226	110,208	17,095	12,188	20,373	24,166
Other Europe	4,183	6,261	12,021	23,883	11,381	3,061	5,140	1,801
Latin America and other Western Hemisphere	796	1,550	33,046	15,400	15,274	3,487	1,607	1,418
South and Central America	399	1,283	1,622	5,334	431	373	182	(D)
Other Western Hemisphere	397	267	31,424	10,066	14,843	3,144	1,425	(D)
Africa.....................	(D)	(D)	(D)	(D)	(D)	(D)	1,738	(D)
Middle East.................	472	447	848	947	(D)	(D)	(D)	(D)
Asia and Pacific.............	23,170	8,688	15,100	40,282	11,383	5,131	11,469	4,800
Australia...................	1,412	2,270	(D)	(D)	4,869	1,565	9,032	2,885
Japan.....................	19,933	3,602	11,696	26,044	5,345	3,275	1,544	986
Other Asia and Pacific........	1,825	2,816	(D)	(D)	1,169	291	893	929

NA Not available.   D Suppressed to avoid disclosure of data of individual companies.   [1] For investments in which more than one investor participated, each investor and each investor's outlays are classified by country of each ultimate beneficial owner.
Source: U.S. Bureau of Economic Analysis, *Survey of Current Business*, June 2005, and previous issues. For most recent copy and historical issues, see <http://www.bea.doc.gov/bea/pubs.htm>.

Table 1282. U.S. Direct Investment Position Abroad, Capital Outflows, and Income by Industry of Foreign Affiliates: 2000 to 2004

[In millions of dollars (1,316,247 represents $1,316,247,000,000). See headnote, table 1283]

Industry	Direct investment position on a historical-cost basis			Capital outflows (inflows (-))			Income		
	2000	2003	2004	2000	2003	2004	2000	2003	2004
All industries, total ...	1,316,247	1,791,891	2,063,998	142,627	119,406	229,294	133,692	171,229	209,338
Mining	72,111	87,697	101,477	2,174	5,426	11,103	13,164	11,274	16,905
Utilities	21,964	21,822	18,985	2,466	-685	-1,138	1,610	2,054	2,086
Manufacturing	343,899	375,250	428,235	43,002	27,825	54,202	42,230	35,981	48,328
Food.................	23,497	23,851	26,021	2,014	2,539	1,613	2,681	3,137	3,227
Chemicals.............	75,807	96,283	107,908	3,812	7,201	11,488	(D)	10,857	13,792
Primary and fabricated metals.................	21,644	22,126	26,328	1,233	-13	2,731	1,536	1,718	2,578
Machinery.............	22,229	21,077	24,543	2,659	2,879	3,250	2,257	2,221	2,873
Computer and electronic products.....	59,909	51,099	58,615	17,303	2,121	6,356	8,860	4,623	5,985
Electrical equipment, appliances, and components	10,005	10,985	12,392	2,100	311	720	1,079	591	1,348
Transportation equip.....	49,887	47,496	48,418	7,814	1,704	-521	4,107	2,335	4,523
Wholesale trade	93,936	121,956	136,949	11,938	11,926	13,803	14,198	18,759	24,145
Information	52,345	49,057	56,422	16,531	4,326	5,343	-964	6,224	9,078
Depository institutions	40,152	62,611	68,100	-1,274	592	285	2,191	2,528	3,247
Finance and insurance	217,086	328,916	370,965	21,659	19,151	29,130	15,210	21,356	27,329
Professional, scientific, and technical	32,868	35,268	42,110	5,441	3,427	6,568	3,548	3,730	5,775
Other industries	441,886	709,314	840,755	40,690	47,419	109,997	42,504	69,322	72,447

D Withheld to avoid disclosure of individual company data.
Source: U.S. Bureau of Economic Analysis, *Survey of Current Business*, July 2005, and earlier issues. See also <http://www.bea.doc.gov/bea/ARTICLES/2005/07July/0705DirectInvest.pdf> (released July 2005).

Table 1283. U.S. Direct Investment Position Abroad on a Historical-Cost Basis by Selected Country: 1990 to 2004

[In millions of dollars (430,521 represents 430,521,000,000). U.S. investment abroad is the ownership or control by one U.S. person of 10% or more of the voting securities of an incorporated foreign business enterprise or an equivalent interest in a unincorporated foreign business enterprise. Negative position can occur when a U.S. parent company's liabilities to the foreign affiliate are greater than its equity in, and loans to the foreign affiliate]

Country	1990	1995	1999	2000	2001	2002	2003	2004
All countries	430,521	699,015	1,215,960	1,316,247	1,460,352	1,616,548	1,791,891	2,063,998
Canada	69,508	83,498	119,590	132,472	152,601	166,473	189,754	216,571
Europe	214,739	344,596	627,754	687,320	771,936	859,378	982,737	1,089,941
Austria	1,113	2,829	3,848	2,872	3,964	4,011	4,920	5,278
Belgium	9,464	18,706	21,756	17,973	22,589	25,727	26,477	27,761
Denmark	1,726	2,161	3,846	5,270	5,160	6,184	6,464	6,618
Finland	544	965	1,379	1,342	1,686	1,722	1,620	2,071
France	19,164	33,358	43,120	42,628	40,125	43,348	48,268	58,927
Germany	27,609	44,242	53,399	55,508	63,396	61,073	68,358	79,579
Greece	282	533	760	795	835	981	1,056	1,255
Ireland	5,894	7,996	25,157	35,903	39,541	51,598	62,547	73,153
Italy	14,063	17,096	17,889	23,484	22,883	23,771	29,611	33,378
Luxembourg	1,697	5,929	22,148	27,849	50,771	62,181	70,025	74,902
Netherlands	19,120	42,113	121,315	115,429	147,687	158,415	186,102	201,918
Norway	4,209	4,741	5,944	4,379	4,446	6,045	7,677	9,104
Portugal	897	1,413	2,188	2,664	2,746	3,093	3,027	3,151
Spain	7,868	10,856	19,970	21,236	28,174	38,001	40,439	45,251
Sweden	1,787	6,816	10,624	25,959	26,374	30,114	34,927	36,399
Switzerland	25,099	31,125	40,532	55,377	63,768	74,229	88,940	100,727
Turkey	522	973	1,792	1,826	1,641	1,869	1,985	2,225
United Kingdom	72,707	106,332	216,638	230,762	228,230	247,952	278,745	302,523
Latin America and other Western Hemisphere	71,413	131,377	253,928	266,576	279,611	289,413	300,690	325,891
South America	22,933	49,170	83,477	84,220	76,809	64,603	70,184	72,584
Argentina	2,531	7,660	18,865	17,488	15,535	11,288	10,948	11,629
Brazil	14,384	25,002	37,184	36,717	32,027	27,598	31,741	33,267
Chile	1,896	6,216	10,177	10,052	10,526	8,928	9,218	10,196
Colombia	1,677	3,506	3,775	3,693	3,122	2,622	2,956	2,987
Ecuador	280	889	1,116	832	579	809	1,082	814
Peru	599	1,335	3,148	3,130	3,197	3,310	3,678	3,934
Venezuela	1,087	3,634	7,385	10,531	10,069	8,671	9,119	8,493
Other	479	928	1,828	1,778	1,755	1,377	1,441	1,264
Central America	20,415	33,493	73,761	73,841	60,716	65,395	67,010	75,433
Costa Rica	251	921	1,493	1,716	1,835	1,803	863	1,098
Honduras	262	68	347	399	227	181	262	339
Mexico	10,313	16,873	37,151	39,352	52,544	56,303	59,070	66,554
Panama	9,289	15,123	33,493	30,758	5,141	5,842	5,538	5,868
Other	299	506	1,277	1,618	970	1,267	1,276	1,574
Other Western Hemisphere	28,065	48,714	96,690	108,515	142,086	159,416	163,496	177,873
Barbados	252	698	3,030	2,141	2,240	1,817	1,022	1,369
Bermuda	20,169	28,374	50,847	60,114	84,969	89,473	85,077	91,265
Dominican Republic	529	330	968	1,143	1,116	983	816	1,041
Africa	3,650	6,017	13,118	11,891	15,574	16,040	18,978	22,259
Egypt	1,231	1,093	2,210	1,998	2,557	2,682	3,518	4,240
Nigeria	-401	629	233	470	260	901	1,080	955
South Africa	775	1,422	3,474	3,562	3,070	3,334	3,754	4,966
Other	2,045	2,873	7,202	5,861	9,687	9,122	10,627	12,097
Middle East	3,959	7,198	10,950	10,863	13,212	15,158	17,363	19,235
Israel	746	1,831	4,777	3,735	5,690	5,726	7,036	6,790
Saudi Arabia	1,899	2,741	3,336	3,661	3,570	4,930	3,513	3,835
United Arab Emirates	409	500	540	683	834	1,087	2,016	2,368
Other	905	2,126	2,298	2,784	3,118	3,415	4,798	6,242
Asia and Pacific	64,716	122,712	190,621	207,125	227,418	270,086	282,370	390,101
Australia	15,110	24,328	35,386	34,838	27,778	39,074	48,858	(D)
China	354	2,765	9,401	11,140	12,081	10,570	11,541	15,430
Hong Kong	6,055	11,768	22,759	27,447	32,494	40,329	37,567	43,743
India	372	1,105	2,390	2,379	2,496	4,232	4,831	6,203
Indonesia	3,207	6,777	8,402	8,904	10,511	(D)	(D)	(D)
Japan	22,599	37,309	55,120	57,091	55,651	66,468	68,097	80,246
Korea, South	2,695	5,557	7,474	8,968	9,977	11,856	13,030	17,332
Malaysia	1,466	4,237	6,222	7,910	7,489	7,101	7,270	8,690
New Zealand	3,156	4,601	4,852	4,271	4,273	3,926	3,886	4,481
Philippines	1,355	2,719	3,517	3,638	5,436	5,964	5,790	6,338
Singapore	3,975	12,140	20,665	24,133	40,764	50,955	50,343	56,900
Taiwan	2,226	4,293	6,744	7,836	9,301	10,144	12,148	(D)
Thailand	1,790	4,283	5,500	5,824	6,176	7,774	7,098	7,747
Other	356	830	2,190	2,746	2,990	(D)	(D)	(D)

D Suppressed to avoid disclosure of data of individual companies.

Source: U.S. Bureau of Economic Analysis, *Survey of Current Business*, July 2005, and earlier issues. See also <http://www.bea.doc.gov/bea/ARTICLES/2005/07July/0705DirectInvest.pdf> (released July 2005).

Foreign Commerce and Aid 827

[In millions of dollars (14,396 represents $14,396,000,000). See text, this section. Negative figures (-) occur when the total of grant returns, principal repayments, and/or foreign currencies disbursed by the U.S. Government exceeds new grants and new credits utilized and/or acquisitions of foreign currencies through new sales of farm products]

Country	1990	1995	1998	1999	2000	2001	2002	2003
Total, net	**14,396**	**12,666**	**14,029**	**18,559**	**17,858**	**12,601**	**17,505**	**23,662**
Investment in financial institutions	1,304	1,517	1,580	1,451	1,500	1,704	1,778	2,169
Western Europe	**-103**	**177**	**317**	**431**	**183**	**220**	**104**	**387**
Austria	-10	-1	(Z)	-	-	-	-	-
Belgium and Luxembourg	-9	-	-	-	-	-	-	46
Denmark	-	-	-	-	-	-	-	-
Finland	-8	-1	(Z)	-	-	-	-	-
France	-15	-	-	-	-	-	-	-
Germany	-338	(Z)	-	-	-	-	-1	-
Iceland	(Z)	-	-	-	-	-	-	-
Ireland	2	-	8	-	-	-	-	44
Italy	-30	(Z)	-	-	-	-	(Z)	-
Netherlands	-	-	-	-	-	-	-	-
Norway	-	-	-	-	-	-	-	-
Portugal	56	-16	26	4	-79	-28	-27	-75
Spain	-122	-59	-37	-28	-19	-19	-19	-19
Sweden	-	-	-	-	-	-	-	-
United Kingdom	-111	-120	-130	-136	-135	-56	-66	-68
Yugoslavia [1]	-39	(X)	-1	-	1	-	-51	231
Former Yugoslavia [1]:								
Bosnia and Herzegovina	(X)	94	236	188	52	115	64	46
Croatia	(X)	9	-11	1	3	18	36	52
Macedonia	(X)	1	7	20	50	29	15	57
Slovenia	(X)	-24	-15	2	2	2	7	7
Former Yugoslavia - Regional [3]	(X)	(Z)	8	21	74	87	128	66
Other and unspecified [3]	520	293	229	355	234	72	17	(Z)
Eastern Europe	**973**	**1,979**	**1,790**	**2,152**	**1,830**	**1,300**	**1,464**	**1,267**
Albania	-	15	16	4	26	38	40	41
Bulgaria	-	6	14	26	46	54	34	46
Czechoslovakia	(Z)	-2	-	-	1	-	-	-
Czech Republic	(X)	3	5	8	11	11	23	8
Estonia	(X)	2	6	4	6	3	-2	18
Hungary	1	36	13	13	12	8	16	7
Latvia	(X)	2	8	9	6	1	11	9
Lithuania	(X)	28	15	4	-16	(Z)	3	12
Poland	912	6	38	24	40	-1	16	19
Romania	79	9	28	10	38	43	48	65
Slovakia	-	2	6	8	7	10	10	13
Soviet Union	-30	(X)	-	-	-	-	-	-
Newly Independent States:								
Armenia	(X)	102	39	35	20	52	54	74
Azerbaijan	(X)	19	6	6	8	15	32	34
Belarus	(X)	50	3	6	1	4	2	(z)
Georgia	(X)	89	28	23	36	49	97	65
Kazakhstan	(X)	17	70	45	42	58	52	49
Kyrgyzstan	(X)	33	30	15	15	32	36	34
Moldova	(X)	19	5	32	32	60	28	22
Russia	(X)	465	444	968	797	280	266	191
Tajikistan	(X)	34	30	6	8	34	18	24
Turkmenistan	(X)	16	3	3	4	8	6	5
Ukraine	(X)	171	172	318	138	195	118	95
Uzbekistan	(X)	1	7	19	22	41	39	51
Former Soviet Union - Regional [3]	(X)	613	603	506	501	295	510	364
Other and unspecified [3]	11	241	200	61	29	10	7	21
Near East and South Asia	**6,656**	**3,025**	**5,045**	**4,378**	**7,658**	**2,520**	**5,656**	**9,811**
Afghanistan	57	10	-	2	5	6	140	548
Bangladesh	181	87	24	65	43	89	45	28
Cyprus	16	6	14	-	-	-	-	-
Egypt	4,976	1,639	2,018	2,093	3,091	1,296	1,689	2,023
Greece	282	261	-240	-145	-169	-153	-218	-318
India	13	48	167	-79	-64	-56	-122	-151
Iran	-	-	-	-	-	-	-	-
Iraq [4]	-7	128	-	-	(Z)	1	(Z)	3,220
Israel	4,380	420	2,842	2,221	3,932	589	3,061	2,742
Jordan	155	129	217	186	317	298	483	1,340
Kuwait	-2,506	-	-	-	-	-	-	75
Lebanon	9	5	2	9	22	60	28	24
Nepal	20	20	20	19	15	27	28	42
Oman	4	4	20	-6	-6	-10	-8	-2
Pakistan	531	-187	-82	79	366	170	445	222
Saudi Arabia	-1,614	-	-	-	-	-	-	-
Sri Lanka	72	27	1	-6	-15	-6	-10	-16
Syria	(Z)	-	-	-	-	-	-	-
Turkey	367	147	-159	-259	-86	-5	-138	-324
United Arab Emirates	-361	-	-	-	-	-	-	-
Yemen (Sanaa)	(X)	(X)	-	-	-	-	-	-
Yemen	43	3	5	10	16	7	5	17
UNRWA [5]	7	103	78	93	97	77	71	124
West Bank-Gaza	1	58	80	88	64	115	143	195
Other and unspecified [3]	29	118	39	10	30	15	14	22

See footnotes at end of table.

U.S. Census Bureau, Statistical Abstract of the United States: 2006

Table 1284. **U.S. Government Foreign Grants and Credits by Type and Country: 1990 to 2003—Con.**

[In millions of dollars. See headnote, p. 828]

Country	1990	1995	1998	1999	2000	2001	2002	2003
Africa	**1,883**	**2,217**	**1,366**	**841**	**1,042**	**1,562**	**2,015**	**2,781**
Algeria	59	755	45	-46	-53	182	-73	-123
Angola	-15	37	38	21	31	43	87	27
Benin	5	14	14	23	22	38	23	23
Botswana	17	18	5	3	1	1	12	(Z)
Burkina	15	23	17	9	7	9	12	2
Burundi	18	39	9	6	3	6	3	18
Cameroon	42	4	6	2	1	3	6	3
Cape Verde	8	11	6	1	1	2	2	1
Chad	24	14	3	2	2	7	3	1
Congo (Kinshasa)	242	1	1	2	9	16	33	1,078
Cote d'Ivoire	18	16	8	11	9	2	32	52
Eritrea	-	9	21	7	48	45	36	23
Ethiopia	57	127	162	44	142	98	87	137
Ghana	14	63	40	38	40	86	48	49
Guinea	16	28	18	22	19	45	41	30
Kenya	115	35	37	31	44	108	50	57
Lesotho	16	13	3	1	1	1	1	1
Liberia	32	67	19	26	19	19	10	13
Madagascar	34	33	44	30	21	63	36	31
Malawi	35	64	23	30	45	41	46	42
Mali	31	31	36	36	50	9	49	50
Mauritania	13	2	4	2	2	5	4	3
Morocco	96	-48	-48	-28	-9	-29	760	-59
Mozambique	83	115	81	74	119	133	105	107
Niger	34	31	13	7	5	5	9	3
Nigeria	156	1	-4	-38	-17	17	45	468
Rwanda	13	138	32	29	26	57	32	36
Senegal	61	24	18	26	27	51	42	44
Sierra Leone	2	11	14	5	10	11	29	36
Somalia	80	26	4	12	7	1	6	10
South Africa	20	112	90	91	68	119	98	113
Sudan	150	11	28	16	17	13	11	41
Swaziland	14	13	14	-	-	-	-	-
Tanzania	51	19	27	22	15	50	44	48
Togo	10	3	2	2	2	2	4	5
Tunisia	44	-4	-19	-22	-19	-18	-12	-17
Uganda	43	56	19	51	92	55	71	85
Zambia	63	27	14	27	44	42	34	51
Zimbabwe	10	29	47	18	23	24	21	23
Other and unspecified [3]	157	246	475	248	168	200	168	269
Far East and Pacific	**39**	**753**	**759**	**1,145**	**550**	**725**	**331**	**760**
Australia	-34	-	-	-	-	-	-	-
Burma	1	-2	-2	-	-	1	4	6
Cambodia	5	39	35	16	23	42	35	32
China	71	136	248	293	167	132	45	4
Hong Kong	-8	73	17	-17	-15	-24	-20	-23
Indonesia	46	25	24	483	270	488	221	821
Japan and Ryukyu Islands	-635	(Z)	-	-	-	-	-	-
Korea, Republic of	-192	-49	-52	330	-132	-215	-134	-137
Laos	(Z)	3	5	4	5	6	7	6
Malaysia	-1	(Z)	2	-	134	184	11	1
Mongolia	-	11	23	14	9	18	20	14
New Zealand	-2	-	-	-	-	-	-	-
Pacific Islands, Trust Territory of the [6]	220	209	175	145	145	206	193	103
Philippines	557	56	297	-34	20	-17	-46	-41
Singapore	(Z)	1	-	-	-	-	-	-
Taiwan	-7	-5	-1	-1	-1	-1	-1	-
Thailand	-19	205	-63	-120	-102	-118	-1	-
Vietnam	1	(Z)	-9	-6	1	10	-27	-50
Other and unspecified [3]	38	51	58	36	26	12	7	9
Western Hemisphere	**2,025**	**485**	**1,033**	**5,120**	**1,173**	**1,380**	**16**	**15**
Argentina	64	-26	-84	-96	-73	-55	710	639
Bolivia	114	101	97	104	136	189	4	18
Brazil	261	-204	90	38	195	119	152	207
Canada	-41	-	-	-	-	-	106	-80
Chile	-32	-24	5	-8	-22	-19	-19	-5
Colombia	-30	5	43	173	33	71	76	148
Costa Rica	108	-28	-27	-37	-34	-31	-27	-42
Dominican Republic	28	-15	-14	-13	-58	-41	-65	-61
Ecuador	61	5	3	14	14	38	75	17
El Salvador	303	119	41	38	27	78	45	53

See footnotes at end of table.

U.S. Census Bureau, Statistical Abstract of the United States: 2006

[In millions of dollars. See headnote, p. 828]

Country	1990	1995	1998	1999	2000	2001	2002	2003
Western Hemisphere—Continued:								
Guatemala	98	39	36	45	49	106	54	41
Guyana	42	10	12	5	5	9	4	4
Haiti	54	156	88	86	63	106	66	64
Honduras	226	77	31	82	100	258	85	49
Jamaica	108	30	-21	-24	-34	-21	-15	-9
Mexico.	140	-198	-127	-118	-123	14	-13	-9
Nicaragua	105	41	50	53	53	152	60	40
Panama [7]	102	8	-20	4,100	-13	-9	(Z)	3
Paraguay	(Z)	1	2	6	4	9	9	11
Peru	93	151	113	101	87	133	109	83
Trinidad and Tobago.	5	-14	205	-39	-19	-21	-26	-31
Uruguay	-3	1	1	2	-2	(Z)	-2	-
Venezuela	-18	-2	5	4	133	2	-8	-7
Other [8] and unspecified [3]	236	251	505	605	652	292	40	145
Other international organizations and unspecified areas [3]	1,619	2,513	2,138	3,141	3,942	3,191	5,447	5,848

X Not applicable. - Represents zero or rounds to zero. Z Less than $500,000. [1] Includes European Atomic Energy Community, European Coal and Steel Community, European Payments Union, European Productivity Agency, North Atlantic Treaty Organization, and Organization for European Economic Cooperation. [2] In 1992, some successor countries assumed portions of outstanding credits of the former Yugoslavia (assignment of the remaining portions is pending). Subsequent negative totals reflect payments to the United States on these assumed credits which were greater than the extension of new credits and grants to these countries. [3] In recent years, significant amounts of foreign assistance has been reported on a regional, inter-regional, and worldwide basis. Country totals in this table may understate actual assistance to many countries. [4] Foreign assistance to Iraq during the 1991-96 period was direct humanitarian assistance to ethnic minorities of Northern Iraq after the conflict in the Persian Gulf. [5] United Nations Relief and Works Agency for Palestine refugees. [6] Excludes transactions with Commonwealth of the Northern Mariana Islands after October 1986; includes transactions with Federated States of Micronesia, Republic of the Marshall Islands, and Republic of Palau. [7] Includes transfer of Panama Canal to the Republic of Panama on December 1999. [8] Includes Andean Development Corporation, Caribbean Development Bank, Central American Bank for Economic Integration, Eastern Caribbean Central Bank, Inter-American Institute of Agricultural Science, Organizations of American States, and Pan American Health Organization.

Source: U.S. Bureau of Economic Analysis, press releases, and unpublished data.

Table 1285. **U.S. Foreign Economic and Military Aid Programs: 1980 to 2003**

[In millions of dollars (9,695 represents $9,695,000,000). For years ending September 30. Economic aid shown here represents U.S. economic aid—not just aid under the Foreign Assistance Act. Major components in recent years include AID, Food for Peace, Peace Corps, and paid-in subscriptions to international financial institutions, such as IBRD, and IDB. Annual figures are gross unadjusted program figures]

Year and region	Total economic and military aid	Economic aid			Military aid		
		Total	Loans	Grants	Total	Loans	Grants
1980	9,695	7,573	1,993	5,580	2,122	1,450	672
1981	10,550	7,305	1,460	5,845	3,245	2,546	699
1982	12,324	8,129	1,454	6,675	4,195	3,084	1,111
1983	14,202	8,603	1,619	6,984	5,599	3,932	1,667
1984	15,524	9,038	1,621	7,417	6,486	4,401	2,085
1985	18,128	12,327	1,579	10,748	5,801	2,365	3,436
1986	16,739	10,900	1,330	9,570	5,839	1,980	3,859
1987	14,488	9,386	1,138	8,248	5,102	953	4,149
1988	13,792	8,961	852	8,109	4,831	763	4,068
1989	14,688	9,860	694	9,166	4,828	410	4,418
1990	15,727	10,834	756	10,078	4,893	404	4,489
1991	16,663	11,904	354	11,550	4,760	428	4,332
1992	15,589	11,242	494	10,748	4,347	345	4,002
1993	28,196	24,054	462	23,593	4,143	855	3,288
1994	15,870	11,940	887	11,053	3,931	770	3,161
1995	15,108	11,295	190	11,105	3,813	558	3,255
1996	13,559	9,589	329	9,260	3,970	544	3,426
1997	13,037	9,171	218	8,953	3,866	298	3,568
1998	14,652	10,847	271	10,576	3,804	100	3,704
1999	17,473	13,411	408	13,003	4,061	152	3,909
2000	17,471	12,704	304	12,400	4,767	-	4,767
2001	16,042	11,569	105	11,464	4,473	-	4,473
2002	20,904	14,937	144	14,793	5,967	4	5,964
2003, total	31,640	19,960	134	19,825	11,681	3,800	7,881
Middle East and North Africa	11,984	6,629	20	6,609	5,355	-	5,355
Sub-Saharan Africa . . .	3,303	3,159	10	3,149	144	-	144
Latin America & Caribbean	2,120	2,066	6	2,060	54	-	54
Asia	2,749	1,977	98	1,879	772	-	772
Oceania	175	174	-	174	1	-	1
Eurasia	1,653	723	-	723	930	-	930
Eastern Europe	4,629	582	-	582	4,047	3,800	247
Western Europe	1,088	1,060	-	1,060	28	-	28
Canada.	24	24	-	24	-	-	-
World not specified . . .	3,914	3,565	-	3,565	350	-	350

- Represents zero or rounds to zero.

Source: U.S. Agency for International Development, *U.S. Overseas Loans and Grants and Assistance from International Organizations*, annual.

[In millions of dollars (17,471 represents $17,471,000,000), except as indicated. For years ending September 30]

Recipient country	2000	2001	2002	2003			
				Total (mil. dol.)	Rank	Economic aid (mil. dol.)	Military aid (mil. dol.)
Total [1]	17,471	16,042	20,904	31,640	(X)	19,960	11,681
Afghanistan	41	78	563	1,300	6	850	450
Albania	69	54	46	56	55	45	11
Angola	103	64	125	157	21	153	4
Armenia	105	115	104	75	40	68	7
Azerbaijan	55	38	64	57	54	46	11
Bahrain	-	-	29	91	32	-	90
Bangladesh	78	153	96	105	24	104	1
Bolivia	240	203	174	208	15	205	3
Bosnia and Herzegovina	174	168	92	89	33	72	17
Bulgaria	49	61	58	58	53	35	24
Cambodia	27	38	48	64	50	61	3
Colombia	1,160	248	541	678	9	657	22
Congo (Kinshasa)	28	59	82	121	23	121	
Croatia	59	65	64	47	63	38	9
Ecuador	82	65	91	89	33	87	2
Egypt	2,043	1,708	2,195	1,753	4	461	1,293
El Salvador	37	113	107	65	49	61	4
Eritrea	37	58	30	103	26	100	3
Ethiopia	270	193	143	600	10	595	5
Georgia	112	135	187	85	35	74	12
Ghana	66	72	54	79	39	78	1
Guatemala	72	75	75	92	30	92	
Guinea	33	37	46	49	61	49	-
Haiti	88	86	58	83	36	83	-
Honduras	46	47	45	71	43	70	1
India	171	156	206	183	19	181	2
Indonesia	242	156	176	200	16	199	1
Iraq	10	-	-	4,262	1	4,117	145
Ireland	-	45	5	50	59	50	
Israel	3,783	2,832	2,793	3,696	3	597	3,098
Jordan	403	266	344	1,595	5	980	615
Kazakhstan	53	68	81	60	51	45	15
Kenya	90	126	114	129	22	127	3
Kyrgyzstan	47	37	78	59	52	51	8
Lebanon	35	52	14	67	48	65	3
Macedonia	60	60	82	74	42	61	13
Madagascar	27	33	32	46	65	46	
Mali	44	41	40	53	57	53	-
Marshall Islands	41	41	50	47	63	47	
Mexico	44	52	93	69	44	68	1
Micronesia	81	82	100	100	27	100	
Mozambique	88	85	67	93	29	90	3
Nepal	21	36	63	55	56	51	4
Nicaragua	34	60	49	69	44	68	2
Nigeria	104	91	108	94	28	93	
Oman	2	2	26	82	37	-	82
Pakistan	6	90	1,077	366	11	140	226
Peru	204	206	287	231	12	229	2
Philippines	80	97	164	225	13	170	54
Poland	22	17	16	3,833	2	2	3,831
Romania	46	64	58	69	44	41	28
Russia	591	814	906	903	8	141	762
Rwanda	38	31	43	48	62	47	1
Senegal	37	33	36	50	59	48	2
Serbia and Montenegro	358	373	332	210	14	207	3
South Africa	53	56	81	92	30	85	7
Sudan	48	65	121	187	18	186	1
Tajikistan	36	62	89	52	58	51	1
Tanzania	43	78	49	81	38	80	
Uganda	76	89	103	179	20	179	-
Ukraine	180	213	244	103	25	77	26
Uzbekistan	34	57	170	75	40	62	14
West Bank/Gaza	122	125	336	192	17	192	
Zambia	35	46	68	68	47	67	1

X Not applicable.   [1] Includes countries not shown separately.

Source: U.S. Agency for International Development, *U.S. Overseas Loans and Grants, annual.*

Table 1287. **U.S. International Trade in Goods and Services: 1997 to 2004**

[In millions of dollars (-107,047 represents $-107,047,000,000).] Data presented on a balance of payments basis and will not agree with the following merchandise trade Tables 1288 to 1297]

Category	1997	1998	1999	2000	2001	2002	2003	2004
TRADE BALANCE								
Total	-107,047	-163,153	-261,201	-375,384	-357,819	-418,038	-489,377	-617,725
Goods	-198,119	-246,696	-346,022	-452,423	-427,215	-482,872	-549,409	-666,183
Services	91,072	83,543	84,821	77,039	69,396	64,834	60,032	48,458
Travel	21,375	14,842	15,838	17,695	11,693	8,503	8,761	10,017
Passenger fares	2,730	127	-1,530	-3,587	-4,707	-2,923	-4,871	-4,407
Other transportation	-1,953	-4,759	-7,223	-11,622	-10,240	-9,361	-13,179	-16,372
Royalties, license fees	24,067	24,391	26,563	26,765	24,385	24,884	28,878	28,459
Other private services	41,692	45,645	50,516	49,568	52,752	53,158	53,618	47,966
Other	4,968	5,220	2,593	317	-2,436	-7,302	-10,982	-14,711
U.S. govt miscel. services. . . .	-1,807	-1,923	-1,936	-2,097	-2,051	-2,125	-2,193	-2,494
EXPORTS								
Total	933,873	932,558	965,473	1,070,054	1,007,580	974,107	1,018,572	1,146,137
Goods	678,366	670,416	683,965	771,994	718,712	681,874	713,761	807,584
Services	255,507	262,142	281,508	298,060	288,868	292,233	304,811	338,553
Travel	73,426	71,325	74,801	82,400	71,893	66,547	65,767	74,663
Passenger fares	20,868	20,098	19,785	20,687	17,926	17,046	15,690	18,835
Other transportation	27,006	25,604	26,916	29,803	28,442	29,166	31,699	37,318
Royalties, license fees	33,228	35,626	39,670	43,233	41,098	44,142	48,084	51,099
Other private services	83,349	91,158	103,523	107,361	116,139	122,594	130,047	142,279
Other	16,675	17,405	15,928	13,790	12,539	11,943	12,713	13,616
U.S. govt miscel. services. . . .	955	926	885	786	831	795	831	743
IMPORTS								
Total	1,040,920	1,095,711	1,226,674	1,445,438	1,365,399	1,392,145	1,507,949	1,763,863
Goods	876,485	917,112	1,029,987	1,224,417	1,145,927	1,164,746	1,263,170	1,473,768
Services	164,435	178,599	196,687	221,021	219,472	227,399	244,779	290,095
Travel	52,051	56,483	58,963	64,705	60,200	58,044	57,006	64,646
Passenger fares	18,138	19,971	21,315	24,274	22,633	19,969	20,561	23,242
Other transportation	28,959	30,363	34,139	41,425	38,682	38,527	44,878	53,690
Royalties, license fees	9,161	11,235	13,107	16,468	16,713	19,258	19,206	22,640
Other private services	41,657	45,513	53,007	57,793	63,387	69,436	76,429	94,313
Other	11,707	12,185	13,335	13,473	14,975	19,245	23,695	28,327
U.S. govt miscel. services. . . .	2,762	2,849	2,821	2,883	2,882	2,920	3,004	3,237

[1] Represents transfers under U.S. military sales contracts for exports and direct defense expenditures for imports.

Source: U.S. Census Bureau, *U.S. International Trade in Goods and Services, December 2004*, Series FT-900(04-12). See also <http://www.census.gov/foreign-trade/Press-Release/2004pr/12/tt900.pdf> (released 10 February 2005).

Table 1288. **U.S. Exports, General Imports, and Trade Balance in Goods: 1980 to 2004**

[In billions of dollars (225.7 represents $225,700,000,000).] Domestic and foreign exports, are f.a.s. value basis; general imports are on customs value basis]

Year	Total goods [1]			Manufactured goods [2, 3]			Agricultural products [4]			Mineral fuels [3, 5]		
	Exports	Imports	Balance	Exports	Imports	Balance	Exports	Imports	Balance	Exports	Imports	Balance
1980 . . .	225.7	245.3	-19.5	160.7	133.0	27.7	41.8	17.4	24.3	8.2	78.9	-70.7
1981 . . .	238.7	261.0	-22.3	171.7	149.8	22.0	43.8	17.2	26.6	10.3	81.2	-70.9
1982 . . .	216.4	244.0	-27.5	155.3	151.7	3.6	37.0	15.7	21.3	12.8	65.3	-52.5
1983 . . .	205.6	258.0	-52.4	148.5	171.2	-22.7	36.5	16.5	19.9	9.8	57.8	-48.0
1983 . . .	205.6	258.0	-52.4	148.7	170.9	-22.2	36.1	16.0	20.2	9.8	57.8	-48.0
1984 . . .	224.0	330.7	-106.7	164.1	230.9	-66.8	37.9	19.3	18.6	9.7	60.8	-51.1
1985 . . .	218.8	336.5	-117.7	168.0	257.5	-89.5	29.3	19.5	9.8	10.3	53.7	-43.4
1986 . . .	227.2	365.4	-138.3	179.8	296.7	-116.8	26.3	20.9	5.4	8.4	37.2	-28.8
1987 . . .	254.1	406.2	-152.1	199.9	324.4	-124.6	28.7	20.3	8.4	8.0	44.1	-36.1
1988 . . .	322.4	441.0	-118.5	255.6	361.4	-105.7	37.1	20.7	16.4	8.5	41.0	-32.5
1989 . . .	363.8	473.2	-109.4	287.0	379.4	-92.4	41.6	21.1	20.5	9.9	52.6	-42.7
1990 . . .	393.6	495.3	-101.7	315.4	388.8	-73.5	39.6	22.3	17.2	12.4	64.7	-52.3
1991 . . .	421.7	488.5	-66.7	345.1	392.4	-47.3	39.4	22.1	17.2	12.3	54.1	-41.8
1992 . . .	448.2	532.7	-84.5	368.5	434.3	-65.9	43.1	23.4	19.8	11.3	55.3	-43.9
1993 . . .	465.1	580.7	-115.6	388.7	479.9	-91.2	42.8	23.6	19.2	9.9	55.9	-46.0
1994 . . .	512.6	663.3	-150.6	431.1	557.3	-126.3	45.9	26.0	20.0	9.0	56.4	-47.4
1995 . . .	584.7	743.4	-158.7	486.7	629.7	-143.0	56.0	29.3	26.8	10.5	59.1	-48.6
1996 . . .	625.1	795.3	-170.2	524.7	658.8	-134.1	60.6	32.6	28.1	12.4	78.1	-65.7
1997 . . .	689.2	870.7	-181.5	592.5	728.9	-136.4	57.1	35.2	21.9	13.0	78.3	-65.3
1998 . . .	682.1	911.9	-229.8	596.6	790.8	-194.2	52.0	35.7	16.3	10.4	57.3	-47.0
1999 . . .	695.8	1,024.6	-328.8	611.6	882.7	-271.1	48.2	36.7	11.5	9.9	75.2	-65.3
2000 . . .	781.9	1,218.0	-436.1	691.5	1,012.9	-321.3	53.0	39.2	13.8	13.4	135.4	-122.0
2001 . . .	729.1	1,141.0	-411.9	640.2	950.7	-310.4	55.2	39.5	15.7	12.7	121.9	-109.2
2002 . . .	693.1	1,164.7	-471.6	606.3	974.6	-368.3	54.8	42.0	12.8	11.7	115.7	-104.0
2003 . . .	724.8	1,257.1	-532.4	627.1	1,027.4	-400.3	61.4	47.5	13.9	14.1	153.3	-139.2
2004 . . .	818.8	1,469.7	-650.9	710.3	1,174.8	-464.4	63.4	54.2	9.2	19.0	206.7	-187.6

[1] Includes nonmonetary gold, military grant aid, special category shipments, trade between the U.S. Virgin Islands and foreign countries and undocumented exports to Canada. Adjustments were also made for carryover. Import values are based on transaction prices whenever possible. [2] Manufactured goods include commodity sections 5-9 under Schedules A and E for 1980-1982 and SITC Rev. 3 for 1983-forward. Manufactures include undocumented exports to Canada, nonmonetary gold (excluding gold ore, scrap, and base bullion), and special category shipments. [3] Data for 1980 exclude trade between the U.S. Virgin Islands and foreign countries. Census data concordances link the 1980-92 trade figures into time series that are as consistent as possible. Import values are for Customs value; these values are based on transaction prices while maintaining a data series as consistent as possible over time. 1991 imports include revisions for passenger cars, trucks, petroleum and petroleum products not included elsewhere. [4] Agricultural products for 1983-forward utilize the latest census definition that excludes manufactured goods that were previously classified as manufactured agricultural products. [5] Mineral fuels include commodity section 3 under SITC Rev. 2 for 1980-1982 and SITC Rev. 3 for 1983-forward.

Source: U.S. International Trade Administration, through 1996, *U.S. Foreign Trade Highlights*, annual; and thereafter, <http://www.ita.doc.gov/td/industry/otea/usfth/aggregate/H04t03.pdf> (released 20 June 2005).

Table 1289.

Table 1289. U.S. Exports and Imports for Consumption of Merchandise by Customs District: 1990 to 2004

[In billions of dollars (393.0 represents $393,000,000,000). Exports are f.a.s. (free alongside ship) value all years; imports are on customs value basis. These data may differ from those in Tables 1288, 1293, and 1294. For methodology, see Foreign Trade Statistics in Appendix III. For methodology, see Foreign Trade Statistics in Appendix III]

Customs district	Exports					Imports for consumption				
	1990	2000	2002	2003	2004	1990	2000	2002	2003	2004
Total [1]	393.0	780.0	693.1	723.7	817.9	490.6	1,205.6	1,152.5	1,250.1	1,460.2
Anchorage, AK	3.7	5.9	7.3	8.4	8.7	0.7	13.4	11.3	9.2	10.5
Baltimore, MD	6.7	6.2	5.1	6.0	7.2	11.2	18.6	19.5	22.7	26.7
Boston, MA	5.6	7.0	6.8	7.0	9.7	12.2	18.7	15.4	16.4	19.2
Buffalo, NY [2]	15.8	38.2	25.7	28.8	33.6	19.2	38.4	34.3	35.9	40.9
Charleston, SC [2]	6.7	12.6	11.9	13.6	15.4	6.8	16.9	17.5	21.0	26.0
Chicago, IL	10.2	21.7	19.6	21.3	25.9	18.3	51.1	53.0	58.3	69.1
Cleveland, OH	4.0	22.7	16.5	17.2	19.0	11.3	36.5	33.3	36.1	44.6
Dallas/Fort Worth, TX	3.4	11.5	11.5	12.3	16.4	4.8	18.8	19.2	22.4	27.8
Detroit, MI	35.6	79.4	86.2	87.6	93.4	37.8	97.6	93.7	98.8	112.2
Duluth, MN	0.8	1.5	1.6	1.7	1.8	3.9	7.0	6.6	7.6	9.0
El Paso, TX	3.9	18.0	16.5	17.5	19.3	5.0	24.1	24.7	25.3	27.8
Great Falls, MT	2.4	5.0	4.6	5.4	6.1	4.7	14.3	14.8	17.5	21.5
Honolulu, HI	0.5	0.7	2.7	2.5	1.8	2.1	2.9	2.1	2.0	2.2
Houston/Galveston, TX	17.6	29.7	29.5	32.1	39.5	21.6	40.9	39.9	48.4	64.4
Laredo, TX	15.2	57.7	48.9	48.6	56.0	10.0	62.7	64.6	66.1	74.4
Los Angeles, CA	42.1	77.6	63.3	67.7	70.8	64.1	150.1	149.5	165.4	191.0
Miami, FL	11.2	31.0	26.3	26.3	30.0	7.1	23.3	22.4	25.0	27.8
Milwaukee, WI	0.1	0.1	0.2	0.2	0.1	1.1	1.5	1.4	1.8	1.5
Minneapolis, MN	0.9	1.4	1.5	1.5	1.7	2.0	4.3	4.4	5.4	5.8
Mobile, AL [2]	1.9	4.0	4.3	4.6	5.0	3.4	7.9	8.1	8.9	11.0
New Orleans, LA	18.0	35.9	32.7	33.6	36.8	24.1	54.0	51.0	59.2	76.2
New York, NY	50.9	79.5	68.4	71.9	80.8	68.0	145.6	140.7	147.5	163.6
Nogales, AZ	2.1	7.3	5.3	5.0	5.9	4.2	14.1	11.7	11.6	12.5
Norfolk, VA [2]	11.7	12.4	11.9	12.3	13.4	7.4	13.6	15.0	17.7	20.0
Ogdensburg, NY	7.9	12.4	10.5	10.4	11.9	9.8	23.7	21.0	21.3	24.2
Pembina, ND	3.4	8.7	7.8	9.2	11.0	4.1	11.0	9.7	9.6	11.1
Philadelphia, PA	4.0	6.0	7.1	7.3	9.0	18.3	28.3	27.3	29.8	38.6
Port Arthur, TX	0.9	1.2	1.1	1.4	2.0	3.2	10.9	10.9	13.7	18.0
Portland, ME	1.7	2.6	2.4	2.8	2.8	4.3	8.7	8.2	8.8	9.3
Portland, OR	5.8	7.2	6.0	6.2	6.7	5.6	12.5	12.7	11.8	13.9
Providence, RI	(Z)	(Z)	(Z)	0.1	0.1	1.3	1.3	1.5	3.1	3.3
San Diego, CA	3.4	12.7	12.9	12.7	14.0	4.3	22.2	22.9	22.8	25.4
San Francisco, CA	23.1	58.3	35.1	33.1	38.2	28.0	68.6	44.3	46.2	54.9
San Juan, PR	2.5	4.8	5.7	8.9	9.7	5.4	11.8	14.8	19.0	19.1
Savannah, GA	7.4	15.9	15.7	17.0	21.6	9.8	26.1	29.5	30.8	38.4
Seattle, WA	32.6	40.4	39.9	39.8	43.5	20.9	40.5	35.9	35.7	43.2
St. Albans, VT	4.0	4.5	3.0	3.0	3.6	5.2	9.4	8.4	9.8	10.5
St. Louis, MO	0.3	1.3	0.8	0.6	0.7	3.0	7.9	6.6	7.9	9.1
Tampa, FL	4.3	4.8	5.8	6.2	7.5	7.0	14.7	14.1	14.6	15.4
Virgin Islands of the U.S.	0.2	0.3	0.4	0.4	0.5	2.1	4.8	3.6	5.0	6.8
Washington, DC	1.1	2.8	2.5	2.4	2.8	0.8	2.6	2.3	2.4	3.3
Wilmington, NC	3.0	2.5	1.7	1.7	1.9	3.3	10.6	11.9	13.2	13.9

Z Less than $50 million. [1] Totals shown for exports reflect the value of estimated parcel post and Special Category shipments, and beginning 1990, adjustments for undocumented exports to Canada which are not distributed by customs district. The value of bituminous coal exported through Norfolk, VA; Charleston, SC; and Mobile, AL, is reflected in the total but not distributed by district. [2] Excludes exports of bituminous coal, which are included in the "Total" line.

Source: U.S. Census Bureau, 1990, U.S. Merchandise Trade: Selected Highlights, Series FT 920, monthly; beginning 2000, U.S. Export History and U.S. Import History on compact disc.

Table 1290. Export and Import Unit Value Indexes—Selected Countries: 2000 to 2003

[Indexes in U.S. dollars, 2000 = 100. A unit value is an implicit price derived from value and quantity data]

Country	Export unit value				Import unit value			
	2000	2001	2002	2003	2000	2001	2002	2003
United States	100.0	99.2	98.2	99.7	100.0	96.5	94.1	96.9
Australia	100.0	98.2	100.0	109.9	100.0	94.3	94.5	103.8
Belgium	100.0	99.3	103.4	120.2	100.0	99.5	102.2	118.3
Canada	100.0	97.8	95.1	105.6	100.0	98.8	98.2	102.0
Finland	100.0	88.3	90.3	105.6	100.0	91.0	96.6	114.7
France	100.0	96.8	98.0	117.6	100.0	95.1	94.7	113.5
Germany	100.0	99.0	101.5	118.3	100.0	97.1	97.2	110.4
Greece	100.0	104.9	112.3	134.8	100.0	106.1	112.1	135.8
Ireland	100.0	98.3	103.2	114.7	100.0	100.0	102.7	115.1
India	100.0	94.3	91.9	(NA)	100.0	96.4	103.7	(NA)
Italy	100.0	101.3	104.5	(NA)	100.0	99.1	100.5	(NA)
Japan	100.0	91.4	87.6	90.9	100.0	90.9	86.8	93.1
Korea	100.0	86.9	83.1	85.1	100.0	90.9	86.8	93.1
Netherlands	100.0	100.4	99.2	(NA)	100.0	91.0	87.5	95.6
New Zealand	100.0	90.3	99.3	111.0	100.0	99.7	103.0	(NA)
Norway	100.0	93.1	93.3	104.3	100.0	93.9	97.0	107.5
Singapore	100.0	92.5	90.5	93.9	100.0	98.2	102.8	116.1
Spain	100.0	99.7	105.1	124.9	100.0	96.5	95.9	99.7
United Kingdom	100.0	95.3	99.2	(NA)	100.0	94.8	95.9	(NA)

NA Not available.

Source: International Monetary Fund, Washington, DC, International Financial Statistics, monthly, (copyright).

Table 1291. U.S. Exports by State of Origin: 2000 to 2004

[In millions of dollars (782,429 represents $782,429,000,000). Exports are on a f.a.s. value basis. Exports are based on origin of movement]

State and other area	2000	2003	2004 Total	2004 Rank	State and other area	2000	2003	2004 Total	2004 Rank
Total	782,429	724,006	819,026	(X)	Missouri	6,497	7,234	8,997	25
					Montana	541	361	565	50
United States	712,055	675,827	769,332	(X)	Nebraska	2,511	2,724	2,316	41
					Nevada	1,482	2,033	2,907	39
Alabama	7,317	8,340	9,037	24	New Hampshire	2,373	1,931	2,286	42
Alaska	2,464	2,739	3,157	37					
Arizona	14,334	13,323	13,423	17	New Jersey	18,638	16,818	19,192	12
Arkansas	2,599	2,962	3,493	32	New Mexico	2,391	2,326	2,046	44
California	119,640	93,995	109,968	2	New York	42,846	39,181	44,401	3
Colorado	6,593	6,109	6,651	27	North Carolina	17,946	16,199	18,115	15
Connecticut	8,047	8,136	8,559	26	North Dakota	626	854	1,008	47
Delaware	2,197	1,886	2,053	43	Ohio	26,322	29,764	31,208	6
Dist. of Columbia	1,003	809	1,164	46	Oklahoma	3,072	2,660	3,178	36
Florida	26,543	24,953	28,982	8	Oregon	11,441	10,357	11,172	23
					Pennsylvania	18,792	16,299	18,487	14
Georgia	14,925	16,286	19,633	11	Rhode Island	1,186	1,178	1,286	45
Hawaii	387	368	405	51					
Idaho	3,559	2,096	2,915	38	South Carolina	8,565	11,773	13,376	18
Illinois	31,438	26,473	30,214	7	South Dakota	679	672	826	48
Indiana	15,386	16,402	19,109	13	Tennessee	11,592	12,612	16,123	16
Iowa	4,466	5,236	6,394	28	Texas	103,866	98,846	117,245	1
Kansas	5,145	4,553	4,931	30	Utah	3,221	4,115	4,718	31
Kentucky	9,612	10,734	12,992	19	Vermont	4,097	2,627	3,283	33
Louisiana	16,814	18,390	19,922	10	Virginia	11,698	10,853	11,631	22
Maine	1,779	2,188	2,432	40	Washington	32,215	34,173	33,793	5
					West Virginia	2,219	2,380	3,262	34
Maryland	4,593	4,941	5,746	29	Wisconsin	10,508	11,510	12,706	20
Massachusetts	20,514	18,663	21,837	9	Wyoming	503	582	680	49
Michigan	33,845	32,941	35,625	4	Puerto Rico	9,735	11,914	13,162	(X)
Minnesota	10,303	11,266	12,678	21	Virgin Islands	174	253	389	(X)
Mississippi	2,726	2,558	3,179	35	Other [1]	60,464	35,457	36,142	(X)

X Not applicable. [1] Includes unreported, not specified, special category, estimated shipments, re-exports, and any timing adjustments.

Source: U.S. Census Bureau, *U.S. International Trade in Goods and Services*, series FT-900, December issues. For most recent release, see <http://www.census.gov/foreign-trade/Press-Release/2004pr/12/#ft900> (released 10 February 2005).

Table 1292. U.S. Agriculture Exports by State: 2000 to 2004

[In millions of dollars (50,743.8 represents $50,743,800,000). Fiscal years]

State	2000	2001	2002	2003	2004	State	2000	2001	2002	2003	2004
U.S.	50,743.8	52,698.2	53,291.2	56,208.9	62,297.3	NE	3,013.4	2,771.4	3,020.4	3,122.6	3,015.0
						NV	16.2	33.4	39.2	34.5	53.4
AL	392.2	395.8	415.5	388.2	567.6	NH	6.3	7.7	6.9	8.1	10.7
AK	0.8	0.8	0.9	1.0	1.0	NJ	103.9	121.0	117.2	146.5	152.0
AZ	718.4	461.1	417.9	453.3	460.4						
AR	980.3	1,187.8	1,212.8	1,444.5	1,900.1	NM	97.4	238.5	227.6	136.7	155.4
CA	6,866.7	7,225.8	7,111.6	8,155.9	9,197.3	NY	475.5	491.8	493.6	453.1	501.7
CO	945.7	879.7	898.3	870.8	762.2	NC	1,317.5	1,430.5	1,467.9	1,299.9	1,637.9
CT	116.3	87.8	69.8	50.3	59.4	ND	1,180.5	1,735.0	2,031.9	1,555.7	1,891.9
DE	113.5	142.7	138.2	115.2	138.8	OH	1,174.4	1,264.9	1,287.3	1,189.7	1,572.0
FL	1,276.5	1,211.8	1,246.9	1,299.0	1,358.7	OK	530.9	520.9	537.2	619.4	808.2
GA	908.8	948.6	1,005.0	923.5	1,275.8	OR	625.5	717.8	683.3	721.6	825.4
HI	78.9	81.6	76.9	70.6	74.9	PA	928.5	1,040.7	955.0	1,008.1	1,048.8
ID	775.9	788.9	767.6	836.1	789.1	RI	2.1	4.6	4.2	3.1	5.9
IL	3,025.7	3,107.0	3,254.3	3,202.5	3,654.4	SC	262.8	308.7	310.6	250.7	386.1
IN	1,402.3	1,592.6	1,750.7	1,562.8	1,858.3						
IA	3,176.5	2,956.6	3,135.7	3,651.1	3,676.3	SD	1,067.4	1,078.8	1,038.2	898.7	1,238.1
KS	3,155.8	2,953.2	3,017.9	2,974.7	2,928.0	TN	488.1	562.1	608.8	661.8	861.0
KY	739.8	1,012.5	969.6	903.7	984.1	TX	3,136.9	2,892.5	2,881.3	3,419.0	3,363.4
LA	426.6	417.3	410.7	475.8	661.4	UT	247.5	252.6	246.7	252.8	229.8
ME	59.9	61.5	59.2	61.3	69.9	VT	16.1	11.2	10.2	30.9	41.9
MD	223.6	263.9	234.1	214.6	248.3	VA	458.7	470.6	464.8	444.8	510.7
						WA	1,561.6	1,836.2	1,794.3	1,912.3	1,886.7
MA	156.5	145.9	137.0	126.1	157.6	WV	30.8	42.6	38.4	34.9	37.6
MI	831.2	778.5	720.4	892.4	919.0	WI	1,377.5	1,504.5	1,453.0	1,407.8	1,369.2
MN	2,275.2	2,299.5	2,166.9	2,699.2	2,891.2	WY	42.8	59.9	54.7	36.0	47.4
MS	604.7	602.8	665.1	792.5	1,140.0						
MO	1,073.6	1,248.5	1,177.8	1,206.7	1,384.9	Unallocated	1,906.2	2,121.9	2,169.8	2,195.6	3,052.7
MT	349.7	325.9	288.1	392.9	436.0						

Source: U.S. Dept. of Agriculture, Economic Research Service, *Foreign Agricultural Trade of the United States (FATUS)*, annual.

Table 1293. U.S. Exports, Imports, and Merchandise Trade Balance by Country: 2000 to 2004

[In millions of dollars (781,917.7 represents $781,917,700,000). Includes silver ore and bullion. Country totals include exports of special category commodities, if any. Data include nonmonetary gold and includes trade of Virgin Islands with foreign countries. For methodology, see Foreign Trade Statistics in Appendix III. Minus sign (-) denotes an excess of imports over exports]

Country [1]	Exports, domestic and foreign					General imports					Merchandise trade balance				
	2000	2001	2002	2003	2004	2000	2001	2002	2003	2004	2000	2001	2002	2003	2004
Total [1]	781,917.7	729,100.3	693,103.2	724,006.3	819,026.2	1,218,022.0	1,140,999.4	1,161,366.0	1,259,705.2	1,470,547.1	-436,104.3	-411,899.1	-468,262.8	-535,698.9	-651,520.9
Afghanistan	8.2	5.8	80.0	60.7	157.7	0.8	0.8	3.3	56.1	24.9	7.4	5.0	76.7	4.6	132.8
Albania	20.9	15.5	14.8	9.7	20.1	7.8	7.3	5.8	4.4	11.4	13.1	8.2	9.0	5.3	8.7
Algeria	861.8	1,037.8	984.4	487.3	972.1	2,724.3	2,701.9	2,360.2	4,752.9	7,409.5	-1,862.5	-1,664.1	-1,375.8	-4,265.6	-6,437.4
Andorra	10.2	8.2	11.0	8.2	11.6	0.3	0.2	0.8	0.3	0.9	9.9	8.0	10.2	7.9	10.7
Angola	225.3	275.9	374.0	491.9	594.2	3,555.3	3,095.9	3,122.7	4,264.3	4,521.2	-3,330.0	-2,820.0	-2,748.7	-3,772.4	-3,927.0
Anguilla	29.9	20.1	19.9	21.3	20.8	1.7	1.8	1.0	1.3	1.2	28.2	18.3	18.9	20.0	19.6
Antigua and Barbuda	138.0	95.5	81.4	127.3	125.3	2.3	3.7	3.5	12.7	4.4	135.7	91.8	77.9	114.6	120.9
Argentina	4,695.6	3,920.2	1,585.4	2,435.4	3,386.0	3,099.5	3,013.4	3,187.3	3,169.3	3,745.5	1,596.1	906.8	-1,601.9	-733.9	-359.4
Armenia	55.6	49.9	111.8	102.8	90.6	23.0	32.9	30.7	37.6	46.1	32.6	17.0	81.1	65.2	44.5
Aruba	291.4	276.5	464.6	355.0	374.4	1,535.5	1,034.0	773.7	963.9	1,776.4	-1,244.1	-757.5	-309.1	-608.9	-1,401.9
Australia	12,482.3	10,930.5	13,085.0	13,103.8	14,270.9	6,438.1	6,477.9	6,478.8	6,413.9	7,544.2	6,044.2	4,452.6	6,606.2	6,689.9	6,726.7
Azerbaijan	2,591.5	2,604.7	2,427.4	1,792.5	1,957.8	3,226.6	3,968.5	3,814.9	4,489.2	5,796.6	-635.1	-1,363.8	-1,387.5	-2,696.7	-3,838.8
Bahamas, The	209.6	64.3	69.6	121.2	158.8	20.9	20.6	34.4	34.4	38.1	188.7	43.7	35.2	86.8	120.7
Bahrain	449.0	432.7	419.3	508.8	300.7	274.6	313.9	449.7	479.4	637.3	174.4	118.8	-30.4	29.4	-336.6
Bangladesh	239.1	306.9	269.1	226.5	289.4	2,417.6	2,359.0	2,134.2	2,073.6	2,302.5	-2,178.5	-2,052.1	-1,865.1	-1,847.1	-2,013.1
Barbados	306.9	286.6	267.6	301.8	347.6	38.6	39.5	34.4	43.5	45.5	268.3	247.1	233.2	258.3	302.1
Belarus	31.1	34.9	19.1	84.1	32.5	104.0	108.2	125.5	215.4	335.9	-72.9	-73.3	-106.4	-131.3	-303.4
Belgium	13,925.7	13,502.3	13,325.8	15,217.9	16,876.7	9,929.3	10,158.4	9,806.8	10,140.7	12,448.5	3,996.4	3,343.9	3,519.0	5,077.2	4,428.2
Belize	208.4	173.2	137.7	199.4	151.7	93.6	97.4	77.7	101.4	107.1	114.8	75.8	60.0	98.0	44.6
Benin	26.4	32.2	35.2	30.2	44.9	2.4	1.3	22.9	0.6	1.5	24.0	30.9	12.3	29.6	43.4
Bermuda	428.5	371.0	415.1	401.2	471.9	39.0	65.6	160.4	15.2	25.1	389.5	305.4	254.7	386.0	446.8
Bolivia	253.0	215.9	192.1	181.8	193.6	184.8	166.4	155.5	184.8	260.8	68.2	49.5	36.6	-3.0	-67.2
Bosnia and Herzegovina	44.1	43.1	31.7	21.2	27.8	17.8	11.9	15.5	11.7	11.2	26.3	31.2	16.2	9.5	16.6
Brazil	15,320.9	15,879.5	12,376.0	11,218.3	13,863.0	13,852.5	14,466.4	15,780.6	17,884.0	21,157.3	1,468.4	1,413.1	-3,404.6	-6,665.7	-7,294.3
Brunei	156.3	104.0	46.3	35.8	49.3	383.8	398.9	287.1	422.5	406.1	-227.5	-294.9	-240.8	-386.7	-356.8
Bulgaria	114.0	108.4	101.4	155.8	171.7	235.6	337.0	339.7	441.4	507.2	-121.6	-228.6	-238.3	-285.6	-335.5
Burkina Faso	15.9	4.4	18.8	11.0	22.0	2.5	5.0	2.9	0.9	0.6	13.4	-0.6	15.9	10.1	21.4
Burma	17.1	11.4	10.1	6.9	11.6	470.7	469.9	356.4	275.7	0.0	-453.6	-458.5	-346.3	-268.8	11.6
Cameroon	59.3	184.0	155.8	90.8	99.6	155.1	101.6	172.1	214.0	308.3	-95.8	82.4	-16.3	-123.2	-208.7
Canada	178,941.0	163,424.1	160,922.6	169,770.0	190,163.4	230,838.3	216,267.8	209,087.6	224,166.1	255,927.9	-51,897.3	-52,843.7	-48,165.0	-54,396.1	-65,764.5
Cayman Islands	354.5	261.8	231.6	309.6	399.5	6.6	6.8	8.8	11.8	14.8	347.9	255.0	222.8	297.8	384.7
Chad	10.8	137.0	127.3	64.4	40.4	4.6	5.7	5.7	22.4	756.2	6.2	131.3	121.6	42.0	-715.7
Chile	3,460.3	3,118.4	2,609.0	2,719.3	3,624.7	3,269.0	3,495.3	3,784.5	3,703.1	4,733.8	191.3	-376.9	-1,175.5	-983.8	-1,109.1
China	16,185.3	19,182.3	22,127.8	28,418.5	34,721.0	100,018.4	102,278.3	125,192.5	152,379.2	196,699.0	-83,833.1	-83,096.0	-103,064.7	-123,960.7	-161,978.0
Colombia	3,671.2	3,583.1	3,582.5	3,754.7	4,504.5	6,968.1	5,710.3	5,604.3	6,385.5	7,289.9	-3,296.9	-2,127.2	-2,021.8	-2,630.8	-2,785.4
Congo (Brazzaville)	81.7	90.0	52.4	78.8	64.8	531.7	473.8	182.1	432.8	857.6	-450.0	-383.8	-129.7	-354.0	-792.7
Congo (Kinshasa)	10.0	18.6	28.1	30.6	66.9	214.8	154.0	204.1	174.5	124.1	-204.8	-135.4	-176.0	-143.9	-57.3
Costa Rica	2,460.4	2,502.3	3,116.5	3,414.2	3,303.7	3,538.7	2,886.1	3,141.8	3,361.6	3,332.9	-1,078.3	-383.8	-25.3	52.6	-29.2
Cote d'Ivoire	94.8	96.8	76.2	102.8	117.9	383.9	333.1	376.4	489.7	714.7	-289.1	-236.3	-300.2	-386.9	-596.8
Croatia	89.9	109.8	78.1	196.8	130.1	141.0	139.0	145.6	180.7	290.8	-51.1	-29.2	-67.5	16.1	-160.7
Cyprus	190.1	267.9	193.4	326.9	96.2	23.4	35.1	25.6	24.8	25.7	166.7	232.8	167.8	302.1	70.5
Czech Republic	735.8	706.1	653.7	672.3	822.0	1,070.2	1,116.2	1,233.4	1,394.3	1,760.9	-334.4	-410.1	-579.7	-722.0	-938.9

See footnotes at end of table.

U.S. Census Bureau, Statistical Abstract of the United States: 2006

[See headnote, page 835]

Country	Exports, domestic and foreign					General imports					Merchandise trade balance				
	2000	2001	2002	2003	2004	2000	2001	2002	2003	2004	2000	2001	2002	2003	2004
Denmark	1,506.8	1,609.2	1,495.9	1,548.4	2,146.9	2,965.0	3,406.7	3,237.3	3,718.4	3,878.1	-1,458.2	-1,797.5	-1,741.4	-2,170.0	-1,731.2
Djibouti	16.8	18.6	58.6	34.3	43.3	0.4	1.0	1.9	0.6	1.0	16.4	17.6	56.7	33.7	42.3
Dominica	37.5	30.7	45.0	34.4	35.9	6.9	5.3	4.7	5.3	2.9	30.6	25.4	40.3	29.1	33.0
Dominican Republic	4,472.8	4,397.6	4,250.1	4,213.6	4,342.9	4,383.3	4,183.4	4,168.9	4,455.1	4,528.4	89.5	214.2	81.2	-241.5	-185.5
Ecuador	1,037.8	1,412.1	1,605.7	1,448.4	1,665.9	2,237.8	2,009.7	2,143.4	2,720.9	4,284.7	-1,200.0	-597.6	-537.7	-1,272.5	-2,618.8
Egypt	3,333.9	3,564.4	2,868.4	2,660.2	3,104.5	887.7	882.0	1,356.0	1,143.8	1,330.0	2,446.2	2,682.4	1,512.4	1,516.4	1,774.5
El Salvador	1,780.2	1,759.5	1,664.1	1,823.8	1,867.8	1,932.9	1,880.2	1,982.3	2,019.4	2,052.6	-152.7	-120.7	-318.2	-195.6	-184.8
Estonia	88.0	57.7	81.5	120.6	133.5	572.9	241.1	220.9	181.6	394.3	-484.9	-183.4	-139.4	-61.0	-260.8
Ethiopia	165.3	61.1	60.5	409.1	459.1	28.7	29.1	25.7	30.5	41.2	136.6	32.0	34.8	378.6	417.9
Fiji	23.0	19.4	19.6	19.6	25.4	146.8	182.3	156.3	175.4	213.4	-123.8	-162.9	-136.7	-155.8	-188.0
Finland	1,570.9	1,554.0	1,534.9	1,713.8	2,066.5	3,250.8	3,393.8	3,447.0	3,598.0	3,891.5	-1,679.9	-1,839.8	-1,912.1	-1,884.2	-1,825.1
France	20,361.5	19,864.5	19,016.2	17,068.2	21,239.6	29,800.1	30,408.2	28,240.1	29,221.2	31,813.8	-9,438.6	-10,543.7	-9,223.9	-12,153.0	-10,574.2
French Guiana	17.0	129.9	249.7	155.7	228.3	2.3	0.4	7.5	112.1	0.2	14.7	129.5	242.2	43.6	228.1
French Polynesia	93.9	83.0	78.9	91.5	93.0	43.9	48.0	44.1	47.9	67.0	50.0	35.0	34.8	43.6	26.0
Gabon	63.5	73.0	65.5	63.0	93.0	2,196.5	1,659.7	1,587.5	1,969.5	2,466.7	-2,133.0	-1,586.7	-1,522.0	-1,906.5	-2,373.7
Gambia, The	9.1	8.4	9.6	26.7	23.1	0.4	0.5	0.3	0.1	0.5	8.7	7.9	9.3	26.6	22.6
Georgia	109.5	105.9	98.8	131.5	226.3	31.9	30.7	17.5	54.0	77.7	77.6	75.2	81.3	77.5	148.6
Germany	29,448.4	29,995.3	26,629.6	28,847.9	31,380.9	58,512.0	59,076.7	62,505.7	68,047.0	77,235.7	-29,064.4	-29,081.4	-35,876.1	-39,199.1	-45,854.8
Ghana	191.2	199.6	192.6	209.4	306.5	204.5	186.9	116.3	81.9	145.5	-13.3	12.7	76.3	127.5	161.0
Gibraltar	15.1	10.4	25.7	1,191.1	137.8	1.4	1.1	1.1		1.4	13.7	9.3	24.6		136.4
Greece	1,221.8	1,293.6	1,151.8	1,191.1	2,063.1	591.4	505.2	546.2	616.0	723.1	630.4	788.4	605.6	575.1	1,340.0
Greenland	1.1	4.7	4.0	3.0	3.6	15.7	28.8	22.6	13.9	14.6	-14.6	-24.1	-18.6	-10.9	-11.0
Grenada	79.5	59.9	56.4	68.4	69.9	27.1	24.1	6.9	7.6	5.1	52.4	35.8	49.5	60.8	64.8
Guadeloupe	85.9	58.8	39.7	45.4	38.6	9.6	10.6	10.5	2.8	3.1	76.3	48.2	29.2	42.6	35.5
Guatemala	1,900.7	1,869.6	2,044.4	2,273.6	2,548.3	2,607.4	2,588.6	2,796.4	2,945.3	3,154.6	-706.7	-719.0	-752.0	-671.7	-606.3
Guinea	68.0	73.3	62.9	35.8	58.5	88.4	87.8	71.6	69.2	64.2	-20.4	-14.5	-8.7	-33.4	-5.7
Guyana	159.2	141.3	128.2	117.2	135.6	139.9	140.3	115.6	118.3	122.7	19.3	1.0	12.6	-1.1	13.0
Haiti	576.6	550.4	573.2	639.8	663.0	296.9	263.1	255.0	332.3	370.7	279.7	287.3	318.2	307.5	292.3
Honduras	2,584.0	2,415.9	2,571.1	2,844.9	3,076.5	3,090.2	3,126.5	3,261.3	3,311.5	3,641.1	-506.2	-710.6	-690.2	-466.6	-564.6
Hong Kong	14,582.0	14,027.5	12,594.4	13,542.1	15,809.2	11,449.0	9,646.3	9,328.2	8,850.4	9,313.6	3,133.0	4,381.2	3,266.2	4,691.7	6,495.5
Hungary	569.1	685.5	687.9	933.8	1,142.1	2,715.2	2,964.6	2,637.4	2,699.3	2,573.6	-2,146.1	-2,279.1	-1,949.5	-1,765.5	-1,431.6
Iceland	255.6	225.4	219.0	242.3	308.4	259.8	232.5	296.9	282.8	274.0	-4.2	-7.1	-77.9	-40.5	34.4
India	3,667.2	3,757.0	4,101.1	4,986.3	6,095.0	10,686.6	9,737.2	11,818.3	13,052.8	15,562.2	-7,019.4	-5,980.2	-7,717.2	-8,066.5	-9,467.2
Indonesia	2,401.9	2,520.6	2,555.8	2,520.1	2,669.1	10,367.0	10,103.6	9,643.3	9,520.0	10,811.1	-7,965.1	-7,583.0	-7,087.5	-6,999.9	-8,142.0
Iran	16.8	8.1	31.8	98.8	85.3	168.8	143.4	156.3	161.2	146.3	-152.0	-135.3	-124.5	-62.4	-61.0
Iraq	10.4	46.2	31.6	315.7	856.1	6,065.9	5,820.3	3,548.2	4,573.8	8,514.5	-6,055.5	-5,774.1	-3,516.6	-4,258.1	-7,658.4
Ireland	7,713.5	7,144.0	6,745.1	7,698.5	8,165.9	16,463.6	18,499.3	22,437.7	25,840.8	27,441.7	-8,750.1	-11,355.3	-15,692.6	-18,142.3	-19,275.8
Israel	7,745.9	7,475.3	7,026.2	6,878.4	9,198.0	12,964.4	11,959.0	12,415.7	12,770.2	14,527.1	-5,218.5	-4,483.7	-5,389.0	-5,891.8	-5,329.2
Italy	11,060.3	9,915.6	10,056.8	10,570.1	10,708.8	25,042.7	23,789.9	24,220.3	25,494.7	28,088.6	-13,982.4	-13,874.3	-14,163.5	-14,866.6	-17,377.8
Jamaica	1,375.8	1,405.5	1,449.3	1,669.6	1,431.6	648.2	460.6	425.4	694.7	320.3	727.6	944.9	1,023.9	974.9	1,111.3
Japan	64,924.4	57,451.6	51,449.3	52,063.8	54,400.2	146,479.4	126,473.3	121,428.7	118,029.0	129,594.7	-81,553.9	-69,021.7	-69,979.4	-65,965.2	-75,194.5
Jordan	316.7	339.0	404.6	404.8	552.2	73.3	229.1	134.6	586.3	1,092.9	243.4	109.9	270.0	-181.5	-540.7
Kazakhstan	124.2	160.3	604.6	168.3	319.4	429.0	351.8	334.6	392.3	538.4	-304.8	-191.5	270.0	-224.0	-219.0
Kenya	237.6	577.7	271.2	196.7	393.8	110.1	128.3	188.6	249.2	352.2	127.5	449.4	82.6	-52.5	41.6

See footnotes at end of table.

U.S. Census Bureau, Statistical Abstract of the United States: 2006

Table 1293. U.S. Exports, Imports, and Merchandise Trade Balance, by Country: 2000 to 2004—Con.

[See headnote, page 835]

Country	Exports, domestic and foreign					General imports					Merchandise trade balance				
	2000	2001	2002	2003	2004	2000	2001	2002	2003	2004	2000	2001	2002	2003	2004
Korea, South	27,830.0	22,180.6	22,575.8	24,098.6	26,333.4	40,307.7	35,181.4	35,571.8	36,963.3	46,162.7	-12,477.7	-13,000.8	-12,996.0	-12,864.7	-19,829.2
Kuwait	787.0	902.4	1,014.7	1,509.1	1,519.6	2,781.2	1,990.7	1,940.4	2,276.8	3,230.6	-1,994.2	-1,088.3	-925.7	-767.7	-1,711.0
Kyrgyzstan	22.8	27.7	31.1	39.1	29.7	1.9	3.3	4.8	11.0	10.8	20.9	24.4	26.3	28.1	18.9
Latvia	133.6	110.5	90.8	124.0	120.9	287.7	144.5	197.0	377.4	364.7	-154.1	-34.0	-106.2	-253.4	-243.8
Lebanon	354.7	418.2	317.4	314.3	462.9	76.8	89.6	61.7	92.3	74.5	277.9	328.6	255.7	222.0	388.4
Lesotho	0.9	0.8	2.0	5.1	5.5	140.3	215.3	321.7	393.3	466.9	-139.4	-214.5	-319.7	-388.2	-461.4
Liberia	43.1	36.8	27.7	33.4	60.6	45.4	42.6	45.8	59.5	84.3	-2.3	-5.8	-18.1	-26.1	-23.7
Liechtenstein	13.9	14.5	14.5	15.9	10.3	278.2	224.2	237.7	261.9	286.1	-264.3	-209.7	-223.2	-246.0	-275.8
Lithuania	59.4	99.8	102.8	162.6	294.8	135.0	164.2	299.6	347.3	482.0	-75.6	-64.4	-196.8	-184.7	-187.2
Luxembourg	397.4	548.6	480.1	279.1	705.6	331.6	305.6	300.0	264.9	291.6	65.8	243.0	180.1	14.2	414.0
Macau	70.5	70.1	79.0	54.6	85.5	1,266.3	1,225.1	1,231.7	1,355.9	1,486.7	-1,195.8	-1,155.0	-1,152.7	-1,301.3	-1,401.2
Macedonia	68.5	32.9	18.6	26.3	21.2	151.8	111.6	73.2	83.7	78.2	-83.3	-78.7	-54.6	-57.4	-57.0
Madagascar	15.4	21.0	15.4	46.4	35.6	157.8	271.6	215.8	383.7	469.2	-142.4	-250.6	-200.4	-337.3	-433.6
Malawi	13.7	12.8	30.1	16.4	21.7	55.4	77.9	70.8	76.9	60.6	-41.7	-65.1	-40.7	-60.5	-39.0
Malaysia	10,937.5	9,357.7	10,343.7	10,920.6	10,896.8	25,568.2	22,340.3	24,008.9	25,437.7	28,185.1	-14,630.7	-12,982.6	-13,665.2	-14,517.1	-17,288.3
Maldives	6.1	6.4	6.6	6.6	9.9	94.1	6.1	12.6	94.4	82.7	-88.0	0.3	-6.0	-87.8	-72.8
Mali	32.0	32.7	11.2	31.5	43.0	9.8	6.1	9.4	2.4	3.7	22.2	26.6	1.8	29.1	39.3
Malta	334.7	258.9	210.1	201.6	182.2	482.4	368.9	309.9	372.8	382.9	-147.7	-110.0	-99.8	-171.2	-200.7
Marshall Islands	60.2	26.5	28.7	28.1	18.4	5.0	5.5	0.7	27.1	12.1	55.2	21.0	28.0	1.0	6.3
Martinique	21.6	23.2	23.7	21.7	28.6	1.7	0.6	0.7	0.6	1.7	19.9	22.6	23.0	21.1	26.9
Mauritania	16.2	24.9	22.9	34.9	77.5	0.3	0.3	0.9	0.9	7.3	15.8	24.6	22.0	34.0	70.2
Mauritius	23.9	29.0	27.5	32.0	28.1	285.9	277.9	280.6	298.1	270.4	-262.0	-248.9	-253.1	-266.1	-242.3
Mexico	111,349.0	101,296.5	97,470.3	97,457.4	110,775.3	135,926.4	131,337.9	134,615.8	138,073.3	155,843.0	-24,577.4	-30,041.4	-37,145.5	-40,615.9	-45,067.7
Micronesia, Federated States of	29.1	30.0	27.2	23.6	24.4	13.7	20.8	15.2	14.3	11.4	15.4	9.2	12.0	9.3	13.0
Moldova	27.3	35.5	30.7	25.2	39.4	105.4	68.3	39.1	42.9	49.4	-78.1	-32.8	-8.4	-17.7	-10.1
Monaco	28.2	15.0	11.4	50.3	18.2	22.9	15.0	15.1	21.6	22.9	5.3	0.0	-3.7	28.7	-4.7
Mongolia	17.7	12.1	66.3	20.7	28.1	116.7	143.8	161.7	183.4	239.1	-99.0	-131.7	-95.4	-162.7	-210.9
Morocco	523.2	282.2	565.4	465.1	523.5	440.8	434.6	392.4	385.2	515.2	82.4	-152.4	173.0	79.9	8.3
Mozambique	57.0	28.4	94.6	62.5	76.4	24.4	7.1	8.5	8.4	10.8	32.6	21.3	86.1	54.1	65.7
Namibia	80.4	255.6	57.8	22.0	72.9	45.0	37.3	57.4	123.2	238.3	35.4	218.3	0.4	-95.2	-165.4
Netherlands	21,836.0	19,484.7	18,310.7	20,702.9	24,286.3	9,670.6	9,515.3	9,848.5	10,971.2	12,604.6	12,165.4	9,969.4	8,462.2	9,731.7	11,681.7
Netherlands Antilles	673.9	816.4	741.4	718.7	872.7	718.7	484.6	361.7	620.4	443.9	-44.8	331.8	379.7	126.7	428.8
New Caledonia	19.3	25.1	36.6	43.2	45.1	31.4	14.6	9.6	12.6	19.4	-12.1	10.5	27.0	30.6	25.6
New Zealand	1,970.3	2,110.5	1,813.1	1,848.8	2,075.7	2,080.2	2,199.2	2,281.6	2,403.4	2,967.3	-109.9	-88.7	-468.5	-554.6	-891.6
Nicaragua	380.1	443.1	437.0	502.8	591.7	588.5	603.6	679.6	769.3	990.5	-208.4	-160.5	-242.6	-266.5	-398.8
Niger	36.5	63.4	40.9	33.6	34.6	7.0	4.6	0.9	4.0	4.0	29.5	58.8	40.0	29.6	30.6
Nigeria	721.8	955.1	1,057.8	1,029.0	1,552.2	10,537.6	8,774.8	5,945.4	10,393.6	16,246.3	-9,815.8	-7,819.7	-4,887.6	-9,364.6	-14,694.1
Norway	1,547.2	1,834.7	1,406.5	1,467.5	1,603.6	5,706.1	5,202.8	5,842.6	5,212.4	6,532.2	-4,158.9	-3,368.1	-4,436.1	-3,744.9	-4,928.6
Oman	199.8	306.2	356.0	323.1	329.7	257.5	420.1	400.6	694.8	418.0	-57.7	-113.9	-44.6	-371.7	-88.3
Pakistan	462.2	541.3	693.4	839.6	1,810.7	2,166.8	2,249.4	2,305.0	2,531.5	2,874.3	-1,704.6	-1,708.1	-1,611.6	-1,691.9	-1,063.6
Panama	1,612.4	1,330.5	1,406.7	1,848.0	1,820.0	307.0	290.7	302.6	301.2	316.1	1,305.4	1,039.8	1,104.1	1,546.8	1,503.9
Papua New Guinea	23.0	22.2	23.2	30.3	42.6	34.5	39.3	90.2	66.1	54.3	-11.5	-17.1	-67.0	-35.8	-11.7
Paraguay	445.8	388.8	432.9	488.8	621.5	40.9	32.6	43.7	53.3	58.6	404.9	356.2	389.2	435.5	562.9
Peru	1,659.9	1,564.3	1,562.5	1,706.8	2,095.4	1,994.9	1,843.8	1,939.3	2,406.8	3,699.8	-335.0	-279.5	-376.8	-700.0	-1,604.4
Philippines	8,799.2	7,660.0	7,276.0	7,992.2	7,071.9	13,934.7	11,325.4	10,979.9	10,060.9	9,141.1	-5,135.5	-3,665.4	-3,703.9	-2,068.7	-2,072.2
Poland	757.2	787.7	686.3	758.7	927.9	1,041.3	952.6	1,108.5	1,325.8	1,828.1	-284.1	-164.9	-422.2	-567.1	-900.8

See footnotes at end of table.

U.S. Census Bureau, Statistical Abstract of the United States: 2006

Table 1293. U.S. Exports, Imports, and Merchandise Trade Balance, by Country: 2000 to 2004—Con.

[See headnote, page 835]

Country	Exports, domestic and foreign					General imports					Merchandise trade balance				
	2000	2001	2002	2003	2004	2000	2001	2002	2003	2004	2000	2001	2002	2003	2004
Portugal	984.2	1,239.7	861.3	862.8	1,046.2	1,578.5	1,555.4	1,672.6	1,967.3	2,243.1	-594.3	-315.7	-811.3	-1,104.5	-1,196.9
Qatar	191.1	335.9	313.9	408.5	454.5	485.6	502.0	484.7	331.3	387.4	-294.5	-166.3	-170.8	77.2	67.1
Romania	232.7	374.5	248.2	366.9	501.6	472.8	519.9	695.1	730.2	852.4	-240.1	-145.4	-446.9	-363.3	-350.7
Russia	2,092.4	2,716.1	2,397.0	2,450.2	2,958.6	7,658.7	6,264.4	6,870.2	8,598.2	11,847.2	-5,566.3	-3,548.3	-4,473.2	-6,148.0	-8,888.6
Samoa	64.0	69.9	7.6	11.1	12.2	5.5	7.3	6.4	4.4	4.7	58.5	62.6	1.2	6.7	7.5
Saudi Arabia	6,234.1	5,957.5	4,780.7	4,596.0	5,245.2	14,364.7	13,272.2	13,149.9	18,068.9	20,923.6	-8,130.6	-7,314.7	-8,369.2	-13,472.9	-15,678.4
Senegal	81.7	79.5	74.6	102.0	89.2	4.2	103.8	3.6	4.5	3.0	77.5	-24.3	71.0	97.5	86.2
Serbia and Montenegro	29.9	66.2	78.1	50.0	143.0	2.3	6.1	9.6	14.6	92.0	27.6	60.1	68.5	35.4	51.0
Singapore	17,806.3	17,651.7	16,217.9	16,515.7	19,600.9	19,178.3	15,000.0	14,802.2	15,158.2	15,305.6	-1,372.0	2,651.7	1,415.7	1,417.5	4,295.2
Slovakia	110.1	69.8	92.7	115.2	131.6	240.8	237.6	260.3	1,013.0	1,213.4	-130.7	-167.8	-167.6	-897.8	-1,081.9
Somalia	4.9	6.6	6.2	7.0	5.9	0.5	0.6	0.3	0.3	0.7	4.4	5.9	5.9	6.7	5.2
South Africa	3,089.5	2,959.6	2,525.5	2,821.2	3,172.0	4,210.1	4,432.6	4,034.1	4,637.6	5,943.5	-1,120.6	-1,473.0	-1,508.6	-1,816.4	-2,771.5
Spain	6,322.3	5,756.0	5,297.9	5,935.3	6,640.5	5,713.3	5,197.3	5,733.0	6,707.3	7,475.8	609.0	558.7	-435.1	-772.5	-835.3
Sri Lanka	204.7	183.0	171.9	154.8	163.9	2,001.9	1,984.2	1,810.4	1,807.4	1,956.9	-1,797.2	-1,801.2	-1,638.5	-1,652.6	-1,792.9
St. Lucia	107.4	86.7	99.5	121.2	103.3	22.3	28.9	19.2	13.0	14.3	85.1	57.8	80.3	108.2	89.0
St. Vincent and the Grenadines	37.9	38.8	40.4	46.5	45.4	8.9	22.5	16.5	4.1	4.1	29.0	16.3	23.9	42.4	41.3
Sudan	17.4	17.0	10.8	26.1	68.1	1.8	3.4	1.4	2.8	3.7	15.6	13.6	9.4	23.3	64.4
Suriname	134.2	155.3	124.8	192.9	178.6	135.2	142.9	132.7	140.1	140.8	-1.0	12.4	-7.9	52.8	37.8
Sweden	4,553.7	3,541.0	3,153.0	3,225.5	3,265.1	9,597.1	8,908.5	9,216.3	11,124.6	12,686.6	-5,043.4	-5,367.5	-6,063.3	-7,899.1	-9,421.5
Switzerland	9,953.6	9,807.3	7,782.5	8,660.1	9,268.3	10,159.9	9,669.6	9,382.0	10,667.9	11,642.7	-206.3	137.7	-1,599.5	-2,007.8	-2,374.3
Syria	226.0	231.4	274.1	214.0	211.3	158.6	158.5	160.8	258.9	267.1	67.4	72.9	113.3	-44.9	-56.4
Taiwan	24,405.9	18,121.6	18,381.8	17,487.9	21,730.9	40,502.8	33,374.5	32,147.9	31,599.9	34,617.4	-16,096.9	-15,252.9	-13,766.1	-14,112.0	-12,886.5
Tajikistan	12.1	28.6	33.1	66.0	55.5	9.0	5.2	1.1	3.1	7.3	3.1	23.4	32.0	62.9	48.2
Tanzania	44.7	64.0	62.7	66.0	127.6	32.2	27.9	24.8	24.2	24.2	12.5	36.1	37.9	41.8	103.4
Thailand	6,617.5	5,989.4	4,860.2	5,841.7	6,363.0	16,385.5	14,727.2	14,792.9	15,180.7	17,577.1	-9,767.8	-8,737.8	-9,932.7	-9,339.0	-11,214.2
Togo	10.6	16.3	13.8	15.2	23.7	6.0	12.6	2.7	5.6	1.6	4.6	3.7	11.1	9.6	22.1
Trinidad and Tobago	1,099.6	1,087.1	1,020.2	1,064.0	1,207.2	2,228.8	2,380.0	2,440.3	4,321.7	5,854.3	-1,129.2	-1,292.9	-1,420.1	-3,257.7	-4,647.1
Tunisia	288.9	276.0	194.8	170.5	258.1	93.9	121.7	93.2	100.1	209.1	195.0	154.3	101.6	70.4	49.0
Turkey	3,720.1	3,094.7	3,113.0	2,904.3	3,361.1	3,041.5	3,054.8	3,516.0	3,787.9	4,935.4	-678.6	39.9	-403.0	-883.6	-1,574.4
Turkmenistan	84.4	248.4	47.1	34.2	294.6	28.0	45.5	59.6	76.4	80.8	56.4	202.9	-12.5	-42.2	213.8
Turks and Caicos Islands	88.6	77.1	53.6	71.9	137.2	5.9	17.7	5.1	6.1	25.8	82.7	69.0	48.5	65.8	130.0
Uganda	28.2	31.7	24.0	42.7	63.7	29.1	17.7	15.3	34.9	25.8	-0.9	14.0	8.7	7.8	38.0
Ukraine	191.0	200.1	254.8	230.8	398.0	872.2	673.6	362.4	282.0	850.2	-681.2	-473.5	-107.6	-51.2	-452.2
United Arab Emirates	2,284.7	2,637.9	3,593.2	3,510.4	4,063.7	971.8	1,194.2	922.9	1,129.0	1,141.8	1,312.9	1,443.7	2,670.3	2,381.4	2,922.0
United Kingdom	41,570.4	40,714.2	33,204.7	33,895.4	35,959.8	43,345.1	41,368.8	40,744.9	42,666.9	46,402.2	-1,774.7	-654.6	-7,540.2	-8,771.5	-10,442.3
Uruguay	536.9	406.3	208.6	328.6	324.4	313.0	227.7	193.2	255.8	580.0	223.9	178.6	15.4	71.0	-255.6
Uzbekistan	157.7	144.9	138.5	256.7	229.7	41.2	53.5	77.1	83.7	88.0	116.5	91.4	61.4	173.0	141.7
Venezuela	5,549.9	5,642.1	4,429.7	2,839.5	4,781.8	18,623.2	15,250.5	15,093.5	17,144.2	24,962.5	-13,073.3	-9,608.4	-10,663.8	-14,304.7	-20,180.6
Vietnam	367.6	460.3	580.2	1,324.4	1,163.4	821.4	1,052.9	2,394.7	4,554.9	5,275.8	-453.8	-592.6	-1,814.5	-3,230.5	-4,112.4
Virgin Islands, British	63.8	74.7	67.4	70.5	232.4	30.9	11.9	40.5	66.1	61.5	32.5	62.8	26.9	35.5	170.9
Yemen	189.4	185.4	366.1	195.3	26.4	255.6	202.4	246.3	12.5	32.5	-66.2	-17.0	119.8	129.2	40.4
Zambia	19.1	31.2	35.7	19.5	7.0	15.6	15.6	19.9	17.3	1.4	1.4	15.6	27.8	7.0	-6.1
Zimbabwe	52.4	31.2	49.3	41.7	47.3	112.4	90.8	102.8	56.6	76.2	-60.0	-59.6	-53.5	-14.9	-28.9

1 Includes timing adjustment and unidentified countries, not shown separately.

Source: U.S. Census Bureau, U.S. International Trade in Goods and Services, December 2004, Series FT-900(04-12) and previous December or final reports. See also <http://www.census.gov/foreign-trade/Press-Release/2004pr/12/#ft900> (released 10 February 2005).

Table 1294. **U.S. Exports and General Imports by Selected SITC Commodity Groups: 2001 to 2004**

[In millions of dollars (729,100 represents $729,100,000,000). SITC = Standard International Trade Classification. For methodology, see Foreign Trade Statistics in Appendix III. n.e.s. = Not elsewhere specified]

Selected commodities	Exports [1]				General imports [2]			
	2001	2002	2003	2004	2001	2002	2003	2004
Total	729,100	693,103	724,006	819,026	1,140,999	1,161,366	1,259,705	1,470,547
Agricultural commodities [3]	53,705	53,115	59,495	61,308	39,544	42,012	47,419	54,264
Animal feeds	4,221	3,824	3,885	3,780	574	605	635	781
Coffee	16	8	5	7	1,357	1,369	1,612	1,868
Corn	4,755	5,108	4,963	6,128	135	137	151	127
Cotton, raw and linters	2,174	2,031	3,219	4,248	27	25	27	18
Hides and skins	1,813	1,594	1,653	1,584	100	84	74	79
Meat and preparations	7,231	6,356	7,261	5,195	4,254	4,269	4,403	5,706
Soybeans	5,429	5,734	7,935	6,685	31	28	47	53
Sugar	3	13	6	4	480	495	535	517
Tobacco, unmanufactured	1,269	1,050	1,035	1,044	710	701	690	690
Vegetables and fruits	7,415	7,607	8,123	8,848	9,517	10,194	11,454	12,804
Wheat	3,375	3,630	3,955	5,158	282	266	141	162
Manufactured goods [3]	577,714	544,913	556,800	609,501	950,679	974,576	1,027,358	1,128,667
ADP equip., office machinery	39,240	30,368	28,852	28,197	75,859	76,877	80,826	93,805
Airplane parts	15,735	14,309	14,524	15,290	6,287	4,986	4,474	4,795
Airplanes	26,961	27,115	23,418	24,847	14,884	12,329	12,327	11,647
Alcoholic bev., distilled	489	505	551	683	3,063	3,273	3,693	4,026
Aluminum	3,253	2,947	2,941	3,797	6,406	6,757	7,238	9,547
Artwork/antiques	1,637	977	1,157	1,316	5,458	5,194	4,398	5,308
Basketware, etc.	3,579	3,842	4,692	5,078	5,591	6,564	7,854	8,425
Chemicals, cosmetics	5,825	5,870	6,557	7,419	3,750	4,195	5,611	6,951
Chemicals, dyeing	3,782	3,860	4,137	4,552	2,478	2,357	2,480	2,669
Chemicals, fertilizers	2,077	2,106	2,341	2,615	1,890	1,619	2,130	2,530
Chemicals, inorganic	5,578	5,464	5,577	6,197	6,153	6,018	7,419	8,273
Chemicals, medicinal	15,031	15,732	18,775	23,341	18,628	24,748	31,516	35,105
Chemicals, n.e.s.	12,382	12,348	12,986	14,539	5,927	6,168	6,857	7,978
Chemicals, organic	16,424	16,406	20,105	25,851	29,712	30,366	32,876	35,213
Chemicals, plastics	18,485	19,380	21,069	25,099	10,401	10,760	12,161	14,224
Cigarettes	2,118	1,466	1,403	1,295	238	316	300	258
Clothing	6,510	5,485	4,960	4,413	63,856	63,803	68,162	72,311
Cork, wood, lumber	3,533	3,364	3,387	3,837	7,968	7,872	7,276	10,607
Crude fertilizers	1,654	1,520	1,582	1,719	1,318	1,275	1,340	1,471
Electrical machinery	72,055	66,948	69,772	73,075	84,670	81,158	82,433	93,280
Fish and preparations	3,069	2,976	3,084	3,513	9,742	10,000	10,930	11,171
Footwear	639	518	495	450	15,234	15,387	15,603	16,505
Furniture and parts	4,255	3,814	3,608	4,058	18,610	21,577	24,356	27,741
Gem diamonds	1,714	1,182	338	950	10,616	12,088	12,931	14,651
General industrial machinery	32,153	30,075	30,115	34,683	33,264	35,200	38,467	45,686
Gold, nonmonetary	4,872	3,244	4,820	4,414	2,079	2,428	2,932	3,996
Iron and steel mill products	5,482	5,252	6,268	7,993	12,449	12,951	11,112	22,404
Lighting, plumbing	1,321	1,333	1,347	1,482	4,895	5,566	6,003	6,812
Metal manufactures, n.e.s.	11,365	11,170	11,218	12,067	15,510	16,681	17,985	21,778
Metal ores; scrap	4,420	4,626	5,646	7,731	3,237	3,101	3,142	4,581
Metalworking machinery	4,703	4,140	4,108	5,963	6,587	5,104	5,335	6,248
Optical goods	3,036	2,132	2,249	2,555	3,455	2,836	2,992	3,530
Paper and paperboard	10,042	9,551	9,814	10,615	14,815	14,435	14,849	16,588
Photographic equipment	3,281	3,529	3,330	3,487	5,596	5,325	5,046	4,903
Plastic articles, n.e.s.	7,065	6,820	6,778	7,364	8,257	9,138	10,216	11,810
Platinum	962	723	481	542	5,240	2,830	2,624	3,506
Power generating machinery	33,577	32,430	31,495	35,714	36,118	33,922	32,485	35,955
Printed materials	4,746	4,429	4,607	4,891	3,721	3,960	4,148	4,507
Pulp and waste paper	3,690	3,842	4,096	4,499	2,630	2,363	2,597	2,940
Records/magnetic media	4,611	4,414	4,473	4,747	4,883	5,279	5,852	6,795
Rubber articles, n.e.s.	1,569	1,423	1,412	1,512	1,979	2,139	2,358	2,733
Rubber tires and tubes	2,287	2,232	2,200	2,525	4,209	4,765	5,258	6,304
Scientific instruments	29,123	27,087	27,998	32,912	21,356	20,884	23,661	28,459
Ships, boats	1,801	1,200	1,172	1,647	1,209	1,325	1,592	2,084
Silver and bullion	234	262	177	271	530	687	801	1,013
Spacecraft	201	509	142	467	71	310	188	39
Specialized industrial machinery	25,747	23,532	23,371	28,825	19,554	18,401	20,841	26,410
Television, VCR, etc.	24,230	19,374	16,851	20,030	62,836	66,212	71,137	87,860
Textile yarn, fabric	10,074	10,263	10,457	11,482	14,616	16,097	17,257	19,505
Toys/games/sporting goods	3,217	2,985	3,155	3,391	20,901	22,067	21,566	22,479
Travel goods	308	277	291	311	4,300	4,402	4,842	5,660
Vehicles	54,347	57,698	60,521	64,646	157,400	168,073	172,578	187,828
Watches/clocks/parts	277	236	242	271	3,048	3,203	3,600	3,789
Wood manufactures	1,568	1,564	1,578	1,791	6,998	7,853	9,289	12,307
Mineral fuel [3]	12,494	11,541	13,691	17,914	121,923	115,748	155,561	204,801
Coal	1,915	1,673	1,621	2,714	1,022	966	1,176	2,418
Crude oil	187	92	155	265	74,293	79,252	101,722	135,999
Petroleum preparations	5,034	6,009	7,057	9,709	24,620	20,748	26,735	37,982
Natural gas	536	995	1,300	2,099	15,417	10,974	20,621	23,168
Re-exports	64,780	63,792	72,319	89,574	(X)	(X)	(X)	(X)

X Not applicable. [1] F.a.s. basis. Exports by commodity are only for domestic exports. [2] Customs value basis. [3] Includes other commodities not shown separately.

Source: U.S. Census Bureau, U.S. International Trade in Goods and Services, Series FT-900(04-12), and previous December or Final reports. See also <http://www.census.gov/foreign-trade/Press-Release/2003pr/12/> (released 10 February 2005).

Foreign Commerce and Aid 839

Table 1295. **United States Total and Aerospace Foreign Trade: 1980 to 2004**

[In millions of dollars (-19,696 represents -$19,696,000,000), except percent. Data are reported as exports of domestic merchandise, including Department of Defense shipments and undocumented exports to Canada, f.a.s. (free-alongside-ship) basis, and imports for consumption, customs value basis. Minus sign (-) indicates deficit]

	Merchandise trade			Aerospace trade						
				Exports						
Year								Civil		
	Trade balance	Imports	Exports	Trade balance	Imports	Total	Percent of U.S. exports	Total	Trans-ports	Military
1980	-19,696	245,262	225,566	11,952	3,554	15,506	6.9	13,248	6,727	2,258
1981	-22,267	260,982	238,715	13,134	4,500	17,634	7.4	13,312	7,180	4,322
1982	-27,510	243,952	216,442	11,035	4,568	15,603	7.2	9,608	3,834	5,995
1983	-52,409	258,048	205,639	12,619	3,446	16,065	7.8	10,595	4,683	5,470
1984	-106,703	330,678	223,976	10,082	4,926	15,008	6.7	9,659	3,195	5,350
1985	-117,712	336,526	218,815	12,593	6,132	18,725	8.6	12,942	5,518	5,783
1986	-138,279	365,438	227,159	11,826	7,902	19,728	8.7	14,851	6,276	4,875
1987	-152,119	406,241	254,122	14,575	7,905	22,480	8.8	15,768	6,377	6,714
1988	-118,526	440,952	322,426	17,860	9,087	26,947	8.4	20,298	8,766	6,651
1989	-109,399	473,211	363,812	22,083	10,028	32,111	8.8	25,619	12,313	6,492
1990	-101,718	495,311	393,592	27,282	11,801	39,083	9.9	31,517	16,691	7,566
1991	-66,723	488,453	421,730	30,785	13,003	43,788	10.4	35,548	20,881	8,239
1992	-84,501	532,665	448,164	31,356	13,662	45,018	10.0	36,906	22,379	8,111
1993	-115,568	580,659	465,091	27,235	12,183	39,418	8.5	31,823	18,146	7,596
1994	-150,630	663,256	512,626	25,010	12,363	37,373	7.3	30,050	15,931	7,322
1995	-158,801	743,543	584,742	21,561	11,509	33,071	5.7	25,079	10,606	7,991
1996	-170,214	795,289	625,075	26,602	13,668	40,270	6.4	29,477	13,624	10,792
1997	-180,522	869,704	689,182	32,239	18,134	50,374	7.3	40,075	21,028	10,299
1998	-229,758	911,896	682,138	40,960	23,110	64,071	9.4	51,999	29,168	12,072
1999	-328,821	1,024,618	695,797	37,381	25,063	62,444	9.0	50,624	25,694	11,820
2000	-436,104	1,218,022	781,918	26,734	27,944	54,679	7.0	45,566	19,615	9,113
2001	-411,899	1,140,999	729,100	26,035	32,473	58,508	8.0	49,371	22,151	9,137
2002	-468,263	1,161,366	693,103	29,534	27,242	56,775	8.2	47,348	21,661	9,427
2003	-532,350	1,257,121	724,771	27,111	25,393	52,504	7.2	44,060	19,434	8,445
2004	-650,812	1,469,864	819,052	31,002	25,815	56,817	6.9	47,325	18,577	9,492

Source: Aerospace Industries Association of America, Washington, DC, *Aerospace Facts and Figures*, annual.

Table 1296. **U.S. Exporting Companies Profile by Company Type and Employment-Size Class: 1992 and 2002**

[(348,960 represents $348,960,000,000). Data are based on economic census and survey data on file at the Census Bureau, administrative records from other government agencies, and documents filed for export clearances]

Company type and employment-size-class	Number of exporters		Known export value [1] (mil. dol.)		Percent of—			
					Number of exporters		Known export value	
	1992	2002	1992	2002	1992	2002	1992	2002
All companies, total	112,854	223,013	348,960	599,839	100.0	100.0	100.0	100.0
No employees	15,534	58,042	9,178	34,178	13.8	26.0	2.6	5.7
1 to 19 employees	51,186	97,352	29,397	41,500	45.4	43.7	8.4	6.9
20 to 49 employees	18,501	29,101	17,005	18,323	16.4	13.0	4.9	3.1
50 to 99 employees	10,505	15,137	13,840	15,585	9.3	6.8	4.0	2.6
100 to 249 employees	8,679	11,424	18,371	26,310	7.7	5.1	5.3	4.4
250 to 499 employees	3,621	4,698	15,055	22,597	3.2	2.1	4.3	3.8
500 or more employees	4,828	7,259	246,114	441,347	4.3	3.3	70.5	73.6
Manufacturers	(NA)	63,100	(NA)	394,632	(NA)	28.3	(NA)	65.8
No employees	(NA)	9,176	(NA)	9,909	(NA)	4.1	(NA)	1.7
1 to 19 employees	(NA)	20,636	(NA)	4,275	(NA)	9.3	(NA)	0.7
20 to 49 employees	(NA)	13,366	(NA)	5,455	(NA)	6.0	(NA)	0.9
50 to 99 employees	(NA)	8,078	(NA)	6,458	(NA)	3.6	(NA)	1.1
100 to 249 employees	(NA)	6,343	(NA)	13,693	(NA)	2.8	(NA)	2.3
250 to 499 employees	(NA)	2,440	(NA)	12,631	(NA)	1.1	(NA)	2.1
500 or more employees	(NA)	3,061	(NA)	342,209	(NA)	1.4	(NA)	57.1
Wholesalers	(NA)	70,886	(NA)	122,907	(NA)	31.8	(NA)	20.5
No employees	(NA)	15,108	(NA)	8,571	(NA)	6.8	(NA)	1.4
1 to 19 employees	(NA)	40,694	(NA)	23,181	(NA)	18.2	(NA)	3.9
20 to 49 employees	(NA)	8,401	(NA)	7,934	(NA)	3.8	(NA)	1.3
50 to 99 employees	(NA)	3,293	(NA)	5,817	(NA)	1.5	(NA)	1.0
100 to 249 employees	(NA)	2,033	(NA)	8,167	(NA)	0.9	(NA)	1.4
250 to 499 employees	(NA)	693	(NA)	4,873	(NA)	0.3	(NA)	0.8
500 or more employees	(NA)	664	(NA)	64,364	(NA)	0.3	(NA)	10.7
Other companies	(NA)	80,676	(NA)	75,843	(NA)	36.2	(NA)	12.6
No employees	(NA)	26,799	(NA)	13,109	(NA)	12.0	(NA)	2.2
1 to 19 employees	(NA)	35,633	(NA)	13,907	(NA)	16.0	(NA)	2.3
20 to 49 employees	(NA)	7,138	(NA)	4,828	(NA)	3.2	(NA)	0.8
50 to 99 employees	(NA)	3,555	(NA)	3,116	(NA)	1.6	(NA)	0.5
100 to 249 employees	(NA)	2,831	(NA)	3,811	(NA)	1.3	(NA)	0.6
250 to 499 employees	(NA)	1,404	(NA)	4,440	(NA)	0.6	(NA)	0.7
500 or more employees	(NA)	3,316	(NA)	32,633	(NA)	1.5	(NA)	5.4
Unclassified companies	(NA)	8,351	(NA)	6,458	(NA)	3.7	(NA)	1.1

NA Not available. [1] Known value is defined as the value of exports by known exporters, i.e., those export transactions that could be matched to specific companies. Export values are on f.a.s. or "free-alongside-ship basis."

Source: U.S. Census Bureau, *A Profile of U.S. Exporting Companies, 1992* and *2002-2003*. See also <http://www.census.gov/foreign-trade/aip/edbrel-0203.pdf> (released 13 July 2005).

Table 1297. Domestic Exports and Imports for Consumption of Merchandise by Selected NAICS Product Category: 2000 to 2004

[In millions of dollars (712,285 represents $712,285,000,000). Includes nonmonetary gold. For methodology, see Foreign Trade Statistics in Appendix III. NAICS = North American Industry Classification System; see text, Section 15]

Product category	2000	2001	2002	2003	2004
Domestic exports, total.	712,285	666,021	629,599	651,687	729,452
Agricultural, forestry and fishery products	29,153	29,666	30,068	34,699	37,830
Agricultural products, total	23,596	24,068	24,827	29,194	31,949
Livestock and livestock products	1,255	1,309	1,020	1,177	963
Forestry products, not elsewhere specified	1,644	1,436	1,419	1,462	1,653
Fish, fresh or chilled; and other marine products	2,658	2,854	2,802	2,866	3,265
Mining, total	6,187	5,403	5,585	6,117	8,677
Oil and gas	1,706	1,261	1,725	2,143	3,001
Minerals and ores	4,481	4,141	3,860	3,973	5,676
Manufacturing, total	644,440	597,101	562,834	577,789	645,104
Food and kindred products	24,966	26,486	25,175	26,795	25,952
Beverages and tobacco products	5,568	4,334	3,559	3,648	3,644
Textiles and fabrics	7,010	7,098	7,397	7,557	8,363
Textile mill products	2,236	1,991	1,875	1,881	2,072
Apparel and accessories	8,104	6,469	5,462	4,923	4,350
Leather and allied products	2,322	2,285	2,049	2,035	2,190
Wood products	4,854	3,944	3,777	3,818	4,249
Paper products	15,539	14,045	13,640	13,965	15,168
Printed, publishing & similar products	4,869	4,867	4,509	4,706	4,983
Petroleum and coal products	8,862	8,214	7,897	9,349	12,579
Chemicals	77,649	76,837	78,049	88,384	105,238
Plastics and rubber products	16,970	15,745	15,383	15,661	17,316
Nonmetallic mineral products	7,830	7,378	6,025	6,069	6,596
Primary metal products	20,126	18,150	15,371	17,877	21,159
Fabricated metal products	21,737	19,547	18,893	18,848	20,821
Machinery, except electrical	85,038	76,572	70,178	69,285	86,264
Computers and electronic products	161,449	134,263	116,243	115,883	122,161
Electrical equipment, appliances and components	25,401	22,764	20,587	20,632	23,606
Transportation equipment	121,701	122,877	123,970	122,246	129,907
Furniture and fixtures	2,882	2,419	2,158	2,349	2,633
Miscellaneous manufactured commodities	19,327	20,815	20,640	21,591	24,795
Special classification provisions	32,505	33,852	31,112	33,109	37,814
Waste & scrap	4,948	4,738	5,081	6,456	8,548
Used or second-hand merchandise	1,950	2,169	1,562	1,808	2,108
Goods returned or reimported	333	310	241	205	152
Special classification provision, not elsewhere specified	25,274	26,635	24,228	24,640	27,006
Imports for consumption, total.	**1,205,339**	**1,132,635**	**1,154,811**	**1,250,097**	**1,460,161**
Agricultural, forestry and fishery products	24,378	23,598	24,327	26,197	27,814
Agricultural products, total	11,771	11,290	11,773	13,035	14,356
Livestock and livestock products	3,085	3,445	3,455	2,782	2,498
Forestry products, not elsewhere specified	1,409	1,158	1,288	1,612	2,019
Fish, fresh or chilled; and other marine products	8,113	7,706	7,811	8,768	8,942
Mining, total	79,841	76,243	76,288	105,662	138,427
Oil and gas	76,166	72,690	72,830	101,800	133,606
Minerals and ores	3,675	3,553	3,458	3,862	4,821
Manufacturing, total	1,040,329	972,669	995,103	1,060,349	1,231,005
Food and kindred products	18,944	19,646	21,110	23,769	27,740
Beverages and tobacco products	8,350	8,723	9,772	10,925	11,652
Textiles and fabrics	7,042	6,336	6,778	6,791	7,387
Textile mill products	7,347	7,580	8,643	9,857	11,707
Apparel and accessories	62,928	62,429	62,313	66,499	70,533
Leather and allied products	21,463	21,865	22,104	22,627	24,541
Wood products	15,388	14,968	15,720	16,581	22,869
Paper products	19,080	18,170	17,528	18,414	20,645
Printed, publishing & similar products	4,197	4,143	4,432	4,699	5,148
Petroleum and coal products	40,156	35,222	31,976	39,161	54,544
Chemicals	76,606	80,681	87,311	102,078	115,246
Plastics and rubber products	17,362	16,887	18,554	20,504	24,085
Nonmetallic mineral products	14,740	13,552	13,547	14,428	16,531
Primary metal products	43,833	36,350	34,356	34,065	56,498
Fabricated metal products	27,974	26,386	28,607	30,068	35,976
Machinery, except electrical	79,366	72,124	68,645	77,344	94,402
Computers and electronic products	250,694	204,950	205,564	212,201	248,033
Electrical equipment, appliances and components	39,567	38,949	39,707	41,914	48,781
Transportation equipment	213,110	212,013	219,186	223,304	239,565
Furniture and fixtures	15,607	15,266	17,492	19,636	22,560
Miscellaneous manufactured commodities	56,577	56,427	61,759	65,484	72,563
Special classification provisions	60,791	60,125	59,093	57,889	62,915
Waste & scrap	1,875	1,590	1,613	1,810	3,054
Used or second-hand merchandise	6,345	5,902	5,668	4,752	5,710
Goods returned or reimported	33,851	34,682	34,981	33,605	34,223
Special classification provision, not elsewhere specified	18,720	17,951	16,831	17,723	19,928

Source: U.S. Census Bureau, U.S. International Trade in Goods and Services, series FT-900, December issues. For most recent, see <http://www.census.gov/foreign-trade/Press-Release/2003pr/12/> (released 10 February 2005) and previous December or final reports.

No. 112.—IMPORTS AND EXPORTS OF MERCHANDISE INTO AND FROM ALASKA: VALUES, 1879 TO 1905.

Year ended June 30—	Imports.			Exports.		
	From United States.[a]	From other countries.	Total.	To United States.	To other countries.	Total.
	Dollars.	Dollars.	Dollars.	Dollars.	Dollars.	Dollars.
1879	317,000	4,791			50,378	
1880	463,000	3,032			31,543	
1881	548,000	10,906			69,183	
1882	585,000	8,484			38,520	
1883	668,000	11,945			28,393	
1884	615,000	4,420			8,438	
1885	853,000	8,944			24,468	
1886	874,000	14,262			8,022	
1887	1,334,000	18,636			7,336	
1888	1,487,000	28,211			23,499	
1889	1,686,000	32,809			200	
1890	1,897,000	24,577			4,682	
1891	1,973,000	23,302			89,073	
1892	2,012,000	15,691			14,185	
1893	2,317,000	37,362			10,211	
1894	2,794,000	80,490			2,663	
1895	3,017,000	55,850			11,520	
1896	3,502,000	72,411			5,358	
1897	8,924,000	96,694			27,205	
1898	13,682,000	175,235			30,705	
1899	9,614,000	196,251			45,729	
1900	18,463,000	385,317			566,347	
1901	13,457,000	557,992			2,534,318	
1902		511,830			2,612,021	
1903	[b]9,599,701	477,463	9,987,164	[c]10,228,569	1,612,128	11,840,697
1904	[b]10,165,110	607,255	10,772,465	[c]10,165,140	1,565,690	11,738,155
1905	[b]11,504,255	1,450,910	12,955,165	[c]10,801,446	1,088,165	11,889,611

[a] Estimated value of merchandise shipped from Pacific coast ports to Alaska from 1879 to 1901. [b] Shipments to Alaska. [c] Shipments from Alaska.

No. 113.—IMPORTS AND EXPORTS OF MERCHANDISE INTO AND FROM PORTO RICO: VALUES, 1887 TO 1905.[a]

Year.[b]	Imports.			Exports.		
	From United States.	From other countries.	Total.	To United States.	To other countries.	Total.
	Dollars.	Dollars.	Dollars.	Dollars.	Dollars.	Dollars.
1887	2,853,065	7,414,445	10,627,510	4,449,654	6,151,437	10,610,091
1888	3,329,728	10,556,306	13,886,034	3,094,389	8,484,892	11,579,281
1889	3,645,785	10,035,577	13,681,362	2,918,988	7,760,362	10,679,350
1890	3,716,263	13,876,119	17,592,322	2,412,070	7,923,581	10,335,651
1891	3,479,418	12,795,079	16,274,497	2,278,862	7,261,127	9,539,989
1892	[c]2,856,003	13,627,751	16,483,754	[d]3,248,007	12,265,571	15,513,641
1893	4,397,614	12,316,621	16,714,238	2,588,256	13,571,048	16,159,304
1894	4,682,725	14,403,611	19,086,336	2,347,869	14,342,322	16,690,191
1895	3,803,307	13,032,146	16,835,453	3,035,209	12,210,430	15,245,639
1896	3,973,855	14,308,835	18,282,690	2,552,174	15,789,256	18,341,430
1897	[c]1,988,888			[d]2,181,024		
1898	[c]1,505,946			[d]2,414,356		
1899	3,951,369	5,851,547	9,805,916	3,457,557	6,698,984	10,156,541
1900[f]	[e]3,096,692	1,069,743	4,165,435	[h]1,195,044	1,402,761	2,597,805
1901[i]	[e]6,861,917	1,952,728	8,814,645	[h]5,883,892	3,002,679	8,886,571
1902[i]	[e]10,882,653	2,326,957	13,209,610	[h]8,378,766	4,055,190	12,433,956
1903[i]	[e]12,245,845	2,203,341	14,449,286	[h]11,051,195	4,037,884	15,089,079
1904[i]	[e]11,210,060	1,958,969	13,169,029	[h]11,722,826	4,543,077	16,265,903
1905[i]	[e]13,974,070	2,562,189	16,536,259	[h]15,683,145	3,076,420	18,709,565

[a] For commerce of the United States with Hawaii, the Philippine Islands, and Porto Rico, see, respectively, pages 230, 231, and 198.
[b] 1887 to 1896 calendar years; from Bulletin No. 13, 1898, Department of Agriculture.
[c] Exports from United States to Porto Rico, fiscal year.
[d] Imports into United States from Porto Rico, fiscal year.
[e] Calendar year; figures include coin and bullion. From report of War Department.
[f] Six months ending June 30.
[g] Shipments to Porto Rico.
[h] Shipments from Porto Rico.
[i] Fiscal years.

Source: Statistical Abstract of the United States: 1905 Edition.

Section 29
Puerto Rico and the Island Areas

This section presents summary economic and social statistics for Puerto Rico, the U.S. Virgin Islands, Guam, American Samoa, and the Northern Mariana Islands. Primary sources are the decennial censuses of population and housing, county business patterns, and the censuses of agriculture, business, manufactures, and construction (taken every 5 years) conducted by the U.S. Census Bureau; the annual *Vital Statistics of the United States*, issued by the National Center for Health Statistics; and the annual *Income and Product* of the Puerto Rico Planning Board, San Juan.

Jurisdiction—The United States gained jurisdiction over these areas as follows: the islands of *Puerto Rico* and *Guam*, surrendered by Spain to the United States in December 1898, were ceded to the United States by the Treaty of Paris, ratified in 1899. Puerto Rico became a commonwealth on July 25, 1952, thereby achieving a high degree of local autonomy under its own constitution. The *U.S. Virgin Islands*, comprising 50 islands and cays, was purchased by the United States from Denmark in 1917. *American Samoa*, a group of seven islands, was acquired by the United States in accordance with a convention among the United States, Great Britain, and Germany, ratified in 1900 (Swains Island was annexed in 1925). By an agreement approved by the Security Council and the United States, the Northern Mariana Islands, previously under Japanese mandate, was administered by the United States between 1947 and 1986 under the United Nations trusteeship system. The Northern Mariana Islands became a commonwealth in 1986.

Censuses—Because characteristics of the Puerto Rico and the Island Areas differ, the presentation of census data for them is not uniform. The 1960 Census of Population covered all of the places listed above except the Northern Mariana Islands (their census was conducted in April 1958 by the Office of the High Commissioner), while the 1960 Census of Housing also excluded American Samoa. The 1970, 1980, 1990, and 2000 Censuses of Population and Housing covered all five areas. The 1959, 1969, and 1978 Censuses of Agriculture covered Puerto Rico, American Samoa, Guam, and the Virgin Islands; the 1964, 1974, and 1982 censuses covered the same areas except American Samoa; and the 1969, 1978, 1987, 1992, and 1997 censuses included the Northern Mariana Islands. Beginning in 1967, Congress authorized the economic censuses, to be taken at 5-year intervals, for years ending in "2" and "7." Prior economic censuses were conducted in Puerto Rico for 1949, 1954, 1958, and 1963 and in Guam and the U.S. Virgin Islands for 1958 and 1963. In 1967, the census of construction industries was added for the first time in Puerto Rico; in 1972, the U.S. Virgin Islands and Guam were covered. For 1982, 1987, 1992, and 1997 the economic censuses covered the Northern Mariana Islands.

Information in other sections—In addition to the statistics presented in this section, other data are included as integral parts of many tables showing distribution by states in various sections of the *Abstract*. See "Puerto Rico and the Island Areas" in the Index. For definition and explanation of terms used, see Section 1, Population; Section 4, Education; Section 17, Agriculture; Section 20, Construction and Housing; Section 21, Manufactures; and Section 22, Domestic Trade.

U.S. Census Bureau, Statistical Abstract of the United States: 2006

Fig. 29.1
Selected Island Areas of the United States

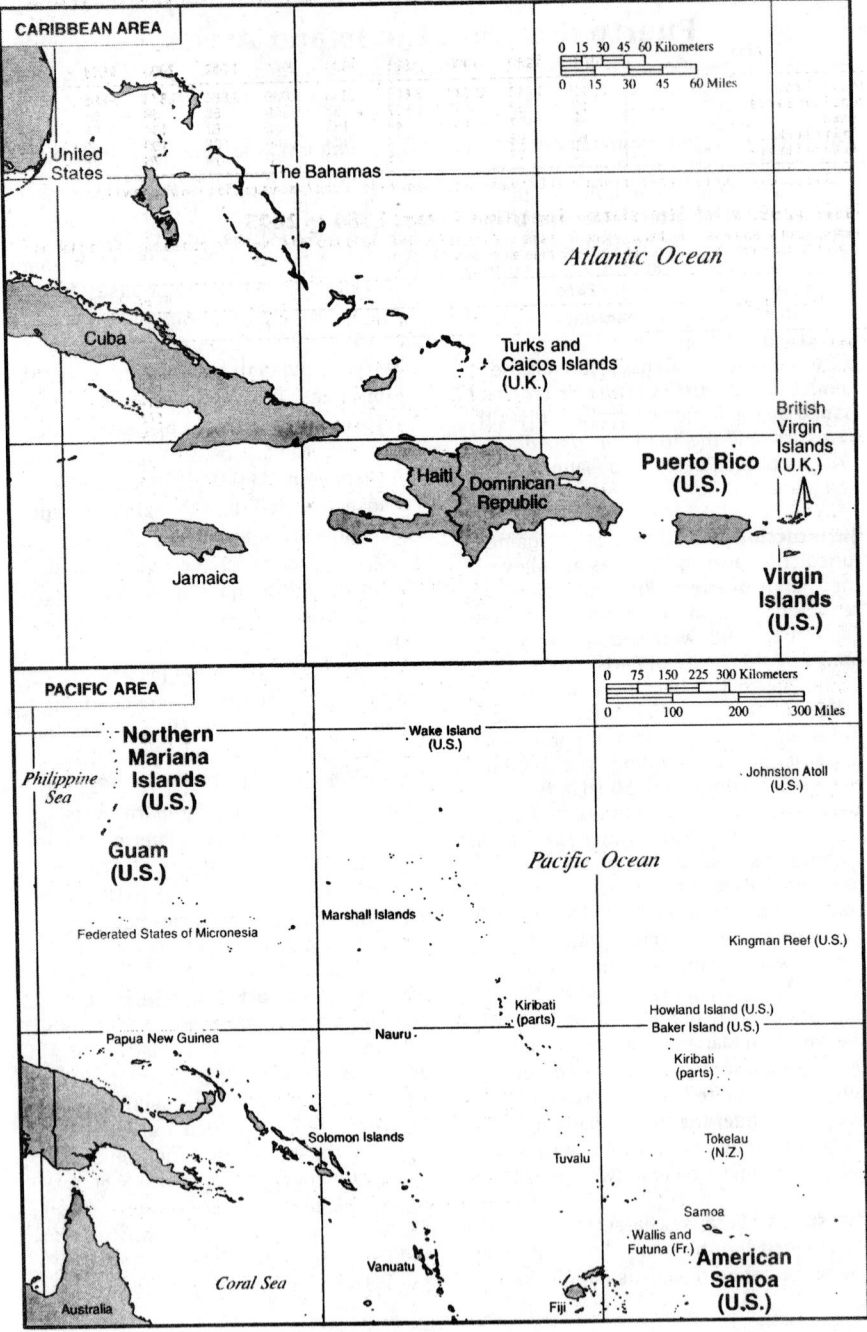

U.S. Census Bureau. Statistical Abstract of the United States: 2006

Table 1298. **Estimated Resident Population With Projection: 1970 to 2010**

[In thousands (2,722 represents 2,722,000). Population as of July 1. Population data generally are de-facto figures for the present territory. Data for 1990 to 2000 are adjusted to the 2000 Census of Population for Puerto Rico only. See text, Section 30, for general comments regarding the data. For details of methodology, coverage, and reliability, see source]

Area	1970	1980	1990	1995	2000	2001	2002	2003	2004	2010, proj.
Puerto Rico	2,722	3,210	3,537	3,683	3,816	3,839	3,860	3,878	3,895	3,985
American Samoa	27	32	47	57	57	58	58	58	58	57
Guam	86	107	134	144	155	158	161	164	166	181
Virgin Islands	63	98	104	114	109	109	109	109	109	108
Northern Mariana Islands	12	17	44	58	70	72	74	76	78	91

Source: U.S. Census Bureau, International Database. See Internet site: <http://census.gov/ipc/www/idbnew.html>.

Table 1299. **Vital Statistics—Specified Areas: 1980 to 2003**

[Births, deaths, and infant deaths by place of residence. Rates for 1980, 1990 and 2000 based on population enumerated as of April 1; for other years, on population estimated as of July 1]

Area and year	Births Number	Births Rate [1]	Deaths Number	Deaths Rate [1]	Infant deaths Number	Infant deaths Rate [2]
Puerto Rico:						
1980	72,986	22.8	20,413	6.4	1,351	18.5
1990	66,417	18.8	25,957	7.3	888	13.4
2000	59,333	15.2	28,369	7.2	574	9.7
2002	52,747	13.7	27,927	7.2	505	(NA)
2003 [3]	49,427	(NA)	28,243	7.3	(NA)	(NA)
Guam:						
1980	2,945	27.8	393	3.7	43	14.6
1990	3,839	28.6	520	3.9	31	8.1
2000	3,766	24.4	648	4.2	22	5.8
2002	3,212	19.9	639	4.0	20	(NA)
2003 [3]	3,286	(NA)	672	4.1	(NA)	(NA)
Virgin Islands:						
1980	2,504	25.9	504	5.2	61	24.4
1990	2,267	21.8	480	4.6	33	14.6
2000	1,564	12.9	641	5.3	21	13.4
2002	1,634	15.0	623	5.7	5	(NA)
2003 [3]	(NA)	(NA)	628	5.8	(NA)	(NA)
American Samoa:						
1997	1,634	27.1	257	4.3	17	(B)
2002	1,627	28.2	294	5.1	25	(NA)
2003 [3]	1,015	(NA)	(NA)	(NA)	(NA)	(NA)
Northern Marianas:						
1998	1,462	21.9	162	2.4	13	(B)
2002	1,290	17.4	163	2.2	9	(NA)
2003 [3]	1,344	(NA)	143	1.9	(NA)	(NA)

B Base figure too small to meet statistical standards of reliability. NA Not available. [1] Per 1,000 population. [2] Rates are infant deaths (under 1 year) per 1,000 live births. [3] Mortality data for 2003 is preliminary.
Source: U.S. National Center for Health Statistics. *Vital Statistics of the United States,* annual; and *National Vital Statistics Reports (NSVR)* and unpublished data. <http://www.cdc.gov/nchs/nvss.htm>.

Table 1300. **Population Characteristics by Area: 2000**

[As of April 1. Based on the Census of Population; see Appendix III. See Table 347 for land area. For definition of median, see Guide to Tabular Presentation]

Item	United States	Puerto Rico	Virgin Islands	Guam	American Samoa	Northern Mariana Islands
Total resident population	281,421,906	3,808,610	108,612	154,805	57,291	69,221
Percent increase, 1990-2000	13.2	8.1	6.7	16.3	22.5	59.7
Male	138,053,563	1,833,577	51,864	79,181	29,264	31,984
Female	143,368,343	1,975,033	56,748	75,624	28,027	37,237
Males per 100 females	96.3	92.8	91.4	104.7	104.4	85.9
Median age (years)	35.3	32.1	33.4	27.4	21.3	28.7
Marital status, persons 15 years and over	221,148,671	2,903,329	80,207	107,649	35,079	53,632
Never married	59,913,370	813,784	32,764	37,711	12,741	22,462
Now married, excludes separated	120,231,273	1,509,403	31,223	57,505	19,519	28,224
Separated	4,769,220	104,897	2,639	1,453	437	916
Widowed	14,674,500	197,123	4,078	4,253	1,570	1,121
Divorced	21,560,308	278,122	9,503	6,727	812	909
Households and families:						
Households	105,480,101	1,261,325	40,648	38,769	9,349	14,055
Family households (families) [1]	71,787,347	1,004,080	26,636	32,367	8,706	9,407
With own children under 18 years	34,588,368	486,409	14,107	19,678	6,297	6,569
Married-couple family	54,493,232	682,804	13,498	22,693	6,596	6,445
With own children under 18 years	24,835,505	337,190	5,905	13,964	5,261	4,526
Female household, no husband present	12,900,103	268,476	10,132	6,284	1,398	1,663
With own children under 18 years	7,561,874	131,584	6,450	3,753	640	1,106
Nonfamily households	33,692,754	257,245	14,012	6,402	643	4,648
Average household size	2.59	2.98	2.64	3.89	6.05	3.66
Average family size	3.14	3.41	3.34	4.27	6.24	4.16

[1] Includes other family types, not shown separately.
Source: U.S. Census Bureau, United States and Puerto Rico: DP-1, "Profile of General Demographic Characteristics: 2000 (area)" and DP-2, "Profile of Selected Social Characteristics Characteristics: 2000 (area)"; Virgin Islands, Guam, and Northern Mariana Islands: "Population and Housing Profile: 2000 (area)". See Internet sites: <http://www.census.gov/population/www/cen2000/islandareas.html> and <http://www.census.gov/census2000/states/pr.html>.

Puerto Rico and the Island Areas 845

Table 1301. **Public Elementary and Secondary Schools by Area: 2002**

[For school year ending in year shown, unless otherwise indicated. (2,152,724 represents $2,152,724,000)]

Item	Puerto Rico	Guam	Virgin Islands	American Samoa	Item	Puerto Rico	Guam	Virgin Islands	American Samoa
Enrollment, fall					School staff				
Elementary (kinder-					Teachers	42,369	(NA)	1,502	943
garten–grade 8). . . .	415,715	(NA)	12,438	10,317	Student support				
Secondary (grades					staff.	3,838	(NA)	107	81
9–12 and post					Other support				
graduates)	167,151	(NA)	5,400	4,146	services staff.	17,868	(NA)	596	153
Staff, fall					Current expendi-				
School district staff. . .	74,553	(NA)	3,036	1,735	tures [1] ($1,000).	2,152,724	(NA)	107,343	46,192

NA Not available [1] Public elementary and secondary day schools.

Source: U.S. National Center for Education Statistics, *Digest of Education Statistics*, annual; and unpublished data. See Internet site <http://nces.ed.gov/edstats>.

Table 1302. **Puerto Rico—Summary: 1980 to 2004**

[3,184.0 represents 3,184,000]

Item	Unit	1980	1990	1995	2000	2001	2002	2003	2004
POPULATION									
Total [1]	1,000	3,184.0	3,512.4	3,641.1	3,808.0	3,827.5	3,849	3,869	3,887
Persons per family	Number. . . .	4.3	3.7	3.5	3.4	3.4	3.4	3.3	3.3
EDUCATION [2]									
Enrollment, total.	1,000	941.4	953.0	932.7	971.4	993.3	1,067.1	1,172.3	1,007.5
Public (except public									
colleges or universities)	1,000	716.1	651.2	621.4	612.3	610.8	603.5	596.3	584.9
Private schools.	1,000	95.2	145.8	145.9	183.7	197.5	272.9	376.2	215.8
College and university	1,000	130.1	156.0	165.4	175.4	185.0	190.7	199.8	206.8
Expenses	Mil. dol. . . .	825.0	1,686.4	2,555.8	4,254.1	4,646.6	4,740.6	4,962.3	5,174.7
As percent of GNP	Percent. . .	7.5	7.8	9.0	10.3	10.5	10.5	10.5	10.3
Public	Mil. dol.. . . .	612.2	1,054.2	1,689.4	3,160.4	3,298.9	3,429.6	3,617.0	3,809.6
Private	Mil. dol.. . . .	212.8	644.2	866.4	1,093.7	1,105.1	1,311.0	1,345.3	1,365.1
LABOR FORCE [3]									
Total [4]	1,000	907	1,124	1,219	1,303	1,293	1,330	1,378	1,392
Employed [5]	1,000	753	963	1,051	1,159	1,158	1,170	1,211	1,234
Agriculture [6]	1,000	38	36	34	24	22	23	25	26
Manufacturing	1,000	143	168	172	159	159	139	136	139
Trade	1,000	138	185	211	239	242	240	257	259
Government	1,000	184	222	232	249	251	261	274	275
Unemployed	1,000	154	161	168	143	135	160	167	158
Unemployment rate [7]	Rate.	17.0	14.0	14.0	11.0	10.5	12.0	12.1	11.4
Compensation of employees	Mil. dol. . . .	7,200	13,639	17,773	23,504	24,389	25,080	26,726	28,282
Average compensation.	Dollar	9,563	14,854	16,911	20,280	21,061	21,436	22,069	22,919
Salary and wages	Mil. dol.. . . .	7,200	13,639	17,773	23,504	24,389	21,859	23,214	24,488
INCOME [8]									
Personal income:									
Current dollars	Mil. dol.. . . .	11,002	21,105	27,378	38,856	41,079	42,039	44,745	46,762
Constant (1954) dollars	Mil. dol.. . . .	3,985	5,551	6,547	8,491	8,714	8,852	9,268	9,564
Disposable personal income:									
Current dollars	Mil. dol.. . . .	10,403	19,914	25,591	36,239	38,405	39,251	41,649	43,610
Constant (1954) dollars	Mil. dol.. . . .	3,768	5,238	6,119	7,919	8,147	8,265	8,626	8,919
Average family income:									
Current dollars	Dollar	14,858	22,232	26,316	34,693	36,491	36,285	35,859	37,990
Constant (1954) dollars	Dollar	5,381	5,847	6,293	7,581	7,741	7,818	7,905	8,120
BANKING [9]									
Assets	Mil. dol.. . . .	10,223	27,902	39,859	58,813	55,701	66,294	74,315	94,427
TOURISM [8]									
Number of visitors	1,000	2,140	3,426	4,087	4,566	4,908	4,364	4,402	4,889
Visitor expenditures	Mil. dol.. . . .	619	1,366	1,828	2,388	2,728	2,486	2,677	3,024
Average per visitor	Dollar	289	399	447	523	556	570	608	619
Net income from tourism	Mil. dol.. . . .	202	383	499	615	663	645	678	733

[1] 1980, 1990, and 2000 enumerated as of April 1; all other years estimated as of July 1. [2] Enrollment for the first school month. Expenses for school year ending in year shown. "Public" includes: Public Preschool, Public Elementary, Public Intermediate, Public High School, Public Post-High School, Public Technological, Public Adult Education, Public Vocational Education, and Public Special Education. "College and university" includes both public and private colleges and universities. [3] Annual average of monthly figures. For fiscal years. [4] For population 16 years old and over. [5] Includes other employment not shown separately. [6] Includes forestry and fisheries. [7] Percent unemployed of the labor force. [8] For fiscal years. [9] As of June 30. Does not include federal savings banks and international banking entities.

Source: Puerto Rico Planning Board, San Juan, PR, *Economic Report of the Governor*, annual. <http://www.gobierno.pr /gprportal/inicio>.

846 Puerto Rico and the Island Areas

Table 1303. Puerto Rico—Gross Product and Net Income: 1990 to 2004

[In millions of dollars (21,619 represents $21,619,000,000). For fiscal years ending June 30. Data for 2004 are preliminary]

Item	1990	1995	2000	2001	2002	2003	2004
Gross product..............	21,619	28,452	41,419	44,047	45,073	47,438	50,320
Agriculture	434	318	529	348	277	314	435
Manufacturing	12,126	17,867	24,079	29,037	31,243	32,501	34,076
Contract construction and mining [1] ... [2]	720	1,006	1,875	1,802	1,648	1,614	1,741
Transportation & other public services [2] ...	2,468	3,276	4,237	4,698	4,948	5,205	5,350
Trade............	4,728	5,989	8,340	8,339	8,623	9,005	9,582
Finance, insurance, real estate	3,896	5,730	9,977	11,294	11,212	12,425	13,024
Services...............	3,015	4,724	6,603	6,982	7,079	7,257	7,899
Government	3,337	4,440	5,478	5,992	6,303	7,006	7,389
Commonwealth............	2,884	3,793	4,601	5,084	5,364	6,006	6,362
Municipalities...........	453	647	877	908	939	1,000	1,027
Rest of the world	-8,985	-14,195	-20,283	-25,162	-26,552	-27,396	-28,522
Statistical discrepancy...........	-121	-703	585	717	292	-493	-654
Net income	17,941	23,653	32,610	34,582	35,852	38,483	41,189
Agriculture	486	442	669	613	544	585	715
Manufacturing	11,277	16,685	22,348	27,390	29,454	30,625	32,169
Mining	26	30	41	45	41	42	43
Contract construction	679	903	1,691	1,578	1,439	1,411	1,522
Transportation & other public services [2] ...	1,778	2,360	2,968	3,159	3,389	3,534	3,642
Trade..............	3,420	4,108	5,752	5,730	5,960	6,141	6,608
Finance, insurance, and real estate	3,280	4,735	8,264	9,252	9,200	10,320	10,836
Services	2,643	4,146	5,682	5,986	6,074	6,215	6,787
Commonwealth government [3].	3,337	4,440	5,478	5,992	6,303	7,006	7,389
Rest of the world	-8,985	-14,195	-20,283	-25,162	-26,552	-27,396	-28,522

[1] Mining includes only quarries. [2] Includes other public utilities, and radio and television broadcasting. [3] Includes public enterprises not elsewhere classified.

Source: Puerto Rico Planning Board, San Juan, PR, *Economic Report of the Governor,* annual. <http://www.gobierno.pr/gprportal/inicio>

Table 1304. Puerto Rico—Transfer Payments: 1990 to 2004

[In millions of dollars (4,871 represents $4,871,000,000). Data represent transfer payments between federal and state governments and other nonresidents. See headnote, Table 1303]

Item	1990	1995	2000	2001	2002	2003	2004
Total receipts	4,871	6,236	8,659	9,317	9,818	10,451	10,618
Federal government	4,649	5,912	7,966	8,528	9,041	9,742	9,804
Transfers to individuals [1]	4,577	5,838	7,868	8,422	8,919	9,619	9,690
Veterans benefits.	349	440	491	490	516	517	520
Medicare.	368	661	1,196	1,262	1,433	1,929	1,998
Old age, disability, survivors (social security)	2,055	2,912	3,863	4,336	4,643	4,739	4,796
Nutritional assistance	880	1,063	1,193	1,208	1,194	1,237	1,241
Industry subsidies	72	74	98	106	123	123	115
U.S. state governments............	18	18	15	11	17	19	16
Other nonresidents............	205	307	679	778	760	690	797
Total payments..............	1,801	2,301	2,763	2,900	3,023	3,229	3,368
Federal government	1,756	2,132	2,693	2,845	2,919	3,085	3,248
Transfers from individuals...........	817	1,052	1,326	1,408	1,456	1,548	1,646
Contribution to Medicare.	97	162	191	205	227	227	258
Employee contribution for social security ..	720	888	1,133	1,200	1,227	1,317	1,383
Transfers from industries	16	49	51	52	64	58	49
Unemployment insurance	247	184	234	233	228	240	226
Employer contribution for social security	675	847	1,081	1,152	1,171	1,240	1,327
Other nonresidents [2]	45	164	70	55	104	144	121
Net balance	3,070	3,935	5,897	6,602	6,796	7,222	7,250
Federal government	2,893	3,780	5,273	5,868	6,123	6,657	6,557
U.S. state governments............	16	13	10	6	-32	-56	-21
Other nonresidents............	162	143	614	728	705	621	714

[1] Includes other receipts and payments not shown separately. [2] Includes U.S. state governments.

Source: Puerto Rico Planning Board, San Juan, PR, *Economic Report of the Governor,* annual. <http://www.gobierno.pr/gprportal/inicio>

Table 1305. Puerto Rico—Merchandise Imports and Exports: 1980 to 2004

[In millions of dollars (9,018 represents $9,018,000,000). Imports are imports for consumption; see text, Section 28]

Item	1980	1985	1990	1995	1997	1998	1999	2000	2001	2002	2003	2004
Imports......	9,018	10,162	16,200	18,969	21,928	21,706	26,697	27,199	27,690	30,511	35,945	37,252
From U.S....	5,345	6,130	10,792	12,213	13,904	13,318	15,949	15,171	14,718	15,675	16,949	18,124
From other...	3,673	4,032	5,408	6,756	8,024	8,388	10,754	11,834	12,972	14,824	18,996	19,128
Exports......	6,576	11,087	20,402	23,573	26,653	31,501	37,779	43,191	46,689	50,641	55,814	54,982
To U.S......	5,643	9,873	17,915	20,986	25,045	28,109	33,173	38,335	40,981	44,907	46,880	45,311
To other	933	1,214	2,487	2,587	1,608	3,392	4,785	4,856	5,708	5,734	8,934	9,671

Source: U.S. Census Bureau, *Foreign Commerce and Navigation of the United States,* annual; *U.S. Trade with Puerto Rico and U.S. Possessions, FT 895;* and, through 1985, *Highlights of U.S. Export and Import Trade, FT990;* thereafter, *FT920* supplement; <http://www.census.gov/foreign-trade/statistics/index.html>.

Table 1306. **Puerto Rico—Economic Summary by Industry: 2002**

[In millions of dollars, (13,980.1 represents $13,980,100,000). Covers establishments with payroll. Employees are for the pay period including March 12. See headnote, Table 739. Based on the County Business Patterns. This annual series is used as a benchmark for statistical series, surveys, and databases between economic censuses. For a description of County Business Patterns; see Appendix III]

Industry	1987 SIC code [1]	Total number of establishments	Number of employees	Annual payroll (mil.dol.)
Total industry....................	(X)	45,642	691,110	13,980.1
Construction industries [2]...........	C	2,251	56,306	957.3
General contractors and operative builders	15	743	27,593	465.7
Manufacturing [2]..................	D	1,893	118,212	3,223.8
Food and kindred products...........	20	267	13,979	310.5
Tobacco products.................	21	5	1,453	36.9
Textile mill products...............	22	21	544	10.5
Apparel and other textile products......	23	175	10,991	145.7
Lumber & wood products............	24	90	1,163	16.2
Furniture and fixtures..............	25	121	1,453	23.8
Paper and allied products...........	26	39	1,971	48.0
Printing and publishing.............	27	189	5,358	156.5
Chemicals and allied products........	28	158	34,189	1,317.8
Petroleum and coal products.........	29	29	1,217	43.7
Rubber and miscellaneous plastic products	30	61	3,636	78.9
Leather and leather products.........	31	15	1,489	20.5
Stone, clay, and glass products.......	32	159	4,403	105.6
Fabricated metal products...........	34	211	5,310	113.8
Industrial machinery and equipment....	35	74	4,771	148.9
Electronic and other electronic equipment	36	75	13,305	289.3
Transportation equipment...........	37	26	1,149	20.2
Instruments and related products......	38	61	9,183	270.5
Miscellaneous manufacturing products...	39	63	1,427	27.7
Wholesale trade [2]................	F	2,747	40,525	1,184.9
Durable goods..................	50	1,552	17,975	517.3
Nondurable goods................	51	1,179	21,782	640.7
Retail trade [2]..................	G	14,455	170,761	2,163.2
Building materials, garden supplies.....	52	908	8,181	167.0
General merchandise stores..........	53	442	21,915	278.4
Food stores....................	54	1,936	28,098	301.7
Automotive dealers and service stations..	55, ex. 554	2,130	17,311	302.4
Gasoline service stations...........	554	1,013	5,192	54.4
Apparel and accessory stores.........	56	1,860	18,074	199.3
Furniture and home furnishings........	57	1,130	8,600	135.1
Eating and drinking places...........	58	3,241	45,420	432.2
Drug stores & proprietary stores.......	591	790	9,473	153.1
Miscellaneous retail...............	59, ex. 591	2,731	19,773	307.2
Service industries [2]..............	I	16,807	218,067	3,948.6
Arrangement of passenger transportation..	472	292	1,797	26.7
Hotels, paradores & motels..........	701	217	13,985	264.7
Personal services................	72	970	5,130	70.0
Business services................	73	2,024	58,406	912.8
Auto repair, services, and parking......	75	1,250	6,022	91.1
Miscellaneous repair services........	76	442	3,509	64.6
Motion pictures.................	78	189	2,163	27.8
Amusement and recreation services.....	79	377	3,364	57.3
Dental laboratories...............	80	5,242	52,302	984.0
Legal services..................	81	1,366	5,914	148.4
Engineering and management services....	87, ex. 872	1,968	18,773	485.6

X Not Applicable.   [1] 1987 Standard Industrial Classification (SIC) code; see text, Section 12.   [2] Includes other industries not shown separately.

Source: U.S. Census Bureau, *County Business Patterns, Puerto Rico,* series CBP/02-53. See also <http://www.census.gov/prod/2005pubs/cbp02-53.pdf> (released May 2005).

Table 1307. **Puerto Rico—Farms and Market Value of Agricultural Products Sold: 2002**

[581,544 represents $581,544,000]

Type of product	Number of farms	Market value ($1,000)	Average value per farm (dol.)	Type of product	Number of farms	Market value ($1,000)	Average value per farm (dol.)
Total.............	17,659	581,544	32,932	Horticultural specialties...	471	66,519	141,229
Crops, including horti-				Grasses other crops	499	11,012	22,069
cultural specialties.......	14,101	250,429	(NA)				
Sugarcane...........	24	614	25,603	Livestock, poultry, and			
Coffee..............	9,108	42,095	4,622	their products..........	5,098	331,115	64,950
Pineapples...........	39	5,754	147,547	Cattle and calves	3,353	36,507	10,888
Plantains............	5,498	47,460	8,632	Poultry and poultry			
Bananas............	3,456	14,426	4,174	products..........	923	78,784	85,357
Grains.............	935	5,471	5,851	Dairy products	363	194,194	534,971
Root crops or tubers	2,236	8,610	3,850	Hogs and pigs........	1,083	9,728	8,983
Fruits and coconuts	3,884	17,940	4,619	Sheep and goats.......	456	680	1,491
Vegetables or melons....	1,288	30,528	23,702	Other	706	11,221	15,893

NA Not available.

Source: U.S. Dept. of Agriculture, National Agricultural Statistics Service, *2002 Census of Agriculture, Volume 1, Geographic Area Series Part 52,* (AC-02-A-52); http://www.nass.usda.gov/census/census02/puertorico/cenpr02.pdf.

Table 1308. Puerto Rico—Agricultural Summary: 1998 and 2002

[1 cuerda = .97 acre]

All farms	Unit	1998	2002	All farms	Unit	1998	2002
Farms	Number. . .	19,951	17,659	Average size of farm			
Farm land.	Cuerdas . .	865,478	690,687	by operator:			
Average size of farm . .	Cuerdas . .	43.4	39.1	Full owners	Cuerdas . .	29.3	26.8
				Part owners	Cuerdas . .	111.7	96.3
Approximate land area . .	Cuerdas . .	2,254,365	2,254,365	Tenants.	Cuerdas . .	75.9	61.1
Proportion in farms . . .	Percent . . .	38.4	30.6	Farms by type of			
				organization:			
Farms by size:				Individual or family . . .	Number. . .	17,887	15,843
Less than 10 cuerdas .	Number. . .	7,759	7,943	Partnership	Number. . .	211	162
10 to 19 cuerdas	Number. . .	4,473	3,847	Corporation	Number. . .	437	595
20 to 49 cuerdas	Number. . .	4,023	3,228	Other	Number. . .	1,416	1,059
50 to 99 cuerdas	Number. . .	1,792	1,282	Farms by value of sales:			
100 to 174 cuerdas . . .	Number. . .	809	590	Less than $1,200	Number. . .	3,307	3,977
175 to 259 cuerdas . . .	Number. . .	421	281	$1,200 to $2,499	Number. . .	3,633	3,471
260 cuerdas or more . .	Number. . .	674	488	$2,500 to $4,499	Number. . .	3,900	3,044
				$5,000 to $7,499	Number. . .	2,408	1,575
Tenure of operator:				$7,500 to $9,999	Number. . .	1,233	1,087
Operators	Number. . .	19,951	17,659	$10,000 to $19,999 . . .	Number. . .	2,366	1,781
Full owners.	Number. . .	15,620	13,693	$20,000 to $39,999. . .	Number. . .	1,247	1,062
Part owners	Number. . .	2,207	2,330	$40,000 to $59,999. . .	Number. . .	405	375
Tenants	Number. . .	2,124	1,636	$60,000 or more	Number. . .	1,452	1,287

Source: U.S. Department of Agriculture, National Agricultural Statistics Service, *2002 Census of Agriculture-Geographic Area Series Part 52, Puerto Rico,* Volume 1, Series AC-02-A-52.

Table 1309. Guam, Virgin Islands, and Northern Mariana Islands—Economic Summary: 2002

[**Sales and payroll in millions of dollars (4,592 represents $4,592,000,000).** Based on the 2002 Economic Census; see Appendix III. Selected kinds of businesses displayed]

Item	Guam	Virgin Islands	Northern Mariana Islands	Item	Guam	Virgin Islands	Northern Mariana Islands
Total: Establishments:	2,926	2,615	1,276	Paid employees [1]	1,920	1,028	849
Sales	4,592	3,961	1,832	Retail trade:			
Annual payroll	846	669	382	Establishments	632	680	297
Paid employees [1]	43,104	28,660	32,790	Sales	1,250	1,217	312
Construction: Establish-				Annual payroll	123	128	29
ments.	244	190	63	Paid employees [1]	7,402	6,653	2,916
Sales	262	286	50	Services:			
Annual payroll	54	91	11	Establishments	(X)	(X)	(X)
Paid employees [1]	3,136	3,050	1,013	Sales	(X)	(X)	(X)
Manufacturing:				Annual payroll	(X)	(X)	(X)
Establishments	49	63	78	Paid employees [1]	(X)	(X)	(X)
Sales	116	173	666	Accommodation & Food			
Annual payroll	32	27	185	Service			
Paid employees [1]	1,155	1,058	16,941	Establishments	392	313	151
Wholesale trade:				Sales	630	331	197
Establishments	187	74	78	Annual payroll	169	92	47
Sales	516	263	123	Paid employees [1]	11,199	5,639	4,304
Annual payroll	43	28	9				

X Not applicable.   [1] For pay period including March 12.
Source: U.S. Census Bureau, *2002 Economic Census of Puerto Rico and the Island Areas; IA02-00A-Guam, IA02-00A-VI, and IA02-00A-NMI.* (Accessed: 18 July 2005); <http://www.census.gov/econ/census02/guide/islandareas.htm>.

Table 1310. Federal Direct Payments: 2003

[In thousands of dollars (5,477,373 represents $5,477,373,000). For fiscal years ending September 30]

Selected program payments	Puerto Rico	Guam	Virgin Islands	American Samoa	Northern Mariana Islands
Direct payments to individuals for retirement and disability [1]	5,477,373	206,531	145,757	40,988	22,320
Social Security:					
Retirement insurance	2,237,235	65,600	83,630	10,571	5,324
Survivors insurance	988,982	27,637	22,451	10,759	4,405
Disability insurance	1,498,216	14,276	17,194	9,825	1,206
Federal retirement and disability:					
Civilian [2]	210,870	58,215	14,942	1,619	5,551
Military.	81,673	28,450	4,582	3,276	1,400
Veterans benefits:					
Service-connected disability. . . .	246,926	9,518	1,498	3,970	516
Other	176,320	1,911	632	886	71
Other direct payments [1].	2,846,715	91,511	106,793	12,216	14,507
Medicare:					
Hospital insurance	566,063	807	14,190	-	-
Supplemental medical insurance . .	995,566	609	10,937	-	-
Food stamp payments	-	53,437	18,494	5,604	7,103
Other	809,966	14,878	8,720	6,612	7,391

- Represents zero or rounds to zero.   [1] Includes other payments, not shown separately.   [2] Includes retirement and disability payments to former U.S. Postal Service employees.
Source: U.S. Census Bureau, *Consolidated Federal Funds Report for Fiscal Year, 2003* (issued September 2004). See also <http://www.census.gov/govs/www/cffr03.html>.

726 STATISTICS OF PRINCIPAL COUNTRIES.

No. 298.—SAVINGS BANKS, INCLUDING POSTAL SAVINGS BANKS: Number of Depositors, Amount of Deposits, and Average Deposits per Deposit Account and per Inhabitant, by Specified Countries.

[Latest data taken from the official reports of the respective countries.]

Country.	Population.	Date of report.	Number of depositors.	Deposits.	Average deposit account.	Average deposit per inhabitant.
				Dollars.	Dollars.	Dollars.
Austria	27,497,000	Dec. 31,1906–7 ª.	5,856,001	1,114,558,951	190.32	40.53
Belgium ᵇ	7,169,000	Dec. 31,1907	2,528,207	162,840,157	64.41	22.71
Bulgaria	4,028,000	Dec. 31,1904	124,007	2,723,182	24.95	.68
Chile	3,400,000	June 30, 1908	198,419	22,876,142	115.29	6.73
Denmark ᶜ	2,600,000	Mar. 31,1907	1,240,739	192,274,881	154.97	73.96
Egypt	11,296,000	Dec. 31,1907	74,179	1,928,749	26.00	.17
France	39,260,000	Dec. 31,1906	12,462,900	921,150,000	73.91	23.46
Algeria	5,232,000	....do......	18,851	878,001	46.58	.17
Tunis	1,898,000	Dec. 31,1907	5,415	1,080,413	199.52	.57
Germany	60,746,000	Dec. 31,1905	17,947,538	3,016,719,512	168.09	49.88
Luxemburg	246,000	Dec. 31,1907	61,049	10,443,220	171.06	42.45
Hungary	20,469,000	Dec. 31,1906	1,632,450	391,666,881	239.93	19.13
Italy	33,910,000	Dec. 31,1907	ᵈ 6,953,078	667,645,797	96.02	19.69
Japan	49,319,000	{Dec. 31,1906 } {Mar. 31,1908 }	ᵉ14,471,560	99,289,016	6.86	2.01
Formosa	3,152,000	{Dec. 31,1906 } {Mar. 31,1907 }	ᶠ 74,635	754,453	10.11	.24
In China and Korea		{Dec. 31,1906 } {Mar. 31,1907 }	ᶠ 61,611	910,889	14.71	
Netherlands	5,672,000	Dec. 31,1906–7 ª.	1,658,985	93,214,669	56.19	16.43
Dutch East Indies	37,020,000	Dec. 31,1906–7 ᶢ.	66,523	5,359,446	80.55	.14
Curaçao	53,000	Dec. 31,1906	1,979	37,604	19.00	.71
Dutch Guiana	78,000	....do......	6,825	261,405	40.06	3.35
Norway	2,321,000	....do......	826,873	108,124,517	130.76	46.59
Roumania ᵇ	6,684,000	Mar. 31,1907	191,070	11,335,516	59.33	1.70
Russia (including Asiatic part).	143,442,000	June 30, 1908	6,376,996	595,598,312	93.40	4.07
Finland	2,934,000	Dec. 31,1907	313,524	38,602,900	123.13	13.16
Spain ⁱ	19,566,000	Dec. 31,1907	469,491	53,553,238	114.07	2.74
Sweden	5,337,000	....do......	1,988,336	187,233,225	94.17	35.08
Switzerland ʲ	3,100,000	1900	1,300,000	193,000,000	148.46	62.26
United Kingdom	44,100,000	Nov.–Dec.,1907ᵏ	12,474,807	1,020,279,595	81.79	23.14
British colonies:						
British India	231,856,000	Mar. 31,1907	1,190,220	47,909,092	40.25	.21
Australian Commonwealth.	4,222,000	1907	1,267,349	215,729,838	170.22	51.10
New Zealand	942,000	Dec. 31,1907	364,422	62,413,169	171.27	66.26
Canada ˡ	6,572,000	Mar. 31,1907	208,234	62,541,892	300.34	9.52
British South Africa	5,341,000	1907	191,754	22,153,520	115.53	4.15
British West Indies	1,736,000	....do......	82,665	5,764,788	69.74	3.32
British colonies, n.e.s.	15,152,000	....do......	194,197	11,852,534	61.03	.78
Total foreign countries.	809,260,000	....	92,884,679	9,342,705,324	100.58	11.54
United States ᵐ	87,496,000	June 30, 1908	8,705,848	3,660,553,945	420.47	41.84
Philippine Islands	8,000,000	....do......	5,389	515,997	95.75	.08
Grand total	904,756,000	....	101,595,916	13,003,775,266	128.00	14.37

ª Figures for private savings banks relate to the end of the calendar year 1906; figures for the postal savings banks relate to the end of 1907, inclusive of deposits in the so-called cheque departments of the Austrian postal savings banks.

ᵇ Data for the state-controlled "Caisse Generale d'Epargne," includes savings deposits with post-offices. In addition, reports are given for three municipal and five private savings banks. On Dec. 31, 1906, the former had 16,461 depositors credited with $1,840,556 of deposits, and the latter 26,584 depositors with $7,896,692 of deposits.

ᶜ Exclusive of 1,597 deposits, amounting to $147,354, held in savings banks in the Faroe Islands. Includes data for savings departments of ordinary banks, which included 141,097 accounts credited with $33,991,526 on Mar. 31, 1907.

ᵈ Exclusive of data for the "Società Ordinarie di credito," and "Società Cooperative di credito," which held savings deposits to the amount of $137,013,060 under date of Dec. 31, 1906.

ᵉ Figures for private savings banks relate to the end of the calendar year 1906; figures for the postal savings banks relate to Mar. 31, 1908.

ᶠ Figures for private savings banks relate to the end of the calendar year 1906; figures for the postal savings banks relate to Mar. 31, 1907.

ᵍ Figures for private savings banks relate to the end of the calendar year 1906; figures for the postal savings banks relate to the end of 1907.

ʰ Figures for the "Case de economie" only.

ⁱ Includes savings deposits in ordinary banks. The "peseta" has been converted at the rate of 17.3 cents. Data taken from "España Economica y Financiera," Sept. 5, 1908.

ʲ Estimates of M. Guillaume de Fatio in the "Journal de Statistique Suisse, 1900, No. 4."

ᵏ Figures for trustee savings banks relate to the year ending Nov. 20; figures for the postal savings banks to Dec. 31.

ˡ Exclusive of data for special private savings banks, which on Mar. 31, 1908, held deposits amounting to $28,574,954. This total does not include the savings deposits in chartered banks ("deposits payable after notice or on a fixed day"), which on Sept. 30, 1908, amounted to $410,332,819.

ᵐ Includes deposits in savings departments of commercial banks in Illinois.

Source: Statistical Abstract of the United States: 1908 Edition.

Comparative International Statistics

U.S. Census Bureau, Statistical Abstract of the United States: 2006

Section 30
Comparative International Statistics

This section presents statistics for the world as a whole and for many countries on a comparative basis with the United States. Data are shown for population, births and deaths, social and industrial indicators, finances, agriculture, communication, and military affairs.

Statistics of the individual nations may be found primarily in official national publications, generally in the form of yearbooks, issued by most of the nations at various intervals in their own national languages and expressed in their own or customary units of measure. (For a listing of selected publications, see Guide to Sources.) For handier reference, especially for international comparisons, the United Nations Statistics Division compiles data as submitted by member countries and issues a number of international summary publications, generally in English and French. Among these are the *Statistical Yearbook*; the *Demographic Yearbook*; *International Trade Statistics Yearbook*; *National Accounts Statistics: Main Aggregates and Detailed Tables*; *Population and Vital Statistics Reports* (quarterly); the *Monthly Bulletin of Statistics*; and the *Energy Statistics Yearbook*. Specialized agencies of the United Nations also issue international summary publications on agricultural, labor, health, and education statistics. Among these are the *Production Yearbook* and *Trade Yearbook* issued by the Food and Agriculture Organization, the *Yearbook of Labour Statistics* issued by the International Labour Office, *World Health Statistics* issued by the World Health Organization, and the *Statistical Yearbook* issued by the Educational, Scientific, and Cultural Organization.

The U.S. Census Bureau presents estimates and projections of basic demographic measures for countries and regions of the world in the *World Population Reports* (WP) series. The *International Population Reports* (Series IPC), and *International Briefs* (Series IB) also present population figures for many foreign countries. Detailed population statistics are also available from the Census Bureau's International Data Base (http:// www.census.gov/ipc/www/idbnew.html>.

The International Monetary Fund (IMF) and the Organization for Economic Cooperation and Development (OECD) also compile data on international statistics. The IMF publishes a series of reports relating to financial data. These include *International Financial Statistics, Direction of Trade*, and *Balance of Payments Yearbook*, published in English, French, and Spanish. The OECD publishes a vast number of statistical publications in various fields such as economics, health, and education. Among these are *OECD in Figures, Main Economic Indicators, Economic Outlook, National Accounts, Labour Force Statistics, OECD Health Data*, and *Education at a Glance.*

Statistical coverage, country names, and classifications—Problems of space and availability of data limit the number of countries and the extent of statistical coverage shown. The list of countries included and the spelling of country names are based almost entirely on the list of sovereign nations, dependencies, and areas of special sovereignty provided by the U.S. Department of State.

In recent years, several important changes took place in the status of the world's nations. In 1990, a unified Germany was formed from the Federal Republic of Germany (West) and the German Democratic Republic (East). The Republic of Yemen was formed by union of the Yemen Arab Republic and the People's Democratic Republic of Yemen. Also in 1990, Namibia, once a United Nations mandate, realized its independence from South Africa.

In 1991, the Soviet Union broke up into 15 independent countries: Armenia, Azerbaijan, Belarus, Estonia, Georgia, Kazakhstan, Kyrgyzstan, Latvia, Lithuania, Moldova, Russia, Tajikistan, Turkmenistan, Ukraine, and Uzbekistan.

In the South Pacific, the Marshall Islands, Micronesia, and Palau gained full independence from the U.S. in 1991.

Following the breakup of the Socialist Federal Republic of Yugoslavia in 1992, the United States recognized Bosnia and Herzegovina, Croatia, Slovenia, and The Former Yugoslav Republic of Macedonia as independent countries.

The Treaty of Maastricht created the European Union (EU) in 1992 with 12 member countries. The EU is not a state intended to replace existing states, but it is more than just an international organization. Its Member States have set up common institutions to which they delegate some of their sovereignty so that decisions on specific matters of joint interest can be made democratically at a European level. This pooling of sovereignty is also called "European integration." The EU has grown in size with successive waves of accessions in 1995 and 2004. The 25 current member of the EU are: Austria, Belgium, Cyprus, Czech Republic, Denmark, Estonia, Finland, France, Germany, Greece, Hungary, Ireland, Italy, Latvia, Lithuania, Luxembourg, Malta, Poland, Portugal, Slovakia, Slovenia, Spain, Sweden, The Netherlands, and the United Kingdom.

In 1992, the EU decided to go for economic and monetary union (EMU), involving the introduction of a single European currency managed by a European Central Bank. The single currency—the euro— became a reality on 1 January 2002, when euro notes and coins replaced national currencies in 12 of the then 15 countries of the European Union (Belgium, Germany, Greece, Spain, France, Ireland, Italy, Luxembourg, The Netherlands, Austria, Portugal, and Finland). Since then, 10 countries have become members of the EU, but have yet to adopt the euro as their national currency.

On January 1, 1993, Czechoslovakia was succeeded by two independent countries: the Czech Republic and Slovakia. Eritrea announced its independence from Ethiopia in April 1993 and was subsequently recognized as an independent nation by the United States. In May of 2002, East Timor won independence from Indonesia, making it the world's newest independent state.

The population estimates and projections used in Tables 1311, 1312, 1314, 1315, and 1318 were prepared by the Census Bureau. For each country, the data on population, by age and sex, fertility, mortality, and international migration were evaluated and, where necessary, adjusted for inconsistencies and errors in the data. In most instances, comprehensive projections were made by the component method, resulting in distributions of the population by age and sex and requiring an assessment of probable future trends of fertility, mortality, and international migration.

Economic associations—The Organization for European Economic Co-Operation (OEEC), a regional grouping of Western European countries established in 1948 for the purpose of harmonizing national economic policies and conditions, was succeeded on September 30, 1961, by the Organization for Economic Cooperation and Development (OECD). The member nations of the OECD are Australia, Austria, Belgium, Canada, Czech Republic, Denmark, Finland, France, Germany, Greece, Hungary, Iceland, Ireland, Italy, Japan, Luxembourg, Mexico, the Netherlands, New Zealand, Norway, Poland, Portugal, Slovakia, South Korea, Spain, Sweden, Switzerland, Turkey, the United Kingdom, and the United States.

Quality and comparability of the data—The quality and comparability of the data presented here are affected by a number of factors:

(1) The year for which data are presented may not be the same for all subjects for a particular country or for a given subject for different countries, though the data shown are the most recent available. All such variations have been noted. The data shown are for calendar years except as otherwise specified.

(2) The bases, methods of estimating, methods of data collection, extent of coverage, precision of definition, scope of territory, and margins of error may vary for different items within a particular country, and for like items for different countries. Footnotes and headnotes to the tables give a few of the major time-periods and coverage qualifications

attached to the figures; considerably more detail is presented in the source publications. Many of the measures shown are, at best, merely rough indicators of magnitude.

(3) Figures shown in this section for the United States may not always agree with figures shown in the preceding sections. Disagreements may be attributable to the use of differing original sources, a difference in the definition of geographic limits (the 50 states, conterminous United States only, or the United States including certain outlying areas and possessions), or to possible adjustments made in the United States' figures by other sources in order to make them more comparable with figures from other countries.

International comparisons of national accounts data—In order to compare national accounts data for different countries, it is necessary to convert each country's data into a common unit of currency, usually the U.S. dollar. The market exchange rates, which are often used in converting national currencies, do not necessarily reflect the relative purchasing power in the various countries. It is necessary that the goods and services produced in different countries be valued consistently if the differences observed are meant to reflect real differences in the volumes of goods and services produced. The use of purchasing power parities (see Table 1328) instead of exchange rates is intended to achieve this objective.

The method used to present the data shown in Table 1328 is to construct volume measures directly by revaluing the goods and services sold in different countries at a common set of international prices. By dividing the ratio of the gross domestic products of two countries expressed in their own national currencies by the corresponding ratio calculated at constant international prices, it is possible to derive the implied purchasing power parity (PPP) between the two currencies concerned. PPPs show how many units of currency are needed in one country to buy the same amount of goods and services that one unit of currency will buy in the other country. For further information, see *National Accounts, Main Aggregates, Volume I,* issued annually by the Organisation for Economic Cooperation and Development, Paris, France.

International Standard Industrial Classification—The original version of the International Standard Industrial Classification of All Economic Activities (ISIC) was adopted in 1948. Wide use has been made both nationally and internationally in classifying data according to kind of economic activity in the fields of production, employment, national income, and other economic statistics. A number of countries have utilized the ISIC as the basis for devising their industrial classification scheme.

Substantial comparability has been attained between the industrial classifications of many other countries, including the United States and the ISIC by ensuring, as far as practicable, that the categories at detailed levels of classification in national schemes fitted into only one category of the ISIC. The United Nations, the International Labour Organization, the Food and Agriculture Organization, and other international bodies have utilized the ISIC in publishing and analyzing statistical data. Revisions of the ISIC were issued in 1958, 1968, and 1989.

International maps—A series of regional world maps is provided on pages 854–860. References are included in Table 1314 for easy location of individual countries on the maps. The Robinson map projection is used for this series of maps. A map projection is used to portray all or part of the round Earth on a flat surface, but this cannot be done without some distortion. For the Robinson projection, distortion is very low along the Equator and within 45 degrees of the center but is greatest near the poles. For additional information on map projections and maps, please contact the Earth Science Information Center, U.S. Geological Survey, 507 National Center, Reston, VA 22092.

U.S. Census Bureau, Statistical Abstract of the United States: 2006

World

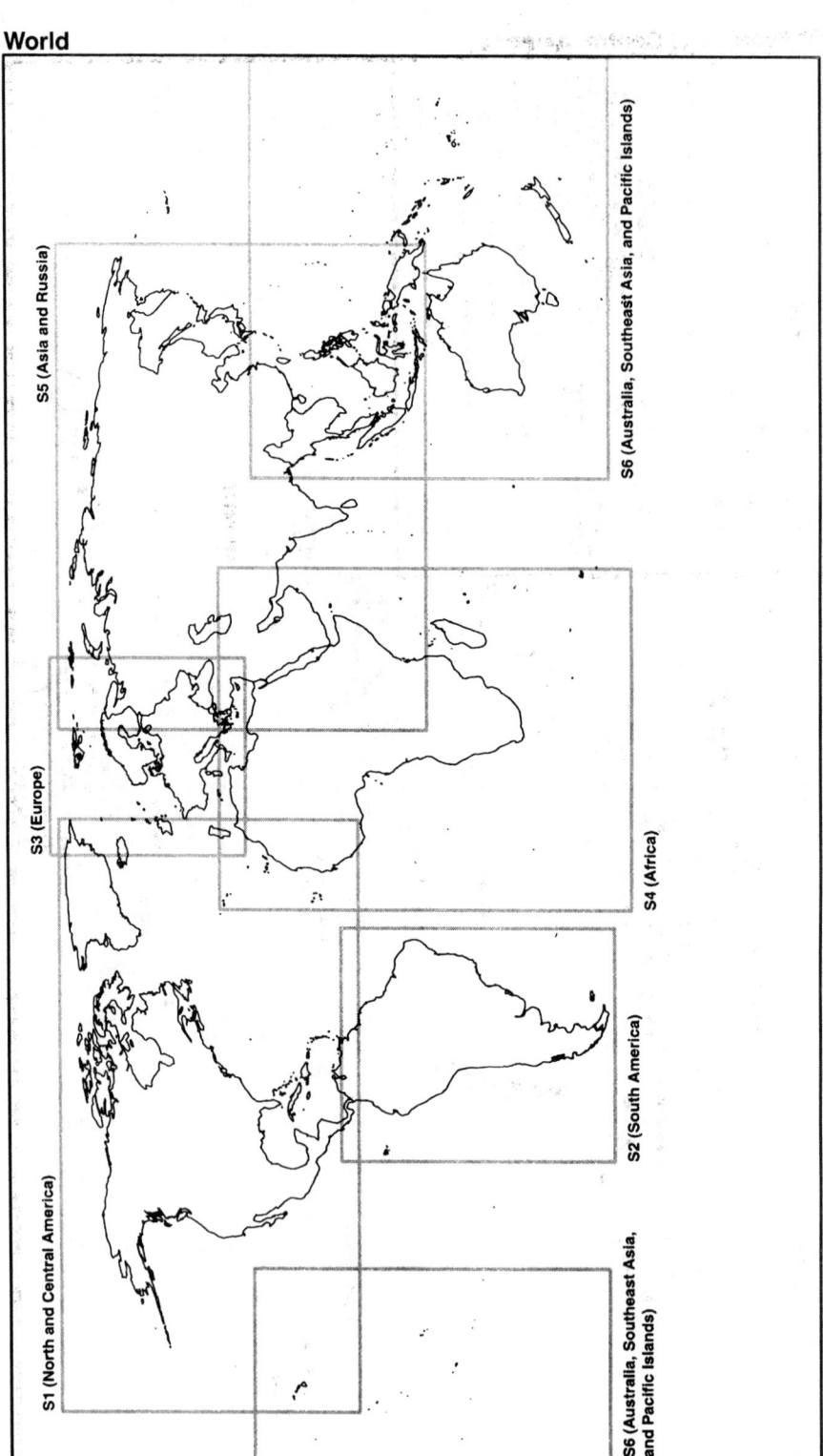

S5 (Asia and Russia)

S6 (Australia, Southeast Asia, and Pacific Islands)

S3 (Europe)

S4 (Africa)

S1 (North and Central America)

S2 (South America)

S6 (Australia, Southeast Asia, and Pacific Islands)

INSET

Atlantic Ocean

The Bahamas

Cuba

Haiti

Jamaica

Caribbean Sea

Gulf of Mexico

United Kingdom (part) (Turks and Caicos Islands)

Dominican Republic

United States (part) (Puerto Rico)

United States (U.S. Virgin Islands)

United Kingdom (part) (British Virgin Islands)

United Kingdom (part) (Anguilla)

Barbuda

Antigua

Dominica

St. Lucia

Grenada

Tobago

Trinidad

Barbados

St. Vincent

St. Kitts and Nevis

United Kingdom (part) (Montserrat)

France (part) (Guadeloupe)

France (part) (Martinique)

Netherlands (part) (Bonaire)

Netherlands (part) (Aruba)

Netherlands (part) (Curaçao)

United Kingdom (part) (Cayman Islands)

Denmark (part) (Greenland)

France (part) (St. Pierre and Miquelon)

United Kingdom (part) (Bermuda)

Atlantic Ocean

SEE INSET

Arctic Ocean

Canada

United States (part)

Gulf of Mexico

Mexico

Belize

Guatemala

El Salvador

Honduras

Nicaragua

Costa Rica

Panama

United States (part) (Alaska)

Pacific Ocean

United States (part) (Hawaii)

U.S. Census Bureau, Statistical Abstract of the United States: 2006

S2 (South America)

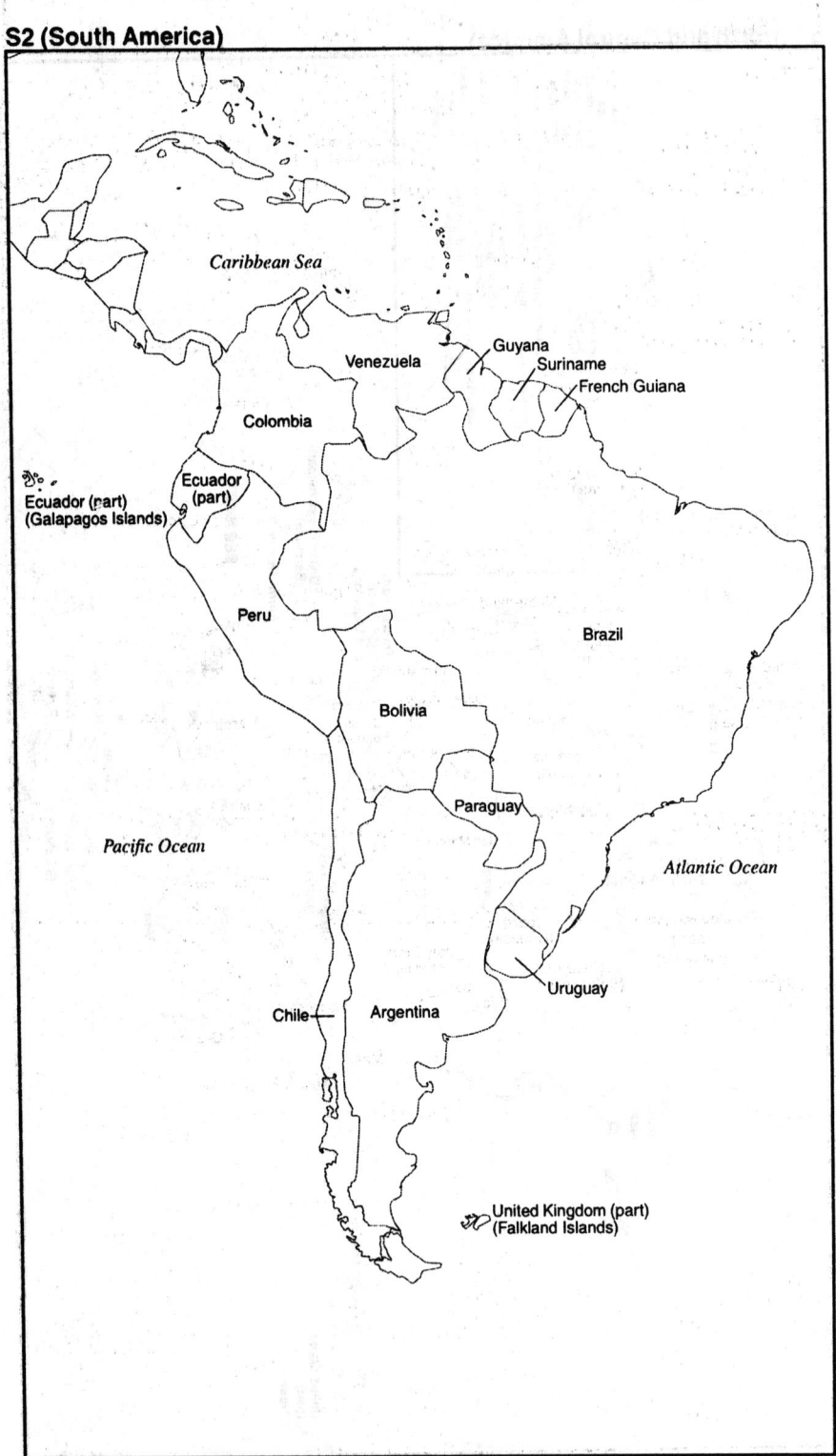

Caribbean Sea

Venezuela

Guyana
Suriname
French Guiana

Colombia

Ecuador (part)
(Galapagos Islands)

Ecuador
(part)

Peru

Brazil

Bolivia

Pacific Ocean

Paraguay

Atlantic Ocean

Uruguay

Chile

Argentina

United Kingdom (part)
(Falkland Islands)

U.S. Census Bureau, Statistical Abstract of the United States: 2006

Norway (part)
(Svalbard)

Arctic Ocean

Iceland

Denmark (part)
(Faroe Islands)

Finland

Norway
(part)

Sweden

Estonia

United Kingdom (part)
(Isle of Man)

Denmark
(part)

Latvia

Russia
(part)

Lithuania

Ireland

Netherlands
(part)

United
Kingdom
(part)

Belarus

United Kingdom (part)
(Guernsey)

Germany

Poland

Ukraine

United Kingdom (part)
(Jersey)

Luxembourg

Belgium

Czech
Republic

Moldova

France
(part)

Switzerland

Slovakia

Atlantic
Ocean

Liechtenstein

Austria

Slovenia

Hungary

Romania

Bosnia &
Herzegovina

Black Sea

San Marino

Croatia

Spain
(part)

Andorra

Monaco

Italy
(part)

Serbia &
Montenegro

United Kingdom
(part)
(Gibraltar)

France
(part)
(Corsica)

Albania

Bulgaria

Portugal
(part)

Spain (parts)
(Balearic Is.)

Italy (part)
(Sardinia)

Italy (part)
(Sicily)

Macedonia

Greece

Malta

Mediterranean Sea

U.S. Census Bureau, Statistical Abstract of the United States: 2006

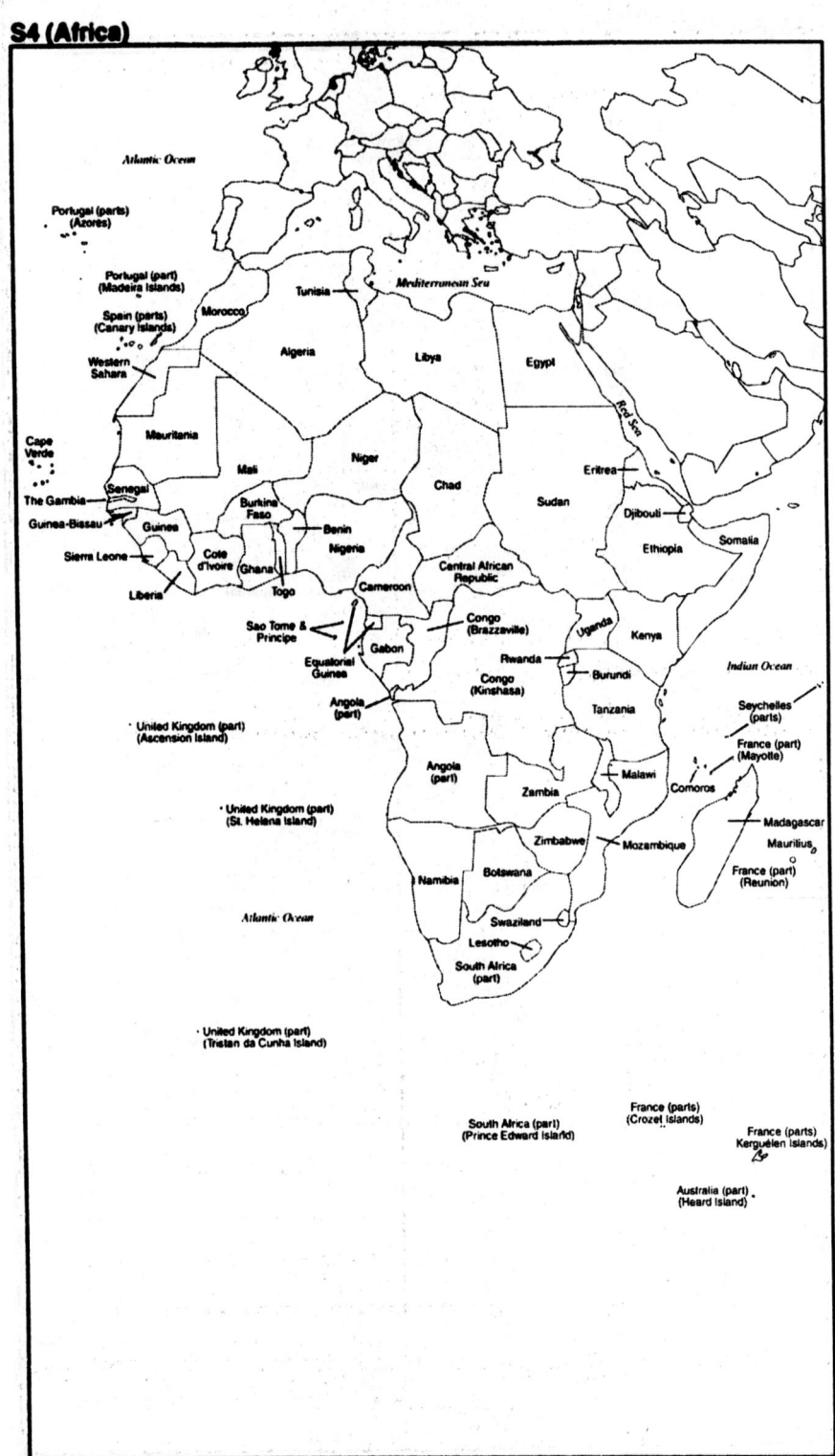

S5 (Asia and Russia)

Arctic Ocean

Pacific Ocean

Russia
(part)

Mongolia

North Korea
South Korea
Japan

Taiwan

Hong Kong
Macau
China (part)
(Hainan)

China
(part)

Bhutan

Bangladesh

Sri
Lanka

Indian Ocean

Nepal

India

Maldives

Kazakhstan

Kyrgyzstan

Uzbekistan

Tajikistan

Turkmenistan

Afghanistan

Pakistan

Caspian Sea

Iran

Azerbaijan

Yemen (part)
(Socotra)

Oman

United Arab
Emirates

Georgia

Armenia

Iraq

Kuwait

Bahrain

Qatar

Saudi
Arabia

Yemen
(part)

Black Sea

Turkey

Syria

Jordan

Red Sea

Cyprus

Lebanon
West Bank
Gaza Strip
Israel

U.S. Census Bureau, Statistical Abstract of the United States: 2006

S6 (Australia, Southeast Asia, and Pacific Islands)

United States (part)
(Midway Islands)

United States (part)
(Johnston Atoll)

Pacific Ocean

Kiribati (parts)

United States (part)
(Jarvis Island)

Kiribati (parts)

France (parts)
(French
Polynesia)

United
Kingdom (part)
(Pitcairn
Islands)

France (parts)
(French Polynesia)

France (parts)
(French Polynesia)

New Zealand (part)
(Cook Islands)

United States (part)
(Howland Island)
United States (part)
(Baker Island)
Kiribati (part)

New Zealand (part)
(Tokelau)

Samoa
United States (part)
(American Samoa)

Niue

Tonga

United States (part)
(Wake Island)

Federated States of Micronesia

Marshall Islands

Nauru

Kiribati (parts)

Tuvalu

France (part)
(Wallis and Futuna)

Fiji

Vanuatu

France (part)
(New Caledonia)

New Zealand
(part)

United States (part)
(Northern Mariana
Islands)
United States (part)
(Guam)

Palau

Philippines

Solomon
Islands

Papua New Guinea

Australia
(part)

Australia
(part)

Burma
Laos
Thailand
Vietnam
Cambodia
Malaysia
Singapore
Brunei

East Timor

Indonesia

Indian Ocean

U.S. Census Bureau, Statistical Abstract of the United States: 2006

Figure 30.1
Net Additions to the World: 2005
In 2005, the world gained 2⅓ people per second

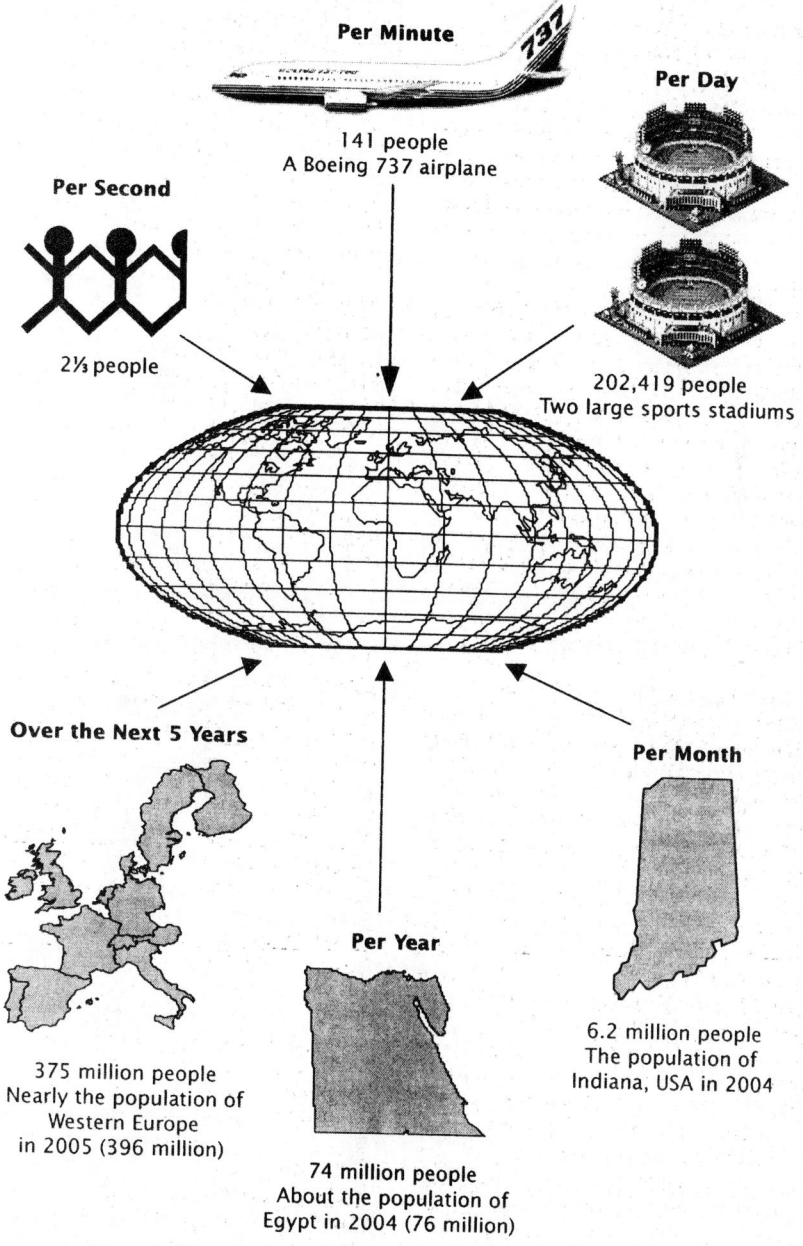

Per Minute

141 people
A Boeing 737 airplane

Per Day

Per Second

2⅓ people

202,419 people
Two large sports stadiums

Over the Next 5 Years

Per Month

Per Year

6.2 million people
The population of
Indiana, USA in 2004

375 million people
Nearly the population of
Western Europe
in 2005 (396 million)

74 million people
About the population of
Egypt in 2004 (76 million)

Source: U.S. Census Bureau, International Programs Center, International Database and
unpublished tables.

Table 1311. Total World Population: 1980 to 2050

[As of midyear (4,453 represents 4,453,000,000)]

Year	Population (mil.)	Average annual[1] Growth rate (percent)	Average annual[1] Population change (mil.)	Year	Population (mil.)	Average annual[1] Growth rate (percent)	Average annual[1] Population change (mil.)
1980.....	4,453	1.7	76.0	2015......	7,203	1.0	73.8
1985.....	4,852	1.7	83.4	2020......	7,563	0.9	69.2
1990.....	5,283	1.6	84.1	2025......	7,898	0.8	63.6
1995.....	5,694	1.4	79.0	2030......	8,206	0.7	58.9
2004.....	6,377	1.2	74.2	2035......	8,493	0.6	54.8
2005.....	6,451	1.2	74.4	2040......	8,759	0.6	50.7
2006.....	6,525	1.1	74.6	2045......	9,004	0.5	46.1
2010.....	6,826	1.1	75.7	2050......	9,224	(NA)	(NA)

NA Not available. [1] Represents change from year shown to immediate succeeding year.

Source: U.S. Census Bureau, International Data Base, "Total Midyear Population for the World: 1950-2050," updated 26 April 2005; <http://www.census.gov/ipc/www/world.html>.

Table 1312. Population by Continent: 1980 to 2050

[In millions, except percent (4,453 represents 4,453,000,000). As of midyear]

Year	World	Africa	North America	South America	Asia	Europe	Oceania
1980	4,453	472	371	242	2,652	694	23
1990	5,283	625	423	296	3,191	721	27
2000	6,082	798	485	348	3,689	730	31
2010	6,826	991	539	393	4,140	728	35
2020	7,563	1,210	593	431	4,571	720	38
2030	8,206	1,449	644	461	4,910	701	41
2040	8,759	1,707	691	481	5,161	676	43
2050	9,224	1,981	732	490	5,332	645	45
PERCENT DISTRIBUTION							
1980	100.0	10.6	8.3	5.4	59.6	15.6	0.5
2000	100.0	13.1	8.0	5.7	60.7	12.0	0.5
2050	100.0	21.5	7.9	5.3	57.8	7.0	0.5

Source: U.S. Census Bureau, "International Data Base" (as of 26 April 2005); <http://www.census.gov/ipc/www/idbnew.html>.

Table 1313. Population and Population Change, by Development Status: 1950 to 2051

[In millions, except percent (2,557 represents 2,557,000,000). As of midyear. Minus sign (-) indicates decrease. The "less developed" countries include all of Africa, all of Asia except 'Japan, the Transcaucasian and Central Asian republics of the New Independent States, all of Latin America and the Caribbean, and all of Oceania except Australia and New Zealand. This category matches the "less developed country" classification employed by the United Nations]

Year	Number World	Number Less developed countries	Number More developed countries	Percent of world Less developed countries	Percent of world More developed countries
POPULATION					
1950	2,557	1,750	807	68.4	31.6
1960	3,041	2,131	910	70.1	29.9
1970	3,709	2,706	1,003	73.0	27.0
1980	4,453	3,372	1,081	75.7	24.3
1990	5,283	4,140	1,143	78.4	21.6
2000	6,082	4,888	1,193	80.4	19.6
2010	6,826	5,602	1,224	82.1	17.9
2020	7,563	6,320	1,243	83.6	16.4
2030	8,206	6,957	1,249	84.8	15.2
2040	8,759	7,513	1,246	85.8	14.2
2050	9,224	7,989	1,235	86.6	13.4
POPULATION CHANGE					
1950-1960...........	484	381	104	78.6	21.4
1960-1970...........	668	575	93	86.1	13.9
1970-1980...........	744	666	78	89.6	10.4
1980-1990...........	830	768	62	92.5	7.5
1990-2000...........	799	748	50	93.7	6.3
2000-2010...........	744	714	31	95.9	4.1
2010-2020...........	737	719	19	97.4	2.6
2020-2030...........	643	637	6	99.0	1.0
2030-2040...........	553	555	-3	100.5	-0.5
2040-2050...........	465	476	-11	102.3	-2.3

Source: U.S. Census Bureau, "International Data Base" (as of 26 April 2005); <http://www.census.gov/ipc/www/idbnew.html>.

Table 1314. Population by Country: 1990 to 2010

[5,282,766 represents 5,282,766,000. Population data generally are de facto figures for the present territory. Population estimates were derived from information available as of fall 2004. See text of this section for general comments concerning the data. For details of methodology, coverage, and reliability, see coverage; and reliability, see source. Minus sign (-) indicates decrease]

Country or area	Map reference	Mid-year population (1,000)				Population rank, 2004	Annual rate of growth,[1] 2000-2010 (percent)	Population per sq. mile, 2004	Area (sq. mile)
		1990	2000	2004	2010, proj.				
World	S0	5,282,766	6,081,528	6,376,863	6,825,750	(X)	1.2	126	50,580,305
Afghanistan	S5	14,669	23,898	28,514	34,505	38	3.7	114	250,000
Albania	S3	3,251	3,474	3,545	3,660	128	0.5	335	10,579
Algeria	S4	25,093	30,409	32,129	34,555	37	1.3	35	919,591
Andorra	S3	53	67	70	74	202	1.0	401	174
Angola	S4	8,291	10,443	11,521	13,262	69	2.4	24	481,351
Antigua and Barbuda	S1	63	66	68	71	204	0.6	402	170
Argentina	S2	33,022	37,498	39,145	41,405	31	1.0	37	1,056,637
Armenia	S5	3,377	3,043	2,991	2,967	133	-0.3	260	11,506
Australia	S6	17,022	19,165	19,913	20,925	52	0.9	7	2,941,285
Austria	S3	7,723	8,113	8,175	8,214	89	0.1	256	31,942
Azerbaijan	S5	7,200	7,748	7,868	8,221	91	0.6	235	33,436
Bahamas, The	S1	257	290	300	311	176	0.7	77	3,888
Bahrain	S4	500	634	678	737	162	1.5	2,836	239
Bangladesh	S5	109,897	130,407	141,340	159,765	8	2.0	2,734	51,703
Barbados	S1	263	273	278	284	178	0.4	1,673	166
Belarus	S3	10,215	10,367	10,311	10,294	78	-0.1	129	80,154
Belgium	S3	9,969	10,264	10,348	10,423	77	0.2	887	11,672
Belize	S1	191	248	274	314	179	2.4	31	8,803
Benin	S4	4,676	6,628	7,438	8,731	95	2.8	174	42,710
Bhutan	S5	1,598	2,005	2,186	2,476	142	2.1	120	18,147
Bolivia	S2	6,574	8,153	8,724	9,499	86	1.5	21	418,683
Bosnia and Herzegovina	S3	4,424	4,035	4,346	4,622	120	1.4	220	19,741
Botswana	S4	1,264	1,607	1,639	1,637	147	0.2	7	226,012
Brazil	S2	151,084	175,553	184,101	195,580	5	1.1	56	3,265,061
Brunei	S6	258	336	365	408	174	1.9	179	2,035
Bulgaria	S3	8,894	7,818	7,518	7,149	92	-0.9	176	42,683
Burkina Faso	S4	8,336	11,309	13,093	15,667	64	3.3	124	105,714
Burma	S5	39,655	44,702	46,520	48,844	26	0.9	183	253,954
Burundi	S4	5,505	6,621	7,516	9,281	93	3.4	759	9,903
Cambodia	S5	9,355	12,466	13,396	14,912	62	1.8	197	68,154
Cameroon	S4	11,779	15,234	16,637	18,780	58	2.1	92	181,251
Canada	S1	27,791	31,278	32,508	34,253	35	0.9	9	3,560,219
Cape Verde	S1	349	401	415	431	172	0.7	267	1,556
Central African Republic	S4	3,084	3,935	4,172	4,567	121	1.5	17	240,533
Chad	S4	6,023	8,316	9,377	11,170	82	3.0	19	486,178
Chile	S2	13,128	15,153	15,824	16,720	60	1.0	55	289,912
China[2]	S5	1,148,364	1,268,853	1,298,848	1,347,563	1	0.6	361	3,600,930
Colombia	S2	32,859	39,686	42,311	46,109	28	1.5	106	401,042
Comoros	S4	429	578	652	773	163	2.9	778	838
Congo (Brazzaville)[3]	S4	2,265	3,102	3,502	4,124	129	2.8	27	131,853
Congo (Kinshasa)[3]	S4	39,064	52,022	58,919	70,757	22	3.1	67	875,521
Costa Rica	S2	3,027	3,711	3,957	4,306	124	1.5	202	19,560
Cote d'Ivoire	S4	11,981	15,563	16,945	19,093	57	2.0	138	122,780
Croatia	S3	4,508	4,411	4,497	4,487	117	0.2	206	21,829
Cuba	S1	10,545	11,134	11,309	11,507	71	0.3	264	42,803
Cyprus	S5	681	758	776	801	159	0.5	217	3,568
Czech Republic	S3	10,310	10,270	10,246	10,202	79	-0.1	337	30,365
Denmark	S3	5,141	5,337	5,413	5,516	108	0.3	331	16,359
Djibouti	S4	366	431	467	526	166	2.0	55	8,486
Dominica	S1	73	72	69	70	203	-0.2	239	290
Dominican Republic	S1	7,078	8,386	8,916	9,735	85	1.5	477	18,680
East Timor	S6	746	847	1,019	1,153	156	3.1	181	5,641
Ecuador	S2	10,318	12,505	13,213	14,245	63	1.3	124	106,888
Egypt	S4	56,694	70,492	76,117	84,348	15	1.8	198	384,344
El Salvador	S1	5,100	6,123	6,588	7,293	99	1.7	823	8,000
Equatorial Guinea	S4	368	473	518	585	165	2.1	48	10,830
Eritrea	S4	2,996	4,357	4,554	5,278	116	1.9	97	46,842
Estonia	S3	1,569	1,380	1,342	1,291	151	-0.7	77	17,413
Ethiopia	S4	48,197	64,690	71,337	81,754	16	2.3	165	432,310
Fiji	S6	738	832	881	958	157	1.4	125	7,054
Finland	S3	4,986	5,169	5,215	5,255	111	0.2	44	117,942
France	S3	56,735	59,382	60,424	61,638	20	0.4	287	210,668
Gabon	S4	937	1,235	1,363	1,543	150	2.2	14	99,486
Gambia, The	S4	949	1,368	1,549	1,831	148	2.9	401	3,861
Georgia	S5	5,426	4,777	4,694	4,601	114	-0.4	174	26,911
Germany	S3	79,380	82,188	82,425	82,283	14	(Z)	609	135,236
Ghana	S4	15,399	19,658	21,483	24,258	50	2.1	242	88,811
Greece	S3	10,130	10,559	10,648	10,750	75	0.2	211	50,502
Grenada	S2	92	89	89	91	197	0.2	683	131
Guatemala	S1	8,001	10,626	11,735	13,405	68	2.3	280	41,865
Guinea	S4	6,279	8,639	9,234	10,758	83	2.2	97	94,927
Guinea-Bissau	S4	996	1,278	1,386	1,564	149	2.0	128	10,811
Guyana	S2	751	755	763	774	161	0.2	10	76,004
Haiti	S1	6,126	7,306	7,942	9,129	90	2.2	746	10,641
Honduras	S1	4,792	6,348	7,007	7,944	97	2.2	162	43,201
Hungary	S3	10,372	10,137	10,032	9,880	80	-0.3	281	35,653
Iceland	S1	255	281	294	309	177	0.9	8	38,707
India	S5	841,655	1,002,708	1,065,071	1,155,011	2	1.4	928	1,147,950
Indonesia	S6	188,005	224,138	238,453	258,825	4	1.4	341	699,548

See footnotes at end of table.

U.S. Census Bureau, Statistical Abstract of the United States: 2006

Table 1314. **Population by Country: 1990 to 2010—Con.**

[See headnote, page 863]

Country or area	Map refer-ence	Mid-year population (1,000)				Popu-lation rank, 2004	Annual rate of growth,[1] 2000-2010 (percent)	Popula-tion per sq. mile, 2004	Area (sq. mile)
		1990	2000	2004	2010, proj.				
Iran	S5	57,036	65,660	67,503	71,861	18	0.9	107	631,660
Iraq	S5	18,135	22,676	25,375	29,672	44	2.7	151	167,556
Ireland	S3	3,508	3,792	3,970	4,250	123	1.1	149	26,598
Israel	S4	4,512	5,842	6,199	6,645	100	1.3	790	7,849
Italy	S3	56,743	57,719	58,057	58,091	23	0.1	511	113,521
Jamaica	S1	2,348	2,615	2,712	2,843	137	0.8	649	4,181
Japan	S5	123,537	126,700	127,333	127,195	9	(Z)	835	152,411
Jordan	S4	3,262	4,999	5,611	6,486	105	2.6	159	35,344
Kazakhstan	S5	16,398	15,032	15,144	15,460	61	0.3	14	1,049,150
Kenya	S4	23,358	29,986	32,982	38,383	34	2.5	150	219,788
Kiribati	S6	71	92	101	115	195	2.3	364	277
Korea, North	S5	20,019	21,648	22,698	23,802	48	0.9	488	46,490
Korea, South	S5	42,869	47,351	48,426	49,568	24	0.5	1,277	37,911
Kuwait	S5	2,142	1,974	2,258	2,788	141	3.5	328	6,880
Kyrgyzstan	S5	4,382	4,851	5,081	5,509	112	1.3	66	76,641
Laos	S5	4,210	5,498	6,068	6,994	102	2.4	68	89,112
Latvia	S3	2,664	2,376	2,306	2,218	140	-0.7	93	24,903
Lebanon	S4	3,147	3,578	3,777	4,056	126	1.3	956	3,950
Lesotho	S4	1,722	2,038	2,039	1,983	144	-0.3	174	11,718
Liberia	S4	2,117	2,694	2,807	3,531	135	2.7	75	37,189
Libya	S4	4,140	5,115	5,632	6,447	104	2.3	8	679,359
Liechtenstein	S3	·29	32	33	35	213	0.8	538	62
Lithuania	S5	3,695	3,654	3,608	3,545	127	-0.3	143	25,174
Luxembourg	S3	383	439	463	498	167	1.3	464	998
Macedonia	S3	1,861	2,015	2,040	2,072	143	0.3	205	9,928
Madagascar	S4	11,522	15,506	17,502	20,993	56	3.0	78	224,533
Malawi	S4	9,287	11,258	12,407	14,309	65	2.4	342	36,324
Malaysia	S6	17,504	21,793	23,522	26,144	46	1.8	185	126,853
Maldives	S5	216	301	339	400	175	2.8	2,930	116
Mali	S4	8,084	10,072	11,126	13,000	72	2.6	24	471,042
Malta	S4	359	390	397	407	173	0.4	3,202	124
Marshall Islands	S6	46	53	58	66	208	2.2	826	70
Mauritania	S4	1,984	2,668	2,999	3,561	132	2.9	8	397,838
Mauritius	S4	1,074	1,179	1,220	1,280	153	0.8	1,710	714
Mexico	S1	84,914	99,927	104,960	112,469	11	1.2	141	742,486
Micronesia, Federated States of	S6	109	108	108	107	194	-0.1	399	271
Moldova	S5	4,398	4,431	4,446	4,535	118	0.2	342	13,012
Monaco	S3	30	32	32	33	214	0.4	41,790	1
Mongolia	S5	2,216	2,601	2,751	3,004	136	1.4	5	604,247
Morocco	S4	24,686	30,122	32,209	35,301	36	1.6	187	172,317
Mozambique	S4	12,656	17,768	19,112	20,673	54	1.5	63	302,737
Namibia	S4	1,471	1,906	2,014	2,077	145	0.9	6	317,873
Nauru	S6	9	12	13	14	223	1.9	1,580	8
Nepal	S5	19,325	24,702	27,071	30,758	40	2.2	513	52,819
Netherlands	S3	14,952	15,908	16,318	16,783	59	0.5	1,245	13,104
New Zealand	S6	3,360	3,820	3,994	4,228	122	1.0	39	103,734
Nicaragua	S2	3,684	4,932	5,360	5,990	109	1.9	115	46,430
Niger	S4	7,945	10,516	11,810	14,054	67	2.9	24	489,073
Nigeria	S4	88,510	114,307	125,744	145,032	10	2.4	358	351,649
Norway	S3	4,242	4,492	4,575	4,676	115	0.4	38	118,865
Oman	S5	1,773	2,533	2,903	3,523	134	3.3	35	82,031
Pakistan	S5	114,578	146,343	159,196	179,592	6	2.0	529	300,664
Palau	S6	15	19	20	22	219	1.4	113	177
Panama	S2	2,390	2,889	3,090	3,393	131	1.6	105	29,340
Papua New Guinea	S6	3,825	4,927	5,420	6,171	107	2.3	31	174,405
Paraguay	S2	4,236	5,586	6,191	7,162	101	2.5	40	153,398
Peru	S2	21,511	25,980	27,544	29,758	39	1.4	56	494,208
Philippines	S6	64,318	79,740	86,242	95,868	12	1.8	749	115,124
Poland	S3	38,119	38,654	38,580	38,464	32	(Z)	328	117,571
Portugal	S3	9,923	10,336	10,524	10,736	76	0.4	297	35,382
Qatar	S5	481	744	840	970	158	2.6	198	4,247
Romania	S5	22,866	22,452	22,356	22,181	49	-0.1	251	88,934
Russia	S5	147,974	146,732	143,974	140,771	7	-0.4	22	6,592,817
Rwanda	S4	6,924	7,507	8,239	9,523	88	2.4	855	9,633
Saint Kitts and Nevis	S1	41	39	39	40	212	0.4	279	139
Saint Lucia	S1	140	156	164	177	190	1.3	696	236
Saint Vincent and the Grenadines	S1	107	115	117	119	191	0.3	895	131
Samoa	S0	170	179	178	176	188	-0.2	162	1,100
San Marino	S3	23	27	29	31	215	1.3	1,230	23
Sao Tome and Principe	S4	119	160	182	219	187	3.1	490	371
Saudi Arabia	S4	16,061	23,153	25,796	29,222	43	2.3	31	829,996
Senegal	S4	7,844	10,324	11,426	13,109	70	2.4	154	74,131
Serbia and Montenegro	S3	9,935	10,850	10,826	10,839	74	(Z)	275	39,435
Seychelles	S4	73	79	81	83	198	0.4	459	176
Sierra Leone	S4	4,221	4,809	5,732	6,580	103	3.1	207	27,653
Singapore	S6	3,047	4,037	4,354	4,701	119	1.5	18,071	241
Slovakia	S3	5,263	5,400	5,424	5,470	106	0.1	288	18,842
Slovenia	S3	1,991	2,011	2,011	2,003	146	(Z)	257	7,819
Solomon Islands	S6	335	466	524	610	164	2.7	49	10,633
Somalia	S4	6,675	7,253	8,305	9,922	87	3.1	34	242,216
South Africa	S4	38,391	44,066	44,448	43,333	27	-0.2	94	471,444

See footnotes at end of table.

U.S. Census Bureau, Statistical Abstract of the United States: 2006

Country or area	Map refer- ence	Mid-year population (1,000) 1990	Mid-year population (1,000) 2000	Mid-year population (1,000) 2004	2010, proj.	Popu- lation rank, 2004	Annual rate of growth,[1] 2000- 2010 (percent)	Popula- tion per sq. mile, 2004	Area (sq. mile)
Spain.	S3	39,351	40,016	40,281	40,549	29	0.1	209	192,819
Sri Lanka	S5	17,193	19,239	19,905	20,832	53	0.8	796	24,996
Sudan	S4	26,627	35,080	39,148	45,485	30	2.6	43	917,375
Suriname	S2	395	429	437	441	170	0.3	7	62,344
Swaziland	S4	885	1,110	1,138	1,119	154	0.1	171	6,641
Sweden	S3	8,601	8,924	8,986	9,074	84	0.2	57	158,927
Switzerland	S3	6,837	7,267	7,451	7,623	94	0.5	485	15,355
Syria	S4	12,436	16,306	18,017	20,606	55	2.3	254	71,062
Tajikistan	S5	5,332	6,441	7,012	8,007	96	2.2	127	55,251
Tanzania	S4	25,138	33,065	36,071	40,382	33	2.0	105	342,100
Thailand	S5	55,197	61,863	63,731	66,303	19	0.7	323	197,595
Togo	S4	3,505	4,712	5,255	6,185	110	2.7	250	21,000
Tonga	S0	92	102	110	123	192	1.8	398	277
Trinidad and Tobago	S2	1,198	1,118	1,084	1,029	155	-0.8	547	1,981
Tunisia	S4	8,207	9,564	9,975	10,583	81	1.0	166	59,985
Turkey	S5	56,085	65,667	68,894	73,322	17	1.1	232	297,591
Turkmenistan	S5	3,668	4,518	4,863	5,431	113	1.8	26	188,456
Tuvalu	S6	9	11	11	13	224	1.5	1,142	10
Uganda	S4	17,074	23,249	26,390	32,500	42	3.4	342	77,108
Ukraine	S5	51,622	49,000	47,310	45,659	25	-0.7	203	233,089
United Arab Emirates	S5	1,951	2,369	2,524	2,763	138	1.5	78	32,278
United Kingdom	S3	57,493	59,522	60,271	61,285	21	0.3	646	93,278
United States	S1	250,132	282,339	293,028	309,163	3	0.9	83	3,539,227
Uruguay	S2	3,106	3,324	3,399	3,491	130	0.5	51	67,035
Uzbekistan	S5	20,624	24,756	26,410	29,280	41	1.7	153	172,741
Vanuatu	S6	154	190	203	221	184	1.5	36	5,699
Venezuela	S2	19,325	23,543	25,017	27,134	45	1.4	73	340,560
Vietnam	S5	67,283	79,060	82,663	87,814	13	1.1	658	125,622
Yemen	S5	12,416	17,479	20,025	24,637	51	3.4	98	203,849
Zambia	S4	7,942	10,117	11,026	12,497	73	2.1	39	285,992
Zimbabwe	S4	10,153	11,751	12,084	12,516	66	0.6	81	149,293
OTHER									
Taiwan[2]	S5	20,279	22,151	22,750	23,562	47	0.6	1,826	12,456
AREAS OF SPECIAL SOVEREIGNTY AND DEPENDENCIES									
American Samoa	S0	47	57	58	57	207	(Z)	754	77
Anguilla	S1	8	12	13	14	222	1.8	370	35
Aruba	S1	67	70	71	73	201	0.5	956	75
Bermuda	S1	58	63	65	67	206	0.7	3,432	19
Cayman Islands	S1	26	38	43	50	211	2.7	429	100
Cook Islands	S0	18	20	21	22	218	0.9	228	93
Faroe Islands	S3	47	45	47	48	210	0.6	86	541
French Guiana.	S2	116	173	191	214	185	2.1	6	34,421
French Polynesia	S0	202	249	266	291	181	1.5	188	1,413
Gaza Strip[4]	S4	643	1,132	1,325	1,651	152	3.8	9,007	147
Gibraltar	S3	29	28	28	28	216	0.2	12,015	2
Greenland	S1	56	56	56	56	209	(Z)	-	131,931
Guadeloupe	S1	378	426	445	468	169	0.9	654	680
Guam	S6	134	155	166	181	189	1.5	795	209
Guernsey	S3	63	64	65	66	205	0.3	868	75
Hong Kong	S5	5,688	6,659	6,855	7,090	98	0.6	17,952	382
Jersey	S3	84	89	91	92	196	0.3	2,003	45
Macau	S6	352	431	445	468	168	0.8	72,081	6
Man, Isle of.	S3	69	73	75	77	200	0.5	329	227
Martinique.	S1	374	415	430	448	171	0.8	1,050	409
Mayotte	S4	90	156	186	231	186	3.9	1,281	145
Montserrat	S1	11	6	9	10	225	4.3	239	39
Netherlands Antilles	S2	189	210	218	228	182	0.8	588	371
New Caledonia	S6	168	202	214	230	183	1.3	30	7,243
Northern Mariana Islands. . . .	S6	44	70	78	91	199	2.6	425	184
Puerto Rico.	S1	3,537	3,816	3,895	3,985	125	0.4	1,126	3,459
Reunion	S4	597	721	766	829	160	1.4	794	965
Saint Helena	S4	7	7	7	8	226	0.6	47	158
Saint Pierre and Miquelon . . .	S1	6	7	7	7	227	0.2	75	93
Turks and Caicos Islands. . . .	S1	12	18	20	24	220	3.0	120	166
Virgin Islands.	S1	104	109	109	108	193	-0.1	805	135
Virgin Islands, British	S1	16	20	22	25	217	2.0	383	58
Wallis and Futuna	S6	14	15	16	17	221	0.9	150	106
West Bank[4]	S4	1,255	2,020	2,311	2,765	139	3.1	1,061	2,178
Western Sahara	S4	191	245	267	301	180	2.1	3	102,703

- Represents or rounds to zero.   X Not applicable.   Z Less than 0.05 percent or less than one person per square mile.
[1] Computed by the exponential method. For explanation of average annual percent change, see Guide to Tabular Presentation.
[2] With the establishment of diplomatic relations with China on January 1, 1979, the U.S. government recognized the People's Republic of China as the sole legal government of China and acknowledged the Chinese position that there is only one China and that Taiwan is part of China.   [3] "Congo" is the official short-form name for both the Republic of Congo and the Democratic Republic of the Congo. To distinguish one from the other the U.S. Department of State adds the capital in parentheses. This practice is unofficial and provisional.   [4] The Gaza Strip and West Bank are Israeli-occupied with interim status subject to Israeli/Palestinian negotiations. The final status is yet to be determined.

Source: U.S. Census Bureau, "International Data Base" (as of 26 April 2005); <http://www.census.gov/ipc/www/idbnew.html>.

Comparative International Statistics 865

Table 1315. Age Distribution by Country: 2004 and 2010

[In percent. Covers countries with 5 million or more population in 2004]

Country or area	2004 Under 15 years old	2004 65 years old and over	2010, proj. Under 15 years old	2010, proj. 65 years old and over	Country or area	2004 Under 15 years old	2004 65 years old and over	2010, proj. Under 15 years old	2010, proj. 65 years old and over
World	28.2	7.2	26.5	7.7	Korea, South	19.7	8.5	16.6	10.4
Afghanistan	44.7	2.4	44.4	2.4	Kyrgyzstan	32.3	6.1	29.4	5.5
Algeria	29.9	4.6	24.8	5.0	Laos	41.9	3.2	40.5	3.1
Angola	43.8	2.8	43.4	2.7	Libya	34.2	4.1	32.9	4.4
Argentina	25.9	10.5	24.1	11.0	Madagascar	44.9	3.1	44.5	2.9
Australia	20.1	12.8	18.7	13.9	Malawi	46.6	2.7	46.2	2.7
Austria	15.9	16.0	14.3	18.1	Malaysia	33.3	4.5	31.0	5.1
Azerbaijan	27.0	7.8	24.5	6.9	Mali	48.0	3.0	48.4	3.0
Bangladesh	33.5	3.4	33.8	3.7	Mexico	31.6	5.5	28.7	6.4
Belarus	16.3	14.5	15.6	13.6	Morocco	32.6	4.9	29.6	5.2
Belgium	17.1	17.3	16.0	17.8	Mozambique	43.5	2.7	41.0	3.0
Benin	44.8	2.3	43.0	2.5	Nepal	39.4	3.6	37.3	3.9
Bolivia	36.4	4.5	32.1	4.9	Netherlands	18.3	13.9	17.2	15.2
Brazil	26.6	5.8	24.0	6.8	Nicaragua	38.1	3.0	33.1	3.4
Bulgaria	14.4	17.1	13.8	17.9	Niger	46.8	2.4	46.9	2.4
Burkina Faso	47.0	2.5	46.3	2.4	Nigeria	42.4	3.0	42.1	3.2
Burma	27.2	5.0	24.9	5.4	Pakistan	40.2	4.1	36.7	4.2
Burundi	46.6	2.6	46.1	2.5	Papua New Guinea	38.3	3.8	36.6	4.1
Cambodia	37.6	3.3	32.9	3.5	Paraguay	38.2	4.8	36.5	5.1
Cameroon	41.9	3.2	40.0	3.4	Peru	32.1	5.1	28.5	5.8
Canada	18.2	13.0	16.7	14.2	Philippines	35.8	3.9	33.2	4.4
Chad	48.0	2.8	47.5	2.7	Poland	16.7	13.1	14.8	13.5
Chile	25.8	7.8	22.7	9.2	Portugal	16.7	16.9	16.3	17.8
China [1]	22.3	7.5	19.6	8.3	Romania	16.2	14.4	15.5	14.7
Colombia	31.0	5.0	28.5	5.7	Russia	15.0	13.8	14.3	13.6
Congo (Kinshasa) [2]	47.6	2.5	46.7	2.5	Rwanda	42.1	2.6	42.6	2.4
Cote d'Ivoire	41.2	2.7	40.1	3.0	Saudi Arabia	38.3	2.3	38.0	2.5
Cuba	20.0	10.1	18.2	11.7	Senegal	41.6	3.0	39.1	3.3
Czech Republic	15.0	14.1	13.5	15.9	Serbia and Montenegro	18.3	14.9	17.5	15.0
Denmark	18.9	15.0	17.9	16.6	Sierra Leone	44.9	3.2	44.5	3.2
Dominican Republic	33.3	5.3	31.2	5.9	Slovakia	17.5	11.7	15.7	12.6
Ecuador	33.9	4.9	31.0	5.4	Somalia	44.7	2.7	45.0	2.5
Egypt	33.4	4.3	31.0	4.9	South Africa	30.9	5.0	27.6	5.8
El Salvador	36.8	5.1	35.0	5.4	Spain	14.4	17.6	14.5	18.4
Ethiopia	44.1	2.7	42.5	2.8	Sri Lanka	24.8	7.0	22.6	8.2
Finland	17.5	15.7	16.2	17.2	Sudan	43.7	2.3	40.7	2.7
France	18.5	16.4	18.0	16.7	Sweden	17.5	17.3	15.5	19.3
Germany	14.7	18.3	13.5	20.4	Switzerland	16.8	15.3	15.4	16.6
Ghana	39.8	3.5	37.0	3.6	Syria	38.0	3.3	35.5	3.4
Greece	14.5	18.6	14.2	19.4	Taiwan [1]	19.9	9.4	18.4	10.4
Guatemala	42.2	3.3	38.6	3.6	Tajikistan	39.2	4.7	36.9	4.1
Guinea	44.4	3.1	44.2	3.2	Tanzania	44.2	2.6	42.6	2.6
Haiti	42.9	3.4	41.6	3.3	Thailand	22.8	7.5	20.4	8.9
Honduras	41.0	3.3	37.4	3.7	Togo	43.0	2.6	41.3	2.8
Hong Kong	14.2	12.5	11.9	13.3	Tunisia	26.0	6.5	22.3	7.2
Hungary	16.0	14.9	14.8	16.0	Turkey	26.6	6.6	23.5	7.3
India	31.7	4.8	29.2	5.3	Uganda	50.2	2.2	49.4	2.1
Indonesia	29.4	5.1	27.6	5.8	Ukraine	15.0	15.8	13.3	15.9
Iran	28.2	4.9	23.4	5.1	United Kingdom	18.0	15.7	16.5	16.4
Iraq	40.3	3.0	38.5	3.0	United States	20.8	12.4	20.0	13.0
Israel	26.7	9.9	25.4	10.0	Uzbekistan	34.1	4.8	31.7	4.3
Italy	14.0	19.1	13.4	20.3	Venezuela	30.5	5.0	26.6	5.7
Japan	14.3	19.0	14.1	22.1	Vietnam	28.8	5.7	24.3	5.7
Jordan	35.2	3.7	30.5	4.3	Yemen	46.6	2.8	46.1	2.5
Kazakhstan	24.4	7.6	21.6	7.6	Zambia	46.7	2.4	45.6	2.3
Kenya	42.4	2.3	42.8	2.2	Zimbabwe	38.0	3.4	36.8	3.6
Korea, North	24.6	7.6	22.2	9.5					

[1] See footnote 2, Table 1314. [2] See footnote 3, Table 1314.

Source: U.S. Census Bureau, "International Data Base" (as of 26 April 2005); <http://www.census.gov/ipc/www/idbnew.html>.

U.S. Census Bureau, Statistical Abstract of the United States: 2006

Table 1316. **Foreign or Foreign-Born Population and Labor Force in Selected OECD Countries: 1990 and 2002**

[**33,383 represents 33,383,000.** In Australia and the United States, the data refer to people present in the country who are foreign born. In the European countries and Japan they generally refer to foreigners and represent the nationalities of residents]

Country	Foreign population [1]				Foreign labor force [2]			
	Number (1,000)		Percent of total population		Number (1,000)		Percent of total labor force	
	1990	2002	1990	2002	1990	2002	1990	2002
United States	(NA)	33,383	(NA)	11.8	11,565	20,964	9.4	14.6
Australia	(NA)	4,566	(NA)	23.2	(NA)	2,438	25.7	24.6
Austria	456	708	5.9	8.8	230	(NA)	7.4	(NA)
Belgium	905	850	9.1	8.2	289	(NA)	7.1	(NA)
Denmark	161	265	3.1	4.9	69	(NA)	2.4	(NA)
France	3,597	(NA)	6.3	(NA)	1,550	(NA)	6.2	(NA)
Germany	5,343	7,336	8.4	8.9	(NA)	(NA)	(NA)	(NA)
Italy	781	1,512	1.4	2.6	(NA)	(NA)	(NA)	(NA)
Japan	1,075	1,852	0.9	1.5	(NA)	(NA)	(NA)	(NA)
Luxembourg	113	171	29.4	38.1	85	(NA)	45.2	(NA)
Netherlands	692	700	4.6	4.3	197	(NA)	3.1	(NA)
Spain.	279	1,324	0.7	3.1	85	(NA)	0.6	(NA)
Sweden	484	474	5.6	5.3	246	(NA)	5.4	(NA)
Switzerland	1,100	1,447	16.3	19.9	670	(NA)	18.9	(NA)
United Kingdom	1,723	2,681	3.2	4.5	882	(NA)	3.3	(NA)

NA Not available. [1] Data are from population registers of foreigners except for France (census), the United Kingdom (Labour Force Survey), Australia (inter-and post-censal estimates), and the United States (Current Population Survey). [2] Includes unemployed except for Italy, Luxembourg, Netherlands, and United Kingdom. Data for Austria, Germany, and Luxembourg are from social security registers, and for Denmark, from the register of population. Data for Italy, Spain, and Switzerland are from residence or work permits. Figures for Japan and Netherlands are estimates. Data for other countries are from labor force surveys.

Source: Organization for Economic Cooperation and Development, Paris, France, *Trends in International Migration* (2004 Edition) (copyright).

Table 1317. **Medical Doctors and Inpatient Care—Selected Countries: 1990 to 2002**

Country	Medical doctors per 1,000 population			Inpatient care					
				Acute care beds per 1,000 population			Average length of stay (days)		
	1990	2000	2002	1990	2000	2002	1990	2000	2002
United States	1.8	2.2	(NA)	3.7	2.9	2.9	9.1	6.8	6.6
Australia	2.2	2.5	(NA)	(NA)	3.8	(NA)	(NA)	16.1	(NA)
Austria	2.2	3.2	3.3	7.1	6.3	6.1	12.8	8.6	8.1
Belgium	3.3	3.9	3.9	4.9	(NA)	(NA)	13.8	(NA)	(NA)
Canada	2.1	2.1	2.1	4.0	3.3	(NA)	13.0	(NA)	(NA)
Czech Republic	2.7	3.4	3.5	8.5	6.6	6.5	15.4	11.4	11.1
Denmark	2.9	3.2	3.3	4.1	3.5	(NA)	8.2	6.0	5.7
Finland	2.4	3.1	3.1	4.3	2.4	2.3	18.2	10.3	10.4
France	3.1	3.3	3.3	5.2	4.1	(NA)	15.1	13.2	(NA)
Germany	(NA)	3.3	3.3	(NA)	(NA)	(NA)	(NA)	(NA)	(NA)
Greece	3.4	4.5	(NA)	4.0	4.0	(NA)	9.9	(NA)	(NA)
Hungary	2.8	(NA)	3.2	7.1	6.3	5.9	12.6	8.9	8.5
Iceland	2.8	3.4	3.6	4.3	(NA)	(NA)	18.3	(NA)	(NA)
Ireland	(NA)	2.2	2.4	3.3	3.0	3.0	7.9	7.4	7.6
Italy	(NA)	4.1	4.4	6.2	4.3	(NA)	11.7	7.7	(NA)
Japan	1.7	1.9	2.0	(NA)	(NA)	(NA)	50.5	39.1	37.5
Korea, South	0.8	1.3	1.5	2.7	5.2	5.7	13.0	14.0	13.0
Luxembourg	2.0	2.5	2.6	6.8	5.9	5.8	17.6	(NA)	(NA)
Mexico	(NA)	1.4	1.5	(NA)	1.1	1.0	4.4	4.3	4.2
Netherlands	2.5	3.2	3.1	4.3	3.5	(NA)	34.1	33.4	(NA)
New Zealand	1.9	2.2	2.1	8.0	(NA)	(NA)	9.4	7.8	7.5
Norway	(NA)	2.9	(NA)	3.8	3.1	3.1	(NA)	8.9	8.4
Poland	2.1	2.2	2.3	6.3	5.1	4.6	12.5	8.9	7.9
Portugal	2.8	3.2	(NA)	3.4	3.3	(NA)	10.8	9.4	(NA)
Slovak Republic	(NA)	3.7	3.6	(NA)	5.9	5.5	(NA)	10.4	9.5
Spain	(NA)	3.1	2.9	3.3	2.8	(NA)	12.2	9.0	(NA)
Sweden	2.9	3.0	(NA)	4.1	2.4	(NA)	18.0	6.4	6.2
Switzerland	3.0	3.5	3.6	6.5	4.1	3.9	(NA)	12.8	12.7
Turkey	0.9	1.3	1.3	2.0	2.2	2.1	6.9	5.9	5.6
United Kingdom	1.5	2.0	2.1	2.8	3.9	3.9	15.7	8.4	8.1

NA Not available.

Source: Organization for Economic Cooperation and Development, Paris, France, *OECD Health Data 2004* (copyright).

Table 1318. Vital Statistics, by Country: 2004 and 2010

[Covers countries with 12 million or more population in 2004]

Country or area	Crude birth rate [1] 2004	Crude birth rate [1] 2010, proj.	Crude death rate [2] 2004	Crude death rate [2] 2010, proj.	Expectation of life at birth (years) 2004	Expectation of life at birth (years) 2010, proj.	Infant mortality rate [3] 2004	Infant mortality rate [3] 2010, proj.	Total fertility rate per woman [4] 2004	Total fertility rate per woman [4] 2010, proj.
United States	14.1	14.2	8.3	8.3	77.4	78.4	6.6	6.2	2.07	2.11
Afghanistan.	47.3	45.1	21.1	18.8	42.5	45.1	166.0	149.3	6.78	6.47
Algeria	17.8	16.7	4.6	4.7	72.7	74.3	32.2	25.7	2.04	1.76
Argentina	17.2	15.8	7.6	7.5	75.7	76.9	15.7	13.1	2.24	2.03
Australia	12.4	11.7	7.4	7.7	80.3	81.0	4.8	4.4	1.76	1.75
Bangladesh.	30.0	27.8	8.5	7.7	61.7	63.9	64.3	54.3	3.15	3.04
Brazil	17.3	15.5	6.1	6.3	71.4	73.0	30.7	24.9	1.97	1.81
Burkina Faso.	46.3	44.2	16.2	14.5	48.0	50.2	94.4	85.2	6.60	6.21
Burma	18.7	16.8	9.9	9.8	60.5	62.1	65.2	55.5	2.08	1.86
Cambodia.	27.0	26.5	9.2	8.6	58.6	60.9	73.0	61.0	3.51	3.10
Cameroon.	34.7	32.2	13.8	12.8	50.7	52.5	66.2	58.5	4.55	4.08
Canada	10.9	10.7	7.7	8.0	80.0	80.7	4.8	4.5	1.61	1.62
Chile	15.8	14.5	5.7	6.1	76.4	77.5	9.1	7.7	2.06	1.90
China [5].	13.0	14.3	6.9	7.1	72.0	73.8	25.3	19.4	1.69	1.80
Colombia	21.2	19.3	5.6	5.6	71.4	73.1	21.7	17.8	2.59	2.44
Congo (Kinshasa) [6]. .	44.4	42.3	13.8	12.3	50.7	52.9	92.6	80.9	6.62	6.11
Cote d'Ivoire	35.9	33.3	15.0	14.5	48.4	49.5	92.5	82.4	4.66	4.20
Ecuador	23.2	20.8	4.3	4.2	76.0	77.2	24.5	19.9	2.78	2.50
Egypt.	23.8	21.3	5.3	5.2	70.7	72.4	33.9	26.7	2.95	2.61
Ethiopia	39.3	35.6	15.3	14.1	48.7	49.8	96.9	86.9	5.44	4.76
France	12.3	11.5	9.1	9.4	79.4	80.3	4.3	4.0	1.85	1.83
Germany	8.5	8.2	10.4	11.0	78.5	79.4	4.2	4.0	1.38	1.42
Ghana	31.8	28.0	10.1	9.1	58.1	60.4	57.7	50.0	4.22	3.57
India	22.8	20.7	8.4	7.9	64.0	66.1	57.9	48.5	2.85	2.55
Indonesia	21.1	18.7	6.3	6.3	69.3	71.1	36.8	30.0	2.47	2.28
Iran	17.1	17.3	5.6	5.6	69.7	71.4	42.9	35.6	1.88	1.73
Iraq	33.1	29.4	5.7	4.9	68.3	70.3	52.7	42.2	4.40	3.76
Italy	9.1	8.0	10.2	10.8	79.5	80.3	6.1	5.4	1.27	1.32
Japan	9.6	8.7	8.8	10.0	81.0	81.6	3.3	3.2	1.38	1.42
Kazakhstan.	15.5	16.7	9.6	9.4	66.1	68.2	30.5	24.9	1.90	1.87
Kenya	40.2	35.3	15.2	11.2	47.2	53.5	63.6	51.8	4.98	4.38
Korea, North	16.8	13.8	7.0	7.5	71.1	72.7	24.8	20.5	2.20	1.90
Korea, South.	10.1	9.5	5.6	6.4	76.7	77.8	6.4	5.7	1.25	1.31
Madagascar	41.9	40.5	11.6	10.1	56.5	58.9	78.5	68.7	5.70	5.47
Malawi	43.8	41.9	19.9	18.2	41.2	42.8	97.9	87.9	6.04	5.66
Malaysia	23.4	22.1	5.1	5.1	72.0	73.6	18.4	15.0	3.10	2.92
Mexico	21.4	19.4	4.7	4.8	74.9	76.3	21.7	17.8	2.49	2.31
Morocco	22.8	20.6	5.7	5.4	70.4	72.1	43.3	34.7	2.81	2.46
Mozambique	36.5	33.3	20.6	22.4	40.9	38.5	132.0	121.9	4.78	4.29
Nepal.	32.0	28.8	9.7	8.7	59.4	61.7	68.8	58.7	4.29	3.73
Netherlands	11.4	10.3	8.7	8.8	78.7	79.6	5.1	4.7	1.66	1.66
Nigeria	40.9	39.5	17.4	15.9	46.5	48.6	100.4	90.9	5.57	5.33
Pakistan	31.2	26.9	8.7	7.5	62.6	64.9	74.4	63.1	4.29	3.46
Peru	21.3	18.9	6.3	6.2	69.2	71.0	33.0	27.2	2.61	2.32
Philippines	25.8	23.2	5.5	5.2	69.6	71.4	24.2	20.2	3.22	2.89
Poland	9.6	10.0	9.7	10.1	74.7	75.9	7.4	6.7	1.23	1.29
Romania	10.7	10.4	11.7	11.9	71.1	72.7	27.2	22.1	1.35	1.40
Russia	9.6	10.3	14.7	15.3	66.8	67.0	16.0	14.1	1.26	1.31
Saudi Arabia	29.7	28.2	2.7	2.5	75.2	76.5	13.7	11.3	4.11	3.77
South Africa	19.1	17.3	20.4	22.7	44.1	42.7	62.8	56.2	2.32	2.02
Spain	10.1	9.5	9.6	10.1	79.4	80.2	4.5	4.2	1.27	1.32
Sri Lanka	15.9	14.8	6.5	6.6	72.9	74.4	14.8	12.5	1.88	1.78
Sudan	35.8	31.8	9.4	8.3	58.1	60.5	64.1	55.2	4.97	4.21
Syria	28.9	25.2	5.0	4.6	69.7	71.5	30.6	25.0	3.61	3.02
Taiwan [5]	12.7	12.0	6.3	6.9	77.1	78.1	6.5	5.9	1.57	1.59
Tanzania	38.6	35.9	17.0	15.3	44.9	47.2	100.6	88.9	5.15	4.62
Thailand	14.1	13.2	6.9	7.3	71.7	73.4	20.8	17.1	1.63	1.65
Turkey	17.2	15.6	6.0	6.1	72.1	73.7	42.6	34.3	1.98	1.82
Uganda	47.5	47.4	13.4	10.6	50.4	56.1	69.5	60.1	6.77	6.57
Ukraine	8.5	9.1	15.1	14.3	68.8	71.1	10.8	9.1	1.15	1.21
United Kingdom	10.9	10.7	10.2	10.0	78.3	79.2	5.2	4.8	1.66	1.66
Uzbekistan	26.1	26.1	8.0	7.4	64.1	66.2	71.3	65.6	2.97	2.80
Venezuela.	19.3	17.8	4.9	5.0	74.1	75.5	23.0	18.9	2.31	2.13
Vietnam	17.2	16.1	6.2	6.2	70.4	71.9	26.8	22.2	1.97	1.80
Yemen	43.2	41.8	8.8	7.4	61.4	63.6	63.3	53.4	6.75	6.23
Zimbabwe.	28.4	26.6	22.0	21.6	39.0	40.2	53.0	49.6	3.23	2.93

[1] Number of births during 1 year per 1,000 persons (based on midyear population). [2] Number of deaths during 1 year per 1,000 persons (based on midyear population). [3] Number of deaths of children under 1 year of age per 1,000 live births in a calendar year. [4] Average number of children that would be born if all women lived to the end of their childbearing years and, at each year of age, they experienced the birth rates occurring in the specified year. [5] See footnote 2, Table 1314. [6] See footnote 3, Table 1314.

Source: U.S. Census Bureau, "International Data Base" (as of 26 April 2005); <http://www.census.gov/ipc/www/idbnew.html>.

U.S. Census Bureau, Statistical Abstract of the United States: 2006

Table 1319. Births to Unmarried Women by Country: 1980 to 2002

[Percent of all live births. For U.S. figures marital status is inferred from a comparison of the child's and parents' surnames on the birth certificate for those states that do not report on marital status. No estimates are included for misstatements on birth records or failures to register births]

Country	1980	1990	1995	2002
United States	18.4	28.0	32.2	34.0
Canada	12.8	24.4	27.6	28.9
Japan	0.8	1.1	1.2	[1]1.7
Denmark	33.2	46.4	46.5	44.6
France	11.4	30.1	37.6	44.3
Germany	(NA)	[2]15.1	16.1	[1]25.0
Ireland	5.0	14.6	22.3	31.1
Italy	4.3	6.5	8.1	[3]9.7
Netherlands	4.1	11.4	15.5	29.1
Spain	3.9	9.6	11.1	21.8
Sweden	39.7	47.0	53.0	56.0
United Kingdom	11.5	27.9	33.6	40.6

NA Not available. [1] Data are for 2001 instead of 2002. [2] Data are for 1991 instead of 1990. [3] Data are for 2000 instead of 2002.

Source: U.S. Bureau of Labor Statistics. "Families and Work Transition in 12 Countries 1980–2001," Monthly Labor Review, September 2003; and unpublished data.

Table 1320. Marriage and Divorce Rates by Country: 1980 to 2002

[Per 1,000 population aged 15–64 years]

Country	Marriage rate				Divorce rate			
	1980	1990	1995	'2002 [1]	1980	1990	1995	2002 [1]
United States [2]	15.9	14.8	13.6	11.7	7.9	7.2	6.8	6.0
Canada	11.5	10.0	8.1	6.8	3.7	4.2	3.9	3.3
Japan	9.8	8.4	9.1	8.8	1.8	1.8	2.3	3.4
Denmark	8.0	9.1	9.9	10.4	4.1	4.0	3.7	4.3
France	9.7	7.7	6.7	7.2	2.4	2.8	3.2	3.3
Germany [3]	(NA)	8.2	7.8	7.1	(NA)	2.5	3.1	3.7
Ireland [4]	10.9	8.3	6.7	7.6	([5])	([5])	([5])	1.0
Italy	8.7	8.2	7.5	6.9	0.3	0.7	0.7	1.1
Netherlands	9.6	9.3	7.7	7.7	2.7	2.8	3.2	3.0
Spain	9.4	8.5	7.5	7.4	(NA)	0.9	1.2	1.5
Sweden	7.1	7.4	6.0	6.6	3.7	3.5	4.0	3.7
United Kingdom	11.6	10.0	8.5	7.3	4.4	4.4	4.5	4.1

NA Not available. [1] Provisional marriage and divorce rates for the United States and Italy; provisional marriage rate for the Netherlands and divorce rate for Spain. U.S. divorce rate is estimated by the Bureau of Labor Statistics. U.S. marriage rate may be understated because of incomplete reporting in Oklahoma. [2] U.S. data include unlicensed marriages in California. [3] Data are for 1991 instead of 1990. [4] Marriages for 2002 are estimated by Eurostat. [5] Divorce not allowed by law prior to 1997.

Source: U.S. Bureau of Labor Statistics, "Families and Work in Transition in 12 Countries, 1980–2001," Monthly Labor Review, September 2003; and unpublished data.

Table 1321. Single-parent Households:1980 to 2004

[In thousands (6,061 represents 6,061,000). For the United Kingdom in 1981, children are defined as those under 15 and those who are 15, 16, or 17 and attended school full-time; for later years, children are defined as those under 16 and those who are 16 or 17 and attend school full-time. For Ireland, children are defined as those under 15. For all other countries, children are defined as children living at home, or away from school, under the age of 18. Data are generally for the entire year, but in some instances they are only for a particular month within the year]

Country and year	Number	Percent of all households with children	Country and year	Number	Percent of all households with children
United States:			Germany:		
1980	6,061	19.5	1991	1,429	15.2
1990	7,752	24.0	1995	2,496	18.8
1995	9,055	26.4	2004	2,466	19.5
2003	10,054	28.0	Ireland: [1]		
Canada:			1981	30	7.2
1981	437	12.7	1991	44	10.7
1991	572	16.2	1996	56	13.8
1996	690	18.7	2002	69	16.7
2001	707	19.3	Netherlands:		
Japan:			1988	179	9.6
1980	796	4.9	1993	180	10.0
1990	934	6.5	1995 [2]	208	11.7
1995	884	6.9	2004 [3]	283	14.6
2000	996	8.3	Sweden:		
Denmark: [1]			1985	117	11.2
1980	99	13.4	1990	151	14.8
1990	117	17.8	1991 [2]	166	15.2
1995	120	18.6	1995	189	17.4
2003	127	19.2	2002	248	23.7
France:			United Kingdom: [4]		
1988	761	11.9	1981	1,010	13.9
1990	755	11.9	1991	1,344	19.4
1995	874	14.0	1994-95	1,617	21.9
2000	1,039	17.1	2003	1,225	18.5

[1] Data are from family-based, rather than household-based, statistics. [2] Break in series. [3] Provisional data. [4] Great Britain only (excludes Northern Ireland).

Source: U.S. Bureau of Labor Statistics, "Families and Work in Transition in 12 Countries, 1980–2001," Monthly Labor Review, September 2003; and unpublished data.

Table 1322. **Percent Distribution of Households by Type and Country: 1980 to 2004**

[Data are generally for the entire year, but in some instances they are only for a particular month within the year]

Year	Total	Married-couple households [1]			Single parent [2]	One-person	Other [3]
		Total	With children [2]	Without children [2]			
United States:							
1980	100.0	60.8	30.9	29.9	7.5	22.7	9.0
1990	100.0	56.0	26.3	29.8	8.3	24.6	11.1
1995	100.0	54.4	25.5	28.9	9.1	25.0	11.5
2003	100.0	51.5	23.3	28.2	9.0	26.4	13.0
Canada:							
1981	100.0	66.8	36.3	30.5	5.3	20.3	7.6
1991	100.0	62.8	29.6	33.2	5.7	22.9	8.6
1996	100.0	60.5	27.8	32.7	6.4	24.2	8.9
2001	100.0	59.4	25.6	33.8	6.1	25.7	8.8
Japan:							
1980	100.0	68.4	42.9	25.6	2.2	19.8	9.5
1990	100.0	65.2	33.1	32.1	2.3	23.1	9.4
1995	100.0	62.8	27.4	35.4	2.0	25.6	9.6
2000	100.0	60.3	23.6	36.7	2.1	27.6	10.0
Denmark: [4]							
1980	100.0	50.3	25.0	25.3	3.9	44.9	1.0
1990	100.0	45.6	19.5	26.1	4.2	49.6	0.6
1995	100.0	44.9	18.2	26.6	4.2	50.4	0.5
2003	100.0	45.7	18.5	27.2	4.4	49.3	0.6
France:							
1982	100.0	67.0	39.7	27.3	4.3	24.6	4.1
1990	100.0	64.9	38.6	26.2	6.6	26.1	2.5
1995	100.0	62.2	35.9	26.3	6.7	28.9	2.3
2000	100.0	60.0	32.8	27.1	7.2	30.8	2.0
Germany:							
1991	100.0	55.3	31.6	23.7	7.1	33.6	4.0
1995	100.0	53.3	29.2	24.0	6.8	34.9	5.1
2000 [5]	100.0	56.8	28.0	28.8	6.0	36.1	1.2
2004	100.0	55.3	26.1	29.2	6.3	37.2	1.2
Ireland:							
1981	100.0	(NA)	(NA)	(NA)	(NA)	16.9	(NA)
1991	100.0	61.6	47.9	13.7	10.6	20.2	7.6
1996	100.0	59.6	44.5	15.1	11.2	21.5	7.7
2002	100.0	59.2	41.4	17.7	11.7	21.6	7.6
Netherlands:							
1988	100.0	64.7	37.3	27.4	5.4	28.7	1.2
1993	100.0	63.1	33.3	29.9	5.0	30.9	1.0
1995 [5]	100.0	61.2	32.6	28.5	5.6	32.6	0.7
2004	100.0	58.8	29.6	29.1	6.2	34.4	0.7
Sweden:							
1985	100.0	54.8	23.8	31.0	3.2	36.1	5.9
1990	100.0	52.1	21.9	30.2	3.9	39.6	4.4
1991 [5]	100.0	52.6	22.4	30.2	4.1	41.2	2.2
1995	100.0	50.7	21.2	29.4	4.6	42.3	2.4
2002	100.0	44.3	17.9	26.4	5.6	47.9	2.2
United Kingdom: [6]							
1981	100.0	65.0	31.0	34.0	5.0	22.0	8.0
1991	100.0	61.0	25.0	36.0	6.0	27.0	6.0
1994-95	100.0	58.0	25.0	33.0	7.0	27.0	8.0
2003 [5]	100.0	56.0	22.0	34.0	5.0	29.0	10.0

NA Not available.   [1] May include unmarried cohabiting couples. Such couples are explicitly included under married couples in Canada, Denmark, Ireland, France, and the Netherlands. For Sweden, all cohabitants are included as married couples. In other countries, some unmarried cohabitants are included as married couples, while some are classified under "other households," depending on responses to surveys and censuses.   [2] Children are defined as unmarried children living at home according to the following age limits: under 18 years old in the United States, Canada, Japan, Denmark, Sweden, and the United Kingdom, except that the United Kingdom includes 15-, 16-, and 17-year-olds in 1981, and 16- and 17-year-olds thereafter only if they are attending school full-time; under 25 years old in France; and children of all ages in Germany, Ireland, and the Netherlands.   [3] Includes both family and nonfamily households not elsewhere classified. These households comprise, for example, siblings residing together, other households composed of relatives, and households made up of roommates. Some unmarried cohabiting couples may also be included in the "other" group. See footnote 1.   [4] From family-based statistics. However, one person living alone constitutes a family in Denmark. In this respect, the Danish data are closer to household statistics.   [5] Break in series.   [6] Great Britain only (excludes Northern Ireland).

Source: U.S. Bureau of Labor Statistics, "Families and Work in Transition in 12 Countries, 1980–2001,"*Monthly Labor Review*, September 2003; and unpublished data.

Table 1323. **Health Expenditures as Percent of GDP by Country: 1980 to 2003**

[In percent. G.D.P. = gross domestic product; for explanation, see text, Section 13, Income]

Country	Total health expenditures					Public health expenditures				
	1980	1990	2000	2002	2003	1980	1990	2000	2002	2003
United States	8.7	11.9	13.1	14.6	15.0	3.6	4.7	5.8	6.6	6.6
Australia	7.0	7.8	9.0	9.3	(NA)	4.4	5.2	6.2	6.3	(NA)
Austria	7.4	7.0	7.6	7.6	(NA)	5.1	5.1	5.3	5.3	(NA)
Belgium	6.4	7.4	8.7	9.1	9.6	(NA)	(NA)	(NA)	(NA)	(NA)
Canada	7.1	9.0	8.9	9.6	9.9	5.4	6.7	6.3	6.7	6.9
Czech Republic	(NA)	4.7	6.6	7.2	7.5	(NA)	4.6	6.0	6.5	6.8
Denmark.	9.1	8.5	8.4	8.8	9.0	8.0	7.0	6.9	7.3	7.5
Finland	6.4	7.8	6.7	7.2	7.4	5.0	6.3	5.0	5.5	5.7
France	7.1	8.6	9.3	9.7	10.1	5.7	6.6	7.1	7.4	7.7
Germany [1]	8.7	8.5	10.6	10.9	11.1	6.8	6.5	8.3	8.6	8.6
Greece	6.6	7.4	9.9	9.8	9.9	3.7	4.0	5.2	5.0	5.1
Hungary	(NA)	(NA)	7.1	7.8	(NA)	(NA)	(NA)	5.0	5.5	(NA)
Iceland	6.2	8.0	9.3	10.0	10.5	5.5	6.9	7.7	8.3	8.8
Ireland	8.4	6.1	6.3	7.3	(NA)	6.8	4.4	4.7	5.5	(NA)
Italy	(NA)	7.9	8.1	8.4	8.4	(NA)	6.3	5.9	6.3	6.3
Japan	6.5	5.9	7.6	7.9	(NA)	4.6	4.6	6.1	6.4	(NA)
Korea, South	(NA)	4.5	4.7	5.3	5.6	(NA)	1.7	2.2	2.7	2.8
Luxembourg	5.9	6.1	5.5	6.1	(NA)	5.5	5.7	4.9	5.2	(NA)
Mexico	(NA)	4.8	5.6	6.0	6.2	(NA)	2.0	2.6	2.7	2.9
Netherlands	7.5	8.0	8.3	9.3	9.8	5.2	5.4	5.2	5.8	6.1
New Zealand.	5.9	6.9	7.8	8.2	8.1	5.2	5.7	6.1	6.4	6.3
Norway	7.0	7.7	7.7	9.9	10.3	5.9	6.4	6.5	8.2	8.6
Poland	(NA)	4.9	5.7	6.0	(NA)	(NA)	4.5	4.0	4.4	(NA)
Portugal	5.6	6.2	9.2	9.3	9.6	3.6	4.1	6.4	6.6	6.7
Slovak Republic	(NA)	(NA)	5.5	5.7	5.9	(NA)	(NA)	4.9	5.1	5.2
Spain	5.4	6.7	7.4	7.6	7.7	4.3	5.3	5.3	5.4	5.5
Sweden	9.1	8.4	8.4	9.2	(NA)	8.4	7.5	7.2	7.9	(NA)
Switzerland	7.4	8.3	10.4	11.1	11.5	(NA)	4.3	5.8	6.4	6.7
Turkey	3.3	3.6	6.6	(NA)	(NA)	1.0	2.2	4.2	(NA)	(NA)
United Kingdom	5.6	6.0	7.3	7.7	(NA)	5.0	5.0	5.9	6.4	(NA)

NA Not available.   [1] Data prior to 1991 are for former West Germany.

Source: Organization for Economic Cooperation and Development, Paris, France, OECD Health Data 2004, 2nd ed. (copyright).

Table 1324. **Average Temperatures and Precipitation—Selected International Cities**

[In degrees Fahrenheit, except as noted. Data are generally based on a standard 30-year period; for details, see source. For data on U.S. cities, see Tables 377-380]

City	January					July				
	Average high	Average low	Warmest	Coldest	Average precipitation (inches)	Average high	Average low	Warmest	Coldest	Average precipitation (inches)
Amsterdam, Netherlands . . .	41	34	57	3	3.1	69	55	90	39	2.9
Athens, Greece	55	44	70	28	1.9	89	73	108	61	0.2
Baghdad, Iraq	58	38	75	25	1.1	110	78	122	61	-
Bangkok, Thailand	89	71	95	54	0.4	90	78	99	72	6.2
Beijing, China	34	17	54	1	0.2	86	72	104	63	8.8
Berlin, Germany	35	26	58	-11	(NA)	73	56	95	41	(NA)
Bogota, Colombia	66	43	84	27	1.9	64	47	82	32	1.8
Brasilia, Brazil	81	64	95	54	(NA)	79	52	97	37	(NA)
Buenos Aires, Argentina . . .	85	64	104	44	4.2	58	41	88	23	2.3
Cairo, Egypt	65	49	86	32	0.2	93	72	108	63	-
Frankfurt, Germany	38	30	56	-4	1.8	75	57	97	38	2.4
Geneva, Switzerland	39	29	57	-2	2.2	77	56	96	41	2.8
Hong Kong, China	67	58	79	43	1.1	89	81	97	70	14.3
Istanbul, Turkey	46	37	64	16	3.7	82	66	100	50	0.7
Jakarta, Indonesia	83	75	92	72	(NA)	88	74	92	67	(NA)
Karachi, Pakistan	76	55	93	39	0.3	89	83	109	68	3.5
Lagos, Nigeria.	82	79	93	64	(NA)	79	76	88	70	(NA)
London, England	45	36	61	15	2.4	72	56	93	45	1.8
Madrid, Spain	51	32	68	14	1.8	90	61	104	46	0.4
Manila, Philippines	86	71	95	61	0.8	88	76	99	70	15.9
Mexico City, Mexico	70	45	86	26	0.3	74	56	86	37	5.1
Montreal, Canada	21	7	52	-31	2.8	79	61	93	43	3.4
Moscow, Russia	21	11	46	-33	1.4	71	55	95	41	3.2
Nairobi, Kenya	77	58	88	45	1.8	71	54	85	43	0.5
New Delhi, India	68	48	85	32	0.9	93	81	111	70	7.9
Paris, France	43	34	59	1	(NA)	75	58	95	41	(NA)
Rio De Janeiro, Brazil. . . .	91	74	109	64	5.3	81	64	102	52	1.8
Rome, Italy.	55	39	64	19	3.2	83	66	100	55	0.6
Seoul, Korea.	33	21	55	-1	(NA)	82	71	97	55	(NA)
Singapore, Singapore	85	73	100	66	9.4	86	76	99	70	5.9
Sydney, Australia	79	65	109	49	4.0	62	44	80	32	2.5
Tel Aviv, Israel.	62	46	84	32	(NA)	87	69	100	50	(NA)
Tokyo, Japan	48	35	66	25	2.0	82	71	95	55	5.3
Toronto, Canada	28	15	59	-24	1.9	79	60	99	45	2.8

- Represents zero.   NA Not available.

Source: U.S. National Oceanic and Atmospheric Administration, Climates of the World.

Comparative International Statistics   871

Table 1325. **Carbon Dioxide Emissions from Consumption of Fossil Fuels by Country: 1990 to 2003**

[In million metric tons of carbon equivalent (5,837 represents 5,837,000,000). Includes carbon dioxide emissions from the consumption of petroleum, natural gas, and coal, and the flaring of natural gas]

Country	1990	1995	1997	1998	1999	2000	2001	2002	2003
World, total.	5,837	6,009	6,249	6,229	6,320	6,504	6,584	6,672	6,862
Australia	72	78	90	92	96	97	101	101	103
Brazil	61	79	88	88	91	94	96	96	96
Canada	131	137	147	148	150	154	155	157	164
China [1]	611	781	829	802	792	827	870	893	966
France	101	102	104	111	109	109	110	110	112
Germany	(NA)	239	239	235	226	231	237	233	230
India	160	236	238	245	254	272	275	276	279
Indonesia	41	58	67	65	72	75	80	85	87
Iran	55	71	79	80	86	87	91	99	101
Italy	113	117	114	119	119	121	121	122	127
Japan	276	298	315	301	308	318	319	325	329
Korea, South	64	107	117	101	114	119	120	126	128
Mexico	82	87	95	100	98	104	102	101	110
Netherlands	56	60	65	65	64	68	75	70	71
Poland	89	84	91	85	89	79	75	75	78
Russia	(NA)	434	397	399	419	424	421	422	438
Saudi Arabia	56	64	69	70	71	79	82	84	89
South Africa	81	94	104	99	102	105	103	104	112
Spain	62	66	72	75	81	86	87	92	93
Taiwan [1]	32	49	56	60	60	68	67	73	76
Thailand	23	43	48	44	46	44	47	49	53
Turkey	35	41	49	50	49	55	50	52	56
Ukraine	(NA)	122	92	91	92	92	89	91	94
United Kingdom	163	151	153	152	150	150	155	152	154
United States	1,364	1,442	1,512	1,521	1,541	1,586	1,563	1,574	1,582

NA Not available.   [1] See footnote 2, Table 1314.

Source: U.S. Energy Information Administration, *International Energy Annual, 2003*. See also <http://www.eia.doe.gov/emeu/iea/carbon.html> (accessed July 2005).

Table 1326. **Educational Attainment by Country: 2002**

[Percent of adult population (persons 25 to 64 years old). Tertiary-type A includes education leading to a BA, Master's or equivalent degree, and advanced research programs]

Country	Upper secondary education or higher	Tertiary-type A attainment	Country	Upper secondary education or higher	Tertiary-type A attainment
United States	87	29	Japan	84	20
Australia	61	20	Luxembourg	57	12
Austria	78	7	Korea, South	71	18
Belgium	61	13	Mexico	13	2
Canada	83	21	Netherlands	66	22
Czech Republic	88	12	New Zealand	76	15
Denmark	80	23	Norway	86	28
Finland	75	16	Poland	47	12
France	65	12	Portugal	20	7
Germany	83	13	Spain	41	17
Greece	50	13	Sweden	82	18
Hungary	71	14	Switzerland	82	16
Iceland	59	20	Turkey	25	9
Ireland	60	16	United Kingdom	64	19
Italy	44	10			

Source: Organization for Economic Cooperation and Development, Paris, France, *OECD in Figures*, 2004 (copyright).

872 Comparative International Statistics

Table 1327. Gross National Income by Country: 1990 and 2003

[61 represents $61,000,000,000. GNI (gross national product, or GNP, in the terminology of the 1968 United Nations System of National Accounts) measures the total domestic and foreign value added claimed by residents. GNI comprises GDP plus net receipts of primary income (compensation of employees and property income) from nonresident sources]

Country	Gross national income [1]				GNI on purchasing power parity basis [2]			
	Total (bil. dol.)		Per capita (dol.)		Total (bil. dol.)		Per capita (dol.)	
	1990	2003	1990	2003	1990	2003	1990	2003
Algeria	61	62	2,440	1,930	107	189	4,280	5,930
Angola	8	10	820	740	15	26	1,570	1,910
Argentina	104	140	3,220	3,810	227	420	6,990	11,410
Australia	302	437	17,720	21,950	278	572	16,320	28,780
Bangladesh	31	55	280	400	107	258	970	1,870
Belarus	(NA)	16	(NA)	1,600	44	60	4,310	6,050
Belgium	185	267	18,520	25,760	181	300	18,140	28,920
Brazil	415	480	2,800	2,720	757	1,326	5,120	7,510
Bulgaria	20	17	2,260	2,130	48	59	5,480	7,540
Burkina Faso	3	4	330	300	6	14	700	1,170
Cambodia	(NA)	4	(NA)	300	(NA)	27	(NA)	2,000
Cameroon	11	10	950	630	19	32	1,600	1,990
Canada	551	774	19,840	24,470	511	950	18,400	30,040
Chile	29	69	2,190	4,360	58	155	4,450	9,810
China [3]	368	1,417	320	1,100	1,488	[4]6,410	1,310	[4]4,980
Colombia	42	81	1,190	1,810	159	286	4,550	6,410
Congo (Kinshasa) [5]	2	2	880	650	2	3	650	730
Cote d'Ivoire	9	11	780	660	15	24	1,270	1,400
Czech Republic	(NA)	73	(NA)	7,150	112	159	10,790	15,600
Ecuador	9	24	900	1,830	26	45	2,510	3,440
Egypt	42	94	810	1,390	121	266	2,310	3,940
Ethiopia	9	6	170	90	27	48	520	710d
France	1,142	1,522	19,620	24,730	1,011	1,652	17,820	27,640
Germany	1,601	2,086	20,160	25,270	1,427	2,279	17,960	27,610
Ghana	6	7	380	320	20	45	1,300	2,190
Greece	79	146	7,770	13,230	114	220	11,260	19,900
Guatemala	8	24	970	1,910	24	50	2,760	4,090
Hong Kong	71	176	12,520	25,860	91	195	15,980	28,680
Hungary	30	64	2,880	6,350	90	140	8,640	13,840
India	331	571	390	540	1,156	3,062	1,360	2,880
Indonesia	111	174	620	810	313	689	1,760	3,210
Iran	141	133	2,590	2,010	204	465	3,740	7,000
Iraq	39	(NA)	2,170	[6]	(NA)	(NA)	(NA)	(NA)
Italy	988	1,243	17,420	21,570	984	1,546	17,360	26,830
Japan	3,349	4,361	27,110	34,180	2,339	3,629	18,930	28,450
Kazakhstan	(NA)	27	(NA)	1,780	76	93	4,620	6,280
Kenya	9	13	380	400	20	33	880	1,030
Korea, South	246	(NA)	5,740	[7]	317	(NA)	7,390	(NA)
Madagascar	3	5	240	290	9	13	740	800
Malawi	2	2	200	160	3	6	410	590
Malaysia	43	96	2,380	3,880	78	222	4,290	8,970
Mali	2	3	270	290	5	11	550	960
Mexico	236	637	2,830	6,230	491	919	5,890	8,980
Morocco	25	39	1,030	1,310	63	119	2,630	3,940
Mozambique	2	4	170	210	7	20	480	1,060
Nepal	4	6	220	240	15	35	840	1,420
Netherlands	280	426	18,710	26,230	264	463	17,670	28,560
Niger	2	2	310	200	5	10	710	830
Nigeria	26	48	270	350	62	123	650	900
Pakistan	43	78	390	520	143	303	1,320	2,040
Peru	17	58	780	2,140	66	138	3,050	5,080
Philippines	45	88	740	1,080	191	379	3,140	4,640
Poland	(NA)	202	(NA)	5,280	215	428	5,640	11,210
Portugal	64	123	6,450	11,800	105	185	10,630	17,710
Romania	40	49	1,730	2,260	124	155	5,340	7,140
Russia	(NA)	375	(NA)	2,610	1,234	1,284	8,320	8,950
Saudi Arabia	118	208	7,490	9,240	162	298	10,240	13,230
Senegal	5	6	720	540	8	17	1,100	1,620
Serbia and Montenegro	(NA)	16	(NA)	1,910	(NA)	(NA)	(NA)	(NA)
Singapore	36	90	11,840	21,230	37	103	12,170	24,180
South Africa	102	126	2,890	2,750	276	464	7,840	10,130
Spain	454	701	11,680	17,040	498	910	12,810	22,150
Sri Lanka	8	18	490	930	31	72	1,880	3,740
Sudan	14	15	570	460	23	59	930	1,760
Sweden	226	259	26,390	28,910	144	239	16,820	26,710
Switzerland	225	299	33,510	40,680	165	237	24,550	32,220
Syria	11	20	940	1,160	25	60	2,090	3,430
Tanzania	5	11	190	300	10	22	410	620
Thailand	84	136	1,520	2,190	199	462	3,580	7,450
Turkey	127	198	2,270	2,800	242	475	4,300	6,710
Uganda	6	6	320	250	12	36	700	1,430
Ukraine	(NA)	47	(NA)	970	368	262	7,080	5,430
United Kingdom	932	1,680	16,190	28,320	940	1,643	16,330	27,690
United States	**5,846**	**11,013**	**23,440**	**37,870**	**5,768**	**10,978**	**23,120**	**37,750**
Uzbekistan	(NA)	11	(NA)	420	30	44	1,480	1,720
Venezuela	52	90	2,650	3,490	89	122	4,580	4,750
Vietnam	9	39	130	480	61	202	920	2,490
Yemen	(NA)	10	(NA)	520	6	16	520	820
Zimbabwe	9	10	880	[7]	22	(NA)	2,140	(NA)

NA Not available. [1] Gross national income calculated using the World Bank Atlas method; for details, see source. [2] See footnote 2, Table 1328. [3] See footnote 2, Table 1314. [4] Estimate based on bilateral comparison between China and the United States. [5] See footnote 3, Table 1314. [6] Estimate: Lower middle income ($766-$3,035). [7] Estimate: Low income ($765 or less).
Source: The World Bank, Washington, DC, World Development Indicators CD-ROM, annual (copyright).

Comparative International Statistics 873

Table 1328. Gross Domestic Product (GDP) by Country: 1995 to 2003

[23,686 represents $23,686,000,000,000. Except as noted, based on the System of National Accounts, 1993: for details, see source]

Country	Current price levels and exchange rates (bil. dol.)					Constant (2000) price levels and exchange rates [1] (bil. dol.)					GDP per capita, 2003 based on current	
	1995	2000	2001	2002	2003	1995	2000	2001	2002	2003	Exchange rates	PPPs [2]
OECD, total [3]	23,686	25,277	24,980	26,104	29,249	22,308	25,277	25,552	25,905	26,480	26,821	27,113
OECD Europe [3][4]	9,253	8,520	8,511	9,303	11,302	7,573	8,520	8,650	8,755	8,839	24,279	24,654
Australia	373	388	369	412	527	333	388	403	415	431	26,361	30,104
Austria	235	194	193	208	255	172	194	195	198	199	31,518	30,674
Belgium	277	228	227	246	304	202	228	230	232	235	29,325	29,627
Canada	582	714	705	727	857	592	714	727	752	767	27,081	30,475
Czech Republic	52	56	61	74	90	54	56	57	58	60	8,864	17,295
Denmark	180	158	159	172	212	142	158	161	162	163	39,333	30,714
Finland	130	120	121	132	161	99	120	121	124	126	30,855	28,595
France [5]	1,553	1,308	1,336	1,437	1,758	1,159	1,308	1,336	1,352	1,358	28,560	28,200
Germany	2,458	1,870	1,886	1,983	2,402	1,724	1,870	1,886	1,887	1,885	29,107	27,565
Greece	118	113	118	133	173	98	113	118	123	128	15,731	20,423
Hungary	45	47	52	65	83	39	47	48	50	52	8,172	15,091
Iceland	7	8	8	9	11	7	8	9	9	9	36,541	29,358
Ireland	67	95	103	120	152	64	95	101	107	111	38,116	33,322
Italy	1,097	1,075	1,090	1,186	1,468	988	1,075	1,094	1,098	1,100	25,273	26,663
Japan	5,304	4,746	4,162	3,972	4,301	4,580	4,746	4,767	4,750	4,876	33,701	28,016
Korea, South	489	512	482	547	605	442	512	531	568	586	12,631	19,279
Luxembourg	18	20	20	21	27	14	20	20	20	21	60,083	54,017
Mexico	286	581	622	648	626	469	581	581	585	592	6,091	9,567
Netherlands	415	371	384	419	513	318	371	376	378	375	31,602	30,427
New Zealand [6]	61	52	52	60	80	48	52	54	56	58	19,799	23,220
Norway	148	167	170	191	221	147	167	171	174	175	48,380	37,108
Poland	132	167	186	191	210	138	167	168	171	177	5,485	11,569
Portugal	107	106	108	121	147	91	106	108	109	107	14,052	18,793
Slovakia	19	20	21	24	33	18	20	21	22	23	6,072	13,165
Spain	584	563	585	657	841	476	563	578	591	606	20,597	25,051
Sweden [6]	248	240	220	242	302	207	240	242	247	250	33,663	28,987
Switzerland [6]	307	246	250	277	322	224	246	249	249	249	43,458	32,629
Turkey	169	199	146	184	240	176	199	184	199	210	3,385	6,971
United Kingdom	1,135	1,438	1,431	1,565	1,796	1,264	1,438	1,471	1,497	1,531	30,246	29,931
United States	7,338	9,765	10,076	10,435	10,951	8,271	9,765	9,839	10,024	10,330	37,622	37,624

[1] Based on constant (1995) price data converted to U.S. dollars using 1995 exchange rates. [2] The goods and services produced in different countries should be valued consistently if the differences observed are meant to reflect real differences in the volumes of goods and services produced. The use of purchasing power parities (PPP) instead of exchange rates is intended to achieve this objective. PPPs show how many units of currency are needed in one country to buy the same amount of goods and services which one unit of currency will buy in the other country. See text of this section. [3] Excluding Czech Republic, Hungary, Poland, and Slovakia. [4] OECD Europe: Austria, Belgium, Denmark, Finland, France, Germany, Greece, Iceland, Ireland, Italy, Luxembourg, Netherlands, Norway, Portugal, Spain, Sweden, Switzerland, Turkey, United Kingdom. [5] Includes overseas departments. [6] Based on System of National Accounts, 1968.

Source: Organization for Economic Cooperation and Development, Paris, France, "National Accounts of OECD Countries annual, Vol. 1"; published July 2005.

Table 1329. Selected International Economic Indicators by Country: 1980 to 2002

[Data cover gross domestic product (GDP) at market prices. Gross fixed capital formation covers private and government sectors except military. Savings data are calculated by deducting outlays—such as personal consumption expenditures, interest paid, and transfer payments to foreigners—from disposable personal income]

Year	United States	France	Germany	Italy	Netherlands	United Kingdom	Japan	Canada
Ratio of gross fixed capital formation to GDP (current prices):								
1980	20.0	23.8	22.6	25.2	22.7	18.7	31.8	23.1
1985	19.4	20.3	19.5	21.8	20.9	18.1	27.8	20.2
1990	17.2	22.6	20.9	21.5	22.5	20.5	32.2	21.3
1995	17.5	18.8	22.4	18.3	20.3	16.3	27.7	17.6
2000	19.9	20.2	21.6	19.8	22.5	16.7	26.2	19.3
2001	19.1	20.1	20.1	19.8	21.9	16.5	25.6	19.9
2002	18.0	19.5	18.4	19.7	21.0	16.1	24.1	19.7
Ratio of savings to disposable personal income:								
1980	10.2	17.2	13.4	27.9	7.8	12.4	19.9	15.6
1985	9.2	14.1	12.1	30.7	5.6	9.8	16.5	15.8
1990	7.8	13.1	13.9	27.8	11.6	8.0	14.0	13.0
1995	5.6	16.0	11.2	22.5	14.9	10.0	11.9	9.2
2000	2.8	15.7	9.8	14.5	6.7	4.3	9.8	4.6
2001	2.3	16.2	10.1	15.4	9.6	5.7	6.9	4.5
2002	3.7	16.7	10.4	16.0	10.7	4.7	5.8	4.2

Source: U.S. Department of Commerce, International Trade Administration, Office of Trade and Economic Analysis, based on official statistics of listed countries.

Table 1330. Average Annual Percent Changes in International Economic Composite Indexes by Country: 1980 to 2003

[Change from previous year; derived from indexes with base 1990 = 100. The coincident index changes are for calendar years and the leading index changes are for years ending June 30, because they lead the coincident indexes by about 6 months, on average. The G-7 countries are United States, Canada, France, Germany, Italy, United Kingdom, and Japan. Minus sign (-) indicates decrease]

Country	1980	1985	1990	1995	1996	1997	1998	1999	2000	2001	2002	2003
LEADING INDEX												
Total, 13 countries	-0.4	2.2	2.1	5.9	1.1	3.4	2.5	1.1	5.6	-0.4	-3.9	2.5
12 countries, excluding U.S.	2.7	4.6	3.8	6.3	1.8	2.8	2.1	1.6	6.7	1.7	-3.2	1.8
G-7 countries	-0.4	2.0	2.0	5.8	1.0	3.3	2.5	0.9	5.3	-0.5	-4.4	2.3
North America	-4.2	-1.0	-0.9	5.4	-	4.3	3.3	0.6	4.1	-3.4	-4.8	3.7
United States	-4.7	-1.4	-1.0	5.2	-0.1	4.4	3.1	0.3	3.8	-4.0	-5.1	3.8
Canada	3.7	4.2	-1.1	7.4	1.1	4.6	6.1	4.0	6.9	3.7	-1.1	2.0
Four European countries	3.1	3.6	1.8	6.3	0.4	1.3	5.7	2.7	4.1	0.5	-5.0	-0.8
France	2.0	0.9	1.5	6.6	-1.1	1.2	6.8	2.0	1.9	-3.7	-7.8	-1.9
Germany	3.1	4.1	4.5	7.3	-0.1	1.9	6.3	5.4	5.7	1.5	-3.6	-0.4
Italy	5.1	6.1	0.2	10.8	0.7	-2.0	10.1	0.4	8.0	2.9		-1.3
United Kingdom	1.8	2.9	-0.3	4.1	2.1	1.8	2.0	2.9	2.5	1.5	-1.3	0.5
Seven Pacific region countries	2.2	5.8	6.1	6.2	3.2	4.1	-1.5	0.2	9.3	3.0	-2.0	4.3
Australia	0.7	7.0	-1.4	6.4	0.9	2.1	4.5	4.5	8.1	-0.8	1.1	2.9
Taiwan[1]	1.1	5.3	4.9	6.6	1.7	8.3	7.4	3.1	8.6	-0.4	2.4	6.2
Thailand	1.3	4.4	12.1	8.7	4.6	-0.7	-3.6	1.0	9.1	2.9	7.0	6.2
Japan	2.3	5.9	6.6	6.0	3.3	4.2	-2.4	-0.9	9.0	3.7	-3.4	4.1
Korea, South	0.6	6.0	6.5	10.5	6.1	4.7	1.3	8.8	15.9	2.6	6.1	6.6
Malaysia	4.8	-1.3	-0.8	4.1	-0.8	1.6	-5.0	-5.6	12.0	-4.8	-1.0	5.6
New Zealand	2.3	3.2	0.8	1.4	1.6	2.9	1.0	1.7	1.7	0.3	2.8	0.9
COINCIDENT INDEX												
Total, 13 countries	0.2	3.7	4.5	2.4	1.9	3.4	1.7	2.6	5.2	-0.7	-1.4	0.6
12 countries, excluding U.S.	2.4	3.6	6.8	1.6	1.3	2.1	-0.7	1.7	5.7	0.5	-0.8	0.9
G-7 countries		3.6	4.5	2.0	1.8	3.3	1.9	2.5	5.1	-1.0	-1.9	0.3
North America	-3.8	4.1	-0.2	4.0	3.2	5.6	6.2	5.2	4.9	-3.1	-2.0	0.2
United States	-4.3	3.7	-0.1	3.8	3.4	5.6	6.1	4.9	4.4	-3.4	-2.2	-0.2
Canada	2.5	10.1	-1.7	5.0	0.3	7.5	7.5	9.4	9.6	-0.7	4.1	2.1
Four European countries	0.8	2.2	5.9	2.5	1.4	3.2	6.1	6.2	9.9	5.2	0.8	0.2
France	-2.0	-1.6	5.7	2.5	0.2	3.5	9.4	8.8	14.2	7.4	-0.2	-1.7
Germany	1.0	2.0	7.2	2.9	-0.4	-	5.0	5.8	7.6	2.0	-2.3	-3.1
Italy	8.7	5.5	9.3	-	4.2	6.2	5.9	8.6	15.1	10.9	6.6	5.3
United Kingdom	-1.2	4.2	0.9	4.1	4.0	6.2	5.0	2.3	4.5	2.9	2.3	3.7
Seven Pacific region countries	3.9	4.4	8.1	0.8	1.3	1.0	-6.2	-2.5	1.6	-3.7	-2.8	1.5
Australia	3.9	8.7	-0.4	8.1	3.5	4.1	6.8	7.9	4.8	-1.0	6.7	6.3
Taiwan[1]	10.2	1.8	5.1	3.8	1.2	6.0	7.8	3.1	4.5	-6.4	1.3	3.1
Thailand	2.9	2.0	11.6	9.7	5.2	-1.6	-6.4	12.6	9.6	7.0	9.6	9.1
Japan	4.3	4.4	8.6	-0.4	0.6	0.6	-6.8	-4.7		-5.0	-4.9	0.7
Korea, South	-4.2	7.1	9.9	8.0	7.1	3.9	-14.7	11.8	13.7	5.3	8.6	2.0
Malaysia	-1.6	-8.5	1.5	3.6	1.3	-1.4	-12.6	-1.9	3.4	-7.8	-7.2	-2.5
New Zealand	0.2	7.4	-1.2	9.5	6.7	1.2	-3.4	5.6	2.7	3.7	6.9	6.4

- Represents or rounds to zero.   [1] See footnote 2, Table 1314.

Source: Foundation for International Business and Economic Research, New York, NY, *International Economic Indicators*, monthly.

Comparative International Statistics   875

Table 1331. **Index of Industrial Production by Country: 1980 to 2004**

[Annual averages of monthly data. Industrial production index measures output in the manufacturing, mining, and electric, gas and water utilities industries. Minus sign (-) indicates decrease]

Country	Index (2000 = 100)								Annual percent change				
	1980	1985	1990	1995	2001	2002	2003	2004	1999-2000	2000-2001	2001-2002	2002-2003	2003-2004
OECD, total.	62.1	67.2	78.4	83.6	97.6	97.8	98.9	102.9	-12.6	-2.4	0.2	1.1	4.0
Australia.	61.3	67.9	79.9	87.0	100.7	103.3	103.8	103.5	-11.1	0.7	2.6	0.5	-0.3
Austria	52.6	57.1	69.0	74.5	102.8	103.6	105.6	112.0	-18.8	2.8	0.8	1.9	6.1
Belgium [1]	70.6	73.5	85.9	86.5	99.0	100.3	101.0	104.3	-8.8	-1.0	1.3	0.7	3.3
Canada.	55.8	64.6	69.1	78.6	96.1	97.5	98.3	101.7	-14.3	-3.9	1.5	0.8	3.5
Czech Republic [1] . . .	(X)	(X)	119.8	90.5	106.5	116.6	123.4	135.6	-4.6	6.5	9.5	5.8	9.9
Denmark.	57.5	70.3	75.8	86.5	101.6	103.0	103.2	103.2	-11.5	1.6	1.4	0.2	-
Finland.	45.6	53.1	60.4	69.3	100.1	102.0	103.2	107.6	-22.5	0.1	1.9	1.2	4.3
France.	76.8	77.2	87.6	87.3	101.1	99.8	99.4	101.6	-11.0	1.1	-1.3	-0.4	2.2
Germany	75.2	77.6	90.7	87.4	100.2	99.2	99.6	102.6	-9.4	0.2	-1.0	0.4	3.0
Greece.	75.6	81.0	83.2	81.7	98.2	99.0	99.3	100.2	-12.4	(NA)	0.8	0.3	0.9
Hungary [1]	69.3	76.1	67.6	59.4	103.6	106.4	113.2	122.6	-29.8	3.6	2.7	6.4	8.3
Ireland	16.8	21.5	30.9	49.6	110.2	118.5	124.3	124.9	-42.7	10.2	7.5	4.9	0.5
Italy	76.8	73.5	86.7	93.1	99.0	97.4	96.9	96.2	-2.8	-1.0	-1.6	-0.5	-0.7
Japan [1]	66.8	79.2	98.5	95.5	93.7	92.6	95.4	100.5	0.2	-6.3	-1.2	3.0	5.3
Korea, South [1]	14.3	23.5	43.1	64.9	100.7	108.8	114.2	126.1	-24.2	0.7	8.0	5.0	10.4
Luxembourg	55.4	67.3	79.5	81.3	103.1	105.2	110.7	117.8	-15.3	3.1	2.0	5.2	6.4
Mexico [2]	56.9	60.1	67.7	70.8	96.6	96.4	96.3	100.0	-25.0	-3.4	-0.2	-0.1	3.8
Netherlands	76.2	76.9	83.9	90.9	100.4	100.1	97.7	100.2	-6.4	0.4	-0.3	-2.4	2.6
New Zealand.	(X)	(X)	83.0	95.0	100.0	104.0	105.0	109.0	-1.0	-	4.0	1.0	3.8
Norway.	46.3	56.2	71.5	90.3	98.7	99.6	95.5	97.4	-7.5	-1.3	0.9	-4.1	2.0
Poland	(X)	74.7	61.0	69.7	100.4	101.8	110.7	124.8	-25.1	0.4	1.4	8.7	12.7
Portugal	54.7	64.5	87.2	84.7	103.1	102.7	102.6	94.6	-15.0	3.1	-0.4	-0.1	-7.8
Spain . . [3], [4]	66.9	69.1	80.6	83.7	98.6	98.7	100.1	101.6	-12.4	-1.4	0.1	1.4	1.5
Sweden [3], [4]	58.4	64.7	74.8	84.0	98.7	98.8	100.2	105.4	-13.5	-1.3	0.1	1.4	5.2
Switzerland.	65.0	67.0	79.0	82.0	99.0	94.0	94.0	99.0	-10.7	-1.0	-5.1	-	5.3
Turkey	30.9	46.0	65.5	80.7	91.3	100.0	108.7	119.4	-13.8	-8.7	9.5	8.7	9.8
United Kingdom	71.6	77.4	87.9	93.4	98.4	96.0	95.8	96.3	-3.9	-1.6	-2.4	-0.2	0.5
United States	54.2	59.1	67.1	77.5	96.4	96.2	96.1	100.1	-18.0	-3.6	-0.2	-0.1	4.2

- Represents or rounds to zero.   NA Not available.   X Not applicable.   [1] Not adjusted for unequal number of working days in the month.   [2] Including construction.   [3] Mining and manufacturing.   [4] Annual figures correspond to official annual figures and differ from the average of the monthly figures.

Source: Organization for Economic Cooperation and Development, Paris, France, *Main Economic Indicators*, monthly (copyright).

Table 1332. **Annual Percent Change in Labor Productivity and Hours Worked by Country: 1995 to 2004**

[Change for period shown. Data are derived from an annual database maintained by the Groningen Growth and Development Centre at the University of Groningen, Netherlands, in association with The Conference Board. For OECD countries and Eastern Europe, estimates are based on gross domestic product per hour worked, converted at purchasing power parities for 2002. Hence, estimates expressed in U.S. dollars at the price level of 2002 are corrected for differences in relative price levels]

Country	Labor productivity		Total hours worked		Country	Labor productivity		Total hours worked	
	1995-2000	2000-2004	1995-2000	2000-2004		1995-2000	2000-2004	1995-2000	2000-2004
All OECD	2.1	2.1	1.1	(Z)	European Union (EU-10, new) [3]	4.0	4.7	(Z)	-1.3
All OECD, excl. United States	2.0	1.7	0.8	0.2	Cyprus	2.5	1.2	1.2	1.5
United States.	2.1	2.9	1.9	-0.4	Czech Republic.	1.9	4.5	-0.7	-1.5
European Union (EU-25, enlarged) [1]	2.1	1.5	0.7	0.1	Estonia	7.5	6.4	-1.8	-0.2
					Hungary	2.3	3.2	1.6	0.4
European Union (EU-15, present) [2]	1.8	1.0	0.9	0.4	Latvia	5.3	7.3	0.1	0.1
Austria.	3.1	1.4	-0.4	-0.2	Lithuania	4.7	11.0	-0.5	-3.4
Belgium	2.8	0.5	-0.1	0.7	Malta.	3.6	-0.3	0.9	0.2
Denmark	2.1	1.4	0.6	-0.1	Poland.	5.2	4.5	(Z)	-1.9
Finland	3.1	2.6	1.6	-0.5	Slovakia	3.9	6.3	-0.2	-1.9
France.	2.4	1.6	0.2	-0.2	Slovenia	3.3	3.0	0.9	0.1
Germany	2.3	1.2	-0.5	-0.7	Other OECD members	2.4	2.2	1.8	0.7
Greece	2.5	2.7	0.9	1.3	Japan	2.3	2.4	-0.9	-0.7
Ireland.	5.8	4.3	3.7	0.9	Australia	2.3	2.2	1.5	1.2
Italy	1.2	-0.4	0.7	1.3	Canada	1.6	1.7	2.5	0.9
Luxembourg	2.7	-0.2	4.3	3.0	Iceland	2.5	3.9	2.5	-1.0
Netherlands	0.6	0.7	3.1	-0.1	Mexico	2.1	0.6	3.2	0.9
Portugal.	2.4	0.6	1.4	(Z)	New Zealand	1.6	1.3	1.0	2.6
Spain	-0.3	(Z)	4.2	2.5	Norway	2.2	2.6	1.4	-0.7
Sweden	2.3	2.6	1.0	-0.6	South Korea	3.7	4.0	0.6	0.7
U.K.	2.1	2.0	1.1	0.3	Switzerland	1.7	1.1	0.3	-0.4
					Turkey	2.9	3.9	1.0	-0.1

Z Less than .05 percent.   [1] Referring to all members of the European Union as of 1 May 2004.   [2] Referring to membership of the European Union until April 2004.   [3] Referring to new membership of the European Union as of 1 May 2004.

Source: The Conference Board, New York, NY, *Performance 2005: Productivity, Employment, and Income in the World's Economies*, by Robert H. McGuckin and Bart van Ark, 2005 (copyright). See also <http://www.conference-board.org/>.

Table 1333. Annual Percent Changes in Consumer Prices, by Country: 2000 to 2004

[Change from previous year. See text of this section for general comments concerning the data. For additional qualifications of the data for individual countries, see source. Minus sign (-) indicates decrease]

Country	2000	2001	2002	2003	2004	Country	2000	2001	2002	2003	2004
United States	3.4	2.2	1.5	1.9	2.0	Kenya	10.0	5.7	2.0	9.8	11.6
Argentina........	-0.9	-1.1	25.9	13.4	4.4	Korea, South	2.2	4.1	2.7	3.6	3.6
Australia	4.5	4.4	3.0	2.8	2.3	Malaysia	1.5	1.4	1.8	1.1	1.5
Austria	2.4	2.7	1.8	1.4	2.1	Mexico	9.5	6.4	5.0	4.6	4.7
Bangladesh	2.4	2.0	3.3	5.7	(NA)	Netherlands	2.5	4.5	3.5	2.1	1.2
Belgium.........	2.5	2.5	1.6	1.6	2.1	Nigeria	14.5	13.0	12.9	14.0	15.0
Bolivia..........	4.6	1.6	0.9	3.3	4.4	Norway	3.1	3.0	1.3	2.5	0.5
Brazil	7.0	6.8	8.5	14.7	6.6	Pakistan	4.4	3.2	3.3	2.9	7.4
Canada.........	2.7	2.5	2.3	2.8	1.8	Peru	3.8	2.0	0.2	2.3	3.7
Chile	3.8	3.6	2.5	2.8	1.1	Philippines	4.4	6.1	3.0	3.0	5.9
Colombia........	9.2	8.0	6.4	7.1	5.9	Portugal	2.8	4.4	3.6	3.3	2.4
Egypt	2.7	2.3	2.7	4.5	11.3	Romania	45.7	34.5	22.5	15.3	11.9
France	1.7	1.7	1.9	2.1	2.1	Russia..........	20.8	21.5	15.8	13.7	10.9
Germany	1.5	2.0	1.4	1.1	1.7	South Africa	5.4	5.7	9.2	5.9	1.4
Ghana..........	25.2	32.9	14.8	26.7	12.6	Spain	3.4	3.6	3.1	3.0	3.0
Greece	3.1	3.4	3.6	3.5	2.9	Sri Lanka	6.2	14.2	9.6	6.3	7.6
Guatemala.......	6.0	7.6	8.0	5.5	7.5	Sweden.........	0.9	2.4	2.2	1.9	0.4
India	4.0	3.7	4.4	3.8	3.8	Switzerland	1.5	1.0	0.6	0.6	0.8
Indonesia........	4.5	11.5	11.9	6.6	6.2	Thailand	1.6	1.6	0.6	1.8	2.8
Iran	14.5	11.3	14.3	16.5	(NA)	Turkey..........	54.9	54.4	45.0	25.3	8.6
Israel	1.1	1.1	5.6	0.7	-0.4	United Kingdom ...	2.9	1.8	1.6	2.9	3.0
Italy	2.5	2.8	2.5	2.7	2.2	Venezuela	16.2	12.5	22.4	31.1	21.8
Japan	-0.7	-0.7	-0.9	-0.3	0.0						

NA Not available.

Source: International Monetary Fund, Washington, DC, *International Financial Statistics*, monthly (copyright).

Table 1334. Comparative Price Levels—Selected OECD Countries: 2005

[Example of data: An item that costs $1.00 in the United States would cost $1.39 (U.S. dollars) in Japan]

Country	United States (U.S. dollar)	Canada (Canadian dollar)	Mexico (Mexican peso)	Japan (yen)	France (euro)	Germany (euro)	Italy (euro)	United Kingdom (pound)
United States	100	98	146	72	83	84	90	85
Australia [1]........	109	107	159	78	91	91	98	85
Austria	118	116	173	85	99	99	106	92
Belgium	116	114	169	83	97	97	104	100
Canada	102	100	149	73	85	85	92	98
Czech Republic	62	61	91	45	52	52	56	86
Denmark.........	152	149	222	109	127	127	137	53
Finland..........	135	133	198	97	113	113	122	128
France	120	117	175	86	100	100	108	114
Germany	119	117	175	86	100	100	107	101
Greece	97	95	142	70	81	81	87	101
Hungary	69	67	100	49	57	57	62	82
Iceland	166	163	243	119	138	139	149	58
Ireland	141	138	205	101	117	118	126	140
Italy	111	109	163	80	93	93	100	119
Japan	139	136	203	100	116	116	125	94
Korea, South	88	86	128	63	73	73	79	117
Luxembourg	117	114	170	84	97	98	105	74
Mexico..........	68	67	100	49	57	57	62	98
Netherlands	118	116	173	85	99	99	106	58
New Zealand [1]....	110	108	161	79	92	92	99	100
Norway..........	153	149	223	110	127	128	137	93
Poland	63	61	92	45	52	52	56	129
Portugal	87	86	128	63	73	73	79	53
Slovakia	62	61	91	45	52	52	56	74
Spain...........	99	97	145	72	83	83	89	52
Sweden	132	129	193	95	110	110	119	84
Switzerland	154	151	224	111	128	129	138	112
Turkey	68	67	99	49	57	57	61	130
United Kingdom ...	118	116	173	85	99	99	106	100

[1] Estimates based on quarterly consumer prices.

Source: Organization for Economic Cooperation and Development, Paris, France, *Main Economic Indicators*, June 2005 (copyright). See also <http://www.oecd.org/dataoecd/48/18/18598721.pdf>.

Table 1335. Gross Public Debt, Expenditures, and Receipts by Country: 1990 to 2004

[Percent of nominal gross domestic product. 2004 data estimated. Expenditures and receipts refer to the general government sector, which is a consolidation of accounts for the central, state, and local governments plus social security. Expenditures, or total outlays, are defined as current outlays plus capital outlays. Receipts cover current receipts, but exclude capital receipts. Nontax receipts consist of property income (including dividends and other transfers from public enterprises), fees, charges, sales, fines, capital transfers received by the general government, etc.)]

Country	Gross debt			Expenditures			Receipts		
	1990	2000	2004	1990	2000	2004	1990	2000	2004
United States [1]	-4.2	1.6	-4.3	37.1	34.2	36.0	32.8	35.8	31.7
Australia	-1.7	[2]0.9	1.1	36.2	[2]35.7	35.5	34.5	36.7	36.6
Austria	-2.4	[2]-1.6	-1.3	52.1	[2]51.5	50.6	49.7	49.8	49.4
Belgium	-6.8	0.2	0.0	53.4	49.3	49.4	46.6	49.5	49.4
Canada	-5.8	2.9	1.3	48.8	41.1	39.4	43.0	44.1	40.7
Czech Republic	(X)	-3.7	-3.0	(X)	42.1	45.9	(X)	38.5	42.9
Denmark	-1.2	2.5	2.3	57.2	54.9	56.3	56.0	57.4	58.6
Finland	5.5	7.1	1.9	48.7	49.1	50.7	54.2	56.1	52.6
France	-2.1	-1.4	-3.7	50.7	52.5	54.4	48.6	51.1	50.7
Germany	-2.0	[2]1.3	-3.6	44.5	[2]45.8	47.7	42.5	47.1	44.0
Greece	-15.7	-4.2	-6.0	50.2	52.1	52.0	34.5	47.9	46.0
Hungary	(NA)	-3.0	-4.5	(NA)	47.9	49.3	(NA)	44.9	44.9
Iceland	-3.3	2.5	0.4	42.7	43.2	47.6	39.3	45.7	48.1
Ireland	-2.8	4.4	1.3	43.2	32.0	34.3	40.4	36.4	35.6
Italy	-11.8	[2]-0.7	-3.1	54.4	[2]46.9	48.6	42.6	46.2	45.5
Japan [3]	2.1	-7.5	-6.1	31.8	38.3	37.3	33.9	30.8	31.2
Korea, South	3.2	5.4	2.9	19.7	23.8	27.3	23.0	29.3	30.2
Netherlands	-5.3	[2]2.2	-2.3	54.8	[2]45.3	48.6	49.4	47.5	46.2
New Zealand	-4.3	3.1	4.2	53.3	35.1	34.1	48.9	38.2	38.3
Norway	2.2	15.6	11.5	54.0	42.7	46.6	56.2	58.2	58.0
Portugal	-6.6	[2]-2.9	-3.0	42.1	[2]45.2	48.4	35.5	42.3	45.4
Spain	-3.9	[2]-0.9	-0.3	43.4	[2]40.0	40.6	39.5	39.1	40.3
Sweden	3.4	5.0	1.2	61.7	57.3	57.1	65.1	62.3	58.3
United Kingdom	-1.6	[2]3.8	-3.4	42.2	[2]37.5	44.1	40.7	41.3	40.7

NA Not available.   X Not applicable.   [1] Receipts exclude the operating surpluses of public enterprises and expenditures include them. [2] Financial balances include substantial one-off revenues from the sale of the mobile telephone licenses. [3] The 2000 expenditures include capital transfers to the Deposit Insurance Company. Receipts include deferred tax payments on postal savings accounts in 2000. In 2002, corporate pension funds were authorized to transfer back to the government the basic part of their employees' pension scheme. This resulted in a capital transfer to the government which reduced the general government financial deficit by 0.1 percentage point of GDP in 2003, and at least by 0.6 percentage point in 2004.

Source: Organization for Economic Cooperation and Development, Paris, France, *OECD Economic Outlook*, December 2004 (copyright).

Table 1336. Percent Distribution of Tax Receipts by Country: 1990 to 2002

Country	Income and profits taxes [2]				Social security contributions			Taxes on goods and services [5]		
	Total [1]	Total [3]	Indi-vidual	Corpo-rate	Total [4]	Employ-ees	Employ-ers	Total [3]	General con-sumption taxes [6]	Taxes on specific goods, ser-vices [7]
United States:										
1990	100.0	45.4	37.7	7.7	25.9	11.0	13.4	17.3	8.0	7.1
2000	100.0	50.9	42.4	8.5	23.3	10.2	11.8	15.8	7.5	6.3
2002	100.0	(NA)	(NA)	(NA)	(NA)	(NA)	(NA)	(NA)	(NA)	(NA)
Canada:										
1990	100.0	48.6	40.8	7.0	12.2	4.4	7.6	25.8	14.1	10.3
2000	100.0	49.2	37.0	11.2	14.1	5.7	8.0	24.4	14.3	8.7
2002	100.0	45.5	35.6	8.7	15.2	6.3	8.5	26.6	15.5	9.6
France:										
1990	100.0	17.2	11.8	5.3	44.1	13.2	27.2	28.4	18.8	8.7
2000	100.0	25.0	18.0	6.9	36.1	9.0	24.8	25.8	16.9	8.2
2002	100.0	24.0	17.4	6.6	37.2	9.3	25.5	25.5	16.8	8.1
Germany:										
1990	100.0	32.4	27.6	4.8	37.5	16.2	19.1	26.7	16.6	9.2
2000	100.0	30.2	25.3	4.8	39.0	17.2	19.2	28.1	18.4	8.8
2002	100.0	28.0	26.0	2.0	40.1	17.6	19.7	29.3	18.1	10.1
Italy:										
1990	100.0	36.5	26.3	10.0	32.9	6.3	23.6	28.0	14.7	10.6
2000	100.0	33.2	25.7	7.5	28.5	5.4	19.8	28.4	15.8	10.0
2002	100.0	32.6	26.2	7.3	30.3	5.9	21.1	25.4	15.1	8.5
Japan:										
1990	100.0	48.5	26.9	21.6	29.0	11.0	15.0	13.2	4.3	7.3
2000	100.0	33.5	20.2	13.2	35.8	13.9	18.2	18.5	8.7	7.7
2002	100.0	49.7	29.6	20.1	0.0	0.0	0.0	32.3	15.1	13.4
United Kingdom:										
1990	100.0	38.3	27.1	11.2	16.7	6.5	9.7	30.5	16.4	12.4
2000	100.0	38.9	29.1	9.8	16.7	6.9	9.6	32.2	18.3	12.4
2002	100.0	37.9	29.9	8.0	17.1	7.0	9.5	32.4	19.1	12.0

- Represents zero.   NA Not available.   [1] Includes property taxes, employer payroll taxes other than Social Security contributions, and miscellaneous taxes, not shown separately.   [2] Includes taxes on capital gains.   [3] Includes other taxes not shown separately.   [4] Includes contributions of self-employed not shown separately.   [5] Taxes on the production, sales, transfer, leasing, and delivery of goods and services and rendering of services.   [6] Primary value-added and sales taxes.   [7] For example, excise taxes on alcohol, tobacco, and gasoline.

Source: Organization for Economic Cooperation and Development, Paris, France, *Revenue Statistics of OECD Member Countries*, annual (copyright).

878   Comparative International Statistics

Table 1337. Household Tax Burden by Country: 2004

[**Percent of gross earnings equivalent to the average production worker**. The tax burden reflects income tax plus employee contributions less cash benefits]

Country	Single person without children	One earner family with two children	Country	Single person without children	One earner family with two children
Australia	24.3	24.3	Korea, South	2.2	1.4
Austria	10.8	8.1	Luxembourg	8.9	0.0
Belgium	26.6	15.2	Mexico	3.0	3.0
Canada	17.8	13.9	Netherlands	8.5	8.3
Czech Republic	11.4	5.3	New Zealand	20.7	20.7
Denmark	30.6	25.4	Norway	20.9	18.0
Finland	24.2	24.2	Poland	6.1	4.1
France	13.1	7.1	Portugal	5.6	0.4
Germany	19.6	-2.8	Slovakia	7.9	-5.3
Greece	0.6	0.6	Spain	12.7	4.3
Hungary	12.4	4.7	Sweden	24.0	24.0
Iceland	25.5	14.0	Switzerland	9.8	5.1
Ireland	10.6	2.2	Turkey	15.4	15.4
Italy	18.6	11.9	United Kingdom	15.9	8.1
Japan	5.9	2.7	United States	16.5	2.4

Source: Organization for Economic Cooperation and Development, Paris, France, *Taxing Wages, 2003-2004*, (copyright).

Table 1338. Income Tax and Social Security Contributions as Percent of Labor Costs: 2004

[Data are for single individual at the income level of the average production worker]

Country	Labor costs [1] (dol.)	Percent of labor costs Total [2]	Income tax	Social security contributions Employee	Employer [3]
Belgium	46,261	54	27	14	14
Germany	42,543	51	20	21	10
Australia	40,630	29	24	-	4
Netherlands	39,614	44	9	26	9
Switzerland	38,213	29	10	11	8
Norway	37,550	37	21	8	8
Denmark	37,788	41	31	11	-
Luxembourg	35,767	32	9	14	9
Canada	37,856	32	18	7	8
Korea, South	36,125	17	2	7	7
Finland	37,174	44	24	6	13
United States	37,606	30	17	8	5
Italy	35,005	46	19	9	18
France	35,443	47	13	14	21
Austria	34,356	45	11	18	16
United Kingdom	36,159	31	16	9	7
Japan	35,103	27	6	12	9
Sweden	34,606	48	24	7	17
Iceland	32,194	30	25	-	4
New Zealand	28,228	21	21	-	-
Ireland	30,236	24	11	5	8
Spain	29,382	38	13	6	19
Czech Republic	19,395	44	11	13	20
Greece	22,138	35	1	16	18
Turkey	20,003	43	15	15	12
Poland	17,319	43	6	25	12
Portugal	16,128	33	6	11	16
Hungary	13,229	46	12	14	20
Mexico	10,278	15	3	2	11

- Represents or rounds to zero.   [1] Adjusted for purchasing power parities, see text of this section. Labor costs include gross wages plus employers compulsory social security contributions.   [2] Due to rounding total may differ one percentage point from aggregate columns for income tax and social security contributions.   [3] Includes reported payroll taxes.

Source: Organization for Economic Cooperation and Development, Paris, France, *Taxing Wages, 2003-2004* (copyright).

Table 1339. Patents by Country: 2004

[Includes only U.S. patents granted to residents of areas outside of the United States and its territories]

Country	Total [1]	Inventions	Designs	Country	Total [1]	Inventions	Designs
Total	87,192	80,022	6,443	Sweden	1,388	1,290	97
				Netherlands	1,537	1,273	50
Japan	37,034	35,350	1,568	Switzerland	1,405	1,277	125
Germany	11,367	10,779	476	Israel	1,091	1,028	47
Taiwan [2]	7,207	5,938	1,268	Australia	1,093	953	114
Korea, South	4,671	4,428	238	Finland	954	918	35
France	3,686	3,380	286	Belgium	678	612	50
United Kingdom	3,905	3,450	406	Austria	575	540	34
Canada	3,781	3,374	398	Denmark	530	414	40
Italy	1,946	1,584	358	Other countries	4,344	3,434	853

[1] Includes patents for botanical plants and reissues, not shown separately.   [2] See footnote 2, Table 1314.

Source: U.S. Patent and Trademark Office, Technology Assessment and Forecast Database.

Table 1340. Civilian Labor Force, Employment, and Unemployment by Country: 1990 to 2004

[125,840 represents 125,840,000. Data based on U.S. labor force definitions (see source) except that minimum age for population base varies as follows: United States, Canada, France, Sweden, and United Kingdom, 16 years; Australia, Japan, Netherlands, Germany, and Italy (beginning 1995), 15 years; and Italy (1990) 14 years]

Year	United States	Canada	Australia	Japan	France	Germany [1]	Italy	Netherlands	Sweden	United Kingdom
Civilian labor force (1,000):										
1990	[2]125,840	14,043	8,440	63,050	[2]24,165	29,410	22,670	6,657	4,594	28,773
2000	[2]142,583	15,632	9,590	66,990	26,078	39,301	23,357	8,149	4,489	28,957
2002	144,863	16,367	9,907	66,240	26,686	39,499	23,728	8,285	4,544	29,340
2003	[2]146,510	16,729	10,092	66,010	26,870	39,591	24,021	8,353	4,567	29,562
2004	[2]147,401	16,956	10,244	65,760	(NA)	39,698	24,065	8,457	4,576	29,748
Labor force participation rate: [3]										
1990	[2]66.5	67.3	64.7	62.6	[2]55.7	55.3	47.2	56.2	67.3	64.4
2000	67.1	65.8	64.4	62.0	56.6	56.7	48.1	64.5	63.8	62.9
2002	66.6	66.7	64.4	60.8	57.2	56.5	48.5	64.7	64.0	62.9
2003	66.2	67.3	64.6	60.3	57.4	56.4	49.1	64.9	64.0	63.0
2004	66.0	67.3	64.7	60.0	(NA)	(NA)	49.1	65.5	63.7	63.0
Civilian employment (1,000):										
1990	[2]118,793	12,956	7,877	61,700	[2]22,081	27,950	21,080	6,267	4,513	26,720
2000	[2]136,891	14,676	8,989	63,790	23,693	36,236	20,969	7,912	4,229	27,373
2002	136,485	15,221	9,271	62,650	24,293	36,061	21,665	8,059	4,310	27,817
2003	[2]137,736	15,579	9,481	62,510	24,293	35,754	21,973	8,035	4,303	28,079
2004	[2]139,252	15,864	9,677	62,630	(NA)	35,796	22,105	8,061	4,276	28,334
Employment-population ratio: [4]										
1990	[2]62.8	62.1	60.4	61.3	[2]50.9	52.6	43.9	52.9	66.1	59.8
2000	64.4	61.9	60.3	59.0	51.5	52.2	43.2	62.7	60.1	59.4
2002	62.7	62.4	60.3	57.5	52.1	51.6	44.3	62.9	60.7	59.6
2003	62.3	63.0	60.7	57.1	51.9	51.0	44.9	62.4	60.3	59.8
2004	62.3	63.4	61.2	57.1	(NA)	(NA)	45.1	62.4	59.5	60.0
Unemployment rate:										
1990	[2]5.6	7.7	6.7	2.1	[2]8.6	5.0	7.0	5.9	1.8	7.1
2000	4.0	6.1	6.3	4.8	9.1	7.8	10.2	2.9	5.8	5.5
2002	5.8	7.0	6.4	5.4	9.0	8.7	8.7	2.7	5.1	5.2
2003	6.0	6.9	6.1	5.3	9.6	9.7	8.5	3.8	5.8	5.0
2004	5.5	6.4	5.5	4.8	9.8	9.8	8.1	4.7	6.6	4.8
Under 25 years old	11.8	12.4	11.6	9.6	21.5	(NA)	(NA)	8.6	17.2	12.3
Teenagers [5]	17.0	17.1	15.8	12.0	26.6	(NA)	(NA)	10.9	22.8	(NA)
20 to 24 years old	9.4	9.6	8.5	9.1	20.4	(NA)	(NA)	6.9	14.9	(NA)
25 years old and over	4.4	5.3	4.1	4.2	8.3	(NA)	(NA)	4.1	5.3	3.3

NA Not available. [1] Unified Germany for 1991 onward. Prior to 1991, data relate to the former West Germany. [2] Break in series. Data not comparable with prior years. [3] Civilian labor force as a percent of the civilian working age population. Germany and Japan include the institutionalized population as part of the working age population. [4] Civilian employment as a percent of the civilian working age population. Germany and Japan include the institutionalized population as part of the working age population. [5] 16-to 19-year-olds in the United States, Canada, France, Sweden, and the United Kingdom; 15-to 19-year-olds in Australia, Japan, Germany, Italy, and the Netherlands.

Source: U.S. Bureau of Labor Statistics, *Comparative Civilian Labor Force Statistics, Ten Countries, 1960-2004*, May 13, 2005. See also <http://bls.gov/fls>.

Table 1341. Percent of Persons Not in Education or at Work by Age Group and Sex: 2002

[Represents those persons not in education and either unemployed or not in the labor force]

Country	15 to 19 years old			20 to 24 years old		
	Total	Male	Female	Total	Male	Female
Australia	7.1	6.9	7.1	13.2	10.3	16.2
Belgium	6.8	7.3	6.4	17.5	15.8	19.2
Canada	6.4	7.2	5.7	13.9	14.0	13.9
Czech Republic	6.0	5.8	6.3	18.1	12.3	24.1
Denmark	2.4	2.3	2.4	7.4	7.0	7.6
Finland	14.9	21.1	7.8	18.8	20.7	17.0
France	3.4	3.6	3.2	14.3	12.6	16.1
Germany	4.7	4.3	5.2	15.9	14.3	17.7
Greece	6.2	5.2	7.3	22.0	15.5	28.2
Hungary	8.0	8.2	7.8	20.3	17.0	23.5
Italy	10.5	10.7	10.3	24.3	21.8	26.8
Luxembourg	3.0	1.7	4.2	7.0	2.6	11.5
Mexico	17.5	7.4	27.4	26.6	6.4	44.8
Netherlands	4.6	4.7	4.5	7.9	6.4	9.5
Poland	3.1	3.5	2.6	25.4	25.2	25.6
Portugal	7.2	7.2	6.8	12.0	8.6	15.3
Spain	7.1	6.9	7.4	15.1	12.4	17.9
Sweden	4.6	5.9	3.3	11.2	11.9	10.6
Switzerland	4.4	(S)	5.0	9.7	6.6	6.0
United States	7.5	7.0	8.0	15.6	12.1	18.9

S Figure does not meet publication standards.

Source: Organization for Economic Cooperation and Development, Paris, France; *Education at a Glance 2004* (copyright).

Table 1342. Unemployment Rates by Country: 2000 to 2004

[**Annual averages.** The standardized unemployment rates shown here are calculated as the number of unemployed persons as a percentage of the civilian labor force. The unemployed are persons of working age who, in the reference period, are without work, available for work and have taken specific steps to find work]

Country	2000	2002	2003	2004	Country	2000	2002	2003	2004
OECD, total	6.3	7.0	7.1	6.9	Ireland	4.3	4.3	4.6	4.5
European Union [1] . . .	7.8	7.7	8.1	8.1	Italy	10.4	9.0	8.6	(NA)
					Japan	4.7	5.4	5.3	4.7
United States	4.0	5.8	6.0	5.5	Korea, South	4.4	3.3	3.6	(NA)
Australia	6.3	6.4	6.1	5.5	Luxembourg	2.3	2.8	3.7	4.2
Austria	3.7	4.2	4.3	4.5	Netherlands	2.9	2.7	3.8	(NA)
Belgium	6.9	7.3	7.9	7.8	New Zealand	6.0	5.2	4.6	(NA)
Canada	6.8	7.7	7.6	7.2	Norway	3.4	3.9	4.5	(NA)
Czech Republic	8.7	7.3	7.8	8.3	Poland	16.4	19.8	19.2	18.8
Denmark	4.4	4.6	5.6	5.4	Portugal	4.1	5.0	6.2	6.6
Finland	9.7	9.1	9.0	8.9	Spain	11.3	11.3	11.3	10.8
France	9.1	8.9	9.5	9.6	Sweden	5.6	4.9	5.6	6.3
Germany	7.8	8.7	9.6	9.8	Switzerland	2.7	3.2	4.2	(NA)
Hungary	6.3	5.6	5.8	5.9	United Kingdom	5.4	5.1	5.0	(NA)

NA Not available.   [1] See footnote 4, Table 1328.

Source: Organization for Economic Cooperation and Development. Paris, France; *Main Economic Indicators*, April 2005 and earlier releases.

Table 1343. Female Labor Force Participation Rates by Country: 1980 to 2003

[**In percent.** Female labor force of all ages divided by female population 15-64 years old]

Country	1980	1990	2000	2003	Country	1980	1990	2000	2003
Australia	52.7	62.1	66.4	66.9	Korea, South	(NA)	51.2	54.3	55.9
Austria	48.7	55.4	62.2	64.7	Luxembourg	39.9	50.7	68.8	82.9
Belgium	47.0	52.4	59.2	59.1	Mexico	33.7	(NA)	42.4	41.9
Canada	57.8	67.6	70.4	73.0	Netherlands	35.5	[1]53.1	65.2	67.0
Czech Republic	(X)	69.1	64.3	63.1	New Zealand	44.6	[1]63.0	67.6	68.8
Denmark	(NA)	78.5	75.9	75.1	Norway	62.3	71.2	76.3	76.1
Finland	70.1	73.8	72.2	72.5	Poland	(NA)	(NA)	59.7	58.1
France	54.4	57.8	62.0	63.9	Portugal	54.3	62.9	67.2	69.4
Germany [2]	52.8	56.7	64.0	65.0	Slovak Republic	(NA)	(NA)	63.0	63.2
Greece	33.0	43.6	50.2	52.0	Spain	32.2	41.2	50.7	53.4
Hungary	(NA)	(NA)	52.5	53.8	Sweden	74.1	[1]80.4	75.0	75.4
Iceland	(NA)	65.6	82.8	81.1	Switzerland	54.1	65.7	70.6	78.0
Ireland	36.3	43.8	56.2	58.2	Turkey	(NA)	36.7	26.9	28.9
Italy	39.6	45.9	46.8	48.8	United Kingdom	58.3	66.5	67.8	68.7
Japan	54.8	60.3	64.2	64.2	**United States**	59.7	[1]68.5	71.7	70.4

NA Not available.   X Not applicable.   [1] Break in series. Data not comparable with prior years.   [2] Prior to 1991, data are for former West Germany.

Source: Organization for Economic Cooperation and Development, Paris, France, *OECD in Figures*, annual (copyright).

Table 1344. Civilian Employment-Population Ratio: 1990 to 2004

[Civilian employment as a percent of the civilian working age population. See headnote, Table 1340]

Country	Women					Men				
	1990	1995	2000	2003	2004	1990	1995	2000	2003	2004
United States	54.3	55.6	57.5	56.1	56.0	72.0	70.8	71.9	68.9	69.2
Canada	54.1	52.6	56.0	58.0	58.3	70.5	66.0	68.1	68.3	68.6
Australia	49.5	50.5	52.5	53.6	53.8	71.4	68.2	68.4	68.1	68.8
Japan	48.0	47.7	46.4	45.3	45.5	75.4	75.0	72.5	69.9	69.6
France	41.6	41.8	44.5	45.7	(NA)	61.4	57.4	59.2	58.7	(NA)
Germany [1]	40.9	42.7	44.4	44.6	(NA)	65.6	63.1	60.6	57.8	(NA)
Italy	29.2	29.1	31.6	34.0	34.2	60.0	56.2	55.8	56.9	57.1
Netherlands	39.4	44.2	52.4	54.2	54.0	67.0	65.9	73.2	70.8	71.0
Sweden	61.8	54.7	56.1	56.8	56.1	70.6	62.1	64.3	63.9	63.1
United Kingdom. . .	50.3	49.8	52.5	53.2	53.5	70.0	64.8	66.9	66.9	66.9

NA Not available.   [1] Unified Germany for 1991 onward. Prior to 1991, data relate to the former West Germany.

Source: U.S. Bureau of Labor Statistics, *Comparative Civilian Labor Force Statistics, Ten Countries, 1960-2004*, May 13, 2005. See also <http://bls.gov/fls>.

Comparative International Statistics   881

Table 1345. Civilian Employment by Industry and Country: 2000 and 2004

[136,891 represents 136,891,000. Data based on U.S. labor force definitions except that minimum age for population base varies as follows: United States, Canada, France, Sweden, and United Kingdom, 16 years; Australia, Germany, Italy, and Japan, 15 years. Industries based on International Standard Industrial Classification; see text of this section]

Industry	United States [1]	Canada [1]	Australia	Japan	France	Germany	Italy	Sweden	United Kingdom
TOTAL EMPLOYMENT (1,000)									
2000, total	**136,891**	**14,759**	**8,989**	**63,790**	**23,695**	**36,236**	**20,969**	**4,217**	**27,677**
Agriculture, forestry, fishing [2] . .	2,464	489	446	3,080	922	959	1,007	122	427
Industry [3]	30,050	3,223	1,901	19,710	5,510	11,897	6,353	999	6,854
Manufacturing [4]	19,644	2,254	1,129	13,180	4,081	8,646	4,796	761	4,752
Services [5]	104,377	11,047	6,642	41,000	17,263	23,380	13,609	3,096	20,396
2004, total	[6]**139,252**	**15,950**	**9,677**	**62,625**	**(NA)**	**35,686**	**22,105**	**4,264**	**(NA)**
Agriculture, forestry, fishing [2] . .	[6]2,232	422	367	2,706	(NA)	864	981	106	(NA)
Industry [3]	[6]27,791	3,437	2,002	17,301	(NA)	10,796	6,650	935	(NA)
Manufacturing [4]	[6]16,484	2,297	1,093	11,466	(NA)	8,090	4,821	683	(NA)
Services [5]	[6]109,229	12,091	7,308	42,618	(NA)	24,026	14,474	3,223	(NA)
PERCENT DISTRIBUTION									
2000, total	**100.0**	**100.0**	**100.0**	**100.0**	**100.0**	**100.0**	**100.0**	**100.0**	**100.0**
Agriculture, forestry, fishing [2] . .	1.8	3.3	5.0	4.8	3.9	2.6	4.8	2.9	1.5
Industry [3]	22.0	21.8	21.1	30.9	23.3	32.8	30.3	23.7	24.8
Manufacturing [4]	14.4	15.3	12.6	20.7	17.2	23.9	22.9	18.0	17.2
Services [5]	76.2	74.8	73.9	64.3	72.9	64.5	64.9	73.4	73.7
2004, total	[6]**100.0**	**100.0**	**100.0**	**100.0**	**100.0**	**100.0**	**100.0**	**100.0**	**100.0**
Agriculture, forestry, fishing [2] . .	[6]1.6	2.6	3.8	4.3	(NA)	2.4	4.4	2.5	(NA)
Industry [3]	[6]20.0	21.5	20.7	27.6	(NA)	30.3	30.1	21.9	(NA)
Manufacturing [4]	[6]11.8	14.4	11.3	18.3	(NA)	22.7	21.8	16.0	(NA)
Services [5]	[6]78.4	75.8	75.5	68.1	(NA)	67.3	65.5	75.6	(NA)

NA Not available. [1] Data for the United States and Canada are based on the 2002 North American Industry Classification System (NAICS). [2] Includes hunting. [3] Includes manufacturing, mining and construction. [4] For Italy, some mining is included in manufacturing. [5] Transportation, communication, public utilities, trade, finance, public administration, private household services, and miscellaneous services. [6] Break in series.

Source: U.S. Bureau of Labor Statistics, *Comparative Civilian Labor Force Statistics, Ten Countries, 1960-2004*, May 2005. See also <http://bls.gov/fls>.

Table 1346. World Food Production by Commodity: 1990 to 2004

[In millions of metric tons (1,768.8 represents 1,768,800,000)]

Commodity	1990	1995	1999	2000	2001	2002	2003	2004
Grains, total	1,768.8	1,710.3	1,871.5	1,839.5	1,872.1	1,809.3	1,817.6	1,854.2
Wheat.	588.0	538.0	585.3	585.8	581.4	580.9	567.0	552.8
Coarse grains.	828.7	801.3	877.5	859.9	892.3	867.9	872.8	912.0
Corn [1]	482.5	559.0	605.4	606.7	590.0	599.0	601.8	623.3
Rice, milled	352.0	371.0	408.7	398.1	398.7	378.3	377.9	389.4
Oils [1]	58.1	76.5	86.4	89.9	90.0	92.8	94.7	101.0
Soybeans [1]	104.1	137.7	159.8	159.9	175.9	185.1	197.1	188.8
Rapeseed [1]	25.1	30.3	35.9	42.6	37.4	36.0	32.5	39.3
Pulses [2]	58.3	55.5	57.0	54.4	54.6	56.5	57.7	61.3
Vegetables and melons [2]	461.7	564.4	695.0	746.0	777.4	809.5	844.0	855.1
Fruits [2]	352.6	409.4	459.8	470.2	470.0	479.4	489.7	497.4
Nuts [2]	4.8	5.7	7.3	7.4	7.5	8.4	8.4	8.4
Beef and pork	117.2	124.4	161.3	160.4	160.6	166.1	167.4	170.8
Poultry	31.5	43.6	61.9	64.5	66.6	68.4	68.2	69.8
Milk	441.3	380.7	380.3	386.8	391.4	402.3	406.6	411.3

[1] Data from U.S. Department of Agriculture, Foreign Agricultural Service, *Production, Supply, & Distribution (PSD) Online.* See also <http://www.fas.usda.gov/psd/psdselection.asp>. [2] Data from Food and Agriculture Organization of the United Nations, Rome, Italy.

Source: U.S. Department of Agriculture, Economic Research Service, *Agricultural Outlook*, monthly.

Table 1347. Fisheries—Commercial Catch by Country: 1990 to 2002

[In thousands of metric tons, live weight (97,854 represents 97,854,000). Catch of fish, crustaceans, mollusks (including weight of shells). Does not include marine mammals and aquatic plants]

Country	1990	2000	2001	2002	Country	1990	2000	2001	2002
World [1]	97,854	130,927	130,651	132,989	Russia	7,808	4,048	3,718	3,334
					Norway	1,745	3,191	3,198	3,297
China [2]	12,095	41,568	42,579	44,320	Philippines	2,210	2,287	2,364	2,474
Peru	6,875	10,665	7,996	8,775	Iceland	1,508	1,986	1,985	2,133
India	3,794	5,685	5,897	5,963	Vietnam	960	1,961	2,009	2,027
United States	5,868	5,174	5,424	5,435	Korea, South	1,745	2,117	2,285	1,966
Indonesia	3,044	4,858	5,137	5,420	Bangladesh	848	1,661	1,781	1,890
Japan	10,354	5,734	5,515	5,271	Mexico	1,401	1,369	1,475	1,524
Chile	5,195	4,692	4,363	4,817	Denmark	1,518	1,578	1,552	1,474
Thailand	2,786	3,643	3,657	3,566	Spain	1,380	1,358	1,397	(NA)

NA Not available.   [1] Includes other countries, not shown separately.   [2] See footnote 1, Table 1314.

Source: U.S. National Oceanic and Atmospheric Administration, National Marine Fisheries Service, *Fisheries of the United States,* annual. Data from Food and Agriculture Organization of the United Nations, Rome, Italy.

Table 1348. Meat Production by Type and Country: 2002 to 2003

[In thousands of metric tons (51,033 represents 51,033,000). Carcass weight basis for beef, veal, and pork. Excludes offals and rabbit]

Country	Beef and veal		Country	Pork [1]		Country	Poultry meat	
	2002	2003, prel.		2002	2003, prel.		2002	2003, prel.
World [2]	51,033	49,975	World [2]	86,451	88,959	World [2]	54,065	54,254
United States	12,427	12,039	China [3]	43,266	45,186	United States	14,467	14,696
European Union . . .	8,138	8,045	European Union . . .	20,938	21,243	China [3]	9,558	9,898
Brazil	7,240	7,385	United States	8,929	9,056	Brazil	7,449	7,645
China [3]	5,846	6,305	Brazil	2,565	2,560	European Union . . .	7,788	7,520
Argentina	2,700	2,800	Canada	1,854	1,882	Mexico	2,157	2,290
Australia	2,089	2,073	Russia	1,630	1,710	India	1,400	1,600
India	1,810	1,960	Poland	1,640	(NA)	Thailand	1,275	1,340
Mexico	1,930	1,950	Japan	1,236	1,259	Japan	1,107	1,127
Russia	1,740	1,670	Korea, South	1,153	1,149	Canada	932	929
Canada	1,294	1,190	Philippines	1,095	1,145	Malaysia	784	835

[1] Includes edible pork fat, but excludes lard and inedible greases (except United States).   [2] Includes other countries, not shown separately.   [3] See footnote 2, Table 1314.

Source: U.S. Department of Agriculture, National Agricultural Statistics Service, *Agricultural Statistics,* annual.

Table 1349. Meat Consumption by Type and Country: 2003 to 2004

In thousand metric tons (12,339 represents 12,339,000). Carcass weight basis for beef, veal, and pork. Broiler (chicken, 16 week-old) weight based on ready-to-cook equivalent]

Country	Beef and veal		Country	Pork		Country	Poultry meat	
	2003	2004 [1]		2003	2004 [1]		2003	2004 [1]
United States	12,339	12,667	China	45,053	47,038	United States	12,539	13,087
European Union [2] . . .	8,315	8,271	European Union [2] . . .	20,043	19,900	China	9,963	9,799
Brazil	6,273	6,400	United States	8,816	8,818	European Union [2] . . .	7,086	7,196
China	6,274	6,627	Russian	2,329	2,199	Brazil	5,729	5,957
Russia	2,378	2,315	Japan	2,373	2,570	Mexico	2,627	2,724
Mexico	2,308	2,419	Brazil	1,957	1,979	Japan	1,841	1,708
Argentina	2,426	2,468	Mexico	1,423	1,556	Russia	1,680	1,610
India [3]	1,521	1,590	South Korea	1,294	1,333	Canada	939	980
Japan	1,325	1,150	Philippines	1,167	1,198	Saudi Arabia	873	890
Canada	1,066	1,020	Canada	1,004	1,063	Malaysia	868	881
Australia	786	755	Taiwan	947	956	India	1,600	1,650
Other Countries	4,061	3,905	Other Countries	2,240	2,033	Other Countries	6,755	6,774

[1] Preliminary data.   [2] European Union-25: Austria, Belgium, Cyprus, Czech Republic, Denmark, Estonia, Finland, France, Germany, Greece, Hungary, Ireland, Italy, Latvia, Lithuania, Luxembourg, Malta, Netherlands, Poland, Portugal, Slovakia, Slovenia, Spain, Sweden, and United Kingdom.   [3] Includes buffalo.

Source: U.S. Department of Agriculture, Foreign Agricultural Service, *Livestock and Poultry: World Markets and Trade,* annual. See also <http://www.fas.usda.gov/dlp/circular/2005/05-04LP/toc.htm>.

Comparative International Statistics   883

Table 1350. World Crop Production Summary: 2003 to 2005

[In millions of metric tons, ($553,920,000), except as indicated]

Commodity	Unit	World[1]	North America United States	North America Canada	North America Mexico	EU-25	Other Europe Russia	Other Europe Ukraine	Asia China	Asia India	Asia Indo-nesia	Asia Pakistan	South America Argen-tina	South America Brazil	Selected Other Australia	Selected Other South Africa	Selected Other Turkey
Wheat:																	
2003-2004	Mil. metric tons	553.92	63.81	23.55	2.40	106.90	34.10	3.60	86.49	65.10	-	19.19	14.00	5.85	26.23	1.54	16.80
2004-2005 prel.	Mil. metric tons	624.51	58.74	25.86	2.40	136.67	45.30	17.50	91.00	72.06	-	19.00	16.00	5.85	21.50	1.70	18.00
Coarse grains:																	
2003-2004	Mil. metric tons	914.17	275.10	26.33	30.10	122.91	30.50	15.60	124.64	37.81	6.35	1.85	18.60	44.88	14.81	10.36	10.34
2004-2005 prel.	Mil. metric tons	1,007.14	319.45	26.44	29.08	150.59	29.55	23.00	137.05	31.99	6.50	1.98	23.90	38.30	10.96	12.54	11.05
Rice (milled):																	
2003-2004	Mil. metric tons	389.47	6.42	-	0.20	1.72	0.29	0.06	112.46	87.00	35.02	4.85	0.74	8.71	0.38	-	0.27
2004-2005 prel.	Mil. metric tons	401.77	7.41	-	0.20	1.86	0.30	0.05	126.00	86.00	34.83	4.92	0.68	8.98	0.25	-	0.33
Total grains[2]:																	
2003-2004	Mil. metric tons	1,857.56	345.33	49.88	32.70	231.53	64.89	19.26	323.59	189.91	41.37	25.89	33.34	59.44	41.42	11.90	27.41
2004-2005 prel.	Mil. metric tons	2,033.42	385.60	52.30	31.68	289.12	75.15	40.55	354.05	190.05	41.33	25.90	40.59	53.13	32.70	14.24	29.37
Oilseeds[3]:																	
2003-2004	Mil. metric tons	334.29	76.60	9.18	0.34	16.44	5.44	4.54	50.85	28.86	1.96	3.76	36.84	53.04	2.27	1.04	2.06
2004-2005 prel.	Mil. metric tons	381.05	96.44	10.81	0.44	21.00	5.32	3.56	58.71	28.75	1.99	5.36	43.43	55.77	2.56	1.06	2.15
Cotton:																	
2003-2004	Mil. 480 lb. bales	95.10	18.26	-	0.36	1.96	-	-	18.26	13.80	0.03	7.75	0.52	6.02	1.70	0.13	4.10
2004-2005 prel.	Mil. 480 lb. bales	119.61	23.25	-	0.63	2.30	-	-	23.25	18.10	0.03	11.30	0.69	6.40	2.80	0.10	4.15

- Indicates no reported or insignificant production. [1] Includes other countries not shown separately. [2] Includes wheat, coarse grains, and rice (milled) shown above. [3] Includes soybean, cottonseed, peanut (in shell), sunflower seed, rapeseed for individual countries. Copra and palm kernel are added to world totals.

Source: U.S. Department of Agriculture, Foreign Agricultural Service. World Agricultural Production, June 2005. See also <http://www.fas.usda.gov/wap/circular/2005/05-06/WldSum.pdf>.

[In thousands of metric tons (28,027 represents 28,027,000). Wheat data are for trade year beginning in July of year shown; rice data are for calendar year; corn data are for trade year beginning in October of year shown. Countries listed are the ten leading exporters or importers in 2004]

Leading exporters	Exports			Leading importers	Imports		
	2000	2003	2004		2000	2003	2004
WHEAT				WHEAT			
United States	28,027	32,287	28,000	China [2]	195	3,749	7,500
Australia	16,682	15,096	17,000	Egypt	6,050	7,295	7,500
Canada	17,351	15,526	15,000	Japan	5,885	5,751	5,700
EU-25 [1]	16,792	10,931	14,500	EU-25 [1]	4,694	5,912	5,500
Argentina	11,396	7,346	11,500	Brazil	7,453	5,559	5,000
Russia	696	3,114	6,000	Indonesia	4,069	4,535	4,400
Ukraine	78	66	3,500	Algeria	5,600	3,933	4,300
Kazakhstan	3,972	4,500	3,200	Korea	3,127	3,434	4,000
India	2,357	5,425	1,500	Mexico	3,066	3,644	3,900
Turkey	1,601	854	1,300	Iraq	3,200	1,925	3,300
RICE				RICE			
Thailand	7,521	10,137	8,500	Nigeria	1,906	1,350	1,400
Vietnam	3,528	4,295	4,200	Philippines	1,175	1,100	1,300
United States	2,541	3,097	3,450	Iraq	959	1,000	1,200
India	1,936	3,000	3,250	EU-25 [1]	1,189	1,000	1,050
Pakistan	2,417	1,800	2,100	Indonesia	1,500	700	1,000
Uruguay	806	804	750	Saudi Arabia	1,053	1,500	1,000
Egypt	705	826	700	Iran	765	950	950
China [2]	1,847	880	500	China [2]	270	1,122	900
Argentina	368	249	400	Senegal	874	850	750
Burma	670	125	300	Cuba	481	639	700
CORN				CORN			
United States	48,329	48,645	46,500	Japan	16,340	16,781	16,800
Argentina	12,229	10,439	13,500	Korea	8,743	8,783	8,500
China [2]	7,276	7,553	4,000	Mexico	5,928	5,707	5,500
Brazil	3,741	5,818	2,000	Taiwan	4,924	4,900	4,700
Ukraine	397	1,238	1,800	Egypt	5,268	3,743	4,300
South Africa	1,415	797	1,500	EU-25 [1]	3,800	5,600	2,500
Romania	50	100	1,000	Malaysia	2,588	2,400	2,400
Thailand	407	726	700	Colombia	1,857	1,999	2,100
Paraguay	386	800	600	Canada	2,843	2,039	2,000
Serbia and Montenegro	50	50	600	Algeria	1,265	1,800	1,900

[1] European Union (EU) has been updated to EU-25 for 2000-2003, but 1995 remains EU-15 data. EU-15: Austria, Belgium, Denmark, Finland, France, Germany, Greece, Ireland, Italy, Luxembourg, Netherlands, Portugal, Spain, Sweden, and United Kingdom. EU-25 added: Poland, Czech Republic, Hungary, Slovakia, Slovenia, Latvia, Lithuania, Estonia, Cyprus, and Malta. [2] See footnote 2, Table 1314.
Source: U.S. Department of Agriculture, Economic Research Service, unpublished data from the PS&D (Production, supply and distribution) database.

Table 1352. **Unmanufactured Tobacco and Cigarettes—Selected Countries: 2000 to 2004**
[6,400 represents 6,400,000. Tobacco is on dry weight basis]

Country	Unmanufactured tobacco (1,000 metric tons)			Country	Cigarettes (bil. pieces)		
	2000	2003	2004		2000	2003	2004
PRODUCTION				PRODUCTION			
World, total	6,400	5,371	5,734	World, total	5,609	5,662	5,530
China [1]	2,295	1,918	2,014	China [1]	1,699	1,793	1,793
Brazil	493	516	757	United States	595	500	498
India	599	595	598	Russia	341	385	380
United States	408	339	358	Japan	258	219	216
Indonesia	157	144	144	Indonesia	233	186	186
				Germany	207	205	185
EXPORTS				Turkey	128	126	130
World, total	2,132	2,049	2,126				
Brazil	342	466	564	EXPORTS			
United States	180	156	164	World, total	843	859	759
China [1]	113	146	157	United States	148	122	119
Malawi	101	121	138	Netherlands	102	105	100
India	123	125	128	Germany	91	106	90
				United Kingdom	111	68	65
IMPORTS				Korea, South	7	31	35
World, total	2,539	2,029	1,873	Hong Kong	28	28	29
Russia	285	293	275	Switzerland	23	23	23
United States	197	261	258	Japan	14	20	20
Germany	263	195	175				
United Kingdom	108	88	100	IMPORTS			
Netherlands	112	110	98	World, total	722	650	637
				Japan	83	83	83
CONSUMPTION				Italy	56	58	70
World, total	5,816	5,935	5,729	France	68	63	63
China [1]	1,235	2,232	2,220	Spain	25	41	43
India	474	488	491	Germany	34	34	32
United States	499	444	436	United Kingdom	69	34	32
Russia	301	294	281	United States	15	23	23
Indonesia	171	151	157				

[1] See footnote 2, Table 1314.
Source: U.S. Dept. of Agriculture, Foreign Agricultural Service, Production, Supply & Distribution Online <http://www.fas.usda.gov/pds /psdselection.asp> (accessed June 2005).

[In thousand cubic meters (12,475 represents 12,475,000)]

Country	Production 2000	Production 2003	Production 2004	Exports 2000	Exports 2003	Exports 2004	Consumption 2000	Consumption 2003	Consumption 2004
SOFTWOOD LOGS									
Australia	12,475	15,003	15,750	988	1,199	1,335	11,488	13,806	14,417
Canada	163,000	180,000	187,000	2,595	4,119	3,514	164,926	179,750	187,286
China [1]	29,891	28,079	29,760	1	-	1	36,288	39,431	41,679
Finland	29,000	29,000	25,700	700	500	370	31,800	34,500	30,830
France	17,000	13,000	13,000	900	500	500	16,210	12,650	12,650
Germany	31,653	21,000	22,000	4,083	3,200	3,300	30,523	20,100	21,000
Japan	14,520	12,605	12,650	2	6	7	26,758	23,066	23,143
New Zealand	15,500	18,540	17,080	6,897	8,081	7,100	8,607	10,464	9,985
Russia	64,000	71,100	72,500	20,000	27,500	28,050	44,000	43,600	44,450
Sweden	30,200	35,000	34,500	1,397	2,000	1,300	35,952	38,000	35,200
SOFTWOOD LUMBER									
Canada	68,557	78,158	81,383	48,607	50,826	55,340	20,719	27,966	26,613
China [1]	3,997	6,761	8,450	88	118	-	4,377	7,726	9,640
Finland	11,750	13,800	13,900	8,000	9,000	8,300	3,750	5,000	5,850
Germany	15,010	15,850	16,500	3,202	3,100	3,500	17,108	16,550	16,700
Japan	16,403	13,550	13,800	2	6	6	25,208	21,621	21,794
Russia	14,000	14,665	15,400	4,500	4,750	5,225	9,500	9,915	10,175
Sweden	14,839	17,000	17,200	11,188	11,600	11,200	3,832	5,550	6,150
TEMPERATE HARDWOOD LOGS									
China [1]	13,187	12,960	13,740	20	8	8	17,970	19,548	20,852
France	9,500	6,500	6,500	1,600	700	700	8,275	6,050	6,050
Russia	22,300	23,800	25,500	8,580	8,995	9,715	13,720	14,805	15,785
TEMPERATE HARDWOOD LUMBER									
China [1]	2,217	3,944	4,930	332	346	350	4,400	6,508	7,635
France	3,000	2,100	2,100	820	370	370	2,530	1,880	1,880
Russia	4,700	4,790	4,890	320	215	235	4,380	4,575	4,655
TROPICAL HARDWOOD LOGS									
Brazil	27,850	29,700	31,790	236	74	60	27,986	29,649	32,110
Indonesia	25,500	26,000	25,000	-	-	-	25,500	26,000	25,000
Malaysia	23,074	21,400	22,500	6,804	5,468	5,650	16,852	15,995	16,950
TROPICAL HARDWOOD LUMBER									
Brazil	14,400	15,910	16,705	901	1,318	1,515	13,656	14,622	15,230
Indonesia	6,600	6,250	6,100	-	-	-	6,600	6,250	6,100
Malaysia	5,589	4,568	4,900	2,901	2,356	2,800	3,973	2,761	2,700

- Represents or rounds to zero.   [1] See footnote 2, Table 1314.
Source: U.S. Department of Agriculture, Foreign Agricultural Service, Production, Supply & Distribution Online <http://www.fas.usda.gov/psd/psdselection.asp> (accessed June 2005).

Table 1354. **World Production of Major Mineral Commodities: 1990 to 2003**
[5,348 represents 5,348,000,000]

Commodity	Unit	1990	2000	2002	2003	Leading producers, 2002
MINERAL FUELS						
Coal	Mil. short tons	5,348	4,931	5,259	5,406	China, United States, India
Dry natural gas	Tril. cu. ft.	73.6	88.3	92.2	95.2	Russia, United States, Canada
Natural gas plant liquids [1]	Mil. barrels [2]	4,632	6,616	7,190	7,530	United States, Saudi Arabia, Canada
Petroleum, crude	Mil. barrels [2]	22,106	24,946	24,376	25,241	Saudi Arabia, Russia, United States
NONMETALLIC MINERALS						
Cement, hydraulic	Mil. metric tons	1,160	1,600	1,800	1,950	China, India, United States
Diamond, gem and industrial	Mil. carats	111	(NA)	134	150	Australia, Botswana, Russia
Nitrogen in ammonia	Mil. metric tons	97.5	109.0	108.0	109.0	China, United States, India
Phosphate rock	Mil. metric tons	162	133	135	137	United States, Morocco and Western Sahara, China
Potash, marketable	Mil. metric tons	28.0	25.3	26.0	28.4	Canada, Russia, Belarus
Salt	Mil. metric tons	183	214	210	210	Canada, China, Germany
Sulfur, elemental basis	Mil. metric tons	58.0	57.2	61.0	62.0	United States, Canada, Russia
METALS						
Aluminum [3]	Mil. metric tons	19.3	24.0	25.9	27.7	China, Russia, Canada
Bauxite, gross weight	Mil. metric tons	113.0	135.0	143.0	146.0	Australia, Guinea, Brazil
Chromite, gross weight [1]	1,000 metric tons	13,200	14,400	13,500	15,500	South Africa, Kazakhstan, India
Copper, metal content [4]	1,000 metric tons	8,950	13,200	13,600	13,600	Chile, Indonesia, United States
Gold, metal content [5]	Metric tons	2,180	2,550	2,550	2,590	South Africa, United States, Australia
Iron ore, gross weight [5]	Mil. metric tons	983	1,060	1,100	1,160	China, Brazil, Australia
Lead, metal content [4]	1,000 metric tons	3,370	3,100	2,910	2,950	Australia, China, United States
Nickel, metal content [4]	1,000 metric tons	974	1,250	1,350	1,400	Russia, Australia, Canada
Tin, metal content [4]	1,000 metric tons	223	238	278	207	China, Peru, Indonesia

NA Not available.   [1] Excludes China.   [2] 42-gallon barrels.   [3] Unalloyed ingot metal.   [4] Mine output.   [5] Includes iron ore concentrates and iron ore agglomerates.

Source: Mineral fuels, U.S. Energy Information Administration, *International Energy Annual, 2003*; nonmetallic minerals and metals, 1990, U.S. Bureau of Mines, thereafter, U.S. Geological Survey, *Minerals Yearbook; Annual Reports*; and *Mineral Commodity Summaries, 2004*.

886   Comparative International Statistics

Table 1355. **World Primary Energy Production by Region and Type: 1980 to 2003**

[In quadrillion Btu (287.7 represents 287,700,000,000,000,000). Btu = British thermal unit. For Btu conversion factors, see source]

Region and type	1980	1985	1990	1995	1998	1999	2000	2001	2002	2003 [1]
World total [2]	287.7	307.1	349.9	364.4	384.5	385.4	397.2	404.5	405.0	417.6
North America	83.3	87.6	91.9	96.0	99.6	98.4	98.7	99.7	99.1	99.1
United States	67.3	67.7	70.8	71.2	72.8	71.7	71.3	71.9	71.0	70.5
Central and South America	12.1	13.7	16.7	21.1	24.8	24.5	26.0	26.0	25.4	25.8
Western Europe	30.5	37.3	38.5	41.7	43.9	44.2	44.3	44.7	44.4	43.9
Eastern Europe and former U.S.S.R.	66.3	75.6	80.7	59.6	57.7	60.0	62.2	64.3	66.2	69.7
Middle East	42.3	25.8	41.0	48.4	54.9	53.9	57.5	56.2	54.3	58.0
Africa	17.4	18.4	21.6	24.2	26.3	26.6	27.8	28.1	28.0	30.1
Asia and Oceania	35.9	48.7	59.4	73.4	77.4	77.8	80.6	85.5	87.4	91.0
Petroleum	133.2	121.2	136.4	141.9	152.3	150.2	156.4	155.6	153.5	159.2
Natural gas	54.7	64.2	75.9	80.2	85.9	87.9	91.4	93.7	95.5	98.7
Coal	71.2	82.2	90.9	88.9	90.9	90.4	91.3	97.1	96.9	100.0
Hydroelectric power	17.9	20.4	22.4	25.4	26.1	26.6	27.1	26.4	26.6	27.2
Nuclear electric power	7.6	15.3	20.4	23.3	24.3	25.1	25.7	26.4	26.7	26.5
Geothermal, solar, wind, wood and waste	0.5	0.8	1.7	2.2	2.7	2.8	3.1	3.2	3.5	3.7

[1] Preliminary. [2] Includes geothermal, solar, and wood and waste energy produced in the United States and not used for generating electricity, not shown separately by type.

Source: U.S. Energy Information Administration, *International Energy Annual, 2003.* See also <http://www.eia.doe.gov/emeu/iea /contents.html>.

Table 1356. **World Primary Energy Consumption by Region and Type: 1980 to 2003**

[In quadrillion Btu (283.4 represents 283,400,000,000,000,000). Btu = British thermal unit. For Btu conversion factors, see source]

Region and type	1980	1985	1990	1995	1998	1999	2000	2001	2002	2003 [1]
World total [2]	283.4	308.6	347.3	365.6	381.9	389.0	399.8	404.0	410.3	421.5
North America	91.8	91.2	100.8	108.8	113.5	115.6	118.3	115.6	117.5	119.1
United States	78.3	76.4	84.6	91.2	95.2	96.8	99.0	96.5	98.1	98.8
Central and South America	11.5	12.4	14.5	17.6	20.1	20.3	20.9	21.2	21.3	21.9
Western Europe	58.5	59.6	64.1	66.3	70.2	70.3	71.6	72.7	72.7	73.6
Eastern Europe and former U.S.S.R.	60.0	69.2	73.0	52.7	48.9	50.0	50.7	51.2	52.1	53.8
Middle East	5.9	8.6	11.3	13.9	16.4	16.8	17.4	18.1	19.1	19.6
Africa	6.8	8.5	9.5	10.6	11.3	11.6	12.0	12.5	12.8	13.3
Far East and Oceania	49.0	59.3	74.1	95.6	101.5	104.4	108.9	112.6	114.9	120.1
Petroleum	131.0	123.1	136.1	142.4	150.6	153.7	155.9	157.3	158.7	162.2
Natural gas	54.0	63.6	75.2	80.9	85.7	87.9	91.3	92.6	95.9	99.1
Coal	70.0	82.6	89.4	89.1	90.3	90.6	94.6	96.1	96.8	100.7
Hydroelectric power	17.9	20.4	22.4	25.4	26.1	26.6	27.1	26.4	26.6	27.2
Nuclear electric power	7.6	15.3	20.4	23.3	24.3	25.1	25.7	26.4	26.7	26.5
Geothermal, solar, wind, wood, and waste	0.5	0.8	1.7	2.2	2.7	2.8	3.1	3.2	3.5	3.7

[1] Preliminary. [2] See footnote 2, Table 1354.

Source: U.S. Energy Information Administration, *International Energy Annual, 2003.* See also <http://www.eia.doe.gov/emeu/iea /contents.html>.

Table 1357. **World Energy Consumption by Region and Energy Source, 1990 to 2001, and Projections, 2010 to 2025**

[In quadrillion Btu (348.4 represents 348,400,000,000,000,000). Btu = British thermal unit. For Btu conversion factors, see source. Energy totals include net imports of coal coke and electricity generated from biomass in the United States. Totals may not equal sum of components due to independent rounding. The electricity portion of the national consumption values consists of generation for domestic use plus an adjustment for electricity trade based on a fuel's share of total generation in the exporting country]

Region and energy source	1990	2000	2001	Projections			
				2010	2015	2020	2025
World, total	348.4	398.9	403.9	470.8	517.3	567.8	622.9
North America	100.6	118.7	115.6	134.5	144.6	155.0	166.6
United States	84.6	99.3	97.0	111.8	119.7	127.9	136.5
Western Europe	59.9	66.8	68.2	71.2	73.8	76.7	79.7
Industrialized Asia	22.3	27.5	27.7	30.6	32.0	33.4	35.1
Eastern Europe and former Soviet Union	76.3	52.2	53.3	59.0	64.3	70.3	75.6
Developing Asia	52.5	80.5	85.0	110.6	129.7	150.5	173.4
Middle East	13.1	20.3	20.8	25.0	27.7	30.7	34.1
Africa	9.3	11.9	12.4	14.6	16.7	19.0	21.5
Central and South America	14.4	21.0	20.9	25.4	28.4	32.2	36.9
Oil	135.1	155.9	156.5	185.4	204.0	223.8	245.3
Natural gas	75.0	91.4	93.1	108.5	122.0	138.8	156.5
Coal	91.6	93.6	95.9	108.0	116.6	126.8	140.2
Nuclear	20.3	25.5	26.4	29.8	31.4	31.8	30.4
Other	26.4	32.8	32.2	39.0	43.2	46.6	50.4

Source: U.S. Energy Information Administration (EIA), *International Energy Outlook 2004.* See also <http://www.eia.doe.gov/oiaf/ieo/pdf /appa1a8.pdf>.

Table 1358. Energy Consumption and Production by Country: 2000 and 2003

[399.8 represents 399,800,000,000,000,000. See text of this section for general comments about the data. For data qualifications for countries, see source]

Country	Primary energy consumed Total (quad. Btu) 2000	2003 prel.	Primary energy consumed Per capita (mil. Btu) 2000	2003 prel.	Dry natural gas production (tril. cu. ft.) 2000	2003 prel.	Crude petroleum production (1,000 barrels per day) 2000	2003 prel.	Coal production (mil. short tons) 2000	2003 prel.
World Total	**399.8**	**421.5**	**6,090**	**6,319**	**88.3**	**95.2**	**68,344**	**69,154**	**4,931**	**5,406**
United States	**99.0**	**98.8**	**282**	**291**	**19.2**	**19.0**	**5,822**	**5,681**	**1,074**	**1,069**
Algeria	1.2	1.3	30	32	2.9	2.9	1,254	1,611	-	-
Argentina	2.7	2.7	37	38	1.3	1.4	761	741	(Z)	(Z)
Australia	4.9	5.1	19	20	1.2	1.3	722	512	338	373
Austria	1.4	1.5	8	8	(Z)	(Z)	19	18	1	1
Bahrain	(Z)	(Z)	(Z)	(Z)	(Z)	(Z)	38	35	-	-
Bangladesh	(Z)	(Z)	138	147	(Z)	(Z)	3	6	-	-
Belarus	1.2	1.2	10	10	(Z)	(Z)	37	37	-	-
Belgium	2.7	2.7	10	10	(Z)	-	-	-	(Z)	(Z)
Brazil	8.6	8.8	172	178	(Z)	(Z)	1,269	1,496	7	6
Bulgaria	(Z)	(Z)	8	8	(Z)	(Z)	(Z)	1	29	30
Burma	(Z)	(Z)	48	49	(Z)	(Z)	12	15	(Z)	(Z)
Canada	13.0	13.5	31	32	6.5	6.5	1,977	2,306	76	68
Chile	1.0	1.1	15	16	(Z)	(Z)	7	6	(Z)	(Z)
China [1]	38.8	45.5	1,275	1,304	(Z)	1.2	3,249	3,409	1,314	1,635
Colombia	1.2	1.2	42	44	(Z)	(Z)	691	541	42	52
Congo (Kinshasa) [2]	(Z)	(Z)	49	53	-	-	26	22	(Z)	(Z)
Cuba	(Z)	(Z)	11	11	(Z)	(Z)	41	55	-	-
Czech Republic	1.7	1.7	10	10	(Z)	(Z)	6	9	72	70
Denmark	(Z)	(Z)	5	5	(Z)	(Z)	363	375	-	-
Ecuador	(Z)	(Z)	12	13	(Z)	(Z)	395	411	-	-
Egypt	2.0	2.3	68	72	(Z)	(Z)	748	618	(Z)	(Z)
Finland	1.2	1.2	5	5	-	-	-	-	-	-
France	10.9	11.2	59	60	(Z)	(Z)	29	24	5	2
Germany	14.3	14.2	82	82	(Z)	(Z)	64	72	226	229
Greece	1.3	1.4	11	11	(Z)	(Z)	5	3	70	75
Hong Kong	(Z)	(Z)	7	7	-	-	-	-	-	-
Hungary	1.0	1.1	10	10	(Z)	(Z)	27	25	15	15
India	13.5	14.0	1,017	1,065	(Z)	(Z)	646	660	370	403
Indonesia	4.1	4.7	212	220	2.4	2.6	1,428	1,151	84	132
Iran	5.0	6.0	66	69	2.1	2.8	3,696	3,743	1	1
Iraq	1.1	(Z)	23	25	(Z)	(Z)	2,571	1,308	-	-
Ireland	(Z)	(Z)	4	4	(Z)	(Z)	-	-	-	-
Israel	(Z)	(Z)	6	6	(Z)	(Z)	(Z)	(Z)	-	-
Italy	7.6	8.0	58	57	(Z)	(Z)	90	96	(Z)	-
Japan	22.3	22.4	127	128	(Z)	(Z)	7	5	3	-
Korea, North	(Z)	(Z)	22	22	-	-	-	-	33	33
Korea, South	7.9	8.6	47	48	-	-	-	-	5	4
Kuwait	(Z)	(Z)	2	3	(Z)	(Z)	2,079	2,178	-	-
Libya	(Z)	(Z)	5	6	(Z)	(Z)	1,410	1,421	-	-
Malaysia	1.9	2.3	23	24	1.5	1.9	690	738	(Z)	(Z)
Mexico	6.3	6.8	99	103	1.3	1.5	3,012	3,371	13	12
Morocco	(Z)	(Z)	29	31	(Z)	(Z)	(Z)	(Z)	(Z)	(Z)
Netherlands	3.8	4.0	16	16	2.6	2.6	29	47	-	-
New Zealand	(Z)	(Z)	4	4	(Z)	(Z)	36	24	4	6
Nigeria	(Z)	(Z)	115	124	(Z)	(Z)	2,165	2,241	(Z)	(Z)
Norway	2.0	1.8	4	5	1.9	2.6	3,197	2,846	(Z)	3
Pakistan	1.9	1.9	143	154	(Z)	(Z)	54	60	3	4
Peru	(Z)	(Z)	26	27	(Z)	(Z)	96	87	(Z)	(Z)
Philippines	1.3	1.3	76	80	(Z)	(Z)	1	14	1	2
Poland	3.6	3.6	39	39	(Z)	(Z)	13	16	179	178
Portugal	1.1	1.1	10	10	-	-	-	-	-	-
Romania	1.6	1.7	22	22	(Z)	(Z)	120	116	32	36
Russia	27.5	29.1	146	143	20.6	21.8	6,479	8,132	265	294
Saudi Arabia	4.8	5.7	22	24	1.8	2.1	8,404	8,848	-	-
Serbia and Montenegro	(Z)	(Z)	11	11	(Z)	(Z)	16	14	38	44
South Africa	4.6	4.9	44	45	(Z)	(Z)	26	30	249	264
Spain	5.5	6.2	41	41	(Z)	(Z)	5	7	26	23
Sweden	2.2	2.1	9	9	-	-	-	-	-	-
Switzerland	1.3	1.3	7	7	-	-	-	-	-	-
Syria	(Z)	(Z)	17	18	(Z)	(Z)	523	464	-	-
Taiwan	3.8	4.2	22	23	(Z)	(Z)	(Z)	(Z)	(Z)	-
Thailand	2.6	3.1	61	63	(Z)	(Z)	110	159	20	21
Trinidad and Tobago	(Z)	(Z)	1	1	(Z)	(Z)	122	135	-	-
Tunisia	(Z)	(Z)	10	10	(Z)	(Z)	79	75	-	-
Turkey	3.2	3.3	68	71	(Z)	(Z)	53	45	70	53
Ukraine	6.0	6.3	50	49	(Z)	(Z)	74	75	69	63
United Arab Emirates	1.8	2.2	3	3	1.4	1.6	2,368	2,348	-	-
United Kingdom	9.7	9.8	59	59	3.8	3.6	2,275	2,093	34	31
Venezuela	2.8	2.9	24	26	(Z)	1.0	3,155	2,335	9	8
Vietnam	(Z)	(Z)	78	81	(Z)	(Z)	316	353	11	18

Z Less than 50 billion cubic feet, 500 barrels per day, or 500,000 short tons.   [1] See footnote 2, Table 1314.   [2] See footnote 3, Table 1314.

Source: U.S. Energy Information Administration, *International Energy Annual.* See also <http://www.eia.doe.gov/emeu/iea/contents.html>.

Table 1359. Net Electricity Generation by Type and Country: 2002

[15,363.1 represents 15,363,100,000,000. kWh=kilowatt hours]

Country	Total [1] (bil. kWh)	Percent distribution Thermal [2]	Hydro	Nuclear	Country	Total [1] (bil. kWh)	Percent distribution Thermal [2]	Hydro	Nuclear
World, total	15,363.1	64.5	17.0	16.6	Korea, South	288.0	59.3	1.1	39.3
Argentina	81.2	48.1	43.8	6.6	Malaysia	70.0	92.5	7.5	-
Australia	209.6	91.2	7.5	-	Mexico	203.7	80.6	12.1	4.5
Austria	62.0	33.0	63.8	-	Netherlands	91.1	90.3	0.1	4.1
Belgium	76.5	38.6	0.5	58.8	New Zealand	39.1	28.0	62.0	-
Brazil	340.1	8.4	83.3	4.1	Norway	128.9	0.4	99.3	-
Bulgaria	41.0	45.3	5.3	49.4	Pakistan	72.4	67.0	30.5	2.5
Canada	582.2	26.7	59.6	12.3	Paraguay	47.8	(Z)	99.9	-
China [3]	1,570.4	80.9	17.3	1.6	Poland	134.0	97.6	1.7	-
Colombia	44.2	22.8	76.0	-	Romania	52.4	59.9	30.3	9.8
Czech Republic . . .	71.8	70.8	3.4	24.8	Russia	864.7	63.3	20.8	15.5
Denmark	36.4	80.6	0.1	-	Saudi Arabia	136.9	100.0	-	-
Egypt	81.6	82.8	17.0	-	Serbia and				
Finland	71.3	41.8	15.0	29.7	Montenegro	31.7	67.4	32.6	-
France	529.1	9.3	11.3	78.4	South Africa	205.7	92.9	1.1	5.8
Germany	548.6	62.3	4.2	28.5	Spain	230.1	58.6	9.9	26.0
Greece	47.2	92.3	5.9	-	Sweden	140.7	4.4	46.8	45.6
Hungary	34.1	60.3	0.6	38.9	Switzerland	63.2	1.6	55.1	40.9
India	563.5	84.9	11.3	3.2	Taiwan [3]	158.5	72.1	4.0	24.0
Indonesia	102.3	84.6	9.6	-	Thailand	102.9	90.9	7.2	-
Iran	132.7	94.0	6.0	-	Turkey	123.3	72.7	27.0	-
Italy	261.1	81.3	15.0	-	Ukraine	163.9	49.3	5.9	44.8
Japan	1,036.2	62.4	7.9	27.1	United Kingdom . . .	360.1	73.7	1.3	23.2
Kazakhstan	55.3	84.1	15.9	-	United States	3,867.2	70.6	6.8	20.2
Korea, North	19.1	45.0	55.0	-	Uzbekistan	46.9	86.6	13.4	-
					Venezuela	85.1	32.7	67.3	-

- Represents zero.   Z Less than 0.05 percent.   [1] Geothermal, solar, wind, and wood and waste generation.   [2] Electricity generated from coal, oil, and gas.   [3] See footnote 2, Table 1314.

Source: U.S. Energy Information Administration, *International Energy Annual 2003.*

Table 1360. Commercial Nuclear Power Generation by Country: 1990 to 2004

[Generation for calendar years; other data as of December (1,743.9 represents 1,743,900,000,000). kWh=kilowatt hours. kW=kilowatt]

Country	Reactors				Gross electricity generated (bil. kWh)				Gross capacity (1,000 kW)			
	1990	2002	2003	2004	1990	2002	2003	2004	1990	2002	2003	2004
Total	368	436	436	436	1,743.9	2,666.7	2,599.3	2,696.2	301,745	380,261	381,185	383,629
United States . .	112	104	104	104	606.4	811.9	797.0	823.8	105,998	104,209	104,425	104,769
Argentina	2	2	2	2	7.0	5.8	1.9	2.9	1,005	1,005	1,005	1,005
Armenia	(NA)	1	1	1	(NA)	2.2	1.9	2.4	(NA)	408	408	408
Belgium	7	7	7	7	42.7	47.3	47.4	47.3	5,740	6,050	6,050	6,101
Brazil	1	2	2	2	2.0	13.8	13.3	11.5	657	2,007	2,007	2,007
Bulgaria	(NA)	6	4	4	(NA)	20	17	17	(NA)	3,760	2,880	2,880
Canada	19	21	21	21	74.0	75.9	75.7	90.9	13,855	15,795	15,396	15,426
China [1]	(NA)	2	2	2	(NA)	14.7	15.0	12.4	(NA)	1,968	1,968	1,968
Czech Republic	(NA)	4	6	6	(NA)	13.3	24.4	26.2	(NA)	1,760	3,722	3,760
Finland	4	4	4	4	18.9	22.3	22.7	22.7	2,400	2,760	2,760	2,760
France	58	59	59	59	314.1	434.7	441.1	448.2	58,862	66,042	66,042	66,042
Germany	22	19	19	18	147.2	164.8	165.1	167.1	23,973	22,365	22,365	21,693
Great Britain . . .	42	25	25	24	68.8	89.6	90.6	77.2	15,274	14,240	14,240	14,000
Hungary	4	4	4	4	13.6	13.9	11.0	11.9	1,760	1,866	1,866	1,866
India	6	14	14	14	6.0	19.5	18.3	16.9	1,330	2,720	2,720	2,770
Italy	2	(NA)	-	-	(NA)	(NA)	(NA)	(NA)	1,132	(NA)	(NA)	(NA)
Japan	40	53	53	52	191.9	313.5	227.1	281.9	31,645	45,907	45,907	45,742
Korea, South . . .	9	18	18	19	52.8	116.5	129.6	129.6	7,616	15,768	15,768	16,768
Lithuania	(NA)	2	2	2	(NA)	13.2	15.5	14.1	(NA)	3,000	3,000	3,000
Mexico	1	2	2	2	2.1	9.7	10.5	9.2	675	1,350	1,350	1,350
Netherlands	2	1	1	1	3.4	3.9	4.0	3.8	540	480	480	480
Pakistan	1	2	2	2	0.4	1.9	1.9	2.1	137	462	462	462
Romania	(NA)	1	1	1	(NA)	5.5	4.9	5.5	(NA)	706	706	706
Russia	(NA)	30	30	30	(NA)	139.7	148.6	142.9	(NA)	22,266	22,266	22,266
Slovakia	(NA)	6	6	6	(NA)	18.2	17.9	17.0	(NA)	2,640	2,640	2,640
Slovenia	1	1	1	1	4.6	5.5	5.2	4.0	664	707	707	707
South Africa	2	2	2	2	8.9	12.6	13.2	14.3	1,930	1,930	1,930	1,930
Spain	10	9	9	9	54.3	63.0	61.9	63.7	7,984	7,870	7,895	7,895
Sweden	12	11	11	11	68.2	68.5	68.4	77.3	10,344	9,844	9,844	9,852
Switzerland	5	5	5	5	23.6	27.1	27.3	26.8	3,079	3,352	3,352	3,352
Taiwan [1]	6	6	6	6	32.9	39.5	38.9	39.5	5,146	5,144	5,144	5,144
Ukraine	(NA)	13	13	15	(NA)	77.9	81.4	85.4	(NA)	11,880	11,880	13,880

- Represents zero.   NA Not available.   [1] See footnote 2, Table 1314.

Source: McGraw-Hill, Inc., New York, NY, *Nucleonics Week*, March issues (copyright).

Comparative International Statistics **889**

Table 1361. **Selected Indexes of Manufacturing Activity by Country: 1990 to 2003**

[1992 = 100. Data relate to employees (wage and salary earners) in Belgium and Italy, and to all employed persons (employees, self-employed workers, and unpaid family workers) in the other countries. Minus sign (-) indicates decrease. For explanation of average annual percent change, see Guide to Tabular Presentation]

Index	United States	Can-ada	Japan	Bel-gium	France	Ger-many	Italy	Nether-lands	Nor-way	Swe-den	United King-dom
Output per hour:											
1990	93.5	93.4	94.4	96.8	93.9	(NA)	96.6	98.7	98.1	94.6	90.1
1995	112.1	112.4	111.0	113.2	114.4	112.3	107.9	117.3	100.7	124.5	106.2
2000	147.6	131.4	135.9	130.8	142.5	128.6	113.5	132.7	106.6	175.5	121.0
2001	149.2	129.1	135.9	132.1	148.0	128.9	114.0	132.5	109.8	171.4	125.1
2002	164.4	134.5	139.0	137.6	155.1	131.6	112.1	135.4	111.7	189.2	127.7
2003	180.4	134.5	154.3	144.0	158.0	135.1	110.9	(NA)	113.5	201.5	134.9
Average annual percent change:											
1995-2000	5.7	3.2	4.1	2.9	4.5	2.7	1.0	2.5	1.1	7.1	2.6
2001-2002	10.2	4.2	2.3	4.2	4.8	2.1	-1.7	2.2	1.7	10.4	2.1
2002-2003	9.7	-	11.0	4.7	1.9	2.7	-1.0	(NA)	1.6	6.5	5.6
Compensation per hour, national currency basis: [1]											
1990	90.5	88.5	90.6	90.1	90.9	(NA)	87.6	89.8	92.3	87.8	83.8
1995	107.3	106.5	108.3	109.2	110.4	117.6	111.3	112.1	109.2	106.8	108.8
2000	134.7	120.5	113.7	120.6	122.8	137.3	127.8	132.0	140.5	136.8	137.6
2001	137.8	124.8	114.6	127.2	128.3	141.4	132.5	138.2	148.9	143.8	144.3
2002	147.1	129.0	122.8	131.8	135.2	144.5	135.7	147.3	157.9	151.7	152.2
2003	159.6	130.7	123.8	137.2	139.1	147.0	140.0	(NA)	164.6	157.2	160.4
Average annual percent change:											
1995-2000	4.7	2.5	1.0	2.0	2.2	3.1	2.8	3.3	5.2	5.1	4.8
2001-2002	6.7	3.3	7.1	3.6	5.4	2.2	2.4	6.5	6.0	5.5	5.5
2002-2003	8.5	1.3	0.8	4.1	2.9	1.7	3.2	(NA)	4.3	3.7	5.4
Real hourly compensation: [2]											
1990	96.1	94.9	95.1	95.2	96.3	(NA)	98.0	95.6	97.7	97.6	92.0
1995	100.1	102.1	106.3	102.2	104.6	107.8	97.4	104.2	102.7	97.9	101.1
2000	112.0	105.8	109.9	104.0	109.5	118.2	99.1	110.2	118.0	120.1	111.9
2001	111.5	106.9	111.7	107.1	112.5	119.4	100.0	110.8	121.4	123.3	115.3
2002	117.1	108.0	120.6	109.2	116.3	120.3	99.9	114.2	127.1	127.0	119.7
2003	124.2	106.4	122.0	111.9	117.2	121.1	100.4	(NA)	129.2	128.8	122.5
Average annual percent change:											
1995-2000	2.3	0.7	0.7	0.3	0.9	(NA)	0.3	1.1	2.8	4.2	2.1
2001-2002	5.0	1.0	8.0	2.0	3.4	0.8	-0.1	3.1	4.7	3.0	3.8
2002-2003	6.1	-1.5	1.2	2.5	0.8	0.7	0.5	(NA)	1.7	1.4	2.3
Unit labor costs, national currency: [1]											
1990	96.8	94.8	95.9	93.0	96.8	(NA)	90.7	91.1	94.2	92.9	93.0
1995	95.7	94.7	97.5	96.4	96.5	104.7	103.2	95.6	108.4	85.8	102.5
2000	91.2	91.7	83.6	92.2	86.2	106.8	112.6	99.5	131.9	77.9	113.7
2001	92.4	96.7	84.4	96.3	86.6	109.7	116.2	104.3	135.6	83.9	115.4
2002	89.5	95.9	88.3	95.7	87.2	109.8	121.1	108.8	141.3	80.1	119.2
2003	88.5	97.2	80.2	95.3	88.0	108.8	126.2	112.6	144.9	78.0	118.9
Average annual percent change:											
1995-2000	-0.9	-0.6	-3.0	-0.9	-2.2	0.4	1.8	0.8	4.0	-1.9	2.1
2001-2002	-3.2	-0.8	4.7	-0.6	0.6	0.1	4.2	4.3	4.2	-4.5	3.3
2002-2003	-1.1	1.4	-9.2	-0.5	1.0	-0.9	4.2	3.5	2.6	-2.6	-0.2
Unit labor costs, U.S. dollar basis: [1, 3]											
1990	96.8	98.1	83.9	89.5	94.1	(NA)	93.3	87.9	93.6	91.3	93.9
1995	95.7	83.4	131.6	105.2	102.5	114.2	78.0	104.8	106.4	70.0	91.6
2000	91.2	74.6	98.4	67.8	64.2	78.7	66.2	73.3	93.0	49.5	97.6
2001	92.4	75.4	88.0	68.7	62.6	78.4	66.2	74.5	93.7	47.3	94.0
2002	89.5	73.8	89.4	72.1	66.5	82.9	72.9	82.1	110.0	48.0	101.4
2003	88.5	83.8	87.7	85.9	80.4	98.3	90.9	101.7	127.2	56.2	110.0
Average annual percent change:											
1995-2000	-0.9	-2.2	-5.7	-8.4	-8.9	-7.2	-3.2	-6.9	-2.7	-6.7	1.3
2001-2002	-3.2	-2.2	1.6	5.0	6.2	5.7	10.0	10.1	17.4	1.6	7.8
2002-2003	-1.1	13.6	-1.9	19.1	20.9	18.6	24.8	23.8	15.6	17.1	8.5
Employment:											
1990	105.4	113.2	97.5	102.5	105.2	(NA)	103.7	100.0	105.2	117.2	115.0
1995	102.8	104.8	90.1	91.9	92.8	86.2	95.8	92.1	107.0	98.0	100.9
2000	102.5	118.2	81.7	88.9	91.6	82.7	96.1	93.1	107.5	98.1	94.1
2001	97.8	116.5	79.6	89.6	92.7	83.0	96.1	92.7	104.5	99.2	89.7
2002	90.6	114.9	75.8	86.0	91.1	81.2	96.9	90.0	103.3	96.4	85.7
2003	86.4	115.5	74.3	83.2	89.1	79.0	97.1	87.3	98.5	93.8	81.9
Average annual percent change:											
1995-2000	-0.1	2.4	-1.9	-0.7	-0.3	-0.8	0.1	0.2	0.1	-	-1.4
2001-2002	-7.3	-1.3	-4.7	-4.0	-1.7	-2.2	0.8	-2.9	-1.2	-2.7	-4.4
2002-2003	-4.7	0.5	-2.0	-3.3	-2.2	-2.7	0.2	-3.0	-4.6	-2.8	-4.5
Aggregate hours:											
1990	105.0	113.5	102.9	104.3	105.6	(NA)	102.9	100.3	103.4	116.4	116.9
2000	103.4	121.3	80.3	91.7	87.2	78.8	100.1	92.5	105.9	107.3	95.0
2001	96.6	118.2	77.7	90.8	86.5	78.2	99.1	92.0	102.3	107.5	90.7
2002	89.7	116.1	74.0	87.2	83.2	76.1	99.7	89.4	99.8	103.0	86.0
2003	85.4	116.3	73.0	84.0	81.3	74.2	99.3	(NA)	94.5	99.2	81.8
Average annual percent change:											
1995-2000	-0.2	2.6	-2.0	-0.1	-1.0	-1.5	0.1	-	-0.1	0.3	-1.3
2001-2002	-7.1	-1.7	-4.8	-4.0	-3.8	-2.7	0.5	-2.9	-2.4	-4.2	-5.1
2002-2003	-4.8	0.1	-1.3	-3.7	-2.3	-2.4	-0.4	(NA)	-5.4	-3.6	-5.0

- Represents or rounds to zero.   NA Not available.   [1] In Canada, France, Sweden, and the United Kingdom, compensation adjusted for employment taxes and government subsidies to estimate the actual labor cost to employers.   [2] Index of hourly compensation divided by the index of consumer prices to adjust for changes in purchasing power.   [3] Indexes in national currency adjusted for changes in prevailing exchange rates.

Source: U.S. Bureau of Labor Statistics, *International Comparisons of Manufacturing Productivity and Unit Labor Cost Trends*, February 25, 2005. See also <http://bls.gov/fls>.

890   Comparative International Statistics

Table 1362. Indexes of Hourly Compensation Costs for Production Workers in Manufacturing by Country: 1990 to 2003

[United States = 100. Compensation costs include pay for time worked, other direct pay (including holiday and vacation pay, bonuses, other direct payments, and the cost of pay-in-kind), employer expenditures for legally required insurance programs and contractual and private benefit plans, and for some countries, other labor taxes. Data adjusted for exchange rates. Area averages are trade-weighted to account for difference in countries' relative importance to U.S. trade in manufactured goods. The trade weights used are the sum of U.S. imports of manufactured products for consumption (customs value) and U.S. exports of domestic manufactured products (f.a.s. value) in 1992; see source for detail]

Area or country	1990	1995	2000	2001	2002	2003	Area or country	1990	1995	2000	2001	2002	2003
United States	100	100	100	100	100	100	Austria	122	148	99	94	98	116
Total [1,2]	81	90	73	68	67	75	Belgium	130	162	111	103	108	126
OECD [3,4]	88	96	78	72	73	81	Czech Republic	(X)	15	15	15	18	21
Europe	[4]116	127	95	90	95	110	Denmark	125	149	117	115	121	146
Asian newly industrializing economies [5]	25	38	36	33	33	34	Finland	144	143	100	98	103	124
Brazil	(NA)	(NA)	18	14	12	12	France	104	113	79	77	81	96
Canada	111	97	85	80	79	88	Germany	(X)	177	116	111	115	136
Mexico	11	9	11	12	12	11	Greece	45	53	(NA)	(NA)	(NA)	(NA)
Australia	89	91	74	66	73	91	Ireland	80	81	66	67	73	87
Hong Kong	22	28	28	28	27	25	Italy	117	93	72	68	71	84
Israel	52	56	59	60	52	53	Luxembourg	109	137	90	85	89	105
Japan	85	138	112	95	88	91	Netherlands	122	141	99	97	102	122
Korea, South	25	43	42	38	43	47	Norway	148	146	116	115	129	144
New Zealand	54	57	41	37	41	51	Portugal	24	30	23	23	24	28
Singapore	25	42	38	36	33	34	Spain	77	75	55	53	56	68
Sri Lanka	2	3	2	2	2	(NA)	Sweden	141	126	104	91	96	115
Taiwan [6]	26	35	32	30	27	27	Switzerland	140	170	108	106	113	127
							United Kingdom	86	81	86	81	85	93

NA Not available. [1] From 1990 to 1995, the 28 foreign economies shown below less Brazil and the Czech Republic; thereafter, all 30 foreign economies. [2] 1990 data are for the former West Germany. [3] Organization for Economic Cooperation and Development; see text of this section. [4] Data for the Czech Republic are not included for 1975-1994. Data for Germany relate to the former West Germany only. [5] Hong Kong, South Korea, Singapore, and Taiwan. [6] See footnote 2, Table 1314.

Source: U.S. Bureau of Labor Statistics, News Release USDL 04-2343, November 18, 2004. See also <http://www.bls.gov/news.release /ichcc.toc.htm>.

Table 1363. Key Global Telecom Indicators for the World Telecommunication Service Sector: 1995 to 2002

[In billons U.S. dollars (779 represents $779,000,000,000), except as noted. All data were converted by annual average exchange rates. Country fiscal year data was aggregated to obtain calendar year estimates]

Indicators	1995	1996	1997	1998	1999	2000	2001	2002, prel.
Telecom market total revenue	779	885	946	1,015	1,123	1,210	1,232	1,295
Telecom telephone services revenue [1]	428	444	437	456	476	477	472	465
Other statistics								
Main telephone lines [2]	689	738	792	846	905	983	1,053	1,129
Mobile cellular subscribers [2]	91	145	215	318	490	740	955	1,155
International telephone traffic minutes [3]	63	71	79	89	100	118	127	135
Personal computers [2]	235	275	325	375	435	500	555	615
Internet users [2]	40	74	117	183	277	399	502	580

[1] Revenue from installation, subscription and local, trunk and international call charges for fixed telephone service. [2] Data are in millions. [3] Including traffic between countries of former Soviet Union.

Source: International Telecommunication Union, Geneva Switzerland, 2004; <http://www.itu.int/ITU-D/ict/statistics/atglance/KeyTelecom99.html>.

Table 1364. Telephones and Computers by Country: 2003

[Rates per 100 persons. See text of this section for general comments about the data. For data qualifications for countries, see source]

Country	Telephone main lines	Cellular phone subscribers	Personal computers [1]	Country	Telephone main lines	Cellular phone subscribers	Personal computers [1]
Argentina	21.88	17.76	8.20	Italy	48.40	101.76	23.07
Australia	54.23	71.95	60.18	Japan	47.19	67.90	38.22
Austria	48.07	87.88	37.41	Korea, South	53.83	70.09	55.80
Belgium	48.92	79.28	31.81	Lebanon	20.00	23.43	10.00
Brazil	22.29	26.36	7.48	Mexico	15.97	29.47	8.30
Bulgaria	38.05	46.64	5.19	Netherlands	61.43	76.76	46.66
Canada	65.14	41.90	48.70	Norway	71.35	90.89	52.83
China [2]	20.90	21.48	2.76	Pakistan	2.66	1.75	0.42
Colombia	17.93	14.13	4.93	Panama	12.20	26.76	3.83
Cuba	6.40	0.31	2.39	Poland	31.87	45.09	14.20
Czech Republic	36.03	96.46	17.74	Russia	25.27	24.93	8.87
Ecuador	12.24	18.92	3.24	Saudi Arabia	15.54	32.11	13.67
Egypt	12.73	8.45	2.91	Singapore	45.03	85.25	62.20
Finland	49.20	90.96	44.17	South Africa	10.66	36.36	7.26
France	56.60	69.59	34.71	Spain	42.91	91.61	19.60
Germany	65.73	78.52	48.47	Sweden	73.57	98.05	62.13
Greece	45.39	90.23	8.17	Switzerland	72.75	84.34	70.87
Guatemala	7.05	13.15	1.44	Taiwan [2]	59.08	114.14	47.14
Hungary	34.86	76.88	10.84	Thailand	10.49	39.42	3.98
India	4.63	2.47	0.72	United Kingdom	59.06	91.17	40.57
Indonesia	3.94	8.74	1.19	United States	62.38	54.58	65.98
Ireland	49.13	87.96	42.08	Venezuela	11.06	27.30	6.09
Israel	45.82	96.07	24.26				

NA Not available. [1] In many countries mainframe computers are used extensively, and thousands of users can be connected to a single mainframe computer; thus the number of PCs understates the total use of computers. [2] See footnote 2, Table 1314.

Source: International Telecommunications Union, Geneva, Switzerland, World Telecommunication Indicators, (copyright). See also <http://www.itu.int/ITU-D/ict/statistics/atglance/main03.pdf>.

Table 1365. **Dow-Jones World Stock Index by Country and Industry: 2000 to 2004**

[Index figures shown are as of December 31. Based on share prices denominated in U.S. dollars. Stocks in countries that impose significant restrictions on foreign ownership are included in the world index in the same proportion that shares are available to foreign investors]

Country and industry	2000	2002	2003	2004	Country and industry	2000	2002	2003	2004
World, total........	210.9	140.5	187.0	214.0	Asia/Pacific	93.0	66.5	92.2	108.6
Americas...........	299.1	199.8	259.8	289.0	Australia	156.0	149.4	218.1	280.7
United States	306.9	204.5	262.7	289.4	Hong Kong........	245.6	156.3	216.8	255.8
Canada	225.3	157.5	238.7	291.2	Indonesia.........	31.2	33.1	55.0	72.5
Mexico	132.2	133.5	175.6	257.3	Japan	88.3	56.5	77.7	90.6
Europe	241.2	152.6	207.9	246.7	Malaysia	88.5	86.1	108.6	120.7
Austria	86.2	104.4	165.2	277.5	New Zealand	96.7	119.8	180.8	235.1
Belgium..........	196.9	154.3	217.3	310.9	Singapore	135.2	97.7	133.2	158.6
Denmark.........	220.1	160.1	239.0	307.8	Thailand	27.2	33.5	80.0	73.0
Finland	1,537.8	671.5	788.0	834.0					
France	252.9	153.8	213.9	250.5	Basic materials.....	96.1	107.9	109.3	105.8
Germany.........	219.1	112.1	180.9	206.8	Consumer goods	183.8	159.6	199.2	226.4
Ireland...........	312.3	236.7	341.4	470.8	Consumer services	192.8	137.8	184.6	209.8
Italy	192.2	123.6	171.0	218.1	Energy	230.7	187.3	234.7	298.2
Netherlands	335.7	199.5	249.8	279.4	Financial	207.1	147.7	201.6	236.3
Norway	151.8	110.8	155.8	228.2	Healthcare.........	329.9	224.6	270.3	287.0
Spain	193.5	142.6	221.9	279.7	Industrial.........	167.1	106.6	146.2	171.2
Sweden	339.0	163.3	261.4	348.9	Technology	552.7	229.6	347.8	355.3
Switzerland	388.8	259.1	344.9	393.8	Telecommunications ...	273.3	147.9	185.6	217.8
United Kingdom	199.8	137.9	177.3	207.3	Utilities	156.0	101.9	128.5	159.3

Source: Dow Jones & Company, Inc., New York, NY, *Dow Jones Indexes*, (copyright).

Table 1366. **Foreign Stock Market Activity—Morgan Stanley Capital International Indexes: 2000 to 2004**

[Index figures shown are as of December 31. January 1, 1970 = 100, except as noted. Minus sign (-) indicates decrease. Based on share prices denominated in U.S. dollars. EM = Emerging Markets]

Index and country	Index			Percent change [1]		Index and country	Index			Percent change [1]	
	2000	2003	2004	2003	2004		2000	2003	2004	2003	2004
ALL COUNTRY (AC)						Sweden	4,240	3,361	4,503	61.0	34.0
INDEXES						Switzerland.........	2,695	2,480	2,822	32.4	13.8
AC World index [2].....	289.8	251.1	284.5	31.6	13.3	United Kingdom.......	1,146	1,006	1,162	27.2	15.5
AC World index except						Hong Kong.........	5,475	4,536	5,479	32.5	20.8
USA [2]	195.4	175.5	207.5	37.5	18.3	Japan	2,552	2,144	2,460	34.6	14.7
AC Asia Pacific [2]......	92.7	87.2	101.4	38.2	16.3	Singapore	2,081	1,820	2,163	34.2	18.8
AC Europe [2]	376.5	321.9	380.1	35.2	18.1						
European Union [2]	361.5	302.6	358.0	35.0	18.3	**EMERGING MARKETS**					
						EM Far East index [4]	123.8	187.9	210.0	44.5	11.8
DEVELOPED						India [6]	114.5	166.4	193.7	74.0	16.5
MARKETS						Indonesia..........	78.2	162.8	235.3	70.0	44.5
World index	1,221	1,036	1,169	30.8	12.8	Korea, South	78.7	163.6	196.2	32.6	20.0
EAFE index [3]	1,492	1,289	1,515	35.3	17.6	Malaysia [6]	160.9	196.9	220.2	23.1	11.8
Europe index	1,378	1,169	1,378	34.8	17.8	Pakistan [6]	44.3	84.5	91.8	31.2	8.6
Pacific index.........	1,832	1,651	1,935	36.3	17.2	Philippines	142.2	113.8	141.2	38.9	24.1
Far East index.......	2,583	2,171	2,501	34.4	15.2	Sri Lanka [6]	36.3	91.0	98.1	42.0	7.8
United States	1,250	1,045	1,137	26.8	8.8	Taiwan [7]	191.7	217.9	232.1	40.0	6.5
Canada	832.5	853.2	1,028.2	52.3	20.5	Thailand	56.9	176.6	169.5	134.2	-4.0
Australia	317.7	441.1	558.6	45.1	26.6						
New Zealand [4]	56.4	107.3	139.3	50.1	29.8	EM Latin America....	1,002	1,101	1,484	67.1	34.8
						Argentina	1,233	933.6	1,163.0	98.5	24.6
Austria	708.3	1,158	1,960	54.5	69.2	Brazil............	869.9	802.0	1,046.6	102.8	30.5
Belgium..........	1,222	1,151	1,606	30.7	39.6	Chile	604.7	800.6	997.3	79.7	24.6
Denmark	2,201	2,252	2,900	46.7	28.8	Colombia [6]	42.1	108.6	245.0	59.0	125.7
Finland [4]	921.8	450.9	468.5	16.7	3.9	Mexico [6]	1,197	1,873	2,716	29.8	45.0
France...........	1,509	1,243	1,446	37.8	16.3	Peru [6]	125.0	344.1	343.4	88.4	-0.2
Germany..........	1,436	1,161	1,328	60.1	14.4	Venezuela [6]	106.1	103.8	151.0	33.6	45.4
Greece	475.8	382.8	540.7	63.2	41.2						
Ireland [4]	308.4	296.5	412.6	39.4	39.2	Czech Republic [8]	79.9	166.4	293.8	54.2	76.6
Italy............	447.2	391.2	503.0	34.8	28.6	Hungary [8]	233.6	352.9	661.8	31.0	87.5
Luxembourg [5].......	491.9	(NA)	(NA)	(NA)	(NA)	Jordan	55.1	113.4	180.4	55.5	59.1
Netherlands	2,177	1,607	1,753	24.5	9.1	Poland [8]	499.0	471.1	747.1	33.1	58.6
Norway	1,181	1,332	1,993	43.8	49.6	Russia [8]	155.2	461.1	479.9	70.3	4.1
Portugal [4].........	127.8	115.8	141.1	39.2	21.9	South Africa [6]	157.6	216.6	304.7	39.8	40.7
Spain	347.1	388.1	486.8	54.3	25.4	Turkey	247.7	231.8	321.0	122.5	38.5

NA Not available. [1] Percent change during calendar year (e.g. December 31, 2000 through December 31, 2000). Adjusted for foreign exchange fluctuations relative to U.S. dollar. [2] January 1, 1988 = 100. [3] Europe, Australasia, Far East index. Comprises all European and Far East countries listed under developed markets plus Australia and New Zealand. [4] January 1, 1988 = 100. [5] MSCI Luxembourg Index discontinued as of March 29, 2002. [6] January 1, 1993 = 100. [7] See footnote 2, Table 1314. [8] January 1, 1995 = 100.

Source: Morgan Stanley Capital International, New York, NY, <http://www.msci.com/equity/index.html> (copyright). This information may not be reproduced or redisseminated in any form without prior written permission from Morgan Stanley Capital International. This information is provided on an "as is" basis. Neither Morgan Stanley or any other party makes any representation or warranty of any kind either express or implied, with respect to this information (or the results to be obtained by the use thereof) and Morgan Stanley expressly disclaims any and all warranties of originality, accuracy, completeness, merchantability and fitness for any particular purpose. The user of this information assumes the entire risk of any use made of the information. In no event shall Morgan Stanley or any other part be liable to the user for any direct or indirect damages, including without limitation, any lost profits, lost savings, or other incidental or consequential damages arising out of use of this information.

Table 1367. Foreign Stock Market Indices: 1980 to 2004

[As of year end. The DAX index is a total return index which includes dividends, whereas the other foreign indices are price indices which exclude dividends]

Year	London FTSE 100	Tokyo Nikkei 225	Hong Kong Hang Seng	Germany DAX-30	Paris CAC-40	Dow Jones Europe STOXX 50
1980	647	7,116	1,477	481	(X)	(X)
1985	1,413	13,113	1,752	1,366	(X)	(X)
1990	2,144	23,849	3,025	1,398	1,518	835
1991	2,493	22,984	4,297	1,578	1,766	1,000
1992	2,847	16,925	5,512	1,545	1,858	1,058
1993	3,418	17,417	11,888	2,267	2,268	1,429
1994	3,066	19,723	8,191	2,107	1,881	1,299
1995	3,689	19,868	10,073	2,254	1,872	1,538
1996	4,119	19,361	13,452	2,889	2,316	1,850
1997	5,136	15,259	10,723	4,250	2,999	2,634
1998	5,883	13,842	9,507	5,002	3,943	3,320
1999	6,930	18,934	16,962	6,958	5,958	4,742
2000	6,223	13,786	15,096	6,434	5,926	4,557
2001	5,217	10,543	11,397	5,160	4,625	3,707
2002	3,940	8,579	9,321	2,893	3,064	2,408
2003	4,477	10,677	12,576	3,965	3,558	2,660
2004	4,814	11,489	14,230	4,256	3,821	2,775

X Not applicable.

Source: Global Financial Data, Los Angeles, CA, <http://www.globalfindata.com>,unpublished data (copyright).

Table 1368. United States and Foreign Stock Markets—Market Capitalization and Value of Shares Traded: 1990 to 2004

[In billions of U.S. dollars (15,104.0 represents $15,104,000,000,000). Market capitalization is the market value of all domestic listed companies at the end of the year. The market value of a company is the share price times the number of shares outstanding. Value of shares traded is the annual total turnover of listed company shares]

Country	Market capitalization				Value of shares traded			
	2000	2002	2003	2004	2000	2002	2003	2004
United States	15,104.0	11,052.4	14,266.3	16,323.7	31,862.5	25,371.3	15,547.4	19,354.9
Argentina	166.1	103.4	38.9	46.4	6.0	1.4	4.9	7.6
Australia	372.8	381.0	585.5	776.4	226.3	294.7	369.8	514.2
Austria	29.9	31.7	54.5	85.8	9.4	5.8	10.8	23.8
Belgium	182.5	127.6	173.6	768.4	38.0	33.8	37.5	70.3
Brazil	226.2	123.8	234.6	330.3	101.3	48.2	60.4	93.6
Canada	841.4	575.3	894.0	1,177.5	634.7	406.1	467.8	653.9
Chile	60.4	47.6	86.3	117.1	6.1	3.1	6.5	11.6
China [1]	581.0	463.1	681.2	639.8	721.5	333.4	476.8	748.3
Denmark	107.7	76.8	128.0	151.3	91.6	51.6	67.0	97.5
Egypt	28.7	26.1	27.1	38.5	11.1	2.6	3.3	5.6
Finland	293.6	138.8	170.3	183.8	206.6	176.5	163.5	220.0
France	1,446.6	967.0	1,355.6	1,857.2	1,083.3	934.8	995.4	1,311.7
Germany	1,270.2	686.0	1,079.0	1,194.5	1,069.1	1,233.1	1,147.2	1,406.1
Greece	110.8	68.7	106.8	125.2	95.1	24.9	38.6	43.5
Hong Kong	623.4	463.1	714.6	861.5	377.9	210.7	331.6	439.0
India	148.1	131.0	279.1	387.9	509.8	197.1	284.8	379.1
Indonesia	26.8	30.0	54.7	73.3	14.3	13.0	14.8	27.6
Iran	34.0	14.3	34.4	47.0	5.0	1.9	5.3	13.3
Ireland	81.9	59.9	85.1	114.1	14.4	32.9	44.0	44.3
Israel	64.1	45.4	75.7	95.5	23.4	55.3	41.6	46.2
Italy	768.4	477.1	614.8	789.6	778.4	539.9	663.2	804.3
Japan	3,157.2	2,126.1	3,040.7	3,678.3	2,693.9	1,573.3	2,273.0	3,430.4
Korea, South	171.6	249.6	329.6	428.6	1,067.7	826.6	682.7	638.9
Luxembourg	34.0	24.6	37.3	50.1	1.2	0.3	0.3	0.4
Malaysia	116.9	123.9	168.4	190.0	58.5	27.6	50.1	59.9
Mexico	125.2	103.1	122.5	171.9	45.3	27.7	23.5	42.8
Morocco	10.9	8.6	13.2	25.1	1.1	0.6	0.7	1.7
Netherlands	640.5	401.5	488.6	622.3	677.2	462.3	463.5	604.2
New Zealand	18.6	21.7	33.1	43.7	10.8	7.5	10.5	15.4
Norway	65.0	67.3	94.7	141.4	60.1	48.9	70.0	135.5
Philippines	51.6	39.0	23.6	28.9	8.2	3.1	2.6	3.7
Poland	31.3	28.8	37.2	71.1	14.6	5.8	8.5	16.6
Portugal	60.7	42.8	58.3	73.4	54.4	20.3	21.4	24.6
Russia	38.9	124.2	230.8	268.0	20.3	36.1	81.0	34.6
Saudi Arabia	67.2	74.9	157.3	306.2	17.3	35.7	159.1	130.8
Singapore	152.8	101.9	145.1	171.6	91.5	56.1	87.9	81.3
Sweden	328.3	177.1	287.5	376.8	390.0	218.5	263.8	412.4
Switzerland	792.3	553.8	725.7	825.8	609.1	656.7	575.6	727.1
Taiwan [1]	247.6	261.5	379.0	441.4	983.5	631.9	592.0	718.6
Thailand	29.5	46.1	118.7	115.4	23.3	47.6	96.6	109.9
Turkey	69.7	34.0	68.4	98.3	179.2	70.7	99.6	147.4
United Kingdom	2,580.0	1,864.1	2,412.4	2,815.9	1,835.3	2,721.3	2,150.8	3,707.2

[1] See footnote 2, Table 1314.

Source: Standard and Poor's, New York, NY, Standard & Poor's Emerging Stock Markets Factbook 2005 (copyright).

Comparative International Statistics 893

Table 1369. Foreign Exchange Rates: 2004

[Foreign currency units per U.S. dollar. Rates shown include market, official, principal, and secondary rates, as published by the International Monetary Fund in *International Financial Statistics*]

Country	Currency	2004	Country	Currency	2004
Afghanistan [1]	Afghanis	3,000.00	Laos	Kip	10,820.0
Albania	Leks	102.65	Latvia	Lats	0.54
Algeria	Algerian Dinars	72.06	Lebanon	Lebanese Pounds	1,507.50
Antigua and Barbuda	E.Caribbean Dollars	2.70	Lesotho	Maloti	6.46
Argentina	Argentine Pesos	2.92	Liberia	Liberian Dollars	54.91
Armenia	Drams	533.45	Libya [1]	Libyan Dinars	1.30
Aruba	Aruban Florins	1.79	Lithuania	Litai	2.78
Australia	Australian Dollars	1.36	Luxembourg [2]	Euro	0.81
Austria [2]	Euro	0.81	Macedonia	Denars	49.41
Bahamas, The	Bahamian Dollars	1.00	Madagascar	Malagasy Ariary	1,868.86
Bahrain	Bahrain Dinars	0.38	Malaysia	Ringgit	3.80
Bangladesh	Taka	59.51	Mali	CFA Francs	528.29
Barbados	Barbados Dollars	2.00	Malta	Maltese Liri	0.34
Belarus [2]	Belarusian Rubel	2,160.26	Mauritania	Ouguiyas	267.00
Belgium [2]	Euro	0.81	Mauritius	Mauritian Rupees	27.50
Belize	Belize Dollars	2.00	Mexico	Mexican Pesos	11.29
Benin	CFA Francs	528.29	Moldova	Lei	12.33
Bolivia	Bolivianos	7.94	Mongolia	Togrogs	1,185.28
Botswana	Pula	4.69	Morocco	Dirhams	8.87
Brazil	Reais	2.93	Mozambique	Meticais	22,581.3
Bulgaria	Leva	1.58	Namibia	Namibia Dollars	6.46
Burkina Faso	CFA Francs	528.29	Nepal	Nepalese Rupees	73.67
Burma [1]	Kyats	5.75	Netherlands [2]	Euro	0.81
Cambodia	Riel	4,016.25	Netherlands Antilles	Guilders	1.79
Cameroon	CFA Francs	528.29	New Zealand	New Zealand Dollars	1.51
Canada	Canadian Dollars	1.30	Nicaragua	Cordobas	15.94
Central African Republic	CFA Francs	528.29	Niger	CFA Francs	528.29
Chad	CFA Francs	528.29	Nigeria	Naira	132.89
Chile	Chilean Pesos	609.37	Norway	Norwegian Kroner	6.74
China [3]	Yuan	8.28	Oman	Rials Omani	0.38
Colombia	Colombian Pesos	2,628.61	Pakistan	Pakistan Rupees	58.26
Comoros	Comorian Francs	396.21	Panama	Balboas	1.00
Congo (Brazzaville) [4]	CFA Francs	528.29	Papua New Guinea	Kina	3.22
Costa Rica	Colones	437.91	Paraguay	Guaranies	5,974.58
Cote d'Ivoire	CFA Francs	528.29	Peru	Nuevos Soles	3.41
Croatia	Kunas	6.04	Philippines	Philippine Pesos	56.04
Cyprus	Cyprus Pounds	0.47	Poland	Zlotys	3.66
Czech Republic	Koruny	25.70	Portugal [2]	Euro	0.81
Denmark	Kroner	5.99	Qatar	Qatar Riyals	3.64
Djibouti	Djibouti Francs	177.72	Romania	Lei	32,636.6
Dominica	E.Caribbean Dollars	2.70	Russia	Russian Rubles	28.81
Dominican Republic	Dominican Pesos	42.12	Rwanda	Rwanda Francs	574.62
Ecuador	U.S. Dollars	25,000.0	Saint Kitts and Nevis	E.Caribbean Dollars	2.70
Egypt	Egyptian Pounds	6.20	Saint Lucia	E.Caribbean Dollars	2.70
El Salvador	Colones	8.75	Saint Vincent and the		
Equatorial Guinea	CFA Francs	528.29	Grenadines	E.Caribbean Dollars	2.70
Estonia	Krooni	12.60	Saudi Arabia	Saudi A. Riyals	3.75
Ethiopia [1]	Birr	8.64	Senegal	CFA Francs	528.29
Euro area (EMU-11) [2]	Euro	0.81	Sierra Leone	Leones	2,701.30
Fiji	Fiji Dollars	1.73	Singapore	Singapore Dollar	1.69
Finland [2]	Euro	0.81	Slovakia	Koruny	32.26
France [2]	Euro	0.81	Slovenia	Tolars	192.38
Gabon	CFA Francs	528.29	South Africa	Rand	6.46
Georgia	Lari	1.92	Spain [2]	Euro	0.81
Germany [2]	Euro	0.81	Sri Lanka	Sri Lanka Rupees	101.19
Greece [2]	Euro	0.81	Sudan	Sudanese Dinars	257.91
Guatemala	Quetzales	7.95	Suriname [1]	Suriname Dollar	2.73
Guyana	Guyana Dollars	198.31	Swaziland	Emalangeni	6.46
Haiti	Gourdes	38.35	Sweden	Swedish Kronor	7.35
Honduras	Lempiras	18.21	Switzerland	Swiss Francs	1.24
Hong Kong	Hong Kong Dollars	7.79	Syria	Syrian Pounds	11.23
Hungary	Forint	202.75	Tanzania	Tanzania Shillings	1,089.33
Iceland	Kronur	70.19	Thailand	Baht	40.22
India	Indian Rupees	45.32	Togo	CFA Francs	528.29
Indonesia	Rupiah	8,938.85	Trinidad and Tobago	TI Dollars	6.30
Iran	Rials	8,613.99	Tunisia	Tunisian Dinars	1.25
Iraq [2]	Dinars	(NA)	Turkey	Liras	1,425,540
Ireland [2]	Euro	0.81	Uganda	Uganda Shillings	1,810.30
Israel	New Sheqalim	4.48	Ukraine	Hryvnias	5.32
Italy [2]	Euro	0.81	United Arab Emirates	Dirhams	3.67
Jamaica	Jamaica Dollars	61.20	United Kingdom	Pounds Sterling	0.55
Japan	Yen	108.19	Uruguay	Uruguayan Pesos	28.70
Jordan	Jordinian Dinars	0.71	Vanuatu	Vatu	111.79
Kazakhstan	Tenge	136.04	Venezuela	Bolivares	1,891.33
Kenya	Kenya Shillings	79.17	Yemen	Yemeni Rials	184.78
Korea, South	Won	1,145.32	Zambia	Zambian Kwacha	4,778.88
Kuwait	Kuwaiti Dinars	0.29	Zimbabwe	Zimbabwe Dollar	4,303.28
Kyrgyzstan	Soms	42.65			

NA Not available. [1] End-of year values were used if annual averages were unavailable. Some values were estimated using partial year data. [2] The euro became the official currency of the 11 Euro Area (EMU) nations on January 1, 1999 and Greece in 2001. [3] See footnote 2, Table 1314. [4] See footnote 3, Table 1314.

Source: U.S. Department of Commerce, International Trade Administration, "Foreign Exchange Rates, 1997-04"; accessed July 2005. Also see <http://www.ita.doc.gov/td/industry/otea/usfth/aggregate/H04T34.html>.

U.S. Census Bureau, Statistical Abstract of the United States: 2006

Table 1370. Reserve Assets and International Transaction Balances by Country: 2000 to 2004

[In millions of U.S. dollars (56,600 represents $56,600,000,000). Assets include holdings of convertible foreign currencies, special drawing rights, and reserve position in International Monetary Fund and exclude gold holdings. Minus sign (-) indicates debits]

Country	Total reserve assets				Current account balance			Merchandise trade balance		
	2000	2003	2004 Total	Currency holdings[1]	2000	2003	2004	2000	2003	2004
United States......	56,600	74,890	75,890	42,720	-411,460	-541,830	(NA)	-449,790	-546,160	(NA)
Algeria..........	12,024	33,125	43,246	43,113	(NA)	(NA)	(NA)	(NA)	(NA)	(NA)
Argentina........	25,147	14,153	18,884	18,007	-8,937	7,390	(NA)	2,452	16,448	(NA)
Australia.........	18,118	32,189	35,803	33,901	-15,481	-30,377	(NA)	-4,813	-15,312	(NA)
Austria..........	14,319	8,470	7,858	6,763	-4,864	-1,363	(NA)	-2,737	1,140	(NA)
Bangladesh	1,486	2,578	3,172	3,171	-306	132	(NA)	-1,654	-2,442	(NA)
Belgium [2]........	[3]9,994	10,989	10,361	7,715	11,381	(NA)	(NA)	2,591	(NA)	(NA)
Brazil...........	32,488	49,111	52,740	52,736	-24,225	4,016	(NA)	-698	24,801	(NA)
Burma..........	223	550	672	672	-212	50	(NA)	-504	578	(NA)
Cameroon	212	640	829	828	(NA)	(NA)	(NA)	-504	(NA)	(NA)
Canada..........	31,924	36,222	34,430	30,167	20,595	17,268	25,870	45,578	41,513	51,734
Chile............	15,035	15,840	15,994	15,495	-898	-1,102	1,390	2,119	3,522	9,019
China [4].........	168,278	408,151	614,500	609,932	20,518	45,875	(NA)	34,474	44,652	(NA)
Colombia ...... [5]	8,916	10,784	13,394	12,769	734	-1,191	(NA)	34,474	435	(NA)
Congo (Brazzaville) [5]	222	35	120	112	648	-3	(NA)	2,037	1,011	(NA)
Cote d'Ivoire......	668	2,231	(NA)	(NA)	-241	583	(NA)	1,486	2,524	(NA).
Denmark	15,108	37,105	39,084	38,196	2,412	6,963	(NA)	6,740	9,697	(NA)
Ecuador.........	947	813	1,070	987	921	-455	(NA)	1,395	-71	(NA)
Egypt..........	13,118	13,589	14,273	14,108	-971	3,743	(NA)	-8,321	-4,201	(NA)
Finland	7,977	10,515	12,318	11,522	8,975	6,829	(NA)	13,684	12,646	(NA)
France..........	37,039	30,186	35,314	29,077	18,580	4,380	(NA)	-3,620	1,040	(NA)
Germany........	[3]56,890	50,694	48,823	39,889	-25,220	54,870	(NA)	57,450	151,660	(NA)
Ghana..........	232	1,353	1,627	1,606	-386	255	(NA)	-830	-714	(NA)
Greece	13,424	4,361	1,191	744	-9,820	-11,225	(NA)	-20,239	-25,606	(NA)
Hungary.........	11,190	12,737	15,908	15,312	-2,900	7,455	(NA)	-2,913	-3,279	(NA)
India	37,902	98,938	126,593	125,164	-2,640	(NA)	(NA)	-14,632	(NA)	(NA)
Indonesia........	28,502	34,962	34,952	34,742	7,985	7,252	(NA)	25,040	23,708	(NA)
Ireland..........	5,360	4,079	2,831	2,324	-593	-2,105	(NA)	25,416	37,807	(NA)
Israel...........	23,281	26,315	27,094	26,616	-671	98	(NA)	-2,883	-2,234	(NA)
Italy............	[3]25,567	30,366	26,408	22,560	-5,781	-20,556	(NA)	9,549	10,201	(NA)
Japan	354,902	663,289	833,891	824,264	119,660	136,220	(NA)	116,720	106,400	(NA)
Kenya	898	1,482	1,519	1,499	-199	68	(NA)	-1,262	-1,143	(NA)
Korea, South	96,131	155,284	198,997	198,175	12,241	12,321	27,613	16,872	22,161	38,161
Kuwait..........	7,082	7,577	8,242	7,347	14,672	7,567	(NA)	13,027	11,261	(NA)
Malaysia	29,523	44,515	66,384	65,409	8,488	13,381	(NA)	20,827	25,711	(NA)
Mexico..........	35,509	58,956	64,141	62,778	-18,191	-8,952	(NA)	-8,003	-5,624	(NA)
Morocco.........	4,823	13,851	16,337	16,107	-501	1,552	(NA)	-3,235	4,345	(NA)
Nepal	945	1,223	1,462	1,453	-299	110	(NA)	-818	-988	(NA)
Netherlands	9,643	11,012	10,102	6,657	6,817	16,403	(NA)	17,427	26,648	(NA)
Nigeria.........	9,911	7,128	16,956	16,955	(NA)	(NA)	(NA)	(NA)	(NA)	(NA)
Norway	20,164	37,220	43,943	42,714	25,851	28,326	34,445	25,975	28,269	33,576
Pakistan.........	1,513	10,941	9,799	9,554	-85	3,573	(NA)	-1,157	-109	(NA)
Peru	8,374	9,777	12,176	12,176	-1,557	-1,061	-72	-455	731	2,728
Philippines	13,047	13,457	12,917	12,780	6,258	3,347	(NA)	3,814	-1,253	(NA)
Poland..........	26,562	32,579	35,324	34,553	-9,998	-4,603	(NA)	-12,308	-5,725	(NA)
Portugal.........	[3]8,909	5,876	5,174	4,631	-11,114	-8,437	(NA)	-13,853	-13,357	(NA)
Romania	3,922	8,040	14,616	14,616	-1,355	-3,311	(NA)	-1,684	-4,537	(NA)
Saudi Arabia......	19,585	22,620	27,291	23,273	14,336	28,085	(NA)	49,843	59,496	(NA)
Singapore	80,132	95,746	112,232	111,498	13,280	28,183	(NA)	12,298	29,323	(NA)
South Africa	6,083	6,456	13,141	12,794	-295	-1,615	(NA)	4,593	3,542	(NA)
Spain	30,989	19,788	12,389	10,481	-19,237	-23,676	(NA)	-34,820	-42,923	(NA)
Sri Lanka........	1,039	2,265	(NA)	(NA)	-1,044	-160	(NA)	-1,044	-872	(NA)
Sudan	247	848	1,626	1,626	-557	-955	-871	440	6	192
Sweden	14,863	19,681	22,129	20,611	6,617	22,844	(NA)	15,215	18,933	(NA)
Switzerland.......	32,272	47,652	55,497	53,634	34,417	43,618	(NA)	2,104	6,961	(NA)
Syria	(NA)	(NA)	(NA)	(NA)	1,061	728	(NA)	1,423	1,332	(NA)
Thailand.........	32,016	41,077	48,664	48,498	9,313	7,963	(NA)	11,701	11,575	(NA)
Trinidad and Tobago. .	1,386	2,451	3,168	2,993	544	(NA)	(NA)	969	(NA)	(NA)
Turkey..........	22,488	33,991	35,669	35,480	-9,819	-7,905	(NA)	-22,410	-14,010	(NA)
United Kingdom ...	[3]43,890	41,850	45,340	39,480	-36,220	-30,470	(NA)	-49,850	-77,500	(NA)
Venezuela	13,088	16,035	18,375	17,867	12,106	11,448	14,575	16,664	16,483	22,053

NA Not available. [1] Holdings of convertible foreign currencies. [2] Balance of payments current account and trade balance data prior to 2002 is for Belgium-Luxembourg. Thereafter, data is for Belgium only. [3] Break in series. Data not comparable to earlier years. [4] See footnote 2, Table 1314. [5] See footnote 3, Table 1314.

Source: International Monetary Fund, Washington, DC, International Financial Statistics, monthly, (copyright).

Comparative International Statistics 895

Table 1371. Foreign Trade—Destination of Exports and Source of Imports for Selected Countries: 2003

[In billions of dollars (3.4 represents $3,400,000,000)]

Country	United States Imports	United States Exports	Canada Imports	Canada Exports	Australia Imports	Australia Exports	Japan Imports	Japan Exports	France Imports	France Exports	Germany Imports	Germany Exports	Italy Imports	Italy Exports	United Kingdom Imports	United Kingdom Exports
Argentina	3.4	2.4	0.3	0.1	0.1	0.1	0.4	0.3	0.5	0.4	1.1	0.8	1.1	0.5	0.4	0.2
Australia	6.7	13.1	1.2	1.0	-	-	15.1	9.9	1.0	2.2	1.1	4.7	1.2	2.6	3.0	3.8
Austria	4.6	1.8	0.7	0.2	0.3	0.0	1.1	1.2	3.6	3.6	23.4	38.9	8.0	6.6	4.4	2.0
Belgium	10.4	15.2	0.8	1.3	0.5	(Z)	1.8	5.8	25.2	27.5	28.7	37.1	12.2	7.7	20.0	17.6
Brazil	19.0	11.2	1.4	0.6	0.4	0.2	2.9	1.9	2.8	1.7	4.3	4.6	2.4	1.8	2.5	1.4
Canada	227.6	169.5	-	-	0.3	0.3	7.5	7.4	2.0	2.7	2.6	5.4	1.4	2.7	6.2	5.3
China	163.3	28.4	13.1	3.4	1.2	1.1	75.5	57.4	15.0	5.2	28.2	20.4	10.8	4.3	14.0	3.2
Colombia	6.8	3.8	0.3	0.2	9.3	5.9	0.2	0.6	0.2	0.4	0.5	0.6	0.4	0.3	0.4	0.2
Czech Republic	1.5	0.7	0.1	0.1	0.0	0.1	0.2	0.6	2.0	2.4	19.6	18.4	1.8	2.8	2.3	1.6
Denmark	3.9	1.5	0.8	0.2	0.1	(Z)	2.4	0.7	2.8	2.8	9.6	12.4	2.1	2.1	4.9	3.6
Egypt	1.2	2.7	0.1	0.2	0.5	0.1	0.1	0.7	0.4	1.1	0.4	-	2.0	1.3	0.7	0.8
Finland	3.8	1.7	0.7	0.2	(Z)	0.2	1.2	1.4	2.5	2.0	5.9	7.5	2.0	1.4	4.3	2.4
France	29.9	17.1	3.5	1.5	2.5	0.3	7.2	7.1	-	-	54.9	78.0	32.3	35.5	32.1	30.2
Germany	69.6	28.8	6.1	2.0	5.2	0.6	14.2	16.4	63.1	53.4	-	-	51.2	40.1	53.8	33.3
Hungary	2.8	0.9	0.1	0.1	0.1	0.8	0.4	1.1	1.7	2.2	13.7	13.3	2.1	3.2	1.9	1.4
India	13.8	5.0	1.0	0.5	0.6	2.2	2.2	2.4	1.4	1.2	2.9	2.7	1.9	1.9	3.5	3.7
Indonesia	10.3	2.5	0.7	0.3	2.7	1.8	16.5	7.2	7.5	0.6	2.4	1.4	1.4	0.4	1.6	0.7
Ireland	26.0	7.7	1.3	0.2	1.1	0.1	3.6	1.9	0.9	2.5	15.7	4.1	4.4	1.5	16.4	20.9
Israel	13.0	6.9	0.4	0.2	0.3	0.1	0.7	0.8	1.1	1.1	1.3	2.5	0.9	1.4	1.4	2.3
Italy	26.7	10.6	3.3	1.0	2.7	1.0	6.1	5.5	33.2	33.2	37.9	53.9	-	-	19.2	13.8
Japan	121.2	52.1	9.8	5.8	10.6	12.8	-	-	11.6	6.0	21.5	13.1	6.0	4.9	13.5	6.1
Luxembourg	0.3	0.3	(Z)	0.1	0.4	0.3	0.1	0.2	1.5	2.0	2.2	5.4	1.2	0.5	1.0	0.5
Mexico	139.7	97.5	8.6	1.6	0.8	0.9	1.8	3.6	0.7	1.6	1.7	5.0	0.3	2.0	0.8	1.1
Netherlands	11.4	20.7	1.2	1.1	0.8	0.1	1.9	11.8	16.8	14.1	46.4	44.1	16.0	6.9	25.6	21.7
Norway	5.5	1.5	3.0	0.7	0.1	(Z)	1.3	0.6	3.1	1.4	7.9	5.0	1.5	1.2	10.8	3.2
Poland	1.4	0.8	0.3	0.1	(Z)	0.1	0.1	0.8	6.9	4.4	17.6	18.2	3.0	5.2	2.6	2.4
Russia	9.1	2.5	0.6	0.2	0.6	1.2	4.2	3.7	2.4	3.2	9.9	13.5	5.8	4.3	4.1	2.3
Saudi Arabia	19.5	4.6	0.6	0.3	0.7	0.9	14.6	2.0	1.0	1.6	1.0	3.6	2.5	1.8	1.3	3.0
South Africa	4.8	2.8	0.4	0.2	0.7	0.4	3.6	3.7	1.6	1.6	3.1	5.5	1.7	1.1	4.9	2.9
Spain	7.1	5.9	0.8	0.6	1.2	0.1	1.4	1.7	27.4	36.5	18.4	36.2	13.8	20.2	13.8	14.3
Sweden	11.5	3.2	1.4	0.2	0.7	0.2	2.0	2.0	4.8	4.9	10.6	15.9	3.9	2.9	7.5	6.2
Switzerland	10.8	8.7	1.0	0.3	2.4	1.5	3.9	16.0	8.0	11.9	20.6	41.9	10.2	11.3	6.4	4.7
Thailand	16.1	5.8	1.3	0.3	3.6	4.8	11.9	13.2	1.6	0.8	2.1	2.1	1.1	0.7	2.8	0.9
United Kingdom	43.7	33.9	6.4	4.3			5.8	16.1	24.4	34.4	35.4	61.4	13.7	20.1	-	-
United States	-	-	**143.7**	**230.6**	**13.4**	**6.1**	**59.0**	**116.1**	**23.7**	**24.8**	**42.2**	**68.7**	**11.6**	**24.8**	**38.7**	**47.5**

- Represents zero.   Z Less than 50,000,000.   NA Not available.   ¹ See footnote 2, Table 1314.

Source: Organization for Economic Cooperation and Development, Paris, France, OECD International Trade by Commodities Statistics, 2003.

Table 1372. International Tourism Arrivals, Expenditures, and Receipts—Leading Countries: 1990 to 2003

[Expenditures and receipts in millions of dollars; arrivals in thousands of visitors (451,336 represents 451,336,000). Receipts are dollars spent by foreign tourists inside the country shown. Expenditures are dollars visitors (same-day visitors and tourists) from a given country of origin spend on tourism outside their country of residence. Excludes international transport receipts]

Country [1]	Arrivals					Expenditures				Receipts				
	1990	2000	2001	2002	2003	2000	2001	2002	2003	1990	2000	2001	2002	2003
World, total [1]	451,336	685,529	683,775	703,018	690,857	436,567	426,207	452,770	493,315	269,458	475,234	462,716	480,341	523,185
France	52,497	77,190	75,202	77,012	75,048	17,906	18,109	19,708	23,576	20,184	30,981	30,363	32,738	37,038
Spain	34,085	47,898	50,094	52,327	51,830	5,476	5,960	6,662	8,285	18,593	30,979	32,691	33,783	41,770
United States	39,362	51,219	46,907	43,525	41,212	64,705	60,200	58,044	56,613	43,007	82,400	71,893	66,728	64,509
Italy	26,679	41,181	39,563	39,799	39,604	15,685	14,795	16,924	20,528	16,458	27,493	25,822	26,873	31,222
China [2]	10,484	31,229	33,167	36,803	32,970	13,114	13,909	15,398	15,187	2,218	16,231	17,792	20,385	17,406
United Kingdom	18,013	25,209	22,835	24,180	24,715	38,262	37,931	41,744	48,477	15,375	21,769	18,864	20,549	22,752
Austria	19,011	17,982	18,180	18,611	19,078	8,512	8,985	9,383	11,761	13,417	9,931	10,259	11,239	14,068
Mexico	17,172	20,641	19,810	19,667	18,665	5,499	5,702	6,060	6,253	5,467	8,294	8,401	8,858	9,457
Germany	17,045	18,983	17,860	17,969	18,392	53,041	51,933	52,483	64,689	14,245	18,637	17,940	18,968	22,984
Canada	15,209	19,627	19,679	20,057	17,534	12,438	12,055	11,679	13,252	6,339	10,778	10,609	10,691	10,579
Hungary	20,510	15,571	15,340	15,870	15,706	1,387	1,456	1,722	2,023	824	3,444	3,770	3,274	3,440
Hong Kong	6,581	13,059	13,725	16,566	15,537	12,502	12,496	12,418	11,447	5,032	5,872	5,905	7,503	7,657
Greece	8,873	13,096	14,057	14,180	13,969	4,558	4,165	2,410	2,386	2,587	9,219	9,476	9,725	10,701
Poland	(NA)	17,400	15,000	13,980	13,720	3,313	3,495	3,202	2,801	358	5,677	4,646	4,314	4,069
Turkey	4,799	9,586	10,783	12,790	13,341	1,713	1,738	1,881	2,113	3,225	7,636	10,067	11,901	13,203
Portugal	8,020	12,097	12,167	11,644	11,707	2,228	2,102	2,255	2,703	3,555	5,243	5,470	5,761	6,937
Malaysia	7,446	10,222	12,775	13,292	10,577	2,075	2,614	2,618	2,846	1,667	5,011	6,863	7,118	5,901
Thailand	5,299	9,579	10,133	10,873	10,082	2,772	2,924	3,303	3,495	4,326	7,483	7,075	7,901	7,822
Netherlands	5,795	10,003	9,500	9,595	9,181	12,191	11,994	13,132	14,609	4,155	7,197	6,708	7,710	9,249
Russia	(NA)	7,030	7,400	7,943	8,015	8,848	9,285	7,301	12,880	(NA)	3,430	3,572	4,167	4,502
Sweden	(NA)	2,746	7,431	7,458	7,627	7,943	6,921	7,370	8,296	2,906	4,064	4,253	5,470	5,304
Croatia	(NA)	5,831	6,544	6,944	7,409	568	606	781	672	1,704	2,758	3,335	3,811	6,376
Saudi Arabia	2,209	6,585	6,736	7,512	7,332	2,918	2,306	1,811	4,166	(NA)	(NA)	(NA)	(NA)	(NA)
Belgium	(NA)	6,457	6,452	6,720	6,690	9,429	9,782	10,173	12,124	3,721	6,592	6,903	6,890	8,130
South Africa	1,029	6,001	5,908	6,550	6,640	2,085	1,878	3,741	2,420	992	2,677	2,569	2,923	4,270
Switzerland	13,200	7,821	7,455	6,868	6,530	6,335	6,256	6,612	7,471	7,411	7,791	7,505	7,888	9,325
Ireland	3,666	6,313	6,543	6,065	6,369	2,590	2,876	2,876	4,709	1,473	2,608	2,790	3,418	3,875
Macao	2,513	5,197	6,134	6,565	6,309	204	192	327	313	315	3,205	3,745	4,440	5,303
United Arab Emirates	973	3,907	4,134	5,445	5,871	3,017	3,319	3,655	3,956	(NA)	1,063	1,200	1,332	1,439
Singapore	4,842	6,917	6,725	6,997	5,705	4,538	5,604	3,867	3,867	4,937	5,229	4,617	4,463	3,998
Japan	3,236	4,757	4,772	5,239	5,212	31,884	26,531	26,656	28,959	3,578	3,373	3,306	3,497	8,848
Tunisia	3,204	5,058	5,387	5,064	5,114	263	273	260	300	948	1,682	1,751	1,523	1,583
Republic of Korea	2,959	5,322	5,147	5,347	4,753	7,132	7,617	7,356	9,998	3,559	6,834	6,384	5,936	5,256
Indonesia	2,178	5,064	5,154	5,033	4,467	3,197	3,406	3,289	3,082	2,105	4,975	5,276	5,285	4,037
Australia	2,215	4,530	4,435	4,420	4,354	6,103	5,700	6,094	7,291	4,088	8,469	8,049	8,577	10,313

NA Not available. [1] Includes other countries not shown separately. [2] See footnote 2, Table 1314.

Source: World Tourism Organization, Madrid, Spain, *Yearbook of Tourism Statistics, 2004* (copyright).

Table 1373. Net Flow of Financial Resources to Developing Countries and Multilateral Organizations: 1995 to 2003

[165,182 represents $165,182,000,000. Net flow covers loans, grants, and grant-like flows minus amortization on loans. Military flows are excluded. Developing countries are designated by Development Assistance Committee as developing. GNP = gross national product]

Type of aid and country	Amount (mil. dol.)					Percent of GNP		
	1995	2000	2001	2002	2003	1995	2000	2003
Total net flows.	165,182	134,485	107,880	73,263	108,545	0.75	0.56	0.39
United States	46,984	25,252	38,618	24,410	37,795	0.65	0.25	0.34
Australia	2,536	1,961	1,290	834	3,010	0.76	0.53	0.61
Austria	906	1,135	836	1,910	1,445	0.39	0.61	0.58
Belgium	-234	2,281	304	1,337	1,221	-0.09	1.00	0.40
Canada.	5,724	6,483	1,538	2,044	4,949	1.04	0.95	0.58
Denmark	1,799	2,176	2,645	1,577	1,896	1.07	1.39	0.91
Finland	604	1,087	1,334	-180	-44	0.50	0.91	-0.03
France	12,477	5,557	16,327	4,729	6,936	0.81	0.43	0.39
Germany	21,197	12,331	6,345	7,207	3,709	0.87	0.66	0.16
Greece	-	229	202	322	403	-	0.20	0.23
Ireland	247	740	735	1,469	2,334	0.46	0.93	1.83
Italy	2,800	10,846	-189	1,399	4,218	0.26	1.01	0.29
Japan	42,295	11,423	13,714	4,659	6,335	0.82	0.24	0.14
Luxembourg	72	129	144	148	201	0.40	0.75	0.84
Netherlands	6,795	6,947	-3,432	-1,487	12,167	1.71	1.85	2.44
New Zealand	166	142	139	164	208	0.31	0.32	0.28
Norway	1,670	1,437	1,485	2,279	3,306	1.16	0.87	1.49
Portugal	395	4,622	1,775	171	1,145	0.38	4.45	0.79
Spain	2,025	23,471	11,523	8,171	6,667	0.37	4.25	0.79
Sweden	2,224	3,952	3,077	2,232	1,255	1.00	1.76	0.42
Switzerland	1,118	2,054	-158	2,234	3,684	0.35	0.80	1.09
United Kingdom	13,382	10,230	9,627	7,634	5,705	1.19	0.72	0.31

- Represents zero.

Source: Organization for Economic Cooperation and Development, Paris, France, *Annual Reports of the Development Assistance Committee* (copyright).

Table 1374. External Debt by Country: 1990 to 2003

[In millions of dollars (28,149 represents $28,149,000,000). Total external debt is debt owed to nonresidents repayable in foreign currency, goods, or services. Total external debt is the sum of public, publicly guaranteed, and private nonguaranteed long-term debt, use of IMF credit, and short-term debt. Short-term debt includes all debt having an original maturity of one year or less and interest in arrears on long-term debt]

Country	1990	2000	2002	2003	Country	1990	2000	2002	2003
Algeria	28,149	25,272	22,800	23,386	Mexico	104,442	150,314	141,264	140,004
Angola	8,594	9,410	10,134	9,698	Morocco	25,017	20,721	18,601	18,795
Argentina	62,233	145,879	132,314	166,207	Nigeria	33,439	31,355	30,476	34,963
Bangladesh.	12,439	15,682	17,037	18,778	Pakistan	20,663	32,779	33,672	36,345
Brazil	119,964	238,793	227,932	235,431	Panama	6,506	7,046	8,298	8,770
Bulgaria	(NA)	10,188	10,462	13,289	Peru	20,064	28,710	28,167	29,857
Cameroon.	6,657	9,277	8,503	9,189	Philippines	30,580	57,429	59,343	62,663
Chile	19,226	37,048	41,945	43,231	Poland	49,364	63,259	69,521	95,219
China [1]	55,301	145,706	168,255	193,567	Romania	1,140	10,498	14,683	21,280
Colombia	17,222	33,934	33,853	32,979	Russia [3]	(NA)	160,027	147,541	175,257
Congo (Kinshasa) [2]	4,947	4,887	5,152	5,516	Serbia and Monte-				
Cote d'Ivoire	17,251	12,138	11,816	12,187	negro [4]	(NA)	11,851	12,688	14,885
Croatia	(NA)	11,344	15,347	23,452	Slovakia	(NA)	12,140	13,013	18,379
Czech Republic	(NA)	21,526	26,419	34,630	South Africa	(NA)	24,861	25,041	27,807
Ecuador	12,107	13,717	16,452	16,864	Sri Lanka	5,863	9,155	9,611	10,238
Egypt.	33,017	29,187	30,750	31,383	Sudan	14,762	15,741	16,389	17,496
Ghana	3,837	6,625	7,338	7,957	Syria	17,259	21,657	21,504	21,566
Hungary	21,202	29,520	34,958	45,785	Tanzania	6,459	7,394	7,244	7,516
India	83,628	99,098	104,429	113,467	Thailand	28,095	79,716	59,212	51,793
Indonesia	69,872	144,407	132,208	134,389	Tunisia	7,690	10,629	12,625	15,502
Iran	9,021	7,982	9,154	11,601	Turkey	49,424	117,431	131,556	145,662
Jordan	8,333	7,354	8,094	8,337	Ukraine	(NA)	12,190	13,555	16,309
Kazakhstan.	(NA)	11,805	17,538	22,835	Uruguay	4,415	8,196	10,736	11,764
Lebanon	1,779	9,856	17,077	18,598	Venezuela	33,171	38,152	32,563	34,851
Malaysia.	15,328	41,941	48,557	49,074	Vietnam	23,270	12,822	13,349	15,817

NA Not available. [1] See footnote 2, Table 1314. [2] See footnote 3, Table 1314. [3] External debt data presented for the Russian Federation prior to 2000 are for the former Soviet Union. The debt of the former Soviet Union is included in the Russian Federation data after 1990 on the assumption that 100 percent of all outstanding external debt as of December 1991 has become a liability of the Russian Federation. Beginning in 2000, the data for the Russian Federation has also been revised to include obligations to members of the former Council for Mutual Economic Assistance and other countries in the form of trade-related credits amounting to $15.4 billion as of the end of 1996. [4] External debt obligations, excluding IBRD, IMF, and short-term, of Bosnia and Herzegovina before 2000 are included under Serbia and Montenegro. Data prior to 2000 refer to the former Socialist Federal Republic of Yugoslavia. Data from 2000 onwards are estimates and reflect borrowing by the former Yugoslavia that are not yet allocated to the successor republics.

Source: The World Bank, Washington, DC, *2005 World Development Indicators CD-ROM* (copyright).

Table 1375. **Foreign Direct Investment Flows in OECD Countries: 2000 to 2002**
[In billions of dollars (1,288.0 represents $1,288,000,000,000). Data are converted to U.S. dollars using the yearly average exchange rate]

Country	Inflows				Outflows			
	2000	2001	2002 [1]	Cumulative, 1994-2003	2000	2001	2002 [1]	Cumulative, 1994-2003
OECD, total.	1,288.0	624.9	535.0	5,174.0	1,235.8	661.9	566.7	6,053.1
Australia.	13.2	4.7	16.5	82.2	0.7	12.2	7.6	57.3
Austria.	8.8	5.9	1.0	41.2	5.7	3.1	5.3	33.6
Belgium-Luxembourg . . .	221.0	84.7	(NA)	762.7	218.4	100.6	(NA)	767.0
Belgium.	(NA)	(NA)	13.1	(NA)	(NA)	(NA)	(NA)	(NA)
Luxembourg	(NA)	(NA)	117.1	(NA)	(NA)	(NA)	11.0	(NA)
Canada	66.8	27.5	21.0	208.1	44.7	36.1	126.2	237.3
Czech Republic.	5.0	5.6	8.5	37.9	0.0	0.2	0.2	1.2
Denmark.	33.8	11.5	6.6	91.7	26.5	13.4	5.7	82.0
Finland.	8.8	3.7	7.9	45.9	24.0	8.4	7.6	72.6
France.	43.3	50.5	48.9	351.6	177.5	86.8	49.5	652.7
Germany	198.3	21.1	36.0	387.0	56.6	36.9	8.6	452.7
Greece	1.1	1.6	0.1	8.7	2.1	0.6	0.7	3.7
Hungary	2.8	3.9	2.8	32.4	0.6	0.4	0.3	3.9
Iceland	0.2	0.2	0.1	1.0	0.4	0.3	0.2	1.5
Ireland	25.8	9.7	24.4	120.0	4.6	4.1	3.1	26.7
Italy	13.4	14.9	14.6	86.5	12.3	21.5	17.1	112.4
Japan	8.3	6.2	9.2	50.5	31.5	38.4	32.3	268.0
Korea, South.	9.3	3.5	2.4	40.9	5.0	2.4	2.6	37.5
Mexico	16.4	26.6	14.4	138.2	(NA)	4.4	1.0	5.4 [2]
Netherlands	63.9	51.9	25.6	286.5	75.6	48.0	34.6	382.8
New Zealand.	1.3	4.2	-0.6	19.9	0.6	0.9	-1.0	2.9
Norway.	6.9	2.0	0.7	35.5	7.6	-1.3	4.2	37.7
Poland	9.3	5.7	4.1	52.0	0.0	-0.1	0.2	1.1
Portugal	6.8	5.9	1.8	25.7	7.5	7.6	3.3	29.2
Spain	37.5	28.0	35.9	183.5	54.7	33.1	31.5	230.1
Sweden	23.2	11.9	11.6	168.2	40.7	6.4	10.7	150.2
Switzerland	19.3	8.9	5.7	81.9	44.7	18.2	7.6	190.4
Turkey	1.0	3.3	1.0	10.6	0.9	0.5	0.2	3.6
United Kingdom.	118.8	52.7	27.8	463.1	233.5	58.9	35.2	878.6
United States	321.3	167.0	72.4	1,349.6	159.2	120.0	134.8	1,331.0

NA Not available. [1] Preliminary. [2] Based on outflow data for 2001 and 2002 only.
Source: Organization for Economic Cooperation and Development, Paris, France, *Financial Market Trends*, June 2004.

Table 1376. **Military Manpower Fit for Military Service, by Country: 2005**
[Covers males ages 15-49]

Country	Number	Country	Number
Afghanistan.	2,662,946	Ireland	814,768
Albania.	668,526	Israel [3]	1,255,902
Algeria	6,590,079	Italy	10,963,513
Argentina	7,316,038	Jamaica	587,006
Australia	4,092,717	Japan	22,234,663
Austria	1,550,441	Kazakhstan	2,473,529
Bahrain.	161,372	Korea, North	4,310,831
Bangladesh	26,841,255	Korea, South	9,932,026
Belarus	1,657,984	Kuwait	737,292
Belgium	1,998,003	Laos.	954,816
Bolivia	1,311,414	Lebanon	821,762
Bosnia and Herzegovina	829,530	Libya	1,291,624
Brazil	33,119,098	Malaysia	4,574,854
Bulgaria	1,302,037	Mexico	19,058,337
Burma [1]	6,512,923	Morocco	6,484,787
Cambodia	1,844,144	Mozambique	1,751,223
Canada.	6,740,490	Netherlands	2,856,691
Chile	3,123,281	New Zealand	809,519
China	281,240,272	Nicaragua	1,051,425
Colombia.	6,986,228	Nigeria	15,053,936
Congo (Kinshasa).	5,851,292	Norway	827,016
Congo (Brazzaville).	360,492	Oman	581,444
Cote d'Ivoire	1,973,265	Pakistan	29,428,747
Croatia	725,914	Peru	4,938,417
Cuba [2]	2,441,927	Philippines.	15,170,096
Czech Republic	1,996,631	Poland	7,740,164
Denmark.	955,168	Russia	21,049,651
Dominican Republic	1,420,693	Saudi Arabia	6,592,709
Ecuador	2,338,428	Singapore	982,368
Egypt	15,540,234	South Africa.	4,927,757
El Salvador	960,315	Spain	7,623,356
Ethiopia	8,072,755	Sudan	5,427,474
Finland	913,617	Sweden	1,493,668
France	11,262,661	Switzerland	1,375,889
Germany.	15,258,931	Syria	3,453,888
Greece	2,018,557	Thailand	10,342,337
Guatemala	2,106,847	Turkey	13,905,901
Honduras	955,019	Ukraine.	7,114,337
Hungary	1,780,513	United Arab Emirates.	526,671
India.	219,471,999	United Kingdom	12,046,268
Indonesia	48,687,234	United States	(NA)
Iran	15,665,725	Venezuela	4,907,947
Iraq	4,930,074	Vietnam	16,032,358

NA Not available. [1] 6,789,720 females ages 15-49 fit for service. [2] 2,396,741 females ages 15-49 fit for service. [3] 1,212,394 females ages 15-49 fit for service.
Source: Central Intelligence Agency, *The World Factbook*, 2005. See also <http://www.cia.gov/cia/publications/factbook/index/html> (accessed July 2005).

Guide to—Sources of Statistics, State Statistical Abstracts, and Foreign Statistical Abstracts

Alphabetically arranged, this guide contains references to important primary sources of statistical information for the United States. Secondary sources have been included if the information contained in them is presented in a particularly convenient form or if primary sources are not readily available. Nonrecurrent publications presenting compilations or estimates that were published later than 2000, or types of data not available in regular series, are also included. Data are also available in press releases.

Valuable information may also be found in state reports, foreign statistical abstracts, which are included at the end of this appendix, and in reports for particular commodities, industries, or similar segments of our economic and social structures, many of which are not included here.

Publications listed under each subject are divided into two main groups: "U.S. Government" and "Nongovernment." The location of the publisher of each report is given except for federal agencies located in Washington, DC. Most federal publications may be purchased from the Superintendent of Documents, U.S. Government Printing Office, Washington, DC, tel. 202-512-1800, (Web site <http://www.access.gpo.gov>. In some cases, federal publications may be obtained from the issuing agency.

Title	Frequency	Paper	Internet PDF	Internet Other Formats
U.S. GOVERNMENT				
Administrative Office of the United States Courts <http://www.uscourts.gov>				
Calendar Year Reports on Authorized Wiretaps (state and federal).	Annual	X	X	X
Federal Court Management Statistics	Annual	X		X
Federal Judicial Caseload Statistics	Annual	X	X	
Judicial Business of the United States Courts	Annual	X	X	
Statistical Tables for the Federal Judiciary	Semiannual	X	X	
Agency for International Development <http://www.usaid.gov>				
U.S. Overseas Loans and Grants and Assistance From International Organizations .	Annual	X	X	
Army, Corps of Engineers <http://www.usace.army.mil>				
Waterborne Commerce of the United States (in five parts)	Annual	X		X
Board of Governors of the Federal Reserve System <http://www.federalreserve.gov>				
Assets and Liabilities of Commercial Banks in the United States H8.	Weekly	X	X	X
Consumer Credit	Monthly	X	X	X
Country Exposure Lending Survey.	Quarterly	X	X	X
Federal Reserve Banks (Monthly review published by each bank)	Monthly	X		
Federal Reserve Bulletin (paper discontinued in 2006).	Quarterly	X	X	
Foreign Exchange Rates	Weekly	X	X	X
Flow of Funds Accounts of the United States: Flows and Outstandings Z1	Quarterly	X	X	X
Industrial Production and Capacity Utilization G17	Monthly	X	X	X
Money Stock and Debt Measures H6	Weekly	X	X	X
Statistical Supplement to the Federal Reserve Bulletin.	Monthly	X		
Bureau of Economic Analysis <http://www.bea.gov>				
Survey of Current Business	Monthly	X	X	
U.S. Direct Investment Abroad: 1999 Benchmark Survey, 2004	Periodic	X	X	
Bureau of Justice Statistics <http://www.ojp.usdoj.gov/bjs>				
American Indians and Crime: A BJS Statistical Profile, 1992–2002, December 2004 .	Periodic	X	X	X
Background Checks for Firearm Transfers.	Annual		X	X
Capital Punishment	Annual	X	X	X
Carjacking, 1993–2002, July 2004	Periodic		X	X
Census of Publicly Funded Forensic Crime Laboratories, 2002, February 2005	Periodic	X	X	X
Census of State and Federal Correctional Facilities, 2000, August 2003	Periodic		X	X
Civil Rights Complaints in U.S. District Courts, 2000, July 2002.	Periodic	X	X	X
Civil Trial Cases and Verdicts in Large Counties, 2001, April 2004	Periodic	X	X	X

Title	Frequency	Paper	PDF	Other Formats
Bureau of Justice Statistics—Con.				
Compendium of Federal Justice Statistics	Annual	X	X	X
Compendium of State Privacy and Security Legislation: 2002, Overview November 20				
Contract Trials and Verdicts in Large Counties, 2001, February 2005	Triennial	X		X
Crime and the Nation's Households	Periodic		X	X
Crimes Against Persons Age 65 or Older, 1993–2002, January 2005	Annual	X	X	X
Criminal Victimization	Periodic		X	X
Cross-National Studies in Crime and Justice, September 2004	Annual	X	X	X
Defense Counsel in Criminal Cases, November 2000	Periodic		X	X
Education and Correctional Populations, January 2003	Periodic	X	X	X
Federal Criminal Case Processing	Periodic	X	X	X
Federal Law Enforcement Officers, 2002, July 2003	Annual		X	X
Felony Defendants in Large Urban Counties, 2000, November 2003	Biennial		X	X
Felony Sentences in State Courts, 2002, December 2004	Biennial	X	X	X
Firearm Use by Offenders, November 2001	Biennial	X	X	X
Hepatitis Testing and Treatment in State Prisons, April 2004	Periodic	X	X	X
Hispanic Victims of Violent Crime, 1993–2000, April 2002	Periodic	X	X	X
HIV in Prisons and Jails	Periodic	X	X	X
Homicide Trends in the United States	Annual	X	X	X
Immigration Offenders in the Federal Criminal Justice System, 2000, August 2002	Annual	X	X	X
Incarcerated Parents and Their Children, August 2000	Periodic	X	X	X
Indicators of School Crime and Safety	Periodic	X	X	X
Intimate Partner Violence, 1993–2001, February 2003	Annual	X	X	X
Jails in Indian Country, 2002, November 2003	Periodic	X	X	X
Justice Expenditure and Employment in the United States, 2001, May 2004	Periodic	X	X	X
Local Police Departments, 2000, January 2003	Periodic	X	X	X
Medical Malpractice Trials and Verdicts in Large Counties, 2001, April 2004	Periodic	X	X	X
Money Laundering Offenders, 1994–2001, July 2003	Periodic	X	X	X
Prevalence of Imprisonment in the U.S. Population, 1974–2001, August 2003	Periodic	X	X	X
Prison and Jail Inmates at Midyear	Annual	X	X	X
Prisoners in 2004	Annual	X	X	X
Probation and Parole in the United States	Annual	X	X	X
Profile of Jail Inmates, 2002, July 2004	Annual	X	X	X
Prosecutors in State Courts, 2001, May 2002	Periodic	X	X	X
Rape and Sexual Assault: Reporting to Police and Medical Attention, 1992–2000 August 2002	Biennial		X	X
Reentry Trends in the United States Current Data Electronic	Periodic	X	X	X
Sheriffs' Offices, 2000, January 2003	Annual		X	X
Sourcebook of Criminal Justice Statistics	Periodic	X	X	X
State Court Prosecutors in Large Districts, 2001, December 2001	Annual	X	X	X
State Court Prosecutors in Small Districts, 2001, January 2003	Periodic	X	X	X
State Court Sentencing of Convicted Felons, 2000 ,June 2003	Periodic		X	X
State Prison Expenditures, 2001, June 2004	Biennial		X	X
Summary of State Sex Offender Registries	Periodic	X	X	X
Survey of DNA Crime Laboratories, 2001, January 2002	Annual	X	X	X
Survey of State Criminal History Information Systems, 2001, September 2003	Periodic		X	X
Survey of State Procedures Related to Firearm Sales	Biennial	X	X	X
Tort Trials and Verdicts in Large Counties, 2001, November 2004	Annual		X	X
Traffic Stop Data Collection Policies for State Police, 2001, December 2001	Periodic	X	X	X
Violent Victimization of College Students, 1995–2002, January 2005	Periodic	X	X	X
Weapon Use and Violent Crime, 1993–2001, September 2003	Periodic		X	X
	Periodic	X	X	X
Bureau of Labor Statistics <http://www.bls.gov>				
College Enrollment and Work Activity of High School Graduates	Annual	X		
Comparative Labor Force Statistics, Ten Countries	Annual	X		
Compensation and Working Conditions	Quarterly	X	X	X
Consumer Expenditure Survey, Integrated Diary and Interview Survey data	Annual	X	X	X
Consumer Prices: Energy and Food	Monthly	X	X	X
CPI Detailed Report	Monthly	X	X	X
Employee Benefits in Private Industry	Annual	X	X	X
Employer Costs for Employee Compensation	Annual	X	X	X
Employment and Earnings	Monthly	X	X	X
Employment and Wages	Annual	X	X	X
Employment Characteristics of Families	Annual	X	X	X
Employment Cost Index	Quarterly	X	X	X
Employment Cost Indexes and Levels	Annual	X	X	X
The Employment Situation	Monthly	X	X	X
Geographic Profile of Employment and Unemployment	Annual	X	X	X
International Comparisons of Hourly Compensation Costs for Production Workers in Manufacturing	Annual	X	X	X
International Comparisons of Manufacturing Productivity and Unit Labor Cost Trends	Annual	X	X	X
Metropolitan Area Employment and Unemployment	Monthly	X	X	X
Monthly Labor Review	Monthly	X	X	X
Occupational Injuries and Illnesses in the United States by Industry	Annual	X	X	X
Occupational Projections and Training Data	Biennial	X	X	X
Producer Price Indexes Detailed Report	Monthly	X	X	X
Productivity Measures for Selected Industries and Government Services	Annual	X	X	X
Real Earnings	Monthly	X	X	X
Regional and State Employment and Unemployment	Monthly	X	X	X
Relative Importance of Components in the Consumer Price Indexes	Annual	X	X	X
Union Members	Annual	X	X	X
U.S. Import and Export Price Indexes	Monthly	X	X	X
Usual Weekly Earnings of Wage and Salary Workers	Quarterly	X	X	X
Work Experience of the Population	Annual	X	X	X

U.S. Census Bureau, Statistical Abstract of the United States: 2006

			Internet	
Title	Frequency	Paper	PDF	Other Formats

Bureau of Land Management
<http://www.blm.gov>

Title	Frequency	Paper	PDF	Other Formats
Public Land Statistics	Annual	X	X	

Census Bureau
<http://www.census.gov>

Title	Frequency	Paper	PDF	Other Formats
2002 Economic Census	Qiunquennial	X	X	X
Comparative Statistics	Quinquennial	X	X	X
Bridge Between NAICS and SIC	Quinquennial	X	X	X
Business Expenses	Quinquennial	X	X	X
Nonemployer Statistics	Annual	X	X	X
Industry Geography	Annual			
Annual Benchmark Report for Retail Trade and Food Services	Annual	X	X	
Annual Benchmark Report for Wholesale Trade	Annual	X	X	X
Annual Survey of Manufactures	Annual	X	X	
Census of Governments	Quinquennial	X	X	
Volume 3, No. 2, Compendium of Public Employment	Quinquennial	X	X	
Volume 4, No. 6, Employee-Retirement Systems of State and Local Governments	Quinquennial	X	X	
Volume 3, No. 1, Employment of Major Local Governments	Quinquennial	X	X	
Volume 4, No. 3, Finances of County Governments	Quinquennial	X	X	
Volume 1, No. 1, Government Organization	Quinquennial	X	X	
Volume 4, No. 1, Public Education Finances	Quinquennial	X	X	
Census of Housing Decennial (2000, most recent)	Decennial	X	X	X
Census of Population Decennial (2000, most recent)	Decennial	X	X	X
CFFR, Consolidated Federal Funds Report	Annual	X	X	X
State and County Areas	Annual	X	X	X
County Business Patterns	Annual		X	X
Current Construction Reports:				
New Residential Construction and New Residential Sales:	Annual	X	X	
Value of Construction Put in Place, C30	Monthly	X	X	
Residential Improvements and Repairs, C50	Quarterly	X	X	
Current Housing Reports:		X	X	
Housing Vacancies, H111	Quarterly	X	X	
Who Can Afford to Buy a House, H121	biennial	X	X	
Market Absorption of Apartments, H130	Quarterly	X	X	
Characteristics of Apartments Completed, H131	Annual	X	X	
American Housing Survey for the United States, H150	Biennial	X	X	
American Housing Survey for Selected Metropolitan Areas, H170	Biennial	X	X	
Current Industrial Reports			X	
Current Population Reports (Series P20)		X	X	X
Consumer Income and Poverty, P60 and Household Economic Studies, P70		X	X	
Alternative Poverty Estimates in the United States: 2003	Periodic	X	X	
Alternative Income Estimates in the United States: 2003	Periodic	X	X	
Income, Poverty, and Health Insurance Coverage in the United States	Annual	X	X	X
Economic Census of Outlying Areas	Quinquennial	X	X	
Federal Aid to States for Fiscal Year	Annual	X	X	X
Global Population Profile: 2002 (Series WP)		X	X	X
International Briefs (Series IB)		X	X	X
International Population Reports (Series IPC)		X	X	X
Manufacturers Shipments, Inventories, and Orders	Monthly	X	X	
Manufacturers Shipments, Inventories, and Orders: 1992–2002	Annual	X	X	
Minority- and Women-Owned Business Enterprises	Quinquennial	X	X	X
Quarterly Financial Report for Manufacturing, Mining, and Trade Corporations	Quarterly	X	X	
Service Annual Survey Report	Annual	X	X	
Survey of Plant Capacity Utilization (Current Industrial Reports, MQ-C1)	Annual	X	X	
U.S. International Trade in Goods and Services: includes cumulative data		X	X	X
U.S. Trade with Puerto Rico and U.S. Possessions (FT 895)	Monthly	X	X	
Vehicle Inventory and Use Survey	Quinquennial	X	X	X

Centers for Disease Control and Prevention, Atlanta, GA
<http://www.cdc.gov>

Title	Frequency	Paper	PDF	Other Formats
Injury Fact Book, 2001–2002		X	X	X
Morbidity and Mortality Weekly Report	Annual	X	X	X

Centers for Medicare and Medicaid Services (CMS)
<http://www.cms.hhs.gov>

Title	Frequency	Paper	PDF	Other Formats
CMS Statistics	Annual	X	X	
Data Compendium	Annual	X	X	
Health Care Financing Review, Medicare and Medicaid Statistical Supplement	Quarterly	X	X	
Health Care Financing Review	Quarterly	X	X	
Trustees Report	Annual	X	X	

Central Intelligence Agency
<http://www.cia.gov>

Title	Frequency	Paper	PDF	Other Formats
World Factbook	Annual	X	X	X

Coast Guard (See Department of Homeland Security)

Comptroller of the Currency
<http://www.occ.treas.gov>

Title	Frequency	Paper	PDF	Other Formats
Quarterly Journal	Quarterly		X	X

Office of the Clerk U.S. House of Representatives
<http://clerkweb.house.gov>

Title	Frequency	Paper	PDF	Other Formats
Statistics of the Presidential and Congressional Election	Biennial		X	X
Official List of Members by State	Periodic		X	X

Council of Economic Advisers
<http://www.whitehouse.gov>

Title	Frequency	Paper	PDF	Other Formats
Economic Indicators	Monthly	X	X	X
Economic Report of the President	Annual	X	X	

902   Appendix I

Title	Frequency	Paper	Internet PDF	Internet Other Formats
Department of Agriculture <http://www.usda.gov>				
Agricultural Chemical Usage	Annual	X	X	X
Agricultural Income and Finance (Situation and Outlook Report)	Quarterly	X	X	X
Agricultural Price Reports	Annual	X	X	X
Agricultural Statistics	Annual	X	X	
Amber Waves	Periodic	X	X	
Catfish Production	Annual	X	X	X
Census of Agriculture	Quinquennial	X	X	X
Cotton Ginnings	Periodic	X	X	
Crop Production Reports	Monthly	X	X	X
Crop Values Report	Annual	X	X	X
Dairy Product Prices	Weekly	X	X	X
Farm Labor	Quarterly	X	X	X
Farms, Land in Farms, and Livestock Operations	Annual	X	X	X
Food Marketing Review, (Agricultural Economic Report No. 743)	Annual	X	X	X
Food Spending in American Households (Statistical Bulletin No. 824)	Annual	X	X	X
Fruit and Vegetable Reports	Periodic	X	X	X
Income, Wealth, and the Economic Well-Being of Farm Households (ERS)	Periodic	X	X	X
Journal of Agricultural Economics Research	Quarterly	X	X	
Livestock and Poultry World Markets and Trade	Annual	X	X	
Livestock Reports	Monthly	X	X	
Milk and Dairy Products Reports	Monthly	X	X	
Poultry and Egg Reports	Weekly	X	X	X
Rural Development Perspectives		X	X	X
Situation and Outlook Reports issued for agricultural exports, cotton and wool, dairy, feed, fruit and tree nuts, agricultural resources, livestock and poultry oil crops, rice, aquaculture, sugar and sweeteners, tobacco, vegetables, wheat, and world agriculture		X	X	
Stock Reports, stocks of grain, peanuts, potatoes, and rice	Periodic	X	X	
Tobacco: World Markets and Trade	Quarterly	X	X	X
Trout Production	Annual			
Usual planting and harvesting dates	Annual	X	X	X
Weekly Weather and Crop Bulletin Report	Periodic	X	X	X
Winter Wheat Seedings	Weekly	X	X	
	Monthly	X	X	X
Department of Agriculture, Food and Nutrition Service <http://www.fns.usda.gov>				
Annual Historical Review	Annual	X		
Characteristics of Food Stamp Households	Annual			
Food and Consumer Service Programs		X	X	X
Department of Agriculture, Natural Resources and Conservation Service <http://www.nrcs.usda.gov>				
National Resources Inventory	Periodic	X		X
Department of Defense <http://www.defenselink.mil/pubs>				
Foreign Military Sales and Military Assistance Facts	Annual			X
Personnel Statistics	Annual		X	
Department of Education <http://www.ed.gov>				
Department of Education, Rehabilitation Services Administration	Annual	X	X	X
Caseload Statistics of State Vocational Rehabilitation Agencies in Fiscal Year	Annual	X	X	X
Department of Health and Human Services <http://www.os.hhs.gov>				
Annual Report	Annual	X		
National Survey on Drug Use & Health	Annual	X	X	X
National Survey of Substance Abuse Treatment Services (N-SSATS)	Annual	X	X	X
Department of Homeland Security (DHS) <http://www.dhs.gov>				
Budget in Brief	Annual	X	X	
Department of Homeland Security, Coast Guard <http://www.uscg.mil/USCG.shtm>				
Fact File		X	X	X
Department of Homeland Security, Office of Immigration Statistics <http://uscis.gov/graphics/shared/statistics/index.htm>				
Yearbook of Immigration Statistics	Annual	X	X	
Department of Housing and Urban Development <http://www.hud.gov>				
Survey of Mortgage Lending Activity	Monthly	X		X
Department of Labor <http://www.dol.gov>				
Annual Report of the Secretary	Annual	X	X	X
Department of State <http://www.state.gov>				
United States Contribution to International Organizations	Annual			X
Department of Transportation <http://www.dot.gov>				
Airport Activity Statistics of Certified Route Air Carriers	Annual	X		X
Annual Report of the Secretary of Transportation		X		
Report of Passenger Travel Between the United States and Foreign Countries	Monthly	X	X	
Transportation Safety Information Report	Quarterly	X		X

| | | | Internet | |
Title	Frequency	Paper	PDF	Other Formats

Department of Transportation—Con.
U.S. International Air Travel Statistics	Annual	X	X	X
Wage Statistics of Class I Railroads in the United States	Annual	X	X	
Air Travel Consumer Report	Monthly	X	X	X

Department of the Treasury
<http://www.treasury.gov>

Department of the Treasury, Alcohol and Tobacco Tax and Trade Bureau (formerly Bureau of Alcohol, Tobacco, and Firearms)
<http://www.atf.treas.gov>
Alcohol and Tobacco Summary Statistics	Annual	X		
Tobacco Products Monthly Statistical Releases		X		

Department of the Treasury, Bureau of Public Debt
<http://www.publicdebt.treas.gov>
Monthly Statement of the Public Debt of the United States	Monthly	X	X	X

Department of the Treasury, Financial Management Services
<http://www.fms.treas.gov>
Active Foreign Credits of the United States Government	Quarterly	X		
Combined Statement of Receipts, Outlays, and Balances	Annual	X	X	X
Monthly Treasury Statement of Receipts and Outlays of the United States Government	Monthly	X	X	X
Treasury Bulletin.	Quarterly	X		X
Financial Report of the United States Government	Annual	X	X	

Department of Veterans Affairs
<http://www.va.gov>
Disability Compensation, Pension, and Death Pension Data	Annual	X		X
Government Life Insurance Programs for Veterans and Members of the Service . . .	Annual	X		X
Selected Compensation and Pension Data by State of Residence	Annual	X		X
Veterans Affairs Annual Accountability Report.	Annual	X	X	X

Drug Enforcement Administration
<http://www.whitehousedrugpolicy.gov>
Drug Abuse and Law Enforcement Statistics	Irregular	X	X	X

Employment and Training Administration
<http://www.doleta.gov>
Unemployment Insurance Claims.	Weekly			X

Energy Information Administration
<http://www.eia.doe.gov>
Annual Energy Outlook	Annual	X	X	X
Annual Energy Review.	Annual	X	X	X
Coal Industry Annual.	Annual		X	X
Cost and Quality of Fuels for Electric Utility Plants	Annual		X	
Electric Power Annual	Annual		X	X
Electric Power Monthly	Monthly	X	X	
Electric Sales, Revenue and Retail Price.	Annual		X	X
Emissions of Greenhouse Gases in the U.S.	Annual		X	
Financial Statistics of Major U.S. Publicly Owned Electric Utilities 2003			X	
International Energy Annual	Annual			X
International Energy Outlook.	Annual		X	X
Inventory of Electric Utility Power Plants in the United States 2000			X	X
Inventory of Nonutility Power Plants in the United States 2000			X	
Monthly Energy Review, 2005	Monthly	X	X	X
Natural Gas 2000 Issues & Trends (Web only).			X	
Performance Profiles of Major Energy Producers	Annual		X	X
Petroleum Marketing Annual	Monthly		X	X
Petroleum Supply Annual, Volume 1.	Annual		X	
Petroleum Supply Annual, Volume 2 (Web only)	Annual		X	
Petroleum Supply Monthly, 2005	Monthly		X	X
Quarterly Coal Report, 2004	Quarterly		X	X
Renewable Energy Annual	Annual		X	
Residential Energy Consumption Survey: Housing Characteristics	Triennial		X	
Residential Transportation Energy Consumption Survey.	Triennial		X	X
State Electricity Profiles, 2002.			X	X
State Energy Data Report	Annual		X	X
State Energy Price and Expenditure Report.	Annual		X	X
U.S. Crude Oil, Natural Gas, and Natural Gas Liquids Reserves	Annual		X	X
Weekly Coal Production, 2005 (Web only).	Weekly		X	X

Environmental Protection Agency
<http://www.epa.gov>
Air Quality Data	Annual			X
Drinking Water Infrastructure Needs Survey.	Periodic	X	X	
Needs Survey, Conveyance and Treatment of Municipal Wastewater Summaries of Technical Data	Biennial		X	
Toxics Release Inventory	Annual		X	X
National Water Quality Inventory: 2000 Report (EPA-841-T-01-001)	Biennial	X	X	

Export-Import Bank of the United States
<http://www.exim.gov>
Annual Report	Annual	X	X	
Report to the U.S. Congress on Export Credit Competition and the Export-Import Bank of the United States.	Annual	X	X	

Farm Credit Administration
<http://www.fca.gov>
Annual Report on the Work of the Cooperative Farm Credit System.	Annual	X	X	
Loans and Discounts of Farm Credit Banks and Associations	Annual	X		

Title	Frequency	Paper	Internet PDF	Internet Other Formats

Farm Credit Administration—Con.

Title	Frequency	Paper	PDF	Other Formats
Production Credit Association: Summary of Operations	Annual	X		
Report to the Federal Land Bank Associations	Annual	X		

Federal Bureau of Investigation
<http://www.fbi.gov>

Title	Frequency	Paper	PDF	Other Formats
Bomb Summary	Annual			
Crime in the United States	Annual	X	X	
Hate Crime Statistics	Annual	X	X	
Law Enforcement Officers Killed and Assaulted	Annual	X	X	

Federal Communications Commission
<http://www.fcc.gov>

Title	Frequency	Paper	PDF	Other Formats
Annual Report	Annual	X	X	
Statistics of Communications Common Carriers	Annual	X	X	

Federal Deposit Insurance Corporation
<http://www.fdic.gov>

Title	Frequency	Paper	PDF	Other Formats
Annual Report	Annual	X	X	
Bank and Thrift Branch Office Data Book	Annual	X	X	X
Quarterly Banking Profile	Quarterly	X	X	
Banking Review	Quarterly	X	X	
Quarterly Historical Statistics on Banking	Quarterly	X	X	
Statistics on Banking				
Summary of Deposits	Annual	X	X	X
Trust Assets of Financial Institutions	Annual	X		X

Federal Highway Administration
<http://www.fhwa.dot.gov>

Title	Frequency	Paper	PDF	Other Formats
Highway Statistics	Annual	X	X	

Federal Railroad Administration
<http://www.fra.dot.gov>

Title	Frequency	Paper	PDF	Other Formats
Accident/Incident Bulletin Summary, statistics, and analysis of accidents on railroads in the United States	Annual	X	X	
Rail-Highway Crossing Accident/Incident and Inventory Bulletin	Annual	X	X	

Fish and Wildlife Service
<http://www.fws.gov>

Title	Frequency	Paper	PDF	Other Formats
Federal Aid in Fish and Wildlife Restoration	Annual	X	X	
National Survey of Fishing, Hunting, and Wildlife Associated Recreation	Quinquennial	X	X	

Forest Service
<http://www.fs.fed.us>

Title	Frequency	Paper	PDF	Other Formats
An Analysis of the Timber Situation in the United States, 1990–2050				X
Land Areas of the National Forest System	Annual	X		X
The 1993 RPA Timber Assessment Update	Periodic			
U.S. Timber Production, Trade, Consumption, and Price Statistics, 2001	Biennial	X	X	

General Services Administration
<http://www.gsa.gov>

Title	Frequency	Paper	PDF	Other Formats
Inventory Report on Real Property Leased to the United States Throughout the World	Annual	X	X	
Inventory Report on Real Property Owned by the United States Throughout the World	Annual	X	X	

Geological Survey
<http://ask.usgs.gov>

Title	Frequency	Paper	PDF	Other Formats
A Statistical Summary of Data from the U.S. Geological Survey's National Water Quality Networks (Open-File Report 83-533)		X		
Mineral Commodity Summaries	Annual	X		
Mineral Industry Surveys	Monthly	X	X	
Minerals Yearbook	Monthly	X	X	X

Internal Revenue Service
<http://www.irs.ustreas.gov>

Title	Frequency	Paper	PDF	Other Formats
Corporation Income Tax Returns	Annual	X	X	X
Individual Income Tax Returns	Annual	X	X	X
IRS Data Book	Annual	X	X	X
Statistics of Income Bulletin	Quarterly	X	X	X

International Trade Administration
<http://www.ita.doc.gov>

Title	Frequency	Paper	PDF	Other Formats
U.S. Foreign Trade Highlights	Annual			X

International Trade Administration, Office of Travel and Tourism
<http://www.tinet.ita.doc.gov>

Title	Frequency	Paper	PDF	Other Formats
Travel Data reports		X		

International Trade Commission
<http://www.usitc.gov>

Title	Frequency	Paper	PDF	Other Formats
Synthetic Organic Chemicals, U.S. Production and Sales	Annual	X	X	

Library of Congress
<http://www.loc.gov>

Title	Frequency	Paper	PDF	Other Formats
Annual Report	Annual	X	X	

Maritime Administration
<http://www.marad.dot.gov>

Title	Frequency	Paper	PDF	Other Formats
Annual Report	Annual	X	X	
Cargo-Carrying U.S. Flag Fleet by Area of Operation	Semiannual	X	X	
Merchant Fleet Ocean-Going Vessels 1,000 Gross Tons and Over	Quarterly	X	X	X
Seafaring Wage Rates	Biennial	X	X	X

Title	Frequency	Paper	PDF	Other Formats
Mine Safety and Health Administration <http://www.msha.gov>				
Informational Reports by Mining Industry: Coal; Metallic Minerals; Nonmetallic Minerals (except stone and coal); Stone, Sand, and Gravel	Annual			X
Mine Injuries and Worktime (some preliminary data)	Quarterly	X		X
National Aeronautics and Space Administration <http://iemp.nasa.gov>				
Annual Procurement Report	Annual	X	X	
The Civil Service Work Force		X	X	
National Center for Education Statistics <http://nces.ed.gov>				
Characteristics of the 100 Largest Public Elementary and Secondary School Districts in the United States	Annual	X		X
College and University Library Survey				X
Computer and Internet Use by Children and Adolescents	Biennial	X	X	
The Condition of Education	Annual	X	X	
Digest of Education Statistics	Annual	X	X	
Earned Degrees Conferred	Annual		X	X
Elementary and Secondary Education	Annual	X	X	X
Faculty Salaries, Tenure, and Benefits	Annual	X		
Fall Enrollment in Degree-Granting Institutions	Annual	X	X	X
Fall Staff in Postsecondary Institutions	Biennial	X	X	
Federal Support for Education	Annual		X	
Financial Statistics of Higher Education	Annual	X	X	
Indicators of School Crime and Safety	Annual	X	X	
National Assessment of Educational Progress	Annual	X	X	
National Education Statistics Quarterly	Quarterly			X
The Nation's Report Card: Mathematics Highlights 2003	Periodic	X	X	
The Nation's Report Card: Reading Highlights 2003	Periodic	X	X	
The Nation's Report Card: Geography 2004	Periodic	X	X	
The Nation's Report Card: Science 2000	Periodic	X	X	
The Nation's Report Card: History 2001	Periodic	X	X	
The Nation's Report Card: Writing 2002	Periodic	X	X	
Private School Survey	Biennial			X
Projections of Education Statistics	Annual	X	X	X
Revenues and Expenditures for Public Elementary and Secondary Education	Annual	X	X	X
School and Staffing Survey	Quadrennial			X
Statistics of Public Elementary and Secondary School Systems, Fall	Annual	X	X	X
Status and Trends in the Education of Blacks		X	X	
National Center for Health Statistics <http://www.cdc.gov/nchs/>				
Ambulatory Care Visits to Physician Offices, Hospital Outpatient Departments, and Emergency Departments	Annual	X	X	
Health: United States	Annual	X	X	
National Hospital Discharge Survey: Annual Summary	Annual		X	
National Vital Statistics Reports (NVRS)	Monthly		X	
Vital and Health Statistics			X	
Series 10: Health Interview Survey Statistics	Annual	X	X	
Series 11: Health and Nutrition Examination Survey Statistics	Irregular	X	X	
Series 13: Data from National Health Care Survey	Irregular	X	X	
Series 14: Data on Health Resources: Manpower and Facilities	Irregular	X	X	
Series 20: Mortality Data	Irregular	X	X	
Series 21: Natality, Marriage, and Divorce Data	Irregular	X	X	
Series 23: Data from the National Survey of Family Growth	Irregular	X	X	
Vital Statistics of the United States	Annual	X	X	
Volume I, Natality	Annual	X	X	
Volume II, Mortality	Annual	X	X	
Volume III, Marriage and Divorce	Annual	X	X	
National Credit Union Administration <http://www.ncua.gov>				
Annual Report	Annual	X	X	
Midyear Statistics	Semiannual	X	X	
Yearend Statistics	Annual		X	
National Endowment for the Arts <http://www.nea.gov>				
National Endowment for the Arts, Annual	Annual			X
The Performing Arts in the GDP, 2002	Periodic	X	X	
Artist Labor Force by State, 2000	Periodic	X	X	
Artist Employment, 2000–2002	Periodic	X	X	
The Arts in the GDP	Periodic	X	X	
Demographic Characteristics of Art Attendance, 2002	Periodic	X	X	
2002 Survey of Public Participation in the Arts	Periodic	X	X	
National Endowment for the Humanities <http://www.neh.gov>				
Budget Request	Annual	X		X
National Guard Bureau <http://www.ngb.army.mil/>				
Annual Review of the Chief	Annual	X	X	
National Highway Traffic Safety Administration <http://www.nhtsa.dot.gov>				
Traffic Safety Facts	Annual	X	X	
The National Library of Medicine (for clinical medical reports) <http://www.nlm.nih.gov>				

906   Appendix I

Title	Frequency	Paper	PDF	Other Formats
The National Library of Medicine (for clinical medical reports)—Con.				
Annual Report	Annual		X	
National Oceanic and Atmospheric Administration				
<http://www.lib.noaa.gov>				
Climates of the World, HCS 6-4.				
Climatological Data, issued in sections for states and outlying areas	Monthly	X		
Climatography of the United States, No. 20, Supplement No. 1, Freeze/Frost Data.	Monthly	X		X
Comparative Climatic Data	Annual	X		X
Daily Normals of Temp, Precip, HDD, & CDD/Clim 84	Periodic			X
General Summary of Tornadoes	Annual			X
Hourly Precipitation Data Monthly with annual summary; for each state	Monthly			X
Local Climatological Data Monthly with annual summary; for major cities	Monthly			X
Monthly Climatic Data for the World	Monthly			X
Monthly Normals of Temp, Precip, HDD, & CDD/Clim 84	Monthly			X
Our Living Oceans	Periodic		X	X
Storm Data	Periodic	X	X	
Weekly Weather and Crop Bulletin National summary	Monthly			X
	Weekly	X	X	
National Park Service				
<http://www.nps.gov>				
Federal Recreation Fee Report	Annual	X		
National Park Statistical Abstract	Annual	X	X	
National Science Foundation				
<http://www.nsf.gov>				
Academic Research and Development Expenditures	Annual	X	X	X
Academic Science and Engineering: Graduate Enrollment and Support	Annual	X	X	X
Characteristics of Doctoral Scientists and Engineers in the United States	Biennial	X	X	X
Characteristics of Recent Science/Engineering Graduates	Biennial	X	X	
Federal Funds for Research and Development	Annual	X	X	
Federal R&D Funding by Budget Function Report	Annual	X	X	X
Federal Science and Engineering Support to Universities, Colleges, and Nonprofit Institutions	Annual	X	X	X
Federal Support to Universities, Colleges, and Nonprofit Institutions	Annual		X	
Graduate Science and Engineering Students and Post-doctorates	Annual		X	X
Immigrant Scientists, Engineers, and Technicians	Annual	X	X	X
International Science and Technology Data Update Report	Annual	X		
National Patterns of Research & Development Resources Report	Annual	X	X	X
Planned R&D Expenditures of Major U.S. Firms, Special Report (NSF 91-306)	Annual	X		
Research and Development in Industry	Annual	X	X	X
Science and Engineering Degrees	Annual	X	X	
Science and Engineering Degrees, by Race/Ethnicity of Recipients, detailed statistical tables	Annual	X	X	
Science and Engineering Doctorates' Awards	Annual			
Science and Engineering Indicators' Report	Biennial	X	X	X
Science and Engineering Personnel: A National Overview Report	Biennial		X	X
Science and Engineering Profiles	Annual	X	X	X
Science and Technology Pocket Data Book Report	Annual	X	X	X
Science Resources Studies Data Brief	Frequent			X
Scientific and Engineering Research Facilities at Universities and Colleges	Biennial		X	X
Scientists, Engineers, and Technicians in Manufacturing Industries, detailed statistical tables	Triennial	X	X	X
Scientists, Engineers, and Technicians in NonManufacturing Industries	Triennial	X	X	X
Scientists, Engineers, and Technicians in Trade and Regulated Industries	Triennial	X	X	X
U.S. Scientists and Engineers	Biennial			
Women, Minorities in Science and Engineering, report	Biennial	X	X	X
	Biennial	X	X	
National Transportation Safety Board				
<http://www.ntsb.gov>				
Accidents; Air Carriers	Annual	X	X	
Accidents; General Aviation	Annual	X	X	
Office of Juvenile Justice and Delinquency Prevention				
<http://ojjdp.ncjrs.org>				
Highlights of the 2002 National Youth Gang Survey (FS-200401)	Annual		X	X
Juvenile Arrests, 2002 (Bulletin, NCJ 204608)	Annual	X	X	X
Victims of Violent Juvenile Crime (Bulletin, NCJ 201628)	Periodic	X	X	X
Office of Management and Budget				
<http://www.whitehouse.gov/omb>				
The Budget of the United States Government	Annual	X	X	
Office of Personnel Management				
<http://www.opm.gov>				
Civil Service Retirement and Disability Fund Report	Annual	X		
Demographic Profile of the Federal Workforce	Biennial	X	X	X
Employment and Trends	Bimonthly	X	X	X
Employment by Geographic Area	Biennial	X	X	X
The Fact Book	Annual	X	X	X
Federal Employment Statistics	Annual			X
Occupations of Federal White-Collar and Blue-Collar Workers	Biennial		X	X
Pay Structure of the Federal Civil Service	Annual		X	X
Statistical Abstract for the Federal Employee Benefit Programs	Annual		X	X
Work Years and Personnel Costs	Annual	X	X	X
Patent and Trademark Office				
<http://www.uspto.gov>				
Commissioner of Patents and Trademarks	Annual	X		X
Technology Assessment and Forecast Reports		X	X	
All Technologies	Annual	X		

Appendix I   907

Title	Frequency	Paper	Internet PDF	Internet Other Formats
Patent and Trademark Office—Con.				
Patenting Trends in the United States.	Annual	X		
State Country.	Annual	X		
Railroad Retirement Board, Chicago, IL <http://www.rrb.gov/default.asp>				
Annual Report	Annual	X	X	
Monthly Benefit Statistics	Monthly	X	X	
Statistical Supplement to the Annual Report	Annual	X	X	
Securities and Exchange Commission <http://www.sec.gov>				
Annual Report	Annual	X	X	
Small Business Administration <http://www.sba.gov>				
Annual Report	Annual	X		X
Handbook of Small Business Data	Annual	X	X	
The State of Small Business.	Annual	X	X	
Social Security Administration <http://www.ssa.gov>				
Annual Statistical Supplement to the Social Security Bulletin.	Annual		X	X
Income of the Population 55 and over	Biennially	X	X	X
Social Security Beneficiaries State and County Data	Annual	X	X	X
Social Security Bulletin	Quarterly	X	X	X
State Assistance Programs for SSI Recipients	Annual	X	X	X
Supplemental Security Income, State, and County Data.	Annual	X	X	X

NONGOVERNMENT

Title	Frequency	Paper	PDF	Other Formats
AAFRC Trust For Philanthropy, Indianapolis, IN <http://www.aafrc.org>				
Giving USA..	Annual	X		
Aerospace Industries Association, Washington, DC <http://www.aia-aerospace.org>				
Aerospace Facts and Figures	Annual	X	X	
Aerospace Industry Year-End Review and Forecast	Annual	X	X	X
Commercial Helicopter Shipments	Triennial	X	X	
Employment in the Aerospace Industry	Monthly		X	
Exports of Aerospace Products	Quarterly	X	X	
Imports of Aerospace Products	Quarterly	X	X	
Manufacturing Production, Capacity, and Utilization in Aerospace and Aircraft and Parts	Monthly	X	X	
Orders, Shipments, Backlog and inventories for Aircraft, Missiles, & Parts.	Monthly	X	X	
Air Transport Association of America, Inc., Washington, DC <http://www.airlines.org>				
Air Transport Association, Annual Report.	Annual	X		
The Alan Guttmacher Institute, New York, NY <http://www.guttmacher.org>				
Perspectives on Sexual and Reproductive Health	Bimonthly	X	X	X
American Bureau of Metal Statistics, Inc., Secaucus, NJ <http://www.abms.com>				
Non-Ferrous Metal Yearbook	Annual	X		
American Council on Education, Washington, DC <http://www.acenet.edu>				
A Fact Book on Higher Education	Quarterly	X		
National Norms for Entering College Freshmen	Annual	X		
American Council of Life Insurers, Washington, DC <http://www.acli.com>				
Life Insurers Fact Book	Annual	X		
American Dental Association, Chicago, IL <http://www.ada.org>				
Dental Students Register	Annual	X		
Distribution of Dentists in the United States by Region and State.	Triennial	X		
Survey of Dental Practice.	Annual	X		
American Forest & Paper Association, Washington, DC <http://www.afandpa.org>				
Annual Statistical Summary of Recovered Paper Utilization	Annual	X	X	
Statistical Roundup.	Monthly	X	X	
Statistics of Paper, Paperboard, and Wood Pulp.	Annual	X		
U.S. Wood Pulp Data Report	Annual	X		
U.S. Forest Facts and Figures.	Annual	X		
American Frozen Food Institute, Burlingame, CA <http://www.affi.com>				
Frozen Food Pack Statistics	Annual	X		
American Gas Association, Washington, DC <http://www.aga.org>				
Gas Facts.	Annual	X		X
American Iron and Steel Institute, Washington, DC <http://www.steel.org>				
Annual Statistical Report	Annual	X		

Title	Frequency	Paper	Internet PDF	Internet Other Formats
American Jewish Committee, New York, NY <http://www.ajc.org>				
American Jewish Year Book	Annual	X		
American Medical Association, Chicago, IL <http://www.ama-assn.org>				
Physician Characteristics and Distribution in the U.S.	Annual	X		
Physician Marketplace Statistics	Annual	X		
Physician Socioeconomic Statistics, 1991–2000		X		
U.S. Medical Licensure Statistics, and License Requirements	Annual	X		
American Metal Market, New York, NY <http://www.amm.com>				
Metal Statistics	Annual	X		
American Osteopathic Association, Chicago, IL <http://www.osteopathic.org/index.cfm>				
American Osteopathic Association Fact Sheet	Biennial	X	X	
American Petroleum Institute, Washington, DC <http://www.api.org>				
The Basic Petroleum Data Book (online subscription)	Annual	X		
Joint Association Survey on Drilling Costs (JA5)	Annual	X		
Petroleum Industry Environmental Report	Annual	X		X
Quarterly Well Completion Report (online subscription)	Quarterly	X		
American Public Transportation Association, Washington, DC <http://www.apta.com>				
Public Transportation Fact Book	Annual	X	X	
Association for Manufacturing Technology, McLean, VA <http://www.amtonline.org>				
Economic Handbook of the Machine Tool Industry, 2003–2004 (online version by subscription only)	Annual			X
Association of American Railroads, Washington, DC <http://www.aar.org>				
Analysis of Class I Railroads	Annual	X		X
Cars of Revenue Freight Loaded	Weekly	X		
Freight Commodity Statistics, Class I Railroads in the United States	Annual	X		X
Yearbook of Railroad Facts	Annual	X		X
Association of Racing Commissioners International, Inc., Lexington, KY <http://www.arci.com>				
Statistical Reports on Greyhound Racing in the United States	Annual	X		
Statistical Reports on Horse Racing in the United States	Annual	X		
Statistical Reports on Jai Alai in the United States	Annual	X		
Book Industry Study Group, Inc., New York, NY <http://www.bisg.org>				
Book Industry Trends	Annual	X		
Consumer Research Study on Book Purchasing	Annual	X		
Boy Scouts of America, Irving, TX <http://www.scouting.org>				
Annual Report	Annual	X		
The Bureau of National Affairs, Inc., Washington, DC <http://www.bna.com>				
Basic Patterns in Union Contracts	Annual	X		
BNAs Employment Outlook	Quarterly	X		
BNAs Job Absence and Turnover	Quarterly	X		
Briefing Sessions on Employee Relations Workbook	Annual	X		
Calendar of Negotiations	Annual	X		
Directory of U.S. Labor Organizations	Annual	X		
National Labor Relations Board Election Statistics	Annual	X		
National Labor Relations Board (NLRB)	Biennial	X		
PPF Survey (Personnel Policies Forum)	Triennial	X		
Union Membership & Earnings Data Book	Annual	X		
Source Book on Collective Bargaining	Annual	X		
BNA Labor PLUS		X		X
BNA Labor Assist		X		X
Carl H Pforzheimer & Co, New York, NY				
Comparative Oil Company Statistics Annual	Annual	X		
Chronicle of Higher Education, Inc., Washington, DC <http://chronicle.com>				
Almanac	Annual	X		
College Board, New York, NY <http://www.collegeboard.com>				
National Report on College-Bound Seniors	Annual	X	X	
Commodity Research Bureau, Logical Systems, Inc., Chicago, IL <http://www.crbtrader.com>				
Commodity Year Book Update Disk	Annual	X		X
CRB Commodity Index Report	Weekly	X		
CRB Commodity Year Book	Annual	X		
CRB Futures Perspective	Weekly		X	
CRB Infotech CD	Monthly	X		X
Electronic Futures Trend Analyzer	Daily	X		
Final Markets	Daily	X		
Futures Market Service (online subscription)	Weekly	X		

Title	Frequency	Paper	Internet PDF	Internet Other Formats
Commodity Research Bureau, Logical Systems, Inc., Chicago, IL— Con.				
Futures Market Service Fundamental & Technical Commentary (online subscription).	Daily	X		
Price Service	Daily	X		
The Conference Board, New York, NY				
<http://www.conference-board.org>				
<http://www.globalindicators.org>				
Business Cycle Indicators.	Monthly	X	X	
Corporate Contributions	Annual	X	X	
Productivity, Employment, and Income in the World's Economies.	Annual	X		
CQ Press, Washington, DC				
<http://www.cqpress.com>				
America Votes	Biennial	X		
Consumer Electronics Association (Electronic Industries Alliance), Arlington, VA				
<http://www.ce.org>				
Electronic Market Data Book.	Annual	X		
Electronic Market Trends	Monthly	X		
Electronics Foreign Trade.	Monthly	X		
The Council of State Governments, Lexington, KY				
<http://www.csg.org/CSG/default.htm>				
The Book of the States	Annual	X	X	
State Administrative Officials Classified by Function	Annual	X		
State Elective Officials and the Legislatures.	Annual	X		
State Legislative Leadership, Committees, and Staff	Annual	X		
Credit Union National Association, Inc., Madison, WI				
<http://www.cuna.org>				
The Credit Union Ranking Report	Annual	X		
Credit Union Services Profile	Annual	X		
Operating Ratios and Spreads	Semiannual	X		
Dow Jones & Co., New York, NY				
<http://www.dj.com>				
Wall Street Journal	Daily	X		
Edison Electric Institute, Washington, DC				
<http://www.eei.org>				
Statistical Yearbook of the Electric Utility Industry	Annual	X		
Editor & Publisher Co., New York, NY				
<http://www.editorandpublisher.com>				
Editor & Publisher.	Monthly	X		
International Year Book	Annual	X		
Market Guide.	Annual	X		
ENO Transportation Foundation, Leesburg, VA				
<http://www.enotrans.com>				
Transportation in America, 2000, with Historical Compendium 1939–1999, 2001 . . .	Periodic	X		
Euromonitor International, London, England				
<http://www.euromonitor.com>				
Consumer Asia.	Annual	X		
Consumer China.	Annual	X		
Consumer Eastern Europe	Annual	X		
Consumer Europe.	Annual	X		
Consumer International	Annual	X		
Consumer Latin America	Annual	X		
European Marketing Data and Statistics	Annual	X		
International Marketing Data and Statistics	Annual	X		
Latin America Marketing Data and Statistics	Annual	X		
World Consumer Expenditure Patterns	Annual	X		
World Consumer Income Patterns	Annual	X		
World Economic Factbook	Annual	X		
World Retail Data and Statistics	Annual	X		
Federal National Mortgage Association, Washington, DC				
<http://www.fanniemae.com>				
Annual Report	Annual	X		
Food and Agriculture Organization of the United Nations, Rome, Italy				
<http://www.fao.org>				
Fertilizer Yearbook	Annual	X		
Production Yearbook	Annual	X		
Trade Yearbook	Annual	X		
Yearbook of Fishery Statistics	Annual	X		
Yearbook of Forest Products.	Annual	X		
The Foundation Center, New York, NY				
<http://www.fdncenter.org>				
Foundation Yearbook.	Annual	X		
General Aviation Manufacturers Association, Washington, DC				
<http://www.gama.aero/home.php>				
Shipment Report.	Quarterly	X		X
Statistical Databook.	Annual	X	X	
Girl Scouts of the USA, New York, NY				
<http://www.girlscouts.org>				
Annual Report	Annual	X	X	

910   Appendix I

U.S. Census Bureau. Statistical Abstract of the United States: 2006

Title	Frequency	Paper	Internet PDF	Internet Other Formats
Health Forum, an American Hospital Association Company, Chicago, IL <http://www.healthforum.com>				
Annual Report	Annual	X		
Hospital Statistics	Annual	X		X
America's Health Insurance Plans, Washington, DC <http://www.ahip.org>				
Source Book of Health Insurance Data	Annual	X		
Independent Petroleum Association of America, Washington, DC <http://www.ipaa.org>				
Domestic Oil and Gas Trends	Monthly	X		
Oil & Natural Gas Production in Your State	Annual	X		X
U.S. Petroleum Statistics	Annual	X		X
Information Today, Inc., Medford, NJ <http://www.infotoday.com>				
American Library Directory	Annual	X		
Bowker Annual Library and Book Trade Almanac	Annual	X		
Institute for Criminal Justice Ethics, New York, NY <http://www.lib.jjay.cuny.edu/cje>				
Criminal Justice Ethics	Semiannual	X		
Insurance Information Institute, New York, NY <http://www.iii.org>				
The Fact Book, Property/Casualty Insurance Facts	Annual	.X	X	
Inter-American Development Bank, Washington, DC <http://www.iadb.org>				
Annual Report	Annual	X	X	
Economic and Social Progress in Latin America	Annual	X		
International Air Transport Association <http://www.iata.org>				
World Air Transport Statistics	Annual	X	X	X
International City Management Association, Washington, DC <http://www.icma.org>				
Compensation: An Annual Report on Local Government Executive Salaries and Fringe Benefits	Annual			X
Municipal Year Book	Annual	X		
International Labour Organization, Geneva, Switzerland <http://www.ilo.org>				
Yearbook of Labour Statistics	Annual	X		
International Monetary Fund, Washington, DC <http://www.imf.org>				
Annual Report	Annual	X	X	X
Balance of Payments Statistics	Monthly	X		
Direction of Trade Statistics	Monthly	X		
Government Finance Statistics Yearbook	Annual	X		
International Financial Statistics	Monthly	X		
Investment Company Institute, Washington, DC <http://www.ici.org>				
Mutual Fund Fact Book	Annual	X	X	
Jane's Information Group, Coulsdon, UK and Alexandria, VA <http://www.janes.com>				
Jane's Air-Launched Weapons	Monthly			X
Jane's All the World's Aircraft	Annual			X
Jane's Armour and Artillery	Annual			X
Jane's Avionics	Annual			X
Jane's Fighting Ships	Annual			X
Jane's Infantry Weapons	Annual			X
Jane's Merchant Ships	Annual			X
Jane's Military Communications	Annual			X
Jane's Military Logistics	Annual			X
Jane's Military Training Systems	Annual			X
Jane's NATO Handbook	Annual			X
Jane's Spaceflight Directory	Annual			X
Joint Center for Political and Economic Studies, Washington, DC <http://www.jointcenter.org>				
Black Elected Officials: A Statistical Summary	Annual	X	X	
McGraw-Hill Construction Dodge, a Division of the McGraw-Hill Companies, New York, NY <http://www.fwdodge.com>				
Dodge Construction Potential (online subscription)	Monthly			X
National Academy of Sciences, Washington, DC <http://www.pnas.org>				
Summary Report Doctorate Recipients from United States Universities	Annual	X		
National Academy of Social Insurance, Washington, DC <http://www.nasi.org/>				
Worker's Compensation, Benefits, Coverage, and Costs	Annual	X	X	
National Association of Home Builders, Washington, DC <http://www.nahb.org>				
Home Builders Forecast (online subscription)	Monthly			X
Housing Economics (online subscription)	Monthly			X

Appendix I 911

Title	Frequency	Paper	Internet PDF	Internet Other Formats
National Association of Home Builders, Washington, DC—Con.				
Housing Market Statistics (online subscription)	Monthly			X
National Association of Latino Elected and Appointed Officials, Washington, DC				
<http://www.naleo.org>				
National Roster of Hispanic Elected Officials.	Annual	X		
National Association of Realtors, Washington, DC				
<http://www.realtor.org>				
Real Estate Outlook: Market Trends & Insights.	Monthly	X		X
National Association of State Budget Officers, Washington, DC				
<http://www.nasbo.org>				
State Expenditure Report	Annual	X	X	
Fiscal Survey of the States	Semi-annual	X	X	
National Association of State Park Directors, Raleigh, NC				
<http://www.naspd.org>				
Annual Information Exchange			X	X
National Catholic Educational Association, Washington, DC				
<http://www.ncea.org>				
Catholic Schools in America	Annual		X	X
U.S. Catholic Elementary and Secondary Schools Staffing and Enrollment	Annual	X		X
U.S. Catholic Elementary Schools and Their Finances.	Biennial			
U.S. Catholic Secondary Schools and Their Finances..	Biennial	X		
National Center for State Courts, Williamsburg, VA				
<http://www.ncsconline.org>				
State Court Caseload Statistics	Annual	X	X	
National Council of Churches USA, New York, NY				
<http://www.ncccusa.org>				
Yearbook of American and Canadian Churches	Annual	X		X
National Education Association, Washington, DC				
<http://www.nea.org>				
Rankings of the States and Estimates of School Statistics	Annual	X	X	
Status of the American Public School Teacher, 2000–2001.	Quinquennial	X	X	
National Fire Protection Association, Quincy, MA				
<http://www.nfpa.org>				
NFPA Journal.	Bimonthly			X
National Golf Foundation, Jupiter, FL				
<http://www.ngf.org>				
Golf Consumer Profile	Annual		X	
Golf Facilities in the U.S.	Annual	X	X	
National Marine Manufacturers Association, Chicago, IL				
<http://www.nmma.org>				
Boating (A Statistical Report on America's Top Family Sport)	Annual	X	X	X
U.S. Recreational Boat Registration Statistics	Annual	X	X	
National Restaurant Association, Washington, DC				
<http://www.restaurant.org>				
Compensation for Salaried Personnel in Restaurants, 2001				
Holiday Dining, 2004				
Quick-Service Restaurant Trends.	Annual	X		
Restaurant Economic Trends (online subscription)	Monthly			X
Restaurant Industry Forecast	Annual	X		
Restaurant Industry in Review.	Annual	X	X	X
Restaurant Industry Operations Report	Annual	X		
Restaurant Industry Pocket Factbook	Annual	X		
Restaurant Industry 2015, 2005.	Annual	X		
Restaurant Performance Index	Monthly	X		X
Restaurant Spending.	Annual	X		
State of the Restaurant Industry Work Force	Annual	X		
Tableservice Restaurant Trends.	Annual	X		
The Economic Impact of the Nation's Eating and Drinking Places	Annual	X		
Hourly Wages for Food Service Occupations	Annual	X		
Research News and Numbers.	Monthy	X		
National Safety Council, Itasca, IL				
<http://www.nsc.org>				
Injury Facts	Annual	X		X
National Sporting Goods Association, Mt. Prospect, IL				
<http://www.nsga.org>				
The Sporting Goods Market in 2004.	Annual	X	X	
Sports Participation in 2003	Annual	X	X	
New York Stock Exchange, Inc., New York, NY				
<http://www.nyse.com>				
Fact Book (online subscription)	Annual	X	X	
The New York Times Almanac, 2004	Annual	X		
Organisation for Economic Cooperation and Development, Paris, France				
<http://www.sourceoecd.org>				
Agricultural Outlook.	Annual	X		X
Bank Profitability: Financial Statements of Banks	Annual	X		X
Central Government Debt: Statistical Yearbook	Annual	X		X
Coal Information.	Annual	X		X

912 Appendix I

Title	Frequency	Paper	PDF	Other Formats
Organisation for Economic Cooperation and Development, Paris, France—Con.				
CO2 Emissions From Fuel Combustion. 1971–2001. 2003 Edition		X		X
Communications Outlook	Annual	X		X
Economic Outlook	Biennial	X		X
Economic Studies	Annual	X		X
Economic Surveys	Annual	X		X
Education at a Glance: OECD Indicators	Annual	X		X
Electricity Information	Annual	X		X
Employment Outlook	Annual	X		X
Energy Balances of Non-OECD Countries	Annual	X		X
Energy Balances of OECD Countries	Annual	X		X
Energy Prices and Taxes	Quarterly	X	X	X
Energy Statistics of NON-OECD Countries	Annual	X	X	X
Energy Statistics of OECD Countries	Annual	X	X	X
Environmental Data Compendium	Annual	X		X
Environmental Outlook		X	X	
External Debt Statistics	Annual			
Financial Market Trends	Triennial	X	X	
Geographical Distribution of Financial Flows to Aid Recipients, 1998–02	Annual	X		
Health Data	Annual	X	X	X
Historical Statistics, 1970–2000, 2001 Edition (discontinued as of 2001)		X	X	X
Information Technology Outlook, 2002 Edition	Biennial	X	X	X
Insurance Statistics Yearbook	Annual	X	X	X
International Development Statistics	Annual			X
International Trade by Commodities	Annual	X	X	
Iron and Steel Industry in 2002, 2004 Edition				
Labor Force Statistics	Annual	X	X	
Main Economic Indicators	Monthly	X	X	
Main Science and Technology Indicators, Volume 2003	Biennial	X	X	
Measuring Globalisation: The Role of Multinationals in OECD Countries, 2001 Edition	Biennial			
Monthly Statistics of International Trade Series A	Monthly	X	X	
National Accounts of OECD Countries	Annual			
Volume I: Main Aggregates		X	X	X
Volume II: Detailed Tables		X	X	X
Natural Gas Information	Annual	X	X	X
Nuclear Energy Data	Annual	X	X	
OECD in Figures	Bimonthly	X		X
Oil Information, 2003 Edition	Annual	X	X	
Oil, Gas, Coal, and Electricity Quarterly Statistics	Quarterly	X	X	
Quarterly Labor Force Statistics (discontinued as of 4th quarter 2004)	Quarterly	X	X	
Quarterly National Accounts	Quarterly	X	X	
Research and Development Statistics		X	X	X
Revenue Statistics of OECD Member Countries	Annual	X	X	
Review of Fisheries in OECD Member Countries	Annual	X	X	
Science, Technology and Industry: Scoreboard, 2003	Biennial	X	X	X
Small and Medium Enterprise Outlook, 2002 Edition	Biennial	X	X	
Structural Statistics for Industry and Services	Annual	X	X	
Taxing Wages	Annual	X	X	
The DAC Journal	Quarterly	X	X	
Trends in International Migration, 2004 Edition	Annual	X	X	
Trends in the Transport Sector, 1970–2002, 2004 Edition		X	X	
Uranium Resources Production and Demand, 2001	Biennial	X	X	
Pan American Health Organization, Washington, DC				
<http://www.paho.org>				
Health Conditions in the Americas	Quadrennial	X	X	X
PennWell Corporation, Tulsa, OK				
<http://www.pennwell.com>				
Offshore (online subscription)	Monthly	X	X	
Oil and Gas Journal (online subscription)	Weekly	X		
Population Association of America, Washington, DC				
<http://www.popassoc.org>				
Demography	Quarterly	X	X	X
Puerto Rico Planning Board, San Juan, PR				
<http://www.jp.gobierno.pr>				
Payments Puerto Rico	Annual	X		
Activity Index	Monthly	X		
Indicators	Monthly	X		
Projections	Annual	X		
Economic Report to the Governor	Annual	X		
Income and Product	Annual	X		
Socioeconomic Statistics	Annual	X		
Radio Advertising Bureau, New York, NY				
<http://www.rab.com>				
Media Facts	Bi-Annual	X	X	
Radio Marketing Guide and Fact Book	Annual	X	X	
Reed Business Information, New York, NY				
<http://www.reedbusiness.com>				
Library Journal	Semimonthly	X		X
Publishers Weekly		X		X
School Library Journal	Monthly	X		X
Regional Airline Association, Washington, DC				
<http://www.raa.org>				

Title	Frequency	Paper	Internet PDF	Internet Other Formats
Regional Airline Association, Washington, DC—Con.				
Statistical Report				X
Magazine	Quarterly			
Securities Industry Association, New York, NY				
<http://www.sia.com>				
Foreign Activity Report	Quarterly	X		
Securities Industry Trends	Periodic	X		
Securities Industry Yearbook	Annual	X		X
Standard and Poor's Corporation, New York, NY				
<http://www.standardandpoors.com>				
Analyst's Handbook	Monthly	X		
Corporation Records	Daily	X		
Daily Stock Price Records	Quarterly	X		
Standard and Poor's Global Stock Market Factbook	Annual	X		
United Nations Statistics Division, New York, NY				
<http://unstats.un.org/unsd/>				
Compendium of Human Settlements Statistics (Series N)	Annual	X		
Demographic Yearbook (Series R)	Annual	X	X	X
Energy Balances and Electricity Profiles (Series W)	Annual	X	X	
Energy Statistics Yearbook (Series J)	Annual	X	X	
Industrial Statistics Yearbook: (Series P)				
Commodity Production Statistics	Annual	X		
International Trade Statistics Yearbook (Series G)	Annual	X		
Monthly Bulletin of Statistics (Series Q)	Monthly	X		
National Accounts Statistics: (Series X)				
Main Aggregates and Detailed Tables	Annual	X		
Analysis of Main Aggregates	Annual	X		
Population and Vital Statistics Report (Series A)	Quarterly	X		
Social Statistics and Indicators (Series K)	Occasional	X		X
The World's Women: Trends and Statistics		X		X
Statistical Yearbook (series; also available in CD-ROM, Series S/CD)	Annual	X		X
World Statistics Pocketbook (Series V)	Annual	X		
United States Telecom Association, Washington, DC				
<http://www.usta.org>				
Statistics of the Local Exchange Carriers	Annual	X		
University of Michigan, Center for Political Studies, Institute for Social Research, Ann Arbor, MI				
<http://www.umich.edu>				
National Election Studies Cumulative Datafile	Biennial	X		X
Warren Communications News, Washington, DC				
<http://www.warren-news.com>				
Cable and Station Coverage Atlas	Annual	X		
Television and Cable Action Update	Weekly	X		
Television and Cable Factbook	Annual	X		X
World Almanac, New York, NY				
<http://www.worldalmanac.com>				
The World Almanac and Book of Facts	Annual	X		
The World Bank Group, Washington, DC				
<http://www.worldbank.org>				
Global Development Finance, 2003	Annual	X		
The Little Data Book		X		
World Bank Atlas, 2003	Annual	X		
World Development Indicators	Annual	X		
World Health Organization, Geneva, Switzerland				
<http://www.who.int>				
Epidemiological and Vital Statistics Report	Monthly	X		
World Health Statistics	Quarterly	X		
World Trade Organization				
<http://www.wto.org>				
International Trade Statistics	Annual	X	X	X

Guide to State Statistical Abstracts

This bibliography includes the most recent statistical abstracts for states published since 1999, plus those that will be issued in late 2005. For some states, a near equivalent has been listed in substitution for, or in addition to, a statistical abstract. All sources contain statistical tables on a variety of subjects for the state as a whole, its component parts, or both. Internet sites also contain statistical data.

Alabama

University of Alabama, Center for Business and Economic Research, Box 870221, Tuscaloosa, AL 35487-0221. 205-348-6191. Fax: 205-348-2951. Internet site <http://cber.cba.ua.edu/>

Economic Abstract of Alabama, 2000.

Alabama Economic Outlook, 2005. Revised annually.

Alaska

Department of Community and Economic Development, Division of Community Advocacy, 550 W. 7th Avenue, Suite 1770, Anchorage, AK 99501-2341. 907-269-4580. Fax: 907-269-4539. Internet site <http://www.dced.state.ak.us/dca/home.htm/>

The Alaska Economic Performance Report, 2004. Online.

Arizona

Economic and Business Research Center, University of Arizona, McClelland Hall, Rm. 103, P.O. Box 210108, Tucson, AZ 85721-0108. 520-621-2155. Fax: 520-621-2150. Internet site <http://www.ebr.eller.arizona.edu/>

Arizona Statistical Abstract, 2003.

Arizona's Economy. Quarterly newsletter.

Arizona Economic Indicators. Semiannual. Online.

Arkansas

University of Arkansas at Little Rock, Institute for Economic Advancement, Economic Research, 2801 South University Avenue, Little Rock, AR 72204. 501-569-8519. Fax: 501-569-8538. Internet site <http://www.aiea.ualr.edu/>

Arkansas State and County Economic Data, 2003. Revised annually.

Arkansas Personal Income Handbook, 2003.

Arkansas Statistical Abstract, 2004. Revised biennially.

California

Department of Finance, 915 L Street, Sacramento, CA 95814. 916-445-3878. Internet site <http://www.dof.ca.gov/HTML/FSDATA/Fshome.htm>

California Statistical Abstract, 2004. Annual. Online only.

Colorado

University of Colorado, University Libraries, 184 UCB, 1720 Pleasant St., Boulder, CO 80309-0184. 303-492-8834. Internet site <http://www.colorado.edu/libraries/govpubs/online.htm>

Colorado by the Numbers. Online only.

Connecticut

Connecticut Department of Economic & Community Development, 505 Hudson St., Hartford, CT 06106. 1-860-270-8000. Internet site <http://www.ct.gov/ecd/site/default.asp>

Connecticut Town Profiles, 2003–2004.

Delaware

Delaware Economic Development Office, 99 Kings Highway, Dover, DE 19901. 302-739-4271. FAX 302-739-2028. Internet site <http://www.state.de.us/dedo/>

Delaware Statistical Overview, 2002–2003.

District of Columbia

Business Resource Center, John A. Wilson Building, 1350 Pennsylvania Avenue, NW, Washington, DC 20004. 202-727-1000. Internet site. <http://brc.dc.gov/resources/facts.asp>

Market Facts and Statistics. Online only.

Florida

University of Florida, Bureau of Economic and Business Research, P.O. Box 117145, 221 Matherly Hall, Gainesville, FL 32611-7145. 352-392-0171, ext. 219. Internet site <http://www.bebr.ufl.edu/>

Florida Statistical Abstract, 2004. 38th ed. Annual. Also available on CD-ROM.

Florida County Perspective, 2004. One profile for each county. Annual. Also available on CD-ROM.

Florida County Rankings, 2004. 11th edition. Annual. Also available on CD-ROM.

Georgia

University of Georgia, Selig Center for Economic Growth, Terry College of Business, Athens, GA 30602-6269. 706-542-4085. Internet site <http://www.selig.uga.edu/>

Georgia Statistical Abstract, 2004–05.

University of Georgia, Center for Agribusiness and Economic Development, 301 Lumpkin House, Athens, GA 30602-7509. 706-542-8938 or 706-542-0760. Fax: 706-542-8934. Internet site <http://www.georgiastats.uga.edu/>

The Georgia County Guide, 2004. Annual.

Hawaii

Hawaii State Department of Business, and Economic Development & Tourism, Research and Economic Analysis Division, Statistics and Data Support Branch, P.O. Box 2359, Honolulu, HI 96804. 808-586-2423. Internet site <http://www2.hawaii.gov/DBEDT/index.cfm>

The State of Hawaii Data Book 2003: A Statistical Abstract. Annual.

Idaho

Idaho Commerce & Labor, 700 West State St., P.O. Box 83720, Boise, ID 83720-0093. 208-334-2650. Internet site <http://www.idoc.state.id.us/data/community/>

County Profiles of Idaho, 2003. Online.

Idaho Community Profiles, 2003. Online.

Profile of Rural Idaho, 1999.

Illinois

Institute of Government and Public Affairs, 1007 W. Nevada Street, Urbana, IL 61801. 217-333-3340. Internet site <http://www.igpa.uiuc.edu/default.htm>

Illinois Statistical Abstract, 2004. Online only.

Indiana

Indiana University, Indiana Business Research Center, Kelley School of Business, Ste 3110, 1275 E. 10th Street, Bloomington, IN 47405. 812-855-4848. Internet site <http://www.stats.indiana.edu/>

STATS Indiana. Online only.

Iowa

Office of Social and Economic Trend Analysis, 303 East Hall, Ames, IA 50010-1070. 515-294-9903. Fax: 515-294-0592. Internet site <http://www.seta.iastate.edu/>

Iowa by the Numbers, 2004. CD-ROM.

State Library of Iowa, State Data Center, Ola Babcock Miller Building, East 12th and Grand, Des Moines, IA 50319. 800-248-4483. Fax: 515-242-6543. Internet site <http://www.silo.lib.ia.us/specialized-services/datacenter/>

Kansas

University of Kansas, Policy Research Institute, 1541 Lilac Lane, 607 Blake Hall, Lawrence, KS 66044-3177. 785-864-3701. Fax: 785-864-3683. Internet site <http://www.ku.edu/pri/>

Kansas Statistical Abstract, 2003. 38th ed. Online only.

Kentucky

Kentucky Cabinet for Economic Development, Division of Research, 300 West Broadway, Frankfort, KY 40601. 800-626-2930. Internet site <http://www.thinkkentucky.comkyedc/resandstat.asp/>

Kentucky Deskbook of Economic Statistics. Online only.

Louisiana

The University of Louisiana at Monroe, 700 University Avenue, Monroe, Louisiana 71209. 318-342-1000. Internet site <http://leap.ulm.edu/>

Louisiana Electronic Assistance Program. Online only.

Louisiana State Census Data Center, Office of Electronic Services, P.O. Box 94095, Baton Rouge, LA 70804-9095. 225-219-4025. Fax: 225-219-4027. Internet site <http://www.louisiana.gov/wps/portal/>

Maine

Maine State Planning Office, #38 State House Station, 184 State Street, Augusta, ME 04333. 800-662-4545. Fax: 207-287-6489. Internet site <http://www.state.me.us/spo/economics/economics/>

Maryland

RESI, Towson University, 8000 York Road, Towson, MD 21252-7097. 410-704-7374. Fax 410-704-4115. Internet site <http://wwwnew.towson.edu/outreach/resi/default.asp/>

Maryland Statistical Abstract, 2003.

Massachusetts

MassCHIP, Massachusetts Department of Public Health, 250 Washington Street, 6th Floor, Boston, MA 02108. 617-624-5629. Internet site <http://masschip.state.ma.us/>

Instant Topics. Online only.

Michigan

Michigan Economic Development Corporation, 300 North Washington Square, Lansing, MI 48913. 517-373-9808. Internet Site <http://medc.michigan.org/miinfo/>

Economic Profiler. Online only.

Minnesota

Minnesota Department of Employment and Economic Development, 1st National Bank Building, 332 Minnesota Street, Suite E200, Saint Paul, MN 55101-1351. 800-657-3858. Internet site <http://www.deed.state.mn.us/factsindex.htm>

Compare Minnesota: Profiles of Minnesota's Economy & Population, 2002–2003.

State Demographic Center, 650 Cedar Street, Saint Paul, MN 55155. 651-296-2557. Internet Site <http://www.demography.state.mn.us/>

Mississippi

Mississippi State University, College of Business and Industry, Division of Research, P.O. Box 5288, Mississippi State, MS 39762. 662-325-3817. Fax: 662-325-8686.

Mississippi Statistical Abstract, 2003.

Missouri
University of Missouri, Economic and Policy Analysis Research Center, 10 Professional Building, Columbia, MO 65211. 573-882-4805. Fax: 573-882-5563. Internet site <http://econ.missouri.edu/eparc/>
Statistical Abstract for Missouri, 2003. Biennial. Online only.

Montana
Census and Economic Information Center, Montana Department of Commerce, 301 S. Park, P.O. Box 200505, Helena, MT 59620-0505. 406-841-2740. Internet site <http://ceic.commerce.state.mt.us/>

Nebraska
Nebraska Department of Economic Development, P.O. Box 94666, 301 Centennial Mall South, Lincoln, NE 68509-4666. 800-426-6505. Fax 402-471-3778. Internet site <http://info.neded.org/>
Nebraska Data Book. Online only.

Nevada
Department of Administration, Budget and Planning Division, 209 East Musser Street, Suite 200, Carson City, NV 89701. 775-684-0222. Fax: 775-684-0260. Internet site <http://www.budget.state.nv.us/>
Nevada Statistical Abstract, 2004. Online only.

New Hampshire
New Hampshire Office of Energy and Planning, 57 Regional Drive, Suite 3, Concord, NH 03301-8519. 603-271-2155. Fax 603-271-2615. Internet site <http://www.nh.gov/oep/>

New Jersey
New Jersey State Data Center, NJ Department of Labor and Workforce Development, P.O. Box 388, Trenton, NJ 08625-0388. 609-984-2595. Fax: 609-984-6833. Internet site <http://www.state.nj.us/labor/lra/>
Labor Market Information. Online only.

New Mexico
University of New Mexico, Bureau of Business and Economic Research, MSC02 1720, Albuquerque, NM 87131-0001. 505-277-2216. Fax 505-277-7066. Internet site <http://www.unm. edu/]bber/>
New Mexico Business, Current Economic Report Monthly.
FOR-UNM Bulletin. Quarterly.

New York
Nelson A. Rockefeller Institute of Government, 411 State Street, Albany, NY 12203-1003. 518-443-5522. Fax: 518-443-5788. Internet site <http://www.rockinst.org/>
New York State Statistical Yearbook, 2004. 29th ed.

North Carolina
Office of Governor, Office of State Budget and Management, 116 West Jones Street, Raleigh, NC 27603-8005. 919-733-7061. Fax 919-733-0640. Internet site <http://www.osbm.state.nc.us/osbm/>
How North Carolina Ranks, 2004. Online only.

North Dakota
University of North Dakota, Bureau of Business and Economic Research, P.O. Box 8369, Grand Forks, ND 58202. 800-225-5863. Fax 701-777-3365. Internet site <http://business.und.edu/bber/>
North Dakota Statistical Abstract. Online only.

Ohio
Office of Strategic Research, Ohio Department of Development, P.O. Box 1001, Columbus, OH 43216-1001. 1-800-848-1300. Internet site <http://www.odod .state.oh.us/research>
Research products and services. Updated continuously.
Ohio County Profiles. Updated periodically.
Ohio County Indicators. Updated periodically.

Oklahoma
University of Oklahoma, Center for Economic and Management Research, Michael F. Price College of Business, 307 West Brooks, Room 3, Norman, OK 73019. 405-325-2933. Fax: 405-325-7688.
Internet site <http://origins.ou.edu/>
Statistical Abstract of Oklahoma, 1999.

Oregon
Secretary of State, Archives Division, Archives Bldg., 800 Summer Street, NE, Salem, OR 97310. 503-373-0701. Fax: 503-378-4118. Internet site <http://www.sos.state.or.us/bbook>
Oregon Blue Book. 2005–2006. Biennial.

Pennsylvania
Pennsylvania State Data Center, Institute of State and Regional Affairs, Penn State Harrisburg, 777 West Harrisburg Pike, Middletown, PA 17057-4898. 717-948-6336. Fax: 717-948-6754 Internet site <http://pasdc.hbg.psu.edu>
Pennsylvania Statistical Abstract, 2004.

Rhode Island
Rhode Island Economic Development Corporation, One West Exchange Street, Providence, RI 02903. 401-222-2601. Internet site <http://www.riedc.com/>
RI Data Bank. Online only.

South Carolina
Budget and Control Board, Office of Research and Statistics, 1919 Blanding Street, Columbia 29201. 803-898-9940. Internet site <http://www.ors2.state.sc.us abstract/index.asp>
South Carolina Statistical Abstract, 2005.

South Dakota
South Dakota State Data Center, Business Research Bureau, The University of South Dakota, 414 E. Clark Street, Vermillion, SD 57069. 605-677-5287. Fax: 605-677-5427. Internet site <http://www.usd.edu /brbinfo/sdc/index.htm>
2003 South Dakota Community Abstracts.

Tennessee
College of Business Administration, The University of Tennessee, Temple Court, Suite 100, 804 Volunteer Blvd., Knoxville, Tennessee 37996-4334. 865-974-5441. Fax: 865-974-3100. Internet site <http://cber.bus.utk.edu/Default.htm>
Tennessee Statistical Abstract, 2003. Biennial.

Texas
Dallas Morning News, Communications Center, P.O. Box 655237, Dallas, TX 75265-5237. 214-977-8261. Internet site <http://www.texasalmanac.com/>
Texas Almanac, 2004–2005.

Texas State Data Center and Office of the State Demographer, Institute for Demographic and Socioeconomic Research, University of Texas at San Antonio, 6900 North Loop, 1604 West, San Antonio, TX 78249-0704. 210-458-6543. Fax: 210-458-6541. Internet site <http://txsdc.utsa.edu/>

Utah
Governor's Office of Planning and Budget, Demographic & Economic Analysis, State Capitol Complex, Suite 210, East Office Building, Salt Lake City, UT 84114-2210. 801-538-1027. Fax: 801-538-1547. Internet site <http://www.governor.utah.gov/dea/>
2005 Economic Report to the Governor. Annual.
Utah Data Guide Newsletter. Quarterly.

Vermont
Department of Employment and Training, Labor Market Information, P.O. Box 488, Montpelier, VT 05601-0488. 802-828-4202. Fax: 802-828-4050. Internet site <http://www.vtlmi.info/>
Vermont Economic-Demographic Profile, 2005. Annual.

Virginia
Weldon Cooper Center, P.O. Box 400206, Charlottesville, VA 22904-4206. 434-982-5582. Fax: 434-982-4596. Internet site <http://www.ccps.virginia.edu/demographics/>
Virginia Statistical Abstract. Online only.

Washington
Washington State Office of Financial Management, Forecasting Division, P.O. Box 43113, Olympia, WA 98504-3113. 360-902-0555. Internet site <http://www.ofm.wa.gov/>
Washington State Data Book, 2003. Biennial.

West Virginia
West Virginia University, College of Business and Economics, Bureau of Business and Economic Research, P.O. Box 6025, Morgantown, WV 26506-6025. 304-293-7831. Fax: 304-293-5652. Internet site <http://www.bber.wvu.edu/>
2004 West Virginia County Data Profiles.
West Virginia Economic Outlook, 2005. Annual.

Wisconsin
Wisconsin Legislative Reference Bureau, P.O. Box 2037, Madison, WI 53701-2037. 608-266-0341 Internet site <http://www.legis.state.wi.us/lrb/bb/>
2003–2004 Wisconsin Blue Book. Biennial.

Wyoming
Department of Administration and Information, Economic Analysis Division, 1807 Capitol Avenue, Suite 206, Cheyenne, WY 82002-0060. 307-777-7504. Fax: 307-632-1819. Internet site <http://eadiv.state.wy.us/>
The Equality State Almanac, 2002.

Guide to Foreign Statistical Abstracts

This bibliography presents recent statistical abstracts for member nations of the Organization for Economic Cooperation and Development and Russia. All sources contain statistical tables on a variety of subjects for the individual countries. Many of the following publications provide text in English as well as in the national language(s). For further information on these publications, contact the named statistical agency which is responsible for editing the publication.

Australia

Australian Bureau of Statistics, Canberra. <http://www.abs.gov.au>.
Year Book Australia. Annual. 2005. With CD-ROM. (In English.)

Austria

Statistik Austria, A-1033 Wien. <http://www.statistik.at/index.shtml>.
Statistisches Jahrbuch Osterreichs. Annual. 2005. With CD-ROM. (In German.) With English translations of table headings.

Belgium

Institut National de Statistique, Rue de Louvain; 44-1000 Bruxelles. <http://statbel.fgov.be/info/linksen.asp>.
Annuaire statistique de la Belgique. Annual. 1995. (In French.)

Canada

Statistics Canada, Ottawa, Ontario, KIA OT6. <http://www.statcan.ca/start.html>.
Canada Yearbook: A review of economic, social and political developments in Canada. 2001. Irregular. (In English.)

Czech Republic

Czech Statistical Office, Sokolovska 142, 186 04 Praha 8; <http://www.czso.cz/>.
Statisticka Rocenka Ceske Republiky 2004. (In English and Czech.)

Denmark

Danmarks Statistik, Sejrogade 11, 2100 Kobenhavn O. <http://www.dst.dk/665>.
Statistisk ARBOG. 2005. Annual. English version available only on Internet and is free of charge at: <www.dst.dk/yearbook>. (Printed version—in Danish only.)

Finland

Statistics Finland, Helsinki. <http://www.stat.fi/tk/tilastotietoaen.html>.
Statistical Yearbook of Finland, Annual. 2004. With CD-ROM. (In English, Finnish, and Swedish.)

France

Institut National de la Statistique et des Etudes Economiques, Paris 18, Bld. Adolphe Pinard, 75675 Paris (Cedex 14). <http://www.insee.fr/fr/home/homepage.asp>.
Annuaire Statistique de la France. Annual. 2003. (In French.) 2004. CD-ROM only.

Germany

Statistische Bundesamt, D-65180 Wiesbaden. <http://www.destatis.de>.
Statistisches Jahrbuch fur die Bundesrepublic Deutschland. Annual. 2004. (In German.)
Statistisches Jahrbuch fur das Ausland. 2004. Statistisches Jahrbuch 2004 Fur die Bundesreublik Deutschland und fur das ausland – CD-ROM.

Greece

National Statistical Service of Greece, Athens. <http:// www.statistics.gr/>.
Concise Statistical Yearbook. 2003. (In English and Greek.)
Statistical Yearbook of Greece. Annual. 2003. (In English and Greek.)

Hungary

Hungarian Central Statistical Office, 1024 Budapest. <http://www.ksh.hu>.
Statistical Yearbook of Hungary, 2003. With CD-ROM. (In English and Hungarian.)

Iceland

Hagstofa Islands/Statistics Iceland; <http://www.hagstofa.is/template41.asp?PageID=251>.
Statistical Yearbook of Iceland. 2004. with CD-ROM. Irregular. (In English and Icelandic.)

Ireland

Central Statistics Office, Skehard Road, Cork. <http://www.cso.ie>.
Statistical Yearbook of Ireland. Annual. 2004. (In English.)

Italy

ISTAT (Istituto Centrale di Statistica); <http://www.istat.it>. Via Cesare Balbo 16 Roma.
Annuario Statistico Italiano. Annual. 2004. With CD-ROM. (In Italian.)

Japan

Statistics Bureau, Ministry of Internal Affairs and Communications Statistical Research and Training Institute Ministry of Internal Affairs and Communications, Japan. <http://www.stat.go.jp/english/data/index.htm>.
Japan Statistical Yearbook. Annual. 2005. (In English and Japanese.)

Korea, South
National Statistical Office, Government
Complex, #920 Dunsan-dong Seo-gu Dae-
jeon 302-701. <http://www.nso.go.kr/>.
Korea Statistical Yearbook. Annual. 2004.
With CD-ROM.
(In Korean and English.)

Luxembourg
STATEC (Service Central de la Statistique et
des Etudes), 13 rue Erasme, B.P. 304,
L-2013, Luxembourg.
.
Annuaire Statistique du Luxembourg.
With CD-ROM. 2004. (In French.)
(Alphabetical numbering system).

Mexico
Instituto Nacional de Estadistica Geografia e
Informatica, Av. Heroe Nacozari Num.
2301 Sur Fracc. Jardines del Parque, CP
20270 Aguascalientes, Ags.
<http://www.inegi.gob.mx/difusion
/ingles/fiest.html>.
*Anuario estadistico de los Estados Unidos
Mexicanos.* Annual. 2002. Also on disc.
(In Spanish.) *Agenda Estadistica 2001.*

Netherlands
Statistics Netherlands, R L Vellekoop.
Prinses Beatrixiaan 428, 2273 X Z Voor-
burg; <http://www.cbs.nl/en/>.
*Statistical Yearbook 2004 of the Nether-
lands.* (In English.)
Statistisch Jaarboek 2004.
With CD-ROM.

New Zealand
Department of Statistics, Wellington.
<http://www.stats.govt.nz/>.
New Zealand Official Yearbook. Annual.
2004. (In English.)

Norway
Statistics Norway, Oslo/Kongsvinger.
<http://www.ssb.no/english/subjects/>.
Statistical Yearbook. Annual. 2004.
(In English.)

Poland
Central Statistical Office al. Niepodleglosci
208, 00-925 Warsaw.
<http://www.stat.gov.pl/english
/index.htm>.
Concise Statistical Yearbook 2003.
(In Polish and English.) *Statistical Year-
book of the Republic of Poland. 2002.*
(In Polish and English.)

Portugal
INE (Instituto Nacional de Estatistica.)
<http://www.ine.pt/indexeng.htm>.
Avenida Antonio Jose de Almeida P-1000-
043 Lisboa.
Anuario Estatistico de Portugal. 2002.
(In Portuguese and English.)

Russia
State Committee of Statistics of Russia,
Moscow. <http://www.gks.ru/eng/>.
Statistical Yearbook. 2004. (In Russian.)

Slovakia
Statistical Office of the Slovak Republic,
Bradacova 7, 852 86 Bratislava.
<http://www.statistics.sk/webdata
/english/index2a.htm>.
Statisticka Rocenka Slovenskej Republiky.
2000. (In English and Slovak.)
With CD-ROM.

Spain
INE (Instituto Nacional de Estadistica);
Paseo de la Castellana, 183, Madrid 16.
<http://www.ine.es/welcoing.htm>.
Anuario Estatistico de Espana.
2002–2003. (In Spanish.)

Sweden
Statistics Sweden, S-11581 Stockholm.
<http://www.scb.se/indexeng.asp>.
Statistisk Arsbok for Sverige. Annual.
2005. With CD-ROM.
(In English and Swedish.)

Switzerland
Bundesamt fur Statistik, Hallwylstrasse 15,
CH-3003, Bern.
Statistisches Jahrbuch der Schweiz.
Annual. 2004. With CD-ROM.
(In French and German.)

Turkey
State Institute of Statistics, Prime Ministry,
114 Necatibey Caddesi, Bakanliklar,
Yenisehir, Ankara.
Statistical Yearbook of Turkey. 1999.
(In English and Turkish.)
Turkey in Statistics. 1999.
(In English only.)

United Kingdom
The Stationary Office; P.O. Box 29, Norwich,
NR3 1GN.
<http://www.statistics.gov.uk/>.
Annual Abstract of Statistics. Annual.
2002. (In English.)

Metropolitan and Micropolitan Statistical Areas: Concepts, Components, and Population

The United States Office of Management and Budget (OMB) defines metropolitan and micropolitan statistical areas according to published standards that are applied to Census Bureau data. The general concept of a metropolitan or micropolitan statistical area is that of a core area containing a substantial population nucleus, together with adjacent communities having a high degree of economic and social integration with that core. Currently defined metropolitan and micropolitan statistical areas are based on application of 2000 standards (which appeared in the Federal Register on December 27, 2000) to 2000 decennial census data. Current metropolitan and micropolitan statistical area definitions were announced by OMB effective June 6, 2003, and subsequently updated as of December 2003 and November 2004.

Standard definitions of metropolitan areas were first issued in 1949 by the then Bureau of the Budget (predecessor of OMB), under the designation "standard metropolitan area" (SMA). The term was changed to "standard metropolitan statistical area" (SMSA) in 1959 and to "metropolitan statistical area" (MSA) in 1983. The term "metropolitan area" (MA) was adopted in 1990 and referred collectively to metropolitan statistical areas (MSAs), consolidated metropolitan statistical areas (CMSAs), and primary metropolitan statistical areas (PMSAs). The term "core-based statistical area" (CBSA) became effective in 2000 and refers collectively to metropolitan and micropolitan statistical areas.

OMB has been responsible for the official metropolitan areas since they were first defined, except for the period 1977 to 1981, when they were the responsibility of the Office of Federal Statistical Policy and Standards, Department of Commerce. The standards for defining metropolitan areas were modified in 1958, 1971, 1975, 1980, 1990, and 2000.

Defining Metropolitan and Micropolitan Statistical Areas—The 2000 standards provide that each CBSA must contain at least 1 urban area of 10,000 or more population. Each metropolitan statistical area must have at least 1 urbanized area of 50,000 or more inhabitants. Each micropolitan statistical area must have at least 1 urban cluster of at least 10,000 but less than 50,000 population.

Under the standards, the county (or counties) in which at least 50 percent of the population resides within urban areas of 10,000 or more population, or that contain at least 5,000 people residing within a single urban area of 10,000 or more population, is identified as a "central county" (counties). Additional "outlying counties" are included in the CBSA if they meet specified requirements of commuting to or from the central counties. Counties or equivalent entities form the geographic "building blocks" for metropolitan and micropolitan statistical areas throughout the United States and Puerto Rico.

If specified criteria are met, a metropolitan statistical area containing a single core with a population of 2.5 million or more may be subdivided to form smaller groupings of counties referred to as "metropolitan divisions."

As of November 2004, there are 361 metropolitan statistical areas and 575 micropolitan statistical areas in the United States. In addition, there are eight metropolitan statistical areas and five micropolitan statistical areas in Puerto Rico.

Principal Cities and Metropolitan and Micropolitan Statistical Area Titles—The largest city in each metropolitan or micropolitan statistical area is designated a "principal city." Additional cities qualify if specified requirements are met concerning population size and employment. The title of each metropolitan or micropolitan statistical area consists of the names of up to three of its principal cities and the name of each state into which the metropolitan or micropolitan statistical area extends. Titles of metropolitan divisions also typically are based on principal city names, but in certain cases consist of county names.

Defining New England City and Town Areas—In view of the importance of cities and town in New England, the 2000 standards also provide for a set of geographic areas that are defined using cities and towns in the six New England states. The New England city and town areas (NECTAs) are defined using the same criteria as metropolitan and micropolitan statistical areas and are identified as either metropolitan or micropolitan, based, respectively, on the presence of either an urbanized area of 50,000 or more population or an urban cluster of at least 10,000 but less than 50,000 population. If the specified criteria are met, a NECTA containing a single core with a population of at least 2.5 million may be subdivided to form smaller groupings of cities and towns referred to as New England city and town area divisions.

Changes in Definitions Over Time—Changes in the definitions of these statistical areas since the 1950 census have consisted chiefly of (1) the recognition of new areas as they reached the minimum required city or urbanized area population and (2) the addition of counties (or cities and towns in New England) to existing areas as new decennial census data showed them to qualify.

In some instances, formerly separate areas have been merged, components of an area have been transferred from one area to another, or components have been dropped from an area. The large majority of changes have taken place on the basis of decennial census data. However, Census Bureau data serve as the basis for intercensal updates in specified circumstances.

Because of these historical changes in geographic definitions, users must be cautious in comparing data for these statistical areas from different dates. For some purposes, comparisons of data for areas as defined at given dates may be appropriate; for other purposes, it may be preferable to maintain consistent area definitions. Historical metropolitan area definitions are available for 1999, 1993, 1990, 1983, 1981, 1973, 1970, 1963, 1960, and 1950.

Excluding Table 26 in the Population section; Table 582 in the Labor Force section; Table 664 in the Income section, and the tables that follow in this appendix, the tables presenting data for metropolitan areas in this edition of the *Statistical Abstract* are based on the 1999 or earlier metropolitan area definitions. For a list of component counties according to the 1999 definition, see Appendix II in the 2002 edition of the *Statistical Abstract* or <http://www.census.gov/population /www/estimates/pastmetro.html>.

Metropolitan and Micropolitan Statistical Areas of the United States

As defined by the U.S. Office of Management and Budget, November 2004

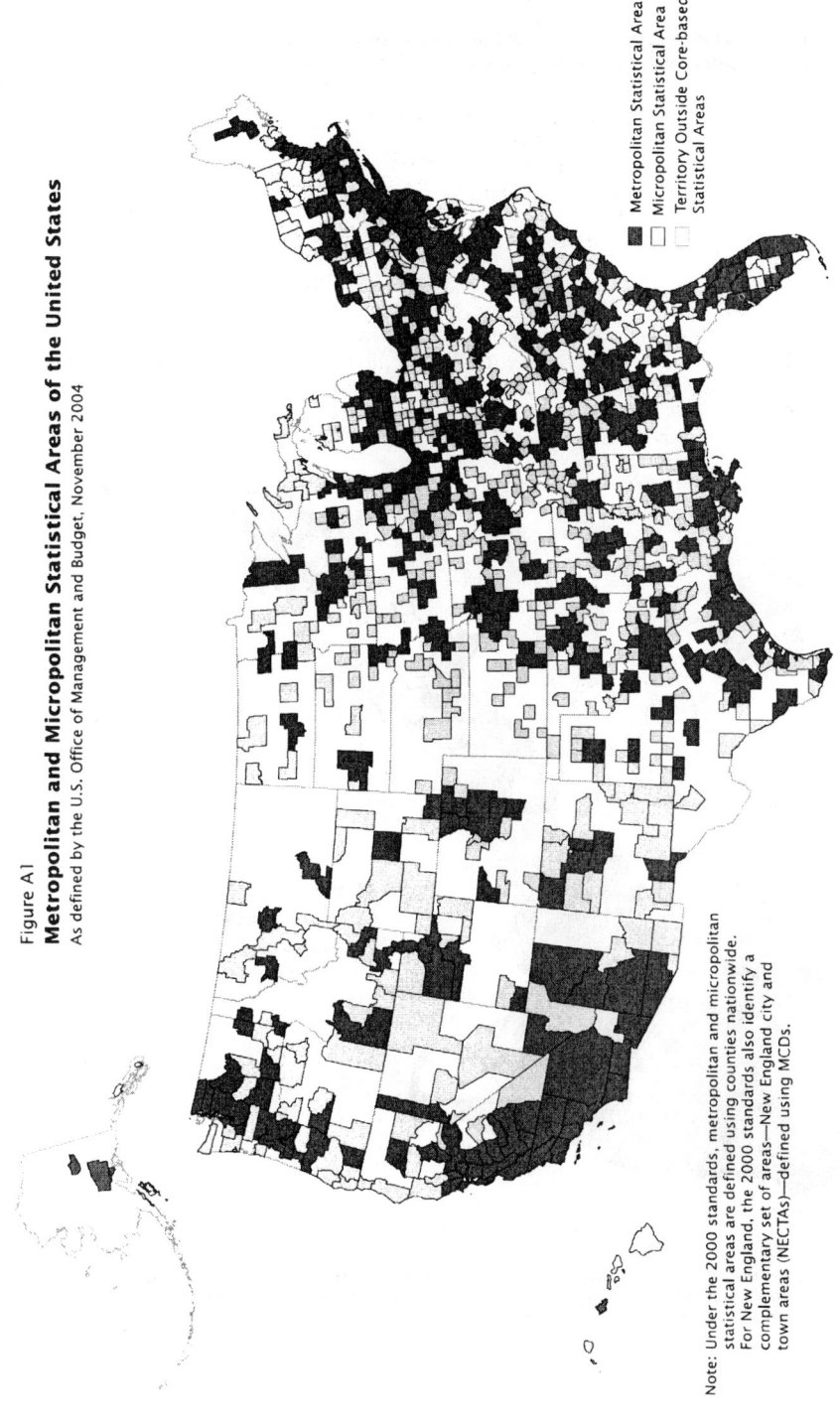

Metropolitan Statistical Area
Micropolitan Statistical Area
Territory Outside Core-based
Statistical Areas

Note: Under the 2000 standards, metropolitan and micropolitan statistical areas are defined using counties nationwide. For New England, the 2000 standards also identify a complementary set of areas—New England city and town areas (NECTAs)—defined using MCDs.

U.S. Census Bureau, Statistical Abstract of the United States: 2006

Metropolitan and Micropolitan New England City and Town Areas (NECTAs)
As defined by the U.S. Office of Management and Budget, November 2004

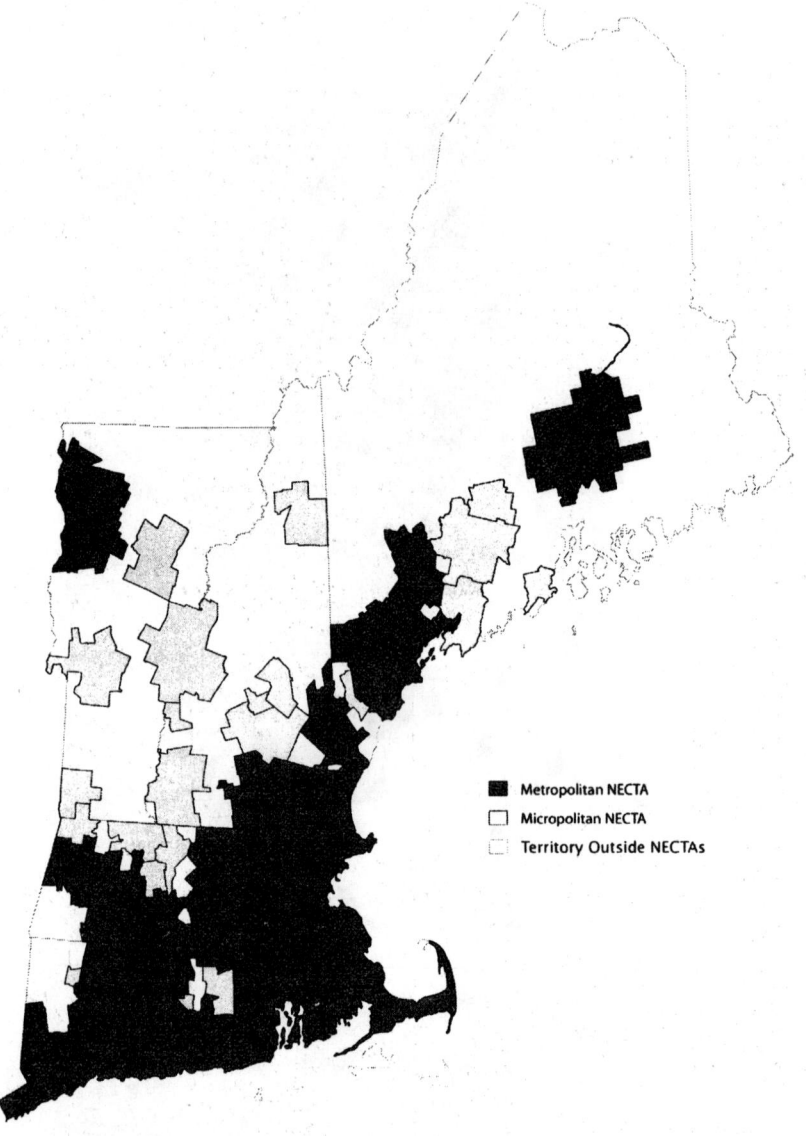

■ Metropolitan NECTA

☐ Micropolitan NECTA

⬚ Territory Outside NECTAs

Note: Under the 2000 standards, metropolitan and micropolitan statistical areas are defined using counties nationwide. For New England, the 2000 standards also identify a complementary set of areas—New England city and town areas (NECTAs)—defined using MCDs.

Table A. Metropolitan Statistical Areas and Components as of November 2004

[Population as of July 2004. 159 represents 159,000. All metropolitan areas are arranged alphabetically]

Metropolitan statistical area Metropolitan division Component county	Population, 2004 (1,000)	Metropolitan statistical area Metropolitan division Component county	Population, 2004 (1,000)	Metropolitan statistical area Metropolitan division Component county	Population, 2004 (1,000)
Abilene, TX	**159**	**Athens-Clarke County, GA** .	**174**	**Baton Rouge, LA, Con.**	
Callahan County, TX . . .	13	Clarke County, GA.	104	East Baton Rouge	
Jones County, TX	20	Madison County, GA . . .	27	Parish, LA.	413
Taylor County, TX	125	Oconee County, GA . . .	29	East Feliciana Parish,	
Akron, OH	**702**	Oglethorpe County, GA .	14	LA	21
Portage County, OH. . . .	155	**Atlanta-Sandy Springs-**		Iberville Parish, LA. . . .	32
Summit County, OH. . . .	547	**Marietta, GA**	**4,708**	Livingston Parish, LA. . .	106
Albany, GA	**163**	Barrow County, GA . . .	56	Pointe Coupee Parish,	
Baker County, GA	4	Bartow County, GA	87	LA	23
Dougherty County, GA . .	96	Butts County, GA.	22	St. Helena Parish, LA . .	10
Lee County, GA.	30	Carroll County, GA. . . .	102	West Baton Rouge	
Terrell County, GA	11	Cherokee County, GA . .	175	Parish, LA.	22
Worth County, GA	22	Clayton County, GA . . .	265	West Feliciana Parish,	
Albany-Schenectady-Troy,		Cobb County, GA	654	LA	15
NY	**845**	Coweta County, GA . . .	105	**Battle Creek, MI**	**139**
Albany County, NY	298	Dawson County, GA . . .	19	Calhoun County, MI. . . .	139
Rensselaer County, NY .	154	DeKalb County, GA. . . .	676	**Bay City, MI**	**109**
Saratoga County, NY . . .	213	Douglas County, GA . . .	107	Bay County, MI	109
Schenectady County,		Fayette County, GA . . .	101	**Beaumont-Port Arthur, TX. .**	**383**
NY.	148	Forsyth County, GA . . .	132	Hardin County, TX	50
Schoharie County, NY . .	32	Fulton County, GA. . . .	814	Jefferson County, TX . . .	248
Albuquerque, NM	**781**	Gwinnett County, GA . . .	701	Orange County, TX	85
Bernalillo County, NM. . .	594	Haralson County, GA . . .	28	**Bellingham, WA**	**180**
Sandoval County, NM . .	102	Heard County, GA	11	Whatcom County, WA . .	180
Torrance County, NM . . .	17	Henry County, GA	160	**Bend, OR**	**134**
Valencia County, NM . . .	69	Jasper County, GA	13	Deschutes County, OR. .	134
Alexandria, LA	**147**	Lamar County, GA. . . .	16	**Billings, MT**	**144**
Grant Parish, LA	19	Meriwether County, GA .	23	Carbon County, MT	10
Rapides Parish, LA	128	Newton County, GA . . .	82	Yellowstone County, MT.	135
Allentown-Bethlehem-		Paulding County, GA . . .	106	**Binghamton, NY**	**249**
Easton, PA-NJ.	**780**	Pickens County, GA. . . .	28	Broome County, NY. . . .	198
Warren County, NJ	110	Pike County, GA	16	Tioga County, NY	52
Carbon County, PA	61	Rockdale County, GA . .	77	**Birmingham-Hoover, AL** . . .	**1,082**
Lehigh County, PA. . . .	326	Spalding County, GA . . .	61	Bibb County, AL	21
Northampton County,		Walton County, GA	72	Blount County, AL	55
PA.	283	**Atlantic City, NJ**	**269**	Chilton County, AL.	41
Altoona, PA	**127**	Atlantic County, NJ	269	Jefferson County, AL . . .	658
Blair County, PA	127	**Auburn-Opelika, AL**	**121**	St. Clair County, AL	70
Amarillo, TX	**236**	Lee County, AL	121	Shelby County, AL.	166
Armstrong County, TX . .	2	**Augusta-Richmond County,**		Walker County, AL.	70
Carson County, TX	6	**GA-SC**	**515**	**Bismarck, ND**	**98**
Potter County, TX	118	Burke County, GA	23	Burleigh County, ND . . .	73
Randall County, TX	109	Columbia County, GA. . .	101	Morton County, ND	25
Ames, IA	**80**	McDuffie County, GA . . .	22	**Blacksburg-Christiansburg-**	
Story County, IA	80	Richmond County, GA . .	196	**Radford, VA**	**151**
Anchorage, AK	**345**	Aiken County, SC	149	Giles County, VA	17
Anchorage Borough, AK.	273	Edgefield County, SC. . .	25	Montgomery County, VA. .	84
Matanuska-Susitna		**Austin-Round Rock, TX.** . . .	**1,412**	Pulaski County, VA	35
Borough, AK.	72	Bastrop County, TX. . . .	69	Radford city, VA	15
Anderson, IN	**131**	Caldwell County, TX. . . .	36	**Bloomington, IN**	**178**
Madison County, IN	131	Hays County, TX.	119	Greene County, IN.	34
Anderson, SC	**174**	Travis County, TX	870	Monroe County, IN.	121
Anderson County, SC. . .	174	Williamson County, TX . .	318	Owen County, IN.	23
Ann Arbor, MI	**339**	**Bakersfield, CA.**	**735**	**Bloomington-Normal, IL** . . .	**158**
Washtenaw County, MI. .	339	Kern County, CA	735	McLean County, IL.	158
Anniston-Oxford, AL	**112**	**Baltimore-Towson, MD**	**2,639**	**Boise City-Nampa, ID**	**525**
Calhoun County, AL. . . .	112	Anne Arundel County,		Ada County, ID	333
Appleton, WI.	**213**	MD	509	Boise County, ID	7
Calumet County, WI. . . .	44	Baltimore County, MD . .	781	Canyon County, ID	158
Outagamie County, WI . .	169	Carroll County, MD	166	Gem County, ID	16
Asheville, NC	**387**	Harford County, MD. . . .	236	Owyhee County, ID	11
Buncombe County, NC. .	216	Howard County, MD. . . .	267	**Boston-Cambridge-Quincy,**	
Haywood County, NC. . .	56	Queen Anne's County,		**MA-NH**	**4,425**
Henderson County, NC . .	95	MD	45	**Boston-Quincy, MA**	**1,810**
Madison County, NC . . .	20	Baltimore city, MD	636	Norfolk County, MA	654
		Bangor, ME.	**148**	Plymouth County, MA. . .	491
		Penobscot County, ME. .	148	Suffolk County, MA	666
		Baton Rouge, LA	**729**		
		Ascension Parish, LA. . .	87		

Metropolitan statistical area Metropolitan division Component county	Popu- lation, 2004 (1,000)	Metropolitan statistical area Metropolitan division Component county	Popu- lation, 2004 (1,000)	Metropolitan statistical area Metropolitan division Component county	Popu- lation, 2004 (1,000)
Boston-Cambridge-Quincy,		**Charlotte-Gastonia-**		**Cleveland-Elyria-Mentor,**	
MA-NH, Con.		**Concord, NC-SC**	1,475	**OH, Con.**	
Cambridge-Newton-		Anson County, NC.....	25	Lake County, OH......	232
Framingham, MA......	1,465	Cabarrus County, NC...	146	Lorain County, OH.....	294
Middlesex County, MA..	1,465	Gaston County, NC....	194	Medina County, OH....	165
Essex County, MA......	739	Mecklenburg County.			
Essex County, MA......	739	NC..............	772	**Coeur d'Alene, ID........**	122
Rockingham County-		Union County, NC....	154	Kootenai County, ID....	122
Strafford County, NH...	411	York County, SC	184		
Rockingham County,				**College Station-Bryan, TX..**	189
NH.............	293	**Charlottesville, VA**	181	Brazos County, TX.....	156
Strafford County, NH...	118	Albemarle County, VA ..	89	Burleson County, TX ..	17
		Fluvanna County, VA...	24	Robertson County, TX..	16
Boulder, CO	279	Greene County, VA....	17		
Boulder County, CO....	279	Nelson County, VA.....	15	**Colorado Springs, CO.....**	576
		Charlottesville city, VA ..	37	El Paso County, CO....	555
Bowling Green, KY	109			Teller County, CO	22
Edmonson County, KY..	12	**Chattanooga, TN-GA......**	490		
Warren County, KY	97	Catoosa County, GA ...	60	**Columbia, MO...........**	151
		Dade County, GA	16	Boone County, MO	141
Bremerton-Silverdale, WA..	239	Walker County, GA	63	Howard County, MO ...	10
Kitsap County, WA......	239	Hamilton County, TN ...	310		
		Marion County, TN.....	28	**Columbia, SC...........**	679
Bridgeport-Stamford-		Sequatchie County, TN..	12	Calhoun County, SC ...	15
Norwalk, CT	903			Fairfield County, SC....	24
Fairfield County, CT....	903	**Cheyenne, WY**	85	Kershaw County, SC ...	55
		Laramie County, WY ...	85	Lexington County, SC ..	231
Brownsville-Harlingen, TX..	372			Richland County, SC ...	335
Cameron County, TX ...	372	**Chicago-Naperville-Joliet,**		Saluda County, SC	19
		IL	9,392		
Brunswick, GA	98	**Chicago-Naperville-Joliet,**		**Columbus, GA-AL........**	280
Brantley County, GA ...	16	**IL**	7,848	Russell County, AL	49
Glynn County, GA	71	Cook County, IL	5,328	Chattahoochee County,	
McIntosh County, GA...	11	DeKalb County, IL	96	GA.............	14
		DuPage County, IL	929	Harris County, GA	27
Buffalo-Niagara Falls, NY ..	1,154	Grundy County, IL	41	Marion County, GA	7
Erie County, NY	936	Kane County, IL	472	Muscogee County, GA ..	183
Niagara County, NY....	218	Kendall County, IL	73		
		McHenry County, IL....	296	**Columbus, IN ....**	73
Burlington, NC	138	Will County, IL........	614	Bartholomew County, IN.	73
Alamance County, NC ..	138	**Gary, IN.............**	692		
		Jasper County, IN	32	**Columbus, OH ....**	1,694
Burlington-South Burling-		Lake County, IN	491	Delaware County, OH ..	143
ton, VT	204	Newton County, IN.....	14	Fairfield County, OH ...	136
Chittenden County, VT..	149	Porter County, IN......	155	Franklin County, OH ...	1,089
Franklin County, VT....	48	**Lake County-Kenosha**		Licking County, OH	153
Grand Isle County, VT ..	8	**County, IL-WI.........**	851	Madison County, OH ...	41
		Lake County, IL.......	693	Morrow County, OH....	34
Canton-Massillon, OH	411	Kenosha County, WI ...	158	Pickaway County, OH ..	54
Carroll County, OH	30			Union County, OH	44
Stark County, OH	381	**Chico, CA..............**	213		
		Butte County, CA.....	213	**Corpus Christi, TX ....**	410
Cape Coral-Fort Myers, FL.	514			Aransas County, TX....	24
Lee County, FL.......	514	**Cincinnati-Middletown,**		Nueces County, TX	318
		OH-KY-IN	2,058	San Patricio County, TX.	68
Carson City, NV	56	Dearborn County, IN ...	49		
Carson City, NV	56	Franklin County, IN ...	23	**Corvallis, OR ....**	79
		Ohio County, IN.......	6	Benton County, OR	79
Casper, WY.............	69	Boone County, KY.....	101		
Natrona County, WY ...	69	Bracken County, KY....	9	**Cumberland, MD-WV......**	101
		Campbell County, KY...	87	Allegany County, MD ...	74
Cedar Rapids, IA........	245	Gallatin County, KY....	8	Mineral County, WV....	27
Benton County, IA	27	Grant County, KY	24		
Jones County, IA......	21	Kenton County, KY	153	**Dallas-Fort Worth-Arlington,**	
Linn County, IA	197	Pendleton County, KY ..	15	**TX**	5,700
		Brown County, OH.....	44	**Dallas-Plano-Irving, TX ..**	3,813
Champaign-Urbana, IL	215	Butler County, OH	347	Collin County, TX......	628
Champaign County, IL ..	184	Clermont County, OH...	189	Dallas County, TX	2,295
Ford County, IL	14	Hamilton County, OH...	815	Delta County, TX......	6
Piatt County, IL.......	16	Warren County, OH ...	189	Denton County, TX	531
				Ellis County, TX.......	129
Charleston, WV..........	308	**Clarksville, TN-KY........**	239	Hunt County, TX	82
Boone County, WV	26	Christian County, KY ...	71	Kaufman County, TX ...	85
Clay County, WV......	10	Trigg County, KY	13	Rockwall County, TX ...	58
Kanawha County, WV ..	195	Montgomery County, TN.	142	**Fort Worth-Arlington, TX.**	1,887
Lincoln County, WV ...	23	Stewart County, TN	13	Johnson County, TX....	143
Putnam County, WV ...	54			Parker County, TX.....	100
		Cleveland, TN...........	107	Tarrant County, TX.....	1,588
Charleston-North Charles-		Bradley County, TN	91	Wise County, TX......	56
ton, SC..............	583	Polk County, TN	16		
Berkeley County, SC ...	150			**Dalton, GA ....**	130
Charleston County, SC..	327	**Cleveland-Elyria-Mentor,**		Murray County, GA	41
Dorchester County, SC..	107	**OH**	2,137	Whitfield County, GA ...	89
		Cuyahoga County, OH ..	1,351		
		Geauga County, OH ...	95	**Danville, IL.............**	83
				Vermilion County, IL....	83

926   Appendix II

Metropolitan statistical area / Metropolitan division / Component county	Population, 2004 (1,000)
Danville, VA	108
Pittsylvania County, VA. .	62
Danville city, VA	46
Davenport-Moline-Rock Island, IA-IL	375
Henry County, IL	51
Mercer County, IL	17
Rock Island County, IL. .	148
Scott County, IA	160
Dayton, OH	846
Greene County, OH	152
Miami County, OH	101
Montgomery County, OH	550
Preble County, OH	43
Decatur, AL	148
Lawrence County, AL	34
Morgan County, AL	113
Decatur, IL	111
Macon County, IL	111
Deltona-Daytona Beach-Ormond Beach, FL	479
Volusia County, FL	479
Denver-Aurora, CO	2,330
Adams County, CO	390
Arapahoe County, CO	523
Broomfield County, CO	43
Clear Creek County, CO	9
Denver County, CO	557
Douglas County, CO	238
Elbert County, CO	22
Gilpin County, CO	5
Jefferson County, CO	526
Park County, CO	17
Des Moines, IA	512
Dallas County, IA	50
Guthrie County, IA	12
Madison County, IA	15
Polk County, IA	393
Warren County, IA	43
Detroit-Warren-Livonia, MI. .	4,493
Detroit-Livonia-Dearborn, MI	2,016
Wayne County, MI	2,016
Warren-Farmington Hills-Troy, MI	2,477
Lapeer County, MI	93
Livingston County, MI	178
Macomb County, MI	823
Oakland County, MI	1,213
St. Clair County, MI	171
Dothan, AL	135
Geneva County, AL	26
Henry County, AL	17
Houston County, AL	93
Dover, DE	139
Kent County, DE	139
Dubuque, IA	91
Dubuque County, IA	91
Duluth, MN-WI	276
Carlton County, MN	34
St. Louis County, MN	198
Douglas County, WI	44
Durham, NC	451
Chatham County, NC	57
Durham County, NC	240
Orange County, NC	118
Person County, NC	37
Eau Claire, WI	153
Chippewa County, WI	59
Eau Claire County, WI	94
El Centro, CA	152
Imperial County, CA	152
Elizabethtown, KY	110
Hardin County, KY	96
Larue County, KY	13
Elkhart-Goshen, IN	192
Elkhart County, IN	192
Elmira, NY	90
Chemung County, NY	90
El Paso, TX	713
El Paso County, TX	713
Erie, PA	282
Erie County, PA	282
Eugene-Springfield, OR	332
Lane County, OR	332
Evansville, IN-KY	348
Gibson County, IN	33
Posey County, IN	27
Vanderburgh County, IN	173
Warrick County, IN	55
Henderson County, KY	45
Webster County, KY	14
Fairbanks, AK	86
Fairbanks North Star Borough, AK	86
Fargo, ND-MN	182
Clay County, MN	53
Cass County, ND	129
Farmington, NM	124
San Juan County, NM	124
Fayetteville, NC	348
Cumberland County, NC	308
Hoke County, NC	39
Fayetteville-Springdale-Rogers, AR-MO	391
Benton County, AR	180
Madison County, AR	15
Washington County, AR	174
McDonald County, MO	22
Flagstaff, AZ	123
Coconino County, AZ	123
Flint, MI	444
Genesee County, MI	444
Florence, SC	197
Darlington County, SC	68
Florence County, SC	130
Florence-Muscle Shoals, AL	142
Colbert County, AL	55
Lauderdale County, AL	88
Fond du Lac, WI	99
Fond du Lac County, WI	99
Fort Collins-Loveland, CO. .	269
Larimer County, CO	269
Fort Smith, AR-OK	282
Crawford County, AR	57
Franklin County, AR	18
Sebastian County, AR	118
Le Flore County, OK	49
Sequoyah County, OK	41
Fort Walton Beach-Crestview-Destin, FL	181
Okaloosa County, FL	181
Fort Wayne, IN	402
Allen County, IN	342
Wells County, IN	28
Fort Wayne, IN, Con.	
Whitley County, IN	32
Fresno, CA	867
Fresno County, CA	867
Gadsden, AL	103
Etowah County, AL	103
Gainesville, FL	239
Alachua County, FL	223
Gilchrist County, FL	16
Gainesville, GA	161
Hall County, GA	161
Glens Falls, NY	128
Warren County, NY	65
Washington County, NY	63
Goldsboro, NC	114
Wayne County, NC	114
Grand Forks, ND-MN	96
Polk County, MN	31
Grand Forks County, ND	65
Grand Junction, CO	127
Mesa County, CO	127
Grand Rapids-Wyoming, MI	768
Barry County, MI	59
Ionia County, MI	64
Kent County, MI	594
Newaygo County, MI	50
Great Falls, MT	80
Cascade County, MT	80
Greeley, CO	219
Weld County, CO	219
Green Bay, WI	295
Brown County, WI	237
Kewaunee County, WI	21
Oconto County, WI	38
Greensboro-High Point, NC	668
Guilford County, NC	439
Randolph County, NC	136
Rockingham County, NC	93
Greenville, NC	161
Greene County, NC	20
Pitt County, NC	141
Greenville, SC	584
Greenville County, SC	401
Laurens County, SC	70
Pickens County, SC	112
Gulfport-Biloxi, MS	253
Hancock County, MS	46
Harrison County, MS	192
Stone County, MS	14
Hagerstown-Martinsburg, MD-WV	245
Washington County, MD	140
Berkeley County, WV	89
Morgan County, WV	16
Hanford-Corcoran, CA.	143
Kings County, CA	143
Harrisburg-Carlisle, PA	519
Cumberland County, PA	221
Dauphin County, PA	253
Perry County, PA	45
Harrisonburg, VA	111
Rockingham County, VA	70
Harrisonburg city, VA	41

Metropolitan statistical area Metropolitan division Component county	Population, 2004 (1,000)
Hartford-West Hartford-East Hartford, CT	**1,185**
Hartford County, CT. . . .	876
Middlesex County, CT . .	162
Tolland County, CT	147
Hattiesburg, MS	**130**
Forrest County, MS	74
Lamar County, MS.	43
Perry County, MS	12
Hickory-Lenoir-Morganton, NC	**353**
Alexander County, NC . .	35
Burke County, NC	89
Caldwell County, NC . . .	79
Catawba County, NC . . .	149
Hinesville-Fort Stewart, GA .	**73**
Liberty County, GA	62
Long County, GA.	11
Holland-Grand Haven, MI . .	**252**
Ottawa County, MI.	252
Honolulu, HI	**900**
Honolulu County, HI. . . .	900
Hot Springs, AR	**92**
Garland County, AR. . . .	92
Houma-Bayou Cane-Thibodaux, LA	**199**
Lafourche Parish, LA . . .	92
Terrebonne Parish, LA . .	107
Houston-Sugar Land-Baytown, TX	**5,180**
Austin County, TX	26
Brazoria County, TX. . . .	271
Chambers County, TX . .	28
Fort Bend County, TX . .	443
Galveston County, TX . .	272
Harris County, TX	3,644
Liberty County, TX.	75
Montgomery County, TX.	362
San Jacinto County, TX .	25
Waller County, TX	35
Huntington-Ashland, WV-KY-OH	**287**
Boyd County, KY.	50
Greenup County, KY . . .	37
Lawrence County, OH . .	63
Cabell County, WV	95
Wayne County, WV	43
Huntsville, AL	**362**
Limestone County, AL . .	69
Madison County, AL. . . .	293
Idaho Falls, ID	**110**
Bonneville County, ID. . .	90
Jefferson County, ID . . .	21
Indianapolis, IN.	**1,622**
Boone County, IN	51
Brown County, IN	15
Hamilton County, IN. . . .	232
Hancock County, IN. . . .	61
Hendricks County, IN . . .	123
Johnson County, IN	126
Marion County, IN.	864
Morgan County, IN.	69
Putnam County, IN	37
Shelby County, IN	44
Iowa City, IA	**137**
Johnson County, IA	116
Washington County, IA. .	21
Ithaca, NY.	**100**
Tompkins County, NY. . .	100

Metropolitan statistical area Metropolitan division Component county	Population, 2004 (1,000)
Jackson, MI	**163**
Jackson County, MI	163
Jackson, MS.	**517**
Copiah County, MS	29
Hinds County, MS	250
Madison County, MS . . .	82
Rankin County, MS	128
Simpson County, MS . . .	28
Jackson, TN	**110**
Chester County, TN	16
Madison County, TN . . .	94
Jacksonville, FL	**1,225**
Baker County, FL	24
Clay County, FL	164
Duval County, FL.	821
Nassau County, FL	63
St. Johns County, FL . . .	152
Jacksonville, NC.	**154**
Onslow County, NC	154
Janesville, WI	**157**
Rock County, WI . . . : . .	157
Jefferson City, MO	**142**
Callaway County, MO. . .	42
Cole County, MO.	72
Moniteau County, MO . .	15
Osage County, MO	13
Johnson City, TN	**187**
Carter County, TN	59
Unicoi County, TN	18
Washington County, TN .	111
Johnstown, PA	**148**
Cambria County, PA. . . .	148
Jonesboro, AR	**112**
Craighead County, AR . .	86
Poinsett County, AR. . . .	25
Joplin, MO	**164**
Jasper County, MO	109
Newton County, MO. . . .	55
Kalamazoo-Portage, MI	**319**
Kalamazoo County, MI . .	241
Van Buren County, MI . .	79
Kankakee-Bradley, IL	**107**
Kankakee County, IL . . .	107
Kansas City, MO-KS	**1,925**
Franklin County, KS. . . .	26
Johnson County, KS . . .	497
Leavenworth County, KS.	72
Linn County, KS	10
Miami County, KS	30
Wyandotte County, KS . .	156
Bates County, MO.	17
Caldwell County, MO. . .	9
Cass County, MO	92
Clay County, MO.	198
Clinton County, MO	21
Jackson County, MO . . .	660
Lafayette County, MO . .	33
Platte County, MO.	81
Ray County, MO	24
Kennewick-Richland-Pasco, WA	**215**
Benton County, WA	156
Franklin County, WA . . .	59
Killeen-Temple-Fort Hood, TX	**346**
Bell County, TX	250
Coryell County, TX.	75
Lampasas County, TX . .	21

Metropolitan statistical area Metropolitan division Component county	Population, 2004 (1,000)
Kingsport-Bristol-Bristol, TN-VA.	**301**
Hawkins County, TN . . .	56
Sullivan County, TN	152
Scott County, VA	23
Washington County, VA .	52
Bristol city, VA.	17
Kingston, NY	**182**
Ulster County, NY	182
Knoxville, TN	**647**
Anderson County, TN. . .	72
Blount County, TN.	114
Knox County, TN.	400
Loudon County, TN	42
Union County, TN	19
Kokomo, IN	**101**
Howard County, IN	85
Tipton County, IN.	17
La Crosse, WI-MN.	**129**
Houston County, MN . . .	20
La Crosse County, WI . .	109
Lafayette, IN.	**182**
Benton County, IN	9
Carroll County, IN	20
Tippecanoe County, IN. .	152
Lafayette, LA	**246**
Lafayette Parish, LA . . .	196
St. Martin Parish, LA . . .	50
Lake Charles, LA	**195**
Calcasieu Parish, LA . . .	185
Cameron Parish, LA . . .	10
Lakeland, FL.	**524**
Polk County, FL.	524
Lancaster, PA	**487**
Lancaster County, PA. . .	487
Lansing-East Lansing, MI . .	**456**
Clinton County, MI.	69
Eaton County, MI.	107
Ingham County, MI	280
Laredo, TX	**219**
Webb County, TX	219
Las Cruces, NM	**186**
Dona Ana County, NM . .	186
Las Vegas-Paradise, NV . . .	**1,651**
Clark County, NV.	1,651
Lawrence, KS	**103**
Douglas County, KS. . . .	103
Lawton, OK	**111**
Comanche County, OK. .	111
Lebanon, PA.	**124**
Lebanon County, PA . . .	124
Lewiston, ID-WA	**59**
Nez Perce County, ID . .	38
Asotin County, WA.	21
Lewiston-Auburn, ME	**107**
Androscoggin County, ME.	107
Lexington-Fayette, KY.	**425**
Bourbon County, KY . . .	20
Clark County, KY.	34
Fayette County, KY	266
Jessamine County, KY. .	42
Scott County, KY	38
Woodford County, KY. . .	24
Lima, OH	**107**
Allen County, OH.	107

U.S. Census Bureau, Statistical Abstract of the United States: 2006

Metropolitan statistical area / Metropolitan division / Component county	Population, 2004 (1,000)
Lincoln, NE	**278**
Lancaster County, NE	262
Seward County, NE	17
Little Rock-North Little Rock, AR	**637**
Faulkner County, AR	95
Grant County, AR	17
Lonoke County, AR	59
Perry County, AR	10
Pulaski County, AR	366
Saline County, AR	89
Logan, UT-ID	**110**
Franklin County, ID	12
Cache County, UT	97
Longview, TX	**200**
Gregg County, TX	115
Rusk County, TX	48
Upshur County, TX	37
Longview, WA	**96**
Cowlitz County, WA	96
Los Angeles-Long Beach-Santa Ana, CA	**12,925**
Los Angeles-Long Beach-Glendale, CA	9,938
Los Angeles County, CA	9,938
Santa Ana-Anaheim-Irvine, CA	2,988
Orange County, CA	2,988
Louisville, KY-IN	**1,201**
Clark County, IN	101
Floyd County, IN	72
Harrison County, IN	36
Washington County, IN	28
Bullitt County, KY	67
Henry County, KY	16
Jefferson County, KY	700
Meade County, KY	28
Nelson County, KY	40
Oldham County, KY	52
Shelby County, KY	37
Spencer County, KY	15
Trimble County, KY	9
Lubbock, TX	**258**
Crosby County, TX	7
Lubbock County, TX	251
Lynchburg, VA	**233**
Amherst County, VA	32
Appomattox County, VA	14
Bedford County, VA	64
Campbell County, VA	52
Bedford city, VA	6
Lynchburg city, VA	65
Macon, GA	**228**
Bibb County, GA	155
Crawford County, GA	13
Jones County, GA	26
Monroe County, GA	23
Twiggs County, GA	10
Madera, CA	**139**
Madera County, CA	139
Madison, WI	**532**
Columbia County, WI	55
Dane County, WI	454
Iowa County, WI	23
Manchester-Nashua, NH	**399**
Hillsborough County, NH	399
Mansfield, OH	**128**
Richland County, OH	128
McAllen-Edinburg-Mission, TX	**658**
Hidalgo County, TX	658

Metropolitan statistical area / Metropolitan division / Component county	Population, 2004 (1,000)
Medford, OR	**193**
Jackson County, OR	193
Memphis, TN-MS-AR	**1,250**
Crittenden County, AR	51
DeSoto County, MS	131
Marshall County, MS	35
Tate County, MS	26
Tunica County, MS	10
Fayette County, TN	34
Shelby County, TN	908
Tipton County, TN	55
Merced, CA	**237**
Merced County, CA	237
Miami-Fort Lauderdale-Miami Beach, FL	**5,362**
Fort Lauderdale-Pompano Beach-Deerfield Beach, FL	1,755
Broward County, FL	1,755
Miami-Miami Beach-Kendall, FL	2,364
Miami-Dade County, FL	2,364
West Palm Beach-Boca Raton-Boynton Beach, FL	1,243
Palm Beach County, FL	1,243
Michigan City-La Porte, IN	**110**
La Porte County, IN	110
Midland, TX	**120**
Midland County, TX	120
Milwaukee-Waukesha-West Allis, WI	**1,515**
Milwaukee County, WI	928
Ozaukee County, WI	86
Washington County, WI	125
Waukesha County, WI	377
Minneapolis-St. Paul-Bloomington, MN-WI	**3,116**
Anoka County, MN	320
Carver County, MN	82
Chisago County, MN	48
Dakota County, MN	379
Hennepin County, MN	1,121
Isanti County, MN	37
Ramsey County, MN	499
Scott County, MN	115
Sherburne County, MN	79
Washington County, MN	217
Wright County, MN	107
Pierce County, WI	38
St. Croix County, WI	74
Missoula, MT	**99**
Missoula County, MT	99
Mobile, AL	**401**
Mobile County, AL	401
Modesto, CA	**498**
Stanislaus County, CA	498
Monroe, LA	**171**
Ouachita Parish, LA	148
Union Parish, LA	23
Monroe, MI	**153**
Monroe County, MI	153
Montgomery, AL	**355**
Autauga County, AL	47
Elmore County, AL	72
Lowndes County, AL	13
Montgomery County, AL	223
Morgantown, WV	**114**
Monongalia County, WV	84
Preston County, WV	30

Metropolitan statistical area / Metropolitan division / Component county	Population, 2004 (1,000)
Morristown, TN	**129**
Grainger County, TN	22
Hamblen County, TN	59
Jefferson County, TN	48
Mount Vernon-Anacortes, WA	**111**
Skagit County, WA	111
Muncie, IN	**118**
Delaware County, IN	118
Muskegon-Norton Shores, MI	**174**
Muskegon County, MI	174
Myrtle Beach-Conway-North Myrtle Beach, SC	**218**
Horry County, SC	218
Napa, CA	**132**
Napa County, CA	132
Naples-Marco Island, FL	**297**
Collier County, FL	297
Nashville-Davidson—Murfreesboro, TN	**1,396**
Cannon County, TN	13
Cheatham County, TN	38
Davidson County, TN	572
Dickson County, TN	45
Hickman County, TN	24
Macon County, TN	21
Robertson County, TN	59
Rutherford County, TN	210
Smith County, TN	18
Sumner County, TN	142
Trousdale County, TN	7
Williamson County, TN	147
Wilson County, TN	98
New Haven-Milford, CT	**846**
New Haven County, CT	846
New Orleans-Metairie-Kenner, LA	**1,320**
Jefferson Parish, LA	454
Orleans Parish, LA	462
Plaquemines Parish, LA	29
St. Bernard Parish, LA	66
St. Charles Parish, LA	50
St. John the Baptist Parish, LA	46
St. Tammany Parish, LA	214
New York-Northern New Jersey-Long Island, NY-NJ-PA	**18,710**
Edison, NJ	2,291
Middlesex County, NJ	785
Monmouth County, NJ	636
Ocean County, NJ	553
Somerset County, NJ	317
Nassau-Suffolk, NY	2,815
Nassau County, NY	1,340
Suffolk County, NY	1,475
Newark-Union, NJ-PA	2,153
Essex County, NJ	797
Hunterdon County, NJ	130
Morris County, NJ	488
Sussex County, NJ	152
Union County, NJ	532
Pike County, PA	54
New York-White Plains-Wayne, NY-NJ	11,450
Bergen County, NJ	903
Hudson County, NJ	606
Passaic County, NJ	500
Bronx County, NY	1,366
Kings County, NY	2,475
New York County, NY	1,563
Putnam County, NY	101
Queens County, NY	2,237
Richmond County, NY	463

Metropolitan statistical area / Metropolitan division / Component county	Population, 2004 (1,000)
New York-White Plains-Wayne, NY-NJ, Con.	
Rockland County, NY...	294
Westchester County, NY.	942
Niles-Benton Harbor, MI ...	**163**
Berrien County, MI....	163
Norwich-New London, CT ..	**266**
New London County, CT	266
Ocala, FL	**291**
Marion County, FL.....	291
Ocean City, NJ	**101**
Cape May County, NJ ..	101
Odessa, TX	**124**
Ector County, TX.....	124
Ogden-Clearfield, UT	**477**
Davis County, UT....	261
Morgan County, UT	8
Weber County, UT.....	209
Oklahoma City, OK	**1,144**
Canadian County, OK ..	96
Cleveland County, OK ..	222
Grady County, OK....	48
Lincoln County, OK....	32
Logan County, OK.....	36
McClain County, OK ...	29
Oklahoma County, OK ..	681
Olympia, WA	**225**
Thurston County, WA...	225
Omaha-Council Bluffs, NE-IA	**804**
Harrison County, IA	16
Mills County, IA.....	15
Pottawattamie County, IA	89
Cass County, NE.....	26
Douglas County, NE	482
Sarpy County, NE	136
Saunders County, NE...	20
Washington County, NE .	20
Orlando-Kissimmee, FL....	**1,862**
Lake County, FL......	261
Orange County, FL	990
Osceola County, FL....	220
Seminole County, FL ...	391
Oshkosh-Neenah, WI	**159**
Winnebago County, WI..	159
Owensboro, KY	**111**
Daviess County, KY...	93
Hancock County, KY ...	8
McLean County, KY....	10
Oxnard-Thousand Oaks-Ventura, CA	**798**
Ventura County, CA....	798
Palm Bay-Melbourne-Titusville, FL	**519**
Brevard County, FL	519
Panama City-Lynn Haven, FL	**158**
Bay County, FL......	158
Parkersburg-Marietta-Vienna, WV-OH	**163**
Washington County, OH	63
Pleasants County, WV .	7
Wirt County, WV	6
Wood County, WV....	87
Pascagoula, MS	**156**
George County, MS...	21
Jackson County, MS ...	135
Pensacola-Ferry Pass-Brent, FL	**437**
Escambia County, FL...	299
Santa Rosa County, FL .	138
Peoria, IL	**368**
Marshall County, IL	13
Peoria County, IL......	182
Stark County, IL	6
Tazewell County, IL	129
Woodford County, IL ...	37
Philadelphia-Camden-Wilmington, PA-NJ-DE-MD.	**5,801**
Camden, NJ	1,238
Burlington County, NJ ..	450
Camden County, NJ....	516
Gloucester County, NJ ..	272
Philadelphia, PA	3,883
Bucks County, PA	618
Chester County, PA ...	466
Delaware County, PA..	555
Montgomery County, PA.	774
Philadelphia County, PA.	1,470
Wilmington, DE-MD-NJ ..	680
New Castle County, DE .	519
Cecil County, MD......	96
Salem County, NJ	65
Phoenix-Mesa-Scottsdale, AZ	**3,715**
Maricopa County, AZ ..	3,501
Pinal County, AZ	214
Pine Bluff, AR	**106**
Cleveland County, AR ..	9
Jefferson County, AR ..	83
Lincoln County, AR	14
Pittsburgh, PA	**2,402**
Allegheny County, PA ..	1,251
Armstrong County, PA ..	71
Beaver County, PA ...	179
Butler County, PA	181
Fayette County, PA ...	146
Washington County, PA.	206
Westmoreland County, PA	369
Pittsfield, MA	**132**
Berkshire County, MA ..	132
Pocatello, ID	**83**
Bannock County, ID...	76
Power County, ID	7
Portland-South Portland-Biddeford, ME.	**511**
Cumberland County, ME.	274
Sagadahoc County, ME .	37
York County, ME	200
Portland-Vancouver-Beaverton, OR-WA	**2,064**
Clackamas County, OR .	363
Columbia County, OR ..	47
Multnomah County, OR .	672
Washington County, OR.	488
Yamhill County, OR ...	91
Clark County, WA	392
Skamania County, WA .	11
Port St. Lucie-Fort Pierce, FL.	**365**
Martin County, FL	138
St. Lucie County, FL ...	227
Poughkeepsie-Newburgh-Middletown, NY.	**664**
Dutchess County, NY ..	293
Orange County, NY ...	370
Prescott, AZ	**191**
Yavapai County, AZ....	191
Providence-New Bedford-Fall River, RI-MA.	**1,629**
Bristol County, MA....	548
Bristol County, RI......	53
Kent County, RI.......	172
Newport County, RI....	85
Providence County, RI ..	642
Washington County, RI..	129
Provo-Orem, UT	**412**
Juab County, UT......	9
Utah County, UT	403
Pueblo, CO	**150**
Pueblo County, CO	150
Punta Gorda, FL	**157**
Charlotte County, FL ...	157
Racine, WI	**194**
Racine County, WI.....	194
Raleigh-Cary, NC	**915**
Franklin County, NC....	54
Johnston County, NC...	142
Wake County, NC	720
Rapid City, SD	**117**
Meade County, SD	25
Pennington County, SD .	93
Reading, PA	**392**
Berks County, PA	392
Redding, CA	**178**
Shasta County, CA	178
Reno-Sparks, NV	**384**
Storey County, NV.....	4
Washoe County, NV....	381
Richmond, VA	**1,154**
Amelia County, VA.....	12
Caroline County, VA....	24
Charles City County, VA.	7
Chesterfield County, VA.	283
Cumberland County, VA .	9
Dinwiddie County, VA..	25
Goochland County, VA .	19
Hanover County, VA....	96
Henrico County, VA....	276
King and Queen County, VA	7
King William County, VA.	14
Louisa County, VA	29
New Kent County, VA...	16
Powhatan County, VA..	26
Prince George County, VA	34
Sussex County, VA	12
Colonial Heights city, VA.	18
Hopewell city, VA.....	22
Petersburg city, VA	33
Richmond city, VA	192
Riverside-San Bernardino-Ontario, CA.	**3,793**
Riverside County, CA...	1,872
San Bernardino County, CA	1,921
Roanoke, VA	**291**
Botetourt County, VA ...	32
Craig County, VA......	5
Franklin County, VA....	50
Roanoke County, VA...	88
Roanoke city, VA......	92
Salem city, VA........	24
Rochester, MN	**175**
Dodge County, MN	19
Olmsted County, MN ..	133
Wabasha County, MN ..	22
Rochester, NY	**1,041**
Livingston County, NY ..	65

Metropolitan statistical area Metropolitan division Component county	Popu-lation, 2004 (1,000)	Metropolitan statistical area Metropolitan division Component county	Popu-lation, 2004 (1,000)	Metropolitan statistical area Metropolitan division Component county	Popu-lation, 2004 (1,000)
Rochester, NY, Con.		**San Antonio, TX, Con.**		**Sioux City, IA-NE-SD.**	**143**
Monroe County, NY	735	Medina County, TX	42	Woodbury County, IA . .	103
Ontario County, NY	104	Wilson County, TX.	37	Dakota County, NE	21
Orleans County, NY. . . .	44			Dixon County, NE	6
Wayne County, NY	94	**San Diego-Carlsbad-San**		Union County, SD	13
Rockford, IL	**335**	**Marcos, CA.**	**2,932**		
Boone County, IL.	48	San Diego County, CA. .	2,932	**Sioux Falls, SD.**	**203**
Winnebago County, IL . .	287			Lincoln County, SD	31
		Sandusky, OH.	**79**	McCook County, SD . . .	6
Rocky Mount, NC	**145**	Erie County, OH	79	Minnehaha County, SD .	157
Edgecombe County, NC.	55			Turner County, SD.	9
Nash County, NC.	91	**San Francisco-Oakland-**			
		Fremont, CA	**4,154**	**South Bend-Mishawaka,**	
Rome, GA.	**94**	Oakland-Fremont-		**IN-MI.**	**318**
Floyd County, GA	94	**Hayward, CA**	**2,464**	St. Joseph County, IN . .	266
		Alameda County, CA . .	1,455	Cass County, MI	52
Sacramento—Arden-		Contra Costa County,			
Arcade—Roseville, CA . . .	**2,017**	CA.	1,009	**Spartanburg, SC**	**264**
El Dorado County, CA . .	173	**San Francisco-San**		Spartanburg County, SC.	264
Placer County, CA.	307	**Mateo-Redwood City,**			
Sacramento County, CA.	1,352	**CA**	**1,689**	**Spokane, WA**	**436**
Yolo County, CA	184	Marin County, CA	246	Spokane County, WA. . .	436
		San Francisco County,			
Saginaw-Saginaw Township		CA.	744	**Springfield, IL.**	**205**
North, MI.	**209**	San Mateo County, CA. .	699	Menard County, IL.	13
Saginaw County, MI. . . .	209			Sangamon County, IL. . .	192
		San Jose-Sunnyvale-Santa			
St. Cloud, MN	**179**	**Clara, CA**	**1,741**	**Springfield, MA.**	**688**
Benton County, MN	38	San Benito County, CA .	56	Franklin County, MA . . .	72
Stearns County, MN. . . .	141	Santa Clara County, CA .	1,685	Hampden County, MA . .	462
				Hampshire County, MA .	154
St. George, UT	**110**	**San Luis Obispo-Paso Rob-**			
Washington County, UT .	110	**les, CA**	**255**	**Springfield, MO.**	**391**
		San Luis Obispo County,		Christian County, MO. . .	64
St. Joseph, MO-KS	**122**	CA.	255	Dallas County, MO.	16
Doniphan County, KS. . .	8			Greene County, MO. . . .	248
Andrew County, MO. . . .	17	**Santa Barbara-Santa Maria,**		Polk County, MO	28
Buchanan County, MO . .	85	**CA**	**402**	Webster County, MO . . .	34
DeKalb County, MO	12	Santa Barbara County,			
		CA.	402	**Springfield, OH.**	**143**
St. Louis, MO-IL [1]	**2,764**			Clark County, OH	143
Bond County, IL	18	**Santa Cruz-Watsonville, CA.**	**251**		
Calhoun County, IL	5	Santa Cruz County, CA .	251	**State College, PA**	**140**
Clinton County, IL	36			Centre County, PA.	140
Jersey County, IL	22	**Santa Fe, NM**	**139**		
Macoupin County, IL. . . .	49	Santa Fe County, NM. . .	139	**Stockton, CA**	**650**
Madison County, IL. . . .	264			San Joaquin County,	
Monroe County, IL.	30	**Santa Rosa-Petaluma, CA.** . .	**468**	CA.	650
St. Clair County, IL	259	Sonoma County, CA . . .	468		
Franklin County, MO . . .	98			**Sumter, SC.**	**106**
Jefferson County, MO . .	210	**Sarasota-Bradenton-Venice,**		Sumter County, SC	106
Lincoln County, MO	46	**FL.**	**652**		
St. Charles County, MO .	321	Manatee County, FL . . .	296	**Syracuse, NY**	**654**
St. Louis County, MO. . .	1,009	Sarasota County, FL . . .	355	Madison County, NY . . .	70
Warren County, MO	28			Onondaga County, NY . .	460
Washington County, MO.	24	**Savannah, GA.**	**311**	Oswego County, NY . . .	124
St. Louis city, MO	343	Bryan County, GA	28		
		Chatham County, GA. . .	239	**Tallahassee, FL.**	**332**
Salem, OR	**369**	Effingham County, GA. . .	45	Gadsden County, FL . . .	46
Marion County, OR	302			Jefferson County, FL . . .	15
Polk County, OR	68	**Scranton—Wilkes-Barre,**		Leon County, FL	244
		PA	**552**	Wakulla County, FL	27
Salinas, CA.	**415**	Lackawanna County, PA.	210		
Monterey County, CA. . .	415	Luzerne County, PA . . .	313	**Tampa-St. Petersburg-**	
		Wyoming County, PA . . .	28	**Clearwater, FL.**	**2,588**
Salisbury, MD	**115**			Hernando County, FL. . .	150
Somerset County, MD . .	26	**Seattle-Tacoma-Bellevue,**		Hillsborough County, FL	1,101
Wicomico County, MD . .	89	**WA**	**3,167**	Pasco County, FL	408
		Seattle-Bellevue-Everett,		Pinellas County, FL	929
Salt Lake City, UT	**1,019**	**WA**	**2,421**		
Salt Lake County, UT. . .	935	King County, WA.	1,777	**Terre Haute, IN**	**169**
Summit County, UT	34	Snohomish County, WA .	644	Clay County, IN.	27
Tooele County, UT.	50	**Tacoma, WA**	**745**	Sullivan County, IN	22
		Pierce County, WA.	745	Vermillion County, IN . . .	17
San Angelo, TX.	**106**			Vigo County, IN.	103
Irion County, TX	2	**Sheboygan, WI**	**114**		
Tom Green County, TX. .	104	Sheboygan County, WI. .	114	**Texarkana, TX-Texarkana,**	
				AR	**133**
San Antonio, TX	**1,854**	**Sherman-Denison, TX.**	**116**	Miller County, AR.	42
Atascosa County, TX . . .	43	Grayson County, TX. . . .	116	Bowie County, TX	90
Bandera County, TX . . .	20				
Bexar County, TX	1,494	**Shreveport-Bossier City,**		**Toledo, OH**	**658**
Comal County, TX	92	**LA**	**382**	Fulton County, OH.	43
Guadalupe County, TX. .	100	Bossier Parish, LA. . . .	104	Lucas County, OH	451
Kendall County, TX	27	Caddo Parish, LA	252	Ottawa County, OH	41
		De Soto Parish, LA	26	Wood County, OH	123

U.S. Census Bureau, Statistical Abstract of the United States: 2006

Metropolitan statistical area / Metropolitan division / Component county	Population, 2004 (1,000)
Topeka, KS	**228**
Jackson County, KS	13
Jefferson County, KS	19
Osage County, KS	17
Shawnee County, KS	172
Wabaunsee County, KS	7
Trenton-Ewing, NJ	**365**
Mercer County, NJ	365
Tucson, AZ	**907**
Pima County, AZ	907
Tulsa, OK	**882**
Creek County, OK	69
Okmulgee County, OK	40
Osage County, OK	45
Pawnee County, OK	17
Rogers County, OK	79
Tulsa County, OK	569
Wagoner County, OK	63
Tuscaloosa, AL	**195**
Greene County, AL	10
Hale County, AL	18
Tuscaloosa County, AL	167
Tyler, TX	**186**
Smith County, TX	186
Utica-Rome, NY	**299**
Herkimer County, NY	64
Oneida County, NY	235
Valdosta, GA	**124**
Brooks County, GA	16
Echols County, GA	4
Lanier County, GA	7
Lowndes County, GA	96
Vallejo-Fairfield, CA	**413**
Solano County, CA	413
Vero Beach, FL	**124**
Indian River County, FL	124
Victoria, TX	**113**
Calhoun County, TX	21
Goliad County, TX	7
Victoria County, TX	86
Vineland-Millville-Bridgeton, NJ	**151**
Cumberland County, NJ	151
Virginia Beach-Norfolk-Newport News, VA-NC	**1,644**
Currituck County, NC	22
Gloucester County, VA	37
Isle of Wight County, VA	33
James City County, VA	56
Mathews County, VA	9
Surry County, VA	7
York County, VA	61

Metropolitan statistical area / Metropolitan division / Component county	Population, 2004 (1,000)
Virginia Beach-Norfolk-Newport News, VA-NC, Con.	
Chesapeake city, VA	215
Hampton city, VA	146
Newport News city, VA	182
Norfolk city, VA	238
Poquoson city, VA	12
Portsmouth city, VA	99
Suffolk city, VA	77
Virginia Beach city, VA	440
Williamsburg city, VA	11
Visalia-Porterville, CA	**402**
Tulare County, CA	402
Waco, TX	**222**
McLennan County, TX	222
Warner Robins, GA	**124**
Houston County, GA	124
Washington-Arlington-Alexandria, DC-VA-MD-WV.	**5,140**
Bethesda-Gaithersburg-Frederick, MD	**1,139**
Frederick County, MD	218
Montgomery County, MD	922
Washington-Arlington-Alexandria, DC-VA-MD-WV	**4,000**
District of Columbia, DC	554
Calvert County, MD	86
Charles County, MD	136
Prince George's County, MD	843
Arlington County, VA	186
Clarke County, VA	14
Fairfax County, VA	1,003
Fauquier County, VA	63
Loudoun County, VA	239
Prince William County, VA	337
Spotsylvania County, VA	112
Stafford County, VA	115
Warren County, VA	34
Alexandria city, VA	128
Fairfax city, VA	22
Falls Church city, VA	11
Fredericksburg city, VA	20
Manassas city, VA	38
Manassas Park city, VA	12
Jefferson County, WV	48
Waterloo-Cedar Falls, IA	**162**
Black Hawk County, IA	126
Bremer County, IA	23
Grundy County, IA	12
Wausau, WI	**128**
Marathon County, WI	128

Metropolitan statistical area / Metropolitan division / Component county	Population, 2004 (1,000)
Weirton-Steubenville, WV-OH	**128**
Jefferson County, OH	71
Brooke County, WV	25
Hancock County, WV	32
Wenatchee, WA	**103**
Chelan County, WA	69
Douglas County, WA	34
Wheeling, WV-OH	**149**
Belmont County, OH	69
Marshall County, WV	35
Ohio County, WV	45
Wichita, KS	**585**
Butler County, KS	62
Harvey County, KS	34
Sedgwick County, KS	464
Sumner County, KS	25
Wichita Falls, TX	**148**
Archer County, TX	9
Clay County, TX	11
Wichita County, TX	127
Williamsport, PA	**119**
Lycoming County, PA	119
Wilmington, NC	**303**
Brunswick County, NC	85
New Hanover County, NC	174
Pender County, NC	45
Winchester, VA-WV	**113**
Frederick County, VA	67
Winchester city, VA	25
Hampshire County, WV	22
Winston-Salem, NC	**442**
Davie County, NC	38
Forsyth County, NC	321
Stokes County, NC	45
Yadkin County, NC	37
Worcester, MA	**779**
Worcester County, MA	779
Yakima, WA	**229**
Yakima County, WA	229
York-Hanover, PA	**402**
York County, PA	402
Youngstown-Warren-Boardman, OH-PA	**590**
Mahoning County, OH	250
Trumbull County, OH	220
Mercer County, PA	120
Yuba City, CA	**151**
Sutter County, CA	87
Yuba County, CA	65
Yuma, AZ	**176**
Yuma County, AZ	176

[1] The portion of Sullivan city in Crawford County, Missouri, is legally part of the St. Louis, MO-IL MSA. The estimate shown here for the St. Louis, MO-IL Metropolitan Statistical Area does not include this area.

Source: U.S. Census Bureau, unpublished data.

932   Appendix II

U.S. Census Bureau. Statistical Abstract of the United States: 2006

Table B. Micropolitan Statistical Areas and Components as of November 2004

[Population as of July 2004. 55 represents 55,000. All micropolitan areas are arranged alphabetically]

Micropolitan statistical area / Component county	Population, 2004 (1,000)	Micropolitan statistical area / Component county	Population, 2004 (1,000)	Micropolitan statistical area / Component county	Population, 2004 (1,000)
Abbeville, LA	55	Astoria, OR	36	Big Rapids, MI	42
Vermilion Parish, LA	55	Clatsop County, OR	36	Mecosta County, MI	42
Aberdeen, SD	39	Atchison, KS	17	Big Spring, TX	33
Brown County, SD	35	Atchison County, KS	17	Howard County, TX	33
Edmunds County, SD	4	Athens, OH	63	Bishop, CA	18
Aberdeen, WA	70	Athens County, OH	63	Inyo County, CA	18
Grays Harbor County, WA	70	Athens, TN	51	Blackfoot, ID	43
Ada, OK	35	McMinn County, TN	51	Bingham County, ID	43
Pontotoc County, OK	35	Athens, TX	79	Bloomsburg-Berwick, PA	83
Adrian, MI	102	Henderson County, TX	79	Columbia County, PA	65
Lenawee County, MI	102	Auburn, IN	42	Montour County, PA	18
Alamogordo, NM	63	De Kalb County, IN	42	Bluefield, WV-VA	107
Otero County, NM	63	Auburn, NY	82	Tazewell County, VA	45
Albany-Lebanon, OR	107	Cayuga County, NY	82	Mercer County, WV	62
Linn County, OR	107	Augusta-Waterville, ME	121	Blytheville, AR	48
Albemarle, NC	59	Kennebec County, ME	121	Mississippi County, AR	48
Stanly County, NC	59	Austin, MN	39	Bogalusa, LA	44
Albert Lea, MN	32	Mower County, MN	39	Washington Parish, LA	44
Freeborn County, MN	32	Bainbridge, GA	29	Bonham, TX	33
Albertville, AL	85	Decatur County, GA	29	Fannin County, TX	33
Marshall County, AL	85	Baraboo, WI	57	Boone, IA	26
Alexander City, AL	52	Sauk County, WI	57	Boone County, IA	26
Coosa County, AL	11	Barre, VT	59	Boone, NC	42
Tallapoosa County, AL	41	Washington County, VT	59	Watauga County, NC	42
Alexandria, MN	35	Bartlesville, OK	49	Borger, TX	23
Douglas County, MN	35	Washington County, OK	49	Hutchinson County, TX	23
Alice, TX	41	Bastrop, LA	31	Bozeman, MT	76
Jim Wells County, TX	41	Morehouse Parish, LA	31	Gallatin County, MT	76
Allegan, MI	112	Batavia, NY	60	Bradford, PA	45
Allegan County, MI	112	Genesee County, NY	60	McKean County, PA	45
Alma, MI	42	Batesville, AR	35	Brainerd, MN	88
Gratiot County, MI	42	Independence County, AR	35	Cass County, MN	28
Alpena, MI	31	Bay City, TX	38	Crow Wing County, MN	59
Alpena County, MI	31	Matagorda County, TX	38	Branson, MO	73
Altus, OK	27	Beatrice, NE	23	Stone County, MO	31
Jackson County, OK	27	Gage County, NE	23	Taney County, MO	42
Americus, GA	37	Beaver Dam, WI	88	Brenham, TX	31
Schley County, GA	4	Dodge County, WI	88	Washington County, TX	31
Sumter County, GA	33	Beckley, WV	79	Brevard, NC	30
Amsterdam, NY	49	Raleigh County, WV	79	Transylvania County, NC	30
Montgomery County, NY	49	Bedford, IN	46	Brigham City, UT	45
Andrews, TX	13	Lawrence County, IN	46	Box Elder County, UT	45
Andrews County, TX	13	Beeville, TX	33	Brookhaven, MS	34
Angola, IN	34	Bee County, TX	33	Lincoln County, MS	34
Steuben County, IN	34	Bellefontaine, OH	47	Brookings, OR	22
Arcadia, FL	35	Logan County, OH	47	Curry County, OR	22
DeSoto County, FL	35	Bemidji, MN	42	Brookings, SD	28
Ardmore, OK	56	Beltrami County, MN	42	Brookings County, SD	28
Carter County, OK	47	Bennettsville, SC	28	Brownsville, TN	20
Love County, OK	9	Marlboro County, SC	28	Haywood County, TN	20
Arkadelphia, AR	23	Bennington, VT	37	Brownwood, TX	38
Clark County, AR	23	Bennington County, VT	37	Brown County, TX	38
Ashland, OH	54	Berlin, NH-VT	40	Bucyrus, OH	46
Ashland County, OH	54	Coos County, NH	34	Crawford County, OH	46
Ashtabula, OH	103	Essex County, VT	7		
Ashtabula County, OH	103				

U.S. Census Bureau, Statistical Abstract of the United States: 2006

Micropolitan statistical area / Component county	Population 2004 (1,000)	Micropolitan statistical area / Component county	Population 2004 (1,000)	Micropolitan statistical area / Component county	Population 2004 (1,000)
Burley, ID	41	**Claremont, NH**	42	**Crowley, LA**	59
Cassia County, ID	21	Sullivan County, NH	42	Acadia Parish, LA	59
Burley, ID, Con.		**Clarksburg, WV**	92	**Cullman, AL**	79
Minidoka County, ID	19	Doddridge County, WV	7	Cullman County, AL	79
Burlington, IA-IL	49	Harrison County, WV	68	**Culpeper, VA**	40
Henderson County, IL	8	Taylor County, WV	16	Culpeper County, VA	40
Des Moines County, IA	41	**Clarksdale, MS**	29	**Danville, KY**	53
Butte-Silver Bow, MT	33	Coahoma County, MS	29	Boyle County, KY	28
Silver Bow County, MT	33	**Clearlake, CA**	64	Lincoln County, KY	25
Cadillac, MI.	47	Lake County, CA	64	**Daphne-Fairhope, AL**	157
Missaukee County, MI	15	**Cleveland, MS**	39	Baldwin County, AL	157
Wexford County, MI	31	Bolivar County, MS	39	**Decatur, IN**	34
Calhoun, GA	49	**Clewiston, FL**	38	Adams County, IN	34
Gordon County, GA	49	Hendry County, FL	38	**Defiance, OH**	39
Cambridge, MD	31	**Clinton, IA**	50	Defiance County, OH	39
Dorchester County, MD	31	Clinton County, IA	50	**Del Rio, TX**	47
Cambridge, OH	41	**Clovis, NM**	46	Val Verde County, TX	47
Guernsey County, OH	41	Curry County, NM	46	**Deming, NM**	26
Camden, AR	33	**Coffeyville, KS**	35	Luna County, NM	26
Calhoun County, AR	6	Montgomery County, KS	35	**De Ridder, LA**	34
Ouachita County, AR	27	**Coldwater, MI**	46	Beauregard Parish, LA	34
Campbellsville, KY	23	Branch County, MI	46	**Dickinson, ND.**	23
Taylor County, KY	23	**Columbia, TN**	75	Billings County, ND	1
Canon City, CO.	47	Maury County, TN	75	Stark County, ND	22
Fremont County, CO	47	**Columbus, MS**	60	**Dillon, SC**	31
Canton, IL.	38	Lowndes County, MS.	60	Dillon County, SC	31
Fulton County, IL.	38	**Columbus, NE**	31	**Dixon, IL.**	36
Cape Girardeau-Jackson, MO-IL	92	Platte County, NE	31	Lee County, IL	36
Alexander County, IL	9	**Concord, NH**	146	**Dodge City, KS**	33
Bollinger County, MO.	12	Merrimack County, NH	146	Ford County, KS	33
Cape Girardeau County, MO	71	**Connersville, IN**	25	**Douglas, GA.**	47
Carbondale, IL	58	Fayette County, IN	25	Atkinson County, GA	8
Jackson County, IL	58	**Cookeville, TN**	98	Coffee County, GA	39
Carlsbad-Artesia, NM	52	Jackson County, TN	11	**Dublin, GA**	56
Eddy County, NM	52	Overton County, TN.	20	Johnson County, GA	10
Cedar City, UT	36	Putnam County, TN.	66	Laurens County, GA	47
Iron County, UT	36	**Coos Bay, OR.**	64	**DuBois, PA.**	83
Cedartown, GA	40	Coos County, OR	64	Clearfield County, PA.	83
Polk County, GA	40	**Corbin, KY**	38	**Dumas, TX**	20
Celina, OH	41	Whitley County, KY	38	Moore County, TX.	20
Mercer County, OH	41	**Cordele, GA**	22	**Duncan, OK**	43
Central City, KY	32	Crisp County, GA	22	Stephens County, OK	43
Muhlenberg County, KY	32	**Corinth, MS**	35	**Dunn, NC**	102
Centralia, IL	41	Alcorn County, MS	35	Harnett County, NC	102
Marion County, IL	41	**Cornelia, GA.**	39	**Durango, CO.**	46
Centralia, WA	72	Habersham County, GA	39	La Plata County, CO	46
Lewis County, WA	72	**Corning, NY**	99	**Durant, OK**	38
Chambersburg, PA	135	Steuben County, NY	99	Bryan County, OK.	38
Franklin County, PA.	135	**Corsicana, TX**	48	**Dyersburg, TN**	38
Charleston-Mattoon, IL	63	Navarro County, TX.	48	Dyer County, TN.	38
Coles County, IL	52	**Cortland, NY.**	49	**Eagle Pass, TX**	50
Cumberland County, IL	11	Cortland County, NY	49	Maverick County, TX	50
Chester, SC	34	**Coshocton, OH.**	37	**East Liverpool-Salem, OH**	112
Chester County, SC.	34	Coshocton County, OH	37	Columbiana County, OH	112
Chillicothe, OH	74	**Crawfordsville, IN**	38	**Easton, MD.**	35
Ross County, OH	74	Montgomery County, IN	38	Talbot County, MD.	35
City of The Dalles, OR	24	**Crescent City, CA**	28	**East Stroudsburg, PA**	159
Wasco County, OR	24	Del Norte County, CA	28	Monroe County, PA	159
		Crossville, TN	50		
		Cumberland County, TN.	50		

934   Appendix II

Micropolitan statistical area / Component county	Population, 2004 (1,000)	Micropolitan statistical area / Component county	Population, 2004 (1,000)	Micropolitan statistical area / Component county	Population, 2004 (1,000)
Edwards, CO	54	**Fort Dodge, IA**	39	**Great Bend, KS**	27
Eagle County, CO	46	Webster County, IA	39	Barton County, KS	27
Lake County, CO	8	**Fort Leonard Wood, MO** ...	44	**Greeneville, TN**	65
Effingham, IL	35	Pulaski County, MO	44	Greene County, TN	65
Effingham County, IL	35	**Fort Morgan, CO**	28	**Greensburg, IN**	25
El Campo, TX	42	Morgan County, CO	28	Decatur County, IN	25
Wharton County, TX	42	**Fort Payne, AL**	67	**Greenville, MS**	60
El Dorado, AR	45	DeKalb County, AL	67	Washington County, MS...	60
Union County, AR	45	**Fort Polk South, LA**	50	**Greenville, OH**	53
Elizabeth City, NC	57	Vernon Parish, LA	50	Darke County, OH	53
Camden County, NC	8	**Fort Valley, GA**	25	**Greenwood, MS**	47
Pasquotank County, NC...	37	Peach County, GA	25	Carroll County, MS	11
Perquimans County, NC...	12	**Frankfort, IN**	34	Leflore County, MS	36
Elk City, OK	19	Clinton County, IN......	34	**Greenwood, SC**	68
Beckham County, OK	19	**Frankfort, KY**	68	Greenwood County, SC...	68
Elko, NV	46	Anderson County, KY ...	20	**Grenada, MS**	23
Elko County, NV	45	Franklin County, KY.....	48	Grenada County, MS.....	23
Eureka County, NV	1	**Freeport, IL**	48	**Guymon, OK**	20
Ellensburg, WA	36	Stephenson County, IL ...	48	Texas County, OK	20
Kittitas County, WA	36	**Fremont, NE**	36	**Hammond, LA**	105
Emporia, KS	39	Dodge County, NE	36	Tangipahoa Parish, LA....	105
Chase County, KS.......	3	**Fremont, OH**	62	**Hannibal, MO**	38
Lyon County, KS........	36	Sandusky County, OH....	62	Marion County, MO	28
Enid, OK	57	**Gaffney, SC**	54	Ralls County, MO	10
Garfield County, OK	57	Cherokee County, SC....	54	**Harriman, TN**	53
Enterprise-Ozark, AL	94	**Gainesville, TX**	39	Roane County, TN	53
Coffee County, AL	45	Cooke County, TX......	39	**Harrisburg, IL**	26
Dale County, AL	49	**Galesburg, IL**	72	Saline County, IL........	26
Escanaba, MI	38	Knox County, IL	54	**Harrison, AR**	44
Delta County, MI........	38	Warren County, IL.......	18	Boone County, AR.......	35
Espanola, NM	41	**Gallup, NM**	72	Newton County, AR......	8
Rio Arriba County, NM...	41	McKinley County, NM	72	**Hastings, NE**	38
Eufaula, AL-GA	31	**Garden City, KS**	39	Adams County, NE	31
Barbour County, AL......	29	Finney County, KS	39	Clay County, NE	7
Quitman County, GA	2	**Gardnerville Ranchos, NV** ..	45	**Havre, MT**	16
Eureka-Arcata-Fortuna, CA .	129	Douglas County, NV	45	Hill County, MT	16
Humboldt County, CA	129	**Georgetown, SC**	60	**Hays, KS**	27
Evanston, WY	20	Georgetown County, SC ..	60	Ellis County, KS	27
Uinta County, WY	20	**Gettysburg, PA**	98	**Heber, UT**	18
Fairmont, MN	21	Adams County, PA	98	Wasatch County, UT	18
Martin County, MN	21	**Gillette, WY**	37	**Helena, MT**	69
Fairmont, WV	56	Campbell County, WY	37	Jefferson County, MT	11
Marion County, WV......	56	**Glasgow, KY**	50	Lewis and Clark County, MT	58
Fallon, NV	24	Barren County, KY	39	**Henderson, NC**	44
Churchill County, NV	24	Metcalfe County, KY.....	10	Vance County, NC.......	44
Faribault-Northfield, MN ...	60	**Gloversville, NY**	55	**Hereford, TX**	19
Rice County, MN........	60	Fulton County, NY.......	55	Deaf Smith County, TX ...	19
Farmington, MO	61	**Granbury, TX**	54	**Hilo, HI**	163
St. Francois County, MO ..	61	Hood County, TX	46	Hawaii County, HI	163
Fergus Falls, MN	58	Somervell County, TX	7	**Hilton Head Island-Beaufort, SC**	157
Otter Tail County, MN	58	**Grand Island, NE**	70	Beaufort County, SC	136
Findlay, OH	74	Hall County, NE	55	Jasper County, SC	21
Hancock County, OH.....	74	Howard County, NE......	7	**Hobbs, NM**	56
Fitzgerald, GA	27	Merrick County, NE	8	Lea County, NM	56
Ben Hill County, GA	17	**Grants, NM**	28	**Homosassa Springs, FL** ...	130
Irwin County, GA........	10	Cibola County, NM	28	Citrus County, FL	130
Forest City, NC	64	**Grants Pass, OR**	80	**Hood River, OR**	21
Rutherford County, NC ...	64	Josephine County, OR....	80	Hood River County, OR...	21
Forrest City, AR	28				
St. Francis County, AR ...	28				

U.S. Census Bureau, Statistical Abstract of the United States: 2006

Micropolitan statistical area Component county	Popu- lation, 2004 (1,000)	Micropolitan statistical area Component county	Popu- lation, 2004 (1,000)	Micropolitan statistical area Component county	Popu- lation, 2004 (1,000)
Hope, AR	33	Keene, NH	77	Lebanon, MO	34
Hempstead County, AR ...	23	Cheshire County, NH.....	77	Laclede County, MO	34
Nevada County, AR......	10				
		Kendallville, IN	47	Lebanon, NH-VT	171
Houghton, MI	38	Noble County, IN........	47	Grafton County, NH......	84
Houghton County, MI.....	36			Orange County, VT......	29
Keweenaw County, MI....	2	Kennett, MO	32	Windsor County, VT	58
		Dunklin County, MO	32		
Hudson, NY	64			Levelland, TX	23
Columbia County, NY ...	64	Keokuk-Fort Madison,		Hockley County, TX......	23
		IA-MO................	44		
Humboldt, TN	48	Lee County, IA	37	Lewisburg, PA	43
Gibson County, TN	48			Union County, PA	43
		Keokuk-Fort Madison,			
Huntingdon, PA	46	IA-MO, Con.		Lewisburg, TN	28
Huntingdon County, PA ...	46	Clark County, MO	7	Marshall County, TN	28
Huntington, IN	38	Kerrville, TX	46	Lewistown, PA	46
Huntington County, IN	38	Kerr County, TX	46	Mifflin County, PA	46
Huntsville, TX...........	62	Ketchikan, AK...........	13	Lexington, NE...........	27
Walker County, TX	62	Ketchikan Gateway		Dawson County, NE	25
		Borough, AK........	13	Gosper County, NE......	2
Huron, SD..............	16				
Beadle County, SD	16	Key West-Marathon, FL....	78	Lexington Park, MD	95
		Monroe County, FL	78	St. Mary's County, MD....	95
Hutchinson, KS..........	64				
Reno County, KS	64	Kill Devil Hills, NC	34	Liberal, KS	23
		Dare County, NC........	34	Seward County, KS......	23
Hutchinson, MN	36				
McLeod County, MN	36	Kingsville, TX...........	32	Lincoln, IL	31
		Kenedy County, TX	(Z)	Logan County, IL........	31
Indiana, PA.............	89	Kleberg County, TX......	31		
Indiana County, PA	89			Lincolnton, NC..........	68
		Kinston, NC	58	Lincoln County, NC......	68
Indianola, MS	33	Lenoir County, NC.......	58		
Sunflower County, MS....	33			Lock Haven, PA	37
		Kirksville, MO...........	29	Clinton County, PA	37
Iron Mountain, MI-WI......	32	Adair County, MO	25		
Dickinson County, MI.....	27	Schuyler County, MO.....	4	Logansport, IN	40
Florence County, WI	5			Cass County, IN	40
		Klamath Falls, OR........	65		
Jackson, WY-ID	26	Klamath County, OR	65	London, KY	56
Teton County, ID	7			Laurel County, KY.......	56
Teton County, WY......	19	Kodiak, AK.............	13		
		Kodiak Island Borough, AK.	13	Los Alamos, NM	19
Jacksonville, IL..........	41			Los Alamos County, NM...	19
Morgan County, IL.......	36	Laconia, NH	61		
Scott County, IL	5	Belknap County, NH	61	Lufkin, TX..............	81
				Angelina County, TX	81
Jacksonville, TX	48	La Follette, TN	41		
Cherokee County, TX	48	Campbell County, TN	41	Lumberton, NC..........	126
				Robeson County, NC.....	126
Jamestown, ND..........	21	La Grande, OR	24		
Stutsman County, ND ...	21	Union County, OR......	24	Macomb, IL.............	32
				McDonough County, IL ...	32
Jamestown-Dunkirk-		LaGrange, GA...........	61		
Fredonia, NY...........	137	Troup County, GA.......	61	Madison, IN	32
Chautauqua County, NY ..	137			Jefferson County, IN	32
		Lake City, FL	62		
Jasper, IN..............	54	Columbia County, FL.....	62	Madisonville, KY.........	47
Dubois County, IN.......	41			Hopkins County, KY	47
Pike County, IN.........	13	Lake Havasu City-Kingman,			
		AZ	180	Magnolia, AR	25
Jennings, LA	31	Mohave County, AZ......	180	Columbia County, AR	25
Jefferson Davis Parish, LA.	31				
		Lamesa, TX	14	Malone, NY.............	51
Jesup, GA	28	Dawson County, TX......	14	Franklin County, NY	51
Wayne County, GA	28				
		Lancaster, SC	63	Manhattan, KS	107
Juneau, AK.............	31	Lancaster County, SC	63	Geary County, KS.......	25
Juneau Borough, AK.....	31			Pottawatomie County, KS..	19
		Laramie, WY............	31	Riley County, KS.......	63
Kahului-Wailuku, HI	138	Albany County, WY	31		
Maui County, HI	138			Manitowoc, WI	82
		Las Vegas, NM	30	Manitowoc County, WI....	82
Kalispell, MT............	81	San Miguel County, NM...	30		
Flathead County, MT.....	81			Mankato-North Mankato,	
		Laurel, MS	84	MN	88
Kapaa, HI..............	62	Jasper County, MS	18	Blue Earth County, MN ...	57
Kauai County, HI........	62	Jones County, MS.......	66	Nicollet County, MN......	31
Kearney, NE	50	Laurinburg, NC..........	36	Marinette, WI-MI	69
Buffalo County, NE	43	Scotland County, NC....	36	Menominee County, MI ...	25
Kearney County, NE	7			Marinette County, WI.....	43
		Lawrenceburg, TN	41		
		Lawrence County, TN	41		

936　Appendix II

Micropolitan statistical area Component county	Popu- lation, 2004 (1,000)	Micropolitan statistical area Component county	Popu- lation, 2004 (1,000)	Micropolitan statistical area Component county	Popu- lation, 2004 (1,000)
Marion, IN	72	**Minden, LA**	41	**New Bern, NC**	115
Grant County, IN	72	Webster Parish, LA	41	Craven County, NC	92
Marion, OH	66	**Mineral Wells, TX**	27	Jones County, NC	10
Marion County, OH	66	Palo Pinto County, TX	27	Pamlico County, NC	13
Marion-Herrin, IL	63	**Minot, ND**	64	**Newberry, SC**	37
Williamson County, IL	63	McHenry County, ND	6	Newberry County, SC	37
Marquette, MI	65	Renville County, ND	2	**New Castle, IN**	48
Marquette County, MI	65	Ward County, ND	56	Henry County, IN	48
Marshall, MN	25	**Mitchell, SD**	23	**New Castle, PA**	93
Lyon County, MN	25	Davison County, SD	19	Lawrence County, PA	93
Marshall, MO	23	Hanson County, SD	4	**New Iberia, LA**	74
Saline County, MO	23	**Moberly, MO**	25	Iberia Parish, LA	74
Marshall, TX	63	Randolph County, MO	25	**New Philadelphia-Dover, OH**	92
Harrison County, TX	63	**Monroe, WI**	35	Tuscarawas County, OH	92
Marshalltown, IA	40	Green County, WI	35	**Newport, TN**	35
Marshall County, IA	40	**Montrose, CO**	37	Cocke County, TN	35
Martin, TN	34	Montrose County, CO	37	**Newton, IA**	38
Weakley County, TN	34	**Morehead City, NC**	62	Jasper County, IA	38
Martinsville, VA	72	Carteret County, NC	62	**New Ulm, MN**	27
Henry County, VA	57	**Morgan City, LA**	52	Brown County, MN	27
Martinsville city, VA	15	St. Mary Parish, LA	52	**Nogales, AZ**	41
Maryville, MO	22	**Moscow, ID**	35	Santa Cruz County, AZ	41
Nodaway County, MO	22	Latah County, ID	35	**Norfolk, NE**	50
Mason City, IA	53	**Moses Lake, WA**	80	Madison County, NE	36
Cerro Gordo County, IA	45	Grant County, WA	80	Pierce County, NE	8
Worth County, IA	8	**Moultrie, GA**	44	Stanton County, NE	7
Mayfield, KY	37	Colquitt County, GA	44	**North Platte, NE**	36
Graves County, KY	37	**Mountain Home, AR**	40	Lincoln County, NE	35
Maysville, KY	31	Baxter County, AR	40	Logan County, NE	1
Lewis County, KY	14	**Mountain Home, ID**	29	McPherson County, NE	1
Mason County, KY	17	Elmore County, ID	29	**North Vernon, IN**	28
McAlester, OK	44	**Mount Airy, NC**	72	Jennings County, IN	28
Pittsburg County, OK	44	Surry County, NC	72	**North Wilkesboro, NC**	67
McComb, MS	53	**Mount Pleasant, MI**	64	Wilkes County, NC	67
Amite County, MS	13	Isabella County, MI	64	**Norwalk, OH**	60
Pike County, MS	39	**Mount Pleasant, TX**	29	Huron County, OH	60
McMinnville, TN	40	Titus County, TX	29	**Oak Harbor, WA**	79
Warren County, TN	40	**Mount Sterling, KY**	42	Island County, WA	79
McPherson, KS	29	Bath County, KY	12	**Oak Hill, WV**	47
McPherson County, KS	29	Menifee County, KY	7	Fayette County, WV	47
Meadville, PA	90	Montgomery County, KY	24	**Ocean Pines, MD**	49
Crawford County, PA	90	**Mount Vernon, IL**	49	Worcester County, MD	49
Menomonie, WI	41	Hamilton County, IL	8	**Ogdensburg-Massena, NY**	111
Dunn County, WI	41	Jefferson County, IL	40	St. Lawrence County, NY	111
Meridian, MS	105	**Mount Vernon, OH**	58	**Oil City, PA**	56
Clarke County, MS	18	Knox County, OH	58	Venango County, PA	56
Kemper County, MS	10	**Murray, KY**	35	**Okeechobee, FL**	39
Lauderdale County, MS	77	Calloway County, KY	35	Okeechobee County, FL	39
Merrill, WI	30	**Muscatine, IA**	55	**Olean, NY**	83
Lincoln County, WI	30	Louisa County, IA	12	Cattaraugus County, NY	83
Mexico, MO	26	Muscatine County, IA	43	**Oneonta, NY**	63
Audrain County, MO	26	**Muskogee, OK**	71	Otsego County, NY	63
Miami, OK	33	Muskogee County, OK	71	**Ontario, OR-ID**	53
Ottawa County, OK	33	**Nacogdoches, TX**	60	Payette County, ID	22
Middlesborough, KY	30	Nacogdoches County, TX	60	Malheur County, OR	31
Bell County, KY	30	**Natchez, MS-LA**	52	**Opelousas-Eunice, LA**	90
Midland, MI	85	Concordia Parish, LA	20	St. Landry Parish, LA	90
Midland County, MI	85	Adams County, MS	33	**Orangeburg, SC**	91
Milledgeville, GA	55	**Natchitoches, LA**	39	Orangeburg County, SC	91
Baldwin County, GA	45	Natchitoches Parish, LA	39		
Hancock County, GA	10				

U.S. Census Bureau, Statistical Abstract of the United States: 2006

Micropolitan statistical area Component county	Popu- lation, 2004 (1,000)	Micropolitan statistical area Component county	Popu- lation, 2004 (1,000)	Micropolitan statistical area Component county	Popu- lation, 2004 (1,000)
Oskaloosa, IA.	22	**Plainview, TX**	36	**Rockland, ME**.	41
Mahaska County, IA	22	Hale County, TX	36	Knox County, ME	41
Ottawa-Streator, IL	154	**Platteville, WI**	50	**Rock Springs, WY**.	38
Bureau County, IL	35	Grant County, WI	50	Sweetwater County, WY . .	38
La Salle County, IL	112				
Putnam County, IL	6	**Plattsburgh, NY**	82	**Rolla, MO**	42
		Clinton County, NY	82	Phelps County, MO	42
Ottumwa, IA	36				
Wapello County, IA	36	**Plymouth, IN**.	47	**Roseburg, OR**.	103
		Marshall County, IN.	47	Douglas County, OR	103
Owatonna, MN	35				
Steele County, MN	35	**Point Pleasant, WV-OH**	57	**Roswell, NM**.	62
		Gallia County, OH.	31	Chaves County, NM	62
Owosso, MI	73	Mason County, WV	26		
Shiawassee County, MI . . .	73			**Russellville, AR**	77
		Ponca City, OK.	47	Pope County, AR	56
Oxford, MS.	41	Kay County, OK	47	Yell County, AR.	21
Lafayette County, MS	41				
		Pontiac, IL	39	**Ruston, LA**	58
Paducah, KY-IL.	98	Livingston County, IL.	39	Jackson Parish, LA	15
Massac County, IL	15			Lincoln Parish, LA.	42
Ballard County, KY	8	**Poplar Bluff, MO**.	41		
Livingston County, KY	10	Butler County, MO.	41	**Rutland, VT**	64
McCracken County, KY . . .	65			Rutland County, VT	64
		Portales, NM.	18		
Pahrump, NV	38	Roosevelt County, NM	18	**Safford, AZ**.	40
Nye County, NV	38			Graham County, AZ.	33
		Port Angeles, WA	68	Greenlee County, AZ.	8
Palatka, FL.	73	Clallam County, WA	68		
Putnam County, FL	73			**St. Marys, GA**.	45
		Portsmouth, OH	77	Camden County, GA	45
Palestine, TX	56	Scioto County, OH	77		
Anderson County, TX	56			**St. Marys, PA**	34
		Pottsville, PA	148	Elk County, PA	34
Palm Coast, FL.	69	Schuylkill County, PA.	148		
Flagler County, FL.	69			**Salina, KS**.	60
		Price, UT	20	Ottawa County, KS	6
Pampa, TX	22	Carbon County, UT	20	Saline County, KS.	54
Gray County, TX.	21				
Roberts County, TX.	1	**Prineville, OR**	21	**Salisbury, NC**	134
		Crook County, OR.	21	Rowan County, NC	134
Paragould, AR	39				
Greene County, AR	39	**Pullman, WA**.	40	**Sanford, NC**	49
		Whitman County, WA.	40	Lee County, NC	49
Paris, TN	32				
Henry County, TN	32	**Quincy, IL-MO**	77	**Sault Ste. Marie, MI**.	39
		Adams County, IL	67	Chippewa County, MI	39
Paris, TX	50	Lewis County, MO.	10		
Lamar County, TX.	50			**Sayre, PA**	63
		Raymondville, TX	20	Bradford County, PA	63
Parsons, KS	22	Willacy County, TX	20		
Labette County, KS.	22			**Scottsbluff, NE**.	37
		Red Bluff, CA	60	Banner County, NE	1
Payson, AZ.	51	Tehama County, CA	60	Scotts Bluff County, NE . . .	37
Gila County, AZ	51				
		Red Wing, MN.	45	**Scottsboro, AL**.	54
Pecos, TX.	12	Goodhue County, MN	45	Jackson County, AL.	54
Reeves County, TX	12				
		Rexburg, ID	43	**Scottsburg, IN**	24
Pella, IA	33	Fremont County, ID	12	Scott County, IN	24
Marion County, IA	33	Madison County, ID. . . .	31		
				Seaford, DE	172
Pendleton-Hermiston, OR . .	85	**Richmond, IN**	70	Sussex County, DE	172
Morrow County, OR.	12	Wayne County, IN.	70		
Umatilla County, OR	73			**Searcy, AR**	71
		Richmond-Berea, KY.	93	White County, AR	71
Peru, IN	36	Madison County, KY . .	76		
Miami County, IN	36	Rockcastle County, KY .	17	**Sebring, FL**.	93
				Highlands County, FL	93
Phoenix Lake-Cedar Ridge,		**Rio Grande City-Roma, TX** .	60		
CA	57	Starr County, TX	60	**Sedalia, MO**	40
Tuolumne County, CA . . .	57			Pettis County, MO.	40
		Riverton, WY	36		
Picayune, MS	52	Fremont County, WY . .	36	**Selinsgrove, PA**	38
Pearl River County, MS . . .	52			Snyder County, PA	38
		Roanoke Rapids, NC.	78		
Pierre, SD.	20	Halifax County, NC	56	**Selma, AL**.	45
Hughes County, SD.	17	Northampton County, NC	22	Dallas County, AL	45
Stanley County, SD.	3				
		Rochelle, IL	54	**Seneca, SC**.	69
Pierre Part, LA	23	Ogle County, IL.	54	Oconee County, SC	69
Assumption Parish, LA . . .	23				
		Rockingham, NC.	47	**Seneca Falls, NY**.	35
Pittsburg, KS	38	Richmond County, NC . .	47	Seneca County, NY.	35
Crawford County, KS.	38				

938 Appendix II

Micropolitan statistical area Component county	Population, 2004 (1,000)	Micropolitan statistical area Component county	Population, 2004 (1,000)	Micropolitan statistical area Component county	Population, 2004 (1,000)
Sevierville, TN	77	**Storm Lake, IA**	20	**Twin Falls, ID**	87
Sevier County, TN.	77	Buena Vista County, IA . . .	20	Jerome County, ID	19
Seymour, IN	42	**Sturgis, MI**	63	Twin Falls County, ID.	68
Jackson County, IN	42	St. Joseph County, MI	63	**Ukiah, CA**	89
Shawnee, OK	67	**Sulphur Springs, TX**	33	Mendocino County, CA . . .	89
Pottawatomie County, OK .	67	Hopkins County, TX.	33	**Union, SC**	29
Shelby, NC	98	**Summerville, GA**	27	Union County, SC	29
Cleveland County, NC	98	Chattooga County, GA. . . .	27	**Union City, TN-KY**	40
Shelbyville, TN	41	**Sunbury, PA**	93	Fulton County, KY.	7
Bedford County, TN.	41	Northumberland County, PA	93	**Union City, TN-KY, Con.**	
Shelton, WA	54			Obion County, TN	32
Mason County, WA	54	**Susanville, CA**	35	**Urbana, OH.**	40
Sheridan, WY	27	Lassen County, CA	35	Champaign County, OH. . .	40
Sheridan County, WY	27	**Sweetwater, TX**	15	**Uvalde, TX**	27
Sidney, OH	49	Nolan County, TX	15	Uvalde County, TX	27
Shelby County, OH	49	**Tahlequah, OK**	44	**Valley, AL**	36
Sierra Vista-Douglas, AZ . . .	124	Cherokee County, OK	44	Chambers County, AL	36
Cochise County, AZ.	124	**Talladega-Sylacauga, AL** . . .	80	**Van Wert, OH**	29
Sikeston, MO	41	Talladega County, AL.	80	Van Wert County, OH	29
Scott County, MO	41	**Tallulah, LA**	13	**Vermillion, SD.**	13
Silver City, NM	29	Madison Parish, LA.	13	Clay County, SD	13
Grant County, NM.	29	**Taos, NM**	31	**Vernal, UT.**	27
Silverthorne, CO	25	Taos County, NM	31	Uintah County, UT.	27
Summit County, CO.	25	**Taylorville, IL**	35	**Vernon, TX**	14
Snyder, TX	16	Christian County, IL.	35	Wilbarger County, TX	14
Scurry County, TX.	16	**The Villages, FL**	61	**Vicksburg, MS**	49
Somerset, KY	59	Sumter County, FL	61	Warren County, MS.	49
Pulaski County, KY	59	**Thomaston, GA.**	28	**Vidalia, GA.**	36
Somerset, PA	80	Upson County, GA	28	Montgomery County, GA . .	9
Somerset County, PA	80	**Thomasville, GA.**	44	Toombs County, GA	27
Southern Pines-Pinehurst, NC	80	Thomas County, GA	44	**Vincennes, IN**	38
Moore County, NC	80	**Thomasville-Lexington, NC** .	154	Knox County, IN	38
		Davidson County, NC	154	**Wabash, IN.**	34
Spearfish, SD	22	**Tiffin, OH**	58	Wabash County, IN	34
Lawrence County, SD	22	Seneca County, OH	58	**Wahpeton, ND-MN.**	24
Spencer, IA.	17	**Tifton, GA.**	40	Wilkin County, MN.	7
Clay County, IA.	17	Tift County, GA	40	Richland County, ND	18
Spirit Lake, IA.	17	**Toccoa, GA.**	25	**Walla Walla, WA**	57
Dickinson County, IA	17	Stephens County, GA	25	Walla Walla County, WA . .	57
Starkville, MS	41	**Torrington, CT**	189	**Walterboro, SC**	40
Oktibbeha County, MS. . . .	41	Litchfield County, CT	189	Colleton County, SC	40
Statesboro, GA.	60	**Traverse City, MI.**	140	**Wapakoneta, OH.**	47
Bulloch County, GA.	60	Benzie County, MI.	17	Auglaize County, OH.	47
Statesville-Mooresville, NC .	137	Grand Traverse County, MI	83	**Warren, PA**	43
Iredell County, NC.	137	Kalkaska County, MI	17	Warren County, PA	43
Staunton-Waynesboro, VA. .	113	Leelanau County, MI	22	**Warrensburg, MO**	51
Augusta County, VA	69	**Troy, AL**	29	Johnson County, MO.	51
Staunton city, VA.	24	Pike County, AL	29	**Warsaw, IN**	76
Waynesboro city, VA	21	**Truckee-Grass Valley, CA** . .	98	Kosciusko County, IN	76
Stephenville, TX	34	Nevada County, CA.	98	**Washington, IN.**	30
Erath County, TX	34	**Tullahoma, TN**	97	Daviess County, IN	30
Sterling, CO	21	Coffee County, TN.	50	**Washington, NC**	46
Logan County, CO	21	Franklin County, TN.	41	Beaufort County, NC	46
Sterling, IL	60	Moore County, TN.	6	**Washington, OH**	28
Whiteside County, IL	60	**Tupelo, MS**	130	Fayette County, OH.	28
Stevens Point, WI	67	Itawamba County, MS	23	**Watertown, SD**	31
Portage County, WI.	67	Lee County, MS	78	Codington County, SD	26
Stillwater, OK	70	Pontotoc County, MS.	28	Hamlin County, SD	6
Payne County, OK	70	**Tuskegee, AL**	23		
		Macon County, AL.	23		

U.S. Census Bureau, Statistical Abstract of the United States: 2006

Micropolitan statistical area Component county	Popu-lation, 2004 (1,000)	Micropolitan statistical area Component county	Popu-lation, 2004 (1,000)	Micropolitan statistical area Component county	Popu-lation, 2004 (1,000)
Watertown-Fort Atkinson, WI	78	**Whitewater, WI**	98	**Wisconsin Rapids-Marshfield, WI**	75
Jefferson County, WI	78	Walworth County, WI	98	Wood County, WI	75
		Willimantic, CT	114	**Woodward, OK**	19
Watertown-Fort Drum, NY . .	111	Windham County, CT	114	Woodward County, OK . . .	19
Jefferson County, NY	111	**Williston, ND**	19		
		Williams County, ND	19	**Wooster, OH**	114
Wauchula, FL	28	**Willmar, MN**	41	Wayne County, OH	114
Hardee County, FL	28	Kandiyohi County, MN	41		
				Worthington, MN	20
Waycross, GA	52	**Wilmington, OH**	42	Nobles County, MN	20
Pierce County, GA	17	Clinton County, OH	42		
Ware County, GA	36			**Yankton, SD**	22
		Wilson, NC	76	Yankton County, SD	22
West Helena, AR	24	Wilson County, NC	76		
Phillips County, AR	24			**Yazoo City, MS**	28
		Winfield, KS	36	Yazoo County, MS	28
West Plains, MO	38	Cowley County, KS	36		
Howell County, MO	38			**Zanesville, OH**	86
		Winona, MN	49	Muskingum County, OH . . .	86
West Point, MS	22	Winona County, MN	49		
Clay County, MS	22				

Z Less than 500.

Source: U.S. Census Bureau, unpublished data.

Appendix III
Limitations of the Data

Introduction The data presented in this *Statistical Abstract* came from many sources. The sources include not only Federal statistical bureaus and other organizations that collect and issue statistics as their principal activity, but also governmental administrative and regulatory agencies, private research bodies, trade associations, insurance companies, health associations, and private organizations such as the National Education Association and philanthropic foundations. Consequently, the data vary considerably as to reference periods, definitions of terms and, for ongoing series, the number and frequency of time periods for which data are available.

The statistics presented were obtained and tabulated by various means. Some statistics are based on complete enumerations or censuses while others are based on samples. Some information is extracted from records kept for administrative or regulatory purposes (school enrollment, hospital records, securities registration, financial accounts, social security records, income tax returns, etc.), while other information is obtained explicitly for statistical purposes through interviews or by mail. The estimation procedures used vary from highly sophisticated scientific techniques, to crude "informed guesses."

Each set of data relates to a group of individuals or units of interest referred to as the *target universe* or *target population*, or simply as the *universe* or *population*. Prior to data collection the target universe should be clearly defined. For example, if data are to be collected for the universe of households in the United States, it is necessary to define a "household." The target universe may not be completely tractable. Cost and other considerations may restrict data collection to a *survey universe* based on some available list, such list may be inaccurate or out of date. This list is called a *survey frame* or *sampling frame*.

The data in many tables are based on data obtained for all population units, *a census*, or on data obtained for only a portion, or *sample*, of the population units. When the data presented are based on a sample, the sample is usually a scientifically selected *probability sample*. This is a sample selected from a list or sampling frame in such a way that every possible sample has a known chance of selection and usually each unit selected can be assigned a number, greater than zero and less than or equal to one, representing its likelihood or probability of selection.

For large-scale sample surveys, the probability sample of units is often selected as a multistage sample. The first stage of a multistage sample is the selection of a probability sample of large groups of population members, referred to as primary sampling units (PSUs). For example, in a national multistage household sample, PSUs are often counties or groups of counties. The second stage of a multistage sample is the selection, within each PSU selected at the first stage, of smaller groups of population units, referred to as secondary sampling units. In subsequent stages of selection, smaller and smaller nested groups are chosen until the ultimate sample of population units is obtained. To qualify a multistage sample as a probability sample, all stages of sampling must be carried out using probability sampling methods.

Prior to selection at each stage of a multistage (or a single-stage) sample, a list of the sampling units or sampling frame for that stage must be obtained. For example, for the first stage of selection of a national household sample, a list of the counties and county groups that form the PSUs must be obtained. For the final stage of selection, lists of households, and sometimes persons within the households, have to be compiled in the field. For surveys of economic entities and for the economic censuses the Census Bureau generally uses a frame constructed from the Census Bureau's Business Register. The Business Register contains all establishments with payroll in the United States including small single establishment firms as well as large multiestablishment firms.

Wherever the quantities in a table refer to an entire universe, but are constructed from data collected in a sample survey, the table quantities are referred to as *sample estimates*. In constructing a sample estimate, an attempt is made to come as close as is feasible to the corresponding universe quantity that would be obtained from a complete census of the universe. Estimates based on a sample will, however, generally differ from the hypothetical census figures. Two classifications of errors are associated with estimates based on sample surveys: (1) *sampling error*—the error arising from the use of a sample, rather than a census, to estimate population quantities and (2) *nonsampling error*—those errors arising from nonsampling sources. As discussed below, the magnitude of the sampling error for an estimate can usually be estimated from the sample data. However, the magnitude of the nonsampling error for an estimate can rarely be estimated. Consequently, actual error in an estimate exceeds the error that can be estimated.

The particular sample used in a survey is only one of a large number of possible samples of the same size which could have been selected using the same sampling procedure. Estimates derived from the different samples would, in general, differ from each other. The *standard error* (SE) is a measure of the variation among the estimates derived from all possible samples. The standard error is the most commonly used measure of the sampling error of an estimate. Valid estimates of the standard errors of survey estimates can usually be calculated from the data collected in a probability sample. For convenience, the standard error is sometimes expressed as a percent of the estimate and is called the relative standard error or *coefficient of variation* (CV). For example, an estimate of 200 units with an estimated standard error of 10 units has an estimated CV of 5 percent.

A sample estimate and an estimate of its standard error or CV can be used to construct interval estimates that have a prescribed confidence that the interval includes the average of the estimates derived from all possible samples with a known probability. To illustrate, if all possible samples were selected under essentially the same general conditions, and using the same sample design, and if an estimate and its estimated standard error were calculated from each sample, then: 1) approximately 68 percent of the intervals from one standard error below the estimate to one standard error above the estimate would include the average estimate derived from all possible samples; 2) approximately 90 percent of the intervals from 1.6 standard errors below the estimate to 1.6 standard errors above the estimate would include the average estimate derived from all possible samples; and 3) approximately 95 percent of the intervals from two standard errors below the estimate to two standard errors above the estimate would include the average estimate derived from all possible samples.

Thus, for a particular sample, one can say with the appropriate level of confidence (e.g., 90 percent or 95 percent) that the average of all possible samples is included in the constructed interval. Example of a confidence interval: An estimate is 200 units with a standard error of 10 units. An approximately 90 percent confidence interval (plus or minus 1.6 standard errors) is from 184 to 216.

All surveys and censuses are subject to nonsampling errors. Nonsampling errors are of two kinds—*random* and *nonrandom*. Random nonsampling errors arise because of the varying interpretation of questions (by respondents or interviewers) and varying actions of coders, keyers, and other processors. Some randomness is also introduced when respondents must estimate. Nonrandom nonsampling errors result from total nonresponse (no usable data obtained for a sampled unit), partial or item nonresponse (only a portion of a response may be usable), inability or unwillingness on the part of respondents to provide correct information, difficulty interpreting questions, mistakes in recording or keying data, errors of collection or processing, and coverage problems (overcoverage and undercoverage of the target universe). Random nonresponse errors usually, but not always, result in an understatement of sampling errors and thus an overstatement of the precision of survey estimates. Estimating the magnitude of nonsampling errors would require special experiments or access to independent data and, consequently, the magnitudes are seldom available.

Nearly all types of nonsampling errors that affect surveys also occur in complete censuses. Since surveys can be conducted on a smaller scale than censuses, nonsampling errors can presumably be controlled more tightly. Relatively more funds and effort can perhaps be expended toward eliciting responses, detecting and correcting response error, and reducing processing errors. As a result, survey results can sometimes be more accurate than census results.

To compensate for suspected nonrandom errors, adjustments of the sample estimates are often made. For example, adjustments are frequently made for nonresponse, both total and partial. Adjustments made for either type of nonresponse are often referred to as *imputations*. Imputation for total nonresponse is usually made by substituting for the questionnaire responses of the nonrespondents the "average" questionnaire responses of the respondents. These imputations usually are made separately within various groups of sample members, formed by attempting to place respondents and nonrespondents together that have "similar" design or ancillary characteristics. Imputation for item nonresponse is usually made by substituting for a missing item the response to that item of a respondent having characteristics that are "similar" to those of the nonrespondent.

For an estimate calculated from a sample survey, the *total error* in the estimate is composed of the sampling error, which can usually be estimated from the sample, and the nonsampling error, which usually cannot be estimated from the

sample. The total error present in a population quantity obtained from a complete census is composed of only nonsampling errors. Ideally, estimates of the total error associated with data given in the *Statistical Abstract* tables should be given. However, due to the unavailability of estimates of nonsampling errors, only estimates of the levels of sampling errors, in terms of estimated standard errors or coefficients of variation, are available. To obtain estimates of the estimated standard errors from the sample of interest, obtain a copy of the referenced report which appears at the end of each table.

Source of Additional Material: The Federal Committee on Statistical Methodology (FCSM) is an interagency committee dedicated to improving the quality of federal statistics <http://fcsm.ssd.census.gov>.

Principal databases—Beginning below are brief descriptions of 35 of the sample surveys and censuses that provide a substantial portion of the data contained in this *Abstract*.

U.S. DEPARTMENT OF AGRICULTURE, National Agriculture Statistics Service

Basic Area Frame Sample

Universe, Frequency, and Types of Data: June agricultural survey collects data on planted acreage and livestock inventories. The survey also serves to measure list incompleteness and is subsampled for multiple frame surveys.

Type of Data Collection Operation: Stratified probability sample of about 11,000 land area units of about 1 sq. mile (range from 0.1 sq. mile in cities to several sq. miles in open grazing areas). Sample includes 42,000 parcels of agricultural land. About 20 percent of the sample replaced annually.

Data Collection and Imputation Procedures: Data collection is by personal enumeration. Imputation is based on enumerator observation or data reported by respondents having similar agricultural characteristics.

Estimates of Sampling Error: Estimated CVs range from 1 percent to 2 percent for regional estimates to 3 percent to 6 percent for state estimates of major crop acres and livestock inventories.

Other (nonsampling) Errors: Minimized through rigid quality controls on the collection process and careful review of all reported data.

Sources of Additional Material: U.S. Department of Agriculture, National Agricultural Statistics Service, USDA's National Agricultural Statistics Service: The Fact Finders of Agriculture, September 1994.

Census of Agriculture

Universe, Frequency, and Types of Data: Complete count of U.S. farms and ranches conducted once every 5 years with data at the national, state, and county level. Data published on farm numbers and related items/characteristics.

Type of Data Collection Operation: Complete census for number of farms; land in farms; agriculture products sold; total cropland; irrigated land; farm operator characteristics; livestock and poultry inventory and sales; and selected crops harvested. Market value of land and buildings, total farm production expenses, machinery and equipment, fertilizer and chemicals, and farm labor are estimated from a sample of farms.

Data Collection and Imputation Procedures: Data collection takes place by mailing questionnaires to all farmers and ranchers. Nonrespondents are contacted by telephone and correspondence follow-ups. Imputations were made for all nonresponse items/characteristics. Coverage adjustments were made to account for missed farms and ranches.

Estimates of Sampling Error: Variability in the estimates is due to the sample selection and estimation for items collected by sample and census nonresponse and coverage estimation procedures. The CVs for national and state estimates are generally very small. The response rate is approximately 81 percent.

Other (nonsampling) Errors: Nonsampling errors are due to incompleteness of the census mailing list, duplications on the list, respondent reporting errors, errors in editing reported data, and in imputation for missing data. Evaluation studies are conducted to measure certain nonsampling errors such as list coverage and classification error. Results from the

evaluation program for the 2002 census indicate the net under-coverage amounted to about 18 percent of the nation's total farms.

Sources of Additional Material: U.S. Department of Agriculture (NASS), 2002 Census of Agriculture, Volume 1, Subject Series C Part 1, Agriculture Atlas of the U.S.; Part 2, Coverage Evaluation; Part 3, Rankings of States and Counties; Part 4, History; Part 5, ZIP Code Tabulation of Selected Items; and Volume 3 Special Studies, Part 1, Farm and Ranch Irrigation Survey; Part 2, Census of Horticultural Specialties; Part 3, Census of Aquaculture.

Multiple Frame Surveys

Universe, Frequency, and Types of Data: Surveys of U.S. farm operators are taken to obtain data on major livestock inventories, selected crop acreage and production, grain stocks, and farm labor characteristics; farm economic data and chemical use data.

Type of Data Collection Operation: Primary frame is obtained from general or special purpose lists, supplemented by a probability sample of land areas used to estimate for list incompleteness.

Data Collection and Imputation Procedures: Mail, telephone, or personal interviews used for initial data collection. Mail nonrespondent follow-up by phone and personal interviews. Imputation based on average of respondents.

Estimates of Sampling Error: Estimated CV for number of hired farm workers is about 3 percent. Estimated CVs range from 1 percent to 2 percent for regional estimates to 3 percent to 6 percent for state estimates of livestock inventories and crop acreage.

Other (nonsampling) Errors: In addition to above, replicated sampling procedures used to monitor effects of changes in survey procedures.

Sources of Additional Material: U.S. Department of Agriculture, National Agricultural Statistics Service), USDA's National Agricultural Statistics Service: The Fact Finders of Agriculture, September 1994.

Objective Yield Surveys

Universe, Frequency, and Types of Data: Surveys for data on corn, cotton, potatoes, soybeans, and wheat, to forecast and estimate yields.

Type of Data Collection Operation: Random location of plots in probability sample. Corn, cotton, soybeans, spring wheat, and durum wheat selected in June from Basic Area Frame Sample (see above). Winter wheat and potatoes selected from March and June multiple frame surveys, respectively.

Data Collection and Imputation Procedures: Enumerators count and measure plant characteristics in sample fields. Production measured from plots at harvest. Harvest loss measured from post harvest gleanings.

Estimates of Sampling Error: CVs for national estimates of production are about 2–3 percent.

Other (nonsampling) Errors: In addition to above, replicated sampling procedures used to monitor effects of changes in survey procedures.

Sources of Additional Material: U.S. Department of Agriculture, National Agricultural Statistics Service), USDA's National Agricultural Statistics Service: The Fact Finders of Agriculture, September 1994.

U.S. BUREAU OF JUSTICE STATISTICS (BJS)

National Crime Victimization Survey

Universe, Frequency, and Types of Data: Monthly survey of individuals and households in the United States to obtain data on criminal victimization of those units for compilation of annual estimates.

Type of Data Collection Operation: National probability sample survey of about 42,000 interviewed households in 203 PSUs selected from a list of addresses from the 1990 census, supplemented by new construction permits and an area sample where permits are not required.

Data Collection and Imputation Procedures: Interviews are conducted every 6 months for 3 years for each household

in the sample; 7,000 households are interviewed monthly. Personal interviews are used in the first interview; the intervening interviews are conducted by telephone whenever possible.

Estimates of Sampling Error: CVs for 2003 estimates are: 3.6 percent for personal crimes (includes all crimes of violence plus purse-snatching crimes), 3.6 percent for crimes of violence; 14.0 percent for estimate of rape/sexual assault counts; 8.7 percent for robbery counts; 3.9 percent for assault counts; 14.5 percent for purse snatching (it refers to purse snatching and pocket picking); 1.9 percent for property crimes; 3.8 percent for burglary counts; 2.1 percent for theft (of property); and 5.9 percent for motor vehicle theft counts.

Other (nonsampling) Errors: Respondent recall errors which may include reporting incidents for other than the reference period; interviewer coding and processing errors; and possible mistaken reporting or classifying of events. Adjustment is made for a household noninterview rate of about 8 percent and for a within-household noninterview rate of 14 percent.

Sources of Additional Material: U.S. Bureau of Justice Statistics, *Criminal Victimization in the United States,* annual.

U.S. Bureau of Labor Statistics

Consumer Expenditure Survey (CE)

Universe, Frequency and Types of Data: Consists of two continuous components: a quarterly Interview survey and a weekly diary or record-keeping survey. They are nationwide surveys that collect data on consumer expenditures, income, characteristics, and assets and liabilities. Samples are national probability samples of households that are representative of the civilian noninstitutionalized population. The surveys have been ongoing since 1980.

Type of Data Collection Operation: The Interview Survey is a panel rotation survey. Each panel is interviewed for five quarters and then dropped from the survey. About 7,500 consumer units are interviewed each quarter. The Diary Survey sample is new each year and consists of about 7,500 consumer units. Data have been collected on an ongoing basis in 105 PSUs since 1996.

Data Collection and Imputation Procedures: For the Interview Survey, data are collected by personal interview with each consumer unit interviewed once per quarter for five consecutive quarters. Designed to collect information that respondents can recall for 3 months or longer, such as large or recurring expenditures. For the Diary Survey, respondents record all their expenditures in a self-reporting diary for two consecutive one-week periods. Designed to pick up items difficult to recall over a long period, such as detailed food expenditures. Missing or invalid attributes or expenditures are imputed. Income, assets, and liabilities are not imputed. The U.S. Census Bureau collects the data for the Bureau of Labor Statistics.

Estimates of Sampling Error: Standard error tables have been available since 2000.

Other (nonsampling) Errors: Includes incorrect information given by respondents, data processing errors, interviewer errors, and so on. They occur regardless of whether data are collected from a sample or from the entire population.

Sources of Additional Material: Bureau of Labor Statistics, Internet site <http://www.bls.gov/cex>.

Consumer Price Index (CPI)

Universe, Frequency, and Types of Data: Monthly survey of price changes of all types of consumer goods and services purchased by urban wage earners and clerical workers prior to 1978, and urban consumers thereafter. Both indexes continue to be published.

Type of Data Collection Operation: Prior to 1978, and since 1998, sample of various consumer items in 87 urban areas; from 1978–1997, in 85 PSUs, except from January 1987 through March 1988, when 91 areas were sampled.

Data Collection and Imputation Procedures: Prices of consumer items are obtained from about 50,000 housing

units, and 23,000 other reporters in 87 areas. Prices of food, fuel, and a few other items are obtained monthly; prices of most other commodities and services are collected every month in the three largest geographic areas and every other month in others.

Estimates of Sampling Error: Estimates of standard errors are available.

Other (nonsampling) Errors: Errors result from inaccurate reporting, difficulties in defining concepts and their operational implementation, and introduction of product quality changes and new products.

Sources of Additional Material: U.S. Bureau of Labor Statistics, Internet site <http://www.stats.bls.gov/cpi/home.htm> and *BLS Handbook of Methods*, Chapter 17, Bulletin 2490.

Current Employment Statistics (CES) Program

Universe, Frequency, and Types of Data: Monthly survey drawn from a sampling frame of over 8 million unemployment insurance tax accounts in order obtain data by industry on employment, hours, and earnings.

Type of Data Collection Operation: In 2004, the CES sample included about 160,000 businesses and government agencies, which represent approximately 400,000 individual worksites.

Data Collection and Imputation Procedures: Each month, the state agencies cooperating with BLS, as well as BLS Data Collection Centers, collect data through various automated collection modes and mail. BLS-Washington staff prepares national estimates of employment, hours, and earnings while states use the data to develop state and area estimates.

Estimates of Sampling Errors: The relative standard error for total nonfarm employment is 0.1 percent.

Other (nonsampling) Errors: Estimates of employment adjusted annually to reflect complete universe. Average adjustment is 0.3 percent over the last decade, with an absolute range from less than 0.05 percent to 0.5 percent.

Sources of Additional Material: U.S.
Bureau of Labor Statistics, Employment
and Earnings, monthly, Explanatory
Notes and Estimates of Errors, Tables
2-A through 2-F.

National Compensation Survey

Universe, Frequency, and Types of Data:
Nationwide sample survey of establishments of all employment size classes, stratified by geographic area, in private industry and state and local government. Data collected include wages and salaries, and employer costs for employee compensation, employment cost index, and employee benefits. Data produced include percent changes in the cost of employment cited in the Employment Cost Index (ECI) and costs per hour worked for individual benefits cited in the Employer Costs for Employee Compensation (ECEC). The survey provides data by ownership (private industry and state and local government), industry sector, major industry divisions, major occupational groups, bargaining status, metropolitan area status, and census region. ECEC also provides data by establishment size class.

Type of Data Collection Operation: Probability proportionate to size sample of establishments. The sample is replaced on a continual basis. Establishments are in the survey for approximately 5 years.

Data Collection and Imputation Procedures: For the initial visit, data are primarily collected in a personal visit to the establishment. Quarterly updates are obtained primarily by mail, fax, and telephone. Imputation is done for individual benefits.

Estimates of Sampling Error: Because standard errors vary from quarter to quarter, the ECI uses a 5-year moving average of standard errors to evaluate published series. These standard errors are available at <http://www.bls.gov/ncs/ect/home.htm>.

Other (nonsampling) Errors: Nonsampling errors have a number of potential sources. The primary sources are (1) survey nonresponse and (2) data collection and processing errors. Nonsampling errors are not measured.

Procedures have been implemented for reducing nonsampling errors, primarily through quality assurance programs. These programs include the use of data collection reinterviews, observed interviews, computer edits of the data, and systematic professional review of the reports on which the data are recorded. The programs also serve as a training device to provide feedback to the field economists, or data collectors, on errors. They also provide information on the sources of error which can be remedied by improved collection instructions or computer processing edits. Extensive training of field economists is also conducted to maintain high standards in data collection.

Sources of Additional Material: Bureau of Labor Statistics, BLS Handbook of Methods, Chapter 8 (Bulletin 2490) and <http://www.bls.gov/ncs>.

Producer Price Index (PPI)

Universe, Frequency, and Types of Data:
Monthly survey of producing companies to determine price changes of all commodities and services produced in the United States for sale in commercial transactions. Data on agriculture, forestry, fishing, manufacturing, mining, gas, electricity, public utilities, wholesale trade, retail trade, transportation, healthcare, and other services.

Type of Data Collection Operation: Probability sample of approximately 30,000 establishments that result in about 100,000 price quotations per month.

Data Collection and Imputation Procedures: Data are collected by mail and facsimile. If transaction prices are not supplied, list prices are used. Some prices are obtained from trade publications, organized exchanges, and government agencies. To calculate index, price changes are multiplied by their relative weights taken from the Census Bureau's 1997 shipment values from their Census of Industries.

Estimates of Sampling Error: Not applicable.

Other (nonsampling) Errors: Not available at present.

Sources of Additional Material: U.S. Bureau of Labor Statistics, *BLS Handbook of Methods*, Chapter 14, Bulletin 2490. U.S. Bureau of Labor Statistics Internet sites <http://stats.bls.gov/ppi>.

BOARD OF GOVERNORS OF THE FEDERAL RESERVE SYSTEM

Survey of Consumer Finances

Universe, Frequency, and Types of Data: Periodic sample survey of families. In this survey a given household is divided into a primary economic unit and other economic units. The primary economic unit, which may be a single individual, is generally chosen as the unit that contains the person who either holds the title to the home or is the first person listed on the lease. The primary unit is used as the reference family. The survey collects detailed data on the composition of family balance sheets, the terms of loans, and relationships with financial institutions. It also gathered information on the employment history and pension rights of the survey respondent and the spouse or partner of the respondent.

Type of Data Collection Operation: The survey employs a two-part strategy for sampling families. Some families were selected by standard multistage area probability sampling methods applied to all 50 states. The remaining families in the survey were selected using statistical records derived from tax returns, under the strict rules governing confidentiality and the rights of potential respondents to refuse participation.

Data Collection and Imputation Procedures: NORC at the University of Chicago has collected data for the survey since 1992. Since 1995, the survey has used computer-assisted personal interviewing. Adjustments for nonresponse are made through multiple imputation of unanswered questions and through weighting adjustments based on data used in the sample design for families that refused participation.

Estimates of Sampling Error: Because of the complex design of the survey, the estimation of potential sampling errors is not straightforward. A replicate-based procedure is available.

Other (nonsampling) Errors: The survey aims to complete 4,500 interviews, with about two thirds of that number deriving from the area-probability sample. The response rate is typically about 70 percent for the area-probability sample and about 35 percent over all strata in the tax-data sample. Proper training and monitoring of interviewers, careful design of questionnaires, and systematic editing of the resulting data were used to control inaccurate survey responses.

Sources of Additional Material: Board of Governors of the Federal Reserve System, "Recent Changes in U.S. Family Finances: Evidence from the 1998 and 2001 Survey of Consumer Finances," *Federal Reserve Bulletin,* January 2003.

U.S. CENSUS BUREAU

2002 Economic Census (Industry Series, Geographic Area Series and Subject Series Reports) (for NAICS sectors 22, 42, 44-45, 48-49, and 51-81)

Universe, Frequency, and Types of Data: Conducted every 5 years to obtain data on number of establishments, number of employees, total payroll size, total sales/receipts/revenue, and other industry-specific statistics. In 2002, the universe was all employer and nonemployer establishments primarily engaged in wholesale, retail, utilities, finance & insurance, real estate, transportation & warehousing, information, education, health care, and other service industries.

Type of Data Collection Operation: All large employer firms were surveyed (i.e., all employer firms above payroll size cutoffs established to separate large from small employers) plus a 5 percent to 25 percent sample of the small employer firms. Firms with no employees were not required to file a census return.

Data Collection and Imputation Procedures: Mail questionnaires were used with both mail and telephone follow-ups for nonrespondents. Data for nonrespondents and for small employer firms not mailed a questionnaire were obtained from administrative records of other federal agencies or imputed. Non-employer data were obtained exclusively from IRS 2002 income tax returns.

Estimates of Sampling Error: Not applicable for basic data such as sales, revenue, receipts, payroll, etc.

Other (nonsampling) Errors: Establishment response rates by NAICS sector in 2002 ranged from 80 percent to 89 percent. Item response rates generally ranged from 50 percent to 90 percent with lower rates for the more detailed questions. Nonsampling errors may occur during the collection, reporting, and keying of data, and due to industry misclassification.

Sources of Additional Material: U.S. Census Bureau, *2002 Economic Census: Industry Series, Geographic Area Series* and *Subject Series Reports* (by NAICS sector), Appendix C and <http://www census.gov/econ/census02/guide /index.html>.

American Community Survey

Universe, Frequency, and Types of Data: Nationwide survey to obtain data about demographic, social, economic, and housing characteristics of people, households and housing units. Covers household population and excludes the population living in institutions, college dormitories, and other group quarters.

Type of Data Collection Operation: Two-stage stratified annual sample of approximately 829,000 housing units. The ACS samples housing units from the Master Address File (MAF). The first stage of sampling involves dividing the United States into primary sampling units (PSUs) most of which comprise a metropolitan area, a large county, or a group of smaller counties. Every PSU falls within the boundary of a state. The PSUs are then grouped into strata on the basis of independent information, that is, information obtained from the decennial census or other sources. The strata are constructed so that they are as homogeneous as possible with respect to social and economic characteristics that are considered important by ACS data users. A pair of PSUs were selected from each stratum. The probability of selection for each PSU in the stratum is

proportional to its estimated 1996 population. In the second stage of sampling, a sample of housing units within the sample PSUs is drawn. Ultimate sampling units (USUs) are housing units. The USUs sampled in the second stage consist of housing units which are systematically drawn from sorted lists of addresses of housing units from the MAF.

Data Collection and Imputation Procedures: The American Community Survey (ACS) is conducted every month on independent samples. Each housing unit in the independent monthly samples is mailed a prenotice letter announcing the selection of the address to participate, a survey questionnaire package, and a reminder postcard. These sample units receive a second (replacement) questionnaire package if the initial questionnaire has not been returned by a scheduled date. In the mail-out/mail-back sites, sample units for which a questionnaire is not returned in the mail and for which a telephone number is available are defined as the telephone nonresponse follow-up universe. Interviewers attempt to contact and interview these mail nonresponse cases. Sample units from all sites that are still unresponsive two months after the mailing of the survey questionnaires and directly after the completion of the telephone followup operation are subsampled at a rate of 1 in 3. The selected nonresponse units are assigned to Field Representatives, who visit the units, verify their existence or declare them nonexistent, determine their occupancy status, and conduct interviews. After data collection is completed, any remaining incomplete or inconsistent information was imputed during the final automated edit of the collected data.

Estimates of Sampling Error: The data in the ACS products are estimates of the actual figures that would have been obtained by interviewing the entire population using the same methodology. The estimates from the chosen sample also differ from other samples of housing units and persons within those housing units.

Other (nonsampling) Errors: Nonsampling Error — In addition to sampling error, data users should realize that other types of errors may be introduced during any of the various complex operations used to collect and process survey data. An important goal of the ACS is to minimize the amount of nonsampling error introduced through nonresponse for sample housing units. One way of accomplishing this is by following up on mail nonrespondents.

Sources of Additional Material: U.S. Census Bureau, American Community Survey Web site available on the Internet, <http://www.census.gov/acs/www/index.html>. U.S. Census Bureau, American Community Survey, Accuracy of the Data documents available on the Internet, <http://www.census.gov/acs/www/UseData/Accuracy/Accuracy1.htm>.

American Housing Survey

Universe, Frequency, and Types of Data: Conducted nationally in the fall in odd numbered years to obtain data on the approximately 121 million occupied or vacant housing units in the United States (group quarters are excluded). Data include characteristics of occupied housing units, vacant units, new housing and mobile home units, financial characteristics, recent mover households, housing and neighborhood quality indicators, and energy characteristics.

Type of Data Collection Operation: The national sample was a multistage probability sample with about 61,000 units eligible for interview in 2003. Sample units, selected within 394 PSUs, were surveyed over a 4-month period.

Data Collection and Imputation Procedures: For 2003, the survey was conducted by personal interviews. The interviewers obtained the information from the occupants or, if the unit was vacant, from informed persons such as landlords, rental agents, or knowledgeable neighbors.

Estimates of Sampling Error: For the national sample, illustrations of the S.E. of the estimates are provided in Appendix D of the 2003 report. As an example, the estimated CV is about 0.2 percent for the estimated percentage of owner-occupied units with two persons.

Other (nonsampling) Errors: Response rate was about 92 percent. Nonsampling errors may result from incorrect or incomplete responses, errors in coding and recording, and processing errors. For the 2003 national sample, approximately 2.2 percent of the total housing inventory was not adequately represented by the AHS sample.

Sources of Additional Material: U.S. Census Bureau, *Current Housing Reports,* Series H-150 and H-170, *American Housing Survey.* <http://www.census.gov/hhes/www/ahs.html>.

Annual Survey of Manufactures

Universe, Frequency, and Types of Data: The Annual Survey of Manufactures (ASM) is conducted annually, except for years ending in 2 and 7 for all manufacturing establishments having one or more paid employees. The purpose of the ASM is to provide key intercensal measures of manufacturing activity, products, and location for the public and private sectors. The ASM provides statistics on employment, payroll, worker hours, payroll supplements, cost of materials, value added by manufacturing, capital expenditures, inventories, and energy consumption. It also provides estimates of value of shipments for 1,800 classes of manufactured products.

Type of Data Collection Operation: The ASM includes approximately 57,000 establishments selected from the census universe of 366,000 manufacturing establishments. Some 27,000 large establishments are selected with certainty, and some 30,000 other establishments are selected with probability proportional to a composite measure of establishment size. The survey is updated from two sources: Internal Revenue Service administrative records are used to include new single-unit manufacturers and the Company Organization Survey identifies new establishments of multiunit forms.

Data Collection and Imputation Procedures: Survey is conducted by mail with phone and mail follow-ups of nonrespondents. Imputation (for all nonresponse items) is based on previous year reports, or for new establishments in survey, on industry averages.

Estimates of Sampling Error: Estimated standard errors for number of employees, new expenditures, and for value added totals are given in annual publications. For U.S. level industry statistics, most estimated standard errors are 2 percent or less, but vary considerably for detailed characteristics.

Other (nonsampling) Errors: Response rate is about 85 percent. Nonsampling errors include those due to collection, reporting, and transcription errors, many of which are corrected through computer and clerical checks.

Sources of Additional Material: U.S. Census Bureau, *Annual Survey of Manufactures,* and Technical Paper 24. <http://www.census.gov/econ/www/mancen.html>

Annual Surveys of State and Local Government

Universe, Frequency, and Types of Data: Sample survey conducted annually to obtain data on revenue, expenditure, debt, and employment of state and local governments. Universe is all governmental units in the United States (about 87,500).

Type of Data Collection Operation: Sample survey includes all state governments, county governments with 100,000+ population, municipalities with 75,000+ population, townships with 50,000+ population, all independent school districts with 10,000+ enrollment in March 2002, all school districts providing college level (postsecondary) education, and other governments meeting certain criteria; probability sample for remaining units.

Data Collection and Imputation Procedures: Field and office compilation of data from official records and reports for states and large local governments; central collection of local governmental financial data through cooperative agreements with a number of state governments; mail canvass of other units with mail and telephone follow-ups of nonrespondents. Data for nonresponses are imputed from previous year data or obtained from secondary sources, if available.

Estimates of Sampling Error: State and local government totals are generally subject to sampling variability of less than 3 percent.

Other (nonsampling) Errors: Nonresponse rate is less than 10 percent for local governments. Other possible errors may result from undetected inaccuracies in classification, response, and processing.

Sources of Additional Material: Publications: <http://www.census.gov/prod/www/abs/govern.html>:U.S. Census Bureau, *Public Employment in 1992,* GE 92, No. 1, *Governmental Finances in 1991–1992,* GF 92, No. 5, and *Census of Governments, 1997 and 2002,* various reports. Web site references: Census of Governments <http://www.census.gov/govs/www/cog2002.html>, <http://www.census.gov/govs/www/cog.html>. Employment—state and local site: <http://www.census.gov/govs/www/apes.html>. Finance—state and local site: <http://www.census.gov/govs/www/estimate.html>.

Census of Population

Universe, Frequency, and Types of Data: Complete count of U.S. population conducted every 10 years since 1790. Data obtained on number and characteristics of people in the U.S.

Type of Data Collection Operation: In 1980, 1990, and 2000, complete census for some items: age, date of birth, sex, race, and relationship to householder. In 1980, approximately 19 percent of the housing units were included in the sample; in 1990 and 2000, approximately 17 percent.

Data Collection and Imputation Procedures: In 1980, 1990, and 2000, mail questionnaires were used extensively with personal interviews in the remainder. Extensive telephone and personal follow-up for nonrespondents was done in the censuses. Imputations were made for missing characteristics.

Estimates of Sampling Error: Sampling errors for data are estimated for all items collected by sample and vary by characteristic and geographic area. The coefficients of variation (CVs) for national and state estimates are generally very small.

Other (nonsampling) Errors: Since 1950, evaluation programs have been conducted to provide information on the magnitude of some sources of nonsampling errors such as response bias and undercoverage in each census. Results from the evaluation program for the 1990 census indicated that the estimated net undercoverage amounted to about 1.5 percent of the total resident population. For Census 2000, the evaluation program indicates a net overcount of 0.5 percent of the resident population.

Sources of Additional Material: U.S. Census Bureau, The Coverage of Population in the 1980 Census, PHC80-E4; *Content Reinterview Study: Accuracy of Data for Selected Population and Housing Characteristics as Measured by Reinterview,* PHC80-E2; *1980 Census of Population,* Vol. 1, (PC80-1), Appendixes B, C, and D. 1990 Census of Population and Housing, Content Reinterview Survey: Accuracy of Data for Selected Population and Housing Characteristics as measured by Reinterview, CPH-E-1; 1990 Census of Population and Housing, Effectiveness of Quality Assurance, CPH-E-2; Programs to Improve Coverage in the 1990 Census, CPH-E-3. For Census 2000, see <http://www.census.gov/pred/www>.

County Business Patterns

Universe, Frequency, and Types of Data: County Business Patterns is an annual tabulation of basic data items extracted from the Business Register, a file of all known single- and multi-location companies maintained and updated by the Census Bureau. Data include number of establishments, number of employees, first quarter and annual payrolls, and number of establishments by employment size class. Data are excluded for self-employed persons, domestic service workers, railroad employees, agricultural production workers, and most government employees.

Type of Data Collection Operation: The annual Company Organization Survey provides individual establishment data for multi-location companies. Data for single establishment companies are obtained from various Census Bureau programs, such as the Annual Survey of

Manufactures and Current Business Surveys, as well as from administrative records of the Internal Revenue Service and the Social Security Administration.

Estimates of Sampling Error: Not applicable.

Other (nonsampling) Error: The data are subject to non-sampling errors, such as industry classification errors, as well as errors of response, keying, and nonreporting.

Sources of Additional Materials: U.S. Census Bureau, *General Explanation of County Business Patterns.*

Current Population Survey (CPS)

Universe, Frequency, and Types of Data: Nationwide monthly sample survey of civilian noninstitutionalized population, 15 years old or over, to obtain data on employment, unemployment, and a number of other characteristics.

Type of Data Collection Operation: Multistage probability sample of about 50,000 households in 754 PSUs in 1996 expanded to about 60,000 households in July 2001. Over-sampling in some states and the largest MSAs to improve reliability for those areas of employment data on annual average basis. A continual sample rotation system is used. Households are in sample 4 months, out for 8 months, and in for 4 more. Month-to-month overlap is 75 percent; year-to-year overlap is 50 percent.

Data Collection and Imputation Procedures: For first and fifth months that a household is in sample, personal interviews; other months, approximately 85 percent of the data collected by phone. Imputation is done for both item and total nonresponse. Adjustment for total nonresponse is done by a predefined cluster of units, by MSA size and residence; for item nonresponse imputation varies by subject matter.

Estimates of Sampling Error: Estimated CVs on national annual averages for labor force, total employment, and nonagricultural employment, 0.2 percent; for total unemployment and agricultural employment, 1.0 percent to 2.5 percent. The estimated CVs for family income and poverty rate for all persons in 1986 are 0.5 percent and 1.5 percent, respectively. CVs for subnational areas, such as states, would be larger and would vary by area.

Other (nonsampling) Errors: Estimates of response bias on unemployment are not available, but estimates of unemployment are usually 5 percent to 9 percent lower than estimates from reinterviews. Six to 7.0 percent of sample households unavailable for interviews.

Sources of Additional Material: U.S. Census Bureau and Bureau of Labor Statistics, *Current Population Survey; Design and Methodology*, (Tech. Paper 63), available on Internet <http://www.census.gov/prod/2002pubs/tp63rv.pdf> and Bureau of Labor Statistics, *Employment and Earnings*, monthly, Explanatory Notes and Estimates of Error, Household Data and *BLS Handbook of Methods*, Chapter 1, available on the Internet <http://www.bls.gov/opub/hom/homch1a.htm>.

Foreign Trade—Import Statistics

Universe, Frequency, and Types of Data: The import entry documents collected by U.S. Bureau of Customs and Border Protection are processed each month to obtain data on the movement of merchandise imported into the United States. Data obtained include value, quantity, and shipping weight by commodity, country of origin, district of entry, and mode of transportation.

Type of Data Collection Operation: Import entry documents, either paper or electronic, are required to be filed for the importation of goods into the United States valued over $2,000, or for articles which must be reported on formal entries. U.S. Bureau of Customs and Border Protection officials collect and transmit statistical copies of the documents to the Census Bureau on a flow basis for data compilation. Estimates for shipments valued under $2,001 and not reported on formal entries are based on estimated established percentages for individual country totals.

Data Collection and Imputation Procedures: Statistical copies of import entry documents, received on a daily basis from ports of entry throughout the

country, are subjected to a monthly processing cycle. They are fully processed to the extent they reflect items valued at $2,001 and over or items which must be reported on formal entries.

Estimates of Sampling Error: Not applicable.

Other (nonsampling) Errors: The goods data are a complete enumeration of documents collected by the U.S. Bureau of Customs and Border Protection and are not subject to sampling errors; but they are subject to several types of nonsampling errors. Quality assurance procedures are performed at every stage of collection, processing and tabulation; however the data are still subject to several types of nonsampling errors. The most significant of these include reporting errors, undocumented shipments, timeliness, data capture errors, and errors in the estimation of low-valued transactions.

Sources of Additional Material: U.S. Census Bureau, FT 900 U.S. International Trade in Goods and Services, FT 925 (discounted after 1996) U.S. Merchandise Trade, FT 895 U.S. Trade with Puerto Rico and U.S. Possessions, FT920 U.S. Merchandise Trade: selected highlights, and Information Section on Goods and Services at <http://www.census.gov/ft900>.

Foreign Trade—Export Statistics

Universe, Frequency, and Types of Data: The export declarations collected by U.S. Bureau of Customs and Border Protection are processed each month to obtain data on the movement of U.S. merchandise exports to foreign countries. Data obtained include value, quantity, and shipping weight of exports by commodity, country of destination, district of exportation, and mode of transportation.

Type of Data Collection Operation: Shipper's Export Declarations (paper and electronic) are generally required to be filed for the exportation of merchandise valued over $2,500. U.S. Bureau of Customs and Border Protection officials collect and transmit the documents to the Census Bureau on a flow basis for data compilation. Data for shipments valued under $2,501 are estimated, based on established percentages of individual country totals.

Data Collection and Imputation Procedures: Statistical copies of Shipper's Export Declarations are received on a daily basis from ports throughout the country and subject to a monthly processing cycle. They are fully processed to the extent they reflect items valued over $2,500. Estimates for shipments valued at $2,500 or less are made, based on established percentages of individual country totals.

Estimates of Sampling Error: Not applicable.

Other (nonsampling) Errors: The goods data are a complete enumeration of documents collected by the U.S. Bureau of Customs and Border Protection and are not subject to sampling errors; but they are subject to several types of non-sampling errors. Quality assurance procedures are performed at every stage of collection, processing and tabulation; however the data are still subject to several types of nonsampling errors. The most significant of these include reporting errors, undocumented shipments, timeliness, data capture errors, and errors in the estimation of low-valued transactions.

Sources of Additional Material: U.S. Census Bureau, FT 900 U.S. International Trade in Goods and Services, FT 925 (discounted after 1996) U.S. Merchandise Trade, FT 895 U.S. Trade with Puerto Rico and U.S. Possessions, FT 920 U.S. Merchandise trade: selected highlights, and Information Section on Goods and Services at <http://census.gov/ft900>.

Monthly Retail Trade and Food Service Survey

Universe, Frequency, and Types of Data: Provides monthly estimates of retail and food service sales by kind of business and end-of-month inventories of retail stores.

Type of Data Collection Operation: Probability sample of all firms from a list frame. The list frame is the Census Bureau's Business Register updated

quarterly for recent birth Employer Identification (EI) Numbers issued by the Internal Revenue Service and assigned a kind-of-business code by the Social Security Administration. The largest firms are included monthly; a sample of others is included every month also.

Data Collection and Imputation Procedures: Data are collected by mail questionnaire with telephone follow-ups and fax reminders for nonrespondents. Imputation is made for each nonresponse item and each item failing edit checks.

Estimates of Sampling Error: For the 2004 monthly surveys, CVs are about 0.5 percent for estimated total retail sales and 1.2 percent for estimated total retail inventories. Sampling errors are shown in monthly publications.

Other (nonsampling) Errors: Imputation rates are about 20 percent for monthly retail and food service sales, and 28 percent for monthly retail inventories.

Sources of Additional Material: U.S. Census Bureau, Current Business Reports, Annual Benchmark Report for Retail Trade and Food Services.

Monthly Survey of Construction

Universe, Frequency, and Types of Data: Survey conducted monthly of newly constructed housing units (excluding mobile homes). Data are collected on the start, completion, and sale of housing. (Annual figures are aggregates of monthly estimates.)

Type of Data Collection Operation: For permit issuing places probability sample of 850 housing units obtained from 19,000 permit issuing places. For non-permit places, multistage probability sample of new housing units selected in 169 PSUs. In those areas, all roads are canvassed in selected enumeration districts.

Data Collection and Imputation Procedures: Data are obtained by telephone inquiry and field visit.

Estimates of Sampling Error: Estimated CV of 3 percent to 4 percent for estimates of national totals, but may be higher than 20 percent for estimated totals of more detailed characteristics, such as housing units in multiunit structures.

Other (nonsampling) Errors: Response rate is over 90 percent for most items. Nonsampling errors are attributed to definitional problems, differences in interpretation of questions, incorrect reporting, inability to obtain information about all cases in the sample, and processing errors.

Sources of Additional Material: All data are available on the Internet at <http://www.census.gov/const/www /newsresconstindex.html>. Further documentation of the survey is also available at that site.

Nonemployer Statistics

Universe, Frequency, and Types of Data: Nonemployer statistics are an annual tabulation of economic data by industry for active businesses without paid employees that are subject to federal income tax. Data showing the number of establishments and receipts by industry are available for the U.S., states, counties, and metropolitan areas. Most types of businesses covered by the Census Bureau's economic statistics programs are included in the nonemployer statistics. Tax-exempt and agricultural-production businesses are excluded from nonemployer statistics.

Type of Data Collection Operation: The universe of nonemployer establishments is created annually as a by-product of the Census Bureau's Business Register processing for employer establishments. If a business is active but without paid employees, then it becomes part of the potential nonemployer universe. Industry classification and receipts are available for each potential nonemployer business. These data are obtained primarily from the annual business income tax returns of the Internal Revenue Service (IRS). The potential nonemployer universe undergoes a series of complex processing, editing, and analytical review procedures at the Census Bureau to distinguish nonemployers from employers, and to correct and complete data items used in creating the data tables.

Estimates of Sampling Error: Not applicable.

Other (nonsampling) Errors: The data are subject to nonsampling errors, such as errors of self-classification by industry on tax forms, as well as errors of response, keying, nonreporting, and coverage.

Sources of Additional Material: U. S. Census Bureau, Nonemployer Statistics: 2002 (Introduction; Coverage and Methodology). See also <http://www.census .gov/epcd/nonemployer/view/cov&meth.htm>

Service Annual Survey

Universe, Frequency, and Types of Data: The U.S. Census Bureau conducts the Service Annual Survey to provide national estimates of revenues, expenses, and e-commerce revenues for taxable and tax-exempt firms classified in selected service industries. Estimates are summarized by industry classification based on the *1997 North American Industry Classification System (NAICS)*. Industries covered by the Service Annual Survey include all or part of the following NAICS sectors: Transportation and Warehousing (NAICS 48–49); Information (NAICS 51); Finance and Insurance (NAICS 52); Real Estate and Rental and Leasing (NAICS 53); Professional, Scientific, and Technical Services (NAICS 54); Administrative and Support and Waste Management and Remediation Services (NAICS 56); Health Care and Social Assistance (NAICS 62); Arts, Entertainment, and Recreation (NAICS 71); and Other Services, except Public Administration (NAICS 81). Data items collected include total revenue, revenue from e-commerce transactions; and for selected industries, revenue from detailed service products, total expenses, and expenses by major type, revenue from exported services, and inventories. Questionnaires are mailed in January and request annual data for the prior year. Estimates are published approximately 12 months after the initial survey mailing.

Type of Data Collection Operation: The Service Annual Survey estimates are developed using data from a probability sample and administrative records. *Service Annual Survey* questionnaires are mailed to a probability sample that is periodically reselected from a universe of firms located in the United States and having paid employees. The sample includes firms of all sizes and covers both taxable firms and firms exempt from Federal income taxes. Updates to the sample are made on a quarterly basis to account for new businesses. Firms without paid employees, or non-employers, are included in the estimates through imputation and/or administrative records data provided by other Federal agencies. Links to additional information about confidentiality protection, sampling error, nonsampling error, sample design, definitions, and copies of the questionnaires may be found on the Internet at <http://www.census .gov/econ/www/servmenu.html>.

Estimates of Sampling Error: Coefficients of variation for the 2003 *Service Annual Survey* estimates range from 0.6% to 2.2% for total revenue estimates computed at the NAICS sector (2-digit NAICS code) level. Sampling errors for more detailed industries are shown in the corresponding publications. The full 2003 *Service Annual Survey* results, including coefficients of variations, can be found at <http://www.census.gov/econ /www/servmenu.html>. Links to additional information regarding sampling error may be found at: <http://www .census.gov/svsd/www/cv.html>.

Other (Nonsampling) Errors: Data are imputed for unit nonresponse, item non-response, and for reported data that fails edits. The percent of imputed data for total revenue for the 2003 *Service Annual Survey* is approximately 14%.

Sources of Additional Material: U.S. Census Bureau, Current Business Reports, *Service Annual Survey*, Census Bureau Web site: <http://www.census.gov /econ/www/servmenu.html>.

U.S. DEPARTMENT OF EDUCATION

National Center for Education Statistics Higher Education General Information Survey (HEGIS), Degrees and Other Formal Awards Conferred. Beginning 1986, Integrated Postsecondary Education Data Survey (IPEDS), Completions

Universe, Frequency, and Types of Data: Annual survey of all institutions and branches listed in the *Education Directory, Colleges and Universities* to obtain data on earned degrees and other formal awards, conferred by field of study, level of degree, sex, and by racial/ethnic characteristics (every other year prior to 1989, then annually).

Type of Data Collection Operation: Complete census.

Data Collection and Imputation Procedures: Data are collected through a Web-based survey in the fall of every year. Missing data are imputed by using data of similar institutions.

Estimates of Sampling Error: Not applicable.

Other (nonsampling) Errors: For 2002–03, approximately 100.0 percent response rate for degree-granting institutions.

Sources of Additional Material: U.S. Department of Education, National Center for Education Statistics, *Postsecondary Institutions in the United States: Fall 2003 and Degrees and Other Awards Conferred: 2002–03*. <http://www.nces .ed.gov/ipeds/>.

National Household Education Surveys Program

Universe, Frequency, and Types of Data: The National Household Education Surveys Program (NHES) is a system of telephone surveys of the noninstitutionalized civilian population of the United States. Surveys in NHES have varying universes of interest depending on the particular survey. Specific topics covered by each survey are at the NHES Web site <http://nces.ed.gov/nhes>. A list of the surveys fielded as part of NHES, each universe, and the years they were fielded is provided below. 1. Adult Education Interviews were conducted with a representative sample of civilian, noninstitutionalized persons age 16 and older who were not enrolled in grade 12 or below (1991, 1995, 1999, 2001, 2003). 2. Before-and After-School Programs and Activities Interviews were conducted with parents of a representative sample of students in grades K through 8 (1999, 2001). 3. Civic Involvement Interviews were conducted with a representative sample of parents, youth, and adults(1996, 1999). 4. Early Childhood Program Participation Interviews were conducted with parents of a representative sample of children from birth through grade 3, with the specific age groups varying by survey year (1991, 1995, 1999, 2001). 5. Household and Library Use Interviews were conducted with a representative sample of U.S. households (1996). 6. Parent and Family Involvement in Education Interviews were conducted with parents of a representative sample of children age 3 through grade 12 or in grades K through 12 depending on the survey year (1996, 1999, 2003). 7. School Readiness Interviews were conducted with parents of a representative sample of 3- to 7-year-old children (1993, 1999). 8. School Safety and Discipline Interviews were conducted with a representative sample of students in grades 6–12, their parents, and the parents of a representative sample of students in grades 3–5 (1993).

Type of Data Collection Operation: NHES uses telephone interviews to collect data.

Data Collection and Imputation Procedures: Telephone numbers are selected using random digit dialing techniques. Approximately 45,000 to 64,000 households are contacted in order to identify persons eligible for the surveys. Data are collected using computer-assisted telephone interviewing (CATI) procedures. Missing data are imputed using hot-deck imputation procedures.

Estimates of Sampling Error: Unweighted sample sizes range between 2,500 and 21,000. The average root design effects of the surveys in NHES range from 1.1 to 4.5.

Other (nonsampling) Errors: Because of unit nonresponse and because the samples are drawn from households with telephone instead of all households, nonresponse and/or coverage bias may exist for some estimates. However, both sources of potential bias are adjusted for in the weighting process. Analyses of both potential sources of bias in the NHES collections have been studied and no significant bias has been detected.

Sources of Additional Material: Please see the NHES Web site at <http://nces.ed.gov/nhes>

U.S. FEDERAL BUREAU OF INVESTIGATION

Uniform Crime Reporting (UCR) Program

Universe, Frequency, and Types of Data: Monthly reports on the number of criminal offenses that become known to law enforcement agencies. Data are collected on crimes cleared by arrest; by age, sex, and race of arrestees and for victims and offenders for homicides; on fatal and nonfatal assaults against law enforcement officers, and on hate crimes reported.

Type of Data Collection Operation: Crime statistics are based on reports of crime data submitted either directly to the FBI by contributing law enforcement agencies or through cooperating state UCR programs.

Data Collection and Imputation Procedures: States with UCR programs collect data directly from individual law enforcement agencies and forward reports, prepared in accordance with UCR standards, to FBI. Accuracy and consistency edits are performed by FBI.

Estimates of Sampling Error: Not applicable.

Other (nonsampling) Errors: Coverage of 93 percent of the population (95 percent in MSAs, 85 percent in "cities outside of metropolitan areas," and 83 percent in nonmetropolitan counties) by UCR Program, through varying number of agencies reporting.

Sources of Additional Material: U.S. Federal Bureau of Investigation, *Crime in the United States,* annual, *Hate Crime Statistics,* annual, *Law Enforcement Officers Killed & Assaulted,* annual, <http://www.fbi.gov/ucr.htm>.

U.S. INTERNAL REVENUE SERVICE

Corporation Income Tax Returns

Universe, Frequency, and Types of Data: Annual study of unaudited corporation income tax returns, Forms 1120,

1120-A, 1120-F, 1120-L, 1120-PC, 1120-REIT, 1120-RIC, and 1120S, filed by corporations or businesses legally defined as corporations. Data provided on various financial characteristics by industry and size of total assets, and business receipts.

Type of Data Collection Operation: Stratified probability sample of approximately 147,000 returns for Tax Year 2002, allocated to sample classes which are based on type of return, size of total assets size of net income or deficit, and selected business activity. Sampling rates for sample classes varied from .25 percent to 100 percent.

Data Collection and Imputation Procedures: Computer selection of sample of tax return records. Data adjusted during editing for incorrect, missing, or inconsistent entries to ensure consistency with other entries on return and to comply with statistical definitions.

Estimates of Sampling Error: Estimated CVs for Tax Year 2002: Returns with assets over $250 million are self-representing. For other returns grouped by assets, CVs ranged from 0.01 percent to 2.16 percent; for amount of net income CV is 0.19 percent.

Other (nonsampling) Errors: Nonsampling errors include coverage errors, processing errors, and response errors.

Sources of Additional Material: U.S. Internal Revenue Service, *Statistics of Income, Corporation Income Tax Returns,* annual.

Partnership Income Tax Returns

Universe, Frequency, and Types of Data: Annual study of unaudited income tax returns of partnerships, Form 1065. Data provided on various financial characteristics by industry.

Type of Data Collection Operation: Stratified probability sample of approximately 34,800 partnership returns from a population of 2.4 million filed during calendar year 2003. The sample is classified based on combinations of gross receipts, net income or loss, and total assets, and on industry. Sampling rates vary from 0.12 percent to 100 percent.

Data Collection and Imputation Procedures: Computer selection of sample of tax return records. Data are adjusted during editing for incorrect, missing, or inconsistent entries to ensure consistency with other entries on return. Data not available due to regulations are not imputed.

Estimates of Sampling Error: Estimated CVs for tax year 2002 (latest available): For number of partnerships, 0.29 percent; business receipts, 0.34 percent; net income, 0.80 percent; net loss, 1.72 percent.

Other (nonsampling) Errors: Processing errors and errors arising from the use of tolerance checks for the data.

Sources of Additional Material: U.S. Internal Revenue Service, *Statistics of Income, Partnership Returns* and *Statistics of Income Bulletin,* Vol. 24, No. 2 (fall 2004).

Sole Proprietorship Income Tax Returns

Universe, Frequency, and Types of Data: Annual study of unaudited income tax returns of nonfarm sole proprietorships, form 1040 with business schedules. Data provided on various financial characteristics by industry.

Type of Data Collection Operation: Stratified probability sample of approximately 50,000 sole proprietorships for tax year 2002. The sample is classified based on presence or absence of certain business schedules; the larger of total income or loss; and size of business plus farm receipts. Sampling rates vary from 0.05 percent to 100 percent.

Data Collection and Imputation Procedures: Computer selection of sample of tax return records. Data adjusted during editing for incorrect, missing, or inconsistent entries to ensure consistency with other entries on return.

Estimates of Sampling Error: Estimated CVs for tax year 2002 are available. For sole proprietorships, business receipts, 0.69 percent; depreciation 1.41 percent.

Other (nonsampling) Errors: Processing errors and errors arising from the use of tolerance checks for the data.

Sources of Additional Material: U.S. Internal Revenue Service, *Statistics of Income, Sole Proprietorship Returns* (for years 1980 through 1983) and *Statistics of Income Bulletin,* Vol. 24, No. 1 (summer 2004, as well as bulletins for earlier years).

Individual Income Tax Returns

Universe, Frequency, and Types of Data: Annual study of unaudited individual income tax returns, forms 1040, 1040A, and 1040EZ, filed by U.S. citizens and residents. Data provided on various financial characteristics by size of adjusted gross income, marital status, and by taxable and nontaxable returns. Data by state, based on 100 percent file, also include returns from 1040NR, filed by nonresident aliens plus certain self-employment tax returns.

Type of Data Collection Operation: Annual 2002 stratified probability sample of approximately 176,000 returns broken into sample strata based on the larger of total income or total loss amounts as well as the size of business plus farm receipts. Sampling rates for sample strata varied from 0.05 percent to 100 percent.

Data Collection and Imputation Procedures: Computer selection of sample of tax return records. Data adjusted during editing for incorrect, missing, or inconsistent entries to ensure consistency with other entries on return.

Estimates of Sampling Error: Estimated CVs for tax year 2002: Adjusted gross income less deficit 0.12 percent; salaries and wages 0.21 percent; and tax exempt interest received 1.78 percent. (State data not subject to sampling error.)

Other (nonsampling) Errors: Processing errors and errors arising from the use of tolerance checks for the data.

Sources of Additional Material: U.S. Internal Revenue Service, *Statistics of Income, Individual Income Tax Returns,* annual.

U.S. NATIONAL CENTER FOR HEALTH STATISTICS (NCHS)

National Health Interview Survey (NHIS)

Universe, Frequency, and Types of Data: Continuous data collection covering the civilian noninstitutionalized population to obtain information on demographic characteristics, conditions, injuries, impairments, use of health services, health behaviors, and other health topics.

Type of Data Collection Operation: Multistage probability sample of 49,000 households (in 198 PSUs) from 1985 to 1994; 36–40,000 households (358 design PSUs) from 1995 on.

Data Collection and Imputation Procedures: Some missing data items (e.g., race, ethnicity) are imputed using a hot deck imputation value. Unit nonresponse is compensated for by an adjustment to the survey weights.

Estimates of Sampling Error: Estimates of Standard Error (SE): For 2003 medically attended injury episodes rates in the past 12 months by falling for: females 29.72 (1.94), and males 26.15 (1.82) per 1,000 population; for 2003 injury episodes rates during the past 12 months inside the home–20.72 (1.18) per 1,000 population.

Other (nonsampling) Errors: The response rate was 93.8 percent in 1996; in 2003, the total household response rate was 89.2 percent, with the final family response rate of 87.9 percent, and the final sample adult response rate of 74.2 percent. (Note: The NHIS sample redesign was conducted in 1995, and the NHIS questionnaire was redesigned in 1997.)

Sources of Additional Material: National Center for Health Statistics, Summary Health Statistics for the U.S. Population: National Health Interview Survey, 2003, Vital and Health Statistics, Series 10 #224; National Center for Health Statistics, Summary Health Statistics for U.S. Children: National Health Interview Survey, 2003, Vital and Health Statistics, Series 10 #223; National Center for Health Statistics, Summary Health Statistics for U.S. Adults: National Health Interview Survey, 2003, Vital and Health Statistics, Series 10 #225; U.S. National Center for Health Statistics, Design and

Estimation for the National Health Interview Survey, 1995–2004, Vital and Health Statistics, Series 2 #130.

National Vital Statistics System

Universe, Frequency, and Types of Data: Annual data on births and deaths in the United States.

Type of Data Collection Operation: Mortality data based on complete file of death records, except 1972, based on 50 percent sample. Natality statistics 1951–71, based on 50 percent sample of birth certificates, except a 20 percent to 50 percent sample in 1967, received by NCHS. Beginning 1972, data from some states received through Vital Statistics Cooperative Program (VSCP) and complete file used; data from other states based on 50 percent sample. Beginning 1986, all reporting areas participated in the VSCP.

Data Collection and Imputation Procedures: Reports based on records from registration offices of all states, District of Columbia, New York City, Puerto Rico, Virgin Islands, Guam, American Samoa, and Northern Marianas.

Estimates of Sampling Error: For recent years, there is no sampling for these files; the files are based on 100 percent of events registered.

Other (nonsampling) Errors: Data on births and deaths believed to be at least 99 percent complete.

Sources of Additional Material: U.S. National Center for Health Statistics, *Vital Statistics of the United States,* Vol. I and Vol. II, annual, and *National Vital Statistics Reports.* NCHS Web site at <http://www.cdc.gov/nchs/nvss.htm>.

National Highway Traffic Safety Administration (NHTSA)

Fatality Analysis Reporting System (FARS)

Universe, Frequency, and Types of Data: FARS is a census of all fatal motor vehicle traffic crashes that occur throughout the United States including the District of Columbia and Puerto Rico on roadways customarily open to the public. The crash must be reported to

the state/jurisdiction and at least one directly related fatality must occur within thirty days of the crash.

Type of Data Collection Operation: One or more analysts, in each state, extract data from the official documents and enter the data into a standardized electronic database.

Data Collection and Imputation Procedures: Detailed data describing the characteristics of the fatal crash, the vehicles and persons involved are obtained from police crash reports, driver and vehicle registration records, autopsy reports, highway department, etc. Computerized edit checks monitor that accuracy and completeness of the data. The FARS incorporates a sophisticated mathematical multiple imputation procedure to develop a probability distribution of missing blood alcohol concentration (BAC) levels in the database for drivers, pedestrians and cyclists.

Estimates of Sampling Error: Since this is census data, there are no sampling errors.

Other (nonsampling) Errors: Fatal motor vehicle traffic crash data are more than 97 percent complete. However, these data are highly dependent on the accuracy of the police accident reports. Errors or omissions within police accident reports may not be detected.

Sources of Additional Material: The FARS Coding and Validation Manual, ANSI D16.1 Manual on Classification of Motor Vehicle Traffic Accidents (Sixth Edition).

Weights and Measures

[For assistance on metric usage, call or write:

Kenneth S. Butcher
NIST
Weights and Measures Division
100 Bureau Drive – Mail Stop 2600
Gaithersburg, MD 20899-2600

Telephone: 301-975-4859 or 4004   FAX: 301-926-0647

E-mail: kbutcher@nist.gov

Internet site <http://www.nist.gov/metric>

Symbol	When you know conventional	Multiply by	To find metric	Symbol
in	inches	2.54	centimeters	cm
ft	feet	30.48	centimeters	cm
yd	yards	0.91	meters	m
mi	miles	1.61	kilometers	km
in^2	square inches	6.45	square centimeters	cm^2
ft^2	square feet	0.09	square meters	m^2
yd^2	square yards	0.84	square meters	m^2
mi^2	square miles	2.59	square kilometers	km^2
	acre	0.41	hectare	ha
oz	ounces [1]	28.35	grams	g
lb	pounds [1]	.45	kilograms	kg
oz (troy)	ounces [2]	31.10	grams	g
	short tons (2,000 lb)	0.91	metric tons	t
	long tons (2,240 lb)	1.02	metric tons	t
fl oz	fluid ounces	29.57	milliliters	mL
c	cups	0.24	liters	L
pt	pints	0.47	liters	L
qt	quarts	0.95	liters	L
gal	gallons	3.78	liters	L
ft^3	cubic feet	0.03	cubic meters	m^3
yd^3	cubic yards	0.76	cubic meters	m^3
F	degrees Fahrenheit (subtract 32)	0.55	degrees Celsius	C

Symbol	When you know metric	Multiply by	To find conventional	Symbol
cm	centimeters	0.39	inches	in
cm	centimeters	0.03	feet	ft
m	meters	1.09	yards	yd
km	kilometers	0.62	miles	mi
cm^2	square centimeters	0.15	square inches	in^2
m^2	square meters	10.76	square feet	ft^2
m^2	square meters	1.20	square yards	yd^2
km^2	square kilometers	0.39	square miles	mi^2
ha	hectares	2.47	acre	
g	grams	.035	ounces [1]	oz
kg	kilograms	2.21	pounds	lb [1]
g	grams	.032	ounces [2]	oz (troy)
t	metric tons	1.10	short tons (2,000 lb)	
t	metric tons	0.98	long tons (2,240 lb)	
mL	milliliters	0.03	fluid ounces	fl oz
L	liter	4.24	cups	c
L	liters	2.13	pints (liquid)	pt
L	liters	1.05	quarts (liquid)	qt
L	liters	0.26	gallons	gal
m^3	cubic meters	35.32	cubic feet	ft^3
m^3	cubic meters	1.32	cubic yards	yd^3
C	degrees Celsius (after multiplying, add 32)	1.80	degrees Fahrenheit	F

[1] For weighing ordinary commodities.   [2] For weighing precious metals, jewels, etc.

Appendix V
Tables Deleted From the
2004–2005 Edition of the Statistical Abstract

U.S. Census Bureau, Statistical Abstract of the United States: 2006

Appendix VI

New Tables

U.S. Census Bureau, Statistical Abstract of the United States: 2006

U.S. Census Bureau, Statistical Abstract of the United States: 2006

U.S. Census Bureau, Statistical Abstract of the United States: 2006

Index

NOTE: Index citations refer to **table** numbers, not page numbers.

NOTE: Index citations refer to **table** numbers, not page numbers.

U.S. Census Bureau, Statistical Abstract of the United States: 2006

NOTE: Index citations refer to **table** numbers, not page numbers.

NOTE: Index citations refer to **table** numbers, not page numbers.

U.S. Census Bureau, Statistical Abstract of the United States: 2006

NOTE: Index citations refer to **table** numbers, not page numbers.

NOTE: Index citations refer to **table** numbers, not page numbers.

NOTE: Index citations refer to **table** numbers, not page numbers.

Carrots 203, 832
Cars. See Automobiles
Cash usage 1173
Cassettes 1131
Casualties, military conflicts 504
Casualty insurance 1212
Catalog and mail order sales . 1016, 1022, 1036, 1020
Catfish 806, 860
Catholic population. See Religion.
CAT scan 168
Cat ownership 1232
Cattle:
   Farm marketings, sales 806, 809
   Imports 815
   Number on farms 835, 836, 838
   Organic 803
   Prices 835
   Production 835, 838
   Slaughter 838
   Value on farms 835
Cauliflower 203, 832
Cayman Islands. See Foreign countries.
Celery 203, 832
Cellular telephones (See also Telephone carriers)
.... 963, 1363
Cement (see also Nonmetallic mineral product manufacturing) 865, 937
   Consumption 866
   Earnings 620
   Employment 620, 866
   Foreign trade 866
   Price indexes 871
   Prices 866
   Production and value 865
   Productivity 622
   World production 1354
Central African Republic. See Foreign countries.
Central America. See Foreign countries.
Central and South American population (His-
   panic origin) 73
Cereal and bakery products:
   Advertising 1109
   Expenditures, prices ... 667, 669, 670, 708, 812
   Foreign trade 1294
Cerebrovascular diseases, deaths . 106, 108, 109, 110, 159, 166, 1199
Certificates of deposit 1159, 1183
Cesarean section deliveries 85, 168
Cesium 866
CFC (Chloroflurocarbon) gases 362
Chad. See Foreign countries.
Charitable contributions (see also Philanthropy) . 473, 475, 570, 571, 574
Charter schools 226
Checking accounts 700, 1159, 1173
Cheese (see also Dairy products)·. 202, 719, 816, 840
Chemical engineering:
   Degrees conferred 782, 784
   Employment 782
   Salary 782
Chemical products 1294
   Producer price indexes 708
   Production 993
   Toxic chemical releases 366, 367, 368
Chemicals manufacturing (see also individual chemicals):
   Capital 757

Chemicals manufacturing (see also individual chemicals): —Con.
   Earnings 620, 971, 973, 981
   Electronic commerce 977
   Employees ... 620, 971, 973, 975, 979, 981
   Establishments 971
   Finances 769
   Foreign trade 975, 1297
   Gross domestic product 651, 970
   Industrial production index 763
   Inventories 983, 984
   Mergers and acquisitions 752
   Multinational companies 771, 772, 773
   Productivity 622
   Profits 768, 769
   Research and development 785, 787
   Shipments 973, 975, 983, 984
   Toxic chemical releases 367
Chemistry (see also Physical sciences):
   Degrees conferred 782, 784
   Employment 604
   Nobel prize laureates 794
   Salary offers 285
Cherries 806, 833
Chicken pox 177
Chickens. See Poultry.
Child abuse 332, 333
Child care .. 568, 569, 604, 606, 609, 708, 960
   Expenditures for 666
Child day care services:
   Earnings 565, 620
   Employees 565, 604, 620
   Establishments 565
   Finances 565, 566
Child support 530, 558, 559
Children (see also Population and Vital statis-
   tics):
   Activity limitation 182
   Adopted 61
   Age and/or sex .. 11, 12, 14, 15, 16, 21, 22
   Aid, social welfare programs 534
   AIDS 179, 180
   Alcohol use 194
   American Indian, Alaska Native population .. 14, 15, 16
   Asian population 14, 15, 16
   Asthma 187
   Black, African-American population .. 14, 15, 16
   Child abuse 332, 333
   Child day care 568, 569, 708
   Child support 530, 558, 559
   Cigarette smoking 194
   College dormitories 68
   Computer use 244, 246, 247
   Congenital abnormalities 166
   Correctional institutions 68
   Cost of raising 666
   Crime, arrests 308, 316
   Deaths and death rates . 104, 105, 108, 109, 180
   Disability status 249
   Drug use 194
   Families in .. 55, 58, 62, 63, 64, 65, 1321
   Food insecurity 199
   Food stamp program 562, 563
   Foreign-born population 45
   Foreign country 1321

NOTE: Index citations refer to **table** numbers, not page numbers.

NOTE: Index citations refer to **table** numbers, not page numbers.

NOTE: Index citations refer to **table** numbers, not page numbers.

U.S. Census Bureau, Statistical Abstract of the United States: 2006

NOTE: Index citations refer to **table** numbers, not page numbers.

NOTE: Index citations refer to **table** numbers, not page numbers.

U.S. Census Bureau, Statistical Abstract of the United States: 2006

NOTE: Index citations refer to **table** numbers, not page numbers.

U.S. Census Bureau, Statistical Abstract of the United States: 2006

NOTE: Index citations refer to **table** numbers, not page numbers.

NOTE: Index citations refer to **table** numbers, not page numbers.

U.S. Census Bureau, Statistical Abstract of the United States: 2006

NOTE: Index citations refer to **table** numbers, not page numbers.

U.S. Census Bureau, Statistical Abstract of the United States: 2006

NOTE: Index citations refer to **table** numbers, not page numbers.

NOTE: Index citations refer to **table** numbers, not page numbers.

NOTE: Index citations refer to **table** numbers, not page numbers.

NOTE: Index citations refer to **table** numbers, not page numbers.

U.S. Census Bureau, Statistical Abstract of the United States: 2006

NOTE: Index citations refer to **table** numbers, not page numbers.

NOTE: Index citations refer to **table** numbers, not page numbers.

NOTE: Index citations refer to **table** numbers, not page numbers.

U.S. Census Bureau, Statistical Abstract of the United States: 2006

NOTE: Index citations refer to **table** numbers, not page numbers.

U.S. Census Bureau, Statistical Abstract of the United States: 2006

NOTE: Index citations refer to **table** numbers, not page numbers.

NOTE: Index citations refer to **table** numbers, not page numbers.

U.S. Census Bureau, Statistical Abstract of the United States: 2006

NOTE: Index citations refer to **table** numbers, not page numbers.

U.S. Census Bureau, Statistical Abstract of the United States: 2006

NOTE: Index citations refer to **table** numbers, not page numbers.

NOTE: Index citations refer to **table** numbers, not page numbers.

NOTE: Index citations refer to **table** numbers, not page numbers.

NOTE: Index citations refer to **table** numbers, not page numbers.

NOTE: Index citations refer to **table** numbers, not page numbers.

NOTE: Index citations refer to **table** numbers, not page numbers.

NOTE: Index citations refer to **table** numbers, not page numbers.

NOTE: Index citations refer to **table** numbers, not page numbers.

U.S. Census Bureau, Statistical Abstract of the United States: 2006

NOTE: Index citations refer to **table** numbers, not page numbers.

NOTE: Index citations refer to **table** numbers, not page numbers.

U.S. Census Bureau, Statistical Abstract of the United States: 2006

NOTE: Index citations refer to **table** numbers, not page numbers.

U.S. Census Bureau, Statistical Abstract of the United States: 2006

NOTE: Index citations refer to **table** numbers, not page numbers.

NOTE: Index citations refer to **table** numbers, not page numbers.

U.S. Census Bureau, Statistical Abstract of the United States: 2006

NOTE: Index citations refer to **table** numbers, not page numbers.

NOTE: Index citations refer to **table** numbers, not page numbers.

U.S. Census Bureau, Statistical Abstract of the United States: 2006

NOTE: Index citations refer to **table** numbers, not page numbers.

U.S. Census Bureau, Statistical Abstract of the United States: 2006

NOTE: Index citations refer to **table** numbers, not page numbers.

U.S. Census Bureau, Statistical Abstract of the United States: 2006

NOTE: Index citations refer to **table** numbers, not page numbers.

NOTE: Index citations refer to **table** numbers, not page numbers.

NOTE: Index citations refer to **table** numbers, not page numbers.

NOTE: Index citations refer to **table** numbers, not page numbers.

U.S. Census Bureau, Statistical Abstract of the United States: 2006

NOTE: Index citations refer to **table** numbers, not page numbers.

U.S. Census Bureau, *Statistical Abstract of the United States: 2006*

NOTE: Index citations refer to **table** numbers, not page numbers.

NOTE: Index citations refer to **table** numbers, not page numbers.

NOTE: Index citations refer to **table** numbers, not page numbers.

U.S. Census Bureau, Statistical Abstract of the United States: 2006

NOTE: Index citations refer to **table** numbers, not page numbers.

NOTE: Index citations refer to **table** numbers, not page numbers.

U.S. Census Bureau, Statistical Abstract of the United States: 2006

NOTE: Index citations refer to **table** numbers, not page numbers.

NOTE: Index citations refer to **table** numbers, not page numbers.